Orient BlackSwan

WordMas

Learner's Dictionary of Modern English

Shreya
Reddy

Chief Lexicographer

BIKRAM K DAS

M.A., Ph.D. (India), M.A. ELT (Lancaster)
formerly:
Professor, Central Institute of English and Foreign Languages, India
Specialist, SEAMEO Regional Language Centre (RELC), Singapore
Associate Professor, National Institute of Education, Singapore
Director, English Language Teaching Institute, Bhubaneswar, India

Chief Editor: USHA AROOR

Project Manager: DURGA RAGHUNATH

Pre-press Coordinator: PREMA NARAYNEN

Project Team

Editorial
Padmaja Anant
Nirmala Krishnaswamy
Nandini Rao

Proofs
Padmaja Anant
Deepika Davidar
Ramaa Kishore
K Latha
Nandini Rao
Vani Vasudevan
D Venkataramanan

Advisory, standardisation
R Sivapriya
S Lalitha

Pronunciation
R Usha
R Vadivelu

Design
Bikram K Das
Durga Raghunath

Design execution
Anand George
J K Sahu

Production
Girish S Mondkar
Henrick A Rose

Illustrations
Mony K

Cover design
Ramakanth Advertising
(P) Limited

Product plan director
B M Mohammed Ali

Brand planning
J Krishnadev Rao
Sheila J Kurian
B Nagalakshmi

Supplementary features and illustrations editors
Prema Naraynen
Durga Raghunath

Contributors
Usha Aroor
Bikram K Das
Nandini Rao
C Rammanohar Reddy

Orient BlackSwan would like to thank Shanta Rameshwar Rao for her editorial help, and the many teachers whose advice and suggestions have helped refine the use-related features of this dictionary. Special thanks are also due to Anand George for his technical support and his extraordinary commitment to the quality and accuracy of the entries.

Orient BlackSwan

WordMaster

WordMaster Learner's Dictionary of Modern English

Orient BlackSwan

ORIENT BLACKSWAN PRIVATE LIMITED

Registered office
3-6-752, Himayatnagar, Hyderabad 500 029 (A.P), INDIA
e-mail: centraloffice@orientblackswan.com

Other offices
Bangalore, Bhopal, Bhubaneswar, Chennai, Ernakulam, Guwahati, Hyderabad, Jaipur, Kolkata, Lucknow, Mumbai, New Delhi, Patna, Pune

First published by Orient Longman Private Limited 2004
Reprinted 2004, (twice), 2006, 2007
First Orient Blackswan impression 2009
Reprinted 2009, 2010

ISBN: 978 81 250 2468 2

Typeset by
Trinity Designers & Typesetters
Chennai 600 041

Printed in India at
Graphica Printers
Hyderabad 500 013

Published by
Orient Blackswan Private Limited
3-6-752, Himayatnagar, Hyderabad 500 029 (A.P), India
e-mail: hyderabad@orientblackswan.com

WordMaster, the new dictionary for the new millennium, is intended essentially for learners of English on the subcontinent, at the middle, secondary and upper secondary levels. It can also serve as a general work of reference.

a contemporary and comprehensive guide

A large number of new words, from areas of knowledge and activity as diverse as information technology, genetics, space exploration and environmental conservation have entered the English language in recent years and passed into common use, thereby enlarging enormously the vocabulary needs of learners. Familiar words are acquiring new meanings and at the same time, many words that are commonly found in dictionaries are becoming obsolete. **WordMaster** contains more than 35,000 headwords, collocations, phrases and idioms which are currently in use and are relevant to present-day needs. It is thus a *contemporary* dictionary.

Like other learners' dictionaries, **WordMaster** is meant to be a comprehensive language-learning guide, providing information not only on the meanings of words but also spelling, pronunciation and grammatical usage. It also provides guidance on stylistic use (e.g. whether a word is used only in informal situations, or whether it carries a negative or an unpleasant meaning) and informs the user of the register or field from which a word comes (e.g. science, technology, medicine).

There are, however, certain innovative features that are unique to **WordMaster** and make it special.

not just a 'meaning finder'

Traditionally, a dictionary has been regarded as a reference book which is consulted only when the need arises. Many users think of a dictionary as just a *meaning finder*, turning to it when they come across an unfamiliar word. The dictionary finds a place of honour in the school or college library but that, unfortunately, is the place to which its use is often restricted. It is seldom that dictionaries are carried into the classroom and used during lessons.

a dictionary for the classroom

WordMaster has been designed as a 'classroom dictionary' which could find a place not only in the learner's schoolbag but also on her or his study-table. It is hoped that learners will feel motivated to turn to the dictionary *continually* while studying their textbooks or working on projects and assignments, and not just when the teacher advises them to do so. For that reason, a number of user-friendly features have been introduced here.

no information overload

First, care has been taken not to overwhelm the user with information. In providing glosses or meanings for words, a selection has been made of the most common meanings and those which learners are most likely to need. Similarly, the simplest and most basic information on grammatical usage has been provided, to understand which no specialised knowledge is required. Convenience, rather than comprehensiveness, has been the goal.

international as well as regional meanings

As most users of **WordMaster** are likely to be from South Asia, several entries present the 'international' meanings as well as, uniquely, the 'regional' meanings that these words have acquired. The words *blouse* and *bless* are examples.

The use of regional names (of places as well as persons) and references to elements of local culture also contribute to the higher 'comfort level' that users of this dictionary are expected to experience. The dictionary also draws attention, where possible, to errors commonly encountered by users of English on the Indian subcontinent.

What makes **WordMaster** particularly easy to use is the fact that here the headwords (the words being glossed) are followed by sentences exemplifying the use of these words in context. The following instance will illustrate the point:

clear contexts of use

di•lemma /dɪ'lemə/ noun, u. *I was planning to go to the cinema with my friend on Sunday but my teacher has invited me to lunch on the same day. I am in a dilemma as I cannot decide whether I should refuse the invitation or disappoint my friend.* = a delicate situation in which one has to choose between two actions or things

The same word is glossed in a popular dictionary as follows:

dilemma / di lem , dai- / n.[C] a situation in which it is very difficult to decide what to do, because all the choices seem equally good or bad: *a moral dilemma*

The example provided in **WordMaster**, it will be noticed, carries an extended context, consisting of two fairly long sentences, as against the short phrase, with minimal context, found in the other dictionary. The context provided in **WordMaster** has been made largely 'transparent' and self-explanatory, so that it is possible for the learner to guess, with reasonable accuracy, what the word might mean. This guess is confirmed when the learner comes, next, to the gloss.

a 'natural' way of learning new words

Two points need to be emphasised here. Firstly, exercises requiring the learner to guess the meanings of unfamiliar words from contexts of use have long been used by teachers in the classroom as an effective technique for learning new words. Secondly, this is how most people learn new words in real life. Most of the words that we can claim to 'know' have been learnt through guessing and not by looking up their meanings in a dictionary. When we meet a word in a meaningful context, we carry away with us an approximate meaning that is sufficient for most uses. Approximate meanings are, in any case, what most dictionaries are able to give us; few words possess a precise, fixed meaning.

Another special feature of **WordMaster** is the arrangement of groups or 'families' of words in clusters. This highlights the connections between words that are related to each other in form as well as meaning. Here is an example.

words in root-based groups

ob•serve /əb'zɜːv/ verb, t. **1** *I observe that there are more scooters than cycles on the road.* = to notice something **2** *'I am happy to see so many students here,' the teacher observed.* = to speak or to make a remark **3** *Have you observed the behaviour of this animal in different conditions?* = to make a scientific study of something [SCIENCE] **4** *The doctors have decided to observe the patient for a week.* = to keep a patient under watch, before or during medical treatment [MEDICINE] **5** *Holi will be observed on the eighteenth of March.* = to celebrate a festival (formal) **6** *Let us observe silence for two minutes.* = to practise some action for a limited period of time (formal)
observation /ɒbzə'veɪʃən/ noun, u. or c. **1** *If you use your powers of observation, you will notice that most people here are below the age of 20.*(u.) = the ability to notice something **2** *Your observations on the teaching in this*

school were well received.(c.) = remarks or comments, specially those made during a speech **3** *Newton discovered the law of gravitation through observation of natural phenomena.*(u.) = the process of studying events in a scientific manner [SCIENCE] **4** *The doctors will keep the patient under observation for a week.*= the process of keeping watch over a patient before or during medical treatment [MEDICINE] **observer** /əb'zɜːvəʳ/ noun, c. **1** *a keen observer of human nature* = a person who can notice things easily **2** *The United Nations is sending observers to the two countries.* = a person who is sent by an organization to some place to keep watch over a situation [TECHNICAL]

The placement of these words in the same cluster informs the learner of the fact that **observation** and **observer** are derivatives of the root-word **observe.** By learning the meaning of **observe**, learners get a convenient foothold which enables them to learn a large number of related words. Such incidental learning is an important aim that **WordMaster** has set itself.

This raises a fundamental question about the way in which most people look at dictionaries. As we suggested earlier, the assumption seems to be that a dictionary is little more than a source of meanings of unfamiliar words and a point of reference for spelling, pronunciation and grammar. When these purposes are achieved, users will put the dictionary away.

a vocabulary and language builder

However, it should be possible to think of a dictionary as a *vocabulary-builder* which one uses not just to know more about words that have already been met, but to build up a stock of words that *could* be used in the future. There is no logical reason why a learner who has used the dictionary to find out the meaning/meanings of **observe** should stop at that word. There could be a natural inclination to browse on, discovering related words in the neighbourhood of the root word. It is expected that the principle of clustering will encourage the habit of browsing and incidental learning, a strategy that many proficient users of dictionaries apply.

WordMaster thus differs in at least two important ways from most dictionaries that are now commonly in use. Both these innovations have resulted from many years of experience gained in the classroom with learners of English as well as their teachers. Both features have been field-tested and have drawn enthusiastic response from learners as well as teachers. It is hoped that they will prove useful to the wider audience to whom this work is now presented.

GRAMMAR LABELS

The following grammatical 'labels' have been used in this dictionary.

noun	a word which 'names' a person, place or 'thing' (e.g. *Shakespeare, Mumbai, chair*)
noun, c. (countable noun)	a noun which refers to things that can be counted and has singular as well as plural forms (e.g. *cup, cups*). Most plurals are formed by adding *-s* or *-es*, but the exceptions are shown, in this dictionary, in brackets and in boldface, after the headword.
noun, u. (uncountable noun)	a noun which refers to things which cannot be counted (e.g. *water, silk*) and which normally have no plural forms
noun, c. or u. (countable or uncountable)	a noun which can be either countable or uncountable, depending on the meaning (e.g. *Five deaths have been reported.*(c.) *Death is inevitable.*(u.))
verb	a word which refers to an action, either physical (e.g. *run, sit*), mental (e.g. *think, know, imagine*) or sensory (e.g. *feel, see*). Verbs have present as well as past tense forms, e.g. *ask/asked* (regular), *run/ran* (irregular). The past tense and past participle forms of irregular verbs are shown in brackets, in boldface, after the word.
verb, t. (transitive verb)	a verb which must be followed by an object, which is usually a noun or a pronoun (e.g. *She likes Mumbai/you*).
verb, i. (intransitive verb)	a verb that does not require an object (e.g. *He slept all day.*)
verb, t. or i. (transitive or intransitive)	a verb which can be either transitive or intransitive [e.g. *I can see a plane.*(t.) *I can see now.*(i.)]
aux. verb (auxiliary verb)	'helping' words which come before verbs and help to shape their meanings (e.g. *can, may, been, have*)
adj. (adjective)	a word which describes a noun (e.g. *red rose, round table*)
adv. (adverb)	a word which 'modifies' a verb (e.g. *He sings sweetly.*)
det. (determiner)	words which describe the nouns before which they are used. They include articles, quantifiers (e.g. *some, little, much*) and demonstratives (e.g. *this, that, these, those*)
pron. (pronoun)	a word which can replace a noun (e.g. *he, she, it*)
poss. pron. (possessive pronoun)	a word which shows 'possession' (e.g. *my, yours, his*)
conj. (conjunction)	a word which joins words, phrases or clauses together (e.g. *and, but*)
prep. (preposition)	a word which is commonly followed by a noun and shows some kind of relationship between the noun and a verb which comes earlier (e.g. *on* in *She sat on the chair.*)
interjec. (interjection)	an exclamation (e.g. *ah!, yes!*)

USAGE LABELS

The following 'stylistic' labels have been used in the dictionary to indicate the attitude (feeling) behind the use of a word, or the situation in which a word is used.

derogatory	a word or phrase which carries an insulting or negative meaning, e.g. *facile*
approving	a word or phrase used in praise or approval, e.g. *perfectionist*
disapproving	a word or phrase which shows the user's attitude of disapproval, e.g. *gimmick, churn out*

not respectful shows lack of respect (usually in South Asian cultural contexts) e.g. *blabber*

old-fashioned not commonly used in modern English, e.g. *array*

literary used to create a 'literary' effect, e.g. *azure*

figurative used with a 'transferred' meaning, e.g. *explode: He exploded when I told him he would not get leave.* ('Explode' is normally used for bombs etc. but is used here to describe the way a person reacts.)

humorous and **polite use** Both these labels are self-explanatory.

formal shows highly careful and correct use of language in 'special' situations, e.g. *abstain*

informal shows relaxed and friendly use of language, e.g. *I am feeling blue.* (= sad)

slang use of language which is permitted only between close friends in very relaxed situations, e.g. *cool* (= nice and likeable)

(USE) These are the words that users are advised not to use as they cause offence, or are not considered suitable in many contexts.

(G) gender-sensitive words that are offensive or not respectful of women and men e.g. *doll, sissy*

REGISTER LABELS

The register (the 'field' or subject from which a word comes) is shown by special labels, printed in small capitals. The labels used are:

BIOLOGY	BUSINESS	CHEMISTRY	COMPUTERS	GEOGRAPHY	GEOMETRY
GRAMMAR	HISTORY	LAW	LITERATURE	MATHEMATICS	MEDIA
MEDICINE	MILITARY	SCIENCE	TECHNICAL		

PRONUNCIATION TABLE

vowels		consonants		diphthongs	
ʌ	but	g	gate	eə	care
ə	asleep	θ	thin	uə	poor
ɜː	curd	ð	that	ai	kite
æ	sad	ʃ	ship	eɪ	cake
ɑː	basket	ʒ	treasure	ɔɪ	toy
e	get	ŋ	ring	əʊ	coat
ɪ	pin	j	yawn	aʊ	blouse
iː	deep	tʃ	chin	ɪə	dear
ɒ	lot	dʒ	join	aɪə	liar
ɔː	sort			**triphthongs**	
ʊ	should			eɪə	mayor
uː	soon			əʊə	mower
				aʊə	hour
				ɔɪə	lawyer

HOW TO USE THE DICTIONARY

This dictionary has been designed as a comprehensive language-learning tool which provides several kinds of information to the user. The diagram below illustrates the kinds of information that have been made available.

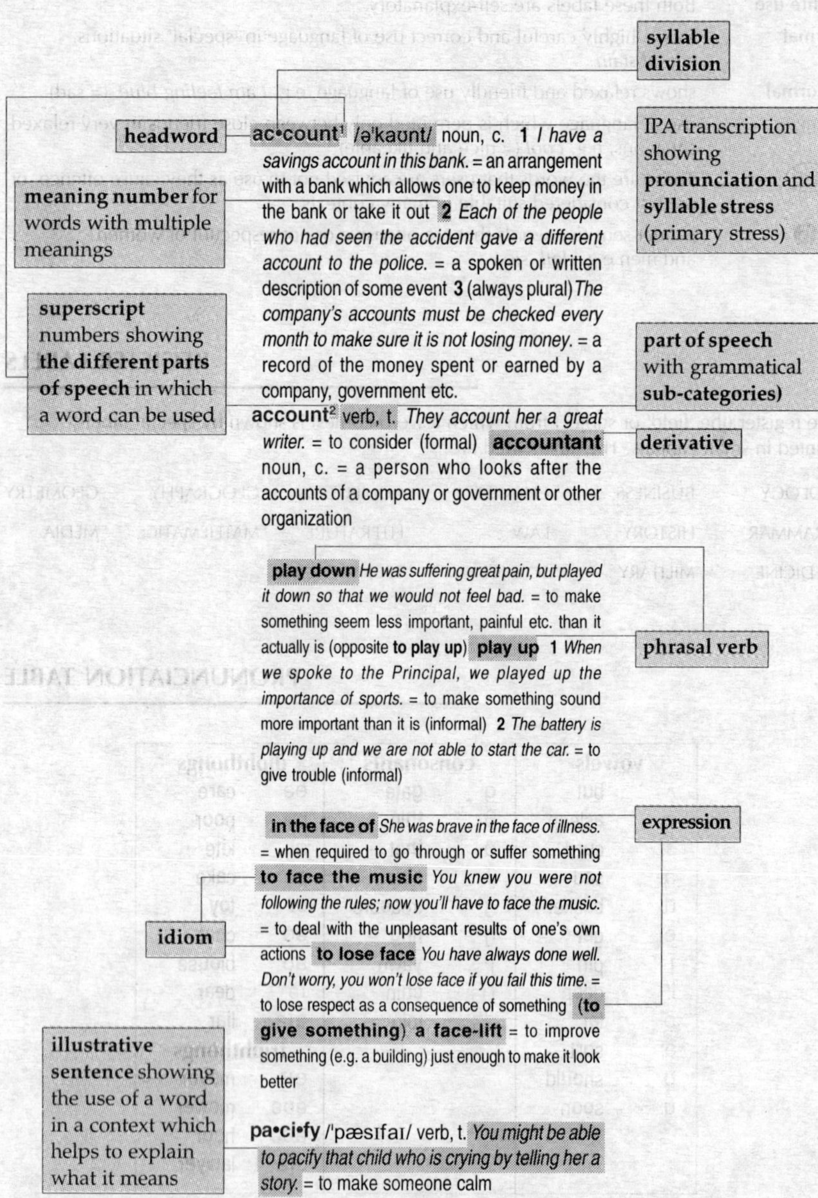

a•cute /ə'kju:t/ adj. **1** *There is an acute shortage of water in the city. All the wells and tanks are dry.* = very great; severe **2** *Dogs have an acute sense of smell and hearing.* = very sharp; keen **3** *an acute angle* = an angle which measures less than 90 degrees [GEOMETRY] (see pic under **angle**)

the meaning in simple English

references to illustrations

cross-reference suggesting comparisons with **synonyms** or **antonyms**

foe•tus (fetus) /'fi:təs/ noun, c. = an unborn baby that is almost fully developed [MEDICINE] (compare **embryo**)

man•go /'mæŋgəʊ/ noun, c. (**mangoes**) or u. **1** (c.) = a kind of fruit that grows in tropical (warm) climates

extra grammatical information showing **irregular** forms (plural, past tense etc.)

nau•se•a /'nɔ:zɪə/ noun, u. = a feeling of sickness that makes one want to vomit (throw up) the food that one has eaten **nauseate** /nɔ:zɪ'eɪt/ verb, t. *The smell of tobacco nauseates me.* = to cause nausea **nauseating** adj. *a nauseating smell* = causing nausea **nauseous** adj.

derived words

cool[1] /ku:l/ adj. **1** *The weather is pleasantly cool.* = neither very hot nor very cold; comfortable **2** *He is always cool when faced with some difficulty.* = calm **3** *When I met my friend yesterday, she seemed rather cool.* = not very friendly **4** *They are really cool people.* = nice and likeable (slang, approving)

contemporary meanings of words

a•moe•ba (ameba) /ə'mi:bə/ noun, c. (**amoebae** or **amoebas**) = a very tiny creature, made up of only one cell, that lives in ponds etc. **amoebic** /ə'mi:bɪk/ adj. e.g., *amoebic dysentery* = caused by amoeba

alternative spelling

re•a•lize (realise) /'rɪəlaɪz/ verb **1** *They went on talking and did not realize that it was getting late.* = to come to understand **2** *I am glad he has realized his dream of becoming a surgeon.* = to achieve

note where necessary on **etymology** (the language from which a word has been borrowed)

am•bi•ence (ambiance) /'æmbiəns/ noun, u. (French) *The hotel on the lake has a charming ambience.* = the character, quality, feeling etc. of a place

nat•ty /'næti/ adj. *natty clothes* = fashionable or stylish (informal)

stylistic label (showing the attitude, situation of use, etc. behind the use of a word)

subject label (showing the field of use from which a word comes)

download verb, t. = to move information from the Internet to the storage system of a computer [COMPUTERS]

mag•net /'mægnɪt/ noun, c. = a piece of iron or steel which can attract (pull towards itself) other pieces of iron or steel **magnetism** noun, u. **1** = the quality that a magnet has of being able to attract pieces of iron or steel **2** *People were attracted to Martin Luther King by his magnetism.* = the power to attract people that some persons have (figurative) **magnetic** /mæg'netɪk/ adj. **1** *This piece of iron has magnetic properties.* = having to do with magnets **2** *Lata Mangeshkar has a magnetic voice.* = very attractive **magnetic field** = the area around a magnet where its effect can be felt [PHYSICS]

clustering (derivatives and compound words are put in the same cluster as the root word to suggest connectedness)

compound words

shit[3] interjec. = an expression of anger or annoyance (USE)

The **DO NOT USE** symbol warns the user that a word is offensive.

chick /tʃɪk/ noun, c. **1** *a day-old chick* = a baby bird, specially a baby chicken **2** = a young woman (slang) (G)

The **GENDER** symbol shows words that may be gender-sensitive (having forms or meanings that are offensive or not respectful to women or men).

bag•gage /'bægɪdʒ/ noun, u. (always singular) = the bags, suitcases etc. that one uses to carry clothes etc. while travelling (also **luggage**)

extra grammatical information shows the restriction on the use of a word

anti- /æntɪ/ prefix meaning **1** opposed to e.g. **anti-aircraft** adj. *an anti-aircraft gun* = directed against an enemy aircraft **2** the opposite of e.g. **anticlockwise** adj. or adv. = in the opposite direction to the movement of the hands of a clock (see pic under **clockwise**) **3** acting to prevent from becoming worse e.g. **antiseptic** adj. = a chemical substance which can fight against infection in a wound caused by bacteria

box draws attention to the root meanings of **prefixes** and **suffixes**

Usage The sentence: *There were a few people in the room.* and the sentence: *There were few people in the room.* have different meanings. **a few** means 'a small number' while, **few** (without **a**) means 'not many'. In the sentence: *Few would believe that...*, **few** means 'hardly anyone'.

The **usage note** focuses on common errors and points out problems in the use of words.

foot

ankle
heel
toe
toenail

illustration with labels

1 Headwords **ac•count**

WORDMASTER provides the spellings, meanings and pronunciations of more than 35,000 entries (words, phrases, expressions and idioms) used in modern English together with grammatical and other kinds of information intended to guide correct and appropriate usage. Each entry is printed in **bold** letters in the dictionary.

WORDMASTER is designed for users (mainly learners at the school and intermediate level) in countries in South Asia. The model of English followed in these countries is, for historical reasons, closer to British English than to American English. Several dictionaries indicate American as well as British spelling, pronunciations, meanings and grammatical usage of words. To keep things simple and to avoid confusion, WORDMASTER provides, in most cases, only the spellings, pronunciations, meanings, etc. which are common on the subcontinent; in some cases, however, alternatives are indicated, specially when these are in wide use.

2 Alternative spellings **ameba**

Alternative spellings have been shown, also in bold print but in brackets, following headwords. We have not always indicated whether the spellings are American or British; it is to be understood that the alternatives are acceptable in the South Asian context.

3 Syllable divisions **ac•count, a•moe•ba**

The word *for* has only one syllable: that is, the entire word can be pronounced with a single 'burst' of air from the lungs. But the word *account* has two syllables (ac + count). There seems to be a 'break' or division after the first syllable and a second burst of air is needed to produce the sound of *count*.

The word *amoeba* has three syllables (*a + moe + ba*). There are other words in the dictionary with four or more syllables.

The headwords in the dictionary indicate also the syllable divisions in words, by means of dots printed between syllables. This information is important for the correct pronunciation of words.

4 Syllable stress /əˈkaʊnt/

In pronouncing the word *account,* we put greater 'stress' or energy on the second syllable (*count*) than on the first (*ac*). This is shown by putting a 'stress mark' before the second syllable. The stress mark is a small vertical line which begins slightly above and to the left of the syllable that is to be stressed. There is no such mark in case a word has only one syllable. 'Syllable stress' is shown together with the transcription used to indicate the pronunciation of a word, which we shall explain next.

5 Pronunciation /əˈkaʊnt/

WORDMASTER uses the International Phonetic Alphabet (IPA) to indicate the pronunciations of words. There is a separate IPA symbol for each vowel and consonant of English and they are explained in a separate table.

Pronunciations are indicated through 'phonemic transcriptions' (a system of writing designed to represent the sounds of languages), which come after the headwords. Before each transcription, as well as after it, you will find a slanting line or 'slash' (/).

Unlike some other dictionaries, WORDMASTER does not indicate American pronunciation. The pronunciations indicated here are the ones most commonly heard in the subcontinent.

IPA transcriptions have not been provided for all the headwords. For example, you will find a transcription for *account*, but not for *accountant*. The reason is that *accountant* is derived from the 'root word' *account* and follows the same stress pattern: the second syllable (*count*) is stressed in both *account* and *accountant*. The basic pronunciation of both words is the same, making a transcription unnecessary for the second word.

But consider the words *magnet* and *magnetic* (which is derived from the root word *magnet*). In *magnet*, the first syllable (*mag*) is stressed but not the second (*net*). In *magnetic*, however, there is a 'stress shift'; the stress moves from the first syllable to the second (*net*). This stress shift changes the pronunciation of *magnetic* completely. The dictionary therefore gives you IPA transcriptions for both words.

The principle followed, therefore, is : IPA transcriptions are provided for derivatives (words derived from root words) only in case there is a stress shift and hence a basic change in pronunciation. (If there is no IPA transcription, you can assume that there is no basic change in the pronunciation.)

6 Superscripts **ac•count**[1]

Many words in English can be used as different 'parts of speech'. For example, *account* can be used as a verb as well as a noun ; *cool* can be used as a verb as well as an adjective. It is easier to learn the meaning and the correct use of a word if one knows which part of speech it is used as.

WORDMASTER uses a system of 'superscripts' (a small number printed above a word) to separate a word which is used as one part of speech from the *same* word (with the same spelling) when it is used as a different part of speech.

Thus, you will find **account**[1] for *account* used as a noun and **account**[2] for the same word used as a verb.

7 Grammatical information verb, t.

Part of speech For each headword, the dictionary shows you the part of speech (noun, adjective, verb etc.) that the word is used as. This information comes after the IPA transcription. We provide, separately, a complete list of all the parts of speech that words in this dictionary could be used as, together with the abbreviations used for each.

Sub-class Verbs are either *transitive* or *intransitive* (though some verbs can be used both transitively and intransitively). Transitive verbs must be followed by objects, but intransitive verbs do not take objects. Not knowing whether a verb is transitive or intransitive can result in grammatical errors. For instance, Asian learners often use expressions such as 'Let us discuss about this subject', turning *discuss*, which should be used as a transitive verb, into an intransitive verb. WORDMASTER tells you whether a verb is transitive (t.) or intransitive (i.), or can be used in both ways (t. or i.).

Nouns are described as being either *countable* (c.) or *uncountable* (u.) Countable nouns, such as *boy* or *tree*, have plural as well as singular forms (*boy/boys, tree/trees*), whereas uncountable nouns such as *milk* generally have no plural form. Countable nouns in the singular form can follow the article *a*, but uncountable nouns cannot. Again, it is important to know if a noun is countable or uncountable in order to use it correctly. WORDMASTER indicates this in each case.

Irregular forms Many verbs form the past tense by the addition of *–ed* : for example *ask–asked*. These are known as *regular verbs.* Other verbs, which are known as *irregular verbs*, seem to follow no fixed pattern in forming past tense as well as participle forms: for example *see–saw–seen* or *run–ran–run*. Whereas learners find it easy to learn the past tense forms of regular verbs by using a simple grammatical rule, they have to remember the different forms of each irregular verb.

In the case of 'regular' nouns, plural forms are formed by simply adding *–s* (e.g. *toy–toys*). The plurals of 'irregular' nouns take different forms (e.g. *mango–mangoes; oasis–oases; sheep–sheep*), each of which has to be learnt separately.
WORDMASTER gives you the past tense and participle forms of irregular verbs and also the plural forms of irregular nouns, in bold letters, in brackets.

Restrictions on usage Some words are used only in the plural form, with *–s* (e.g. *scissors* or *trousers*). Some other words are used only in the singular form and can never have a plural form (e.g. *luggage* or *equipment*). Such restrictions on the use of words are also indicated.

8 Multiple meanings

A large number of English words have 'multiple meanings'. Some of these are closely related to each other; others may be far removed from one another. Each of these meanings is indicated by a number (1,2,3 etc.) The meanings of words (word-glosses) are given in language which is made as simple as possible, using only very 'common' words.

9 Illustrative sentences or examples

We come now to what is undoubtedly a unique feature of WORDMASTER.

Most dictionaries provide the gloss or meaning first, followed by the illustrative sentence. In WORDMASTER, the sentence or phrase illustrating the use of that word is provided first, *before* the meaning is given. For example, the headword *pacify* (used as a transitive verb) is followed by this sentence: *You might be able to pacify that child, who is crying, by telling her a story.* The context that is provided helps to make the meaning of *pacify* as self-explanatory and 'transparent' as possible. It is intended that the dictionary user should be able to make a very good 'guess'about the meaning of the word being glossed. The guess is later confirmed when the user reads the gloss which follows.

The ability to guess the meanings of new words from the contexts in which they are found is important for language learners, and many new words are learnt in this way. WORDMASTER encourages users to develop this ability.

10 Stylistic labels (informal), (not respectful)

An expression such as *Let's hang around* would be used only in *informal* speech or writing – for example in a relaxed conversation between friends – and not in a *formal* context (for example, during a business meeting). It is important for language learners to know the distinction between formal and informal use to be able to use words *appropriately,* as required by the situation.

11 Register labels [COMPUTERS], [PHYSICS]

A word such as *RAM,* which has come into common use now, is taken from the 'register' , or 'field', of computers. WORDMASTER provides such information for a large number of words.

12 Usage notes

Being specially designed for the use of South Asian learners, WORDMASTER provides useful information on points of grammatical usage which commonly cause problems for such learners. (The note on *discuss about* focuses on one such problem area.)

CONTENTS

aA

a, **A** /eɪ/ the first letter of the English alphabet

a /e/ or /eɪ/ indef. article **1** *Give me a pen.* = one (any pen, not a particular pen) **2** *Akash earns Rs 500 a month.* = in each month **3** *Milk is sold at Rs 12 a litre.* = for each litre **4** *A triangle has three sides.* = All (triangles have three sides).

a- prefix meaning **1** not e.g. **apolitical** adj. = not political **2** in a certain manner or in a certain condition e.g. **aloud** adv. = in a loud manner **alive** adj. *I am lucky to be alive.* = in a living condition

a•back /ə'bæk/ adv. **to be taken aback** *My friend was taken aback when he was told that his scooter had been stolen.* = to be shocked or greatly surprised by some unexpected or unpleasant event (slightly old-fashioned)

ab•a•cus /'æbəkəs/ noun, c. = a simple instrument used, especially in China and Japan, to carry out mathematical calculations, consisting of a wooden frame holding a number of metal rods on which small wooden balls can be moved up, down or across

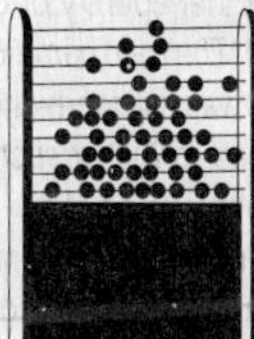

abacus

a•ban•don /ə'bændən/ verb, t. **1** *The dog had been abandoned on the highway but the young boy gave it a home.* = to leave someone or give up a thing (e.g. a house) forever **2** *The cricket match had to be abandoned because of rain.* = to discontinue; to stop and not start again **abandoned** adj.

a•bate /ə'beɪt/ verb, i. *The storm has abated, so it is safe to go out now.* = to decrease in force (formal)

ab•bre•vi•ate /ə'bri:vieɪt/ verb, t. *We usually abbreviate Indian Institute of Technology to IIT.* = to make a word or name shorter by dropping some letters **abbreviation** /əbri:vi'eɪʃən/ noun, c. = the shortened form of a word or name

ab•di•cate /'æbdɪkeɪt/ verb, i. or t. **1** *The king decided to abdicate and lead the life of an ordinary citizen.*(i.) = to give up an important official position, especially that of a king or queen [HISTORY] **2** *It is the duty of the government to make sure that children receive education. No government should abdicate this responsibility.*(t.) = to give up a right or duty (formal)

ab•do•men /'æbdəmən/ noun, c. = the front part of the body, below the chest and above the waist [BIOLOGY]

ab•duct /əb'dʌkt/ verb, t. *The criminals have abducted the child.* = to take someone away unlawfully and by force; to kidnap

aber•ra•tion /æbə'reɪʃən/ noun, u. *He is usually talkative, but of late he has been very quiet. I find an aberration in his behaviour.* = a change, usually temporary, in one's usual way of thinking or behaving

a•bet /ə'bet/ verb, t. (**abetted**) *The police suspect some well-known people of abetting crime in the city.* = to encourage and help in something that is wrong or against the law [LAW]

to aid and abet = to encourage crime or some illegal activity

a•bey•ance /ə'beɪəns/ noun, u. *The law against the giving and receiving of dowries was kept in abeyance for some years but is being revived now.* = the condition of not being in use for a time (formal)

ab•hor /əb'hɔ:ʳ/ verb, t. (**abhorred**) *I abhor it when people throw garbage on the streets.* = to hate or dislike strongly **abhorrence** noun, u. *His abhorrence for violence of any kind is well known.* = deep dislike or hatred

a•bide /ə'baɪd/ verb, t. or i. (used in negative sentences and questions) *I can't abide rude behaviour in anyone.*(t.) = to tolerate (formal, old-fashioned)

to abide by *I promise to abide by your decision.* = to obey or follow

a•bil•i•ty /ə'bɪlɪti/ noun, c. (**abilities**) or u. **1** *Only human beings have the ability to speak. No animal can do this.*(u.) = the power to do something **2** *Tagore had great ability as a writer.*(u.) = skill **3** *He has many different abilities. He can sing as well as dance.*(c.) = skill, talent

ab•ject /'æbdʒekt/ adj. **1** *abject poverty* = extreme; of as low quality as possible (referring to the condition in which someone lives) **2** *He offered an abject apology as he had been rude to us.* = showing that one is very ashamed and sorry

a•ble /'eɪbəl/ adj. **1** *We were able to find your house with difficulty.* = to be successful in doing something **2** *My daughter is only five years old, but she is already able to use the computer.* = to have the knowledge or skill required to do something **3** *He is an able writer and is getting better and better.* = skilful; good at doing something

-able /-əbl/ suffix added to verbs to describe some quality that a person or thing has e.g. **1** *a washable sari* = something which can be washed **2** *a lovable person* = a person who is easy to love

ab•norm•al /æb'nɔ:məl/ adj. **1** *Usually it never*

rains in March, but this March we have already had 100 mm of rain. This weather is quite abnormal. = different from what happens usually; unusual **2** *My neighbour's son is only 13, but he is already 200 cm tall and weighs 100 kg. His growth is quite abnormal.* = different from what is common, in a way that may be harmful or dangerous.

a•board[1] /ə'bɔ:d/ prep. *There are 300 passengers aboard this plane.* = on (inside) a bus, ship, train or plane

aboard[2] adv. *As the train is about to leave, all the passengers on the platform are advised to get aboard.* = into a bus, ship, train or plane.

a•bode /ə'bəʊd/ noun (usually singular) = one's home (literary or humorous)

a•bol•ish /ə'bɒlɪʃ/ verb, t. *The government has abolished child marriage. Now a girl cannot marry if she is below 18.* = to stop or put an end to something by law **abolition** /æbə'lɪʃən/ noun, u. = the act of stopping something through an order

a•bom•i•na•ble /ə'bɒmɪnəbəl/ adj. *Conditions in the camp were so abominable that many of the students fell sick.* = very bad or unpleasant **the abominable snowman** = a large hairy man-like animal said to live in the Himalayan mountains (also **yeti**)

ab•o•rig•i•nal /æbə'rɪdʒɪnəl/ adj. *The Santhals are an aboriginal tribe which has been living in Orissa for thousands of years.* = people who have been living in a place from the earliest times [TECHNICAL]

a•bort /ə'bɔ:t/ verb, t. or i. **1** = to lose a baby which is born too early **2** *The doctors had to abort the baby as the mother was very ill.*(t.) = to cause a baby to be born before the due time so as to end its life **3** *Our picnic had to be aborted because of the heavy rain.*(t.) = to stop or give up some activity because of some problem or danger **abortion** noun, c. or u. = the action of ending the life of an unborn baby, especially when done intentionally **abortive** adj. *The prisoners tried to escape by climbing over the wall but they were caught. The attempt was abortive.* = (an action that is) unsuccessful because it has to be given up before it can be completed

a•bound /ə'baʊnd/ verb, i. *The Nilgiri mountains abound in medicinal plants of different kinds.* = to be full of; to contain in large quantities (old-fashioned)

a•bout[1] /ə'baʊt/ prep. **1** *This is a book about cricket.* = on the subject of **2** *Education is about a search for truth.* = what something aims to do

about[2] adv. **1** *Rina is about ten years old.* = a little more or less than a given number **2** *The meeting is about to begin.* = going to happen very soon

a•bove[1] /ə'bʌv/ prep. **1** *Our classroom is above the library which is on the ground floor.* = in a higher place than **2** *If you are above 18, you can vote.* = more than **3** *I know that Thomas is completely honest. He is above suspicion.* = beyond

above[2] adv. *The shop is not on this floor. It is on the floor above.* = on a higher level

above[3] adj. *For the above reasons, we have decided to offer you this job.* = mentioned earlier (in a letter etc.) **above board** adj. *The lease of the theatre was open and above board. Only the signed amount was paid.* = honest and open; not secret or hidden

a•bra•sive /ə'breɪsɪv/ adj. *His abrasive manner offended me and I walked out of the meeting.* = rude and unpleasant

a•breast /ə'brest/ adv. *It is difficult for two people to walk abreast on this narrow path.* = side by side and moving in the same direction

to keep abreast of *Our teachers try to keep abreast of the most recent developments in computer science.* = to know the latest facts on some subject

a•bridge /ə'brɪdʒ/ verb, t. *This book has more than 1,000 pages. We have to abridge it to about 300 pages.*= to make something, usually a book, shorter

a•broad /ə'brɔ:d/ adv. **1** *My brother lives abroad but I prefer to live in India.* = in another country **2** *I am going abroad next month. I will go first to Japan and then to America.* = to another country or countries

a•brupt /ə'brʌpt/ adj. **1** *The train came to an abrupt halt, although the station was still far away.* = sudden; not expected **2** *He spoke to me in such an abrupt manner that I felt hurt.*= rude and unfriendly **abruptly** adv. = suddenly and without warning

ab•scess /'æbses/ noun, c. = a swelling in the body which is full of pus [MEDICINE]

ab•scond /əb'skɒnd/ verb, i. *The police are looking for them but they can't find them as they are absconding.* = to hide somewhere because one has done something wrong [LAW]

ab•sence /'æbsəns/ noun, u. *We really felt Rani's absence when she left our school. She was such a cheerful girl.* = the fact of someone or something not being found in the usual place

ab•sent[1] /'æbsənt/ adj. *Navin comes to school every day but today he is absent as he is sick.*= not found in the place where one is expected to be

absent[2] /əb'sent/ verb, t. (+ self) *You must not absent yourself from class if you want to learn the subject.* = to stay away from a place knowingly **absentee** /æbsən'ti:/ noun, c. = a person who is absent **absent-minded** adj. *Our uncle is so absent-minded that he can't even remember his children's names.* = so concerned with one's thoughts that one cannot remember things, or notice what is happening

ab•so•lute /'æbsəlu:t/ adj. *I have absolute trust in my doctor and will do whatever she tells me to do.* = complete; total **absolute zero** noun, u. = the lowest temperature that is thought to be possible [PHYSICS/ CHEMISTRY]

ab•sorb /əb'sɔ:b/ verb, t. **1** *Trees absorb water from the soil through their roots.* = to draw in liquid slowly; to soak up **2** *A tin roof absorbs a lot of heat from the sun.* = to take in **3** *The larger company absorbed the smaller companies.* = to make a part of itself **4** *I have read the book but I have not had the time to absorb it.* = to understand something thoroughly **5** *I was absorbed in the book and didn't hear you call.* = to fill the attention of **absorbent** adj. *Cotton is absorbent but nylon isn't.* = material that can absorb water or some other liquid easily [TECHNICAL] **absorbing** adj. *The book is so absorbing that you won't be able to put it down once you start reading it.* = very interesting **absorption** /əb'sɔ:pʃən/ noun, u. = the process of soaking up water or some other liquid [PHYSICS]

ab•stain /əb'steɪn/ verb, i. **1** *As my doctor asked me to abstain from smoking, I gave it up.* = to keep away from something that one enjoys, because it is harmful (formal) **2** *When the members of Parliament were asked to vote on the new bill, some members abstained.* = not to take part in voting in parliament

ab•stract[1] /'æbstrækt/ adj. *Beauty is only an abstract idea; you cannot see or touch it.* = something that cannot be seen, touched etc.; not concrete

abstract[2] noun, c. *Please send us an abstract of the paper you have written, in not more than 150 words.* = a short summary of an article, book, speech etc., containing only the important points

abstract[3] /əb'strækt/ verb, t. = to make an abstract of a speech, article, book etc. **abstract art** noun = art (usually painting) which has little relation to the real world and uses private symbols etc.

ab•surd /əb'sɜ:d/ adj. *Your idea of building a cinema in the middle of the jungle is absurd.* = foolish and making no sense; ridiculous

a•bun•dance /ə'bʌndəns/ noun, sing or u. **1** *Apples grow in abundance in Kashmir*(u.) = in large quantities; in plenty **2** *Rice can be grown only in places which have an abundance of rainfall.* (sing.) = a lot of **abundant** adj. = plentiful

a•buse[1] /ə'bju:s/ noun, c.or u. **1** *abuse of power*(c.) = wrong use of something; misuse **2** *In many countries the abuse of children is punishable by law.*(u.) // *abuse of animals* = cruelty or harmful treatment which may be physical, sexual or emotional in nature **3** *If you call someone stupid, they may take it as an abuse.*(c.) = a bad word, used to insult someone

a•buse[2] /ə'bju:z/ verb, t. **1** *You should not abuse the freedom that I have given you by coming late to the office.* = to make wrong use of something good **2** *He says that you abused him by calling him names.* = to use bad language so as to insult someone **drug abuse** noun, u.= causing harm to one's health by using opium, heroin or other drugs

a•bys•mal /ə'bɪzməl/ adj. *The film was of such abysmal quality that most people walked out of the cinema.* = very bad **abysmally** adv.

a•byss /ə'bɪs/ noun, c. *As we drove up the mountain, there were huge rocks on one side and a steep abyss on the other.* = a very deep hole or ditch

AC abbr. of **alternating current** = a flow of electricity that changes direction regularly and at a rapid rate (The supply of electric power to homes, factories etc. is by AC current.) (see also **DC**)

ac•a•dem•ic[1] /ækə'demɪk/ adj. **1** *academic standards* = connected with education **2** *What we would eat if we were vegetarians is a purely academic question because we are not vegetarians!* = something that is not very likely to happen in real life; not related to practical situations

academic[2] noun, c. *Two of my sisters are academics. One is a professor of mathematics and the other a professor of history.* = a person who teaches at a college or university **academic year** noun, c. = the period (e.g. June to May of the following year) when there are courses at a school, university or college

a•cad•e•my /ə'kædəmi/ noun, c. (**academies**) **1** *The Indian Military Academy in Dehra Dun trains officers for the army.* = a college or school where special training is given **2** *the Academy of Fine Arts* = a group of people who make up an organization interested in the advancement of art, music, science etc.

ac•cede /æk'si:d/ verb, i. **1** *The students begged the Principal to give them a holiday and he finally acceded to their request.* = to agree to a request or suggestion (formal) **2** *Akbar acceded to the throne of Delhi after the death of his father, Emperor Humayun.* = to take up an important position (formal) **3** *The state of Travancore acceded to the Indian Union in 1947.* = to join a group of people, countries etc. (formal) [HISTORY]

ac•cel•e•rate /ək'seləreɪt/ verb, i. *The runner started slowly, but after about 200 m he accelerated and started to run fast.* = to increase the speed at which someone or something is moving **acceleration** /əkselə'reɪʃən/ noun, u. = the rate at which a car, train or other vehicle increases its speed [SCIENCE] **accelerator** /ək'seləreɪtər/ noun, c. = the pedal in a car which the driver presses with his/ her foot to make the car go faster

ac•cent /'æksent/ noun, c. or u. **1** *Most of us speak English with a regional accent.*(c.) = a way of speaking usually connected with a country, area or social group [TECHNICAL] **2** *When one is driving the accent should be on safety, not speed.*(u.) = special importance or attention given to something

ac•cen•tu•ate /æk'sentjʊeɪt/ verb, t. *The dark background accentuates the brightness of the picture.* = to make something more noticable (more easily seen)

ac•cept /ək'sept/ verb, t. **1** *The teacher happily accepted the books which the students gave her for the class library.* = to willingly receive something which is offered **2** *For a long time she could not accept the fact of her failure in the examination.* = to recognize as being true or right **acceptable** adj. **1** *Writing an exam with a pencil is not acceptable in some schools.* = something that one can allow **2** *The Hindi you speak sounds different, but it is acceptable.* = good enough for a given purpose

ac•cess[1] /'ækses/ noun, u. *The only access to this room is through a window.* = the way by which one can enter or reach a place (formal)

access[2] verb, t. **1** *access a file* = to find amidst a group of other things (formal) **2** *There is something wrong with my computer. I cannot access the data which I had stored in its hard disk.* = to find information which has been stored in a computer [COMPUTERS] **accessible** /ək'sesɪbəl/ adj. **1** *Puri is easily accessible from Bhubaneswar.* = easy to reach **2** *The Prime Minister is very accessible to the public.* = easy to meet, even though occupying an important position

ac•ces•sion /ək'seʃən/ noun, u. *the queen's accession to the throne* = the process or event by which one comes to a high position specially that of a king or queen (formal) [HISTORY]

ac•ces•so•ry /ək'sesəri/ noun, c. (**accessories**) *I have bought some accessories for my new car: a radio, a pair of fog lights and a set of seat-covers.*= an extra item that is added to something to make it more attractive or useful

ac•ci•dent /'æksɪdənt/ noun, c. or u. **1** *Fifteen people were injured in an accident on the highway.*(c.) = something that happens by chance or by mistake, in which people may be injured or killed **2** *I had not met my friend for many years, but yesterday I met him on the street, purely by accident.*(u.)= something that happens by chance **accidental** /æksɪ'dentəl/ adj. = happening by chance and not planned **accident-prone** adj. *an accident-prone person* = one who keeps having accidents

ac•claim[1] /ə'kleɪm/ noun, u. *He received international acclaim for his beautiful dancing.* = strong approval; praise (formal)

acclaim[2] verb, t. **1** *Her novels have been critically acclaimed for their artistic quality.* = to praise **2** *She has been acclaimed leader by all the members of the party.* = to make a public announcement accepting someone as one's leader

ac•cli•ma•tize (acclimatise) /ə'klaɪmətaɪz/ verb, t. or i. **1** *Since you plan to go to the North Pole, you should first acclimatize yourself by spending a few weeks in a cold place.*(t.) = to slowly become used to a new climate [TECHNICAL] **2** *When we moved to this hot place my wife fell ill frequently. Over time, she has become acclimatized.*(i.) = to adjust or get used to

ac•co•lade /'ækəleɪd/ noun, u. (usually plural) *The new film has received high accolades from critics and we hope it will be liked by the public as well.* = praise (old-fashioned)

ac•com•mo•date /ə'kɒmədeɪt/ verb, t. *This car can accommodate six passengers.* = to have enough space for **accommodation** /əkɒmə'deɪʃən/ noun, u.= place to live or work in **accommodating** adj. *Our teachers will do everything possible to help you. They are very accomodating.* = agreeing to do or provide what somebody wants

ac•com•pa•ny /ə'kʌmpəni/ verb, t. (**accompanied**) **1** *Let me accompany you to the shop.* = to go with **2** *Study the text that accompanies this picture.* = to be found together with **3** *I will accompany you on the tabla when you sing.* = to play on a musical instrument while someone else is singing **accompaniment** noun, c. or u. **1** *Mango pickle makes a good accompaniment to an Indian meal.*(c.) = something which is usually or often found with something else **2** *He provided accompaniment on the tabla while she sang.*(u.) = music which is played on an instrument at the same time as a song [TECHNICAL] **accompanist** /ə'kʌmpənɪst/ noun, c.= a musician who plays on a musical instrument while someone else sings

ac•com•plice /ə'kʌmplɪs/ noun, c. *The police arrested the thief as well as his accomplice.* = a person who helps someone in committing a crime [LAW]

ac•com•plish /ə'kʌmplɪʃ/ verb, t. *She was able to accomplish a lot in the last two weeks by working through the nights.* = to be able to do something important; to achieve **accomplished** adj. *My sister is an accomplished dancer and has won many prizes.* = good at something; skilled **accomplishment** noun

ac•cord /ə'kɔːd/ noun, c. (no plural) or u. **1** *Earlier, my friend and I could never agree on anything but now there is perfect accord between us.*(u.) =

agreement or understanding (formal) **2** *The two countries signed a peace accord, bringing the war to an end.*(c.) = a political agreement between two countries; a treaty

accordingly /əˈkɔːdɪŋlɪ/ adv. **1** *The teachers wanted the school to look clean at all times, and the students have cleaned it up accordingly.* = in keeping with what has been said or done **2** *The government decided to send a hundred doctors to the villages and, accordingly, many doctors have been transferred.* = as a result

according to /əˈkɔːdɪŋ tə/ prep. **1** *This house has been designed according to your needs.* = in keeping with **2** *I don't like Kolkata but, according to my brother, it is the finest city in the world.*= in the opinion of

ac•count[1] /əˈkaʊnt/ noun, c. **1** *I have a savings account in this bank.* = an arrangement with a bank which allows one to keep money in the bank or take it out **2** *Each of the people who had seen the accident gave a different account to the police.* = a spoken or written description of some event **3** (always plural) *The company's accounts must be checked every month to make sure it is not losing money.* = a record of the money spent or earned by a company, government etc.

account[2] verb, t. *They account her a great writer.* = to consider (formal) **accountant** noun, c. = a person who looks after the accounts of a company or government or other organization

account for **1** *Rahim had no sleep last night and this accounts for the fact that he looks so tired this morning.* = to be the cause of **2** *The police would like to know where you were between 7.00 and 9.00 p.m. yesterday, when the house was burgled. Can you account for your movements during this time?* = to give a satisfactory explanation for something **on account of** *Sheela came late to school on account of the rain.* = because of

ac•coun•ta•ble /əˈkaʊntəbəl/ adj. *When the school takes the children on a picnic, the teachers are accountable to the parents for the children's safety.* = having to explain something to someone if it goes wrong; responsible

ac•cu•mu•late /əˈkjuːmjʊleɪt/ verb, t. or i. **1** *He built a school with the money he had accumulated over fifty years.*(t.) = to collect more and more of something over a period of time (formal) **2** *If you don't clean this room every day, a lot of dust will accumulate.*(i.) = to increase slowly and gather in some place **accumulation** noun

ac•cu•rate /ˈækjʊret/ adj. *I need an accurate measurement of this room.* = exactly correct **accuracy** noun, u. = the quality of being accurate

ac•cuse /əˈkjuːz/ verb, t. *Homi accused me of copying his work.* = to say (charge) that someone has done something wrong **accusation** /ækjʊˈzeɪʃən/ noun, u. = the act of accusing someone **accused** noun

ac•cus•tomed /əˈkʌstəmd/ adj. (+ to) *As I have never lived in England before, it will take me some time to get accustomed to this climate.*= to become used to something; to get adjusted

AC/DC device noun = a machine that can run on both alternating current (AC) or direct current (DC)

ace[1] /eɪs/ noun, c. **1** *In our game of bridge, my opponent played the ten of hearts and I played the ace.* = a playing card which has only a single 'spot' (club, diamond, heart or spade) and usually has the highest value **2** *The company is lucky to have a manager like Fatima. She is a real ace.* = a person who is very good at his/her work (informal) **3** = (in tennis) a very fast, strong serve which is not returned

ace

ace[2] adj. *an ace pilot* = a highly skilled pilot

a•ce•tate /ˈæsɪteɪt/ noun = a chemical substance made from acetic acid, often used to produce a kind of artificial cloth [CHEMISTRY]

ache[1] /eɪk/ noun, c. *I have a headache.* = pain in some part of the body. (Note the use of the article.)

ache[2] verb, i. *I laughed so much that my stomach ached.* = to feel a continuous, dull pain

a•chieve /əˈtʃiːv/ verb, t. *India achieved independence in 1947 after many years of struggle.* = to be successful in doing something **achievement** noun, c. or u. **1** *His double century in the cricket match was a great achievement.*(c) = something important that one has been able to do **2** *a great sense of achievement.*(u.) = the successful doing or finishing of something **high achiever** noun = a person who produces very good results, specially in studies

ac•id[1] /ˈæsɪd/ noun, c. or u. **1** = a type of chemical substance that contains hydrogen and forms a salt when combined with an alkali; it may destroy things it touches [CHEMISTRY] **2** (u.) = a word used to refer to LSD, a dangerous drug

acid[2] adj. *This fruit has a slightly acid taste.* = sour **acidic** /əˈsɪdɪk/ adj. = having the quality of an acid **acid rain** adj. = rain which contains harmful acids

acid test adj. *Will the new government be able to reduce poverty? That will be the acid test.* = a test which will prove whether something is as valuable as it is supposed to be

ac•knowl•edge /ək'nɒlɪdʒ/ verb, t. **1** *The driver of the car acknowledged that the accident took place because of his carelessness.* = to accept, or admit, that something is true **2** *I must acknowledge the help I have received from my wife in writing this book.* = to state, in speech or writing, that one has been helped **3** *The bank has acknowledged receipt of the letter which I sent last week.* = to write and tell a person that you have received a letter from him/her **acknowledgement** /ək'nɒlɪdʒmənt/ noun, c. or u. **1** (u.) = the act of admitting that something is true **2** (c.) = a statement thanking people for help received **3** (c.) = a letter confirming the arrival of a package etc.

ac•ne /'ækni/ noun, u. = a skin condition that makes pimples (raised infected spots) appear on the face

a•cous•tic /ə'kuːstɪk/ adj. *The acoustic nerve carries sound from the ear to the brain.* = connected with sound or the sense of hearing [TECHNICAL] **acoustics** noun, u. (always plural) **1** *The music concert has been arranged in this room because the acoustics here are very good.* = the qualities of a room which influence the quality of the sounds that are heard in it **2** = the scientific study of sound (a branch of physics) [SCIENCE]

ac•quaint /ə'kweɪnt/ verb, t. **1** *I am acquainted with the manager of the office, but I don't know him very well.* = to know a person (or thing) slightly but not very well **2** *I will need some time to acquaint myself with all the facts of this case.* = to find out or collect information about something (formal) **acquaintance** noun, c. or u. **1** (c.) = someone that one knows, but not very well **2** *acquaintance with computers*(u.) = slight knowledge of someone or something

ac•quire /ə'kwaɪəʳ/ verb, t. **1** *My friend has finally acquired a car.* = to get something one did not have before, and usually, has worked hard to get (formal) **2** *The government plans to acquire this land for a new hospital.* = to take possession of land or property through an order (referring to an action by the government) **3** *She has acquired a lot of experience as a teacher.* = to get, over a period of time **acquisition** /ækwɪ'zɪʃən/ noun, c. or u. **1** (u.) = the act of acquiring, or taking possession of, land by the government **2** *The company is really happy with its new acquisitions, including the six new computers.*(c.) // *I heard you have bought a car. Let me see your latest acquisition.*(c.) = something acquired

ac•quit /ə'kwɪt/ verb, t. (**acquitted**) *The judge acquitted the prisoner of murder as no one had actually seen him commit it.* = to decide that someone who is being tried in a court is not guilty of doing something wrong [LAW]

a•cre /'eɪkəʳ/ noun, c. = an area of land measuring approximately 4047 square metres or 4840 square yards

ac•ro•nym /'ækrənɪm/ noun, c. *UNO is an acronym for United Nations Organization.* = a word made up by choosing the first letter of each word in a name

a•cross[1] /ə'krɒs/ prep. **1** *Don't walk across the road now as there is too much traffic.* = from one side to the other **2** *The school is just across the road.* = on the opposite side

across[2] adv. **1** *When we reached the river, we did not find a boat. So we swam across.* = to the other side **2** *The room is 4 m long and 2 m across.* = wide

act[1] /ækt/ verb, t. or i. **1** *The police must act now to check crime in the city.*(t.) = to do something; to take action **2** *This new drug will act on the organisms which cause malaria.*(t.) = to have an effect **3** *She is not really unhappy. She is only acting.*(i.) = pretending **4** *He is usually very quiet, but today he just can't stop talking. I don't know why he is acting in this strange way.*(i.) = behaving **5** *Javed Khan acts the part of a doctor in this new film.*(t.) = to play a certain role or part in a film, play etc.

act[2] noun, c. **1** *The girl saved a little boy from drowning in the river. She has been given a medal for this act of bravery.* = something that someone has done **2** *the Income Tax Act* = a law passed by parliament **3** *Act 5, Scene 2* = one of the main divisions of a stage play **to catch someone in the act** *The pickpocket was caught in the act.* = while actually doing something **act of God** = a storm, flood etc. which is caused by natural forces and cannot be controlled by human beings [LAW]

act•ing[1] /'æktɪŋ/ adj. *The director of the Institute is away but the acting director can see you.* = someone who is asked to do a job while the person who usually does that job is away

acting[2] noun, u. = the profession of working in films, the theatre etc.

ac•tion /'ækʃən/ noun, c. or u. **1** *You have made many promises, but have done nothing yet. It looks as if you believe only in talk, not action.*(u.) = doing something **2** *You have lost those valuable documents and I must hold you responsible for this action.*(c.) = something that is done by a person **3** *The rocks under the waterfall have become smooth because of the action of the falling water.*(u.) = effect **4** *Garbage is piling up on the roads. Please take some action* *soon.*(u.) = do something to correct a situation **action-packed** adj. = a film, match etc. which has a lot of exciting events

in action 1 *Five soldiers were killed in action.* = while fighting [TECHNICAL] 2 *He looks lazy and slow when he is relaxing, but have you seen him in action?* = in an active state, doing things one is good at in an energetic way **to be out of action** *The lift will be out of action until they change the cable.* = of something or someone, to be injured, in a state of repair, etc. and therefore unable to do its/their work **'Lights! Camera! Action! '** = a call made by the director of a film to the crew to start filming a scene

ac•tiv•ate /'æktɪveɪt/ verb, t. 1 *If you press this button you will activate the bell and it will start ringing.* = to make something, especially an electric system, active; to bring to use [TECHNICAL] 2 *The law against blackmarketing has not been used for a long time but the government will activate it again.* = to bring back to usc

ac•tive[1] /'æktɪv/ adj. 1 *You will never find them sitting idle and doing nothing. They are always active.* = doing something or ready to do something 2 *an active volcano* = able to produce the typical effects, or act in a typical way [TECHNICAL] 3 *Your plan is under active consideration.* = being done at the present time (formal)

active[2] noun *In the sentence 'Rahim wrote a letter', 'wrote' is in the active voice.* = used to refer to the form of the verb when the subject is the doer of the action [GRAMMAR]

ac•tiv•ist /'æktɪvɪst/ noun, c. *She is an animal rights activist.* = a person who wants to bring about some social or political change and works hard for that change

ac•tiv•i•ty /æk'tɪvɪti/ noun, c. (**activities**) or u. 1 *The town is usually quiet, but now that it is holiday time, people are arriving and there is a lot of activity.*(u.) = things being done 2 *I would like to take part in some cultural activities such as drama and music.*(c.) = something that one does or takes part in as a hobby, especially for interest

ac•tor /'æktər/ noun, c. = a man or a woman who takes part in films, plays or television **actress** noun, c. (**actresses**) = a woman who plays a role in a film, play etc.

> **Usage** The word **actor** is now commonly used to refer to a woman as well as a man.

ac•tu•al /'æktʃuəl/ adj. *Before the election there were rumours that our party would lose, but when the actual results came in, it was found that we had won.* = real, not imaginary **actually** adv. *He looks about 20, but he's actually 45.* = in fact

ac•u•punc•ture /'ækjuːpʌŋktəʳ/ noun = a method of treating disease and relieving pain by pushing fine steel needles into parts of the body, first used in China [MEDICINE]

a•cute /ə'kjuːt/ adj. 1 *There is an acute shortage of water in the city. All the wells and tanks are dry.* = very great; severe 2 *Dogs have an acute sense of smell and hearing.* = very sharp; keen 3 *an acute angle* = an angle which measures less than 90 degrees [GEOMETRY] (see pic under **angle**)

AD /eɪ'diː/ abbrv. of **anno domini** (Latin) = years since the birth of Christ (see also **BC**)

ad•a•mant /'ædəmənt/ adj. *Though I begged her to change her mind, Mona was adamant and refused to come with me to Delhi.* = not willing to change one's mind

Adam's apple noun, c. = the swelling in the front part of the neck which moves up and down when a person speaks or swallows something (informal)

a•dapt /ə'dæpt/ verb, t. or i. 1 *He adapted the engine in his car so that it could run on petrol, diesel or gas.*(t.) = to make a change in something so that it is able to work in new or different conditions; to modify for new needs 2 *Camels do not need much water. They have adapted very well to life in the desert.*(i.) = to go through a process of change which helps one to face new conditions; to adjust **adaptable** adj. = able to adapt or adjust easily, so that one can face new conditions without any difficulty **adaptation** /ædæp'teɪʃən/ noun, c. or u. *The film 'Godan' is an adaptation of Premchand's novel.*(c.) = something produced by changing the original, for a special purpose

a•dapt•or /ə'dæptər/ noun, c. = a device that allows the connection of more than one electrical device (e.g. an electric iron and a toaster) to a source of electricity

add /æd/ verb, t. 1 *If you add 6 to 4, you get 10.* = to increase a number by another number so as to get a total [MATHEMATICS] 2 *Please add my name to the list of speakers.* = to include something which was not there earlier **added** adj. *added sugar* = something which is added to increase what is already there

to add fuel to the fire = to make a bad situation worse **to add insult to injury** = to give a person, who is already feeling unhappy or hurt about something, a reason to feel insulted as well

ad•der /'ædəʳ/ noun = a kind of poisonous snake found in parts of Europe, Africa and Asia

ad•dict /'ædɪkt/ noun, c. *Those men and women don't just take drugs, they are addicts.* = a person who has got into a (usually bad) habit which he/she cannot get out of (derogatory) **addiction** /ə'dɪkʃən/ noun, c. or u. = a habit which one cannot shake off easily (e.g. **drug addiction**) **addictive** adj. = a substance (e.g. coffee, drugs) the use of which, if done regularly, can become a habit

ad•di•tion /əˈdɪʃən/ noun, c. or u. **1** (u.) = the process by which numbers are added **2** *Additions are made to the list from time to time.*(c.) = something added

in addition to *In addition to being a good cook, he is also a good singer.* = besides

additional adj. *The house has only one room. We may need an additional room for the children.* = more than the number which already exists; extra

ad•di•tive /ˈædɪtɪv/ noun, c.= a chemical that is added to something (e.g. food) to improve it or make it last longer [TECHNICAL]

ad•dress[1] /əˈdres/ noun, c. (**addresses**) **1** = the name, number etc. of the place where one lives or works and where letters etc. can be sent **2** *After the guests had arrived, the president read out his welcome address.* = a formal speech made on a special occasion to a group

address[2] verb, t. **1** *You should address the judge as 'Your Honour'.* = to speak or write to someone, using a particular title or rank **2** *You can address your questions to the children in this audience as the programme is for them.* = to speak or write with a particular person or group in mind (formal) **addressee** noun, c.= the person to whom a letter, parcel etc. is sent

ad•ept /ˈædept/ adj. *Chitra is very adept at repairing machines.* = highly skilled

ad•e•quate /ˈædɪkwɪt/ adj. *He earns only a few hundred rupees a month and this is not adequate for the family.* = enough; sufficient

ad•here /ədˈhɪəʳ/ verb, i. **1** *The stamp did not adhere to the envelope as there was no glue on the back.* = to stick to something else with the help of glue (formal) **2** *In times of difficulty, it is not easy to adhere to one's beliefs.* = to stay with something and not change one's mind

ad•he•sive /ədˈhiːsɪv/ noun, c. = a subtance such as glue that can stick or cause something to stick [TECHNICAL]

ad hoc /æd ˈhɒk/ adj. (Latin) *The captain for the next match will be selected by an ad hoc committee.* = created or set-up for a special purpose and not permanent

ad•ja•cent /əˈdʒeɪsənt/ adj. *The bank and the post-office are adjacent to each other.* = next to; touching each other **adjacent angle** = an angle which has a common arm with another angle which lies next to it

ad•jec•tive /ˈædʒɪktɪv/ noun, c. *In the sentence 'She is a shy woman', the word 'shy' is an adjective.* = a word that describes or tells us more about a noun [GRAMMAR]

ad•join /əˈdʒɔɪn/ verb, t. or i. *Our house adjoins theirs, with only a low wall between the two houses.*(i.) = to be next to (see also **adjacent**)

ad•journ /əˈdʒɜːn/ verb, t. or i. **1** *The judge decided to adjourn the trial to the following Monday.*(t.) = to stop a meeting, trial etc. for a short period **2** *The court will now adjourn.*(i.) = to stop working for some time

ad•junct /ˈædʒʌŋkt/ noun, c. *The Planning Commission is not a part of the government but it is an important adjunct to the government.* = something that is added on to something else but is not considered a part of it

ad•just /əˈdʒʌst/ verb, t. or i. **1** *Can you adjust the sound on the TV?*(t.) = to make a slight change in something in order to make it work better **2** *He has fallen sick again. He cannot adjust to this cold climate.*(i.) = to change oneself in order to be better able to face a new situation; to adapt **adjustable** adj. *You can increase or decrease the height of an adjustable chair.* = (of something) which can be changed to different positions, settings or levels **adjustment** noun, c. or u. *We had to make a few small adjustments to the programme as some people were not happy with it.*(c.) = a small change, made to suit the conditions

ad•min•is•ter /ədˈmɪnɪstəʳ/ verb, t. **1** *The British divided India into a number of provinces so that they could administer the country better.* = to rule or manage a government, company etc. **2** *The doctor administered a life-saving drug to the patient.* = to give (formal) **3** *The Chief Justice administered the oath of office to the new ministers.* = to make someone promise something officially **administration** /ədmɪnɪˈstreɪʃən/ noun, c. or u. **1** *the administration of the country* = the management of the affairs of a government or company **2** *the company administration.*(c.) = the group of people managing a government, company etc. **administrative** /ədˈmɪnɪstrətɪv/ adj. *My duties in this school are mainly administrative. I don't have to teach.* = related to the management of a government, company etc. **administrator** /ədˈmɪnɪstreɪtəʳ/ noun, c. = a person whose job is administration

ad•mi•ral /ˈædmərəl/ noun, c. = a senior rank in the navy

ad•mi•ra•tion /ædmɪˈreɪʃən/ noun, u. *I have great admiration for our teacher.* = a feeling of respect

ad•mire /ədˈmaɪəʳ/ verb, t. = to think of someone with pleasure and respect **admirer** noun, c. *He is an admirer of Ravi Shankar.* = a person who admires someone

ad•mis•si•ble /əd'mɪsɪbəl/ adj. *evidence admissible in a court of law* = something that can be accepted or considered [LAW]

ad•mis•sion /əd'mɪʃən/ noun, c. or u. **1** *My daughter has been given admission to the medical college.*(u.) = permission to enter or join a college, school, club etc. **2** *The thief has made an admission of his crime.*(c.) = a statement accepting that something is true; a confession **admission fee** = the cost of entrance to a park, museum etc.

ad•mit /əd'mɪt/ verb, t. (**admitted**) **1** *The Principal has agreed to admit my child to her school.*(t.) = to allow someone to enter or join an organization **2** *The thief has admitted that she stole my car.*(t.) = to agree, or accept, that something (usually bad) is true **3** *The facts admit no other explanation.* = allow

ad•mon•ish /əd'mɒnɪʃ/ verb, t. *The teacher admonished the students for not bringing their textbooks to class.* = to tell someone gently that you do not like something that he/she has done (formal)

a•do /ə'du:/ noun, u. *Without further ado, let me now invite the Chief Guest to inaugurate the meeting.* = delay or unnecessary activity (old-fashioned)

ad•o•les•cence /ædə'lesəns/ noun, u. = the period of life between the ages 13 and 17 when one is neither a child nor an adult **adolescent** adj. = a person who is going through the period of adolescence

a•dopt /ə'dɒpt/ verb, t. **1** *As my uncle has no children of his own, he plans to adopt a child.* = to accept someone else's child as one's own through a legal process **2** *Some Indian farmers have adopted the Japanese method of growing rice.* = to take and use (compare **adapt**) **3** *to adopt a tough approach to indiscipline* = to begin to have **adoption** noun, u. = the act of adopting someone or something

a•dore /ə'dɔːr/ verb, t. **1** *He adores his elder sister.* = to have deep love and respect for a person or an animal **2** = to worship (a supernatural power or being) **adorable** adj. *What an adorable child!* = attractive; lovable **adoration** /ædə'reɪʃən/ noun, u. = the act of adoring someone

a•dorn /ə'dɔ:n/ verb, t. *The room was adorned with beautiful paintings.* = to make something look more beautiful; to decorate (formal)

ad•re•na•lin /ə'drenəlɪn/ noun = a chemical substance produced inside the body when one is angry, excited or frightened, which causes the heart to beat faster [BIOLOGY]

a•drift /ə'drɪft/ adj. **1** *When the ship sank, some of the passengers got into a lifeboat. For six days they were adrift.* = driven about aimlessly by the sea or wind **2** *Last year, when she had no work and no one to guide her, she felt she was adrift.* = going on without any purpose or direction

a•dult[1] /'ædʌlt/ noun, c. = a fully-grown person or animal, especially a person over the age of 18 or 21

adult[2] adj. **1** *It is difficult to tame an adult lion.* = a fully grown person or animal **2** *This is an adult film.* = meant for adults only

a•dul•ter•ate /ə'dʌltəreɪt/ verb, t. *People adulterate milk by adding water to it.* = to make a substance impure or of poorer quality by the addition of something of lower quality (disapproving)

a•dul•ter•y /ə'dʌltəri/ noun, u. = a sexual relationship between a married person and someone who is not their husband/wife (disapproving)

ad•vance[1] /ədvɑ:ns/ noun, c. or u. **1** *Our army has checked the enemy's advance.*(u.) = forward movement (usually of soldiers) **2** *The advance of television in the last ten years has been remarkable*(u.) = development or progress **3** *The discovery of a new planet is a great advance in science.*(c.) = a step forward **4** *The company has given me an advance of Rs 10,000 to buy a scooter.*(c.) = money paid to someone for some purpose earlier than it is due

advance[2] verb, t. **1** *The cheetah advanced on the deer.* = to move forward towards someone/something **2** *The editor of the magazine took every opportunity to advance the cause of art.* = to support and help **3** *Ms Shah advanced the time of the meeting.* = to bring forward to an earlier date or time

advance[3] adj. *I am sending you an advance copy of my note to read before the meeting.* = something which is sent ahead (earlier than something else, which is to follow)

ad•van•tage /əd'vɑ:ntɪdʒ/ noun, c. or u. *Michael Jordan's great height gives him an advantage over other basketball players.*(c.) = some quality or condition that helps someone to be successful or to do better than others **advantageous** /ædvən'teɪdʒəs/ adj. *It is advantageous for a basketball player to be tall.* = giving an advantage to someone

to take advantage of **1** *We should take advantage of the fine weather and go on a picnic.* = to make good use of something for one's benefit **2** *You are taking advantage of his kindness.* = to use in a way which is not proper or fair (disapproving)

ad•vent /'ædvent / noun, u. *People travelled in horse carriages before the advent of the motor car.* = the arrival or coming of an important invention, event, person etc. (formal)

ad•ven•ture /əd'ventʃər/ noun, c. or u. **1** *Our trip to the Simlipal forest, where we were chased by a wild elephant, proved to be quite an adventure.*(c.) = an experience or event that is exciting and somewhat dangerous **2** *An explorer's life is one of adventure.*(u.) = excitement and risk **adventurous** adj. = fond of adventure

ad•verb /ˈædvɜːb/ noun, c. *In the sentence 'Rahul walks slowly', the word 'slowly' is used as an adverb.* = a word or a group of words that describes a verb, an adjective or another adverb **adverbial** /ədˈvɜːbiəl/ adj. *an adverbial phrase* = a word or group of words that is used as an adverb [GRAMMAR]

ad•ver•sa•ry /ˈædvəsəri/ noun, c. (**adversaries**) *We will use every possible means to win over our adversary.* = opponent, enemy (formal)

ad•verse /ˈædvɜːs/ adj. *I do not have an office or a desk. I will not be able to work in such adverse conditions.* = unfavourable; going against; opposing **adversity** /ədˈvɜːsɪti/ noun, u. *a period of adversity.* = a situation in which you have many difficulties and everything seems to go against you

ad•ver•tise /ˈædvətaɪz/ verb, t. or i. *You must advertise your car if you want to attract buyers.*(t.) // *The food in this restaurant is so good that it does not need to advertise.*(i.) = to make something known to the public through newspapers, television etc. **advertisement** /ədˈvɜːtɪsment/ noun, c. = a notice of something to be sold, a job to be filled etc. in a newspaper, poster or on television

ad•vice /ədˈvaɪs/ noun, u. *Take my advice and study hard if you want to do well in the examination.* = an opinion given by one person to another on how to behave or act

ad•vise /ədˈvaɪz/ verb, t. *I advise you to give up smoking at once.* = to give advice to someone **advisable** adj. *It is advisable to wear a helmet while driving a two-wheeler.* = sensible; wise **adviser** noun, c. (**advisor**) = a person who gives advice to someone important, or to students (e.g. *adviser to the Prime Minister, student adviser*)

ad•vo•cate[1] /ˈædvəkeɪt/ verb, t. *Our party advocates compulsory education for children.* = to support

advocate[2] noun, c. **1** *Sona has engaged a famous advocate to defend him in court.* = a lawyer who argues in favour of the person who hires him or her **2** *Our President is an advocate of free trade.* = a person who supports some cause or idea

aer•i•al[1] /ˈeəriəl/ noun, c. = a wire or metal rod, usually fixed on top of a house or car, to receive radio or television signals (also **antenna**)

aerial[2] adj. **1** *This is an aerial photograph of Delhi, taken from a height of 30,000 ft.* = taken from the air **2** *an aerial battle* = taking place in the air

aero- /eərəʊ/ prefix, meaning 'connected with the air' e.g. **aer•o•dy•nam•ic** /eərəʊdaɪˈnæmɪk/ adj. *This new car has an aerodynamic design.* = related to the flow of air over and around a moving object

aer•o•bic /eəˈrəʊbɪk/ adj. = a biological process that takes place in the presence of air or oxygen [BIOLOGY] (opposite **anaerobic**)

aer•o•bics /eəˈrəʊbɪks/ noun (always plural) = physical exercises designed to make the heart and lungs stronger [TECHNICAL]

aer•o•gramme /ˈeərəgræm/ noun, c. = a sheet of paper on which a letter can be written and sent by air without an envelope (see **airmail**)

ae•ro•sol /ˈeərəsɒl/ noun, c. **1** = a metal container in which some liquid can be stored under pressure and forced out in the form of a spray (tiny drops) **2** = particles (solid or liquid) suspended in a gas (e.g. smoke, fog) [TECHNICAL]

aerosol

aes•the•tic /iːsˈθetɪk/ adj. *The beautiful paintings in Raj's room show that he has good aesthetic sense.* = related to the appreciation of beauty and art **aesthetics** noun (always plural) = the study of the principles of art and beauty

af•fa•ble /ˈæfəbəl/ adj. *Maria has many friends because of her affable nature.* = friendly and likeable

af•fair /əˈfeəʳ/ noun, c. **1** *The manager had so many important affairs to attend to that he did not know where to start.* = a matter that requires attention or action to be taken **2** *His affair with a colleague was a secret until yesterday.* = an emotional relationship between two people who are not married to each other, although at least one of them is married (informal, generally disapproving)

state of affairs (always plural) *an awkward state of affairs* = a situation which is present at a particular time

af•fect /əˈfekt/ verb, t. **1** *If you spend so much time watching television, it will affect your studies.* = to have an effect or influence on something **2** *She was deeply affected when she heard that her friend had been injured.* = to feel pain, sorrow etc. **3** *She affected illness so that she would not have to go to school.* = to pretend to feel, have or do (disapproving)

af•fec•ta•tion /æfekˈteɪʃən/ noun, u. *When Bimal speaks English, he tries to sound like a foreigner. His accent is just an affectation.* = behaviour which does not come naturally but is 'put on', like a pose (derogatory)

af•fect•ed /əˈfektɪd/ adj. *an affected smile* = unnatural

af•fec•tion /ə'fekʃən/ noun, u. *She greeted me with great affection, as if I was her own child.* = gentle love **affectionate** adj. = loving

af•fi•da•vit /æfɪ'deɪvɪt/ noun, c. = a written statement which is true and may be used as evidence in a court of law [LAW]

af•fil•i•ate /ə'fɪlieɪt/ verb, t. or i. *Our college has been affiliated to Tribhuvan University.* = to join or be connected to a larger group or organization **affiliation** /əfɪli'eɪʃən/ noun, u. = permission to join a larger group or organization

af•fin•i•ty /ə'fɪnɪti/ noun, u. *The two neighbouring countries share a strong affinity.* = a close and natural relationship or connection

af•firm /ə'fɜːm/ verb, t. *The government affirmed its intention to make education compulsory for children below the age of 14.* = to declare; to state that something is true

af•fir•ma•tive[1] /ə'fɜːmətɪv/ noun, u. *When I asked him if he would like to join us, his answer was in the affirmative.* = saying or meaning 'yes' (formal)

affirmative[2] adj. *an affirmative smile* = an action showing that you agree or mean 'yes'

af•fix[1] /'æfɪks/ noun, c. = a group of letters added to a word, either at the beginning (prefix, e.g. *dis*-count) or at the end (suffix, e.g. count-*less*), to form a different word [TECHNICAL]

affix[2] verb, t. *Please affix a stamp to the envelope.* = to stick, to attach (formal)

af•flict /ə'flɪkt/ verb, t. *The people who live in this area have been afflicted with a strange disease.* = to cause to suffer in the body or mind **affliction** noun, c. or u. = something causing suffering or pain; a disease

af•flu•ent /'æflʊənt/ adj. *They come from an affluent family, but there was a time when they had very little money.* = having plenty of money; rich **affluence** noun, u. = wealth, prosperity

af•ford /ə'fɔːd/ verb, t. **1** *Now that we have saved some money, we can afford a holiday in Nepal.* = to be able to buy something or spend money on something **2** *I am afraid I can't afford to sleep tonight as I have important work to do.*= to be able to do something without loss or damage

af•fo•res•ta•tion /əfɒrɪ'steɪʃən/ noun, u. = the process of planting a large number of trees on bare land

af•front[1] /ə'frʌnt/ noun, c. *The remark you have just made about my honesty is a personal affront.* = deliberate insult

affront[2] verb, t. (**affronted**) *Her rude remark affronted me.* = to insult openly

a•flame /ə'fleɪm/ adj. *Someone dropped a burning match on the carpet and soon the entire building was aflame.* = on fire (also **ablaze**)

a•float /ə'fləʊt/ adj. *Water was pouring into the boat through a large hole but we managed to keep it afloat.* = floating on the surface of water

a•foot /ə'fʊt/ adj. *Plans are afoot to close down the factory.* = being prepared or planned (referring usually to something unpleasant)

a•fraid /ə'freɪd/ adj. **1** *Don't be afraid, I am not going to hurt you.* = being in a state of fear **2** *I didn't tell you of his illness as I was afraid the news would upset you.* = thinking that something bad may happen **3** *I'm afraid we are going to be late for the meeting.* = sorry about something that has happened or is likely to happen (polite use)

a•fresh /ə'freʃ/ adv. *The essay you wrote is full of mistakes. You will have to do it afresh.* = once more; again (formal)

Af•ri•can[1] /'æfrikən/ noun, c. = a person from Africa

African[2] adj. = something that is connected with Africa **African American** noun, c. = an American whose ancestors came from Africa

af•ter /'ɑːftə'/ prep. **1** *I would like to have some coffee after my breakfast.* = when something (an event or time) has been completed **2** *I am facing one problem after another.* = following continuously **3** *The police are after the thief.* = in search of **4** *After the way he treated me, I will not visit him ever again.* = because of **5** *After all my care in packing it, the clock arrived broken.* = in spite of **6** *The road was named after his mother.* = with the name of **after-effect** noun, c. (usually plural) *I ate so much at the party that I am feeling the after-effects now.* = the effect, usually unpleasant, of doing something, that remains after the cause is gone **aftermath** /'ɑːftəmæθ/ noun, u. *The storm is over but now, during the aftermath, people are afraid to come out of their homes.* = the period following a bad event such as a war, storm etc. **afternoon** noun, c. or u. = the period between noon (12.00) and evening **afterthought** noun, c. *This part of the house was not in the original plan. It has been added as an afterthought.* = something that is not planned at first but is thought of, added or done later **afterwards** adv. *I can't talk to you during the meeting but I will talk to you afterwards.* = later

a•gain /ə'gen/ adv. **1** *He was here yesterday and he is here again today.* = one more time **2** *She had been ill for sometime but now she is well again.* = as before **3** *He might go to Kandy, but then again he might not.* = on the other hand **4** *I've told you again and again not to disturb her.* = repeatedly

a•gainst /ə'genst/ prep. **1** *I am against using animals for experiments.* = not in favour of **2** *He lost* *the election because most people voted against him.* = in opposition to **3** *She was sitting with her back against the wall.* = supported by **4** *The children have been vaccinated against polio.* = as a defence or protection from **5** *This picture looks very good against that wall.* = having something as a background

against all odds (**odds** always plural) *He managed to complete the work against all odds.* = despite all chances that it would not happen **against the law** *It is against the law to carry explosives in an aircraft or train.* = not legal **to go against someone's wishes** = to do something which is the opposite of what someone wishes you to do **to go against the grain** *I was forced to tell a lie in order to protect him but it went against the grain.* = against one's principles or beliefs

age[1] /eidʒ/ noun, c. or u. **1** *My grandfather died at the age of 92.*(c.) = the number of years that one has lived **2** *The man has reached middle age.*(u.) = a period in one's life **3** *Age has made me wise.*(u.) = the state of being old **4** *Many strange creatures lived on the earth before the Ice Age.*(c.) = a particular period in history (usually in capitals) **5** *It has been an age since we last met.*(c.) = a long time (informal) **6** *I haven't met you in ages.* (usually plural) = a very long time (informal)

age[2] verb, t. or i. **1** *He seems to have aged a lot in the last two years.*(i.) = to become older or to look older **2** *His strenuous life has aged him.*(t.) = to cause someone to become older **age-group** noun, c. *a book written for the 12–14 age-group* = a group of people who are between two particular ages **age-limit** noun, c. = the age below which or above which one is not considered suitable for something

to act one's age = to behave in a mature and sensible way **to come of age** = to reach the stage of maturity in one's biological growth; to reach the age of (usually) 18 or 21, when one can take on responsibilities, vote etc. **to feel one's age** = to feel old

age•ing[1] /'eɪdʒɪŋ/ noun, u. *It is said that Vitamin E can slow ageing.* = the process of growing older

ageing[2] adj. *The airline company wants to replace its ageing planes.* = something that is very old and no longer very useful

a•gen•cy /'eɪdʒənsɪ/ noun, c. (**agencies**) = an organization which represents other companies, stocks their products, provides information of their behalf etc. e.g. **employment agency** = a company that brings people in touch with jobs **advertising agency** = a company that helps to sell products by informing people about them **news agency** = an organization that collects news and sells it to different newspapers, televison stations etc.

a•gen•da /ə'dʒendə/ noun, c. *What is the agenda for today's meeting?* = a list of the subjects to be discussed at a meeting

a•gent /'eɪdʒənt/ noun, c. **1** *My brother works as an agent for an insurance company.* = a person who works for a company and helps to get business for the company by meeting people **2** *Soap is used as a cleaning agent.* = something that is used to produce a certain result

ag•gra•vate /'ægrəveɪt/ verb, t. *There was some trouble yesterday between two groups of students and someone aggravated the situation by shouting at one of the leaders.* = to make a bad situation worse (formal)

ag•gre•gate[1] /'ægrɪgeɪt/ noun, c. *The examination results are out. My daughter has an aggregate of 720 marks out of 800.* = total

aggregate[2] verb, t. or i. *Could you please aggregate your marks.*(t.) = to total up

ag•gres•sion /ə'greʃən/ noun, u. *The argument would not have ended in a fight if one of the groups had not attacked the other. It was an act of agression.* = the starting of a quarrel or fight by one side attacking or being violent with the other; a situation in which one country decides to start a war against another

ag•gres•sive /ə'gresɪv/ adj. **1** *He is always fighting with other children. He is an aggressive child.* = always ready to fight (disapproving) **2** *The government has started an aggressive programme to ensure education for all.* = something done in a forceful and energetic manner, to make sure that results are produced (not disapproving)

ag•gres•sor /ə'gresəʳ/ noun, c. = a person or country that starts a fight or war with another person or country

ag•grieved /ə'gri:vd/ adj. *He is feeling aggrieved because he was not made the captain of the team.* = feeling hurt or unhappy because one has been unfairly treated

a•ghast /ə'ga:st/ adj. *We were aghast at the sight of the damage that the earthquake had caused.* = shocked; filled with surprise or fear

a•gile /'ædʒaɪl/ adj. **1** *The cheetah is an agile animal which can run at a speed of 100 km an hour.* = able to move quickly and easily; nimble **2** *Einstein had an agile mind.* = able to think very quickly **agility** /ə'dʒɪlɪti/ noun, u. = quick and easy movements

ag•i•tate /'ædʒɪteɪt/ verb, t. or i. **1** *We are peaceful people. Don't agitate us unnecessarily.*(t.) = to make someone feel angry, anxious or nervous **2** *We are agitating for free midday meals for school children.*(i.) = to work for or against some political or social cause by creating public opinion **agitation** /ædʒɪ'teɪʃən/ noun, c. or u. **1** (c.) = a public movement in support of or against some political or social cause **2** *He was in* *a state of great agitation.*(u.) = mental unrest **agitator** noun, c. **1** = a person who tries to build up public support for or against some political or social cause through speeches, writings etc. **2** = a machine for shaking or mixing things

ag•nos•tic /æg'nɒstɪk / adj. = a person who is not sure if God exists (compare **atheist**)

a•go /ə'gəʊ/ adj. *The house was built only 20 years ago, but it looks old already.* = before now; in the past

a•gog /ə'gɒg/ adj. *The children are agog with excitement as they are going on a picnic.* = full of excitement and expectation (old-fashioned)

ag•o•ny /'ægəni/ noun, c. or u. *My brother broke his leg when he fell down the stairs and was in agony.*= very great pain of body or mind **agonize (agonise)** /'ægənaɪz/ verb, t. or i. **1** *I accepted the offer of the job after agonizing over it for weeks.*(i.) = to think about or feel something deeply and painfully **2** *He agonized me by asking me to accompany him again and again.*(t.) = to cause agony to someone **agonizing (agonising)** adj. *an agonizing decision* = something that causes great pain, anxiety

a•grar•i•an /ə'greəriən/ adj. *The farmers are happy with the government's agrarian policies.* = connected with land and agriculture [TECHNICAL]

a•gree /ə'griː/ verb, i. or t. **1** *I asked my friend to lend me his motorcycle but he didn't agree.*(i.) = to say 'yes' to something **2** *We both agree that she is a very good writer.*(t.) = to have the same idea or opinion (opposite **disagree**) **3** *What you are telling us about the accident doesn't agree with the report that was published in the newspapers.*(i.) = to be the same as; to match **4** *The fruit did not agree with me. It gave me a stomach upset.* = to cause indigestion **agreeable** adj. **1** *I suggested we go to the zoo and he was agreeable to my suggestion.* = ready to accept **2** *Everyone in the school likes him because of his agreeable nature.* = friendly **agreement** noun, c. or u. **1** *We are in total agreement with you about the quality of this painting, and have decided to buy it.*(u.) = a situation in which two or more people share the same opinion **2** *The strike has been called off as the workers and the management of the company have reached an agreement.*(c.) = an arrangement or understanding made between people, groups or companies **3** = a legal document which records the fact that two people or groups have agreed to something

ag•ri•cul•ture /'ægrɪkʌltʃər/ noun, u. = the science or activity of farming and growing crops

agro- /ægrəʊ/ prefix meaning 'connected with farming' e.g. **agro-industry, agro-business**

ah /ɑː/ interjec. *Ah, there you are!* = a cry of pain, surprise, joy, dislike etc.

a•ha /ɑː'hɑː/ interjec. *Aha, so that's what it meant!* = a cry of joy, surprise, satisfaction, amusement etc.; a way of saying that one has found out about something one didn't know

a•head[1] /ə'hed/ adv. *The guide walked ahead to show us the way.* = in front

ahead[2] adj. **1** *The road ahead was full of potholes.* = in front **2** *Let us see what changes lie ahead.* = in the future **3** *The time in New Delhi is five and a half hours ahead of the time in London.* = in advance of

to get ahead = to do well; to succeed **go ahead** *Once I had satisfied everyone that the plan was safe, they asked me to go ahead.* = to go on to do something because it is all right to do so

AI abbr. of **Artificial Intelligence**

aid[1] /eɪd/ noun, c. or u. **1** *Many people living outside the country offered aid to the workers who had lost their jobs.*(u.) = help and support **2** *A good dictionary is a useful aid in learning English.*(c.) = something that gives help

aid[2] verb, t. *Education aids the development of a person's character.* = to give support to; to help

aide /eɪd/ noun, c. (French) = a person who is employed to help an important official

AIDS /eɪdz/ abbr. of **Acquired Immune Deficiency Syndrome** noun = an illness which destroys the natural system of protection that the body has against disease

ai•ling /'eɪlɪŋ/ adj. *My father has been ailing from malaria.* = suffering from some illness **ailment** noun, c. = an illness, especially one which is not very serious

aim[1] /eɪm/ verb, t. or i. **1** *The photographer aimed his camera at the tigers.*(t.) = to point an object (a gun or camera) at someone **2** *The factory aims to produce more cars this year.*(i.)= to plan to do something

aim[2] noun, c. or u. **1** *The competitors took aim at the target.*(u.)= the action of pointing something at someone **2** *The aim of this meeting is to decide how we should welcome the Chief Guest.*(c.) = purpose **aimless** adj. *aimless talk* = without purpose or direction

air[1] /eə/ noun, c. or u. **1** (u.) = the mixture of gases surrounding the earth, which we breathe **2** *The balloon rose slowly into the air.*(u.) = the space above the earth **3** *There was an air of excitement as the concert was about to begin.*(c.) = general feeling; mood

air[2] verb, t. **1** *We have called this meeting to air our views.* = to make one's ideas, opinions etc. known **2** *You can air your clothes on the balcony.* = to dry or remove smells from clothes etc. by putting them out in the open air **3** *The programme is to be aired* *this evening on the radio.*= to broadcast on radio or television **air travel** = travel in a plane **by air** *I am going to Patna by air.* = in a plane **to be like a breath of fresh air** *Her cheerful voice was like a breath of fresh air in that crowded shop.* = to bring a feeling of freshness **to walk on air** *When we saw her, she had heard about her success and was walking on air.* = to be in a great state of happiness about something one has achieved, or praise one has heard **to clear the air (with someone)** = (in a situation where there is a dispute or disagreement with someone) to work things out so that a level of understanding is reached **a (lot of) hot air** *They talked about many things they would do, but it was a lot of hot air.* = statements, promises etc. which cannot be believed (informal, not respectful)

air•base /'eəbeɪs/ noun, c. = a place where military planes land and take off

air•borne /'eəbɔ:n/ adj. **1** *The airborne cargo to Europe consists mainly of fresh flowers.* = sent or carried by air **2** *Our plane is now airborne.* = no longer on the ground but in the air

Air Chief Marshal noun = the highest rank in the air force

air conditioner noun = a machine that keeps a building, car, bus etc., cool and comfortable in hot weather

air•craft /'eəkrɑ:ft/ noun, c. (singular as well as plural) = a flying machine of any kind **aircraft carrier** noun, c. = a fighting ship that can carry aircraft and has a wide, flat surface (deck) on which aircraft can land and take off

air force noun = the part of a country's defence force that fights from the air, using aircraft

air gun noun, c. = a gun which uses the pressure of air to fire a bullet

air hostess noun, c.= a woman who looks after the comfort and safety of passengers on an aircraft

air•ing /e'ərɪŋ/ noun, u. *Give the sheets an airing.* = the drying of sheets, clothes etc. in the open air to remove smells from them

air•lift[1] /'eəlɪft/ verb, t. *We airlifted food to the drought-hit areas.* = to carry people or goods to a place by air, especially to or from a place that is difficult to reach

airlift[2] noun, c. = the act of carrying people or goods to a place by air

air•line /'eəlaɪn/ noun, c. = a company that regularly carries people or goods by air **airliner** noun, c. = a large aircraft used to carry passengers

air•mail /'eəmeɪl/ noun, u. = letters, parcels etc. sent by air

air•port /'eəpɔ:t/ noun, c. = a place where aircraft can land and take-off and which has buildings for the use of passengers etc.

air raid noun, c. = an attack by military aircraft

airs /eəz/ noun, c. (always plural) *Don't give yourself such airs.* = unnatural behaviour intended to show one's importance to others (derogatory)

air•sick•ness /'eəsɪknəs/ noun, u. = a feeling of sickness, often leading to vomitting, caused by the movement of an aircraft in the air

air•space /'eəspeɪs/ noun, u. = the air or sky above a country, which is regarded as the property of that country

air strip noun, c. = a place where aircraft can land but where there are no buildings for passengers etc., as in an airport

air•tight /'eətaɪt/ adj. *Make sure that you store food in an air-tight container.* = something which does not allow air to get in or out

air-worthy adj. = able to fly without the fear of failing or not working while in the air (used to refer to aircraft)

air•y /'eəri/ adj. = a building, room etc. which allows air to get in easily

aisle /aɪl/ noun, c. = the passage between rows of seats in a bus, plane, cinema etc.

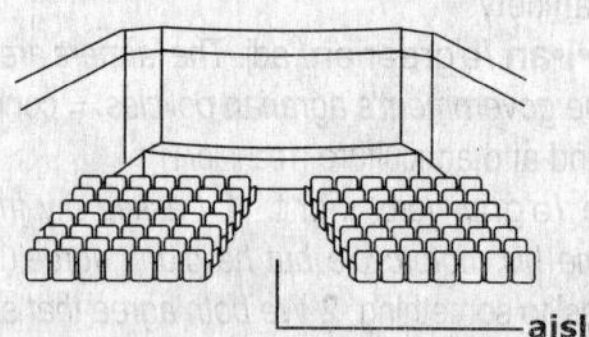

a•jar /ə'dʒɑ:/ adj. *We didn't close the door fully but left it ajar.* = slightly open

a•kin /ə'kɪn/ adj. *His role in the class is akin to that of a monitor.* = similar to; like each other

a•la•carte /a: la: 'ka:t/ adj. (French) *an a la carte lunch in a restaurant* = a meal (ordered in a restaurant) in which each dish (item of food) carries a separate price

a•lac•ri•ty /ə'lækrɪtɪ/ noun, u. *When he was offered Rs 1,000 for his old bicycle, he accepted the offer with alacrity.* = great willingness or eagerness (formal)

a•larm[1] /ə'lɑ:m/ noun, c. or u. **1** *She ran out in alarm when the curtains caught fire.*(u.) = fear and anxiety caused by the possibility of danger **2** *He raised an alarm when he saw an unknown person entering the house.*(c.) = a warning of danger

alarm[2] verb, t. *Don't alarm the animals by talking, or they will run away.* = to fill with fear and anxiety **alarming** adj. *Pollution in the cities is rapidly increasing. This is alarming.* = something that causes anxiety and worry **alarmist** noun = a person who always expects danger and makes other people feel anxious by giving them frequent warnings **alarm**

clock noun = a clock which can be made to ring at a particular time to wake up a sleeping person

to give a false alarm = a warning (of something unpleasant) that turns out to be either unnecessary or untrue

to have no cause for alarm = to have no reason to worry about something

a•las /ə'læs/ interjec. expressing sadness

al•be•it /ɔːl'biːɪt/ conj. *Conditions in the factory are improving, albeit slowly.* = although (formal)

al•bi•no /æl'biːnəʊ/ noun, c.= a person or animal with pale white skin, light-coloured hair and pinkish eyes caused by the lack of colouring matter (pigment) in the body [BIOLOGY]

al•bum /'ælbəm/ noun, c. = a book used for pasting in collections of stamps, photographs etc.

al•bu•men /'ælbjʊmɪn/ noun = a substance found in the colourless part of an egg which turns white when cooked

al•che•my /'ælkəmi/ noun = a science which was practised hundreds of years ago, especially in the Middle Ages, concerned with finding a way to turn cheaper metals into gold **alchemist** noun, c. = a person who practised alchemy

al•co•hol /'ælkəhɒl/ noun, u. **1** = a chemical substance present in wine, beer etc. which can make a person drunk if taken in large quantities **2** = any stong drink which contains alcohol **alcohol dependence** noun = a medical condition in which a person gets into the habit of taking alcohol regularly and cannot give up the habit [MEDICINE] **alcoholic** /ælkə'hɒlɪk/ adj. or noun, c. **1** *an alcoholic drink* (adj.) = something containing alcohol **2** (noun, c.) = a person who cannot give up the habit of drinking alcohol (derogatory)

a•lert[1] /ə'lɜːt/ adj. *Our dog is very alert and barks whenever it sees an unknown person.* = quick to act when one sees or hears something; watchful

alert[2] noun, c. *The army has been put on high alert.* = a state of readiness to face danger

alert[3] verb, t. *Our neighbours alerted us to the fact that thieves were active in the area.* = to inform someone that there may be some danger

to be on the alert *When you are in a forest, you should always be on the alert.* = ready to act quickly on seeing or hearing something **to sound the alert** = to give a warning signal

al•gae /'ældʒiː/ noun, c. (plural of **alga**) = tiny green plants found in or near water [BIOLOGY]

al•ge•bra /'ældʒɪbrə/ noun = a branch of mathematics in which letters and signs are used to represent values and numbers [MATHEMATICS]

a•li•as[1] /'eɪliəs/ noun, c. (**aliases**) *The actor was travelling secretly under an alias.* = a false name

alias[2] adv. *This is a photograph of the dangerous criminal Kumar Chalees, alias Bablu.* = also known as

al•i•bi /'ælɪbaɪ/ noun, c. (**alibies**) *The police wanted to arrest Sanjay as they suspected that he had burgled Vijay's house. But Sanjay had an alibi. On the day of the burglary he had been away in Mumbai attending a meeting.* = a reason for saying that someone who is accused of a crime could not have committed the crime because he/she was in some other place when the crime was committed [LAW]

a•li•en[1] /'eɪliən/ noun, c. = a person belonging to a foreign country or (as shown in films) another planet (also **foreigner**)

alien[2] adj. *This kind of dress is alien to our culture.* = something that is so different as to cause dislike or opposition **alienate** verb, t. *The increase in the price of tickets has alienated soccer fans, and most of them have decided to stay away from the match.* = to cause someone to become unfriendly or to lose their support **alienation** noun, u. *I have lived outside this country for so many years now that I have a feeling of alienation when I return here.* = a feeling of not being a part of one's surroundings

a•light /ə'laɪt/ verb, i. *When we reached Amritsar the train stopped and we alighted from our coach.* = to get off a train, bus etc. on reaching the end of a journey (formal or literary)

a•lign /ə'laɪn/ verb, t. **1** *You will have to align your desk with the other desks in the classroom.* = to arrange or form into a line **2** *Many countries have aligned themselves with others in the war against terrorism.* = to think along the same lines as someone else **alignment** noun, u. *Please check the alignment of the front and rear wheel of the scooter.* = the state of being in the same line as something else

a•like /ə'laɪk/ adv. *The sisters are so much alike, it is difficult to say who is who.* = like each other; similar

al•i•men•ta•ry ca•nal /ælɪmentəri kə'næl/ noun, c. = the tube leading from the mouth to the stomach and onward, through which food passes and is digested [BIOLOGY]

al•i•mo•ny /'ælɪməni/ noun, u. = money paid regularly under the orders of a court by a man or a woman to his/her former partner after a divorce [LAW]

a•live /ə'laɪv/ adj. **1** *The fish which I caught an hour ago is still alive.* = living; not dead **2** *The debate was kept alive by the newspapers.* = active; open

al•ka•li /'ælkəlaɪ/ noun, c. (**alkalies**) = a chemical substance which can combine with an acid to form a salt [CHEMISTRY] (opposite **acid**) **alkaline** adj. = having the quality, taste etc. of an alkali [CHEMISTRY]

all[1] /ɔːl/ det. **1** *The cat drank all the milk. There is none left for you.* = the whole of something. **2** *All my* *friends came to see me on my birthday.* = every one

all² adv. *She was left all alone in the house.* = completely; wholly

all³ pron. *All are invited to the party.* = everybody; everything; everyone **all-clear** noun, c. *When the entire group had crossed the rocky stream, the all-clear signal was given.* = a signal (e.g. the blowing of a whistle) given to show that some danger is over **all-inclusive** adj. *Your salary will be Rs 5,000 a month, all-inclusive.* = including everything **all out** *We must make an all out effort to win this match.* = using every possible strength and effort **all over** = everywhere **all-purpose** adj. *an all-purpose knife* = something that can be used for several different purposes **all-rounder** noun, c. = a person who can do a number of things well or play a number of games equally well.

all along *He pretended to be my friend when all along he did not like me.* = during the time that something is happening (informal) **all the (quicker)** *If you can get an autorickshaw, you will reach the station all the quicker.* = even more (quickly etc.) **all too (soon) ...** *It was a wonderful evening but it was over all too soon.* = very **above all** *You need to work hard and observe the rules of the college, but above all you should enjoy being here.* = most importantly **all in all** *The weather was bad and the food did not arrive on time, but all in all we had a good time.* = everything considered **after all** *Don't be too strict with the boy; after all he is just a child.* = (a phrase meaning 'you should consider that') **(not) at all** *'Thank you for the gift.' 'Not at all.'* = a expression used to respond to an expression of thanks **All that glitters is not gold.** = Things that seem good are not necessarily so.

> **Usage** **all** cannot be used in negative sentences to mean 'not all' or 'none' e.g. *All of them did not come.* or *All of them do not agree with you.* These sentences should read: *Not all of them came. / Not all of them agree with you.* (= none), *None of them came. / None of them agrees with you.*

Al•lah /ə'lɑːh/ noun, u. = the word used in Islam to address God

al•lay /ə'leɪ/ verb, t. *The doctor allayed my fears by telling me I was not suffering from any disease.* = to reduce someone's doubts, fears etc.; to calm (formal)

al•le•ga•tion /ælɪ'geɪʃən/ noun, c. *If you bring an allegation of corruption against someone you should be able to provide some proof.* = a statement that charges someone with wrong-doing but which is not supported by proof [LAW]

al•lege /ə'ledʒ/ verb, t. = to state that something wrong has been done without being able to prove it **allegedly** adv.

al•le•giance /ə'liːdʒəns/ noun, u. *You owe allegiance to the country in which you live.* = loyalty, respect and support for a leader, country, idea etc.

al•le•go•ry /'ælɪgəri/ noun, c. (**allegories**) = a poem, story, etc. in which the characters and actions represent certain good or bad qualities [LITERATURE]

al•ler•gy /'ælədʒi/ noun, c. (**allergies**) or u. *Dust gives me a headache. The doctors think I have an allergy to it.* = a condition of being highly sensitive to something that is eaten, breathed in or touched in a way that causes pain or suffering [MEDICINE] **allergic** adj. *I am allergic to dust.* = having an allergy to something

al•le•vi•ate /ə'liːvieɪt/ verb, t. *It is a doctor's duty to help sick people and alleviate their suffering.* = to make less; to relieve pain (formal)

al•ley /'æli/ noun, c. (**alleys**) = a very narrow street or path between buildings

al•li•ance /ə'laɪəns/ noun, c. or u. **1** *The two parties have formed an alliance to fight the election.* (c.) = an agreement or understanding between two persons, groups or countries for a common purpose **2** *The truck drivers are planning a strike in alliance with the railway workers.* (u.) = in partnership with; together with

al•lied /'ælaɪd/ adj. **1** *We became close friends because of our allied interests.* = joined together by some common bond or interst **2** *We are meeting to discuss the effect of the cyclone and allied matters.* = related

al•li•ga•tor /'ælɪgeɪtə^r/ noun, c. = a large reptile (animal belonging to the lizard family) living in or near lakes, rivers etc. in parts of America and China (see also **crocodile**)

al•lit•er•a•tion /əlɪtə'reɪʃən/ noun, u.= the repetition of the same sound in a line of poetry (e.g. 'the slithering of slimy snakes') [LITERATURE]

al•lo•cate /'æləkeɪt/ verb, t. *The government has allocated a large sum of money for relief in the cyclone-affected areas.* = to set apart for a particular purpose; to earmark **allocation** noun u. or c. **1** (u.) = the act of allocating something **2** (c.) = something that has been allocated

al•lot /ə'lɒt/ verb, t. **1** *The teacher has allotted this desk to me.* = to give something to someone through an order **2** *Fifteen marks have been allotted for this question on grammar.* = given as a share out of a larger amount **allotment** noun, u. = **1** the act or system of allotting **2** = a share of something, e.g. money

al•lo•trope /'ælətrəʊp/ noun, c. = two or more forms of a chemical element that differ in physical properties but exhibit the same chemical behaviour (diamond and graphite are allotropes of carbon) [CHEMISTRY]

al•low /ə'laʊ/ verb, t. **1** *I will allow you to leave the room now.* = to let someone do something; to permit (opposite **disallow**) **2** *Children below the age of 12 are not allowed into the cinema.* = given permission to enter **3** *The referee did not allow the goal as the player was off-side.* = to accept something as correct or valid

al•low•ance /ə'lɑʊəns/ noun, c. or u. **1** *Our employees get a travel allowance of Rs 500 every month.*(c.) = money paid regularly to someone to cover travel, petrol, medical expenses etc. **2** *She didn't do well in her test. Please make allowance for the fact that she was ill.*(u.) = the act of taking some fact into consideration

al•loy /'ælɔɪ/ noun, c. *Brass is an alloy of copper and tin.* = a metal which is a mixture of two or more metals [CHEMISTRY]

al•lude /ə'lu:d/ verb,i. *When Rahul said that he would always be grateful to a friend who had helped him, he was clearly alluding to you.* = to speak about someone in an indirect way (formal) **allusion** /ə'lu:ʒən/ noun, c. = the act of alluding to someone (speaking indirectly about someone)

al•lur•ing /ə'ljʊərɪŋ/ adj. *The offer you have made is so alluring that I can't refuse it.* = not easy to refuse; tempting

al•lu•vi•al /ə'lu:viəl/ adj. = a type of soil which is very good for growing crops and is generally left behind by rivers. [GEOGRAPHY]

al•ly /'ælaɪ/ noun, c. (**allies**) = a person, group, country etc. that helps and supports another person, group etc.

al•ma ma•ter /'ælmə 'meɪtə/ noun, c. (Latin) = the school, college or university that one attended

al•ma•nac /'ɔ:lmənæk/ noun, c. = a list of the days in a year, showing the time of sunrise, sunset, changes in the moon etc.

al•might•y /ɔ:l'maɪti/ adj. = able to do everything; all-powerful (**the Almighty** = God)

al•mond /'ɑ:mənd/ noun = the seed of a kind of fruit tree which is eaten as a nut

al•most /'ɔ:lməʊst/ adv. *My foot slipped and I almost fell as I was coming down the stairs.* = nearly; not quite

alms /ɑ:mz/ noun, u. (always plural) = money, food etc. given to poor people (old-fashioned)

a•loft /ə'lɒft/ adv. *The flag was flying aloft.* = high up (literary)

a•lone[1] /ə'ləʊn/ adv. *He has no relations or friends. He lives alone.* = without or away from anyone else

alone[2] adj. *You alone can do this task.* = only **to go it alone** (informal) = to do something by oneself, without anyone's help **to leave well alone** = to not disturb or try to change someone or something

a•long[1] /ə'lɒŋ/ prep. **1** *We walked along the path until we came to the end.*= from one end to the other **2** *They are planting some fruit trees along this road.* = in line with the length of something

along[2] adv. **1** *When I went to Kolkata, I took my brother along.* = together with oneself **2** *She skipped along, singing loudly.* = forward; on

a•loof /ə'lu:f/ adj. *He doesn't like to play with the other boys. He keeps aloof.* = keeping oneself separate and at a distance from others

a•loud /ə'laʊd/ adv. *The children were asked to read the poem aloud.* = so that one can be heard

al•pha /'ælfə/ noun, c. = the first letter (α) in the Greek alphabet

al•pha•bet /'ælfəbet/ noun, c. = the complete set of letters used in writing a language, e.g. from a to z (in English) **alphabetical** adj. *In a dictionary, the words are arranged in alphabetical order.* = in the same order in which letters are found in the alphabet (a, b, c, d etc.) **alpha-numeric** adj. *an alpha-numeric keyboard* = containing letters as well as numbers

Usage The letters 'a', 't', 'x' etc. are **letters** of the alphabet, not 'alphabets'.

al•pine /'ælpaɪn/ adj. e.g. *alpine climate* = connected with the Alps or other high mountains [GEOGRAPHY]

al•read•y /ɔ:l'redi/ adv. **1** *When I reached the station I found that the train had already left.* = by or before a certain time **2** *Is he here already?* = so early (an expression used in negative sentences and questions)

Al•sa•tian /æl'seɪʃən/ noun, c. = a big dog with long thick black and yellow fur

al•so /'ɔ:lsəʊ/ adv. *When you go to school, you should carry your textbooks and also your exercise books.* = as well as; besides **also-ran** noun, c. = a person who takes part in a competition but does not win any prize (informal)

al•tar /'ɔ:ltər/ noun, c. = a flat, raised piece of stone or wood in a temple, church etc. on which things that are offered to God are placed

al•ter /'ɔ:ltər/ verb, i. or t. **1** *This city has altered a lot since I was here last.*(i.) = to change (formal) **2** *This shirt is too big for you. It needs to be altered.*(t.) = to change the measurement of a piece of clothing **alteration** /ɔ:ltə'reɪʃən/ noun, u. **1** = a change which is made to something **2** = the act of changing something

al•ter•ca•tion /ɔ:ltə'keɪʃən/ noun, c. or u. *There*

was an altercation between the two soccer teams when a player hurt a member of the opposing team. = a noisy disagreement or fight

al•ter•nate[1] /ɔːl'tɜːnɪt/ adj. **1** *Yesterday it rained and today there is sunshine. We seem to be having alternate days of rain and sunshine.* = two things that happen by turn, first one and then the other **2** *My brother goes to work only on alternate days. He rests on Mondays, Wednesdays and Fridays.* = every second hour, week, day, month etc; one of every two

al•ter•nate[2] /'ɔːltənɪt/ verb, i. *The weather in Goa alternates between rain and sunshine.* = to change from one to the other by turn

al•ter•na•tive[1] /ɔːl'tɜːnətɪv/ noun, c. *If you don't want to go swimming, let me suggest an alternative. You can stay at home and read.* = something that one can choose to do or have in place of something else

alternative[2] adj. *We travelled from Kolkata to Delhi through Kanpur, but returned by an alternative route, through Nagpur.* = which can be chosen in place of something else **alternative medicine** noun = a system of health-care based on traditional systems of medicine in place of Western or dominant system: e.g. homeopathy, ayurved etc.

al•though /ɔːl'ðəʊ/ conj. *Although my daughter was ill, she won the race.* = in spite of the fact that

al•ti•tude /'æltɪtjuːd/ noun, c. or u. **1** (u.) = the height of a mountain, place or aircraft above sea-level **2** *At high altitudes I feel very sick.*(c.) = at a great height above sea level **altimeter** noun, c. = an instrument fitted to an aircraft which can measure the height at which it is flying

al•to•geth•er /ɔːltə'geðə/ adv. **1** *This car is altogether new. It was bought only this morning.* = completely, thoroughly **2** *It was very hot but the trip was not altogether bad.* = on the whole **3** *How many people are there altogether?* = counting the total number **to be in the altogether** = to be naked (slang)

al•tru•ism /'æltruːɪzəm/ noun, u. *People who donate money to charitable causes do it out of a sense of altruism.* = willingness to help others without thinking of one's own interests **altruist** noun, c. = a person who helps others unselfishly

al•u•min•i•um /æljʊ'mɪniəm/ noun, u. = a light, silvery-white metal (**aluminum**, in American English)

a•lum•nus /ə'lʌmnəs/ noun, c. (**alumni**) (Latin) = a former student of a school, college or university

al•ways /'ɔːlwɪz/ adv. **1** *The sun always rises in the east.* = at all times **2** *I will be your friend always.* = for ever **3** *She is always late for meetings.* = very often, as a habit (disapproving)

am /əm/ or /æm/ verb, i. = first person, singular, present tense form of the verb **be** (e.g. *I am a human being.*)

AM abbr. of **amplitude modulation** noun = a method of broadcasting sound by radio in which the strength of sound waves varies [TECHNICAL] (compare **FM**)

a.m. abbr. of **ante meridiem** (Latin) = before mid-day. (used to refer to times of the day before noon e.g., *9.00 a.m.*) (see also **p.m.**)

a•mal•gam /ə'mælgəm/ noun, c. **1** *Each of us is an amalgam of good and bad qualities.* = a mixture of different things **2** = a mixture of different metals, one of which is mercury [CHEMISTRY] **amalgamate** verb, t. *Three different companies will be amalgamated into a single unit .* = to join two or more groups together; to unite or merge

a•mass /ə'mæs/ verb, t. *She has amassed a large amount of money by writing stories for films.* = to gather a large amount of money, power etc. (formal)

am•a•teur /'æmətəʳ/ noun, c. *an amateur photographer* = a person who takes part in sports, drama, films etc. because he/she is interested in doing it but does not receive money for it; not professional **amateurish** adj. *His singing was very amateurish.* = something done without skill; not in a professional manner (derogatory)

a•maze /ə'meɪz/ verb, t. *Ravi had been an average student but he amazed us by getting the top position in the final exam.* = to cause great, usually pleasant, surprise **amazing** adj. *an amazing book* = causing surprise because of quality or quantity

am•bas•sa•dor /æm'bæsədəʳ/ noun, c. = a person who is sent by the government of his/her country to a foreign country to represent his/her government

am•ber /'æmbəʳ/ noun, u. = a hard yellowish substance formed from the sap (juice) of trees, often used to make ornaments

ambi- /æmbɪ/ prefix meaning 'both' or 'double' e.g. **am•bi•dex•trous** /æmbɪ'dekstrəs/ adj. = (a person who is) able to use both hands equally well

am•bi•ence (**ambiance**) /'æmbiəns/ noun, u. (French) *The hotel on the lake has a charming ambience.* = the character, quality, feeling etc. of a place

am•big•u•ous /æm'bɪgjʊəs/ adj. *When I asked Sarah if she would come with me, she just smiled. It was an ambiguous reply.* = something which can have more than one meaning and is therefore confusing or intended to confuse (opposite **unambiguous**)

am•bi•tion /æm'bɪʃən/ noun, u. or c. *Now that Jamila has been admitted into a medical college, she can fulfil her ambition of becoming a doctor.*(u.) = a strong desire to do something **ambitious** adj. **1** = (having) a strong desire for wealth, success, power **2** *an ambitious programme* = something that has been done with a strong desire to get good results

am•ble /ˈæmbəl/ verb, i. = to walk slowly, in a relaxed way

am•bu•lance /ˈæmbjʊləns/ noun, c. = a motor vehicle used to carry sick or wounded people to a hospital

am•bush[1] /ˈæmbʊʃ/ verb, t. *The tiger hid in the tall grass and ambushed the deer.* = to attack someone from a place of hiding

ambush[2] noun, c. *The herd of deer was trapped in the ambush.* = an attack made from a place of hiding

ameba see **amoeba**

a•men /ɑːˈmen/ interjec. = 'may this come true'; often used at the end of a prayer

a•me•na•ble /əˈmiːnəbəl/ adj. *I asked him to become my partner in the business, but he was not amenable to my suggestion.* = willing to listen and be influenced

a•mend /əˈmend/ verb, t. *to amend the constitution* = to correct; to change for the better **amendment** noun, c. = the act of making a change in a law or rule

a•mends /əˈmendz/ noun, c. (**to make amends**) *He was in a bad mood throughout the journey, but he made amends by showing us great kindness when we reached his house.* = to show that one is sorry by saying or doing something which pleases

a•me•ni•ty /əˈmiːnɪti/ noun, c. (**amenities**) *What amenities does this hotel provide for its guests?* = a thing or condition that makes a journey, stay etc. more comfortable

A•mer•i•can[1] /əˈmerɪkən/ noun, c. = a person from United States of America or the American continent

American[2] adj. *an American sandwich* = something connected with the United States of America **Americanism** /əˈmerɪkənɪzəm/ noun, c. = a use of English which is typically American **American Indian** noun, c. = a person who belongs to the race which was living in America originally (The term 'native American' is now preferred. 'Red Indian' is considered derogatory and has gone out of use.) **americanize (americanise)** /əˈmerɪkənaɪz/ verb, t. *Ali is completely americanized in his speech and manners as he has many American friends.* = to change someone or something so as to give them an American quality

am•e•thyst /ˈæmɪθɪst/ noun, c. = a costly purple stone used for making ornaments

a•mi•a•ble /ˈeɪmiəbəl/ adj. *He is an amiable person and is liked by everyone.* = friendly and pleasant

am•i•ca•ble /ˈæmɪkəbəl/ adj. *We are happy that the dispute between the two neighbours has been settled in an amicable manner.* = something done in a friendly and peaceful manner

a•mid /əˈmɪd/ prep. *The thief managed to escape amid the confusion.* = in the middle of (formal) (also **amidst**)

a•mi•no-ac•id /əˈmiːnəʊˈæsɪd/ noun, c. = a chemical substance present in any kind of protein (living matter), which is very necessary for life [BIOLOGY]

a•miss /əˈmɪs/ adj. *Why is everyone angry? What is amiss?* = wrong (formal/literary)

to take something amiss = to misunderstand and be angry or offended by something

am•me•ter /ˈæmɪtəʳ/ noun = an instrument that can measure the strength of an electrical current in amperes [PHYSICS]

am•mo•ni•a /əˈməʊniə/ noun = a gas which has a very strong, sharp smell and is used for making fertilizers and explosives [CHEMISTRY]

am•mu•ni•tion /æmjʊˈnɪʃən/ noun, u. (always singular) = bullets, shells etc. which can be fired from a gun or cannon

am•ne•sia /æmˈniːzɪə/ noun, u. *He has forgotten the names of all his friends, He seems to be suffering from amnesia.* = loss of memory [TECHNICAL]

am•nes•ty /ˈæmnɪstɪ/ noun, u. or c. *The government has granted amnesty to the hospital workers who were arrested last week for going on strike.* = an act of forgiveness, usually by the government, for people who have done something wrong or illegal connected with a country or its people [LAW]

a•moe•ba (ameba) /əˈmiːbə/ noun, c. (**amoebae** or **amoebas**) = a very tiny creature, made up of only one cell, that lives in ponds etc. **amoebic** /əˈmiːbɪk/ adj. e.g., *amoebic dysentery* = caused by amoeba

a•mok /əˈmɒk/ adv. *The elephant ran amok and killed a number of people.* = out of control and violent

a•mong /əˈmʌŋ/ prep. **1** *The house is hidden among a clump of coconut trees.* = surrounded by; in the middle of **2** *She is among the few who helped me when I needed help.* = one of several **3** *Please discuss this problem among yourselves.* = between the members of a group (also **amongst**)

a•mor•al /eɪˈmɒrəl/ adj. *Very young children are generally amoral.* = having no understanding of the difference between right and wrong

am•o•rous /ˈæmərəs/ adj. *He has an amorous nature. Whenever I meet him he seems to be in love with someone.* = connected with the feeling of love; falling in love easily

a•mor•phous /əˈmɔːfəs/ adj. *My plans for the future are still rather amorphous. I don't know what I'll do.* = without a fixed shape or form

a•mount[1] /ə'maʊnt/ noun, c. *She has given large amounts of money to charitable causes.* = a quantity of something

amount[2] verb, i. *Our travel expenses this month amount to Rs 10,000.* = to add up to

am•pere /'æmpeəʳ/ noun, c. = a measure of the quantity of electricity flowing past a point [PHYSICS]

am•phib•i•an /æm'fɪbiən/ noun, c. = an animal that can live both in water and on land (e.g. a frog) [BIOLOGY] **amphibious** adj. = able to live in water as well as on land

am•ple /'æmpəl/ adj. *I gave you ample time to finish your homework but you still haven't completed it.* = enough or more than enough (formal)

am•pli•fy /'æmplɪfaɪ/ verb, t. (**amplified**) **1** *He made a very short statement but said he would amplify it later.* = to make something larger (formal) **2** *He amplified his remarks with some new statistics.* = to explain in greater detail **amplifier** noun, c. = an instrument that makes an electric current stronger or music louder

am•pu•tate /'æmpjʊteɪt/ verb, t. = to cut off a limb (hand or leg) of a person through a surgical operation, often in order to save the person's life [MEDICINE] **amputation** /æmpjʊ'teɪʃən/ noun, c. = the act of cutting off a person's limb

a•muse /ə'mju:z/ verb, t. *You are looking sad today so I will tell you a funny story to amuse you.* = to make a person smile or laugh by doing or saying something funny **amusing** adj.= something that can amuse **amusement** noun, u. or c. **1** = the state of being amused (being made to smile or laugh by something funny) **2** = things which can entertain (make someone feel happy) **amusement park** noun, c. = a place where children can have fun by riding on machines and playing games of skill or chance

an /ən/ indef. article used before words that begin with a vowel sound e.g. *an egg* = one

-an /ən/ suffix meaning 'a person who is from some place' or 'a person who does a particular kind of work' etc. e.g. *a Brazilian* = a person from Brazil *a musician* = a person whose profession is to produce music etc.

an- /ən/ prefix meaning 'without' e.g. **anaerobic** = without oxygen; **anaesthetic (anesthetic)** = without feeling etc.

a•nach•ro•nis•m /ə'nækrənɪzəm/ noun, c. *Although there are palaces and forts in India, living in them is an anachronism now.* = something that is out of place in the present period of time

an•a•con•da /ænə'kɒndə/ noun = a large South American snake that hunts other animals by crushing them to death

a•nae•mi•a (anemia) /ə'ni:miə/ noun = an unhealthy medical condition in which a person does not have enough hemoglobin (red cells) in the blood **anaemic** adj. = sufffering from anaemia

an•aes•the•si•a (anesthesia) /ænɪs'θi:ziə/ noun = the state of being unconscious and feeling no pain as the result of getting an anaesthetic **anaesthetic** /ænɪs'θetɪk/ noun = a chemical substance used to make a person feel no pain either in a limited area (local) or in the whole body (general) [MEDICINE] **anaesthetist** /ə'ni:sθɪtɪst/ noun, c. = a doctor who gives an anaesthetic to a patient

a•nal /'eɪnəl/ adj. = related to, or near, the **anus**

an•al•ge•sic /ænəl'dʒi:zɪk/ noun, c. = a substance (e.g. aspirin) that helps one to reduce or feel no pain though one is conscious [MEDICINE]

a•nal•o•gy /ə'nælədʒi/ noun,c. *The poet offers an analogy between the moon and the face of his beloved.* = a comparison between two different things, sometimes used to explain an idea

an•a•lyze (analyse) /'ænəlaɪz/ verb, t. *Our English teacher taught us how to analyze a sentence when studying grammar.* = to examine or study something by dividing it into its parts **analysis** /ə'nælɪsɪs/ noun, u. or c. (**analyses**) **1** = an examination done by dividing something into separate parts **2** *The editorial in the newspaper gave us an excellent analysis of the news.* = a close examination of something, together with opinions and judgements **analyst** /ænəlɪst/ noun *a political analyst* = a person who makes an analysis of political situations **analytic** /ænəl'ɪtɪk/ adj. *a person with an analytic mind.* = good at methods of analysing and examining things in detail (also **analytical**) **in the final analysis** = when everything has been considered

an•ar•chy /'ænəki/ noun, u. *There was anarchy in the country for some time after the war but now there is order.* = lawlessness and social or political disorder caused by the absence of an effective government **anarchic** adj.

a•nat•o•my /ə'nætəmi/ noun **1** = the science which deals with the structure of the body and its parts **2** *We are studying the anatomy of a frog.* = the manner in which the body of a person or animal is made up **3** *She has a nice anatomy.* = body (informal, humorous) **anatomical** /ænə'tɒmɪkəl/ adj. = related to anatomy **anatomist** /ə'nætəmɪst/ noun, c. = a person who is skilled in anatomy

an•ces•tor /'ænsəstəʳ/ noun, c. *Though I live in Bihar now, my ancestors came from a village in Bengal.* = a member of one's family who lived long ago and from whom one is descended **ancestral** /æn'sestrəl/ adj. *ancestral home* = something that is connected with one's ancestors **ancestry** /'ænsestrɪ/ adj. **1** = the family a person comes from **2** = used to refer to all one's ancestors together **ancestor worship** noun, u. = the practice of praying to one's ancestors and regarding them as sacred

an•chor[1] /'æŋke'/ noun, c. **1** *The ship lost its anchor and was carried away by the ocean currents.* = a heavy piece of iron, usually with two arms, which can be lowered into the water to keep a ship from moving **2** *The opening batsman was the anchor for the Indian side.* = a person who provides support and a feeling of safety for others (also **sheet-anchor**) **3** = a person who appears in a television programme and helps to connect the different parts of the programme (also **anchor-person** or **host**)

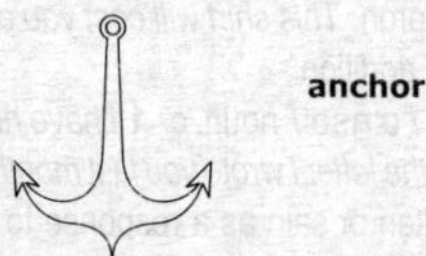
anchor

anchor[2] verb, i. or t. **1** *The ship anchored about a mile away from the shore.*(i.) = to keep a boat or a ship in a fixed position by lowering the anchor **2** *He anchors the top-rated music show.*(t.) = to work as the anchor for a television programme

an•cient /'eɪnʃənt/ adj. *This is an ancient monument built in the eighth century.* = very old; of or from a long time ago

and /ənd/ conj. **1** *bread and butter* = a word that joins two words or parts of a sentence together **2** *I ate my dinner and went to sleep.* = afterwards **3** *Drink this and you will feel less tired.* = as a result

and so on *They served us tea, took our bags upstairs, made us comfortable, and so on.* = a phrase which means 'and similar things' **And to think that ...** *She promised to get the tickets but didn't bother. And to think we depended on her!* = an expression of disappointment **And why are you late?** = an expression of displeasure (not respectful)

an•ec•dote /'ænɪkdəʊt/ noun, c. *Let me tell you an anecdote about my first year in school.* = a short, amusing or interesting story about a person/event

a•new /ə'nju:/ adv. *The school building has been repaired anew.* = once again, but in a new or different way (formal, literary) (see also **afresh**)

an•gel /'eɪndʒəl/ noun, c. **1** = a supernatural being who is a messenger sent by God (referred to in religious texts, stories etc.) **2** *You are a real angel!* = a kind person (informal) **angelic** /æn'dʒəlɪk/ adj. *an angelic face* = having a very innocent or beautiful quality

an•ger[1] /'æŋgə'/ noun, u. *His anger at being left out of the team was understandable.* = strong feeling which can make a person violent

anger[2] verb, t. or i. *It angered us to see how people littered the park with plastic bags.*(t.) = to make someone angry **angry** adj. = feeling anger

an•gle[1] /'æŋgəl/ noun, c. **1** = the space between two lines that meet, measured in degrees [GEOMETRY] **2** *Let us discuss this question from another angle.* = point of view

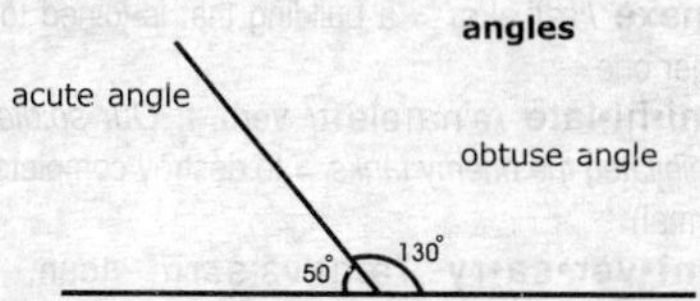

angles

angle[2] verb, i. = to try to catch fish with a fishing-rod **to angle for something** = to work towards an objective by well thought out means

Anglo- /æŋgləʊ/ prefix meaning 'connected with England or the people of England' e.g. **Anglo-Indian** noun, c. or adj. **1** (noun, c.) = a person who has English as well as Indian ancestors **2** *Anglo-Indian schools* (adj.) = run by the Anglo-Indian community **Anglo-Saxon** noun, c. or u. **1** (c.) = a person belonging to the Anglo-Saxon tribe, which lived in England in early times, from about AD 600 **2** (u.) = the language used by the Anglo-Saxon people

an•guish /'æŋgwɪʃ/ noun, u. *She was in anguish after she hurt her foot.* = very great pain or suffering of the mind

an•gu•lar /'æŋgjʊlə'/ adj. *an angular face/body* = having a sharp outline or shape; not rounded

an•i•mal[1] /'ænɪməl/ noun, c. = a living creature (e.g. a lion) which, unlike a plant, has five senses and is able to move when it wants to

animal[2] adj. **1** *animal fat* = something from or connected with an animal **2** *animal desire* = of the body, not of the spirit or mind **animal husbandry** noun = the science and practice of looking after animals for the production of milk and meat

an•i•mate[1] /'ænɪmɪt/ adj. = something which has life (opposite **inanimate**)

an•i•mate[2] /'ænɪməɪt/ verb, t. *Laughter animated his face* = to put life into something **animated** adj. **1** *an animated discussion* = full of energy; lively **2** *an animated cartoon* = pictures that appear to be moving **animation** /æni'meiʃən/ noun u. **1** = the making of films, computer games, advertisements etc. using pictures and models that appear to move [TECHNICAL] **2** = the quality of being lively and full of energy

an•i•mos•i•ty /'ænɪ'mɒsɪti/ noun, u. *A small*

quarrel has developed into great animosity between the two groups. = powerful, often active hatred

an•ions /'ænaɪəns/ = an ion with a negative charge [CHEMISTRY]

an•kle /'æŋkəl/ noun, c. = the joint between the foot and the leg (see pic under **foot**) **anklet** noun, c. = an ornament worn around the ankle

an•nex /ə'neks/ verb, t. *The East India Company annexed Bengal after defeating the Nawab.* = to take control and possession of a place by force

an•nexe /'æneks/ = a building that is joined to a larger one

an•ni•hi•late /ə'naɪəleɪt/ verb, t. *Our soldiers annihilated the enemy tanks.* = to destroy completely (formal)

an•ni•ver•sa•ry /ænɪ'vɜːsəri/ noun, c. (**anniversaries**) *On 15 August1997, India celebrated the fiftieth anniversary of its independence.* = a special day which falls an exact year or number of years after something important has happened

An•no Dom•i•ni /ænəʊ 'dɒmɪnaɪ/ see **AD**

an•no•ta•te /'ænəteit/ verb, t. *an annotated edition of Shakespeare's plays* = to add short notes explaining a text

an•nounce /ə'naʊns/ verb, t. *The station master announced that the train would arrive 20 minutes late.* = to make something known to the public **announcement** noun, c. or u. **1** (c.) = a statement giving the public information about something that has happened or is going to happen **2** (u.) = the act of announcing something **announcer** /ə'naʊnsə[r]/ noun, c. = a person who reads the news, or introduces people etc. on television, or at public functions

an•noy /ə'nɔɪ/ verb, t. *The continuous noise outside my house really annoys me.* = to trouble and cause irritation **annoyance** noun, c. or u. **1** (c.) = something that annoys **2** (u.) = the state of being annoyed

an•nu•al[1] /'ænjuəl/ adj. **1** *The annual function of the school will be held next month.* = happening once a year or every year **2** *What is the company's annual expenditure on telephone calls?* = of or for one year

annual[2] noun, c. **1** = a plant that lives only for one year or season **2** *a photography annual* = a book produced once a year

an•nul /ə'nʌl/ verb, t. (**annulled**) *Their marriage has been annulled by the court.* = to declare officially that a marriage, agreement etc. has ended and has no legal force [LAW]

an•ode /'ænəʊd/ noun, c. = a positive pole or end of an electrical battery, which collects electrons [TECHNICAL]

a•nom•a•ly /ə'nɒməlɪ/ noun, u. or c. (**anomalies**) *The land is rich in nutrients, and yet the farmers have problems with crops. This is a strange anomaly.*(u.) = a situation that is very unusual and difficult to explain or accept **anomalous** adj. *an anomalous situation* = very unusual and difficult to explain or accept

a•non•y•mous /ə'nɒnɪməs/ adj. *anonymous phone calls // an anonymous poem* = from or by someone whose name is not known (sometimes abbreviated as **anon.**)

an•o•rex•i•a /ænə'reksɪə/ noun = a kind of illness which causes a person to lose all desire for food [MEDICINE] **anorexic** adj. *an anorexic person* = suffering from anorexia

an•oth•er[1] /ə'nʌðə[r]/ det. **1** *Would you like to have another cup of tea?* = one more of the same kind **2** *Is there another way of reaching this place?* = a different one

another[2] pron. *This shirt will cost you another Rs 50.* = more; in addition

an•swer[1] /'ɑːnsə[r]/ noun, c. **1** *I have not received an answer to the letter I wrote you last month.* = something that is written or said as a response to a question or statement **2** *The answer is 29.* = something that is arrived at as a result of thinking or calculation **3** *We don't have a simple answer to the problem of pollution.* = solution

answer[2] verb, t. or i. **1** *Will you answer my question?* (t.) = to speak in reply **2** *Why don't you answer?*(i.) = to speak **3** *He answers the description given by my friend.*(t.) = to be as described **answerable** adj. *The teachers will be answerable to parents if the results are generally poor.* = required to explain or defend one's actions; responsible

answer back = to reply rudely **answer for** *If something goes wrong with the plan you will have to answer for the delay.* = to take or accept the responsibility for something **to have all the answers** = to know how to handle most situations

ant /ænt/ noun, c. = a small insect which lives in social groups **ant-eater** = an animal with a long, sticky tongue that eats ants

an•tag•o•nis•m /æn'tægənɪzəm/ noun, u. *The new plan was unsuccessful because of the antagonism between the planners.* = enmity, opposition or hatred between people or groups **antagonist** noun, c. = one who opposes (fights against) another person or cause; opponent **antagonize (antagonise)** verb, t. = to cause someone to become an enemy or an opponent

An•tarc•tic /æn'tɑːktɪk/ noun, u. = the very cold southernmost part of the world (see pic under **earth**)

an•te- /'æntɪ/ prefix meaning 'before' (earlier than some other event) e.g. **antenatal** = before a baby is born

an•te /'æntɪ/ noun = the amount of money which one bets in a game of cards (slang)
to up the ante = to increase the amount of risk in something that one is doing, in the hope of getting greater rewards

an•te•ced•ent /æntɪ'si:dənt/ noun, c. **1** = an event which comes before another event **2** = a noun which has been used earlier, to which a pronoun refers [GRAMMAR]

an•te•ced•ents /æntɪ'si:dənts/ noun (always plural) *I can't employ him before checking his antecedents.* = past record

an•te•lope /'æntɪləʊp/ noun, c. = a kind of deer

ante•na•tal /æntɪ'neɪtəl/ adj. (Latin) *the antenatal care of expectant mothers* = before the birth of a baby (compare **post-natal**)

an•ten•na /æn'tenə/ noun, c. (**antennae**) **1** = thin hair-like organs, growing in pairs on the head of an insect with the help of which it can feel **2** = a metal stick fixed on a building, car etc. to catch radio or television signals (see also **aerial**)

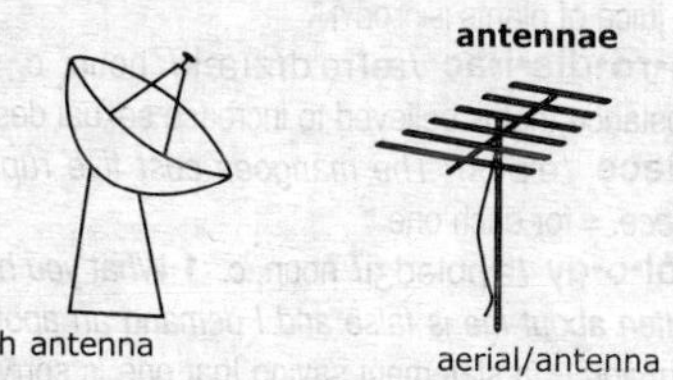

an•ter•i•or /æn'tɪəriə^r/ adj. = the front part of something [BIOLOGY] (opposite **posterior**)

an•them /'ænθəm/ noun, c. *the national anthem* = a ceremonial song of praise

an•ther /'ænθə^r/ noun, c. = the male part of a flower which contains pollen (see pic under **flower**)

an•thol•o•gy /æn'θɒlədʒi/ noun, c. = a collection of poems, stories or other writings, often on the same subject, that have been chosen from several books or writers and published together as a book [LITERATURE]

an•thrax /'ænθræks/ noun = a serious infectious disease which causes fever and death in cattle, sheep and other animals and can also attack human beings [MEDICINE]

an•thro•pol•o•gy /ænθrə'pɒlədʒi/ noun = the science which studies the human race, its origins, beliefs, customs, social organization etc. **anthro pological** /ænθrəpə'lɒdʒɪkəl/ adj. = connected with anthropology **anthropologist** /ænθrə'pɒlədʒɪst/ noun, c. = a person who has studied anthropology and made it his/her profession

anti- /æntɪ/ prefix meaning **1** opposed to e.g. **anti-aircraft** adj. *an anti-aircraft gun* = directed against an enemy aircraft **2** the opposite of e.g. **anticlockwise** adj. or adv. = in the opposite direction to the movement of the hands of a clock (see pic under **clockwise**) **3** acting to prevent from becoming worse e.g. **antiseptic** /æntɪ'septɪk/ adj. = a chemical substance which can fight against infection in a wound caused by bacteria

an•ti•bi•o•tic /æntɪbaɪ'ɒtɪk/ noun, c. = a medicinal substance produced by tiny living plants which is used to fight infections in the body caused by harmful bacteria

an•ti•bod•y /'æntɪbɒdɪ/ noun, c. = a substance produced in the body which fights disease [BIOLOGY]

an•ti•ci•pate /æn'tɪsɪpeɪt/ verb, t. **1** *I knew there was trouble at the factory. But I did not anticipate a strike.* = to think that something is likely to happen; to expect **2** *We anticipated a water shortage by carrying bottled water with us.* = to act in order to prevent something which one expects will happen **anticipation** noun

an•ti•cli•max /æntɪ'kiaɪmæks/ noun, c. *To be back at home after a week of trekking in the jungle is such an anticlimax.* = something ordinary and unexciting coming after something exciting

an•tics /'æntɪks/ noun (always plural) *Everyone laughed at his antics in the classroom.* = foolish and silly behaviour

an•ti•dote /'æntɪdəʊt/ noun, c. *an antidote for snake-bite* = a substance that fights against the effect of a poison, or prevents disease [MEDICINE]

an•ti•freeze /'æntɪfri:z/ noun, u. = a chemical substance which prevents water from freezing (turning into ice) and is therefore added to the water used to cool the engines of motor vehicles, in very cold weather

an•tip•a•thy /æn'tɪpəθi/ noun, u. or c. *My parents never allowed us to smoke. Their antipathy to smoking was well known.* = a fixed or strong dislike (formal)

an•tique[1] /æn'ti:k/ adj. *antique furniture* = made in an earlier period of time and therefore considered rare and valuable

antique[2] noun, c. *a valuable antique* = an object that is of value because it was made long ago

an•tiq•ui•ty /æn'tɪkwɪti/ noun, u. or c. **1** *a Mughal fort of great antiquity*(u.) = state of being very old **2** *The museum contains many priceless antiquities.*(c.) = things that are very old and have historical value

an•ti-so•cial /æntɪ'səʊʃəl/ adj. **1** *anti-social behaviour* = going against the rules of society and likely to harm others **2** = not wanting to be friendly

an•tith•e•sis /æn'tɪθəsɪs/ noun, c. (**antitheses**) *Love is the antithesis of hate.* = the direct opposite

ant•ler /'æntlə^r/ noun, c. = one of the two branched horns of a stag (male deer)

an•to•nym /'æntənim/ noun, c. *'Sad' is the antonym of 'happy'.* = a word that is opposite in meaning to another word (see also **synonym**)

a•nus /'eɪnəs/ noun. = the opening in the body through which solid waste matter is passed out

an•vil /'ænvɪl/ noun, c. = a heavy iron block on which metal is placed and hammered to give it a required shape

anx•i•e•ty /æŋ'zaɪəti/ noun, c. (**anxieties**) or u. **1** *We hear we may have a test any time next week. This is causing great anxiety to all of us.*(u.) = the feeling of nervousness and discomfort that one has when one thinks that something unpleasant, fearful or difficult may happen **2** *Can't you forget your anxieties and enjoy yourself?*(c.) = worries; troubles

anx•ious /'æŋkʃəs/ adj. **1** *You must be anxious to know the results.* = feeling nervous and worried **2** *He is always anxious to help people.* = wishing strongly to do something; eager

an•y /'eni/ det. or pron. **1** *Do you have any friends in this town?*(det.) **2** *I don't have any money to give you.* = some (used in questions or negative sentences) **3** *Have you read any book on this subject?*(det.) = a; one **4** *He will need any help that he can get.* = as much as possible **anyhow** adv. **1** *She had thrown her books about the room anyhow.* = carelessly **2** *He had asked me not to visit them, but I visited them anyhow.* = in spite of something **3** *Anyhow, I went to his house, and ...* = an expression used while continuing a story **anyone** pron. **1** *Anyone will be able to show you the way to my house.* = any person; all persons **2** *I don't want anyone to know this.* = any person (used in questions or negative sentences) **anything** pron. *I don't want anything from you. // Is there anything in that box?* = not a single thing (used in negative sentences and questions) **anyway** adv. **1** *He told me not to go, but I went anyway.* = in spite of **2** *Well, anyway, what happened next ...* = 'to get on with my story' **anywhere** adv. **1** *You can sit anywhere.* = in any place **2** *Did you go anywhere yesterday?* = to any place (used in questions) **3** *anywhere from 40 to 60 students* = any number or amount

a•or•ta /eɪ'ɔːtə/ noun = the largest artery (blood vessel) in the body, carrying blood from the heart to different parts of the body [BIOLOGY]

a•part /ə'pɑːt/ adv. **1** *The houses in this row are wide apart.* = separated by a distance **2** *The mechanic took the engine of my car apart.* = into separate parts **3** *Apart from you, does anyone think they can't finish the homework on time?* = other than; except for

a•part•heid /ə'paːteɪt/ noun = the political and social system that existed in South Africa for a long time and ended only in about 1990, under which black people (belonging to African races) were kept separate from white people (of European descent) and treated as inferior [TECHNICAL]

a•part•ment /ə'pɑːtmənt/ noun, c. (American) = a set of rooms in a building which includes a kitchen and a bathroom; a flat (see also **flat, house**)

ap•a•thy /'æpəθi/ noun, u. *Very few people came to vote. There was apathy to the election* = absence of feeling or interest

ape[1] /eɪp/ noun, c. = a large monkey without a tail, e.g. chimpanzee, gorilla

ape[2] verb, t. *He tries to ape your manner of speaking.* = to copy in an unsuccessful way (derogatory)

ap•er•ture /'æpətʃə^r/ noun, c. = a hole or narrow opening, especially one that allows light into a camera

a•pex /'eɪpeks/ noun, c. **1** *the apex of the pyramid* = the top or the highest point of something **2** *She is at the apex of her career as a singer.* = the highest or most successful point

a•phid /'eɪfɪd/ noun = a kind of insect that lives on the juice of plants [BIOLOGY]

aph•ro•dis•i•ac /æfrə'dɪzɪæk/ noun, c. = a substance that is believed to increase sexual desire

a•piece /ə'piːs/ *The mangoes cost five rupees apiece.* = for each one

a•pol•o•gy /ə'pɒlədʒi/ noun, c. **1** *What you have written about me is false and I demand an apology from you.* = a statement saying that one is sorry for having done something **2** *He is a good poet. But what he sent me to read was an apology for a poem.* = a poor copy or substitute **apologize** (**apologise**) verb, i. = to make or offer an apology to someone

a•pos•tle /ə'pɒsəl/ noun, c. **1** = one of the twelve followers of Jesus Christ who went from place to place telling people about him **2** *Gandhiji was an apostle of peace.* = one who believes strongly in something and wants others to share his/her belief

a•pos•tro•phe /ə'pɒstrəfi/ noun, c. **1** *You should spell 'don't' with an apostrophe after the 'n'.* = a punctuation mark, or sign, used in writing to show that a letter or numbers (e.g. '90s for 1990s) has been dropped **2** *'John's' is spelt with an apostrophe.* = the same sign, used to show possession

ap•pal /ə'pɔːl/ verb,t. (**appalled**) *We were appalled by the news of the accident.* = to shock deeply (formal)

ap•pa•ra•tus /æpə'reɪtəs/ noun, u. *special diving apparatus* = the things (instruments, tools etc.) one needs to do a particular piece of work with

ap•par•el /ə'pærəl/ noun, u. *sports apparel* = clothes or dress of a special type (formal)

ap•par•ent /ə'pærənt/ adj. **1** *It became apparent*

to us that he could not speak Hindi when he answered all our questions in English. = easily seen or understood; evident **2** *There is only an apparent improvement in the child's behaviour.* = something that seems (appears) to be true but is not true **apparently** adv. **1** *Apparently, the new hockey coach is a good teacher. Everyone seems to be happy with her.* = It seems that (but one cannot be sure) **2** *He looked at us blankly; apparently he did not recognise us.* = it is clear (that) **3** *She greeted us but didn't help us. Apparently, she was busy.* = it seems that (but one cannot be sure)

ap•peal[1] /ə'pi:l/ noun, c. or u. **1** *Relief workers have sent out an appeal for money to help the refugees.*(c.) = a strong request for help, support, money etc. **2** *Such books have no appeal for me.*(u.) = attraction **3** *I will lodge an appeal with the Supreme Court for a review of this case.*(c.) = a request made to a higher court of justice to change some decision of a lower court [LAW]

appeal[2] verb, i. **1** *Relief workers have appealed to the public for supplies.* = to make an appeal **2** *A book without pictures may not appeal to young children.* = to attract **3** *Have you appealed to the Supreme Court?* = to make an appeal on a legal matter **appealing** adj. **1** *The idea of going on a picnic tomorrow is quite appealing.* = attractive **2** *appealing eyes* = asking for pity or help **sex-appeal** noun, u. = the physical attraction that a man feels towards a woman or a woman towards a man (informal)

ap•pear /ə'pɪə/ verb, i. **1** *We did not expect to see anyone on that lonely road, but suddenly a man appeared.* = to be seen **2** *You appear to be worried about something.* = to seem **3** *You will have to appear in court tomorrow.* = to be present for some official purpose **appearance** /ə'pɪərəns/ noun, u. or c. **1** *She made an appearence when the party was about to end.*(c.) = the act of appearing, so that one is seen **2** *Your whole appearance is untidy.*(u.) = the way one looks; outward qualities

ap•pease /ə'pi:z/ verb, t. *The shopowner apologized to the angry customer to appease him.* = to try to calm or please someone by doing or saying something nice

ap•pend /ə'pend/ verb, t. *The writer appended a short note to the article she had written.* = to add something written to the end of a longer piece of writing (formal) **appendage** /ə'pendɪdʒ/ noun, u. = something that is added on to something else which is more important

ap•pen•dix /ə'pendɪks/ noun **1** = a small bag which is attached to the intestines (the tube in the body through which food passes) and which does not have a clearly known use in the human body [BIOLOGY] **2** = a part, usually at the end of a book, which gives extra information **appendicitis** /əpendɪ'saɪtɪs/ noun = a condition in which the appendix becomes infected and has to be removed through an operation [MEDICINE]

ap•pe•tite /'æpətaɪt/ noun, c. or u. *I don't want to eat now. I have no appetite.*(u.) = desire to eat

ap•pe•tiz•er (appetiser) /'æpɪtaɪzə^r/ noun, c. = something eaten or drunk before a meal in order to increase the appetite **appetizing (appetising)** adj. *an appetizing smell* = causing desire, especially for food

ap•plaud /ə'plɔ:d/ verb, t. or i. *The audience applauded when the actors appeared on the stage.*(t.) = to praise by striking one's hands together; to clap **applause** /ə'plɔ:z/ noun, u. = loud praise expressed by an audience by clapping

ap•ple /'æpəl/ noun, c. = a hard, round fruit with juicy white flesh, and red, green or yellow skin

to be the apple of somebody's eye = to be a great favourite

ap•pli•ance /ə'plaɪəns/ noun, c. *an electrical appliance* = a machine, instrument or tool (e.g. an electric heater) which is used for some purpose

ap•pli•ca•tion /æplɪ'keɪʃən/ noun, c. or u. **1** *I have sent in my application for leave to the office.*(c.) = a written request **2** *Computers have many applications.*(c.) = a practical use of something **3** *He is very intelligent, but lacks application.*(u.) = careful or continuous attention to work **4** *Your wound will heal quickly after the application of this ointment.*(u.) = the use of a medicinal substance to cover a part of the body

ap•ply /ə'plaɪ/ verb, t. or i. **1** *Have you applied for a job?*(i.) = to make a request in writing for something **2** *Can you apply this formula to solve the equation?*(t.) = to make use of something for some purpose **3** *You should apply this ointment on the wound.*(t.) = to spread or gently rub something over a part of the body **4** *This rule will not apply in your case.*(i.) = to be used in order to reach a decision **5** *You must apply yourself to your studies with greater sincerity.*(t.) = to work hard and carefully (formal) **applicable** /ə'plɪkəbəl/ adj. *This rule is applicable only to those above the age of 65.* = to have an effect for **applicant** /'æplɪkənt/ noun, c. = a person who has applied for something (e.g. a job)

ap•point /ə'pɔɪnt/ verb, t. **1** *We have appointed a new manager.* = to choose someone for a job **2** *Let us appoint a day for our next meeting.* = to fix a date or time for a meeting **appointment** noun, c. or u. **1** *Can I make an appointment to see the doctor tomorrow?*(c.) = a time or date fixed for a meeting with someone important **2** *Your appointment as head teacher has been approved.* = selection for a particular post

ap•por•tion /ə'pɔ:ʃən/ verb, t. **1** *The money from the sale of the house will be apportioned among the four owners.* = to divide and share out (specially money or blame) among several people or things (formal) **2** *Both of you cut down the tree but we find it dificult to apportion the blame.* = to say who should be blamed more and who less

ap•pre•ci•ate /ə'pri:ʃieɪt/ verb, t. or i. **1** *I am happy that you have learnt to appreciate poetry.*(t.) = to understand and enjoy something fully **2** *I really appreciate the help you gave me when I was in trouble.*(t.) = to be thankful for something **3** *This building has appreciated in value from Rs 1 to 2 million over five years.*(i.) = to increase in value over time **appreciation** /əpri:ʃi'əɪʃən/ noun, u. **1** = understanding of the good qualities or worth of something **2** *appreciation of a poem* = a discussion of the qualities of something **3** *I appreciate the point that you make, but I don't agree.* = to understand **appreciative** /ə'pri:ʃətɪv/ adj. *an appreciative audience* = showing appreciation (opposite **unappreciative**)

ap•pre•hen•sion /æprɪ'henʃən/ noun, u. *We waited for the results with a great deal of apprehension.*(u.) = anxiety; worry

ap•pre•hen•sive /æprɪ'hensɪv/ adj. *He was apprehensive that the match would be cancelled because of rain.* = anxious and nervous

ap•pren•tice[1] /ə'prentɪs/ noun, c. = a person who is learning some trade while attached to a skilled person of the same trade

apprentice[2] verb t. *I am apprenticed to a motor mechanic.* = to be working under someone as a part of one's training

ap•proach[1] /ə'prəʊtʃ/ verb, t. **1** *The road was deserted but as we approached Delhi, the traffic increased dramatically.* = to come nearer to something **2** *Did my friend approach you to ask for your opinion?* = to meet someone in order to make a request **3** *The two scientists approached the problem differently.* = to deal with a situation in a certain way

approach[2] noun, c. or u. **1** *The tiger's approach frightened the deer away.*(u.) = the act of coming nearer **2** *All approaches to the airport have been sealed off by the police.*(c.) = a road or path which leads to some place **3** *We need a new approach to the teaching of English.* = a way of doing something

ap•proa•cha•ble /ə'prəʊtʃəbəl/ adj. **1** *You will find the tutor a very approachable person.* = easy to speak to; accessible **2** *There is no road connecting the town to the lake. It is not approachable.* = able to be reached

ap•pro•pri•ate[1] /ə'preʊpriət/ adj. *You have given an appropriate answer to the question.* = suitable and correct (opposite **inappropriate**)

appropriate[2] /ə'preʊpriəɪt/ verb, t. **1** *The secretary had appropriated the club's money for his own use.* = to take something illegally or without permission (also **misappropriate**) (disapproving) **2** *The government plans to appropriate this land for a new hospital.* = to take something (usually by a legal process) and use it for a particular purpose (not disapproving)

ap•prove /ə'pru:v/ verb, i. or t. **1** *I do not approve of your eating in bed.*(i.) = to think of something as good or wise **2** *The Cabinet has approved the plan.*(t.) = to agree officially to something **approval** noun, u. *You cannot build a house on this land without the Corporation's approval.* = official permission

ap•pro•ver /ə'pru:vər/ noun, c. *One of the accused persons has turned approver.* = a person who takes part in some crime along with others but later agrees to help the police by giving evidence against the others [LAW]

ap•prox•i•mate[1] /ə'prɒksɪmɪt/ adj. *The approximate distance between Cuttack and Puri is 80 km.* = nearly correct but not exact; rough (opposite **accurate, exact**)

ap•prox•i•mate[2] /ə'prɒksɪmeɪt/ verb, t. *The cost of this new project will approximate Rs 800 crore.* = come close to

ap•ri•cot /'eɪprɪkɒt/ noun, c. = a round, soft fruit, with orange or yellow furry skin and a stone inside

A•pril /'eɪprɪl/ noun = the fourth month of the year **April Fool's Day** = the first day in April, when some people like to play tricks on others

a•pron /'eɪprən/ noun, c. **1** = a piece of clothing worn over one's clothes to keep them clean **2** = the place near the runway where planes are parked before they take off or after they land

apt /æpt/ adj. **1** *an apt reply* = suitable; appropriate **2** *This old car is apt to break down.* = likely to

ap•ti•tude /'æptɪtju:d/ noun, c. or u. *This child has an aptitude for music.*(c.) = a natural skill or ability to learn

a•quar•i•um /ə'kweəriəm/ noun, c. (**aquariums** or **aquaria**) = a glass box, or a large building filled with water and having glass windows, in which fish and/or other sea animals are kept to be seen

A•quar•i•us /ə'kweərɪəs/ noun, u. = the sign of the zodiac represented by the symbol of a person pouring water from a pot (see pic under **zodiac**)

a•quat•ic /ə'kwætɪk/ adj. *acquatic plants; acquatic*

sports = living in, or happening in or on water

Ar•ab /'ærəb/ noun, c. = a person, especially one from Northern Africa or the Arabian peninsula, whose language is Arabic **Arabic** /'ærəbɪk/ noun, u. = the language or writing of the Arabs **Arabic numeral** noun, c. = the signs used to show the numbers 1, 2, 3, in English and many other languages (see also **Roman numerals** I, II,)

ar•a•ble /'ærəbəl/ adj. = land which can be used for growing crops

ar•bi•tra•ry /'ɑːbɪtrəri/ adj. **1** *You must follow the rules. You can't act in an arbitrary manner.* = doing whatever you want without caring about rules or the feelings of others **2** *I had to choose one of the candidates, but as I knew nothing about any of them, my choice was quite arbitrary.* = not done in a systematic manner; not based on reason but personal opinion

ar•bi•trate /'ɑːbɪtreɪt/ verb, i. or t. *The committee is going to arbitrate the dispute between the employees and the management of the factory.*(t.) = to help in settling a dispute between two parties especially at their request [LAW]

arc /ɑːk/ noun, c. *The sun moves in an arc across the sky.* = a part of a circle or any curved line

ar•cade /ɑː'keɪd/ noun, c. *a shopping arcade* = a covered area or passage in which there are shops

arch- /ɑːtʃ/ prefix meaning 'the highest', or 'greatest' e.g. **archbishop** /ɑːtʃ'bɪʃəp/ noun, c. = a highly ranked Christian priest **arch enemy** /ɑːtʃ 'enəmi/ = the main enemy

arch[1] /ɑːtʃ/ noun, c. = the curved top part of a doorway, window, bridge etc.

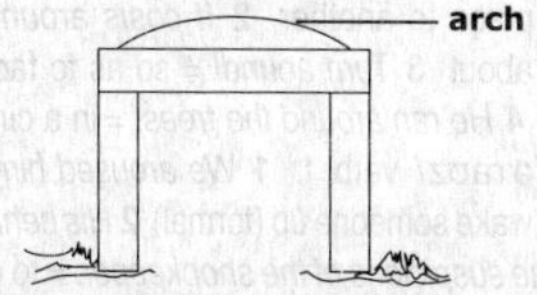

arch[2] verb, t. or i. *The rainbow arched across the sky.* = to form the shape of an arch

ar•chae•ol•o•gy (archeology) /ɑːki'ɒlədʒi/ noun = the study of the buried remains of houses, pots, tools etc. from earlier times **archaeologist (archeologist)** noun, c. = a person who practises archaeology

ar•cha•ic /ɑː'keɪ-ɪk/ adj. *a book written in archaic language* = very old and no longer in use

ar•cher /'ɑːtʃəʳ/ noun, c. = a person who shoots arrows with a bow **archery** /'ɑːtʃəri/ noun = the art or sport of shooting arrows with a bow

ar•chi•pel•a•go /ɑːkɪ'peləgəʊ/ noun, c. = a group or chain of islands stretching across the sea

ar•chi•tec•ture /'ɑːkɪtektʃəʳ/ noun, u. = the art and science of building, including designing, planning and decorating **architect** /'ɑːkɪtekt/ noun, c. = a person who designs buildings etc.

ar•chives /'ɑːkaɪvz/ noun (always plural) **1** = a place where documents (papers, records, reports, etc.) of historical importance are stored **2** = the documents which are stored in such a place

Arc•tic /'ɑːktɪk/ adj. *the Arctic zone* = related to the very cold, northernmost part of the world (see also **Antarctic**) (see pic under **earth**)

ar•dent /'ɑːdənt/ adj. *Raghu is an ardent trekker. He goes on at least four treks a year.* = eager; very strong and active

ar•dour /'ɑːdəʳ/ noun, u. *The two women spoke with great ardour about the duties of a citizen.* = strong feeling (literary) (see also **passion**)

ar•du•ous /'ɑːdjuːəs/ adj. *an ardous journey* = tiring and needing a lot of effort

are /əʳ/ verb, i. *Umesh and Naresh are brothers.* = the present tense, plural form of **be**

ar•e•a /'eəriə/ noun, c. or u. **1** = the size of a flat surface, measured by multiplying its length by its breadth (compare **volume**) **2** *There are no schools in this area.*(c.) = a part of a town or country; region **3** *He is very well read in the area of classical music.*(c.) = a subject or field of activity **area code** noun, c. = a set of numbers added before a telephone number to make a telephone call to a particular city, town etc. within a country

a•re•na /ə'riːnə/ noun, c. *a sports arena* = a closed area used for sports, entertainment etc.

ar•gu•a•ble /'ɑːgjʊəbəl/ adj. *The umpire declared the batsman out but it was an arguable decision.* = doubtful; a statement for or against which a reason or argument can be given **arguably** adv. *Delhi is arguably the most well-planned city in the country.* = something which can be stated (argued) but is not necessarily true

ar•gue /'ɑːgjuː/ verb, t. or i. **1** *Do as I tell you and don't argue.*(i.) = to use words to disagree **2** *Some of the students argued during the debate that travel should be a necessary part of education.*(i.) = to provide reasons for/against something **3** *This lawyer will argue your case in court.*(t.) = to reason strongly in support of someone (a client) in a court of law [LAW]

argument /'ɑːgjʊmənt/ noun, c. or u. **1** c. = a reason given in support of some statement **2** *You should use argument, not violence, to settle your dispute.*(u.) = the use of reason **argumentative** /ɑːgjʊ'mentətɪv/ adj. *an argumentative person* = fond of arguing and not willing to accept what others say (derogatory)

-arian suffix meaning 'one who is connected with something', e.g. *librarian, vegetarian* = one who is connected with or believes in something

ar•id /'ærɪd/ adj. *arid climate* = having so little rain as to be dry and not suitable for agriculture

Ar•ies /'eəriːz/ noun, u. = the sign of the zodiac represented by the symbol of a ram (male sheep) (see pic under **zodiac**)

ar•ise /ə'raɪz/ verb, i (**arose, arisen**) *A new problem may suddenly arise.* = to come into being; to appear

ar•is•toc•ra•cy /ærɪ'stɒkrəsi/ noun, u. or c. (**aristocracies**) = people who are thought to belong to the highest social class **aristocrat** /'ærɪstəkræt/ noun, c. = a person who belongs to the aristocracy

a•rith•me•tic /ə'rɪθmətɪk/ noun = the science of numbers **arithmetical** /ərɪθ'metɪkəl/ adj. = connected with arithmetic **arithmetic progression** noun, c. = a set of numbers (3, 5, 7, 9...) in which a fixed number must be added to each number to get the next one [MATHEMATICS]

arm[1] /ɑːm/ noun, c. **1** *She carried the paper under her arm.* = one of the two upper limbs of a human being **2** *One of the arms of the chair is broken.* = something that has the shape of a human arm **3** *an arm of the government* = a branch or department

arm[2] /ɑːm/ verb, t. or i. **1** *Our soldiers will be armed with automatic rifles.*(i.) = supplied with weapons (opposite **disarm**) **2** *The country has to arm itself for war.*(t.) = to prepare to fight **armband** /'aːmbænd/ noun, c. = a band of cloth worn around the arm (below the shoulder) to show the wearer's official position or to show that the wearer is in mourning (expressing sorrow over the death of a friend etc.) **armchair** noun, c. = a chair which has supports for the arms (see pic under **chair**)

to twist somebody's arm = to force somebody to do something **to welcome somebody with open arms** *Though she had left the school two years ago her friends welcomed her with open arms when she returned.* = to accept somebody or something happily

ar•ma•da /ɑː'mɑːdə/ noun, c. = a collection or fleet of armed ships

ar•ma•ture /'ɑːmətʃəʳ/ noun, c. = the part of a generator consisting of a piece of metal with wire wound around it, that goes round and round in order to produce electricity [TECHNICAL]

armed /ɑːməd/ adj. *an armed guard* = having or using weapons **armed forces** noun, c. (always plural) = the members of the army, navy and air force, who use weapons to protect their country

ar•mi•stice /'ɑːmɪstɪs/ noun, c. = an agreement made during a war to stop fighting, usually for some time

ar•mour /'ɑːməʳ/ noun, u. = a strong covering, usually made of steel, which protects a soldier, or a horse during fighting **armoured car** noun = a military vehicle protected by steel armour

arm•pit /'aːmpɪt/ noun, c. = the hollow space behind the arm, below the shoulder

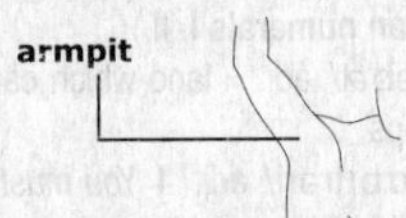

arms /ɑːmz/ noun, c. (always plural) *Many people feel public money is better spent on protecting wildlife than on arms.* = weapons **arms race** noun, c. = a competition between countries which are not friendly towards each other to produce more and better weapons

to be up in arms *The public was up in arms over the rise in the price of petrol.* = to object or protest angrily **to keep someone at arm's length** = to keep a formal or not very close friendship with someone

ar•my /'ɑːmi/ noun, c. (**armies**) = the military forces of a country, especially those trained to fight on land

a•ro•ma /ə'rəʊmə/ noun, u. *the aroma of freshly-cooked food* = a strong and pleasant smell **aromatic** /ærə'mætɪk/ adj. *aromatic spices used in cooking* = having a strong, usually pleasant smell

a•round[1] /ə'raʊnd/ prep. **1** *There is a high wall around our house* = on all sides of **2** *His clothes were lying around the house.* = in different parts of **3** *He lives somewhere around Delhi.* = in some place near

around[2] adv. **1** *Do you know your way around?* = from one place to another **2** *It costs around fifty rupees.* = about **3** *Turn aound!* = so as to face the other way **4** *He ran around the trees.* = in a circle

a•rouse /ə'raʊz/ verb, t. **1** *We aroused him from sleep.* = to wake someone up (formal) **2** *His behaviour aroused the suspicions of the shopkeeper.* = to cause something to become active **3** = to cause sexual excitement

ar•range /ə'reɪndʒ/ verb, t. or i. **1** *Please arrange these books on the table.* **2** *Arrange the names in alphabetical order.*(t.) = to put things in a desired order **3** *Let us arrange for a taxi to take us to the station.*(i.) = to plan or fix up something in advance **arrangement** /ə'reɪndʒmənt/ noun, c. or u. **1** *She is making all the arrangements for the school play.*(c.) = plans for things that are to be done **2** *a beautiful flower arrangement* = something that has been put in a pleasing order

ar•ray[1] /ə'reɪ/ noun, c. or u. **1** *A glittering array of film stars was present at the cricket match.*(c.) = a large group of people or things which attracts attention **2** *ceremonial array*(u.) = colourful or attractive clothes worn on a special occasion (old-fashioned)

array[2] verb, t. **1** *The books were neatly arrayed on shelves at the bookfair.* = to arrange neatly, so that something can attract attention **2** *The students were arrayed in robes for their graduation ceremony.* = to be dressed in fine clothes (formal)

ar•rears /ə'rɪəz/ noun (always plural) **1** *You must pay up the arrears of rent for the last three months.* = money which should have been paid but has not been paid **2** = work that is still to be done

to be in arrears = to be late in paying up money

ar•rest[1] /ə'rest/ verb, t. **1** *The police officer was able to arrest the thief in a few hours.* = to seize (catch hold of) someone using the power of the law **2** *arresting the spread of a disease* = to bring to an end; to stop

arrest[2] noun, c. or u. *to make an arrest* = the act of arresting or being arrested

ar•rive /ə'raɪv/ verb, i. **1** *We arrived in Kochi at 7.00 a.m.* = to reach a place at the end of a journey (opposite **depart**) **2** *The day of the wedding has arrived.* = to come; to happen **3** *He worked very hard, and now he has finally arrived.* = to be successful **arrival** noun, u. or c. **1** u. = the act of arriving at a place **2** *the new arrival* (c.) = a person or thing that has arrived at some place for the first time; a newly-born child

arrive at *We finally arrived at the answer.* = to reach something

ar•ro•gant /'ærəgənt/ adj. *They were so arrogant that they did not even greet us.* = proud and having no respect for others **arrogance** noun, u. = the quality of being arrogant; pride of a kind which is not liked

ar•row /'ærəʊ/ noun, c. **1** *hunting with bow and arrows* = a thin, straight stick, pointed at one end and with feathers at the other end which is fired from a bow (see pic under **quiver**) **2** = a sign like an arrow, used to show direction or the position of something

arrow-root noun, u. = the flour made from the root of a tropical plant

ar•se•nal /'ɑːsənəl/ noun, c. **1** = a government building where weapons are made or stored **2** = a stock of weapons

ar•se•nic /'ɑːsənɪk/ noun = a highly poisonous chemical substance, sometimes used for killing rats

ar•son /'ɑːsən/ noun = the crime of setting fire to a building in order to damage it or cause destruction

art /ɑːt/ noun, c. or u. **1** *Dancing is an art.*(c.) = an activity requiring skill, through which the love of beauty is expressed **2** *Art makes life beautiful.*(u.) = the expression of beauty **artist** /'ɑːtɪst/ noun, c. = a person who produces works of art (painting, music etc.) **artistic** /ɑː'tɪstɪk/ adj.= concerning or typical of art or artists **artiste** /ɑː'tiːst/ noun, c. = a professional singer, dancer, actor etc. who takes part in a show **art critic** noun, c. = a person who knows a great deal about art and writes books, articles, etc. expressing his/her views on the work of artists **art gallery** noun, c. (**galleries**) = a place where paintings are hung up on the walls so that people can look at them

ar•te•fact (artifact) /'ɑːtɪfækt/ noun, c. = any object made by human hands

ar•te•ry /'ɑːtəri/ noun, c. (**arteries**) = a blood vessel inside the body that carries blood from the heart to the different parts of the body [BIOLOGY] **arterial** /ɑː'tɪəriəl/ adj. **1** *arterial blood* = blood from an artery **2** *an arterial road* = an important road which carries a lot of traffic

art•ful /'ɑːtfəl/ adj. *He is very artful and always manages to get what he wants.* = clever; cunning (derogatory)

ar•thri•tis /ɑː'θraɪtɪs/ noun = a disease which causes pain and swelling in the joints of the body [MEDICINE]

ar•ti•cle /'ɑːtɪkəl/ noun, c. **1** *All the articles in this shop are expensive.* = objects; things **2** *Have you completed the article you were writing?* = a piece of writing on a particular subject, in a magazine or newspaper **3** *The words 'a', 'an' and 'the' are articles in English.* = a word used before a noun [GRAMMAR]

ar•tic•u•late[1] /ɑː'tɪkjʊlət/ adj. *The speaker was very articulate and presented her arguments forcefully.* = able to express oneself clearly and effectively

articulate[2] /ɑː'tɪkjʊleɪt/ verb, t. **1** *The speaker tried his best to articulate his feelings but was not very successful.* = to express one's thoughts and feelings clearly **2** *The sound 's', as in the word 'sit', is articulated with the tip of the tongue touching the back of the teeth.* = to pronounce or to produce a sound used in speech **3** *The fingers on the human hand are articulated.* = to join together in a way that allows free movement of the parts [TECHNICAL/MEDICINE]

ar•ti•fact (artefact) /'ɑːtɪfækt/ noun, c. *The National Museum in Delhi contains gold and silver ornaments and other artifacts from the Indus Valley Civilization.* = an object made by human hands which has special historical or cultural value

ar•ti•fi•cial /ɑː'tɪfɪʃəl/ adj. **1** *The room was decorated with artificial flowers made of plastic.* = a copy of something natural, produced by human beings (opposite **natural**) **2** *His behaviour is very artificial. I* *never know if he means what he says.* = false and lacking in sincerity (derogatory) **artificial insemination** noun, u. = the process of putting male seed into a female with the help of instruments, so that the female can produce a baby **artificial respiration** noun, u. = the process of forcing air into the lungs of someone who has stopped breathing by pressing on his/her chest, so that he/she can breathe again

ar•til•le•ry /ɑːˈtɪləri/ noun, u. **1** = big guns (cannon), mounted on wheels or motor vehicles **2** = the part of the army that uses tanks and big guns in battle

ar•ti•san /ɑːtɪˈzæn/ noun, c. = a person who does skilled work with his/her hands, e.g. a carpenter (compare **craftsperson**)

arts /ɑːts/ noun, c. (always plural) **1** *the fine arts* = the different branches of art (specially painting, sculpture, etc.) **2** = the study of subjects which are not considered to be a part of science e.g. history, literature; the humanities

Ar•y•an[1] /ˈeəriən/ noun = speakers of Indo-European or Indo-Iranian languages who are believed to have come into India from Central Asia about 4000 years ago

Aryan[2] adj. = related to the Aryans

as[1] /əz/ adv. *He is as old as my father* = equally; like

as[2] prep. *Kalidas became famous as a poet when he was only 18.* = in the form of

as[3] conj. **1** *She has not come to see you as she is sick.* = because **2** *I saw her as she was getting out of the bus.* = while; when

as if/as though *This report looks as if/as though it has been written in a hurry.* = to appear or to look like something

asap (ASAP) abbr. of **As Soon As Possible** = a phrase used in informal notes to remind someone that something needs to be done urgently

as•bes•tos /æsˈbestəs/ noun, u. = a kind of mineral from which building material used for the roofs of houses, and protective clothing against heat are made (considered dangerous for health)

as•cend /əˈsend/ verb, t. or i. *We ascended the stairs. // The road ascended the mountain in a series of sharp bends and curves.*(t.) = to climb; go to a higher level from a lower level (formal) (opposite **descend**)

as•cent /əˈsent/ noun, c. or u. **1** *Our ascent up the mountain was slow.* (u.) = the act of climbing **2** *Be careful, there is a steep ascent here.*(c.) = an upward slope; a way up

as•cer•tain /æsəˈteɪn/ verb, t. *The detectives are trying to ascertain who exactly was present at the house during the crime.* = to find the truth; to become sure of the facts (formal)

as•cet•ic[1] /əˈsetɪk/ noun, c. = a person who avoids all pleasures and comforts for religious reasons

ascetic[2] adj. *leading an ascetic life* = like that of an ascetic

ASCII abbr. of **American Standard Code for Information Interchange** = a coding scheme that assigns numeric values to letters, numbers, punctuation marks etc. [COMPUTERS]

as•cribe /əˈskraɪb/ verb, t. *No one knows who wrote the Mahabharata but it is generally ascribed to the sage Vyasa.* = to believe something to be the work of someone (compare **attribute**)

ASEAN abbr. of **Association of South East Asian Nations**

a•sep•tic /eɪˈseptɪk/ adj. *Every operation theatre should be aseptic.*= made clean so that no germs are present (compare **antiseptic**) [MEDICINE]

a•sex•u•al /eɪˈsekʃuəl/ adj. *Asexual reproduction takes place in many plants.* = without sexual union [TECHNICAL]

ash[1] /æʃ/ noun, u. (usually plural **ashes**) *the ashes from the fire* = the soft grey powder that remains after something has been burnt

ash[2] /æʃ/ noun, c. or u. **1** = a kind of tree that grows in cold climates **2** = the wood of the ash tree

a•shamed /əˈʃeɪmd/ adj. *I am ashamed to tell you that I lied.* = unwilling to talk or to face people because of some bad thing that one has done

ash•en /æʃən/ adj. = ash-coloured (a grey or pale colour)

ash•tray /ˈæʃtreɪ/ noun, c. = a small container in which the ash from a burning cigarette etc. can be shaken off and collected

A•sian[1] /ˈeɪʃən/ noun, c. = a person who belongs to some country in Asia

Asian[2] adj. *Asian culture* = related to Asia **Asian American** noun, c. = a person who is an American but whose ancestors belonged to Asia

a•side[1] /əˈsaɪd/ adv. *Will you please step aside and let the children pass?* = to the side

a•side[2] noun, c. *'How foolish!' the man said in an aside.* = a remark made in a low voice and not meant to be heard

ask /ɑːsk/ verb, t. or i. **1** *'Where do you live?' the man asked me.*(t.) = to request someone to give an answer **2** *Could I ask you for a glass of water?*(t.) = to request or invite **3** *When the bell rang the teacher asked the students to stop writing.* = to order

to ask for trouble *Walking at night on a lonely road is asking for trouble.* = to act in a way that will definitely lead to trouble

as•kew /əˈskjuː/ adj. *His tie was somewhat askew, so he straightened it.* = not straight (referring to a cap or tie worn by someone) (old-fashioned)

a•sleep /ə'sli:p/ adj. *The boy was fast asleep in class.* = sleeping (opposite **awake**)

as•par•a•gus /ə'spærəgəs/ noun = the stem of a kind of plant which is eaten as a vegetable

as•pect /'æspekt/ noun, c. **1** *She discussed every aspect of the problem before taking a decision.*= one way of looking at a many-sided subject or problem **2** *In the sentence 'The boy is writing', the verb 'write' is in the progressive aspect.* = the form of the verb e.g. 'is writing' or 'has written', which shows whether an action is complete or still in progress [GRAMMAR]

as•per•sion /ə'spɜ:ʃən/ noun, u. **to cast aspersions on someone** *She cast aspersions on her roommate's cooking by saying that she often had to go out and eat in a restaurant.* = something said against someone directly or indirectly (often used humorously)

as•phalt /'æsfælt/ noun, u. = a black, sticky material which becomes firm when it hardens and is used for laying the surface of roads

as•phyx•i•a /æs'fɪksiə/ noun = the state of not being able to breathe [MEDICINE] **asphyxiate** verb, t. or i. = to prevent someone from breathing or to be unable to breathe **asphyxiation** noun, u.

as•pire /ə'spaɪə/ verb, i. *He aspires to win this tournament.* = to have a strong desire or to direct one's efforts towards an important aim or goal (formal) **aspirant** /'æspɪrənt/ noun, c. = a person who has a strong desire to get something important **aspiration** /æspɪ'reɪʃən/ noun, c. or u. = a strong desire to do or get something

as•pirin /'æsprɪn/ noun = a drug that lessens pain and fever

ass /æs/ noun, c. **1** = an animal like a horse but smaller (compare **donkey, mule**) **2** = the bottom part of the body on which one sits (slang) **3** *Don't be an ass.* = a foolish person (informal)

as•sail /ə'seɪl/ verb, t. *The members of the defeated team were assailed with angry shouts from the crowd.* = to attack forcefully with actions, words or feelings **assailant** /ə'seɪlənt/ noun, c. = a person who attacks someone

as•sas•sin•ate /ə'sæsɪneɪt/ verb, t. *Mahatma Gandhi was assassinated in 1948.* = to murder an important person for political reasons (compare **murder, kill**) **assasin** noun, c. = one who murders for political reasons or for a reward **assassination** /əsæsɪ'neɪʃən/ noun, u. = the act of assassinating someone

as•sault[1] /ə'sɔ:lt/ noun, c. or u. *The army launched an assault on the enemy forces.*(c.) = a sudden and violent attack

assault[2] verb, t. *He was assaulted by a band of robbers when he was walking down a dark lane.* = to attack someone physically; to strike or hit

as•sem•ble /ə'sembəl/ verb, t. or i. **1** *Do you know how to assemble a watch?*(t.) = to put something together by joining its separate parts **2** *The children assembled in the hall for prayers.*(i.) = to come together in a group

as•sem•bly /ə'semblɪ/ noun, c. **1** *He has become a member of the state assembly.* = the group of people who make laws **2** *The new members of the club were asked to introduce themselves to the assembly.* = a group of people who have gathered together for some purpose **assembly-line** noun, c. = an arrangement of workers and machines where the work (the thing being made) is placed on a moving belt and passed on from one worker to another, with each worker doing part of the work until it is complete (e.g. a car)

as•sent[1] /ə'sent/ verb, i. *The President of India has given her assent to the new budget proposals.* = to agree in official capacity to an idea or suggestion (see also **consent**)

assent[2] noun, u. *We are waiting for the President's assent.* = the act of agreeing officially to something (opposite **dissent**)

as•sert /ə'sɜ:t/ verb, t. **1** *He asserted his opinion strongly.* = to state strongly **2** *Assert your authority!* = to act with force so as to show one's power, control, etc. **assertion** noun, c. = a strong statement or claim **assertive** adj. = a person who likes to state or defend his or her ideas strongly

as•sess /ə'ses/ verb, t. *They assessed the value of the house to be two lakh rupees.* = to calculate or judge the value, quality, cost etc. of something **assessment** noun, c. or u. = judgement; the act of assessing something **continuous assessment** noun, u. = a system of conducting tests at different times to judge student-performance throughout the year, instead of at a single final examination **internal assessment** noun, c. or u. = a system of testing in which the performance of students is judged by their own teachers and not by outsiders

as•set /'æset/ noun, c. **1** *Homi is an excellent cricketer and a great asset to his team.* = a person who is of great value **2** *All high-income tax payers have been asked to declare their assets.* = property, cash etc. which a person owns and is valuable

as•sid•u•ous /ə'sɪdjʊəs/ adj. *Scientists have been carrying out assiduous research to study the effects of this new drug.* = showing or doing hard and careful work (formal)

as•sign /ə'saɪn/ verb, t. *I have been assigned the task of taking notes from the Director's speech.* = to give; to entrust **assignment** noun, c. or u. **1** *She is* *going to South America on a special assignment.*(c.) = a duty given to someone **2** (u.) = the act of assigning something to someone

as•sim•i•late /ə'sɪmɪleɪt/ verb, t. **1** *Our neighbourhood has assimilated people from many different cultures.* = to make something a part of oneself **2** *Have you assimilated all the facts of this case?* = to learn and understand completely **3** *Food is assimilated in the stomach and the intestines.* = digested and taken into the body [BIOLOGY]

as•sist /ə'sɪst/ verb, t. or i. *A team of researchers assisted the scientist in her project.*(t.) = to help someone in doing something (formal) **assistance** noun, u. = help and support **assistant** noun, c. or adj. = one who helps someone in his/her work and is under the direction of that person

as•so•ci•ate[1] /ə'səʊʃieɪt/ verb, t. **1** *I would like to associate myself with the activities of this group.*(t.) = to join someone in doing something, as a friend or partner **2** *I always associate Agra with the Taj Mahal.*(t.) = to connect one thing with another in one's thoughts (opposite **dissociate**)

associate[2] noun, c. *He is my friend and business associate.* = a person who is a partner in some business, work etc.

associate[3] adj. *Sahana is an Associate Professor at the university.* = of almost equal rank as someone else (e.g. a Professor)

as•so•ci•a•tion /əsəʊsi'eɪʃən/ noun, c. or u. **1** *We want to form an association of animal lovers.*(c.) = an organised group of people who work together for some common purpose **2** *This house has many pleasant associations for us.*(c.) = things one connects with an object, situation etc. **3** *Her association with the university ended when she went abroad.*(u.) = relationship

as•sort•ed /ə'sɔːtɪd/ adj. *I have bought a basket of assorted fruits for you: some mangoes, apples, grapes etc.*= things of different types mixed together

as•sume /ə'sjuːm/ verb, t. or i. **1** *I assume that you are interested in this play.*(i.) = to believe something to be true, without asking for proof **2** *The President will assume office tomorrow.*(t.) = to take up a new responsibility **assumption** noun, c. or u. = something that is taken to be true, without any proof being required

as•sure /ə'ʃʊə/ verb, t. **1** *I assure you that you will be safe in this house.* = to give someone confidence and remove that person's fears, doubts etc. **2** *Hard work will assure your success in the examination.* = to make something certain; to ensure **assurance** noun, c. or u. **1** (c.) = a promise of help, support etc. to give a person confidence **2** *The new student has gained tremendous assurance in the last two months and is no longer nervous.*(u.) = confidence; belief in oneself **assured** /ə'ʃʊəd/ adj. or noun, c. *Your future in this profession is assured.* (adj.) = safe; certain to be good

as•te•risk /æ'stərɪsk/ noun, c. = a sign or symbol that looks like a star (*), used in writing and printing to draw the reader's attention to something

as•ter•oid /'æstərɔɪd/ noun, c. = one of many small minor planets (found between Mars and Jupiter)

asth•ma /'æsmə/ noun = a disease that sometimes makes breathing difficult **asthmatic** /æs'mætɪk/ adj. or noun, c. **1** *an asthmatic attack*(adj.) = caused by asthma **2** *an asthmatic*(noun, c.) = a person who suffers from asthma

as•tig•ma•tis•m /ə'stɪgmətɪzəm/ noun = a condition of the eye in which one cannot see clearly because the shape of the eyeball has changed [MEDICINE]

as•ton•ish /ə'stɒnɪʃ/ verb, t. *We did not think he would do well in the examination, but his excellent results astonished us.* = to cause great surprise **astonishing** adj. = highly surprising **astonishment** noun, u. = great surprise

as•tound /ə'staʊnd/ verb, t. *The news of your defeat in the quiz astounded me.* = to cause extreme surprise together with shock **astounding** adj. = causing extreme surprise

a•stray /ə'streɪ/ adv. **1** *It is easy to go astray in the forest.* = to lose one's way **2** *His plans went astray because of his wrong calculations.* = off the right path or way

a•stride /ə'straɪd/ prep. *He was sitting astride the horse.* = with a leg on each side

astro- /'æstrəʊ/ prefix meaning 'concerning the stars or space' e.g. **astrology** /ə'strɒlədʒi/ noun = the art of telling a person's future using calculations based on the positions of the planets **astrologer** noun, c. = a person who practises astrology **astrological** /æstrə'lɒdʒɪkəl/ adj. = connected with astrology

as•tro•naut /'æstrənɔːt/ noun, c. = a person who travels into space using a spacecraft

as•tron•o•my /ə'strɒnəmi/ noun = the scientific study of the universe and of the sun, moon, planets etc. **astronomer** noun, c. = a person who studies and practices astronomy **astronomical** /æstrə'nɒmɪkəl/ adj. **1** *an astronomical telescope* = connected with astronomy **2** = very large

as•tute /ə'stjuːt/ adj. *Ms Shukla is an astute lawyer.* = very clever and able to understand and judge what is going on; shrewd

a•sy•lum /ə'saɪləm/ noun, u. or c. **1** (u.) = protection and shelter given by one country to people of another country who have left it for political reasons **2** *a lunatic asylum*(c.) = a shelter for people who are mentally unsound (old-fashioned and now considered offensive)

at /ət/ prep. **1** *Write your name at the top of the page.* = a point in space **2** *We shall meet at 5.00 p.m.* = an exact point in time **3** *Shoot at this target.* = in the direction of **4** *I laughed at his joke.* = in answer to something **5** *Mangoes are being sold at Rs 20 a kg.* = showing rate or price **6** *She is very good at English.* = an activity that one is doing or a subject that one is studying

a•the•is•m /'eɪθiɪzəm/ noun = the belief that there is no God **atheist** /eɪθi'ɪst/ noun, c. = a person who does not believe that God exists

ath•lete /'æθli:t/ noun, c. = a person who takes part in athletics **athlete's foot** noun, u. = a disease caused by a kind of fungus which makes the skin between the toes crack

ath•let•ic /æθ'letɪk/ adj. **1** *an athletic competition* = connected with athletics **2** *He leads a very athletic life.* = physically active **athletics** noun (always plural) *High jump and discus throw are common events in athletics.* = physical exercises and sports which require speed, strength etc.

at•las /'ætləs/ noun, c. = a book containing maps

ATM abbr. of **Automated Teller Machine** noun = a machine controlled by a computer, from which a person who has a bank account can withdraw (take out) money by using a card and entering a personal identification number (PIN)

at•mo•sphere /'ætməsfɪə/ noun, c. or u. **1** = the mixture of gases which surrounds the earth and certain other planets or stars **2** *The atmosphere in this town is very tense because of the strike.*(u.) = the general feeling that a place has or produces **atmospheric** /ætməs'ferɪk/ adj. *atmospheric pressure* = connected with the earth's atmosphere

at•om /'ætəm/ noun, c. *hydrogen atom* = the smallest particle of an element that still has the same qualities and can combine with other substances **atom bomb** noun, c. = a bomb which is made to explode by splitting the atoms of a radioactive metal such as uranium or plutonium

a•tom•ic /ə'tɒmɪk/ adj. *an atomic explosion* = connected with atoms **atomic energy** noun, u. = the power or energy produced by splitting an atom which can then be used to produce electricity etc. (see also **nuclear energy**)

a•tone /ə'təʊn/ verb, i. *He tried to atone for his rudeness by sending her flowers.* = to show that one is sorry for having done something wrong by doing a good deed as a kind of repayment or self-punishment (formal)

a•troc•i•ty /ə'trɒsɪti/ noun, c. (**atrocities**) **1** *History tells us of many atrocities committed against people, especially in wars.* = an act of extreme cruelty **2** *The new film is so bad that I can only describe it as an atrocity.* = something that is so bad that it cannot be tolerated **atrocious** /ə'trəʊʃəs/ adj. **1** = extremely cruel **2** *The food in this restaurant is atrocious.* = shockingly bad

at•ro•phy[1] /'ætrəfi/ verb, i. (**atrophied**) *The muscles of his legs have atrophied and he cannot walk.* = to become weak and unfit for use especially through lack of blood or lack of use

atrophy[2] noun, u. = the condition of a part of the body becoming unfit for use through lack of blood or use [MEDICINE]

at•tach /ə'tætʃ/ verb, t. **1** *I have attached my photograph to the application.* = to fix or connect (join) two things together **2** *If you don't pay back the money you have borrowed from the bank, your house will be attached.* = to seize or take possession of someone's property as payment for an unpaid debt **attached** *We are very attached to our dog.* = fond of someone or something in such a way that one does not want to leave them or make them unhappy **attachment** /ə'tætʃmənt/ noun, c. or u. **1** *This mixer has an attachment which can be used for making bread.*(c.) = a part of a machine which can be attached to it when required **2** *I have great attachment to the town where I was born.*(u.) = love of or fondness for something

attache (case) /ə'tæʃeɪ/ noun, c. = a small box or case with a handle, used for carrying papers

at•tack[1] /ə'tæk/ verb, t. **1** *The wounded tiger attacked the hunter.* = to use violence against someone **2** *The newspaper article attacked the government's economic plan.* = to write or speak strongly against someone or something **3** *A new disease has attacked the people in this area.* = to cause harm or damage **4** *He attacked the task given to him with great determination.* = to begin a piece of work with great spirit

attack[2] noun, c. **1** *We were able to push back the enemy attack.* = an act of violence **2** *The speaker made a severe attack on the industries that pollute the environment.* = strong criticism **3** *My wife had an attack of asthma last night.* = a sudden and usually short period of illness

at•tain /ə'teɪn/ verb, t. *Buddha went to the forest and meditated for many years so that he could attain wisdom.* = to gain or reach something after a long effort (formal) **attainment** noun, u. or c. **1** (u.) = the act of attaining (getting) something **2** *Your attainments as a writer will always be remembered.*(c.) = something great or important that one has been able to do; achievement

at•tempt[1] /ə'tempt/ verb, t. *I did not have time to attempt all the questions in the examination.* = to try to do something

attempt[2] noun, c. *He climbed the mountain at the second attempt.* = an effort made to do something

at•tend /ə'tend/ verb, t. or i. **1** *Did you attend the lecture yesterday?*(t.) = to be present at; to go to **2** *Why aren't you attending to my words?*(i.) = to pay attention to **3** *Who is attending to this patient?*(t.) = to look after **attendance** noun, u. **1** = the act of attending (going to) classes etc. **2** = the number of people present (at a meeting etc.) **attendant** noun, c. = one whose duty is to look after someone

at•ten•tion /ə'tenʃən/ noun, u. **1** *Pay attention to my lecture.* = the act of keeping the mind fixed on something **2** *This sick child needs a lot of attention.* = care **3** *Your bad behaviour has been brought to my attention.* = notice **4** *The soldiers are standing at attention.* = in a straight and stiff position [MILITARY] **attentive** adj. = paying great attention

at•test /ə'test/ verb, t. *Ask a government officer to attest your signature on this application form.* = to declare that something is true or genuine [LAW]

at•tic /'ætɪk/ noun, c. = a room just below the roof of a building, in which things can be stored (compare **loft**)

at•tire[1] /ə'taɪər/ noun, u. *dressed in ceremonial attire* = clothes (formal, old-fashioned)

attire[2] verb, t. *attired in ceremonial dress* = to put on clothes (formal, old-fashioned)

at•ti•tude /'ætɪtju:d/ noun, c. *Your attitude towards the people of this village is negative.* = how one feels about someone or something

at•tor•ney /ə'tɜ:ni/ noun, c. (American) = a lawyer **attorney general** noun, c. = the chief lawyer who works for the government (see also **lawyer**)

at•tract /ə'trækt/ verb, t. **1** *The child's beautiful smile attracted us.* = to cause admiration or a feeling of love etc. **2** *This magnet attracts iron.* = to draw or pull towards itself **attraction** noun, u. or c. **1** (u.) = the power to attract someone **2** *What are the main attractions in this city?*(c.) = places or objects which people want to visit or see **attractive** adj. *an attractive smile* = someone or something which attracts

at•tri•bute[1] /'ætrɪbju:t/ noun, c. *One of her many attributes is intelligence.* = a good quality

attribute[2] /ə'trɪbju:t/ verb, t. **1** *I attribute my success to hard work.* = to believe that something is the result of some action **2** *This play is generally attributed to Shakespeare, although no one is sure if he actually wrote it.* = to believe that a piece of work (writing etc.) has been done by someone

at•tune /ə'tju:n/ verb, t. (**to be attuned to something**) *He sleeps all day and works all night, but I am not attuned to his style of working.* = to be used to something

a•typ•i•cal /eɪ'tɪpɪkəl/ adj. *Most people are happy when they are praised, but she becomes angry. This is very atypical behaviour.* = not common or usual; not typical [SCIENCE]

au•ber•gine /'əʊbəʒi:n/ noun = a kind of vegetable, also known as egg-plant or brinjal (in India)

auc•tion[1] /'ɔ:kʃən/ noun, c. *I bought this old table at an auction for only Rs 30.* = a meeting where things are sold to the person who offers the highest price

auction[2] verb, t. *The bank is going to auction this property.* = to sell something through an auction

au•da•cious /ɔ:'deɪʃəs/ adj. **1** *He made an audacious attempt to climb Mount Everest without the help of oxygen.* = very brave but full of risk **2** *How can you ask such a bold question? You are very audacious!* = rude and disrespectful (disapproving) **audacity** /ɔ:'dæsɪtɪ/ noun, c. = the quality of being audacious (both meanings)

au•di•ble /'ɔ:dɪbəl/ adj. = something that can be heard (opposite **inaudible**)

au•di•ence /'ɔ:diəns/ noun, c. *A large audience turned up for the show.* = the people who listen to or watch a performance, e.g. a musical programme, drama, film show etc.

au•di•o- /'ɔ:diəʊ/ prefix meaning 'connected with sound' e.g. **audiovisual** /ɔ:diəʊ'vɪʒuəl/ adj. = something that can be seen as well as heard (e.g. a television programme)

au•dit[1] /'ɔ:dɪt/ verb, t. *I have to audit the office accounts.* = to make an official examination of the accounts of a company etc.

audit[2] noun, c. *We are going through an audit.* = an examination of accounts **auditor** noun, c. = a person whose job it is to carry out an audit

au•di•to•ri•um /ɔ:dɪ'tɔ:riəm/ noun, c. = a large room or hall where people can sit and listen to or watch a performance

au•di•to•ry /'ɔ:dɪtəri/ adj. *auditory nerve* = connected with hearing or with the ears

aug•ment /ɔ:g'ment/ verb, t. *The teacher augmented the students' knowledge by making them do interesting projects.* = to cause something to increase or become more complete by adding something to it (formal)

Au•gust /'ɔ:gəst/ noun, c. = the eighth month of the year

aunt /ɑ:nt/ noun, c. = the sister of one's father or mother or the wife of one's uncle

au•ra /'ɔ:rə/ noun, c. *An aura of sadness hung around the old, ruined house.* = an effect or feeling that surrounds a place or a person

au•ral /'ɔ:rəl/ adj. *You need some aural practice.* = of or received through hearing (see also **oral**)

au•ri•cle /'ɔ:rɪkəl/ noun, c. *the left auricle of the heart* = one of the two hollow spaces at the top part of the heart which receives blood from the various parts of the body (see also **ventricle**) [BIOLOGY]

aus•pic•es /'ɔ:spɪsɪz/ noun (always plural) *This meeting is being held under the auspices of the Red Cross Society of India.* = with the help, support and favour of (formal)

Australian /ɒstreɪliən/ noun, c. = a person who belongs to Australia

aus•ter•i•ty /ɔ:'sterɪti/ adj. *The company has adopted austerity measures to save money. No one is allowed to travel by air now.* = the practice of not using luxurious things or spending money freely

au•then•tic /ɔ:'θentɪk/ adj. *This is an authentic Rabindranath Tagore painting.* = genuine; real, not false

au•thor[1] /'ɔ:θə^r/ noun, c. = the writer of a book, article, story etc.

author[2] verb, t. *Who has authored this book?* = to write (formal)

au•thor•i•ty /ɔ:'θɒrɪti/ noun, c. or u. **1** *The school authorities have decided to change the textbooks.*(c.) = a person or group that has the power to control something **2** *By whose authority have you entered this building?*(u.) = the power to control or command **3** *She is an authority on stamps.*(c.) = a person who knows a great deal about some subject and whose views are treated with respect **authoritative** /ɔ:'θɒrɪtətɪv/ adj. *an authoritative map of Delhi* = something which provides information that can be trusted **authoritarian** /ɔ:θɒrɪ'teəriən/ adj. *He is very authoritarian in the way he deals with his children.* = a person who wants everyone to obey him/her (often disapproving)

au•thor•ize (authorise) /'ɔ:θəraɪz/ verb, t. *I have authorized my mother to receive the parcel on my behalf.* = to give formal permission to someone for a purpose **authorization (authorisation)** /ɔ:θəraɪ'zeɪʃən/ noun, u. *a letter of authorization* = a paper which shows that someone has been authorized to do something

au•to- /ɔ:təʊ/ prefix meaning 'self' e.g. **autobiography** /ɔ:təbaɪ'ɒgrəfi/ noun, c. = an account of one's own life written by oneself

au•toc•ra•cy /ɔ:'tɒkrəsɪ/ noun **1** = government by a ruler who has unlimited power **2** = a country that is ruled in this way

au•to•crat /'ɔ:təkræt/ noun, c. = a ruler with unlimited power

au•to•graph /'ɔ:təgrɑ:f/ noun, c. = the name of a famous person, signed by the person himself/herself at the request of an admirer

au•to•mat•ic /ɔ:tə'mætɪk/ adj. *an automatic watch* = a machine that works by itself **automation** /ɔ:tə'meɪʃən/ noun, u. = the use of machines which do not require human beings to make them work

au•to•mo•bile /'ɔ:təməbi:l/ noun, c. = a vehicle which has an engine or motor and can run on its own power; a motor car (see **car**)

au•ton•o•my /ɔ:'tɒnəmi/ noun, u. *The university has complete autonomy.* = the right or power to control its own working (to manage one's own affairs) without interference from anyone else **autonomous** adj. = someone or something which has autonomy

au•top•sy /'ɔ:tɒpsɪ/ noun, c.(**autopsies**) = the examination of a dead-body carried out to discover the cause of death [LAW/MEDICINE] (see also **post-mortem**)

au•tumn /'ɔ:təm/ noun, c. = the season that comes between summer and winter

aux•il•ia•ry /ɔ:g'ziljəri/ adj. *The nursing department is an auxiliary wing of the hospital.* = something that gives support **auxiliary verb** noun, c. *In the sentence 'I can help you', 'can' is an auxiliary verb* = a helping verb that supports the main verb [GRAMMAR]

a•vail /ə'veɪl/ verb, t. (+self) *I would like to avail myself of this opportunity to improve my English.* = to make good use of something (very formal, old-fashioned)

to little/no avail *We searched for his house all night, but to no avail.* = without succeeding

a•vai•la•ble /ə'veɪləbəl/ adj. *You can't have mangoes now. They are available only during the summer.* = can be got or bought

av•a•lanche /'ævəlɔ:ntʃ/ noun, c. = a large mass of snow and ice which crashes down the side of a mountain

av•ant garde[1] /ævɑ:ŋ'gɑ:rd/ noun, u. (used with either plural or singular foms of verbs) (French) *Paris has been the traditional home of the artistic avant garde.* = the group of writers, musicians, artists etc. whose work presents the latest and most original ideas and styles

avant garde[2] adj. *avant garde cinema* = containing the latest ideas and styles

av•a•rice /'ævərɪs/ noun, u. = extreme desire to become rich; greed

a•venge /ə'vendʒ/ verb, t. *He swore to avenge the*

murder of his friend. = to punish someone for some harm that has been done to oneself; to take revenge (literary)

av•e•nue /'ævənju:/ noun, c. = a straight, wide road, often with trees growing on both sides, especially one that leads to a house

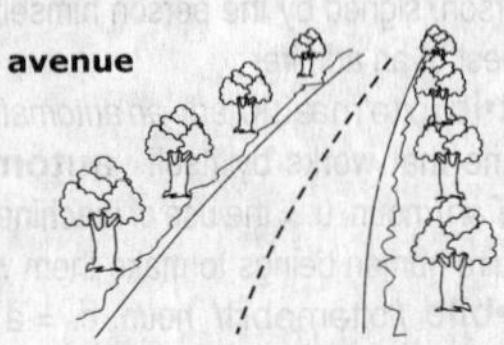

av•e•rage[1] /'ævərɪdʒ/ noun, c. *The average of 3, 5 and 13 is 7.* = the number that one gets by adding two or more numbers or figures and then dividing the total by the number of figures added

average[2] adj. **1** *The average age of the children in this class is eight years, although some children are much older and some much younger.* = the number that one gets by calculating the average **2** *This is very average performance. You could have done much better.* = of a poor standard

a•verse /ə'vɜ:s/ adj. *I am averse to the idea of making children study for long hours.* = disliking or opposed to something (formal)

a•ver•sion /ə'vɜ:ʃən/ noun, c. *I have an aversion to tobacco.* = a strong dislike or hatred for

a•vert /ə'vɜ:t/ verb, t. *My car almost hit a scooter, but I averted an accident by applying the brakes.* = to prevent something bad from happening; to avoid

a•vi•a•ry /'eɪviəri/ noun, c. = a large, closed space for keeping birds

a•vi•a•tion /eɪvi'eɪʃən/ noun *I am taking lessons in aviation in order to become a pilot.* = the science or practice of flying an aircraft

av•id /'ævɪd/ adj. *He is an avid reader of Shakespeare.* = extremely eager or interested

av•o•ca•do /ævə'kɑ:dəʊ/ noun = a kind of tropical fruit with a thick green or purple skin, soft yellow green flesh and a large stone inside

a•void /ə'vɔɪd/ verb, t. **1** *The driver of the car tried to avoid a truck but he hit a tree.* **2** *You should avoid the mid-day sun.* = to miss or keep away from

a•wake[1] /ə'weɪk/ verb, t. or i. (**awoke, awoken**) *I awoke when the alarm clock rang.*= to come out of sleep

awake[2] adj. *If you are awake, why don't you talk to me?* = not sleeping **awaken** verb, t. **1** *The child awakened to the sound of the bell.* = to cause someone who has been sleeping to become awake **2** *Most people have now been awakened to the danger of AIDS.* = to cause someone to understand something (figurative)

a•ward[1] /ə'wɔ:d/ verb, t. *The school awarded her the first prize.* = to give a prize to

award[2] noun, c. *I have received an award of Rs 5,000.* = prize or reward

a•ware /ə'weəʳ/ adj. *Are you aware of the rules for the competition?* = to have knowledge and understanding of something **awareness** noun, u. = the state of being aware of something

a•way /ə'weɪ/ adv. **1** *We are leaving this town and going away.* = from one place to another **2** *Kolkata is still 20 km away.* = at a distance of **3** *Our house was washed away in the flood.* = out of existence **4** *He put the camera away.* = in a safe place

to do away with *The college is going to do away with the second computer lab.* = to get rid off

awe /ɔ:/ noun, u. *He lives in awe of his father.* = fear mixed with respect and wonder **awe-inspiring** adj. *The Himalayan mountains are truly awe-inspiring.* = causing a feeling of awe

aw•ful /'ɔ:fəl/ adj. **1** *There is an awful smell coming from the drain.* = very bad and unpleasant; terrible (derogatory) **2** *I have an awful lot of work to do.* = very great (informal, not derogatory) **awfully** adv. *It's awfully hot!* = very (informal)

awk•ward /'ɔ:kwəd/ adj. **1** *He has a very awkward walk.* = lacking skill and beauty; clumsy **2** *There was an awkward silence in the room when we walked in.* = uncomfortable, embarassing

axe[1] /æks/ noun, c. = a tool which has a heavy metal blade on the end of a long wooden handle, used for cutting trees down

axe[2] verb, t. *As the company has no money to pay the workers, 300 jobs are going to be axed.* = to be removed or taken away (informal)

ax•i•om /'æksiəm/ noun, c. = a rule or principle that is acepted as true without questioning [MATHEMATICS] **axiomatic** /æksiə'mætɪk/ adj. = something that does not need proof; self-evident

ax•is /'æksɪs/ noun, c. (**axes**) *The earth rotates on its own axis.* = the imaginary line through the centre of a body around which the spinning body moves (see pic under **earth**)

ax•le /'æksəl/ noun, c. = the bar or rod connecting the two wheels of a cart or carriage, on which the wheels turn

aye /aɪ/ noun, c. or u. *I'll say aye to that!* = yes (old-fashioned or humorous) **ayes** noun (always plural) *The ayes have it.* = the members (of parliament etc.) voting in favour of something (opposite **nays**)

a•zure /æʒəʳ/ adj. = bright blue in colour, like the sky (literary)

bB

b, B /biː/ the second letter in the English alphabet
b. abbr. of **born in the year** (*Seema Gurung, b.1947*)
B.A. abbr. of **Bachelor of Arts** = a first university degree in Arts
bab•ble[1] /ˈbæbəl/ verb, i. or t. *The man babbled in his sleep but we could not understand what he was saying.* = to talk in a way that is hard to understand, specially while sleeping (sometimes not respectful)
babble[2] noun, c. *I heard a babble of voices from the other room.*= the confused sound of many people speaking at the same time
ba•boon /bəˈbuːn/ noun, c. = a large monkey with a face like a dog's, found in Africa or South Asia
ba•by[1] /ˈbeɪbɪ/ noun, c. (**babies**) or adj. = a very young child or animal
baby[2] verb, t. *Don't baby your children. They are old enough to look after themselves.* = to treat someone like a baby and give too much protection **baby-sit** verb, i. = to do the work of a baby-sitter **baby-sitter** noun, c. = a person who is paid to look after babies or children while their parents are away **baby-talk** noun **1** = the sounds produced by a baby when it is learning to talk **2** = the kind of language a grown-up person sometimes uses when talking to a baby
bach•e•lor /ˈbætʃələʳ/ noun, c. **1** = an unmarried person, usually a man **2** = a person who has a Bachelor's degree (BA, BSc etc.)
ba•cil•lus /bəˈsɪləs/ noun, c. (**bacilli**) = any of several forms of bacteria which can cause disease **bacillary** /ˈbæsɪləri/ adj. *bacillary dysentery* = caused by a bacillus
back[1] /bæk/ noun, c. = the part of the body which is opposite the chest, from the neck to the spine
back[2] adj. *My friend likes to sit in the back row in class.*= the part that is opposite the front
back[3] verb, t. or i. **1** *Scientists are suggesting different methods of saving water, but we will back anyone who can offer us a cheap and simple method.*(t.) = to support or help, specially with money **2** *The car was backing slowly.*(i.) = to move backwards
back[4] adv. *The show was cancelled so I came back home.* = in or to the place where one was before **backing** noun, u. *We cannot manage this school without the backing of parents.* = support **back to back** = people standing or sitting facing opposite directions, with the backs touching or close **back to front** = wearing a garment in such a way that the front part is at the back **to have at the back of one's mind** = to be thinking about something while also thinking about something else that is more important **to do something behind someone's back** *They spoke about her poor performance behind her back.* = to speak or do something against someone without letting that person know (disapproving) **to know something like the back of one's hand** *He has been to Mysore so many times that he knows it like the back of his hand.* = to know something very well **to take a back seat** *She no longer wants to manage the company. She is happy to take a back seat.* = to allow somebody else to play a more important role than oneself (informal) **to back down** *You have fought for human rights for so long, don't back down now.* = to give up supporting a cause **to back out** = to decide not to do something **to back (up) someone or something** **1** *I am going to state my opinion. Will you back me up?* = to support or show that something is true **2** *Careful! The bus is backing up into the bay.* = to move backwards **3** = to make a copy of a computer programme or file in case the original is affected [COMPUTERS]
back-biting /ˈbækbaɪtɪŋ/ noun, u. *If you have something to say against me, why don't you say it when I am present? I don't like your habit of back-biting.* = talking against someone when that person is absent
back•bone /ˈbækbəʊn/ noun, c. **1** = the spine or the set of bones in the middle of the back **2** *a person with backbone* = strength of mind or character (figurative)
back•fire /ˈbækfˈaɪər/ verb, i. *His plan to make money in the stock market backfired and he lost all the money he had.* = to have an effect opposite to that which was planned or intended
back•ground /ˈbækgraʊnd/ noun u. or c. **1** *This is a photograph of my wife. You can see our house in the background.*(u.) = the scenery or some object which is behind the main object in a photograph, painting etc. **2** *Tell us about your background.*(c.) = the things which help to make a person who he/she is e.g. family, education, experience etc. **3** *Although he is very wellknown, he likes to remain in the background.*(u.) = a position in which one is not easily seen or noticed by others
back•lash /ˈbæklæʃ/ noun, c. *The government's efforts to set up more industries here may produce a backlash among the farmers.* = a strong reaction against something that is being done or planned
back•log /ˈbæklɒg/ noun, c. *As our factory was closed for six months there is a huge backlog of orders.* = work that should have been done earlier but has not been done
back•wa•ter /ˈbækwɔːtər/ noun, c. **1** = (also plural) a lagoon (lake) which is connected to the sea **2** (also

plural) *Nothing ever happens in this small town. It is just a backwater.* = an out-of-the way place, not affected by new ideas (derogatory)

back•yard /bæk'jɑːd/ noun, c. = an open space at the back of a house, used for drying clothes etc.

bac•te•ri•a /bæk'tɪəriə/ noun, c. (plural of **bacterium**) = tiny living creatures which cannot be seen by the human eye, some of which can cause disease **bacterial** adj. = connected to or caused by bacteria **bacteriology** /bæktɪəri'ɒlədʒi/ noun = the scientific study of bacteria and the diseases caused by them

bad /bæd/ adj. **1** *a bad person* = not good **2** *a bad smell* = not pleasant **3** *a bad cold* = serious **4** *a bad heart* = unhealthy **bad blood** noun *There is bad blood between our families.* = relations which are not friendly **bad debt** noun = money which someone has borrowed and will not be able to pay back

too bad *It's too bad you missed the show.*= unfortunate (informal) **not bad** *'What was the show like?' 'Not bad.'* = quite good (informal) **to go bad** = to become rotten, to be spoilt

badge /bædʒ/ noun, c. *a police officer's badge* = a piece of metal, silk etc. worn to show a person's rank, membership etc.

bad•ger /'bædʒər/ verb, t. *We badgered our uncle to take us to the film, and in the end he agreed.* = to ask for something in a manner which is likely to cause annoyance (informal)

baf•fle /'bæfəl/ verb, t. *The question was so unexpected that I was baffled and could not answer.* = to confuse or puzzle someone so that one does not know what to do or say

bag[1] /bæg/ noun, c. **1** *a shopping bag* = a container made of cloth, leather etc. **2** *a bag of potato chips* = the amount contained in a bag

bag[2] verb, t. **1** *Has the rice been bagged?* = to put or store something in a bag **2** *We went hunting and I bagged two rabbits.* = to catch or shoot an animal while hunting **3** *He bagged the last two wickets.* = to do something outstanding in a sports competition or match (informal) **baggy** adj. *baggy trousers* = very loose-fitting

bag•gage /'bægɪdʒ/ noun, u. (always singular) = the bags, suitcases etc. that one uses to carry clothes etc. while travelling (also **luggage**)

bail[1] /beɪl/ noun, u. or c. **1** *The prisoner was released on bail.*(u.) = money deposited on behalf of a prisoner, under the order of a court, as a condition for being allowed to go out of jail until the day he/she has to appear in court **2** (c.) = either of two small pieces of wood placed on top of the stumps in the game of cricket

bail[2] verb, t. *I have come to bail you out.* = to deposit money with the court so that a prisoner can be allowed to leave

to bail out *We had no money to pay off our debts, but he bailed us out by lending us Rs 10,000.* = to help someone out of a difficult situation, especially by providing money

bait[1] /beɪt/ noun, u. or c. **1** = food used to attract and catch fish or other animals **2** *Free gifts are often used as bait to attract customers.* = something that is used to persuade or attract

bait[2] verb, t. **1** *to bait a fish-hook* = to set a bait (often a worm or small fish) on the end of fish-hook, so that some fish might try to eat it and get hooked (caught) **2** *He didn't agree at first to work for us, but we baited him by offering a good salary.* = to tempt or attract someone by offering something as a bait (informal, figurative) **3** *Please let us stop baiting her. She is getting very angry.* = to say things with the intention of making someone angry (informal, figurative)

bake /beɪk/ verb, t. *to bake a cake* = to cook food in an oven, using dry heat **baker** noun, c. = a person who bakes and sells bread, cakes etc. **bakery** noun, c. (**bakeries**) = a shop where bread, cakes, biscuits etc. are baked and sold

bal•ance[1] /'bæləns/ noun, c. or u. **1** = an instrument used for weighing things **2** *He did not see the last step and lost his balance and fell.*(u.) = the state of remaining steady (not falling) **3** *My mother gave me Rs 50. I spent Rs 20 and returned the balance to her.*(u.) = something which is left over (formal) **4** *I called the bank to ask what my balance was.* = the money in someone's account in a bank at any given time

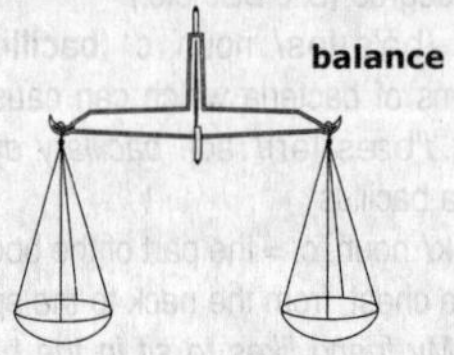
balance

balance[2] verb, t. *The dog in the circus can balance a ball on its nose.* = to keep something steady

to keep one's balance = to remain calm without giving way to some strong feeling **to have a balanced view** = to accept that there may be truths on both sides in a conflict

bal•co•ny /'bælkəni/ noun, c. (**balconies**) = an open space projecting from a building, where people can stand or sit

bald /bɔːld/ adj. **1** = having no hair on the head **2** *a bald statement* = plain and without any additions, sometimes so plain as to be harsh

bale[1] /bəil/ noun, c. *a bale of cotton* = a quantity of something (e.g. cotton, straw) tied tightly into a bundle

B

bale[2] verb, t. = to remove water from a boat by hand **to bale out** verb *The pilot managed to bale out before the aircraft crashed.* = to escape from an aircraft with the help of a parachute

ball /bɔːl/ noun, c. **1** = a round object used for playing some games **2** = a social occasion when men and women dance together **ball bearing** noun = a ball made of hard steel which is put between moving parts to make a machine work smoothly **ball pen** noun, c. = a pen which has a small ball at one end through which the ink passes as the pen writes

to be on the ball *It's good to work with her. She's really on the ball.* = full of energy and taking action quickly (informal, approving) **to have a ball** = to enjoy oneself (informal) **to set the ball rolling** = to start an activity that involves many people **to have the ball in one's court** *We've discussed the matter and the ball is in your court now.* = to be in a position to decide and take the next step in a plan of action, usually involving two persons or groups (informal)

bal•lad /'bæləd/ noun, c. = a simple story in the form of a poem or song

bal•last /'bæləst/ noun, u. = heavy material carried in a ship to keep it steady while at sea

bal•let /'bæleɪ/ noun, c. = a kind of dance with music which tells a story **ballerina** /bælə'riːnə/ noun, c. = a female ballet dancer

bal•loon[1] /bə'luːn/ noun, c. = a small bag made of strong, light material which is filled with air and used as a toy

balloon[2] verb, i. **1** *Her face ballooned when a wasp stung her on the cheek.* = to swell up and grow round like a balloon **2** *We had better go slow on the expenditure. The costs are ballooning.* = to grow in a way that causes alarm

bal•lot /'bælət/ noun, u. *Voting in the election will be through secret ballot.* = a system of secret voting in which voters indicate on a piece of paper (ballot paper) who they are voting for and drop the paper into a box (ballot box)

balm /bɑːm/ noun, u. = an oily liquid with a strong but pleasent smell which is rubbed into the body to draw out pain

bam•boo[1] /bæm'buː/ noun, u. or c. = a tall, thin but hard plant belonging to the grass family

bamboo[2] adj. *a bamboo screen* = something made of bamboo

bam•boo•zle /bæm'buːzəl/ verb, t. *I was bamboozled into buying a ticket for a film I did not want to see.* = to trick or cheat in a small, often harmless way (informal)

ban[1] /bæn/ verb, t. (**banned**) *The government has banned the sale of cigarettes to children.* = to prevent or stop something by an order

ban[2] noun, c. *There is a ban on smoking in cinema houses.* = an order banning something

ba•nal /bə'nɑːl/ adj. *The dialogues and songs in the film are so banal that one gets bored.* = uninteresting and dull; of poor quality

ba•na•na /bə'nɑːnə/ noun, c. = a long, curved fruit with a yellow skin and soft white flesh **banana republic** noun = a small country which depends very much on agriculture, has no industries and has a weak and corrupt government (derogatory)

band[1] /bænd/ noun, c. **1** *a rubber band* = a thin, narrow ring of rubber or elastic material used to hold things together **2** *The snake was black, with yellow bands.* = a coloured line or ring that stands out against a background of a different colour **3** *a band of thieves* = a group of people who work together for some common purpose **4** *a musical band* = a group of musicians who play together but on different instruments

band[2] verb, i. *People with the same interests usually band together.* = to form a band or group **band-master** noun, c. = the chief musician in a musical band

ban•dage[1] /'bændɪdʒ/ noun, c. = a long and narrow piece of cloth or other material used to cover a wound in order to protect it

bandage[2] verb, t. = to cover with a bandage

ban•dit /'bændɪt/ noun, c. = a member of an armed group of robbers who attack travellers

bane /beɪn/ noun, c. *Drinking is the bane of his life.* = something that causes continual trouble or harm; curse

bang[1] /bæŋ/ noun, c. **1** *I heard the bang of a gun.* = a sudden, loud sound **2** *Walk carefully on the slippery floor or you might fall and get a bang on your nose.* = a blow

bang[2] verb, t. **1** *She banged the door shut.* = to push something with force, making a loud noise **2** *He banged the car into a tree.* = to strike or hit something with force

to be bang on *Her answer to my question was bang on.* = exactly correct (informal) **to go off with a bang** **1** *The gun went off with a bang.* = to make a loud sound **2** *The meeting went off with a bang.* = to be very successful (informal) **to be bang opposite** adj. *Our school is bang opposite the hospital.* = exactly opposite (informal)

ban•gle /'bæŋgəl/ noun, c. = a band made of glass, metal, etc. worn around the wrist

ban•ish /'bænɪʃ/ verb, t. *The film is about traitors who are banished from their country and never allowed to return.* = to punish someone for political reasons by sending him/her out of the country for ever

bank[1] /bæŋk/ noun, c. **1** *the State Bank* = a place where money is kept and paid out on demand **2** *the* *bank of the river* = land along the side of a river **3** *a blood bank* = a store of something to be used later **4** *The plane went into a sharp bank before it climbed.* = a sharp turn

bank² verb, t. or i. **1** *Please bank this money for me.*(t.) = to put money in a bank **2** *I know I can bank on you. You will never let me down.*(i.) = to depend on **3** *The aircraft banked sharply and turned around.*(i.) = (referring to an aircraft) to make a sharp turn, so that one wing is lower than the other [TECHNICAL] **bank account** noun = an arrangement made with a bank for keeping money in the bank or taking it out when required **bank-balance** noun = the amount of money that one has in one's bank account at any given time **bank-rate** noun = the rate of interest which a bank pays a customer

bank•rupt /ˈbæŋkrʌpt/ adj. *He is completely bankrupt and cannot pay back the money he borrowed from you.* = having no money at all

ban•ner /ˈbænəʳ/ noun, c. **1** = flag **2** = a long piece of cloth on which a sign is painted, usually carried between two poles **banner headlines** noun, c. (generally plural) = news printed in very large letters at the top of a page in a newspaper, so that it can easily attract attention

ban•quet /ˈbæŋkwɪt/ noun, c. = a formal dinner for many people given to honour some important person, where speeches are made

ban•tam /ˈbæntəm/ noun, c. **1** = a kind of chicken of very small size **2** = a person who is very small in size (derogatory)

ban•ter /ˈbæntəʳ/ noun, u. *I thought the group was having a serious discussion but it was actually a lot of banter.* = friendly comments and jokes

ban•yan /ˈbænjən/ noun, c. = a large tree found in India, the branches of which grow downwards and form new roots

bap•tize (baptise) /bæpˈtaɪz/ verb, t. = to perform a religious ceremony by which someone joins the Christian religion **baptism** noun, c. or u. = the ceremony by which one is baptized

bar¹ /bɑːʳ/ noun, c. **1** *a wooden bar; a bar of chocolate* = a piece of wood, metal or some other material that is greater in length than in breadth **2** *window bars* = the straight rods which are fixed across a window, gate etc. to prevent people from getting in or out **3** *a coffee-bar; a salad-bar* = a counter or shop where coffee or drinks, food etc. are served **4** *a bar of music* = a sequence of notes sung or played **5** *the bar* = a group of barristers (lawyers) (Note the article.) [LAW] **barbell** noun, c. = a thick steel rod with a round, heavy weight at each end, used for physical exercise

bar² verb, t. (**barred**) **1** *Allow the guests to pass and don't bar the way.* = to prevent someone from moving **2** *You may be barred (debarred) from appearing at the examination if you are found using unfair means.* = to stop someone from doing something

to be behind bars (always plural) = to be in prison (informal)

barb /bɑːb/ noun,c. **1** = the sharp, curved point of a fish-hook or arrow **2** *His speech was so full of barbs that most people felt uncomfortable.* = a remark which is clever or witty but meant to hurt **barbed** adj. *barbed words* = something which has barbs and can cause pain **barbed wire** noun = a wire with short, sharp points on it, used for making fences to keep people, cattle etc. out

bar•bar•i•an /bɑːˈbeəriən/ noun, c. = an offensive way of referring to a person who is thought to be uncivilized, or a crude person who behaves in a manner which society does not approve of (derogatory) USE **barbaric** adj.**1** *a barbaric murder* = very cruel **2** *barbaric customs* = very cruel and violent

bar•be•cue¹ /ˈbɑːbɪkjuː/ noun, c. **1** = a metal frame which is used to cook meat, vegetables etc. over an open fire **2** = an open-air party at which meat, vegetables etc. cooked on a barbecue are served

barbecue² verb, t. *I will barbecue the chicken.* = to cook something on a barbecue

bar•ber /ˈbɑːbəʳ/ noun, c. = a person whose job is to cut and style men's hair, shave beards etc.

bar code noun, c. = a label on a product consisting of thick and thin vertical lines, which has information (e.g. price, batch number) which a computer can read

bar code

bard /bɑːd/ noun, c. = poet (literary)

bare¹ /beəʳ/ adj. **1** *a bare body* = without clothes, shoes or any covering **2** *a bare mountain* = without trees, grass etc. **3** *Give me the bare facts of the case.* = only the facts without any addition **4** *Our library looks so bare. There are very few books in it.* = containing very few things (often disapproving)

bare² verb, t. **1** *The dog bared its teeth.* = to show by removing the covering, usually as a sign of anger **2** *to bare oneself* = to become naked **3** *The newspaper has bared all the facts.* = to make public in a daring way **bare-faced** adj. *a bare-faced lie* = said without any sense of shame **barefoot** adv. or adj. = not wearing shoes or socks

to do something with one's bare hands *He held the snake with his bare hands.* = without using any protection or weapon **the bare minimum** *Rs 5,000 is the bare minimum we need to start the animal shelter.* = the lowest possible amount of money, number of things etc. required to do something

barely /ˈbeəlɪ/ adv. *She is barely 20 years old.* = hardly; only just

bar•gain[1] /ˈbɑːgɪn/ noun, c. **1** *I bought this computer for only Rs5,000. It was a real bargain.* = something which one has bought very cheaply, much below its real value **2** *Let's make a bargain. You help me with maths and I'll help you with history.* = an agreement between two people where one agrees to do something in return for something done by the other person

bargain[2] verb, i. **1** *When I go shopping, I like to bargain with the shopkeeper.* = to try to reduce the price of something that one is buying; to haggle **2** *Talks are going on between the employees and the management. Both sides are expected to bargain hard.* = to try to get the most favourable terms for an agreement; to negotiate

barge[1] /bɑːdʒ/ noun, c. = a large boat with a flat bottom which is used to carry heavy goods

barge[2] verb, i. *He barged into the room without knocking.* = to push one's way into a house, party, meeting etc. without an invitation (informal)

bar•i•tone /ˈbærɪtəʊn/ noun, c. = a low, deep voice in which some male persons sing (see also **bass** and **tenor**) [MUSIC]

bark[1] /bɑːk/ noun, u. or c. **1** *the bark of a tree*(u.) = the hard outer covering of a tree **2** *the bark of a dog*(c.) = the sharp, loud sound made by a dog

bark[2] verb, i. **1** *Does your dog bite, or does it only bark?* = to make the sound that a dog makes **2** *The conductor barked angrily at me because I couldn't find my ticket.* = to speak in a rough, angry voice (figurative, not respectful)

bar•ley /ˈbɑːli/ noun, u. = a kind of cereal or grain, produced by the barley plant **barley water** noun, u. = a light, sweet drink made from barley

barn /bɑːn/ noun, c. = a large building on a farm, used for storing crops or keeping farm animals

ba•rom•e•ter /bəˈrɒmɪtəʳ/ noun, c. = an instrument that measures air pressure and can be used to predict weather changes

bar•rack /ˈbærək/ verb, t. *The speaker was barracked by the crowd when he talked about all the wonderful things he was doing.* = to shout at someone in order to make fun of him/her

bar•racks /ˈbærəks/ noun, c. (always plural) *police barracks* = a building or group of buildings where soldiers or police personnel live

bar•rage /ˈbærɑːʒ/ noun, c. **1** = a dam built across a river to provide water for farming **2** *an artillery barrage* = the continuous firing of many heavy guns **3** *When I returned home late, I had to face a barrage of questions.* = many questions asked in an attacking or anxious manner

bar•rel /ˈbærəl/ noun, c. **1** *the barrel of a gun* = the long tube-like part of a gun through which bullets are fired **2** *a barrel of wine* = a wooden container for wine, oil etc. with curved sides and a flat top and bottom

bar•ren /ˈbærən/ adj. **1** = the condition in which the female (of a plant or animal) cannot bear fruit or produce young ones **2** *barren land* = land on which crops do not grow

bar•ri•cade[1] /ˈbærɪkeɪd/ noun, c. *The police have put up a barricade on the road leading to the airport.* = a temporary wall put up on a road to prevent the movement of people

barricade[2] verb, t. *The police have been ordered to barricade this road.* = to put up a barricade

bar•ri•er /ˈbærieʳ/ noun, c. **1** = a wall or fence that prevents the movement of people **2** *When one is visiting a new country the language barrier is difficult to overcome.* = something that cannot be seen but prevents movement or separates people

bar•ring /ˈbɑːrɪŋ/ prep. *Every seat in the class has been taken barring this one.* = except for

bar•ris•ter /ˈbærɪstə/ noun, c. = a lawyer who practises law or is allowed to practise law in a British court

bar•row /ˈbærəʊ/ noun, c. *a wheelbarrow* = a small cart on wheels

bar•ter /ˈbɑːtəʳ/ verb, t. *The people in my village usually barter rice for all the things they need.* = to exchange goods for other goods, without using money

base[1] /beɪs/ noun, c. **1** *the base of the statue* = the lowest part of something **2** *Sanskrit is the base for many Indian languages.* = the starting-point or origin **3** *an army base* = the place from where an activity is controlled **4** = a chemical with a pH of more than 7 [CHEMISTRY]

base[2] verb, t. **1** *We will base our future plans on your report.* = to use something as the starting-point for something else **2** *Our company is based in Kathmandu but has branches all over the world.* = to have an office in some place from where everything is controlled

base[3] adj. *base deeds* = low or bad (derogatory)

base•ball /ˈbeɪsbɔːl/ noun, u. = a ball game very popular in America, in which a player has to run around four bases after hitting the ball, in order to complete a run

baseball

base•less /ˈbeɪslɪs/ adj. *The news about the postponement of the examinations is baseless. Someone is trying to fool us.* = without any base (foundation) and therefore not to be trusted

base•line /ˈbeɪslaɪn/ noun, c. **1** *Using 1995 as the baseline, the government is calculating how much the price of sugar is rising every year.* = a particular point or line which is used as the starting-point when making comparisons or measurements **2** = the line at each end of a tennis court which marks its limit [TENNIS]

base•ment /ˈbeɪsmənt/ noun, c. = the part of a building which is below street level

base met•al noun, c. = a metal such as iron or lead which is not regarded as precious

bash[1] /bæʃ/ noun, c. **1** *The woman gave the attacker a bash on the head with her handbag.* = a hard blow **2** *I have never played tennis, but I would like to have a bash at it.* = a trial attempt (informal) **3** *We are having a bash at my house tomorrow as it is my daughter's birthday.* = a party (informal)

bash[2] verb, t. *I stepped on the brakes but the car behind bashed into my car.* = to hit very hard

bash•ful /ˈbæʃfəl/ adj. *This present is for you. Please take it and don't be so bashful.* = shy

basic[1] /ˈbeɪsɪk/ adj. **1** *Food and shelter are basic needs.* = the most necessary **2** *My basic salary is Rs 1000, with a house-rent allowance of Rs 700 a month.* = without anything being added **basics** noun (always plural) *Children must be taught the basics: reading, writing and arithmetic.* = the most necessary things

BASIC[2] noun = a simple computer language

basis /ˈbeɪsɪs/ noun, c. *Is there any basis for this report?* = the facts on which something is based

bas•il /ˈbæzəl/ noun, c. = a kind of plant with sweet-smelling leaves which are used in cooking, similar to (but not the same as) the leaves of the Indian tulsi plant

ba•sin /ˈbeɪsən/ noun, c. **1** = a container for liquids, usually round and with a wide mouth, generally used for washing **2** *the Mahanadi basin* = the land area surrounding a river, from which water runs down into the river

bask /bɑːsk/ verb, i. **1** *If you go to the Sunderban forests, you will see crocodiles lying on the river bank, basking in the sun.* = lying or sitting lazily, enjoying the warmth of the sun **2** *I can see you are still basking in your teacher's approval.* = to enjoy the good feelings you have when someone admires or likes you

bas•ket /ˈbɑːskɪt/ noun, c. **1** = a round, light container made of thin strips of bamboo, plastic etc. **2** *a basket of fruit.* = the things that are contained in a basket **basketball** noun, u. = a game played between teams of five players in which each tries to score points by putting the ball into the opponent's 'basket'

to put all one's eggs in one basket = to put everything at risk by depending on one thing only rather than keeping many possibilities open

bass /beɪs/ noun, u. = the lowest and deepest voice which a male singer can have (music) (see also **baritone** and **tenor**)

bas•tard /ˈbɑːstəd/ noun, c. **1** = a child of parents who are not legally married (old-fashioned, derogatory) **2** = a word of abuse used for someone whom one does not like (USE)

bat[1] /bæt/ noun, c. **1** *a cricket bat* = a piece of wood with a special shape, used for hitting a ball in games like cricket and tennis **2** *a flying bat* = a small mouse-like animal with wings that is active at night

bat[2] verb, i. *The Indian team will bat first.* = to hit the ball with the bat; to have a turn to use the bat **batsman** noun, c. = a cricket player who is batting or is known for his skill in batting (**batter** in the game of baseball)

to not bat an eyelid *She did not bat an eyelid when I told her that she had won the lottery.* = to show no surprise or shock when something extraordinary happens

batch /bætʃ/ noun, c. (**batches**) **1** *a batch of freshly-baked bread* = a quantity of some material that is produced at the same time **2** *a new batch of students* = a group of people considered to form a single set

bath[1] /bɑːθ/ noun, c. or **1** *I am going for a bath now.* = the act of washing the whole body to clean it **2** *a fibre-glass bath* = a large tub in which one lies or sits down to wash one's body **3** *a bedroom with an attached bath* = bathroom **4** *The steel sheet has to be cleaned in an acid bath.* = a liquid used for some special purpose

bath[2] verb, t. *Would you like to bath the baby?* = to give someone a bath **bathing suit** noun, c. = a short, light dress which is worn while bathing or swimming

bathe /beɪð/ verb, i. or t. **1** *The doctor has told me to bathe my eyes with this medicine.*(t.) = to cover completely with some liquid as a treatment for some infection **2** *Have you bathed?*(i.) = to have a bath **3** *The mountains were bathed in sunlight.*(i.) = to be covered with something (figurative)

B

bath•room /'bɑːθruːm/ noun, c. a place for bathing which also contains a toilet

ba•tik /bə'tiːk/ noun, u. **1** = a process of creating coloured designs on cloth by covering the remaining parts (which are not to be coloured) with wax **2** = the printed cloth created through this process

ba•ton /'bætɒn/ noun, c. **1** = a short, thin stick used by the conductor (leader) of a musical group to guide the other musicians **2** = a short stick used as a weapon by a policeman or army officer **3** = a stick which is passed on by one runner in a team to the next runner, in a relay race

bat•tal•ion /bə'tæljən/ noun, c. = a group of 500–1000 soldiers forming part of a larger unit (see also **company** and **brigade**)

bat•ter[1] /'bætəʳ/ noun, u. or c. **1** *mixing batter for a cake*(u.) = a mixture of flour, sugar, eggs etc. used in cooking **2** (c.) = a batsman in the game of baseball

batter[2] verb, t. *The thieves battered the door down.* = to damage or break something by continuous beating **battered** adj. *a battered person* = someone who has been treated with cruelty or violence

bat•ter•ing-ram noun = a large, heavy piece of wood used in wars long ago to break down the gates or walls of an enemy fort

bat•ter•y /'bætəri/ noun, c. (**batteries**) or u. **1** *a battery for a flashlight*(c.) = a device (simple machine) used to produce and store electricity **2** *a battery of guns*(c.) = a number of big guns which are fired together during a battle **3** = a set of small box-like cages in which hens lay eggs for mass sale **4** *The men were arrested for assault and battery.*(u.) = the crime of hitting other people

bat•tle[1] /'bætl/ noun, c. *A fierce battle is on between our troops and the enemy's.* = a fight, especially between armies in a war

battle[2] verb, i. or t. *The fire-brigade had to battle against the flames for more than six hours.*(i.) // *They battled the flames all day.*(t.) // *She battled against cancer for many years.* = to fight or struggle against **battle-cry** noun, c. = words used by soldiers while fighting, to give themselves courage **battlefield** noun, c. = a place where a battle has taken place **battleship** noun, c. = a large warship with many big guns

to fight a losing battle = to do something in which you are not likely to be successful

baw•dy /'bɔːdi/ adj. *telling bawdy stories* = (stories, jokes or songs) about sex, told in a humorous manner

bawl /bɔːl/ verb, t. and i. **1** *They bawled at me in a way which frightened me.*(i.) = to shout at someone angrily **2** *That baby has been bawling all night.* = to cry noisily (informal, not respectful)

bay[1] /beɪ/ noun, c. *the Bay of Bengal* = a sea surrounded by land on three sides

bay[2] verb. i. *The dogs started to bay loudly as they caught the smell of the jackal.* = to make the long, deep cry of a hunting-dog

bay leaf noun, c. = a kind of sweet-smelling dried leaf used in cooking

bay•o•net[1] /'beɪənɪt/ noun, c. = a sharp knife that can be fixed to the end of a gun or rifle

bayonet[2] verb, t. = to drive a bayonet into someone

ba•zaar /bə'zɑː/ noun, c. **1** = a market place in an Asian country **2** *a church bazaar* = a special sale arranged by the members of a group, usually for some charitable purpose

BBC abbr. of **British Broadcasting Corporation** = a company set up by the British government that produces radio and television programmes

BC abbr. of **before Christ** = a system of naming the dates of events that took place before the birth of Christ (see A.D.)

be[1] /biː/ aux. verb. present tense forms **is, am, are;** *He is my friend.*(singular); *I am a doctor.*(singular); *They / we / you are students.*(plural) past tense forms **was, were**; *He / I was a student.*(singular); *They / we / you were students.*(plural) progressive form (**be + ing**) *He is being asked; I am being asked; They / we / you are being asked.* passive form: (**be + en**) *He is beaten; I am beaten; They / we / you are beaten.*

be- /biː/ prefix **1** *I want to befriend him.* = to make or treat as **2** *The sea is becalmed.* = to be in the stated condition

beach[1] /biːtʃ/ noun, c. = a long stretch of sand along the sea

beach[2] verb, t. *Have you beached your boats?* = to run or drive a boat onto the beach

bea•con /'biːkən/ noun, c. **1** = a light or fire which is lit on top of a tower or hill to guide ships at sea **2** *The lives of good people should be a beacon for all of us.* = something that guides or sets an example to be followed (figurative)

bead /biːd/ noun, c. **1** *a string of beads* = a small piece of glass or stone, usually round, with a hole in it through which a piece of thread or wire can be pushed to form a necklace **2** *beads of sweat* = a drop of liquid

beak /biːk/ noun, c. = the bony front part of the mouth of a bird

beak•er /'biːkəʳ/ noun, c. **1** = a drinking cup with a wide mouth and no handle **2** = a glass container for liquids, used in a science laboratory (see pic under **laboratory equipment**)

beam[1] /biːm/ noun, c. **1** = a large, long and heavy piece of wood, steel etc. which supports the roof of a building **2** = the long metal arm of a balance used for weighing things, from which the scales are hung **3** *a beam of light* = light shining in a line or band e.g. a moonbeam

beam[2] verb, i. **1** *He was beaming with delight at the news of his victory.* = to smile brightly and happily **2** *Doordarshan will beam this news across the world.* = to broadcast (send out) a programme over radio or television [TECHNICAL]

bean /biːn/ noun, c. **1** *soya bean* = the edible seed of a type of climbing plant **2** *coffee beans* = the seeds of certain plants which look like beans **bean sprouts** noun, c. (usually in plural) = a very young plant that is beginning to grow and is often eaten without cooking

to be full of beans = full of enthusiasm and energy (informal) **to spill the beans** = to tell someone about something that should have been kept a secret (informal)

bear[1] /beəʳ/ noun, c. **1** = a large, heavy animal with thick and rough fur **2** = a person who sells away her or his shares in the stock-market, expecting that their prices will fall [TECHNICAL] (opposite **bull**)

bear[2] verb, t. or i. (**bore, borne**) **1** *This chair cannot bear such a heavy load. It is sure to break.*(t.) = to carry; to support **2** *I can bear a lot of pain.*(t.) = to suffer without complaining; to endure **3** *We are willing to bear a part of the cost, not all of it.* = to pay for something willingly **4** *bear a child* = to give birth to a baby (formal, old-fashioned) **5** *The document bears no names.* = to have or carry (formal) **bearable** adj. *Is the pain bearable?* = something unpleasant that one can bear without too much suffering

bear up *How have you been bearing up since your fall?* = to manage with courage and determination **to bear (someone) a grudge** = to have constant negative feelings towards someone because of something which happened in the past **to bear the brunt of** *The captain bore the brunt of the media's attack when the team lost the series at home.* = to face the full force of something unpleasant **to bear something in mind** *She will bear your advice in mind for the future.* = to remember something, usually advice or a warning, in such a way that it is useful when needed

beard[1] /bɪəd/ noun, c. = the hair growing on the face and neck

beard[2] verb, t. *The manager is trying to avoid me, but I am going to beard him over the matter of my promotion.* = to face or oppose someone without fear (informal)

to beard the lion in his den = to face or challenge someone in a place where he/she is known to be strong or powerful

bear•er /'beərəʳ/ noun, c. **1** *He is the bearer of bad news.* = a person who carries or brings something **2** = a waiter (a person who serves food or drinks, specially in a club)

bear•ing /'beərɪŋ/ noun, c. or u. **1** *I admire her upright bearing.*(u.) = the manner in which a person stands or moves **2** *Whatever she says at this meeting will have an important bearing on our decision.*(c.) = influence **3** *a ball bearing* = a part of a machine, containing small steel balls, which helps moving parts work more easily

bear•ish /'beərɪʃ/ adj. *The market is bearish now.* = in a situation where the prices of shares are expected to fall (opposite **bullish**) [TECHNICAL]

beast /biːst/ noun, c. **1** = a four-footed animal **2** *What a beast you are!* = a person that one does not like (figurative, informal) **beastly** adj. *Your behaviour is beastly.* = unpleasant and cruel **beast of burden** noun, c. **1** = an animal that is used to carry loads e.g. a horse, donkey, camel etc. **2** *I am little more than a beast of burden in this office.* = a person who is given too much work (figurative)

beat[1] /biːt/ verb, t. **1** *The man was beating the carpet with a stick to dust it.* = to hit or strike someone or something again and again **2** *Our hockey team can beat theirs.* = defeat **3** *His heart is still beating.* = working

beat[2] noun, c. **1** *the beat of a drum* = the regular sound produced by the heart or by a drum, machine, etc. **2** *The music has a strong beat.* = the regular pattern of sounds in music or poetry; rhythm **3** *the policeman's beat* = the path that a police-person follows while on duty

to beat about the bush = to talk about something for a long time without getting to the main point or purpose **to be off the beaten track** = to be in a place or path that is not used by many **Can you beat that?** *She has been sleeping for about twelve hours. Can you beat that?* = Isn't that remarkable? (informal, approving or disapproving) **to beat the heat/rush etc.** *I think I'll beat the crowds at the shops by going early.* = to be successful in doing something by taking some immediate action (informal)

beat•er /'biːtəʳ/ noun, c. **1** *an egg-beater* = an instrument used to beat (stir) something **2** = a person whose job it was to beat the forest and drive out wild animals so that they could be hunted

beau /bəʊ/ noun, c. (**beaux, beaus**) (French) = a woman's lover (old-fashioned)

beau•ty /'bjuːti/ noun, u. or c. (**beauties**) **1** *I am admiring the beauty of the mountain.*(u.) = the quality in someone or something that attracts a person **2** *She was a great beauty, and we were proud of her.*(c.) = a woman who has beauty (old-fashioned) **3** *The beauty of this suitcase is that you can take it wherever you go.* = advantage (informal) **beautiful** adj. = someone or something that has beauty **beautify**

B

verb = to make something or someone beautiful **beauty contest** noun = a competition to judge the most beautiful women in a group **beauty queen** noun = a woman who has won a prize in a beauty contest **beauty parlour** noun = a place where people are given special treatment for the face, hair, hands etc. to make them look more attractive **beautician** /bjuːˈtɪʃən/ noun, c. = a person whose job is to make the face, skin, hands etc. look more beautiful

be•cause /bɪˈkɒz/ conj. *I could not come because it was raining.*= for the reason that

beck /bek/ noun **(to be at someone's beck and call)** *If you don't tell people how busy you are, you will have to be at their beck and call.* = to be always available or ready to serve someone

be•come /bɪˈkʌm/ linking verb (**became**) **1** *Nirmal became the class monitor.* = to come to be something that one was not earlier **2** *I am becoming rather worried about your fever.* = to start feeling something one wasn't feeling earlier **becoming** adj. *That new dress looks very becoming.* = beautiful (old-fashioned)

bed[1] /bed/ noun, c. **1** *He sleeps on a hard bed.* = a piece of furniture used for sleeping on **2** *the bed of the river* = the bottom **3** *a bed of concrete* = the foundation on which something stands **4** *flower bed* = an area in a garden where flowers are planted

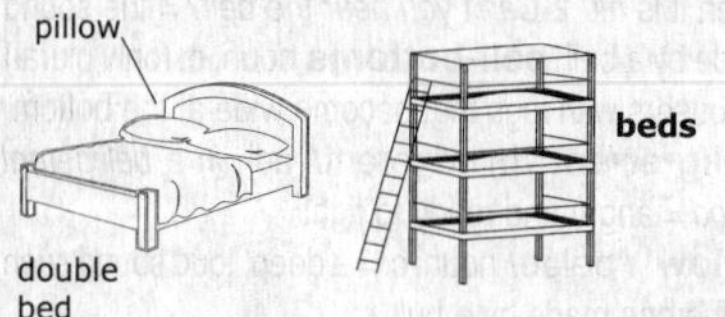

bed[2] verb, t. (**bedded**) *I have to bed the machine in a layer of concrete.* = to fix something in a base or foundation **bedbug** noun, c. = an insect which sucks blood and can be found in dirty beds **bedfellow** noun, c. **1** = a person who shares one's bed **2** = a close companion or partner in some business or other activity (informal) **bedlinen** noun, u. = bedsheets, pillow covers etc. that are used with a bed **bedpan** noun, c. = a container for body wastes used by persons who are sick or old or unable to get out of bed **bedridden** adj. = a state in which a person is unable to get out of bed because of long illness **bedrock** noun, u. **1** = the layer of solid rock deep down inside the earth over which other layers of soil are found **2** *The company is successful because it is well managed. Efficiency is the bedrock of its success.* = the principle which is the foundation for something **bedsore** noun, c. = a painful place on a person's skin caused by lying in bed for a long time **bedspread** noun, c. = a decorative cloth cover for a bed **bed-wetting** noun, u.= a condition in which someone, e.g. a child, passes urine in bed while asleep

to bed down = to make a person or animal comfortable for the night **to get up on the wrong side of the bed** = to be in a bad temper or mood (informal) **bed of roses** noun, c. *Life is not a bed of roses. You will have to work hard to succeed.* = something that is very comfortable

bed•lam /ˈbedləm/ noun, c. *If the teacher leaves the class alone for a few minutes, there is bedlam by the time she returns!* = a place where there is a lot of noise and confusion (informal)

bee /biː/ noun, c. = a stinging insect that makes honey from the juice of flowers and lives in large groups **beehive** noun, c. = a nest or box in which bees live **beeline** noun *At the party Rajesh didn't talk to anybody but made a beeline for the food.* = the most direct route to something (informal, often disapproving)

beef[1] /biːf/ noun, u. = the meat of a cow or ox **beefy** adj. *a beefy actor* = a very big, strong and often fat person (informal)

beef[2] verb, i. *He is always beefing about the long hours he works.* = complaining (informal)

been[1] /bɪn/ aux verb *He has been playing tennis* – doing something for some time, but not any longer

been[2] verb, i. *I have been to America three times.* = gone and come back from

beep /biːp/ noun, c. *I heard the beep of the scooter horn.* = a short, sharp sound, not very loud **beeper** noun, c. = an instrument which makes a beeping sound to inform someone that he/she is wanted on a telephone by a caller; a **pager**

beer /bɪəʳ/ noun, u. or c. **1** (u.) = a drink with a bitter taste, made from grain, which contains a low amount of alcohol **2** *Would you like a beer?*(c.) = a glass, mug or bottle of beer

beet /biːt/ noun = a red root vegetable from which beet sugar is made

bee•tle /ˈbiːtl/ noun, c. = a kind of insect which has a hard covering over its body

be•fore[1] /bɪˈfɔːʳ/ prep. or conj. **1** *I was here before the guests arrived.* (conj.) **2** *You must come before 12 o'clock.* (prep.) = earlier than **3** *The ghost suddenly appeared before me.* = in front of **4** *You will have to appear before the selection committee.* = for a particular purpose **5** *You should put duty before pleasure.* = in a more important position than something else

before[2] adv. *Have we met before?* = on an earlier occasion **beforehand** adv. *I had been informed beforehand that you were coming.* = in advance

be•friend /bɪ'frend/ verb, t. *Mr Sinha befriended me when I first came to Kolkata as a student.* = to become somebody's friend, especially someone who is younger or needs help

beg /'beg/ verb, i. or t. **1** *You seem to be a strong and healthy person. Why are you begging on the streets?*(i.) = asking people for food, money etc. because you are poor **2** *My daughter begged to go on the picnic with her friends.*(t.) = to ask for something with great eagerness or anxiety

to beg somebody's pardon **1** = to say that one is sorry **2** = to ask someone to repeat what he/she said **3** = a way of announcing that one is going to disagree

beg•gar /begəʳ/ noun, c. = a person who lives by begging

be•gin /bɪ'gɪn/ verb, t. or i. (**began, begun**) *We shall begin our show in 10 minutes.*(t.)= to start at a particular time or in a particular way **beginner** noun, c. *You swim quite well for a beginner.* = a person who is just beginning to do something **beginning** noun, c. *Let us go back to the beginning of this story.* = the point at which something begins

to begin with *We can't do the project. To begin with, we have no one to help us.* = to state or introduce the first point or reason for something

be•half /bɪ'hɑːf/ noun, u. **(on behalf of)** *I am writing this letter on behalf of a friend, who is in hospital.* = for; in the interests of

be•have /bɪ'heɪv/ verb, i. or t. **1** *My friend has been behaving strangely ever since he won the lottery.*(i.) = acting in a certain way **2** *I want you to behave yourself. No talking, whispering or laughing!*(t.) = to act in a manner which is thought to be proper and socially acceptable

be•hav•iour /bɪ'heɪvjəʳ/ noun, u. *We can study the behaviour of wild animals in a zoo.* = the way in which someone or something acts

be•head /bɪ'hed/ verb, t. = to cut off someone's head, especially as a punishment

be•hind[1] /bɪ'haɪnd/ prep. or adv. **1** *She is hiding behind this door.* = at the back of **2** *Some countries are behind others in economic development.* = in a less advanced position **3** *Don't worry, we are all behind you in this struggle.* = in support of **4** *Who is behind the attack?* = responsible for causing

behind[2] noun, u. *a kick in the behind* = the back part of the body; the **buttocks** (slang)

be•hold /bɪ'həʊld/ verb, t. *Behold her, yon solitary highland lass!* = to look at (old-fashioned and literary)

beige /beɪʒ/ noun, u. or adj. = (of) a dull, yellowish-brown colour

be•ing[1] /'biːɪŋ/ noun, u. or c. **1** *a human being*(c.) =a living creature **2** *When did the earth come into being?*(u.) = existence

being[2] aux. verb *The house is being repaired.* = progressive form of **be**, showing action in progress [GRAMMAR]

belch[1] /beltʃ/ noun, c. = the sound produced when one allows gas from the stomach to pass out through the mouth (also **burp**)

belch[2] verb, t. or i. *The chimneys of the factories are belching smoke.*(t.) = to throw out with force

be•lief /bɪ'liːf/ noun, c. or u. **1** *My belief in God is very strong.*(u.) = strong religious faith **2** *My belief in your leadership has been shaken.*(u.) = trust, confidence **3** *I share many of your beliefs.*(c.) = an idea that is strongly held and has a powerful influence on a person's behaviour

be•lieve /bɪ'liːv/ verb, t. **1** *Please believe me. I am telling you the truth!* = to consider something or someone to be true **2** *I believe we have met before, Mr Misra.* = to think or suppose **believable** adj. *a believable story* = something that can be believed **believer** noun **1** *a true believer* = one who accepts or follows a certain religion or ideal **2** *a believer in the value of hard work* = one who accepts a certain idea

to believe in something *I believe in rebirth.*= to have strong faith in (something)

bell /bel/ noun, c. **1** = a piece of metal, round and hollow or flat in shape, which makes a ringing sound when it is hit **2** *Can't you hear the bell?* = the sound made by a bell **bell-bottoms** noun, c. (only plural) = trousers with legs that become wide at the bottom

bel•lig•er•ent /bɪ'lɪdʒərənt/ adj. *in a belligerent mood* = angry and ready to fight

bel•low[1] /'beləʊ/ noun, c. = a deep, loud sound such as the one made by a bull

bellow[2] verb, i. or t. *to bellow with anger* = to shout in a deep, loud voice

bel•lows /'beləʊz/ noun, c. (always plural) = a hollow bag, usually made of leather, used for blowing air into a fire

bel•ly /'beli/ noun, c. (**bellies**) **1** = the stomach; the part of the human body between the chest and the legs (informal) **2** *the minerals lying in the belly of the earth* = the inside of something **3** *the belly of an aircraft* = the curved lower surface **belly-button** noun, c. = the mark or sunken spot in the belly where the child was attached to the mother before birth; the navel (slang) **belly-dance** noun, c. = a kind of dance usually performed by women, using movements of the belly **belly-landing** noun, c. = the act of landing an aircraft on its belly when it is unable to land on its wheels

be•long /bɪ'lɒŋ/ verb, i. **1** *Why should I leave this*

B

city? I belong here. = to feel that one is a part of something or in the right place **2** *This house belongs to Mr Mishra.*= to be the property of **belong to** *I belong to a well-known family of musicians.* = to be a member of **belongings** noun, c. (always plural) *I lost all my belongings in the fire.* = things which belong to one, and which can be moved; possessions

be•lov•ed[1] /bɪˈlʌvɪd/ noun (no plural) *Madhuri is very happy because she is going to marry her beloved.* = a person who is loved very much

beloved[2] adj. *Shah Jahan built the Taj Mahal in memory of his beloved wife.* = greatly loved

be•low[1] /bɪləʊ/ prep. **1** *My exercise book is just below the pile of books. You will see it if you lift the books.* = on a lower level **2** *Your work has been below average.* = less than **3** *I am still below the age of retirement.* = younger than

below[2] adv. *The show is free for children aged three and below.* = less than

belt[1] /belt/ noun, c. **1** = a band, usually made of leather or plastic, worn around the waist to hold up trousers, skirts etc. **2** = a circular band made of rubber or leather which drives some part of a machine or moves things from one place to another **3** *Bihar, Orissa and Madhya Pradesh form the mineral belt of the country.* = a part of a country that is known for something

belt[2] verb, t. **1** *Please belt up your overcoat.*= to tie up with a belt **2** *He belted the next ball for a six.* = to hit very hard (informal)

to hit someone below the belt = to attack someone in an unfair manner **to belt out a song** = to sing in a very loud voice **to tighten one's belt** = to prepare oneself to face a difficult time, specially a time of financial difficulty

bench /bentʃ/ noun, c. **1** *The teacher made me stand on the bench.* = a long wooden seat on which several people can sit **2** *The lawyer addressed the bench.* = the seat where the judge sits in a law court **3** *The lawyer has been raised to the bench.* = the position of a judge **benchmark** noun *Your book will be a benchmark for all future writers.* = something which is used as a standard by which other things of a similar kind are judged

bend[1] /bend/ verb, t. or i. *You will have to bend this pipe to make it fit.* = to force something into a shape different from the one it had earlier

bend[2] noun, c. *Walk straight on until you come to a bend in the road.* = a curve in a road or river

be•neath /bɪˈniːθ/ prep. or adv. **1** *The ship sank beneath the waves.*(prep.) = below **2** *It is beneath my dignity to ask for money.* (prep.) = not worthy of

ben•e•fac•tor /ˈbenɪfæktəʳ/ noun, c. = one who helps others, specially with money **beneficent** /bɪˈnefɪsənt/ adj. = kind and generous (formal)

ben•e•fit[1] /ˈbenɪfɪt/ verb, t. *This new medicine will surely benefit the patient.* = to help or to provide some advantage

benefit[2] noun, u. or c. *This new rule gives us no benefit.*(u.)=help; advantage **beneficial** /benɪˈfɪʃəl/ adj. = something which gives benefit (help) **beneficiary** noun, c. (**beneficiaries**) *Farmers will be the main beneficiaries of the government's new policy on agriculture.*= one who gains some benefit (advantage)

be•nev•o•lent /bɪˈnevələnt/ adj. *a benevolent ruler* = kind and helpful to others

be•nign /bɪˈnaɪn/ adj. **1** = kind and gentle **2** *a benign tumour* = a disease which is not dangerous to life (opposite **malignant**)

be•reav•ed /bɪˈriːvd/ adj. = a person who has suffered a bereavement or loss **bereavement** noun, u. or c. *His wife's death has shattered him. I don't know how I can comfort him in his bereavement.* = the state of having lost someone whom one loved especially because of death

be•reft /bɪˈreft/ adj. *After losing his job, he is bereft of all hope.*= completely without; having lost

ber•i•ber•i /beriˈberi/ noun, u. = a disease that attacks the nerves, caused by the lack of vitamin B

ber•ry /ˈberi/ noun, c. (**berries**) = a small, soft fruit with seeds (e.g. *strawberry*)

ber•serk /bɜːˈsɜːk/ adj. **(to go berserk)** *Why are you tearing up your books? Have you gone berserk?* = almost mad with anger or grief (informal)

berth[1] /bɜːθ/ noun, c. **1** *I have a lower berth in this compartment.* = a sleeping place in a train or ship **2** = a place in a harbour where a ship can stop and be tied up

berth[2] verb, t. *The ship will berth here.* = to find a place to stop

be•side /bɪˈsaɪd/ prep. *Come and sit beside me.* = next to; by the side of

to be beside the point *That you were late by only five minutes is beside the point. Why were you late at all?* = having nothing to do with the main point **to be beside oneself** *He was beside himself with anger.*= to lose control of oneself due to anger, fear, etc.

be•sides[1] /bɪˈsaɪdz/ prep. *There were many people at the meeting besides the three directors.* = in addition to

besides[2] adv. *I don't want to go. Besides, I am too tired.* = in addition; also

be•seige /bɪˈsiːdʒ/ verb, t. *The enemy troops have beseiged our town. We can't get out through any of the gates.* = to surround a place so that the people inside cannot come out

best[1] /best/ adj. *She is the best student in the class.* = of the highest quality or level

best[2] adv. *Which of these shirts do you like best?* = the most

best[3] noun, u. *She tried her best to make us come for her brother's wedding.* = the most that one can do **best man** = a person who attends a marriage ceremony as a close friend of the bridegroom **best-seller** = a book which a large number of readers buy over a period of time

bet[1] /bet/ noun c. *I made a bet with my friend that Sri Lanka would win.* = an agreement to risk money or something valuable on the result of a future event

bet[2] verb, i. or t. *I bet that it will rain today.*(t.) // *Do you want to bet?*(i.) = to enter into an agreement to risk money or something valuable on the result of a future event

be•ta /'bi:tə/ noun = the second letter of the Greek alphabet represented by the symbol β

be•tel /'bi:tl/ noun, c. **1** = a leaf wrapped around pieces of pink or red nut (betel nut) and chewed in parts of India and South East Asia **2** = the leaf of the betel plant

be•tray /bɪ'treɪ/ verb, t. **1** *to betray one's country* = to be false to someone who has faith in you **2** *The man betrayed no fear when the robbers surrounded him.*= to show feeling **betrayal** noun, u. *a betrayal of our trust* = the act of betraying someone or something

bet•ter[1] /'betəʳ/ adj. (**good – better – best**) **1** *I am a good cook but my brother is a better cook.* = of higher quality **2** *Are you feeling better today?* = improved in health **3** *I have been waiting here for the better part of an hour.* = almost all of the stated time

better[2] adv. *This machine can run on kerosene, but it works better on petrol.* = in a better way

better[3] verb, t. *Lalit scored 99 in mathematics in the last examination but this time he has scored 100. He has bettered his own record.* = to do better than; to improve on **better half** noun, c. = one's wife or husband (informal, humorous)

be•tween /bɪ'twi:n/ prep. **1** *My shop is between the post office and the hospital.* = in the space that separates two things **2** *Meet me between five and six this evening.* = a point of time that separates two other points of time **3** *The Rajdhani Express runs between Delhi and Kolkata.* = from one place to another place **4** *He divided the money between his two children.* = giving equal amounts of something to two or more people

bev•er•age /'bevərɪdʒ/ noun, c. = a liquid drink other than water (e.g. tea, coffee)

be•ware /bɪ'weəʳ/ verb, i. *The sign on his gate says: Beware of the dog!* = be very careful (formal, used as a warning)

be•wil•der /bɪ'wɪldəʳ/ verb, t. *His sudden change in mood from happy to very sad was bewildering.* = to confuse and surprise

be•yond /bɪjɒnd/ prep. or adv. **1** *Our school is beyond the city limits.*(prep.) = on the other side of **2** *The mangoes on the tree are beyond my reach.*(prep.) = too far away **3** *I have read nothing on this subject beyond this book.*(prep.) = other than **4** *My house is at the end of the road, with nothing beyond.*(adv.) = coming after

bi- /'baɪ/ prefix meaning **1** two, twice or double e.g. **bi•cy•cle** /'baɪsɪkəl/ noun, c. = a vehicle with two wheels **2** both e.g. **bi•lin•gual** /baɪ'lɪŋgwəl/ adj. or noun, c. **a** *a bilingual dictionary*(adj.) = using two languages **b** *He is a bilingual.*(noun, c.) = a person who can speak or write two languages

bi•as[1] /'baɪəs/ noun, c. or u. *This newspaper has a bias against our team. They always find fault with us.* = a fixed opinion which someone has about a person or group, either in favour or against

bias[2] verb, t. *Umpires have to be fair at all times. No one should try to bias an umpire's judgement.* = to cause someone to form a bias (a fixed opinion) either in favour of or against someone

bib /bɪb/ noun, c. = a piece of cloth tied under a baby's chin to protect its clothes while eating or drinking

Bi•ble /'baɪbəl/ noun **1** *the Holy Bible* = the holy book of the Christians **2** *This book is a bible for actors.* = a book which is read and respected by all those belonging to a profession, group etc. **biblical** /'bɪblɪkəl/ adj. *a biblical character/reference* = someone or something connected with the Bible

biblio- /bɪbliəʊ/ prefix meaning 'connected with books' e.g. **bib•li•og•ra•phy** /bɪbli'ɒgrəfi/ noun, c. (**bibliographies**) = a list of the books and articles which have been used in preparing a book or article

bi-cen•te•na•ry /baɪsen'ti:nərɪ/ noun = a day that celebrates the completion of 200 years of something important

bi•ceps /'baɪseps/ noun, c. (singular as well as plural) = the large muscle on the front of the upper arm

bick•er•ing /'bɪkərɪŋ/ verb, i. *Why are you and I always bickering over small things? Let's be friends.* = quarrelling, not very seriously, over unimportant things

bid[1] /bɪd/ verb, t. or i. (**bade**) **1** *I want to bid Rs 50,000 for that painting.* = to offer a price to buy something at an auction **2** *Many foreign oil companies will bid for the contract to look for oil in the Arabian Sea.* = to try to win a contract by asking the lowest price for doing something **3** *Let me bid you goodbye* *now.* = to say or wish; to offer a greeting (formal) **4** *I bid you enter.* = to order someone to do something (old fashioned)

bid[2] noun, c. **1** *I have received two bids for this painting* = an offer (of a price) to buy something at an auction **2** *I am going to make a bid for the contract.* = an offer to do something for a certain price **3** = a statement (in some card games e.g. bridge) of the number of points that a player thinks he/she will win **bidding** noun, u. **1** *He cleaned up this room at my bidding.* = orders; command (formal) **2** *The bidding can begin now.* = the process of making offers to buy something at an auction

to make a bid for something = to try to get something

bi•er /bɪəʳ/ noun, c. = a frame fitted with wheels on which the body of a dead person is placed before it is buried or cremated

bi•fo•cal /baɪ'fəʊkəl/ adj. *a bifocal lens* = a pair of spectacles with lenses that are divided into two parts — a lower part for reading and an upper part for looking at things far away

bi•fur•cate /'baɪfəkeɪt/ verb, i. *The road bifurcates at Pipli. One branch leads to Konark and the other to Puri.* = to divide into two branches (used for roads, rivers, etc.)

big /bɪɡ/ adj. (**bigger**, **biggest**) **1** *a big house* = large **2** *He is a big name in cricket.* = famous **3** *The big day has come.* = specially important **4** *a big waste of time* = complete **5** *a big liar* = constant, frequent **6** *He's a big boy now, and knows what he is doing.* = mature, grown up **big bang theory** noun = the idea that all the stars and planets were parts of a single mass of material which exploded into many pieces [ASTRONOMY] **the Big Four** = China, the US, UK and Russia, which are believed to be the most influential world powers **big game** noun, u. = large animals such as tigers which were hunted for sport **big gun/shot** = a very important person (slang) **big-mouth** noun = a person who loves to talk, mostly about himself/herself; a person who is unable to keep a secret (informal) **big wig** noun = an important person in a company, government etc. (informal, disapproving)

to be too big for one's boots = to try to show oneself as being very important or powerful, when this is not the case (informal) **big deal** *So you have won a free ticket to the film show. Big deal!* = an expression of sarcasm, making fun of someone who thinks he/she has achieved something great, when that is not the case (informal) **to be no big deal** *It is true that I walked all the way to deliver the parcel but it was no big deal.* = to not be very important or difficult (slang) **to think big** **1** *If you want to set up a factory, you should have a large one. I want you to think big!* = to plan to do things on a large scale **2** = to be broad-minded and tolerant

big•a•my /'bɪɡəmɪ/ noun, u. = the situation of having two wives at the same time, which is against many codes of law [LAW]

big•ot /'bɪɡət/ noun, c. = a person who thinks that only his/her opinions and beliefs, especially about religion, politics and race, are right, and others' beliefs are wrong

bike /baɪk/ noun, c. = bicycle or motorcycle (informal)

bi•ki•ni /bɪ'kiːni/ noun, c. (**bikinies**) = a very small, two-piece swimsuit for women

bi•lat•er•al /baɪ'lætərəl/ adj. *a bilateral agreement* = an agreement between two groups or parties that must be observed by both sides

bile /baɪl/ noun, u. **1** = a yellowish green liquid produced in the body by the liver, which helps to digest fat [MEDICINE] **2** *We can't publish your article criticizing our leader. It is too full of bile.* = bitter feelings expressed in speech or writing (figurative)

bil•i•ous /'bɪljəs/ adj. = a condition in which one feels unwell because of having too much bile in the blood, usually as a result of eating oily food

bill[1] /bɪl/ noun, c. or **1** *Here is the bill for the things you have bought from our shop.* = one or more pieces of paper which have a list of the items sold in a shop, or work done, and their cost **2** *The parliament will vote today on the Reservation for Women Bill.* = a plan for a new law on which a parliament has to vote **3** *a five-dollar bill* = the word used in America for a currency note **4** = the beak of a bird

bill[2] verb, t. *The doctor will bill you for his services.* = to send a bill to someone for payment

bil•li•ards /'bɪljədz/ noun, u. = a game played on a table covered with felt, in which small but heavy balls are hit with a long stick (cue) against each other or into pockets at the sides and corners of the table

bil•lion /'bɪljən/ noun, c. = the number represented by 1,000,000,000 (a thousand million)

bil•low[1] /'bɪləʊ/ noun, c. = a large wave in the sea (literary)

billow[2] verb, t. *The national flag is billowing in the wind.* = to be driven by the wind, like a wave

bi-month•ly /baɪ'mʌnθlɪ/ adj. or noun, c. *a bi-monthly magazine* = something that appears after two months

bin /bɪn/ noun, c. *a garbage bin* = a large container used for collecting waste material or for storing things

bi•na•ry /'baɪnərɪ/ adj. **1** = made up of two parts **2** *a binary system* = a system of counting which uses only the numbers 0 and 1 (used in designing computers)

bind /baɪnd/ verb, t. or i. (**bound**) **1** *We will bind the* *plant to a pole to hold it up.*(t.) = to tie with a rope or string **2** *All my poems have been bound together into a book.*(t.) = to stitch together into a book **3** *This rain will help to bind the soil.*(t.) = hold together; strengthen **4** *The mixture of corn and vegetables will bind if you add mashed potatoes to it.*(i.) = to stick together when made into a ball or other shape **5** *You will be bound by this law.*(t.) = to force someone to obey a law or rule **6** *Our love for our country binds us together.*(t.) = to unite in a common feeling or goal **binder** noun, c. = a person whose job is to bind books (**book binder**) **binding** adj. or noun, u. **1** *The agreement is binding on both sides.*(adj.) = to have the power to be obeyed or followed [LAW] **2** = the cover of a book (noun)

bin•go /'bɪŋgəʊ/ noun, u. = a game of chance where a caller reads out numbers that may be marked on cards selected at random. The winner is the first one to have all the numbers in his/her card called out.

bi•noc•u•lars /baɪ'nɒkjʊləz/ noun, c. (always plural) *a pair of binoculars* = an instrument which has two tubes or eye-pieces (one for each eye), used for making things which are at a distance look bigger and closer

bi•no•mi•al /baɪ'nəʊmɪəl/ noun or adj. = an expression in mathemantics that has two numbers or letters joined by a + or - sign e.g. (a+b) or (x-7)

bio- /baɪəʊ/ prefix meaning 'connected with living things' e.g. **biochemistry** /baɪəʊ'kemɪstri/ noun, u. = the scientific study of the chemical processes connected with living things

bi•o•da•ta /'baɪəʊdeɪtə/ noun, u. = a record of the important events and achievements in one's life e.g. one's education, usually sent by people seeking jobs (also **cv**)

bi•o-de•gra•da•ble /baɪəʊdɪ'greɪdəbəl/ adj. *Plastic is not bio-degradable, but paper is.* = material which can be broken down by bacteria present in the soil and air into products which do not cause harm to the environment

bi•og•ra•phy /baɪ'ɒgrəfɪ/ noun, c. (**biographies**) = a written account of a person's life **biographer** noun = a person who writes an account of a person's life **biographic** adj.

bi•ol•o•gy /baɪ'ɒlədʒi/ noun = the scientific study of living things **biological** /baɪə'lɒdzɪkəl/ adj. = connected with living things **biological clock** noun = the natural process by which development takes place in living creatures according to a fixed time table **biological warfare** noun = the use of living things (germs, bacteria etc.) to harm or destroy an enemy **biologically** adv.

bio•mass /'baɪəumæs/ noun, u. = organic matter obtained from plants or animals (e.g. dead leaves, dung etc.) which can be used to produce gas etc.

bi•op•sy /'baɪɒpsɪ/ noun, u. or c. = a medical test in which small pieces of a diseased organ are removed and tested for cancer etc.

bi•o•sphere /'baɪəʊsfɪər/ noun, u. = the part of the world in which life can exist

bio-technology /baɪəʊtek'nɒlədʒɪ/ noun, u. = the use of living things (bacteria etc.) in industry, agriculture etc. for manufacturing or producing things

bi•par•tite /baɪ'pɑːtaɪt/ adj. *a bipartite leaf* = divided into two parts

bi•ped /'baɪped/ noun, c. = an animal that has two legs

bi•plane /'baɪpleɪn/ noun, c. = an aircraft which has two sets of wings, one above the other

birch /bɜːtʃ/ noun, c. = a tree common in northern countries, with smooth wood and thin branches

bird /bɜːd/ = a two-legged creature with feathers. (Most birds can fly.) **bird-brained** adj. = a person who is not very intelligent (informal, disrespectful) **bird-watcher** noun = a person who studies the habits of wild birds by watching them in their natural surroundings **bird of prey** = a bird that kills and eats small animals or other birds e.g. the eagle **bird's-eye view** *From this height you can get a bird's-eye view of the whole city.* = a view from above or from the sky

a bird in the hand is worth two in the bush. *You already have a job. Why do you want to resign and look for another job? Remember, a bird in the hand is worth two in the bush.*= something that one already has or is sure to get and therefore must not give up while trying to get something else **birds of a feather** = people who have the same interests, hobbies etc. **killing two birds with one stone** = to get two results through the same action **bird of passage** = a person who does not stay in one place or in one job for a long time **the bird has flown** *The police heard that a dangerous criminal was hiding in a hotel in the city and went there to arrest him. But the bird had already flown.* = to escape before one is caught (referring to an evil or dangerous person) **the birds and bees** = a humorous reference to sex education (explaining the idea of sex, birth etc. to very young children without causing shock)

birth /bɜːθ/ noun, c. and u. **1** *We celebrated the birth of the new baby.* = the action or process of being born **2** *Jayant Singh is a person of royal birth.* = origin; the family one comes from **3** *This day marks the birth*

B

of our country's freedom. = beginning **birth certificate** noun, c. = a record of the date, time, place etc. of one's birth, which can be used as a proof of age **birth control** noun, u. = the process of controlling and limiting the number of children born in a family through the use of various methods of **contraception** **birthmark** /'bɜ:θmɑ:k/ noun, c. = a mark found on the skin of a new-born baby which is special in some way **birthplace** /'bɜ:θpleɪs/ noun, c. = the place where one was born **birth rate** /'bɜ:θreɪt/ noun, c. = the number of children born in a country or group in a particular year, for every hundred or thousand persons in the population **birthright** /'bɜ:θraɪt/ noun (singular only) *Freedom is the birthright of the citizen of any country.* = a right or rights that one has because one is born in a particular country

birth•day /'bɜ:θdeɪ/ noun, c. = the day of the month on which a person was born

bis•cuit /'bɪskɪt/ noun, c. **1** = a flat, thin piece of cake, which is hard or crisp and generally sweet **2** = a whitish brown colour

bi•sect /baɪ'sekt/ verb, t. *The line AB bisects the line XY.* = to divide into two equal parts [GEOMETRY]

bi•sex•u•al /baɪ'sekʃuəl/ adj. or noun *a bisexual plant* = something that is male as well as female [BIOLOGY]

bish•op /'bɪʃəp/ noun, c. = **1** a Christian priest who has a high rank (see also **archbishop**) **2** = one of the pieces used in the game of chess, which can be moved only diagonally (from one corner of the board to the opposite corner) but for any number of squares (known as 'pheel' or elephant in Indian versions of chess)

bi•son /'baɪsən/ noun, c. = a large animal, similar to an Indian buffalo, once found in large numbers in North America

bit /bɪt/ noun, c. **1** *The floor was covered with bits of paper.* = a small piece or quantity of something **2** = a thin piece of metal that is put inside the mouth of a horse and used to control its movements **3** *I am a bit tired.* = a little (informal) **4** = the smallest unit of information that can be stored in a computer's memory (see also **byte**) [COMPUTERS] **5** *I have a bit of news to give you.* = some **6** *I'd like to rest for a bit.* = a short while **7** *a bit of pineapple* = a small part of something larger **8** *I've heard the song many times and particularly like the bit when the piano comes in.* = part **9** *'Were you afraid when he told us the ghost story?' 'Not a bit.'* = not at all (informal) **10** *The railway station was not far, but it was a bit of a nuisance walking all the way with heavy bags.* = not very much, but enough to cause a problem (used to refer to unpleasant things)

to do one's bit = to help as much as one can in something in which others are also helping **bits and pieces** *I see that you've packed. It'll take me some time to get my bits and pieces together.* = small items which have to be put away, packed, taken etc. (informal) **bit by bit** *He had no friends at first but bit by bit he made a number of friends.* = slowly **to be a bit much** *Borrowing the car for a day was all right, but asking to keep it for a week was a bit much.* = to be not right or fair; to go too far (informal) **blown to bits** = to shatter (as the result of an explosion) **to champ at the bit** = to get impatient to start some activity **to take a bit of doing** *The house is lovely but will take quite a bit of doing before we move in.* = to have work that is difficult to do

bitch[1] /bɪtʃ/ noun, c. **1** = a she-dog (the female of a dog) **2** = a word used to describe a woman who is considered bad-tempered, unfair, or having a bad character (derogatory) USE

bitch[2] verb, i. *He loves to bitch about his office whenever he gets the chance.* = to complain in a way which others think is not correct (derogatory) USE

bite[1] /baɪt/ verb, t. or i. (**bit, bitten**) **1** *The dog will bite you if you go too close.*(t.) // *That dog doesn't bite.*(i.) = to cut or attack someone or something using the teeth **2** *The fish are not biting today.*(i.) = not accepting the bait (food put on the hook to attract fish)

bite[2] noun, c. **1** *He took a big bite out of the apple.* = a piece which has been cut out of something by the teeth **2** *I haven't had a bite to eat all day.* = something to eat **biting** /'baɪtɪŋ/ adj. **1** *The biting wind outside made us stay indoors.* = sharply cold **2** *biting words* = harsh and hurtful **bitten** /'bɪtən/ verb, t. *bitten by a dog* = to receive a bite from some animal

to bite one's tongue = to try to prevent oneself from saying something that may cause unpleasantness etc. **to bite somebody's head off** = to snap or answer someone in a very angry way (informal) **to bite the hand that feeds one** *I have been helping Mohan for years, but he is now turning against me. How can he bite the hand that feeds him?* = to harm someone who has helped you **to bite off more than one can chew** = to attempt more than one can manage to do

bit•ter /'bɪtə^r/ adj. **1** *Coffee has a bitter taste.* = sharp and slightly unpleasant taste (opposite **sweet**) **2** *Winters in Canada are bitter.* = very sharply cold (opposite **mild**) **3** *We had a bitter experience on the train.* = unpleasant and painful (opposite **pleasant** or **happy**) **4** *This is the bitter truth.* = hard to accept **5** *a bitter enemy* = causing deep hatred **bitterly** adv. **1** *We complained bitterly to the tour operator about how badly the tour had been organized.* = in a strong way, in order that attention is paid to what is said **2** *It* *was bitterly cold in the hills.* = sharply **bitterness** noun, u. *Although he has suffered so much, he has no bitterness.* = feelings of hatred or dislike **bitter-sweet** adj. *I have bitter-sweet memories of childhood.* = pleasant but mixed with sadness

to the bitter end *Although our soldiers were tired, we fought to the bitter end.* = to the end, which may be unpleasant (sometimes humorous) **a bitter pill (to swallow)** = something which is very unpleasant or hurtful but which one has to put up with

bi•tu•men /ˈbɪtʃʊmɪn/ noun, u. = a hard, sticky substance used for making roads

bi-week•ly /baɪˈwiːklɪ/ *a bi-weekly magazine* = something that appears once in two weeks; fortnightly

bi•zarre /bɪˈzɑː/ adj. *Your friend walked into the room and suddenly started jumping all over the furniture. His behaviour was really bizarre.* = odd or strange in an unusual way (disapproving)

blab•ber /ˈblæbəʳ/ verb, t. *She blabbered on about the book she is writing, though I wasn't really interested.* = to talk foolishly and too much (derogatory, not respectful)

black[1] /blæk/ adj. **1** *black hair* = dark **2** *black coffee* = without milk **3** = member of a race/group which is dark-skinned; a member of an African group (see box) **4** *black poetry* = written by or about Afro-Caribbean groups **5** *black and white film/camera/television* = not in colour but in black, white and grey tones **6** *The windows were black with soot and we had to clean them.* = very dirty **7** *We had a good year last year, but now things are looking black.* = without hope **8** *a black look* = full of hate and anger

black[2] noun, u. *She was dressed in black.* = in black clothes (often a sign of mourning)

(to be) in the black *Our company was losing money, but now we are in the black.* = making profits (opposite **in the red**) **to black out** **1** = to faint (informal) **2** *They blacked out the words they didn't want us to read.* = to cover with black ink so that something cannot be read **in black and white** *Are you willing to put this in black and white?* = in writing (which can have legal value) **black sheep** *the black sheep of the family* = a person who is a cause of disappointment or misery to others connected with him/her

> **Usage** The adjective **black** needs to be used with care. It may be useful to remember the following:
>
> **black,** when referring to the African races, is a technical word. The terms African American (USA) and Afro-Caribbean (UK) are now preferred.
>
> The terms **negro** and **coloured** are now considered offensive.
>
> There is a growing trend in favour of avoiding the use of **black** to mean bad, inferior or unpleasant.

black arts /ˈblækɑːts/ noun = the use of supernatural powers to tell the future or to control events (also black magic) (often derogatory)

black belt /ˈblækbelt/ noun, c. *He is a black belt in judo and karate.* = a person who is an expert in judo, karate or other martial arts

black•bird /ˈblækbɜːd/ noun, c. = a small black bird found in Europe and America

black•board /ˈblækbɔːd/ noun, c. = a board with a black surface which a teacher uses to write on with chalk etc. (The word '**chalkboard**' is often used instead of **blackboard**)

black com•e•dy /ˈblækˈkɒmɪdi/ noun, c. (**-comedies**) = a drama, film or book which is funny but which also brings out the dark and unpleasant side of human life [TECHNICAL]

black hole /ˈblæk həʊl/ noun, c. = an area in outer space into which everything nearby, including light, is sucked in and cannot escape because of a strong gravitational field [TECHNICAL/ASTRONOMY]

black•list /ˈblæklɪst/ noun, c. = a list of people, companies, etc. who are to be avoided and with whom no business is to be done

black magic /ˈblækmædʒɪk/ noun, u. = see **black arts** (opposite **white magic**)

black•mail /ˈblækmeɪl/ verb, t. *They saw him drunk one night and are now trying to blackmail him and get some money out of him.* = to try to get money out of someone by threatening to reveal (make known) something bad or unpleasant about that person

black•mar•ket[1] /ˈblækmɑːkɪt/ noun, c. *He sells cinema tickets in the black market.*

blackmarket[2] verb, t. *He blackmarkets cinema tickets.* = selling things at a price higher than what is legal, or in a hidden and secret manner

black•out /ˈblækaʊt/ noun, c. **1** *There are no lights in the house. There is a blackout.* = a period of darkness when there is no supply of electric power **2** *She had a temporary blackout and fell down.* = loss of consciousness or memory for a short time

black•smith /ˈblæksmɪθ/ noun, c. = a person who makes and repairs things made of iron

blad•der /ˈblædəʳ/ noun, c. **1** *the urinary bladder* = a bag inside the body in which urine collects before it is passed out **2** *a football bladder* = a bag made of rubber or other material which can be filled with air or some liquid

blade /bleɪd/ noun, c. **1** *the blade of a knife*; *a razor blade* = the flat, sharp part of a knife or razor which can cut **2** *a blade of grass* = a long, flat leaf of grass

blame[1] /bleɪm/ verb, t. *The government blamed the driver of the train for the accident.* = to hold someone responsible for something bad that happens

B

blame[2] noun, u. *The blame will come to you if something goes wrong.* = the responsibility for something bad that happens **blameless** adj. = free from blame or guilt; innocent

bland /blænd/ adj. **1** *This curry is so bland that I cannot eat it.* = without taste (often derogatory) **2** *This book is very bland.* = not very interesting; very ordinary

blank[1] /blæŋk/ adj. **1** *Give me a blank sheet of paper.* = empty, with no writing, pictures etc. on it **2** *When I asked him a question he looked blank.* = not showing understanding or feelings

blank[2] noun, c. *Fill in the blanks using suitable words.* = an empty space or line on which something has to be written **blank cheque** noun, c. = a cheque which has been signed but in which the amount to be paid is not mentioned and can be filled in later

to go blank *I knew the answer to the question but when the examiner asked me, I went blank.* = to fail to speak the necessary words at an important time as a result of shock, fear, nervousness etc. **to blank something out** **1** = to erase or cover something written so that it can no longer be read **2** = to take a decision to forget something unpleasant, sad etc.

blan•ket[1] /'blæŋkɪt/ noun, c, **1** *It is very cold tonight. I need a blanket to cover myself.* = a heavy covering made of wool, used as protection from the cold **2** *There was a blanket of snow on the ground.* = a thick covering (figurative)

blanket[2] adj. *I have blanket permission from the Principal to invite anyone I like to the function.* = unlimited (formal)

blank verse noun, u. = poetry which has rhythm but no rhyme (in which the last word in a line does not match the sound of the last word in the previous line) [LITERATURE]

blare[1] /bleəʳ/ verb, i. *The horns of the cars were blaring so loudly that I almost became deaf.* = to make a loud, harsh sound

blare[2] noun, u. *the blare of trumpets* = the sound made by horns, trumpets etc.

blasé /'blɑːzeɪ/ adj. (French) *I thought he would be very excited about the new computer, but he was quite blasé.* = not showing interest or happiness when expected to do so

blas•phe•my /'blæsfɪmi/ noun, c. (**blasphemies**) or u. = a statement showing lack of respect to God or things that are considered holy **blaspheme** /blæs'fiːm/ verb, i. = to talk disrespectfully about God or things people consider holy

blast[1] /blɑːst/ noun, c. **1** *Many people were injured in the bomb blast.* = explosion **2** *There was a blast of hot air from the desert.* = sudden and strong movement of wind **3** *a blast of the trumpet* = the loud sound produced by some musical instruments

blast[2] verb, t. **1** *The engineers are going to blast this rock with dynamite.* = to break something into pieces by using an **explosive** substance **2** *The television was blasting away all morning.* = making a loud, unpleasant sound **3** *I was blasted for delivering the package late.* = to be scolded strongly (informal) **blast-furnace** noun, c.= a tower in which iron ore is melted to take out metal **blast-off** noun = the exact moment when a rocket is fired and leaves the ground

bla•tant /'bleɪtənt/ adj. *Why did you go away when I had ordered you to stay? You should be punished for this blatant act of disobedience.* = something done deliberately and without shame, in a way that everyone can see

blaze[1] /bleɪz/ noun, c **1** *The tiny flames grew into a blaze.* = a sudden bright flame **2** *The firemen were able to control the blaze.* = a large, strong and dangerous fire **3** *a blaze of anger // a blaze of colour* = a violent or sudden burst of anger or colour (figurative) **blazing** adj.

blaze[2] verb, i. **1** *There was a fire blazing in the fireplace.* = to burn brightly **2** *The room was blazing with sunshine.* = to be very bright (figurative)

to blaze a trail = to do something good which had not been done before **to be blazed all over** *The story of the crime was blazed all over the newspapers.* = written about in a newspaper, magazine etc. in a bold, detailed way

blaz•er /'bleɪzə/ noun, c.= a jacket (coat) usually made of woollen cloth, which carries the special sign (emblem) of a team, club, school etc.

bleach[1] /bliːtʃ/ verb, t. *We use ammonia gas to bleach paper and make it look white.* = to use some chemical or sunlight to take away the colour of something and make it look white or pale

bleach[2] noun, u. = a chemical used to bleach something **bleaching-powder** noun, u. = a whitish powder used to bleach things and also to kill germs

bleak /bliːk/ adj. **1** *I got only 10 marks in the test. The chances of my passing the final examination look bleak.* = not hopeful or encouraging **2** *The house had not been repaired or painted for years and looked bleak.* = causing a feeling of sadness; depressing

blear•y /'blɪəri/ adj. *He had not slept all night and looked bleary-eyed.* = (of the eyes or face) showing tiredness due to lack of sleep etc.

bleat[1] /bliːt/ verb, i. *He was bleating something in a shrill voice.* = to make the sound made by sheep or goats or to speak in a thin, high-pitched voice (not respectful)

bleat[2] noun, c. = the noise made by a goat or sheep

bleed /bliːd/ verb, i. or t. **1** *His nose was bleeding.*

(i.) = to lose blood **2** *They have been bleeding the company for years, and now there is nothing left.*(t.) = to rob someone or something of money **3** *I will have to bleed the brakes of your car.*(t.)= to draw out liquid or air from a machine to make it work properly **bleeding-time** noun, u. = the time taken by the blood flowing from a fresh wound to dry up and stop flowing [MEDICINE]

bleep[1] /bli:p/ noun, c. = a long, high-pitched sound given out repeatedly by a machine to attract attention

bleep[2] verb, i. = to produce a bleeping sound **bleeper** noun, c. = a small machine carried in the pocket which makes a bleeping sound (usually to show that someone wants to speak to you on the telephone)

blem•ish[1] /ˈblemɪʃ/ noun, c. or u. *Her beautiful face was without a blemish.*(c.) = some fault that spoils the loveliness or perfect quality of someone or something

blem•ish[2] verb, t. *Her good record has been blemished by the mistake she made.* = to spoil

blend[1] /blend/ verb, t. **1** *You have to blend flour, sugar and eggs to make a cake.* = to mix two or more things together **2** *The flowers blend well with the blue walls.* = to produce a pleasant effect when brought together

blend[2] noun, c. *This is a blend of Indian and western music.* = something produced by mixing things together **blender** = a small electric machine used in the kitchen to turn solid things into liquids for cooking or as soups or juices (also **mixer**)

bless /ˈbles/ verb, t. **1** *Please come to the wedding and bless the bride and the bridegroom.* = to express a wish that God may protect or bring happiness to someone (done by older relatives etc. on the occasion of a wedding, birthday etc.) **2** *You have been blessed with a daughter.* = to be lucky enough to have **blessed** adj. **1** *blessed music* = having a calming effect **2** *Who's the blessed person who took my book?* = a word used to show that one is mildly annoyed (often humorous) **blessing** noun, c. or u. *You have my blessings.*= good wishes expressed by an older person for approval, support etc. for a younger person

to count one's blessings (always plural) = to believe that one is fortunate to have what one has **a blessing in disguise** *The rain was a blessing in disguise because we were forced to stay indoors and complete our work.* = something that looks as if it will spoil, stop, delay etc. something but which turns out to be an unexpected source of help

blight[1] /blaɪt/ noun, u. *onion blight* = any disease that affects plants

blight[2] verb, t. *The crops have been blighted by some strange disease. // Her life has been blighted by illness.* = spoil; damage (figurative)

blind[1] /blaɪnd/ adj. **1** *a blind person* = not able to see (see note) **2** *a blind corner in the road* = a place at which it is difficult to see what lies ahead **3** *blind belief // blind faith* = very strong but not supported by reason **4** *blind anger/rage* = very strong and without reason

blind[2] verb, t. or i. **1** *I was blinded by the headlights of the car.*(t.) = to be made unable to see, temporarily **2** = to make someone sightless by an act of violence

blind[3] noun, c. *a window blind* = a piece of cloth or other material used to cover a window **blinding** adj. **1** *the blinding headlights of a car* = so bright as to cause the eyes to shut **2** *a blinding headache* = causing so much pain and discomfort as to make it difficult for one to concentrate on anything **blind alley** noun, c. (**alleys**) = a narrow lane with no way out at the other end; a dead-end **blindfold** noun, c. or verb, t. **1** (noun) = a piece of cloth tied over someone's eyes so that he/she is unable to see **2** (verb) = to tie a blindfold over someone's eyes **blind spot** noun, c. **1** = a part of the road just behind you that you cannot see when driving a car **2** *Modern art is my blind spot.* = a person or thing that one cannot understand or accept

to be blind to something *He is blind to her faults.* = unable or unwilling to accept or understand something, usually because of love or trust **to be as blind as a bat** = to be unable to see properly (humorous) **to turn a blind eye to something** *She knew I had made a mistake but decided to turn a blind eye to it.* = to choose to not take notice of something wrong

Usage Other phrases are now preferred when referring to someone who cannot see. (**Blind** is sometimes considered too direct and not respectful.)
visually challenged (formal)
not sighted
vision-impaired

blink[1] /blɪŋk/ verb, i. or t. **1** *Please don't blink your eyes when the doctor is trying to examine them.*(t.) = to shut and open one's eyes quickly **2** *The traffic lights are blinking.*(i.) = to go on and off repeatedly

blink[2] noun, c. *The camera caught the blink.* = the act of closing and opening the eyes quickly

blink•ers /blɪŋkərz/ noun, c. (always plural) *the horse's blinkers* = small pieces of leather fixed on either side of a horse's head, allowing the animal to look only straight ahead and not to either side **blinkered** adj. *blinkered opinions* = fixed ideas which prevent one from seeing things from a different point of view

to wear blinkers = to have fixed ideas or opinions **on the blink** *The washing machine is on the blink so I will* *have to wash the clothes by hand.* = out of order (informal) **to happen in the blink of an eye** = in an extremely short time

blip /blɪp/ noun, c. = a very short sound or image produced once or several times by an electrical machine e.g. a machine that records the heartbeats of a person

bliss /blɪs/ noun, u. *Listening to classical music on the radio is his idea of bliss.* = perfect happiness

blis•ter[1] /'blɪstəʳ/ noun, c. **1** = a small swelling in the skin, filled with liquid, caused by burning, rubbing etc. **2** *a blister in the paint* = a bump or swelling in any surface, filled with liquid (like a blister)

blis•ter[2] verb, i. or t. *The heat was so great that the paint on the walls of the building blistered.* = to swell up (like a blister)

blitz /blɪts/ noun (German) **1** *The German Air Force carried out a blitz on England during the war.* = a heavy attack of planes from the air, made on an enemy **2** *We are planning a publicity blitz.* = a period of great activity for some special purpose (informal)

bliz•zard /'blɪzəd/ noun, c. = a heavy snow-storm

bloat•ed /'bləʊtɪd/ adj. *The bloated body of a dead animal floated down the river.* = greatly swollen

blob /blɒb/ noun, c. **1** *a blob of paint on the page* = a drop of some liquid that forms a round mark **2** *He was out for a blob in this match.* = zero (informal)

bloc /blɒk/ noun, c. *the Communist bloc* = a group of nations or people who have come together for a common cause

block[1] /blɒk/ noun, c. **1** *a block of stone* = a large, solid piece of stone, wood etc. **2** *a block of flats* = a building containing many flats **3** *He has a block in one of his arteries.* = something that prevents movement or flow (also **blockage**) **4** = in a game or sport, a move made to prevent the opponent from moving forward (towards the goal)

block[2] verb, t. *Please allow us to pass and do not block the way* = to make it difficult to pass **block booking** = a situation in which a number of seats in a cinema etc. are booked by a group **blockbuster** noun, c. = a highly successful film or book (informal) **block capitals** noun (always plural) *Write your name in block capitals on the application form.* = large capital letters (also **block letters**)

block•ade /blɒ'keɪd/ noun, c. = the process of stopping people or goods from moving in or out of a place by surrounding it with troops, ships etc.

blonde /blɒnd/ noun, c. *a blonde* = a woman or man with hair of very light colour

blood /blʌd/ noun, u. **1** = the red liquid carried by the veins and arteries in the body **2** *a man of royal blood* = family **blood-bank** noun, c. = a place where blood is stored and can be used by people who have lost blood after an accident or operation **bloodbath** noun, c. = the killing of many people together; a massacre **blood count** noun, c. = a medical examination of a person's blood to test if it contains the right amounts of all the blood cells **blood-curdling** adj. *a blood-curdling story* = extremely frightening **blood donor** noun, c. = a person who gives blood to someone who is in need of blood (see **blood transfusion**) **blood group** noun, c. = one of the four groups or classes (A, B, AB, O) into which human blood can be divided, depending on the presence or absence of certain substances **blood poisoning** noun, u. = a serious condition in which the blood is infected with bacteria **blood pressure** noun, u. = the force with which blood travels through the body because of the action of the heart **blood relation** noun, c. = a person who has been born into the same family as someone else **blood sport** noun, c. = the hunting and killing of animals for pleasure **bloodstain** noun, c. = a mark (on clothes, weapons etc.) left by blood **blood transfusion** noun, c. = the process of putting blood into the body of a person who is in need of blood **blood type** noun, c. (see **blood-group**) **blood vessel** noun, c. = any of the tubes through which blood flows inside the body

to kill someone in cold blood = after careful planning and in a cruel manner **flesh and blood** = the member of one's own family **to make one's blood boil** *The sight of cruelty to animals makes my blood boil.* = to make one very angry

blood•y /'blʌdi/ adj. **1** *He hit a lamp-post and came home with a bloody nose.* = with blood all over **2** *a bloody fool!* = a word used in anger to describe someone or something (informal, derogatory) **bloody-minded** adj. *You seem to enjoy saying 'No' to everything. Why are you so bloody-minded?* = one who opposes the wishes of others for no good reason (derogatory)

bloom[1] /bluːm/ noun, c. *a beautiful rose bloom* = a flower that has opened out (is not a bud)

bloom[2] verb, i. **1** *I will make the garden bloom again.* = to produce flowers **2** *She seems to be blooming after her holiday.* = to look very healthy (figurative) **3** *I am glad to see your business blooming.* = to prosper (be successful)

blos•som[1] /'blɒsəm/ noun, c. *an apple blossom* = the flower of a tree or bush from which a fruit can be produced

blossom[2] verb, i. **1** *The mango trees are blossoming.* = to produce flowers from which fruits will come **2** *Let our friendship blossom into something meaningful.* = grow

blot[1] /blɒt/ noun, c. **1** *an ink blot* = a drop of liquid (specially ink) that makes something look dirty **2** *This theft has left a blot on your record.* = a thing that spoils someone's opinion of you

blot[2] verb, t. *You have blotted the paper so badly that I can't read what you have written.* = to make blots on something **blotting paper** noun, u. = a kind of thick and soft paper used to remove ink blots

to blot one's copybook = to spoil the good name one enjoyed before

blouse /blaʊz/ noun, c. **1** = a garment that covers the upper part of a woman's body, generally reaching above the waist, worn with a sari **2** = a loose garment for the upper part, of a woman's body, worn with skirts or trousers

blow[1] /bləʊ/ verb, i. or t. **1** *The wind is blowing hard.*(i.) = to move air forcefully in a strong current **2** *The wind blew down all the trees.*(t.) = to make something move by the power of the wind **3** *Ask the children to blow up the balloons.*(i.) = to fill something with air from the lungs, coming out of the mouth **4** *Use a handkerchief when you blow your nose.*(t.) = to clean one's nose by sending a strong breath through it **5** *We blew our money on a new television set.*(t.) = to spend money on something without thinking about it (informal) **6** *The lights went out because the fuse blew.*(i.) = to stop working because of some fault in the electrical circuit **7** *By doing no study, you've blown your chances of doing well in the exam.*(t.) = to spoil one's chance of something good happening

blow[2] noun, c. **1** *He gave me a blow on the jaw.* = a hard hit given with the hand or a weapon **2** *Her death was a big blow to me.* = sudden shock or disappointment

to blow out = to put out a fire or flame **to blow over** *The quarrel has now blown over.* = to come to an end after going on for some time **to blow up 1** *blow up rock with dynamite* = to break or destroy something by using an explosive **2** *blow up a photograph* = to make something, especially a photographic image, larger (informal) **3** *They saw the mess in the room and blew me up.* = to scold (informal) **to blow something out of proportion** = to make something look much more serious than it really is **to blow hot and cold** = to have opinions which are always changing and even opposite to each other (informal) **to blow one's mind** *The special effects in the film are so good that they will blow your mind.* = to fill someone with wonder and admiration (informal) **to blow something sky-high** = to destroy something completely **to blow one's own trumpet** = to talk very highly of oneself and one's achievements **a blow-by-blow account** = a detailed description of some event

blow•er /'bləʊə^r/ noun, c. = a large fan which can produce a strong current of air

blub•ber /'blʌbə^r/ noun, u. = the fat from the body of an animal, specially a whale

blud•geon /'blʌdʒən/ noun, c. = a short, heavy stick used as a weapon

blue[1] /blu:/ adj. **1** *the blue sky* = a colour e.g. of a clear sky on a sunny day **2** *I am feeling very blue.* = sad (informal)

blue[2] noun **1** = the colour blue **2** *the Blues* = a type of slow, sad music **3** *a cricket blue* = a person who has played for Cambridge or Oxford University **blue-bird** noun, c. = a small, blue singing bird **blue-blooded** adj. = from a royal or noble family **blue-bottle** noun, c. = a large, blue-coloured fly (insect) **blue-eyed boy** noun, c. *the Principal's blue-eyed boy* = a male person who is a great favourite of someone important (informal, sometimes disapproving) **blue film** noun, c. = a film showing sex, which is seen secretly (informal) **blue jeans** noun, c. (used only in plural form **jeans**) = trousers made of thick cloth, often blue in colour, which can stand a lot of rough use **blueprint** noun, c. = a drawing showing the plan for building a house or machine

to get the blues = to be sad and without hope, usually for a short period **once in a blue moon** *We don't like crowded places much so we go to the cinema only once in a blue moon.* = very seldom, very rarely **out of the blue/a bolt from the blue** *She wrote to us out of the blue.* = happening very unexpectedly and causing great surprise (informal) **to do something until one is blue in the face** *I advised them until I was blue in the face, but they wouldn't listen.* = to make a great effort to argue, advise, console etc. but without success

bluff[1] /blʌf/ verb, i. or t. *He says he has won a free holiday abroad but I think he is only bluffing.*(i.) = to try to cheat or trick someone by pretending falsely to be (or do) something

bluff[2] noun, c. or u. *If he tells you that he can create trouble for you, don't believe him. It's only a bluff.* = a false statement made to impress or frighten someone

blun•der[1] /'blʌndə^r/ noun, c. *I made a terrible blunder! I switched the computer off without saving my file.* = a foolish but serious mistake

blunder[2] verb, i. *Sometimes one can blunder out of ignorance.* = to make a foolish but serious mistake

blunt[1] /blʌnt/ adj. **1** *You can't cut vegetables with this knife. It's blunt.* = not sharp enough to cut **2** *Your blunt talk will get you into trouble.* = honest; saying exactly what one thinks and therefore likely to hurt another's feelings

blunt[2] verb, t. *I don't want to go on the picnic. The bad weather has blunted my desire to go out.* = to make something less sharp or strong

blur[1] /blɜ:/ noun, c. *I can't see the house clearly*

B

because it is too far away. It looks like a blur from here. = something which does not have a clear shape

blur[2] verb, t. *The mist has blurred everything. I can't see the house clearly.* = to make something less clear and not easy to see

blurb /blɜːb/ noun, c. *The blurb on the cover of the book calls it 'The best guide to restaurants in the city'.*= a short description of a book, usually printed on the cover, intended to make people want to read it

blurt /blɜːt/ verb, t. *When the policeman threatened to arrest him, he blurted out the truth.* = to speak suddenly and without thinking, because of fear, excitement etc.

blush[1] /blʌʃ/ verb, i. *He blushed when I told him he looked very handsome.* = to become red in the face because one feels embarassed (uncomfortable), nervous etc.

blush[2] noun, c. *Your words brought a blush to his cheeks.* = the red colour appearing on the cheeks of a person when he/she feels embarrassed, because of good things said

blus•ter /'blʌstə/ verb, i. = to speak in a loud uneven voice in a boastful way

boa con•stric•tor noun, c. = a large snake seen in South America that crushes (constricts) its prey

boar /bɔːʳ/ noun, c. = a male pig

board[1] /bɔːd/ noun, c. **1** = a piece of wood which is usually square or rectangular and flat **2** *The Board of Directors of the company* = the group of people who control a company **3** *I am paying Rs 500 a month for my board.* = the cost of food supplied in a hostel, guest-house etc.

board[2] verb, i. **1** *I will board the train at Nagpur.* = to get into a bus, plane, train or ship **2** *I am boarding in the boy's hostel now.* = to get food in a hostel etc. **boarder** noun, c. = a person who lives in a boarding-house or hostel **boarding card** = a card given to a passenger on an aircraft to show that he/she has the right to board (enter) **board game** noun, c. = a game played by moving counters (small, flat, round pieces of plastic etc.) on a board (usually made of thick paper) e.g. Ludo or Snakes and Ladders **boarding (house)** noun = a private house or a building where one can get accommodation and food at a cheap price **board meeting** noun = a meeting where the Directors of a company come together **board room** noun = the room in which meetings are held **boarding school** noun, c. = a school which provides living accommodation for its students

to board something up *The entrance to the building has been boarded up.* = to cover something with boards (flat pieces of wood) to show that it is out of use, being repaired etc.

boast[1] /bəʊst/ verb, i. or t. **1** *He is always boasting about the big house he lived in when he was a child.*(i.) = to talk in a way that is intended to give others an unreal idea of one's greatness or importance (derogatory) **2** *This town boasts a zoo and a botanical garden.*(t.) = to have (not derogatory)

boast[2] noun, c. *Can you live up to your boast that you score a century in every match?* = an expression of self-praise **boastful** adj. = fond of boasting

boat /'bəʊt/ noun, c. = a vessel, usually small and open to the sky, in which one can travel across short stretches of water

to be in the same boat (as someone else) *Both Hema and I are without jobs, so we are in the same boat.* = to be going through an unpleasant or difficult experience which is similar to someone else's **to burn one's boats** *Our music teacher decided to act in films but she knew she was burning her boats. If she failed, she would never be able to return to the school.* = to give up something that one has in an attempt to get something better or more attractive

bob /bɒb/ verb, i. or t. **1** *The boat was floating, but the waves made it bob up and down.*(i.) = to move up or down quickly, specially in water **2** *She has bobbed her hair. It used to be very long.*(t.) = to cut one's hair short

bod•y /'bɒdi/ noun, c. (**bodies**) **1** *You should have a healthy mind in a healthy body.* = the physical structure of a human being or animal **2** *bodies recovered from the plane crash* = a dead person **3** *She had a rash on her arms and legs but not on her body.* = the part of one's physical structure which does not include the limbs and head **4** *Shakespeare has left behind a large body of work.* = a large collection or volume **5** *The houses of Parliament are elected bodies.* = a group of people working together for some purpose **6** *heavenly bodies // foreign bodies* = object **7** *The body of the car was damaged in the accident but nothing happened to the engine.* = the part of a car, bus or plane inside which passengers sit **bodily** adj. *I hope you didn't suffer any bodily harm.* = of the body **body-blow** noun, c. **1** = a hit received by a boxer (in the sport of boxing) on the body (below the neck and not on the arms) **2** = any serious loss or disappointment suffered by a person **body-building** noun, u. = a sport in which one tries to build one's muscles through exercise, usually by lifting heavy weights **body-builder** noun, c. = a person who takes part in the sport of body-building **bodyguard** noun, c. = a person whose job is to protect an important person **body language** noun, u. = the use of the body to express one's feelings without the use of words (informal) **body odour (also b.o.)** noun, u. = the unpleasant smell given out by the body of a person, because of too much perspiration etc.

bog[1] /bɒg/ noun, c. = an area of soft, wet ground, usually covered with plants, into which one's feet sink; marshy land

bog[2] verb, t. *Our efforts to bring relief to the people of Ersama got bogged down because we ran out of funds.* = to get stuck up or to be held up, so that one is unable to do anything

to get bogged down = to be unable to move ahead or make progress

bog•gle /ˈbɒgəl/ verb, i. **1** *He boggled when someone suggested that he should pay for the dinner.* = to hesitate or refuse to do something **2** *The mind boggles when one tries to imagine the state of the world's forests at the end of this century.* = to become completely confused, shocked and unable to think

bo•gus /ˈbəʊgəs/ adj. *casting a bogus vote* = false, not genuine (generally used to talk about votes, documents etc.)

boil[1] /bɔɪl/ verb, t. or i. **1** *Please boil some water for the tea.*(t.) = to heat a liquid until it begins to turn into a gas **2** *The water has begun to boil.*(i.) = to reach the boiling point

boil[2] noun, c. = a painful swelling on the skin **boiler** noun, c. = a large vessel in which water is heated to provide hot water, heat or steam **boiling point** = the temperature at which a liquid starts to boil and turn into gas

to boil down to something *You have sent us a three page letter, but what it all boils down to is that you don't want to participate in the competition.*= the main point or substance

bois•ter•ous /ˈbɔɪstərəs/ adj. *The atmosphere in the classroom was so boisterous that the teacher had to stop the lesson.*= happy and noisy and full of energy (disapproving)

bold /bəʊld/ adj. **1** *Come on, don't be afraid! You must be bold.*= brave **2** *You shouldn't talk to your teacher like that! How can you be so bold?*= disrespectful and rude (disapproving) **3** *The painter has used very bold lines in this painting.* = strong and clear **boldface** noun, u. = thick black letters used in printing to make something prominent

bol•ster[1] /ˈbəʊlstəʳ/ noun, c. = a long, cylinder-shaped pillow

bolster[2] verb, t. *The excellent monsoon this year has bolstered agricultural production.* = to help or to increase

bolt[1] /bəʊlt/ noun, c. **1** = a long metal screw that slides into a metal nut **2** = a metal bar that slides across a door or window to prevent anyone from getting in **3** *a bolt of lightning* = a sudden, very bright flash of lightning

bolt[2] verb, t. or i. **1** *Please bolt the door.*(t.) = to make a door or window safe by sliding the bolt across it. **2** *The horse bolted when the cracker burst.*(i.) = to run, usually in fear or to escape from something

a bolt from the blue = see under **blue** **bolt upright** = to sit or stand absolutely straight **to lock the stable after the horse has bolted** = to do something so late that it has no effect

bomb[1] /bɒm/ noun, c. **1** = a metal container which has some explosive and small pieces of metal that will explode when thrown or dropped

bomb[2] verb, t. **1** *bomb enemy positions* = to attack with bombs, specially from the air **2** *We thought the new film would be successful, but it bombed.*(i.) = to be unsuccessful and cause a big loss (referring to a book or film) (informal) **bomber** /ˈbɒməʳ/ noun, c. = a plane or person that carries bombs and explodes them on a position occupied by an enemy **bombshell** /ˈbɒmʃel/ noun, c. *The organiser dropped a bombshell by announcing that the tournament had been cancelled.*= a piece of news which is not pleasant and which causes great surprise (informal)

bom•bard /bɒmˈbɑːd/ verb, t. **1** *bombard the city* = to attack continuously with big guns or with bombs **2** *She bombarded me with questions.* = to ask so many questions or give so much information that one becomes confused (informal) **bombardment** noun, u. = an attack carried out with big guns

bo•na•fi•de /bəʊnəˈfaɪdi/ adj. *Lunch will be served to bonafide passengers travelling by this train.*= genuine and legal **bonafides** noun (always plural) *The police asked me to establish my bonafides.* = proof of being genuine (formal)

bo•nan•za /bəˈnænzə/ noun, c. *The film proved to be a real bonanza for the producer.* = something that brings in great profit

bond[1] /bɒnd/ noun, c. **1** *There is usually a close bond between those who are in the same class for many years in school.* = a feeling of unity or friendship **2** *I have signed a bond to serve this company for at least three years.* = a legal document on which an agreement between two parties is recorded **3** *I have invested my money in government bonds.* = a paper in which a government or company promises to pay back, with interest, money which has been lent **4** (always plural) = ropes, chains etc. which are used to tie someone up and make him/her a prisoner [LITERARY]

bond[2] verb, i. or t. **1** *You can bond these two pieces of wood together by using this paste.*(t.) = to join together in such a way that the parts are stuck firmly together **2** *The broken pieces will take about an hour to bond.*(i.) = stick together **3** *In school, we students bonded just by spending so much time together.*(i.) = to become close and trusting friends with someone **bonds** noun, c. (always plural) = ropes, chains etc. which are used to tie someone up and make him/her a prisoner **bonded** adj. *bonded labour* = forced to work for someone under a bond (agreement) and having no freedom **bonding** noun, u. *bonding between a parent and a child* = the formation of a bond (a loving relationship) **bondage** noun, u. *living in bondage* = the state of being a slave (not having any freedom)

bone[1] /bəʊn/ noun, c. or u. **1** *He fell and broke a bone in his leg.*(c.) = a hard part of the body inside the skin and flesh **2** = the material in the bone

bone[2] verb, t. *Will you please bone this chicken?* = to remove the bones from the body of an animal before cooking it **bone china** noun, u. = pottery (cups, plates etc.) made of very fine white clay mixed with the bones of animals **bone dry** adj. = perfectly dry **bone lazy/idle** = very lazy or idle **bone meal** noun, u. = the powdered bones of animals, used as fertilizer

to become a bone of contention = something that causes a quarrel **to have a bone to pick** *I have a bone to pick with you. You invited everyone else to your party but forgot to invite me. Why?* = to have something to complain about **to make no bones about (doing) something** = to do something in an open and honest way without trying to hide anything **to feel something in one's bones** *She could feel it in her bones that the trip was going to fail.* = to be very sure that something will happen, even through there is no way of proving that it will

bon•fire /ˈbɒnfaɪəʳ/ noun, c. = a large fire which is lit in the open

bon•net /ˈbɒnɪt/ noun, c. **1** = a round covering for the head, tied under the chin, usually won by babies **2** = the metal cover over the engine of a car

to have a bee in one's bonnet *Saif eats only raw vegetables. He has a bee in his bonnet about eating only uncooked food, which is rich in vitamins.* = to have a fixed idea in one's mind about something

bon•sai /ˈbɒnsaɪ/ noun, u. (Japanese) = the art of growing trees in a pot in such a way that they do not reach their full size

bo•nus /ˈbəʊnəs/ noun, c. *We will be paid a thousand rupees extra this month as a Christmas bonus.* = extra payment made to a worker, in addition to the usual pay

book[1] /bʊk/ noun, c. **1** *I am writing a book on the temples of Orissa.* = sheets of paper fastened together as something which can be read or written in **2** *Can you find his name in the company's books?* (always plural) = records

book[2] verb, t. *I have booked two tickets for tonight's show.* = to buy or arrange for something in advance **2** *The police have booked him for murder.* = to write down a charge against someone in the police records **booking** noun, c. *I have made a booking for tonight's show.* = reservation **book-keeping** noun, u. = the act of or the system for keeping accounts in a company or office **bookworm** noun, c. = a person who is very fond of reading books and takes little interest in other things (derogatory)

to be booked up *We couldn't get a room in any hotel as they were all booked up.* = (of a hotel, cinema show etc.) a situation where rooms are all occupied or reserved, in advance **to be in someone's good books** = to be liked or favoured by someone whose opinion is important **to read someone like a book** = to be able to know someone's innermost thoughts easily **to throw the book at someone** = to lose one's temper (informal) **to live/go by the book** = to do something strictly according to the rules (often disapproving)

boom[1] /bu:m/ verb, i. **1** *The drums are booming.* = to make a deep and loud sound which can be heard over a long distance **2** *Business in this town is booming.* = to grow quickly

boom[2] noun, c. (no plural) **1** *the boom of the guns* = loud sound **2** *Our town is going through a period of boom.* = quick growth **a boom town** noun = a place where people suddenly grow rich

boo•mer•ang[1] /ˈbu:məræŋ/ noun, c. = a curved stick made of wood which makes a circle when thrown and returns to the thrower, used in hunting by Australian aborigines

boomerang[2] verb, i. *Your habit of blaming people will boomerang on you some day.* = (referring to some undesirable action) to harm the person who is trying to harm others

boon /bu:n/ noun, c. **1** *ask for a boon* = a wish made before God, asking for something (old-fashioned) **2** *Having a doctor near our house is a real boon for us.* = something that is a very great help

boost[1] /bu:st/ verb, t. *Our books are not selling. Can you think of something that can boost our sales?* = to push up from a lower position; to cause an increase in something

boost[2] noun, c. *The help you offered me yesterday gave my hopes a big boost.* = a push upwards; encouragement **booster** noun, c. *a booster dose of a medicine* = something that boosts (increases the effect of) something else

boot[1] /bu:t/ noun, c. **1** = thick and heavy shoes made of leather or rubber **2** = the covered space at the back of a car where luggage can be stored

boot[2] verb, t. or i. **1** *boot the ball*(t.) = to kick **2** *He was booted out of the office.*(t.) = to dismiss someone from a job in an undignified way (informal, not respectful) **3** *The computer has to be booted before it will start working.*(i.) = to load a programme into the memory of a computer in order to make it ready to work [COMPUTERS] **boot-legger** noun, c. = a person who makes and sells alcoholic drinks illegally

to boot up = to switch a computer on and get one of its programmes working [computers] **to give someone the boot** = to ask someone to leave a job (informal, not respectful) **to get too big for one's boots** = to think too highly of oneself

booth /buːð/ noun, c. **1** = a temporary shop set up at a fair to sell things **2** *a phone booth* = a small enclosed space

boot•y /'buːti/ noun, u. = valuable things which a thief steals, or an army takes away from another country

booze[1] /buːz/ noun, u. = strong alcoholic drink (informal)

booze[2] verb, i. = to have strong alcoholic drinks (informal)

bor•der[1] /'bɔːdəʳ/ noun, c. **1** *Her sari had a red border.*= the edge of a garment **2** *the border between India and Tibet* = the line separating two countries or states **3** *Let's give this picture a border.* = a line or pattern which gives a picture etc. a frame

border[2] verb, t. *Tibet borders India in the north.* = to share a border with **borderline** adj. or noun **1** *The pass-mark in English is 30 but you got 29. Yours was a borderline case.*(adj.) = to lie on the border between two different classes **2** *the borderline between India and China* (noun) = the line on the map which separates two countries

to border on *Their argument bordered on a fight.* = to be very near a point which is an extreme form of somehing

bore[1] /bɔːʳ/ verb, t. **1** *We will have to bore a tube-well here.* = to make a hole in something **2** *His speech was so dull that it bored the audience.* = to make someone lose interest

bore[2] noun, c. **1** *He is such a bore that everyone avoids him.* = a person who talks in a dull and uninteresting way and bores everyone (derogatory) **2** *a 12-bore gun* = the measurement of the hole inside the barrel of a gun **bored** adj. *I got very bored with the film.* = with no more interest in something **boredom** /'bɔːdəm/ noun, u. = the state of being bored by something **boring** adj. = dull and uninteresting

born /bɔːn/ adj. *Amitabh Bachchan was born in 1947.* = to begin life; to come out of one's mother's body or out of an egg and be a separate living being

born and bred *I was born and bred in Mumbai.* = to be born and to spend a good part of one's early life in a place **a born (singer)** = having a natural talent for something **to not be born yesterday** *Don't try to fool me. I wasn't born yesterday.* = to have enough experience of the world not to be tricked or cheated easily

borne /bɔːn/ verb, t. (past participle of **bear**) *Our efforts have borne fruit at last.* = to produce results **air-borne** adj. = things that are carried by air or sent to a place by air **water-borne** adj. *water-borne diseases* = things that are carried by water

bor•row /'bɒrəʊ/ verb, t. *I want to borrow your car for a few days as my car is being repaired.*= to take something (e.g. money, a pen) from someone for a short time, with the intention of returning it **borrower** noun, c. = a person who borrows something from someone

bos•om /'bʊzəm/ noun, c. *He hugged me to his bosom.* = chest; a woman's breasts

boss[1] /bɒs/ noun, c. = a person who is your employer or your senior and who supervises your work (informal)

boss[2] verb, t. *Don't try to boss me around.* = to act like someone's boss (to give orders to someone) (informal) **bossy** adj. *a bossy person* = someone who likes to give orders to others (derogatory)

bot•a•ny /'bɒtəni/ noun = the scientific study of plants **botanical** /bə'tænɪkəl/ adj. *a botanical garden* = connected with plants or the study of botany **botanist** /'bɒtənɪst/ noun, c. = a scientist who studies plants [BIOLOGY]

botch /bɒtʃ/ verb, t. *Although he is a good actor, he botched up the show tonight.* = to do a very bad job of something; to spoil (informal)

both[1] /bəʊθ/ det. *Both the girls have come.* = (of two) one as well as the other

both[2] pro. *Are the girls here? I want to meet both.* = the two persons (see usage note under **all**)

both•er[1] /'bɒðəʳ/ verb, t. **1** *He is busy. Don't bother him now.* = to disturb or trouble someone **2** *Don't bother to return the book. I have read it already.* = to trouble oneself **3** *Rushing to work in the morning really bothers her.* = to cause worry or anxiety **4** *Is he angry? Well, I wouldn't bother about that too much.* = pay attention in an anxious way **5** *Is the noise on television bothering you?* = distracting or disturbing in an unpleasant way

bother[2] noun, u. *I am going to give you a bit of bother.* = small trouble (polite use)

to not be bothered *I told him he should buy our tickets soon, but he wasn't bothered.* = to not care about something; to ignore advice on purpose **to be hot and bothered** = to be disturbed or upset about something

B

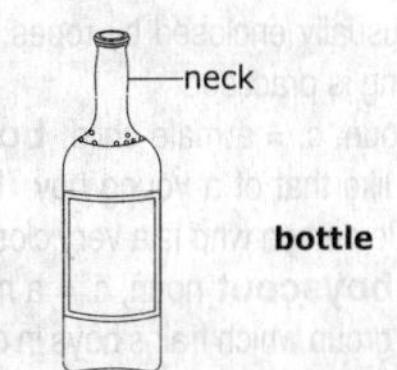

bot•tle[1] /'bɒtl/ noun, c. **1** = a container for a liquid having a long, thin neck **2** *He drank a bottle of milk.*= =the amount of liquid contained in a bottle

bottle[2] verb, t. *We have to bottle the orange juice.* = to put something into a bottle **bottle-feed** verb, t. = to feed a baby with milk from a bottle, in case the mother is not able to feed the baby with her own milk **bottle green** adj. = a deep green colour **bottle-neck** noun, c. *We have a bottleneck in the factory as many of our employees are sick.* = something that slows down work or the flow of something (e.g. traffic)

to bottle up (**one's feelings**) *He didn't want to cry in front of us and so he bottled up his feelings.* = to prevent oneself from expressing sadness, fear, anger etc. because one does not want others to see it

bot•tom[1] /'bɒtəm/ noun, c. **1** *a cooking-pot with a copper bottom* = the lowest part of something **2** *the bottom of the sea* = the ground beneath a sea or river **3** *Don't be sitting on your bottom all the time! Get up and do some work.* = the part of the body that one sits on (informal)

bottom[2] verb *The price of rice has bottomed out. It is sure to go up now.* = to reach the lowest point **bottomless** adj. *the bottomless sea* = very deep

bottom-line noun, u. *We have reached an agreement with the workers. The bottom-line is that the strike will be called off and work will start from tomorrow.* = the most important result or the most important point

to get to the bottom of *We must get to the bottom of this mystery.* = to try to find out what causes something unpleasant **to touch/hit rock bottom** *The price of onions has hit rock bottom.* = to reach a level which cannot get lower (informal) **to bottom out** = (of something which one buys) to touch the lowest price level

bou•gain•vil•le•a /bu:gən'vɪliə/ noun, u. = a climbing plant which grows in hot countries and produces flowers of very bright colour

bough /baʊ/ noun, c. = the biggest or main branch of a tree

boul•der /'bəʊldə'/ noun, c. = a large stone or a large and heavy rock

boule•vard /'bu:lvɑ:d/ noun, c. = a wide, straight street with trees on both sides

bounce /baʊns/ verb, i. and t. **1** *The ball bounced off the wall and came back to him.*(i.)= to jump up or back after hitting something solid **2** *She bounced up and down on the bed.*(t.) = to jump up and down on an elastic or springy surface **3** *Your cheque has bounced.*(i.) = to be returned or refused by a bank **bouncy** adj.

bound[1] /baʊnd/ noun, c. *He went over the wall. with a single bound.* = a big leap or jump

bound[2] verb, i. **1** *The leopard bounded over the fence.* = to jump **2** *The thief was bound with ropes.* (past tense of **bind**) = to tie up someone with a rope **3** *a book bound in leather* (past tense of **bind**) = having a stiff or thick cover **4** *India is bounded on the east by the Bay of Bengal.* = to be enclosed by something; to have something as a boundary **5** *We were water-bound after the heavy rain.* = surrounded and limited by

bound[3] adj. **1** *Where are you bound?* = going to **2** *The company is bound by Indian laws.* = obliged or required to do something **3** *It's bound to rain today.* = certain; sure **boundless** adj. *the boundless ocean* = having no limits

out of bounds (always plural) *We can use the swimming pool, but the football field is out of bounds for us.* = a place where one is not allowed **by leaps and bounds** *He was slow to understand maths at first, but with help his ability improved by leaps and bounds.* = to grow (especially improve) at a fast pace

bound•a•ry[1] /'baʊndəri/ noun, c. (**boundaries**) or adj. **1**= something that separates one area from another **2** *to hit a boundary* = to hit a ball across the line that marks the limit of a playing field so as to score 4 runs (in cricket)

boundary[2] adj. *the boundary wall* = something that marks the limit of an area

boun•ty /'baʊnti/ noun, u. *The king's bounty to the poor people was famous.* = the quality of being generous and kind

bou•quet /bəʊ'keɪ/ noun, c. = flowers, tied together and presented to someone on a special occasion

bour•geois /'bʊəʒwɑ:/ adj. (French) **1** = related to or belonging to the middle class **2** = someone who is too attached to material things (derogatory)

bout /baʊt/ noun, c. **1** *I have just recovered from a bout of fever.* = attack of a disease **2** *a bout of drinking* = a short period of activity

bou•tique /bu:'ti:k/ noun, c. (French) = a small shop that sells fashionable and expensive clothes or other items of personal use

bo•vine /'bəʊvaɪn/ adj. *bovine population* = something that has to do with cows

bow[1] /baʊ/ verb, i. or t. *He bowed his head in prayer.* = to bend the upper part of the body or head as a sign of respect

bow[2] noun *He made a deep bow.* = the act of bending the body or head to show respect

bow[3] /bəʊ/ noun, c. **1** = a weapon, which has a curved piece of wood held in place by a tight string, used for shooting arrows **2** = a long, thin piece of wood with a number of strings tied across it, used for playing a musical instrument with strings (e.g., a violin) **3** *a ribbon tied into a bow* = a knot made by folding a piece of string or ribbon into two curved pieces, which are then tied together **bow-legged** adj. *a bow-legged person* = having the legs curved in the shape of a bow **bow-tie** noun = a short piece of silk cloth, tied into a bow, worn by men around the neck as a decoration

to bow out *Raju bowed out of the team.* = to withdraw (give up one's place) **to have a second string to one's bow** *He has lost his job, but he can earn his living by painting pictures. He has a second string to his bow.* = some extra skill or ability, in addition to the main one

bow•els /'baʊəls/ noun, c. (plural form) **1** = the intestines (tubes inside the body through which food passes) **2** *Coal is dug out of the bowels of the earth.* = the inside part

bowl[1] /bəʊl/ noun, c. **1** = a deep, round vessel or container **2** *a bowl of milk* = the amount of liquid contained in a bowl

bowl[2] verb *Kumble has bowled six overs.* = to throw the ball at a batsman in the game of cricket

bowl•er noun, c.= a person who bowls (cricket) **bowling** noun, u. = a game in which a heavy ball is rolled along the ground and made to hit and knock down a number of wooden pins

to bowl someone over **1** *I was bowled over by the speeding bicycle.* = to be knocked down **2** *I was bowled over by his singing.* = to be surprised in a very pleasant way (informal) **to bowl someone out** = (in cricket) to make a batsman leave the game

box[1] /bɑks/ noun, c. **1** *a box full of books* = a container, usually square or rectangular, either open or with a lid, in which articles are kept **2** *a box of chocolates* = the contents of a box

box[2] verb, t. **1** *We have to box these mangoes and send them to the market.* = to pack something in a box **2** *to box one's ears* = to hit someone with a closed fist, as in the sport of boxing **box-office** noun = a place where tickets for a cinema show, play etc. are sold

box•er /'bɑksəʳ/ noun, c. = a person who takes part in the sport of boxing **boxing** noun, u. = a sport in which two players try to hit each other with gloves worn over their hands while remaining inside an enclosed area **boxing day** = the day after Christmas (i.e. 26 December) **boxing-ring** noun = the area, usually enclosed by ropes, in which the sport of boxing is practised

boy /bɔɪ/ noun, c. = a male child **boyish** *boyish looks* adj. = like that of a young boy **boy-friend** noun = a male person who is a very close friend (see **girl-friend**) **boyscout** noun, c. = a member of an international group which trains boys in character and self-help (see **girl guide**)

boy•cott[1] /'bɔɪkɒt/ verb, t. *We have decided to boycott this shop.* = to stay away from or to firmly avoid buying or supporting something

boycott[2] noun, c. *We have started a boycott of this shop.* = the act of boycotting

bra /brɑː/ noun, c. (short form of **brassiere**) = an inner garment worn by women which supports the breasts

brace[1] /breɪs/ noun, c. **1** *The doctor has asked me to wear a brace to support my back.* = something which is used or worn to provide support **2** = a metal wire stretched across the teeth to provide support and make them straight

brace[2] verb, t. **1** *We will have to brace the walls if we want to save this old house.* = to use a support **2** *Brace yourself for the bad news.* = to prepare oneself to react to something unexpected and unpleasant

brace•let /'breɪslɪt/ noun, c. = a band of metal, usually of gold or silver, usually worn around or near the wrist

brac•es /'breɪsəz/ noun (always plural) = a pair of elastic bands worn over the shoulders by men and used to hold up their trousers (also **suspenders**)

brack•et /'brækɪt/ noun, c. **1** *Fix this bracket on the wall.* = a piece of metal, wood etc. which can be fixed to a wall and from which something can be hung **2** *The meanings of the words are given in brackets.* (often plural) = a sign, in the form ( ) or [ ], used to enclose a piece of information

brack•ish /'brækɪʃ/ adj. *The water of the lake is brackish.* = impure water which has a salty taste

brag /bræg/ verb, i. *He is always bragging of the wonderful things he did in America.* = to boast or praise oneself in a manner which is not liked by others (derogatory)

braid[1] /breɪd/ noun, c. *The girl wore her hair in a braid.* = a length of something (e.g. hair) which is produced by twisting together several lengths; a plait

braid[2] verb, t. *Let me braid your hair.* = to twist or weave something into a braid

Braille /breɪl/ noun, u. = a system of writing or printing using raised marks on paper, which blind people can read by touching with their fingers

brain /breɪn/ noun, c. **1** = the organ, found inside the head, which controls thought and feeling and every part of the body **2** *He has a good brain.* = mind **3** *We*

B

are sending our best brains to the contest. = persons with good minds (informal) **brain-child** noun (no plural) *This magazine was the brain-child of our former Principal.* = somebody's idea or invention which has been successful **brain drain** noun, u. *India is suffering a brain drain as many of our leading scientists are leaving the country.* = the loss suffered by a country when people with high intelligence leave it to work elsewhere **brain-scan** noun, c. = a picture of the brain used by doctors to test if there is any defect in a person's brain which needs treatment **brain-storm** verb, i. *Before you start writing your essay, I would like you to brainstorm in groups and come up with some interesting ideas.* = to discuss and exchange ideas quickly in a group so as to come up with new ideas **brainwash** verb, t. *I don't want the ads on television to brainwash me into buying things I don't need.* = to try to make someone believe what you want him/her to believe **brainwave** noun *We were feeling very gloomy because we hadn't solved the problem. Then one of us had a brainwave.* = a clever idea which suddenly comes to someone **brainy** /'breɪni/ adj. = very clever; intelligent

brake[1] /breɪk/ noun, c. (usually plural) *The brakes on my car are not working.*= the part of a vehicle (car, motor-cycle, bicycle etc.) that is used to stop or slow down the vehicle

brake[2] verb, i. *A man suddenly appeared in front of our car and we had to brake to avoid hitting him.* = to stop a vehicle by using the brakes

branch[1] /brɑːntʃ/ noun, c. (**branches**) *the branch of a tree* = a part that grows out of and divides from something

branch[2] verb *This narrow road branches off from the main highway.* = to form a branch

brand[1] /brænd/ noun, c. *When I have to buy tooth-paste, I buy only Smyle, which is my favourite brand.* = the name given to a product, by which it is known to customers

brand[2] verb, t. *When he was a child he was sent to jail, and this experience branded him for life.* = to leave a painful mark on one's body or mind **brand new** adj. *a brand-new shirt* = something that has just been bought and not used at all **branded** adj. *I buy only branded tooth paste.* = a product with the name and label of a company which is well-known and trusted

bran•dy /'brændi/ noun, u. or c. (**brandies**) = a strong alcoholic drink made from the juice of grapes

brash /bræʃ/ adj. *Don't be so brash when you talk to your elders. Show them a little respect.* = rude and proud; disrespectful (derogatory)

brass /brɑːs/ noun, u. = a yellow metal which is a mixture of copper and zinc **brassy** adj. **1** = like brass: yellow, hard etc. **2** *brassy music* = loud and harsh **3** = a person who is seen as too bold, loud etc. (disapproving)

brat /bræt/ noun, c. = a child who has been spoilt and behaves badly (informal)

bra•va•do /brə'vɑːdəʊ/ noun, u. *He pretended he was not afraid of snakes, but the moment he saw one all his bravado disappeared.* = a false show of courage

brave[1] /breɪv/ adj. *our brave soldiers* = fearless and full of courage

brave[2] verb, t. *The ship sailed on, braving the huge waves* = to face danger without fear

brawl /brɔːl/ noun, c. *a drunken brawl* = a fight, usually in a public place, which is noisy and uncontrolled

brawn /brɔːn/ noun, u. *more brawn than brains* = large body frame and muscular strength **brawny** adj. = big and strong

bray[1] /breɪ/ noun, u. = the sound produced by a donkey, or any sound like it

bray[2] verb, i. = to produce a sound like that produced by a donkey

bra•zen /'breɪzən/ adj. *a brazen act of cheating* = done openly without shame

breach[1] /briːtʃ/ noun, c. **1** *a breach of promise* = an action which breaks or goes against a promise made earlier **2** *a breach of peace* = an act which breaks or disturbs peace **3** *a breach in a road* = an opening or a break, caused by a flood

breach[2] verb, t. *The enemy defences have been breached by our soldiers.* = to open up or break down something

bread /bred/ noun, u. **1** *a loaf of bread* = food made by baking a mixture of flour, water, salt etc. **2** *to earn one's bread* = money earned for work done (figurative) **bread crumb** noun, c. = a very small piece of bread **bread-fruit** noun, u. = the fruit of a kind of tree that is said to taste like bread **bread-winner** noun, c. = the head of a family or a member of the family who earns money to support the family

to be someone's bread and butter *Music is my bread and butter.* = something that helps to provide a living **to know which side of one's bread is buttered** = to be able to get the maximum benefit or advantage from a situation

breadth /bredθ/ noun, u. *the breadth of a football field* = the distance from one side to the other

break[1] /breɪk/ verb, t. or i. (**broke, broken**) **1** *I dropped the glass and broke it. // How did you break your leg?* (t.) = to cause something hard to divide into pieces by striking it against some hard object or allowing it to fall etc. **2** *I dropped the clock and broke it.*(t.) = to damage something so that it does not work. **3** *If you break the peace you will be arrested.*(t.) =

disturb **4** *We will break our journey in Kolkata. // He broke his fast with a glass of orange juice.*(t.) = to discontinue or interrupt something, either for a short time or permanently **5** *She will try to break the high-jump record.*(t.) = to improve upon **6** *How did the cup break?*(i.) = fall and divide into pieces **7** *Some thieves broke into the shop last night.*(t.) = to enter by force

break[2] noun, u. **1** *The sun shone through a break in the clouds.* = an opening or gap **2** *There is a break in your service from 1998 to 1999.* = a period of discontinuity **3** *We have been working for two hours. Let us take a break.*= a period of rest. **4** *He has been very unlucky. He deserves a break now.*= a bit of good luck (informal) **breakaway** *the breakaway group* = a small group that separates itself from the main group

to break down **1** *Our car broke down on the road.* = to fail or stop working (referring to a machine) **2** *He broke down and cried when he got the sad news.* = to lose control over one's feelings **to break out** *War has broken out between the two countries.*= something unpleasant that begins suddenly **to break even** *Our company lost a lot of money last year, but this year we were able to break even.* = to have neither loss nor profit in business **breakthrough** noun *The discovery of penicillin was a real breakthrough in medicine.* = a new discovery that brings about a very big improvement or change **to break the ice** *As we did not know each other, we did not speak for a long time. Finally, I broke the ice by offering him a cigarette.* = to remove the feeling of awkwardness or nervousness between people who do not know each other **to break new ground** = to do something entirely new **to break something off** *We have broken off our friendship.*= to end a relationship suddenly

break•fast /'brekfəst/ noun, u. or c. = the first meal with which one starts the day

breakdown /'breikdaun/ noun, c. **1** *She had a breakdown and had to go on long leave.* = a condition in which one is mentally disturbed and is not able to do even basic things **2** *The car has had several breakdowns. Let's not keep it.* = a situation in which a car, bus etc. or machinery stops working **3** *I studied the bill the hospital gave me and asked them to give me a breakdown of the expenses.* = a list made item by item

breast /brest/ noun, c. **1** = the part of a woman's body that produces milk **2** = the upper part of the body (chest) **breast-bone** noun = the big bone in the middle of the chest, to which most of the ribs are attached **breastfeed** verb = to feed a baby with milk from the breasts, not from a bottle **breast pocket** noun = the pocket stitched to the upper part of a coat or shirt **breast stroke** noun = the movement of the arms across the chest made while swimming with one's back facing upwards

to make a clean breast of something = to confess that one has done something wrong, committed a crime etc.

breath /breθ/ noun, u. or c. **1** *Take a deep breath.*(c.) = the act of taking air into the lungs and bringing it out again through the nose or mouth **2** *He has lost his breath.*(u.) = air which is taken into the lungs **breathless** adj. *I ran up the stairs but I was breathless when I reached the top.* = breathing with difficulty **breathtaking** adj. *The beauty of the mountain was really breathtaking.* = causing very great wonder or surprise

a breath of fresh air **1** *Let's go out for a breath of fresh air* = a rest from some work that one has been doing **2** *When she came into the room, it was like a breath of fresh air* = a welcome change **to take one's breath away** *The Taj Mahal is so beautiful that it will take your breath away.* = to make someone unable to speak because of surprise or wonder **to speak under one's breath** = to speak in a very low voice **to catch one's breath** *I did a lot of work in the morning, then stopped to catch my breath.* = to stop to relax after a spell of activity **to hold one's breath** *She held her breath as she opened the letter.* = to pause or wait with anxiety, hoping that what will happen will be good **to (not) waste one's breath** *Don't give him any more advice. You're wasting your breath.* = making an effort (to advise, convince etc.) which will not serve any purpose

breathe /bri:ð/ verb, i. or t. **1** (i.) = to draw (take) air into the lungs and out again **2** *He was breathing fire when he spoke.*(t.) = to give out a strong feeling **breather** noun, u. *We have been working since seven. Let's take a breather now.* = a short pause during work, for rest (informal)

to breathe one's last = to die **to breathe a sigh of relief** = to relax after a period of anxiety **to breathe down someone's neck** *I will complete the work, please stop breathing down my neck.* = to keep watching or advising to see if someone is doing something properly etc. (informal, not respectful)

breed[1] /bri:d/ verb, t. or i. (**bred**) **1** *We breed horses.*(t.) = to keep animals or plants for the purpose of producing and developing young animals or new plants **2** *Last year we had only two rabbits but now we have a hundred. They are breeding fast.*(i.) = producing babies and increasing in number

breed[2] noun *I have an improved breed of cattle on my farm.* = a new type or class of some animal, produced by using scientific methods

breeze[1] /bri:z/ noun, c. *There was a gentle breeze blowing.* =a gentle wind

breeze[2] verb, i. **1** *He breezed in suddenly while I was reading a book.* = to move quickly and lightly, in a happy mood (informal) **2** *She breezed through the* *book in just a few minutes.* = to complete some task quickly and without much effort

brev•i•ty /'brevɪti/ noun, u. *The Chief Guest stayed with us for only two minutes and then left. We were disappointed at the brevity of his speech and his visit.* = shortness relating to something written or spoken

brew[1] /bru:/ verb, t. or i. **1** *Let me brew some tea for you.*(t.) = to prepare some drink (usually beer or tea/coffee) **2** *Let the tea brew for a few minutes in the tea-pot before you pour it out.*(i.) = to be allowed to soak in hot water so as to become stronger in taste **3** *I think there is some trouble brewing in the office.*(i.) = starting

brew[2] noun, c. *The brew that she produced had a very good taste.* = a drink (usually beer or tea/coffee) produced through the process of brewing **brewer** noun, c. = a person who makes beer **brewery** noun, c. (**breweries**) = a place where beer is made

bri•be[1] /braɪb/ verb, t. = to pay money to someone so that he/she will agree to do something illegal or improper

bribe[2] noun, c. = money being paid or taken for doing something illegal or improper **bribery** noun, c. = the act of giving and taking bribes

bri•ck /brɪk/ noun, c. = a piece of hard clay which has been baked in the sun or in an oven(kiln) and is used for building houses **brick-layer** noun, c. = a workman who joins bricks together to build something **brickyard** noun, c. = a place where bricks are made

to drop a brick *When the Chief Justice arrived, I dropped a brick by addressing him as the Chief Minister.* = to say or do something that causes embarassment **to come down on someone like a ton of bricks** = to be angry and to blame someone strongly (informal)

bri•de /braɪd/ noun, c. = a woman who is going to be married or has just been married **bridegroom** /'braɪdgru:m/ noun, c. = a man who is going to be married or has just been married

bri•dge[1] /brɪdʒ/ noun, c. **1** = a structure which is put up across a river etc. and over which vehicles can run **2** = a kind of card game **3** = the bony part of the nose

bridge[2] verb, t. *The engineers are going to bridge the river.* = to build a bridge across a river etc.

to bridge the gap *bridge the gap between dream and reality* = to make a connection between two things of an opposite nature or to remove the difference between these **to build bridges** = to try to improve the relationship between two people (or groups) who are not getting on with one another

bri•dle[1] /'braɪdl/ noun, c. = leather bands put on a horse's head to control its movements

bridle[2] verb, t. **1** *Please bridle the horse.*= to place a bridle on a horse before riding it **2** *The young soldiers are getting restless but they will have to be bridled.* = to bring someone or something under control **3** *We bridled at the way she insulted us.* = to be angry and to show it but not be able to do anything

brief[1] /bri:f/ adj. *His letter was brief and to the point.* = short

brief[2] **1** verb, t. *Let me brief you on the main points to be discussed at this meeting.* **2** *The lawyer has been briefed on the facts of the case.* = to give instructions or necessary information to someone (specially to a lawyer) [LAW]

brief[3] noun, c. *I speak only for myself. I do not hold a brief for anyone.* = the authority to represent someone or to speak on behalf of someone **briefcase** noun, c. = a small box with a handle, usually made of leather or plastic, in which important papers are kept **briefing** noun, u. = the act or process of giving information or instructions to someone before an important event **briefs** noun (always plural) = a man's or woman's underwear covering the lower part of the body (informal)

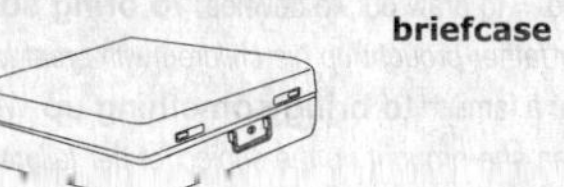
briefcase

bri•gade /brɪ'geɪd/ noun, c. **1** = a group of about 5000 soldiers who are part of an army **2** *the Fire Brigade* = an organisation created to carry out a special duty, such as fighting fires **brigadier** /brɪgə'dɪə^r/ noun, c. = a senior officer in the army, above the rank of colonel

bri•ght /braɪt/ adj. **1** *bright lights* = giving out strong light; shining **2** *bright colours* = strong and easily seen **3** *a bright student* = very intelligent **4** *a bright future* = full of hope **brighten** verb, t. *That picture hanging on the wall really brightens the room.* = to make something look bright and colourful

to look on the bright side of something = to look at the positive side of a bad situation

bril•liant /'brɪljənt/ adj. **1** *brilliant sunshine* = very bright **2** *a brilliant student* = highly intelligent **3** *a brilliant novel* = outstanding; highly successful (informal) **brilliance** /'brɪljəns/ noun, u. = the quality of being brilliant

brim[1] /brɪm/ noun, c. *The cup was full to the brim.* = the top edge of a cup, glass or bowl or the lower part of a hat

brim[2] verb, i. **1** *Her eyes were brimming with tears.* = full (of tears) and about to flow down **2** *The cup is brimming over.* = to be full to the top and about to overflow

brine /braɪn/ noun, u. = water containing salt, used for preserving food (preventing food from going bad)

bring /brɪŋ/ verb, t. (**brought**) **1** *Bring me a glass of water.* = to carry or come with something from one place to another **2** *A visit to the seaside brings peace.* = to cause; to lead to **3** *The smell of ripe mangoes brought a lot of flies.* = to attract **4** *To make tea, you must bring the water to the boil.* = to create the conditions in which something can happen **bringing up** (also **upbringing**) noun = the care which parents or guardians give to growing children

to bring about *The floods brought about great destruction.* = to cause (used in a negative situation) **bring down** *The public is demanding that the government bring down the price of milk.* = to lower the cost etc. of something or to make something fall (e.g. a building) **to bring forward** *The date of the election has been brought forward from December to August.* = to move something closer to the present time **to bring off** *Tendulkar had hit the ball very hard but Mahanama brought off a wonderful catch.* = to succeed in doing something difficult (informal) **to bring out** *A good teacher can help to bring out the intelligence of a child.* = to draw out; to develop **to bring someone up** *Our father brought up his children with great love.* = to look after a family **to bring something up** *We were eating when she brought up the subject of her failure.* = to start to talk about something which is unpleasant or sad

bri•nk /brɪŋk/ *The two countries were on the brink of a war last year.* = very near to the point at which something bad or dangerous can happen; the edge of something

brisk /brɪsk/ adj. *We will take a brisk walk.* = quick and active

bris•tle[1] /ˈbrɪsl/ noun, c. **1** *My toothbrush has nylon bristles.* = the short, stiff hairs (taken from an animal or made of nylon etc.) fixed on top of a brush **2** *There are some ugly bristles on your chin.* = short hairs

bristle[2] verb **1** *The tiger's fur bristled.* = hair or fur that stands up stiffly to show that one is angry, annoyed etc. **2** *The place where the meeting was held bristled with armed policemen.*= to be full of something

Brit•ish /ˈbrɪtɪʃ/ adj. = from or related to Great Britain

brit•tle /ˈbrɪtl/ adj. *Glass is brittle but plastic is not.* = something that is hard but can break into pieces easily

broach /brəʊtʃ/ verb, t. *I want to ask for a rise in my salary, but I do not know how to broach the topic.* = to introduce or bring up a topic (subject) during a conversation

broad /brɔːd/ adj. **1** *a broad river* = wide and large when measured from one side to the other (opposite **narrow**) **2** *a broad-minded person* = one who is prepared to respect the ideas of others; generous (opposite **narrow-minded**) **3** *Give me a broad idea of the town where you lived earlier.* = general; not detailed **broaden** verb, t. = to make something broader

broad•band /ˈbrɔːdbænd/ noun, u. = a radio-or television-related system which allows several programmes to be broadcast at the same time [TECHNICAL]

broad•cast[1] /ˈbrɔːdkɒːst/ noun, c. *Have you heard the news broadcast today?* = a programme presented on radio or television

broadcast[2] verb, t. **1** *Doordarshan will broadcast a commentary on the cricket match.* = to present a programme on radio or television **2** *I am going to broadcast the good news to all my friends.* = to make something known to a lot of people (informal) **broad gauge** noun = a railway track where the distance between the two steel rails on which trains run is 5.5 feet **broad jump** noun = an item in a sports meet where competitors are required to jump across a pit full of sand (also **long jump**)

bro•cade /brəˈkeɪd/ noun, u. = expensive cloth woven out of silver or gold thread

broc•co•li /ˈbrɒkəli/ noun = a vegetable that looks like a cauliflower but is green in colour

bro•chure /ˈbrəʊʃəʳ/ noun, c. *a brochure on tourism in India* = a small, thin book (**booklet**) containing pictures and photographs and describing the attractions or services that a place offers

broil /brɔɪl/ verb, t. = to cook something, specially meat, without water or oil, using direct heat **broiler** noun = a young chicken which has a lot of meat and has been specially bred for broiling

broke /brəʊk/ adj. *I can't buy shoes for my children as I am broke.* = having no money at all (informal) **broken** adj. **1** *a broken window* = damaged **2** *a broken promise* = not kept **3** *speaking in broken English* = incorrect or ungrammatical

bro•ker /ˈbrəʊkəʳ/ noun, c. = a person who arranges to buy and sell things for others, specially shares in companies

bron•chi•tis /brɒŋˈkaɪtɪs/ noun, u. = an illness that affects the lungs and causes coughing

bronze[1] /brɒnz/ noun, u. = a mixture of two metals, copper and tin, that has a reddish-brown colour

bronze[2] adj. *bronze-coloured hair* = having a reddish brown colour **bronze medal** noun, c. = a medal (a round, flat piece of metal) given as a prize to a person who comes third in a sports event

brooch /brəʊtʃ/ noun, c. (**brooches**) = an ornament usually worn by women, which is pinned on to a dress

brood[1] /bruːd/ noun, c. *a brood of chickens* = a family of young ones, specially birds

brood[2] verb, i. *Don't brood over your performance in*

B

the test. It's over! = to keep worrying about something unpleasant that has happened

brook /brʊk/ noun, c. = a small stream

broom /bru:m/ noun, c. = a brush with a long handle, used to sweep floors

broth /brɒθ/ noun, u. = thick soup containing meat and vegetables

broth•el /'brɒθəl/ noun, c. = a place where sex workers live and work

broth•er /'brʌðəʳ/ noun, c. = a male person who is born of the same parents as oneself **brother-in-law** noun, c. (**brothers-in-law**) = the brother of one's wife or husband or the husband of one's sister

brotherly /'brʌðəlɪ/ adj. *He gave me a brotherly hug.* = loving (like that of a brother)

brow /braʊ/ noun, c. = the forehead **browbeat** verb, t. *Don't try to browbeat me into voting for you.* = to force someone to obey by using strong words

brown[1] /braʊn/ adj. = the colour of soil or earth

brown[2] verb, t. *I will have to brown the meat.* = to cook something so that it gets a brown colour

browse /braʊz/ verb, i. **1** *cows browsing in the fields* = to feed on grass, young plants etc. (used for cattle) **2** *Let me browse through the book.* = to read through parts of a book in order to get an idea of what it contains **3** *browsing the Net* = searching different addresses or websites on the Internet and looking for information [COMPUTERS]

bruise[1] /bru:z/ verb, t. *I fell down and bruised my leg.* = to cause an injury to some part of the body so as to leave a mark, without breaking the skin

bruise[2] noun, c. *There is a bruise on my hand where he hit me with a stick.* = a dark mark left on the skin where one has been hit

bru•nch /brʌntʃ/ noun, c. = a meal which is either a late breakfast or an early lunch (**breakfast + lunch**)

bru•nette /bru:'net/ noun, c. = a person (usually a woman) with hair of a black or dark brown colour (see also **blonde**)

brunt /brʌnt/ noun, u. *The captain of the cricket team which lost had to bear the brunt of the blame.* = the most difficult and painful part of an unpleasant reaction to something

brush[1] /brʌʃ/ noun, c. (**brushes**) **1** *a toothbrush // paint-brush* = an instrument used to clean, paint etc which has a handle to which bristles (stiff hairs) made of nylon or animal hair are attached **2** *I had a brush with my senior this morning.* = a small quarrel or argument (informal)

brush[2] verb, t.or i. *Have you brushed your teeth?*(t.) = to clean something with a brush

to brush aside/off *The Manager brushed all our objections aside and bought new furniture for the office.* = to pay no attention to something **to brush up on something** *It would be a good idea to brush up on your computer skills before you attend the interview.* = to refresh one's knowledge of something quickly for a certain purpose

brute /bru:t/ noun, c. **1** = a large, wild animal **2** = a person who behaves like an animal **brutal** /'bru:təl/ adj. *a brutal murder* = very cruel

B.Sc. abbr. of **Bachelor of Science** = a first degree in Science

bub•ble[1] /'bʌbəl/ noun, c. *The child is blowing soap bubbles.* = a hollow ball of liquid containing air or gas

bubble[2] verb, i. *The pot of rice is bubbling on the stove.* = to form bubbles or to make the sound of bubbles rising in a liquid

buck[1] /bʌk/ noun, c. *a black buck* = a male deer

buck[2] verb, i. or t. *The horse is bucking.*(i.) = jumping with all four feet off the ground.

to buck up = to cheer up (to stop feeling sad) (informal)

to pass the buck *Don't pass the buck to me.* = responsibility (slang)

buck•et /'bʌkɪt/ noun, c. = an open container with a wide mouth and a handle, used for carrying liquids

to kick the bucket = to die (slang, often humorous, not respectful)

buck•le[1] /'bʌkəl/ noun, c. *a silver buckle for a belt* = something which fastens the two ends of a belt

buckle[2] verb, t. *You should buckle your belt.* = to hold something in place with the help of a buckle

to buckle down to something *You must buckle down to your work.* = to settle down to serious work

bud /bʌd/ noun, c. = a very young flower which has not yet opened up its petals **budding** adj. *a budding poet* = just beginning to develop

bud•dy /'bʌdi/ noun, c. (**buddies**) = a good friend (informal)

budge /bʌdʒ/ verb, i. or t. **1** *The man stood in the middle of the road and refused to budge although I sounded my horn.*(i.) = to move **2** *I can't budge this heavy bookshelf. Please help me.*(t.) = to cause something to move slightly (informal)

bud•get[1] /bʌdʒɪt/ noun, c = a plan made by the government for the amount of money to be spent by it and the amount of money to be collected through taxes, borrowing etc.

budget[2] verb, t. *You have to budget your time carefully.* = to plan how much time, money etc. one is going to spend on something

buff[1] /bʌf/ adj. *a buff-coloured shirt* = of a pale yellow colour

buff[2] noun, c. *She is a cricket buff.* = a person who is very interested in something and knows a lot about it.

buff[3] verb, t. *The brass statues have been buffed and* *they are shining.* = to polish something made of metal and make it shine

buf•fa•lo /ˈbʌfələʊ/ noun, c. (**buffaloes**) = a large, black animal belonging to the family of cattle

buff•er /ˈbʌfəʳ/ noun, c. **1** = a spring-loaded part on the front and back of a railway carriage which saves it from damage if it hits another carriage **2** = a country which lies between two other countries that are fighting or may fight **3** *We have stocked 20 bags of rice as a buffer in case of any shortage of food.* = something extra that can serve one in case of need **4** = extra space in the memory of a computer in which data is temporarily stored [COMPUTERS]

buf•fet[1] /ˈbʌfɪt/ verb, t. (usually passive) *The small ship was buffeted by the waves and the wind.* = to be tossed by the force of something (literary)

buf•fet[2] /ˈbʊfeɪ/ noun **1** *We will have a buffet lunch.* = food placed on a table, which people serve themselves and eat while standing up **2** = a carriage in a train or a place where one can buy food

buf•foon /bəˈfuːn/ noun, c. = a foolish person who tries to be funny (derogatory)

bug[1] /bʌg/ noun, c. **1** *a bed-bug* = a small insect **2** *I found a bug attached to my telephone.* = an electronic instrument used to listen secretly to something being said **3** *There seems to be a bug in my computer system.* = a problem which prevents a machine from working properly **4** *a flu bug* = an infection, usually of the stomach, which one can pass on to others (informal)

bug[2] verb, t. **1** *Tell me, what is bugging you?* = to annoy continuously or to cause worry (slang) **2** *My telephone has been bugged.* = to fit a bug (an electronic listening device) inside a room or to a telephone, without the knowledge of the users, so as to listen to them secretly

bu•gle /ˈbjuːgəl/ noun, c. = a small musical instrument made of brass, used for calling soldiers to a parade

build[1] /bɪld/ verb, t. or i. (**built**) **1** *We plan to build a house on this piece of land.* = to construct or make **2** *This exercise will build your muscles.* = to develop **3** *Anger was building in the group.*(i.) = growing stronger

build[2] noun, u. *He has a very attractive build.* = shape of the body **builder** noun = a person who builds something (usually houses which are sold to people) **building** noun, c. = a permanent structure with walls and a roof, usually made of bricks and concrete **building block** noun, c. (**blocks**) **1** = a toy, which has many small pieces which can be joined together by a child to form a building **2** *Words are the building blocks of language.* = the pieces out of which something is built or made (figurative) **built-in** adj. *Our bedroom has built-in cupboards.* = something which forms a fixed part of a building and cannot be taken out **built-up** adj. *This is a built-up area now, although it used to be an open field.* = covered with buildings

to build on something *Our school already had a good reputation and we were able to build on it.* = to use something as a base for **to build up one's strength** = to become stronger as a result of eating nourishing food etc.

bulb /bʌlb/ noun, c. **1** *an electric bulb* = a round, hollow piece of glass, inside which there are very thin wires which give out light when an electric current is passed through them **2** *the bulb of a lily plant* = the round (bulb-shaped) root of certain plants

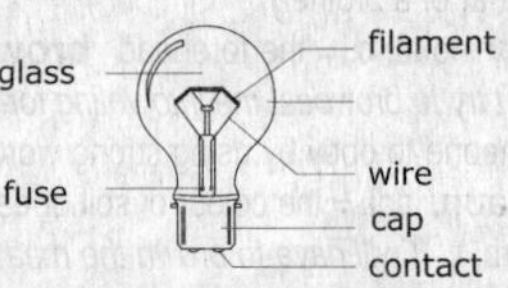

bulge[1] /bʌldʒ/ verb, i. *My school bag is so full it has started to bulge.* = to swell and curve outwards; to hang out

bulge[2] noun, c. *There is a bulge in your shirt pocket. You seem to have a wallet in that pocket.* = a swelling caused by pressure from inside

bulk /bʌlk/ noun, u. **1** *It is difficult to fit the bulk of his huge body in this small chair.*= large size and shape **2** *The bulk of the work has been completed.* = the greater part of something **3** *He buys sugar in bulk.* = in large quantities **bulky** adj. = big in size

bull /bʊl/ noun, c. = the male of a cow or certain other types of animals (e.g. **a bull-elephant**) **bulldog** noun, c. = a fierce dog with very powerful jaws and a short body, originally bred in England **bull's-eye** noun, c. (**-eyes**) = the circle at the centre of a round target, at which people who are taking part in a shooting-competition with guns or bows and arrows, aim **to hit the bull's-eye** = to be completely successful in doing something **bullfighting** noun = a sport, very popular in Spain and parts of South America, in which a man tries to kill a bull with a sword after making it tired **bullshit** /ˈbʊlʃɪt/ noun, u. *You are talking absolute bullshit.* = nonsense (informal, slang, derogatory) **bulldozer** noun, c. = a powerful machine fitted with a movable blade, used for levelling the earth and moving large rocks etc.

bul•let /ˈbʊlɪt/ noun, c. = a piece of metal which is fired with great force from a gun **bullet-proof** adj. *a bullet-proof car* = something made out of a material which a bullet cannot penetrate (enter)

B

bul•le•tin /ˈbʊlətɪn/ noun, c. *a news bulletin* = a short printed notice or news report **bulletin board** noun, c. = a notice board

bul•lock /ˈbʊlək/ noun, c. = the male of a cow which cannot breed (produce young ones)

bul•ly[1] /ˈbʊli/ noun, c. (**bullies**) **1** = a person who likes to hurt or frighten weaker or timid persons **2** = someone who acts like a bully; a powerful country which tries to put pressure on countries which are less powerful

bully[2] verb, t. (**bullied**) *Don't try to bully me.* = to act like a bully

bul•wark /ˈbʊlwək/ noun = a strong protecting wall

bum[1] /bʌm/ noun = the part of the body on which one sits (slang)

bum[2] verb, t. *Can I bum a ride in the bus?* = to ask to enjoy something without paying for it (slang)

bump[1] /bʌmp/ verb, t. *My car bumped into a wall.* = to hit something with force

bump[2] noun, c. **1** *He slid down the stairs and fell with a loud bump.* = the sound produced when something heavy hits a hard surface **2** *Be careful; there is a bump on this road.* = a raised, uneven area on a flat surface **3** *to fall and get a bump* = a swelling of the skin as the result of an injury **bumpy** adj. *a bumpy road* = uneven and full of bumps

to bump into someone *I bumped into an old friend the other day.* = to meet unexpectedly (informal) **to bump someone off** = to murder someone (slang)

bumper[1] /bʌmpəʳ/ noun, c. = horizontal bars fixed at the front and back of a car to protect it in case of accidents

bumper[2] adj. *We are expecting a bumper crop this year.* = of unusually large size or amount

bun /bʌn/ noun, c. **1** = a small, round and sweet loaf of bread **2** *hair coiled into a tight bun* = hair tied up into a large, round knot at the back of the head

bunch[1] /bʌntʃ/ noun, c. (**bunches**) **1** *a bunch of bananas* = a group of things which are similar and are tied together or growing at the same time **2** *The students came in a bunch.* = group

bunch[2] verb, i. *The boys were all bunched together in one corner.* = to gather together in a bunch

bun•dle[1] /bʌndl/ noun, c. or verb, t. *a thick bundle of sticks* = a number of things tied together with rope, string etc. or in a piece of cloth

bundle[2] verb, t. **1** *The thief was arrested and bundled into a police van.* = to move someone in a rough manner **2** *She bundled all her clothes together and left.* = to put things together untidily and hurriedly

bun•ga•low /ˈbʌŋgələʊ/ noun, c. (Hindi) = a house built on one level only, often with a sloping roof

bun•gle[1] /ˈbʌŋgəl/ verb, t. *I had asked the carpenter to make a table for me, but he bungled the job.* = to spoil something by doing or planning it badly

bungle[2] noun, u. *This job is a complete bungle. You will have to do it again.* = a piece of work that has been done badly

bunk /bʌŋk/ noun, c. *the upper bunk in a compartment* = a narrow bed fixed to a wall, on a train or ship

bun•ker /ˈbʌŋkəʳ/ noun, c. **1** = a place for storing coal, especially in a ship **2** = an underground shelter for soldiers during a war

bun•ny /ˈbʌni/ noun, c. (**bunnies**) = the word for 'rabbit' often used by small children

buoy[1] /bɔɪ/ noun, c. = an object floating in water, which is fixed to the bottom of the sea to warn ships of the presence of rocks

buoy[2] verb, t. *When I go for a swim, I take a rubber tube to buoy me up.* = to help someone to float; to support **buoyant** /ˈbɔɪənt/ adj. **1** *Cork is a buoyant material.* = something that floats on water **2** *I am in a buoyant mood.* = feeling light and cheerful (figurative)

bur•den[1] /ˈbɜːdn/ noun, c. *He is carrying a heavy burden on his back.* = load

burden[2] verb, t. *Don't burden me with your problems.* = to put a load or responsibility on someone

bu•reau /ˈbjʊərəʊ/ noun, c. (**bureaux** or **bureaus**) (French) **1** = a large writing table with a top which folds in or out **2** *the Central Bureau of Investigation (C.B.I.)* = an office or department **bureaucracy** /bjʊəˈrɒkrəsi/ noun, c. (**bureaucracies**) = the system of running a government with the help of permanent officials; the Civil Service **bureaucrat** /ˈbjʊərəkræt/ noun, c. = a member of a bureaucracy (sometimes derogatory)

bur•glar /ˈbɜːgləʳ/ noun, c. = a person who enters a house etc. illegally with the purpose of stealing, especially at night **burglary** /ˈbɜːgləri/ noun, c. (**burglaries**) = the act or crime of trying to break into a house with the intention of stealing **burglar alarm** noun = an electronic device that produces a loud warning noise when a burglar tries to enter

bur•ly /ˈbɜːli/ adj. *a burly policeman* = having a large and sturdy build

burn[1] /bɜːn/ verb, i. or t. **1** *The fire is burning.*(i.) = to give out heat and light **2** *The house is burning.*(i.) = to be on fire **3** *This generator burns kerosene.* = to consume (use) **4** *He is burning his father's money.* = to waste (figurative)

burn[2] noun, c. *She has a burn on her hand.* = a mark produced by burning **burner** noun, c. = a device that burns gas or some other fuel and produces a flame, used in cooking **burnt** adj. **burning** adj. *burning ambition* = strong

to burn up *This air-conditioner is burning up a lot of electricity.* = using in an excessive or wasteful way **to burn oneself out** = to spoil or destroy one's health as a result of working too hard (informal) **to burn one's fingers** = to lose money or suffer some other loss by trying to do something new **to burn a hole in one's pocket** = to buy something which costs a lot of money (informal) **to burn one's bridges** (see **burn one's boats**)

burp /bɜːp/ verb, i. = to get rid of gas in the stomach through the mouth, usually with a sound (informal)

bur•row[1] /ˈbʌrəʊ/ noun, c. *a rabbit's burrow* = a hole in the ground made by an animal, in which it lives

burrow[2] verb, t. *The bulldozer burrowed its way through the rock.* = to dig into something

bur•sar /ˈbɜːsər/ noun, c. = an officer in a school or college who has the responsibility of collecting fees etc.

burst[1] /bɜːst/ verb, i. or t. **1** *The balloon burst with a loud bang.*(i.) = to break open or break apart suddenly with force, under pressure **2** *The river burst its banks.*(t.) = to break

burst[2] noun, c. **1** *There is a burst in the dam, through which the water is pouring out.* = an opening **2** *We usually do no work in the office, but whenever there is a new project there is a great burst of activity.* = a period of sudden activity etc.

to burst out crying/laughing = to laugh/cry etc. suddenly and without being able to control oneself **to burst into flames** = to catch fire suddenly **to be bursting with energy** = to have a lot of energy (informal)

bur•y /ˈberi/ verb, t. **1** = to place a dead body into a grave, under the earth **2** *Someone buried a box full of gold coins in this place, hundreds of years ago* = to hide something inside the earth

to bury the hatchet *Sudhir and Mohan were bitter enemies, but now they have decided to bury the hatchet.* = to stop being enemies and become friends

bus[1] /bʌs/ noun, c. (**buses**) = a large motor-vehicle that carries passengers

bus[2] verb, t. *We will bus the children to school.* = to send by bus **bus depot** noun, c. = a place where buses are kept and where passengers can board (get into) them **bus pass** noun = a ticket which allows a passenger to use a bus for a period, usually one month **bus stop** noun = a place where buses stop to allow passengers to get off or on

bus

bush /bʊʃ/ noun, c. (**bushes**) or u. **1** *a rose bush*(c.) = a low plant, with many stems growing close together **2** *the African bush*(u.) = a part of a country thickly covered with wild bushes **bushed** adj. *I feel bushed after the race.* = deeply tired (informal) **bushy** adj. *a bushy beard* = growing thickly (like a bush)

busi•ness /ˈbɪznɪs/ noun, u. **1** *We do business with cotton growers.* = the activity of buying and selling **2** *A teacher's business is to teach.* = profession; responsibility **3** *I am tired of this whole business.* = affair; matter **4** *Let us get down to business.* = serious matters **business card** noun = a card carried by someone, which has his/her name, address, telephone number etc. (also **visiting-card**) **business class** noun = the front row of seats on an aircraft, where better service is provided to passengers, at a higher price **businessperson** (also **businessman, businesswoman**) noun, c. = a person who carries on some kind of business (buying and selling) **business studies** noun = a course of studies at a university in business management or commerce

to be in business = to be able to start doing something because one has everything one needs to do it (informal) **to be none of anybody's business** *Why do they want to know where we went? It's none of their business.* = a strong, impolite way of telling someone that something does not concern them (not respectful) **to mean business** *She spoke about her plans in a casual way but we knew she meant business.* = to be serious about doing something, even if it causes problems **like nobody's business** *We had just met but got on like nobody's business.* = very well or very badly (informal)

bust /bʌst/ noun, c. *a marble bust of Mahatma Gandhi* = a statue or photograph of a person showing only the head, shoulders and upper chest

bus•tle[1] /ˈbʌsəl/ verb, i. *She is always bustling through the corridors.* = to rush about busily and in a great hurry

bustle[2] noun, u. *I enjoy the noise and bustle of this town.* = great activity

bus•y[1] /ˈbɪzi/ adj. **1** *I am busy now, but I will be free after an hour.* = engaged in work; having a lot of work to do **2** *a busy town* = full of activity **3** *The telephone line is busy.* = engaged

busy[2] verb, t. *As he had no other work to do, he busied himself writing letters.* = to engage oneself in doing something

but[1] /bət/ conj. **1** *I wanted to eat something, but there was no food in the house.* = suggesting that conditions are not favourable **2** *She is ill but cheerful.* = suggesting a contrast, or something unexpected **3** *They have not one but three houses.* = instead **4** *But for her, I would not have passed the test.* = only because of **5** *I would have helped you but...* = a way of suggesting, without actually saying it, that something cannot be done, won't happen etc.

but[2] prep. **1** *There is no one here but me.* = except **2** *He lives in the last house but one.* = one house away from the last house

but[3] adv. *Don't be angry with him. He is but a child.* = only

bu•tane /'bju:teɪn/ noun = a kind of gas used for cooking

butch•er[1] /'bʊtʃəʳ/ noun, c. **1** = a person who sells meat **2** = a cruel person who causes the death of many people

butcher[2] verb, t. **1** *The goats have been butchered.* = to kill an animal for sale as food **2** = to kill in a bloody, cruel manner

but•ler /'bʌtləʳ/ noun, c. = a man who is in charge of all others who work in a house

butt[1] /bʌt/ verb, t. *The goat butted me in the stomach.* = to strike someone with the head or horns

butt[2] noun, c. **1** *the butt of a rifle* = the thick, lower end of something **2** *Pick up the cigarette butts.* = the unsmoked part of a cigarette **3** *the butt of a joke* = a person that people make fun of **4** *Get off your butt.* = slang for 'buttocks' or the part of the body one sits on (not respectful)

but•ter[1] /'bʌtəʳ/ noun, u. = a fairly solid, yellowish substance prepared from milk, which is rich in fat and can be spread on bread etc.

butter[2] verb, t. *Has the bread been buttered?* = to spread butter on bread **butterfingers** noun = a person who keeps on dropping things which he/she is carrying **buttermilk** noun, u. = the liquid that remains after butter has been taken out of milk

to butter somebody up *He isn't someone you can butter up.* = to keep someone pleased by flattery

but•ter•fly /'bʌtəflaɪ/ noun, c. (**butterflies**) **1** = an insect with beautiful coloured wings **2** *Don't be such a butterfly.* = a person who lives only for pleasure

but•tock /'bʌtək/ noun, c. (usually plural **buttocks**) = the fleshy part of the body above the legs, on which a person sits

but•ton[1] /'bʌtn/ noun, c. **1** = a small, round disc which is stitched to one part of a garment (dress) and passed through a hole in another part, so as to join them together **2** *the 'stop' button on a cassette player* = a part of a machine which one presses to make the machine work

button[2] verb, t. *Please button up your coats.* = to use the buttons on a garment to hold the garment close to the body **buttonhole** noun, c. or verb, t. **1** (noun) = the hole cut into a shirt, coat etc. through which a button passes **2** *She buttonholed me as I was going for lunch and kept talking for half an hour.*(verb) = to stop someone and force him/her to join a conversation (informal)

bux•om /'bʌksəm/ adj. *a buxom lady* = a woman who is thought to be plump (a little fat) in an attractive way

buy /baɪ/ verb, t. (**bought**) **1** *I will buy a new shirt today*(t.) = to get something by paying money for it **2** *The judge won't buy your story.*(t.) = to believe; accept (informal) **buyer** noun, c. = a person who buys or wants to buy something, usually for a company **buyer's market** noun = a situation in which there are a lot of goods in the market and buyers can get things at a low price

to be a good buy = something of good value which one gets at a cheap price (informal) **to buy up** *They have bought up all the houses in the street.* = to buy things (e.g. food, property) in quantity quickly (informal) **to buy time** = to ask for more time to do something

buzz[1] /bʌz/ verb, i. *The bees are buzzing.* = making the continuous sound that bees make

buzz[2] noun (always singular) **1** *Can you hear the buzz?* = the sound of buzzing **2** *Give him a buzz.* = a telephone call (informal)

buz•zard /'bʌzəd/ noun = a kind of large bird, like a hawk, that kills and eats other birds

buzz•er /'bʌzəʳ/ noun, c. = a signal that makes a buzzing sound

buzz•word /'bʌzwɔ:d/ noun *E commerce is the new buzzword in the world of computers.* = something new and fashionable that everyone is talking about

by /baɪ/ prep. **1** *He was bitten by a snake.*= referring to the doer of an action **2** *Send this letter by airmail* = through the use of **3** *You should be here by 10.00 a.m.* = not later than **4** *Don't stand by the window.*= near **5** *He walked by but did not stop.* = past **6** *Bats fly by night.* = during **7** *I caught him by the throat.* = the part of the body being held

by- /'baɪ/ prefix meaning 'something that is less important' e.g. **by-election** noun = a special election held between main elections, to fill a position whose holder has died or left

by•gone /'baɪgɒn/ adj. *in bygone years* = past and over long ago

to let bygones be bygones = to forgive and forget past quarrels

by•law /'baɪlɔ:/ noun, c. = a law made not by the national government but by a local authority

by•pass[1] /'baɪpɑ:s/ noun **1** *the Agra bypass* = a road that goes round a busy city or other area in order to avoid the heavy traffic **2** *bypass surgery* = an operation done to send blood from the heart through new blood-tubes outside the heart, as the old ones are blocked

bypass[2] verb, t. *Since he refuses to meet us, we will* *bypass him and go straight to the manager.* = to avoid or go round someone

by-prod•uct /ˈbaɪprɒdʌkt/ noun *Wax is obtained as a by-product during the process of refining crude oil into petrol.* = something additional (extra) that is obtained during the process of making something else

by•stand•er /ˈbaɪstændəʳ/ noun, c. = a person who stands near and watches some event but does not take part in it

by•word /ˈbaɪwɜːd/ noun, c. *Dr Ambedkar became a byword for the fight against social injustice.* = the name of a person who becomes a symbol of a certain quality

bye /baɪ/ interjec. or noun. **1** *Bye for now!* = goodbye; farewell **2** *The umpire has signalled a bye.*(noun) = a run scored in cricket without the batsman having played the ball

byte /baɪt/ noun, c. = a unit of information stored by a computer, equal to eight bits [COMPUTERS]

cC

c, C /siː/ the third letter of the English alphabet
c. abbr. of **circa** (adv.) (Latin) *Amitabh Dev was born c. 1947* = about; approximately (in the year)
cab /kæb/ noun, c. **1** = taxi **2** = the front part of a truck, where the driver sits
cab•a•ret /ˈkæbəreɪ/ noun, c. = a performance of dance and music given at a restaurant, usually at night
cab•bage /ˈkæbɪdʒ/ noun, c. = a round vegetable consisting of layers of fleshy green leaves
cab•in /ˈkæbɪn/ noun, c. **1** = a small, one-roomed house built of cheap materials **2** = an enclosed area in a workplace **3** *the pilot's cabin* = the small room at the front of an aircraft where the pilot sits
cab•i•net /ˈkæbɪnɪt/ noun, c. **1** *the cabinet of ministers* = the group of important ministers in a government, which takes most decisions **2** *a steel cabinet* = a piece of furniture with shelves and doors, used for storing things; an almirah or cupboard
ca•ble[1] /ˈkeɪbəl/ noun, c. **1** = a thick, strong rope made of steel wires **2** *telephone cable* = a set of wires used to send or receive telephone or telegraph messages **3** *I have received a cable from my son in London.* = a message sent from one country or city to another by telegraph
cable[2] verb, t. *I am going to cable my sister in Nagpur.* = to send a message by telegraph **cable car** noun, c. = a small coach/car which hangs from thick high cables and carries passengers **cable television** noun, u. = a system of receiving additional television channels through cables, on extra payment
cache /kæʃ/ noun, c. *The army found a large cache of weapons in the militant's camp.* = a secret store of weapons, food etc. **cachè memory** noun, u. = the extra memory, or ability to store information, which is available in a computer [COMPUTERS]
cack•le[1] /ˈkækəl/ noun, c. **1** = the sound made by a hen **2** *cackle of laughter* = the short, high pitched sound which some people make when laughing
cackle[2] verb, i. *The man cackled when I told him a funny story.* = to make a cackling sound while laughing
cac•oph•o•ny /kəˈkɒfəni/ noun, u. = an unpleasant mixture of loud sounds (opposite **harmony**)
cac•tus /ˈkæktəs/ noun, c. (**cactuses** or **cacti**) = a plant that grows in dry places and has thick fleshy leaves with sharp needle-like thorns
cad /kæd/ noun, c. *Don't be such a cad!* = a person who has no principles and behaves in a crude manner (old-fashioned, derogatory)
ca•dav•er /kəˈdævə/ noun, c. = the dead body of a human being [MEDICINE]
CAD/CAM /ˈkædkæm/ abbr. of **Computer Assisted Design/ Computer Assisted Manufacture** = the use of computers to design and manufacture industrial goods e.g. motor cars [COMPUTERS]
ca•det /kəˈdet/ noun, c. = a person who is being trained to join the armed forces or police
cad•mi•um /ˈkædmiəm/ noun = a poisonous soft, bluish-white metal
ca•dre /ˈkɑːdəʳ/ noun, c. = a group of trained and skilled people who belong to the same political party or profession
cae•sar•e•an (cesarian) /siˈzeəriən/ noun = an operation in which a pregnant woman's womb is cut open surgically and the baby removed, when a normal birth is difficult or impossible [MEDICINE]
ca•fe /ˈkæfeɪ/ noun, c. = a restaurant where light meals and drinks are served
caf•e•te•ri•a /kæfɪˈtɪəriə/ a restaurant, usually in a college, factory etc. where customers serve themselves instead of having food served to them (see also **self-service**)
caf•feine /ˈkæfiːn/ noun = a substance present in tea and coffee which makes a person feel more energetic **decaffeinated coffee/tea** noun = coffee/tea from which caffeine has been removed
cage[1] /keɪdʒ/ noun, c. *a bird cage* = an enclosure made of steel wires or bars inside which animals or birds are kept
cage[2] verb, t. *The lion has been caged.* = to put an animal or bird into a cage
ca•jole /kəˈdʒəʊl/ verb, t. *They cajoled me into driving them to Bangalore although I didn't want to go.* = to get someone to do something by using praise (sometimes false)
cake[1] /keɪk/ noun, c. or u. *a birthday cake* = a sweet made by baking a mixture of flour, eggs, butter etc.
cake[2] verb, i. *His shoes were caked with mud.* = to cover thickly
a piece of cake *Passing the test was a piece of cake.* = something that is very easy to do (informal) **to sell like hot cakes** = sell very quickly **to have one's cake and eat it too** *Ramesh has sold his car to a friend, but he still uses it every day. He wants to have his cake and eat it too!* = to take unfair advantage of a situation
ca•lam•i•ty /kəˈlæmɪti/ noun, c. (**calamities**) *If the monsoon fails again this year, it will be a calamity.* = an event which causes great suffering and loss
cal•ci•um /ˈkælsiəm/ noun = a white metal that is present in bones, lime etc. **calcify** verb, t. or i. = to become hard because of the presence of calcium [MEDICINE]

cal•cu•late /ˈkælkjʊleɪt/ verb, t. **1** *You can measure the length and breadth of this piece of land and calculate its area.* = to find out a certain quantity or amount by using mathematical processes **2** *The new road is calculated to increase the flow of traffic.* = to do something with a purpose in mind **calculation** noun, c. or u. = the act or the result of calculating something **calculated risk** adj. = a chance taken or a choice made with full knowledge of the risks, dangers etc. involved but with a hope of success or gain

cal•cu•la•tor /ˈkælkjʊleɪtəʳ/ noun, c. = an instrument used to perform calculations using numbers (addition, multiplication, percentages etc.)

cal•cu•lus /ˈkælkjʊləs/ noun = a branch of mathematics which studies ways of calculating quantities which change, for example the speed of falling objects [MATHEMATICS]

cal•en•dar /ˈkælɪndəʳ/ noun, c. = a list showing the days and months of the whole year **calendar year** noun = a complete year of 365 days from January to December

calf /kɑːf/ noun, c. (**calves**) **1** = the young of a cow or elephant **2** = the fleshy part at the back of the leg, between the knee and ankle

cal•i•brate /ˈkælibreɪt/ verb, t. = to set up an instrument (e.g. a parking meter, a taxi meter) in such a way that it accurately measures distance travelled, weight etc.

call[1] /kɔːl/ verb, t. or i. **1** *Didn't you hear your mother call (you)? You must go at once.*(t.) = to order someone to come **2** *I called him late last night and he sounded sleepy.*(t.) = to speak to someone on the telephone **3** *Laila is ill and the neighbour calls every day.*(i.) = to visit **4** *Let us call a meeting as the matter is important.*(t.) = organise, arrange **5** *We shall call this child Vinay.*(t.) = to give a name to someone; to address someone by a certain name **6** *I can't call the house beautiful, though it is quite spacious.*(t.) = to consider or think

call[2] noun, c. **1** *We heard a call for help.* = a loud cry or shout **2** *The Minister is waiting for the President's call.* = order **3** *There is a call for you.* = someone wishing to speak on the telephone **4** *There is no call for panic.* = reason **5** *The doctor is out. She is on a call.* = a professional visit by a doctor to see a patient **to call for someone or something** = to order/ask for **to call a spade a spade** = to say exactly what one thinks without putting it delicately **to call (someone's) bluff** = to force someone, who claims to be able to do something, either to prove that he/she can really do it, or admit that he/she cannot do it **to call for a celebration** *This is good work and calls for a celebration.* = to deserve **to call the shots** (always plural) = to be in control; to give the orders (informal) **to call to order** *She called the meeting to order.* = to announce the start of a meeting **to call to mind** = to remember something **to call it a day** *I'm tired. Let's call it a day.* = to stop doing something that one has been doing (informal) **to be on call** *Although Dr Khan is at home today, he is on call at the hospital.* = to be available if needed **to call off** = to cancel **to call on** *We called on her the other day.* = to visit for a short while **to call someone up** *We need to talk to her urgently. Could you call her up?* = to make a telephone call

cal•lig•ra•phy /kəˈlɪgrəfi/ noun, u.= the art of producing beautiful handwriting

call•ing /ˈkɔːlɪŋ/ noun (only singular) **1** a person's trade or work **2** *He was interested in many things but had a calling to help the disabled.* = a strong urge or desire to do something for the benefit of others

cal•li•pers /ˈkælɪpəz/ noun, c. (always plural) **1** = an instrument used to measure the thickness or diameter of objects **2** = metal supports for the leg used by a person whose legs are not strong

cal•lous /ˈkæləs/ adj. *The child asked for help but you walked away. How could you be so callous?* = without any feeling for others; unkind or unhelpful

cal•low /ˈkæləʊ/ adj. *Don't be guided by him. He is a callow person.* = young and without experience or wisdom

calm[1] /kɑːm/ adj. *The sea is calm today, so we can go swimming.* = quiet and peaceful; free from excitement

calm[2] verb, t. *She was able to calm the child who had been crying for hours.* = to make someone calm

cal•o•rie /ˈkæləri/ noun, c. *A glass of milk contains 300 calories.* = a measure of the amount of energy contained in a quantity of a certain kind of food

ca•lyx /ˈkælɪks/ noun, c. (**calyxes** or **calyces**) = the ring of green leaves which protects the petals of a flower [BOTANY]

cam•el /ˈkæməl/ noun, c. = an animal with a long neck and long legs that can live in the desert

cam•cor•der /ˈkæmkɔːdəʳ/ noun, c. = (trademark) a portable video camera which can record as well playback pictures

cam•e•ra /ˈkæmərə/ noun, c. = an instrument used for taking photographs or producing films or television pictures

camera

cam•ou•flage[1] /'kæməflɑːʒ/ noun, u. *Some lizards can change colour as a form of camouflage, to protect themselves from their enemies.* = the use of colours, shapes etc. to hide a person or thing by making him/it look no different from the surrounding grass, trees, rocks etc. so that an enemy cannot find him or it

camouflage[2] verb, t. *The soldiers camouflaged their jeep by tying the branches of trees over it.* = to hide something by using camouflage

camp[1] /kæmp/ noun, c. *an army camp* = a place where tents or huts have been put up for people to live in for a short time **camp-follower** noun, c. = a person who faithfully follows the leader of a political or religious group

camp[2] verb, i. *Let us camp here for the night.* = to set up a camp (usually a tent)

cam•paign[1] /kæm'peɪn/ noun, c. *an election campaign* = a set of planned political, military or business activities done in order to get a desired result

campaign[2] verb, i. *The women are campaigning for equal rights.* = to take part in a campaign; to support a cause

cam•phor /'kæmfəʳ/ noun, u.= a white substance with a strong smell which is burnt by Hindus at religious ceremonies. It is also used to keep insects away.

cam•pus /'kæmpəs/ noun, c. = the grounds of a university, college or school

can[1] /kən/ or /kæn/ aux. verb (**could**) **1** *I can speak French.* = to be able to do something **2** *You can sit here.* = to have permission **3** *Can we go home?* = to be allowed to do something **4** *Can I have some water, please?* = to make a request **5** *They can be quite strict. // It can get really warm here.* = showing that something may happen (see also **may**)

can[2] /kæn/ noun, c. = a sealed (closed) metal container in which liquids or food can be kept

can[3] verb, t. (**canned**) *The tomatoes have to be canned.* = to preserve food by putting it inside a can from which air has been removed **can opener** noun, c. = a kind of knife with a sharp blade which is used to cut open a metal can

ca•nal /kə'næl/ noun, c. = an artificial stream which carries water to the fields where crops are being grown

ca•nar•y /kə'neəri/ noun, c. (**canaries**) = a small, yellow singing bird, often kept as a pet

can•cel /'kænsəl/ verb, t. **1** *The authorities have decided to cancel the parade.* = to give up (call off) an activity which has been planned **2** *Please cancel this cheque.* = to cross out something which has been written by drawing a line through it, so that it has no value

can•cer /'kænsəʳ/ noun, u. or c. *Many of the patients in the hospital are suffering from cancer of the throat.*(u.) *// There is a cancer in my stomach.*(c.) = a diseased growth in the body which can cause death **Cancer** noun, u. = a sign of the zodiac, represented by a crab (see pic under **zodiac**) **Tropic of Cancer** noun = an imaginary line drawn around the earth, north of the equator (see pic under **earth**)

can•did /'kændɪd/ adj. *You may not like what I have just told you, but I had to be candid.* = truthful and frank, even when it is unpleasant to tell the truth (formal)

can•di•date /'kændɪdɪt/ noun, c. **1** *I am a candidate for this post.* = a person who wants to be chosen for, or elected to, a certain position **2** *Candidates are not allowed to talk during the examination.* = a person who is appearing at a test or examination

can•dle /'kændl/ noun, c. = a long piece of solid wax with a thread inside which gives out light when it is burnt **candle-stick** noun, c. = a holder for a candle

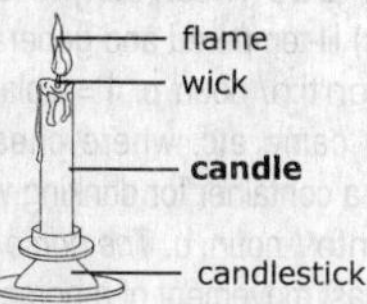

to not hold a candle to something *This may be a beautiful building, but it cannot hold a candle to the Taj Mahal.* = not to be good enough when compared with something else **to burn the candle at both ends** *Arun became ill as he was working too hard. This is what happens when one burns the candle at both ends.* = to work very hard without rest

can•dy /'kændi/ noun, u. or c. (**candies**) (American) = a sweet prepared by boiling sugar together with other substances e.g. chocolate

cane[1] /keɪn/ noun, c. or u. **1** *a sofa made of cane* (u.) **2** *The officer swung his cane as he walked.*(c.) = a kind of hard, tall grass which can be used to make furniture or be used as a stick

cane[2] verb, t. **1** = to hit with a cane **2** *These chairs need to be caned.* = to fit a chair with a seat made of woven cane, so that someone can sit on it

ca•nine /'keɪnaɪn/ adj. **1** = (an animal) belonging to the dog family **2** *canine teeth* = the two long and pointed teeth, like those of a dog, growing from the upper jaw

can•is•ter /'kænɪstəʳ/ noun, c. = a large metal container used for holding solids, gases or liquids

can•na•bis /'kænəbɪs/ noun = a drug produced from a kind of plant, known as the Indian hemp plant (also **hashish** or **marijuana**)

can•ni•bal /'kænɪbəl/ noun, c. = a human being or animal that eats the flesh of his/her/its own kind

can•non[1] /'kænən/ noun, c. (**cannons** or **cannon**) = a large, powerful gun, often mounted on a carriage with wheels or fixed to an aircraft

cannon[2] verb, i. *Our car skidded and cannoned into a tea stall.* = to hit something with force while moving **cannon fodder** noun, u. = a soldier of low rank who is pushed without any thought for his/her safety into a battle where he/she is sure to be killed

can•not /'kænət/ aux. verb (**can + not**) *I am so sorry I cannot accept your invitation.* = not be able to (formal; informal **can't**)

can•ny /'kæni/ adj. *a canny businessperson* = a very careful and clever person who cannot easily be fooled or tricked

ca•noe /kə'nu:/ noun, c. = a long narrow boat, pointed at both ends

ca•no•py /'kænəpɪ/ noun, c. (**canopies**) = a cover, usually made of thick cloth, fitted above a bed or an open terrace etc.

can•tan•ker•ous /kæn'tæŋkərəs/ adj. = (a person who is) ill-tempered and generally unkind

can•teen /kæn'ti:n/ noun, c. **1** = a place in a school, factory, army camp etc. where cheap meals are available **2** = a container for drinking water

can•ter /'kæntəʳ/ noun, u. *The horse is moving at a canter.* = the fast movement of a horse (faster than a **trot** but slower than a **gallop**)

can•ti•le•ver /'kæntɪli:vəʳ/ noun, c. = an arm-like beam that hangs out from an upright post or wall and is used to support a heavy weight e.g. a bridge

can•to /'kæntəʊ/ noun, c. (**cantos**) = a large sub-division of a long poem [LITERATURE]

can•ton•ment /kæn'təʊnmənt/ noun, c. = a part of a town or city, created by the British government in India, which has been set apart for the use of the army and is looked after by army authorities

can•vas /'kænvəs/ noun, u. or c. **1** *a canvas tent* (u.) = a kind of strong, thick cloth used for making tents or bags, or for paintings etc. **2** *The artist is displaying a number of his canvases at the exhibition.*(c.) = a finished painting done on canvas

can•vass /'kænvəs/ verb, t. or i. *I am canvassing votes for my brother, who is contesting the election.*(t.) = to go from place to place meeting people and asking them for votes or orders for something that one is trying to sell

can•yon /'kænjən/ noun, c. = a deep, narrow valley between high mountains

cap[1] /kæp/ noun, c. **1** = a soft, close fitting covering for the head **2** *He has been awarded the India cap.* = a cap which shows a certain position, membership of a team etc. **3** *the cap on a bottle* = a protective covering used to close a bottle etc. **4** *The government has put a cap on this project.* = an upper limit for the amount of money that can be spent

cap[2] verb, t. (**capped**) **1** *The clouds have capped the mountains.* = to cover the top of **2** *Can you cap that story?* = to improve on what someone has said or done (informal) **3** *He has been capped for the next test match.* = selected for a team

ca•pa•ble /'keɪpəbəl/ adj. **1** *Rajiv Sahay proved to be a capable leader.* = able **2** *He is quite capable of managing this company.* = having the power, skill or other qualities needed to do something

ca•pac•i•ty /kə'pæsɪti/ noun, u. **1** *The fuel tank of this car has a capacity of 50 litres.* = the amount that something can hold **2** *The hall was filled to capacity.* = the largest number or quantity possible **3** *He is going to America in his capacity as Finance Minister.* = a particular position of responsibility **4** *She has great managerial capacity.* = ability or skill

cape /keɪp/ noun, c. **1** = a loose-fitting coat without sleeves worn over one's dress **2** *Cape Horn* = a piece of land sticking out into the sea

ca•per[1] /'keɪpəʳ/ noun, c. *The children were dancing and cutting capers.* = a playful, jumping movement

caper[2] verb, i. *The children were capering happily through the corridors.* = to jump about in a happy and playful manner

ca•pil•la•ry /kə'pɪləri/ noun, c. (**capillaries**) **1** = a very fine, hair-like tube **2** = one of the very thin tubes in the body through which blood flows [BIOLOGY] **capillary force/attraction** noun = a natural force which causes water or other fluid to rise up in a tube (e.g. sap rising up the trunk of a tree) against the force of gravity

cap•i•tal[1] /'kæpɪtəl/ noun, c. **1** *New Delhi is India's capital.* = the place where the government of a country or state is located **2** *I started my business with a capital of only Rs 5000.* = money required to start a business or industry

capital[2] adj. **1** *Murder is a capital offence.* = punishable by death **2** *Write your name in capital letters.* = A, B, C etc. and not a, b, c **3** *It was a capital idea.* = excellent **capital punishment** noun = the legal process of punishment by death [LAW]

cap•i•tal•is•m /'kæpɪtl-ɪzəm/ noun, u. = an economic system based on private ownership of industry, free buying and selling and little control of the economy by the state (compare **communism**, **socialism**) **capitalist** noun, c. **1** = a person who supports the system of capitalism **2** = a person who uses his or her money or borrows money to set up a business or industry

ca•pit•u•late /kə'pɪtʃʊleɪt/ verb, i. *Germany capitulated in 1945 when the American and Russian armies surrounded Berlin.* = to accept defeat in a war; to surrender (formal)

C

ca•price /kə'pri:s/ noun, c. *Why do you keep changing your job every month? I am tired of your caprices.* = sudden change of mind or behaviour seemingly without any reason (disapproving) **capricious** adj. *The weather is capricious these days. The mornings are bright and sunny but every afternoon there is rain.* = changing often and suddenly

Cap•ri•corn /'kæprɪkɔ:n/ noun, u. **1** = a sign of the zodiac, represented by a goat (see pic under **zodiac**) **2** *the Tropic of Capricorn* = an imaginary line running around the earth, south of the equator (see also **Tropic of Cancer**)

cap•si•cum /'kæpsɪkəm/ noun = a vegetable belonging to the family of chillies, larger in size than a chilli and round (also **bell-pepper**)

cap•size /kæp'saɪz/ verb, i. *The ship capsized in the storm and sank.* = to turn over (turn upside-down)

cap•sule /'kæpsju:l/ noun, c. **1** *a capsule of vitamin B* = a measured amount of medicine inside a soft cover made of gelatine, which is swallowed (see pic under **medicine**) **2** = the part of a spaceship where the pilots live and work from, which separates from the rocket after it has been launched

cap•tain[1] /'kæptɪn/ noun, c. **1** *India's cricket captain* = the leader of a team or group **2** = the commander of a ship or aircraft **3** = an officer of middle rank in the army, navy or airforce

captain[2] verb, t. *Who is going to captain our basketball team?* = to lead

cap•tion /'kæpʃən/ noun, c. = words written above or below a picture describing what the picture contains

cap•tive[1] /'kæptɪv/ adj. **1** *The terrorists were arrested and held captive for many years.* = kept in prison **2** *captive animals in the zoo* = kept in a closed space and not allowed to move about freely

captive[2] noun, c. *The captive is well looked after.* = a person who has been made prisoner in a war **captivity** /kæp'tɪvɪti/ noun, u. *These animals are living in captivity in the zoo.* = the state of being captive **captivate** /'kæptɪveɪt/ verb, t. *I was captivated by the beauty of Kashmir.* = to attract and charm completely **captivating** adj. *the captivating beauty of the Pinjore Gardens* = highly attractive

cap•ture[1] /'kæptʃər/ noun, u. *the capture of the city* = the act of taking possession of a place usually after victory in a war

capture[2] verb, t. **1** *Two foreign spies have been captured.* = to make a person or animal a prisoner **2** *It was a small country and was easily captured.* = to take control of something by force after defeating an enemy **3** *The poet has captured the beauty of the Chilika Lake in this poem.* = to put something in words or pictures so that its beauty is never lost

car /kɑ:r/ noun, c. **1** *a motor car* = a vehicle used for carrying a small number of passengers **2** *the dining-car on a train* = a carriage which forms part of a train **car-jack** noun, c. *We suffered a car-jack on the highway.* = to be stopped and forced to give up one's car (see also **hi-jack**) **car park** noun, c. = an area where a car can be left, usually on payment, while the owner is busy working, shopping etc.

ca•ra•pace /'kærəpeɪs/ noun, c. = the protective hard outer shell of tortoises, crabs etc.

car•at /'kærət/ noun, u. **1** *22-carat gold ornaments* = a measure of the purity of gold (Pure gold is said to be *24*-carat gold.) **2** *a 300-carat diamond* = a measure of the weight of a precious stone, equal to *200* milligrams

car•a•van /'kærəvæn/ noun, c. **1** *a trading caravan* = a group of people, usually traders, who travelled together in the old days, using horses or camels **2** *a motor caravan* = a large vehicle which is towed (pulled) by a motor car, and in which people can sleep, cook etc. when going for a holiday

car•bo•hy•drate /kɑ:bəʊ'haɪdreɪt/ noun, c. = a substance present in food which contains carbon, hydrogen and oxygen, and provides energy to the body e.g. sugar, rice etc.

car•bon /'kɑ:bən/ noun = an element (simple substance) which is found in pure form in diamonds **carbon copy** noun, c. = a copy of a document produced with the help of carbon paper **carbon-dating** noun, u. = a scientific method of calculating the age of a very old object by measuring the amount of carbon present in it **carbon monoxide** noun = a highly poisonous gas produced by the engines of motor cars, trucks etc. **carbon paper** noun, u. = a sheet of thin paper which has a coating of carbon material on one side and can be used between sheets of writing paper to produce copies of documents

car•cass (carcase) /'kɑ:kəs/ noun, c. (**carcasses, carcases**) = the dead body of an animal

car•cin•o•gen /kɑ:'sɪnədʒən/ noun, c. = having the effect of producing cancer **carcinogenic** adj. leading to or causing cancer [MEDICINE]

card /kɑ:d/ noun, c. **1** *playing card* (**cards**) = one of a set of *52* small pieces of stiff paper with different markings, used to play various card games **2** *business (visiting) card* = a small, stiff piece of paper or plastic carrying the name, address, telephone number etc. of a person **3** *greeting card* = a piece of paper sent to someone on a special occasion (e.g. a birthday or festival), often with a printed message, carrying the sender's good wishes

to be on the cards (always plural) *The teachers think a change in the syllabus is on the cards.* = likely, possible

car•da•mom /'kɑːdəməm/ noun = a kind of spice, used to give flavour to food, produced from the small seeds of a climbing plant grown in the hills of South India, Indonesia etc.

card•board /'kɑːdbɔːd/ noun, u. = thick, stiff paper used for making boxes, covers of books etc.

card catalogue noun, c. = a set of cards which provide information about the books in a library, such as the titles of books, the names of the authors and publishers etc.

car•di- /kɑːdi/ prefix meaning 'related to the heart' e.g. **car•di•ac** /'kɑːdi-æk/ adj. *cardiac failure; cardiac surgery* = connected with the heart or with heart disease **cardiac surgeon** noun = a surgeon who performs operations of the heart or blood vessels **cardiogram** /'kɑːdɪəgræm/ noun, c. = a graphic recording which shows the working of the heart **cardiologist** /kɑːdɪ'ɒlədʒɪst/ noun, c. = a doctor who uses medicines to treat patients who have diseases or problems of the heart **cardiology** noun, u. = the study and treatment of medical conditions of the heart

car•di•gan /'kɑːdɪgən/ noun, c. = a short coat, knitted with woollen thread, open in front, with buttons

car•di•nal[1] /'kɑːdɪnəl/ noun, c. = a Catholic priest of very high rank , next only to that of the Pope

cardinal[2] adj. *Secularism is one of the cardinal principles behind the Indian Constitution.* = most important **cardinal numbers** noun = numbers that show quantity but not order (1, 2, 3 etc. but not 1st, 2nd 3rd etc.) (see also **ordinal**) **cardinal points of the compass** noun = the four main directions: north, south, east and west

card index noun, c. = a box containing a number of cards, each one of which carries some information, arranged in order

cardsharp noun, c. (**card sharps**) = a person who makes his/her living by cheating people at card games (informal)

care[1] /keəʳ/ noun, c. or u. **1** *Your mother needs a lot of care because she's old.*(u.) = the process of looking after someone e.g. someone old or sick **2** *I will take care of the dog while you are away.*(u.) // *You will look after the dog with care, won't you?* = responsibility for looking after and protecting someone or something **3** (always plural) *His cares have made him old.*(c.) = things that cause worry or unhappiness **4** *You should do your work with greater care* (u.) = serious attention and effort **5** *Cross the road with care.*(u.) = attention to safety

care[2] verb, i. **1** *When my neighbours lost their house in the fire, they did not seem to care at all.* = to feel worried or anxious about something **2** *She cares a lot about her grandfather.*(i.) = to be attached to or fond of someone or something **3** *'Would you care for some more tea?' 'No thanks, I don't care for tea at all.'* = to want or like something (used only in questions or negative sentences) **4** *She doesn't care about wealth and fame.* = to consider something important **5** *'Take an umbrella. You'll get wet in the rain.' 'I don't care!'* = to be concerned or bothered **careful** adj. **1** *A careful driver will never drive fast on crowded roads.* **2** *She is very careful with her money.* = giving a lot of thought to safety, so as to avoid accidents, loss etc.; cautious (opposite **careless**) **3** *They have done a careful study of all the facts in this case.* = giving a lot of attention to detail; thorough **carefully** adv. **intensive care unit (ICU)** = a division in a hospital which looks after patients who are seriously ill or who are recovering from surgery etc.

to not care less *I know I'm right. I couldn't care less what others think.* = to not be bothered about what others think of one or what one is doing

> **Usage** *Does he care for his brother?* = to have affection or a liking for
> *Will he care for his brother if he falls ill?* = look after
> *Does he care about the job?* = to have respect for or consider important
> *Don't worry, his brother will take care of the arrangements.* = be responsible for

ca•reer /kə'rɪəʳ/ noun, c. **1** *She takes her career as a doctor seriously.* = a job or profession that one is trained for **2** *He had a brilliant career as a student.* = a record of achievements **career counselling** noun = the process of giving advice to a student about the courses of study or profession which he/she should follow

care•free /'keəfriː/ adj. *She leads a carefree life, without any worries.* = free from worries and anxieties

car•ess[1] /kə'res/ verb, t. *They caressed the baby.* = to give someone a gentle, loving touch or kiss

caress[2] noun, c. (**caresses**) = the act of caressing

care•taker /'keəteɪkəʳ/ noun, c. **1** = a person who is paid to look after a building etc. **2** = a person who looks after a house while the owner is away **caretaker-government** noun, c. = a government which holds office for a short time, before a new government is formed

car•go /'kɑːgəʊ/ noun, u. or c. (**cargoes**) *The ship is carrying a cargo of iron ore.*(c.) = the load of goods carried by a ship, plane or truck

car•i•ca•ture[1] /'kærɪkətʃʊəʳ/ noun, c. or u. = a humorous picture or description of (usually) a (well-

C

known) person in which some quality is made to stand out (see also **cartoon**)
caricature[2] verb, t. *He caricatured his friends in a drawing he had made.* = to produce a caricature of someone
car•ies /ˈkeəriz/ noun, u. = decay of the teeth [MEDICINE]
car•nage /ˈkɑːnɪdʒ/ noun, u. *There was great carnage during the riots of 1947.* = killing and wounding of people
car•nal /ˈkɑːnəl/ adj. *carnal pleasures* = something that is related to the physical side of life, especially sex
car•na•tion /kɑːˈneɪʃən/ noun = a sweet-smelling flower, usually red or white
car•ni•val /ˈkɑːnɪvəl/ noun, c. = a time of public merry-making, with feasting, drinking, dancing, colourful processions etc.
car•ni•vore /ˈkɑːnɪvɔːʳ/ noun, c. = a flesh-eating animal **carnivorous** /kɑːˈnɪvərəs/ adj. *a carnivorous animal or plant* = flesh-eating
ca•rol /ˈkærəl/ noun, c.= song of welcome, joy and praise sung at Christmas time around the theme of the birth of Christ
carp[1] /kɑːp/ noun, c. = a kind of fresh-water fish
carp[2] verb, i. *Stop carping about the food!* = to complain continuously and unnecessarily about something (disapproving)
car•pen•ter /ˈkɑːpɪntəʳ/ noun, c. = a person who makes or repairs wooden objects **carpentry** noun, u. = the art or profession of a carpenter
car•pet[1] /ˈkɑːpɪt/ noun, c. = a covering for floors made of heavy woollen or cotton material
carpet[2] verb, t. *The hall has been carpeted.* = to cover with a carpet **carpeting** noun, u. = the material used for making carpets
car•riage /ˈkærɪdʒ/ noun, c. or u. **1** = a vehicle that runs on wheels, especially a horse-drawn vehicle(c.) **2** *a railway carriage*(c.) = a coach that forms part of a train **3** *the carriage of goods by road or by railway*(u.) = the act or process of carrying something from one place to another
car•ri•er /ˈkæriəʳ/ noun, c. **1** *a carrier of goods* = someone or something that carries goods from one place to another **2** *The anopheles mosquito is a carrier of malaria.* = a person or thing that spreads a disease **carrier bag** noun, c. = a paper or plastic bag in which something bought from a shop is carried away by a customer **carrier pigeon** noun, c. = a pigeon which is trained to carry messages written on tiny pieces of paper, from one place to another
car•rot /ˈkærət/ noun, c. **1** = the swollen, orange coloured root of a plant which is eaten as a vegetable **2** *We were made to study all day, but the carrot offered to us was that we would be taken to the cinema in the evening.* = a reward promised to someone for doing something (informal)
car•ry /ˈkæri/ verb, t. or i. **1** *These trucks carry eggs to markets in Kolkata.*(t.) = to move something from one place to another **2** *The germs of plague are carried by rats.*(t.) = to spread; to pass from one person to another **3** *The weight of the roof is carried by these pillars.*(t.) = to support **4** *Today's newspaper carries an article about the strike.*(t.) = to contain **5** *This crime carries a heavy penalty.*(t.) = to have something attached **6** *We could not hear you as your voice did not carry.*(i.) = to travel across a space **7** *The bill introduced by the Law Minister in Parliament was carried.*(i.) = to pass a law in Parliament **8** *A good leader should be able to carry his supporters.*(t.) = to win the support of **9** *When you are adding 2 to 9, you have to carry 1.*(t.) = to move a number into the next column when adding numbers **10** *The computer carries a two-year warranty.*(t.) = to come with **11** *In our shop, we sometimes carry fresh fruit.*(t.) = to have for sale **12** *She carries herself well.*(t.) = hold oneself, walk etc. in a smart and attractive manner **13** *It's sad that he has to leave the job, but we can't carry him any more.* = to keep someone who doesn't work hard or well in a job, a team etc.
to get carried away *I am sorry that I got carried away after hearing his speech.* = to get excited and lose control of oneself for a short time **to carry the day** *We did not expect India to win but the excellent batting by Tendulkar carried the day.* = to bring victory **to carry off** **1** *She carried off her part in the drama quite well.*= to perform **2** *Your daughter carried off most of the prizes in the competition.* = to win (informal) **to carry something out** *We carried out my aunt's wishes and took our uncle to the seaside.* = to fulfil or complete **to carry weight** *Their opinions carry a lot of weight.* = to be valued and listened to with respect **to carry something too far** = to overdo something (e.g. a trick played on someone, a punishment) so that its effects become unpleasant or get out of control **to carry on (doing something)** *We tried to attract his attention but he carried on writing.* = to continue to do something, often in a way that is annoying to others **to carry on and on** *We expected her to stop, but she carried on and on until everyone got bored.* = to go on speaking (informal, disapproving)
cart[1] /kɑːt/ noun, c. = a wooden vehicle with two wheels, pulled by an animal or a human being
cart[2] verb, t. *The farmer carted his rice to the market.* = to carry in a cart **cart-load** noun, c. = the quantity of something that can be carried in a cart **cart-wheel** noun, c. = a fast circular movement, like that of a wheel, performed by someone to show joy or

excitement, in which the person first balances on his/her hands, holding the legs straight up, then turns over so as to land on the feet **(to turn a cartwheel)**

car•ti•lage /'kɑːtɪlɪdʒ/ noun, u. or c. = the strong elastic substance attached to the bone present in certain parts of the body that gives shape and support (e.g. the ears or the lower part of the nose, as well as inside bone-joints)

car•tog•ra•pher /kɑː'tɒgrəfəʳ/ noun, c. = a person who produces maps **cartography** noun, u. = the science and art of producing maps

car•ton /'kɑːtn/ noun, c. = a box made of thick, strong paper in which goods are packed

car•toon /'kɑː'tuːn/ noun, c. = a humorous drawing published in a newspaper or magazine or on film, generally about something which is in the news (see also **caricature**)

cart•ridge /'kɑːtrɪdʒ/ noun, c. **1** = a tube made of thick paper or metal, which is filled with gunpowder or some other explosive material and fired from a gun **2** = a replaceable or refillable container which stores some substance e.g. an ink-cartridge which stores ink **cartridge-paper** noun, u. = strong, thick white paper used for drawing

carve /kɑːv/ verb, t. **1** = to make something out of wood or stone by cutting away pieces of the material **2** *He has carved out a place for herself as a television actor.* = to create a career for oneself through hard work (figurative) (compare **emboss,** see also **engrave**) **carving** noun, c. *a stone carving* = something that has been carved out of stone or wood **carving knife** noun = a knife used to cut meat etc. into small pieces which can be eaten

cas•cade[1] /kæ'skeɪd/ noun, c. = a small waterfall [LITERATURE] (compare **cataract** meaning **2**)

cascade[2] verb, i. *The rain cascaded down the tin roof.* = to come down with force, like a waterfall

case /keɪs/ noun, c. **1** *The judge decided three cases today.* = a legal matter which is decided in a law court **2** *There have been three cases of malaria in this village.* = an example of something **3** *You seem to have a strong case.* = the facts or arguments supporting one side in a dispute **4** *I have brought three cases of books for you to read.* = a large box made of wood or cardboard **5** *the book in the showcase* = a cupboard with a glass front in which things are out on display **6** *'Me' is the accusative case of 'I', while 'my' is the possessive case.* = a change in the form of a noun or pronoun, to show its relationship with the other words in a sentence [GRAMMAR] **case history** noun, c. (**histories**) *The doctor is taking your friend's case-history.* = a record of the health problems that one has had in the past [MEDICINE] **case-study** noun, c. (**-studies**) = a piece of research based on the detailed study of one or a few individuals

in that case *They don't seem to be interested in our plan. In that case, let's not discuss it with them.* = if so

cash[1] /kæʃ/ noun, u. *I cannot pay you in cash but I can give you a cheque.* = money in the form of bank-notes or coins

cash[2] verb, t. *You can cash this cheque at a bank.* = to get cash in return for a cheque **cash book** noun, c. = a register in which the daily accounts (the money received or spent) of a company are maintained **cash crop** noun, c. = a crop grown for sale rather than for the personal use of the grower (e.g. cotton)

hard cash *They own many houses, but need hard cash.* = actual money in hand (not in a bank, or in the form of cheque etc.) **cash on delivery** (also **COD**) an arrangement in which one pays for goods only after they are delivered **to cash in** *The new Director is a friend of mine and will help you. You should cash in on this opportunity.* = to take full advantage of a situation (informal) **to pay cash down** = to pay in cash immediately, without delay

cash•ier /kæ'ʃɪəʳ/ noun, c. = a person in charge of money and payments in an office, bank etc.

ca•shew /'kæʃuː/ noun, u. = a kind of tree that produces a small, curved nut (cashew nut)

ca•si•no /kə'sɪːnəʊ/ noun, c. = a place where people can gamble

cask /kɑːsk/ noun, c. = a container for liquids (usually wine) made of wood

cas•ket /'kɑːskɪt/ noun, c. = a small box used for keeping ornaments, valuable papers etc.

cas•se•role /'kæsərəʊl/ noun, c. or u. **1** (c.) = a deep covered dish in which food can be cooked **2** (u.) = the food cooked in a casserole

cas•sette /kə'set/ noun, c. = a plastic container that holds magnetic tape, which can be fitted into a cassette player (audio or video taperecorder) **cassette-player** noun, c. = a taperecorder or a video tape recorder which can record and/or play back sounds and/or visuals recorded on a cassette

cast[1] /kɑːst/ noun, c. **1** *This film has a very powerful cast.* = the people who act in a film or play **2** *a single cast of the net* = the act of throwing a fishing net into the water **3** *a plaster cast* = a hard covering put over a broken bone to keep it in place so that it can heal **4** *a bronze cast* = see **cast**[2] meaning **6**

cast[2] verb, t. **1** *The fisherman cast his net into the sea.* = to throw (literary) **2** *to cast one's vote* = to drop (into a box) **3** *Your involvement in a case of cheating has cast some doubts on your honesty.* = to cause; to raise (formal) **4** *Snakes cast off their skin every year.* = to throw off (see also **cast-off**) **5** *Shah Rukh Khan has been cast in the new film.* = to give someone an acting part in a film or play **6** *The artist is casting a bronze statue of the great leader.* = to make a metal object by pouring hot, liquid metal into a specially shaped container (**mould**) **cast iron** noun, u. = a type of iron which is hard but brittle (can break easily), used for making furniture etc. **cast-off** noun, c. = an unwanted object (usually clothing) which may be given away

caste /kɑːst/ noun, u. or c. (u.) = a social class or group which a person is considered a member of

cast•er (castor) /ˈkɑːstəʳ/ noun, c. = small wheel fixed to the base of a piece of furniture, so that it can be moved easily

cast•i•gate /ˈkæstɪgeɪt/ verb, t. *I was castigated for losing the money collected for charity.* = to punish or scold in a strong way (see also **chastise**) (formal)

cas•tle /ˈkɑːsəl/ noun, c. **1** = a large and strong building, usually made of stone, used in former times to defend a place from enemy attack **2** = one of the pieces used in the game of chess, which can move any number of squares but only forwards, backwards or sideways (also known as rook)

cas•tor /ˈkɑːstəʳ/ noun, u. **1** = the small seeds of a plant from which oil is produced **2** see **caster**

cas•trate /kæˈstreɪt/ verb, t. = to remove the sex organs of a male animal or person so that it/he cannot reproduce

cas•u•al /ˈkæʒuəl/ adj. **1** *We had a casual meeting of the Board this morning* = informal; not official **2** *He is wearing casual clothes.* = informal; not meant for formal occasions **3** *I am only a casual reader of poetry.* = not serious or thorough **4** *a casual worker in a factory* = one who is employed only for a short period; not regular

cas•u•al•ty /ˈkæʒuəlti/ noun, c. (**casualties**) = a person seriously injured or killed in a war, accident etc. **casual leave** (**CL**) a short spell of leave, not planned in advance, often taken for personal reasons

cat /kæt/ noun, c. = a small animal often kept as a pet **big cats** noun = wild animals belonging to the cat family e.g. lion, tiger etc. **cat-call** noun, c. *During the show the actors received many cat-calls from the audience.* = a whistle or other rude noise made during a stage show, game etc. by members of the audience to show their displeasure

to let the cat out of the bag = to make a secret known to others **to rain cats and dogs** = to rain heavily

cat•a•logue[1] /ˈkætəlɒg/ noun, c. = a list of things (e.g. the books in a library or goods available in a shop) arranged in such a way that they can be easily found

catalogue[2] verb, t. *I have to catalogue the new books that have just been bought for the library.* = to enter something into a catalogue

cat•a•lyst /ˈkætəlɪst/ noun, c. **1** *Platinum dioxide is used as a catalyst.* = a substance that helps to speed up a chemical process but does not undergo any change itself [CHEMISTRY] **2** *The arrival of Mahatma Gandhi from South Africa served as a catalyst in India's struggle for freedom.* = an event that helps to bring about or speed up other events (figurative)

cat•a•ma•ran /kætəməˈræn/ noun, c. = a kind of boat which has two hulls (bodies) joined together

cat•a•pult[1] /ˈkætəpʌlt/ noun, c. **1** = a small Y-shaped stick to which a rubber band is tied, used to shoot small stones **2** = a fighting machine used in former times to throw heavy stones etc. at the enemy

catapult[2] verb, t. *This film will catapult the new actor to instant fame.* = to cause someone to rise quickly in a profession etc.

cat•a•ract /ˈkætərækt/ noun, c. **1** = a condition of the eye which prevents a person from seeing clearly **2** = a large waterfall (compare **cascade**)

ca•tas•tro•phe /kəˈtæstrəfi/ noun, c. *First we had a cyclone that killed thousands of people and now we have floods. We are facing one catastrophe after another.* = a sudden and unexpected natural event that causes suffering and destruction (also **calamity**)

catch[1] /kætʃ/ noun, c. (**catches**) **1** *The wicket-keeper took a wonderful catch.*(c.) = the act of taking hold of a moving object in the air **2** *the catch from the sea*(u.) = the quantity of something, especially fish, which one has been able to get **3** *There is no catch on this door.* = a hook that keeps a door shut, so that it cannot be opened from the outside **4** *Why are they selling the car so cheap? There must be a catch!* = some hidden problem or difficulty **5** *There was a catch in his voice when he spoke about his childhood.* = a change in the voice which shows emotion

catch[2] verb, t. or i. (**caught**) **1** *Catch the ball when I throw it to you.*(t.) = to get hold of some object which is moving through the air **2** *The police have caught the thieves.*(t.) = to get hold of someone, especially after a chase **3** *Cats like to catch mice.*(t.) = to hunt and kill **4** *You must go at once if you want to catch the train.*(t.) = to be in time for something **5** *You will catch a cold.*(t.) = to get an infection or illness **6** *Your new dress will catch everyone's eye.*(t.) = to attract or draw attention **7** *I am sorry but I did not catch what you said.*(t.) = to hear or understand **8** *The old wooden building can catch fire easily.*(t.) = to start to burn **9** *The sleeve of my shirt caught in the bolt of the window.*(i.) = to get stuck or hooked **catching** adj. *Chicken pox is very catching.* = a disease or infection that spreads easily (informal)

to catch on *This new film song is sure to catch on quickly.* = to become popular (informal) **to catch sight of (to catch a glimpse of) someone** *I caught sight of them at the crowded railway station, and waved.* = to see suddenly **to catch someone doing something** *He caught them trying to read his letters.* = to see someone doing something they should not be doing **to catch up with something or someone** 1 *You can start walking to school, I will catch up with you.* 2 *When she returned to school she stayed back to catch up with the lessons she had missed when she was ill.* = to reach a position or part which others have reached before you

catch•ment /ˈkætʃmənt/ noun, u. 1 = an area from which a river or lake gets its water 2 *a catchment area for a school* = an area from where a school is able to get many students

catch•word /ˈkætʃwɜːd/ noun, c. *'Swadeshi' became a catchword during the freedom movement.* = a word or phrase that is repeated regularly by a political party or newspaper and becomes a kind of slogan to attract people

catch•y /ˈkætʃɪ/ adj. *a catchy song* = something that can easily catch on (become popular)

cat•e•gor•i•cal /kætɪˈgɒrɪkəl/ adj. *The Minister made a categorical statement saying that he is not going to resign.* = very definite, showing no doubt at all

cat•e•go•ry /ˈkætəgəri/ noun, c. (**categories**) *The students in this school belong to two categories: boarders and day-scholars.* = the different classes into which people or things can be divided **categorize (categorise)** verb, t. *My friend has a law degree but he does not want to be categorized as a lawyer. He prefers to call himself a social worker.* = to be put in a certain category or class

ca•ter /ˈkeɪtəʳ/ verb, i. or t. 1 *I have asked Mayfair Restaurant to cater at my son's wedding.*(i.) = to provide food for guests at a party or function 2 *The new school will cater to the needs of the people of this locality.*(i.) = to meet the need for something

cat•er•pil•lar /ˈkætəpɪləʳ/ noun, c. = an insect with many legs that turns later into a moth or butterfly **caterpillar track** noun *Army tanks run on caterpillar tracks.* = a kind of metal chain on which a vehicle moves (instead of wheels)

ca•the•dral /kəˈθiːdrəl/ noun, c. = a very large, beautifully decorated church built of stone

cath•e•ter /ˈkæθɪtəʳ/ noun, c. = a very thin, flexible tube which is pushed into the body of a person who is ill or disabled and through which measurements can be made or liquids can be put in or taken out to help in medical treatment [MEDICINE]

cath•ode /ˈkæθəʊd/ noun, c. = the negative terminal (end) of an electrical device (machine) such as a battery (compare **anode**)

Catholic /ˈkæθəlɪk/ noun or adj. = a person who follows the Roman Catholic religion

cath•o•lic /ˈkæθəlɪk/ adj. *He has very catholic tastes in music. He enjoys Western as well as African and Indian music.* = able to take interest in many different things

CAT scan (**CT scan**) /ˈkætskæn/ noun, c. = an advanced x-ray image which shows features of the body and is used to detect the presence, of a disease, e.g. cancer

cat•tle /ˈkætl/ noun, u. (always plural) = large four-footed farm animals (cows, bulls, oxen, buffaloes)

cat•ty /ˈkætɪ/ adj. *They are always making catty remarks about their friends.* = unkind and full of bad feeling (informal, derogatory)

cat•walk /ˈkætwɔːk/ noun, c. = a narrow, raised platform for people to walk on, especially models at a fashion-show or workers in a factory

cau•cus /ˈkɔːkəs/ noun, c. = a small group of people within a political party who hold the same views

caul•dron /ˈkɔːldrən/ noun, c. = a large, round metal cooking-pot

cau•li•flow•er /ˈkɒlɪflaʊəʳ/ noun, c. or u. = a vegetable which is a collection of tiny white flowers surrounded by thick green leaves

cause[1] /kɔːz/ noun, c. 1 *Someone dropped a burning cigarette on the carpet and that was the cause of the fire.*= a person, thing or event that makes something happen 2 *Do you have any cause to complain?* = reason 3 *I am fighting for a good cause.* = some principle that one believes in

cause[2] verb, t. *We want to know what caused this accident.* = to be the cause of something **root cause** noun *The root cause of the pollution in the city is the large number of old vehicles.* = the main or basic reason for something negative

to make common cause with *The people living on this street made common cause in fighting noise pollution.* = to come together for the purpose of working for a cause or belief

cau•sal /ˈkɔːzəl/ adj. *Doctors believe that there is may be causal connection between smoking and cancer of the lungs.* = serving as a cause (reason) for something

caus•tic /ˈkɔːstɪk/ adj. 1 *Hydrochloric acid is highly caustic.* = something that can burn the skin 2 *caustic remarks* = something that hurts one's feelings

cau•tion[1] /ˈkɔːʃən/ noun, u. or c. 1 *Advise the children to use caution when crossing the street.*(u.) = great care and attention, in order to be safe from danger (formal) 2 *The policeman let us off with a* *caution but told us we would be arrested if we exceeded the speed limit again.*(c.) = warning

caution[2] verb, t. **1** *Let me caution you to carry a torch when you go out at night.* = to warn against possible danger **2** *The policeman cautioned me for driving very fast.* = to warn someone who has been doing something wrong not to do it again **cautious** adj. *I don't think he will lend you a thousand rupees as he is very cautious with money.* = careful to avoid risks

cav•al•ry /ˈkævəlri/ noun, u. **1** = (in former days) soldiers who fought on horse-back **2** = (in modern times) the branch of the army that uses tanks or other armoured vehicles

cave /keɪv/ noun, c. = a deep natural hollow place in the side of a mountain or hill or under the ground **cave-man** noun, c. (**-men**) = a person who lived in caves in very ancient times **cave-dweller** = a person who acts in a rough, violent manner G (figurative) **cavern** /ˈkævən/ noun, c. = a large cave (literary)

cav•i•ty /ˈkævɪti/ noun, c. (**cavities**) *a cavity in one's tooth* = a hole or hollow space in something solid

caw[1] /kɔː/ noun, c. = the sound produced by a crow

caw[2] verb, i. = to make a cawing sound

cc abbr. of **cubic centimetre(s)** *a car with a 1000 cc engine* = the unit for measuring volume in the metric system

CD abbr. of **compact disc** = a small disc (flat, round piece) of metal coated with plastic, on which a large amount of information can be stored for use in a computer **CD-ROM** abbr. of **Compact Disc with Read-Only Memory** = a CD which can only be read but cannot be rewritten or erased [COMPUTERS]

cease /siːs/ verb, i. or t. *You are ordered to cease all further imports of drugs.*(t.) = to stop (formal) **cease-fire** noun, u. *Both sides have agreed to a cease-fire.* = an agreement between the two sides in a war to stop fighting

ce•dar /ˈsiːdəʳ/ noun, c. or u. = a tree which produces soft, light brown wood

cede /siːd/ verb, t. *to cede territory to the enemy* = to give up a piece of land to another country after defeat in a war (formal)

cei•ling /ˈsiːlɪŋ/ noun, c. **1** *The room has a very high ceiling.* = the inner surface of the top of a room **2** *The government has fixed a ceiling on the price of wheat.* = an upper limit

cel•e•brate /ˈseləbreɪt/ verb, t. *India celebrates its Independence Day on the fifteenth of August.* = to mark a special event or occasion by organising some activity **celebrated** adj. *a celebrated writer* = famous **celebrity** /səˈlebrɪti/ noun, c. (**celebrities**) *This actor is already a celebrity at the age of twenty.* = a famous person

cel•e•ry /ˈseləri/ noun, u. = the soft, greenish stem of a plant eaten as a vegetable

ce•les•ti•al /sɪˈlestiəl/ adj. *Ancient astronomers studied the sun and other celestial bodies.* = heavenly (often literary)

cel•i•bate /ˈselɪbət/ adj. = a person who keeps away from sexual activity **celibacy** noun, u. = the state of being celibate

cell /sel/ noun, c. **1** *a bone cell* = the smallest part into which a living thing can be divided **2** *a prison cell* = a tiny room in a prison or monastery in which only one person can live **3** *a torch cell* = a small electrical battery in which electrical energy is stored **4** *the espionage cell* = a small group of people working within a larger department **cellular** adj. = something that is made up of many tiny cells in an electronic circuit (e.g. a cellular phone)

cel•lar /ˈseləʳ/ noun, c. *a wine cellar* = an underground room used for storing wine etc.

cel•lo /ˈtʃeləʊ/ noun, c. = a large stringed instrument, like a violin, played with a bow

cel•lo•phane /ˈseləfeɪn/ noun, u. = transparent soft plastic material used to make bags, wrap food etc.

cell•phone /ˈselfəʊn/ noun, c. = a cellular phone (a mobile telephone)

cel•lu•lose /ˈseljʊləʊz/ noun, u. = the substance, from which the cell walls of plants are made [BIOLOGY]

Cel•si•us /ˈselsiəs/ noun = a scale of temperature in which the freezing point of water is 0 degrees, and the boiling point 100 degrees (also known as the **Centigrade** scale)

ce•ment /sɪˈment/ noun, u. = a mixture of lime and clay which becomes hard when mixed with water and allowed to dry, used in building houses etc.

cem•e•tery /ˈsemɪtri/ noun, c. (**cemeteries**) = a piece of land in which people are buried after death

cen•o•taph /ˈsenətɑːf/ noun, c. = a building set up in memory of a dead person

cen•sor[1] /ˈsensəʳ/ noun, c. *The Board of Censors has passed the new film.* = an official who examines films, books, magazines etc. and has the power to remove anything that is offensive or thought to be in bad taste

censor[2] verb, t. *The government must censor the film before it can be shown to anyone.* = to examine through a censor **censorship** noun, u. = the system set up by some authority to censor and control films, books, newspapers etc.

cen•sure[1] /ˈsenʃəʳ/ noun, u. *The opposition brought a censure motion against the government.* = the act of expressing disapproval or criticism

censure[2] verb, t. *This action of the government was censured in Parliament by the opposition parties.* = to express strong criticism and disapproval (especially in parliament)

cen•sus /ˈsensəs/ noun, u. *In India, a census is taken once in ten years.* = an official counting of the population

cent /sent/ noun, c. = a coin which has the value of the hundredth part (0.01) of a dollar

cen•te•na•ry /senˈtiːnəri/ noun, c. *This year we celebrate the birth centenary of one of our great leaders.* = a day or year which comes exactly 100 years after a particular event

Cen•ti•grade /ˈsentəgreɪd/ noun see **Celsius**

cen•ti•me•tre /ˈsentɪmiːtəʳ/ noun = a unit for measuring length, equal to the hundredth part of a metre (abbr. as cm)

cen•ti•pede /ˈsentɪpiːd/ noun, c. = a small insect with many legs

cen•tral /ˈsentrəl/ adj. **1** *the central government* = belonging to the centre or located (placed) at the centre **2** *the central point in the speech* = most important **centralize (centralise)** verb, t. = to bring something under a central authority (opposite **de-centralize**) **centre of gravity** noun, c. = the point at which the entire weight of an object seems to be concentrated

cen•tre[1] **(center)** /ˈsentəʳ/ noun, c. **1** *the centre of a circle // Mumbai is India's most important business centre.* = a place where a lot of activity goes on **2** *I think her views are left of centre.* = a position in politics where one takes a moderate (middle) position (neither **left** nor **right**)

centre[2] verb, t. **1** *The left-out has centred the ball.* = to hit the ball to the centre of the field, in the game of football or hockey **2** *Please centre the table on the floor.* = to place at the centre

to centre round *Our hopes are centred round our niece who shows a lot of promise.* = to place one's hope or trust in someone **to centre on something** *This test centres on the topic of climate.* = to be mainly about something

cen•tri•fu•gal /sentrɪˈfjuːgəl/ adj. *When a car is going round a curve at high speed, there are powerful centrifugal forces acting on it.* = moving or pulling in a direction away from the centre [PHYSICS] (opposite **centripetal**) **centrifuge** /ˈsentrɪfjuːdʒ/ noun, c. = a machine in which a container of liquid is made to spin very fast, so that any solids present in the liquid get separated from it. (A centrifuge is used to separate cream from milk.)

cen•tri•pe•tal /sentrɪˈpiːtəl/ adj. = moving towards the centre (opposite **centrifugal**)

cen•tu•ry /ˈsentʃəri/ noun, c. (**centuries**) **1** = a period of 100 years **2** = 100 runs made by a cricket player

ce•ram•ic /sɪˈræmɪk/ adj. *a ceramic vase* = made of clay which is 'fired' in a special oven (also **china**)

ce•ram•ics /sɪˈræmɪks/ noun, u. or c. (always plural) **1** = the process by which pots or other objects made of clay are baked (burnt) in an oven until they become hard **2** = objects that are made by this process

ce•re•al /ˈsɪəriəl/ noun, c. or u. **1** (c.) = a plant from which food grains are produced e.g. rice, wheat, millet **2** (u.) = food made from rice, wheat, maize or other grains

cer•e•bral /ˈserɪbrəl/ adj. **1** *cerebral haemorrhage* = related to the brain **2** *a cerebral writer* = calling for the use of one's intellect rather than emotions

cer•e•mo•ny /ˈserɪməni/ noun, c. (**ceremonies**) or u. *a wedding ceremony*(c.) = an action or event which has a special social or religious importance and is performed according to an established set of rules **ceremonial** /serɪˈməʊniəl/ adj. *The President uses this car only on ceremonial occasions such as Republic Day.* = something which is connected with a ceremony

cer•tain /ˈsɜːtn/ adj. **1** *I am certain that India will win this match, because we have never lost at Kolkata.* = having no doubt **2** *Our team is certain to win.* = sure **3** *Please make certain that you lock all the doors before you leave.* = to be absolutely sure **certainly** adv. **1** *We will certainly reach late.* = without doubt **2** *'Could you help me carry this bag?' 'Certainly.'* = of course ('Certainly not' is a firm, unpleasant way of refusing) **certainty** noun, u. *I can state with absolute certainty that we are on the wrong train.* = the state of being free from doubt

cer•tif•i•cate /səˈtɪfɪkət/ noun, c. *Your date of birth, according to your birth certificate, is 5 July 1985.* = an official document which proves that the facts stated by someone are true **certify** /ˈsɜːtɪfaɪ/ verb, t. *You must ask a senior government official to certify that you belong to this state.* = to declare that something is true or correct

ces•sa•tion /seˈseɪʃən/ noun, u. *There is peace now after the cessation of fighting.* = a short pause or stop (formal)

cess•pit /ˈsespɪt/ noun, c. **1** = a pit (hole in the ground) in which waste material from houses is collected **2** = a place in which there is a lot of corruption (figurative)

chafe /tʃeɪf/ verb, t. or i. **1** *The shoe is chafing the skin on my foot.*(t.) = to rub painfully against something **2** *He is chafing at the delay in starting the match.*(i.) = to become impatient

C

chaff /tʃɑːf/ noun, u. *The chaff from the rice is fed to cows.* = the outer skin (cover) of a grain of rice etc.

chain[1] /tʃeɪn/ noun, c. or u. **1** *The dog is tied up with a chain. // He gave her a silver chain.*(c.) = a number of metal rings connected to each other to form a length of metal used to tie something, or as an ornament **2** *The Himalayas are a chain of mountains.*(c.) = a row of connected mountains [GEOGRAPHY] **3** *They own a chain of restaurants.*(c.) = a number of shops etc. which are owned by the same person or company

chain[2] verb, t. *You should chain the dog when you have visitors.* = to tie someone or something up with a chain **chain-smoker** noun, c. = a person who is in the habit of smoking a large number of cigarettes continuously **chain reaction** noun, c. = a number of events or chemical reactions related to each other in such a way that each one leads to the next **to be in chains** = to be a slave or in prison

chair[1] /tʃeəʳ/ noun, c. **1** *a wooden chair* = a piece of furniture with four legs and a back on which one sits **2** *The meeting was declared closed by the chair.* = the chairperson or someone who is presiding over a meeting **3** *The university has set up a chair in Indian philosophy.* = a position of professor at a university **4** *She is the Chair, Department of History.* = the head of a department in a university

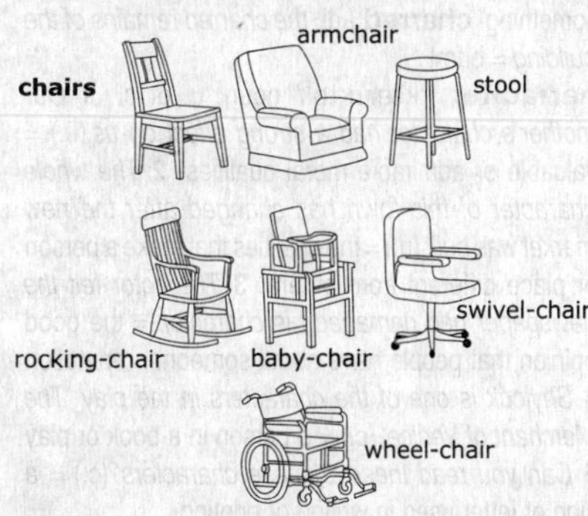

chair[2] verb, t. *I will request the senior teacher to chair this meeting.* = to act as the chairperson at a meeting **chairman/chairwoman** noun (see **chairperson**)

chair•per•son /'tʃeəpɜːsən/ noun, c. = a person who controls the activities at a meeting. (The term **chairperson** is preferred because it includes women and men.)

chalk /tʃɔːk/ noun, u. **1** = a chemical substance (calcium carbonate) often found in rocks **2** *a piece of chalk* = soft material used for writing on a chalkboard (blackboard) **to chalk up** *Our football team has chalked up three victories in a row.* = to score a victory **to chalk out** = to plan in advance **to be as different as chalk from cheese** = to be completely different

chal•lenge[1] /'tʃælɪndʒ/ noun, c. or u. **1** *India has accepted the challenge by Sri Lanka.*(c.) = an invitation to play against someone **2** *Writing a book on the forest tribes of India must have been a real challenge.*(c.) = something that is difficult to do and brings out the best qualities in a person

challenge[2] verb, t. **1** *This order of the government can be challenged in a court of law.* = to question the legality of something **2** *She has challenged me to play three games of chess with her.* = to invite someone to play in a match against you

chal•lenged /'tʃælɪndʒd/ adj. *There are special books for the visually challenged.* = the word 'challenged' is used together with *-ly* adverbs in words such as 'visually challenged' (blind), and 'mentally challenged' (having a mental disability) as a non-discriminating word for persons with a disability

cham•ber /'tʃeɪmbəʳ/ noun, c. **1** *the judge's chamber* = a large room set apart for some special purpose **2** *the four chambers of the heart, the oil-chamber in the engine of a car* = an enclosed space inside a body or machine **Chamber of Commerce** noun, c. = a group of important businesspersons who sometimes advise the government on business matters **chamber-pot** noun, c. = a closed metal container, used by persons who are sick and unable to go to the toilet (bathroom) (old-fashioned)

cha•me•le•on /kə'miːliən/ noun, c. = a small lizard which can change its colours to match the surroundings (see also **camouflage**)

cham•pagne /ʃæm'peɪn/ noun, u. = an expensive colourless wine which produces bubbles when poured out, generally drunk to celebrate something

cham•pi•on[1] /'tʃæmpiən/ noun, c. **1** *Pete Sampras is the tennis champion this year.* = a person who has defeated everyone else in one or more tournaments **2** *Meera Roy is a champion of women's rights.* = a person who fights for or strongly supports a cause, principle or movement

champion[2] verb, t. *Mr Shah has agreed to champion our cause.* = to support strongly **championship** noun, u. *the Wimbledon championship* = a tournament (competition) held to decide who should be the champion

chance[1] /tʃɑːns/ noun, c. **1** *You will be given a chance to speak.* = opportunity **2** *You are going to the station so late that there is no chance of your catching the train.* = possibility **3** *I met my old friend by chance on the train.* = unexpectedly

chance[2] adj. *This was a chance meeting.* = something that happens unexpectedly and has not been planned

chance[3] verb, t. **1** *I chanced to be present at the meeting when the Prime Minister arrived.* = to happen by chance (without planning) **2** *Do you want to contest the election? All right, you can chance it.* = to take a risk **chancy** adj. *Tendulkar played a chancy innings and was lucky to get so many runs.* = full of risks (informal)

Chan•cel•lor /ˈtʃɑːnsələʳ/ noun, c. *The Chancellor of the University* = an official who has a very high rank

chan•de•lier /ʃændəˈlɪəʳ/ noun, c. = a large, decorated holder for candles or electric lights, made of glass, that hangs from the ceiling

change[1] /tʃeɪndʒ/ noun, c. or u. **1** *You will find a change in our syllabus.*(c.) = the act or result of bringing in something new or different **2** *I am tired of watching television. Let us go to the cinema for a change.*(u.) = something different **3** *I bought a pen for Rs 35. I gave the shop keeper Rs 50 and he returned Rs 15 as change.*(u.) = money returned when the amount given is more than the value of the goods bought **4** *Keep some loose change in your purse.*(u.) = coins of low value **5** *He was looking cheerful, for a change.*(u.) = unusually (The phrase expresses relief about a situation.) **6** *We normally go for a walk by the river, but last evening we walked through the park. It made a nice change.*(u.) = difference

change[2] verb, t. or i. **1** *We must change the syllabus and introduce new textbooks.*(t.) = to make things different **2** *Your clothes are dirty. I think you should change.*(i.) = to put on different clothes **3** *In the story, the man changes into a tree by magic.*(i.) = to stop being what one normally is and become something else **to change over** *We were using an electric stove but have now changed over to gas.* = to start using completely different methods, equipment etc. **to change hands** *The shop now has a different name. Maybe it has changed hands.* = to be managed by new owners **to change for the better** = to show a change in one's behaviour which others think is an improvement

chan•nel[1] /ˈtʃænəl/ noun, c. **1** *You will have to dig a channel for the rain-water to flow away.* = a passage for a liquid to flow through **2** *Let us watch the cricket match on the sports channel.* = a band of electro-magnetic waves on which a particular television programme is carried **3** *the English Channel* = a narrow sea connecting two larger seas or oceans **4** *Your application must come through the official channel.* = the route (path) through which information passes in an office

channel[2] verb, t. *The government's money is now being channelled into agricultural development.* = to direct (put) one's money or energy into a particular kind of activity **channelize (channelise)** verb

chant[1] /tʃɑːnt/ noun, c. *She taught us some chants.* = the sound of words being chanted

chant[2] verb, t. **1** *The priests were chanting prayers.* = to recite or sing words which have a religious importance or where a special effect is intended **2** *The crowd was chanting slogans.* = to repeat words continuously in a sing-song way

cha•os /ˈkeɪɒs/ noun, u. *There was chaos at the railway station when people heard the train was cancelled.* = a state of complete disorder and confusion **chaotic** /keɪˈɒtɪk/ adj. *The traffic on these roads is chaotic.* = without any order

chap[1] /tʃæp/ noun, c. *He is a nice chap.* = a man or boy (informal)

chap[2] verb, t. *The hot dry wind chapped her skin.* = to cause the skin to crack because of dryness

chap•a•ti /tʃəˈpɑːtɪ/ noun, c. (**chapatis, chapaties**) = a round, flat piece of bread made out of whole wheat and cooked on a flat iron pan

chap•el /ˈtʃæpəl/ noun, c. = a small church (compare **cathedral**)

chap•ter /ˈtʃæptəʳ/ noun, c. = one of the main parts into which a long book can be divided

char /tʃɑːʳ/ verb, t. **(charred)** *The fire has charred the building.* = to leave the black marks of burning on something **charred** adj. *the charred remains of the building* = burnt

char•ac•ter /ˈkærɪktəʳ/ noun, u. or c. **1** *Our mother's character had a strong effect on us.*(u.) = valuable or admirable moral qualities **2** *The whole character of this town has changed after the new market was built.*(u.) = the qualities that make a person or place different from others **3** *The actor felt the newspaper had damaged his character.* = the good opinion that people have about someone; reputation **4** *Shylock is one of the characters in the play 'The Merchant of Venice'.*(c.) = a person in a book or play **5** *Can you read these Chinese characters?*(c.) = a sign or letter used in writing or printing **to be a person of character** = to have strong principles which are admired by others

char•ac•ter•is•tic[1] /kærɪktəˈrɪstɪk/ noun, c. *Punctuality is one of the characteristics of the people working in this office.* = some quality by which one can easily recognize a person or thing

characteristic[2] adj. *You can find the characteristic smell of tandoori chicken in this restaurant.* = some quality that can always be expected or found in a person or thing

char•ac•ter•ize (characterise) /ˈkærɪktəraɪz/ verb, t. *A small head and large ears characterize the*

African elephant, while the Indian elephant has a large head and smaller ears. = to be characteristic (typical) of something

cha•rade /ʃə'rɑːd/ noun *Your friend is not really angry with you; she is only putting on a charade of being angry.* = behaviour which can be easily seen to be false

cha•rades /ʃə'rɑːdz/ noun (always plural) = a game in which people try to guess words (e.g. the title of a film) through the silent actions performed by other players

char•coal /'tʃɑːkəʊl/ noun, u. = the black substance formed when wood is burnt in a closed container with little air, which can be used as fuel

charge[1] /tʃɑːdʒ/ noun, c. or u. **1** *The charge for a room in this hotel is Rs 250 a night.*(c.) = the price asked for something **2** *Who is in charge of this office?*(u.) = control **3** *He has been arrested on a charge of robbery.*(c.) = a spoken or written statement saying that someone has done something wrong **4** *There is no charge in this battery.*(u.) = electrical energy; power

charge[2] verb, t. or i. **1** *The doctor will charge you Rs 100 as fees.*(t.) = to ask for payment **2** *The crowd charged into the building.*(i.) = to rush forward usually to attack **3** *The police have charged him with theft.*(t.) = to state that someone has done something wrong; to accuse **4** *You will have to charge this battery.*(t.) = to put electrical energy into something **charge-sheet** noun, c. = a record of the charges made by the police against a person who will then be tried in a court **charge card** noun, c.= a kind of credit card which allows the customer to buy something and pay for it later

char•i•ot /'tʃæriət/ noun, c. = a light horse-drawn carriage, usually with two wheels, used in battles and races in former times **charioteer** /tʃæriə'tɪə[r]/ noun, c. = the driver of a chariot

cha•ris•ma /kə'rɪzmə/ noun, u. *Our leader was loved by the people and had great charisma.* = some special quality which attracts love and respect **charismatic** /kærɪz'mætɪk/ adj. *a charismatic leader* = having charisma

char•i•ty /'tʃærɪti/ noun, u. or c. (**charities**) **1** *She gives a lot of money to charity.*(u.) = *money or help given to people who are poor, sick etc.* **2** *He gives some money each month to a number of charities.*(c.) = a society or organisation that collects money to help poor people **3** *She helps people out of charity.*(u.) = sympathy and kindness **charitable** adj. **1** *a charitable person* = kind and generous in helping the poor or someone in need **2** *One should take a charitable view of his past misdeeds.* = sympathetic, willing to forgive **3** *a charitable fund* = something that is related to charity (giving help to the poor)

charm[1] /tʃɑːm/ noun, u. or c. **1** *The woman has great charm and is liked by everybody.*(u.) = the power to attract and please others **2** *a good luck charm*(c.) = something magical which brings good or bad luck

charm[2] verb, t. **1** *He can charm anybody with his smile.*(t.) = to create a good effect on someone **2** *We were charmed by their kindness.* = very pleased **3** *We felt charmed by the music.* = to feel the powerful effect of something

chart[1] /tʃɑːt/ noun, c. *Here is a chart showing the names of the villages with schools.* = a piece of paper containing some information, usually in the form of tables, diagrams etc.

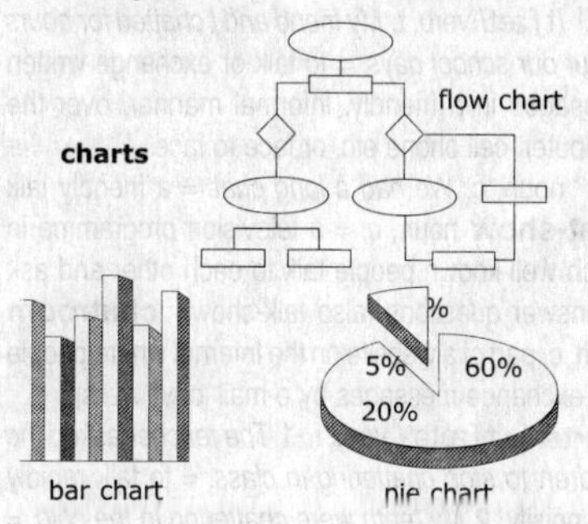

chart[2] verb, t. *This article charts the performance of the Sri Lankan cricket team during the last two years.* = to give some information in the form of a chart **charts** (always plural) *A.R. Rahman has been in the charts for weeks.* = a list of best-selling records compiled every week

char•ter[1] /'tʃɑːtə[r]/ noun, c. = an official document which describes the rights, duties etc. given to a person or company

charter[2] verb t. (**chartered**) **1** *to charter a plane* = to hire a plane, bus etc. for some special purpose **2** = to give a charter to **chartered** adj. *chartered bus* = hired for a special purpose **chartered accountant** noun, c. = an accountant who has been given a charter (license to practise)

chase[1] /tʃeɪs/ verb, t. **1** *The policeman chased the thief but could not catch him.* = to follow someone in order to catch **2** *He chased the dog away.* = to make someone leave or go away

chase[2] noun, c. or u. *The criminals were caught by the police after a long chase.* = the act of chasing someone

chas•m /'kæzəm/ noun, c. **1** = a deep crack or opening in the earth **2** *There was a chasm between the two groups after their quarrel.* = a break in friendship (figurative)

chas•sis /ˈtʃæsi/ noun, c. = the framework on which the body of a motor car is built

chaste /tʃeɪst/ adj. **1** *a chaste person* = not indulging in sexual activity which is considered improper or immoral **2** *written in chaste Hindi* = simple and not highly decorative **chastity** /ˈtʃæstɪti/ noun, u. = the state of being chaste

chas•ten /ˈtʃeɪsən/ verb, t. *The tragic death of his friend has chastened him and made him a better person.* = to cause a person to improve as a result of suffering or punishment (formal)

chas•tise /tʃæˈstaɪz/ verb, t. *They were chastised for using bad language.* = to punish severely (see also **castigate**)

chat[1] /tʃæt/ verb, t. *My friend and I chatted for hours about our school days.* = to talk or exchange written messages in a friendly, informal manner, over the computer, cell phone etc. or face to face

chat[2] noun, c. *We had a long chat.* = a friendly talk **chat-show** noun, c. = a television programme in which well-known people talk to each other and ask or answer questions (also talk-show) **chatroom** noun, c. part of a website on the Internet where people can exchange messages by e-mail [COMPUTERS]

chat•ter[1] /ˈtʃætəʳ/ verb, i. **1** *The teacher asked the children to stop chattering in class.* = to talk rapidly and noisily **2** *My teeth were chattering in the cold.* = to knock together and make a sound because of cold, fear etc.

chatter[2] noun, u. *Stop the chatter!* = rapid and noisy talk **chatterbox** noun, c. = *What a chatterbox he is!* = a person who loves to talk (informal)

chauf•feur /ˈʃəʊfəʳ/ noun, c. (French) = a person who is paid to drive someone's car

chau•vin•is•m /ˈʃəʊvɪnɪzəm/ noun, u. **1** *Why don't you admit that our country often does wrong things? I don't like your chauvinism.* = supporting one's own country blindly **2** *male chauvinism* = a strong, unreasonable belief that a specific gender, language, religion, way of living etc. is superior to another **chauvinist** noun, c. *A chauvinist like you will always find fault with other countries* = a person who always supports his own country, gender, religion, language etc. (derogatory)

cheap /tʃiːp/ adj. **1** *Vegetables become cheap in winter but are expensive in summer.* = low in price **2** *We felt uncomfortable when they started telling cheap jokes.* = vulgar and in bad taste

> **Usage** The word cheap (when referring to the price of something) must be used with care because of the possible confusion between meanings.

> **Usage** *He got a cheap ticket to Lucknow.* = low in price (shows approval)
> *That dress was really cheap.* = low in price (shows approval)
> *That was a cheap dress.* = not suitable for the occasion (shows disapproval)

cheap•skate /ˈtʃɪːpskeɪt/ noun c. = a person who spends or gives unwillingly; a miser (informal)

cheat[1] /tʃiːt/ verb, t. **1** *You must be careful in dealing with them or they will cheat you.*(t.) = to make someone suffer a loss by doing something dishonest e.g. deliberately selling a defective car to a customer **2** *cheating at examinations* = to do something which is illegal or wrong knowingly

cheat[2] noun, c. *The police have arrested the cheat.* = a person who cheats others

check[1] /tʃek/ verb, t. **1** *The conductor will check your ticket.* = to examine something to see if it is correct **2** *You should check your temperature every morning.* = to observe (see) **3** *We have been able to check smuggling at the border.* = to stop

check[2] noun, c. or u. **1** *The police have come here to make a check.*(c.) = an examination to see that everything is all right **2** *The doctor has managed to keep the disease in check.*(u.) = under control **3** (usually plural) *The shirt had large blue checks.* = a pattern of squares **4** (see **cheque**) **checked** adj. *He was wearing a checked shirt.* = having a pattern of squares (checks) **5** *You will have to move your king as it is under check.* = an attack on the king in the game of chess **check in** noun, c. (**check ins**) = the act of reporting one's arrival at a hotel or airport counter **check out** noun, u. = the act of signing out one's departure from a hotel **checklist** noun, c. *The mechanics who repair an aircraft have to go through a long checklist, to make sure that it is ready to fly.* = a complete list of all the checks (examinations) to be made **checkmate** verb, i. *Your king has been checkmated!* = to surround the king, in the game of chess, so that it cannot be moved and is defeated **checkpoint** noun, c. *When you drive around the city at night you will have to go through a number of police checkpoints.* = a place where a check (examination) is made on people, traffic, goods etc. **check-up** noun, c. *I have to go to the hospital every month for a check-up.* = a general medical examination

cheek /tʃiːk/ noun, u. **1** = the soft part of the face below the eye **2** *I did not like his behaviour at all. In fact, I have never seen such cheek!* = disrespectful behaviour which makes one feel angry (informal) **cheeky** adj. *Don't be cheeky with me!* = showing disrespectful behaviour (informal)

C

cheep /tʃi:p/ noun, c. = the thin, high-pitched sound produced by young birds

cheer[1] /tʃɪə/ verb, t. or i. **1** *He looks sad. Let us cheer him up.*(t.) = to take away one's sadness and make him/her feel happy **2** *The crowd cheered loudly when Tendulkar scored a century.*(i.) = to shout in praise or encouragement **Cheer up!** interjec. = an expression used to encourage a person not to be sad or gloomy

cheer[2] noun, c. or u. *Can you hear the cheers of the crowd?*(c.) = a shout of praise or encouragement

to be in good cheer *I met them yesterday. They were in good cheer.* = a happy state of mind

cheer•ful /'tʃɪəfʊl/ adj. *He is always cheerful. I have never seen him look sad.* = happy

cheese /tʃi:z/ noun, u. or c. = a solid food produced from milk through the action of bacteria

chee•tah /'tʃi:tə/ noun, c. = a large spotted animal of the cat family which can run very fast, now found only in Africa but formerly also in India

chef /ʃef/ noun, c. (French) = a highly skilled cook who works in a hotel or restaurant (compare **cook**)

chem•is•try /'kemɪstri/ noun = scientific study of the natural substances which different things are made up of and the manner in which these substances combine with each other **chemical** adj. or noun, c. **1** *a chemical process*(adj.) = connected with chemistry **2** *Potassium chloride is a chemical.*(noun) = a substance that is used in chemistry **chemist** noun, c. **1** = a scientist who specialises in the study of chemistry **2** = a person who owns or works in a shop where medicines are sold

chem•o•ther•a•py /ki:məʊ'θerəpi/ noun = the use of chemicals (medicines) to treat cancer [MEDICINE]

cheque /tʃek/ noun, c. = a piece of paper which is used to order a bank to pay someone a certain sum of money (**check** in America) **blank cheque** noun, c. = a cheque which has been signed by the person making a payment but in which the amount of money to be paid has not been filled in **crossed cheque** noun, c. = a cheque across which the person making the payment has drawn a pair of lines to tell the bank that money cannot be paid directly to the payee (the person who is to be paid) but only into his/her bank account

chequered /'tʃekəd/ adj. **1** *a chequered table-cloth* = having a pattern of squares of two usually contrasting colours **2** *He had a chequered career as an athlete.* = mixed; both good and bad

cher•ish /tʃerɪʃ/ verb, t. *I shall always cherish the present you have given me.* = to attach great value to something; to love and care for

cher•ry /'tʃeri/ noun, c. (**cherries**) = a small, red, fleshy fruit

chess /tʃes/ noun = a game said to have begun in India, in which two players play against each other with 16 pieces (chessmen) which are moved according to fixed rules across a chess-board on which there are 32 squares of black and white colour alternatively

chest /tʃest/ noun, c. **1** = the upper front part of the body **2** = a large, strong box used for storing things

chew /tʃu:/ verb, t. *You must chew your food well before you swallow it.* = to crush food with the teeth **chewing gum** noun = a soft, sticky substance with a sweet taste which is meant to be chewed but not swallowed **to chew the cud** = the habit which cows have of bringing half-eaten food up from the stomach into the mouth and chewing it

to chew on something *Let's not be in a hurry, let's chew on the subject.* = to think about something carefully **to bite off more than one can chew** = to take up something which turns out to be more difficult, large etc. than one imagined

chic /ʃi:k/ adj. (French) *She always wears chic clothes.* = stylish and fashionable

chick /tʃɪk/ noun, c. **1** *a day-old chick* = a baby bird, specially a baby chicken **2** = a young woman (slang) Ⓖ **chick pea** noun = the edible seed of a plant belonging to the pea family ('gram', in India)

chick•en /'tʃɪkɪn/ noun, c. or u. **1** *Buy a chicken for dinner.*(c.) = a common bird bred for meat or laying eggs **2** *Would you like a piece of chicken?*(u.) = the meat of a chicken **chicken-feed** noun, u. *You are paying me only a hundred rupees for doing this job? This is chicken feed!* = a small and unimportant sum of money **chicken-hearted** adj. = cowardly and without courage

to chicken out *He had agreed to come with me into the forest but he chickened out at the last minute.* = to decide not to do something because of fear (informal, derogatory)

chicken pox /'tʃɪkɪnpɒks/ noun, u. = a disease, common among children, marked by fever and marks appearing on the skin

chide /tʃaɪd/ verb, t. (**chided** or **chid**) *The Warden of the hostel will chide you if you return to the hostel late.* = to scold

chief[1] /tʃi:f/ noun, c. *a tribal chief* = the leader or head of a group of people or an organisation (figurative)

chief[2] adj. **1** *the chief tutor* = having the seniormost position **2** *Rice is our chief crop.* = most important; main

child /tʃaɪld/ noun, c. (**children**) **1** *a small child* = a young human being **2** *my only child* = son or daughter **3** *a child of the age of television* = product **childhood** noun, u. = the time of being a child **childish** adj. **1** *Don't be childish. Act like an adult!* =

behaving in a manner unsuitable for a grown-up person (derogatory) **2** *He spoke in a childish voice.* = like that of a child (not derogatory) **child-like** adj. *I like him for his child-like nature.* = simple and innocent, like a child; lovable (compare **childish**) **child's play** noun, u. *Solving this problem will be child's play for me.* = something very easy to do

chill[1] /tʃɪl/ noun, c. **1** *I got wet in the rain and caught a chill.* (c.) = an illness marked by running of the nose, coughing etc. **2** *There was a chill in the air.* = coldness

chill[2] verb, t. **1** *Please chill this milk in the refrigerator.* = to make something cold **2** *I was chilled by the story of the murder.* = to feel fear

chill[3] adj. *There is a chill wind blowing.* = cold **chilly** adj. = somewhat cold but not very cold

chilli /'tʃɪli/ noun, c. (**chillies**) = the fruit of a kind of plant with a very hot taste which is used in cooking [also chili, chile (American English)]

chime[1] /tʃaɪm/ noun, c. *Can you hear the chimes of the clock?* = the soft musical sound produced by a set of bells or a clock (chiming clock) which has a special device to make the sound of bells

chime[2] verb, i. *The clock chimed softly and woke me up.* = to make a chiming sound

chim•ney /'tʃɪmni/ noun, c. = a hollow pipe rising above the roof of a building, factory or ship, through which smoke and hot gases from a fire pass out into the air

chim•pan•zee (chimp) /tʃɪmpæn'zi:/ noun, c. = a large, highly intelligent ape (tail-less monkey) found in Africa

chin /tʃɪn/ noun, c. = the bony part of the face below the mouth

chi•na /'tʃaɪnə/ noun, u. **1** *cups made of china* = a hard white substance like glass made by baking clay at high temperatures, used for making cups, dishes etc. **2** *Where do you keep your expensive china?* = plates, cups etc. made of china (also **porcelain, ceramic**)

chink /tʃɪŋk/ noun, c. *The sunlight came in through a chink in the door.* = a narrow crack or opening

chip[1] /tʃɪp/ noun, c. **1** *I was hit in the eye by a flying chip of wood. // We used marble chips for the floor.* = a small piece of wood or stone which has been broken off from a larger piece **2** *a potato chip* = a long thin piece of potato fried in oil (called **potato crisp** in Britain) **3** *microchip* = a tiny piece of silicon or other **semiconductive** material which forms part of a computer and stores information, performs calculations etc. [COMPUTERS]

chip[2] verb, i. or t. *This stone chips easily.* = to break off into one or more smaller pieces **to chip in 1** *I wish you wouldn't chip in when I'm talking.* = to enter into or to interrupt a conversation **2** *He wanted the book badly, so we all chipped in and bought it for him.* = to join others in raising money for some purpose **a chip off the old block** = a person who has some talent, good quality etc. which her/his parent is known to have **to have a chip on one's shoulder** = to continue to feel angry because of something that happened in the past

chirp[1] /tʃɜ:p/ noun, c. *the chirp of a mynah* = the short, sharp sound produced by a small bird or insect

chirp[2] verb, i. = to make a sound that is like the chirp of a bird **chirpy** adj. *You are very chirpy today. Have you received some good news?* = happy and cheerful (informal)

chis•el[1] /'tʃɪzəl/ noun, c. = a metal tool with a sharp cutting edge, used to carve (cut into) wood, stone etc. (see pic under **tools**)

chisel[2] verb, t. = to cut something with a chisel **chiselled** adj. *chiselled features* = very sharp (as if cut with a chisel) (used to describe a person's features)

chit /tʃɪt/ noun, c. **1** *a chit of paper* = a small piece of paper torn out of a bigger piece **2** = a young girl who is thought to be disrespectful to older people (derogatory)

chit-chat noun, c. *friendly chit-chat* = informal and light conversation (informal)

chiv•al•rous /'ʃɪvəlrəs/ adj. *The two women had run out of money, but luckily they met a chivalrous young man who helped them out.* = (a man who is) kind, polite and helpful to women (old-fashioned) **chivalry** noun, u. = the quality of being chivalrous

chlo•rine /'klɔ:ri:n/ noun, u. = a greenish-yellow gas with a strong smell **chlorinate** verb, t. = to put chlorine gas into something, especially water, in order to kill the germs which may be present

chlo•ro•form /'klɒrəfɔ:m/ noun, u. = a liquid which easily turns into a gas and is used to make a person unconscious before a surgical operation (see also **anaesthesia**)

chlo•ro•phyll /'klɒrəfɪl/ noun, u. = the substance present in the leaves of plants that makes them green

choco•late[1] /'tʃɒklɪt/ noun, u. **1** *a bar of chocolate* = a sweet brown substance made from **cocoa** which is mixed with milk, sugar and other substances and eaten as a sweet **2** = a drink made from chocolate **3** = the brown colour that chocolate has

chocolate[2] adj. *a chocolate-coloured dress* = having a brown colour

choice[1] /tʃɔɪs/ noun, c. or u. **1** *What would you like to eat? You have a choice between fish and chicken.* (c.) = the chance to choose between different things **2** *Mr Naidu has proved to be a good choice as Mayor.* (u.) = a person or thing which is chosen out of several

choice[2] adj. *He offered us some choice mangoes from his garden.* = of very good quality

choir /ˈkwaɪəʳ/ noun, c. (used with plural or singular verb) *The choir is/are singing tonight.* = a group of people who sing together in a church

choke[1] /tʃəʊk/ noun, c. *If you cannot start the car in the morning, use the choke.* = a device that chokes (blocks) the supply of air to the engine of a car, making it easier to start the engine when it is cold

choke[2] verb, i. or t. **1** *There was so much smoke in the room that I almost choked*(i.) = to have difficulty in breathing **2** *She choked with emotion when she got news of her daughter's illness.*(t.) = to be unable to speak because of some strong emotion **3** *The garbage has choked the drain.*(t.) = to fill up and block

chol•e•ra /ˈkɒlərə/ noun = a serious disease carried by germs present in water which causes diarrhoea and vomiting

cho•les•te•rol /ˈkəlestərɒl/ noun, u. = a substance found in certain kinds of food e.g. eggs, butter etc. which, when present in the body in a large quantity, settles on the inside walls of arteries and can cause them to get narrow, blocked etc.

choose /tʃuːz/ verb, t. and i. (**chose**) **1** *The Nature Club chose Nazir as its secretary.*(t) = to select (pick out) one from a number of things, people or possibilities **2** *She chose not to attend the meeting* (t.) = to decide to do something **choosy** adj. *He is very choosy about clothes.* = very careful about choosing; difficult to please

chop[1] /tʃɒp/ noun, c. **1** *a chop on the arm* = a short, sharp blow **2** *I am cooking a chicken chop.* = a small piece of meat which contains a bone

chop[2] verb, t. (**chopped**) *Can you chop some onions for the curry?* = to cut something, into small pieces with a sharp tool such as a knife or axe **chopper** noun, c. **1** = a heavy, sharp knife used for cutting meat or wood **2** = a helicopter (slang) **chopsticks** noun, c. = a pair of long thin sticks which people in some Asian countries (e.g. China, Japan) use to hold food while eating **chopping board** noun, c. = a flat piece of wood, plastic etc. on which vegetables are placed to be chopped

chord /kɔːd/ noun, c. **1** = a combination of musical notes [MUSIC] **2** = a straight line joining two points in a curve [GEOMETRY]

to strike a chord = to be reminded of something because of similarities

chore /tʃɔːʳ/ noun, c. *I have many household chores to do.* = work which has to be done regularly, specially in the house (informal)

chor•e•og•ra•phy /kɒrɪˈɒgrefi/ noun = the art of dancing or arranging dances for films or the stage

cho•rus /ˈkɔːrəs/ noun, c. **1** = a group of people singing together **2** = the lines in a song which are repeated several times, in between the other lines **3** *voices shouting in chorus* = something said or shouted together by people in a crowd (compare **chant**)

Christ /kraɪst/ noun = Jesus Christ, the founder of the Christian religion **Christian** noun, c. = a follower of Jesus Christ **Christian era** noun, u. = the modern calendar followed by most countries, which begins with the year in which Christ was born

chris•ten /ˈkrɪsən/ verb, t. = to perform a ceremony at which a baby is made a member of the church and given a name

Christ•mas /ˈkrɪsməs/ noun, c. = a festival celebrated on 25 December to mark the birth of Christ **Christmas tree** noun, c. = a small tree, real or artificial, which is decorated with lights, coloured paper etc. and put up in homes, shops etc. for the Christmas festival

chro•mi•um /ˈkrəʊmiəm/ noun = a metal that is mixed with iron and used for making steel and for covering metal objects with a shining, protective surface that does not rust (**chromium plating**)

chro•mo•some /ˈkrəʊməsəʊm/ noun, c. = a tiny thread-like body present in all living cells, which passes on the nature, physical qualities etc. of the parents to the child [BIOLOGY] (see also **X chromosome**, **Y chromosome** and **DNA**)

chron•ic /ˈkrɒnɪk/ adj. *My wife suffers from chronic asthma.* = a disease that continues for a long time

chron•i•cle /ˈkrɒnɪkəl/ noun, c. *The Babarnamah is a chronicle of events that happened in Emperor Babar's time.* = a record of historical events

chron•o•log•i•cal /krɒnəˈlɒdʒɪkəl/ adj. *I will talk to you about the Mughal kings in chronological order, starting with Babar.* = arranged according to the order of time (from the earliest to the last)

chrys•a•lis /ˈkrɪsəlɪs/ noun, c. (**chrysalises**) = one of the stages in the life of an insect, when it is covered with a hard shell [BIOLOGY]

chry•san•the•mum /krɪˈsænθɪməm/ noun = a garden plant with large, brightly coloured flowers

chub•by /ˈtʃʌbi/ adj. *a chubby baby* = a healthy person, usually a baby or young adult, who is slightly fat in a way that is pleasing (informal)

chuck /tʃʌk/ verb, t. *Can you chuck the ball to me?* = to throw (informal)

chuck•le[1] /ˈtʃʌkəl/ verb, i. *He chuckled to himself as he read the funny poem.* = a quiet laugh

chuckle[2] noun, c. *She seems to have found something funny. Can you hear her chuckles?*(c.) = the sound one makes when chuckling

chug[1] /tʃʌg/ verb, i. (**chugged**) *The old steam locomotive chugged slowly up the mountain.* = to make a sound like that of a person breathing hard, while moving (used for steam engines)

chug[2] /tʃʌg/ noun, c. *The chug of the old steam locomotive* = the sound made by a steam engine

chum /tʃʌm/ noun, c. = a good friend (used specially among schoolboys) **chummy** adj. *The two boys are very chummy.* = friendly (with each other) (informal)

chunk /tʃʌŋk/ noun, c. **1** *a large chunk of bread* = a thick piece **2** *The new car took a large chunk out of my salary.* = a large part of something **chunky** adj.

church /tʃɜːtʃ/ noun, c. (**churches**) **1** = a place where Christians worship **2** *He has decided to join the church.* = the profession of a Christian priest (see also **cathedral**) **churchyard** noun, c. = an open space around a church where people who have died are buried

churn[1] /tʃɜːn/ verb, t. or i. **1** *We churn milk to make butter.*(t.) = to cause some liquid (water, milk etc.) to shake violently; to separate butter from milk by shaking the milk **2** *This writer churns out at least three books every year.*(t.) = to produce in large quantities and without too much thought (informal, disapproving)

churn[2] noun, c. *a cream churn* = a container in which milk is kept for churning

chute /ʃuːt/ noun, c. **1** *the garbage chute in a building* = a sloping passage down which things may be dropped or made to slide down **2** = a **parachute** (informal)

CIA abbrv. of **Central Intelligence Agency** = a government organization in America whose responsibility it is to collect secret information

ci•ca•da /sɪˈkɑːdə/ noun *the chirping of cicadas* = an insect that makes a continuous high singing sound

CID abbr. of **Criminal Investigation Department** = the branch of the police force that investigates crime

ci•gar /sɪˈgɑːʳ/ noun, c. = a thick roll (tube) of dried and uncut tobacco leaves, which is smoked

cig•a•rette /sɪgəˈret/ noun, c. = a thin paper tube filled with finely cut tobacco, which is smoked

C-in-C abbr. of **Commander-in-Chief** = the highest post in the army (now replaced in India by **Chief of Army Staff**)

cin•der /ˈsɪndəʳ/ noun, c. *Clean out the cinders from the fireplace. // The chapatis were burnt to a cinder.* = a small piece of burnt or partly burnt wood, coal etc.

cin•e•ma /ˈsɪnɪmə/ noun, u. or c. **1** *the only cinema in town*(c.) = a building in which people can sit and watch a film (movie) **2** *Do you enjoy watching cinema?* (u.) = films (in general) **3** *I have been working in cinema all my life.*(u.) = the art or industry of making films **cinematography** /sɪnɪməˈtɒgrəfi/ noun, u. = the art or science of using a camera to make films

cin•na•mon /ˈsɪnəmən/ noun = the sweet-smelling bark of a tree, used as a spice to give flavour to food

ci•pher[1] /ˈsaɪfəʳ/ noun, u. **1** = the number zero (0) **2** *He felt he was a cipher in the company.* = a person who has no importance at all **3** *The police caught the foreign spy sending a wireless message in cipher.* = a system of secret writing (also **code**)

cipher[2] verb, t. *Have you ciphered the message?* = to put a message into cipher (code) (opposite **decipher**)

cir•cle[1] /ˈsɜːkəl/ noun, c. **1** = a flat area enclosed by a curved line on which every point is at an equal distance from the centre (see pic under **shapes**) **2** *children standing in a circle* = something that has the shape of a circle **3** (always plural) *move in the highest circles* = a group of people who are united by some common interest

circle[2] verb, t. **1** *The teacher circled each spelling mistake with red ink.* = to draw or make a circle around something; to encircle **2** *The pigeons were circling overhead.* = to move in a circle **vicious circle** noun = a situation where one unpleasant thing leads to one or more unpleasant things which then lead back to the original situation, making it worse

to come full circle = an expression which describes a situation in which, after many moves forward, one comes back to the starting point

cir•cuit /ˈsɜːkɪt/ noun, c. **1** *We made a circuit of the entire school compound on our bicycles.* = a path that forms a complete circle around an area **2** *The lights went out because of a break in the electrical circuit.* = the complete circular path of an electrical current **circuit-breaker** noun, c. = a switch that can stop the supply of electricity for reasons of safety **circuitous** adj. *Why are you taking this circuitous route to Kolkata? You can go by a much shorter route.* = a long and roundabout path to some place instead of a shorter and more direct path **closed circuit television** noun, c. = a television system generally used in factories, shops etc. as part of a security system in which pictures are sent by wire to a few receivers only **the (tennis) circuit** (always singular) = a series of tournaments that players regularly take part in

cir•cu•lar[1] /ˈsɜːkjʊləʳ/ noun, c. *This is a circular from the office on the new school timings.* = a printed notice that is sent to many people for their information

circular[2] adj. *a circular table* = round in shape

cir•cu•late /ˈsɜːkjʊleɪt/ verb, t. **1** *Blood circulates through the body.* = to flow round and round along the same path **2** *The news has been circulated to all our agents.* = spread widely **circulation**

/sɜːkjʊˈleɪʃən/ noun, u. **1** *The circulation of blood in your body is poor.* = the flow of a liquid round and round, along the same path **2** *All 500-rupee notes will be taken out of circulation.* = the movement of money from one person to another **3** *This newspaper has a daily circulation of 100,000.* = the number of copies of a newspaper or magazine sold every day

cir•cum•cise /ˈsɜːkəmsaɪz/ verb, t. = to cut off the loose skin at the end of the male sex organ (**foreskin**) for religious or medical reasons

cir•cum•fer•ence /səˈkʌmfərəns/ noun, c. or u. = the length around the outside of a circle [MATHEMATICS] (see also **perimeter**)

cir•cum•stance /ˈsɜːkəmstæns/ noun, c. (usually plural) *What were the circumstances that forced you to sell your house?* = the conditions in which a certain action or event takes place

cir•cum•vent /ˈsɜːkəmvent/ verb, t. *We were afraid the lack of manpower would force us to close down the factory, but we were able to circumvent that problem.* = to avoid a problem by going around it

cir•cus /ˈsɜːkəs/ noun, c. **1** = a company that travels from place to place entertaining people by performing different acts of skill and courage, some with trained animals **2** *Connaught Circus* = a circle formed in a place where several roads meet

cir•rho•sis /sɪˈrəʊsɪs/ noun = a life-threatening disease of the liver [MEDICINE]

cir•rus /ˈsɪrəs/ noun, u. = light white clouds seen at a great height [GEOGRAPHY] (see also **cumulus**)

cis•tern /ˈsɪstən/ noun, c. = a container for storing water

cit•a•del /ˈsɪtədel/ noun, c. **1** = a strong fort built near or above a city for its protection (also **fort**) **2** *The Supreme Court is the last citadel of justice.* = a place where something can be protected or kept safe

cite /saɪt/ verb, t. *Can you cite figures to prove that crime is increasing in the city?* = to mention or quote something in order to support one's statement

citation /saɪˈteɪʃən/ noun, u. or c. **1** = a quotation from a book or other source, often in support of a statement **2** = an official statement describing why a person has been given an award or honour

cit•i•zen /ˈsɪtɪzən/ noun, c. *a citizen of India* = a person who belongs to a certain country and has the right to vote there **citizenship** noun, u. *I have applied for German citizenship.* = the state of being a citizen

cit•rus /ˈsɪtrəs/ noun, u. *The doctor has advised me to eat oranges or other citrus fruits.*= fruits of the orange or lemon family

cit•y /ˈsɪti/ noun, c. **(cities)** = a large group of houses, shops, offices, educational institutions etc., much larger than a town, where many people live and work

civ•ic /ˈsɪvɪk/ adj. *Mumbai has many civic amenities.* = related to a city or life in a city **civics** noun = the study of the rights and duties of a citizen, the political system of a country etc.

civ•il /ˈsɪvəl/ adj. **1** *the civil laws of a country* = laws that relate to disputes or quarrels between private citizens **2** *a civil marriage* = a marriage performed according to the common system of laws, not the rules laid down by a religion **3** *Be civil to him even if he is rude.* = polite (formal) **civil defence** noun, u. = protection of the ordinary citizens of a country from the enemy during a war **civil disobedience** noun, u. = a non-violent way of forcing a government to change its laws by refusing to pay taxes etc., made popular by Mahatma Gandhi **civil engineering** noun = the design and construction of buildings, roads, bridges etc. **civil rights** noun, c. = the rights which all citizens of a country have **civil services** noun (always plural) = the people who work for the government, not including the military services or armed forces **civil war** noun, c. = a war fought between two groups belonging to the same country

ci•vil•ian /sɪˈvɪljən/ noun or adj. = an ordinary citizen who does not belong to any military service

ci•vil•i•ty /sɪˈvɪlɪti/ noun, u. *He treated us with great civility.* = politeness; courtesy

civ•i•li•za•tion (civilisation) /sɪvəl-aɪˈzeɪʃən/ noun, u. *the Indus Valley civilization* = a human society that exists in a place at a particular time and has reached a high level of development **civilize** /ˈsɪvəl-aɪz/ verb, t. *I wish someone would civilize the children in the class next door. They are so unruly!* = to teach someone to behave in a more orderly and polite manner

claim[1] /kleɪm/ noun, c. *He has a claim to this property.* = a legal right

claim[2] verb, t. **1** *If the train is cancelled we can claim the money that we paid for our tickets.* = to ask for or demand something **2** *They claimed that their ancestors were kings.*= to declare something to be true, specially something that is disputed (questioned) by someone else **3** *The earthquake claimed hundreds of lives.* = to destroy **claimant** /ˈkleɪmənt/ noun, c. = a person who makes a claim

clam•ber /ˈklæmbəʳ/ verb, i. *We managed to clamber up the mountain.* = to climb with difficulty using hands and feet

clam•my /ˈklæmi/ adj. *clammy weather* = cold, wet and sticky

clam•our[1] /ˈklæməʳ/ noun, u. *a clamour of angry voices* = loud, continuous shouting

clamour[2] verb, i. *The students were clamouring for*

a holiday. = to demand strongly and noisily

clamp[1] /klæmp/ noun, c. *Use a clamp to hold the piece of wood while you are cutting it.* = a tool that has a long screw with a handle, used for holding things together

clamp[2] verb, t. **1** *Clamp the two pieces of wood together until the glue is dry.*(t.) = to hold things together with a clamp **2** *The government has clamped a ban on this film.* = to force someone to obey a law

clamp-down[1] /'klæmpdaʊn/ noun, c. *The government has ordered a total clamp-down on public meetings.* = an order by the government stopping people from doing or saying something

clamp•down[2] verb, i. *The police has clamped down on gambling.* = to stop or prevent something by strict action

clan /klæn/ noun, c. = a group of people who belong to the same family or to related families and usually support each other strongly **clannish** adj. *The people in this village are very clannish and will not welcome strangers.* = staying united as a group, specially against outsiders (disapproving)

clan•des•tine /klæn'destɪn/ adj. *a clandestine meeting* = something done secretly, usually against the law

clang /klæŋ/ noun, u. *the clang of hammers* = the sound produced when a metal object is struck by another metal object

clank[1] /klæŋk/ noun, u. *the clank of metal chains being dragged* = the sound made by a heavy metal object being moved or dragged

clank[2] verb, i. *The old steam engine clanked away in one corner.* = to produce a sound like that of a heavy metal object being moved or dragged

clap[1] /klæp/ noun, c. **1** *The players gave the captain a clap when the match was over.* = the sound made when people strike their hands together to show approval **2** *a clap on the back* = a friendly and light blow **3** *a sudden clap of thunder* = a loud sound, similar to that of a clap

clap[2] verb, i. or t. **1** *The audience clapped when the actor finished his speech.*(i.) = to strike the palms of the two hands together with a loud sound, to show that something has been liked **2** *The captain of the team clapped the bowler on the back.*(t.) = to strike lightly with an open hand in a friendly and encouraging manner

clap-trap /'klæptræp/ noun, u. *He spoke a lot of clap-trap which impressed no one.* = empty and insincere talk or writing (informal, derogatory)

clar•i•fy /'klærɪfaɪ/ verb, t. *I could not understand the last point in your speech. Could you please clarify it?* = to make something clear and easy to understand

clarification /'klærɪfɪ'keɪʃən/ noun, u. = a statement made to explain something or remove doubts

clar•i•net /klærɪ'net/ noun, c. = a musical instrument like a large flute

clar•i•on /'klæriən/ noun, u. = (the sound made by) a kind of trumpet used in former times to inform people that there was danger from an enemy **clarion call** noun, c. *The Prime Minister's speech was a clarion call to the nation.* = a clear call to do one's duty (figurative, formal)

clar•i•ty /'klærɪti/ noun, u. *He spoke with such clarity that everyone was able to understand him.* = the quality of being clear

clash[1] /klæʃ/ verb, i. **1** *The two armies clashed near the border.* = to strike against or to run into each other; to get into opposition or to fight **2** *As your wedding clashes with my examination, I will not be able to come.* = to happen at the same time as some other event thereby, preventing someone from taking part in both **3** *Your shirt clashes with the colour of your skirt.* = to not match or look good with

clash[2] noun, u. **1** *There was a clash between the two groups.* = a disagreement which may or may not lead to violence **2** *The heavy metal plate fell to the ground with a loud clash.* = a loud, confused noise **3** *the clash of cymbals* = a loud resounding noise made when a pair of **cymbals** are struck together

clasp[1] /klɑːsp/ verb, t. *He clasped the suitcase tightly with both hands as if he was afraid someone might take it away.* = to hold something strongly

clasp[2] noun, c. **1** *She held her baby's hand in a strong clasp.* = the action of holding tightly **2** *I bought a leather belt with a metal clasp.* = a piece of metal that holds two things together

class /klɑːs/ noun, c. **(classes)** or u. **1** *Ostriches belong to a class of birds without wings.*(c.) = one of the groups into which something can be divided, specially for scientific study **2** *middle class* = one of the groups into which society is divided, which are considered to be at the same economic, political etc. level **3** *These students belong to my class.*(c.) = a group of students who are taught together **4** *When does the next class begin?*(c.) = lesson **5** *I am travelling second class.*(u.) = a division of the passengers on a train or plane, according to the amount charged as fare **6** *I have a second class degree.*(u.) = the quality of performance in an examination **classification** /klæsɪfɪ'keɪʃən/ noun, u. = the process of dividing things into different classes, specially for scientific study **classify** /'klæsɪʃaɪ/ verb, t. = to arrange into different classes **classless** adj. *a classless society* = not divided into classes **classmate** noun, c. = a person who is in the same class, in school or college, as someone else

clas•sic[1] /'klæsɪk/ noun, c. *'Meghadootam' is one of the classics of Indian literature.* = a great piece of art or literature which is considered very important

classic[2] adj. **1** *a classic film* = very great; good enough to be recognized as a classic **2** *a classic joke* = having all the qualities one expects to find **classical** adj. *Bharatanatyam is one of the classical dances of India.* = something (specially dance, music, literature etc.) that has come down to us from ancient times and is based on a well-known system of principles or rules

clat•ter[1] /'klætəʳ/ verb, i. *The metal tray clattered down the stairs.* = to produce a loud ringing sound while moving or falling

clatter[2] noun, u. *the clatter of dishes* = loud noise produced by hard objects hitting each other

clause /klɔːz/ noun, c. **1** *In the sentence 'I know Roy, but I don't know his brother', 'but I don't know his brother' is a clause.* = a part of a sentence that contains a subject and a verb [GRAMMAR] **2** *Our agreement contains a clause relating to payment of salaries to workers.* = a part of an agreement or contract [LAW]

claus•tro•pho•bia /klɔːstrə'fəʊbiə/ noun, u. *She can't use the lift because she suffers from claustrophobia.* = strong fear, which cannot be easily overcome, of being shut up in a closed space **claustrophobic** adj. = suffering from claustrophobia

claw[1] /klɔː/ noun, c. **1** = the long, sharp, pointed nails on the feet of a bird or animal **2** = the limb of an insect or sea animal which can be used to hold objects or for self-defence

claw[2] verb, t. *The leopard clawed the hunter's face.* = to tear or cut with one's claws

clay /kleɪ/ noun, c. *bricks made of clay* = heavy, soft earth or mud which becomes hard when dry, from which pots, bricks etc. can be made

clean[1] /kliːn/ adj. **1** *Her house is always spotlessly clean.* = free from dirt or dust **2** *a clean sheet of paper* = not yet used **3** *a clean life* = morally blameless **4** *clean humour* = containing nothing offensive

clean[2] verb, t. **1** *Someone has dropped some ink on the floor. Please clean it.* = to make something free from dirt, dust, stains etc. **2** = to remove a virus from a computer [COMPUTERS] **cleanliness** noun **cleaning** adj. *cleaning fluid* = something which cleans **cleaner** noun, c. **1** = a person who is paid to clean a building **2** *a vacuum cleaner; a liquid cleaner* = a machine or substance used to clean things **clean-shaven** adj. = a man who has removed the hair growing on his face

to come clean *Although she denied that she had broken the vase, in the end she came clean and admitted her fault.* = to admit one is guilty **to clean out** *The thieves broke into my room and cleaned out the place.* = to steal everything (informal) **to make a clean breast of something** = to confess **to clean forget** *I'm sorry, I clean forgot to bring your book.* = to forget completely (informal) **to take someone to the cleaner's 1** = to scold someone bitterly or harshly **2** = to deceive someone and take all their money

cleanse /klenz/ verb, t. **1** *The nurse cleansed the patient's wounds with some spirit.* = to make a cut, wound etc. clean and free from germs **2** *to cleanse one's thoughts* = to make something pure and free from evil (figurative)

clear[1] /klɪəʳ/ adj. **1** *The water is so clear that you can see the stones on the river bed.* = easy to see through **2** *clear skin* = free of marks or spots **3** *a clear sky* = free from clouds **4** *a clear style of speaking/writing* = easy to understand **5** *a clear case of murder* = obvious; leaving no doubts **6** *She is very clear about her future plans.* = certain; not in any doubt

clear[2] adv. *He spoke out loud and clear.* = in a clear manner

clear[3] verb, i. or t. **1** *The sky has cleared. There are no clouds.*(i.) = to become clear **2** *Please clear your table of all papers.*(t.) // *The road has been cleared of snow and is now open to traffic.*(t.) = to make clean or safe by removing something **3** *The judge cleared the prisoner of all the charges that had been brought against him.*(t.) = to declare a person to be free of any guilt (wrong-doing) **4** *Your tour programme has been cleared by the Managing Director.*(i.) = to approve or give official permission for something **5** *The athlete cleared two metres in the long jump event.*(t.) = to jump over something without touching it **clear-cut** adj. *His ideas are always very clear-cut.* = definite; free from confusion or doubt **clear-sighted** adj. *clear-sighted policy* = having a clear picture of the future

to clear out *We were making so much noise in the bus that the conductor asked us to clear out.* = to leave at once (not respectful) **to clear up** *Please clear up before you leave.* = to make a place neat

clear•ance /'klɪərəns/ noun, u. **1** *I have received clearance from the government to start a new school.* = official permission to do something **2** *There was a clearance of only a few inches between the bridge and the top of the bus.* = the distance or gap between an object and some other object passing under or beside it **clearance sale** noun, c. = a time when a shop sells goods cheap so as to get rid of as many things as possible

clear•ing /'klɪərɪŋ/ noun, c. = an area of land from which all trees have been cut away

cleave /kliːv/ verb, t. (**cleaved, cleft** or **clove**) = to split or divide something into two or more parts by a hard blow (old-fashioned) **cleft** /kleft/ adj. *a cleft upper lip* = split or divided

cleft pal•ate /kleft pælət/ noun, c. = a defect which some babies have from birth, in which the palate (top of the mouth) is divided and not properly formed, leading to difficulty in speaking

clem•en•cy /ˈklemənsi/ noun, u. *an appeal for clemency* = mercy; a lighter punishment [LAW]

cler•gy /ˈklɜːdʒi/ noun, u. (used with a plural verb) = Christian priests

clerk /klɑːk/ noun, c. = a person whose job is to keep records or accounts or do general office work, under the orders of a higher official **clerical** /ˈklerɪkəl/ adj. **1** *a clerical post* = that of a clerk **2** *clerical duties* = that of a priest

clev•er /ˈklevəʳ/ adj. **1** *a clever child* = intelligent and quick to learn **2** *a clever trick* = something that requires intelligence **3** *He is very clever with his hands* = skillful at doing things **4** *Don't try to be clever with me!* = using one's intelligence to take advantage of someone (disapproving)

cli•chè /ˈkliːʃeɪ/ noun, u. = a common saying or idea that is repeated so often that it loses its meaning (derogatory)

click[1] /klɪk/ noun, c. **1** *The key turned in the lock with a soft click.* = a low, sharp and short sound **2** *I used a double click to open the file.* = pressing the button of the mouse while using a computer [COMPUTERS]

click[2] verb, t. or i. **1** *The soldiers clicked their heels as they came to attention.*(t.) = to make the sound of a click **2** *The photographer clicked the shutter of his camera after asking us not to move.*(t.) = to take a photograph, using a camera **3** *He clicked the button of his mouse.* = to press the button of the mouse in order to select a command, item from the menu etc. [COMPUTERS] **4** *I was trying to understand how the mixer worked and suddenly it all clicked into place!*(i.) = to suddenly become clear or to be understood (informal) **5** *I am sure this new song will click.*(i.) = to be successful (slang)

cli•ent /ˈklaɪənt/ noun, c. *This lawyer never takes money from a poor client.* = someone who pays a professional person (e.g. a lawyer or chartered accountant) for some work

cliff /klɪf/ noun, c. = the high, very steep side of a rock **cliff-hanger** noun, c. *India needed four runs to win the match, and there was only one more ball left in the last over. We were so excited! It was a real a cliff-hanger of a match.* = a competition in which the result remains uncertain till the end or a story or film in which one cannot be sure of the end till the last moment

cli•mate /ˈklaɪmɪt/ noun, u. *Singapore has a damp climate.* = the kind of weather found round the year **climatic** /klaɪˈmætɪk/ adj. *climatic conditions* = related to the climate

cli•max /ˈklaɪmæks/ noun, u. **1** *The climax of the film comes when the hero rescues the heroine after fighting off six of his enemies.* = the most exciting or interesting part of a story or film, usually coming near the end (opposite **anti-climax**) **2** = the highest point of sexual pleasure (see also **orgasm**)

climb[1] /klaɪm/ verb, t. or i. **1** *Tenzing climbed Mount Everest in 1956.*(t.) // *She climbed the stairs slowly.*(t.) = to go up to the top or towards the top of a mountain, staircase etc. **2** *After the plane left the ground, it climbed steeply.*(i.) = to rise continuously **3** *The boy climbed the tree to pluck some mangoes.*(t.) = to go up from a lower to a higher position, using the hands and feet

climb[2] noun, u. **1** *The hill did not look very steep, but it was a difficult climb.* = something that one climbs **2** *On this road you will find a steep climb for the next two kilometres.* = a steep slope or rise

clinch[1] /klɪntʃ/ verb, t. *I did not think I would get the contract as many others were trying, but finally I was able to clinch the deal.* = to be able to settle or close a business matter successfully (informal)

clinch[2] noun, c. *in a tight clinch* = a position in which two people hold each other tightly with their arms around each other; an embrace (informal)

cling /klɪŋ/ verb, i. (**clung**) **1** *The children clung to their mother in fear.* = to hold on tightly to someone **2** *His shirt was wet with perspiration and clung to his back.* = to stick to something **3** *to cling to a belief* = to refuse to stop believing in something even when there is a strong reason to do so **cling-wrap film** noun, u. = thin, transparent plastic material used to cover and protect food by holding it tightly in place

clin•ic /ˈklɪnɪk/ noun, c. *the doctor's clinic* = a place where medical help is available (compare **hospital**) **clinical** adj. **1** *a clinical test* = relating to a clinic or hospital **2** *He takes a very clinical view of the whole affair.* = without having any personal feelings

clink[1] /klɪŋk/ noun, c. *the clink of wine glasses* = the sound produced when pieces of glass or metal strike each other lightly

clink[2] verb, t. or i. *Let us clink our glasses and drink a toast.*(t.) = to make the soft, musical sound produced when two pieces of glass or metal strike each other lightly

clip[1] /klɪp/ noun, c. **1** *a paper clip* = a small piece of metal or plastic used to hold sheets of paper; hair or other light objects together **2** *The barber gave me a clip.* = a hair-cut (informal) **3** *They showed us a clip from a new film at the Film Society meeting.* = a short piece (of a film etc.) which has been cut out of a longer piece **4** *a clip on the ear* = a gentle blow (informal)

clip[2] verb, t. **1** *Clip the sheets of paper together.* = to fasten or hold together with a clip **2** *The barber will clip your hair.* = to cut with scissors or some other sharp instrument to make something look shorter and neater **3** = to hit (informal)

clip•ping /ˈklɪpɪŋ/ noun, c. *newspaper clipping* = an item of news (e.g. a news report) cut out from a newspaper and kept for future use

clique /kliːk/ noun, c. *The clique in the office will not allow anyone to work peacefully.* = a small group inside a larger group which works for its own interests and does not admit outsiders (derogatory)

cloak[1] /kləʊk/ noun, c. **1** *a long, loose coat, worn on top of other clothes* **2** *Their friendly behaviour was only a cloak for their selfish intentions.* = something that acts as a cover and hides something unpleasant

cloak[2] verb, t. *As he cloaked his evil intentions behind his sweet words many people trusted him.* = to hide one's thoughts, feelings etc. from others **cloak-and-dagger** adj. *a cloak-and-dagger operation* = relating to secret and mysterious activities, usually involving spies **cloak-room** noun,c. = a room in a public building, e.g. a railway station or airport, where one can leave one's belongings for a short time and get them back later on payment

clob•ber /ˈklɒbəʳ/ verb, t. = to beat severely

clock[1] /klɒk/ noun, c. *an alarm clock* = an instrument used to show the time, which is hung on a wall or placed on a table etc. and not worn on the body like a watch

clock[2] verb, t. *The runner from Africa clocked 9.6 seconds for the 100 m race.* = to show or record the time taken by someone to do something, using a stop-watch **clockwise** adv. *The screw has to be turned clockwise in order to tighten it.* = in the direction in which the hands of a clock move (opposite **anticlockwise**) **clockwork** noun, u. *a clockwork toy* = something which has a spring inside and has to be wound up like a clock in order to make it work

clockwise

anticlockwise

to work round the clock = all day and night **to clock in** = to report the time of one's arrival for work at a factory, office etc. **to clock up** *She clocked up forty hours this week.* = to work for a certain number of hours for which one gets credit **to put the clock back** *When we visited the house in which we had lived as children, we felt we had put the clock back.* = to return to the past (figurative) **to work against the clock** *We had only two hours to decorate the building before the chief guest's arrival, but we were able to do it by working against the clock.* = to work very fast in order to complete a job before a certain time

clod /klɒd/ noun, c. **1** *a clod of earth* = a lump or large piece of earth, clay etc. **2** = a person thought to be dull and unintelligent (not polite)

clog[1] /klɒg/ noun, c. (usually plural) = one of a pair of shoes made of wood

clog[2] verb, t. (**clogged**) *The drain has been clogged with rubbish.* = to cause something to get blocked or choked

clone[1] /kləʊn/ noun, c. = a plant or animal which has been produced by scientists from a single cell taken from the parent plant or animal and has exactly the same qualities

clone[2] verb, t. *Scientists have been able to clone sheep and cattle.* = to produce a plant or animal which is a clone of another plant or animal

close[1] /kləʊz/ verb, t. **1** *Please close the door.* = to cause something to shut (opposite **open**) **2** *It is time for you to close your speech.* = to end

close[2] noun, c. *Our story has come to a close.* = end

close[3] adj. **1** *The station is close to our college.* = near **2** *He is a close friend.* = near in relationship **3** *I am going to keep a close watch on all your activities.* = careful **4** *It was a close contest between the two swimmers.* = a competition where the result is decided by a small difference

close[4] adv. *We live very close to the hospital.* = near **closed** adj. *The door was closed. I don't know if he was in the room.* = shut **close-fisted** adj. *a close-fisted person* = unwilling to spend money; miserly **a close call** *My car almost hit the tree, but luckily we escaped. It was a close call.* = something unpleasant that nearly happened but did not happen (also **close shave**) **to draw to a close** *The school play drew to a close with the singing of a song.* = to come to an end **to close something down** *They had to close down the shop as there were not many customers.* = to stop doing something permanently

clos•et /ˈklɒzɪt/ noun, c. = a cupboard built into a wall going all the way from the floor to the ceiling **a closet socialist** noun = a person who doesn't want his or her political views to be known publicly

clot[1] /klɒt/ noun, c. *a blood clot* = a half-solid mass formed from some liquid, usually blood

clot[2] verb, i. (**clotted**) *The blood flowing from his wound had clotted.* = to form a semi-solid mass, usually of blood or other liquids

cloth /klɒθ/ noun, u. *a piece of cotton cloth* = material woven from cotton, silk or woollen yarn (thread) and used for making garments

clothe /kləʊð/ verb, t. *In winter, we should clothe ourselves in woollen garments.* = to provide clothes for; to dress

clothes /kləʊðz/ noun, u. (always plural) *Have you bought any new clothes this year?* = garments (e.g. shirts, trousers, t-shirts, skirts)

cloth•ing /'kləʊðɪŋ/ noun, u. *This shop sells woollen clothing.* = clothes (formal)

cloud[1] /klaʊd/ noun, c. **1** *There are dark clouds in the sky.* = very small drops of water floating high in the sky **2** *Thick clouds of smoke hung over the scene of the fire.* = something (smoke or dust) that looks like a cloud **3** *The clouds of war are gathering around us.* = something that causes unhappiness or fear (figurative)

cloud[2] verb, t. **1** *The sky has clouded over.* = to become covered with clouds **2** *Old age has clouded his memory.* = to cause something to become dim or faint **cloudburst** noun, c. = a sudden and heavy shower of rain **cloud nine** noun *She was on cloud nine when she heard how well she had done in the exam.* = very happy (informal) **cloudy** adj. *cloudy skies* = covered with clouds

to leave under a cloud *It is sad that after doing such good work, they had to leave under a cloud.* = to be forced to leave a job etc. on the charge of having done something dishonest

clout[1] /klaʊt/ noun, c. or u. **1** *a clout on the head*(c.) = a blow **2** *political clout*(u.) = influence or power (informal)

clout[2] verb, t. = to hit hard

clove /kləʊv/ noun, c. (usually plural) = the dried flower of a plant, used as a spice to add taste to food

clown[1] /klaʊn/ noun, c. **1** *the clown in a circus* = a person who works in a circus and makes people laugh by putting on strange clothes and doing funny things **2** *Don't be such a clown.* = someone who behaves in a silly (foolish) manner (disapproving)

clown[2] verb, i. *Please stop clowning and listen to me.* = to act in a light-hearted or foolish manner (usually disapproving) **clownish** adj. *clownish behaviour* = absurd and foolish (derogatory)

club[1] /klʌb/ noun, c. **1** *the Debating Club* = a group of people who meet regularly for some common purpose or interest **2** = a thick, heavy stick, thicker at the top end, used as a weapon **3** *a golf club* = one of a set of metal or wooden sticks used in the game of golf **4** *the eight of clubs* (always plural) = a playing card marked with one or more black, three-leafed figures

club[2] verb, t. **1** = to beat with a heavy stick (club) **2** *Cleaning the house and clearing the garbage are two separate matters. Let's not club them.* = to join or merge (informal) **3** *The students clubbed together to buy a present for their teacher.* = to share the cost of something with others (informal) (also **pool**)

clubfoot noun = a defect which some babies are born with, in which the foot is badly shaped or twisted out of position

cluck /klʌk/ verb, i. or t. **1** *The mother hen clucked to her chicks.*(i.) = to make the sound that a hen makes when sitting on an egg or calling her chicks **2** *She clucked her disapproval.* (t.) = to make a sound using one's tongue to show disapproval or sympathy

clue[1] /klu:/ noun, c. **1** *If you want to solve this crossword puzzle, you must study the clues which are printed below it.* **2** *The police have found a number of clues, including some fingerprints, which may help them to catch the murderer.* = some object or information that helps to find the answer or solution to a question or mystery

clue[2] verb, t. *How did you get clued to the answer?* = to provide someone with a clue or hint

to be clued in (**to clue someone in**) *She is very clued in about low-fat diets.* = to be well-informed on subjects in which knowledge has to be gathered from several sources (informal)

clump[1] /klʌmp/ verb, i. = to walk with slow and noisy steps, as a result of having an artificial leg, wearing a heavy shoe etc.

clump[2] noun, c. or u. **1** *The thief hid in a clump of bushes.*(c.) = a number of trees or bushes growing very close to each other **2** *I heard the clump of the policeman's heavy boots.*(u.) = the sound of heavy and slow footsteps

clum•sy /'klʌmzi/ adj. **1** *His movements are clumsy now, but he will soon become a good dancer.* = awkward and ungraceful in movements and actions **2** *a clumsy attempt to shift the blame to someone else* = something that is not done with skill and is not successful

clus•ter[1] /'klʌstəʳ/ noun, c. *mangoes hanging from trees in thick clusters* = a number of things of the same kind which grow or are found together; a bunch

cluster[2] verb, i. *The boys clustered together to read the letter from their friend in Kenya.* = to gather together in a group or bunch

clutch[1] /klʌtʃ/ verb, t. *As she boarded the bus, the lady clutched her bag tightly.* = to hold tightly so as not to lose something

clutch[2] noun, c. **1** *His clutch was not very strong and he fell from the branch.* = the act of clutching or holding something tightly **2** *a clutch of eggs* = a number of eggs laid by a bird at one time **3** *the clutch on a motor-*

car = the part of a motorcar or motorcycle which allows the engine to get connected to or disconnected from the wheels on which the vehicle moves **clutches** noun, c. (always plural) *We fell into the clutches of some thieves.* = control or power of an undesirable kind

clut•ter[1] /'klʌtə'/ verb, t. or i. **1** *Don't clutter your room unnecessarily.*(t.) **2** *His room is always cluttered with books.*(i.) = to make a place untidy by filling it up with unnecessary things

clutter[2] noun, u. **1** *I took out a bagful of clutter from our room.* = things scattered about in an untidy fashion **2** *There are far too many ideas in this paragraph. It is difficult to cut through the clutter and get to the main idea.* = badly organised ideas which fill up one's mind, or one's writing, creating confusion

cm abbr. of **centimetre** = a unit of length equal to the hundredth part of a metre

co- /kəʊ/ prefix meaning together e.g. **co-exist** verb, t. *co-exist* = to exist or live together with another living being

c/o abbr. of **care of** (on a postal address)

Co. abbr. of **company** (e.g. Liberty Shoe Co.)

coach[1] /kəʊtʃ/ noun, c. (**coaches**) **1** *The coach will take you to the airport* = a comfortable bus **2** *I have reserved a berth in the Kolkata coach of the Rajdhani Express* = a railway carriage which forms a part of a train **3** *a cricket coach* = a person who trains players or athletes for games, competitions etc.

coach[2] verb, t. *He coaches students for the Joint Entrance Examination.* = to train or teach students, but usually not in a regular school or college

co•ag•u•late /kəʊ'ægjʊleɪt/ verb, i. *The blood from the wound coagulated to form a sticky mass.* = to change from a liquid into a solid state through some chemical action; to **clot** [TECHNICAL]

coal /kəʊl/ noun, u. or c. **1** *a railway wagon loaded with coal* (u.) = a black substance dug out of the earth which is burnt to give heat **2** *a burning coal from the fire* (c.) = a piece of coal **coalfield** noun, c. = an area where there is a large amount of coal buried under the earth **coal mine** noun, c. = a mine (underground pit) from which coal is taken out **coal tar** noun, u. = a thick, black, sticky liquid produced by heating coal without air, generally used to prepare the surface of roads (also **tar**)

to carry coals to Newcastle (always plural) *His company plans to sell its cars in America, where all the big car factories are located. This is a case of carrying coals to Newcastle.* = to take goods to a place where they are already available in plenty **to haul someone over the coals** (always plural) = to speak to someone very angrily for something they have done wrong (informal)

co•a•lesce /kəʊə'les/ verb, i. *A number of small groups have coalesced to form a large club.* = to join together to form a single group or mass; to merge (formal)

co•a•li•tion /kəʊə'lɪʃən/ noun, u. *a coalition of several parties* = a union of separate political parties for a common purpose

coarse /kɔːs/ adj. **1** *a shirt made from coarse cloth* = thick and rough **2** *a coarse person* = having a rough nature, lacking in education, grace etc. (used to describe a person) **3** *coarse language* = crude and vulgar

coast[1] /kəʊst/ noun, c. *The Bay of Bengal lies along the eastern coast of India.* = land which lies close to the sea

coast[2] verb, i. *The children coasted down the hill on their bicycles.* = to move smoothly without making any effort, especially down a hill **coastal** adj. *India's coastal belt* = on or near the coast **coastguard** noun, u. or c. **1** (u.) = a branch of the navy or police force that guards the coast of a country from attack as well as smuggling etc. **2** (c.) = a person belonging to the **coastguard** **coastline** noun, c. = the shape of a coast, as seen from the air or on a map [GEOGRAPHY]

coat[1] /kəʊt/ noun, c. **1** *a woollen coat* = a garment with long sleeves **2** *a dog's coat* = the fur or hair that covers the skin of an animal **3** *a coat of paint* = a covering of some material spread over a surface

coat[2] verb, t. *The table has been coated with red oxide paint.* = to cover a surface with a coat of some paint material **coating** noun, u. *There is a thick coating of dust on the furniture.* = a layer (of dust, paint etc.) on or over a surface

co-author verb, t. = to write a book, paper etc. together with someone else

coax /kəʊks/ verb, t. *The mother coaxed her child to go to sleep by promising to read her stories in the morning.* = to try to make someone agree to do something through kind words, a promise of some reward etc.

cob•ble /'kɒbəl/ verb, t. **1** = to repair shoes **2** *We hurriedly cobbled together a programme for the Prime Minister's visit to the village.* = to make or put together something quickly

cob•bler /'kɒblə'/ noun, c. = a person who repairs shoes and other leather objects

co•bra /'kəʊbrə/ noun, c. = a poisonous snake found in Asia and Africa which can spread the skin of its neck to form a hood

cob•web /'kɒbweb/ noun, c. **1** = a fine net made of sticky threads produced by a spider **2** *cobwebs in the mind* = confused ideas which do not allow a person to think clearly (figurative)

co•caine /kəʊ'keɪn/ noun = an addictive drug, used in former times to reduce pain

coc•cyx /'kɒksɪks/ noun = the small bone at the end of the backbone or spine (also **tailbone**)

cock[1] /kɒk/ noun, c. **1** = a fully-grown male chicken or other kind of bird **2** *a stop-cock* = a tap or valve that controls the flow of some liquid **3** = the male sex organ (slang) (USE)

cock[2] verb, t. **1** *The dog cocked its ears when it heard the sound of approaching footsteps.* = to raise or lift up a part of the body **2** *to cock a gun* = to make a gun ready for firing by raising its hammer **cock-and-bull story** *When I asked him why he was late, he gave me a cock-and-bull story about an accident he had met with.* = an impossible story told as if it was true **cock-eyed** adj. **1** = (a person who has) eyes that are turned to one side or towards each other (also **squint-eyed**) **2** *cock-eyed ideas* = foolish (informal) **cock fight** noun, c. = a fight between two cocks (male birds) arranged by people who bet money on the winner **cocksure** adj. *She always looks so cocksure that one feels surprised when she sometimes makes mistakes.* = having so much confidence in oneself as to cause irritation in others (derogatory)

to cock a snook at someone = to show one's lack of respect for someone

cock•a•too /kɒkə'tu:/ noun, c. = a kind of parrot found in Australia, with a crest (bunch of feathers) on its head, which often imitates human voices

cock•pit /'kɒkpɪt/ noun, c. = the part of a plane or racing car where the pilot or driver sits

cock•roach /'kɒkrəʊtʃ/ noun, c. = a large brown insect that lives in wet and dirty places, considered a pest

cock•tail /'kɒkteɪl/ noun, c. **1** = a drink which is a mixture of several kinds of alcoholic and non-alcoholic drinks **2** *a fruit cocktail* = a mixture of different kinds of fruit, seafood etc. **3** = a combination of several different things put together for a purpose e.g. *a cocktail of drugs* (= medicines) for the treatment of a disease

co•coa /'kəʊkəʊ/ noun, u. **1** = a kind of brown powder produced from the seeds of the cacao plant, used in making chocolate or other sweets **2** = a drink made from this

co•co•nut /'kəʊkənʌt/ noun, c. = a large nut (hard fruit) obtained from a tall tree, which contains soft white flesh which is eaten or dried and used to produce coconut oil

co•coon /kə'ku:n/ noun, c. = the covering made of silky threads which protects an insect when it is not fully grown (e.g. the silk-worm from which we get silk)

cod /kɒd/ noun c. or u. **1** (c.) = a kind of large sea-fish **2** *fried cod* (u.) = the flesh of the cod

code[1] /kəʊd/ noun, c. **1** *sending messages in code* = a system used for sending secret messages which cannot be understood by anyone except the sender and the receiver **2** *criminal code // dress code // traffic code // code of conduct* = a set of laws or rules; prescribed rules for dress, behaviour etc.

code[2] verb, t. *Have you coded the message?* = to change an ordinary message into a code (opposite **de-code**) **codify** verb, t. (**codified**) *Have the rules for the office been codified?* = to arrange a set of rules into a proper system which can be put into writing

co•ed•u•ca•tion /kəʊedjʊ'keɪʃən/ noun, u. = a system of education in which boys and girls or men and women go to the same school or college **coeducational** adj. *a coeducational school* = for both girls and boys

co•erce /kəʊ'ɜ:s/ verb, t. *to coerce someone into leaving* = to make an unwilling person agree to do something by using some kind of force or pressure

co-ex•ist /kəʊɪg'zɪst/ verb, i. *It is possible but difficult for large and powerful countries to co-exist.* = to live together peacefully or at the same time (used of countries, groups of people etc.)

cof•fee /'kɒfi/ noun, u. **1** = a brown powder made from the seeds of the coffee plant, used to make a hot or cold drink **2** = a drink made from this

cof•fers /'kɒfɜ:z/ noun, c. (always plural) *The coffers are empty.* = a large,strong box used for keeping money, gold, or other valuable objects; a store of money (usually figurative)

cof•fin /'kɒfɪn/ noun, c. = a wooden box in which the body of a dead person is placed before it is buried

cog /kɒg/ noun, c. = a metal tooth in a wheel in a machine which has many teeth and is driven or moved by another such wheel

a cog in the wheel = a person who is a small and unimportant part of a very large organization

co•gent /'kəʊdʒənt/ adj. *He gave us a cogent reason for not taking part in the debate.* = a very strong or forceful argument which everyone is able to accept; convincing

cog•i•tate /'kɒdʒɪteɪt/ verb, i. *I will have to cogitate carefully upon this matter before I can decide.* = to think seriously and carefully about something (formal)

cog•nate /'kɒgneɪt/ adj. *Oriya and Bangla are cognate languages.* = closely related to each other

cog•ni•tion /kɒg'nɪʃən/ noun, u. *Scientists use their cognition to discover the laws of nature.* = the ability to know or understand things by using one's powers of reasoning **cognitive** adj. *Develop your cognitive skills instead of learning things by heart.* =

related to the mind or the ability to think and reason

cognizance (cognisance) /ˈkɒgnɪzəns/ noun, u. *We have no cognizance of the new tax laws.* = knowledge or understanding of something (formal) [LAW]

to take cognizance of something = to take something into consideration while deciding something (legal)

co•here /kəʊˈhɪəʳ/ verb, c. **1** *Can the groups cohere much longer if they each pull in a different direction?* = to stay together; to remain united **2** *In the first sentence of this paragraph you talk about cricket and in the next sentence you talk about films. These two sentences do not cohere.* = to be logically connected to each other **coherent** adj. **1** *I could easily understand his speech because it was logical and coherent.* = wellconnected and logical and therefore easy to understand **2** *The man was so frightened that his speech was barely coherent.* = capable of being understood (opposite **incoherent**) **cohesion** noun, u. **1** *There is no cohesion in your arguments.* = logical connection and unity **2** *There is great cohesion among the members of this group.* = ability to stay united **cohesive** adj. **1** *a cohesive policy* = forming a well connected whole **2** *a cohesive device* = a word such as 'and', 'however,' etc. which connects sentences or parts of sentences

co•hort /ˈkəʊhɔːt/ noun, c. *a cohort of teachers* = a group of people who are of the same age or have the same number of years in service etc.

coif•fure /kwɒˈfjʊə/ noun, u. (French) = a way of arranging or dressing one's hair; hairstyle

coil[1] /kɔɪl/ verb, i. or t. *The snake coiled itself round the tree.*(t.) = to form one or more tight rings around something; to curve one's body in sleep so that one's knees touch or are close to one's stomach

coil[2] noun, c. **1** *a coil of rope* = a connected set of rings into which a rope or wire can be wound for storing easily **2** *an electrical coil* = wire which has been wound into a continuous circular shape and is used to carry an electrical current

coin[1] /kɔɪn/ noun, c. = a small, thin, flat piece of metal, used as money

coin[2] verb, t. *To make us laugh, he coined the word 'constabulate', meaning 'to make someone a constable'!* = to create a new word or expression **coinage** noun, c. *The word 'website' is a recent coinage.* = a word or expression which has recently been created

co•in•cide /ˈkəʊɪnsaɪd/ verb, i. **1** *India's Independence Day, 15 August, coincides with the date on which Sri Aurobindo was born.* = to happen at the same time as something else **2** *Your views on bringing up children coincide with mine.* = to be the same as

coincidence /kəʊˈɪnsɪdəns/ noun, c. *I did not plan to arrive in Delhi on your birthday. It was just a coincidence.* = two things happening at the same time by chance and not as a result of planning

coir /kɔɪəʳ/ noun, u. *a coir mat* = the rough, hair-like outer covering of the coconut, used for making ropes, mats etc.

co•i•tus /ˈkəʊɪtəs/ = the act of sexual union [MEDICINE]

coke /kəʊk/ noun, u. **1** = the solid substance which remains after gas has been removed from coal by heating **2** = cocaine (slang)

col•an•der /ˈkʌləndəʳ/ noun, c. = a round pan with many holes in the bottom, used for separating some solid substance from a liquid e.g. in order to make soup

cold[1] /kəʊld/ adj. **1** *a cold wind* = having a low or lower than usual temperature **2** *a cold welcome* = not friendly or pleasant (figurative)

cold[2] noun, u. **1** *It is so cold here that I need my woollens.* = low temperature **2** *I have a bad cold.* = an illness of the nose or throat, which generally happens in cold weather

cold[3] adv. **1** *The food has gone cold.* = not warm enough to be eaten **2** *The story of his sufferings left me cold.* = with no feeling of sympathy **cold-blooded** adj. **1** *Snakes are cold-blooded animals.* = having a body temperature that changes according to the temperature outside **2** *a cold-blooded murder* = cruel; showing complete lack of feeling **cold comfort** noun, u. *It is cold comfort to know that I am not the only person to fail in the examination.* = something that does not give much comfort or consolation **cold-hearted** adj. *a cold-hearted person* = unkind; without feelings **cold storage** noun, u. **1** *vegetables kept in cold storage* = a place where vegetables, fruits etc. can be kept at a low temperature for a long time so that they do not go bad **2** *My plans to write the novel have gone into cold storage as I am not free now.* = the condition of being put aside for future action (figurative) **cold war** noun, c. *The two countries seem to be planning a cold war.* = unfriendly relations between countries without actual fighting

to develop cold feet *The two friends had planned to play in the cricket match, but one of them developed cold feet and decided to stay at home.* = loss of courage or confidence just before doing something that has been planned **to give someone the cold shoulder** *When she suddenly became arrogant, all her friends started to give her the cold shoulder.* = unfriendly or unsympathetic treatment given deliberately as a way of showing one's disapproval **to be left out in the cold** = to be ignored

col•ic /ˈkɒlɪk/ noun, u. = severe pain in the stomach or intestines

col•lab•o•rate /kə'læbəreɪt/ verb, i. *Many countries are collaborating with the United Nations in the task of restoring peace.* = to work together with someone for some purpose **collaboration** /kəlæbə'reɪʃən/ noun, c. *Collaboration between the two countries will continue for some time.* = the action of collaborating (working together) **collaborator** noun, c.

col•lage /'kɒlɑːʒ/ noun, u. (French) *a collage of paintings* = a picture made by pasting many different pictures or other objects on the same surface

col•lapse[1] /kə'læps/ verb, i. or t. **1** *The building collapsed after the heavy rain.*(i.) = to fall down suddenly because of loss of strength or support **2** *The patient collapsed after the operation.*(i.) = to lose strength or to be near the point of death [MEDICINE] **3** *The peace talks collapsed because there was too much disagreement.*(i.) = to fail **4** *You can collapse this bicycle and carry it in your car.*(t.) = to fold something or to make it smaller so that it occupies less space

collapse[2] noun, u. *the collapse of the bridge* = the state or act of collapsing (breaking down) **collapsible** adj. *collapsible gates* = something that can be collapsed (folded to occupy less space)

col•lar[1] /'kɒlə'/ noun, c. **1** = the part of a shirt, coat etc. that goes round the neck **2** = a band or ring put round an animal's neck in order to be able to chain it or hold it, or to indicate its owner, address etc.

collar[2] verb, t. *We collared the thief just as he tried to climb over the wall.* = to catch and hold; to seize (informal) **blue collar (job)** = a job held by persons who work with their hands, usually in a factory **white collar (job)** = a job held by someone (e.g. a bank manager or clerk) who works at a desk in an office and is not required to get his/her hands dirty **collar bone** noun, c. = one of the two bones in the human body that join the ribs to the front of the shoulder bone (also **clavicle**)

col•lat•e•ral /kə'lætərəl/ noun, u. *I want a loan from the bank but I do not have any property to offer as collateral.* = something (e.g. a building, gold) which the lender can sell in case a loan cannot be paid back

col•league /'kɒliːg/ noun, c. *my colleague in the office* = a person who works in the same place or in the same profession as someone else

col•lect /kə'lekt/ verb, t. or i. **1** *A large crowd collected outside the cinema.*(i.) = to come together in one place and form a group or mass **2** *Please collect all the books lying on the desk and arrange them on the shelves.*(t.) = to bring together in one place **3** *He collects stamps.*(t.) = to gather objects over a long period of time as a hobby **4** *Have you collected your clothes from the laundry?* = to take away or to receive something **5** *The government will collect sales tax from all shops.* = to ask for or obtain payment of money, taxes etc. **collection** noun, c. or u. **1** *Let me show you my collection of stamps*(c.) = a set of things of the same kind that have been collected by someone as a hobby **2** *The municipality is responsible for the collection of garbage from the roads.*(u.) = the act of collecting (gathering) something

col•lec•tive[1] /kə'lektɪv/ adj. *Keeping this building clean is a collective responsibility.* = something that is or should be shared by a group of people

collective[2] noun, c. **1** *collective farm* = a large farm owned by the government and managed jointly by a group **2** *collective noun* = a word such as 'committee' or 'government', which can refer either to a group of people (together) or to its members (individually) and can be used either with the singular or plural form of a verb e.g. *the committe is/are of the opinion that...* [GRAMMAR]

col•lec•tor /kə'lektə'/ noun, c. **1** *a stamp collector* = one who collects things as a hobby **2** *the collector of the district* = a senior government official who is in charge of the administration of a district

col•lege /'kɒlɪdʒ/ noun, c. = an institution where education at a higher or professional level is offered and which is part of a university

col•lide /kə'laɪd/ verb, i. *Our bus collided with a truck, but there was no serious damage.* = to come together or strike against something with force **collision** noun, c. or u. **1** *a collision between the two cars* = the act of colliding (crashing into one another) **2** *The two leaders seem to be headed for a collision.* = a serious disagreement (figurative)

col•lie•ry /'kɒljəri/ noun, c. (**collieries**) = coal mine

col•lo•qui•al /kə'ləʊkwiəl/ adj. *This play about people in a village is written in colloquial language.* = language used by ordinary people for everyday purposes **colloquialism** noun, c. or u. *When we say that someone has 'hit the hay' (gone to bed), we are using a colloquialism.*(c.) = a word or expression used in colloquial language

col•lude /kə'luːd/ verb, i. *He was arrested as they suspected that he was colluding with criminals.* = to act together with someone, usually for doing something illegal **collusion** noun, u. = a secret agreement between people for doing something illegal

col•on /'kəʊlən/ noun, c. **1** = the large intestine; the last part of the tube inside the body through which food has to pass [MEDICINE] **2** *Use a colon here instead of a full stop.* = a punctuation mark used in writing, shown as two dots, one above the other (:)

colo•nel /'kɜːnəl/ noun, c. = an officer of middle rank in the army (between that of **major** and **brigadier**)

co•lo•ni•al /kə'ləʊniəl/ adj. or noun, c. **1** *Britain was a colonial power in the nineteenth century.*(adj.) = used to describe the governing style and activities of a country which set up colonies in other countries, usually far away, and ruled over them **2** *a colonial attitude* (adj.) = an approach to governing another country by force in the belief that it is not capable of managing its government, trade etc. (generally derogatory) **3** *a colonial* (noun) = a person who has lived for a long time in a colony but is not a member of the local population

co•lo•ni•a•lis•m /kə'ləʊnɪəlɪzəm/ noun, u. = the practice of a country's having colonies in other countries

col•o•ny /'kɒləni/ noun, c. (**colonies**) **1** *The French set up a colony in Pondicherry nearly 200 years ago.* = a country or area under the political control of another country which is usually far away **2** = a group of people who leave their own country and make their home in another country **3** *the railway colony in Kharagpur* = a part of a city or town where people who work in the same organisation etc. have their homes **colonize (colonise)** verb, t. = to set up a colony in another country

co•los•sus /kə'lɒsəs/ noun, u. **1** *The country is a colossus when compared to the tiny islands near its coast.* = something which is very large, a giant **2** *Amitabh Bachchan is a colossus in the world of entertainment.* = a person who has very great importance **colossal** adj. *a colossal statue* = of very great size

col•our[1] /'kʌlə^r/ noun, u. or c. **1** *Books for children are usually printed in colour.*(u.) = the quality in an object which allows us to see it as red, green, blue etc. **2** *I need a brush and some colours.*(c.) = the material that an artist uses to paint **3** *The political problems in some countries are related to colour.* = the colour of a person's skin which shows which race he/she belongs to **4** *Tourists love Rajasthan because they find a lot of colour here.* = the special qualities of a place, such as the customs of the people, the way in which they dress etc. which make it interesting

colour[2] verb, t. **1** *Anshika loves to colour pictures.* = to put colour into something using pencils, paints, crayons etc. **2** *He should not let one unpleasant experience colour his opinion of them.* = to influence or change a person's judgement **colourblind** adj. = (a person who is) unable to see the difference between certain colours because of a defect in the eyes **coloured** adj. *a coloured person* = a person who does not belong to the European, Asian or African race (This is an offensive use—terms like Asian African-American etc. are used to refer to people belonging to different racial groups.) **colour scheme** = the arrangement of colours in a room, picture etc.

colt /kəʊlt/ noun, c. = a young male horse

col•umn /'kɒləm/ noun, c. **1** *a stone column* = a pillar in a building used as a support for the roof **2** *a column of smoke* = something that looks like a pillar **3** *a column of marching soldiers* = a large number of rows of people, vehicles etc. following one behind the other **4** *a column on a page* = one of two or more divisions on a page of print, lying side by side **5** *a weekly column in a newspaper* = an article by a particular writer, usually on a particular subject, that appears regularly in a newspaper or magazine **columnist** /'kɒləmnɪst/ noun, c. = a writer who regularly writes a column for a newspaper or magazine

co•ma /'kəʊmə/ noun, u. *to lie in a coma* = a state of long and deep unconsciousness, caused by disease, shock etc.

comb[1] /kəʊm/ noun, c. **1** = a piece of plastic, metal etc. with a row of fine teeth, used to make the hair look tidy **2** *a rooster's comb* = the crown-like, brightly coloured growth on the head of a rooster, parakeet etc. **3** *a comb of honey* = a piece of a beehive with honey in it

comb[2] verb, t. **1** *Comb your hair before you go out!* = to use a comb to arrange the hair **2** *We combed the beach for a blue shell, but couldn't find it.* = to search very hard and with great care

com•bat[1] /'kɒmbæt/ noun, u. or c. **1** *These soildiers are new and have very little experience of combat.*(u.) = fighting in a war **2** *Many doctors are engaged in the combat against disease.*(u.) = fight

combat[2] verb, t. *The army has been called in to combat terrorism.* = to fight against **combatant** /'kɒmbətənt/ noun, c. = a person who takes part in a combat (fight) **combative** adj. = willing to fight or argue; high-spirited

com•bine /kəm'baɪn/ verb, t. **1** *This song combines Western and Indian music.* = to bring together **2** *The two parties have combined to fight the election.* = to come together **3** = a large business organisation formed by the union of several smaller companies **combination** /kɒmbɪ'neɪʃən/ noun, u. or c. **1** *Every person is a combination of good and bad qualities.*(c.) = a mixture of two or more things **2** *These two singers sing very well in combination.*(u.) = the state of singing, acting etc. together **3** *This is a good combination to wear.* = a set of things used together

com•bus•tion /kəm'bʌstʃən/ noun, u. *The combustion of oxygen in air forms carbon dioxide gas.* = the act of burning or catching fire **internal combustion engine** noun = a kind of engine in which the gas formed by mixing petrol or diesel with air is burnt inside the engine and not outside it

come /kʌm/ verb, i. **1** *Please come to this table.* = to move towards the speaker or to a particular place. **2** *The train has come.* = to arrive **3** *Her hair is so long that it comes to her waist.* = to reach **4** *He came second in the examination.* = to be in a particular position **5** *How did you come to be in Indonesia when the cyclone started?* = happen **6** *This shirt comes in six different colours.* = to be offered or available for sale to customers **7** *I did not like coffee at first but I have come to enjoy it.* = to begin **8** *The water in the river came up to my knees.* = to reach as far as **9** *The letter 'C' comes before the letter 'E' in the English alphabet.* = to have the position of **10** *My shoelace came undone.* = to become **11** *If I don't have a spoon, I use a fork or whatever comes to hand.* = to be available **12** *Their needs should come before ours.* = be taken care of **13** *to come* = to reach a sexual climax (orgasm) (infomal, slang)

to come about *How did this quarrel between the two of you come about?* = to happen; to begin **come along** *How is the book you are writing coming along?* = to advance or progress (informal) **come apart** *The old book came apart in my hands as I turned over the pages.* = to break into parts or pieces **comeback** *Rajiv Kumar had stopped acting in films but now he has made a comeback.* = a return to a former position of importance **come off** *The wedding will come off next month.* = to take place **come round** **1** *He was unconscious but now he has come round.* = to regain consciousness **2** *They disagreed with us at first, but finally came round to our point of view.* = to begin to think the same way as, after a period of doubt or disagreement **3** *She's angry now, but don't worry, she'll come round.* = become less angry, upset, critical etc. **to come to** *She had fainted, but came to in a few seconds.* = to become conscious after a state of unconsciousness **to come down on** *The government will come down heavily on people who do not pay taxes.* = to punish **to come down with** *He has come down with chicken pox.* = to catch some disease **to come up to (something)** *The play did not come up to my expectations.* = match, fulfil **to come up with** *We thought for a long time and then came up with a solution.* = to arrive at **to come to rest** *The tyre rolled across the road and down the hill, and finally came to rest near a rock.* = to come to a stop after a period of movement (used of machines etc.) **to come true** *I hope all that the astrologer says will come true.* = become real **to come of age** = to reach the age at which one is sexually mature or can be put in a position of responsibility (e.g. made the ruler of a country) **to come by** **1** *Good books are hard to come by.* = to find or get **2** *How did you come by that sprain in your leg?* = get, receive **to come up in the world** = to reach a higher position than one had in the past **to come to grips with something** *You won't learn mathematics unless you come to grips with it.* = deal with something seriously **to come up against** *We thought everything was going smoothly until we came up against a serious problem.* = to have trouble one was not expecting

com•e•dy /'kɒmɪdi/ noun, u. or c. (**comedies**) = a kind of play, film etc. which is amusing (makes people laugh) and ends happily **comedian** /kə'mi:diən/ noun, c. *Johny Lever is such a good comedian that one look at his face is enough to make you laugh.* = an actor or performer whose job it is to make people laugh

com•et /'kɒmɪt/ noun, c. = a heavenly body in space that moves around the sun and looks like a falling star, usually with a bright tail

com•fort[1] /'kʌmfət/ noun, u. or c. **1** *He had a hard life as a child, but lives in comfort now.*(u.) = the state of being free from worry, pain etc. and having one's bodily needs taken care of **2** *My children are a great comfort to me in my old age.*(c.) = a person or thing that gives hope or strength

comfort[2] verb, t. *She has recently lost her father. Let us comfort her.* = to try to give a person strength and hope **comfortable** adj. **1** *This is a very comfortable chair.* = something that gives comfort (freedom from worry, pain etc.) **2** *The patient is feeling comfortable after the operation.* = free from pain

com•ic[1] /'kɒmɪk/ adj. *He is a great comic artiste.* = someone or something that causes laughter

comic[2] noun, c. *Many children and adults enjoy reading comics.* = a magazine or newspaper meant for children, containing pictures which tell a story **comical** adj. *The wind blew his hat off and he was running after it, trying to catch it. It was a comical sight.* = funny in a strange way **comic strip** noun, c. = a short series of pictures which tell an amusing story

com•ma /'kɒmə/ noun, c. = a punctuation mark or sign used in writing, shown as (,), indicating a short pause while reading

com•mand[1] /kə'mɑ:nd/ verb, t. **1** *The general commanded his soldiers to move back.* = to order someone to do something **2** *She gave up singing a long time ago, but still commands respect.* = to deserve and get

command[2] noun, u. or c. **1** *His commands must be obeyed.* (c.) = an order **2** *Captain Kohli is in command of this ship.*(u.) = in control **commander** noun, u. = a person who controls a group of soldiers,a ship, a plane etc. **commandment** noun, c. *the Ten Commandments* = a law or rule believed to come from God

com•man•do /kə'mɑ:ndəʊ/ noun, c. (**commandos**) = a member of a special fighting force which is trained to go into action at short notice and to fight in dangerous situations

com•mem•o•rate /kə'meməreɪt/ verb, t. *This statue commemorates the brave young men who gave up their lives to make India free.* = to remember or to remind people of someone or something that is important and deserves to be remembered

com•mence /kə'mens/ verb, i. *The examination will commence at 9 a.m.* = to begin (formal)

com•mend /kə'mend/ verb, t. *The students were commended highly for their excellent performance in the examination.* = to praise **commendation** /kɒmən'deɪʃən/ noun, u. *The boys who helped the police in fighting the crime received a commendation from the government.* = a letter of praise given to someone for doing something good

com•men•su•rate /kə'menʃərɪt/ adj. *He was given a job commensurate with his abilities.* = equal to; in keeping with; matching

com•ment[1] /'kɒment/ noun, c. or u. **1** *Please read this essay and write your comments in the margin.*(c.) = an opinion expressed (given) about someone or something **2** *I listened to his speech without comment.*(u) = the act of making a comment

comment[2] verb, t. *I would like to comment on some of the things that the writer describes in this book.* = to make a comment (express an opinion)

com•men•ta•ry /'kɒməntəri/ noun, c. (**commentaries**) **1** *a commentary on the writings of Nehru* = a book which explains and makes comments on another book **2** *a sports commentary* = a description of an event given, with comments (opinions), over radio or television while the event is taking place **commentator** /kɒmən'teɪtəʳ/ noun, c. *a cricket commentator* = a person who gives or writes a commentary on an event, a book etc.

com•merce /'kɒmɜːs/ noun, u. *Mumbai is an important centre of commerce.* = trade or business **commercial** /kə'mɜːʃəl/ adj. *the commercial capital of India* = related to commerce (business) **commercial vehicle** noun = a truck or bus, used for business purposes **commercialize** verb, t. *Friendship has been commercialized by greeting cards and gifts.* = turned into a business (often derogatory)

com•mis•sion[1] /kə'mɪʃən/ noun, c. or u. **1** *The salesperson earns a commission of 10 per cent on each book that he sells.*(c.) = an amount of money paid to a salesperson or agent for selling something, usually based on the value of the thing sold **2** *A commission was set up by the government to suggest how education could be improved.*(c.) = a group of people specially appointed to examine some problem and write a report **3** *This architect has received a commission to design a new hotel.*(c.) = a responsibility or job given to someone

commission[2] verb, t. *The artist has been commissioned to make a marble statue of Dr Ambedkar.* = to appoint someone to do something; to give a commission (job) to someone **commissioner** noun, c. *the Revenue Commissioner* = a senior government official in charge of a department

com•mit /kə'mɪt/ verb, t. (**committed**) **1** *commit a serious crime* = to do something wrong or illegal **2** *They will be committed to prison.* = to be sent to prison **3** *The Green Tree Club is committed to the cause of tree-planting.* = to give complete support to some cause **4** *I can't commit myself to picking you up tomorrow.* = to make a promise which obliges one to do something **5** *Please commit this poem to memory.* = to learn something by heart; to memorize **commitment** noun, c. or u. **1** *I made a commitment to my teacher that I would complete this essay tonight.*(u.) = a promise to do something **2** *I don't want to adopt this dog as I don't want any commitments.*(c.) = some responsibility that one feels obliged to take up

com•mit•tee /kə'mɪti/ noun, c. *The government has appointed a committee to look into this matter.* = a small group of people chosen by a larger group to do something

com•mode /kə'məʊd/ noun, c. = a seat used as a toilet (old-fashioned)

com•mo•di•ous /kə'məʊdiəs/ adj. *a commodious house* = having a lot of space (formal)

com•mod•i•ty /kə'mɒdɪti/ noun, c. (**commodities**) = something (generally an agricultural product) that is used regularly and also traded in the market

com•mo•dore /'kɒmədɔːʳ/ noun, c. = a senior officer in the navy or airforce

com•mon /'kɒmən/ adj. **1** *Tigers used to be common in the forests of Orissa.* = found often and in many places **2** *The common person will be hit by the rising prices.* = average; ordinary; not wealthy **3** *This boundary wall is common to both of us.* = shared by two or more people **common denominator** noun, c. **1** *The fractions 4/5 and 3/5 have a common denominator, which is 5.* = a number by which two or more other numbers are divided [MATHEMATICS] **2** *The common denominator which unites all of us is the love of our country.* = a belief shared by all the members of a group **common noun** *'Boy' is a common noun but 'Asif' is a proper noun.* = a noun that does not name a particular person, place or thing [GRAMMAR] **common room** noun, c. = a room in a school or college building which is meant for the use of all the students or teachers, when they want to relax

common sense noun, u. *You can solve this problem by just using your common sense.* = the ability to understand and judge things correctly, which comes from practical experience **the Commonwealth** noun = an asociation of countries which were formerly parts of the British Empire, to encourage trade and friendly relations among its members

to have something in common with someone *My brother and I have nothing in common. He likes to have lots of friends, while I like to be alone.* = some quality which two people share

com•mo•tion /kə'məʊʃən/ noun, u. *There was a commotion in the school when the inspector arrived.* = noisy and excited movement and activity

com•mu•nal /'kɒmjʊnəl/ adj. *communal riots* = something related to, or based on, the existence of different racial, religious or language groups (communities)

com•mune[1] /'kɒmju:n/ noun, c. **1** = a group of people who live and work together and help one another for each other's good **2** = a group of families and individuals who live and work together as a team to run farms, factories etc. for the government

commune[2] /kə'mju:n/ verb, i. *I often go to the seaside as I like to commune with nature.* = to exchange thoughts and feelings with someone without using language

communion /kə'mju:njən/ noun, u. *Don't disturb them. They are holding communion with nature.* = the process of sharing or exchanging deep ideas and feelings, specially of a religious nature (formal)

com•mu•ni•cate /kə'mju:nɪkeɪt/ verb, t. or i. **1** *You should be able to communicate your ideas to your readers.* = to make one's ideas and feelings known to others(t.) **2** *She can communicate very well.*(i.) = to speak or write in order to share one's ideas or feelings with others **3** *Many of the patients in the hospital communicated the disease to their families.*(t.) = to pass on a disease **communicable** adj. *a hospital for the treatment of communicable diseases* = things (ideas, diseases, etc.) which can be communicated (passed on from one person to another) **communication** /kəmju:nɪ'keɪʃən/ noun, u. or c. **1** *There is no communication between Meena and her friend. Has something happened?*(u.) = sharing of ideas or feelings, mainly through speaking **2** *E-mail is now the most economical means of communication.*(u.) = sending messages **3** *I have received a communication from the Director.*(c.) = a message, letter etc. (formal) **communications** noun (always plural) *Communications between Kolkata and the neighbouring cities have been cut off completely because of the floods.* = the various means of travelling, moving goods or sending messages from one place to another by road or railway, telephone, telegraph etc. **communicative** /kə'mju:nɪkətɪv/ adj. **1** *You will find that she is very communicative and will gladly share information with you.* = very willing to talk or to give information **2** *poor communicative skills* = related to communication

Communism /'kɒmjʊnɪzəm/ noun = a political system in which the means of production are owned or controlled by the state **communist** noun, c. = a person who believes in communism

com•mu•ni•ty /kə'mju:nɪti/ noun, c. or u. (**communities**) (used wth singular or plural verb) **1** *a member of the Parsi community* = a group of people united by a common culture, religion, language etc. **2** *We are all interested in the welfare of the community.* = society as a whole

com•mute /kə'mju:t/ verb, i. or t. **1** *He has to commute between Delhi and Noida by bus every day.*(i.) = to travel a long distance regularly between one's home and place of work **2** *She has decided to commute her pension into a one-time payment.*(t.) = to exchange one thing (specially one form of payment) for another **commuter** noun, c. = a person who commutes to work

com•pact[1] /'kɒmpækt/ adj. **1** *a compact car* = small but neat and well designed **2** *The houses are built in a compact group.* = closely packed

compact[2] noun, c. **1** *We have made a compact never to complain about each other.* = an agreement **2** *a powder compact* = a small, flat container for face powder **compact disc** noun, c. = a small disc (flat circular piece) of metal coated with plastic, on which high-quality sound can be recorded or large quantities of data stored (see also **CD**)

com•pa•ny /'kʌmpəni/ noun, u. or c. (**companies**) **1** *the Bata Shoe Company*(c.) = a group of people who combine together for business **2** *I enjoy your company*(u.) = being together with someone **3** *We are expecting company tonight.*(u.) = guests **companion** /kəm'pænjən/ noun, c. *The woman is ill and cannot live alone. She needs a companion.* = a person who stays and helps another person and is a friend to him/her

com•pare /kəm'peəʳ/ verb, t. **1** *Let us compare India and China as developing countries. Which one has made greater progress?* = to examine or judge one thing against another, in order to bring out the points of similarity and difference **2** *The poet compares the face of his beloved to the moon.* = to try to find similarity between things which are not really similar **comparison** /kəm'pærɪsən/ noun, u. or c. **1** *The teacher drew a comparison between the* *two countries.* = the act of comparing two things or people **2** *There is no comparison between the two cities. The one we live in is far better.* = the result of comparing two things **comparable** /'kɒmprəbəl/ adj. *These two train fares are not comparable. One is Rs 1000 and the other only Rs 300.* = (things or people) that can be compared to each other (opposite **incomparable**) **comparative** /kəm'pærətɪv/ adj. **1** *I am making a comparative study of colour terms in Hindi and English.* = something that makes a comparison between two things **2** *'Better' is the comparative form of the adjective 'good'.* = the form of an adjective used in comparing only two things (see **superlative**)

com•part•ment /kəm'pɑːtmənt/ noun, c. *I am travelling in a second class compartment.* = one of the parts into which a space can be divided **water-tight compartment** *You cannot keep sports and education in water-tight compartments. There is a close connection between the two.* = a complete separation between two things that are connected to each other

com•pass /'kʌmpəs/ noun, c. or u. (**compasses**) **1** *a magnetic compass* = an instrument with a needle that always points north **2** *a pair of compasses* = an instrument which has two 'legs' and is used for drawing circles, measuring distances on a map etc. (always plural)

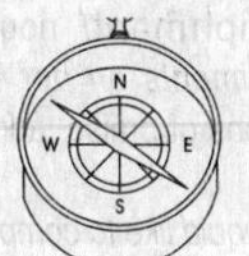

compass

com•pas•sion /kəm'pæʃən/ noun, c. *The Buddhist religion asks us to show compassion to all living creatures, including animals.* = sympathy and pity **compassionate** adj. **1** *a highly compassionate person* = showing compassion (pity) **2** *The judge decided that the thief, who was old and sick, should be set free on compassionate grounds.* = something done out of sympathy and pity

com•pat•i•ble /kəm'pætɪbəl/ adj. **1** *Although we come from different countries, we like the same kind of music and the same books. We are fully compatible.* = able to live and work together in agreement (opposite **incompatible**) **2** *The new software is not compatible with my old computer.* = able to work or be used together

com•pat•ri•ot /kəm'pætriət/ noun, c. = a person who belongs to the same country as another (formal)

com•pel /kəm'pel/ verb, t. *We like to play in the evening but our uncle compels us to study.* = to force a person to do something which he/she is not willing to do **compulsion** noun, u. **1** *A group of children came to me and demanded some money for a picnic, but I refused to pay under compulsion.* = force or influence used to make a person do something **2** *I had given up sweets, but this evening I felt a sudden compulsion to have some.* = a strong desire which is difficult to control **compulsive** adj. **1** *I felt a compulsive need to have a sweet.* = a desire which becomes a compulsion (difficult to control) **2** *She is a compulsive tea-drinker.* = a person who suffers from some compulsion **compulsory** /kəm'pʌlsəri/ adj. *In Singapore, military training is compulsory for all male university students.* = something which must be done and from which there is no escape; obligatory

com•pen•sate /'kɒmpənseɪt/ verb, t. *The airline will pay Rs 2 lakh to the families of people who died in the air crash, to compensate them for their loss.* = to give something (especially money) to someone to make up for some loss that he/she has suffered because of some action for which one is responsible **compensation** /kɒmpən'seɪʃən/ noun, u. = something (especially money) given to someone to compensate him/her for some loss

com•pere[1] /'kɒmpeəʳ/ verb, t. *We hear an artist is coming to compere the dance programme.* = to introduce the people who take part in some show (on stage, radio etc.) and the items they are going to present etc.

compere[2] noun, c. *a compere* = a person who comperes (introduces) a show

com•pete /kəm'piːt/ verb, i. *The well-known runner, P.T. Usha, will compete in the next Asian Games.* = to take part in a competition and try to win prizes

com•pe•tence /'kɒmpɪtəns/ noun, c. *You have asked him to translate the report into Hindi, but are you sure of his competence?* = ability to do something that one is required to do **competent** adj. *Homi will be able to write this report in English. He is quite competent in English now.* = having the ability or skill required to do something

com•pe•ti•tion /kɒmpɪ'tɪʃən/ noun, c. or u. **1** *a dance competition.*(c.) = a test in which different people take part to show which one of them can do something better than the others **2** *I do not enjoy competition.*(u.) = the act of competing with others **competitive** /kəm'petɪtɪv/ adj. **1** *We should try to sell our shirts at a competitive price.* = something that helps or allows one to compete with others **2** *They are very competitive by nature.* = fond of competiting **competitor** noun, c. = a person who takes part in a competition

com•pile /kəm'paɪl/ verb, t. *He is compiling a list*

of doctors practising in this city. = to collect and put together facts, information etc. from different sources in the form of a report or book **compiler** noun, c. = a person who compiles information etc. for a book, e.g. a compiler of a dictionary **compilation** /kɒmpɪˈleɪʃən/ noun, u. **1** *This book is a compilation of articles by different authors.* = collection **2** *I want to thank everyone who has helped me in the compilation of this book.* = the act of compiling a book

com•pla•cent /kəmˈpleɪsənt/ adj. *I know we are well prepared for the test, but let's not be too complacent.* = feeling pleased and satisfied with oneself without enough reason; not feeling worried at a time when one should feel worried; smug (disapproving) **complacency** noun, u. = the state of being complacent

com•plain /kəmˈpleɪn/ verb, i. or t. *Last week my mother was ill and in great pain, but she never complained.* = to express feelings of annoyance, unhappiness, suffering etc. **complaint** noun, c. **1** *Some of the boys in your class have made a complaint against you to the Principal.* = a statement, written or spoken, expressing annoyance, unhappiness etc. caused by someone or something **2** *My telephone is not working, I have to register a complaint.* = a report about something that is not working, is defective etc. **3** *a stomach complaint* = illness

com•ple•ment /ˈkɒmplɪment/ noun, c. **1** *My friend and I went to the cinema and then we had dinner in a good restaurant. It was a perfect complement to a very enjoyable evening.* = something which, when added to something else, makes it complete or perfect **2** *In the sentence 'Sajida is my friend', the word 'friend' is used as a complement.* = a noun that comes after a verb and helps to complete the meaning of the sentence [GRAMMAR] **complementary** /kɒmplɪˈmentəri/ adj. **1** = making something complete **2** *complementary angles* = a pair of angles which measure a total of 90 degrees [GEOMETRY] **3** *complementary colours* = colours which result in grey or white when mixed [TECHNICAL]; colours which are not in sharp contrast, e.g. green and blue

com•plete[1] /kəmˈpliːt/ adj. **1** *I want to buy the 'Complete Works of William Shakespeare'. Do you have it?* = full, with no part missing **2** *My essay is now complete.* = finished **3** *His decision to leave the city came as a complete surprise.* = total

complete[2] verb, t. **1** *I have to complete my homework.* = to finish **2** *I need a picture of a cobra to complete my collection of Indian snakes.* = to add something which is missing in order to make it whole

com•plex[1] /ˈkɒmpleks/ adj. **1** *Countries like ours have many complex problems.* = difficult to understand and deal with **2** *Water is brought from the river to the fields through a complex system of canals.* = made up of many different but closely connected parts **3** *'I have many friends who read books' is a complex sentence.* = consisting of a main clause and one or more subordinate clauses [GRAMMAR]

complex[2] noun, c. **1** *I have a small shop in the new shopping complex.* = a group of buildings which contains a number of shops, restaurants, houses etc. **2** *suffer from an inferiority complex* = unconscious fears, desires, feelings etc. which influence the behaviour of a person **complexity** /kəmˈpleksɪti/ noun, u. *a problem of great complexity* = something which has the quality of being complex (difficult to understand and deal with)

com•plex•ion /kəmˈplekʃən/ noun, u. *a smooth complexion* = the natural colour and look of the skin, especially the face

com•pli•cate /ˈkɒmplɪkeɪt/ verb, t. *My friend does not have a cycle and has to take a bus which is always crowded. And now, to complicate matters, the buses are not running as the drivers are on strike.* = to make things more difficult to deal with **complicated** adj. **1** *This is a very complicated topic and I can't explain it in a single class.* = something that is difficult to understand **2** *a complicated machine* = having many connected parts

com•pli•ment[1] /ˈkɒmplɪmənt/ noun, c. *The dancer received compliments on her wonderful performance.* = expressions of praise, admiration or respect

compliment[2] verb, t. *I would like to compliment you on the wonderful work you have done.* = to praise someone **complimentary** /kɒmplɪˈmentəri/ adj. **1** *Thank you for your complimentary remarks.* = (remarks) expressing praise, admiration etc. **2** *I am sending you two complimentary tickets for the show.* = (tickets) given free, as a favour or sign of respect

com•ply /kəmˈplaɪ/ verb, i. *Although we may not agree with the rule, we must comply with it.* = to obey an order or rule **compliance** noun, u. *compliance with the law* = obedience **compliant** adj. *a compliant person* = one who is too willing to listen to others and do as they say (derogatory)

com•po•nent /kəmˈpəʊnənt/ noun, c. *As some of the components needed to make these cars are not available here, we have to import them.* = a part that is used, together with other parts, to make a machine, e.g. a motor car

com•pose /kəmˈpəʊz/ verb, t. **1** *The famous musician, Ravi Shankar, will compose the music for this film.* = to create a piece of music or poetry

C

2 *Don't be so upset. Please compose yourself.* = to make someone, especially oneself, calm (formal) **3** *The book has already been composed and will be printed soon.* = to make a book ready for printing **4** *Carbon dioxide is composed of one part of carbon and two parts of oxygen.* = to be made up of **composer** noun, c. = a person who composes (creates) music

com•pos•ite /'kɒmpəzɪt/ adj. *This is a composite group which has people from different parts of India.* = a combination of different people or things

com•po•si•tion /kɒmpə'zɪʃən/ noun, u. or c. **1** *She teaches us composition.*(u.) = the art or skill of writing **2** *The teacher will correct your composition and return to you.*(c.) = a piece of writing **3** *We don't know enough about the composition of this poem to say where and how it was written.* = the act of composing (writing) a poem or a piece of music **4** *This is a new composition by the musician, L. Ramani.*(c.) = a piece of music or poetry composed by someone **5** *Scientists are carrying out experiments to find out the composition of the planet Mars.*(u.) = the combination of various parts or materials from which something is made

com•post /'kɒmpɒst/ noun, u. *You can make compost from cowdung, rotting leaves and other waste material.* = a mixture of different materials, mostly rotting leaves, grass etc. used as a fertilizer, to make the soil richer

com•po•sure /kəm'pəʊʒə^r/ noun, u. *He started his speech confidently but lost his composure when people in the audience started walking out.* = the state of being composed (calm)

com•pound[1] /'kɒmpaʊnd/ noun, c. **1** *The school has a large compound.*(c.) = an area enclosed by a wall or fence and containing a number of buildings **2** *Water is a compound, produced by combining the elements hydrogen and oxygen.* = a chemical substance made up of at least two different **elements** (simple substances) [CHEMISTRY]

compound[2] verb, t. *We were late for school and compounded the problem by forgetting our school bags in the bus.* = to make something which is bad, even worse **compound word/sentence** noun = a word or sentence produced by combining two words or clauses [GRAMMAR] **compound fracture** noun, u. = a break in a bone which causes it to cut through the flesh and skin, making an open wound **compound interest** noun = interest calculated on the principal (the sum of money originally lent) as well as the interest earned

com•pre•hend /kɒmprɪ'hend/ verb, t. *I cannot comprehend what they are saying as I don't know their language.* = to understand (formal) **comprehensible** adj. *The language of the essay is quite comprehensible.* = something that can be understood (opposite **incomprehensible**) **comprehension** noun, u. *Have you understood the main points of this essay? Let me ask you a few questions to check your comprehension.* = the ability to understand

com•pre•hen•sive /kɒmprɪ'hensɪv/ adj. *Your answer to this question leaves out many things. We need a more comprehensive answer.* = including everything; thorough

com•press /kəm'pres/ verb, t. *Your answer runs into fifteen pages. It should be compressed into three pages.* = to force a substance, piece of writing etc. into less space **compressor** noun, c. = a machine that can compress air or gas

com•prise /kəm'praɪz/ verb, t. *The Northeastern Region comprises the states of Nagaland, Mizoram, Manipur and Arunachal Pradesh.* = to be made up of

com•pro•mise[1] /'kɒmprəmaɪz/ noun, c. or u. *Some of us wanted to travel by train and some by bus. Finally we reached a compromise and travelled part of the way by bus.* = an agreement reached between two individuals or groups after a quarrel or dispute, in which each person or group agrees to some of the demands of the other

compromise[2] verb, i. or t. **1** *Harinder wanted Rs 700 for his old bicycle but I thought it was worth no more than Rs 500. Finally, we compromised on a price of Rs 600.*(i.) = to reach a compromise **2** *When you speak in parliament, make sure you don't compromise your principles by saying things you do not believe in.*(t.) = to do something which brings shame, disrespect or dishonour to one

compulsion, compulsory, compulsive see **compel**

com•punc•tion /kəm'pʌŋkʃən/ noun, u. *The student did not have the slightest compunction in missing his classes.* = a feeling of guilt or shame that stops one from doing something wrong (generally used in negative sentences)

com•pute /kəm'pju:t/ verb, i. or t. *We need to compute how much money we have to pay as rent.* = to calculate **computation** /kɒmpjʊ'teɪʃən/ noun, u. *According to my computation, the journey and stay together cost us Rs 2000.* = the act of calculating something (formal) **computer** /kəm'pju:tə/ noun, c. = an electronic machine that can store and recall information and do various kinds of computation (calculation), according to the programme which is supplied **computerize (computerise)** verb, t. *The bank has computerized* *all its operations.* = to use or to start using computers to do some work

com•rade /ˈkɒmrɪd/ noun, c. **1** *We have been comrades in the air force for many years.* = a close companion who shares some difficult work or danger **2** = the title by which a member of the Communist Party is addressed by other members of the party

con[1] /kɒn/ noun, c. (always plural) *Before you decide to change your job, you should think carefully about the pros and cons.* = the points for and against an idea

con[2] verb, t. *They conned us out of a lot of money.* = to cheat or trick someone after winning his/her confidence (trust) (informal, derogatory)

con[3] adj. *He is a con man.* = a professional cheat who first creates trust and then cheats (slang)

con•cave /kɒnˈkeɪv/adj. *a concave mirror* = something that curves inwards (opposite **convex**)

con•ceal /kənˈsiːl/ verb, t. *The security guards at the airport searched all visitors to make sure they had not concealed any weapons under their clothes. // He is able to conceal his feelings.* = to hide

con•cede /kənˈsiːd/ verb, t. **1** *He insisted that he had used the word correctly, but conceded his mistake after we showed him its meaning in the dictionary.* = to accept or admit something as correct or true, generally unwillingly **2** *The bowler conceded 15 runs in that over.* = to be forced to give away something that one does not want to give

con•ceit /kənˈsiːt/ noun, u. *He generally doesn't talk to people, but that's because he is shy, not because of conceit.* = the quality of thinking too highly of oneself; pride **conceited** adj. a conceited person = thinking too highly of himself; arrogant

con•ceive /kənˈsiːv/ verb, t. or i. **1** *Scientists first conceived the idea of a computer about 200 years ago.*(t.) *// Can you conceive of life without electricity?* = to think of; to imagine **2** *The doctors had said she could never have a baby, but she conceived last month.*(i) = to become pregnant **conceivable** adj. *It is conceivable that one day we shall be able to fly to New York in just two hours.* = something that can be imagined or thought of; possible (opposite **inconceivable**)

con•cen•trate[1] /ˈkɒnsəntreɪt/ verb, i. or t. **1** *Don't spend so much time worrying. You must concentrate on your work.* = to direct one's thoughts, efforts, attention etc. towards a particular activity or purpose **2** *All the new schools are concentrated around Sitaranagar Gardens.* = to come together in or around a place

concentrate[2] noun, c. = a substance which has been produced by removing all or some of the water present in some natural substance, e.g. orange juice

concentrated adj. *The bottle contains concentrated orange juice. You will have to mix one litre of water to make six glasses of juice.* = something (usually a liquid) which has been made thicker or stronger by removing water from it **concentration** /kɒnsənˈtreɪʃən/ noun, u. **1** *One needs great concentration if one is trying to study in a noisy place.* = the ability to keep one's attention fixed on something in spite of distractions **2** *There is a concentration of people from the North-east in this part of Delhi.* = a gathering of many people in one place

con•cen•tric /kənˈsentrɪk/ adj. = circles which have a common centre

con•cept /ˈkɒnsept/ noun, c. or u. *Please explain the concept of evaporation to me.*(c.) = idea or principle **conception** /kənˈsepʃən/ noun, u. **1** *His conception of exercise was just a short walk around the block!* = understanding or idea (of something) **2** *the time of conception* = the beginning of a new life within the mother **conceptual** /kənˈseptʃuəl/ adj. *The conceptual abilities of a child develop rapidly between the ages of 2 and 4 years.* = relating to the formation of concepts (ideas) in the mind

con•cern[1] /kənˈsɜːn/ verb, t. **1** *This article concerns cruelty to animals.* = to be about **2** *Don't read this letter. It does not concern you.* = to be of importance or interest to **3** *Please don't concern yourself with this problem. Let others think about it.* = to worry about something (sometimes not respectful)

concern[2] noun, c. **1** *Your health is of great concern to me.* = importance **2** *Your poor health is causing concern to all of us.* = worry **3** *They are looking after the family concerns.* = business activity **concerned** adj. **1** *Your parents are greatly concerned about your health.* = anxious; worried **2** *Please send this application to the officer concerned.* = someone who deals with a particular matter **concerning** /kənsɜːnɪŋ/ adj. *This is a letter concerning the new building.* = about (formal)

> **Usage** The two meanings of 'concerned' are often confused. 'Send this application to the concerned officer' would mean 'to the officer who is worried or anxious', but is often used to mean 'Send it to the officer who is dealing with this matter.' The correct expression would be 'the officer concerned.'

con•cert /ˈkɒnsət/ noun, c. or u. **1** *I have bought tickets for the concert by Madhup Mudgal.*(c.) = a musical performance by one or many musicians **2** *Three volunteer groups are working in concert to help the people in this area.*(u.) = together **concerted** adj. *The schools are making a concerted* *effort to stop the use of animals in scientific experiments.* = something that is planned and done together

con•ces•sion /kən'seʃən/ noun, u. or c. **1** *The shopkeeper has agreed to give me a concession on the price of these articles.* = a reduction in price **2** *The two brothers quarrelled over a piece of land, but the elder brother finally made a concession and let the younger have it.* = something that is given up or agreed to after a dispute, which helps one of the groups

conch /kɒntʃ/ noun, c. (**conches**) = the large, twisted shell of a sea-animal, which produces a loud sound when air is blown through it, sometimes used in Hindu religious ceremonies

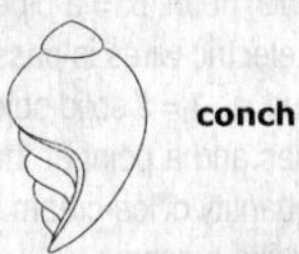
conch

con•cil•i•ate /kən'sɪlieɪt/ verb, t. *The school was unable to give us funds for the Nature Club, but they conciliated us by giving us a large library of books and nature magazines.* = to do something to remove the disappointment, anger or mistrust which someone has been feeling **conciliation** /kənsɪli'eɪʃən/ noun, u. *The people are ignoring the government's attempts at conciliation.* = the act or process of conciliating **conciliatory** /kən'sɪliətəri/ adj. *a conciliatory gesture* = something done in order to conciliate (please)

con•cise /kən'saɪs/ adj. *I need a concise report on the event, in not more than a page.* = short but clear

con•clude /kən'klu:d/ verb, t. or i. **1** *The meeting concluded at eight and everyone left.*(i.) = to come to an end **2** *I concluded my speech by thanking everyone.*(t.) = to bring something to an end **3** *The judge concluded that the accused was not guilty.* = to reach a decision or judgement after examining the facts **conclusion** noun, c. or u. **1** *The conclusion of the novel was very powerful.* = end **2** *After you have discussed the important points in your essay, you should write the conclusion in the last paragraph.* = the final opinion or judgement that one arrives at after considering all the facts **3** = the last paragraph in an essay that sums up (compare **inference**) **conclusive** adj. *We have conclusive evidence that she is innocent.* = something that helps one to reach a definite conclusion (judgement or decision) and removes all doubts (opposite **inconclusive**)

con•coct /kən'kɒkt/ verb, t. **1** *They should have told us the truth instead of concocting a story to explain why they were late.* = to make up something false in order to deceive, or avoid a problem (informal, derogatory) **2** *He concocted a refreshing drink from milk, mango juice and sugar.* = to produce something by mixing a number of things together (informal) **concoction** noun, c. **1** *He gave me a tasty concoction of tea, honey and ginger.* = something that is produced from a mixture of several things **2** *The story we heard was just a concoction.*(c.) = an untrue story; a lie

con•com•i•tant /kən'kɒmɪtənt/ adj. *I hope that we shall never have another war, with all its concomitant suffering.* = something that is a necessary part of something else and cannot be separated from it

con•cord /'kɒŋkɔ:d/ noun, u. *concord between countries* = peace and understanding (opposite **discord**)

con•crete /'kɒŋkri:t/ noun, u. **1** *a house with a concrete roof* = a mixture of cement, sand, small stones and water which becomes hard on drying, used in the construction of buildings etc. **2** *Food is something concrete; happiness is not.* = something real which one can see, touch etc. (opposite **abstract**) **3** *Please don't talk vaguely. I want a concrete description from you.* = clear and definite **concrete jungle** noun = a city which is full of ugly concrete buildings, without any green trees or open spaces (derogatory)

con•cu•bine /'kɒŋkjʊbaɪn/ noun, c. = a woman who lives with and has sexual relations with a man, but is not married to him (old-fashioned, usually derogatory)

con•cur /kən'kɜ:/ verb, i. *I fully concur with you in this decision.* = agree (formal) **concurrent** adj. **1** *My views on this subject are concurrent with yours.* = in agreement **2** *The meeting in Mysore was concurrent with the meeting in Patna.* = happening at the same time (formal)

con•cus•sion /kən'kʌʃən/ noun, u. *She received a hard knock on the head when she fell and suffered a concussion.* = damage to the brain caused by a blow to the head, shock etc. usually temporary

con•demn /kən'dem/ verb, t. **1** *The cutting down of the trees has been condemned by everyone.* = to say strongly that some action is wrong **2** *The prisoner was condemned to a seven-year jail sentence.* = to state the punishment for a guilty person **3** *This old bus has been condemned and cannot be used any more.* = to declare something unfit for use **condemnation** /kɒndəm'neɪʃən/ noun, u. = the act of condemning someone or something

con•dense /kən'dens/ verb, t. or i. **1** *The publisher has asked me to condense this novel to a hundred* *pages.*(t.) = to make a book, report etc. shorter **2** *The steam rising from the kettle will condense to form drops of water.*(i.) = to form drops of liquid by the cooling of warm air or gas **condensation** /kɒnden'seɪʃən/ noun, u. **1** = the tiny drops of liquid that collect on a cold surface when steam cools **2** = the result of shortening a report, book etc. **condensed milk** noun, u. = milk which has been made thick by boiling away the water **condenser** noun, c. = a machine that changes a gas into its liquid form, used in refrigerators, air-conditioners etc.

con•de•scend /kɒndɪ'send/ verb, i. *They were our neighbours and friends, but after they became famous, they didn't condescend to call or visit us.* = to do something beneath one's position (derogatory, sometimes humorous)

con•di•ment /'kɒndɪmənt/ noun, c. (usually plural) *You will need some special condiments to make mango chutney.* = substances which are used to add taste to food (old-fashioned, formal)

con•di•tion /kən'dɪʃən/ noun, u. or c. **1** *This wall is in a very poor condition and must be repaired at once.*(u.) = the state of health, fitness or readiness for use **2** *I will attend the meeting on the condition that I am not asked to speak!*(u.) = only if **3** *The agreement spells out the conditions on which the strike may be called off.*(c.) = something that is necessary for something else to happen **4** *You are appointed on the following terms and conditions.*(c.) = rules of service **5** *a heart condition* = an illness or defect in some part of the body **conditional** adj. *Your admission to the higher class is conditional on your passing the exam.* = depending on the fulfillment of some condition (formal)

con•do•lence /kən'dəʊləns/ noun, u. *a message of condolence* = an expression of sympathy for someone whose relative or friend has died

con•dom /'kɒndəm/ noun, c. = a rubber covering worn over the male sex organ during sexual intercourse as a means of birth control or protection against disease

con•done /kən'dəʊn/ verb, t. *I cannot condone your disturbing the peace of the neighbourhood, even if it is for a good cause.* = to excuse; to treat a wrong action as harmless

con•du•cive /kən'dju:sɪv/ adj. *The atmosphere in the hospital is not conducive to rest. People are talking loudly all the time.* = likely to produce or lead to something

con•duct[1] /'kɒndʌkt/ noun, u. *Why is my conduct not satisfactory? Have I done anything wrong?* = behaviour (formal)

con•duct[2] /kən'dʌkt/ verb, t. **1** *They conducted the meeting so well that everyone had a chance to speak.* = to direct or lead **2** *I hope the children conducted themselves well while the visitors were here.* = to behave **3** *Copper can conduct electricity but rubber cannot.* = to allow electricity or heat to pass through [PHYSICS] **4** *Zubin Mehta will conduct the orchestra.* = to guide or lead a group of musicians who are playing a piece of music

con•duc•tor /kən'dʌktə^r/ noun, c. **1** = a person who directs or guides a group of musicians **2** = a person who collects fares (money) from passengers on a bus or checks their tickets on a train **3** = a substance that allows electricity or heat to pass through it easily [PHYSICS]

con•duit /'kɒndɪt/ noun, c. = a pipe through which water or a set of electric wires is passed

cone /kəʊn/ noun, c. **1** = a solid object with a round base, circular sides and a point at the top **2** *an ice-cream cone* = a quantity of ice-cream inside an edible container shaped like a cone

con•fec•tion•e•ry /kən'fekʃənəri/ noun, u. = sweets

con•fed•e•ra•cy /kən'fedərəsi/ noun, c. (**confederacies**) *Several of the countries in East Africa have formed a confederacy.* = a union of groups or states with political objectives

con•fer /kən'fɜ:/ verb, i. *They have not come to any decision; they are still conferring.* = to talk together and exchange opinions (formal)

con•fe•rence /'kɒnfərəns/ noun, c. or u. *A conference of language teachers from all parts of the country will be held in Hyderabad.*(c.) = a meeting at which a group of people can exchange ideas on a subject

con•fess /kən'fes/ verb, t. **1** *Let him confess to the crime only if he is sure he is guilty.* = to make a statement admitting or accepting that one has done something wrong **2** *Thank you for suggesting that we invite Arun. I confess I hadn't thought of it.* = to admit that one has missed or omitted something **3** = to make one's faults known to God through a priest

con•fes•sion /kən'feʃən/ noun, c. or u. **1** = a statement confessing one's crimes, faults etc. **2** = a part of a religious ceremony at which a person admits his or her sins to a priest [TECHNICAL]

confidant /'kɒnfɪdænt/ noun, c. *She is a close confidant of mine. I tell her everything.* = a person to whom one tells one's secrets

con•fide /kən'faɪd/ verb, t. or i. *He confides all his secrets to me.* = to talk secretly or privately to a person that one trusts about one's secret or personal matters **confidence** /'kɒnfɪdəns/ noun, u. **1** *I don't have the confidence to make a public speech.*(u.) = a certain calmness which comes from knowing that one can do something well **2** *Let me tell you something in strict confidence.*(u.) = in the hope or belief that something will not be told to others **confidence trick** noun, c. = a trick played on someone by first winning that person's confidence (trust) and then cheating him/her (see also **con**)

con•fi•dent /ˈkɒnfɪdənt/ adj. **1** *I am confident of winning the election.* = having a belief in one's own ability to do something **2** *a confident smile* = showing confidence

con•fi•den•tial /kɒnfɪˈdenʃəl/ adj. *a confidential report* = something that is to be kept secret

con•fine /kənˈfaɪn/ verb, t. **1** *Let us confine our remarks to the subject we are discussing.* = to keep within limits; restrict **2** *The animals in the zoo are confined in their cages.* = to shut or keep in a small space **confinement** noun, u. **1** *Animals become sick if they are kept in confinement.* = the state of being confined (shut up in a small space) **2** *She has gone to the hospital for her confinement.* = the time during which a woman who is about to give birth is helped to prepare for the event [TECHNICAL]

con•firm /kənˈfɜːm/ verb, t. **1** *I must say I didn't believe the news until Zarina confirmed it.* = to support something (a statement, belief etc.) by stating that it is true or correct **2** *He had a temporary job with us but he has just been confirmed.* = to give or get formal approval to continue to work in an organisation **confirmation** /kɒnfəˈmeɪʃən/ noun, u. = something that confirms; the act of confirming

con•fis•cate /ˈkɒnfɪskeɪt/ verb, t. *If you play music in class, the teacher may confiscate your tape-recorder.* = to take possession of something as a punishment, sometimes with an intent to return it if behaviour etc. improves

con•fla•gra•tion /kɒnfləˈgreɪʃən/ *All the books in the library were destroyed in the conflagration.* = a very large fire (formal)

con•flict[1] /ˈkɒnflɪkt/ noun, c. or u. **1** *Conflicts between the two armies are quite common.*(c.) = a fight **2** *a conflict between countries* = disagreement as a result of sharp differences in points of view **3** *I couldn't decide which book to buy. There was such a conflict in my mind.*(u.) = a situation in which two opposing ideas or courses of action exist in a person's mind **4** *There were many conflicts in the neighbourhood over the problem of garbage.*(c.) = fight, argument

conflict[2] /kənˈflɪkt/ verb, t. *Your views on this subject conflict with mine. I am sorry we cannot agree.* = to be in opposition to; to disagree

con•flu•ence /ˈkɒnfluəns/ noun, u. *a confluence of rivers* = a meeting of rivers [GEOGRAPHY]

con•form /kənˈfɔːm/ verb, i. *We may not agree with some of the rules, but we will have to conform to them.* = to accept and obey a set of rules etc. **conformist** noun, c. = a person who follows or obeys a set of rules or social customs without questioning them (disapproving) **conformity** noun, u. = agreement with established rules

con•found /kənˈfaʊnd/ verb, t. *The unexpected results of the election confounded all of us.* = to confuse and surprise

con•front /kənˈfrʌnt/ verb, t. **1** *The two armies confronted each other on the battlefield.* = to stand face to face with the intention of fighting or arguing **2** *At first he claimed to be innocent, but when he was confronted with evidence of his guilt he confessed that he had committed the crime.* = to challenge or question strongly something that has been said **confrontation** /kɒnfrənˈteɪʃən/ noun, u. or c. *Let's not have a confrontation with the other group when we can discuss the matter peacefully.* = an unpleasant situation in which someone is openly opposed

con•fuse /kənˈfjuːz/ verb, t. **1** *Some of you want her to stay and others are asking her to go. Please don't confuse her.* = to cause someone to become uncertain about what to do or think **2** *I always confuse you with your brother. You look completely alike.* = to be unable to tell the difference between two things **confusion** noun, u. **1** = a state of not knowing what to think or do **2** = general disorder

con•geal /kənˈdʒiːl/ verb, i. = (of blood) to become thick, sticky and almost solid

con•ge•ni•al /kənˈdʒiːniəl/ adj. *I like living in Bhopal. The surroundings are very congenial.* = pleasant and in agreement with one's nature

con•gen•i•tal /kənˈdʒenɪtəl/ adj. *a congenital defect* = something (especially some disease) that exists from the time of birth

con•ges•ted /kənˈdʒestɪd/ adj. **1** *This road is always congested with traffic.* = crowded and full **2** *Your lungs are congested.* = blocked

con•glom•e•rate /kənˈglɒmərɪt/ = a large business house

con•glom•e•ra•tion /kənglɒməˈreɪʃən/ noun, u. *The article presents a conglomeration of ideas from many writers.* = a collection of many different things gathered together

con•grat•u•late /kənˈgrætʃʊleɪt/ verb, t. *Let me congratulate you on your victory.* = to express one's pleasure to someone because of some happy event or something achieved by him/her

con•gre•gate /ˈkɒngrɪgeɪt/ verb, i. *A large crowd*

had congregated at the airport to welcome the poet. = to gather together

con•gress /ˈkɒŋgres/ noun, c. *the annual congress of scientists* = a formal meeting of professional people to exchange information **Congress** noun = the highest law-making body in the U.S.A.

co•nif•er•ous /kəˈnɪfərəs/ adj. *a coniferous forest* = trees which grow in high places and remain green throughout the year

conj. abbr. of **conjunction**

con•jec•ture[1] /kənˈdʒektʃəʳ/ noun, c. or u. *I am not sure how many students have applied for admission. The number reported is only a conjecture.*(c.) = a guess

conjecture[2] verb, t. *The students conjectured that the examination would be an easy one.* = to guess

con•ju•gal /ˈkɒndʒʊgəl/ adj. *conjugal matters* = connected with marriage

con•junc•tion /kənˈdʒʌŋkʃən/ noun, c. *In the sentence 'I went home and had a good rest.', the word 'and' is a conjunction.* = a word such as 'and', 'but' etc. which joins together words or groups of words [GRAMMAR]

con•junc•ti•vi•tis /kəndʒʌŋktɪˈvaɪtɪs/ noun, u. = a painful disease of the eye which causes redness and swelling [MEDICINE]

con•jure /ˈkʌndʒəʳ/ verb, t. or i. *The magician conjured a chicken out of his hat.*(t.) = to produce by magic, or as if by magic **conjurer** (**conjuror**) noun, c. = a person who practises magic as a profession; a magician

a name to conjure with *Sunil Gavaskar is a name to conjure with in the world of cricket.* = a person with a great reputation

conk /kɒŋk/ verb, t. *If someone conked you, you could get badly injured.* = to hit on the head in order to harm (slang)

con•nect /kəˈnekt/ verb, t. **1** *This road connects Guntur to Vijayawada.* = to join two things or places to each other **2** *I shall always connect this house with the happy days of my childhood.* = to think of some thing or place together with something else; to associate **3** *Can you connect me to the Principal?* = to join through a telephone line **connection** noun, c. **1** *Rail and road connections between Delhi and the neighbouring towns have been cut.*(c.) = anything that connects **2** *Doctors believe there is a connection between smoking and cancer of the lungs.*(c.) = a relationship between two things (where one is often a cause for the other) **3** *He has many political connections.*(c.) = some important person that one knows or is related to

con•nive /kəˈnaɪv/ verb, i. *The thieves connived with the guards to rob the bank.* = to work together secretly with someone to do something wrong

con•nois•eur /kɒnəˈsɜːʳ/ noun, c. (French) *a connoiseur of poetry* = a person who has love for as well as deep knowledge of something which is thought to have value (e.g. art, music)

con•no•ta•tion /kɒnəˈteɪʃən/ noun, c. (often used in plural form) *The name Aman has a pleasant connotation and makes one think of joy and peace.* = some meaning or idea, pleasant or unpleasant, favourable or unfavourable, that is connected with a word, in addition to its usual meaning

con•quer /ˈkɒŋkəʳ/ verb, t. **1** *The king wanted to conquer the western part of the country and add it to his empire.* = to win and take land by force **2** *You have to conquer your fear of ghosts.* = succeed in ending or dealing with a problem **3** *Hillary and Tenzing conquered Mount Everest in 1955.* = to gain control over something **conqueror** noun, c. = a person who conquers a city or country

con•quest /ˈkɒŋkwest/ noun, u. or c. **1** (u.)= the act of conquering **2** (c.) = something that has been conquered

con•science /ˈkɒnʃəns/ noun, u. *I have never been fair to you and my conscience troubles me.* = an inner feeling that tells one the difference between right and wrong

con•sci•en•tious /kɒnʃiˈenʃəs/ adj. *She is such a conscientious worker that she will always complete any task which you give her.* = doing one's work with great care and sincerity

con•scious /ˈkɒnʃəs/ adj. **1** *He was severely injured but remained conscious.* = to be able to think, feel and understand what is happening **2** *I am conscious of the fact that I have not done my best.* = to be aware of something; to know or understand **consciousness** noun, u. = the ability to think, feel, understand etc.

con•se•crate /ˈkɒnsɪkreɪt/ verb, t. **1** *The new church will be consecrated today.* = to perform a religious ceremony to make something holy **2** *He has consecrated his life to the service of the country.* = to give up or set apart something for a noble purpose

con•sec•u•tive /kənˈsekjʊtɪv/adj. *You must come here on three consecutive days—today, tomorrow and the day after tomorrow.* = following each other without a break

con•sen•sus /kənˈsensəs/ noun, u. *A decision can be taken only after a consensus has been reached.* = agreement among the people in a group

con•sent[1] /kənˈsent/ noun, u. *They wanted to build a room upstairs and I have given them my consent.* = agreement or permission

consent[2] verb, i. *The students asked for a holiday on Friday and the Principal consented.* = to agree to something when one is in a position to refuse

con•se•quence /'kɒnsɪkwəns/ noun, c. (sometimes plural) *You have been neglecting your studies and now you may have to suffer the consequence.* = the result of some action **consequently** adv. = as a result; therefore

con•serve /kən'sɜːv/ verb, t. *If we do not conserve water, there will be a serious shortage in a few years.* = to save; to stop something from being wasted or destroyed

con•ser•va•tion /kɒnsə'veɪʃən/ noun, u. *the conservation of our forests* = action taken to prevent something from being wasted or destroyed **conservationist** noun, c. = a person who is active in conserving natural things such as water, forests etc.

con•ser•va•tive /kən'sɜːvətɪv/ adj. **1** = bound to old and familiar ways of thinking or doing things when other, newer, ways are available (generally disapproving) **2** *a conservative style of dressing* = not in fashion, traditional (generally disapproving) **a conservative estimate** *The school will need about Rs 70,000 for the new bicycle stand, and that is just a conservative estimate.* = kept intentionally low with the aim of being careful

con•sid•er /kən'sɪdə/ verb, t. **1** *I consider him a brave person, even though he may not seem to be so.* = to have an opinion about someone or something **2** *I hope you will consider my application for the job.* = to think about; to examine **3** *When you consider the fact that this is only his first film, I would say Hrithik is a fine actor.* = to take something into account when making a judgement **consideration** /kənsɪdə'reɪʃən/ noun, u. **1** *I am sending in my application for your consideration.* = careful thought; examination (formal) **2** *Sheela shows a lot of consideration for her parents.* = care for the feelings of others **3** *What train you take should not be a consideration when the important thing is to get to Sultanpur.* = a fact to be thought about seriously **4** *For a small consideration, they can help you clear the weeds in the garden.* = payment for work done or help taken (formal, somewhat old-fashioned)

con•sid•e•ra•ble /kən'sɪdərəbəl/ adj. *We have lived in Kolhapur for a considerable length of time.* = fairly large in size, amount or degree (see also **inconsiderable**)

con•sid•er•ate /kən'sɪdərət/ adj. *She is very considerate and never phones us after nine at night.* = careful to think about the feelings and convenience of others (opposite **inconsiderate**)

con•sign /kən'saɪn/ verb, t. **1** *I have already consigned the books to you by air-mail.* = to send something to someone **2** *The old files were consigned to the flames.* = put into (generally used of something which is no longer needed) **3** *The man was consigned to prison on the orders of the court.* = to put someone in an unpleasant place or situation **consignee** noun = a person to whom something is sent **consignment** noun, c. = things which are sent or received together, for purposes of trade

con•sist (of) /kən'sɪst/ verb, t. *The North American continent consists of Canada, the U.S.A. and Mexico.* = to be made up of (compare **comprise**)

con•sis•tent /kən'sɪstənt/ adj. *Saurav has scored at least 50 runs in every match. He is very consistent as a batsman.* = not changing frequently in what one says, believes or does; steady and dependable (opposite **inconsistent**)

con•sole /'kɒnsəʊl/ verb, t. *When she failed in the examination we tried to console her but it was difficult.* = to give sympathy or comfort to one who is unhappy **consolation** /kɒnsə'leɪʃən/ noun, u. = sympathy or comfort given to someone who is unhappy **consolation prize** noun, c. = a prize given to someone who is not successful in winning an important prize in a competition, in order to give him/her some comfort and encouragement

con•sol•i•date /kən'sɒlɪdeɪt/ verb, t. **1** *The company consolidated its position by doubling its sales.* = to make oneself stronger **2** *There were three small bookshops in the city, but now they have been consolidated into one large shop.* = to combine a number of things together to form something larger **consolidation** /kənsɒlɪ'deɪʃən/ noun, u. **1** = the act or the result of becoming stronger **2** = the act of joining a number of smaller things together to form something larger

con•so•nant /'kɒnsənənt/ noun, c. *All the letters of the English alphabet except 'a', 'e', 'i', 'o' and 'u' are consonants.* = a letter representing a speech sound which is produced by blocking the flow of air through the mouth (compare **vowel**)

con•sort[1] /'kɒnsɔːt/ noun, c. *The Emperor Shah Jahan built the Taj Mahal in memory of his consort, Noor Jahan.* = the wife or husband of a ruler (formal, old-fashioned)

consort[2] verb, t. *I am surprised to find that you consort with such people.* = to keep company with people who are not good (formal)

con•sor•ti•um /kən'sɔːtiəm/ noun, c. (Latin) (**consortiums** or **consortia**) *The new steel plant is being put up by a consortium of international companies.* = a combination of different companies which have joined together

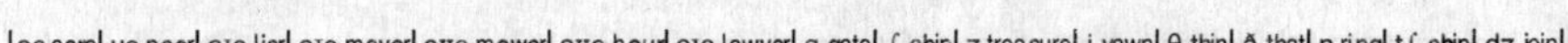

| eə care| ʊə poor| aɪə liar| eɪə mayor| əʊə mower| aʊə hour| ɔɪə lawyer| g gate| ʃ ship| ʒ treasure| j yawn| θ thin| ð that| ŋ ring| tʃ chin| dʒ join|

con•spic•u•ous /kən'spɪkjuəs/ adj. *All my friends are here except Saif. He is conspicuous by his absence.* = attracting attention; standing out from the others because of some difference

con•spi•ra•cy /kən'spɪrəsi/ noun, u. = a secret plan made by two or more people to do something illegal

con•spi•ra•tor /kən'spɪrətə[r]/ noun, c. = a person who takes part in a conspiracy

con•spire /kən'spaɪə[r]/ verb, i. *They conspired to cheat the bank by encashing some forged cheques.* = to plan with one or more persons to do something wrong

con•sta•ble /'kʌnstəbəl/ noun, c. = a member of the police force having the junior most rank (compare **policeman**, **officer**)

con•stant[1] /'kɒnstənt/ adj. **1** *The temperature of Mumbai has remained constant at 31 degrees Celsius for the whole week.* = showing no change **2** *There is constant trouble in our neighbourhood.* = happening all the time **3** *a constant friend* = faithful

constant[2] noun, c. *The area of a circle can be calculated by multiplying the square of its radius by π (pi), which is a constant, equal in value to 3.142.* = a number or quantity which does not change [MATHEMATICS] (compare **variable**)

con•stant•ly /'kɒnstəntlɪ/ adv. *He constantly complains to his neighbours about their playing music too loud.* = repeatedly; every now and then

con•stel•la•tion /kɒnstə'leɪʃən/ noun, c. = a group of stars, some of which have names e.g. Orion

con•ster•na•tion /kɒnstə'neɪʃən/ noun, u. *The train arrived but when she found that her parents were not on it, she was filled with consternation.* = shock, worry and fear

con•sti•pa•tion /kɒnstɪ'peɪʃən/ noun, u. = a condition in which a person is unable to empty the bowels

con•sti•tu•en•cy /kən'stɪtʃuənsi/ noun, c. (**constituencies**) = a part of a country from which a person is elected to the state assembly or the national parliament

con•sti•tu•ent /kən'stɪtʃuənt/ adj. or noun, c. *Madras University has 320 constituent colleges.*(adj.) = things that make up a whole

con•sti•tute /'kɒnstɪtju:t/ verb, t. *About 120 colleges in different parts of Kerala constitute Calicut University.* = to form or make up something

con•sti•tu•tion /kɒnstɪ'tju:ʃən/ noun, u. **1** *the Constitution of India* = the system of laws and principles, generally in written form, according to which a country is governed **2** *I have a very strong constitution. I almost never fall ill.* = the condition of a person's health **3** *the constitution of the state of Jharkhand* = the act of setting up or establishing something

con•strain /kən'streɪn/ verb, t. *Our ability to help people is constrained by a lack of funds.* = to hold back or check someone from doing something (formal)

con•strained /kən'streind/ adj. *As she was among strangers, her manner was rather constrained.* = not natural and relaxed

con•straint /kən'streɪnt/ noun, c. *This school has to work under a number of constraints, the most serious being the lack of good teachers.* = something that checks or prevents someone from doing something

con•strict /kən'strɪkt/ verb, t. *Blood cannot flow freely through the body when the blood vessels become constricted.* = to make something narrow **constriction** noun, u. *constriction of the arteries* = narrowing

con•struct /kən'strʌkt/ verb, t. *They are constructing a large hospital near my house.* = to build **construction** noun, u. or c. **1** *The house is under construction, I don't know when it will be complete.* (u.) = the process of building or being built **2** *This tower is part of a new construction.*(c.) = something that has been built

con•struc•tive /kən'strʌktɪv/ adj. *He made some very constructive suggestions for the improvement of the school.* = helpful (opposite **destructive**)

con•strue /kən'stru:/ verb, t. *Her loud manner is often construed as rudeness.* = to find a different and negative meaning for something that is stated (formal)

con•sul /'kɒnsəl/ noun, c. = a person appointed by the government to serve in a city in a foreign country and help the citizens of his/her own country who may be living or working there

con•su•late /'kɒnsjʊlət/ noun, c. = the office of the consul

con•sult /kən'sʌlt/ verb, t. *You look tired and pale. You should consult your doctor.* = to go to someone, usually an expert in some profession, for advice, help etc. **consultant** noun, c. = a person who can be consulted for professional advice **consultation** /kɒnsəl'teɪʃən/ noun, u. **1** = a meeting held by people who want to take each other's advice etc. **2** = the act of consulting someone e.g. a doctor, a lawyer

con•sume /kən'sju:m/ verb, t. **1** *The people of this state consume more rice than wheat.* = to eat or drink (formal) **2** *Our office consumes a lot of paper.* = to use up **3** *This project is consuming all my time.* = to take up (formal) **4** *The building was consumed by the flames.* = to be burnt

con•sum•er /kən'sju:mər/ noun, c. = a person who is thought of as a buyer or user of a product or a service

[TECHNICAL] **consumer durables** noun = large products (e.g. computers, chairs, washing machines) which are not bought by a customer frequently **consumer goods** noun = articles of clothing, food etc. which are regularly used by people in their homes

con•sum•er•ism /kən'sjuːmərɪzəm/ noun. = the belief or practice which supports and encourages the buying of products and services

con•sum•mate[1] /'kɒnsəmeɪt/ verb, t. **1** *Ten years of hard work will be consummated when this book is published.* = to complete or make something perfect **2** *Her husband has been unable to consummate the marriage.* = to complete a marriage by having sex [LAW]

consummate[2] /'kɒnsəmet/ adj. *He is a consummate musician.* = complete and perfect **consummation** /kɒnsə'meɪʃən/ noun, c. **1** *This new book is the consummation of ten years of hard work.* = the highest point or the completion of something **2** = the act of consummating a marriage by having sex

con•sump•tion /kən'sʌmpʃən/ noun, u. *The consumption of alcohol is increasing.* = the act of using something (usually by eating or drinking) or the amount that is used

con•tact[1] /'kɒntækt/ noun, u. or c. **1** *When we came out of the warm room, contact with the cold air made us shiver.*(u.) = the act of feeling or touching something **2** *I am in regular contact with my friends in other parts of the world.* = the condition of being able to meet or get information from someone through the telephone, e-mail, letters etc. **3** *I have a number of useful business contacts in Japan.*(c.) = a person whom one knows and can get help from

contact[2] verb, t. *I have not been able to contact my son in America.* = to reach or to get in touch with someone by telephone, letters, e-mail etc.

contact lens noun, c. (**contact lenses**) = a lens made of transparent plastic which is worn inside the eye, just over the eye-ball, and helps the wearer to see more clearly

con•ta•gious /kən'teɪdʒəs/ adj. *Chicken pox is contagious.* = a disease which can be passed from one person to another by touch or through the air (compare **infectious**)

con•tain /kən'teɪn/ verb, t. **1** *This box contains important letters.* = to hold **2** *This tablet contains some calcium.* = to have something as a part **3** *He could not contain his joy when I gave him the good news.* = to check; to hold back

con•tain•er /kən'teɪnəʳ/ noun, c. = a box, bottle or any other object used to contain (hold or store) something

con•tam•i•nate /kən'tæmɪneɪt/ verb t. or i. *The water of the river has been contaminated by poisonous chemicals from factories.*(t.) = to make something impure and harmful by mixing polluting matter **contaminant** noun, c. = something that contaminates

con•tam•i•na•tion /kəntæmɪ'neɪʃən/ noun, u. = the act or result of contaminating something

con•tem•plate /'kɒntəmpleɪt/ verb, t. **1** *I am contemplating buying a house closer to the city.* = to think deeply about or to plan a future course of action **2** *She was contemplating the beautiful sunset.* = to look at something quietly and calmly **contemplation** /kɒntəm'pleɪʃən/ noun, u. *He spends an hour on the beach every morning in contemplation.* = the act of thinking deeply and calmly; meditation

con•tem•po•ra•ry[1] /kən'tempərəri/ adj. *I am teaching a course on contemporary literature.* = belonging to the present time; modern

contemporary[2] noun, c. (**contemporaries**) *My mother and hers were contemporaries, but they never met.* = a person of the same age or living at the same time as another

con•tempt /kən'tempt/ noun, u. *Instead of showing contempt for their dishonest ways, why don't you try to correct them?* = total lack of respect; strong dislike **contemptible** adj. *contemptible behaviour* = deserving contempt **contemptuous** adj. *a contemptuous laugh* = expressing contempt

con•tend /kən'tend/ verb, i. **1** *The two countries are contending for the gold medal in hockey.* = to compete **2** *I have to contend with many difficulties in my effort to stop people from using plastic bags.* = struggle; fight against **3** *The lawyer contended that his client was innocent.* = to claim; to state strongly **contender** noun, c. *Korea and Germany are strong contenders for the gold medal.* = one who takes part in a competition **contention** noun, u. *It is my contention that learning things by heart does not help.* = claim

a bone of contention *The playground which lies between the two schools has become a bone of contention between them because both want to use it at the same time.* = something over which there is a dispute or difference of opinion

con•tent[1] /kən'tent/ adj. *She is perfectly content with her present job.* = happy and satisfied (opposite **discontent**)

content[2] verb, t. *You should content yourself with one cup of coffee in the morning.* = to limit oneself to; to be satisfied with

content[3] /'kɒntent/ noun, c. or u. **1** (always plural) *Are you familiar with the contents of this book?*(c.) =

a list of the topics or ideas found in a book, speech etc. **2** *Beer has an alcohol content of about four per cent.*(u.) = the amount of a substance present in something **3** (always plural) *The customs officer wants to examine the contents of your suitcase.*(c.) = the things inside

con•test[1] /'kɒntest/ noun, c. *a drawing contest* = an event in which people are required to show their skill at something in order to win prizes; competition

contest[2] /kən'test/ verb, t. **1** *I plan to contest the elections.* = to compete for **2** *The house belonged to us, but they contested our claim.*= to question; to say something is not what it is claimed to be **contestant** noun, c. = a person who takes part in a contest

con•text /'kɒntekst/ noun, c. **1** *'He could have taken a short cut to the market, but he chose a circuitous route instead and had to walk abut eight kilometres.' Can you guess from the context what 'circuitous' means?* = the words surrounding a particular word, which help one to understand its meaning **2** *She said I had not been very helpful. Do you know what context she was referring to?* = the conditions in which some event takes place

con•tin•ent /'kɒntɪnənt/ noun, c. = one of the seven main land masses on the earth **continental** /kɒntɪ'nentl/ adj. = belonging to or found on a continent **continental drift** noun, u. = the very slow movement of the continents across the earth **continental shelf** noun, u. = the land lying under the sea, around the edges of a continent [GEOGRAPHY]

con•tin•gen•cy /kən'tɪndʒənsi/ noun, u. *We are facing a number of problems and should be prepared for any contingency.* = something that may or may not happen, but will cause a problem if it does happen

con•tin•gent[1] /kən'tɪndʒənt/ adj. *My moving to Surat is contingent on my getting a job there.* = depending on something which is uncertain (formal)

contingent[2] noun, c. *the Indian contingent at the Olympic Games* = group or team

con•tin•u•al /kən'tɪnjʊəl/ adj. *I am tired of your continual complaints about the food.* = something unpleasant or bad which is repeated again and again, with or without a break, over a period of time (derogatory)

con•tin•ue /kən'tɪnju:/ verb, i. or t. **1** *The Olympic Games will begin on 15 September and continue till 1 October.*(i.) = to go on without a break **2** *We will continue this story next week.*(t.) = to start something again after a break **3** *You are requested to continue as the Secretary of the club until the next election.*(i.) = to remain; to stay

con•tin•u•ous /kən'tɪnjʊəs/ adj. *The rain has been continuous for the past week.* = something that goes on without a break over a period of time. (not derogatory) **continuation** /kəntɪnju'eɪʃən/ noun, u. = the act of continuing **continuity** /kɒntɪ'nju:ɪti/ noun, u. *There should be continuity between the different parts of your story.* = unbroken connection

con•tort /kən'tɔ:t/ verb, i. *People who are experts in yoga can contort their bodies into difficult postures.* = to twist or bend something out of its natural shape

con•tour /'kɒntʊə^r/ noun, c. **1** *You can clearly see the contours of the coast of Tamil Nadu from the air* = shape; outline **2** *a contour map of India* = a line drawn on a map showing all the places which are at the same height [GEOGRAPHY]

con•tra- /kɒntrə/ prefix meaning 'against' or 'opposite' e.g. **con•tra•cep•tive** /kɒntrə'septɪv/ noun, c. or adj. = a device or drug which is used to prevent pregnancy

con•tra•band /'kɒntrəbænd/ noun, u = goods which cannot be brought into a country legally

con•tra•cep•tion /kɒntrə'sepʃən/ noun, u. = the process or action of using contraceptives to prevent birth

con•tract[1] /kən'trækt/ verb, i. or t. **1** *A piece of metal becomes longer when it is heated but contracts when it is cooled.*(i.) = to become smaller or shorter (opposite **expand**) **2** *I have contracted an engineer to build my new house.*(t.) = to enter into a contract with someone **3** *He has contracted malaria.* = to become ill (formal)

contract[2] /'kɒntrækt/ noun, c. or u. *to enter into a contract*(c.) = a written agreement between two people or groups which is binding in law **contraction** /kən'trækʃən/ noun, u. or c. = the process of becoming smaller

con•trac•tor /kən'træktə^r/ noun, c. = a person who enters into a contract to do some work, especially building jobs

con•tra•dict /kɒntrə'dɪkt/ verb, t. *We knew what he was saying was false but we did not contradict him.* = to declare something to be wrong or untrue; to say the opposite of what someone else says **contradiction** noun, c. = a statement which contradicts (goes against) another statement made earlier **contradictory** adj. *a contradictory statement* = something which contradicts something else

con•trap•tion /kən'træpʃən/ noun, c. *She built herself a car. It was a strange-looking contraption!* = a strange-looking machine (derogatory or humorous)

con•tra•ry /'kɒntrəri/ adj. *My doctor thinks I am suffering from malaria but another doctor has given me a contrary opinion.* = different and opposite

C

con•trast[1] /ˈkɒntrɑːst/ noun, c. *Juhi's brother is shy and quiet, but Juhi is bold and friendly. What a contrast there is between the two!* = complete difference **contrast**[2] /kənˈtrɑːst/ verb, t. *In this article, the writer contrasts China with India and shows how different the two countries are.* = to compare two things so as to point out the differences between them

con•tra•vene /kɒntrəˈviːn/ verb, t. *The police officer explained that I had contravened the law by driving without a licence.* = to break or go against a law **contravention** noun, u. = the act of going against a law

con•trib•ute /kənˈtrɪbjuːt/ verb, t. **1** *They contributed a lot of money to the local hospital.* = to give money for a good cause **2** *He has contributed an article to the Hindustan Times.* = to write and send an article to a newspaper or magazine **3** *Goa's excellent beaches have contributed to its popularity as a tourist centre.* = to help in bringing about something **contribution** /kɒntrɪˈbjuːʃən/ noun, c. **1** = money contributed to a cause **2** = the work done or the effort put in by someone to bring about a certain result

con•trive /kənˈtraɪv/ verb, i. *With great difficulty I contrived to find a job.* = to succeed in doing something with difficulty

con•trived /kənˈtraɪvd/ adj. *They were too polite to say that they didn't like the film but the enjoyment on their faces was contrived.* = achieved with effort; not natural

con•trol[1] /kənˈtrəʊl/ verb, t. **1** *Mr Shah controls the supply of water to our building.* = to guide or direct **2** *I know you feel angry but please try to control your emotions.* = hold back

control[2] noun, c. *He has good control of the car.* = the power, skill or ability to guide and direct someone or something

con•tro•ver•sy /ˈkɒntrəvɜːsi, kənˈtrɒvəsi/ noun, u. or c. (**controversies**) *There is a controversy about whether students should have holidays before exams.* = a dispute in which opposite opinions are expressed strongly **controversial** /kɒntrəˈvɜːʃəl/ adj. *The rule about not allowing pets in the park was controversial.* = something that causes a controversy

con•va•lesce /kɒnvəˈles/ verb, i. *She is convalescing after her illness.* = to get better after an illness **convalescence** noun, u. = the period of time during which one is convalescing after an illness

con•vec•tion /kənˈvekʃən/ noun, u. = the movement in a gas or liquid caused by heating or cooling [CHEMISTRY]

con•vene /kənˈviːn/ verb, t. *to convene a meeting* = to organise (arrange) a meeting or social event **convener** noun, c. = one who convenes a meeting

con•ve•ni•ence /kənˈviːnɪəns/ noun, u. or c. **1** *The hotel is close to the railway station and the shops. You will like it for its convenience.*(u.) = the quality of being convenient. **2** *This house has all modern conveniences.*(c.) = things which make life more comfortable **convenient** adj. *Which date do you think would be most convenient for our next sports day?* = suited to one's needs

con•vent /ˈkɒnvənt/ noun, c. = a place where Christian nuns (women who have given their lives to religious work) live, teach etc.

con•ven•tion /kənˈvenʃən/ noun, u. and c. **1** *All the countries of the world have signed the Geneva Convention.*(c.) = a formal agreement between countries **2** *Everyone who comes to the annual meeting is required to dress formally. That is the convention.*(u.) = a generally accepted but unwritten rule of social behaviour **3** *This is a convention of doctors.*(c.) = a meeting of a group for a special purpose **conventional** adj. *They are very conventional in their eating habits.* = wanting to follow the usual customs and standards, sometimes too closely in the opinion of others (often disapproving) (opposite **unconventional**)

con•verge /kənˈvɜːdʒ/ verb, i. *The four roads converge at the hospital.* = to come together at a common point (opposite **diverge**)

con•ver•sant /kənˈvɜːsənt/ adj. *I am not conversant with these roads as I have come here for the first time.* = having knowledge of something; familiar (formal)

con•ver•sa•tion /kɒnvəˈseɪʃən/ noun, u. or c. *I had an interesting conversation with a man I met on the train.*(c.) = friendly social talk; a chat **conversational** adj. *I have joined a course in conversational French.* = the kind of informal language which is used in conversation

con•verse[1] /kənˈvɜːs/ verb, i. *Let us converse in Hindi so that everyone understands us.* = to talk together

converse[2] /ˈkɒnvɜːs/ noun, u. *Cloudy days are warm days but the converse is not always true.* = the reverse (opposite) of something that has been said

con•ver•sion /kənˈvɜːʃən/ noun, u. or c. **1** *The conversion of Indian rupees to American dollars can be done only at a bank.* = the act of converting (changing) **2** *conversions to other religions*(c.) = the act of changing one's religion

con•vert[1] /kənˈvɜːt/ verb, t. or i. **1** *I want to covert my Indian rupees into Nepali rupees.*(t.) = to change **2** *convert to Buddhism* = to change one's religion

convert[2] /ˈkɒnvɜːt/ noun, c. = a person who has changed his/her religion and accepted a new religion

con•ver•ti•ble /kənˈvɜːtɪbəl/ adj. *a convertible bed that becomes a sofa* = something that can be changed easily into something else

con•vex /ˈkɒnveks/ adj. *a convex mirror* = curving outwards (opposite **concave**)

con•vey /kənˈveɪ/ verb, t. **1** *These railway wagons convey coal from the mines to the steel plant.* = to carry from one place to another **2** *I hope this letter conveys my feelings of joy.* = to express **conveyance** noun, u. *We will provide conveyance to take you to the station.* = a means of transport

con•vict[1] /kənˈvɪkt/ verb, t. *convict someone on a charge of murder* = to decide (by a judge) that someone is guilty of doing something wrong (opposite **acquit**)

convict[2] /ˈkɒnvɪkt/ noun, c. = a person who has been convicted (found guilty of some crime) and sent to jail, usually for a long period **conviction** /kənˈvɪkʃən/ noun, u. or c. **1** *The accused will appeal against his conviction.*(u.) = the act of being judged to be guilty **2** *It is my firm conviction that the government can start more schools.*(c.) = strong belief

con•vince /kənˈvɪns/ verb, t. *You don't believe what I am telling you. Let me try to convince you.* = to cause someone to believe that what you are saying is true; to persuade **convincing** adj. *Your arguments are quite convincing. I believe you.* = able to convince

con•vo•ca•tion /kɒnvəˈkeɪʃən/ noun, c. = a meeting at which students of a university who have graduated are given their degrees

con•voy /ˈkɒnvɔɪ/ noun, c. = a group of ships or cars sailing or driving together to protect each other, specially from enemy attack during a war

con•vul•sion /kənˈvʌlʃən/ noun, c. (usually plural) (**convulsions**) = violent shaking of the body caused by some illness

coo /kuː/ verb, i. *The pigeons cooed all night.* = to make a low, soft sound like that of a pigeon

cook[1] /kʊk/ verb, t. or i. **1** *Are you cooking chicken curry for us?* (t.) // *He doesn't cook often, he eats out.*(i.) = to prepare food for eating by using heat **2** *The chicken should cook for at least half an hour.* (i.) = to go through the process of cooking

cook[2] noun, c. *He is an excellent cook.* = one who cooks

to cook up an excuse = to offer a false reason for doing or not doing something (informal, derogatory) **Too many cooks spoil the broth.** = if too many people get involved in doing something it is not likely to succeed

cook•er /ˈkʊkəʳ/ noun, c. = a device (machine) used for cooking food, usually run on electricity or gas

cook•e•ry /ˈkʊkərɪ/ noun, u. = the art of cooking **cookery book** noun, c. = a book which tells one how to cook different kinds of food

cool[1] /kuːl/ adj. **1** *The weather is pleasantly cool.* = neither very hot nor very cold; comfortable **2** *He is always cool when faced with some difficulty.* = calm **3** *When I met my friend yesterday, she seemed rather cool.* = not very friendly **4** *They are really cool people.* = nice and likeable (slang, approving)

cool[2] verb, t. *The water flowing through these pipes cools the engine.* = to keep something at a low temperature **coolly** adv. = without much interest **coolness** noun **cooling** adj. *cooling lotion* = something which cools

to keep one's cool = to stay calm **to lose one's cool** = used in a situation in which one becomes angry suddenly

coo•lant /ˈkuːlənt/ noun, c. or u. = a liquid which is used to cool a machine (e.g. the engine of a car) while working

coop /kuːp/ noun, c. *a chicken coop* = a cage in which birds, specially chickens, are kept

cooped up = to be kept in a small space, or to have the feeling of being kept in a small space, without the freedom to move about

co•op•e•rate /kəʊˈɒpəreɪt/ verb, i. *We can finish this job in a day, if all of you co-operate with me.* = to work together for a common purpose **cooperation** /kəʊɒpəˈreɪʃən/ noun, u. **1** *It was cooperation and hard work that made the programme such a success.* = the act of working together for a common purpose **2** *I do hope I can get your cooperation.* = willingness to work together for a common purpose

co•op•e•ra•tive[1] /kəʊˈɒpərətɪv/ adj. *He is usually very cooperative so he should agree to help you.* = willing to work together with or to help someone

cooperative[2] noun, c. *We are going to form a students' cooperative.* = a shop or company which is owned and run by a group with a common purpose

co•or•di•nate /kəʊˈɔːdɪneɪt/ verb, t. *I have been asked to coordinate the work of three different departments.* = to make different groups of people, who usually work independently, work together for a common purpose **coordination** /kəʊɔːdɪˈneɪʃən/ noun, u. **1** *We should have better coordination if we are to finish this job in time.* = the process by which different groups of people work together **2** *To be a good athlete you need excellent coordination of all your muscles.* = the working together of different muscles in performing a movement

cop /kɒp/ noun, c. = a police officer (slang)

cope /kəʊp/ verb, i. *We are usually able to finish our work in time, but when we get a lot of extra work we* *are often unable to cope.* = to deal successfully with a difficult situation

cop•i•er /'kɒpiəʳ/ noun, c. = a machine (a photocopier) which make photographic copies of documents, books etc.

co•pi•lot /'kəʊpaɪlət/ noun, c. = a person who helps the captain (chief pilot) of an aircraft to fly it

co•pi•ous /'kəʊpiəs/ adj. *The harvest was excellent, thanks to the copious rains.* = plentiful; abundant

cop•per /'kɒpəʳ/ noun = a soft, reddish metal used for making electric wires etc.

cop•ra /'kɒprə/ noun, u. = the dried flesh of the coconut from which coconut oil is made

cop•u•late /'kɒpjʊleɪt/ verb, i. = to join together in an act of sex (formal) **copulation** /kɒpjʊ'leɪʃən/ noun, u. or c. = the act of copulating

cop•y[1] /'kɒpi/ noun, c. (**copies**) **1** *I have a copy of the letter which I wrote to you last month in case it didn't reach you.* = something which looks exactly like another **2** *Did you get your copy of 'Frontline' yesterday?* = a single issue of a magazine, newspaper, book etc.

copy[2] verb, t. **1** *Will you please copy this article for me?* = to make a copy of something **2** *Please don't copy the way I talk, I feel bad.* = to follow an example; to imitate **3** *Any candidate found copying in the examination will be asked to leave.* = to cheat at an examination by copying an answer from a book or from someone else **4** *I hope the ideas in the article are your own, and that you didn't copy them.* = to borrow and use **copybook** noun, c. = a book containing sheets of paper on which people can write **copycat** noun, c. = a person who copies (imitates) someone else without thinking (informal; derogatory)

copyright /'kɒpiraɪt/ noun, u. = the right given by the law to claim some material (e.g. a book, film, painting etc.) as one's property

cop•y•writ•er /'kɒpiraɪtəʳ/ noun, c. = a person who writes the words for an advertisement

cor•al /'kɒrəl/ noun, u. = a white, pink or red stone-like substance formed from the shells (outer coverings) of very small sea animals, often used for making jewellery

cord /kɔːd/ noun, c. = a length of thick string or rope

cor•di•al[1] /'kɔːdiəl/ adj. *We extend a very cordial welcome to our guest.* = warm and friendly

cordial[2] noun, u. *lime-juice cordial* = a drink made from fruit juice

cor•don[1] /'kɔːdn/ noun, c. = a ring formed by a number of people to protect someone

cordon[2] verb, t. *The police have cordoned off the area.* = to surround an area so that no one can enter it

cor•du•roy /'kɔːdjʊrɔɪ/ noun, u. = a kind of thick cotton cloth with thin parallel raised lines on it

core[1] /kɔːʳ/ noun, u. or c. **1** *the core of an apple* = the hard central part of certain fruits, containing the seeds **2** *The core of India's wealth is from agriculture.* = the most important or central part of something

core[2] adj. *core idea // core curriculum // core business* = main or central; most important

core[3] verb, t. *I have to core these apples.* = to remove the core of some fruit

co•ri•an•der /kɒri'ændəʳ/ noun, u. = a spice made from the dried seeds of a plant, used especially in Indian cooking

cork[1] /kɔːk/ noun, u. or c. **1** (u.)= the soft bark of a kind of tree, known as the cork tree **2** (c.) = a piece of this material which is used to close the mouth of a bottle

cork[2] verb, t. *Let me cork the bottle.* = to close the mouth of a bottle with a cork

cork-screw /'kɔːkskruː/ noun, c. = a long, twisted piece of metal, like a screw, with a handle, used to pull corks out of bottles

cor•mo•rant /'kɔːmərənt/ noun, c. = a fish-eating sea bird which was trained by the people of China, in former times, to catch fish

corn /kɔːn/ noun, u. **1** = the edible seeds of certain types of plants such as maize, millet and barley **2** = a painful area of hard skin formed on the foot by the rubbing of a shoe etc. **cornflakes** noun, u. = seeds of the maize plant, roasted and beaten flat, often eaten with milk for breakfast

cor•ner[1] /'kɔːnəʳ/ noun, c. **1** *a corner of the room* = the point at which two sides, lines, roads etc. meet **2** *We live in a little-known corner of the country.* = a part of a larger area **3** *Please don't push me into a corner, I will find it difficult to defend myself.* = a difficult situation from which it is hard to get out

corner[2] verb, t. **1** *I am so sorry he has been cornered.* = to force someone into a difficult or dangerous situation (informal) **2** *The two big companies have cornered the market in petroleum.* = to gain control of

cor•ner•stone /'kɔːnəstəʊn/ noun, c. **1** = a stone set in one of the bottom corners of a building which is usually put in place by a special guest at a ceremony **2** *I believe that hard work is the cornerstone of success.* = something of great importance, on which everything else is based

co•rol•la•ry /kə'rɒləri/ noun, c. (**corollaries**) *If cricket continues to be the most popular game in India, the corollary is that all other games will be neglected.* = a result which follows naturally from something else

co•ro•na /kə'rəʊnə/ noun, c. = the bright ring of light seen around the sun when the moon passes in front of it during an eclipse

cor•o•na•ry /ˈkɒrənəri/ adj. = having to do with the heart **coronary thrombosis** noun = the stopping of the supply of blood to the heart, causing a heart attack (see **clot, heart attack**) [MEDICINE]

cor•o•na•tion /kɒrəˈneɪʃən/ noun, u. or c. = the ceremony at which a new king or queen is crowned

cor•po•ral[1] /ˈkɔːpərəl/ adj. *corporal punishment* = physical (of the body)

corporal[2] noun, c. = a very junior officer in the army

cor•po•ra•tion /kɔːpəˈreɪʃən/ noun, c. **1** *the Life Insurance Corporation of India* = a company which is legally permitted to run a business **2** *the Municipal Corporation of Delhi* = a group of people responsible for maintaining and looking after a city or town

cor•po•re•al /kɔːˈpɔːriəl/ adj. *I have food and shelter to look after my corporeal needs, but I wish there were some good libraries here!* = related to the body and not the spirit or mind (formal)

corps /kɔːʳ/ noun, c. (used with singular or plural verb) *the National Cadet Corps (NCC)* = a trained group of people

corpse /kɔːps/ noun, c. = the dead body of a human being

cor•pu•lent /ˈkɔːpjʊlənt/ adj.= very fat (formal)

cor•pus /ˈkɔːpəs/ noun, c. (**corpora**) **1** *a corpus of Urdu plays* = a collection of writings of a special kind **2** *Our dictionary is based on a corpus of one million words.* = the material on which a piece of work is based [TECHNICAL]

cor•pus•cle /ˈkɔːpəsəl/ noun, c. *white and red blood corpuscles* = the red or white cells which make up the blood

cor•rect[1] /kəˈrekt/ verb, t. *I'd like you to correct me when I make a mistake.* = to point out and set right a mistake

correct[2] adj. **1** *This is the correct answer.* = without a mistake; based on facts **2** *Although he was very correct in his behaviour, we found him very unfriendly.* = according to rules or customs **correction** noun, u. or c. = the act of correcting

cor•re•la•tion /kɒrɪˈleɪʃən/ noun, u. *Doctors believe that there may be a correlation between smoking and cancer of the lungs.* = a shared relation of cause and effect between two separate things **correlate** verb, t. = to show that there is a correlation between two things (e.g. smoking and lung cancer)

cor•re•spond /kɒrɪˈspɒnd/ verb, i. **1** *This blue spot on the map corresponds to the lake that you now see.* = to be in agreement with; to match **2** *Have you been corresponding regularly with your brother in Germany?* = to exchange letters with

cor•re•spon•dent /kɒrɪˈspɒndənt/ noun, c. **1** *She is a good correspondent but she has not written to me recently.* = someone with whom one regularly exchanges letters **2** *a newspaper correspondent* = one who writes regularly for a newspaper

cor•re•spon•ding /kɒrɪˈspɒndɪŋ/ adj. *With the coming of summer, there was a corresponding scarcity of water.* = happening at the same time in a way that is related; matching

cor•ri•dor /ˈkɒrɪdɔːʳ/ noun, c. **1** = a passage between two rows or rooms or connecting two buildings **2** = a narrow piece of land that stretches out into another country

cor•rob•o•rate /kəˈrɒbəreɪt/ verb, t. *The report was quite correct and was corroborated by a few other people.* = to provide further proof or support for something that was said or reported earlier, with some proof being given (formal)

cor•rode /kəˈrəʊd/ verb, t. *The steel body of the old ship has been badly corroded by sea-water.* = the slow wearing away and destruction of metal by the action of some chemical, over a period of time **corrosion** noun, u. = the process by which something gets corroded **corrosive** adj. = something that causes corrosion

cor•ru•ga•ted /ˈkɒrəgeɪtɪd/ adj. *a sheet of corrugated iron* = something that has long rows of wave-like folds

cor•rupt[1] /kəˈrʌpt/ adj. *a corrupt organisation* = bad and dishonest, specially in matters concerning money

corrupt[2] verb, t. or i. *Power can corrupt good people.*(t.) = to make someone dishonest and bad; to spoil **corrupted** adj. = of a computer hard disk, floppy disk etc., to have parts which are damaged or not working **corruption** noun, c. = the state of being corrupt

cor•tege /kɔːˈteɪʒ/ noun = a funeral procession

cor•ti•sone /ˈkɔːtɪzəʊn/ noun = a powerful substance used as a medicine, usually for stiffness and pain in the muscles and joints

cos•met•ic[1] /kɒzˈmetɪk/ noun, c. (usually plural) (**cosmetics**) = a substance (e.g. powder, eyeliner, lipstick) which is intended to improve a person's looks

cosmetic[2] adj. **1** *a cosmetic lotion* = something that has the quality of a cosmetic **2** *This old house has not been repaired and still leaks. The owners have only made a few cosmetic changes.* = dealing only with the outward appearance and not the real problem

cos•mo•pol•i•tan /kɒzməˈpɒlɪtən/ adj. *Mumbai is probably India's most cosmopolitan city. You find people from all parts of the country living and working here.* = consisting of people from different parts of the country or the world

cos•mos /ˈkɒzmɒs/ noun = the solar system (the

C

sun, stars and planets) and the entire universe considered as an ordered system ruled by scientific laws **cosmic** adj. *Some astrologers claim that they can control the stars, planets and other cosmic forces.* = relating to the cosmos (universe) **cosmonaut** noun, c. = a person who travels through space in a spaceship (also **astronaut**)

cos•set /ˈkɒsɪt/ verb, t. *They have cossetted the dog so much that it cannot feed itself.* = to give too much attention or care to a person or animal (disapproving)

cost[1] /kɒst/ noun, c. or u. **1** *The cost of petrol has gone up again.*(u.) = the amount of money that one has to pay for something; price **2** *Our costs have come down and so we can lower our prices.*(c.) = the amount of money that one has to spend in manufacturing (making) something **3** *He saved the children from the fire at the cost of his own life.*(u.) = something that one has to give up in order to save someone or to get something else

cost[2] verb, t. **1** *This shirt costs Rs 300.* = to have a price of **2** *He will tell you next week how much we will have to spend on the repairs. He will have to cost everything first.* (t.) = to calculate the cost of something **cost-effective** adj. *It will not be cost-effective to make these shirts in Chennai. We can get them made more cheaply in Gandhinagar.* = having as low a cost as possible in order to get the highest profit or benefit **costly** adj. = having a high cost

at all costs (always plural) *She must pass this test at all costs, otherwise she can't get her licence.* = so important that it must be done **to cost the earth (to cost an arm and a leg)** *It cost us the earth to get the house repaired.* = to require a large sum of money (informal) **to count the cost** = to be aware of the benefits as well as risks before one undertakes something **to sell/buy something at cost** = at the price at which something is made/manufactured, that is, without a margin of profit

co-star[1] /ˈkəʊ stɑːʳ/ noun, c. *Shah Rukh Khan has Kajol as his co-star in this film.* = a famous actor or actress who appears together with another famous actor in a film or television programme

co-star[2] verb, i. *Kajol and Shah Rukh Khan co-star in this film.* = to appear together in a film

cos•tume /ˈkɒstjʊm/ noun, u. or c. **1** *At the Republic Day celebrations, the children wore the traditional costumes of the different states of India.* = the clothes or dress typical of a country or time **2** *The costumes in this film are of the 16th century.* = the clothes worn by actors in a film, play or other performance **costume jewellery** noun, u. = jewellery made from cheap materials but looking very expensive

co•sy /ˈkəʊzi/ adj. *a cosy room in a corner of the house* = comfortable and giving a feeling of being friendly

cot /kɒt/ noun, c. **1** = a light bed which can be carried easily **2** abbr. for **cotangent** [TRIGONOMETRY]

co•te•rie /ˈkəʊtəri/ noun, c. *a coterie of writers* = a small, close group of people with common interests

cot•tage /ˈkɒtɪdʒ/ noun, c. = a small house in the countryside, usually away from the city **cottage industry** noun, u. or c. (**industries**) = an industry which can be set up by a few people, working with simple tools, and does not require a large factory, heavy machines etc.

cot•ton /ˈkɒtn/ noun, u. = the soft white fibre (hair-like substance) produced by the cotton plant, from which cotton cloth is made

couch[1] /kaʊtʃ/ noun, c. (**couches**) = sofa; a long,comfortable seat with a back and sometimes arms

couch[2] verb, i. *The letter was couched in friendly language.* = to express in a certain kind of language, usually in writing (formal)

cou•gar /ˈkuːgəʳ/ noun, c. = a kind of lion found in North and South America (also **puma** or **mountain lion**)

cough[1] /kɒf/ verb, i. **1** *The child has been coughing all night.* = to push out air noisily and with force through the throat, usually because of some discomfort in the throat **2** *They expected me to cough up the money for the celebration.* = to be forced to pay all the expenses for something (informal, disapproving)

cough[2] noun, u. or c. **1** *He has a bad cough.* = an illness which leads to frequent coughing **2** *I heard a soft cough behind me.* = the sound of coughing, usually produced to attract someone's attention in a polite way

could /kəd/ aux. verb (past tense of **can**) **1** *He could sing very well when he was young.* = was able to (in the past) **2** *You could have helped me (but you didn't).* = it was possible **3** *I could pay you back if I had some money.* = be able to do something if some condition is met **4** *Could you give me some water?* = a request which is made with some hesitation

coun•cil /ˈkaʊnsəl/ noun, c. (used with singular or plural verbs) *the Council of Ministers* = a group of people with the power to make laws and take important decisions

coun•sel[1] /ˈkaʊnsəl/ noun, c. **1** = a lawyer who acts for someone in a court of law **2** = advice (old-fashioned or literary)

counsel[2] verb, t. = to advise **counsellor** noun, c.= advisor

count[1] /kaʊnt/ verb, i. or t. **1** *The child has learnt to count upto twenty.*(i.) = to say the numbers in the correct order **2** *Please count the number of children who are present in the class.*(t.) = to find the total number of objects or people in a group **3** *We were thirty, counting the driver of the bus.*(t.) = including **4** *You didn't do what I advised you to do. Maybe what I say doesn't count.*(i.) = to not be important, valuable or worth taking note of; not to be added e.g. points or goals in a game **5** *In this word-game, every word you make with the letters 'q', 'x' and 'z' counts as an extra point.*(t.) = to have a certain value

count[2] noun, u. or plural **1** *At the last count, there were 55 people in the building.*(u.) = an act of adding **2** (always plural) *He was tried in court but found innocent on all counts.* = in respect of every charge or accusation [LAW] **3** (always plural) *It was a pity that the new car which the company manufactured failed on all counts.* = in all ways **countable** adj. = which can be counted

to count on *I am not going to have much help at the meeting and am counting on yours.* = to depend on; to trust **to count (oneself) lucky, fortunate etc.** = to believe and be thankful that one is lucky etc. **to lose count of something** *I have lost count of the number of times I have missed the bus.* = to do something very often (referring to some action that causes some loss or harm) **to count one's chickens before they are hatched** = to think of the gains from doing something even before one has done enough to expect such gains

countdown /'kaʊntdaʊn/ noun = the act of counting backwards in seconds (e.g. from ten to zero) to mark an important event e.g. the firing of a rocket

coun•te•nance[1] /'kaʊntɪnəns/ noun, c. = face [LITERARY]

countenance[2] verb, t. *I cannot countenance such bad behaviour.* = to accept or tolerate (formal)

counter- /'kɒuntə^r/ prefix used with an adjective, noun or verb **1** working against something and preventing it from happening e.g. **counter-productive** adj. *If you force him to work harder, your effort will be counter-productive. He will stop working.* = something which produces an effect opposite to what was intended or planned **2** to act against something harmful and prevent it from happening e.g. **counteract** verb, t. *This medicine will counteract the effect of the poison.* = to act against **3** an equally strong etc. response to something e.g. **counter-attack** noun, c. = an attack on an enemy made in reply to an attack by the enemy **4** something that is attached to or matches something else e.g. **counterfoil** noun, c. = a part of a printed receipt, cheque etc. which is torn off and kept as a record **5** an equal who has the same job or position in another group, system, company etc. e.g. **counterpart** noun, c. *General Malik, the chief of the Indian army, is meeting General Musharraf, his counterpart in the Pakistan army.* = a person who is of the same rank, or doing the same job as another person, but in a different place

count•er[1] /kaʊntə^r/ noun, c. **1** *the ticket counter* = a long, narrow table in a shop or office where things are kept for sale or where money is paid **2** *a counter in the game of Ludo* = a small, thin, round, coloured piece of plastic which a player moves on a board or uses in place of money in certain games

counter[2] verb, t. *counter an argument* = to take some action to oppose or defend oneself against something

counter[3] adj. or adv. *Everything they did went counter to my advice.* = opposite to or against

coun•ter•feit[1] /'kaʊntəfɪt/ adj. *a counterfeit coin* = (something which is) made as a copy of something else, in order to cheat someone

counterfeit[2] verb, t. = to make a copy of something in order to cheat someone

coun•ter•sign /'kaʊntəsaɪn/ verb, t. or i. *The Secretary has signed this cheque and now the President has to countersign it.* = to sign a paper aready signed by someone else in order to make it legal or effective

count(able) noun = a noun which refers to things which can be counted, and which generally has a plural as well as singular form e.g. boy/boys (opposite **uncountable**) [GRAMMAR]

coun•try[1] /'kʌntri/ noun, c. or u. (**countries**) **1** *Laos is a country in Asia.*(c.) = an area of land with its own government, national flag, laws etc. **2** *We want to get out of the city and spend some time in the country.*(u.) = open land outside a town or city **3** *Maharashtra is cotton country.*(u.) = an area which has a special quality or is known for something

country[2] adj. *a country house* = related to the country, not a town or city

coun•try•man (country-person) /'kʌntrimən/ noun, c. (**-men**) = someone who belongs to the same country as another person

coun•try•side /'kʌntrɪsaɪd/ noun, u. = open land outside a town or city

coup /kuː/ noun, c. (French) *Of the two groups in the City Council, one was in favour of a shopping centre while the other wanted a park. Finally, the second group staged a coup and got the park approved.* = a clever action or move that brings success or victory **coup d' etat** /kuːdeɪ'tɑː/ noun (French) = a sudden change of government through the use of force

cou•ple[1] /'kʌpəl/ noun, c. **1** *a loving couple* = husband and wife **2** *This house has a couple of bedrooms.* = two (informal) **3** *I had a couple of drinks.* = a few

couple[2] verb, i. or t. *The two railway carriages were* *coupled.* = to join together; to connect

coup•ling /ˈkʌplɪŋ/ noun, c. **1** = a device that joins two things, specially two railway carriages, together **2** = an act of sexual union

coup•let /ˈkʌplɪt/ noun, c. = a pair of lines in a poem which rhyme (end with the same sound) and usually contain a complete idea

cou•pon /ˈkuːpɒn/ noun, c. *You can use this coupon to get a cup of tea at the canteen.* = a ticket that one purchases and uses later to obtain something, instead of making payment in cash

cour•age /ˈkʌrɪdʒ/ noun, u. *We admired her courage in fighting the terrible disease.*= the quality of being brave, having no fear **courageous** adj. = brave

cou•ri•er[1] /ˈkʊrieʳ/ noun, c. = a person or company which carries letters, papers, parcels etc. from one place to another on payment

courier[2] verb, t. = to send a letter etc. through a courier

course[1] /kɔːs/ noun, c. **1** *Let us follow the course of the river.* = the path along which someone or something moves **2** *In the course of the year we learnt many new things.* = the passage of time **3** *a course of lectures* = a set of **4** *a four-course dinner* = a dish (preparation of food) served as a part of a meal

course[2] adv. *Of course you can come!* = certainly

court[1] /kɔːt/ noun, u. or c. **1** = a place where law cases are heard and judged **2** *The lawyer addressed the court.*(u.) = judge **3** *a badminton court*(c.) = an area marked off by lines for the playing of certain games **4** *Emperor Akbar's court*(c.) = the officials who served a king or queen in former times (also **courtiers**)

court[2] verb, t. **1** *He is courting us in order to get some favour.* = to pay special attention to someone in order to get something out of him/her **2** *You are courting danger by riding on the steps of the crowded bus.* = to risk by taking unnecessary chances **3** = (said of a man) to try hard to get a woman to agree to marry one (old-fashioned)

court-mar•tial[1] /kɔːt ˈmɑːʃəl/ noun, c. (**courts-martial** or **court-martials**) = a military court which tries people belonging to the armed forces

court-martial[2] verb, t. = to try someone in a court-martial

court•yard /ˈkɔːtjɑːd/ noun, c. = an open space in the middle of a house, with walls on all sides

cour•te•ous /ˈkɜːtiəs/ adj. = showing courtesy; very polite

cour•te•sy /ˈkɜːtɪsi/ noun, u.= polite and kind behaviour

cous•in /ˈkʌzən/ noun, c. = the son or daughter of an uncle or aunt

cov•e•nant /ˈkʌvənənt/ noun, u. = a formal agreement between two or more people

cov•er[1] /ˈkʌvəʳ/ verb, t. or i. **1** *We use this piece of cloth to cover the table.*(t.) = to place something on top of some object in order to protect or hide it **2** *A thick layer of dust covered the furniture.*(t.) = to lie along the surface of something **3** *This book covers the recent war in Bosnia.*(t.) = to deal with **4** *We covered the distance from Delhi to Agra in two hours.*(t.) = to go from one place to another **5** *It is almost the end of the year and we haven't covered all the topics we are supposed to study.*(t.) = to teach or learn, as part of a list **6** *When our history teacher was absent, another teacher covered for her.*(i.) = to take someone's place temporarily and do her/his work (informal) **7** *Your car is not covered for accidental damage.*(i.) = insured

cover[2] noun, c. or u. **1** *a bed-cover*(c.) = something that protects by covering **2** *the cover of a book* = the front or back page of a book or magazine **3** *It is raining. Let us take cover under this tree.*(u.) = shelter **coverage** noun, u. *The newspaper gave excellent coverage of the cricket match.*= the amount of space given by a newspaper to reports of a particular event **covering letter** noun, c. = a letter sent with another letter or an application etc. to explain it or to give additional information

under cover of *The thieves escaped under cover of darkness.* = hidden by **to cover up something** *You don't have to cover up your mistakes. We understand why you made them.* = to hide in order to stop something bad from becoming known **to cover up** *It's cold outside. You had better cover up well.* = dress well in order to protect oneself from cold weather **to take cover** *It is raining, let us take cover.* = to find shelter

cov•ert /ˈkʌvət/ adj. *He has a covert fear of crowds.* = something that one does not express or do openly; hidden (opposite **overt**)

co•vet /ˈkʌvɪt/ verb, t. *covet someone's job* = to want strongly to possess things, specially things that belong to others **covetous** adj. = always wanting to possess things; greedy

cow[1] /kaʊ/ noun, c. = a fully grown, female farm animal

cow[2] verb, t. *Don't be cowed by their threats.* = to be frightened (informal)

cow•ard /ˈkaʊəd/ noun, c. *She may seem to be a coward, but in fact she is brave.* = a person who has no courage and is always afraid **cowardice** noun, u. = the quality of being cowardly or showing cowardly behaviour **cowardly** adj. = having the qualities of a coward

cow•boy /ˈkaʊbɔɪ/ noun = a person who works on a farm where there are a lot of cows (specially in

America) and looks after them

cow•er /ˈkaʊəʳ/ verb, i. *Our dog is afraid of this man and always cowers before him.* = to bend low and draw back in fear or shame

cow•herd /ˈkaʊhɜːd/ noun = a person who looks after a herd (large group) of cows while they are grazing (roaming about in the fields and eating grass)

cow•rie /ˈkaʊri/ noun, c. (**cowries**) = the shell (outer covering) of a small sea-animal that was used as money in the old days

cox /kɒks/ noun, c. = a person who guides and controls a rowing boat, specially during a race

coy /kɔɪ/ adj. *coy behaviour* = pretending to be shy (used for a woman) Ⓖ

co•zy adj. see **cosy**

CPU abbr. of **Central Processing Unit** noun = the brain of a computer that deals with information

crab /kræb/ noun, c. or u. **1** (c.) = a small sea animal with a thick shell and five pairs of legs **2** (u.) = the flesh of a crab

crab

crack[1] /kræk/ verb, t. **1** *The cup will crack if you pour boiling water into it.* = to break without splitting into parts **2** *crack a joke* = to tell a joke (informal) **3** *His voice cracked as he told us the sad part of the story.* = a sudden change in the tone or loudness of a person's voice

crack[2] noun, c. **1** *There is a crack in the glass.* = a line showing where something hard has broken without splitting into parts **2** *a crack of thunder* = a loud sound **3** *We made so many cracks about her voice that she is feeling hurt.* = a quick, usually unkind, joke **4** *a crack on the head* = a blow **5** = a very pure form of the addictive drug **cocaine** (slang) **cracked** adj. = a little mad (informal)

at the crack of dawn = very early in the morning **to have a crack at something** *I have never played this game before, but I'm going to have a crack at it.* = to attempt (informal) **to crack up** *It is true that you have problems, but if you don't calm down, you will crack up.* = to lose control over one's mind and body (informal) **to get cracking** *We don't have much time left to study, so let's get cracking.* = to start working hard suddenly and with determination (informal) **to crack down on someone or something** *The police cracked down on the gang of thieves.* = to take sudden and strong action to stop an illegal activity

crack•er /ˈkrækəʳ/ noun, c. **1** = a kind of biscuit made without sugar **2** = one of the different kinds of fireworks normally used on festive occasions which bursts with a loud sound when it is lit

crack•le /ˈkrækəl/ verb, i. *The fire is crackling.* = the sharp sound produced by burning wood or coal

crack•pot /ˈkrækpɒt/ noun, c. = a person who has strange or foolish ideas (informal)

cra•dle[1] /ˈkreɪdl/ noun, c. **1** = a small bed for a baby **2** *India is one of the cradles of human civilization.* = the place where something begins

cradle[2] verb, t. *The mother cradled the baby in her arms.* = to hold gently

craft /krɑːft/ noun, u. or c. **1** *He is learning the carpenter's craft.*(c.) = trade; work that needs skill **2** *He used a lot of craft to make us buy the expensive table.*(u.) = clever behaviour which is intended to mislead or deceive (disapproving) **3** (plural **craft**) = a boat, ship or airplane **crafts** noun (always plural) *arts and crafts* = traditional things, made usually with one's hands **crafts(wo)man (crafts person)** noun, c. = a highly skilled worker

-craft /ˈkrɑːft/ suffix used **1** to name a vehicle e.g. **aircraft, spacecraft** and **2** with a special skill e.g. **stagecraft, metal craft**

craft•y /ˈkrɑːfti/ adj. = clever and able to cheat (derogatory) **craftsmanship** noun, u. = the skill used in making something beautiful by hand

crag /kræg/ noun, c. = a high rock

cram /kræm/ verb, t. or i. **1** *Twelve people were crammed into a taxi.*(t.) = to crowd or force someone or something into a small space **2** *It is not a good idea to cram for the examination.*(i.) = to prepare for an examination by getting things by heart (informal)

cramp[1] /kræmp/ noun, c. *He is suffering from a cramp in the leg.* = severe pain from the sudden tightening of a muscle, which makes movement difficult

cramp[2] verb, t. *We are cramping his talent by not listening to his ideas.* = to limit or restrict something; to prevent something or someone from developing or growing **cramps** noun (always plural) = great pain in the stomach **cramped** adj. *a cramped room* = having very little space

crane[1] /kreɪn/ noun, c. **1** = a machine that is used to lift heavy weights **2** = a water-bird with long legs and a long neck

crane[2] verb, t. *He craned his neck to get a better view of the parade.* = to stretch out one's neck in order to get a better view

cra•ni•um /ˈkreɪnɪəm/ noun, c. = the skull; the round, hollow bone at the top of the head that protects the brain [MEDICINE]

crank[1] /kræŋk/ noun, c. **1** = a handle used to turn a wheel; a part of a machine which changes forward-and-backward movement in a straight line into a circular movement **2** *She had some wonderful ideas* *but most people did not listen to her because they thought she was a crank.* = a person with strange but strong ideas on some subject (informal, not respectful)

crank[2] verb, t. *Let us crank up this old car.* = to start an engine by turning a crank (handle) **cranky** adj. *The child is becoming cranky.* = bad-tempered (informal)

crap /kræp/ noun, u. **1** = solid waste from the bowels (slang) **2** *You are talking absolute crap!* = nonsense (slang)

crash[1] /kræʃ/ verb, i. or t. **1** *The plane crashed into a high mountain.*(i.) = to have an accident by striking something noisily and with force **2** *If we go so fast we'll crash the car.*(t.) = to cause a noisy accident **3** *The waves crashed against the rocks.*(i.) = to hit something noisily and with force **4** *The bank has crashed.*(i.) = to suffer great loss of money or the failure of business **5** *The computer has crashed.*(i.) = to stop working **6** *The buffaloes crashed through the sugarcane fields.*(i.) = to walk noisily, destroying things in one's path

crash[2] noun, c. or u. **1** *a plane crash*(c.) = a violent accident **2** *We heard the crash of thunder.*(u.) = loud noise **crash course** noun, c. *We are doing a crash course in Japanese.* = a course of study which has to be completed in a very short time and therefore needs great effort by students **crash-helmet** noun = a strong covering for the head worn by motor-cyclists to protect the head in case of an accident

crass /kræs/ adj. *Those crass remarks of yours really hurt us.* = showing no respect for the feelings of others; coarse

crate[1] /kreɪt/ noun, c. *a crate of soft drinks* = a box used to carry bottles containing some liquid

crate[2] verb, t. *We will have to crate these bottles.* = to pack into crates

cra•ter /'kreɪtə^r/ noun, c. **1** = the round and hollow mouth of a volcano **2** = a deep hole in the ground made by a heavy falling object or bomb

crave /'kreɪv/ verb, t. or i. **1** *The doctor has put her on a diet, so she is craving for food.*(i.) = to have an uncontrollable desire to eat, smoke, or to drink something, especially something which is bad for one **2** *He hasn't smoked for a month, so he craves a cigarette.*(t.) = to have a very strong desire for something (usually something that is harmful) **3** *We crave your presence at the meeting.*(t.) = request deeply (old-fashioned, formal/sarcastic) **craving** noun, u. or c. *He had a strong craving for sweets when he was on a diet.* = very strong, uncontrollable desire for something

crawl[1] /krɔːl/ verb, i. **1** *The baby is beginning to crawl.* = to move very slowly on one's hands and knees **2** *Your kitchen is crawling with cockroaches.* = to be full of something unpleasant

crawl[2] noun, u. *The cars are moving at a crawl.* = very slow speed

cray•on /'kreɪən/ noun, c. = a stick of soft coloured chalk used for painting pictures

craze /kreɪz/ noun, u. *This new song has become a craze among young people.* = something that suddenly becomes very popular or fashionable, but only for a short time (informal) **crazy** adj. **1** *You must be crazy if you think I am going to see the film again.* = slightly mad or stupid (informal) **2** *She is crazy about Hindi films.* = deeply fond of something (informal) **crazily** adv.

creak[1] /kriːk/ verb, i. *The doors are creaking because no one has put oil in the hinges.* = to make the sound that a badly-oiled door makes when it is opened

creak[2] noun, c. *The door opened slowly with a loud creak.* = the sound made by a creaking door **creaky** adj. = making a creaking sound

cream[1] /kriːm/ noun, u. **1** = the solid layer, containing fat, that rises to the top of milk after it has been boiled **2** *The cream of India's scientists once worked in this laboratory.* = the best

cream[2] verb, t. *We have to cream the milk.* = to remove the layer of cream

cream[3] adj. *He was wearing a cream silk shirt.* = of the colour of cream (very light yellow) **cold cream** noun, u. = a thick, sweet-smelling substance used mostly by women to protect the skin during winter

crease[1] /kriːs/ noun, c. **1** *His trousers have been freshly ironed and the creases are very sharp.* = the lines made in cloth or paper by pressing with a hot iron, folding etc. **2** *The batsman was inside his crease and was declared not out.* = a line drawn in front of the wicket, in the game of cricket, marking the area within which a batsman is allowed to move

crease[2] verb, i. or t. *This dress creases very easily.*(i.) = to become pressed into folds or creases

cre•ate /kri'eɪt/ verb, t. *Who created the universe? // You have created a new high jump record.* = to produce something that was not there before

cre•a•tion /kri'eɪʃən/ noun, c. or u. **1** *This painting is my daughter's creation.* = something, particularly a work of art, which has been created (made) **2** *Poets know the pains of creation.*(u.) = the process by which something is created. **creative** adj. = having the imagination or skill required to create something **creator** noun, c. = God; someone who creates something **creativity** /krɪəɪ'tɪvɪtɪ/ noun, u. = the ability to produce something beautiful by using one's imagination or skill

crea•ture /'kriːtʃə^r/ noun, c.= something that is living **creature comforts** noun (always plural) = the things that make life comfortable

crè•che /kreʃ/ noun, c. = a place where very young children are looked after while their parents are working

cre•den•tials /krɪˈdenʃəlz/ noun, c. (always plural) *The police will check your credentials before letting you in.* = papers which provide proof of a person's identity (name, position etc.)

cred•i•ble /ˈkredɪbəl/ adj. *Your report on the incident seems quite credible.* = something or someone that can be believed **credibility** /kredɪˈbɪlɪti/ noun, u. *We always say we'll finish our work in time but never do. Our credibility is in doubt.* = the quality of being credible (worthy of being believed)

cred•it[1] /ˈkredɪt/ noun, u. or c. **1** *If you don't have enough money to buy the car, you can get it on credit.*(u.) = a system which allows one to buy something and pay for it later **2** *He has Rs 5000 to his credit.*(u.) = the amount of money a person has in a bank **3** *She deserves credit for training the basketball team.*(u.) = praise **4** *You will earn five credits for completing this course successfully.*(c.) = a measure of the work completed by a student at an American university

credit[2] verb, t. **1** *Please credit this money to my bank account.* = to deposit (put) money in one's bank account **2** *What you are saying is difficult to credit. It sounds impossible.* = to believe **3** *Do you think I would do something so stupid? You should credit me with some commonsense.* = to accept that someone has some good quality

cred•i•ta•ble /ˈkredɪtəbəl/ adj. *The child has been ill but her performance at school has been quite creditable.* = good; something that deserves praise

cred•i•tor /ˈkredɪtəʳ/ noun = a person to whom one owes money

credit card noun = a plastic card which can be checked by a computer and allows one to get things on credit and pay for them later through a bank

cred•u•lous /ˈkredjʊləs/ adj. *a very credulous person* = one who is very willing or ready to believe things (disapproving)

creed /kri:d/ noun, c. **1** *Anyone can be a member of the Citizen's Action Group, regardless of their creed.* = the system of beliefs and principles which one follows **2** = religion and religious beliefs

creek /kri:k/ noun, c. = a small body of water (pond or lake)

creep[1] /kri:p/ verb, i. *The snake was creeping across the field.* = moving with the body close to the ground

creep[2] noun, c. = a person who is not liked because she/he offers false praise in the hope of getting favours (slang) **creeps** noun (always plural) *The dark cave gave me the creeps.* = a feeling of fear (informal) **to make one's flesh creep** to have a feeling of fear or dislike (informal)

creep•er /ˈkri:pəʳ/ noun, c. = a plant which climbs up trees or walls or grows along the ground

cre•mate /krɪˈmeɪt/ verb, t. = to burn the body of a dead person **cremation** noun, u. or c. = the ceremony of burning a dead person

crem•a•to•ri•um /kreməˈtɔ:riəm/ = a building in which dead people are cremated

cre•ole /ˈkri:əʊl/ noun, c. **1** = a language which is a mixture of a European language (e.g. English or French) and some other language, used in some parts of the world **2** = a person of mixed European and African blood

cre•scen•do /krɪˈʃendəʊ/ noun, u. *The sound of the music rose to a crescendo.* = a gradual increase in force or loudness (of music)

cres•cent /ˈkresənt/ noun, c. or adj. *the crescent moon* (adj.) = a curved shape which is part of a circle, like that of the moon at certain times of the month (see pic under **shapes**)

crest /krest/ noun, c. **1** = the bright feathers growing on top of a bird's head **2** *the crest of the hill* = the top (of a hill etc.) **3** *the University crest* = a special printed sign used on the top of letters etc.

crest•fal•len /ˈkrestfɔ:lən/ adj. *He looks completely crestfallen after losing the election.* = disappointed; sad

crev•ice /ˈkrevɪs/ noun, c. = a narrow crack or opening in a rock

crew /kru:/ noun, c. (used with singular or plural verb) = the group of people who work on a ship or aircraft **crew cut** noun = hair which has been cut very short

crib[1] /krɪb/ noun, c. = a bed for a baby or a very young child

crib[2] verb, i. = to copy from someone else during an examination (slang)

crick /krɪk/ noun, c. *I have a crick in my neck and I can't turn my head.* = a painful condition of the neck or back which makes movement difficult

crick•et /ˈkrɪkɪt/ noun, u. **1** = an outdoor game brought to India by the British, played between teams of 11 players **2** = a small insect which makes a loud noise by rubbing its wings together **cricketer** noun = a cricket player

crime /kraɪm/ noun, c. or u. = an action which is against the law and for doing which one can be punished **criminal** noun, c. = a person who has committed a crime **criminal act** noun, c. = an act which is considered to be a crime **criminal law** noun = the laws related to crime and the punishment of crime

crim•son /'krɪmzən/ adj. = of a deep red colour

cringe /krɪndʒ/ verb, i. **1** *The dog was afraid of me and cringed when I went near it.* = to bend low and move back out of fear **2** *You should behave with dignity and not cringe before the boss.* = to show too much respect to someone who is important or powerful (disapproving)

crin•kle[1] /'krɪŋkəl/ verb, i. or t. **1** *The letter had been read by so many people, folded and unfolded so many times, that it had got crinkled and was difficult to read.* = to become covered with many fine lines or folds **2** *The baby crinkled its eyes.* = to make the eyes look smaller or narrower, usually to express happiness

crinkle[2] noun, c. = a fine line or fold which forms on paper or cloth that has been crushed (pressed many times) **crinkly** adj. *crinkly paper* = having many crinkles (folds)

crip•ple[1] /'krɪpəl/ noun, c. = a person who has lost the use of one or more limbs (arms and legs)

cripple[2] verb, t. **1** *The accident crippled him, but he is as energetic as ever.* = to make someone a cripple **2** *The rains have failed and crippled agriculture in this region.* = to damage or harm seriously

cri•sis /'kraɪsɪs/ noun, c. (**crises**) *Even when they were going through a crisis they looked cheerful.* = a time of great danger or uncertainty

crisp[1] /krɪsp/ adj. **1** *The biscuits are crisp.* = stiff, hard and brittle (easy to break into pieces) **2** = (of paper money, sheets of paper, starched fabric) stiff, bright and clean **3** = (of fruit and vegetables) hard in a way which shows freshness and high quality **4** *a crisp style* = (of writing) achieving a good effect using very few words; (of speaking) clear, brief and not very friendly

crisp[2] noun, c. (usually plural) = a thin slice of fried potato which is hard and can break

cri•te•ri•on /kraɪ'tɪəriən/ noun, c. (**criteria**) *The most important criterion for selecting officers for the army is physical fitness.* = a standard by which one judges something or someone

crit•ic /'krɪtɪk/ noun, c. **1** *He is a well-known film critic.* = a person who is an expert on some subject (e.g. music, films etc.) and whose views and opinions on the subject, published in books, magazines or newspapers, are respected **2** *She is one of your worst critics.* = a person who finds fault with someone **critical** adj. **1** *Her critical opinions are greatly respected.* = relating to opinions or judgements about both the good and bad qualities of something **2** *I know I am very critical of the books you write but I am only trying to help.* = finding fault with **3** *The patient is in a critical condition.* = a situation in which there is danger and risk and things could either improve or get worse **4** *The nuclear reactor has gone critical.* = (of a nuclear reactor) in a condition in which, once started, chain reactions occur on their own [PHYSICS] **critically** adv.

crit•i•cis•m /'krɪtɪsɪzəm/ noun, u. or c. **1** *We are studying the history of literary criticism.* = judgement passed on a work of art by a critic **2** *Some criticism is good but too much will make us feel discouraged.* = unfavourable judgement or opinion **criticize (criticise)** verb, t. **1** *They criticized my style of dressing.* = to point out the bad points of something **2** *I asked her to criticize my acting.* = to make a judgement about both the good and bad points of something

cri•tique /krɪ'ti:k/ noun, u. = a piece of writing in a book or magazine which makes a judgement of some writer's work

croak[1] /krəʊk/ verb, i. *The frogs are croaking after the rain.* = to make the deep, hoarse cracking noise made by frogs

croak[2] noun, c. **1** = the sound that a frog makes **2** = to die (slang, not respectful)

crock•e•ry /'krɒkəri/ noun, u. = cups, plates, dishes, etc. made of glass or china clay

croc•o•dile /'krɒkədaɪl/ noun, c. = a large reptile (animal belonging to the lizard family) with very thick skin that lives in rivers or lakes **crocodile tears** noun (always plural) *Don't shed crocodile tears, we know you are not really sad.* = a false show of grief

crook /krʊk/ noun, c. **1** *The police were on the trail of the crooks for a long time.* = a dishonest person or a criminal (informal) **2** *He held the walking stick in the crook of his arm.* = a point where there is a bend **crooked** adj. **1** *a crooked road* = full of bends and turns; not straight **2** *a crooked person* = dishonest

croon /kru:n/ verb, t. or i. *The mother was crooning to her baby.*(i.) = a style of singing in which the voice is soft and low **crooner** noun, c.

crop[1] /krɒp/ noun, c. **1** *We grow three crops of rice on this land every year.* = a product (e.g. wheat) grown on land **2** = the quantity of wheat, rice, coffee etc. produced at a time on a person's land **3** *The barber gave me a crop.* = hair cut very short **4** = a whip used by horse-riders

crop[2] verb, t. **1** *The tea bushes are cropped every year.* = to cut the top of some plant **2** *He had his hair cropped.* = to cut very short

crore /krɔ:r/ noun, c. = a number represented by 10,000,000 (ten million), in use in India and Pakistan

cross[1] /krɒs/ noun, c. (**crosses**) **1** a mark made by drawing one line across another, in the shape **+** or **X**, often used to show that something is incorrect

2 = anything which has this shape **3** = the symbol (sign) of the Christian religion (often capital) **4** = a medal in the form of a cross given to soldiers for courage in war **5** *This dog is a cross between an Alsatian and a Doberman.* = a mixture of two different kinds of animals or plants

cross[2] adj. *My brother was cross when I woke him up from deep sleep.* = angry in a way that is not serious

cross[3] verb, t. or i. **1** *Don't cross the road now. It is dangerous to do so.*(t.) = to go across (from one side to the other) **2** *The two roads cross each other.*(t.) = to meet and continue on the other side **3** *I waved when my friend and I crossed each other on the pavement.*(i.) = to walk in the opposite direction to someone **4** *When I make a mistake in my written work, I cross it out and write the word or words again.*(t.) = to draw a line across something written to show that it is a mistake **5** *Please don't cross me now. I'm in a bad mood.*(t.) = to oppose someone (say or do something against his/her wish) **6** (t.) = (in worship etc.) to make the sign of the cross **7** = to make a symbol of two parallel lines in the top left corner of a cheque to show that money is to be paid into someone's bank account and not directly **8** *The two kinds of rice have been crossed to produce a new variety of rice.*(i.) = to breed (unite) one kind of animal or plant with a different kind of animal or plant so as to produce a new kind of animal or plant **crossly** adv. **crossbreed** noun, c. = an animal or plant produced by crossing two different kinds of animals or plants **cross-country** adj. or adv. **1** *a cross-country race*(adj.) = a race across open country or fields **2** *They ran cross-country* (adv.) **cross-examine** verb, t. *The defending lawyer will cross-examine the witness.* = to question a witness in court for the second time, after he/she has already been questioned once by the lawyer for the other side **cross-eyed** adj. = unable to focus both eyes on some object (also **squint-eyed**) (informal, disrespectful) **cross-check** verb, t. *I am not sure the information you have given me is correct. I must cross-check with someone else.* = to become certain aboout the correctness of something by checking from one or more sources **cross-legged** adv. *sitting cross-legged* = sitting with the legs folded and one leg placed across the other **crossroads** noun, c. (always plural) **1** = a place where two roads cross each other **2** = a point at which a difficult decision must be taken **cross-section** noun, c. **1** *a cross-section of the stem of a young plant* = a very thin slice or piece of something (e.g. the stem of a plant) obtained by cutting across its length, which can be studied under a microscope **2** *a cross-section of the student population* = a sample (example) of something which gives a good idea of the whole **to talk at cross purposes** (always plural) *My brother and I never agree and are always talking at cross purposes.* = to be unable to understand each other because each one is talking about a different thing **to have a cross to bear** = to have a problem which causes great difficulty and sadness and which one cannot get rid of **to cross swords with someone** = to fight or oppose someone whose views are well known to everyone **to keep one's fingers crossed** = to hope that something will turn out well (The gesture is based on the supersitition that if one's fingers are crossed, it will keep off bad luck.) **to not cross one's bridges before one comes to them** = to plan to face difficulties only if and when they happen and not before **to reach a crossroads** = to come to a point where a difficult decision has to be made **to cross one's mind** *It crossed my mind that I was the only one who hadn't been invited to the meeting.* = to think of something suddenly

cross•ing /'krɒsɪŋ/ noun, c. = a place where people usually go across a river or a road

cross•word (puzzle) /'krɒs'wɜ:d/ noun, c. = a game in which words have to be fitted into spaces in a numbered square, using clues (hints) which are given

crotch /krɒtʃ/ noun = the place where the legs of a human being join the trunk (the main body)

crouch /kraʊtʃ/ verb, i. *The runners are crouching for the start of the race.* = to lower the body close to the ground by bending the knees and the back, in preparation for jumping forward suddenly

crow[1] /krəʊ/ noun, c. = a large black bird which has a typical hoarse cry

crow[2] verb, i. **1** = to make the loud, hoarse sound produced by a crow **2** *Stop crowing about your victory in the competition.* = to boast (talk proudly about oneself) (disapproving)

crow•bar /'krəʊba:r/ noun, c. = a thick iron rod used to lift heavy objects off the ground or to break open boxes etc.

crowd[1] /kraʊd/ noun, c. = a large number of people gathered together but not in an orderly way

crowd[2] verb, t.or i. **1** *The boy has fainted. Please don't crowd round him.*(i.) = to come together in such large numbers that there is not enough space **2** *People watching the procession crowded the streets.*(t.) = to gather in large numbers **crowded** adj. = filled with people

crown[1] /kraʊn/ noun, c. **1** = an ornament for the head, usually made of gold, generally worn by a king or queen as a sign of royal power **2** *This is a story about a man who was not born a king but claimed the crown.* = the title or position of a king **3** *the crown of the head* = the highest or topmost part of something **4** *He is the winner of the singles crown in tennis.* =

C

title or prize

crown[2] verb, t. **1** *The new king will be crowned soon.* = to go through a religious ceremony which makes a person a king or queen **2** *Her efforts were crowned with success.* = to be given the highest reward **3** *We took the wrong route to the station, lost our tickets, and to crown it all, we got on the wrong train.* = to come as the last and worst misfortune in a series of misfortunes (informal) **crown prince** noun = the person who is to become the next king of a country

cru•cial /ˈkruːʃəl/ adj. *India needs two more runs to win this match, and there is only one ball left in this over. This is the most crucial moment of the game.* = the most important; decisive; something on which a decision or result depends

cru•ci•ble /ˈkruːsɪbəl/ noun, c. **1** = a small vessel, usually made of clay, in which things can be heated to a very high temperature in the science laboratory for an experiment (see pic under **laboratory equipment**) **2** *During World War II many countries passed through the crucible of suffering.* = a severe test which can prove the quality of something

cru•ci•fix /ˈkruːsɪfɪks/ noun, c. = a small figure of Jesus Christ on the cross **Crucifixion** noun, u. = the death of Jesus Christ on the cross **crucify** verb, t. **1** = to kill a person by nailing him/her to a cross and letting him/her die slowly **2** = to punish or attack someone without mercy; to destroy someone's reputation (informal)

crude[1] /kruːd/ adj. **1** *crude oil* = something which is in a raw or natural state **2** *a crude person* = thought to be lacking grace, good manners or education **3** *living in a crude house in the jungle* = made or built without skill; rough **4** *a crude estimate of the cost* = not exact; rough

crude[2] noun, u. *India will buy 5 million barrels of crude from Iraq.* = crude oil which has to be refined into petroleum products **crudity** noun, u. = the quality of being crude

cru•el /ˈkruːəl/ adj. **1** *The World Wildlife Society was set up to teach people not to be cruel to animals.* = without kindness or mercy **2** *It was a cruel shock to him when he found he had lost his job.* = causing great pain and sadness **cruelty** noun, u. = the quality of being cruel

cruise[1] /kruːz/ verb, i. *The plane was cruising at a speed of 500 kilometres per hour.* = to move at a fast and steady speed on a long journey (used for ships, planes, cars etc.)

cruise[2] noun, c. *We are going on a cruise on the Indian Ocean.* = a slow, gentle sea-voyage (on a ship) taken for pleasure

crumb /krʌm/ noun, c. = a very small piece of bread, cake etc.

crum•ble[1] /ˈkrʌmbəl/ verb, i. or t. *These old houses are crumbling because they have not been repaired for many years.*(i.) = to fall apart; to become weak and decayed **2** *You must crumble the bread and mix it with the milk.*(t.) = to break into pieces

crum•ple /ˈkrʌmpəl/ verb, t. or i. **1** *He was so angry on reading the letter that he crumpled it into a ball and threw it out of the window.*(t.) = to cause something soft to develop wrinkles as a result of pressure, squeezing into a ball etc. **2** *She was quite strong, but when they accused her unfairly she crumpled.*(i.) = to collapse and become weak in an emotional situation **crumpled** adj. *a crumpled piece of paper* = with folds and wrinkles as a result of squeezing or (with garments) with use

crunch[1] /krʌntʃ/ verb, t. *I can hear you crunching peanuts.* = to chew or crush food noisily with the teeth

crunch[2] noun, u. or c. **1** *We heard the crunch of feet on the ground.* = the sound produced when something is crunched (pressed down hard or rubbed against something) **2** *a cash crunch* = severe shortage

when it comes to the crunch *She opposes our ideas and does not support our plans, but when it comes to the crunch, she really helps.* = a time when things are especially difficult

cru•sade /kruːˈseɪd/ noun, c. **1** = a war fought in the name of religion **2** *He is carrying on a crusade against rash driving.* = action taken to fight for a good cause or against something bad

crush[1] /krʌʃ/ verb, t. **1** *The bones in his foot were crushed when a heavy rock fell on it.* = to break into pieces by pressing with great force **2** *crush a revolt* = to defeat completely by using force **3** *I have just ironed the shirt. Fold it properly, or you will crush it again.* = to loose smoothness and develop wrinkles **4** *Ayurvedic medicines are now made by crushing herbs in a machine.* = grinding or putting under pressure to make into a paste or powder

crush[2] noun, u. or c. **1** *The huge crowd pushed forward and some people were injured in the crush.* = the pressure caused by people being crowded together **2** *pineapple crush* = a drink made from crushed fruit mixed with water **3** *She had a crush on one of her teachers.* = a feeling (in a very young person) of being in love with an older person, which does not last (informal)

crust /krʌst/ noun, u. or c. **1** *the crust of a loaf of bread.*(u.) = the hard outer surface of a loaf of bread **2** *the crust of the earth*(u.) = the top layer **crusty** adj.

crus•ta•cean /krʌˈsteɪʃən/ noun, c. = an animal with a hard, protective shell e.g. a crab

crutch /krʌtʃ/ noun, c. (**crutches**) **1** = a stick with a cross-piece that is held under the arm, used as a support by people who have difficulty in walking **2** = something which supports or helps one at a time of weakness, but may not be necessary

crux /krʌks/ noun, u. *I am trying to understand the crux of the problem.* = the most important or core part

cry[1] /kraɪ/ verb, i. or t. **1** *She is crying because she failed in the examination.*(i) = to express sorrow or happiness etc. with tears and sobs **2** *The man cried out in pain.* = to make a loud sound expressing pain(t.) **3** *'I can't find my friend!' the boy cried.*(i.) = to shout loudly **4** *Did you hear the jackals crying?*(i.) = to make the natural sound produced by an animal

cry[2] noun, c. or u. (**cries**) **1** *If you are feeling unhappy, you should have a good cry. It will make you feel better.*(u.) = the action of expressing sorrow through tears, in order to make one's sorrow less **2** *I heard a cry of pain from behind the bushes. It was a wounded cat.*(c.) = a loud sound expressing pain, fear etc. **3** *the cry of jackals* = the natural sound made by certain animals **cry baby** noun = a person who can be made to cry very easily (disapproving)

to cry over spilt milk = to waste time feeling unhappy about something which is over **to cry wolf** = to call for help unnecessarily, when there is no danger or need for help **to be a far cry from something** *I didn't like the novel he wrote recently. It is a far cry from the wonderful book he wrote ten years ago.* = to be bad or of poor quality in comparison to something else **to cry off something** *He had promised to help us with money, but cried off at the last moment.* = to not fulfil a promise or agreement to do something (informal) **a crying shame** = a great pity, or cause for shame (informal)

cryp•tic /ˈkrɪptɪk/ adj. *When I asked the teacher how I had done in the examination, he offered only a cryptic comment.* = short and difficult to understand; not clearly expressed

crys•tal[1] /ˈkrɪstl/ noun, u. or c. **1** (u.) = a kind of transparent rock that looks like glass; glass of very high quality **2** *sugar crystals* (c.) = a solid of very regular shape formed when a liquid containing the solid is allowed to cool

crystal[2] adj. *Your explanation is crystal clear.* = very clear and easy to understand **crystallize** verb, i. **1** *The sugar has crystallized.* = to form crystals **2** *My ideas were vague at first but are now beginning to crystallize.* = to take a definite shape and become clear **crystal gazing** verb, t. or i. = to try to look into or make guesses about the future

cub /kʌb/ noun, c. = a young animal (used for tigers, lions and other meat-eating animals)

cub•by•hole /ˈkʌbihəʊl/ noun, c. = a small enclosed space used to store things, or a very small room in a building (informal)

cube /kjuːb/ noun, c. **1** = a solid object (e.g. an ice cube) with six faces or sides, each of which is a square (equal in length and breadth) (see pic under **shapes**) **2** *The cube of two (2^3) is eight.* = any number *multiplied by itself twice (2x2x2)* [MATHEMATICS] **cube root** noun *The cube root of 27 is three.* = the number which, when multiplied by itself twice, gives a certain number (3x3x3 = *27*) [MATHEMATICS] **cubic** adj. *This tank has a volume of 60 cubic metres* = the measurement of the volume (inside space) of something obtained by multiplying its length by its breadth and then by its height **cubical** adj. = having the shape of a cube

cu•bi•cle /ˈkjuːbɪkəl/ noun, c. = a part of a large room which has been divided into a number of smaller rooms

cu•bit /ˈkjuːbɪt/ noun, c. = the length of the human arm from the wrist to the elbow, used as a convenient measure of length

cuck•oo[1] /ˈkʊkuː/ noun, c. = a small brown or black bird which sings sweetly and is said to lay its eggs in the nest of some other bird

cuckoo[2] adj. *Have you gone cuckoo?* = mad (slang) **cuckoo clock** noun, c. = a clock which has a bird inside that comes out on the hour every hour and makes a sound like that of a cuckoo

cu•cum•ber /ˈkjuːkʌmbəʳ/ noun, u. or c. = a long green, tube-like vegetable which is usually eaten raw in a salad etc.

cud /kʌd/ noun, u. *chewing the cud* = food that has already been eaten and is then brought up by a cow from the stomach, to be chewed and eaten a second time

cud•dle /ˈkʌdl/ verb, t. *cuddling the baby* = to hold close to the body and embrace lovingly **cuddly** adj. *a cuddly baby* = someone (e.g. a baby) that one would like to cuddle (informal)

cud•gel[1] /ˈkʌdʒəl/ noun, c. = a short but thick and heavy stick, used as a weapon; a club

cudgel[2] verb, t. = to beat with a cudgel

to take up cudgels for (on behalf of) someone = to support someone in a quarrel or dispute

cue /kjuː/ noun, c. **1** *Please give me a cue when it is my turn to speak.* = a sign made to a person taking part in a play etc., informing him/her that it is his/her turn to speak or perform some action **2** *The end of the leader's speech was the cue for his supporters to start shouting slogans.* = some action or event that becomes a signal for something else to happen

cuff[1] /kʌf/ noun, c. = the end of the sleeve (the part that covers the arms) of a shirt

cuff[2] verb, t. *When I was cuffed on the head, my spectacles fell off.* = to hit lightly with the open hand **to speak off the cuff** = to speak without any previous preparation or planning (an **off-the-cuff remark**)(informal)

cui•sine /kwɪ'zi:n/ noun, n. or c. (French) *In this restaurant we serve Chinese cuisine.* = food cooked in the special style of a region or country

cul•i•na•ry /'kʌlɪnəri/ adj. *What lovely food you make! I really admire your culinary skills.* = connected with cooking or the kitchen

cull /kʌl/ verb, t. **1** *There are so many deer in this forest that if there is a drought, we may have to cull some of them.* = to kill some of the animals in a group, usually the weakest ones, in a planned way so that the rest may be able to get enough food **2** *The quotations in this book are culled from many sources.* = to select and put together

cul•mi•nate (in) /'kʌlmɪneɪt/ verb, t. *The series of meetings culminated in the signing of an agreement. // Their disagreement culminated in a serious quarrel.* = to result or end in; to come to a point where the development of something reaches its final or highest stage

cul•mi•na•tion /kʌlmɪ'neɪʃən/ noun, u. *I got my M.Sc. degree today. This was the culmination of my student career.* = the highest point or the final stage of something

cul•pa•ble /'kʌlpəbəl/ adj. *The guard fell asleep and everything was stolen. This was a case of culpable neglect of duty.* = some action that deserves to be blamed or punished

cul•prit /'kʌlprɪt/ noun, c. *My watch has been stolen and I know who the culprit is.* = a person who has committed some crime

cult[1] /kʌlt/ noun, c. or u. = a small group of people within a religion who worship in a way which is considered different (sometimes derogatory)

cult[2] adj. *This musician has become a cult figure.* = a fashion or style in art, music etc. that becomes extremely popular and attracts people, almost like a religion

cul•ti•vate /kʌltɪveɪt/ verb, t. **1** *We must cultivate the land, not allow it to go bare and dry.* = to prepare soil for agriculture and to grow crops on it **2** *You should cultivate a taste for classical music.* = to develop through study, training etc. **3** *He thinks you sincerely like him but it is clear that you are only cultivating him.* = to try to develop good relations with someone in the hope of getting some benefit (disapproving) **cultivation** /kʌltɪ'veɪʃən/ noun, u. = the act or process of cultivating

cul•ture /'kʌltʃə'/ noun, u. or c. **1** *I am studying Islamic culture.* = the customs, beliefs, art, literature, music etc. special to a group of people **2** *They are a family with culture and education.*(u.) = values and ways of behaving which people consider good **3** *I am interested in fish culture.*(u) = the raising of plants and animals for commercial use **4** *The scientist is preparing a culture of the bacteria that produces cholera.*(c.) = a group of bacteria or other germs grown in the laboratory for some scientific purpose **cultured** adj.**1** *a cultured person* = a person who is interested in art, music, literature etc. **2** *a cultured pearl* = something made in artificial conditions

cul•vert /'kʌlvət/ noun, c.= a pipe under a road through which water can flow

cum /kʊm/ prep. *This room is our kitchen-cum-dining room.* = as well as; combined with (something that serves two purposes)

cum•ber•some /'kʌmbəsəm/ adj. *Bangalore has a very cumbersome system for the numbering of houses.* = something that is difficult to use

cum•in /'kʌmɪn/ noun, u. = the seeds of a plant used as a spice in cooking

cu•mu•la•tive /'kju:mjʊlətɪv/ adj.**1** *If you go on drinking so much coffee, you will cause cumulative damage to your liver and stomach.* = something that goes on increasing **2** *the cumulative total* = a number arrived at after adding a series of numbers

cu•mu•lus (clouds) /'kju:mjʊləs/ noun or adj. = thick white clouds that look like piles of cotton

cu•nei•form /'kju:nɪfɔ:m/ adj. = the system of writing used by the people of ancient Mesopotamia

cun•ning[1] /'kʌnɪŋ/ adj. *The taxi drivers were cunning and did not give us information about buses.* = very clever and likely to cheat (derogatory)

cunning[2] noun, u. *They used a lot of cunning to buy that lovely house at a low price.* = cleverness used to deceive someone **cunningly** adv.

cup[1] /kʌp/ noun, c. **1** = a container, usually round and with a handle, from which one drinks milk, coffee etc. **2** *Please have the medicine with a cup of milk.* = the quantity that can fill a cup **3** *the Beighton Cup for hockey* = a prize in the shape of a large cup, made of some metal, given to the winner of some sports tournament **4** *the cup of the pitcher plant* = something that has the shape of a cup

cup[2] verb, t. (**cupped**) **1** *to cup one's hands* = to hold one's hands together, palms facing up, in the shape of a cup, as for example, to receive a ball which is thrown **cupful** noun, c. *two cupfuls of milk* = the amount of liquid or substance a cup can hold **to be (not be) one's cup of tea** *Watching football on television is very much my cup of tea. I'm never too sleepy to watch it..* = something that one enjoys doing

cup•board /'kʌbəd/ noun, c. = a piece of furniture

with shelves and doors, made of metal or wood, used for storing clothes, books etc.

cu•pid•i•ty /kjʊ'pɪdɪti/ noun, u. = a strong desire for money; greed (derogatory)

cur /kɜː'/ noun, c. **1** = a dog **2** = a person that one does not like (old-fashioned)

cu•ra•tor /kjʊ'reɪtə'/ noun, c. = a person who manages a museum

curb[1] /kɜːb/ verb, t. *The government is trying to curb the rise in the price of petrol.* = to control and keep under check

curb[2] noun, c. **1** *This new law will act as a curb on the use of drugs.* = something that can check or control **2** = the raised edge or border of a pavement (also **kerb**) (American)

curd /kɜːd/ noun, u. (**curds**) = the thick, solid substance that is obtained from milk when it turns sour due to the action of bacteria, used as food (also **yoghurt**)

cur•dle /'kɜːdl/ verb, i. **1** *The milk has curdled.* = to turn sour and form curds (small solid pieces floating in liquid) due to the action of bacteria **2** *The roaring of the tigers in the forest made my blood curdle.* = to cause great fear

cure[1] /kjʊə'/ verb, t. **1** *This medicine will cure you of your illness.* = to help a person get rid of an illness or disease **2** *The fish has been cured by adding salt and drying it in the sun.* = to preserve food (prevent it from going bad) by adding salt etc.

cure[2] noun, u. or c. *He is still looking for a cure for his illness.*(c.) = a method of treatment that can cure a person (a course of medicines, massage etc.) **curable** adj. *a curable disease* = a disease that can be cured **curative** adj. *The leaves of this plant have curative properties for a damaged liver.* = having the power to cure disease

cur•few /'kɜːfjuː/ noun, u. *The government has imposed curfew on the streets from 9.00 p.m. to 5.00 a.m.* = an order passed by the government forcing everyone to stay inside their homes at certain times, to prevent any trouble

cu•ri•o /'kjʊəriəʊ/ noun, c. = an object of art, usually small, kept for display

cu•ri•os•i•ty /kjʊəri'ɒsɪti/ noun, u. or c. **1** *Curiosity is at the root of all scientific discoveries.*(u.) = the desire to learn or find out about new things **2** *Her curiosity about who our friends are is annoying.* = the desire to know something one does not know in a way that other people do not like (disapproving) **3** *This old wooden house is quite a curiosity.*(c.) = a strange and unusual object

cu•ri•ous /'kjʊəriəs/ adj. **1** *I don't know the result of last night's cricket match. I am curious to know who won.* = having the desire to learn something that one does not know about **2** *He is always curious about what we are doing.* = interested in information about something in a way that is not liked by others **3** *It is curious that your friend never told us his name.* = strange and unusual

curl[1] /kɜl/ noun, c. **1** *The baby's head is covered with thick curls.* = a small roll of hair that has a curved shape **2** *a curl of smoke* = something that looks like a curl

curl[2] verb, i. or t. **1** *His hair curls.*(i.) = to form a curl **2** *The hair-dresser will curl your hair.*(t.) = to cause something to form a curl **3** *The jasmine creeper curled round the bamboo pole.* = to make a ring round something **curly** adj. *curly hair* = having curls

to curl up **1** *The kitten curled up in my lap and went to sleep.* = to lie in a relaxed position in which one's body is in a curve, with the knees bent and close to the chest **2** *However much I try to straighten the pages of the calendar, they curl up.* = (of cloth, paper etc.) to turn inwards at the edges or corner

cur•rant /'kʌrənt/ noun, c.= a dried grape, used to make food sweet

cur•ren•cy /'kʌrənsi/ noun, u. or c. (**currencies**) **1** *Could we pay in American currency?*(u.) = the type of money used in a country **2** *Rumours about the postponment of the exam are gaining currency.*(u.) = the situation of being accepted or believed by many people

cur•rent[1] /'kʌrənt/ adj. *You will get Rs 3000 a month in the current year and Rs 4000 a month starting next year.* = happening now (at the present time)

current[2] noun, c. or u. **1** *There is a strong current in the middle of the river.* = a mass of liquid that flows at a greater speed through a larger body of the same liquid **2** *an electrical current*(c.) = a flow of electricity **currently** adv.

current account noun, c. = an account in a bank from which money can be taken out at any time and which does not earn any interest

cur•ric•u•lum /kə'rɪkjʊləm/ noun, u. or c. (**curriculums** or **curricula**) *Computer Applications is now taught as part of the school curriculum.* = the details of the different subjects taught in a school or college at any given level **curriculum vitae** /kərɪkjʊləm 'viːtaɪ/ noun, c. (also **CV**) = a written summary of the details of a person's life, such as name, age, educational qualifications, sent along with a job application (also **bio-data** or **resumè**)

cur•ry[1] /'kʌri/ noun, u. or c. (**curries**) *chicken curry* (u.) = meat or vegetables with sauce cooked in the Indian style, with spices

curry[2] verb, t. *The vegetables have to be curried.* =

cooked into a curry

to curry favour = to try to win someone's support through flattery (false praise)

curse[1] /kɜːs/ verb, t. or i. **1** *The wizard cursed the king, saying he would lose his kingdom.* = to ask for bad luck to be brought down on someone, using some supernatural or magical power; to express the wish that someone may have bad luck **2** *He was cursing even in his sleep.* = to use bad language; to swear **3** *I am cursed with a poor memory.*(i.) = to suffer because of someone or something

curse[2] noun, c. **1** *The old witch put a curse on me.* = a piece of black magic which brings bad luck to someone **2** *This railway crossing, which is closed most of the time, is a curse to people in a hurry.* = something that causes suffering and trouble or inconvenience

cur•sive /ˈkɜːsɪv/adj. *cursive writing* = flowing writing, in which the different letters in a word are joined together

cur•sor /ˈkɜːsəʳ/ noun, c. = a small mark or line which moves on the screen of a computer system and points to the place where some entry is being made [COMPUTERS]

cursor

cur•so•ry /ˈkɜːsəri/ adj. *I have not had time to read the report carefully. I had only a cursory glance at it this morning.* = done quickly and without close attention to detail

curt /kɜːt/ adj. *He's usually friendly, but when I spoke to him his reply was curt.* = brief in a way which is unfriendly or showing displeasure

cur•tail /kɜːˈteɪl/ verb, t. *The government's plans to start more schools have had to be curtailed as there is no money.* = to shorten; to reduce or make less

cur•tain /ˈkɜːtn/ noun, c. **1** = a length of cloth hung over a door or window to keep out sunlight, or to prevent someone from looking in **2** = the heavy screen hanging in front of the stage where a play is being performed

curve /kɜːv/ noun, c. **1** = a line which is not straight but forms part of a circle **2** *a curve in the road* = a bend **curvature** noun, u. *the earth's curvature* = the state of being curved or the degree to which something is curved

cush•ion[1] /ˈkʊʃən/ noun, c. **1** = a stitched bag filled with cotton or other soft material on which a person can lie, lean on or sit **2** *He needs Rs 200 for the journey and about Rs 50 for food etc. Let's give him Rs 100 more as a cushion.* = money which can help in unexpected situations or an emergency

cushion[2] verb, t. *When her mother died her friends tried to cushion the shock by taking her with them on a quiet holiday.* = to reduce the force of something unpleasant **cushy** adj. *a cushy job* = comfortable and requiring little effort (informal)

cus•tard /ˈkʌstəd/ noun, u.= a kind of pudding, usually yellow, made with cornflour and milk

cus•to•dy /ˈkʌstədi/ noun, u. **1** *I will leave the child in your custody.* = care and protection **2** *The thief is now in police custody.* = being guarded by the police

cus•to•dian /kʌˈstəʊdiən/ noun, c. = one who is responsible for looking after or taking care of someone or something

cus•tom /ˈkʌstəm/ noun, c. or u. *It is our custom to invite friends for a feast whenever our team wins.*(u.) = something that is done regularly by the members of a group **customary** adj. = something that has become a custom **custom-made** adj. *a custom-made computer* = specially made for some important customer

cus•tom•er /ˈkʌstəməʳ/ noun, c. = a person who buys something from a shop or uses a service (e.g. a courier service)

cus•toms /ˈkʌstəms/ noun, u. (always plural) **1** *I paid Rs 5000 as customs duty on the computer I brought from Singapore.* = tax due on things which are brought into a country from another country **2** *I have to go through customs.* = an office where travellers are required to pay tax on goods which they have brought into the country

cut[1] /kʌt/ verb, t. or i. **1** *Use this knife to cut the vegetables.*(t.) = to use a sharp instrument such as a knife to separate a small piece (of something) from the main part **2** *I have cut my finger.*(t.) = to make a narrow opening or wound with a sharp instrument, either accidently or on purpose **3** *This knife does not cut.*(i.) = to be able to cut **4** *They have cut train fares by half in the holiday season on some routes.*(t.) = reduce **5** *I had just started to speak when he cut me angrily.*(t.) = to interrupt suddenly **6** *The baby has cut her first tooth!*(t.) = to make something appear **7** *She has cut a new record.*(t.) = to make a record of music

cut[2] noun, c. **1** *I have a cut in my hand.* = a wound which is the result of cutting **2** *I like the cut of your clothes.* = style **3** *They want their cut of the profits.* = share (in something dishonest) (informal, disapproving) **4** = a clever stroke in tennis etc. **5** *cut in salary* = reduction **6** *a power cut* = a halt in the supply of electricity, usually temporarily **7** *That unkind cut was not necessary.* = a cruel remark **8** = (usually plural) parts of a film which are not needed and are removed when the film is edited

to cut off *They have cut off water supply here for a while.* = to stop the flow or delivery of something or of a service **to be cut off from something** *We were happy in the farm house but were cut off from the excitement of being in a city.* = to not be able to have or reach something as a result of something else **to cut down something** = to take away by cutting down e.g. a tree **to cut down on (something)** = to reduce something for one's benefit **to cut back** *The hotel wants to cut back on the air-conditioning as it is expensive.* = to reduce the expenditure on something **to cut something short** *She had to cut her speech short because it was getting late for everyone.* = to reduce the time taken to make a speech, take a walk etc. for a reason **to be cut out for something** *She acts so well. She's really cut out for films or television.* = to have a talent or skill for something (informal) **to be a cut above something** = to be better than (informal) **to cut something fine** *You are supposed to catch the 8.45 train. Aren't you cutting it fine by leaving for the station at 8.30?* = to make very little allowance in time to achieve something **to cut a sorry figure** to behave in a manner which is disappointing and embarassing to others because it is below one's expectations **to cut corners** = in a difficult situation, to take steps to reduce money etc. spent on something **to cut the crap** *I don't have time to listen to a long account so could you cut the crap and tell me the important part.* = an impatient way of telling someone to leave out unnecessary details and get to the main point (slang)

cute /kju:t/ adj. *What a cute child!* = pretty and lovable (informal)

cu•ti•cle /'kju:tɪkəl/ noun, u. = the covering of thick skin near the fingernails

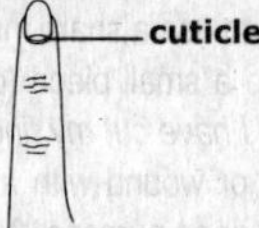

cut•lass /'kʌtləs/ noun, c. = a short, curved sword

cut•le•ry /'kʌtləri/ noun, u. = knives, forks and spoons used for eating

cut•let /'kʌtlɪt/ noun, c. = a small piece of meat with the bone attached; meat or vegetables cut into very fine pieces, covered with flour or bread crumbs and fried

CV abbr. for **curriculum vitae**

cutting[1] /'kʌtɪŋ/ adj. **1** *a cutting remark* = unkind and hurtful **2** *a cutting wind* = sharp and cold in a way that is painful

cutting[2] noun, c. **1** *a newspaper cutting* = an article, news item etc. which is cut out of a newspaper **2** = a part of a plant, usually the stem with buds, used to make a new plant from a 'mother' plant

cy•a•nide /'saɪənaɪd/ noun, u. = a strong poison

cy•ber•net•ics /saɪbə'netɪks/ noun = the study of the way in which information is stored and used by machines as well as the human brain [COMPUTERS] **cyber cafe** noun = a shop where a number of computers are available for the use of customers, specially people wanting to use the Internet **cyber space** noun = a term used in stories (fiction) to refer to a vast space where messages and visual materials are sent through the Internet

cy•cle[1] /'saɪkəl/ noun, c. **1** *the cycle of seasons* = a series of connected events which are repeated over and over again in the same order **2** = short fom of **bi-cycle** (a vehicle with two wheels)

cycle[2] verb, i. *We will cycle to the market.* = to go somewhere on a bicycle **cyclic** adj. = happening in cycles (repeated over and over again) **cyclist** noun, c. = a person who rides a bicycle **cycling** adj.

cy•clone /'saɪkləʊn/ noun, c. = a very powerful wind or storm which moves round and round in a circle

cy•clops /'saɪklɒps/ noun = a giant with only one eye, mentioned in stories from ancient Greece

cy•clo•style /'saɪkləstaɪl/ verb, t. *Please cyclostyle 500 copies of this notice.* = to make copies of a document from a master-copy produced by a special copying machine (also **mimeograph**)

cyl•in•der /'sɪlɪndər/ noun, c. **1** = a tube-shaped hollow or solid structure with a circular base and straight sides **2** *a cylinder of cooking-gas* = a hollow steel container used for storing some gas **3** *a cylinder in a petrol engine* = a hollow tube inside a petrol or diesel engine within which the piston moves **cylindrical** adj. = having the shape of a cylinder

cym•bal /'sɪmbəl/ noun, c. (usually plural) (**cymbals**) = one of a pair of flat metal plates with handles which are struck together to produce a musical sound (used in India during prayers)

cyn•ic /'sɪnɪk/ noun, c. = a person who has a low opinion of most people and most things **cynical** adj. *He is always making cynical remarks.* = like a cynic

cyst /sɪst/ noun, c. = a growth in the body which has liquid substance inside it

cy•tol•o•gy /saɪ'tɒlədʒi/ noun, u. = the scientific study of cells

czar /zɑːr/ noun = the title given in former times to the king who ruled over Russia

dD

D

d, D the fourth letter of the English alphabet

d. = abbr. of **died** (*Jawaharlal Nehru, d.1964*)

dab[1] /dæb/ verb, t. *The nurse dabbed the child's face with a towel.* = to touch lightly and gently

dab[2] noun, c. *She gave the wall a final dab of paint.* = a light touch

dab•ble /ˈdæbəl/ verb, i. *I dabbled in politics for a few years when I was a student.* = to take part in something but not seriously (sometimes derogatory)

dad /dæd/ noun, c. = father (informal)

daf•fo•dil /ˈdæfədɪl/ noun, c. = a yellow flower that grows in spring in cold countries

daft /dɑːft/ adj. *What a daft plan! It will never work.* = foolish or slightly mad (informal)

dag•ger /ˈdægəʳ/ noun, c. = a short pointed knife, with two sharp edges, used as a weapon (see pic under **knife**)

dai•ly[1] /ˈdeɪli/ adj. *the daily newspaper* = appearing every day

daily[2] adv. *There is a bus service from Delhi to Agra daily.* = every day

dain•ty /ˈdeɪnti/ adj. *a dainty child* = small, pretty and delicate

dair•y[1] /ˈdeəri/ noun, c. (**dairies**) = a place where milk, butter, cheese etc. are produced

dairy[2] adj. *dairy animals* = connected with the production of milk

dais /ˈdeɪs/ noun, c. = a raised platform on which speakers can stand or sit

dai•sy /ˈdeɪzi/ noun, c. (**daisies**) = a small white flower with a yellow centre

dam[1] /dæm/ noun, c. = a high wall built across a river to store water

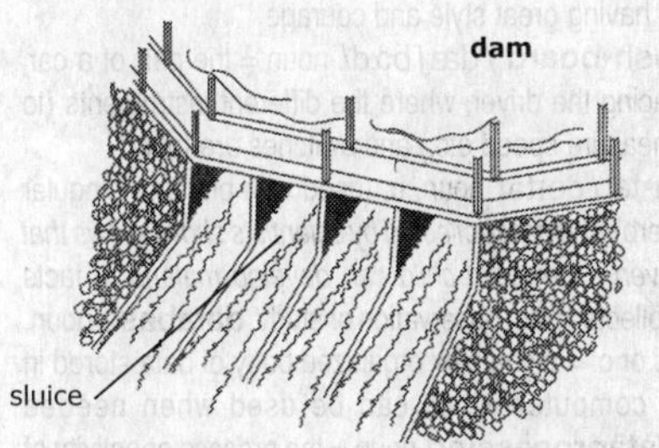

dam[2] verb, t. (**dammed**) *The engineers have dammed (up) the river.* = to build a dam across a river

dam•age[1] /ˈdæmɪdʒ/ verb, t. *The fire damaged the school building.* = to cause harm or loss

damage[2] noun, u. *We have to repair the damage caused by the storm.* = the harm done **damages** noun, u. (always plural) *The court ordered the magazine to pay damages of Rs 10,000 to the actor for publishing a false report about him.* = money paid to someone for some loss that has been caused, usually to his/her reputation

Dame /deɪm/ noun, c. **1** = a British title of honour given to a woman (formal) (see also **Sir**) **2** *Do you know that dame?* = woman (slang) G

damn[1] /dæm/ verb, t. **1** *Someone left the gate open and the cows have come in. Damn him!* = a swear word expressing anger USE **2** *The critics have damned the new film.* = to declare something to be bad

damn[2] adj. *a damn fool.* = a swear-word used to give force to a statement, good as well as bad (informal)

damn[3] adv. *She played damn well in the match.* = a swear word used to give force to a statement, usually in a positive sense (informal) USE

damn[4] interjec. *Oh damn! I've lost my watch.* = a swear word used to express anger or disappointment (informal) USE

to not give a damn *We thought he would be unhappy when we stopped being friends but he didn't give a damn.* = to not be interested at all in something (informal) **to damn with faint praise** = to praise someone unwillingly and without sincerity **to do one's damndest** = to try very hard to do something (informal) **to know damn-all** = to know nothing (about something) (informal)

damp[1] /dæmp/ adj. *a damp towel* = a little wet

damp[2] noun, u. *The damp in the air causes breathing problems.* = wetness **dampen** /ˈdæmpən/ verb, t. **1** *Could you dampen the fabric a little before ironing it?* = to make slightly wet with water **2** *He was feeling excited about his new job and not even the bad weather could dampen his spirits.* = to reduce the strength of good feelings

dam•sel /ˈdæmzəl/ noun, c. = a young woman of noble birth [LITERATURE]

dance[1] /dɑːns/ verb, i. *Do you like to dance?* = to move one's body to the rhythm of music

dance[2] noun, c. **1** *This is my last dance of the evening.* = the act of dancing **2** *Odissi is a classical dance.* = a style or kind of dancing **dancer** noun, c. = a person who dances, usually as a profession

dan•druff /ˈdændrəf/ noun, u. = a condition of the scalp (the thin skin on top of the head) which causes bits of dry skin to form in the hair

dan•dy /ˈdændi/ noun, c. (**dandies**) = a man who likes to wear costly clothes that attract attention (disapproving)

dan•ger /ˈdeindʒəʳ/ noun, u. or c. **1** *Don't cross the* *street now. There is danger from speeding cars.*(u.) = the possibility of harm or loss **2** *Open man-holes in the road are a danger to everyone.*(c.) = a thing that can cause harm **dangerous** adj. *Boxing is a dangerous sport.* = able or likely to cause harm

dan•gle /ˈdæŋgəl/ verb, t. or i. **1** *The man sat on the wall dangling his legs.*(t.) = to make something hang or swing loosely **2** *The bunch of keys dangled from a chair.* (i.) = to hang

dank /dæŋk/ adj. *The rooms in this old building are very dank after the rains.* = damp (wet and cold in an unhealthy way)

dap•per /ˈdæpəʳ/ adj. *Our players looked very dapper on the field.* = smart; neat in appearance (used for men)

dap•pled /ˈdæpəld/ adj. *The blue sky was dappled with patches of white clouds.* = marked with spots or patches of different colour or of light and shadow

dare[1] /deəʳ/ aux. verb **1** *I dare not go there now.* **2** *Dare I ask what brings you here?* = to have the courage to do something (used only in negative sentences and questions)

dare[2] verb, i. or t. *He who dares, wins.*(i.) = to be brave enough to do something where others are afraid and uncertain

daring[1] /ˈdeərɪŋ/ adj. *He is a daring hunter.* = brave and ready to face danger

daring[2] noun, u. *Our soldiers showed great daring.* = courage

> **Usage** When **dare** is used as an auxiliary verb, it is followed by another verb, without 'to' e.g. *I dare go no further.* But when **dare** is used as a main verb, it is followed by 'to' e.g. *How can you dare to say such a thing?* (The meaning is much the same.) 'Need' is also used as both an auxiliary and a main verb, in the same way.

Don't you dare! = a warning given to someone not to do something (informal) **How dare you!** = an expression showing anger because someone has done something you don't like (informal) **to dare someone** *I dare you to wear this bright purple shirt.* = to challenge someone to do something risky or likely to cause disapproval

dark[1] /dɑːk/ adj. **1** *This room is so dark that you can hardly see anything.* = without light **2** *There is a dark side to the happy story I told you.* = hidden and unpleasant **3** *He was wearing a dark red shirt.* = a deeper form of some colour **4** *a dark person* = used to describe a person, the colour of whose skin is a deep colour, or in some cultures, a person whose eyes and skin or hair are brown or black (opposite **fair**)

dark[2] noun, u. *Some birds can see in the dark.* = the absence of light; darkness **darken** verb, t. or i. *Can you darken this part of the painting a little more?*(t.) = to make something darker **darkness** noun, u. **darkroom** = a room without any light that is used to produce photographs from film [TECHNICAL]

to be (kept) in the dark *They told everyone about their plans, but I was kept in the dark.* = to not be told what is happening **to keep someone in the dark** = not to let someone know what is happening (on purpose) **a dark horse** = a person whose abilities are not known or have not been tested (often derogatory) **the dark(er) side of life** = the unhappy or the evil side of life

dar•ling[1] /ˈdɑːlɪŋ/ noun, c. **1** *The child is a little darling.* = someone who is very lovable (easy to love) (informal) **2** *Darling, let's go out.* = a term used to address a person one loves (informal)

darling[2] adj. *This is my darling daughter.* = much loved

darn /dɑːn/ verb, t. *My mother is darning my old clothes.* = to use a needle and thread to mend clothing or cloth which is torn

dart[1] /dɑːt/ verb, i. *The man darted through the corridor after the postman, who had just left.* = to run quickly

dart[2] noun, c. = a small arrow with a sharp point, sometimes fired from a gun **darts** noun = a popular indoor game in which players throw darts at a circular board (dartboard)

dash[1] /dæʃ/ verb, i. or t. **1** *He dashed across the road.*(i.) = to run quickly and suddenly **2** *The waves dashed against the rock with great force.*(i.) = to strike with force **3** *India's hopes of winning the match were dashed by the rain.*(t.) = to destroy

dash[2] noun, c. or u. **1** *The prisoner made a dash for freedom while the guards were asleep.*(c.) = a quick and sudden run **2** *The curry needs a dash of chilli.*(u.) = a small amount (informal) **3** = a mark, shown as (—), used in writing or printing to show a break in a sentence

dash•ing /ˈdæʃɪŋ/ adj. *the dashing hero of the film* = having great style and courage

dash•board /ˈdæʃbɔːd/ noun = the part of a car, facing the driver, where the different instruments (to measure speed etc.) and switches are found

da•ta /ˈdeɪtə/ noun, u. (used with plural or singular verb) *The data collected by scientists show/shows that even a newborn child can develop malaria.* = facts collected from observation or study **database** noun, u. or c. = a complex organized body of data stored in a computer which can be used when needed **dataprocessing** noun = the process or activity of using a computer to carry out different operations on a database in order to get the desired result

date[1] /deɪt/ noun, c. **1** *The date today is 2 October 2002.* = the time as shown by the number of the day, the month and the year **2** = the fruit of the date palm **3** *I have a date with my doctor this evening.* = an arrangement to meet someone at a particular time (informal) **4** *She is going on a date with Asif.* = a social meeting between a man and a woman (informal) **5** *She is going out with her date.* = a person, usually of the opposite sex, with whom one has arranged a social meeting (informal)

date[2] verb, t. or i. **1** *Historians have found an ancient book on Tibet, written thousands of years ago. They are trying to date it.*(t.) = to discover the date (time) of something very old **2** *Please remember to date your letter.*(t.) = to write the date on something **3** *This book was written in 1900 but it still hasn't dated.*(i.) = to become old-fashioned and out of place in the present time **4** *He is dating this girl.* = to meet a person, usually of the opposite sex, socially (informal) **dated** adj. *Your cap looks rather dated.* = old-fashioned

out-of-date (outdated) = not modern; old-fashioned **up-to-date** = modern; upto the present time

daub /dɔːb/ verb, t. *The walls of the house have been daubed with black paint.* = to cover a surface with something sticky (e.g. paint or mud) but in a careless way

daugh•ter /ˈdɔːtəʳ/ noun, c. = someone's female child **daughter-in-law** noun, c. = the wife of one's son

daunt /dɔːnt/ verb, t. *He is going to face an interview, but he does not look daunted.* = to lose courage or to cause loss of courage (literary)

dawn[1] /dɔːn/ noun, c. or u. **1** *You will have to wake up at dawn.*(u.) = the time just before sunrise **2** *India is witnessing the dawn of the age of cyber technology.*(c.) = the beginning of a new period that brings hope or improvement

dawn[2] verb, i. *The day is dawning.* = beginning (figurative)

to dawn on (upon) *It suddenly dawned on me that my friends were making fun of me.* = to begin to realize (understand) something

day /deɪ/ noun, c. **1** *the seven days of the week* = a period of 24 hours **2** *She works all day and comes home at night.* = the period between sunrise and sunset **3** *Such things never happened in my day.* = a point or period of time in the past **daydream** /ˈdeɪdriːm/ noun, c. = thoughts of pleasant things not connected with reality

at the end of the day = when everything has been considered **to call it a day** *He has played for India for 13 years, and now he has decided to call it a day.* = to bring something to an end **from one day to the next** = on two days which follow each other **to make someone's day** = to give someone reason to feel happy **to have a field day** *The media has had a field day writing about the business family's problems.* = to enjoy doing something successfully **to have had one's day** *He has had his day and should now retire.* = to have enjoyed a period of success which is now over (informal, derogatory)

dazed /deɪzd/ adj. *He looked dazed after the accident.* = in a shocked or confused state

to be in a daze *The news of my accident left my parents in a daze.* = to be in a shocked or confused state

daz•zle[1] /ˈdæzəl/ verb, t. *The light from her torch shone on my eyes and dazzled me.* = to make someone unable to see because of a strong light shining on their eyes

dazzle[2] noun, u. *Don't be led away by the dazzle of money.* = attraction (disapproving)

DC abbr. of **Direct Current** (noun) = an electrical current that flows in one direction only (compare **AC**)

DDT noun = a poisonous chemical used to kill insects, especially mosquitoes

dead[1] /ded/ adj. **1** *a dead person* = not living **2** *The telephone is dead.* = not working **3** *Anglo-Saxon is a dead language.* = no longer used **4** *I want to move to another house. The neighbourhood here is really dead.* = quiet and without activity in a way which is boring

dead[2] noun, u. *He came to see me in the dead of the night.* = the quietest part of

dead[3] adv. **1** *I am dead tired.* = completely (informal) **2** *The test was dead easy.* = very (informal) **dead end** noun **1** = a point at the end of a street beyond which one cannot go **2** = a situation which does not allow a person to make progress (figurative) **3** *I have reached a dead end in my efforts to write a novel.* = a point from where one cannot move forward **deadwood** noun, c. *There is a lot of deadwood in the book you wrote, which must be removed.* = something which has lost its usefulness or value (figurative)

to go dead **1** *The machine went dead suddenly.* = to stop working **2** *My foot has suddenly gone dead.* = (of parts of the body) to feel no pain, cold, warmth etc. **as dead as a door-nail** = completely without life (informal) **dead on time** = exactly on time (informal) **over my dead body** *'I'd like you to meet them and apologise.' 'Over my dead body!'* = a strong way of refusing to do something (informal) **to be a dead loss** = a great and complete loss **to not be caught dead doing something** *She wouldn't be caught dead wearing silk.* = to refuse to do something because it is against one's principles or because one doesn't like doing it (informal)

dead•en /ˈdedən/ verb, t. *I was in great pain, but the injection helped to deaden it.* = to reduce in strength (so that pain etc. are hardly felt)

dead•line /ˈdedlaɪn/ noun, c. *The deadline for completing this report is 5.00 p.m. tomorrow.* = the date or time before which something must be completed

dead•lock /ˈdedlɒk/ noun, c. *a deadlock in the peace talks* = a point in a discussion from where no progress can be made

dead•ly /ˈdedlɪ/ adj. **1** *AIDS is a deadly disease.* = very dangerous; capable of causing death **2** *a deadly song* = very good (slang)

deaf /def/ adj. **1** *a deaf child* = unable to hear **2** *He was deaf to all my requests.* = unwilling to listen **deafen** verb, t. *We were deafened by the loud music.* = to lose one's hearing temporarily because of a very loud sound

to fall on deaf ears *My request that we go to a play instead of a film fell on deaf ears, and we had to go to the film.* = (referring to a request or suggestion) to not be given attention

> **Usage** A person is generally referred to now as 'hearing-impaired', not 'deaf'.

deal[1] /diːl/ verb, i. or t. (**dealt**) **1** *He deals in readymade garments.*(t.) = to trade; to buy and sell **2** *Will you please deal the cards?*(t.) = to give out playing cards to the players in a game **3** *He dealt his enemy a heavy blow with his sword.*(t.) = to strike (formal)

deal[2] noun, c. **1** *I will sell you sugar and you can sell me cotton. That is a deal.* = a business arrangement which helps both sides (informal) **2** *He lost a good deal of money last week.* = a large quantity **dealer** noun, c. = a person who buys or sells something

(to be no) big deal **1** *I walked all the way from the railway station because I couldn't get a bus or taxi. It was no big deal.* = not a great or difficult thing (informal) **2** *'I helped with the cooking last night.' 'Big deal!'* = a way of telling someone that something they did does not call for praise or importance **a raw deal** = unfair or unjust treatment (informal)

dean /diːn/ noun, c. = a senior professor at a university who is in charge of a department or school

dear[1] /dɪəʳ/ adj. **1** *a dear friend* = greatly loved **2** *Dear Sir* = a formal opening for a letter **3** *She is very dear to me.* = valuable, precious **4** *In times of war, sugar and rice become very dear.* = expensive

dear[2] noun, c. *That child is such a dear! Everyone loves her.* = a person who is very lovable (informal)

dear[3] interjec. *Oh dear! I've lost my pen.* = an expression of mild irritation (displeasure)

dearth /dɜːθ/ noun, u. *There is a dearth of young people in this office. Most of us are old.* = a lack of; shortage

death /deθ/ noun, u. **1** *death caused by heart failure* = the end of life **2** *the death of the kingdom* = the end (figurative) **death rate** noun = the number of people dying in a year for every 1,000 people in the country **death trap** noun, c. *This new highway is a death trap.* = something that is highly dangerous and can cause death **death warrant** noun = an official order to put someone to death, usually for committing some crime

a matter of life and death = a matter of very great importance (informal) **to be the death of someone** *You didn't come home until midnight and I was so worried. You'll be the death of me!* = a way of telling someone they have caused you a lot of anxiety (informal) **to be at death's door** = to be very near the point of death **to be bored to death** = to be very bored (informal)

de•ba•cle /deɪˈbɑːkəl/ noun, u. *Our cricket team lost eight wickets for 40 runs. It was a batting debacle.* = a sudden failure; collapse (formal)

de•bar /dibɑːʳ/ verb, t. (**debarred**) *She was debarred from writing the exam because she had not attended all the classes.* = to prevent someone from doing something

de•base /dɪˈbeɪs/ verb, t. *You have debased the medical profession by demanding so much money from poor patients.* = to lower the value of something which is thought of as noble or precious (formal)

de•bate[1] /dɪˈbeɪt/ noun, c. = an argument or discussion at which some subject or topic is talked about by at least two persons or groups, each expressing a different point of view

debate[2] verb, t. *People are debating the long-term effects of heavy exercise.* = to argue about an issue

de•bauch /dɪˈbɔːtʃ/ noun, c. = a person who is immoral or unacceptable to most people, especially in behaviour related to alcohol and sex

de•bil•i•ty /dɪˈbɪlɪti/ noun, u. = weakness of body or mind caused by disease or poor health [TECHNICAL]

deb•it[1] /debɪt/ verb, t. = to take money out of a bank account (opposite **credit**) [TECHNICAL]

debit[2] noun, u. = a record of money being taken out of an account

deb•o•nair /debəˈneəʳ/ adj. *a debonair young man* = very cheerful, handsome and stylish (used only to describe men)

deb•ris /deˈbriː/ noun, u. *The building was pulled down last year but the debris is still lying on the road.* = the remains of a building that has been destroyed or has fallen

debt /det/ noun, u. or c. **1** *I borrowed Rs 10,000 last month to buy a scooter. I will have to pay off this debt soon.*(c.) = money which has been borrowed and has to be repaid **2** *I am deeply in your debt for your help to me when I was in trouble.*(u.) = a feeling of owing something to someone

to be in someone's debt = to feel grateful to someone **to run into debt** = to be forced to borrow money **a bad debt** = used to describe the fact that money which someone has borrowed from you will not be returned

de•but /'deɪbjuː/ noun, u. *The young actor made his debut in the film 'Kaho Na Pyar Hai'.* = first public appearance

deca- /dekə/ prefix meaning 'ten' e.g. **dec•ade** /'dekeɪd/ noun, c. = a period of ten years

de•cap•i•tate /dɪ'kæpɪteɪt/ verb, t. = to cut off someone's head

de•cay[1] /dɪ'keɪ/ verb, i. **1** *The dentist pulled out two of my teeth which had decayed.* = to become rotten **2** *My health has decayed with age.* = to get into a worse condition than before

decay[2] noun, c. *You can find decay everywhere in this old city.* = the process or the effect of gradually becoming worse **decadent** /'dekədənt/ adj. *a decadent culture* = without the good qualities it had earlier

de•cease /dɪ'siːs/ noun, u. *This property will go to your son on your decease.* = death [LAW] **deceased** noun = a dead person

de•ceive /dɪ'siːv/ verb, t. *I always thought my business partner was honest, but he has deceived me.* = to trick or cheat someone by pretending to be good, honest etc. **deceit** noun, u. *They have become rich through deceit.* = the quality of being dishonest **deceitful** adj. = dishonest **deception** noun, u. = the act of deceiving someone **deceptive** adj. *She looks capable, but appearances are deceptive.* = something that can deceive; misleading

de•cent /'diːsənt/ adj. **1** *In our part of town, it is not considered decent to wear a sleeveless shirt.* = proper; socially acceptable (opposite **indecent**) **2** *She's such a decent person, she would never say anything about us which isn't true.* = kind and having a good moral sense **3** *He earns a decent salary.* = fairly good, respectable **decency** noun, u. **1** *She had the decency to admit that she had made a mistake.* = the quality of being fair-minded **2** = socially acceptable conduct, especially connected with sex

de•cen•tral•ize (decentralise) /diː'sentrəlaɪz/ verb, t. *The Reserve Bank had an office only in Delhi, but now it has been decentralized and will have offices in every state.* = to move a government or business from one central place to several different places (opposite **centralize**) [TECHNICAL]

dec•i•bel /'desɪbel/ noun, c. *The sound produced by a motorcycle measures more than 120 decibels.* = a measure of the loudness of a sound [PHYSICS]

de•cide /d'ɪsaɪd/ verb, t.or i. **1** *I may go to Darjeeling for my holiday or I may go to Kerala. I have not decided yet.*(i.) = to make a choice or to make up one's mind to do something **2** *The government has decided to transfer you to Assam.*(t.) = to make up one's mind to do something

dec•i•mal /'desɪməl/ noun, c. **1** *the decimal system* = based on the number 10 **2** *You can write the number either as 2½, using a fraction, or as 2.5, using a decimal point.* = a mark, shown as (.), which tells us that a number is being expressed as a fraction of 10 [MATHEMATICS]

dec•i•mate /'desɪmeɪt/ verb, t. *The deer population in the forest was decimated by the fire.* = to destroy a large part of something (formal)

de•ci•pher /dɪ'saɪfə[r]/ verb, t. *The police department is trying to decipher this letter.* = to try to find the meaning of something that is not clear (see also **code** or **cipher**)

decision /dɪ'sɪʒən/ noun, u. **1** *We are waiting for your decision.* = the act of making up one's mind **2** *The umpire has given his decision. The batsman is out!* = judgement

decisive /dɪ'saɪsɪv/ adj. **1** *Sri Lanka has won the match by 200 runs. This is a decisive victory.* = something that leaves no doubt in anyone's mind **2** *Manoj takes too long to choose his clothes. He should be more decisive.* = able to come to a decision quickly (opposite **indecisive**)

deck[1] /dek/ noun, c. **1** *the deck of a ship* = the uppermost open level of a ship; one of the floors of a ship or bus built at different levels **2** *a deck of cards* = a complete set of 52 playing cards

deck[2] verb, t. *The students have decked out the school building with coloured lights for Republic Day.* = to decorate (literary)

de•clare /dɪ'kleə[r]/ verb, t. **1** *Have we as a group declared our policy on the use of nuclear weapons? / / Once a country declares war, there is no escape from it.* = to make something known to the public **2** *I declare this meeting closed.* = to make a formal announcement of an event **3** *The customs officer asked me to declare the things I had brought from Singapore.* = to give to an officer a list of the things for which tax has to be paid **4** *The Sri Lankan captain declared the innings.* = to end a batting innings, in the game of cricket, before all the players in the side are out **declaration** /deklə'reɪʃən/ noun, u. = the act of declaring something **declarative** /dɪ'klærətɪv/ adj. *'I like tea' is a declarative sentence, but 'Do you like tea?' is an interrogative sentence.* = a sentence that has the form of a statement [GRAMMAR]

de•cline[1] /dɪ'klaɪn/ verb, i. **1** *The British empire was at its height in the nineteenth century, but by 1945 its power had declined.* = to become less or weaker;

to go from a better to a worse position **2** *I requested the film star for her autograph but she declined.* = to refuse

decline[2] noun, u. **1** *The decline of the kingdom began when many wars had weakened it.* = a period or process of declining (going from a good to a bad position) **2** *The birth rate in Kerala is showing a decline.* = reduction; decrease

de•code /diːˈkəʊd/ verb, t. = to find out the meaning of something which is written in a code (see **decipher**) [TECHNICAL]

de•com•pose /diːkəmˈpəʊz/ verb, i. or t. **1** *The body of the dead animal is decomposing.*(i) = to decay; to rot [TECHNICAL] **2** (t.) = to make a chemical compound etc. break up into simple parts [CHEMISTRY]

dec•o•rate /ˈdekəreɪt/ verb, t. **1** *We will decorate the house with potted plants.* = to make something look more beautiful or attractive **2** *He was decorated with a medal for his courage.* = an honour given in a formal ceremony **decorative** adj. = used for decorating **decoration** /dekəˈreɪʃən/ noun, u. or c. **1** (u.) = the act of decorating something **2** (c.) = something that decorates

de•co•rum /dɪˈkɔːrəm/ noun, u. *There should be no shouting at the meeting. We must maintain decorum.* = correct or proper behaviour which is socially approved of (formal) **decorous** /ˈdekərəs/ adj. = acceptable and correct; in keeping with decorum (opposite **indecorous**)

de•coy /ˈdiːkɔɪ/ noun, c. *A policeman, dressed as a shopkeeper, was used as a decoy to trap the gang of thieves.* = something or someone that is used to trap and catch an animal or a person

de•crease[1] /ˈdiːkriːs/ verb, t. *If India's exports are decreasing, there is cause for alarm.* = to become less

decrease[2] noun, u. *There is a decrease in our exports.* = the fact of becoming less (opposite **increase**)

de•cree[1] /dɪˈkriː/ verb, t. *The government has decreed that no medical college can run without proper laboratory facilities.* = to order officially (formal)

decree[2] noun, u. = an official order by the government

de•crep•it /dɪˈkrepɪt/ adj. *a decrepit old house* = in a poor and weak condition due to age

de•cry /dɪˈkraɪ/ verb, t. *People have been decrying his books for years, but I enjoy them.* = to say bad things about someone or something

ded•i•cate /ˈdedɪkeɪt/ verb, t. **1** *Mahatma Gandhi dedicated his life to the cause of India's freedom.* = to offer or give something to a cause or a person **2** *We need a dedicated telephone line for our Internet connection.* = meant only for a particular kind of use [COMPUTERS & TECHNICAL] **dedication** /dedɪkeɪʃən/ noun, u. or c. **1** *She always works with great dedication.*(u.) = giving oneself up completely to the work that one is doing **2** *The dedication at the beginning of the book shows how much the writer loved his wife.*(c.) = the words at the beginning of a book offering it to someone

de•duce /dɪˈdjuːs/ verb, t. *You look tired and your eyes are red. I can deduce that you haven't slept at all.* = to reach a conclusion on the basis of some evidence (formal)

de•duct /dɪˈdʌkt/ verb, t. *The examiner may deduct marks if you use too many abbreviations.* = to take away something from a larger amount (formal)

de•duc•tion /dɪˈdʌkʃən/ noun, u. or c. **1** *I have used deduction to come to this conclusion.*(u.) = the process of deducing something (see **deduce**) (opposite **induction**) **2** *Your deduction that he has been delayed because of heavy traffic is quite logical.*(c.) = something that is deduced **3** *The deduction of two marks from his test score will teach him to be more careful.*(u.) = something that is deducted (taken away)

deed /diːd/ noun, c. **1** *They have done many good deeds, such as building hospitals where treatment is free.* = something that one does **2** *I have signed a deed giving this property to my children.* = a legal document that shows ownership of some property [LAW]

deem /diːm/ verb, t. *I deem it an honour to be your friend.* = to consider (formal) **deemed** adj. *a deemed university* = considered to be

deep[1] /diːp/ adj. **1** *The river is deep.* = a long way down from the top **2** *The forest is deep.* = a long way from the outside to the centre **3** *deep-blue sky* = of a strong and dark colour **4** *a deep voice* = low **5** *deep sleep* = not easily awakened **6** *in deep trouble* = serious **7** *She looks simple but is quite a deep person.* = having thoughts and feelings that one does not know about

deep[2] adv. **1** *I was so deep in thought, I did not hear the children come in.* = involved or absorbed **2** *deep in debt* = so much that it is not easy to come out of it **deep fry** verb = to fry some food, keeping it completely covered in oil **deep freeze** noun = a machine that keeps food at a very low temperature so that it does not get spoilt

to go off the deep end = to become very angry at something **to be in deep water** = to be in serious trouble

deer /dɪəʳ/ noun, c. (**deer**) = a large grass-eating animal

de•face /dɪˈfeɪs/ verb, t. *The walls of the Red Fort have been defaced by people who write their names across them.* = to spoil the way something looks by making dirty marks on its surface (formal, disapproving)

de•fac•to /dəɪˈfæktəʊ/ adj. (Latin) *The army took de facto control of the country.* = in actual fact, though not legally or officially (opposite **de jure**)

de•fame /dɪˈfeɪm/ verb, t. *He is out to defame you and has been talking against you for years.* = to spoil someone's reputation by saying false things about him/her

de•fault[1] /dɪˈfɒlt/ verb, i. *She took a loan from the bank and had to pay back Rs 5,000 every month, but this month she has defaulted on the payment as she had no money.* = to fail to do something (e.g. repaying a loan) that one is required to do by law or by a contract [TECHNICAL]

default[2] noun, u. **1** *Mehek was not on the list for the scholarship, but got it by default as the person who had been selected joined another college.* = something that is allowed to happen because something else does not happen **2** *This computer uses Windows 95 as default.* = a set of instructions built into a computer program which it will follow unless different instructions are given [COMPUTERS]

de•feat[1] /dɪˈfiːt/ verb, t. **1** *India defeated Australia in a one-day match.* = to win in a game, fight, vote etc. **2** *Our plans were defeated by the lack of money.* = to prevent something from becoming successful

defeat[2] noun, u. or c. *Australia's defeat in the match was unexpected.*(c.) = the fact of being defeated

de•fe•cate /ˈdefɪkeɪt/ verb, t. = to get rid of solid waste from the body (formal)

de•fect[1] /dɪˈfekt/ noun, c. or u. **1** *These clothes are being sold very cheaply because they have some manufacturing defects.*(c.) = fault; something missing or wrongly done **2** *a hearing defect*(u.) = problem

defect[2] verb, i. = to leave a political party and join an opposing party

de•fend /dɪˈfend/ verb, t. **1** *Are you trained to defend yourself if someone attacks you?* = to keep someone or something safe from danger **2** *This lawyer will defend you in court.* = to speak for someone who has been accused of committing some crime **defence** noun, u. or c. **1** *When her mother was criticized she leapt to her defence.*(u.) = the act of defending **2** *We have planted thousands of trees as a defence against storms.*(c.) = a means of defending something **3** *The defence will try to prove that the accused is not guilty.* = the lawyer or lawyers who are defending an accused person in a court of law [LAW] **4** = the military weapons used for protecting a country

de•fen•sive /dɪˈfensɪv/ adj. **1** *The army took up a defensive position on the mountain.* = suitable for protecting oneself from an attack **2** *You need not be so defensive. I am not finding fault with your work.* = prepared to protect oneself from criticism

to be on the defensive = to expect an attack and to be prepared for it **to become defensive** = to try to defend your actions even when you are not being criticized

de•fer /dɪˈfɜːʳ/ verb, t. (**deferred**) *Today's meeting has been deferred to next week.* = to delay until a later date; postpone (formal)

de•fi•cient /dɪˈfɪʃənt/ adj. *The food we eat is deficient in vitamins.* = not containing enough of something

de•fi•cit /ˈdefɪsɪt/ noun, u. *The harvest was poor this year and we expect a deficit of 200 million tonnes of foodgrains.* = the amount by which something is less than what is required or expected

de•file /dɪˈfaɪl/ verb, t. *The water of the lake has been defiled by the garbage that is being thrown into it.* = to make something dirty or impure (formal)

de•fine /dɪˈfaɪn/ verb, t. **1** *We define 'zoo' as a place where wild animals are kept.* = to give the meaning of a word **2** *The rules of the game have been defined in the manual.* = to show or explain the nature of something clearly **defined** adj. *It was dark and although I could see something in the room, it was not clearly defined.* = having a clear shape (so that one can tell what it is)

def•i•nite /ˈdefɪnɪt/ adj. *Everyone has suggestions about when we can fix up the meeting. Now let's think of a definite date.* = clear and exact; fixed **definite article** noun, c. *In the sentence 'The old man has arrived', 'the' is a definite article.* = the word 'the', used to talk about a particular person, place or thing [GRAMMAR]

def•i•ni•tion /defɪˈnɪʃən/ noun, u. or c. *Can you give me the definition of the term 'isosceles triangle'?* = the meaning of a word or phrase or idea

de•flate /diːˈfleɪt/ verb, t. or i. **1** *Someone pricked the balloon with a pin and deflated it.*(t.) = to become smaller by losing air (opposite **inflate**) [TECHNICAL] **2** *The singer felt deflated when someone said that she had a poor voice.* = to become less self-confident or proud; to feel let down (figurative)

de•flect /dɪˈflekt/ verb, t. or i. **1** *The ball hit the door of the car and got deflected.* = to change direction after hitting something **2** *Sports deflected her from her studies.* = to turn one's attention away from something

de•for•es•ta•tion /diːfɒrɪˈsteɪʃən/ noun = the act of cutting down trees (opposite **afforestation**) [TECHNICAL]

de•form /dɪˈfɔːm/ verb, t. *His fingers have become deformed after the accident.* = to spoil the original shape or appearance of something; to lose original shape

de•fraud /dɪˈfrɔːd/ verb, t. *defraud the bank of Rs 5 million* = to cheat [LAW]

deft /deft/ adj. *He moves quickly. He is a deft fielder.* = skilful and quick

de•funct /dɪˈfʌŋkt/ adj. *This is a defunct railway station. No one uses it now.* = not in use; dead and forgotten (formal)

de•fuse /diːˈfjuːz/ verb, t. **1** *to defuse a bomb* = to remove the fuse of a bomb (the part that causes the bomb to explode) so that it cannot cause any harm **2** *to defuse a dangerous situation* = to remove the cause of trouble and make a situation calmer (figurative)

de•fy /dɪˈfaɪ/ verb, t. **1** *I told them to stay at home and help but they defied me and went to the cinema instead.* = to act on purpose against someone's wishes or orders; to disobey **2** *AIDS is spreading rapidly and has defied all attempts to control it.* = to defeat; to make something unsuccessful

de•gen•e•rate /dɪˈdʒenəreɪt/ verb, i. *The meeting degenerated into a quarrel when people lost their tempers and started shouting.* = to change from a higher or better state into a lower or worse state (formal)

de•gen•e•ra•tion /dɪdʒenəˈreɪʃən/ noun, u. = the loss of quality or value

de•grade /dɪˈgreɪd/ verb, t. **1** *Please don't degrade me by criticising me in front of my friends.* = to cause someone to lose respect **2** *If dead plants or animals are left to rot in the soil, they slowly get degraded into simple chemicals which make the soil richer.* = to change from a higher form of matter to a lower or simpler form due to the action of bacteria [TECHNICAL] **degradable** (**biodegradable**) adj. *The government has banned the use of plastic bags because plastics are not biodegradable.* = something which can be broken down by the action of bacteria into simple substances which do not harm the soil [TECHNICAL]

de•gree /dɪˈgriː/ noun, c. or u. **1** *Water boils at 100 degrees centigrade.* **2** *Angle ABC measures 70 degrees.*(c.) = a unit for the measurement of temperatures or angles [GEOMETRY] **3** *He has received the B.A. degree.*(c.) = a title given by a university to a student who has passed an examination **4** *There is always a degree of danger in rock climbing.*(u.) = a certain level or amount

by degrees *She has been ill and is now getting back her strength by degrees.* = in a slow and gradual way

de•hy•dra•te /diːhaɪˈdreɪt/ verb, t. *Dehydrated potatoes can be stored for a long time.* = to remove water from something in order to make it last longer [TECHNICAL] **dehydrated** adj. *dehydrated food* = artificially drained of water and dried in order to preserve **dehydration** noun, u. *You must drink a lot of water in summer or you will suffer dehydration.* = loss of water from the body [MEDICINE]

de•i•fy /ˈdiːɪfaɪ/ verb, t. (**deified**) *Our leader never wanted people to deify him.* = to turn someone into a god or an object of worship (formal)

deity /ˈdiːɪti/ noun, c. (**deities**) = a god or goddess (formal)

de•jec•ted /dɪˈdʒektɪd/ adj. *She is very dejected after losing the match.* = sad because of disappointment

de jure /diːˈdʒʊəri/ adj. (Latin) *the de jure ruler of the country* = in law, but not in fact (compare with **defacto**)

de•lay[1] /dɪˈleɪ/ verb, t. or i. **1** *The meeting was to be held at 10 o' clock, but we have delayed it by an hour.*(t.) = to move something to a later time **2** *We could not come in time as we were delayed by the heavy traffic.*(t.) = to make someone late

delay[2] noun, c. or u. **1** *I'm sorry, there will be a delay of half an hour in today's programme.* = the time by which an event is moved back **2** *He promised to do the work without delay.*(u.) = letting more time pass **3** *Delays are expected on all south-bound trains.*(c.) = (used especially of travel by train, air, bus etc. and traffic) going beyond the time stated for something to happen

del•e•gate[1] /ˈdelɪgɪt/ noun, c. = someone who is chosen to speak or vote for a group at a meeting; a representative

delegate[2] /ˈdelɪgeɪt/ verb, t. *I have delegated part of my duty to a junior colleague.* = to give one's powers or rights to someone for a short time

de•lete /dɪˈliːt/ verb, t. *I don't want my name to be included in this list. Please delete it.* = to remove something that has been written or printed (formal) **deletion** noun, u. or c. **1** = the act of deleting **2** = something that has been deleted

de•lib•e•rate[1] /dɪˈlɪbərət/ adj. *I stepped on his foot accidentally, but he thought it was deliberate.* = something (often unpleasant) that is done knowingly; on purpose

deliberate[2] /dɪˈlɪbərəɪt/ verb, t. *The senior members of the club will meet to deliberate who should be made the next president.* = to discuss and consider carefully before making a decision (formal)

del•i•ca•cy /ˈdelɪkəsi/ noun, c. (**delicacies**) or u. **1** *Biriyani is considered a delicacy.*(c.) = food that is loved but is generally expensive **2** *She acted with great delicacy in this matter.* = with great care not to offend

de•li•cate /ˈdelɪkɪt/ adj. **1** *These glasses are very delicate. They must be packed carefully or they will break.* = something that can break easily and therefore needs careful handling **2** *a delicate child* = falling sick frequently **3** *a Kashmiri shawl with delicate embroidery* = made with great skill **4** *The reason for his divorce is a delicate matter.* = something that should be treated or talked about with great care **5** *The food has a delicate taste.* = gentle; not strong

de•li•cious /dɪˈlɪʃəs/ adj. *What delicious food!* = tasty and enjoyable

de•light[1] /dɪˈlaɪt/ noun, u. or c. **1** *My children find great delight in feeding the dog.*(u.) = joy **2** *Have you visited the delights of this city?*(c.) = something that gives delight

delight[2] verb, t. or i. **1** *This is a wonderful book which will delight your children.*(t.) = to give great pleasure **2** *He delights in playing with children.*(i.) // *She delights in teasing animals.*(i.) = to take pleasure in doing something, either pleasant, or unpleasant and unkind **delightful** adj. *We spent a delightful evening telling each other jokes.* = filled with pleasure

de•lin•quent[1] /dɪˈlɪŋkwənt/ noun, c. = someone, usually very young, who breaks the law [LAW]

delinquent[2] adj. *a delinquent child* = a young person who has broken the law

de•lir•i•um /dɪˈlɪriəm/ noun, u. or c. **1** *The man had high fever and was talking in a delirium.*(u.) = a dream-like state often caused by illness **2** *He was in a delirium of joy.*(c.) = a very excited state **delirious** adj. *He was delirious with fever.* = in a state of delirium

de•liv•er /dɪˈlɪvəʳ/ verb, t. or i. **1** *The postman delivers letters to our homes.*(t.) = to bring or carry to the place requested **2** *He delivered a fine speech.*(t.) = to say something in a formal way **3** *The doctor delivered the baby in the hospital.*(t.) = to help in the birth of [MEDICINE] **4** *I hope the chairperson delivers on his promise.*(i.) = to do/give something promised **5** *She delivered a hard thump on the door as it was stuck.*(t.) = give with force **6** *She was in great pain and prayed to be delivered from it.*(t.) = to save from harm (formal)

de•liv•er•y /dɪˈlɪvərɪ/ noun, u. **1** *The next postal delivery is at 3.00 p.m.* = the act of delivering something, specially letters etc. **2** *My sister had a painless delivery.* = birth of a baby **3** *The delivery of your speech was brilliant.* = style of speaking

del•ta /ˈdeltə/ noun, c. **1** = the fourth letter of the Greek alphabet, written as (Δ,δ) **2** = a piece of land shaped like a triangle, formed at the place where a river divides into smaller rivers before it falls into the sea [GEOGRAPHY]

de•lude /dɪˈluːd/ verb, t. *to delude people with sweet words* = to deceive by misleading **delusion** noun, u. or c. *He is under the delusion that everyone admires him, but we know that it is not true.*(c.) = false idea or impression

de•luge[1] /ˈdeljuːdʒ/ noun, u. or c. **1** *There was a lot of damage to houses in the deluge.*(u.) = a great flood **2** *The film star received a deluge of letters.*(c.) = a very large number of something (humorous)

deluge[2] verb, t. *The organisers of the show were deluged with requests for tickets.* = to be flooded with, all at the same time

de•luxe /dɪˈlʌks/ adj. *a deluxe room in a hotel* = of very high quality and therefore expensive

de•mag•ne•tize (demagnetise) /diːˈmægnətaɪz/ verb, t. = to take away the magnetic qualities of a magnet or piece of metal (opposite **magnetize**) [TECHNICAL]

dem•a•gogue /ˈdeməgɒg/ noun, c. = a political leader who can attract crowds through the ability to speak with great emotion, not with logic and argument (formal, derogatory)

de•mand[1] /dɪˈmɑːnd/ verb, t. **1** *The employees demanded an increase in their pay.* = to ask strongly for something **2** *This old car demands repairs urgently.* = to be in great need of

demand[2] noun, c. or u. **1** *We are unable to fulfill your demands.*(c.) = something that is demanded **2** *There is great demand for Sri Lankan tea all over the world.*(u.) = desire on the part of a group of people for something **demanding** adj. *My new job is very demanding.* = requiring a lot of attention and effort **to be in demand** *During festivals, sweets are greatly in demand.* = to be wanted by many people **to make demands on** *I think you should try and work by yourself and not make such demands on my time.* = to expect or use a great deal of something e.g. time

de•mar•cate /ˈdiːmaːkeɪt/ verb, t. *The boundary between the two countries is clearly demarcated.* = to mark the limits of something [LAW]

demi- prefix meaning 'half' or 'partly' e.g. **a demi-god**

de•mise /dɪˈmaɪz/ noun, u. *He became the chairperson of the company on the demise of his father.* = death (formal) [LAW]

de•mo•bi•lize (demobilise) /diːˈməʊbɪlaɪz/ verb, t. = to send soldiers home after the end of a war (opposite **mobilize**)

de•moc•ra•cy /dɪˈmɒkrəsi/ noun, u. or c. (**democracies**) **1** (u.) = the system of having an elected government **2** *India is the world's largest democracy.*(c.) = a country which has an elected government

dem•o•crat•ic /deməˈkrætɪk/ adj. **1** *a democratic government* = based on a system of democracy **2** *a democratic workplace* = having or supporting equal rights and the same rules/standards for all persons

de•mog•ra•phy /dɪˈmɒgrəfi/ noun = the study of

changes (births, deaths etc) in a human population **demographic** /deməˈgræfɪk/ adj.= connected with the study of population

de•mo•lish /dɪˈmɒlɪʃ/ verb, t. *Builders will demolish the old market and build a new block of apartments here.* = to pull down

de•mon /ˈdiːmən/ noun, c. = an evil, supernatural being or a cruel person

dem•on•strate /ˈdemənstreɪt/ verb, t. or i. **1** *The engineer demonstrated the use of the tractor to the farmers.*(t.)= to show how something is done **2** *We are going to take out a procession to demonstrate against the new tax laws.*(i.) = to make a public show of a strong feeling or opinion **demonstration** /demənˈstreɪʃən/ noun, u. or c. **1** *He gave us a demonstration of how the pump works.* = an example of showing how something is done **2** *About 10,000 people took part in the demonstration.* = a public expression of strong feeling

de•mor•al•ize (demoralise) /dɪˈmɒrəlaɪz/ verb, t. *The defeat by the Sri Lankan team has demoralized the Indian cricket players.* = to make someone lose courage and confidence

de•mote /dɪˈməʊt/ verb, t. *The Manager has been demoted to the rank of Assistant Manager.* = to lower someone in rank or position (opposite **promote**)

den /den/ noun, c. **1** *the tiger's den* = the home of a wild animal **2** *a den of thieves* = a place where secret, illegal activity goes on **3** *My brother is in his den.* = a small, comfortable room in a house where one can be alone (slang)

de•ni•al /dɪˈnaɪəl/ noun, u. or c. **1** *the denial of the report* = the act of saying that something is not true (informal) (see **deny**) **2** *We are upset by the government's denial of permission to set up a new factory.* = the act of refusing to give something

den•im /ˈdenɪm/ noun, u. = strong and thick cotton cloth used for making jeans, jackets etc. (see **blue-jeans**)

de•nom•i•na•tor /dɪˈnɒmineitəʳ/ noun, c. *In the fraction 3/5, 5 is the denominator.* = the number by which a whole is divided into parts [MATHEMATICS]

de•note /dɪˈnəʊt/ verb, t. *The word 'teacher' denotes someone who helps us to learn .* = to carry a certain meaning **denotation** /diːnəʊˈteɪʃən/ noun, u. = the meaning actually carried by a word, rather than the ideas that are suggested by it [TECHNICAL] (see **connotation**)

de•nounce /dɪˈnaʊns/ verb, t. *The newspapers denounced the government's plan to cut down trees in order to build a new road.* = to express strong opposition to something **denunciation** noun, u. = the action of denouncing something or someone

dense /dens/ adj. **1** *Traffic on the roads is very dense in the morning.* = many things crowded closely together **2** *Why are you acting so dense? What I am saying is very easy to understand.* = not intelligent; stupid (informal)

dent[1] /dent/ noun, c. **1** *There is a dent in my car where it was hit by a scooter.* = a hollow place in a metal surface, damaged after being hit with force, but not broken **2** *I tried hard to persuade him to save, but didn't make a dent on him.* = an impression made as a result of persuasion etc. to make a person do something (informal)

dent[2] verb, t. *The car was badly dented in the accident.* = to make a dent

den•tal /ˈdentəl/ adj. *Don't neglect your dental health. Look after your teeth.* = connected with the teeth **dentist** noun, c. = a doctor who looks after teeth **dentures** noun (used in plural form only) = false teeth

de•nude /dɪˈnjuːd/ verb, t. *The cyclone has uprooted millions of trees. The whole area is denuded of trees.*= to take away the natural covering of something and leave it bare (formal)

de•ny /dɪˈnaɪ/ verb, t. **1** *We were told that Robert had chicken pox but Robert denies this.* = to refuse to accept something, usually something unpleasant, as true **2** *They denied him permission to enter the country though he applied many times.* = to refuse to give or allow

de•o•do•rant /diːˈəʊdərənt/ noun, c.= something that is used on the body to prevent unpleasant body smells

de•part /dɪˈpɑːt/ verb, i. *The train to Chennai will arrive at 8.15 and depart at 8.35.* = to leave a place (formal) **departure** noun, u. or c. **1** = the act of departing (leaving a place) **2** *The meeting will take place on a Sunday. This is a departure from the usual practice*(n.) = done differently from what is usual or has happened before

de•part•ment /dɪˈpɑːtmənt/ noun, c. **1** *the Department of Biology* = a division or branch of a government, business, university etc. which deals with a particular activity or subject **2** *I will organise the event, but the tickets are your department.* = an activity that is the special responsibility of a person (informal)

de•pend /dɪˈpend/ verb, i. **1** *If Arun says he will help you, he will keep his word. You can depend on* *him.* = to have trust or confidence in someone **2** *This school gets no help from the government. It depends entirely on the fees received from the students.* = to be supported by **3** *Whether you do well in the exam or not will depend on the effort you put in.* = to be decided by **dependant** noun, c. *Until he finds a job, he is a dependant. // The widow has two dependants whom she has to support.* = a person who depends on someone else for everything he/she needs **dependable** adj. *She'll do the job well. She's very dependable.* = someone or something which one can trust or depend on

it/that depends *'Are you leaving tonight or tomorrow?' 'That depends.'* = a way of replying to someone that something depends on something else (informal)

dependent /dɪˈpendənt/ adj. *The patient has breathing problems and is dependent on a supply of oxygen.* = needing the support of someone or something

de•pict /dɪˈpɪkt/ verb, t. *This painting depicts an urban scene in India 150 years ago.* = to show; to represent (formal)

de•plete /dɪˈpliːt/ verb, t. *As we continue to use great amounts of energy, the earth's coal reserves are getting depleted every day.* = to make something less (formal)

de•plore /dɪˈplɔːʳ/ verb, t. *When the Indian team lost the match, the crowd started throwing plastic bottles at the players. I deplore such behaviour.* = to express strong dislike or disapproval

de•ploy /dɪˈplɔɪ/ verb, t. **1** = to put soldiers in position, ready to fight **2** *deploy our resources* = to use something in order to get results [TECHNICAL]

de•port /dɪˈpɔːt/ verb, t. *Some foreigners who were smuggling drugs into the country have been arrested. They will be deported.* = to send someone, usually a foreigner, out of the country for breaking the law or not having the legal right to be there [LAW] **deportation** /depəˈteɪʃən/ noun, u. = the act of sending someone out of the country [LAW]

de•pose /dɪˈpəʊz/ verb, i. *The revolutionaries deposed the dictator.* = to remove a ruler from power [TECHNICAL]

de•pos•it[1] /dɪˈpɒzɪt/ verb, t. **1** *I want to deposit this money in my bank account.* = to put money in a bank **2** *Each year the river gets flooded and deposits a lot of mud on the fields.* = to leave behind **3** *Please deposit your books at the counter before you enter the library* = to put something down at a stated place (formal)

deposit[2] noun, c. **1** *What is the amount of the deposit you have made?* = money paid into a bank **2** *There is a deposit of some white substance at the bottom of this bottle of juice.* = solid matter that sinks to the bottom of a liquid **3** *You can take away six bottles of the drink, but you will have to pay a deposit of Rs 5 for each bottle which will be refunded when you return the empty bottles.* = money paid as a part of the price at the time of buying or renting something, which can be returned to the buyer later

dep•ot /depəʊ/ noun, c. **1** = a place where things are stored; a warehouse or godown **2** *a bus depot* = a place where buses are parked and repaired

de•pre•ci•ate /dɪˈpriːʃieɪt/ verb, i. *Earlier, one American dollar was equal to Rs 42 but now it is worth much more. The rupee has depreciated quite a lot.* = to lose value (opposite **appreciate**) **depreciation** noun, u. = the process by which something which has value e.g. a building or a car, loses some of this value because it gets old or because of market conditions

de•press /dɪˈpres/ verb, t. **1** *His friend's failure in the exam has depressed him.* = to make someone unhappy **2** *The telecom strike has depressed business activity.* = to make something less active **3** *Please depress this lever to flush the toilet.* = to press down (formal) **depressed** adj. *She was depressed about moving to another city but soon cheered up.* = very unhappy **depressing** adj. *We found the film very depressing and felt sad for a long time.* = saddening, with a sense of little hope **depression** noun, u. **1** = a condition in which one feels depressed **2** *The water from the rains had collected in the depression on the road.* = a point in a road, etc. where the level is lower before it levels up again **3** *The depression during times of war results in a lot of hardship.* = a period in which business activity is low **4** *a depression over the Bay of Bengal* = a weather condition caused by low atmospheric pressure which may result in rain etc. [GEOGRAPHY]

de•prive /dɪˈpraɪv/ verb, t. *The breakdown in the power supply forced us to close the cinema and deprived us of our only means of entertainment.* = to take away something which one needs or has a right to

depth /depθ/ noun, u. or c. (see **deep**) **1** *The depth of the river is six metres.* = the distance from the surface or top to the bottom (see pic under **dimension**) **2** *The depth of feeling in this poem is remarkable.* = the extent (of feeling, knowledge etc.)

in-depth *We have made an in-depth study of this problem.* = going deeply into some question; thorough study **to be out of one's depth** *Ten minutes into the discussion on nuclear physics, I realised that I was out of my depth.* = to be unable to understand something because one does not know enough about it

dep•u•ta•tion /depjʊ'teɪʃən/ noun, c. or u. *A deputation from the employees' union will meet the manager.* = a small group of people who are asked by a larger group to represent them at a meeting etc.; a delegation **depute** /dɪ'pjuːt/ verb, t. *As the principal was busy, she deputed one of the teachers to attend the meeting.* = to appoint someone to do something in place of oneself **deputy** /'depjʊti/ noun, c. (**deputies**) *I am attending this meeting as the Manager's deputy.* = a person who is deputed by someone to take his/her place and is next in rank to that person

de•rail /diː'reɪl/ verb, t. *The train was derailed when it hit a bus at a railway crossing.* = to cause a train to run off the track [TECHNICAL]

de•ranged /dɪ'reɪndʒd/ adj. *a mentally deranged person* = completely unbalanced in mind (formal)

der•e•lict /'derɪlɪkt/ adj. *a derelict building/ship* = badly broken down and no longer in use

de•ride /dɪ'raɪd/ verb, t. *You may not like her poetry, but you don't have to deride it.* = to make fun of; to ridicule

de•rive /dɪ'raɪv/ verb, t. **1** *He derives most of his income from land.* = to get something from some source; to obtain **2** *This word is derived from Sanskrit.* = to come from something; to have as its origin (starting point) (formal) **derivative** /dɪ'rɪvətɪv/ noun, c. or adj. **1** *The word 'incomparable' is a derivative of the word 'compare'.*(noun, c.) = something which is developed from something else [TECHNICAL] **2** *His writing is derivative. He gets all his ideas from other writers.*(adj.) = not original; taken from other sources (derogatory) **derivation** [MATHEMATICS, SCIENCE]

de•rog•a•to•ry /dɪ'rɒgətəri/ adj. *The actor is angry because the magazine published a derogatory article about him.* = showing total lack of respect

de•scend /dɪ'send/ verb, t. or i. *The Ganga descends from the Himalayas to the plains below.* = to come down from a higher to a lower level (opposite **ascend**) **descendant** /dɪ'sendənt/ noun, u. *The Maharaja of Jaipur is said to be a descendant of Maharana Pratap.* = one who belongs to the same family as somebody who lived a long time ago (a grandson, great-grandson etc.) [HISTORY]

de•scribe /dɪ'skraɪb/ verb, t. *The police inspector asked me to describe the man who had attacked me.* = to tell what someone or something is like **description** /dɪ'skrɪpʃən/ noun, u. or c. *Here is a description of the person who will meet you at the railway station. She is tall, has long hair and wears glasses.*(c.) = something we write or say that describes someone or something

des•e•crate /'desɪkreɪt/ verb, t. *He doesn't want to descrate the church by using it for a political meeting.* = to misuse something which is holy

des•ert[1] /'dezət/ noun, c. = a large area of sand which is bare because of low rainfall, and where there is very little vegetation

de•sert[2] /dɪ'zɜːt/ verb, t. or i. **1** *Most people think he has deserted his family, but he has gone to the city only to look for a better job.*(t.) = to leave someone or something for whom (or which) one is responsible, usually for ever **2** *Minutes before the debate my confidence deserted me.*(t.) = to leave at a difficult time **3** = to leave the army without permission **deserter** noun, c. = a person who runs away without permission after joining the army [TECHNICAL]

de•serve /dɪ'zɜːv/ verb, t. *He earns about Rs 2,000 a month, but he deserves much more.* = to be worthy of receiving

des•ic•cate /'desɪkeɪt/ verb, t. = to make something dry [TECHNICAL]

de•sign[1] /dɪ'zaɪn/ verb, t. *I have asked an architect to design a house for me. // He designed a wonderful cover for the book.* = to plan something that is to be made or built

design[2] noun, c. or u. **1** *Let me show you the design for the new building.*(c.) = the plan or drawings for something that is to be built **2** *The carpet has a floral design*(u.) = a decorative pattern **designs** noun (always plural) *I trusted them until I realised they had designs on my money.* = plans which have an evil purpose (disapproving)

des•ig•nate[1] /'dezɪgneɪt/ verb, t. *She has been designated president of the club.* = to choose or name someone for a particular position

designate[2] noun *the president designate* = a person who has been chosen or named to take up a certain position but has not yet taken it up **designation** /'dezɪg'neɪʃən/ noun, u. or c. *My designation at the office is Director of Planning.* = title

de•sire[1] /dɪ'zaɪə^r/ verb, t. **1** *She desires that you meet her this evening.* = to want or wish (formal, old-fashioned) **2** = to be eager to have sexual relations with

desire[2] noun, c. or u. **1** *I hope that every desire of yours will be fulfilled.*(c.) = wish **2** = a powerful wish to have sex with someone **desirable** adj. *a highly desirable quality* = looked for when judging someone's skills etc. **desired** adj. *the desired aim* = something that was wished for or wanted

to leave a lot to be desired *His behaviour at work leaves a lot to be desired.* = not to have some important quality or skill (derogatory)

de•sist /dɪ'zɪst/ verb, i. *He asked his friend to desist* *from spending so much money on clothes.* = to stop doing something (formal)

desk /desk/ noun, c. = a table at which one reads or writes **desktop (computer)** noun = a small computer meant for use in the home or office **desktop publishing (DTP)** = printing and publishing books, magazines etc. with the use of a desktop computer and a printer

des•o•late /ˈdesələt/ adj. *She has built her house in a desolate place where no one ever goes.* = lonely and producing a feeling of sadness (literary)

de•spair[1] /dɪˈspeəʳ/ verb, i. *You may have failed in the examination but you should not despair. I am sure you will do better next time.* = to give up hope

despair[2] noun, u. *We were filled with despair when our house was destroyed in the fire.* = a feeling of losing all hope **desperate** /despərɪt/ adj. **1** *The woman is in a desperate situation as she has no money and no one to help her.* = hopeless **2** *She is desperate for work.* = ready to do anything to change the situation one is in **3** *The prisoners made a desperate attempt to escape.* = full of risk and done as a last attempt, because of a loss of hope

de•spise /dɪˈspaɪz/ verb, t. *I despise people who tell lies.* = to have an extremely low opinion of someone

de•spite /dɪˈspaɪt/ prep. *He came to the meeting despite the rain.* = in spite of

de•spon•dent /dɪˈspɒndənt/ adj. *He has not written the examination because he is despondent about passing.* = completely without hope for the future; expecting little improvement

des•pot /ˈdespɒt/ noun, c. *Our captain never listens to anyone and does whatever he likes. He is quite a despot.* = a person who has total control and uses it unjustly (disapproving)

des•sert /dɪˈzɜːt/ noun, u. or c. = something sweet which is served after a meal

des•ti•na•tion /destɪˈneɪʃən/ noun, u. or c. *The train has reached its destination.* = the place to which one is going or something is sent

des•ti•ny /ˈdestɪni/ noun, u. or c. *Nothing can stop me from becoming a great leader. This is my destiny.* = one's fate or what one is born to do or become in life

des•ti•tute /ˈdestɪtjuːt/ adj. *Many people lost their homes in the cyclone and have become destitute.* = without food, clothing, shelter etc. or the money to buy them

de•stroy /dɪˈstrɔɪ/ verb, t. *The fire has destroyed the building.* = to damage something so badly that it cannot be repaired **destroyer** noun, c. = a small and fast warship

destruction /dɪˈstrʌkʃən/ noun, u. = the act of destroying **destructive** adj. = something or someone that causes destruction

des•ul•to•ry /ˈdezəltəri/ adj. *We were sitting idly, having a desultory conversation.* = aimless; without a plan

de•tach /dɪˈtætʃ/ verb, t. *The boy is unhappy because he has been detached from his friends.* = to separate someone or something from a larger group/thing **detachment** noun, u. *His detachment has helped him get over his sorrow.* = the quality of being able to keep one's feelings separated from the situation one is in

de•tail[1] /ˈdiːteɪl/ noun, c. *Tell me everything that happened at the meeting. I want all the details.* = the extra and small points or facts and not just the main things

detail[2] verb, t. *He detailed the plans which had been made for the picnic.* = to give the details of something

de•tain /dɪˈteɪn/ verb, t. **1** *The teacher detained the student after class because he had not done his homework.* = to prevent someone from leaving **2** *I am sorry to be late. I was detained by the heavy traffic.* = to delay **detention** noun, c. = the act of detaining someone, specially a student after school as a punishment

de•tect /dɪˈtekt/ verb, t. *The police detected some fingerprints on the door-handle which may reveal the identity of the burglar.* = to find or discover something through careful observation **detective** noun, c. = a person whose job it is to search for information that will help the police to catch a criminal

de•ter /dɪˈtɜːʳ/ verb, t. (**deterred**) *The fear of injury deters me from taking part in active sports.* = to stop someone from doing something through fear, punishment etc. (formal)

det•er•gent /dɪˈtɜːdʒənt/ noun, c. = a soapless chemical substance that cleans clothes, floors etc.

de•te•ri•o•rate /dɪˈtɪəriəreɪt/ verb, i. *Rahim's health is deteriorating because of long hours of work in the sun.* = to become worse

de•ter•mi•na•tion /dɪtɜːmɪˈneɪʃən/ noun, u. = the ability to decide and act firmly according to one's decision **determine** /dɪˈtɜːmɪn/ verb, t. **1** *I am determined to complete the trek to Annapurna.* = to make up one's mind to do something **2** *Let us determine how much plastic waste is dumped in the city every day.* = to find out accurately **3** *The patient's age will determine the kind of treatment the doctors give her.* = to control or influence **determined** adj. *Anu is such a determined person that she is bound to succeed in her efforts.* = strongly focused on what one wants to do

de•ter•rent /dɪˈterənt/ noun, c. = something that

deters (stops one from doing something) **deterrent punishment** noun = heavy punishment given to someone to discourage others from doing something wrong [LAW] **deterrence** noun, u.

de•test /dɪ'test/ verb, t. *I detest having to make polite conversation.* = to dislike strongly

de•throne /dɪ'θrəʊn/ verb, t. = to remove someone (a king or a queen) from power [HISTORY]

det•o•nate /'detəneɪt/ verb, t. *They detonated a mine to blow up the bridge.* = to cause something to explode [TECHNICAL]

de•tour /'di:tʊə/ noun, c. *The road to the airport is very crowded. We will have to make a detour.* = a longer and roundabout journey to reach a place in order to avoid something

de•tract /dɪ'trækt/ verb, t. *You have written an excellent essay, but there are many spelling mistakes which detract from the quality of the writing.* = to reduce or lessen the value of something (formal)

det•ri•ment /'detrɪmənt/ noun, u. *It is not possible to set up a chemical factory near a town without detriment to the health of the people.* = harm or damage (formal) **detrimental** /detrɪ'məntəl/ adj. = able to cause harm

dev•a•state /'devəsteɪt/ verb, t. **1** *The storm devastated hundreds of villages.* = to destroy **2** *She was devastated when she lost her job.* = in a poor mental condition as a result of a great shock **devastating** adj. = causing great destruction or mental shock

de•vel•op /dɪ'veləp/ verb, t. or i. **1** *The automobile industry is developing rapidly.*(i.) = growing as planned **2** *She has developed into an excellent tennis player over the years.* = to grow into **3** *Education helps children to develop.*(i) = to bring out the best qualities of someone or something **4** *I liked your essay, but you should develop your last point a little more.*(t.) = to think out in detail **5** *The photographer has to develop the negatives.*(t.) = to cause pictures to appear on a film [PHOTOGRAPHY] **development** noun, u. or c. **1** *Foreign trade will help a country's economic development*(u.) = the process of developing (growing) **2** *What's the latest development in your office?*(c.) = a new event or piece of news **3** *There has been very little development in the treatment of some diseases of the eye.* = progress in research which helps solve a problem

de•vi•ate /'di:vieɪt/ verb, i. *He goes for a walk at five o' clock every morning and never deviates from this routine.* = to do something which is different from the expected or the normal thing **deviation** /dɪvɪ'eɪʃən/ noun, c. or u. = the act of deviating

de•vice /dɪ'vaɪs/ noun, c. **1** *My car is fitted with a device which allows me to use the mobile phone while I am driving.* = a machine or instrument which is used for a special purpose **2** *We planned a device to get him to write the letter.* = a way of achieving a goal which is clever and not straightforward

dev•il /'devəl/ noun, c. = an evil spirit or a wicked person

between the devil and the deep sea = facing a choice between two things which are equally unpleasant **to give the devil his/her due** *Though his behaviour on the tennis court is terrible, I must admit that he is a great player. After all, you have to give the devil his due!* = to be fair and just, even to a person who one otherwise cannot praise or admire **Talk of the devil!** = used to express surprise when someone who has just been mentioned arrives unexpectedly (informal)

de•vi•ous /'di:viəs/ adj. *He is such a devious person that you can never know what he is planning.* = clever but dishonest in a hidden way (disapproving)

dev•ise /dɪ'vaɪz/ verb, t. *Our scientists have devised a new computer which can talk.* = to build or do something new, using great intelligence or skill

de•void /dɪ'vɔɪd/ adj. His *speech was dull and devoid of humour.* = without; lacking in a particular quality

de•volve /dɪ'vɑlv/ verb, t. *While Amar is in hospital, his work will devolve on his deputy.* = to fall on or to pass on to someone else (formal)

de•vote /dɪ'vəʊt/ verb, t. *My mornings are devoted to physical exercise.* = to set apart for some purpose; to give a lot of attention to **devoted** adj. *a devoted parent* = very loving and caring in a steady way **devotee** /devə'ti:/ noun, c. **1** = a follower of God or a religious leader **2** *a devotee of detective fiction* = a person who has great love for or interest in something (humourous) **devotion** noun, u. = great fondness or love, specially in religious matters

de•vour /dɪ'vaʊə^r/ verb, t. *When I am hungry I can devour a large meal.* = to eat quickly and in large quantity when one is very hungry (used for emphasis or to create humour)

de•vout /dɪ'vaʊt/ adj. *a devout follower* = very religious and not questioning anything

dew /dju:/ noun, u. = small drops of water which collect on grass, leaves etc. during the night

dex•ter•i•ty /dek'sterɪti/ noun, u. *Our artists, who produce beautiful paintings, have great dexterity.* = skill **dexterous** /'dekstərəs/ adj. = possessing dexterity

di•a•be•tes /dɑiə'bi:ti:z/ noun = a disease in which the body is unable to control the level of sugar in the blood [MEDICINE] **diabetic** /dɑɪə'betɪk/ noun, c. or adj. = someone who suffers from diabetes

di•a•bol•i•cal /daɪəˈbɒlɪkəl/ adj. *a diabolical plan* = very evil and cruel

di•ag•nose /ˈdaɪəgnəʊz/ verb, t. *The doctors diagnosed his disease as malaria.* = to find out and say what disease someone is suffering from [MEDICINE] **diagnosis** /daɪəgˈnəʊsɪs/ noun, u. = the act of diagnosing a disease

di•ag•o•nal /daɪˈægənəl/ noun, c. = a line joining the two opposite corners of a four-sided figure [GEOMETRY] **diagonally** adv. *He walked diagonally across the room.* = from one corner to the opposite corner

di•a•gram /ˈdaɪəgræm/ noun, c. = a figure or scientific drawing which explains something e.g. the parts of the ear

dial[1] /daɪəl/ noun, c. **1** *the dial of a clock* = the face of an instrument, on which time, temperature, measure etc. are shown **2** *the dial of a telephone* = the part of a telephone on which the numbers are shown

dial[2] /daɪəl/ verb, t. *dial a number* = to push buttons or turn a disc on a telephone to make a phone call

di•a•lect /ˈdaɪəlekt/ noun, c. = the variety of a language spoken in one part of a country, which is different from other forms of the same language spoken elsewhere in the country [TECHNICAL]

di•a•logue /ˈdaɪəlɒg/ noun, u. or c. **1** *He has written the dialogue for the new film.*(c.) = the talk between the different characters in a book, play or film **2** *India and America have entered into a dialogue.*(u.) = an exchange of ideas and opinions, usually on a political issue

di•a•me•ter /daɪˈæmɪtəʳ/ noun, c. = the straight line joining one point on a circle to another point and passing through the centre of the circle [GEOMETRY]

di•a•mond /daɪəmənd/ noun, c. or u. **1** = a very hard and expensive precious stone used in jewellery **2** = the shape of a figure with four sides, pointed at the top and bottom **3** = a playing card with this figure printed on it **diamond jubilee** noun = a day which marks the completion of 60 years after some important event

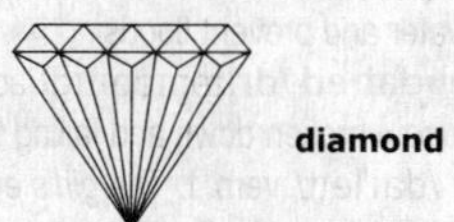

diamond

di•a•phragm /ˈdaɪəfræm/ noun, c. **1** = the muscle inside the body that separates the lungs from the stomach and helps one breathe [BIOLOGY] **2** = any piece of thin material inside a machine which stretches tightly across an opening

di•ar•rhoe•a /daɪəˈrɪə/ noun, u. = an illness in which waste matter in liquid form passes out of the bowels very frequently [MEDICINE]

di•a•ry /ˈdaɪəri/ noun, c. (**diaries**) = a book which has some space for every day of the year, in which one can write about the events that take place on that day

dice[1] /daɪs/ noun, c. (plural form of **die**) = small six-sided pieces of wood, bone or plastic, on each side of which there are dots to show numbers from one to six, used in playing certain games

dice[2] /daɪs/ verb, t. *Dice the chicken.* = to cut a vegetable or meat into small, square pieces for cooking

di•chot•o•my /daɪˈkɒtəmi/ noun, u. *There is a clear dichotomy in the group on the issue of using nuclear arms.* = a division of something into two opposite parts; opposing views on a subject

dic•tate /dɪkˈteɪt/ verb, t. or i. **1** = to tell or read something aloud so that another person can write it down or record it with the help of a machine **2** *Why do you want to dictate how I should run the house?* = to give orders and force someone to obey **dictation** noun, u. or c. **1** = the act of dictating **2** = something that is read out or spoken for another person to write down or type **dictator** noun = a ruler who has complete power and whom everyone is forced to obey

dic•tion /ˈdɪkʃən/ noun, u. **1** = the choice of words, specially in poetry **2** = the way in which somebody pronounces words

dic•tion•a•ry /ˈdɪkʃənəri/ noun, c. (**dictionaries**) = a book that contains a list of words in alphabetical order in the same language or in another language, together with their meanings, pronunciation, examples to show their use etc.

di•dac•tic /daɪˈdæktɪk/ adj. *This is a didactic poem which teaches us the importance of patriotism.* = something that tries to teach or is connected with education

die[1] /daɪ/ verb, i. (**died**) **1** = to stop living **2** *My faith in you will never die.* = (of a feeling) to disappear or stop

die[2] noun, c. **1** *We use dies to make these plastic chairs.* = a piece of metal used to press something into a certain shape **2** = one of a pair of dice, used in a game

The die has been cast = the decision has been made and cannot be changed **to die down** = to become less strong **to die out** = (of fashions, beliefs etc.) to disappear completely **to die for something** = to have a great desire for something (informal) **to be dying to do something** *I'm dying to see my baby cousin.* = to have a great wish to do something (informal) **to die for** *The ice-cream he makes is to die for.* = very wonderful or good (informal) **to die with one's boots on (to die in harness)** = to die while still active **to die away** *The sound was loud at first, then it died away.* = to become gradually less and come to an end

die•sel /'di:zəl/ noun, u. = heavy mineral oil that is burnt instead of petrol in car or truck engines **diesel engine** = a kind of engine used in trucks, buses etc. that burns diesel oil (named after its inventor, Rudolf Diesel)

diet[1] /'daɪət/ noun, u. or c. **1** *You need a balanced diet to stay healthy*(u.) = the food and drink that one takes **2** *He has gone on a diet to lose weight.*(c.) = the limited amount of food that one takes when trying to lose weight

diet[2] verb, i. *The doctors have advised him to diet.* = to control one's diet in order to lose weight

di•ffer /'dɪfər/ verb, i. **1** *My uncle and aunt differ very much in their nature. One is quiet while the other loves to talk.* = to be unlike **2** *We differ in our views on Hindi films.* = to disagree **difference** noun, u . or c. **1** *It is easy to see the difference between the two boys. One is tall while the other is short.* = the quality or qualities that make a person or thing different from another **2** *A train ticket to Kolkata costs Rs 300 while a bus ticket costs only Rs 180. The difference is quite a lot.* = the amount by which one thing is more or less than another **3** *I hear there has been some difference between your professor and you.* = disagreement or quarrel **different** adj. **1** *This is a different shirt from the one you wore this morning.* = not the same **2** *Mohsin and his brother are very different in their looks. One is tall while the other is short.* = not of the same kind **3** *I am getting letters from different places.* = separate

to make no difference **1** *It makes no difference whether you go tonight or tomorrow.* = to not be important **2** *I went all the way to be with them, but it didn't make any difference to them.* = to not have the effect that was desired (derogatory) **to make a difference** *I was feeling very low, and your cheerful telephone call made a great difference.* = a change in one's mood, feelings etc. for the better

dif•fi•cult /'dɪfɪkəlt/ adj. **1** *We expected the test to be easy but it was quite difficult.* = not easy **2** *He is such a difficult person that no one wants to work with him.* = hard to deal with; not easily made happy **3** *I am going through a difficult time.* = full of problems **difficulty** noun, u. or c. (**difficulties**) **1** *She walks with difficulty.*(u.) = great effort; not easily **2** *She has financial difficulties.*(c.) = trouble or problem

dif•fi•dent /'dɪfɪdənt/ adj. *He feels diffident about speaking to a large audience.* = lacking confidence in one's ability

dif•fuse /dɪ'fju:z/ verb, i. or t. *The lovely smell of roses diffused the room.* = to spread out in all directions **diffusion** noun, u.= the process of spreading gradually

dig[1] /dɪg/ verb, t. or i. (**dug**) *We have to dig a hole to plant this tree.*(t.) = to make a hole in the ground

dig[2] noun, c. *The remark that Hari made was a dig at me.* = something said to make fun of someone

to dig one's own grave = to cause serious trouble for oneself **to dig in** = to help oneself to food; to start eating (informal) **to dig one's heels in** = to refuse to change one's mind **to dig something out** = **1** to find something by searching (informal) **2** to get information from someone who is unwilling to give that piece of information (informal)

di•gest[1] /daɪ'dʒest/ verb, t. **1** *I can't digest rich food.*= to cause food to be changed into a form which the body can use **2** *The lecture was interesting. But it was too much to digest all at once.* = to understand thoroughly (figurative)

digest[2] noun, c. *He has made a digest of all the reports on this case.* = summary or abstract

di•git /'dɪdʒɪt/ noun, c. *Telephone numbers in most cities have seven or eight digits.* = a number from 0 to 9 **digital** adj. **1** *a digital watch* = showing quantities in the form of numbers and not points on a scale (opposite **analogue**) [TECHNICAL] **2** *a digital compact disc // a digital recording* = an electronic system that uses 0 and 1 to store sound or information

dig•ni•ty /'dɪgnɪti/ noun, u. **1** *She was feeling angry, but behaved with great dignity.* = a calm and serious manner which wins respect **2** *Everyone came to the meeting in formal wear, in keeping with the dignity of the occasion.* = seriousness and importance **dignitary** /'dɪgnɪtəri/ noun, c. (**dignitaries**) = a person in a high position

to be beneath/below one's dignity *I did not reply to the insulting remark because it was beneath my dignity.* = not in keeping with one's self-respect

di•gress /daɪ'gres/ verb, i. *You were telling us about the cricket match. Don't digress and start talking about your children.* = to move away from a subject **digression** noun, u. or c. *This is a digression from the subject.* = something that is not connected to what is being talked or written about

dike (**dyke**) /daɪk/ noun, c. = a wall built to hold back water and prevent floods

di•lap•i•dat•ed /dɪ'læpɪdeɪtɪd/ adj. *a dilapidated old house* = broken down and falling to pieces

di•late /daɪ'leɪt/ verb, t. *The girl's eyes dilated with fear while she saw the horror movie.* = (of eyes, body organs etc.) to grow larger or wider

di•lemma /dɪ'lemə/ noun, u. *I was planning to go to the cinema with my friend on Sunday but my teacher has invited me to lunch on the same day. I am in a dilemma as I cannot decide whether I should refuse the invitation or disappoint my friend.* = a delicate situation in which one has to choose between two actions or things

di•li•gent /ˈdɪlɪdʒənt/ adj. *If a student is diligent she can do well in the examination even if it is difficult.* = hardworking (formal)

dil•ly-dal•ly /dɪlɪˈdælɪ/ verb, i. *We must be at the station at 8 p.m. to catch the Delhi train. Get ready at once and don't dilly-dally* = to waste time unnecessarily (informal)

di•lute /daɪˈluːt/ verb, t. *You have to dilute the milk with water or the baby will not be able to digest it.* = to make a liquid thinner or weaker by mixing it with some other liquid

dim[1] /dɪm/ adj. **1** *I could not read the paper as the light was too dim.* = not bright (referring to a light) **2** *I saw the dim shape of a building in the distance.* = not clear **3** *The chances of our winning are dim.* = not hopeful **4** *a dim person* = not intelligent (informal, not respectful)

dim[2] verb, t. *Please dim your lights.* = to make less bright

to take a dim view of something = to disapprove

di•men•sion /daɪˈmenʃən/ noun, u. or c. **1** *The dimensions of this room are: length 5 metres, breadth 3.5 metres and height 2.5 metres* = measurement of the length, width or height **2** *We must discuss this problem in all its dimensions.* = an aspect (side) of a problem **dimensional** adj. *a three dimensional photograph* = having or appearing to have the stated number of dimensions (sides)

dimension

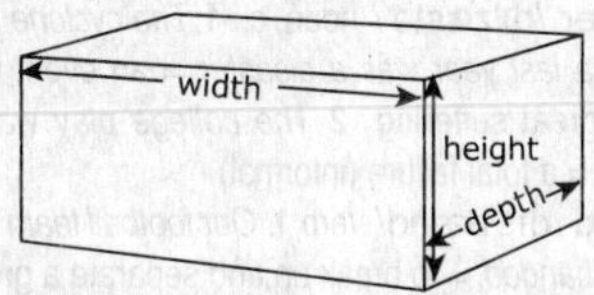

di•min•ish /dɪˈmɪnɪʃ/ verb, i. or t. *The singer's popularity has greatly diminished in the last two years. Her cassettes are not selling.* = to become less or reduce

di•min•u•tive /dɪˈmɪnjtɪv/ adj. *a diminutive house* = very small (formal)

dim•ple /ˈdɪmpəl/ noun, c. *the dimples in his cheeks* = the small hollow places formed in the cheeks usually when one smiles

din[1] /dɪn/ noun, u. *There was such a din in the room that I couldn't hear a word of the speech.* = continuous loud noise

din[2] verb, t. *She must pass the examination this time. You will have to din this into her ears.* = to repeat something frequently and in a slightly unpleasant way so as to make someone remember it (informal)

dine /daɪn/ verb, i. = to eat dinner (formal)

to dine out = to eat dinner in a restaurant

ding-dong[1] /ˈdɪŋdɒŋ/ adj. *a ding-dong battle* = noisy and exciting (informal)

ding-dong[2] noun, u. *I could hear the ding-dong of the bells in the clock tower* = the sound of bells

din•ghy /ˈdɪŋgi/ adj. = a small boat with a sail

din•gy /ˈdɪndʒi/ noun, c. *a dingy room* = dirty, dull-looking and dark

din•ner /ˈdɪnəʳ/ noun, c. or u. **1** (u.) = the main meal of the day, usually taken in the evening **2** *We are having a dinner tomorrow in the students' honour.*(c.) = a formal occasion when people have dinner together

di•no•saur /ˈdaɪnəsɔːʳ/ noun = a very large animal belonging to the family of reptiles (lizards) which lived on the earth several million years ago and then disappeared

dint (by dint of) /dɪnt/ noun, u. *He became a successful lawyer by dint of hard work.* = by means of

dip[1] /dɪp/ verb, t. **1** *He dipped his hand in the water.* = to lower something into a liquid briefly **2** *The sun dipped below the trees.* = to go down

dip[2] noun, c. **1** *Let us go for a dip in the sea.* = a quick bathe in a river or sea **2** *There has been a dip in the price of gold.* = a drop or fall **3** *I am making a cheese dip.* = a thick sauce into which food (e.g. vegetables, chips) can be dipped to give it better taste

to dip into a book = to read something from a book without paying much attenion to it **to dip into one's savings** = to use a part of the money one has saved

diph•ther•i•a /dɪfˈθɪəriə/ noun = a severe bacterial disease which affects the throat [MEDICINE]

di•plo•ma /dɪˈpləʊmə/ noun, c. *She has a Diploma in Education.* = an educational qualification that one can generally get after the completion of a course at a university

dip•lo•mat /ˈdɪpləmæt/ noun, c. **1** = a person who represents his/her country in a foreign country (e.g., an ambassador) **2** = a person who has great skill in dealing with people and getting them to agree **diplomacy** /dɪˈpləʊməsi/ noun, u. = the art or skill of being a diplomat **diplomatic** /dɪpləˈmætɪk/ adj. **1** *He belongs to the diplomatic service.* = connected with the branch of a government that deals with foreign countries **2** *I asked Prem an awkward question and he gave me a very diplomatic answer.* = done carefully, so as not to hurt someone's feelings

dire /daɪəʳ/ adj. *Our theatre group has no money and is in dire need of funds.* = very great; urgent

to be in dire straits = to be in great difficulty, especially about money

di•rect[1] /dɪˈrekt/ verb, t. **1** *Who is going to direct the new film?* = to guide or control **2** *The question was directed at the captain.* = to be aimed at something or someone **3** *The judge directed the police to free the accused at once.* = to order

direct[2] adj. **1** *I am taking the direct flight to Delhi.* = going straight from one point to another **2** *I want a direct answer from you.* = straight and clear **3** *Your illness is a direct result of your poor eating.* = without any other reason coming between

direct current see **DC**

di•rec•tion /daɪˈrekʃən, dɪ-/ noun, u. or c. **1** *The school has made great progress under the direction of the new principal.* = control and guidance **2** *The batsman hit the ball in the direction of the square leg boundary.* = towards **3** *I am waiting for the technician's directions.* = information or instruction (often plural)

di•rect•ly /daɪˈrektlɪ, dɪ-/ adv. **1** *Our school is directly opposite the hospital.* = exactly **2** *We have decided to buy books directly from the publishers.* = straight (without making use of others) **3** *I am flying to Delhi directly, not through Kolkata.* = by a straight route **4** *He came directly on receiving your call.* = at once

di•rec•tor /dɪˈrektə, daɪ-/ noun, c. **1** = a person who runs a company etc. **2** = a person who is in charge of a film or play

di•rec•to•ry /daɪˈrektərɪ, dɪ-/ noun, c. (**directories**) *the telephone directory* = a list of names arranged in alphabetical order

dirge /dɜːdʒ/ noun, c. = a slow, sad song or poem about the death of someone [LITERATURE]

dirt /dɜːt/ noun, u. *There was a lot of dirt on top of the old cupboard.* = unclean matter **dirt cheap** adj. = very cheap (informal)

dirt•y[1] /dɜːtɪ/ adj. **1** *a dirty room* = not clean **2** *a dirty joke* = referring to sex in a rude or unpleasant way (informal)

dirty[2] verb *Don't dirty your clothes.* = to make something dirty

to give someone a dirty look = to look at someone angrily and show them that you don't like them or what they are doing **to do someone's dirty work** = to do the necessary but unpleasant/dull etc. work that someone else does not want to do (informal) **to treat someone like dirt** = to show no respect for someone **to do the dirty on someone** = to treat someone unfairly or dishonestly (informal)

dis- /dɪs/ prefix meaning 'not' or 'the opposite of' e.g.

disability /dɪsəˈbɪlɪtɪ/ noun, c. or u. *They should have better arrangements in the theatre for people with a disability.*(c.) = a state of being unable to use one's hands, legs etc. from birth or as the result of an illness or injury

dis•able /dɪsˈeɪbəl/ verb, i. or t. *He was disabled in the war.*(i.) = to be unable to use a part of the body properly because of injury or disease **disabled** noun = those who are disabled

dis•a•gree /dɪsəˈgriː/ verb, i. **1** *I disagree with you. I don't think your idea will work.* = to have a different or opposite opinion **2** *These two reports seem to disagree.* = to be different from each other

dis•ap•pear /dɪsəˈpɪəʳ/ verb, t. *There are no trees left in the city after the storm. They have all disappeared.* = to go out of sight; to stop existing **disappearance** noun, c or u. = the act of disappearing

dis•ap•point /dɪsəˈpɔɪnt/ verb, t. *I expect you to come early. I hope you won't disappoint me.* = to make someone unhappy/sad because what was hoped for was not done **disappointed** adj *I was disappointed with the film. I had expected it to be good.* = unhappy because what one expects does not happen **disappointing** adj *a disappointing music concert* = making one feel unhappy because one expected something better

dis•ap•prove /dɪsəˈpruːv/ verb, i. or t. *He disapproves of people smoking in the office.* = to have a low opinion of someone or something

dis•arm /dɪsˈɑːm/ verb, t. or i. *The soldiers who refused to obey orders have been disarmed.* = to take away the weapons from a soldier, criminal etc. **disarmament** noun, u. = giving up one's weapons

dis•ar•ray /dɪsəˈreɪ/ noun, u. *We have just moved into this house and all our things are lying in complete disarray.* = a state of untidiness and lack of order

dis•as•ter /dɪˈzɑːstəʳ/ noun, c. **1** *The cyclone that hit Orissa last year was a disaster.* = an event that causes great suffering **2** *The college play was a disaster.* = a total failure (informal)

dis•band /dɪsˈbænd/ verb, t. *Our football team has been disbanded.* = to break up and separate a group that has been together

dis•burse /dɪsˈbɜːs/ verb, t. *I have received Rs 10,000 which I will disburse to the employees.* = to pay out (formal)

disc (**disk**) /dɪsk/ noun, c. **1** = a round and flat object **2** = a piece of cartilage between the bones of the back **floppy/compact disk** = a round or square object used to store data, music etc. electronically [COMPUTERS]

dis•card /dɪsˈkɑːd/ verb, t. *I have discarded these old shoes.* = to throw away something that has become useless

di•scern /dɪˈsɜːn/ verb, t. *I looked all around but I could see nothing. At last I discerned the house in the distance.* = to see or understand something with difficulty (literary)

di•scern•ing /dɪˈsɜːnɪŋ/ adj. *This shop has rare books for discerning readers.* = possessing good taste in clothes, food, music, books etc.

dis•charge[1] /ˈdɪstʃɑːdʒ/ verb, t. **1** *This drain discharges dirty water from the factory into the river.* = to let out or pour out **2** *Don't you think he has discharged his duties very efficiently?* = to perform a duty (formal) **3** *The doctor discharged the patient from the hospital.* = to allow someone to go; especially from a hospital **4** *The battery has been discharged.* = to lose electrical energy

discharge[2] noun, u. **1** *The discharge of water from the river is highest during the monsoon.* = the amount of a gas or liquid that is discharged (given out) **2** *The patient went home after his discharge.* = the action of being discharged

di•sci•ple /dɪˈsaɪpəl/ noun, c. = a follower of a religious teacher

dis•ci•pline[1] /ˈdɪsɪplɪn/ noun, u. or c. **1** *Discipline is very important in the army.*(u.) = training which produces obedience (opposite **indiscipline**) **2** *Political Science and Economics are the disciplines taught in this college.*(c.) = a subject taught in a university or college

discipline[2] verb, t. *She thought the students needed to be disciplined.* = to develop discipline through training; to punish someone in order to correct him/her

dis•claim /dɪsˈkleɪm/ verb, t. *The newspapers reported that the tigers had died due to the carelessness of the zoo staff, but the director of the zoo has disclaimed responsibility for their death.* = to state that one has nothing to do with something; to deny (formal)

dis•close /dɪsˈkləʊz/ verb, t. *The judge ordered the police to disclose the name of the person who had given them information.* = to reveal or give out some information

dis•col•our /dɪsˈkʌlə/ verb, t. *The paintings have become discoloured.* = to change the colour of something; to lose colour often because of age, dirt etc.

dis•con•cert /dɪskənˈsɜːt/ verb, t. *The loss of my valuable books disconcerted me completely.* = to cause someone to become upset and worried

dis•con•nect /dɪskəˈnekt/ verb, t. **1** *Our telephone has been disconnected as the bill was not paid.* = to cut off **2** *I got disconnected while I was talking on the phone.* = to break the telephone connection between two people **disconnected** adj. *I can't write a report from disconnected bits of information.* = not connected with something else

dis•con•so•late /dɪsˈkɒnsəlɪt/ adj. *She is disconsolate because she can't find her dog.* = very sad and without hope (literary)

dis•con•tent•ed /dɪskəˈntentid/ adj. *No matter how well he did, he always looked discontented.* = not satisfied; unhappy

dis•con•tin•ue /dɪskənˈtɪnjuː/ verb, t. or i. *I had joined the M. A. course but I will have to discontinue as I have no time to study.* = to stop or give up

dis•cord /ˈdɪskɔːd/ noun, u. **1** *There was so much discord between the two students sharing the room that one of them decided to move out.* = lack of understanding and agreement **2** = lack of harmony in the notes played in music **discordant** adj = the state of not being in tune with or matching something

dis•count[1] /dɪsˈkaʊnt/ noun, c. *This scooter costs Rs 40,000 but I paid only Rs 34,000 as I got a special discount of 15 per cent.* = a reduction made in the original price of something

discount[2] verb, t. *You should discount the stories that you hear of his bravery during the war. He is just an ordinary person.* = to regard as unimportant or unlikely to be true

dis•cour•age /dɪsˈkʌrɪdʒ/ verb, t. **1** *Ravi felt discouraged when his application was rejected.* = to lose hope (opposite **encourage**) **2** *You should discourage him from criticizing his teachers.* = to stop someone from doing something

dis•course /ˈdɪskɔːs/ noun, u. = a serious speech or discussion

dis•cour•te•ous /dɪsˈkɜːtiəs/ adj. *It was discourteous of you not to visit her when she was ill.* = showing bad manners or lack of courtesy

dis•cov•er /dɪsˈkʌvəʳ/ verb, t. *Who discovered penicillin?* = to find or learn something for the first time

dis•cov•e•ry /dɪsˈkʌvərɪ/ noun, c. or u. **1** *the discovery of pencillin.*(c.) = the act of finding for the first time **2** *Many people believe that education is a process of discovery.*(u.) = understanding something through observation, experience etc.

dis•creet /dɪˈskriːt/ adj. *You can talk to him freely. He is very discreet and will never tell anyone what you said to him.* = careful in dealing with people and showing good judgement (opposite **indiscreet**) **discretion** /dɪˈskreʃən/ noun, u. = the quality of being discreet

di•screp•an•cy /dɪˈskrepənci/ noun, generally u. *Your report is totally different from his. Why is there such a discrepancy?* = difference which is striking

di•scrim•i•nate /dɪˈskrɪmɪneɪt/ verb, i. **1** *The written test will discriminate between the good and the average candidates.* = to bring out the difference between people or things **2** *I don't discriminate among my students. All of them are the same for me.* = to favour one person or group over another **discrimination** /dɪskrɪmɪˈneɪʃən/ noun, u. *discrimination against women.* = the system of treating one group unjustly or unfairly **discriminatory** /dɪˈskrɪmɪnətəri/ adj. *discriminatory rules* = showing unfair favour to one group and disfavour to another

di•scuss /dɪ'skʌs/ verb, t. *The writer discusses the events that led to the war.* = to talk or write about something from several different points of view (The verb 'discuss' is never followed by the preposition 'about')

dis•dain /dɪs'deɪn/ noun, u. *I know you don't agree with her views, but you don't have to treat them with such disdain.* = feeling of contempt and disrespect (formal)

dis•ease /dɪ'ziːz/ noun, u. or c. *AIDS is a deadly disease.* = illness caused by some infection or disorder in the body

dis•fig•ure /dɪs'fɪgə^r/ verb, t. *People have disfigured the walls by writing on them.* = to spoil the appearance of something

dis•grace[1] /dɪs'greɪs/ verb, t. *You have disgraced the family by your bad manners.* = to bring shame or loss of name

disgrace[2] noun, u. *She left the job in disgrace as she was found to be dishonest.* = the loss of honour as the result of some wrong action

dis•grunt•led /dɪs'grʌntld/ adj. *The students are disgruntled because you didn't allow them to watch the cricket match.* = a little angry and dissatisfied because of not getting what one wants

dis•guise[1] /dɪs'gaɪz/ verb, t. *The prisoner disguised himself as a woman and escaped from prison.* = to change one's appearance in order to trick or cheat someone

disguise[2] noun, c. *In the play he put on the disguise of a woman.* = a dress, make-up etc., which is used to prevent people from knowing who one is

dis•gust[1] /dɪs'gʌst/ noun, u. *The sight of the rubbish lying on the road filled me with disgust.* = strong feeling of dislike caused by something that is unpleasant or ugly

disgust[2] verb, t. *Your habit of not combing your hair disgusts me.* = to cause a strong feeling of dislike

dish[1] /dɪʃ/ noun, c. **1** *Food was served in silver dishes.* = a vessel, usually round, used to serve food **2** *a meat dish* = an item of food cooked in a particular way

dish[2] verb, t. **1** *Will you dish out the food?* = to serve food (informal) **2** *He loves to dish out advice to people.* = to offer something which is not welcome (informal, disapproving)

dis•heart•en /dɪs'hɑːtn/ verb, i. *I hope the Indian team will not be disheartened by this defeat.* = to cause someone to lose hope

di•shev•elled /dɪ'ʃevəld/ adj. *You shouldn't go for an interview looking so dishevelled.* = untidy in one's appearance, dress etc. (disapproving)

dis•hon•our[1] /dɪs'ɒnə^r/ noun, u. *You brought dishonour to the family by running away from the fight.* = shame

dishonour[2] verb, t. *The bank has dishonoured your cheque.* = to refuse to pay out money on a cheque

dis•il•lu•sion /dɪsɪ'luːʒən/ verb, t. *They think life in big cities is always wonderful. I don't want to disillusion them.* = to make someone stop having hope or a good impression about something

disillusioned adj. *I thought this was a very good school but I feel disillusioned after joining it.* = feeling disappointed on learning the truth about someone or something

dis•in•clined /dɪsɪn'klaɪnd/ adj. *He has been asking me to join karate classes, but I feel disinclined to do so.* = not willing

dis•in•fect /dɪsɪn'fekt/ verb, t. = to clean with some chemical which destroys germs [TECHNICAL]

dis•in•for•ma tion /dɪsɪnfə'meɪʃən/ noun, u. = false information deliberately given out to mislead people

dis•in•her•it /dɪsɪn'herɪt/ verb, t. = to take away from someone the legal right to receive one's property after one's death [LAW]

dis•in•te•grate /dɪs'ɪntɪgreɪt/ verb, i. **1** *The ancient piece of pottery disintegrated in his hands when he held it.* = (of something hard or crisp) to break up into pieces **2** *The empire disintegrated when the emperor died.* = to break up because of political problems

dis•lo•cate /'dɪsləkeɪt/ verb, t. *I fell down the stairs and dislocated my shoulder.* = to put something (specially a bone) out of its proper place [MEDICINE]

dis•lodge /dɪs'lɒdʒ/ verb, t. *The nail had been hammered in so hard that we could not dislodge it from the wall.* = to move someone or something out of a fixed position

dis•mal /'dɪzməl/ adj. *a dismal future.* = sad and hopeless

dis•man•tle /dɪs'mæntəl/ verb, t. *The factory shed was dismantled and moved to another place.* = to take something apart (into pieces)

dis•may[1] /dɪs'meɪ/ noun, u. *When we were told that another storm was expected, we were filled with dismay.* = sadness and disappointment

dismay[2] verb, t. *The news that our friends were leaving town dismayed us.* = to cause sadness and disappointment (formal)

dis•miss /dɪs'mɪs/ verb, i. or t. **1** = to remove from a job **2** *The teacher dismissed the class.* = to send someone away (so that the person can go home etc.) **3** *The judge dismissed the case.* = to decide that a court case should not continue, usually because of the lack of evidence [LAW]

dis•mount /dɪs'maʊnt/ verb, i. = to get off a horse or bicycle or something that one rides

dis•or•der /dɪs'ɔ:dəʳ/ noun, u. **1** *Books and clothes lay scattered everywhere. The house was in complete disorder.* = an untidy state **2** *He suffers from a stomach disorder.* = any illness in which the mind or body is not working properly

dis•or•gan•ized (disorganised) /dɪs'ɔ:gənaɪzd/ adj. *Your essay is very disorganized. There is no link between one point and another.* = lacking proper order or arrangement (opposite **organized**)

dis•own /dɪs'əʊn/ verb, t. **1** = to stop accepting someone as one's own or as one's legal responsibility [LAW] **2** *I disown responsibility for damaging the walls.* = to say that one has not done something

dis•pa•rate /'dɪspərɪt/ adj. *You cannot compare China and India. The situation in the two countries is quite disparate.* = different; difficult to compare **disparity** noun, u. = difference; a state of not being equal to something

dis•patch (despatch) /dɪ'spætʃ/ verb, t. *Have you dispatched the letters?* = to send out (formal)

dis•pel /dɪ'spel/ verb, t. *The rains came and dispelled the heat.* = to make something, especially a feeling, disappear

dis•pen•sary /dɪ'spensəri/ noun, c. (**dispensaries**) = a place where medicines are given to people who need them

dis•pense /dɪ'spens/ verb, t. **1** = to give out medicines etc. to a number of people (formal) **2** *Let's dispense with this chair since we no longer need it.* = to give away and manage without (formal)

di•sperse /dɪ'spɜ:s/ verb, t. or i. *The police used tear gas to disperse the crowd.*(t.) = to separate and move in different directions

dis•place /dɪs'pleɪs/ verb, t. *The flood displaced thousands of people from their homes.* = to make someone or something move out from their/its usual place **displacement** noun, u. = the amount of liquid which is made to flow out when a solid object is lowered into the liquid etc. [PHYSICS]

dis•play[1] /dɪ'spleɪ/ verb, t. *The shops are displaying beautiful silk saris to attract customers.* = to put up for show (formal)

display[2] noun, c. or u. **1** *They have put up an attractive display of books.*(c.) = an arrangement of things put on show **2** *a sudden display of affection* (u.) = a show of feeling

dis•pose /dɪ'spəʊz/ verb, t. *I have disposed of all my old clothes.* = to get rid of **disposable** adj. *We have to get some disposable paper plates and cups for our picnic.* = something that is used only once and then thrown away **disposal** noun, u. **1** *The municipality is responsible for the disposal of garbage from the city.* = the act of getting rid of something (formal) **2** *I will place my car at your disposal.* = available for someone's free use (formal)

dis•pos•sess /dɪspə'zes/ verb, t. *The refugees who left their homes were dispossessed of all their property.* = to take away someone's possessions

dis•pro•por•tion•ate /dɪsprə'pɔ:ʃənɪt/ adj. *He earns Rs 5,000 a month but spends Rs 2,000 on clothes—quite a disproportionate amount!* = a lot more (or less) in relation to something else

di•spute[1] /dɪ'spju:t/ verb, t. or i. **1** *disputing over land*(i.) = to argue or quarrel about something for a long time **2** *I dispute the results of his research. His figures are wrong.*(t.) = to disagree about the correctness of something

dispute[2] noun, c. or u. *There is an old dispute between the two partners over this question.*(c.) = a strong disagreement or argument

dis•qual•i•fy /dɪs'kwɒlɪfaɪ/ verb, t. *Some athletes who took part in the Olympic Games were disqualified for taking drugs.* = to declare someone unfit to take part in games, exams or other events which have rules and standards

dis•re•gard /dɪsrɪ'gɑ:d/ verb, t. *Please disregard the notice you have received about the meeting tomorrow. The meeting is cancelled.* = to pay no attention to something (formal)

dis•rupt /dɪs'rʌpt/ verb, t. *Some people tried to disrupt the meeting by walking out.* = to break up; to cause disorder, generally on purpose

dis•sect /dɪ'sekt/ verb, t. **1** = to cut up the body of a plant, animal or human being in order to study it [TECHNICAL] **2** *I dissect the news in the newspapers every morning.* = to study carefully

dis•sent[1] /dɪ'sent/ verb, i. *One of the judges dissented with the views of the other two judges.* = to disagree with the opinion of the majority

dissent[2] noun, u. *One of the judges gave a note of dissent.* = refusal to agree (formal)

dis•ser•ta•tion /dɪsə'teɪʃən/ noun, u. or c. = a thesis; a long, written discussion of a topic produced for a higher university degree

dis•ser•vice /dɪ'sɜ:vɪs/ noun, u. *He did the nation a disservice by helping the enemy.* = a harmful action

dis•si•pate /'dɪsɪpeɪt/ verb, t. *Don't dissipate all your energy in games. Remember, your studies are more important.* = to waste (formal)

dis•so•ci•ate /dɪ'səʊʃieɪt/ verb, t. *It is difficult to dissociate politics from sports.* = to separate or keep apart

dis•solve /dɪ'zɒlv/ verb, i. or t. **1** *Salt dissolves in* *water.*(t.) = to change into a liquid form by mixing with some liquid **2** *Parliament has been dissolved.*(i.) = to break up or end an association or group

dis•suade /dɪ'sweɪd/ verb, t. *She was planning to go on a very dangerous journey but I managed to dissuade her.* = to advise someone not to do something

dis•tance[1] /'dɪstəns/ noun, u. or c. **1** *The distance between Calcutta and New Delhi is 1,500 kilometres.*(c.) = the space which separates two points **2** *I saw a house in the distance.*(u.) = far away **3** *They were good friends but there is a distance between them now.* = a situation in which two people stop being friends

distance[2] verb. *He distanced himself from us after he left the company.* = to become less friendly (figurative)

to keep one's distance = to stay away from someone on purpose, usually because one does not want to get very friendly or because one has had an unpleasant experience with the person

distant /'dɪstənt/ adj. **1** *a distant place* = far away **2** *a distant relation* = not close **3** *His behaviour was rather distant.* = not very friendly

in the not-too-distant past = not very long ago

dis•taste•ful /dɪs'teɪstfəl/ adj. *The pictures in his room are rather distasteful.* = not in good taste; not pleasant (disapproving)

dis•til /dɪ'stɪl/ verb, t. **1** = to make a liquid pure by turning it into a gas by boiling and then turning it back into a liquid by cooling **2** = to prepare alcoholic drinks by this method **distillery** noun, c. (**distilleries**) = a factory which makes alcoholic drinks

dis•tinct /dɪ'stɪŋkt/ adj. **1** *The state of Bihar has been divided into two distinct parts.* = completely different and separate **2** *Your handwriting is not distinct.* = clearly seen or heard

dis•tinc•tion /dɪ'stɪŋkʃən/ noun, u. or c. **1** *There should be a clear distinction between those who are likely to be chosen for the team and those who are not going to be chosen.*(c.) = something that separates or marks a difference between two things **2** *He has won great distinction as a writer.* = honour **3** *He passed the examination with distinction.*(u.) = producing very good results **4** *She is a singer of great distinction.* = high quality

to draw a distinction *We need to draw a distinction between growing trees and growing trees of one kind.* = to keep things separate

dis•tinc•tive /dɪ'stɪŋktɪv/ adj. *She has very distinctive handwriting.* = clearly marking something as different from others

dis•tin•guish /dɪ'stɪŋgwɪʃ/ verb, t. **1** *You can easily distinguish a shark from other fish by the tail-fin.* = to recognize; to be able to see the difference between two or more things or people **2** *He has distinguished himself as a writer.* = to become famous **distinguished** adj. = well known in a way which is admired or deserved

dis•tort /dɪ'stɔːt/ verb, t. *The report in the newspaper has completely distorted the speech I made last night.* = to give a false account of something; to damage out of shape

dis•tract /dɪ'strækt/ verb, t. *The attention of the students was distracted by the music being played over a loudspeaker.* = to turn away someone's attention from something **distraction** noun, u. or c. *It is difficult to concentrate on studies. Television is such a distraction.* = something that takes away one's attention from what one is doing

to drive someone to distraction = to cause confusion of the mind **to love someone to distraction** = to love very much (informal)

dis•tress[1] /dɪ'stres/ noun, u. *She was in distress over the loss of her friend.* = great suffering of the mind or body

distress[2] verb, t. *I was distressed by the unkind remarks he made about me.* = to suffer deep pain of the mind **distressing** adj.

dis•trib•ute /dɪ'strɪbjuːt/ verb, t. **1** *We distribute sweets to children on Republic Day.* = to divide and give out **2** *Their tea gardens are distributed over a number of districts in Assam.* = to spread out over an area

dis•trust /dɪs'trʌst/ verb, t. *I distrust her because she does not always speak the truth.* = to have no faith or trust in

dis•turb /dɪ'stɜːb/ verb, t. **1** *Don't disturb me when I am working.* = to do something which makes it difficult for someone to keep their mind on their work or to continue working **2** *Don't disturb the arrangement of the chairs.* = to change or upset **3** *I was disturbed by the news of your illness.* = to feel anxious or worried **4** *He had hired a few criminals to disturb the peace in the town.* = to cause trouble (disapproving) **disturbance** noun, u. *The police had to be called in as there was some disturbance in the city.* = disorder or trouble

dis•use /dɪs'juːs/ noun, u. *The house is in poor condition because of disuse.* = (of houses, machines, language etc.) the state of not being in use

ditch[1] /dɪtʃ/ noun, c. (**ditches**) *The car fell into a ditch.* = a hollow or hole in the ground

ditch[2] verb, t. *He got bored with the relationship and ditched her.* = to let someone down by not doing what was promised; in a relationship where one loves a man or woman, to leave her/him for someone else (slang)

dith•er /ˈdɪðəʳ/verb, i. *After dithering for a long time she has decided to become a journalist.* = to not be able to make up one's mind about something

dit•to /ˈdɪtəʊ/ noun, u. *I spent Rs 50 on sweets and ditto on soft drinks* = the same (informal)

dive[1] /daɪv/ verb, t. **1** *The girl dived off the rock into the sea.* = to jump into the water in a controlled movement so as to land head first **2** *The scientists are diving to explore the bottom of the sea.* = to go under the surface of the water **3** *The goalkeeper dived and collected the ball.* = to make a sudden quick jump, head first

dive[2] noun, c. *She made a graceful dive into the swimming pool.* = an act of diving

di•verge /daɪˈvɜːdʒ/ verb, i. *Our views on education diverge. He wants to teach through English while I am keen on the mother-tongue.* = to move in different directions **divergent** adj. = moving in different directions

di•verse /daɪˈvɜːs/ adj. *The children in this group come from diverse family backgrounds.* = different from each other

diversify /daɪˈvɜːsɪfaɪ/ verb, i. or t. *Our company produces only motorcars, but now we have decided to diversify. We will also produce scooters and mopeds.*(i.) = to take up a number of different business activities

diversion /daɪˈvɜːʃən/ noun, u. or c. **1** *The road is being repaired so you will have to take a diversion.*(c.) = a path that turns away from the usual route **2** *The diversion of the river has made this area fertile.*(u.) = the act of diverting or turning something aside **3** *Cinemas are one of the main diversions in cities.*(c.) = something that amuses and entertains people

di•vert /daɪˈvɜːt/ verb, t. *The money which is now being spent on weapons should be diverted to education and health programmes.* = to turn something away from one direction or thing to another

di•vest /daɪˈvest/ verb, t. *divest the minister of all his powers* = to take away someone's position, rights, property etc.

di•vide /dɪˈvaɪd/ verb, t. **1** *The money in the box will be divided among the three of us.* = to distribute; to share so that each person gets something **2** *The teacher divided the class into groups.* = to make into different groups or parts **3** *You can divide 21 by 7.* = to see how many times a number is found in another number **4** *I divide my time between work and family.* = to use for different purposes **5** *Our quarrel over where the new building should be built has divided us.* = to stop being friendly

dividend /ˈdɪvɪdend/ noun, c. **1** = a share of the profits made by a company which is paid to shareholders **2** = a number which is divided by another number

di•vine /dɪˈvaɪn/ adj. = having to do with God **divinity** noun, c. = the state or quality of being divine (a god)

di•vi•sion /dɪˈvɪʒən/ noun, u. or c. **1** *The division of India took place in 1947*(u.) = the act of dividing (separating into different parts) **2** *The state contains four main divisions.*(c.) = a part into which something is divided **3** *There is division within the team.*(u.) = difference of opinion **4** *He passed in the second division.* = class **5** = the process by which a number can be divided **6** = one of the parts into which an army is divided **divisible** adj. *22 is divisible by 11* = (a number) that can be divided by another number (opposite **indivisible**)

di•vi•sor /dɪˈvaɪzəʳ/ noun, c. *If we divide 27 by 3, 27 is the dividend while 3 is the divisor.* = a number by which another number is divided

di•vorce[1] /dɪˈvɔːs/ verb, t. **1** = to bring a marriage to an end through a court of law **2** *Your ideas are divorced from reality.* = to have no connection with

divorce[2] noun, u. or c. **1** *He wants a divorce from his wife.*(c.) = the official ending of a marriage through a court of law **2** *In any work we do, it is difficult to divorce the easy from the difficult parts.* = to see a difference between two things; to separate

di•vulge /daɪˈvʌldʒ/ verb, t. *You must promise not to divulge my plans to anyone.* = to give out a secret (formal)

diz•zy /ˈdɪzi/ adj. *He felt dizzy when he sat on the merry-go-round.* = an uncomfortable feeling of losing one's balance and going round and round

do[1] /duː/ aux. verb **1** *How much do you know?* **2** *You do not know me.* **3** *Yes, I do know the answer.* = auxiliary verb, used along with a main verb to form questions and negative sentences or in short sentences for emphasis **4** *He plays golf, and so do I.* = used to replace another verb

do[2] verb, t. or i. **1** *What is the Board doing about noise pollution?*(t.) = to perform an action, activity or task **2** *What do you do for your food?* = arrange, organise **3** *How are you doing in your studies?*(i.) = to make progress **4** *My car does 60 kilometres per hour.*(t.) = to be capable of producing **5** *One litre of paint will do for this wall.*(i.) = to be enough **6** *Do remember to take an umbrella.*(t.) = a way of stressing that something should be done **7** *'Don't you like watching television?' 'I do.'*(i.) = used as an answer to don't, or in place of a verb to follow **8** *If you take up French, you'll have to do it for four years.*(t.) = study (as part of a course) **9** *Let's go to that restaurant. They do good Bengali food there.*(t.) = make (food) (informal)

do[3] noun *We are having a do to celebrate our victory.* = a party (informal) **do-gooder** noun = a person who tries to help others but is not very practical or effective (derogatory)

to do up (something) *We are going to do up her room so that she feels happy when she's back from hospital.* = to decorate or make a place look pleasant (informal) **to do with 1** *Have you any ice? I could do with a cold drink.* = to need something (informal) **2** *The film is to do with the horrors of war.* = about; connected with; on the subject of (formal) **to do or die** = to do everything possible to succeed **to be up and doing** = to be active after a period of illness or rest (informal) **to do someone in** = to kill (informal) **to do someone out of something** *By not letting me know, they did me out of the chance of getting a wonderful job.* = to make sure that someone does not get what she/he needs or deserves **to do without** *There were no onions in the house so we did without.* = to manage without something that is fairly important or necessary **to have nothing to do with someone** *They cheated me in that shop, and now I'll have nothing to do with them.* = to make up one's mind not to be friendly with, work with, buy from etc. someone

do•cile /'dəʊsaɪl/ adj. *She will do whatever you ask. She is a very docile person.* = quiet and willing to obey (sometimes derogatory)

dock[1] /dɒk/ noun, c. **1** = a place where ships are loaded and unloaded or repaired **2** *the prisoner in the dock* = the place in a court of law where a prisoner is made to stand

dock[2] verb, t. *The ship has been docked.* = to put a ship into a dock for unloading, repairs etc.

doc•tor[1] /'dɒktə^r/ noun, c. **1** = a person who treats sick people **2** = a person who has a Ph.D. degree

doctor[2] verb, t. *The contract papers have been doctored.* = to change a document in a dishonest way (disapproving)

doc•trine /'dɒktrɪn/ noun, c. *the doctrine of rebirth* = principle or set of beliefs that one is taught by a religion or a political party

doc•u•ment[1] /'dɒkjʊmənt/ noun, c. *Do you have documents to prove that you are the owner of this house?* = a legal or official paper

document[2] verb, t. *The war of 1914 has been well documented.* = to record an event in the form of documents or to prove something with the help of documents

documentary /dɒkjʊ'mentəri/ noun = film, TV or radio programme that gives information about a certain subject

dod•der /'dɒdə^r/ verb, i. = to walk slowly and unsteadily due to old age

dodge /dɒdʒ/ verb, t. **1** *He tried to dodge the blow but he was hit on the shoulder.* = to move aside quickly in order to avoid getting hit **2** *I asked him if he was getting married but he dodged the question.* = to avoid something (e.g. a question, by not answering it)

doe /dəʊ/ noun, c. = a female deer

dog[1] /dɒg/ noun, c. = a small four-legged animal often kept as a pet

dog[2] verb, t. *He has been dogged by bad luck.* = to be followed by (informal) **dog-eared** adj. *a dog-eared exercise book* = a book or exercise book whose pages have become bent at the corners due to heavy use

dog tired = extremely tired (informal) **a dog in the manger** *You don't enjoy television yourself and you won't allow your children to watch television. You are a real dog in the manger!* = someone who does not want others to use or enjoy something even though he/she does not enjoy or want it **to lead a dog's life** = to lead an unhappy life, full of troubles **to let sleeping dogs lie** = not to do anything to disturb a situation which was rough and difficult but is now peaceful **a dog-eat-dog situation** = a highly competitive situation in which people take advantage of each other

dogged /'dɒgɪd/ adj. *She worked in a dogged way to fulfil her ambitions.* = very determined (usually approving) **doggedly** adv.

dog•ge•rel /'dɒgərəl/ noun, c. = a badly written poem without much meaning

dog•ma /'dɒgmə/ noun, c.= a belief (generally connected with religion) that one is expected to follow without questioning **dogmatic** adj. *a dogmatic person* = not willing to give up one's beliefs

dol•drums /'dɒldrəmz/ noun, u. (always plural) = a part of the ocean where sailing ships were unable to move (in the old days) as there was no wind to drive them

to be in the doldrums *The jute industry is in the doldrums now.* = to be in a state of inactivity (when nothing happens)

dole /dəʊl/ noun, u. = money paid by the government (in some countries) to people who are without jobs

to dole out *She doled out food to her children.* = to give in small quantities to someone who is in need, or in a weak position (informal, derogatory)

doll /dɒl/ noun, c. **1** = a figure, usually that of a small child, baby or adult, used as a toy **2** = a word sometimes used by men to describe an attractive woman **3** = a word sometimes used to refer to a good-looking but not very intelligent woman (derogatory) Ⓖ

dol•lar /'dɒlə^r/ noun, c. = the unit of money used in America, Canada, Australia, New Zealand, Hong Kong and Singapore

to bet one's bottom dollar = to be very certain that one is right (informal) **to look like a million dollars** = to look very attractive (informal)

dol•phin /'dɒlfɪn/ noun = a highly intelligent mammal that lives in the sea

dolt /dəʊlt/ noun, c. = a stupid person (derogatory)

do•main /də'meɪn/ noun, c. **1** *It is difficult to explain how some people are able to tell the future. Such things lie outside the domain of science.* = an area of activity or knowledge **2** = a set of Internet addresses that end with the same name [COMPUTERS]

dome /dəʊm/ noun, c. **1** = a round roof on a building **2** *the dome of someone's head* = something round, shaped like a dome

do•mes•tic /də'mestɪk/ adj. **1** *domestic problems* = having to do with the home or family **2** *a domestic flight* = within the country (opposite **international**) **domestic animals** = animals which are kept in the home or on a farm e.g. dogs, cats, cows **domestic science (home science)** = the study of the skills required in the home e.g. cooking **domesticate** verb, t. = to tame or train an animal so that it can live in the home along with human beings

dom•i•cile /'dɒmɪsaɪl/ noun, u. *His domicile is New Delhi, India, though he is working in America.* = the place to which a person belongs or where he/she lives

dom•i•nate /'dɒmɪneɪt/ verb, t. or i. **1** *Sachin Tendulkar has dominated the game of cricket in India.* = to have the most important position in **2** *When I am in a meeting with you, I never get a chance to speak. You dominate every meeting.* = to control or rule **dominant** adj. *The dominant theme in his poetry was love for his motherland.* = most noticeable or important

dom•i•neer•ing /dɒmɪ'nɪərɪŋ/ adj. *My partner in business is so domineering that he wants to decide everything for me.* = ruling over others without any consideration for their feelings (derogatory)

do•min•ion /də'mɪnjen/ noun, u. or c. **1** *Akbar's dominion extended over the whole of India.*(u.) = power and control **2** *Bengal was a part of Akbar's dominion.*(c.) = kingdom

don /dɒn/ noun, c. = the powerful leader of a gang of criminals

do•nate /dəʊ'neɪt/ verb, t. *My neighbour has donated a lot of money to charity.* = to give away something, especially money, for a good cause; to give one's blood, organs etc to someone medically in need

donation noun, c. = something, especially money that is donated

don•key /'dɒŋki:/ noun, c. **1** = an animal like a horse but smaller, with larger ears **2** = a silly or foolish person

doo•dle[1] /'du:dl/ verb, t. *He was doodling away in his notebook, paying little attention to the lecture.* = to draw, not seriously, lines, figures etc. while thinking of something else

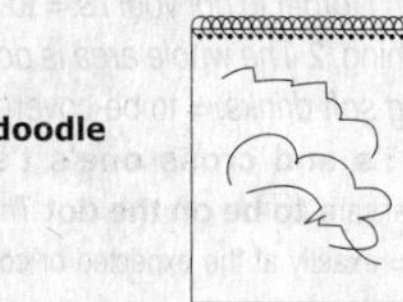

doodle[2] noun, c. *The sheet of paper was covered with doodles.* = things that are drawn while doodling

doom[1] /du:m/ noun, u. *The soldiers knew that they were sure to be killed yet they marched cheerfully to their doom.* = death or destruction that cannot be avoided (literary)

doom[2] verb, t. *Our hopes for a lasting peace are doomed.* = to face certain destruction **Doomsday** noun = the day when the world will come to an end, as some religions believe

door /dɔ:^r/ noun, c. = a flat block of wood, metal or plastic which opens or closes the entrance to a building etc. **doorbell** noun = a bell that visitors to a house can ring to announce their presence **doorkeeper** noun = a person who guards the entrance to a building

to show someone the door = to ask an unwelcome guest to leave **to shut the door in someone's face** = to refuse to listen or talk to someone **to answer the door** = to open the door to allow someone to come in **behind closed doors** = in a secret manner

dope[1] /dəʊp/ noun, u. **1** = an illegal drug, such as marijuana (ganja) (slang) **2** = a stupid person (derogatory, slang)

dope[2] verb, t. *The man has been doped.* = to give a drug to a person or animal in order to make him/her unconscious

dor•mant /'dɔ:mənt/ adj. **1** *a dormant volcano* = inactive (not active) **2** = (of genes, infection etc.) hidden and not active but likely to become active in certain situations [BIOLOGY]

dor•mi•to•ry /'dɔ:mɪtəri/ noun, c. (**dormitories**) = a large hall in which several people can sleep

dor•sal /'dɔ:səl/ adj. *the dorsal fin of a fish* = on or near the back of an animal [BIOLOGY] (see pic under **fish**)

dose[1] /dəʊs/ noun, c. *Give him just one dose of the medicine.* = a measured amount of medicine

dose[2] verb, t. *We dosed our child with cough syrup.* = to give medicine to someone (often derogatory)

dos•si•er /ˈdɒsieɪ/ noun, c. *The police maintains dossiers on all important people.* = a set of secret papers containing detailed information about someone or something

dot[1] /dɒt/ noun, c. = a small round mark or spot **dot-com** = an abbreviation used on the Internet to show that one is referring to a commercial organisation (business company) [COMPUTERS]

dot[2] verb, t. **1** *Don't forget to dot your i's.* = to put a dot on or over something **2** *The whole area is dotted with little shops selling soft drinks.* = to be covered with

to dot one's i's and cross one's t's = to do something with great care **to be on the dot** *The meeting began on the dot.* = exactly at the expected or correct time (informal)

do•tage /ˈdəʊtɪdʒ/ noun, u. *in one's dotage* = second childhood; the period of old age when one's mind does not work clearly

dote /dəʊt/ verb, t. *They are loving parents and dote on their children.* = to have great love for someone, to the point where it becomes a weakness

doub•le[1] /ˈdʌbəl/ adj. **1** *The spelling of the word 'door' is: 'd', 'double o', 'r'* = containing two of something, or the same thing twice **2** *We need a double bed.* = something meant for two people **doubly** adv.

double[2] noun, c. or u. **1** *You don't want to sell this painting for Rs 50? Very well, I'll give you double.*(u.) = twice the amount **2** *That man is your double.*(c.) = a person who looks very much like another **double-dealer** noun = a person who is dishonest, generally in business dealings (derogatory)

double[3] verb, t. *I will double your salary if I like your work.* = to make something twice the original amount or size **double-cross** verb, t. *The thief double-crossed his partners by informing the police about them.* = to betray or cheat someone with whom one has agreed to do something dishonest **double-check** = to check something twice in order to be sure **double-book** = a seat in a train, plane, cinema etc. is double-booked when it has been given to two persons (instead of to one)

at/on the double *Please come here. On the double!* = very quickly and without delay (informal) **to double as** *Karishma is a young girl in the film. She also doubles as the girl's mother.* = to have a second use or job (in addition to the first one) **to double up/over** **1** *He suddenly doubled up and clutched his stomach.* = to bend at the waist in a sharp movement as a result of sudden pain **2** *We doubled up listening to the story.* = to laugh **to be bent double** = (of trees, persons etc.) to be bent down sharply as a result of age, force etc.

doubt[1] /daʊt/ verb, t. **1** *He says he is 21, but I doubt it.* = to question the truth of something **2** *Although there are dark clouds in the sky, I doubt if it will rain this evening.* = to consider something unlikely or uncertain

doubt[2] noun, c. or u. **1** *I have some doubts about the accuracy of this report.*(c.) = lack of trust or confidence **2** *His honesty was never in doubt.*(u.) = a state of uncertainty **doubtful** adj. **1** *I am doubtful if she will come on time.* = feeling doubt **2** *His coming is doubtful.* = uncertain **3** *She gave us a doubtful report.* = something that cannot be trusted **doubting Thomas** *Don't be such a doubting Thomas.* = a person who does not believe things easily (informal)

to give someone the benefit of the doubt = to think well of somebody even though there seems to be something against him/her

dough /dəʊ/ noun, u. = the mixture of flour, water, salt, sugar etc. from which bread, pies, chapatis etc. are made

dour /dʊəʳ/ adj. *a dour person* = one who does not speak or smile often and does not change his/her mind easily

douse (**dowse**) /daʊs/ verb, t. *to douse a fire* = to put out a fire by throwing water on it

dove /dʌv/ noun, c. = a bird, the white species of which is considered a symbol of peace

dovetail /ˈdʌvteɪl/ verb, t. **1** = to join two pieces of wood by using a special kind of joint, called a dovetail **2** *Each of you is writing a separate report, but I would like you to dovetail your reports so that I can get a complete picture.* = to join or fit two or more things together skilfully

dow•dy /ˈdaʊdi/ adj. *a dowdy dress* = unattractive and old-fashioned (derogatory)

down[1] /daʊn/ prep. **1** *We ran down the hill.* = from a higher place to a lower place **2** *He was walking down the road.* = along **3** *We are rowing down the river.* = with the current

down[2] adv. **1** *The sun is going down.* = to a lower position **2** *I bent down to pick up the sheet of paper.* =towards a lower position such as the floor, ground etc. **3** *You should lie down.* = from a standing or sitting to a lying position **4** *Our profits are going down.* = to a lower level **5** *Will you walk down to the market with me?* = away from a place **6** *Write down his address.* = on paper

down[3] adj. **1** *She has been down since he lost his job.* = depressed (informal) **2** *This is the down train from Howrah.* = going away from **3** *The computer system is down.* = not working temporarily

down[4] verb, t. **1** *Our hockey team has downed the Australins.* = to defeat **2** *He downed his coffee quickly.* = to swallow some liquid

down[5] noun, u. = the soft feathers covering the skin of a young bird **down-and-out** adj. *My friend is down-and-out these days.* = going through a period of bad luck, with no money, opportunity etc. **downcast** adj. = feeling sad **downgrade** verb, t. *The Manager has been downgraded to the rank of Assistant Manager.* = to bring down in position or importance **download** verb, t. = to move information from the Internet to the storage system of a computer [COMPUTERS] **down payment** noun *I have to make a down payment of Rs 25,000 on the car which I am buying.* = a part of the full price of something, the rest to be paid later **downplay** verb, t. *The newspapers are trying to downplay the importance of this meeting.* = to make something seem less important than it really is **downpour** noun = a heavy shower of rain **Down's syndrome** noun = a biological condition which results in a person's being born with disabilities that are mental as well as physical [MEDICINE] **down-to-earth** adj. *a very down-to-earth person* = practical and honest **downtown** noun (American) = the important business area in a city **downtrodden** adj. *downtrodden people* = treated badly by those who are in power

to come down in the world = to lose one's social position **to be down with something** *She is down with the flu.* = to suffer from some disease **to be down for something** = to be included in a list of people taking part in a competition **to down tools** = to stop working

doy•en /ˈdɔɪən/ noun, c. *Rabindranath Tagore was the doyen of Bengali poets.* = the seniormost and most respected member of a group (usually of teachers or writers)

doze[1] /dəʊz/ verb, i. *I dozed off while riding in the bus.* = to sleep lightly

doze[2] noun, u. *He had a quick doze.* = short and light sleep (informal)

doz•en /ˈdʌzən/ noun, c. *a dozen eggs* = a group of 12

drab /dræb/ adj. *a drab brown dress* = dull and uninteresting

draft[1] /drɑːft/ noun, c. **1** *I am preparing the first draft of my speech.* = the first rough form of something which is written **2** *a bank draft* = a written order given to a bank, asking for a payment to be made

draft[2] verb, t. *I am drafting a report for the committee.* = to prepare a draft (informal)

drag[1] /dræg/ verb, t. **1** *Several trees fell across the road but they have been dragged away.* = to pull something heavy along a surface **2** = to move something across the screen of a monitor using a mouse [COMPUTERS]

drag[2] noun, u. **1** *The meeting was such a drag that we left.* = something dull and uninteresting **2** *An aircraft has to overcome a powerful drag when it is flying.* = the force of air which prevents forward movement [TECHNICAL] **3** *a drag show* = a performance in which a man is dressed as a woman (slang)

to drag one's feet = to be deliberately slow in doing something **to drag on** = to go on for too long a period of time **to drag up** *Why do you want to drag up those terrible times?* = to remind someone of something unpleasant which has been forgotten

dra•gon /ˈdrægən/ noun, c. = an imaginary large animal, found in stories, that breathes fire **dragonfly** noun, c. = a large insect with large, thin wings

drain[1] /dreɪn/ verb, t. **1** *The water in the pond has been drained. It is dry now.* = to make something dry by removing liquid from it **2** *We will dig a channel to drain the water away.* = to allow water to flow away **3** *With one gulp he drained his glass.* = to drink all the liquid in the glass

drain[2] noun, c. **1** *The drain is choked with garbage.* = a pipe or channel which allows water to flow away **2** *The amusement park is running well but it is a big drain on our resources.* = something that uses up something else

to go down the drain = to be wasted, (referring to money)

dra•ma /ˈdrɑːmə/ noun, u. or c. **1** *He is writing a drama for television.*(c.) = a piece of writing that is acted out **2** *He is an authority on Sanskrit drama.*(u.) = literature in the form of plays **3** *high drama in court.*(u.) = interesting or exciting events **dramatic** /drəˈmætɪk/ adj. **1** *a dramatic situation* = exciting **2** *a dramatic change or increase* = sudden and often unexpected **3** *a dramatic display of anger* = showing excessive emotion **dramatically** adv. **dramatist** /ˈdræmətɪst/ noun, c. = a person who writes plays **dramatize** verb, t. *The novel is being dramatized.* = to change a book into a drama so that it can be acted out **dramatics** /drəˈmætɪks/ noun (always plural) = the study of things connected with drama, e.g. acting

drape /dreɪp/ verb, t. *The table was draped with a tablecloth.* = to cover with cloth

dras•tic /ˈdræstɪk/ adj. *We are making small changes in the school syllabus. No one likes a drastic change.* = something done suddenly that produces a powerful effect

draught[1] **(draft)** /drɑːft/ noun, c. *Don't stand in the draught. You will catch a cold.* = a moving current of cold air

draught[2] adj. *He gulped down a draught of water.* = the amount of water, tea or other liquid that one swallows at one single time

draughts /ˈdrɑːfts/ noun = an indoor game for two

persons, played on a black and white board with 12 round pieces

draw[1] /drɔː/ verb, t. or i. (**drew, drawn**) **1** *The boy drew a large mountain.*(t.) = to create a picture using a pencil, pen or other instrument, but not a brush **2** *The students are learning to draw.*(i.) = to make pictures **3** *The horse drew the cart along the road.*(t.) = to pull **4** *draw water from the well*(t.) = to take out **5** *The match drew a big crowd.*(t.) = to attract **6** *India drew the match.* = to end a game without losing or winning **7** *to draw conclusions* = to reach some result **8** *How much money have you drawn from the bank?* = to take something out from a source where it is stored or available **9** *In times of trouble, she draws a lot of courage from her friends.* = to take **10** *The time for the exam is drawing near.* = to come close

draw[2] noun, c. **1** *The match ended in a draw.* = a match, competition etc. in which neither of the teams wins **2** *The professor is always a big draw at workgroups.* = someone or something that attracts people **3** *He won the prize in a lucky draw.* = lottery

to draw up *We drew up a list of people we wanted to invite.* = to prepare **to draw a blank** *The police were trying to find out who the leader of the gang is, but they drew a blank.* = to be unsuccessful in getting information **to draw the line** *I don't mind playing cards for fun, but I draw the line at gambling.* = to fix a limit beyond which one does not wish to do something **to draw (someone) out** *The boy was shy but I managed to draw him out and we talked for a long time.* = to make someone speak freely **to draw something up** = to prepare plans for some activity

drawback /ˈdrɔːbæk/ noun, c. *The book you have written is a good one, but there's one drawback. It's too long.* = disadvantage; something that spoils an otherwise good thing

drawer /ˈdrɔːr/ noun, c. = a kind of box without a lid, which fits into a table and can slide in and out, and is used to store things

drawing /ˈdrɔːɪŋ/ noun, c. or u. **1** *This is a drawing of the new building.*(c.) = a picture made with pencils, crayons etc. and not with a brush **2** *We teach our students drawing.*(u.) = the art of making pictures **drawing room** noun, c. = the room in a house where visitors are received (also **living room**)

drawl[1] /drɔːl/ verb, i. or t. = to speak very slowly, stretching the vowels

drawl[2] noun = a very slow style of speaking

dread[1] /dred/ verb, t. *I dread examinations.* = to be very afraid of (formal)

dread[2] noun, u. *I have a dread of examinations.* = great fear of something **dreadful** adj. *I got the dreadful news of the train accident.* = something that is sad or unpleasant

dream[1] /driːm/ noun, c. **1** *I had a strange dream last night.* = something that one thinks of or imagines while asleep **2** *I have dreams of an India where there will be no poverty.* = something that one wants very much to happen but which may not happen

dream[2] verb. i. or t. (**dreamt** or **dreamed**) **1** *Last night I dreamt that I was in New York.* = to have a dream while asleep **2** *When did I say that I would give you Rs 1,000? You must be dreaming!* = to imagine something **dreamer** noun, c. = a person who has talent and imagination, but is not very practical or down-to-earth

beyond one's wildest dreams = more than one had hoped for **to dream up something** = to think of an excuse for not doing something

drear•y /ˈdrɪəri/ adj. *Nothing interesting ever happens here. Life is dreary.* = dull and boring **dreariness** noun, u.

dredge /dredʒ/ verb, t. *The engineers are dredging the river as it is not deep enough for ships to pass.* = to dig up mud or sand from the bottom of a river or sea in order to make it more deep **dredger** noun, c. = a special kind of ship which is used to dredge a river or sea

drench /drentʃ/ verb, t. *I got drenched in the rain and caught a cold.* = to become completely wet

dress[1] /dres/ verb, i. or t. **1** *We will leave in ten minutes. Please get dressed.*(i.) = to put clothes on oneself or someone else; to put on clothes suitable for going out in etc. **2** *She dressed for the journey.*(i.) = to wear clothes for a particular purpose or occasion **3** *The doctor is dressing his wounds.*(t.) = to clean a wound and tie a bandage over it [MEDICINE] **4** *Please dress the chicken.* = to clean and prepare for cooking

dress[2] noun, c. **1** *That's a pretty dress.* = a garment or item of clothing worn by a girl or woman **2** *the national dress of Nepal* = a specific style of clothes **dress circle** noun = the first row of seats in a cinema or theatre **dress rehearsal** noun, u. = the final rehearsal of a drama before it is shown to an audience, in which the actors wear the clothes they are supposed to wear on stage

to be dressed in one's Sunday best = to be wearing one's best clothes for some special occasion **to be dressed to kill** = to be wearing very attractive clothes (informal) **to dress something up** *They dressed up the computer to make it look new.* = to make something look more attractive than it really is **to give someone a dressing-down** = to scold someone

> **Usage** The noun **dress** is a word for a particular item of clothing worn by girls or women. A man's clothes would not be described as a dress.

Usage A sari is a form of dress but it cannot be referred to as 'a dress'.

The verbs **dress, wear** and **put on** often get confused. We usually **put on** a garment with sleeves, a neck etc (e.g. a blouse, a shirt). We don't **put on** a sari, we **wear** it.

dressing /'dresɪŋ/ noun, u. or c. **1** *She enjoys dressing.*(u.) = the act of putting on clothes **2** *Put a clean dressing on the wound.*(c.) = material used to cover a wound [MEDICINE] **3** *salad dressing* = a mixture of oil and spices used to add taste to food **dressing table** noun, c. = a table fitted with a mirror and drawers, used by a person who is dressing

drib•ble[1] /'drɪbəl/ verb, i. or t. **1** *Saliva was dribbling from the baby's mouth.*(i.) = to allow some heavy liquid to flow out slowly in drops **2** *The centre half dribbled the ball to the left out.*(t.) = to keep the ball moving while running, in the game of football or hockey, with the help of short pushes or kicks

dribble[2] noun, c. **1** *a thin dribble of saliva* = a thin flow; a trickle **2** *a fast dribble* = the act of dribbling the ball in hockey or football

dri•ft[1] /drɪft/ verb, i. **1** *The boat is drifting down the river.* = to float along slowly, driven by the wind or current **2** *The work started well but now we seem to be drifting.* = to move with no sense of direction **3** *The younger people are drifting away from the villages to the towns.* = to move away slowly

drift[2] noun, c. *I couldn't get the drift of your speech.* = the general meaning **driftwood** noun = wood from trees which is carried along by rivers

drill[1] /drɪl/ noun, c. or u. **1** *a carpenter's drill.*(c.) = a machine used to make a hole in something (see pic under **tools**) **2** *The teacher led the students through a drill.*(c.) = physical exercise **3** *I am giving the students a drill in the vowels of English.* = practice which involves repetition **4** *a fire drill* = practice of what should be done in an emergency

drill[2] verb, t. *The thieves drilled a large hole in the wall and entered the room.* = to use a drill to make a hole

drink[1] /drɪŋk/ verb, t. or i. (**drank, drunk**) **1** *You should drink more milk.*(t.) = to take some liquid into the stomach through the mouth **2** *He drinks too much.*(i.) = to take alcoholic liquids (disapproving)

drink[2] noun, c.or u. **1** *Would you like a soft drink?*(c.) = a cup etc. of a hot or cold liquid (e.g. orange juice) which one drinks **2** *Have a drink before you go.* = an alcoholic liquid

to drink up something *It's late, please drink up your coffee.* = to drink something fast and finish it **to drink like a fish** = to be very fond of alcoholic drinks **to drink in something** *We drank in the beauty of the sunset.* = to look at or listen to something with great enjoyment or eagerness

drip[1] /drɪp/ verb, i. or t. *Water is dripping from the roof.*(i.) = to fall in drops

drip[2] noun, c. **1** *You can hear the drip from the tap.* = the sound of water falling in drops **2** *The man who was hurt in the accident has been given a drip.* = some liquid which is allowed to flow into a person's veins slowly in tiny drops (containing some medicine or chemical which the body needs) [MEDICINE] **drip-dry** adj. = clothing that becomes smooth after drying and does not need to be ironed after washing

drive[1] /draɪv/ verb, t. or i. (**drove, driven**) **1** *My brother will drive the car.*(t.) = to control a moving vehicle **2** *Can you drive?*(i.) = to be able to control a moving vehicle, specially a car **3** *He drove us out of the house because we were singing very loudly.*(t.) = to force someone to leave a place **4** *His depression drove him to drink.*(i.) = to force a person to do something, usually bad **5** *The batsman drove the ball over the fielder's head.*(t.) = to hit hard

drive[2] noun, c. or u. **1** *Let us go for a drive.*(c.) = a ride in a vehicle, especially a car, taken for pleasure **2** = a narrow road leading to a building **3** *He works hard but he has no drive.*(u.) = great energy or strong desire to succeed **4** *Our club is running a membership drive.*(c.) = a campaign **5** *a disk drive* = a part of a computer that reads and stores information [COMPUTERS] **6** *Hunger is a powerful drive* = a need of the body which has to be satisfied **driver** = a person who drives a car **drive-in restaurant** noun = a restaurant that people can use without getting out of their cars **driving** verb = the action of controlling a car **driving licence** an official card or book which allows one to drive in public places

to drive a hard bargain = to get something which is to your advantage by bargaining **to drive something home** = to make a point very clear **to drive at something** = to suggest something indirectly **to be in the driving seat** = to be in control

driz•zle[1] /'drɪzəl/ verb, i. *We expect heavy rain but it is only drizzling now.* = to rain in very fine and small drops

drizzle[2] noun, c. *We had a light drizzle.*(c.) = a very light shower of rain

drom•e•da•ry /'drɒmədəri/ noun (**dromedaries**) = a type of camel with only one hump on its back

drone[1] /drəʊn/ verb, i. **1** *The generator droned all night, making sleep impossible.* = to make a low, deep humming sound like that of a bee **2** *The speaker droned on, though no one was listening.* = to talk for a long time in a low and dull voice

drone[2] noun, u. **1** *The singer's voice was accompanied by the drone of the tanpura.* = a continuous low sound **2** = a male bee

droop /druːp/ verb, i. **1** *The plants are drooping from the heat.* = to bend or hang down **2** *We started the work happily but by the evening our spirits were drooping.* = to become low or sad

drop[1] /drɒp/ verb, t. or i. **1** *Don't drop the glasses. They will break.*(t.) = to allow something to fall from a height **2** *The price of gold has dropped.*(i.) = to come down to a lower level **3** *I have dropped the idea of going to America.*(t.) = to give up **4** *He has been dropped from the team.*(i.) = to leave out **5** *My friend dropped in this morning.*(i.) = to visit someone unexpectedly **6** *I will drop you at the station.* = to take someone to some place (usually in a car)

drop[2] noun, c. or u. **1** *Take only two drops of this medicine.* = an amount of liquid that falls in one round mass **2** *There was a big drop in temperature.* = fall **dropper** noun, c. = a small glass tube with a rubber bulb at one end, used for measuring out liquids (e.g. medicines) in drops (see pic under **laboratory equipment**) **drops** = a liquid that is put into the eyes, ears or nose

to drop in on someone = to visit someone unexpectedly **to drop a hint** = to suggest something indirectly **to drop a brick** = to say something foolish or embarassing which makes others feel uncomfortable **to drop off** = to fall asleep **to drop out** = to stop going to classes or to give up some activity **to drop the subject** = to stop discussing something because it might make someone who may hear what is being said unhappy **to let a matter drop** = to agree to stop discussing something **to drop someone a line** = to write someone a letter (informal) **to drop names** = to mention the names of well-known people, or those in high positions, as a way of showing to others that one knows them (informal, disapproving) **at the drop of a hat** *He can sing at the drop of a hat.* = without having a strong reason to do something (informal)

droppings /ˈdrɒpɪŋz/ noun (plural only) *bird droppings* = small bits of solid waste matter from birds or animals **drop-out** noun, c. = someone who leaves a school or college without going through the course of study fully

drought /draʊt/ noun, u. = a long period without rain

drove /drəʊv/ noun, c. *a drove of sheep* = a group of farm animals moving together

drown /draʊn/ verb, i. or t. **1** (i.) = to die by going under the surface of water and being unable to breathe **2** *His voice was drowned by the shouts from the crowd.*(t.) = to make so much noise that something or somebody cannot be heard

drow•sy /ˈdraʊzi/ adj. *I feel drowsy after the heavy meal.* = sleepy; in a state just before one falls asleep

drudge[1] /drʌdʒ/ verb, i. *I have been drudging in this office for two years.* = to do hard but dull work for little money

drudge[2] noun, c. *I am just a drudge in this office.* = a person who has to drudge **drudgery** noun, u. = hard and uninteresting work

drum[1] /drʌm/ noun, c. **1** = a musical instrument consisting of a piece of thin leather stretched over a hollow, round frame which makes a sound when it is struck with the hand or a stick **2** *an oil drum* = a round metal container for liquids **3** = a part of a machine that looks like a drum

drums

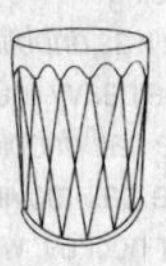

drum[2] verb, i. or t. *He drummed on the table with his fingers.* = to produce a sound like that of a drum **drummer** noun, c. = a professional musician who play on drums **drumstick** **1** = the lower part of the leg of a chicken **2** = the long, stick-like fruit of tree, which is eaten as a vegetable

to drum something into one's ears = to keep on repeating something so that one remembers **to beat one's own drum** = to say things in praise of oneself **to drum something into somebody** = to repeat an idea until it has been clearly understood

drunk[1] /drʌŋk/ adj. *He was so drunk that he could hardly walk.* = under the influence of alcohol

drunk[2] verb, t. *He has drunk all the milk.* = past participle form of **drink**

dry[1] /draɪ/ adj. **1** *The fields are dry because there is no rain.* = without any water or moisture; not wet **2** *Tamil Nadu has gone dry.* = not allowing the sale of alcoholic drinks **3** *This is a very dry document.* = uninteresting **4** *dry chapatis* = eaten without anything else; without oil

dry[2] verb, t. **1** *She is drying her clothes.* = to put out in such a way that it becomes dry **2** *Could you dry the dishes?* = to wipe something which has been washed until there is no moisture on it **dryclean** verb, t. = to clean clothes with some chemical instead of water **dry dock** noun, c. = a place where a ship can be repaired after all the water has been pumped out **dry humour** = humour which sounds like something said seriously

as dry as dust = very dull and uninteresting **a dry cough/sneeze** = a cough/sneeze which does not produce any liquid from the mouth or nose **to be home and dry** = to complete something successfully **to dry up** **1** *The river has dried up.* = (of a river, lake etc.) to be completely without water **2** *The actor was just about to say her lines when she dried up.* =to be unable to say what one was supposed to say (out of nervousness) (informal)

du•al /ˈdjuːəl/ adj. *My son has an American passport as well as an Indian passport. He has dual citizenship.*= double; having to do with two things

dub /dʌb/ verb, t. or i. **1** *D. N. West has been dubbed 'Do Nothing West' because he has done nothing for the team.*(t.) = to call somebody by a name **2** *The English film will be dubbed in Hindi.*(i.) = to create new sounds for a film so that what was said originally in one language is now heard in another language

du•bi•ous /ˈdjuːbiəs/ adj. **1** *I had agreed to her plan but now I am a little dubious about the whole thing* = doubtful **2** *a dubious reputation* = something that causes doubt about one's honesty etc.

duck[1] /dʌk/ noun, c. **1** = a small species of water-bird, often farmed for its eggs or meat **2** *He scored a duck in this match.* = zero (informal)

duck[2] verb, i. or t. *The boy ducked to avoid being hit.* (i.) = to move or lower one's head or body quickly in order to avoid a blow **duckling** noun, c. = a small, young duck

to take to something like a duck to water = to learn something very easily and quickly **like water off a duck's back** = having no effect on someone

duct /dʌkt/ noun, c. = a thin, narrow tube or pipe that carries a liquid, gas etc. [TECHNICAL] **ductless gland** noun = a part inside the body which produces some chemical needed by the body and allows it to flow directly into the blood, and not through a duct (tube) e.g. the pituitary gland

duc•tile /ˈdʌktaɪl/ adj. *Aluminium is a ductile metal.* = having the quality of taking any required shape easily; being easy to work with [TECHNICAL]

dud /dʌd/ noun, c. *a dud coin* = something that is found to be of no use or value (informal)

due[1] /djuː/ adj. **1** *I must repay all the money which is due to the bank.* = something which is owed to someone (has to be paid back) **2** *You should show due respect to your teachers.* = proper or correct; belonging to someone as a right **3** *The train is due to arrive at 10.00.* = expected **4** *His victory was due to the hard work he put in.* = because of (formal)

due[2] noun, c. or u. **1** *You should clear all your dues.*(c.) = money that is owed to someone and has to be paid back **2** *I have not done you a favour by giving you a promotion; this was your due.*(u.) = something that belongs to someone as a right

in due course = at the proper time

du•el /ˈdjuːəl/ noun, c. = a fight between two people (formerly used to refer to a fight with chosen weapons to settle an argument)

du•et /djuˈet/ noun, c. = a song in which two people sing or play, often at the same time

duke /djuːk/ noun, c. *the Duke of Edinburgh* = a British person of high rank, lower only than that of the king or queen (see also **duchess**)

dull[1] /dʌl/ adj. **1** *a dull person* = not intelligent **2** *You cannot cut the vegetables with that dull knife.* = not having a sharp edge **3** *The match has been dull so far.* = not interesting or exciting **4** *He has painted the walls a dull grey colour.* = not bright

dull[2] verb, t. *The doctor gave me an injection to dull the pain.* = to reduce or make less **dullard** noun,c. = a dull person

to have never a dull moment = to have something interesting going on **dull as ditch-water** = uninteresting

dumb /dʌm/ adj. **1** = not able to speak **2** *The man chose to be dumb.*= unwilling to speak **3** *How can you be so dumb?* = stupid (informal) **dumbfound** verb, t. *The new player dumbfounded his critics by scoring a century in his first match.*= to surprise someone so much that he/she is unable to speak

to strike someone dumb = to shock someone greatly in a pleasant or unpleasant way

dum•my[1] /ˈdʌmi/ noun, c. (**dummies**) **1** *They have put up a dummy in the shop to display new clothes.* = a figure of a human being used to show new clothes **2** = a stupid person (informal, American)

dummy[2] adj. **1** *This company has a dummy manager.* = something or somebody that is there only for show, but has no power to do anything (not respectful) **2** = a pacifier used to keep a baby calm

dump[1] /dʌmp/ verb, t. **1** *The truck dumped the sand just in front of my house.* = to unload something in a careless manner **2** *The film company dumped the actor because she was absent most of the time.* = to get rid of (not respectful) **3** *When countries produce more goods than they need, they try to dump them on other countries.* = to sell something in a foreign market at a very cheap price [TECHNICAL]

dump[2] noun, c. *This lake has become a rubbish dump for the whole city.* = a place for dumping waste material **dumper** noun, c. = a special kind of truck with a container that can be raised to unload sand etc. **dumpling** = a kind of cake having meat etc. inside it

dumpy /ˈdʌmpɪ/ adj. *a dumpy little man* = short and fat

dunce /dʌns/ noun, c. = a person considered stupid; a slow learner

dune /djuːn/ noun, c. *sand dune* = a small hill made of sand, found near the sea or in a desert

dung /dʌŋ/ noun, u. = solid waste matter produced by an animal, often used as a fertilizer

D

dun•geon /ˈdʌndʒən/ noun, c.= an underground jail or prison in a castle

dunk /dʌŋk/ verb, t. *He dunked the piece of bread in his tea.* = to dip bread etc. into a liquid to make it soft for eating (informal)

dupe /djuːp/ verb, t. *He duped all of us and ran away with our money.* = to cheat or trick someone

du•plex /ˈdjuːpleks/ noun, c. **1** = a flat which has rooms on two floors **2** = a small house which has one common wall with a neighbouring house

du•pli•cate[1] /ˈdjuːplɪkət/ adj. *This is a duplicate key for your scooter.* = of exactly the same kind

duplicate[2] noun, c. **1** *This key is a duplicate.* = something that is an exact copy of something else **2** *Fill out this application form in duplicate.* = two copies which are exactly the same

duplicate[3] /ˈdjuːplɪkeɪt/ verb, t. *I will have to duplicate this key.* = to make a duplicate

du•pli•ci•ty /djuːˈplɪsɪti/ noun, u. *The company lost money due to the manager's duplicity.* = the quality of being dishonest (formal, disapproving)

du•ra•ble /ˈdjʊərəbəl/ adj. *These shoes are extremely durable.* = able to last (stand use for a long time)

du•ra•tion /djʊˈreɪʃən/ noun, u. *You will not be allowed to go home for the duration of your trial.* = the period during which something continues (formal)

dur•ess /djʊˈres/ noun, u. *The thief admitted his crime to the police, but his statement was made under duress.* = use of threats or force

dur•ing /ˈdjʊərɪŋ/ prep. **1** *It is very hot during the day but cool at night.* = all through a period of time **2** *I had to go out once during the examination.* = at one point within a longer period of time

dusk /dʌsk/ noun, u. = the time just before night when the sun sets and it is nearly dark

dust[1] /dʌst/ noun, u. *The table is covered with dust.* = the fine, dry powder produced by small grains of earth, coal etc.

dust[2] verb, t. **1** *Please dust the table.* = to take away dust from a surface, by wiping etc. **2** *The doctor is dusting the wound with antiseptic powder.* = to put light powder on something **dusty** = covered with or full of dust **duster** noun, c. = a piece of cloth used to remove dust from a surface or to clean a blackboard on which something has been written with chalk **dustbin** noun, c. = a container with a lid in which rubbish is collected before it is thrown away

to kick up the dust = to create an argument or quarrel **to wait for the dust to settle** = to wait for a situation to become clear after a period of confusion **to bite the dust** = to come to an unsuccessful end

duty /ˈdjuːti/ noun, u. or c. (**duties**) **1** *It is the duty of a soldier to protect his country from the enemy.*(u.) **2** *My duties include teaching and cooking lunch for the students.*(c.) = work that one is expected or supposed to do **3** *You will have to pay duty on the computer you have brought from Singapore.* = tax **dutiful** adj. = willing to do one's duty

dwarf[1] /dwɔːf/ noun, c. (**dwarfs** or **dwarves**) = a person who is much shorter in height than the average person (considered offensive at present)

dwarf[2] adj. *a dwarf variety (of a tree)* = a person, animal or plant of much less than the usual height or size

dwarf[3] verb, t. *Our house has been dwarfed by the tall new building which has come up next to it.* = to make something look very small by comparison

dwell /dwel/ verb, i. (**dwelt**) = to live somewhere (old-fashioned, literary)

dwin•dle /ˈdwɪndl/ verb, i. *The population of this village is fast dwindling as many people are leaving.* = to become less or weaker

dye[1] /daɪ/ noun, c. (**dyes**) = colour or paint, made from chemicals or vegetable matter, used to colour something **dyed** adj. *a dyed shirt* = put into dye so that its colur changes

dye[2] verb, t. *I will have to dye this shirt as it has lost its colour.* = to give colour to something by using a dye

dyke /daɪk/ noun, c. see **dike**

dy•na•mic /daɪˈnæmɪk/ adj. *We have a dynamic leader.* = active, full of energy, new ideas etc.

dy•na•mics /daɪˈnæmɪks/ noun. **1** *You need to understand the dynamics of social change in the community.* = the ways in which people or things interact **2** = the scientific study of the forces involved in movement [PHYSICS]

dy•na•mite /ˈdaɪnəmaɪt/ noun, u. = a strong explosive mixture made of nitroglycerine

dy•na•mo /ˈdaɪnəməʊ/ noun, c. = a machine that can produce electrical energy from some other form of energy e.g. wind or water energy (also **generator**)

dy•nas•ty /ˈdɪnəsti/ noun, c. (**dynasties**) = a series of rulers belonging to the same family [HISTORY]

dys•en•te•ry /ˈdɪsəntəri/ noun = an uncomfortable condition of the body which causes a person to empty his/her bowels frequently and to produce blood

dys•lex•i•a /dɪsˈleksiə/ noun = a problem in reading caused by difficulty in seeing the differences between the shapes of letters (e.g. between 'b' and 'd') [TECHNICAL] **dyslexic** adj.

dys•pep•sia /dɪsˈpepsiə/ noun = a condition in which one is unable to digest food [MEDICINE]

eE

e, E /iː/ the fifth letter of the English alphabet
e- = 'electronic', or based on, as in *e-mail, e-commerce, e-banking* etc. [COMPUTERS]
each /iːtʃ/ det. or pron. *Each of the boys carried a flag.* = every single one (out of two or more)
ea•ger /ˈiːgəʳ/ adj. *She is so eager to play in the match that she is using all her free time to practise.* = full of keen interest **eagerly** adv.
ea•gle /ˈiːgəl/ noun, c. = a very large meat-eating bird **eagle-eyed** adj. *Our eagle-eyed soldiers spotted the enemy.* = having keen (good) eyesight, like an eagle (literary)
ear /ɪəʳ/ noun, c. **1** = the part of the body we use for hearing **2** *He has an ear for music.* = the ability to recognize sounds **3** *an ear of wheat* = the top part of a plant that carries grains **eardrum** noun, c. = a piece of thin, tightly stretched skin inside the ear which allows us to hear sounds **earlobe** /ˈɪəˌləʊb/ noun, c. = the soft, fleshy part at the bottom of one's ear **earmark** verb, t. *I have earmarked this money for our holiday in Goa.* = to keep aside for a particular purpose **earring** noun, c. = a piece of jewellery worn on the ear

to be all ears *She looked bored when I met her but was all ears when I told her we would both be going to Delhi.* = listening with keen attention (informal) **to have an ear to the ground** = to be very well informed about things that are happening around one **to play something by ear** *I'm not sure what we can do if the plan fails. Let's play it by ear.* = to be guided by one's feelings or instincts while reacting to a situation, instead of following a fixed plan **to play (a musical instrument) by ear** = to play a piece of music by depending on one's memory rather than reading the music as one plays **to turn a deaf ear** = to decide not to attend to advice or a call for help

ear•ly[1] /ˈɜːli/ adj. **1** *He gets up early in the morning.* = at the beginning of a period of time e.g. the morning or night **2** *The train was due at 7.00 but it arrived at 6.50. It was ten minutes early.* = arriving or happening before the expected time **3** *When did early life on earth begin?* = first or near the first **4** *They taught him to read at an early age.* = young
early[2] adv. **1** *They arrived early for dinner.* = before the expected time **2** *Can you call me early tomorrow?* = towards the start of the day, week etc.
earn /ɜːn/ verb, t. **1** *I earn Rs 5000 a month.* = to get money in return for work **2** *Yuvraj Singh has earned his place in the Indian team.* = to get something that one deserves **3** = to get money as interest on money in the bank **earnings** /ˈɜːnɪŋʒ/ noun, u. (always plural) **1** *The family's earnings were insufficient.* = money earned through work **2** = money earned by a company or government; income
ear•nest[1] /ˈɜːnɪst/ adj. *Tara and Ketan will be successful in any job as they are very earnest about their work.* = serious about things
earnest[2] noun, u. *When I called him an ass, I was only joking. I did not mean it in earnest.* = seriousness
earth[1] /ɜːθ/ noun, u. **1** = the planet on which we live **2** *I need two baskets of earth to fill up this hole.* = soil

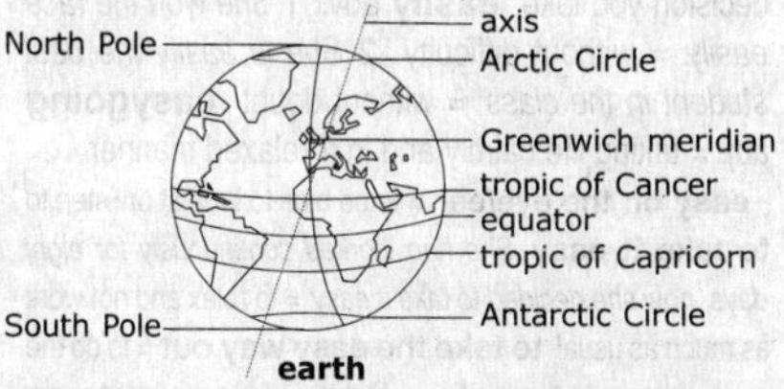

earth

earth[2] verb, t. *You must earth the machine or you will get a shock.* = to make an electrical machine safe by connecting it to the ground with a wire [TECHNICAL] **earthenware** /ˈɜːθənweəʳ/ noun, u. = cups, pots etc. made of baked clay

to come down/ bring someone down to earth = to be forced to deal with the hard realities of a situation

earth•quake /ˈɜːθkweɪk/ noun, c. = a sudden and violent shaking of the earth's surface
ease[1] /iːz/ noun, u. **1** *He lives a life of ease and doesn't do much.* = comfort **2** *She passed the examination with ease.* = without much difficulty or effort
ease[2] verb, t. or i. **1** *The doctor gave me an injection to ease the pain.*(t.) = to reduce or make less **2** *He eased the car into the garage.*(t.) = to move something slowly and carefully **3** *Take this medicine. After an hour, the pain will ease.*(i.) = (of pain, situations, the climate etc.) to become less strong or unpleasant

to ease off *The headache will ease off once you take this medicine.* = to become weaker or less intense **to ease up** = to become less focused or severe on someone **to be at ease** = to feel comfortable **to stand at ease** = a command given to soldiers to make them stand with their feet apart and hands behind their backs, in a relaxed way [MILITARY] **to put one's mind at ease** = to become more relaxed and to stop feeling nervous about something

ea•sel /ˈiːzəl/ noun, c. = a wooden frame used to hold a picture while it is being painted
east /iːst/ noun = the direction in which the sun rises **eastern** adj. *the eastern states of India* = of the east

easterly adj. **1** *travelling in an easterly direction* = towards the east **2** *an easterly wind* = from the east **eastward** adv. *flying eastward* = towards the east **the East** noun = the eastern part of the world, specially Asia

Eas•ter /'i:stə'/ noun = a Christian festival held in March or April to mark Christ's being crucified and coming back to life

ea•sy /'i:zi/ adj. **1** *It is easy to learn French.* = not difficult **2** *He has an easy life.* = comfortable and free from trouble **3** *I was rather anxious last night but am easy now.* = in a calm and relaxed state **4** *'Shall we go out or eat here?' 'I'm easy.'* = I will accept whatever decision you take **easily** adv. **1** *She won the race easily.* = without difficulty **2** *She is easily the best student in the class.* = without doubt **easygoing** adj. = taking life calmly and in a relaxed manner

easy on the eye/ear = to be nice to look at or listen to **to take it easy** *She had worked continuously for eight days, now she decided to take it easy.* = to relax and not work as much as usual **to take the easy way out** = to do the easy rather than the best or right thing (disapproving) **to go easy on something** *The doctor wants me to go easy on sweets.* = to be careful about something one usually has or does a lot of, or often **easier said than done** = easy to talk about but not so easy to do **to get off easy** *I thought my seniors would scold me for not doing my work properly, but I got off easy. They only gave me gentle advice.* = to get less strong punishment than one expected (informal)

eat /i:t/ verb, i. and t. (**ate, eaten**) = to take in food through the mouth; to have a meal **eatable** adj. *The food was barely eatable.* = good enough to be eaten (compare **edible**)

to eat out = to have a meal in a restaurant instead of eating at home **Eat up!** =an expression encouraging someone, generally a child etc. to eat all the food given to him/her **to eat humble pie** =to be forced to admit that one was wrong and to apologize **to eat one's words** = to take back one's words when one is proved wrong **to have someone eating out of one's hand** = to get someone to do anything that one wants them to do because one is loved, is charming etc. **to eat into** *The long meeting has eaten into our lunch break.* = to use up of more time or money than was planned

eaves•drop /'i:vzdrɒp/ verb, i. *I am sorry I was trying to eavesdrop when your father was talking to you.* = to listen secretly to what other people are saying (disapproving)

ebb[1] /eb/ verb, i. **1** *The tide is ebbing.* = to flow away from the shore (used to describe the flow of sea-water) **2** *His strength ebbed away and he became very weak.* = to become less (figurative, literary)

ebb[2] noun, u. **1** *The tide is at an ebb.* = the flow of sea-water away from the shore **2** *Government activities are at a low ebb.* = a state when nothing is happening

eb•o•ny[1] /'ebəni/ noun, u. = a kind of tree that produces hard, dark wood

ebony[2] adj. **1** = made of ebony wood **2** = very dark-coloured

ec•cen•tric[1] /ɪk'sentrɪk/ adj. *The eccentric young man lives in a house with 50 cats.* = a person with very unusual habits or behaviour

eccentric[2] noun, c. *He is an eccentric.* = an eccentric person

ECG abbr. of **electrocardiogram** noun = a drawing made by a machine that traces the electrical activity of the heart [MEDICINE]

ech•o[1] /'ekəʊ/ noun, n. (**echoes**) *If you clap your hands inside this room, you will hear an echo.* = a sound which is repeated because it is sent back off a surface

echo[2] verb, i. or t. **1** *The sound echoed around the room.*(i.) = to be heard as an echo **2** *This book echoes all your ideas.*(t.) = to repeat or imitate

e•clec•tic /ɪ'klektɪk/ adj. *The system of education in this school is eclectic. It combines ideas taken from many different countries.* = not following a single set of ideas but combining ideas taken from different sources

e•clipse[1] /ɪ'klɪps/ noun, c or u. **1** (c.) = the darkness caused by the moon coming between the sun and the earth (**solar eclipse**) or the earth coming between the sun and the moon (**lunar eclipse**) **2** *The rise of the general meant the eclipse of the king.*(u.) = loss of power and influence

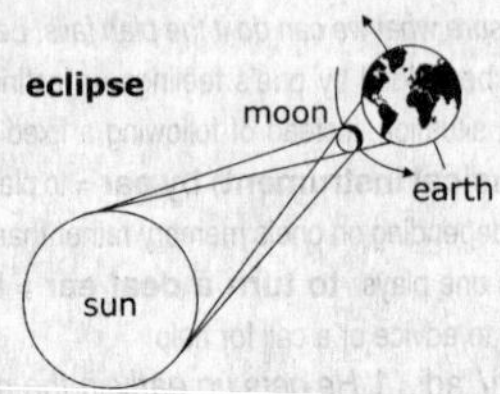

eclipse[2] verb, t. *Her reputation as a novelist has now eclipsed that of her famous grandfather.* = to do better than someone else; to surpass

e•col•o•gy /ɪkɒlədʒi/ noun = the scientific study of the natural surroundings in which plants, animals and human beings live, and the effect that they have on each other

ec•o•nom•ic /ɪkə'nɒmɪk/ adj. **1** *The economic policies of the government are not very effective.* = having to do with economics **2** *The company gave up the idea of making cars as it would not be economic.* = profitable

ec•o•nom•i•cal /ɪkə'nɒmɪkəl/ adj. *It is more economical to travel by bus than by train.* = using money, time etc. in a better way, without waste

ec•o•nom•ics /ɪkə'nɒmɪks/ noun = the scientific study of the ways in which wealth is produced and used

e•con•o•mize (economise) /ɪ'kɒnəmaɪz/ verb, i. *We must economize on petrol.* = save

e•con•o•my /ɪ'kɒnəmi/ noun, u. or c. (**economies**) **1** *India's economy is growing fast.*(c.) = the economic system of a country (its trade, industry, agriculture etc.) **2** *All of us must practise economy now.*(u.) = the careful use of money

ec•sta•sy /'ekstəsi/ noun, u. *The beautiful music created a feeling of ecstasy in the audience.* = a very strong feeling of joy **ecstatic** /ɪk'stætɪk/ adj. *The children were ecstatic when their mother gave them ice cream.* = feeling great joy

ec•ze•ma /'eksɪmə/ noun, u. = a skin disease causing swelling and blisters [MEDICINE]

ed•dy[1] /'edi/ noun, c. (**eddies**) *The boat was caught in an eddy and spun round and round.* = a circular movement of water or wind

eddy[2] verb, i. *The smoke eddied round the kitchen.* = to move round and round

edge[1] /edʒ/ noun, c. **1** *The knife has a sharp edge.* = the thin, sharp cutting part of a knife **2** *The flowers grew along the edge of the pond.* = the outer part, where something ends; the border

edge[2] verb, t. **1** *For the carnival, he wore a yellow shirt edged with orange.* = to form the edge or border of something **2** *We edged our way out of the crowded meeting as we did not want to disturb anyone.* = to move sideways slowly, so as not to be noticed **edgeways** adv. **1** *The desk was so big that it had to be carried in edgeways.* = sideways **2** *They were both talking so much that we couldn't get a word in edgeways.* = in between (informal)

to be on edge *Everyone else in the room was relaxed but she was clearly on edge.* = nervous and anxious **to have an edge over (someone)** *In our violin class, Shama has an edge over us because she's been learning to play for several years.* = to have an advantage over someone else based on skill, experience etc. **to take the edge off something** *His kind words took the edge off the deep sadness we were feeling.* = to make emotion, taste, pain etc. less strong or sharply felt

ed•i•ble /'edɪbəl/ adj. *The fruits of the banyan tree are not edible.* = which can safely be eaten; non-poisonous (see also **eatable**)

> Usage **eatable** is used to comment on the taste of food while **edible** is used to comment on the safety of eating something.

e•dict /'i:dɪkt/ noun, c. *The emperor Ashoka issued an edict ordering his subjects to be kind to animals.* = a public order issued by someone in power

ed•i•fice /'edɪfɪs/ noun, c. = a fine, large building, such as a palace (formal or literary)

ed•i•fy /'edɪfaɪ/ verb, t. *I hope the lecture you heard this morning has edified your mind.* = to improve someone's mind or character (formal)

ed•it /'edɪt/ verb, t. *You will need to edit this book before it is published.* = to prepare a book or article for printing by correcting mistakes, leaving out certain parts etc. **edition** /ɪ'dɪʃən/ noun, c. *the first edition of a book* = the form in which a book appears when it is published **editor** /'edɪtə^r/ noun, c. **1** = a person who edits a book or article **2** = a person who is in charge of a newspaper or magazine **editorial** /edɪ'tɔ:rɪel/ noun = an opinion given by the newspaper on an important subject

ed•u•cate /'edjʊkeɪt/ verb, t. = to teach; to develop someone's mind and character **educated** /edjʊ'keɪtɪd/ adj. **1** *an educated woman* = a person who has had a good education and is knowledgable **2** *an educated guess* = a guess based on knowledge and therefore likely to be correct **education** /edjʊ'keɪʃn/ noun, c. or u. **1** (u.) = the formal process of educating people in schools, colleges, universities etc. **2** *I went to university to complete my education in public health.*(c.) = someone's learning or experience in a particular field

eel /i:l/ noun, c. *as slippery as an eel* = a long fish that looks like a snake

ee•rie /'ɪəri/ adj. *The old, deserted house has an eerie atmosphere.* = strange and causing fear

ef•face /ɪ'feɪs/ verb, t. *This is an old coin. Unfortunately, you can't read the writing on it because it has been effaced.* = to destroy the surface of something so that the writing etc. on it is removed [TECHNICAL]

ef•fect[1] /ɪ'fekt/ noun, c. or u. **1** *The advertising campaign has had no effect on the sales of this product.* = result **2** *This rule comes into effect next year.* = use or practice

effect[2] verb, t. *The architect has effected a number of changes in the plan.* = to bring about; to cause (formal) **effective** adj. *The mosquito coil has been quite effective.* = producing the desired result **effects** noun **1** (always plural) *The Customs officer will check your personal effects.* = belongings **2** *The film had some wonderful special effects.* = images and sounds in a film, on stage etc. which are unusual

to take effect *The medicine you have taken for your headache will take effect soon.* = (of medicines etc.) to show results **with immediate effect** *Nina will take over as* *the senior teacher with immediate effect.* = immediately; from the time of speaking (formal) **words to that effect** *Sonali said she had been unfair, or words to that effect.* = to give a general idea of what a person said rather than the exact words

ef•fem•i•nate /ɪˈfemɪnət/ adj. = having the looks or qualities of a woman (used to refer to a man) (derogatory)

ef•fer•ves•cence /efəˈvesəns/ noun, u. *If you put a little sodium bicarbonate in a glass of water it will produce effervescence.* = little bubbles of gas produced in a liquid because of some chemical action [CHEMISTRY] **effervesce** verb, i. = to produce an effervescent reaction **effervescent** adj. **1** = a liquid that gives out bubbles **2** *He is in an effervescent mood.* = cheerful and excited (used to refer to a person)

ef•fi•ca•cious /efɪˈkeɪʃəs/ adj. *The new medicine proved to be efficacious. The patient was cured in two days.* = having the power to produce good results (used to refer to a medicine or a course of action) (formal)

ef•fi•cient /ɪˈfɪʃənt/ adj. *We have an efficient manager. The office is doing well.* = able to work well and produce good results

ef•fi•gy /ˈefɪdʒi/ noun, c. (**effigies**) *The angry protestors took out an effigy of the leader.* = the figure or likeness of some person made out of wood, old clothes etc. used to show disrespect

ef•flu•ent /ˈefluənt/ noun, c. (usually plural) or u. *The effluents from the factories are being poured into the river and are polluting it.* = harmful waste material from factories, etc. that is poured out into rivers or seas [TECHNICAL]

ef•fort /ˈefət/ noun, u. or c. **1** *I was able to lift the heavy iron bar with great effort.*(u.) = the use of strength (of the body or the mind) **2** *The school is making an effort to increase the number of books in the library.*(c.) = an attempt to do something difficult

ef•fron•te•ry /ɪˈfrʌntəri/ noun, u. *I wonder how he had the effrontery to criticise you after all the help you gave him.* = the boldness to do something without feeling any shame (disapproving)

ef•fu•sive /ɪˈfjuːsɪv/ adj. *He gave us an effusive welcome even though he didn't know us well.* = showing a lot of feeling, often without sincerity

e.g. abbr. of **exempli gratia** (Latin) = for example

e•gal•i•tar•i•an /ɪgælɪˈteəriən/ adj. *an egalitarian society* = treating everyone as equal

egg[1] /eg/ noun, c. or u. **1** *an ostrich egg*(c.) = a round or oval object with a hard shell which comes out of a female bird, snake etc. and contains the unborn baby of the animal **2** *I had egg curry for lunch.*(u.) = eggs used as food

egg[2] verb, t. *My friends egged me on to take part in the debate although I was not very keen.* = to encourage strongly (informal) **egghead** noun, c. = a person who is interested only in books and studies and not in practical things (derogatory) **eggplant** noun = the fruit of a plant, usually round, purple, green or white, also known as 'brinjal' or 'aubergine'

to put all one's eggs in one basket *If you want to have a good programme, you should invite a number of speakers instead of just one. It is never wise to put all your eggs in one basket.* = to depend completely on only one thing

e•go /ˈiːgəʊ/ noun, u. *His ego was hurt when he was not selected for the team.* = the good opinion that one has of oneself **egocentric** /ɪgəʊˈsentrɪk/ adj. *She is an egocentric person.* = thinking only of oneself **egoism** /ˈɪgəʊɪzm/ noun, u. *Your egoism is what has made you so unpopular.* = the quality of thinking only of oneself (also **egotism**) **egoist** noun = a person who thinks only of him/herself (also **egotist**)

eight /eɪt/ noun = the number written as 8

eigh•teen /eɪˈtiːn/ noun = the number written as 18

eigh•ty /ˈeɪti/ noun = the number written as 80

ei•ther[1] /ˈaɪðəʳ/ det. **1** *The Principal wants either Sally or Sheila to read out the speech.* = one or the other of two **2** *We have a house with a garden on either side.* = both

either[2] pron. *We have sweets as well as ice cream. You can have either.* = one or the other

either[3] adv. *I have not read this book and my sister hasn't read it either.* = one as well as the other (used only in negative sentences)

either[4] conj. *Either Philip or his brother will come here tomorrow.* = one or the other

e•jac•u•late /ɪˈdʒækjʊleɪt/ verb, i. **1** = to throw out sperm (male seed) with force from the body [BIOLOGY] **2** = to cry out or speak suddenly

e•ject /ɪˈdʒekt/ verb, t. or i. **1** *The warden of the hostel ejected some students who were causing trouble.*(t.) = to throw out forcibly from a place (formal) **2** *The pilot ejected from the falling plane.*(i.) = to leave or come out of something with force [TECHNICAL] **3** = to remove a disk or tape from a device such as a cassette player

eke /iːk/ verb, t. *She eked out her small income by doing extra work in the evenings.* = to make a small supply (of money, food etc.) last longer by being careful (old-fashioned)

to eke out a living = to make just enough money to live on (old-fashioned)

e•lab•o•rate[1] /ɪˈlæbərət/ adj. *They made elaborate arrangements for the long train journey.* = done with great care, going into details

e•lab•o•rate[2] /ɪˈlæbəreɪt/ verb, i. or t. *Could you*

please elaborate further on what you have just told us?(i.) = to add more details

e•lapse /ɪ'læps/ verb, i. *Three months have elapsed since she left town.* = to pass (referring to a period of time) (formal) [LAW]

e•las•tic /ɪ'læstɪk/ adj. *an elastic belt* = able to return to its original size and shape (referring to things made of material such as rubber)

e•lat•ed /ɪ'leɪtɪd/ adj. *They were elated when their team won.* = full of joy

el•bow /'elbəʊ/ noun, c. **1** = the joint between the upper arm and the lower arm (forearm) **2** *an elbow joint* = a piece of metal, shaped like an elbow, which connects two pipes etc.

el•der[1] /'eldə'/ adj. *my elder brother* = the older of two people (specially a brother or sister)

elder[2] noun, c. *a village elder* = a person who is respected because of his or her age and wisdom and has an important position **elderly** adj. = old or nearing old age

e•lect[1] /ɪ'lekt/ verb, t or i. **1** *The party elected a new president.*(t.) = to choose by voting **2** *He elected to return to India.*(i.) = to decide to do something (formal)

elect[2] adj. *The prime minister elect* = someone who has been elected to a certain position **election** noun, u. = the process by which someone is elected (through voting) **electorate** noun, u. = the people who vote or have the right to vote in an election

e•lec•tive /ɪ'lektɪv/ adj. or noun *an elective (subject)* = a subject which one can choose to study or not to study

e•lec•tric /ɪ'lektrik/ adj. *an electric clock* = something that is operated by electricity **electrical** adj. *an electrical engineer* = connected with electricity **electrician** /ɪlek'trɪʃən/ noun, c. = a person who repairs electrical machines etc. **electrification** /ɪlektrɪfɪ'keɪʃən/ noun, u. = the bringing of electricity to a place

e•lec•tri•ci•ty /ɪlek'trɪsɪti/ noun = the power or energy produced by a battery or generator (dynamo); a kind of energy which can be used to provide heat, light etc.

e•lec•tro•cu•tion /ɪlektrə'kju:ʃən/ noun = death caused by an electrical current passing through the body

e•lec•trode /ɪ'lektrəʊd/ noun, c. = one of the two points (terminals) at which a current enters or leaves an electrical machine [SCIENCE]

e•lec•trol•y•sis /ɪlek'trɒlɪsɪs/ noun = the separation of a liquid into its chemical parts by passing an electrical current through it [SCIENCE]

e•lec•tro•mag•net /ɪlektrəʊ'mægnɪt/ noun, c. = any material (usually metal) around which a wire is wound, that acts like a magnet when a current passes through the wire [TECHNICAL]

e•lec•tron /ɪ'lektrɒn/ noun, c. = a tiny particle (piece) of matter which forms part of an atom and carries a negative electrical charge (compare **proton, neutron**) [SCIENCE]

e•lec•tron•ic /ɪlek'trɒnɪk/ adj. *an electronic calculator* = a machine that works by using the flow of electrons **electronics** noun **1** = the science that deals with the behaviour of electrons **2** = the application of this science in making electronic machines e.g. computers

el•e•gant /'elɪgənt/ adj. *an elegant swimmer* = graceful and stylish

el•e•gy /'elɪdʒi/ noun, c. (**elegies**) = a poem or song expressing sorrow at the death of someone [LITERATURE]

el•e•ment /'elɪmənt/ noun, c. **1** *Water is a compound made up of the two elements, hydrogen and oxygen.* = a substance which cannot be broken up into some other substance but can combine with other elements to form substances called compounds [CHEMISTRY] **2** *There is an element of truth in what he says.* = a small amount **3** *Luck is an important element in a person's success.* = a part of something **elements** noun, c. (always plural) **1** *I will teach you the elements of mathematics.* = the first things to be learnt about a subject **2** *The elements seem to be in an angry mood.* = the things that make up the weather (sun, wind, clouds, rain etc.) (figurative, literary)

to be in one's element = to feel very comfortable and happy

el•e•men•ta•ry /elɪ'mentəri/ adj. *a textbook of elementary mathematics* = simple and easy; concerned with the first things to be learnt

el•e•phant /'elɪfənt/ noun, c. = a large and strong animal with curved teeth (tusks) and a long nose, called a trunk

el•e•vate /'elɪveɪt/ verb, t. **1** *He has been elevated to the post of judge.* = to raise or lift to a higher position (formal) **2** *This book will elevate your mind.* = to improve **elevation** /ˌelɪ'veɪʃən/ noun, u. or c. **1** *Darjeeling is situated at an elevation of 1,000 m above sea level.*(c.) = height above sea level [GEOGRAPHY] **2** *I congratulated her on her elevation to the position of a judge.*(u.) = the act or result of raising someone to a higher position (formal) **3** *I have asked the architect to draw a front elevation of the house he is going to build for me.*(c.) = a drawing showing how a building will look from the front or from one side [TECHNICAL] **elevator** noun, c.= a machine that carries people and goods to a higher level in a building; a lift

e•le•ven /ɪ'levən/ noun **1** = the number written as 11 **2** *the Sri Lanka eleven* = a sports team made up of

11 players **eleventh hour** *We were getting ready for the examination, but it was cancelled at the eleventh hour.* = at the very last moment (informal)

elf /elf/ noun, c. (**elves**) = a small creature with pointed ears that plays tricks on people (in stories)

e•li•cit /ɪ'lɪsɪt/ verb, t. *The police have been questioning the prisoner and trying to elicit the names of the other people who were involved in the crime.* = to try to get information or a reaction from someone (formal)

el•i•gi•ble /'elɪdʒɪbəl/ adj. **1** *You are not eligible for the job as you do not have the required experience.* = fulfilling the necessary conditions for something **2** *an eligible boy/girl* = suitable to be chosen, especially for marriage

e•lim•i•nate /ɪ'lɪmɪneɪt/ verb, t.**1** *Malaria was very common here in the past, but the health authorities have managed to eliminate it.* = to remove or get rid of completely **2** *They were eliminated from the competition in the first round and had to go back home.* = to be out of a contest after being defeated

e•lite[1] /eɪ'li:t/ noun, u. *clothes for the elite* = people belonging to the highest or richest class

elite[2] adj. *an elite group* = of the highest class

e•lix•ir /ɪ'lɪksə^r/ noun, u. or c. *He is very relaxed after his holiday. It has proved to be an elixir for his depression.* = something that has a magical power to cure

elk /elk/ noun, c. = a kind of deer found in some cold countries

el•lipse /ɪ'lɪps/ noun, c. = a geometrical shape that is oval (egg-shaped) **elliptical** adj. *The earth moves in an elliptical path around the sun.* = oval or egg-shaped

elm /elm/ noun, c. = a large tree that produces hard wood and has broad leaves

el•o•cu•tion /elə'kju:ʃən/ noun = the art of speaking clearly and effectively in public

e•lon•gate /'i:lɒŋgeɪt/ verb, t. *Look at this picture of Mr Thakur which the artist has drawn. It doesn't look like him; the nose is elongated.* = to make something look longer than it really is

e•lope /ɪ'ləʊp/ verb, i. *The young man and woman decided to elope and get married.* = to run away and get married secretly, usually without the knowledge of the parents

el•o•quent /'eləkwənt/ adj. *He made an eloquent speech in praise of the new film.* = expressing one's ideas effectively and in rich language, so that the listeners are influenced (formal)

else /els/ adv. **1** *She had nothing else to say.* = more **2** *He left but everyone else stayed on.* = other than **or else** **1** *Do not stay up late, or else you will wake up late and miss your bus.* = otherwise; if not **2** *Finish your work or else...* = an expression used to warn someone of an unpleasant result that awaits them

e•lu•ci•date /ɪ'lu:sɪdeɪt/ verb, t. or i. *I'm sorry, but I could not understand your lecture. Could you elucidate the main points?* = to explain or make something clear (formal) (also **explain**)

e•lude /ɪ'lu:d/ verb, t. *The thief was able to elude the police by hiding inside a well.* = to escape being caught by using a clever plan

e•ma•ci•a•ted /ɪ'meɪʃieɪtɪd/ adj. *The children look emaciated because they have just recovered from typhoid.* = thin and weak from hunger or illness (formal)

e-mail[1] /i:meɪl/ noun, c. = a system of sending and receiving messages from one computer to another, usually through a modem and telephone line (short for electronic mail [COMPUTERS]

e-mail[2] verb, t. *I e-mailed him yesterday and received his reply within five minutes.* = to send an e-mail

e•man•ci•pate /ɪ'mænsɪpeɪt/ verb, t. *Winning the right to vote emancipated women all over the world.* = to give freedom or political rights to someone (formal)

em•balm /ɪm'bɑ:m/ verb, t. = to treat a dead body with spices or chemicals so that it will not decay

em•bank•ment /ɪm'bæŋkmənt/ noun, c. = a wide wall built of stones or earth to stop a river from overflowing

em•bar•go[1] /ɪm'bɑ:gəʊ/ noun, c. *There is an embargo on the sale of ivory.* = an official order forbidding trade in something

embargo[2] verb, t. *The government has embargoed trade in sandalwood.* = to put an embargo on something; to ban

em•bark /ɪm'bɑ:k/ verb, i. **1** *We embarked at Mumbai and disembarked at Karachi.* = to get on a boat, ship or aircraft **2** *He plans to become a writer after retiring. It is brave of him to embark on a completely new career.* = to start something new (formal)

em•bar•rass /ɪm'bærəs/ verb, t. *My colleague embarrassed me at the meeting by remarking about the clothes I was wearing.* = to make someone feel uncomfortable or ashamed

em•bas•sy /'embəsi/ noun, c. (**embassies**) *the American embassy in India* = the office in which the ambassador and officials of some country work in a foreign country (see **ambassador**)

em•bed /ɪm'bed/ verb, t. *The arrow was embedded in the tree trunk and could not be removed easily.* = to fix something strongly and deeply into something else

em•bel•lish /ɪm'belɪʃ/ verb, t. *The queen's dress was embellished with diamonds and rubies.* = to decorate; to make something more beautiful by adding something to it (formal)

em•ber /ˈembəʳ/ noun, c. = a piece of burning wood or coal from a fire which has died down

em•bez•zle /ɪmˈbezəl/ verb, t. *The police asked the bank cashier how much he had embezzled from the bank.* = to steal money that belongs to someone else and has been placed in one's care **embezzlement** noun, u. = the act of embezzling money [LAW]

em•bit•ter /ɪmˈbɪtəʳ/ verb, t. *He has tried his hand at many tasks and failed; this has embittered him against society.* = to make someone feel bitter (sad and angry) over a long period of time **embittered** adj. *None of the plans she suggested had succeeded. She left the job a very embittered woman.* = with feelings of sadness and anger

em•blem /ˈembləm/ noun, c. *The Ashoka pillar, with its four lions, is India's national emblem.* = a symbol or sign

em•bo•dy /ɪmˈbodi/ verb, t. *This poem embodies the poet's love for his beloved.* = to express or give form to (formal) **embodiment** noun

em•boss /ɪmˈbɒs/ verb, t. *Your name has been embossed on this metal plate.* = to make a raised pattern of letters, numbers etc. on metal, paper etc. by pressing the material from behind

em•brace /ɪmˈbreɪs/ verb, t. or i. **1** = to express one's love for someone by holding the person tightly and putting one's arms around him/her **2** *He has embraced Buddhism.*(t.) = to adopt (a religion, way of thinking etc.) (formal) **3** *This book embraces all aspects of India's economic policy.*(t.) = to include or cover

em•broi•der /ɪmˈbrɔɪdəʳ/ verb, t. or i. **1** *She embroidered the tablecloth with a beautiful pattern of flowers.* = to make patterns on a piece of cloth using a needle and thread **2** *Don't try to embroider the report. Let me have the facts.* = to try to improve a story or report by adding imaginary details (disapproving) **embroidery** noun, u. or c. (**embroideries**) = a design made on cloth by using a needle and thread

em•bry•o /ˈembriəʊ/ noun, c. = the unborn baby of a human being, animal, bird or plant (compare **foetus**)

e•mend /ɪˈmend/ verb, t. *The printing mistakes in the book have been emended.* = to correct the mistakes in a book before printing it (compare **amend**)

em•e•rald /ˈemərəld/ adj. noun, c. or u. = (the colour of) a green precious stone

e•merge /ɪˈmɜːdʒ/ verb, i. **1** *The chick emerged from the egg.* = to come out of; to appear **2** *Several surprising facts have emerged from the study.* = to become known as a result of

e•mer•gen•cy /ɪˈmɜːdʒənsi/ noun, u. or c. (**emergencies**) *In case of a fire or any other emergency, you should dial the number 101 on the telephone and ask for help.* = an unexpected and dangerous situation which must be dealt with at once **to be in a state of emergency** = a situation in which the government has to take some action immediately to help or protect the people (e.g. after an earthquake)

e•met•ic /ɪˈmetɪk/ noun, c. or u. = a substance or medicine which causes a person to throw up (vomit) food from the stomach [MEDICINE]

em•i•grate /ˈemɪgreɪt/ verb, i. *Ameena is planning to emigrate to South Africa.* = to leave one's country and settle in some other country (compare **immigrate**) **emigrant** noun, c. = a person who emigrates

em•i•nent /ˈemɪnənt/ adj. *She is such an eminent poet that she needs no introduction.* = famous

e•mir /eˈmɪəʳ/ noun, c. (amir or ameer) = a ruler of an Arab country or kingdom

em•is•sa•ry /ˈemɪsəri/ noun, c. (**emissaries**) = a person who is sent on a mission (asked to do some special work or deliver a official message) (formal)

e•mit /ɪˈmɪt/ verb, t. *The car is emitting a lot of smoke.* = to give out or send out **emission** noun, u. = something that is given out (formal) (usually smoke or harmful gas from a factory etc.)

e•mol•li•ent /ɪˈmɒlɪənt/ noun, c. = a substance (usually medicine) that is rubbed on the skin to soften it and reduce soreness [MEDICINE]

e•mol•u•ment(s) /ɪˈmɒljʊmənt/ noun, u. (usually plural) = money paid or received for work; wage or salary (formal)

e•mo•tion /ɪˈməʊʃən/ noun, u. or c. *The song is full of emotion and makes us want to cry.*(u.) = a strong feeling such as love, anger or fear **emotional** adj. *a very emotional scene* = having to do with emotion (feeling)

em•pa•thy /ˈempəθi/ noun, u. *A good actor needs a lot of empathy to play different roles.* = the ability to enter into the feelings of another person

em•pe•ror /ˈempərəʳ/ noun, c. = the ruler of an empire (a large kingdom)

em•pha•sis /ˈemfəsɪs/ noun, u. or c. (**emphases**) *In this office,. the emphasis is on work, not talk.* = special attention given to something to bring out its importance **emphasize (emphasise)** verb, t. *The cricket coach emphasized the importance of fitness.* = to give special importance to something

em•pir•i•cal /ɪmˈpɪrɪkəl/ adj. *The doctor has treated many cases of malaria, and his approach is entirely empirical.* = guided by practical experience rather than theories **empirically** adj. = using an empirical approach

em•ploy /ɪmˈplɔɪ/ verb, t. *The school will employ*

E

three new teachers. = to appoint (to get someone to do some work) **employee** noun, c. = someone who is appointed to do some work **employer** noun, c. = someone who employs people

em•pow•er /ɪm'paʊəʳ/ verb, t. *The people of this village are not aware of their rights as most of them are illiterate. We must give them some education to empower them.* = to give political rights or power to people

emp•ty[1] /'empti/ adj. **1** *Her glass is empty. Fill it up.* = containing nothing **2** *I am tired of your empty promises.* = without meaning or purpose

empty[2] verb, t. *The building emptied at once when someone shouted 'Fire!'* = to become empty

to do something on an empty stomach = to do something before taking any food

e•mu /'i:mju:/ noun, c. = a large bird which cannot fly, found in Australia

EMU abbr. of **Economic and Monetary Union** = the system where many countries of Europe (which constitute the European Union) come under the same currency, called the **euro**

em•u•late /'emjʊleɪt/ verb, t. *Your father was a great singer. You should try to emulate his achievements.* = to try to do as well as some other person (formal)

e•mul•sion /ɪ'mʌlʃən/ noun, c. = a mixture of two liquids which do not normally mix with each other e.g. oil and water [TECHNICAL]

en•a•ble /ɪ'neɪbəl/ verb, t. *The money you have given me will enable me to buy a few books that I need.* = to give someone the ability (means) to do something

en•act /ɪ'nækt/ verb, t. *The parliament has enacted a new law.* = to make or pass a law (referring to the government or parliament)

e•nam•el[1] /ɪ'næməl/ noun, u. **1** = a kind of paint; a hard, glass-like substance which is used to cover the surface of metal objects (e.g. pots and pans) **2** the hard, white outer surface of the tooth

enamel[2] verb, t. *I am going to enamel this flower vase.* = to cover with enamel

en•am•oured /ɪ'næməd/ adj. *He is so enamoured of his garden that he does not want to move to another house.* = taken with, having a strong liking for something or someone (literary)

en bloc /ɒn 'blɒk/ adv. (French) *They left the meeting en bloc.* = all at the same time; together

en•case /ɪn'keɪs/ verb, t. *His feet were encased in expensive leather shoes.* = to be surrounded or covered with (formal and old-fashioned)

en•chant /ɪn'tʃɑ:nt/ verb, t. *She was enchanted by the natural beauty of Leh.* = to fill someone with delight (see also **enrapture**) **enchanting** adj.= charming

en•cir•cle /ɪn'sɜ:kəl/ verb, t. = to form a circle around something or someone; to surround

en•close /ɪn'kləʊz/ verb, t. **1** *The school is enclosed by a high wall.* = to surround with a fence or wall in order to keep people out **2** *I enclose a copy of my story with this letter.* = to put something in an envelope together with a letter **enclosure** noun, c. **1** *the visitors' enclosure* = an enclosed area **2** = something that is enclosed with a letter

en•code /ɪn'kəʊd/ verb, t. **1** *Please encode this message.* = to put a message into code (a secret writing system) **2** = to change a message into a form a computer can read (opposite **decode**) [TECHNICAL]

en•com•pass /ɪn'kʌmpəs/ verb, t. **1** *Modern history encompasses a wide range of topics.* = to include or cover **2** *This village is encompassed by high mountains.* = to surround (formal)

en•core /'ɒŋkɔ:/ noun, c. or u. **1** *The audience liked the song so much that the singer had to come back for three encores.*(c.) = a repetition of a song, dance, etc. by a singer or dancer which is demanded by the audience **2** = the word ('Encore!' = again) used by an audience to ask for a repeat of a song, act etc.

en•coun•ter[1] /ɪn'kaʊntəʳ/ verb, t. *You will encounter many problems on this job.* = to face or meet with something unpleasant (problems, difficulties etc.) (formal)

encounter[2] noun, c. *I had a frightening encounter with a wild elephant while I was walking through the forest.* = an unexpected meeting with someone or something

en•cour•age /ɪn'kʌrɪdʒ/ verb, t. *My coach always encouraged me to work very hard.* = to give confidence or hope to someone

en•croach /ɪn'krəʊtʃ/ verb, i. **1** *The municipality plans to pull down the houses of people who have encroached on government land.* = to occupy by force something that does not belong to you [LAW] **2** *I hope I am not encroaching on your time.* = to occupy more of something than one should (formal)

en•cum•ber /ɪn'kʌmbəʳ/ verb, t. *It is difficult to travel when one is encumbered with a lot of luggage.* = to be loaded or weighed down with something that prevents free movement or action (formal) **encumbrance** noun, c. or u. = something that is a burden and does not allow free movement [LAW]

en•cy•clo•pe•di•a (encyclopaedia) /ɪnsaɪklə'pi:diə/ noun, c. = a book or set of books containing information on many subjects or topics usually arranged in alphabetical order

end[1] /end/ noun, c. **1** *the end of the road.* = the last part or point **2** *the end of a story* = the conclusion

3 *a means to an end* = aim or purpose 4 *a cigarette end* = a piece that is left over

end[2] verb, t. or i. *The meeting ended at midnight.*(i.) = to come to a finish

end in *The match ended in a draw.* = to have something as the final result **end up** *After watching the movie and going out for dinner, my friends ended up at my house. // I studied science in college but ended up becoming an artist.* = to come to a certain state after doing something else **to be at a loose end** = to have nothing to do **to make both ends meet** = to have just enough money for one's needs

en•dan•ger /ɪn'deɪndʒəʳ/ verb, t. *He has endangered our safety by making us travel in a boat without life jackets.* = to put someone in danger **endangered species** noun, c. = a plant or animal that is in danger of not existing anymore and has to be protected

en•dear /ɪn'dɪəʳ/ verb, t. *Her sweet nature endeared her to everyone.* = to cause someone/oneself to be loved

en•deav•our[1] /ɪn'devəʳ/ noun, u. or c. *Our endeavours to clean up this city have been successful.* = attempt (formal)

endeavour[2] verb, t. *You should endeavour to improve yourself in many ways.* = to try (formal)

en•dem•ic /en'demɪk/ adj. *Malaria is endemic in many parts of India and Africa.* = found regularly and commonly in a place (generally referring to diseases) [TECHNICAL]

en•dorse /ɪn'dɔːs/ verb, t. 1 *I endorse your action in refusing to pay a bribe.* = to support an action, opinion etc. 2 *to endorse a cheque* = to sign one's name on the back of a cheque in order to let the bank know that it is genuine **endorsement** noun, c. or u. 1 *The people of the colony gathering to listen to the leader's speech can be seen as an endorsement of her record.*(c.) = an action that conveys public support for a person or thing 2 *Rahul Dravid has signed an endorsement for a well-known brand of shoes.*(c.) = an official agreement that makes a famous person agree to advertise a product

en•dow /ɪn'daʊ/ verb, t. 1 = to create a charitable fund for a school, hospital etc. 2 *She is endowed with great artistic talent.* = to possess some good quality from birth (formal) **endowment** noun, u. or c. = a fund created by someone to help a school, hospital etc. [LAW]

en•dure /ɪn'djʊəʳ/ verb, t. 1 *As a soldier, you must be able to endure discomfort and pain.* = to put up with an uncomfortable or painful situation without complaining 2 *The Taj Mahal is 400 years old and we believe it will endure for at least another 400 years.* = to last **endurance** noun, u. *She suffered great pain but never complained. We were surprised at her endurance.* = the ability to bear pain

en•e•my /'enəmi/ noun, c. (**enemies**) 1 *He has many friends and very few enemies.* = someone who hates a person and wishes to harm him/her 2 *The enemy is advancing across the border.* = the army of a country that one is fighting against (generally used in singular)

to be your own worst enemy = to be in the habit of doing something that harms you more than anyone else

en•er•gy /'enədʒi/ noun, u. or c. (**energies**) 1 *She can work all day and all night without getting tired. I don't know where she gets her energy from.* = the ability to do a lot of work 2 *India is trying to develop the use of wind energy.* = power which can be used to drive machines etc. **energetic** /ˌenə'dʒetɪk/ adj. = full of energy

en•force /ɪn'fɔːs/ verb, t. *The government is going to enforce the new law against the use of child labour.* = to cause a rule or law to be put into practice

en•gage /ɪn'geɪdʒ/ verb, t. 1 *We have engaged a computer specialist.* = to employ 2 *The children will have to be engaged throughout the day.* = to take up one's time, attention etc. **engaged** adj. 1 *He is engaged to Shahina.* = (the state of) having agreed to marry someone 2 *They are engaged in talks with the foreign officials.* = busy in doing something 3 *The telephone line is engaged.* = not free **engagement** noun, u. or c. 1 *His engagement has been announced.* = an agreement to marry someone 2 *I can't come to your party as I have another engagement.* = an arrangement to meet someone or do something

en•gine /'endʒɪn/ noun, c. 1 *This car has a powerful engine.* = a machine that produces power 2 *a train pulled by a steam engine* = a locomotive (a vehicle that pulls a train)

en•gi•neer[1] /endʒɪ'nɪəʳ/ noun, c. *a civil engineer* = a person who designs and builds houses, roads, machines etc.

engineer[2] verb, t. 1 *The new super-highway has been engineered by a Japanese company.* = to build something requiring great skill 2 *They engineered a strike in the factory.* = to cause something (generally unpleasant) to happen through secret planning (disapproving)

en•grave /ɪn'greɪv/ verb, t. = to cut pictures, words etc. on wood, stone or metal (compare **emboss**, see also **carve**)

en•gross•ed /ɪn'grəʊst/ adj. *She was so engrossed in her work that she did not hear the ringing of the alarm.* = having one's attention completely filled or occupied with something **engrossing** adj. *an engrossing book* = very interesting

en•gulf /ɪn'gʌlf/ verb, t. *The house was completely engulfed by the flames.* = to swallow up and destroy (formal)

en•hance /ɪn'hɑːns/ verb, t. *This blue shirt will enhance his good looks.* = to increase the value or beauty of something or someone (formal)

e•nig•ma /ɪ'nɪgmə/ noun, c. *I know nothing about my neighbour. He is an enigma to me.* = someone or something that is difficult to know or understand **enigmatic** /ɪ'nɪgmætɪk/ adj. = mysterious

en•joy /enɪg'mtɪ/ verb, t. *I enjoy Hindi songs; they fill me with joy.* = to get pleasure from **enjoyable** adj. *a very enjoyable film* = able to give pleasure

en•large /ɪn'lɑːdʒ/ verb, t. *The photograph is very small. Ask the studio to enlarge it.* = to make something, usually a photograph or a document, bigger **enlargement** noun, u. = something that has been made bigger

en•light•en /ɪn'laɪtn/ verb, t. *I knew nothing about astronomy but your talk has enlightened me.* = to cause to understand (formal)

en•list /ɪn'lɪst/ verb, t. or i. **1** *I had to enlist the support of all my friends in order to make this meeting a success.*(t.) = to ask people for help **2** *All the young men in this village want to enlist because our country has been attacked.*(i.) = to join the army

en•liv•en /ɪn'laɪvən/ verb, t. = to make things more active or interesting

en masse /ˌɒn'mæs/ adv. (French) *They decided to resign en masse.* = all together; in a crowd

en•meshed /ɪn'meʃt/ verb, t. *I needed their help, but they were so enmeshed in problems of their own that I wasn't able to ask them.* = to be caught in something that one cannot get out of (like being caught in a net or mesh) (formal)

e•nor•mous /ɪ'nɔːməs/ adj. *an enormous crowd* = very large **enormity** /ɪ'nɔːmɪtɪ/ noun, u. *I have realised the enormity of the problem that faces us. I will need everybody's help.* = great size or seriousness (used to refer to problems, difficulties, crimes etc.)

e•nough[1] /ɪ'nʌf/ det. or pron. **1** *There is enough food for all of us.* (det.) **2** *I don't want any more rice. I have eaten enough.*(pron.) = as much as is required

enough[2] adv. **1** *He was kind enough to show me the way to the station.* = to the extent required **2** *He plays well enough for a beginner.* = quite well, but not very well

en•quire /ɪn'kwaɪəʳ/ verb, i. *We need to enquire about buses to Pondicherry.* = to ask for information (also **inquire**)

en•rage /ɪn'reɪdʒ/ verb, t. *They were enraged when they saw how laboratory animals were being treated.* = to make someone very angry

en•rap•ture /ɪn'ræptʃəʳ/ verb, t. *The beautiful music enraptured the audience.* = to fill someone with great joy (literary)

en•roll /ɪn'reʊl/ verb, t. *The school plans to enroll 500 students this year.* = to make someone a member (of a school, group etc.)

en route /ˌɒn'ruːt/ adv. (French) *We stopped at Agra en route to Delhi.* = on the way to

en•sue /ɪn'sjuː/ verb, i. *Many people were still trying to get into the train when it started moving, and a lot of confusion ensued.* = to follow as a result (formal)

en•sure /ɪn'ʃʊəʳ/ verb, t. *You must go to the stadium early to ensure that you get a ticket for the match.* = to make sure of something

en•tail /ɪn'teɪl/ verb, t. *Success entails a lot of hard work.* = to require; to make something necessary

en•tan•gle /ɪn'tæŋgəl/ verb, t. *The bird got entangled in the net and couldn't fly away.* = to get caught or mixed up in something

en•ter /'entəʳ/ verb, t. or i. **1** *He entered the room with some hesitation.*(t.) = to go into **2** *She is entering the medical profession.*(t.) = to join **3** *The receptionist entered my name in his diary.*(t.) = to write down **4** *She has entered a new phase in her life now that she has started working.*(t.) = to begin **5** *The competition is open. Anyone above the age of 12 can enter.*(i.) = to take part in a contest **entrance** noun, u. or c. **1** (c.) = a gate or door by which people enter a place **2** *People were waiting for the lead actor's entrance.*(u.) = the act of entering **3** *They were refused entrance to the restaurant because they were wearing shorts.*(u.) = permission to enter **entry** noun, u. or c. (**entries**) **1** *The new students are celebrating their entry into the university.*(u.) = the act of becoming a part of something **2** *She made an entry in her diary.*(c.) = something that is written down **3** *We are making a list of all the entries to the competition.* = the people entering a competition **4** *They were not allowed entry into the examination hall.*(u.) = the right to enter a place

en•trant /'entrənt/ noun, c. *a new entrant to the legal profession* = a person who joins a profession or a competition (formal)

en•ter•prise /'entəpraɪz/ noun, u. or c. **1** *He does not have a job now but I am sure he will find one. He has a lot of enterprise.*(u) = willingness to take risks and do things that are difficult or new **2** *The company is about to start a new enterprise.*(c.) = a business **enterprising** adj. *a very enterprising woman* = one who has enterprise

en•ter•tain /entə'teɪn/ verb, t. **1** *The singer entertained the crowd for two hours.* = to keep someone interested and amused by a public performance **2** *We are entertaining a few guests this* *evening.* = to receive guests and offer them food etc. **3** *We are not entertaining any new applications.* = to receive or accept **entertainment** noun, u. **1** *The company will spend Rs 1000 on the entertainment of guests.* = the act of entertaining (guests) **2** *The film was not very good as a form of art, but it was good entertainment.* = a film or public performance that entertains (keeps the audience interested) **entertaining** adj.

en•thral /ɪn'θrɔːl/ verb, t. (**enthrall**) *The concert was so good that it completely enthralled the audience.* = to hold the attention and interest of someone completely, as if by magic (see also **enrapture**) (literary)

en•throne /ɪn'θrəʊn/ verb, t. = to make someone a king or to put one in a position of great power (formal)

en•thuse /ɪn'θjuːz/ verb, t. *The new science teacher is very good. He is able to enthuse his students.*(t.) = to create a strong interest in **enthusiasm** /ɪn'θjuːzɪˌæzəm/ noun, u. *Our cricket players were full of enthusiasm when they left for Australia.* = a strong desire to do something **enthusiastic** /ɪnθjuːzɪ'ætɪk/ adj. = full of enthusiasm

en•tice /ɪn'taɪs/ verb, t. *Advertisements entice people into buying more things than they need.* = to draw or attract someone into doing something (often disapproving) **enticing** adj. = so attractive that it is difficult to stay away from it

en•tire /ɪn'taɪə^r/ adj. **1** *I have cleaned the entire house today.* = the whole of something, with nothing left out **2** *I am in entire agreement with you.* = complete; total **entirely** adv. *This is entirely the responsibility of the students.* = completely

en•ti•tle /ɪn'taɪtl/ verb, t. **1** *This ticket entitles you to a reserved seat on the train.* = to give someone the right to do or have something **2** *The book is entitled 'Travels with a Donkey'* = to give a title to a book

en•ti•ty /'entɪti/ noun, u. or c. (**entities**) *Sikkim has become a part of India. It is no longer a separate entity.* = something that has an independent existence

en•to•mol•o•gy /ˌentə'mɒlədʒi/ noun = the scientific study of insects **entomologist** noun [BIOLOGY]

en•trails /'entreɪlz/ noun (always plural) = the parts inside the body of an animal, specially the bowels (the organs that carry food away from the stomach)

entrance, entrant, entry see **enter**

en•treat /ɪn'triːt/ verb, t. *I entreat you to help me.* = to beg **entreaty** adj. *He paid no attention to my entreaty.* = act of entreating (formal)

en•trench /ɪn'trentʃ/ verb, t. *The soldiers are now entrenched on the mountain and it will be difficult for the enemy to push them back.* = to be established in a strong position from which one cannot easily be moved or removed (formal)

en•tre•pre•neur /ɒntrəprə'nɜː^r/ noun, c. (French) = a person who makes money by starting a new business, specially one in which there may be some risk (see **enterprise**)

en•trust /ɪn'trʌst/ verb, t. *I entrust the house to you. Please look after it while we're away.* = to make someone responsible for something

en•twine /ɪn'twaɪn/ verb, t. *The rose creeper was entwined around the mango tree.* = to twist round and round

e•nu•mer•ate /ɪ'njuːməreɪt/ verb, t. *He enumerated the reasons for not wishing to leave the country.* = to make a count of; to name things, one by one from a list (formal)

e•nun•ci•ate /ɪ'nʌnsieɪt/ verb, t. **1** *The actor read out her part from the script, enunciating the words clearly.* = to pronounce words carefully and clearly **2** *When the student was invited to speak, he enunciated his ideas very clearly.* = to state clearly (compare **propound**) **enunciation** noun, c. or u.

en•vel•op /ɪn'veləp/ verb, t. *The house was enveloped in flames.* = to wrap up or cover completely

en•vel•ope /'envələʊp/ noun, c. = a paper container for a letter

envy[1] /'envi/ verb, t. *She is so talented that I sometimes envy her.* = to have a negative feeling about someone because of some quality or possession that he/she has and that you wish you had

envy[2] noun, u. *His palatial house attracts the envy of many people.* = the feeling of envy **enviable** adj. = something that can cause envy **envious** adj. = having the feeling of envy

en•vi•ron•ment /ɪn'vaɪərənmənt/ noun, c. **1** *growing up in a pleasant environment* = the social and physical conditions or surroundings in which people live, which have an effect on their bodies and minds **2** = the natural surroundings (air, water, soil etc.) in which living things exist **3** = the operating system in a computer, on the base of which software programs are developed e.g. *a Windows environment* [COMPUTERS] **environmental** /ɪnvaɪrən'məntəl/ adj. *Sheila is very interested in environmental issues and wants to write about them after she finishes college.* = relating to the effect of human activity on the environment **environmentalist** noun, c. = a person who is active in trying to protect the environment

en•vis•age /ɪn'vɪzɪdʒ/ noun, t. *I can envisage a time when not a single tree will be left in this city.* = to imagine; to see as a possibility (formal)

en•voy /'envɔɪ/ noun, c. = a person who is sent to a

foreign country to represent his or her own country (formal) (compare **emissary**)

en•zyme /'enzaɪm/ noun, c. = a chemical substance produced by plants or animals, which helps to bring about chemical changes [BIOLOGY, CHEMISTRY]

e•phem•e•ral /ɪ'femərəl/ adj. *His fame as an actor was ephemeral. In a few years he was forgotten.* = lasting for a very short time

ep•ic[1] /'epɪk/ noun, c. = a very long poem written in ancient times, describing heroic deeds [LITERATURE]

epic[2] adj. *an epic battle* = very long and full of events

ep•i•centre /'epɪsentə^r/ noun, c. = the centre of an area on the earth's surface where the force of an earthquake is felt [TECHNICAL]

ep•i•cure /'epɪkjʊə^r/ noun, c. = a person who is knowledgeable about food and loves good food

ep•i•dem•ic /epɪ'demɪk/ noun, c. *There is a cholera epidemic in the state.* = a disease that is passed on to a large number of people or animals at the same time

ep•i•gram /'epɪgræm/ noun, c. = a short, clever and amusing remark

ep•i•lep•sy /'epɪlepsi/ noun, u. = a disorder of the brain which causes violent shaking of the body or unconsciousness [MEDICINE]

ep•i•logue /'epɪlɒg/ noun, c. = the last part of a book or play that comments on what has gone before [LITERATURE]

ep•i•sode /'epɪsəʊd/ noun, c. **1** *This is the last episode of the television programme.* = a part of a story which contains a number of such parts **2** *That is an episode which I'd like to forget.* = an event or incident

e•pis•tle /ɪ'pɪsəl/ noun, c. = a very long and important letter [LITERATURE]

ep•i•taph /epɪtɒ:f/ noun, c. = something written in praise of a dead person, usually on a piece of stone above his/her grave

ep•i•thet /'epɪθet/ noun, c. *We always use the epithet 'the Great' when talking about the emperor Akbar.* = a word or expression that describes someone or a quality in them

ep•i•tome /ɪ'pɪtəmi/ noun, u. *Her collection of paintings is the epitome of good taste.* = the finest example of some desirable quality

e•poch /'i:pɒk/ noun, c. *The death of Mahatma Gandhi marked the end of an important epoch in our history.* = a period of history during which certain important events take place

e•qual[1] /'i:kwəl/ adj. *Roshni and I are of equal age. We are both 17.* = the same in size, rank, quality, etc.

equal[2] noun, c. *equals in the department* = a person of the same quality, rank etc.

e•quate /ɪ'kweɪt/ verb, t. *You can't equate fame with pcpularity.* = to treat two things as equal or the same

e•qua•ni•mi•ty /i:kwə'nɪmɪti/ noun, u. *She has many serious problems, but she is facing them with great equanimity.* = calmness of mind (formal)

e•qua•tor /ɪ'kweɪtə^r/ noun = an imaginary line drawn around the middle of the earth, dividing the earth into a northern and a southern half [GEOGRAPHY] (see pic under **earth**)

e•ques•tri•an /ɪ'kwestriən/ adj. *He is going to take part in the equestrian events at the Olympic games.* = connected with horse riding [TECHNICAL]

e•qui•lat•e•ral /i:kwɪlætərəl/ adj. *an equilateral triangle* = having all sides equal in length [GEOMETRY] (see pic under **triangles**)

e•qui•lib•ri•um /i:kwɪ'lɪbriəm/ noun, u. **1** *She was riding her bicycle well but she suddenly lost her equilibrium and fell.* = balance (in science, the state of balance between opposing forces) **2** *She lost her equilibrium when she was criticized and became very angry.* = mental balance; the state of remaining calm

eq•uine /'ekwaɪn/ adj. = having to do with horses

e•qui•nox /'i:kwɪnɒks/ noun = one of the two days in the year (21 March and 22 September) when day and night are of equal length [GEOGRAPHY]

e•quip /ɪ'kwɪp/ verb, t. *People who go trekking in the Himalayas have to be equipped with special clothing and boots.* = to supply with the knowledge, tools etc. necessary for doing something **equipment** noun, u. (no plural) = the things needed for a particular activity

e•quiv•a•lent[1] /ɪ'kwɪvələnt/ adj. *He changed Rs 5000 into an equivalent amount in US dollars.* = equal

equivalent[2] noun, u. *Is there any equivalent of the English word 'silly' in your language?* = something that has the same value or meaning

e•quiv•o•cal /ɪ'kwɪvəkəl/ adj.= (words) carrying a doubtful or double meaning

era /'ɪərə/ noun, c. *the Christian era* = a period of history which is named after and counted from some important event (e.g. the birth of Christ)

e•rad•i•cate /ɪ'rædɪkeɪt/ verb, t. *The government is trying to eradicate crime.* = to remove completely (formal)

e•rase /ɪ'reɪz/ verb, t. **1** *You should erase the words you have written on this page.* = to remove or rub away the marks of writing **2** *We are trying to erase the painful memories of the defeat.* = to remove **eraser** noun, c. = a rubber (used to rub out writing from paper)

e•rect[1] /ɪ'rekt/ verb, t. *We will erect a statue of our leader.* = to build; to fix in an upright position

erect[2] adj. *You should always walk erect and not with your back bowed.* = standing up straight; upright

e•rec•tion /ɪˈrekʃən/ noun, u. or c. **1** *the erection of a statue* = the act of putting up a statue, building etc. **2** = the process of the male sex organ becoming hard because of sexual excitement [MEDICINE]

e•rode /ɪˈreʊd/ verb, t. *The river has been eroding its banks for years.* = to wear away; to eat into **erosion** noun, u. *We are planting trees to check the erosion of the soil.* = the process of the soil being worn away by the action of water or wind [GEOGRAPHY]

e•rot•ic /ɪˈrɒtɪk/ adj. *erotic feelings* = having to do with love and sex

err /ɜːʳ/ verb, i. *To err is human.* = to make mistakes (old-fashioned)

er•rand /ˈerənd/ noun, c. *My friend sent me to the bank on an errand.* = a journey made at the personal request of a relative, friend etc. to carry a message or deliver or bring something back

er•rat•ic /ɪˈrætɪk/ adj. *He played a very erratic game.* = uneven (sometimes good and sometimes bad)

er•ro•ne•ous /ɪˈrəʊnɪəs/ adj. *I thought you could be trusted, but I find my assumption was erroneous.* = incorrect; wrong (formal)

er•ror /ˈerəʳ/ noun, c. *There is an error in your calculations. Can you do them again?* = mistake

er•u•dite /ˈerʊdaɪt/ adj. *Our teacher is highly erudite.* = well-read and learned (formal) **erudition** /erʊˈdɪʃən/ noun, u. = learning; scholarship

e•rupt /ɪˈrʌpt/ verb, i. **1** *The volcano erupted and poured out hot lava into the valley below.* = to explode and pour out fire (referring to a volcano) **2** *Celebrations erupted in the city after our victory in the World Cup.* = to burst or break out suddenly (figurative) **eruption** noun

es•ca•late /ˈeskəleɪt/ verb, i. **1** *The fighting was not very serious at first but it later escalated into a war.* = to grow into something big or serious **2** *The cost of living has escalated.* = to rise **escalator** /eskəˈleɪtəʳ/ noun, c. = a moving staircase driven by a machine

es•ca•pade /ˈeskəpeɪd/ noun, u. *The boys were told not to go into the jungle as it is full of snakes. However, they disobeyed the order. Luckily, no harm resulted from their escapade.* = an exciting adventure, done in disobedience of the rules

es•cape[1] /ɪˈskeɪp/ verb, i. or t. **1** *The prisoners have escaped from jail.*(i.) = to get away or get out of an enclosed space; to become free **2** *We narrowly escaped an accident.*(t.) = to avoid something dangerous or unpleasant. **3** *This letter has escaped your notice.*(t.) = to miss

escape[2] noun, c. *The prisoners made a daring escape.* = an act of escaping **escapist** noun, c. *He has given up his job and joined an ashram in the Himalayas. I think he is just an escapist.* = a person who tries to run away from duty or from reality (derogatory)

es•chew /ɪsˈtʃuː/ verb, t. *You should eschew bad habits such as smoking.* = to avoid or keep away from (formal)

es•cort[1] /ˈeskɔːt/ verb, t. *Six policemen escorted the prisoner when he was taken to the court for his trial.* = to go along with someone in order to protect or show the way etc.

escort[2] noun, c. *I don't need an escort. I can travel alone.* = someone who escorts

Es•ki•mo /ˈeskɪməʊ/ noun, c. = a person belonging to the Eskimo community, which lives in the cold countries near the North Pole (old-fashioned) (Eskimos now prefer to be called Inuits)

es•o•ter•ic /esəˈterɪk/ adj. *an esoteric religion* = something secret and mysterious and known only to a few people

es•pe•cial (**special**) /ɪˈspeʃəl/ adj. *He is an especial friend of mine.* = not ordinary (formal)

Es•pe•ranto /espəˈræntəʊ/ noun = a language created in the nineteenth century for international use, which did not become popular

es•pi•o•nage /ˈespiənɒːʒ/ noun, u. *The police have arrested a number of foreigners who were engaged in espionage.* = the activity of spying (trying to find out secrets about other countries)

es•say[1] /ˈeseɪ/ noun, c. *Write an essay on 'The Festivals of India'.* = a piece of writing on some subject, usually done for a course of studies

essay[2] verb, t. = to try or attempt (old-fashioned)

es•sence /ˈesəns/ noun, u. **1** *The essence of all religions is love and tolerance.* = the central or most important part of something **2** *vanilla essence* = a substance from a plant or fruit, having the smell or taste of that plant or fruit

es•sen•tial /eˈsenʃl/ adj.**1** *Water is essential for life.* = absolutely necessary **2** *It is essential that you tell him that you think.* = very important **3** *Rice is an essential ingredient in pulao.* = basic and important **essentials** noun (always plural) *She didn't pack too many things for the journey, only the essentials.* = very necessary things **essentially** *He may find fault with us but he is essentially a good person.* = for the most part; overall

es•tab•lish /ɪˈstæblɪʃ/ verb, t. **1** *This university was established in 1858.* = to set up or create **2** *He has established his reputation as a lawyer.* = to be firmly settled **3** *The detective has established the facts of the case.* = to prove beyond doubt **4** *Has the conference helped the countries establish good trade relations?* = to begin **establishment** noun, c. or

E

u. **1** *We have an establishment here as well as one in Chennai.*(c.) = an organisation or a place equipped for business, living etc. **2** *We consider the establishment of peace and order important in this town.*(u.) = the act of creating or setting up something **the Establishment** (usually capital) = the organisations and people who have the most power and influence in a country

es•tate /ɪ'steɪt/ noun, c. **1** *I have a plot of land in the new industrial estate.* = a large piece of land containing a number of buildings, built according to a plan **2** = the property which a person leaves behind on his/her death **fourth estate** noun = journalists and the television channels, newspapers, magazines, radio stations etc. that they work for

es•teem /ɪ'sti:m/ noun, u. *She was held in high esteem by all her colleagues.* = great respect (formal)

estimable /'estiməbəl/ adj. *an estimable person* = deserving respect

es•ti•mate[1] /'estɪmeɪt/ verb, t. *I estimate the number of people present at the meeting at 5000.* = to judge or calculate the size, value etc. of something; to guess

estimate[2] /'estɪmɪt/ noun, c. *The estimate you prepared for the new building was quite accurate.* = calculation of the expected cost **estimated** /estɪ'meɪtɪd/ adj. *The estimated cost of the travel arrangements is Rs 2500.* = approximate; according to calculations which are close to the actual cost **estimation** noun, u. = what has been estimated or the act of estimating

es•trange /ɪ'streɪndʒ/ verb, t. *He has been estranged from his brother after their quarrel.* = to be no longer on friendly terms with someone (formal)

es•tu•a•ry /'estʃuəri/ noun, c. (**estuaries**) = the wide mouth of a river at the point where it meets the sea [GEOGRAPHY]

et•ce•te•ra (etc.) /et'setərə/ abbr. as **etc.** *We will need some rice, oil, vegetables, etcetera* = and so on

etch /etʃ/ verb, t. or i. = to cut a picture out of a metal plate, using acid, so as to print from it (compare **emboss**, **carve**) **etching** noun, c.= a picture printed by this process

e•ter•ni•ty /ɪ'tɜ:nɪti/ noun, u. *Many believe that a person's soul never dies but lives for all eternity.*= time which has no end (figurative) **eternal** adj. *The body dies but the soul is eternal.*= lasting for ever; without beginning or end

e•ther /'i:θə^r/ noun, u. **1** *The sun's rays travel to us through the ether.* = the thin air which is believed to be present in outer space **2** a kind of gas used earlier as an anaesthetic, to put a person to sleep before an operation

e•the•re•al /ɪ'θɪəriəl/ adj. *The ethereal beauty of Rajasthan made me feel that it did not belong to this world.* = unearthly and delicate, like that of a spirit or fairy (literary)

Ethernet™ /'ɪ:θənet/ noun = a system in which many computers in an area are connected to each other through wires

e•th•ic /'eθɪk/ noun, u. = a system of moral behaviour which tells people what to do and what not to do **ethics** noun = the study of moral principles **ethical** adj. *You may want to evade paying taxes because so many are doing it, but it is not ethical.* = morally acceptable

eth•nic /'eθnɪk/ adj. *ethnic culture* = typical of a race or tribe **ethnology** /eθ'nɒlədʒi/ noun = the scientific study of the different human races

et•i•quette /'etɪket/ noun, u. *You should observe etiquette and give up your seat on the bus to an elderly person.* = the rules of polite and correct behaviour

et•y•mol•o•gy /etɪ'mɒlədʒi/ noun = the study of the history, origins and changing meanings of words

eu•ca•lyp•tus /ju:kə'lɪptəs/ noun = a kind of tree that grows in Australia and Asia, which produces a strong-smelling oil used as medicine (also **gum-tree**)

eu•lo•gy /'ju:lədʒi/ noun, u. or c. (**eulogies**) *The poet composed a eulogy to love.* = a speech or piece of writing praising someone or something [LITERATURE]

eu•nuch /'ju:nək/ noun, c. = a man who has had his testicles removed

eu•phe•mis•m /'ju:fɪmɪzəm/ noun, u. or c. *When we say 'passed away' instead of 'died', we are using a euphemism.* = the use of a milder, less unpleasant word or expression in place of a harsh term

eu•pho•ri•a /ju:'fɔ:riə/ noun, u. *The whole family was in a state of euphoria after I harvested our first crop.* = a feeling of happiness and excitement

Eu•ra•sian /jʊ'reɪʒən/ noun or adj. = a person of mixed European and Asian blood (also **Anglo-Indian**)

euro /'jʊ:reʊ/ noun = the common unit of currency used in most European countries

eu•tha•na•si•a /ju:'fɔ:riə/ noun = the practice, legal in some countries, of allowing a person who has an incurable disease to die without suffering; the belief that people who are very ill should be allowed to die if they choose to (also **mercy-killing**)

e•va•cu•ate /ɪ'vækjueɪt/ verb, t. *The village near the border was evacuated during the war.* = to take all the people away from a place to protect them from danger (formal) **evacuation** /ɪvækju'eɪʃən/ noun = the process of evacuating people from a building, area etc.

e•vade /ɪ'veɪd/ verb, t. *When I asked her if she would marry me, she evaded the question.* = to avoid

evasion *The government is trying to check tax evasion.* = the act of evading (not paying) taxes **evasive** adj. *He gave me an evasive answer.*= not direct; trying to hide the truth

e•val•u•ate /ɪ'væljueɪt/ verb, t. *The management will evaluate the work of all the people in the office.* = to judge the quality of something **evaluation** /ɪvælju'eɪʃən/ noun, c. or u.

e•van•gel•ist /ɪ'vændʒɪlɪst/ noun, c. = a person who tries to teach others the importance of having faith in Christianity **evangelical** /ɪvæn'dʒelɪkəl/ adj.

e•vap•o•rate /ɪ'væpəreɪt/ verb, i. or t. *If you allow the water to boil too long, all of it will evaporate.*(i.) = to allow water to change into steam and disappear [PHYSICS] **evaporation** /ɪvæpə'reɪʃən/ noun, u.

eve /i:v/ noun, u. **1** *New Year's Eve* = the day or the night just before an important occasion **2** *We are meeting on the eve of the celebration.*= the time before an important event (old-fashioned)

e•ven[1] /'i:vən/ adj. **1** *The surface of the playground is not even.* = flat and smooth **2** *India won the first match and Sri Lanka won the second. Now the two sides are even.* = equal **3** *The numbers 4,6 and 8 are even numbers.* = a number which can be divided by 2 **4** *an even-tempered person* = calm, not showing sharp changes in emotion

even[2] adv. **1** *She goes to the library every day. She goes there even on Sundays.* = which is more than one might expect. ('Even', used as an adverb, makes a statement seem stronger or more surprising.) **2** *It was hot yesterday but it is even hotter today.* ('Even' makes the comparison stronger) **3** *I consider him shy, even unfriendly.* = used for emphasis

even[3] **(out)** verb, t. *The price of petroleum keeps going up or down frequently. We hope it will even out soon.* = to become level **even-handed** adj. *A teacher should not have favourites. She must be even-handed in awarding marks to students.* = just or fair **even if** *I will go to the Himalayas even if I have to take leave for a month.* = used for emphasis to say that one will do something, whatever the cost **even though** *Even though I have a master's degree I would like to apply for another one.* = used to begin a statement

to get even with somebody = to punish someone by causing them as much unhappiness as they have caused you

eve•ning /'i:vnɪŋ/ noun, c. or u. = the time of the day just before and a few hours after sunset

e•vent /ɪ'vent/ noun, c. **1** *A famous veena player is visiting our school tomorrow.The newspapers will cover this event.* = something that happens **2** *The Indian team going to the Olympic Games will take part in only a few events.* = a particular item (e.g. long jump) in a sports competition

e•ven•tual /ɪ'ventʃuəl/ adj. *Our students will visit every home and teach the older people to read and write. You may not see much change at first, but the eventual benefit will be great.* = happening at last as a result **eventually** adv. *When she started a new business she lost money at first, but eventually she made a profit.*= at last; finally

ev•er /'evə^r/ adv. (used to give emphasis to expressions) **1** *Have you ever been to Paris?* = at any time **2** *He came to India thirty years ago and has lived here ever since.*= always **3** *Thank you ever so much!* **4** (used in questions which begin with *when, what, who*) *Whatever do you mean?* = showing surprise **5** *I'll follow you whereever you go.* = used for emphasis with 'how', 'what', 'where'etc.

ev•ery /'evri/ det. **1** *Every student must do the homework.* = each or all (more than two) **2** *She comes every week.*= once in each (week) **3** *We made every attempt to win.*= as much as possible **everybody (everyone)** *Raise your hand, everybody!* = every person **everyday** adj. *These are my everyday clothes* = for daily use, not for special occasions

every now and then *Every now and then she visits her parents in Ooty.* = sometimes but not very often

eve•ry•thing /'evrɪθɪŋ/ **1** *Everything is ready.* = all things **2** *Money isn't everything* = the most important thing

eve•ry•where /'evrɪˌweər/ adv. *I have looked for it everywhere.* = in all places

e•vict /ɪ'vɪkt/ verb, t. *My tenant hasn't paid his rent for six months. I will have to evict him.*= to make a person (officially) leave a place [LAW] **eviction** noun, u.

ev•i•dence /'evɪdəns/ noun, u. *You say you saw a man from Mars. Do you have any evidence to prove it?* = something that supports or proves a statement [LAW] **evident** adj. *It is quite evident that you are confused.*= clear

to be in evidence *When we arrived at the gathering there were no guests in evidence.* = to be seen or noticed.

e•vil[1] /'i:vəl/ adj. *She plays an evil character in the movie.* = causing trouble or harm; wicked

evil[2] noun, u. or c. *There is a little evil in all of us.*(u.) = something that makes us do bad things

e•vince /ɪ'vɪns/ verb, t. *He evinced great interest in my paintings.* = to show (formal)

e•voke /ɪ'vəʊk/ verb, t. *My visit to the village where I was born evoked many memories.* = to produce; to call up **evocative** adj. *This book describing Lucknow was evocative of many memories of my childhood.* = producing memories and feelings

evocation noun, u.

e•volve /ɪ'vɒlv/ verb, i. or t. *Scientists do not believe now that humans have evolved from apes.* = to develop gradually **evolution** /iːvə'luːʃən/ noun, u. *the evolution of the aeroplane* = the gradual development of something from something else that came earlier and was simpler

ewe /juː/ noun, c. = a fully grown female sheep (opposite **ram**)

ex- /ɪks/ prefix meaning 'formerly but not now' e.g. *the ex-Captain*

ex•a•cer•bate /ɪg'zæsəbeɪt/ verb, t. *This medicine has exacerbated the pain instead of reducing it.* = to make something that was already bad worse (formal)

ex•act[1] /ɪg'zækt/ adj. *The exact distance from Bhubaneswar to Puri is 57.3 km.* = precise,correct

exact[2] verb, t. *to exact a high rent* = to get (specially money) by force **exactly** adv. *Her age is exactly 33 years and 5 months.*= precisely (opposite **roughly** or **approximately**) **exacting** adj. *The work of a pilot is very exacting.*= demanding much care and attention

ex•ag•ge•rate /ɪg'zædʒəreɪt/ verb, i. or t. *The newspaper exaggerated when it reported that 10,000 people were present at the meeting. Actually, there were about 2000.*(i.) = to say that something is larger, better etc. than it really is **exaggeration** /ɪgzædʒə'reɪʃən/ noun, c. = a comment that makes something seem bigger, better or more important than it actually is

ex•alt /ɪg'zɔːlt/ verb, t. **1** *The critics exalted the new film to the skies, saying it was the best film ever made.* = to praise highly (literary) **2** *The judge was exalted to the rank of Chief Justice.* = to raise a person in rank

ex•am•ine /ɪg'zæmɪn/ verb, t. **1** *The doctor will examine your throat.* = to look at closely in order to find out something **2** *The lawyer examined the witness.* = to ask questions in court **3** *This professor will examine your paper.* = to test or evaluate (find out how good or bad something is) **4** *He wanted to take part in the protest march, but felt he needed time to examine his feelings.* = think about carefully with a view to reaching a decision **examination** /ɪg,zæmɪ'neɪʃən/ noun, u. or c. *The examination is over.* = the act of examining

ex•am•ple /ɪg'zɑːmpəl/ noun, u. or c. **1** *This is an example of the temple paintings of the twelfth century.* = a particular object, taken from a number of things of the same kind, which shows what the others are like **2** *Saif forgot to answer one of the questions in the examination. This is an example of his carelessness.* = something that supports or proves a general rule **to set an example** *Ann did such good work in the office that she set an example for the others.* = to provide a model for others to follow **to make an example of someone** = to punish someone so that others will be afraid to behave in the same way

ex•as•per•ate /ɪg'zɑːspəreɪt/ verb, t. *Vijay is unwilling to do anything I tell him to do. His laziness exasperates me.* = to make someone feel mildly angry and impatient

ex•ca•vate /'ekskəveɪt/ verb, t. *Some historians are excavating a hill near Hoshangabad, where an ancient city once stood.* = to dig out and uncover something that has been covered for a long period by the earth [TECHNICAL] **excavation** /ekskə'veɪʃən/ noun, u. or c. **1** (u.) = the act of excavating **2** = something that has been uncovered by excavating

ex•ceed /ɪk'siːd/ verb, t. *Your speed on the highway exceeded 100 km per hour.* = to be greater than; to go beyond the limit that is allowed (formal)

ex•cel /ɪk'sel/ verb, i. *My daughter excels in studies as well as sports.*= to be very good at; to do better than others in something

ex•cept[1] /ɪk'sept/ prep. *He invited all his friends except me.* = leaving out; not including

except[2] conj. *I know nothing about this matter except what my friends told me.* = but only

except[3] verb, t. *Everyone will be rewarded. No one will be excepted.* = to leave out **exception** noun, c. *an exception to the rule* = something that marks a difference from the usual set of rules, practices etc. **to make an exception** = to deal with something in a way that is different from the usual **to take exception** = to dislike something because it makes one angry or irritated **with the exception of** = used while saying that a certain person is not included in what one is saying

ex•cerpt /'eksɜːpt/ noun, c. = a short piece taken from a book, film, piece of music etc.

ex•cess[1] /ɪk'ses/ noun, u. or c. **1** *There is an excess of violence in the new film.* = something more than what is reasonable **2** *The company's profits are in excess of Rs 50 crore.* = more than

excess[2] adj. *You will have to pay for excess baggage.* = over and above the limit which is allowed

ex•change[1] /ɪks'tʃeɪndʒ/ verb, t. *I have a blue shirt which I would like to exchange for a yellow one.* = to give something and receive something in return

exchange[2] noun, u. or c. **1** *There is a lot of cultural exchange between the two countries.* = an example of giving and receiving **2** *a telephone exchange* = a place where telephone connections are made **3** *stock exchange* = a place where shares in companies are bought and sold **4** *She went on exchange to London.* = an arrangement, usually between two countries, in which persons from each country visit the other country

ex•che•quer /ɪks'tʃekəʳ/ noun, u. = the government treasury; that part of the government which is responsible for collecting taxes and paying out money

ex•cise /'eksaɪz/ noun, u. = tax paid to the government on goods produced or sold in the country (e.g. on alcoholic drinks)

ex•cite /ɪk'saɪt/ verb, t. *The umpire's decision, which went against the home team, excited the crowd.*= to have strong feelings of joy, anger, etc. and lose one's calmness **excitement** noun, u. = the state of being excited **exciting** adj. *The match was exciting.* = causing excitement

ex•claim /ɪk'skleɪm/ verb, t. *'We have won the match!' the captain exclaimed as the last run was scored.* = to speak out loudly and suddenly with strong feeling **exclamation** /ekskləˈmeɪʃən/ noun, c. **exclamation mark** noun, c. = the mark (!) used while writing to show that someone is saying something suddenly and loudly

ex•clude /ɪk'sklu:d/ verb, t. *The selectors have decided to exclude him from the team.*= to leave out or keep out **exclusive** adj. **1** *an exclusive club* = one that excludes (keeps out) people not belonging to a certain group etc. **2** *This car is for your exclusive use.* = limited to only that person **3** *The hotel charges Rs 300 a day, exclusive of food.* = not including

ex•crete /ɪk'skri:t/ verb, t.= to pass waste matter out of the body [BIOLOGY] **excretion** noun, u. = the act or process of excreting something **excrement** /'ekskrɪmənt/ noun, u. = solid waste matter passed out from the bowels

ex•cru•ci•a•ting /ɪk'skru:ʃieɪtɪŋ/ adj. *I have an excruciating headache.* = very intense (referring to pain)

ex•cur•sion /ɪk'skɜ:ʃən/ noun, c. *The students are going on an excursion to Darjeeling.* = a journey made for pleasure or study by a number of people travelling together

ex•cuse[1] /ɪk'skju:z/ verb, t. **1** *Please excuse me for coming late.* = to pardon or forgive someone for a fault or mistake **2** *May I be excused from football practice today?* = to free someone from a duty **3** *Excuse me, where are you from?* = a polite expression used to ask a question, etc.

excuse[2] noun, c. **1** *The work must be completed today, and I won't accept any excuses.* = a reason, true or false, given for not doing something **2** *I am thinking of an excuse to leave this meeting.* = a reason, true or false, for doing something

to make an excuse = to give an explanation of why one hasn't done something **to excuse oneself** = to ask that one be allowed to leave or not attend a meeting, party etc.

ex•e•cra•ble /'eksɪkrəbəl/ adj. *The food in this restaurant is execrable. We should not eat here again.* = very bad (a very strong expression of disapproval)

ex•e•cute /'eksɪkju:t/ verb, t. **1** = to punish someone legally for a serious crime by taking his/her life [LAW] **2** *Please make sure that my orders are executed satisfactorily.*= to carry out an order or perform a piece of work **execution** /eksɪ'kju:ʃən/ noun, u. **1** = the act of executing (killing) a person as a legal punishment [LAW] **2** = the carrying out of an order

ex•e•cu•tive /ɪg'zekjʊtɪv/ noun, c. = a person in a high position in government or business who has to make and carry out decisions

ex•em•pla•ry /ɪg'zempləri/ adj. **1** *Her conduct as a student has been exemplary.* = fit to be copied as an example **2** *exemplary punishment* = intended to serve as a warning to others (disapproving)

ex•emp•lify /ɪg'zemplɪfaɪ/ verb, i. *This poem by Kalidasa exemplifies Sanskrit literature at its best.* = to be an example of something

ex•empt /ɪg'zempt/ verb, t. *The students have been exempted from payment of fees because of their excellent performance.*= to free someone from some duty, payment,etc. imposed on others

ex•er•cise[1] /'eksəsaɪz/ noun, c. or u. **1** *I want you to work out these five exercises.*(c.) = a question to be answered by a student for practice **2** *a military exercise* = an action performed by the military (army, navy or airforce) during peace-time, as practice for fighting

exercise[2] verb, i. or t. **1** *You should exercise regularly.*(i.) = to take physical exercise **2** *The Supreme Court exercised its power to overrule the decision of the High Court.*(t.) = to use a power, right, etc.

ex•ert /ɪg'zɜ:t/ verb, t. **1** *Don't exert yourself so much. You will become tired.* = to use up one's energy or strength **2** *She exerts great influence on me. I always seek her advice.* = to produce an effect

ex•hale /eks'heɪl/ verb, i. = to breathe out (opposite **inhale**)

ex•haust[1] /ɪg'zɔ:st/ verb, t. **1** *The long walk has exhausted him.* = to make one tired **2** *I have exhausted all my money.* = to use up completely

exhaust[2] noun, u. *Some gas is leaking from the exhaust.* = the pipe which allows used (burnt) gas to escape from a machine (also **exhaust-pipe**) **exhausting** adj. *an exhausting meeting* = something that makes one tired

ex•haus•tive /ɪg'zɔ:stɪv/ adj. *Your answer to this question was very exhaustive.* = thorough and complete; covering all aspects of a question

ex•hib•it[1] /ɪg'zɪbɪt/ verb, t. *We will exhibit our new* *cars next month at the Car Show.* = to show something to the public

exhibit[2] noun, c. *This lobster, which is from the crustacean family, is the first exhibit.* = something which is put on show, in a laboratory, museum or law court **exhibition** /ˌeksɪˈbɪʃən/ noun, u. or c. = a public show of objects

ex•hil•a•rate /ɪgˈzɪləreɪt/ verb, t. *You should take a walk by the seaside every morning. It will exhilarate you.* = to make someone feel cheerful and full of energy **exhilaration** /ɪgzɪləˈreɪʃən/ noun

ex•hort /ɪgˈzɔːt/ verb, t. *The coach exhorted the athlete to complete the race even though she was tired.* = to urge or advise strongly

ex•hume /ɪgˈzjuːm/ verb, t. = to dig up or unearth something, especially a dead body [TECHNICAL]

ex•i•gen•cy /ˈeksɪdʒənsi/ noun, c. (**exigencies**) or u. *The government has asked officials to be prepared for any exigency, as we are expecting floods after the heavy rains.* = a difficult situation which requires immediate action; an emergency

ex•ile[1] /ˈeksaɪl/ verb, t. *They had committed great crimes against the country, so the king exiled them.* = to send someone out of the county for political reasons

exile[2] noun, u. or c. **1** *living in exile*(u.) = forced absence from the country for political reasons **2** *She is a political exile.*(c.) = a person who has been exiled

ex•ist /ɪgˈzɪst/ verb, i. *Many strange animals lived on this earth millions of years ago but some of them do not exist now.* = to live **existence** noun, u. *Do you believe in the existence of ghosts?* = the state of existing

ex•it[1] /ˈegzɪt/ noun, u. *Where is the exit?* = the way out of a place

exit[2] verb, i. *Let us exit before the crowd arrives.* = to get out; to leave (humorous)

ex•o•dus /ˈeksədəs/ noun, u. *There is an exodus of people from the villages into Mumbai.* = a large number of people moving out of a place

ex•of•fi•ci•o /eksəˈfɪʃiəʊ/ adj. (Latin) *The Education Minister is exofficio President of the Board of Governors.*= because of one's official position (and not as an individual)

ex•on•e•rate /ɪgˈzɒnəreɪt/ verb, t. *Everyone said he was guilty of the crime, but he was tried and the court has exonerated him.* = to free someone from blame (formal)

ex•orb•i•tant /ɪgˈzɔːbɪtənt/ adj. *I did not buy the book as I found the price exorbitant.* = too great (referring to costs, demands etc.)

ex•or•cize (exorcise) /ˈeksɔːsaɪz/ verb, t. **1** = to drive out an evil spirit from a person or place [TECHNICAL] **2** *He has been able to exorcize his fears.* = to drive out; to get rid of

ex•o•tic /ɪgˈzɒtɪk/ adj. **1** *There are several kinds of exotic plants in the Botanical Garden.* = from a different country **2** *She loves travelling to exotic places such as Siberia.* = exciting and unusual, because connected to a foreign country **exotica** noun = unusual objects collected from foreign countries

ex•pand /ɪkˈspænd/ verb, i. or t. *The metal tube expanded from 32 cm to 42 cm.* = to become bigger or to make something bigger **expansion** noun, u. = the act of expanding **expanse** noun, u. *a huge expanse of water* = a wide space of water or land

ex•pa•ti•ate /ɪkˈspeɪʃieɪt/ verb, t. *We invited the writer to expatiate on her story.* = to speak or write at length about something (see also **elaborate**)

ex•pat•ri•ate[1] (**expat**) /eksˈpætriət/ noun, c. = a person who is living outside his/her own country

expatriate[2] verb, t. = to force a person to leave his/her own country [TECHNICAL]

ex•pect /ɪkˈspekt/ verb, t. **1** *I expect that it will rain tonight.* = to think or believe that something will happen **2** *I am expecting a letter from him.* = to wait for something to happen **3** *I am expecting some guests.* = to wait for a visit from someone **4** *You can't expect our neighbour to come on time. He is always late.* = to hope for or wish for something

ex•pe•di•ent /ɪkˈspiːdiənt/ adj. *I thought it expedient to end my speech as the audience was becoming restless.* = (an action that is) advisable or wise, in a certain situation (formal)

ex•pe•dite /ˈekspɪdaɪt/ verb, t. *They are very slow in appointing new teachers. Can we do something to expedite the process?* = to make something happen more quickly (formal)

ex•pe•di•tion /ekspɪˈdɪʃən/ noun, c. *My friend is going on a scientific expedition to the South Pole.* = a journey undertaken for some purpose, especially exploration, research or war

ex•pel /ɪkˈspel/ verb, t. (**expelled**) *The student was expelled from school for bad behaviour.* = to drive out or send out **expulsion** noun, u. = the act of expelling someone or something

ex•pend /ɪkˈspend/ verb, t. *Don't expend all your energy on cooking.* = to spend; to use up (formal) **expenditure** /ɪkˈspendɪtʃə/ noun, u. *The company's expenditure on entertainment is very high.* = the act of spending money on something

ex•pense /ɪkˈspens/ noun, u. *I managed to get these old books at great expense.* = cost **expenses** noun, c. (always plural) *What are your expenses on travel?* = the amount of money spent for a particular purpose **expensive** adj. = costly

ex•pe•ri•ence /ɪkˈspɪəriəns/ noun, u. or c. **1** *She*

has five years' experience of teaching. = the knowledge or skill that comes from doing something **2** *My journey along the backwaters of Kerala was an unforgettable experience.*(c.) = something interesting that happens to one and has an effect on the mind

ex•per•i•ment[1] /ɪk'sperɪmənt/ noun, c. or u. *He is conducting an experiment to find out if chimpanzees can learn to count.*(c.) = a trial made to learn something or prove the truth of an idea

experiment[2] verb, i. *Our scientists are experimenting with new kinds of crops.* = to carry out an experiment **experimental** /ɪksperɪ'məntəl/ adj. = connected with an experiment

ex•pert[1] /'ekspɜːt/ noun, c. *He is an expert on African languages.* = a person with deep and special knowledge of something

expert[2] adj. *I am going to her for expert advice.* = having special knowledge or skill **expertise** noun, u. *We need your expertise to run this company.* = the skill or special knowledge that an expert has

ex•pire /ɪk'spaɪəʳ/ verb. **1** *My friend has expired.* = to die (formal) **2** *The time limit has expired.* = to come to an end; to run out

ex•plain /ɪk'spleɪn/ verb, t. **1** *Can you explain the meaning of this poem?* = to make something clear, so that one can understand **2** *I want you to explain why you forgot to do your homework.* = to give reasons for something going wrong (used as a warning or a threat of punishment) **explanation** /ɪksplə'neɪʃən/ noun, u. *The packet was not delivered on time. We have to ask the courier for an explanation.* = a statement giving reasons for something going wrong
to explain oneself = to give an explanation of why you have done something, to another person who is angry with you

ex•ple•tive /ɪk'spliːtɪv/ noun, c. = a word or expression used to express some strong feeling, which is generally avoided in polite talk

ex•pli•cit /ɪk'splɪsɪt/ adj. **1** *You are driving too fast, although I gave you explicit instructions to drive carefully.*= something which is expressed in a clear and direct way (referring to statements, rules etc.) **2** = (of a book or film) describing sex or violence openly

ex•plode /ɪk'spləʊd/ verb, i. or t. **1** *The cracker exploded, injuring one person.* = to blow up or burst **2** *She exploded when the boss told her she would not get leave.* = to become very angry and shout loudly etc. (figurative) **explosion** noun, u. *a loud explosion* = an example of something exploding

ex•ploit[1] /'ɪksplɔɪt/ verb, t. **1** *The mineral resources of Maharashtra have not been fully exploited.* = to make use of something for profit **2** *He can donate money for the cause, but don't exploit his generous nature.* = to take advantage of; to use unfairly for one's own profit (derogatory)

exploit[2] noun, c. (often plural) *Tell us about your latest exploits in China.* = an adventure; a brave and successful act

ex•plore /ɪk'splɔːʳ/ verb, t. **1** *Before I do anything else, I am going to explore the rooms in this house.*= to travel through a place with the purpose of finding something new **2** *She has promised to explore the possibility of finding a job for you.* = to look into; to examine **exploration** /ɪksplə'reɪʃən/ noun, c. or u. **explorer** noun, c.

ex•po•nent /ɪk'spəʊnənt/ noun, c. *She is the greatest living exponent of the Kuchipudi style of dance.* = someone who practices a form of art or supports a belief

ex•port[1] /ɪk'spɔːt/ verb, t. *India exports tea to Russia.* = to send goods out of a country for sale

export[2] noun, c. *Tea is one of our most important exports.* = something that is exported

ex•pose /ek'spəʊz/ verb, t. **1** *I don't think you should expose your head to the sun.* = to uncover; to display (show) **2** *The baby should not be exposed to the cold wind.*= to leave something open and unprotected **3** *Students who go to universities abroad are exposed to many new ideas.*= to be brought in contact with new ideas etc. **4** *The report has exposed the real reason behind the failure of the project.* = to make a secret or a guilty person known **5** *I have to expose a roll of film.* = to use a roll of film to take photographs [TECHNICAL] **exposure** noun, u. or c. **1** *If you take off your clothes here you may be arrested for indecent exposure.*(u.) = the act of showing or displaying **2** *The plant died of exposure.*(u.) = the result of being left unprotected against the sun etc. **3** *Exposure to science has helped many students.*(u.) = the result of being brought in contact with **4** *The exposure of their contacts with criminals forced them to resign.* = the result of making something known to the public **5** *This film allows 36 exposures.* = photographs taken on a roll of film [PHOTOGRAPHY]

ex•po•si•tion /ekspə'zɪʃən/ noun, u. **1** *The writer presented an exposition of his new book.* = an act of explaining something **2** *There will be an exposition of classical dances next month.* = a show; an exhibition

ex•pound /ɪk'spaʊnd/ verb, t. *The scientist expounded his ideas at the conference.* = to explain in detail (formal) (see also **enunciate**)

ex•press[1] /ɪk'spres/ verb, t. *This poem expresses love for nature.* = to show a feeling or opinion through words, actions etc.

express[2] noun, c. *To save time, I am travelling by the Coromandel Express.* = a fast train which stops at few stations

express[3] adj. *Send this letter by express delivery.* = fast

ex•pres•sion /ɪk'spreʃən/ noun, u. or c. **1** *The constitution allows freedom of expression.*(u.) = speaking or writing to express one's opinions and feelings make known **2** *She puts a lot of expression into her dancing.*(u.) = feeling **3** *The expression 'born with a silver spoon' is very meaningful in his case.* = a word or group of words **expressive** adj. *an expressive face* = showing feeling

ex•pro•pri•ate /ɪk'sprəʊprieɪt/ verb, t. *The government expropriated his property as it was needed for a hospital.* = to take away something owned by another [TECHNICAL]

ex•punge /ɪk'spʌndʒ/ verb, t. = to remove something from a book or a written record (formal)

ex•pur•gate /'ekspəgeɪt/ verb, t. *The judge has ordered the publisher to expurgate the objectionable parts of the book.* = to remove or cut out the objectionable parts of a book (formal)

ex•qui•site /ɪk'skwɪzɪt/ adj. *an exquisite poem* = extremely beautiful and well-made

ex•tem•pore[1] /ɪk'stempəri/ adj. *an extempore speech* = (a speech) made without any previous preparation

extempore[2] adv. *She spoke extempore.* = without any previous preparation

ex•tend /ɪk'stend/ verb, t. **1** *The road is being extended from the station to the airport.* **2** *Her five year term is being extended.* = to make something longer in space or time **3** *He extended his hand to me.* = to stretch out **4** *We are happy to extend an invitation to you.* = to offer **5** *This lake extends over a very large area.* = to spread out or stretch out **extension** noun, u. or c. **1** *The extension of the road will be completed soon.* = the act of making something longer **2** *We are constructing an extension to the canteen.* = something that is added on **3** *The officer was given an extension.* = an additional period of service

ex•tent /ɪk'stent/ noun, u. **1** *This map shows the extent of the forest.* = the area over which something extends (stretches out) **2** *We were surprised at the extent of his knowledge.* = range **3** *To some extent, you are right.* = to some degree **extensive** adj. *the extensive campus* = large

to a certain extent = partly but not fully **to a large extent** *The complaints about the movie was to a large extent correct.* = to a great degree but not fully

ex•te•ri•or[1] /ɪk'stɪəriə^r/ noun, u. or c. *I need to get the exterior of this building painted.* = the outside or outer surface of a building etc.

exterior[2] adj. *Please paint the exterior walls only, not the inside.* = outer (opposite **interior**)

ex•ter•mi•nate /ɪk'stɜːmɪneɪt/ verb, t. *The government has failed to exterminate mosquitoes.* = to kill all the people or creatures in a place (formal)

ex•ter•nal /ɪk'stɜːnl/ adj. *This ointment is for external use only.* = on the outside of something (opposite **internal**)

ex•tinct /ɪk'stɪŋkt/ adj. *You cannot find the dodo anywhere in the world. It has become extinct.* = no longer in existence **extinction** noun, u.

ex•tin•guish /ɪk'stɪŋgwɪʃ/ verb, t. *Please extinguish all the lights before you leave.* = to put out a fire or switch off a light (formal)

ex•tol /ɪk'stəʊl/ verb, t. *He has been extolling the virtues of Goa as a holiday resort.* = to praise very highly

ex•tort /ɪk'stɔːt/ verb, t. *This gang has been extorting money from all the shopkeepers in this area.* = to get something (specially money) by using threats or violence

ex•tra[1] /'ekstrə/ adj. *It is very cold tonight. May I have an extra blanket?* = additional; more than what is usual or necessary.

extra[2] noun, c. **1** *He is appearing as an extra in this film. He is a part of the crowd.* = an actor who has a very small part in a film **2** (usually plural) *The computer comes with some extras such as a printer and some CDs.* = things given away with an item **3** *I was happy to do the work overnight. I don't want to be paid extra.* = any more, anything additional **4** *The book costs Rs 200. The CD-Rom will be extra.* = additional and not included **5** *She looked pleased to see me, and was extra happy when she saw the baby.* = more than expected (informal) **extra-curricular** adj. = activities such as sports, debating, drama etc. which are carried out in a school or college but are outside the curriculum (subjects which are taught) **extra-sensory perception (ESP)** = the power to know or feel things without the use of the five senses (sight, smell, hearing, taste, touch) which some people are said to have

ex•tract[1] /ɪk'strækt/ verb, t. **1** *We grow lemon grass on this farm, from which we extract a kind of oil.* = to take out some substance from some raw material **2** *The dentist extracted my tooth.* = to pull out [TECHNICAL] **3** *The police extracted a confession from the criminal who had been arrested.* = to force someone to admit or promise something by using force

extract[2] /'ekstrækt/ noun, c. **1** *Vanilla essence is an extract prepared from flowers.* = a substance taken out from some raw material **2** *I shall read out an extract from this book.* = a short passage taken from a book

ex•tra•dite /'ekstrədaɪt/ verb, t. *The criminal was extradited from Thailand to India.* = to send someone who is thought to be guilty of some crime from the country in which he/she is living to the country that wants to place the person on trial [LAW] **extradition** /ɪkstrə'dɪʃən/ noun

ex•tra•ne•ous /ɪk'streɪniəs/ adj. *Your article on birds should deal with things related to birds, and not introduce extraneous topics.* = not related to the subject being talked or written about

extra•or•di•na•ry /ɪk'strɔːdənəri/ adj. **1** *extraordinary kindness* = much more than what is ordinary (common or usual) **2** *What an extraordinary sight this is!* = strange and unusual

ex•trav•a•gant /ɪk'strævəgənt/ adj. **1** *extravagant habits* = wasteful, specially of money **2** *The scientist has been making extravagant claims for his new invention.* = more than what is reasonable **extravagance** noun, u. = the quality, or an example, of being extravagant

ex•treme[1] /ɪk'striːm/ adj. **1** *These plants will die in the extreme cold.* = very great; of the highest degree possible **2** *Ladakh lies in the extreme north of India.* = the (northern) most

extreme[2] noun, c. *You should avoid all extremes of temperature.* = the limits (highest or lowest) **extremity** /ɪk'stremɪtɪ/ noun, c. (**extremities**) = the last or furthest points or parts of something

ex•tri•cate /'ekstrɪkeɪt/ verb, t. **1** *She has been able to extricate herself from the financial problems she had got into.* = to set someone (or oneself) free from a difficult or dangerous situation (formal) **2** *More than ten injured people were extricated from the bus which had been wrecked in the accident.* = to pull out with some difficulty

ex•tro•vert /'ekstrəvɜːt/ noun, c. *You will always find her with a crowd of friends. She is an extrovert.* = a person who loves to have social contact with others (opposite **introvert**) [SCIENCE]

ex•u•be•rant /ɪg'zjuːbərənt/ adj. *He is always in an exuberant mood when we have a social gathering.* = extremely cheerful and excited

ex•ude /ɪg'zjuːd/ verb, t. *The rubber tree exudes a thick white sap from which rubber is made. // to exude happiness* = to give out or produce (formal) [TECHNICAL]

ex•ult /ɪg'zʌlt/ verb, i. *The tennis player's fans exulted when she won the match.* = to show great happiness

eye[1] /aɪ/ noun, c. **1** = the part of the body that we see with **2** *He has an eye for beauty.* = the ability to know the value of something **3** *the eye of a needle* = the small hole in a needle through which a thread can pass

eye[2] verb, t. *He has been eyeing your pen for quite some time.* = to have a desire to take away something which belongs to someone else **eyeball** /'aɪbɔːl/ noun, c. = the whole of the eye, including the part inside the head, which is like a ball in shape **eyeballs** noun *We had over 2 million eyeballs and the television programme was a great success.* = a measure of the people who are attracted to a television programme or visit a website on the Internet [COMPUTERS] **eyebrow** noun, c. = the line of hairs growing above the eye **eye contact** noun = the action of looking straight into someone's face **eyelash** noun, c. (**-lashes**) = the small hairs growing along the edge of the eyelid **eyelid** noun, c. = the piece of skin covering the eye, which can move up and down **eye-opener** noun, c. *Her acting in this film was a real eye-opener.* = something which causes great surprise and makes you realise the truth about something **eyesore** noun, c. *The new station building is an eye-sore.* = something which is ugly to look at and can be seen by many people **eyewash** noun, u. *You work very hard, but what you say about not stopping to eat is a lot of eyewash.* = nonsense; something said to mislead people (informal) **eyewitness** noun, c. *He is an eyewitness to the murder.* = a person who has seen something happen and can tell the judge about it in a law court

a good eye for *She has a good eye for detail.* = to be very skilful at something **to keep an eye on (someone or something)** = to watch someone's behaviour carefully **to keep one's eyes open** = to keep looking for something that you hope to find **to not believe one's eyes** = to think something so impossible that it seems unreal **an eye for an eye** = to seek revenge for some loss or damage that one has suffered **to keep one's eye peeled** *We need to find a small shop on a very crowded street. Let's keep our eyes peeled.* = to prepare to look very carefully for something **to not be able to take your eyes off something** = to find something very attractive or interesting **to have a good eye for something** *Nina has a good eye for pictures.*= to have the ability to see or notice something **to do something with one's eyes open** = to get involved in something with care and a full knowledge of the consequences and problems

e-zine /iːziːn/ noun, c. = a magazine that one can read in electronic form on a computer screen (short for electronic magazine) [COMPUTERS]

fF

f, F /ef/ the sixth letter of the English alphabet

F abbr. for **Fahrenheit** *Water freezes at 32ºF.*

fa•ble /ˈfeɪbəl/ noun, c. or u. = a short story that teaches a lesson (moral) and in which animals are usually the main characters (compare **myth, legend**)

fab•ric /ˈfæbrɪk/ noun, c. or u. *a shirt made of cotton fabric.*(u.) = the material out of which a dress is made

fab•ri•cate /fæbrɪˈkeɪt/ verb, t. **1** *We have to fabricate the metal frame for this desk.* = to make by joining together [TECHNICAL] **2** *They fabricated a story about the work they had done.*= to make up or invent a false story about someone or something (derogatory) **fabrication** noun, u. or c. **1** (u.) = the act of building something **2** *This story is a complete fabrication.*(c.) = something that has been made up falsely

fab•u•lous /ˈfæbjʊləs/ adj. **1** *fabulous jewellery* = very beautiful (informal) **2** *We had a fabulous holiday.* = so great or wonderful that it is hard to believe or describe (informal)

fa•ça•de /fəˈsɑːd/ noun, c. (French) **1** *the façade of a building* = the front [TECHNICAL] **2** *They wear a façade of goodness but are really unpleasant people.* = a false appearance or show

façade

face¹ /feɪs/ noun, c. **1** = the front part of the head, including the forehead, nose, ears, lips and chin **2** *the face of the clock* = the front part of something

face² verb, t. **1** *The building faces the main road.* = to stand opposite to something **2** *We are facing a problem with the water supply.* = to have to deal with **3** *The building is faced with marble.* = to cover the front part of something with a different material **faceless** adj. *a faceless crowd* = without individual character **facial** adj. *facial hair* = connected with a person's face **at face value** noun, u. *Take it at face value.* = as seen from the outside, without one's going deeply into it

face to face *a face to face talk* = direct **in the face of** *She was brave in the face of illness.* = when required to go through or suffer something **to face the music** *You knew you were not following the rules; now you'll have to face the music.* = to deal with the unpleasant results of one's own actions **to lose face** *You have always done well. Don't worry, you won't lose face if you fail this time.* = to lose respect as a consequence of something **to put on a brave face** *She was very upset when she lost her job, but she put on a brave face.* = to act as if one is not sad, depressed etc. in order to make a situation seem better **on the face of (it)** *On the face of it, the plan looks all right, but I have my doubts.* = from the outside or from what one can see/tell at first **(to give something) a face-lift** = to improve something (e.g. a building) just enough to make it look better

fa•cet /ˈfæsɪt/ noun, c. **1** *the facets of a diamond* = one of many sides of a precious stone **2** *There are several facets to this problem.* = different sides to be considered (thought about)

fa•ce•tious /fəˈsiːʃəs/ adj. *This is a serious occasion. Your facetious remarks are out of place.* = humorous in a foolish way (derogatory)

fa•cile /ˈfæsaɪl/ adj. **1** *When they were asked to suggest some new ideas for the school magazine, they could only come up with some facile plans.* = easily done; not requiring much thought or effort (derogatory) **2** *a facile win* = easily obtained or done

fa•cil•i•ta•te /fəˈsɪlɪteɪt/ verb, t. *The new highway will facilitate travel across the country.* = to make something easier; to help

fa•cil•i•ty /fəˈsɪlɪti/ noun, u. or c. (**facilities**) **1** *She has great facility with languages.*(u.) = ability to do things easily and well (formal) **2** (generally plural) *Our school does not have library facilities.*(c.) = something that helps one or provides an advantage **3** *Could I use the facilities, please*? = a polite way of referring to a toilet (formal)

fac•sim•i•le /fækˈsɪmɪli/ noun, c. *This is a facsimile of a letter written by Tipu Sultan to the British representative.* = an exact copy, not the original (The word **fax** comes from fascimile.) [LAW]

fact /fækt/ noun, c. *You have been getting a lot of wrong information. Now here are the facts.* = something that is true or correct; the truth **factual** adj. *a factual account of the war* = based on things that actually happened **in fact** **1** *She expected it to rain, but in fact it was very sunny.* = actually **2** *I know very little about whales; in fact I know almost nothing.* = really (said for emphasis and contrast)

fac•tion /ˈfækʃən/ noun, c. = a group within a large group or political party

fac•tor /ˈfæktəʳ/ noun, c. **1** *Her illness was a major factor in her leaving school.* = something that can influence a result in a negative or positive way **2** = a whole number by which a larger number can be divided (2, 4, 5, 10 are factors of 20) [MATHEMATICS]

fac•to•ry /ˈfæktəri/ noun, c. (**factories**) *a tyre factory* = a place where goods are produced (in large numbers) with the help of machines

fac•ul•ty /ˈfækəlti/ noun, c. (**faculties**) **1** *He has lost the faculty of speech, which is special to human beings.* = the power or natural ability **2** *the Faculty of Science* = a branch of learning in a university (faculty can also mean teaching staff)

fad /fæd/ noun, c. *Many people want to listen to pop music, but this is only a passing fad.* = an interest in something that will not remain for a long time (informal, derogatory)

fade /feɪd/ verb, i. or t. **1** *I could hear her very clearly at first but suddenly her voice faded away.*(i.) = to become less strong **2** *These curtains have faded because of the strong sunlight falling on them.*(t.) = to become lighter in colour

fae•ces (feces) /ˈfiːsiːz/ noun, u. = solid waste material from the bowels [MEDICINE]

fag /fæg/ noun, c. = a cigarette (informal) **fagged** adj. = tired

fag•got /ˈfægət/ noun, c. = a bunch of small sticks which can be used as fuel

Fah•ren•heit /ˈfærənhaɪt/ noun = a scale of temperature in which the freezing point of water is 32 degrees and its boiling point 212 degrees

fail /feɪl/ verb, i. or t. **1** *Don't worry, you won't fail in the examination.*(i.) // *I'm sorry you failed the driving test.*(t.) = to be unsuccessful in something **2** *The examiners don't want to fail you.*(t.) = to decide that someone should not pass an examination **3** *The monsoon has failed us again.*(t.) = to disappoint **4** *My business has failed.* (i.) = to be unsuccessful **failure** noun, u. or c. **1** *the failure of the experiment* = the act of failing **2** *The holiday was a failure. We could not relax at all.* = someone or something that has failed **without fail** *You must come at 7.00 tomorrow, without fail.* = certainly, with no possibility of not (coming) etc.

faint[1] /feɪnt/ verb, i. *He fainted when he heard the news, and we had to call the doctor.* = to lose consciousness

faint[2] adj. **1** *We heard a faint sound.* = not strong or clear **2** *There is only a faint chance of her coming.* = very small

fair[1] /feəʳ/ adj. **1** *The decision by the referee was fair.* = just; impartial **2** *He won the election by fair means.* = honest (opposite **unfair**) **3** *He has a fair knowledge of Russian.* = quite good **4** *We expect fair weather today.* = bright and sunny **5** *They don't know everything about our plans, but they have a fair idea.* = rough

fair[2] noun, c. **1** *Elephants are sold at the Sonepur fair.* = a market, generally in the countryside, that is held at regular intervals; a (usually) large exhibition of books, garments etc. **2** *a trade fair* = an event at which many people display and sell their goods **fair play** = treatment or behaviour that is fair and just

fairly /feəlɪ/ adv. **1** *She felt that she had not been treated fairly.* = in a just way **2** *She is fairly good at art.* = quite

fai•ry /ˈfeəri/ noun, c. (**fairies**) = an imaginary creature that looks like a small human being and has wings and magical powers **fairy tale** noun, c. **1** = a story about fairies **2** = a story that is hard to believe

faith /feɪθ/ noun, u. or c. **1** *I have great faith in her.*(u.) = strong trust or belief **2** *I am a follower of the Buddhist faith.*(c.) = religion **faithful** adj. **1** *a faithful friend* = showing loyalty **2** *This is a faithful account of what happened at the meeting.* = true in every detail **3** = to be loyal to one's partner (in a relationship)

fake[1] /feɪk/ verb, t. **1** *She faked illness in order to avoid travelling.* = to pretend to be feeling something when one is not (usually derogatory) **2** *The police arrested him for faking bank notes.* = to produce false copies of something for a reason

fake[2] noun, c. *not really a doctor but a fake* = a person or thing that is not really what he/she/it is supposed to be

fake[3] adj. *a fake watch* = not genuine but a copy of the real thing

fal•con /ˈfɔːlkən/ noun, c. = a bird with pointed wings that can be trained to hunt other birds or small animals

fall[1] /fɔːl/ verb, i. (**fell, fallen**) **1** *He fell off a tree and hurt himself.* = to come down from a higher to a lower place **2** *The price of gold has fallen.* = to become less **3** *The city fell to the attack of the planes.* = to be conquered or defeated **4** *Thousands of soldiers fell in the war.* = to be killed **5** *Ramzan falls on a Monday this year.* = to happen

fall[2] noun, c. **1** *I had a fall and broke my leg.* = an act of falling **2** *There is a big fall in the price of gold.* = a decrease or reduction **3** = American English for autumn **fallout** noun, u. *the fallout from the nuclear test at Pokhran* = the dangerous radioactive matter that is left floating in the air after a nuclear explosion **to fall about** *The story was so funny that all of us fell about laughing.* = to laugh a lot and with great enjoyment (informal) **to fall apart** *Our science project made good progress at first, then it just fell apart.* = to fail or not work out **to fall back on** *As no buses were available, I had to fall back on my old bicycle.* = to be forced to use something as nothing else is available **to fall for** **1** *She fell for the trick we played on her on April Fool's Day.* = to believe that something is true, not knowing that a trick is being played on you **2** = to fall in love with someone (informal)

to fall in with *I wasn't sure I wanted to do what they suggested, but I had to fall in with their plans.* = agree to be a part of **to fall out** *We fell out over a small matter, but are now friends again.* = to quarrel **to fall through** *Sadly, our trip to Silent Valley fell through.*= to be given up or not to happen

fal•la•cy /ˈfæləsi/ noun, u. or c. (**fallacies**) *It is a fallacy to think that girls are cleverer than boys or that boys are cleverer than girls.* = a false idea or belief **fallacious** /fəˈleɪʃəs/ adj. *a fallacious belief* = something that is a fallacy

fal•li•ble /ˈfælɪbəl/ adj. *It is possible that my calculation is wrong. I admit that I am fallible.* = able or likely to make mistakes (opposite **infallible**)

fal•low /ˈfæləʊ/ adj. *fallow land* = land on which crops have not been grown for a few years so that the quality of the land will improve

false /fɔːls/ adj. **1** *That story is false. I don't believe it.*= not true or correct **2** *We both like praise, so let's not show any false modesty.* = insincere or dishonest **3** *false teeth* = not real, artificial **false alarm** = a warning of something bad which does not happen **falsify** /ˈfalsɪfaɪ/ verb, t. *falsify a report or a statement* = to change something (usually true) and make it untrue

fal•ter /ˈfɔːltəʳ/ verb, i. **1** *The old man's footsteps faltered as he walked towards the door.* = to move or speak unsteadily because of weakness or uncertainty **2** = to lose confidence

fame /feɪm/ noun, u. *Her fame as a writer spread quickly.* = the condition of being well known

fa•mil•i•ar /fəˈmɪliəʳ/ adj. **1** *An old man carrying a basket of vegetables on his head is a familiar sight in this part of the city.* = common; known to everyone **2** *I am not familiar with these roads. Please show me the way.* = having a thorough knowledge of **3** *He acted so familiar with us that we felt uncomfortable.* = friendly in a way that may not be welcome (disapproving) **familiarity** /fəmɪlɪˈærɪti/ noun, u. *Her familiarity with the roads of the city is very useful.* = knowledge of or close relationship with

fam•i•ly /ˈfæməli/ noun, c. (**families**) **1** *Our family consists of my parents, my aunt and myself.* = a group of people related to each other by blood or marriage **2** *Cats and lepoards are part of the same family.* = a group of animals, birds etc. which have some common characteristics (e.g. shape of head and body, style of movement, claws, feeding habits) **3** = a term used to refer to a class of computers [COMPUTERS] **family planning** = controlling the number of children who are born by using different methods of birth-control **family tree** = a diagram which traces the relationship between members of a family, usually over a long period starting from the past

fa•mine /ˈfæmɪn/ noun, u. or c. *There was a famine as we had no rain for three years and many people were unable to get any food.*(c.) = serious shortage of food over a long period in a large area

famished /ˈfæmɪʃt/ adj. *I feel famished. Let us eat now.* = very hungry; suffering from hunger

fa•mous /ˈfeɪməs/ adj. *a famous writer* = very well known

fan[1] /fæn/ noun, c. **1** *a ceiling fan; a palm-leaf fan* = an instrument or machine that causes air to flow **2** *an Amitabh Bachchan fan* = an admirer or supporter of some famous person (informal)

fan[2] verb, t. **1** *It is very hot in this room. Let's fan ourselves with these newspapers.* = to use a fan or something like a fan to cause air to flow **2** *fan the fires of hatred* = to cause bad feelings to grow (figurative, literary)

fa•nat•ic /fəˈnætɪk/ noun, c. *Mahatma Gandhi was deeply religious but he was not a fanatic. He respected all religions.* = a person with very strong views, especially on religion and politics, who is not prepared to listen to people who do not agree with him/her **fanatical** adj. *a person with fanatical views* = extremely strong and unreasonable, sometimes dangerously so **fanaticism** noun, u. = the quality one finds in a fanatic

fan•cy[1] /ˈfænsi/ noun, u. or c. (**fancies**) **1** *A poet can see many strange things in his fancy.*(u.) = imagination **2** *I have taken a fancy to that kind of coffee.*(c.) = a liking not based on reason (informal)

fancy[2] verb, t. **1** *Do you fancy a holiday in Kashmir?* = want or wish for (informal) **2** *I can't fancy going all the way to Mumbai just to see a film star!* = to imagine (informal) **3** *They left Nagpur without telling anyone. Fancy that!* = an expression of mild disapproval meaning 'Just imagine!' (informal) **4** *Do you think he fancies her?* = to be sexually attracted to a person (informal)

fancy[3] adj. *Please show me some ordinary shoes—nothing fancy.* = ornamented (highly decorated); not ordinary **fancy dress** = clothes worn, often as part of a competition, to dress up as someone different **to fancy oneself** = to have a very high opinion of oneself (informal)

fan•fare /ˈfænfeəʳ/ noun, u.**1** = a short, loud piece of music played to introduce a person or an event **2** *The film festival started with much fanfare.* = the excitement before an important event (figurative)

fang /fæŋ/ noun, c. *the tiger's fangs* = the long, sharp tooth of an animal

fan•tas•tic /fænˈtæstɪk/ adj. **1** *He told me a fantastic story about a journey he had made to the* *moon.* = unreal and impossible **2** *We saw the garden he had created. It was fantastic!* = unbelievably good (informal)

fan•ta•sy /'fæntəsi/ noun, u. or c. (**fantasies**) **1** *She lives in a world of fantasy.*(u.) = imagination **2** *This story is a fantasy.*(c.) = something unreal that has been imagined or made up

far[1] /fɑːʳ/ adj. **1** *Mumbai is very far from Delhi.* = a long way off **2** *She is a visitor from a far country.* = a long way off; distant **3** *The final version of the novel was far better than the first draft.* = much (better, worse etc.)

far[2] adv. **1** *We had not gone far when the car broke down.* = a long way **2** *How far is the station from the school?* = at what distance **far-fetched** adj. *She gave me a really far-fetched excuse to explain why she had been absent.* = something that is difficult to believe **far-reaching** adj. *The work they did on wild-life protection had a far-reaching influence.* = having great influence or effect **far-sighted** adj. *a far-sighted leader* = able to see or think of the future effects of present actions

so far *We have had problems with electricity but so far the water supply has been good.* = up to the time of speaking **to go far** **1** *A 100-rupee note doesn't go far these days.* = to be able to buy many things; to be enough **2** *She is a promising young writer and should go far.* = to be successful **to go too far** *It all began as a harmless joke but we went too far and made him angry.* = to do something to such an extent as to cause an unpleasant situation

farce /fɑːs/ noun, c. or u. **1** (c.) = a kind of light and humorous play [LITERATURE] **2** *The queues at that ticket counter are a farce. People can join the queue at any point they like.* = some action that is done only for show, without any result being expected and usually to mislead (informal) **3** *a farce of a lecture* = a poor, disappointing version of something (informal)

fare[1] /feəʳ/ noun, c. *The train fare from Kolkata to Delhi is Rs 600.* = the amount of money that is paid to travel by train or air

fare[2] verb, i. *They fared very well in the examination.* = to perform; to be successful

fare•well[1] /feə'wel/ noun, c. *We said farewell to our friends when they left town.* = good bye

farewell[2] adj. *a farewell speech* = expressing good wishes to someone who is leaving

farm[1] /fɑːm/ noun, c. = an area of land used for growing crops or raising animals

farm[2] verb, t. *I plan to farm this land.* = to grow crops or rear animals on a piece of land **farmer** noun, c. = a person who owns or works on a farm

to farm out *This factory has very few workers, so it has to farm out some of its work to other factories.* = to send out work which one is supposed to do, to other people

fart /'fɑːʳt/ verb i. = to force the wind (gas) out of one's bowels (not polite)

far•ther[1] (**further**) /'fɑːðəʳ/ adj. *Kolkata is very far from this town, but Delhi is even farther.* = more far

farther[2] (**further**) adv. *The government has no money to go any farther with this new project.* = forward; ahead

> **Usage** Either **farther** or **further** can be used in a sentence such as: *Farther/Further down the street, you will find the cake shop.* Both are used to talk about real distances and places. **Further** has also the sense of 'higher' or 'more' e.g. *further education.*

fas•ci•nate /'fæsɪneɪt/ verb, t. *Indian culture has fascinated people all over the world.* = to charm; to have a powerful influence on **fascinating** /fæsɪ'neɪtɪŋ/ adj. *You have written a fascinating novel.* = very interesting **fascination** noun, u. = great attraction

fas•cis•m /'fæʃɪzəm/ noun = a political system in which the government, under a strong leader, has complete power and control over industry, education etc. and allows no opposition **fascist** noun, c.

fash•ion[1] /'fæʃən/ noun, c. **1** *You find many men and women colouring their hair now. This is the new fashion.*(c.) **2** *Narrow trousers are no longer in fashion.*(u.) = a way of dressing or behaving that is popular at a given time **3** *She speaks in a strange fashion.*(u.) = manner; way of doing something

fashion[2] verb, t. *She fashioned a beautiful dress out of the old sari.* = to make (literary) **fashionable** adj. *a fashionable woman; a fashionable hair-style* = following the latest fashion

fast[1] /fɑːst/ adv. **1** *She runs very fast.* = quickly **2** *He is fast asleep.* = sleeping deeply **3** *The door was stuck fast. We couldn't open it.* = in such a way that it cannot move or be moved

fast[2] adj. **1** *This is a fast train.* = moving quickly **2** *The clock is 10 minutes fast.* = ahead of the correct time **3** *The colour on this shirt is fast.* = not easily washed away **4** *fast film.* = (used about photographic film) very sensitive to light and therefore used to shoot in poor light

fast[3] verb, i. *My grandmother fasts once a week.* = to eat no food as a part of a religious ritual, for medical reasons etc

fast[4] noun. *Are you well enough to keep a fast?* = the practice of going without food

fasten /fɑːsən/ verb, t. *Have you fastened the door properly?* = to close or join together **fastener** /fɑːsənəʳ/ noun, c. = a thing that fastens

fas•tid•i•ous /fæ'stɪdiəs/ adj. *He is so fastidious*

about his food that he never eats out.= difficult to please; always finding fault with things (see also **fussy**) (slightly derogatory)

fat[1] /fæt/ adj. **1** *a fat boy* = having a lot of fat (see below) on one's body (descriptive, but can be impolite or disrespectful) **2** *We were charged a fat fee for express delivery.* = very high (informal) **3** *We have a fat chance of winning against such a good team!* = no or hardly any (chance) (informal)

fat[2] noun, u. or c. **1** *You must get rid of all the fat around your waist.*(u.) = the heavy flesh under the skin which is formed from food that is not used up by the body **2** *A balanced diet should contain some fat, to supply energy to the body.* = food which provides energy but is stored in the body as fat if not burnt up through exercise **fatten** verb, t. = to make an animal fat before it is ready to be killed and eaten

the fat's in the fire = the situation has suddenly turned as bad as it could become **to live off the fat of the land** = to have the best things, often at the expense of others, without doing much or any work (derogatory)

fa•tal /ˈfeɪtl/ adj. **1** *The bite of some snakes can be fatal.*= something that causes death **2** *a fatal mistake* = causing a bad result which cannot be set right (figurative)

fate /feɪt/ noun, u. **1** *He wanted to become a doctor, but fate made him an actor.* = the supernatural power that is believed to control events **2** *A dam is being built across the river and 200 villages will disappear under the water. The fate of the people who live there is uncertain.* = the future **fateful** adj. *a fateful day* = a very important day that has far-reaching consequences (usually negative) **fatalism** noun = the belief that all events are controlled by fate

fa•ther /ˈfɑːðəʳ/ noun, c. **1** = the male of the parents **2** *Dr Ambedkar was the father of the Indian Constitution.* = the person who produces or begins something **3** = the title sometimes given to Christian priests **father figure** = an older man on whom one depends for guidance or advice (figurative) **father-in-law** *(fathers-in-law)* = the father of one's wife or husband

fa•thom[1] /ˈfæðəm/ noun, c. = a measure of the depth of water, equal to six feet or 1.8 metres

fathom[2] verb, t. *I am unable to fathom the meaning of the poem.* = to understand completely

fa•tigue[1] /fəˈtiːg/ noun, u. **1** *After marching for 50 km the soldiers collapsed from fatigue.* = very great tiredness **2** *We found some cracks in the wings of the aircraft which had been caused by metal fatigue.* = a defect or weakness in a mechanical part that develops after long use [TECHNICAL]

fatigue[2] verb, t. *The long period of study has fatigued me.* = to make someone very tired (formal)

fault[1] /fɔːlt/ noun, c. **1** *This computer does not work. There must be a fault in the machine.* = something wrong; a defect **2** *One of her faults is her forgetfulness.* = something for which one is likely to be blamed **3** = a crack in the rocky surface of the earth [GEOGRAPHY] **4** = a service in tennis that is not according to rules [SPORTS]

fault[2] verb, t. *She read out the passage so well that it was difficult to fault her.* = to find a fault in someone **faultless** adj. *That was a faultless dance performance.* = perfect **faulty** adj. *a faulty connection* = having faults

fau•na /ˈfɔːnə/ noun, u. *Scientists are studying the fauna found in these jungles.* = the animals living in or around a place (see also **flora**) [BIOLOGY]

fa•vour[1] /ˈfeɪvəʳ/ noun, u. or c. **1** *I want to ask you for a favour. May I use your suitcase?*(c.) = a kind act done to the person who is asking **2** *We are trying to decide where to go for our picnic and most of the students are in favour of Jabalpur.*(u.) = a preference (liking) for someone or something over another **3** *I'm out of favour with my friend after our last argument.* = appoval; good opinion **4** *I don't think you should show favour to just a few and neglect the others.*(u.) = unfairly kind treatment shown to a person, to the disadvantage of others

favour[2] verb, t. **1** *I favour resting on weekends over going out.* = to show a preference for someone or something **2** *She doesn't really favour us, but everyone thinks she does because she is nice to us.* = to be seen to show unfair support of or preference for someone **3** *All of us except Martin favour the idea of building another room.* = approve

in (someone's) favour *The judge decided the case in my favour.* = to one's advantage

favourite[1] /ˈfeɪvərɪt/ noun, c. *The baby is everyone's favourite.* = a person or thing that one likes the most

favourite[2] adj. *He is my favourite actor.* = someone or something that is loved more than others **favouritism** noun, u. = the practice of showing special favour to one person and being unfair to others (derogatory)

fawn[1] /fɔːn/ noun, c. = a young deer

fawn[2] verb, i. *You will always find the artist surrounded by a few of her followers who fawn on her.* = to give a lot of attention to someone in order to win his/her favour (derogatory)

fear[1] /fɪəʳ/ noun, u. or c. *She has a great fear of dogs, especially big ones.* = the feeling that one may be harmed or in danger

fear[2] verb, t. **1** *She fears snakes and scorpions.* = to be afraid of **2** *I fear war may break out any day on.* =

to be anxious or worried about something **3** *It's going to be a hot day, I fear.* = to think that something unpleasant might happen **fearful** adj. **1** *We ran into a fearful storm.* = causing fear **2** *I was fearful of missing the train.* = afraid (opposite **fearsome**)

fea•si•ble /ˈfiːzɪbəl/ adj. *Most people think it is not feasible to have a garden inside the house but I say it is.* = possible; something that can be done

feast[1] /fiːst/ noun, c. = a large meal or a public meal shared by many people

feast[2] verb, t. **1** = to arrange a feast for someone **2** *We feasted our eyes on the beautiful collection of paintings.* = to enjoy (figurative)

feat /fiːt/ noun, c. *The little boy ran all the way from his house to the school, more than five kilometres away. It was quite a feat.* = an action that deserves to be noticed because it requires a lot of courage, strength, skill etc.

fea•ther /ˈfeðəʳ/ noun, c. = the light covering that grows on a bird's body, specially the wings
a feather in one's cap = some achievement that one can be proud of **birds of a feather** = people of the same kind (usually bad) (usually derogatory) **to feather one's nest** = to make oneself rich, often through corrupt or dishonest means (derogatory)

fea•ture[1] /ˈfiːtʃəʳ/ noun, c. **1** *In the dark, I could see a woman standing near the door, but I could not make out her features.* = parts of the face (eyes, nose, lips etc.) **2** *Noise, dust and smoke are now common features of life in the city.* = an important or noticeable part or quality of something **3** *Have you read the feature on police dogs in this Sunday's newspaper?* = a long article appearing in a newspaper

feature[2] verb, t. or i. *The new film features Aishwarya Rai and Salman Khan.* = to have or include

Feb•ru•a•ry /ˈfebruəri/ noun = the second month of the year

fed /fed/ verb, t. past tense of **feed**
fed up *I am fed with up with this place.* = bored and tired (informal)

fed•e•ra•tion /fedəˈreɪʃən/ noun, c. or u. **1** *The different states in India are parts of a federation.*(c.) = a group of states joining into a single group, but with each state keeping control of some matters [TECHNICAL] **2** *the Federation of Students' Unions*(c.) = a group of societies or unions that have joined together **3** (u.) = the process of joining together to form a larger group **federal** /ˈfedərel/ adj. *a federal system of governance* = relating to a federation **federalism** noun = the belief in political, fiscal etc.

fee /fiː/ noun, c. **1** *The doctor charges a fee of Rs 50.* = a sum of money paid for professional services **2** = the cost of entrance/membership etc.

fee•ble /ˈfiːbəl/ adj. *He has grown feeble with age.* = weak; without energy or power **feeble-minded** adj. *a feeble-minded person* = not having a strong mind

feed[1] /fiːd/ verb, t. or i. (**fed**) **1** *Did you feed the cats? They look hungry.*(t.) = to give food to **2** *Monkeys feed on fruits and nuts.*(i.) = to eat **3** *The mother is feeding her baby.*(t.) = to give milk from one's breast **4** *Don't feed us with all these foolish ideas.*(t.) = to fill someone's mind in a way that is not welcome (disapproving) **5** *We have to feed the data into our computers.*(t.) = to type in or copy in [COMPUTERS]

feed[2] noun, u. or c. *We have to buy some feed for the cattle.*(u.) = food for animals

feed•back /ˈfiːdbæk/ noun, u. *Although the books have been in use in schools for many years, we have received no feedback on their quality.* = information received about the result of some action taken, which is passed back to the persons responsible, so that necessary changes or corrections can be made

feel[1] /fiːl/ verb, t. or i. (**felt**) **1** *I feel great happiness when I reach home after a day's work.* (t.) = to experience **2** *I feel some pain in my back.*(t.) = to suffer **3** *My new shirt feels like cotton, but it may be a blend.*(i.) = to produce a certain effect when touched etc. **4** *In the dark, he felt his way along the corridor.*(t.) = to get to know of something by touching **5** *I feel Saturdays should be holidays.*(t.) = to have an opinion **6** *Do you feel like having a drink?* (t.) = to have a wish for

feel[2] noun, u. **1** *This blanket has a rough feel.* = the sensation caused by touching something **2** *I am getting the feel of this new scooter.* = knowledge of something gained by using it or experiencing it **feeler** noun, c. **1** = a sense organ in certain animals used while searching for food or sensing danger [BIOLOGY] **2** *They sent out feelers that they would need help ahead of the meeting.* = a hesitant message sent out in advance in order to know what people think, usually before a proper request is made (informal) **feeling** noun, u. or c. **1** *He has no feeling in the leg.*(u.) = the ability or power to feel pain etc. **2** *He had a sudden feeling of hunger.*(c.) = emotion or sensation **3** *I have a feeling that the plan will work.*(c.) = knowledge that something will or is likely to happen **feelings** noun (usually plural) *He gave us the bad news with no consideration for our feelings.* = capacity to feel hurt or unhappy

feign /feɪn/ verb, t. *He feigned shyness to avoid meeting us.* = to pretend to have a quality or condition

feint /feɪnt/ noun, c. *The boxer made a feint with his left hand and then hit his opponent with his right.* = to make a false attack or blow to draw the opponent's attention away from the real danger

fe•li•ci•tate /fɪˈlɪsɪteɪt/ verb, t. *There will be a meeting to felicitate him on winning the Green Peace award.* = to express happiness at something good that has happened to someone **felicitations** /felɪsɪˈteɪʃəns/ noun, c. = good wishes

fe•li•ci•ty /fɪˈlɪsɪti/ noun, u. **1** = happiness or luck (literary) **2** *He writes with great felicity.* = the ability to use the right words (formal)

fe•line[1] /ˈfiːlaɪn/ noun, c. *Lions and tigers are felines.*(c.) = members of the cat family

feline[2] adj. *feline grace* = like a cat

fell verb **1** = the past tense of **fall** **2** (t.) = to cut down a tree

fel•low[1] /ˈfeləʊ/ noun, c. **1** *He is a jolly good fellow.* = person (informal) **2** *She is a Fellow of the Royal Society.* = a member of a learned society [TECHNICAL]

fellow[2] adj. *One must have sympathy for one's fellow students.* = (those who are) like oneself **fellowship** noun, c. or u. **1** *a spirit of fellowship*(c.) = the quality of sharing the joys and sorrows of others **2** *He has received Fellowship of the Royal Society.*(u.) = the honour of being a member of a learned society **3** = a scholarship at a university, with some teaching duties

fe•lo•ny /ˈfeləni/ noun, c. (**felonies**) (American) *Murder is a felony.* = a serious crime [LAW]

felt noun, u. = a kind of thick cloth made from wool, used for making hats or covering the tops of tables

felt-tip pen noun. = a pen with a felt tip (made of thick fur or wool), having a firm end rather than a nib

fe•male[1] /ˈfiːmeɪl/ noun, c. **1** *a mature female* = a woman or animal which is able to produce eggs or babies **2** = a way of referring to a woman which is casual and disrespectful (derogatory) Ⓖ

female[2] adj. *a female artist* = being a woman or a girl

fem•i•nine /ˈfemɪnɪn/ adj. **1** *He used a feminine voice on the phone to make us think it was his sister.* = like that of a woman or as expected of a woman (sometimes derogatory) **2** *'Lioness' is the feminine form of 'lion'.* = a form of a word that shows whether we are referring to a man or a woman (or a male or a female) [GRAMMAR]

fem•i•nis•m /ˈfemɪnɪzəm/ noun = the belief that women should have the same rights, opportunities, ways of being judged etc. as men, and that this process should be given attention **feminist** noun, c. = a person who works actively for women's rights

fence /fens/ noun, c.**1** = a light wall, usually made of wire stretched between poles, used to divide two pieces of land **2** = a person who receives and sells stolen goods (slang)

to sit on the fence = to avoid taking sides in a quarrel or dispute

fend /fend/ verb, i. or t. **to fend for oneself** *You are now old enough to fend for yourself.* = to look after oneself **to fend off someone or something** *As I was not feeling well, my parents fended off all callers and visitors.* = to keep someone or something away (informal)

fen•der /ˈfendəʳ/ noun, c. **1** = something used to prevent damage in case of an accident caused by striking against something e.g. the bumpers on a motorcar **2** (American) = the mudguards of a car

fen•u•greek /ˈfenjuːgrɪk/ noun = a kind of seed used for flavouring food ('methi' in some Indian languages)

fer•ment[1] /ˈfɜːment/ verb, t. or i. **1** *Whisky is made by fermenting barley.*(t.) = to allow alcohol to be produced from sugar as a result of action by bacteria **2** *To make idlis, you should allow the batter to ferment overnight.*(i.) = to cause a substance to rise as a result of bubbles of carbon-dioxide gas forming due to the action of bacteria

ferment[2] noun, u. *ferment in the country* = a state of political and social excitement as a result of change **fermentation** /fɜːmenˈtəɪʃən/ noun

fern /fɜːn/ noun = a kind of flowerless green plant with feather-like leaves

fe•ro•cious /fəˈrəʊʃəs/ adj. *a ferocious dog* = violent and likely to attack

fer•ret[1] /ˈferɪt/ noun, c. = a small cat-like animal which hunts rabbits by entering the holes in which they live, and driving them out

ferret[2] verb, i. *We have been looking into old trunks and cupboards to ferret out photographs of our childhood.* = to find something by searching carefully (informal)

fer•rous /ˈferəs/ adj. *ferrous metals* = containing iron (opposite **non-ferrous**) [CHEMISTRY]

ferry[1] /ˈferi/ noun, c. (**ferries**) *When the new bridge is built across the river, no one will use the ferry.* = a boat or ship in which people regularly cross a river or stretch of sea

ferry[2] verb, t. (**ferried**) *The boat ferried us across the river.* = to carry across a river in a boat

fer•tile /ˈfɜːtaɪl/ adj. **1** *fertile land* = land on which crops and fruit can be grown easily and in large quantities **2** = able to produce young one (referring to plants, animals or human beings) (opposite **infertile** or **sterile** or **barren**) **3** *She has a fertile imagination.* = very active in imagining things; full of ideas (humorous)

fer•ti•lize (fertilise) /ˈfɜːtɪlaɪz/ verb, t. **1** = to bring about the union of male seeds with the female eggs in a plant or animal, through which young are produced [TECHNICAL] **2** *The land has to be fertilized.* = to put natural/artificial substances on the land to make plants grow better **fertilizer (fertiliser)** /fɜːtɪˈlaɪzəʳ/ noun, u. or c. = a substance that makes land more fertile

fer•vent /ˈfɜːvənt/ adj. *He has a fervent desire to start a school.* = strong (referring to a wish or belief) **fervour** noun, u. *She spoke with great fervour.* = strength of feeling

fes•ter /ˈfestəʳ/ verb, i. **1** *The wound in his leg has been festering for a long time.* = to become infected and diseased (referring to a wound or cut) **2** *A feeling of dissatisfaction has been festering in our minds.* = to become bitter and angry (referring to a feeling) because it is not dealt with well

fes•ti•val /ˈfestɪvəl/ noun, c. **1** = an event (usually religious) which is often marked by great public celebration **2** *a dance festival* = a public performance (show) of dances, films etc. held at some place

fes•toon[1] /feˈstuːn/ noun, c. = a chain made of coloured paper, cloth etc. which is hung from a high place, usually to celebrate something

festoon[2] verb, t. = to decorate with festoons

fetch /fetʃ/ verb, t. **1** *Could you please go to the post office and fetch me some stamps?* = to go to another place and bring back something from it **2** *This car should fetch at least Rs 30,000.* = to be worth a certain price

fete /feɪt/ noun, c. = an outdoor gathering for enjoyment, where money is raised for charitable purposes through the sale of articles, games etc.

fet•id /ˈfiːtɪd/ adj. *a fetid smell* = having a very unpleasant smell

fet•ish /ˈfetɪʃ/ noun, c. *He makes such a fetish of cleanliness that he cleans his room three times a day.* = something to which one gives too much importance and attention

fet•ter[1] /ˈfetəʳ/ noun, c. (generally plural **fetters**) *shake off one's fetters* = something that binds or ties down and prevents one from becoming free

fetter[2] verb, t. *We feel fettered by these rules.* = to restrict or limit (one's) freedom

feud[1] /fjuːd/ noun, c. *There is an old feud between the two families.* = a feeling of anger or a serious dispute often over a long time, between two families or groups, likely to lead to frequent fighting

feud[2] verb, i. *the two feuding families* = to take part in a feud

feu•dal /ˈfjuːdl/ adj. *the feudal system* = belonging to a social system existing in former times, in which a rich and powerful landowner, who received large areas of land from the king, gave away some of it to people of lower rank, who offered him their services in return [HISTORY]

fe•ver /ˈfiːvəʳ/ noun, c. or u. *I have a fever.*(c.) // *Stomach infections are often accompanied by fever.*(u.) = a condition of the body caused by some illness when the temperature of the body rises above the normal level **feverish** adj. **1** *to feel feverish* = feeling unwell, as if one has or is about to have a fever **2** *at a feverish pace* = very fast and with great excitement

few[1] /fjuː/ noun. *Most people are busy with their jobs. Few have time to relax.* = not many

few[2] pron. *He asked me for some eggs but I had very few left.* = not many

few[3] det. **1** *She has few friends.* = not many **2** *She has a few friends.* = at least a small number

> **Usage** The sentence: *There were a few people in the room.* and the sentence: *There were few people in the room.* have different meanings.
> **a few** means 'a small number' while, **few** (without **a**) means 'not many'. In the sentence: *Few would believe that...,* **few** means 'hardly anyone'.

fez /fez/ noun, c. = a round fur hat with a flat top

fi•an•ce /fiˈɒnseɪ/ noun, c. (French) = a man to whom a woman is engaged to be married **fiancee** noun, c. (same pronunciation) = a woman to whom a man is engaged to be married

fi•as•co /fiˈæskəʊ/ noun, c. (**fiascos**) *We expected a lot from this meeting but it proved to be a fiasco.* = a total failure

fib[1] /fɪb/ noun, c. = a lie (false statement) which is not very important

fib[2] verb, i. *Are you fibbing?* = to tell a fib

fi•bre (fiber) /ˈfaɪbəʳ/ noun, u. or c. **1** *a muscle fibre*(c.) = a thread-like part of the body of a plant or animal **2** *Cotton is a natural fibre.*(c.) = a substance containing fine threads, used for making cloth, rope etc. **3** (u.) = a thread-like substance in certain kinds of food which helps the body to get rid of waste matter easily **fibreglass** noun, u. = light but strong material made from glass fibres, used for making tennis racquets, boats etc. **fibre optics** noun **1** = the use of very thin wires, made of fibre glass, to carry telephone signals with the help of light waves [TECHNICAL] **2** *a fibre-optic cable*(adj.) = using fibre optics

fick•le /ˈfɪkəl/ adj. **1** *a fickle friend* = not dependable; likely to change one's mind suddenly, especially in love or friendship (derogatory) **2** *The weather is fickle.* = (of weather) changing all the time; not steady

fic•tion /ˈfɪkʃən/ noun, u. **1** = a novel or short story that is about imaginary events and characters and not something that really happened **2** *a piece of fiction* = something that is false and should not be believed (compare **fact**)

fi•ddle[1] /ˈfɪdl/ noun, c. **1** = a musical instrument with strings that is played like a violin **2** *an accounts fiddle* = dishonest or illegal work done in money-related matters (informal, derogatory)

fiddle[2] verb, i. **1** = to play on the violin (old-fashioned) **2** *Stop fiddling with the thermometer. You'll drop it.* = to play with something by holding it in the hands **3** *This report has been fiddled with.* = to change the facts in a document in a dishonest way (disapproving) **to play second fiddle to someone** = to play a relatively unimportant part in some activity helping a more important person (informal) **fit as a fiddle** = perfectly healthy (informal)

fi•del•i•ty /fɪˈdelɪti/ noun, u. **1** *Heads of organizations must be sure about the fidelity of those who work for them.* = the quality of being loyal and faithful to someone **2** *The fidelity of this recording is exceptional.* = the faithfulness of a copy to the original object or event (commonly used about music. See **hi-fi**)

fi•dget /ˈfɪdʒɪt/ verb, i. *Please stop fidgeting. It makes me think you are not listening.* = to move one's body in a restless manner so as not to sit or stand still

field[1] /fiːld/ noun, c. **1** *a rice field* = an area of land used for growing crops **2** *a football field* = an open area used for games etc. **3** *He is an expert in the field of European languages.* = a branch of knowledge **4** *magnetic field* = an area affected by or included in something [PHYSICS]

field[2] verb, t. **1** *Ganguly fields the ball and throws it back to the bowler.* = to catch or stop a ball in the game of cricket **2** *India will field the same team in the next match.* = to use for a contest **field work** noun, u. = scientific or social study done outside a laboratory or classroom to collect **data** on a subject

fiend /fiːnd/ noun, c. **1** = a wicked person in a legend **2** *a fiend for work* = a person who is very keen about something (informal) **fiendish** adj. *He laughed with fiendish delight.* = showing great excitement and keenness in a cruel and unpleasant way

fierce /fɪəs/ adj. **1** *a fierce dog* = angry and violent **2** *fierce competition* = very strong or great

fi•er•y /ˈfaɪəri/ adj. *a fiery temper* = with a capacity to get angry very quickly

fife /faɪf/ noun, c. = a musical instrument like a trumpet

fif•teen /ˌfɪfˈtiːn/ noun, c. = the number represented by 15 (5+10)

fifth[1] /fɪfθ/ noun, c. *a fifth of the property* = one part of something which has been divided into five equal parts

fifth[2] adj. *the fifth house in the row* = coming after the first four

fif•ty /ˈfɪfti/ noun, c. = the number represented by 50 (5x10) **fifty-fifty** adj. *She has a fifty-fifty chance of being chosen for the play.* = an equal chance (of winning or losing, getting or not getting etc.)

fig /fɪg/ noun, c. = a kind of fruit with many seeds which is often eaten dried

fight[1] /faɪt/ noun, c. **1** *This is not a fight, it's a friendly argument.* = a dispute or argument that may lead to physical violence **2** *We need your support in the fight against pollution.* = struggle, usually against something harmful or evil

fight[2] verb, t. or i. (**fought**) **1** *The soldiers have fought in many wars.*(t.) = to take part in a war **2** *They are always fighting.*(i.) = quarrelling (with or without the use of violence) **3** *We must fight corruption.*(t.) = to oppose or resist **4** *I had to fight my nervousness before I went on stage.* = to struggle to prevent an emotion from being felt, or seen by others **5** *fight the election* = compete with someone for votes, a job etc. **to be fighting fit** = to be in very good health (informal) **to have a fighting chance** = to have a fairly good chance of winning, suceeding etc. **to fight shy of something** = to try to avoid doing something which is seen as difficult or uninteresting

fight•er /ˈfaɪtəʳ/ noun, c. **1** = a person who takes part in a fight or likes to fight **2** = a small and fast military aircraft that can destroy enemy aircraft during an aerial battle

fig•ment /ˈfɪgmənt/ noun, c. *He was sure he had seen a creature from another planet but we told him it was only a figment of his imagination.* = something that one believes to be true but is not real

fig•u•ra•tive /ˈfɪgjʊrətɪv/ adj. *When I say music is sweet, I am using a figurative expression. Actually, music has no taste.* = a word or expression that is not to be understood in its exact meaning but used to give an imaginative effect. (see **figure of speech**)

fig•ure[1] /ˈfɪgəʳ/ noun, c. **1** = the shape of the whole body **2** *I could see a blue figure in the distance.* = a person who is not clearly visible because she/he is far away, in poor light etc. **3** *You can find many beautiful carved figures on the walls of the temple at Mt Abu.* = a human being or animal shown in a painting, statue or carving **4** *Jawaharlal Nehru was an important political figure of his time.* = personality **5** (usually plural) *Write the amount to be paid in figures as well as words.* = the numbers from 0 to 9 **6** *In this figure, you can see how the building will look from the top.* = a diagram (drawing) used to explain something

figure[2] verb, i. or t. **1** *Politics does not figure in his writing.*(i.) = to be a part of **2** (American) *I figured she would be here.*(t.) = to guess (informal)

figurehead /ˈfɪgəhed/ noun, c. *He is only a*

figurehead. He does not have any influence on the decisions taken. = the head of a government or organisation who has an official position but no power

figure of speech noun, c. *The expression 'blue-eyed boy' is only a figure of speech.* = words used for the sake of effect without depending on their exact meaning

fi•la•ment /'fɪləmənt/ noun, c. **1** *the filament inside an electric bulb* = a very thin thread or piece of wire that produces light when electricity is passed through it (see pic under **bulb**) **2** = a thin long part of the stamen that supports the anther in a flower [BOTANY]

filch /fɪltʃ/ verb, t. *Someone has filched my box of paints.* = to steal something of not very high value, secretly (informal)

file[1] /faɪl/ noun, c. **1** *a steel file* = a metal tool with a rough face, used for cutting away hard surfaces or making them smooth **2** = a folder made of stiff material in which papers on a subject can be arranged or clipped together **3** *a confidential file* = a collection of papers on a given subject kept together in a folder **4** *single file* = a line or row of people, one behind the other **5** = some information on a subject stored in a computer [COMPUTERS]

file[2] verb, t. **1** *I have to file this piece of wood before I can polish it.* = to make something smooth with the help of a file **2** *Let me file this report.* = to store in a file

fi•li•al /'fɪliəl/ adj. *The emperor built this monument in memory of his father, as a filial duty.* = relating to a son or daughter (literary)

fil•i•gree /'fɪlɪgriː/ noun, u. = fine threads produced from silver or gold which are used to make ornaments

filings /'faɪlɪŋs/ noun, c. *iron filings* = very fine pieces of metal, like dust, which are left behind when a metal surface is rubbed with a file

fill /fɪl/ verb, t or i. **1** *Fill this bottle with water.*(t.) = to put into a container or space as much as it will hold; to make full **2** *We have to fill this vacant post.*(t.) = to place someone in a position that is empty **3** *His eyes filled when I told him the sad story.*(i.) = to become full with tears

to fill up *Let us fill the tank up with petrol.* = to make completely full **to fill in** *You will have to fill in this application form.* = to complete or make entries in **to fill out** **1** *Have you filled out the form?* = to complete (same as **fill in**) **2** *He has really filled out.* = to become fat (informal) **to eat one's fill** *We have eaten our fill and can't have any more!* = as much as one requires or can take **to have one's fill of something** *I've had my fill of film songs.* = to have so much of something that one does not want any more of it

fil•let[1] /'fɪlɪt/ noun, c. *a fish fillet* = a piece of fish or meat from which the bones have been removed

fillet[2] verb, t. *I will have to fillet this fish.* = to remove the bones from

fil•ly /'fɪli/ noun, c. (**fillies**) = a young female horse (compare **colt**)

film[1] /fɪlm/ noun, u. or c. **1** *The water in the lake is covered with a film of oil.*(u.) = a thin layer of some material which forms a kind of skin, covering a surface **2** *I have loaded a roll of film in my camera as I want to take some photographs.*(u.) = a thin sheet of plastic material covered with chemicals which are sensitive to light and can be used to take photographs (photographic film) **3** *Have you seen the new film directed by Shyam Benegal?*(c.) = movie; a story or play recorded on film and meant to be shown in a cinema or on television

film[2] verb, t. *Ramanand Sagar and Sanjay Khan have filmed many epics for television.* = to produce a film for cinema or television **filmstar** = a well-known actor or actress in films **filmy** adj. *a filmy silk sari* = thin and translucent

fil•ter[1] /'fɪltə^r/ noun, c. **1** *a water-filter* = a device (machine) which removes impurities from liquids or gases which are passed through it **2** *colour filter* = lightly coloured glass used in photography to change the quality of light passing through it, so that special effects are achieved

filter[2] verb, t. *We will have to filter this water.* = to clean or make pure by passing through a filter

filth /fɪlθ/ noun, u. = dirty matter (derogatory)

fin /fɪn/ noun, c. **1** = a wing-like part on the back and sides of a fish which it uses to swim **2** = a flat, thin part that sticks out at the edge of an aircraft/vehicle, helping it to move faster

fi•nal[1] /'faɪnəl/ noun, c. *We are playing the final tomorrow.* = the last and most important match in a tournament

final[2] adj. *the final examination* = last; coming at the end **finalist** noun c. = one of the people or teams in the finals **finalize (finalise)** verb, t. *I have finalized the arrangements for my holiday.* = to complete and make certain **finally** adv. = lastly

fi•nance[1] /'faɪnæns/ noun, u. or c. **1** *I need some finance to start a new business.*(u.) = money used for running a business **2** *the Ministry of Finance* = the department that controls the money earned and spent by the government **3** (always plural) *the finances of the company* = the amount of money a company, government etc. is able to spend

finance[2] verb, t. *The bank has agreed to finance my business.* = to provide money for a business etc.

find[1] /faɪnd/ noun, c. *He is India's new batting find.* = something good that has been discovered (found) (informal)

F

find[2] verb, t. (**found**) **1** *Geologists have found oil under the Arabian Sea.* = to discover, especially by searching **2** *Did you find the gold ring which had been lost?* = to recover (get back) something which was lost **3** *I have always found him very helpful.* = to come to know something through experience

all found *He gets Rs 5,000 a month all found.* = including everything that one is supposed to get (referring to the money one is paid for work done)

fine[1] /faɪn/ noun, c. *You have to pay a fine of Rs 500.* = an amount of money paid as punishment

fine[2] verb, t. *You will be fined for breaking the law.* = to be made to pay a fine

fine[3] adj. **1** *This is a fine poem.* = of good quality **2** *We need some fine needles.* = very thin **3** *a fine difference between two things* = very hard to tell apart **4** *We are having fine weather.* = bright and sunny

fine[4] adv. *I will have to look at the book again to understand the fine points.* = difficult to notice or understand **fine arts** = music, painting, poetry etc. **finery** noun, u.= beautiful clothes and ornaments **fine tune** verb *The picture on the television screen is not clear. You will have to fine tune it.* = to make small adjustments that improve something

A fine thing to do! = an expression showing displeasure over some activity **to cut (something) very fine** = *Our train was to leave at 5.00, and we reached the station at 4.58. That was really cutting it fine.* = to allow very little time before some event (informal)

fin•ger /ˈfɪŋgəʳ/ noun, c. **1** = one of the five movable parts at the end of each hand **2** *a finger of land* = something that has the shape of a finger **fingerprint** noun, c. = the mark left by one's fingers, which can be used to find out who has committed a crime **fingertip** noun, c. = the part at the end of one's fingers

to have a finger in every pie = to have a part in everything that is going on **to keep one's fingers crossed** = to hope for the best **to have something at one's fingertips** *She has the facts at her fingertips.* = to have complete knowledge of something **to put one's finger on something** *You've put your finger on it!* = to place or identify something exactly (informal) **to have green fingers** = to have a talent for making plants grow **to not lift a finger** *There was so much work to do, but she did not lift a finger to help us.* = to not help even a little (disapproving) **to not lay a finger on someone** = to not harm or punish someone, especially by beating or hitting them **to burn one's fingers** = to experience failure or to suffer as a result of trying out a new idea, a new business venture etc. and consequently not want to try again **to let something slip through one's fingers** = to waste an opportunity by not doing anything about it **to give someone the finger** = to insult someone by showing them the back of your fist with the middle finger pointing upwards (informal) USE

fin•i•cky /ˈfɪnɪki/ adj. *You should not be so finicky about your food.* = caring too much about unimportant matters (**fastidious**) (disapproving)

fin•ish[1] /ˈfɪnɪʃ/ noun, u. **1** *The race had a close finish.* = end **2** *The marble statue is crude. It lacks finish.* = the quality that one finds in something that has been done with great skill

finish[2] verb, t. **1** *I have finished my homework.* = to complete or end **2** *The tailor has to finish the coat this evening.* = to do the last things needed to make something perfect or complete **3** *The food is finished.* = to be used up **4** *Please let me borrow your pen after you have finished with it.* = to have no further use for something

to be finished = to be very tired physically or emotionally (informal) **to finish with (something or someone)** *They are always quarrelling with me. I have finished with them.* = to not wish to continue a relationship (informal)

fi•nite /ˈfaɪnaɪt/ adj. *We can't go on spending money on this project. Our resources are finite.* = having a definite limit or size (opposite **infinite**)

fir /fɜːʳ/ noun = a kind of tall, straight tree that grows in cold countries

fire[1] /faɪəʳ/ noun, u. or c. **1** *The house is on fire.*(u.) = in flames **2** *Let us light a fire.*(c.) = burning wood or coal used to warm people or a house **3** *Our soldiers came under fire.* = shooting of bullets

fire[2] verb, t. **1** = to shoot bullets from a gun **2** *The potter fired the clay pots that she had made.* = to bake pots by putting them in a heated oven **3** *His brave words fired the crowd.* = to fill someone with strong feelings of anger or courage **4** *My colleague has been fired.* = to dismiss from service (informal) **fire brigade** noun, c. = a group of people whose job it is to put out harmful or dangerous fires **fire-engine** = a vehicle carrying equipment for putting out large fires **fireplace** noun, c. = a part of a room in a house where a fire can be lit to keep the room warm

fireplace

to catch fire = to start to burn from contact with a flame, etc. **to play with fire** = to do something dangerous **to come under fire** = to be blamed for something

firearm noun, c. = a gun that can be carried **firefly** noun, c. = an insect that gives out light from its body **fireproof** adj. = something that cannot be burnt or badly damaged by heat **fireworks** noun (always plural) = objects that are filled with special chemicals and give out bright coloured lights or produce a loud sound when the wick is lit (used on festivals and special occasions)

firm[1] adj. **1** *This house has been built on a firm foundation of rock.* = strong and solid **2** *He kept a firm grip on his father's arm.* = strong and sure **3** *My decision is firm.* = strong and not changing

firm[2] /fɜːm/ noun, c. *Our firm makes medicines.* = a business company

fir•ma•ment /'fɜːməmənt/ noun, u. = sky (literary)

first[1] /fɜːst/ noun. *He got a first in the examination.* = a first class (informal)

first[2] pron. *She was the first to sing.* = before all the others

first[3] adv. *Sit down first, and then we can talk.* = before other things happen

first[4] det. **1** *She was the first speaker.* = before anyone else **2** *This is my first visit to Delhi.* = something that never happened earlier **3** *The first years in a new job are the most difficult.* = at the beginning **4** *This is the first thing to remember when you are starting your work.* = most important **first aid** = treatment given to a person injured in an accident or suddenly taken ill, before professional medical help is available **first-class** *a first-class meal* = of the highest quality **first class** = the most expensive method of travel **first floor** **1** = the rooms in a building just above the ground level (in British English and more commonly used in India) **2** = the rooms at the ground level (American English, now becoming popular in India) **firsthand** *a firsthand report* = information given by someone directly involved in an incident **first name** *Mr Sinha's first name is Ramesh.* = the part of the name which comes first, before the surname **first-rate** *This is a first-rate book.* = of the highest quality (informal)

to be on first name terms with someone = to be very friendly with someone, so that you can address him/her by the first name **to put someone or something first** *In all matters, he puts his family first.* = to consider most important

fis•cal /'fɪskəl/ adj. *the government's fiscal policy* = having to do with public money, specially the taxes collected by the government

fish[1] /fɪʃ/ noun, u. or c. (**fish** or **fishes**) **1** *He caught several fish/we saw three little fishes.*(c.) = an animal that lives in water **2** *Would you like some more fish?*(u.) = the flesh of a fish, used as food

fish[2] verb, i. **1** *They were fishing in the river.* = to catch or try to catch fish **2** *He was fishing around inside the cupboard.* = to search for something (informal) **fisherman** noun = a person who catches fish for a living or as a hobby **fishy** adj. **1** *a fishy smell* = like that of a fish **2** *There is something fishy about this story.* = something that causes doubt or suspicion; dishonest (informal)

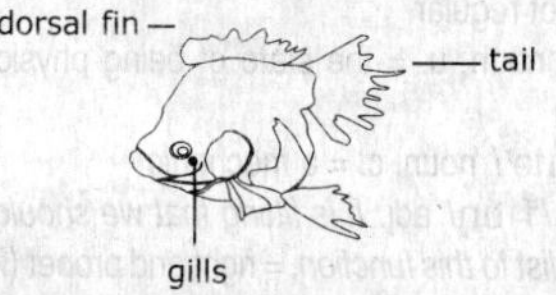

a cold fish = a person who is not friendly and does not show her/his feelings (derogatory) **to feel like a fish out of water** = to feel uncomfortable because one is in unfamiliar or unfriendly surroundings **to fish for compliments** = to try to make someone say something good about you **to fish in troubled waters** = to try to gain something from the troubles of other people **to fish out something** = to bring something out of its place after a search

fis•sion /'fɪʃən/ noun, u. *The first atom bomb made use of the fission of uranium atoms.* = the process of dividing or breaking up the central part (nucleus) of an atom into smaller parts (opposite **fusion**) [PHYSICS]

fis•sure /'fɪʃər/ noun, c. = a long deep crack in the earth

fist[1] /fɪst/ noun, c. *He clenched his fist.* = the shape of the hand with the fingers tightly clenched (closed)

fist[2] verb, t. *The goalkeeper fisted the ball away.* = to hit with one's fist **tight-fisted** adj. = a person who does not like to spend money; a miser

fit[1] /fɪt/ noun, u. **1** *This shirt has a nice fit.* = the way in which something fits a person's body **2** *She feels she is about to have a fit.* = a condition which causes a sudden violent, uncontrollable shaking of the body **3** *He screamed in a fit of anger.* = a violent feeling which does not last for a long time **4** *He had a fit when I told him what had happened.* = an outburst of anger

fit[2] verb, t. or i. **1** *These trousers don't fit (me). They are too tight.*(t.) = to be of the right size **2** *Your experience fits you for this job.*(t.) = to be suitable for a purpose **3** *They are fitting new locks to the doors.*(t.) = to put into place **4** *That piece fits here.*(i.) = to be in the correct position

fit[3] adj. **1** *This book is not fit to be published.* = suitable for a given purpose **2** *He is very fit, although he is 70.* = healthy and strong

by fits and starts *I study by fits and starts* = not regularly (informal) **to fit in** = to be accepted and be part of a social group **to fit the bill** = to be exactly what is required

fit•ful /'fɪtfʊl/ adj. *Her attendance in school has been fitful.* = not regular

fit•ness noun, u. = the state of being physically fit (healthy)

fit•ter /'fɪtəʳ/ noun, c. = a mechanic

fit•ting[1] /'fɪtɪŋ/ adj. *It is fitting that we should invite the novelist to this function.* = right and proper (formal)

fitting[2] noun (usually plural) = something that is fitted into a house/building after it has been built e.g. electrical fittings

five /faɪv/ noun = the number represented by *5* **fiver** noun, c. = a 5-rupee note or coin **five-star** *a five-star hotel* = of the highest quality **high fives** = the action of raising one's hand high, with the fingers open, to strike the open palm of a partner or teammate, to express joy at something good that happens in a match or game

fix[1] /fɪks/ noun, c. *We are in a fix. Can you help us?* = a difficult situation (informal)

fix[2] verb, t. **1** *The goalposts were fixed in place at the two ends of the football field.* = to put something firmly in place so that it cannot be moved or shaken **2** *His salary was fixed at Rs 1000 a month.* = decided finally **3** *I will have to fix the scooter, it is giving me some trouble.* = to repair (informal) **4** *The match has been fixed for next Monday.* = to arrange **5** *The match has been fixed.* = to make a dishonest arrangement by which the result of a match is decided before the match (informal) **6** *Is he giving you trouble? I'll fix him.* = to deal harshly with someone, as a kind of punishment

fix•a•tion /fɪk'seɪʃən/ noun, c. *a fixation about cleanliness* = a very strong, sometimes unhealthy, feeling about something [TECHNICAL]

fixed adj. *He works on a fixed salary.* = not changing

fix•ture /'fɪkstʃəʳ/ noun, c. **1** *The house will be rented out with all fittings and fixtures.* = something that is fitted into a building and is a necessary part of it **2** = a sporting event arranged for a particular day

fizz /fɪz/ noun, u. *All the fizz has gone from that bottle of lemonade.* = the bubbles of gas in a liquid

fiz•zle out /'fɪzəl aʊt/ verb, i. *The celebrations fizzled out completely.* = to come to a poor or weak end (informal)

flab•ber•gast /'flæbəgɑːst/ verb, t. (usually passive) *I was flabbergasted when I heard that your brother had left his job.* = to cause great surprise or shock (informal)

flab•by /'flæbi/ adj. = having too much of fat instead of muscle

flac•cid /'flæsɪd/ adj. *The plants are not growing properly. Their stems have become flaccid.* = soft and weak; not firm [TECHNICAL]

flag[1] /flæg/ noun, c. *the national flag* = a piece of cloth, usually rectangular in shape, with some pattern on it, fixed to a pole (the flagpole)

flag[2] verb, i. or t. (**flagged**) **1** *We are flagging as we have been working continuously for eight hours.*(i.) = to become tired and weak **2** *I have flagged this document so that you can find it easily when you are going through the file.* = to put a flag (a small piece of paper) on something so that it can be picked out easily from others

to flag something down *I flagged down a passing taxi.* = to stop a vehicle by waving at the driver **to keep the flag flying** = to bring honour to one's country while taking part in a contest etc.

fla•grant /'fleɪgrənt/ adj. *She was driving at 100 km an hour on a road where the speed limit is 40 km per hour. The police arrested her for this flagrant violation of the traffic rules.* = open and without shame or responsibility (formal)

flair /fleəʳ/ noun, u. *He has a flair for writing.* = a natural ability

flak /flæk/ noun, u. **1** *The enemy planes faced heavy flak as they flew in to attack the city.* = firing from guns that shoot from the ground at flying aircraft **2** *Our school had to face a lot of flak for changing the dates of the exams.* = criticism or opposition (informal)

flake /fleɪk/ noun, c. *corn flakes* = a light, flat piece of some material, shaped like a leaf

flam•boy•ant /flæm'bɔɪənt/ adj. **1** *He dresses in bright and flamboyant clothes.* = showy; attracting a lot of attention **2** = used to describe a person's personality, sometimes disapprovingly, when he/she is very loud and confident

flame[1] /fleɪm/ noun, c. or u. *the flame of the candle*(u.) = the burning gas rising from a fire, candle or lamp (see pic under **candle**)

flame[2] /fleɪm/ verb, i. *The candle is flaming brightly.* = to burn and give out light **flammable** /'flæməbəl/ adj. (American) = something which can be set on fire (compare **inflammable**) [TECHNICAL]

fla•min•go /flə'mɪŋgəʊ/ noun, c. (**flamingoes** or **flamingos**) = a tall waterbird with pink feathers and long thin legs

flange /flændʒ/ noun, c. = the raised edge of the flat wheel of a railway carriage, made in such a way that it will not run off the steel track on which it moves [TECHNICAL]

flank[1] /flæŋk/ noun, c. **1** = the side of an animal's body **2** *The enemy attacked the left flank of our army.* = one side of a moving army or a team (in games such as football)

flank[2] verb, t. *The buildings flank the road.* = to lie along one flank (side) of something

flan•nel /ˈflænəl/ noun, u. = soft woollen cloth with a slighty furry (hairy) surface

flap[1] /flæp/ noun, c. *the flap of an envelope* = a wide, flat part of something that is fixed on one side and hangs down and covers an opening

flap[2] verb, t. or i. *The bird is flapping its wings.*(t.) = (of wings) to move up and down in the air, making a sound

flare[1] /fleəʳ/ noun, c. **1** *the flare of a candle* = sudden brightening of light **2** *The sailors on the ship fired flares into the sky.* = a very bright light used by sailors or soldiers as a signal

flare[2] verb, i. *lanterns flaring brightly* = to burn brightly
to flare up *Trouble has flared up in the city.* = to start suddenly

flash[1] /flæʃ/ noun, c. (**flashes**) **1** *There was a flash of lightning.* = a sudden quick bright light **2** *a news flash* = a short news report received by radio, telephone etc. **3** *a photo flash* = a bright light used for taking photographs in the dark

flash[2] verb, i. or t. **1** *The lightning flashed suddenly.*(i.) = to shine for a short time **2** *Something flashed past my window.*(i.) = to move quickly **3** *We have flashed the news to New Delhi.*(t.) = to send a message by radio, telephone etc. **flasher** noun **1**= a light signal that goes off and on regularly **2** = a man with a sick mind who is in the habit of showing his private parts very quickly to others (slang) **flashback** noun, c. = a part of a cinema that goes back in time to show something that happened earlier [TECHNICAL] **flashlight** noun, c. = an electric torch **flashy** adj. *flashy clothes, flashy sports car* = very bright and colourful, attracting attention
in a flash = very quickly **a flash in the pan** = success that comes by a lucky chance

flask /flɑːsk/ noun, c. **1** = a container or bottle used for carrying liquids such as tea etc. (A **vaccum flask** keeps liquids hot or cold) **2** = a bottle used for mixing chemicals in a laboratory [CHEMISTRY]

flat[1] /flæt/ adj. **1** *a flat surface* = smooth and level **2** *a flat tyre* = without any air inside **3** *The story of the film is flat.* = dull and uninteresting **4** *The batteries are flat.* = without any electrical charge **5** *The drink is flat.* = not fresh; without bubbles **6** *We asked her if she would like to come on a trip with us and her answer was a flat no!* = very strong and not allowing any argument or discussion (informal)

flat[2] noun, c. *a three-roomed flat* = an apartment (set of rooms) **flat rate** = an amount that includes everything

flat•ter /ˈflætəʳ/ verb, t. **1** *Don't try to flatter me.* = to praise someone insincerely in order to please him/her **2** *I was very flattered that they liked my design the best.* = to feel happy because one has been praised or honoured **3** *This dress flatters you.* = to bring out the best in someone

flat•u•lence /ˈflætjʊləns/ noun, u. = gas in the stomach [MEDICINE]

flaunt /flɔːnt/ verb, t. *flaunt one's wealth* = to show publicly something that you think others will admire (derogatory)

fla•vour[1] /ˈfleɪvəʳ/ noun, c. **1** *ice cream with a chocolate flavour* = taste **2** *The film will give you a flavour of Hyderabad.* = an idea of the quality or character of a thing

flavour[2] verb, t. *You can flavour your cakes with chocolate.* = to give flavour (taste) to something **flavouring** noun, u. = something that is added to food to give it a special taste **flavour of the month** = a humorous way of refering to an item of fashion which does not last long

flaw[1] /flɔː/ noun, c. *The painting is beautiful but unfortunately there is a slight flaw in it.* = a small defect

flaw[2] verb, t. *The beauty of the finely carved table is flawed by the scratch on it.* = to spoil the perfect quality of something **flawless** adj. = without any defect; perfect

flea /flɪː/ noun, c. = a small insect without wings that sucks blood from animals and can spread disease among human beings

fleck /flek/ noun, c. **1** *a blue dress with white flecks* = a small mark **2** *a fleck of dust* = a small particle of something

fledg•ling /ˈfledʒlɪŋ/ noun, c. **1** = a very young bird that is just beginning to fly **2** *a fledgling poet* = a person who is just beginning a career

flee /fliː/ verb, i. or t. (**fled**) = to escape some danger by running away

fleece[1] /fliːs/ noun, u. = the wool growing on a sheep (literary)

fleece[2] verb, i. *Don't buy things in these shops. They fleece customers.* = to be cheated or asked to pay too much for something (informal)

fleet[1] /fliːt/ noun, c. **1** = a number of fighting ships which sail together, under a single commander **2** *a fleet of cars* = a large number of

fleet[2] adj. *a fleet runner* = very fast (also **fleet-footed**) **fleeting** adj. **1** *I have grown old with the fleeting years.* = passing quickly (literary) **2** *I caught only a fleeting glimpse of the film star.* = a brief look at someone who passes by quickly

flesh /fleʃ/ noun, u. the soft substance, including muscles and fat, that covers the bones and lies under the skin; meat **fleshy** adj. **1** *the fleshy part of the leg* = having many soft thick layers **2** = fat (humorous)
flesh and blood **1** *The pain is more than flesh and blood can bear* = human nature **2** *They are my own flesh*

F

and blood = relatives **in the flesh** *Have you seen Hema Malini, the actress, in the flesh.* = in reality (formal) **to make one's flesh creep** = to frighten **to flesh something out** = to make something (usually a piece of writing) longer by adding more details **flesh wound** = a wound that is not very deep

flex[1] /fleks/ verb, t. *I got up and flexed my limbs.* = to bend and move

flex[2] noun, c. *a length of flex* = electric wire

flexible adj. **1** *Metal wires are flexible, but wood is not.* = something that can be bent easily without breaking **2** *Our timings are flexible.* = something that can be changed easily to suit different conditions (opposite **inflexible**)

flick[1] /flɪk/ noun, c. *I brushed away the dirt with a flick of my fingers.* = a short, light movement

flick[2] verb, t. *The horse flicked the flies away with its tail.* = to strike lightly with a quick small movement

flicks noun, u. (always plural) *I am going to the flicks.* = a cinema show (slang)

flick•er[1] /ˈflɪkəʳ/ verb, i. *The candle flame flickered in the wind.* = to burn or shine unsteadily

flicker[2] noun, c. **1** *the flicker of a candle* = the weak, shaking light given out by a candle before it goes out **2** *I had a last flicker of hope.* = a feeling of hope, doubt etc. that stays for a short time (figurative)

flight /flaɪt/ noun, u. or c. **1** *I want to photograph an eagle in flight.*(u.)= the act of flying **2** *a flight of people from the city, trying to escape the heat wave*(c.) = the act of running away or escaping **3** *I am taking the next flight to Delhi.*(c.) = a journey in an aircraft **4** *a flight of ducks*(c.) = a number of birds flying together in a group **5** *a flight of stairs*(c.) = a set of stairs **flightless** adj. *The ostrich is a flightless bird.* = having no wings and therefore unable to fly [TECHNICAL]

flim•sy /ˈflɪmzi/ adj. **1** *flimsy material* = light and thin; not strong **2** *He gave us a flimsy excuse for not being able to attend the function.* = something that is hard to believe; not convincing

flinch /flɪntʃ/ verb, i. *The child flinched when his father raised a hand.* = to show fear or pain through one's expressions or movements

fling /flɪŋ/ verb, t. (**flung**) **1** *She flung the ball so hard that it hit the window and broke it.* = to throw with great force **2** *He flung himself on the bed.* = to throw carelessly and with great force

flint /flɪnt/ noun, u. or c. = a kind of hard stone which produces sparks when rubbed against a piece of steel or another stone and was used in former times to light fires

flip /flɪp/ verb, t. (**flipped**) **1** *The umpire flipped the coin in the air.* = to throw or toss something up into the air, so that it turns over again and again **2** *She flipped the pages of the book.* = to turn over

flip•pant /ˈflɪpənt/ adj. *You can't call this school a jail. We don't like such flippant remarks.* = trying to be light-hearted and funny when one is expected to be serious (derogatory)

flip•per /ˈflɪpəʳ/ noun, c. *the flippers of a whale* = the limb of a large sea-animal, such as a whale, used for swimming through the water

flirt /flɜːt/ verb, i. *I was not flirting with you, I was just being friendly.* = to act in a way that lets the other person know you find them sexually attractive

flit /flɪt/ verb, i. *The butterfly flits from one flower to another.* = to fly or move lightly and quickly

float[1] /fləʊt/ verb, i. or t. **1** *Cork floats on water.*(i.) = to stay at the top of a liquid without sinking below the surface **2** *The balloon floated through the air.*(i.) = to be carried by the wind without falling to the ground **3** *Children celebrate this festival by floating little boats on the water.* **4** *The ship sank in the sea last year but now they are trying to float it again.*(t.) = to cause something to float **5** *She has floated a new company.*(t.) = to start a new business

float[2] noun, c. *Fishermen use floats to keep their nets in place when they are fishing.* = a light object that floats on the water **floating** adj. *Mumbai has a large floating population.* = not fixed but moving in and out of a city, village etc.

flock[1] /flɒk/ noun, c. **1** *a flock of sheep* = a group of sheep, goats or birds **2** = a large crowd of people (informal)

flock[2] verb, i. *Thousands of birds flock around the lake in winter.* = to gather together

Birds of a feather flock together. = People with similar natures, interests etc. like to seek one another's company.

floe /fləʊ/ noun, c. (**floes**) *an ice floe* = a large mass of ice floating in the sea (compare **iceberg**)

flog /flɒg/ verb, t. = to punish by beating a person or animal with a whip or stick **flogging** noun = punishment given by beating with a whip or stick

to flog a dead horse = to waste one's time by trying to talk about something in which people are no longer interested

flood[1] /flʌd/ noun, u. or c. **1** *All the rivers are in flood.*(u.) = the presence of too much water in a river, causing it to flow over its banks **2** *We have received a flood of letters.*(c.) = a large number or amount (informal)

flood[2] verb, t. *The Gandak river floods hundreds of villages in Bihar every year after the rains.* = to cause a flood

floor[1] /flɔːʳ/ noun, c. **1** *There is a lot of dust on the floor.* = the surface on which one stands, inside a building **2** *My room is on the second floor of this* *building.* = level; storey **3** *the floor of the ocean* = the bottom-most part

floor[2] verb, t. **1** *His reply was so astonishing that I didn't know what to say. I was completely floored!* = to be at a loss for word's because of surprise, admiration etc. (informal) **2** *The new building has to be floored.* = to provide with a floor

to go through the floor **1** = to fall very low (of prices, etc.) **2** *When I started to speak, I couldn't remember what I wanted to say. I wanted to go through the floor!* = to feel deeply embarassed **to have the floor** = to have an opportunity to speak

flop[1] /flɒp/ noun, c. *The meeting proved to be a big flop.* = something that does not succeed; a failure (informal)

flop[2] verb, i. **1** *He was so tired that he just flopped into bed.* = to fall heavily; to collapse **2** *The new film has flopped.* = to be unsuccessful (informal)

floppy /ˈflɒpi/ adj. *floppy clothes* = soft and loose **floppy disk** noun, c. = a piece of soft plastic coated with a magnetic substance, on which information from a computer can be stored [COMPUTERS] (compare **hard disk**)

flo•ra /ˈflɔːrə/ noun, u. = plant life; the plants growing naturally in and around a place (compare **fauna**) [BIOLOGY]

flo•rid /ˈflɒrɪd/ adj. **1** *She writes in a florid style.* = highly decorative and trying to attract attention; flowery (derogatory) **2** *a florid complexion* = having a red face (often a sign of poor health)

florist /ˈflɒrɪst/ noun, c. = a person who sells flowers

flo•til•la /fləˈtɪlə/ noun, c. = a group of small ships or boats

flot•sam /ˈflɒtsəm/ noun, u. = the waste material floating about in the sea or washed up on the beach

flounce[1] /flaʊns/ noun, c. = a piece of cloth used to decorate a dress

flounce[2] verb, i. *I tried to explain the problem but he wasn't willing to listen and flounced out of the house.* = to rush away angrily (informal)

floun•der /ˈflaʊndəʳ/ verb, i. **1** *He did not know how to swim and floundered in the water until someone helped him out.* = to move helplessly and with difficulty through water, mud, snow etc. **2** *The speaker forgot what she had to say and started to flounder.* = to lose control while speaking or doing something requiring skill

flour /flaʊəʳ/ noun, u. = grain (wheat, rice etc.) in powdered form, used for making bread etc.

flour•ish[1] verb, i. or t. **1** *They are doing well. Their business is flourishing.*(i.) = to be successful or to grow in a healthy manner; to prosper **2** *He flourished his M.A. degree certificate in our faces.*(t.) = to hold in the hand and wave about with energy to indicate control, power etc.

flourish[2] /ˈflʌrɪʃ/ noun, c. *sign with a flourish* = a showy movement or gesture that attracts attention; a decorative curl made while writing

flout /flaʊt/ verb, t. *By not wearing uniform, you've flouted the rules of the school.* = to go against; to not accept

flow[1] /fləʊ/ noun, u. *the flow of blood from a wound* = the action or process of flowing

flow[2] verb, i. *The river flows past this town.* = to move smoothly as in a stream **flow chart** noun, c. = a kind of diagram (drawing) which explains the different steps that one has to go through to complete an action [TECHNICAL] (see pic under **chart**)

flow•er[1] /ˈflaʊəʳ/ noun, c. = the part of a plant, often brightly coloured, that produces seeds or fruit

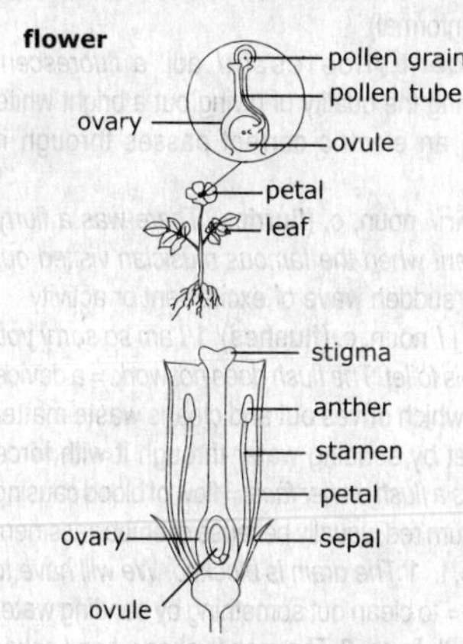

cross-section of a **flower**

flower[2] verb, i. **1** *The plants are beginning to flower.* = to produce flowers **2** *allow someone's talent to flower* = to develop (used of skill, personality etc.) **flowerbed** = an area in a garden where flowers are grown **flowerpot** noun, c. = a pot filled with earth, in which a plant can be grown

flow•er•y /ˈflaʊərɪ/ adj. *a flowery style* = a way of writing or speaking using rich and fanciful language (derogatory)

flu /fluː/ noun, u. = short form of **influenza** (a disease which causes cold and fever) (informal)

fluc•tu•ate /ˈflʌktʃueɪt/ verb, i. *The price of tea fluctuates. Last month it was Rs 200 a kilo but this month it has gone up to Rs 400.* = to rise or fall from time to time; to change

fluency /ˈfluːənsɪ/ noun, u. = the quality or skill of being fluent (see below)

flu•ent /ˈfluːənt/ adj. **1** *He is fluent in English as* *well as Hindi.* = able to speak and write well and easily **2** *She has a fluent style of singing.* = effortless and easy

fluff /flʌf/ noun, u. = soft and light waste material from cotton or wool that is often found floating in the air as dust

flu•id[1] /ˈfluːɪd/ noun, c. or u. *Petroleum is a fluid.* = liquid (compare **solid**)

fluid[2] adj. **1** *When hot steel is poured out of a furnace it is fluid, but later it becomes solid.* = having the form and qualities of a liquid **2** *Our plans for the future are still fluid.* = uncertain; not fixed

fluke /fluːk/ noun, c. *I am not a good tennis player, but I managed to win in straight sets by a fluke.* = a lucky chance (informal)

flum•mox /ˈflʌməks/ verb, t. *The interviewer asked me such a difficult question that I was flummoxed.* = to be unable to decide what to say or do; to be confused (informal)

flu•o•res•cent /flʊəˈresənt/ adj. *a fluorescent lamp* = having the quality of giving out a bright white light when an electric current passes through it [TECHNICAL]

flur•ry /ˈflʌri/ noun, c. (**flurries**) *There was a flurry of excitement when the famous musician visited our school.* = a sudden wave of excitement or activity

flush[1] /flʌʃ/ noun, c. (**flushes**) **1** *I am so sorry you can't use this toilet. The flush does not work.* = a device (machine) which drives out and cleans waste matter from a toilet by sending water through it with force **2** *There was a flush on her face.* = flow of blood causing the face to turn red, usually because of embarrassment

flush[2] verb, t. **1** *The drain is blocked. We will have to flush it out.* = to clean out something by sending water through it with force **2** *The man flushed when I asked him why he was late.* = to become red in the face due to a rush of blood, caused by anger, nervousness, pride etc.

flush[3] adj. **1** *The door is flush with the wall.* = exactly on the same level as something else **2** *The company is flush with money.* = having a lot of money which can be used (informal)

flus•ter /ˈflʌstəʳ/ verb, t. *People asked me so many questions at the meeting that I was flustered and unable to answer them.* = to make someone nervous and confused

flute /fluːt/ noun, c. = a musical instrument in the shape of a thin pipe (usually made of bamboo) with a number of holes, into which the musician blows air from the mouth

flut•ter[1] /ˈflʌtəʳ/ noun, u. or c. **1** *The actor's entry on the stage caused a flutter.*(u.) = a wave of excitement **2** *a flutter in the signal*(c.) = a brief break or weakening in force

flutter[2] verb, i. or t. **1** *The bird fluttered its wings.*(t.) = to move the wings up and down without flying **2** *The flag is fluttering in the breeze.*(i.) = to shake and wave backwards and forwards, up and down

flux /flʌks/ noun, u. *The school is moving to a new building and everything is in a state of flux.* = quick movement as a result of change

fly[1] /flaɪ/ (**flies**) noun, c. **1** = a kind of insect with wings **2** = the front opening in a pair of trousers, shorts, etc which is fastened with a zip or buttons

fly[2] verb, i. or t. (**flew, flown**) **1** *The bird can fly.*(i.) = to move through the air by using its wings **2** *She likes to fly kites.*(t.) = to cause something to move through the air **3** *The door flew open.* = to move quickly and with force **4** *They both flew into a temper.* = to become angry suddenly and quickly (informal) **5** *I am late for class. I must fly.* = run; move quickly (informal)

a fly in the ointment = something that spoils the pleasure of a happy occasion **to fly the flag** = to show that one is proud of one's country, one's workplace etc. (informal) **to fly off the handle** = to get very angry suddenly (informal) **to not hurt a fly** *He wouldn't hurt a fly.* = to be a very gentle, kind person **to fly by the seat of one's pants** = to manage a situation by making guesses and working on the basis of one's instincts or feelings rather than by being knowledgeable about it (informal, often disapproving) **to go fly a kite** = to go away (an expression of anger) (informal, disrespectful)

fly•ing[1] /ˈflaɪ-ɪŋ/ noun, u. *I love flying.* = the act of flying (travelling in an aircraft)

flying[2] adj. **1** *a flying bird* = moving through the air **2** *a flying visit* = a very short visit **3** *a flying start* = a very good beginning (informal) **flying doctor** = a doctor who visits patients in distant places by aircraft **flying fish** = a fish found in the Tropics, with winglike fins for moving fast through the air **flying saucer** noun = a mysterious flying object, which some people claim to have seen, shaped like a saucer (plate), carrying creatures from some other planet **flying squad** noun = a group of police officers who are always ready to go into action when needed **fly-leaf** noun, c. = an unprinted page at the beginning of a book **flyover** noun, c. = a bridge that allows one road to pass on top of another road **flywheel** noun, c. = a heavy wheel fitted to a machine that helps the machine to work at a steady speed because of its weight

to pass with flying colours = to do very well at an examination

foal /fəʊl/ noun, c. = a very young horse

foam[1] /fəʊm/ noun, u. *sea-waves covered with foam* = the bubbles seen on top of a liquid

foam[2] verb, i. *The sick cow was foaming at the mouth.*

= to produce foam **foam rubber** = soft rubber which is full of air-bubbles, used for making cushions etc.

fob /fɒb/ noun, c. = a short chain to which a pocket-watch is attached

to fob something off on someone = to cheat someone by selling them something which is worthless or of very little value (informal)

fo•cus[1] /ˈfəʊkəs/ noun, u. **1** = the point at which rays of light or sound meet after reflection or refraction [PHYSICS] **2** *The focus of the article was the importance of conserving our forests.* = the subject which receives greatest attention **3** *In this photograph you are out of focus.* = not clearly seen (in a photograph)

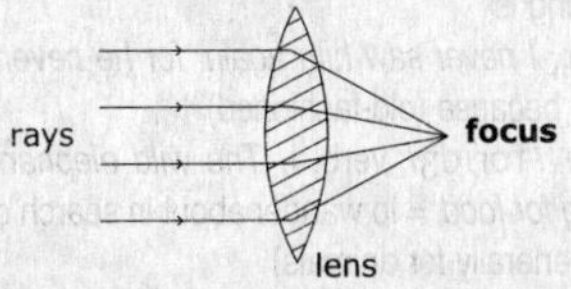

focus[2] verb, t. **1** *Please focus your camera on this building.* = to adjust the lens of a camera so that something is sharply seen in a photograph **2** *We are going to focus on the languages of India.* = to give special attention to

fod•der /ˈfɒdəʳ/ noun, u. = food for cattle, horses etc.

foe /fəʊ/ noun, c. = enemy (literary)

foe•tus (fetus) /ˈfiːtəs/ noun, c. = an unborn baby that is almost fully developed [MEDICINE] (compare **embryo**)

fog[1] /fɒg/ noun, u. = tiny drops of water hanging low in the air, which make it difficult to see clearly **foggy** adj. *We were not able to drive in the foggy weather.* = to not be clear because of fog

fog[2] verb, t. (**fogged**) *My glasses have become fogged. I can't see clearly.* = to become covered with tiny drops of water from the air

fo•gey /ˈfəʊgi/ noun, c. (**fogies**) *an old fogey* = a person with old-fashioned and fixed ideas (derogatory)

foi•ble /ˈfɔɪbəl/ noun, c. *My grandmother collects different kinds of dolls. This is her only foible.* = a strange habit or a weakness in one's character

foil[1] /fɔɪl/ noun, u. *If you wrap your food in aluminium foil you can keep it fresh.* = metal which has been beaten into very thin paper-like sheets

foil[2] verb, t. *Some thieves were trying to rob a bank but the police foiled their attempt.* = to cause someone to fail in doing something

foist /fɔɪst/ verb, t. **1** *If they don't want you in their party, you shouldn't foist yourself on them.* = to force someone to accept something against their wishes **2** *They foisted this damaged computer on me.* = to deceive someone by selling him or her something which is bad

fold[1] /fəʊld/ noun, c. **1** *The piece of paper is covered with folds.* = the lines made in paper or cloth by folding it **2** *a sheep fold* = a shelter for sheep or cattle

fold[2] verb, t. **1** *Fold this sheet of paper in the middle.* = to bend and press one part of something on another **2** *This is a folding chair. You can fold it up and carry it easily.* = to bend or close something so that it takes up less space **3** *The show folded up after a week.* = to close down suddenly (informal) **folder** noun, c. = a piece of cardboard that is folded to hold papers

to return to the fold = to come back to the place or the group to which one belongs

fo•li•age /ˈfəʊli-ɪdʒ/ noun, u. = the leaves of a plant or tree (formal)

folk[1] /fəʊk/ noun, u. or c. **1** *folk from a nearby village* (u.) = people belonging to the same place or country, who generally have the same lifestyle **2** *Good bye, folks!*(c.) = people (generally used for one's relations or friends) (informal)

folk[2] adj. *I love folk music.* = something that relates to a community or particular region and has existed for a long time **folklore** noun = the study of the habits, beliefs etc. of a group of people in earlier times

fol•lic•le /ˈfɒlɪkəl/ noun, c. = a small hole in the skin out of which a single hair grows [BIOLOGY]

fol•low /ˈfɒləʊ/ verb, t. or i. **1** *The letter 'B' follows the letter 'A'.*(t.) // *Lead, and I shall follow.*(i.) = to come after someone or something **2** *Please follow the lecture.*(t.) = to pay attention to something **3** *Can you follow what he is saying?*(t.) = to understand **4** *You should follow her advice.*(t.) = to accept **5** *We live in the same city but it does not follow that we speak the same language.*(i.) = to be a necessary result of something **follower** noun, c. = a person who supports another person, belief etc. **following** noun **1** = a group of supporters **2** *The following have been selected for the team.* = those who are about to be mentioned

fol•ly /ˈfɒli/ noun, u. or c. (**follies**) *You must suffer for your folly.*(u.) = foolishness (formal)

fo•ment /fəʊˈment/ verb, t. **1** *to foment trouble* = to cause or encourage a troublesome situation **2** *The doctor has asked me to foment my back with hot water as it is hurting.* = to apply heat to some part of the body to take away pain [MEDICINE]

fond /fɒnd/ adj. **1** *She is fond of sweets.* = to have a great liking for something **2** *fond parents* = affectionate

fon•dle /ˈfɒndl/ verb, t. = to touch gently in a loving or sexual way

font /fɒnt/ noun, c. *Use 10-point Courier font to type this document.* = the shape, size and style of the letters

F

used in printing something (also sometimes spelt **fount**) [TECHNICAL]

food /fuːd/ noun, u. or c. = something which is eaten **food-chain** = a series of plants and animals each dependent on the next for their food

fool[1] /fuːl/ noun, c. **1** = a person without understanding or sense; a stupid person **2** *a mango fool* = a sweet made with fruit and cream

fool[2] verb, t. or i. **1** *I thought you couldn't speak our language, but I find you can. You fooled us!* = to trick or mislead someone, sometimes in fun **2** *I was not serious when I said I would not come. I was only fooling.* = joking and not speaking seriously **foolish** adj. = without good sense **foolhardy** adj. = careless; taking unnecessary risks **foolproof** adj. = something which is so simple or clear or well-planned that it cannot go wrong **foolscap** noun, u. or adj. = writing paper of large size

to live in a fool's paradise = to believe that everything is all right when there are actually many problems

foot[1] /fʊt/ noun, c. (**feet**) **1** = the lowest part of the leg **2** *the foot of the hill* = the lowest part of something **3** = a length of 12 inches or 30.48 cm

foot
ankle
heel
toe
toenail

foot[2] verb, t. **1** *We will have to foot it back to the hostel.* = to walk (informal) **2** *Don't worry, I will foot the bill for this dinner.* = to pay for something (informal)

foot•age /ˈfʊtɪdʒ/ noun, u. = the amount of film that has been used to shoot something and is now to be used for broadcasting etc. [TECHNICAL] **football** noun, u. = a game played between two teams containing 11 players each, in which a leather ball is kicked across a field into a goal (see also **soccer**) **foothill** noun = a low hill at the bottom of a high mountain **footlights** noun (usually plural) = the row of lights along the front edge of a stage on which a play is being presented **footnote** noun, c. = a note at the bottom of a page in a book, explaining something or adding some information **footpath** noun, c. = a path, on either side of the main road, for pedestrians **footprint** noun, c. = a mark left by someone's foot or shoe on the ground **footwear** noun, u. = shoes etc. worn on the feet

foot-and-mouth disease = a serious disease which can attack cattle **to have both feet on the ground** = to act in a sensible manner and not have any wild ideas **to put one's foot down** = to use one's authority to stop something from happening **to put one's foot in one's mouth** = to say something which causes embarassment without one's intending it

fop /fɒp/ noun, c. = a man who takes too much interest in clothes and in his own appearance (derogatory)

for[1] /fəʳ/ or /fɔːʳ/ prep. **1** *Here is a piece of cake for you.* = showing that something is to be given to someone **2** *What is this switch for?* = showing the use of something or how it works **3** *Use this cream for lessening the pain.* = to help or make something less **4** *Are you for or against jogging?* = in support of something **5** *He was sent to China for some work.* = because of **6** *I bought this TV set for Rs 6,000.* = by giving a certain price **7** *I am going to America for 14 days.* = showing a length of time **8** *He slept for two hours.* = showing a distance/length of time **9** *She is very bold for her age.* = showing how unusual/difficult something is

for[2] conj. *I never saw him again, for he never came back.* = because (old-fashioned)

for•age /ˈfɒrɪdʒ/ verb, i. *The wild elephants are foraging for food.* = to wander about in search of food (used generally for animals)

for•ay /ˈfɒreɪ/ noun, c. *The film star likes to remember his foray into politics.* = an attempt to take up some activity different from what one does usually (formal)

for•bid /fəˈbɪd/ verb, t. (**forbade, forbidden**) *We were forbidden to go out by ourselves because we were not old enough.* = to order someone not to do something

force[1] /fɔːs/ noun, u. or c. **1** *I had to use force to break open the door.*(u.) = strength, power or violence **2** *the police force* (c.) = a group of people trained for a particular kind of work **3** = a power that causes movement or changes it (e.g. magnetic force)

force[2] verb, t. **1** *She forced the door open.* **2** *He forced me to keep still when we watched the mystery film.* = to use one's strength, power or influence to do something or make someone do something **3** *She forced herself to see the doctor though she didn't want to.* = to make oneself do something that one does not want to do **forceful** adj. *He made a forceful speech.* = powerful **forcible** adj. *a forcible attempt to enter the house* = using force

for•ceps /ˈfɔːseps/ noun, c. (always plural) = an instrument used by doctors to hold something firmly

ford /fɔːd/ noun, c. = a place where a river can be crossed on foot as the water is not very deep

fore- /fɔːʳ/ a prefix meaning **a.** before in time e.g. **forecast** noun, c. or verb, t. **1** *weather forecast*(noun, c.) = a statement made about something that is going to happen in the future **2** *I forecast a rise in the price of gold.*(verb, t.) = to tell what is going to happen in the future **b.** in front of e.g. **foreground** noun, c. or verb, t. **1** (noun, c.) = the front part of a scene in a picture or photograph (opposite **background**) **2** (verb, t.) = to make something look specially prominent or important

fore•arm /'fɔ:rɑ:m/ noun, c. = the lower part of the arm, from the wrist to the elbow

fore•father /'fɔ:ˌfɑ:ðəʳ/ noun, c. = a person from whom one is descended (a grandfather, great-grandfather etc.); (also **ancestor**)

fore•front /'fɔ:frʌnt/ noun, u. *She is always in the forefront of the fight against pollution.* = in a leading positions in front

fore•head /'fɒrɪd/ noun, c. = the front part of the face, above the eyes and below the hair

foreign /'fɒrɪn/ adj. **1** *a foreign language* = relating to a country that is not one's own **2** *A foreign body has got into his eye, causing redness.*= something that has entered inside the body but should not be there **foreigner** noun, c. = a person who belongs to a foreign country

fore•man /'fɔ:mən/ noun, c. = a person who leads a group of workers (also **foreperson**)

fore•most /'fɔ:məʊst/ adj. *the foremost university in the country* = the most important; leading

foren•sic /fə'rensɪk/ adj. *forensic medicine* = scientific methods used to find out more about a crime and how it was commited **forensic evidence/ material** = items such as blood, hair, finger prints, which provide information about a crime

fore•see /fɔ:'si:/ verb, t. *I don't foresee any problems in your visit to Delhi.* = to think of what is going to happen in the future **foreseeable** adj. *This city will keep on growing in the foreseeable future.* = as far as one can look into the future

fore•sha•dow /fɔ:'ʃædəʊ/ verb, t. *The death of 12 tigers in the zoo foreshadows the total destruction of our wildlife.* = to give an indication (sign) of what is going to happen in the future (formal)

fore•sight /'fɔ:saɪt/ noun, u. *He had the foresight to carry an umbrella with him.* = the wisdom to be prepared for the future

forest /'fɒrɪst/ noun, c. = a large piece of land covered with trees **forestry** noun = the science of planting and preserving (taking care of) forests

fore•stall /fɔ:'stɔ:l/ verb, t. *My neighbour wanted to buy this car but I forestalled him by buying it myself.* = to prevent someone from doing something by doing it first

fore•tell /fɔ:'tel/ verb, t. = to tell what is going to happen in the future

for•ever /fər'evəʳ/ adv. *I shall be your friend forever.* = for all time

fore•warn /fɔ:'wɔ:n/ veb, t. = to warn someone of coming danger

fore•word /'fɔ:wɜ:d/ noun, c. = a printed note at the beginning of a book which says something about the book

for•feit /'fɔ:fɪt/ verb, t. *Please return this hired bicycle by 10 o'clock tomorrow, otherwise you may have to forfeit the money you paid as a deposit.* = to give up something or have something taken away as the result of some wrong action (formal)

forge[1] /fɔ:dʒ/ noun, c. = a large fire in which metal objects are heated and shaped in a blacksmith's shop

forge[2] verb, t. **1** *The blacksmith is forging a sword.* = to make something by heating a piece of metal in a forge **2** *India is forging ahead in the field of information technology.* = to make quick progress **3** *They were arrested for trying to forge 100-rupee notes.* = to make a copy of something in order to cheat someone **forgery** noun, c. *She was arrested for forgery.* = the crime of copying something in order to cheat someone

for•get /fə'get/ verb, t. (**forgot**, **forgotten**) **1** *I forgot to return the book to the library.* = to fail to remember something **2** *Forget your troubles and be cheerful !* = to stop thinking about something

for•give /fə'gɪv/ verb, t. or i. (**forgave**, **forgiven**) = to give up the feeling of anger that one has against someone who has done you some harm **forgiveness** noun, u. = the act of forgiving someone

forgo /fɔ:'gəʊ/ (**forwent, forgone)** verb, t. *You will have to forgo your holiday to get the work completed in time.* = to give up something pleasant (formal)

fork[1] /fɔ:k/ noun, c. **1** = an instrument used to hold food and carry it to the mouth, having a handle at one end and two or more points at the other **2** *a fork in the road* = a place where something long (e.g. a tree, road or river) divides into two branches

fork[2] verb, i. *The road forks at this point.* = to divide into two parts or branches

for•lorn /fə'lɔ:n/ adj. *The child that had lost its mother had a forlorn look on its face.* = sad and lonely

form[1] /fɔ:m/ noun, u. or c. **1** *The building is circular in form.* = shape **2** *The hotel offers different forms of recreation.*(c.) = kind or type (of something) **3** *Fill in this form.*(c.) = a piece of printed paper with empty spaces in which information can be filled in

to be in good form = to be in a state of health and fitness

form[2] verb, t. **1** *The potter forms the clay into beautiful objects.* = to give shape to **2** *Rice and dal form the main ingredients of our diet.* = to make up

for•mal /'fɔ:məl/ adj. *You have to wear formal clothes for the party on Republic Day.* = ceremonial; according to accepted customs **formality** /fɔ:'mælɪti/ noun, c. (**formalities**) *You have to go through some formalities before you can start work in this office.* = an action done in keeping with some rules

for•ma•lin /'fɔ:mələn/ = a solution of formaldehyde

in water used to destroy bacteria and preserve specimens in a laboratory [CHEMISTRY]

for•mat[1] /ˈfɔːmæt/ noun, u. or c. **1** *The format for the new book has been decided.* = the size and shape in which a book, magazine etc. is produced **2** *Do you like the format of the new television show?* = the arrangement or general plan of something

format[2] verb, t. *I will have to format this file.* = to arrange something in a particular manner so that information can be stored in it [COMPUTERS]

for•ma•tion /fɒˈmeɪʃən/ noun, u. **1** *formation of lines.* = shaping or making **2** *The birds are flying in a v-formation.* = arrangement

for•mer /ˈfɔːməʳ/ adj. **1** *These things were done in former times but are not done now.* **2** *He is the former Principal of this school.* = earlier but not at present **3** *Mr Sinha and Mr Mishra have arrived. The former (Mr Sinha) is a lawyer while the latter (Mr Mishra) is an engineer.* = the person or thing that was referred to earlier (compare **latter**)

for•mi•da•ble /ˈfɔːmɪdəbəl/ adj. **1** *a formidable problem* = causing fear, anxiety etc. **2** *The other team had a formidable record. We have to be prepared for a tough game.* = difficult to defeat or deal with

for•mula /ˈfɔːmjʊlə/ noun, c. (**formulas** or **formulae**) **1** = a general law or fact that is expressed in a short form by a group of letters, numbers etc. **2** = a way of showing how elements combine to form a chemical compound [CHEMISTRY] **3** *Have you learnt the secret formula for making this drink?* = a set of instructions for doing or making something

for•sake /fəˈseɪk/ verb, t. (**forsook, forsaken**) = to desert; to leave or give up someone that one is supposed to take care of (old fashioned)

for•swear /fɔːˈsweəʳ/ verb, t. (**foreswore, foresworn**) *I hear you have foresworn fast driving.* = to make a promise to give up or stop doing something

fort /fɔːt/ noun, c. = a strongly made building used for the defence of a city (in former times) **fortress** noun, c. (**fortresses**) = a large fort **fortify** verb, t. *Our defences have been fortified.* = to make something stronger

forte /ˈfɔːtɪ/ noun (usually u.) *She is not very good at English. Marathi is her forte.* = something that one is specially good at

forth /fɔːθ/ adv. *He went forth to win fame as a singer.* = forward; out into the world (literary) **forthcoming** adj. **1** *Wait for our forthcoming publication.* = expected in the near future **2** *I asked several people to help, but no volunteer was forthcoming.* = ready **forthright** adj. *She is honest and forthright, but some people may find her rude.* = straightforward; expressing one's thoughts and feelings openly

forthwith adv. *Please go there forthwith. It's an emergency.* = at once, without delay [LITERARY]

for•ti•tude /ˈfɔːtɪtjuːd/ noun, u. = the courage to bear pain or face difficulties without complaining

fort•night /ˈfɔːtnaɪt/ noun, c. = a period of two weeks (14 days) **fortnightly** adj. or adv. = once every fortnight

for•tu•i•tous /fɔːˈtjuːɪtəs/ adj. **1** *My meeting with Komal was entirely fortuitous, I wasn't expecting to see him.* = happening by chance; accidental (formal) **2** *It was fortutious that we didn't sell our house last year.* = lucky

for•tune /ˈfɔːtʃʊn/ noun, u. or c. **1** *She had the good fortune to be born in a family of poets.* = luck **2** *He made a fortune by selling paper toys.* = a lot of wealth **fortune-teller** = a person who can make a prediction of what will happen in the future **fortunate** adj. *I was fortunate in having good teachers.* = having good luck

forty /ˈfɔːti/ noun = the number represented by 40 (4x10) **forty winks** noun = a short nap (sleep) taken in the afternoon (humorous)

fo•rum /ˈfɔːrəm/ noun, c. (**forums** or **fora**) *This newsletter provides a forum in which students can discuss their problems.* = a place where public matters can be raised or discussed; a meeting held to discuss problems

for•ward[1] /ˈfɔːwəd/ adv. **1** *We will march forward.* = ahead **2** *She brought forward some new arguments.* = into a prominent place

forward[2] adj. *a very forward way of thinking* = advanced in development, ahead of its time (compare **backward**)

for•ward[3] verb *I will forward your letter to the editor.* = to send a letter, e-mail etc. from one address to another

fos•sil /ˈfɒsəl/ noun, c. **1** = a part of a plant or animal that lived very long ago, which has become hard like a rock **2** = a person with very old-fashioned ideas (humorous) **fossil fuel** = a substance found inside the earth, such as coal or petroleum, which is formed from a plant or animal that lived long ago, and can be burnt **fossilize** verb, i. = to become a fossil

fos•ter /ˈfɒstəʳ/ verb, t. *The Sahitya Akademi was set up to foster the growth of Indian literature.* = to encourage something to grow or develop; to promote **foster-parents** = people who look after someone else's child and bring it up as their own

foul[1] /faʊl/ noun, c. *The referee declared a foul.* = an action that is against the rules, in the sport of football, boxing etc.

foul[2] verb, t. *Factories must not foul the air.* = to make something dirty or impure

foul[3] adj. **1** *a foul smell* = bad; unpleasant **2** *foul weather* = stormy

found /faʊnd/ verb, t. (**founded**) **1** *This university was founded in 1857.* = to start or set up something; to establish **2** *This film is founded on a real-life story.*= based on **foundation** /faʊn'deɪʃən/ noun, u. or c. **1** *The foundation of this university took place in 1857.*(u.)= the act of starting something **2** *A good foundation in maths is necessary for studying economics.* = that on which something is based **3** (always plural) *This house has solid foundations.*(c.) = the part of a building, below the ground, which supports or holds it up **4** *foundation cream* = a cream that is used as a base upon which other cosmetics are applied **5** *The Fulbright Foundation* = an organisation, often named after the founder, that runs and supports projects, and gives out money for special purposes **founder** /'faʊndər/ noun, c. = a person who starts or sets up something

foun•dry /'faʊndri/ noun, c. (**foundries**) = a place where metal is melted down and poured into moulds (different shapes) to make different objects or parts for machines

foun•tain /'faʊntɪn/ noun, c.**1** = a device (arrangement) used in gardens, parks etc. that causes a stream of water to shoot up with force **2** *There was a fountain of sparks when the display of fireworks began.* = the pattern which is formed when something is thrown into the air with force **fountain pen** = a writing instrument which holds ink inside its body and allows it to flow slowly down into a metal nib

four /fɔːr/ noun = the number represented by 4 **four-letter word** = a word, often consisting of four letters, that is not used in polite conversation **foursome** = a group of four people who get together to play some game requiring four players

four•teen /fɔː'tiːn/ noun = the number represented by 14 (4+10)

fowl /faʊl/ noun, c. = a bird (especially chicken) that can be eaten

fox[1] /fɒks/ noun, c. (**foxes**) = a wild animal like a small dog, said to be very clever, which was hunted by people on horseback in former times

fox[2] verb, t. **1** *He foxed me into giving him a loan.* = to trick or deceive mildly (informal) **2** *I was foxed by this question.* = to be puzzled (unable to understand) (informal)

foy•er /'fɔɪeɪ/ noun, c. = the large, high entrance hall to a hotel or cinema building

frac•as /'frækɑː/ noun = a noisy quarrel in which many people take part, sometimes leading to a fight (formal)

frac•tion /'frækʃən/ noun, c. **1** = a number which is less than 1 or a part of 1 (e.g. 2/3) **2** *These lovely paintings are only a fraction of the collection they have in the studio.* = a small part

frac•ture[1] /'fræktʃər/ noun, c. *I have a fracture in my leg.* = the breaking of a bone in the body

fracture[2] verb, t. *He has fractured his arm.* = to break a bone in the body

fra•gile /'frædʒaɪl/ adj. **1** *a fragile china cup* = something that can break easily and needs to be handled with great care **2** *fragile health* = delicate and weak

frag•ment[1] /'frægmənt/ noun, c. *The glass bowl dropped from my hand and shattered into fragments.* = a small piece into which something breaks

fragment[2] verb, t. *Some of the states are being broken up and this may fragment the whole country.* = to divide or break up into smaller parts **fragmentation** /frægmən'teɪʃən/ noun, u. = the process of breaking up something into small parts **fragmentary** adj. = forming a part of something larger

frag•rance /'freɪgrəns/ noun, u. *the fragrance of roses* = an attractive or pleasant smell **fragrant** adj.

frail /freɪl/ adj. *He is very frail after his illness.* = weak and delicate **frailty** noun, c. or u. **1** (u.) = the condition of being frail **2** *One of his frailities is anger.*(c.) = a weakness in one's character

frame[1] /freɪm/ noun, c. **1** *a photo frame* = a border or case which surrounds something **2** *the bicycle frame* = the part which supports something and around which it is built **3** *He has a strong frame.* = body

frame[2] verb, t. **1** *You will have to frame this picture.* = to put a frame (border) around something **2** *Frame a sentence using the word "anxious"* = to make or produce **3** *The man is not guilty of this crime but has been framed by his neighbours.* = to produce false proof to show that someone is guilty of a crime (informal) **framework** noun, c. *This is the framework of the wooden shed.* = the structure that offers the basic support

franc /fræŋk/ noun = a unit of money used in France, Belgium and Switzerland

fran•chise[1] /'fræntʃaɪz/ noun, u. or c. **1** *adult franchise*(u.) = the right to vote **2** *They hold a franchise for an American company that makes shoes.*(c.) = a special right given by a company to someone to sell the goods made by it, using the name of that company

franchise[2] verb, t. *We are going to franchise people to sell our products.*(t.) = to give someone a franchise

frank /fræŋk/ adj. *a frank discussion* = free and open; direct and truthful

fran•tic /'fræntɪk/ adj. *She was making frantic efforts* *to attract our attention but we were busy talking.* = very anxious; excited

fra•ter•nal /frəˈtɜːnəl/ adj. *fraternal feelings* = like that of a brother; brotherly **fraternity** noun, c. (**fraternities**) *a fraternity of doctors* = brotherhood; an association of people with common interests or a common profession

fraud /frɔːd/ noun, u. or c.**1** = the crime of cheating someone **2** = a person who cheats others or pretends to be what he or she is not

fraught /frɔːt/ adj. *fraught with danger* = full of

fray[1] /freɪ/ noun, c. *He loves to join a fray.* = a quarrel or fight (literary)

fray[2] verb, t. *My shirt has become frayed with use.* = to become worn out

freak[1] /friːk/ noun, c. *Our cow gave birth to a freak—a calf with six legs.* = something unnatural

freak[2] adj. *We had freak rains last night. It never rains at this time of the year.* = unusual or unnatural

freckle /ˈfrekəl/ noun, c. = a small brown mark on the face or skin

free[1] /friː/ adj. **1** *You are free to go.* = able to do as one wishes; not under the control of someone else **2** *Are you free now ?* = not busy **3** *Admission to the park is free.* = without cost **4** *The bathroom is free now.* = not in use **5** *The dancer's movements are very free.* = natural; graceful **6** *Please don't touch the free end of the wire.* = the part which is loose, unattached

free[2] verb, t. **1** *We have been asked to free the prisoner.* = to make someone free **2** *My friend freed me from having to cook for nine people.* = to allow someone not to do something that he/she is unwilling to do **free of charge** *You have to pay for the room, but the food is free of charge.* = that which one does not have to pay for **free enterprise** = business in which there are not many trade controls, specially by the government **free kick or throw** = a chance to kick or throw the ball (in football or basketball) given to one team when some player in the other team breaks a rule **free speech** = a situation (in a country) when one is allowed to speak out one's thoughts or beliefs without fear of the law

of one's own free will = doing whatever one wants to do **to make free with something** *He made free with my bicycle.* = to use something without permission or without looking after it well (disapproving) **to free up (space)** *If we move this cupboard, we can free up some space for the chairs.* = make (space etc.) available by moving something

-free /ˈfriː/ suffix (added to a noun) meaning 'something which does not contain a certain substance' e.g. *caffeine-free, pollution-free* = not having caffeine, conditions of pollution etc.

free•bie /ˈfribi/ noun, c. (**freebies**)= something you get free when you buy something else (informal, American)

free•dom /ˈfriːdəm/ noun, u.or c. **1** *India won its freedom in 1947.* = the state of being free and not governed by an outside power **2** *freedom from hunger, anxiety etc.* = the absence of something unpleasant **3** *They give their children a lot of freedom.* = When one has freedom, one can do what one wants. **freedom (of speech** etc.) = the freedom to do something without the control of the government, or some other institution **freedom fighter** = a person who takes part in a movement to free her/his country from being ruled by another country

freehand /ˈfriːhænd/ adj. = a drawing done without the help of any instruments **freehold** /ˈfriːhəʊld/ noun = land which one is allowed to own without any conditions or time limit

freelance /ˈfriːlɑːns/ noun or adj. = a person who works (e.g. as a writer or journalist) for anyone who pays/him her and not for a single employer

freeze[1] /friːz/ (**froze**, **frozen**) noun. **1** = to change from water into ice **2** *The meat has been frozen.* = to preserve food by keeping it at very low temperature **3** *There is a freeze on admissions.* = a fixing or control of something by an organisation (informal)

freeze[2] verb, t. (**froze**, **frozen**) **1** *The photographer froze when she saw a tiger about to jump at her.* = to be unable to move out of fear or surprise **2** *The prices of foodgrains have been frozen.* = fixed at a certain level by the government **freezer** noun, c. = a machine in which food can be stored at a very low temperature **freezing point** noun, u. = the temperature (0ºC) at which water turns into ice (compare **boiling point**)

freight /freɪt/ noun, u. **1** = goods carried by railways, trucks etc. **2** = the money paid for carrying goods

French[1] noun **1** = the language spoken in France and related countries **2** = the people of France

French[2] adj. *French wine, cheese etc.* = made in or in the style of France

fre•net•ic /frɪˈnetɪk/ adj.**1** *frenetic with joy* = highly excited **2** *work at a frenetic pace* = done with great speed and energy (informal)

fren•zy /ˈfrenzi/ noun, c. *The football players got into a frenzy before the match.* = a state of great excitement or anxiety

fre•quent /ˈfriːkwənt/ adj. *frequent attacks of malaria* = happening often or repeatedly **frequency** noun, u. or c. **1** *The frequency of accidents on this road has gone up.* = the rate at which something happens or is repeated **2** *The radio signals are sent out at very high frequency.* = the rate at which something is repeated (e.g. oscillations of a pendulum) [TECHNICAL, PHYSICS]

fres•co /ˈfreskəʊ/ noun, c. (**frescos**) = a painting done on a wall

fresh /freʃ/ adj. **1** *fresh fruit* = food that has just been gathered and is in good condition; not frozen or tinned **2** *fresh water* = not containing salt **3** *fresh air* = pure **4** *Our players are fresh.* = not tired; in good physical condition **5** *The teacher seems to be quite fresh.* = new to a profession **6** *Don't get fresh with me!* = too free with someone of the opposite sex (informal, disapproving)

fret /fret/ verb, i. *Don't fret. Everything will be all right.* = to worry without reason

fretsaw /ˈfretsɔː/ noun, c. = an instrument used for cutting out pieces from a thin sheet of wood so as to produce an ornamental design (fretwork)

fric•tion /ˈfrɪkʃən/ noun, u. **1** *There is friction between the road and the wheels of a car.* = the natural force that makes it difficult for things to move freely over or through each other [PHYSICS] **2** *The rope has become worn out because of friction.* = rubbing **3** *There is some friction between the two groups.* = bad feeling or enmity

Fri•day /ˈfraɪdi/ noun = the sixth day of the week, between Thursday and Saturday

fridge /frɪdʒ/ noun, c. = short form of **refrigerator** (a machine which keeps food at a low temperature in order to preserve it)

friend /frend/ noun, c.= a person whom one knows well and likes, but who may not be a relative **friendly** adj. *a friendly person* = pleasant and welcoming in the way a friend would be (opposite **unfriendly**)

-friendly suffix (added to a noun) meaning 'something which supports or encourages someone' e.g. *user-friendly software* = that which helps or supports the user

friendship noun, u. or c. *No one can destroy our friendship.* = the state of being a friend to someone

fri•gate /ˈfrɪgɪt/ noun, c. = a small, fast fighting-ship

fright /fraɪt/ noun, u. *He gave me a fright by suddenly shouting in my ear.* = a feeling of fear (not very great) **frighten** verb, t. = to cause a feeling of fear in someone

fri•gid /ˈfrɪdʒɪd/ adj. **1** *a frigid expression* = not friendly or enthusiastic, very formal **2** = unable to enjoy sex (generally referring to women)

frill /frɪl/ noun, c. **1** *a dress with frills* = a decorative edge or border for a dress **2** *I just want a scooter that moves—no frills.* = something that is not necessary but adds to the beauty

fringe /frɪndʒ/ noun, c. **1** *a fringe of hair* = a straight, short border of hair over one's forehead or threads hanging from curtains etc. **2** *We have a small house on the fringes of the town.* = the edge; the part farthest from the centre **fringe benefits** noun = the extra advantages that one gets from working in a certain position, in addition to the salary **fringe group** noun = a small group that has broken away from the main party

frisk /frɪsk/ verb, t. **1** *The security staff have to frisk all passengers before allowing them to enter the aircraft.* = to search someone for hidden weapons, etc. by passing one's hands over the body **2** *The rabbits are frisking about happily.* = to run and jump about playfully

frit•ter /ˈfrɪtəʳ/ verb, t. *Don't fritter away all your energy on such useless activities.* = to waste (derogatory)

friv•o•lous /ˈfrɪvələs/ adj. *The interviewer asked you a serious question. You should not have given her such a frivolous reply.* = light-hearted and silly; not serious (derogatory)

fro /frəʊ/ (**walking to and fro**) adv. = from one place to another and back (old-fashioned)

frock /frɒk/ noun, c. = a dress for a young girl or a priest

frog /frɒg/ noun, c. = a small hairless animal that lives in the water as well as on land (compare **toad**)

frogman noun, c. = an expert diver who can remain and move about under water for a long time with the help of special equipment

frolic[1] /ˈfrɒlɪk/ verb, i. *The children frolicked in the playground.* = to play happily

frolic[2] /ˈfrɒlɪk/ noun, c. (**frolicked**) *The children are having a frolic.* = game

from /frəm/ or /frʌm/ prep. **1** *This is the train from Delhi.* = starting at **2** *This is a letter from my father.* = sent or given by **3** *Chapatis are made from whole wheat.* = out of **4** *The school is five km from the station.* = showing distance **5** *She suffers from asthma.* = because of **6** *The price range is from Rs 60 to 80.* = to show the point at which something (price, figure etc.) starts

frond /frɒnd/ noun, c. = the leaf of a palm tree

front[1] /frʌnt/ noun, u. **1** *This is the front of the building.* = the most forward part **2** *Our soldiers are going to the front.* = the place where fighting is taking place **3** *We must put on a brave front.* = appearance

front[2] adj *Two of her front teeth were removed.* = of or at the front

up front *When we decided to buy the house, we paid the owner a part of the money up front.* = to make an advance payment as an indication that one is definitely interested in something

fron•tier /ˈfrʌntɪəʳ/ noun, c. *the frontier between India and Pakistan* = the line joining two countries

F

frost[1] /frɒst/ noun, u. = little particles of ice formed on cold surfaces at very low temperatures (below 0ºC) e.g. inside a refrigerator

frost[2] verb, i. *The windows are frosted up.* = to get covered with frost **frostbite** noun, u. = swelling of a person's limbs because of extreme cold temperature

froth /frɒθ/ noun, u. = the bubbles formed on top of sea-waves or liquids (e.g. beer) (see also **foam**)

frown[1] /fraʊn/ verb, i. = to draw the eyebrows together, causing lines to appear on the forehead, to show anger or displeasure

frown[2] noun, c. = the expression of anger or displeasure through the act of frowning

fru•gal /'fru:gəl/ adj. *a person of frugal habits* = careful about spending money; economical, simple

fruit[1] /fru:t/ noun, c. (**fruits** or **fruit**) or u. **1** (c.) = the part of a plant or tree which contains its seeds and is often used as food **2** *This is the fruit of your labours.*(u.) = result

fruit[2] verb, i. *The tree has begun to fruit.* = to produce fruit **fruitful** adj. = producing good results (opposite **fruitless**)

frus•trate /frʌ'streɪt/ verb, t. **1** *We had planned to go on a picnic, but the bad weather has frustrated our plans.* = to defeat; to prevent something from being fulfilled **2** *The film show has been cancelled three times. I feel so frustrated!* = to cause someone to feel disappointed or dissatisfied

fry /fraɪ/ verb, t. = to cook something in hot oil

fudge /fʌdʒ/ noun, u. = a kind of soft sweet

fuel[1] /'fju:əl/ noun, u. or c. = something that can be burnt to produce heat and energy

fuel[2] verb, t. *Our economy is fuelled by exports.* = to provide fuel for; to provide the power that makes something work (figurative)

fu•gi•tive /'fju:dʒɪtɪv/ noun, c. = a person who is trying to escape or run away from the police or some danger

ful•crum /'fʊlkrəm/ noun, c. = the support on which a lever moves [TECHNICAL]

ful•fil /fʊl'fɪl/ verb, t. **1** *I have fulfilled my promise.* = to complete or carry out **2** *I have fulfilled my ambition.* = to achieve **3** *This hospital fulfills a great need.* = to meet or satisfy

full /fʊl/ adj. **1** *The bottle is full.* =holding as much as something can **2** *Her answers were full of mistakes.* = having a lot of something **3** *I want a full report on the function.* = not leaving any details out **4** *She ran at full speed.* = the maximum possible **full-blown** *He has full blown measles.* = the worst or most developed form **full-length** *This is a full-length film.* = as compared to a short film (less than 90 mins) **full stop** = a mark that shows the end of a sentence **full-time** adj. or adv. *He is a full-time student.* = for the regular number of hours (opposite **part-time**) **fulltime** noun, u. = the end of the time set for a match e.g. football

fum•ble /'fʌmbəl/ verb, i. **1** *The speaker was fumbling for words.* = to search for something in a clumsy manner **2** *The fielder fumbled with the ball and dropped the catch.* = to handle something without skill

fume[1] /fju:m/ noun, c. (usually plural) *The room was full of tobacco fumes.* = heavy and strong-smelling gas given out by something that is burning and can be dangerous if inhaled

fume[2] verb, i. *He was fuming with rage because he had not been invited to speak.* = to be very angry (informal)

fu•mi•gate /'fju:mɪgeɪt/ verb, t. *You should fumigate this room regularly to get rid of the germs.* = to clear a room of harmful bacteria by using some chemical which produces smoke or gas

fun[1] /fʌn/ noun, u. *We had great fun at the picnic.* = enjoyment or pleasure

fun[2] adj. *She is a fun person.* = someone with whom one can enjoy themselves (slang) **funny** adj. **1** *Let me tell you a funny joke.* = amusing, humorous; something that makes one laugh **2** *A funny thing happened as I was coming to school.* = strange, unexpected

func•tion[1] /'fʌŋkʃən/ noun, u. or c. **1** *The function of the censors is to make sure that a film is suitable for the audience.* = the duty given to someone **2** *We had a function at school today. Many guests were invited.* = a special event at which many people are present

function[2] verb, i. *The computer is not functioning.* = to work (formal)

fund[1] /fʌnd/ noun, c. *We have started a fund for retired teachers.* = a sum of money set apart for some special purpose

fund[2] verb, t. *The government will fund this project.* = to provide money for some activity

fun•da•men•tal[1] /fʌndə'mentl/ adj. *The system of education needs some fundamental changes.* = deep; basic; producing an effect on the complete nature of something

fundamental[2] noun (generally plural) *If you want to become a musician you will have to first learn the fundamentals of music.* = the first things; the rules or principles on which something is based **fundamental rights** = the rights which are given to every citizen of a country **fundamentalist** noun = a person who believes that the rules of a religion must be followed exactly

fu•ne•ral /ˈfjuːnərəl/ noun, u. or c. = a religious ceremony at which a dead person is buried or cremated (burnt) **funereal** /fjuːˈnɪːrɪəl/ adj. = sad; relating to a funeral (literary)

fun•gus /ˈfʌngəs/ noun, c. (**fungi** or **funguses**) or u. = a kind of plant that is not green and is without flowers or leaves (e.g. a mushroom) (Some fungi may be harmful.)

fun•nel[1] /ˈfʌnəl/ noun, c. **1** = an object in the shape of a tube which is wide and round at the top and narrow at the bottom, used for pouring liquids into vessels with narrow mouths (see pic under **laboratory equipment**) **2** *the funnel of a ship* = a long metal chimney through which smoke comes out of the engine that drives a ship

funnel[2] verb, t. *All the money is being funnelled into cricket. There is nothing left for other games.* = to pour into something; to use only for a limited purpose

fur /fɜːʳ/ noun, u. = the thick hair that covers the skin of some animals **furry** adj. = having a lot of fur

fur•bish /ˈfɜːbɪʃ/ verb, t. *The house is being furbished and a lot of new furniture has been bought.* = to improve the appearance of something that is old and worn-out

furl /fɜːl/ verb, t. *The umbrella is furled after it has been used.* = to roll up or fold (opposite **unfurl**)

fur•long /ˈfɜːlɒŋ/ noun, c. = a measure of distance, equal to 220 yards (210)

fur•nace /ˈfɜːnɪs/ noun, c. = a place or container in a factory or steam engine where a fire is kept burning at very high temperature, in which metals and other substances are heated

fur•ni•ture /ˈfɜːnɪtʃəʳ/ noun, u. (always singular) = beds, tables, chairs, cupboards etc. that are needed to make a house comfortable

fur•nish /ˈfɜːnɪʃ/ verb, t. **1** *You will have to furnish the new house before you can move in.* = to provide furniture for a building **2** *Can you furnish us with all the information we need?* = to supply or provide

fu•ro•re /fjʊˈrɔːri/ noun, u. *There was a furore when the umpire declared the batsman out.* = anger and excitement among a crowd

fur•row /ˈfʌrəʊ/ noun, c. = a long, narrow mark or cut in the earth made by a plough

fur•ther[1] /ˈfɜːðəʳ/ adv. *Delhi is further away from Kolkata than Lucknow.* = more far

further[2] adj. *I have nothing further to say.* = more

further[3] verb, t. *India should do everything possible to further the cause of peace.* = to help something to become successful

fur•tive /ˈfɜːtɪv/ adj. *The furtive manner in which the man behaved made me suspicious.* = secret and not open or direct; trying to escape being noticed

fu•ry /ˈfjʊəri/ noun, u. *the fury of the storm* = very great anger **furious** /ˈfjʊəriəs/ adj. **1** *They were furious when they came back and found the house locked.* = very angry **2** *He ran at a furious speed.* = very strong; great (informal)

fuse[1] /fjuːz/ noun, c. **1** *The fuse in the electric cooker has blown and that's why it is not working.* = a very thin piece of wire, placed in an electric device (machine) or system, which melts if too much current passes through it and thus shuts off the current, protecting the device [TECHNICAL] **2** *The bomb had a short fuse.* = a string or pipe which carries fire to an explosive article and causes it to blow up

fuse[2] verb, i. **1** *The wire has fused.* = to melt **2** *We will have to fuse these two pieces of metal.* = to join together by using heat

to be on a very short fuse = to be in the habit of becoming angry very easily

fusion noun, u. = the process of joining together (of metal etc.) [TECHNICAL, PHYSICS]

fu•se•lage /ˈfjuːzəlɑːʒ/ noun = the main body of an aircraft, within which passengers sit

fuss[1] /fʌs/ noun, u. . *Don't make such a fuss because you lost those notes. You can write them again.* = unnecessary impatience, excitement, anger

fuss[2] verb, i. **1** *They like to fuss over their cooking.* = to give a lot of attention to **2** *Don't fuss. Everything will be all right.* = to behave in a worried, anxious manner (informal) **fussy** adj. **1** = nervous and excitable **2** *He is very fussy about his food.* = paying too much attention to small details (disapproving)

fu•tile /ˈfjuːtaɪl/ adj. *a futile search* = producing no result; useless

fu•ture[1] /ˈfjuːtʃəʳ/ noun, u. **1** *Would you like to know your future?* = the time which is to come **2** *I see no future in this business.* = chance of success in future **3** *the future tense* = the form of a verb that expresses what may happen in the time to come [GRAMMAR] **futuristic** /fjuːtʃəˈrɪstɪk/ adj. *a futuristic building* = an appearance that suggests how things will look in the future

future[2] adj. *future events* = relating to the future

fuzz /fʌz/ noun, u. = a mass of thin hair or hair-like substance **fuzzy** adj. *a fuzzy picture* = not very sharp or clear

gG

g, G /dʒi:/ the seventh letter of the English alphabet

gab /gæb/ noun **(the gift of the gab)** *He has the gift of the gab. He can convince people of anything.* = the talent to talk well and fluently in a way which impresses people (informal)

gab•ble /'gæbəl/ verb, i. *I could hear her gabbling away at the meeting but I couldn't understand a word she was saying.* = to speak so fast that one cannot be understood (informal, humorous or not respectful)

gad /gæd/ verb, i. *Stop gadding around and settle down to work.* = to travel from one place to another aimlessly, looking for enjoyment (informal, humorous or not respectful)

gad•get /'gædʒɪt/ noun, c. *He has invented a gadget that keeps rats away by producing a loud noise.* = a small machine or device that is invented and used for a particular purpose (informal)

gaffe /gæf/ noun, c. *I made a gaffe by asking her how much money she earned in a month.* = an unintended social mistake which causes embarrassment (informal)

gag[1] /gæg/ verb, t. or i. **1** (t.) = to prevent someone from speaking by putting a piece of cloth, etc. into his/her mouth **2** *No one knows what is happening as the newspapers have been gagged.*(t.) = to pass an order usually in court preventing someone from expressing his/her views (informal) **3** *The rice had such a foul smell that I gagged when I tried to eat a handful.*(i.) = to be unable to swallow and to be about to vomit (informal)

gag[2] noun, c. **1** *The thieves stuffed a gag into his mouth.* = a piece of cloth put inside someone's mouth to prevent him/her from speaking **2** *The comedian produced some stale gags that everyone had heard before. No one found him funny.* = a joke or funny story (informal)

ga•ga /'gɑːgɑː/ adj. *The people are going gaga over the new action movie.* = having a strong attraction for someone or something (informal and often disapproving))

gag•gle /'gægəl/ noun, c. *a gaggle of school-children* = a noisy group

gai•e•ty /'geɪɪti/ noun, u. *The guests were enjoying themselves, but suddenly there was a loud explosion, putting an end to their gaiety.* = feeling of cheerfulness and enjoyment (old-fashioned)

gain[1] /geɪn/ verb, t. **1** *I will not gain anything from selling this house.* = to obtain something useful e.g. money, power, access etc. **2** *They managed to gain entry into the cricket pavilion.* = to get into a place etc. by making an effort **3** *He is gaining weight.* = to have an increase in **4** *My watch is gaining two minutes every day.* = to work too fast by a given amount of time (used for a watch or clock)

gain[2] noun, u. or c. *He made a gain of Rs 1,000 when he sold his new car.* = the act of making a profit

to gain ground *The protest against cruelty to animals is gaining ground.* = (of an idea, belief etc.) to become stronger

gainful adj. *You should take up some gainful employment.* = something which helps one to earn money

gain•say /geɪn'seɪ/ verb, t. *You may not like her, but you cannot gainsay her ability as a leader.* = to refuse to accept something as true (used in negative sentences only) (formal)

gait /geɪt/ noun, u. *a majestic gait* = manner of walking

ga•la /'gɑːlə/ adj. *The celebration was a gala event.* = very grand and colourful

gal•ax•y /'gæləksi/ noun, c. (**galaxies**) **1** = a large group of stars which makes up a part of the universe **2** *a galaxy of poets* = a group of famous people

gale /geɪl/ noun, c. = a very strong wind **gale of laughter** *There was a gale of laughter from the next room.* = sounds of laughter coming in a wave

gall /gɔːl/ noun, u. **1** = a bitter, greenish liquid produced in the body by the gall-bladder, which helps to digest fats present in food (also **bile**) **2** *I wonder how he had the gall to insult his teacher.* = bad manners for which a certain kind of courage is needed (disapproving)

gal•lant /'gælənt/ adj. *our gallant soldiers* = brave

gal•le•ry /'gæləri/ noun, c. (**galleries**) **1** *an art gallery* = a large building where works of art are put up for show **2** *a seat in the gallery* = rows of seats fixed on top of high wooden or metal frames, from which people can watch a game (e.g. a cricket match) or a show in a theatre, for which a lower price is usually charged

to play to the gallery = to try to win praise from the common people

gal•ley /'gæli/ noun, c. (**galleys**) **1** = a long, low ship, rowed by slaves and used as a fighting-ship in former times **2** = the kitchen in a ship or aircraft

gal•li•vant /'gælɪvænt/ verb, i. *You can't spend your whole life gallivanting around the country. You must settle down to work.* = to move around looking for enjoyment (see also **gad**) (humorous)

gal•lon /'gælən/ noun, c. = a measure for liquids, equal to 4.5 litres, formerly used in India but now used only in USA (3.8 L = 1 American gallon)

gal•lop[1] /'gæləp/ noun, c. (no plural) *The horse*

moved at a gallop. = the fastest movement of a horse, when all four legs come off the ground at the same time

gallop[2] verb, i. *The horse galloped away.* = to move at a gallop

gal•lows /ˈgæləʊz/ noun, c. (only plural) = a wooden frame used to hang criminals, usually as a punishment for murder

Gallup poll /ˈgæləp pəʊl/ noun, u. = a method used to guess the result of an election before it is made known, by making a count of the opinions of groups of people who are going to vote or have already voted

ga•lore /gəˈlɔːʳ/ adj. *The actor has admirers galore in all parts of the country.* = in large number

galosh /gəˈlɒʃ/ noun, c. (only in plural form **galoshes**) = rubber boots worn on top of ordinary shoes to protect them from rain or snow

gal•va•nize (galvanise) /ˈgælvənaɪz/ verb, t. **1** *The sheets of iron have been galvanized.*= to pour a covering of zinc over a sheet of iron or steel with the help of electricity, so that the metal will not rust **2** *The announcement of the dates for the examination galvanized the students into action.* = to shock or force someone who has not been active into action

gam•bit /ˈgæmbɪt/ noun, c. *the opening gambit in a game of chess* = a clever and risky move, or action, by a player in a game of chess or by someone taking part in a conversation etc. in order to gain an advantage over an opponent

gam•ble[1] /ˈgæmbəl/ verb, i. *She loves to gamble although she always loses money.* = to take part in betting or to take a risk in the hope of making a profit

gamble[2] noun, c. *When we decided to start a new business, we were not sure if it would succeed. It was a gamble.* = an action which is risky

game[1] /geɪm/ noun, c. or u. **1** *She is good at outdoor games such as cricket.*(c.) = a sport or activity in which the players compete with one another **2** *We have just finished a game of bridge.*(c.) = a particular example of a sport **3** *There is no game left in these rivers now.*(u.) = wild animals including birds and fish which are hunted for food or as a form of sport

game[2] adj. *If you want me to join you on this picnic, I am game.* = willing to do something (informal) **big game** noun, u. = large animals, such as tigers, which were hunted for sport

to play games with someone *I don't want you to play games with me. Please tell me exactly what you are planning.* = to act with a dishonest purpose or in an unfair way in order to get what you want (informal) **to give the game away** = to do something to spoil what is a secret or a surprise

gamut /ˈgæmət/ noun, u. *She is such a good actor that she can present the whole gamut of emotions, from anger to love.* = the whole range of something

gang[1] /gæŋ/ noun, c. **1** *a gang of thieves* = a group of people working on something, usually something criminal **2** *Where is the rest of your gang?* = a group of friends (informal)

gang[2] verb, i. *They have all ganged up against me.* = to form a group to fight against someone

gang•ling /ˈgæŋglɪŋ/ adj. *a gangling youth* = very tall and thin and therefore jerky or not graceful in movement (informal)

gangplank noun, c. = a long, narrow piece of wood which forms a movable bridge from a ship to the shore (also **gangway**)

gang•rene /ˈgæŋgriːn/ noun, u. = the decay of some part of the body caused by the lack of blood supply to that part [MEDICINE]

gangster /ˈgæŋstəʳ/ noun, c. = a member of a group of dangerous criminals

gang•way /ˈgæŋweɪ/ noun, c. **1** = a movable bridge leading to a ship or aircraft **2** = a path between two rows of seats in a cinema or on a bus (also **gangplank**)

gaol /dʒeɪl/ noun, c. = jail (prison) (old-fashioned) **gaoler** noun = a guard in a prison

gap /gæp/ noun, c. **1** *There is a large gap between two of his front teeth.* = a space between two things **2** *There is a wide gap between the rich and the poor in some countries.* = a difference between people or groups of people **3** *I could not understand your speech fully. There was an information gap. // There is a generation gap between my children and me.* = failure to understand or appreciate something because of incomplete information, being much older or younger than someone else etc.

gape /geɪp/ verb, i. **1** *When the screen covering the beautiful statue was removed the audience gaped at it in wonder.* = to look at someone or something in surprise or wonder, usually with the mouth open **2** *His old shoes are gaping at the toes.* = to come apart and be wide open

ga•rage /ˈgærɑːʒ/ or /gəˈrɑːʒ/ noun, c. **1** = a building in which motor vehicles are kept **2** = a place where motor vehicles are repaired

gar•bage /ˈgɑːbɪdʒ/ noun, u. **1** = leftover food, used paper and other waste material which needs to be thrown away **2** *He spoke a lot of garbage.* = nonsense (informal)

gar•bled /ˈgɑːbəld/ adj. *She gave us a garbled account of the meeting which was held last night.* = confusing and difficult to understand

gar•den[1] /ˈgɑːdn/ noun, c. = a piece of land on which flowers or vegetables are grown

garden[2] verb, i. *He likes to garden in the evening.* = to do work in a garden, growing flowers, vegetables etc.

gar•gle[1] /ˈgɑːgəl/ verb, i. *The doctor has asked me to gargle with salt water as I have a sore throat.* = to wash the throat and mouth with some liquid by blowing air from the lungs through the liquid, held in the mouth and throat, but not swallowing it

gargle[2] noun, c. *You should use a salt water gargle.* = a liquid which one gargles with

gar•ish /ˈgeərɪʃ/ adj. *garish clothes* = having very bright colours which hurt the eyes (derogatory)

gar•land[1] /ˈgɑːlənd/ noun, c.= a closed chain of flowers which is put around the neck of someone to whom respect is being shown

garland[2] verb, t. *He was garlanded on the occasion of his visit.* = to place a garland, usually of flowers, round a person's neck

gar•lic /ˈgɑːlɪk/ noun, u. = pods from a plant with a strong smell and taste, used to give flavour to food

gar•ment /ˈgɑːmənt/ noun, c.= an item (piece) of clothing e.g. a shirt (formal, literary)

gar•ner /ˈgɑːnəʳ/ verb, t. = to collect and store something

gar•net /ˈgɑːnɪt/ noun, c. or u. = a purple gemstone which is used in jewellery

gar•nish[1] /ˈgɑːnɪʃ/ noun, u = some material, usually some vegetable or fruit cut into small pieces, which is put on top of a dish of cooked food to give it flavour or to make it look more attractive

garnish[2] verb, t. *Garnish the fried chicken with some chopped onions.* = to decorate food by using a garnish

gar•ret /ˈgærɪt/ noun, c. = a small and not very comfortable room at the top of a building

gar•ri•son[1] /ˈgærɪsən/ noun, c. **1** = a group of soldiers who are defending a place **2** = a camp in which soldiers live

garrison[2] verb, t. *The city has been garrisoned.* = to send soldiers to defend a place against an enemy during a war

gar•ru•lous /ˈgærələs/ adj. *a garrulous person* = (a person who is) in the habit of talking too much

gar•ter /ˈgɑːtəʳ/ noun, c. = an elastic band worn around the leg to keep a sock in place (not commonly used now)

gas[1] noun, u. or c. *Oxygen is a gas.*(c.) // *We use gas to cook our food.*(u.) = a substance which is not solid or liquid and usually cannot be seen

gas[2] /gæs/ verb, t. or i. (**gassed**) **1** (t.) = to use some kind of poisonous gas to kill someone **2** *Don't sit there gassing all day. Do some work!*(i.) = to talk without any purpose. (slang) **gas-bag** noun = a person who loves to talk **gaseous** adj. = in the form of a gas **gas mask** noun = a covering worn over the face which protects the wearer from dangerous gases present in the air

gash[1] /gæʃ/ verb, t. *He fell off the bicycle and gashed his leg.* = to cut or wound deeply

gash[2] noun, c. *The blood was flowing from a gash in her leg.* = a deep cut or wound

gas•ket /ˈgæskɪt/ noun, c. = a thin and flat piece of rubber, paper etc. which is put between two parts of a machine so that no steam, air or liquid can escape from it [TECHNICAL]

gas•o•line /ˈgæsəliːn/ noun, u. = petrol (also **gas**) (American)

gasp[1] /gɑːsp/ verb, i. **1** *The man had been running hard and was gasping for breath.* = to breathe quickly and with difficulty **2** *The audience gasped in surprise when the two famous film stars appeared on the stage.* = to draw in one's breath suddenly with a sound because of surprise, wonder etc.

gasp[2] noun, c. **1** *He was breathing in quick gasps.* = a quick, short breath **2** *There was a gasp of surprise from the audience when the film stars appeared.* = the action of drawing in breath suddenly

gas•tric /ˈgæstrɪk/ adj. *gastric pain* = having to do with the stomach [MEDICINE] **gastritis** /gæsˈtrɪtɪs/ noun = infection of the stomach which causes pain **gastronomy** /gæsˈtronəmɪ/ noun, u. = the art and science of appreciating good food

gate /geɪt/ noun, c. = a frame on hinges which closes an opening in a fence or wall and can be moved to allow people to enter or leave **gatecrasher** noun, c. = an uninvited guest

gath•er /ˈgæðəʳ/ verb, t. or i. **1** *The children wandered through the park gathering flowers.*(t.) = to bring things together; to collect **2** *A crowd gathered outside the stadium.*(i.) = to come together in large numbers (referring to people) **3** *I gather you are contesting the next election.* = to get information or find out about something

gauche /gəʊʃ/ adj. *His gauche behaviour at the party made us feel ashamed.* = not socially correct or acceptable behaviour

gau•dy /ˈgɔːdi/ adj. *a gaudy piece of jewellery* = very bright and showy (see also **garish**)

gauge[1] /geɪdʒ/ verb, t. **1** *We use a special thermometer to gauge the temperature of the air outside the aircraft.* = to measure **2** *I am afraid you have not been able to gauge the situation correctly.* = to judge or understand something (formal)

gauge[2] noun, c. **1** *a rain-gauge* = an instrument used for measuring the size, speed etc. of something **2** *narrow-gauge railway // a cupboard made of 16-guage steel* = a measurement of the distance between two things or of the thickness of something [TECHNICAL]

gaunt /gɔːnt/ adj. *a tall, thin person with gaunt cheeks* = thin and bony looking; ill or hungry

gaunt•let /ˈgɔːntlɪt/ noun, c. = a glove (covering for the hand) made of metal, used by soldiers to protect themselves in former times

to pick up the gauntlet = to accept a challenge **to run the gauntlet** = to expose oneself to some danger

gauze /gɔːz/ noun, u. **1** = very thin, net-like cloth, used as a bandage to cover a wound **2** *a wire gauze* = a kind of light screen or net, woven out of thin metal wires, on which a container can be placed and heated, for an experiment in science

gawk /gɔːk/ verb, i. *He stood gawking at the 120-storey building.* = to look at someone or something in a foolish way, usually in surprise (informal) **gawky** adj. *Her gawky movements made everyone look at her curiously.* = awkward and clumsy in movement

gay[1] /geɪ/ noun, c. = a person, generally a man, who is homosexual (attracted to a person of the same sex as oneself)

gay[2] adj. **1** = bright and colourful (old-fashioned, out of use now) **2** *a gay magazine* = for homosexual persons

gaze[1] /geɪz/ verb, i. *He sat on the beach, gazing at the sunset.* = to look on with wonder or pleasure at something for a long time

gaze[2] noun, u. *I could not meet his gaze and had to look away.* = a long, steady look

ga•ze•bo /gəˈziːbəʊ/ noun, c. = a place in a garden or on top of a hill where one can sit and admire the scenery

ga•zelle /gəˈzel/ noun, c. = a kind of antelope (deer) that moves fast

ga•zette /gəˈzet/ noun, c. = a newspaper published by the government, containing important notices, orders etc.

gear /geaʳ/ noun, u. or c. **1** *the gears in a motorcar* = a set of wheels with teeth which allows a machine (e.g. a motorcar) to run at different speeds **2** *sports gear*(u.) = the equipment (tools, shoes, clothing etc.) needed or used for a special activity such as mountain-climbing, swimming under water, playing games such as hockey and football etc.

to gear up to do something *We are gearing up for water shortage in our city.* = to make preparations for something which will happen **to be geared to something** *The production of motor cars is geared to the demand. When more people want to buy cars, the factories produce more cars, but when the demand is low, the factories produce fewer cars.* = to plan a course of action which will suit a particular condition or need

geck•o /ˈgekəʊ/ noun = a small animal of the lizard family, commonly found in houses in warm countries

gel•a•tine /ˈdʒelətiːn/ noun = a clear substance produced by boiling the bones of animals, used for making jelly

gem /dʒem/ noun, c. **1** = a precious stone such as a diamond, which has been cut and can be used in making jewellery **2** *He is a gem of a friend.* = a person who is given high value because of some special quality or skill (figurative)

gen•der /ˈdʒendəʳ/ noun, u. or c. **1** *The pronoun 'he' is masculine in gender while the pronoun 'she' is feminine.* = the form of a word which shows whether it refers to someone or something that is male (e.g. 'man' or 'boy') or female (e.g. 'woman' or 'girl') [GRAMMAR] **2** *The government makes no gender distinctions in selecting officers. There are women as well as men working in important posts.* = differences based on the sex of a person (male or female)

gene /dʒiːn/ noun, c. = a part of a living cell that helps to pass on the qualities of the parent (father or mother) to its young ones **genetic** /dʒɪˈnetɪk/ adj. *Many forms of diabetes are genetic.* = something that is passed on through the genes from the parent to the child (also **hereditary**) **genetics** noun, u. = the study of genes and how they carry the qualities of the parent to the child **genetic code** noun = the arrangement of genes in a cell that controls the development of living things **genetic engineering** noun = the process of bringing about a change in the nature of the genes so as to control the qualities of the child that is produced by the parent **genetically modified crops** noun = plants (usually plants which produce foodgrains such as wheat etc.) which have been changed through genetic engineering so that they can produce more than normal plants (sometimes abbreviated as GMC)

ge•ne•al•o•gy /dʒiːniˈælədʒi/ noun, u. or c. (**genealogies**) = the study of the history of a family showing how its members are related to each other

gen•e•ral[1] /ˈdʒenərəl/ noun, c. = an officer of very high rank in the army

general[2] adj. **1** *There is a general feeling that the roads in the city need to be improved.* = having to do with all or most of the people; widespread **2** *This school provides a good general education but if you want to learn more about computers you should go to a technical school.* = dealing with common things but not limited to something special **3** *This book gives a general description of the people living in Thailand.* = not detailed, but dealing with the main things **general election** noun = an election in which all the voters in a country vote to elect a government **generalize (generalise)** verb, i. *You cannot* *generalize that everyone has a television set just because a few people in the building do.* = to form a rule or principle that can apply to a large number of people or things by looking at only a few examples **generalization (generalisation)** /dʒenərelaɪ'ʒeɪʃən/ noun, u. or c. = a statement made about a large group of people or things by looking at just a few examples

gen•e•rate /'dʒenəreɪt/ verb, t. *The new dam will generate 5000 megawatts of electricity.* = to produce (formal)

gen•e•ra•tion /dʒenə'reɪʃən/ noun, c. or u. **1** *The new generation of students is more interested in technology than in the arts.*(c.) = people of about the same age living at a particular time **2** *Our family has been living in this village for at least five generations.* = the period of time during which a person can grow up from a child into an adult and produce children, roughly equal to 25 years **3** *The generation of electricity has gone up as many new dams have been built.*(u.) = the act of producing something **generation gap** noun = the difference in the ideas, feelings etc. of young people and older people, often leading to a poor understanding of each other **new generation** *new generation computers* = (of machines), new versions which are capable of meeting new needs

generator /'dʒenəˌreɪtəʳ/ noun, c. = a machine that produces electricity (also **dynamo**)

ge•ner•ic /dʒɪ'nerɪk/ adj. **1** *'Panthera' is the generic name given to a class of large cats, to which leopards belong.*= referring to a whole group of things and not to a particular thing **2** *In the USA, doctors are allowed to prescribe only generic drugs, not medicine sold under a particular brand name.* = belonging to a class of drugs (medicines) and not having a special trade name e.g. Crocin

gen•e•rous /'dʒenərəs/ adj. **1** *He is a very generous person and has given a lot of money to charitable organizations.* = kind and willing to help by giving away money etc. **2** *He gave me a generous helping of rice.* = large

gen•e•sis /'dʒenɪsɪs/ noun, u. *The speaker explained the genesis of Hindustani music.* = the beginning or origin of something (formal)

ge•ni•al /'dʒi:niəl/ adj. *She is such a genial person that everyone likes her.* = having a friendly and cheerful attitude

ge•nie /'dʒi:ni/ noun, c. = a spirit with magical powers, found in Arabian fairy tales

gen•i•tal /'dʒenɪtəl/ adj. = having to do with the sex organs

gen•i•tals noun, c. (always plural) = the sex organs that are on the outer part of a person's body

gen•i•tive /'dʒenɪtɪv/ noun or adj. *'His' is the genitive or possessive form of the pronoun 'he'.* = the form of a noun or pronoun which shows possession or ownership [GRAMMAR]

ge•ni•us /'dʒi:niəs/ noun, c. (**geniuses**) or u. **1** *The boy is a musical genius and I am sure he will become a great singer.*(c.) = a person born with very great ability or intelligence **2** *This beautiful painting is a work of genius.*(u.) = very great and unusual ability or skill

gen•o•cide /'dʒenəsaɪd/ noun = the deliberate killing of a whole race of people

genome /'dʒi:nəʊm/ = the sum of all the genes that are found in living beings [TECHNICAL]

gen•re /'ʒɒnrə/ noun, c. *The novel is the most popular genre in modern literature.* = a class of literature, art, film or music which follows a particular form

gen•teel /dʒen'ti:l/ adj. *genteel manners* = polite and refined in a way that is thought to belong to a high social class **gentility** noun, u. = the quality of being genteel

gen•tle /'dʒentl/ adj. **1** *She is too gentle a person to hurt you.* = kind and careful not to hurt people **2** *gentle exercise* = not violent or requiring much effort

gen•tle•man /'dʒentlmən/ noun, c. (**gentlemen**) **1** = a polite man, seen as dignified and as someone who behaves well with others (somewhat old-fashioned) **2** *Gentlemen, can I have your attention?* = used to refer the men in a gathering

gen•try /'dʒentri/ noun, u. *The gentry of the town have been invited to the function.* = people belonging to the higher social classes (old-fashioned)

gen•u•ine /'dʒenjuɪn/ adj. **1** *Is this a genuine painting by the great painter Van Gogh or is it only a copy?* = real; actually being what something or someone or supposed to be **2** *a genuine person* = very honest and sincere

ge•nus /'dʒi:nəs/ noun, c. (**genera**) = a biological group or class to which an animal or plant belongs (see also **species**) [BIOLOGY]

geo- prefix meaning having to do with the Earth e.g. **ge•og•ra•phy** /dʒi'ɒgrəfi/ noun **1** = the study of the things found on the Earth's surface, physical features, climate, vegetation etc. **2** *The geography of this city, lying next to a mountain, is very attractive.* = the way in which a place is arranged

ge•o•cen•tric /dʒi:əʊ'sentrɪk/ adj. *The astronomer Copernicus proved that the universe was not geocentric.* = having the Earth as the centre

ge•ol•o•gy /dʒi'ɒlədʒi/ noun = the study of the materials which make up the Earth e.g. rocks, minerals, soil etc.

ge•om•e•try /dʒi'ɒmɪtri/ noun = the branch of mathematics which deals with lines, surfaces, angles and shapes (e.g. a circle, a triangle) **geometric (geometrical)** /dʒɪə'metrɪk/ adj. **1** = having to do with geometry **2** *geometrical patterns* = formed by lines or regular patterns only and not showing living things (human beings, animals etc.) **geometric progression** noun *The numbers 2,6,18,54 etc. form a geometric progression.* = a set of numbers in which each number is multiplied or divided by a fixed number in order to get the next number [MATHEMATICS] (compare **arthimetical progression**)

ge•ra•ni•um /dʒe'reɪniəm/ noun, c. = a small plant which produces red, pink, or white flowers, commonly found in gardens

ge•ri•at•rics /dʒeri'ætrɪks/ noun = the branch of medicine which deals with the treatment and care of old people **geriatric** adj. *a geriatric ward in a hospital* = having to do with the treatment and care of old people

germ /dʒɜːm/ noun, c. *This disease is caused by a germ.* = a very tiny living thing that can cause disease **germ cell** noun *Scientists are collecting germ cells from rice plants in order to produce new kinds of rice.* = a cell (small part of a plant or animal) which can grow into a new plant or animal **germ warfare** noun = the use of germs during a war to kill enemy soldiers (also **biological warfare**) **germicide** noun, c. = a chemical that can kill germs [TECHNICAL]

ger•mi•nate /'dʒɜːmɪneɪt/ verb, i. *These seeds will germinate if they are kept in a warm and damp place.* = to cause a seed to grow [TECHNICAL]

ger•und /'dʒerənd/ noun, c. *In the sentence 'I love eating.' the word 'eating', is a gerund.* = a verb ending in 'ing' which is used as a noun in a sentence. [GRAMMAR]

ges•ta•tion /dʒe'steɪʃən/ noun, u. *A human foetus has a gestation period of nine months.* = the time during which the child develops inside the mother's body (before it is born) [BIOLOGY]

ges•ti•cu•late /dʒe'stɪkjʊleɪt/ verb, i. *I saw her gesticulating from a distance but I don't know what she was trying to say.* = to use movements of the arms and hands in order to express some meaning (formal)

gesture[1] /'dʒestʃəʳ/ noun, c. **1** *She made an angry gesture by shaking her fist.* = the use of movements of the body, specially the hands, to express a certain meaning **2** *It was not necessary for him to invite me home for a meal, but he did so. It was a kind gesture on his part.* = an action done to express a certain feeling, usually pleasant

gesture[2] verb, i. *She asked me to sit down and gestured towards the chair.* = to make a gesture to express some meaning

get /get/ verb, t. or i. (**got**) **1** *She got the first prize.*(t.) = to receive or obtain **2** *I've got a brand new car.*(t.) = to have something **3** *Get me a chair.*(t.) = to bring or fetch **4** *She got an attack of influenza last week.*(t.) = to suffer from some illness **5** *We got to the station in time.*(t.) = to reach **6** *He is getting too old to run.*(t.) = to become **7** *I got him to clean the house.*(t.) = to cause something to happen **8** *I don't get you.*(t.) = to understand **9** *Let's go home before it gets too hot.* = becomes **get-together** = an informal meeting of friends **get-up** *The new book has a nice get-up.* = something done to make the appearance of a book etc. attractive

> **Usage** The participle form of **get** is **gotten** in American English. (e.g. *I have gotten a new car.*) The participle form is **got** in British English. (e.g. *I have got a new car.*)

to get about *How do you manage to get about when you are in the village?* = to move from place to place **to get something across** *Were you able to get your ideas across to your students?* = to make oneself understood **to get along** *Do you get along with your seniors?* = to have a good relationship with someone **to get around** *My grandfather is very old. He doesn't get around the house very much.* = to move about or go somewhere **to get at** *What are you getting at? Will you explain what you mean?* = to suggest or say something indirectly **to get away** *I'd like to get away from the city and go somewhere quiet.* = to escape **to get away with something** *Their child does so many naughty things, but she gets away with it.* = to be able to escape punishment for doing something wrong because one is loved, very important etc. **to get by** *I find it difficult to get by on my salary.* = to manage (to have enough money for one's needs) **to get down to** *I must get down to work now.* = to begin something seriously **to get off** *I jumped a traffic light, but I was lucky to get off with just a warning.* = to be lucky enough to escape punishment **to get through** = to be successful in an examination or in reaching someone on the telephone **to get over** **1** *I was really sad when I failed but have got over it.* = to feel better after an experience of sorrow, shock, disappointment etc. **2** *She had a very bad backache but has now got over it.* = to recover from an illness **to get round** *The news has got round that he is leaving his job.* = to be known to many people (used to refer to a matter which is generally not favourable to the person)

gey•ser /'giːzəʳ/ noun, c. **1** = a stream of water, usually hot, which shoots up with force out of the ground from time to time **2** = a machine, working on electricity or gas, usually found in the bathrooms of houses, which stores and produces hot water

ghast•ly /ˈgɑːstli/ adj. **1** *He made such a ghastly speech that everyone in the audience walked out.* = very bad **2** *A truck collided with a motorbike. It was a ghastly accident.* = something that is very unpleasant to look at and causes fear

ghee /giː/ noun, u. = cooking fat made from butter

gher•kin /ˈgɜːkɪn/ noun, c. = a kind of green vegetable like a cucumber, which is usually pickled in salt water or vinegar before eating

ghet•to /ˈgetəʊ/ noun, c. (**ghettos** or **ghettoes**) = an overcrowded part of a city where people belonging to a particular community or group live together in poor conditions

ghost /gəʊst/ noun, c. = the spirit of a dead person which is said to be able to appear in different forms **ghostwriter** noun = a person who is paid to write a book for someone else, using that person's name

ghoul /guːl/ noun = an evil spirit which is said to eat the dead bodies of human beings

giant /ˈdʒaɪənt/ noun, c. = an imaginary wicked or sometimes friendly creature that has the shape of a very large and powerful human being (found in children's stories)

gib•ber•ish /ˈdʒɪbərɪʃ/ noun, u. *I can't understand a word of what you are saying. You are talking gibberish!* = meaningless nonsense (derogatory)

gib•bet /ˈdʒɪbɪt/ noun, c. = a wooden post from which criminals were hanged in former times (see also **gallows**)

gib•bon /ˈgɪbən/ noun, c. = a kind of small ape found in parts of Asia

gibe /dʒaɪb/ noun, c. *The gibes you made at the Director in your speech were not liked by many.* = an unkind remark intended to make someone appear foolish

gib•lets /ˈdʒɪblɪts/ noun, u. (only plural) = the heart, liver and other organs of a bird (e.g. a chicken) which are removed before cooking but are often eaten separately

gid•dy /ˈgɪdi/ adj. *I feel giddy whenever I travel by boat.* = feeling unsteady, as though everything was turning round and round and one was about to fall

gift /gɪft/ noun, c. **1** *This pen is a birthday gift for your daughter.* = present **2** *She has a gift for music.* = a special talent or ability that one is born with

gi•gan•tic /dʒaɪˈgæntɪk/ adj. *a gigantic crowd* = very large; huge

gig•gle[1] /ˈgɪgəl/ verb, i. *Stop giggling! This is a serious matter.* = to laugh in a foolish way because of being nervous or embarrassed

giggle[2] noun, c. *You can hear her giggles.* = the sound made while giggling

gild /gɪld/ verb, t. *If you gild these silver ornaments, they will look as if they are made of gold.* = to cover something with a thin coating of gold **gilt** noun, u. = the thin covering of gold which is put on something (usually an ornament made of cheaper metal)

gill /gɪl/ noun, c. = an organ (body part) in the head of a fish, on either side of the mouth, through which the fish gets oxygen present in the water (see pic under **fish**)

gim•let /ˈgɪmlɪt/ noun, c. = a tool used by a carpenter to make holes in wood, through which screws can be fitted

gim•mick /ˈgɪmɪk/ noun, c. *A company that makes toothpaste is offering a free trip to Singapore as a prize, but this is only a sales gimmick.* = an idea intended to draw the attention of people, usually in order to sell something (disapproving)

gin /dʒɪn/ noun, u. = a strong alcoholic drink which is usually colourless and looks like water

ging•er /ˈdʒɪndʒəʳ/ noun, u. = the root of a plant which is used as a spice to give a hot taste to food

gip•sy (**gypsy**) /ˈdʒɪpsi/ noun, c. (**gipsies**) = a member of a group of people who have no fixed home and travel from place to place

gi•raffe /dʒɪˈrɑːf/ noun = an African animal with a very long neck and legs, yellowish-brown in colour, with black spots

gir•der /ˈgɜːdəʳ/ noun, c.= a strong and heavy beam (thick piece of metal) made of steel, which supports a bridge or the roof of a building

gir•dle /ˈgɜːdl/ verb, t. *The mountain girdles the town of Dehra Dun.* = to form a ring around something

girl /gɜːl/ noun, c. **1** = a very young woman **2** *I am taking my little girl to school.* = daughter **girlfriend** noun = a woman who has a close relationship with a man

girth /gɜːθ/ noun, u. *This old tree has a girth of five metres around the trunk.* = the measurement of the thickness of something around its middle part

gist /dʒɪst/ noun, u. *I don't have time to read this long report. Just give me the gist.* = the main points, without the details

give /gɪv/ verb, t. or i. (**gave**, **given**) **1** *My parents gave me an encyclopedia for my twelfth birthday.*(t.) = to cause or allow someone to own something **2** *Give her the present which you bought her for her birthday.*(t.) = to hand over **3** *I will give you a week to complete this task.*(t.) = to allow **4** *This cow gives two litres of milk a day.*(t.) = to produce or supply **5** *He gave a loud cry and fell down.*(t.) **6** *She will give the welcome address.* = to speak **7** *The noise from these machines gave me a headache.*(t.) = to create or produce **8** *Please give me five more minutes to complete the work.*(t.) = to allow **9** *The look on his face gave me the feeling that he was angry with me.*(t.) = to create a certain effect **10** *The plastic bench gave* *a little after many people had sat on it.*(i.) = to change shape because of pressure **giveaway** noun *I can guess who wrote this letter, even though the writer's name is missing. The handwriting is a clear giveaway.* = something that makes a secret known, without its intending to do so

give and take *A friendship can last only when there is give and take between the friends.* = willingness to accept the wishes or ideas of the other person **to give in** *For a long time I refused to see the film but finally gave in.* = to let something happen after a period of preventing it from happening **to give as good as one gets** = to give someone the same kind of unpleasant treatment that he/she gives you **to give off** *The chutney was stale and gave off a bad smell.* = to create or produce noise, light, smell etc. **to give up** **1** *I gave up swimming when I developed a pain in my legs.* = to stop doing something that one does often **2** *I really think you should give up smoking.* = to stop doing something that is bad for one's health

gizzard /'gɪzəd/ noun = a small bag of muscle inside the stomach of a bird in which food is broken up into tiny pieces with the help of small stones which the bird has swallowed

gla•cier /'glæsiə^r/ noun, c. = a river of ice high up on a mountain (from which a river has its source)

glad /glæd/ adj. *I am glad to see you in good health.* = happy

glade /gleɪd/ noun, c. = an open space surrounded by trees

glad•i•a•tor /'glædieɪtə^r/ noun, c. = a trained fighter who was made to fight, in ancient Rome, against other gladiators or wild animals, for the entertainment of crowds that came to watch such fights

glam•our /'glæmə^r/ noun, u. *People are attracted to filmstars because of their glamour.* = a quality, attributed to rich, famous or beautiful people, which has a strong attractions for ordinary people

glance[1] /glɑːns/ verb, i. *She glanced at her watch and saw that she was late for the meeting.* = to take a quick, short look

glance[2] noun, c. *One glance at his face told me how angry he was.* = a quick, short look

gland /glænd/ noun, c. *The salivary gland helps us to digest our food.* = a small organ of the body that produces a kind of chemical substance that enters the blood and has some effect on the working of the body

glare[1] /gleə^r/ verb, i. *The man stood there, saying nothing but glaring at me angrily.* = to look hard and long at someone in anger

glare[2] noun, u. **1** *His angry glare frightened me.* = a hard look of anger **2** *The glare of the lights was so strong that I was blinded for a minute.* = the brightness of a strong light that hurts the eyes **glaring** adj. *Forgetting to print the chief guest's name on the invitation card was a glaring mistake.* = (something bad) that is very easily noticed or seen; shocking

glass /glɑːs/ noun, u. or c. (**glasses**) **1** *a sheet of glass* (u.) = a hard, transparent material that is brittle (breaks easily) and is made by melting sand and other chemicals at very high temperature **2** *a wine glass*(c.) = a small container for liquids that one drinks from, usually made of glass **3** *You should drink a glass of milk every morning.*(c.) = the amount of liquid that can be held by a glass (meaning 2) **glasses** noun, c. (only plural, following 'a pair of') *I must get a new pair of glasses from the optician.* = spectacles; two pieces of specially cut glass, plastic etc. in a frame, worn over the ears and nose, which help a person to see more clearly

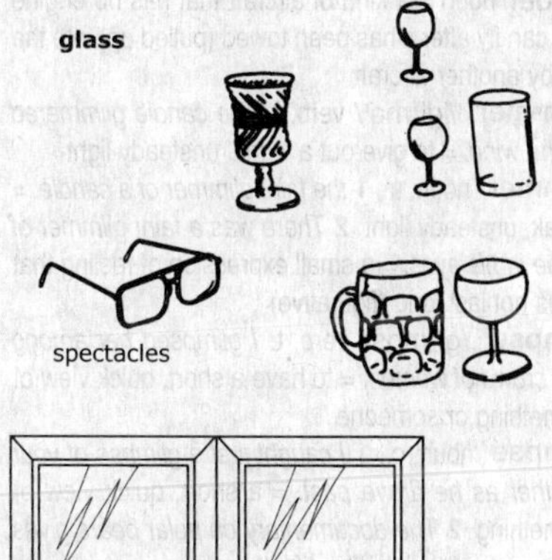

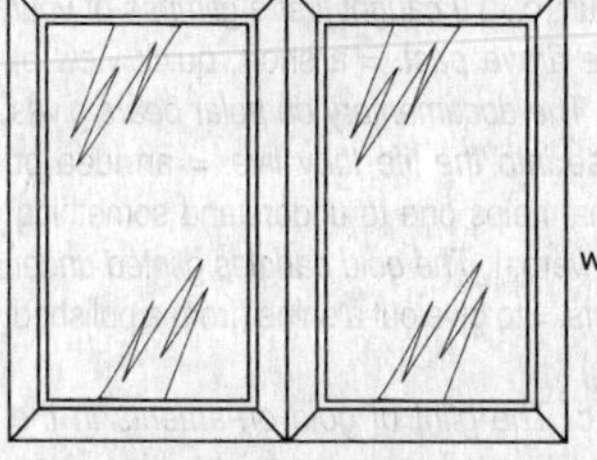

glaze[1] /gleɪz/ noun, u. *These clay pots have a beautiful glaze.* = a shiny glass-like surface which an object made of clay (earth) gets when it is heated to a very high temperature

glaze[2] verb, t. **1** *The potter will glaze these pots by baking them in a special oven.* = to put a glaze (shiny surface) on a pot **2** *These windows have to be glazed.* = to fit a door or window frame with glass

gleam[1] /gliːm/ verb, t. *We saw a light from the village gleaming in the darkness.* = to shine faintly

gleam[2] noun, u. **1** *the soft gleam of a candle* = a soft, gentle light that shines for a short time **2** *There was a gleam of hope in his eyes.* = a sudden expression of feeling in someone's eyes

G

glean /gliːn/ verb, i. *These facts have been gleaned from a number of newspaper articles.* = to gather facts or information from different sources (formal)
glee /gliː/ noun, u. *The children clapped their hands in glee.* = joy (literary)
glen /glen/ noun, c. = a valley between mountains (commonly used in Scotland or Ireland)
glib /glɪb/ adj. *I don't trust him at all. He is far too glib.* = able to talk easily and cleverly and to persuade others, though not always truthful or sincere (disapproving)
glide /glaɪd/ verb, i. **1** *The boat glided across the calm waters of the lake.* = to move lightly and effortlessly across a surface **2** *The eagles glided in circles through the air.* = to move through the air without beating the wings or using the power of an engine (used to describe the flight of a bird or aircraft) **glider** noun = a kind of aircraft that has no engine but can fly after it has been towed (pulled up) into the air by another aircraft
glim•mer[1] /ˈglɪməʳ/ verb, i. *The candle glimmered in the wind.* = to give out a weak, unsteady light
glimmer[2] noun, u. **1** *the faint glimmer of a candle.* = weak, unsteady light **2** *There was a faint glimmer of hope in his eyes.* = a small expression of feeling that does not last long (figurative)
glimpse[1] /glɪmps/ verb, t. *I glimpsed her among the crowd of women.* = to have a short, quick view of something or someone
glimpse[2] noun, c. **1** *I caught just a glimpse of your brother as he drove past.* = a short, quick view of something **2** *The documentary on polar bears gives one a glimpse into the life they live.* = an idea or experience that helps one to understand something
glint[1] /glɪnt/ verb, i. *The gold bangles glinted under the bright lights.* = to give out a shine (from a polished metal surface)
glint[2] noun, c. *The glint of gold ornaments in the jeweller's shop dazzled me.* = the bright shine given out by polished metal
glis•ten /ˈglɪsən/ verb, i. *Her forehead glistened with drops of sweat.* = to give out the shine that comes from a wet surface
glitch /glɪtʃ/ noun, c. (**glitches**) *The engine of the car won't start. There must be a glitch in the electrical system.* = a fault in a machine or a computer program that prevents it from working properly (informal)
glit•ter[1] /ˈglɪtəʳ/ verb, i. **1** *The diamonds in her ring glittered brilliantly.* = to shine in small flashes **2** *His eyes glittered when I promised to publish his story.* = to shine with excitement
glitter[2] noun, u. **1** *The glitter of sunlight on the water was dazzling.* = small flashes (not continuous) **2** *Most people are attracted by the glitter of films.* = excitement (see also **glamour**)
gloat /gləʊt/ verb, i. *It's nice that you won the match but I don't think you should gloat over your victory.* = to feel superior because of something that one has achieved and to talk about it in a boastful and unpleasant manner
globe /gləʊb/ noun, c. **1** = any round object shaped like a ball **2** = a round object representing the Earth, with a map of the different oceans and continents printed on it **3** = the Earth (the planet we live on) **global** adj. **1** *Everyone fears the possibility of a global war.* = something that relates to all the countries of the world **2** *We should have a global picture of the water problem.* = relating to every part of something **globalization (globalisation)** /gləʊbəlalaɪˈzəʃən/ noun, u. *the globalization of India's economy* = the process or result of becoming a part of some system that operates all over the world or in many countries
gloom /gluːm/ noun, u. **1** *We couldn't find our way in the gloom.* = darkness **2** *She was filled with gloom when she heard of the accident.* = sorrow
glory[1] /ˈglɔːrɪ/ noun, u. **1** *Her achievements as a writer have brought glory to the country.* = honour and fame **2** *The temple at Khajuraho had been neglected for years, but now it has been restored to its former glory.* = greatness and beauty
glory[2] verb, t. *When India became independent in 1947, the people were very happy. They gloried in their new freedom.* = to get happiness from (formal, literary)
gloss[1] /glɒs/ verb, t. **1** *The editor of the book has glossed all the difficult words.* = to explain the meaning of a word **2** *In her presentation the Director tried to gloss over the company's poor sales figures.* = to mention but not go into great detail, so as to cover up something (derogatory)
gloss[2] noun, u. or c. (**glosses**) **1** *The new car looks shiny and attractive now, but in a few months the gloss will be gone.*(u.) = shine and brightness **2** *I don't know what the word 'adumbrate' means. Could you give me a gloss for the word?*(c.) = an explanation of the meaning of a word (see also **glossary**) **glossary** noun, c. (**glossaries**) = a note in a book explaining the meanings of difficult or unfamiliar words **glossy** adj. = shining brightly
glove /glʌv/ noun, c. = a covering for the hand, made of leather, wool, rubber etc. which has separate coverings for each finger
glow[1] /gləʊ/ verb, i *Heat this piece of iron in the fire until it begins to glow.* = to give out light and heat without flames

glow[2] noun, u. *The glow from the burning pieces of coal lit up his face.* = the reddish light given out by something that is burning without flames **glow-worm** noun = an insect that gives out a faint green light from its body

glow•er /'glaʊəʳ/ verb, i. *I have never seen a more unfriendly person than Umang. He never smiles or speaks to anyone; he just stands there glowering.* = to look at someone in an angry and unfriendly manner

glu•cose /'gluːkəʊs/ noun, u. = sugar in pure form, found in fruits and needed by the body for energy

glue[1] /gluː/ verb, t. *You will have to glue the two pieces of wood together.* = to join together by using glue

glue[2] noun, u. = a substance which sticks (joins) things together

glum /glʌm/ adj. *Why do you look so glum? Have you had bad news?* = unhappy and depressed

glut /glʌt/ noun, u. *We had such a good harvest this year that there is a glut of rice now.* = a greater supply of something than is needed; excess

glut•ton /'glʌtn/ noun, c. **1** *He is such a glutton that he eats two whole chickens for breakfast.* = a person who eats too much (derogatory) **2** *He is a glutton for hard work.* = a person who is always willing to do something difficult and unpleasant (approving)

gly•ce•rine /'glɪsərɪn/ noun, u. = a thick, colourless sweet liquid made from animal or vegetable fat and used for preparing medicines, soap or explosives

gnarl•ed /nɑːld/ adj. *a gnarled old banyan tree; a gnarled old man* = rough in appearance due to old age and exposure to sun and wind

gnash /næʃ/ verb, t. *She gnashed her teeth in anger.* = to express anger by bringing the teeth in the upper and lower jaws together with force

gnat /næt/ noun, c. = a small flying insect like a bee, that can sting

gnaw /nɔː/ verb, t. *The dog kept gnawing at a bone.* = to chew or bite repeatedly at something hard

gnome /nəʊm/ noun, c. = a magical creature found in children's stories that looks like a little old man with a beard and a pointed hat and lives underground

gnu /nuː/ noun, c. = a kind of large deer found in the southern part of Africa

go /gəʊ/ verb, i. (**went**, **gone**) **1** *I want you to go.* = to leave a place; to depart **2** *You can go there by bus.* = to travel **3** *The milk has gone sour.* = to become **4** *This road goes to the airport.* = to extend to (reach as far as) a place **5** *Two goes into six three times.* = to divide a number exactly **6** *My old car went for Rs 10,000.* = to be sold for a certain price **7** *She will go far.* = to be very successful **8** *A 100 rupee note doesn't go very far these days.* = to be able to buy things **9** *Which school do you go to?* = to be part of an institution **10** *Where does this road go?* = lead; take one to **11** *Now that I have had some rest, my headache is starting to go.* = (of a condition) to be there no longer **12** *Half her time goes in travelling to work and back.* = (of money, time etc.) to be spent **13** *The box can be placed here, but that heavy suitcase goes under the table.* = to be placed **go-cart** noun, c. = a small carriage for a baby, pushed by hand **go-kart** noun, c.= a tiny racing car with an open body

to go about something *I would like to open an account in this bank but I don't know how to go about it.* = to do something for the first time **to go back on one's word** = to break a promise or agreement **to go it alone** = to do something without help from anyone **to go ahead** **1** *My parents did not want me to apply for a job in Delhi, but I went ahead anyway.* = to do something, often something which others don't want you to do **2** *I like your idea. Go ahead.* = giving someone permission to do something, in an encouraging way **to go down with (measles etc.)** *She went down with measles.* = to suffer a temporary illness (informal) **to go into something** **1** *The lawyer went into the details of the case.* = to study closely **2** *A lot of hard work has gone into building this hospital.* = to spend on (used to talk about effort, time, money etc.) **to go off** **1** = (of a bomb) to explode; (of a siren etc.) to sound or make a loud noise **2** *The lights have gone off.* = (of lights, machinery etc.) to stop working **3** *The rice we made yesterday has gone off.* = to get spoilt or go bad **to (not) go on** **1** *The work is difficult, but we have to go on.* = to continue to do something that is not easy to do **2** *The chief guest has not come, but let's go on.* = to start or continue an activity **3** *'I want to tell you a secret.' 'Go on.'* = said to encourage someone to begin or continue doing something **to go on and on** = to talk or complain about something for such a long time that everyone is tired of listening **to go over** *Let's go over the speech once more. // Let's go over the fire alarm rules.* = to study, practise or revise something in order to be better prepared **go around** *Is there enough food to go around?* = to be enough in quantity or numbers **to go through with something** *I don't think I can go through with this diet.* = to do something which one has decided to do even after knowing that there are problems **to go through the roof** **1** *She went through the roof when I told her what I had spent on the clothes I bought.* = to be very angry suddenly (informal) **2** *The prices of television sets have gone through the roof.* = (of the value of something), to become higher than ever (informal) **to go without** *There was no milk in the market, so the children had to go without.* = to manage without something, usually something which is important or necessary, or which one thinks is important

goad /gəʊd/ verb, t. *He doesn't like travelling, so if*

G

you want him to join you on the trip you will have to goad him into it. = to force or persuade someone into doing something which he/she does not like to do

goal /geʊl/ noun, c. **1** *Her goal is to become a famous writer.* = aim or purpose **2** *He scored a goal in the fifth minute.* = a point scored in the game of football or hockey by hitting the ball between two posts (**goal-posts**) which are guarded by a player of the opposite team (the **goalkeeper**)

goat /gəʊt/ noun, c. = an animal with long hair and horns which is kept on farms for its meat as well as milk

gob•ble /ˈgɒbəl/ verb, t. *Don't gobble your food.* = to eat very quickly and noisily (not respectful)

gob•let /ˈgɒblɪt/ noun, c. = a drinking-cup without a handle from which wine is drunk

gob•lin /ˈgɒblɪn/ noun, c. = an imaginary creature found in fairy stories, which is supposed to be small and ugly and fond of playing tricks on people

god /gɒd/ noun, c. = a supernatural being that people worship **God** noun (no plural) = the supreme being who is believed to have created the universe and everything in it

go•down /ˈgəʊdaʊn/ noun, c. = a warehouse; a large shed in which things are stored before they are sold

goggles noun, c. (only plural, following "pair of") = a pair of large and often coloured glasses in a frame, worn to protect the eyes from the sun, dust etc.

goi•tre /ˈgɔɪtəʳ/ noun = a kind of sickness in which the front part of the neck gets swollen [MEDICINE]

go•ing[1] /ˈgəʊɪŋ/ verb, i. = the progressive form of 'go'

going[2] noun **1** *I don't like your going there.* = the act of leaving **2** *You have done most of the work. That's good going!* = progress

going[3] adj. *That's the going rate for a two-bedroom flat.* = at the present time

gold[1] /gəʊld/ noun, u. = a soft yellow metal used for making ornaments as well as coins (money), the possession of which is supposed to make a person rich

gold[2] adj. *gold earrings* = made of gold **gold medal** noun = the top prize in a competition **golden** adj. **1** *a golden ring* = made of gold **2** *golden hair* = looking like gold **3** *a golden chance* = very favourable **golden age** noun = a period of time in the past which is supposed to have brought great happiness, prosperity etc. **golden handshake** noun = a large amount of money given to someone on their leaving a job **golden jubilee/wedding** = something celebrated at the end of 50 years **golden oldie** = popular music or a song which though played or written long ago, is still liked very much **golden rule** = a principle or rule that one is advised to follow

as good as gold *I thought my children would not behave themselves, but they were as good as gold.* = (used of children or humorously), behaving in a manner which one approves of

golf /gɒlf/ noun, u.= an outdoor game played across a very large playing area (**golf-course**) in which a small, hard, white ball is hit with long sticks (clubs) into a number of holes in the ground, with each player trying to use as few strokes (hits) as possible

gon•do•la /ˈgɒndələ/ noun, c. = a kind of long, narrow boat used to move along the canals of Venice, in Italy

gone[1] adj. *They were waiting at the bus stop a moment ago. Now they are all gone.* = not at a certain place anymore

gone[2] past participle of **go**

gong /gɒŋ/ noun, c. = a piece of round metal which makes a deep, loud sound when it is hit with a hammer (a piece of wood)

good[1] /gʊd/ adj. (**better**, **best**) **1** *a good child* = someone or something that is liked because of his/her/its qualities **2** *Milk is good for children.* = useful, healthy or helpful **3** *He's good at games.* = possessing skill or ability to do something well **4** *He has always been good to his customers.* = kind and helpful **5** *Be good!* = well-behaved (generally spoken to a child) **6** *He had a good look at the car.* = careful; thorough **7** *We have travelled a good distance.* = a fair amount **8** *The knife may be old but it's still good.* = (of a tool, instrument etc.) able to work satisfactorily

good[2] noun, u. *Third umpires were introduced into cricket for the good of the game.* = something that will make something better **Good morning / Good afternoon / Good evening** = expressions used to greet someone during the period of the day mentioned **Good night** = an expression used to take leave of someone during the evening or night **Goodbye** = an expression used when someone leaves or you leave **Good Samaritan** = a person who helps people who may be in trouble **goody-goody** adj. *He's always trying to be goody-goody.* = trying to impress others through polite or good behaviour, which is often not sincere (derogatory) **goodish** adj. **1** = good but not as good as one wants or expects **2** *a goodish distance* = used in the sense of 'fairly', to talk about distance, quality or amount

for good *He gave up smoking for good.* = forever, permanently **to be no good (to not be very good) at something** *I'm no good at needle work.* = to not be able to do something well **to be in someone's good books** = to be thought of favourably by someone whose opinion matters **to be onto a good thing** = to be able to manage well without spending or taking too much trouble (informal, disapproving) **Oh, good!** 'I've just finished the work.' 'Oh good!' = a phrase used to mean that the speaker is happy about something you have said or done **to do someone a world of good** *Why don't you go on a holiday? It will do you a world of good.* = to help someone improve their mental and physical health **to put in a good word for someone** *Could you put in a good word for me?* = to help someone who is hoping to get a job, receive a favour etc., by saying something favourable about the person to the person who will judge her/him **It's a good thing** *It's a good thing I took my umbrella, it rained so hard.* = used to express satisfaction, relief etc. that one had or did something (and did not suffer as a result of not doing or having it) **That's a good one!** *You mean you're going to be the lead actor in Mr Johar's next film? That's a good one!* = used to show that you don't believe something (informal)

goods /gʊdz/ noun, u. (only plural) **1** *consumer goods* = things which are sold in the market **2** *the carriage of goods by trucks* = heavy articles carried in trucks or trains

goose /guːs/ noun, c. (**geese**) = a bird like a duck, but larger in size, which is eaten as well as kept for its eggs

goose•ber•ry noun, c. (**-berries**) = a kind of fruit with a slightly sour taste that grows on a bush

gore[1] /gɔːʳ/ verb, t. *Don't go near the bull or it may gore you.* = to wound someone with the horns or tusks (used to describe an attack by a bull or elephant)

gore[2] noun, u. = thick blood (literary not common now)

gorge[1] /gɔːdʒ/ noun, u. = a deep, narrow valley cut by a river flowing through a mountain

gorge[2] verb, t. *He ate a whole basketful of mangoes at the farm. The way he gorged himself was disgusting.* = to eat too much food (disapproving)

gor•geous /ˈgɔːdʒəs/ adj. **1** *She looks gorgeous in that red dress.* = very attractive **2** *The drive through the hills was gorgeous.* = very pleasant

go•ril•la /gəˈrɪlə/ noun = a large ape found in parts of Africa

gos•pel /ˈgɒspəl/ noun, c. **1** *the Gospel according to St. John* = one of the four accounts of the life and teachings of Jesus Christ, each believed to have been written by one of his followers **2** *She is trying to preach a new gospel.* = a new religious faith or new line of thinking

gos•sip /ˈgɒsɪp/ noun, u, c. **1** *People read film magazines because they contain a lot of gossip about film stars.* = stories about the private lives and activities of other people, especially famous people, which present them in a bad light and are often untrue **2** = a person who enjoys talking about others

Goth•ic /ˈgɒθɪk/ adj. = having to do with the Goths (a race of people who lived in Germany and the neighbouring countries hundreds of years ago) **Gothic architecture** noun = a style of building, seen specially in old churches, that was popular in Western Europe about six hundred years ago, which made use of tall pillars and long, pointed arches and high ceilings

gourd /gʊəd/ noun, c. = a class of vegetables, very common in India, which have thick skins covering soft flesh (e.g. bitter-gourd, sweet-gourd, snake-gourd etc.)

gour•mand /ˈgʊəmənd/ noun, c. = a person who is very fond of eating and drinking (slightly disapproving)

gour•met /ˈgʊəmeɪ/ noun, c. = a person who thinks of food and cooking as an art and has a deep knowledge of food and wine

gout /gaʊt/ noun = a kind of disease that old people often suffer from, in which the joints of the knees, fingers and toes swell up and become painful

gov•ern /ˈgʌvən/ verb, t. *The British governed India for more than 200 years.* = to rule a country **government** noun, u. or c. **1** (c.) = the group of people who rule a country or state **2** (c.) = the act of ruling a country **governess** noun, c. (**governesses**) = a woman teacher who (in former times) lived as a member of the family and looked after the education of the children **governor** noun, c. = a person who is supposed to be the head of the government of a state, but may have little political power

gown /gaʊn/ noun, c. **1** = a long dress for a Western woman, worn on formal occasions **2** = a loose, black garment worn over the other clothes by lawyers as a sign of their profession (formal)

grab /græb/ verb, t. **1** *The thief grabbed my suitcase and ran.* = to take hold of something with a sudden, strong grip; to snatch **2** *I'll grab a sandwich on my way to work.* = to eat something quickly because one is in a hurry (informal) **3** *grab an opportunity* = to take advantage of something by acting quickly

grace[1] /greɪs/ noun, u. **1** *She moves with amazing grace.* = beauty of movement, specially in dance **2** *He had the grace to congratulate his opponent who had defeated him in the debate.* = behaviour which is generous and fair as may be expected of a person with good manners **3** *The bank has allowed us a month's grace to pay up the loan.* = extra time allowed for making a payment which is due by a certain date

grace[2] verb, t. *The famous poet has agreed to grace our meeting with his presence.* = to give honour to someone or something (formal) **graceful** adj. *a graceful dancer* = having grace (beauty of movement) **gracious** adj. *a gracious host* = polite and kind

grade[1] /greɪd/ verb, t. **1** *Have you finished grading the examination papers?* = to examine or give grades to **2** *These eggs have been graded 'Extra Large', 'Large' and 'Medium', according to size.* = to divide into different classes

grade[2] noun, c. **1** *She is a writer of the highest grade.*=a particular level or class, in quality **2** (often plural) *Your grades in the examination have been excellent.*= results in an examination, usually shown by the letters 'A', 'B', etc. instead of marks, following the American system

gra•di•ent /'greɪdiənt/ noun, u. or c. *The road up the mountain has a gradient of one in 10 (10%).* = a measure of the slope or degree of steepness of a road or railway

grad•u•al /'grædʒuəl/ adj. **1** *Five years ago 560 children were born in this town and this year the number has fallen to 540. There seems to be a gradual decrease in the number of births.* = slow, not high in numbers **2** *The hill has a gradual slope. We can climb it without difficulty.* = not steep **gradually** adv.

grad•u•ate[1] /'grædʒueɪt/ verb, i. **1** *He is going to graduate from the university this month.* = to get a university degree **2** *We will have to graduate this flask.* = to make marks on something so that it can be used to make measurements [TECHNICAL]

grad•u•ate[2] /'grædʒuɪt/ noun, c. = a person who has completed a first university degree (B.A., B.Sc., B.Com. etc.) **graduate studies** = post graduate programmes of study in a university (American)

graf•fi•ti /græ'fi:ti/ noun, u. *The walls are covered with graffiti whenever there is an election.* = drawings or writings on a wall, usually of a political nature

graffiti

graft[1] noun, c. or u. or **1** = a piece cut from one tree or plant and allowed to grow on another plant **2** = a piece of healthy skin taken from one part of the body and fixed on to a damaged part and allowed to grow to form new skin **3** *He has been arrested for graft.* = bribery (the giving or receiving of money for some dishonest purpose)

graft[2] /grɑ:ft/ verb, t. = to produce a graft (meanings **2** or **1** above) **grafting** noun, c. *He is quite an average person, but he has succeeded in business through grafting.* = hard and patient work **grafter** noun, c. *He is not a great batsman but he manages to score many runs. He is a successful grafter.* = a person who succeeds through patient and hard work, without having great talent

grain /greɪn/ noun, c. or u. **1** *a grain of rice*(c.) = a single seed from a plant producing rice, wheat etc. **2** *a grain of sand*(c.) = a single, very small piece of some hard substance **3** *The government's warehouses are full of grain from last year's harvest.*(u.) = food in the form of grains of rice, wheat, etc. **4** *The piece of wood has a very fine grain.*(u.) = the natural arrangement of fibres (long thread-like substances) in a piece of wood or rock

to go against the grain = to have to do something which is against one's nature or character

gram /græm/ noun, u. **1** = a measure of weight equal to a thousandth part of a kilogramme (1000g = 1kg) **2** *gram flour* = a kind of foodgrain produced by a plant of the pea family, popular in India (also **chick pea**)

gram•mar /'græmə^r/ noun, u. or c. **1** = the rules by which words change their forms (e.g. 'boy' into 'boys' or 'ask' into 'asked') and combine with other words to form sentences(u.) **2** = the study of such rules(u.) **3** = a book containing a description of such rules(c.)

gram•o•phone /'græməfəʊn/ noun, c. = an old-fashioned machine that plays music from records (large circular disks made of plastic) using a needle (also **record player**)

gra•na•ry /'grænəri/ noun, c. (**granaries**) = a building where grain is stored

grand /grænd/ adj. **1** *The new building looks grand.* = very impressive in appearance; splendid **2** *The party was a grand success.* = very great **grandfather** noun, c. = father's father or mother's father **grandfather clock** = a tall, old-fashioned clock that is placed on the floor **grandchild** noun, c. = son or daughter of one's son or daughter **Grand Slam** = a complete set of championships in a year of some sport e.g. tennis

gran•deur /'grændʒə^r/ noun, u. *It is difficult to describe the grandeur of the Himalayas in words.* = very great beauty and power

grandstand noun = the rows of covered seats in a stadium from which people watch a match

gra•nite /'grænɪt/ noun, u. = a kind of very hard stone which can be polished and used for floors, etc.

gran•ny /'græni/ noun, c. (**grannies**) = a grandmother or a very old woman (informal)

grant[1] /grɑ:nt/ verb, t. **1** *I had requested the government to transfer me to a city and the government has granted my request.* = to officially accept or agree to a request, wish etc. **2** *The judge granted me a pardon.* = to give **3** *I grant that he is intelligent, but he is not very hardworking.* = to accept something as correct or true

grant[2] noun, c. *The university has received a grant of Rs 10 million.* = money given by the government for a particular purpose

to take someone or something for granted *You should have taken my permission before spending my money. You shouldn't take me for granted.* = to act according to a fixed idea or belief about someone or something, without making sure that it is correct

gran•ule /'grænju:l/ noun, c. = a very tiny piece of some solid substance

grape /greɪp/ noun, c. or u. **1** = a small,round fruit produced by a vine (climbing plant) that is full of juice from which wine can be made **2** *grape salad*(u.) = something made from grapes **grapefruit** noun, c. = a large round fruit with a thick skin belonging to the citrus family, which includes oranges and lemons

graph /grɑ:f/ noun, c. *This is a graph showing the rise in the number of road accidents over the last five years.* = a mathematical diagram which shows how two different quantities (numbers of things) are related to each other [TECHNICAL]

graphic /græfɪk/ adj. **1** *Today's newspaper contains a graphic report on yesterday's train accident.* = very clear, detailed and life-like (making the reader feel as though he/she was actually present) **2** *the graphic arts* = connected with the drawing of pictures

graphics noun (only plural) *computer graphics* = writing or drawing produced by a computer or an artist (a graphic artist) e.g. for the cover of a book

graph•ite /'græfaɪt/ noun, u. = a soft, shiny black substance which is a form of carbon, put inside pencils used for writing or drawing

grap•ple /'græpəl/ (+ with) verb, t. **1** *The guard grappled with the thief and threw him to the ground.* = to take hold of someone or something and struggle with him/her/it **2** *We will have to grapple with the problem of drug abuse.* = to face a difficult situation boldly (figurative)

grasp[1] /grɑ:sp/ verb, t. **1** *The woman grasped the rope and pulled herself up.* = to take hold of something with the hands **2** *I was unable to grasp his lecture.* = to understand (formal)

grasp[2] noun, u. *The man held the child in a firm grasp.* = a hold with the hands or arms

grass /grɑ:s/ noun, u.= different kinds of plants with narrow green leaves that grow along the ground and are eaten by cattle, sheep etc. **grasshopper** noun, c.= a kind of small insect which can hop (jump) high **grassroots** noun *If you want to help the country, you will have to start by working at the grassroots level.* = the ordinary people

to not let grass grow under one's feet = to not allow anything to delay or postpone what one is doing (approving)

grate[1] /greɪt/ verb, t. **1** *Please grate these carrots.* = to rub something, specially pieces of fruit, vegetable, cheese etc. against a rough sheet with holes (called a **grater**) so that it is broken up into fine pieces **2** *The two cars grated against each other as they tried to pass on the narrow street.* = to rub against something hard, producing an unpleasant sound

grate[2] noun, c. *Put the logs of wood across the grate and then light the fire.* = the iron bars across a fireplace on top of which pieces of wood or coal are placed in order to start a fire **grating** noun, u. = the metal bars which protect a window or a hole in the ground

grate•ful /'greɪtfəl/ adj. *I shall always be grateful for the help you gave me when I was ill.* = feeling thankful to someone for some help or favour

grat•i•fy /'grætɪfaɪ/ verb, t. (**gratified**) **1** *I am gratified to hear that my book has been liked.* = to give pleasure or happiness (formal) **2** *She always wanted to travel around the world and now that she has become a pilot she can gratify that desire.* = to satisfy or fulfil (a desire)

gra•tis /'grætɪs/ adv. or adj. *If you need advice, I can give you some, gratis.*(adv.) = free of cost; without payment (humourous)

grat•i•tude /'grætɪtju:d/ noun, u. *I don't expect any gratitude for the help I gave you. I was happy to help.* = the feeling of being grateful (thankful) for some help

gra•tu•i•tous /grə'tju:ɪtəs/ adj. *I don't want any gratuitous advice from you.* = not needed or wanted, unncessary in a particular situation (not respectful)

gra•tu•i•ty /grə'tju:ɪti/ noun, u. = a sum of money (a tip) paid to someone as a gift on retiring from service, or a small amount of money that you give someone who serves you

grave[1] /greɪv/ noun, c. = the place in the ground where a dead person has been buried

grave[2] adj. **1** *a grave injury* = serious and needing immediate attention **2** *Why do you look so grave? You should relax!* = serious or solemn (formal)

grav•el /'grævəl/ noun, u. *a gravel path* = small stones mixed with sand, used for making a path etc.

grav•i•ty /'grævɪti/ noun, u. **1** *The force of gravity prevents humans from floating in the air.* = the force with which the earth attracts things towards itself or makes objects fall to the ground **2** *Many people have complained that the building is not safe. The owners should understand the gravity of the situation and get the building repaired.* = the seriousness or importance of a situation which makes some action necessary (formal) **3** *The chairperson wanted to laugh when someone made a joke, but she had to maintain her* *gravity.* = the state of being serious and dignified (formal)

grav•i•tate /'grævɪteɪt/ verb, i. **1** *All falling objects gravitate towards the centre of the earth.* = to be attracted by the earth's gravity **2** *People from the villages are gravitating to the towns, attracted by the possibility of finding jobs.* = to move towards a place because of some attraction

gra•vy /'greɪvi/ noun, u. = the juice which collects in a pot in which meat or vegetables are being cooked

graze /greɪz/ verb, i. **1** *The cattle are grazing in the fields.* = to feed on grass **2** *He has gone out to graze the cattle.* = to lead cattle or other animals into fields where there is grass **3** *He fell off his bicycle and grazed his hands.* = to injure lightly by rubbing the skin against something hard **4** *The two cars grazed each other.* = to touch lightly while passing

grease[1] /gri:s/ noun, u. **1** *The mechanic applied some grease to the wheels of the bicycle to make them run more smoothly.* = a thick oily substance used to make the moving parts of machine run more smoothly **2** = animal fat that becomes soft while cooking

grease[2] verb, t. *The wheels of the bicycle don't run smoothly. You will have to grease them.* = to put grease on something

to grease somebody's palm = to pay a bribe to someone to get something done

great[1] /greɪt/ adj. **1** *The population of Delhi is very great.* = large **2** *Shelley was a great poet.* = of very high quality **3** *This is a great day for me.* = important **4** *Akbar the Great* = famous or well known

great[2] noun, c. *Kapil Dev will be remembered as an all-time great.* = a person who deserves to be famous

greed /gri:d/ noun, u. *I have already paid you Rs 10,000 but you are not satisfied. Is there no limit to your greed?* = strong desire to have more and more money, power, food etc. **greedy** adj. *You have had three helpings of chicken already, and you still want more. Don't be so greedy.* = having a strong desire for food (derogatory)

green[1] /gri:n/ adj. **1** *the green leaves of a tree* = the colour of leaves and grass, which is a mixture of yellow and blue **2** *Many writers are now interested in debating green issues.* = connected with the protection of the environment (the natural surroundings in which we live) **3** *When we were growing up, we were too green to understand the horrors of war.* = young, not experienced **4** *green mangoes* = not ripe

green[2] noun, u. *They are playing cricket on the village green.* = open field or meadow where grass grows

green[3] verb, t. *The government plans to green this whole area.* = to plant trees in an area where there are no trees or few trees **green card** noun = a document that allows a person from some other country to work and live in the USA **greens** noun, u. (only plural) = leafy green vegetables which are cooked and eaten **greengrocer** noun = a person who sells vegetables (old-fashioned) **greenhouse** noun = a building made of glass in which plants are grown in controlled conditions (temperature, amount of water etc.) **greenhouse effect** noun = the increase in the temperature of the air surrounding the earth because of the presence of harmful gases which do not allow heat to escape **greenie** = a person who is interested in protecting the environment (informal) **green light** (**green signal**) noun *We need the green light from you before we can begin today's programme.* = permission to begin some activity (informal)

greet /gri:t/ verb, t. *He greeted me warmly when we met this morning.* = to welcome someone on meeting them with words or actions **greeting** noun, u. or c. *The usual greeting when you meet someone at Christmas time is 'Merry Christmas!'* = the words used to greet someone

gre•gar•i•ous /grɪ'geəriəs/ adj. *It is difficult for a gregarious person like you to live all alone.* = liking the company of others; sociable

gre•nade /grɪ'neɪd/ noun, c. = a small bomb which is thrown by hand or fired from a gun

grey (**gray**) /greɪ/ adj. **1** *The sky looks grey because of the rain clouds.* = a dull colour which is a mixture of black and white **2** *He is turning grey.* = getting grey hair because of old age **greymarket** noun *The greymarket for computers is growing.* = copies or imitations of goods made by well-known manufacturers which are sold at a cheaper price and of whose quality one cannot be sure **grey matter** noun = brains; intelligence (informal)

grey•hound /'greɪhaʊnd/ noun, c. = a kind of dog with a thin body and long legs that can run very fast and is used for racing

grid /grɪd/ noun, c. **1** *The principal drew a grid on the blackboard to explain the new timetable to the teachers.* = a set of squares arranged in rows and columns, used to present some information **2** = a set of metal bars set across each other, forming small squares **3** = a set of numbered squares printed on a map, with the help of which the position of any place on the map can be found **4** *the power grid* = a network of connected wires by which electric power produced in one part of the country can be sent to another part when needed

grid•dle /'grɪdl/ noun, c. = a round iron plate which can be heated over a fire and is used to bake bread, chapatis etc. using dry heat

grief /gri:f/ noun, u. = great sorrow, specially at the death of a loved person
to be grief stricken = to feel very great grief (sorrow) **to come to grief** *Her plans came to grief.* = to come to an unhappy end; (of ships, planes etc.) to be destroyed (formal) **good grief!** *Good grief! I've lost my suitcase!* = an expression used to show that one is unpleasantly surprised

grieve /gri:v/ verb, i. *He is grieving for his friend, who died on this day a year ago. // I am grieved to see you in this sad condition.* = to feel or express grief (sorrow) (formal)

griev•ance /'gri:vəns/ noun, u. or c. *The workers felt they were not being paid enough money, but no one listened to their grievance.* = a complaint about some loss or injustice which one has suffered

grill[1] /grɪl/ verb, t. = to cook something, usually meat, under or over direct heat

grill[2] noun, c. **1** = a device, usually run on electricity or gas, which can grill food (cook it by direct heat) **2** = (see **grille**)

grille /grɪl/ noun, c. **1** = a metal frame with bars running across it, often arranged in different patterns, used to protect a door or window **2** = the bright metal bars covering the radiator at the front end of a motor car

grim /grɪm/ adj. **1** *She is looking very grim today. She hasn't smiled even once.* = looking serious and worried, as though expecting some trouble or difficulty **2** *There is some grim news in today's newspapers.* = causing fear or anxiety

gri•mace[1] /grɪ'meɪs/ verb, i. *He grimaced with pain when the doctor gave him an injection.* = to express pain or sorrow by twisting the face into an unnatural expression

grimace[2] noun, c. *He made a grimace as the doctor pushed the needle into his arm.* = the twisting of the face to express pain

grime /graɪm/ noun, u. *You are covered with grime; have a good bath and clean up.* = thick black dirt (old-fashioned)

grin[1] /grɪn/ verb, i. (**grinned**) *The boy grinned when he saw his friend.* = to produce a wide and happy smile showing one's teeth

grin[2] noun, c. = a wide smile, stretching from one side of the face to the other showing one's teeth

grind[1] /graɪnd/ verb, t. (**ground**) **1** *We grind wheat into flour in order to make bread.* = to break something up into very fine pieces or powder by pressing between two hard surfaces **2** *This knife has lost its sharp edge. You will have to grind it.* = to make a knife sharp by rubbing it against a hard stone **3** *I ground my cigarette into the ashtray.* = to rub (something) against a surface with force

grind[2] noun, u. *I find it a terrible grind to work in this office for 14 hours.* = hard and uninteresting work **grinder** noun = a machine which grinds things (e.g. wheat or coffee) into powder **grindstone** noun = a rough stone against which a knife is rubbed to make it sharp
to grind to a halt *The train ground to a halt.* = to stop, producing a lot of noise and shaking (of a train, bus etc.)

grip[1] /grɪp/ verb, t. **1** *The road is very slippery. Grip my hand tightly or you may fall.* = to take hold of something tightly **2** *This book is so interesting that it grips you completely.* = to take hold of one's attention

grip[2] noun, u. **1** *Although the man was old and weak, I was surprised by the strength of his grip when he held my hand.* = the action of gripping (holding) something **2** *The city is in the grip of a heat wave.* = suffering from the strong effects of something **3** *The team is losing its grip on the match.*= the power to control

gripe[1] /graɪp/ verb, i. *He is always griping about the hot weather.* = to complain (informal, disapproving)

gripe[2] noun, c. *My gripe is that you never pay any attention to my suggestions.* = complaint (informal)

gris•ly /'grɪzli/ adj. *The newspapers had a grisly picture of the people who were wounded in the war.* = (something that is) unpleasant because it deals with violence or bloodshed

grit /grɪt/ noun, u. **1** = small pieces of stone or some other hard substance **2** *The runner completed the 10,000 metre race although she was feverish and could barely stand. I admired her grit.* = courage or determination which enables a person to do something difficult

groan[1] /grəʊn/ verb, i. *The sick man was groaning in pain.* = to make a deep sound expressing pain, suffering, disappointment etc.

groan[2] noun, c. *There were groans of disappointment from the crowd when Sehwag was bowled with the very first ball.* = the sound produced when someone groans

gro•cer /'grəʊsə^r/ noun = a person who sells foodstuffs (rice, sugar, tea, oil etc.) or other things used in the home regularly (e.g. soap, toothpaste etc.) **grocery** noun, u. or c. (**groceries**) = the things sold by a grocer

groin /grɔɪn/ noun, c. = the place where the legs join the body

groom[1] /gru:m/ verb, t. **1** *We are grooming them to head the organisation.* = to choose and prepare or train someone for a special position or responsibility **2** *He grooms himself well. You will never find him looking untidy.* = to take good care of one's appearance by dressing well (old-fashioned) **3** *grooming a horse* = to clean an animal, especially a horse, by brushing

G

groom[2] noun, c. **1** = bridegroom (a man who is about to get married or has just been married) **2** = a person who takes care of horses

groove /gru:v/ noun, c. **1** *The window slides in this groove when it is opened or closed.* = a long, hollow cut in a piece of wood or metal in which something moves **2** *The wheels of the bullock carts moving along this road have made deep grooves in it.* = a deep mark in a surface, caused by pressure

grope /grəʊp/ verb, i. *She groped about in the dark, trying to find the light switch.* = to try to find something that one cannot see by stretching out one's hands to touch things

to grope one's way somewhere = to try to find one's way in the dark by touching things, because one cannot see

gross[1] /grəʊs/ noun, c. = 12 dozen or 144 (in number)

gross[2] verb, t. *The new film has grossed more than 5 million in the first week.* = to earn as profit

gross[3] adj. **1** *My gross salary, including all allowances, is Rs 10,725 a month.* = total; before something is taken away **2** *The doctor who did not attend to the patient in time has been guilty of gross negligence.* = something that is seriously wrong and cannot be excused **3** *I am shocked by your gross behaviour.* = rough and improper **4** *He has put on so much weight that he looks quite gross.* = fat and ugly

gro•tesque /grəʊ'tesk/ adj. *You will find a grotesque picture hanging on the wall, showing a man with ten heads and enormous teeth sticking out like tusks. // The old man looks quite grotesque when he tries to dress like a teenager.* = strange and unnatural in appearance, causing fear or laughter

grot•to /'grɒtəʊ/ noun, c. (**grottos** or **grottoes**) = a small cave

grouch[1] /graʊtʃ/ verb, i. *Stop grouching about your exam!* = to complain in a bad-tempered manner (informal)

grouch[2] noun, c. **1** *I am tired of your grouches.* = complaints **2** *What a grouch you are!* = a person who keeps complaining about things

ground[1] noun, u. or c. **1** *The ground is very hard here. It will be difficult to dig a hole.*(u.)= the solid surface of the earth **2** *This is sandy ground.*(u.)= soil **3** *a football ground*(c.) = a piece of land used for a particular purpose **4** *The professor covered a lot of ground during her talk.*(u.) = information relating to some subject **5** (always plural) *What are your grounds for saying that we should move out of this house?*(c.) = a reason for saying something (formal) **6** (always plural) *Let us take a walk around the grounds.*(u.) = the area surrounding a building

ground[2] /graʊnd/ verb, t. (**grounded**) **1** *The ship grounded as the water was not very deep.* = to hit the bottom of the sea or river (used to refer to a ship) **2** *The aircraft has been grounded as there is some problem with the engine.* = to prevent an aircraft from flying **ground floor** noun, c. = the lowest floor of a building, built at the ground level (known as the **first floor** in American English) **groundless** adj. *Your fears are quite groundless.* = without reason or cause **groundnut** noun = the nut (seed) of a plant which grows under the ground and produces a kind of oil **groundwork** noun, u. *I have completed the groundwork for my new book and. now I can start writing it.* = the work done as preparation for something

to be on familiar ground = to be talking/writing about a subject that one knows well **to be on dangerous ground** = to be in a position in which one is likely to say, do or write something which may prove to be risky

group[1] /gru:p/ verb, t. *We can group these plants together as none of them have green leaves.* = to place or arrange in a group (usually for the purpose of study)

group[2] noun, c. **1** *a group of children* = a number of persons or objects gathered together at one place or time **2** *Hawks and eagles belong to a group of hunting birds.* = class

grouse /graʊs/ noun, c. **1** = a kind of small brown bird which is commonly eaten **2** *He has a grouse against you. It seems you insulted him once.* = complaint or grievance (informal)

grove /grəʊv/ noun, c. *a mango grove* = an area where fruit trees (usually of the same kind) have been planted

gro•vel /'grɒvəl/ verb, i. (**grovelled**) *I hate to see you grovel for a role in the film. You should behave with greater dignity.* = to show too much respect or humility to someone who is in power or can give you something you want (disapproving)

grow /grəʊ/ verb, t. or i. (**grew, grown**) **1** *Coconut trees grow best in sandy soil.*(i.)= to survive and increase in size;(used about plants) to develop **2** *I am happy to see how tall you have grown.*(i.) = to become bigger or taller **3** *She grows rice on her land.*(t.) = to cause or allow something to survive and increase in size **4** *Her savings have grown.*(i.) = to become greater in quantity or number **5** *He is growing bald.*(i.) = to become **growth** noun, u. or c. **1** *The growth of these plants is quite normal.*(u.) = the process of becoming larger in size **2** *the growth of unemployment*(u.) = increase **3** *The doctor found a growth inside his mouth.*(c.) = a part of the body that grows in an unnatural way [MEDICINE] **grown-up** noun, c. or adj. **1** *We have no grown-ups to look after the children.* (noun) = an adult person **2** *The child is* *trying to act grown up.*(adj.) = behaving or looking like an adult

growl[1] /graʊl/ verb, i. *The dog growls at strangers.* = to make a deep sound in the throat expressing anger or suspicion

growl[2] noun, c. *The dog's growls don't frighten me.* = the sound of growling

grub /grʌb/ noun, c. or u. **1** (c.) = a young insect, after it has just come out of its egg, looking like a worm **2** *Have you had your grub?*(u.) = food (informal)

grub•by /'grʌbi/ adj. *Your clothes look grubby. Get them washed.* = dirty (informal)

grudge[1] /grʌdʒ/ noun, c. *He has a grudge against you as he feels you got the job that should have gone to him.* = a deep dislike of someone, caused by the feeling that he/she has done you some harm

grudge[2] verb, t. **1** *They grudged her the high salary they paid her.* = to give something unwillingly **2** *I don't grudge you your success.* = to feel unhappy at something good that happens to someone else

gruel /'gru:əl/ noun, u. = the watery liquid that collects on top of rice which has been boiled and is often used as food

gruel•ling /'gru:elɪŋ/ adj. *I feel tired after the gruelling car race.* = something that requires a lot of effort and makes one tired

grue•some /'gru:səm/ adj. *a gruesome murder* = very horrible and violent

gruff /grʌf/ adj. *He always speaks to us in such a gruff manner that we are frightened.* = rough and angry

grum•ble[1] /'grʌmbəl/ verb, i. *She is always grumbling about being made to work too hard.* = to complain in a quiet but bad-tempered manner

grumble[2] noun, c. *I am tired of listening to your grumbles.* = a complaint

grump•y /'grʌmpi/ adj. *She is always grumpy on Monday mornings, when she has to return to the office after a weekend.* = bad-tempered and complaining (informal)

grunt[1] /grʌnt/ verb, i. *When I asked him whether he would come for dinner, he just grunted.* = to make a deep sound in the throat expressing dissatisfaction or an unwillingness to talk

grunt[2] noun, c. = the sound made by a pig or a similar sound made by a human being

gua•no /'gwɑ:nəʊ/ noun, u. = dried waste matter passed out of the intestines of seabirds, from which fertilizer (a chemical that helps plants grow well) is made

gua•ran•tee[1] /gærən'ti:/ noun, c.or u. *There is a one-year gurantee on this new car. If anything goes wrong during this time, the car will be replaced by the manufacturer.* = a written agreement or promise made by the maker of an article to repair or replace it if a defect is found

guarantee[2] verb, t. *I guarantee that this watch has no defect.* = to provide a guarantee for the quality of something that is sold

guard[1] /gɑ:d/ verb, t. *We have hired a person to guard the house at night and prevent thieves from breaking in. // Guard the prisoner well and make sure that he does not escape.* = to keep watch over something or someone in order to keep it/him/her protected and safe, or to prevent him/her from escaping

guard[2] noun, c. *The guards have been ordered not to allow anyone to enter this house.* = a person or group of persons who guard (keep watch over) someone or something **guarded** adj. *When the newspaper reporter asked the film star a question about her private life, she gave him a guarded reply.* = careful; not saying too much

guard•i•an /'gɑ:diən/ noun, c. *The boy's parents live in the USA, so I look after him as his guardian.* = a person who has been appointed to look after a child that is not his/her own

gua•va /'gwɑ:və/ noun, c. = a small round tropical fruit (growing in warm or hot places) with white or pink flesh

guer•ril•la[1] (**guerilla**) /gə'rɪlə/ noun, c. = a fighter who is not a regular soldier and is (usually) fighting against the government and who attacks the enemy in small groups, while hiding from them

guerrilla[2] adj. *guerrilla war* = a war fought by guerrilla fighters

guess[1] /ges/ verb, t. *I can only guess why she wants to leave the job.* = to try to form a judgement or an opinion or to find the answer to a question without being sure of it

guess[2] noun, c. *I don't know how much you paid for that old car but I can make a guess.* = an attempt to find an answer to a question to which one does not know the correct or exact answer **guesswork** noun = the act of guessing about something **guesstimate** = an estimate of something based on a guess

a wild guess = a guess made without much thinking **Guess what!** *Guess what! I've forgotten the book again!* = an expression of surprise mixed with joy or sarcasm (informal, often humorous) **to be anybody's guess** *When he will finish the work is anybody's guess.* = no one knows the answer (informal, humorous) **to keep someone guessing** **1** *We won't tell them what happens at the end of the play. Let's keep them guessing.* = to not reveal or tell what is going to happen **2** = to not tell one's partner in a romantic relationship whether it will end in marriage, be a permanent one etc.

guest /gest/ noun, c. **1** *I am expecting two guests who will stay with me for couple of days.* = a person who is invited by someone (the host) for a meal or to spend some time in his/her house **2** = a person who is staying at a hotel

guf•faw[1] /gəˈfɔː/verb, i. *We guffawed at her silly plan.* = to laugh loudly and rudely

guffaw[2] noun, c. *There was a guffaw when I sang out of tune.* = a burst of loud and rude laughter

guide[1] /gaɪd/ verb, t. **1** *I don't know the way to the station. I shall be grateful if you could guide me there.* = to show someone the way by leading him/her to it **2** *The driver guided the bus carefully through the narrow streets.* = to control or direct **3** *I'm really very confused. Please guide me.* = advise

guide[2] noun, c. **1** *The guide will take us around the town and show us all the interesting places.* = a person who is paid to take tourists or visitors around places of interest **2** *This book is a useful guide to classical Indian music.* = a book which introduces or teaches a new subject **the Guides** noun = an organization of girls who are trained to help people in need

guile /gaɪl/ noun, u. *a person with a lot of guile* = cleverness which is used for bad purposes e.g. to cheat people

guil•lo•tine[1] /ˈgɪlətiːn/ noun, c. **1** = an instrument consisting of a large heavy blade (knife) sliding down between two wooden posts, used in France in the eighteenth century to punish criminals by cutting off their heads **2** = an order or ruling given by the speaker, bringing some discussion in the parliament to an end

guillotine[2] verb, t. = to cut off someone's head, using a guillotine

guilt /gɪlt/ noun, u. **1** *The man was tried in court for murder, but he was set free because his guilt could not be proved.*= responsibility for doing something wrong or against the law **2** *I have such a sense of guilt about not helping my friend when she was ill.* = the feeling produced by the knowledge that one has done something wrong **guilty** adj. *You are guilty of murder.* = found to have done something wrong

guinea pig noun, c. **1** = an animal which looks like a small rabbit and is commonly used for scientific experiments or tests **2** *The doctors are testing a new medicine and we are the guinea-pig.* = used figuratively about human beings on whom something new is tested

guise /gaɪz/ noun, c. *It is said that Haroon-al-Rashid, the ruler of Baghdad, often went round the city at night in the guise of a beggar, in order to find out what was happening in his kingdom.* = outward appearance or dress

gui•tar /gɪˈtɑːr/ noun, c. = a musical instrument with six strings and a long narrow stem attached to a larger flat body, played with the fingers

gulf /gʌlf/ noun, c. **1** *the Persian Gulf* = a stretch of deep sea partly surrounded by land **2** *There is a wide gulf between our views on music, which can never be bridged.* = difference or gap between the way people think, feel or live

gull /gʌl/ noun = a kind of large bird commonly found near the sea

gul•let /ˈgʌlɪt/ noun = the pipe leading down the throat from the mouth to the stomach, through which food passes

gul•li•ble /ˈgʌlɪbəl/ adj. *Why did you believe them when they promised you a job? You are too gullible!* = very willing to believe others and therefore easily tricked

gul•ly /ˈgʌli/ noun, c. (**gullies**) **1** = a small narrow valley cut through the side of a hill by heavy rain or a storm **2** = a fielding position in cricket close to the batsman, on the off side and between point and slip

gulp[1] /gʌlp/ verb, t. **1** *The man gulped down his tea and ran to catch the bus.* = to swallow large amounts of food or drink quickly **2** *She gulped when I asked her what she was doing in my room.* = to make a sudden swallowing movement, out of nervousness or surprise

gulp[2] noun, c. *He finished his coffee in a single gulp.* = a large mouthful which is swallowed

gum[1] /gʌm/ verb, t. *This envelope has to be gummed before it can be mailed.* = to stick something with gum or to put gum on something

gum[2] noun, c. or u. **1** *She is bleeding from the gums.*(c.) = the pink firm area covering the jaws in which the teeth are rooted **2** *This gum is taken from a eucalyptus tree.*(u.)= a sticky substance obtained from a plant or tree and used for sticking things together **3** = chewing gum or bubble gum **gumboots** noun (always plural) = large boots made of rubber which are worn when walking through muddy areas

gun[1] noun, c. = a weapon which is either held in the hands or fixed to a frame, from which bullets or shells can be fired

gun[2] /gʌn/ verb, t. **1** *The driver gunned the engine of her car before the race.* = to make the engine of a car run very fast **2** *The enemy soldiers were gunned down by our troops.* = to shoot down with guns

gur•gle[1] /ˈgɜːgəl/ verb, i. *The rain water gurgled through the drains.* = to flow with a bubbling sound

gurgle[2] noun, u. *I can hear the gurgle of the stream flowing down the hillside.* = the sound made by flowing water

guru /ˈgʊruː/ noun, c. = a teacher or religious leader or a person who is respected for his/her ideas

gush[1] /gʌʃ/ verb, i. **1** *Blood gushed from the cut in my head.* = to flow out with force, in large quantities **2** *I didn't like the way he gushed about your book.* = to praise excitedly and in a way which seems to have the purpose of flattering someone (disapproving)

gush[2] noun, u. *The doctor tried to stop the gush of blood by applying pressure.* = the flow of liquid in large quantities **gushing** adj. *a gushing speech* = expressing some feeling very strongly but without much sincerity

gust /gʌst/ noun, c. *a gust of wind* = a strong, sudden rush of air

gusto /'gʌstəʊ/ noun, u. *He talked with great gusto.* = energy and enjoyment

gut[1] /gʌt/ noun, c. or u. **1** (c.) = the intestines (tubes inside the body below the stomach, through which food passes) **2** (u.) = strong thread made from the intestines of sheep

gut[2] verb, t. (**gutted**) **1** = to remove the intestines, stomach etc. of an animal before cooking it **2** *The building was gutted by the fire.* = to destroy completely (used to describe the effects of fire) **gut feeling** noun *I have a gut feeling that we are going to win this match, although everyone thinks we will lose.* = a strong natural feeling, not based on reason **guts** noun, u. **1** = intestines or bowels **2** *I thought you were a timid person, afraid of getting into a fight, but I see you have guts.*(always plural) = courage and determination (informal)

to hate someone's guts = to dislike the fact that someone is bold, clever etc. (informal)

gut•ter /'gʌtə^r/ noun, c. = a drain through which rainwater or dirty water flows **guttersnipe** noun, c. = a poor child from the lowest social class (derogatory) **gutter press** noun = newspapers which print shocking stories about the private lives of people

gut•tur•al /'gʌtərəl/ adj. *a guttural sound* = a sound which seems to come from the back of the throat

guy /gaɪ/ noun, c. *He's a good guy.* = man or woman (informal)

guz•zle /'gʌzəl/ verb, t. or i. *He has been guzzling icecream and soft drinks all evening.* = to eat or drink quickly and greedily (informal)

gym•kha•na /gʒɪm'kɑːnə/ noun, c. = a sports club

gym•na•sium /dʒm'neɪziəm/ noun, c. (**gynasiums** or **gymnasia**) = a place where people can perform physical exercises, using equipment of different kinds **gymnastics** /dʒɪm'næstɪks/ noun, u. (only plural form) = physical exercises requiring balance and skill, done indoors e.g. swinging from parallel bars or rings

gy•nae•col•o•gy (**gynecology**) /gaɪnɪ'kɒlədʒi/ noun = the branch of medicine which deals with the diseases and medical conditions of women

gyp•sum /'dʒɪpsəm/ noun = a soft white chalk-like substance, from which plaster of paris is made

gy•rate /dʒaɪ'reɪt/ verb, i. = to turn round and round at great speed while staying in one place (literary)

gy•ro•scope /'dʒaɪrəskəʊp/ noun = an instrument which helps to keep balance in a ship or aircraft, consisting of a heavy wheel which spins very fast inside a frame

G

hH

h, H /eɪtʃ/ the eighth letter of the English alphabet

ha /hɑː/ interjec. = an expression of surprise, interest, amusement etc.

ha•bit /ˈhæbɪt/ noun, c. or u. **1** *She has a habit of biting her fingernails when she is thinking.*(c.) = some action that one performs regularly, often without knowing that one is doing it **2** = special clothing worn by nuns, monks etc. **habitual** /həˈbɪtʃuəl/ adj. **1** *He is a habitual smoker.* = doing something as a habit **2** *She greeted us with her habitual friendliness.* = usual **habituate** verb, i. *I am habituated to twenty cups of tea a day.* = to do something regularly as a habit **habit-forming** adj. *Tea and coffee are habit-forming.* = likely to result in a habit if done regularly (see also **addiction, addictive**)

to break a habit *He used to smoke 20 cigarettes a day but he has been able to break the habit. Now he doesn't smoke at all.* = to give up a bad habit **from force of habit** *He is rich now and has many servants, but he still cooks his own food from force of habit.* = doing something that one has been in the habit of doing, although it is no longer necessary

hab•i•ta•ble /ˈhæbɪtəbəl/ adj. *This house is not habitable.* = fit to be lived in (formal)

hab•i•tat /ˈhæbɪtæt/ noun, u. *The habitat of the whale is the deep waters of the Pacific Ocean.* = the natural home in which a living creature is found [BIOLOGY]

hab•i•ta•tion /hæbɪˈteɪʃən/ noun, u. or c. **1** *Some of the people who have approached us do not have proper habitations.*(c.) = a place to live in; a home (formal) **2** *This old house is no longer fit for human habitation.*(u.) = the act of living in a place (formal)

hack[1] /hæk/ verb, t. or i. **1** (t.) = to cut with an axe or knife, using force **2** *Someone has hacked into the data files in my computer system.*(i.) = to break through the security system that protects data on a computer network, without the permission or knowledge of its users [COMPUTERS] (see also **hacker**)

hack[2] noun, c. *No one takes his newspaper reports seriously. He is just a hack.* = a low-paid writer, usually working for a newspaper (derogatory, not respectful)) **hacker** noun, c. *An unknown hacker broke into our computer system and destroyed our database.* = someone who hacks into a computer system (informal) **hacksaw** noun, c. = a saw (a metal blade with teeth) used for cutting metal

hack•ney (+carriage) /ˈhækni/ noun, c. = a horse-drawn carriage which one can hire

hack•neyed /ˈhæknid/ adj. *The story of the film is the hackneyed one about the two brothers who get separated in childhood.* = something which has been repeated so often that it has lost its freshness and meaning (derogatory)

hae•mo•glo•bin (hemoglobin) /hiːməˈgləʊbɪn/ noun = the substance in blood which makes it red in colour [MEDICINE]

hae•mo•phil•i•a (hemophilia) /hiːməˈfɪliə/ noun = a disease which causes a person to bleed for a long time after receiving a cut because the blood does not **clot** (thicken and stop flowing) [MEDICINE]

haem•or•rhage (hemorage) /ˈhemərɪdʒ/ noun, c. = a flow of blood which causes a lot of blood to be lost [MEDICINE]

hag /hæg/ noun, c. = an ugly old woman who is unpleasant (derogatory)

hag•gard /ˈhægəd/ adj. *He returned from his month-long expedition into the forest looking tired and haggard.* = weak and unwell, because of overwork or lack of sleep

hag•gle /ˈhægəl/ verb, i. *We haggled over the price of the old car for a long time, but finally agreed on a price.* = to bargain or to argue over the price of something

haiku /ˈhaɪkuː/ noun = a Japanese poem of three lines [LITERATURE]

hail[1] /heɪl/ noun, c. = rain which turns into little balls of ice because of sudden cooling

hail[2] verb, t. **1** *He hailed an autorickshaw from a distance.* = to shout to someone in order to attract his/her attention **2** *The film has been hailed as a masterpiece.* = to praise strongly and publicly

hair /heəʳ/ noun, u. or c. = the thread-like parts growing from the body of an animal or the body, head and face of a human being **hairy** adj. = with hair or full of hair **hairdo** noun, c. (**hair-dos**) = the way in which a person's hair is styled by a hair-dresser (informal) **hairdresser** noun, c. = a person who styles the hair (cuts it and makes it look attractive) of a man or woman **hairpin bend** noun, c. = a sharp, U-shaped curve in a road going up or down a hill **hair-raising** adj. *a hair-raising experience* = something that causes excitement mixed with fear

to split hairs = (always plural) in an argument or disagreement, to go into details which seem unimportant **to keep one's hair on** = to not lose one's temper, to keep calm (informal) **to not turn a hair** *I told Lisa she had failed in the test, but she didn't turn a hair.* = to not let others know one is bothered by unpleasant news (informal, disapproving) **to tear one's hair** = to react angrily or nervously to a situation **to let one's hair down** = to relax and enjoy oneself after having done hard work over a long period (informal) **to get in someone's hair** = to upset someone's calmness by annoying them (informal) **to make one's hair stand on end** = to put one into a state of great fear (informal)

hale /heɪl/ adj. **(hale and hearty)** *He has recovered from his illness and looks hale and hearty.* = in good health

half[1] /hɑːf/ noun, c. **(halves)** *Take one half of the apple and give me the other half.* = one of the two equal parts of something

half[2] adj. *The bottle is half full.* = partly but not completely

half[3] det. *She will be here in half an hour.* = one of the two equal parts into which something is or can be divided **halve** /hɑːv/ verb, t. = to divide into two equal parts **half-baked** adj. *Your half-baked ideas won't work.* = ideas or plans which have not been fully thought out **half-mast** adv. *The national flags are flying at half-mast because our leader is dead.* = the lowering of a flag to a position near the centre of the flag-pole, as a sign of national sorrow

to not do something by halves = to do something very carefully **to go halves** = to share equally the amount one pays for something (informal)

hall /hɔːl/ noun, c. **1** = a large room **2** = the room that is just inside the entrance of a building

hal•le•lu•jah /hælə'ljuːjə/ interjec. (Hebrew) = an expression of praise and thanks to God

hal•low /'hæləʊ/ verb, t. = *This ground has been hallowed by the blood of the heroes who died here for their country.* = to make something holy (formal)

hal•lu•ci•na•tion /həluːsɪ'neɪʃən/ noun, u. *He claims that he saw the ghost of his great-grandfather last night but I think it was just a hallucination.* = something imaginary that one believes to be real, often because one has taken a drug or is ill

ha•lo /'heɪləʊ/ noun, c. **(halos or haloes)** **1** = a ring of bright light painted around the head of a holy person **2** = a circle of light seen around the moon or sun in very misty weather

halt[1] /hɔːlt/ verb, i. or t. **1** *'Halt!' the guard shouted at us as we came near the actor's residence.*(i.) = to stop **2** *The driver halted the train as the track was being repaired.*(t.) = to bring something to a stop

halt[2] noun, c. *The train came to a halt at the station.* = a stop or pause that doesn't last very long

hal•ter /'hɔːltə^r/ noun, c. **1** = a strap around the neck that holds a woman's dress in place **2** = the rope or leather band tied around the head of a horse, by which it is led

halve see under **half**

ham[1] /hæm/ noun, u. or c. **1** *We had ham and eggs for breakfast.*(u.) = meat from the upper part of the leg (the buttock and thigh) of a pig, which has been preserved with salt or by smoking it over a fire **2** *After the cyclone all the telephone lines were blown down, but some hams provided valuable help by sending information over the radio.*(c.) = a person who sends and receives wireless messages over the radio as a hobby, using his/her own equipment ('ham' is an abbreviation for 'amateur radio operator'.) [TECHNICAL] **3** (c.) = an actor who puts too much expression or movement into his or her acting) (derogatory)

ham[2] verb, i. *He likes to ham when he is acting.* = to act with too much expression, movement etc. (in a film or on the stage) (derogatory) **hamburger** noun, c. = an item of food consisting of two buns (pieces of round bread), between which is placed meat that has been ground (broken into very fine pieces) and cooked over a fire

hamster /'hæmstə^r/ noun, c. = an animal that looks like a small rat, often kept as a pet

hamstring[1] /'hæmstrɪŋ/ noun = the thick tendon (thick strong cord) at the back of the leg, connecting the muscle in the thigh to the bone in the lower leg

hamstring[2] verb, t. **(hamstrung)** *The government is unable to do anything; it is hamstrung by the lack of funds.* = to be made powerless and unable to act

ham•let /'hæmlɪt/ noun, c. = a small village

ham•mer[1] /'hæmə^r/ noun, c. = a tool consisting of a heavy piece of metal (the head) fitted to a wooden handle, used to drive metal nails into wood or to hit things with force in order to break them up into small pieces

hammer[2] verb, t. *These nails have to be hammered into the wood.* = to hit something with a hammer (see pic under **tools**)

to hammer an idea *You have to hammer this idea into her head if you want her to remember it.* = to keep on repeating something until it is understood or has some effect

ham•mock /'hæmək/ noun, c. = a kind of bed or seat made of strong cloth or ropes, which can be hung between two trees or two posts or from a hook in the ceiling

ham•per[1] /'hæmpə^r/ noun, c. = a large basket with a lid, generally used to carry food for a picnic

hamper[2] verb, t. *The work of building new roads has been hampered by the shortage of labour.* = to cause difficulty in doing something

hand[1] /hænd/ noun, c. **1** = the lowest part of the arm, below the wrist and including the fingers **2** *the hands of the clock* = the pointer or needle of a watch or clock which shows the time **3** *She writes a beautiful hand.* = handwriting **4** *a farmhand* = a person who does hard physical work on a farm **5** *He's an old hand* *at this kind of work.* = a person with skill or experience **6** *Give him a big hand!* = applause, welcome or encouragement given by clapping the hands

hand[2] verb, t. **1** *Hand me that pen, please.* = to give or put into someone's hand **2** *Please take this letter and hand it over to your neighbour.* = to deliver or give **3** *Will you hand out these sweets to the children?* = to distribute **handbag** noun = a small bag used by a woman to carry money etc. **handbill** noun = a small printed advertisement **handbook** noun = a book which introduces a new subject or tells one how to do something **handbrake** noun = a device (simple machine) in a car which is used to stop the car and is worked by the hand (and not foot) **handcuffs** noun = a pair of metal rings connected by a chain, which are put around the wrists of a prisoner **second-hand** adj. = something that has had an owner earlier

to ask for someone's hand = to express a desire to marry someone **to be at hand** = to be available or nearby **to get out of hand** = to get out of control **to lend a hand** = to help someone do a piece of work **to live from hand to mouth** = to have just enough money for one's needs **to have a hand in something** *I think Nita had a hand in the fact that we didn't go on the school picnic.* = to have a part or role in seeing that something unpleasant happens or something good does not happen **to win hands down** = to win completely and in a big way (informal)

han•di•cap[1] /'hændikæp/ noun, c. **1** = the absence of a physical or mental ability (see usage note) **2** *Not knowing German is a handicap if you are working in Germany.* = something that puts a person at a disadvantage **3** *He is such a good player that we will have to set him a handicap if we want to give the others a chance.* = a way of making a sports competition more equal (and therefore more interesting) by giving some disadvantage to a strong competitor

> **Usage** the phrase 'differently abled' is preferred when referring to a person with a handicap.

handicap[2] verb, t. *I am handicapped by my inability to use a computer.* = to put someone at a disadvantage or to be at a disadvantage

han•di•craft /'hændikrɑːft/ noun, c. *Weaving and pottery are our most common handicrafts.* = the production of articles of common use by hand, requiring great skill

handiwork /'hændɪwɜːk/ noun, u. **1** *an exhibition of drawings and other handiwork by schoolchildren* = work done by hand, requiring skill **2** *The table lamp had been knocked over when we returned home. I think it must be the handiwork of our cats.* = the result, specially the bad result, of someone's action (disapproving)

hand•ker•chief /'hæŋkətʃɪf/ noun, c. (**-chiefs or -chieves**) = a small piece of cloth used to wipe one's face or fingers

han•dle[1] /'hændl/ noun, c. *an umbrella with a long handle* = a part of an object which is used to hold it or carry it in the hand

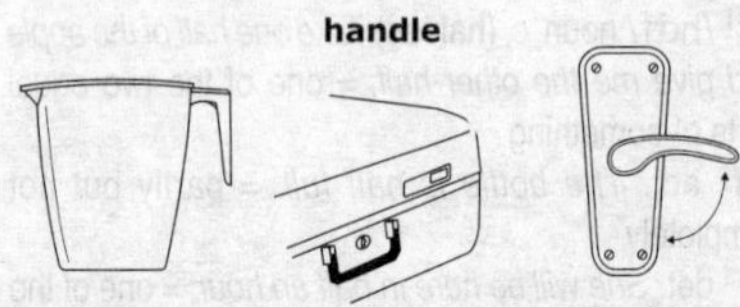

handle[2] verb, t. **1** *Please handle this watch carefully. It is very expensive.* = to hold or to touch with the fingers and hands **2** *This is a dangerous situation and you should call in the police to handle it.* = to deal with, control or manage **handlebars** noun, c. (always plural) **1** = the part of a bicycle or motorcycle which the rider holds with his/her hands **2** = large U-shaped moustaches which stretch on either side and turn up slightly at the ends, looking like the handlebars of a bicycle

hand•some /'hænsəm/ adj. **1** *a handsome man* =good-looking (more often used to describe a man than a woman) **2** *a handsome salary* = fairly large; decent

han•dy[1] /'hændi/ adj. *She is quite handy with a set of carpenter's tools.* = possessing good skills at using the hands

handy[2] adv. *Keep a pen and a sheet of paper handy when you receive a telephone message.* = nearby; in a place which can be easily reached **handyman** noun, c. = a person who does various kinds of repair jobs in the house

to come in handy = to be useful

hang /hæŋ/ verb, t. or i. (**hung or hanged**) **1** *Please hang this picture from that nail on the wall.*(t.) = to fix something in such a way that the lower part is free to move or swing about **2** = to kill somebody or oneself by putting a rope around the neck and allowing the body to hang without touching the ground

to get the hang of something *You may never have driven a jeep before, but you will soon get the hang of it.* = to learn how to do something that needs skill, generally by doing it for some time **to hang around** *He is always hanging around the railway station.* = to wait or stay near a place without having any clear purpose (informal, sometimes disapproving) **to hang out with someone** *He's always happy when he's hanging out with his friends.* = spending time with, often without a purpose (informal) **to hang up** =

to end a telephone conversation by putting the receiver down **to hang fire** *The plan we sent them is still hanging fire.* = to be delayed or blocked (used to refer to plans and proposals) **Hang on!** *Hang on! I just remembered something.* = used to ask someone to wait or to show that one has remembered something important (informal) **to leave something hanging in the air** = to leave something that someone hopes to have an answer to, uncertain

> **Usage** 'hang' takes the past tense form 'hanged' only when referring to a 'hanging' (the punishment given in some countries to someone who has committed a murder or a very serious crime.)

hangar /'hæŋəʳ/ noun, c. = a large building in which aircraft are kept when they are not in use or are being repaired

hanger /'hæŋəʳ/ (**coathanger**) noun, c. = a frame made of wood, plastic or metal which is pushed inside the shoulders of a coat or shirt so that it will keep its shape **hanger-on** noun, c. = someone who attaches himself/herself to an important person in the hope of getting some benefit or advantage from him/her **hangout** noun, c. *This restaurant is my favourite hangout.* = a place that one likes to visit, where one can often be found

hanging /'hæŋɪŋ/ noun, c. or u. = the punishment sometimes given to a person for committing a murder or some other very serious crime

hangover /'hæŋəʊvər/ noun, c. **1** = the headache and feeling of being unwell that one has after drinking too much alcohol **2** *Some people say that our love for the English language is a hangover from the British rule.* = the long-lasting effect of something that happened earlier

han•ker /'hæŋkəʳ/ verb, t. (+ after) *She is very lonely and hankers after friendship.* = to have a strong wish for something which one cannot get **hankering** noun, c. = a strong wish for something; longing

hank•y-pank•y /hæŋki 'pæŋki/ noun, u. *When you find people in the office whispering to each other, it is likely that there is some hanky-panky going on.* = behaviour which is not correct or proper (disapproving)

hap•ha•zard /hæp'hæzəd/ adj. = without a plan or done in an unplanned manner

hap•less /'hæpləs/ adj. *a hapless person* = unlucky (literary)

hap•pen /'hæpən/ verb, i. **1** *This accident happened while the car was trying to overtake a bus.* = to take place **2** *I just happened to be at the party she attended.* = to be somewhere or to do something by chance **3** *What will happen if the exam is advanced? // I pulled the alarm chain but nothing happened. The train did not stop.* = to produce some result or effect

hap•py /'hæpi/ adj. **1** *The child looks happy.* = feeling or showing pleasure **2** *I am happy that you have passed the examination.* = feeling pleasure because of something good **3** *By a happy chance, he was passing by when my car broke down on the road.* = fortunate **happiness** noun, u. = the state of being happy **happy-go-lucky** adj. *a happy-go-lucky person who never looks worried* = having no worries, specially about the future

har•a•ki•ri /hærə'kɪri/ noun (Japanese) = a way of killing oneself with a sword, by cutting the stomach open, formerly used in Japan as a means of saving one's honour

to commit harakari = to do something unwise which causes great harm to oneself (figurative)

ha•rangue[1] /hə'ræŋ/ noun, c. *The visiting professor delivered a long harangue to the gathering.* = a loud speech in which one tries to convince others of his/her opinion

harangue[2] verb, t. *The leader harangued his opponents.* = to attack or blame someone in a speech

har•ass /'hærəs/ verb, t. *The judge ordered the policeman to stop harassing the shopkeepers.* = to trouble someone repeatedly

har•bin•ger /'hɑːbɪndʒəʳ/ noun, c. *The dark clouds in June are harbingers of the monsoon.* = messenger; someone or something that tells us what is going to happen (literary)

har•bour[1] /'hɑːbəʳ/ noun, c. *The ship entered the harbour.* = a part of the sea near the shore, where the water is calm and where ships can take shelter

harbour[2] verb, t. **1** *The police can arrest you for harbouring a dangerous criminal.* = to give protection or shelter to someone who is bad **2** *Don't harbour such unkind thoughts about me.* = to keep some unpleasant thought in one's mind and not allow them to go

hard[1] /hɑːd/ adj. **1** *Diamond is hard.* = difficult to break **2** *This is a hard question to answer.* = difficult **3** *He received a hard blow.* = powerful **4** *She is a hard worker.* = able to do a lot of work **5** *She has a hard life.* = full of difficulties **6** *He is very hard on his children.* = strict **7** *hard water* = water containing large amounts of certain minerals, which makes it unsuitable for drinking or washing clothes

hard[2] adv. **1** *She works hard.* = putting in a lot of effort **2** *It is raining hard.* = heavily **hard and fast** adj. *This is not a hard and fast rule.* = something that cannot be changed **hardback** (**hard cover**) noun = a book with a thick, strong cover **hard-boiled** adj. = an egg boiled until the yellow part is solid **hard**

copy noun = a copy of a document which has been printed out from a computer on paper (opposite **soft copy**) **hard disk** noun = the part of a computer (inside the machine) in which information is stored (compare **floppy disk**) **hard drink** (**hard liquor**) noun = a drink which contains a lot of alcohol (e.g. whisky) **hard feelings** noun = feelings of anger or hatred towards someone **hard-hitting** adj. *a hard-hitting article in a magazine* = a piece of writing or speech which is very powerful and effective **hardware** noun, u. **1** = iron nails, screws, tools etc. made of metal **2** = the mechanical parts of a computer (compare **software**)

to be a hard act to follow = something which is so good that one cannot improve on it easily **to give somebody a hard time** = to make a situation difficult for somebody (informal) **to be hard up** = to have too little money (informal) **to be hard-pressed to do something** *She was hard-pressed to explain why she had stayed away from school for a week.* = to find it difficult to do something

hard•ly /ˈhɑːrdli/ adv. **1** *I hardly ever see you these days—may be once a year.* = almost not **2** *He is hardly able to manage on his salary.* = only with great difficulty **3** *I had hardly begun writing when the bell rang.* = only just (soon after)

har•dy /ˈhɑːrdi/ adj. *Banyan trees are very hardy.* = able to bear cold, pain, etc. and to survive in difficult conditions

hare /heəʳ/ noun, c. = an animal like a rabbit, but bigger and able to run very fast **hare-brained** adj. *a hare-brained idea* = impractical and foolish **harelip** noun = a physical condition that some people are born with, in which the upper lip is divided into two parts because it does not develop properly

hark /hɑːk/ verb, i. *Hark! Someone is knocking on the door.* = to listen (literary)

to hark back = to talk about things that happened much earlier (old-fashioned, literary)

har•le•quin /ˈhɑːlɪkwɪn/ noun, c.= a character who appears in some children's plays wearing very bright and colourful clothes, and plays tricks on others

harm[1] /hɑːm/ verb, t. *Don't be afraid of the dog. He won't harm you. // You will be glad to know that the storm has not harmed your house at all.* = to cause some injury or damage to someone or something

harm[2] noun, u. *The article accusing me of being corrupt did a lot of harm to my reputation.* = damage or injury caused by something **harmful** adj. *Smoking is harmful to health.* = something that causes harm (opposite **harmless**)

har•mo•ny /ˈhɑːməni/ noun, u. **1** *What beautiful harmony the singers produced!* = a pleasing union of musical sounds or colours **2** *People of different religions should live together in harmony.* = peace and agreement with each other **3** *Your ideas are not in harmony with mine.* = a state of agreement **harmonize (harmonise)** verb, i. or t. *Your voices don't harmonize when you are singing.*(i.) = to combine or blend together in a pleasant way **harmonium** noun = a musical instrument in which sounds are produced by forcing air to pass through thin pieces of metal called reeds

har•ness[1] /ˈhɑːnɪs/ verb, t. **1** *The horses have to be harnessed to the carriage.* = to put leather straps around the neck and body of a horse so that it can pull something e.g. a carriage **2** *The river has been harnessed to produce electricity.* = to control and use a natural force for a particular purpose

harness[2] noun, u. *The horses need a new harness.* = ropes or bands of leather used to tie a horse

to die in harness = to die while one is still working actively

harp[1] /hɑːp/ noun, c. = a musical instrument in which sounds are produced by plucking (pulling at) metal wires or strings of different length

harp[2] verb, t. (**+ on**) *She is always harping on the subject of clothes, to remind her husband to buy her a new sari.* = to talk repeatedly or continually about something

har•poon /hɑːˈpuːn/ noun, c. = a long, sharp spear with a rope tied to it at one end, which is used to hunt whales and other large sea animals

har•row[1] /ˈhærəʊ/ noun, c. = a tool with several sharp teeth used by farmers to break up the soil before planting seeds

harrow[2] verb, t. *The soil has to be harrowed.* = to break up the soil by using a harrow **harrowing** adj. *We went through a harrowing experience when the storm hit our city.* = causing great suffering; upsetting

harsh /hɑːʃ/ adj. **1** *harsh words* = unkind and unfair **2** *Although I believe in discipline, I try not to be harsh with my students.* = strict, severe **3** *The weather in Canada can be quite harsh in winter.* = difficult to live in **4** *She spoke in a harsh tone and made us feel angry.* = unpleasant to hear **harshness** noun

har•vest[1] /ˈhɑːvɪst/ verb, t. *The farmers are harvesting the rice crop.*= to gather a crop from the fields

harvest[2] noun, c. or u. **1** *The farmers have returned home after the harvest.* = the act of harvesting crops **2** *We are expecting a good harvest this year.* = the quantity of the crops that are harvested (gathered)

hash /hæʃ/ noun, u. = a meal containing meat cut up into small pieces **re-hash** noun *The musical programme put up on Republic Day was a re-hash of* *last year's programme.* = old and stale material presented a second time

to make a hash of something *I had asked him to arrange a party but he made a hash of the arrangements.* = to do something very badly (informal)

hash•ish /ˈhæʃɪʃ/ noun, u. = a harmful drug prepared from the hemp plant

has•sle[1] /ˈhæsəl/ noun, c. *I am facing so many hassles at home that I am unable to sleep.* = a situation which causes a lot of worry

hassle[2] verb, t. *Please don't hassle me now as I am studying.* = to annoy or trouble

haste /heɪst/ noun, u. *She left the house in such haste that she forgot to tie up her shoe laces.* = something done very quickly, when there is not enough time **hasten** /ˈheɪsən/ verb, i. or t. **1** *He spilled some ink on his friend but hastened to apologize.*(i.) = to move quickly in order to do something **2** *The service in this restaurant is very slow. Could you do something to hasten it?*(t.) = to cause something to happen more quickly

hat /hæt/ noun, c. = a high or raised covering for the head **hat-trick** noun, c. = three successes of the same type during a match or game in a sport (e.g. three batsmen given out to successive balls (one after the other) by the same bowler, in cricket) [TECHNICAL]

to take one's hat off to someone = to express admiration for someone **to talk through one's hat** = to talk nonsense

hatch[1] /hætʃ/ verb, t. or i. **1** *On this poultry farm, eggs are hatched in a machine called an incubator.*(t.) = to cause a young chick to come out of the egg **2** *The chicks hatched this morning.*(i.) = to come out of an egg **3** *The thieves hatched a plan to steal the Kohinoor diamond.*(t.) = to prepare a secret plan to do something bad

hatch[2] noun **1** *The workers threw the boxes of oranges down the hatch into the waiting trucks.* = an opening in a wall or floor through which things can pass **2** = the door in an aeroplane

hatchback /ˈhætʃbæk/ noun, c. = a car which does not have a separate space at the back for storing luggage but in which a door at the back opens upward

hatchery /ˈhætʃəri/ noun, c. (**hatcheries**) = a place where eggs, specially fish-eggs, are hatched

hatch•et /ˈhætʃɪt/ noun, c. = an axe with a short handle, used as a a tool for cutting things down or as a weapon **hatchet-man** noun = a person who is paid by someone to attack or kill an enemy

hate[1] /heɪt/ verb, t. **1** *I love being with people but I hate crowds.* = to have a strong dislike for someone or something **2** *I hate to disturb you but can I have five minutes of your time?* = a polite way of saying that one is sorry for something that one is doing

hate[2] noun, u. or c. *There was a look of hate in his eyes. It frightened me.*(u.) = strong dislike (also hatred)

haugh•ty /ˈhɔːti/ adj. = proud; thinking oneself to be better than others

haul[1] /hɔːl/ verb, t. *Two locomotives haul this train up the mountain to Darjeeling.* = to pull with some effort or difficulty

haul[2] noun, c. **1** *The fishermen had a big haul of fish.* = the amount of fish caught in a net **2** *The thieves got away with a big haul.* = stolen goods

to haul someone in = to arrest someone for some crime **to haul someone up** *I was hauled up for losing the keys of the office.* = to ask someone to explain why a mistake has been made (informal) **to haul someone over the coals** = to speak angrily or very severely to someone for making a mistake **to be a long haul** = something that will take a long time

haunch /hɔːntʃ/ noun, c. (**haunches**) = hips or buttocks

haunt[1] /hɔːnt/ verb, t. **1** *This house is said to be haunted by the ghost of an old woman.* = to be visited by a ghost (the spirit of a dead person) **2** *That unhappy episode has haunted me for years.* = to be always in the mind and to cause unhappiness

haunt[2] noun, c. *You will often find Komal and his friends chatting away under a tree on the river bank. It is their favourite haunt.* = a place which a person visits frequently **haunted** adj. *a haunted house* = believed to be visited by ghosts or in which ghosts are said to live **haunting** adj. *This song from the film 'Devdas' has a haunting melody which keeps ringing in your ears.* = something strange, beautiful or having a quality which remains in one's thoughts

have[1] /həv/ verb, t. (**had**) **1** *We have three houses in the city.* = to own **2** *They have short tempers.* = to show as part of one's character or personality **3** *These rooms have marble floors.* = to contain or include **4** *They have malaria.* = to suffer from **5** *We have no hopes of passing the examination.* = to feel or keep in the mind **6** *He had some rice for lunch.* = to eat or drink something **7** *He had a bath before he went to bed.* = to perform some action **8** *She had a baby last month.* = to give birth to **9** *We have to meet the Principal.* =to be required or forced to do something

have[2] aux. verb *She has broken the high jump record.* = used with the participle forms of verbs to form the perfect tense, showing the completion of some action

haves /ˈhævz/ noun = the rich people in a country or society **have-nots** noun = the poor people in a country or society

ha•ven /ˈheɪvən/ noun, c. *This little pond by the farm* *has become a haven for birds.* = a place where one can find peace and safety

hav•er•sack /'hævəsæk/ noun, c. = a bag which can hang from one's shoulder and in which one can carry things

hav•oc /'hævək/ noun, u. *The flood washed away many villages and caused havoc in the state.* = serious damage or destruction

hawk[1] /hɔ:k/ noun, c. = a meat-eating bird which can be trained to hunt other birds or small animals

hawk[2] verb, t. *This man hawks pens and books in trains.* = to sell things by travelling from place to place (sometimes used in place of the word 'sell' in a way which is not respectful) **hawker** noun, c. = a person who travels from place to place and sells things

to watch someone like a hawk = to watch someone very carefully

haw•thorn /'hɔ:θɔ:n/ noun = a small tree which produces white flowers and red berries

hay /heɪ/ noun, u. = grass which has been cut and dried and is used to feed cattle **hay fever** noun = an illness caused by dust from plants which produces a bad cold **haystack** noun = a large pile of hay, stored for cattle to eat

to go haywire *All our arrangements for the party went haywire.* = to end in a state of confusion (informal) **to hit the hay** *We're all tired. Let's hit the hay.* = go to sleep (informal) **to make hay while the sun shines** = to make the best use of an opportunity (a chance to do something)

haz•ard[1] /'hæzəd/ noun, c. *Smoking is a serious health hazard.* = danger or risk

hazard[2] verb, t. *I don't know the answer to your question but I will hazard a guess.* = to say or do something when there is a risk of making a mistake **hazardous** adj. *A soldier's profession is hazardous.* = dangerous or risky

haze /heɪz/ noun, u. *It is not possible to see anything through this haze.* = light mist or dust or smoke, through which one cannot see clearly **hazy** adj. **1** = not allowing one to see **2** *She has only a hazy idea of the problems faced by the people. She should spend more time here.* = unclear; vague

ha•zel /'heɪzəl/ noun = a small tree or bush which produces a kind of nut (**hazelnut**)

he[1] /hi:/ pron. *I asked Mike to come but he refused.* = the male person or animal already referred to (spoken about earlier)

he[2] noun, c. (singular) *If you see a lion with a thick mane around the head, you can be sure that it is a he.* = a male

head[1] /hed/ noun, c. **1** *She lifted her head to look up.* = the part of the body containing the eyes, ears, nose, mouth etc. **2** *He has a lot of creative ideas in his head.* = mind or brain **3** *the Head of the Department* = the person who controls something; the leader **4** *She was standing at the head of the stairs.* = the upper part **5** = the part of a tape-recorder, videotape player etc. that comes in contact with the tape and changes the electronic signal into sounds/ pictures

head[2] verb, t. **1** *He heads the the group of doctors.* = to lead **2** *She has just returned from the station and now she is heading for the market.* = to travel in a certain direction **3** *The centre-forward headed the ball into the goal.* = to hit the ball with the head in the game of football **headache** noun, c. *She has a headache.* = a pain in the head (Notice the use of the article.) **head-hunter** noun, c. **1** = a person who (in former times) killed his enemies and cut off their heads, as a sign of victory **2** = a person who is paid to find suitable people for particular jobs (figurative) **head-on** adj. or adv. **1** *a head-on collision between a car and a truck.*(adj.) = (an accident) in which the front part of one vehicle hits the front part of another vehicle **2** *I had serious differences with my senior. For a long time I avoided an argument, but finally I had to take him head-on.*(adv.) = a difference of opinion which is expressed openly **headphones** noun (always plural) = a piece of equipment worn over the ears that allows one to listen to music etc. from a music player, computer etc. without others hearing it **headstrong** adj.= a person who does whatever he or she wants to do, paying no attention to advice given by others **heady** adj. *Victory in the match gave our players a heady feeling.* = giving a feeling of joy and excitement

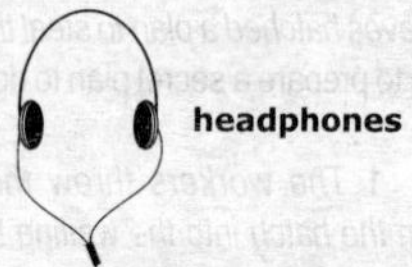
headphones

to bite someone's head off = to answer in a very angry and rude way **to go to someone's head** *I hope all that success hasn't gone to his head.* = to make someone very proud **to have a good head for something** = *She has a good head for numbers.* = to be able to understand or do something easily **to not make head or tail of something** = to not be able to understand something

headline[1] /'hedlaɪn/ noun, c. = the words printed in large letters at the top of an article in a newspaper which give readers an idea of the important news

headline[2] verb, t. *The newspapers headlined the Sri Lankan team's victory in Sydney.* = to present a piece of news in a headline, to make it look important

heads /heds/ noun *There was a toss before the cricket match, and the Indian captain called 'Heads!'* = the side of a coin which often has the picture of a man or woman, animal etc. on it (opposite **tails**)

heal /hi:l/ verb, i. or t. **1** *My wounds have healed and I can walk again.*(i.) = to become healthy once more **2** *This new medicine will heal the pain in your shoulder.*(t.) = to cure or make healthy

health /helθ/ noun, u. *Some exercise is necessary for one's health.* = the state of being well in body and mind and free of disease **health food** noun = food that is supposed to be specially good for one's health usually because it does not contain chemicals **healthy** /'helθɪ/ adj. **1** *She is a very healthy child.* = strong and not falling ill often **2** *He has healthy teeth.* = in good condition **3** *There was healthy competition between the students in the class.* = sensible and in the right spirit

to drink (to) someone's health = to drink some liquid (usually containing alcohol) at a feast or social gathering while expressing a wish that someone may enjoy good health

heap[1] /hi:p/ noun, c. *The books lay in a heap on the bed.* = an untidy pile of things lying on top of each other

heap[2] verb, t. *He heaped rice and dal on his plate and sat down to eat.* = to pile up in a large quantity

hear /hɪə^r/ verb, t. or i. (**heard**) **1** *I can hear the crying of a baby.*(t.) // *He can't hear very well after his illness.*(i.) = to receive or to be able to receive sounds through the ears **2** *I hear you have been given a promotion.*(t.) = to be told or informed **3** *The judge will hear your case next week.*(t.) = to listen to arguments in a court of law in order to come to a decision [LAW] **hearing** noun, u. or c. **1** *How good is your hearing?*(u.) = the power or ability to receive sounds through the ears **2** *The judge gave me a patient hearing.*(c.) = an act of listening carefully to someone [LAW] **3** *The hearing of your case is fixed for tomorrow.*(u.) = a trial of a case before a judge [LAW] **hearing aid** = a small electric machine fitted inside or over the ear, which helps a person to hear by making sounds louder **hearsay** adj. *A person cannot be sent to jail unless there is strong evidence against him. Hearsay evidence is not enough.* = something which is said by someone, but for which there is no proof

to hear from *I have not heard from them for over a year now.* = to receive a telephone call, letter etc. from someone

hearse /hɜ:s/ noun, c. = a carriage used to carry a dead person

heart /hɑ:t/ noun, c. **1** *You have a weak heart. You must be careful not to work too hard.* = the organ inside the chest which pumps blood to different parts of the body **2** *You should do what your heart tells you to do.* = feelings or emotions **3** *The Reserve Bank forms the heart of India's banking system.* // *Now we come to the heart of the matter.* = the central or most important part of something **4** (always plural) *the Queen of Hearts* = one of a set of 13 playing cards, out of a total of 52 cards, on which a heart-shaped figure is printed in red **heartache** noun, u. = feeling of sorrow **heartbreak** noun, u. = deep sorrow or disappointment **hearten** verb, t. *We were heartened by India's victory in the test match.* = to cause someone to feel happy; to encourage **heartfelt** adj. *Please accept my heartfelt thanks.* = sincere (from the heart) **heartthrob** noun, c. *Hrithik Roshan is the latest heartthrob of film lovers.* = a very attractive person to whom people are easily attracted **heart-to-heart** adj. = open and sincere and hiding nothing **hearty** adj **1** *a hearty welcome* = friendly and sincere **2** *a hearty breakfast* = large and filling

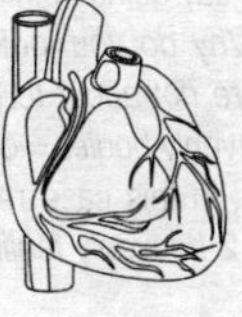
heart

from the bottom of one's heart *I think your work is excellent, and I say that from the bottom of my heart.* = in a very sincere and deep way. **to not have the heart to do something** = to be unable to do something unkind or to hurt someone **to do something to one's heart's content** = to do something to the maximum level of enjoyment **to do something with a heavy heart** = to carry out something while feeling very sad about it

hearth /hɑ:θ/ noun, c. = the place where a fire is lit in a room to keep it warm in winter

heat[1] /hi:t/ noun, u. *The heat becomes unbearable in Delhi during the summer.* = the degree of hotness; temperature

heat[2] verb, t. *The food has become cold. Please heat it up.* = to make something hot **heater** noun, c. = a machine that is used to heat water or a room etc. **heating** noun, u. = a system that makes a house, a building etc. warm **heatstroke** /'hi:tstrəʊk/ noun, c. = weakness and tiredness, with fever, resulting from exposure to the hot sun

the heat of the moment = a state of great anger or excitement

heats /hi:ts/ noun, c. (always plural) *Eight runners are competing in the first heats of the 200 metres race, of whom two will go to the final.* = a race or sports competition which is held before the final round, to select the competitors for the final

H

hea•then /ˈhiːðən/ noun, c. = a person who is not a Christian or who does not belong to any of the major religions (old-fashioned)

hea•ther /ˈheðəʳ/ noun, u. = a small bush which grows wild on open land

heave[1] /hiːv/ verb, t. or i. **1** *We had to heave the steel cupboard up the stairs.*(t.) = to lift, push or pull something with great effort **2** *His chest heaved as he tried to breathe.*(i.) = to rise and fall regularly

heave[2] noun, c. *One last heave will be required to lift this box up the stairs.* = the act of heaving (pushing or pulling)

to heave a sigh of relief = to breathe out slowly and loudly when one is glad that something is over

heaven /ˈhevən/ noun, u. or c. (**heavens**) **1** *the gods in heaven* (*Heaven*) = the place where God or the gods are supposed to be and where the souls of good people are thought to be taken after they die **2** *We had a wonderful holiday this weekend. It was heaven to lie in bed all day doing nothing.*= a state of great happiness **3** *Why do you look so worried? Surely, the heavens are not about to fall.* = the sky **heavenly** adj. **1** *heavenly bodies* = connected with the sky or with space, in this case referring to the sun, moon, stars etc. **2** *heavenly feeling* = a feeling of great pleasure

heav•y /ˈhevi/ adj. **1** *The box is so heavy that I can't lift it.* = having great weight **2** *We can expect heavy rains today.* **3** *You will have to pay a heavy fine.* **4** *There is heavy traffic on the roads.* = of great force, amount or degree **5** *Her last lecture made for heavy listening.* = serious, difficult or in some cases boring **heavy metal** noun, u. = a kind of rock music played very loudly on electric guitars etc.

to make heavy weather of something = to make something appear much more difficult than it is

heck•le /ˈhekəl/ verb, t. *The minister was heckled by the crowd when he tried to make a speech.* = to prevent a person from speaking by shouting and making unfriendly remarks

hec•tare /ˈhekteəʳ/ noun, c. = a unit of measurement of land, equal to about 2.5 acres (10,000 sqm)

hec•tic /ˈhektɪk/ adj. *I had a hectic day in the office today. I could not get a moment's rest.* = full of excitement and hurried activity

hedge[1] /hedʒ/ noun, c. = a row of bushes or small trees separating one piece of land from another

hedge[2] verb, i. *She is hedging and not telling us the truth.* = to not give a direct answer to a question

to hedge one's bets = to reduce the risk of making a mistake by keeping several choices open

hedge•hog /ˈhedʒhɒg/ noun, u. = a small animal which has sharp quills (needles) on its back to protect it from other animals

heed[1] /hiːd/ verb, t. *You should heed the advice of your teachers.* = to pay attention to something or to take something seriously (formal)

heed[2] noun, u. *You must pay heed to your teacher's advice.* = careful attention (formal)

heel /hiːl/ noun, c. **1** = the rounded back part of the foot (see pic under **foot**) **2** = the part of a shoe or sock that covers the heel of the foot **3** *high-heeled shoe* = the raised part of a shoe under the heel of one's foot

hef•ty /ˈhefti/ adj. **1** *a hefty policeman* = a big and strong person **2** *a hefty fine* = large in amount (informal)

he•gem•o•ny /hɪˈgeməni/ noun, u. = the control of one state over another

heif•er /ˈhefəʳ/ noun, c. = a young female cow which has not yet produced a calf (young one)

height /haɪt/ noun, u. **1** *He is 1.75 m in height // The height of the mountain is 8,000 m.* = the measurement of something from top to bottom (see pic under **dimension**) **2** *Her height helps her when she plays basketball.* = the quality of being tall **3** *At the height of winter we travelled to the Arctic.* = the strongest part of something

hein•ous /ˈheɪnəs/ adj. *a heinous crime* = wicked and shameful

heir /eəʳ/ noun, c. = a person to whom the property of a dead person goes by law

heir•loom /ˈeəluːm/ noun, c. *That old painting which you see in my room is a family heirloom bought by my great-grandmother many years ago.* = a valuable object that is passed on by persons to their children or other relatives in a family

hel•i•cop•ter /ˈhelɪkɒptəʳ/ noun, c. = a small aircraft without wings that flies with the help of large metal blades fixed on top, which turn very fast and make it go straight up into the air

he•li•um /ˈhiːliəm/ noun = a kind of gas that is lighter than air and does not burn and is used to fill balloons [CHEMISTRY]

hell (**Hell**) /hel/ noun **1** = a place to which, it is believed in some religions, bad people are sent by God when they die **2** *Our lives have become hell because of the noise caused by the construction outside.* = a condition of great suffering

to give somebody hell = to speak very strictly or angrily to someone (informal) **to run/hurt/bleed etc. like hell** = to happen very strongly or very badly (informal) **to get the hell out of somewhere** = to get out of a place quickly, usually because otherwise, something unpleasant will happen (slang) **one hell of a (good film)** = a way of saying something or someone is very good

Hel•len•ic /he'lenɪk/ adj. *Hellenic culture* = having to do with ancient Greece

hello /hə'ləʊ/ interjec. **1** *Hello Sarah! How are you this morning?* = an expression used as a friendly greeting **2** *Hello, is that 247235?* = a word often used to begin a conversation on the telephone **3** *Hello, could you please tell me how to get to the station?* = a word often used to draw someone's attention, in order to ask for help etc.

helm /helm/ noun, u. or c. **1** = the wheel which controls the movement of a ship at sea **2** *The Principal has been at the helm of this school for the last ten years.* = the position from which one controls or guides something (figurative)

hel•met /'helmɪt/ noun, c. = a covering for the head, made of metal or plastic, which protects the head from injury (see pic under **visor**)

help[1] /help/ verb, t. or i. **1** *My friend helped me to clean up the house.*(t.) = to do part of the work which another person is supposed to do **2** *My friends helped me with money when I did not have a job.*(t.) = to do something for another person which makes life easier or better **3** *Can I help you to some more chicken?* **4** *She helped herself to some ice cream.*(t.) = to give food to someone or to oneself **5** *You can call the doctor if you like but that won't help.*(i.) = to make things better

help[2] noun, u. or c. **1** *I am grateful for your help with the cooking.*(u.) = the act of helping **2** *Your instructions were a great help–I was able to open the box easily.*(c.) = someone or something that helps **3** *I've found a help to cook for me in the morning.*(c.) = a person who does some work for one regularly **helpful** adj. *Her advice was very helpful.* = useful

helpless /'helplɪs/ adj. *He felt quite helpless when his wife died. // I feel helpless without my mobile phone.* = to not be able to take care of oneself or manage well **helping** noun, c. *Let me give you another helping of ice-cream.* = an amount of food given to someone

helter-skelter /heltə^r 'skeltə^r/ adv. *He ran helter-skelter to school, with the buttons of his shirt undone and his shoelaces untied.* = in a great hurry or in a state of disorder

hem[1] /hem/ noun, c. *the hem of a dress* = the edge of a piece of cloth that is folded and stitched

hem[2] verb, t. (**to hem in**) *This piece of land is completely hemmed in by buildings.* = to surround on all sides

hemi- /hemɪ/ prefix meaning 'half' e.g. **hemisphere** /'hemɪsfɪə^r/ noun, c. **1** = half of a sphere (any round object) **2** *the northern hemisphere* = one half of the Earth, north or south of the equator

hemp /hemp/ noun, u. = a kind of plant from which ropes can be made and from which the drug **cannabis** is produced

hen /hen/ noun, c. **1** = a female bird which lays eggs **2** *a hen-sparrow* = the female of any kind of bird

hence /hens/ adv. **1** *Your boss needs your help urgently, hence the phone call.* = for this reason (formal) **2** *You will receive a notice from our office two days hence.* = from this time or from this place

henceforth adv. *You will henceforth take your orders from the Prime Minister, not the President.* = after this time; from now on

hench•man /'hentʃmən/ noun, c. (**-men**) = a faithful supporter of a person who may be asked to do violent or illegal things for the person he supports (derogatory)

hen•na /'henə/ noun, u. = a kind of plant from the leaves of which a red dye (colour) is produced and which is used to colour the hair, beard, fingernails etc.

hep•a•ti•tis /hepə'taɪtɪs/ noun = a disease of the liver which causes the eyes and skin to turn yellow (also **jaundice**) [MEDICINE]

hepta- /heptə/prefix meaning 'seven' e.g. **heptagon** /'heptəgən/ noun, c. = a geometrical figure (shape) with seven sides

her[1] /hər/ det. *Mrs Rao and her daughter* = of or belonging to some woman

her[2] pron. *I was looking for Asha, but could not find her.* = object form of the pronoun 'she' (referring to a woman)

herself /hə'self/ pron. **1** *She will do it herself.* = without anyone's help **2** *She wasn't herself yesterday.* = in her normal state of mind or body

her•ald[1] /'herəld/ verb, t. *The appearance of dark clouds heralds the coming of the monsoon.* = to announce; to tell of something that is going to happen (literary)

herald[2] noun, c. *The cuckoo is a herald of spring.* = someone or something that tells us of something that is going to happen soon (literary)

herb /hɜːb/ noun, c. = a small plant from which some medicine can be produced or which can be used to improve the taste of food e.g. mint **herbal** adj. *herbal medicine // herbal oil* = made of or using herbs

her•bi•vore /'hɜːbɪvɔː^r/ noun, c. = an animal that only eats plants and not other animals (opposite **carnivore**) [BIOLOGY]

her•bi•vor•ous /hɜː'bɪvərəs/ adj. *a herbivorous animal* = plant-eating (see also **carnivorous, insectivorous, omnivorous**)

Her•cu•le•an /hɜːkjʊ'liːən/ adj. *a Herculean task* = requiring very great effort or strength (literary)

herd[1] /hɜːd/ noun, c. *a herd of wild elephants* = a group of animals of the same kind which live together

herd[2] verb, t. **1** *He is employed to herd cattle.* = to look after animals in a herd **2** *The teachers herded the school-children into the bus.* = to guide or direct a group of children etc.

here /hɪəʳ/ adv. **1** *Come here!* **2** *I live here.* = to or at a place **3** *Here they come!* = used at the beginning of a sentence to draw attention to something

hereafter /hiər'a:ftəʳ/ adv. = from now on

hereby /hɪəbai/ adv. *I hereby declare this meeting closed.* = by doing or saying this

he•red•i•ta•ry /hɪ'redɪtəri/ adj. *a hereditary disease* = something which can be passed on from a parent to a child through the genes (see **gene, genetic**)

her•e•sy /'herəsɪ/ noun, c. (**heresies**) *Galileo's statement that the earth is round and not flat was regarded as a heresy by the people of his time.* = a statement or belief that goes against what most people think to be true and is considered punishable **heretic** noun, c. = a person who questions or challenges a belief that most people accept as the truth

her•i•tage /'herɪtɪdʒ/ noun, u. *School children should be given an idea of our country's great heritage in art, music and culture.* = the history or traditions of a country or group, considered to be of special value

her•met•ic /hɜ:'metɪk/ adj. *a hermetic seal in a pump* = fitting so closely together that no air can pass through [TECHNICAL]

her•mit /'hɜ:mɪt/ noun, c. = a person who lives in isolation (away from others) in order to lead a spiritual or religious life

her•nia /'hɜ:niə/ noun, c. = a break or weakness in the tissue covering the abdomen (front part of the body) which allows the intestine to move out of its natural place [MEDICINE]

he•ro /'hɪərəʊ/ noun, c. (**heroes**) **1** = a person who is admired for some great or good quality such as bravery, courage etc. **2** *It is difficult to say who the hero of the film is.* = the main or central character in a play or film **heroics** noun *He has been talking a lot but has done nothing for the people. We are tired of his heroics.* = actions which appear very brave or grand but mean nothing (derogatory)

her•o•in /'herəʊɪn/ noun = a drug which can be used to remove pain but is often used by drug-addicts to produce a false feeling of pleasure or happiness

her•o•ine /'herəʊɪn/ noun, c. = the leading female character in a film or play etc.

he•ron /'herən/ noun = a type of bird with long legs and a long neck that lives near water

her•ring /'herɪŋ/ noun, c. = a type of fish that lives in the sea and swims in large groups

a red herring noun = a subject or topic which is introduced to draw attention away from the main topic

hes•i•tate /'hezɪteɪt/ verb, i. *Mr Rao has been offered a job in Germany, but he is hesitating to accept the offer because he is not sure if his children will be happy there.* = to be unwilling to decide or to do something because one is not sure if it is the right thing to do

hes•si•an /'hesiən/ noun, u. = rough cloth made from jute, used for making sacks (bags in which rice etc. are carried)

he•te•ro- /hetərəʊ/ prefix meaning **1** different e.g. **heterodox** adj. *He has very heterodox views on religion.* = different from or going against the ideas which are commonly accepted (opposite **orthodox**) **2** other (opposite **homo-**) e.g. **heterogenous** (see below)

het•e•ro•ge•ne•ous /'hetərəʊ'dʒi:niəs/ adj. *Mumbai has a heterogeneous population, consisting of people from different parts of the country.* = made up of things that are very different from each other (opposite **homogeneous**)

heterosexual /'hetərə'sekʃuəl/ adj. = attracted sexually to someone of the opposite sex (opposite **homosexual**)

heu•ris•tic /hjʊ'rɪstɪk/ adj. *a heuristic process of learning* = learning based on the discoveries that one makes through personal experience

hew /hju:/ verb, t. (**hewed**, **hewn**) *We have to hew down a few trees.* = to cut down something with the help of an axe (literary)

hexa- /heksə/ prefix meaning six e.g. **hexagon** /'heksəgən/ noun, c. = a geometrical figure with six sides (see pic under **shapes**)

hey /heɪ/ interjec. *Hey! Come here at once!* = an expression used to attract someone's attention or to express surprise etc. (informal)

hey•day /'heɪdeɪ/ noun, u. *In its heyday the company owned six floors of the building. Now it owns just one.* = the time of greatest power, influence etc.

hey•pres•to /heɪ 'prestəʊ/ interjec. = done very quickly as if by magic

hi /haɪ/ interjec. *Hi, how are you Shilpa?* = an expression used as a greeting (a short form of 'hello') (informal)

hi•a•tus /haɪ'eɪtəs/ noun, u. *The party has come back to power in Maharashtra after a hiatus of six years.* = a gap or break (formal)

hi•ber•nate /'haɪbəneɪt/ verb, i. *It is said that bears hibernate during winter.* = to go into a long sleep in order to save energy [BIOLOGY] **hibernation** /haɪbə'neɪʃən/ noun

hi•bis•cus /haɪ'bɪskəs/ noun = a plant that

produces large, brightly-coloured flowers

hic•cup /ˈhɪkʌp/ noun, c. (usually plural **hiccups**) **1** *The boy is having hiccups and can't speak.* = a sharp sound caused by a sudden difficulty in breathing, sometimes due to eating or drinking something too quickly **2** *The new factory has not gone into production yet because of some hiccups.* = a small problem that causes a delay (figurative)

hide[1] /haɪd/ verb, t. or i. (**hid, hidden**) **1** *I have hidden the money under my bed.*(t.) = to put something in a place where it cannot be seen or found **2** *The boy is hiding behind the screen.*(i.) = to put oneself in a place where one cannot be seen **3** *She was disappointed when she learnt that she had failed but she managed to hide her disappointment.*(t.) = to cover up a feeling and not make it known

hide[2] noun, c. or u. **1** *We built a hide among the trees from which we could photograph the tigers.*(c.) = a place where a person can hide in order to photograph animals, birds etc. without being seen by them **2** *India exports buffalo hides to Europe.*(c.)= the skin of an animal from which leather is made **hide-and-seek** noun = a children's game in which some players hide while others look for them **hidebound** adj. *a hide-bound person* = not willing to accept changes (derogatory)

hid•e•ous /ˈhɪdiəs/ adj. **1** *a hideous painting* = extremely ugly **2** *a hideous sight* = causing one to feel upset, shocked etc.

hi•er•ar•chy /ˈhaɪrɑːki/ noun, c. (**hierarchies**) or u. *There are many people above me in the government hierarchy.* = a system in which people or things are grouped and arranged into higher and lower ranks or positions

hi•e•ro•glyph•ics /haɪrəˈglɪfɪks/ noun (always plural) = a system of writing used in ancient times in Egypt in which pictures (hieroglyphs) represented words

hig•gle•dy-pig•gle•dy /hɪgəldi ˈpɪgəldi/ adv. or adj. *Things were lying higgledy-piggledy all over the room.* = in a state of disorder (informal)

high[1] /haɪ/ adj. **1** *a high building* = raised well above the ground **2** *a building that is 100 ft high* = having a particular height **3** *high prices* = above the usual level or amount of something

high[2] adv. **1** *The bird was flying high in the sky.* = at a high position **2** *How high can you sing?* = used to talk about pitch in sound **3** *The ball flew high into the air.* = to a high level

high[3] noun, c. **1** *The kidnapping cases reached an all time high last year.* = high level or point (informal) **2** *Deep sea diving gave me a real high.* = the excitement and pleasure that one gets from doing something they like (informal) **Highness** noun = a title used to address a king or queen or a person from a royal family **high-rise** adj. = a building which is very tall and has several floors **high-sounding** adj. = words which seem to be very important but carry little meaning (derogatory) **high-strung** (**highly-strung**) adj. = nervous and easily excited **high school** noun, c. or u. = a school for children who are above 13 years of age **high-tech** adj. = using the most modern technology **high tide** noun, u. = a rise in the level of water in the sea **high-and-mighty** adj. = proud and arrogant in behaviour **highbrow** noun, c. = a person who is interested in things that ordinary people may find too serious or dull e.g. *highbrow cinema* (opposite **low-brow**) **High Commissioner** noun = a person who acts as the ambassador or representative of a Commonwealth country in another Commonwealth country **High Court** = a court that is a level above an ordinary court, and lower than the Supreme Court **high fidelity** (**hi-fi**) adj. = machines which can record and playback musical sounds which are very close to the original sounds in quality **high flier** noun = a person who is very ambitious and clever and is likely to be successful in his/her plans (informal) **high-handed** adj. = using one's power without thinking of the feelings of other people

highlands /ˈhaɪləndz/ noun = an area where there are many mountains [GEOGRAPHY]

high•light[1] noun, c. *The television programme presented the highlights of yesterday's cricket match.* = the most important or interesting events or points, selected from something bigger

highlight[2] verb, t. *Can you highlight the main points in your paper?* = to select and draw particular attention to something **highlighter** /ˈhaɪlɑɪtəʳ/ noun = a pen with a coloured felt tip which is used to highlight text which is important, to be noted etc. (When highlighted the text can be seen through the band of coloured ink)

hi-jack /ˈhaɪdʒæk/ verb, t. *The plane was hijacked on its way across the Pacific.* = to take control of something (usually an aircraft) by force and use threats of violence to make some political demand

hike[1] /haɪk/ verb, t. or i. **1** *I shall go hiking in Nagarkot next month.*(i.) = to go on a long walk through the countryside (see also **hitch-hike**) **2** *The government has hiked the price of petrol once more.*(t.) = to raise or increase (informal)

hike[2] noun, c. **1** *Will you come with me on a hike?* = a long walk **2** *There has been another price hike.* = an increase in the price of something (informal)

hi•lar•i•ous /hɪˈleəriəs/ adj. *Mehmood was an excellent comedian who made several hilarious films.*

= (of things and events), causing a lot of laughter and enjoyment

hill /hɪl/ noun, c. = a raised area of land, not very high **hillock** /'hɪlək/ noun, c. = a small hill

to be over the hill = to be no longer young or good at something (informal, not respectful)

hilt /hɪlt/ noun, c. = the handle of a sword or knife

him /ɪm/ pron. *If you see Tapan, tell him that I am going to congratulate him.* = the object form of 'he', the pronoun used to refer to a male person or animal **himself** pron. **1** *He hurt himself while moving the desk.* = the form of the pronoun 'he' (called the reflexive form) which shows that an action produces some effect on the doer of the action **2** *He wrote this himself.* = the use of the reflexive pronoun for emphasis (he and no one else)

hind[1] /haɪnd/ adj. *The horse stood on its hind legs.*= at the back (opposite **front**)

hind[2] noun, c. = a female deer **hind-sight** noun, u. *In hind-sight, we can say that we made a number of mistakes in planning our programme.* = understanding the nature of some event only after it has taken place

hin•der /'hɪndə^r/ verb, t. *The match was hindered by rain.* = to stop or delay something or to prevent it from happening **hindrance** noun, u. *There should be no hindrance in our programme.* = something or someone that hinders

Hin•du[1] /'hɪndu:/ noun, c. = a person who follows the Hindu religion

Hindu[2] adj. = having to do with the Hindu religion or the people who follow that religion **Hinduism** noun = the set of beliefs followed by Hindus

hinge[1] /hɪndʒ/ noun, c. = a part consisting of two flat pieces of metal joined together, which can be fitted to a door and which allows the door to swing freely

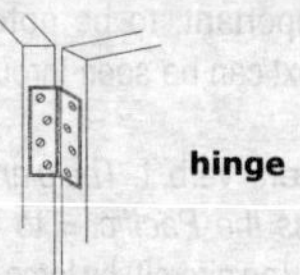

hinge

hinge[2] verb, t. *The door is hinged at three places.* = to be fitted with a hinge

to hinge on (upon) *The success of a student in the examination hinges on the amount of study that he or she puts in.* = to depend on

hint[1] /hɪnt/ verb, i. *My mother said she was going to give us a surprise and hinted that she might cook some biryani for us.* = to suggest or to say something indirectly

hint[2] noun, c. **1** *She dropped a hint that she might leave town soon, and so we should look for someone else to take her place.* = an indirect suggestion or statement **2** *There is a hint of winter in the air. It is beginning to get cold.* = a small sign

hin•ter•land /'hɪntəlænd/ noun, u. *Mumbai is India's most important business centre, with a rich hinterland.* = the area that lies behind a port or city and is far away from the sea or rivers (informal)

hip /hɪp/ noun, c. = the round,fleshy part of the body above the legs and below the waist **hip pocket** noun, c. = a pocket at the back of a pair of trousers

hip•pie (**hippy**) noun, c. = a person who does not accept the usual values and way of life of society. (In the 1960's, hippies were known by the clothes they wore, their long hair etc.)

hip•po•pot•a•mus (**hippo**) /hɪpə'pɒtəməs/ noun (**hippopotamuses** or **hippopatami**) = a large African animal which lives in or near water

hire[1] /haɪə^r/ verb, t. *I don't have a car so I will have to hire a taxi to take me to Pune.* = to get the use of something for a limited time by making a payment (also **rent** in American English)

hire[2] noun, u. *We have some bicycles for hire.*= the act of hiring something **hireling** noun, c. = a person who is willing to work for anyone for payment (derogatory) **hire-purchase** noun, u. = a system which allows one to buy something without paying the full price, but by making small payments (instalments), usually every month

his[1] /ɪz/ det. *Utpal has invited me to his house.* = belonging to him (to a male)

his[2] pron. *I am told Rakesh has bought a car but I did not know this car was his.* = possessive form (showing possession or ownership) of the pronoun 'he', used to refer to a male person or animal

hiss[1] /hɪs/ verb, i. or t. **1** *The snake hissed angrily when the boys surrounded it.*(i.) = to make a sound by allowing air to pass out of the mouth continuously with force **2** *The crowd hissed the fielder when he dropped an easy catch.*(t.) = to make a hissing sound in order to show displeasure, anger etc.

hiss[2] noun, c. (**hisses**) *The pressure-cooker gave a hiss.* = the sound made while hissing

his•to•ry /'hɪstəri/ noun, u. or c. (**histories**) **1** *We are studying American history.*(u.) = the record of past events which have had an important effect on a society or country; the study of such events **2** *I am writing a history of Indian classical music.*(c.) = a study or record of the development of something **3** *The doctor will have to look at the patient's medical history before he can make a diagnosis.*(u.) = the events or facts to do with a person or thing **historian** noun, c. = a person who studies history or writes about it **historic** adj. *The Quit India movement was historic.* = important and likely to become a part of history **historical** adj. *historical research* = connected with the study of history **case-history** noun, c. = a record of the health problems that a person has had, maintained by a doctor

to go down in history = to become a part of history

his•tri•on•ic /hɪstri'ɒnɪk/ adj. *The actor has a lot of histrionic talent.* = connected with acting (on the stage or in films) (formal) **histrionics** noun, u. *He pretended to be very happy when he saw me. I was quite impressed by his histrionics.* = insincere or false behaviour which reminds one of drama seen on the stage (derogatory)

hit[1] /hɪt/ verb, t. **(hit)** **1** *The ball hit him on the leg.* = to strike with the hand or some other object **2** *The car went off the road and hit a tree.* = to strike against something with force **3** *The increase in the price of diesel will hit all of us.* = to have a bad effect on **4** *Tendulkar has hit a century.* = to score runs or points in a game **5** *What she said made me angry. Later it hit me that she was only joking.* = to realise the truth of something (informal)

hit[2] noun, c. **1** *He got a hit on the jaw.* = a blow **2** *This new film will be a hit.* = a great success **3** *How many hits did the site get today?* = a visit to a website by someone using the internet [COMPUTERS] **hit-and-run** adj. *a hit-and-run accident* = an accident in which the driver of a car etc. does not stop to help someone who may have been injured but runs away to avoid trouble with the police

to hit it off with someone = to get on well or successfully with someone (informal) **to hit the nail on the head** = to say or do just the right thing **to hit the roof** *My friend will hit the roof when she finds out I have lost her watch.* = to be very angry (informal) **to not know what hit one** *He was very angry. We didn't know what had hit us!* = to be unprepared for something unpleasant (informal, often humorous)

hitch[1] /hɪtʃ/ verb, t. **1** *The bullocks were hitched to the cart.* = to join or attach to something **2** *hitching a ride* = to get a free ride (see **hitch-hike**, below)

hitch[2] noun, c. (**hitches**) *There has been a slight hitch in the programme which will cause some delay.* = problem or difficulty **hitch-hike** verb, t. *He hitch-hiked his way from Mumbai to Delhi.* = to get a free ride in a car or truck, after standing by the road-side and signalling to the driver to stop

to get hitched = to get married to someone (slang)

hith•er /'hɪðə^r/ adv. *Come hither!* = here; to this place (old-fashioned) **hitherto** adv. *Hitherto, we have been sending our rice to America, but from now on we will send it to Japan.* = until this time (in the past)

HIV abbr. of **human immuno-deficiency virus** noun = the virus that is considered to cause **AIDS**

hive /haɪv/ noun, c. **1** *a beehive* = a box in which bees are kept or a nest which they build, usually in a high place **2** *Mumbai is a hive of trade and industry.* = a very busy place (figurative)

to hive off verb *The group has hived off its cement-producing units and sold them to another company.* = to separate a company from a larger business group

ho interjec. *Ho there!* = an expression used to attract someone's attention or to express surprise etc. **ho ho** interjec. = an expression used to show, often in a superior way, that one does not believe something

hoard[1] /hɔ:d/ verb, t. *People have been hoarding rice because they have been told there may be a shortage of food.* = to store or stock up something (food, money etc.) secretly in a larger quantity than is required

hoard[2] noun, c. *He has a large hoard of money in an underground room in his house.* = a secret store of something valuable

hoard•ing /'hɔ:dɪŋ/ noun, c. = a large signboard, usually mounted on high pillars by the side of a road, carrying an advertisement

hoarse /hɔ:s/ adj. *a hoarse voice* = a voice that has become rough or weak because of a cold or shouting too much

hoar•y /'hɔ:ri/ adj. *Her hair is hoary with age.* = gray or white (literary)

hoax /həʊks/ noun, c. (**hoaxes**) *Someone telephoned the police to report that a man had been killed, but the call proved to be a hoax.* = a trick played on someone by giving false information

hob /hɒb/ noun, c. = the flat top of a gas or electric stove on which pans are kept (used for cooking)

hob•ble /'hɒbəl/ verb, i. *He hurt his leg in a football match and was able to hobble home with some difficulty.* = to walk painfully and with difficulty as a result of some injury (informal)

hob•by /'hɒbi/ noun, c. (**hobbies**) *Her hobby is collecting stamps.* = something that one enjoys doing and does in one's spare time **hobby-horse** noun, c. **1** = a toy horse, usually made of wood, on which a child can ride **2** *As soon as you talk to him he will bring up the topic of banning cricket in this country, which is his hobby-horse.* = a favourite subject or idea to which a person keeps returning (figurative)

hob•gob•lin /hɒb'gɒblɪn/ noun, c. = a goblin (wicked and ugly fairy, found in children's stories) that loves to play tricks on people

hobnob /'hɒbnɒb/ verb, i. *She is always trying to hobnob with important people, in the hope of getting some favours from them.* = to try to have a good relationship with someone in an important position. (derogatory)

H

hock /hɒk/ verb, t. *I had to hock my gold ring as I needed some money urgently.* = to pawn (to leave something valuable with a money-lender in return for money that one has borrowed) (informal)

hock•ey /'hɒki/ noun = a game with eleven players on each side in which a small ball is hit across a field with long sticks curved at the bottom

ho•cus-po•cus /həʊkəs 'peʊkəs/ noun, u. *In India there are many holy men who say they can perform miracles, such as curing disease, by using their spiritual powers. My friend does not believe in miracles and thinks all this is just hocus-pocus.* = the use of tricks to cheat or confuse people

hodge-podge see **hotch-potch**

hoe[1] /həʊ/ noun, c.= a tool used in the garden which has a long handle and is used to break up the soil and remove unwanted plants

hoe[2] verb, t. = to use a hoe

hog[1] /hɒg/ noun, c. **1** = a fat pig **2** *Don't be such a hog!* = a greedy person who eats too much (figurative)

hog[2] verb, t. *She hogs the bathroom every morning and does not allow anyone else to use it.* = to use something in a selfish manner and not allow anyone else to use it (informal) **road-hog** noun, c. = the driver of a motor-car who tries to occupy the whole of the road without caring for the safety of other drivers

to go the whole hog = to do something thoroughly and completely

hoist[1] /hɔɪst/ verb, t. *hoisting a flag* = to raise, lift or pull something up

hoist[2] noun, c. = a machine used for lifting heavy objects

to be hoist with one's own petard = to be trapped or caught by one's own trick (old-fashioned)

hold[1] /həʊld/ verb, t. **(held, held) 1** *Hold the knife in your right hand and the fork in your left when you eat.* = to grip (catch something in the hand so that it does not slip out) **2** *The roof is held up by these two stone pillars.* = to support **3** *When the teacher asked a question some of the students held up their hands.* = to keep in a particular position **4** *The police are holding the two men in jail.* = to prevent someone or something from moving or getting out **5** *Hold your breath for one minute.* = to control **6** *This bottle holds one litre of milk.* = to contain **7** *Can we hold the meeting in this room?* = to have a meeting or event **8** *The views that she holds don't agree with ours.* = to have an opinion **9** *She is talking on the other line. Can you please hold?* (i.) = to ask a person who is on the telephone to wait until the person one wants to talk to is ready

hold[2] or noun, u. **1** *He caught hold of the thief and pushed him down to the floor.* = the act of holding someone or something **2** *She has a strong hold on the party.* = control **hold-all** noun = a large bag for carrying clothes or bedding **holder** noun *a cigarette-holder* = something which holds or contains an object **holding** noun = a piece of land that one possesses

to hold something against someone = to think badly of someone because of something that happened in the past **to hold back 1** *I wanted to show that I was hurt but I held back because it was not the right time.* = to not express one's feelings **2** *They needed my help but I held back because it was going to take up a lot of my time.* = to be unwilling to do something **to hold out** = to continue in spite of difficulties **to hold up 1** *The traffic was held up by the procession.* = to delay something by blocking it **2** = to rob someone **to be left holding the baby** = to be left, usually suddenly, in a position where others make one take up a responsibility which one does not want to take up **Hold it! 1** = an expression used to ask someone to stop doing something or wait (informal) **2** = an expression used to stop someone saying something or to interrupt them **to not hold (much) water** *I'm afraid your explanation does not hold much water.* = to not sound true or possible **to hold one's own** *He's a shy person but when anyone tries to argue with him, he can hold his own.* = to look after or protect oneself well in an argument etc.

hole /həʊl/ noun, c. **1** *She is digging a hole in order to plant a tree.* = an empty space in something solid **2** *The rabbit quickly jumped into its hole.* = the home in which a small animal lives, inside a tree or the ground **3** = the small opening in a golf course into which a ball must be hit [TECHNICAL] **4** *What a hole!* = a small, dark room (derogatory, informal)

to hole up = to hide from someone

hol•i•day[1] /'hɒlɪdi/ noun, c. **1** *We have been working hard for a week. We will take a holiday tomorrow.* = a day of rest **2** *We are going to Cochin for a holiday.* = a period of enjoyment spent in a place away from one's home or place of work

holiday[2] verb, i. *They are holidaying in Karnataka.* = to travel to some place for a holiday

ho•lis•tic /həu'lɪstɪk/ adj. = looking at or treating things as a whole, and not in parts

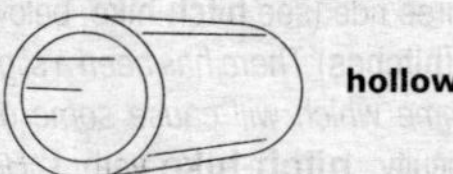

hollow

hol•low[1] /'hɒləʊ/ adj. **1** *Her gold bangles look solid, but in fact they are hollow.* = having an empty space inside **2** *hollow cheeks* = referring to parts of the face to suggest poor health

hollow[2] noun *The house had been built in a hollow at the foot of a hill.* = an area which is at a lower level than the surrounding areas

hollow[3] verb, t. *We will have to hollow out this log of wood.* = to make something hollow

hol•o•caust /ˈhɒləkɔːst/ noun, c. *The entire city was destroyed by a fire and thousands of people died in the holocaust.* = some event that causes terrible destruction and loss of life, specially by burning

hol•o•gram /ˈhɒləgræm/ noun, c. = a picture which seems to be three-dimensional (solid)

hol•ster /ˈhəʊlstəʳ/ noun, c. = a leather holder for a pistol (small gun) that is worn on a belt

holy /ˈhəʊli/ adj. *The Ganga is said to be a holy river.* = connected with God; good and pure

ho•mage /ˈhɒmɪdʒ/ noun, u. *Our history books tell us that Akbar ruled over the whole of India and that the smaller kings, whom he had defeated in battle, paid him homage.* = great respect shown to someone, specially a ruler

home[1] /həʊm/ noun, c. **1** *This little house is my home, where I live with my family.* = the place where one lives **2** *India is the home of the Gir lion.* = the place in which an animal or plant lives or where it was first found **3** *The game of chess had its home in India.* = the place where something started **4** *an aged people's home* = a place where old people, children etc. are looked after

home[2] adj. **1** *He has a happy home life.* = connected with one's home and family **2** *The senior minister looks after home affairs.* = connected with one's own state or country **3** *This match will be played on home ground.* = belonging to one of the teams

home[3] adv. **1** *He didn't get home until midnight.*= where one lives **2** *Turkey took the penalty corner and hit the ball home.* = into the correct position **home-body** noun, c. = a person who likes to stay at home **homecoming** noun, c. = an occasion on which someone returns home after a long time **homely** adj. **1** *a homely meal* = simple and good **2** *a homely person* = not good looking (not respectful) **home-maker** noun, c. = a person in a family who looks after the house, cooks etc. (The word is used in preference to 'housewife'. It refers to both men and women.) **home rule** noun, u. = political control of a country by the people whose home it is and not by people from another country **homesick** adj. = having a strong desire to return to one's own family or country **homestead** noun or adj. = the piece of land on which a home is built as well as the building **home truth** noun, c. = a fact about someone which is not very pleasant to hear **homework** = school work done outside the class **a homing pigeon** = a pigeon used to carry messages, which knows exactly where its home is and always returns to that place (also **carrier pigeon**)

to home in on something = to reach a correct answer to a problem **to be at home with something** *He's completely at home with the subject of childcare.* = to know something very thoroughly and to be comfortable with it **to make oneself at home** = to makes oneself feel comfortable and relaxed in a place one is not familiar with or one would tend to behave formally in (informal) **to be home and dry** = to complete something successfully

ho•me•op•a•thy /həʊmiˈɒpəθi/ noun = a system of medicine in which some substance which can cause a disease is used to treat a disease similar to it

hom•i•cide /ˈhɒmɪsaɪd/ noun, u. or c. **1** = an act of murder (deliberate killing of a human being) **2** = a person who has murdered someone

hom•i•ly /ˈhɒmɪli/ noun, c. (**homilies**) *a long homily* = a long talk giving advice to someone (not respectful)

ho•mo- /həʊməʊ/ prefix meaning 'the same' e.g. **homogeneous** /həʊməˈdʒiːniəs/ adj. *These twelve villages have a homogeneous population.* = made up of things of the same kind (opposite **heterogeneous**)

homologous /həˈmɒləgəs/ = identical in position, structure etc. to something else [TECHNICAL]

ho•mo•nym /ˈhɒmənɪm/ noun, c. *The words 'bear', meaning 'to suffer', and 'bear', referring to the animal, are homonyms.* = words having the same spelling and sound but different meanings

hom•o•phone /ˈhɒməfəʊn/ noun, c. *The words 'dew' and 'due' are homophones.* = words having the same sound but different spellings and meanings

Ho•mo sa•pi•ens /həʊməʊ ˈsæpɪenz/ noun = a member of the human race as it exists now [TECHNICAL]

ho•mo•sex•u•al /həʊməˈsekʃuəl/ noun, c. = a person who is attracted to a person of the same sex (opposite **heterosexual**)

hone /həʊn/ verb, t. *The knife has been beautifully honed.* = to give a sharp edge to a knife or sword

hon•est /ˈɒnɪst/ adj. *an honest businessman* = one who can be trusted and is not likely to steal or cheat **honesty** noun, u. = the quality of being honest

hon•ey /ˈhʌni/ noun, u. = the sweet golden liquid produced by bees from the juice of flowers **honeycomb** noun, c. = a little container with six sides, made of wax and produced by bees, in which honey is stored

hon•ey•moon[1] /ˈhʌnɪmuːn/ noun, c. = a holiday taken by a man and a woman just after their marriage

honeymoon[2] verb, i. *They are honeymooning in Europe.* = to go somewhere on a honeymoon

honk[1] /hɒŋk/ noun, u. = the sound made by the horn of a car or by a wild goose

honk[2] verb, i. *The driver of the car honked his horn loudly.* = to make a honking sound

honorarium /ɒnəreəriəm/ noun, u. = money paid

to a person holding an honorary job for which there is no salary

hon•or•ar•y /ˈɒnərəri/ adj. *The Chairperson of the company is not paid a salary. She holds an honorary position.* = a job or position for which a regular salary is not paid **honorary degree** = a university degree given to someone as an honour, without having to take courses, pass examination etc.

hon•our[1] /ˈɒnəʳ/ noun, u. or c. **1** *Mahatma Gandhi received great honour as a leader of people not only in India but all over the world.*(u.) = great respect and love which is publicly expressed **2** *It was an honour to receive the prize.*(c.) = something that one does with pride and pleasure

honour[2] verb, t. **1** *We have arranged this function to honour our brave soldiers who fought in the war.* = to show respect **2** *The bank will honour this cheque.* = to accept **honours** (**Honours**) noun *He passed the B.A. degree with Honours in Sanskrit.* = a university degree with special attention given to one subject **honourable** adj. **1** *an honourable profession* = having dignity and deserving respect **2** *an honourable person* = having a high sense of moral behaviour **3** *an honourable agreement* = fair and just to all who are involved **honourably** adv.

hood /hʊd/ noun, c. **1** = a covering for the head and neck, which leaves the face open **2** *the hood of a cycle rickshaw* = a covering made of cloth, fitted over a wooden frame, which covers the top of a vehicle and can be raised or lowered **3** *the hood of a car* = American English for **bonnet** (the metal covering over the engine of a car)

-hood /ˈhʊd/ suffix meaning **1** state e.g. *childhood* **2** group e.g. *brotherhood*

hood•lum /ˈhuːdləm/ noun, c. = a person who is hired to do some violent criminal act

hood•wink /ˈhʊdˌwɪŋk/ verb, t. *He hoodwinked me into paying him Rs 1,000.* = to cheat or trick someone

hoof /huːf/ noun, c. (**hoofs** or **hooves**) = the hard, bony part at the end of the foot of a horse, cow or deer

hook[1] /hʊk/ noun, c. **1** *a fish hook* = a piece of metal with a curved and often pointed end, from which something can be hung or which can be used to catch or to lift something **2** = a hit made by swinging the bat in a curve (cricket)

hook[2] verb, t. **1** *Can you hook up the child's dress?* = to fasten (close or tie up) something by using one or more hooks **2** *She has hooked a big fish.* = to catch with a hook **3** *Ganguly has hooked the ball for a six.* = to hit the ball in cricket so as to send it high to one side **hooker** noun, c. = a sex-worker (slang, not respectful) **hookworm** noun, c. = a kind of worm which lives inside the intestines of a human being or animal

by hook or by crook = to do something using any means possible **off the hook** = (used about a telephone) when the receiver (top part) is not in place, preventing calls from being received **to be (get) hooked** = to be trapped (to get into an unpleasant situation and not be able to get out)

hoo•li•gan /ˈhuːlɪgən/ noun, c. = a person who acts in a rough and violent way in public

hoop /huːp/ noun, c. = a circular band or ring made of metal or plastic, which is put around the top of a wooden barrel

hoot[1] /huːt/ noun, c. **1** *the hoot of an owl* **2** *the hoot of a car horn* = the sound made by an owl or a similar sound made by the horn of a motor-car **3** *The audience greeted the actor with a hoot.* = loud sounds or laughter produced by a group of people to show that they do not like something

hoot[2] verb, i. **1** *The driver hooted his horn.* = to make a hooting sound **2** *The audience hooted the speaker.* = to show disrespect or displeasure by making a loud sound or by laughing

hop[1] /hɒp/ verb, i. (**hopped**) **1** *The bird hopped from one branch to another.* = to give a small jump (used to describe the movement of birds and small animals e.g. frogs) **2** *The children were hopping across the field* = to jump on one leg (used for human beings) **3** *He hopped into the car.* = to get into or out of a vehicle very quickly

hop[2] noun, c. *She cleared the ditch with a hop.* = the act of jumping **hopping flight** noun = a journey made in an aircraft which stops at a number of places which are not very far from each other

Hop it! = a rude way of asking someone to go away **to be hopping mad** = to be very angry (informal)

hope[1] /həʊp/ verb, t. or i. *He hopes to pass the examination in the first division.* = to believe strongly that something good will happen because there is some reason to believe this

hope[2] noun, u. or c. *The patient's condition is getting worse, but the doctors have not given up hopes of his recovery.* = the expectation or belief that something good will happen

hope•ful adj. **1** *We are hopeful that the minister will come on time.* = feeling hope **2** *The patient has opened his eyes. This is a hopeful sign.* = something that causes hope **hopeless** adj. **1** *This is a hopeless situation. We have lost nine wickets and still need 150 runs to win.* = something that gives no cause for hope **2** *I am quite hopeless as a singer.* = lacking in skill

to dash somebody's hopes = to completely destroy somebody's belief **to hope against hope** = to continue to expect something good, even when it seems unlikely **to hope for the best** = to expect something good to happen, when it seems unlikely

horde /hɔːd/ noun, c. = a large, noisy and moving crowd

ho•ri•zon /həˈraɪzən/ noun = the line at which the sky and the earth seem to meet

horizontal /hɒrɪˈzɒntl/ adj. *Keep the piece of wood in a horizontal position.* = flat or level with the ground (compare **vertical, perpendicular**)

horizontal

to expand one's horizons (always plural) = to be able to get more knowledge or experience

hor•mone /ˈhɔːməʊn/ noun, c. = a kind of chemical produced inside the body which gets mixed with the blood and has some effect on the growth, development etc. of the body [BIOLOGY]

horn /hɔːn/ noun, c. or u. **1** *the horns of a cow*(c.) = one of a pair of bony, pointed parts growing on the head of a cow, buffalo, goat, deer etc. **2** = a musical instrument made of metal that is played by blowing into it **3** *the horn of a motorcar*(c.) = the part in a motor-car, truck etc. that makes a loud sound to warn others

to take the bull by the horns = to face a difficult situation with courage **to be on the horns of a dilemma** = to not know what to do in a particular situation

hor•net /ˈhɔːnɪt/ noun, c. = a black and yellow insect like a bee, which has a painful sting

hor•o•scope /ˈhɒrəskəʊp/ noun, c. = a chart or diagram showing the positions of the planets at the time when a person was born, from which it is believed that the person's future can be told

hor•ror /ˈhɒrəʳ/ noun, u. or c. **1** *The news that 30,000 people had been killed in the earthquake filled us with horror.*(u.) = a feeling of shock, fear, anxiety and dislike **2** *The television programme showed us the horrors of the earthquake.*(c.) = something that causes a feeling of shock, disgust or great fear **3** *horror movie* = a film that creates horror by showing ghosts and other supernatural things **horrible** adj. **1** *a horrible accident* = causing horror **2** *horrible handwriting* = very bad **horrify** verb, t. (**horrified**) *The news of the earthquake horrified us.* = to cause a feeling of horror

hors d'oeu•vre /ɔː ˈdɜːv/ noun, c. (French) = appetizer (food served in small quantities at the beginning of a meal to add to the enjoyment of the meal)

horse¹ /hɔːs/ noun, c. = a large, strong animal that people ride on or use to draw carts and carriages

horse² verb, i. *Stop horsing around!* = to waste time in rough play or rough behaviour (slang) **horseman/horsewoman** noun, c. = a person who is skilled at riding horses **horsepower** noun, u. *This car can develop 80 horsepower* = a measure of the power that an engine can produce **horse-sense** noun, c. *You need a little horse-sense to deal with this situation* = common sense **horse-trading** noun, u. = a process by which two persons or two parties try to reach an agreement, by giving away something and getting something in return

straight from the horse's mouth *The newspaper reporter got the news of the cricketer's retirement straight from the horse's mouth.* = information given directly by someone connected with some event

hor•ti•cul•ture /ˈhɔːtɪkʌltʃəʳ/ noun = the science of growing fruits, flowers and vegetables

hose¹ /həʊz/ noun, c. **1** = a thick pipe or tube made of rubber or plastic, through which water can flow with force **2** = thick socks (see **hosiery**)

hose² verb, t. *She is hosing the car down.* = to use a hose to wash something or to provide water for a plant etc.

ho•sier•y /ˈhəʊzjəri/ noun, u. = clothing made by knitting threads on a machine e.g. underwear, tee-shirts, socks etc.

hos•pi•tal /ˈhɒspɪtl/ noun, c. = a place where people who are ill receive medical treatment

hos•pi•tal•i•ty /hɒspɪˈtælɪti/ noun, u. *Mr Sharma always looks after people who are travelling through Delhi. He is well-known for his hospitality.* = the quality of being friendly and welcoming and looking after guests well **hospitable** /hɒsˈpɪtəbəl/ adj. *Mr Sharma is a very hospitable person.* = friendly and welcoming to guests

host¹ /həʊst/ noun, c. **1** = a person who receives guests and provides them with food etc. **2** *the host on a television programme* = a person who introduces other performers on a television programme **3** *If you buy a new computer you will receive a host of prizes from the dealers.* = a large number **4** = an animal or plant on which another animal or plant feeds [TECHNICAL] (compare **parasite**)

host² verb, t. *He is hosting a dinner for a hundred guests.* = to act as a host at a party or on a television show etc. **hostess** noun, c. = a woman who is a host **airhostess** noun, c. = a woman who serves food and drink to passengers on an aircraft and looks after them

hos•tage /ˈhɒstɪdʒ/ noun, c. *The robbers have kidnapped two of our students and are holding them as hostages.* = a person who is captured and held

H

prisoner by criminals or terrorists and used to bargain with his/her relatives and friends, so that the criminals can get what they want

hos•tel /'hɒstəl/ noun, c. = a place where students can live and eat together

hos•tile /'hɒstaɪl/ adj. *The people living in this city are hostile to the idea of the new bridge and will never agree to it.* = unfriendly; showing extreme dislike

hot[1] /hɒt/ adj. **1** *Bhubaneswar becomes very hot in summer.* = having a high degree of heat **2** *The people of Andhra Pradesh like hot food.* = food which contains a lot of chilli and causes a burning feeling in the mouth **3** *He has a hot temper.* = excitable and easily made angry **4** *He fled a hot situation.* = difficult to deal with **5** *He is the hot favourite to win this tournament.* = very popular **6** *hot news* = fresh and exciting (figurative)

hot[2] verb, i. (**hotted**) *The series of matches between India and Australia started tamely but is hotting up now.* = to become exciting (informal) **hot air** noun *His speech was full of hot air* = high-sounding but meaningless talk **hotbed** noun *Delhi has become a hotbed of crime.* = a place where a lot of bad things happen **hot-blooded** adj. *a hot-blooded person* = easily made angry **hot dog** noun = a sausage (meat which has been cut into very fine pieces and packed inside a thin piece of animal skin) which is placed between two long pieces of bread and eaten **hothouse** noun = a building which is kept warm and in which certain kinds of plants are grown (see also **greenhouse**) **hotline** noun = a direct telephone link between heads of governments which can be used when a serious problem arises or there is danger of war **hot water bottle** noun, c. = a rubber container that is filled with water and put in a bed to warm it

to get into hot water = to get into trouble **to sell like hot cakes** = to sell quickly **to blow hot and cold** = to say or do things which contradict each other **to go hot and cold** = to be in a situation where one is very anxious or very afraid **to be too hot to handle** = a situation which is very unpleasant or dangerous **to be a hot ticket** = to be a popular actor, singer etc. who is greatly admired and who everyone wants to see (informal)

hotch potch (**hodge-podge**) /'hɔːtʃ'pɔːʃ/ noun, u. *The new book by Mr Verma is a hotch-potch of ideas taken from different writers.* = a confusing mixture of different things, without any order (derogatory)

ho•tel /həʊ'tel/ noun, c. = a place where travellers can get rooms to stay in for a short time as well as meals for a sum of money **hotelier** noun, c, = a person who owns a hotel

hound[1] /haʊnd/ noun, c. = a hunting dog

hound[2] verb, t. *The filmstar was hounded by the press for details about her new movie.* = to be troubled or followed continuously by someone (informal)

hour /aʊəʳ/ noun, c. **1** = a period of 60 minutes **2** *Pondicherry is two hours away.* = the distance one can travel in 60 minutes **3** (always plural) *We can examine the account after hours.* = working hours (the period during which a shop or office is open)

house[1] /haʊs/ noun, c. **1** = a building in which people belonging to a family live **2** *a cinema house* = a building used for a particular purpose **3** = one of the groups into which the children studying in a school are divided, specially for purposes of competition in sports **4** *The Prime Minister informed the House that relief operations had started in the region.* = one of the divisions of Parliament

house[2] /haʊs/ verb, t. **1** *This building houses the National Library.* = to provide space for **2** *We will have to house 10,000 refugees urgently.* = to provide shelter for **house arrest** noun = a situation in which a person who is suspected of having done something wrong is not allowed by the police to leave his or her house **house-broken** adj. = a pet animal which has been trained not to make the house dirty by passing urine etc. inside it **housebreaking** noun = the act of entering someone's house for the purpose of stealing **house coat** noun = a long dress worn by women while working inside the house **household** noun = the members of the family living together in a house **household name** noun = very well known and popular **housekeeping** noun **1** = the action of managing a house and taking care of the people living in it **2** = the job of looking after the rooms, the facilities, services etc. in a hotel **house-proud** adj. = a person who likes to keep his/her house clean and tidy **house surgeon** noun = a doctor who is receiving training in a hospital **house-warming** noun = a party given on moving into a new house **housewife** noun = a woman who looks after her family and the house they live in and who does not go out to work (The term **homemaker** is now preferred as being more respectful and as referring to both men and women.)

to be on the house = paid for by the restaurant, hotel etc. that one is visiting **to get on (with someone) like a house on fire** = to be very good friends with someone and have a lot in common with them **to put one's house in order** = to organize things neatly **to bring the house down** = to give a performance (on a stage etc.) which is greatly liked by everyone (informal)

hov•el /'hɒvəl/ a place which is small and dirty and

which people believe is unsuitable for living in (derogatory)

hover /'hɒvəʳ/ verb, i. *The birds hovered in the air over the fields.* = to remain in the air in one place without moving **hovercraft** noun = a kind of aircraft without wings that can fly over land or water, keeping very close to the surface and supported by a strong downward current of air

how[1] /haʊ/ adv. **1** *How can I become a member of this club?* = in what way **2** *Your father was ill. How is he now?* = in what condition

how[2] conj. *I will never forget how you helped me.* = the fact that **How are you? / How do you do?** = a form of greeting used when meeting someone **How's that?** = an expression used by a player on the field in the game of cricket, asking the umpire to decide whether a batsman of the opposite team is out

how•ev•er /haʊ'evəʳ/ adv. **1** *She is very ill. However, she is sure to come to your party next week.* = in spite of; nevertheless (used to add a comment) **2** *This man is likely to leave the job, however much we pay him.* = in whatever way **3** *However did you manage to find that book?* = how; in what way

how•it•zer /'haʊɪtsəʳ/ noun, c. = a very heavy gun which can fire shells over a long distance

howl[1] /haʊl/ verb, i. *The dogs howled when they caught the scent of a stranger.* = to produce a long, loud, sound expressing anger, pain etc. (generally used to describe the sound produced by a dog, wolf etc. but also sometimes by a human being)

howl[2] noun, c. *I heard a howl of anger from the next room, in which the meeting was going on.* = the sound produced when howling **howler** noun, c. = a mistake committed by someone, generally while writing, which makes people laugh

HTML abbr. of **Hypertext Mark-Up Language** = a system of codes used to mark text, pictures, colour etc. so that they can be seen as web pages [COMPUTERS]

hub /hʌb/ noun, c. **1** *The hub of a wheel* = the central part of a wheel, around which it turns **2** *Mumbai is the hub of commerce in India.* = a busy centre of activity

hub•bub /'hʌbʌb/ noun, u. *What a hubbub there is in this market!* = a mixture of loud noises

hud•dle[1] /'hʌdl/ verb, i. *As It was very cold inside the room we huddled together to keep warm.* = to crowd together, forming a group or pile

huddle[2] noun, c. *They stood in a huddle, whispering.* = a large number of people or things forming an untidy group or pile

hue /hju:/ noun, c. **1** *This flower has a beautiful golden hue.* = colour (literary) **2** *Politicians of every hue are now busy trying to win votes.* = type or kind **hue and cry** *There was a hue and cry when the price of petrol went up.* = an expression of public anger or opposition to something

huff[1] /hʌf/ verb, i. *The old ladies huffed and puffed as they climbed up the stairs.* = to breathe loudly and with some effort

huff[2] noun, u. *The man walked off in a huff because you did not invite him to stay on after the meeting.* = a state of being displeased or angry

hug[1] /hʌg/ verb, t. (**hugged**) **1** *The mother hugged her child lovingly.* = to hold someone or something tightly in the arms, close to the body **2** *The road from Puri to Konark hugs the coast.* = to stay near

hug[1] noun, c. *Give the child a hug!* = the act of holding someone close as an expression of love

huge /hju:dʒ/ adj. **1** *a huge person* = very large **2** *The book was a huge success.* = very great **3** *She gets a huge allowance.* = a very large amount

hulk /hʌlk/ noun, c. **1** *We saw the hulk of an old ship tied up close to the shore.* = the body of an old ship or some other vehicle which is no longer in use and is in a bad condition **2** *What a hulk that boy is!* = a large person (disrespectful)

hull /hʌl/ noun, c. = the main body of a ship, which floats on water

hul•la•ba•loo /hʌləbə'lu:/ *Don't make such a hullabaloo! You can be heard down the corridor.* = a loud noise produced by many voices

hum[1] /hʌm/ verb, t. or u. (**hummed**) **1** *Can you hear the bees humming around the beehive?*(i) = to make a continuous low sound **2** *If you don't know the words of the song, you can hum it to us.*(t) = to sing without moving the lips **3** *The market was humming with activity.*(i) = to be full of activity

hum[2] noun, u. *We heard the hum of a car's engine in the distance.* = a continuous low sound

hu•man[1] /'hju:mən/ adj. **1** *Human intelligence is higher than that of any computer.* = belonging to or having to do with a human being **2** *human qualities* = feelings, emotions (e.g. pity) and often weaknesses (e.g. jealousy) that humans commonly have **3** *the human side of Sylvia* = connected with qualities of kindness, pity etc. **4** *a human error* = a mistake made by a person, not a machine

human[2] noun, c. *It is said that the earliest humans lived in Africa about a million years ago.* = a member of the human race; a person

hu•mane /hju:'meɪn/ adj. *a very humane person* = kind and sympathetic

humanitarian /hjumæni'teəriən/ adj. *The Red Cross does a lot of humanitarian work in the developing countries of the world.* = something done to improve the lives of human beings who are suffering

H

hu•man•i•ties /hjuː'mænɪtiz/ noun = the study of literature, history, philosophy etc. (and not science)

humanity /hju'mænɪti/ noun, u. **1** *crimes against humanity* = human beings **2** *The children injured in the riots were treated with great humanity.* = kindness

hum•ble[1] /'hʌmbl/ adj. **1** *Although she is a famous person, she is very humble.* = not thinking that one is better than others; not proud **2** *The big shop had humble beginnings.* = ordinary or small

humble[2] verb, t. *We were humbled by our defeat in the match.* = to cause someone to lose pride **humility** noun, u. = the quality of being humble (not thinking that one is better than others)

hum•bug /'hʌmbʌg/ noun, u. or c. **1** *What you said in you speech was a lot of humbug.*(u.) = nonsense or something that should not be believed (informal) **2** (c.) = a person who pretends to be what he/she is not

hum•drum /'hʌmdrʌm/ adj. *We live very humdrum lives in this little town, without any excitement.* = very ordinary and dull

hu•mid /'hjuːmɪd/ adj. *The climate in Chennai is very humid as it is near the sea.* = containing a lot of water-vapour (tiny, invisible drops of water present in the air); damp (wet) **humidity** /hjuː'mɪdɪti/ noun, c. *The humidity of the climate in Mumbai makes one feel tired.* = the quality of being humid

hu•mil•i•ate /hjuː'mɪlieɪt/ verb, t. *My boss humiliated me by shouting at me in front of all my colleagues.* = to cause someone to feel ashamed or to lose respect **humiliation** /hjuːmɪlɪ'eɪʃən/ noun, u. = the feeling of shame, embarassment

hu•mour[1] /'hjuːməʳ/ noun, u. *Anyone who can make jokes about themselves must have a good sense of humour.* = the ability to make people laugh and to enjoy something that is funny

humour[2] verb, t. *Will you have to humour your seniors at work?* = to keep someone happy by doing what he or she wants (derogatory) **humorous** adj. *a humorous film* = able to make people laugh, funny **humorist** noun, c. = a person who can make people laugh, specially by writing funny things

hump /hʌmp/ noun, c. **1** *Camels have large humps on their backs.* = a round part which stands out **2** *The road has many humps.* = a part of a road surface which is raised and forces cars etc. to slow down

hu•mus /'hjuːməs/ noun = the substance, made up of dead plants, leaves etc. which makes the soil rich [TECHNICAL]

hunch[1] /hʌntʃ/ noun, c. (**hunches**) *I was not sure how many people were coming to this meeting but I had a hunch that many people would come.* = an idea based on some feeling rather than on facts, which often turns out to be right (informal)

hunch[2] verb, t. *She lay in bed reading a book, hunched up under the electric light.* = to pull the body into a rounded shape **hunchback** /'hʌntʃbæk/ noun, c. = a person whose back is bent and who has a growth (a hump) sticking out from the back

hun•dred /'hʌndrɪd/ noun, c. = the number represented by 100

hun•ger[1] /'hʌŋgəʳ/ noun, u. **1** *That was a good meal, but I don't know if your hunger has been satisfied.* = the desire for food **2** *People are dying of hunger.* = lack of food **3** *She has a hunger for knowledge.* = a strong desire to get something

hunger[2] verb, i. *She hungers for justice.* = to have a strong desire for something (literary) **hungry** adj. *Are you hungry?* = wishing to eat; feeling hunger

hunk /hʌŋk/ noun, c. **1** *a hunk of bread* = a thick piece of some food **2** *What a hunk!* = a man with an attractive and muscular body (informal)

hunt[1] /hʌnt/ verb, t. **1** *Tigers hunt deer and other small animals.* = to chase and kill an animal for food **2** *Are crocodiles still hunted in India*? = to search out, chase and kill an animal for sport (enjoyment) **3** *He is hunting for a textbook of physics.* = to search for

hunt[2] noun, c. **1** *The villagers have started a hunt for the missing child.* = the act of searching for someone or something **2** *a tiger hunt* = an act of chasing wild animals, in order to kill them **hunter** noun, c. = a person or animal that hunts wild animals for food or sport

to hunt something or someone down = to search for and find

hur•dle[1] /'hɜːdl/ noun, c. **1** *The government has to face many hurdles in carrying out its programmes.* = something that creates a difficulty or prevents one from doing something **2** *I am competing in the 110 metres hurdles race.* = a wooden frame that one has to jump over in a race

hurdle[2] verb, t. *He hurdled the gate with a single jump.* = to jump over something without touching it

hurl /hɜːl/ verb, t. = to throw something heavy with an effort

to hurl abuse (accusations) at someone = to shout at someone in an insulting manner

hur•ly-bur•ly /'hɜːli bɜːli/ noun, u. *I am tired of the hurly-burly of the city. I prefer the peace of the countryside.* = noisy activity

hur•ray (hurrah) /hʊ'reɪ/ interjec. *Hurray! It's raining!* = an expression of joy

hur•ri•cane /'hʌrɪkən/ noun, c. = a violent storm with strong winds and rain

hur•ry[1] /'hʌri/ verb, i. or t. (**hurried**) **1** *She hurried to catch the postman who had just left the house.*(i.) = to move or do something quickly **2** *The meeting is* *going very slowly. Can you hurry things up?*(t.) = to make things happen more quickly

hurry[2] noun, u. **1** *He left in a great hurry.* = using quick movements or actions **2** *We have plenty of time to reach the airport. There is no hurry.* = need to be quick

hurry up *Hurry up or we'll miss the bus.*= to do something quickly (informal)

hurt[1] /hɜːt/ verb, t. or i. **1** *She fell off the bicycle and hurt her leg.*(t.) = to cause some injury (damage) to the body **2** *My arm hurts.*(i.) = to feel pain **3** *I am hurt by your unkind remarks.*(t.) = to feel pain in the mind **4** *Cigarette companies will be hurt by the new law banning smoking.* = to suffer loss

hurt[2] noun, u. *Your letter of apology cannot take away the hurt to my feelings.* = damage or injury

hur•tle /'hɜːtl/ verb, i. *The cyclist hurtled down the road.* = to move on a bicycle, in a car etc. with great speed

hus•band[1] /'hʌzbənd/ noun, c. = the man to whom a woman is married

husband[2] verb, t. *We will have to husband our resources carefully or we will never be able to complete this project.* = to use carefully or to make the best use of something without wasting it (formal, old-fashioned) **husbandry** (**animal husbandry**) noun, u. = a branch of farming which tells us how to make the best use of land, forests, cattle etc.

hush[1] /hʌʃ/ noun, u. *There was a hush in the auditorium as she got up to speak.* = silence

hush[2] verb, t. *Can you hush the baby, please? We are disturbed by its crying.* = to cause someone to become silent (informal) **hush-hush** adj. *a hush-hush affair* = something which is planned or done secretly, without letting anyone know (informal, derogatory) **hush-money** noun, u. = money paid to someone to prevent something unpleasant or shameful from becoming known

husk[1] /hʌsk/ noun, c. **1** = the dry outer covering of some seed or fruit **2** *He has taken everything, leaving only the husk behind.* = the useless part of something (figurative)

husk[2] verb, t. *The paddy has to be husked.* = to remove the husk (outer covering) of grain (also **de-husk**)

hus•ky[1] /'hʌski/ adj. **1** *We could not hear her clearly as she spoke in a very husky voice.* = somewhat rough and difficult to hear (referring to a person's voice) **2** *a husky person* = big and strong

husky[2] noun, c. (**huskies**) = a large working dog with thick fur which is used (in the very cold countries near the North Pole) to pull sledges over the ice (see also **sledge**)

hus•sy /'hʌsi/ noun, c. (**hussies**) = a woman who is very bold and impolite (derogatory) Ⓖ

hus•tle[1] /'hʌsəl/ verb, t. *The workers in this factory are very slow. You will have to hustle them.* = to cause someone to move or work fast

hustle[2] noun, u. *You will find a lot of hustle and bustle in the city when there is an election.* = hurried activity

hut /hʌt/ noun, c. = a small building, usually with one room only, made of simple and cheap materials

hutch /hʌtʃ/ noun, c. (**hutches**) *a rabbit hutch* = a small box or cage in which rabbits or other small animals are kept as pets

H

hy•a•cinth /'haɪəsɪnθ/ noun = a kind of plant which produces sweet-smelling flowers **water hyacinth** noun = a kind of plant with large, thick leaves which grows wild in ponds and other watery places

hy•brid /'haɪbrɪd/ noun or adj. *This new animal in the zoo, called a 'liger', is a hybrid. Its father is a lion and its mother a tiger.*(noun) = a plant or animal produced from parents of different breeds

hy•drant /'haɪdrənt/ noun, c. = a water-tap set up on a street to supply water for public use, specially to put out fires

hy•draul•ic /haɪ'drɒlɪk/ adj. *The car has hydraulic brakes.* = made to work by the pressure of water, oil or some other liquid [TECHNICAL]

hy•dro- /haɪdrəʊ/ prefix meaning connected with water e.g. **hydrophobia** /haɪdrə'fəʊbiə/ noun = a disease which causes, among other things, fear of water (also known as **rabies**) [MEDICINE]

hy•dro•car•bon /haɪdrə'kɒːbən/ noun, c. = a chemical in which hydrogen and carbon are combined e.g. petrol [CHEMISTRY]

hy•dro•e•lec•tric /haɪdreʊɪ'lektrɪk/ adj. *a hydro-electric powerstation* = electricity produced by making use of the power of falling water

hy•dro•gen /'haɪdrədʒən/ noun = a gas that is lighter than air, has no smell or colour, burns very easily and produces water when combined with oxygen **hydrogen bomb** noun = a very powerful bomb which explodes when atoms of hydrogen are made to fuse (join) together

hy•ena (hyaena) /haɪ'iːnə/ a wild animal somewhat like a dog which eats the bodies of dead animals and has a cry that sounds like a human laugh

hy•giene /'haɪdʒiːn/ noun = the science which deals with the prevention of disease through special attention to cleanliness **hygienic** adj. = very clean and therefore healthy

hymn[1] /hɪm/ noun, c. = a prayer in the form of a song

hymn[2] verb, t. = to sing a hymn or prayer

hy•per- /haɪpəʳ/ prefix meaning **1** more than usual e.g. **hyperactive** adj. *a hyperactive child* = more active than is usual and therefore unable to sit quietly (technical or derogatory) **2** 'too much' e.g. **hypersensitive** adj. = unusually sensitive (having feelings which are very easily hurt) (derogatory)

hy•per•bo•le /haɪ'pɜːbəli/ noun, u. *Calling someone 'an ocean of wisdom' is an example of hyperbole.* = describing something by means of exaggeration (making something appear bigger, better etc. than it really is) [LITERATURE]

hyperlink noun, c. = a line or place in an electronic document that is connected to another document or page [COMPUTERS]

hy•phen /'haɪfən/ noun, c. = a short line which joins words together e.g. 'hyper-active' **hyphenate** verb, t. = to put a hyphen between two words to join them together

hyp•no•tize (hypnotise) /'hɪpnətaɪz/ verb, t. = to control the mind and actions of a person by putting him/her into a dream-like state **hypnosis** noun, c. = the dream-like state created by hypnotizing a person **hypnotist** noun, c. = a person who can hypnotize people

hy•po- /'haɪpəʊ/ prefix meaning 'less than usual' or 'too little' (opposite of **hyper**)

hy•po•chon•dri•a /haɪpə'kɒndriə/ noun = the state of worrying too much about one's own health **hypochondriac** adj. = a person who suffers from hypochondria

hy•po•crite /'hɪpəkrɪt/ noun, c. = a person who says one thing but does something very different or pretends to be something that he/she is not

hypocrisy /hɪ'pɒkrɪsi/ noun = the quality of being a hypocrite

hy•po•der•mic /haɪpə'dɜːmɪk/ adj. *a hypodermic needle* = something which is used for an injection (allowing some medicine to pass directly into the blood through a hollow needle which makes a small hole in the skin)

hy•po•te•nuse /haɪ'pɒtɪnjuːz/ noun, c. *the hypotenuse of a right-angled triangle* = the longest side in a triangle in which one angle measures 90 degrees [GEOMETRY]

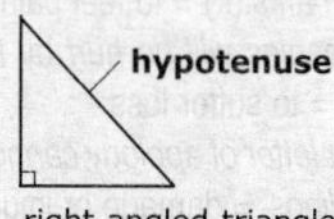

hy•poth•e•sis /haɪ'pɒθɪsɪs/ noun, c. (**hypotheses**) *The scientist Galileo put forward the hypothesis that the earth is round, at a time when everyone else believed that the earth was flat.* = an idea which is suggested as a possible explanation for something that is observed (seen), but which has not been tested or proved **hypothetical** /haɪpə'θetɪkəl/ adj. *What I would do if I were the Prime Minister of India is only a hypothetical question, because I will never become the Prime Minister!* = something that is based on ideas and situations that are not real

hys•te•ri•a /hɪ'stɪəriə/ noun = a condition of the mind and body which causes a person to become very excited and to laugh or weep without reason **hysterical** adj. = in a state of hysteria

i, I /aɪ/ the ninth letter of the English alphabet

I /aɪ/ pron. *I am doing something important.* = a word used by a person who is speaking to refer to himself or herself

i•bex /'aɪbeks/ noun, c. (**ibexes** or **ibex**) = a kind of wild goat found in the mountains of Europe

ibis /'aɪbɪs/ noun, c. (**ibises** or **ibis**) = a large bird with a long downward-curving beak

ice[1] /aɪs/ noun, u. = water which has been cooled to a very low temperature and frozen (made solid)

ice[2] verb, t. = to add ice to something in order to cool it **icy** adj. **1** *an icy wind* = extremely cold **2** *icy roads* = covered with layers of ice **3** *His manner was so icy that we felt like going away.* = cold and unfriendly **Ice Age** noun = a time, very long ago, when large parts of the earth were covered with ice **iceberg** noun, c. = a large mountain of ice floating in the ocean **ice cream** noun, u. or c. = a kind of sweet made from milk or cream, sugar and flavouring etc which has been kept at very low temperature and has become almost solid

to break the ice = to do something at a gathering where people are meeting for the first time, to make them feel more comfortable and friendly **to put something on ice** *Since we haven't received the money for the project, let's put it on ice.* = to stop work on a plan or idea or put it away for a while, usually for a reason (informal) **to cut no ice** *They were strongly against the plan, and all our explanations cut no ice with them.* = to not succeed in making someone feel that something is worthwhile, good etc. or to have no effect on someone (informal)

i•ci•cle /'aɪsɪkəl/ noun, c. = a long stick of ice formed when water falling from a height freezes

ic•ing /'aɪsɪŋ/ noun, u. = a coating of sugar, chocolate etc. which covers a cake

i•con (**ikon**) /'aɪkɒn/ noun, c. **1** = a small sign on a computer screen which has a certain meaning and can be used to make the computer carry out some instruction [COMPUTERS] **2** *Elvis Presley was an icon of rock n' roll music.* = a person who is popular, admired and well remembered **3** = a picture of a god or a holy person used for religious purposes **iconoclast** /aɪ'kɒnəklæst/ noun, c. = a person who speaks against the things (mostly religious) that most people believe in and respect

ID /aɪ'di:/ noun, c. **1** = abbreviation of identity card (see **identity**) **2** *e-mail id* = one's e-mail address e.g. sheela2@vsnl.com

i•dea /aɪ'dɪə/ noun, c. **1** *Our new leader is a man with many exciting new ideas.* = thought or plan for doing something in a particular way **2** *'Let's go on a picnic tomorrow.' 'That's an excellent idea!'* = a plan for a possible course of action **3** *Can you give me some idea of the climate in Singapore?* = information or knowledge which is not detailed or exact **4** *When I went to drama school, the idea was to become an actor.* = purpose, aim

to have no idea (only singular) *'Do you know why Sanat is absent today?' 'I have no idea?'* = to not have information about something **to (not) be one's idea of something** *Watching a film is not my idea of an enjoyable evening.* = opinion **to have some (a rough) idea** = to have a little knowledge about something

i•deal[1] /aɪ'dɪəl/ adj. *Darjeeling is the ideal place for a holiday.* = perfect

ideal[2] noun, c. **1** *Sachin Tendulkar is my ideal of what a good cricketer should be.* = a perfect example of some quality that one values **2** (always plural) *She is a person with high ideals.* = high principles, values or standards of behaviour **idealism** noun, u. = the quality of believing in ideals **idealist** noun, c. = a person with high ideals which may not be suitable for the real or practical world (sometimes derogatory)

i•den•ti•ty /aɪ'dentɪti/ noun, u. or c. (**identities**) *The man who was injured in the accident has lost his memory. The police is trying to find out his identity.* = who or what a person is (details such as name, age, profession, address etc.) **identity card (ID card)** noun, c. = a card or piece of paper carrying a person's name, photograph etc. which can help prove his/her identity **identify** verb, t. **1** *I don't know who you are. Is there anyone here who can identify you?* = to point out someone's identity **2** *Could we identify someone who can help us with this project?* = select, for a purpose **identification** /aidentifi'keiʃən/ noun, u. **1**= the act of identifying someone **2** *Can you produce some identification?* = some document (official paper) which can identify a person **identical** /aɪ'dentɪkəl/ adj. *Leela and Anita are identical twins.* = very strongly alike

i•de•ol•o•gy /aɪdi'ɒlədʒi/ noun, u. or c. (**ideologies**) = ideas which form a way of thinking and acting on which a political or economic system is based

id•i•om /'ɪdiəm/ noun, c. **1** *'To cut no ice' is an idiom which means 'to have no effect on someone'* = an expression which carries a special meaning, which is different from the meanings of the individual words **2** *The characters in this film speak in the idiom of Mumbai.* = the way in which a language is used by the people belonging to a particular group or area

I

idiomatic /ɪdiə'mætɪk/ adj. *'To cry wolf' is an idiomatic expression which means 'to give a false alarm'.* = containing an idiom or having the form of an idiom

id•i•ot /'ɪdiət/ noun, c. *What an idiot I've been!* = a foolish person (derogatory)

i•dle[1] /'aɪdl/ adj. **1** *Get up and start working. I don't like idle people.* = not doing any work **2** *The machines are idle because there is no electricity.* = not producing anything

idle[2] verb, i. **1** *Why are you idling away your time?* = to waste time doing nothing **2** *The engine of my car is very quiet when it is idling.* = running very slowly and not being made to do useful work (used for an engine)

i•dol /'aɪdl/ noun, c. **1** = a statue or picture which is worshipped as a god **2** *Sachin Tendulkar is the idol of many young people who love cricket.* = someone who is loved and respected by many people **idolize (idolise)** verb, t. = to show someone very great respect in the belief that she/he is perfect

if /ɪf/ conj. **1** *I will come to your party if you invite me.* = only on condition that **2** *If she asks for payment, please give her this cheque.* = in case **3** *Do you know if he is coming to the meeting? // She asked if I had eaten.* = whether (used to ask a reported question, following the verbs 'know', 'remember' 'wonder' or 'ask') **4** *He's an interesting person, if a little strange.* = even though **5** *If I've said anything wrong, please forgive me.* = used to talk about a possibility **6** *If you don't mind, I'll leave now.* = used to express a hope that someone will not respond negatively to something **ifs and buts** noun (always plural) *I want this work to be completed by this evening. No ifs and buts!* = excuses for not doing something (informal) **if only** *If only I had taken the train, I would have been in Lucknow by now.* = an expression used to express sadness that something was not done, or that something didn't happen

> **Usage** The phrase **if suppose** in *If suppose I take up the job* is incorrect. Use either **if** or **suppose**, depending on what you want to say.

-ify suffix meaning **1** = to become or do something e.g. **qualify, beautify, modify** **2** = to cause a particular emotion e.g. **terrify**

ig•loo /'ɪgluː/ noun, c. = a house made of blocks of ice

ig•ne•ous /'ɪgnɪəs/ adj. *Volcanic regions abound in igneous rocks.* = a type of rock formed when volcanic lava solidifies

ig•nite /ɪg'naɪt/ verb, t. or i. *The engine of the car starts when a mixture of petrol and air is ignited.*(t.) = to burn or cause something to burn **ignition** /ɪg'nɪʃən/ noun, u. = the action or process of making something burn

ig•no•rant /'ɪgnərənt/ adj. *Don't you know what the capital of France is? How can you be so ignorant!* = not knowing something that one is supposed to know **ignorance** noun, u. = the state of being ignorant

ig•nore /ɪg'nɔːʳ/ verb, t. *When I ask you to do something, please listen. Don't ignore me.* = to pay no attention to someone or something

i•gua•na /ɪ'gwɑːnə/ noun, c. = a very large lizard found in parts of South America

il- /ɪl/ prefix meaning 'not' e.g. **il•lit•e•rate** /ɪ'lɪtərət/ adj. *an illiterate person* = not able to read or write (opposite **literate**) **illiteracy** noun, u. = the state of being illiterate

ill[1] /ɪl/ adj. **1** *He cannot come because he is ill.* = in poor health **2** *I don't have any ill feelings towards you.* = unpleasant, usually because of something bad done to one **3** *Ill health has kept him from coming to work.* = bad or poor (health)

ill[2] adv. **1** *an ill-fitting dress // an ill-fed cat // The animal was ill treated.* = badly; not properly or in a cruel way (generally with **treat**) **2** *It was sad that they spoke ill of a friend who had done so much for them.* = unfavourably (formal)

ill[3] noun, c. **1** *Many great people have worked to remove the social ills of their time.* = (often plural) a custom which causes misery and difficulty to some **2** *Is education the cure for all ills?* = problems and difficulties

ill at ease *He is shy and quite ill at ease among strangers.* = not comfortable

> **Usage** One can *fall ill* (become ill) or be *seriously* (= very) *ill*. One is *taken ill* when an illness strikes suddenly. A person is *terminally ill* when she/he has an illness which is certain to lead to death. Note that *'She is serious.'* cannot be used to mean *'She is seriously ill.'*

il•le•gal /ɪ'liːgəl/ adj. *It is illegal to drive a car without a licence.* = not legal, against the law (opposite **legal**)

il•le•gi•ble /ɪ'ledʒəbəl/ adj. *Your handwriting is so bad, it is almost illegible.* = impossible or difficult to read (opposite **legible**)

il•le•git•i•mate /ɪlɪ'dʒɪtɪmət/ adj. **1** *an illegitimate child* = born to parents who are not married to each other **2** *an illegitimate procedure* = not allowed by the law or the rules (opposite **legitimate**)

il•li•cit /ɪ'lɪsɪt/ adj. *There is an illicit trade in tiger skins.* = against the law and done secretly

ill•ness /'ɪlnɪs/ noun u. or c. (**illnesses**) *My cousin* could not come on holiday because of his illness.(u.) = state of being unhealthy, either physically or mentally

il•lo•gi•cal /ɪ'lɒdʒɪkəl/ adj. = not supported by logic or reason (opposite **logical**)

il•lu•mi•nate /ɪ'lu:mɪneɪt/ verb, t. **1** *Government buildings are illuminated on the occasion of Republic Day.* = to decorate with lights for a special occasion **2** *There are no electric lights inside the temple. The place is illuminated by oil lamps.* = to provide or give light to **3** *This book will illuminate you on the benefits of yoga.* = to give knowledge or understanding (formal) **illumination** /ɪlu:mɪn'eɪʃən/ noun, u. **1** *There will be no illumination of buildings on Republic Day this year because of the earthquake and floods in the country.* = the act of decorating with lights **2** *You cannot read the writing on the walls because of the poor illumination.* = the amount of light that is available **illuminating** /ɪ'lu:mɪneɪtɪŋ/ adj. *a highly illuminating talk* = something that brings better knowledge and understanding

il•lu•sion /ɪ'lu:ʒən/ noun, u. *This town seems to be peaceful, but that is only an illusion. As a matter of fact, there are many problems here.* = something that is different in reality from what it appears to be on the surface

il•lus•trate /'ɪləstreɪt/ verb, t. or i. **1** *I have asked a famous artist to illustrate my book.*(t.) = to create pictures for a book which are connected with its contents **2** *We listened to many stories that illustrate the courage of our soldiers.* = to give an example of something **illustration** /ɪləs'treɪʃən/ noun, u. or c. **1** = a picture that is part of a book **2** = an example

im- /ɪmɪ/ prefix meaning 'not' e.g. **impossible** /ɪm'pɒsɪbəl/ adj. *It is difficult but not impossible for you to become a dancer.* = something that cannot be done (opposite **possible**)

im•age /'ɪmɪdʒ/ noun, c. **1** = a statue or picture which is worshipped (see **icon**) **2** *a clean image* = the picture or idea that people have in their minds of someone or something **3** *You can see your own image in a mirror.* = the picture or reflection of some object as seen in a mirror or through the lens of a camera **4** *The poet uses an image of the sun when talking about the hero.* = a picture in words created by the special use of language in poetry **imagery** noun, u. = the special use of language in poetry to create pictures in words

i•ma•gine /ɪ'mædʒɪn/ verb, t. **1** *Imagine that you are a person living in the eighth century and describe a typical day in your life.* = to think of something that is not real as if it was real **2** *You cannot imagine my surprise at meeting you in this strange place.* = to form an idea or a picture in the mind **3** *You are the leader of this group, I imagine.* = to suppose or think (sometimes disapproving) **4** *Is this lovely garden real or am I imagining it?* = having an unreal idea in one's mind **imagination** /ɪmægɪn'eɪʃən/ noun, u. **1** *The artist who painted this picture must have had a wonderful imagination.* = the ability to think of something which is not real and to use this ability to create art or literature **2** *These problems that you complain about are nothing but your imagination.* = something that is not real (often derogatory) **imaginary** /ɪ'mægɪnəri/ adj. *The places and characters in this novel are all imaginary.* = not real or actual **imaginative** adj. = having the ability to use the imagination to create something

im•bal•ance /ɪm'bæləns/ noun, u. *There is an imbalance in the student population. We have many more boys than girls.* = more of one than of the other (opposite **balance**)

im•i•tate /'ɪmɪteɪt/ verb, t. *Sawan can imitate Amitabh Bachchan's voice.* = to copy **imitation** /ɪmɪ'teɪʃən/ noun, c. or u. or adj. **1** *Alfred did a wonderful imitation of Amitabh Bachchan.*(noun) = the act of imitating someone **2** *This sofa has a covering of imitation leather.*(adj.) = something that is a copy of something else

im•mac•u•late /ɪ'mækjʊlɪt/ adj. **1** *His clothes always look immaculate.* = neat, bright and clean **2** *Her manners are immaculate.* = without a fault; perfect

im•ma•ture /ɪmə'tʃʊə^r/ adj. *Although he is sixty years old, his behaviour is often immature.* = not wise, as may be expected of a grown-up person (opposite **mature**)

im•me•di•ate /ɪ'mi:diət/ adj. **1** *The man is bleeding and needs immediate medical attention.* = without any delay **2** *I have a lot of relatives, but my immediate family consists of my wife, her mother, my two children and myself.* = nearest, closest

im•mense /ɪ'mens/ adj. **1** *The lake covers an immense area, we can hardly see the other side.* = (of space or size of objects) very large **2** *The holiday did me an immense amount of good.* = a great deal

im•merse /ɪ'mɜ:s/ verb, t. **1** *The wood has to be immersed in a solution of water and chemicals.* = to make something sink into a body of water or other liquid, so that it is fully covered **2** *He was so immersed in reading the book that he didn't notice when we left.* = to be deeply involved in some activity (figurative)

im•mi•grate /'ɪmɪgreɪt/ verb, i. = to come to live in a different country (opposite **emigrate**) **immigrant** noun, c. *Thousands of immigrants enter America each year from different parts of the world.* = someone who enters a country from abroad with the intention of settling there (opposite **emigrant**) **immigration** /ɪmɪ'greɪʃən/ noun, u. = the act of entering another country in order to settle there (opposite **emigration**)

im•mi•nent /'ɪmɪnənt/ adj. *There are dark clouds gathering in the sky. A storm is imminent.* = likely to take place soon

im•mo•bile /ɪ'məʊbaɪl/ adj. *He is unhappy because he has broken a leg and cannot get out of bed. He hates to be immobile.* = not able to move (opposite **mobile**) **immobilize (immobilise)** verb, t. *When he broke his leg the doctor put it in a plaster so as to immobilize it, so that the bones would heal quickly.* = to prevent someone or something from moving

im•mor•al /ɪ'mɒrəl/ adj. *You must not steal, even if you are desperate. Stealing is immoral.* = not in keeping with the principles of morality (right conduct or behaviour) (opposite **moral**)

im•mor•tal /ɪ'mɔ:təl/ adj. *He did not want his dog to die. He wanted it to be immortal. // immortal works of art* = someone or something that will never die or lose value and importance (opposite **mortal**)

im•mune /ɪ'mju:n/ adj. *A child who has had small pox once will never get it again. Her body becomes immune to small pox.* = protected against something and not harmed by it **immunity** noun, u. *A person who has had chicken pox once develops immunity to the disease.* = the quality of being protected against something

imp /ɪmp/ noun, c. **1** = a supernatural being in stories that causes trouble to others **2** = a very naughty child (informal)

im•pact /'ɪmpækt/ noun, u. **1** *When the two trains hit each other, the impact was so great that one of the trains was badly damaged.* = the force with which one object hits another object **2** *If the price of diesel goes up, it will have an impact on the price of food.* = effect or influence (usually bad)

im•pair /ɪm'peə^r/ verb, t. *The earthquake has impaired industry in these parts, as many factories have been destroyed.* = to harm; to hinder (formal)

im•par•tial /ɪm'pɑ:ʃəl/ adj. *Judges cannot favour either of the two sides in a dispute. They must be impartial.* = fair; not giving help or support to either side (opposite **partial**)

im•passe /'ɪmpæs/ noun, u. *Our efforts to solve the problem reached an impasse and we could not go further.* = a point at which no progress is possible; a dead end

im•pa•tient /ɪm'peɪʃənt/ adj. *His father has promised to send him to America next year but he wants to go at once. He is getting impatient.* = restless from a sense of being eager to do something, and therefore unwilling to accept delay (opposite **patient**) **impatience** noun, u.

im•pede /ɪm'pi:d/ verb, t. *Our journey by car was impeded by the poor condition of the roads.* = to hinder or to prevent someone from doing something smoothly or easily **impediment** noun, c. = something that impedes or hinders

im•pend•ing /ɪm'pendɪŋ/ adj. *The students are preparing seriously for the impending examination.* = about to take place (formal)

im•pen•e•tra•ble /ɪm'penɪtrəbəl/ adj. *The forests are so thick in the Sunderban area that they are almost impenetrable.* = something which cannot be penetrated or entered into

im•per•a•tive /ɪm'perətɪv/ adj. **1** *There is a serious shortage of water and it is imperative that we organise supplies immediately.* = absolutely necessary; something that must be done at once (formal) **2** *'Stop!' is an example of an imperative sentence.* = a sentence that has the form of a command [GRAMMAR]

im•per•fect /ɪm'pɜ:fɪkt/ adj. *Please don't be angry if I make a mistake. Remember, we are all imperfect.* = having a fault or something which prevents someone/something from being completely perfect (opposite **perfect**)

im•pe•ri•al /ɪm'pɪəriəl/ adj. *an imperial power* = having to do with an emperor or an empire

im•per•son•al /ɪm'pɜ:sənəl/ adj. *Hundreds of people work in this office but no one ever talks to you or even smiles at you. The atmosphere is quite impersonal.* = not having or showing personal feelings or connection (disapproving) (opposite **personal**)

im•per•ti•nent /ɪm'pɜ:tɪnənt/ adj. *Don't be impertinent when you talk to your teacher. Show her respect.* = talking or answering in a disrespectful way

im•per•vi•ous /ɪm'pɜ:vɪəs/ adj. *This piece of leather will not allow water to pass through it. It is impervious to moisture.* = (of material) not allowing liquid etc. to pass through

im•pe•tus /'ɪmpɪtəs/ noun, u. *The government is giving loans to farmers in this area in order to provide an impetus to agriculture.* = a push forward; something that helps or encourages people to do something

im•plant /'ɪmplɑ:nt/ noun, c. *a heart implant* = something that has been put in place artificially inside the body

im•ple•ment[1] /'ɪmplɪmənt/ noun, c. *We need better farming implements in order to grow more rice on this land.* = a tool or instrument

implement[2] verb, t. *The new government policy on education will not be easy to implement.* = to carry out or put into action

im•plore /ɪm'plɔːʳ/ verb, t. *I implore you to help me as I am in great difficulty.* = to beg someone strongly to do something

im•ply /ɪm'plaɪ/ verb, t. (**implied**) *He said he didn't enjoy his visit to our city. Was he implying that we did not look after him well?* = to not say something directly but to say something with a hidden meaning

im•po•lite /ɪmpə'laɪt/ adj. *It was impolite of you not to reply to my letter.* = not showing good manners

im•port[1] /ɪm'pɔːt/ verb, t. **1** *India imports petroleum from West Asia.* = to receive or bring something into a country from another country **2** = to transfer or move a document, information etc from one computer to another, or one program to another [COMPUTERS]

import[2] noun, u. or c. **1** *India's imports, including petroleum and textiles, have increased this year.*(c.) = things that are imported (opposite **export**) **2** *The import of our leader's speech was that most of us will have to give some time to cleaning up the neighbourhood.*(u.) = a meaning which is not expressed directly (formal)

im•por•tant /ɪm'pɔːtənt/ adj. **1** *Rice is the most important foodgrain for the people of this state.* = having special value **2** *a very important person (VIP)* = having great influence or power **importance** noun, u. *You will be paid well but you will have to work hard. The company attaches great importance to work.* = special attention given to something

im•pose /ɪm'pəʊz/ verb, t. or i. **1** *The government is going to impose a new tax on all professional people.*(t.) = to pass an order to make someone do something (formal) **2** *impose strict discipline*(t.) = to make someone accept something which is not liked **3** *It is kind of you to invite me to stay in your house, but I don't want to impose on you.*(i.)= to give unnecessary trouble to someone **imposition** /ɪmpə'zɪʃən/ noun, u. *the imposition of a new tax* = the act of imposing something **imposing** /ɪm'pəʊzɪŋ/ adj. *The government buildings in New Delhi are very imposing.* = large in size and grand in appearance

im•pos•tor /ɪm'pɒstəʳ/ noun, c. = someone who makes people believe he/she is someone or something that he/she is not, usually for dishonest purposes (derogatory)

im•pov•e•rish /ɪm'pɒvərɪʃ/ verb, t. **1** *The earthquake has impoverished many people in this area and they have lost everything they had.* = to make someone poor **2** *The soil will be impoverished by the use of chemicals.* = to reduce in quality or strength

im•press /ɪm'pres/ verb, t. **1** *The new batsman impressed everyone with his fine batting.* = to cause someone to have a good opinion about you **2** *Please impress upon her that this task has to be completed by tomorrow.* = to make someone understand the importance of something **impression** noun, u. or c. **1** *Your speech created a good impression.* = an effect on the mind created by someone or something **2** *You can see the impression of his shoes clearly in the mud.* = a pattern or mark made by putting pressure on a surface **impressive** adj. *Younis played an impressive innings in this match.* = something that makes a good and strong impression (see meaning **1** for **impress**)

im•pris•on /ɪm'prɪzən/ verb, t. *You can be imprisoned for careless driving.* = to put someone in prison or jail **life imprisonment** noun = punishment given to a criminal by putting him/her in prison for the whole of his/her life

im•prop•er /ɪm'prɒpəʳ/ adj. **1** *Many people think it is improper if you do not take off your footwear when entering someone's house.* = behaviour which is not morally or socially accepted **2** *improper activities* = criminal or unlawful (opposite **proper**) **3** *an improper suggestion* = connected with sex

im•prove /ɪm'pruːv/ verb, t. or i. **1** *Your handwriting is very bad. You must improve it.*(t.) = to make something better **2** *Is the patient's condition improving?*(i.) = to become better **improvement** noun, u. *The patient's condition is showing some improvement.* = the state of becoming better

im•pro•vise /'ɪmprəvaɪz/ verb, i. or t. *The actor forgot the words she was supposed to speak on the stage and had to improvise.*(i.) = to be forced to do something that one had not prepared for, sometimes because of something unexpected happening

im•pu•dent /'ɪmpjʊdənt/ adj. *You were very impudent when you asked your teacher why he had not given you better marks.* = rude and disrespectful

im•pulse /'ɪmpʌls/ noun, c. or u. *We went shopping and bought a lot of clothes on an impulse.*(c.) = a sudden decision to do something, often considered unnecessary and unwise **impulsive** /ɪm'pʌlsɪv/ adj. *He is such an impulsive person that you can never know what he will do next.* = likely to decide or do something suddenly without thinking about it carefully

in- /ɪn/ prefix meaning not e.g. **inaccurate** /ɪn'æekjʊrɪt/ adj. *Your report was inaccurate. There were only a hundred people at the meeting but you said there were more than a thousand.* = not exact (opposite **accurate**)

in[1] /ɪn/ prep. **1** *The book is in my bag.* = inside or within **2** *There are 45 students in this class.* = as a part of **3** *She passed the B.A. examination in 1986.* = during **4** *The girl in blue is my daughter.* = wearing a certain kind of dress **5** *She spoke in French.* = by means of or through (used of a language)

in[2] adv. **1** *Come in!* = into a space, from the outside **2** *The doctor is in.* = present in a place

in[3] adj. *The new restaurant is the in-place now.* = popular and fashionable (informal)

in•a•bil•i•ty /ɪnə'bɪlɪti/ noun, u. *My inability to attend the meeting was because of my illness.* = lack of power or ability to do something

in•ac•ces•si•ble /ɪnək'sesɪbəl/ adj. *It is not possible to get to the top of the hill. As there are no roads, it is inaccessible.* = difficult or impossible to reach (opposite **accessible**)

in•ad•e•quate /ɪn'ædɪkwɪt/ adj. *We had cooked five kilograms of rice but this proved to be inadequate as there were more than 50 guests.* = not enough (opposite **adequate**)

i•nane /ɪ'neɪn/ adj. *an inane speech* = foolish and meaningless

in•au•di•ble /ɪn'ɔːdɪbəl/ adj. *His voice was almost inaudible.* = something that cannot be heard (opposite **audible**)

in•au•gu•rate /ɪ'nɔːgjʊreɪt/ verb, t. *We have invited a film actor to inaugurate the new building.* = to open a new building or to start a public event

in•born /ɪn'bɔːn/ adj. *Human beings have an inborn ability to use language.* = present from birth

in•cal•cu•la•ble /ɪn'kælkjʊləbəl/ adj. *Rabindranath Tagore was one of our greatest writers. The value of his contribution to Indian literature is incalculable.* = something that cannot be measured or calculated because it is too great

in•ca•pa•ble /ɪn'keɪpəbəl/ adj. *He is so honest that he is incapable of telling a lie.* = not able to do something (opposite **capable**)

in•car•na•tion /ɪnkɑː'neɪʃən/ noun, u. or c. = the coming of a divine being to earth in the form of a human being **reincarnation** noun, u. = the act of being born again

in•cense[1] /'ɪnsens/ noun *You can get the sweet smell of incense burning in the temple.* = a substance used in religious ceremonies which has a fragrant smell when burnt

in•cense[2] /ɪn'sens/ verb, t. *I was so incensed by their bad behaviour that I had to ask them to leave.*(t.) = to be made very angry by something (formal)

in•cen•tive /ɪn'sentɪv/ noun, u. or c. *We had to work over two weekends, but as an incentive, we had a week's holiday.* = something that encourages a person to do more work or to do something with more interest

in•ces•sant /ɪn'sesənt/ adj. *We were unable to leave the house because of incessant rain.* = something that does not (or does not seem to) stop

in•cest /'ɪnsest/ noun, u. = sexual relations between near relatives in a family e.g. between a man and his sister, considered unnatural and forbidden [LAW]

inch[1] /ɪntʃ/ noun, c. = a unit of measuring length, equal to 2.54 centimetres

inch[2] verb, i. *The cars inched their way along the crowded street.* = to move slowly in small stretches with difficulty

in•ci•dent /'ɪnsɪdənt/ noun, c. = an event or happening

in•ci•den•tal /ɪnsɪ'dəntəl/ adj. *Let us first plan the main events in the programme. We can fill in the incidental details later.* = something that is not very important and happens together with something else that is more important **incidentally** adv. *She is a wonderful singer. Incidentally, her mother was a famous violinist.* = 'By the way'

in•cin•e•rate /ɪn'sɪnəreɪt/ verb, t. *The garbage removed from these houses is incinerated every day.* = to destroy waste or unwanted material by burning **incinerator** noun, c. = a large electric oven that is used to destroy unwanted things by burning them

in•ci•sion /ɪn'sɪʒən/ noun, c. or u. *The surgeon started the operation by making an incision in the patient's abdomen.* = a cut; the act of making a cut **incisive** adj. *A member of the audience asked the speaker a very incisive question which he was unable to answer.* = sharp and cutting **incisor** noun, c. = one of the broad, flat teeth in the front part of the mouth, which are used for cutting food into small pieces

in•cite /ɪn'saɪt/ verb, t. *incite a revolt* = to cause or encourage someone to do something wrong

in•cli•na•tion /ɪnklɪ'neɪʃən/ noun, u. or c. **1** *Whenever he feels the inclination to travel, he goes to the Himalayas.*(u.) = desire **2** *He has an inclination to avoid people of his own age.*(c.) = a natural tendency or feeling which makes one behave in a certain way **3** *There is a slight inclination in the road here as we are going up the hill.*(u.) = slope

in•cline /ɪn'klaɪn/ verb, i. **1** *She thinks our plan is bad, and I am inclined to agree.* = to feel a desire to do something **2** *He inclined his head to show that he was thinking.* = to make something move downwards or sideways

in•clude /ɪn'kluːd/ verb, t. **1** *The dictionary includes a number of illustrations.* = to contain as a part **2** *Please include my name in the list of people who will be invited.* = to put in or to consider as part of a group etc. **inclusion** noun, u. = the act of including something or someone in a list etc.

in•co•her•ent /ɪnkəʊ'hɪərənt/ adj. *She was crying and I could not understand what she was trying to* say. *She was quite incoherent.* = unable to express oneself clearly or to express ideas in a logical way (opposite **coherent**)

in•come /ˈɪŋkʌm/ noun, u. or c. = the money that is earned or received on a regular basis, for work done

in•com•pa•ra•ble /ɪnˈkɒmpərəbəl/ adj. *The beauty of the Himalayas is incomparable.* = so good that it cannot be compared to anything else (opposite **comparable**)

in•com•pe•tent /ɪnˈkɒmpɪtənt/ adj. *I knew she was lazy, but I didn't know she was incompetent as well. How can she help us then?* = not having the ability to do something (opposite **competent**)

in•com•pre•hen•si•ble /ɪnkɒmprɪˈhensɪbəl/ adj. *an incomprehensible book* = something that one cannot understand (opposite **comprehensible**)

in•con•clu•sive /ɪnkənˈkluːsɪv/ adj. *The match between the two teams was inconclusive. Neither team won.* = not leading to a clear result (opposite **conclusive**)

in•con•se•quen•tial /ɪnkɒnsɪˈkwenʃəl/ adj. *Nothing depends on the result of this test. It is quite inconsequential.* = of no or very little importance for the future

in•con•sid•er•ate /ɪnkənˈsɪdərɪt/ adj. *She came all the way to see you, and you didn't even look at her. How could you be so inconsiderate?* = uncaring about the feelings of others (opposite **considerate**)

in•con•sis•tent /ɪnkənˈsɪstənt/ adj. **1** *What you do is quite inconsistent with what you think.* = not in agreement with (formal, disapproving) **2** *He is very inconsistent as a batsman. He may score a century in one match and make a low score in the next three matches.* = changing all the time; not steady (opposite **consistent**)

in•con•spic•u•ous /ɪnkənˈspɪkjʊəs/ adj. *He always sits in an inconspicuous place in the last row because he does not want to be noticed.* = not attracting attention (opposite **conspicuous**)

in•con•ve•ni•ent /ɪnkənˈviːnɪənt/ adj. *Why do you want to have the meeting on a Sunday? It is very inconvenient for me.* = causing trouble or discomfort (opposite **convenient**)

in•cor•po•rate /ɪnˈkɔːpəreɪt/ verb, t. *You should incorporate the ideas I am suggesting into your speech.* = to include as a part of something larger

in•cor•rup•ti•ble /ɪnkəˈrʌptɪbəl/ adj. *an incorruptible officer* = a person who can never be made to do something dishonest (opposite **corruptible**) (approving)

in•crease[1] /ɪnˈkriːs/ verb, i. or t. **1** *The number of people who own computers is increasing.*(i.) **2** *They will soon increase the price of petrol.*(t.) = to make or become greater

increase[2] /ˈɪŋkriːs/ noun, u. *There is a slight increase in the price of sugar.* = rise (opposite **decrease**)

in•cred•i•ble /ɪnˈkredɪbəl/ adj. **1** *I am sure you are lying. Your story is incredible!* = hard to believe (opposite **credible**) **2** *What an incredible collection of paintings you have!* = unbelievably wonderful (informal) **incredulous** /ɪnˈkredjʊləs/ adj. *As the policeman listened to my story, he looked quite incredulous.* = not willing to believe something (opposite **credulous**)

in•cu•bate /ˈɪŋkjʊbeɪt/ verb, t. **1** = to keep an egg at a certain temperature until the young one comes out of it **2** *The chicken pox virus takes at least two weeks to incubate.* = to lie hidden inside the body while growing, before appearing as a disease [MEDICINE] **incubator** noun, c. = a machine which keeps eggs warm and helps the young ones to grow in them or a machine which keeps babies born before time in a safe and warm environment

in•cur•a•ble /ɪnˈkjʊərəbəl/ adj. *an incurable disease* = something that cannot be cured or set right (opposite **curable**)

in•debt•ed /ɪnˈdetɪd/ adj. *I am indebted to my parents who worked hard so that I could get a good education.* = in someone's debt; grateful to someone for something

in•de•cent /ɪnˈdiːsənt/ adj. *This film should be banned as it contains some indecent songs and dances.* = vulgar and in bad taste (opposite **decent**)

in•de•ci•sion /ɪndɪˈsɪʒən/ noun, u. *Do you want to go by bus or by train? Your indecision is making us nervous.* = the state of not being able to decide something

in•deed /ɪnˈdiːd/ adv. **1** *That was an exciting match indeed!* = in fact; really (an expression used to make a statement more forceful) **2** *'They are the most powerful people in the country.' 'Indeed!'* = an expression showing that one is surprised, or that one does not believe what is said

in•de•pen•dent /ɪndɪˈpendənt/ adj. **1** *an independent country* = not ruled or controlled by someone else **2** *She has a very independent nature and she accepts no help from her parents.* = not taking help or advice from anyone (opposite **dependent**) **independence** noun, u. *India gained independence in 1947.* = the quality or state of being independent

in•dex /ˈɪndeks/ noun, c. **1** = an alphabetical list at the end of a book showing the pages on which particular words, names etc. can be found (plural **indexes**) **2** *The cost of living index has gone up by 200 per cent in the last six months.* = a number used

I

to measure the cost of something by comparing it to the cost at some other time (plural **indices** or **indexes**) **3** *It is said that the face is the index of the mind.* = something by which something else can be judged or measured (plural **indices** or **indexes**) **index finger** noun = the finger next to the thumb, which is generally used to point at something

in•di•cate /ˈɪndɪkeɪt/ verb, t. *Your silence indicates that you agree with me.* = to show **indication** /ɪndɪˈkeɪʃən/ noun, u. or c. *The presence of dark clouds in the sky is an indication of rain.*(u.) = a sign which informs us of something that is going to happen **indicator** noun, c. = a light on the front and rear of a car, bus etc. which shows the direction in which the car is going to turn

in•dif•fer•ent /ɪnˈdɪfərənt/ adj. **1** *In the past they were always happy when I visited them but now they seem quite indifferent.* = having no feelings about something or someone **2** *We were hoping that Tendulkar would bat well as usual, but he gave an indifferent performance.* = not very good; mediocre (ordinary)

in•di•ge•nous /ɪnˈdɪdʒənəs/ adj. *Tea is not indigenous to India. It was brought into this country from China 300 years ago.* = something that belongs naturally to a place and has not been brought in from outside

in•di•ges•tion /ɪndɪˈdʒestʃən/ noun, u. *If you eat a lot of spicy food, you will get indigestion.* = illness or pain caused when the stomach is not able to deal with food that has been eaten

in•dig•nant /ɪnˈdɪgnənt/ adj. *She was indignant when she was told we hadn't bought her a ticket for the film we were all going to.* = to be angry or unhappy because of something wrong or unjust

in•di•go /ˈɪndɪgəʊ/ noun **1** = a plant from which a purple dye or colour was produced and used (in former days) for dyeing (colouring) cloth **2** = a dark purple colour

in•di•rect /ɪndɪˈrekt/ adj. **1** *You are planning to go from Kolkata to Delhi via Bhopal. Why are you taking such an indirect route?* = not straight but round about **2** *My senior asked me if I was feeling bored in the office. This was an indirect way of telling me that he was not happy with my work.* = something that carries a meaning which can be understood but which is not expressed openly and in a straightforward manner **indirect object** noun *In the sentence 'Mohan asked his teacher a question', the phrase 'a question' is the direct object while 'his teacher' is the indirect object.* = the person or the thing to whom (or to which) something is done [GRAMMAR] **indirect speech** noun *The sentence 'Navin said, "Salma, I want a piece of bread"' is in direct speech, while the sentence 'Navin told Salma that he wanted a piece of bread' is in indirect speech.* = the words of a speaker as reported by someone else and not presented exactly as used by the speaker (also **reported speech**) [GRAMMAR]

in•dis•creet /ɪndɪˈskriːt/ adj. *I was somewhat indiscreet when I told my aunt that she looked very old.* = not very careful about the things one says (opposite **discreet**)

in•di•spen•sa•ble /ɪndɪˈspensəbəl/ adj. *Mr Mishra is our best teacher. In fact, he is absolutely indispensable. If he leaves the school, all our students will go away.* = someone or something that one cannot do without (opposite **dispensable**)

in•dis•posed /ɪndɪˈspəʊzd/ adj. *The minister cannot come to the meeting as he is indisposed.* = not well (formal)

in•dis•pu•ta•ble /ɪndɪˈspjuːtəbəl/ adj. *The fact that India and Sri Lanka have some of the greatest batsmen in the world today is indisputable.* = something that one cannot doubt but has to agree with (opposite **disputable**)

in•dis•tinct /ɪndɪˈstɪŋkt/ adj. *Your face looks indistinct in this photograph.* = not clearly seen or heard (opposite **distinct**)

in•di•vid•u•al[1] /ɪndɪˈvɪdʒʊəl/ noun, c. *Each individual in a group is a little different from the others.* = a single person or thing, taken separately and not as part of a group

individual[2] adj. *Each student in the class gets individual attention from the teachers.* = something which is meant for or given to one member of a group but may not be suitable for others

in•di•vis•i•ble /ɪndɪˈvɪzəbəl/ adj. = something that cannot be split up or divided into parts (opposite **divisible**)

In•do- /ɪndəʊ/ prefix meaning having to do with India e.g. **Indo-Anglian** adj. *an Indo-Anglian writer* = a person who is an Indian but writes in English **Indo-European** adj. *an Indo-European language* = one of a family of languages that includes many of the languages of Europe as well as the languages of India (e.g. Sanskrit and German)

in•door /ˈɪndɔːʳ/ adj. *Table tennis is an indoor game.* = happening inside a building (opposite **outdoor**) **indoors** adv. *It is very hot outside. We will have to remain indoors.* = inside a house or other building (opposite **outdoors**)

in•duce /ɪnˈdjuːs/ verb, t. **1** *I wanted to keep the matter secret but my friends induced me to reveal it to them.* = to persuade someone to do something against her/his will **2** *This medicine may induce sleep.* = to cause or bring about

in•dulge /ɪn'dʌldʒ/ verb, t. or i. **1** *Don't indulge your children too much or they will get spoilt.*(t.) = to give too much love to someone and allow him/her to do whatever he/she wants **2** *He sometimes indulges in gambling.*(i.) = to allow oneself to do something for enjoyment, specially something that is considered bad or harmful (formal) **indulgence** noun, u. **1** *The children are getting spoilt through your indulgence.*= the habit of allowing someone to do what he/she wants (disapproving) **2** *Indulgence in drinking is bad for one's health.* = the habit of doing something harmful for enjoyment (formal)

in•dus•try /'ɪndəstri/ noun, u. or c. (**industries**) **1** *the textile industry in Gujarat*(c.) = the production of goods by factories **2** *The people of this region are known for their industry.*(u.) = habit of working hard (also **industriousness**) **industrial** /ɪn'dʌstrɪəl/ adj. *industrial development* = connected with industry **industrialist** noun, c. = a person who sets up a factory to produce something **industrious** adj. *a very industrious person* = hard working

in•ed•i•ble /ɪn'edəbəl/ adj. *inedible food* = something which cannot be eaten because it is spoilt, too spicy etc. or because it is not suitable for eating

in•ef•fec•tu•al /ɪnɪ'fektʃuəl/ adj. *He wanted to bring about some improvement in the school but his efforts proved to be ineffectual.* = not achieving the desired result (also **ineffective**)

in•ef•fi•cient /ɪnɪ'fɪʃənt/ adj. *She tries her best but she is very inefficient at work.* = not able to work in a satisfactory way or not able to produce good results (referring to a person or a machine) (opposite **efficient**)

inert /ɪ'nɜːrt/ adj. **1** *The government has become inert. Nothing is getting done.* = unable to act **2** *Nitrogen is an inert gas.* = a chemical on which other chemicals produce no reaction or effect [CHEMISTRY]

in•er•tia /ɪ'nɜːʃə/ noun, u. **1** *The car kept moving due to its own inertia even when the engine was switched off.* = the natural force which keeps an object moving or at rest unless some other force acts on it [PHYSICS] **2** *No work is being done in this office. There is complete inertia.* = absence of movement or activity (derogatory)

in•es•sen•tial /ɪnɪ'senʃəl/ adj. *Please remove all inessential furniture from the room.* = not needed or necessary (opposite **essential**)

in•ev•i•ta•ble /ɪ'nevɪtəbəl/ adj. *The weather office thinks a storm is inevitable but we hope they are wrong.* = (something that is) bound to happen and cannot be avoided

in•ex•cu•sa•ble /ɪnɪk'skjuːzəbəl/ adj. *Your rude behaviour at the meeting was inexcusable.* = something that cannot be excused

in•ex•pe•ri•enced /ɪnɪk'spɪəriənst/ adj. *The new teacher is not able to control her class as she is inexperienced.* = lacking experience (the ability to do something well that comes through long practice) (opposite **experienced**)

in•fant[1] /'ɪnfənt/ noun, c. = a very small child that has not learnt to talk or walk

infant[2] adj. *infant food* = something meant for or connected with an infant

in•fan•try /'ɪnfəntri/ noun, u. or c. (**infantries**) = soldiers who fight on foot

in•fat•u•a•tion /ɪnfætʃu'eɪʃən/ noun, u. *This is not a case of true love; it is only infatuation.* = a state of being foolishly in love with someone which usually does not last very long (derogatory) **infatuated** adj.

in•fect /ɪn'fekt/ verb, t. *We can't drink water from this river. It has become infected as there are insects floating in it.* = to make food or water unsafe because of the presence of germs which can cause disease **infection** noun, u. = a disease caused by germs which can be carried from one person to another through the air or through water **infectious** adj. **1** *an infectious disease* = a disease that can be passed through the air or water from one person to another **2** *Her laughter is infectious.* = something that can carry a feeling (usually of happiness) to other people (figurative)

in•fer /ɪn'fɜːr/ verb, t. (**inferred**) *I infer from your letter that you are not happy in this city as you have asked for a transfer.* = to make a judgement or to form an opinion based on something that one has come to know (formal) **inference** /'ɪnfərəns/ noun, u. *No one except you entered this room last night. So I can say by inference that you must have been the one who switched on the television.* = the act of inferring something (making a judgement or forming an opinion based on some evidence)

in•fe•ri•or /ɪn'fɪəriər/ adj. *I think this pen is cheap becuase it is inferior to the other one.* = less good than something else; of a lower quality **inferiority** /ɪnfɪəri'ɒrɪti/ noun, u. = the fact of being inferior or having a feeling of being inferior **inferiority complex** noun = a feeling, which is often not correct, that makes a person believe that he/she is not as good as others [TECHNICAL]

in•fer•no /ɪn'fɜːnəʊ/ noun, c. *a burning inferno* = a place where fires are burning, causing great heat

in•fer•tile /ɪn'fɜːtaɪl/ adj. **1** *infertile land* = unable to produce crops **2** *an infertile person* = unable to have children (opposite **fertile**)

in•fest /ɪn'fest/ verb, t. *This house is infested with rats.* = to be full of pests (e.g. rats, insects) that cause harm to human beings

in•fi•del /'ɪnfɪdl/ noun, c. = someone who follows a religion or has a set of religious beliefs different from one's own

in•fi•del•i•ty /ɪnfɪ'delɪti/ noun, u. = the act of not being faithful, specially to one's husband or wife (opposite **fidelity**) [LAW]

in•fil•trate /'ɪnfɪltreɪt/ verb, t. **1** *Our soldiers managed to infiltrate the enemy position.* = to get secretly into a place held by the enemy **2** *It is possible that foreign spies have managed to infiltrate the army.* = to enter secretly into an organisation belonging to an enemy, with the intention of doing some harm **infiltration** /ɪnfɪl'treɪʃən/ noun, u. = the act of infiltrating **infiltrator** noun, c. = a person who infiltrates into a place or an organisation

in•fi•nite /'ɪnfɪnɪt/ adj. **1** *The universe is infinite.* = something that has no end or limit (opposite **finite**) **2** *He took infinite trouble to look after us when we stayed with him.* = endless, with great attention to detail **infinity** /ɪn'fɪnɪti/ noun, u. **1** = an imaginary number which is too great to be calculated [MATHEMATICS] **2** = a distance too great to be calculated

in•fin•i•tive /ɪn'fɪnɪtɪv/ noun, c. *In the sentence 'I want to go', 'to go' is the infinitive form of the verb 'go'* = a form of a verb which is used after 'to' and can follow a noun or another verb [GRAMMAR]

in•flam•ma•ble /ɪn'flæməbəl/ adj. *The old building, which was made of wood and other inflammable materials, caught fire at once.* = something which can catch fire and burn easily **inflammatory** adj. *an inflammatory speech* = a message, spoken or written, that can create strong feelings of anger and violence in others

in•flam•ma•tion /ɪnflə'meɪʃən/ noun, u. = a painful swelling in the body, caused by some infection

in•flate /ɪn'fleɪt/ verb, t. *The balloons were inflated and hung from the ceiling.* = to fill up something with air and make it swell out **inflation** noun, u. = a rise in the prices of things, which brings down the value of money and makes people poorer

in•flect /ɪn'flekt/ verb, t. **1** *We can inflect the word 'boy', which is singular, to 'boys', which is plural.* = to change the form of a word in order to express a different meaning [GRAMMAR] **2** *You should inflect your voice carefully if you want to sound cheerful.* = to change the tone (sound) of one's voice in order to express a certain feeling

in•flex•i•ble /ɪn'fleksɪbəl/ adj. *You can never make him change his mind once he decides to do something. He is completely inflexible.* = not willing to bend or to change one's mind (opposite **flexible**)

in•flict /ɪn'flɪkt/ verb, t. *A heavy fine was inflicted on us when we took photographs by flash light in the ancient building.* = to force something unpleasant on someone (formal or legal)

in•flu•ence[1] /'ɪnflʊəns/ verb, t. *If your students do not study, you will have to explain to them why they must study. Good teachers should be able to influence their students.* = to have an effect on the thinking and behaviour of someone

influence[2] noun, u. *Although I am his mother, I have no influence on him and he does what he likes.* = the power to make someone think or act in a certain way **influential** /ɪnflu'enʃəl/ adj. **1** *The book was very influential.* = producing a lot of effect on people **2** *an influential member of the committee* = important and able to make others listen

in•flu•en•za /ɪnflu'enzə/ noun = a sickness which causes fever, head-ache and cold (also **flu**)

in•form /ɪn'fɔːm/ verb, t. *He does not know that the school is closed tomorrow. Will you please inform him?* = to give someone knowledge of something which he/she did not have (formal) **information** /ɪnfə'meɪʃən/ noun, u *I did not have the information that the school is closed today, or I would not have come.* = facts which give us knowledge of or about something **Information Technology** noun, u. = the use of computers to collect, store and use information (also **IT**)

in•for•mal /ɪn'fɔːməl/ adj. **1** *The new Director had an informal discussion with her colleagues over lunch.* = a meeting, discussion etc. held in a friendly atmosphere (as if among friends) **2** *I want you to wear informal clothes when you come to the meeting.* = suitable for ordinary, everyday occasions but not for official occasions

informant /ɪn'fɔːmənt/ noun, c. **1** = a person who is part of a criminal group and who reveals its secrets to the police, other groups etc. **2** *My informant tells me that there is no Hindi word for 'computer'.* = a person who helps someone who is making a study of a language or culture by giving him/her some information about the language or culture

informer /ɪn'fɔːmə^r/ noun, c. = a person who gives secret information to the police on criminal activities (often derogatory)

infra- /ɪnfrə/ prefix meaning 'below' or 'beyond' e.g. **infra-red rays** noun = rays of light which cannot be seen but which produce heat **infrastructure** noun, u. = the things which help an industry to work smoothly, such as roads, telephone systems, supply of electricity and water etc.

in•fringe /ɪn'frɪndʒ/ verb, t. *infringe the law* = to

break or go against a law **infringement** noun, u. = the act of breaking a law

in•fu•ri•ate /ɪn'fjʊərieɪt/ verb, t. *They feel infuriated when they see people smoking.* = to make someone very angry

in•ge•ni•ous /ɪn'dʒi:nɪəs/ adj. *He has come up with an ingenious plan to export mangoes to China.* = very clever **ingenuity** /ɪndʒə'nju:ɪti/ noun, u. *It required great ingenuity to design a car that can run on hydrogen gas, but she was able to do it.* = skill and intelligence

in•gen•u•ous /ɪn'dʒenjʊəs/ adj. *He is so ingenuous that anyone can cheat him.* = simple and easily influenced (often derogatory)

in•glo•ri•ous /ɪn'glɔ:riəs/ adj. *an inglorious defeat in the cricket match* = shameful; bringing dishonour (opposite **glorious**)

in•got /'ɪŋgət/ noun, c. *a steel ingot* = a lump of metal shaped like a brick

in•grained /ɪn'greɪnd/ adj. *She has a deeply ingrained dislike of travel.* = something that has been fixed deeply into one's mind or nature

in•gra•ti•ate /ɪn'greɪʃieɪt/ verb, t. *The man is trying to ingratiate himself with his seniors, so that he can get a promotion.* = to try to win someone's favour through flattery

in•grat•i•tude /ɪn'grætɪtju:d/ noun, u. *I will always remember the help you gave me. I will never be guilty of ingratitude.* = the quality of not being grateful (opposite **gratitude**)

in•gre•di•ent /ɪn'gri:diənt/ noun, c. *You need a number of ingredients to make this sweet, mainly sugar and milk.* = something that is used, along with other things, to make something (specially in cooking)

in•hab•it /ɪn'hæbɪt/ verb, t. *The Paraja tribe inhabits the mountains of western Orissa.* = to live in a place (formal) **inhabitant** noun, c. *The Asian lion is an inhabitant of the forests of Gujarat.* = a person or an animal which lives in a certain place

in•hale /ɪn'heɪl/ verb, t. or i. *When you are smoking, others may inhale the smoke.* = to take in something into the lungs, along with one's breath

in•her•ent /ɪn'hɪərənt/ adj. *Most children have an inherent fondness for sweet foods such as ice cream.* = something that is built into one's nature or is naturally present in something

in•her•it /ɪn'herɪt/ verb, t. *As you have no family, who will inherit your property?* = to receive something, specially property, from someone who has died **inheritance** noun, u. = something (usually property or money) that has been inherited

in•hib•it /ɪn'hɪbɪt/ verb, t. *A hot climate can inhibit the development of sports in a country.* = to make something difficult, or to hold back or prevent it **inhibition** /ɪnhɪ'bɪʃən/ noun, c. *She has no inhibitions about showing her anger when necessary.* = a feeling of shyness which checks one from doing something that one would like to do

in•hu•man /ɪn'hju:mən/ adj. **1** *suffer inhuman treatment* = very cruel, without feelings of mercy **2** *The cry of anger that went up from the crowd when the police started firing was almost inhuman.* = not having a human quality

in•im•i•ta•ble /ɪ'nɪmɪtəbəl/ adj. *Asha Bhonsle's singing style is inimitable.* = something that is so good that it cannot be copied

i•ni•tial[1] /ɪ'nɪʃəl/ adj. *When she first came to this school, she was very shy. But after she got over her initial shyness, she became very friendly.* = something that happens or is found at the beginning

initial[2] noun, c. *Mr Ahmed's initials are S.A. They stand for Saif Ali.* = single letters used at the beginning of a person's name, as an abbreviation (short form) of the first and middle names

i•ni•ti•ate /ɪ'nɪʃieɪt/ verb, t. **1** *The government is initiating a new programme for the education of tribal children.* = to start or begin **2** *Robert was initiated into our club today.* = to make someone a member of a group after a certain ceremony **initiation** /ɪnɪʃɪ'eɪʃən/ noun

i•ni•tia•tive /ɪ'nɪʃətɪv/ noun, u. **1** *You should not be guided by others. You should use your own initiative.* = the ability, usually liked by people, to take a decision on one's own and start some activity oneself, without depending on others **2** *No one has thought of putting up a play. Let's take the initiative and suggest it.* = the first step which starts a chain of actions or events

in•ject /ɪn'dʒekt/ verb, t. *The doctor injected an antibiotic into his hip.* = to use a syringe or special needle to put some liquid into someone's body **injection** noun, u. or c. **1** = the act of injecting someone **2** = the liquid that is injected into someone

in•jure /'ɪndʒə/ verb, t. **1** *Five people were injured in the accident but luckily no one was killed.* = to harm or cause damage to the body of a living being **2** *The article in today's newspaper will injure his chances of victory in the election.* = to spoil **injury** noun, u. or c. (**injuries**) *He has suffered an injury in the head.* = the damage done to someone or something **injurious** adj. *Smoking is injurious to health.* = harmful

ink[1] /ɪŋk/ noun, u. or c. = the coloured fluid or liquid substance used in writing, printing or drawing

ink[2] verb, t. **1** *The cyclostyling machine has to be inked before it can be used to print something.* = to put ink on something **2** *The artist draws the outlines of the picture with a pencil and inks in the details later.* = to complete a drawing by using ink **inky** adj. **1** *inky hands* = covered with ink **2** *an inky blue sky* = dark (usually dark blue) **inkjet printer** noun = a machine using a special technology, used to print computer documents [COMPUTERS]

ink•ling /ˈɪŋklɪŋ/ noun, u. *I didn't have the slightest inkling that you were planning to come here today.* = idea or hint of something that is going to happen

in•land[1] /ˈɪnlənd/ adj. *inland trade in food grains* = happening inside a country

inland[2] adv. /ɪnˈlænd/ *We will be travelling inland.* = towards the centre of the country, away from the coast

in-laws /ˈɪnlɔːz/ noun, c. (often plural) = people who are related to one through marriage (e.g. father-in-law)

in•lay /ˈɪnleɪ/ noun, u. *The table is made of teak wood, but it has an inlay of ivory.* = a pattern made with some material placed inside an object made of a different material

in•let /ˈɪnlet/ noun, c. **1** = a narrow arm of the sea reaching into the coast **2** = a pipe or opening through which water or some other liquid can enter (opposite **outlet**)

in•mate /ˈɪnmeɪt/ noun, c. *One of the inmates of the jail has escaped.* = someone who has to stay in a prison or hospital for the mentally ill along with others (formal)

inn /ɪn/ noun, c. = a small hotel; (usually an old-style place) where a traveller can find a room to sleep in

in•nate /ɪˈneɪt/ adj. *The people of Indonesia have an innate sense of politeness. They will never speak rudely to anyone.* = some quality that is natural to one

in•ner /ˈɪnəʳ/ adj. **1** *The inner rooms in this house do not receive sunlight.* = on the inside (opposite **outer**) **2** *The poet's words have an inner meaning.* = hidden; not expressed openly

in•nings /ˈɪnɪŋz/ noun, c. (always plural) *India scored 150 runs in their first innings.* = the time during which a cricket team or a single player from the team is batting (**inning** = the time taken by a team to bat in the game of baseball)

in•no•cent /ˈɪnəsənt/ adj. **1** *The man was sent to prison, although he was innocent.* = not guilty of doing anything wrong **2** *Everyone was angry with him, although he had made just an innocent remark.* = not intended to cause unhappiness etc.; harmless

in•noc•u•ous /ɪˈnɒkjʊəs/ adj. *The dog looks ferocious, but it is really quite innocuous.* = not able to cause harm or hurt one's feelings

in•no•vate /ˈɪnəveɪt/ verb, i. *Our manager wants every meeting to begin with a recitation of humorous poems to create a happy mood. He loves to innovate.* = to introduce or try out new ideas **innovation** /ɪnəˈveɪʃən/ noun, u. = a new idea that brings about a change

in•nu•me•ra•ble /ɪˈnjuːmərəbəl/ adj. *the innumerable stars in the sky* = too many to be counted

i•noc•u•late /ɪˈnɒkjʊleɪt/ verb, t. *inoculate the child against small pox* = to treat a person or animal against some disease by injecting a weak form of the same disease (a vaccine) into the body, to create immunity

in•op•por•tune /ɪnˈɒpətjuːn/ adj. *She came to see me at a very inopportune time, when I was arguing loudly with my uncle.* = not suitable or convenient (opposite **opportune**)

in•or•gan•ic /ɪnɔːˈgænɪk/ adj. *Most farmers use inorganic fertilizers, such as potassium nitrate, which damage the soil. They should be advised to use cowdung or other organic fertilizers.* = not obtained from an animal or plant (opposite **organic**)

in•put[1] /ˈɪnpʊt/ noun, c. **1** *If you want the factory to produce more goods, you should provide more inputs, such as raw materials, money, labour etc.* = things that must be supplied or put into an industry etc. to make it work **2** *I can't work on this essay without some inputs from you.* = ideas, advice, guidance etc. which help one develop a plan or improve it

input[2] verb, t. (**inputted** or **input**) *I want you to input this data into the computer.* = to feed (put) information into a computer [COMPUTERS]

in•quest /ˈɪŋkwest/ noun, c. = an inquiry held by a court to find out how someone died or why a crime took place [LAW]

in•quire (**enquire**) /ɪnˈkwaɪəʳ/ verb, i. *Please phone the railway station and inquire when our train is arriving.* = to ask for information (formal) **inquiry** (**enquiry**) noun, u. or c. (**inquiries**) = the act of inquiring

in•quis•i•tive /ɪnˈkwɪzɪtɪv/ adj. *You shouldn't be so inquisitive about what she told me. It's a secret.* = interested in knowing about other people and their private affairs (disapproving)

in•sane /ɪnˈseɪn/ adj. *insane with grief* = mad; mentally unbalanced **insanity** noun, u. = madness

in•scribe /ɪnˈskraɪb/ verb, t. *The names of the soldiers who died in the war have been inscribed on a marble slab.* = to write, print or engrave something as a permanent record **inscription** noun, u. = writing which has been inscribed on stone etc.

in•scru•ta•ble /ɪnˈskruːtəbəl/ adj. *You can never know what she is thinking. The expression on her face is inscrutable.* = something that is a mystery and cannot be understood

in•sect /ˈɪnsekt/ noun, c. = a small invertebrate animal with six legs e.g. a cockroach **insecticide** /ɪnˈsektɪsaɪd/ noun, u. or c. = a chemical substance used for destroying insects [TECHNICAL]

insect

in•se•cure /ɪnsɪˈkjʊəʳ/ adj. *My position in the company is insecure.* = shaky; not safe

in•sen•si•tive /ɪnˈsensɪtɪv/ adj. **1** *How can you think of going on a holiday when millions of people are suffering? How can you be so insensitive?* = not caring about the feelings or sufferings of others **2** *He feels no pain when you pinch him in the arm. His body seems to have become insensitive to pain.* = having no power to feel pain etc.

in•sep•a•ra•ble /ɪnˈsepərəbəl/ adj. *The two friends are inseparable. You will always find them together.* = something or someone that cannot be separated (taken away) from something else

in•sert /ɪnˈsɜːt/ verb, t. *Please insert the disk in the disk drive.* = to put or push an object into something else **insertion** noun, u. = the act of inserting or putting something into something else

insert
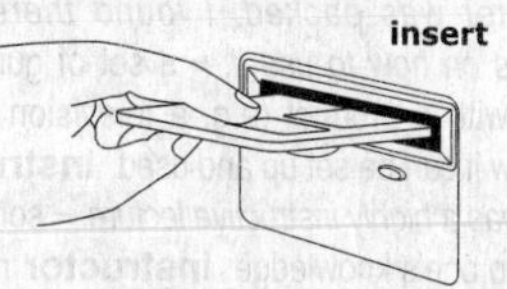

in-service /ɪn sɜːvɪs/ adj. *in-service training for teachers* = something that takes place during the time when one is working

in•side[1] /ɪnˈsaɪd/ prep. **1** *The book is inside the bag.* = within **2** *No one is allowed inside the departure area in an airport except the passengers.* = into an area or region which is specially protected **3** *She could feel the baby moving inside her.* = in one's body

inside[2] adv. **1** *The children are sleeping inside.* = indoors; inside a room or house **2** *He looks brave but has real fears inside.* = in a way that other people cannot see

inside[3] adj. *You will find his picture on an inside page of the newspaper.* = near the middle

inside[4] noun, c. **1** *The inside of the building is very dirty, although the outside looks clean.* = the part that is inside (away from the open air) **2** *inside information* = information or knowledge that is secret and known only to a few **insider** noun, c. = a term used to refer to a person who is considered part of a group or organization (opposite **outsider**) **insides** noun (always plural) *I have a pain in my insides.* = stomach (informal)

to turn something inside out *We had to turn the house inside out to find the gold bangle.* = to look for something anxiously and thoroughly and in the process move objects, papers etc. so that they are not in their usual place **to know something inside out** *I know my history lessons inside out.* = to know a subject etc. in great detail **inside information** (also **inside story**) = information or details about something or someone which are hidden and known to only a few

in•sight /ˈɪnsaɪt/ noun, u. or c. **1** *She showed great insight in understanding our problem.*(u.) = the natural ability to understand or judge a situation **2** *Our teacher's lesson gave us new insights into life in ancient times.*(c.) = special and sudden knowledge or understanding

in•sig•ni•a /ɪnˈsɪgniə/ noun, c. *The Ashoka pillar with the four lions is our national insignia, which you will find on all currency notes.* = a sign or symbol of official power

in•sig•nif•i•cant /ɪnsɪgˈnɪfɪkənt/ adj. *an insignificant position* = unimportant or having no meaning (opposite **significant**)

in•sin•u•ate /ɪnˈsɪnjʊeɪt/ verb, t. *Why are you asking me if I know what happened to your books? Are you insinuating that I took them?* = to suggest something unpleasant by making an indirect remark **insinuation** /ɪnsɪnjʊˈeɪʃən/ noun, u. = the act of insinuating something

in•sip•id /ɪnˈsɪpɪd/ adj. *You can add some chillies to your food if you find it insipid.* = without taste

in•sist /ɪnˈsɪst/ verb, i. or t. **1** *He insisted on making a long speech, even though everyone was ready to leave.* = to demand that something must happen or be done **2** *He insists that he is innocent, although many people think he is guilty.* = to state something strongly

in•so•lent /ˈɪnsələnt/ adj. *You have been very insolent to your teacher. You must be more respectful.* = rude and showing lack of respect

in•sol•u•ble /ɪnˈsɒljʊbəl/ adj. **1** *Chalk is insoluble in water, but salt is soluble.* = not capable of dissolving in a liquid [CHEMISTRY] **2** *Who killed him? The murder remains an insoluble mystery.* = incapable of being solved (explained or understood)

in•som•nia /ɪnˈsɒmniə/ noun, u. = a condition in which one is unable to sleep [MEDICINE]

in•spect /ɪnˈspekt/ verb, t. *I want to inspect your class and see how well you teach.* = to examine something thoroughly in order to judge its quality **inspection** noun, u. = the act of inspecting something **inspector** noun, c. = a person whose job it is to inspect something

in•spire /ɪn'spaɪəʳ/ verb, t. **1** *The example of our fearless leaders inspired many Indians to struggle for the freedom of this country.* = to create in someone the desire to do something good **2** *The novel I wrote was inspired by the story you told me.* = to create a new idea on the basis of which a work of art or literature is created **inspiration** /ɪnspɪ'reɪʃən/ noun, u. = the courage or desire to do something good by following an example

in•sta•bil•i•ty /ɪnstə'bɪlɪti/ noun, u. *The government may fall any day, as our leaders are fighting among themselves. The instability of the government is disturbing.* = the state of being easily shaken off balance (opposite **stability**)

in•stall /ɪn'stɔːl/ verb, t. **1** *A new governing body has been installed in the school.* = to set up or put in power **2** *We have installed air-conditioners in the building.* = to set up a machine for use **3** *Shall I install the new software in your computer?* = to save a program on the hard disk of a computer [COMPUTERS] **installation** /ɪnstɒ'leɪʃən/ noun, u. or c. **1** *the installation of a new government* = the act of installing something **2** *a military installation* = a military base (a place which is used and protected by the military)

in•stal•ment /ɪn'stɔːlmənt/ noun, c. *I have taken a loan from a bank to buy a car. It will have to be repaid in forty instalments.* = a sum of money paid at regular intervals to repay a loan or as a part of the price of something that has been bought

in•stance /'ɪnstəns/ noun, c. *Can you give me an instance of a student who has passed the high school examination at the age of thirteen?* = example

in•stant[1] /'ɪnstənt/ noun, c. (usually singular) *He vanished in an instant.* = a very short period of time

instant[2] adj. *I always use instant coffee.* = something that can be done or made in an instant (in a very short time) **instantaneous** /ɪnstən'teɪnəɪs/ adj. *When I asked him a question, his answer was instantaneous.* = happening at once

in•stead /ɪn'sted/ adv. *I can't go to the meeting. My son can go instead (of me).* = in place of

in•step /'ɪnstep/ noun = the upper, middle part of the foot

in•sti•gate /'ɪnstɪgeɪt/ verb, t. *instigate people to stay away from work* = to say something which encourages someone to do something wrong

in•stil /ɪn'stɪl/ verb, t. (**instilled**) *My teacher instilled the quality of patience in us.* = to help someone think in a certain way, have certain attitudes etc.

in•stinct /'ɪnstɪŋkt/ noun, u. or c. *When baby turtles come out of their eggs, they start crawling towards the sea, driven by some instinct.* = a natural feeling that causes an animal or human being to behave in a certain way, without having to think or to learn from someone else **instinctive** /ɪn'stɪŋktɪv/ adj. *Dogs and cats have an instinctive mistrust of strangers.* = something that happens by instinct

in•sti•tute[1] /'ɪnstɪtjuːt/ noun, c. *the Indian Institute of Technology* = an organisation (usually connected with education or research) that is set up for some special purpose

institute[2] verb, t. *The Board of Governors has decided to institute a gold medal, to be given to the best student each year.* = to set up **institution** /ɪnstɪ'tjuːʃən/ noun, c. **1** *The Regional Research Laboratory in Hyderabad is a well-known institution.* = an organisation which has existed for some time **2** *The institution of marriage must be respected.* = custom or tradition; something that has existed for a long time

in•struct /ɪn'strʌkt/ verb, t. **1** *I have been asked to instruct him in classical music.* = to teach (formal) **2** *The teacher instructed the students to wait after the bell went.* = to order someone to do something **instruction** noun, u. or c. **1** *I give the class instruction in the art of painting.* = the act of teaching **2** *Those are the instructions our teacher gave us.* = orders, usually from a person in authority **3** (always plural) *When I opened the box in which the new toaster was packed, I found there were instructions on how to use it.* = a set of guidelines which go with a product (e.g. a television set) to explain how it can be set up and used **instructive** adj. *That was a highly instructive lecture.* = something that adds to one's knowledge **instructor** noun, c. = a teacher

in•stru•ment /'ɪnstrəmənt/ noun, c. **1** *Biologists need a microscope and other instruments for their profession.* = a tool which helps one in carrying out some highly skilled or scientific work **2** *a musical instrument* = something which can be used to produce musical sounds **3** *All of us must to try to be instruments of peace.* = someone or something which seems to be used by some higher force for some purpose **instrumental** /ɪnstrə'mentəl/ adj. **1** *Many freedom fighters were instrumental in bringing freedom to India.* = being part of the cause for something **2** *instrumental music* = music produced by instruments only, without any human voices

in•suf•fi•cient /ɪnsə'fɪʃənt/ adj. *The food was insufficient for so many people. Several people remained hungry.* = not enough for a particular purpose (opposite **sufficient**)

in•su•lar /'ɪnsjʊləʳ/ adj. *You appreciate only Indian things and dislike anything that is foreign. You shouldn't be so insular.* = interested only in things belonging to one's own group, country etc.; narrow-minded (disapproving) **insularity** /ɪnsjʊ'lærɪti/ noun, u. = the quality of being insular

in•su•late /'ɪnsjʊleɪt/ verb, t. **1** *The electric cables are insulated with a covering of thick rubber.* = to cover something with some material so as to prevent electricity, heat, sound etc. from getting out or getting in **2** *His family lives far away from the city, among the mountains, and is insulated from all the dust and noise.* = to protect a person or thing from the unpleasant effects of the surroundings **insulation** /ɪnsjʊ'leɪʃən/ noun, u. = material which insulates e.g. rubber

in•suit[1] /ɪn'sʌlt/ verb, t. *They had invited me to dinner and I felt very insulted when I got there and found they had gone out.* = to be rude to someone or to treat them disrespectfully

insult[2] /'ɪnsʌlt/ noun, c. *I felt unable to take such an insult.* = a rude or offensive remark or action

in•sur•ance /ɪn'ʃʊərəns/ noun, u. *My new car is covered by insurance.* = an agreement signed by a company to pay money to someone in case of an accident, death etc. **insure** /ɪnʃʊəʳ/ verb, t. *My car is insured against accidents.* = to protect someone or something against accidents, death etc. by signing an agreement with an insurance company

in•sur•moun•ta•ble /ɪnsə'maʊntəbəl/ adj. *insurmountable problems* = (problems) that cannot be overcome or dealt with

in•tact /ɪn'tækt/ adj. *I was told that your house had been damaged in the earthquake, but I was happy to see that it is still intact.* = whole; not damaged or broken into small pieces

in•take /'ɪnteɪk/ noun, u. *This school usually admits 100 new students every year but this year the intake has gone up to 150.* = the number that is taken in

in•tan•gi•ble /ɪn'tændʒebəl/ adj. *Although this city is dirty and overcrowded, there is an intangible feeling of joy that one gets by living here.* = something that one can feel but cannot show or describe

in•te•ger /'ɪŋtɪdʒəʳ/ noun, c. *The number 5 is an integer but 5.3 is not an integer.* = a whole number [MATHEMATICS]

in•te•grate /'ɪntɪgreɪt/ verb, t. **1** *Many people who left India and settled in other countries have not been able to integrate fully into those societies.* = to join and become part of a larger group **2** *The districts of Koraput and Malkangiri are to be integrated into a single district.* = to join together **integral** /ɪn'tegrəl/ adj. *Science and mathematics are an integral part of the school curriculum.* = something that cannot be left out **integrity** noun, u. **1** *She may not work very hard, but no one can doubt her integrity.* = honesty and strength of character **2** *We must protect the integrity of our nation.* = the state of being united and not split into many parts

in•tel•lect /'ɪntɛɪlekt/ noun, u. *a man of high intellect* = the ability to think and reason intelligently (see **intelligent**)

in•tel•lect•u•al[1] /ɪntə'lektʃuəl/ noun, c. *She is an intellectual and will give us some fresh ideas to think about.* = someone who is highly educated, intelligent and has the ability to work with complex ideas

intellectual[2] adj. **1** *an intellectual debate* = connected with intelligent thinking **2** *He does not like any intellectual activity.* = something that has to do with the use of the mind

in•tel•li•gence /ɪn'telɪdʒəns/ noun, u. **1** *This is a test of intelligence.* = the ability to think well **2** = secret information about the activities of an enemy country [MILITARY] **intelligent** adj. *a highly intelligent student* = having a quick and clever mind

in•tel•li•gi•ble /ɪn'telɪdʒəbəl/ adj. *His talk was not intelligible.* = something heard or read which can be understood (opposite **unintelligible**)

in•tend /ɪn'tend/ verb, t. *She intended to come to the special class but unfortunately she fell ill and could not come.* = to have a plan or purpose in one's mind to do something **intention** noun, u. or c. = some plan that one has for doing something (also intent) **intentional** adj. *intentional damage* = something done knowingly, on purpose

in•tense /ɪn'tens/ adj. *He has an intense desire to learn about computers.* = very strong **intensify** verb, i. or t. *The storm seems to be intensifying. I hope we won't have another cyclone.*(i.) = to become stronger **intensive** adj. *The syllabus contains one book for intensive study and two other books for extensive reading.* = concentrated; requiring a lot of attention or effort

in•ter- /ɪntəʳ/ prefix meaning 'between' or 'among' e.g. **in•ter•act** /ɪntər'ækt/ verb, i. *Television personalities like to interact with the public.* = to meet or come in touch with someone so as to know his/her mind as well as to have an effect on him/her

in•ter•cept /ɪntə'sept/ verb, t. *The police intercepted a wireless message which a foreign spy was trying to send.* = to catch and stop something from reaching someone

in•ter•change /ɪntə'tʃeɪndʒ/ verb, t. *We have interchanged the engines of the two cars.* = to put or use one thing in place of another

in•ter•com /'ɪntəkɒm/ noun, c. = a telephone system used to talk to someone in the same building or in a place nearby

I

in•ter•course /ˈɪntəkɔːs/ noun, u. **1** *sexual intercourse* = an act of sex between two people **2** = an exchange of ideas or feelings between people

in•ter•de•pen•dent /ɪntədɪˈpendənt/ adj. *India and Pakistan are interdependent in their trade relations. They need our sugar and we need their cotton.* = depending on each other

in•terest[1] /ˈɪntrɪst/ noun, u.or c. **1** *He was reading your letter with great interest.*(u.) = willingness to give attention to something **2** *The book had no interest for me.*(u.) = some quality that can hold one's attention and make one read, listen etc. more carefully **3** *Music is one of my many interests.*(c.) = something that one likes to do **4** *The bank charges interest at 15 per cent on loans.*(u.) = a charge made for lending money

interest[2] verb, t. *Your plan to start a new factory does not interest me.* = to hold someone's attention **interesting** adj. *an interesting story* = something that holds one's interest and attention

in•ter•fere /ɪntəˈfɪəʳ/ verb, i. *Please do not interfere when I am advising her. Let me do the talking.* = to come in between two people; to take part in something that one is not concerned with (derogatory) **interference** noun, u. = the act of interfering

in•ter•im /ˈɪntərɪm/ adj. *The government will build many new roads in this area, but as an interim measure some of the old roads will be repaired.* = something done immediately or within a short time, as part of something larger that is to be done later

in•te•rior /ɪnˈtɪəriəʳ/ noun, c. *The interior of the house will be painted in bright colours.* = the inside part

in•ter•jec•tion /ɪntəˈdʒekʃən/ noun *'Oh!' is an interjection that expresses pain.* = a word or phrase (group of words) that expresses some strong feeling [GRAMMAR]

in•ter•link /ɪntəˈlɪŋk/ verb, t. *Kolkata and Delhi are interlinked by road as well as by railway.* = to join two things together

in•ter•mis•sion /ɪntəˈmɪʃən/ noun, u. *There will be a short intermission of ten minutes after this dance.* = interval

in•ter•mit•tent /ɪntəˈmɪtənt/ adj. *We had intermittent rain yesterday. It rained heavily in the morning and again in the evening, but not in the afternoon.* = something that happens for a time, stops, and begins again

in•tern /ɪnˈtɜːn/ verb, t. *The judge said that the persons who were being tried should be interned.* = to make someone go to prison or to limit someone's freedom [LAW] **internship** noun, u. = the period during which a person is under training in a hospital, school etc.

in•ter•nal /ɪnˈtɜːnəl/ adj. **1** *Although he had no wounds on his body, he was bleeding from some internal injury.* = something happening inside the body **2** *I am the internal examiner for this paper.* = someone who belongs to an organisation and is not brought in from outside

in•ter•na•tion•al /ɪntəˈnæʃənəl/ adj. *The Olympic Games, held once in four years, are an international competition in sports.* = something happening among two or more different countries

In•ter•net /ˈɪntənet/ noun, u. = (always capital) a system that connects people using computers in different parts of the world (see also **the Net**)

in•ter•pret /ɪnˈtɜːprɪt/ verb, t. **1** *Mr Li Peng spoke in Chinese and someone interpreted his speech in English.* = to put the words spoken in one language into a different language **2** *She said nothing when I asked her if she agreed with me, but I interpret her silence to mean that she has no objection.* = to try to find a meaning for something **interpretation** /ɪntəpreˈteɪʃən/ noun, u. or c. = the act of interpreting **interpreter** /ɪnˈtɜːprɪtəʳ/ noun, c. = a person who interprets (usually a speech given in one language into a different language)

in•ter•ro•gate /ɪnˈterəgeɪt/ verb, t. *The police are interrogating the man who was arrested last night to find out who was helping him in this crime.* = to ask a lot of questions in order to find out something (formal) **interrogation** /ɪntereˈgeɪʃən/ noun, u. = the act of interrogating (asking questions) **interrogative** /ɪntərˈɒgətɪv/ adj. *'What is your name?' is an interrogative sentence.* = a sentence in the form of a question [GRAMMAR]

in•ter•rupt /ɪntəˈrʌpt/ verb, t. **1** *Please don't interrupt me when I am speaking. You will have a chance to speak when I have finished.* = to stop someone in the middle of doing or saying something **2** *At the interview they asked him why his studies were interrupted for two years.* = to stop a process in the middle, for a period of time

in•ter•sect /ɪntəˈsekt/ verb, i. *The two lines AB and XY intersect at the point O.* = to meet or to cut each other [GEOMETRY] **intersection** noun, c. = a place where two roads cross each other

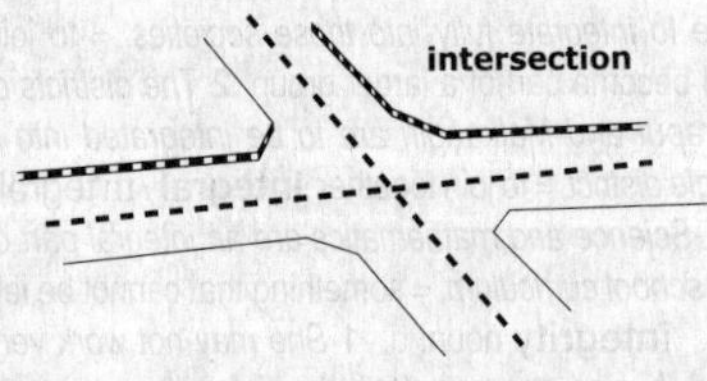

in•ter•sperse /ɪntə'spɜ:s/ verb, t. *It was a very serious film, although it was interspersed with some humorous scenes.* = to put something here and there in the middle of something different (formal)

in•ter•val /'ɪntəvəl/ noun, c. **1** *There will be an interval of 20 minutes after the first part of the film.* = a break in time, usually in a film or play or in school, between two events or activities **2** *The school bell rings at 40-minute intervals.* = at the end of every hour, 30 minutes etc. **3** *The flower pots have been placed at regular intervals.* = equal spaces between two objects **4** *I drink water at regular intervals.* = equal periods of time

in•ter•vene /ɪntə'vi:n/ verb, i. *My two sons were arguing and I was forced to intervene.* = to come between two people in order to stop something unpleasant **intervention** noun, u. = the act of intervening

in•ter•view[1] /'ɪntəvju:/ noun, c. *We will have a written examination as well as an interview to select a new manager. // A press interview has been arranged for the Prime Minister.* = a meeting at which someone has to face questions asked by a number of people, who may be trying to find out if he/she is suitable for a job, or to find out about his/her ideas and opinions, in order to write a report for a newspaper

interview[2] verb, t. *The Chairperson of the company will interview the candidates.* = to ask questions at an interview

in•tes•tine /ɪn'testɪn/ noun (often plural **intestines**) = the long tube which carries waste food away from the stomach and out of the body [BIOLOGY]

in•ti•mate[1] /'ɪntɪmɪt/ adj. **1** *Seema and I have been intimate friends since our schooldays.* = very close and friendly **2** *She shared her most intimate thoughts with me.* = very personal, not revealed to others easily **3** *intimate contact* = connected with having sexual relations

intimate[2] /'ɪntɪmeɪt/ verb, t. *He intimated a desire to be left alone.* = to convey or to express a wish indirectly (formal)

in•tim•i•date /ɪn'tɪmɪdeɪt/ verb, t. *Why are you looking at me angrily? Are you trying to intimidate me?* = to frighten by using threats

in•to /'ɪntə/ prep. **1** *She walked into the room suddenly.* = to enter **2** *He developed into a successful writer.* = to become **3** *They ran into a tree.* = used when an object is hit or touched **4** *When I went into high school, I was only twelve years old.* = move to something new and become closely involved in it **5** *Cut the carrots into small pieces.* = in order to make **6** *'What is two into two?' 'Four.'* = to multiply numbers **to run into someone** = to meet someone unexpectedly **to be into something** *He is into computers now.* = interested in (informal)

in•tol•e•ra•ble /ɪn'tɒlərəbəl/ adj. *The noise on the street is intolerable.* = something that one cannot bear (opposite **tolerable**) **intolerant** adj. *If you are so intolerant of our ideas, how can we work together?* = not willing to accept differences in ways of thinking and behaving **intolerance** noun, u.

in•to•na•tion /ɪntə'neɪʃən/ noun, u.= rise or fall in the level of the voice, in order to bring out a particular meaning [TECHNICAL]

in•tox•i•cant /ɪn'tɒksɪkənt/ noun, u. = something which can make one drunk (e.g., alcohol) [TECHNICAL] **intoxicate** verb, t. *These drinks can intoxicate you, be careful.* = to make a person drunk

in•tra- /ɪntrə/ prefix meaning 'inside' or 'within' e.g. **in•tra•ve•nous** /ɪntrə'vi:nəs/ adj. *an intravenous injection* = given into a vein

in•tran•si•tive /ɪn'trænsɪtɪv/ adj. *The verb 'is' is intransitive, but 'like' is transitive.* = a verb that does not take an object [GRAMMAR]

in•trep•id /ɪn'trepɪd/ adj. *We must be thankful to our intrepid soldiers who are fighting the enemy.* = fearless (literary)

in•tri•cate /'ɪntrɪkɪt/ adj. **1** *intricate carving* = full of fine details **2** *The film we saw last night has a very intricate plot. There are so many characters in the story and so many things happen to them that it is difficult to follow the story.* = full of fine details and therefore difficult to understand

in•trigue[1] /ɪn'tri:g/ noun, u. *They succeeded in their plot because of cunning and intrigue.* = the art of planning and doing things secretly and dishonestly (derogatory)

intrigue[2] verb, t. *I am greatly intrigued by the stories he tells about all the strange places he has visited.* = to find something very interesting and mysterious

in•trin•sic /ɪn'trɪnsɪk/ adj. *Your plan has intrinsic merit, but you have not thought about all the details.* = something that is in-built (a part of the nature of someone or something) (see **inherent**)

in•tro•duce /ɪntrə'dju:s/ verb, t. **1** *Let me introduce you to each other. This is my sister-in-law, Mohini, and this is my friend Hamid.* = to get two or more people to meet each other for the first time **2** *The railways were introduced into India by the British in 1812.* = to bring in for the first time **3** *The government is introducing a ban on the sale of cigarettes to children.* = to bring in a new law **4** *I must introduce you to the pleasure of gardening.* = to tell someone about a skill, a hobby etc. for the first time **introduction** /ɪntrə'dʌkʃən/ noun, u. = the act of introducing someone or something

in•tro•spect /ɪntrə'spekt/ verb, i. *I want you to*

I

introspect and think about the mistakes you have made. = to examine or look into one's own thoughts and feelings **introspection** noun, u. = the act of introspecting (examining oneself)

in•tro•vert /ˈɪntrəvɜːt/ noun, c. *He is such an introvert that he does not like to mix with anyone.* = a person who is concerned only with his/her own thoughts and does not like social relationships with others (often disapproving) (opposite **extrovert**) [TECHNICAL]

in•trude /ɪnˈtruːd/ verb, i. *You seem to be very busy. I hope I am not intruding on your time.* = to enter something without being invited

in•tu•i•tion /ɪntjʊˈɪʃən/ noun, u. *My intuition tells me that this man cannot be trusted, though I know nothing about him.* = the ability to get to know something without using the methods of reasoning **intuitive** adj. = based on intuition

in•un•date /ˈɪnəndeɪt/ verb, t. *After the heavy rain, the river overflowed and inundated the neighbouring villages.* = to flood; to cover under water

in•vade /ɪnˈveɪd/ verb, t. *Alexander the Great invaded India in 326 BC.* = to enter a country with the intention of fighting a war **invasion** noun, u. = the act of invading a country

in•va•lid[1] /ˈɪnvəliːd/ noun, c. = a person who is disabled and in poor health for a long time

invalid[2] /ɪnˈvælɪd/ adj. **1** *Your passport is invalid.* = not acceptable for use, usually because of some legal problem **2** *The reasons stated by you for the failure of the project are invalid.* = not based on good reasoning and therefore not acceptable

in•val•ua•ble /ɪnˈvæljʊbəl/ adj. *The help you gave me on the project proved to be invaluable. I am really grateful to you.* = something that has such great value that its value cannot be measured

in•var•i•a•ble /ɪnˈveəriəbəl/ adj. *The food in this restaurant is always good. Its quality is invariable.* = something that does not change **invariably** adv. *He is invariably busy when I visit him.* = always

in•vent /ɪnˈvent/ verb, t. **1** *The gramophone was invented by Thomas Edison.* = to create or produce something for the first time **2** *She always invents an excuse for being late.* = to think of a story or plan which is not true, usually so as to mislead people **invention** noun, u. or c. **1** = the act of inventing something **2** = something that has been invented by someone **inventive** adj. *He has an inventive mind.* = having the ability to invent or to think of something new

in•ven•tory /ˈɪnvəntri/ noun, c. (**inventories**) = a list of the things found in a factory, office etc.

in•verse (+ proportion, ratio) /ɪnvɜːs/ adj. *The older he becomes, the less wise he seems to be. His age and his wisdom seem to be in inverse proportion.* = opposite to each other [TECHNICAL]

in•vert /ɪnˈvɜːt/ verb, t. *If you invert the glass, all the water in it will spill out.* = to turn something upside down or in the opposite direction **inverted** adj. = turned upside down **inverted comma** noun, c. = a printed or written mark which looks like a comma turned upside down (') and is used to show the actual words of a speaker

in•vest /ɪnˈvest/ verb, t. or i. *He has invested money in many companies.* = to put money into some business

in•ves•ti•gate /ɪnˈvestɪgeɪt/ verb, t. or i. *to investigate a murder* = to try to get information about something or to find out the truth about something

in•vi•gi•late /ɪnˈvɪdʒɪleɪt/ verb, t. or i. *He has been asked to invigilate the examination.* = to keep watch over the people who are taking an examination so as to prevent cheating **invigilator** noun, c. = a person who invigilates an examination

in•vin•ci•ble /ɪnˈvɪnsɪbəl/ adj. *The cricketers thought they were invincible, but they were defeated in the very first match.* = one who cannot be defeated

in•vis•i•ble /ɪnˈvɪzəbəl/ adj. *The germs which cause cholera are so small that they are invisible to the human eye.* = something that one cannot see (opposite **visible**)

in•vite /ɪnˈvaɪt/ verb, t. **1** *My friend has invited me to his lecture.* = to ask someone to come to a social event **2** *When the speaker had finished his talk, the Chairman invited questions from the audience.* = to ask for or request **invitation** /ɪnvɪˈteɪʃən/ noun, u. or c. **1** = a written or spoken request asking someone to come for some social event **2** = the act of inviting someone

in•voice[1] /ˈɪnvɔɪs/ noun, c. = a list of goods supplied, stating quantity and price

invoice[2] verb, t. = to send an invoice (bill) to someone

in•voke /ɪnˈvəʊk/ verb, t. **1** *The priest chanted a mantra invoking God's blessings.* = to pray to a divine power for help **2** *The government invoked the Internal Security Act to arrest the leaders of the strike.* = to bring some law into use for a particular purpose **3** *I invoke your help.* = to ask for **invocation** /ɪnvəˈkeɪʃən/ noun, u. or c. *This is an invocation to the god of light.* = prayer

in•vol•un•ta•ry /ɪnˈvɒləntəri/ adj. *an involuntary act* = something done without conscious intention or effort

in•volve /ɪnˈvɒlv/ verb, t. **1** *You shouldn't get involved in local politics.* = to become connected with or mixed up with something **2** *I didn't know that* *arranging a picnic involved so much hard work.* = to require; to have something as a necessary part

in•ward /ˈɪnwəd/ adj. *All the cars are taking people away from the city but there is no inward traffic.* = moving towards the inside

i•o•dine /ˈaɪədiːn/ noun, u. = a substance that is found in sea-water and is used by doctors to prevent the infection of wounds

i•on /ˈaɪən/ noun = an atom which can carry a positive or negative electrical charge [CHEMISTRY]

i•o•ta /aɪˈəʊtə/ noun, u. *There is not even an iota of truth in the report.* = a very small amount (used in negative sentences only)

IQ abbr. of **Intelligence Quotient** = a measure of the intelligence of a person, where normal intelligence is represented by 100

ir- /ɪr/ prefix meaning 'not' e.g. **ir•re•place•a•ble** /ɪrɪˈpleɪsəbəl/ adj. *Our teacher is irreplacable.* = someone who is too valuable to be replaced by someone else

i•rate /aɪˈreɪt/ adj. *an irate letter* = very angry about something (formal)

ir•i•des•cent /ɪrɪˈdesənt/ adj. *the butterfly's iridescent wings* = having colours that seem to change in the light (literary)

i•ris /ˈaɪərɪs/ noun **1** = a kind of yellow or purple flower **2** = the coloured ring which surrounds the pupil (central part) of the eye [BIOLOGY] (see pic under **eye**)

irk /ɜːk/ verb, t. *I was irked by his silly question.* = to make someone feel angry or annoyed (old-fashioned)

i•ron[1] /ˈaɪən/ noun, u. or c. **1** (u.) = a common metal used in making steel **2** *an electric iron*(c.) = a heavy object which becomes hot and is used to take wrinkles out of clothes

iron[2] verb, t. *to iron clothes* = to use an iron to take wrinkles out of clothes

to iron out one's differences = to remove differences of opinion between people through talk

i•ron•y /ˈaɪərəni/ noun, u. *Saying 'You are a big help!' to someone who has given you no help at all is an example of irony.* = the use of words to carry a meaning which is the opposite of what they seem to mean [LITERATURE] **ironic** /aɪˈrɔːnɪk/ adj. *It is ironic that the man you dislike is the only person who can help you now.* = something that is the opposite of what one would expect or hope for

ir•ra•tion•al /ɪˈræʃənəl/ adj. *Your fear of ghosts is irrational.* = based on fanciful thoughts, not on reason (opposite **rational**)

ir•rel•e•vant /ɪˈreləvənt/ adj. *Why did you speak on classical music when you were asked to speak on films? Everything that you said was irrelevant.* = not related to the topic being discussed or to the situation that exists (opposite **relevant**)

ir•rep•a•ra•ble /ɪˈrepərəbəl/ adj. *The damage caused to these houses by the floods is irreparable.* = something that cannot be repaired or put right (formal)

ir•re•proa•cha•ble /ɪrɪˈprəʊtʃəbəl/ adj. *Everyone likes her because her manners are irreproachable.* = something that one cannot find fault with

ir•re•spec•tive /ɪrɪˈspektɪv/ adv. *This book can be enjoyed by everyone, irrespective of age.* = without reference or regard to something

ir•re•spon•si•ble /ɪrɪˈspɒnsəbəl/ adj. *He never does anything that he is asked to do. I find him totally irresponsible.* = one who has no sense of responsibility (does not think that it is his duty to do certain things and do them properly) (disapproving)

ir•rev•o•ca•ble /ɪˈrevəkəbəl/ adj. *Any judgement by the Supreme Court is irrevocable.* = something that cannot be changed or taken back (formal)

ir•ri•gate /ˈɪrɪgeɪt/ verb, t. *We must irrigate these fields to grow more wheat.* = to supply water to land for agriculture [TECHNICAL]

ir•ri•tate /ˈɪrɪteɪt/ verb, t. *Your habit of laughing foolishly without reason irritates me.* = to make someone feel angry

is /ɪz/ verb, i. (**was**) *Navroze is our leader.*= third person, singular, present tense form of the verb 'be'

is•land /ˈaɪlənd/ noun, c. = a piece of land surrounded on all sides by water [GEOGRAPHY]

i•so•bar /ˈɑɪsəbɑːʳ/ noun, c. = a line on a map joining places which have the same atmospheric pressure [GEOGRAPHY]

i•so•late /ˈaɪsəleɪt/ verb, t. *Your child has chicken pox. We must isolate him from the other children so that no one else gets the disease.* = to keep someone separate or apart from others [TECHNICAL]

i•sos•ce•les /aɪsɒsəliːz/ adj. *an isosceles triangle* = a triangle that has two sides of equal length [GEOMETRY] (see pic under **triangles**)

is•sue[1] /ˈɪʃuː/ noun, c. **1** *The issue we are discussing now is how to control our expenses.* = the subject being discussed **2** *'India Today' magazine has brought out a special issue on the unusual hobbies people have.* = something which is produced or published to be sold

issue[2] verb, t. *The Prime Minister's office will issue a statement on the subject.* = to produce or come out with

isth•mus /ˈɪsməs/ noun *the isthmus of Panama* = a narrow piece of land surrounded by water that connects two larger pieces of land [GEOGRAPHY]

it /ɪt/ pron. **1** *He told me to read this book but I haven't read it.* = referring to some non-living object that has been mentioned before **2** *It is raining.* = making a statement about the weather **3** *It is wonderful to be young.* = an empty (dummy) subject which refers back to the real subject of the verb, which comes later **4** *'Hello, is that Veena speaking? It's me, Arun.'* = used, specially in telephone conversations, to show who is speaking **5** *It was Anne who asked me to come.* = used to make the subject of the sentence look more important

that's it *You've left our train tickets at home? That's it, now we can't take the train!* = an expression of anger or irritation used to show that something cannot go ahead as planned (informal) **someone is 'it'** **1** *If you're looking for a good actor, Mary is it.* = the person/thing we are looking for or the right person or thing **2** *'The word you want is archeology'. 'That's it, thanks!'* = the right answer

IT abbr. of **Information Technology** = the science of computers

i•tal•ics /ɪ'tælɪks/ noun *All the examples given in this dictionary are printed in italics.* = sloping letters used in printing

itch[1] /ɪtʃ/ verb, i. *My back is itching. Can you scratch it for me?* = to feel uncomfortable, making one want to scratch

itch[2] noun, c. **1** *an itch in the back* = an uncomfortable feeling which makes one want to scratch **2** *I have an itch to travel.* = a strong desire (informal)

i•tem /'aɪtəm/ noun, c. *The next item on our programme is an Odissi dance by Madhavi Mudgal.* = a single thing which is part of a list of other things

i•tin•e•ra•ry /aɪ'tɪnərəri/ noun, c. (**itineraries**) = a plan for a journey (formal)

i•vo•ry /'aɪvəri/ noun, u. **1** = the bony substance of which the tusks of an elephant are made **2** = the slightly yellow colour that ivory has **ivory tower** noun *You live in an ivory tower. You don't know what is happening in the world outside.* = a situation in which someone does not know about the problems and difficulties of ordinary people (disapproving)

i•vy /'aɪvi/ noun, u. = a kind of climbing plant with large leaves

jJ

j, J /dʒeɪ/ the tenth letter of the English alphabet

jab[1] /dʒæb/ verb, t. (**jabbed**) **1** *The doctor jabbed a needle into my arm.* = to push something hard and pointed into something **2** = to hit someone with a short, straight, movement of the hand

jab[2] noun, c. *a jab in the stomach* = a sudden blow or push with some hard object

jab•ber[1] /ˈdʒæbəʳ/ verb, i. *The man jabbered away in his excitement, and no one could understand him.* = to talk quickly but not clearly

jabber[2] noun, u. *meaningless jabber* = fast and meaningless talk

jack[1] /dʒæk/ noun, c. **1** = a machine used for lifting a heavy weight, such as a car, in order to change the tyre etc. (see pic under **tools**) **2** = a playing card with the picture of a man on it, greater in value than the ten but smaller than the queen (see also **cards**)

jack[2] verb, t. *You will have to jack up the car.* = to lift with the help of a jack **jackass** noun, c. **1** = a male ass or donkey **2** = a person who behaves foolishly (informal) **jack-boot** noun = a large and heavy boot which covers the leg up to the knee

jack-of-all-trades *He is a jack-of-all-trades: a gardener, carpenter and cook, all in one.* = a person who can do many different kinds of work, but may not be good at any of them (mildly derogatory) **jack in the box** = a toy in the form of a box, containing the head of a man mounted on a spring, which jumps out suddenly when the box is opened

jack•al /ˈdʒækɔːl/ noun, c. = a wild animal belonging to the dog family which eats the dead bodies of animals killed by other hunting animals

jack•et /ˈdʒækɪt/ noun, c. **1** = a short coat with sleeves, worn with trousers (A 'coat' or 'over-coat' is usually worn over a jacket, and is longer.) **2** *The potatoes have been roasted in their jackets.* = the skin of a potato **life jacket** noun, c. = equipment made of plastic and filled with air which, is worn on the upper part of the body, to help one float in water

jacket

jack-knife /ˈdʒæknaɪf/ noun, c. (**-knives**) = a knife with a blade that folds into the handle

jack•pot /ˈdʒækpɒt/ noun, c. the biggest prize in a lottery or competition

to hit the jackpot = to be very successful

ja•cuz•zi /dʒəˈkuːzi/ noun, c. **(jacuzzi)** = a machine fitted to a bath-tub or swimming pool which can create a strong current of water with many bubbles

jade /dʒeid/ noun, u. = a semi-precious green stone from which jewellery or statues can be made

ja•ded /ˈdʒeɪdɪd/ adj. *We have seen so many films in the last two weeks that we feel jaded. Maybe we should do something else!* = a condition of being tired and bored, especially after one has had too much of a good thing

jag•ged /ˈdʒægɪd/ adj. *When metal had not been discovered, people used stones with jagged edges as knives.* = having a rough, uneven edge with sharp points

jag•u•ar /ˈdʒægjʊəʳ/ noun, c. = a large wild cat found in Central and South America that looks like a leopard

jail[1] /dʒeɪl/ noun, c. *The thief was sent to jail.* = a place where criminals are kept as part of their punishment; prison (old-fashioned) (also **gaol**)

jail[2] verb, t. *He was jailed for four years.* = to put in jail

jam[1] /dʒæm/ noun, u. (American **jelly**) **1** *pineapple jam* = a thick, sweet substance prepared from the juice of fruit, boiled with sugar, generally eaten with bread **2** *Our bus was caught in a traffic jam.* = a thick crowd of people or vehicles through which it is difficult to move

jam[2] verb, t. or i. (**jammed**) **1** *The roads are jammed all the way to the airport.*(t.) = to fill with people/ vehicles so that it is difficult to move **2** *This window is jammed; I can't open it.*(i.) = stuck, immobile **jam-packed** adj. *a jam-packed stadium* = very crowded **jam session** noun, c. = a music (jazz or rock) performance in which the music played has not been practised beforehand

to be in a jam = to be in a difficult position (informal)

jan•gle[1] /ˈdʒæŋgəl/ noun, u. *I could hear the jangle of bells from a kilometre away.* = the sound made by metal striking metal

jangle[2] verb, i. *The bunch of keys tied to the end of her sari jangled as she walked.* = to produce the loud sound of metal striking metal

Jan•u•a•ry /ˈdʒænjʊəri/ noun = the first month of the calendar year

jar[1] /dʒɑːʳ/ noun, c. **1** *a jar filled with sweets* = a bottle with a wide mouth and cover, generally made of glass or stone, used for storing things **2** *a jar of honey* = the amount of something e.g. oil, jam, which can be put in a jar **3** *The car came to a halt suddenly, giving us a jar.* = an unpleasant shaking sensation

jar[2] verb, i. (**jarred**) *The loud music jarred on my ears.* = to produce an unpleasant or disturbing effect on someone (referring to a sound)

jar•gon /ˈdʒɑːgən/ noun, u. *This textbook of surgery is written in medical jargon.* = the use of a language by the members of a particular professional group, with words and expressions that are special to that subject or profession

jas•mine /ˈdʒæzmɪn/ noun, u. = a climbing creeper; the white, scented flower of the plant

jaun•dice /ˈdʒɔːndɪs/ noun, u. = a disease caused by infection of the liver which makes the skin and the eyes look yellow

jaunt /dʒɔːnt/ noun, c. *The members of the club have gone on a jaunt to the seaside.* = a short journey taken for pleasure (informal) **jaunty** /ˈdʒɔːnti/ adj. *She was in a jaunty mood as she stood waving to us from the train.* = cheerful and happy

jav•e•lin /ˈdʒævəlɪn/ noun, c. = a light spear which can be thrown through the air over a long distance, once used as a weapon but now used only in sports competitions

jaw /dʒɔː/ noun, c. **1** *He has lost four of the teeth on his upper jaw.* = the bony parts in the face in which the teeth are set **2** (always plural) *The lion opened his jaws wide.* = the mouth of a fierce animal

for one's jaws to drop *Our jaws dropped when we saw the magnificent building.* = to be greatly and suddenly surprised or shocked, often as a response to something pleasant

jay /dʒeɪ/ noun, c. = a bird of the crow family

jay•walk /ˈdʒeɪwɔːk/ verb, i. *Any pedestrian found jaywalking across this street can be fined by the police.* = to cross the street in a dangerous manner, at a place where one is not supposed to cross **jaywalker** noun, c. = a person who jaywalks

jazz[1] /dʒæz/ noun, u. = a kind of music with a strong rhythm (beat or regular sound of drums) first made popular by African Americans

jazz[2] verb, t. *I've jazzed up my cupboard with photographs of my recent holidays.* = to make something brighter or more enjoyable (informal) **jazzy** adj. **1** = having a sound like that of jazz music **2** *I bought a jazzy bike yesterday.* = something that calls attention to itself, usually by its bright colour (informal)

jeal•ous /ˈdʒeləs/ adj. **1** *He was jealous because she won the quiz while he did not even qualify.* = unhappy because someone else has something you like but cannot get **2** *She is jealous of her new plants and does not let anybody else water them.* = possessive (not willing to allow someone else to share something) **3** *a jealous wife/husband* = not willing to allow the person one loves to show romantic interest in another person

jealously adv. *He protected the reputation of his family jealously.* = to try hard to keep something protected

jeal•ous•y /ˈdʒeləsi/ noun, c. or u. = a strong negative emotion which makes one unhappy when someone else has something that one wants for oneself (compare **envy**)

jeans /dʒiːnz/ noun, c. (always plural; following '*a pair of*') = trousers made of strong, thick material, for rough or informal use

jeep /dʒiːp/ noun, c. = a small, open car used for travelling across rough ground

jeer /dʒɪəʳ/ verb, i. or t. *The crowd jeered when the captain of the team was bowled out with the first ball.*(i.) = to make fun of someone by laughing noisily

Jekyll and Hyde noun = two very different personalities found in the same person

jel•ly /ˈdʒeli/ noun, u. *mango jelly* = a sweet made from fruit juice and sugar, which is solid but soft, less thick than jam and translucent (like glass) (compare **jam**)

to turn to jelly *My legs turned to jelly when I tried to run out of the reach of the dog.* = (of one's limbs etc.) to become useless, usually out of fear

jel•ly•fish /ˈdʒelɪfɪʃ/ noun, u. = a sea-animal which has a soft, transparent body

jelly fish

jeopardize (jeopardise) /dʒepədaɪz/ verb, t. *The lawyer jeopardized his reputation when he agreed to defend a criminal.* = to put something in a risky situation

jeopardy /ˈdʒepədi/ noun, u. *By missing the rehearsals, Rahul has put his chances of playing the lead role in jeopardy.* = at risk; in danger (formal)

jerk[1] /dʒɜːk/ verb, t. *The man was about to be run over by a truck, but I caught his arm and jerked him away.* = to pull suddenly

jerk[2] noun, c. **1** *The train came to a stop with a jerk.* = a short, quick backward movement **2** (American) = a stupid person (slang)

jer•kin /ˈdʒɜːkɪn/ noun, c. = a short jacket which fits tightly around the waist

jerry can /ˈdʒerɪkæn/ noun, c. = a large container with flat sides used for storing liquids

jer•sey /ˈdʒɜːzi/ noun, c. (**jersies**) *a football jersey* = a shirt worn by a player in a game, which shows which team he/she is playing for (also **jumper**, **pullover**, **sweater**)

jest[1] /dʒest/ verb, i. *I was jesting when I said I could walk on a tight rope.* = to joke; to create fun by talking in a light-hearted manner

jest[2] noun, c. *He called you an ass, but it was only a jest.* = joke **jester** noun, c. = a person whose job it was (in former times) to make people laugh

Je•su•it /'dʒezjuɪt/ noun, c. = a Christian priest belonging to a religious group known as the Society of Jesus

Jesus Christ = see **Christ**

jet[1] /dʒet/ noun, c. **1** *a four-engined jet* = an aircraft driven by jet engines (see below) **2** *a jet of water* = a fast, narrow stream of some liquid or gas which comes out through a small opening with force

jet[2] verb, i. (**jetted**) **1** *Water jetted from the pipe with force.* = to flow out in a narrow stream with force **2** *He spends most of his time jetting around the world.* = to travel by air at high speed **jet-black** noun, u. = very dark black in colour **jet engine** noun, c. = an engine that drives an aircraft forward by pushing out a jet (stream) of hot air and gases with great force in the opposite direction **jet lag** noun, u. = the tiredness that a traveller feels after flying at high speed in a jet aircraft to a different part of the world, where the time is different from what it is in the place where the journey began **jet-propelled** adj. *a jet-propelled aircraft* = driven by jet engines **jet set** noun, u. = the group of rich and fashionable people, in any society, who travel a lot (informal)

jet•sam /'dʒetsəm/ noun, u. = waste material thrown out of a ship and floating towards the shore (see also **flotsam**)

jet•ti•son /'dʒetɪsən/ verb, t. *The aircraft was carrying too heavy a load, so the pilot decided to jettison some of the petrol in the tanks to make the aircraft lighter.* = to throw out

jet•ty /'dʒeti/ noun, c. (**jetties**) = a platform built out into the water, for the use of passengers getting into or out of a ship

Jew /dʒuː/ noun, c. = a person following the beliefs of Judaism

jew•el /'dʒuːəl/ noun, c. **1** = a costly stone such as a diamond or ruby which is set in a gold ornament (e. g. a ring) **2** = an ornament that contains a number of jewels **3** *He is a jewel of a man.* = a person or thing of great value (figurative, informal) **jewellery** noun, u. (always singular) = ornaments such as necklaces and bangles usually made of gold, with or without stones **jeweller** noun, c. = a person who makes jewellery

the jewel in the crown = the most precious or outstanding item in a collection

jibe (gibe) /dʒaɪb/ noun, c. = a remark which makes fun of someone

jif•fy /'dʒɪfi/ noun, u. *Please wait, I'll be back in a jiffy.* = a very short while (informal)

jig[1] /'dʒɪg/ noun, c. **1** = a quick dance **2** = a piece of equipment which holds a tool in position

jig[2] verb, t. or i. (**jigging**) = to dance a jig

jig•gle /'dʒɪgəl/ verb, t. or i. *Don't jiggle the tray or the tea will spill.*(t.) = to move something in short, quick movements (informal)

jig•saw /'dʒɪgsɔː/ noun, c. = a tool with a metal blade used for cutting out thin pieces of wood to make a design **jigsaw puzzle** noun, c. = a picture which is pasted on top of a piece of wood and then cut into many small pieces. These pieces are separated and have to be fitted back together to make the complete picture.

jilt /dʒɪlt/ verb, t. *This man promised to marry my friend but now he has jilted her.* = to be false to a person one loves or to refuse to marry a person after having promised to do so

jin•gle[1] /'dʒɪŋgəl/ noun, u. or c. **1** *You can hear the jingle of the little bells on the dancer's feet as she walks.*(u.) = the sweet sound produced by small bells or two pieces of metal striking each other **2** *She writes jingles for television to advertise toothpaste.*(c.) = short and simple songs played over the radio or television to advertise some product

jingle[2] verb, i. *The bells on the dancer's feet jingled merrily.* = to produce a sweet sound, like that of small bells

jing•o•is•m /'dʒɪŋgəʊɪzəm/ noun, u. = the belief that one's country is better than all others (derogatory)

jinn (djinn) /dʒɪn/ noun, c. = a supernatural spirit, found in fables from Muslim countries (also **genie**)

jinx[1] /dʒɪŋks/ noun, c. *Our holidays in Patna seem to have a jinx on them. We never enjoy them.* = something that brings bad luck

jinx[2] verb, t. *First we lost our bags, and then we missed our train. This holiday is jinxed!* = to be troubled by bad luck

jit•ters /'dʒɪtəz/ noun, u. (always plural) *She always gets the jitters just before an examination.* = anxiety or nervousness before an important event

jive /dʒaɪv/ verb, i. = to dance to the sound of fast music

job /dʒɒb/ noun, c. or singular **1** *He has a full-time job in an office.*(c.) = regular paid employment **2** *The carpenter has done a good job.*(c.) = a piece of work **3** *It's your job to water these plants.* (singular) = duty **4** *When you have completed all the jobs, log off.*(t.) = something specific done by a computer e.g. calculations or sorting **jobless** adj. = unemployed (Note: This does not mean 'idle' or 'free to do what someone wants'.)

to make a good/bad job of something = to do something well/badly **to be out of a job**= to be unemployed **to do the job** *I need a fork but this spoon will do the job.* = to serve the purpose in a particular situation

jock•ey /'dʒɒki/ noun, c. = a person who is paid to ride horses in races

joc•u•lar /'dʒɒkjʊləʳ/ adj. *a jocular remark* = intended to cause laughter

jog[1] /dʒɒg/ verb, i. **1** *He jogs every morning.*= to run slowly for exercise **2** *He will remember everything if you jog his memory.* = to shake gently; nudge (figurative)

jog[2] noun, u. **1** *Will you come with me for a jog?* = a slow run **2** *Give him a jog and wake him up.* = a shake

john /dʒɒn/ noun, c. (American) = a toilet or lavatory (informal)

join[1] /dʒɔɪn/ verb, t. or i. **1** *This road joins New Delhi to Gurgaon.*(t.) = to connect or bring together **2** *You can start the dinner. I will join you later.*(t.) = to become united with **3** *The two roads join at this point.*(i.) = to meet **4** *I am joining the Officers' Club.*(t.) = to become a member of **5** *We had to join a long queue.* = to stand at the end of a line

join[2] noun, c. *The carpenter has repaired the broken chair so cleverly that you can't see the join.* = the place where two things are joined together

join in *Will you join in with us and celebrate Anu's promotion?* = to participate **to join hands with someone** *Parvez and I have joined hands to set up a restaurant.* = to set up plans to work with someone else (sometimes in a cause which is not approved of)

joint[1] /dʒɔɪnt/ noun, c. **1** *I have a pain in my knee joint.* = the place where two bones are joined together in the body **2** *The long pipe has a number of joints.* = a place where things are joined or a part that joins things **3** = a place regularly visited by someone for food etc. of an unhealthy kind (derogatory) **4** = a cigarette containing marijuana (slang)

joint[2] adj. *a joint family/decision/account* = shared by two or more people; of several people

joist /dʒɔɪst/ noun, c. = a metal beam which supports some part of a building

joke[1] /dʒəʊk/ noun, c. **1** = a short funny story about someone or something **2** *Someone played a joke on him by pretending to be his long lost friend.* = a trick played on someone to create laughter **3** *The dress was something of a joke.* = something which is not a good example of something or someone who is not taken seriously **4** *practical joke* = a joke/trick played on someone that is amusing for others

joke[2] verb, i. *I don't like anyone joking with me while I am working.* = to speak in a light-hearted and non-serious manner **joker** noun, c. **1** = a person who likes to joke **2** = an extra card in a pack of cards, which can be given any value

to play a joke on somebody = to fool someone for the amusement of others **to take a joke** *He gets irritated very easily. He can't take a joke.* = to not be able to laugh at a joke about/on oneself

jol•ly[1] /'dʒɒli/ adj. *a jolly old man* = cheerful and happy

jolly[2] adv. *We had a jolly good time.* = very (informal)

jolt[1] /dʒəʊlt/ verb, t. or i. **1** *The train jolted so much that we could not sleep.*(i.) = to move roughly, shaking from side to side **2** *I was jolted out of my sleep by the sound of the door being banged.* = to wake or surprise in a sudden and unpleasant way (often figurative)

jolt[2] noun, c. *The news of India's defeat in the match gave me a jolt.* = shock or blow

jos•tle /'dʒɒsəl/ verb, t. *The film stars were jostled by the crowd during the shooting of the film.* = to push someone roughly

jos•tling /'dʒɒslɪŋ/ noun, u. *The jostling in the bus caused him to feel sick.* = the pressure which one feels inside a crowded vehicle

jot[1] /dʒɒt/ verb, t. (**jotted**) *Can you jot down the main points of his speech?* = to write quickly

jot[2] noun *There is not even a jot of truth in the report you have sent.* = a very small amount (used in negative sentences only) **jotting** noun, c. *Let me show you the jottings I made from your speech.* = a short note, written quickly

jou•le /dʒuːl/ noun, c. = a unit of work/energy [PHYSICS]

jour•nal /'dʒɜːnəl/ noun, u. **1** *This is the new journal of the Computer Society of India.* = a serious magazine containing articles by experts or people doing research **2** *He maintains a journal in which he puts down all his personal thoughts.* = diary

journalism /'dʒɜːnəlɪzəm/ noun, u. = the profession of writing for newspapers, magazines, televison or the Internet **journalist** noun, c. = a person who has made journalism his/her profession

jour•ney[1] /'dʒɜːni/ noun, c. **1** *We are going on a long journey by train, from Kanyakumari to New Delhi.* = a trip from one place to another, usually by land **2** *The journey of life teaches us many valuable lessons.* = experience (figurative) (see also **travel**)

journey[2] verb, i. *We will journey from Ahmedabad to Guwahati.* = to go on a journey (formal and somewhat old-fashioned)

jo•vi•al /'dʒəuvɪəl/ adj. *Our jovial host kept all of us amused with her jokes.* = cheerful and friendly

jowls /dʒaʊls/ noun, u. (always plural) = the skin/area below the cheeks

joy /dʒɔɪ/ noun, u. or c. **1** *The birth of a daughter filled us with joy.*(u.) = great happiness **2** *My children are a joy to me in my old age.*(c.) = someone or something that causes great happiness

joy•ous /'dʒɔɪəs/ adj. = full of joy (formal) [LITERATURE]

joy-ride = a ride in a car or plane, taken for

enjoyment **joy-stick** noun, c. = a handle by which one can control the movement of something, especially an aircraft

jub•i•lant /ˈdʒuːbɪlənt/ adj. *He is jubilant because he managed to complete the test in an hour.* = very happy about something that has happened

ju•bi•lee /ˈdʒuːbɪliː/ noun, c. = a celebration marking some special date on which something important happened many years ago

Ju•da•is•m /ˈdʒuːdeɪ-ɪzəm/ = the religion followed by the Jews

judge[1] /dʒʌdʒ/ noun, c. *The judge will decide the case.* = an official who decides law cases in a court

judge[2] verb, t. *She has been asked to judge the flower show.* = to choose the winner in a competition **judgment** (**judgement**) noun, u. or c. **1** *The judgment has been signed by the judge.*(u.) = the official decision given by a judge in a court of law **2** *His judgment of people is generally correct.*(u.) = the ability to form an opinion about people or things **3** *The lawyer referred to a judgment by the Supreme Court.*(c.) = a decision taken earlier by a judge which can act as an example for other judges **Day of Judgement** (often capitals) noun = the day on which, according to some religious beliefs, God will judge our deeds

ju•di•cia•ry /dʒuːˈdɪʃəri/ noun, u. = the branch of the government that deals with law and justice **judicial** adj. = dealing with judges and courts of law

ju•di•cious /dʒuːˈdɪʃəs/ adj. *a judicious decision* = wise (formal)

ju•do /ˈdʒuːdəʊ/ noun, u. = a martial art (sport that teaches one to protect oneself against an attacker) that began in Japan and Korea (see also **jujitsu** and **karate**)

jug /dʒʌg/ noun, c. = a container with a handle, used for storing and pouring out liquids (also **pitcher**)

jug•ger•naut /ˈdʒʌgənɔːt/ noun **1** = a large vehicle used for carrying loads **2** = a very powerful force which no one can check

jug•gle /ˈdʒʌgəl/ verb, t. *The clown in the circus can juggle four balls at the same time.* = to keep several objects up in the air by throwing them up, catching them and throwing them up again

to juggle the accounts = to arrange or make changes in something cleverly, usually to cheat someone (derogatory)

ju•gu•lar /ˈdʒʌgjʊləʳ/ noun, c. *the jugular vein* = one of the two large veins inside the neck carrying blood from the head to the heart

to go for the jugular = to attack someone dangerously with the intention of causing serious harm

juice[1] /dʒuːs/ noun, u. *You should drink a glass of orange juice every morning.* = the liquid from fruit, vegetables or meat

juice[2] verb, t. *He is juicing an orange for you.* = to take the juice out of something **juicy** adj. **1** *a juicy apple* = full of juice **2** *a juicy piece of news* = interesting (usually relating to improper behaviour) **juicer** noun, c. = a machine used to take the juice out of fruit and vegetables

ju•jit•su /dʒuːˈdʒɪtsuː/ noun, u. = a martial art (sport which teaches one to defend oneself against an attacker) which began in Japan (see also **judo** and **karate**)

juke•box /ˈdʒuːk bɒks/ noun, c. = a machine, often inside a restaurant, that plays a selected piece of music when a coin is put into it

Ju•ly /dʒʊˈlaɪ/ noun = the seventh month of the year, between June and August

jum•ble[1] /ˈdʒʌmbəl/ verb, t. *The books and papers inside the room have been jumbled up and are lying in an untidy heap.* = to mix up in a disorderly fashion

jumble[2] noun, u. *There is an untidy jumble of things lying on the floor.* = a mixture of things without any order **jumble sale** noun, c. = a sale of used articles, usually to raise money

jum•bo /ˈdʒʌmbəʊ/ adj. *a jumbo jet* = very large in size

jump[1] /dʒʌmp/ verb, i. or t. **1** *The thief jumped over the fence when he saw that the lights in the house were on.*(i.) = to push oneself up into the air, over or across something **2** *He jumped the fence.*(t.) = to cross or go over something by jumping **3** *He jumped from one topic to another during his lecture.*(i.) = to move suddenly from one point to another (figurative) **4** *The price of petrol jumped from Rs 15 to Rs 30 a litre.*(i.) = to rise sharply and suddenly

jump[2] noun, c. **1** *That was a beautiful jump.* = an act of jumping **2** *There is a big jump in the price of fertilizer.* = sudden rise **jump-start** verb, t. **1** *to jump start a car* = to start a car by connecting its battery to that of another car, so that a strong electric current is produced **2** *to jump start a new industry* = to do something in order to help something to work better **jumpsuit** = a single whole-body garment that covers the upper body and the legs

to jump out of one's skin = to move suddenly in surprise or shock (informal) **to jump the gun** = to start doing something before the proper time (informal) **to jump the traffic lights** = to disobey a red (stop) traffic signal and drive on (informal) **to jump the queue** = to take an unfair advantage over others in a situation in which one is required to wait for one's turn (informal)

jump•er /ˈdʒʌmpəʳ/ noun, c. **1** *a high jumper* = a person who jumps **2** = a woollen garment that covers the upper half of the body

jump•y /ˈdʒʌmpi/ adj. *She is feeling more and more*

J

jumpy as the examination draws near. = nervous and excited (informal)

junc•tion /ˈdʒʌŋkʃən/ noun, c. or u. *Kharagpur is an important junction where the railway lines from Kolkata, Mumbai and Chennai meet.*(c.)= a place where roads, railway lines,etc. meet or join **junction box** noun, c. = a box where various electrical wires are joined

junc•ture /ˈdʒʌŋktʃəʳ/ noun, u. *It looks like we will easily win the match, and at this juncture the captain should declare the innings.* = a particular point of time which is very important (formal)

June /dʒuːn/ noun = the sixth month of the year, between May and July, usually the hottest in India

jun•gle /ˈdʒʌŋgəl/ noun, c. = thick tropical forest **concrete jungle** = an area (usually a city) that has many buildings and very little open ground (disapproving) **jungle gym** noun, c. = a framework of metal or wood that can be climbed (usually used by children)

ju•ni•or[1] /ˈdʒuːnɪəʳ/ adj. **1** *He is a junior salesman in the store.* = of low or lower rank (opposite **senior**) **2** *She is junior to me by two years.* = younger in age or having fewer years in service or having joined a school or college later than someone else

junior[2] noun, c. (abbr. as **Jr** or **Jnr**) (American) *George Bush, Junior (George Bush, Jr.)* = the younger of two people in the same family who have the same name **junior school** = a school for children aged 5 to 10 years **junior college** = a college for students preparing to enter a bachelor's degree course

ju•ni•per /ˈdʒuːnɪpəʳ/ noun, c. = an evergreen bush that has sharp leaves and small berries, used for making gin

junk[1] /dʒʌŋk/ noun, c. or u. **1** *Throw out all this junk. You don't need it.*(u.) = old and unwanted things **2** *a Chinese junk*(c.) = a kind of sailing ship with square sails, used in China

junk[2] verb, t. (**junked**) *You should junk all this old furniture.* = to get rid of something that is not needed **junk food** noun, u. = food that is not healthy **junk mail** noun, u. = letters, advertisements etc. sent to people who have not asked for them and do not want them **junk jewellery** noun, u. = jewellery that is eye-catching but of little value **junkie** (also **junky**) noun, c. **1** = a person who is addicted to drugs (slang) **2** *a video game junkie* = a person who watches television, plays video games, uses the computer etc. a great deal (humorous)

jun•ket /ˈdʒʌŋkɪt/ noun, c. **1** = an unnecessary journey or trip made by a government official and paid for by public money (derogatory) **2** = a pudding made with milk

jun•ta /ˈdʒʌntə/ noun, u. *the military junta in a neighbouring country* = a (military) government that comes to power without an election

Ju•pi•ter /ˈdʒuːpɪtəʳ/ noun (always capital) one of the planets of the **solar system**

jur•is•dic•tion /dʒʊərɪsˈdɪkʃən/ noun *This case does not lie within the jurisdiction of the High Court and should not have been decided by it.* = the power to decide a law case (formal)

ju•ris•pru•dence /dʒʊərɪsˈpruːdəns/ noun = the study of the principles of law

jury /ˈdʒʊərɪ/ noun, c. (**juries**) = a group of people from the public, who may not know much about law, who are chosen to hear a case in a court of law and give a decision on it (The jury system is common in the U.S.A., but no longer found in India.) **jurist** noun, c. = a person who is an expert in law

just[1] /dʒəst/ adv. **1** *The accident took place just at this spot.* = exactly **2** *He has just arrived.* = only a short time ago **3** *She is just a child.* = no more than **4** *I don't know where he went. He seems to have just disappeared.* = completely **5** *I know he has come a long way, but he'll just have to wait.* = an expression used to say something strongly **6** *She thinks she has packed just about everything she needs for the trip.* = almost **7** *I was just about to send you the e-mail when you called.* = to be about to do something very soon **8** *to be just as good/bad as something else* = equally **9** *The bus arrived just as I was leaving the bus-stop.* = at the same time **10** *I just can't bear that noise.* = really; used to stress something

just kidding = a way of telling someone not to worry and that one was joking (kidding) about something **just like that!** *She left her job, just like that!* = without giving something importance, thinking of others' feelings etc. (informal, disapproving)

just[2] /dʒʌst/ adj. *That is a just and fair decision.* = right and proper

jus•tice /ˈdʒʌstɪs/ noun, u. **1** *The man was innocent, and we are happy that he has been set free. Justice has been done.* = the right and proper thing **2** *The police must arrest this criminal and bring him to justice.* = the power of the law **Justice** noun *Mr Justice Misra* = the title by which a judge is addressed

jus•ti•fy /ˈdʒʌstɪfaɪ/ verb, t. *You have spent Rs 10,000 to buy paper for the office. How can you justify this expenditure?* = to give a good reason for something; to explain **justifiable** /dʒʌstɪˈfaɪəbl/ adj. *justifiable expense* = something that has a good reason **justification** /dʒʌstfɪˈkeɪʃən/ noun, u or c. *What is the justification for your action?*(c.) = a reason for doing something

jut /dʒʌt/ verb, i. (**jutted**) *The lighthouse has been* *built on a rock which juts out into the sea.* = to stick out or extend into

jute /dʒuːt/ noun, u. = a fibre (thread-like material) produced by a plant, from which ropes and sacks are made

ju•ve•nile /'dʒuːvənaɪl/ adj. *a juvenile person* = a very young person, no longer a child but not an adult

juvenile delinquency noun, c. = the committing of crimes by very young people [LAW]

jux•ta•pose /dʒʌkstə'pəʊz/ verb, t. *If you juxtapose these two paintings, you will see how different one is from the other.* = to place side by side or close together (formal)

J

kK

k, K /keɪ/ the eleventh letter of the English alphabet

K abbr. of **Kelvin** noun = a unit for measuring temperature (0º centigrade = –273º K)

ka•lei•do•scope /kə'laɪdəskəʊp/ noun, c. = a toy consisting of a tube with pieces of coloured glass and mirrors fitted inside, which shows different patterns in the mirrors when the tube is turned around **kaleidoscopic** /kəlaɪdəs'kɒpɪk/ adj. = colourful, having great variety

kan•ga•roo /kæŋgə'ruː/ noun = an animal found in Australia which hops along on its powerful back legs and carries its babies in a pouch in its stomach

ka•o•lin /'keɪəlɪn/ noun = a kind of white clay (earth) used for making fine pots as well as medicines

ka•ra•o•ke /kærɪ'əʊkɪ/ noun (Japanese) = a form of entertainment in which one sings while musical accompaniment as well as the words of the song are provided by a machine

ka•ra•te /kə'rɑːti/ noun, u. = a kind of martial art, originally from Japan and Korea, which teaches one to defend oneself against an attacker (see also **judo, jujitsu, kung fu**)

ka•yak /'kaɪæk/ noun, c. = a light, narrow covered boat which usually seats only one person

ke•bab /kə'bɑːb/ (also **kabab**) noun, u. or c. = small pieces of meat cooked over a fire on a thin bamboo or metal stick (see also **barbecue**)

keel /kiːl/ noun, c. = a long, straight piece of wood or metal which holds the bottom of a ship together and over which the frame of the ship is built
to keel over = to fall over sideways

keen /kiːn/ adj. **1** *She is keen to study computer technology in Germany.* = having a deep interest in doing something **2** *He has such a keen mind that he can learn any new subject.* = sharp; good at understanding **3** *a keen knife* = having a sharp edge

keep /kiːp/ verb, t. or i. (**kept**) **1** *You can keep the pen I lent you. You need not return it to me.*(t.) = to continue to have something in one's possession, without the need to return it **2** *He keeps a huge dog.*(t.) = to have/own and look after an animal **3** *They invited me over and kept me in great comfort for a week.*(t.) = to look after someone with care **4** *This blanket will keep you warm.*(t.) = to cause to remain in a particular state **5** *He keeps writing letters to me.*(t.) = to continue to do something **6** *He kept his word to me.*(t.) = to fulfill **7** *I'm afraid this food won't keep very long.*(i.) = to remain in good condition
to keep off *I've been asked to keep off red meat because it isn't healthy for me.* = to avoid something (informal) **to keep up** *I can cycle quite fast, but cannot keep up with my sister.* = to be as fast, good etc. as someone else in an activity (informal) **to keep (something) up** *You've done a wonderful job. Keep it up!* = an expression used to encourage someone who is doing good work (informal) **to keep one's head** = to remain calm in a difficult situation (informal) **to keep one's shirt on** = to stay calm and not get angry (informal) **to keep to something** *Try to keep to the subject.* = to not move away from something one is discussing, or to stick to a promise **to keep something to oneself** = to not share information, a secret etc. with others **to keep to oneself** *He has few friends and usually keeps to himself.* = to not be interested in meeting other people **to keep out of something** = to choose not to be involved in something which is likely to create trouble **to keep up one's spirits** = to try to be cheerful in a situation which causes sadness, low feelings etc. **for keeps** *This book is yours for keeps.* = for all time (informal) **keeping up with the Joneses** = trying to live as well as someone who has more money, is more stylish etc. (disapproving)

> **Usage** **keep** and **put**
> 'keep' is used to indicate the position occupied by something permanently or over a long period of time e.g. 'I keep my books in this cupboard' 'Put', on the other hand, indicates a temporary position e.g. 'Put the book on the table.'

keep•er /'kiːpəʳ/ noun, c. or suffix *a shopkeeper* = someone who is in charge of something

keg /keg/ noun, c. = a small wooden **barrel** that can hold liquids

ken•nel /'kenəl/ noun, c. = a shelter (small house or hut) for a dog

kerb /kɜːb/ noun = a raised space along the side of a street, built at a slightly higher level, for people to walk on

ker•chief /'kɜːtʃɪf/ noun, c. = a square piece of cloth used to cover the head and neck (see also **handkerchief**)

ker•nel /'kɜːnəl/ noun, c. **1** = the inside part of a nut, which is eaten e.g. a groundnut **2** *Let us get to the kernel of this problem.* = the central or most important part (figurative)

ker•o•sene /'kerəsiːn/ noun, u. = thin, colourless oil made from petroleum, used for providing light or heat

ketch•up /'ketʃəp/ noun, u. = a thick, red sticky liquid made by boiling tomatoes with sugar, salt and spices, used as an accompaniment to food

kettle /'ketl/ noun, c. = a pot with a handle and a lid

as well as a spout (a narrow curved mouth for pouring liquids), in which water can be heated

the kettle calling the pot black = a person with a bad reputation trying to give someone else a bad name

key[1] /kiː/ noun, c. **1** *the key to the front door* = a piece of metal which, when inserted (put into) a lock and turned, can close or open the lock **2** *the keys of a typewriter or a piano* = a part of a machine that is pressed down to make the machine work **3** = a book or a part of a book that has answers to questions in the same book or a different book **4** = (in an atlas, diagram etc.) a table which tells one what the colours, symbols, lines etc in a map stand for

key[2] adj. *Now watch carefully; this is the key scene.* = the most important

key[3] verb, t. (**keyed**) *The data has to be keyed into the computer.* = to enter data (information) into a computer using the keyboard, so that it can be read again, printed or sent out **keyboard** noun, c. = the part of a typewriter, computer, piano etc. which has one or more rows of keys which are pressed down to make the machine work **keynote** noun, u. *The keynote for this conference is the prevention of violence against women.* = the main topic or point **keynote address** = a speech which introduces the main topic for a meeting, conference etc. **keyring** noun, c. = a small ring made of metal which is used to keep keys in one place **keyhole** noun, c. = the hole in a door where the key is inserted **keyword** noun, c. = a word used when searching the Internet for information about a particular subject [COMPUTERS]

to be keyed up *When we heard that we might spot a tiger on the night safari, we were keyed up.* = excited and nervous

kha•ki[1] /ˈkɑːki/ adj. *Policepersons in India usually wear khaki uniforms.* = light yellowish-brown in colour

khaki[2] noun, c. *He looked very smart in his new khakis.* = trousers meant for informal wear (to be worn on ordinary, everyday occasions)

kib•butz /kɪˈbʊts/ noun, c. (**kibbutzim** or **kibbutzes**) = a farm or factory in Israel where people live and work together

kick[1] /kɪk/ verb, t. *He kicked the ball into the goal with his left foot.* = to hit with the foot

kick[2] noun, c. **1** *The centre-forward scored a goal with a powerful kick.* = a hit or strong push given with the foot **2** *He gets a kick out of watching wrestling on television.* = a feeling of great interest or excitement (informal) **kick-back** noun = bribe or money paid dishonestly to someone for doing something

to kick off *The match kicked off at nine.* = to start some activity (informal) **to get a kick out of something** *They get a kick out of watching violence in films.* = to get great pleasure and excitement, sometimes by being unkind or unfeeling, in doing something (informal) **to kick the bucket** = to die (slang, humorous or not respectful) **to kick a habit** *When I asked him if he still smoked, he said he had kicked the habit.* = to give up a bad habit (informal) **to kick somebody out** = to remove somebody (from a job) or to make them leave (informal, not respectful) **to kick-start something** = to make something start working again (figurative) **to kick up a fuss** = to complain vigorously about something, especially when it is not necessary to do so (informal) **to do something for kicks** = to do something, especially something filled with danger, for the excitement it creates (informal)

kid[1] /kɪd/ noun, c. **1** = the baby of a goat **2** *What's the kid doing?* = a child or a very young person (informal)

kid[2] verb, t. (**kidded**) *You must be kidding! Don't try to kid me.* = to joke with someone or to play a trick on someone (informal) **kid stuff** = something that is very easy to do (informal)

kid•nap /ˈkɪdnæp/ verb, t. (**kidnapped**) *The boy was kidnapped by a gang of criminals.* = to take away a person by force, usually for a ransom (money demanded for returning him/her)

kid•ney /ˈkɪdni/ noun, c. = an organ (working part) inside the body of an animal or human being, which separates waste matter from the blood, in the form of urine **kidney bean** noun, c. = kidney-shaped beans, usually red or dark, eaten as a vegetable

kill[1] /kɪl/ verb, t. **1** *Hunters have killed all the tigers in this forest.* = to cause someone's death, usually by violence **2** *We had planned a picnic, but the rain killed it.* = to put an end to something (informal) **3** *My feet are killing me.* = to cause great discomfort (informal)

kill[2] noun, c. *The tiger is sitting over its kill.* = an animal that has been killed by another animal for food **killer** noun = something (e.g a disease) or someone who kills **killing** adj. *We though we would enjoy the trek but it was killing.* = something that makes one very tired (informal) **killer whale** = a species of whale with distinct black and white markings **killjoy** noun, c. *Our group leader is a killjoy; he refuses to allow us to go trekking alone.* = a person who spoils the pleasure of others

to kill time = to find something to do in order to make time pass quickly (informal) **to kill somebody for doing something** *My sister will kill me if I ruin her rose bush.* = be very angry (informal) **to kill someone with kindness** = to be greatly or excessively kind to someone (informal) **The suspense is killing me** = to be very anxious to know how something will end (informal) **to kill two birds with one stone** = to achieve two purposes with a single effort **to be dressed to kill** = to wear (fashionable) clothes in an excessive way, or dress in such a

K

way that people notice you (informal) **to make a killing** = to earn a lot of money very quickly (informal)

kiln /kɪln/ noun, c. *a brick kiln* = a closed space in which bricks made of clay are baked (heated until they become hard)

ki•lo- /ˈkiːləu/ prefix meaning 'thousand' e.g. **kilobyte** = a unit for measuring the amount of information that can be stored in a computer, equal to 1000 bytes **kilogram** (abbr. as **kg**) noun, c. = a unit of weight, equal to 1000 grams **kilohertz** (abbr. as **kHz**) = a unit for measuring the frequency of radio waves, equal to 1000 hertz **kilometre** (abbr. as **km**) noun, c. = a unit of distance, equal to 1000 metres **kilowatt** (abbr. as **kw**) noun, c. = a unit for measuring energy, equal to 1000 watts

kilt /kɪlt/ noun, c. = a kind of short pleated skirt traditionally worn by men in Scotland

ki•mo•no /kɪˈməʊnəʊ/ noun, c. = a long, loose dress with wide sleeves worn by the Japanese

kin /kɪn/ noun, u. = members of one's family; relatives (slightly old-fashioned)

kind[1] /kaɪnd/ adj. *He is a kind man who has helped many people.* = one who cares about the happiness or feelings of people (opposite **unkind**)

kind[2] noun, u. **1** *Tigers and lions are animals of the same kind, belonging to the cat family.* = a group or class whose members share some qualities; type or sort **2** *Are you saying I told her our secret? I did nothing of the kind!* = sort; of the nature of the activity being talked about **3** *I'm not the kind of person who lets people down.* = type **kind-hearted** adj. *The kind-hearted milk-seller gave the poor woman some extra milk.* = having a kind nature **kindness** noun, c. = the quality of being kind; caring about others and helping them

in kind *You need not pay me cash for the rice I have supplied to you. You can pay me in kind. I'd love some coconuts from your tree.* = payment made through things, often of the same type, instead of money **kind of** **1** *A cougar is a kind of wild cat.* = an expression used when one wants to explain something not familiar in words that are easy to understand **2** *It was kind of bad.* = an expression used in place of details which one does not want to reveal or which one cannot (or does not want to) describe

kin•der•gar•ten /ˈkɪndəgɑːtn/ noun, u. = a school for very young children, usually four to six years old) (compare **junior school**)

kin•dle /ˈkɪndl/ verb, t. **1** *Let us collect some wood and kindle a fire.* = to cause something to burn **2** *I spoke to the group of students on the benefits of yoga, but I was unable to kindle much interest among them.* = to cause someone to feel interested

ki•net•ic /kɪˈnetɪk/ adj. *A car that is moving possesses kinetic energy.* = related to movement [TECHNICAL] (compare **potential energy**)

king /kɪŋ/ noun, c. **1** *the King of Nepal* = the male ruler of a country, usually the eldest son of the former king **2** *Gautam is the oil king.* = a rich and powerful businessperson **3** *Your king is under attack!* = the most important piece in the game of **chess** **4** *Play the king of hearts.* = a playing card bearing the picture of a king **kingly** adj. *kingly behaviour* = generous, just and dignified, of the kind expected of a king **kingdom** noun, c. **1** *the kingdom of Thailand* = a country ruled by a king or queen **2** *the animal kingdom* = one of the main classes into which living things are divided

kingfisher /ˈkɪŋkɪʃəʳ/ noun, c. = a small bird that catches and eats fish from lakes, rivers etc. (see pic under **bird**) **king-size** adj. *a king-size pack* = larger than the usual size **king-pin** noun = the most important person in a group, on whom the success of some activity depends

kink /kɪŋk/ noun, c. *You should straighten out the rope and remove the kinks.* = a twist or knot in one's hair, a piece of rope etc. **kinky** adj. **1** *kinky hair* = hair that has tight curls **2** *a kinky mind* = having some quality which makes a person behave differently from most others (often derogatory)

kins•man /ˈkɪnzmən/ noun, c. (**kinsmen**) = relative (The word 'kinsman' is generally avoided as it seems to favour the male sex or gender.)

ki•osk /ˈkiːɒsk/ noun, c. = a small shop selling newspapers, cigarettes etc.

kip•per /ˈkɪpəʳ/ noun, c. = a kind of fish that has been dried over the smoke from a fire and salted so that it will not go bad

kiss[1] /kɪs/ verb, t. *She kissed the child goodnight.* = to touch someone with the lips as a sign of love or friendship

kiss[2] noun, c. *give someone a kiss* = an act of kissing

kiss of life = to help a person who is not breathing, usually someone who has almost drowned, start breathing again by placing one's mouth on his/her mouth and start blowing in air **to kiss something goodbye** *If you don't send in a letter asking for leave, you may have to kiss the job goodbye.* = to lose a job, an opportunity etc. through one's own carelessness (informal, humorous)

kit /kɪt/ noun, c. *I forgot to pack my shaving kit.* = the equipment, tools etc. that one needs for a particular purpose or job **kit bag** noun, c. = a long narrow bag in which soldiers or sailors carry the things they need every day

kitch•en /ˈkɪtʃɪn/ noun, c.= a room in which food is cooked **kitchenette** noun, c. = a very small kitchen

kite /kaɪt/ noun, c. **1** = a piece of thin paper or silk, mounted on a light frame, which is tied to the end of a long piece of string (thread) and can be made to fly with the help of the wind **2** = a meat-eating bird (also **hawk**)

go fly a kite *When I suggested that we try to repair the old car he told me to go fly a kite.* = to dismiss an idea as being unrealistic (informal, not respectful)

kitsch /kɪtʃ/ noun, u. *There are a lot of paintings in his room. He thinks they are beautiful, but I think they are just kitsch.* = things used for decoration that are of poor artistic quality (have little value as art) (derogatory)

kit•ten /'kɪtən/ noun, c. = the young of a cat

kit•ty /'kɪti/ noun **1** *I am putting Rs 100 in the kitty.* = money collected from every member of a group and put together, to be used for some common purpose **2** = money collected from each player in a card game, which is taken by the winner **3** = the informal way of calling a cat

ki•wi /'ki:wi:/ noun, c. = a large bird found in New Zealand, which has very small wings and cannot fly **kiwi fruit** = a sour fruit which has a rough brown skin and is green inside

klep•to•ma•ni•a /kleptə'meɪnɪə/ noun = a disease of the mind that causes a strong desire to steal **kleptomaniac** noun, c. = a person who suffers from kleptomania

knack /næk/ noun, u. *At first he was unable to use a computer but now he has got the knack.* = a special skill which partly comes from practice (informal)

knead /ni:d/ verb, t. *To make chappatis, we must first knead some flour with water.* = to mix flour thoroughly with water using the fingers and the palm

knee /ni:/ noun, c. = the joint between the thigh and the lower leg **kneecap** noun, c. = the bone at the front of the knee joint **knee-deep** adj. **1** *The water is only knee-deep.* = upto the level of the knee **2** *knee-deep in trouble* = quite a lot of something **knee-jerk** adj. *knee-jerk reaction* = behaviour which is not based on careful thought but on instinct (a natural reaction to a situation)

to learn at someone's (one's mother's) knee = to learn something while still a baby **on bended knee** *I ask you, on bended knee, not to write that letter.* = a way of pleading with someone (figurative) **to bring someone or something to their knees** **1** *In the war that took place the smaller country was defeated and brought to its knees.* = to suffer a bad and sometimes shameful defeat in a war **2** = to be placed at a very low level through repeated failure

kneel /ni:l/ verb, i. (**knelt**) *Some people kneel while praying to God.* = to fold one's legs and sit with the weight of the body resting on the knees

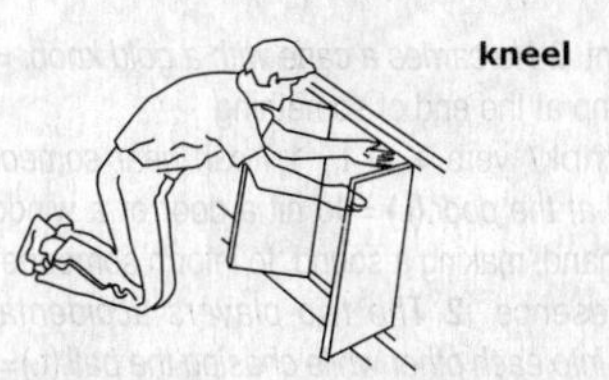

knell /nel/ noun, u. = the sound of a bell ringing slowly to mark a sad occasion, such as a death

knick•ers /'nɪkəz/ noun, c. (always plural) = an undergarment for women worn around the waist and covering the top part of the legs (informal)

knick-knack /'nɪk næk/ noun, c. *She bought some knick-knacks for the house.* = a small decorative object for the house (informal)

knife[1] /naɪf/ noun, c. (**knives**) = a tool which has a sharp metal blade with a handle, used for cutting things

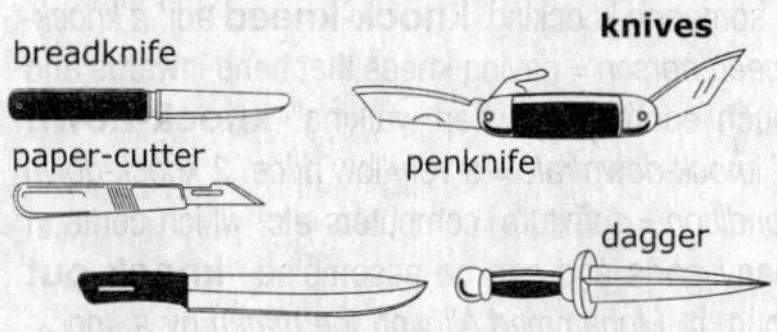

knife[2] verb, t. *The thief knifed her when she raised an alarm.* = to injure somebody with a knife (also **stab**)

to have one's knife in someone = to have a strong, sharp feeling of hate towards someone (informal)

knight[1] /naɪt/ noun, c. **1** = a person of high rank (in the Middle Ages) who fought on horse-back **2** = one of the pieces in the game of **chess**, shaped like the head of a horse, which moves two squares forward or backwards and one square to the left or right **3** = a man given the title of 'Sir' as an honour by a British king or queen

knight[2] verb, t. *The famous singer, Paul McCartney, was knighted. He is now Sir Paul McCartney.* = to receive the title of 'Sir', as an honour, from the British king or queen

knit /nɪt/ verb, t. or i. (**knitted** or **knit**) **1** *My brother is knitting a pullover for me.*(t.) = to make a garment (e.g. a sweater) by joining threads into a kind of net, using long needles (knitting needles) **2** *He had broken three of his ribs but the bones are knitting together.* = to join **knitting** noun, u. *I am very poor at knitting.* = the act of making things with needles and wool **knitting needle** noun, c. = a long needle used for knitting (see pic under **needles**) **knitwear** noun, u. = clothes made with wool or thread joined in rows

to knit one's eyebrows = to move the eyebrows close together to show worry, deep thought etc.

knob /nɒb/ noun, c. **1** *the knobs on the television set* = a round button used to control the working of an instrument **2** *He carries a cane with a gold knob.* = a round lump at the end of something

knock[1] /nɒk/ verb, i. or t. **1** *I can hear someone knocking at the door.*(i.) = to hit a door or a window with the hand, making a sound, to inform someone of one's presence **2** *The two players accidentally knocked into each other while chasing the ball.*(t.)= to hit against **3** *The children knocked down the chair when they ran across the room.*(t.) = to make something fall down by the action of hitting against it (also **knock over**) (see also to **knock someone down** below) **4** *If the engine knocks, you may have to take it to a mechanic.*(i.) = to make a noise (of machinery, an engine etc.) **5** *knock down a wall* = to cause a structure to fall **6** *knock a nail into the wall*(t.) = to hit a surface so that an object (e.g. a nail) goes in

knock[2] noun, c. *I hear a knock at the door.* = the sound of someone knocking **knock-kneed** adj. *a knock-kneed person* = having knees that bend inwards and touch each other when walking **knock-down** **1** *knock-down rate* = a very low price **2** *knock-down condition* = furniture, computers etc. which come in many parts and can be assembled **knock-out** noun, c. *Mohammad Ali won the match by a knock-out.* = a victory in a boxing match won by hitting the opponent so hard that he cannot get up again

to knock (something) around 1 = to do small things which help one relax (informal) **2** *We started the meeting by knocking a few ideas around.* = to have a discussion in which people respond to or offer ideas (informal) **to knock someone down** = to hit a person while driving a car, bus etc. **to knock something down** **1** *They knocked down the price of the book by Rs 100 and so I was able to buy it.* = to lower the price of something (informal) **2** *The ideas I suggested were all knocked down.* = to reject (informal) **to knock off** *Let's not work late, let's knock off early.* = to stop doing some work in order to rest etc. (informal) **to knock somebody off** = to murder (informal) **to knock somebody up** = to have sex with someone (slang) USE **to knock something off** = to steal, usually a small object **to knock someone out** **1** = (in boxing etc.), to make someone unconscious **2** = in a game, to defeat someone **to take a knock** *Her confidence in herself has taken a knock.* = to suffer a setback (referring to one's feelings etc.)

knoll /nəʊl/ noun, c. = a small, round hill [LITERATURE]

knot[1] /nɒt/ verb, t. (**knotted**) *The prisoner knotted some bedsheets together to make a rope and escaped from the prison by climbing down it.* = to join two pieces of rope, string etc. by tying their ends together

knot[2] noun, c. **1** *I need help to open this knot.* = a joint in a rope or string where two ends are tied together **2** *She tied her hair in a knot.* = hair that is twisted into a round ball at the back of the head **3** *The ship is sailing at a speed of 20 knots.* = a unit for measuring the speed of a ship, equal to about 1.85 km per hour **4** *This piece of wood cannot be used because there are too many knots in it.* = a hard mass formed in a piece of wood at a place where a branch joins the tree

to tie the knot = to marry (informal, often humorous) **to tie oneself up in knots** = to become very confused while trying to describe or explain something, so that what one is saying is not clear **to have a knot in one's stomach** = to feel as if there were something hard in one's stomach, as a result of fear or anxiety

know /nəʊ/ verb, t. or i. (**knew**, **known**) **1** *I know a number of European languages besides English.*(t.) // *Do you know where the manager's room is?*(t.) = to have a knowledge of a certain subject, way of doing something etc. **2** *I know their family very well.*(t.) = to be familiar with **3** *I know he will come today.*(t.) = to feel very sure of something **4** *She knew that she was going to miss the bus.*(i.) = to understand something **5** *Sodium chloride is also known as 'common salt'.* = to be given a name **known** adj. **1** *a known criminal* = having a reputation, either good or bad **2** *a known difficulty* = something which one is familiar with **know-all** noun, c. (American **know-it-all**) = a person who behaves as if he/she knows everything (derogatory) **know-how** noun, u. *We are setting up a factory to manufacture scooters. We will get the know-how from Japan.* = the knowledge or skill needed to do something

to know a thing or two *She knows a thing or two about cars.* = to have knowledge about something as a result of experience (informal) **to know something backwards** (or **inside out**) = to have detailed knowledge about something (informal) **Well, what do you know!** *Well, what do you know, he wants to act in films!* = an expression of surprise, mixed with ridicule **Heaven/God/Goodness knows** **1** *God knows how he finished the race as he had a corn on his foot.* = a way of saying you don't know (informal) **2** *Heaven knows, the city needs this rain.* = used to emphasise a statement (informal) **you know** **1** *The bathroom was, you know, not very clean.* = an expression used to delay mentioning a detail which is unpleasant **2** *That's not a nice thing to say, you know.* = used to stress a point one is making **3** *'How did you spend the weekend?' 'Well, you know, I relaxed.'* = used to say that one wants to continue talking but can't think of the next word **you never know** *You never know, she might learn to love the music that she now says she hates.* = a phrase used to indicate (sometimes with the intention of making fun) that you don't know what will happen in the future **one should have known** *He should have known it would take more than four hours.* = an expression of mild annoyance used to show that someone should have been aware of something **to know perfectly well** *Why did you take that road? You know perfectly well it is damaged.* = an expression used to show that one is annoyed because someone did not realise something simple and obvious **to (not) know something from something else** 1 *He doesn't know snakes from worms.* = to not be able to tell the difference between two things which are similar in some ways 2 = to be unable to tell the difference between two opposite things e.g. right from wrong, hope from despair **How should I know?** *'Is our teacher in today?' 'How should I know?'* = a reply used to show that one cannot be expected to be aware of something (not respectful)

know•ing /ˈnəʊɪŋ/ adj. *a knowing smile* = showing that you know what somebody is really thinking **knowingly** adv. 1 *He winked knowingly at us.* = in a way that shows that one knows something which is a secret or is embarrassing 2 *I made her angry, knowingly.* = deliberately; with full knowledge

knowl•edge /ˈnɒlɪdʒ/ noun, u. 1 *He has a good knowledge of Kannada.* = what one knows or has learnt through study 2 *This incident should have been brought to my knowledge.* = the state of being informed about something **knowledgeable** adj. *She is very knowledgeable about dogs.* = knowing a lot about something

general knowledge = a knowledge of important facts and figures relating to various subjects **common knowledge** *It is common knowledge that plants should not be disturbed at night.* = something that people generally know **working knowledge** *I have a working knowledge of French.* = to have very basic and limited knowledge of a language, a computer program etc. but enough to manage **to the best of one's knowledge** *I don't know when railways were introduced into Sri Lanka. To the best of my knowledge, it was the late nineteenth century.* = used to show that one is not absolutely sure of something **without one's knowledge** *They borrowed my car without my knowledge when I was away.* = describing a situation in which one does not know something has taken place or is taking place

knuck•le /ˈnʌkəl/ noun, c. = the joint where a finger joins the hand

to knuckle down = to start working hard **to knuckle under** = to be forced to accept the orders of a more powerful person (informal)

ko•a•la /kəʊˈɑːlə/ noun = an Australian animal that is furry, looks like a small bear and lives on eucalyptus trees

kohl /kəʊl/ noun, u. = a black substance used to darken the eyes and make them look more attractive

Ko•ran /kɔːˈrɑːn/ noun, c. = the holy book of the Muslims

ko•sher /ˈkəʊʃəʳ/ adj. *kosher meat* = food which has been prepared and cooked according to the rules of the Jewish religion

kow-tow /kaʊˈtaʊ/ verb, i. *You shouldn't kow-tow to them.* = to show too much respect to someone or to obey his/her wishes completely (informal)

ku•dos /ˈkjuːdɒs/ noun, u. *The director of the film earned kudos by winning the highest award.* = praise or glory

kung•fu /kʌŋˈfuː/ noun = a martial art (art of self-defence) that started in China (see also **judo, karate, jujitsu**)

K

lL

l, L /el/ the twelfth letter of the English alphabet

l **1** = abbr. of 'litre' **2** = abbr. of 'large' (size) **3 L** = used to denote 'learner' on vehicles etc.

lab /læb/ = abbr. of **laboratory** noun, c.

la•bel[1] /'leɪbəl/ noun, c. *There is no label on this bottle, so I can't tell what there is in it.* = a piece of paper fixed to a bottle etc. which gives information about its contents (what is inside)

label[2] verb, t. (**labelled**) **1** *You should label the bottle clearly.* = to fix a label on a bottle or other container so that one knows what is inside it **2** *They have been labelled unfriendly by their neighbours.* = to be described as

la•bor•a•tory /lə'bɒrətri/ noun, c. (**laboratories**) = a place where scientific research is carried out or where scientists test or prepare materials (e.g. medicines)

la•bour[1] /'leɪbə^r/ noun, u. **1** *It took many years of labour to build the Taj Mahal.* = hard work **2** *We need skilled labour to run this factory.* = workers **3** *Reena is going into labour today.* = the act of giving birth to a baby

labour[2] verb, i. or t. **1** *You will have to labour to pass the examination.*(i.) = to work hard (formal, old-fashioned) **2** *The truck loaded with rice bags laboured up the hill.*(i.) = to move slowly and with great effort **3** *Don't labour the point.*(t.) = to keep on arguing or talking unnecessarily about something **labourer** noun, c. = a paid worker **Labour** noun, u. = a political party (in Britain) that believes in social equality of opportunity and supports the rights of workers **laboured** adj. *He made a laboured speech, halting after every sentence.* = showing signs of doing something with great effort and difficulty **labour union** noun, c. = a group which protects the interests of workers in a factory etc. (the number of hours they work, the pay they receive etc.)

la•bo•ri•ous /lə'bɔːrɪəs/ adj. *Making lunch for so many people was a laborious job.* = something that needs a lot of labour or hard work

Lab•ra•dor /'læbrədɔː^r/ noun, c. = a big black or golden dog, often used as a guide dog for blind people

lab•y•rinth /'læbərɪnθ/ noun, c. **1** = a place or a building which is difficult to get out of because it has many paths meeting and crossing each other **2** = the inner ear [BIOLOGY]

lac /læk/ noun, u. **1** = a resin-like substance that is secreted by an insect **2** = the number represented by 100,000 (also **lakh**)

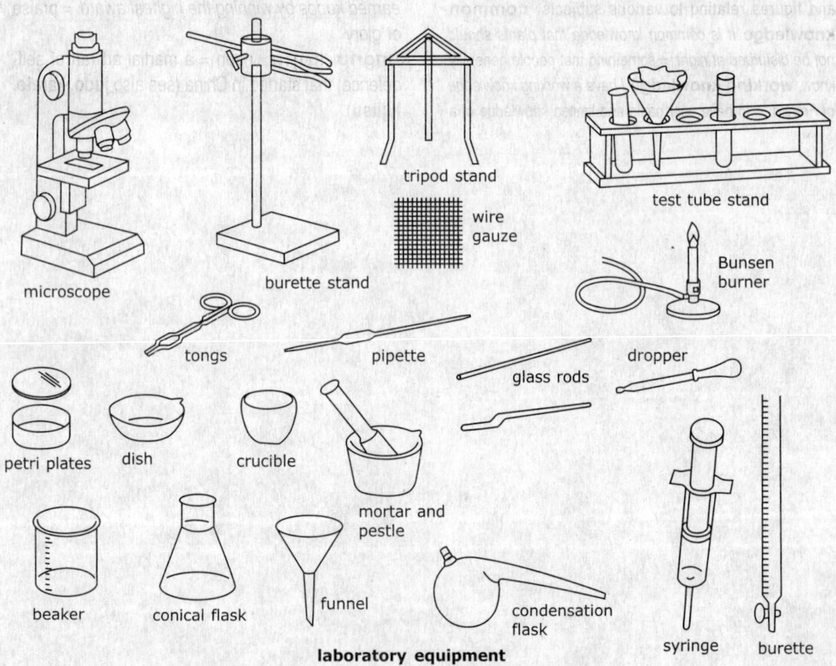

laboratory equipment

lace[1] /leɪs/ noun, u. or c. **1** *The curtains in her room are made of silk lace.*(u.) = decorative cloth made from fine thread **2** *Tie up your shoelaces.*(c.) = a string or thread used to tie up a shoe, so that it fits properly

lace[2] verb, t. **1** *Lace your shoes.* = to tie the laces on a shoe **2** *The orange juice has been laced with gin.* = to add a small amount of some alcoholic drink to a drink that does not contain alcohol (informal)

la•ce•rate /ˈlæsəreɪt/ verb, t. *He lacerated his knee when he fell.* = to tear or cut roughly **laceration** /læsəˈreɪʃən/ noun, u. = a wound in which the skin is torn and cut up

lack[1] /læk/ verb, t. *The concert was good but lacked pace.* = to be without something or not to have enough of something

lack[2] noun, u. *There was a lack of sympathy in his words when he scolded the child.* = the state of not having enough of something **lacking** adj. *Food and warm clothes were lacking when help arrived after the earthquake.* = missing, absent **lacklustre** adj. *This actor usually acts well but he has given a lacklustre performance in his new film.* = dull and boring

lack•a•dai•si•cal /lækəˈdeɪzɪkəl/ adj. *You should take your studies more seriously. Your whole approach to study is lackadaisical.* = lazy; not showing enough interest or effort

la•con•ic /ləˈkɒnɪk/ adj. *She made a laconic speech, although we thought she would have much to say.* = very brief (short); using very few words

lac•quer /ˈlækər/ noun, u. = a kind of transparent paint which appears as a shiny surface on wood or metal

lac•ta•tion /lækˈteɪʃən/ noun, u. = the production of milk by an animal or human mother **lactating** adj. *a lactating cow* = able to produce milk

lac•tose /ˈlæktəʊs/ noun, c. = a kind of sugar found in milk (see also **glucose, fructose**)

la•cu•na /ləˈkjuːnə/ noun, c. (**lacunae** or **lacunas**) *There is a lacuna in your report. You have written nothing about the work we did last month.* = gap; something that should have been there but is missing (formal)

lad /læd/ noun, c. = boy or young man (informal)

lad•der /ˈlædər/ noun, c. = two long pieces of bamboo, metal or rope which are joined to each other by a number of steps (**rungs**), used for climbing up the side of a building etc.

la•den /ˈleɪdn/ adj. *The ship is laden with coal.* = heavily loaded

la•dle[1] /ˈleɪdl/ noun, c. = a large, round and deep spoon with a long handle, used usually for serving liquid food (milk, soup, curry etc.)

ladle[2] verb, t. *He ladled out the soup.* = to serve some liquid/solid food with a ladle

la•dy /ˈleɪdi/ noun, c. (**ladies**) = woman (polite, old-fashioned, sometimes formal) **Lady** noun *Lord Emsworth and Lady Sarah* = (in Britain) the title of a woman who has the rank of a peer or who is the wife of a peer or knight **the ladies** (short for **ladies' room**) = a toilet, only for the use of women **ladybird** noun, c. = a small, round, bright red insect **lady'sfinger** noun, c. = a name used in some Asian countries for a kind of long green vegetable (also **okra**)

> **Usage** The word lady tends to be used because it is considered by some to be more respectful, e.g. 'Only ladies were allowed.' It is now generally considered old-fashioned. Many people now prefer the word 'woman' as in, for example, a *woman scientist*, a *woman doctor*.

lag[1] /læg/ verb, i. *They are lagging behind in the three-legged race.* = to move or develop more slowly than someone else; to fall behind

lag[2] noun, u. *There was a lag between his exposure to the cold and his catching flu.* = delay or gap; the period of time between two events **laggard** /ˈlægəːd/ noun, c. *This laggard is always the last to finish his work.* = a lazy person who works very slowly (derogatory) **jet lag** = see under **jet**

la•ger /ˈlɑːgər/ noun = a kind of light beer (light alcoholic drink)

la•goon /ləˈguːn/ noun, c. = a lake of sea water separated from the sea by a barrier (wall) of sand or rock

laid /leɪd/ verb = past tense or participle of **lay**

to be laid-back *He is very laid-back though he has a train to catch in ten minutes.* = relaxed, not anxious **to be laid up** *laid up with a sore throat* = to be forced to stay indoors due to an illness **to be laid low** *He was laid low by a rare kind of fever.* = to be made weak, usually by an illness

lair /leər/ noun, c. *the leopard's lair* = den; a place where a wild animal lives

lais•sez-faire /leseɪˈfeər/ noun, u. (French) = free enterprise; a system in which the government does not control the business activities of private companies

lake /leɪk/ noun, c. = a large area of fresh water, surrounded by land

lakh (**lac**) /læk/ noun, c. = a number equal to a hundred thousand (100,000)

la•ma /ˈlɑːmə/ noun, c. = the title of a Tibetan Buddhist spiritual leader

lamb /læm/ noun, c. or u. **1** (c.) = the young one of a sheep **2** (u.) = the meat of a lamb, used as food

lam•bent /ˈlæmbənt/ adj. *The candle burnt with a lambent flame.* = giving out a soft light (literary)

lame[1] /leɪm/ adj. **1** *The man became lame after he*

L

broke his leg in an accident. = unable to walk properly **2** *Don't give me such a lame excuse for your absence.* = weak, difficult to believe as being true

lame[2] verb, t. *The man was lamed in the accident.* = to make someone lame

la•ment[1] /lə'ment/ verb, i. or t. *She is lamenting the death of her friend who was killed in the war.* = to express sorrow (unhappiness) over something (formal)

lament[2] noun, u. *This song is a lament on the death of the brave soldiers.* = an expression of sorrow

lam•i•nate[1] /'læmɪneɪt/ verb, t. *The top of this table has been laminated with a sheet of plastic.* = to cover with a thin sheet of plastic

laminate[2] noun, u. = material (usually plastic) used to cover a surface

lamp /læmp/ noun, c. = a device (a simple machine) which gives light, using oil, gas or electricity (see pic under **lights**) **lamp post** noun, c. = a tall post on which a light is fixed, usually to light up roads **lamp-shade** noun, c. = a covering placed on and around a lamp to lessen the brighteness and to make it look beautiful

lam•poon /læm'puːn/ verb, t. *The writer of the article lampoons the people in power.* = to write something attacking and making fun of someone

LAN abbr. of **Local Area Network** = a system in which computers are connected within a local space e.g. an office [COMPUTERS]

lance[1] /lɑːns/ noun, c. = a long spear (stick with a sharp metal point) used as a weapon in former times by soldiers fighting on horseback

lance[2] verb, t. *The surgeon is going to lance the boil in my leg and take out the pus.* = to cut open a wound (formal) **lancer** noun, c. = a soldier who fought with a lance (in former days)

lan•cet /'lɑːnsɪt/ noun, c. = a sharp knife used by a surgeon or doctor to perform an operation

land[1] /lænd/ noun, u. or c. **1** *After sailing across the ocean for three months, Columbus returned to land.*(u.) = the solid, dry part of the earth's surface **2** *The farmer chose to sow cotton on his land.*(u.) = an area of ground owned as property **3** *She is travelling to a distant land.*(c.) = country **4** (always capital) *Land of the Rising Sun* = a name for a country used when giving a unique description **5** *homeland; motherland* = suffix (coming at the end of a word)

land[2] verb, t. or i. **1** *The pilot landed the plane safely.*(t.) **2** *The plane has landed.*(i.) = to cause an aircraft to come down to the earth from the sky or to bring something down (e.g. a kite) **3** *The soldiers landed on the beach near Chennai.*(i.) = to come from the water to the land **4** *He landed himself in serious trouble.*(t.) = to put someone or oneself in a difficult situation **landfill** noun, c. = a place where garbage is buried **landlady** noun, c. (**-ladies**) = a woman who owns a building and earns rent from it (The word *house-owner* is now preferred to *landlady* or *landlord* as it represents both men and women.) **landlocked** adj. *Nepal is a landlocked country.* = a country which is completely surrounded by other countries and cut off from the sea **landlord** noun, c. = a man who owns a building and earns rent from it **landmark** noun, c. **1** *You can easily reach my house by using the railway station as a landmark.* = a place or building which can be used to tell one's position (where one is) **2** *The 15th of August, 1947 is a landmark in India's history.* = an important event in the life of a person or the history of a country **landmine** noun, c. = a bomb hidden in or on the ground which explodes when a person or vehicle passes over it

land•scape[1] /lændskeɪp/ noun, u. or c. **1** *The landscape around Kandy is very beautiful.*(u.)= scenery (natural objects seen in or around a place) **2** *He has painted many beautiful landscapes.*(c.) = a painting or a picture which shows natural objects (mountains, rivers etc.)

landscape[2] verb, t. *We have asked a famous architect to landscape the new building.* = to make the surroundings of a place more natural and attractive

land•slide[1] /'lændslaɪd/ noun, c. = a natural fall of earth down the side of a mountain

landslide[2] adj. *a landslide victory* = an unexpected and very large victory, usually in an election (figurative)

lane /leɪn/ noun, c. **1** = a narrow road **2** *a four-lane highway* = one of the parallel parts into which a wide road is divided for the easy movement of traffic

lan•guage /'læŋgwɪdʒ/ noun, u. or c. **1** *It is said that only human beings possess language.*(u.) = a system of expressing meanings through words and sentences used by human beings **2** *She can speak six languages.*(c.) = a particular system for expressing meanings through words, used by the people of a particular country **3** *a computer language*(c.) = a system of signs or words used to design a program for a computer **4** *The report was in medical language and very difficult to understand.* = the words and phrases connected with a particular subject e.g. medicine, law **5** *He was angry and used terrible language.* = words which cause offence (informal) **language laboratory** noun, c. = a room fitted with a number of tape-recorders, in which learners of a language can practise listening to or speaking the language

lan•guid /'læŋgwɪd/ adj. *Her movements are languid.* = slow and lazy but in a graceful way (literary)

lan•guish /ˈlæŋgwɪʃ/ verb, i. **1** *languish in prison* = to remain in a condition of suffering **2** *The plants are languishing for lack of water.* = to become weak (literary)

lank /læŋk/ adj. *Her hair is dark but lank.* = straight and lifeless (used to refer to a person's hair) **lanky** adj. = tall and thin (used to refer to a person's body)

lan•tern /ˈlæntən/ noun, c. = a container of metal and glass with a lamp or candle inside, used to provide light

lap[1] /læp/ noun, u. or c. **1** *The mother held the child in her lap.*(u.) = the part of a person's body between the waist and the knees, when seated **2** *The coach asked them to run three laps round the track.*(c.) = a complete round of a circular field **3** *You can hear the lap (lapping) of the waves on the shore.*(u.) = the sound of waves striking the shore (which is like that of an animal drinking water)

lap[2] verb, t. or i. (**lapped**) **1** *The thirsty tiger lapped up the water from the stream.* = to drink by taking up liquid with quick movements of the tongue **2** *The runner who came first in the race lapped most of the other runners.* = to be ahead of a competitor in a race by one or more complete laps of the track **3** *The waves lapped against the boat.*(i.) = to make a gentle sound as water hits against something **lapdog** noun, c. **1** = a very small pet dog **2** = a person who follows/ imitates someone else all the time (derogatory) **laptop** noun, c. = a small computer which can be carried around

to lap something up **1** *The comic actor did not give a very clever speech but the audience lapped it up.* = to enjoy something e.g. music, greatly, even when it is not very good (informal) **2** = to enjoy an item of food and eat it fast (informal)

la•pel /ləˈpel/ noun, c. = the front part of a jacket or coat, which is connected to the collar

lapse[1] /læps/ noun, c. **1** *He is suffering from a lapse of memory.* = a temporary fault or mistake **2** *I asked him a question but he answered after a lapse of two minutes.* = a gap; passage of time

lapse[2] verb, i. *Your membership has lapsed because you did not pay the membership fee.* = to come to an end

lar•ce•ny /ˈlɑːsəni/ noun, u. = an act of stealing (theft) (formal)

lard /lɑːd/ noun, u. = the fat of an animal used in cooking

lar•der /ˈlɑːdəʳ/ noun, c. = a room where food is stored (also **pantry**)

large /lɑːdʒ/ adj *a large house* = bigger than usual in size or number

to be at large *The hungry tiger is at large.* = free; not under control (used for a dangerous person or animal) **by and large** *By and large, the meeting was a success.* = on the whole (if not completely)

lar•gesse /lɑːˈdʒes/ noun, u. *The rich business houses have been distributing largesse to the poor people in the villages.* = something given to someone out of kindness or generosity

lark /lɑːk/ noun, c. **1** = a kind of singing bird **2** *The boys had a lark by dressing up as ghosts and giving their classmates a fright.* = something done as a joke (informal)

lar•va /ˈlɑːvə/ noun, c. (**larvae**) = a kind of worm (crawling insect) that grows into an adult insect (e.g. a mosquito, ant or butterfly)

lar•ynx /ˈlærɪŋks/ noun, u. = the part of the human body, inside the throat (neck), that is used to produce the sounds we use while speaking **laryngitis** /lærɪnˈdʒaɪtɪs/ noun, u. = infection of the larynx that causes pain and swelling and sometimes temporary loss of the ability to speak

la•ser /ˈleɪzəʳ/ noun, c. = a machine that produces a narrow and very powerful beam of light which can cut through metal and other hard substances and can also be used to perform surgical operations inside the brain etc. **laser disc** = a disc on which information is recorded and read with a laser beam (see also **compact disc**) [TECHNOLOGY] **laser printer** noun = a machine that is used, together with a computer, to print on paper by using a beam of light

lash[1] /læʃ/ verb, t. or i. **1** (t.) = to hit with a whip **2** *Pokhra was lashed by strong winds last night.*(t.) = to hit hard (as if with a whip) **3** *He lashed out at those who had blamed him unfairly.*(i.) = to attack using strong words or language **4** *The tiger lashed its tail from side to side.*(t.) = to move violently **5** *The boat was lashed to a tree on the bank.*(t.) = to tie something firmly with a rope to something else

lash[2] noun, c. (**lashes**) **1** = a hit given with a whip **2** *The girl has long lashes.* = eyelashes (the hairs growing out of the folds of skin covering the eye)

lass /læs/ noun, c. (**lasses**) = a girl or young woman (informal) (compare **lad**)

las•si•tude /ˈlæsɪtjuːd/ noun, u. = the feeling of laziness that one has when tired

las•so /ləˈsuː/ noun, c. = a rope with one end knotted (tied) into a ring, which can be slipped and tightened around the neck of an animal (e.g. a cow or horse) to prevent it from running away

last[1] /lɑːst/ det. **1** *Your friend is sitting in the last row.* = behind everyone else **2** *I got the last ticket.* = the only thing remaining **3** *I saw her last night.* = most recently; on an occasion nearest to the present

last[2] adv. **1** *She came in last.* = behind all the others **2** *I met him last at the bus-stop.* = most recently; on an

L

occasion nearest to the present

last[3] pron. **1** *She was the last to hand in her essay.* = after everyone else **2** *He ate the last of the biscuits.* = the only thing remaining

last[4] verb, i. **1** *This storm won't last.* = to remain or continue for some time **2** *I expected these shoes to last for many years.* = to remain in good condition **lastly** adv. *Lastly, I would like to check if we have packed our raincoats.* = finally (mentioning the last point in a list) **lasting** adj. *This book and its beautiful photographs will give us lasting joy.* = continuing for a long time **the last straw** = some problem or difficulty which comes after many other problems or difficulties, making a situation very difficult to handle (see also **straw**) **last word** = the final word or expression that gives one victory in an argument

to have the last laugh = to be proved correct or victorious in the end **as a last resort** *There was a transport strike and it was difficult to walk to the station, so as a last resort we had to ask our neighbour to take us in her car.* = the thing that has to be done or used because everything else has failed **to do something in the last minute** = to do something at the final moment before something finishes or is about to start (generally disapproving) **to be the last person** *Sheila is the last person we thought would be a doctor.* = to be or do something that people don't expect you to do (informal) **the last thing** *It was a bad day anyway and the last thing we wanted was for the lights to go off.* = something that is not wanted or not welcome (informal) **to be on its last legs** = (of furniture, equipment etc.) in very poor condition and not likely to last **to not hear the last of something** *They have been boasting about their mountain climbing and I fear we haven't heard the last of it.* = used to express the feeling that something unpleasant, or a problem, has not ended (informal, often humorous) **to be the last word** *The film was the last word in acting.* = to be the best or most advanced (informal)

latch[1] /lætʃ/ noun, c. (**latches**) *He lifted the latch and opened the gate.* = a metal bar used to fasten (close) a door or gate

latch[2] verb, t. *Please latch the door.* = to fasten(close) with a latch **latch-key** noun, c. = a key that opens the door of a house leading to the outside **latch-key child** = a child whose parents are often away at work and who has to open the door herself or himself when coming back from school etc. (often used to express concern for a child who is not getting enough support from its parents)

to latch on to something = to begin to understand something (informal) **to latch on to someone** = to become too friendly with someone and refuse to leave him/her (disapproving)

late[1] /leɪt/ adj. **1** *The train was late.* = arriving or happening after the expected time **2** *She is writing a book about her late husband.* = a person who died recently

late[2] adv. **1** *The train arrived late.* = arriving or happening after the expected time **2** *He arrived late at night.* = in the last part of **late-comer** adj.= someone who arrives late

lately /'leɪtli/ adv. *The child has been avoiding her friends lately.* = recently

later /'leɪtə'/ *I am busy now, but I will talk to you later.* = after some time

latest /'leɪtəst/ adj. *the latest fashion* = the most recent

la•tent /'leɪtənt/ adj. *Education should bring out the latent talent of a child.* = something that lies hidden

lat•e•ral /'lætərəl/ adj. *This photograph gives you a lateral view of the new building.* = from the side **lateral thinking** noun = the ability to think of an unexpected answer or solution to a problem

la•tex /'leɪteks/ noun, u. = the thick, milky juice produced by the rubber plant (from which rubber is made)

lathe /leɪð/ noun, c. = a machine on which a piece of metal or wood can be given a desired shape by turning it round and round at speed and pressing it against a sharp tool

la•ther[1] /'lɑːðə'/ noun, u. = the thick foam produced by shaking a mixture of soap and water

lather[2] verb, i. *He lathered his face before he started to shave.* = to cover with lather

Latin /lætɪn/ adj. **1** = the language spoken in ancient Rome **2** = any country that speaks a language derived from Latin e.g. Italian, Spanish, French etc. **Latino** noun = a person from a South American country where Spanish is spoken, who has moved to the U.S.A. (informal) (also **Hispanic**)

lat•i•tude /'lætɪtjuːd/ noun, u. or c. **1** *Kanyakumari, the southernmost tip of India, has a latitude of 15 degrees north.*(c.) = the distance north or south of the equator, measured in degrees **2** *Companies have been given a lot of latitude in the matter of hiring and firing people.*(u.)= freedom to do something

lat•rine /lə'triːn/ noun, c. = a pit or hole dug in the ground for use as a toilet (lavatory) in an army camp etc.

lat•ter[1] /'lætə'/ noun *Ms Verma and Mr Misra were my teachers in school. The latter taught me Mathematics.* = the second of two people or things that have just been mentioned (opposite **former**)

latter[2] adj. *He started out as a policeman but became a farmer towards the latter part of his life.* = later (opposite **earlier**)

lattice /lætɪs/ noun, c. = a frame of wood or metal

with bars across it which is used as a support for creepers or as a fence

laud /lɔːd/ verb, t. *She was lauded for saving the child from falling into the well.* = to praise (formal) **laudable** adj. = worthy of praise **laudatory** adj. *a laudatory review* = expressing praise

laugh[1] /lɑːf/ verb, i. *Why are you laughing? Do you find my remarks funny?* = to express happiness or amusement by making a sound while breathing out with force (compare **smile, giggle**)

laugh[2] noun, c. **1** *His laugh was loud enough to be heard downstairs.* = the act of laughing **2** *She thinks her speech was a great success, but actually it was a laugh.* = something that cannot be taken seriously; a joke (informal) **laughable** adj. *a laughable mistake* = making people laugh; funny **laughingly** adv. *My mother laughingly reminded me of how I tried to trim the cat's whiskers when I was a child.* = to laugh while you say something **laughter** noun, u. = the action of laughing

to laugh at someone/something *I hope you won't laugh at the story I've written.* = to make fun of **to have the last laugh** = (see **last**) **to burst out laughing** = to laugh suddenly, with great enjoyment **to be no laughing matter** *Missing my train that night was no laughing matter. I had to wait until the next morning.* = to be a serious matter **to do something for a laugh** = to do something as a joke or in fun (informal)

launch[1] /lɔːntʃ/ verb, t. **1** *The new ship will be launched today.* = to put a new ship into the water for the first time **2** *We are launching a new programme today.* = to begin something new

launch[2] noun, u. or c. (**launches**) **1** *You are invited to the launch.*(u.) = the ceremony of launching something (showing something publicly for the first time) **2** *a motor launch*(c.) = a large motor-boat which carries passengers

laun•der /ˈlɔːndəʳ/ verb, t. = to wash or clean clothes

to launder money = to do something in order to make money which has been earned dishonestly, appear legal

laundry /ˈlɔːndrɪ/ noun, c. or u. **1** (u.) = a shop where clothes are washed or cleaned **2** *Where do you send your laundry?*(u.) = clothes which need to be washed or cleaned **launderette** /lɒndəˈrət/ noun, c. = a shop where one can launder (wash) one's own clothes in an automatic washing-machine by putting some coins into the machine (also **laundromat**)

laur•e•ate /ˈlɔːriɪt/ noun, c. *the Nobel laureate in Economics* = someone who has won a specially high honour **poet-laureate** noun = a poet who is given a special position by the king or queen of England and is required to write poems to mark special occasions

laur•el /ˈlɒrəl/ noun, c. = a small tree with green leaves (In former times, in Greece, a champion sports person was honoured by having a crown of laurel leaves placed on his head.) **laurels** noun (always plural) *The laurels for this match were won by Mahanama.* = honour or prize for some achievement

la•va /ˈlɑːvə/ noun, u. = red-hot liquid rock that flows from of a volcano

lav•a•to•ry /ˈlævətəri/ noun, c. (**lavatories**) = a **toilet**

lav•en•der[1] /ˈlævɪndəʳ/ noun = a plant which produces sweet-smelling blue-pink flowers

lavender[2] adj. = purple colour, like that of the flowers of lavender

lav•ish[1] /ˈlævɪʃ/ adj. *She did not want a lavish party for her birthday, so they had only samosas and mango juice.* = very grand; generous and expensive

lavish[2] verb, t. *She lavished attention on her pet cat.* = to give someone a lot of care, love, attention, praise etc.

law /lɔː/ noun, c. or u. **1** *There is a law against child marriage in most countries.*(c.) = a rule made by the government which everyone in a country must obey **2** *Everyone should be equal in the eyes of the law.*(u.) = the complete set of rules made by the government which controls the behaviour (actions) of the people in a country **3** *He is studying law at the university.*(u.) = the study of the laws of a country and the principles used in making these laws **4** *The law of gravitation was first stated by Isaac Newton.*(c.) = the statement of a principle which can explain or help to understand the things that commonly happen in nature **law-abiding** adj. = honest and always obeying the law **lawless** *a lawless city* = where the law is not respected or feared **lawsuit** /lɔːsjuːt/ noun, c. = a problem presented in court, by a person or organization (not the police) for a decision **lawyer** noun, c. = a person who has studied law and is trained to represent people in court or to write business agreements etc.

lawn /lɔːn/ noun, c. = a piece of land, usually surrounding a building, which is covered with grass that has been carefully mown (cut) **lawn mower** noun, c. = a machine that is used to mow (cut) grass

lax /læks/ adj. *The discipline in this school is very lax. The teachers should have more control over the students.* = not having enough control

lax•a•tive /ˈlæksətɪv/ *Castor oil is used as a laxative.* = a substance or a medicine that helps a person to get rid of the solid waste matter in the intestines easily (compare **emetic**)

lay[1] /leɪ/ verb, i. or t. (**laid**) (also past tense of **lie**) **1** *The friends of the injured man lifted him out of the* *car and laid him on the ground.*(i.) = to put down carefully in a flat position **2** *The Minister will lay the foundation of the new library building.*(t.) = to start a new building **3** *Please lay the table for dinner.*(t.) = to make things ready on a table for the beginning of a meal **4** *The hen lays eggs.*(t.) = to produce an egg **5** = to have sex with a woman (slang) (USE)

lay² adj. *a lay person* = not specially trained for a profession (**layperson**) noun, c. *This book on agriculture has been written in language that the layperson cannot understand.* = a person who has no special training in some subject or for some kind of work **layout** noun, u. *The layout of the new shopping complex has been designed by a famous architect.* = a plan or design for a building etc.

to lay down arms = to accept defeat in a war and stop fighting **to lay someone off** *He has been laid off because business has been poor.* = to stop employing a worker, usually because there is not enough work or because the employer cannot afford to pay him/her **to lay a hand/finger on** *I don't want you to lay a finger on my brother.* = to hurt **to lay claim to** *She approached the court and laid claim to the designs prepared by the official architect.* = to say that one owns something **to lay down one's life** = to sacrifice one's life for some cause **to lay down the law** = to make the rules about something clear (informal) **to lay someone's fears to rest** = to reassure **to lay out** *The gardens and the pools have been beautifully laid out by the architect.* = to arrange and present buildings, gardens etc. **to lay one's cards on the table** = to talk honestly or frankly to someone

lay•er /'leɪəʳ/ noun, c. *The table is covered with a thick layer of dust.* = a quantity of some substance that has been spread out over an area

la•zy /'leɪzi/ adj. *The children are becoming lazy. You must ask them to help more.* = not willing to work (disapproving) **lazybones** noun (always plural) = a person who is lazy (informal, not polite)

lbw abbr. of **leg before wicket** = a decision taken by the umpire in the game of cricket, in which a batsman is said to be out when he is hit on the leg by a ball that would otherwise have hit the stumps (wicket) [SPORTS]

LCD abbr. of **Liquid Crystal Display** noun, c. = a screen showing text or pictures passing through liquid using electricity [TECHNOLOGY]

lead¹ /lɪ:d/ verb, t. (**led**) **1** *The teacher led the new children to their classroom.* = to walk in front of someone so as to show him/her the way **2** *This road leads to the airport.* = to go in the direction of **3** *Saurav Ganguly will lead the Indian team in this match.* = to be in command of a group **4** *The Sri Lankan team is leading by 120 runs.* = to be ahead of someone in a competition or game **5** *She leads a very active life.* = to live a certain kind of life

lead² noun, u. **1** *We don't know what to do in this situation. We are waiting for someone to give us a lead.* = a suggestion (idea) or an example that tells or shows someone what should be done **2** *The Indian team is now in the lead.* = a winning position

lead³ adj. *She is the lead singer in this song.* = the most important

lead⁴ /led/ noun, u. **1** = a soft metal used in electrical batteries etc. **2** = a thin black stick inside a pencil, that makes it write **leaded** adj. *leaded petrol* = containing lead (opposite **unleaded** or **lead-free**)

leader /'li:dəʳ/ noun, c. = a person who guides others (shows them the way) or is in command of a group **leadership** noun, c. *Under his leadership the team played very well.* = the position or quality of a leader **a leading question** noun, c. = a question (specially a question asked in court by a lawyer) asked in such a way that the expected answer is suggested [LAW]

leaf /li:f/ noun, c. (**leaves**) **1** *a banana leaf* = the flat, green part of a plant or tree which is joined to the stem or to a branch (see pic under **leaf**) **2** *the leaf of a book* = a sheet of paper in a book which is printed on both sides **leafy 1** *a leafy part of the city* = with a large number of trees **2** *leafy vegetables* = (vegetables) with a lot of leaves or made up of leaves e.g. cabbage

leaflet /'li:flɪt/ noun, c. = a piece of printed paper folded into a small book, which contains an advertisement for something and is generally given away free

to leaf through *While waiting for the bus I leafed through a magazine.* = to read quickly parts of a book/magazine, usually in a casual manner **to turn over a new leaf** = to begin a new and improved part of one's life

league¹ /li:g/ noun, c. **1** *India has joined the international cricket league.* = a group of sports teams which play matches against each other to decide which team is the best **2** *the League of Nations // League for Safe Driving* = a group of countries or people joining together for a common purpose or cause

league² verb, i. *All the opposition parties have leagued together against the government.* = to join together for a common purpose or cause

leak¹ /li:k/ verb, i. **1** *Water is leaking into the boat through a hole in the bottom.* = to flow into or out of something through a small opening, usually creating a problem (used to refer to the flow of a liquid or gas) **2** *Someone must have leaked this report to the newspapers.* = to make something secret known to the public (informal, derogatory)

leak² noun, c. *There is a small leak in the boat.* = a

small opening through which some liquid or gas can flow into or out of something **leakage** noun, c. **1** *Water got into the boat because of a leakage* = an example of quantity of something that is leaking (e.g. oil, water) **2** = information that is given out, often on purpose, in order to spoil chances of success **leaky** /li:kɪ/ adj. *a leaky tap* = something that leaks

lean[1] /li:n/ verb, i. (**leaned** or **leant**) **1** *We leaned forward as we climbed the mountain, to balance the heavy loads we were carrying on our backs.* = to slope or tilt (bend forwards or backwards) from an upright position **2** *He sat on the floor, leaning against the wall.* = to support oneself in a sloping position, putting the weight of the body on something

lean[2] adj. **1** *He used to be fat, but he is quite lean now.* = thin (often approving) **2** *This has been a lean year for the film industry. Most films did not earn much money.* = earning little profit **3** *They eat only lean meant.* = food, especially meat, without natural fat in it

leap[1] /li:p/ verb, i. (**leapt** or **leaped**) **1** *She leapt over the wall before the dog caught up with her.* = to jump over or across something **2** *He leaped to defend his leader.* = to move quickly to do something

leap[2] noun, c. *The tiger crossed the stream with a single leap.* = a sudden, big jump **leap year** noun, c. = a year which comes once in four years, in which the month of February has 29 days instead of 28

by/in leaps and bounds = very quickly and successfully (informal) **a leap in the dark** = an action taken without thinking of the consequences **to leap at** *She leapt at her father's offer to drop her at school.* = to accept eagerly (informal) **to leap out at one** *This colour leaps out at you from the shelf.* = to stand out from the surroundings (informal)

learn /lɜ:n/ verb, t. (**learnt** or **learned**) **1** *She is learning French in school.* = to gain knowledge of some subject or to gain skill in doing something, as a result of teaching or experience **2** *I learn that you are now a successful lawyer.* = to get information about something **3** *He has learnt to respect the advice of friends.* = to come to understand something **learned** /'lɜ:nɪd/ adj. *a learned professor* = one who has gained a great deal of knowledge **learner** noun, c. **1** = a person who is learning **2** = a person learning to drive a vehicle (abbr. as **L**) **learning** noun, u. = knowlege that is gained by studying (see also **knowledge**)

lease[1] /li:s/ noun c. *The government has given me this plot of land on a 99-year lease.*(c.) = a written legal agreement by which a piece of land or a building is given to someone for a fixed period, in return for payment

lease[2] verb, t. *I have leased this building for ten years.* = to take or give something (e.g. a building) on lease

leash[1] /li:ʃ/ noun, c. *You have to keep the dog on a leash.* = a piece of rope etc. used to tie up and control an animal

leash[2] verb, t. *He leashed the dog to the post.* = to tie up an animal with a leash (opposite **unleash**)

least[1] /li:st/ det. or pron. *This student gave me the least trouble. // This is the least I can do for you.* = the smallest amount

least[2] adv. *She is the least fussy of all the sisters.* = less than all the others

at least **1** *At least let me help clean the vessels.* = if nothing else **2** *at least eight people* = a minimum of **in the least** *The rain has not affected her spirit in the least.* = hardly; at all **last but not least** *Last but not least, I must thank my wife for all the help she has given me.* = something that is important though it is mentioned last

lea•ther /'leðəʳ/ noun, u. = the skin of an animal that has been dried and treated with chemicals and from which shoes, bags etc. can be made

leave[1] /li:v/ verb, t. or i. (**left**) **1** *We must leave this city tomorrow.*(t.) **2** *Are you ready to leave?*(i.) = to go away from a place **3** *I have left this job.*(t.) = to give up **4** *I have left my glasses at home.*(t.) = to go without taking something **5** *The accident left a scar on his face.*(t.) = to cause to remain as an effect **6** *I can hear music from the next room. Did you leave the television on?* = to make something remain on, off, hot etc. **7** *Please do not leave any food on your plate.* = to let food remain on a plate because one is full or does not like it **8** *Could you leave the windows open, there's a nice breeze.* = to let something stay as it is **9** *You can leave the children with me on Thursday. I'll be happy to look after them.* = to place children etc. for a short while with someone who will look after them **10** *Leave your watch with her.* = to give someone something which needs mending or watching **11** *Do not worry about the cooking, leave it to me.* = I will be responsible for it **12** *They had left some food for me in the fridge.* = to place or put something in a place where someone can take or use it **13** *Aruna had left a message for me on the answering machine.* = used with a spoken/written message or letter which is put in a place where it can be found/heard **14** *When she died she left me her lovely books.* = to receive something which someone wanted you to have after their death

leave[2] noun, u. **1** *He has taken a month's leave.* = a period of time during which one is not working **2** *He wrote this article in the newspaper without my leave.* = permission (formal)

to leave something or someone alone *Leave*

the tree alone; don't cut it. = to let something stay as it is; to not disturb someone or something, or not cause someone more sadness, anxiety etc by being with them **to leave no stone unturned** *They left no stone unturned to make the programme a success.* = to make every effort possible **to leave out** *The team for the next match has been announced but my friend has been left out.* = to not include (when counting or giving something) **to leave word with someone** = to give someone a message for someone else **to be left over** *Is there any of that delicious rice left over?* = (of food, money etc.) to last after most of it has been eaten, spent etc. (adj. **leftover** food) **to leave somebody cold** *It was an interesting novel but it left me cold.* = to not make one feel any strong emotion of happiness, fear, sadness etc. (informal) **to leave a bad taste in one's mouth** *We became friends again but our quarrel left a bad taste in my mouth.* = to feel a sense of unpleasantness when you remember something in the past **to get left behind** **1** = when competing with someone else, to do less well **2** *His book on ancient temples in Nepal leaves all other books behind.* = (of work, books, art etc.) to be so good as to make one forget the worth of other, similar things (informal)

lea•ven[1] /ˈlevən/ noun, u. = a substance (e.g. yeast) that is added to a mixture of flour and water to make bread more soft

leaven[2] verb, t. = to add yeast to a mixture of flour and water (old-fashioned)

lech•er•ous /ˈletʃərəs/ adj. *lecherous behaviour* = having too much interest in sex (derogatory)

lec•ture[1] /ˈlektʃəʳ/ noun, c. *Did you listen to the professor's lecture on the relationship between music and mathematics?* = a serious and learned talk given on some subject, especially as a part of university teaching

lecture[2] verb, i. or t. **1** *Dr Misra will lecture on Romantic poetry today.*(i.) = to give a lecture on some subject **2** *They love to lecture their children.*(t.) = to talk seriously to someone, usually giving that person some advice or warning with good intentions but which they may find unpleasant or tiresome (informal, often humorous) **lecturer** noun, c. = a person who lectures (teaches) at a university

ledge /ledʒ/ noun, c. *window ledge* = a narrow shelf or platform built into a wall, just above or below a window

LED abbr. of **Light Emitting Diode** noun, c. *LED display* = characters (words and figures) displayed through light in electronic equipment

led•ger /ˈledʒəʳ/ noun, c. = a large book in which the accounts of a company, bank etc. are kept

leech /liːtʃ/ noun, c. (**leeches**) **1** = a small insect that lives in wet places and fixes itself to the skin of animals or humans, sucking their blood **2** = a person who does no work but supports himself/herself by getting money or help from someone else (derogatory)

leek /liːk/ noun, u. = a vegetable with long green shoots that is often eaten raw

leer[1] /lɪəʳ/ noun, c. *The man had a leer on his face which made me very angry.* = an unpleasant smile which expresses crude and vulgar enjoyment

leer[2] verb, i. = to look at someone with a leer

left[1] /left/ adj. **1** *He writes with his left hand.* = the side of the body where the heart is (opposite **right**) **2** *He took a left turn when he came to the crossroads.* = in the direction indicated (shown) by one's left hand

left[2] adv. *She is turning left.* = towards the left side

left[3] noun, u. **1** *Please turn to the left.* = the left side or direction **2** *The parties on the left are opposed to free trade.* = political parties which favour **socialism** or **communism** **left-handed** adj. = a person who does most things with his/her left hand (also **lefty** or **southpaw** (American English) (opposite **right-handed**) **left luggage** = a place where luggage carried by passengers on trains, planes etc. can be left and looked after for a short period **leftover** = the remaining part **leftovers** (always plural) = food left uneaten, that may be eaten at a later meal

a left-handed compliment = something which seems to be said in praise of a person, but is really criticism (an unfavourable remark)

leg[1] /leg/ noun, c. or u. **1** *He cannot walk as he has an injured leg.*(c.) = a limb of a human being or an animal which supports the body and is used in walking or running **2** *chicken leg.*(u.) = the leg of a bird or animal used as food **3** *We will have to travel by boat for the next leg of our journey.*(c.) = a part of a journey or competition **4** *The batsman hit the ball to square leg.*(u.) = the side of the cricket field which is to the left of a right-handed batsman as he stands facing the bowler. [SPORTS] (also **leg-side**; opposite **off-side** or **off**)

leg[2] verb, i. *Since I missed the last bus from the railway station I had to leg it home.* = to walk (informal)

-legged suffix *three-legged table* = used to describe the number of legs an object has

leg•a•cy /ˈlegəsi/ noun, c. (**legacies**) **1** *He left all his property as a legacy for his family when he died.* = money or property that one receives from a person who has died **2** *India has a rich legacy of classical music.* = something of value that is passed on from one generation to the next and belongs to everyone

le•gal /ˈliːgəl/ adj. **1** *It is not legal for a person below the age of 18 to drive a car.* = allowed by law **2** *I need some legal advice.* = related to law (compare **legitimate**) **legalize (legalise)** verb, t. *After the wedding ceremony, they went to the registrar to* *legalize their marriage.* = to make something legal (allowed by law) **legal tender** noun = money which can be used within a country

le•gend /ˈledʒənd/ noun, c. or u. **1** (c.) = an ancient story (which may not be true) about brave people and their noble deeds **2** *Mahatma Gandhi became a legend during his lifetime.* = a person who becomes famous for his/her achievements **legendary** adj. **1** *the legendary Vinoo Mankad* = a person who becomes very famous and is remembered by many people **2** *a legendary character* = not real but belonging to a legend (a story)

le•gi•ble /ˈledʒɪbəl/ adj. *I can read your handwriting quite easily. It is perfectly legible.* = can be read easily

le•gis•la•ture /ˈledʒɪsleɪtʃəʳ/ noun, u. = the branch of the government that makes laws, e.g. the parliament (Lok Sabha) **legislate** verb, i. *The parliament has legislated for the privatization of industries owned by the government.* = to make new laws **legislator** noun, c. = a person who is responsible for making new laws (e.g. a member of parliament)

le•git•i•mate /lɪˈdʒɪtɪmɪt/ adj. **1** *a legitimate child* = born of parents who are legally married (opposite **illegitimate**) **2** *The demand for higher pay made by the employees is perfectly legitimate.* = proper; allowed by the law or the rules

lei•sure /ˈleʒəʳ/ noun, u. *I like to paint whenever I have some leisure.* = free time **leisurely** adv. *a leisurely walk* = done without any hurry

le•mon[1] /ˈlemən/ noun, c. or u. **1** (c.) = a yellow fruit which produces sour juice **2** *Should I add some lemon to your tea?*(u.) = the juice of a lemon

lemon[2] adj. *She was wearing a lemon kurta.* = light yellow in colour, like that of a lemon (also **lemon-yellow**) **lemon squash** = a drink made from lemon juice and sugar, which is mixed with water

le•mur /li:məʳ/ noun, c. = a small animal that looks like a monkey and is active only at night, found in Madagascar (an island to the right of central Africa)

lend /lend/ verb, t. (**lent**) **1** *Can you lend me your pen? I will return it to you at the end of the day.* = to give someone something or to allow someone to use something belonging to you for a period of time, on the understanding that it will be returned **2** *The bank lends money at an interest of 12 per cent.* = to give out money for a period of time in order to earn interest **3** *The presence of the detective lent some glamour to the party.* = to add some quality to something

to lend a hand = to help someone in doing something
to lend an ear = to listen patiently and sympathetically

length /leŋθ/ noun, u. or c. **1** *The length of this field is 200 metres.*(u.)= the measurement of something from one end to the other **2** *I am surprised at the length of your answer.*(u.) = the quality of being too long **3** *She spoke at length.*(u.) = using many words **4** *Tie up the parcel with a length of rope.*(c.) = a piece of **lengthen** verb, t. = to make something longer **lengthy** adj. *a lengthy report* = very long (derogatory)

le•ni•ent /ˈli:niənt/ adj. *The thief should have been sent to jail for at least five years, but as the judge was lenient, he sentenced the thief to only six months in prison.* = kind and not strict in punishing people

lens /lenz/ noun, c. (**lenses**) *The lens of my camera has become dirty.* = a piece of curved glass or plastic which can bend rays of light. (used in cameras, telescopes, spectacles etc.)

Lent /lənt/ noun = the period of 40 days before Easter, during which Christians usually fast and pray

len•til /ˈlentl/ noun, u. (usually plural **lentils**) = the dried seeds of plants belonging to the family of beans, used as food ('daal', eaten by people in India)

Le•o /ˈli:əʊ/ noun = the fifth sign of the zodiac, represented by a lion (see pic under **zodiac**)

leop•ard /ˈlepəd/ noun, c. = a large and fierce animal belonging to the cat family, which is yellow in colour with many black spots, found in parts of India and Africa

lep•re•chaun /ˈleprɪkɔ:n/ noun, c. = a fairy which looks like a short old man, common in old fairy tales from Ireland

lep•ro•sy /ˈleprəsi/ noun, u. = a disease in which the skin of human beings loses sensation and which affects their limbs, faces etc. **leper** noun, c. = a person suffering from leprosy

les•bi•an /ˈlezbiən/ noun, c. = a woman whose sexual partner is another woman

le•sion /ˈli:zən/ noun, c. = a wound or injury [MEDICINE]

less[1] /les/ det. or pron. **1** *I would like less sugar in my tea.*(det.) **2** *I can't eat so much rice. Could you please give me a little less?*(pron.) = a smaller amount; not so much **3** *You will find less cars on the road now than we had last year.*(det.) = a smaller number

less[2] adv. *He is less educated than his brothers.* = not as much as

less[3] prep. *The conductor returned Rs 10 to me less the bus fare of Rs 2.50.* = after subtracting (taking away) something **lessen** verb, t. *This medicine will lessen the pain.* = to make less **lesser** adj. *Though they sing together, Nitin is clearly the lesser singer of the two.* = not as good or important as someone else (not used with 'than')

les•son /ˈlesən/ noun, c. *The teacher is giving a language lesson.* = a period during which something is taught to someone, especially in a school classroom **to be taught a lesson** *I hope your defeat in the election has taught you a lesson.* = some piece of wisdom that one learns through experience **to teach someone a lesson** *They have been giving us a lot of trouble. We must teach them a lesson now.* = to make someone who has been making things difficult or unpleasant suffer, usually just enough to make them stop

lest /lest/ prep. *The little girl would not accept my help in climbing the ladder, lest I should call her a baby.* = in order that something should not happen (formal)

let[1] /let/ verb, t. (**let**) **1** *Please let him go home.* = to allow **2** *Let us (Let's) go to the cinema tonight.* = used to make a suggestion **3** *Let AB be a straight line, and let X be its middle point.* = used to make a supposition in mathematics **4** *We are letting (out) our house.* = to give on rent

let[2] noun, c. *That service was a let!* = a service in the game of tennis that must be re-played because the ball has hit the top of the net [SPORTS]

to let someone down = to disappoint someone **to let on** *The secretary wouldn't let on what happened at the meeting.* = to reveal; to let somebody know something (informal) **to let up** *If the storm lets up we can continue our trek.* = to cease; to stop (even for a short while) **to let oneself go** *I felt shy about having a stylish haircut. Then I let myself go and had one.* = to make a decision to do something that one would normally not feel free to do because others will talk (informal) **to let something ride** **1** = to decide not to react angrily etc. to something someone has said (informal) **2** = to decide not to act at once on a decision (informal) **to let someone have it** = to scold someone strongly (informal)

le•thal /'li:θəl/ adj. *a lethal blow* = something that can cause death (compare **fatal**)

leth•ar•gy /'leθədʒi/ noun, u. *The lethargy I feel is probably due to the heat.* = the state of being lazy and not wanting to work **lethargic** adj.

let•ter /'letəʳ/ noun, c. **1** = a written message sent through the post **2** *the letters of the alphabet* = a written or printed sign that represents a speech sound e.g. the letter 'b', as in 'ball' **letter-box** noun, c. = a box in which letters are dropped, so that they may be collected by a postman or by the person to whom the letters have been sent **letterhead** noun, c. = the name and address of the person who is sending a letter, printed at the top of a sheet of paper **letter of credit** (**LC**) = an official letter from a bank allowing someone to borrow money from another bank, specially in a foreign country

let•tuce /'letɪs/ noun, u. = a vegetable with large, soft green leaves which are usually eaten in salads

leu•co•cyte /'lu:kəsaɪt/ noun, c. = white blood corpuscles (the white cells in the blood which fight infection [MEDICINE]

leu•ke•mia (leukemia) /lu:'ki:miə/ noun, c. = a disease which causes the presence of too many white cells in the blood and not enough red cells, causing weakness [MEDICINE]

lev•el[1] /'levəl/ adj. **1** *The football field is perfectly level.* = having a flat surface, no part of which is higher than another part **2** *Our plane is level with the mountains.* = at the same height as **3** *I will try my level best to come.* = the very best that one can do (informal)

level[2] noun, c. **1** *The top of this mountain is 5,000 metres above sea-level.* = the surface of the sea, which is used as a reference for measuring the height of a place **2** *This house has been built on two levels.* = at different heights above the surface of the ground **3** *The uniform is worn by workers at all levels.* = in different positions

level[3] verb, t. *The mountain had to be levelled before the new road could be built across it.* = to make flat **level crossing** noun, c. = a place where a road crosses a railway track, with gates that can be raised or lowered **level-headed** adj. = calm and balanced

le•ver /'li:vəʳ/ noun, c. **1** = a simple machine used for lifting or moving heavy objects. It consists of a straight metal rod, which is fixed at a point, called the fulcrum. One end of the rod is pushed underneath the object to be lifted while the other end is pressed down **2** = a metal rod or handle which is connected to a machine and can be pushed down to make the machine start working

lev•i•tate /'levɪteɪt/ verb, i. = to rise and float in the air **levitation** /levɪ'teɪʃən/ noun = the action of levitating (floating in the air)

lev•i•ty /'levɪti/ noun, u. *This is a serious matter. I am surprised that you can treat it with such levity.* = lack of seriousness; light-heartedness (formal)

lev•y[1] /'levi/ verb, t. (**levied**) *The government will levy a tax on alcoholic drinks.* = to demand and collect taxes

levy[2] noun, c. (**levies**) *The government has imposed a levy on petrol.* = a tax or payment demanded by the government

lewd /lu:d/ adj. *People want the government to ban this film as it contains a number of lewd songs.* = vulgar and in bad taste; suggesting crude thoughts of sex

lex•i•con /'leksɪkən/ noun, u. or c. **1** (singular) *the lexicon of a language* = the total stock of words in a language **2** (c.) = a dictionary or list of words with their meanings **lexical** adj. *the lexical meaning* = having to do with words **lexicography** /leksɪ'kɔ:grəfi/ noun = the act of preparing a dictionary

li•a•bil•i•ty /laɪə'bɪlɪtɪ/ noun, u. or c. **1** *If a worker is injured while working, it is the company's liability.*(c.) = something for which one is legally responsible **2** *The company's liabilities are much greater than its assets.*(c.) = debts; money that has to be paid to various people **3** *Our family house in the village has become a liability.*(u.) = a burden (a load that one is forced to carry)

li•a•ble /'laɪəbəl/ adj. **1** *He is liable to laugh loudly when he is amused.* = likely to do something **2** *If you drive a car without a licence you are liable to be fined.* = likely to be punished

li•aise /li'eiz/ verb, i. *My job as the secretary is to liaise with all the employees of the company.* = to create and to keep up a working relationship with someone

li•ai•son /li'eɪzən/ noun, u. **1** *There is close liaison between the hospital staff and the health workers in the village.* = close working relationship between two people or two groups of people (sometimes derogatory) **2** = a sexual relationship between a man and a woman who are not married to each other

li•ar /'laɪə[r]/ noun, c. = a person who tells lies

li•bel /'laɪbəl/ noun, u. or c. (u.) *Rehan sued the magazine for libel.*(u.) // *a libel action suit*(c.)= something that is written or spoken falsely against someone and can damage that person's reputation

lib•e•ral[1] /'lɪbərəl/ adj. **1** *a liberal mind* = having respect for the ideas and feelings of others **2** *This university offers a liberal education.* = encouraging the development of the mind, but not necessarily useful for a profession **3** *There was a liberal supply of ice cream at the party.* = plentiful

liberal[2] noun, c. *He is known to be a liberal in politics.* = a person with a liberal mind who does not have extreme views **liberal arts** noun = subjects such as literature, history etc. which help the development of the mind and knowledge of the world (rather than technical skills and abilities) **liberalization (liberalisation)** /lɪbərəlaɪ'zeɪʃən/ noun *economic liberalization* = the act of making something more open and less controlled by the government

lib•e•rate /'lɪbəreɪt/ verb, t. = to free someone, usually from prison

lib•er•ty /'lɪbəti/ noun, u. or c. (**liberties**) **1** *We fought for liberty from foreign rule.* = freedom, specially of the mind **2** *He has given me liberty to speak.* = permission

to take liberties with someone = (generally of a man) to behave in a way which seems too friendly (and therefore crude) with someone, especially a woman

Libra /'li:brə/ noun = the seventh sign of the zodiac, represented by a pair of scales (see pic under **zodiac**)

li•bra•ry /'laɪbrəri/ noun, c. (**libraries**) = a place where many books are kept and are available for use by members of the public

li•cence /'laɪsəns/ noun, u. or c. **1** *driving licence*(c.) = an official paper or document giving someone permission to do something (e.g. drive a motor car) **2** *Freedom of speech should not turn into licence.*(u.) = too much freedom that can cause harm (derogatory)

license verb, t. *The government has licensed the sale of fruit-based drinks.* = to give someone a licence to do something (to allow or give permission for)

lick /lɪk/ verb, t. or i. **1** *The dog licked my face.*(t.) = to move the tongue across the surface of something **2** *The tiger licked up the water from the stream.*(t.) = to drink by using quick movements of the tongue (also **lap**) **3** *The other team played splendidly; we were licked.*(i.) = to lose, specially a game (informal)

to lick one's wounds = to suffer quietly after being defeated in something

lid /lɪd/ noun, c. *The cooking pan has a glass lid.* = a cover for a box, pot or an open container

to take the lid off something = to make something which is unpleasant and should be kept secret, known to everyone

lie[1] /laɪ/ verb, i. **1** (past tense **lied**) *She lied to you when she told you she was a doctor. She is actually a school teacher.* = to make an untrue statement **2** (**lay, lain**) *He was lying on the ground.* = to be in a flat position, spread out on a flat surface **3** *You should lie down and take rest.* = to place one's body in a flat position **4** *The city lay in ruins after the earthquake.* = to be in a certain condition (as described) **5** *The school lies ahead.* = to be in a certain place or position

lie[2] /laɪ/ noun, c. *He told you a lie when he said he had cycled 50 km.* = an untrue statement or a falsehood **lie detector** noun, c. = an instrument that can show whether a person is lying or telling the truth

to lie around *When there is so much work to be done, don't lie around doing nothing.* = to be doing nothing **to lie low** = to try not to be noticed **to lie in wait for someone** = to wait in a place where one cannot be seen, in order to surprise and attack someone **to not take something lying down** *They insulted me and I am not going to take it lying down.* = to decide to take revenge because you have been insulted, hurt etc.

lieu (in lieu of) /lju:/ noun, u. *In lieu of the help I gave her, she offered to look after my baby.* = in place of; in exchange for

lieu•ten•ant /lef'tenənt/ noun, c. = an officer in the army or navy who has a junior rank (below the rank of captain)

life /laɪf/ noun, u. or c. (**lives**) **1** *A plant has life but a stone is lifeless.*(u.) = the energy present in a living

L

plant or animal that makes it grow, produce offspring (young ones) etc. **2** *Scientists think there may be life on the planet Mars.*(u.) = forms of matter in which life (meaning **1**) is present **3** *Life is not all work. There should be place for enjoyment too.*(u.) = the quality of human existence **4** *A soldier must be prepared to sacrifice his life for his country.*(c.) = the state of being alive **5** *My grandfather had a long life. He died at the age of 93.*(c.) = the period between birth and death **6** *On a Sunday, you will find no sign of life in this place.*(u.) = activity, movement **lifebelt** noun, c. = a ring made of some material that will float, found on a ship or boat, which a person can wear around the body to prevent him/her from sinking (see also **life jacket** under **jacket**) **lifeboat** noun, c. = a small boat carried on a ship to help passengers to escape in case the ship sinks **life-cycle** noun, c. = the changes or developments that a living thing goes through in the course of its life (e.g. from the egg of an insect to the fully-grown animal) **life history (life story)** noun = the story and details of somebody's life **life insurance** noun = money paid to a company regularly so that if (and when) one dies, the company pays a large amount of money to one's relatives (see also **insurance**) **life jacket** (see under **jacket**) **life-like** = looking real **lifeline** noun **1** = a rope used to save somebody from drowning **2** *My work is my lifeline.* = anything that is very important for life or being alive (figurative) **lifelong** = forever; for as long as one lives **life sentence** noun = the punishment of staying in prison for 14 years **lifesize** adj. *lifesize statue* = the same size as the original **lifespan** noun, u. = the period of time for which a human being, animal or plant can expect to remain alive **lifestyle** noun, c. = the manner in which one lives

full of life = lively; enjoying life **to take someone's life** = to kill someone

lift[1] /lɪft/ verb, t. or i. **1** *This suitcase is very heavy. You won't be able to lift it.*(t.) = to raise; to carry something from a lower to a higher level **2** *The government should lift the ban on foreign films.*(t.) = to remove or take away **3** *The fog has lifted.*(i.) = to rise or move up

lift[2] noun, c. **1** *You can use the lift to go to the fifth floor.* = a machine in a building which carries people up or down, from one floor to another (**elevator** in American English) **2** *I can give you a lift in my car.* = a free ride in a vehicle **3** *As the air rushes past the wings of a flying aircraft, it produces lift.* = a force that carries something upwards [PHYSICS] **4** *My new hairstyle has given me a lift.* = a good feeling (informal) **lift-off** noun, u. = the beginning of the flight of a spacecraft (a vehicle that can carry a person through space)

lig•a•ment /ˈlɪgəmənt/ noun, c. = a band of tissue that joins bones to each other or to muscles

lig•a•ture /ˈlɪgətʃə/ noun, c. = a kind of thread used by a surgeon during an operation to tie-up a blood vessel and prevent loss of blood [MEDICINE]

light[1] /laɪt/ noun, u. or c. **1** *I can't read the book as there is not enough light.*(u.) = the form of energy that allows one to see **2** *Switch on the light.*(c.) = a lamp that uses oil or electrical energy to produce light **3** *I thought she was an unhelpful person but after she helped her grandmother cross the road, I began to see her in a better light.*(c.) = the way in which one sees or thinks of someone or something **4** *Some new facts about this case have come to light.*(u.) = the condition of becoming known

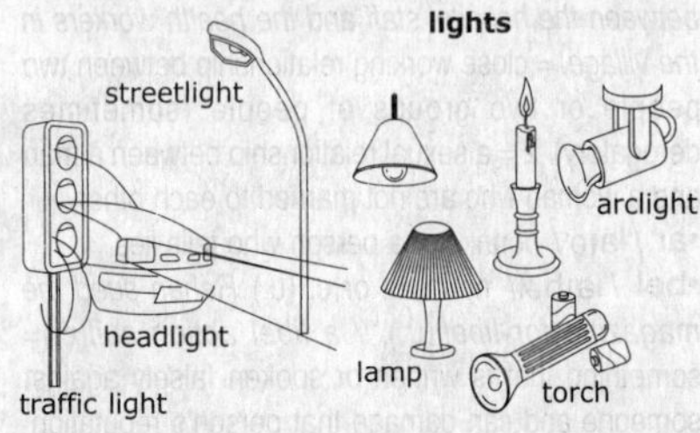

light[2] verb, t. (**lit** or **lighted**) **1** *We must light a fire. It's very cold in this room.* = to cause something start burning **2** *Please light the candle.* = to cause something to give out light **3** *The house is lit by two powerful lights.* = to give light to

light[3] adj. **1** *She wears clothes of a light colour.* = not dark **2** *The suitcase is very light. It must be empty.* = not heavy **3** *Give me some magazines for light reading.* = not serious **4** *The patient should be given only light food.* = easy to digest **light-house** noun, c. = a tower built near the sea, with a powerful light on top to guide ships **light year** noun, c. = 9.46×10^{12} km, the distance through which light can travel in one year (a unit for measuring the distance of a star from the earth or another star) [PHYSICS] **lighten** verb, t. = to make something lighter

the light at the end of the tunnel = something that offers hope, after a long period of disappointment or difficulty **to make light of** = not to take something very seriously or to do something very easily **to throw light on** = to explain; to make clear **in a lighter note** *We have been talking about Professor Shreshta's achievements. On a lighter note, let me tell you a story about him.* = a phrase used to suggest that one has been talking on serious matters and is now going to talk about something humorous

light•ning /ˈlaɪtnɪŋ/ noun, u. = a powerful flash of light in the sky caused by electrical energy passing from one cloud to another or from a cloud to the earth

lig•nite /lɪgnaɪt/ noun, u. = a kind of soft coal

like[1] /laɪk/ verb, t. **1** *I like reading books.* = to be fond of or to love someone or something **2** *I would like (to have) a cup of tea.* = to want **3** *I would like to go to Australia this summer.* = to wish to do something

like[2] prep. **1** *His house is just like mine.* = similar to (having the same quality as) **2** *He jumps like a kangaroo.* = in the same manner as **3** *To make a puppet we can use everyday materials like string, cardboard, nails etc.* = for example

like[3] noun, c. **1** *We will never see his like as a musician in a thousand years.* = someone who can be compared to **2** (always plural) *I don't think we should listen to the likes of him.* = someone like him (used only when the person referred to is not liked or respected)

like[4] adj. *She and I have like minds.* = of the same kind **likely** adj. *It is likely that he will come today as it is sunny.* = probable (something that can be expected) **likelihood** noun, u. *Do you see the dark clouds in the sky? There is a strong likelihood of rain.* = probability (a strong possibility that something will happen) **like-minded** adj. = having the same ideas **likeness** noun, u. *His brother and he have a family likeness.* = resemblance (quality of looking like each other) **likewise** adv. *She gave away all her books when the examination was over and advised me to do likewise.* = to do the same thing **liking** noun, u. *He has a great liking for sweets.* = fondness

li•lac[1] /'laɪlək/ noun, c. = a kind of sweet-smelling flower which is light purple in colour

lilac[2] adj. *a lilac dress* = having the light purple colour of a lilac flower

lilt /lɪlt/ noun, u. *The song has a pleasant lilt.* = a musical pattern of rising and falling sound **lilting** adj. *a lilting tune* = having a lilt

lil•y /'lɪli/ noun, c. (**lilies**) = a plant with large flowers of different colours (red, white, pink etc.)

limb /lɪm/ noun, c. **1** = a leg or arm (of a human being or animal) **2** = the branch of a tree

lim•ber[1] /'lɪmbəʳ/ verb, i. *The runners are limbering up before the start of the race.* = to stretch and loosen up the muscles of the body before a race etc.

limber[2] adj. *the limber body of the dancer* = supple (moving and bending easily)

lim•bo /'lɪmbəʊ/ noun, u. **1** = a place which is neither one of happiness (like heaven) nor a place of sorrow (like hell), in the existence of which some religious groups believe **2** *He is in limbo now, waiting for the results of the examination to be published.* = a state of uncertainty

lime /laɪm/ noun, u. or c. **1** (c.) = a kind of fruit which produces sour juice, like a lemon **2** (u.) = calcium carbonate (a white substance, which is a mixture of calcium, carbon and oxygen, and is used for giving a white colour to houses) **limestone** noun, u. = a kind of rock containing calcium, which has important industrial uses

limelight /'laɪmlaɪt/ noun, u. **1** = a very bright light produced by heating lime in a flame, which was used in the old days to light up a stage when a play was being performed **2** *Although she is a wellknown dancer, she does not enjoy being in the limelight.* = the centre of public attention (figurative)

lim•e•rick /'lɪmərɪk/ noun, c. = a humorous poem which has five lines

lim•it[1] /'lɪmɪt/ noun, c. **1** *This fence marks the northern limit of my property.* = the farthest point or boundary **2** *You cannot be selected for this trek if you are more than 65 years old. There is an age limit.* = the greatest or smallest amount or number that is allowed

limit[2] verb, t. *We will limit the number of guests invited to this party to 50.* = to keep within a certain size, number etc. **limitation** /lɪmɪ'teɪʃən/ noun, u. or c. *This cassette player has a limitation. It does not work on battery cells.*(c.) = a disadvantage; something that one cannot do

limited adj. **1** *limited powers* = having limits **2** *For a limited peiod, our computers will be sold for a discount.* = not very long (period of time) **3** *I'd like to help but am limited by the fact that I'm not too well myself.* = to be prevented from doing something (because of a problem) **limited company** (**Ltd.**) noun, c. = a business company which is required by law to pay back all debts, but only to the limit of the money owned by the company

lim•ou•sine /'lɪməziːn/ noun, c. = a very big and comfortable motor car (sometimes abbreviated to 'limo')

limp[1] /lɪmp/ verb, i. *He is limping because he has hurt his leg.* = to walk unevenly, with difficulty

limp[2] noun, u. *She walks with a limp.* = slow and painful movement

limp[3] adj. *Your shirt looks rather limp. You should use some starch.* = weak; without stiffness (opposite **crisp**)

lim•pet /'lɪmpɪt/ noun, c. = a small sea-animal that clings (holds on tightly) to the rock where it lives, under the water

lim•pid /'lɪmpɪd/ adj. *The water of this stream is so limpid that you can see the rocks lying on the bottom.* = clear and transparent

line[1] /laɪn/ noun, c. **1** *Draw a line five centimetres in length.* = a long, narrow mark drawn on a surface **2** *Your essay should not be more than ten lines in length.* = a row of words on a printed page **3** *I want all* *of you to stand in line.* = a row (side by side or one behind the other) **4** *Please put out the clothes on the line to dry.* = a piece of rope or string, generally used to dry clothes (also **clothes-line**) **5** *Sorry, I can't hear you clearly. There must be something wrong with the line.* = a telephone wire or connection **6** *Ustad Amjad Ali Khan comes from a long line of musicians.* = the members of a family who follow each other in time **7** *All railway lines are closed for repairs.* = a railway track **8** (generally singular) *He's in the medical line.* = profession **9** *Her talk was along religious lines.* = (always plural) dealing with a certain subject **10** *online* = connected through the Internet with another computer (opposite **offline**)

line[2] verb, t. **1** *A child cannot write on a sheet of paper unless it has been lined.* = to draw lines on something **2** *The crowds lined both sides of the street as the Prime Minister drove past in his car.* = to form a line or row **3** *Ask the tailor to line this cloth with silk material.* = to cover the inner surface of something with some material (see **lining**) **linear** /ˈlɪniəʳ/ adj. *In English, the arrangement of letters in a word is linear.* = coming one after the other and forming a line **linesman** noun, c. (**linesmen**) (also **linesperson**) = a person whose duty is to stay near the boundary line (in the game of tennis, football or hockey) and help the referee or umpire to decide if the ball has gone out of play and who hit it out of play

along these/those lines *Her phone message was not very clear but it was something along these lines—.* = used when offering a general idea of something, the details, of which are not known or understood **to fall into line** *She's very new to the job and does not know it well. She'll soon fall into line, I expect.* = to start doing the things that a company or organization expects you to do **somewhere along the line** *Samir started the essay with great energy, but somewhere along the line he lost interest.* = while doing something

lin•en /ˈlɪnɪn/ noun, u. **1** = soft cloth made from a special kind of fibre **2** *table/bed linen* = cloth used to cover a table or a bed

liner /ˈlaɪnəʳ/ noun, c. *an ocean liner/airliner* = a large ship or aircraft used by a company to carry passengers

lin•ger /ˈlɪŋgəʳ/ verb, i. **1** *It's time for us to go to the theatre. Don't linger, or we'll be late.* = to remain in some place instead of going; to delay the action of going **2** *I can't forget the wonderful party we had on your birthday. The memory of that party still lingers.* = to stay on (instead of disappearing)

lin•ge•rie /ˈlænʒəriː/ noun, u. = underclothes used by women

lin•go /ˈlɪŋgəʊ/ noun, u. *I am sorry, but I don't speak your lingo.* = language (slang)

lin•guis•tics /lɪŋˈgwɪstɪks/ noun, u. = the study of the development, grammar etc. of a single language or all languages **linguistic** adj. *linguistic development* = having to do with language **linguist** noun, c. **1** = a person who studies linguistics **2** = a person who is good with languages

lingua franca /lɪŋgwə ˈfræŋkə/ noun, c. *Hindi serves as a lingua franca in many parts of this country.* = a language which joins people (a language used for communication between people who ordinarily speak different languages)

lining /ˈlaɪnɪŋ/ noun, c. *The woollen coat has a silk lining.* = material that is used to cover the inner surface of a dress

link[1] /lɪŋk/ verb, t. *This road links Delhi to Agra.* = to join together or connect

link[2] noun, c. **1** *All telephone links between Nellore and its neighbouring cities have been cut off because of the storm.* = something which connects **2** *One of the links in this chain has rusted.* = a single ring in a chain **linkage** noun, u. *There is no linkage between the sentences in this paragraph.* = connection between things

li•no•le•um /lɪˈnəʊliəm/ noun, u. = a stiff material used for covering floors

lin•seed /ˈlɪnsiːd/ noun, u. = the seed of a kind of plant, from which linseed oil is produced. (Linseed oil is mixed with paint to make it thinner, so that it can be spread more easily.)

lint /lɪnt/ noun, u. **1** = soft cotton cloth used to cover and protect wounds **2** = fibres from cloth which stick to other clothes, while washing etc.

lin•tel /ˈlɪntl/ noun, c. = a piece of stone or concrete above a door or window

lion /ˈlaɪən/ noun, c. = a large wild animal belonging to the cat family, sometimes called the 'king of beasts (animals)' **lionize (lionise)** verb, t. *The students lionize their English teacher, Mr Prahlad.* = to give special respect and love to someone

lip /lɪp/ noun, c. or u. **1** *He has thick lips.*(c.) = one of the two edges of the mouth, where the skin is of a slightly different colour **2** *Don't give me any of your lip or you will be sorry!*(u.) = rude or insulting talk (informal) **lip-reading** noun = the action of watching the movements made by someone's lips while speaking, so as to guess what the person is saying (often used by people who are not able to hear) **lip-service** noun, u. *She does not agree with her supervisor on many issues but pays him lip-service.* = to appear to like or support someone without actually liking or supporting him/her (disapproving) **lipstick** noun, u. or c. = a piece of soft wax-like substance, shaped like a small stick, used to colour the lips

liq•ueur /lɪˈkjʊəʳ/ noun, u. or c. = a kind of sweet alcoholic drink that is taken in a small quantity, specially after a meal

liq•uid[1] /ˈlɪkwɪd/ noun, c. or u. *Water is a colourless liquid.*(c.) = a substance which is neither solid nor a gas, can be seen and has no fixed shape

liquid[2] adj. *The patient can only have liquid food.* = in the form of liquid **liquid assets** noun *She owns a lot of property but she has no liquid assets.* = the things that one possesses in the form of money or something which can easily be changed into money **liquidize (liquidise)** verb, t. = to change something solid (specially fruits and vegetables) into liquid form **liquidizer** noun, c. = a machine that can crush fruits and vegetables into liquid form **liquidate** verb, t. **1** = to kill or destroy **2** *The company lost so much money that it had to be liquidated.* = to close down a business which is losing money **liquidation** noun

liq•uor /ˈlɪkəʳ/ noun, u. = a strong alcoholic drink, e.g. whisky or rum

lir•a /ˈlɪərə/ noun, c. (**liras** or **lire** /lireɪ/) = the unit of money used in Italy

lisp[1] /lɪsp/ verb, i. *The child lisps and cannot speak clearly.* = to speak in a manner that cannot be clearly understood, because of difficulty in producing certain sounds

lisp[2] noun, u. *He speaks with a lisp.* = the habit or action of lisping

lis•som (lissome) /ˈlɪsəm/ adj. *The dancer has a lissom body.* = graceful in movement and without much fat (used to describe the body of a woman)

list[1] /lɪst/ noun, c. *a long shopping list.* = a number of names (of people or things) written one below the other

list[2] verb, t. *Please list the names of the boys who are going on the picnic tomorrow.* = to make a list of things or people

lis•ten /ˈlɪsən/ verb, i. *I enjoy listening to new film songs.* = to hear something with attention **listener** noun, c. *She is a good listener.* = a person who listens to someone who is speaking

list•less /ˈlɪstləs/ adj. *The students are feeling listless because of the heat.* = without energy or interest in doing something (see also **lethargy, languor**)

lit•e•rate /ˈlɪtərɪt/ adj. *All the women in this village are literate.* = able to read and write (opposite **illiterate**) **literacy** noun, u. *The level of literacy in this part of the country is quite high.* = the state of being literate

lit•e•ral /ˈlɪtərəl/ adj. **1** *She is not tall in the literal sense, but she stands out in the class because of her personality.* = the surface meaning that a word or expression has, without considering any additional or hidden meanings (opposite **figurative**) **2** *This is a literal translation in English of a Hindi poem.* = word for word, not related to deep meanings **literally** adv. **1** *These people are literally starving. They have had no food for almost two days.* = in fact or in reality; taking a word in its literal (factual) meaning **2** *The classroom is literally flooded with paper airplanes.* = in effect, although not in reality (used to give extra force to a colourful expression) (informal)

lit•e•ra•ture /ˈlɪtərətʃəʳ/ noun, u. or c. **1** (u.) = written books which have high artistic value **2** *He is studying American literature.*(c.) – the study of the great books produced in a country or during a period of time **3** *The literature on the treatment of cancer is vast.*(u.) = the books, articles etc. on a given subject **literary** adj. *She speaks in a highly literary style.* = belonging to literature and not the everyday use of language

lithe /laɪð/ adj. *A runner should have a lithe body.* = supple (able to bend or move easily)

lithium /ˈlɪθiəm/ noun, u. = a very light metallic element, used for making batteries, aluminium etc.

lit•i•ga•tion /lɪtɪˈgeɪʃən/ noun, u. = the process by which a case is settled (decided) in a court of law **litigate** /ˈlɪtɪgeɪt/ verb, i. = to take some matter to a law court for a decision [LAW]

lit•mus /ˈlɪtməs/ noun, u. = a substance which turns pink when it touches acid and blue when it touches alkali [CHEMISTRY]

li•tre /ˈliːtəʳ/ noun, c. (American **liter**) = a unit for measuring volume (the amount of liquid present in a container), equal to 1000 ccs

lit•ter[1] /ˈlɪtəʳ/ noun, u. or c. **1** *After we have eaten our lunch, let us clean up the litter and throw it into the garbage bin.* = waste material that has been thrown away carelessly **2** *a litter of kittens* = young animals that are born to a mother at the same time

litter[2] verb, t. **1** *Don't litter the streets.* = to throw or scatter litter (waste material) **2** *The book is littered with printing mistakes.* = to be full of or covered with (figurative)

lit•tle[1] /ˈlɪtl/ det. **1** *He has little time for friends now.* = not much **2** *You can come and talk to me about your problems. I have a little time now.* = some

little[2] adj. **1** *I have a little house in the village.* = small in a way that can be liked **2** *They had a nice little fight. // a sweet little kiss // poor little Maya* = 'Little' is used to show that one is making fun of something or does not like the situation ('a nice little fight') or that one likes it ('a sweet little kiss') or that one feels sorry for someone in a superior way ('poor little Maya')

little[3] adv. **1** *Can you give me some rice. I want just a little.* = a small amount **2** *His new film is little more* *than a mixture of all the other films he has made.* = not much more than **3** *I write to her very little now.* = not often

lit•to•ral /ˈlɪtərəl/ adj. = an area of land lying next to the sea [GEOGRAPHY]

live[1] /lɪv/ verb, i. **1** *My parents live in a village.* = to have one's home in **2** *No humans can live for long periods in Antarctica because of the cold.* = to have life; to survive **3** *to live an exciting life* = to spend one's time in a certain way

live[2] /laɪv/ adj. *You can see a live rhinoceros in the zoo.* = something that has life; alive

live[3] adv. *This interview with the football coach is being televised live.* = seen and heard on television at the same time as it is happening (not recorded) **lively** /laɪvli/ adj. *a lively dance // a lively speech* = full of life (energy and movement); interesting **livelihood** /ˈlaɪvlihʊd/ noun, u. *He earns his livelihood by writing songs.* = the way in which one earns money

to live and let live = to allow others to do what they want to do **to live on something** *We lived on bread and jam for a week.* = to survive using something **to live up to** *I am finding it difficult to live up to my sister's reputation as a sportsperson.* = to match; to achieve **to live with** *Anand has to live with the fact that he is not as good a cook as his brother.* = to accept , though not happily **to live like a king** = to live a life of luxury

li•ver /ˈlɪvəʳ/ noun, u. or c. **1** (c.) = the large organ (working part) in the body that keeps the blood clean and produces bile **2** *fried chicken liver*(u.) = the liver from an animal's body, used as food

liv•e•ry /ˈlɪvəri/ noun, u. or c. (**liveries**) = the special uniform worn by people working in the service of a company or a person

livestock /ˈlaɪvstɒk/ noun, u. (only singular) = animals kept on a farm (cattle, sheep, goats etc.)

li•vid /ˈlɪvɪd/ adj. *livid with anger* = in a very angry state; furious

living[1] /ˈlɪvɪŋ/ adj. **1** *He is my only living relation.* = alive at the present time **2** *She is a living encyclopaedia of science.* = something that has life (used to express admiration or respect)

living[2] noun, u. *He earns his living by painting pictures.* = money needed for survival (to live on) **living room** noun, c. = the main room in a house where people generally receive guests (also **drawing room** or **sitting room**)

li•zard /ˈlɪzəd/ noun, c. = an animal belonging to a class of animals that have a rough or hard skin and four short legs and a tail, and lay eggs

lla•ma /ˈlɒmə/ noun, c. = an animal that looks like a camel and is found in South America

load[1] /ləʊd/ noun, c. **1** *The heavy load may be too much for this small car.* = something heavy that has to be carried from one place to another in a vehicle or by an animal or a human being **2** *She has a heavy teaching load this term.* = the amount of work that one is required to do **3** *This pillar is bearing the entire load of the roof.* = weight

load[2] verb, t. or i. **1** *We have to load the truck with potatoes.* = to put a load (something that has to be carried) into or on a vehicle **2** *Load the gun/camera.* = to put bullets into a gun in order to fire or to put a film into a camera in order to take photographs **3** *The program will take 20 minutes to load.*(i.) = to transfer a program from some source into the memory of a computer **4** *This is the second load in the washing machine.* = set of clothes to be washed **loaded** adj. **1** *a loaded camera/gun* = carrying a film, gun powder, bullets etc. **2** *a loaded train* = full of people **3** *They don't have to worry. They are loaded.* = very wealthy (informal) **4** *a loaded statement* = full of hidden and usually negative information or meaning **download** = to store information received, through the Internet in one's computer [COMPUTERS] **upload** = (the opposite of **download**) to transfer information, text etc. from a computer to a server, making it possible for it to be sent to another computer

loaf[1] /ləʊf/ noun, c. (**loaves**) *a loaf of bread* = a fairly large piece of bread which is baked in an oven and can be cut into smaller pieces (slices)

loaf[2] verb, i. *You are not supposed to loaf when all your friends are working.* = to waste time by doing no work (informal) **loafers** noun **1** = shoes that one can easily slip one's feet into and which do not need to be tied/buckled on **2** = a person who loafs

loam /ləʊm/ noun, u. = dark-coloured soil (earth) that contains a lot of humus (dead and rotten leaves from plants etc.) and is very good for farming, growing crops/plants

loan[1] /ləʊn/ noun, c. or u. **1** *She has taken a loan of Rs 20,000 from the bank.*(c.) = money which is lent out for a period of time and has to be repaid, generally with interest **2** *This bicycle is on loan from my neighbour.* = the act of lending or having something lent

loan[2] verb, t. **1** *The bank will loan you money to start your shop.* = to give money on loan **2** *My friend has loaned me his car.* = to allow someone to use something for a period of time **loan word** noun, c. *Although 'station' is originally an English word, it has become a loan word in Hindi.* = a word that is taken from one language into another

loath /ləʊð/ adj. *He was very loath to allow me to use his car.* = reluctant; unwilling to do something (formal)

loathe /ləʊθ/ verb, t. *I loathe her habit of leaving the* *wet towel on the floor.* = to hate or dislike someone or something strongly **loathing** noun, u. *His rudeness filled me with loathing* = a strong feeling of dislike **loathsome** adj. = something that causes loathing

lob[1] /lɒb/ verb, t. (**lobbed**) *He lobbed the ball high over my head into the far end of the court. // He lobbed the ball into the goal.* = to hit the ball in a slow, high curve (in the game of tennis or football)

lob[2] noun, c. *I was unable to return the lob.* = a ball that has been lobbed (in tennis)

lob•by[1] /'lɒbi/ noun, c. (**lobbies**) **1** *The guests are waiting in the hotel lobby.* = a wide hall or passage leading inside from the entrance (in a hotel, cinema etc.) **2** *The government is under pressure from the farmers' lobby to increase the price of foodgrains.* = a group of people who represent a certain interest (e.g. farming, industry, trade etc.) and who try to influence the policy of the government so that it will help them

lobby[2] verb, i. *Your party should lobby for higher government spending on primary education.* = to try to influence people in power so that they will support one's interests (informal)

lobe /ləʊb/ noun, c. **1** *the ear lobes* = the soft fleshy parts at the bottom of each ear **2** *the lobes of the brain/lungs* = the rounded parts into which an organ of the body is divided [TECHNICAL]

lob•ster /'lɒbstəʳ/ noun, c. or u. **1** (c.) = a sea-animal with two claws, eight legs and a hard shell **2** (u.) = the meat of the lobster, used as food

lo•cal[1] /'ləʊkəl/ adj. **1** *We took the patient to the local hospital as there was no time to take him to the big hospital in the city, 50 km away.* = belonging to the place where one lives **2** *The operation was done under local anaesthesia.* = something that affects only one part of the body and not the whole of it

local[2] noun, c. *He is a local.* = a person who belongs to an area and has not come from some place outside (informal) **locality** /ləʊ'kælɪti/ noun, u. or c. (**localities**) *There is no telephone booth in this locality.*(u.) = a particular area, usually small, that one is talking about **localize** /'ləʊkəlaɪz/ verb, t. *There was a danger that cholera would spread from this village to the entire district, but the doctors have been able to localize the disease.* = to keep something undesirable limited to a small area

locale /ləʊ'kɑːl/ noun, c. *a scenic locale* = a place where something special happens, such as the action in a book or film

lo•cate /ləʊ'keɪt/ verb, t. **1** *The new cement factory will be located in Dhenkanal.* = to set up something in a certain place **2** *I put my keys somewhere in this room, but I cannot locate them now.* = to find the position of something **location** noun, u. or c. **1** *We are looking for a suitable location for our new restaurant.*(c.) = place **2** *This new film about Hyderabad will be shot on location.*(u.) = the actual place where some event is supposed to take place

loch /lɒk/ noun, c. = a lake (in the language of Scotland) or part of a sea located near land

lock[1] /lɒk/ noun, c. *I put a lock on the suitcase so it would not open accidentally.* = a simple device (machine) used to keep a door, cupboard etc. closed, and which can be opened with a key

lock[2] verb, t. *Please lock the door/box.* = to close a door or the lid of a box etc. by using a lock so that it can only be opened with the help of a key **locker** noun, c. = a small cupboard fitted with a lock, in which things can be kept safely **lock-out** noun, c. *There is a lock-out in the factory. All the workers have gone home.* = the closing of a factory by its owner to force workers to stop work **locksmith** noun, c. = a person who makes or repairs locks and keys **lock-up** noun = a small prison

lock•et /'lɒkɪt/ noun, c. = a small piece of jewellery which can be fixed to a chain worn around the neck

lo•co•mo•tive /ləʊkə'məʊtɪv/ noun, c. = a railway engine which pulls trains

lo•cust /'ləʊkəst/ noun, c. = an insect which flies in large swarms (groups) and attacks and destroys crops in fields

lodestone /'ləʊdstəʊn/ noun, c. = a piece of stone which contains iron and has the qualities of a magnet **lodestar** = the pole star, used to help find direction

lodge[1] /lɒdʒ/ verb, i. or t. **1** *My son is lodging with some friends.*(i.) = to stay in a place for a short time by paying rent **2** *The woman next door lodges students.*(t.) = to provide someone with a place to stay in for a short time **3** *The bullet that was fired at him lodged in his chest.*(i.) = to become fixed in some position **4** *I want to lodge a complaint against the manager of this hotel.*(t.) = to make an official statement or complaint (formal, legal)

lodge[2] noun, c. **1** *I have a room in a lodge.* = a place where rooms are available on rent for a short time **2** *a hunting lodge* = a small building which is used only occasionally **lodger** noun, c. = a person who pays rent to stay in some place

loft[1] /lɒft/ noun, c. *This room has a loft where you can store your belongings.* = a space above the ceiling of a room where things can be stored

loft[2] verb, t. *The batsman lofted the ball over the square*

L

leg boundary. = to hit a ball high into the air, especially in the game of cricket

lof•ty /ˈlɒfti/ adj. **1** = high or tall **2** *lofty ideals* = of very high moral quality; noble

log[1] /lɒg/ noun, c. **1** *a log of wood* = a part or whole of the trunk or branch of a tree which has been cut down **2** *The driver of the truck has to enter the details of each journey in his log.* = a written record of the journeys made by a vehicle (car, ship or aircraft)

log[2] verb, t. (**logged**) **1** *This old bus has logged more than 300,000 kms.* = to travel a certain distance, which is recorded in writing **2** *This forest has been so heavily logged that there are no trees left.* = to cut down trees in a forest in order to get logs of wood **logbook** noun, c. = a book in which all the details of a car or other vehicle which is in use are recorded **log in/on** verb = to start using a computer system, especially to 'surf' the Internet **log out/off** verb = to end a period of using a computer system, especially the Internet

log•a•rith•m (log) /ˈlɒgərɪðəm/ noun *The logarithm of 100 in base 10 is 2.* = a number which shows how many times a number (called the base) has to be multiplied by itself to produce another number [MATHEMATICS]

log•ger•heads /ˈlɒgəhedz/ noun *My friend and I were at loggerheads, trying to decide which of us would serve first in a game of tennis.* = a state of serious disagreement (not being able to agree) about something

lo•gic /ˈlɒdʒɪk/ noun, u. **1** *He is a student of logic.* = the scientific study of the methods of reasoning (thinking) used by human beings **2** *The logic of her arguments was very clear.* = the manner of reasoning **3** *I don't see the logic of paving the space around the building. All the rain water will be wasted.* = a way of thinking which is based on good judgement **logical** adj. **1** *The scientist produced some very logical arguments to show that a car would not be able to travel at a speed greater than that of sound.* = well thought-out and argued, according to the rules of logic **2** *If you expect people to help you, you must be prepared to help them. This is only logical.* = reasonable (based on good reasoning)

lo•gis•tics /ləˈdʒɪstɪks/ noun, u. *We expect 50 guests for the wedding next week. We will have to find accommodation for them as well as provide food. It is going to be difficult to manage the logistics.* = the planning and organization necessary to do something difficult and complicated successfully

lo•go /ˈləʊgəʊ/ noun, c. (**logos**) = *The logo of the Chrysler Daimler-Benz company, which makes the famous Mercedes cars, is a star with three points inside a circle.* = trademark (a picture or sign that a business company puts on the things that it produces, and by which it is known)

loin /lɔɪn/ **1** (always plural, **loins**) = the part of the body below the stomach and above the legs **2** = the meat of an animal from the back and near the tail

loi•ter /ˈlɔɪtəʳ/ verb, i. *The police will arrest anyone who is found loitering near the school, between 10 a.m. and 4 p.m.* = to stand or wait in a public place, without a reason or purpose

loll /lɒl/ verb, i. *He was lolling in his easy chair in the garden, listening to the song of the birds.* = to lie or sit in a relaxed position

lol•li•pop /ˈlɒlipɒp/ noun, c. = a kind of sweet made of hardened sugar, which is fixed to a small, thin stick and is usually licked

lone /ləʊn/ adj. *The lone goal in the second half of the game helped France win the match.* = solitary; a single thing or person **lonely** adj. **1** *He lives all alone in a big house, with no one to talk to. He feels very lonely.* = unhappy because of being alone **2** *Her house is on a very lonely road. There is hardly any traffic.* = without people nearby **loner** noun, c. = a person who likes to live or work alone

long[1] /lɒŋ/ adj. **1** *Her long hair came down to her waist.* = having a large length, or larger than the average, from one end to the other **2** *You will have to walk a long way to reach the station. It is more than 8 km away. // We met after a very long time—more than 20 years!* = a great distance or period of time **3** *The room is 10 m long and 4 m broad.* = the measurement of an object from one end to another, at the point where this measurement is greatest

long[2] adv. *This meeting won't take long. // Anu couldn't stay long at the party; she had to leave by 8 p.m.* = a long time or for a long time

long[3] verb, i. *I long to see my mother again. I haven't seen her in seven years.* = to want something very strongly **longing** noun, c. *He has a longing for Indian sweets.* = a strong desire for something **long-drawn-out** adj. *a long-drawn-out argument* = elaborate and lasting for a long time **long-hand** noun, u. = writing done by hand, using a pen or pencil, and not using shortened forms, or done with the help of a typewriter or other machine (opposite **short-hand**) **long-lasting** adj. *a long-lasting quarrel* = which has been going on for a long time **long-lost** adj. *In the film the long-lost brothers met each other in the last scene.* = not having seen someone for a long time or someone who is lost **long-winded** adj. *He made a long-winded speech.* = going on too long and using too many words (derogatory) **longish** adj. *He wrote me a longish letter.* = fairly long but not too long (informal)

to go a long way *She is sincere about her work; she will definitely go a long way and will be successful in her career.* = to achieve; to succeed (approving) **before long** = after a short time **so long** = an expression that is used instead of 'goodbye' **long ago** = very far back in the past

lon•gev•i•ty /lɒnˈdʒevɪti/ noun, u. *If you visit Hunza Valley, which is in the north-western part of Pakistan, you will come across many people who are more than a 100 years old. Scientists are trying to discover the secret of their longevity.* = long life (formal)

lon•gi•tude /ˈlɒndʒɪtju:d/ noun, c. or u. = the position of a place on the surface of the earth, measured (in degrees) east or west of an imaginary line running through Greenwich in England (compare **latitude**)

loo /lu:/ noun, c. = toilet or lavatory (informal)

look[1] /lʊk/ verb, i. **1** *Look at this photograph. Can you recognize the boy in the picture? // He looked up and saw his daughter waving at him from the window.* = to use one's eyes in order to see something or to turn one's eyes in some direction in order to see something **2** *I am looking for the book I was reading last night.* = to search for something **3** *You look very angry. What's the matter?* = to seem or appear to be

look[2] noun, c. **1** *He took another look at the house.* = the action of using one's eyes in order to see **2** *a loving look // an angry look* = the expression of some feeling through the eyes or face **3** *This house has the look of a prison.* = appearance **looks** noun (always plural) *He has grown old, but he hasn't lost his looks.* = attractive apperance **look-alike** noun, c. *An Amitabh Bachchan look-alike presented a dance from one of his films.* = someone who looks very much like some famous person **Look out!** = a warning to somebody to be careful **looking-glass** noun, c. = mirror

to look after = to take care of **to look around** = to search for something **to look down on** = to have a low opinion about someone **to look forward to** *I look forward to your next visit.* = to expect with pleasure **to look into something** *I'm looking into the reasons for my students always coming late on Fridays.* = to examine, with a view to getting an answer **to look on** = to watch something happening without taking part in it **to look up** *Things are looking up now for the Indian team.* = to improve **to look up someone (to look someone up)** = to visit someone **to look up something (to look something up)** *Look this word up in the dictionary.* = to get information about something from a book **to look out for something** *Could you look out for a second-hand computer for me?* = to be alert; so that one can notice or find something quickly **to look through someone** = to pretend not to notice someone **to look as if** *She looks as if she is going to faint.* = to give the impression of something **to give someone a look** = to make it clear to someone that one is angry (informal) **If looks could kill (I'd be dead)** = an expression used to describe a very angry look given by someone (informal, often humorous)

loom[1] /lu:m/ noun, c. = a machine on which cloth is woven from threads

loom[2] verb, i. *A strange figure suddenly loomed out of the darkness.* = to be seen, but not very clearly, so as to appear large and frightening

loop[1] /lu:p/ noun, c. *Let me show you how to tie your shoelace. Take one end of the lace, form a loop, and then tie it up with the other end into a knot, which will not slip.* = a piece of string, wire or rope that has been bent into a curved or round shape, with the ends almost touching or crossing each other

loop[2] verb, i. **1** *Take this rope and loop it around the tree.* = to make a loop with a rope or string **2** *The river loops around the hill.* = to curve into the shape of a loop **loophole** noun, c. *The judge who was trying the criminals in court had to set them free because of some loophole in the law.* = a weakness or defect in a set of rules or laws which allows someone to escape punishment

loose /lu:s/ adj. **1** *One of the buttons on your shirt is loose. It may fall off.* = not firmly fixed in place **2** *The shirt you are wearing is very loose. It is too big for you.* = not fitting tightly **3** *Be careful. The dog is loose.* = not tied up or kept in a closed space and therefore free to run about **4** *This is a loose translation of a Hindi poem.* = not exact **5** *a loose character* = immoral **6** *loose stool/motions* = solid waste which, because of a bad stomach condition, has a lot of fluid matter in it **loose change** noun = coins that one carries in a purse, wallet etc. **loose-fitting** *loose-fitting clothes* = (of clothes) not tight and sticking to the body

loosen /ˈlu:sən/ verb, t. **1** *My belt is uncomfortably tight. I want to loosen it.* = to make something less tight **2** *The government has loosened its control on the press.* = to have less control

to be at a loose end = to have no fixed work to do **to let (an animal) loose** = to free an animal by disconnecting its collar from the chain **to tie up loose ends** *We have agreed on all the conditions for the sale of the house but still have to tie up some loose ends.* = to attend to smaller details after the major points have been taken care of in a legal matter

loot[1] /lu:t/ noun, u. *The robbers broke into the bank and took away Rs 50,000 in bank notes. The loot was divided among the members of the gang.* = something valuable, specially money, which has been stolen or obtained illegally

loot[2] verb, t. *The robbers looted the shop last night.* = to rob

lop /lɒp/ verb, t. (**lopped**) *The branches of the tree have been lopped off.* = to cut something off, especially the branches of a tree

lope /ləʊp/ verb, t. *The leopard loped away when our jeep went too close to the tree under which he was lying.* = to run easily, with long steps

lop-sided /lɒp'saɪdɪd/ adj. *Economic development in this country has been lop-sided. While industry has grown, agriculture has not progressed at all.* = not equally balanced; having one side heavier or bigger than the other (informal)

lo•qua•cious /ləʊ'kweɪʃəs/ adj. *He is such a loquacious person that it is difficult to make him stop talking.* = talkative (fond of talking a lot)

lord[1] /lɔːd/ noun, c. **1** = a man of noble or high birth in British society **2** *Lord* = a way of referring to God **3** *Lord Swraj Paul is visiting India.* = a title given by the King or Queen of England to someone, which is used as part of his name (see also **Lady**) **4** *The meeting of the media lords was postponed.* = a person who is powerful in a particular field

lord[2] verb, t. *She likes to lord it over her juniors.* = to behave in a proud and rude manner, giving orders to others

lore /lɔːʳ/ noun, u. *The knowledge of medicinal herbs which can cure many diseases is an important part of tribal lore.* = traditional knowledge which is not written down but is passed on from one generation to the next

lor•ry /'lɒri/ noun, c. (**lorries**) = a heavy truck

lose /luːz/ verb, t. (**lost**) **1** *I have lost my pen. I can't find it anywhere.* = to no longer possess (have) something because one does not know where it is or because it has been taken away **2** *Arun may lose the race.* = to fail to win **3** *He has lost weight.* = to have less of something **4** *He has lost his father.* = to no longer have as a result of death **5** *The children lost their way in the forest.* = to be unable to find one's way **6** *The clock is losing time.* = to work too slowly

loser /'luːzəʳ/ noun, c. **1** *The winner will get the trophy and the loser will get a gift cheque.* = a person who loses **2** = a person who is unsuccessful in life (derogatory)

to lose sleep = to worry about something **to lose track** *I have lost track of the story because I had to answer the telephone four times.* = to not know something fully **to lose one's heart** = to fall in love (informal) **to lose one's temper** = to become angry **to lose face** = to do something which makes people lose their respect for you (see also **face**)

loss /lɒss/ noun, u. or c. (**losses**) **1** *He reported the loss of his watch to the police.*(u.) = the fact of losing (no longer having) someone or something **2** *The company has suffered a loss of Rs 5 crore this year.*(c.)= a situation in which one spends more money than one earns

lost[1] /lɒst/ verb, t. or i. (also see **lose** above) = the past tense of **lose**

lost[2] adj. **1** *There is a notice in the newspaper about a lost child.* = someone or something that cannot be found by the parents, owner etc. **2** *We got lost in the forest.* = unable to find one's way **3** *The memory of the lost match will haunt the captain for years.* = something that was not won **lost property** noun = any article that has been found and is not claimed by the person who has lost it

Get lost! = a rude way of telling a person to go away **a lost cause** = an idea or belief that does not have much chance of succeeding **I am lost (I've lost you)** *Can you start the story again? I'm lost.* = to be confused and uncertain **to be lost for words** = to be unable to speak because one is very sad, happy, shocked etc. **to be lost to the world** = to be deeply asleep (informal) **He/she has lost it!** = has become mad or crazy (slang, not respectful)

lot[1] /lɒt/ det. (**lots**) **1** *He has a lot of (lots of) money.* = a large amount (when used with u. nouns) **2** *She has a lot of (lots of) friends.* = a large number (when used with c. nouns)

lot[2] noun, c. or u. **1** *How many mangoes do you have? I'll eat the lot.*(u.) = the whole quantity or number **2** *I am expecting another lot of guests tomorrow.*(c.) // *When is the next lot of cars coming in?*(c.) = a group or set of people or objects **3** *We will draw lots to decide the winner.*(c.) = a system of deciding something by chance (see also **lottery**)

lo•tion /'ləʊʃən/ noun, u. or c. = liquid medicine for the skin or hair

lot•te•ry /'lɒtəri/ noun, c. (**lotteries**) *He won the first prize in the lottery.* = a system in which numbered tickets are sold and prizes given to the winning tickets, which are chosen by chance

lo•tus /'ləʊtəs/ noun, c. = a large pink or white flower that grows in water **lotus-eater** noun, c. = a person who lives in his own dream world, away from the real world

loud /laʊd/ adj. **1** *a loud sound* = a sound that is strong and easily heard over a long distance **2** *a loud person* = one who tries to attract everyone's attention through his or her appearance, behaviour etc. **loud-mouth** noun = a person who talks too much and is disliked **loud-speaker** noun, c. = a kind of machine that makes sounds louder, so that they can be easily heard over a distance

lounge[1] /laʊndʒ/ noun, c. *The guests are waiting in the lounge.* = a room in a hotel or house where one can sit comfortably

lounge[2] verb, i. *He was lounging on the sofa.* = to sit or lie comfortably

louse /laʊs/ noun, c. (**lice**) = a small insect that lives on the skin or in the hair of human beings or animals **lousy** adj. *That was a lousy film we saw today.* = very bad (informal)

lout /laʊt/ noun, c. *You are behaving like a lout!* = a crude person

lou•vre /'lu:vəʳ/ noun, c. = a thin, sloping piece of metal, glass or plastic that is fixed in a frame covering a window, which can be raised or lowered to allow more or less light or air to come in

love[1] /lʌv/ verb, t. *We love our parents deeply. // I love travelling to new places.* = to have a strong feeling of fondness or liking for someone or something

love[2] noun, u. or c. **1** (u.) = the feeling of fondness for someone **2** *The young man has fallen in love.*(u.) = a feeling of fondness mixed with attraction for someone of the opposite sex **3** *She was the love of his life.*(c.) = a person who is loved by someone; something (e.g. rock-climbing) which one loves to do **4** *Gopichand is leading 8-love in this game.*(u.) = a score of no (zero) points in games like tennis, badminton **lovely** adv. *a lovely flower* = very beautiful/nice **lover** noun, c. = a person whom one loves and has sexual relations with **lovable** adj. *a lovable child* = something or someone which can easily be loved and which is pleasant **love-letter** noun, c. = a letter written by/ to the person one loves

to make love (to someone) = to have sex with someone **(not) for love or money** *I won't part with my favourite book for love or money!* = a way of saying that nothing will make one do something (informal)

low[1] /ləʊ/ adj. **1** *You can jump over this wall easily. It is quite low.* = not high above the ground or floor **2** *low profits* = small in value **3** *He spoke in a low voice.* = not loud **4** *She has a low opinion of your ability as a leader.* = not favourable **5** *How could you use such a low trick to win the race?* = dishonourable or dishonest

low[2] adv. *He sank low into the bath tub.* = into a low position

low[3] noun, c. *The price of gold reached an all-time low.* = a low level **lowly 1** (adj.) = of a low rank or position **2** *lowly paid job* (adv.) = of a small degree or level **low-brow** noun = a person who is not interested in books, art, literature etc. (derogatory) (opposite **high-brow**) **low-down** noun *The newspaper reporter gave us the low-down on the secret deal with a foreign country.* = correct and secret information about something (informal) **low down** adj. *They are such low down people, I don't want to be friends with them.* = having no good qualities **low-land** noun = an area of land that is lower than the surrounding area and is usually covered with water **low-pitched** adj. *a low-pitched voice* = deep (voice) **low profile** noun *keep a low profile* = the state of not drawing too much attention to oneself **low tide** noun = the time when the water is at a low level on the sea-shore (opposite **high tide**)

to lie low = to hide or be quiet at a time when someone wants to catch you or to involve you in something you don't want to be a part of **highs and lows** *'How do you like your job?' 'It's full of highs and lows.'* = good times as well as unpleasant times

low•er[1] /'ləʊəʳ/ adj. *He fell off a tree, but he was not hurt as he had fallen from one of the lower branches.* = not as high as something else

lower[2] verb, i. **1** *Mandeep had been carrying the suitcase on his head, but he lowered it to the ground as he approached his coach.* = to bring down to a lesser (smaller) height **2** *The sky is lowering. We are going to have a storm.* = to look dark and threatening (used to refer to the sky or the weather) **lower case** noun = letters of the alphabet written or printed in the usual small form and not in capitals (a, b, c etc. and not A, B, C) **Lower House** noun = one of the two divisions of the parliament that has more members and more power (e.g. the Lok Sabha, in the Indian parliament)

loy•al /'lɔɪəl/ adj. *The two friends remained loyal to each other even when their classmates tried to create a misunderstanding between them.* = faithful to one's friends, leader, country etc. **loyalty** noun, u. = the quality of being loyal

loz•enge /'lɒzɪndʒ/ noun, c. *cough lozenge* = a small sweet, often containing some medicine, that melts slowly in the mouth

L-plate noun = a board with the capital letter **L** that is hung on a vehicle to signal that the driver is learning to drive

LPG abbr. of **Liquid Petroleum Gas** = a gas used for burning as fuel in kitchen stoves, automobiles etc. and usually packed in metal cylinders

LSD noun = abbr. for *lysergic acid*, **diethylamide** a dangerous drug that can cause a person to hallucinate (imagine things that do not really exist) (see also **acid**)

Ltd. abbr. of **Limited** (usually for a business company) (see under **limit**)

lu•bri•cant /'lu:brɪkənt/ noun, u. or c. = an oily substance that is put into a machine (e.g. the engine of a car) to help the parts of the machine work more smoothly and easily **lubricate** verb, t. *You haven't lubricated the car for a long time.* = to put a lubricant into a machine to make it work more smoothly **lubrication** /lu:brɪ'keɪʃən/ noun, u. = the process of using a lubricant in a machine

lu•cid /'lu:sɪd/ adj. **1** *He writes in a lucid style.* =

L

clear and easy to understand **2** *His mind remains lucid, even though he is more than a 100 years old.* = able to understand clearly **lucidity** /luː'sɪdɪti/ noun, u. = the quality of being lucid (clear)

luck /lʌk/ noun, u. **1** *She won the quiz as much through luck as skill.* = fate; the force that makes either good or bad things happen by chance **2** *Keep this picture. It will bring you luck.* = good fortune (some force that brings success) **lucky** adj. *You are lucky to be studying in a good school.* = having good fortune or good luck

to be down on one's luck = to be unlucky/unfortunate

lu•cra•tive /'luːkrətɪv/ adj. *a lucrative job* = profitable; bringing in plenty of money

lu•di•crous /'luːdɪkrəs/ adj. *You look ludicrous in that red velvet coat, with all the gold lace on it.* = ridiculous; something that causes people to laugh at you

lug /lʌg/ verb, t. (**lugged**) *He lugged the heavy suitcase up the stairs.* = to lift or carry with difficulty (informal)

lug•gage /'lʌgɪdʒ/ noun, u. (only singular) *He is carrying a lot of luggage on this journey.* = the boxes, bags, suitcases etc. (full of clothes etc.) that one carries on a journey (also **baggage**)

luke•warm /luːk'wɔːm/ adj. **1** *Drink lukewarm water, not hot water.* = slightly warm **2** *When I asked him to join our club his response was rather lukewarm.* = not showing much interest

lull[1] /lʌl/ verb, t. *The soft music lulled the child to sleep.* = to cause sleep or rest in a gentle way

lull[2] noun, u. *There is a lull in the market. It will get busy after February.* = a short period when there is no activity and things are quiet **lullaby** noun, c. (**lullabies**) = a song that one sings to make a child sleep

lum•ba•go /lʌm'beɪgəʊ/ noun, u. = a kind of sickness that causes pain in the lower back

lum•bar /'lʌmbəʳ/ adj. *lumbar vertebra* = belonging to the lower part of the back [MEDICINE]

lum•ber[1] /'lʌmbəʳ/ noun, u. **1** *We have no place in the house to store the old, broken furniture and all the other lumber.* = useless and unwanted things **2** = timber (wood from trees, used for making furniture etc. or as firewood)

lumber[2] verb, i. *He lumbered slowly up the stairs, carrying a heavy suitcase.* = to move in a heavy, awkward manner **lumberjack** noun, c. = a person whose job is to cut down trees in the forest

lu•mi•nous /'luːmɪnəs/ adj. *You can see the road signs clearly at night because they are painted with luminous paint.* = able to shine in the dark

lump[1] /lʌmp/ noun, c. **1** *You should mix the flour thoroughly with water or it will form lumps.* = a mass of something solid, which has no particular shape **2** = a small growth or swelling on the body

lump[2] verb, t. *There is nothing you can do to improve things in this city. You will just have to lump it!* = to accept something unpleasant without complaining (informal)

lunacy /'luːnəsi/ noun, u. = a condition of madness (sickness of the mind), which people believed (in the old days) to be caused by the moon **lunatic** noun, c. **1** = a very foolish person **2** = a mad person (no longer used)

lu•nar /'luːnəʳ/ adj. *a lunar eclipse* = having to do with the moon

lunch[1] /lʌntʃ/ noun, c. or u. = a meal eaten in the middle of the day

lunch[2] verb, i. *He is lunching at the restaurant.* = to eat lunch **lunch-box** noun, c. (**lunch-boxes**) = a container in which lunch is packed **lunchtime/lunch hour** noun, u. = the time during which lunch is eaten

lung /lʌŋ/ noun, c. = one of two organs in the body, inside the chest, which are used in breathing

lunge[1] /lʌndʒ/ verb, i. *She lunged forward to catch the ball.* = to move forward suddenly, in order to attack or catch (in a game)

lunge[2] noun, c. *He made a sudden lunge at me.* = a sudden attacking movement

lurch[1] /lɜːtʃ/ verb, i. *The bullock cart lurched slowly down the road.* = to move with a slow, unsteady movement

lurch[2] noun, u. *The cart gave a sudden lurch.* = a lurching movement

to leave someone in the lurch = to not help someone at a time of difficulty

lure[1] /lʊəʳ/ verb, t. *He was lured to Mumbai in the hope of becoming a film star.* = to attract by making a promise, which is usually false

lure[2] noun, u. *the lure of money* = attraction (usually of a dangerous kind)

lu•rid /'lʊərɪd/ adj. **1** *The house was painted in lurid colours.* = very bright and colourful, but not in an attractive manner **2** *The newspaper contains all the lurid details of the murder.* = shocking, having unpleasant details

lurk /lɜːk/ verb, i. *lurking in the shadows* = to wait quietly and secretly, specially before attacking or doing something violent

lus•cious /ˈlʌʃəs/ adj. *There are luscious mangoes growing on the trees, waiting to be plucked and eaten.* = full of juice and having a sweet taste

lush /lʌʃ/ adj. **1** *The fields look green and lush during the rainy season.* = covered thickly with grass or other small plants **2** *a lush dress* = looking very expensive and luxurious

lust[1] /lʌst/ noun, u. or c. **1** (u.) = very strong, uncontrolled sexual desire **2** *the lust for power*(u.) = very strong desire for something

lust[2] verb, i. *He lusts after power.* = to desire very strongly **lustful** adj. = full of lust (strong desire)

lus•tre /ˈlʌstəʳ/ noun, u. **1** *the lustre of diamonds* = very bright shine **2** = honour or glory

lus•ty /ˈlʌsti/ adj. *a lusty shout* = full of life and energy (not to be confused with **lustful**)

lux•u•ri•ant /lʌgˈzjʊəriənt/ adj. *There is luxuriant grass growing in these fields.* = growing healthily and in great amounts (not to be confused with **luxurious**)

luxury /ˈlʌkʃəri/ noun, u. or c. (**luxuries**) **1** (u.) = very great comfort **2** *Going to the cinema is a luxury which I cannot afford.*(c.) = something that is very pleasant but not necessary **luxurious** /lʌgˈzjʊəriəs/ adj. *a luxurious hotel* = very comfortable and expensive

lymph /lɪmf/ noun, u. = clear watery liquid present inside the body which is a part of the bloodstream

lynch /lɪntʃ/ verb, t. = to take hold of someone who has done something wrong and to kill him/her without a trial (used to refer to some action by a crowd or mob)

lynx /lɪŋks/ noun = a kind of fierce wild cat

lyre /laɪəʳ/ noun, c. = a U-shaped musical instrument with strings, used by the people of Ancient Greece

lyr•ic[1] /ˈlɪrɪk/ noun, c. = a short, musical poem expressing some personal feeling

lyric[2] adj. *lyric poetry* = having the qualities of a lyric **lyrical** adj. = a feeling of joy and admiration expressed in a very personal way **lyrics** noun = the words of a song, especially one written for a film etc. **lyricist** /ˈlɪrɪsɪst/ noun, c. = a person who writes the words for songs

L

mM

m, M /em/ **1** the thirteenth letter of the English alphabet **2** (always capital) = medium (size) **3** = abbr. of metre **4** = abbr. of million

MA abbr. of **Master of Arts** = a university degree higher than **BA**

ma'am /mæm/ noun = short form of **madam** (see below)

ma•ca•bre /mə'kɑːbrə/ adj. (French) *I have heard a macabre story about a woman who died here and whose ghost haunts this house.* = connected with death and causing fear

mac•a•ro•ni /mækə'rəʊni/ noun, u. = a kind of Italian food made from flour, in the shape of small hollow tubes (also **pasta**)

ma•caw /mə'kɔː/ noun = a brightly-coloured bird of the parrot family, found in South America

mace /meɪs/ noun, c. or u. **1** (c.) = a heavy stick with a rounded end, used as a weapon **2** (u.) = a spice made from nutmeg, a sweet-smelling nut

Mach /mɑːk/ noun = the speed of a flying aircraft measured in relation to the speed of sound (The speed of sound is Mach 1.) [TECHNICAL]

ma•chine[1] /mə'ʃiːn/ noun, c. **1** *a washing machine* = an instrument which is used to do some kind of work, often replacing human labour **2** *I want you to think about what I've said, not be a machine.* = a person who does something without thinking about it, and often without stopping (informal)

machine[2] verb, t. *This metal part for a motorcar engine has to be machined carefully.* = to make something with the help of a machine **machinery** noun, u. (no plural) **1** *The machinery for the new factory has been imported from Japan.* = machines in general, used for different purposes **2** *I don't understand the machinery of this new car.* = the way in which a machine works **3** *political machinery* = system (figurative) **machine gun** noun, c. = a gun which fires bullets very quickly **machine-readable** adj. *The price of each book is printed on the cover, in machine-readable form.* = in a way that can be read and understood by a computer, using a system of **bar-codes** (thick and thin lines) and a **scanner**

ma•cho /'mætʃəʊ/ adj. *He always dresses and acts in a macho fashion.* = trying to look and act in a way which is thought to be very manly (strong and brave) (informal)

mack•e•rel /'mækərəl/ noun = a kind of sea fish

mack•in•tosh /'mækɪntɒʃ/ noun, u. = a kind of long waterproof coat used to protect people from rain (also **raincoat**)

mac•ro- /'mækrəʊ/ prefix meaning **1** = large e.g. **macro-economics** = the study of large systems or concepts in economics **2** whole e.g. **macrocosm** noun = the whole universe (of which the earth is a part)

mad /mæd/ adj. **1** *a mad person* = suffering from sickness of the mind **2** *Indians are mad about cricket.* = very fond of (informal) **3** *She was mad at being made to wait for two hours.* = very angry (American English) (informal) **4** *You must be mad to go out in this rain without an umbrella.* = without sense (informal) **madness** noun. **madden** verb, t. *The tiger was maddened by the bullet wound in its shoulder.* = to drive someone or an animal mad with anger or pain **maddening** adj. *The pain in my leg is maddening.* = causing much suffering **mad-cap** adj. *He has some mad-cap idea about walking all the way to Delhi.* = foolish and not very practical (informal)

> **Usage** It is now considered generally more respectful to use the terms 'mentally challenged' or 'mentally ill' instead of 'mad.'

to work/run/dance etc. **like mad** *I worked like mad on the story I was writing.* = to do something at great speed and with great effort (informal) **a mad rush** *There was a mad rush at the railway station when the train came in.* = disorganized movement by a crowd, with a lot of pushing etc. (informal)

mad•am (Madam) /'mædəm/ noun *Madam, may I come in?* = a respectful way of addressing or talking to a woman one does not know, or with whom one wants to be formal (the short form is **Ma'am**)

made = see under **make**

Ma•donn•a /mə'dɒnə/ noun = Mary, the Mother of Jesus Christ (in the Christian religion)

mael•strom /'meɪlstrəm/ noun, c. *The boat was caught in a maelstrom.* = a place in a river where the water moves round and round with great force and can suck objects down

maes•tro /'maɪstrəʊ/ noun, c. (Italian) **1** *Ravi Shankar, the sitar maestro* = a very great musician **2** = a person who is famous in any field of activity

ma•fia /'mɑːfiə/ noun, c. (Italian) = a gang of criminals

mag•a•zine /mægə'ziːn/ noun, c. **1** = a thin book containing pictures, articles etc. published every week, fortnight or month **2** *the magazine of a rifle* = the hollow part of a gun into which bullets are fed (placed) before they are fired

ma•gen•ta /mə'dʒentə/ adj. *a magenta sunset* = dark purple **magenta** noun.

mag•got /ˈmægət/ noun, c. = a small worm which grows out of the egg of a fly and develops into a fly when fully grown

ma•gic /ˈmædʒɪk/ noun, u. **1** = the use of supernatural forces (spirits etc.) to make strange things happen (also **black magic**) **2** = the use of clever tricks, such as making things disappear, by an entertainer (a person who provides enjoyment for people) (also **white magic**) **magician** /ˈmædʒɪʃən/ noun, c. = a person who can do magic (both meanings)

ma•gis•trate /ˈmædʒɪstreɪt/ noun, c. = a government official who has the power to judge law cases

mag•nan•i•mous /mægˈnænɪməs/ adj. *She made a magnanimous donation to the school.* = kind-hearted and generous (formal)

mag•nate /ˈmægneɪt/ noun, c. *a business magnate* = a rich and powerful businessperson

mag•ne•sia /mægˈniːʃə/ noun = a kind of white powder used in medicines for the stomach

mag•ne•sium /mægˈniːzɪəm/ noun = a common silvery metal which is used in fireworks etc.

mag•net /ˈmægnɪt/ noun, c. = a piece of iron or steel which can attract (pull towards itself) other pieces of iron or steel **magnetism** noun, u. **1** = the quality that a magnet has of being able to attract pieces of iron or steel **2** *People were attracted to Martin Luther King by his magnetism.* = the power to attract people that some persons have (figurative) **magnetic** /mægˈnetɪk/ adj. **1** *This piece of iron has magnetic properties.* = having to do with magnets **2** *Lata Mangeshkar has a magnetic voice.* = very attractive **magnetic field** = the area around a magnet where its effect can be felt [PHYSICS]

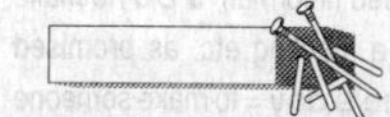

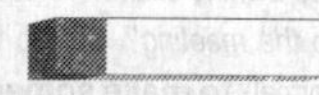

mag•nif•i•cent /mægˈnɪfɪsənt/ adj. *He lives in a magnificent house which has more than 50 rooms.* = very beautiful and grand

mag•ni•fy /ˈmægnɪfaɪ/ verb, t. (**magnified**) *This lens will magnify the small letters on the page so that you can read them easily.* = to make something look larger than it is **magnification** /mægnɪfɪˈkeɪʃən/ noun, u. = the process of making something look larger, using some equipment **magnifying glass** noun, u. = a thick piece of glass, curved on both sides, used to make things look larger so that they can be seen clearly

magnitude /ˈmægnɪtjuːd/ noun, u. *There were at least 50,000 people present at the meeting. The magnitude of the crowd surprised us.* = large size

mag•no•li•a /mægˈnəʊliə/ noun = a kind of large flower which grows on a tree and has a pleasant smell

mag•pie /ˈmægpaɪ/ noun, c. (**magpies**) = a kind of bird with black and white feathers that is said to be attracted by bright and shining objects

ma•hog•a•ny /məˈhɒgəni/ noun = a kind of hard and costly wood having a reddish-brown colour, used for making furniture

maid /meɪd/ noun, c. *kitchen maid* = a woman who is employed to work in a house or hotel, generally to keep it clean

maid•en[1] /ˈmeɪdn/ noun, c. = a young, unmarried girl (old-fashioned, literary) Ⓖ

maiden[2] adj. *The new member of parliament will make her maiden speech today.* = the first; something done for the first time **maiden over** noun, c. = an over (in cricket) in which no runs are scored [SPORTS]

mail[1] /meɪl/ noun, u. **1** *I want to send this letter by registered mail.* = the postal system through which letters etc. are sent **2** *Have you received any mail today?* = letters, e-mail etc.

mail[2] verb, t. *Please mail this letter at the post office.* = to send a letter, e-mail etc. through the postal or the computer system (see also **e-mail**)

maim /maɪm/ verb, t. *Several young men from this village, who were in the army, were killed or maimed during the war.* = to wound very badly so as to make one unfit to use a certain part of the body

main[1] /meɪn/ adj. *The main reason for his success is his ability to work hard.* = most important

main[2] noun, c. (always plural) *There will be no supply of water today as the mains are being repaired.* = a large pipe or cable (wire) carrying water, gas or electricity to buildings **mainland** noun *The island of Rameshwaram is connected to the mainland by a bridge.* = the large piece of land which makes up a country (This does not include the islands around it) **mainframe** noun, c. = a very large, powerful computer that is the centre of a computer system [COMPUTERS] **mainly** adv. **1** *This dish uses mainly potatoes. // We travelled mainly by bus.* = mostly **2** *Her illness was caused mainly by her working in the sun.* = the most important reason for something **mainstay** noun, u. *Agriculture is the mainstay of this country.* = something that provides the most important means of support for the people **mainstream** noun = *Bhagwan Verma was a good poet, but he does not belong to the mainstream of Hindi literature.* = a tradition in literature, science etc. which most people follow

main•tain /meɪnˈteɪn/ verb, t. **1** *Your car is in poor condition. You must maintain it properly.* = to take care of something and to keep it in good condition **2** *This* shop has maintained its reputation for selling goods of high quality.* = to keep up; to continue as before **3** *He maintains a large family.* = to look after and support **maintenance** /ˈmeɪntənens/ noun, u. **1** *The maintenance of this old house costs at least Rs 10,000 a month.* = the act of keeping something in good condition **2** *The judge ordered him to pay his wife Rs 10,000 every month towards maintenance, after they were divorced.* = money paid to a former husband or wife regularly by his/her former wife or husband, under the orders of a court

maize /meɪz/ noun, u. = a kind of plant grown by farmers, the seeds of which are eaten, generally in the form of flour (also **corn**)

ma•jes•ty /ˈmædʒɪsti/ noun, u. *It is difficult to describe the majesty of these high mountains.* = beauty that has a powerful effect on the mind **Majesty** noun *Your Majesty* = a title used to address or talk about a king or queen **majestic** /meˈdʒestɪk/ adj.

ma•jor[1] /ˈmeɪdʒəʳ/ adj. *India has more than 2,000 languages but there are 20 major languages, as well as minor languages spoken by a few people.* = one of the main or most important (opposite **minor**)

major[2] noun, c. **1** *He is 18 years old and a major now.* = a person who has reached the age at which one is recognized in law as being a fully-grown person **2** *The parade was led by Major Singh.* = an officer of middle rank in the army (higher than Captain but lower than Colonel)

major[3] verb, i. *My daughter is majoring in Economics.* = to study something at a university as the most important subject

majority /məˈdʒɒrɪtɪ/ noun, u. **1** *The majority of the students want a holiday tomorrow.* = the greater number (opposite **minority**) **2** *She won the election by a large majority.* = margin or difference between two quantities

make[1] /meɪk/ verb, t. (**made**) **1** *My father is making chapatis for us.* = to produce something **2** *He has made an agreement with his publishers. // He made several good suggestions.* = to perform an action **3** *Don't eat this mango. It will make you sick.* = to cause something to happen **4** *He makes a lot of money.* = to earn **5** *We made it to the station in time.* = to reach **6** *Five and two make seven.* = to add up to a total **7** *Our teacher made us study very hard.* = to cause someone to do something by force **8** *This leafy tree makes an excellent shelter against the sun.* = to be good or suitable for a purpose **9** *She was made a director of the company.* = to give a person a some responsibility in an organization

make[2] noun, u. or c. **1** *He sells cars of different make.*(u.) **2** *You can find many makes of watches in this shop.*(c.) = a product manufactured by a particular company and sold under a certain name

make-believe[1] /ˈmeɪkbɪˈliːv/ noun, u. *He lives in a world of make-believe* = imagination

make-believe[2] adj. *a make-believe world* = false and imaginary; something that has no connection with reality

makeshift /ˈmeɪkʃɪft/ adj. *We did not have a house, so we found makeshift accommodation in a tea-shop.* = something done to meet an urgent need, in the absence of something better

make-up /ˈmeɪkʌp/ noun, u. = powder, lipstick etc. used on the face to make a person look more attractive; used by actors to make them appear like the characters they are playing, or to look suitable for the camera

to make do *We don't have a car, so we must make do with a bicycle.* = to manage with something (in the absence of something else which is required) **to make off with** *The thieves made off with a huge amount of cash.* = to steal **to make the most of something** *Make the most of your meeting with the well-known writer.* = to take full advantage of a chance or opportunity **to make up 1** *When the principal asked him why he was late, he made up a story about his father falling ill suddenly.* = to invent a story or excuse (disapproving) **2** *Have they made up with each other after the fight they had?* = to go back to being friends again after a fight, argument etc. **to make up for something** *She is a poor speaker, but she makes up for it by writing beautifully.* = to compensate for something (to have something good to offer which takes away the effect of something bad) **to make it 1** *We thought we were going to be late but we made it.* = used when one reaches or gets to a place in time for something and feels relief (informal) **2** *Only three students made it in the exam.* = to succeed (informal) **3** *Did he make it to the meeting?* = to go to a meeting etc. as promised (informal) **to make someone's day** = to make someone happy by doing something which gives them happiness (informal) **Make it snappy!** = an instruction to someone to do something fast (informal) **to make (something) out 1** *make out a cheque* = to prepare a cheque etc. addressed to someone who has to be paid **2** *There was so much noise outside the classroom that we couldn't make out what the teacher was saying.* = to be hardly able to see, hear, read etc. something

mal- prefix meaning bad or badly e.g. **mal•ad•just•ed** /mæləˈdʒʌstɪd/ adj. *The boy has been unhappy ever since he came to this school. He seems to be maladjusted.* = not able to accept the people or things around oneself and therefore not happy (often disapproving)

mal•a•dy /ˈmælədi/ noun, u. or c. (**maladies**) *He*

suffers from a strange malady.(c.) = sickness or disease

ma•laise /mə'leɪz/ noun, u. *The patient has a feeling of malaise though he is not suffereing from any disease.* = a general feeling of being unwell, for which there may be no reason (formal)

ma•lar•ia /mə'leəriə/ noun = a common disease carried by mosquitoes which causes high fever and pain

male[1] /meɪl/ adj. = belonging to the sex that does not give birth to young ones

male[2] noun, c. *There are only two males in this herd of elephants.* = a male person or animal **male chauvinist** noun, c. = a person who believes that men are superior to women

ma•lev•o•lent /mə'levələnt/ adj. *Some malevolent power seems to be ruling our fate and making us suffer.* = evil or harmful (opposite **benevolent**)

mal•formed /mæl'fɔːmd/ adj. *The baby was born with a malformed hand which had seven fingers.* = an incorrectly or unusually shaped part of the body

mal•func•tion /mæl'fʌŋkʃən/ noun, u. *There is some malfunction in the engine of the car. I can't start it.* = some fault in the working of a machine etc.

mal•ice /'mælɪs/ noun, u. *There is a lot of malice in this piece of writing. The author seems to hate everyone.* = hatred or anger **malicious** /mə'lɪʃəs/ adj. *malicious look* = full of anger and hatred

ma•lign /mə'laɪn/ verb, t. *The film magazine has been maligning the actor.* = to talk or write unkindly about someone

ma•lig•nant /mə'lɪgnənt/ adj. **1** *a malignant person* = evil and harmful **2** *a malignant tumour* = an unnatural growth that can turn into cancer and lead to death [MEDICINE]

ma•lin•ger /mə'lɪŋgəʳ/ verb, i. *My driver is on leave. He says he is ill but I am sure he is malingering.* = to avoid work by pretending to be sick (derogatory)

mall /mɔːl/ noun, c. = a large shopping centre

mal•le•a•ble /'mæliəbəl/ adj. *Silver and lead are malleable metals. They can be beaten into thin, flat sheets.* = something that can be beaten or pressed flat [SCIENCE]

mal•let /'mælɪt/ noun, c. = a heavy wooden hammer

mal•nu•tri•tion /mælnjʊ'trɪʃən/ noun, u. *These children are weak and sickly. They have been suffering from malnutrition.* = poor health caused by lack of food

mal•prac•tice /mæl'præktɪs/ noun, u. or c. *Many students were caught copying in the examination and the police had to be called in to check malpractice.*(u.) = something done dishonestly or in an illegal manner [LAW]

malt /mɔːlt/ noun, u. = grain (wheat, barley etc.) that has been kept in water until it begins to sprout (grow) and then dried and used for making some drink (usually alcoholic)

mam•mal /'mæməl/ noun, c. = an animal that does not lay eggs (except for the duck-billed platypus) but gives birth to babies and feeds them with milk which it produces (e.g. dogs, human beings) **mammary** /'mæmərɪ/ adj. *Whales have large mammary glands.* = producing milk [BIOLOGY]

mam•moth[1] /'mæməθ/ noun = a kind of large, hairy elephant that lived on earth very long ago but is no longer found

mammoth[2] adj. *She drives to the office in a mammoth car.* = very large

man[1] /mæn/ noun, c. (**men**) or u. **1** *a young man* (c.) = an adult (fully-grown) human male **2** *Man has caused a lot of damage to the surroundings in which he lives.*(u.)= the human race as a whole, including women (see note below) **3** *Our men are unhappy because they have not been paid for the last six months.*(u.) = a worker

man[2] verb, t. (**manned**) *The new factory will be manned by workers from Korea.* = to provide with workers (*operated, run* or *managed* are expressions preferred today) **man-eater** noun, c. = an animal that eats human flesh **right-hand (man)** noun = a trusted adviser or follower **manhandle** verb, t. **1** *The photographer complained that he had been manhandled by the police.* = to treat someone roughly or with violence (derogatory) **2** *The steel cupboard had to be manhandled up the stairs.* = to move something heavy, using the strength of human beings **man-hole** noun, c. = an opening, fitted with a lid (cover), through which a worker can enter to repair a drain etc. **man-made** adj. = made by human beings, not found naturally (*human-made, artificial* or *synthetic* are preferred expressions) **man-power** = workers needed to do a piece of work **man-slaughter** noun, u. = the crime of killing someone, but not on purpose (not deliberately)

Usage As **man** in the following contexts seems to refer to only male human beings, it is now considered polite or correct to use words which include both men and women. The following are recommended:

humans or **human beings**, as in *Humans* (instead of *Man*) *have been great inventors.*

man (verb) replace with **manage** or *run*, as in *The shop is managed by* (not **manned by**) *seven people.*

man-hours *person hours*

man-made *human-made*

chairman/salesman/businessman etc. *chairperson, salesperson, businessperson* etc.

M

the man in the street = the ordinary or average person **a man of the world** = a wise or clever person with a lot of experience **Oh man!** (or **Man!**) = an expression used to show that one likes or is enjoying something (slang)

man•age /ˈmænɪdʒ/ verb, t. or i. **1** *She managed the company so well that it made a huge profit.*(t.) = to look after something; to be in control of **2** *I don't have much experience of cooking but I think I can manage just for today.*(i.) = to be able to do something though not very well **3** *I can't give you Rs 10,000 but perhaps I could manage a thousand.*(t.) = to be able to find something **manageable** adj. *The political situation in the state is difficult but manageable.* = something that can be managed (controlled) **management** noun, u. **1** *The company succeeded because of good management.* = the way in which a company, a business, one's time etc. are managed (controlled), or the act of managing them **2** *The management has decided to start another school.* = the group of people who manage a business etc. **manager** noun, c. **1** = a person who manages (looks after or controls) a business etc. **2** = a person who is in charge of a sports team (e.g. in cricket, football)

Man•da•rin /ˈmændərɪn/ noun = the official form of the Chinese language which is used in and around the capital, Beijing

man•date /ˈmændeɪt/ noun, u. or c. *The party that wins the largest number of seats in the election gets the people's mandate to form the government.* = the right or power to rule, given by the people especially after an election **mandatory** adj. *It is mandatory for all house-owners to pay municipal tax.* = compulsory; something that must be done (formal)

man•di•ble /ˈmændɪbəl/ noun = the bone that forms the movable lower jaw of an animal or human being (also **jaw-bone**) [BIOLOGY]

man•do•lin /mændəˈlɪn/ noun = a musical instrument with eight strings (somewhat like a guitar)

mane /meɪn/ noun, c. *the lion's mane* = the long hair around the face of a male lion or the hair on the back of a horse's neck

man•ga•nese /ˈmæŋgəniːz/ noun = a kind of metal used in making steel

mange /meɪndʒ/ noun = a skin disease that attacks animals, especially cats and dogs **mangy** adj. *a mangy cat* = suffering from mange

man•ger /meɪndʒəʳ/ noun, c. = a large open container in which food is given to horses or cattle

man•gle /ˈmæŋgəl/ verb, t. *His hand was badly mangled when he accidentally put it into a machine which was running.* = to cut up or tear into pieces so that something can no longer be recognized

man•go /ˈmæŋgəʊ/ noun, c. (**mangoes**) or u. **1** (c.) = a kind of fruit that grows in tropical (warm) climates **2** *mango pudding*(u.) = the flesh or juice of a mango used as food

man•grove /ˈmæŋgrəʊv/ noun = a kind of tree that grows near the water and has thick roots growing down from the branches

ma•ni•a /ˈmeɪniə/ noun, u. **1** = a dangerous disorder of the mind (e.g. kleptomania, a mental condition which makes someone want to steal) [MEDICINE] **2** *a mania for watching horror films* = a very strong desire to do something (informal) **maniac** noun, c. **1** = a person suffering from some mania (disorder of the mind) **2** *She drives like a maniac.* = a person who does not understand what danger is (derogatory) **manic** adj. *He is suffering from manic depression.* = having to do with some mania [MEDICINE]

man•i•cure /ˈmænɪkjʊəʳ/ noun, u. or c. = beauty treatment for the hands and the fingernails

man•i•fest[1] /ˈmænɪfest/ verb, t. *Malaria manifests itself in the form of high fever and severe headache.* = to appear in a certain form; to be seen (formal)

manifest[2] adj. *The failure of the government to control crime is quite manifest.* = something that can be clearly seen **manifesto** /mænɪˈfestəʊ/ noun, c. (**manifestos**) = a written statement produced by a political party, usually before an election, to let people know about its beliefs, plans etc.

man•i•fold[1] /ˈmænɪfəʊld/ adj. *She has manifold problems. She has lost her job, and her husband and daughter are ill.* = of many kinds (formal)

manifold[2] noun, c. = a pipe through which gas can escape from the engine of a motorcar [TECHNICAL]

ma•nil•a /məˈnɪlə/ noun, u. or c. *a manila envelope* = thick, strong brown paper

ma•nip•u•late /məˈnɪpjʊleɪt/ verb, t. **1** *He has become unpopular but he is able to manipulate the crowd so that they still say nice things about him.* = to control or influence something in a clever manner for one's own advantage (derogatory) **2** *The surgeon tried to set the broken bones in my arm by manipulating them.* = to do something with the hands that requires great skill **manipulative** adj.

mankind /mænˈkaɪnd/ noun *Have computers really benefited mankind?* = human beings in general (The preferred word today is **humankind** or **people**. See note after **man**)

man•ner /ˈmænəʳ/ noun, c. (usually singular) *The children like the manner in which you teach.* = the way or method of doing something **manners** noun, u. (always plural) *Why are you so rude? Didn't they teach you any manners at school?* = polite or good behaviour **mannerism** noun, c. *The speaker had a very irritating mannerism. He kept saying 'Do you* *follow me?' after each sentence.* = a peculiar way of behaving or speaking that becomes a habit (derogatory)

ma•noeu•vre[1] **(maneuver)** /mə'nu:vəʳ/ verb, t. **1** *The driver manoeuvered the car through the crowded street.* = to move or turn something skilfully and in a controlled manner **2** *He knows how to manoeuvre his way through the world of politics.* = to do something clever and often dishonest in order to gain an advantage (derogatory)

manoeuvre[2] noun, c. **1** *The army will be carrying out manoeuvres in the desert this week.* = a military movement (of soldiers, tanks etc.) done for training purposes **2** *He will try everything possible to defeat me in the election but I think I will be able to check his manoeuvres.*(c.) = a clever and often dishonest action intended to gain an advantage over someone (derogatory) **manoeuvrable (maneuverable)** adj. *The new car is highly manoeuverable and can be turned around even in this narrow lane.* = something that can be easily moved or turned in a controlled manner

man•or /'mænəʳ/ noun, c. = a large house, with land around it (formal)

man•sion /'mænʃən/ noun, c. = a large house

man•tle /'mæntl/ noun, c. **1** = a loose and long coat without sleeves, worn in former times **2** = the part of the earth between the centre and the surface [TECHNICAL]

man•u•al[1] /'mænjuəl/ adj. *He is so used to working on a computer that he can no longer work on a manual typewriter.* = done or used by the human hand

manual[2] noun, c. *I am preparing a manual for teachers.* = a book which tells someone how to do something (e.g. how to teach, how to repair a radio)

man•u•fac•ture[1] /mænjʊ'fæktʃəʳ/ verb, t. *We have several factories in India which manufacture motorcars.* = to make or produce something in large quantities with the help of machines

manufacture[2] noun, u. *The manufacture of steam locomotives has been stopped now.* = the act or process of producing something

ma•nure /mə'njʊəʳ/ noun, u. *Cowdung is used as manure.* = waste matter produced by animals which is used to make land fertile (so that it can produce better crops)

man•u•script /'mænjʊskrɪpt/ noun, c. = a book written by hand or typed (on a typewriter or computer), before it has been printed (abbr. **ms**)

many[1] /'meni/ det. *He has many dogs.* = several, a large number

many[2] pron. *He asked me to bring all my friends to his party, but unfortunately I do not have many.* = a large number (of)

Mao•ri /'maʊri/ noun = a person belonging to the Maori tribe, the aboriginal tribe of New Zealand

map[1] /mæp/ noun, c. *You can find Pokhra on any map of Nepal.* = a picture of the earth's surface, showing mountains, rivers, the position of states, cities etc. [GEOGRAPHY]

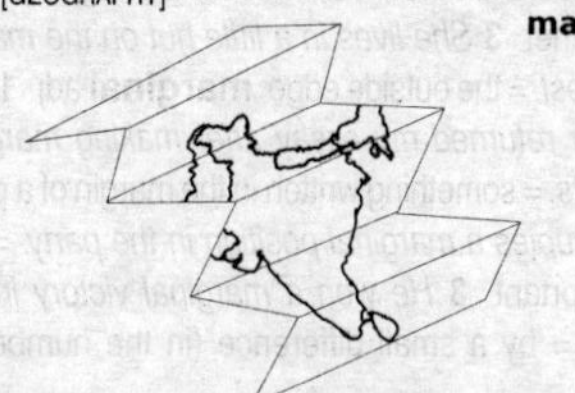
map

map[2] verb, t. (**mapped**) *The western part of this state has not been mapped yet.* = to make a map of something

to map out *We have to map out the route we are taking.* = to plan something **to put something on the map** = to make an unknown place known to everyone

ma•ple /'meɪpəl/ noun, u. = a kind of tree, common in America and Canada, which produces sweet juice from which maple sugar is made

mar /mɑ:ʳ/ verb, t. (**marred**) *The scar on her cheek mars the beauty of her face.* = to spoil or make less perfect

mar•a•thon[1] /'mærəθən/ noun = a long-distance race of about 26 miles (42 km)

marathon[2] adj. *He made a marathon speech.* = very long and needing much effort (figurative)

ma•raud•ing /mə'rɔ:dɪŋ/ adj. *The gang of robbers has gone on a marauding raid.* = moving about with the intention to rob or kill **marauder** noun, c. = one who robs or kills

mar•ble /'mɑ:bəl/ noun, u. or c. **1** *The Taj Mahal is built of white marble.* = a kind of soft stone, white or coloured, which is used to make buildings, floors etc. **2** = a coloured glass ball, used in the game of marbles (see below) **marbles** noun = a game played by rolling small, coloured glass balls on the ground

to lose one's marbles = to become mentally unwell (informal, not respectful)

march[1] /mɑ:tʃ/ verb, i. *The soldiers will march through the streets of the capital on Republic Day.* = to walk with strong and regular steps, usually in a group

march[2] noun, c. *a peace march* = an act where a large group of people walk together in an organized way, often to support or oppose something

mare /meəʳ/ noun, c. = a fully-grown female horse **mare's nest** = a discovery which turns out to be useless

mar•ga•rine /mɑdʒə'ri:n/ noun = a kind of food that looks like butter but is made from vegetable oil

M

mar•gin /ˈmɑːdʒɪn/ noun, c. **1** *Someone has written his name in the left margin on this page of the book.* = the blank area (with no printing on it) down the side of the page of a book, near either edge **2** *The Sri Lankan team defeated the Australians by a margin of 250 runs.* = difference; the amount by which one thing is greater than another **3** *She lives in a little hut on the margin of the forest.* = the outside edge **marginal** adj. **1** *The professor returned my essay after making marginal comments.* = something written in the margin of a page **2** *He occupies a marginal position in the party.* = not very important **3** *He won a marginal victory in the election.* = by a small difference (in the number of votes)

mari•gold /ˈmærɪgəʊld/ noun = a kind of ball-shaped yellow flower, often used for making garlands

mar•i•jua•na /mærɪˈwɑːnə/ noun = a kind of drug made from the dried leaves and stems of a plant known as cannabis or Indian hemp ('bhang')

mari•nate /ˈmærɪneɪt/ verb, t. *The meat should be marinated in lemon juice or yoghurt for six hours before it is cooked.* = to keep meat in a mixture of oil, lemon juice or vinegar and some spices for some time before cooking it, in order to make it soft and give it a particular taste **marinade** noun, u. = the mixture of oil, lemon juice and spices etc. which is used to marinate meat

ma•rine /məˈriːn/ adj. *a marine animal* = living in the sea or obtained from the sea **mariner** noun, c. = a sailor (literary)

mar•i•tal /ˈmærɪtəl/ adj. *marital bliss* = having to do with marriage

mar•i•time /ˈmærɪtaɪm/ adj. *England was once a great maritime power and English ships were found in every port in the world.* = having to do with the sea and with ships

mark[1] /mɑːk/ noun, c. **1** *He walked across the clean floor, leaving the marks of his dirty feet on it. // She carries the marks of small pox on her face.* = a spot or cut on a surface **2** *He has the highest marks in history.* = a figure (usually between 0 and 10 or 0 and 100) which shows how well one has done in an examination or a competition **3** *He folded his hands when he greeted me, as a mark of respect.* = sign or symbol **4** *You should use an exclamation mark after the word 'Oh'.* = a written sign which carries a certain meaning **5** *He aimed at the target and fired, but the bullet missed its mark.* = the object that one aims at **6** *This shirt, which I bought in Gemany, cost 200 marks.* = the unit of money used in Germany and some neighbouring countries

mark[2] verb, t. **1** *His face has been marked by small pox.* = to make a mark that spoils the appearance of something **2** *The teachers are marking examination papers.* = to give marks to **3** *This sign-board marks the spot where 200 people were killed.* = to show the position of **4** *All the novels written by this writer are marked by great sympathy for women.* = to carry the sign of **5** *Can you mark the questions that you cannot answer?* = to put a sign to indicate something **6** *He is such a good forward that he is marked by two people.* = to stay close to a player of the opposing team so that he or she cannot score easily [SPORTS] **marked** adj. **1** *There is a marked improvement in the condition of the patient.* = easily noticed or seen **2** *His enemies have threatened to harm him. He is a marked person.* = a person whose life is in danger

to mark time **1** = to make the movements of marching while remaining in the same place **2** = to be doing something without making progress **quick/slow off the mark** = quick or slow to start something **mark up** = to increase the price of something, sometimes so that one does not lose money while offering a discount **to not be up to the mark** *Her singing is not up to the mark.* = to not be as good as expected (informal) **On your marks!** = a command asking runners in a race to get ready to run

marker /mɑːkəʳ/ noun, c. = a pen, piece of paper etc. that marks clearly because it is thick or of a different colour

mar•ket[1] /ˈmɑːkɪt/ noun, c. **1** *Please get some fresh vegetables from the market.* = a place where things are bought and sold **2** *These shirts are made for the European market.* = an area or country where there is a demand for goods **3** *There is no market now for classical music.* = demand for particular goods

market[2] verb, t. *We market our clothes mainly in the Arab countries.* = to offer for sale **marketing** noun *He teaches marketing at the Institute of Business Management.* = the science which tells one how to sell one's products in the market

marks•man /ˈmɑːksmən/ noun, c. (**-men**) = a person who can shoot well with a gun

mar•lin /ˈmɑːlɪn/ noun = a kind of large fish which lives in the sea

mar•ma•lade /ˈmɑːməleɪd/ noun, u. = a kind of jam made with the skin of oranges (see also **jam**)

ma•roon[1] /məˈruːn/ noun = a dark red colour

maroon[2] adj. *a maroon shirt* = of a maroon colour

maroon[3] verb, t. *It rained so heavily that all the roads were flooded and we could not leave the village. We were marooned there for a week.* = to be left in a place with no means of getting away or leaving

mar•quee /mɑːˈkiː/ noun, c. = a large tent used for public meetings etc.

mar•row /ˈmærəʊ/ noun, u. = the soft substance found inside hollow bones

mar•ry /ˈmæri/ verb, t. or i. (**married**) **1** *Rehana married Ashok.*(t.) // *Ashok decided to marry.*(i.) = to become the husband of a woman or the wife of a man through a religious or legal ceremony **2** *The Bishop of Kolkata will marry the young couple.*(t.) = to perform a religious or legal ceremony through which a man and a woman are married to each other **marriage** /ˈmærɪdʒ/ noun, u. or c. **1** *The marriage of my daughter will be performed next month.*(c.) = the ceremony through which two people get married to each other **2** *I am not ready for marriage yet. I will wait for another five years.*(u.) = the state of being married **3** *a marriage of minds* = coming together **marriageable** adj. *of marriageable age* = suitable (legally) for marriage **married** adj. *He is a married man.* = having a wife or husband

Mars /mɑːz/ noun **1** = one of the planets in the solar system [PHYSICS] **2** = the Roman god of war, to whom soldiers prayed (in the old days) for victory in battle **Martian** adj. = having to do with the planet Mars

marsh /mɑːʃ/ noun, c. or u. = low, soft land that is partly covered with water (see also **swamp**)

mar•shal[1] /ˈmɑːʃəl/ noun, c. = an officer of the highest rank in the British or Indian army (Field Marshal) or air-force (Air Chief Marshal)

marshal[2] verb, t. (**marshalled**) *The teacher marshalled the little children onto the stage.* = to lead

mar•su•pi•al /mɑːˈsuːpiəl/ noun *The kangaroo is a marsupial.* = a class of animals, to which the kangaroo belongs, which carry their babies in a pouch (bag) in the front part of their bodies [BIOLOGY]

mar•tial /ˈmɑːʃəl/ adj. *The band was playing martial music as the soldiers started their parade.* = having to do with war or fighting **martial arts** noun = sports such as judo, karate, kung-fu etc. which teach a person how to defend himself/herself from an attacker, often without using weapons **martial law** noun = the rule of a country by the military forces (army, navy, etc.)

mar•ti•ni /mɑːˈtiːni/ noun = a kind of alcoholic drink produced by mixing different drinks (see also **cocktail**)

mar•tyr[1] /ˈmɑːtəʳ/ noun, c. *Bhagat Singh, who was hanged by the British, is honoured in India as a martyr.* = a person who gives up his/her life for a noble cause, such as the freedom of the country

martyr[2] verb, t. *The British government martyred Bhagat Singh.* = to kill someone so as to make a martyr of him/her **martyrdom** noun, u. = the act of becoming a martyr

mar•vel[1] /ˈmɑːvəl/ verb, i. *She dances so beautifully that one can only marvel at the beauty of her movements.* = to look at something or someone with great wonder, surprise and admiration

marvel[2] noun, c. *The Taj Mahal was built about 400 years ago, but it remains a marvel even today.* = something that causes great wonder, surprise and admiration **marvellous** adj. *She has a marvellous memory. She can remember hundreds of telephone numbers.* = causing great wonder, surprise or admiration

Marx•is•m /ˈmɑːksɪzəm/ noun = the political ideas of Karl Marx, on which communism is based, which looks at history as a struggle between different social classes (see also **communism, socialism, capitalism**)

mas•ca•ra /mæˈskɑːrə/ noun, u. = a substance used to colour the eye-lashes (see also **eye-lashes**)

mas•cot /ˈmæskət/ noun, c. *The mascot of the Indian football team is a baby elephant.* = an animal, object or person that is supposed to bring good luck and becomes a symbol (sign)

mas•cu•line /ˈmæskjʊlɪn/ adj. **1** *'Lion' is masculine while 'lioness' is feminine.* = belonging to the class of words which are used to name or talk about a male animal or person [GRAMMAR] **2** *masculine looks* = having the qualities that are thought to be attractive in a man

mash[1] /mæʃ/ verb, t. *Please boil and mash some potatoes for our dinner.* = to crush a soft substance after cooking

mash[2] noun, u. *He prepared some grain mash to feed the cows.* = a soft mixture of grain and water **mashed** adj. *mashed potatoes* = crushed into a soft mass

mask[1] /mɑːsk/ noun, c. *The robbers wore masks over their faces so that they would not be recognized.* = a covering for the face or a part of the face, to hide or protect it

mask[2] verb, t. **1** *The strong smell of onions completely masked the flavour of the other vegetables.* = to hide or prevent from being smelt, heard, seen etc. **2** *Although she was angry, she kept smiling. She knows how to mask her feelings.* = to hide one's true feelings, thoughts etc. so that others cannot see them

ma•so•chism /ˈmæsəkɪzəm/ noun = a psychological condition in which one finds pleasure by suffering pain or giving oneself pain (opposite **sadism**)

ma•son /ˈmeɪsən/ noun, c. = a person who works with bricks, stone, cement etc. to construct buildings

mas•que•rade[1] /mæskəˈreɪd/ verb, i. *The robbers entered the bank by masquerading as policemen.* = to pretend to be

masquerade[2] noun, u. *He pretends to be my friend but he is really my enemy. Anyway, I can see through his masquerade.* = the action of pretending (formal)

mass[1] /mæs/ noun, u. or c. (**masses**) **1** *There is* *a great mass of sand lying on the road. It should be removed.*(c.) = a pile or heap of some solid substance **2** *There were masses of people around the cricket stadium.* = a large number **3** *Any substance, whether solid, liquid or gas, has mass.*(u.) = weight [PHYSICS] **4** *The priest will say mass.* = a religious ceremony that is a part of Christian worship

mass[2] adj. *The gang of criminals has been accused of mass murder.* = of a large number of people

mass[3] verb, i. *The crowds massed around the cricket stadium.* = to gather together in a large number **masses** noun (always plural) *Most films are made for the entertainment of the masses.* = the largest class of people in a society (sometimes derogatory) **mass media** noun = newspapers, radio, television and cinema, which can be used to spread information quickly among the masses **mass production** noun = the making of large numbers or quantities of some product with the help of machines

mas•sa•cre[1] /ˈmæsəkəʳ/ verb, t. = to kill a number of helpless people or animals in a cruel manner

massacre[2] noun, c. *a massacre of innocent people* = the killing of many helpless people or animals in a cruel manner

mas•sage[1] /ˈmæsɑːʒ/ verb, t. *The football coach massaged the knee of the player who had been injured in the match.* = to press or rub someone's body with the arms, hands, fingers and sometimes feet, so as to take away pain

massage[2] noun, c. or u. *The coach gave the player a massage.*(c.) = the act of massaging someone **masseur** /ˈmæsɜːʳ/ noun, c. = a person whose profession is to massage people

mas•sive /ˈmæsɪv/ adj. *Her house is surrounded by massive walls. // a massive heart attack* = very large or great (also **huge**)

mast /mɑːst/ noun, c. **1** *a ship with three masts* = a long, upright pole, usually made of wood, which carries the sails on a ship **2** = a metal or wooden pole from the top of which a flag can be flown

to fly a flag at half-mast = to lower a flag from its usual position at the top of a mast to show respect to a dead leader etc.

mas•tec•to•my /mæˈstektəmi/ noun = an operation done to remove the breast of a woman who has cancer (of the breast)

master[1] /ˈmɑːstəʳ/ noun, c. **1** *He is one of the great masters in the field of music.* = a person who has gained very great skill in doing something **2** *He is the master of the house.* = the man who owns or controls something (old-fashioned) **3** *We are getting a new master to teach mathematics.* = a male teacher **4** *master copy // master tape* = an original from which copies can be made

master[2] adj. *He is a master cook.* = having very great skill in doing something

master[3] verb, t. *She has mastered the art of painting on walls.* = to become very skilful in doing something **master key** noun = a key which can open many different locks **master of ceremonies** noun, c. = a person who is in charge of the programme at a social gathering (a party etc.) and makes announcements etc. (abbr. **MC**) **masterpiece** noun, c. = a piece of work (writing, painting etc.) done with very great skill

mat /mæt/ noun, c.= a rough and strong covering for the floor, often made of straw, which is also used for sleeping on **matted** adj. *long, matted hair* = forming a thick, untidy layer (like a mat) **table mat** noun, c.= a small piece of cloth or plastic which is put under the plates that people eat from, in order to protect the surface of the table

mat•a•dor /ˈmætədɔːʳ/ noun, c. = bull-fighter; a person whose profession is to fight bulls, as a sport, which is popular in Spain and parts of South America

match[1] /mætʃ/ noun, c. (**matches**) **1** *a football match* = a game or sports event in which teams compete **2** *There is only one match left in this box of matches.* = a thin stick made of soft wood, one end of which is covered with some substance which burns easily when it is rubbed against a hard surface **3** *I have found one red sock, but I cannot find its match.* = something which is just like another **4** *Sachin Tendulkar is a great batsman, but he has met his match in Brian Lara, who is also a great batsman.* = a person who is equal to, or as good as, someone else **5** *He is trying to find a match for his daughter.* = a person of the opposite sex to whom someone may be married (old-fashioned)

match[2] verb, t. or i. **1** *The colour of the curtains should match the colour of the walls.*(t.) // *Her sari and blouse don't match.*(i.) = to be like something else in colour, design etc. **2** *There is no other runner who can match him in speed.*(i.) = to be the equal of **3** *The chairs in the classroom have to be light to match the little children's needs.* = to be suitable for a purpose **4** *We'll have to match the space to the number of people who will sit there.* = to be enough for **matchbox** noun, c. = a box that contains matches, for lighting a fire (meaning **2**, **match**[1])

mate[1] /meɪt/ noun, c. **1** *Manu and Salil are childhood mates.* = a friend (informal) **2** *The carpenter has come with his mates.* = a person that one works with (informal) **3** *The tiger has found a mate.* = one of a pair of animals, one of which is a male and the other a female **4** *He is the first mate on this ship.* = an officer on a ship who is junior to the captain

mate[2] verb, i. or t. = used of animals, to have sex for the purpose of producing young ones (also **breed**)

ma•te•ri•al[1] /mə'tɪəriəl/ noun, u. or c. **1** *This coat is made of thick woollen material.*(u.) = cloth **2** *We cannot repair the house as we have no building materials.*(c.) = a substance which is used to make some object **3** *I am collecting material for my research.*(u.) = information which can go into a book

material[2] adj. **1** *We need money to satisfy our material needs.* = relating to wordly objects (e.g. food) **2** *This fact is not very material to our case.* = important **materialism** noun, u. **1** = the desire to possess things which can be bought with money (generally derogatory) **2** = the belief that only material things (which can be seen, touched etc.) exist and there is no such thing as the 'spirit' **materialist** noun = a person who is interested only in material things and not in spiritual matters **materialize (materialise)** verb, i. *She had hoped to become a good scientist some day, but her hopes have not materialized.* = to become real

ma•ter•nal /mə'tɜːnl/ adj. **1** *The tigress has strong maternal instincts. She will fight to protect her cubs.* = related to the state of being a mother **2** *She is my maternal grandmother.* = related to a person through his/her mother (compare **paternal**) **maternity** adj. **1** *maternity clothes* = connected with the act or condition of giving birth to a baby **2** = connected with the act or condition of being a mother [LAW]

math•e•mat•ics /mæθə'mætɪks/ noun = the science that deals with numbers, shapes or quantities

ma•ti•n•ee /'mætɪneɪ/ noun = the performance of a play or a film during the afternoon **matinee idol** noun = an actor who is very popular

ma•tri•arch /'meɪtriɑːk/ noun, c. = a mother or grandmother who heads a family **matriarchy** noun = a system in which property is handed down from the mother to her daughters (also **matriarchal system**)

ma•tric•u•late /mə'trɪkjʊleɪt/ verb, i. = to pass out of the school system and join the university

mat•ri•mo•ny /'mætrɪməni/ noun, u. *to be united in matrimony* = the state of being married **matrimonial** /mætrɪ'məʊnɪəl/ adj. or noun. *a matrimonial advertisment* = connected with marriage

ma•tron /'meɪtrən/ noun, c. **1** = a woman who is in charge of a group of children in a school or of other women (in a hospital, prison etc.) **2** = a strong woman who commands people (derogatory) Ⓖ

matt /mæt/ adj. *a photograph with matt finish* = having a dull and not a shiny surface

mat•ter[1] /'mætəʳ/ noun, c. or u. **1** *We are discussing an important political matter.*(c.) = a subject which is being dealt with or talked about **2** *What's the matter? Why is everyone so excited?*(u.) = trouble or problem **3** *All the things we see around us are made up of matter.*(u.) // *We have to think of a way to get rid of all the dirty matter in this factory.* = substance **4** *We thought he would take long, but he was back in a matter of minutes.* = only a short time

matter[2] verb, i. *It really matters to me that you have come all this way just to see me.* // *I have missed my train, but it doesn't matter. There is another train after two hours.* = to be important (often used in negative sentences)

a matter of life and death = something that is extremely urgent **a matter of opinion** = something that people do not agree on **matter-of-fact** *He spoke about his adventures in a very matter-of-fact tone.* = dealing with facts only, without any feelings **as a matter of fact** *You think he is not a good singer, but as a matter of fact he is quite good.* = in reality **no laughing matter** = something that should be taken very seriously

matt•ress /'mætrɪs/ noun, c. (**mattresses**) = a kind of mat made of thick, strong cloth, which is filled with soft material such as cotton and spread on top of a bed, for someone to sleep on

mature[1] /mə'tʃʊəʳ/ adj. **1** *These mango trees are five years old. They are mature and will produce fruit this year.* = fully grown and developed (physically) **2** *Although she is only 16 she has a mature mind. She will do nothing without thinking carefully about it.* = having a fully developed mind (opposite **immature**)

mature[2] verb, i. **1** *These mango trees will mature this year and start producing fruit.* = to grow up physically **2** *She has matured a lot during these two years.* = to grow mentally (in the way one thinks etc.) **maturation** /mætʃʊ'reɪʃn/ noun = the process of becoming mature **maturity** /mə'tʃʊrɪti/ adj. = the state of being mature

maud•lin /'mɔːdlɪn/ adj. *singing maudlin songs* = sad in a foolish way (specially when drunk)

maul /mɔːl/ verb, t. *The tiger dragged the hunter into the bushes and mauled him badly.* = to wound or hurt badly (used to describe an attack by an animal)

mau•so•le•um /mɔːsə'liːəm/ noun, c. *The Taj Mahal is a mausoleum built by an emperor for his queen.* = a large tomb, like a palace, built over the grave of a dead person

mauve /məʊv/ noun = a light purple colour

mav•e•rick /'mævərɪk/ noun, c. *He is quite a maverick, and very few people can understand him.* = a person who is always different from others in his/her behaviour

M

maw /mɔ:/ noun, c. *the maw of the tiger* = the mouth of a fierce animal (old-fashioned)

mawk•ish /'mɔ:kɪʃ/ adj. *The film had some mawkish scenes in which a son expresses love for his mother by weeping on her shoulder.* = showing emotion or love in a manner which is thought to be silly (derogatory)

max•im /'mæksɪm/ noun, c. *They followed the maxim 'Charity begins at home.'* = a short saying that is meant to guide people in their behaviour

max•i•mum[1] /'mæksɪməm/ noun, u. or c. (**maxima** or **maximums**) *You can score a maximum of 100 marks in the physics examination.*(c.) = the highest number or amount which is possible

maximum[2] adj. (opposite **minimum**) *The maximum temperature today was 42 degrees Celsius.* = the highest or greatest **maximize (maximise)** verb, t. *Our profits were very low this year. We must think of a plan to maximize our profits next year.* = to make something as large as possible

may /meɪ/ aux. verb **1** *You may (can) sit down now.* = expressing permission to do something **2** *It may rain today.* = expressing possibility **3** *May you live to be a hundred!* = expressing a wish **4** *She may be slow but she does things so perfectly.* = expressing the idea that while the statement made in the first part of the sentence may or may not be true, the statement made in the second part is certainly true **May** noun = the fifth month of the year, between April and June **May Day** noun = the first day in May, which is celebrated as International Labour Day, to honour workers all over the world **mayday** noun = the international signal asking for help, sent out from a ship or an aircraft which is in trouble

may•hem /'meɪhem/ noun, u. *When the umpire declared te batsman out, there was a lot of mayhem in the stadium.* = trouble and confusion

may•on•naise /meɪə'neɪz/ noun, u. = thick white sauce made with eggs, oil and vinegar, to be eaten with salads

may•or /meə^r/ noun, c. = an elected official who is in charge of the administration of a city

maze /meɪz/ noun, c. = a complicated system of paths through which people walk, trying to find their way out, as a kind of entertainment (also **labyrinth**)

a maze

MC abbr. of **Master of Ceremonies** (see **master**)

MD abbr. of **1** *Doctor of Medicine* = a higher degree in Medicine, given after the first degree of MBBS **2** *Managing Director* = the person who manages a business or a company

me /mi:/ pron. *She likes me.* = object form of the pronoun 'I'

mead•ow /'medəʊ/ noun, c. = an open field covered with wild grass, in which cattle can graze (eat grass)

mea•gre /'mi:gə^r/ adj. *She has to manage on a meagre salary.* = very small in quantity or value

meal /mi:l/ noun, c. or u. **1** *He eats only two meals a day—breakfast and dinner.*(c.) = the food eaten at a particular time of the day **2** *bone meal*(u.) = something (specially some grain) which has been crushed into a powder **3** *a square meal* = a meal which satisfies one's hunger

mean[1] /mi:n/ adj. **1** *He is so mean that he never gives money to any charity.* = unwilling to give or share **2** *She was very mean not to thank you for the present.* = unkind **3** *The mean temperature in Bhubaneswar in June is 39 degrees Celsius.* = average

mean[2] noun, c. **1** *The mean of 5, 9 and 13 is 9.* = average **2** *Parents must find a mean between too much kindness to children and too much strictness.* = something that is between two extremes

mean[3] verb, t. **1** *The expression 'to pass away' means 'to die'.* = to express or carry a certain meaning (see under **meaning**) **2** *My parents mean a lot to me.* = to have importance **3** *I meant to come yesterday, but I could not come.* = to intend to do something **meaning** noun, u. or c. **1** *The meaning of the word 'travel' is 'to go from one place to another'.* = what a word or an expression stands for or conveys **2** *Education has little meaning for the poor who hardly get anything to eat.* = importance **meaningful** adj. *He plays a very meaningful part in this new film.* = important **meanwhile** *It is now only 11 a.m. and our next class begins at 12.30 p.m. Meanwhile, we can have a quick lunch.* = in the time between two events or at the same time as something is happening

to mean business *When our basketball coach asked us to do some exercises after the game, we thought she was joking, but she meant business.* = to be serious about something that one plans to do **to mean well** = to have good intentions **I mean to say** *He is useless as a wicket-keeper. I mean to say, he shouldn't have dropped that easy catch.* = an expression of disapproval, used to soften the effect of something stronger that was said earlier

means /mi:nz/ noun (always plural) **1** *The most comfortable means of travelling there is by train.* = a method or way of doing something **2** *She has been living beyond her means.* = income; the money that one has

by all means *'Shall we sell the building?' 'By all means?'* = an expression used to convey complete agreement with something that has been proposed or suggested **to live beyond one's means** = to be spending more money on oneself than one should spend **a means to an end** = something done in order to achieve a desired result

me•an•der /mi'ændəʳ/ verb, i. **1** *The river meanders between these hills and flows down to the sea.* = to flow slowly along a winding (not straight) path (used to describe the flow of a river or stream) **2** *We like to meander through the streets of Varanasi.* = to walk slowly and aimlessly (literary)

mea•sles /'miːzəlz/ noun (always plural) = a kind of sickness which produces fever and small red spots on the face and body and is highly infectious

measly /'miːzlɪ/ adj. *a measly amount* = very small (derogatory)

mea•sure¹ /'meʒəʳ/ verb, t. **1** *The engineers measured the height of the mountain before building a road across it.* = to find out the size, length, height etc. of something, using standard units such as metres, kilograms etc. **2** *The ladder which was used to climb the wall measured 13 feet in length.* = to have a certain size

measure² noun, u. or c. **1** *He sold me 12 measures of rice.*(c.) = a container which is used to measure out a quantity of some thing **2** *He is not very intelligent but he has a certain measure of cleverness.*(u.) = amount or degree (formal) **3** (usually plural) *The government is taking measures to check the smuggling of drugs.*(c.) = an action taken to bring about a certain result **measurable** adj. = something that can be measured **measured** adj. *She spoke in a measured voice.* = carefully chosen or planned **measurement** noun, u. or c. **1** (u.) = the act of measuring something **2** (c.) = the length, height etc. of something that is found by measuring it

short measure = less than the correct amount **to get the measure of someone** = to understand someone's nature correctly **to measure up** *We thought we would give him a chance to do some other kind of work but he didn't measure up.* = to be good enough

meat /miːt/ noun, u. **1** = the flesh of an animal or bird, used as food **2** *He spoke a lot, but there was no meat in his argument.* = ideas that may be considered important (figurative) **meaty** adj. **1** *meaty piece of chicken* = containing a lot of meat **2** *a meaty book* = having a lot of ideas which make one think (figurative)

Mec•ca /'mekə/ noun **1** = the holiest city for Muslims **2** *Varanasi seems to be a Mecca for all foreigners visiting India.* = a place that everyone wants to visit

me•chan•ic /mɪ'kænɪk/ noun, c. = a person who has skill in repairing machines

mechanics (mechanics) /mɪ'kænɪks/ noun **1** *He teaches us mechanics.* = a branch of physics that deals with the effect of physical forces on objects **2** *The new principal knows a lot about the mechanics of running a college.* = the way in which something is done **mechanism** /'mekənɪzəm/ noun, u. *My watch has stopped. There must be something wrong with its mechanism.* = the parts of a machine that allow it to work **mechanize (mechanise)** verb, t. = to replace people with machines to do a certain work

med•al /'medl/ noun, c. *She won the gold medal for swimming.* = a round, flat piece of metal given to the winner of a competition as a prize **medallion** /mə'dæliən/ noun, c. = a large, round and flat piece of metal worn around the neck as a decoration

med•dle /'medl/ verb, i. **1** *Two of my neighbours are quarrelling. I could have stopped the quarrel but I don't like to meddle in the affairs of other people.* = to take too much interest in things that do not concern one (derogatory) **2** *The television was working perfectly until you started to meddle with it.* = to interfere in the working of something **meddlesome** adj. *a meddlesome person* = one who likes to meddle in the affairs of other people

me•di•a /'miːdiə/ noun, u. (always plural, but used with either singular or plural forms of verbs) *The media plays/play an important part in educating the public.* = newspapers, television and radio, through which information can be spread (see also **medium, mass media**) **media studies** noun = the study of the media (television etc.) and its use as an academic subject

me•di•an /'miːdɪən/ noun, c. **1** = the middle value in a series of numbers arranged in a certain order **2** = a straight line passing through the vertex of a triangle to the mid-point of the opposite side [MATHEMATICS]

me•di•ate /'miːdieɪt/ verb, i. *My two neighbours quarrelled and I was forced to mediate between them.* = to act as a peacemaker or referee between two opposing sides

me•di•cine /'medsən/ noun, c. or u. **1** *The leaves of the neem tree make an excellent medicine for any skin disease.*(c.) = some substance that can cure a disease **2** *He is studying medicine at the university.*(u.)

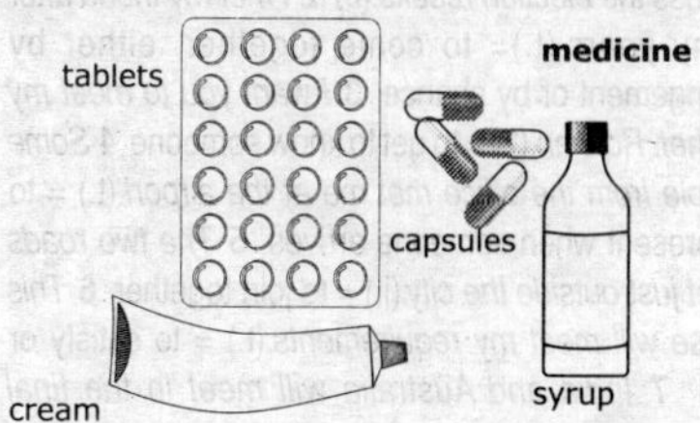

M

= the science that deals with the treatment of diseases **medical** /ˈmedɪkəl/ adj. *a medical book* = dealing with the science of medicine **medication** /medɪˈkeɪʃn/ noun, u. *The patient is asleep. He is under medication.* = the medicines given to treat a disease **medicinal** /mɪˈdɪsənəl/ adj. *She grows medicinal plants in her garden.* = something that can be used to prepare medicines

me•di•e•val (mediaeval) /mediˈiːvəl/ adj. = the middle period in history (from about AD1100 to AD1500)

me•di•o•cre /miːdiˈəʊkər/ adj. *He gave a mediocre performance in the match.* = neither very good nor very bad; ordinary

me•di•ta•tion /medɪˈteɪʃən/ noun, u. *She is always calm because she practises meditation.* = the art of making the mind calm by clearing it of unnecessary thoughts and fixing it on a single thought **meditate** /ˈmedɪteɪt/ verb, i. = to practise meditation **meditative** adj. = showing deep thought

me•di•um[1] /ˈmiːdiəm/ adj. *He is of medium height, about 160 cm.* = of middle size, quality etc.

medium[2] noun, c. (**media** or **mediums**) **1** *Air is the medium through which sound travels. If there is no air, you will not be able to hear any sounds.* = a substance which is necessary for something to exist or for something to happen [SCIENCE] **2** *In this school, we use Hindi as the medium of teaching.* = the language used in doing something **3** *She uses dance as the medium to express her feelings.* = something which is used as the means by which one does something or expresses oneself (see also **media**) **4** = a person who is said to be able to receive messages from the spirits of dead people (also **spiritualist**) **medium wave** = radio signals with a wave length of between 100 and 1,000 metres

med•ley /ˈmedli/ noun, c. **1** *The city of New York contains a medley of people from different parts of the world.* = a mixture of different kinds of things or people **2** = a piece of music made up of many songs or tunes played one after the other

meek /miːk/ adj. *He is so meek that I have never seen him getting angry.* = gentle and non-violent **meekness** noun, u.

meet[1] /miːt/ verb, t. or i. (**met**) **1** *We are meeting to discuss the election results.*(i.) **2** *I met my friend after many years.*(t.)= to come together, either by arrangement or by chance **3** *I want you to meet my brother, Roshan.*(t.) = to get to know someone **4** *Some people from the office met me at the airport.*(t.) = to be present when someone arrives **5** *The two roads meet just outside the city.*(i.) = to join together **6** *This house will meet my requirements.*(t.) = to satisfy or fulfil **7** *India and Australia will meet in the final match.*(i.) = to play against each other

meet[2] noun, c. *We are organizing a sports meet next month.* = a gathering of people, specially for a sports event **meeting** noun, c. *There will be a meeting of scientists from 16 countries in Tokyo.* = a coming together of people for some purpose

there is more to something than meets the eye = something is deeper or more interesting than it appears to be **to meet someone halfway** = to reach an agreement with someone by agreeing to something and getting something in return

> **Usage** In British English, the expression used is 'to meet someone', whereas in American English the expression is 'to meet with someone'. (The British usage is more common in India.)

meg•a- /megə/ prefix meaning **1** one million times (of a given number) e.g. **meg•a•byte** /ˈmegəbaɪt/ noun = a unit for measuring the amount of information that a computer can store, equal to more than one million 'bytes', abbr. as MB [COMPUTERS], **megahertz** noun = a unit for measuring how many million times an electrical current can flow in one second, abbr. as MHz [PHYSICS] **2** = very large e.g. **mega-store** noun = a very large shop

meg•a•phone /ˈmegəfəʊn/ noun, c. = an instrument shaped like a tube with a wide mouth, used for making one's voice sound louder

mel•an•chol•y[1] /ˈmelənkəli/ noun, u. *He is suffering from melancholy.* = a feeling of sadness

melancholy[2] adj. *a melancholy piece of music.* = producing sadness **melancholia** /melənˈkəʊlɪə/ noun = a sickness of the mind that makes one feel sad for no particular reason **melancholic** adj. = suffering from melancholia (formal)

mel•ee /ˈmeleɪ/ noun, u. *A big crowd rushed into the hall and she was trapped in the melee.* = a large and uncontrolled crowd

mel•li•flu•ous /mɪˈlɪfluəs/ adj. *mellifluous music* = sweet (used to describe music or some sound)

mel•low[1] /ˈmeləʊ/ adj. **1** *As a young man he was always ready to quarrel but he has become mellow with age.* = gentle or wise as a result of aging or experience (used to describe the behaviour of people) **2** *This room will be beautiful if painted with mellow colours.* = having a smooth and gentle appearance **3** *Cheese becomes mellow with age.* = (about certain kinds of food or wine) having a gentle taste; not too strong

mel•low[2] verb, i. or t. *As you can see, the leader of the party has mellowed with age.*(i.) = to become mellow (wise and gentle)

mel•o•dra•ma /'melədrɑːmə/ noun, u. or c. *Many Indian films are full of melodrama.*(u.) = a kind of drama or film containing a lot of emotion, with exciting and sudden events and characters who are either very good or very evil **melodramatic** /melədrə'mætɪk/ adj.

mel•o•dy /'melədi/ noun, u. or c. (**melodies**) = a song or tune **melodious** /mə'ləʊdɪəs/ adj. = having a sweet sound

mel•on /'melən/ noun, u. or c. = a kind of fruit containing soft, juicy flesh

melt /melt/ verb, i. or t. **1** *If you leave ice on the floor, it will melt after some time.*(i.) = to turn from a solid substance into a liquid due to the action of heat **2** *The artist will melt some wax and pour the molten wax into a hollow mould, to form a statue.*(t.) = to cause a solid substance to turn into a liquid by heating it **3** *I shouted out to the man, but he just melted into the crowd.*(i.) = to disappear **4** *She was feeling very angry with the children, but when she saw them her heart melted.*(i.) = to be suddenly filled with softer feelings **melting point** noun *The metal lead has a melting point of only 85 degrees C.* = the temperature at which a solid substance will turn into a liquid **melting pot** noun *India has been a melting pot of different races and cultures for thousands of years.* = a place where different races, cultures etc. come together and become one

mem•ber /'membəʳ/ noun, c. *He is a member of our family.* = a person belonging to a family, club etc.

mem•brane /'membreɪn/ noun, c. *There is a fine membrane inside the ear which allows us to hear sounds.* = a very soft and thin piece of skin, specially inside the body [BIOLOGY, TECHNICAL]

me•men•to /mɪ'mentəʊ/ noun, c. (**mementos**) = a small object which reminds one of a special event or occasion (e.g. a visit to a well-known place etc.) (also **souvenir**)

mem•o /'meməʊ/ noun, c. (**memos**) abbr.of **memorandum** /meməʊ'rændəm/ noun, c. (**memoranda** or **memorandums**) **1** = a written message sent by one person to another in the same company etc. **2** = a note to remind someone of something that needs to be done **memorandum of understanding (MOU)** noun = an informal legal agreement between two companies etc.

mem•oirs /'memwɑːʳz/ (always plural) noun *Have you read the memoirs of the late Sarojini Naidu?* = a record of the life of a famous person, written by the person himself/herself

mem•o•ry /'meməri/ noun, u. or c. (**memories**) **1** *The old woman has an excellent memory. She remembers all the events of her childhood.*(c.) = the ability to remember things **2** *Can you recite the poem from memory?*(u.) = the store of things (in the mind) that are remembered **3** *I have some very pleasant memories of my stay in Patna.*(c.) = something that one can remember **4** *How much memory does your computer have?*(u.) = the part of the computer where information is stored [COMPUTERS] **5** *We built a hospital in memory of all those who died in the war.*(u.) = the act of remembering someone who has died **memorable** /'memərəbəl/ adj. *The day of my wedding will always remain memorable.*= something that is worth remembering because of its importance **memorabilia** /memərəbɪliə/ noun, u. *If you visit the Bradman Museum, you will see some memorabilia, including his watch and a pair of gloves which he used.* = small objects which are collected because they remind us of a famous person or an interesting event **memorial** /mɪ'mɔːriəl/ noun, c. = a monument (stone building etc.) built in memory of a famous person **memorize (memorise)** /'meməraɪz/ verb, t. *Can you memorize these telephone numbers?* = to learn something by heart so that it can be easily remembered when required

to have a memory like a sieve = to be unable to remember anything

men•ace /'menɪs/ noun, u. *Our village is facing a menace from frequent floods.* = danger or threat **menacing** adj. *a menacing voice* = threatening or fearsome

men•a•ge•rie /mɪ'nædʒəri/ noun, c. = a private zoo

mend[1] /mend/ verb, t. *This man mends broken pots and pans.* = to repair

mend[2] noun, c. *Her old coat has a mend near the shoulder.* = a place where something has been mended (repaired)

on the mend *She was very depressed after her illness but she is on the mend now.*= to be improving in health (informal)
to mend one's ways = to get rid of one's bad habits

men•di•cant /'mendɪkənt/ noun, c. = a person, usually a religious person, who goes from place to place begging for alms

me•ni•al /'miːnɪəl/ adj. *menial jobs* = heavy and uninteresting work, not requiring skill, below one's dignity

Usage 'menial' was used formerly to refer to a person working as a helper in a house. This use is now considered offensive.

men•in•gi•tis /menɪn'dʒaɪtɪs/ noun = a serious disease which attacks the outer part of the brain [MEDICINE]

M

men•o•pause /'menəpɔ:z/ noun = the time when a woman stops having menstrual periods **menses** /'mensi:z/ noun = the flow of blood from the part of the body (uterus) where a baby can develop (also **menstrual period**) **menstruate** /'menstrueɪt/ verb, i. = to have menstrual periods **menstruation** /menstru'eɪʃən/ noun = the process of having menstrual periods

men•su•ra•tion /mensjʊə'reɪʃən/ noun = the branch of mathematics which deals with the measurement of length, area, volume etc.

men•tal /'mentl/ adj. *The psychologist is studying the child's mental development.* = having to do with the mind **mental age** *The patient is 14 years old but has a mental age of five.* = (generally used to refer to a person whose mind has not developed properly) the power of thinking that one would expect to find in a person of a certain age [SCIENCE] **mental hospital** noun = a hospital where people with mental illness are treated

to have a mental block about something = to be unable or unwilling to think about something (disapproving)

men•tal•i•ty /men'tælɪti/ noun, u. or c. (**mentalities**) *a criminal mentality* = the way in which a person's mind works

men•thol /'menθɒl/ noun = a solid white substance which has a strong smell and is used as a medicine

men•tion[1] /'menʃən/ verb, t. *Mr Verma mentioned you but did not tell me much about you.* = to speak about someone in a few words, without giving details

mention[2] noun, c. *Mr Verma made a mention of you when we met last month.* = a short remark about someone or something, without details

men•tor[1] /'mentɔ:r/ noun, c. *I have learnt many things from him and regard him as my mentor.* = a person who guides and advises someone regularly, particularly about work

mentor[2] verb, t. *I am mentoring these young boys.* = to give advice and help to someone **mentoring** noun, u.

men•u /'menju:/ noun, c. **1** = a list of the different dishes (items of food) that are available in a restaurant **2** = a list of the different choices available in a computer programme, which appear on the screen [COMPUTERS]

me•ow (**miaow**) /mi'aʊ/ noun = the crying sound made by a cat

mer•can•tile /'mɜ:kəntaɪl/ adj. *You should have some knowledge of mercantile law if you want to start a business.* = having to do with trade

mer•ce•na•ry[1] /'mɜ:sənəri/ noun, c. (**mercenaries**) = a professional soldier who is willing to fight for anyone who will pay him or her

mercenary[2] adj. *a mercenary attitude to work* = interested only in money (derogatory)

mer•chant /'mɜ:tʃənt/ noun, c. = a person who buys and sells goods, usually in large amounts **merchant navy** noun = ships belonging to a country which are used for trading, not war

mer•chan•dise /'mɜ:tʃəndaɪz/ noun, u. *They have a lot of merchandise in their shop.* = things which are offered for sale (also **goods**)

mer•cy /'mɜ:si/ noun, u. *The judge showed mercy to the criminal and allowed her to go free.* = kindness shown when one has the power to make a person suffer **merciful** adj. *a merciful judge* = showing mercy (pity) **merciless** adj. *the merciless killing of people* = showing no mercy **mercy killing** noun. = the painless killing of someone, generally by using a powerful drug, who is suffering from a disease that cannot be cured (also **euthanasia**)

to be at someone's mercy = to be helpless

mer•cu•ry /'mɜ:kjʊri/ noun = a silvery, liquid metal, used in thermometers (instruments that measure temperature) **mercurial** /mɜ:'kjʊəriəl/ adj. *She has a mercurial temper and becomes angry easily.* = quick and active; changing very quickly

Mercury /'mɜ:kjʊri/ noun **1** = the messenger of the gods, in stories from ancient Rome **2** = the planet nearest to the sun

mere /mɪər/ adj. *He is only 10 years old—a mere child.* = nothing more than **merely** adv. *I was merely joking when I said that he should become the next Prime Minister.* = only (formal)

merge /mɜ:dʒ/ verb, i. or t. **1** *The rivers Ganga and Yamuna merge at Allahabad.*(i.) = to meet and become one **2** *The princely states merged into the Union of India in 1947.* = to become a part of **merger** noun, u. *The merger of the publishing company and the film company was completed last year.* = the act of merging (joining together to become one)

me•rid•i•an /mə'rɪdiən/ noun, c. = an imaginary line drawn on the surface of the earth which passes through both the North Pole and the South Pole and helps to mark the position of a place on the map [GEOGRAPHY]

me•ringue /mə'ræŋ/ noun, u. = a kind of light cake made from sugar and the white part of eggs

mer•it[1] /'merɪt/ noun, u. or c. **1** *My sister got a scholarship entirely through her own merit and not through somebody's help.*(u.) = the quality of being good at something (e.g. studies or professional work) for which one deserves praise **2** *We have received a number of paintings for the art competition. Each painting will be judged on its merits.*(c.) = a good quality

merit[2] verb, t. *Your proposal is so well-researched that it merits consideration.* = to deserve

meritorious /merɪ'tɔ:riəs/ adj. *a meritorious student* = having merit

mer•maid /'mɜ:meɪd/ noun, c. = an imaginary creature which has the upper body of a woman and the tail of a fish

mer•ry /'meri/ adj. *He is always merry, although he has many problems.* = cheerful and happy **merry-go-round** noun = a machine which turns round and round in a circle and has toy animals on which children can ride **merry-making** noun, u. = feasting, dancing, singing etc. done for enjoyment

mesh[1] /meʃ/ noun, u. or c. (**meshes**) **1** *We have fitted the windows with wire mesh so that no mosquitoes can enter.*(u.) = a piece of material made from steel wires or plastic threads woven into a net, with small spaces between the wires **2** *The fish were caught in the meshes of the net.*(c.) = the spaces between the threads in a net

mesh[2] verb, i. *I don't think I can work in this company for long. My ideas and those of the others don't mesh.* = to fit together (used to describe ideas etc.)

mes•mer•ize (mesmerise) /'mezməraɪz/ verb, t. *I was mesmerized by his beautiful song.* = to capture the attention of someone completely

mess[1] /mes/ noun, c. or u. **1** *I am having all my meals in the students' mess.*(c.) = a room in a students' hostel or army officers' camp etc. where meals are served **2** *When the students moved out of the hostel, it was a complete mess.*(u.) = a state of untidiness and disorder **3** *The director has left the company in a mess.*(u.) = a troubled situation

mess[2] verb, t. or i. *Don't mess up my room.*(t.) = to leave things in an untidy state **messy** adj. *The room is very messy.* = untidy

mess around with something = to play with something in a careless way (informal) **to create a mess** **1** = to make something dirty or untidy **2** = to cause trouble or confusion for others **to make a mess of something** = to spoil something **to mess with someone** *You shouldn't mess with him. He is a dangerous person.* = to cause trouble to someone (informal)

mes•sage[1] /'mesɪdʒ/ noun, c. **1** *Your sister came to see you while you were away. She has left a message for you.* = a piece of information that is passed on to someone **2** *This book has a message for readers.* = an important idea that a picture, book, poster etc. is trying to pass on

message[2] verb, t. *Could you message me tonight to let me know how you are?* = to send a message to someone on a mobile telephone

messenger /'mesɪndʒə^r/ noun, c. = a person who brings a message (old-fashioned)

to get the message *I get the message! You want me to leave!* = to be able to understand something, usually something not very pleasant, which is not said clearly or directly

Mess•iah /mɪ'saɪə/ noun, c. = a great religious leader who is believed to have the power to save the world

me•ta- /metə/ prefix meaning 'beyond the normal' e.g. **met•a•phys•ics** /metə'fɪzɪks/ noun = a branch of philosophy that deals with the nature of existence **metaphysical** adj. **1** = relating to metaphysics **2** *metaphysical ideas* = dealing with abstract questions, such as 'What is death?'

me•tab•o•lism /mɪ'tæbəlɪzəm/ noun *As one grows older, the body's metabolism slows down.* = the chemical processes in the body, specially those processes by which the body gets energy from food

me•tal /'metl/ noun, c. or u. *Silver and copper are metals.* = a substance obtained from minerals (different kinds of rock inside the earth) through which heat and electricity can travel easily

me•tal•lic /mɪ'tælɪk/ adj. *a metallic substance* = having the qualities of metal or made of metal **metallurgy** /mɪ'tælədzi/ noun = the scientific study of metals and the process by which they can be produced **metallurgist** noun, c. = a person who studies or practises metallurgy [CHEMISTRY]

met•a•mor•pho•sis /metə'mɔ:fəsɪs/ noun, c. (**metamorphoses**) *All insects go through a process of metamorphosis in which there are several stages.* = a complete change from one form into another [BIOLOGY]

met•a•phor /'metəfə^r/ noun, c. *When I say you are a wolf in sheep's clothing, I am using a metaphor.* = the use of literary language, common in poetry, to describe someone or something by making an indirect comparison with something else, without using words such as 'like' or 'as', which are generally used to make comparisons between different things (see also **simile**) **metaphorical** /metə'fɒrɪkəl/ adj.

mete /mi:t/ verb, t. *mete out severe punishment* = to give or to order punishment (formal)

me•te•or /'mi:tiə^r/ noun, c. = a piece of rock or other matter, thought to have come from some outer space, that falls through space and produces a bright light as it burns on coming in contact with the earth's atmosphere (the layer of air surrounding the earth) (also **falling star** or **shooting star**) **meteorite** /'mi:tiəraɪt/ noun, c. = a meteor that lands on the earth without getting totally burnt up **meteoric** /mi:tɪ'ɒrɪk/ adj. *Amir Khan has had a meteoric career in films.* = like a meteor (gaining very great success in a very short time) (approving)

me•te•o•rol•o•gy /mi:tiə'rɒlədʒi/ noun = the science which studies weather conditions (wind, rain

M

etc.) **meteorologist** noun = a scientist who studies or practises meterorology

me•ter[1] /'mi:tə^r/ noun, c. = a machine which measures the amount of electricity, water etc. that has been used

meter[2] verb, t. *We are going to meter the supply of electricity.* = to measure with the help of a meter

me•thane /'mi:θeɪn/ noun = a gas that can be burnt to produce heat and is produced by the rotting of organic matter (something that was once part of a living plant or animal)

me•thod /'meθəd/ noun, c. or u. **1** *The teacher used the translation method to teach English.*(c.) = a planned way of doing something **2** *I don't find much method in the way things are done in this office.*(u.) = proper planning **methodical** /mɪ'θɒdɪkəl/ adj. *She is very methodical in her work.* = doing things carefully and in a planned way **methodology** /meθə'dɒlədʒɪ/ noun, u. *Can you describe the methodology that you used in carrying out this research?* = a system or a set of methods used to do something or to study a particular subject

to have method in one's madness = to have a good reason for some action, even though it seems foolish or not done in an orderly way

methyl alcohol /'meθɪl 'ælkəhɒl/ = alcohol mixed with a poisonous substance got from wood etc.

meth•yl•at•ed spir•it /meθɪleɪtɪd spɪrɪt/ noun, u. = alcohol which has been mixed with some poisonous substance so that it cannot be drunk, and is used for other purposes such as fuel or for mixing paints etc.

me•tic•u•lous /mɪ'tɪkjʊləs/ adj. *She is always meticulous in her work and never makes a mistake.* = extremely careful and paying great attention to details

me•tre /'mɪtə^r/ noun **1** = a unit for measuring length, originally used in France but now used in most countries, equal to 100 cm **2** *This poem has been written in iambic metre.* = the regular arrangement of sounds in poetry, which produces a certain kind of rhythm (pattern of strong and soft sounds) **metric** adj. *the metric system of measurement* = using the metre, kilometre, kilogramme etc. as units of measurement

met•ro /'metrəʊ/ noun, c. **1** = abbr. of **metropolis** **2** = an underground railway system used in large cities (also **subway**) **metropolis** /mɪ'trɒpəlɪs/ noun, c. (**metropolises**) *Delhi, Mumbai, Chennai and Kolkata are the four Indian metropolises.*= a very large and important city **metropolitan** adj. *a metropolitan centre* = relating to a metropolis

met•tle /'metl/ noun, u. *Tendulkar made a poor start and was almost bowled with the first ball, but he proved his mettle by scoring a brilliant century.* = courage and ability shown during a competition

mew[1] /mju:/ noun = the sound made by a cat

mew[2] verb, i. *The cat mewed when it saw its master.* = to make the sound that a cat makes

mez•za•nine /'mezəni:n/ noun = a small floor in a building that comes between the bottom (ground) floor and the next higher floor

mg abbr. of **milligram**

ml abbr. of **millilitre**

mi•ca /'maɪkə/ noun = a kind of mineral (rock) from which a glass-like substance can be produced, which is not damaged by heat

mi•cro- /'maɪkrəʊ/ prefix meaning very small (opposite **macro-**) e.g. **mi•crobe** /'maɪkrəʊb/ noun, c.= a living thing which is so small that it cannot be seen with the naked eye and which can cause disease

mi•cro•bi•ol•o•gy /maɪkrəʊbaɪ'ɒlədʒɪ/ noun = the scientific study of very small living things, such as bacteria

micro•computer /'maɪkrəʊkəmpju:tər/ noun, c. = a computer of very small size (old-fashioned)

mi•cro•cos•m /'maɪkrəʊkɒzəm/ noun, u. *In this tiny colony you can find people from all parts of India. It is a microcosm of our vast country.* = something very small which represents all the qualities of something that is much larger (opposite **macrocosm**)

mi•cro•or•gan•ism /maɪkrəʊ'ɔ:gənɪzəm/ noun, c. = a very tiny living creature e.g. a bacterium [BIOLOGY]

mi•cro•phone /'maɪkrəfəʊn/ noun, c. (also **mike**) = an instrument that receives sound waves and converts them into electrical waves, which can again be converted into sound waves through an amplifier and loud speakers

mi•cro•pro•ces•sor /'maɪkrəʊprəʊsesə^r/ noun, c. = the 'brain' of a computer that controls its working [COMPUTERS]

mi•cro•scope /'maɪkrəskəʊp/ noun, c. = an instrument that can make extremely small objects or living things look much larger, so that they can be studied by scientists (see pic under **laboratory equipment**) **microscopic** /maɪkrəs'kɒpɪk/ adj. *a microscopic creature* = so small that it can be seen only with the help of a microscope, not with the naked eye

mi•cro•wave /'maɪkrəʊweɪv/ noun, c. = a form of electrical energy having a very short wavelength, which can be used to send wireless messages and also for cooking food **microwave oven** noun = a machine operated by electricity, which can cook or heat food very quickly, using microwaves

mid- /ˈmɪd/ prefix meaning 'middle' e.g. **mid-day** noun = the middle part of the day (12.00 noon) **midnight** noun = the middle of the night (12 o'clock at night) **mid-point** noun, c. = a point which is at or near the centre **midway** adv. *Our farm lies midway between Pune and Mumbai.* = in the middle, between two places **mid-week** noun = the middle days of the week (Tuesday, Wednesday and Thursday)

mid•dle[1] /ˈmɪdl/ noun, u. *There are three houses along this road, and my house is the one in the middle.* = the point or position which is almost at the centre, with something on either side

middle[2] adj. *the middle house* = in the central or a nearly central position (compare **centre**) **middle age** noun, u. = the period of life between youth and old age (roughly from the age of 40 to 55) **Middle Ages** noun = the period of history between AD 1100 and AD 1500 (see also **Medieval Period**) **middling** adj. *'How was the play?' 'Oh, middling.'* = (of events, food etc.) neither very good nor very bad (mildly derogatory) **middle class** noun or adj. = the name given to a social group of people who are employed in different professions (e.g. teaching, banking etc.) and do not belong to either the very rich **upper class** or the **working class**, which is employed in doing heavy work in factories etc. **middleman (middle person)** noun, c. = a person who buys something from a producer (e.g. a farmer) and sells it at a profit to a shop-keeper or a consumer (a user of the product) **middle school** noun, c. = a school for children above primary school and below secondary school

in the middle of nowhere = a long way from any town, village etc.

midge /mɪdz/ noun, c. = a small insect which sometimes bites

mid•get[1] /ˈmɪdʒɪt/ noun, c. = a person of very small height (not respectful)

midget[2] adj. *a midget car* = of very small size

midst /mɪdst/ noun, u. *She remained calm in the midst of all her troubles.* = in the middle of; surrounded by (old-fashioned)

midwife noun, c. (**midwives**) = a woman who is not a doctor but helps women who are about to give birth

mien /miːn/ noun, u. *We were impressed by his dignified mien.* = the expression on a person's face or his/her whole appearance (literary)

might[1] /maɪt/ aux. modal verb (sometimes considered to be the past tense of **may**) *He might come tomorrow.* = expressing slight possibility

might[2] noun, u. *He threw the ball with all his might.* = strength **mighty** adj. *the mighty Roman Empire* = powerful and strong

mi•graine /ˈmiːgreɪn/ noun, u. = a kind of sickness which produces very painful headaches

mi•grate /maɪˈgreɪt/ verb, i. **1** *Every winter, thousands of birds migrate from Central Asia to the Chilka Lake.* = to travel regularly, in certain seasons, from one part of the world to another (used to describe the movement of animals, birds, fish etc.) **2** *I am planning to migrate to America.* = to move away from one's country or home to some other place (see also **immigrate**) **migration** noun, u. = the act of migrating (meaning **1**) **migrant** /ˈmaɪgrənt/ noun, c. = a person or animal that migrates to another place **migratory** /maɪgrəɪtəri/ adj. = used about birds, animals etc. that travel from one part to another during a particular time of the year

mike /maɪk/ see **microphone**

mild /maɪld/ adj. **1** *He is a mild person who does not like to argue with anyone.* = gentle and peace-loving **2** *She has mild fever.* = not very severe (strong) and not causing much discomfort **mildly** adv. **mildness** noun.

mil•dew /ˈmɪldjuː/ noun, u. *old furniture covered with mildew* = a kind of fungus (very tiny plant) that grows on things that have been kept for a long time in warm and wet conditions (e.g. bread or leather shoes)

mile /maɪl/ noun, c. = a unit for measuring distances, equal to about two km **mileage** /ˈmaɪlədʒ/ noun, u. **1** *This car has a mileage of 20,000 miles.* = the distance that a vehicle has travelled **2** *This car returns a mileage of 10 km to a litre of petrol.* = the distance that a vehicle is able to travel on a given amount of fuel **3** *The film star donated a lakh of rupees to a charity but got a lot of mileage out of this.* = advantage or benefit **mile-stone** noun **1** = a small stone pillar by the side of a road, showing the distance to the next important city **2** *The defeat of the Australian team by the Indians was a milestone in the history of Indian sports.* = an important event

mi•lieu /ˈmiːljɜː/ noun, c. (**milieux** or **milieus**) *Fifty years ago, girls were treated as inferior to boys, but this is not possible today. We live in a different social milieu.* = the physical and social surroundings or conditions in which one lives

mil•i•tant[1] /ˈmɪlɪtənt/ adj. *He has a militant attitude and fights for everything.* = ready to fight or use violence

militant[2] noun, c. = a person who uses violence in politics

mil•i•ta•ry[1] /ˈmɪlɪtəri/ noun, u. *The military had to be called in to control the situation as the police was unable to control it.* = the army

military[2] adj. *a military government* = having to do with the fighting forces (army, navy, air force)

M

mil•i•tate /ˈmɪlɪteɪt/ verb, i. *The fact that you were once in jail will militate against you when you apply for a job.* = to go against; to be something which will be seen as negative (formal)

mi•li•tia /mɪˈlɪʃə/ noun, u. = people who are trained to fight to defend their country or keep law and order when required, but who do not belong to the army

milk[1] /mɪlk/ noun, u. **1** = a white liquid produced by female animals and human beings to feed their babies **2** *The milk from the rubber tree is used to produce rubber.* = the thick white sap or juice produced by certain kinds of trees that looks like milk

milk[2] verb, t. **1** *Do you know how to milk cows?* = to get milk from a cow or other animal **2** *to milk a snake* = to draw out poison from a snake [TECHNICAL] **milkshake** noun = a thick cold drink with some flavour (e.g. chocolate) made from milk **milky** adj. = made from milk or looking like milk

to milk a situation *He wants to milk the water shortage by selling buckets of water at a very high price.* = to take advantage (often dishonestly) of a situation and profit by it **to milk someone** = to get as much money as possible from someone

mill[1] /mɪl/ noun, c. **1** *a flour mill* = a simple machine which is used to crush wheat or other kinds of grain into flour, from which bread can be made **2** *a textile mill* = a factory in which a certain type of product is made

mill[2] verb, t. *This wheat has to be milled.* = to crush grain into flour in a mill **millstone** noun, c. **1** = one of the two circular stones between which grain is crushed into flour **2** *Why don't you do some work instead of hanging like a millstone round my neck?* = someone or something which puts a heavy responsibility or burden on a person

to mill about *There was a large crowd milling about the airport.* = to be moving aimlessly

mil•len•ni•um /mɪˈleniəm/ noun, c. (**millennia** or **millenniums**) **1** = a period of 1,000 years **2** *We are all waiting for the millenium to arrive.* = an ideal period of time, when everyone can expect to be happy

mil•let /ˈmɪlɪt/ noun = a kind of cereal (foodgrain)

milli- /ˈmɪlɪ/ prefix meaning 'one-thousandth' e.g. **millimetre** = one thousandth of a metre

mil•lion /ˈmiljən/ noun, c. **1** = a number equal to 1,000,000 **2** (always plural) *Millions of people attended the conference in Brazil* = a very large number (informal) **millionaire** noun, c. = a very rich person

mil•li•pede /ˈmɪlɪpiːd/ noun, c. = a small insect with many legs

mi•me[1] /maɪm/ noun, u. **1** *I was very hungry, but as I didn't know Spanish, I couldn't tell anyone what I wanted. Finally, I had to use mime to ask for food!* = the use of actions and gestures without words to express a certain meaning **2** = a kind of play with actions and facial expressions in which no one speaks

mime[2] verb, t. *The actor mimed the movements of a man who was drunk.* = to show something through actions and gestures, not with words

mim•ic[1] /ˈmɪmɪk/ verb, t. (**mimicked**) *The television host mimics the famous film star in his television programme.* = to copy the speech or actions of some well-known person to make people laugh

mimic[2] noun, c. *Suresh is an excellent mimic.* = an actor who mimics people **mimicry** noun, u. = the art of mimicking people

min abbr. of **1** = minutes **2** = minimum

min•a•ret /mɪnəˈret/ noun, c. *There is a minaret at each corner of the Taj Mahal.* = a tall, thin tower, usually built as part of a mosque

mince[1] /mɪns/ verb, t. *I have to mince some meat to make kheema curry.* = to chop (cut) a piece of meat or vegetables into very fine pieces, using a heavy knife or a cutting machine known as a mincer

mince[2] noun, u. *I need some mince for my cooking.* = meat which has been minced **mincingly** *to walk mincingly* = to walk taking very short steps (often disapproving)

not to mince one's words *Not to mince one's words, I think he is very lazy.* = to use strong instead of mild language to talk about something unpleasant (generally used in negative sentences) **to make mincemeat out of someone** = to destroy or defeat someone completely (informal)

mind[1] /maɪnd/ noun, c. or u. **1** *He has a sharp mind.*(c.) = the abililty to think or reason **2** *She has a good mind for science.* = the way in which one thinks or feels **3** *His name slips my mind now.* = memory **4** *Your mind is not on your work.* = attention

mind[2] verb, t. **1** *You should always mind the advice of your elders.* = pay attention to (formal) **2** *Mind out! There's a man with a ladder! // Mind your head!* = a warming given to someone to be careful as there may be some danger **3** *Who is minding the baby?* = to take care of **4** *I don't mind your singing while I am working.* = to have no objection to something **5** *Would you mind opening the window, please?* = expressing a request **mindful** /ˈmaɪndfʊl/ adj. *Are you mindful of the fact that you have to pick up your father from the station tomorrow?* = able to remember something that one has to do **mindless** adj. *mindless anger* = without any thought **mind-boggling** adj. *The size of the crowd at the film festival was mind-boggling.* = something that causes great wonder and surprise **mind-reader** noun, c. = a person who is said to know what is in the mind of another person

to be in two minds *I am in two minds about whether to go to Delhi in the summer.* = to not be sure about what one should do **to be out of one's mind** *You're going out in this stormy weather? You must be out of your mind!* = a way of telling someone they are doing something foolish (informal) **to bring to mind** = to remember **to make up one's mind** *I wasn't sure earlier but I've now made up my mind to apply for the job.* = to reach a decision **to put someone's mind at rest** *He was worried that I was travelling without any money, but I put his mind at rest by telling him I had enough.* = to make someone stop worrying about something **to mind one's own business** *Why do you want to know more about their plans? I think we should mind our own business.* = to not interfere in the affairs of others (impolite and not respectful if used as a command) **to blow someone's mind** *The music they played really blew my mind.* = to fill one with wonder (informal) **Never mind!** = don't worry, it's all right **to keep an open mind** *Should young people start jobs at twenty? I have an open mind on the subject.* = to not be rigid and fixed in one's thinking so that one is able to look at many points of view **to have a closed mind** = the opposite of having an **open mind** (see earlier) **to know one's mind** = to know exactly what one wants to do **to speak one's mind** = to say exactly what one thinks or believes is right, even if it may hurt someone's feelings **It's all in the mind** = a way of saying that one's feelings and attitudes towards someone or something are influenced by certain beliefs in the mind, and that one can change them if one wants to

-minded a suffix meaning 'having a certain kind of mind' e.g. **narrow-minded** = unable to see things, except in one way

mine[1] /maɪn/ possessive pron. *This book is mine.* = belonging to me

mine[2] noun, c. **1** *a coal mine* = a deep hole in the earth from which coal or other mineral substances are dug out (see **mineral**, below) **2** *an anti-tank mine* = a kind of bomb used to destroy an enemy, which is placed inside the water or below the ground and explodes (bursts) when it is hit by a ship or when someone steps on it

mine[3] verb, t. **(mined)** **1** *We are mining the hillside for gold.* = to dig a mine (hole in the earth) in order to look for minerals **2** *Coal used to be mined here, but there is no coal left now.* = to take something out of a mine **3** *This stretch of road has been heavily mined by the enemy.* = to place a mine (bomb) somewhere **miner** noun, c. = a person who works in a mine (to take out minerals) **mining** noun = the industry of taking minerals out of the earth **minefield** noun, c. = an area in which mines (bombs) have been placed by an enemy

a mine of information = able to give information about many things

min•e•ral /ˈmɪnərəl/ noun, c. = a chemical substance that is formed naturally inside the earth and obtained from a mine **mineralogy** /mɪnəˈrælədʒɪ/ noun = the scientific study of minerals **mineral oil** noun = oil obtained from inside the earth (petroleum) **mineral water** noun = water that comes from inside the earth and has minerals (natural chemicals present in the earth) mixed in it which make it good for health

min•gle /ˈmɪŋgəl/ verb, i. *If you want to be successful as a politician you must learn to mingle with the crowd.* = to mix closely with other things or people

mi•ni- /mɪni/ prefix meaning 'small' e.g. **mini-bus** noun, c. = a bus of very small size, carrying only a few passengers **mini-skirt** noun, c. = a skirt (dress) worn below the waist that is very short in length

min•i•a•ture[1] /ˈmɪnɪtʃər/ adj. *The child is playing with a miniature truck.* = a very small copy of a larger object

miniature[2] noun, c. *She collects miniatures painted by Moghul artists.* = a very small painting of a person

min•i•mum[1] /ˈmɪnɪməm/ noun, u. or c. (**minima** or **minimums**) *Your contribution to this project has been minimum. You must work harder.*(u.) = very little

minimum[2] adj. *The minimum age for getting a driving licence is 18 years.* = the lowest or smallest number or amount possible **minimize (minimise)** verb, t. *We are spending too much money in running this office. We will have to minimize our expenses.* = to bring to a minimum **minimal** adj. *minimal expenditure* = as little as possible

min•is•cule /ˈmɪnɪskjuːl/ adj. *The dish was hot even though he had used only a miniscule amount of chilli.* = extremely small (also **minuscule**) (often humorous)

min•is•ter[1] /ˈmɪnɪstər/ noun, c. **1** *He is the Minister for Home Affairs.* = a politician who is a member of the government and is put in charge of a particular department **2** *He is studying to become a minister.* = a Christian priest

minister[2] verb, i. *Mother Teresa spent most of her life ministering to the poor and sick.* = taking care of someone who needs help **ministry** noun, c.

M

(**ministries**) **1** *The leader of the largest party has been asked to form the new ministry.* = the government **2** *the Ministry of Defence* = a government department which is under a minister **3** = the service of the church

mink /mɪŋk/ noun, c. or u. **1** (c.) = a small animal which has thick, brown fur (hair covering the skin) **2** *a mink coat* = the fur of the mink, which is used to make very expensive coats for women

min•now /'mɪnəʊ/ noun, c. = a kind of very small fish

mi•nor[1] /'maɪnəʳ/ adj. *He is considered a minor poet, but I love his work.* = not important when compared to others (opposite **major**)

minor[2] noun, c. *As she is only 12, she is still a minor.* = a person who has not reached the age at which one legally becomes an adult (grown-up person)

min•strel /'mɪnstrəl/ noun, c. = a travelling musician who, in the old days, went from place to place singing songs of bravery

mint /mɪnt/ noun, u. or c. **1** *mint sauce*(u.) = a plant with small, green leaves which have a strong but pleasant smell and are used to add flavour to food **2** *the government mint*(c.) = a place where coins (to be used as money) are made for the government

to mint money *He is a successful lawyer now and is minting money.* = to earn a lot of money

mi•nus[1] /'maɪnəs/ prep. or noun, c. (**minuses**) **1** *Seven minus three equals four.* (7-3 = 4). = made less by the number stated **2** *The temperature outside the aircraft is -55º Centigrade.* = below (less than) zero

minus[2] noun, c. (**minuses**) **1** *You have to put a minus before the number 55.* = a minus sign, showing that a number is less than zero **2** *As a batsman he has a number of minuses.* = weaknesses or disadvantages

minus[3] adj. *Her lack of experience goes against her. It is a minus factor.* = a disadvantage

min•ute[1] /'mɪnɪt/ noun, c. **1** *There are 60 minutes in an hour.* = a division of time **2** *This will be over in a minute.* = a very short time **3** *This angle measures 35 degrees and 15 minutes.* = a unit for measuring an angle (A degree is divided into 60 minutes.) [GEOMETRY] **4** *The chairperson has asked me to write the minutes of this meeting.* = an official record of what takes place at a meeting

minute[2] verb, t. *I want you to minute all that I have said on this point.* = to include in the minutes (official record) of a meeting

minute[3] /maɪ'nju:t/ adj. **1** *The Chairperson and the Secretary had some minute differences over the selection of candidates.* = very small **2** *She was able to describe the book in minute detail.* = very exact

any minute/moment now *Listen! Any minute now, we'll hear the door bang.* = very soon (informal)

mir•a•cle /'mɪrəkəl/ noun, c. **1** = a wonderful action performed by some supernatural power **2** *Everyone in the bus escaped, though it rolled over twice. What a miracle!* = something surprising and wonderful that cannot be explained **miraculous** /mɪ'rækjʊləs/ adj. *He has had a miraculous cure.* = like a miracle

mi•rage /'mɪrɑ:ʒ/ noun, c. **1** = a strange effect produced by the movement of hot air in a desert, which makes people imagine that they are seeing things which are not there **2** *He has been chasing wealth all his life, but it is a mirage that he is unable to hold on to.* = something that one tries very hard to achieve, but without success (figurative)

mir•ror[1] /'mɪrəʳ/ noun, c. = a piece of glass which reflects light and produces an image (picture) of whatever is in front of it

mirror[2] verb, t. (**mirrored**) *The writings of Jonathan Swift mirror the English society of the eighteenth century.* = to show something as it really is, as if in a mirror **mirror image** noun = an image (picture) seen in a mirror, in which the right side becomes the left side and the left side becomes the right side

mirth /mɜ:θ/ noun, u. *The play we saw on television last night produced a lot of mirth.* = laughter

mis- /mɪs/ prefix meaning **1** 'wrong' e.g. **misconduct** noun, u. = wrong behaviour **2** wrongly e.g. **mis-spell** /mɪs'spel/ verb, t. (**mis-spelled** or **mis-spelt**) = to spell a word wrongly

misbehave /mɪsbɪ'heɪv/ verb, i. = to behave badly

miscalculate /mɪs'kælkjʊleɪt/ verb, i. or t. = to make a wrong calculation about the time, money etc. required for something

miscarriage /mɪs'kærɪdʒ/ noun, u. = the accidental birth of a baby before the expected time, resulting in its death (compare **abortion**) [MEDICAL] **miscarry** verb, i. = to have a miscarriage

mis•cel•la•ne•ous /mɪsə'leɪniəs/ adj. (abbr. **misc**) *I need Rs 1,000 a month to pay house rent, Rs 2,000 for food and Rs 1,000 for miscellaneous expenses.* = of different kinds

mis•chief noun, u. **1** *What mischief has the child been up to?* = childish behaviour that is bad or wrong, but causes no serious harm **2** *He couldn't harm me by writing against me in the papers, so now he is planning some new mischief.* = damage or harm done knowingly by a grown-up person (disapproving)

mis•con•cep•tion /mɪskən'sepʃən/ noun, u. = a wrong idea that one has about something

misconstrue /mɪskən'stru:/ verb, t. = to put a wrong meaning on one's words (formal)

mis•de•mea•nour /mɪsdɪ'mi:nəʳ/ noun, u. = a crime or an offence which is not very serious

mi•ser /ˈmaɪzəʳ/ noun, c. = a person who is very careful with money and does not like to spend it
mis•e•ra•ble /ˈmɪzərəbəl/ adj. **1** *He is feeling miserable in this new city as he has no friends.* = very unhappy **2** *We were working in miserable conditions.* = likely to cause suffering **3** *a miserable little room* = very small or poor in quality
mis•fit /mɪsˈfɪt/ noun, c. *I feel I am a misfit in this gathering of famous writers.* = a person who is unable to fit into (to adjust to or accept) a certain situation
mis•for•tune /mɪsˈfɔːtʃən/ noun, u. or c. = a piece of bad lack
mis•giv•ing noun, c. or u. *When the doctor told me my child needed heart surgery, I was full of misgivings.* = a doubt or fear which may prove to be wrong
misguide /mɪsˈgaɪd/ verb, t. = to teach someone wrong or bad things
mis•hap noun, c. = accident
mish•mash /ˈmɪʃmæʃ/ noun, u. *This new film is a mishmash of at least three other well-known films.* = a mixture of things taken from different sources (informal)
misinform /mɪsɪnˈfɔːm/ verb, t. = to deliberately give wrong information to someone
mis•in•ter•pret /mɪsɪnˈtɜːprɪt/ verb, t. = to put a wrong meaning on something that is said or done (see also **misconstrue**)
mis•judge /mɪsˈdʒʌdʒ/ verb, t. *I thought he was hard-working but he turned out to be lazy. I had misjudged him completely.* = to form a wrong judgement or opinion about someone
mis•lead /mɪsˈliːd/ verb, t. (**misled**) *You misled me by telling me there was very little work in this office. I find I have to work for 10 hours a day.* = to cause someone to think or act in a wrong manner (see also **misguide**)
mismanage /mɪsˈmænɪdʒ/ verb, t. = to manage or control an organization (a company or a school etc.) badly
mis•place /mɪsˈpleɪs/ verb, t. = to put something in a place where it cannot be found again (also **mislay**)
mis•print /ˈmɪsprɪnt/ verb, t. = to make a mistake in printing
mis•quote /ˈmɪskʊəʊt/ verb, t. *I said he has 14 children, not 40. You are misquoting me.* = to report the words of a person wrongly
mis•read verb, t. *When the audience clapped, the speaker thought they liked his speech. He misread their reaction; actually, they wanted him to stop.* = to read something wrongly or to understand something wrongly
mis•rep•re•sent verb, t. *The accident took place because the brakes failed, not because the driver fell asleep. You are misrepresenting the facts.* = to give a wrong picture of something
mis•rule noun, u.= bad government by a ruler
miss[1] /mɪs/ verb, t. (**missed**) **1** *The wicket-keeper missed a simple catch. // The ball just missed the leg stump. // If you don't rush to the station at once you will miss your train.* = to be unable to catch, hit, meet etc. something **2** *I am missing my children. They are away in Mahe.* = to feel unhappy at the absence of someone or something
miss[2] noun, c. (**misses**) *The wicket-keeper jumped, but could not catch the ball. That was a narrow miss!* = a failure to catch, hit etc. something **missing** adj. **1** *a missing tile* = not found or not where it should be **2** *a missing person* = a person who cannot be found but has not been reported killed **3** *Fill in the missing letters to complete the word.* = which should be there but is not **the missing link** = some creature (which has never been found) which might have been like an ape, but from which human beings might have developed
miss[3] noun, c. (**misses**) *Miss Gurung teaches us history.* = the form of address used for an unmarried woman (**Ms** is now preferred by many women as a form of address.)

miss out *You will miss out on the boat ride if you stay at home.* = to not be able to do or enjoy something **to give something a miss** = to decide not to do something (an activity, an event etc.) **to miss the bus (boat)** = to lose a good chance by hesitating or being too slow
mis•sile /ˈmɪsaɪl/ noun, c. **1** = any object (e.g. a stone) thrown through the air, which could cause damage or injury **2** *a ballistic missile* = a flying weapon which can be aimed at a distant target (the place or object that one wants to hit and destroy)
mis•sion /ˈmɪʃən/ noun, c. **1** *They went on a long tour of Nepal. Their mission was to teach children about basic health.* = a duty or purpose for which someone is sent somewhere **2** *My mission in life is to help people to read and write.* = the work that one believes one has been born to do as a duty **3** *A trade mission from Nepal is visiting New Delhi.* = a group of people who are sent to a foreign country for a special purpose **4** *This school is run by the Catholic mission.* = a religious organization **5** *a space mission* = a very special journey made by a spacecraft **missionary** noun, c. (**missionaries**) = a person who works for a religious organization and tries to make others understand his/her religion
mist[1] /mɪst/ noun, u. or c. = a kind of cloud made up of tiny drops of water floating in the air, close to the ground
mist[2] verb, i. *I could not see anything as my spectacles had misted over.* = to be covered with tiny drops of water, like a mist

M

mis•take[1] noun, c. or u. = something that has been done wrongly or should not have been done at all

mistake[2] verb, t. (**mistook, mistaken**) *Sita looks so much like her twin sister Gita that most people mistake one for the other.* = to fail to recognize someone or something correctly

mis•ter /ˈmɪstəʳ/ noun *Mister Jones is my neighbour.* = a form of address for a man (abbr. **Mr**)

mis•tress /ˈmɪstrɪs/ noun, c. (**mistresses**) **1** *She is the mistress of this house.* = a woman who controls or owns something (old-fashioned) **2** *The school has a new mistress.* = a woman teacher (old-fashioned)

mis•trust verb, t. *They mistrust me because I have lied several times.* = to have no trust in someone

mis•un•der•stand /mɪsʌndəˈstænd/ verb, t. (**misunderstood**) = to understand someone wrongly **misunderstanding** noun, c. or u. = a situation in which something has not been understood correctly

misuse verb, t. = to use something wrongly or badly

mite /maɪt/ noun, c. = a small insect

mit•i•gate /ˈmɪtɪgeɪt/ verb, t. *There is a move to plant neem trees in our neighbourhood. This will mitigate the effect of pollution from diesel fumes.* = to make something less bad or less harmful

mit•ten /ˈmɪtn/ noun, c. = gloves worn on the hands, which do not have separate coverings for each finger

mix[1] /mɪks/ verb, t. or i. **1** *You can mix lime juice with water.*(t.) = to combine different things together, so that they cannot be separated easily **2** *I want you to mix with all the guests.*(i.) = to talk in a friendly way with other people

mix[2] noun, c. **1** *There was a mix of people from many different professions at the meeting.* = a combination or group made up of different things or people **2** *an idli mix* = a special powder that contains the different things required to make a dish etc. **mixture** noun, c. or u. **1** *We use a mixture of sugar, lemon juice and water to make lemonade.*(c.) = a combination of different things **2** *This bottle contains cough mixture.*(u.) = a medicine produced by combining a number of chemicals together **mixed** adj. **1** *I got a mixed response from the audience.* = both good and bad **2** *I had a mixed group of classmates in school.* = made up of different kinds of people or things **mixed economy** noun = a country where some of the business is run by the government (the public sector) and some by private companies (the private sector)

mixed blessing *Television has proved to be a mixed blessing.* = something that is harmful as well as useful **to be mixed up** = to be confused and not know what to do **to get mixed up with** *She had a quiet life so far, but suddenly she's got mixed up with people who smoke and drink.* = to get involved in something unpleasant **mixed bag** *We have received many paintings for our art competition, but it is a mixed bag.* = containing a number of things, not all of the same quality

mix•er /ˈmɪksəʳ/ noun, c. = an electrical machine used (mostly in the kitchen) to mix substances together (also **blender**)

mne•mo•nic /nɪˈmɒnɪk/ noun, c. *Whenever I forget how many days there are in a particular month, I recite the poem 'Thirty days has September etc.' to myself. It is an excellent mnemonic.* = something that helps one to remember something

MO abbr. of **money-order** = money sent through the postal system

moan[1] /məʊn/ verb, i. **1** *The sick man moaned in pain.* = to make a low sound expressing pain or sorrow **2** *Stop moaning! You are very comfortable here.* = to complain unnecessarily (informal)

moan[2] noun, c. *I heard a soft moan from the sick patient in the hospital.* = the sound of moaning

moat /məʊt/ noun, c. = a ditch (long, deep hole) filled with water, surrounding a fort or castle (see **fort**), intended to stop enemies from entering

mob /mɒb/ noun, c. = a large and uncontrolled crowd that could cause trouble

mo•bile[1] /ˈməʊbaɪl/ adj. *We are using a mobile home to travel around the country. // a mobile phone* = something that can move easily or be moved from place to place

mobile[2] noun, c. **1** *You will find a beautiful mobile hanging from the roof of this building.* = a piece of decoration made up of small parts tied to wires or strings, which can move in the wind **2** *She is using a mobile to speak to her friend.* = a mobile phone (a telephone that one can carry around and use from any place) (also **cell phone**) **mobility** /məʊˈbɪlɪti/ noun, u. *I have lost my mobility after I broke my leg in an accident.* = the quality of being mobile (able to move about) **mobilize (mobilise)** /ˈməʊbɪaləɪz/verb, t. **1** *We have mobilized to protest against the noise of the diesel engines in our locality.* = to organize people in support of something **2** *The army is being mobilized.* = to make an army ready for war

moc•ca•sin /ˈmɒkəsɪn/ noun, c. = a shoe made of soft leather which can be slipped on and does not need to be tied up

mock[1] /mɒk/ verb, t. *You shouldn't mock someone who seems to be less intelligent than you.* = to make fun of someone

mock[2] adj. **1** *We are staging a mock parliament.* = something that is a copy of something else (the real thing) **2** *a mock entrance test* = something that is held as a preparation before the real thing is to happen

mock-up noun, c. = a model or copy of something that is going to be built **mockery** noun, u. **1** *Some people laughed when I danced badly, but I was not disturbed by their mockery.* = the act of mocking or laughing at someone **2** *You have made a mockery of the examination by using unfair means.* = to take away the value of something and turn it into a joke

mo•dal /'məʊdl/ noun, c. *'Can', 'may', 'will', 'shall', etc. are all modals.* = an auxiliary (helping) verb that expresses permission, possibility etc. [GRAMMAR]

mode /məʊd/ noun, c. **1** *The mode of teaching in this school is rather old-fashioned.* = a way of doing something **2** *The tape-recorder is now in the playback mode. It can play a cassette but cannot record anything.* = the manner in which a machine, which can do different things, is working at a particular time **3** *Narrow trousers are now the mode.* = fashion

mo•del[1] /'mɒdl/ noun, c. **1** *This is a cardboard model of the new school that will be built.* = a small but exact copy of a building, machine etc. to show what it will look like **2** *She works as a model for a fashion designer.* = a good-looking person who appears on a stage or platform in new clothes designed by someone so that people interested in buying such clothes can see what they look like **3** *The artist is looking for a model.* = a person who is paid to be painted by an artist or photographed by a photographer **4** *We have followed the British model in planning the Indian parliamentary system.* = a system or a design which can be copied by someone else **5** *She is a model for other teachers.* = someone who can serve as a good example for others to copy **6** *We want to buy a car of this model.* = a particular type of vehicle made by a company during a particular year

model[2] adj. *She is a model teacher.* = serving as an example for others to copy

model[3] verb, t. **1** *This artist models statues of birds and animals out of clay.* = to make or shape something **2** *She models clothes for a fashion designer.* = to work as a model so that people can see clothes of new design

mo•dem /'məʊdəm/ noun, c. = an instrument that connects a computer to a telephone line and allows communication to the Internet [COMPUTERS]

mod•e•rate[1] /'mɒdərɪt/ adj. **1** *He lives in a house of moderate size.* = neither very large nor very small **2** *This political party has moderate views.* = not at one extreme or the other but somewhere in the middle

moderate[2] /'mɒdəreɪt/ verb, t. **1** *They are asking for too much money. They should moderate their demands.* = to make something less strong **2** *I have been asked to moderate the questions that have been set for the examination.* = to review or check the questions set (by someone else) for an examination, making sure that they are not too difficult (used in education to ensure that standards of judging or testing are uniform)

moderate[3] noun, c. = a person whose political views are not at one extreme or the other **moderator** /mɒdə'reɪtə^r/ noun, c. **1** = a person who acts as a referee in a dispute, argument or debate **2** = a person who moderates the questions set for an examination

mo•dern /'mɒdn/ adj. **1** *a history of modern India* = belonging to the present time **2** *a modern institution* = having the technology, systems etc. of the present times **modernize (modernise)** verb, t. *We must modernize our system of education.* = to make something suitable for the needs of the present time

mod•est /'mɒdɪst/ adj. **1** *Although she is a famous writer, she is so modest that she never talks about her achievements.* = not speaking too much of one's good qualities **2** *I have been given a modest increase in my salary.* = not very large (often disapproving) **modesty** noun, u. = the quality of being modest

mo•di•cum /'mɒdɪkəm/ noun, u. *He doesn't have even a modicum of dishonesty. // There is not even a modicum of truth in this report.* = a very small amount (mostly used in negative sentences) (formal, somewhat old-fashioned)

mod•i•fy /'mɒdɪfaɪ/ verb, t. *We are going to modify the design of this house by adding an extra bedroom.* = to change slightly **modification** /mɒdɪfɪ'keɪʃn/ noun, u. **1** = the act of modifying (changing) something **2** = a change that has been made to something **modifier** /'mɒdɪfɪə/ noun = a word (e.g. an adverb) that changes the meaning of or has an effect on another meaning

mod•ule /'mɒdju:l/ noun, c. *The new English course is designed in the form of modules, which a student can choose from at different times.* = a small independent part or unit which can be combined with other parts to make a larger structure or arrangement

mod•u•late /'mɒdjʊleɪt/ verb, t. *He has a powerful voice but he should learn how to modulate it.* = to control the strength of a sound

mo•dus op•e•ran•di /məʊdəs ɒpə'rændi/ noun (Latin) *Police detectives use a very clever modus operandi to catch criminals.* = a method of doing something

modus vivendi /məʊdəs vɪ'vendi/ noun (Latin) *There was some dispute between the two brothers over property, but now they have worked out a modus vivendi to live together in peace.* = an arrangement by which people can live or work together in peace

mo•gul /'məʊgəl/ noun, c. *He owns 25 factories and is a powerful business mogul.* = an important, rich and powerful person (informal)

M

moist /mɔɪst/ adj. *The soil is moist after the rain.* = slightly wet **moisten** /'mɔɪsn/ verb, t. *She moistened a towel and wiped the child's face with it.* = to make something wet **moisture** /'mɔɪstʃəʳ/ noun, u. *There is a lot of moisture in the air. It may rain today.* = wetness (water or some other liquid in the form of very tiny drops) **moisturize (moisturise)** verb, t. *This lotion (medicine for the skin) will moisturize your skin.* = to take away the dryness from something **moisturizer** /mɔɪstʃə'raɪzəʳ/ noun, c. = a liquid or cream that makes the skin less dry

mo•lar /'məʊlə/ noun, c. = the large teeth at the back of the mouth which are used to break up food while chewing

mo•las•ses /mə'læsɪz/ noun, u. (always plural) = the thick, dark and sweet substance produced by boiling the juice of sugarcane

mold /məʊld/ noun, u. = see **mould** (below)

mole /məʊl/ noun, c. **1** = a small animal that looks like a rat and makes its home under the ground **2** = a spy who gives secret information, usually to the police (informal) **3** *She has a mole on her cheek.* = a small, raised mark, usually black, on a person's skin **4** = a unit used to measure how much of a substance there is [CHEMISTRY] **mole-hill** noun, c. = a small pile of earth dug up by a mole while making its home under the ground

to make a mountain out of a mole-hill = to make something which is unimportant appear to be very important by talking a lot about it

mol•e•cule /'mɒlɪkju:l/ noun, c. *A molecule of hydrogen contains two atoms.* = the smallest part into which a chemical substance can be divided without losing its natural qualities, usually consisting of two or more atoms [CHEMISTRY] (compare **atom**) **molecular** /mə'lekjʊləʳ/ adj. *molecular weight* = relating to a molecule

mo•lest /mə'lest/ verb, t. = to harm a child or a woman sexually **molestation** /məʊle'steɪʃən/ noun, u. = the act of molesting someone

mol•li•fy /'mɒlɪfaɪ/ verb, t. *She was very angry with me, but I mollified her by inviting her to dinner.* = to make a person less angry

mol•lusc /'mɒləsk/ noun, c. = a kind of animal that has a very soft body covered with a hard shell e.g. a snail or an oyster [BIOLOGY]

mol•ten /'məʊltən/ adj. *molten steel* = something solid which melts and becomes liquid due to great heat

mo•lyb•de•num /mə'lɪbdənəm/ noun = a kind of white metal that is sometimes mixed with steel

mom /mɒm/ noun, c. = mother (also **mum** or **mummy**) (informal)

mo•ment /'məʊmənt/ noun, c. **1** *I will be back in a moment.* = a very short period of time **2** *The actor arrived at just that moment.* = a particular point of time **3** *She is going to speak on a matter of great moment.* = importance (formal) **momentary** adj. a momentary loss of memory = lasting for just a moment **momentous** /məʊ'mentəs/ adj. *a momentous event* = very important (formal)

the moment of truth = a moment when something very important or dramatic happens **at the moment** *She can't come to the door now. She's busy at the moment.* = now **at any moment** = very soon after the present time **at the last moment** *The meeting is planned, but Mr. Alvarez may change his mind about it at the last moment.* = just in time before something happens **for the moment** *I know we need better chairs in the classroom, but for the moment, could you manage with the ones we have?* = only for the present time, but not later **to have one's moments** = to feel happy, important etc. only at certain times, but not always

mo•men•tum /məʊ'mentəm/ noun, u. **1** = the mass (weight) of an object mutiplied by its velocity (speed) [PHYSICS] **2** *The driver tried to stop the train by applying the brakes, but the train had so much momentum that it could not be stopped at once and rolled along for nearly two kilometres.* = the force that a moving object has, because of which it cannot be stopped at once

mon•arch /'mɒnək/ noun, c. = the ruler of a country (king or queen) **monarchy** noun, u. or c. (**monarchies**) **1** (u.) = the system of rule by a king or queen **2** (c.) = a country which is ruled by a king or queen

mon•as•tery /'mɒnəstri/ noun, c. (**monasteries**) = a place where monks (people who have chosen to spend their lives in serving their religion) live (see also **monk**) **monastic** /mə'næstɪk/ adj. *a monastic life* = like that of a monk

mon•e•ta•ry /'mʌnɪteri/ adj. = having to do with money

mon•ey /'mʌni/ noun, u. **1** *I need some money to buy food.* = coins, bank-notes etc. which can be used to buy things **2** *He has a lot of money.* = wealth **money-changer** noun, c. = a person who can exchange the money used in one country for the money used in a different country **money-lender** noun = a person who gives out loans on interest **money-spinner** noun = a book or film etc. which earns a lot of money for the writer or producer (informal)

to get one's money's worth = to get complete value for the money that one has spent **to come into big**

money = to get a lot of money from some source, usually by inheriting money from someone who has died (informal) **to have money to burn** = to be careless with money because one is very rich (disapproving) **money for jam** = money which is earned very easily, without much effort **to put one's money where one's mouth is** = to provide proof to support something that one is saying **hush money** = money paid as a bribe, to keep something secret (informal) **money talks** = an expression used to suggest that if one has money, one has power and can get/do what one wants

mon•goose /ˈmɒŋguːs/ noun, c. (**mongooses**) = a small animal found in India (and other tropical countries) that kills snakes

mon•grel /ˈmʌŋgrəl/ noun, c. = a dog whose parents belong to different breeds and is not considered valuable

mon•i•tor[1] /ˈmɒnɪtəʳ/ verb, t. *The Election Commission is sending a team of officials to three states to monitor the elections there.* = to watch something carefully over a period of time so as to make sure that nothing goes wrong

monitor[2] noun, c. **1** *You can see the pictures on the monitor.* = an instrument with a screen on which pictures or words can be shown, used as part of a computer system [COMPUTERS] **2** *The teacher has made me the monitor for this class.* = a pupil who is chosen by the teacher to help him/her in keeping order in the class

monk /mʌŋk/ noun, c. = a person (generally a man) who joins a religious group and leads a life of prayer and service to religion (compare **nun**)

mon•key[1] /ˈmʌŋki/ noun, c. = a small, tree-climbing animal with a long tail

monkey[2] verb, i. *Who asked you to monkey with this machine?* = to handle something (specially a machine) carelessly because of not knowing enough about it (informal) **monkey business** *I don't want any of your monkey business.* = behaviour which is not honest or acceptable and is often secret **monkey-nut** = a peanut or groundnut

mon•o- /mɒnəʊ/ prefix meaning one or single e.g. **mo•no•chrome** /ˈmɒnəkrəʊm/ adj. *We have arranged an exhibition of monochrome photographs.* = having no colours other than black and white

mono noun or adj. *Is your new cassette player a stereo or a mono?* = a machine which produces sounds that seem to come from only one direction (see also **stereo**)

mo•nog•a•my /məˈnɒgəmi/ noun, u. = the custom of having only one wife or husband at one time (opposite **bigamy** or **polygamy**) **monogamous** adj.

mon•o•graph /ˈmɒnəgrɑːf/ noun, c. = a short book written on a single subject, usually to report some research

mon•o•lin•gual[1] /mɒnəʊˈlɪŋgwəl/ noun, c. = a person who knows and can use only one language

monolingual[2] adj. *a monolingual dictionary* = using only one language (opposite **bilingual** or **multilingual**)

mon•o•lith /ˈmɒnəlɪθ/ noun, c. = a single large, tall block of stone, put up for religious purposes by people who lived long ago **monolithic** /mɒnəˈlɪθɪk/ adj. *a monolithic state* = something (usually a company or a governnment) which becomes too large and powerful and does not allow any differences (derogatory)

mon•o•logue /ˈmɒnəlɒg/ noun, c. or u. = a long speech by one person only (opposite **dialogue**) (sometimes derogatory)

mo•nop•o•ly /məˈnɒpəli/ noun, u. or c. (**monopolies**) *The railways are a government monopoly.*(u.) = a business which is controlled by a single person or group, with no competition from anyone else **monopolize (monopolise)** verb, t. *The large company wants to monopolize the telecommunications industry.* = to have full control over something and allow no competition

mon•o•rail /ˈmɒnəʊreɪl/ noun, c. = a train which runs on or hangs from a single rail (railway track)

mon•o•syl•la•ble /mɒnəˈsɪləbəl/ noun, c. *The word 'send' is a monosyllable but 'sending' has two syllables.* = a word which has only one syllable (see **syllable**) **monosyllabic** /mɒnəsɪˈlæbɪk/ adj. *a monosyllabic word* = having one syllable only

mon•o•the•is•m /ˈmɒnəʊθiːɪzəm/ noun, u. = the belief that there is only one god (opposite **polytheism**)

mo•no•tone /ˈmɒnətəʊn/ noun, c. *He was speaking in a dull monotone that made us feel sleepy.* = a way of speaking in which the voice never rises or falls and therefore sounds dull **monotonous** /məˈnɒtənəs/ adj. *The film was very monotonous.* = not containing variety (change) and therefore dull

mo•nox•ide /məˈnɒksaɪd/ noun, u. or c. = a chemical which contains only one atom of oxygen in each molecule [CHEMISTRY]

mon•soon /mɒnˈsuːn/ noun, c. **1** = a season in the Indian subcontinent and parts of South Asia when there is very heavy rain **2** = a wind that brings heavy rain

mon•ster /ˈmɒnstəʳ/ noun, c. **1** = an imaginary creature (appearing in children's stories) that is very large and frightening **2** *The tiger was an absolute monster.* = an animal of unusually large size **3** *The man is a monster.* = a very evil or wicked person (figurative) **monstrosity** /mɒnˈstrɑsɪti/ noun, u.

M

The new office building is a monstrosity. = something very large and ugly **monstrous** /ˈmɒnstrəs/ adj. **1** *Your behaviour at the meeting was monstrous.* = very bad **2** *a monstrous elephant* = of unusually large size

month /mʌnθ/ noun, c. = one of the 12 parts into which a year is divided **monthly** adj. = happening every month

mo•nu•ment /ˈmɒnjʊmənt/ noun, c. = an object (usually a stone building, tower etc.) built to remember a person or an important event **monumental** /mɒnjʊˈməntl/ adj. *a monumental piece of writing* = very great or important **historical monument** = an old building or place which is important in the history of a country

moo[1] /muː/ noun, c. = the sound made by a cow

moo[2] verb, i. = to make a sound like a cow

mood /muːd/ noun, c. **1** *He is in a happy mood now.* = the way one feels at a particular time **2** *The sentence 'Go home at once!' is in the imperative mood.* = the form of the verb which shows whether a sentence is to be understood as a statement (indicative), a question (interrogative) or a command (imperative) [GRAMMAR] **moody** adj. *a very moody person* = having moods that change easily and often

moon[1] /muːn/ noun **1** = the heavenly body that moves around the earth and shines at night **2** *the moons of Jupiter* = a heavenly body that moves around planets other than the earth

moon[2] verb, i. *Stop mooning around and settle down to some work!* = to spend time doing nothing (informal) **moonless** adj. = dark, with no moon in the sky **moon-beam** noun, c. = a ray of light that comes from the moon **moonlight** noun, u. = the light of the sun, reflected by and seeming to come from the moon **moonlight** verb, i. *She is a teacher in a school but she is also moonlighting and doing other jobs.* = to have more than one job, without the knowledge of the employer **moonstruck** adj. *You must be moonstruck!* = slightly mad

to be over the moon = to feel extremely happy about something **to cry for the moon** = to wish strongly for something that one cannot get **to promise someone the moon** = to promise to do something that one cannot possibly do or to give someone something that one cannot give

moor[1] /mʊəʳ/ noun, c. = an open area of land covered with rough grass

moor[2] verb, t. *We will moor the boat here.* = to tie up a boat or ship to something on the land (e.g. a tree) so that it cannot move **moorings** noun, c. (generally plural) **1** *The ship broke loose from its moorings.* = the place to which a ship is moored (tied) **2** *This generation has lost its emotional moorings.* = something that keeps a person steady and balanced

Moor = a person from Morocco (an Arab country in northern Africa)

moose /muːs/ noun, c. = a kind of large deer found in North America

moot point /ˈmuːt pɔɪnt/ noun, c. *It is a moot point whether the banning of violent programmes on television will reduce crime.* = a question which has not been decided and over which there can be a debate

mop[1] /mɒp/ noun, c. **1** = a long stick with a number of loose cotton threads hanging from one end, used to clean floors **2** *a mop of hair* = a mass of untidy hair on someone's head

mop[2] verb, t. **1** *You have spilled some ink on the floor. Please mop it up.* = to clean with a mop **2** *She kept mopping his face with a towel.* = to wipe (clean with a piece of cloth) **a mopping-up operation** noun *The army is engaged in mopping-up operations across the border.* = an attack carried out by soldiers to mop up (remove completely) any enemies remaining in an area

to mop up = to clean something using a mop etc. from a surface

mope /məʊp/ verb, i. *Stop moping over your defeat.* = to continue to be unhappy about something

mo•ped /ˈməʊped/ noun, c. = a light motorcycle or a bicycle fitted with an engine

mo•raine /məˈreɪn/ noun, u. = masses of earth or rock lying on the edges of a glacier [GEOGRAPHY] (see also **glacier**)

mo•ral[1] /ˈmɒrəl/ adj. *We expected our leaders to be honest and just and to have high moral values.* = based on principles of right and wrong behaviour etc.

moral[2] noun, c. *The moral of this story is that you should always think before you speak.* = something that one learns from a story or an incident about the right way to act or behave **morals** noun (always plural) *He will do anything to win. He has no morals.* = the rules or standards for good behaviour which a person is supposed to have **morality** /məˈræləti/ noun, u. *the morality of using nuclear weapons* = standards of good or honest behaviour **moralize (moralise)** /ˈmɒrəlaɪz/ verb, i. *He loves to moralize, though he seldom practises what he preaches.* = to talk about the importance of morality etc. without doing anything about it (derogatory)

mo•rale /məˈrɑːl/ noun, u. *The morale of our company is very high after achieving the sales target.* = the level of confidence or courage in an army, team etc.

mor•a•to•ri•um /mɒrəˈtɔːriəm/ noun, c. (**moratoria**) *The government has declared a* *moratorium on the testing of nuclear weapons.* = the stopping of something for a limited period of time

mor•bid /ˈmɔːbɪd/ adj. *My brother loves reading murder stories. I don't know why he has such a morbid interest in the subject.* = having an unhealthy interest in unpleasant subjects, specially things connected with death or disease (disapproving) **morbidity** /mɒˈbɪdɪti/ noun, u. **1** = the quality of being morbid **2** = (of a person with a disease), the tendency for the disease to worsen [MEDICINE]

more[1] /mɔːʳ/ det. **1** *This class has 25 boys and 13 girls. There are more boys than girls in this class.* = a larger number **2** *You have given me only five rupees for a meal. I need some more money.* = an additional amount

more[2] pron. *I don't have enough money. I need some more.* = an additional number or amount

more[3] adv. *He should practise more if he wants to play for his country. // She is more hardworking than her brother.* = to a greater extent or degree

more and more *There are more and more restaurants in the city.* = an increasing number or amount **not any more** = not any longer **more or less** *This is more or less the number of people coming to the party.* = roughly, approximately

morgue /mɔːg/ noun, u. = a place where dead bodies are kept, specially in cases of unnatural death (also **mortuary**)

morn /mɔːn/ noun = literary form of "morning"

morning /ˈmɔːnɪŋ/ noun, c. or u. = the first part of the day, from sunrise to noon

mo•ron /ˈmɔːrɒn/ noun, c. = a very stupid person (not polite) (informal)

mo•rose /məˈrəʊs/ adj. *Why do you look so morose? What's wrong?* = sad; depressed

moreover conj. or adv. *He is very hard-working. Moreover, he is completely honest.*(conj.) = in addition to what has been said

mor•pheme /ˈmɔːfiːm/ noun, c. *The word "books" contains two morphemes : book + -s* = the smallest meaningful part into which a word can be divided [GRAMMAR] **morphology** /mɔːˈphɒlədʒi/ noun = the study of the morphemes of a language [TECHNICAL]

mor•phine /ˈmɔːfiːn/ noun, u. = a drug made from opium, which is used by doctors to lessen pain (also **morphia**)

mor•sel /ˈmɔːsəl/ noun, c. *a morsel of bread* = a very small piece of food

mor•tal[1] /ˈmɔːtl/ adj. **1** *All human beings and animals are mortal.* = bound to die; not living forever (opposite **immortal**) **2** *He has a mortal wound in the chest.* = likely to cause death **3** *She is in mortal danger.* = very great (figurative)

mortal[2] noun, c. *It is said that the gods sometimes come down from heaven to live with mortals.* = a human being who, by nature, will be born and will die

mortality /mɔːˈtælɪti/ noun, u. or c. (**mortalities**) **1** *The death of my father reminded me of my own mortality.*(u.) = the quality of being mortal **2** *A large number of mortalities resulted from the accident.*(c.) = a death caused by some accident, war etc.

mor•tar /ˈmɔːtəʳ/ noun, u. or c. **1** *This building is made from brick and mortar.*(u.) = a mixture of sand, cement and water, used to join bricks together **2** (c.) = a heavy gun used in war **3** *a mortar and pestle*(c.) = a hard bowl, made of stone or clay, in which something can be ground (crushed into powder), using a short stick called a **pestle** (see pic under **laboratory equipment**)

mort•gage[1] /ˈmɔːgɪdʒ/ verb, t. *I need a loan from the bank to start a business. I will have to mortgage my house in order to get the loan.* = to give up the ownership of a building or piece of land for a certain period in return for a loan of money

mortgage[2] noun, u. *This house is on mortgage with the bank.* = an agreement by which one borrows money in return for some property (buildings or land)

mor•ti•fy /ˈmɔːtɪfaɪ/ verb, t. *I was mortified to find that when I stood up to read my speech, I had forgotten my spectacles.* = to feel great shame and embarrassment (formal) **mortification** /mɒtɪfɪˈkeɪʃən/ noun, u. *To my mortification, I discovered that I had no money to pay for my bus ticket.* = feeling of shame

mor•tu•a•ry /ˈmɔːtʃuəri/ noun, c.= a building where dead bodies are kept (see also **morgue**)

mo•saic[1] /məʊˈzeɪ-ɪk/ noun, u. or c. = a pattern made by using many small pieces of coloured stone or glass in a background of a different colour

mosaic[2] adj. *a mosaic floor* = made with small pieces of coloured stone

mos•que /mɒsk/ noun, c. = a place of worship for Muslims

mos•qui•to /məˈskiːtəʊ/ noun, c. (**mosquitoes**) = a small flying insect that sucks blood

moss /mɒs/ noun, u. = tiny green plants that are soft and grow in wet places (on rocks, tree-trunks, walls etc.) **mossy** adj.

a rolling stone gathers no moss = A person who is always moving from one job to another can never become rich or successful.

most[1] /məʊst/ det. *Most men tell lies.* = nearly all

most[2] pron. *I like all my friends but I like Mohan the most.* = more than the others

most[3] adv. **1** *This is the most beautiful painting in the room.* = more than the others **2** *I shall be most grateful for your help.* = very

M

at the most *At the most, a hundred people will come to our meeting.* = the maximum number **for the most part (mostly)** 1 = almost completely 2 = nearly always **to make the most of something** = to take as much advantage of a situation as possible

-most suffix meaning 1 greatest e.g. **uppermost** adj. *The thought of meeting you was uppermost in my mind.* = having greater importance than anything else 2 farthest from a point e.g. **southernmost** adj. *Kanya Kumari is the southernmost point on the mainland of India.* = farther to the south than anything else

mote /məʊt/ noun, c. = a very small particle (piece) of dust

mo•tel /məʊˈtel/ noun, c. = a hotel by the side of a road, meant for the use of motorists (people travelling in motorcars) (motel = motor + hotel)

moth /mɒθ/ noun, c. = an insect like a butterfly that flies at night and is attracted by lights **moth-ball** noun = a small, white ball made of a chemical with a very strong smell, which protects clothes by driving moths away **moth-eaten** adj. 1 *moth-eaten clothes* = damaged by moths 2 *moth-eaten furniture* = in very poor condition

mo•ther[1] /ˈmʌðəʳ/ noun, c. 1 *This is the boy's mother.* = a female human being or animal that has given birth to a child (young one) 2 *Poverty is the mother of crime.* = the cause of (figurative) 3 *I have the mother of all stomach upsets!* = the worst kind of something (informal)

mother[2] verb, t. *Mr Mulay has a number of dogs at home and he mothers them lovingly.* = to take care of and protect like a mother **mother-board** noun, c. = the central part of a computer that controls all the other parts [COMPUTERS] **mother-in-law** noun, c. = the mother of one's wife or husband **motherland** = the country of your birth to which you have strong emotional ties **mother tongue** noun, c. = the first language that a baby hears and learns to speak at home

mo•tif /məʊˈtiːf/ noun, c. (French) *These new curtains have a flower motif.* = pattern or design

mo•tion[1] /ˈməʊʃən/ noun, u. or c. 1 *The train is in motion.*(u.) = the act or process of moving 2 *The Leader of the Opposition introduced a motion in the parliament.*(c.) = a suggestion or proposal made at a meeting (formal) 3 *The doctor asked the sick man if his motions were regular.*(c.) = the act of emptying the bowels of solid waste matter (a term normally used by doctors)

motion[2] verb, i. *The policeman motioned the driver of the car to stop.* = to signal with a movement of the hand **motion-picture** noun = a cinema film

to go through the motions of something = to do something only because one has to do it, without any interest **to put something in motion** = to start a process or a machine

mo•ti•vate /ˈməʊtɪveɪt/ verb, t. *Although Indrajeet is very lazy, he may agree to work for you if you motivate him by giving him interesting work.* = to give someone a strong reason for wanting to do something **motivation** /məʊtɪˈveɪʃən/ noun, u. *She is intelligent but she lacks the motivation to work hard.* = desire or need to do something **motive** /ˈməʊtɪv/ noun, c. *The man who was killed had no enemies. The police are trying to find out what motive anyone could have for killing him.* = the reason for doing something

mot•ley /ˈmɒtli/ adj. *The film-star is always followed by a motley crowd of admirers.* = of many different kinds (derogatory)

mo•tor[1] /ˈməʊtəʳ/ noun, c. *The motor of my electric pump has been damaged.* = the machine or engine that drives something or makes something work

motor[2] adj. 1 *the motor industry in India* = connected with cars (also **automobile** or **auto**) 2 *My friend is unable to move his left arm and leg. The doctors say he has lost motor control of the left half of his body.* = having to with the muscles that help the body to move (see also **muscle**)

motor[3] verb, i. *We will motor down to Chennai for the holidays.* = to travel in a motorcar **motorist** noun, c. = a person who drives a motorcar **motorized** adj. *a motorized bicycle* = fitted with a motor **motorbike** noun = motorcycle

mot•to /ˈmɒtəʊ/ noun, c. (**mottoes** or **mottos**) *The motto of the Government of India is 'Satyameva Jayate'* (the truth alone conquers) = a short sentence or phrase that expresses a principle or objective of a company, organization etc.

mould[1] /məʊld/ verb, t. *These chairs have been moulded out of sheets of plastic by a special machine. // A good school will mould the character of its students.* = to make or shape something (to give it a shape)

mould[2] noun, c. 1 *These wax candles, which are shaped like apples, are made by melting wax and pouring it into an apple-shaped mould.* = a hollow container with a particular shape into which some liquid or soft substance is poured, so that when the substance becomes hard it takes the shape of the container 2 *The piece of bread is covered with mould. You can't eat it.* = a soft greenish material (which is made up of tiny plants) that grows on food such as bread or cheese which has been kept too long in a warm, wet place (also **mold**) **mouldy** adj. = covered with mould

moult /məʊlt/ verb, i. *Birds moult each year before winter.* = to lose feathers, hair or skin during certain seasons of the year (used in connection with birds and animals)

mound /maʊnd/ noun, c. **1** = a pile of earth, stones etc. **2** *He served me a mound of rice.* = a large pile of something (informal if used humorously)

mount[1] /maʊnt/ verb, t. **1** *He mounted his horse and rode away.* = to get on a horse, bicycle etc. **2** *You will have to mount these stairs to reach the rooms above.* = to climb **3** *Excitement mounted in the stadium as Tendulkar neared his century.* = to rise **4** *The company is mounting a sales campaign to increase the sales of their products. // The army mounted an attack on the enemy.* = to organize (plan and carry out) some activity **5** *You should mount these photographs in an album.* = to fix or place in a position where something can be easily seen

mount[2] noun, c. *Mount Everest* = a word used as part of the name of a mountain (abbr. **Mt.**)

moun•tain /ˈmaʊntɪn/ noun, c. **1** = a raised part of the earth's surface, higher than a hill, the top part of which is often covered with snow **2** *I have a mountain of examination papers to correct.* = a very large amount (figurative) **mountainous** adj. = full of mountains **mountaineering** /maʊntɪˈnɪərɪŋ/ noun, u. = the sport or skill of climbing high mountains **mountaineer** noun, c. = a person who climbs high mountains

mourn /mɔːn/ verb, t. or i. *He is mourning the death of his mother.* = to feel or express grief at the death of someone **mournful** adj. *a mournful glance* = very sad **mourner** noun, c. = a person who is present at somebody's funeral (the ceremony held to mourn someone's death)

mouse /maʊs/ noun, c. (**mice**) **1** = a small animal like a rat, but smaller in size **2** (plural **mouses**) = a small instrument that is connected to a computer and clicked to make the computer do various things [COMPUTERS] **mouse-trap** noun, c. = a simple device (machine) used to catch mice

mous•tache /məˈstɑːʃ/ noun, c. = the hair which grows above a man's upper lip

mouth[1] /maʊθ/ noun, c. **1** = the opening in the face of a human being through which food is taken into the body **2** *the mouth of a volcano* = an opening **3** = the point where a river falls into a sea [GEOGRAPHY]

mouth[2] /maʊð/ verb, t. *He can't sing, so he just mouthed the words while the others sang.* = to move one's lips as if speaking or singing, without making any sound **mouthful** noun, c. **1** *She drank a mouthful of tea.* = a small quantity of food or drink taken in the mouth **2** *Your name is quite a mouthful!* = a word that is hard to say **mouth-organ** noun, c = a musical instrument that is played by holding it between the lips and blowing air through it (also **harmonica**) **mouth-piece** noun, c. **1** = the part of a musical instrument or telephone that is held in or near the mouth **2** *This newspaper is the mouth-piece of the Chief Minister.* = a newspaper or a person that expresses the opinions of someone (derogatory) **mouth-watering** = (about food) very attractive and giving one a desire to eat

-mouthed suffix meaning speaking in a certain way e.g. **1 loud-mouthed** = speaking very loudly **2 foul-mouthed** = using bad language

to make one's mouth water 1 = (about food) to look or smell so good that one wants to eat it at once **2** = to want to get something which looks very attractive (figurative) **to put one's foot in one's mouth** = to say something carelessly, making a mistake **to be down in the mouth** *Although he had not failed in the test, he looked very down in the mouth.* = to look very unhappy **to have a big mouth (to be all mouth)** = to be very fond of talking or boasting **to keep one's mouth shut** = to say nothing or to stop talking **to (not) look a gift horse in the mouth** = to not look critically at something one gets free **to put words in someone's mouth** = to state falsely that someone said something **to shoot one's mouth off** = to talk carelessly, without thinking **to live from hand to mouth** = to have barely enough money for one's needs **by word of mouth** *The new restaurant is getting known by word of mouth.* = only through speaking and not writing

move[1] /muːv/ verb, i. or t. **1** *The train is moving.*(i.) *// Please move your chair closer to the table.*(t.) = to change position or to change the position of something **2** *Work is moving fast in the office now.* = to progress **3** *We were moved by the courageous story.*(t.) = to cause a person to feel pity or sadness **4** *The Chairperson moved that we should adjourn the meeting to the next week.*(t.) = to make a suggestion or proposal at a meeting **5** *He moves mostly in political circles.*(i.) = to mix with people of a certain type **6** *We will move to our new house tomorrow.*(i.) = to change the place one lives in

move[2] noun, c. **1** *He was afraid to move, in case the guards should see him.* = an act of moving one's body **2** *It is your move now!* = the act of changing the position of a piece in the game of chess **3** *That was a clever move!* = an action done to get some result **movement** noun, u. or c. **1** *My legs hurt so much that movement has become difficult.*(u.) = the act of moving from one place to another **2** *She has joined the movement to resist the building of dams.*(c.) = a group of people working together for a common cause **3** *a movement away from globalization* (u.) = a change in

M

the way people think **4** *My watch is assembled in India but it has a Japanese movement.* = the system of parts inside a watch or clock that make it work **movable** adj. *a movable tent* = something that can be moved

to make a/no move 1 *If you make a move, the animal will attack you.* = to make any movement of the body **2** *We should make a move. It's past nine.* = to leave a place (informal) **3** *Although we begged them so many times, they made no move to help.* = to take action **to move in 1** *He couldn't find a room to stay in and so he moved in with us.* = to come to live in someone else's house with them, either permanently or for a period **2** *We've just moved in and don't know our neighbours.* = to begin to live in a new house **to move out** = to leave one's home **to get moving** *We have a lot of dishes to wash up. Let's get moving.* = to do something without further delay (informal) **to be on the move** *I'm not able to get them on the phone because they're always on the move.*= to be travelling or going somewhere (informal) **to move heaven and earth** *We had to move heaven and earth to see that the ugly new building did not come up.* = to work very hard to achieve a purpose in which there are many difficulties (informal) **movers and shakers** = used to refer to people who have the power and influence to make things happen

mo•vie /'mu:vi/ noun, c. = a cinema **film** **movie-star** = a filmstar

moving /'mu:viŋ/ adj. *a moving story* = causing deep feelings

mow /məʊ/ verb, t. (**mowed**, **mown**) *We have to mow the grass.* = to cut grass or food-producing plants growing in a field **mower** noun, c. = a machine that can cut grass

MP /'em'pi:/ abbr. of **1** *Member of Parliament* **2** *Military Police*

Mr /'mɪstəʳ/ abbr. of **Mister** = a title used with the name of a man

Mrs /'mɪsɪz/ = a title used with the name of a woman who is married

Ms /mɪz/ = a title used with the name of a woman who does not wish to be called either 'Miss' (an unmarried woman) or 'Mrs' (a married woman)

ms abbr. of **1** = **manuscript** **2** = multiple sclerosis [MEDICINE]

Mt abbr. of **Mountain** (e.g. Mt. Everest)

much[1] /mʌtʃ/ det. (used only in negative sentences and questions) **1** *We don't have much money.* = a lot of **2** *She is not much of a speaker, but she writes well.* = (not) very good

much[2] pron. *He asked me if I had any money and I told him I didn't have much.* = a lot of; a large amount (used in questions and negative sentences only)

much[3] adv. *The man is much taller than I had expected.* = by a large amount or degree

muck[1] /mʌk/ noun, u. *The roads were covered with muck.* = dirt or mud (informal)

muck[2] verb, t. *I mucked up my car when I was driving through the village roads.* = to make something dirty or to spoil something (informal)

mu•cus /'mju:kəs/ noun, u. = the thick, slippery liquid found inside certain parts of the body e.g. the nose or the throat **mucous** adj.

mud /mʌd/ noun, u. *The roads are covered with thick mud during the rainy season.* = earth (soil) which is very wet and sticky

mu•ddle[1] /'mʌdl/ noun, c. *His books and clothes were lying all over the room in a complete muddle.* = a state of confusion and disorder **muddled** adj.

muddle[2] verb, t. **1** *I had arranged all my files in order and now someone has muddled them up.* = to create a state of disorder and confusion **2** *Your explanation was so confusing that it muddled everyone.* = to cause someone to feel confused (also **muddle-headed**)

to muddle along = to continue working in a confused manner **to muddle through** = to be successful in doing something in spite of making mistakes and not having a clear plan

muddy[1] /'mʌdɪ/ adj. *muddy water* = covered with or containing mud

muddy[2] verb, t. (**muddied**) *You have muddied the floor by walking across it with your muddy shoes on.* = to make something dirty with mud

mues•li /'mju:zli/ noun, u. = a mixture of grain, nuts, dried fruit etc. generally eaten with milk for breakfast

mu•ezzin /mu:'ezɪn/ noun, c. = a man who calls Muslims to prayer from a **mosque**

muff /mʌf/ verb, t. *The wicket-keeper muffed an easy catch.* = to miss (to fail to catch) (informal)

muf•fle /'mʌfəl/ verb, t. **1** *The engine of a motorcar is fitted with a box, called the silencer or muffler, which muffles the sound of the engine.* = to make a sound less loud **2** *She muffled up her head and neck in a woollen shawl.* = to cover oneself so as to keep warm **muffler** noun, c. **1** = a device (machine) which muffles sounds (makes them less loud) **2** = a piece of woollen material used to cover up the neck in winter

muf•ti /'mʌfti/ noun, c. or u. **1** (c.) = a person who has the position of a religious leader in an Islamic country **2** *The army officers came in mufti when they were invited to a party.*(u.) = ordinary clothes, not uniform

mug[1] /mʌg/ noun, c. **1** *She is drinking tea from a mug.* = a round container with a handle, generally larger than a cup, from which one drinks a hot liquid **2** *You are such a mug that anyone can cheat you.* = a foolish or simple person (informal)

mug[2] verb, t. *The businessman was mugged on the street by a gang.* = to rob a person in a public place after using violence (slang) **mugging** noun, c. = the act of robbing someone (slang) **to mug something up** = to learn something by heart (usually before an examination) **mugger** /'mʌgəʳ/ noun, c. = a person who mugs (robs) someone

muggy *muggy weather* = unpleasantly warm and humid

mul•berry /'mʌlbəri/ noun = a berry (fruit) of dark purple colour

mulch[1] /mʌltʃ/ noun, u. = dead leaves, wood chips etc. which are spread over the soil to prevent it from becoming too dry

mulch[2] verb, t. = to cover with mulch

mule /mju:l/ noun, c. = an animal which has a donkey as its father and a mare (female horse) as its mother and is used for carrying heavy loads **mulish** adj. *a mulish person* = having the quality of stubbornness (refusing to see other's points of view), which is said to be present in all mules (figurative)

mull /mʌl/ verb, t. *I would like to mull over your suggestion before I decide what to do.* = to ponder (think about something for a time)

mul•lah /mʊlɑ:h/ noun, c. = a Muslim religious teacher

mul•li•ga•taw•ny /mʌlɪgə'tɔ:ni/ noun = a kind of soup made from pepper and other spices, very popular among the British who lived in India

mul•ti- /mʌltɪ/ prefix meaning 'many' e.g. **multilateral** /mʌltɪ'lætərəl/ adj. *a multilateral agreement* = having many sides (having to do with more than two groups or nations)

mul•ti•lin•gual /mʌltɪ'lɪŋgwəl/ adj. *multilingual translation* = speaking or able to speak more than two languages

mul•ti•media /mʌ'ltɪmi:dɪə/ adj. *a multimedia presentation* = showing pictures together with sounds and printed texts

mul•ti•na•tion•al /mʌltɪ'næʃənəl/ adj. *a multinational company* = a company which has offices and factories etc. in many different countries

mul•ti•ple[1] /'mʌltɪpəl/ adj. *He suffered multiple injuries in the accident.* = many

multiple[2] noun, c. *Sixteen is a multiple of 4* = a number which one gets by multiplying one number by another number (16 = 4x4) **multiply** /'mʌltɪplaɪ/ verb, t. **1** *If you multiply 9 by 3, you get 27.* = to add a number to itself many times (27 = 9+9+9) **2** *The number of schools in this town is multiplying fast.* = to grow in number **multiplication** /mʌltɪplɪ'keɪʃn/ noun, u. *The teacher has given the students some exercises in multiplication.* = the process of mutiplying numbers (in arithmetic) (compare **division**, **addition**, **subtraction**) **multiplication tables** noun = a list of numbers which small children are made to learn by heart, which tells them which numbers one gets by mutiplying numbers from 1 to 12 by other numbers

mul•ti-sto•reyed adj. *a multi-storeyed building* = having several storeys (levels of floors)

mul•ti•tude /'mʌltɪtju:d/ noun, c. *He has a multitude of problems.* = a very large number

mum[1] /mʌm/ adj. *The police inspector asked the thief hundreds of questions, but he remained mum.* = silent; refusing to speak (informal)

mum[2] noun, c. = mother (informal)

mum•ble /'mʌmbəl/ verb, i. *When I asked him what he was doing in my room, he could only mumble in reply.* = to speak unclearly and in a low voice so that the words are difficult to understand

mumbo-jumbo /mʌmbəʊ 'dʒʌmbəu/ noun *The holy man told me he could cure my fever by chanting some prayers. However, I have no faith in such mumbo-jumbo.* = something done to create a mysterious or magical effect, often in the name of religion (derogatory)

mum•my /'mʌmi/ noun, c. (**mummies**) **1** = mother **2** *The National Museum has the mummy of an Egyptian princess who died 4,000 years ago.* = a dead body that has been treated with chemicals so that it will not decay (become rotten), as was done in ancient Egypt **mummify** verb, t. (**mummified**) = to turn a dead body into a mummy by treating it with chemicals

mumps /mʌmps/ noun, u. = a kind of sickness, common among children, which causes fever and painful swellings in the neck

munch /mʌntʃ/ verb, t. *The teacher was angry because I was munching peanuts in class.* = to chew or eat something noisily, with strong movements of the jaw

mun•dane /mʌn'deɪn/ adj. *People think a bus conductor's job is mundane but I really like it.* = connected with everyday life; dull (formal/literary)

mu•ni•ci•pal•i•ty /mju:nɪsɪ'pælɪti/ noun, c. (**municipalities**) **1** = a city or town which has its own local government (to keep it clean etc.) **2** = the group of people who manage the affairs of a city or town **municipal** /mju:'nɪsɪpəl/ adj. *a municipal building* = having to do with a municipality

mu•ni•tion•s /mju:'nɪʃənz/ noun, u. (always plural) = weapons used in war (guns, bombs etc.)

mu•ral /'mjʊərəl/ noun, c. = a large painting done on a wall

mur•der[1] /'mɜ:dəʳ/ verb, t. *The police thought he had been murdered but he had died a natural death.* = to kill a human being deliberately

murder[2] noun, u. or c. **1** *The police have arrested him on a charge of murder.*(u.) = the crime of

M

murdering someone **2** *A murder was committed here last night.*(c.) = a particular case of murder (compare **kill, assassinate**) **murderous** adj. *a murderous attack* = very violent and possibly leading to death **murderer** noun, c. = a person who commits murder **to get away with murder** = to be allowed to do whatever one wants without being punished or warned

mur•ky /ˈmɜːki/ adj. **1** *The water of the river used to be very clear, but it has turned murky.* = dark and dirty **2** *a murky past* = unpleasant and shameful (figurative)

mur•mur[1] /ˈmɜːməʳ/ verb, i. or t. **1** *Stop murmuring. I can't hear what you are saying.*(t.) = to speak in a soft, low voice **2** *Everyone in the office is murmuring about my habit of shouting angrily at people.*(i.) = to complain about something, but not openly

murmur[2] noun, c. *Can you hear the murmur of the waves gently touching the shore?* = a soft, low sound

muscle[1] /ˈmʌsəl/ noun, u. or c. **1** *He has no fat on his body, only muscle.*(u.) // *There are three large muscles in the human arm.*(c.) = the thread-like material, covering the bones, which makes up the flesh of an animal or human being and which can contract (grow tight) to cause movement of the body **2** *They have a lot of financial muscle.*(u.) = power or influence (figurative)

muscle[2] verb, i. *The guards tried to stop him but he muscled his way in.* = to enter a place by force **muscular** /ˈmʌskjʊləʳ/ adj. *a muscular body* = having a lot of big muscles **muscle-man** noun, c. = a person with a strong body who is paid to protect his employer, using violence when necessary (slang)

muse[1] /mjuːz/ verb, i. *He was musing about the holiday he had just returned from.* = to think about something deeply and for a long time

muse[2] noun, c. **1** *the nine Muses* = a goddess (in stories from Ancient Greece) who represents some branch of art (e.g. poetry, painting, music etc.) **2** *He is writing very bad poetry now. His muse seems to have left him.* = inspiration (the force that makes a person do something well)

mu•seum /mjuːˈziːəm/ noun, c. = a building where objects which have historical, scientific or artistic value are kept and shown to the public

mush /mʌʃ/ noun, u. **1** *He boiled the rice for such a long time that it became mush.* = food which is soft and sticky **2** *The new novel she has written is nothing but mush.* = writing which is full of sentiment (feelings of love, pity etc. which are not very deep) (derogatory)

mush•room[1] /ˈmʌʃruːm/ noun, c. or u. **1** (c.) = a kind of plant without leaves, shaped like a small umbrella, which grows very fast **2** *Would you like some mushroom?*(u.) = the flesh of the mushroom, used as food

mush•room[2] verb, i. *Hundreds of English-medium public schools have mushroomed all over the country.* = to grow very quickly and in an uncontrolled manner (informal, derogatory)

mushroom

mu•sic /ˈmjuːzɪk/ noun, u. *Do you like Western music?* = an arrangement of sounds produced by the human voice or by musical instruments which gives pleasure to the listener

musical[1] /ˈmjuːzɪkəl/ adj. **1** *a musical voice* = pleasant to hear (like music) **2** *a musical person* = interested in or having a talent for music

musical[2] noun = a film or play that has many songs or dances in it **musician** /mjuˈzɪʃən/ noun, c. = a person who produces music, either by singing or by playing a musical instrument **music system** = a number of machines (usually consisting of a cassette player or **CD** (Compact Disc) player, an amplifier and two or more speakers) connected to each other, which are used to play recorded music **musical chairs** = a game in which the players move round and round a number of chairs (one less than the number of players) placed in a circle while music is being played, but have to find and sit down quickly in an empty chair when the music stops

musk /mʌsk/ noun, u. = a natural substance produced by a kind of deer (the musk-deer) which has a very strong smell and is used for making perfume

mus•ket /ˈmʌskɪt/ noun, c = a kind of gun used in former times **musketeer** /mʌskɪˈtiəʳ/ noun, c. = a soldier who used a musket to fight

Mus•lim /ˈmʊslɪm/ noun, c. = a follower of the prophet Mohammed, the founder of Islam

mus•lin /ˈmʌzlɪn/ noun, u. = very fine cotton cloth, for which the weavers of India were famous in former times

muss /mʌs/ verb, t. *The wind mussed up his hair.* = to make something untidy

mus•sel /ˈmʌsəl/ noun, c. = a kind of sea-animal with a hard shell and soft flesh which is eaten

must[1] /məst/ aux. modal verb **1** *You must go to school every day.* = it is necessary to do this **2** *That must be the postman, bringing our letters.* = it is very probable (likely) that this is so

must[2] noun, c. (no plural) *Warm clothes are a must if you are planning to go to Darjeeling.* = something that is absolutely necessary

mus•tang /ˈmʌstæŋ/ noun, c. = a wild horse of small size, found in America

mus•tard /ˈmʌstəd/ noun, u. a kind of plant that produces bright yellow flowers and seeds which have a hot taste and are used as a spice (to add taste to food) **mustard gas** noun = a poisonous gas which was sometimes used during World War I (1914–1918)

mus•ter /ˈmʌstəʳ/ verb, i. or t. **1** *The soldiers will muster here every morning for parade.*(i.) = to gather together **2** *I wanted to ask my teacher for permission to come back late after the holidays, but I could not muster enough courage to speak to her.*(t.) = to gather

mus•ty /ˈmʌsti/ adj. *The room has a musty smell as it was kept locked for years.* = the unpleasant smell that comes from old and slightly wet things

mu•ta•tion /mjuːˈteɪʃən/ noun, u. or c. *These tiny creatures living in the water have undergone mutation.* = a process of change in a living plant or animal **mutate** verb, i. or t. *mutated virus* = to change biologically **mutant** /ˈmjuːtənt/ noun, c. = a living thing which has undergone a change and become different

mute[1] /mjuːt/ noun, c. = a person who is unable to speak

mute[2] adj. **1** *mute admiration* = silent; without words **2** = the state of an electronic device when it does not make any noise [TECHNICAL] **muted** adj. *The minister's speech was greeted with muted applause.* = not very loud; soft

mu•ti•late /ˈmjuːtɪleɪt/ verb, t. **1** *The bodies of our soldiers were mutilated by the enemy.* = to damage a person's body by removing a part **2** *The editor has mutilated my story by trying to change it.* = to spoil (figurative)

mu•ti•ny[1] /ˈmjuːtɪni/ verb, i. *Some Indian soldiers mutinied against their British officers in 1857.* = to disobey; to try to take away power from someone who is in charge

mutiny[2] noun, c. (**mutinies**) or u. *The First War of Independence (1857) was earlier called the Sepoy Mutiny.* = an act of mutiny **mutineer** /ˈmjuːtɪnɪəʳ/ noun, c. = a person who takes part in a mutiny

mut•ter[1] /ˈmʌtəʳ/ verb, t. or i. *She was muttering something under her breath.*(t.) = to speak angry or complaining words in a low voice which cannot be heard clearly

mutter[2] noun, u. *I could hear the mutter of voices.* = the sound of someone muttering

mut•ton /ˈmʌtn/ noun, u. = meat from a sheep or goat

mu•tu•al /ˈmjuːtʃuəl/ adj.**1** *I will help you if you help me. The agreement should be mutual.* = done by both sides or felt by both sides, in an action in which two people or two groups take part **2** *Abraham is our mutual friend.* = common to two people or shared by two people

muz•zle[1] /ˈmʌzəl/ noun, c. **1** *the muzzle of a horse* = the front part of the head of an animal (usually a horse or a dog) **2** *the muzzle of a gun* = the front part of the barrel of a gun (the tube through which bullets are fired) **3** *You should put a muzzle on the dog so that it does not bite anyone.* = a covering put around the mouth of a dangerous animal to prevent it from biting

muzzle[2] verb, t. **1** *Have you muzzled the dog?* = to put a muzzle around the mouth of an animal **2** *The newspapers refuse to be muzzled by anyone.* = to force someone to keep silent (figurative, derogatory)

my /maɪ/ det. **1** *She is my mother.* = belonging to me **2** *My! My! What a nice dress you are wearing!* = an expression showing surprise or pleasure, sometimes to make fun of the person one is talking to

my•nah /ˈmaɪnə/ noun = a dark-coloured bird that can learn to copy human voices

my•o•pi a /maɪˈəʊpiə/ noun = a defect in the eye which makes a person unable to see things which are far away (also **near-sightedness** or **short-sightedness**) **myopic** adj = suffering from myopia

myr•i•ad /ˈmɪriəd/ noun, c. *He has a myriad followers.* = a very large number (formal)

myr•tle /ˈmɜːtl/ noun = a small tree with shiny green leaves

my•self /maɪˈself/ reflexive pron. **1** *I saw myself in the mirror.* = used when an action done by a person affects the same person **2** *I'll do it myself, I don't need your help.* = without any help from others

all by myself **1** = alone, without anyone else **2** = without anyone else's help

mys•te•ry /ˈmɪstəri/ noun, u. or c. (**mysteries**) *No one knows who killed the woman. The police is trying to solve the mystery.*(c.) // *He likes stories of adventure and mystery.*(u.) = something strange or unknown that has not been or cannot be fully explained or understood **mysterious** /mɪˈstɪərɪəs/ adj. *mysterious sounds at night* = full of mystery **mystify** /ˈmɪstɪfaɪ/ verb, t. (**mystified**) *The police is mystified by this strange murder.* = to make someone unable to understand or explain something **mystique** /mɪˈstiːk/ noun, u. *There is a certain mystique attached to the new kind of yoga she is teaching.* = a special quality that makes something appear mysterious and attractive (often disapproving)

mys•ti•cis•m /ˈmɪstɪsɪzəm/ noun = the belief that one can understand the hidden nature of God and of truth through prayer or meditation and not through

M

reasoning **mystic** noun, c. = a person who practises mysticism

myth /mɪθ/ noun, c. or u. **1** = an ancient story that deals with the early history of a group of people in a literary way **2** = something that is generally believed but is not true **mythology** /maɪ'θɔːlədʒi/ noun, u. = myths in general **mythical** /'mɪθɪkəl/ adj. *a mythical event* = relating to a myth (also mythological)

nN

n, N /en/ the fourteenth letter of the English alphabet
n, short form of '**and**' (e.g. *bread 'n' butter*) (informal)
nab /næb/ verb, t. (**nabbed**) *The police nabbed the thief.* = to catch a criminal (informal)
na•dir /'neɪdɪəʳ/ noun, u. *Our party reached its nadir in 1977, when almost all its leaders were defeated in the election.* = the lowest point of power or importance
nag[1] /næg/ verb, i. or t. **1** *Oh all right, I'll buy you a new dress. Now, will you stop nagging?*(i.) = to annoy or trouble someone constantly by complaining or asking him/her to do something **2** *I don't know how to solve this problem. It has been nagging me all week.*(t.) = to cause worry for a long time (informal)
nag[2] noun, c. **1** = a horse which is in poor physical condition (informal) **2** = a person who is in the habit of nagging (The word 'nag' was often used to describe a bad-tempered woman who constantly quarrelled with her husband. This use is considered offensive now.)
G
nail[1] /neɪl/ noun, c. **1** *I need a large nail to hang this picture from.* = a thin piece of metal, usually iron, one end of which is pointed and the other end flat so that it can be hammered (hit with a hammer), which is used to join two pieces of wood together etc. **2** *a fingernail* = the thick, hard covering over the soft flesh at the end of a finger or toe

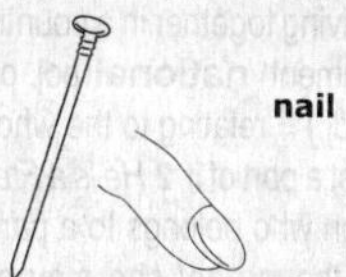
nail

nail[2] verb, t. **1** *We have to nail these pieces of wood together.* = to fix or join something with a nail **2** *The police suspected he was involved in smuggling, but they weren't able to nail him.* = to prove that someone is guilty of a crime **nail-biting** *The match between India and Australia came to a nail-biting finish.* = very exciting **nail polish** = thick, coloured liquid used to paint the nails of the fingers and toes to make them look attractive
to hit the nail on the head = to say something that is exactly correct (informal)
na•ïve /naɪ'iːv/ adj. **1** *He is so naïve that he will believe anything you tell him.* = simple and willing to believe anything **2** *You thought everyone would donate large sums of money to the charity. How naïve of you!* = having little experience of life
na•ked /'neɪkɪd/ adj. **1** *a naked person* = without any clothes covering the body (also **nude**) **2** *The forest becomes quite naked during the summer.* = without leaves or trees **3** *Let me tell you the naked truth.* = with nothing kept hidden (figurative)
with the naked eye = without the help of any instrument that could help one to see more clearly
name[1] /neɪm/ noun, c. or u. **1** *His name is Ramesh Bhatia.*(c.) = the word or words used to call someone **2** *She has a name as a writer.*(c.) = reputation; fame
name[2] verb, t. **1** *I have named this child Ismail.* = to give a name to someone **2** *He has been named in the police report as one of the persons suspected of the murder.* = to mention **3** *She has been named the next Indian ambassador to China.* = to appoint someone to a high position **namely** adv. *I would like to discuss one other matter: namely, the appointment of the captain for the team.* = that is to say (often abbreviated as **viz.**) **namesake** noun, c. *Would you like to meet your namesake, Amitabh?* = a person who has the same name as someone else **first name** *Your name appears on the passenger list as Ambani Dinesh, with the first name coming after the last name.* = the name by which a person is usually addressed by his/her family and friends **last name** = the name given to every member of a family (also **surname** or **family name**)
to be quite a name *He is quite a name in the world of sports.*= a well-known person (informal) **to call someone names** (always plural) *She may have been angry with me but why did she have to call me names.* = to use offensive or insulting language while talking to someone or about someone else (informal) **to drop names** = to mention the names of famous or important people during a conversation, with the intention of showing that one knows them personally (informal, disapproving) **to get a good/bad name for something** *This fruit shop has a bad name for selling overripe fruit.* = to be known for something **the name of the game** *You can't expect to become a good singer in just one week. Practice is the name of the game.* = what one must do in order to achieve something (informal) **You name it!** *This shop sells everything—clothes, computers, watches. You name it!* = anything that one can think of (informal)
nan•ny /'næni/ noun, c. (**nannies**) = a woman who is employed to take care of a small child in a family and who usually lives in the same house (see also **nurse**) **nanny goat** noun, c. = a female goat (compare **billy goat**)
nano- /'nænəu/ a prefix for a unit of measurement equal to a thousand millionth e.g. **nanosecond** = a thousand millionth of a second
nap[1] /næp/ noun, c. *I like to take a nap in the*

N

afternoon. = a short sleep during the day

nap[2] verb, i. (**napped**) *Would you like to nap?* = to take a nap

to catch someone napping = to find someone in a state of not being prepared for something (informal)

na•palm /ˈneɪpɑːm/ noun = a substance made from petrol which burns very easily and can be used to start a fire when dropped as a bomb from an aircraft

nape /neɪp/ noun *the nape of the neck* = the back of the neck

nap•kin /ˈnæpkɪn/ noun, c. **1** *a baby's napkin* = a piece of cloth or paper lined with cotton wrapped around the waist and thighs of a baby, in which the waste matter from the baby's body can be collected (formal) (also **nappy**, **diaper**) **2** *a dinner napkin* = a piece of cloth or paper used to protect one's clothes and to wipe one's fingers and mouth while eating

nappy (nappies) = see **napkin** (meaning **1**) (informal)

nar•cis•sus /nɑːˈsɪsəs/ noun = a kind of white or yellow flower **narcissism** noun = the quality of being too much in love with oneself **Narcissus** = a character in a story from ancient Greece, a very handsome young man who fell in love with his own beauty and was unable to love anyone else

nar•cot•ic /nɑːˈkɒtɪk/ noun, u. or c. or adj. = a drug such as cocaine or opium which can be used to cause sleep and lessens pain when used in small quantities but can cause great harm when taken regularly and in larger quantities

nar•rate /nəˈreɪt/ verb, t. *He narrated the story of his life.* = to tell a story or to describe an event or a number of events (formal) **narration** noun, u. = the act of narrating something **narrator** noun, c. = a person who narrates something (tells a story) **narrative** /ˈnærətɪv/ noun, c. **1** = a story or description of events which is narrated **2** = the skill of telling stories

nar•row[1] /ˈnærəʊ/ adj. **1** *a narrow lane* = having a small distance from one side to the other, in comparison with the length (opposite **wide**) **2** *The ship moved into the harbour before the storm broke. It was a narrow escape.* = very close to a bad or dangerous situation **3** *We lost the match, but it was a narrow defeat.* = a victory or defeat in a game, contest etc. in which the two sides get almost the same amount of success **4** Everyone expects us to be fair. Let us not take a narrow view of the matter. = referring to an attitude in which, e.g. while judging someone or something, one considers only some things and not others, on purpose (derogatory) narrowly adv.

narrow[2] verb, t. (**narrowed**) **1** *The river narrows at this point.* = to become narrow (less wide) **2** *The differences between us have narrowed.* = to become less sharp or strong **narrow gauge** = a railway track which has less than the usual width (opposite **broad gauge**) **narrow-minded** *a narrow-minded person* = unwilling to accept ideas, customs etc. which are different from one's own (opposite **broad-minded**)

to narrow something down *The president of the party has narrowed down the list of candidates to five.* = to reduce to a smaller number in order to fix a limit on something

NASA /ˈnæsə/ abbr. of **National Aeronautics and Space Administration** = the department of the American government that controls space travel and research

na•sal[1] /ˈneɪzəl/ noun, c. *'m' and 'n' are nasals.* = a speech sound made through the nose [TECHNICAL]

nasal[2] adj. *a nasal voice* = coming through the nose or having to do with the nose

nas•cent /ˈnæsənt/ adj. *A few people in the village are trying to stop the practice of child labour. It is only a nascent movement now, but it will spread.* = newly started and therefore small, but likely to grow (formal)

nas•tur•tium /nəˈstɜːʃəm/ noun = a garden plant that produces flowers of different colours

nas•ty /ˈnɑːsti/ adj. **1** *There's a nasty smell from the drain outside.* = unpleasant **2** *The shopkeeper was rude and behaved in a nasty manner.* = rude **3** *She has a nasty cut above the eye.* = dangerous or painful **4** *He played a nasty trick on me.* = immoral or wicked

na•tion /ˈneɪʃən/ noun, c. *The whole nation went wild with joy when our team won the World Cup.* = a group of people living together in a country and having their own government **national** adj. or noun **1** *the national team* (adj.) = relating to the whole country or nation and not just a part of it **2** *He is a French national.* (noun) = a person who belongs to a particular nation (country), even though he/ she may be living in a different country **national park** = an area that is specially looked after by the government and visited by many people for its natural beauty **nationality** /næʃəˈnælɪti/ noun, c. or u. *She lives in Singapore, but she has Pakistani nationality.* = membership of a nation, while living in another country **nationalism** noun, u. **1** = great love for one's country and the feeling that it is better than other countries (sometimes derogatory) (compare **jingoism**) **2** = the strong interest of a group of people sharing the same beliefs in having a separate country **nationalistic** /næʃənəˈlɪstɪk/ adj. = believing that one's country is better than other countries and having a poor view of other countries (disapproving) **nationalize (nationalise)** /ˈnæʃənəlaɪz/ verb, t. *The banks in the country have been nationalized.* = to give control of a business or industry to the central government of a country

na•tive[1] /ˈneɪtɪv/ noun, c. **1** *She is a native of Bastar in Chhatisgarh.* = a person who was born in a certain place **2** *the natives* (often plural) = the people originally living in a place, whose country is ruled by others (derogatory and offensive)

native[2] adj. **1** *He is visiting his native land.* = the place of one's birth **2** *The pepper plant is native to India.* = belonging to a place from the beginning and not brought in from outside (also **indigenous**)

na•tiv•i•ty /nəˈtɪvɪti/ noun, u. = birth (the act of being born) **Nativity** noun = the birth of Jesus Christ, the founder of the Christian religion

NATO /ˈneɪtəʊ/ abbr. of **North Atlantic Treaty Organization** = a group of European countries, together with U.S.A and Canada, which give military help to each other under a treaty (agreement)

nat•ter /ˈnætəʳ/ noun, u. *I couldn't bear to listen to their natter for too long.* = light talk (not about serious matters); chatter (informal)

nat•ty /ˈnæti/ adj. *natty clothes* = fashionable or stylish (informal)

nat•u•ral /ˈnætʃərəl/ adj. **1** *I admire the natural beauty of this place. // a natural lake // natural disasters* = belonging to or caused by nature (the natural world) and not made by humans (opposite **artificial, man-made**) **2** *It is natural to feel nervous before an interview.* = usual; something that can be expected **3** *She has a natural talent for drawing.* = something that one has been born with **4** *natural parents* = parents who have given birth to one **5** *His laughter on stage was so natural.* = done without any special effort **6** *They keep posing for photographs and I want them to look natural.* = normal and not putting on a special smile etc. for the camera **7** *natural protein* = from natural sources, not created with chemicals or with no chemicals added **naturalist** noun, c. = a person who studies nature, specially plants and animals, in natural (real) surroundings and not in a laboratory **naturalize (naturalise)** verb, t. **1** *He was born in Japan but was naturalized after he had lived in the U.S for 20 years.* = to make a person who was born somewhere else a citizen of a country **2** *Tobacco was brought to India from Europe and naturalized here.* = to bring a plant or animal to a new home **naturally** adv. **1** *She has lost her gold watch. Naturally, she is upset.* = the expected result of something **2** *My skin is naturally dry.* = as a gift from nature **3** *He spoke so naturally on stage, we didn't realise he was nervous.* = in a calm and relaxed manner **4** *Cooking comes naturally to everyone in his family.* = without any obvious effort; easily **naturalness** noun, u. **Naturalism** noun = the belief that people should be shown, in literature, art etc. as they really are and not as we imagine them to be **natural gas** noun = a gas (usually methane) which is present inside the earth or sea and can be taken out and used for different purposes **natural history** = the study of plants, animals, rocks etc. **natural resources** = the land, water, mineral deposits etc that a country has **natural sciences** = the study of biology, chemistry and physics

na•ture /ˈneɪtʃəʳ/ noun, u. or c. **1** *He is a great lover of nature.* = things that are not made by man (e.g. mountains, lakes, forests) **2** *She has a friendly nature.*(u.) = character **3** *We have to study the nature of the soil before we decide which crops we should grow here.*(u.) = the qualities that make someone or something different from others **4** *I don't read writings of this nature.*(c.) = type **5** *By its very nature, a snake will not attack unless it is in danger.* = behaviour that an animal or human being is born with and does not have to learn **naturopath** /ˈnætʃərəʊpæθ/ noun = a person who treats illness by using herbs, plants, roots etc. (and not artificial medicines) **naturopathy** /ˈnætʃərəʊpəθi/ noun **human nature** *It's human nature to feel hurt when someone says something insulting.* = the qualities that one is born with

the call of nature = the need to empty out waste matter from the body at once **by nature** *He is an anxious person by nature.* = born with a certain quality **to let nature take its course** *He is suffering from a disease which the doctors don't know how to treat. We will have to let him recover by himself and let nature take its course.* = to allow things to happen without doing anything to control them

-natured /ˈneɪtʃəd/ suffix used to describe a person's character e.g. **good-natured** /gʊd ˈneɪtʃəd/

naught (nought) /nɔːt/ noun = nothing; nil or zero (old-fashioned use)

naugh•ty /ˈnɔːti/ adj. **1** *a naughty child* = behaving badly and not listening to others (used to describe the behaviour of a child) **2** *The film has some naughty scenes.* = improper but not in a serious way (informal)

nau•se•a /ˈnɔːzɪə/ noun, u. = a feeling of sickness that makes one want to vomit (throw up the food that one has eaten) **nauseate** /nɔːzɪˈeɪt/ verb, t. *The smell of tobacco nauseates me.* = to cause nausea **nauseating** adj. *a nauseating smell* = causing nausea **nauseous** adj.

nau•ti•cal /ˈnɔːtɪkəl/ adj. *Distances at sea are measured in nautical miles.* = relating to ships, sailors or the sea

na•vel /ˈneɪvəl/ noun, c. = the small depressed

(deeper) area in the middle of a person's stomach which marks the place where the baby was attached to the mother before birth by the umbilicus (umbilical cord) (informal) (also **belly-button**)

nav•i•gate /'nævɪgeɪt/ verb, i. or t. **1** *The captain navigated the ship across the Atlantic Ocean.*(t.) = to guide or direct a ship or aircraft across the sea or the sky **2** *Please use the map to navigate while I drive.* = to use a map to find a route to some place **navigable** adj. *The river is not navigable as the water is not deep enough.* = deep or wide enough for a boat or ship to travel in (used to describe a river or sea) **navigation** /nævɪ'geɪʃən/ noun = the art and science of guiding a ship or aircraft safely across the sea or sky **navigator** noun, c. = the officer who plans the course (path) that a ship is supposed to follow at sea; a person who reads the map and guides the driver in a car rally

na•vy /'neɪvi/ noun, c. (**navies**) **1** = the branch of a country's military forces that defends the country against attack by sea **2** = a group of ships belonging to a country **naval** adj. *a naval officer* = having to do with the navy **navy blue** noun or adj. = a dark blue colour

nay /neɪ/ noun, c. = no (old-fashioned) (opposite **aye** or **yea**) **nays** noun, c. (always plural) = persons who vote against something in the parliament

NB abbr. of **nota bene** (Latin) = note well (a hint that something which is being read is important)

NCO abbr. of **Non-commissioned Officer** = a junior officer in the army, below the rank of lieutenant

NE abbr. of **north-east**

Ne•an•der•thal /ni'ændətɑːl/ noun = a race of early human beings who lived in Europe during the Stone Age, before 12,000 BC

near[1] /nɪəʳ/ prep. *My house is near the station.* = close to; not far from

near[2] adj. **1** *Our village is quite near.* = not far away; close **2** *a near relation* = closely related **3** *Her singing was near perfect.* = almost **nearest** adj.

near[3] adv. *They live quite near.* = not far away

near[4] verb, t. *We could see people running as we neared the town. // The time is nearing six.* = to approach (to come closer to something) **nearest** adj. **1** *I'm nearest to the station so I will receive her.* = most close **2** *We called only the nearest relatives to the wedding.* = the most closely related **3** *I calculated the fare to the nearest ten rupees and paid the taxi Rs 40 instead of Rs 37.* = the round figure closest to the amount **nearly** adv. *We have nearly reached the school.* = almost **Near East** noun = the countries in Africa and Asia lying close to Europe (e.g. Morocco, Turkey) (opposite **Far East**)

to be nowhere near *She said that the Taj Mahal was built in the twelfth century, but she was nowhere near the correct answer.* = not at all close to something (a number, place etc.) **to be a near thing/miss** *He just missed running over a dog which ran suddenly into the middle of the road. It was a near thing.* = an accident that one avoids narrowly **to be near to doing something** = to almost do something e.g. marry someone, refuse an offer of a job, but not actually do it in the end

neat /niːt/ adj. **1** *Her handwriting is very neat.* = tidy; well-ordered, with everything in its proper place **2** *He drinks his whisky neat.* = with nothing added to it (used to refer to alcoholic drinks) **neatly** adv.

neb•u•la /'nebjʊlə/ noun, c. (**nebulae**) = a cloud of dust and gas seen in space, among the stars **nebulous** adj. *nebulous ideas* = having no clear shape; vague

ne•ces•sa•ry /'nesɪsəri/ adj. *Water is necessary for life. // It is necessary to switch off the fan when you leave a room.* = something that one must have or do; essential **necessity** /ne'sesɪti/ noun, u. or c. (**necessities**) **1** *This house is too small. I feel the necessity for a larger house.*(u.) = the condition of being necessary **2** *A fan has become a necessity because of the hot weather.*(c.) = something that is necessary **necessitate** verb, t. = to make something necessary (formal)

neck[1] /nek/ noun, c. **1** *The giraffe has a long neck.* = the part of the body connecting the head to the shoulders **2** *the neck of the shirt* = the part that goes around the neck **3** *the neck of a bottle* = the long portion that is just below the mouth (opening) (see pic under **bottle**)

neck[2] verb, i. = to have close physical contact without having sex (informal/slang, old-fashioned) **neck-tie** (**tie**) noun, c. = a long, narrow piece of cloth worn around the neck, under the collar of the shirt, and tied in a knot at the front

neck and neck = to be equal to someone in a race or some kind of competition **to be upto one's neck in trouble** = to have too much of something that one does not like (e.g. trouble) **a pain in the neck** *Please don't give him our telephone number. He's a pain in the neck.* = someone who annoys you (informal) **to stick one's neck out** *They are having a fight and I'd like to help but don't want to stick my neck out.* = to do something which could lead to avoidable trouble

necklace /'neklɪs/ noun, c. = a chain made of gold or some other material which is worn round the neck

nec•tar /'nektəʳ/ noun, u. **1** = a drink said to be taken by the gods (in stories from ancient Greece or India) **2** = the juice of flowers collected by bees, from which honey is made

née /neɪ/ adj. *Mrs Sinha née Roy* = a word used to

show that a woman had a certain surname (family name) before her marriage

need[1] /ni:d/ noun, u. or c. **1** *As he does not have a bicycle he has to walk to his office, which is six kilometres away. He feels the need for a bicycle.*(u.) = a condition in which one does not have something which one must have in order to live comfortably **2** *As we have a holiday tomorrow there is no need for you to go to school.*(u) = something that must be done

need[2] verb, t. *I need some aspirin for my headache.* = to feel that one must have something

need[3] aux. (modal) verb *You need not go.* = do not have to do something (used in negative sentences or questions) **needful** adj. *He had asked me to fill the form, but I haven't had time to do the needful.* = whatever has to be done **needy** adj. *a needy person* = poor

nee•dle[1] /'ni:dl/ noun, c. **1** = a long, thin piece of metal used for sewing (stitching) clothes, having a sharp point at one end and a hole at the other end (called the 'eye' of the needle) through which a thread can be passed **2** *an injection needle* = a thin, hollow metal tube with a sharp point which is pushed into somebody's skin when a liquid medicine has to be injected (put inside the body) **3** *the needle of a compass* = a long, thin metal pointer fitted to a scientific instrument

needles

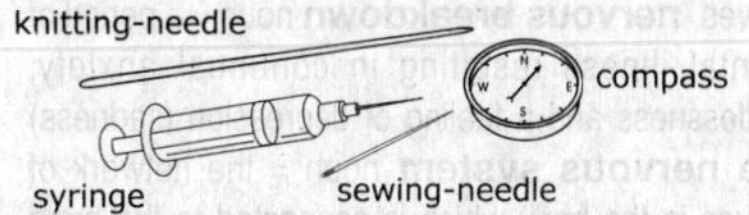

needle[2] verb, t. *His friends are always needling him because he is soft-hearted and cries easily.* = to trouble or annoy someone by making jokes or unkind remarks (informal) **needlework** noun = work like sewing or embroidery

to look for a needle in a hay-stack = to search for something which is very small and therefore difficult to find

ne•gate /nɪ'geɪt/ verb, t. *You say you want to be my friend, and then you tell all our neighbours that I can't be trusted. Your action negates your own words.* = to go against or to cancel out the effect of something **negation** noun, u. **1** *You should not have refused to help these poor children. This is a negation of all the good work you did earlier.* = the act of negating (cancelling out)something **2** *He is making a study of negation in Hindi.* = the different ways of saying 'no' in a language

neg•a•tive[1] /'negətɪv/ adj. **1** *When I asked him if he could lend me his camera, his answer was in the negative. // 'He can sing' is an affirmative sentence but 'He can't sing' is a negative sentence.* = expressing 'no' (refusing something, not agreeing to something, saying that something is not true etc.) **2** *She is very negative in the way she sees things.* = seeing only the bad or unpleasant side of things; not hopeful **3** *a negative quantity* = less than zero (e.g. - 5) **4** *Her blood was tested for malaria, but the test proved to be negative.* = showing that something tested for is not present [MEDICINE] **5** *a negative charge* = (of an electrical current) describing the direction in which the current is flowing [TECHNICAL]

negative[2] noun = a piece of film from which a photograph can be made **negative pole** = the end opposite the positive end of a magnet [PHYSICS]

ne•glect[1] /nɪ'glekt/ verb, t. **1** *If you spend so much time on games you will neglect your studies.* = to give too little attention or care to someone or something **2** *He neglected to switch off the lights before locking up the office.* = to fail to do something that should have been done, because of carelessness or forgetfulness

neglect[2] noun, u. *The plants in the garden died because of neglect.* = the action or condition of neglecting something **neglectful** adj. = careless or forgetful

neg•li•gee /'neglɪʒeɪ/ noun, c. = a very light dress worn at night by a woman who is getting ready to go to bed

neg•li•gent /'neglɪdʒənt/ adj. *The guards should have made sure that all the doors were properly locked, but they were negligent. That is why the thieves got in.* = neglectful; careless or forgetful in doing something **negligence** noun, u. *The guards who forgot to lock the doors at night should be punished for negligence.* = the action of neglecting something (being careless or forgetful) **negligible** adj. *She has been injured in the accident but the injuries are negligible.* = very slight (small) and not worth thinking about

ne•go•ti•ate /nɪ'gəʊʃieɪt/ verb, t. or i. **1** *I am negotiating a business agreement with a company in Japan.*(t.) // *We are negotiating with the management, and we hope they will agree to raise our salaries.*(i.) = to talk to a person or group in order to reach an agreement of some kind **2** *The car was going so fast that it ran off the road while trying to negotiate a curve.*(t.) = to move or travel along a path **negotiable** adj. **1** *I have told you how much I expect for my car, but the price is negotiable.* = something that can be negotiated (changed after discussion) **2** *The village roads are not negotiable during the rainy season.* = not fit for travelling on **negotiation**

N

/nɪgəʊʃɪ'eɪʃən/ noun, u. or c. *The negotiation has been successful.* = the act of negotiating (having discussions about) something

ne•gro /'ni:grəʊ/ noun, c. (**negroes**) = a person with dark skin, belonging to an African race. (The word 'negro' is now generally considered offensive. The terms now preferred are, 'African American' (in the U.S.A) or 'person of African origin') USE

neigh /neɪ/ noun, c. = the sound made by a horse

neigh•bour /'neɪbə^r/ noun, c. *She loves chatting to her neighbour across the fence.* = someone who lives near the place where one lives **neighbourhood** noun, u. or c. **1** *There are no shops in the neighbourhood.*(u.) = the area surrounding the place where one lives **2** *This is a quiet neighbourhood.*(u.) = a part of a town or city where a group of people live, close to each other **neighbouring** adj. *The roads in the neighbouring town are better than ours.* = being next to or near something **neighbourly** adj. *Let me give you some neighbourly advice.* = friendly (coming from a neighbour)

nei•ther[1] /'naɪðə^r/ det. *Neither Mohini nor Hema won the prize. It went to Saina.*

neither[2] pron. *I asked you to read both books but you have read neither.* = not one and not the other (of two)

neither[3] adv. *I didn't get the prize and neither did my friend.* = also not

neither[4] conj. *Neither he nor his brother got the prize.* = not one or the other

nem•e•sis /'nemɪsɪs/ noun = *He made millions by cheating people but he finally met his nemesis and was sent to jail.* = punishment or misfortune that is deserved and cannot be escaped from

neo- /ni:əʊ/ prefix meaning **1** new e.g. **neoclassical** /ni:əʊ'klæsɪkəl/ adj. *a neo-classical building* = made or built recently, but in the classical style (a style that was popular long ago) **2** coming after e.g. **neocolonialism** /ni:əʊkə'ləʊnɪəlɪzəm/ noun, u. = the attempt by some powerful countries in modern times to control other countries, as was done by the colonial countries several hundred years ago

ne•o•lith•ic /ni:ə'lɪθɪk/ adj. = belonging to the New Stone Age (about 10,000 years ago)

ne•ol•o•gis•m /ni:'ɒlədʒɪzəm/ noun, c. *The word 'program', when used to talk about computers, is a neologism that was not known twenty years ago.* = a word or phrase that has been newly created or given a new meaning

ne•on[1] /'ni:ɒn/ noun *neon gas* = a kind of gas that is inert (on which nothing has any effect)

neon[2] adj. *neon lights* = very bright lights in different colours, made of glass tubes filled with neon gas, which are used to advertise different products

neph•ew /'nevju:/ noun, c. = the son of one's brother or sister (compare **niece**)

ne•phri•tis /nɪ'fraɪtɪs/ noun = a disease that affects the kidneys **nephrology** noun = the study of diseases of the kidneys

nep•o•tis•m /'nepətɪzəm/ noun, u. *They have given highly paid jobs to all their relations. Someone should speak out against this nepotism.* = the misuse of power by giving unfair advantages to one's relatives and friends

Nep•tune /'neptju:n/ noun = one of the planets in the solar system, named after the god of the ocean (in stories from ancient Rome)

nerd /nɜ:d/ noun, c. = a person who is dull and not very fashionable (informal, derogatory)

nerve /nɜ:v/ noun, c. or u. **1** *the sciatic nerve*(c.) = a thread-like structure (part) inside the body which carries feelings of pain etc. to the brain from different parts of the body **2** *He had the nerve to make me wait for two hours.* = the foolish kind of courage that makes a person do something rude or disrespectful (informal) **nerves** noun *He had a sudden attack of nerves before the interview.* = loss of courage or confidence **nervous** adj. **1** *I am always nervous before an examination.* = slightly afraid and worried **2** *She has a nervous disorder.* = connected with the nerves **nervous breakdown** noun = a period of mental illness resulting in continual anxiety, restlessness and a feeling of depression (sadness) **the nervous system** noun = the network of nerves in the body which is connected to the brain and carries messages from and to the brain

to get on someone's nerves = to make someone irritated and angry **to lose one's nerve** *At the driving test, they asked me so many questions that I lost my nerve and did badly.* = to lose the courage one had in the beginning

nest[1] /nest/ noun, c. *a bird's nest* = a home built by a bird, usually out of twigs (small branches of trees) or bits of straw or grass, in which it lays its eggs and keeps its chicks (young ones) until they have grown up

nest[2] verb, i. *The birds are nesting in the mango trees.* = to build a nest **nest-egg** noun *The money she got on her retirement is her nest egg.* = money saved by someone for future use **nestling** noun, c. = a young bird that has not left its nest (literary)

nes•tle /'nesəl/ verb, t. *The child nestled its head on the soft pillow.* = to lie in a warm and comfortable position

net[1] /net/ noun, c. **1** *a nylon net.* = material made from threads or wires tied or woven together so as to leave open spaces in between, allowing gases, liquids or small objects to pass through (also **netting**) **2** *We caught the fish in a net.* = an object made from netting material tied or woven into a net, used to stop something from passing through **3** *a tennis net* = a net used in games such as tennis, table-tennis, volley-ball, badminton etc. in which a player loses a point if the ball is hit into the net **4** *surfing the Net* = an abbreviation for the Internet [COMPUTERS]

net[2] verb, t. (**netted**) **1** *We netted a large fish.* = to catch in a net **2** *He netted two goals.* = to score a goal (in the game of football or hockey) by hitting a ball into the net at the back of the goal-post

net[3] adj. *The company made a net (nett) profit of five lakhs this year.* = the total amount remaining after everything that should have been deducted has been deducted

to surf/browse the Net = to get into the Internet system and view pages or sites on the World Wide Web

neth•er /ˈneðəʳ/ adj. *He lives in a room somewhere in this huge building.I don't know where his room is, probably somewhere in the nether regions.* = lower or hidden (humorous)

net•work[1] /ˈnetwɜːk/ noun, c. *The railways form a large network. // a television network* = a large system made up of many similar parts that are connected to each other so as to allow movement or communication between or along the parts

network[2] verb, i. *The different television channels are networking together.* = to form a network, so as to communicate with each other

neu•ral•gia /njʊˈrældʒə/ noun = pain in the body caused by some damage to the nerves

neuro- /njʊˈrəʊ/ prefix meaning 'having to do with the nerves' e.g. **neurology** /njʊˈrɒlədʒi/ noun = the branch of medicine which deals with disorders of the nervous system in the body **neurologist** noun, c. = a doctor who practises neurology

neu•ro•sis /njʊˈrəʊsəs/ noun = a disorder of the mind causing great anxiety and fear **neurotic** adj. or noun = (a person who is) suffering from neurosis

neuron noun, c. = a cell that carries messages from the various parts of the body to the brain and back [BIOLOGY]

neu•ter[1] /ˈnjuːtəʳ/ adj. *The pronoun 'he' is masculine, 'she' is feminine, but 'it' is neuter in gender.* = a word that is neither masculine in gender (that is, referring to a male person or animal) nor feminine (referring to a female person or animal) [GRAMMAR]

neuter[2] verb, t. = to remove the sex organs of a male animal

neu•tral[1] /ˈnjuːtrəl/ adj. *I don't like or dislike them. I have neutral feelings about them.* = neither in favour of something nor against it; having no strong feelings or opinions about something **2** *We did not join one group or the other. We remained neutral.* = not helping either side in a war or a dispute **3** = neither acidic nor basic [CHEMISTRY]

neutral[2] noun, u. or c. **1** *The car is not moving because it is in neutral.*(u.) = the condition when no power is being carried from the engine of a car to the wheels, because the gears are not connected to each other (see also **gear**) **neutrality** /njuːˈtrælɪti/ noun, u. = the state of being neutral in a war

neutralize (neutralise) /ˈnjuːtrəlaɪz/ verb, t. **1** *Our salaries have been raised, but the cost of food has also gone up, neutralizing the effect of the raise.* = to take away the effect or value of something **2** = to make a country remain neutral during a war

neu•tron /ˈnjuːtrɒn/ noun, c. = a very tiny piece of matter inside an atom, which carries no electrical charge (see also **electron, proton**)

nev•er /ˈnevəʳ/ adv. **1** *I don't know anything about London as I have never been there.* = not at any time **2** *'He told me your secret.' 'Never!'* = used to say that something could not have happened, and that you don't believe it **nevertheless** adv. *It is raining heavily. Nevertheless, I must go for the meeting because people are expecting me.* = in spite of that (formal)

never mind *'I'm sorry, there's no dinner left for you.' 'Never mind. I can go and get some.'* = an expression meaning, 'It does not matter. Don't worry.' **you never know** *Nihar doesn't want to go with the others to the cinema, but you never know, he may change his mind.* = an expression used to show that someone's behaviour cannot be predicted (informal, humorous)

new /njuː/ adj. *The book is so new that very few people have read it.* = produced (made) very recently **2** *This car is new, not second-hand.* = not used or owned by anyone before **3** *She doesn't like this house, so she is thinking of moving into a new one.* = different **4** *I don't find it easy to learn a new language.* = not known or experienced before **5** *Look, there are some new leaves on the bush!* = (of something which grows) just appeared or developed **6** *My house has a new number now.* = changed from the old **7** *We are new to this city.* = recently arrived **8** *The water problem has been solved, but we have a new problem now.* = another, fresh; one that wasn't there before **newly** adj. *a newly-painted car* = recently (not very long ago) **newborn** adj. = recently born (referring to a baby) **newcomer** noun = a person who has just come to a place **new-fangled** adj. *I don't like your new-fangled ideas about teaching meditation to children.* = new but not necessarily better (derogatory) **new**

N

moon = the time when the moon first appears and can hardly be seen **New Testament** noun = the part of the Bible that tells us about Jesus Christ **New Year's Day** noun = the first day in January, which marks the beginning of a new year

as good as new *He has repaired the table. It looks as good as new.* = almost as if it were new **to feel like a new person** – to feel in a better state of health than one felt before **What's new?** *'He came late to class this morning.' 'He did? So what's new?'* = this is only to be expected and I am not surprised at all (slang, derogatory)

news /nju:z/ noun, u. **1** *What's the news in the papers today?* = information or reports about recent events **2** *the 9 o'clock news* = a programme on radio or television which presents the news **news agency** noun, c. = a company that supplies news to newspapers, television and radio channels **newscaster** noun, c. = a person who presents the news on radio or television (also **news-reader**) **newsflash** = a piece of news (on television or radio), which is important and therefore shown by breaking the regular reading of the news [MEDIA] **newsletter** noun, c. = a printed sheet containing news, published and sent to readers regularly by post **newspaper** = large sheets of printed paper containing news, articles, advertisements usually published and sold everyday **newsworthy** adj. *We didn't report your speech in the newspaper as we didn't think it was newsworthy.* = something which is interesting or important enough to be published as news

to break the news = to be the first to give someone the news **to make the news** = to do something which gets reported in the newspaper, on television etc. **to be in the news** = to be talked about in an important way by newspapers, television etc. **No news is good news.** = a way of hoping, especially when one is expecting unpleasant news, that not getting any news will mean that things are all right **That's news to me!** *You're leaving the city? That's news to me!* = an expression used to show that one is surprised or annoyed because one has not been told something **to be bad news** I don't think we should deal with them. They're bad news. = to be likely to cause trouble or be unpleasant (informal)

next[1] /nekst/ det. *There are no seats left in the first row but there is a seat in the next row.* = nearest or closest to something in time or space, with nothing in between

next[2] adv. **1** *The school is next to the shopping centre.* = nearest to **2** *Which song will you sing next?* = just after the present one **next door** adv. *She lives next door.* = in the house next to this one

next to nothing *He knows next to nothing about music.* = almost nothing

NGO abbr. of **Non-governmental Organization** = an organization usually not connected directly with the government but engaged in doing social work

nib /nɪb/ noun, c. *The pen has a steel nib.* = a flat and pointed piece of metal at the end of a pen, through which ink flows down to the paper while writing

nib•ble[1] /'nɪbəl/ verb, t. **1** *The boy does not seem to be hungry. He is only nibbling at his food.* = to take small and repeated bites of food **2** *The mouse nibbled through the rope.* = to cut something with the teeth

nibble[2] noun, c. *She took a nibble from the piece of bread.* = a small bite

nice /naɪs/ adj. **1** *It rained yesterday but today the weather is nice.* = pleasant **2** *He is a really nice person.* = friendly **3** *You should be nice to your students.* = kind; good **nicely** adv. **1** *He will help you if you speak to him nicely.* = politely **2** *The motorbike was running nicely until we suddenly ran out of petrol.* = in a good way, as expected **nicety** noun, c. (**niceties**) *The two companies have come to a broad agreement, but their lawyers will have to examine all the niceties.* = small details which have to be looked at carefully

a nice bit ot trouble (mess) etc. *That was a nice bit of trouble you got into!* = 'Nice' is used here to mean exactly the opposite—bad or unpleasant (informal) **Nice work!** = a way of praising someone (informal)

niche /ni:ʃ/ noun, c. (French) **1** = a hollow place in a wall, where one can keep a statue or something beautiful for people to see **2** *He has found his niche as the only writer of science fiction in Hindi.* = a special position that one occupies **niche market** *He makes glass furniture for a niche market.* = a limited number of buyers who are prepared to buy a very special kind of product

nick[1] /nɪk/ verb, t. **1** *I accidentally nicked my face while shaving.* = to cut **2** *Someone has nicked my watch.* = to steal (informal)

nick[2] noun, c. *There are some nicks in the door where the dog scratched the wood with its claws.* = a small cut in a surface

in the nick of time *The doctor arrived in the nick of time, or the patient would have died.* = just in time

nick•el /'nɪkəl/ noun = a hard, silvery white metal which is often mixed with steel so that it will not rust **nickel-plating** = a thin, shiny coating of nickel put on top of another metal with the help of an electric current

nick•nack (**knick-knack**) /'nɪk næk/ noun, c. *His house is full of little nicknacks which he has collected over many years.* = a small decorative object

nick•name /'nɪkneɪm/ noun, c. *Saurav Ganguli's nickname is 'Maharaj' (king)* = a name by which a person is called affectionately by members of his/ her family and close friends

nic•o•tine /ˈnɪkəti:n/ noun, u. = a poisonous, habit-forming substance which is present in tobacco

niece /ni:s/ noun, c. = the daughter of one's brother or sister or husband's or wife's brother or sister

niff /nɪf/ noun, u. *The room carries a niff of stale food.* = a bad or unpleasant smell (informal)

nif•ty /ˈnɪfti/ adj. *That's a nice little wooden table you have made. A nifty piece of work, I must say!* = something attractive or effective (informal)

nig•gard•ly /ˈnɪgədli/ adj. **1** *a niggardly person* = not willing to spend money or do anything to help anyone **2** *She made me a niggardly offer for my car, so I didn't agree to sell it to her.* = very small in amount; miserly (informal)

nig•gling /ˈnɪgəlɪŋ/ adj. *I have a niggling doubt that we left the house without locking the door properly.* = something that annoys or troubles one for a long time (referring to an idea or feeling)

nigh /naɪ/ adv. *The time to go is nigh.* = near (old-fashioned or poetic)

night /naɪt/ noun, u.or c. **1** *The sun is about to set. Soon it will be night.*(u.) // *We have booked a room in the hotel for two days and one night.*(c.) = the part of the day (period of 24 hours) when the sun cannot be seen and it is dark **2** *I want to see the new play on the opening night.*(c.) = the evening on which some special event takes place **night-blindness** noun = a defect in the eyes resulting in the inability to see clearly in poor light **night-club** noun = a place that people visit at night for entertainment (to eat, drink and watch a performance of dance and music) **night-life** noun = the entertainment that is available in night-clubs etc. **night-shift** noun, c. = the part of the day (usually between 10.00 at night and 8.00 in the morning) when a person works in a factory, hospital etc. **night-soil** noun = waste matter from human bodies, which may be used for agriculture **nightie** noun, c. (**nighties**) = a dress worn by a woman in bed (informal)

a late night = a night when one goes to bed very late **good night** = said before one goes to bed **last thing at night** *Please have this medicine last thing at night.* = just before one goes to bed **to (work) nights 1** *He's at home in the day. He works nights now.* = to work, go for a walk, exercise etc. on a regular basis at night (informal) **2** *The baby cried nights.* = every night or often (informal) **to stay up all night** *We stayed up all night watching the football match on television.* = to choose not to sleep and to work etc. instead

nigh•tin•gale /ˈnaɪtɪŋgeɪl/ noun, c. = a kind of bird that sings very sweetly

night•mare /ˈnaɪtmeəʳ/ noun, c. **1** = a bad or frightening dream **2** = a frightening or unpleasant experience

nil /nɪl/ noun, u. *India lost the football match by five goals to nil.* = zero; nothing

nim•ble /ˈnɪmbəl/ adj. **1** *She is so nimble that she runs ahead of everyone else in a race.* = quick in movement (literary) **2** *He has a nimble mind.* = quick in thinking

nim•bus /ˈnɪmbəs/ noun or adj. *nimbus clouds* = a dark cloud that usually brings rain [GEOGRAPHY]

nine /naɪn/ noun or det. or pron. = the number after eight and before ten **ninth** det. = coming after eight things or people **nine days' wonder** *The actor's first film was a hit, but all his other films were flops. His popularity proved to be a nine days' wonder.* = an event that causes excitement for a short time and is then forgotten

nine•teen /naɪnˈti:n/ noun or det. = the number coming after 18 and before 20

to speak nineteen to the dozen = to speak very fast, without stopping

nine•ty /ˈnaɪnti/ noun = the number obtained by mutiplying 9 by ten (9x10 = 90)

nip[1] /nɪp/ verb, t. *The dog nipped me in the leg.* = to bite lightly

nip[2] noun, u. or c. **1** *There is a nip in the air.*(u.) = a slight feeling of coldness **2** *He took a nip of whisky.*(c.) = a small amount of some strong alcoholic drink

to nip something in the bud = to stop something unpleasant, such as a fight, when it is just starting and has not been able to grow **to nip across** *I nipped across to buy a loaf of bread.* = to go somewhere quickly (informal)

nip•ple /ˈnɪpəl/ noun, c. **1** = the raised part on a woman's breast or the chest of a female mammal, through which a baby can suck milk from the mother **2** = a piece of rubber shaped like a nipple, fitted to the end of a bottle, through which a baby sucks milk **3** *a grease nipple* = an opening in a machine through which oil or grease can be put into the machine

nip•py /ˈnɪpi/ adj. **1** *The weather is nippy.* = cold (informal) **2** *He is a nippy runner.* = fast (informal)

nir•va•na /nɪrˈvɑ:nə/ noun = the state of being free from all pain, sorrow and desire (in Hinduism and Buddhism)

nit /nɪt/ noun, c. = a small insect or its egg sometimes found in a person's hair **nit-picking** noun, u. *My senior in the office has such a habit of nit-picking that he is never satisfied with my work.* = the habit of paying too much attention to small faults (derogatory)

ni•tro•gen /ˈnaɪtrədʒən/ noun = a kind of colourless gas which forms 78 per cent of the air that we breathe **nitrate** noun, u. or c. = a chemical which is rich in nitrogen and can be used as fertilizer **nitric acid**

N

noun = a very powerful acid which can destroy substances and is used in making explosives

ni•tro•gly•ce•rine /naɪtrəʊ'glɪsərɪn/ noun = a powerful explosive, also known as dynamite, used to blow up rocks etc.

nit•ty-grit•ty /nɪti'grɪti/ noun *We have talked in general terms about the new project. Let us come to the nitty gritty now.* = the practical and basic details that have to be considered in planning something (informal)

no[1] /nəʊ/ det. **1** *We have no sugar. // He has no time.* = not any **2** *No smoking!* = used in warning signs **3** *It's no distance at all from my house to the railway station.* = hardly any (very little)

no[2] adv. **1** *'Will you come to the play tonight?' 'No, I'm not feeling well.'* = an answer expressing refusal or disagreement **2** *She has no more than two or three friends.* = not any **3** *We ordered food from the restaurant and in no time, it was delivered to our house.* = hardly any

no[3] noun, c. *Can you give me a clear no or a yes by tomorrow?* = an answer expressing disagreement **no-ball** = a ball bowled by a bowler (in cricket) that is against the rules and is not counted

no, no **1** *'He left without telling me.' 'No, no, he's left you a note.'* = a way of stressing that something is not what one thinks it is; a way of disagreeing **2** *'No, no, you can't go in.'* = a way of strongly stopping someone from doing something **3** *I'm sorry, but I can't join your club. That's a total no no.* = something that one will never agree to do (informal) **no-man's land** = an area of land which falls between two countries and is not controlled by either country **no-nonsense** *She is famous for her no-nonsense approach to company management.* = practical and efficient (interested only in getting things done) (approving) **a no-win situation** = a difficult situation which can have no solution, no matter what one does **no good/use** *It's no good going to the station now. The train will have left.* = it is pointless to do something **Oh no!** *'I had a fall and broke my arm.' 'Oh no!'* = a way of reacting to news of something unpleasant that has happened to someone, or to show that one is disappointed **to not take no for an answer** *You're going on the trip with us, and we'll not take no for an answer.* = to make a request in such a way that the person requested cannot refuse (informal)

No•bel prize /nəʊbel 'praɪz/ noun = a prize given by a group of people in Sweden and founded by Alfred Nobel, the inventor of dynamite (nitroglycerine), for outstanding work in science, medicine, literature, economics and efforts to bring peace to the world

no•ble[1] /'nəʊbəl/ adj. **1** *I am glad you've taken up the noble cause of teaching disabled children.* = something that should be praised or admired because it is based on high moral principles **2** *a person from a noble family* = (in the past) having a high position in society (old-fashioned)

noble[2] (**noble man**) noun, c. = a member of the nobility **nobility** noun, u. = the class of rich, land-owning families which, in former times, were close to the rulers of the country (see also **aristocracy**) **noble gas/metal** noun, c. = any of the gases or metals that do not react with other chemicals or with the air [CHEMISTRY]

no•bod•y[1] /'nəʊbədi/ det. *Nobody came to see me when I was in hospital.* = no one

nobody[2] noun, c. *I'm just a nobody.* = a person without any position or importance (informal)

noc•tur•nal /nɒk'tɜːnl/ adj. *Owls are nocturnal birds. They hunt only at night.* = having to do with the night (active only during the night)

nod[1] /nɒd/ verb, i. (**nodded**) *The teacher nodded when I asked him if I could leave the meeting. // She nodded at me when we met on the street.* = to move one's head down and up again to show agreement or to greet someone

nod[2] noun, c. *He gave me a nod. // Our plan was given the nod.* (Note the use of 'a' and 'the') = a movement of the head to show agreement or greeting (figurative in the second example)

node /nəʊd/ noun, c. **1** *a leaf node* = a place where things are joined (e.g. the place where a leaf joins the stem or branch of a plant or a tree) [BOTANY] **2** *a lymph node* = a lump, especially at the meeting point of two bones in the human body [ZOOLOGY] (also **nodule**) **nodal** adj. **1** = having to do with a node (a place where things are joined) **2** *a nodal organization* = an important part of a network or system which connects or brings things together

noise /nɔɪz/ noun, u. or c. *The noise of traffic on the streets is enough to make you deaf.*(u.) = unwanted, unpleasant and loud sounds **noisy** adj. *These streets are very noisy. // The class is very noisy.* = full of noise or making a lot of noise

no•mad /'nəʊmæd/ noun, c. = a member of a tribe which has no permanent home but keeps moving from place to place **nomadic** adj.

nom•de•plume /nɒmdə'pluːm/ noun, c. (French) *Samuel L. Clemens wrote under the nom de plume of Mark Twain.* = pen name (the false name used by a writer)

no•men•cla•ture /nəʊ'meŋklətʃə[r]/ noun, u. = the system used, specially in science, to name things

nom•i•nal /'nɒmɪnl/ adj. **1** *He is the nominal ruler of the state, but the real ruler is his mother.* = only in name but not in reality **2** *I sold the car to my brother for a nominal payment of one rupee.* = very small compared to the expected price or value

nom•i•nate /'nɒmɪneɪt/ verb, t. *The class has nominated me for the post of class leader.* = to name or suggest someone officially for a position **nomination** /nɒmɪ'neɪʃən/ noun, u. = the act of nominating someone to a position **nominee** /'nɒmɪni:/ noun, c. = a person who is nominated

nominative /'nɒmɪnətɪv/ noun *'I' is the nominative form of the pronoun while 'me' is the dative form.* = the form of a noun or pronoun which shows that it is the subject of a sentence [GRAMMAR]

non- /nɒn/ prefix meaning not e.g. **non-addictive** /nɒn'ædɪktɪv/ adj. *Coffee is non-addictive.* = something that does not lead to the formation of a habit

no•na•ge•nar•i•an /nəʊnədʒə'neəriən/ noun, c. = a person who is in his nineties (between 90 and 99 years old)

non-alcoholic adj. = not containing alcohol

non-aligned adj. *a meeting of non-aligned countries* = not a member of any group or supporting any other country

non•cha•lant /'nɒnʃələnt/ adj. (French) *He remained nonchalant even when he had lost all his money.* = calm and showing no anxiety or care

non-committal adj. *She was non-committal when we asked her if she would like to accompany us on our tour.* = not expressing a clear or definite opinion

non-con•duc•tor /nɒnkən'dʌktr/ noun, c. = a substance that does not allow electricity or heat to pass through it

non-con•form•ist adj. = a person who lives and thinks in a way that is different from that of other people

non•de•script /nɒndɪskrɪpt/ adj. *a nondescript person* = very ordinary; having no special quality which can be noticed (derogatory)

none[1] /nʌn/ det. *None of my friends lives in this neighbourhood.* = not even one

none[2] pron. **1** *My sister has three children but I have none.* = not any **2** *Half a loaf of bread is better than none at all.* = not anyone or anything

none the wiser *I was none the wiser for having gone to the travel agent. He did not give me any useful information.* = not knowing any more than before

non-entity noun, c. (**nonentities**) *He was treated as a nonentity, though he had many talents.* = a person without any importance or position (derogatory)

none•the•less /nʌnðə'les/ adv. *He does not visit people often. Nonetheless, he is very popular with his neighbours.* = in spite of that (also **nevertheless**)

non-fiction noun, u. = writing that is about real and not imaginary people, things or events

non•plus /nɒn'plʌs/ verb, t. (**nonplussed**) *I was completely nonplussed by the question asked at the interview.* = to cause someone to feel confused and not know what to say or do

non-proliferation noun, u. *a treaty for the non-proliferation of nuclear weapons* = not allowing something (specially the ability to make and use nuclear weapons) to spread among many countries

non-resident adj. *She is a non-resident Indian (NRI).* = a person who does not live in the country where he or she was born or of which he or she is a citizen

non•sense /'nɒnsəns/ noun, u. *Stop talking nonsense!* = speech or writing without sense (meaning)

non-starter noun, c. *The idea of using gas to run all the buses in the country is a non-starter.* = an idea which has no chance of succeeding (informal)

non-stick adj. *a non-stick frying-pan* = having an inner surface coated with some chemical to which food will not stick

non-stop adj. *a non-stop flight* = without a pause or stop

non-vegetarian noun or adj. **1** (noun) = a person who eats meat or fish as well as vegetables **2** *non-vegetarian food* (adj.) = containing meat or fish

non-verbal adj. *non-verbal communication* = without the use of words, written or spoken

non-violence noun, u. = the belief that no violence (use of force) should be used in politics, religion or living

noo•dle /'nu:dl/ noun, u. (usually plural **noodles**) = food made from flour, in the form of long, thin threads

nook /nʊk/ noun, c. *She likes to sit in a nook in the garden, reading a book.* = a small space which is hidden or shelterd

in every nook and corner/cranny = every place

noon /nu:n/ noun, u. or c. = the middle of the day (12 o'clock) (compare **midnight**)

noose /nu:s/ noun, c. *the hangman's noose* = a ring formed by the end of a rope which becomes tight when the rope is pulled

nope /nəʊp/ adv. *'Will you come with me?' 'Nope.'* = no (slang)

nor /nɔ:ʳ/ conj. *'I like Kolkata. It's neither too crowded, like Mumbai, nor too expensive, like Delhi.'* = used, together with **neither**, before the second or last of a set of negative choices

norm /nɔ:m/ noun, c. **1** *He said we should never use bad language because it went against the norms of polite behaviour.* = a standard of behaviour (way of doing things) that is accepted by most people **2** *We will accept two children as the norm for a family.* = standard; something which is used to measure or judge other things of the same kind

nor•mal[1] /'nɔ:məl/ noun, u. *The temperature in the month of May should be about 35 degrees Celsius*

N

but this year it is 43 degrees— eight degrees above normal.* = what is usual or expected (opposite **abnormal**)

normal[2] adj. **1** *The normal temperature of the human body is 23 degrees Celsius.* = average or usual **2** *a normal baby* = in good physical and mental health **normality** /nɒ'mælɪtɪ/ noun, u. *There was some trouble in the city last week but now normality has returned.* = the usual state of things (also **normalcy**) **normalize (normalise)** /'nɔːməlaɪz/ verb, t. *Relations between the two warring countries have been normalized.* = to go back to the normal (usual) condition

north /nɔːθ/ noun = one of the four directions (north, south, east and west), which is the direction in which the left arm of a person will point if he/she stands facing the rising sun (east) **northern** adj. *the northern states of India* = in the north or belonging to the north **North Atlantic Drift** = a warm water current in the Atlantic Ocean that affects the climate of Europe [GEOGRAPHY] **northerly** adj. **1** *northerly winds* = coming from the north **2** *We marched off in a northerly direction.* = towards the north **north-east** noun = the direction that is half-way between north and east **north-eastern** adj. = belonging to the north-east **north-west** noun = the direction that is half-way between north and west **North Pole** noun = the most northern point on the surface of the earth (see pic under **earth**) **northern lights** noun = bands of brightly coloured light seen in the night sky in countries near the North Pole (also known as **aurora borealis**)

nose[1] /nəʊz/ noun, c. **1** = the part of the face above the mouth, which stands out from the rest of the face and with the help of which we are able to smell and breathe **2** *the nose of the aircraft* = the narrow and pointed front end of something

nose[2] verb, i. or t. **1** *She nosed the car into the traffic.*(t.) = to move ahead slowly and carefully **2** *I don't like other people nosing into my affairs.*(i.) = taking an interest in something that does not concern you (informal, derogatory) **3** *I found him nosing about the house.*(t.) = to look for or search for something which does not concern you **nosy** adj. *a nosy person* = one who is interested in things that do not concern him/her (informal, derogatory) **nose-bag** = a bag containing grain, hung around the head of a horse

to poke one's nose into someone's affairs = to take an interest in things which do not concern one (informal) **to do something under someone's nose** *She learnt later that they had planned the robbery under her nose, and she didn't know!* = openly (without trying to hide something) (informal) **to turn one's nose up at something** = to not want to do something because one thinks oneself to be too good for it **to cut off one's nose to spite one's face** = to do something in a mood of anger, even if it is unpleasant or harmful to oneself (figurative)

nose•dive /'nəʊzdaɪv/ verb, i. *The aircraft nose-dived into the sea.* = to drop straight down at great speed from a height with the nose (front part) pointing downwards

nos•tal•gia /nɒ'stældʒə/ noun, u. *I have a strong feeling of nostalgia when I think of the little town where I grew up.* = fondness (love) for something belonging to the past **nostalgic** adj. *He feels nostalgic about the place where he lived as a child.* = full of nostalgia

nos•tril /'nɒstrɪl/ noun, c. = one of the two openings at the end of one's nose, through which one breathes

not /nɒt/ adv. **1** *She is not ready as yet. Could you wait a few minutes?* = a word used to express a negative meaning **2** *Is he planning to go to the meeting or not?* = a word which replaces a whole expression and carries a meaning opposite to what was stated earlier **3** *'Do you think it will rain today?' 'I think not.'* = a short negative answer **4** *Shall we buy this computer or not?* = the negative of two possibilities **not at all** *'Thank you for coming.' 'Not at all.'* = a reply often given to an expression of thanks (also *'You are welcome!'*) **notwithstanding** prep. *He is still very popular in this city, notwithstanding all the bad reports being published about him.* = in spite of (formal)

no•ta•ry /'nəʊtəri/ noun, c. (**notaries**) = a public official who has the legal authority to witness a document, as proof that it is genuine (also **notary public**)

no•ta•tion /nəʊ'teɪʃən/ noun, c. = a system of written symbols used in mathematics or music

notch[1] /nɒtʃ/ noun, c. (**notches**) **1** *He cut a notch in the branch of a tree.* = a V-shaped cut made in a hard surface **2** *Many people think that as an actor, Amitabh Bachchan is several notches above all the new actors.* = an imaginary point on a scale by which values are compared

notch[2] verb, t. *The hockey team notched up a victory in the first match.* = to record a gain or an achievement

note[1] /nəʊt/ noun, c. **1** *Have you made notes from the professor's lecture?* = a written record, usually based on a book that one has read or a talk that one has listened to, which helps one to remember what one has read or heard **2** *I have received a note from the secretary.* = a short letter **3** *a bank note* = a piece of printed paper which can be used as money **4** = a musical sound **5** *There was a note of sadness in his voice.* = something which shows (one's) feelings

note[2] verb, t. **1** *Please note that no children are allowed at the meeting.* = to pay special attention to something and to remember it **2** *Please note this telephone number in your diary.* = to make a written record of **notable** /ˈnəʊtəbl/ adj. *This book is notable for its description of Tibetan customs.* = so interesting as to deserve attention and mention **notepaper** noun, u. = special paper used to write letters or notes **noteworthy** adj. *He did not say anything noteworthy in his talk.* = deserving attention or notice

to take note of something = to pay special attention to something and remember it

note•book /ˈnəʊtbʊk/ noun, c. **1** = a book, which is used to write things (class notes, accounts etc.) in so that they can be referred to later **2** = a portable computer (a laptop) [COMPUTERS]

noth•ing[1] /ˈnʌθɪŋ/ det. *She said nothing new.* = not anything

nothing[2] pron. **1** *Nothing has happened.* = not anything **2** *There's nothing happening in the town hall tonight.* = the absence of something, e.g. a television programme **3** *We can't expect him to repair the cycle for nothing.* = no payment **4** *I gave him a lot of advice, but for nothing.* = serving no purpose

nothing[3] adv. *She's nothing like you describe her. You said she was unfriendly, but she was very friendly.* = not at all

to have nothing to do with someone *He was my friend once upon a time, but I have nothing to do with him now.* = to have no connection with someone or something **to want nothing to do with someone** *She has let us down and we want nothing to do with her.* = to not want any connection with a person, usually for a reason **nothing but** *She does nothing but paint all day.* = only **nothing much** *'What did you do in Bangalore last weekend?' 'Nothing much.'* = not a lot **It's nothing** *'You helped us so much. Thank you!' 'Oh, it was nothing.'* = a way of replying to thanks by saying something isn't or wasn't difficult to do (informal) **nothing to it** *Of course you can drive a bus. There's nothing to it.* = an expression meaning 'It's quite easy to do.' (informal) **nothing on earth** **1** *Nothing on earth can be as good as this song.* = an expression meaning that something is the best there is (informal) **2** *The ice cream tasted like nothing on earth.* = so bad that it cannot be described (informal)

no•tice[1] /ˈnəʊtɪs/ noun, c. **1** *The notice on the board says that the school will be closed tomorrow.*(c.) = a written statement giving information to the public **2** *The bank has sent me a notice saying it will take me to court if I don't pay up the loan.*(c.) = a warning or information about something that is going to be done **3** *This matter should have been brought to my notice. Why wasn't I told?*(u.) = attention

notice[2] verb, t. *I notice that you have got new curtains for your room.* = to observe (see) something or to pay special attention to something **noticeable** adj. *There is a noticeable improvement in the patient's condition.* = something that can be easily observed (seen) **notice-board** noun, c. = a large board usually fixed on a wall, on which notices are put up so that people can read them (also **bulletin board**)

no•ti•fy /ˈnəʊtɪfaɪ/ verb, t. (**notified**) *All the students have been notified of the change in the timetable.* = to inform through a written notice (formal) **notification** /nəʊtɪfɪˈkeɪʃən/ noun, u. or c. **1** = the act of notifying or sending a notice to someone **2** = a notice given to someone

no•tion /ˈnəʊʃən/ noun, c. *I had the notion that he and you were related to each other.* = a vague (not clear or exact) idea or piece of information which often proves to be wrong **notional** adj. *She is the notional head of the department, although she can't take important decisions.* = something that exists only as an idea, not in reality

no•to•ri•ous /nəʊˈtɔːriəs/ adj. *This shop has become notorious for selling stolen goods.* = famous for something bad **notoriety** /nəʊtəˈrɑɪəti/ noun, u. = the state of being notorious

nought /nɔːt/ noun, c. = zero **noughts and crosses** = a game played on a piece of paper in which two players write either 0 or X in a pattern of nine squares, and the player who gets three noughts or three crosses in a straight line wins

noun /naʊn/ noun, c. *The words 'plate' and 'truth' are both nouns.* = a word that names a person (e.g. Asif), a place (e.g. New Delhi), a thing (e.g. a chair) or a quality or idea (e.g. beauty) [GRAMMAR]

nour•ish /ˈnʌrɪʃ/ verb, t. **1** *You should nourish the children by giving them plenty of milk and fruits.* = to provide food so as to keep someone or something healthy (formal) **2** *to nourish new ideas* = to support and encourage **nourishment** noun, u. *Are the children getting enough nourishment?* = food given to someone or something to maintain good health

no•va /ˈnəʊvə/ noun, c. (**novas** or **novae**) = a bright star [PHYSICS]

no•vel[1] /ˈnɒvəl/ noun, c. *He is writing a novel about the war.* = a long story about imaginary people and events

novel[2] adj. *That's a novel idea! No one has thought of it before.* = new and original **novelist** noun, c. = a person who writes a novel

nov•el•ty /ˈnɒvəlti/ noun, c. **1** = the quality of being new and original **2** = a small object that is not very expensive

No•vem•ber /nəʊˈvembəʳ/ noun = the eleventh

N

month of the year, between October and December

nov•ice /ˈnɒvɪs/ noun, c. *I can tell from the way you are driving that you are a novice.* = a beginner; a person who has little skill in or experience of doing something

now /naʊ/ adv. **1** *I want you to go now, not later.* = at this time; at present **2** *She has been a doctor for ten years now.* = from the beginning to the present time **3** *We will have some games now.* = very soon **4** *I want you to phone him now, please.* = immediately **5** *Now, whom did you want to meet?* = used to introduce a statement or question **nowadays** adv. *It doesn't usually rain much here but we are getting a lot of rain nowadays.* = at the present time, in comparison with the past

now and then *She calls me now and then.* = occasionally **for now** *Yes we do need a scooter, but for now let's manage with a bicycle.* = for the present **now for** *I have eaten a big meal. Now for a good nap!* = an expression used to refer to something that one is going to do next **any day now** *My friend is getting married soon and I should be receiving an invitation to the wedding any day now.* = soon **now or never** *There's no time to think about applying for a job. It's now or never.* = a way of saying 'the right time is this, not later.' (informal) **What is it now?** *This is the third time you have telephoned me this morning. What is it now?* = said to mean 'Why are you disturbing me again?' (showing annoyance at being disturbed repeatedly)

nox•ious /ˈnɒkʃəs/ adj. *When diesel oil is burnt in an engine, some noxious gases are produced.* = harmful or poisonous (formal)

noz•zle /ˈnɒzəl/ noun, c. *There is a plastic nozzle fitted to the end of the rubber pipe.* = a short, pointed piece of metal or plastic fitted to the end of a pipe, so that the flow of liquid or gas through the pipe can be controlled and directed towards a particular point

nu•ance /ˈnjuːɑːns/ noun, c. *A word can have many meanings, and a good dictionary tries to show the different nuances in the meanings of words.* = a very small difference in meaning which is difficult to describe

nu•cle•us /ˈnjuːklɪəs/ noun, c. (**nucleuses** or **nuclei**) **1** *the nucleus of an atom* = the central part of an atom, made of protons, neutrons and electrons [PHYSICS] **2** *the nucleus of a cell* = the central part of a cell (the smallest part into which a living substance can be divided) [BIOLOGY] **3** *I am setting up a new team of scientists, and I want the two of you to form its nucleus.* = the most important or central part of an organization or group, around which it can grow **nuclear** /ˈnjuːklɪə^r/ adj. **1** *nuclear weapons* = having to do with nuclear energy (the powerful energy which is produced when the nucleus of an atom is divided or joined to the nucleus of another atom) **2** = having to do with the nucleus in an atom **nuclear disarmament** noun = the giving up of nuclear weapons by an agreement between countries **nuclear power-station** noun = a power station (place where electrical energy is produced) which uses nuclear energy to produce electricity **nuclear reactor** noun = a powerful device that contains many parts and produces nuclear energy **nuclear weapon** noun, c. = a bomb which can produce very great destruction because it uses nuclear energy

nude[1] /njuːd/ adj. = naked (with no clothes on the body)

nude[2] noun, c. = a painting or a photograph of a naked person which is a work of art **nudity** noun, u. = the state of being nude

nudge[1] /nʌdʒ/ verb, t. *He nudged me to remind me that it was time to leave the meeting.* = to give someone a gentle push, usually with the elbow, to attract his/her attention or to remind him/her of something

nudge[2] noun, c. *She gave me a nudge.* = a gentle push with the elbow

nug•get /ˈnʌgɪt/ noun, c. **1** *a nugget of gold* = a rough lump of some precious metal found in the earth **2** *a nugget of advice* = a very useful and valuable piece of advice (figurative, humorous)

nui•sance /ˈnjuːsəns/ noun, c. (no plural) *The heavy traffic on this road is a real nuisance.* = someone or something that causes annoyance (a feeling of anger) or trouble

null /nʌl/ adj. *null value* = zero; nil **null and void** adj *The agreement between us is null and void now.* = having no legal value

numb[1] /nʌm/ adj. *It was so cold that my hands became numb.* = without the ability to feel anything (especially pain)

numb[2] verb, t. *The doctor will give you an injection of morphine to numb the pain.* = to take away the ability to feel pain **numbness** noun, u.

num•ber[1] /ˈnʌmbə^r/ noun, c. **1** *Five is a number.* = a written symbol (sign) representing a unit which forms part of the system of counting and calculating **2** *He lives at Number 13, Race Course Road.* = a number which shows the position of something in a list **3** *a number of houses* = quantity or amount **4** *'Cow' is singular in number, but 'cows' is plural.* = a change in the form of a noun or pronoun which tells us whether the word refers to one person or thing (singular) or more than one (plural) [GRAMMAR] **5** *Do you have her number?* = telephone number **6** *We sold all the back numbers of the magazine.* = (of magazines and journals), copies published earlier

number[2] verb, t. **1** *Have you numbered the pages of the book?* = to give a number to **2** *He is ill and his days are numbered.* = limited in number (not many are left) (informal) **even number** = 2 and multiples of the number 2 **odd number** = 1, 3, 5, 7, 11 etc. **number-crunching** = the use of a calculating machine or computer to do a large number of difficult calculations **number plate** = a metal plate at the front or back of a vehicle which shows its registration number (the official number given to a vehicle by the government)

to have a head for numbers = to be good at making calculations, estimates and at finance **any number of** *There are any number of reasons why she's angry.* = a way of saying there are many reasons for something (informal) **Your number is up** **1** *You haven't done your work? Your number is up!* = a way of saying that someone will suffer the reasons for doing or not doing something **2** = a way of saying that someone will die (informal, not respectful)

nu•me•ral /'nju:mərəl/ noun, c. *Seven is a numeral* = a symbol (sign) that represents a number **numeracy** noun, u. = the ability to understand and work with numbers **numerate** adj. *He is a numerate person.* = able to work with numbers (to add, subtract etc.) **numerator** noun, c. *In the fraction ¾, the numerator is three.* = the number which is above the line in a fraction (compare **denominator**) **numerical** /nju:'merɪkəl/ adj. *a numerical problem* = having to do with numbers **numerous** adj. *He has numerous problems.* = many

nu•mis•mat•ics /nju:mɪz'mætɪks/ noun = the study of coins (specially old coins which have historical value)

nun /nʌn/ noun, c. = a woman who has joined a religious group and spends her life in prayer or the service of her religion (see also **monk**) **nunnery** noun = a house in which nuns live together

nup•tial /'nʌpʃəl/ adj. = connected with the ceremony of marriage **nuptials** noun (always plural) *The nuptials are over and the wedding feast can begin now.* = wedding ceremony (old-fashioned)

nurse[1] /nɜ:s/ noun, c. **1** *a nurse in a hospital* = a person who is trained to take care of sick or old people **2** *a child's nurse* = a woman who looks after a very young child (see also **nanny**)

nurse[2] verb, t. **1** *He likes to nurse sick people.* = to take care of **2** *The mother was nursing her baby.* = to feed with milk from the breast **3** *The baby was nursing at the mother's breast.* = to suck milk from the breast **nursing** noun, u. = the profession or job of being a nurse **nursing home** noun, c. = a private hospital where people who have health problems can be looked after

nur•se•ry /'nɜ:səri/ noun, c. (**nurseries**) **1** = a room in a house where a child sleeps or plays **2** = a place where small children are taken care of while their parents are working (also **nursery school**) **3** = a place where plants are grown and sold **nursery rhyme** noun, c. = a short, well-known song or poem for children

nur•ture[1] /'nɜ:tʃər/ verb, t. *My parents nurtured me with great love.* = to take care of and protect someone or something and help him/her/it to grow (literary)

nurture[2] noun, u. *A child will become weak without proper nurture.* = care and protection while growing

nut /nʌt/ noun, c. **1** *a cashew nut* = the dry seed of a plant, which is protected by a hard shell (cover) **2** *nuts and bolts* = a small piece of metal with a hole in it, through which a bolt (a long piece of metal, which is used as a screw) can be pushed, in order to fix or tighten something (see pic under **tools**) **3** *He is a real nut.* = a slightly mad person (informal, humorous or approving) **nuts** adj. *You've spent so much money on the house. You must be nuts.* = slightly mad (also **nut-case**) (humorous or not respectful, slang) **nutcracker** noun, c. = a tool used for cracking open the hard shell of a nut **nutmeg** noun, u. = a kind of nut with a sweet smell which is powdered and used as a spice **nutshell** noun, u. **1** = the hard outer covering of a nut **2** *Let me have the facts of the case in a nutshell.* = in brief (in a few words)

nu•tri•tion /nju:'trɪʃən/ noun, u. *These plants don't look very healthy. They need more nutrition.* = food which is necessary to stay healthy **nutrient** noun, c. *This soil is very fertile because it is rich in nutrients.* = a substance which a plant, animal or human being can use as food, to stay healthy [TECHNICAL]

nuz•zle /'nʌzəl/ verb, t. *The horse nuzzled its young one lovingly.* = to touch or rub gently with the nose (used to describe the behaviour of an animal)

ny•lon /'naɪlɒn/ noun, u. = an artificial (human-made) fibre from which clothing, ropes etc. can be made

nymph /nɪmf/ noun, c. = a goddess or female spirit, mentioned in stories from ancient Greece and Rome, that is supposed to live in a natural thing such as a tree, river, lake etc. [LITERATURE]

N

oO

o, O /əʊ/ the fifteenth letter of the English alphabet
O interjec. *O King!* = a form of address (literary)
o' prep. *Jack o' London* = of (literary)
oak /əʊk/ noun, c. or u. **1** (c.) = a large tree that grows in cold countries **2** (u.) = the wood of the oak tree
oar /ɔːʳ/ noun, c. = a long pole with a wide, flat blade at one end, which is held in position at some point on the side of a boat and used to row the boat
o•a•sis /əʊˈeɪsɪs/ noun, c. (**oases**) = a place in a desert where there is water which helps trees to grow
oath /əʊθ/ noun, c. or u. *He has sworn an oath to tell the truth.*(c.) = a promise
oats /ˈəʊts/ noun = a kind of cereal or foodgrain
o•bei•sance /əʊˈbeɪsəns/ noun, u. or c. *He made an obeisance to the king by bowing three times.*(c.) = respect shown to an important person by bending the upper part of the body (formal, old-fashioned)
o•bese /əʊˈbiːs/ adj. *an obese person* = fat in an unhealthy way [MEDICINE] **obesity** noun, u. = the state of being obese
o•bey /əʊˈbeɪ/ verb, t. *Children should obey their parents.* = to do what one is told to do **obedient** adj. *an obedient child* = a person who is willing to obey (opposite **disobedient**)
o•bit•u•a•ry /əˈbɪtʃuəri/ noun, c. (**obituaries**) *I came to know of the famous dancer's death when I read the obituary in today's paper.* = a report printed in a newspaper informing people that someone has died, together with an account of the dead person's life
ob•ject¹ /ˈɒbdʒɪkt/ noun, c. **1** *He held a small wooden object in his hand.* = a thing that can be seen or felt **2** *The object of my visit is to inform you that you have been selected for the job.* = purpose; aim **3** *In the sentence 'Prema saw a tiger', the noun 'tiger' is the object of the verb 'saw'.* = a noun or pronoun that usually follows a verb in a sentence and represents the thing or person to whom something (some action) is done [GRAMMAR] **4** *Our teacher was the object of our admiration.* = a person who is given love, respect etc.
object² /əbˈdʒekt/ verb, i. *I object to your keeping birds in cages.* = to speak against something that you do not like or do not agree with **objection** noun, c. *There were objections from several students when the dates for the examination were changed without notice.* = a statement showing disagreement with something or unhappiness over something **objectionable** adj. *objectionable behaviour* = thought to be improper (wrong)
ob•jec•tive¹ /əbˈdʒektɪv/ noun, c. *My objective is to complete the project in two weeks.* = aim (something that one wants to do)
objective² adj. *A judge must be objective while making a judgement.* = not guided by personal feeling; fair and considering only the facts available (opposite **subjective**)
o•blige /əˈblaɪdʒ/ verb, t. or i. **1** *I was obliged to move out of the house as the owner wanted to move in.*(t.) = to make it necessary for someone to do something; to compel **2** *If you need help with the heavy boxes, I would be happy to oblige.*(i.) = to do someone a favour; to help someone **obliging** adj. *an obliging person* = willing to help **obligation** /ɒblɪˈgeɪʃən/ noun, c. or u. **1** *It is the obligation of every citizen to vote in the election.*(u.) = a duty that one must perform **2** *I am under an obligation to him as he helped me find a job.* = a situation in which one feels bound to help someone because of some help received in the past **obligatory** /əˈblɪgətəri/ adj. *It is obligatory for you to vote.* = which must be done (opposite **optional**)
o•blique /əˈbliːk/ adj. **1** *an oblique line* = sloping (not straight) **2** *He made an oblique remark hinting that I had hurt him.* = indirect
o•blit•er•ate /əˈblɪtəreɪt/ verb, t. *A powerful king ruled this city hundreds of years ago but all traces of his kingdom have been obliterated.* = to wipe out or remove completely (formal)
o•bliv•i•on /əˈblɪvɪən/ noun, u. **1** *Nothing remains of that powerful kingdom. It has gone into oblivion.* = the state of being completely forgotten (formal, literary) **2** = the state of being unaware of anything around you **oblivious** adj. *The tiger was creeping through the tall grass towards the deer, but the deer was oblivious of the danger.* = not aware of something (not in a position to know)
ob•long /ˈɒblɒŋ/ adj. = a figure with four straight lines (at 90º to each other), but longer than it is broad (see also **rectangle**)
ob•nox•ious /əbˈnɒkʃəs/ adj. *They have an obnoxious habit of reading letters meant for other people.* = very unpleasant (disapproving)
ob•scene /əbˈsiːn/ adj. *an obscene picture* = dirty or indecent, especially in matters related to sex **obscenity** noun, u. or c. (**obscenities**) **1** (u.) = the fact of being obscene (indecent) **2** *His language is full of obscenities.*(c.) = an obscene (bad) word or action
ob•scure¹ /əbˈskjʊəʳ/ verb, t. *The article in the*

newspaper praises the new leader but obscures the fact that he was once in jail for cheating. = to hide or cover up something

obscure[2] adj. **1** *His ideas on education are so obscure that no one knows exactly what he is trying to say.* = not clear; difficult to understand **2** *This article was printed in some obscure newspaper which no one has heard about.* = not well known

ob•serve /əb'zɜːv/ verb, t. **1** *I observe that there are more scooters than cycles on the road.* = to notice something **2** *'I am happy to see so many students here', the teacher observed.* = to speak or to make a remark **3** *Have you observed the behaviour of this animal in different living conditions?* = to make a scientific study of something [SCIENCE] **4** *The doctors have decided to observe the patient for a week.* = to keep a patient under watch, before or during medical treatment [MEDICINE] **5** *Holi will be observed on the 18th of March.* = to celebrate a festival (formal) **6** *Let us observe silence for two minutes.* = to practise some action for a limited period of time (formal) **observation** /ɒbzə'veɪʃən/ noun, u. or c. **1** *If you use your powers of observation, you will notice that most people here are below the age of 20.*(u.) = the ability to notice something **2** *Your observations on the teaching in this school were well received.*(c.) = remarks or comments, specially those made during a speech **3** *Newton discovered the law of gravitation through observation of natural phenomena.*(u.) = the process of studying events in a scientific manner [SCIENCE] **4** *The doctors will keep the patient under observation for a week.* = the process of keeping watch over a patient before or during medical treatment [MEDICINE] **observer** /əb'zɜːvər/ noun, c. **1** *a keen observer of human nature* = a person who can notice things easily **2** *The United Nations is sending observers to the two countries.* = a person who is sent by an organization to some place to keep watch over a situation [TECHNICAL] **observant** adj. *If you had been more observant, you would have noticed that Naseer looked rather pale.* = able to observe (notice) things quickly

observatory /əb'zɜːvətəri/ noun, c. (**observatories**) = a building from which scientists can watch the stars etc. with the help of telescopes and other scientific instruments

ob•sess /əb'ses/ verb, t. *You should not let the idea of becoming a film star obsess you. You need to complete your studies.* = to completely fill someone's mind, so that he/she is unable to think of anything else **obsession** noun, u. or c. *The Internet has become an obsession with him. He spends at least six hours every day on the computer.*(c.) // *Her obsession with clothes is worrying.*(u.) = something that fills one's mind completely and takes up most of his/her time (disapproving) **obsessive** adj. *an obsessive interest in films* = being an obsession (derogatory)

ob•so•lete /'ɒbsəliːt/ adj. *The Long Playing record (LP) has become obsolete. The new recording systems are much more modern.* = out of date and not suitable for use at the present time or on modern equipment (also **out-of-date**)

ob•sta•cle /'ɒbstəkəl/ noun, c. *Not knowing how to swim is an obstacle to becoming a captain on a ship.* = something that prevents progress or movement

ob•stet•rics /əb'stetrɪks/ noun = the branch of medicine that deals with the process of childbirth [MEDICINE] **obstetrician** /əbste'trɪʃən/ noun, c. = a doctor who helps a woman deliver (give birth to) a child

ob•sti•nate /'ɒbstɪnət/ adj. *The boy is so obstinate that he won't listen to anyone.* = not willing to change one's mind or follow anyone's advice (also **stubborn**) (disapproving)

ob•struct /əb'strʌkt/ verb, t. *The man stood in the middle of the road, obstructing the flow of traffic.* = to block or prevent someone or something from moving **obstruction** noun, c. or u. *The traffic on the road could not move because there were many obstructions.*(c.) = something that obstructs (blocks); obstacle

ob•tain /əb'teɪn/ verb, t. *You cannot obtain the medicine that you want without a prescription.*(t.) = to get (formal)

ob•tru•sive /əb'truːsɪv/ adj. *The room was beautifully decorated, except for the bright yellow curtains. They were far too obtrusive.* = too easily noticed, in a way that is not liked (opposite **unobtrusive**) (disapproving)

ob•tuse /əb'tjuːs/ adj. **1** *The boy is so obtuse that it is difficult to make him understand anything.* = slow to understand (formal) **2** *an obtuse angle* = measuring more than 90º but less than 180º [GEOMETRY] (see pic under **angle**)

ob•vi•ous /'ɒbvɪəs/ adj. *You were unable to answer a single question. It was obvious that you hadn't prepared for this test.* = easy to see or understand **obviously** adv. *He obviously knows this city very well —he can find his way around easily.* = clearly (can be easily seen)

oc•ca•sion[1] /ə'keɪʒən/ noun, c. or u. **1** *The minister visited our village last month but on that occasion he stayed only for a few minutes.*(c.) = a time when something happens **2** *There is an important meeting*

O

going on. This is not the occasion to raise your demands.(u.) = a suitable time for doing something **3** *The farewell party was a memorable occasion.*(c.) = a special gathering, event etc. **occasional** adj. *We get only occasional rain in this part of the country.* = happening only sometimes; not regular **occasionally** adv. *We visit Colombo occasionally.* = not very frequently, only sometimes

oc•cult[1] /ˈɒkʌlt/ adj. *It is said that some people have occult powers which make it possible for them to perform magical deeds.* = mysterious and magical

occult[2] noun, u. *They are very interested in the occult.* = supernatural forces, usually considered evil

oc•cu•py /ˈɒkjʊpaɪ/ verb, t. (**occupied**) **1** *Our new house is almost ready. We will occupy it next month.* = to move into and take possession of a place **2** *The Japanese army occupied Singapore in 1942.* = to take possession of a place by using military force **3** *Cricket occupies all my spare time.* = to fill up a space or period of time **4** *He can't talk to you now. He is occupied.* = busy (formal) **occupant** noun, c. *The occupants of the house are away on a vacation.* = a person who occupies (lives in) a house **occupation** /ɒkjʊˈpeɪʃən/ noun, u. or c. **1** *Her occupation is that of a motor mechanic.* = profession or trade (what one does to earn a living) **2** *Singapore was under Japanese occupation from 1942–1945.* = the act of occupying (taking possession of) a place **3** *Swimming is a healthy occupation.* = something done to spend time **occupational** adj. *Soldiers often get injured when they are fighting a war. This is an occupational risk.* = connected with an occupation (profession) **occupational therapy** noun = the treatment of illness by giving the patient some work to do [MEDICINE]

oc•cur /əˈkɜːʳ/ verb, i. (**occurred**) **1** *Many people were injured in the train accident which occurred last night.* = to happen or take place (formal) **2** *Uranium occurs in some parts of Kerala. // The word 'living' occurs three times in this paragraph.* = to be found **3** *It never occured to me that I could enter through the back door.* = to come to one's mind **occurrence** noun, u. or c. **1** *We must do everything possible to prevent the occurrence of such accidents.*(u.) = the process of happening (formal) **2** *The accident was not unusual. Such accidents are common occurrences.*(c.) = something that happens

o•cean /ˈəʊʃən/ noun, c. **1** = a mass of salt water that covers large parts of the earth's surface **2** (always capital) *the Pacific Ocean* = one of the five oceans into which the water on the earth's surface is divided **ocean-going** adj *an ocean-going ship* = a ship large enough to sail on the sea **oceanic** /əʊʃɪˈænɪk/ adj. = having to do with oceans **oceanography** /əʊʃəˈnɒgrəfi/ noun = the scientific study of the ocean

o•chre[1] **(ocher)** /ˈəʊkəʳ/ noun = a reddish-yellow colour

ochre[2] adj. = of an ochre colour

o'clock /əˈklɒk/ adv. *It is seven o'clock now.* = an expression used to tell the time, used only with the numbers from one to twelve

oc•ta•gon /ˈɒktəgən/ noun, c. = a geometrical figure (shape) which has eight sides [GEOMETRY]

oc•tane /ˈɒkteɪn/ noun *My car uses 95-octane petrol.* = a measure of the quality of petrol and the amount of power it can produce [TECHNICAL]

oc•tave /ˈɒktɪv/ noun, c. *This singer's voice has a range of three octaves.* = a scale (comprising eight musical notes) in music which measures how low or high a singer's voice can go [TECHNICAL]

Oc•to•ber /ɒkˈtəʊbə/ noun = the tenth month of the year, between September and November

oc•to•ge•nar•i•an /ɒktəʊdʒɪˈneəriən/ noun, c. = a person in his/her eighties (between 80 and 89 years of age)

oc•to•pus /ˈɒktəpəs/ noun = an animal that lives in the deep waters of the sea and has eight tentacles (arms) with which it catches its prey (animals hunted for food)

odd /ɒd/ adj. **1** *When he saw me he hid behind a sofa. I found his behaviour very odd.* = strange or peculiar; different from what is usual **2** *She does odd jobs in her spare time.* = not regular and not continuing all day **3** *You're wearing odd slippers.* = not one of a pair **4** *'Do you like James Bond?' 'No, but I watch the odd Bond film.'* = occasional (now and then) (informal) **odd number** noun, c. *1, 3 and 5 are odd numbers.* = a number that cannot be divided by 2 **odds** noun, c. (always plural) **1** *The Sri Lankan team is playing so well that the odds are it will beat the South Africans.* = the probability that something will happen **2** *The two senior managers were at odds for some time but now they seem to agree on most things.* = in disagreement with one another (informal) **odd-jobs person** noun = a person who has no permanent job but is paid to do various small jobs for different people **odd man out** noun *Which of the following words is the odd man out : (1) chair (2) table (3) actor (4) door?* = a person or thing that is different from the others in a group **odds and ends** noun *I have to pick up the odds and ends which are still lying around the house.* = small things that do not have much value **odds-on favourite** *The Pakistan team, which has won this tournament three times in the last four years, is the odds-on favourite.* = expected by most people to win **against**

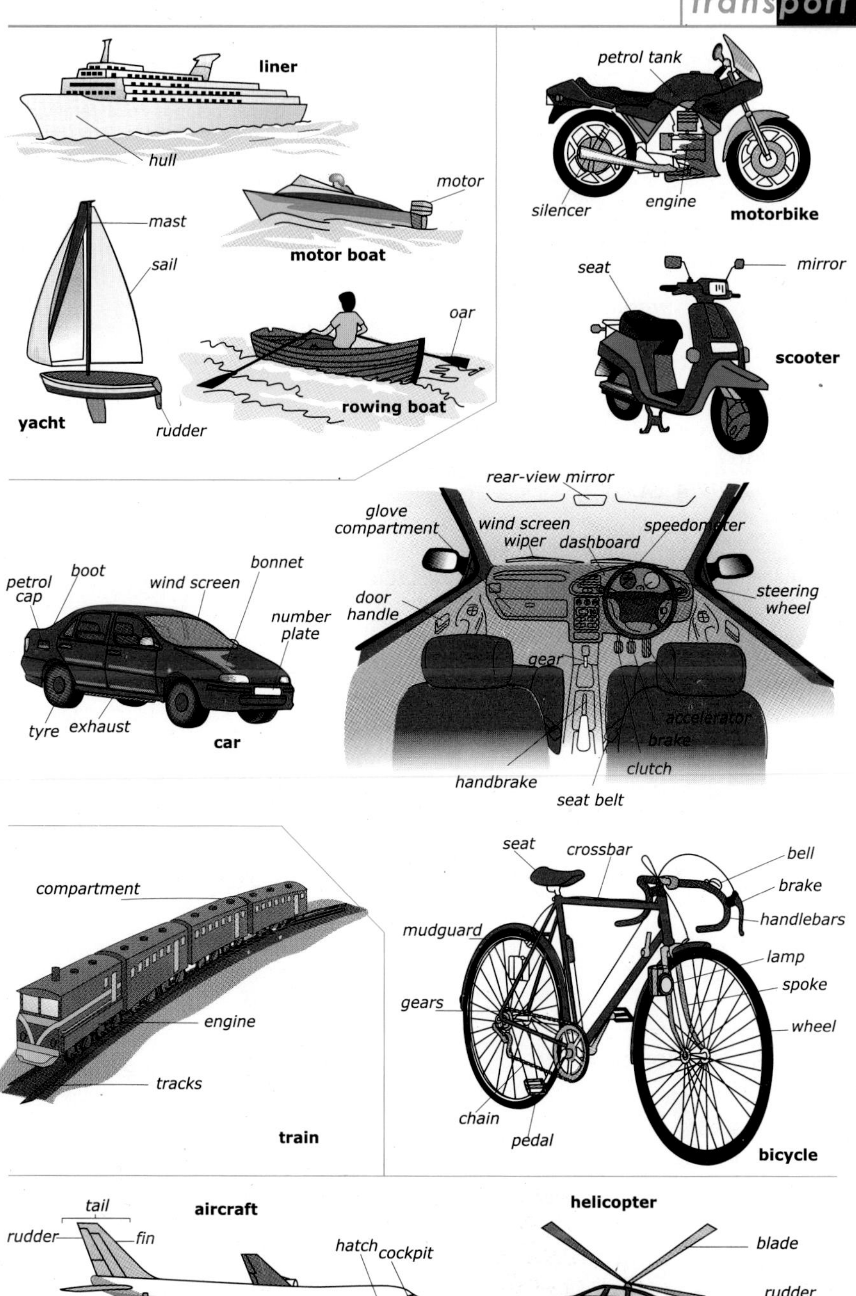
liner
hull
motor
motor boat
mast
sail
yacht
rudder
oar
rowing boat
petrol tank
silencer
engine
motorbike
seat
mirror
scooter
rear-view mirror
glove compartment
wind screen wiper
dashboard
speedometer
door handle
steering wheel
gear
accelerator
brake
clutch
handbrake
seat belt
petrol cap
boot
wind screen
bonnet
number plate
tyre
exhaust
car
compartment
engine
tracks
train
seat
crossbar
bell
brake
handlebars
mudguard
lamp
spoke
gears
wheel
chain
pedal
bicycle
tail
aircraft
rudder
fin
hatch
cockpit
wing
nose
jet engine
helicopter
blade
rudder

The **taxonomic organization** of species is **hierarchical.** Each species belongs to a genus, each genus belongs to a family, and so on through order, class, phylum, and kingdom. Modern **taxonomy** recognizes five kingdoms into which the estimated five million species of the world are divided.

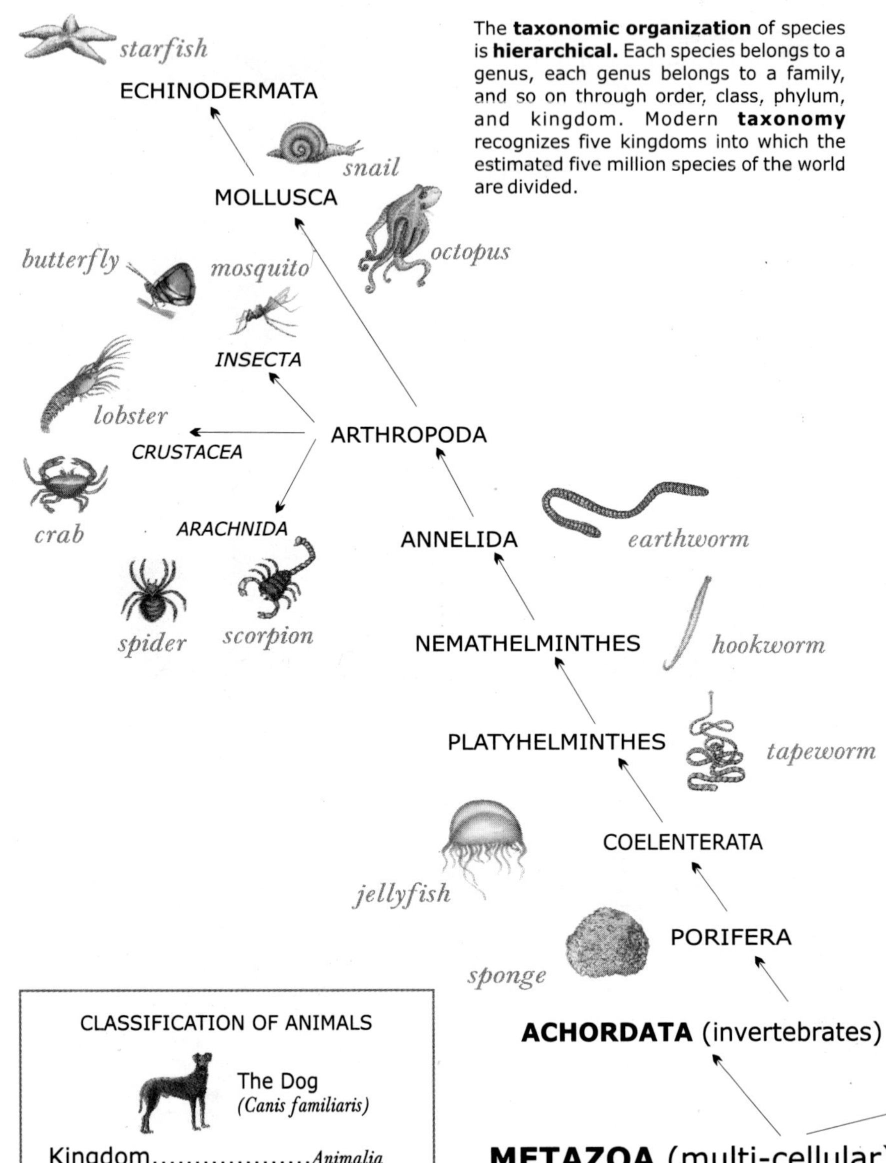

CLASSIFICATION OF ANIMALS

The Dog
(Canis familiaris)

Kingdom.................. *Animalia*
Phylum.................... *Chordata*
Class...................... *Mammalia*
Order...................... *Carnivora*
Family..................... *Canidae*
Genus...................... *Canis*
Species.................... *familiaris*

THE ANIMAL

Carolus Linnaeus, an eighteenth century Swedish botanist, devised the system of **binomial nomenclature** used for naming species. In this system, each species is given a two-part Latin name.

By convention, the genus name is capitalized, and both the genus and species name are italicized. e.g. *Canis familiaris* or simply *C. familiaris*.

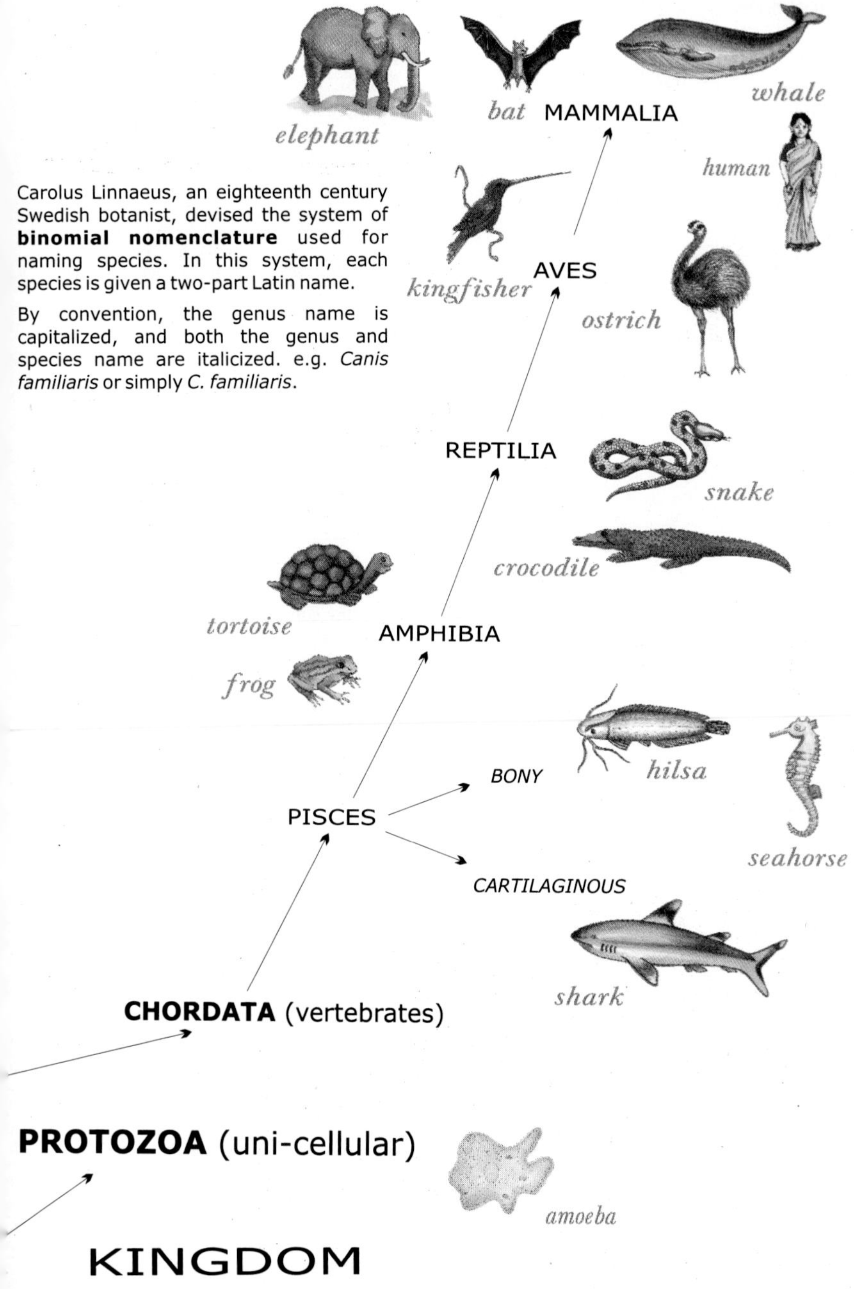

PROTOZOA (uni-cellular)

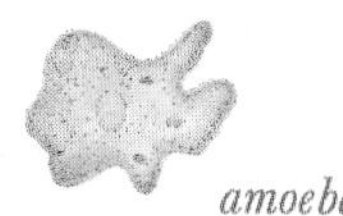
amoeba

KINGDOM

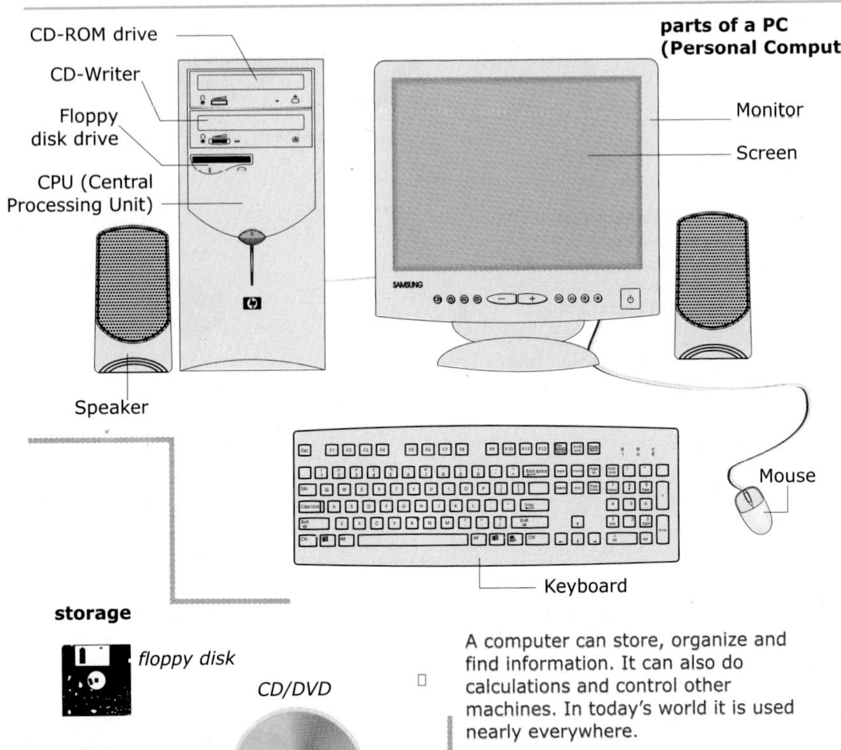

storage

floppy disk

CD/DVD

zip disk

A computer can store, organize and find information. It can also do calculations and control other machines. In today's world it is used nearly everywhere.

The part that makes the entire system of the computer work is called the **processor.**

Each computer stores programs, games, documents etc. on its **hard disk.** If information is to be carried from one computer to another it can be stored on a **floppy disk,** a **zip disk** or a **CD** (Compact Disc).

When a computer is open the **RAM** (Random Access Memory) allows the user to access information, give commands and complete an operation within the computer. The RAM is the main memory of the computer.

A computer can be used to view many media. The **CD-ROM drive, speakers, sound card** and **DVD-drive** allow a user to listen to music, watch movies etc. on the computer.

A **printer** is required to print documents, pictures etc. onto a document. A **scanner** is used to scan pictures or documents into a computer.

For a computer to be **interactive** it must have an **OS** (Operating System). Once an OS is loaded onto a system then **software packages** can be **installed** too. The software programs (a series of commands) have many applications that can be used in **word processing, designing, spreadsheet work, data entry** etc.

The Internet

This is a large **network** of computers that allows many people all over the world to communicate with each other, find information and present information to as many viewers who can **access** the network.

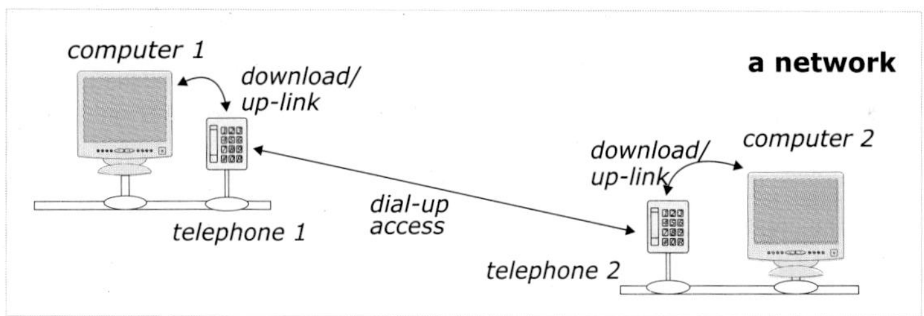

The **World Wide Web** lets you **download** information onto your home computer and store it through a **browser.** *You can also send* **e-mail** *through this network.*

A **modem** allows you to get onto this network. A browser accesses **homepages, websites, search engines** etc. that have information that you may want to download, receive, send or just read.

Once a browser window is open you will have to type in a **URL/address** of a particular web site to go to it. A URL on the world wide web is of the form– **http://www orientlongman.com.**

home page

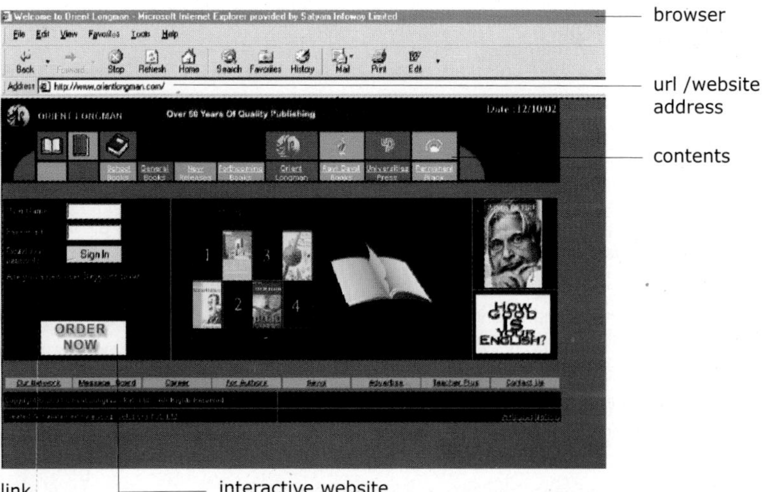

FIRST AID FUNDAMENTALS

First aid is not a replacement for medical attention. It is an **informed awareness** of what an **untrained** person should do (and should not do) until the patient is in the hands of a doctor. These simple measures aim to keep the patient in the best possible condition until professional medical help is received.

The most important rules

#1 Keep calm. Take charge of the situation. Clear away crowds, if they surround the patient. Take help from able people who remain to assist.

#2 Listen to the history of the situation. Pay special attention to the **symptoms.** Examine the patient for signs. This will help you **diagnose** the problem with greater accuracy.

#3 If the injuries are serious, send someone to telephone for medical help. Give an accurate report of the problem.

#4 Provide the correct first aid treatment.

#5 Await professional medical help after this. If the patient is able to travel and needs further medical attention, send him/her to a doctor or hospital.

YOUR FIRST AID KIT SHOULD HAVE

- A roll of cotton
- Various bandages: rolls of **gauze,** strips of cloth to make slings, sticker bandages, adhesive tape
- A box of **sterile** dressings individually wrapped, to cover open **wounds**
- A pair of scissors
- A pair of tweezers
- Safety pins
- A sharp knife
- A flashlight with spare batteries
- Thermometer
- Eye-dropper
- Pack for ice
- Petroleum jelly
- Burn ointments
- Pain relievers
- **Antiseptic** preparations (**salves** like Dettol, iodine, mercurochrome, alcohol)
- Tablets for indigestion, **allergic reactions**, headaches, and other illnesses that the owner is prone to
- Glucose powder
- Medicated soap
- Clean towel
- First Aid Manual

++ Drugs do not last indefinitely. They may lose their potency, or their components may recombine harmfully. All prescription drugs have an expiry date. Discard drugs immediately after this date.

++ Keep your First Aid Kit unlocked, to prevent searching for the keys when it is needed.

SOME FIRST AID TIPS

CHOKING

Choking means that something – food or a foreign body – is plugging the windpipe, so that the patient cannot breathe. If the airway is completely blocked, the victim may die in less than five minutes. Acting fast is crucial. The **Heimlich Manouevre** is the most effective first aid measure for choking. This is what you have to do.

1. Make a fist with one hand and place the thumb-side against the victim's abdomen, above the navel and below the ribcage.

2. Grasp your fist with the other hand and press it forcefully into the abdomen with a quick upward thrust. Repeat this several times until the stuck object is ejected.

Remember: Do not squeeze the person with your arms. This could damage the ribs. To avoid squeezing, keep your arms bent at the elbow.

DROWNING

If the patient is not breathing, begin **artificial respiration** at once. Do this in rapid succession:

1. **Place the patient on his or her back. Do not do this if you suspect a broken neck.**
2. Place the palm of one hand on the forehead of the patient and tilt the head back. Place the fingers of the other hand under the chin and lift to bring it forward. This position prevents the airway from becoming obstructed by the tongue.

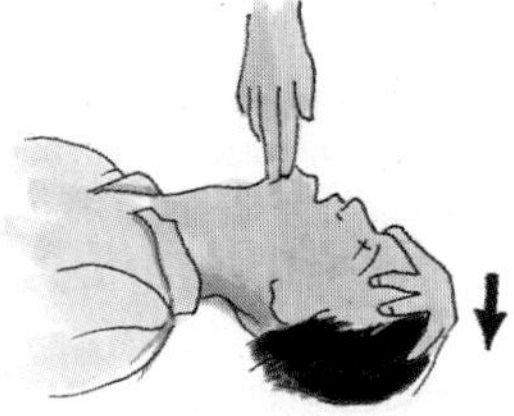

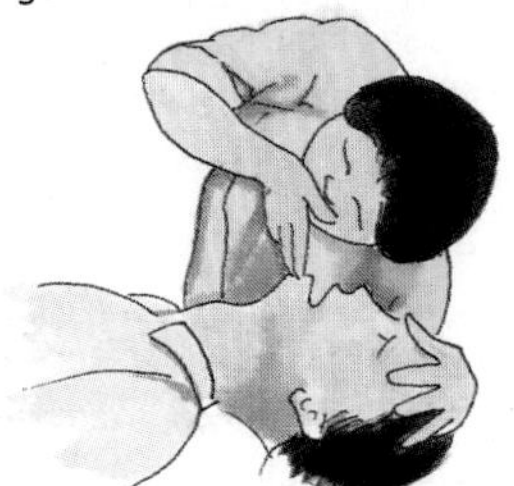

3. Watch the patient's chest for signs of breathing. Place your cheek near the patient's mouth and nose to feel any exhaled air. If there is none, move to step 4.
4. Use the thumb and index finger of the hand that is on the patient's forehead to pinch the patient's nostrils closed. Remember to continue to maintain the proper tilt of the head.
5. Place your mouth over the victim's and give two full breaths. Take a deep gulp of air between the two. Each ventilation should cause the patient's chest to rise and fall. If this fails to happen, try adjusting the patient's head. If this too fails, perhaps the victim's airway is obstructed (see CHOKING).

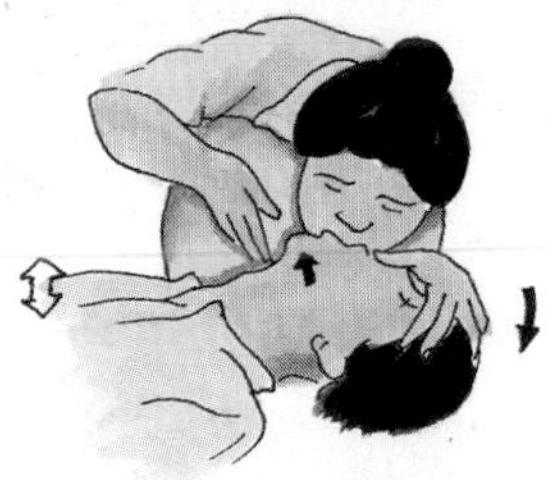

6. If you can revive the patient's breathing, feel the carotid pulse for signs of a pulse rate. If there is no pulse, take the patient to a qualified practitioner to administer Cardio-pulmonary Resuscitation (CPR). If there is a pulse but no breathing, begin steady mouth-to-mouth breathing.

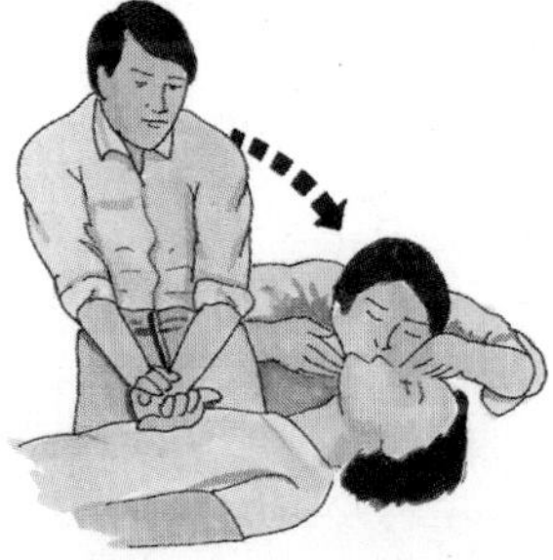

7. For this, place your mouth over the patient's and breathe hard. Remove your mouth to let the patient exhale while you take another deep breath. Repeat this procedure every five seconds, until the patient starts to breathe on his/her own.
8. Send for an ambulance meanwhile and keep the patient lying down even after revival. Use a blanket, sheet or jacket to keep the patient warm.

Our language, in the ways in which we choose to use it, reveals our attitudes to people, animals, situations and things. Among these attitudes are prejudice, bias and decisions to discriminate against someone or something. Just as language has the power to raise and enrich our thinking, it has the unhappy capacity to offend, create biases and stereotypes. Language is never completely free of bias, but if we want to aim to be fair in a society that is diverse and multicultural, our choice of words becomes important.

We commonly discriminate against others on the grounds of sex, religion, race, marital status, sexual preferences, disability (both mental and physical) and the kind of work they do. We also deal with structures and levels in society. In the books we read and the things we say, there is a growing tendency for humans to consider themselves the centre of the universe and therefore many of us habitually see the world through adult human eyes. Terms which express sexism, hatred, contempt and 'differentness' are common in both formal and informal language. **WordMaster** frequently highlights discriminatory usage and guides users about alternatives.

These pages look at some standard words and phrases which have gained acceptance or are welcomed. They look at language which is *inclusive* and which aims to cut across, for example, race, sex and disability. Except where such distinctions are in some way necessary to our meaning, it is important to avoid using them.

'man' words

Male-centred words have been standard usage for years. In such examples, we need language that represents both men and women, or in which gender is absent unless its use is significant to the meaning.

Avoid	**Use**
man as in	
1 ***Man** has seen many wars.*	humans, the human race, human beings
2 *Let's find the **man** who can do this job.*	person
mankind	humankind, people, men and women
one-man show	one-person show, solo performance
the man in the street	the average person, ordinary people
businessman	businessperson
craftsman	craftsperson
chairman	chairperson
fisherman	fisher
handyman	repairer
layman	layperson
milkman	milk supplier
postman	postal worker
salesman	salesperson, sales worker, sales attendant
man-made	artificial, synthetic, fabricated
manpower	workforce, staff, human resources
man hours	work hours, project hours
manning (the shop)	managing, looking after

using bias-free and inclusive language

jobs and positions

The terms on the right offer alternatives which are generally non-discriminatory and which in some cases are dignity-giving. Unless essential to the context, gender labels are either unimportant or discriminatory.

Avoid	**Use**
housewife	homeworker
air hostess	flight attendant
salesgirl	salesperson, sales attendant
actress, authoress, manageress	actor, author, manager
lady doctor	doctor, woman doctor
cleaning woman	cleaner, help, office/house cleaner
career girl	professional

terms of address

Mr, Ms (*instead of* Mrs or Miss)

Dr Mehta (*not* Dr Mrs Mehta)

Professor D'souza (*not* Professor Mrs D'souza)

disability

People with disabilities are often viewed *through* these disabilities, and sometimes only as having a disability. We need language which is inclusive and which does not direct attention to the disability where this is not necessary. Terms such as 'retard', 'cretin', 'nutcase', 'psycho' and 'cripple' are insulting and derogatory.

Labels with *the* (such as 'the disabled', 'the handicapped', 'the deaf', 'the blind') tend to view people as if they were part of a single mass with no other identity. Terms such as *disabled persons*, *persons with a disability*, *physically disabled people*, *blind people* or *people with visual impairment* are considered more objective and respectful. A 'mentally retarded person' is a *person with an intellectual disability*, 'a paraplegic' is similarly *a paraplegic person*, 'epileptics' are *persons with epilepsy* etc.

non-human-centred ways of 'seeing' the world

We look at the world through adult human eyes, and often as if there were no other way of viewing it! Land is described in terms of its value to us, because crops can be grown on it, because it is suitable for the construction of buildings or because the weather suits us.

Similarly, animals are described as *dangerous* or *harmless*. They are classified as *domestic* and *wild*. We see them as being 'useful' or 'not useful' to us. When we refer to a *poisonous snake*, we are not talking about venom-carrying, we mean that it has poison which can kill human beings.

We need to find ways to describe things in their own terms and in their own right, not necessarily as connected to us and dependent on our judgement.

cricket

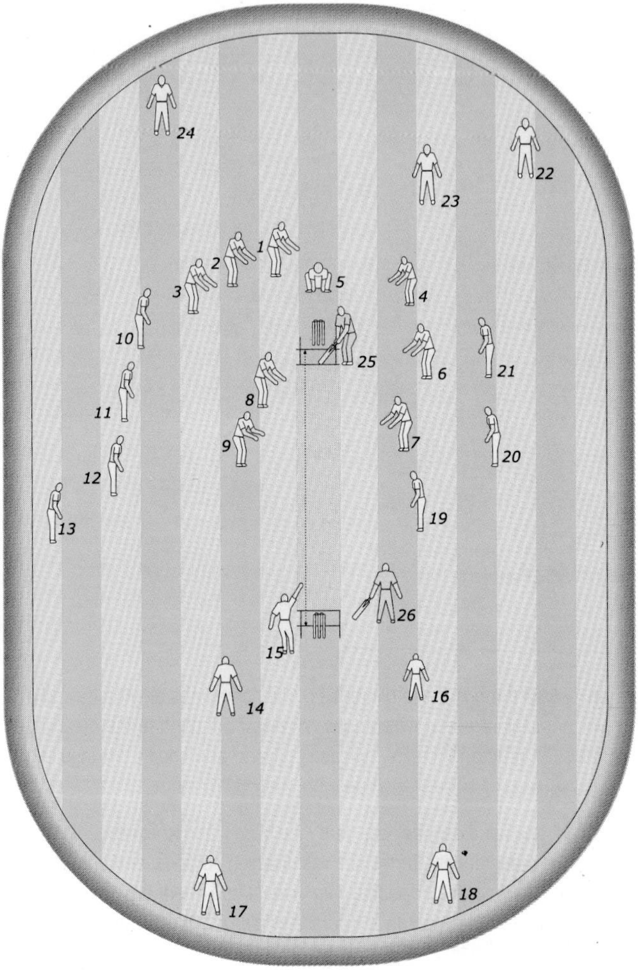

1 1st slip
2 2nd slip
3 3rd slip
4 leg slip
5 wicket keeper
6 short leg
7 forward short leg
8 silly point
9 silly mid-off
10 gully
11 point
12 cover
13 extra cover
14 mid-off
15 bowler
16 mid-on
17 long-off
18 long-on
19 silly mid-on
20 mid-wicket
21 square leg
22 fine leg
23 long leg
24 third man
25 striker
26 non-striker

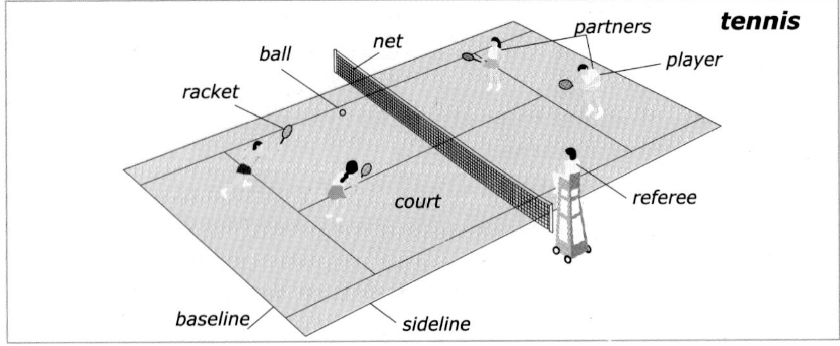

soccer & athletics

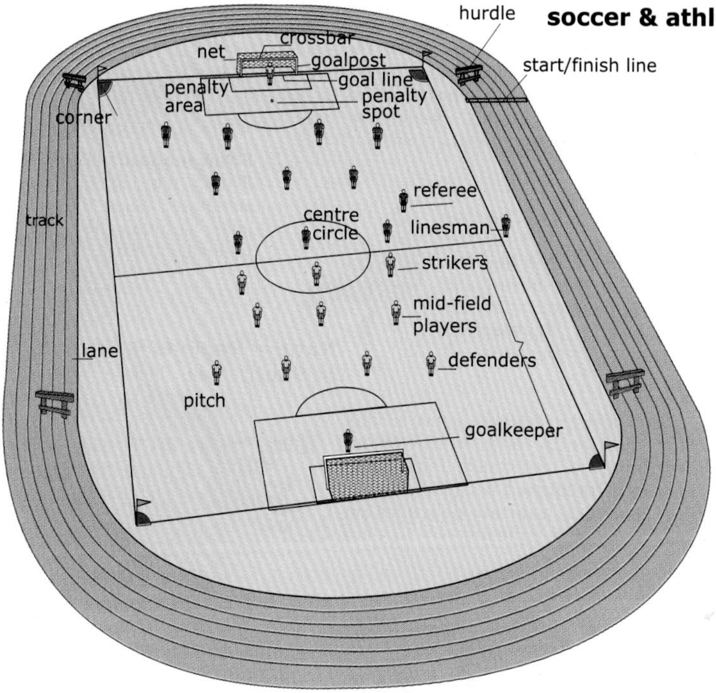

hurdle
net
crossbar
goalpost
goal line
start/finish line
penalty area
penalty spot
corner
referee
track
centre circle
linesman
strikers
mid-field players
lane
defenders
pitch
goalkeeper

swimming

the crawl
breaststroke
backstroke
diving

sports equipment

net/basket
boxing gloves
cricket bat
tennis racket
hockey stick
weights
golf club
trainers (AmE sneakers)
weights
football
tennis ball
shuttlecock
table tennis bat
rugby ball

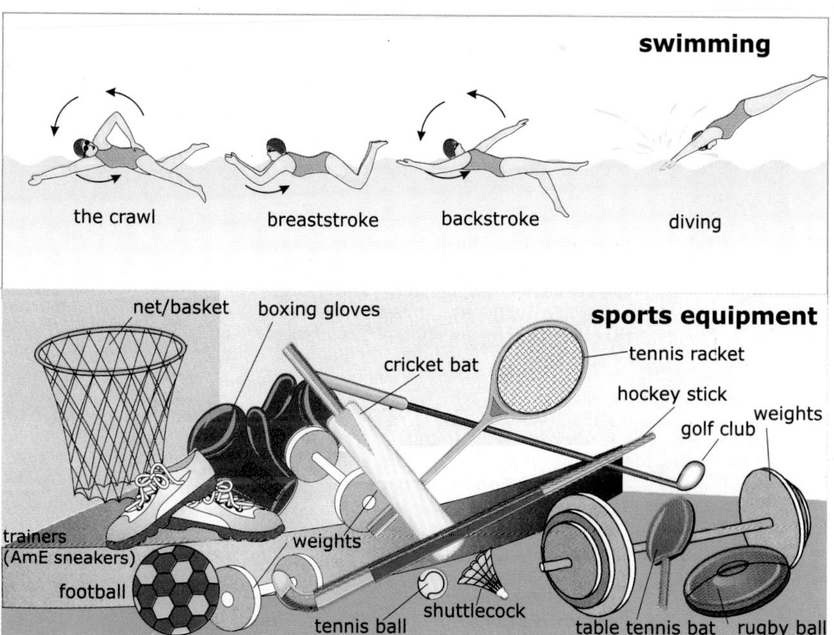

Musk deer *(Moschus moschiferus)* are a tiny species of deer found in the high reaches of the Himalaya, in Kashmir and Nepal. The male of the species is **persecuted** for its musk gland, which is used **commercially** to make perfumes.

Snow leopards *(Panthera uncia)* live in the high ranges of the Himalaya. When they move into lower altitudes, they are **killed** for their valuable **fur**.

The **Great Indian bustard** *(Choriotis nigriceps)* is a low-flying, fast-running bird found in **arid** regions like the Rann of Kutch, the Thar desert and some parts of the Deccan plateau. Hunting and **habitat destruction** threaten the future of this bird.

Natural Regions of South Asia

Sarus cranes *(Grus antigone)* inhabit the **wetlands** and **marshes** of northern and west-central India. Their future is threatened because of over-hunting and **habitat degradation** due to intensive agriculture.

The **Asiatic lion** *(Panthera leo persica)* was once common in western Asia. Excessive **hunting** has confined it to one small **sanctuary** in the forests of Gir, where only a few hundred lions survive.

The reclusive **Lion-tailed macaque** *(Macaca silenus)* lives in the dense **rainforests** of the Western Ghats. Large-scale **felling** of these forests is **threatening** the **survival** of this species.

The **Slender loris** *(Loris tardigradus)* is found in the jungles of southern India and Sri Lanka. **Poachers** capture these animals alive for the **pet trade.** Lorises are also killed for their large eyes, which are locally said to have **medicinal value**, as a cure for eye diseases.

The **Nilgiri tahr** *(Hemitragus hylocrius)* is confined to only two **protected** regions: one in the high altitudes of the Nilgiris and the other in Eravikulam. Only a few thousand animals remain in the wild.

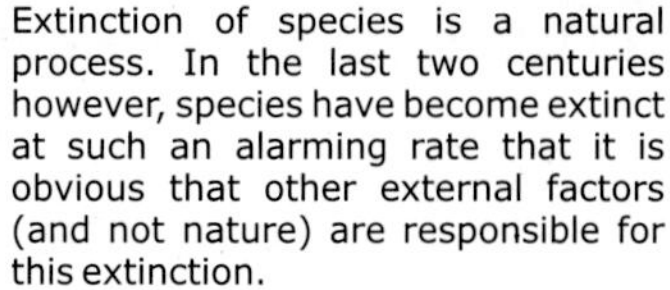

Red pandas *(Ailurus fulgens)* are found in the high **temperate** forests of the Himalaya, from Nepal and Sikkim up to southern China. Little is known about these reclusive creatures.

Tigers *(Panthera tigris)* numbered about 40,000 at the turn of the twentieth century. Rampant hunting and **habitat fragmentation** have now brought their numbers down to two or three thousand. Tigers are now **locally extinct** in many areas.

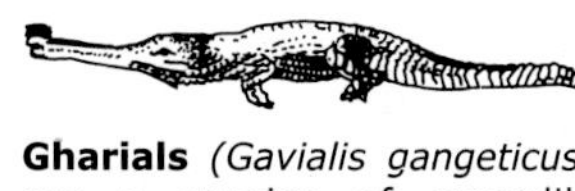

Gharials *(Gavialis gangeticus)* are a species of crocodile **endemic** only to India. **Wild populations** are now confined to only a few rivers in the north.

The **One-horned rhinoceros** *(Rhinoceros unicornis)* is now found only in the floodplains of the Brahmaputra. It faces the threat of almost certain **extinction**. Two reasons can be attributed to its present status: **poaching** for its valuable horn and habitat loss.

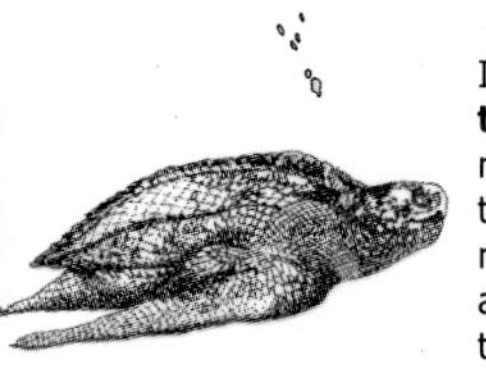

In South Asia, **Leatherback sea turtles** *(Dermochelys coriacea)* nest mainly on the undisturbed beaches of the Andaman and Nicobar Islands. Large numbers are killed every year when they are caught in the nets of **fishing** trawlers. Leatherbacks are expected to go extinct in the next ten years.

The **Great Indian hornbill** *(Buceros bicornis)* inhabits the dense forests of the lower Himalaya and the Western Ghats. Timber-logging in these areas has **depleted** the forest area, resulting in a rapid decline in the species.

Extinction of species is a natural process. In the last two centuries however, species have become extinct at such an alarming rate that it is obvious that other external factors (and not nature) are responsible for this extinction.

When the population of a species drops so low that its survival in the wild is doubtful and extinction seems imminent, it is considered an **endangered species**.

How does a species become endangered?

A species can become extinct if:

1 it is hunted extensively for pleasure, or poached for its meat, skin and other body parts.

2 people encroach upon its natural habitat for agricultural and industrial development. This usually leads to degradation of forest area and 'habitat fragmentation'.

3 new or 'exotic' species of flora and fauna are introduced into its territory. Such experiments often prove harmful to endemic plants and animals.

Every year, about 3000 species all over the world are said to become extinct due to development, agriculture and other human activities.

The formation of protected areas like sanctuaries and national parks has helped sustain the survival of some species.

To learn about the endangered species of the world, look up this website: http://www.redlist.org

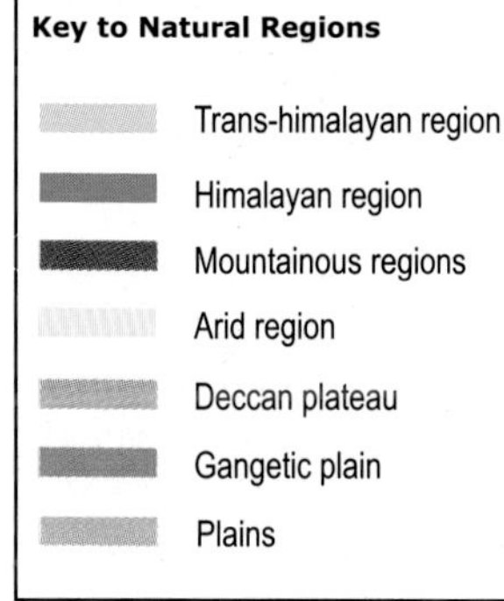

Disclaimer: The map of South Asia is not drawn to scale.

1 What are human rights?

All children, women and men have human rights which entitle them to live with dignity (true worth or self-respect). People have a right to **justice**; a right to equality, whatever their religion, **caste** or **gender**; a right to adequate food which keeps them in good health; a right to basic education; a right to clean air and water.

Human rights are **basic** rights that all people in all countries have. There are rights in every aspect of life. There are civil and political rights; economic, social and cultural rights; and rights for children.

These rights are sometimes guaranteed (or promised) by **laws** passed by governments.

Some basic human rights

Civil and political rights

1 The right to life
2 No **discrimination** based on gender, colour, religion, language or caste
3 The right to freedom from **slavery**
4 The right to freedom from **arbitrary arrest**
5 The right to free speech
6 The right to vote

The right to vote

Economic rights

1 The right to work
2 The right to food
3 The right to shelter
4 The right to medical care
5 The right to equal pay for equal work for men and women

The right to equal pay for equal work for men and women

Social and cultural rights

1 The right to freedom of religion and belief
2 The right to a clean environment
3 The right to form **trade unions**
4 The right to property
5 The right to marry

Children's rights

1 The right to education
2 The right to health services
3 The right not to be separated from the child's parents
4 The right to an **adequate standard of living**
5 The right to protection against **exploitation**

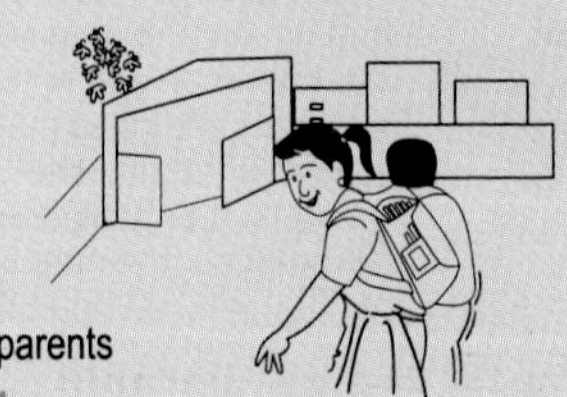

The right to education

People all over the world have been concerned with human rights. Human rights have **evolved** over many centuries. They were widely recognized (accepted) and expanded in the twentieth century.

Some milestones on the path to Universal Human Rights

- The Kalinga War (c 250 BC): Emperor Ashoka banned war, **capital punishment** and torture
- Magna Carta in England (1215 AD): The first step to defining the **freedoms** and rights of free persons and the Church
- Eighteenth-century European philosophy of 'humanism' (or a belief in human values and dignity): **Awareness** of rights and **responsibilities** of humans
- French Revolution (1789): '**Declaration** of the Rights of Man'
- American War of Independence (1776–1783): American **Constitution** and its Bill of Rights assured basic rights for citizens: freedom of speech, of press and **association**, right to **legal** process and freedom from cruel punishment
- Nineteenth Century: International agreements banned the slave trade
- Russian (or Bolshevik) Revolution (1917): Affirmed the **fundamental** rights of citizens, especially workers
- 1903: The Women's Social and Political Union (Great Britain) demanded rights for women, especially the right to vote. In 1920, the United States gave women the right to vote. In 1928, women in Great Britain won the right to vote.
- 1948: Adoption of the United Nations (UN) Universal Declaration on Human Rights
- Mid-twentieth century: End of **colonialism**. Many newly independent countries, such as India, adopted the rights set out in the Universal Declaration of Human Rights.
- 1989: Adoption of the UN Convention on the Rights of the Child
- 1990: **Apartheid** ends in South Africa; all South Africans have equal rights
- 1992: UN Rio **Charter** (or statement of rights) on Environment and Development: the right to a clean environment and development

the suffragettes demand the right to vote

a racist signboard: discrimination on the basis of colour

2 Universal Declaration on Human Rights (UDHR)

The first global recognition of human rights was **contained** in the UDHR, which was adopted by the UN in 1948. The UDHR is not an international **treaty** (agreement) which can be enforced, but it lists 30 human rights that countries **pledge** to **honour**. A few of the 30 rights are:

1. All human beings are born free and equal in dignity and rights. (Article 1)
2. No one shall be subjected to torture. (Article 5)
3. Everyone has the right to a **nationality**. (Article 15)
4. Everyone has the right to freedom of thought and religion. (Article 18)
5. Everyone has the right to education. (Article 26)

3 Enforcement of human rights

Governments of all countries recognize human rights. But not all countries give the same importance to all civil, political, economic, social and cultural rights. Governments of countries where elections are held regularly do guarantee the right to vote and the freedom of speech. But few governments implement the right to food.

4 Rights and responsibilities

Human rights also contain responsibilities. The right to free speech is a basic right. The responsibility is not to **abuse** this right by expressing hate against people of certain communities, religions or castes.

Right to freedom of spee

5 Constitutions

The Constitution of all countries guarantee rights to people. The Constitution of india guarantees all Indians some fundamental rights. All citizens have a right to equal treatment before the law. Citizens cannot be discriminated against on the grounds of religion, caste, sex or place of birth. The Constitution guarantees the freedom of speech, the right to assemble (form trade unions) and the freedom to travel and live anywhere in the country.

The Constitution also contains the 'Directive Principles of State Policy'. These are meant to direct or guide the government in improving the **welfare** of citizens. The government is not legally bound to enforce them. The Directive Principles include free and compulsory education for all children.

Right to seek redress

When governments do not honour human rights, like the right to freedom from arbitrary arrest, citizens have the right to seek **redress**. The National Human Rights Commission was set up in 1993 to hear complaints and investigate cases of **violation** of human rights.

The Constitution and laws passed by the Central and State Governments guarantee many human rights. But citizens do not always know their rights. People can exercise their rights only if they are aware of them. Schools, colleges, newspapers, books, television, websites and non-governmental organizations provide information on human rights.

Websites

To learn more about human rights, you could look up these websites:

1 UN Universal Declaration on Human Rights:
http://www.un.org/Overview/rights.html

2 National Human Rights Commission (INDIA):
http://nhrc.nic.in/

3 Rights of the Child:
http://www.unhchr.ch/html/menu3/b/k2crc.htm

4 UN Resources on Environment for Children:
http://www.unep.org/Documents/Default.asp?DocumentID=295

all odds *Everyone thought she would lose, but she won her case against all odds.* = something that was believed by everyone to be impossible but becomes a reality

ode /əʊd/ noun, c. *Ode to the West Wind* = a long poem written in praise of a person or thing [LITERATURE]

o•di•ous /'əʊdɪəs/ adj. *He is such an odious person that no one wants to be his friend.* = very unpleasant (formal)

o•dour /'əʊdəʳ/ noun, u. or c. *They keep cows in a shed close to my bedroom. I can get the odour of cow-dung every night.* = a strong smell, usually unpleasant **odourless** adj. = having no smell

od•ys•sey /'ɒdɪsi/ noun, c. *Our trek in the Himalayas was not a picnic; it was an odyssey.* = a long and adventurous journey (literary)

oe•soph•a•gus /ɪ'sɒfəgəs/ noun = a tube inside the body leading from the mouth to the stomach, through which food passes [BIOLOGY]

oes•tro•gen /'iːstrədʒən/ noun = a hormone (chemical substance) produced in the ovaries (the part of the body that produces eggs) of women as well as female animals, which is responsible for the female qualities of a person [BIOLOGY]

of /əv/ **or** /ɒːv/ prep. **1** *the residence of the Prime Minister* = belonging to **2** *a crown of gold* = made of **3** *a kilogram of sugar* = amount or quantity **4** *a book of short stories* = containing **5** *the 18th of March* = a day in a month **6** *the front of the house* = showing position **7** *the courage of a lion* = typical of or connected with **8** *the result of the match* = relating to **9** *a man of great wisdom* = having some quality

off[1] /ɒf/ prep. **1** *She got off the bus. // He took all his books off the table.* = away from **2** *Her house is off the main road.* = at some distance from **3** *He is off meat and sweets now.* = not taking (eating or drinking) something

off[2] adv. **1** *They drove off.* = out of or away from **2** *He took his jacket off.* = removed from **3** *I am off!* = starting to go away

off[3] adj. **1** *The fans are off.* = not working (opposite **on**) **2** *The meeting is off.* = stopped or cancelled **3** *The milk has gone off.* = to go bad (referring to food)

off and on *I meet her off and on, though we are neighbours.* = sometimes, not always **off limits** *The school laboratory is off limits for students under ten.* = some place which one is not allowed to enter **well/badly off** = to have or not have a lot of money **off-the-record** *What I have told you about them was off-the-record.* = not to be quoted or reported to anyone **off the shelf** *She buys her clothes off the shelf.* = ready-made; whatever is easily available

off- /ɒf/ prefix meaning **1** not on e.g. **off-duty** /'ɒf'djuːti/ *off-duty officer* = not on duty **2** away from e.g. **off-centre** /ɒf'sentə/ adv. or adj. *The button is off-centre.* = not in the centre

off-colour /'ɒf'kʌləʳ/ adj. *The singer seems to be off-colour today.* = not well (physically) or not in one's usual form

offhand /'ɒfhænd/ *You have asked me how many members this club has. I am not sure of the exact figure, but offhand I would say, about a hundred.* = without taking time to prepare an answer

off•load /'ɒfləʊd/ verb, t. *We managed to offload the ugly and useless furniture.* = to get rid of something unwanted

off-putting adj. *I found his arrogant manner rather off-putting.* = unpleasant and causing dislike

off•shoot /'ɒfʃuːt/ noun, c. *Our school is an offshoot of the Delhi Garden School.* = branch

off•side /ɒf'saɪd/ adv. or adj. *The referee decided that the centre-forward was off-side*(adv.) = in a position where a player should not be (in football and hockey)

off•spring /'ɒfsprɪŋ/ noun, u. (no plural) *They have no offspring.* = child or children (formal)

of•fence /ə'fens/ noun, c. or u. **1** *Robbery is a serious offence.*(u.) = crime; an act of breaking the law **2** *Your words have caused offence.*(u.) = the act or the effect of hurting someone's feelings

of•fend /ə'fend/ verb, t. *Your remarks have offended her and she is feeling very unhappy.* = to hurt someone's feelings

of•fend•er /ə'fendəʳ/ noun, c. = one who commits an offence (a crime) or breaks a law **offensive** adj. or noun, u. or c. **1** *I find your remarks offensive.*(adj.) = unpleasant or causing one to feel insulted **2** *Our army has gone on the offensive.*(noun, u.) = the action of attacking someone first without waiting to be attacked

to take offence = to feel very angry or upset at what someone has said

of•fer[1] /'ɒfəʳ/ verb, t. **1** *The company has offered him a job.* = to ask someone whether he/she would like to take something that one is in a position to give **2** *He offered to drive me to the airport in his car.* = to express willingness to do something **3** *Your letter offers me some hope.* = to give **4** *He is offering prayers.* = to give to God

offer[2] noun, c. or u. **1** *She says she will pay Rs 30,000 for my old car. Her offer is so attractive that I can't refuse it.*(c.) = something that one agrees or promises to do **2** *These shirts are on offer.*(u.) = on sale at a price lower than usual (also **special offer**) **offering** noun, c. *She placed her offerings on the altar.* = something that is given, especially to God

of•fice /'ɒfɪs/ noun, c. or u. **1** *The company has its*

O

offices in Birganj and Pokhra.(c.) = a place where people work for a company, government etc. **2** *Let us go to the booking office and buy tickets.*(c.) = a place where a particular service is offered **3** *She holds the office of secretary in the company.*(u.) = a position of responsibility **official** /ˈəfɪʃəl/ noun, c. or adj. **1** *He is an official in the Education Department.*(noun) = a person who works for the government or a company and has some power or authority over others **2** *an official letter*(adj.) = connected with the work of or accepted by a government or company **3** *We will have a new Principal in May. This announcement is official.*(adj.) = as declared to the public (opposite **unofficial**) **officer** noun, c. *an army officer // a customs officer* = a person in the army or government who commands (leads) people or does an important job **officialese** noun, u. *The government's reply to my letter was written in officialese which no one could understand.* = the style of writing often used by government officials which is difficult for some to understand (derogatory) **officiate** verb, i. *She is the Assistant Director but she is officiating as the Director of the company.* = to perform the duties of an official for a short period, in the absence of someone who is supposed to perform those duties

of•ten /ˈɒfən/ or /ˈɒftən/ adv. **1** *The doctor comes here quite often, at least once a week.* = many times **2** *How often do you clean your refrigerator?* = frequently

every so often *He is in the habit of forgetting to reply to letters, so his wife has to remind him every so often.* = quite often **more often than not** = usually

o•gle /ˈəʊgəl/ verb, t. = to look at someone with sexual interest, in a manner which is usually not liked (derogatory)

o•gre /ˈəʊgəʳ/ noun, c. **1** = a fierce giant, found in stories meant for children **2** = a frightening or unpleasant person (figurative, often humorous)

oh /əʊ/ interjec. **1** *'I came back home at two last night.' 'Oh!'* = an expression of surprise, fear or pain **2** *Oh King, please grant my wish!* = a form of address

ohm /əʊm/ noun = a unit for measuring electrical resistance (the amount of electrical energy that can pass through a substance) [PHYSICS]

oil[1] /ɔɪl/ noun, u. or c. **1** (u.) = thick liquid containing fat, obtained from plants, animals or from the inside of the earth, used for cooking, burning, making machines run smoothly etc. **2** *medicinal oils*(c.) = different kinds of oil

oil[2] verb, t. *The wheels of the bicycle have to be oiled.* = to put oil on or into something **oily** adj. **1** *oily food* = containing a lot of oil **2** *a person with oily manners* = polite in an unpleasant way (figurative, derogatory) **oil-field** noun, c. = an area where oil can be found inside the earth or under the sea **oil painting** noun, c. = a picture made with paints which are mixed with oil **oil slick** noun, c. = a large film (sheet) of oil floating on top of the water in a sea or lake, which can kill all the plants and animals in the water **oil tanker** noun, c. = a special kind of ship or truck that is used to carry oil **oil-well** noun, c. = a hole dug deep into the ground or the sea from which oil can be taken out

oint•ment /ˈɔɪntmənt/ noun, u. = a kind of medicine containing oil or wax, which is rubbed into the skin to heal a wound or a sore

o•kay[1] /əʊˈkeɪ/ adj. *Your plan seems to be okay.* = all right; acceptable (also o.k. or ok) (informal)

okay[2] adv. **1** *The car is running okay now.* = correctly (in the right manner) (informal) **2** *Okay, I will come with you to the meeting.* = very well (expressing agreement or consent) (informal)

okay[3] verb, t. *The Director has okayed the plan. Now we can start the project.* = to accept or to approve (give permission for) (informal)

okay[4] noun, c. *I have the Director's okay for my plan.* = approval (permission to do something) (informal)

ok•ra /ˈɒkrə/ noun = a kind of long, thin, green vegetable (also **lady's finger**)

old /əʊld/ adj. **1** *an old man; an old temple* = having lived or existed for many years **2** *an old coat* = in use for a long time **3** *an old friend* = having continued in a relationship for a long time **4** *a three-year old child* = having reached a certain age (which is stated) **5** *She went back to her old job after she had tried out a number of new jobs.* = former, earlier **6** *This is an old model.* = something belonging to the past (opposite **new, modern**) **7** *There's some old curd in the fridge.* = made a long time ago (opposite **fresh**) **8** *an old quarrel* = something which has been going on for a long time **old age** = the last part of one's life belonging to **old boy** noun, c. *He is an old boy of this school.* = a former student of a school or college (also **alumnus**) **old-fashioned** adj. *an old-fashioned dress* = not very common or popular at the present time **old guard** noun, c. *He is a member of the old guard in the Farmer's Party.* = a group of people in an organization who have been there for a long time and who do not like change **old hand** noun, c. *She is an old hand at teaching.* = a very experienced person **Old Testament** noun = the different books which form parts of the Bible, dealing with events before the birth of Jesus Christ **old-timer** noun, c. = a person who has been in a particular place, position or organization for a long time **old wives' tale** noun = an old belief or idea that is not considered to be based on fact (derogatory)

o•le•an•der /əʊli'ændə^r/ noun = a kind of plant that produces flowers which are pink or white in colour

ol•fac•to•ry /ɒl'fæktəri/ adj. *The olfactory sense in dogs is highly developed. They can smell things from a great distance.* = having to do with the sense of smell (the ability to smell things) [BIOLOGY]

ol•i•gar•chy /'ɒlɪgɑːki/ noun, u. or c. (**oligarchies**) = government by a small group of powerful people

ol•ive /'ɒlɪv/ noun u or c. **1** (u.) = a kind of tree that grows mostly in countries near the Mediterranean Sea (Italy, Spain, Greece etc.) and produces the olive fruit, from which we get olive oil **2** (c.) = the fruit of this tree, used as food **olive branch** noun *holding out the olive branch* = a sign of peace **olive green** noun = a kind of dull-green colour that is commonly seen in military uniforms (clothes worn by soldiers)

O•lym•pics /ə'lɪmpɪks/ noun = an international sports competition that was originally held in Greece and is now held once in four years in different parts of the world (also Olympiad)

o•me•ga /'əʊmɪgə/ noun = the last letter of the Greek alphabet, represented by the sign Ω

ome•lette /'ɒmlɪt/ noun, c. = a dish (item of food) made by beating the liquid inside an egg into a kind of froth (foam), which is then fried in hot oil or butter

o•men /'əʊmən/ noun, c. *Some people believe that if a black cat crosses your path when you are about to start on a journey, that is a bad omen.* = a sign of something, either good or bad, that is going to happen in the future

om•i•nous /'ɒmɪnəs/ adj. *We are going to have a storm. There are ominous black clouds gathering in the sky.* = giving a warning of something bad that is going to happen (formal, literary)

o•mit /əʊ'mɪt/ verb, t. (**omitted**) *Debasis played for India in the last two matches but he will not play in the next match. He has been omitted from the team.* = to leave out (not include) someone or something (formal) **omission** noun, u. or c. **1** *We are sorry about your omission from the team.*(u.) = the act of omitting someone or something (formal) **2** *Kumble's name has not been included in the team. This is a surprising omission.*(c.) = someone or something that is omitted (left out) (formal)

omni- /'ɒmnɪ/ prefix meaning 'all' e.g. **om•ni•bus** /'ɒmnɪbəs/ noun, c. (**omnibuses**) or adj. **1** (noun) = bus (old-fashioned) **2** *a Premchand omnibus* (noun) // *an omnibus edition of Premchand's works*(adj.) = a book containing many of the writings produced by a single author, which have already been published separately elsewhere

om•nip•o•tent /ɒm'nɪpətənt/ adj. *an omnipotent ruler* = all-powerful (having unlimited power)

omnipresent /ɒmnɪ'presənt/ adj. = present everywhere

om•ni•vo•r•ous /ɒm'nɪvərəs/ adj. = eating everything (an animal that eats any kind of food, meat as well as vegetables etc.) (compare **carnivorous, herbivorous**)

on[1] /ɒn/ prep. **1** *The book is on the table.* = above a surface and touching it **2** *He has ink marks on his hands.* = covering **3** *He had the dog on a leash.* = connected to **4** *This is a book on yoga.* = relating to (about) **5** *He is on the Board of Governors.* = working for; a member of **6** *This tractor runs on kerosene oil.* = by means of **7** *The shops are open on Sunday.* = the time when something happens **8** *On hearing of his father's death I sent him a letter.* = after

on[2] adv. **1** *He walked on.* = continuously, without stopping **2** *If you walk on you will reach the station.* = further **3** *She is on a diet.* = to be using or having a particular kind of food **4** *The lights are on.* = working

not on *You can't say whatever you like and hurt the feelings of people. That's not on!* = to not be acceptable (informal) **(to) go on 1** *There's something in the box. Go on, open it.* = a way of encouraging someone to do something **2** *I'll be a little late. Go on, and don't wait for me.* = to keep walking, moving etc. **3** *'I've fallen in love.' 'Go on, you're joking!'* = a way of expressing surprise (informal) **to go on and on** *I've listened patiently to your words of advice. Please don't go on and on.* = to keep saying something and cause the other person to feel annoyed (derogatory) **on someone** *The lunch is on me. You paid the last time.* = to pay for something **on and off** *I hear from her on and off, she has so much to do!* = not in a regular and continuous way

on•look•er /'ɒnlʊkə^r/ noun, c. = a person who watches something happening without taking part in it

on•set /'ɒnset/ noun, u. *The storm last night announced the onset of the monsoon.* = the start or beginning

on•slaught /'ɒnslɔːt/ noun, u. *The army made an onslaught on the enemy position.*= a violent attack

once[1] /wʌns/ adv. **1** *I have seen her only once.* = one single time **2** *He was an actor once.* = at some time in the past

once[2] noun, c. *Let me drive your car just this once.* = one time

once[3] conj. *Once you begin reading this book, you won't be able to put it down.* = from the moment that

once and for all *Let me say this once and for all: you are not going to eat any more sweets.* = for the last time **once upon a time** = at some time in the past (words commonly used to begin a story for children) **at once** *She is very sick. Please come at once.* = immediately **once in a blue moon** *She writes to me once in a blue moon.* = very rarely (informal)

O

one[1] /wʌn/ det. **1** *He has two daughters and one son.* = the number 1; single **2** *One day the king had a dream.* = on a particular occasion **3** *One Aloke Sinha wants to meet you.* = a person not known to the speaker but calling herself/himself by a certain name **4** *He is the one person who can help you.* = only

one[2] pron. **1** *He has asked me to look for a house but I can't find one.* = the person or thing mentioned earlier **2** *One should respect one's teachers.* = any person (formal) **3** *Ramesh is the one with brown hair.* = the particular person who is described **4** *She is the one who wrote the lovely poem.* = the person who has already been mentioned **5** *You're not a guest. You are one of us.* = part (of a group); belonging to a group **one-off** adj *I will repair your computer free, but only on a one-off basis.* = something that will be done only once and not repeated **one-sided** adj. *The match between Bangladesh and South Africa was very one-sided.* = unequal (with one side much stronger than the other) **one-time** adj. *She was a one-time captain of the team.* = former (in the past but not now) **one another** = each other **one-upmanship** noun, u. = a competition in which one person tries to do better than someone else **one-way** adj. **1** *a one-way street* = moving or allowing movement in only one direction **2** *a one-way ticket* = only travelling to a place, not back to the place from where you left (opposite **return**)

one-to-one *The two leaders will have a one-to-one meeting.* = between two people only **to be one up on someone** = to have an advantage over someone in a test, game etc. (informal)

o•ne•rous /ˈɒnərəs/ adj. *As the company's secretary he has to perform many onerous duties.* = difficult (referring to a task or duty) (formal)

on•ion /ˈʌnjən/ noun, c. or u. **1** (c.) = a round vegetable with a very strong smell, which grows under the ground and is used as a spice to add taste to food **2** *I don't like onion in my food.*(u.) = the same vegetable used as food

on•line /ˈɒnlaɪn/ adv. *I will find the information online.* = connected to the **Internet** [COMPUTERS]

on•ly[1] /ˈəʊnli/ adj. **1** *He is my only child.* = with no others of the kind stated **2** *He wears only the costliest clothes.* = nothing else but

only[2] adv. *I have only two days more to complete the film.* = no more than

only[3] conj. *I would like to teach the poor children; only, I don't have the time.* = but for the fact that

on•o•mat•o•poe•ia /ɒnəmætəˈpiːə/ noun *The phrase 'the buzzing of bees' is an example of onomatopoeia.* = the use of a word (e.g. 'buzzing') which imitates (copies) a natural sound (e.g. the sound made by a bee) [LITERATURE]

on•to /ˈɒntuː/ prep. *She stepped onto the plane from the step-ladder.* = moving from one position to another

to be onto somebody *He is planning to cheat us, but I am onto him.* = to know what someone is planning to do (generally used of something unpleasant) (informal) **to be onto something** *They are onto a cure for malaria.* = to have found out something that could lead to a good result (informal)

on•tol•o•gy /ɒnˈtɒlədʒi/ noun = the branch of philosophy which deals with the nature of existence [TECHNICAL]

o•nus /ˈəʊnəs/ noun, u. *There are several people helping us on the project, but the onus is on me as the leader.* = the duty or the responsibility of doing something [LAW]

on•yx /ˈɒnɪks/ noun = a kind of semi-precious stone that has many shades of colour, commonly used to make jewellery and paperweights

oo•dles /ˈuːdlz/ noun, u. (always plural) *She has oodles of energy.* = a lot of (slang, humorous)

ooze[1] /uːz/ verb, i. or t. *Blood is oozing from his wound.*(i.) = to flow out slowly (used for a thick liquid)

ooze[2] noun, u. *My legs were caught in the ooze.* = wet mud in which things can get stuck

o•pal /ˈəʊpəl/ noun = a kind of precious stone that is white but contains traces (faint marks) of other colours as well

o•paque /əʊˈpeɪk/ adj. *Glass is usually transparent, but some kinds of glass are opaque.* = not allowing light to pass through or not allowing one to see through it (opposite **transparent**) [TECHNICAL]

OPEC abbr. of **Organization of Petroleum Exporting Countries** = a group of countries which produce petroleum (oil), and control its price around the world

o•pen[1] /ˈəʊpən/ adj. **1** *The door is open.* = not shut or closed; allowing someone to enter or pass through **2** *an open magazine* = allowing someone to read what is printed on the pages **3** *an open field* = not surrounded by walls; allowing one to pass freely **4** *The post-office is open.* = allowing people to enter and get the services they need

open[2] verb, t. or i. **1** *Please open the door.*(t.) = to cause something to become open, allowing someone to enter **2** *The door opened.*(i.) = to become open **3** *I opened the conference by making a short speech.*(t.) = to start **4** *The post-office opens at 10.00.*(i.) = to begin working **5** *Please open the file and read the story.*(t.) = to start a file or program so as to read or work on it [COMPUTERS] **6** *This room opens on to the courtyard.*(i.) = to lead directly to **opener** noun, c. **1** *a bottle-opener* = a thing that is used to open something **2** = the batsman who opens the innings for his team in cricket [SPORTS] **open-air** adj. *an open-air cinema* = in the open-air (outside a building, not inside) **open-and-shut** adj. *This murder is an open-and-shut case for the police.* = easy to solve or prove **open-ended** adj. *an open-ended discussion* = with nothing decided in advance (beforehand) **open-eyed** adj. *She was open-eyed with wonder when she saw the Taj Mahal for the first time.* = with eyes wide open in surprise or wonder **open-heart surgery** noun = an operation in which the heart is made to stop beating for some time and is cut open to be examined and repaired **open house** noun = a day when the public can visit a school, organization etc. meet the people there and see how it works etc. **Open University** noun = a university which allows people to study at home or in their free time, through lessons given through radio or television or sent through the post

with open arms *The new teacher was welcomed with open arms.* = showing that one is pleased to welcome something or someone **to open fire** = to shoot at someone or something **open up** **1** *At first she was silent but then she opened up.* = to become willing to talk about something **2** = to make a business less controlled **(out) in the open** *The secret was out in the open. We were happy that everyone now knew what was happening.* = known to everyone as a result of being revealed or told **to have an open mind** *I don't like large cities, but I'm moving to Mumbai with an open mind.* = without prejudice or negative thinking; willing to accept something

opening[1] /'əʊpnɪŋ/ noun, c. or u. **1** *There is an opening in the wall, through which you can enter.*(c.) = gap; a clear space **2** *The opening of a new school will help the people of this area.*(u.) = the act of starting something **3** *There is an opening in the advertising company for an artist.*(c.) = a job that is available and can be applied for

opening[2] adj. *I liked her opening speech at the conference. // Saurav Ganguly is our opening batsman.* = something or someone that opens (begins or starts) something

op•e•ra /'ɒpərə/ noun, c. = a kind of musical drama in which the story is told mainly through songs

op•e•rate /'ɒpəreɪt/ verb, t. or i. **1** *He has been hired to operate the computer system in the office.*(t.) = to make something (specially some machine) work **2** *The trains are operating once again.*(i.) = to work **3** *The surgeon will operate tomorrow.*(i.) = to perform a surgical operation (to cut open someone's body in order to remove a diseased part etc.) **4** *The company operates in three cities.*(i.) = to do business **operation** /ɒpə'reɪʃən/ noun, u. or c. **1** *The machines are in operation.*(u.) // *Have you understood the operation of these new machines?*(u.) = the state or process of working **2** *The operation has been successful.*(c.) = the act of cutting open a person's body, performed by a surgeon **operator** noun, c. **1** *the projector operator in a cinema // a telephone operator* = a person who operates a machine (makes it work) **2** *He is a clever operator.* = a person who is very clever and usually dishonest in business matters in a way that people don't usually like (also **smooth operator**) (derogatory) **operational** adj. *The factory is fully operational now.* = in a working condition **operative** /'ɒpərətɪv/ adj. **1** *This new rule will become operative next month.* = to start working and producing an effect **2** *a post-operative check* = connected with a medical operation **operating system** noun = a set of programs that controls the way in which other programs in a computer work and the way a user interacts with the computer [COMPUTERS] **operating theatre** noun = a room in which operations are performed

oph•thal•mo•lo•gy /ɒfθæl'mɒlədʒi/ noun = the branch of medicine that deals with the eyes and their diseases **opthalmic** /ɒf'θælmɪk/ adj. = having to do with the eyes [MEDICINE]

o•pin•ion /ə'pɪnjən/ noun, c. or u. **1** *In my opinion, this is not the right time to start a new business.*(c.) = an idea that someone has or expresses about someone or something, based mainly on feelings and beliefs rather than facts **2** *My doctor thinks I may have an ulcer, but I am going to get a second opinion.* = professional judgement or advice **opinionated** adj. *She is so opinionated that she never takes anyone's advice.* = too sure that one's opinion is always right (formal, derogatory) **opinion poll** noun, c. = a system of voting in which people are asked to give their opinion on some subject so that a representative statement based on common beliefs may be made

to have a low/high/good/bad opinion of someone/something = to think well or poorly of someone or something

o•pi•um /'əʊpɪəm/ noun = a drug which produces sleep, made from the seeds of the poppy plant **opiate** noun, c. = a drug that contains opium (formal)

op•por•tu•ni•ty /ɒpə'tju:nɪti/ noun, c. (**opportunities**) or u. *Arundhati Roy is visiting our school tomorrow and all the students will have an opportunity to meet her.*(c.) = chance; an occasion or situation which makes it possible to do something that one wants to do **opportune** /'ɒpətju:n/ adj. **1** *I was waiting for the opportune moment to ask you for a favour.* = the correct time for doing something

O

2 *You visited the office at an opportune time. We were looking for someone exactly like you.* = favourable **opportunist** /ɒpə'tju:nɪst/ noun, c. *Last year you were supporting Mr Singh, but now that Mr Rao is the new President of the club, you have become a supporter of Mr Rao. What an opportunist you are!* = a person without fixed principles, who makes use of every opportunity (favourable situation) to gain something (derogatory) **opportunistic** adj.

op•pose /ə'pəʊz/ verb, t. 1 *When a teacher suggested that the examination should be postponed, others opposed him.* = to disagree and to speak against an opinion (idea) expressed by someone 2 *India will oppose Australia in this match.* = to compete with or fight against **opposed** adj. **(opposed to something)** *He has always been opposed to smoking.* = believing strongly that something is harmful or wrong **opponent** /ə'pəʊnənt/ noun, c. *I am facing a strong opponent in the election.* = one who fights against or competes with someone **opposition** noun, u. 1 *My plan had to be given up because of the opposition from several people.* = the act of opposing something or someone (speaking against an opinion expressed by someone) (formal) 2 *India will face strong opposition in the next match as they are going to play against South Africa.* = the people who are fighting against or competing with someone (formal) **the Opposition** noun = the group of members in the parliament who are not in the government

op•po•site[1] /'ɒpezɪt/ noun *'Old' is the opposite of 'young'.* = something that is completely different from something else

opposite[2] adj. *When I praised the child and said he had done some good work, my friend the opposite view and said it was not really good.* = as different as possible

opposite[3] prep. *He lives opposite the market.* = facing (just in front of)

op•press /ə'pres/ verb, t. = to treat in a cruel way and make someone suffer by not allowing them the rights that others have **oppression** noun, u. *The people have decided to fight against the king's oppression.* = the action of oppressing someone (ruling in a cruel way) **oppressor** noun, c. = one who oppresses someone **oppressive** adj. *The heat is oppressive.* = causing suffering or pain

opt /ɒpt/ verb, t. *I could have been a doctor but I opted to become a painter instead.* = to choose to do something (formal) **option** noun, c. *You can go either to Mumbai or to Goa for your holiday. You have an option.* = the freedom to choose between two different things **optional** adj. *You will have to study mathematics and physics. Those are compulsory subjects. But you can take geography as an optional subject.* = something that one is free to choose or not to choose (opposite **compulsory**)

op•tic /'ɒptɪk/ adj. *the optic nerve* = having to do with the eyes **optical** adj. *This man repairs microscopes and other optical instruments.* = having to do with vision (the act of seeing something) **optician** /ɒp'tɪʃən/ noun, c. = a person who makes and sells spectacles (which help people to see more clearly) **optics** noun = the science of light, vision and sight [PHYSICS]

op•ti•mist /'ɒptɪmɪst/ noun, c. *He is such an optimist that he believes it will not rain today, even though it has been raining for the past week.* = a person who always hopes for the best (opposite **pessimist**) **optimism** noun, u. *I think we will have to call off our picnic as it is bound to rain. I see no reason for optimism.* = the quality of being an optimist (hoping for the best) **optimistic** /ɒptɪ'mɪstɪk/ adj. *I feel very optimistic about being admitted to the college.* = having very strong hopes

op•ti•mum /'ɒptɪməm/ adj. *Under optimum conditions this factory can produce 1,000 cars a day, but at present we are producing only 200 cars.* = most favourable or best (most likely to bring success) (also optimal)

op•u•lence /'ɒpjʊləns/ noun, u. *There is too much opulence in the way this room has been decorated. I prefer something more simple.* = a show of wealth or luxury (formal, often disapproving) **opulent** adj. *They own an opulent house with 25 rooms.* = very rich; grand

or /ə^r/ conj. 1 *You can go now or later.* = indicating more than one possibility 2 *Do as I say or you will be in serious trouble.* = otherwise; if not 3 *He is the sardar, or chief, of this tribe.* = which is to say (in other words) 4 *I have visited the city museum six or seven times.* = used between numbers which are close together so that one gets a general idea of the number

or•a•cle /'ɒrəkəl/ noun, c. 1 = a person with supernatural powers, able to tell the future (in ancient Greece) 2 = anyone who tries to say what is likely to happen in the future

o•ral /'ɔ:rəl/ adj. 1 *After the written examination you will have an oral test.* = spoken (and not written) 2 *The dentist will advise you on oral hygiene.* = having to do with the mouth (formal) **orally** adj. *Take this medicine orally.* = through the mouth (formal)

or•ange[1] /'ɒrɪndʒ/ noun, c. or u. 1 (c.) = a round, juicy fruit which is reddish-yellow in colour 2 (u.) = the flesh or juice of the same fruit, used as food

orange[2] adj. *an orange sari* = of the colour of an

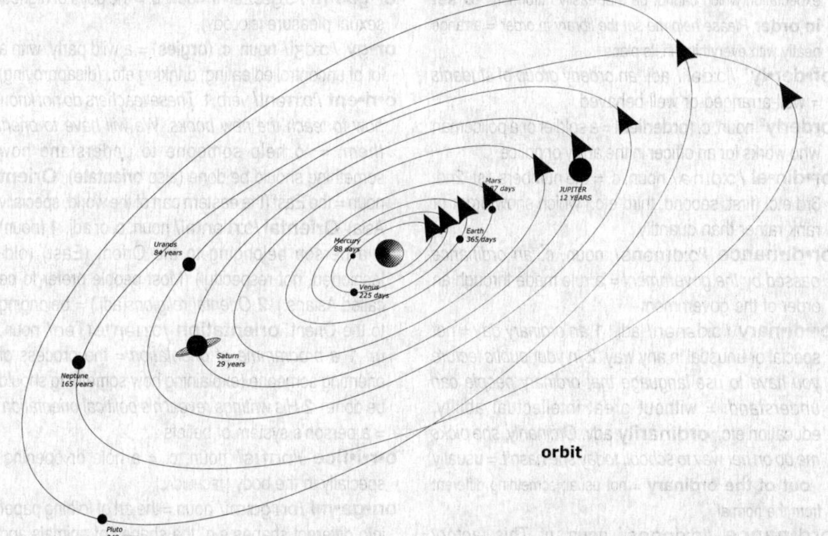

orbit

orange (reddish-yellow)

o•rang•u•tang /ɔːræŋuːˈtæŋ/ noun = a large ape with reddish-brown hair, found in Borneo and Sumatra

or•a•tor /ˈɒrətə^r/ noun, c. *President Radhakrishnan was one of the greatest orators of his time. When he spoke, people listened in absolute silence.* = a person who has great skill in the art of speaking in public (to a large audience) (formal) **oration** noun, c. *Jawaharlal Nehu's speech in parliament welcoming India's independence was one of the greatest orations of all time.* = a public speech (formal)

or•bit[1] /ˈɔːbɪt/ noun, c. *the earth's orbit around the sun* = the curved path followed by a planet (e.g. the earth) or a space-craft (a vehicle moving in space) as it goes round something else

orbit[2] verb, t. *The earth orbits the sun once in 365 days.* = to move in an orbit around something

or•chard /ˈɔːtʃəd/ noun, c. = a garden containing fruit trees

or•ches•tra /ˈɔːkɪstrə/ noun, c. = a large group of musicians who play together on different musical instruments **orchestrate** verb, t. *We are going to have a conference here next month. You will have to orchestrate all the programmes.* = to plan and manage (look after) some activity which requires a number of people to work together, so as to get the best results

or•chid /ˈɔːkɪd/ noun = a kind of flower with an unusual shape and beautiful, bright colours

or•deal /ɔːˈdiːl/ noun, c. *We had to climb many hills to reach the village. It was a real ordeal.* = a difficult and painful experience

or•der[1] /ˈɔːdə^r/ verb, t. **1** *The teacher ordered the student to stand up.* = to give a command which must be obeyed because of one's position **2** *I ordered some tandoori chicken for my friend. // I have ordered some new books for the library.* = to ask for something to be bought, supplied, made etc. in return for payment **3** *Your essay is very loosely written. It seems you have not been able to order your ideas properly.* = to arrange things neatly

order[2] noun, u. or c. **1** *I have received an order from the government asking me to go to Delhi for a meeting.*(c.) = a command **2** *The children were shouting at the top of their voices and the teacher was trying hard to maintain order in the classroom.*(u.) = a condition in which rules are obeyed, so that it is possible for work to go on (opposite **disorder**) **3** *In a dictionary, the words whose meanings are being explained are arranged in alphabetical order.*(u.) = sequence (the arrangement of names etc. in a list, with one name following another according to a certain system) **4** *The telephone was not working yesterday but today it is in order.*(u.) = in a working condition **5** *The waiter at the restaurant took our order.*(c.) = a request by a customer for something to be brought or made on payment **Order! Order!** interjec. = an expression used to announce the start of a meeting

to order someone around/about = to tell others what they must do (disapproving) **out of order** *The stereo is out of order. We can't listen to any music.* = to not be in working condition **a tall order** *Do you really expect me to work two days without a break? That's a tall order!* = an

O

expectation which cannot be met easily (informal) **to set in order** *Please help me set the library in order.* = arrange neatly with everything in its place

or•der•ly[1] /'ɔːdəli/ adj. *an orderly group of students* = well-arranged or well-behaved

orderly[2] noun, c. (**orderlies**) = a soldier or a policeman who works for an officer in the army or police

or•din•al /'ɔːdɪnəl/ noun, c. = the numbers 1st, 2nd, 3rd etc. (first, second, third etc.) which show order or rank rather than quantity

or•di•nance /'ɔːdɪnəns/ noun, c. *an ordinance passed by the government* = a rule made through an order of the government

or•di•nary /'ɔːdənəri/ adj. **1** *an ordinary day* = not special or unusual in any way **2** *In your public lecture you have to use language that ordinary people can understand.* = without great intellectual ability, education etc. **ordinarily** adv. *Ordinarily, she picks me up on her way to school, today she hasn't.* = usually **out of the ordinary** = not usual; something different from the normal

ord•nance /'ɔːdnəns/ noun, u. *This factory produces ordnance for the army.* = weapons needed by the army for fighting, specially cannons (big and heavy guns mounted on wheels)

ore /ɔː'/ noun, c. or u. *iron ore* = rock or earth from which metals (e.g. iron, copper) can be obtained

or•gan /'ɔːgən/ noun, c. **1** *The heart, liver, lungs, etc. are important organs.* = an inner part of the body which has a special function (purpose) **2** *This newspaper is the organ of the Weavers' Party.* = a newspaper which represents the views or policies of a group **3** *She plays the organ.* = a large musical instrument containing pipes of different length, through which air is blown to produce musical sounds

or•gan•is•m /'ɔːgənɪzəm/ noun, u. or c. = a living thing which is made up of many parts **organic** /ɔː'gænɪk/ adj. *organic fertilizer* = having to do with living things or produced by living things (opposite **inorganic**)

or•gan•ize (organise) /'ɔːgənaɪz/ verb, t. **1** *You must organize your thoughts in order to write a good essay.* = to arrange the different parts of something properly so that they fit together and work well **2** *We are organizing a birthday party for you.*= to make arrangements for **organization (organisation)** /ɔːgənaɪ'zeɪʃən/ noun, c. or u. **1** *People for Animals is a large organization, with branches in every state.*(c.) = a group which has people working at different levels for a common purpose **2** *The organization of an advertising campaign requires a lot of effort as well as money.*(u.) = the action or process of arranging things or putting things together for some purpose

or•gas•m /'ɔːgæzəm/ noun, u. = the point of highest sexual pleasure [BIOLOGY]

or•gy /'ɔːdʒi/ noun, c. (**orgies**) = a wild party, with a lot of uncontrolled eating, drinking etc. (disapproving)

o•ri•ent /'ɔːrɪənt/ verb, t. *These teachers do not know how to teach the new books. We will have to orient them.* = to help someone to understand how something should be done (also **orientate**) **Orient** noun = the East (the eastern part of the world, specially Asia) **Oriental** /ɔːrɪ'əntəl/ noun, c. or adj. **1** (noun) = a person belonging to the Orient (East) (old-fashioned, not respectful) (Most people prefer to be called Asians.) **2** *Oriental religions*(adj.) = belonging to the Orient **orientation** /ɔːrɪən'teɪʃən/ noun, u. **1** *a programme of orientation* = the process of orienting someone (explaining how something should be done) **2** *His writings reveal his political orientation.* = a person's system of beliefs

o•r•i•fice /'ɒrɪfɪs/ noun, c. = a hole or opening, specially in the body [TECHNICAL]

ori•ga•mi /ɒrɪ'gɑːmi/ noun = the art of folding paper into different shapes e.g. the shapes of animals and birds, which began in Japan

or•i•gin /'ɒrɪdʒɪn/ noun, c. or u. *This dictionary explains the origins of English words, many of which have come from Indian languages.*(c.) = the point, place or thing from which something begins

o•rig•i•nal[1] /ə'rɪdʒɪnəl/ adj. **1** *The original meaning of the word 'villain' was 'one who owns a villa, or a house', but now 'villain' has come to mean 'a bad or wicked person'.* = the earliest or first **2** *I like your essay very much. It is really original.* = new and fresh; different from others

original[2] noun, c. *This painting is an original by the famous artist, Jamini Roy. It is not a copy. // I have a copy of the letter. Where is the original?* = something from which copies can or have been made (also, for documents, **top copy**) **originality** /ərɪdʒɪ'nælɪti/ noun, u. *The writer was praised for her originality.* = the quality of being original (new and different from others) **originate** /ə'rɪdʒɪneɪt/ verb, i. *The river Ganga originates in a glacier in the Himalayas.* = to start from something (formal)

or•na•ment[1] /'ɔːnəment/ noun, c. or u. **1** *The jeweller makes gold ornaments.*(c.) = rings, bangles, necklaces etc. made of gold or other costly materials, worn mostly by women in order to look more beautiful **2** *I want a simple wooden chair, without any ornament.*(c.) = decoration; something that is added to an object to make it look more beautiful, though not more useful

ornament[2] verb, t. *Several beautiful paintings by Van Gogh ornament his drawing room.* = to add beauty to something **ornamental** /ɔːnə'mentəl/ adj. *ornamental furniture* = having a lot of decoration, but not serving a useful purpose

or•nate /ɔː'neɪt/ adj. *furniture of ornate design* = having a lot of decoration; ornamental

or•ni•thol•o•gy /ɔːnɪ'θɒlədʒi/ noun = the scientific study of birds **ornithologist** noun, c. = a person who studies or practises ornithology

or•phan[1] /'ɔːfən/ noun, c. *He lost both his parents and became an orphan at the age of five.* = a person, specially a child, whose parents are dead

orphan[2] verb, t. *The war has orphaned many children.* = to cause someone to become an orphan **orphanage** noun, c. = a place in which orphans live and are taken care of

or•tho•don•tist /ɔːθə'dɒntɪst/ noun, c. = a dentist (doctor who takes care of the teeth) who helps people with crooked teeth by straightening them

or•tho•dox /'ɔːθədɒks/ adj. *He is very orthodox in his religious views and does not want any new ideas to be brought in.* = holding beliefs or ideas which have been accepted by most people for a long time

or•thog•ra•phy /ɔː'θɒgrəfi/ noun, u. *English orthography is very different from the Chinese system of writing.* = a system of spelling

or•tho•pae•dics (orthopedics) /ɔːθə'piːdɪks/ noun = the branch of medicine that deals with the care of the bones and joints

Os•car /'ɒskəʳ/ noun = a prize given in the U.S.A. each year for making and acting in films

os•cil•late /'ɒsɪleɪt/ verb, t. **1** *The pendulum of the clock oscillates once in each second.* = to move from side to side [PHYSICS] **2** = to move from one direction to another as in radio waves [TECHNICAL] **3** = to move between extreme feelings of e.g. happiness or sadness **oscillation** /ɒsɪ'leɪʃən/ noun, c. **1** = the action of oscillating **2** = one complete movement from side to side [TECHNICAL]

os•mo•sis /ɒz'məʊsɪs/ noun = the process by which liquids pass slowly through a membrane (a solid substance with very tiny holes, through which liquids or gases can pass) [SCIENCE]

os•ten•si•ble /ɒ'stensɪbəl/ adj. *We don't know why he left the job. The ostensible reason was that he had started a business of his own but the real reason was that he had got a job in Delhi.* = what seems to be; appearing to be real but not real (referring to a reason for doing something) (formal, disapproving)

os•ten•ta•tion /ɒstən'teɪʃən/ noun, u. *We will be married in a very simple ceremony. We don't like ostentation.* = a show of wealth (formal, derogatory) (formal) **ostentatious** adj. *an ostentatious person* = having a liking for ostentation (show) (formal, disapproving)

os•tra•cize (ostracise) /'ɒstrəsaɪz/ verb, t. *The family ostracized her because she changed her religion.* = to stop accepting someone as a member of a group because of something he/she has done (formal)

os•trich /'ɒstrɪtʃ/ noun, c. (**ostriches**) = a very large bird, found in Africa, which has beautiful feathers but cannot fly

oth•er[1] /'ʌðəʳ/ det. **1** *I don't want the red book. Give me the other book.* = different from the one which is being referred to **2** *Do you need any other books?* = more or additional

other[2] pron. **1** *If you don't like this shirt, you can try the other.* = the second of two **2** *Although he is very busy, he always tries to help others.* = not the same as oneself **otherwise** adv. or conj. **1** *She thinks she is a good actor, but most people think otherwise.*(adv.) = in a different way **2** *He is lazy, but otherwise he has the qualities of a good manager.*(adv.) = apart from that **3** *You must work hard, otherwise you will not succeed.*(conj.) = if not; or else

in other words = that is to say

ot•ter /'ɒtəʳ/ noun, c. = an animal with thick fur (hair) that looks like a large rat and is very good at swimming and catching fish

ouch /aʊtʃ/ interjec. *Ouch! That hurts!* = an expression of pain (informal, sometimes humorous)

ought /ɔːt/ aux. (modal) verb (used with **to**) **1** *You ought to look after your old parents.* = should (to have the moral duty to do something) **2** *My house ought to have been repaired last year, but I had no money.* = which would have been the right thing to do **3** *The new film ought to have a good sale.* = should (that is what one expects)

ounce /aʊns/ noun, c = a unit of weight equal to about 28.35 gms (abbreviated as oz)

our /aʊəʳ/ det. *This is our house.* = belonging to us **ours** pron. *This house is ours.* = belonging to us **ourselves** pron. **1** *We saw ourselves on television the other night.* = us ('We saw us') **2** *We bought ourselves a new house.* = for us ('We bought for us') **3** *We cooked everything ourselves.* = without help from anyone

oust /aʊst/ verb, t. *You would have been the next president of the club. Why did you have to oust the present one?* = to force someone out and take his/her place or position

out[1] /aʊt/ adv. **1** *He opened the door and walked out.* = away from the inside **2** *Please give out the sweets to the children.* = to a number of people **3** *He*

O

read out the names from the list. = in a loud voice **4** *The batsman has been given out.* = no longer allowed to play **5** *There will be a lot of excitement when the new book is out.* = published; released to the public **6** *Scarves are out this season.* = not in fashion any more **7** *Wednesday is out, maybe we can have dinner on Friday.* = not acceptable or possible (informal)

out[2] adj. **1** *The doctor is out. Please have a seat.* = not in the place where one expects to find someone **2** *The results of the examination are out.* = to be seen or known by many people

out- /'aʊt/ prefix meaning **1** outside e.g. **outdoor** /aʊtdɔːʳ/ adj. *outdoor swimming pool* = found or done in the open (opposite **indoor**) **2** beyond e.g. **outskirts** /'aʊtskɜːts/ noun, u. (always plural) *She has built her house on the outskirts of the city.* = beyond or further than the central parts **3** greater than e.g. **outnumber** /aʊt'nʌmbəʳ/ verb, t. *Our soldiers outnumbered the enemy troops.* = to be more in number than

out•break /'aʊtbreɪk/ noun, u. *There has been an outbreak of cholera in the city.* = a sudden appearance or beginning of something bad

out•burst /'aʊtbɜːst/ noun, u. *He started shouting in an outburst of anger.* = a sudden and strong expression of some feeling

out•cast /'aʊtkɑːst/ noun, c. = a person who has been forced out of a group for his/her views or behaviour

out•class /aʊt'klɑːs/ verb, t. *The Australian team completely outclassed the Indian team.* = to be much better than

out•come /'aʊtkʌm/ noun, c. *We are waiting for the outcome of the examination which was held last month.* = result (formal)

out•cry /'aʊtkraɪ/ noun, c. (**outcries**) *There was an outcry from several famous musicians when an unknown musician was given the title of Bharat Ratna.* = a public protest or expression of anger

out•dat•ed /aʊtdeɪtɪd/ adj. *Your ideas on education are out-dated.* = no longer in use or no longer accepted (also **obsolete**)

out•do /aʊt'duː/ verb, t. (**outdid**, **outdone**) *Last year we put up a lovely play, but the one we put up this year outdid it.* = to do better than someone else, or oneself at another point in time

out•fit /'aʊtfɪt/ noun, c. **1** *We are buying new outfits for the cricket team.* = a set of the things, specially clothes, needeed for some activity **2** *I want to join your outfit.* = a group of people working together (informal, sometimes not respectful)

out•go•ing /aʊtgəʊɪŋ/ adj. *This meeting is being held to bid farewell to the outgoing Principal.* = (one who is) leaving or giving up a position

out•grow /aʊt'grəʊ/ verb, t. (**outgrew**, **outgrown**) *The boy has outgrown his clothes.* = to grow too big or old for something

out•ing /'aʊtɪŋ/ noun, c. *We are going to the zoo for an outing.* = a pleasure trip

out•land•ish /aʊt'lændɪʃ/ adj. *He came to the meeting wearing outlandish clothes.* = strange (disapproving)

out•law[1] /'aʊtlɔː/ noun, c. *The filmstar was kidnapped by an outlaw.* = a person who has broken the law and is trying to avoid punishment

outlaw[2] verb, t. *The government has outlawed the trade in ivory.* = to declare that something is against the law

out•lay /'aʊtleɪ/ noun, c. *The government is making an outlay of Rs 200 crore on the new factory.* = money spent for some purpose

out•let /'aʊtlet/ noun, c. or u. **1** *The outlet pipe allows you to empty the tank when you want to clean it.* = a pipe through which some gas or liquid can be taken out **2** *The child has so much energy that she needs some outlet, such as sports.* = some activity which allows a person to release (take out) his/her feelings, energy etc. **3** *The company is starting a new outlet to sell its shoes.* = a shop through which the products of a company are sold

out•line[1] /'aʊtlaɪn/ noun, c. **1** *As it was getting dark, I could not see the house clearly but I could see its outline.* = the lines showing the shape of some object **2** *You should produce an outline of your essay before you start writing it.* = the main ideas, without the details

outline[2] verb, t. *The leader of the group outlined his plans to his followers.* = to explain or describe the main ideas or points, without the details

out•live /aʊt'lɪv/ verb, t. *The old king, who died at the age of 115, outlived all his children.* = to live longer than someone else

out•look /'aʊtlʊk/ noun, u. **1** *He has a healthy outlook on life.* = the way in which one thinks about something **2** *What is the outlook for the weather today? Do you think it will rain?* = the possibility that something may happen; what one may expect

out•put /' tpʊt/ noun, u. or c. **1** *He works eighteen hours a day but produces little output.*(u.) = something that is produced after some effort (formal) **2** = the data, results etc. given out by a computer [COMPUTERS] (compare **input**)

out•rage[1] /'aʊtreɪdʒ/ noun, u. *How could you write such horrible things about me? This is an outrage!* = an action that hurts one's feelings or causes pain

outrage[2] verb, t. *The government's action in closing* *down this school has outraged the feelings of the public.* = to cause hurt or anger **outrageous** /aʊt'reɪgəs/ adj. *outrageous behaviour* = shocking, not acceptable

out•side[1] /aʊt'saɪd/ noun, u. *The outside of the house looks more modern than the inside.* = the outer part of something

outside[2] adj. *You can enter the house through an outside door.* = on the outside

outside[3] adv. *It is raining outside.* = on the outside

outsider noun, c. *No one tells me anything about the school because they think I am an outsider.* = a person who does not belong to a group or is not accepted as a member of a group **outside chance** adj. = not very likely **outside interests** adj. = having nothing to do with work

out•spo•ken /aʊt'spəʊkən/ adj. *People respect him because he is outspoken and not afraid to tell the truth.* = expressing one's feelings openly, without fear (sometimes disapproving)

out•source /'aʊtsɜːs/ verb, t. *American software companies are outsourcing a lot of their work to companies in India.* = to arrange for another person, company etc. to do some work for one's company

out•stand•ing /aʊt'stændɪŋ/ adj. **1** *an outstanding student* = much better than others **2** *outstanding payments* = not paid, completed etc.

out•weigh /aʊt'weɪ/ verb, t. *He is lazy but honest. His good qualities outweigh his faults.* = to be greater in value than something else

out•wit /aʊt'wɪt/ verb, t. = to do something more clever than someone and get an advantage over them

o•va /'əʊvə/ noun, c. (plural of **ovum**) = the eggs produced by a woman or female animal, from which a baby is born **ovary** noun, c. (**ovaries**) = the part of the body of a woman or female animal that produces eggs **ovulate** /'ɒvjʊleɪt/ verb, i. = to produce eggs inside the body, before they are fertilized

o•val /'əʊvəl/ adj. *an oval table* = egg-shaped (see pic under **shapes**)

o•va•tion /əʊ'veɪʃən/ noun, u. *When Ganguly scored his century the crowd gave him a standing ovation.* = happiness expressed by a crowd by clapping, shouting etc.

ov•en /'ʌvən/ noun, c. = a kind of box in which food is baked (cooked) by heating the air inside

o•ver[1] /'əʊvə^r/ prep. **1** *Our plane is flying over the city of Agra.* = above **2** *He wears a coat over his sweater.* = on top of **3** *There is a bridge over the river.* = from one side to the other **4** *We travelled over a large part of Uttar Pradesh.* = in many parts of **5** *Ashoka ruled over the whole of India.* = in control of **6** *He has read over 3,000 books on this subject.* = more than **7** *I received this news over the telephone.* = by means of

over[2] adv. **1** *The wind was so strong that it blew the tree over.* = down **2** *You can come over to our house whenever you like.* = across **3** *The child rolled over in its sleep.* = from one side to another **4** *This book is meant for children of five and over.* = more than **5** *If you make a mistake you will have to type it over again.* = once more

over[3] adj. *The examination is over.* = finished

over[4] noun, c. *He bowled a maiden over.* = a set of six or eight balls from the same direction, by the same bowler [SPORTS]

over- /'əʊvə/ prefix meaning **1** much more than usual e.g. **overload**[1] /əʊvə'ləʊd/ verb, t. *This truck is meant to carry only five tonnes of coal but you have put more than eight tonnes on it. You have overloaded the truck.* = to put too much load (weight) on someone or something **overload**[2] noun, u. *There is an overload of three tonnes on this truck.* = the amount by which a load exceeds (is more than) the correct load **2** too much e.g. **overdo** /əʊvə'duː/ verb, t. (**overdid**, **overdone**) *I had asked him to cook a good meal for the guests, but he has overdone things and cooked 15 dishes.* = to do more than is required **3** completely e.g. **overjoyed** /əʊvə'dʒɔɪd/ adj. *He was overjoyed when he heard that all the children in the class had passed the examination.* = extremely happy **4** outer e.g. **overcoat** /'əʊvəkəʊt/ noun **5** extra e.g. **overtime** /'əʊvətaɪm/ noun, adv. **6** above e.g. **overcast** /əʊvə'kɑːst/ adj. *The sky is overcast. I think it will rain.* = to be covered with dark clouds

over-act /əʊvər'ækt/ verb, i. *Dilip Kumar has over-acted in this film.* = to act in an unnatural way in a film or drama (disapproving)

o•ver•all[1] /əʊvər'ɔːl/ adj. *He is in over-all charge of the office.* = including everything

overall[2] adv. *He has many faults but overall, he is a good worker.* = when everything is considered

o•ver•awe /əʊvər'ɔː/ verb, t. *I was so overawed by her personality that I could not say a word to her.* = to be unable to speak out of respect or fear

o•ver•bear•ing /əʊvə'beərɪŋ/ adj. *an overbearing manner* = proud and trying to take control of others (derogatory)

o•ver•charge /əʊvə'tʃɑːdʒ/ verb, t. *The house-owner wants me to pay a rent of Rs 1000 for this tiny house. I feel he is overcharging me.* = to ask someone to pay more than he/she should pay (disapproving)

o•ver•come /əʊvə'kʌm/ verb, t. (**overcame**) **1** *The soldiers overcame the enemy.* = to defeat **2** *I managed to overcome my shyness and acted in the* *school play.* = of a habit, a sickness, a disability etc., to bring oneself out of it successfully by effort and determination

o•ver•crowd•ed /əʊvə'kraʊdɪd/ adj. *The bus is overcrowded. It is carrying more than 70 passengers.* = to have too many people within a space

o•ver•dose /'əʊvədəʊs/ noun, c. *The doctor had asked him to take some aspirin for his headache and he took six tablets. That was a big overdose.* = too much of some medicine

o•ver•draft /'əʊvədrɑːft/ noun, c. *The bank has allowed him an overdraft of Rs 20,000.* = a sum of money which a bank allows a person to draw (take out), which is more than the money which he/she has put into the bank

o•ver•es•ti•mate /əʊvər'estɪmeɪt/ verb, t. *I had thought I would need Rs 3,000 to get my car repaired but I actually spent less than 2,000. I had over-estimated the expenses.* = to estimate (calculate) that an amount required for some purpose will be greater than it actually is

o•ver•flow /əʊvə'fləʊ/ verb, t. or i. (**overflowed**) *There was so much rain this year that the river overflowed its banks.*(t.)= to flow over the edges of something

o•ver•haul[1] /əʊvə'hɔːl/ verb, t. **1** *We will have to overhaul this car. It is badly in need of repair.* = to examine something thoroughly and repair it if necessary **2** *He had a slow start in the race, but after that he ran so fast that he overhauled the other runners.* = to come from behind and to get ahead of someone (also **overtake**)

overhaul[2] noun, c. *The car is running very well after the overhaul.* = the act of repairing something throughly

o•ver•head /əʊvə'hed/ adv. or adj. *The kites are flying overhead.*(adv.) = above one's head **overhead projector** noun, c. = a machine that projects (throws) pictures on a wall, at a level higher than the heads of the people who are looking at the pictures **overheads** noun, c. (always plural) *Our company is losing money because of the high overheads.* = money which has to be spent regularly to keep a business running

o•ver•hear /əʊvə'hɪəʳ/ verb, t. (**overheard**) *I overheard the Principal telling the teachers that Rahim has come first in the exam.* = to hear accidentally something which one is not supposed to hear

o•ver•in•dulge /əʊvərɪn'dʌldʒ/ verb, i. *I overindulged at the party and had about eight helpings of ice-cream. As a result, I am ill today.* = to have too much of something that one likes, especially food and drink

o•ver•land /əʊvə'lænd/ adv. *We will take a flight to Chennai and then travel overland to Madurai.* = across the land (by train, bus, or car and not by air or sea)

o•ver•lap[1] /əʊvə'læp/ verb, t. or i. *I worked in this college from 1970 to 1975, whereas you worked here from 1973 to 1980. These two periods overlap.*(i.) = to cover a part of something and to go beyond it

overlap[2] noun, u. or c. *There is a slight overlap between the roof of this house and the roof of the next house.*(u.) = the amount by which one thing overlaps (goes beyond) something else

o•ver•look /əʊvə'lʊk/ verb, t. **1** *His house, which is on top of a hill, overlooks the town.* = to have or provide (give) a view of something from above **2** *I made a spelling mistake in my essay but the teacher did not point it out. She must have overlooked it.* = to miss or not to notice either knowingly or unknowingly **3** *Please overlook my faults.* = to pay no attention to

o•ver•night /əʊvə'naɪt/ adv. **1** *We will stay overnight in Kolkata.* = for the night **2** *She opened a new shop overnight.* = very quickly; suddenly **overnight** adj. **an overnight journey** = requiring the whole of the night

o•ver•pop•u•lat•ed /əʊvə'pɒpjʊleɪtɪd/ adj. *Most people think Delhi is over-populated.* = to have too many people living in a place

o•ver•pow•er /əʊvə'paʊəʳ/ verb, t. *The man was overpowered by the two thieves and they took away his wallet.* = to defeat completely through greater strength

o•ver•rate /əʊvə'reɪt/ verb, t. *His reputation as a singer is overrated. Actually, he is an ordinary singer.* = to have too high an opinion of someone or something

o•ver•re•act /əʊvəri'aekt/ verb, i. *The writer over-reacted and became very angry when someone pointed out a mistake in her writing.* = to become angry or upset over a small thing

o•ver•ride[1] /əʊvə'raɪd/ verb, t. (**overrode**, **over-ridden**) *The members of the club had decided to go to Puri for the picnic but the president of the club overrode them and said they would go to Goa instead.* = to use one's official position to take a decision that goes against some other decision (also **overrule**)

override[2] noun, c. = a device that can be used to make something continue to work if the electricity or the electronic functions fail

o•ver•run /əʊvə'rʌn/ verb, t. (**overran**, **overrun**) *The fields are overrun by grasshoppers.* = to conquer by spreading over something in great numbers

o•ver•seas /əʊvə'siːz/ adv. *She is being sent overseas for training.* = to a foreign country

o•ver•see /əʊvə'siː/ verb, t. (**oversaw**, **overseen**)

The new manager will oversee the setting up of the new factory. = to look after something and make sure that it is done properly

o•ver•shad•ow /əʊvəˈʃædəʊ/ verb, t. *Shabana Azmi acted quite well in the film but Rakhee overshadowed her.* = to do much better than someone else

o•ver•sight /ˈəʊvəsaɪt/ noun, u. or c. *I checked the accounts carefully but I didn't notice that there was a mistake on the last page. It was an oversight.* = failure to notice something that one should have noticed

o•ver•sleep /əʊvəˈsliːp/ verb, i. **(overslept)** *She overslept and was late for the cinema.* = to sleep longer than one should have

o•ver•step /əʊvəˈstep/ verb, t. *You are only the manager of this company, working under the Managing Director. You have overstepped your authority by hiring so many new workers.* = to go beyond the limits of something e.g. one's power or authority

o•vert /ˈəʊvɜːt/ adj. *Many people liked my plan but no one gave me overt support.* = (some action that is) done openly and not in a hidden or secret way (opposite **covert**)

o•ver•take /əʊvəˈteɪk/ verb, t. (**overtook, overtaken**) *Our car is so fast that it can easily overtake all the other cars.* = to go faster than or to come from behind and pass something or someone that is moving slower

o•ver•throw /əʊvəˈθrəʊ/ verb, t. (**overthrew, overthrown**) *The Americans fought against British rule and overthrew it after the War of Independence.* = to defeat and remove from power

o•ver•turn /əʊvəˈtɜːn/ verb, i. or t. **1** *The car overturned but no one was hurt.*(i.) = to turn upside down **2** *The Supreme Court overturned the High Court's judgement.*(t.) = to go against what someone else has decided earlier (specially someone who is in a less powerful position)

o•ver•view /ˈəʊvəvjuː/ noun, c. *I will present an overview of the work done by us during the year.* = a short account of something giving only the main points, without the details

o•ver•weight adj. /əʊvəˈweɪt/ *The child is only six years old but he weighs 75 kg. He is overweight.* = weighing more than is usual

o•ver•whelm /əʊvəˈwelm/ verb, t. *The Sri Lankan team overwhelmed the Australian team and defeated it by an innings and 200 runs.* = to defeat completely by using much greater force **overwhelming** adj. *The Australians secured an overwhelming victory over the Sri Lankans.* = very great

o•ver•work /əʊvəˈwɜːk/ noun, u. *He has been working 15 hours a day for the last three months and has become ill due to overwork.* = too much work

o•vip•ar•ous /əʊˈvɪpərəs/ adj. *Some snakes are oviparous—they lay eggs; but other snakes are viviparous. They give birth directly to young ones.* = (animals) which lay eggs (opposite **viviparous**) [BIOLOGY]

ovum, ovulate = see **ova**

owe /əʊ/ verb, t. **1** *You owe me Rs 500, which you borrowed last year. When are you going to return the money?* = to have to pay back money which was taken as a loan **2** *You owe a lot to the teachers who taught you when you were a child.* = to be grateful for something that was received

owl /aʊl/ noun, c. = a bird with large eyes that is active mostly at night (see pic under **bird**)

own[1] /əʊn/ det. *You must travel by your own car and not by taxi.*

own[2] pron. *She has no children of her own.* = belonging to oneself and not to someone else

own[3] verb, t. **1** *She owns a house in the city.* = to possess or have **2** *I must own that this essay was written by my brother and not by me.* = to admit (formal, old-fashioned) **owner** noun, c. *He is the owner of the house I live in.* = a person to whom something belongs

to own up *They are looking for the person who broke the window. Why don't you own up?* = to admit that one has done something wrong (informal) **to come into one's own** *She was helping backstage in all our plays, but as an actor she has finally come into her own.* = to have the opportunity to do something that one is specially good at **to hold one's own** *Though she was in the company of experienced tennis players, she held her own and played very well.* = to prove to be as good as others

ox /ɒks/ noun, c. (**oxen** or **oxes**) = a male animal belonging to the family of cattle (cows and bulls) which has had its sex organs removed (also **bullock**)

ox•y•gen /ˈɒksɪdʒən/ noun = a gas present in the air which is necessary for all forms of life **oxygenate** verb, t. *Blood from different parts of the body is oxygenated in the lungs.* = to make blood pure by adding oxygen to it **oxide** noun, c. *nitrous oxide* = a compound in which oxygen is combined with some other chemical element e.g. copper oxide **oxidize (oxidise)** verb, t. or i. *If you leave a piece of iron lying on the ground, it will oxidize and form rust.*(t.) = to combine with oxygen

oy•ster /ˈɔɪstəʳ/ noun, c. or u. = a kind of animal with a hard shell living in the water, inside which pearls are sometimes found

o•zone /ˈəʊzəʊn/ noun = a form of oxygen (There is a layer of ozone above the earth's surface which protects it from harmful radiation.)

O

pP

p, P /pi:/ the sixteenth letter of the English alphabet

p. abbr. of **1 page** (referring to the number of a page in a book) **2 paise** = (India) **3 pence** (U.K) = units of money

pa /pɑ:/ noun = a form of address for one's father (informal)

PA noun abbr. of **Personal Assistant** (e.g. *PA to the Chief Minister*)

pace[1] /peɪs/ noun, u. or c. **1** *He walked at a slow pace.* = speed **2** *The bowler measured off 20 paces and started his run.* = a step taken by a person

pace[2] verb, i. or t. **1** *The guards paced up and down outside the bank.*(i.) = to walk with slow and regular steps **2** *The runner who is in the lead has been asked to pace the other runners.*(t.) = to set the speed for someone who is running **pace bowler** noun = a fast bowler [CRICKET] **pacemaker** noun = a small electrical machine fitted inside the chest of a person with a weak heart, in order to make it beat at the normal speed

pach•y•derm /'pækɪdɜ:m/ noun = an animal with a thick skin e.g. an elephant [BIOLOGY]

pac•i•fis•m /'pæsɪfɪzəm/ noun, u. = the belief that war is always bad and must be avoided **pacifist** noun, c. = a person who believes in pacifism **pacify** verb, t. *You might be able to pacify that child who is crying by telling her a story.* = to make someone calm **pacifier** noun, c. = a piece of rubber given to a baby to suck in order to make it calm

pack[1] /pæk/ verb, t. or i. **1** *I have to pack as I am leaving for Delhi tonight.*(i.) // *Pack these books in cardboard boxes.*(t.) = to put one's belongings (clothes, books etc.) into boxes,suitcases etc for storing or before travelling **2** *Pack a lunch for the journey.* = put food etc. into a box to be eaten later **3** *On the day of the match, thousands of fans packed the stadium.*(t.) = to fill up a space completely **4** *Pack some salt around the trunk of the coconut tree.* = to arrange and press something against or around something in order to protect it or treat it

pack[2] noun, c. **1** *Don't forget to carry a pack of playing cards for this long journey.* = a whole set of cards etc. **2** *a pack of cigarettes* = a small,light container in which a number of the same things have been packed (stored) **3** *a pack of wolves* = a group of wild animals that hunt together

to pack (somebody) off *We packed the children off so we could rest after our illness.* = to send someone away quickly so that they do not cause any trouble (informal, disrespectful) **to send someone packing** = to send someone away in a forceful way, without respect (informal) **to pack up 1** *It's late. Let's pack up.* = to bring the work one is doing to an end and leave (informal) **2** *My computer's packed up. Can I use yours?* = (of a machine) to stop working and be in need of repair (informal)

pack•age[1] /'pækɪdʒ/ noun, c. *He has received a package of books from America.* = (see **packet**)

package[2] verb, t. *If you want to sell your products, you must package them more attractively.* = to display something in an attractive package for sale **package deal** noun, c. = an agreement containing a number of conditions (things that must be agreed to) **package tour** noun = a plan for a tour (a holiday spent away from one's home) which includes a number of things (e.g. stay in a hotel, meals etc.) in addition to the cost of travelling, so that one does not have to pay separately for them **a software package** noun = a group of (software) items which together form a set for a specific purpose e.g. the Windows package

pack•et /'pækɪt/ noun, c. *a packet of sweets* = a number of things put together in a single container (also **package**)

pact /pækt/ noun, c. *The two countries made a pact to help each other if there was a war.* = agreement (usually between countries)

pad[1] /pæd/ noun, c. **1** *a letterpad* = sheets of paper held together and used for writing, drawing etc. **2** *The doctor covered the wound with a cotton pad.* = soft material (cotton, cloth etc.) put inside something (e.g. a dress) or used to cover something to make it more comfortable or to give it shape **3** = the soft fleshy part on the lower side of the foot of some animals (e.g. dogs, cats)

pad[2] verb, t. (**padded**) **1** *The tailor has padded the shoulders of my jacket.* = to put a pad inside a garment (dress) in order to make it more comfortable or to give it shape **2** *He has padded his essay and made it rather long, but he does not have much to say.* = to make a piece of writing or speech longer by using more words than are necessary **3** *He padded about the house in cloth slippers, so as not to disturb anyone.* = to walk slowly and carefully without making any sound **padding** noun, u. **1** = soft material used to make pads **2** = words used unnecessarily in a piece of writing or speech

pad•dle[1] /'pædl/ noun, c. = a short pole with a wide, flat blade at one end, which is held in the hands and used to row a boat (make it move through the water)

paddle[2] verb, t. or i. (**paddled**) **1** *She paddled the boat gently along the river.*(t.) = to row a boat using a paddle **2** *The dog paddled through the water.*(i.) = to swim by using the feet, as a dog or duck does **3** *The children were paddling happily in the sea.*(i.) = to walk about in water which is not deep

pad•dy /'pædi/ noun, u. or c. (**paddies**) **1** *paddy seedlings* = rice that is still growing on a plant and has not become ripe **2** (u.) = ripe grains of rice from which the husk (outer covering) has not been removed **3** *rice paddies*(c.) = a field in which rice is grown (This use is not common in India.)

pad•lock[1] /'pædlɒk/ noun, c. = a large lock used to fasten (close) a door, box, bicycle etc., which can be removed when not required

padlock[2] verb, t. *padlock the front door* = to close with a padlock

pa•dre /'pɑ:dri/ noun, c. = a Christian priest

pa•gan /'peɪgən/ noun, c. **1** = a word used in former times to describe a person who was not a Christian and who worshipped many gods and goddesses (derogatory) **2** = a person with no religion (who often follows beliefs/practices that do not belong to any of the main religions of the world) (derogatory)

page[1] /peɪdʒ/ noun, c. **1** *a page from a book* = one side of a printed sheet of paper in a book etc. **2** = the text or images seen on a computer screen at a time **3** = a boy who works for a hotel or club and carries messages (old-fashioned)

page[2] verb, t. *Page the doctor. We need him at once.* = to call someone, using a loudspeaker or a pager (paging machine) **pager** noun, c. = a small machine like a telephone, which can be carried in the pocket and which rings when the owner of the machine is paged (called) by someone

pag•eant /'pædʒənt/ noun, c. *On Republic Day each year, there is a colourful pageant on the streets of Delhi.* = a public show held on special occasions, in which people move in a procession

pa•go•da /pə'gəʊdə/ noun, c. = a Hindu or Buddhist place of worship found in India, Srilanka or East Asia

pain[1] /peɪn/ noun, u. or c. **1** *He felt a severe pain when he hit himself on the knee.*(c.)= feeling of suffering or discomfort caused by an injury or illness **2** = a feeling of sadness caused by something unpleasant

pain[2] verb, t. or i. **1** *Does it pain?*(i.) = to feel pain in some part of the body **2** *It pains me that you no longer think I am your friend.*(t.) = to feel sad about something **painful** adj. *It was very painful to get up after I fell from the swing.* = causing pain **painless** *My tooth was taken out in a painless way.* = without causing pain **painkiller** noun, c. = a medicine which takes away pain **pains** noun, u. (always plural) *The man has taken good care of us and we should pay him something extra for his pains.* = hard work or effort **painstaking** adj. *It took four months of painstaking effort for Satish to finish the painting.* = careful, patient and hardworking

to take pains (always plural) *She took great pains to make sure we were comfortable.* = to take great trouble to do something **a pain in (the neck)** = someone who gives a person a lot of trouble or annoys them (informal)

paint[1] /peɪnt/ noun, u. or c. = liquid colouring matter which is spread over a surface or a picture to colour it

paint[2] verb, t. **1** *He is painting the door blue.* = to put paint on a surface or a picture so as to give it a colour **2** = to put colouring material on one's face or fingernails **paints** (always plural) = tubes or blocks of painting material **painting** noun, c. *That's a beautiful painting of the Taj Mahal!* = a picture drawn by an artist, using paints **painter** noun, c. **1** = a person who paints surfaces such as doors, houses, cars etc. **2** = an artist who makes paintings **paintbrush** = a brush used to dip into paint and spread over a wall etc.

to paint a sad/gloomy/rosy etc. picture of something *Sawan painted a gloomy picture of the hospital, so I decided not to go there for my operation.* = to talk about something in a certain way in order to create a certain kind of feeling **to paint the town red** = to have a good time dancing, eating etc. in a way which makes people notice

pair[1] /peə^r/ noun, c. **1** *a pair of birds* = two animals of the same kind which live together, one of which is a male and the other a female **2** = people who are connected in some way e.g. a pair of singers **3** *a pair of shoes* = two things of the same kind which are used together **4** *a pair of trousers* = something made out of two similar parts which are joined together

pair[2] verb, t. *to pair someone with someone else* = to form a pair by bringing two people or two things together

pal /pæl/ noun, c. = a close friend (informal) **pally** adj. *He is trying to be pally.* = friendly (informal)

pal•ace /'pælɪs/ noun, c. = a very large building in which a king, queen or president lives **palatial** /pə'leɪʃəl/ adj. *a palatial building* = very large and grand, like a palace

pal•an•quin /pælən'ki:n/ noun, c. = a carriage without wheels, carried on the shoulders of human beings, in which people ride

pal•ate /'pælɪt/ noun **1** = the top inside part of the mouth **2** *This food is sure to please your palate.* = desire for good food **palatable** adj. **1** *palatable food* = having good taste **2** *He did not find my advice palatable.* = acceptable (to one's liking) **palatal** adj. *a palatal sound* = a sound produced while making some part of the tongue touch the palate [TECHNICAL]

pale[1] /peɪl/ adj. **1** *He looks pale and sickly.* = having

P

little colour in the face or skin **2** *a pale blue dress* = light in colour

pale[2] verb, i. **1** *He paled when he saw the blood on my face.* = to become pale as a result of blood flowing away from the face, usually because of fear or surprise **2** *The beauty of Switzerland pales in comparison to that of Pokhra in Nepal.* = to appear less when compared to something else

pal•e•o•lith•ic /pæliəʊ'lɪθɪk/ adj. = belonging to the Stone Age (the time, very long ago, when people did not know how to use metals and made weapons and tools out of stone)

pal•e•on•tol•o•gy (palaeontology) /pælien'tɒlədʒi/ noun, c. = the study of **fossils** (plants or animals that died thousands of years ago and have turned into stone)

pal•ette /'pælɪt/ noun, c. = a curved piece of wood on which an artist mixes the paints which he/she uses to paint pictures

pall[1] /pɔ:l/ verb, i. *I used to enjoy tandoori chicken but I have been eating it so often that the taste has palled.* = to become less attractive because of having or doing something repeatedly

pall[2] noun, c. **1** = a large piece of cloth used to cover a dead body or a coffin (the box in which a dead body is kept) **2** *The city was covered by a pall of darkness.* = covering **pallbearer** noun, c. = a person who carries a dead person or a coffin on his/her shoulder during a funeral (the ceremony of burying or cremating a person after death)

pal•li•a•tive /'pæliətɪv/ noun, c. *You should not use painkillers when you get a headache. A painkiller is only a palliative.* = something that reduces pain or suffering but does not cure a disease or get rid of a problem

palm /pɑ:m/ noun, c. **1** *a coconut palm* = a tree belonging to the family of palms (tall, thin trees with a bunch of large leaves at the top) **2** *the palm of the hand* = the soft, fleshy part of the hand between the fingers and the wrist which is covered with many lines **palm top** = a small hand-held computer that can be carried in the pocket [COMPUTERS]

to carry off the palm = to win the top prize in a competition **to read someone's palm** = to tell someone about the future by examining the lines in the palm of the hand **to palm something off** *The shop-keeper managed to palm off a damaged radio to one of his customers.* = to get rid of something which is bad or unacceptable (informal)

palm•ist•ry /'pɑ:mɪstrɪ/ noun, u. = the practice of telling a person's future by examining the lines on the palm of his/her hand **palmist** noun = a person who practises palmistry

pal•pa•ble /'pælpəbəl/ adj. **1** *He told me that he owned many houses in the city, but I could see that it was a palpable lie.* = obvious (which one can see at once) **2** *The people looked relaxed, but the feeling of anxiety was quite palpable.* = something that can almost be touched or felt

pal•pi•ta•tion /pælpɪ'teɪʃən/ noun, c. *The doctor listened to the palpitation of my heart through his stethoscope.* = the sound of a person's heart beat beating at an unusually high speed **palpitate** /'pælpɪteɪt/ verb, i. *Why is your heart palpitating?* = to beat very fast (used to describe a person's heartbeat)

pal•sy /'pɔ:lzi/ noun *cerebral palsy* = a condition that affects the brain and causes loss of feeling in the limbs

pal•try /'pɔ:ltri/ adj. *a paltry salary of Rs 150 a month* = so small as to have no value

pam•per /'pæmpə[r]/ verb, t. *You are pampering your children by giving them too many toys.* = to give someone too much attention or love

pam•phlet /'pæmflɪt/ noun, c. *a political pamphlet* = a small printed book or sheet dealing with some matter of public interest **pamphleteer** /pæmfli'tɪə[r]/ noun, c. = a person who writes pamphlets, specially on political matters

pan[1] /pæn/ noun, c. **1** *a frying pan* = a metal pot used for cooking **2** *the pan of a balance* = a small container at each end of a balance in which something which is to be weighed is placed

pan[2] verb, i. or t. (**panned**) **1** *The camera panned slowly from one end of the room to the other.*(i.) = to move a camera (while making a film) slowly from one side to another, in order to produce a sense of movement **2** *The new book written by this author has been panned by all the critics.*(t.) = to criticize (to say that something is bad) (informal)

pan- /pæn/ prefix meaning 'including all' e.g. **pan-Indian** *a pan-Indian language* = a language that is spoken in all parts of India

pan•a•ce•a /pænə'sɪə/ noun, c. *I don't agree that education is a panacea for all evils. We face many problems.* = something that one thinks (not very wisely) can solve most problems or cure most diseases (often disapproving)

pa•nache /pə'næʃ/ noun, u. *She spoke with such panache that everyone applauded her speech.* = a stylish and graceful manner of doing things

pan•cake /'pæŋkeɪk/ noun, c. = a kind of thin, flat cake

pan•cre•as /'pæŋkriəs/ noun = an organ near the stomach which produces insulin, a chemical that controls the amount of sugar in the blood [BIOLOGY]

pan•da /'pændə/ noun = a large black and white animal that looks like a bear, found in China

pan•de•mo•ni•um /pændɪˈməʊniəm/ noun, u. *When there is no teacher in the class, the children shout and run about wildly, creating pandemonium.* = noise and disorder

pan•der /ˈpændəʳ/ verb, t. *Some magazines pander to the low tastes of their readers by printing gossip about film stars.* = to give someone what he/she wants, even when you know this is wrong (disapproving)

Pan•do•ra's box /pændɔːrez ˈbɒks/ noun = a source of trouble

to open a Pandora's box *Leave that problem alone. You will open a Pandora's box if you talk about it.* = to do something which creates a number of unwanted problems

pane /peɪn/ noun, c. *a window pane* = a sheet of glass fitted to a window

pan•e•gyr•ic /pænɪˈdʒɪrɪk/ noun, c. *The newspaper published a panegyric on the writer, calling him the father of the modern novel.* = something written or spoken to praise someone highly

pan•el /ˈpænl/ noun, c. **1** *a concrete wall decorated with teak panels* = a piece of wood or some other material fixed over a surface of a different material **2** *the control panel on an aircraft* = a board into which different controls (instruments, switches etc.) for a machine are fitted **3** *a panel of experts* = a group of people chosen to perform some special work (e.g. to hold an interview to select someone for a job) **panelist** noun, c. = a person who is chosen to be a member of a panel (special group)

pang /pæŋ/ noun, c. *pangs of hunger* = a sharp pain **pangs of love** (always plural) = the unhappiness which someone in love feels when separated from the loved one (figurative)

pan•ic[1] /ˈpænɪk/ noun, u. or c. (always singular) *It is true that we are late but there is no cause for panic.*(u.) // *Some people created a panic by shouting that the house was on fire.*(c.) = sudden and very great fear or anxiety for which there is usually no reason

panic[2] verb, i. *Don't panic! We are perfectly safe here.* = to feel fear in a sudden and uncontrolled way **panicky** adj. *Don't get so panicky!* = to be in a state of panic (informal)

to push the panic button = to raise an alarm or do something in haste as a result of being in a state of panic (informal) **a panic sale** = a sale made in haste, usually because one is afraid that the price will come down further and the seller will suffer a loss

pan•o•ra•ma /pænəˈrɑːmə/ noun, c. **1** *As our plane was flying low, we could enjoy the beautiful panorama of the green forest spread below us.* = a view of a wide area of land, seen from a height **2** *This novel presents a panorama of life in the eighteenth century.* = an account or description of something vast (very big and wide)

pan•sy /ˈpænzi/ noun, c. (**pansies**) **1** = a garden plant that produces small, flat flowers of different colours **2** = a man who behaves like a woman (slang, derogatory)

pant[1] /pænt/ verb, i. *The girl was panting as she had been running to catch the bus.* = to breathe fast, taking short breaths

pant[2] noun, c. = a short, quick breath

pan•ta•loons /pæntəˈluːnz/ noun, c. (always plural) = loose fitting trousers worn by men in earlier times

pan•the•ism /ˈpænθiɪzəm/ noun = a religion based on the worship of Nature **pantheist** noun, c. = one who worships Nature

pan•the•on /ˈpænθiən/ noun, c. *The ancient Greeks had a pantheon of gods and goddesses of whom Zens was the king.* = the complete set of gods worshipped by the followers of a religion which believes in more than one god

pan•ther /ˈpænθəʳ/ noun, c. = a fierce wild animal belonging to the cat family, similar to a leopard

pan•to•mime /ˈpæntəmaɪm/ noun, c. = a play (drama) based on a fairy story and produced for children, especially during Christmas

pan•try /ˈpæntri/ noun, c. (**pantries**) = a small room in a house, next to the kitchen, where food is stored

pants /pænts/ noun, c. (always plural) = trousers or shorts (informal)

pap /pæp/ noun, u. = very soft food given to babies or sick people

pa•pa /pəˈpɑː/ noun, c. = a form of address used for one's father (informal)

pa•pa•ya /pəˈpaɪə/ noun = a kind of yellow fruit that grows on a tall tree in warm climates (also **pawpaw**)

pa•per[1] /ˈpeɪpəʳ/ noun, u. or c. **1** (u.) = the material used for writing or printing books etc. **2** *an evening paper*(c.) = newspaper **3** *an examination paper*(c.) = a set of printed questions given out to someone who is taking an examination **4** *papers presented at a conference*(c.) = something written on a subject, meant to be read out at a conference or printed in a journal or book **5** *government papers*(c.) = record or document

paper[2] verb, t. *The walls are being papered.* = to cover something with paper **paperweight** noun, c. = a small object that is heavy enough to weigh down loose papers so that the wind does not carry them away **paperwork** noun, u. *They have agreed to our offer on the phone but you will have to take care of the paperwork.* = the work of writing reports,documents etc. and keeping them in files **paper qualifications** adj. **1** = relating to one's

P

education, the degree one has etc. **2** = qualifications (degrees etc.) on paper, as against one's actual practical experience (often derogatory)

papiermâché /pæpieɪˈmæʃeɪ/ noun, u. *toys made of papiermâché* = paper which has been boiled into a soft mass and then made hard, used for making different objects e.g. toys

pap•ri•ka /ˈpæprɪkə/ noun = a red powder made from a kind of chilli which is not very hot, used to add taste and colour to food

pa•py•rus /pəˈpaɪərəs/ noun = a kind of water-plant from which paper was made in Egypt in ancient times

par /pɑːʳ/ noun, u. **1** *If you compare these two bowlers, you will find they are at par.* = of the same level or quality; equal **2** *He usually bowls well but today his bowling was below par.* = below or less than the usual level or standard (informal) **3** *The shares of this company are selling at par.* = the same value at which a share was first bought by someone [TECHNICAL] **4** = the number of strokes taken by a player to hit a golf ball into a hole [SPORTS]

par excellence /pɑːrˈeksəlɑːns/ adj. (French) *Anju George is our ace athlete, par excellence.* = without an equal

parity /ˈpærɪti/ noun, u. *Our football team has been working hard to achieve parity with the other teams.* = the state of being equal to someone else

para- /pærə/ prefix meaning **1** beyond e.g. **paranormal** /pærəˈnɔːməl/ adj. *paranormal phenomena* = beyond science; not explainable by science **2** almost but not fully qualified for something e.g. **paramedic** /pærəˈmedɪk/ noun, c. = a person who is trained to give some medical help at the place of an accident but is not a doctor

par•a•ble /ˈpærəbəl/ noun, c. *Buddha and Christ used parables to teach their followers.* = a simple story which teaches a lesson

pa•rab•o•la /pəˈræbələ/ noun, c. = a curved line which is like the path of a bullet fired from a gun, or a ball when thrown in the air, which then falls towards the earth [TECHNICAL]

par•a•chute /ˈpærəʃuːt/ noun, c. = a large, round piece of nylon cloth shaped like an umbrella, to which ropes are tied and with the help of which a person can drop slowly to the ground from a flying aircraft without getting hurt **parachutist** noun, c. = a person who is trained to drop from an aircraft, using a parachute **paratrooper** /pærəˈtruːpəʳ/ noun, c. = a soldier who is carried in an aircraft to a place where a battle is being fought and who then drops out of the aircraft with the help of a parachute

parachute

pa•rade[1] /pəˈreɪd/ noun, c. *a military parade* = a ceremony in which people march together in front of people who are watching them

parade[2] verb, t. **1** *The general is parading his troops.* = to cause soldiers to march together in a parade **2** *We know how clever you are. There is no need for you to parade your cleverness.* = to make a show of something (figurative, derogatory)

par•a•dise /ˈpærədaɪs/ noun, u. **1** = heaven (the place to which the souls of good people are thought to be sent after death, as a reward for being good) **2** *This lake is a paradise for bird lovers.* = a place where one can freely do something that one likes to do

par•a•dox /ˈpærədɒks/ noun, c. *'Let us make haste slowly.' This statement may look like a paradox, but it is true.* = a statement which seems impossible as it combines two opposite things, but which is true **paradoxical** /pærəˈdɒksɪkəl/ adj.

par•af•fin /ˈpærəfɪn/ noun, u. = kerosene (a term commonly used in Britain)

par•a•gon /ˈpærəgən/ noun, c. *a paragon of wisdom* = a model or perfect example of some good quality (often humorous)

par•a•graph /ˈpærəgrɑːf/ noun, c. = a group of sentences which are connected to each other and are generally on the same topic

par•a•keet /ˈpærəkiːt/ noun, c. = a kind of parrot

par•al•lel[1] /ˈpærəlel/ adj. *These two lines are parallel.* = running side by side but always at the same distance from each other (referring to two or more lines)

parallel[2] noun, c. **1** *I want you to draw a parallel.* = a line which runs parallel to another line **2** *This city is full of life. The only parallel I can think of is Delhi.* = something that is similar to (like) something else

parallel[3] verb, t. (**paralleled**) *Mumbai is full of life. The only city which can parallel it is Delhi.* = to be similar to something else **parallelogram** /pærəˈleləʊgræm/ noun, c. = a geometrical figure with four sides, having its opposite sides parallel and equal to each other (see also **rectangle**) (see pic under **shapes**) **parallel port** noun, c. = a special kind of socket at the back of a computer through which the computer can be connected to a printer, scanner, another computer etc.

pa•ral•y•sis /pəˈrælɪsɪs/ noun, u. *He has been suffering from paralysis since his accident.* = damage caused to the brain or the nervous system, resulting in the loss of feeling and the inability to move some or all parts of the body **paralyze (paralyse)** /'pærəlaɪz/ verb, t. **1** *She injured her spine in an accident and is paralyzed.* = to suffer from paralysis **2** *Work has been paralyzed by the strike.* = to cause something to stop working (figurative)

par•a•mil•i•tary /pærə'mɪlɪtərɪ/ noun or adj. *The government is sending the Border Security Force and other paramilitary forces to maintain law and order at the border.*(adj.) = not belonging to the regular army but doing almost the same kind of work

par•a•mount /'pærəmaʊnt/ adj. *the paramount ruler of a country* = highest, greatest or most important (formal)

par•a•noi•a /pærə'nɔɪə/ noun = a disease of the mind which makes a person believe that he/she is likely to be harmed by someone and so cannot trust anyone **paranoiac** noun, c. = a person who suffers from paranoia **paranoid** /'pærənɔɪd/ adj. *He is becoming paranoid.* = suffering from paranoia

par•a•pet /'pærəpɪt/ noun, c. = a low wall at the edge of a roof

par•a•pher•na•li•a /pærəfə'neɪliə/ noun, u. (always singular) *The magician has come with all his paraphernalia and will put up a magic show for the children.* = all the things that are needed for some activity

par•a•phrase[1] /'pærəfreɪz/ noun, c. *I couldn't understand a word of her speech. Can you give me a paraphrase?* = a re-telling or rewriting of something in simpler language

paraphrase[2] verb, t. *Please paraphrase the speech for us.* = to make a paraphrase of something

par•a•ple•gic /pærə'pliːdʒɪk/ noun, c. = a person who is unable to use the lower part of the body

par•a•psy•chol•o•gy /pærəsaɪ'kɒlədʒɪ/ noun = the study of things that are beyond psychology (things that cannot be fully explained by science such as telepathy) (the ability to know another person's thoughts) etc.

par•a•site /'pærəsaɪt/ noun, c. **1** = a plant or animal that lives by getting the food that it needs from another plant or animal **2** = a person who does nothing to earn his or her living but depends on others **parasitic** /pærə'sɪtɪk/ adj. **1** = (of a plant or animal) living off another plant, animal etc. [BIOLOGY] **2** = (of a person) dependant on someone else's money, food, shelter etc. and doing nothing in return (derogatory)

par•a•sol /'pærəsɒl/ noun, c. = a kind of umbrella used by a lady

par•a•ty•phoid /pærə'taɪfɔɪd/ noun = a disease that is almost like typhoid, but less serious

par•boil /'pɑːbɔɪl/ verb, t. *The rice has been parboiled.* = to boil something (specially rice) for a short time

par•cel[1] /'pɑːsəl/ noun, c. **1** *I have received a parcel of books.* = an object or a number of objects wrapped in cloth or paper so that it can be easily carried or sent by post **2** *a parcel of land* = a piece of land

parcel[2] verb, t. (**parcelled**) **1** *I want to buy these books. Will you please parcel them for me?* = to make into a parcel **2** *My land is to be parcelled out and given to my two children.* = to divide

parched /pɑːtʃt/ adj. *There has been no rain for two years and the land is parched.* = completely dry

parch•ment /'pɑːtʃmənt/ noun, u. = a kind of thin leather, made from the dried skin of sheep or goats, used in former times for writing on

par•don[1] /'pɑːdn/ verb, t. *He has not helped me at, but I will pardon him this time.* = to excuse someone who has done something wrong, without punishing him/her

pardon[2] noun, c. *The judge granted him a pardon.* = freedom from punishment

pardon[3] interjec. *Pardon, can you please repeat what you said?* = used to ask a person to repeat what he or she said because one did not hear it **pardonable** adj. *Your offence is pardonable.* = some wrong action that is not very serious and can be pardoned

pardon me for (something) = used when one is about to do something rude e.g. interrupting **I beg your pardon** **1** *'I almost made you fall. I beg your pardon.'* = a formal way of saying that one is sorry **2** *'Did you come today?' 'I beg your pardon?' 'I said, "Did you come today?"'* = a request made to ask someone to repeat something said earlier which could not be heard clearly **3** *'That was a silly thing to say.' 'I beg your pardon!'* = a way of telling someone you don't like what they are saying

pare /peəʳ/ verb, t. **1** *You can use this knife to pare apples.* = to remove or cut away the thin skin or covering of something with a sharp knife **2** *We have to pare our costs down to the minimum.* = to cut down or reduce

par•ent[1] /'peərənt/ noun, c. = one's mother or father **single parent** = a woman or man who is separated from his/her partner and bringing up a child or children on her/his own

parent[2] adj. *The parent company in the U.S.A. has taken control of the Indian branch.* = a business company that sets up branches in other countries **parental** /pə'rentl/ adj. *I have many parental duties.* = of a parent **parentage** /'peərɪntɪdʒ/ noun, u. *She is an Indian citizen but has Sri Lankan parentage.* = the origin of the parents who have given

P

birth to a child **parenthood** noun, u. *They are very happy that they have had a child at last and are really enjoying parenthood.* = the state of being a parent **parenting** noun, u. *You must learn the art of parenting if you want your children to be well-behaved.* = the duties performed by a parent (e.g. education of the children)

pa•ren•the•sis /pə'renθɪsɪs/noun, c. (usually plural **parentheses**) *Mrs Sen is my aunt (mother's sister). The nature of our relationship is explained in the parenthesis.* = the bracket (punctuation mark) that is put before as well as after a word or expression which is used to explain or comment upon another word used in the same sentence

par•ish /'pærɪʃ/ noun, c. = an area which has a church of its own

parity see **par**

park[1] /pɑːk/ noun, c. *a public park* = a large piece of land, usually covered with grass or trees, used by the public for recreation **theme park** = see **theme**

park[2] verb, t. *You can park your car here.* = to leave a car in a place when it is not being used **parking lot** noun, c. = a place where many vehicles are parked

Par•kin•son's dis•ease /'pɑːkɪnsənz/ noun, u. = a disease that some old people suffer from, which causes the limbs to become very weak over time and to shake

par•lia•ment /'pɑːləmənt/ noun, u. or c. = the main law-making body in a country, consisting of members who are directly or indirectly elected by the people **parliamentarian** /'pɑːləmen'teərɪən/ noun, c. = a member of a parliament **parliamentary** /pɑːlə'mentərɪ/ adj. *a parliamentary committee* = relating to the parliament

par•lour /'pɑːləʳ/ noun, c. *a video parlour // beauty parlour* = a shop which sells a special kind of article or offers a special service

pa•ro•chi•al /pə'rəʊkiəl/ adj. *This newspaper is rather parochial. It does not cover issues outside our locality.* = narrow-minded; interested only in people with whom one is directly connected (derogatory)

par•o•dy /'pærədi/ noun, c. (**parodies**) or u. *This new film is a clever parody of the famous film 'Sholay'.* = a book, drama or film which creates humour by copying a well-known book, play or film

pa•role /pə'rəʊl/ noun, u. *The prisoner has been allowed to go home on parole.* = freedom given to a prisoner before the period of his/her stay in jail has ended, on condition that he/she should behave well

par•ri•cide /'pærɪsaɪd/ noun, c. = a person who is guilty of killing his/her own father

par•rot[1] /'pærət/noun, c. = a bird with bright green feathers that can often be taught to copy the sounds of human speech

parrot[2] verb, t. *He was merely parroting your words.* = to copy or repeat the words or ideas of another person without understanding their meaning fully (derogatory)

par•ry /'pæri/ verb, t. (**parried**) **1** *parry a blow* = to escape a blow by a quick movement or by blocking (stopping) the blow **2** *He parried the journalists' questions with clever replies.*(t.) = to avoid answering questions by asking another question or providing a clever reply

pars•ley /'pɑːsli/ noun = a small plant with green leaves, used to give taste to food

part[1] /pɑːt/ noun, c. or u. **1** *Divide this cake into four parts.*(c.) = a piece into which something can be divided **2** *I have to buy some parts for my car.*(c.) = a piece of a machine which helps to make it work **3** *He is taking part in the competition.*(u.) = a share in some activity **4** *He plays the part of a lawyer in this film.*(c.) = role; the character that an actor tries to represent in a drama or film **5** *You have heard only one part of the story.* = some of or a portion of something

part[2] verb, i. or t. **1** *I am afraid you and I have to part.*(i.) = to be separated from each other **2** *You will have to part with this house.* = to be forced to give up something **3** *The curtains parted and the drama began.*(i.) = to spread out (move away from each other) **4** *She parts her hair in the middle.*(t.) = to separate the hair on the head along a line

part[3] adj. *I am only part-owner of this house.* = of only a part (not the whole) **parts** noun (always plural) **1** *the northern and southern parts of the country* **2** *He does not belong to these parts.* = an area or region in a country **3** *He is a man of parts.* = many different skills **part(s) of speech** noun = the different classes into which the words of a language are divided e.g. noun, verb etc.

to part with *When I left the university I had to part with all my books, because I could not carry them back home.* = to give up or give away something **the better part of (something)** *I've been in this school for the better part of twelve years.* = for the greater part of a period of time **in part** *I agree with her in part, but not everything she says is acceptable.* = to some extent, not totally **to be part and parcel of something** *Referring to books in the library is part and parcel of learning.* = to be an essential activity included in something **to part company** **1** = to bring a friendship, marriage etc. to an end **2** = to stop agreeing with someone on an important subject

par•take /pɑː'teɪk/ verb, i. *I want you to partake of this food.* = to have some food or drink (old-fashioned)

par•tial /'pɑːʃəl/ adj. **1** *The meeting was a partial success. It went off quite well, but we had a few* *problems.* = in part (not completely) **2** *I am partial to chocolate cake.* = showing special liking for something or someone **partiality** /pɑːʃi'æliti/ noun, u. = the quality of being partial (showing special favour to someone or something) **partially** adv. **1** *The building was partially hidden by the trees.* = partly **2** *We were treated very partially and given all the comforts while the others were not.* = in a good way as a result of being liked (disapproving)

par•tic•i•pate /pɑː'tɪsɪpeɪt/ verb, i. *All the children will participate in the school play.* = to take part in some activity **participant** noun, c. = one who takes part in some activity

par•ti•ci•ple /'pɑːtɪsɪpəl/ noun, c. *In the sentence 'He has already eaten', 'eaten' is a participle.* = a form of a verb which is non-finite (does not show whether it is in the past tense or present tense) and often ends in '-en' [GRAMMAR]

par•ti•cle /'pɑːtɪkəl/ noun, c. **1** *a particle of dust* = a very tiny piece of something **2** *In the sentence 'I can't put up with this nonsense', the word 'up' is a particle.* = a small word which is generally a preposition, adverb or conjunction and is often used together with a verb [GRAMMAR]

par•tic•u•lar /pə'tɪkjʊlər/ adj. **1** *Are you looking for a particular book for your child, or would you be in interested in just any book?* = something special, considered separately from others **2** *He is very particular about the clothes he wears.* = taking a lot of care in choosing something; choosy **particularly** adv. *I was happy to see you, but I was particulary happy to see your parents.* = especially **particulars** noun, u. (always plural) *I will look for your lost child. Please give me the name and other particulars.* = detailed information about something or someone

part•ing[1] /'pɑːtɪŋ/ noun, u. or c. **1** *Parting from one's friends is painful.*(u.) = the situation when two people (usually two people who like or love each other) leave each other for a period of time or permanently **2** *the parting in a person's hair*(c.) = the line on the head where the hair is parted (divided into two parts)

parting[2] adj. *parting words* = done or spoken at the time of parting (going away)

par•ti•tion[1] /pɑː'tɪʃən/ noun, u. or c. **1** *Many books have been written about the partition of India in 1947.*(u.) = the act of dividing a country into two or more parts **2** *The large hall can be divided into two smaller rooms by using a wooden partition.*(c.) = a wall made of thin wood, cloth etc. that can be easily removed and is used to separate one room from another

partition[2] verb, t. *The brothers decided to partition the family property.* = to divide into two or more parts

part•ly /'pɑːtli/ adv. **1** *I didn't go to school partly because I was ill but also because I was tired.* = to some extent **2** *The ground was partly cemented.* = not fully

part•ner[1] /'pɑːtnər/ noun, c. **1** *He will be my partner in the tennis match.* = one who joins or helps someone in carrying out an activity that is shared between two or more people **2** *This firm has four partners.* = one of the owners of a business who shares the profit or loss with other owners **3** = the person one lives with or is married to

partner[2] verb, t. *She is going to partner me in this match.* = to be one's partner in some activity **partnership** noun, u. or c. **1** *Rahim and Sheila set up a business in partnership.*(u.) = the state of being a partner in some activity **2** *The second wicket partnership between Sehwag and Tendulkar was worth 150 runs.*(c.) = an activity, usually in a game, which two players perform together as partners **3** *The terms of the partnership have been drawn up by a lawyer.*(c.) = a business agreement between two or more partners

par•tridge /'pɑːtrɪdʒ/ noun, c. = a kind of game-bird, hunted for its meat

par•ty[1] /'pɑːti/ noun, c. (**parties**) **1** *There were many guests at the party.* = a social gathering when people come together to eat, drink and enjoy themselves **2** *A party of teachers is visiting our school.* = group **3** *She is starting a new political party.* = a group of people who have the same political ideas and aims and who engage in political activity

party[2] verb, i. *We have won the match. Now we must party.* = to celebrate something by having a party (informal)

pass[1] /pɑːs/ verb, t. or i. **1** *I passed him on the road as I was coming here.*(t.) // *I passed his house.*(t.) // *A train just passed.*(i.) = to reach and move away from something or someone who may be going in the same direction or in a different direction or not moving at all **2** *The car was trying to pass our bus, but the road was too narrow.*(t.) = to overtake; to go ahead of someone by moving faster **3** *The storm will soon pass.*(i.) = to come to an end **4** *He passed the ball to me.*(t.) = to give or send **5** *How do you pass the time?*(t.) = to spend time **6** *He has passed the test.*(t.) = to be successful in a test or examination **7** *Your work is of such poor quality that I cannot pass it.*(t.) = to accept as being satisfactory **8** *The Parliament has passed the new law.*(t.) = to be accepted officially by the parliament

pass[2] noun, c. (**passes**) **1** *She has a railway pass, so she does not need a ticket.* = an official document which allows a person to do something e.g. travel in a

P

bus or train without payment **2** *Many foreign travellers came to India through the Khyber Pass.* = a gap in a chain of mountains which allows a traveller to cross easily **3** *He has managed a pass in the examination.* = a successful result in an examination **4** *He sent a pass to me.* = the act of passing (giving) the ball to another player, in the game of football, hockey, basketball etc. **passbook** noun, c. = a small book which shows how much money a person puts into or takes out of a bank **passable** adj. *He has written a passable book.* = not of high quality but just good enough to be accepted

to pass away (also **to pass on**) = to die (polite use) **to pass down** *This shawl has been passed down from my grandmother to me.* = to give something to someone who will keep it after you die **to pass the buck** = to shift a responsibility to someone else (disapproving) **to pass out** = to become unconscious (also **faint**) **to pass off** *She got her mother to write an essay, but passed it off as her own.* = to make people believe that something is genuine, when it is not **to pass for** *She is only 9, but she can pass for 15 because of her height.* = to seem to be something that one is not **to pass something on** *Could you please pass on this message to your sister?* = to give someone something that you have been asked to give **pass it on** *There is no history class today. Pass it on.* = a way of asking someone to tell others a piece of information you gave them **to pass up** *By not sending in an application, I passed up a good chance to compete for a scholarship.* = to let an opportunity go, on purpose **to make a pass at someone** = to show sexual interest in someone (disapproving)

pas•sage /ˈpæsɪdʒ/ noun, c. or u. **1** *There is a passage which connects the library to the main building.*(c.) = a narrow connecting path **2** *Please read through this passage from the book.*(c.) = a part of a longer piece of writing or speech **3** *The passage of heavy vehicles over this old bridge is not allowed.*(u.) = the action of going across, along or over something **4** *The passage of time will make you forget your grief.* = the flow of time

pas•sen•ger /ˈpæsɪndʒəʳ/ noun, c. *a passenger in a bus* = a person who travels in a vehicle but is not driving or working on it

pas•sion /ˈpæʃən/ noun, u. or c. **1** *He spoke with great passion.*(u.) = strong feeling **2** *You should learn to control your passions.*(c.) (always plural) = a very strong feeling (of love, anger etc.) which may drive a person to do something improper or wrong **3** *He has a passion for Alphonso mangoes.*(c.) = very strong liking (informal) **passionate** adj. **1** *a passionate speech* = full of emotion (feeling) **2** *a passionate person* = easily influenced by passions (desires) **passionately** adv.

pas•sive[1] /ˈpæsɪv/adj. **1** *He remained passive at the meeting and did not say a word.* = not doing or saying anything **2** *'Australia defeated India' is an active sentence, but when you make it passive, it becomes 'India was defeated by Australia'.* = a sentence in which the subject is the person or thing to whom or on which some action is done [GRAMMAR]

passive[2] noun, u. *This sentence is in the passive.* = the passive form (also **passive voice**) **passive smoking** noun = breathing in smoke from cigarettes etc. that other people are smoking **passivize** verb, t. = to change a sentence or verb into the passive form [GRAMMAR]

pass•port /ˈpɑːspɔːt/ noun, c. = an official document given by the government to a person who is a citizen of that country, to show that he/she has permission to leave or enter the country

pass•word /ˈpɑːswɜːd/ noun, c. **1** = a secret word which must be spoken by a person before he/she is allowed to enter a place **2** = a secret sign (group of letters, numbers etc.) which a person must use in order to get into a computer system

past[1] /pɑːst/ noun, u. **1** *Typewriters now seem a thing of the past.* = the time before the present **2** *'Ate' is past, while 'eat' is present.* = the form of a verb which shows whether we are talking about something that happened before the present time [GRAMMAR] **3** *I know nothing about his past.* = a part of one's life that is over

past[2] adj. **1** *In past years, the monsoon always arrived in June.* = before the present time **2** *Summer is past and the rains have come.* = over; ended **3** *He is the past president of the party.* = former

past[3] prep. **1** *We drove past the hospital and came to the school.* = further than; beyond **2** *The show begins at twenty minutes past six.* = after

pas•ta /ˈpæstə/noun, u. = Italian food made in different shapes from wheat flour

paste[1] /peɪst/ noun, u. **1** *She made a paste by mixing some flour and water.* = a thick mixture of a liquid and some solid substance **2** *Use a little paste to stick the paper to the wooden surface.* = a sticky mixture used to stick paper to something

paste[2] verb, t. **1** *I have pasted the posters on the wall.* = to stick paper to some surface with paste **2** = to move text, pictures or files to a document within a computer from elsewhere [COMPUTERS]

pas•tel[1] /ˈpæstəl/ noun, u. or c. *The artist used pastels to produce this painting.*(c.) = a stick of paint used for making pictures, produced by mixing some colour to a soft material

pastel[2] adj. *a pastel blue sari* = having a very light shade of some colour

pas•teur•ized (-ised) /ˈpæstʃəraɪz/ adj. = some liquid (usually milk) which has been heated to a high temperature (but not boiled) so as to kill the harmful bacteria present in it **pasteurization** /pæstʃəraɪˈzeɪʃn/ noun = the action of pasteurizing something

pas•time /ˈpɑːstaɪm/ noun, c. *Watching television is her only pastime.* = something done to make the time pass more pleasantly (also **hobby**)

pas•tor /ˈpɑːstəʳ/ noun, c. = a Christian priest who is the head of a church group **pastoral** adj. **1** *pastoral duties* = having to do with a pastor (priest) **2** *We lead a simple pastoral life on our farm.* = having to do with the countryside (open and peaceful places away from the busy cities) **pastoral poetry** noun = poetry which describes the joys of living a natural life, away from the city

pas•try /ˈpeɪstri/ noun, c. (**pastries**) = a small cake

pas•ture[1] /ˈpɑːstʃəʳ/ noun, u. or c. = a piece of grassy land where sheep or cows feed

pasture[2] verb, t. *Where do you pasture your sheep?* = to allow animals to feed on grass in a pasture

pat[1] /pæt/ noun, c. **1** *She gave the child a loving pat on the back.* = a gentle touch with the fingers and palm of the hand, to express affection, friendliness etc. **2** *a pat of butter* = a small, flat piece of some substance (usually butter)

pat[2] verb, t. (**patted**) *He patted the dog on the head.* = to tap someone several times with an open hand as a way of showing love, encouragement etc.

patch[1] /pætʃ/ noun, c. (**patches**) **1** *The dog was white, with black patches.* = a small area on a surface that is different in colour from the surrounding areas **2** *He has patches all over his old trousers.* = a piece of material used to cover up a torn or damaged part **3** *a vegetable patch* = a small piece of land where something is grown

patch[2] verb, t. **1** *Have you patched the hole in your trousers?* = to put a patch on a torn or damaged part **2** *The brothers had quarrelled but they have patched up their differences now.* = to end a quarrel **patchwork** noun, u. or c. *Your essay is a patchwork of passages taken from different books.* = something made by joining several pieces together (derogatory)

not a patch on *The new restaurant is not a patch on the old one.* = not as good as **to go through a bad patch (to hit a bad patch)** = to go through a period of difficulty

pa•tel•la /pəˈtelə/ noun = the knee-cap (bone over the knee joint) [BIOLOGY]

pa•tent[1] /ˈpeɪtənt/ noun, c. *The inventor of this new washing machine has been given a patent on his invention.* = the right given to an inventor (someone who has made something new) to make a product in large quantities, while stopping others from making it without the inventor's permission

patent[2] verb, t. *The inventor of the machine has patented it.* = to get a patent on a new invention

patent[3] adj. *It is quite patent that he is telling a lie.* = obvious; easy to see **patently** adv. **patent medicine** noun = a medicine which can be manufactured by only one company, which has a patent on it

pa•ter•nal /pəˈtɜːnəl/ adj. *our paternal home* = belonging to one's father or having to do with one's father (compare **maternal**) **paternalism** noun, u. = the practice of protecting and looking after people like a father, often without giving them the freedom to grow (often derogatory) **paternity** noun, u. *The paternity of the child was established through a DNA test.* = the fact of being the biological father of a child [LAW]

path /pɑːθ/ noun, c. **1** *We walked along a narrow jungle path.* = a way made on the ground for people to walk on **2** *The aircraft followed a path through the clouds.* = the direction that something is moving in **3** *My sister is a nurse. She has chosen the path of sacrifice.* = the career or profession that one follows (figurative)

pa•thet•ic /pəˈθetɪk/ adj. **1** *I heard the drowning woman's pathetic cries for help, and was able to save her.* = causing one to feel pity and sadness **2** *Our performance in this match was pathetic and we deserved to lose.* = of poor quality (informal, derogatory)

pa•thol•o•gy /pəˈθɒlədʒi/ noun = the study of the tiny living things (bacteria or germs etc.) that cause many diseases **pathologist** noun, c. = a doctor who studies the germs that cause diseases **pathological** /pæθəˈlɒdʒɪkəl/ adj. **1** *a pathological test* = connected with pathology **2** *pathological liar* = unable to control one's behaviour, because of some weakness of the mind

pa•thos /ˈpeɪθɒs/ noun, u. *The film was so full of pathos that most people in the audience were crying when it ended.* = a feeling of pity and sorrow [LITERATURE]

pa•tience /ˈpeɪʃəns/ noun, u. *He has great patience with children and never gets angry with them.* = the ability to remain calm in a difficult or unpleasant situation

pa•tient[1] /ˈpeɪʃənt/ adj. *Please be patient. The bus will arrive in a few minutes.* = calm and not upset because of some delay

patient[2] noun, c. *She is a patient in this hospital.* = a person who receives medical treatment from a doctor

pa•tri•arch /ˈpeɪtriɑːk/ noun, c. = the oldest and most respected man in a family or a community (compare **matriarch**) (formal)

P

pat•ri•ot /'pætriət/ noun, c. = a person who has great love for his/her country and is willing to make sacrifices to defend it **patriotic** /pætrɪ'ɒtɪk/ adj. *a patriotic young woman* = having deep love for one's country **patriotism** /'pætrɪətɪzm/ noun, u. = the quality that a patriot has

pa•trol[1] /pə'trəul/ verb, t. (**patrolled**) *The police is patrolling this area to make sure that there are no violent incidents.* = to go round an area to see that there is no trouble

patrol[2] noun, c. or u. **1** *The police patrol will begin tonight.*(u.) = the act of patrolling an area **2** *The police patrol is well armed.*(c.) = a group of policemen or soldiers who are patrolling an area

pa•tron /'peɪtrən/ noun, c. *She is a great lover of art and you will find her at every art exhibition. I wish we had more such patrons of art.* = a person who supports (usually with money) a good cause, such as that of art **patronage** noun, u. *The artists are looking for government patronage.* = the support given by a patron **patronize (patronise)** verb, t. **1** *I have been patronizing this shop for years and I buy all my requirements here.* = to support a business by buying things etc. (formal) **2** *You may know more about music, while I am just a beginner but that doesn't mean you can patronize me.* = to show by one's behaviour that one is better or more important than someone else (derogatory) **patronizing (patronising)** adj. = behaving as if one were superior to someone else (derogatory)

pat•ter[1] /'pætəʳ/ noun, u. *the gentle patter of raindrops falling on the leaves* = the soft sound made when something falls lightly and repeatedly on a surface

patter[2] verb, i. *The children pattered down the corridor.* = to run or walk softly, making a pattering sound

pat•tern /'pætən/ noun, c. or u. **1** *The curtains have a floral pattern.*(c.)= a regular arrangement of lines, shapes and colours on a surface, which makes it look attractive **2** *I find no pattern to the weather. It's raining one day and bright and sunny the next.* = a regular arrangement of events which one can predict

pat•ty /'pæti/ noun, c. (**patties**) *a meat patty* = food cut into small pieces and cooked

pau•ci•ty /'pɔːsɪti/ noun, u. *There is a paucity of people who may be willing to join the army.* = shortage or lack of something (formal)

paunch /pɔːntʃ/noun, c. (**paunches**) = a fat stomach which bulges (sticks out) (not respectful)

pau•per /'pɔːpəʳ/ noun, c. *She was once a rich woman but now she is a pauper.* = a very poor person (old-fashioned)

pause[1] /pɔːz/ verb, i. *He paused in the middle of a sentence to take a sip of water.* = to stop for a short time

pause[2] noun, c. *We will continue our discussion after a brief pause.* = a short break in some activity **pause button** noun = the button in a video player etc. that stops playing or recording, for a short time

pave /peɪv/ verb, t. = to cover a surface with something hard and flat e.g. tiles **pavement** /'peɪvmənt/ noun, c. = the raised path along each side of a street, on which people can walk

pa•vil•ion /pə'vɪljən/ noun, c. **1** *a sports pavilion* = a building inside a sports field, where the players and people watching a game can sit **2** *a pavilion at an exhibition* = a light building, meant for temporary use, where objects of interest can be shown to the public

paw[1] /pɔː/ noun, c. **1** *the tiger's paw* = the lower part of the foot of an animal which has claws (nails) **2** *Keep your paws off me!* = the hand of a human being (humorous)

paw[2] verb, t. **1** *The horse was restless and pawed the ground impatiently.* = to touch or rub a surface with the paw or hoof (referring to an animal) **2** = to touch someone in a rough and sexually improper manner (disapproving)

pawn[1] /pɔːn/ noun, c. **1** = the least important piece in the game of chess, which can be moved only one square forward **2** = someone who has no power or importance and is used by someone else for his/her own advantage

pawn[2] verb, t. *As I had no money, I had to pawn my watch in order to pay for the train ticket.* = to borrow money from a pawnbroker (see below) by leaving something of value with him/her, on the understanding that it will be returned when the money is paid back **pawnbroker** noun, c. = a person who lends money to people after taking something of value from them

pay[1] /peɪ/ verb, t. or i. (**paid**) **1** *How much did you pay for your new watch?* = to give money to someone in return for something that one has bought or some service that one has received **2** *I have to pay my taxes.* = to give money that is due to someone **3** *The school will pay for itself in five years.* = to produce a profit **4** *I want to pay him a visit.* = to make **5** *Pay attention to what I say!* = to listen

pay[2] noun, u. = salary; money received in exchange for work **payable** adj. *This cheque is payable at any branch of the State Bank of India.* = can be exchanged for money **payee** /pei'iː/ noun, c. = a person who is paid (who gets some money) **payment** noun, u. or c. **1** *You must make the payment today.*(u.) = the act of paying money **2** *You have to make monthly payments of Rs 3000 for the* *car you have bought.*(c.)= an amount of money that is paid **pay phone** noun = a public telephone that one can use on payment of money

to pay one's respects to somebody = to meet somebody as a sign of respect **to pay tribute to somebody or something** = to do something special (say, sing etc.) in order to show respect **to pay (someone) back** 1 *Please lend me Rs 50. I will pay you back soon.* = to return the money that one has borrowed **2** *You have made me look foolish today, but I'll pay you back someday.* = to do something harmful or insulting to someone so that they are put in the same position as you are now **pay off** *All your patience will pay off when your results are declared.* = to produce a favourable result (informal) **to pay your way through (college)** = to work and earn money to pay for one's education **to pay through the nose** = to spend a lot of money on something, much more than one thinks is right **to pay someone off** = to give someone money in order that they do not reveal (let someone know about) something wrong or illegal that one has done

PC abbr. of **1 Personal Computer** = a small computer which one can use at home **2 political correctness** = a way of thinking, speaking or writing that does not offend people

pea /pi:/ noun, c. = the small, round, green seed of a plant which is eaten as a vegetable

peace /pi:s/ noun, u. **1** *I hope the agreement will bring peace to the country.* = a state (condition) when there is no fighting or violence **2** *I don't have peace of mind on this job.* = freedom from worry; a state of calmness **peaceful** adj. *The election meeting was peaceful, although we expected some trouble.* = free from trouble or violence

peach[1] /pi:tʃ/noun, c. (**peaches**) = a fruit which has a reddish yellow colour and soft, juicy flesh

peach[2] adj. **1** *a peach coloured sari* = a light pink colour **2** *He is a peach of a person.* = having qualities that one can admire (informal)

pea•cock /'pi:kɒk/noun, c. = a large bird with beautiful bluish-green feathers, specially in its tail, which is India's national bird

peak[1] /pi:k/ noun, c. **1** *We reached the peak of the mountain.* = the top of a mountain **2** *Examination fever is at its peak now.* = the highest or strongest point

peak[2] verb, i. *I hope the atheletes peak in time for the Olympic games.* = to reach the highest point of one's ability etc.

peak[3] adj. *The traffic on this road during peak hours is really heavy.* = at the point of greatest activity

peal[1] /pi:l/ noun, c. *a peal of thunder* = a loud, long sound

peal[2] verb, i. *The bells are pealing.* = to produce a loud ringing sound

pea•nut /'pi:nʌt/ noun, c. = a kind of edible nut that grows under the ground, from which oil is produced (also **groundnut** or **monkeynut**) **peanuts** (always plural) *I am paid peanuts!* = a very small sum of money which has almost no value (derogatory)

pear /peəʳ/ noun, c. = a sweet, juicy fruit

pearl /pɜ:l/ noun, c. = a shiny substance, often in the shape of a small ball, found inside some oysters, which has value as a precious stone and is used in making jewellery **pearl diver** noun, c. = a person who dives into the sea looking for oysters which may contain pearls

peas•ant /'pezənt/ noun, c. = a farmer who owns a small piece of land on which he/she grows crops so that his/her family can be fed

peat /pi:t/ noun, u. = a kind of mud which is found in bogs (wet places) and can be burnt like coal as it contains a lot of plant matter

peb•ble /'pebəl/ noun, c. = a small, round, smooth stone found on riverbeds or on the seashore

peck[1] /pek/ verb, i. or t. **1** = to strike or eat with the beak (referring to a bird) **2** *She is only pecking at her food, not eating anything.* = taking food in very small quantities, without any interest

peck[2] noun, c. = a light kiss (informal)

pec•tin /'pektɪn/ noun, u. = a kind of chemical used for making jams and jellies, which is present in some fruits

pec•to•ral /'pektərəl/ adj. *pectoral muscles* = the muscles in the chest, below the shoulders

pe•cu•li•ar /pɪ'kju:liəʳ/ adj. *He has a peculiar habit of taking a bath in the middle of the night. // The sauce has a peculiar taste. Maybe it has gone bad.* = strange and unusual, often in an unpleasant way **peculiarity** /pɪkju:lɪ'ærɪti/ noun, u. or c. (**peculiarities**) **1** (u.) = the quality of being peculiar **2** (c.) = a strange or unusual habit that a person has **peculiarly** adv. *This route is peculiarly different.* = more than what is usual

ped•a•go•gy /'pedəgɒdʒi/ noun, u. = the activity of teaching, specially young children

ped•al[1] /'pedl/ noun, c. *Press the brake pedal when you want to stop the car.* = a flat piece of metal, fitted to a motorcar or a bicycle, which is pressed down with the foot to drive it or to control its working

pedal[2] verb, i. or t. *He pedalled down the road to the shop.*(i.) = to drive a bicycle by using its pedals

pe•dan•tic /pɪ'dæntɪk/ adj. *You should not be so pedantic about small grammatical mistakes.* = worried too much about rules or unimportant details (derogatory)

ped•dle /'pedl/ verb, t. **1** *He goes around the city peddling ice cream.* = to go from place to place trying

P

to sell something **2** = to sell illegal drugs **3** = to sell something which does not have much value

ped•es•tal /ˈpedɪstəl/ noun, c. = the base on which a statue stands

to put someone on a pedestal = to think of someone, as nobler, better and higher than he or she actually is (disapproving)

pe•des•tri•an[1] /pɪˈdestriən/ noun, c. *There are so many cars on this road that it has become dangerous for pedestrians.* = a person who walks on a road

pedestrian[2] adj. *a very pedestrian style of writing* = dull and lacking in imagination (derogatory) **pedestrian crossing** noun, c. = a place where pedestrians are allowed to cross a street (also **zebra crossing**)

pe•di•at•rics (paediatrics) /piːdɪˈætrɪks/ noun = the branch of medicine which deals with the treatment of children's diseases **pediatrician (paediatrician)** /pidɪˈætrɪʃən/ noun, c. = a doctor who treats children's diseases

ped•i•cure /ˈpedɪkjʊəʳ/ noun, u. or c. = care of the feet and the nails growing on the feet (see also **manicure**)

ped•i•gree[1] /ˈpedɪgriː/ noun, u. or c. *He has bought an Alsatian dog with a pedigree.* = a written record of the family history (who the parents, grandparents etc. were) of a human being or an animal

pedigree[2] adj. *a pedigree dog* = an animal which has a pedigree

pee[1] /piː/ verb, i. = to urinate (slang, not polite)

pee[2] noun, u. = the act of urinating (slang, not polite)

peek[1] /piːk/ verb, i. *She tried to peek through the curtains at the guests.* = to take a quick look without letting others know

peek[2] noun, c. *Take a peek.* = the act of peeking **a peak preview** = a viewing of a film which is not yet showing at the cinemas for a small and special audience

peel[1] /piːl/ verb, t. or i. **1** *Can you peel this orange for me? // The nurse peeled off my bandages.*(t.) = to remove the skin or outer covering from a fruit, vegetable or some other object **2** *The paint on the building is beginning to peel.*(i.) = to lose part of the surface

peel[2] noun, u. *You can use orange peel to make marmalade.* = the skin of a fruit or vegetable which has been removed

to keep one's eyes/ears peeled = to keep a careful watch or listen for something very carefully

peep[1] /piːp/ verb, i. **1** *The child peeped out of the window.* = to take a quick look **2** *The sun peeped through the clouds.* = to appear for a short time

peep[2] noun, c. *He had a peep at the book before the examination began.* = a quick short look **peeping Tom** noun = a man who has a bad habit of peeping at people, specially women, in an offensive manner, through doors etc. (derogatory)

peer[1] /pɪəʳ/ verb, i. *She was peering at the letter, trying to make out from the handwriting who the writer could be.* = to look very carefully at something by narrowing one's eyes

peer[2] noun, c. *The child should be put in the same class as her peers.* = a person of the same age or position as someone else **peer group** noun = a group of people, specially children, who are of the same age or educational level **peerless** adj. *Her beauty is peerless.* = with nothing to equal it

peeve /piːv/ verb, t. *I felt peeved when she did not return my phone call.* = to feel angry or to cause someone to feel angry

peg[1] /peg/ noun, c. **1** *My trousers are hanging from the peg on the wall. // We will hammer the tent pegs into the ground and then put up our tent.* = a short piece of wood or metal fixed to a wall or driven into the ground, used for hanging things from, tying things to etc. **2** *a peg of whisky* = a measure of the amount of some alcoholic drink that one consumes (takes)

peg[2] verb, t. **1** *I have pegged the bookshelf to the wall.* = to fix with a peg **2** *The price of oil has been pegged to the 1999 level.* = to fix the price of things at a certain level **off the peg** *He buys his clothes off the peg.* = ready-made; not specially made to fit somebody

to have somebody pegged = to know exactly what a person's character is (informal)

pe•jor•a•tive /pɪˈdʒɒrətɪv/ adj. *Don't call me a donkey! Don't you know the word is pejorative?* = (of the use of a word or language in general) carrying a negative or unpleasant meaning

pe•kin•ese /piːkɪˈniːz/ noun = a small dog with a wide face and long, silky hair

pel•i•can /ˈpelɪkən/ noun = a large bird with a long beak, the lower part of which looks like a bag

pel•let /ˈpelɪt/ noun, c. **1** *a paper pellet* = a small ball-like mass of some substance **2** = a small piece of lead which is fired from a gun

pelt[1] /pelt/ verb, t. **1** *The spectators pelted the players with plastic water bottles.* = to attack someone by throwing a large number of things quickly **2** *The rain pelted down and we all had to run into the house.* = to rain very heavily **3** *The students pelted past us to catch the bus.* = to run very fast

pelt[2] noun, c. *the pelt of a leopard* = the skin of a dead animal, before it has been dried and made into leather

pel•vis /ˈpelvɪs/ noun = the framework of bones below the waist, to which the bones of the leg are joined **pelvic** adj. *a pelvic fracture* = of the pelvis

pen[1] /pen/ noun, c. **1** *a ballpen* = an instrument used for writing **2** *a cattle pen* = a small area enclosed with a fence, in which animals, specially cattle, are kept **3** *play pen* = a small place, sometimes a cot, enclosed by a frame, in which a baby can play safely

pen[2] verb, t. **1** *She has penned me a letter at last.* = to write (old-fashioned) **2** *The sheep have been penned in.* = to shut animals in a pen **penfriend** noun, c. = a person whom one has made friends with by writing letters, but has not met **penknife** noun, c. (**pen-knives**) = a small knife with a blade that can fold up **penname** noun, c. = the false name under which a writer may write (see also **nom de plume** or **pseudonym**)

penknife

pe•nal /ˈpiːnl/ adj. *Criminals are punished under the country's penal laws.* = relating to crime and its punishment

penalize (-ise) /ˈpiːnəlaɪz/ verb, t. **1** = to punish someone for breaking a law or a rule **2** *The teacher penalized the student for his bad handwriting by deducting five marks.* = to punish or to put someone at a disadvantage

penalty /ˈpenltɪ/ noun, u. or c. (**penalties**) **1** *There will be a penalty of Rs 500 if you are caught driving a car on the wrong side of the road.*(c.) = a punishment for breaking a law or rule, often in the form of a fine (an order to pay money as punishment) **2** *The referee awarded a penalty as the centre-forward fouled a player inside the penalty area.* = a punishment given to a player or team for breaking a rule in a game

pen•ance noun, u. *He once shot a bird and felt so sorry that he gave up meat as penance.* = the action of doing something to show that one is sorry for something wrong that one has done

pen•cil /ˈpensəl/ noun, c. = a writing object made of wood or metal, which has a stick of some soft material inside that leaves marks on paper

pen•dant /ˈpendənt/ noun, c. = a small object worn around the neck with a chain

pend•ing[1] /ˈpendɪŋ/ adj. *My case has not been decided yet by the judge; it is still pending.* = undecided

pending[2] prep. *We will allow you to continue working, pending the orders for your transfer.* = until (while waiting for)

pen•du•lum /ˈpendjʊləm/ noun, c. *the pendulum of a clock* = a rod or a piece of string with a weight at the bottom, which hangs from a fixed point and can swing freely from side to side (Old-fashioned clocks had pendulums to make sure they kept correct time.)

pen•e•trate /ˈpenɪtreɪt/ verb, t. or i. **1** *The bullet penetrated the door.*(t.) = to enter into something or pass through something **2** *The poem was difficult to penetrate.*(i.) = to be understood (figurative) **penetration** /penɪˈtreɪʃən/ noun, u. = the action of penetrating (entering into) something **penetrating** adj. **1** *He gave us a penetrating look when we entered the room late.* = a steady, long look intended to make a person feel uncomfortable **2** *She asked some penetrating questions during the presentation.* = intelligent and forcing one to think

pen•guin /ˈpeŋgwɪn/ noun, c. = a large sea bird living in Antarctica that cannot fly but is very good at swimming under the water

pen•i•cil•lin /penɪˈsɪlɪn/ noun = a powerful antibiotic (medicine that can destroy many kinds of bacteria which cause disease and infection) made from a kind of fungus

pe•nin•su•la /pɪˈnɪnsjʊlə/ noun, c. *the Deccan peninsula* = a piece of land almost completely surrounded by water

pe•nis /ˈpiːnɪs/ noun, c. = the sex organ of a male animal or human being

pen•i•tent /ˈpenɪtənt/ adj. *After he had hit the dog, he felt penitent and promised never to hurt it again.* = feeling very sorry for something wrong that one has done, which one realises to be wrong

penitentiary /pənɪˈtenʃəri/ noun, c. (**penitentiaries**) = a kind of prison where people who have committed small crimes are given a chance to improve their behaviour

pen•ny /ˈpeni/ noun, c. (**pennies** or **pence**) = the smallest unit of money used in Britain (1 pound = 100 pence) **penniless** adj. *a penniless writer* = a person without money **penny-pincher** noun, c. = a person who does not like to spend money; a miser

pen•sion /ˈpenʃən/ noun, c. = an amount of money which one receives every month after one has retired (stopped working), from a former employer **pensioner** noun, c. = a person who has stopped working and is getting a pension

pen•sive /ˈpensɪv/ adj. *He was in a quiet and pensive mood after he heard of his friend's illness.* = thoughtful and sad

penta- prefix meaning 'five' e.g. **pen•ta•gon** /ˈpentəgən/ noun, c. = a geometrical figure (shape) with five equal sides (see pic under **shapes**)

Pentagon noun = a building in Washington, the capital of the U.S.A., from which the American defence forces (army, navy and air-force) are controlled

pen•tam•e•ter /pen'tæmɪtə^r/ noun = a line of poetry which contains five main beats (loud or strong sounds)

pentathlon /pen'tæθlən/ noun, c. = a sports competition in which there are five events (see also **decathlon**)

pent•house /'penthaʊs/ noun, c. = a set of rooms built on top of a tall building covering the entire area of the floor below

pent-up adj. *She has no one to speak to in this place. So she never gets a chance to express her pent-up feelings.* = (feelings) that one cannot express freely, which one is forced to keep within oneself

pe•nul•ti•mate /pi'nʌltɪmɪt/adj. *This is the penultimate match. The winning team will go to the final.* = just before the last or final event; the semi-final event in a tournament (formal)

pe•num•bra /pɪ'nʌmbrə/ noun = a slightly dark area surrounding an area of complete darkness, called the umbra [PHYSICS]

pen•u•ry /'penjʊri/ noun, u. *The man lives in complete penury. He has no money even to buy food.* = very great poverty (state of being poor)

pe•o•ny /'pi:əni/ noun = a garden plant with white or pink flowers

peo•ple[1] /'pi:pəl/ noun, c. **1** *I don't know many people in this city.* = more than one person **2** *The Prime Minister spoke to the people on television.* = the citizens of a country **3** *The French are a very artistic people.* = the whole of a nation **4** *Are all your people coming for your wedding?* = relatives

people[2] verb, t. *Singapore is peopled by groups from various nationalities.* = to live in a place **peoples** noun (always plural) *the peoples of the world* = the different nations

pep /pep/ noun, u. *He never seems to get tired. He is always full of pep.* = energy and high spirits (informal) **pep pill** noun, c. = a medicine or drug which gives one energy for a short time **pep talk** noun, c. *The captain gave his players a pep talk before the match.* = a short talk which gives the listeners courage or the desire to win (informal)

pep•per[1] /'pepə^r/ noun, u. = a kind of spice with a hot taste, made from the small, round seeds of a plant

pepper[2] verb, t. *The article was peppered with quotations from famous writers.* = containing a lot of **peppery** adj. **1** *The peppery taste of the curry made my throat burn.* = hot (like that of pepper) **2** *He has a peppery temper.* = easily made angry **pepper-and-salt** adj. *pepper-and-salt coloured moustaches* = a mixture of black and white

pep•per•mint /'pepəmɪnt/ noun = a kind of sweet made from the mint plant

pep•sin /'pepsɪn/ noun = a kind of juice produced in the stomach that helps to break down and digest food **peptic ulcer** noun, c. = a kind of wound that forms inside the stomach of a person who has too much acid in the stomach

per /pə^r/ prep. **1** *He earns Rs 3000 per month.* = in each **2** *These eggs cost Rs 20 per dozen.* = for each **per annum** /pər 'ænəm/ adv. *a salary of Rs 1.5 lakh per annum* = in each year **per capita** /pər 'kæpitə/ adv. *the per capita income of the country* = for each person **per cent** /pə 'sent/ adv. *You will have to pay 10 per cent interest on this loan.* = for each hundred

per•am•bu•la•tor /pə'ræmbjʊleɪtə^r/ noun, c. = a small carriage with wheels in which a baby can be taken out into the fresh air (formal) (also **pram**)

per•ceive /pə'si:v/ verb, t. *I perceive a slight improvement in the patient's condition. // I now perceive what the writer is trying to say.* = to be able to see or to understand **perception** /pə'sepʃən/ noun, u. **1** = the action of perceiving (understanding) something **2** *With her keen perception the teacher understood the students' problems.* = the ability to look at things and understand them well **perceptible** adj. *I see no perceptible change in his behaviour.* = which can be easily perceived (seen) **perceptive** adj. *Your comments on the book were highly perceptive.* = showing very good understanding

perch[1] /pɜ:tʃ/ verb, i. **1** *The bird perched on the highest branch of the tree.* = to come to rest (used to refer to a bird) **2** *His cottage was perched on a high rock.* = to be in a certain position on top of something high

perch[2] noun, c. **1** *The bird found a perch on the highest branch of the tree.* = a resting place for a bird **2** *From his perch on the roof-top he could see the procession clearly.* = a high position

per•co•late /'pɜ:kəleɪt/ verb, i. **1** *Rain-water percolates through the soil and forms large pools below the ground.* = to pass slowly through some material which has very small holes **2** *Very little news of the peace talks percolated to the public.* = to reach (figurative) **percolator** /pɜ:kə'leɪtə^r/ noun, c. = an electrical machine used for making coffee by allowing boiling water to percolate (pass) through powdered coffee

per•cus•sion /pə'kʌʃən/ noun, u. = the sound produced by a musical instrument such as a tabla or drum, caused by striking a tightly stretched piece of leather with the fingers and hands or with a stick **percussionist** noun, c. = a musician who plays some kind of percussion instrument, e.g. a drum

pe•remp•to•ry /pə'remptəri/ adj. *You should not*

have dismissed her in that peremptory manner, without listening to her point of view. = not polite or friendly (as if giving an order to someone and expecting to be obeyed)

pe•ren•ni•al /pə'reniəl/ adj. **1** *Shortage of water is a perennial problem in the city.* = permanent; lasting for ever **2** *a perennial plant* = a plant that lives for more than two years (compare **annual**, **biennial**) [BIOLOGY]

per•fect[1] /'pɜːfɪkt/ adj. **1** *The weather is just perfect for a picnic—not too hot and not too cold.* = without any fault **2** *Rati is perfect for the job.* = exactly right **3** *She is a perfect novice at the job.* = complete **4** = the form of a verb which tells us whether an action may be thought of as complete, e.g. 'He has done his homework.' [GRAMMAR]

perfect[2] /pə'fekt/ verb, t. *She has perfected her singing.* = to make something perfect **perfection** /pə'fekʃən/ noun, u. *You should aim at perfection in your dancing.* = the state of being perfect (having no defects) **perfectionist** noun, c. = a person who does things as well as he or she possibly can and expects others to do the same (generally approving) **perfectly** adv. **1** *They gave us perfectly cooked curry.* = in a perfect or beautiful way **2** *He had a perfectly good reason for being late.* = very

per•fo•rate /'pɜːfəreɪt/ verb, t. *The doctor medically perforated the patient's lung to let the fluid out.* = to make a hole or holes in something **perforation** /pɜːfə'reɪʃən/ noun, c. *The sheets of paper have perforations down the middle, so that they can easily be torn into two.* = a small hole or line of holes

per•form /pə'fɔːm/ verb, t. or i. **1** *I am happy to see that you have performed all the tasks which were given to you.*(t.) = to do something; to carry out or complete a piece of work **2** *The students are performing a play on the stage.*(t.) = to present a show before an audience **3** *All our players performed well in this match.*(i.) = to do something that requires skill **performance** noun, u. **1** *Our hockey team's performance in this match was brilliant.* = the manner of doing something **2** *Pandit Chaurasia, the famous flute player, will give a performance at the Rabindra Bhavan this evening.* = a public show **performer** noun, c. **1** = a person who performs (gives a show before an audience) (sometimes not respectful) **2** *a good performer* = a person who takes part in an exam, test etc.

per•fume /'pɜːfjuːm/ noun, u. **1** *the perfume of roses* = a very pleasant smell **2** *a bottle of French perfume* = a liquid made from flowers etc. which has a very pleasant smell and is used mainly by women to give their bodies an attractive smell

per•func•to•ry /pə'fʌŋktəri/ adj. *The examiner was in a hurry and examined the answer-papers in a perfunctory manner.* = careless and hurried (formal)

per•haps /pə'hæps/ adv. *He is twenty, perhaps twentyfive years old.* = possibly; maybe

per•il /'perɪl/ noun, u. or c. *The man realized he was in peril when he saw a leopard about to jump on him.*(u.) // *My father had fought in the mountains and he often told us about the perils of war.*(c.) = great danger(s) **perilous** adj. *The journey to Mansarovar, across high mountains, is perilous.* = dangerous

pe•rim•e•ter /pə'rɪmɪtə[r]/ noun, u. *The perimeter of the school compound is protected by a fence.* = the border or outer edge of an area of land

pe•ri•od /'pɪəriəd/ noun, c. **1** *He spent a period of five years in China.* = a length of time **2** *Many great poets were born during the Mughal period.* = a particular length of time in the history of a country etc. **3** *The geography teacher will meet us in the third period.* = a part of the school time-table **4** = the time of the month when a woman loses blood from her body (see also **menses**) **5** (American) *There should be a period at the end of the sentence.* = fullstop **periodic** /pɪəri'ɒdɪk/ adj. *We have periodic tests in this school.* = happening regularly, after a certain length of time (also **periodical** adj.) **periodical** noun, c. = a magazine that appears after a regular period of time, e.g. once in a month (formal) **periodic table** noun = a list of all the chemical elements arranged in a table depending on the number of positively charged particles (protons) they have [CHEMISTRY]

pe•riph•e•ry /pə'rɪfəri/ noun, c. (**peripheries**) or u. *Our school is on the periphery of the city.* = the outer edge of an area; the less important part, away from the centre **peripheral** adj. *Listening to music is a peripheral interest of mine.* = not as important as something else

per•i•scope /'perɪskəʊp/ noun, c. = an instrument consisting of a long tube fitted with mirrors, which allows one to see something that is above him/her. (Used by people in submarines to look at ships sailing on the surface of the sea.)

per•ish /'perɪʃ/ verb, i. **1** *Many people perished in the train accident.* = to die (referring to people or animals) (often literary) **2** *The vegetables perished while they were being transported.* = to become spoilt or rotten (referring to food) **perishable** adj. = something that can easily get spoilt or rotten (referring to food)

per•ju•ry /'pɜːdʒəri/ noun, u. = the crime of telling a lie in court after promising to tell the truth [LAW] **perjurer** noun, c. = one who commits perjury

perk[1] /pɜːk/ noun, c. *She gets a good salary as well*

P

as lots of perks, such as money for books. = an advantage or benefit that one gets from one's work, in addition to one's salary (informal) (formal = **perquisite**)

perk[2] verb, i. *He was looking rather sad, but he perked up when I told him that he had won a prize.* = to become more cheerful **perky** adj. = cheerful and full of life

perm[1] /'pɜːm/ (abbr. of **permanent wave**) noun, c. = waves or curls put in a woman's hair, using a chemical process, so that they will last for several months

perm[2] verb, t. *The hair dresser will perm your hair.* = to give someone a perm

per•ma•nent /'pɜːmənənt/ adj. *The job he has been given is only for a year, but it may become permanent.* = lasting forever or for a long time **permanence** noun, u. = the quality of being permanent

per•man•ga•nate /pə'mæŋgənɪt/ noun, u. = a chemical having a dark purple colour, used for disinfecting (killing harmful germs) (also **potassium permanganate**)

per•me•ate /'pɜːmieɪt/verb, i. or t. **1** *Water permeated through tiny cracks in the roof.*(i.) = to pass through (referring to some liquid or gas) **2** *The smell of stale food permeates the entire building.*(t.) = to fill; to be present everywhere (formal) **permeable** adj. *Sandstone is permeable to water.* = allowing some substance (usually a liquid or gas) to pass through it

per•mis•sion /pə'mɪʃən/noun, u. *The Chairman has given me permission to speak.* = the act (done by a person in authority) of allowing someone to do something **permissive** adj. *Society has become more permissive now than it was a hundred years ago.* = allowing a lot of freedom in matters of behaviour (disapproving)

per•mit[1] /pə'mɪt/ verb, t. (**permitted**) *Please permit her to enter the room.* = to allow someone to do something (formal)

permit[2] /'pɜːmɪt/ noun, c. *I have a permit allowing me to travel.* = an official document allowing someone to do something, especially for a certain period of time

per•mu•ta•tion /pɜːmjʊ'teɪʃən/ noun, u. or c. *We have six kinds of vegetables. You can have any three kinds for lunch or dinner. Let us try out different permutations and see what we enjoy best.* = one of the ways in which a number of things can be arranged in a group [MATHEMATICS]

per•ni•cious /pə'nɪʃəs/ adj. *The pernicious effects of smoking are becoming clear now.* = extremely harmful (formal)

per•ox•ide /pə'rɒksaɪd/ noun = a liquid that is used to kill germs and make face and hair colour lighter (also **hydrogen peroxide**)

per•pen•dic•u•lar[1] /pɜːpən'dɪkjʊləʳ/ adj. *The wall should be perfectly perpendicular.* = making an angle of 90 degrees with the ground

perpendicular[2] noun, c. = a line which makes an angle of 90 degrees with another line

per•pe•trate /'pɜːpɪtreɪt/ verb, t. *The evil king perpetrated many crimes during his reign.* = to do something wrong or illegal (formal) **perpetrator** noun, c. = one who has committed a crime or done something wrong or evil

per•pet•u•al /pə'petʃuəl/ adj. **1** *Mt Everest is covered in perpetual snow.* = permanent; having no end **2** *The perpetual chatter in the classroom made the teacher angry.* = continuing for a long time (formal, often derogatory) **perpetuate** verb, t. *We must do something to end poverty. We can't allow it to be perpetuated.* = to make something continue for ever (formal) **perpetuity** /pɜːpi'tjuːiti/ noun, u. *The government has allowed us to keep this land in perpetuity.* = for all time (formal)

per•plex /pə'pleks/ verb, t. *He is very friendly one day but the next day he will not even recognize you. His behaviour will perplex you.* = to cause confusion (failure to understand) **perplexed** adj.

per se /pɜː'seɪ/ adv. *Watching television is not a bad thing per se, but it can hinder the development of reading.* = by itself (not considered along with other things)

per•se•cute /'pɜːsɪkjuːt/ verb, t. = to treat someone cruelly and make him/her suffer for racial, religious or political reasons **persecution** /pɜːsɪ'kjuːʃən/ noun, u. *persecution of the freedom fighters.* = the act or the effect of being persecuted

per•se•vere /pɜːsɪ'vɪəʳ/ verb, i. *When you are learning yoga, you may often feel discouraged and want to give up, but you should persevere.* = to go on trying to do something in spite of difficulties **perseverance** noun, u. = the quality that makes a person persevere (go on trying)

Per•sian /'pɜːʃən/ noun, c. or u. **1** = a person who belongs to Persia (Iran) **2** = the language of Iran

per•sist /pə'sɪst/ verb, i. **1** *The teacher asked the student not to talk in class, but the student persisted.* = to go on doing something even when asked not to do it **2** *We are trying to remove malaria completely but it still persists.* = to continue to exist **persistent** adj. **1** *I told the salesperson that I did not want to buy anything but she was persistent.* = continuing to do something that is not liked or that one is told not to do (derogatory) **2** *She has a persistent cough* = something undesirable that will not go away easily **persistence** noun

per•son /ˈpɜ:sən/ noun, c. or u. **1** *This car can seat four persons.* = people; human beings in general **2** *I like her as a person, though she is not a good teacher.* = individual; a human being with certain qualities that make him/her different from others **3** *The police searched his person and found some drugs.* = body **4** *first/second/third person* = a form of a pronoun or verb that indicates whether the speaker is referring to himself/herself, or to the listener, or to someone else [GRAMMAR] **5** *businessperson/chairperson* = someone who works in business or is the head of a company

per•son•a•ble /ˈpɜ:sənəbəl/ adj. *He is very personable. You will like him.* = having an attractive appearance or character (formal)

personal /ˈpɜ:sənəl/ adj. **1** *This is a personal letter. I can't let you read it.* = private; belonging to or meant for one person only **2** *The minister made a personal appeal to the public.* = done by a particular person and not by somebody else **3** *We offer personal service at our bank.* = paying special attention to each individual **personal computer (PC)** noun, c. = a small computer, generally for the use of one person **personal pronoun** noun, c. *'I', 'you' and 'he' are personal pronouns.* = a pronoun that refers to some person such as the speaker or the person being spoken to [GRAMMAR]

to get personal with somebody = to make a remark about someone's appearance or character (disapproving) **in person** *You will have to come in person if you want to vote.* = yourself

per•son•al•i•ty /pɜ:səˈnælɪti/ noun, u. or c. **1** *a leader with a powerful personality*(u.) = having qualities of character which have an effect on other people **2** *Many personalities have been invited to the meeting.*(c.) = a person who is wellknown to the public **personality cult** noun = the belief that the personality (character) of a leader is more important in politics than the party or its views

per•son•i•fy /pəˈsɒnɪfaɪ/ verb, t. *She personifies kindness.* = to think of someone as being the perfect example of some quality **personification** /pəsɒnɪfɪˈkeɪʃən/ noun, u. **1** = the act of personifying something (thinking of someone as human) **2** *personification of evil* = a person who is a perfect example of some quality

per•son•nel /pɜ:səˈnel/ noun, u. (plural **personnel**) *We need trained personnel for this factory.* = the persons working for an organization

per•spec•tive /pəˈspektɪv/ noun, u. or c. **1** *Don't allow your troubles to conquer you. Try to see things in the right perspective.*(u.) = the sensible and balanced way of looking at things **2** *He brings a fresh perspective to this discussion.* = an individual view or way of seeing something **3** *This drawing shows the new building in perspective.*(u.) = a drawing of an object which gives it depth (some objects appearing farther away than others)

per•spi•ra•tion /pɜ:spɪˈreɪʃən/ noun, u. = sweat (the bodily fluid that flows out through the skin after one has done some physical exercise) **perspire** /pɜ:ˈspaɪr/ verb, i. = to produce sweat from the body (formal)

per•suade /pəˈsweɪd/ verb, t. *He did not want to come for the picnic, but the other boys persuaded him to come.* = to make someone change his/her mind, or to believe or do something, through repeated requests, arguments etc. **persuasion** /pəˈsweɪzən/ noun, u. *We had to use a lot of persuasion before he agreed to come.* = the act or skill of persuading someone **persuasive** adj. *persuasive arguments* = having the power to persuade someone

pert /pɜ:t/ adj. *a pert young girl* = energetic and amusing in a bold and likeable way

per•tain (to) /pəˈteɪn/ verb, i. *These documents pertain to the agreement that has been signed.* = to relate to; to be connected with (formal) **pertinent** /ˈpɜ:tɪnənt/ adj. *This question is not pertinent to the matter we are discussing. It is about something else.* = connected directly with something that is being discussed (formal)

per•turb /pəˈtɜ:b/ verb, t. *We may have lost the match, but this defeat does not perturb me.* = to disturb; to cause someone to feel worried (formal) **perturbed** adj.

pe•ruse /pəˈru:z/ verb, t. *I'll give you the book and you can peruse it when you find the time.* = to read through something carefully (formal)

per•vade /pəˈveɪd/ verb, t. *A feeling of sadness pervaded the movie.* = to fill something or to spread through every part (referring to ideas, feelings etc.) **pervasive** adj. *The influence of television is so pervasive that even small children in villages have begun to talk like Amitabh Bachchan.* = spreading to every part (of a country etc.)

per•verse /pəˈvɜ:s/ adj. *Why do you continue to smoke twenty cigarettes a day when most people have given up smoking? Your behaviour seems quite perverse.* = deliberately continuing to do or believe in something that is known to be wrong or is not liked by other people (derogatory) **perversion** noun, u. or c. **1** *sexual perversion* = an action or type of behaviour that is considered unacceptable or unnatural by most people or by the law **2** *The judge allowed the prisoner, who had killed his wife, to go free. This was a perversion of justice.* = a wrong or unacceptable form of something (e.g. truth, justice) (formal)

P

pervert /pə'vɜ:t/ noun, c. = a person whose behaviour (especially sexual behaviour) is thought to be unnatural and unacceptable

pe•so /'peɪsəʊ/ noun, c. (**pesos**) = a form of money used in Spain and countries which were once controlled by Spain

pes•si•mist /'pesɪmɪst/ noun, c. *She is such a pessimist that she believes it will rain on the day of the match.* = one who sees only the dark (unpleasant) side of things and believes that the future will be bad (opposite **optimist**) **pessimism** noun, u. = the quality of being a pessimist

pest /pest/ noun, c. **1** = a plant, insect or small animal that causes damage to crops **2** *You are such a pest. You always come here to ask for something when I am busy.* = a person whose presence annoys someone (informal)

pes•ter /'pestə^r/ verb, t. *When you visit the temple lots of vendors will pester you to buy their goods.* = to annoy or trouble someone by making demands, specially for money

pesticide /'pestɪsaɪd/ noun, u. = a chemical that is used to destroy pests

pes•ti•lence /'pestɪləns/ noun, u. = a disease such as cholera that spreads quickly and causes many deaths (literary)

pes•tle /'pesəl/ noun, c. = a heavy piece of wood, stone etc. that is used to crush (break up) a solid substance into powder

pet[1] /pet/ noun, c. *He keeps a parrot as a pet.*

pet[2] adj. *He has a pet rabbit.* = an animal that is kept in the home as a companion

pet[3] verb, t. (**petted**) *The mother petted her child.* = to touch with the hands in a loving way **pet name** noun, c. = the name by which someone is lovingly called by friends or members of the family

pet•al /'petl/ noun, c. *a rose petal* = the leaf-like parts of a flower, which are usually brightly coloured (see pic under **flower**)

pet•er (out) /'pi:tə^r/ verb, i. *Interest in wild-life conservation is in danger of petering out.* = to come to an end gradually

pe•tite /pə'ti:t/ adj. *a petite woman* = small in an attractive way (referring to a woman) Ⓖ

pe•ti•tion[1] /pɪ'tɪʃən/ noun, c. **1** *The citizens of the town have signed a petition protesting against the building of a new hotel.* = a written request or demand made to the government, signed by many persons **2** *The High Court had sentenced the man to five year's imprisonment, but he has sent a petition to the Supreme Court asking for a review of his case.* = an official letter sent to a court of law, asking for a review of a law case [LAW]

petition[2] verb, t. *The citizens are going to petition the government for a reduction in taxes.* = to make or send a petition **petitioner** noun, c. = a person who makes a petition

pet•rel /'petrəl/ noun, c. = a kind of sea-bird that feeds by diving into the water

pet•ri•fy /'petrɪfaɪ/ verb, t. or i. (**petrified**) **1** *These pieces of stone are really trees that grew in this forest five million years ago and have become petrified.*(i.) = to turn into stone **2** *The tiny child stood still, petrified with fear, as the tiger crept slowly towards it.*(t.) = to be unable to move or act (as if made of stone) because of extreme fear (figurative)

pe•tro•le•um /pɪ'trəʊliəm/ noun, u. = the thick, dark mineral oil that is taken out of the earth and used for making petrol, plastics and other chemicals **petrol** /'petrəl/ noun, u. = the thin, colourless liquid that is produced from petroleum and used as fuel for motor-car engines etc. **petrochemical** /petrəʊ'kemɪkəl/ noun, c. = a chemical substance that is produced from petroleum and used for manufacturing plastics etc. **petrol station** noun, c. = a place where one can get petrol and other things (lubricants etc.) for a car

pet•ti•coat /'petikəʊt/ noun, c. = a woman's undergarment tied round the waist for saris, or covering the body from the shoulders to the knees for dresses

pet•ty /'peti/ adj. **1** *She read through the report quickly, ignoring the petty details.* = small and unimportant (in comparison to larger, more important things) **2** *She can be so petty that she will quarrel with you over five rupees.* = small-minded **petty cash** noun, u. = an amount of money kept in an office for making small payments

pet•u•lant /'petʃʊlənt/ adj. *The girl was so petulant that she refused to talk to anyone.* = bad-tempered and childish for no reason (formal)

pe•tu•ni•a /pɪ'tju:niə/ noun = a garden plant with white or red flowers

pew /pju:/ noun, c. = a seat, like a bench, for people to sit on while in a church

pew•ter /'pju:tə^r/ noun, u. = a silvery metal made by mixing lead and tin

pH = a measure of the amount of alkali or acid in a substance [CHEMISTRY]

phag•o•cyte /'fægəsaɪt/ noun, c. = a blood-cell which protects the body by killing harmful bacteria [MEDICINE]

pha•lanx /'fælæŋks/ noun, c. (**phalanxes**) = a group of policemen or soldiers marching close together for attack or defence

phal•lus /'fæləs/ noun, c. = an image, usually made

of stone, of the male sex organ, which is worshipped in some religions as a symbol (sign) of the power of creation

phan•tom /ˈfæntəm/ noun, c. = a ghost

pha•raoh /ˈfeərəʊ/ noun, c. = one of many kings who ruled in Ancient Egypt

phar•ma•col•o•gy /fɑːməˈkɒlədʒi/ noun = the science which studies the effects of different drugs and medicines on the body [TECHNICAL]

phar•ma•cy /ˈfɑːməsi/ noun, u. or c. (**pharmacies**) **1** (u.) = the study of how drugs and medicines are made **2** (c.) = a shop where medicines are sold **pharmacist** noun, c. = a person who mixes or makes medicines (also **chemist**) **pharmaceutical** /fɑːməˈsjuːtɪkəl/ adj. *a pharmaceutical company* = connected with the making of medicines

phar•ynx /ˈfærɪŋks/ noun = the tube which connects the mouth and nose to the throat **pharyngitis** /færɪŋˈdʒɑɪtɪs/ noun = infection of the pharynx, causing swelling and pain

phase[1] /feɪz/ noun, u. or c. **1** *The first phase of the project has been completed.* = a stage or step in a series of events or a process of development **2** *the phases of the moon* = the different shapes which the moon seems to have at different times as it rotates in orbit around the earth

phase[2] verb, t. *The project will be phased carefully.* = to divide something into phases or stages

phase in = to start using something gradually (in stages etc.) over a period **phase out** *The bus company will take a year to phase out the old buses and introduce new buses.* = to remove something gradually by phases (stages)

Ph.D abbr. of **Doctor of Philosophy** = an advanced degree given by a university, to a person who has done some original research in a specific area of a subject

pheas•ant /ˈfezənt/ noun (**pheasant** or **pheasants**) = a kind of game-bird (a bird that is hunted for its meat)

phe•nom•e•non /fɪˈnɒmɪnən/ noun, c. (**phenomena**) **1** *Eclipses of the sun and moon are natural phenomena, although people believed at one time that they were caused by supernatural forces.* = something that happens regularly as part of a natural process but appears unusual or strange and has scientific interest **2** *A batsman like Don Bradman is born once in a hundred years. He was a phenomenon.* = a very unusual or special person or event (figurative) **phenomenal** adj. *Rathi played a phenomenal game of chess.* = unusual and wonderful

phi•al /ˈfaɪəl/ noun, c. (American) = a small bottle in which liquid medicines are kept

phi•lan•thro•pist /fɪˈlænθrəpɪst/ noun, c. = a person who likes to help people who are poor or in trouble, specially by giving away money

phi•lat•e•list /fɪˈlætəlɪst/ noun, c. = a person who collects stamps **philately** = stamp collecting [TECHNICAL]

phi•los•o•phy /fɪˈlɒsəfi/ noun, u. or c. (**philosophies**) **1** = the study of the nature and meaning of reality and existence, knowledge, goodness etc. **2** *What is the philosophy behind the new political movement?* = a system of beliefs and principles which guides some action **philosopher** noun, c. = a person who studies philosophy or thinks about the meaning of life etc. **philosophical** /fɪləˈsɒfɪkəl/ adj. **1** *a philosophical question* = concerning philosophy **2** *She was calm and philosophical about not being accepted by the university.* = not worrying and remaining calm about something bad that happens **philosophize (philosophise)** /fɪˈlɒsəfaɪz/ verb, i. = to think like a philosopher **philosopher's stone** noun = an imaginary substance which could turn a cheap metal into gold

phlegm /flem/ noun, u. = the thick liquid (mucous) produced inside the nose, throat etc. when one has a cold **phlegmatic** /flegˈmætɪk/ adj. *a phlegmatic person* = calm and not easily excited (formal)

pho•bi•a /ˈfəʊbiə/ noun, c. or u. = strong and unreasonable fear of some kind, which one cannot get over easily

-phobia /fəʊbɪə/ a suffix added to nouns to mean **1** complete dislike of something e.g. **arachnophobia** noun = a hatred of spiders **2** a dislike or deep fear of something that could be a mental illness e.g. **pyrophobia** noun = a fear of fires

phoe•nix /ˈfiːnɪks/ noun = an imaginary bird which lives for 500 years and then burns itself and is born again from its own ashes (referred to in ancient stories)

to rise like a phoenix from the ashes = to be revived (brought back into active life) after going through a period of difficulty or suffering

phone[1] /fəʊn/noun, c. = telephone

phone[2] verb, t. *I phoned him last night.* = to call or speak to someone over the telephone **phone card** noun, c. = a card that one can use to make calls from a public booth

to tap someone's phone = to listen secretly to conversations on someone's telephone, using special electronic instruments **phone in** = a television or radio programme where one can phone the station and make a request, ask question etc. on the phone

pho•neme /ˈfəʊniːm/ noun, c. *The words 'bat' and 'mat' are pronounced in the same way, except for the difference between the first sound ('b') in 'bat' and the first sound ('m') in 'mat'. So we can say that 'b' and 'm'*

P

are phonemes in English. = the smallest unit of sound that can make one word different from another word [TECHNICAL] **phonemics** /fəˈniːmiks/ noun = the study of the phonemes in a language

pho•net•ics /fəˈnetɪks/ noun = the scientific study of the sounds used in human speech (also **phonology**) **phonetic** adj. *phonetic symbols* = special symbols (signs) used to represent the actual sounds of human speech **phonetician** /fəʊnəˈtɪʃən/ noun = a person who studies or practises phonetics

pho•ney[1] (phony) /ˈfəʊni/ noun, c. (American) *Her accent is phoney.* = someone who pretends to be something that he/she is not in reality; a fraud (informal)

phoney[2] adj. *They are fighting a phoney war.* = false; not real

phono- /ˈfəʊnəʊ/ a prefix used to mean 'connected with sound' i.e. phonics e.g. **pho•no•graph** /ˈfəʊnəgrɑːf/ noun, c. = an old-fashioned instrument that plays music from records (discs made of plastic) (also **gramophone**)

phos•pho•rus /ˈfɒsfərəs/ noun = a yellowish substance that gives out a faint light in the dark **phosphorescent** /fɒsfəˈreʃɪnt/ adj. *Sea waves have a phosphorescent quality.* = shining faintly in the dark

pho•to- /fəʊtəʊ/ a prefix meaning **1** connected with light e.g. **photosensitive** *photosensitive screen* = affected by light **2** to do with photographs e.g. **pho•to•cop•y** /ˈfəʊtəkɒpi/ noun, c. or verb, t. = a copy of something or to make a copy

pho•to /ˈfəʊtəʊ/ noun, c. (**photos**) = see **photograph** (informal)

pho•to•cop•i•er /ˈfəʊtəʊkɒpɪəʳ/ noun, c. = a machine that makes photographic copies of something

pho•to•graph[1] /ˈfəʊtəgrɑːf/ noun, c. = a picture made by using a camera and photographic film (a thin sheet of plastic, coated with chemicals which change colour when light falls on them)

photograph[2] verb, t. *I want to photograph this building.* = to make a photograph **photography** /fəʊˈtɒgrəfi/ noun, u. = the art and science of making photographs **photographer** noun, c. = a person who makes photographs **photographic** /fəʊtəˈgræfɪk/ adj. **1** *a photographic exhibition* = having to do with photographs **2** *a photographic memory* = able to remember things very clearly **photoelectric** adj. = using electricity that is produced by the effect of light [PHYSICS] **photogenic** /fəʊtəʊˈdʒenɪk/ adj. *a photogenic face* = looking very good in a photograph

pho•to•syn•the•sis /fəʊtəʊˈsɪnθɪsɪs/ noun, u. = the process by which plants are able to make their own food in the presence of sunlight [BIOLOGY]

phrase /freɪz/ noun, c. *'On the face of it' is a phrase meaning 'without going deep into some matter'.* = a group of words which are commonly used together and can form part of a sentence [GRAMMAR] **phrasal** adj. = having to do with a phrase **phrasal verb** noun, c. *'Put up with' is a phrasal verb which means 'to tolerate'.* = a phrase made up of a verb together with one or more prepositions or adverbs, which has a meaning somewhat different from that of the verb taken by itself [GRAMMAR] **phrase book** noun, c. = a book which is used by tourists visiting a foreign country and contains sentences in the language of that country which may be frequently required or used **phraseology** /freɪzɪˈɒlədʒi/ noun, u. = the way in which words are used (or arranged) to talk or write about a particular subject (formal)

phy•lum /ˈfaɪləm/ noun, c. (**phyla**) = a family or group of animals or plants which have certain things in common [BIOLOGY]

phys•i•cal /ˈfɪzɪkəl/ adj. **1** *You need physical exercise.* = relating to the body **2** *She is more interested in the physical development of the village than in its spiritual development.* = having to do with material things required for the body, such as money, food, housing etc. **3** *Let me describe the physical properties of hydrogen. It is a colourless gas, lighter than air, having no smell, which burns easily.* = having to do with qualities which can be seen, smelt, measured etc. **4** *Don't get physical!* = having the habit of touching other people in a sexual way **5** *a physical science* = an area connected with physics **physical education** noun = the study of the body and its care through exercise, sports etc. **physical geography** noun = the study of the surface of the earth, its shape, the rivers, mountains etc. (compare **political geography**)

phy•si•cian /fɪˈzɪʃən/ noun, c. = a doctor who treats diseases through medicines

phys•ics /ˈfɪzɪks/ noun = the science that deals with different forms of matter and natural forces such as light, electricity, heat etc. **physicist** noun, c. = a scientist who studies physics

phys•i•ol•o•gy /fɪzɪˈɒlədʒi/ noun = the study of how the different parts of living things of various animals, plants etc. work

phys•i•o•ther•a•py /fɪziəʊˈθerəpi/ noun = the treatment and care of the body through exercise, massage etc. **physiotherapist** noun, c. = a person who practises physiotherapy

phy•sique /fɪˈziːk/ noun, u. = the form of the human body

pi /paɪ/ noun **1** = a letter of the Greek alphabet, represented by the sign π **2** *The circumference of a circle is given by the formula 2 πr ,where the value of π is 22 / 7 or 3.14.* = a constant (a quantity which does not change) in mathematics, used for making certain calculations (It is the distance around a circle divided by its width.) [GEOMETRY]

pi•an•o /pi'ænəʊ/ noun, c. (**pianos**) = a large musical instrument in which sounds are produced when small hammers are made to hit strings (metal wires) of different length **pianist** /'piːənɪst/ noun, c. = a professional musician who plays the piano

pick[1] /pɪk/ verb, t. **1** *The selectors have picked twelve players for the team.* = to choose or select out of a larger group or number **2** *The girls are picking flowers in the garden.* = to gather (or take from a particular place) **3** *Don't pick your nose!* = to clean the nose by using one's finger (informal, disapproving)

pick[2] noun, u. **1** *Which shirt would you like? You can take your pick.* = the thing that one would like to choose **2** *Kumble is the pick of the Indian bowlers.* = the best **picky** adj. *She is very picky about food.* = choosy (careful to pick or choose only certain things) (informal) (see also **fussy**) (sometimes disapproving) **pick-axe** noun, c. = a tool which has a wooden handle and a metal head with two sharp points, and is used for digging up a hard surface **pickpocket** noun = a person who steals things from other's bags, pockets etc.

to pick someone's brains *I am taking part in the debate tomorrow and I would like to pick your brains.* = to get or take ideas from someone (informal) **to pick a lock** *The thief entered the house after picking the lock on the front door.* = to open a lock by using some instrument other than the key of the lock **to pick someone's pocket** = to steal money from someone's pocket **to pick a quarrel** = to start a quarrel with someone **to pick on somebody** *She keeps picking on her friend and teases him because he cannot sing well.* = to behave unfairly by teasing someone in an unkind way (informal) **to pick someone out** = to choose someone from a group **to pick up** = to improve and get better after an illness **to pick someone up** *We have requested our neighbour to pick us up from school.* = to collect someone, usually in a car etc. **to pick someone/something up** **1** *I picked up my dog and gave him a hug.* = to lift something from the ground **2** *I cannot pick up your signal here; let me go out into the open.* = to receive an electronic signal, television picture, radio sound etc. **3** *I picked up some Chinese cooking skills during this course.* = to learn a skill, language etc. (informal) **to pick up a book or packet** = to buy or collect **to take one's pick** *They sell many kinds of pens here. Take your pick.* = to choose from a variety of things (informal)

pick•et /'pɪkɪt/ verb, t. *The workers are picketing the factory as they are demanding better working conditions.* = to stand near the entrance to a factory, shop etc. and prevent people from entering, until a issue with the employers has been settled

pick•le[1] /'pɪkəl/ noun, c. or u. = fruit or vegetables which have been kept in a mixture of oil, vinegar, spices and salt for sometime and are used to add taste to food

pickle[2] verb, t. *I am going to pickle these mangoes.* = to make a pickle out of something

pic•nic /'pɪknɪk/ noun, c. *We are going on a picnic to the Botanical Gardens.* = a visit by a family or a group to an attractive outdoor spot, during which food is taken to be eaten outside

pic•ture[1] /'pɪktʃər/ noun, c. **1** *The child is drawing a picture of the monkeys in the zoo.* = a painting or drawing **2** *I can't see you in this picture.* = photograph **3** *The picture on the TV screen is rather faint.* = the image that appears on a television screen **4** *This book presents an exciting picture of life in the Himalayas.* = a description that provides an image in the mind

picture[2] verb, t. **1** *Can you picture the scene which the writer describes?* = to imagine **2** *In this painting the artist has pictured Napoleon leading his army into battle.* = to show in a painting or drawing **picture book** noun = a children's book that has many pictures and some text and generally tells a story **picture postcard** = a postcard with a picture of photograph on its front **pictorial** /pɪk'tɔːriəl/ adj. *a pictorial magazine* = containing pictures or showing something through pictures

to get the picture *You've been trying to meet me all day. I get the picture: you want a day off, don't you?* = to understand the truth about something (informal) **to be the picture of health** = to be very healthy

pic•tur•esque /pɪktʃə'resk/ adj. **1** *The people living in the villages of Rajasthan look very picturesque in their bright clothes.* = interesting and colourful in an old-fashioned way **2** *The writer uses picturesque language to describe the beauty of the lake.* = very clear, vivid and beautiful (words in this case)

pid•dle /'pɪdl/ verb, i. = to urinate (pass water) (slang) **piddling** adj. *piddling details* = small and unimportant (informal, derogatory)

pid•gin /'pɪdʒɪn/ noun, u. or c. = a language which is a mixture of two or more languages and is used for conversation among people who do not know each other's language

pie /paɪ/ noun, c. = a kind of cake which has an outer crust (covering) filled with fruit or meat

to have a finger in every pie = to play a part in many different activities (disapproving)

P

piece[1] /piːs/ noun, c. **1** *Give me a piece of that cake.* = a small part of something solid, which has been broken or cut off **2** *He has lost some of his important pieces, including the bishop and the knight.* = a small object used to play a game such as chess **3** *She wrote an excellent piece on the music festival.* = an article in a newspaper or magazine **4** *Can you play that piece again?* = a single composition of music, art etc.

piece[2] verb, t. *Several people who witnessed the accident gave different accounts of what happened. The police is trying to piece the facts together.* = to join the different pieces (parts) and make something complete **piecemeal** adj. or adv. *This large painting was made by a number of artists, working piecemeal.*(adv.) = doing something a bit at a time

a piece of cake *Passing this examination will be a piece of cake for me.* = something which is very easy to do (informal) **to give somebody a piece of one's mind** = to speak to someone very angrily telling them exactly what/how one feels **to go to pieces** = to feel like one has lost control and is unable to go to work or complete regular tasks easily (informal) **to take something to pieces** *The watch-repairer took the watch to pieces.* = to open up something (e.g. a clock) so that one gets the separate parts which make it up

pied /paɪd/ adj. = having feathers of different colours (used to describe a bird)

pier /pɪə[r]/ noun, c. = a kind of bridge that extends from the land into the water, where boats can stop to let their passengers get off or get on

pierce /pɪəs/ verb, t. **1** *I pierced my finger accidentally with the needle when I was trying to mend my shirt.* = to pass through something solid (of an object having a sharp point) **2** *The sun's rays pierced the clouds.* = to pass through sharply **piercing** adj. *a piercing wind* = so strong that it can pierce (pass through) something

pi•e•ty /'paɪəti/ noun, u. = deep respect for one's religion and for God **pious** /'paɪəs/ adj. *a pious person* = having great piety

pig /pɪg/ noun, c. **1** = a farm animal which has a fat body and short legs **2** *a greedy pig* = an offensive word for an unpleasant person who eats too much or does not care for the feelings of others (informal, derogatory) **piggy** noun, c. (**piggies**) = a word used by a child to refer to a pig **piggyback** /'pɪgibæk/ verb, i. *The government plans to start 300 new schools and our project to train teachers can piggy-back on the government's programme.* = to ride on the back of someone or something; to take advantage of something that is happening to do what you want to do **piggy bank** /'pɪgibæŋk/ noun, c. = a small toy made of clay, glass etc. in the shape of a pig, in which children drop coins to learn the habit of saving money **pig-headed** adj. *a pig-headed person* = stubborn (not willing to change one's thinking easily) **pig iron** noun, u. = an impure form of iron produced by heating iron-ore (the rock from which iron is obtained) in a furnace **piglet** noun, c. = a very young pig **pigsty** noun, c. (**pigsties**) **1** = a hut or shed in which pigs are kept **2** *This house has become a pig-sty.* = a very dirty and badly kept place (derogatory) **pigtail** noun, c. = hair on the head of a person which is twisted together into a kind of rope and tied with a ribbon or piece of string

to pig out = to eat a great deal at a meal (informal)

pi•geon /'pɪdʒɪn/ noun, c. = a kind of bird often found sitting on the roofs of old buildings, which is kept as a pet and also sometimes used to carry messages from one place to another **pigeon-hole**[1] noun, c. = a small space or compartment into which a box is divided (by using thin walls or partitions) and hung on a wall, so that letters etc. meant for different people can be kept in it **pigeon-hole**[2] verb, t. *You need different kinds of people to run a hospital. In fact, it is difficult to pigeon-hole them.* = to put something or someone in a class or category, separate from other classes or categories

pig•ment /'pɪgmənt/ noun, u. or c. **1** = a coloured substance from which paint is made **2** = the substance in the human body which gives colour to the skin, hair etc. **pigmentation** /pɪgmən'teɪʃn/ noun, u. *Her skin has lost its pigmentation and become white.* = the colouring matter present in the skin (formal)

pi•lau (pilaf) /'piːlaʊ/ noun, u. = a kind of food made with rice, meat, vegetables, nuts etc. popular in India and other Asian countries (also **pulao**)

pile[1] /paɪl/ noun, c. **1** *There is a large pile of books on the table.* = a number of things of the same kind, placed on top of each other **2** *The new building will be supported by concrete piles.* = a heavy pillar driven into or built into the ground, supporting a building, bridge etc.

pile[2] verb, t. **1** *He piled the books on top of the table.* = to put things on top of each other to make a pile **2** *The work in the office is piling up.* = to increase or grow into something big **pile driver** noun, c. = a machine which is like a very big hammer and is used to drive piles into the ground, before a building comes up, supported on the piles **pile-up** noun, c. = a road traffic accident in which cars, buses etc. crash into each other

to pile into *The school children piled into the bus once the doors opened.* = to get into a place or car etc. in large numbers **to pile on** **1** *The citizens have piled on the pressure and the government will have to solve the water* *problem soon.* = to increase (e.g. the demands one makes in order to get a result) **2** *I feel awkward when she piles on praise like that.* = to say something in an excessive way (so that it does not seem sincere) (informal, derogatory)

piles /paɪlz/ noun = a condition of the body in which the blood vessels near the anus (the opening at the lower end of the intestines) become swollen and painful (also **haemorrhoids**)

pil•fer /'pɪlfəʳ/ verb, t. *The cashier has been pilfering money from the office.* = to steal things in small quantities or of little value

pil•grim /'pɪlgrɪm/ noun, c. = a person who travels to a place of religious importance **pilgrimage** noun, u. or c. **1** = a journey to a place of religious importance, made by a pilgrim **2** = a place which is visited by a pilgrim

pill /pɪl/ noun, c. *a headache pill* = a small, solid piece of some medicine which is usually swallowed and not chewed (also **tablet**)

a bitter pill to swallow = an unpleasant situation that is difficult to accept (figurative)

pil•lage /'pɪlɪdʒ/ verb, t. = to plunder or loot (to rob, using violence)

pil•lar /'pɪləʳ/ noun, c. **1** = a tall, upright column (post) made of stone or concrete which supports the roof of a building **2** *She is one of the pillars of this community.* = a person who helps or supports a group (figurative)

pil•li•on[1] /'pɪljən/ noun, c. *You can drive the motorcycle and I will sit on the pillion.* = the second seat on a motorcycle or scooter, behind the driver's seat.

pillion[2] adv. *He was riding pillion.* = on the pillion of a motorcycle

pil•low /'pɪləʊ/ noun, c. *a feather pillow* = a cloth bag filled with cotton, feathers or some other soft material, which is used to support the head while sleeping (see pic under **bed**) **pillow-case/-cover** noun = a cloth bag used to cover a pillow

pi•lot[1] /'paɪlət/ noun, c. **1** *an airline pilot* = a person who controls an aircraft while it is flying **2** *a river pilot* = a person who has detailed knowledge of a river or some other stretch of water and who guides a ship while it is passing through this stretch **3** *This project is only a pilot.* = something which is taken up in advance of a large project or programme, in order to test whether it will be successful

pilot[2] verb, t. **1** *Capt. Wijeratne is piloting this aircraft.* = to control an aircraft while it is flying **2** *pilot a ship* = to guide a ship through a stretch of water **3** *The Home Minister will pilot the new act through the Parliament.* = to make sure that a new law is accepted by the Parliament

pilot[3] adj. *a pilot project* = something which is done as a trial for something else that is to follow

auto(matic) pilot noun = a machine, controlled by a computer, which can take over the control of an aircraft while the human pilot is resting **pilot error** noun = an accident to an aircraft caused by some mistake of the pilot **pilot lamp** noun = a small light (usually red) on a machine which burns to show that the machine is working

pimp /pɪmp/ noun, c. = a person who acts as an agent, supplying and finding customers for sex workers (not respectful)

pim•ple /'pɪmpəl/ noun, c. = a small, round infected spot on the skin, which may be full of pus

pin[1] /pɪn/ noun, c. *You can use a pin to hold the papers together.* = a small piece of metal with a sharp point, like a small needle, which is used to hold pieces of cloth or paper together

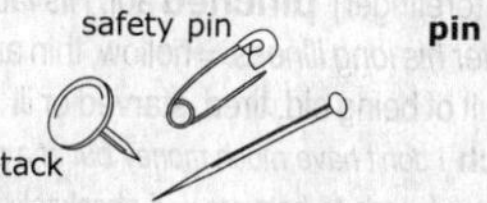

pin[2] verb, t. (**pinned**) **1** *She pinned the two pieces of paper together.* = to fasten or join together with a pin **2** *The older boy pinned the younger boy to the floor.* = to hold in a certain position so that one cannot get up or move **pin-prick** noun, c. **1** *The injection was like a pin-prick.* = a quick, short pain that one feels when a needle is pushed into the skin **2** *My seniors in the offfice sometimes test my patience through little pinpricks.* = something that causes a minor irritation (makes one feel angry or upset) **pin-up** noun, c. = A picture of an attractive and well-known woman or man (e.g. a film-star) which is pinned-up on a wall by an admirer. A pin-up can also be a picture of usually, a woman with revealing clothes **pincode** = a postal number which identifies the area and city in which one lives (compare **zip code**)

you could hear a pin drop = used to emphasize how quiet a place is **to pin one's hopes on something** = to hope very much that something will be successful because everything else has failed **to pin someone down** *He won't tell us how to proceed unless we pin him down.* = to force someone to speak about something clearly, with all the details

PIN abbr. for 'personal identification number,' a number used by the owner of a credit-card, bank account etc. and not known to anyone else for security reasons

pin•cer /'pɪnsəʳ/ noun, c. *The crab uses its pincers to protect itself from enemies.* = one of the two hand-like parts, ending in sharp points, which some animals (crabs, lobsters, scorpions etc.) have and which they use to hold their food or to protect themselves **pincers** noun (always plural) = a metal tool that looks like a pair of scissors, with two short and curved movable parts which can be used to hold and pull a nail out of a piece of wood (see **pliers**)

pinch[1] /pɪntʃ/ verb, t. or i. **1** *Her grandmother pinched her cheek playfully.*(t.) = to squeeze a person's flesh between the thumb and forefinger, either in play, to express affection, or in anger, causing pain **2** *The child's fingers got pinched in the door.*(t.) = to be caught between two hard surfaces **3** *The new shoes are pinching.*(i.) = to press tightly and cause pain **4** *Someone has pinched my watch.*(t.) = to steal (informal)

pinch[2] noun, c. **1** *She gave her friend a playful pinch.* = the act of pinching someone **2** *He added a pinch of salt to the curry.* = a small amount of some powdery substance (as much as can be picked up between the thumb and forefinger) **pinched** adj. *His face looked pinched after his long illness.* = hollow, thin and drawn in as a result of being old, tired, starved or ill

at a pinch *I don't have much money but at a pinch I can always ask my friends to help me.* = if absolutely necessary (informal) **to take something with a pinch of salt** *You say you will give up smoking. I take that with a pinch of salt.* = to not believe something completely, often because of an earlier experience (informal) **to feel the pinch** *Prices are going up and we are all feeling the pinch.* = to feel suffering or hardship

pine[1] /paɪn/ noun **1** *a pine tree* = a kind of tree with thin, sharp leaves that grows in high or cold places **2** = the wood of this tree

pine[2] verb, i. **1** *He hasn't seen his children in the last ten years and he is pining for them.* = to suffer in the mind because one cannot have something that one would strongly wish to have **2** *She has been pining away ever since she moved away from her house.* = to feel very sad and become weak as a result

pine•ap•ple /ˈpaɪnæpəl/ noun = a kind of yellow, juicy fruit that is covered with a thick skin

ping /pɪŋ/ noun, u. *We heard the ping of bullets as they whistled over our heads.* = a short, sharp sound

ping-pong /ˈpɪŋpɒŋ/ noun = the game of table tennis

pin•ion /ˈpɪnjən/ verb, t. *The policeman caught hold of the thief and pinioned his arms.* = to hold someone by the arms so as to prevent movement (formal)

pink[1] /pɪŋk/ noun = a very pale red colour

pink[2] adj. *pink cheeks* = the colour pink

pin•na•cle /ˈpɪnəkəl/ noun, c. **1** *Lata Mangeshkar has reached the pinnacle of fame as a singer.* = the highest point **2** = a pointed rock or the top of a mountain

pin•point[1] /ˈpɪnpɔɪnt/ verb, t. *The police knows roughly the area in which the robber lives, but they have not been able to pinpoint its exact location.*(t.) = to find or show the exact position of something

pinpoint[2] adj. *She hit the target with pinpoint accuracy.* = very accurate

pint /paɪnt/ noun, c. *a pint of milk* = a measure of the amount of liquid which a container can hold, equal to about half a litre **pint-sized** adj. *a pint-sized person* = very small (not respectful)

pi•o•neer[1] /paɪəˈnɪəʳ/ noun, c. *Jagdish Chandra Bose was a pioneer in the field of science.* = a person who is the first to take up some new activity (an area of knowledge etc.) and is followed by others

pioneer[2] verb, t. *Homi Bhabha pioneered research in the field of nuclear physics in India.* = to be the first to take up a new activity **pioneering** adj. *Sir C.V. Raman did pioneering research in physics.* = used to describe something (e.g. research, an idea, a method) which is done for the first time and changes the way people think etc.

pious see **piety**

pip[1] /pɪp/ noun, c. **1** *an orange pip* = the small seed of a fruit, e.g.an orange **2** *the pips on an army officer's uniform* = the stars, made of metal or plastic, which are put on the shoulders of the uniform (military dress) worn by an army officer, and which show his/her rank

pip[2] verb, t. (**pipped**) *P.T. Usha almost won the 200 m race, but she was pipped at the finishing line by Shiny Abraham.* = to defeat or to be defeated narrowly by someone in a race or competition (informal)

pipe[1] /paɪp/ noun, c. **1** *a water pipe* = a tube (long piece of hollow, round metal or plastic) through which some liquid or gas can flow **2** *a tobacco pipe* = a short, hollow tube with a round container at one end which is used for smoking tobacco

pipe[2] verb, t. **1** *The water that we get in our homes is piped all the way from the Mahanadi river, 200 km away.* = to be carried through pipes (referring to some liquid or gas) **2** *'Welcome to our school!' a little child piped.* = to speak in the high, energetic voice children use (informal) **pipe dream** noun, c. = an idea or plan which cannot be put into practice (derogatory) **pipeline** noun, c. = a long line of thick pipes through which water, oil or gas can be carried over long distances in a large quantity or volume **piped music** = recorded music played in e.g. a plane, a shop

to pipe down *Why are the people outside shouting? Please ask them to pipe down.* = to stop making a noise (informal, not respectful)

pi•pette /pɪˈpet/ noun, c. = a thin glass tube which can be used to suck up measured quantities of some liquid and is used for carrying out experiments in chemistry (see pic under **laboratory equipment**)

pip•ing[1] /ˈpaɪpɪŋ/ noun, u. **1** *The piping in this house is old and needs to be changed.* = the system of pipes **2** *The cushion covers are decorated with blue piping.* = a narrow piece of cloth which is folded into a tube and used to decorate something

piping[2] adj. *The food was served piping hot.* = very hot (referring to food)

pi•pul (peepul) /ˈpiːpʌl/ noun = a large tree with spade- shaped leaves commonly found in India

pique[1] /piːk/ noun, u. *He left the meeting in a pique because he was not allowed to speak.* = a feeling of displeasure caused when one thinks one has been insulted

pique[2] verb, i. *She felt piqued because her name was not in the guest list.* = to feel hurt and displeased

pi•ra•nha /pɪˈrɑːnjə/ noun = a kind of fish found in South America which will attack and eat up any animal that enters the water in which the fish lives

pi•rate[1] /ˈpaɪrət/ noun, c. **1** = a sea-robber (a person who attacks and robs ships at sea) **2** = a person who copies and sells a product made by someone else, without having the permission or the right to do so

pirate[2] verb, t. *A recording company has pirated the songs of Lata Mangeshkar.* = to copy or sell the work done by someone else (e.g. a writer or a singer) without having the right or the permission to do so **piracy** noun, u. **1** = robbery at sea, committed by a pirate **2** = the action of pirating (copying illegally) something such as books, tapes etc.

Pis•ces /ˈpaɪsiːz/ noun = the sign of the zodiac which is represented by two fish (see pic under **zodiac**)

piss[1] /pɪs/ noun, u. = urine (slang)

piss[2] verb, i. = to urinate

piss off *I was tired of listening to them and asked them to piss off.* = an offensive way of asking someone to leave **to be pissed off** = to react to something in a way that shows that one is disappointed, displeased or unhappy with something (slang)

pis•ta•chi•o /pɪˈstɑːʃiəʊ/ noun = a small, green nut with a very pleasant taste often used in making sweets

pis•til /ˈpɪstl/ noun, c. = the central, female part of a flower which produces seeds [BIOLOGY] (compare **stamen**)

pis•tol /ˈpɪstəl/ noun, c. = a very small gun which can be carried in the pocket and aimed and fired with one hand

pis•ton /ˈpɪstən/ noun, c. = a part of an engine that fits tightly in a hollow tube called a cylinder and moves up and down to make the engine work

pit[1] /pɪt/ noun, c. **1** *We dug a pit and buried all the garbage in it.* = a hole dug in the ground **2** *The miners have gone down into the pit.* = a coal-mine **3** *There are some pits in this steel plate.* = a small mark or hole in a surface **4** = a large hard seed in a fruit e.g. a date

pit[2] verb, t. (**pitted**) **1** *His face has been pitted by disease.* = to make holes or pits in something **2** *India has been pitted against South Africa in the opening match.* = to make someone compete against someone else **pitfall** noun, c. *A politician has to be prepared at all times to face pitfalls.* = an unexpected danger or difficulty

to be the pits *This restaurant is the pits. Let's not eat here again.* = to be very bad (slang)

pitch[1] /pɪtʃ/ noun, u. or c. **1** *a cricket pitch*(c.) = an area marked out for playing some game **2** *Lata Mangeshkar sings at a very high pitch.*(u.) = the degree of highness or lowness of a voice while singing or speaking **3** *Violence has reached a high pitch in the city.*(u.) = level or degree

pitch[2] verb, t. or i. **1** *Let us pitch our tent under these trees.*(t.)= to put up a tent or a camp **2** *The ship pitched violently as the storm hit us.*(i.) = to move in such a way that the front part goes up and down (describing the movement of a ship or aircraft) **3** *Everyone liked the talk because the speaker had pitched it at just the right level.*(t.) = to adjust or set the level of a speech or a piece of writing so that it can be understood by most people **4** *Pitch the ball to me.*(t.) = to throw a ball through the air at someone **5** *The bowler pitched the ball very close to the batsman.*(t.) = to make the ball hit the ground when bowling in sports like cricket, baseball etc. **6** *She pitched forward and fell when the bus-driver used the brakes suddenly.* = to move as a result of some other action so as to fall, or nearly fall

pitch[3] adj. *It was pitch-dark inside the room.* = completely dark

to pitch in = to join someone in doing something **a pitched battle** = a battle fought (in the old days) at a fixed place (usually an open field)

pitch•er /ˈpɪtʃəʳ/ noun, c. **1** *a pitcher full of water* = a container, usually made of clay, that holds some liquid **2** *a baseball pitcher* = a player who pitches (throws) the ball in the game of baseball

pitch•fork /ˈpɪtʃfɔːk/ noun, c. = a tool with a long handle and two thin metal arms, generally used by farm workers to lift and move hay

pith /pɪθ/ noun, u. **1** = the soft, white substance found at the centre of the stems of certain plants **2** *You seem to have some good ideas for the development of this village. Now let us get to the pith.* = the central or most important part of an idea, argument etc. **pithy** adj. *Your ideas are pithy.* = having pith or substance and said in few words (something that can be taken seriously)

P

pit•tance /ˈpɪtəns/ noun, u. *I was paid a pittance for doing the work.* = a very small amount of money (not very generous) (derogatory)

pi•tu•i•ta•ry /pɪˈtjuːɪtəri/ noun *the pituitary gland* = a small organ (working part of the body) at the lower end of the brain, which produces some hormones (chemicals) that affect the growth and sexual development of the body

pit•y[1] /ˈpɪti/ noun, u. *How can you leave the dog out in the rain. Have you no pity?* = sorrow at the suffering of another living being and a desire to help

pity[2] verb, t. (**pitied**) *Arjun got soaked in the rain. I pity him.* = to feel sorry for someone **piteous** adj. *a piteous cry for help* = causing pity **pitiable** adj. *The house is in a pitiable condition.* = deserving pity (also pitiful) **pitiless** adj. = having or showing no pity

for pity's sake *For pity's sake! Please get up. Its seven o' clock.* = said to show annoyance **What a pity** *I couldn't meet her children when she came to town. What a pity!* = to say that something is unfortunate

pi•vot[1] /ˈpɪvət/ noun, c. **1** *the pivot in a machine* = the fixed central point or part in a machine around which something turns (goes round) or balances **2** *Agriculture is the pivot of our economy.* = the most important part, on which everything depends (figurative)

pivot[2] verb, t. **1** *You can make this chair revolve (turn round and round). It pivots on this large screw.* = to turn around a fixed point **2** *The political system of the country pivots on the strength of the economy.* = to depend on **pivotal** adj. *She played a pivotal role when her country won the tennis cup.* = most important

pix /pɪks/ noun, c = pictures (informal)

pix•el /ˈpɪksəl/ noun, c. = the smallest part of an image on the computer screen [COMPUTERS]

pix•ie /ˈpɪksi/ noun, c. (**pixies**) = a kind of fairy (in stories for children) who can do magic

piz•za /ˈpiːtsə/ noun, u. or c. = a thick, round piece of bread which is baked with cheese, tomatoes etc. on it

plac•ard /ˈplækɑːd/ noun, c. *Ahmed waited at the airport carrying a placard with his colleague's name.* = a large notice, supported on a pole, carried in a public place to attract attention

pla•cate /pləˈkeɪt/ verb, t. *She placated her angry friend with a nice letter.* = to do something to take away a person's anger (formal)

place[1] /pleɪs/ noun, c. **1** *This is the place where the battle was fought.* = a particular area or spot **2** *Is there place for us to sit inside? // I'm sorry we can't offer you any of the jobs. All the places have been filled.* = a position or seat (in a car etc.) that can be used or a job in a company **3** *I have found a place in the college hockey team.* = a chance to play for a team, study in a college etc. **4** *Please put the book back in its place.* = usual position **5** *This boy came first in the examination, and that girl took second place.* = position after the end of an exam or race etc. **6** *The answer is 7.583, calculated to the third decimal place.* = the position of a figure to the right of the decimal point **7** *She has a really nice place in a quiet part of the town.* = home (informal)

place[2] verb, t. **1** *He placed the book on top of the desk.* = to put down **2** *The new officer will be placed in the accounts department.* = to find a job for **3** *I have placed an order for a new car.* = to give **4** *Your face looks familiar, but I can't place you.* = to remember someone fully **placement** noun **1** = the art of finding a place to work **2** = a temporary job

to be all over the place *His books were all over the place.* = everywhere (in a way which makes it difficult to find something) **to be in someone's place** *If I was in your place I would go to school today.* = to be in another's situation **in the first place** *No, I didn't go to school on Tuesday. In the first place, I wasn't even in town.* = used when one is listing out reasons why something happened (informal) **to put someone in their place** = to let someone know that they are not the cleverest or the skilful at something **to feel out of place** = to feel uncomfortable in a situation **to be in place** *Are all the things in the new house in place?* = in a suitable position **in place of** *In place of the film we wanted to show, we are performing a play.* = instead of **to do something in someone's place** *She couldn't attend the meeting, so I went in her place.* = instead of the person who is originally supposed to do something **to fall into place** *When the detective saw the letter, everything suddenly fell into place.* = to become clear (used of something e.g. a mystery, in which the facts are not clear at first) **to not be one's place** *It is not my place to talk about the company's faults. I'm very new here.* = I should not be saying this as I am too junior etc. **to be going places** = to become successful in one's job (informal)

pla•ce•bo /pləˈsiːbəʊ/ noun, c. (**placebos**) *The doctors have given him a placebo, and it seems to work.* = a substance that is not a medicine but is believed to be a medicine by the patient

pla•cen•ta /pləˈsentə/ noun, c. = the flesh-like material which joins the baby, before its birth, to the mother (also **umbilical cord**)

pla•cid /ˈplæsɪd/ adj. *a placid lake* = calm and peaceful

pla•gi•a•ris•m /ˈpleɪdʒərɪzəm/ noun, u. or c. **1** *His new book is mostly a copy of a novel by Tagore. I never thought he would turn to plagiarism.*(u.) = the practice of taking ideas or words from the work of another writer, composer etc. and using them as one's own, without admitting that one has done so **2** *This is clearly a plagiarism.*(c.) = an idea or expression that one writer has taken from another, without admitting that he/she has done so **plagiarize (plagiarise)** verb, t. = to commit an act of plagiarism **plagiarist** noun, c. = a writer who plagiarizes another writer

plague[1] /pleɪg/ noun = a disease carried by fleas (insects) which live on rats, causing high fever, swellings on the body and, often, death

plague[2] verb, t. *The state has been plagued by natural disasters throughout the year.* = to cause trouble, suffering etc.

plain[1] /pleɪn/ adj. **1** *She looks beautiful even in plain clothes.* = simple and without any decoration or show **2** *a plain girl* = not good-looking (derogatory) **3** *It is quite plain that you have not studied for the examination.* = obvious (easy to see) **4** *I think the time for plain speaking has come.* = frank (without trying to hide anything) **5** *I need some plain paper.* = without lines **6** *plain chocolate // plain flour* = only the substance (chocolate, flour etc.) mentioned, without anything added to it

plain[2] noun, c. (also plains) *The city lies in the middle of a large plain.* = a large piece of flat land **plainclothes** adj. *The Prime Minister is always surrounded by plainclothes guards.* = not wearing police or army uniform (dress) while on duty **plainly** adv. *She did not speak to us. Plainly, she was angry or hurt.* = clearly **plain English** **1** = clear, simple English which is not difficult to understand **2** = a movement to make the English used in legal, medical etc. documents free of expressions which are difficult to understand (except by specialists in that field) so that it can reach more people [TECHNICAL]

plain sailing noun, u. *At first I found it difficult to do the work, but once I had practised, it was plain sailing.* = a situation that presents no difficulties **to make something plain** *I would like to make it plain that I am not trying to sell you anything.* = to make something clear so that the other person does not misunderstand

plain•tiff /'pleɪntɪf/ noun, c. = a person who brings a plaint (a complaint) to a court [LAW]

plain•tive /'pleɪntɪv/ adj. *a plaintive song* = expressing sorrow (literary)

plait /plæt/ noun, c. = a kind of rope made by twisting strands of hair or threads together

plan[1] /plæn/ noun, c. or u. **1** *The government has come up with a new plan to bring clean drinking water to villages.*(c.) // *The work is progressing according to plan.*(u.) = a set of decisions about some future actions, to be taken up for a particular purpose **2** *The architect has prepared the plans for the new building.*(c.) = a drawing of a building that will come up in the future

plan[2] verb, t. (**planned**) **1** *They plan to visit China next year.* = to decide some future event or activity **2** *The new cinema complex is very badly planned.* = to design something (e.g. a building)

plane[1] /pleɪn/ noun, c. **1** = aircraft **2** *I would like to discuss this matter with you on a personal plane.* = level **3** *The carpenter uses a plane to make surfaces smooth.* = a tool used by carpenters to make a wooden surface flat and smooth

plane[2] adj. *a plane surface* = completely flat [TECHNICAL]

plane[3] verb, t. *The table has many bumps. We must plane it.* = to use a plane to make a surface smooth

pla•net /'plænɪt/ noun, c. = a heavenly body that moves in an orbit or fixed path around a star, such as the sun **planetarium** /plænɪ'teəriəm/ noun, c. = a building fitted with a special machine that is like a film projector, which can show pictures of the sky at night and the movements of the different stars and planets, on the curved roof of the building which represents the night sky

plank /plæŋk/ noun, c. = a long, narrow and flat piece of wood from which different wooden objects can be made

plank•ton /'plæŋktən/ noun = tiny forms of animal or plant life found in the sea, rivers or lakes, which become food for many kinds of fish

plant[1] /plɑːnt/ noun, c. **1** *a rice plant* = a living thing with roots and leaves, smaller than a tree **2** *an industrial plant* = a factory **3** *processing plant* = machinery used for some industrial purpose **4** = a person who pretends to be part of an audience, group etc. but who has actually been placed there to observe things, ask the questions one wants asked etc. (often derogatory)

plant[2] verb, t. **1** *We have to plant more trees.* = to put a plant or tree or the seed of a plant or tree in the ground, so that it can grow **2** *She planted herself in front of the ticket counter, waiting for it to open.* = to position oneself somewhere firmly (humourous, informal) **3** *The terrorists planted a bomb under the bridge.* = to place something secretly in a place **4** *The police found some drugs in his suitcase. Someone must have planted them there.* = to hide something illegal in someone's luggage, clothes etc. to make the person appear guilty **plantation** /plæn'teɪʃən/ noun, u. or c. **1** *tree plantation*(u.) = the action of planting trees **2** *a coffee plantation*(c.) = a large area of land used for growing crops for profit **planter** noun, c. **1** *a tea planter* = someone who owns a plantation or is in charge of it **2** = a pot in which a plant can be planted

P

plan•tain /'plæntɪn/ noun, c. or u. = a fruit which is like a banana

plaque /plɑːk/ noun, u. or c. **1** *a wall plaque*(c.) = a small, flat piece of stone or metal fitted into a wall, on which there is some writing in memory of an important person or event **2** (u.) = the yellowish substance (bacteria) that forms on teeth

plas•ma /'plæzmə/ noun, u. **1** *blood plasma* = the liquid part of blood in which the red or white blood-cells float [BIOLOGY] **2** = a kind of gas contained inside a star that is still hot and has not become solid [PHYSICS] **plasma panel/display** = a large electronic display board which is connected to a computer and can be used in public places

plas•ter[1] /'plɑːstəʳ/ noun, u. or c. **1** *The plaster on the walls of the old building is peeling off.*(u.) = a mixture of sand and cement used to cover the bricks in a wall or building **2** *I have broken my arm. The doctor will put a plaster on it.*(c.) = a cloth bandage containing a powder (called gypsum or plaster of paris), which becomes hard when water is added to it (A plaster is used to hold a broken bone in position so that it can join properly.) **3** *Put a plaster on the cut on your forehead.*(c.) = a small bandage which covers a wound and can stick to the skin, so that it will not fall off

plaster[2] verb, t. **1** *The brick wall has to be plastered.* = to cover with a mixture of sand and cement **2** *The doctor plastered my broken arm.* = to put a broken limb (arm or leg) in a plaster (bandage) **3** *The news of your victory was plastered all over the newspapers.* = to be written about in great detail **plastered** adj. *The man was thoroughly plastered.* = drunk (informal)

plas•tic[1] /'plæstɪk/ noun, u. or c. **1** *This factory produces plastics.* = an artificial chemical substance which can be used to make objects of different kinds, in different shapes (e.g. chairs or buckets) **2** *We accept both cash and plastic.* = a credit card that one can use instead of money for paying things (informal)

plastic[2] adj. **1** *This material is very plastic.* = something which can be moulded into different shapes and keeps these shapes **2** *a plastic smile* = artificial or not sincere **plastic explosives** noun, c. = a soft chemical material from which a bomb can be made and which can be given different shapes by pressing with the fingers **plastic surgery** noun *His face has been so badly burnt that he will need plastic surgery. // The filmstar has undergone plastic surgery to improve the shape of her nose.* = the repairing or improving of a damaged or badly shaped part of the body by taking skin or bone from some other part and allowing it to grow in the damaged or unsatisfactory part [MEDICINE]

plas•ti•cine /'plæstɪsiːn/ noun, u. = a soft, clay-like substance in different colours, from which children make toy animals or other toy objects

plate[1] /pleɪt/ noun, u. or c. **1** *a dinner plate* = a round, flat vessel usually made of glass, china or plastic, from which food is eaten **2** *Scientists tell us that the earth is made up of huge plates which move very, very slowly. It is the movement of these plates that causes earthquakes.*(c.) = large, flat pieces of hard rock of which the earth's surface is made **3** *This statue is made of lead, covered with gold plate.*(u.) = a thin covering of some metal, usually gold or silver, over some cheaper metal **4** *a plate in the skull // a number plate* = a piece of metal that is used to protect something [MEDICINE] or to provide information

plate[2] verb, t. *The jeweller will plate these silver ornaments with gold.* = to cover thinly with some metal **plateful** noun, c. = the amount of food that a plate will hold **platter** noun, c. = a large plate (vessel) in which food is served

to hand something to someone on a plate or silver platter = to make it very easy for someone to get something which is usually hard to get **to have too much on one's plate** = to have too many things to worry about or deal with

pla•teau /'plætəʊ/ noun, c. (**plateaus** or **plateaux**) **1** *the Deccan plateau* = a large piece of level (flat) land which is higher than the land surrounding it [GEOGRAPHY] **2** *She was improving steadily as an artist, but she seems to have reached a plateau now.* = a stage in one's development or growth during which there is no change or further development

plate•let /'pleɪtlɪt/ noun, c. = small cells in the blood that help it to clot

plat•form /'plætfɔːm/ noun, c. **1** *a railway platform* = a raised, flat surface built on one side of a railway track, so that passengers can easily get into or out of trains **2** *the speaker's platform* = a low table on which a speaker stands while talking to an audience, so that he/she is at a height and can be seen by people sitting at the back **3** *The candidate has made clean water supply her election platform.* = an idea or a cause which a politician adopts (makes his own) in order to fight an election **4** *The Citizens' Club provides a platform for discussion on many topics.* = a place where one gets a chance to express one's opinions **5** *We are using the Windows platform for our work.* = a software system which supports a number of programs [COMPUTERS]

pla•ti•num /'plætɪnəm/ noun = precious white metal from which jewellery is made and which is also used by some chemical industries

pla•ti•tude /'plætɪtjuːd/ noun, c. *I am tired of*

hearing you repeat these platitudes endlessly. = a statement that contains some truth but which is so well-known (e.g. 'Honesty is the best policy') that no one wants to hear it being repeated (derogatory)

pla•toon /plə'tu:n/ noun, c. = a small group of soldiers

plat•y•pus /'plætɪpəs/ noun = an animal found in Australia that has a beak and feet like that of a duck, lays eggs but feeds its young ones with milk

plau•si•ble /'plɔ:zɪbəl/ adj. *He may be telling us the truth. His story sounds plausible.* = seeming to be true or reasonable (referring to a statement or argument) (opposite **implausible**)

play[1] /pleɪ/ verb, i. or t. **1** *The children are playing in the garden.*(i.) // *They are playing hide-and-seek.*(t.) = to do something for amusement **2** *India will be playing Australia in the next match.*(t.) = to compete against someone in a sporting competition **3** *He likes to play the radio in the morning.*(t.) = to turn something on **4** *He is playing his flute.*(t.) = to produce music on a musical instrument **5** *Shah Rukh Khan plays a young poet in this film.*(t.) = to perform a role in a drama or film **6** *He played a trick on us.*(t.) = to do something funny, clever or dishonest

play[2] noun, u. or c. **1** *We are going to see the new play.*(c.) = drama (a piece of writing turned into a story with dialogues and action and presented by actors) **2** *Play in the match has been stopped because of rain.*(u.) = the activity done during a game or sport **3** *My niece is more interested in play than in study.* = activity done for amusement, specially by children **4** *the play button* = a button on a video cassette recorder or music player etc. that allows one to run a tape **player** noun, c. **1** = one who takes part in a game, either as an individual or as a member of a team **2** *a record player* = an electronic instrument that can run a tape **3** *a piano player* = one who plays a musical instrument **4** *'Softwise' is one of the players in the software industry.* = one of the important companies in an industry [BUSINESS] **playground** noun, c. = an area or large piece of land where people (specially children) can play **playschool** noun, c. = a school for very young children, where they learn through play **playwright** noun, c. = a person who writes plays (dramas)

play down *He was suffering great pain, but played it down so that we would not feel bad.* = to make something seem less important, painful etc. than it actually is (opposite **to play up**) **play up** **1** *When we spoke to the Principal, we played up the importance of sports.* = to make something sound more important than it is (informal) **2** *The battery is playing up and we are not able to start the car.* = to give trouble (informal) **to play one's cards right** = to handle or plan a situation cleverly so that the results help one later **to play second fiddle** = to have to act/be in a position lower to someone else (informal) **to not play ball** *She wanted Ravi to accompany her to the station but he would not play ball.* = to not do something that someone wants you to do (informal) **to play the fool** = to behave in a foolish way **to play something by ear** = to act according to the situation or circumstances, instead of having a fixed plan **to play one's cards close to one's chest** = to tell nothing about one's plans to anyone **to play to the gallery** = to do something that will please most people (disapproving) **to play on words** = to use words with more than one meaning (see **pun**) **to play along** *She did not really agree with what her companion said but she played along.* = to act as though you agree with someone because you want to avoid a quarrel **to play hard to get** = (in a sexual relationship) to behave as if one does not care for the other person in order to attract him/her more **to play it cool** *Don't worry, you are bound to get promoted soon. Just play it cool!* = to remain calm while doing something necessary to achieve your goal (informal) **to play safe** = to not take unnecessary risks in something that one is trying to do **to play games** *Stop playing games and tell me what is really on your mind.* = to do something to mislead or confuse another person, without revealing your real intention **to play the game** = to act in an honest and honourable way **to play for time** *He says he would like to discuss things with you but he is not really interested in reaching an agreement. He is only playing for time.* = to delay matters so that one gets more time to carry out one's plans

play•back[1] /'pleɪbæk/ noun, u. **1** *a playback singer* = the action of using a singer to sing the songs that an audience thinks an actor is singing **2** = a recording on videotape etc. can be viewed by going to the starting point

playback[2] adj. *a playback singer* = a person who in the making of a film, actually sings the song(s) that the actor in the film appears to be singing

pla•za /'plɑ:zə/ noun, c. = an open area in a town or a group of shops in the centre of town where there is a market

plea /pli:/ noun, c. **1** *She made a strong plea for giving the children a holiday.* = a serious request **2** *He didn't come to work on the plea that he had fever.* = excuse

plead /pli:d/ verb, t. **1** *The students pleaded that they should be allowed to go home as they had not gone home for a whole year.* = to ask for something very strongly and seriously **2** *The prisoner engaged a lawyer to plead her case.* = to present a case before a judge on behalf of someone

pleas•ant /'plezənt/ adj. **1** *The weather is pleasant in Bangalore throughout the year.* = enjoyable or

P

comfortable **2** *She is quite a pleasant person to talk to.* = friendly and likeable **pleasantry** noun, c. (usually plural **pleasantries**) *The two associates exchanged pleasantries before settling down to serious talk.* = light and polite talk

please[1] /pli:z/ verb, t. **1** *I will buy this sari for my friend. I am sure it will please her.* = to make someone feel happy or satisfied **2** *You can choose any book that you please.* = to want

please[2] interjec. *Please sir, may I be excused?* = making a polite request **pleased** adv. *She seemed very pleased with her new sandals // we were so pleased to see you.* = to be happy or satisfied about something **pleasing** adj. *That sari has a pleasing colour.* = likeable

if you please = used to make a polite request (formal) **Yes please** *'Would you like some orange juice?' 'Yes please.'* = to accept politely **Please yourself** *If you don't want to do what I'm telling you to do, please yourself.* =a way of telling someone, with some irritation, that because they haven't taken your advice they can do what they want

plea•sure /'pleʒə^r/ noun, u. **1** *His face lit up with pleasure when he saw his children.* = happiness **2** *She likes to combine work with pleasure.* = relaxation or some activity that helps to make the mind light **3** *What a pleasure it is to meet you after all these years!* = something that causes happiness

to have the pleasure *Could I have the pleasure of your company for dinner tonight?* = an expression used to invite someone (formal) **to take pleasure in something** = to enjoy doing something very much **with pleasure** *'Could you help me cook dinner?' 'With pleasure.'* = used to say that you would be happy to do something that you are requested to do

pleat[1] /pli:t/ noun, c. *trousers with pleats* = a long, flat fold in a dress

pleat[2] verb *to pleat a sari* = to make pleats in a piece of cloth

pledge[1] /pledʒ/ verb, t. *The people pledged to come forward and work wholeheartedly to remove poverty and hunger.* = to make a solemn promise

pledge[2] noun, c. = a solemn promise

plen•ty[1] /'plenti/ noun, u. **1** *Poverty has its problems but so does plenty.* = the state of being rich **2** *He used to be poor but now he has wealth in plenty.* = in large quantities

plenty[2] pron. *I don't need any more money for the journey. I have plenty.* = enough or a large quantity **plentiful** adj. *We have a plentiful supply of food.* = more than enough (opposite **scarce**) **plenitude** noun, u. *He has a plenitude of wealth.* = plenty or a great amount (old-fashioned, literary)

pli•a•ble /'plaɪəbəl/ adj. **1** *Silver is a very pliable metal.* = something that can be easily bent without breaking **2** *She is old-fashioned but quite pliable.* = willing to accept new ideas **3** = easily influenced or persuaded (sometimes derogatory)

pli•ers /'plaɪəz/ noun, c. (always plural) = a tool that looks like a pair of scissors and is used to hold something or to cut pieces of wire (see **pincers**) (see pic under **tools**)

plight /plaɪt/ noun, u. *The children were cold. He was so sorry to see their plight that he gave them all the warm clothes he had.* = a condition or situation that is sad and serious and causes pity

plinth /plɪnθ/ noun, c. = the base (lower part) of a building or column, which is partly under the ground and supports the upper part

plod /plɒd/ verb, i. (**plodded**) **1** *They plodded along, tired after the day's work.* = to walk slowly and with difficulty **2** *She is plodding away at her task.* = to work steadily but without much interest **plodder** noun, c. *Don't expect much from her. She is just a plodder.* = a slow and not very intelligent person who can work hard (derogatory)

plonk /plɒŋk/ verb, t. *She plonked the heavy suitcase down on the bed.* = to put down or drop something heavy or to sit down, usually with a noise (informal)

plop /plɒp/ noun, c. *The stone fell into the water with a plop.* = the soft sound made when something solid drops into a liquid

plot[1] /plɒt/ noun, c. **1** *The plot of the film is rather complicated.* = the connected events which make up a story **2** *a plot to slow down work* = a secret plan to do something **3** *I have been given a small plot in the new township.* = a piece of land

plot[2] verb, t. (**plotted**) **1** *They plotted to make her give them money.* = to make a secret plan to do something **2** *The captain of the ship plotted his course carefully.* = to mark on a map a route that is to be taken by a ship or plane **3** = to mark points on a **graph**

plough[1] /plaʊ/ verb, t. *ploughing the land* = to turn the soil over before seeds are planted

plough[2] noun, c. = a tool used by farmers to break up the soil before seeds are planted in it, consisting of a wooden frame to which a metal blade is attached for cutting up the soil

to plough back = to put the money earned through a business back into the business **to plough into** = to crash into something because one is driving a car etc. without care or attention **to plough on** = to continue to work hard at something **to plough through** *We ploughed through the many cars on the road.* = to move through something with difficulty

ploy /plɔɪ/ noun, c. *He quickly tried to think of a ploy* *to make his aunt buy him a new shirt.* = a clever or confusing trick (derogatory)

pluck[1] /plʌk/ verb, t. **1** *There are lots of ripe mangoes on the trees. We should pluck them now.* = to gather flowers, fruit etc. growing on a tree or plant by pulling them out **2** *Can you pluck out the grey hairs on my head?* = to pull out and remove something which is not wanted **3** *The sitar player produces musical sounds by plucking the strings of the sitar.* = to pull repeatedly

pluck[2] noun, u. *He lost one of his legs in the war but he is not worried. He has plenty of pluck.* = courage and determination (informal) **plucky** adj. *a plucky fighter* = a person who has pluck (courage)

plug[1] /plʌg/ noun, c. **1** *The bath-tub has an opening in the bottom, to allow the water to flow out. But you can use a rubber plug to close the opening.* = a piece of rubber,metal etc. which is used to close a hole or an opening in a container so that nothing can get out or get in **2** *an electrical plug* = a small plastic object with two or three metal pins attached to it which, when pushed into small openings in a wall etc. connects a machine using electricity (e.g. a television set) to wires through which an electric current is flowing

plug[2] verb, t. *The water is leaking out through this hole. Can you plug the hole with some cement?* = to close or block a hole or an opening so that something cannot get out or get in

to plug in *Please plug in the computer.* = to connect an electrical appliance to a supply of electricity **to pull the plug on something** = to stop something by no longer providing money or support of some other kind

plum[1] /plʌm/ noun, c. or u. **1** (c.) = a kind of round, juicy fruit with a hard seed **2** (u.) = a colour close to red

plum[2] adj. *She has a plum job.* = very desirable (informal)

plum•age /'plu:mɪdʒ/ noun, u. *Some parrots have very colourful plumage.* = the feathers of a bird **plume** noun, c. **1** *The king's crown is decorated with peacock plumes.* = a large feather from a bird, used to decorate something **2** *a plume of smoke* = something that looks like a large feather (e.g. a long and thin cloud)

plumb[1] /plʌm/ verb, t. *The ancient philosophers of India tried to plumb the mysteries of life.* = to study something deeply in order to understand it (formal)

plumb[2] adj. *The wall that you are building is not straight. It should be plumb.* = perfectly vertical (upright) and not sloping backwards or forwards

plumb[3] adv. *The ball hit him plumb on the nose.* = exactly

to plumb the depths *This director's first film was bad, but with his second film he has really plumbed the depths.* = to reach the lowest level of something

plumb•er /'plʌməʳ/ noun, c. = a person who fits water-pipes in a building or repairs water-pipes, taps etc. **plumbing** noun, u. = the complete system of pipes, taps etc. in a building through which water is supplied

plum•met /'plʌmɪt/ verb, i. **1** *The aircraft plummeted suddenly after one of its wings was damaged in the storm.* = to fall with great speed from a height **2** *The share prices plummeted this week.* = to fall sharply (become lower in value)

plump /plʌmp/ adj. **1** *a plump baby* = fat in a pleasant way **2** *a plump cushion* = large and round

plun•der[1] /'plʌndəʳ/ verb, t. *Armies plundered Eastern Europe during the war and carried away many valuable objects.* = to rob by taking away something forcibly, specially during a war

plunder[2] noun, u. = things taken away by thieves or robbers

plunge[1] /plʌndʒ/ verb, i. **1** *The boy jumped off the high rock and plunged into the sea below.* = to move forwards or downwards suddenly with force **2** *The temperature in Delhi is supposed to plunge this week.* = to fall much lower **3** *She opened the car and plunged into the house.* = to move fast and with force into something

plunge[2] noun, u. *He took a plunge into the water.* = an act of jumping suddenly into water **plunger** noun, c. *the plunger of an injection syringe* = a part of a machine that moves up and down

to take the plunge = to decide suddenly to do something (especially to get married) after hesitating for a time (informal) **to plunge in** **1** = to start doing something with great enthusiasm **2** *to plunge a needle in* = to quickly push something in **to plunge into** *The country has plunged into a crisis after the drought.* = to suddenly be put into an unpleasant situation

plu•ral[1] /'plʊərəl/ noun, u. or c. *'Children' is the plural of 'child'* = a form of a word which shows that we are talking of more than one person or thing (opposite **singular**) [GRAMMAR]

plural[2] adj. *'They' is a plural pronoun.* = the plural form of a word

plus[1] /plʌs/ prep. *Two plus five equals seven.* = added to

plus[2] noun, c. (**pluses**) **1** *The fact that you know many*

P

languages is a plus on this job. = an advantage (informal) **2** *You should use a plus to show that you are adding two numbers to each other.* = a mathematical sign represented by **+**

plus[3] adj. **1** *Your long experience will be a plus factor.* = desirable (informal) **2** *He has to retire as he is sixty-plus now.* = more than **3** *A+* (said as A plus). = a grade which is higher than A etc.

plush[1] /plʌʃ/ adj. *plush surroundings* = luxurious (very comfortable and expensive looking)

plush[2] noun, u. *The seats in the cinema are covered with plush.* = a kind of soft cloth with short hair-like threads covering its surface

Plu•to /'plu:təʊ/ noun = a planet in the solar system, which is very far away from the earth and at the farthest distance from the sun

plu•to•ni•um /plu:'təʊnɪəm/ noun = a kind of (**radio-active**) metal that is used to produce nuclear energy (energy produced by breaking up the atoms of a substance)

ply[1] /plaɪ/ noun, c. (**plies**) or adj. *three-ply wool; a six-ply nylon tyre* = a measure of the thickness or strength of a material, depending on the number of threads or lengths of material (called plies) which are woven together to form the material

ply[2] verb, i. or t. *Buses are plying on the new highway.* (i.) = to move along a road or route (used to refer to the movement of vehicles) **2** *He plies a taxi on this route.*(t.) = to drive a vehicle that carries passengers

to ply someone with something = to keep giving someone a lot of food, drinks, presents etc.

ply•wood /'plaɪwʊd/ noun, u. = wooden board (thin, flat material) made by joining several thin sheets of wood together with glue

pm abbr. of **post meridiem** = sometime after 12.00 noon

pneu•mat•ic /nju:'mætɪk/ adj. *a pneumatic lift* = worked by the pressure of air (referring to machines)

pneu•mo•ni•a /nju:'məʊniə/ noun = a serious disease that attacks the lungs and causes breathing difficulties

poach /pəʊtʃ/ verb, t. or i. **1** *There are not many tigers left as people have been poaching tigers for many years.*(t.) = to catch or kill animals in an illegal way for profit (derogatory) **2** (t.) = to cook an egg or fish in boiling water **3** *The company is poaching senior managers from its rival companies.* = to persuade someone to leave another company or group and join yours (informal) **poaching** noun, u. *The government is trying to stop poaching.* = the illegal catching or killing of animals **poacher** noun, c. = a person who poaches (catches or kills animals illegally)

pock•et[1] /'pɒkɪt/ noun, c. **1** *a shirt pocket* = a piece of cloth stitched into a small bag in which objects can be kept, which is attached to a shirt, coat or other garment (dress) **2** (always singular) *I will pay for this meal out of my own pocket.* = supply of money **3** *We drove into a pocket of mist as we were going up the hill.* = a small area (figurative)

pocket[2] verb, t. *She pocketed the charge and didn't return any to her mother.* = to take or keep money for oneself, often dishonestly **pocket-book** noun, c. **1** = a small book which can be carried in the pocket **2** = a purse (handbag) for a woman (American) **pocket calculator** = a calculator that is small enough to be carried in one's pocket **pocket money** noun, u. = money given by parents to a child to spend as he/she likes

to pick someone's pocket = to steal a person's wallet

to be in each other's pockets = used of two people who spend too much time together (disapproving or humorous)

pock•mark /'pɒkmɑ:k/ noun, c. = a small, hollow mark on the skin of a person who suffered from chicken-pox or acne **pock-marked** adj. = covered with pock-marks

pod /pɒd/ noun, c. *like two peas in a pod* = a long, hollow part of a plant that contains the seeds of the plant

podg•y /'pɒdʒi/ adj. *a podgy little child* = short and fat (informal, less offensive than **fat**)

po•di•um /'pəʊdɪəm/ noun, c. *the speaker's podium* = a raised area on which a person can stand so that he/she is easily seen by others

po•em /'pəʊɪm/ noun, c. = a piece of writing which has an imaginative and musical quality, in which the lines are not continuous (running on from one line to the next without stopping)

po•et /'pəʊɪt/ noun, c = a writer of poems **poetry** noun, u. **1** *He will be remembered for his poetry.* = the art or skill of writing poems **2** *the English poetry of the nineteenth century* = the poems written during a certain time or in a certain country or by a certain person **poetic** adj. *poetic langage* = having to do with poetry or poets **poetic justice** noun = the punishment or rewarding of a person (which is often shown in a story) because it is what they deserve **poetic licence** noun = the freedom given to a poet or writer to change facts, in order to make his/her writing more attractive **Poet Laureate** noun = an important poet who is specially honoured by being requested to write for special occasions

poi•gnant /'pɔɪnjənt/ adj. *She told us the poignant story of how she had to start work at the age of sixteen.* = causing sadness or pity

point[1] /pɔɪnt/ noun, c. or u. **1** *The needle has a* *sharp point.*(c.) = a sharp end which can prick (break) the skin **2** *It was at this point that our car broke down yesterday.* = a particular place, position or moment **3** *She ran the 100m in 11.(point) 2 secs.* = the way in which a number is referred to, using the decimal system **4** *Can you suggest a few points for my essay?* = an idea or fact that can be included in a speech or piece of writing **5** *Each team gets two points for winning a match and one point if a match ends in a draw.* = a unit for recording the score in a game or sports competition **6** *What are her strong points?* = a quality of somebody or something

point[2] verb, i. or t. **1** *When I asked the child where her father was, she pointed at a man sitting in the last row.*(i.) = to show where someone or something is by holding out a finger **2** *You should never point a knife at anyone, even if it is to say something.*(t.) = to aim at **3** *The needle of a magnetic compass points north.* = to show a certain direction **point-blank 1** *at point-blank range* = (of a bullet fired from a gun) from a very close position **2** *They asked me point-blank if I had told others the secret.* = in a sharp, direct way which can cause surprise or offence (informal) **pointed** adj. **1** *a pointed nose* = having a sharp end **2** *a pointed remark* = spoken in a meaningful or critical way **pointer** noun, c. **1** *The teacher used a pointer to show where Dehradun was on the map.* = a long, thin piece of wood that is used to draw attention to something **2** *I have just joined this school. You have been here for a long time, so can you give me a few pointers?* = a tip (words of advice) (informal) **3** = a kind of hunting dog **pointless** adj. *We are already an hour late so it is pointless going to the meeting now.* = without use/purpose **point of order** noun, c. *The Leader of the Opposition raised a point of order during the Lok Sabha debate.* = a short speech made at a meeting to say that some rule has not been followed or should be followed

beside the point *We admire her for her bravery. That she is young is beside the point.* = not important or relevant **to make a point of something** *Although it was only an informal meeting, he made a point of welcoming us.* = to make sure that one does something which is noticed **point of view** *You may not agree but this is my point of view.* = a certain way of looking at something **to the point** = (said of writing or speeches) just right or said well enough to convey clearly what needs to be said or written **up to a point** *What you say is true up to a point.* = not fully but partly **a sore point** *Which route to take to work has become a sore point between us.* = a point of constant argument or disagreement **to miss the point** = to not understand the main idea of something **What's the point?** *It's over now. We can't do anything, what's the point of talking about it?* = used to indicate that some action is not likely to be useful

poise /pɔɪz/ noun, u. **1** *I have never seen her lose her poise at meetings, no matter how strongly she is attacked.* = balance or the state of remaining calm **2** *The dancer has remarkable poise.* = a balanced way of moving **poised** adj. **1** *She always looks poised.* = calm and balanced **2** *The man is dangerously ill—poised between life and death.* = in an uncertain position between two opposite things **3** *The cat is poised to strike at the mouse.* = ready to do something

poi•son[1] /ˈpɔɪzən/ noun, u. or c. *some poison in the bottle* (u.) // *Carbon monoxide is a deadly poison.*(c.) = a substance that can cause illness or death if you eat, drink or breathe it

poison[2] verb, t. **1** *In the story, the queen poisoned the apple before giving it to Snow White.* = to use poison to harm or kill someone **2** *The chemicals from the factory are poisoning the water of the river.* = to make something impure so that it turns into a poison **3** *Some people think that television is poisoning the minds of children.* = to have a bad influence on someone's mind **poisonous** adj. **1** *a poisonous snake* = containing or being able to produce poison **2** *poisonous gas* = likely to kill

poke[1] /pəʊk/ verb, i. or t. **1** *She poked my elbow with her pen.*(t.) = to push a pointed object into something or someone **2** *She poked her head out of the window.*(i.) = to stretch something through or out of an opening

poke[2] noun, u. *I gave him a poke in the ribs with my finger.* = an act of poking (pushing something pointed into someone)

pok•er /ˈpəʊkəʳ/ noun, c or u. **1** (c.) = a metal rod used to shake up the pieces of coal in a fire so that they will burn better **2** (u.) = a kind of card game played for money **poker-faced** adj. *a poker-faced person* = having no expression at all on the face

to poke fun at someone = to make fun of someone **to poke one's nose into something** = to take an interest in some matter that does not concern you

po•lar /ˈpəʊləʳ/ adj. **1** *a polar bear* = having to do with either the North or the South Pole of the earth **2** *polar differences* = exactly opposite to each other (formal)

po•la•ri•ty /pəˈlærɪti/ noun, u. (**polarities**) = the state of having two opposite ends or poles (referring to a magnet etc.) [PHYSICS]

Po•lar•oid[1] /ˈpəʊlərɔɪd/ adj. *Polaroid lenses for sun-glasses*(adj.) = glass which has been treated in a special way so that the light passing through it causes no harm to the eyes (used for making sun-glasses etc.)

P

Polaroid[2] noun = (trademark) a camera that produces photographs immediately

pole /pəʊl/ noun, c. **1** *The roof of the hut is supported by wooden poles.* = a long, straight stick of wood or bamboo that is used to support something **2** *We are at opposite poles in our views on education.* = opinions or views which are opposite to (completely different from) each other **3** *the poles of the earth* = the two opposite ends of the earth's surface (the North and South Poles) PIC/169 **4** *the poles of a magnet* = the two ends of a magnet, having opposite powers of attraction **pole star** noun = a very bright star seen at night in the northern part of the sky **pole-vault** noun = a kind of sport in which a person is required to vault (jump) over a high bar, using a long pole **pole-vaulter** noun, c.

to be poles apart *They don't like the same kind of music. In fact they are poles apart in their taste.* = (of people's tastes, opinions, personality) to be so different that there is nothing in common

po•lice[1] /pə'li:s/ noun, u. (generally used with plural forms of verbs but also with singular forms) *The police have/has arrested the criminals.* = a group of persons whose duty is to protect the lives and property of people and to make everyone obey the law

police[2] verb, t. *The security guards have been policing the factory during the strike.* = to guard a place **police station** noun = a building used as an office by the police **police state** noun = a government which controls political freedom and uses the police to make sure that people are obeying rules (derogatory)

pol•i•cy /'pɒlɪsi/ noun, u. or c. (**policies**) **1** *It is the policy of this government to be on friendly terms with our neighbours.*(u) = a set of ideas and beliefs that guides the actions of a group or an individual **2** *an insurance policy*(c.) = a document showing that a person has an agreement with an insurance company under which the company will pay him/her money in case of some loss, accident, death etc. **3** *She has a policy of letting people know what she will do.* = a set of beliefs

po•li•o /'pəʊliəʊ/ noun = a serious disease, more common among children, which can cause paralysis (inability to move one's arms and legs)

pol•ish[1] /'pɒlɪʃ/ noun, u. **1** *wax polish for a car* = a substance which, when rubbed on or spread over a surface, makes it shine **2** *The table has a good polish.* = a smooth and shiny surface **3** *He lacks polish.* = refined (good) manners or quality

polish[2] verb, t. **1** *I am going to polish my car today.* = to make a surface bright and shiny by rubbing or spreading some polish over it **2** *Please practise harder and polish your typing skills before you attend the interview.* = to improve a skill by working harder at it **polished** adj. **1** *The singer gave a polished performance* = done with great skill (referring to work done by an artist) **2** *He is very polished in his behaviour.* = having good manners

to polish off *He polished off a whole chicken.* = to eat something quickly and completely (informal, often disapproving)

po•lite /pə'laɪt/ adj. *She is so polite that she will never say a word until you have finished speaking.* = having or showing good manners (opposite **rude**) **politely** adv. *She politely refused her friend's invitation to dinner.* = to say something in a polite way **politeness** noun

pol•i•tic /'pɒlɪtɪk/ adj. *It would not be politic on your part to refer to this unfortunate incident again.* = wise

pol•i•tics /'pɒlɪtɪks/noun **1** *She is very active in politics and hopes to become a minister some day.* = the activity of taking part in public affairs and using such activity to try to take control of the government **2** *He is a student of politics.* = the study of the principles of government (also **political science**) **3** *There is a lot of politics in the office.* = activity within a particular group by which some people try to gain some advantage over others (often derogatory) **political** /pə'lɪtɪkəl/ adj. **1** *Many of India's political institutions, such as the parliament and the law courts, have been set up on the British model.* = having to do with public affairs and the government of a country **2** *The company's decision to appoint a new director is purely political.* = done to bring some advantage **political geography** noun = the study of the way in which continents are divided into countries etc. rather than the physical features marking them (mountains, rivers etc.) (compare **physical geography**) **politician** /pɒlɪ'tɪʃən/ noun, c. **1** = a person who has made politics (public affairs) his/her profession **2** = a clever person who works always for his/her own interests

pol•ka dot /'pɒlkə dɒt/ noun, c. = a printed design for dress material (cloth for dresses) consisting of large circular dots on a background of different colour

poll[1] /pəʊl/ noun, c. **1** *We are conducting a poll to find out how many people think India should sign a treaty to ban nuclear tests.*(c.) = an attempt to find out the opinions of people on some matter by asking them questions **2** *a defeat at the polls* (always plural) = the process of voting in an election **3** *The poll has been quite heavy in this election.*(u.) = number of votes cast (given)

poll[2] verb, t. *Our candidate polled only 2000 votes.* = to receive votes in an election **polling** noun, u. **1** *Polling begins tomorrow.* = the process of voting at an election **2** *The polling on the website indicates that this was a popular programme.* = the act of asking people for their opinion on something **polling booth** noun, c. = a place where people can cast their votes

pol•len /'pɒlən/ noun, u. = the yellow dust produced by the male part of a flower which, when carried by the wind or by an insect (e.g., a bee) to the female part, causes it to produce seeds from which a new plant can grow **pollinate** verb, t. *Bees help to pollinate flowers.* = to carry pollen from one flower to another so that it produces seeds **pollination** /pɒlɪ'neɪʃən/ noun, u.

pol•lute /pə'luːt/ verb, t. *The Yamuna has been polluted by chemical waste from factories.* = to make something impure or unfit for use **pollution** noun, u. = the process of polluting air, water, land etc. (making it impure) [BIOLOGY] **pollutant** noun, c. *The chemical factories are discharging dangerous pollutants into the Yamuna.* = a substance that pollutes something or makes it impure

po•lo /'pəʊləʊ/ noun = a game, said to have been started in India hundreds of years ago, in which players on horseback try to hit a small ball with a long stick to score goals **polo neck** noun *a shirt with a polo neck* = a garment (e.g. a shirt or sweater) with a round collar that forms a circle around the neck

pol•y- /pɒlɪ/ prefix meaning many e.g. **pol•y•gon** /'pɒlɪgən/ noun, c. = a geometrical figure (shape) with four or more sides

pol•y•es•ter /pɒlɪ'estə/ noun = a kind of artificial material from which clothes can be made

pol•y•syl•la•ble /'pɒlɪsɪləbəl/ noun *The word 'photographic' is a polysyllable.* = a word that has more than one syllable (see also **syllable**)

pol•y•tech•nic /pɒlɪ'teknɪk/ noun, c. = a college where technical education is given in many different subjects or areas so that it can be used in practical work

pol•yp /'pɒlɪp/ noun, c. **1** = a very small animal that lives in water **2** = a small growth in the body that is generally harmless

pom•e•gran•ate /'pɒmɪgrænɪt/ noun, c. = a kind of round fruit with a thick skin and small juicy seeds inside

pomp /pɒmp/ noun, u. *Republic Day is celebrated in Delhi with a lot of pomp.* = a show of solemnity (seriousness) **pompous** adj. = behaving in a serious manner, as if to show one's importance (derogatory)

pond /pɒnd/ noun, c. = an artificial lake

pon•der /'pɒndəʳ/ verb, i. or t. *She pondered how to make the best use of the money she had won in the lottery.*(i.) // *I cannot answer you immediately. I need time to ponder the matter.*(t.) = to think over a matter carefully for some time (formal; literary or old-fashioned)

pon•toon /pɒn'tuːn/ noun, c. = a hollow metal container built like a boat, which floats in water and is used as a support for a floating bridge

po•ny /'pəʊni/ noun, c. (**ponies**) = a horse of small size

poo•dle /'puːdl/ noun, c. = a kind of dog with thick, curling hair which is often cut in a special way

pooh /puː/ interjec. *Pooh! What does he know about cricket?* = an expression of mild contempt (old-fashioned) **pooh-pooh** verb, t. (**pooh-poohed**) *When I asked her whether she would like to meet the singer, she pooh-poohed the idea.* = to dismiss an idea (to say that it is not a good idea) (informal)

pool[1] /puːl/ noun, c. **1** *There is a liitle pool in the forest where the animals come to drink.* = a small area of still water **2** *a pool of blood* = a small amount of some liquid **3** = a swimming pool **4** *a car pool* = things belonging to different people which are shared by the members of a group **5** = a game in which balls are hit with sticks (cues) into holes in a table (Pool is similar to billiards but played on a smaller table.)

pool[2] verb, t. *We will have to pool our resources.* = to bring together and share (money, ideas, equipment etc.)

poor[1] /puəʳ/ adj. **1** *They are very poor and cannot afford to go to school.* = without money **2** *We had poor rainfall last year.* = much less than usual **3** *His handwriting is poor.* = not good **4** *Poor girl! She has broken her leg just before a match!* = expressing sympathy or pity for someone **5** *He is in poor health and needs to see a doctor.* = bad, well below normal

poor[2] noun, u. *You should help the poor.* = the poor people **poorly** adv. or adj. **1** *A poorly done job.*(adv.) = not very well **2** *After the spell of flu, she is feeling rather poorly.*(adj.) = in a weak state of health

a poor second *In the race, she finished a poor second.* = a very long way behind the person or thing that has come first

pop[1] /pɒp/ verb, i. or t. (**popped**) **1** *The rubber balloon popped when the baby stepped on it.*(i.) = to burst with a short, low sound **2** *Your sister popped in while you were in the bathroom.*(i.) = to come in suddenly (informal) **3** *I will pop this letter into the letter box.*(t.) = to drop

pop[2] noun, u. *The balloon burst with a soft pop.* = the low sound of something bursting without much force

pop[3] adj. *pop music* = short for 'popular' and modern (informal) **pop art** noun = a form of modern painting based on popular or 'pop' culture, which shows

P

common subjects (e.g. advertisements) from everyday life **pop culture** noun = the popular culture of the modern age, specially popular among young people **pop music** noun = modern popular music, which is generally loud and has a strong rhythm and simple words that are easy to remember **popcorn** noun, u. = seeds of corn (maize) which are heated until they pop (swell up and burst) and are eaten with salt **pop-eyed** adj. *He was pop-eyed with wonder when he saw the Taj Mahal.* = having one's eyes wide open because of surprise or wonder (informal) **pop-gun** noun = a toy gun that fires small objects with a pop (low sound) **pop-up** adj. or noun **1** *This book has pop-up pictures.* = made in such a way that something that is inside will pop up (jump up or out) **2** = used to describe a box or menu that appears suddenly on a computer screen when one clicks the mouse [COMPUTERS]

to pop off = to die unexpectedly (informal, humorous and not respectful)

Pope /pəʊp/ noun = the head of the Roman Catholic religion (also pontiff)

pop•lar /ˈpɒpləʳ/ noun = a tall, thin tree that grows very straight

pop•lin /ˈpɒplɪn/ noun = a kind of cotton cloth

pop•py /ˈpɒpi/ noun, c. (**poppies**) or u. = a plant with white or bright-red flowers (Opium is produced from one kind of poppy plant which has white flowers)

pop•u•lar /ˈpɒpjʊləʳ/ adj. **1** *The new film star, Hrithik Roshan, is very popular with youngsters.* = liked by many people **2** *The popular feeling about our leader is that she is a gentle person, with a fine sense of humour.* = common **popularity** /pɒpjʊˈlærɪti/ noun, u. *Asha Bhonsle's popularity has grown with the years.* = the quality of being liked, enjoyed or supported by a lot of people **popularize (popularise)** /ˈpɒpjʊləraɪz/ verb, t. *Cricket has been popularized by television.* = to make something popular **popular opinion** noun = what most or many people think

by popular demand *By popular demand, the rock group is playing in the city again.* = because many people wanted something

pop•u•la•tion /pɒpjʊˈleɪʃən/ noun, u. or c. *India's population is now over one billion. // The tiger population in Corbett National Park is slowly increasing.* = the number of people or animals living in an area or a particular group of something **populate** /ˈpɒpjʊleɪt/ verb, t. *The islands in the Pacific Ocean are populated by people belonging to the Polynesian race.* = to live in an area **populous** adj. *Mumbai is a populous city.* = having a large population (formal)

por•ce•lain /ˈpɔːslɪn/ noun, u. or adj. = made of porcelain (a special kind of clay which is heated in an oven until it melts and forms a glass-like material) (also **china**)

porch /pɔːtʃ/ noun, c. (**porches**) = a covered entrance to a building (see also **portico**)

por•cu•pine /ˈpɔːkjʊpaɪn/ noun = an animal whose entire body is covered with sharp, pointed quills (feather-like growths) which protect it from enemies (also **hedgehog**) (see pic under **quill**)

pore[1] /pɔːʳ/ noun, c. *the pores in a person's skin* = a tiny opening in the skin through which sweat (liquid produced by the body) comes out

pore[2] verb, i. *He has been poring over her letter for two hours.* = to study (read with great attention) something that has been written **porous** /ˈpɔːrəs/ adj. *Drinking water is often kept in pots made of porous clay, so that the water is cool.* = a material which has tiny pores or holes through which a liquid can pass

pork /pɔːk/ noun, u. = the meat of a pig when used as food

por•nog•ra•phy /pɔːˈnɒgrəfi/ noun, u. = pictures or writing intended to cause sexual excitement (disapproving) **porn** noun, u. = a short form of the word 'pornography'

por•poise /ˈpɔːpəs/ noun = an animal that lives in water and is a mammal (giving birth to young ones and feeding them with milk) but smaller than the dolphin

por•ridge /ˈpɒrɪdʒ/ noun, u. = soft food prepared by boiling some grain (usually oats or wheat) in water or milk, often eaten for breakfast

port /pɔːt/ noun, c. **1** *the port of Mumbai* = a place where ships can stop and load or unload goods or people **2** *a computer with two parallel ports* = an opening in a computer through which it can be connected to a monitor (screen), printer etc. **port-hole** noun = a circular window in the side of a ship, covered with glass

por•ta•ble /ˈpɔːtəbəl/ adj. *a portable computer* = something that can be easily carried from one place to another

por•tal /ˈpɔːtəl/ noun, c. = a website through which one can connect with the Internet [COMPUTERS] **portals** noun, u. (always plural) = a large entrance to a building [LITERATURE]

por•tend /pɔːˈtend/ verb, t. *The black clouds in the sky portend a storm.* = to be a sign or warning of something that is coming (formal)

por•ter /ˈpɔːtəʳ/ noun, c. = a person who is paid to carry heavy objects, such as the suitcases of travellers

port•fo•li•o /pɔːtˈfəʊliəʊ/ noun, c. (**portfolios**) **1** a file (a large cover shaped like a book, made of card-board or plastic, inside which loose sheets of paper can be kept) **2** *The minister has been given two important portfolios.* = a department under the charge of a minister in the government **3** *The painter showed us her portfolio of drawings.* = a collection of drawings etc. carried inside a portfolio (cover) **4** = a particular selection of **shares** owned by a person or an organization

por•ti•co /ˈpɔːtɪkəʊ/noun, c. (**porticos**) = a covered entrance to a building (formal) (see also **porch**)

por•tion[1] /ˈpɔːʃən/ noun, c. **1** *I live in the front portion of this building.* = a part of something larger **2** *A portion of my savings will go towards buying the bicycle.* = a share of something **3** *Could I have another portion of chicken please?* = (used about food) a quantity of something

portion[2] verb, t. *The teacher portioned out the sweets among the children.* = to divide

port•rait /ˈpɔːtrɪt/ noun, c. **1** = a painting, drawing or photograph of a person **2** = the printout from a computer such that the height is greater than the width [COMPUTERS]

por•tray /pɔːˈtreɪ/ verb, t. *This film portrays the life of Dr Ambedkar.* = to represent (show)

pose[1] /pəʊz/ verb, i. or t. **1** *After the meeting we were asked to pose for a group photograph.*(i.) = to sit or stand in a certain way without moving in order to be photographed or painted **2** *He has posed a difficult question.*(t.) = to ask a question, create a challenge etc. **3** *He is not really unhappy. He is only posing.*(i.) = to pretend (to behave in a false or unnatural manner)

pose[2] noun, c. **1** *The film star was photographed in several different poses.* = a position in which one stands or sits in order to be photographed or painted **2** *His unhappiness is only a pose. Actually, he is quite happy.* = an act of pretending (showing false or unnatural behaviour)

posh /pɒʃ/ adj. *a posh house filled with expensive furniture* = fashionable and expensive (informal)

po•si•tion[1] /pəˈzɪʃən/ noun, c. or u. **1** *The sentry has been ordered not to move fom his position.*(c.) = a place where someone or something stands (is located) **2** *He was sitting in a comfortable position.*(c.) = the way in which one sits or stands **3** *I am not in a position to accept your offer.*(u.) = situation **4** *Your daughter got the highest position in the examination.*(c) = rank **5** *She has applied for a position in the company.*(c.) = job

position[2] verb, t. *George positioned himself outside the door so that he could keep an eye on everyone who was leaving.* = to put someone or oneself in a certain place

pos•i•tive /ˈpɒzɪtɪv/ adj. **1** *We were not sure if the company would accept our plan, but as their reply is positive we can go ahead with the plan.* = expressing acceptance or agreement (opposite **negative**) (formal) **2** *I am positive that the man who spoke to you on the telephone was the one who called yesterday.* = certain (formal) **3** *We haven't been on good terms with our neighbour but now there are some positive developments.* = giving cause for hope (formal) **4** *Why do you always say that we are going to lose? I want you to be more positive.* = hopeful **5** *His blood was tested this morning for malaria and the result was positive.* = showing the presence of a disease etc. **6** *'Big' is the positive form of the adjective while 'bigger' is the comparative form.* = the simple form of an adjective, which shows that no comparison is being made [GRAMMAR] **positively** adv. **1** *I was positively touched by the present my aunt gave me.* = without a doubt **2** *If you approach the problem positively, you will be able to solve it quickly.* = to think about the good things in a situation, rather than the bad things **3** *She spoke cautiously for the first five minutes but continued more positively for the next half hour.* = confident and strong **4** *I positively dislike travelling by air.* = used to emphasize something that one feels strongly about **positive discrimination** noun = the practice of showing special favour to people who have been unfairly treated in the past in order to make up for past injustice

pos•sess /pəˈzes/ verb, t. *Do you possess a scooter?* = to own or have something (formal) **possessed** adj. *He was shouting and screaming as if posessed.* = under the control of some evil spirit **possession** noun, u. or c. **1** *The government will give you this land as you are already in possession.*(u.) = the state of owning or holding something, specially a piece of land or a building **2** *She lives simply and does not have many possessions.*(c.) = the things that own possesses (owns) **possessive** adj. **1** *Rajan is so possessive of his camera that he does not let anyone use it.* = not willing to share something with someone because one loves it very much **2** *'My' and 'mine' are the possessive forms of the pronoun 'I'.* = the grammatical form of a word which shows ownership [GRAMMAR]

pos•si•ble /ˈpɒsɪbəl/ adj. **1** *It is possible for you to get a job in the new company.* = something that can happen or can be done **2** *It is possible for the price of wheat to come down soon.* = something that may or may not happen **possibly** adv. **1** *'Can you come with me to the shops today?' 'Possibly.'* = may be **2** *I will let you know as soon as I possibly can.* = used to say that one is trying very hard to do something **possibility** noun, u. or c. (**possibilities**) **1** *There*

P

is every possibility of your winning this election.(u.) = likelihood (a good chance of something happening) **2** (always plural) *This house is in poor condition now, but it has possibilities.*(c.) = the ability to become better **3** *This city offers many possibilities of things we could do today.*(c.) = one of many things that can be done

pos•sum /ˈpɒsəm/ noun = a kind of tree-climbing animal found in America

post- /pəʊst/ a prefix meaning **1** after e.g. **post•grad•u•ate** /pəʊstˈgrædjʊɪt/ noun or adj. *a post-graduate degree*(adj.) = a higher degree given to a person after he/she has already become a graduate and received the first degree (B.A., B.Sc. etc.) **2** later than e.g. **post-dated** /pəʊstˈdeɪtɪd/ verb, t. *Could you give me a postdated cheque?* = to put a date on a cheque that is later than the current date (the date on which the cheque is written out)

post[1] /pəʊst/ noun, c. or u. **1** *Please tie the dog to the post.*(c.) = a thick piece of wood fixed into the ground **2** *I will send the books by post.*(u.) = the system by which letters, parcels etc. are sent **3** *The post has just arrived.*(u.) = letters etc. sent by post **4** *She was offered the post of Manager.*(c.) = job or position

post[2] verb, t. **1** *Please post this letter at once.* = to send letters etc. by post **2** *The new officer has been posted to Kolkata.* = to send a person to a particular place to work **3** *Please post this paper on the notice-board.* = to put up a notice on a wall or notice-board **postcard** noun, c. = a card on which one can write a letter and send it by post **post code** noun *The post code for Bhubaneswar is 571007* = a number which is given to every post office in the country, so that letters can easily be sent through it (also **pin code** or **zip code**) **postman** noun, c. = a person who collects letters, packages etc. from a post office and delivers them to every house **post office** noun = a place where work connected with the postal system e.g. selling stamps, collecting letters which have to be sent to different places etc. is done **postage** noun, u. **1** *How much postage do I have to pay to send this letter to America?* = the amount of money required to send something by post **2** = the correct number of stamps for a letter, package etc. **postal** adj. *Postal charges may go up soon.* = having to do with the system of sending letters etc.

post•er /ˈpəʊstəʳ/ noun, c. = a picture or photograph of a large size that is put up usually to inform or advertise an event, show etc.

pos•te•ri•or[1] /pɒˈstɪəriəʳ/ noun, u. = the back part of the body, on which a person sits (the bottom) (formal or humorous)

posterior[2] adj. *a posterior view of the building* = relating to the back part of something

pos•ter•i•ty /pɒˈsterɪti/ noun, u. *The letters written by Mahatma Gandhi during his lifetime have been preserved for posterity in a museum.* = people born at a later time (formal)

post•hu•mous /ˈpɒstjʊməs/ adj. *Some of India's great leaders received posthumous awards of 'Bharat Ratna' several years after their death.* = happening after the death of a person (formal)

post-meridiem /pəʊst məˈrɪdiəm/ adv. = a time after 12 o'clock in the day, usually abbreviated as **pm**

post•mor•tem /pəʊstˈmɔːtəm/ noun **1** = an examination of the dead body of a person done after his/her death, to find out the cause of death (also **autopsy**) **2** *We had a post-mortem after the exam to find out why we had done badly.* = a discussion to find out why something produced bad results (figurative)

post•pone /pəʊsˈpəʊn/ verb, t. *The examination was to begin tomorrow but it has been postponed to next week.* = to delay an event so that it takes place at a later time

post•script /ˈpəʊstskrɪpt/ noun = a short message added to a letter or e-mail at the end

pos•tu•late /pɒstʃʊˈleɪt/ verb, t. *Copernicus first postulated that the earth moved around the sun.* = to suggest something as being possible or likely, for the sake of argument or experiment (formal)

pos•ture /ˈpɒstʃəʳ/ noun, u. or c. **1** *You should always sit with your back and shoulders straight. That is the correct posture.*(u.) = the position in which one keeps one's body while sitting or standing **2** *I had hoped that we could reach an agreement, but he took a very rigid posture.*(u.) = a way of behaving or thinking (formal)

post•war /pəʊstˈwɔːr/ adj. or adv. *European cinema grew very fast in the postwar years.*(adj.) = the period after a war

pot[1] /pɒt/ noun, c. or u. **1** *a cooking-pot*(c.) = a container made of clay, metal etc. in which liquids or solids are kept, specially for cooking **2** *I need a pot of tea.*(c.) = the amount of liquid that can be held in a pot **3** *He has pots of money.*(c.) (always plural) = a very large amount of something, usually money (not respectful) **4** *The police caught him smoking pot.*(u.) = marijuana (a dangerous drug) (slang)

pot[2] verb, t. *He is potting the plants so that he can carry them to his new home.* = to put a plant in a pot **pot-belly** noun = a paunch (a fat stomach that sticks out or hangs like a pot) **pot-boiler** noun = a book or film of rather poor quality, written or produced to earn money quickly **pothole** noun, c. = a hole in the surface of a road **pot luck** noun or adj. *Come over to my house this evening and let us have a pot* *luck dinner.*(adj.) = a meal where people eat whatever food is available, without specially cooking anything

po•ta•ble /ˈpəʊtəbəl/ adj. *Is this water potable?* = suitable for drinking (formal)

po•tas•si•um /pəˈtæsɪəm/ noun = a kind of metal which is present in the bodies of all living things **potash** noun = a chemical containing potassium, which is used as a **fertilizer**

po•ta•to /pəˈteɪtəʊ/ noun, u. or c. (**potatoes**) = a kind of very popular vegetable that grows under the soil and has a brown or yellow skin **potato crisp** noun = a very thin, round and flat piece of potato that has been dried and then fried in oil (On the subcontinent, potato crisps are often called potato chips.)

po•tent /ˈpəʊtənt/ adj. **1** *The doctor gave me a potent medicine. I was cured quickly.* = very strong or powerful **2** = able to have sex (used to describe a man) (opposite **impotent**) **potency** adj. *The potency of this new medicine has not been tested.* = power or effectiveness (ability to produce the desired effect)

po•ten•tial[1] /pəˈtenʃəl/ adj. *He is the potential captain of the team.* = something that can happen in future, if not at the present time

potential[2] noun, u. *This young writer has a lot of potential.* = possibility for growth or development **potentially** adv. *This illness could become potentially very dangerous.* = possibly (happening in the future) **potential energy** *Water stored behind a dam possesses potential energy.* = the energy stored in a body because of the position it is in [PHYSICS] (compare **kinetic energy**)

po•tion /ˈpəʊʃən/ noun = a liquid that is used as a medicine or is considered magical (in stories)

pot•ter /ˈpɒtəʳ/ noun, c. = a person who makes pots out of clay **pottery** noun, u. = pots and other objects made out of clay

pot•ty /pɒti/ noun, c. (**potties**) or adj. = a small pot, made of plastic or metal, into which a child can empty his/her bowels (informal)

pouch /paʊtʃ/ noun, c. (**pouches**) **1** = a small bag made of leather or cloth **2** *The monkey stores its food in a pouch inside its cheeks.* = a fold of skin which is like a bag

poul•tice /ˈpəʊltɪs/ noun, c. = a bandage containing some soft substance which is used to cover the skin and can take away pain or a swelling

poul•try /ˈpəʊltri/ noun, u. or c. (**poultries**) **1** *We will buy some poultry for our farm.*(u.) = farm birds such as hens, ducks etc. which are kept for their eggs and meat **2** = meat from hens, ducks etc.(u.) **3** *She runs a poultry.*(c.) = a farm on which poultry is kept

pounce /paʊns/ verb, i. **1** *The tiger pounced on the deer.* = to attack and catch hold of someone or something with a sudden jump **2** *The reporters pounced on the film actor's remarks.* = to jump on to something (figurative)

pound[1] /paʊnd/ noun, c. **1** *This cake weighs one pound.* = a unit of weight equal to about half a kilogramme **2** *He earns 5000 pounds a year.* = a unit of money used in Britain (symbol £) **3** *Stray cattle which have no homes are put in the pound.* = a place where stray animals (cows, dogs etc. which have no master or home) are kept

pound[2] verb, t. or i. **1** (t.) = to beat rice with a wooden stick so that the husk (outer covering) is separated from the grain or to beat and crush something into powder **2** *His heart was pounding with fear.*(i.) = beating very fast

to get/demand your pound of flesh = something that you insist on having even if it causes the other person suffering (from Shakespeare's 'Merchant of Venice')

pour /pɔːʳ/ verb, t. or i. **1** *Pour some water out of the jug.*(t.) = to cause some liquid to flow out of a container by tilting it (making one side higher than the other) **2** *The rain poured down on us.*(i.) = to flow steadily and in a large quantity

to pour oil on troubled waters = to prevent some trouble by making people calm **to pour something down the drain** = to waste something (money, time etc.) **to pour cold water on something** = to react to something in a negative way, discouraging others **to pour out** *She poured out her troubles to us.* = to tell somebody everything that you feel

pout[1] /paʊt/ verb, i. *Why are you pouting? Is it because you were not given a chance to play?* = to push the lips forward so as to show displeasure (used mostly to describe the behaviour of a child or young girl)

pout[2] noun, c. = an act of pouting

pov•er•ty /ˈpɒvəti/ noun, u. *living in poverty* = the state of being very poor and not being able to pay for food, clothing etc.

POW abbr. of **Prisoner of War** = a soldier who has been captured by the enemy and is kept in a special prison

pow•der[1] /ˈpaʊdəʳ/ noun, u. *talcum powder // chilli powder* = a solid substance in the form of very small and fine grains

powder[2] verb, t. **1** *Please powder these tablets.* = to crush or break up something solid into powder **2** *powder one's nose* = to put powder on something

pow•er[1] /ˈpaʊəʳ/ noun, u. or c. **1** *As head of the company she has a lot of power.*(u.) = influence or control over others **2** *Human beings have the power of speech.*(u.) = ability to do something **3** *Many trees* were blown down by the power of the wind. // I will need a computer with more power.(u.) = strength, force or speed **4** *The lights are not on because there is no power.*(u.) = electrical energy **5** *The engine of your car has very little power.*(u.) = the ability to do some work (e.g. move a vehicle) **6** *The lenses of your spectacles have high power.*(u.) = the ability to make things look bigger or more clear **7** *a foreign power*(c.) = country **8** *Two to the power of three is 8.* ($2^3 = 8$) = the number of times a number must be multiplied by itself [MATHEMATICS]

power[2] verb, t. *This bicycle is powered by a small petrol engine.* = to supply power to something **power cut/failure** noun = a period when there is no supply of electricity **power point** noun, c. = a source from which a supply of electrical energy can be obtained to make an electrical appliance work **powerful** adj. **1** *a powerful leader* = having a lot of power or influence **2** *You need powerful legs to run a 5 km race.* = physically very strong **powerless** /ˈpaʊəlɪs/ adj. = lacking strength or power **powerhouse** noun, c. **1** = a kind of factory where there are machines which produce power (electrical energy) (also power station or power plant) **2** *The creative director is a powerhouse of ideas.* = a person who is good at producing ideas **power of attorney** noun = the power given to someone through a legal agreement to act on behalf of (take some action for) someone else because they are ill or too old [LAW] **power-steering** noun *a car with power-steering* = a device (machine) which allows the driver of a car to steer (control the direction of) a car with little effort by using the power of the engine

to be in power = (of a political party) to be in control of the government **to do everything within one's power** = to do everything that one possibly can **to exercise one's power** = to use one's authority or influence

-powered /paʊəd/ suffix meaning driven by the power of e.g. **solar-powered** adj. *solar-powered engine* = driven by the power of the sun

pox /pɒks/ noun = small pox (a disease which leaves marks, called pock-marks, on the face)

PR abbr. of **Public Relations** = the branch of a government or company that deals directly with the public and receives complaints, inquiries etc.

prac•ti•cal[1] /ˈpræktɪkəl/ adj. **1** *He has a degree in Business Management but he lacks practical experience of managing a company.* = having to do with action in actual conditions and not just ideas **2** *She is a very practical person who knows how to deal with difficult situations.* = effective (able to do things well or get things done) **3** *I want a practical pair of shoes.* = one that serves a purpose well and can be taken care of easily

practical[2] noun, c. *We have a Chemistry practical next week.* = a lesson or an examination which requires a person to perform some task **practically** adv. **1** *We visit them practically every day.* = nearly; almost **2** *I will do everything practically possible to come to see you in Kochi.* = that which can be done **practical joke** noun, c. *He played a practical joke on me on April Fool's Day by telling me that I had won a prize in a lottery.* = a trick played on someone which causes some humour **practicable** adj. *The Supreme Court has ordered the government to clean up the Yamuna river within six months, but most people think this is not practicable.* = something that is possible to do

for all practical purposes *For all practical purposes, he is the boss in the office* = in actual fact, though not officially

prac•tice /ˈpræktɪs/ noun, u. or c. **1** *You need more practice if you want to sing well.*(u.) = frequent repetition of an activity in order to become better at it **2** *This sounds like a good idea, but can it be put into practice?*(u.) = the actual doing of something (as different from just thinking about it) **3** *The doctor has a very good practice.*(u.) = business **4** *It is common practice in Japan to greet one by bowing.*(c.) = a common or usual tradition or custom

to be out of practice = to not be skilful at doing something because one has not done it for a while **practice makes perfect** = doing an activity regularly can make one very good at it

prac•tise /ˈpræktɪs/ verb, t. or i. **1** *You must practise every morning if you want to become a singer.*(i.) // *You will have to practise your drawing.* (t.) = to perform an action repeatedly in order to gain some skill **2** *She plans to practise law.*(t.) = to work as a lawyer or doctor **3** *Most of our money is gone and we will have to practise economy.*(t.) = to bring into use **practised** adj. *a practised radio jockey* = very skilled at something **practising** adj. *a practising lawyer/Catholic/Hindu/Muslim etc.* = a person who actively follows a religion or is in a profession

to practise what you preach *If you want others to be tidy you must practise what you preach.* = to do what you want others to do

prac•ti•tion•er /prækˈtɪʃənəʳ/ noun, c. *a medical practitioner* = a person who works in a profession

prag•mat•ic /prægˈmætɪk/ adj. *We need a pragmatic approach to this problem, not one based on theory.* = dealing with a situation in a practical way, which suits present conditions, instead of following a fixed idea (formal) **pragmatism** noun, u. = the quality of being pragmatic **pragmatist** noun, c.

prai•rie /'preəri/ noun, c. = a large grassy plain (flat area) without trees, in North America

praise[1] /preɪz/ verb, t. *The Principal praised the teacher for her excellent lesson.* = to speak highly of someone or something

praise[2] noun, u. *The new film has received high praise from critics.* = something said or written to show that one thinks highly of someone or something **praiseworthy** adj. *Your attempt to clean up this dirty city is praiseworthy.* = something that deserves praise (formal)

pram /præm/ noun, c. short form of 'perambulator' = a baby-carriage (a small carriage in which a baby can be taken out)

prance /prɑːns/ verb, i. **1** *The horses were prancing impatiently.* = to jump by raising first the front legs and then the back legs high into the air (referring to the movement of a horse) **2** *The children were prancing around the garden.* = to move quickly or happily, with a lot of energy

prank /præŋk/ noun, c. *School children like to play pranks on their friends.* = a playful trick that causes no harm **prankster** noun, c. = a person who plays pranks

prat•tle[1] /'prætl/ verb, i. *The child prattled endlessly about everything that had happened in school that day.* = to talk for a long time in the way that children often do (approving)

prattle[2] noun, c. *I get bored with his foolish prattle.* = meaningless or pointless talk (derogatory)

prawn /prɔːn/ noun, c. or u. **1** (c.) = a small sea-animal with a hard shell and ten legs **2** *fried prawn*(u.) = the meat of a prawn, used as food

pray /preɪ/ verb, i. **1** = to communicate with (speak to) God, either silently or aloud **2** *We prayed for rain.* = to wish for something strongly **prayer** noun, c. = the words used in speaking to God **prayer book** noun, c. = a book that contains religious prayers

pre- /priː/ prefix meaning before e.g. **pre-cooked** adj. *pre-cooked food* = food which has been cooked earlier and only has to be warmed up before it is eaten

preach /priːtʃ/ verb, i. or t. **1** (i.) = to give a religious talk, usually with the intention of making someone accept your religion **2** *She always preaches the benefits of regular exercise.*(t.) = to try to convince people of something **3** *Please stop preaching to me. I know what to do.*(i.) = to give someone advice on how to behave (disapproving)

pre•am•ble /priː'æmbəl/ noun, c. = a statement made before a speech or a piece of writing to explain what follows

pre•ar•range /priːə'reɪndʒ/ verb, t. *It had been pre-arranged that everyone would clap when he finished his speech.* = to arrange in advance

pre•car•i•ous /prɪ'keəriəs/ adj. *The government may fall at any time. It is in a precarious position.* = dangerous; unsafe

pre•cau•tion /prɪ'kɔːʃən/ noun, c. *We were advised to take a course of medicines as a precaution against malaria.* = some action taken in advance to guard against possible danger **precautionary** adj.

pre•cede /prɪ'siːd/ verb, t. *The meeting was preceded by a welcoming song.* = to happen before something else (formal) **preceding** adj. *I could not attend the meeting on 18 August because I had been ill the preceding day.* = coming just before (formal)

pre•ce•dent /'presɪdənt/ noun, c. *The boss said he would grant me leave to go home for my brother's wedding, but he did not want others in the office to use this as a precedent.* = something that has happened earlier and is used as an example to decide something at a later time

pre•cincts /'priːsɪŋkts/ noun, u. (always plural) *You will find a few eating places within the precincts of the university.* = the area surrounding a building or a group of buildings (formal)

pre•cious /'preʃəs/ adj. **1** *This is a very precious necklace.* = worth a large amount of money **2** *a precious photograph* = much loved **3** *a precious old coin* = very rare **precious metal** noun = a metal which is very rare and valuable and is used in making jewellery **precious stone** noun = a gem (an expensive stone such as a diamond or ruby) used in jewellery

pre•ci•pice /'presɪpɪs/ noun, c. = a steep, high cliff

pre•cip•i•tate[1] /prɪ'sɪpɪteɪt/ verb, t. or i. **1** *War between Spain and England was bound to take place some day, but the attack by an English ship precipitated the war.*(t.) = to make something happen sooner than expected **2** *Mixing hydrocholic acid with sodium nitrate causes sodium chloride to precipitate.*(i.) = to cause a solid matter to separate from a liquid through some chemical action [CHEMISTRY]

precipitate[2] /prɪ'sɪpɪtɪt/ noun, c. *Sodium chloride is obtained as a precipitate if hydrochloric acid is mixed with sodium nitrate.* = some solid matter that has been separated from a liquid through chemical action [CHEMISTRY]

pré•cis /'presiː/ noun, u. (French) = a shortened form of a speech or piece of writing, containing only the main points

pre•cise /prɪ'saɪs/ adj. *Don't write that 4,000 people were present at the meeting when there were only 2,000. Your reporting should be precise.* = exact or correct (formal) **precisely** adv. **1** *Your answer*

P

should be in 30 words precisely. = exactly **2** *'So if we don't take the bus we won't reach the show on time?' 'Precisely.'* = used to express agreement **precision** noun, u. *I expect greater precision in your reporting.* = the quality of being precise (exact)

pre•con•ceive /priːkən'siːv/ adj. *You should not come to this meeting with pre-conceived ideas.* = ideas or opinions about something that one has formed in advance without enough information

pre-con•di•tion /priːkən'dɪʃən/ noun, c. *If you want to come to an agreement with him, there should be no pre-conditions.* = something that must be agreed to before something else can happen

pre•cur•sor /prɪ'kɜːsə^r/ noun, c. *The first calculating machine, built in the eighteenth century, was the precursor to the modern computer.* = something that comes before something else and prepares the way for it

pre-date /priː'deɪt/ verb, t. *The use of stone pre-dates the use of iron.* = to come earlier in history than something else

pred•a•tor /'predətə^r/ noun, c. *There are a few leopards in this forest, but no other predators.* = a wild animal that hunts and kills other animals **predatory** adj. *Owls are predatory birds.* = having the qualities of a predator

pre•dic•a•ment /prɪ'dɪkəmənt/ noun, u. *His pocket had been picked and all his money was gone. He did not know what to do in such a predicament.* = a difficult situation that leaves one confused (formal)

pred•i•cate /'predɪkɪt/ noun, c. *In the sentence 'The policeman caught the thief', 'caught the thief' is the predicate while 'the policeman' is the subject.* = the part of a sentence which tells us something about the subject [GRAMMAR]

pre•dict /prɪ'dɪkt/ verb, t. *Most weather forecasters try to predict rainfall patterns.* = to know or say in advance that something will happen **prediction** noun, u. or c. *Ranjit made a prediction that Sri Lanka would win the World Cup.*(c.) = something that is predicted (told in advance)

pre•dom•i•nant /prɪ'dɒmɪnənt/ adj. *Spanish is the predominant language in South America.* = having greater importance than others (formal)

pre•empt /priː'empt/ verb, t. *We were planning to meet the Chief Minister to request him to start a new school, but we find that our plans have been pre-empted. He has already given orders for the building of the school.* = to make an action by some other person unnecessary or ineffective by doing it first

preen /priːn/ verb, t. **1** *The parrot was preening its feathers.* = to clean with one's beak (referring to a bird) **2** *preening herself in front of the mirror* = to make oneself look tidy (referring to people)

pre-exist /priːɪg'zɪst/ verb, i. *Scientists believe that some intelligent animals, similar to humans, pre-existed on Earth before the first human beings appeared.* = to exist (live) before something else

pre-fab•ri•cate /priː'fæbrɪkeɪt/ verb, t. = to construct some of the parts of a building, such as the roof, pillars, doors and windows, in advance and then fit them into the building

pref•ace[1] /'prefɪs/ noun, c. *The writer explains in his preface how this book was written.* = an introduction to a book that comes before the main book (compare **foreword**)

preface[2] verb, t. *The speaker prefaced his speech with a few remarks thanking us for inviting him.* = to say or write something as an introduction

pre•fect /'priːfekt/ noun, c. = a student in a school who is given authority to control younger students

pre•fer /prɪ'fɜː^r/ verb, t. *Would you like some tea, or would you prefer coffee?* = to choose one thing over another **preferable** /'prefəreɪbəl/ adj. *I don't mind having tea, but coffee would be preferable.* = better **preference** noun, u. or c. *We can offer you tea, coffee or soft drinks. What is your preference?*(c.) = choice (greater liking for one thing rather than another)

> **Usage** One prefers something **to** something else, not **than.**

pre•fix[1] /'priːfɪks/ noun, c. *The prefix 'un-' means 'not'.* = a group of letters that carries a certain meaning and can be attached (fixed) to the beginning of a word

prefix[2] verb, t. *You can prefix 'im-' to the word 'possible'.* = to attach a prefix to the beginning of a word

preg•nant /'pregnənt/ adj. **1** *a pregnant woman* = having a child inside the body (referring to a female animal or human being) **2** *His words were pregnant with meaning.* = full of hidden meaning **pregnancy** noun, u. *She is in the third month of pregnancy.* = the condition of being pregnant

a pregnant pause = a pause (usually in a conversation) that is heavy and full of meaning (informal, humorous)

pre•his•to•ry /priːhɪ'stəri/ noun = the period of time of which there is no reliable (recorded) history **prehistoric** adj. = belonging to prehistory

prej•u•dice[1] /'predʒədɪs/ noun, c. or u. **1** *He does not enjoy talking to us because he has a prejudice against people who don't speak Hindi.*(c.) = a strong dislike of someone or something, for which there is no good reason **2** *The new law discourages racial*

prejudice.(u.) = hatred of people belonging to a different religion, race etc.
prejudice[2] verb, t. **1** *Please don't prejudice the judges. Let them decide for themselves.* = to influence in an unfair way **2** *Your habit of mumbling may prejudice your chances at the interview.* = to harm
pre•lim•i•na•ry /prɪˈlɪmɪnəri/ adj. *The preliminary examination will be held in March and the final examination in July.* = happening before some other event which is more important
prel•ude /ˈpreljuːd/ noun, c. **1** *The result of this election may be a prelude to great political change in the coming months.* = something that announces (tells us) that a more important event is to follow **2** = a short piece of music played before a longer piece that is to follow
pre•ma•ture /ˈprematjʊəʳ/ adj. *Keats died at the age of 29. His premature death deprived the world of a great poet.* = something that happens or is done before the natural or proper time
prem•i•er[1] /ˈpremiəʳ/ adj. *She is the hockey team's premier player.* = most important (formal)
premier[2] noun, c. *The premier will speak in parliament tomorrow.* = Prime Minister (informal)
prem•i•ere[1] /ˈpremieəʳ/ noun, c. *I have come to attend the premiere of the new film.* = the very first show of a film or play
premiere[2] verb, i. *The film will premiere next week.* = to have a premiere
prem•ise /ˈpremɪs/ noun, c. (always singular) *She based her research on the premise that the population would increase in the next five years.* = a piece of reasoning upon which an argument/research/ experiment is based
prem•is•es /ˈpremɪsəz/ noun, u. (always plural) *We have decided to rent out these premises to a bank.* = a building with its surrounding land
pre•mi•um /ˈpriːmɪəm/ noun, u. or c. (**premiums** or **premia**) **1** *You have not paid the premium on this insurance policy.*(c.) = money paid for an insurance policy **2** *Many cars are selling at a premium these days.*(u.) = money paid over and above the usual price in order that something becomes available when demanded **3** *A Masters degree in microbiology is at a premium now.*(u.) = having a higher value than usual
pre•mo•ni•tion /premәˈnɪʃən/ noun, c. *a premonition of death* = a feeling that something bad is going to happen
pre•na•tal /priːˈneɪtәl/ adj. *a hospital for the pre-natal care of mothers* = relating to the period or state before a child is born
pre•oc•cu•pa•tion /priːɒkjʊˈpeɪʃən/ noun, c. or u. *Cricket is his main preoccupation now.* = something that occupies (fills up) one's attention or time **pre-occupied** adj. *When I said 'Hello' to Ravi, he was too preoccupied to answer me.* = having one's mind fixed on something else
prep /prep/ abbr. of 'preposition' or of 'preparatory' as in 'prep school'
pre-paid /priːˈpeɪd/ adj. *She has sent me two pre-paid tickets for the film festival next week.* = something for which the price has been paid in advance
pre•pare /prɪˈpeəʳ/ verb, t. or i. **1** *Can you prepare tandoori chicken?* (t.) = to make or cook **2** *I want you to prepare for the test next week.*(i.) = to study in order to pass an examination or be ready for a future event **3** *Have you prepared your students for the examination?* (t.) = to get ready for some future event **preparation** /prәpәˈreɪʃən/ noun, u. or c. **1** *The cook has produced a wonderful preparation of chicken masala.*(c.) = something that has been produced or cooked (formal) **2** (always plural) *The preparations for the meeting are complete.*(c.) = things which are done to get ready or to get something ready for a future event **3** *Your preparation for the examination seems to be satisfactory.*(u.) = the act of getting ready or the state of being ready **preparatory** /prɪˈpærәtri/ adj. *a preparatory meeting* = done in order to get ready for something
prep•o•si•tion /prepәˈzɪʃən/ noun, c. *In the phrase 'a bird in hand', the word 'in' is a preposition.* = a word that is used before a noun or pronoun and shows the connection of that word to some other word [GRAMMAR]
pre•pos•ter•ous /prɪˈpɒstərәs/ adj. *Why should I give you Rs 10,000 for the old bicycle? Your demand is preposterous.* = completely unreasonable and not worth considering
pre-school /ˈpriːskuːl/ noun = a kind of school to which a very young child is sent, mainly to learn through play, before she or he joins a regular school
pre•scribe /prɪˈskraɪb/ verb, t. **1** *The doctor has prescribed this medicine for my cough.* = to say or write what medicine a sick person should take **2** *The law prescribes imprisonment for cheating someone.* = to say with authority what should be done in a certain situation (formal) **prescription** noun, c. or u. **1** *Take the doctor's prescription to the medicine shop.*(c.) = a piece of paper on which a doctor has written the names of the medicines which a sick person should take, after examining him/her **2** *The government has banned the prescription of certain medicines.*(u.) = the act of prescribing
pres•ence /ˈprezəns/ noun, u. *Your presence at the meeting made it interesting.* = the fact of being present (at a place) (opposite **absence**) **presence**

P

of mind noun *He showed great presence of mind by calling up the police as soon as the thieves broke into his neighbour's house.* = the ability to act quickly and calmly in a difficult situation

present[1] /'prezənt/ noun, c. or u. **1** *This ring is a present from my sister.* = gift (something given to someone) (formal) **2** *I'm sorry I can't lend you any money at present.* = now (at the time of speaking) **3** *The verb 'eats' is in the present.* = the form of a verb which shows that we are talking about an action that takes place regularly, and at the time one is speaking [GRAMMAR]

present[2] adj. **1** *Your son was present at the meeting.* = at a certain place **2** *Is this your present address?* = at this time **3** *The verb 'eats' is in the present tense.* = the form of a verb which shows that we are talking about an action that takes place regularly, at the time or when one is speaking ('now') [GRAMMAR]

present[3] /prɪ'zənt/ verb, t. **1** *My sister has presented this ring to me.* = to give as a gift **2** *The minister will present the prizes to the students.* = to give away something at a special ceremony **3** *The theatre group in the school is presenting a new play.* = to show to the public **4** *Allow me to present the Director of this Institute, Professor Raha.* = to introduce formally **5** *I will present this paper at the conference.* = to read out to an audience

pre•sen•ta•ble /prɪ'zentəbəl/ adj. *The house is very dirty. It is not presentable.* = fit to be shown to someone who one doesn't know too well **presentation** /prɪzen'teɪʃən/ noun, u. **1** *The presentation will be in the evening after all the matches are completed.* = the act of giving away prizes **2** *His presentation of the company's performance was excellent.* = the way in which something is explained, shown etc. **present participle** noun, c. *In the sentence 'He is sleeping', 'sleeping' is the present participle form of the verb 'sleep'.* = a form of a verb produced by adding '-ing' to it, which shows that some action is in progress at the present time, and which can also be used as an adjective e.g. 'a sleeping child' [GRAMMAR] **present perfect** noun *In the sentence 'She has eaten', 'has eaten' is in the present perfect.* = the form of a verb produced (generally) by adding '-en' to it, which shows that an action has been completed [GRAMMAR]

pre•serve[1] /prɪ'zɜːv/ verb, t. **1** *This house is more than a hundred years old but it looks new. The owner has preserved it well.* = to keep something in good condition for a long time **2** *The government must preserve the old monuments in Delhi.* = to protect from harm or damage

preserve[2] noun, u. *mango preserves* = fruit boiled with sugar and spices so that it can be kept for a long time **preservation** /prəzə'veɪʃən/ noun, u. *The government spends a lot of money on the preservation of historical buildings.* = the act of preserving something (keeping in good condition) **preservative** /prɪ'zɜːvətɪv/ noun, c. or u. *Some preservatives have been added to the ice-cream so that it can be kept for a long time.*(c.) = a chemical which is added to food to prevent it from going bad quickly

pre-set /priː 'set/ verb, t *You can pre-set the alarm clock at night so that it will ring in the morning and wake you up.* = to set or adjust something in advance

pre•side /prɪ'zaɪd/ verb, i. *The Education Minister will preside at the meeting.* = to control or be in charge of a meeting or some other activity

pres•i•dent /'prezɪdənt/ noun, c. **1** *the President of India* = a person who has the highest political position in a country where there is no king **2** *the president of a company* = the head of a business company **presidential** /prəzɪ'denʃəl/ adj. **presidency** noun, u. = the office (position) of a president

press[1] /pres/ noun, c. (**presses**) or u. **1** (u.) = newspapers and the people working for various newspapers **2** *He owns a small printing press.*(c.) = a machine used for printing books etc. **3** *Can you give my shirt a press?*(u.) = the act of pressing a garment with a hot iron to remove wrinkles

press[2] verb, t. **1** *The bell will ring when you press this switch.* = to push something downwards **2** *Shall I press your trousers?* = to give a smooth surface or a sharp fold to a garment by using a hot iron **3** *She pressed me to stay on and have dinner with her.* = to urge (to request someone repeatedly to do something) **press conference** noun, c. = a meeting of journalists with an organization, the government etc., when some information has to be given out to the press

to be hard pressed for time to do something = to find something very difficult to complete etc. because one is very busy **to press charges** = to complain officially (to the police) about someone or something **to press on ahead** *They pressed on with the preparations for the function though it was raining.* = to continue to do something even though it is difficult to do

pres•sure /'preʃəʳ/ noun, u. **1** *The pressure of the wind drives this machine. // Water flows through these pipes at high pressure.* = the force with which something drives or hits something else **2** *We are putting pressure on them to start a new school here.* = something said repeatedly to make someone do something **3** *I am working under a lot of pressure.* = conditions which make the mind troubled **pressurize (pressurise)** verb, t. *We must* *pressurise the chemical companies to stop polluting the environment.* = to use influence to try to get something done **pressure-cooker** noun, c. = a vessel (pot) with a tight-fitting lid in which food can be cooked very quickly because of the pressure of steam **pressure-group** noun, c. = a group of people which tries to use its political influence to get something done

pres•tige /pre'stiːdʒ/ noun, u. *Teachers have a lot of prestige in society.* = value and respect **prestigious** adj. *a highly prestigious institution* = having a lot of prestige (value and respect)

pre•sume /prɪ'zjuːm/ verb, t. or i. **1** *I presume that Khalid is coming for the meeting tomorrow because he has not told anyone that he cannot come.* = to suppose; to believe that something is true even though one is not certain **2** *I cannot presume to tell you how to run your office.* = to have the courage to do something which one has no right to do (formal) **presumption** noun, u. = *Your presumption that the examination will be announced tomorrow is correct.* = the act of presuming something **presumptuous** adj. *It was presumptuous of Harsha to think that just one telephone call from him would make all of us rush to his birthday party.* = not showing enough respect to someone while thinking too highly of oneself (derogatory)

pre•sup•pose /priːsə'pəʊz/ verb, t. *Why do you presuppose that your team is going to win the match? You may lose.* = to believe in advance that something is going to happen

pre•tence /prɪ'tens/ noun, u. or c. *She was not able to continue the pretence of enjoying the concert.*(u.) = a false show

pre•tend /prɪ'tend/ verb, t. or i. **1** *He pretends to be a good singer but I know that he is quite bad.*(t.) = to try to appear falsely as something which one is not **2** *I know that this is not a palace and you are not a queen but let us pretend.*(i.) = to imagine something, as part of a game

pre•text /'priːtekst/ noun, c. *Seema left on the pretext that she had an appointment with the doctor.* = a false reason given for doing something

pret•ty[1] /'prɪti/ adj. *What a pretty dress that is!* = good-looking, attractive

pretty[2] adv. *It's pretty hot today!* = quite, but not very (to a large extent or degree) (informal) **prettily** adv.

not a pretty sight *I looked at the injury on his knee. It was not a pretty sight.* = not at all pleasant to see (informal, sometimes humorous) **to be not just a pretty face** = (said in defence of someone) to have qualities or skills which are worth considering, not just good looks **pretty-pretty** *'Do you like this room?' 'Not much. It's too pretty-pretty.'* = too highly decorated and therefore not pleasing

pre•vail /prɪ'veɪl/ verb, i. **1** *The custom of child marriage still prevails in some parts of the country.* = to continue to exist **2** *Don't lose hope! I am sure that justice will prevail in the end.* = to win **prevailing** adj. *It is not possible for me to work in the prevailing conditions.* = found at a certain time

prev•a•lent /'prevələnt/ adj. *The tradition of sending one's eldest son into the army is prevalent in this part of the country.* = quite common

pre•vent /prɪ'vent/ verb, t. **1** *Satish was determined to become an actor and nobody could prevent him from going into films.* = to stop or check someone from doing something **2** *We advise people to wear helmets to prevent serious injuries.* = to stop something from happening **prevention** noun, u. *We are distributing medicines for the prevention of malaria.* = the act of preventing (checking) something **preventive** noun, c. or adj. *Neem leaves are an excellent preventive against cholera.* = something that helps to prevent (stop) something bad from happening

pre•view[1] /'priːvjuː/ verb, t. *The director of the new film has invited us to preview it before it is released next week.* = to view (see) a new film, play etc. before it is shown to the public

preview[2] noun, c. *We will have a preview of the film.* = an occasion when something is previewed

pre•vi•ous /'priːvɪəs/ adj. *He could not come for the meeting because he fell and broke his leg the previous day.* = happening or coming earlier (formal)

prey /preɪ/ noun, u. (always singular) *Smaller animals, such as deer, are the natural prey of tigers.* = animals which are hunted and killed by other animals

to prey on/upon **1** *Tigers usually prey on deer.* = to kill for food **2** *The fear of failing in the test always preyed on her mind.* = to cause worry

price[1] /praɪs/ noun, u. or c. **1** *The price of this book is Rs 50.* = the amount of money for which something is sold or bought; cost **2** *A deduction of two marks is the price you pay for submitting your homework late.* = an unpleasant thing that happens because one has not done what one was supposed to

price[2] verb, t. *This book is priced at Rs 150.* = to fix the price of something **priceless** adj. *This painting is 500 years old and it is priceless.* = so valuable that its price cannot be calculated **price-tag** noun, c. = a piece of paper attached to an article which shows its price **pricey** adj. *This dress is rather pricey. I don't think I can buy it.* = high-priced (informal)

at any price *I was determined to go to Mumbai this weekend at any price.* = whatever the consequences or preparations necessary **not at any price** = to never want to do something **at a price** *Mangoes are out of season but* *you can get them at a price.* = for a lot of money **to be beyond price** *This harmonium is my great-grandmother's. It is beyond price.* = to be so precious that no price can be set on it **to pay the price** *I allowed him to have his way and now I am paying the price.* = to suffer for something one did with good intentions

prick[1] /prɪk/ verb, t. *The doctor pricked the girl's finger with a needle and collected a drop of her blood for a test.* = to make a very small hole in something with a pointed object

prick[2] noun, c. **1** *The doctor gave her finger a prick.* = the act of pricking (making a small hole) **2** *She felt a prick.* = a sudden sharp pain caused by some pointed object **prickly** adj. **1** *This damp, hot climate causes prickly heat to appear on the skin.* = causing a feeling of discomfort **2** *a prickly person* = becoming angry or irritated easily

pride see **proud**

priest /priːst/ noun, c. = a person, usually a man, who performs religious duties for a group of people

prig /prɪg/ noun, c. = a person who is very careful about obeying the rules of correct behaviour and considers himself/herself superior to others (derogatory)

prim /prɪm/ adj. *Why are you so prim and proper? You don't allow people to shout or laugh in your house.* = very correct and proper in behaviour and easily shocked by anything rude

pri•ma•ry /'praɪmərɪ/ adj. **1** *The primary occupation of the people in this village is agriculture.* = chief or main **2** *He goes to a primary school.* = having to do with the earliest period in one's life **3** *The experiment is in a primary stage of development.* = early; not advanced **primarily** /praɪ'mærɪli/ adv. *Yes, we do sell some medicines here, but we are primarily a grocery shop.* = mainly **primary colour** noun, c. = each of the three colours red, yellow and blue, from a mixture of which all other colours can be produced

pri•mate /'praɪmeɪt/ noun, c. = a member of the most developed group of mammals including monkeys, apes and human beings

prime[1] /praɪm/ noun, c. *The young soldiers were in the prime of life.* = the best or strongest part or time

prime[2] adj. *He is selling off some prime property.* = of the highest value or importance

prime[3] verb, t. *The students were primed for the test by their teachers.* = to prepare or make someone ready to face a test etc. **prime minister** (abbr. **PM**) noun, c. = the most important minister and the head of the government in countries which follow the parliamentary system of government **prime number** noun, c. *13 is a prime number.* = a number which can be divided only by itself or by 1 [MATHEMATICS] **prime time** noun = the time (usually in the evening) when the highest number of people are watching television **a prime example** *a prime example of untidiness* = having all the qualities that represent something **a prime suspect** = to be the main person who is thought to have done something

prim•er /'praɪmə^r/ noun, c. **1** = a textbook for very young children **2** = a kind of paint which is spread on a surface before the main painting is done

pri•me•val (primaeval) /praɪ'miːvəl/ adj. *the primeval forests of the Sunderbans* = very ancient (old)

prim•i•tive /'prɪmɪtɪv/ adj. **1** *Primitive people lived in caves.* = at the earliest stage of development [HISTORY] **2** *Living conditions in this town are primitive.* = old-fashioned and not comfortable (derogatory)

prim•rose /'prɪmrəʊz/ noun, c. = a kind of garden plant that produces light yellow flowers

prince /prɪns/ noun, c. = the son of a king or queen

prin•cess /prɪn'ses/ noun, c. (**princesses**) = the daughter of a king or queen

prin•ci•pal[1] /'prɪnsɪpəl/ adj. *Rice is the principal food here.* = chief or main

principal[2] noun, c. *She is our principal.* = the head of an educational institution **principally** adv.

prin•ci•ple /'prɪnsɪpəl/ noun, c. or u. **1** *Freedom of speech is one of the most important principles of democracy.*(c.) = a truth or belief on which something is based **2** *I cannot accept this present from you. It would go against my principles.*(c.)= a rule which guides one's behaviour

in principle *In principle, I agree with your suggestion but we will have to disuss some points.* = in a large sense, but not in the details

print[1] /prɪnt/ verb, t. **1** *We print textbooks here.* = to produce a book, newspaper, magazine etc. on paper using a machine and ink **2** *We will print the story in the front page.* = to make something appear in a newspaper, book, magazine etc. **3** = to decorate with a coloured pattern, using a block of wood or metal into which the pattern has been cut **4** = to make a photograph from a negative

print[2] noun, u. or c. **1** *This book is available in large print for people with poor eyesight.*(u.)= the letters and words which appear in a newspaper, book or magazine **2** *You can see the prints of his car tyres on the wet sand.*(c.) = a mark made on a surface by some object pressing down on it **3** *The photographer has made two prints of this photograph.*(c.) = a copy of a picture or photograph **4** *Your sari has a very attractive print.*(u.) = a decorative design on a dress **printing** noun, u. **printable** adj. (usually negative) *When he gets angry he uses language which is not printable.* = fit to be heard or read by others (also **unprintable**) (often humorous) **printer** noun, c. **1** = a machine which prints out information from a computer [COMPUTERS] **2** = a person whose job is to print books etc. **printing press** noun = a machine that is used for printing newspapers, books etc. **print out** noun, c. or u. = a document from a computer that is printed onto a paper [COMPUTERS] **in print** *Is this book in print any more?* = still being printed and sold **out of print** = to not be published any more and hence not available in the market

pri•or /'praɪəʳ/ adj. *I cannot come to the meeting as I have some prior engagements.* = from before; relating to an earlier time or event (formal)

pri•or•i•ty /praɪ'ɒrɪti/ noun, u. or c. **1** *Your studies must have priority over sports.*(u.) = greater importance than something else **2** *You should know what your priorities are.*(c.) = matters that need more attention than others

pris•m /'prɪzəm/ noun, c. = a piece of transparent glass with three sides which can bend rays of light passing through it and can also break up white light into different colours

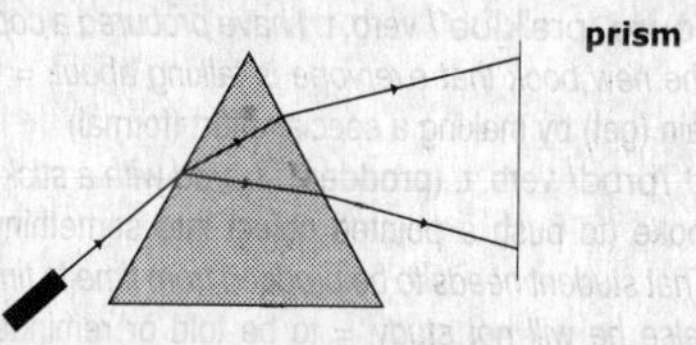
prism

pris•on /'prɪzən/ noun, c. or u. = a place where people who have committed some crime are sent as a punishment (also **jail**) **prisoner** noun, c. = a person who is sent to prison as a punishment for committing some crime **prisoner-of-war** (abbr. **POW**) noun, c. = a soldier who has been caught by the enemy during a war and is kept in a special prison

pri•vate[1] /'praɪvɪt/ adj. **1** *These are my private letters. You should not read them.* = personal and not meant to be shared with anyone **2** *This is his private library which no one else is allowed to use.* = meant to be used by a particular person and not others **3** *This used to be a government factory but it has now become private.* = not owned or managed by the government [TECHNICAL] **4** *She is a very private person, and has very few friends.* = not wanting to share one's feelings with others (often disapproving)

private[2] noun, c. *He is a private in the army.* = a soldier having the lowest rank in the army **private detective** noun = a person who is not a policeperson but can be hired to do a policeperson's work, such as trying to find out who committed a certain crime **private enterprise** noun = a business which is not owned or managed by the government **privacy** /'prɪvəsɪ/ noun, u. **1** *We have no privacy here because our neighbours can easily look into our house.* = the state of being away from other people, so that one can freely do what one likes without being disturbed or seen by others **2** *The actor must have his privacy.* = the state of not being under public attention

pri•va•tize (privatise) /'praɪvətaɪz/ verb, t. *to privatize a company.* = to sell a government-owned company to private owners (people who are not part of the government) **privatization (privatisation)** /praɪvitaɪ'zeɪʃən/ noun = the process by which government-owned companies are sold to private owners

in private *I would like to talk to you in private.* = alone

priv•i•lege /'prɪvɪlɪdʒ/ noun, u. or c. *to enjoy many privileges* = a special right or advantage given to a person or group **privileged** adj. **1** *Members of the royal family were privileged people.* = having many privileges **2** *I am privileged to speak to this audience.* = fortunate

priv•y /'prɪvi/ adj. *He is privy to all our secrets.* = sharing secret knowledge (formal)

prize[1] /praɪz/ noun, c. *She won a prize for her painting.* = a reward given to someone for winning a competition, race etc. or for doing some good act

prize[2] verb, t. *We prize the help given by you to this school.* = to put a high value on something

pro- /prəʊ/ prefix meaning **1** in favour of e.g. *a pro-China policy*(adj.)= to be in favour of China **2** in place of e.g. *pro-Vice Chancellor* = to be acting in place of Vice Chancellor

pros and cons noun (always plural) *Before you decide to join politics, you should consider the pros and cons carefully.* = the reasons for and against doing something

PRO abbr. of **Public Relations Officer** noun = an officer in a government or private company who deals with the public, giving them information etc.

prob•a•ble /'prɒbəbəl/ adj. *It is highly probable that India will beat Sri Lanka in this match.* = likely or expected to happen **probability** /prɒbə'bɪlɪti/ noun, u. or c. **1** *There is a strong probability of India's winning.* = likelihood; the state of being probable **2** = the chance that an event might occur e.g. calling 'Heads' or 'Tails' correctly when flipping a coin [MATHEMATICS]

pro•ba•tion /prə'beɪʃən/ noun, u. **1** *The new teacher is still on probation.* = the process of being on trial before one is selected for a job **2** *a year's probation* = the period for which one is on probation

probe[1] /prəʊb/ verb, t. *The engineer will probe the causes of the collapse of the building.* = to examine or look into some matter

probe[2] noun, c. or u. **1** = a long, thin metal instrument used to examine some part of the body **2** *The government has set up a probe into these charges of corruption.* = a careful search or inquiry

prob•lem /ˈprɒbləm/ noun, c. **1** *We are facing several problems in our work. The biggest problem is the shortage of money. // That car is a constant problem.* = something that presents a difficulty and needs attention **2** *The teacher has given us a problem to solve.* = a question which needs careful thinking to answer **problematic** /prɒbləˈmætɪk/ adj. *Teaching this new book in class will be problematic.* = causing problems (difficulties)

pro•bos•cis /prəˈbɒsɪs/ noun, c. (**probosces**) **1** = the long, movable nose that some animals (e.g. an elephant or rhinoceros) have **2** = the long, tube-like mouth of some insects e.g. mosquitoes [BIOLOGY]

pro•ceed /prəˈsiːd/ verb, i. **1** *The construction is proceeding according to plan.* = to go ahead or to continue (formal) **2** *After cutting the vegetables Samir proceeded to fry them.* = to do the next thing after something has been completed (formal) **procedure** noun, u. or c. *We must follow the correct procedure when filing a law case.*(c.) = a set of actions which have to be carried out while doing something

proceedings /prəˈsiːdɪŋs/ (always plural) noun, c. **1** *The director of the film was shooting a battle scene and the journalists watched the proceedings with interest.* = the actions that form part of some interesting event **2** *A member of parliament is expected to know parliamentary proceedings.* = the rules or activities which are followed in a particular place

pro•ceeds /ˈprəʊsiːdz/ noun, c. (always plural) *The proceeds from this film show will be given away to charitable organisations.* = the money collected from the sale of something or from some activity

pro•cess[1] /ˈprəʊses/ noun, u. or c. (**processes**) **1** *This state is going through a process of economic and political change.*(u.)= a series of connected actions or events which may or may not be planned or controlled but which lead to a certain result **2** *Steel is produced from iron ore by using the hot-strip rolling process.*(u.) = a connected set of actions that are done in a planned and controlled way in order to produce a desired result

process[2] verb, t. **1** *The university has not processed your application yet.* = to put something through a process (a set of actions or decisions guided by certain rules) **2** *The data has to be processed.* = to examine or analyse with the help of a computer some information that has been collected (data-processing) [COMPUTERS] **3** = to print a photograph from film [TECHNICAL] **procession** /prəʊˈseʃən/ noun, u. or c. = a number of people, vehicles etc. that walk or move slowly as part of some ceremony (e.g. a wedding procession) **processor** /ˈprəʊsesəʳ/ noun, c. = a machine that is used to carry out some process e.g. a microprocessor (in a computer) that carries out the central functions in a computer

in the process *She had gone to the airport to see her uncle off and in the process she ran into an old friend.* = while doing something else (formal) **to be in the process of doing something** *I am in the process of writing a report.* = to be busy or occupied doing something

pro•claim /prəˈkleɪm/ verb, t. *The government has proclaimed a national holiday.* = to make something known to the public **proclamation** /prɒkləˈmeɪʃən/ noun, c. *a proclamation announcing the dates of the election* = an official statement made for the public

pro•cras•ti•nate /prəˈkræstɪneɪt/ verb, i. *Stop procastinating and start preparing for the examination.* = to keep on delaying some activity (formal) **procrastination** /prəkræstɪˈneɪʃən/ noun, u. = the action of procrastinating

pro•cure /prəˈkjʊəʳ/ verb, t. *I have procured a copy of the new book that everyone is talking about.* = to obtain (get) by making a special effort (formal)

prod /prɒd/ verb, t. (**prodded**) **1** *prod with a stick* = to poke (to push a pointed object into something) **2** *That student needs to be prodded from time to time or else he will not study.* = to be told or reminded repeatedly to do something (figurative) **prodding** noun

prod•i•gy /ˈprɒdɪdʒi/ noun, c. (**prodigies**) *a violin prodigy* = a genius (a person with unusual intelligence or ability)

pro•duce[1] /prəˈdjuːs/ verb, t. **1** *Sri Lankan farmers produce the finest tea.* = to grow **2** *This factory produces 200,000 motorcycles a year.* = to make **3** *A lioness can produce two cubs in a year.* = to give birth to **4** *The test did not produce any result.* = to lead to **5** *Produce the line AB to the point X.* = to make a line longer until it reaches a point [MATHEMATICS] **6** = to plan and control the making of a film, play etc.

prod•uce[2] /ˈprɒdjuːs/ noun, u. *Farmers are not able to get a good price for their produce.* = something that has been grown or made on a farm

prod•uct /ˈprɒdʌkt/ noun, c. **1** *The main products of Kashmir are apples, woollen carpets and shawls.* = something that is grown on the land or produced (made) by hand or in a factory **2** = a number that is obtained by multiplying two or more numbers together [MATHEMATICS] **3** = a compound that is obtained when two other substances are changed by a chemical action (reaction) [CHEMISTRY] **4** *Ranjit is a product of* *the Ahmedabad School of Art.* = someone who has been trained to do something in a certain way

pro•duc•tion /prəˈdʌkʃən/ noun, u. or c. **1** *India has started the production of computer chips.*(u.) = the process of making something **2** *The production of cement has increased.*(u.) = the amount of something that is produced **3** *This play is the theatre group's latest production.*(c.) = something that has been made by someone **productive** adj. *I am very productive in the morning.* = someone or something that is able to produce a lot of things **productivity** /prɒdʌkˈtɪvɪti/ noun, u. *The productivity of the paint factory is low.* = the ability to produce goods

Prof. /prɒf/ abbr. of **professor** (informal)

pro•fess /prəˈfes/ verb, t. **1** = to follow a certain religion **2** *Why did you profess agreement with the idea when you actually didn't think it would work?* = to claim something, without being sincere (formal)

pro•fes•sion /prəˈfeʃən/ noun, u. or c. **1** *He is a lawyer by profession.*(u.) // *He wants to change his profession.*(c.) = work or employment that requires special education or training **professional**[1] adj. *The doctor has a lot of professional experience.* = relating to a profession **2** *He is a professional singer.* = doing something as a profession (for a living) and not as a hobby **3** *The doctor is highly professional in his behaviour.* = showing the best qualities that one would expect in a member of a profession **professional**[2] noun, c. **1** = a person who does something as a profession (opposite **amateur**) **2** *He is a real professional.* = having high professional standards **professionalism** noun, u. *We are impressed by the professionalism of the airport staff.* = high standards of professional behaviour

pro•fes•sor /prəˈfesəʳ/ noun, c. = a university or college teacher who has the highest rank **professorship** noun, c. = the position held by a professor

pro•fi•cient /prəˈfɪʃənt/ adj. *She started learning French only a year ago but has become quite proficient in the language.* = skilled; able to do something well **proficiency** noun, u. *He has excellent proficiency in French.* = skill; abilility to do something well

pro•file[1] /ˈprəʊfaɪl/ noun, u. or c. **1** *Can you draw her profile?*(u.) = a side view of something, specially of a person's face **2** = a short description of someone

profile[2] verb, t. *The writer of this book has profiled the people of this state in a very interesting manner.* = to write about someone or to draw a picture of someone

to keep a low profile = to stay away from the attention of the public because of fear, shame, shyness etc.

prof•it[1] /ˈprɒfɪt/ noun, c. or u. *He bought a car for Rs 25000 and sold it for Rs 35000, making a good profit.*(u.) = money gained from a business or by selling something at a higher price than what one paid for it

profit[2] verb, i. or t. *The steel industry will profit from the new import laws.* = to earn a profit or to gain some advantage **profitable** adj. *Writing books for children is highly profitable.* = producing a lot of profit **profitability** /prɒfɪtəˈbɪlɪtɪ/ noun, u. *Last year our company made a profit of 50 crores but this year the profit was only 25 crores. The profitability of the company has gone down.* = the ability to produce profits **profit and loss account** = the statement of a company that shows how much it earns and spends

prof•li•gate[1] /ˈprɒflɪgɪt/ noun, c. *His father was such a profligate that he spent all his money on horse-racing.* = a person who is careless with his money

profligate[2] adj. *profligate spending of money* = careless

pro•found /prəˈfaʊnd/ adj. **1** *He has profound knowledge of his subject.* = deep **2** *The book left a profound impression on my mind.* = strong

pro•fuse /prəˈfjuːs/ adj. **1** *profuse bleeding* = in great quantity **2** *She was profuse in thanking me for the help with her project.* = generous (ready to give freely) **profusion** noun, u. *There is a profusion of roses in the garden.* = a great amount of something (formal)

prog•e•ny /ˈprɒdʒəni/ noun, u. (used with plural forms of verbs) *His progeny have none of his wicked qualities.* = children (formal)

prog•no•sis /prɒgˈnəʊsɪs/ noun, u. (**prognoses**) **1** *The doctor's prognosis is that the patient will be cured in a few days.* = a doctor's judgement of what is likely to happen to a patient [MEDICINE] **2** *Our factories have stopped working. The prognosis for the future is bad.* = a judgement or opinion of what is likely to happen in the future (formal)

pro•gram[1] /ˈprəʊgræm/ noun, c. *a computer program* = a set of instructions (orders) given to a computer in a special language which the computer can follow, to make it do something [COMPUTERS]

program[2] verb, t. (**programmed**) *I have to program the computer.* = to write or supply a program for a computer **programmer** noun, c. = a person who writes programs for a computer

pro•gramme[1] /ˈprəʊgræm/ (**program** in American English) noun, c. **1** *What is the programme for today's meeting?* = a list of the things to be done on a particular occasion **2** *I like to watch sports programmes on television.* = a show or performance presented on radio or television **3** *The government has an extensive*

P

programme for the improvement of schools in villages. = plans for future activities

programme[2] verb, t. (**programmed**) *We have programmed the video recorder to start recording at 8.30 pm.* = to plan or arrange some activity in a certain way

Usage 'program' is used in British English only to refer to the use of computers. In India, the American convention of using only 'program' is gradually becoming popular.

pro•gress[1] /'prəʊgres/ noun, u. **1** *The progress of the car through the muddy roads was slow.* = advance or forward movement **2** *Last year the boy had got only 50 in English but this year he has scored 75. He seems to be making good progress.* = improvement **3** *Don't disturb the students while the class is in progress.* = the process of continuing

progress[2] /prə'gres/ verb, i. (**progressed**) **1** *Is the work progressing or are you still making plans?* = to move forward **2** *The doctor thinks the patient is progressing well.* = to improve in health **progress report** noun = a statement that comments on the performance or progress that a person has made over a certain period of time (especially school students) **progression** noun, u. *The numbers 4,12 and 36 are in geometric progression.* = a set of numbers that progress (increase) in a certain way [MATHEMATICS] **progressive** adj. **1** *In 1999 only 25 per cent of our students had passed. In the year 2000, 38 percent passed whereas in 2001, 47 percent of the students have passed. There is progressive improvement in the results.* = improving continuously **2** *a progressive magazine* = supporting new ideas especially in politics and education

pro•hib•it /prə'hɪbɪt/ verb, t. *The library rules prohibit talking inside the library.* = to stop or prevent someone from doing something **prohibition** /prəʊhɪ'bɪʃən/ noun, u. **1** = the action of prohibiting (stopping) something **2** *Prohibition* = an order by the government stopping the sale or use of alcoholic drinks **prohibitive** /prəʊ'hɪbɪtɪv/ adj. *The price of fish is so prohibitive that we have not been able to buy any for more than three months now.* = preventing or discouraging something

proj•ect[1] /'prɒdʒekt/ noun, c. *The teacher has given the class a science project.* = a piece of work which has to be done and which requires skill and careful planning

pro•ject[2] /prə'dʒekt/ verb, i. or t. **1** *The building has a large balcony which projects three feet from the wall.*(i.) = to stick out; to extend beyond a certain point **2** *You can project the pictures on this screen, using a projector.*(t.) = to cause light to be thrown on a surface **3** *She projects herself as having a lot of self-confidence.*(t.) = to represent (show) someone or something (or oneself) to others in a certain way, so as to produce a certain kind of impression **4** *The government has projected an expenditure of Rs 5 lakh for the repair of this building.*(t.) = to plan for the future **projector** noun, c. = a machine which makes large pictures appear on a screen or a flat surface like a wall **projection** noun, c. **1** *a projection from the wall of a building* = something that sticks out **2** *the company's projection for next year's expenditure* = plans for the future

pro•lif•ic /prə'lɪfɪk/ adj. **1** *Rabbits are prolific breeders. A pair of rabbits can produce 100 young ones in a year.* = able to produce many young ones **2** *She is a prolific writer. She has already produced 25 novels.* = able to produce a lot of work

pro•logue /'prəʊlɒg/ noun, c. **1** = an introduction to a poem or play **2** = an event that leads to something more important or serious (see also **prelude**)

pro•long /prə'lɒŋ/ verb, t. *The patient's breathing has stopped, but the doctors are using a heart-lung machine to prolong his life.* = to make something last longer

to prolong one's agony = to not tell something that a person is anxious to hear

prom•e•nade /prɒmə'nɑːd/noun, c. = a wide path, often facing the sea, along which people take walks

prom•i•nent /'prɒmɪnənt/ adj. **1** *She has a very prominent nose.* = sticking out **2** *He has a prominent birthmark on his neck.* = easily noticed or seen **3** *She is one of our most prominent writers.* = important and well-known **prominence** noun, u. **1** = the quality of being prominent (important or easily noticed) **2** *The newspaper gives too much prominence to her speeches.* = importance

pro•mis•cu•ous /prə'mɪskjʊəs/ adj. = having sex with many different partners **promiscuity** /premɪs'kʊɪtɪ/ noun, u. = the quality of being promiscuous

prom•ise[1] /'prɒmɪs/ verb, t. or i. **1** *I promise that you will be taken to the market tomorrow.*(t.) // *I am sure he will come. He has promised.*(i.) = to tell someone that you will surely do something **2** *She promises to be a great singer.*(t.) = to give cause for hope

promise[2] noun, c. or u. **1** *He has made a promise to pay back the money when I need it.*(c.) = a statement that something will surely be done or not done **2** *She shows great promise as a singer.*(u.) = a sign that something good will happen **promising** adj. *a* *promising hockey player* = showing signs of becoming very good or reaching the highest levels of something **to break a promise** = to not do something one has said one would do **to promise someone the moon** = to make a promise that is difficult or impossible to fulfill **Promises, promises!** *You're going to help me clean the house on Sunday? Promises, promises!* = a humorous or sarcastic way of saying that one doesn't believe someone will keep her/his promise

prom•on•tory /'prɒmәntәri/ noun, c. = a long, narrow piece of land stretching out into the sea [GEOGRAPHY]

pro•mote /prә'mәʊt/ verb, t. **1** *My son has been promoted to Class 5. // My sister has been promoted to the post of General Manager.* = to put someone in a higher class or position **2** *The government is trying to promote the use of paper bags instead of plastic bags.* = to actively help or encourage someone to do something **3** *He is promoting a new company that will manufacture pumps.* = to support the formation of a new company with money etc. **promotion** noun, u. or c. **1** *Your promotion was well deserved.* = the result of being promoted to a higher position **2** *Our toothpaste is not selling well. We should have a promotion to increase sales.* = something done to increase the sale or use of a product **promoter** noun = a person who raises money for an event or for a new business

prompt[1] /prɒmpt/ adj. **1** *Prompt treatment of disease can save lives.* = done quickly, without delay **2** *He was prompt in replying to my letter. I got his reply the next day.* = quick to do something

prompt[2] verb, t. **1** *My unhappiness prompted me to speak.* = to cause **2** *If the actor forgets his lines you will have to prompt him.* = to remind an actor of the words which he/she is supposed to speak in a drama **3** *Let him try to answer my question. I don't want you to prompt him.* = to suggest to someone what he/she should say

prompt[3] noun, c. **1** *I have forgotten my lines. Can you give me a prompt?* = a reminder of what an actor is supposed to say **2** = a sign that appears on a computer screen informing one that it has finished a task and is ready for some more instructions [COMPUTERS] **promptly** adv. **1** *I sent her an e-mail and she replied promptly.* = without delay **2** *We left the party promptly at 7 o'clock.* = at the exact time

prone[1] /prәʊn/ adj. **1** *The men in our family are prone to heart conditions.* = likely to suffer from **2** *prone to lying* = likely to do something undesirable

prone[2] adv. *He was lying prone on the ground.* = flat on the ground, with the face down

prong /prɒŋ/ noun, c. *the two prongs of a fork* = one of two or more thin, pointed pieces of metal which is joined to another piece of the same kind **a two-pronged (double-pronged) attack** = an attack on an enemy which comes from two directions at the same time

pro•noun /'prәʊnaʊn/ noun, c. *In the sentence 'Mohsin is my brother but I don't like him', 'my', 'I', and 'him' are pronouns.* = a word that can be used in place of a noun [GRAMMAR]

pro•nounce /prә'naʊns/ verb, t. **1** *The word 'knee' is pronounced 'nee'.* = to produce the sound of a word or letter **2** *The judge pronounced the prisoner not guilty.* = to make a declaration (an official statement) [LAW] **pronunciation** /prәnʌnsɪ'eɪʃәn/ noun, u. or c. **1** *What is the pronunciation of the word 'psychology'?* = the way in which a particular word is pronounced (spoken) **2** *Your pronunciation suggests that you are from Maharashtra.* = the way in which a particular person pronounces (speaks) a word or a language **pronounced** adj. *He walks with a pronounced limp.* = easily seen or noticed **pronouncement** noun, u. = an official declaration made by a person who has the authority to do so (see meaning 2 for **pronounce**)

proof /pru:f/ noun, u. or c. **1** *Do you have any proof to show that you are the owner of this car?*(u.) = a fact or a document which can show beyond doubt that something is true **2** *I would like to check the proofs of the book which is being printed.*(c.) = a copy of something which is being printed, made so that mistakes in printing can be corrected **3** = a test or steps of reasoning to prove a hypothesis [MATHEMATICS] **proof-read** verb, t. = to check a proof for mistakes

-proof suffix meaning 'able to resist the action of something' e.g. *waterproof, soundproof* etc.

prop[1] /prɒp/ noun, c. **1** *The roof of this old building is supported by bamboo props.* = a support which holds up something **2** *The drama was put up on a bare stage, without any props.* = an object that is used in a play or film to help the audience imagine the scene

prop[2] verb, t. (**propped**) *The old roof had to be propped up to stop it from falling.* = to use a prop to support something

prop•a•gan•da /prɒpә'gændә/ noun, u. = information (which may be false), usually for political purposes, given out to people to make them think the way you want them to think **propagandist** noun, c. = a person whose job is to produce propaganda

prop•a•gate /'prɒpәgeɪt/ verb, t. **1** *He is going to U.S.A. to propagate yoga.* = to cause an idea to spread **2** *The bamboo plant propagates itself by putting out new shoots every year.* = to increase by producing young

P

pro•pane /ˈprəʊpeɪn/ noun = a kind of gas used for cooking and heating buildings

pro•pel /prəˈpel/ verb, t. (**propelled**) *Many buses in Delhi are propelled by CNG (Compressed Natural Gas).* = to drive a machine and make it move forward **propeller** noun, c. = a machine with moving blades which looks like a fan and propels (drives) a ship or aircraft **propellant** noun, c. = any fuel (substance that can be burnt) which propels (drives) a machine, such as a rocket **propulsion** noun

prop•er /ˈprɒpəʳ/ adj. **1** *It was not proper on your part to be out when our guests arrived.* = right or correct **2** *I don't have a proper home. I am living in a hotel.* = real or actual **properly** adv. *Please paint the house properly. // Please check the papers properly.* = throughly; in the way that is correct **proper fraction** noun, c. *¾ is a proper fraction.* = a fraction in which the numerator (number above the dividing line) is smaller than the denominator (number below the dividing line) (opposite **improper fraction**) [MATHEMATICS] **proper noun** noun, c. *'Mohan' and 'Kolkata' are proper nouns, while 'cat' is a common noun.* = a word which is the name of a particular person or place and is spelt with a capital letter [GRAMMAR]

prop•er•ty /ˈprɒpəti/ noun, u. or c. (**properties**) **1** *This land is the school's property. We will have to ask the school before we use it.*(u.) // *This is valuable property.*(c.) = something (usually a piece of land or a building) which is owned by (belongs to) someone **2** *One of the properties of hydrogen is that it is lighter than air.*(c.) = a quality by which something can be recognised

proph•et /ˈprɒfɪt/ noun, c. **1** = a person who brings a message from God and causes it to spread in the form of a religion **2** *He had said that India would win, and India won. He proved to be quite a prophet!* = a person who is able to tell the future correctly **prophecy** noun, c. *Her prophecy about the growth of the computer industry proved to be accurate.* = a statement saying that something is going to happen in the future **prophesy** verb, i. or t. *Can you prophesy who is going to win the match next week?* = to say what is going to happen in the future **prophetic** /prəˈfetɪk/ adj. *His words proved to be prophetic. It rained the next day, just as he had prophesied.* = correctly saying what is going to happen

pro•por•tion /prəˈpɔːʃən/ noun, u. or c. **1** *This doll's head is too small in proportion to the rest of its body. // The proportion of unmarried to married men is very high in this group.* = the size or amount of something when compared to that of something else **2** *She is able to save only a small proportion of her salary.* = part or share **proportional** adj. *Your share in the company's profits will be proportional to the amount of work that you put in.* = in proportion to (also **proportionate**) **proportions** noun, u. (always plural) *The proportions of the new library building are impressive.* = size and shape

to blow things out of proportion = to make a situation seem more serious that it actually is **to have a sense of proportion** = to be able to see and understand a situation correctly

pro•pose /prəˈpəʊz/ verb, t. **1** *I propose Rakesh Khanna's name for the post of president.* = to put forward formally for consideration by other people **2** *I propose to go to Pokhra for my holidays.* = to plan **3** *to propose marriage* = to ask someone to marry you **proposal** noun, c. **1** *We have received a proposal from the Bangladesh government for a joint meeting.* = suggestion or plan **2** = the act of formally asking someone to marry you

pro•pound /prəˈpaʊnd/ verb, t. *Einstein propounded the Theory of Relativity.* = to put forward a theory (new idea) for consideration (formal)

pro•pri•e•tor /prəˈpraɪətəʳ/ noun, c. = the owner of a business (formal)

pro•sa•ic /prəʊˈzeɪk/ adj. *a prosaic person* = having little imagination; dull and uninteresting

pro•scribe /prəʊˈskraɪb/ verb, t. *The government has proscribed this book as it is likely to corrupt the minds of young readers.* = to ban (to declare something illegal) (compare **prescribe**) (formal)

prose /prəʊz/ noun, u. = the use of language in its ordinary, everyday form (compare **poetry** or verse)

pro•se•cute /ˈprɒsɪkjuːt/ verb, t. *The police will prosecute him for breaking traffic rules.* = to bring a charge in a law court against someone who has broken the law [LAW]

pro•se•cu•tion /prɒsɪˈkjuːʃən/ noun, u. **1** *The government has ordered the prosecution of motorists who disobey traffic rules.* = the act of prosecuting someone who has broken the law **2** *She is the lawyer for the prosecution.* = the person or persons who try to show in court that a person is guilty (compare **defence**) **prosecutor** /ˈprɒsɪkjuːtəʳ/ noun, c. = a lawyer who works for the government and prosecutes people who break the law (also **public prosecutor**)

pros•o•dy /ˈprɒsədi/ noun, u. = the study of the patterns of sound in poetry

pros•pect[1] /ˈprɒspekt/ noun **1** (only singular) *I like the prospect of visiting Goa for a short holiday.* = the possibility of something happening **2** (always plural) *You should accept this job.The prospects are quite good here.* = opportunities for improvement etc.

prospect[2] /prəˈspekt/ verb, i. *Several companies*

are prospecting for oil in the Arabian Sea. = to search for minerals (gold, silver, oil etc.) which may be present inside the earth or under the sea **prospective** /prɒ'spektɪv/ adj. *He is the prospective manager of the new office. He has just been interviewed for the job.* = likely to become **prospectus** /prə'spektəs/ noun, c. = a printed statement put out by a business or educational organisation, describing the advantages which it offers

pros•per /'prɒspəʳ/ verb, i. *He was very poor five years ago but now he owns a large house in the city. He has prospered.* = to become successful and rich **prosperous** adj. *She is a prosperous businessperson, the owner of a dozen factories.* = successful and rich **prosperity** /prɒ'sperɪti/ noun, u. *The rains have brought prosperity to the farmers.* = success and wealth

pros•ti•tute /'prɒstɪtju:t/ noun, c. = a sex worker, especially a woman, who offers sex for money (The preferred term is **sex worker**.)

pro•tect /prə'tekt/ verb, t. **1** *Our defence forces (army, navy and airforce) protect this country from enemy attack.* = to keep safe from harm or injury; to guard **2** *Every country has to protect its industries.* = to help an industry by putting a tax on goods made by companies outside the country which are imported (brought into the country) **protection** noun, u. **1** *I always carry an umbrella for my own protection against the rain.* = the state of being protected **2** *The seat-belts in a car are a protection in case of an accident.* = something that protects **protective** adj. **1** *The outer shell of a bird's egg is a protective covering for the young chick inside.* = offering protection **2** *The lion is very protective of her cubs.* = wishing to protect **protectionism** noun, u. = the system of protecting the industries of a country by charging taxes on imported goods

prot•é•gé /'prɒteʒeɪ/ noun, c. (French) *She is a protégé of the the great singer Nalin Basu.* = a person who is helped by someone who is very powerful and influential

pro•tein /'prəʊti:n/ noun, u. or c. *Cheese contains a lot of protein.*(u.) = a substance which is present in such foods as meat, cheese, beans, etc. and which is necessary to build up the body

pro•test[1] /prə'test/ verb, i. or t. *When the students were told the examination would be held earlier than announced, they protested.*(i.) // *The students protested the teacher's decision.*(t.) = to complain (express one's unhappiness or dissatisfaction) against something which one does not like or agree with

protest[2] /'prəʊtest/ noun, c. or u. *strong protests*(c.) // *The workers shouted slogans in protest against the management's decision.*(u.) = an act of protesting (complaining or disagreeing) **Protestant** /'prəʊtestənt/ noun, c. = a person who follows the Protestant faith (the beliefs followed by Christians who do not accept the authority of the Pope or the Roman Catholic Church)

proto- /prəʊtəʊ/ prefix meaning **1** the first e.g. **prototype** /'prəʊtətaɪp/ noun, c. *the prototype of a new aircraft* = the first or earliest form of a new machine, which will be improved upon and developed **2** earliest e.g. **protoplasm** /'prəʊtəplæzəm/ noun, u. = the substance which is present in the cells of all living things and which is the earliest form of life [BIOLOGY]

pro•to•col /'prəʊtəkɒl/ noun, u. **1** *Protocol requires that when the president of another country visits India, he or she should be welcomed on arrival by the President of India, who is of equal rank.* = the fixed rules of behaviour which are used on special occasions by the representatives of different countries; behaviour and work rules prescribed in a company or an organization such as the armed forces **2** = the original written version of an agreement **3** = a set of rules that controls the flow of information from one computer to another [COMPUTERS]

pro•ton /'prəʊtɒn/ noun, c. = a smaller part of an atom which carries a positive electrical charge (see also **electron**, **neutron**)

protoplasm, prototype see **proto-**

pro•to•zo•a /prəʊtə'zəʊə/ noun, c. (always plural, used with plural verbs) = very tiny living things having only one cell

pro•tract /prə'trækt/ verb, t. *There is no need to protract this quarrel. Let us end it now.* = to stretch or extend something (to make it continue for a long time) **protractor** noun, c. = an instrument, usually in the form of a half-circle, used for measuring an angle in degrees [TECHNICAL]

pro•trude /prə'tru:d/ verb, i. *Your handkerchief is protruding from the pocket of your shirt.*= to stick out **protrusion** noun, u. or c. **1** (u.) = the act of protruding **2** *There is a protrusion on the back of his hand.*(c.) = something which protrudes (sticks out)

proud /praʊd/ adj. **1** *He has become very proud. He thinks he is better than all of us because he has a university degree.* = thinking too highly of oneself (derogatory) **2** *She is too proud to ask for another's help.* = having respect for oneself (not derogatory) **3** *I am proud of my students.* = getting pleasure or satisfaction, with good reason, from something with which one is connected **pride** noun, u. **1** *You have many good qualities but your pride makes people think badly of you.* = the quality of being proud (thinking too

P

highly of oneself) (derogatory) **2** *We take pride in our reputation for being honest.* = the feeling of satisfaction or pleasure that one gets by doing something good **3** *Nina Kansaker is the pride of the acting group.* = the most valuable person or thing **4** *a pride of lions* = a group of lions, containing males as well as females, that live and hunt together

to pride oneself on doing something *This city prides itself on its cleanliness.* = to feel happy about something with which one is connected

prove /pru:v/ verb, t. **1** *I can prove that this tree is 300 years old.* = to show beyond doubt that something is true, by producing facts etc. **2** *He has proved a good choice.* = to show that one is able to do something which he/she is required to do

prov•erb /'prɒvɜ:b/ noun, c. *'A rolling stone gathers no moss' is a well-known proverb in English.* = a short, well-known and widely used saying which expresses some truth or wisdom **proverbial** /prə'vɜ:bɪəl/ adj. *The hospitality of the Arab people is proverbial.* = very well-known and widely spoken about

pro•vide /prə'vaɪd/ verb, t. *This hotel provides a free breakfast along with the room.*(t.) = to supply (to allow someone to have or use) **to provide for** verb **1** *She has a large family to provide for.* = to support, specially with money **2** *We expect 200 guests but we have provided for 500.* = to make arrangements for **provided** adv. *She agreed to drive the jeep to Mussourie provided someone sat beside her and told her the way.* = a condition that says something can be done only if something else happens **provident** /'prɒvɪdent/ adj. *provident fund* = providing support for the future, usually in the form of money (formal) **provision** /prə'vɪzən/ noun, u. **1** *The government has made no provision for the education of girls in this village.* = the act of providing (supplying) something for other's use **2** *She made provision for the children's lunch at a friend's house because she was away on work.* = preparation for some future need **3** *One of the provisions in this agreement is that the landlord must give three months' notice to the tenant.* = a condition in an agreement or a law (also proviso) **provisions** noun, u. (always plural) *We have run out of provisions. We must get some rice and vegetables from the market.* = food supplies **provisional** adj. *A provisional government has been set up, which will look after the state until the elections are held.* = temporary (for the present time only)

prov•i•dence (Providence) /'prɒvɪdəns/ noun, u. *He could have been badly injured in the accident but he was saved by providence.* = the protection that God is thought to provide to all human beings

prov•ince /'prɒvɪns/ noun, c. **1** *The Mughal rulers had divided India into a number of provinces.* = a part of a country or kingdom, which has its own system of administration but is controlled by the system at the centre **2** *I cannot talk to you on Western music. That lies outside my province.* = an area of knowledge with which one is connected **provincial** /prə'vɪnʃəl/ adj. **1** *a system of provincial government* = relating to a province **2** *He is very provincial in his views and it is difficult to get him to agree with anyone.* = narrow-minded and old-fashioned (derogatory)

pro•voke /prə'vəʊk/ verb, t. *He tried to provoke me by saying I was always making mistakes, but I remained calm.* = to try to make a person angry or to cause a certain reaction **provocation** /prɒvə'keɪʃən/ noun, u. *I remained calm in spite of her provocation.* = the act of provoking someone **provocative** /prə'vɒkətɪv/ adj. *He made a provocative statement at the meeting, saying that we had no loyalty to our country.* = having the power to provoke (cause anger or other strong feelings)

prow /praʊ/ noun, u. *the prow of a boat* = the pointed front part of a boat or ship (also **bow**) (compare **stern**)

prow•ess /'praʊɪs/ noun, u. *sporting prowess* = ability or strength

prowl /praʊl/ verb, i. or t. **1** *The leopard prowled about the village at night.*(i.) = to move quietly, looking for prey **2** *The police found the thieves prowling the streets at night.*(t.) = to move quietly without making a sound, usually for some illegal purpose

prox•im•i•ty /prɒk'sɪmɪti/ noun, u. *There are no shops in the proximity of our home. We have to go a long way to buy the things that we need.* = nearness (the area immediately surrounding some place)

prox•y /'prɒksi/ noun, c. (**proxies**) or u. **1** *I was not able to attend the meeting, but I asked a friend to be my proxy.*(c.) = a person who represents or acts on behalf of another person **2** *Members of this club are allowed to vote by proxy.*(u.) = the system of using a proxy (someone who represents you or acts on your behalf)

prude /pru:d/ noun, c. = a person who is easily shocked by rude things, especially things connected with sex (slightly derogatory) **prudery** noun, u. = the quality of being a prude

pru•dent /'pru:dənt/ adj. *Why did you trust an unknown person with your money? You should have been more prudent.* = careful or wise **prudence** noun, u. = carefulness or wisdom that saves one from doing something harmful

prune[1] /pru:n/ noun, c. = a dried plum (fruit)

prune[2] verb, t. *These rose plants have to be pruned regularly.* = to cut, remove or shorten the branches of a plant or tree

pry /praɪ/ verb, i. or t. (**pried**) **1** *Let's not pry into their affairs.*(i.) = to try to find out about someone else's private affairs **2** *He pried open the door with an iron bar.*(t.) = to use force to open a door or a box

psalm /sɑːm/ noun, c. = a song or poem used in Christian worship

pseu•do- /sjuːdəʊ/ prefix meaning 'false' e.g. **pseudo** noun, c. *What pseudos they are!* = a person who is not sincere or honest and pretends to be something which he/she is not (informal, derogatory)

pseu•do•nym /'sjuːdənɪm/ noun, c. = a false name, specially a pen-name used by a writer

psy•che /'saɪki/ noun, u. = the human mind or soul (formal) **psychic** adj. = having unusual powers of the mind that cannot be scientifically explained, which makes a person know what another is thinking

psy•chi•a•try /saɪ'kaɪətri/ noun = the study of the diseases of the mind and their treatment [MEDICINE] **psychiatrist** noun, c. = a doctor who treats diseases of the mind

psycho- a prefix meaning 'connected with the mind' e.g. **psy•chol•o•gy** /saɪ'kɒlədʒi/ noun = the scientific study of the mind and the way it works **psychological** /saɪkə'lɒdʒɪkəl/ adj. *a psychological film* = dealing with the mind or its working **psychologist** /saɪ'kɒlədʒɪst/ noun, c. = a person who studies or teaches psychology

psy•cho•a•nal•y•sis /saɪkə-ənælɪsɪs/ noun, u. = treatment of disorders of the mind by analysing (examining) a person's experiences, memories, dreams etc. **psycho-analyst** noun, c. = a person trained in psycho-analysis

psy•cho•path /'saɪkəpæθ/ noun, c. = a person with a disturbed mind who can easily commit violent crimes

psy•cho•sis /saɪ'kəʊsɪs/ noun, u. = serious disorder of the mind that may cause a person to lose touch with reality and affect their personality **psychotic** noun, c. = a person who suffers from psychosis

psy•cho•so•mat•ic /saɪkəʊsə'mætɪk/ adj. *Asthma is thought to be a psychosomatic disease.* = caused mainly by anxiety (fear in the mind)

pub /pʌb/ noun, c. short form of 'public house' = a place where alcoholic drinks can be sold and bought

pu•ber•ty /'pjuːbəti/ noun, u. = the age at which a boy or girl reaches sexual maturity and is able to produce children

pu•bic /'pjuːbɪk/ adj. *pubic hair* = having to do with the sex organs

pub•lic[1] /'pʌblɪk/ adj. **1** *Public opinion on this subject is very important.* = having to do with people in general **2** *This is a public library.* = for the use of everyone (opposite **private**) **3** *a course in public policy* = connected with the government

public[2] noun, u. (no plural form, but can be used with singular or plural forms of verbs) **1** *The public is/are losing interest in the theatre.* = people in general **2** *In this college there is no public for poetry.* = people who are interested in something or have something in common

to be public knowledge = to be known to many people **to go public** **1** = to let something that was a secret become well-known **2** = of a commercial organization, to put up its shares for sale to the public [BUSINESS] **to be in the public eye** = to be seen on television, in the newspapers etc.

pub•lic•i•ty /pʌ'blɪsɪti/ noun, u. *The new film is getting a lot of publicity in the media.* = public notice or attention **publicize (publicise)** /'pʌblɪsaɪz/ verb, t. *We are trying to publicize the new book so that people will buy it.* = to bring to the notice of the public **public address system** noun = an arrangement of microphones, loud-speakers etc. used to make the voice of a speaker louder so that it can be heard by many people at a meeting etc. **public health** noun = the health care provided by the government **public sector** (always singular) noun = the industries or services in a country which are owned and managed by the government **public works** noun (always plural) = the building of roads, bridges, buildings etc. by the government for the use of the public

pub•lish /'pʌblɪʃ/ verb, t. **1** *Orient Longman publishes many kinds of books including medical books.* = to print, produce and sell books, magazines etc. **2** *The report will be published next week.* = to make known to the public **publisher** noun, c. = a person or a company which publishes books, magazines etc. **publishing** noun, u. = the business of making books, newspapers etc. ready to print and sell **publication** /pʌblɪ'keɪʃən/ noun, u. or c. **1** (u.) = the act or business of publishing books etc. **2** *This is our latest publication.*(c.) = a book, magazine etc. that has been published **3** *We are waiting for the publication of the election results.*(u.) = the act of making something known to the public

pud•ding /'pʊdɪŋ/ noun, u. or c. **1** = a sweet dish prepared from rice, milk, eggs, fruit etc **2** = any sweet eaten at the end of a meal

pud•dle /'pʌdl/ noun, c. *I stepped into a puddle and got some mud on my trousers.* = a small amount of water, especially rain, which collects on the ground

pu•er•ile /'pjʊəraɪl/ adj. *He has written many books on religion but I find them rather puerile.* = childish and silly (derogatory)

P

puff[1] /pʌf/ verb, i. or t. **1** *He was puffing as he ran up the hill.*(i.) = to breathe quickly and heavily as a result of some exercise etc. **2** *puff a cigarette*(i.) = to breathe in and out while smoking **3** *He puffed smoke into the air.*(t.) = to blow or to breathe out smoke

puff[2] noun, c. **1** *He took a long puff at his cigarette.* = the act of puffing (breathing in or out while smoking) **2** *A puff of wind blew away the paper.* = a sudden rush of air, smoke etc. **3** *She applied some powder on her cheeks with a puff.* = a ball of soft material used for putting talcum powder on the skin **puffy** adj. *His eyes looked puffy. Maybe she had been crying.* = swollen

puf•fin /'pʌfɪn/ noun, c. = a kind of sea-bird found in the North Atlantic region

pug /pʌg/ noun, c. = a kind of dog that is very small in size and has a wide, flat face

puke[1] /pju:k/ verb, i. *The fish had such a bad smell that it made me puke.* = to vomit or throw up (informal)

puke[2] noun, u. *There was puke all over her clothes.* = vomit (food that is thrown up from the stomach) (informal)

pull[1] /pʊl/ verb, t. **1** *The horse was pulling a cart. // If you pull this rope the bell will ring.* = to cause something to move forward or move towards you **2** *The dentist pulled out my tooth.* = to remove or to take something out of its usual place **3** *Tendulkar pulled the ball over the boundary.* = to hit the ball high [SPORTS] **4** *She pulled her thigh muscle while rowing the boat.* = to damage a muscle because of putting in too much effort

pull[2] noun, c. **1** *He gave the rope a pull.* = the act of pulling something towards yourself **2** *the earth's gravitational pull* = a force that makes something move in a certain direction **pull-over** noun, c. = a sweater (woollen garment) that is worn by pulling it down over one's head **pull-out** noun, c. = a part of a book or magazine, which can be taken out and forms a separate part (another small book)

to pull off = to succeed in doing something unexpected **to pull through** = to come out of a difficult or dangerous situation, e.g. an illness **to pull a fast one on someone** = to cheat or deceive someone by using a trick (informal) **to pull someone's leg** = to make fun of someone in a gentle way **to pull one's weight** = to do a large share of some work as is expected **to pull oneself together** = to start to behave calmly and control one's feelings **to pull strings** = to use one's influence or power to gain an advantage

pul•let /'pʊlɪt/ noun, c. = a young hen

pul•ley /'pʊli/ noun, c. = a machine consisting of a wheel over which a rope or chain passes, which can be used to lift heavy things

pul•mo•na•ry /'pʊlmənəri/ adj. *the pulmonary artery* = having to do with the lungs [MEDICINE]

pulp[1] /pʌlp/ noun, u. **1** *Paper is made from bamboo pulp.* = a substance which has been boiled until it becomes very soft, almost liquid **2** = the soft, inner part of a fleshy fruit

pulp[2] verb, t. *The bamboo is pulped by boiling it.* = to turn some substance into pulp **pulp fiction** noun = cheaply produced stories, mostly romantic

pul•pit /'pʊlpɪt/ noun, c. = a small raised platform in a church, on which the priest stands as he speaks to the worshippers in the church

pul•sar /'pʌlsɑːʳ/ noun, c. = a very small star that sends out radio waves [TECHNICAL]

pulse[1] /pʌls/ noun, u. or c. **1** (u.) = the movement of blood through the arteries (blood vessels leading away from the heart) in jerks, caused by the beating of the heart **2** *Telephone systems in India use a pulse.*(u.) = a short burst of electrical energy, which is repeated regularly

pulse[2] verb, i. *Blood pulses through the arteries.* = to move or flow steadily **pulsate** /pʌl'seɪt/ verb, i. *The music pulsated through the room.* = to move or shake with a regular rhythm; to vibrate **pulses** (always plural) = the seeds of some plants that are cooked and eaten

pul•ver•ize (pulverise) /'pʌlvəraɪz/ verb, t. **1** *The glass dish fell from the top of the building and was pulverized.* = to break or crush into powder **2** *The Australians pulverized the Indian team.* = to defeat very badly (figurative)

pu•ma /'pju:mə/ noun, c. = a large wild animal belonging to the cat family that looks like a lion and is found in South America

pum•ice /'pʌmɪs/ noun, u. = a kind of soft stone that is used for rubbing or cleaning things

pum•mel /'pʌməl/ verb, t. (**pummelled**) *Rohan pummelled the boxing bag with his fists.* = to hit repeatedly

pump[1] /pʌmp/ noun, c. **1** *a bicycle pump* = a machine that can force a liquid, such as water, or a gas, into or out of some place **2** *He had black leather pumps on his feet.* = a kind of light shoe without laces

pump[2] verb, t. *We have to pump water out of the well.* = to use a pump (machine) to lift or move a liquid or a gas

pump•kin /'pʌmpkɪn/ noun, c. = the large, round fruit of a plant that is eaten as a vegetable

pun[1] /pʌn/ noun, c. *In Shakespeare's play 'The Merchant of Venice', Shylock makes a pun when he says that Antonio's blood will be on his sole but not on his soul.* = humour or a special effect created by playing with the meanings or spellings of words

pun[2] verb, i. (**punned**) *Shakespeare often puns on words.* = to play with words

punch[1] /pʌntʃ/ noun, c. or u. **1** *He hit an excellent shot and punched the air in excitement.*(c.) = to hit something with one's fist **2** (c.) = a machine which can make holes in paper, metal etc. **3** *fruit punch* (u.) = a kind of drink made by mixing different kinds of juice together

punch[2] verb, i. or t. **1** *He punched the pillow many times in anger.* = to hit with a closed fist **2** *The conductor punched my ticket.*(t) = to make a hole in something, using a punch (machine) **punch-line** noun, c. = the last few words in a story or joke, which make it interesting or funny

punc•tu•al /'pʌŋktʃuəl/ adj. *She is always punctual. I have never known her to be late for class.* = doing something at exactly the right time

punc•tu•a•tion /pʌŋktʃu'eɪʃən/ noun, u. *The punctuation is wrong in this sentence. You should have used a comma here, not a semi-colon.* = the system of signs, including commas, semi-colons, full-stops etc. used to separate sentences, phrases etc. from each other in a piece of writing **punctuate** /'pʌnklʃueɪt/ verb, t. *How should I punctuate this part of my essay?* = to use punctuation to separate sentences etc.

punc•ture[1] /'pʌŋktʃəʳ/ noun, c. *a puncture in the tyre* = a small hole through which some gas or liquid can escape

puncture[2] verb, t. *The nails lying on the road punctured the car tyres.* = to make a hole in something

pun•gent /'pʌndʒənt/ adj. *Garlic has a pungent smell.* = strong and sharp (referring to a taste or smell)

pun•ish /'pʌnɪʃ/ verb, t. *The teacher punished the student for disturbing the class by asking him to leave.* = to cause someone to suffer for doing something wrong **punishable** adj. *Driving without a licence is a punishable offence.* = which can be punished under the law **punishment** adj. **1** *The punishment for late submission is to deduct two marks.* = the action taken to punish someone **2** *This motorcycle can take a lot of punishment.* = rough treatment **punishing** adj. *It was a punishing trip. I didn't have a day's rest.* = something that makes one very tired

punk /pʌŋk/ noun, c. **1** = a kind of rock music of the 1940's and 1980's which was violently against tradition **2** = a person who colours his or her hair and wears unusual clothes with metal etc. as a sign of independence (fashionable some years ago but not now)

punt /pʌnt/ noun, c. = a long, narrow boat with a flat bottom which is moved by using a long stick that pushes against the bottom of a river

pu•ny /'pju:ni/ adj. *a man with a puny body* = small and weak (often derogatory)

pup /pʌp/ noun, c. = the term used for the baby of certain animals e.g. a seal **puppy** noun, c. (**puppies**) = the baby of a dog **puppy love** noun = love between a very young boy and a very young girl, which often does not last (derogatory)

pu•pa /'pju:pə/ noun, c. (**pupas** or **pupae**) = an insect which is in the middle stage of its development, shortly before it is fully developed

pu•pil /'pju:pəl/ noun, c. **1** *The teacher has 50 pupils.* = a person, specially a child, who is learning something **2** *the pupil of the eye* = the small, dark opening in the centre of the eye through which light passes into the eye (see pic under **eye**)

pup•pet /'pʌpɪt/ noun, c. **1** = a toy figure of a human being or animal, usually made of wood, that can be made to move by pulling strings tied to it **2** *a puppet minister* = someone whose actions are controlled by someone else (derogatory) **puppeteer** /pʌpɪ'tɪər/ noun, c. = a person who makes and operates puppets and presents shows in which puppets are used

pur•chase[1] /'pɜ:tʃɪs/ verb, t. *We have to purchase some gifts for the children who are coming to the party.* = to buy (formal)

purchase[2] noun, u. or c. **1** *The purchase of books has been stopped by the government.*(u.) = the act of purchasing (buying) **2** *This car was an excellent purchase.*(c.) = something that has been bought

pur•dah /'pɜ:də/ noun *The women of the royal family lived in purdah.* = the system of not allowing women to appear in public either by making them stay at home or covering their faces, especially when men are present

pure /pjʊəʳ/ adj. **1** *This ring is made of pure silver.* = not mixed with anything else **2** *He saw me by pure accident.* = complete **3** *She has a pure white sari.* = not mixed with any other colour **4** *I am learning pure mathematics.* = theoretical not practical **5** *His mind is pure.* = free from evil **purify** verb, t. = to make something pure **purification** /pjʊrɪfɪ'keɪʃən/ noun, u. = the process of making something pure

pu•ree /'pjʊəreɪ/ noun, u. *We use tomato puree to make our curries.* = some fruit or vegetable which has been turned almost into a liquid, by boiling or using a machine (called a blender or liquidizer)

purge /pɜ:dʒ/ verb, t. **1** *The leader of the group decided to purge the members who had been speaking against him.* = to get rid of something or someone; to drive out **2** *to purge oneself through penance* = to make oneself clean **3** *This medicine may purge you.* = to clear out the waste matter inside the bowels (intestines) (see also **purgative**)

P

purgative noun, c. *Castor oil is a purgative.* = a substance or a medicine that helps to clear out waste matter from the bowels

purl /pɜ:l/ verb, i. = to make a backward stitch in knitting

pur•ple /ˈpɜ:pəl/ noun = a colour produced by mixing red and blue colours **a purple passage/patch** = an unexpectedly fine piece of writing in the middle of something that is very dull

pur•port[1] /ˈpɜ:pɔ:t/ noun, u. *I could not understand the purport of your letter.* = meaning or intention (formal)

purport[2] verb, t. *He purports to be very close to the Prime Minister.* = to claim to be (formal)

pur•pose /ˈpɜ:pəs/ noun, u. or c. **1** *The purpose of my letter was to warn you of danger.*(u.)= the reason for doing something **2** *This soap can be used for different purposes.*(c.) = the use to which something is put **3** *He worked with a sense of purpose.*(u.) = a definite aim **purposeful** adj. *Our discussion was purposeful.* = having a clear purpose or aim **purposely** adv. *I purposely did not invite you to my party.* = intentionally; knowingly

purr[1] /pɜ:ʳ/ verb, i. (**purred**) *A cat purrs when it is happy. // The engine of my car is purring nicely.* = to make a continuous low sound, like that made by a cat when it is happy

purr[2] noun, u. *Can you hear the purr of the engine?*

purse[1] /pɜ:s/ noun, c. = a flat bag, usually made of leather, in which money (usually in the form of notes) is carried

purse[2] verb *to purse one's lips* = to press one's lips into a thin line to show that one does not like something

purs•er /ˈpɜ:səʳ/ noun, c. = an officer on a ship or aircraft who keeps accounts and looks after the comfort of passengers

pur•sue /pəˈsju:/ verb, t. *The police pursued the thief.* = to chase or to run after someone with the intention of catching him/her

pur•suit /pəˈsju:t/ noun, u. = the action of pursuing (chasing) someone

pur•view /ˈpɜ:vju:/ noun, c. *This matter does not come within the purview of the Defence Ministry. The Prime Minister has to decide it.* = the limit of one's authority, knowledege

pus /pʌs/ noun, u. = the thick, whitish-yellow liquid that sometimes forms in a wound or infected part of the body

push[1] /pʊʃ/ verb, t. or i. **1** *He pushed the cupboard against the wall.*(t.) *// Don't push! I will fall.*(i.) = to cause something to move away from oneself by using force **2** *I know you will never complete this job unless I push you.*(t.) = to force someone to do something **3** *We are trying to push this new product in the market.*(t.) = to bring something to the notice of people [TECHNICAL]

push[2] noun, u. **1** *Let us give the car a push.* = the act of pushing something **2** *He has a lot of push. I expect him to be very successful.* = the energy or determination required to do something (informal) **push-over** noun = someone who can be easily defeated

to be pushed for time *I'm sorry I can't help. I'm pushed for time.* = to not have enough time (informal) **to push someone around** = to give someone orders in a rude way **to push for** *We are trying to push for a bus-stop in our neighbourhood.* = to try to get something, usually something good or useful

put /pʊt/ verb, t. **1** *Put the book on the table.* = to place or move something from one place to another **2** *You have put too much salt in the curry.* = to add **3** *Put some ointment on the wound.* = to apply or spread **4** *Can you put that in simple language?* = to express **5** *Put inverted commas around the word 'tree'* = to write **6** *I'd put her first, not last, among the talented writers.* = to place or rank

to put aside = to save (specially money) **to put off** **1** *We put off the journey by a day.* = to delay or move to a later date **2** *I liked them but their bad manners put me off.* = to make someone not like someone or something **to put something/someone down** **1** = to put what one is holding down **2** *I'll put that down on paper.* = to write something **3** *I'll put down Rs 500 as a first payment.* = to pay a certain amount as an initial cost of something **4** *The cat was very sick and had to be put down.* =to cause an animal to die because it is old or sick **5** = to tell somebody that they are not good enough at something **to put somebody or something up** **1** *Put your hand up if you can help us with the play.* = to hold or lift something up **2** = to build something (e.g. a tent) **3** *put up a picture/poster* = to fix something, on a wall, board etc. **4** *I would be happy to put you up for a few days.* = to provide temporary accomodation (living space) to someone **to put a stop to something** *We have wasted a lot of time arguing. Let's put a stop to it.* = to bring an activity which is considered harmful or not welcome to an end **to put something behind one** = to decide by agreement, to stop thinking about a problem, disappointment or failure **to put something down to something else** *Paul is looking worried. I put it down to his fear of writing exams.* = to say that a feeling, way of behaving etc. is caused by something else **How shall I put it?** *She's a very—how shall I put it?—impatient person.* = an expression used to suggest that the speaker is looking for the correct words to say, or words that will not cause unhappiness

pu•tre•fy /ˈpjuːtrɪfaɪ/ verb, i. = (of meat or something organic) to become rotten (formal) **putrefaction** /pjuːtrɪˈfækʃən/ noun, u. = the process of becoming rotten

pu•trid /ˈpjuːtrɪd/ adj. *putrid meat* = rotten and giving out a bad smell

putt /pʌt/ verb, t. (**putted**) = to hit the ball in the game of golf

put•ty /ˈpʌti/ noun, u. = a soft material used in fixing a sheet of glass to a window

puz•zle[1] /ˈpʌzəl/ verb, t. **1** *His letter puzzles me. I don't know what he is trying to say.* = to make someone confused (unable to understand something) **2** *I am trying to puzzle out the meaning of this letter.* = to make an effort to try to find out the meaning of something or the solution to a problem etc.

puzzle[2] noun, c. *Can you solve this crossword puzzle?* = a game or a toy which forces a person to think hard **puzzled** adj. *She looked puzzled when I asked her where the pencil was.* = confused

PVC abbr. of **polyvinylchloride** = a kind of plastic material used to make pipes etc.

py•ja•mas /pəˈdʒɑːməz/ noun (always plural) **1** = a dress worn when going to bed, consisting of a short jacket (coat) and a pair of loose trousers **2** = any loose-fitting clothes worn when going to bed and (therefore) not considered suitable for formal use

py•or•rhoe•a /paɪəˈriːə/ noun = a disease which causes bleeding from the teeth and gums [MEDICINE]

pyr•a•mid /ˈpɪrəmɪd/ noun, c. **1** = a solid geometrical shape, consisting of a square base and four triangular sides that meet at a point **2** *an Egyptian pyramid* = a very large stone building in the shape of a pyramid, used as a tomb for a king, found in Egypt

pyre /paɪəʳ/ noun, c. *a funeral pyre* = a pile of wood on which a dead body is kept for burning

py•thon /ˈpaɪθən/ noun, c. = a very large and powerful snake that has no poison but kills its prey by winding its body round it, crushing it and swallowing the prey

P

qQ

q, Q /kju:/ the seventeenth letter of the English alphabet

QED abbr. of **quod erat demonstrandum** (Latin) = which was to be proved (commonly written after the proof given for a theorem) [GEOMETRY]

quack /kwæk/ noun, c. **1** = the sound made by a duck **2** = a person who has not been trained as a doctor but who pretends to be one (derogatory)

quad- /kwɒd/ prefix meaning four e.g. **quad•ran•gle** /'kwɒdræŋgəl/ noun, c. = a courtyard (open space surrounded by buildings on four sides) which forms part of a college or university campus **quadrangular** /kwɒ'dræŋguləʳ/ adj. *a quadrangular cricket tournament* = limited to four teams or sides

quad•rant /'kwɒdrənt/ noun, c. = a quarter (fourth part) of a circle

quad•ru•ped /'kwɒdrʊped/ noun, c. *The horse is a quadruped.* = an animal with four legs

quad•ru•ple[1] /'kwɒdrʊpəl/ noun, c. *100 is the quadruple of 25* = a number which is four times as great as another number

quadruple[2] verb, t. *We plan to quadruple the number of schools in this town.* = to multiply something by four **quadruplicate** noun, u. *You have to submit your application in quadruplicate* = in four copies (compare **duplicate, triplicate**)

quail[1] /kweɪl/ noun, c. (**quail** or **quails**) or u. (u.) = a type of small bird, once hunted for its meat and now raised on farms

quail[2] verb, i. *He quailed when he was suddenly asked to go on stage.* = to feel or show great fear (literary)

quaint /kweɪnt/ adj. *a quaint custom* = something which seems strange and unusual to others

quake[1] /kweɪk/ verb, i. **1** *The earth quaked.* = to shake (referring to the earth) **2** *The actor quaked when the director asked him to leap into the water.* = to shake with fear or cold (referring to a person) (literary)

quake[2] noun, c. *We felt a small quake last night.* = earthquake (informal) **Quaker** noun = a member of a Christian religious group which believes in leading a very simple life

qual•i•fy /'kwɒlɪfaɪ/ verb, i. or t. (**qualified**) **1** *The Sri Lankan team beat the Australian team and qualified for the final round of the tournament.*(i.) = to prove oneself suitable for something **2** *The MBBS degree qualifies you to practise as a doctor.*(t.) = to make someone suitable for something **3** *He said he would like to qualify the statement he had made earlier.*(t.) = to change something that one has said earlier etc. by making it less strong, less general etc. **4** *An adjective qualifies a noun.*(t.) = to describe the qualities of something [GRAMMAR] **qualification** /kwɒlɪfɪ'keɪʃən/ noun, c. or u. **1** *The MBBS degree is a necessary qualification for practising medicine.*(c.) = a degree or a form of training that makes one suitable for some job etc. **2** (u.) = the act of qualifying for something

qual•i•ty /'kwɒlɪti/ noun, u. or c. (**qualities**) **1** *I am not satisfied with the quality of this shirt. I want something better.*(u.) = the extent to which something is good **2** *She is honest and hard-working and has many good qualities.*(c.) = something that makes a person or thing different from others **qualitative** /'kwɒlɪtətɪv/ adj. *We want to see a qualitative improvement in your work.* = having to do with the quality of something (as different from quantity or exact measurement) **quality control** = the system of checking goods, services etc. to make sure the quality is acceptable **quality time** = time spent happily, especially with one's children, free from worries

qualm /kwɑ:m/ noun, c. (usually plural) *I have serious qualms about sending my child alone to school in the public bus.* = a feeling that one may be doing something wrong

quan•da•ry /'kwɒndəri/ noun, c. *He has been offered an attractive job in Mumbai, but he does not want to leave Kolkata. He is in a quandary.* = the state of not being able to decide what to do; dilemma (formal)

quan•ti•ty /'kwɒntɪti/ noun, u. or c. (**quantities**) *She has written more than 20 books, but they are all badly written. She should be told that quantity is not important in writing.*(u.) // *Large quantities of foodgrain have been sent to states where there is a shortage.*(c.) = an amount or number that can be counted, weighed etc. **quantifier** noun, c. *In the expression 'a lot of money', the phrase 'a lot of' is used as a quantifier.* = a word or phrase that shows quantity [GRAMMAR] **quantify** verb, t. *You say that the students are improving. Can you quantify that statement and tell me what percentage of the students got pass marks?* = to express something as a quantity (something that can be measured, counted etc.) **quantitative** adj. *We are doing a quantitative survey of the schools in this district. We would like to know how many schools there are, how many teachers are working in those schools etc.* = concerned with quantity (the measurement of how much, how many etc.)

quan•tum /'kwɒntəm/ noun, u. or c. (**quanta or**

quantums) *What is the quantum of money that you need to complete this building?*(u.) = a quantity (amount) that is needed or wanted (formal) **quantum leap** noun *India has taken a quantum leap forward in information technology.* = sudden and great progress **quantum theory** noun = the theory that energy (e.g. heat or light) travels from a source in fixed quantities [PHYSICS]

quar•an•tine[1] /'kwɒrənti:n/ noun, u. *The child is suffering from chicken pox. He must be kept in quarantine for six weeks.* = the period during which a person suffering from an infectious disease is separated from other people to prevent the infection from spreading

quarantine[2] verb, t. *The patient will be quarantined.* = to put a person in quarantine

quark /kwɑ:k/ noun, c. = a very small particle (piece of matter) that forms part of an atom [PHYSICS]

quar•rel[1] /'kwɒrəl/ verb, i. (**quarrelled**) *The two children were quarrelling over a toy.* = to disagree or argue angrily about something

quarrel[2] noun, c. *There was a quarrel between the two brothers.* = the act of quarrelling **quarrelsome** adj. *a quarrelsome person* = one who is in the habit of quarrelling (derogatory)

quar•ry[1] /'kwɒri/ noun, c. **1** *a stone quarry* = a place, usually in the side of a hill, from which stone or minerals are dug out **2** *The leopard is chasing its quarry.* = an animal or a person that one is chasing or hunting

quarry[2] verb, t. (**quarried**) *Marble is quarried in Rajasthan.* = to dig (stone or minerals) out of a quarry

quart /kwɔ:t/ noun, c. = a unit for measuring the amount of liquid that a container can hold, equal to about one litre

quar•ter /'kwɔ:tə[r]/ noun, c. **1** *Give me a quarter of that cake.* = one part out of four equal parts into which something is or can be divided **2** *This is the rent for the first quarter of 2001.* = a period of three months **3** *We received some help from an unexpected quarter.* = a place or person **4** *We shall offer no quarter to those who break the law.* = mercy **5** (always plural) *I am living in government quarters.* = accommodation (a place to live in) **quarter-final** noun, c. = a match in a tournament played just before the semi-final match **quarterly** adj. *a quarterly magazine* = appearing four times a year (once in three months)

quartz /kwɔ:ts/ noun, u. = a kind of mineral which is used in making electronic watches etc.

quasi- /'kweɪzɑɪ/ a prefix meaning **1** partly but not wholly e.g. **quasi-official** *a quasi-official inquiry* = only partly official **2** not genuine or real e.g. **quasi-science** = not real science that can be proved

qua•ver[1] /'kweɪvə[r]/ verb, i. *His voice quavered when he spoke about the death of his dog.* = to shake (referring to someone's voice) because of nervousness, sadness etc.

quaver[2] noun, u. *He spoke with a quaver.* = a shake in the voice

quay /ki:/ noun, c. = a place on the bank of a river where boats load and unload goods

quea•sy /'kwi:zi/ adj. *The movement of the ship through the rough sea made me feel queasy.* = wanting to vomit or throw up

queen /kwi:n/ noun, c. **1** = a woman who rules over a country or is the wife of a king **2** *a beauty queen* = a woman who wins the highest prize in a competition **3** *the queen bee* = the most powerful insect, which is a female, in a group of insects **4** = the most powerful piece in the game of chess, positioned next to the king at the beginning of a game **5** = a playing card with the picture of a queen on it

queer /kwɪə[r]/ adj. **1** *He has a queer habit. He always sleeps in a sitting position.* = strange and unusual (disapproving) **2** *She told the doctor she was feeling slightly queer.* = unwell **3** *The old man is a little queer.* = slightly mad **4** = a homosexual person (also **gay**) (The word 'queer' is now generally not used with this meaning as it causes offence.)

to queer someone's pitch = to spoil someone's chances of success

quell /kwel/ verb, t. **1** *The British rulers quelled the Indian War of Independence in 1857.* = to put down by force (referring to a revolt or mutiny) (formal) **2** *You have quelled our doubts.* = to end

quench /kwentʃ/ verb, t. **1** *Drink this lemon juice. It will quench your thirst.* = to satisfy one's thirst **2** *The fire has been quenched.* = to put out a fire

quer•u•lous /'kwerʊləs/ adj. *She asked me in a querulous tone, 'Why can't I leave now?'* = complaining

que•ry /'kwɪəri/ noun, c. (**queries**) *Have I answered your query?* = a question usually based on a doubt (formal)

quest /kwest/ noun, c. *I have been searching all the bookshops for a copy of the book. My quest has ended at last.* = a long search (literary)

ques•tion[1] /'kwestʃən/ noun, c. **1** *'Where do you live?' is a question. // He asked me a question which I was unable to answer.* = a sentence or phrase which needs a reply, used to get information, clarify a doubt etc. **2** *the question of better services at railway stations* = a matter that has to be decided or acted upon **3** (usually plural) *The accident raises questions about the safety of travelling by train.* = doubts or uncertainty

question[2] verb, t. **1** *The police are questioning the man who was arrested last night.* = to ask questions to find out something **2** *I question your ability to lead*

Q

this team. = to raise doubts about something **questionable** adj. *His ability to lead the team is questionable.* = something that can be doubted **question mark** noun **1** = the sign of punctuation (?) used after a question **2** *There is a question mark over the future of this government.* = doubt or uncertainty **questionnaire** /kwestʃə'neəʳ/ noun, c. = a set of written questions given to a large number of people to answer, in order to get some information

without question *Without question, this is the most beautiful garden I've seen.* = without any doubt **no question** (**of something happening**) *There is no question of our allowing you to travel alone. You are too young.* = something that will definitely not happen **out of the question** *You want to leave now? That's out of the question. You haven't finished your work.* = not permitted or possible (Note that **the** must be used.)

queue[1] /kjuː/ noun, c. *There is a long queue at the ticket counter.* = people standing one behind the other in a line and waiting for their turn to receive some service etc.

queue[2] verb, i. *Please queue up if you want to buy tickets.* = to form a queue

to jump the queue = to get ahead of someone who has been standing in a queue for a longer time than one, or to try to get something before it is one's turn to get it

quib•ble[1] /'kwɪbəl/ verb, i. *The two men were quibbling over the amount of lime juice that should be added to the soup.* = to argue continuously over something that is not very important

quibble[2] noun, c. *I have a small quibble over the quality of the food. It is not hot enough.* = complaint

quick[1] /kwɪk/ adj. **1** *He is quick to learn new ways of cooking.* = able to do things in a very short time **2** *We had a quick dinner before we left for the airport.* = done in a short time

quick[2] adv. *Come quick! I have something wonderful to show you.* = fast; with great speed **quickly** adv. **quicken** verb, i. or t. *Changes in education are usually slow, but with the coming of computers the changes have quickened.*(i.) = to become quicker or faster

quick-lime /'kwɪk-laɪm/ noun, u. = lime (calcium oxide)

quicksand /'kwɪksænd/ noun, c. or u. *Be careful! There is quicksand here.*(u.) = wet sand which sucks in anyone who tries to walk over it

quick-silver /'kwɪksɪlvəʳ/ noun = the liquid metal called mercury

qui•et /'kwaɪət/ adj. **1** *The house is very quiet now that the children are sleeping. // The market is quiet now because of the long holiday.* = silent or without much activity **2** *I was impressed by his quiet confidence.* = without attracting much attention or making much noise **3** *She's a quiet person.* = not given to talking much **quieten** verb, t. *Can you quieten the children? They are making too much noise.* = to make someone quiet

to keep quiet *I didn't really know the answer, so I kept quiet.* = to stay silent for a reason **to keep something quiet** *We're planning a party for them but we want to keep it quiet.* = to not talk to many people about something that one wishes to keep secret **on the quiet 1** *She works in a laboratory but has been writing a novel on the quiet.* = in such a way that no one gets to know about it (approving) **2** *He has a job but has been working for others on the quiet.* = secretly in order that others do not know (derogatory)

quill /kwɪl/ noun, c. **1** = the long feather of a bird, which was used as a pen in former times **2** = a sharp, needle-like growth found on the back of a porcupine (see also **porcupine**)

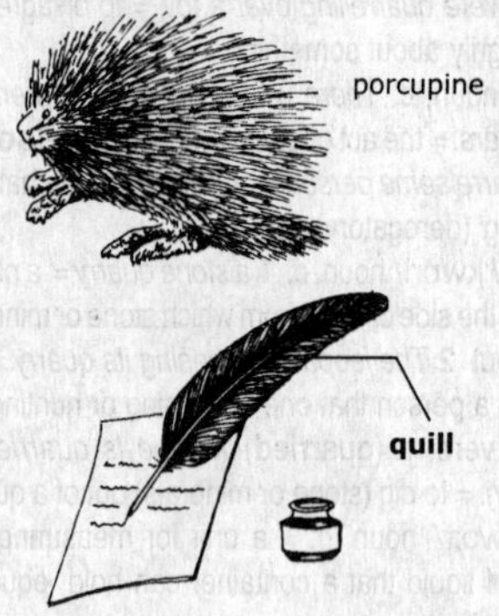

quilt /kwɪlt/ noun, c. = a large bag, filled with cotton or other soft material, used as a cover to keep one warm in bed

quin- /kwɪn/ prefix meaning five e.g. **quintet** noun, c. = a group of five singers singing together **quin•tu•plet** /'kwɪntjʊplɪt/ noun, c. = one of five children born of the same mother at the same time

quip[1] /kwɪp/ noun, c. *The man who made the quip that 'A fool and his money are soon parted' must have been very intelligent.* = remark or statement which is witty and amusing

quip[2] verb, t. = to make a quip

quirk /kwɜːk/ noun, c. *One of his quirks is that he always goes to bed with his glasses on, may be so that he can see his dreams more clearly!* = a habit which is thought to be strange

quit /kwɪt/ verb, t. (**quit**) **1** *I do not work in this school any more. I have quit my job.* = to give up something and leave **2** *We quit the place at nine.* = to leave a place **quitter** noun, c. *She is a fighter, not a quitter.* = a person who runs away from a difficult situation

quits adj. *He defeated me in the first match, but I defeated him in the next match. Now we are quits.* = equal; on the same level (informal)

quite /kwaɪt/ adv. **1** *She was quite right in asking you to leave.* = very; completely **2** *It was quite a good film, but it could have been better.* = to some extent, but not completely **3** *'He is a good bowler.' 'Quite!'* = an expression of agreement

quiv•er[1] /ˈkwɪvəʳ/ noun, c. *He has several arrows in his quiver.* = a cylinder-like container for carrying arrows

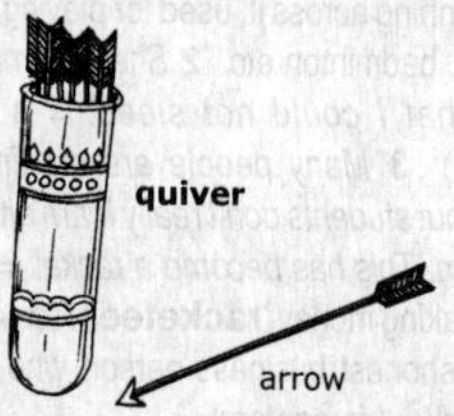

quiver[2] verb, i. *He was quivering with anger and we had to calm him down.* = to shake, specially with anger or excitement

quiz /kwɪz/ noun, c. (**quizzes**) *The school won many prizes in the science quiz.* = a competition in which people are asked questions which they have to answer to win

quiz[2] verb, t. (**quizzed**) *The teacher quizzed the student to find out why he was late.* = to ask questions

quizzical /ˈkwɪzɪkəl/ adj. *His father gave him a quizzical look when he came home with a parcel in his hand.* = seeming to ask a question without saying anything in words (describing an expression or a look)

quo•rum /ˈkwɔːrəm/ noun, u. *Since we have a quorum, we can continue with our meeting.* = the minimum number of people required for holding a meeting, starting a group etc.

quo•ta /ˈkwəʊtə/ noun, c. *Our state has not received its quota of rice from the Central Government.* = an amount that is given to someone as his/her/its share

quote[1] /kwəʊt/ verb, t. **1** *The teacher quoted a line from a poem to show that time does not stand still.* = to repeat, in speech or writing, the words used by some other speaker or writer **2** *The lawyer quoted an earlier decision by the Supreme Court in support of his argument.* = to mention as an example

quote[2] noun, c. **1** *'Do unto others as you would that they did unto you' is a famous quote from the Bible.* = words from a speech or a book that are quoted by someone **2** (always plural) *The word 'leader' has been put in quotes.* = quotation marks (punctuation marks which show that someone's words are being quoted)

quotation /kwəʊˈteɪʃən/ noun, c. *This is a quotation from one of the plays of Shakespeare.* = a quote (see meaning **1**, above, for **quote**)

quo•tient /ˈkwəʊʃənt/ noun, c. *When you divide 108 by 9, the quotient is 12.* = a number obtained by dividing one number by another [MATHEMATICS]

Q

rR

r, R the eighteenth letter of the English alphabet

R abbr. of 'river' e.g. *R. Ganga*

rab•bi /'ræbaɪ/ noun, c. = a Jewish priest

rab•bit /'ræbɪt/ noun, c. = a small animal with long ears, often kept as a pet

rab•ble /'ræbəl/ noun, u. = a noisy crowd that can become violent (derogatory) **rabble-rouser** noun, c. = a speaker who can make a crowd of people excited or violent through his/her speeches (informal, derogatory)

ra•bies /'reɪbi:z/ noun = a disease causing uncontrollable behaviour that attacks dogs and some other animals and can be passed on to other animals or human beings through the bite of an animal suffering from the disease

ra•bid /'ræbɪd/ adj. **1** *a rabid dog* = suffering from rabies **2** *a rabid supporter of vegetarianism* = having very strong feelings or opinions which one is not willing to give up (derogatory)

race[1] /reɪs/ noun, c. **1** *He is taking part in the 200 m race.* = a competition to see who can run the fastest **2** = one of the groups into which human beings can be divided according to their physical qualities (colour of skin, type of hair etc.)

race[2] verb, t. **1** *I will race you to the school gates.* = to compete in a race **2** *He raced the engine of his motorcycle.* = to cause something (e.g. the engine of a car) to run or work at great speed

race•course /'reɪskɔ:s/ noun, c. = a circular field used for horse-racing

ra•cial /'reɪʃəl/ adj. *racial discrimination* = having to do with a person's race or happening between people of different races **racism** /'reɪsɪzəm/ noun = the belief that people belonging to a certain race are superior to people belonging to other races (derogatory) **racist** noun, c. = a person who believes that people belonging to his/her race are superior to people belonging to other races (derogatory)

ra•cy /'reɪsɪ/ adj. *He writes racy stories* = interesting and full of excitement (informal)

rack[1] /ræk/ noun, c. (usually used in compound words) *a shoe-rack* = a shelf or frame made of metal or wood, on which shoes, books etc. can be kept

rack[2] verb, t. *Her body was racked with pain.* = to cause great suffering

to rack one's brains = to think deeply in order to find an answer to a question

rack•et (racquet) /'rækɪt/ noun, c. **1** *a tennis racket* = a frame made of metal or wood, with nylon strings running across it, used for playing games such as tennis, badminton etc. **2** *She was making such a racket that I could not sleep.* = a loud noise (informal) **3** *Many people are starting computer courses but students don't really learn anything useful from them. This has become a racket.* = a dishonest way of making money **racketeer** /rækɪ'tɪə^r/ noun, c. = a dishonest business-person who is mixed up with a racket (derogatory)

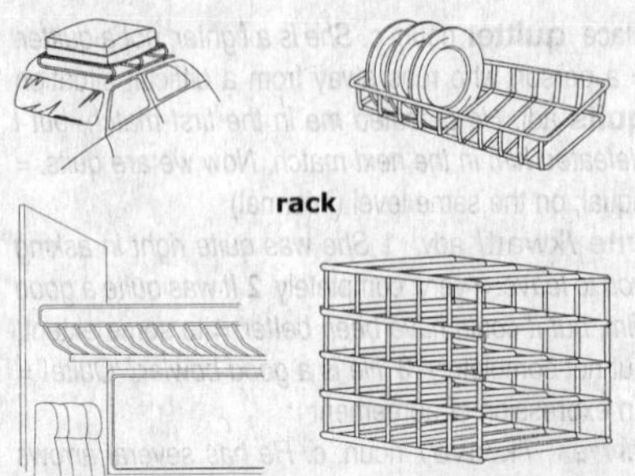
rack

ra•dar /'reɪdɑ:ʳ/ noun = an instrument which uses radio waves to find the position of a solid object (e.g. an aircraft) on the ground or in the air

ra•dial[1] /'reɪdɪəl/ adj. *radial roads* = coming out in straight lines from a central point (like a **radius**)

radial[2] noun, c. *radial tyre* = a tyre for a motor-car in which the steel or nylon cords (wires) that hold the tyre together run across the body of the tyre (like lines drawn from the centre) and not along it, as in an ordinary tyre

ra•di•ant /'reɪdiənt/ adj. **1** *She had a radiant smile when she received her M.A. degree.* = bright and shining, like the sun **2** *radiant energy* = producing heat and light [PHYSICS] **radiantly** adv.

ra•di•ate /'reɪdieɪt/ verb, t. **1** *The sun radiates heat and light.* = to give out energy (heat, light etc.) **2** *He radiates confidence.* = to send out in a strong way (figurative) **3** *These two roads radiate from the Town Hall.* = to come from a central point and spread in straight lines in different directions (like a **radius**) **radiation** /reɪdi'eɪʃən/ noun, u. **1** = the process of radiating heat, light etc. **2** *nuclear radiation* = rays sent out by radioactive substances which are dangerous and destroy living cells **3** *ultraviolet radiation* = rays carrying heat and light **4** *radiation therapy* = an approach to treating cancer and other diseases using rays

radiator /'reɪdɪeɪtəʳ/ noun, c. **1** = a system of pipes through which hot water flows, used for heating buildings in cold climates **2** = a system of pipes through which water flows, used to keep the engine of a car cool

ra•di•cal /ˈrædɪkəl/ adj. **1** *radical reform in education* = complete and bringing about great change **2** *He is very radical in his political views.* = favouring deep or complete change (political, in this case)

ra•di•o /ˈreɪdiəʊ/ noun, c. or u. **1** (c.) = a device (machine) that can receive electromagnetic waves sent out through the air and change them into sound waves, which can be heard **2** *The police department uses radio to send messages.*(u.) = the system of sending and receiving messages with the help of radio sets (also **wireless**)

ra•di•o•ac•tive /reɪdiəʊˈæktɪv/ adj. *Uranium is a radioactive substance.* = having the quality of radioactivity (see below) **radioactivity** noun, u. = the quality that some substances (e.g. metals such as radium, uranium, plutonium etc.) have of giving out energy which can be harmful to living things, through the breaking up of their atoms

ra•di•ol•o•gy /reɪdiˈɒlədʒɪ/ noun = a branch of medicine which deals with the use of radioactive substances such as radium, for treating cancer and other diseases (see **radioactive**) **radiologist** noun, c. = a doctor who practises radiology [MEDICINE]

ra•di•o-te•le•scope /reɪdiˈɒtelɪskəʊp/ noun = an instrument which can follow the movements of the stars by receiving the electro-magnetic waves given out by them

ra•dish /ˈrædɪʃ/ noun, c. = a small, red root vegetable with a sharp taste which is used in salads

ra•di•um /ˈreɪdiəm/ noun = a kind of metal which is highly radioactive (gives out energy through the breaking up of atoms) and is often used for treating cancer etc. (symbol Ra) [CHEMISTRY]

ra•di•us /ˈreɪdiəs/ noun, c. (**radii**) **1** = a line drawn from the centre of a circle to its circumference (the curved line which forms the boundary of the circle) (compare **diameter**) [GEOMETRY] **2** *All schools within a radius of 20 km from the city will be closed because of the cholera epidemic.* = an area surrounding a certain point **3** = the shorter bone in the arm that connects the wrist to the elbow [MEDICINE]

raf•fia /ˈræfiə/ noun, u. = a thread-like material obtained from the stems of palm leaves, used for making baskets etc.

raf•fle[1] /ˈræfəl/ noun, c. = an arrangement by which money is raised for some charitable purpose by selling tickets with numbers on them, some of which are chosen to win prizes (also **lottery**)

raffle[2] verb, t. *We are going to raffle this car.* = to give something away as a prize in a raffle

raft[1] /rɑːft/ noun, c. = a floating platform made by tying planks of wood together

raft[2] verb, i. or t. *The men are rafting down the river.* = to travel along a river on a raft or to transport goods by raft

raf•ter /ˈrɑːftəʳ/ noun, c. = a large wooden beam that supports the roof of a building

rag[1] /ræg/ noun, c. **1** *She used a rag to wipe the oil off her fingers.* = a small piece of old cloth or other waste material **2** (generally plural) *The beggar was dressed in rags.* = old and torn clothes

rag[2] verb, t. *The second year students are planning to rag the new students.* = to play rough tricks on someone, specially a new student in a school or college, often as part of a welcoming ceremony (informal) **ragbag** noun *This newspaper is only a ragbag of stale news.* = a confusing mixture of things (derogatory) **ragging** noun = the action of playing rough and often unpleasant tricks, usually on someone who is new to an organisation (informal)

rage[1] /reɪdʒ/ noun, u. or c. **1** *The fact that she had been left out of the team filled Ramya with rage and she stamped out of the room.*(u.) = great anger **2** *He flew into a rage on reading the report.*(c.) = a sudden feeling of great anger

rage[2] verb, i. (usually at/against) **1** *He raged at the bus driver for driving carelesly.* = to speak or shout in anger **2** *The storm raged for two days.* = to continue with great force or violence

to be the rage *Blue jeans are the rage now, specially among college students.* = to be in fashion (informal)

rag•ged /ˈrægɪd/ adj. **1** *ragged clothes* = old and torn **2** *The actor gave a ragged performance in this film.* = of poor quality (referring to work done by someone)

raid[1] /reɪd/ verb, t. **1** *The soldiers raided the enemy camp.* = to carry out a quick attack on an enemy with the intention of causing damage **2** *The police raided the hotel where the smugglers were hiding.* = to search a place for a criminal or to check some illegal activity (referring to a visit by the police etc.)

raid[2] noun, c. **1** *The soldiers carried out a raid on the enemy camp.* = a quick attack **2** *The police conducted a raid on the house, looking for drugs.* = a visit by the police without warning to look for something illegal

rail[1] /reɪl/ noun, c. or u. **1** *The garden is fenced off with rails.*(c.) = a long, thin, straight piece of metal (usually steel), used for different purposes e.g. to form the top part of a fence or to cover the side of a staircase to prevent people from falling over the side **2** (usually plural) *The train ran off the rails but, luckily, there was no damage.*(c.) = one of two long thin pieces of metal, fixed to the ground, on which the wheels of a train move(c.) **3** *We are travelling to Kolkata by rail.*(u.) = the railway system

rail[2] verb, i. *In his speech he railed against injustice.* =

R

to complain or protest in an angry manner (formal)

rail-head /ˈreɪlhed/ noun, c. *If you visit Mussorie, your rail-head will be Dehra Doon.* = a railway station beyond which trains do not run [TECHNICAL]

rail•ing /ˈreɪlɪŋ/ noun, u. = a protecting fence put around an open space e.g. along the sides of the roof of a building or the side of a staircase

rail•way /ˈreɪlweɪ/ noun, c. = the system used to carry goods and people by trains which run on metal rails (see meaning **2** for **rail**[1]) (also **railroad**) **railway station** noun, c. = a place where railway trains stop so that people can get off or get on

rain[1] /reɪn/ noun, u. or c. **1** *We had heavy rain this morning.* = drops of water falling from clouds in the sky **2** (always plural) *The rains have arrived.* = the season during which there is rain

rain[2] verb, i. *It rained last night.* = to fall in the form of rain **rainbow** /ˈreɪnbəʊ/ noun, c. = a band of seven colours, curving in a semicircle, which sometimes appears in the sky after a shower of rain **raincoat** noun, c. = a long coat, usually made of rubber or plastic, which protects the person who is wearing it from rain **rainforest** noun, c. = a very thick tropical forest growing in a place which has heavy rainfall **rain gauge** noun, c. = an instrument used to measure the amount of rainfall in a place

to rain blows (curses) on someone = to hit or abuse someone repeatedly in anger **to rain cats and dogs** = to rain heavily (informal) **to take a rain check** (American) *I can't come to your party this evening, but I will take a rain check on it.* = to put off an invitation or an offer made to you for a later, more convenient time

raise[1] /reɪz/ verb, t. **1** *The teacher asked the students to raise their hands if they knew the answer to her question.* = to lift or move something upwards **2** *He has been raised from the rank of secretary to that of president.* = to promote (move to a higher position or rank) **3** *The house-owner wants to raise the rent for this house.* = to increase **4** *I have raised Rs 5,00,000 for the charity.* = to collect **5** *They were raised in Kerala.* = to bring up and take care of a child or an animal **6** *I would like to raise the question of my transfer.* = to bring up for discussion **7** *Your speech has raised some doubts in my mind.* = to cause something to appear

raise[2] noun, c. *He has done well on the job and has been given a raise.* = an increase in salary (American)

to raise one's eyebrows = to show disapproval or surprise **to raise hell** = to create a lot of trouble by shouting etc. (informal)

rai•sin /ˈreɪzən/ noun, c. or u. = a sweet dried grape, used in making cakes etc.

raison•d'être /reɪzɒnˈdetrə/ noun (French) *After the death of his wife, his children are his raison d'être.* = the reason for one's existence

rake[1] /reɪk/ noun, c. *The farmer used a rake to level the ground.* = a tool with a long handle and a number of metal points at one end, used for making the earth level, removing dead leaves etc.

rake[2] verb, t. *The farmer raked the soil.* = to use a rake to make the earth level

to rake in *They rake in at least half a million of rupees every month.* = to earn a lot of money (informal, not respectful) **to rake something up** *His quarrel with his brother is almost forgotten. Why do you want to rake it up?* = to talk about something that has been forgotten so as to remind someone of it

ral•ly[1] /ˈræli/ noun, c. (**rallies**) **1** *A student rally will be held outside the Vice-Chancellor's office.* = a large public meeting of people who support a particular idea or political cause **2** *I am taking part in the Mumbai–Pune car rally.* = a cross-country motorcar race **3** *There were several long and exciting rallies in the tennis match.* = a long and continuous exchange of shots between players, in a game such as tennis, table-tennis or badminton

rally[2] verb, t. or i. (**rallied**) **1** *They are trying to rally support against drunken driving.*(t.) = to bring together or to come together in order to support a cause **2** *Last night the patient was in a bad condition but she has rallied this morning.*(i.) = to improve in condition; become healthier, stronger etc.

to rally round/around someone = to get together and help a person who is in some kind of trouble

ram[1] /ræm/ noun, c. **1** = a fully grown male sheep (opposite **ewe**) **2** *a hydraulic ram* = a machine with a moving part which can put pressure on something **3** *a battering ram* = a long, heavy wooden pole which, in former times, was pushed with force against a solid object, such as a door or wall, in order to break it down

ram[2] verb, t. (**rammed**) **1** *The two cars rammed into each other.* = to run into something with force **2** *The loose earth has to be rammed down before we can build something on it.* = to press down on something with force **3** *You are welcome to your views, but you don't have to ram them down our throats.* = to force someone to accept an idea (informal) **ram-rod** noun = a stick used to ram (push) gunpowder into an old-fashioned gun or cannon

to ram something home = to emphasize a point in order to make sure that it is understood **to be straight/stiff as a ram-rod** = to sit or walk upright, keeping one's back very straight (old-fashioned, disapproving)

RAM /ræm/ abbr. of **Random Access Memory** = the ability of a computer to store information in such a way that it can be recovered in any order [COMPUTERS]

ram•ble[1] /'ræmbəl/ verb, i. **1** *We love to ramble through the fields.* = to walk for pleasure **2** *I'm sorry I keep rambling on about my grandchildren.* = to talk aimlessly for a long time

ramble[2] noun, c. *We went for a ramble through the fields.* = a long walk taken for pleasure **rambling** adj. *a long and rambling speech* = without any order or plan (derogatory)

ram•i•fy /'ræmɪfaɪ/ verb, i. *He had one little grocery shop in the beginning but now his business has ramified and he has over thirty.* = to spread by branching out in many directions

ram•i•fi•ca•tion(s) /ræmɪfɪ'keɪʃən/ noun, c. (usually plural) **1** *The new law on pollution will have widespread ramifications.* = an unexpected result or consequence of something which affects many people **2** = the branches of a business, organization etc.

ramp /ræmp/ noun, c. *The mechanic drove the car up the ramp, so that he could carry out some repairs on the car.* = a sloping platform which leads from a lower to a higher level (A ramp is also provided so that wheelchair users can move about easily in public places.)

ram•page /ræm'peɪdʒ/ verb, i. *The herd of wild elephants rampaged through the jungle.* = to rush around wildly (formal)

to go on the rampage *The angry crowd went on the rampage, burning down and looting shops.* = angry and excited behaviour by a crowd

ram•pant /'ræmpənt/ adj. *Corruption is rampant in many departments.* = spreading everywhere and difficult to check (referring to something unpleasant e.g. crime, disease)

ram•part /'ræmpɑ:t/ noun, c. (usually plural) (**ramparts**) = wide, high walls made of earth or stone, protecting a fort or city

ram•shack•le /'ræmʃækəl/ adj. *an old, ramshackle bus* = in very poor condition and in need of repair (referring to a building or vehicle)

ranch /rɑ:ntʃ/ noun, c. = a large farm in N. America or Australia where cattle, sheep etc. are bred

ran•cid /'rænsɪd/ adj. *rancid butter* = having a bad, usually sour, smell and taste (referring to oil, butter etc. that is not fresh)

ran•cour /'ræŋkə^r/ noun, u. *Although they were very unkind to me I feel no rancour towards them.* = feeling of hatred or anger (formal)

R & D abbr. of **Research and Development** = the activity of carrying out research or trying out new ideas, so as to develop new products for a company etc.

ran•dom[1] /'rændəm/ noun *He walked through the shops, buying things at random to give to his friends.* = done without a clear plan or design

random[2] adj. *The company has taken up a random survey to find out what people think of its new soap.* = a method of collecting facts or opinions in which anyone has a chance of being picked up to take part **to do something at random** = without any clear plan

range[1] /reɪndʒ/ noun, c. **1** *the Himalyan range*(c.) = a chain or line of mountains **2** *The temperature in Delhi varies in a range of 3–42 degrees centigrade.* = the limits within which something can change **3** *This shop stocks a wide range of children's clothing.* = a group of similar things, from which one can choose **4** *The mountain was beyond the range of my camera.* = the distance to which a gun can shoot or a camera can take clear pictures **5** *a shooting range* = an area where people can practice shooting or test new weapons

range[2] verb, i. **1** *The temperature in Delhi ranges from 3–42 degrees centigrade.* = to change between certain limits **2** *The tigers ranged freely through the hills. // Our discussion ranged over a wide variety of subjects.* = to move about or wander freely **range-finder** noun, c. = an instrument used to find the distance between a photographer and some object which is being photographed, or between a gun and some object which is being fired at

rang•er /'reɪndʒə^r/ noun, c. **1** *a forest ranger* = a forest guard who protects the trees and animals in the forest **2** = a policeperson who protects the law (American)

rank[1] /ræŋk/ noun, c. **1** *The Air Chief Marshal has the highest rank in the airforce.* = position **2** *The soldiers are marching in ranks.* = a line or row (of soldiers etc.)

rank[2] verb, t. **1** *How would you rank these three poets?* = to arrange or place people or things in a certain order, according to quality, size etc. **2** *He ranks among the best writers in the country.* = to occupy or have a certain position (among a group)

rank[3] adj. **1** *The garden has become rank.* = having too thick a growth of plants (old-fashioned) **2** *He is a rank beginner.* = complete

rank and file = the ordinary or common people in an organisation (not respectful) **to close ranks** = to unite or come together to face a difficulty

ran•kle /'ræŋkəl/ verb, i. *Her unkind comment about my dance performance still rankles.* = to continue to cause pain or bitterness

ran•sack /'rænsæk/ verb, t. **1** *She ransacked the cupboard to look for a document.* = to search thoroughly, often causing damage **2** *The robbers ransacked the village.* = to rob by searching in a rough and violent way

R

ran•som[1] /ˈrænsəm/ noun, u. = money demanded by or paid to a kidnapper (a person who is holding someone illegally as a prisoner) to free the person being held (see also **hostage**)

ransom[2] verb, t. *The kidnapped army officer was ransomed and returned safely.* = to set someone free by paying a ransom

rant /rænt/ verb, i. *The man ranted on about how wicked the world had become.* = to talk in a loud and excited way, without making much sense (disapproving)

rap[1] /ræp/ verb, i. or t. (**rapped**) **1** *He rapped the table with a ruler.* = to knock or hit in a sharp or quick manner **2** *The magistrate rapped the police for not doing their work properly.* = to rebuke (speak harshly, pointing out some mistake) **3** *rap out orders* = to speak quickly and in a sharp (angry) voice

rap[2] noun, c. **1** = a light blow on a hard surface **2** *a rap on the window glass* = the sound produced by striking something in a sharp quick way **3** = a kind of song in which the singer speaks the words quickly

to take the rap *It was she who came home late, but I had to take the rap.* = to take the blame for something wrong that someone else has done (informal)

rape[1] /reɪp/ verb, t. = to force a person to have sex by using violence or threats

rape[2] noun, u. or c. = the act or crime of raping a person

rap•id /ˈræpɪd/ adj. *The change in our village in the last two years has been rapid. We have four wells and six pumps now.* = happening very fast **rapids** noun, c. (always plural) = a part of a river where the water moves very fast over rocks

ra•pi•er /ˈreɪpiəʳ/ noun, c. = a long, thin sword with a sharp point (often used figuratively e.g. *a rapier tongue*)

rap•port /ræˈpɔː/ noun, u. *The teacher has good rapport with her students.* = close understanding or good relationship with someone

rap•proche•ment /ræˈprɒʃmɒŋ/ noun, u. (French) *rapprochement between the two warring countries* = a better understanding between two people or groups that have not been friends for some time (formal)

rapt /ræpt/ adj. *We listened to her speech with rapt attention.* = giving one's whole mind to something so that one does not notice anything else

rap•ture /ˈræptʃə/ noun, u. **1** *We looked at the garden in rapture.* = a great feeling of wonder (literary) **2** (often plural **raptures**) *The children were in raptures when the circus clowns appeared.* = very great joy **rapturous** adj. *The film star was greeted with rapturous applause when he arrived.* = expressing great joy

rare /reəʳ/ adj. **1** *Tigers are becoming increasingly rare in India.* = not seen very often **2** *The air on top of a high mountain is rare.* = thin and light (referring to air) **3** (American) *I like to eat meat which is cooked rare.* = not cooked very much **rarity** noun, u. or c. (**rarities**) *Woman taxi drivers are still a rarity.*(c.) = something that is rare (difficult to find) **rare earth** noun = a radioactive metal such as uranium which is found inside the earth (see **radioactive**)

rar•e•fied /ˈreərɪfaɪd/ adj. *The air is rarefied at a height of 30,000 feet.* = thin and low in oxygen (referring to air)

rar•ing /ˈreərɪŋ/ adj. *The children are raring to go to the cinema.* = very eager to do something (informal)

ras•cal /ˈrɑːskəl/ noun, c. **1** = a person who cheats others **2** *Your son has hidden my shoes somewhere. Where is the little rascal?* = a person, generally a child, who plays tricks on others but is liked

rash[1] /ræʃ/ adj. *You are driving too fast.You should not be rash.* = careless; doing things without thinking of the possible danger or harm that may result **rashly** adv

rash[2] noun, c. (**rashes**) **1** *There is a rash on the child's face.* = a red mark appearing on the skin, caused by some illness e.g. measles **2** *Yesterday was a quiet day in the office, but today we had a rash of orders.* = a great many, coming at nearly the same time

rasp /rɑːsp/ verb, t. or i. *Her voice is so harsh that it rasps on one's nerves.*(i.) = to have an unpleasant effect on someone (referring to a person's voice)

rasp•ber•ry /ˈrɑːzbəri/ noun = a kind of sweet, juicy red berry (fruit) that grows on a bush

rat[1] /ræt/ noun **1** = an animal with a long tail, larger than a mouse, that causes a lot of damage, specially to food grains **2** *He is such a rat!* = a person who is not loyal in matters of work and friendship (derogatory, informal)

rat[2] verb, i. (**ratted**) **1** *We trusted him with all our secrets and never dreamt that he would rat on us some day.* = to betray someone, generally by giving out secrets (informal, derogatory) **2** *The farmers use these dogs for ratting.* = to hunt rats **rat race** noun *Life in the city is often a rat race.* = an unpleasant competition which has no end (derogatory) **rat-snake** noun = a kind of large snake which has no poison and which hunts rats

to smell a rat = to suspect that something is wrong

rate[1] /reɪt/ noun, u. or c. **1** *Our boat is moving at the rate of six kilometres per hour.*(u.) = a way of measuring something by relating one quantity (e.g. speed) to another quantity (e.g. time) **2** *We are paying very high rates for this work.*(c.) = level of payment

rate[2] verb, t. **1** *His teachers rate him high.* = to express an opinion or judgement about something or someone **2** *He rates a special mention in your report.* = to deserve (to be worthy of something) **rating** noun *Many viewers gave the new show a high rating.* = a record of how much something is appreciated or liked

at any rate *Most students like Hindi films. At any rate, the ones I know do.* = an expression used to qualify or explain what one has said earlier

ra•ther /'rɑːðə^r/ adv. **1** *a rather hot day* = to some extent (less strong than **very**) **2** *He is happy to see you; or rather, he is excited to see you.* = more exactly or more correctly **3** *I would rather read than watch television.* = preferably (wishing to do something more than something else)

rat•i•fy /'rætɪfaɪ/ verb, t. (**ratified**) *The agreement was ratified at the meeting today.* = to approve a written agreement (to decide that it should remain in force) by voting or signing (formal)

ra•ti•o /'reɪʃiəʊ/ noun, c. (**ratios**) *The ratio of boys to girls in this school is 3:2.* = the relation between two quantities represented by numbers, to show how much larger one is than the other

ra•ti•on[1] /'ræʃən/ verb, t. *The government has rationed the supply of kerosene. Each family will get five litres a month.* = to control or limit the supply of something

ration[2] noun, u. or c. **1** (always singular) *Have you received your ration of rice?* = the amount of something that one is allowed to take **2** (always plural) *We have used up all our rations.*(c.) = supply of food

ra•tion•al /'ræʃənəl/ adj. **1** *I don't think he will be upset by what has happened. He is rational and will understand the situation.* = having the ability to think and work things out logically (formal) **2** *The magician produced a gold watch out of the air. Some people believe that he performed a miracle, but I am sure there is a rational explanation.*= something that can be explained through logic (by connecting events to natural causes) (formal) **rationalist** noun, c. = a person who believes that everything can be explained through reason (the ability to think) **rationalize (rationalise)** verb, t. **1** *When he lost the election, he tried to rationalize his defeat by saying that it is not good for one person to remain in power always.* = to try to find an explanation or an excuse for something, knowing that it may not be true **2** *rationalize the transport system* = to make changes in something so that it is better organized and works better

ra•tio•nale /ræʃə'nɑːl/ noun, u. *There must be a rationale for making English compulsory in schools.* = a reason for doing or deciding to do something (formal)

rat•tan /rə'tæn/ noun, u. = a kind of cane from South East Asia, used for making furniture

rat•tle[1] /'rætl/ noun, c. **1** = a child's toy, consisting of a hollow tube, usually made of metal, with a number of small, solid objects inside, which make quick, sharp sounds when the toy is shaken **2** *There was a loud rattle as the tray containing the cups and saucers slipped from my hand.* = a noisy sound produced by things falling, breaking etc.

rattle[2] verb, i. or t. **1** *The wind made the windows rattle.*(i.) = to cause something to shake and produce quick, sharp sounds, like those made by a rattle **2** *The old car rattled along the road.*(i.) = to move while making sounds like a rattle **3** *The insulting letter from my senior rattled me.*(t.) = to make someone feel uneasy or angry **rattlesnake** noun = a kind of highly poisonous snake found in North America, having small bony rings on its tail which produce a rattling sound when the snake is about to attack **rattle-trap** noun = an old car or bus that produces a lot of rattling noises while moving (informal)

to rattle something off *She rattled off all the names of the hockey players in the Indian team.* = to speak from memory without thinking for too long (sometimes disapproving)

rau•cous /'rɔːkəs/ adj. *raucous laughter* = having a loud, rough and unpleasant sound

raunch•y /'rɔːntʃi/ adj. *raunchy jokes* = connected with sex, meant to be exciting (disapproving)

ra•vage /'rævɪdʒ/ verb, t. *ravaged by an earthquake* = to destroy something or to damage it badly **ravages** noun (always plural) = the signs of destruction left behind by a fire, storm etc.

rave /reɪv/ verb, i. **1** *The man was raving angrily about the transport problems in the city.* = to talk wildly, in an excited manner **2** *All the critics are raving about the new film.* = to praise something very highly **rave review** noun = something written about a new book, film etc. which praises it highly (informal)

ra•ven /'reɪvən/ noun, c. = a bird which looks like a crow but is completely black in colour

rav•e•nous /'rævənəs/ adj. *You haven't eaten anything since yesterday. You must be ravenous.* = very hungry (literary or formal)

ra•vine /rə'viːn/ noun, c. = a deep, narrow valley between mountains [GEOGRAPHY]

ra•vi•o•li /rævi'əʊli/ noun = an Italian dish consisting of small balls made of flour, filled with meat and served with sauce

ra•vish /'rævɪʃ/ verb, t. **1** *We were ravished by the beauty of Kashmir.* = to fill with great joy or delight **2** *The village was ravished by the invading army.* = to plunder (rob) **3** = to rape a woman (old-fashioned or literary) **ravishing** adj. *a ravishing smile* = causing great delight

R

raw[1] /rɔː/ adj. **1** *raw vegetables* = not cooked **2** *raw cotton* = a substance which is in its natural state **3** *raw materials* = natural materials from which things are produced in a factory **4** *What we have is raw data, we will have to organize it.* = not organized into a form that can be used **5** *a raw worker* = a person who has not been properly trained **6** *The raw power in his shot took the ball over the boundary line.* = pure (not mixed with anything else) **7** *The skin on your wounds is still raw.* = not fully healed and therefore painful **a raw deal** noun *The workers were given a raw deal by the management.* = unfair treatment

ray /reɪ/ noun, c. **1** *a ray of light* = a narrow beam or line of light or some other form of energy **2** *a ray of hope* = a small bit **3** *a sting ray* = a kind of fish with a flat body and a long tail

ray•on /ˈreɪɒn/ noun = an artificial material made from plants, out of which clothes can be made

raze /reɪz/ verb, t. *The building was razed by the fire.* = to destroy a building, town etc. completely

ra•zor /ˈreɪzəʳ/ noun, c. = a kind of knife with a sharp edge, used to remove hair from the face, head etc. **razor blade** noun, c. = a thin piece of steel with one or two sharp edges, which can be fitted into a safety razor (a special kind of razor) and thrown away after it has been used several times **razor-sharp** adj. *a razor-sharp mind* = very intelligent or clever

re /riː/ abbr. of 'with reference to' (used in business letters to remind the person receiving the letter of something)

re- (usually in verbs) prefix meaning **1** again e.g. **reappear** verb, i. *The sun had disappeared behind a cloud but it has reappeared now.* = to be seen again **2** again in a new and more improved way e.g. **rewrite** verb, t. *to rewrite an essay* = to write again in a better way **3** back to a state that something was in before e.g. **reactivate** verb, t. *We reactivated the machine.* = to make something active again

reach[1] /riːtʃ/ verb, t. **1** *We will reach Delhi on Saturday.* = to get to or arrive at a place **2** *She reached across the table to pick up the book.* = to stretch out a hand or an arm in order to get something **3** *Can you reach that box on the top shelf of the cupboard?* = to be able to touch something by stretching out an arm **4** *I have not been able to reach him on his phone.* = to get in touch with someone **5** *The argument has reached a stage where neither person is going to listen to the other.* = to move up to a particular state or level

reach[2] noun, u. **1** *The light switch is beyond the child's reach.* = the distance to which one can stretch one's arm **2** *The school is within easy reach of the station.* = the distance that one has to travel to get to a place

re•act /riˈækt/ verb, t. **1** *When I asked him what the matter was he reacted by bursting into tears.* = to behave in a particular way in answer to something **2** *Hydrochloric acid reacts with sodium to form common salt.* = to go through a chemical change [CHEMISTRY] **reaction** noun, u. or c. **1** *What was her reaction when you told her that her friend was ill?* = the manner (way) of behaving in response to something **2** *Action and reaction are equal and opposite.* = the force produced by a body (object) when some other force acts upon it [PHYSICS] **3** = a chemical change produced by substances acting on each other (see meaning **2** for **react**)

re•ac•tion•a•ry /riˈækʃənəri/ adj. = opposed to any social or political change (disapproving)

reactor /riˈæktəʳ/ noun, c. *a nuclear reactor* = a machine which produces nuclear energy in a controlled way by breaking down or joining together the atoms of a substance such as plutonium

read /riːd/ verb, t. or i. **1** *The child has learnt to read.*(i.) = to recognize printed or written letters and words and to understand the meanings they carry **2** *I have read the report in today's newspaper.* (t.) = to go through something printed in a book, newspaper etc. and get information from it **3** *This poem reads well.*(i.) = to have or produce a certain effect when it is read (referring to something that is written or printed) **5** *The thermometer reads 44 degrees centigrade.*(t.) = to record or show (referring to something measured by an instrument) **6** *My son is reading law at Delhi University.*(t.) = to study a subject at a university in order to get a degree **7** *I read his remarks to mean that he wants to be the next captain of the team.*(t.) = to interpret (to get a certain meaning from something that is said or written) **8** *My computer cannot read the disk you sent me.* = to be able to access information on a disk [COMPUTERS] **readable** adj. **1** *This is a very readable book.* = interesting, easy or enjoyable to read **2** *Your handwriting is perfectly readable.* = which can be read without difficulty (also **legible**) **machine-readable** adj.= printed in a form that can be read by a machine and fed into a computer **reader** noun, c. **1** *a newsreader* = one who reads something, either silently to himself/herself, or aloud to an audience **2** *an English reader* = a textbook used for teaching a language **3** = a person who teaches in a university or college and has a rank next lower to that of a professor **readership** noun, u. *Her books have wide readership.* = the number or kind of people who regularly read something **read out** noun, c. or verb. = information obtained from a computer, either in printed form or on a monitor (screen)

to read up = to find out more information on a particular subject by reading (informal) **to read between the lines** = to find hidden meanings in something **to read somebody like a book** = to be able to make out easily what a person is thinking or feeling

read•ing /'ri:dɪŋ/ noun, u. or c. **1** *Reading is what I like best when I am alone.*(u.) = the act of reading the matter **2** *The professor gave us a lot of reading to do.*(u.) = books, journals, articles etc. that make up the matter to be read **3** *What's your reading of the situation?*(c.) = one's opinion or what one has understood **4** *the thermometer reading*(c.) = the number that an instrument shows while measuring something

re•ad•just /ri:ə'dʒʌst/ verb, t. or i. *The sound from the radio is not loud enough. Can you readjust the volume?*(t.) = to adjust something again (to make a change in the way something is working so that it works better)

read•y[1] /'redi/adj. **1** *She is ready to go to school.* = prepared to do something **2** *I am ready to help you.* = willing **3** *She has a ready wit.* = quick (slightly old-fashioned) **4** *He looked ready to cry.* = about to cry, laugh etc.

ready[2] verb, t. (**readied**) *Let us ready the house for the boss's visit.*= to make something ready **ready-made** adj. **1** *ready-made clothes* = not specially made for someone but made in advance, to be sold in a shop (referring to clothes) (also **ready-to-wear**) **2** *ready-made opinions* = not original but borrowed from someone else (derogatory) **ready-money/cash** noun = money that is available for immediate use **readiness** noun, u. = the state of being ready (prepared) to do something

at the ready *The filmstar will be here for only a few minutes. If you want to photograph her, keep your cameras at the ready.* = ready to be used at short notice **rough and ready** *I don't know the exact rate of exchange between dollars and pounds, but a rough and ready calculation is two dollars to a pound.* = not exact or perfect but good enough for quick use

re•a•gent /ri'eɪdʒənt/ noun, c. *Sulphuric acid is often used as a reagent in chemistry.* = a chemical substance that acts on some other chemical substance [CHEMISTRY]

real /rɪəl/ adj. **1** *Is that diamond real, or is it only a piece of glass that looks like a diamond?* = genuine (not false) **2** *Is the film based on a real incident or an imaginary story?* = something that exists; not imaginary **3** *He looks like a real scholar.* = (used for emphasis) having qualities one would expect **real estate** noun, u. *He owns a lot of real estate in the city, including two houses and some shops.* = property in the form of buildings **realism** noun, u. *Satyajit Ray's films have a lot of realism. The characters in his films are ordinary people that you meet every day.* = the quality of showing life as it really is, without any falsehood **realistic** /rɪə'lɪstɪk/ adj. **1** *You know very well that you can't become a film star. You should be realistic.* = accepting things as they are and being sensible **2** *The dinosaurs in the film were very realistic.* = not real but seeming real **reality** /rɪ'ælɪtɪ/ noun **1** *All his paintings show imaginary places. He seldom deals with reality.* = what is real or that which exists **2** *We had heard wonderful things about London, but the reality was quite disappointing.* = the real nature of something **3** *He looks very tall in the photograph but in reality, he is of average height.* = in person

re•a•lize (realise) /'rɪəlɑɪz/ verb **1** *They went on talking and did not realize that it was getting late.* = to come to understand **2** *I am glad he has realized his dream of becoming a surgeon.* = to achieve **realization** /rɪəlɪ'zeɪʃən/ noun, u. = the act of realizing something

real•ly /'rɪəli/ adv. **1** *Can you really stand on your head?* = truly; actually **2** *It was really cold in that room.* = rather, very **Really?** *'I can run almost two km in a minute.' 'Really?'* = (depending on the tone used) an expression used to show surprise and admiration **Well really!** = an expression used to show surprise and displeasure

realm /relm/ noun, c. **1** *the ruler of the realm* = kingdom (a country ruled by a king or queen) **2** *Such things happen only in the realm of imagination, not in real life.* = the world of imagination, science etc. (literary)

ream /ri:m/ noun, c. = a quantity of paper (about 500 sheets in the US and 480 in Britain)

reap /ri:p/ verb, t. *When the crop is ripe the farmers will reap it.* = to cut and gather a crop of grain (compare **sow, harvest**)

re•ar[1] /ri:ə'r/ noun, u. *In most cars the engine is in front, but in this car the engine is at the rear.* = the back part of something

rear[2] adj. *The rear seat of the car is more comfortable than the front seat.* = at the back

rear[3] verb, i. or t. **1** *The horse suddenly reared.*(i.) = to lift the front legs off the ground and balance on the back legs (referring to a four-legged animal) **2** *The snake reared its head.*(t.) = to raise or lift a part of the body **3** *He rears goats on his farm.*(t.) = to raise (to take care of a human child or baby animal until it is fully grown) **rear-view mirror** = a mirror in a vehicle which enables a driver to see the traffic etc. behind the vehicle

re•ar•range /ri:ə'reɪndʒ/ verb, t. *We will rearrange the furniture in this room.* = to arrange again (to put

R

things in positions different from those in which they were before)

rea•son[1] /'ri:zən/ noun, c. or u. **1** *The reason for my absence from the meeting yesterday is my child's illness.*(c.) = a fact or situation that explains why something happened **2** *I expect you to use your reason when you are faced with a problem.*(u.) = the ability to think and come to conclusions

reason[2] verb, t. *I reasoned that you would not be able to come as it was raining heavily.* = to come to a conclusion or judgement based on some fact **reasonable** adj. **1** *I think she will let you keep the book for another month. She is a reasonable person.* = willing to understand the problems of others (referring to people) **2** *He wants Rs 20,000 for this car. That is a reasonable price.* = fair (not too much) **reasonably** adv. *It was a reasonably comfortable journey.* = fairly; enough to satisfy one but not fully **reasoning** noun, u. *In my reasoning, there is no chance of your winning this election.* = an opinion that one forms after considering all the facts

reason with = to talk to somebody in order to convince him/her

re•as•sure /ri:ə'ʃʊə/ verb, t. *I would like to reassure you that no one is going to blame you for our defeat.* = to give hope or comfort to someone who is feeling anxious or worried

re•bate /'ri:beɪt/ noun, c. *The telephone company will give you a rebate of Rs 50 if you pay your bill before the end of the month.* = a reduction in the payment to be made

re•bel[1] /rɪ'bel/ verb, i. (**rebelled**) *He rebelled against his parents and left home.* = to refuse to obey someone who has power or authority

rebel[2] /'rebəl/ noun, c. *He has become a rebel and is fighting against the people in power.* = a person who fights against the government because he or she wants change

re•bel•lion /rɪ'beljən/ noun, u. or c. = the act of rebelling against someone **rebellious** adj. *She is rebellious by nature and never listens to her teachers.* = not ready or willing to follow what an authority or society asks one to do

re•birth /rɪ:'bɜ:θ/ noun, u. = the process of being born again (formal)

re•boot /rɪ:'bu:t/ verb, t. = to make a computer work again after it has failed to work for some reason [COMPUTERS]

re•bound[1] /'rɪ:baʊnd/ verb, i. *The ball rebounded after hitting the wall.* = to bound (jump up) again or to jump back after hitting something

rebound[2] /rɪ'baʊnd/ noun, u. *The fielder caught the ball on the rebound.* = the action of jumping back after hitting something

re•buff[1] /rɪ'bʌf/ noun, c. *His attempts to become friendly with the girl next door met with a rebuff.* = rejection; an unfriendly answer to an offer of help, friendship etc.

rebuff[2] verb, t. *The child rebuffed our attempts to become friendly with her.* = to reject or turn back

re•build /rɪ:'bɪld/ verb, t. *We have to rebuild the houses which were damaged in the storm.* = to build again or to repair

re•buke[1] /rɪ'bju:k/ verb, t. *The judge rebuked the police for their unfair treatment of the prisoner.* = to speak in a harsh or angry manner to someone for something done by him/her which is not liked (formal)

rebuke[2] noun, c. = the action of rebuking someone

re•but /rɪ'bʌt/ verb, t. (**rebutted**) *One of the speakers said that women would not be able to do the job and I had to rebut his argument.* = to reply to an argument and to show that it is wrong (formal) **rebuttal** noun, u. = the act of rebutting an argument

re•cal•ci•trant /rɪ'kælsɪtrənt/ adj. *The girl refuses to obey her teachers. We are worried about her recalcitrant behaviour.* = refusing again and again to obey or to accept a situation (formal)

re•call /rɪ'kɔ:l/ verb, t. **1** *I cannot recall your name.* = to remember something **2** *He was recalled to the side for the series against Australia.* = to ask a person to return

re•cant /rɪ'kænt/ verb, t. *George Orwell, the famous writer, was a Communist at first but later recanted his belief in Communism.* = to declare that one has given up a belief that one had earlier in a religion, political idea etc.

re•ca•pit•u•late /ri:kə'pɪtʃʊleɪt/ verb, t. *Let me recapitulate the main points of the speech.* = to say again, repeating the main points of something said earlier (formal) (also **recap**)

re•cap•ture /ri:'kæptʃər/ verb, t. *The thief escaped from prison but was recaptured.* = to catch someone who had escaped

re•cast /ri:'kɑ:st/ verb, t. **1** *This essay has to be recast.* = to write, plan etc. something again, giving it a new shape **2** = to change the cast (the actors taking part) of a film or play

re•cede /rɪ'si:d/ verb, i. *The water in the river has begun to recede after the flood.* = to go back or to become less (formal) **a receding hairline** = used about a person's appearance when hair stops growing in the front

re•ceipt /rɪ'si:t/ noun, u. or c. **1** *I will reply at once on receipt of your letter.*(u.) = the act of receiving (getting) something **2** *Please give me a receipt to show that I have paid you Rs 500.*(c.) = a document showing that one has received money or some other thing from someone

re•ceive /rɪ'siːv/ verb, t. **1** *He has not received the letter which you wrote him.* = to get **2** *She does not receive presents from friends on her birthday.* = to accept something from someone **3** *Three of us went to the airport to receive our cousins.* = to meet and welcome

re•ceiv•er /rɪ'siːvə^r/ noun, c. **1** *a telephone receiver* = an instrument (telephone, radio etc.) used for receiving messages **2** = a person appointed by a court to take charge of a business which is about to close down [LAW]

re•cent /'riːsənt/adj. *This library was set up only last month. It is a recent addition to the college.* = having happened only a short time ago **recently** adv. = not very long ago

re•cep•ta•cle /rɪ'septəkəl/ noun, c. = a vessel or container in which something (usually some liquid) can be kept (formal)

re•cep•tion /rɪ'sepʃən/ noun, u. or c. **1** *She got a very friendly reception on her first day at work.* = a public welcome **2** *I got married last week. We had the reception at a nearby hotel.* = a party given on a special occasion **3** *I have signed the hotel register at the reception.* = the office that receives (welcomes) visitors at a hotel or office **receptionist** noun, c. = a person whose duty is to receive visitors or guests in a hotel etc.

re•cep•tive /rɪ'septɪv/ adj. *She's very receptive. She always listens to any new ideas her friends have.* = willing to accept something (usually an idea or a comment)

re•cess /rɪ'ses/ noun, c. **1** *The school has a 15-minute recess at 11.30 a.m.* = a period of rest (see also **interval**) **2** *There is a recess in the wall where we can fit a bookshelf.* = a hollow space in a wall where a cupboard etc. can be fitted

re•ces•sion /rɪ'seʃən/ noun, u. *The country is going through an economic recession and many people are out of work.* = a period when there is less trade or industrial production in a country

re•charge /riː'tʃɑːdʒ/ verb, t. = to charge again (to put back electrical energy into a battery which has lost its energy)

to recharge one's batteries = to get back one's energy and strength

re•ci•pe /'resɪpi/ noun, c. *a recipe for making masala dosa* = a set of instructions for cooking a particular kind of food

re•cip•i•ent /rɪ'sɪpiənt/ noun, c. *Pandit Ravi Shankar is a recipient of the 'Bharat Ratna' award.* = a person who is given something (formal)

re•cip•ro•cal /rɪ'sɪprəkəl/ adj. **1** *Pakistan and India have entered into a reciprocal trade agreement. Pakistan will import sugar from India while India will import cotton.* = two-sided (something that happens between two parties and is of benefit to both) **2** *the reciprocal of 7 is 1/7* = the number obtained by dividing 1 by a certain number [MATHEMATICS]

re•cip•ro•cate /rɪ'sɪprəkeɪt/ verb, t. *I am happy that you want to be friends with us again; we reciprocate your feelings.* = to give something in exchange for something received (formal)

re•cite /rɪ'saɪt/ verb, t. *The little child recited a nursery rhyme.* = to say something, especially a poem or song, from memory **recital** noun, u. or c. *a music recital* = a performance of music or dance

re•ci•ta•tion /resɪ'teɪʃən/ noun, u. *Did you enjoy the recitation of your poem by the children?* = the act of reciting something (usually a poem)

reck•less /'rekləs/ adj. *a reckless driver* = careless and not thinking about the danger or harm that can be caused by one's actions (see also **rash**)

reck•on /'rekən/ verb, t. **1** *Scientists reckon that about 3 million years ago the Himalayas lay under the ocean.* = to believe something as the result of making a calculation (formal) **2** *It is an hour since he called. I reckon he is not coming.* = to guess (informal) **reckoning** noun, u. *Scientists had predicted that we would have a normal monsoon last year but their reckoning proved to be wrong.* = calculation

to be out of the reckoning = to not be among those likely to be chosen or to win

re-claim /rɪ'kleɪm/ verb, t. **1** *The government had taken possession of his property, but he has been able to reclaim it.* = to ask for and get back something that had been taken away **2** *This piece of land has been reclaimed from the sea.* = to make land fit for use (again)

re•cline /rɪ'klaɪn/ verb, i. *recline against the cushions* = to lie back in a comfortable position **reclining** adj. *a reclining position* = leaning back comfortably

re•cluse /rɪ'kluːs/ noun, c. *He is a recluse and does not like to meet anyone.* = a person who likes to live alone, away from others (disapproving)

rec•og•nize (recognise) /'rekəgnaɪz/ verb, t. **1** *I met an old friend after 30 years. She looked so different that I could not recognize her.* = to be able to know again someone or something that one knew earlier **2** *The new government of Croatia has been recognized by all the countries of the world. // He is recognized as a leading poet.* = to accept something or someone as legal or worthy of respect **recognition** /rekəg'nɪʃən/ noun, u. **1** *He has changed beyond recognition.* = the state of being

R

recognized **2** *She never got the recognition she deserved as a poet.* = the act or the fact of being recognized (accepted as legal or worthy of respect)

re•coil /rɪˈkɔɪl/ verb, i. **1** *The gun recoiled with great force when it was fired.* = to spring back when fired (referring to a gun) **2** *He recoiled with fear when he saw a snake on his bed.* = to jump back suddenly out of fear or dislike

re•col•lect /rekəˈlekt/ verb, t. *I don't recollect what happened on my first day at school.* = to remember after some effort (see also **recall**)

rec•om•mend /rekəˈmend/ verb, t. *The new film by Aamir Khan is very good. I recommend it.* = to praise someone or something strongly as being suitable for something **recommendation** /rekəmenˈdeɪʃən/ noun, u. or c. **1** *I went to see the film on your recommendation. I agree that it is very good.*(u.) = the act of recommending someone or something **2** *We gave him the job because he had several favourable recommendations.*(c.) = a letter recommending someone for a job (saying that he/she is suitable and should be chosen)

rec•on•cile /ˈrekənsaɪl/ verb, t. or i. **1** *The two friends had quarrelled but now they are reconciled.*(i.) = to become friends again **2** *You say you love animals and yet you support their use for scientific experiments. How do you reconcile these two positons?* = to find agreement between two opposite ideas or situations **3** *I didn't like the idea of living in a noisy neighbourhood, but now I am reconciled to it.* = to accept something that one cannot change easily

reconciliation /rɪˈkɒneɪsəns/ noun, c. *There was a reconciliation last week between the two brothers who had not been on speaking terms for years.* = the act of being reconciled (becoming friends again)

re•con•nais•sance /rɪˈkɒnsɪəns/ noun, u. *The soldiers were sent out to make a reconnaisance.* = to go near an enemy position in order to find out something (number, position etc.) about the enemy, before a battle begins; an advance party that goes out to study a situation before it is dealt with [TECHNICAL]

re•con•sid•er /rɪːkənˈsɪdər/ verb, t. *Your application was turned down by the authorities but they will reconsider it, if you apply again.* = to consider (think about) something again, with the possibility of changing one's mind

re-con•struct /riːkənˈstrʌkt/verb, t. **1** *The government will reconstruct this building.* = to build something again after it has been damaged **2** *The police team is visiting the place where the accident took place. They are trying to reconstruct the accident.* = to make something happen again artificially so that people can understand how it could have happened

rec•ord[1] /rɪˈkɔːd/ verb, t. **1** *I have recorded everything that you said yesterday.* = to write down something on paper so that it can be preserved or read later **2** *I have recorded the Director's speech.* = to make a copy of sounds and visuals (with the help of a recording machine) so that they can be heard or seen again (e.g. on an audiocassette or video tape) **3** *A rainfall of 170 mm was recorded yesterday.* = to measure with the help of instruments

record[2] /ˈrekɔːd/ noun, c. **1** *The police have a complete record of the criminal's movements.* = a written statement of facts etc. **2** *He has broken the long jump record.* = the best achievement by anyone in the past, specially in sports or studies **3** *a gramophone record* = a piece of plastic on which sound is stored, so that it can be heard again

record[3] adj. *He completed the race in record time.* = better than anyone had done in the past **recorder** noun, c. = a machine for recording sound **recording** noun, c. or u. **1** (c.) = sounds or pictures put on tape etc. **2** *a recording session* = the process of putting music onto a cassette, CD etc.

to go on record *She went on record to say that the programme did not interest her.* = to say something officially so that it may be reported or written as one's having said it [MEDIA] **off the record** *I did support his ideas at the meeting, but off the record, I don't think they will be accepted.* = to say something unofficially which cannot be repeated as your having said it [MEDIA] **to set the record straight** = to correct a mistake by finding out the true facts

re•count /rɪːˈkaʊnt/ verb, t. **1** *The government will recount the votes cast in the election.* = to count again **2** *We want you to recount your days as Principal of this college.* = to tell the story of something that happened earlier

re•coup /rɪˈkuːp/ verb, t. *He had lost a lot of money but he has recouped his losses.* = to get back (again) something that one had lost, especially money or one's health

re•course /rɪˈkɔːs/ noun, u. *You have no hope of getting your money back unless you have recourse to the law.* = to take help from the police, law etc. or to do something that one would normally not do (formal)

re•cov•er /riːˈkʌvəʳ/ verb, t. or i. **1** *The police have recovered the stolen car.*(t.) = to get back (again) something that had been lost, stolen or taken away **2** *She is recovering from her illness.* = to return to a state of good health after illness **recovery** noun, u. = the state of recovering or having recovered

re•cre•ate /riːkriˈeɪt/ verb, t. **1** *The art director of the film recreated a part of the Red Fort in order to shoot the film.* = to make an exact copy of something

2 *Can you recreate the scene for us?* = to make something happen again (see **reconstruct**)

re•cre•a•tion /rekri'eɪʃən/ noun, u. **1** *We are going to have a park for the recreation of children.* = enjoyment, specially during free time **2** = the act of recreating something

re•crim•i•na•tion /rɪkrɪmɪ'neɪʃən/ noun, u. or c. (usually plural **recriminations**) *There were bitter recriminations after our team lost the match.* = the act of people quarrelling and blaming each other

re•cruit[1] /rɪ'kru:t/ verb, t. *The hospital will recruit 50 new doctors this year.* = to give employment (work) to someone

recruit[2] noun, c. *He is a new recruit to the army.* = someone who has just joined the army or some other service

rec•tan•gle /'rektæŋgəl/ noun, c. = a geometrical figure with four straight sides, in which the opposite sides are of equal length and the angles are of 90 degrees [GEOMETRY] (see pic under **shapes**) **rectangular** /rek'tæŋgjʊlə/ adj. = having the shape of a rectangle

rec•ti•fy /'rektɪfaɪ/ verb, t. *There is some fault in the car. Can you rectify it?* = to remove a defect and set something right (formal)

rec•tor /'rektəʳ/ noun, c. **1** = a Christian priest **2** = the head of a school or college

rec•tum /'rektəm/ noun = the last part of the intestines, near the **anus** [MEDICINE] **rectal** adj. *rectal cancer* = having to do with the rectum

re•cum•bent /rɪ'kʌmbənt/ adj. *In Bangkok you can see a huge statue of Gautam Buddha in a recumbent posture.* = lying down (formal)

re•cu•pe•rate /rɪ'kju:pəreɪt/ verb, i. *She has recuperated after her illness.* = to become healthy again after an illness (formal)

re•cur /rɪ'kɜ:ʳ/ verb, i. (**recurred**) *We must make sure that such accidents do not recur.* = to happen again

re•cy•cle /ri:'saɪkəl/ verb, t. *Don't throw away the old newspapers. We can recycle them.* = to use again (to treat some material which has already been used in such a way that it can be used again) **recyclable** adj. = capable of being recycled **recycling** noun, u. = the process by which something is recycled

red[1] /red/ adj. *a red rose* = the colour which blood has

red[2] noun **1** *If you mix red and blue you get purple.* = the colour red **2** *He is a Red.* = a communist or left-wing person **redden** verb, t. **1** = to turn red **2** =to be embarassed **redalert** noun, u. *The police have been put on red alert.* = a state of high readiness to deal with a dangerous situation **red-blooded** adj. = young and strong and full of high spirits (referring to people) **red blood cell** noun, c. = a cell in the blood which carries oxygen and gives red colour to blood **red carpet** noun *She received the red carpet treatment in her old school after she became a famous writer.* = a special welcome given to an important guest **the Red Cross** noun = an international organisation that looks after sick and wounded people during a war or after a natural disaster **red-letter day** noun = a specially happy and important day in the life of a person **red light** noun = a red light used to show the presence of danger or to order vehicles to stop **red-light district** (**area**) noun = a part of a city where sex-workers do their work **red meat** noun = the dark-coloured meat from a large animal such as a goat or cow, which is supposed to be less healthy than white meat from a chicken, specially for people with high blood pressure **red pepper** noun = chilies which have been dried and powdered for use in cooking **red-tape** noun *This project has been delayed because of red-tape.* = complicated rules that delay action unnecessarily **Red Indian** noun = a member of one of the tribes which were the earliest inhabitants of North America

> **Usage** The term 'Red Indian' is no longer used as it is considered offensive. It has been replaced by 'Native American.'

to be caught red-handed = to be caught while trying to do something illegal **a red-herring** = a subject which is brought up during a discussion in order to draw attention away from the topic being discussed **to be in the red** = to suffer loss of money and be in debt **to see red** *When I heard he had let us down again, I saw red.* = to be very angry (informal)

re•deem[1] /rɪ'di:m/ verb, t. **1** *The minister had promised, before the election, to build a school in this village and he has redeemed his promise.* = to carry out or fulfil a promise **2** *Everyone thought she was selfish and heartless, but she has redeemed herself by helping so many people.* = to regain the good opinion of people after having lost it **3** = get something back by paying for it **Redeemer** noun, c. = the word used for Jesus Christ who, according to the Christian religion, was sent by God to redeem (save) the human race from sin and evil **redemption** noun, u. = the act of redeeming (saving) someone

re•do /rɪ:'du:/ verb, t. *Your essay has been badly written. You will have to redo it.* = to do something again, improving on what was done earlier

re•do•lent /'redələnt/ adj. *The chicken curry was redolent of saffron and other wonderful spices.* = smelling of something pleasant (literary)

R

re•dress /rɪ'dres/ verb, t. *The government arrested him unjustly, but now the Supreme Court has ordered that he should be set free. The injustice has been redressed.* = to put right something that had been done wrongly or unjustly (formal)

re•duce /rɪ'dju:s/ verb, t. *The teacher reduced the boy's marks from 65 to 50.* = to make less **reduction** noun, u. or c. *There has been some reduction this year in the number of deaths from cholera.*(u.) = the fact of becoming less of the action of making something less

to reduce someone to tears = to make someone cry by saying something hurtful **to be reduced to something** *He lost a lot of money in business and was reduced to borrowing money from friends.* = to reach a point where one is forced to do something which is hurtful to one's pride or dignity

re•dun•dant /rɪ'dʌndənt/ adj. *We have 50 people working here but we need only 30. Twenty of them are redundant.* = not needed; more than necessary (formal) **redundancy** noun, u. = the condition of being redundant

reed /ri:d/ noun, c. **1** = a thin, grass-like plant that grows in wet places **2** *the reeds of a harmonium* = a thin piece of metal in a musical instrument that produces a musical sound by vibrating (shaking) when a stream of air is blown over it **reedy** adj. *a reedy voice* = thin or high

reef /ri:f/ noun, c. (**reefs**) *a coral reef* = a line or chain of rocks in the sea, not far from the shore **reef knot** noun = a kind of double knot made in a rope or string, so that it will not slip or open easily

reek[1] /ri:k/ verb, i. *Their breath reeked of onions.*= to smell of something unpleasant

reek[2] noun, u. *You can get the reek of stale food in the kitchen.* = a strong and unpleasant smell

reel[1] /ri:l/ noun, c. *a reel of cotton thread* = a cylindrical object, usually made of wood or metal, on which thread, wire, cinema film etc. can be wound (also **spool**)

reel[2] verb, t. or i. **1** (t.) *The boy reeled in the kite which he had been flying.* = to make a piece of thread shorter by winding it around a reel **2** *The runners reeled into the stadium, tired after their 26 km marathon race.*(i.) = to walk unsteadily **3** *My head is reeling.*(i.) = to feel unsteady, because of shock or some sickness

to reel off *She reeled off the names of the members.* = to repeat quickly from memory (informal)

re-el•ect /ri:ɪ'lekt/ verb, t. *She has been re-elected to parliament.* = to elect again

ref. /ref/ abbr. of 'with reference to', used in a business letter or document to remind the receiver (the person getting the letter) of some other letter written earlier

re•fer /rɪ'fɜ:'/ verb, t. or i. (**referred**) **1** *You should refer to the dictionary when you are not sure of the spelling of a word.* = to go to someone or something in order to get some information **2** *The new plan has been referred to the Managing Director of India for his opinion.* = to send something to another person for information or for an opinion **3** *In her speech, the speaker referred to the recent killing of tigers by poachers.*(i.) = to mention or speak about something

ref•er•ee[1] /refə'ri:/ noun, c. **1** *a football referee* = a person who is in charge of a match or game and who makes sure that the rules are being followed by the players **2** = a person who is asked to write a reference for someone (see meaning **3** for **reference**)

referee[2] verb, t. *I have been asked to referee this match.* = to act as a referee in a match

ref•er•ence /'refərəns/ noun, u. or c. **1** *These dictionaries are kept in the library for reference.*(u.) = the act of using something to get some information **2** *The editorial made a reference to the water problem in the city.*(c.) = the act of referring to (mentioning) something **3** *I am writing a reference for one of my students, who wants to study in Sri Lanka.*(c.) = a letter or document giving information about someone's character, achievements etc. so as to help that person in getting a job etc. **reference book** noun, c. = a book such as a dictionary or atlas which one uses when some information is needed **reference library** noun, c. = a collection of reference books in a library, which must be used inside the library and cannot be taken out

ref•e•ren•dum /refə'rendəm/ noun, c. (**referenda** or **referendums**) or u. *to hold a referendum* = the taking of votes to decide an important course of action

re•fill[1] /ri:'fɪl/ verb, t. *The petrol tank is empty. It has to be refilled.* = to fill up again

refill[2] /'ri:fɪl/ noun, c. **1** *I have to buy a refill for my pen.* = a small container of ink which is fitted into a pen so that it can be used to write again **2** *He emptied his glass and asked for a refill.* = some more of the same drink **refillable** /rɪ'fɪləbəl/ adj. = used to describe an object (e.g. a battery cell, a printing cartridge etc.) which can be refilled and used again

re•fine /rɪ'faɪn/ verb, t. *Sugar is made by refining sugarcane juice.* = to make something more pure by removing other substances from it **refinery** noun, c. (**refineries**) = a factory in which a substance (e.g. oil taken out of the earth) is refined, so as to make it more pure or to make other products from it **refinement** noun, c. or u. **1** *The computers made 20 years ago were difficult to use but the computers of today have many refinements.*(c.) = an improvement which makes something better **2** *a woman of great* *refinement*(u.) = the qualities of good manners and behaviour that are expected in a person

re•flect /rɪˈflekt/ verb, t. **1** *A mirror reflects light.* = to throw back light, heat etc. **2** *She has taken many photographs of temples in India. This reflects her interest in Indian culture.* = to show **3** *You should reflect carefully on this problem before you come to a decision.* = to think carefully **reflection** /rɪˈflekʃən/ noun, u. or c. **1** *You can see the reflection of the clouds in the water.*(u.) = an image or picture of something seen in water or in a mirror **2** *The manner in which you dress is a reflection of your taste.*(c.) = a sign of what something is like **3** *I have come to this decision after a great deal of reflection.*(u.) = thinking **4** *This book contains Gandhiji's reflections on Indian politics.*(c.) = thoughts expressed in a book **5** *What I said about this city was not meant as a reflection.*(c.) = an unfavourable opinion about something **reflective** /rɪˈflektɪv/ adj. *a reflective person* = having the habit of reflecting (thinking deeply)

re•flec•tor /rɪˈflektəʳ/ noun, c. **1** = an object or surface that reflects light, sound etc. **2** = a small piece of plastic or glass fitted on the back of a bicycle that can be seen at night when light shines on it

re•flex[1] /ˈriːfleks/ noun, c. *When a child suddenly ran across the road in front of my car, I was able to brake in time. Fortunately, my reflexes were good.* = the ability to react quickly to a situation without having to think about what one is doing

re•flex[2] adj. *a reflex action* = connected with one's reflexes (see **reflex**[1]) **reflex angle** noun, c. = an angle of more than 180º [GEOMETRY] (compare **acute angle, obtuse angle**)

re•flex•ive /rɪˈfleksɪv/ adj. *The sentence "He hurt himself" contains a reflexive pronoun, "himself".* = the use of a word to show that an action done by a person has some effect on the same person [GRAMMAR]

re•form[1] /riːˈfɔːm/ verb, i. or t. **1** *Earlier, he turned violent easily, but now he has completely reformed.*(i.) = to change for the better **2** *We will have to reform the system of education.*(t.)= to make something better by bringing in some change

reform[2] noun, c. or u. **1** *She made many reforms in the way in which the school was run.*(c.) = a major change which improves the way in which something is run or managed **2** *The booking system for train tickets needs reform.*(u.) = a basic change which results in improved services, facilities etc. **Reformation** /refəˈmeɪʃən/ noun, u. = an important event in the history of Europe in the sixteenth century, when the Protestant Church broke away form the Catholic Church

re•fract /rɪˈfrækt/ verb, t. = to cause rays of light to bend and change direction (used in connection with water, glass etc.) [PHYSICS] **refraction** noun, u. = the change in the direction in which light is travelling, when it passes from one substance (e.g. air) into a different substance (e.g. water) [PHYSICS]

re•frain[1] /rɪˈfreɪn/ verb, i. *Please refrain from talking in the library.* = to stop oneself from doing something (formal)

refrain[2] noun, c. *The song has a refrain which means 'Be careful, take care.'* = a part of a song, which is repeated several times (especially at the end of each verse)

re•fresh /rɪˈfreʃ/ verb, t. **1** *I was tired after the match but the cup of tea has refreshed me.* = to make one feel energetic **2** *You seem to have forgotten your promise. Let me refresh your memory.* = to remind someone of something **refresher course** = a course given to bring the knowledge of a group of people on a particular subject up to date **refreshing** adj. *Normally we have classes indoors but today we had a class under the trees. It made a refreshing change.* = welcome in a way that is fresh and different **refreshment** /rɪˈfreʃmənt/ noun, c. (usually plural **refreshments**) *We will serve refreshments to the passengers once the plane takes off.* = light food and drink

re•fri•ge•rate /rɪˈfrɪdʒəreɪt/ verb, t. = to cool food to a very low temperature so that it will not go bad quickly **refrigerator** noun, c. = a machine in which food can be kept at a very low temperature so that it does not go bad **refrigerant** noun, c. = a kind of gas which is used in refrigerators

ref•uge /ˈrefjuːdʒ/ noun, u. *When the king was chased by his enemies, he took refuge in a cave.* = shelter (a place where one is protected from danger)

re•fu•gee /refjʊˈdʒiː/ noun, c. = a person who has been forced to leave his/her home or country and look for refuge (shelter) in another place

re•fund[1] /rɪˈfʌnd/ verb, t. *As the shirt you bought is damaged, the shop will refund the price to you.* = to return or give back money which was received earlier

refund[2] noun, c. *I have received a refund from the shop for the sari I returned to them.* = money which has been refunded

re•fuse[1] /rɪˈfjuːz/ verb, t. or i. **1** *The director offered her a part in the play, but she refused.*(i.) = to say 'no' or to be unwilling to do something **2** *The government has refused him permission to leave the country.*(t.) = not to allow

refuse[2] /ˈrefjuːs/ noun, u. *industrial refuse* = garbage or rubbish (waste material that is thrown out) **refusal** /rɪˈfjuːzəl/ noun, u. = the act of refusing something

re•fute /rɪˈfjuːt/ verb, t. *He argued that dogs are more* *loving than cats, but she was able to refute his argument easily.* = to prove that an argument is false or incorrect (formal)

re•gain /rɪ'geɪn/ verb, t. *She was very ill but she has regained her health.* = to get back (again) something that one had lost

re•gal /'ri:gəl/ adj. *He gave us a regal welcome.* = very grand; fit for a king (literary)

re•gale /rɪ'geɪl/verb, t. *He regaled us with wonderful stories of adventure.* = to entertain someone, specially by telling stories

re•ga•lia /rɪ'geɪliə/ noun, u. *The students appeared in colourful regalia on the occasion of their convocation.* = clothes used on a special or ceremonial occasion (old-fashioned)

regard[1] /rɪ'gɑ:d/ noun, u. **1** *I have great regard for my professor.* = respect **2** *I am writing to you with regard to the matter we discussed last week.*= in connection with

regard[2] verb, t. **1** *Everyone regards him highly.* = to respect **2** *I don't want to discuss this matter with you. I regard it as closed.* = to consider **3** *She regarded him with curiosity.* = to look at someone in a certain way **regarding** prep. *I am writing to you regarding the matter we discussed last week.* = about ; in connection with (used in business letters) (slightly old-fashioned and formal) **regardless** adv. **1** *Although they had little money, they carried on regardless and bought some expensive clothes.* = without worrying about or caring for something **2** = without reference to something **regards** noun, u. (always plural) *I send you my warm regards.* = good wishes (used in friendly letters)

re•gat•ta /rɪ'gætə/ noun, c. = an event with many races between sailing or rowing boats

re•gen•e•rate /rɪ'dʒenəreɪt/ verb, i. *The lizard has lost its tail but it will regenerate.* = to grow back again **regeneration** /rɪdʒenə'reɪʃən/ noun, u. = the process by which something regenerates

re•gent /'ri:dʒənt/ noun, c. = a person who rules a kingdom in place of the real king or queen

reg•gae /'regeɪ/ noun = a very popular kind of music that started in the West Indies

re•gime /reɪ'ʒi:m/ noun, c. *Many Indians were sent to jail for writing against the British regime.* = a particular kind of government

re•gi•men /'redʒɪmɪn/ noun, c. *The doctor has prescribed a strict regimen of diet and exercise for the patient.* = a set of rules about diet, exercise etc. that a patient is asked to follow in order to improve his/her health

re•gi•ment /'redʒɪmənt/ noun, c. = a large group of about 1,000 soldiers, commanded by a **colonel** **regimental** /redʒɪ'məntəl/ adj. *a regimental dinner* = having to do with a regiment **regimentation** /redʒɪmən'teɪʃən/ noun, u. *Each teacher should be allowed to teach in a way that suits him or her. There should be no regimentation.* = a system which forces everyone to behave in the same way (generally derogatory)

re•gion /'ri:dʒən/ noun, c. *These people belong to the north-eastern region.* = a large area or part of a country **regional** adj. *We are going to have a regional committee for each game.* = having to do with a region

re•gis•ter[1] /'redʒɪstə^r/ noun, c. or u. **1** *Students must sign the attendance register.*(c.) = a book of large size containing a list or official record **2** *These books are written in a scientific register.*(c.) = the style of writing or speaking used by people belonging to a particular profession or studying a particular subject [TECHNICAL]

register[2] verb, t. **1** *You will have to register your new car before you can drive it on the roads.*= to get something entered into official records **2** *The thermometer registered 50 degrees Centigrade.*= to show (used for a thermometer or other measuring instrument) **3** *register surprise* = show emotion **registration** /redʒɪs'treɪʃən/ noun, u. = the act of registering something **registrar** /'redʒɪstrɑ:^r/ noun = a person who is in charge of office records

re•gress /rɪ'gres/ verb, i. *We thought he had become mature with age, but he has actually regressed.* = to go back to a kind of behaviour which is connected with a less developed state **regressive** adj. *a regressive policy* = going ino a less developed state than before

re•gret[1] /rɪ'gret/ verb, t. *I have always regretted the fact that I did not take more interest in sports when I was young.* = to feel sorry or upset about something

regret[2] noun, c. *I have no regrets about losing the match.* = a feeling of sadness or disappointment **regrettable** adj. *It is regrettable that we could not meet when I was in Chennai.* = something that one should be sorry about (formal)

reg•u•lar /'regjʊlə^r/ adj. **1** *She is very regular in coming to classes. I have never known her to be absent.* = always doing what one is expected to do (opposite **irregular**) **2** *I am a regular user of this bus.* = doing something very often **3** *His heart-beat is regular.* = happening again and again at equal intervals (gaps) of time **4** *Your apppointment is not regular.* = done according to the usual rules; straightforward and honest **5** *'Ask' is a regular verb, but 'see'is an irregular verb.* = a verb whose past tense is not formed in the usual way, by adding '-ed'

[GRAMMAR] **regularize (regularise)** /ˈregjʊlərɑɪz/ verb *She has been working as a temporary teacher for the last six months, but her appointment will be regularized now.* = to make something that has been going on for some time official

reg•u•late /ˈregjʊleɪt/ verb, t. *Although many people want to see the Taj Mahal on the first day of the new year, the police have to regulate the number of visitors. Only a fixed number are allowed in at a time.* = to control or keep in check **regulation** /regjʊˈleɪʃən/ noun, u. or c. **1** = the act of regulating (controlling) something **2** *There is a police regulation controlling the speed of vehicles on the city roads.*(c.) = an official order or rule, used to regulate (control) something **regulator** noun, c. *The speed of the ceiling fan is controlled by a regulator.* = an instrument that controls the working of a machine

re•gur•gi•tate /rɪˈgɜːdʒɪteɪt/ verb, t. **1** = to bring food up again from the stomach into the mouth after swallowing it [TECHNICAL] **2** *The students regurgitated the notes which their teacher had dictated.* = to repeat something from memory without understanding it (figurative, derogatory)

re•ha•bil•i•tate /riːhəˈbɪlɪteɪt/ verb, t. *The people who lost their homes in the earthquake have been rehabilitated.* = to bring back again to a good condition or situation after a period of suffering; to provide a home to someone who has lost his/her home

re•hash[1] /riːˈhæʃ/ verb, t. *He has produced a new book by rehashing all his old writings.* = to use old ideas again in a slightly different form (derogatory)

rehash[2] noun, u. *This new book is just a rehash of all his old writings.* = a repetition of old ideas in a slightly different form

re•hearse /rɪˈhɜːs/ verb, t. *The actors are rehearsing their parts before the drama is staged.* = to practise something (e.g. a drama, speech, a piece of music etc.) before it is done publicly **rehearsal** noun, u. or c. *We will have a rehearsal of the play this evening.*(c.) = the act of rehearsing (practising) something

reign[1] /reɪn/ verb, i. **1** *Emperor Akbar reigned for more than 50 years during the sixteenth century.* = to rule over a country as a king or queen [HISTORY] **2** *Australia reigns in cricket.* = to be much better than anyone else in some activity (figurative)

reign[2] noun, c. or u. *The Taj Mahal was built during Shah Jehan's reign.* = the period during which a king or queen rules

re•im•burse /riːɪmˈbɜːs/ verb, t. *The company will reimburse the money that you spent last month on travelling.* = to pay back money to someone who has had to spend money for some official purpose (formal)

rein[1] /reɪn/ noun, c. (usually plural **reins**) *The horse will stop if you pull the reins.* = a narrow band made of leather, tied to the head of a horse and used to control its movements

rein[2] verb, t. **1** *You will have to rein in the horse.* = to make a horse move more slowly by using the reins **2** *The students are spending too much time watching television. We should rein them in.* = to control a person's behaviour (figurative)

re•in•car•nate /riːɪnkɑːˈneɪt/ verb, i. or t. *He is so violent that I feel he will reincarnate as a tiger.* = to be born again or to cause someone or something to be born again **reincarnation** noun, u. **1** = the action of being born again **2** *She believes she is the reincarnation of a sage of ancient times.* = someone who has been born again

rein•deer /ˈreɪndɪə^r/ noun (plural **reindeer**) = a kind of deer with large horns, found in cold countries near the North Pole

re•in•force /riːɪnˈfɔːs/ verb, t. **1** *There were only 50 soldiers on our side, but as there were more than 500 enemy soldiers, it became necessary to reinforce our troops.* = to add strength to an army or other group by sending more men, weapons etc. **2** *Let us reinforce the wall with an extra layer of concrete.* = to add strength or support to something **reinforcement** noun, u. or c. **1** (u.) = the action of making something stronger **2** *The general asked for reinforcements when he found himself outnumbered by the enemy*(c.) = more soldiers or weapons etc. sent to make an army stronger **reinforced concrete (cement)** = cement which has been made stronger by putting steel rods inside, before the cement becomes hard

re•in•state /riːɪnˈsteɪt/ verb, t. *The officer had been asked to leave but she has been reinstated.* = to put someone back (again) in a former position or job (formal)

re-issue /riːˈɪʃuː/ verb, t. *The book was out of print but it has been re-issued.* = to print a book again

re•it•e•rate /riːˈɪtəreɪt/ verb, t. = to say again (to repeat a statement many times)

re•ject[1] /rɪˈdʒekt/ verb, t. *If you do not send in your application in time, the admissions committee will reject it.* = to turn down or refuse to accept someone or something

re•ject[2] noun, c. *The rejects are being sold at half the usual price.* = a thing or person that is not good enough (not polite when used about a person) **rejection** noun, u. = the action of rejecting someone or something

re•joice /rɪˈdʒɔɪs/ verb, i. *We rejoice at the victory of our team.* = to feel great happiness about something

R

(literary) **rejoicing** noun, u. *There was great rejoicing when our team won.* = great happiness or joy shown usually by a group of people

re-join /riː'dʒɔɪn/ verb, t. or i. *He has re-joined his party.* = to join again after having left

re•join•der /rɪ'dʒɔɪndəʳ/ noun, c. *I was so angry on getting his letter that I sent him a rejoinder at once.* = a strong reply

re•ju•ve•nate /rɪ'dʒuːvəneɪt/ verb, t. *He looks rejuvenated after his holiday in Goa.* = to make someone feel or look young again

re•kindle /riː'kɪndl/ verb, t. = to light a fire again

re•lapse[1] /rɪ'læps/ verb, i. *The patient was improving but he has relapsed.* = to return to a poor state of health after some improvement

relapse[2] noun, u. *The patient has suffered a relapse.* = a return to poor health after some improvement

re•late /rɪ'leɪt/ verb, t. **1** *There was a lot of rain last week and this week we have had many two-wheeler accidents. Can we relate these two things?* = to try to find a connection between two things **2** *Can you relate what happened at the meeting yesterday?* = to tell (usually a story) (formal) **related** adj. **1** *He and I are related. He is married to my sister.* = having some family connections **2** *The rise in the price of vegetables is related to the rise in petrol prices.* = having some connection with something that is being discussed **relation** /rɪ'leɪʃən/ noun, u. or c. **1** *What you are saying has no relation to the matter we are discussing now.*(u.) = connection **2** *That man is a distant relation. His mother is my husband's cousin.*(c.) = a person with whom one has some family connection **relationship** noun, c. **1** *a loving relationship between two sisters* = a friendly or loving connection **2** *He wanted to have a relationship with her.* = a friendship based on sex **3** *The relationship between the two teams is improving.* = the way in which people feel about each other **4** *Is there a relationship between smoking and cancer?* = a connection, usually one of cause and effect

rel•a•tive[1] /'relətɪv/ noun, c. *I have invited all my relatives to my son's wedding.* = relation (a member of one's family)

relative[2] adj. *Although the bus was overcrowded it was air-conditioned, and we travelled in relative comfort.* = as compared to someone or something else **relative clause** noun *In the sentence 'I have read the book which you published last week', 'which you published last week' is a relative clause.* = a clause (group of words containing a finite verb) that is connected to the rest of the sentence by 'who', 'which' or 'that' [GRAMMAR]

Re•la•ti•vi•ty /relə'tɪvɪtɪ/ noun = the idea that time, mass (weight) and energy are related to each other and change with the speed of light [PHYSICS]

re•lax /rɪ'læks/ verb, i. or t. **1** *You have been working hard for the last five hours. You should relax now.*(i.) = to make one's mind and body free and comfortable **2** *Please relax the muscle in your arm, otherwise I will not be able to inject this medicine.*(i.) = to make something less tight or stiff **3** *The company has a strict rule against smoking on the premises, and they will not relax it under any circumstances.* = to be less strict in making someone obey a law or rule **relaxation** /riːlæk'seɪʃən/ noun, u. **1** *relaxation of import laws* = the act of relaxing a law or rule (making it less strict) **2** *She plays chess for relaxation.* = something done for enjoyment in one's free time

re•lay[1] /riː'leɪ/ verb, t. **1** *He phoned us and wanted us to relay the news to others.* = to pass on something (e.g. some information) from one person to the next **2** *Doordarshan will relay the cricket match from Harare.* = to send or carry a television or radio programme from one place to another

relay[2] noun, c. *The Olympic flame was brought from Greece to Australia by a relay of runners.* = one part of a team of people who help to carry something by passing it on from one person to the next **relay race** noun = a race in which each runner of a team runs only for a part of the total distance, allowing the next runner to continue

re•lease[1] /rɪ'liːs/ verb, t. **1** *The judge ordered the police to release the prisoner.* = to set free [LAW] **2** *The new book on birds will be released next week.* = to show a new book or film to the public for the first time **3** *He released the string and the bird flew away.* = to let go of something **4** *The name of the winner has not been released.* = to let some information be known to the public

release[2] noun, u. **1** *The judge ordered the release of the prisoner.* = the act of setting someone free [LAW] **2** *Many important guests were invited to the release of the new film.* = the public showing of a new film or book for the first time

rel•e•gate /'relɪgeɪt/ verb, t. *This rocking chair was once everyone's favourite but now it has been relegated to the storeroom.* = to push someone or something down to a lower or less important position (formal) **relegation** /relɪ'geɪʃən/ noun = the act of relegating someone or something

re•lent /rɪ'lent/ verb, i. **1** *The storm caused a lot of destruction in the last two days but it seems to be relenting now.* = to become less severe or strong **2** *At first, her parents would not allow her to go to the party with her friends but later they relented.* = to agree to something that has been refused previously

relentless adj. *The rain has been pouring down for four weeks now. It is relentless.* = continuous and strong; (of attitudes) showing no mercy

rel•e•vant /ˈrelɪvənt/ adj. *We are discussing cricket and you suddenly start talking about films. What you are saying is not relevant.* = connected with the subject being discussed (opposite **irrelevant**)

re•ly /rɪˈlaɪ/ verb, t. **1** *Our city relies on the river nearby for its supply of water.* = to depend on **2** *She is very honest. You can rely on her.* = to trust **reliable** adj. *My watch is reliable. It always shows the correct time.* = (someone or something) that can be trusted **reliance** noun, u. = the state (condition) of depending on something **reliant** adj. *India is heavily reliant on agriculture.* = depending on something

re•lic /ˈrelɪk/ noun, c. *The ruined temple at Hampi is a relic of Karnataka's past.* = something old that still survives and reminds one of the past **relics** noun (always plural) *Buddha's relics have been kept in a temple in Sri Lanka.* = parts from the body or clothing of a dead person, considered holy, preserved in his/her memory

relief /rɪˈliːf/ noun, u. or c. **1** *This medicine will give you relief from pain.*(u.) = freedom from pain, sorrow etc. **2** *The government is sending relief to the people who have lost their homes in the earthquake.*(u.) = help given to people in trouble **3** *I am going off-duty now. My relief has arrived.*(c.) = a person who takes over a duty from someone else **4** *The building was lit up brightly and stood out in high relief.*(u.) = standing out clearly from the background **relief map** noun, c. = a map of a country in which the high areas (mountains etc.) stand out from the lower areas [GEOGRAPHY]

re•lieve /rɪˈliːv/ verb, t. **1** *This medicine will relieve the pain in your chest.* = to make one's suffering less **2** *This guard is on duty until 8.00 in the morning, after which another guard will relieve him.* = to take up some duty from someone else, making him/her free

re•li•gion /rɪˈlɪdʒən/ noun, u. or c. **1** *It is said that all human beings need religion to give them hope.*(u.) = belief in the existence of the soul and God or gods **2** *India is the home of some of the oldest religions in the world.*(c.) = a particular system of belief or practice in worshipping God or gods **religious** adj. **1** *a religious ceremony* = connected with religion **2** *a religious person* = having deep faith in religion

re•lin•quish /rɪˈlɪŋkwɪʃ/ verb, t. *He relinquished his kingdom and lived as an ordinary citizen.* = to give up power, wealth etc. (formal)

re•lish[1] /ˈrelɪʃ/ verb, t. *This book has been beautifully written. I am sure you will relish it.* = to enjoy or like very much

relish[2] noun, u. **1** *He ate the salad with great relish.*= enjoyment; usually of food **2** *She served her guest some relish, along with rice and curry.* = something that adds taste to food, e.g. pickles or sauce

re•live /ˈriːlɪv/ verb, t. *When I see old photographs, I often relive my childhood.* = to remember and experience (feel) something again in the mind

re•lo•cate /riːləʊˈkeɪt/ verb, t. *We had set up our factory in Mumbai but we will have to relocate it to Pune.* = to find a new place for someone or something

re•luc•tant /rɪˈlʌktənt/ adj. *I enjoyed my holiday in Lucknow so much that I was reluctant to return to Delhi.* = unwilling or unhappy to do something **reluctance** noun, u. *I returned from my holiday with great reluctance.* = unwillingness to do something **reluctantly** adv.

re•main[1] /rɪˈmeɪn/ verb, i. **1** *The cake has been eaten. Only a small piece remains.* = to be left behind when everything else is gone **2** *He remained seated when everyone else stood up.* = to continue doing something

re•main•der /rɪˈmeɪndəʳ/ noun, u. **1** *I have eaten up most of the oranges. You can have the remainder.* = what remains (is left) **2** *If you divide 14 by 4, you get 3 as the quotient and 2 as the remainder.* = the number that is left when one number is divided by another number [MATHEMATICS]

re•mains /rɪˈmeɪnz/ noun, u. (always plural) *Here you see the remains of the king's palace.* = the part of something that remains (is left) behind when everything else is gone

re•make[1] /riːˈmeɪk/ verb, t. *The producer is going to remake this film.* = to make something again, especially a film

remake[2] noun *This is a remake of the popular film "Sholay".* = a film made on the basis of an older one

re•mand /rɪˈmɑːnd/ verb, t. *The judge ordered her to be remanded to police custody.* = to send to prison to await trial [LAW]

re•mark[1] /rɪˈmɑːk/ verb, t. *'This meeting should end quickly,' the Chairperson remarked.* = to say something, especially something that one has just thought of or noticed

remark[2] noun, c. *They made rude remarks about those who were late.*= a spoken or written opinion or comment **remarkable** adj. *She has a remarkable sense of humour. She makes everyone laugh.* = unusual; worth talking about **remarkably** adv.

rem•e•dy[1] /ˈremɪdi/ noun (**remedies**) or u. *This new medicine is a remedy for cancer.*(c.) // *There is no easy remedy for violence.*(u.)= something that can cure a disease or take away the effects of something unpleasant

R

remedy[2] verb, t. *The house is in terrible shape, but we can remedy the situation.* = to change something and make it better (also **remediate**) **remedial** /rɪ'mi:diəl/ adj. *remedial classes* = something that can be used to set right or cure

re•mem•ber /rɪ'membəʳ/ verb, t. **1** *Can you remember when we last met?* = to bring back to mind **2** *Please remember to call me.* = to not forget

re•mind /rɪ'maɪnd/ verb, t. *I may forget to visit him. Will you remind me?* = to cause someone to remember something **reminder** noun, c. *We have received a reminder from the telephone company to pay up our dues.* = something that makes one remember to do something

rem•i•nisce /remɪ'nɪs/ verb, i. *When the two friends met after 20 years, they reminisced about old times.* = to think or talk happily about the past (formal) **reminiscence** noun, c. (usually plural **reminiscences**) *The old actor plans to publish his reminiscences.* = a book in which one writes about past events and memories

re•mis•sion /rɪ'mɪʃən/ noun, u. *He feels better now. There has been a remission of his fever.* = a period when something, specially an illness, becomes less severe.

re•mit /rɪ'mɪt/ verb, t. (**remitted**) **1** *I have to remit Rs 500 to my brother who lives in a village.* = to send money by post (formal) **2** *He was sentenced to 5 years imprisonment, but the court has remitted his sentence.* = to free someone from punishment or reduce the punishment [LAW]

rem•nant /re'mnənt/ noun, c. **1** *The tailor threw away the remnants after he had stitched a shirt out of the piece of cloth.* = the small pieces of cloth that are left over after a garment has been made out of a piece of some material **2** = part that remains

re•mo•del /ri:'mɒdəl/ verb, t. *He has remodelled his house.* = to give something a new shape or appearance

re•mon•strate /'remənstreɪt/ verb, i. *The students remonstrated when the teacher scolded them for coming late to class.* = to complain or protest (formal)

re•morse /rɪ'mɔ:s/ noun, u. *The emperor Ashoka was filled with remorse when he saw that thousands of soldiers had been killed in the war started by him.* = a feeling of sorrow for having done something wrong (literary)

re•mote /rɪ'məʊt/ adj. **1** *Kalinga was a powerful kingdom in the remote past. // Electricity has not reached the remote villages of this state.* = distant (far away) in time or space **2** *I don't have the remotest idea what you are talking about.* = slight (small) **3** *I tried to talk to them but they were very remote.* = not friendly (figurative) **remotely** adv. **remoteness** noun, u. **remote control** noun = an instrument which allows one to control a machine (e.g. a television set) from a distance

a remote chance *You have very little time but there is a remote chance that you will catch the train.* = not very likely to happen but only just possible

re•move /rɪ'mu:v/ verb, t. **1** *Please remove the garbage from the road.* = to take away from one place to another **2** = to dismiss somebody from a position **removal** noun, u. **1** *the removal of restrictions* = the act of removing (taking away)something **2** = carrying things from one place to another

re•mu•ne•rate /rɪ'mju:nəreɪt/ verb, t. *You will be remunerated for the work that you have done.* = to pay someone for work done (formal) **remuneration** /rɪmju:nə'reɪʃən/ noun, u. = money paid for work done **remunerative** /rɪ'mju:nəreɪtɪv/ adj. *This job is not very remunerative. I get paid very little.* = well-paid

re•nais•sance /rɪ'neɪsəns/ noun, u. *Bengal had a renaissance in the nineteenth century, when many great writers and philosophers appeared.* = re-birth (a period when art, culture etc. are revived or brought back to life) **Renaissance** noun *the European Renaissance* = the period in the history of Europe between the 14th and 17th centuries, when many great works of art and literature were produced [HISTORY]

re•nal /'ri:nəl/ adj. = having to do with the **kidneys** [MEDICINE]

re-name /ri:'neɪm/ verb, t. *Madras has been renamed Chennai.* = to give something a new name

rend /rend/ verb, t. (**rent**) = to tear up (old-fashioned, literary)

ren•der /'rendəʳ/ verb, t. **1** *You will have to render accounts for the money you have spent.* (formal, old-fashioned) **2** *You have rendered great service to the country.* = to give or to perform (formal) **rendering** noun, u. or c. **1** *Lata Mangeshkar gave a wonderful rendering of a bhajan by Meerabai.* = a performance of a piece of music (also **rendition**) **2** *This is an English rendering of a Hindi novel by Premchand.* = translation

ren•dez•vous /'rɒndɪvu:/ noun, c. (French) **1** *He is going to the cinema for a rendezvous with his girl-friend.* = a private and often secret meeting with someone **2** *This new restaurant has become a popular rendezvous for college students.* = a place where people like to meet

ren•e•gade /'renɪgeɪd/ noun, c. = a person who leaves a certain political or religious group to join another group with completely different views

re•new /rɪ'nju:/ verb, t. **1** *You will have to renew* *your membership of this club, which ended last week.*= to start something again after a break **2** *The brief holiday renewed my spirits.* = to give fresh strength and energy

re•nounce /rɪ'naʊns/ verb, t. *He renounced politics and devoted his life to social work.* = to give up something for ever (formal)

ren•o•vate /'renəveɪt/ verb, t. *This old building will be renovated.* = to bring something back into good condition by repairing it **renovation** /renə'veɪʃən/ noun, u.

re•nown /rɪ'naʊn/ noun, u. *Lata Mangeshkar has won great renown as a singer.* = fame (literary) **renowned** adj. *Jagjeet Singh is a renowned singer.* = famous

rent[1] /rent/ verb, t. **1** *We are renting out this house to a bank.*= to allow someone to use something in return for regular payment **2** *We will have to rent a building for our new office.* = to be allowed to use something by paying money regularly for its use

rent[2] noun, u. or c. **1** *The rent for the house in which I live now is Rs 1000 a month.* = money paid regularly for the use of something (also **rental**) **2** = a large hole in a piece of cloth (old-fashioned, literary)

re•o•pen /riː'əʊpən/ verb, t. or i. *The school is closed for the summer vacation. It will reopen in July.* = to open or begin again

re•or•gan•ize (reorganise) /riː'ɔːgənaɪz/ verb, t. = to organize again (to change the way in which something works or the position in which something is, so as to make it work better)

re•pair[1] /rɪ'peəʳ/ verb, t. *My watch is not working. I need to get it repaired.* = to make something work again

repair[2] noun, c. (usually plural) *The car is difficult to start and gets heated easily. It needs repairs.* = something that has to be done to fix something (make it work)

re•par•tee /repɑː'tiː/ noun, c. *Urvashi is known for her sense of humour. Whenever she gets into a discussion, she comes up with an excellent repartee.* = a quick and clever reply given to someone during a conversation or debate

re•past /rɪ'pɑːst/ noun, c. *I have had an excellent repast. I can't eat anything more.* = a meal (formal, literary)

re•pat•ri•ate /riː'pætrieɪt/ verb, t. = to send someone or something (e.g. money) back (again) to one's country

re•pay /rɪ'peɪ/ verb, t. **1** *Can you repay the money by Friday?* = to give back money that is owed **2** *You have helped me a lot in these difficult times. How can I repay your kindness?* = to give in return for kindness, help etc.

re•peal /rɪ'piːl/ verb, t. = to officially put an end to a law (formal)

re•peat[1] /rɪ'piːt/ verb, t. **1** *Do not repeat this mistake.* = to do something again **2** *Please do not repeat what you've heard in this room to anyone.* = to say something again

re•peat[2] noun, c. *I've seen this episode before. It is a repeat.* = something that is shown or done again **repetition** /repɪ'tɪʃən/ noun, u. or c. = the act of repeating something (derogatory) **repetitive** adj.

to repeat oneself = to say the same thing over and over again

re•pel /rɪ'pel/ verb, t. (**repelled**) **1** *The enemy attack on our camp was repelled by our brave soldiers.* = to drive back by force **2** *She was repelled by their noisy behaviour.* = to cause a strong feeling of dislike **repellant** noun, u. or adj. *mosquito repellant* (noun) = a substance that drives things away or keeps them away

re•pent /rɪ'pent/ verb, t. or i. *He had said very unpleasant things about me, but, as he repented and said he would never do this again, I excused him.* = to feel and show that one is sorry for having done something wrong (formal) **repentant** adj. *He was repentant after he lost his temper unnecessarily.* = feeling or showing that one is sorry for having done something wrong

re•per•cus•sion /riːpə'kʌʃən/ noun, c. (usually plural) *The President's speech criticizing the government has had strong repercussions on the country.* = strong and far-reaching effect

re•per•toire /'repətwɑːʳ/ noun, c. *She has a huge repertoire of jokes. She can tell you a funny story whenever you ask her to do so.* = stock (referring to the plays, songs, jokes etc. that someone performs or produces regularly)

re•phrase /riː'freɪz/ verb, t. = to say something again using different words

re•place /rɪ'pleɪs/ verb, t. **1** *Saif will replace Robert in the next match.* = to take the place of someone **2** *Please replace the book on the shelf.* = to put something back in its correct place

replay /riː'pleɪ/ verb, t. **1** = to play a match or a game again **2** = to play back something that has been recorded (on a recording machine)

re•plen•ish /rɪ'plenɪʃ/ verb, t. *We have used up all our food. We will have to replenish it.* = to re-fill or put back food etc. which has been used up (formal) **replenishment** noun

rep•li•ca /'replɪkə/ noun, c. *This is a replica of the Taj Mahal.* = a close copy **replicate** verb, t. *American scientists will replicate an experiment which was carried out last week in India.* = to do something

R

in exactly the same way as something done earlier **replication** /replɪ'keɪʃən/ noun

re•ply[1] /rɪ'plaɪ/ verb, i. (**replied**) *He has not replied to my letter yet.* = to answer

reply[2] noun, c. (**replies**) or u. *He gave her a polite reply.*(c.) = something said as an answer

re•port[1] /rɪ'pɔːt/ verb, t. or i. **1** *Have you reported the theft of your car to the police?*(t.) = to give information about something **2** *She has been reporting on the World Cup for five years now.*(i.) = to write in the newspaper giving information about some event **3** *Please report at the office on time.*(i.) = to come to a certain place and let others know that one is there (formal)

report[2] noun, c. **1** *The sports committee should give us a more detailed report.* = a piece of writing which gives information about some event etc. **2** *There was a loud report when the tyre burst.* = the noise of an explosion or gun being fired **reporter** noun, c. = a person who writes regularly about events for a newspaper (formal) (compare **journalist**) **reported speech** noun *The sentence 'She asked me 'What's your name?' becomes 'She asked me what my name was' in reported speech.*= the words of a speaker as reported by some other person (see also **indirect speech**) [GRAMMAR] **reportedly** = according to what is known unofficially

re•pose[1] /rɪ'pəʊz/ verb, i. **1** *The old woman reposed peacefully on her bed, tired after her work.* = to lie down and rest (formal, literary) **2** *We repose a lot of hope in these discussions.* = to put trust, hope etc. in something (formal)

repose[2] noun, u. *The statue of Buddha has a look of perfect repose.* = calmness or peace

re•pos•i•to•ry /rɪ'pɒzɪtəri/ noun, c. (**repositories**) *a repository of historical documents* = a place where things are stored

rep•re•hen•si•ble /reprɪ'hensɪbəl/ adj. *Why did you start a fight during the meeting? Your behaviour was reprehensible.* = of a kind which invites great blame (formal)

rep•re•sent /reprɪ'zent/ verb, t. **1** *She represented her country in the Olympic Games.* = to speak or do something on behalf of someone or in their place **2** *This map represents the extent of the Moghul empire during Akbar's reign.* = to show **representation** /reprɪzen'teɪʃən/ noun, u. *This sculpture is a representation of the country's struggle for freedom.* = something that represents (shows) something **representative** /reprɪ'zentətɪv/ noun, c. *Mrs Roy was the group's representative at the conference.* = a person who speaks or acts on behalf of someone

re•pres•sion /rɪ'preʃən/ noun, u. *emotional repression* = the act of not allowing the natural expression of feelings [TECHNICAL] **repressive** adj. *a repressive government* = not allowing freedom (disapproving)

re•prieve /rɪ'priːv/ noun, c. *The President of India granted the prisoner a reprieve and he was set free.* = an official order stopping or delaying some punishment [LAW]

rep•ri•mand[1] /'reprɪmɑːnd/ verb, t. *The judge reprimanded the police for taking the sick man to jail.* = to express strong disapproval (dislike) of some action (formal)

reprimand[2] noun, c. = a strong expression of disapproval

re•print /riː'prɪnt/ verb, t. = to print something (e.g. a book) again, after all the copies printed earlier have been sold

re•pri•sal /rɪ'praɪzəl/ noun, c. or u. *When one of our cities was bombed by the enemy our air force bombed two of their cities as a reprisal.* = punishment given to someone in return for some wrong or harm done to you (formal)

re•proach[1] /rɪ'prəʊtʃ/ verb, t. *The teacher reproached her for not completing the work on time.* = to blame someone in a way that shows your unhappiness over something that has been done (or not done)

reproach[2] noun, u. or c. *We received a reproach from our teacher for not doing as well as she wanted.*(c.) = an expression of disapproval (not liking something)

re•pro•cess /riː'prəʊses/ verb, t. *Uranium which has been used in a nuclear reactor can be re-processed.* = to treat a substance in such a way that it can be used again (see also **recycle**)

re•pro•duce /riːprə'djuːs/ verb, t. **1** = to make a copy of something **2** = to produce young ones (babies) [BIOLOGY] **reproduction** /rɪprə'dʌkʃən/ noun, u. or c. **1** = the act of producing young ones **2** *The quality of reproduction of the black and white photographs in this book is not very good.*(u.) = the process of making a copy of something **3** (c.) = a copy of a work of art or music

re•prove /rɪ'pruːv/ verb, t. *He reproved the young children for breaking the window.* = to express disapproval of some action (see also **reprimand**) (formal)

rep•tile /'reptaɪl/ noun, c. = a member of a family of animals including snakes and lizards which lay eggs and have scales covering their bodies [BIOLOGY]

re•pub•lic /rɪ'pʌblɪk/ noun, c. = a country which has a system of government by elected representatives of the people and is usually headed by a President (compare **monarchy**)

re•pu•di•ate /rɪˈpjuːdieɪt/ verb, t. *You say I am lying but I strongly repudiate the accusation.* = to deny something (to say that something is false or unjust) (formal)

re•pug•nant /rɪˈpʌgnənt/ adj. *He enjoys watching violent films, which I find repugnant.* = causing a feeling of very deep dislike (formal) **repugnance** noun

re•pulse /rɪˈpʌls/ verb, t. **1** *Our soldiers repulsed the enemy attack.* = to push or drive back **2** *She has been repulsing all offers of partnership.* = to refuse strongly **repulsive** adj. *Most people find frogs repulsive but I love them.* = causing strong dislike

rep•u•ta•tion /repjʊˈteɪʃən/ noun, u. or c. *Sachin Tendulkar enjoys an international reputation as a great batsman.* = an opinion (usually good) that most people have about someone or something **reputed** adj. *Sanath Jayasuriya is a reputed batsman.* = well known

to live up to one's reputation = to act in a way that people have come to expect

re•quest[1] /rɪˈkwest/ verb, t. *I request you to let me leave early as I am not well.* = to ask for something in a very polite way

request[2] noun, c. *We are making a request for a more powerful computer.* = the act of asking for something (more formal than **ask**)

re•quire /rɪˈkwaɪəʳ/ verb, t. **1** *I have enough money for the journey. I do not require more.* = to want or need **2** *The college rules require students to pay their fees by the fifth of the month.* = to expect and demand (formal) **requirement** noun, c. *If you want me to find a house for you, you should let me know your requirements.*(c.) = the details of something that one needs or wants

to meet the requirements of something *You must have a B.A. degree in order to join the M.A. classes. Do you meet this requirement?* = to have something that is needed for some purpose

re•qui•site /ˈrekwɪzɪt/ adj. *Have you got the requisite papers for your driving licence?* = needed for a particular purpose **requisition** /rekwɪˈzɪʃən/ noun, c. *We have sent a requisition for some new computers for this office.* = a formal demand or request for something which is needed

re•run[1] /riːˈrʌn/ verb, t. = to run a video or a recorded television programme or film again

re-run[2] noun, c. = a repeat showing of a television serial etc. which has been shown before

re•sched•ule /riːˈʃedjuːl/ verb, t. *The meeting was to have been held in March but it has been rescheduled. It will now be held in November.* = to fix a later date or time for an event than was first planned

res•cue[1] /ˈreskjuː/ verb, t. *This brave boy rescued a child who was drowning in the river.* = to save from danger or harm

rescue[2] noun, u. *The rescue of the drowning child made us happy.* = the act of saving someone from danger or harm

to come/go to someone's rescue = to help someone who is in trouble or danger

re•search[1] /rɪˈsɜːtʃ/ noun, u. *Scientists are carrying out research to find a cure for cancer.* = a serious and detailed study of some subject done to get new information or reach a new understanding

research[2] verb, t. *Scientists are researching the medicinal properties of these plants.* = to carry out research into something

re•semb•le /rɪˈzembəl/ verb, t. *The girl resembles her brother.* = to look like someone or something **resemblance** noun, u. *He has a strong resemblance to his mother.* = the quality of looking like someone else

re•sent /rɪˈzent/ verb, t. *Why did the officer fail me in the driving test when all the others passed? I resent that!* = to feel hurt and angry because one has been treated unfairly **resentment** noun, u. *to feel resentment* = the feeling of being angry or hurt **resentful** adj. **resentfully** adv.

re•serve[1] /rɪˈzɜːv/ verb, t. *Please reserve a berth for me on the Rajdhani Express.* = to have something set apart for a special purpose or for the use of a particular person

reserve[2] noun, u. or c. **1** *Don't use up all the food. Keep something in reserve for unexpected guests.*(u.) = a quantity of something (e.g. food or money) which is stored or kept for future use **2** *Bangladesh has huge reserves of natural gas.*(c.) = a store of something which has not been used but can be used in future **3** *Yuvraj has been selected for the team but he will not be playing. He is the reserve.*(c.) = an extra player in a team **4** *a game reserve*(c.) = a forest in which wild animals and plants are protected by law and cannot be hunted **5** *He will not say anything even if he is unhappy with you. He has a lot of reserve.*(u.) = the quality of keeping one's feelings under check (control) and saying very little **reservation** /rɪzəˈveɪʃən/ noun, c. or u. **1** *Do you have a reservation on this train?* = an arrangement by which something is kept apart for the use of a particular person **2** (always plural) *I have some reservations about his appointment as captain of the team.* = feelings of doubt **reserved** adj. *He is a very reserved person and does not like to talk much.* = unwilling to express one's feelings (mildly derogatory)

res•er•voir /ˈrezəvwɑː/ noun, c. = an artificial lake

R

in which water is stored for use by a city etc.

re•set /riː'set/ verb, t. **1** *The dates for the examination have been re-set.* = to fix a different date or time for something (see also **re-schedule**) **2** *Your watch is 20 minutes behind the correct time. Please re-set it.* = to change the time shown by a watch or clock **3** *The surgeon will re-set the broken bones in my leg.* = to put a broken bone back in place

re-set•tle /riː'setl/ verb, t. = to find a home (again) for someone who has lost his/her home

re•shuf•fle /riː'ʃʌfəl/ verb, t. *The Prime Minister has reshuffled his cabinet.* = to move people into different jobs or positions

re•side /rɪ'zaɪd/ verb, i. *He resides in America but visits India every year.* = to live in a place (formal)

res•i•dence /'rezɪdəns/ noun, u. *I have been to her office but never to her residence.* = home (the building in which one lives) (formal)

res•i•dent[1] /'rezɪdənt/ noun, c. *She is a resident of Shakti Nagar.* = a person who lives in a place

resident[2] adj. *She is not resident in India.* = living in a place **residential** /rezɪ'dənʃəl/ adj.

res•i•due /'rezɪdjuː/ noun, u. or c. *The white residue at the bottom of the kettle is calcium which has been left behind when the water boiled.* = the substance that remains behind after some process, e.g. boiling [TECHNICAL] **residual** adj. *Most of the problems have been solved but there are a few residual problems.* = remaining; left over

re•sign /rɪ'zaɪn/ verb, i. *She has resigned as the chairperson of the committee as she had too many other things to do.* = to give up a job or position

res•ig•na•tion /rezɪg'neɪʃən/ noun, u. **1** *He is unhappy with the job and has handed in his resignation.* = the act of resigning or giving up a job **2** *He has accepted his loss with resignation.* = the state of accepting something unpleasant without complaining

to resign oneself to something = to accept something unpleasant that cannot be avoided

re•sil•i•ent /rɪ'zɪliənt/ adj. **1** *Rubber is a resilient substance.* = able to return to its former shape or condition when pressure is taken away **2** *She was very unhappy when she lost her mother, but her resilient nature helped her to get over her sorrow.* = able to deal with and recover quickly from the effects of illness, shock or unhappiness **resilience** noun, u. *He has great resilience. See how quickly he has recovered from his illness!* = the quality of being resilient

re•sin /'rezɪn/ noun, u. **1** = a yellow solid substance that is made from the thick sap (juice) which comes out of certain trees **2** = a substance used in making plastics [CHEMISTRY]

re•sist /rɪ'zɪst/ verb, t. **1** *Our soldiers resisted the enemy attack.* = to oppose or fight against something **2** *Concrete buildings can resist earthquakes if they are designed correctly.* = to remain unharmed by something **3** *She is so fond of icecream that she can't resist it.* = to force oneself to stay away from something that one likes **resistance** noun, u. **1** *Our soldiers offered strong resistance to the enemy.* = the act of resisting (fighting against) something **2** *The greater the speed of the aircraft, the higher the resistance of the wind.* = the force which opposes something **3** *Old people do not have much resistance to disease.* = the ability to remain unharmed by something **4** = the power of a substance to not conduct heat or electricity [PHYSICS] **resistant** adj. *My watch is resistant to water.* = able to resist something

re•sit /riː'sɪt/ verb, t. *If you don't pass the examination you will have to re-sit it.* = to take an examination again

res•o•lute /'rezəluːt/ adj. *She is a resolute person. When she decides to do something, she always does it.* = determined (having strong determination)

res•o•lu•tion /rezə'luːʃən/ noun, c. or u. **1** *We are happy about the resolution of this old family dispute.*(u.) = the action of finding a way out of a difficult situation **2** *The members of the club passed a resolution to elect a new president.*(c.) = a formal decision by a group, reached after a vote **3** *She has made a resolution to give up smoking.*(c.) = something that one strongly decides to do

re•solve[1] /rɪ'zɒlv/ verb, t. **1** *It is time for us to resolve our differences and live together peacefully.* = to settle; to find a way of ending a difficult situation **2** *I have resolved not to go to his house again, though he has invited me many times.* = to make a decision which one is determined not to change **3** *The members of the club resolved to elect a new president.* = to decide formally at a meeting

resolve[2] noun, u. *Your support has strengthened my resolve to fight environmental pollution.* = determination (strong desire to do something) (formal)

res•o•nance /'rezənəns/ noun, u. **1** = the sound caused in an object by sound waves which are produced by some other object with the same **frequency** [PHYSICS] **2** *His voice has a lot of resonance.* = sound which has the quality of being deep and clear

res•o•nate /'rezəneɪt/ verb, i. **1** *The sound from the loudspeakers made the glass panes of the window resonate.* = to cause resonance **2** *His deep voice resonated through the hall.* = to be heard loudly and clearly **3** *His ideas resonated with the people and he won the elections easily.* = to be of the same opinion as someone else

re•sort[1] /rɪ'zɔːt/ noun, c. *Darjeeling is a popular*

holiday resort. = a place where people go for a holiday

resort[2] verb, i. *You must settle this matter peacefully. Do not resort to force or violence.* = to make use of something, usually bad, to get what one wants

to be the last resort = if everything else fails

re•sound /rɪˈzaʊnd/ verb, i. *The entire stadium resounded with the sound of clapping when he completed his century.* = to echo (to be filled with sound) **resounding** adj. *India won a resounding victory over the Australian team.* = very great

re•source /rɪˈzɔːs/ noun, c. **1** (usually plural) *India is rich in natural resources such as coal.* = wealth **2** *I have used up all my resources and have nothing left.* = something (e.g. money) that one possesses and can use in time of need **resourceful** adj. *He is a very resourceful person and knows how to get out of difficult situations.* = able to find ways of dealing with situations **resourcefully** adv.

re•spect[1] /rɪˈspekt/ noun, u. or c. **1** *Children should have respect for their parents.*(u.) = politeness and honour shown towards someone or something that is considered important **2** (always plural) *Please convey my respects to your father.*(u.) = good wishes **3** *In Mumbai, people are so busy that no one has time for friends or neighbours. Kolkata is better in this respect.*(c.) = a particular point or detail

respect[2] verb, t. **1** *I respect her for her courage.* = to show honour to someone or to something that is considered important **2** *I respect your opinions.* = to show consideration for something **respectful** adj. *He is always respectful towards his teachers.* = showing respect **respectable** adj. **1** *a respectable person* = having qualities or a social position which people consider good or important **2** *Sri Lanka managed to put up a respectable total in this match.* = quite good

re•spect•ive /rɪˈspektɪv/ adj. *Ravi lives in Mumbai while Anil is from Kolkata. After this meeting they will return to their respective homes.* = belonging to the person with whose name it has been mentioned earlier **respectively** adv. *Ravi and Anil have been appointed captain and vice-captain of the team respectively.* = each one separately, in the order mentioned earlier (Ravi has been appointed captain and Anil vice-captain)

res•pi•ra•tion /respɪˈreɪʃən/ noun, u. = the action of breathing (formal) [BIOLOGY] **respirator** noun, c. = a device that helps a person to breathe over a long period of time when he or she cannot do so by themselves [MEDICINE] **respiratory** /respɪˈreɪtəri/ adj. *She has some respiratory problems.* = connected with breathing **respire** verb, i. = to breathe

res•pite /ˈrespɪt/ noun, u. *He has been working since morning and needs some respite.* = rest; a period of relaxation (formal)

re•splen•dent /rɪˈsplendənt/ adj. *On Republic Day, Delhi is resplendent with lights.* = bright and shining (literary)

re•spond /rɪˈspɒnd/ verb, i. **1** *He has not responded to my letter yet.* = to reply in speech or writing **2** *She responded to my request by giving me Rs 1,000 immediately.* = to react to something **3** *The patient seems to be responding well to this new medicine. He is much better today.* = to get better as a result of treatment **response** noun, c. or u. **1** *I have received a response to my letter.*(c.) = reply **2** *The public response to the appeal by the farmers has been very encouraging.*(u.) = reaction **responsive** adj. *She is very responsive to new ideas.* = willing to accept **respondent** noun, c. = a person who has to answer a charge in a law court [LAW]

re•spon•si•ble /rɪˈspɒnsɪbəl/ adj. **1** *You are both responsible for the school gardens.* = having the duty of looking after something **2** *The driver of the bus is responsible for this accident.* = being the cause of something bad or unpleasant (disapproving) **3** *She is a very responsible person. You can be sure that she will complete this work in time.* = trustworthy (one who can be trusted to do what he/she is asked to do) (opposite **irresponsible**) **responsibility** /rɪspɒnsɪˈbɪlɪti/ noun, u. or c. (**responsibilities**) **1** *She has been given the responsibility of making arrangements for the conference.*(c.) = the duty of looking after something **2** *The responsibility for this accident has to be decided by the judge.*(u.) = the blame or fault (for causing something unpleasant) **3** *He should develop a sense of responsibility.*(u.) = the quality of being trustworthy

rest[1] /rest/ verb, i. or t. **1** *The athlete is resting after the race.*(i.) = to have freedom from work, specially after doing something that makes one tired **2** *You can rest your feet on this table.*(t.) = to support

rest[2] noun, u. **1** *She is tired and is taking a rest.* = a period of freedom from work **2** *The ball rolled along the ground for a few feet and then came to rest.* = the condition of not moving **3** *This chair is very comfortable because it has a high backrest.* = a support for something **4** *You can keep one of these books for yourself and return the rest.* = what is left

to rest on something *The success of this project rests on that one important condition.* = to depend on **to let something rest** = to not talk about something any more so that there is peace, food feeling etc. **to put one's mind at rest** *The exam results put his mind at rest.* = to cause one to stop worrying

R

re-state /riː'steɪt/ verb, t. *I did not understand your argument. Can you re-state it?* = to say or write something again in a different way so that it can be understood (see also **rephrase**)

res•tau•rant /'restərɒnt/ noun, c. = a place where food is served and where people can usually sit and eat

res•tive /'restɪv/ adj. *People are becoming restive because of the rumours that a war may begin soon.* = nervous and therefore unable to keep still (formal)

rest•less /'restlɪs/ adj. *The child is so restless that it can't sit still for more than a minute.* = unable to keep still; moving about

rest•room /'rest ruːm/ noun = a toilet in a public place e.g. a hotel, airport (American English)

re•store /rɪ'ɪstɔː/ verb, t. **1** *There was some trouble in the city yesterday but peace has been restored now.* = to bring or put back what has been taken away **2** *The government will need to spend a lot of money to restore the Ajanta cave paintings.* = to bring something (specially an old building) back to its original condition

re•strain /rɪ'streɪn/ verb, t. *You should have restrained her from shouting at the meeting.* = to check (control) or prevent someone or oneself from doing something (formal) **restraint** noun, u. or c. **1** *I am glad you did not reply when that man shouted at you. You showed great restraint.*(u.) = the quality of being able to control oneself **2** *The government has imposed restraints on the press. Newspapers are not allowed to report violent incidents.*(c.) = something that checks or controls

re•strict /rɪ'strɪkt/ verb, t. *The officials plan to restrict the number of people entering the stadium.* = to control and put a limit on something **restriction** noun, u. or c. *The state government has imposed a restriction on the sale of liquor.*(c.) = something done to control and put a limit on something

re•struc•ture /riː'strʌktʃər/ verb, t. *The company is being restructured.* = to arrange a system (e.g. a company or a political party etc.) again, in a different and better way (see also **reorganize**)

re•sult[1] /rɪ'zʌlt/ noun, u. or c. **1** *This accident is the result of careless driving.* = something that happens because of something else **2** (always plural) *The results of the examination are out.* = a report on the success or failure of someone in an examination or a competition **3** = what one sees or finds out by doing an experiment

result[2] verb, i. **1** *The delay in the arrival of one train resulted in the delay of several others.* = to lead to some result; to cause **2** *The defeat of the Indian team resulted from poor fielding.* = to be caused by

re•sume /rɪ'zjuːm/ verb, t. or i. *The match has been stopped because of rain but we will resume after lunch.*(i.) = to begin again after a halt **resumption** noun, u. *Many people left the stadium when the match was stopped, but they returned after its resumption.* = the act of resuming something (starting again after a halt) (formal)

re•su•mé /'rezjʊmeɪ/ noun, c. (French) **1** *He gave us a resumé of the match.* = summary **2** *Please send in your resumé along with your application.* = a record of the things that one has done or achieved, which one uses when applying for a job etc. (also **curriculum vitae** or **cv**) [TECHNICAL]

re•sur•gence /rɪ'sɜːdʒəns/ noun, u. *the resurgence of nationalism* = the powerful return of something (ideology, art etc.)

re•sur•rect /rezə'rekt/ verb, t. *the dying art of puppet theatre has been resurrected.* = to bring something back to life or activity **Ressurrection** noun = coming back to life (Christians believe that Jesus Christ was resurrected after he had been crucified.)

re•sus•ci•tate /rɪ'sʌsɪteɪt/ verb, t. *The patient had stopped breathing and we thought he was dead but the doctors managed to resuscitate him.* = to revive (to bring a person who had stopped breathing back to life) [MEDICINE]

re•tail[1] /rɪ'teɪl/ verb, t. *She retails tea after buying it in large quantities from the tea gardens.* = to sell something directly to customers for their use

retail[2] adj. *He owns a retail shop.* = a shop which sells things directly to customers for their use **retailer** noun, c. = a business person who sells things directly to customers through a shop

re•tain /rɪ'teɪn/ verb, t. *He has sold most of his property but still retains a small house in the city. // I would go mad if I had to live in this crowded city. How do you manage to retain your cheerfulness?* = to be able to keep something without losing it **retainer** noun, u. = a fixed sum of money paid to someone (instead of a salary) in order to have their continued help **retention** noun, u. *His feet are swollen because of the retention of fluid in the body.* = the process of keeping something without getting rid of it **retentive** adj. *a retentive memory.* = able to retain or keep things for a long time

re•tal•i•ate /rɪ'tælieɪt/ verb, i. *When the hospital lowered the salaries of the nurses they retaliated by staying away from work.* = to return ill treatment with a similar act (to do something bad to someone who has done something bad to you) **retaliation** /rɪtæli'eɪʃən/ noun, u. = the act of retaliating **retaliatory** adj.

re•tard /rɪ'tɑːd/ verb, t. *The development of this region has been retarded by the lack of communications.* = to cause something to slow down **retarded** adj. *retarded growth* = developing at a much slower rate than normal

retch /retʃ/ verb, i. *The food was so bad that it made me retch.* = to make sounds like vomitting but not throw up food

re•tell /riː'tel/ verb, t. = to tell a story again in a different way

re•think /riː'θɪŋk/ verb, t. *Our plan may not succeed. We will have to rethink it.* = to think about (a plan etc.) something again, in order to change it

ret•i•cent /'retɪsənt/ adj. *The girl is very reticent. She hardly speaks to anyone.* = shy and unwilling to speak to others

ret•i•na /'retɪnə/ noun = the area at the back of the eye that receives light and sends images to the brain, allowing us to see things [BIOLOGY]

ret•i•nue /'retɪnjuː/ noun, c. *The President and his retinue of officials.* = a group of people who travel with someone very important

re•tire /rɪ'taɪə^r/ verb, i. **1** *A government employee has to retire on reaching the age of 60.* = to give up working on reaching a certain age **2** *It is 10 o'clock now and it is time for me to retire.* = to go to bed (old-fashioned) **retired** adj. *retired persons* = someone who has retired **retirement** noun, u. **1** = the act of retiring (giving up one's profession) **2** = the period after one has retired

re•tort[1] /rɪ'tɔːt/ verb, i. *When he asked me rudely why I was late, I retorted by saying that it was none of his business.* = to give an angry, disrespectful or humorous reply

retort[2] noun, c. **1** *an angry retort* = an angry or amusing reply **2** = a glass bottle with a long, bent neck, in which chemicals are heated [TECHNICAL]

re•trace /rɪ'treɪs/ verb, t. **1** *Last month some people attacked my neighbour and stole things from his house. The police are trying to retrace the events that took place that night.* = to go back again to something that happened in the past, in order to find out what happened (see also **reconstruct**) **2** *She was lost in the large city and was unable to retrace her way back home.* = to go back the way one came

re•tract /rɪ'trækt/ verb, t. **1** *A cat can retract its claws but a dog cannot.* = to draw in or to pull back [TECHNICAL] **2** *The witness told the magistrate earlier that he had seen the man being robbed, but now he has retracted his statement.* = to take back a statement that one had made earlier (formal) **retractable** adj. *Leopards have retractable claws.* = which can be pulled up or in (see meaning **1** for **retract**)

re-tread /'riːtred/ verb, t. *to retread an old tyre* = to put back (again) the tread (the thick covering of rubber which comes in contact with the road) on a worn-out tyre

re•treat[1] /rɪ'trækt/ verb, i. *Napoleon's army was forced to retreat from Russia because of the fierce winter.* = to move back from a place (usually a place where fighting is taking place)

retreat[2] noun, u. or c. **1** *The retreat of Napoleon's army led to his downfall.*(u.) = the act of retreating (moving back) **2** *Every summer, I go to Rishikesh, where I have a retreat among the hills.*(c.) = a place to which one can go when one needs peace or safety **3** = a period of time spent in prayer and meditation, generally away from routine

to beat a (hasty) retreat = to run away before something one doesn't want happens (humorous)

re•trench /rɪ'trentʃ/ verb, i. or t. **1** *We spent a lot of money on the new factory, but we must retrench now as we are losing money.*(i.) = to reduce (cut) costs **2** *We had taken on 500 workers for the factory but we will have to retrench 200 of them as the business is running into loss.*(t.) = to dismiss someone from a job as a means of saving money

re•tri•al /riː'traɪəl/ noun, c. *The court ordered a retrial because some new evidence was found.* = new or fresh trial for a person whose crime has already been judged in a court of law [LAW]

re•trieve /rɪ'triːv/ verb, t. **1** *I have to retrive my luggage from the train.* = to get something back from a place where one had left it **2** *Can you retrieve the data that was stored in the computer?* = to find and bring back [COMPUTERS] **3** *The company lost a lot of money last year but has managed to retrieve its position.* = to get back (again) into a better position

retro- prefix meaning 'back' e.g. **retrospective** /retrə'spektɪv/ adj. or noun, u. *retrospective cinema*(adj.) = concerning the past **2** from an earlier point in time e.g. **retroactive** /retrəʊ'æktɪv/ adj. *The new law against smuggling will have retroactive effect.* = coming into effect from an earlier date (referring to a law or rule) (also **retrospective**)

ret•ro•spect /'retrəspekt/ noun, u. *In retrospect, I can say that my decision to quit my job was a mistake.* = thinking in the present about something that happened in the past **retrospection** /retrə'spekʃən/ noun, u. *Retrospection can sometimes be pleasant, but it usually makes one sad.* = the action of thinking about the past **retrospective** noun, c. or adj. **1** *The Film Society is arranging a retrospective of Raj Kapoor films.*(noun) = a series of old films, usually made by the same director or having the same actor, which are shown to

R

an audience **2** *retrospective effect* (adj.) = looking back, applying to the past

re•turn[1] /rɪˈtɜːn/ verb, i. or t. **1** *I shall return to Chennai on the 10th of March.*(i.) = to go back to a place **2** *The postal services will return to normal tomorrow.*(i.) = to go back to usual activity **3** *If the pain returns, phone me.*(i.) = (of a medical symptom) to come back **4** *She has still not returned my book.*(t.) = to give back something one had taken **5** *I have contacted them and left a message but they haven't returned my call.*(t.) = to make a telephone call in answer to an earlier call **6** (t.) = to hit the ball back in tennis [SPORT]

return[2] noun, u. or c. **1** *I'll call you on my return from Delhi.*(u.) = the act of going or coming back to a place **2** (c.) = (in tennis) the action of hitting the ball back **3** (usually plural) *What are the returns on this investment?* = the profit that one gets back **4** = the key on the computer keyboard which is pressed to move to the next line [COMPUTERS] **return ticket** = a ticket which allows one to return to the place from which one started

in return *I helped her settle down in her new house and, in return, she looked after my cat when I was away.* = receiving help as a result of having helped someone **on someone's return** *I know she's out, but on her return, could you ask her to call me.* = when someone returns or comes back home, to the office etc. **Many happy returns (of the day)!** = a greeting on the occasion of someone's birthday

re•u•nite /riːjuːˈnaɪt/ verb, t. **1** *The two brothers have been reunited after 20 years of separation.* = to come together again **2** *East and West Germany have been reunited.* = to be joined together and become one again

re•use /riːˈjuːz/ verb, t. *These old envelopes can be re-used.* = to use again (see also **recycle**)

re•vamp /riːˈvæmp/ verb, t. *revamp the examination system* = to make again; to give something a new shape (see also **reorganize, restructure**)

re•veal /rɪˈviːl/ verb, t. **1** *He did not reveal the names of his friends to the police.* = to make a secret known **2** *The x-ray revealed a crack in her finger.* = to show what was hidden before **revealing** adj. **1** *in a revealing dress* = allowing those parts of the body to be seen which most people believe should be kept hidden **2** *This film provides some revealing insights into the customs of the people of Nepal.* = allowing something that was secret or unknown to be known

rev•el /ˈrevəl/ verb, i. (**revelled**) *They revelled all night to celebrate their victory.* = to enjoy oneself by drinking, dancing etc. (old-fashioned) **revelry** noun, u. = wild and noisy enjoyment

rev•e•la•tion /revəˈleɪʃən/ noun, u. or c. **1** *We always thought he had no interest in sports. It was a revelation to us that he had been a famous cricketer once.*(u.) = the making known of something that had been kept hidden or secret **2** (c.) (usually plural) = information about someone's life, career, thoughts etc. which surprises others

re•venge /rɪˈvendʒ/ noun, u. *I have been insulted in public. I must have revenge!* = harm done to someone as a punishment for harm that he/she did to you (compare **avenge**)

to take revenge = to act against someone with the intention of hurting or destroying, as a reaction to damage done to oneself

rev•e•nue /ˈrevɪnjuː/ noun, u. *The government's revenue from the sale of tobacco has fallen this year.* = the income which the government receives from taxes

re•ver•be•rate /rɪˈvɜːbəreɪt/ verb, i. *The sound of thunder reverberated through the valley.* = to echo (to be thrown back and heard again and again); referring to a sound as it bounces off surfaces (literary) **reverberation** /rɪvəbəˈreɪʃən/ noun, c. (usually plural) **1** *The reverberations faded away gradually.* = echoes (sounds which are heard again and again) **2** *The arrest of the leader produced strong reverberations.* = the effect, usually unpleasant, of some action (figurative)

re•vere /rɪˈvɪər/ verb, t. *The world revered Mahatma Gandhi, who was thought to be the greatest leader of his age.* = to give great respect to someone

rev•e•rence /ˈrevərəns/ noun, u. *My reverence for the Buddha has grown with the years.* = great respect, mixed with love **Reverend** noun = a term of respect used for a Christian priest or a Buddhist monk

rev•e•rie /ˈrevəri/ noun, c. (**reveries**) or u. = a pleasant dream-like state while awake

re•ver•sal /rɪˈvɜːsəl/ noun, u. or c. **1** *the reversal of the High Court's decision*(u.) = the act of reversing something (changing to its opposite) **2** *We are shocked by this reversal which the Indian team has suffered.*(c.) = defeat (formal)

re•verse[1] /rɪˈvɜːs/ verb, t. or i. **1** *We can't go forward as the road ahead is blocked. We will have to reverse.*(i.) = to move backwards **2** *The High Court ordered the release of the prisoner, but the Supreme Court has reversed the High Court's judgement.*(t.) = to change a decision or judgement to its opposite [LAW] **3** *Will you reverse the page of the book you are reading?*(t.) = to turn something back

reverse[2] noun, u. **1** *The car is moving in reverse.* = a backward direction **2** *This five-rupee coin has the Ashoka pillar on the reverse.* = the other side or back of something **3** *I had asked him not to eat fried food, but he did the reverse.* = the opposite of what is suggested **4** *Our army has met with a reverse.* =

defeat or set-back **reversible** adj. *a reversible jacket* = (of a garment) which can also be worn inside out

to say in reverse order = to say something backwards (starting at the end)

re•vert /rɪ'vɜːt/ verb, i. **1** *If the new system does not work we will revert to the old one.* = to go back to an earlier condition (formal) **2** *We were discussing cricket before we started talking about films. Shall we revert to our original topic?* = to go back to an earlier topic of conversation (formal) **3** *This property will revert to the government at the end of the lease.* = to become the property of a former owner again [LAW]

review[1] /rɪ'vjuː/ verb, t. **1** *The examiners will review the cases of all candidates who failed by less than five marks.* = to consider and judge something again, possibly in order to change an earlier decision **2** *Let us review last week's work.* = to look back at and assess (judge) something **3** = to write an article commenting about something that happened earlier

review[2] noun, c. **1** *There will be a review of your performance at the end of the month.* = the examining of something in order to suggest possible changes **2** = an article in a newspaper, magazine etc. that comments on the quality of content of a book, film etc.

re•vise /rɪ'vaɪz/ verb, t. **1** *There are many mistakes in your essay. Please revise it carefully.* = to read through something again in order to make corrections or improvements **2** *I have revised my opinion about them.* = to change a plan, an opinion etc. usually as a result of thinking again (usually from unfavourable to favourable) **3** *I have revised chapters 8–10 and am now ready to write the exam.* = to study a subject again carefully for an examination, interview etc. **revision** noun, u. or c. = the act of revising something that had been written earlier

re•vi•tal•ize (revitalise) /riː'vaɪtəlaɪz/ verb, t. *The Film Club has been revitalized after Ms Gupta took over as its president.* = to put life or energy again into something

re•vive /rɪ'vaɪv/ verb, t. *We have to revive our club, which has been inactive for many years.* = to bring back (again) to life or activity

re•voke /rɪ'vəʊk/ verb, t. *The government has revoked its earlier order.* = to officially cancel or take back an order or a decision (formal)

re•volt[1] /rɪ'vəʊlt/ verb, i. or t. **1** *to revolt against the government*(i.) = to refuse to obey someone in power and to take violent action against him/her **2** *Do you think people will revolt?*(i.) = protest **3** *His behaviour is so crude that it revolts me.*(t.) = to shock or to cause disgust (very strong dislike)

revolt[2] noun, u. or c. *a revolt against the tax laws* = an act of revolting **revolting** adj. *revolting habits* = causing disgust or contempt

rev•o•lu•tion /revə'luːʃən/ noun, u. or c. **1** *The French Revolution completely changed the political map of Europe.* = a sudden and very great change, specially a violent change in the system of government **2** *The coming of the Internet has brought about a revolution in education.* = a complete change in the ways of thinking etc. **3** *The earth completes one revolution around the sun in 365 days.* = a complete circular movement around a fixed point **revolutionary** adj. or noun **1** (adj.) = connected with revolution **2** *revolutionary changes in the system of education.*(adj.) = producing large or dramatic changes **3** (noun) = a person who supports revolution

re•volve /rɪ'vɒlv/ verb, i. *The earth revolves on its axis once in 24 hours.* = to turn around a central line or point, like a wheel

to revolve around someone or something **1** = to depend completely on someone or something **2** *Her life revolves around her children.* = to consider someone or something as being very important in one's life

re•volv•er /rɪ'vɒlvə^r/ noun, c. = a small gun, in which the bullets are kept in a container that revolves (turns round and round)

re•vul•sion /rɪ'vʌlʃən/ noun, u. *The sight of garbage lying on the streets fills me with revulsion.* = a feeling of disgust (formal)

re•ward[1] /rɪ'wɔːd/ noun, c.or u. **1** *The promotion to Chief Chef from Junior Chef was a reward for Mr Thakur's efforts.* = something of value given to someone in return for doing some good work **2** = money or something equal to money given to someone who helps one find something that is lost, or the police to find someone who has been taken away by force or is missing, or a criminal who is in hiding

reward[2] verb, t. *She was rewarded with a promotion.* = to give someone a reward **rewarding** adj. *Teaching has been a very rewarding profession for me.* = (of a job or activity) that gives a lot of satisfaction, but possibly not much money

re•word /riː'wɜːd/ verb, t. *I have re-worded my letter to the bank.* = to say or write something again using different words (see also **rephrase, re-state**)

re•work /riː'wɜːk/ verb, t. *You should re-work the novel you are writing.* = to change something (e.g. a piece of writing) and put it in a different form (see also **re-do**)

re•write /riː'raɪt/ verb, t. = to write something again but in a different and better way

rhe•sus /'riːsəs/ noun = the common monkey found in northern India **rhesus factor (rh factor)** noun

R

= a substance found in the red blood cells of many people, the presence (positive) or absence (negative) of which in the blood of parents can prove to be dangerous for a new-born baby [BIOLOGY]

rhet•o•ric /ˈretərɪk/ noun, u. = the art of speaking in public in such a way that is convincing or makes a strong impression **rhetorical** /rɪˈtarɪkəl/ adj. *She has great rhetorical skill.* = connected with rhetoric (the art of speaking) **rhetorical question** noun *He asked 'Is there anyone in this crowd who does not want India to be prosperous?' It was just a rhetorical question, of course.* = a question which does not need an answer, but is asked in order to create an effect

rheu•ma•tis•m /ˈruːmətɪzəm/ noun = a disease that causes pain and stiffness in the joints and muscles of the body [MEDICINE] **rheumatic** /ruːˈmætɪk/ adj. *rheumatic fever* = having to do with rheumatism

rhi•no•ce•ros /raɪˈnɒsərəs/ noun (also **rhino**) = a large animal with a very thick skin and either one or two horns on its nose, found in parts of Africa and Asia

rhi•zome /ˈraɪzəʊm/ noun = a plant of the family to which ginger belongs, which grows along or under the ground and has roots and stems growing from it [BIOLOGY]

rhom•bus /ˈrɒmbəs/ noun = a geometrical figure with four sides of equal length, but with none of its angles measuring 90 degrees [GEOMETRY] (see pic under **shapes**)

rhyme[1] /raɪm/ verb, i. *In the poem "Jack and Jill went up the hill", the words "Jill" and "hill" rhyme.* = to have a sound that is almost the same as the sound of another word (referring to a word at the end of a line of poetry) [LITERATURE]

rhyme[2] noun, c. *Do you know this rhyme?* = a short and simple poem, having lines that rhyme **nursery rhyme** = a simple poem with rhyme (e.g. *"Twinkle, twinkle little star..."*) that is taught to and recited by very young children

rhyth•m /ˈrɪðəm/ noun, c. *The dancer danced to the rhythm of the tabla.* = a regular and repeated pattern of sounds (specially in music or poetry) **rhythmic** adj. *the rhythmic beating of the heart* = having rhythm

rib[1] /rɪb/ noun, c. **1** *He broke a rib when he fell from the motorcycle.* = one of the bones running around the chest of a human being or an animal **2** *an umbrella with steel ribs* = a curved piece of metal or wood that forms the frame of an umbrella or a boat

rib[2] verb, t. (**ribbed**) *The girl who always comes to school with her pet cat was ribbed by her fellow-students.* = to make fun of someone in a friendly way (informal) **rib cage** noun, c. = the arrangement of ribs in the body that surrounds and protects the lungs

rib•ald /ˈrɪbəld/ adj. *a ribald joke* = humorous in a crude manner and often related to sex (usually referring to a story or a joke)

rib•bon /ˈrɪbən/ noun, c. = a long, narrow piece of silk or some other material, used to tie up or decorate things or used in a typewriter to print out words on paper

ri•bo•fla•vin /raɪbəʊˈfleɪvɪn/ noun = the scientific name for vitamin B2 (a chemical substance that is important for health and is found in meat, milk etc.) [MEDICINE]

rice /raɪs/ noun, u. **1** = a plant belonging to the grass family, grown in wet and warm places, the seeds of which are eaten **2** = food made with rice

rich /rɪtʃ/ adj. **1** *a rich person* = having a lot of money, property etc. **2** *Soya beans are rich in protein.* = containing a lot of some substance (which is mentioned) **3** *The food is very rich.* = containing a lot of oil or spices **4** *rich soil* = land that is very good for growing crops **5** *a rich red* = colour that is deep and strong **6** *rich Chinese silk* = very expensive and lovely to look at **richness** noun, u. **richly** adv. **1** *a richly polished floor* = beautifully **2** *a richly embroidered sari* = containing a lot or plenty of something **3** *You richly deserve comfort in your old age.* = greatly **riches** noun, u. (plural only) *He likes to show off his riches to the whole world.* = wealth (old-fashioned)

rick•ets /ˈrɪkɪts/ noun = a disease that some children suffer from, caused by the lack of vitamin D, resulting in the bones becoming weak **rickety** adj. *a rickety old chair* = weak and likely to break

rick•shaw /ˈrɪkʃɔː/ noun, c. = a carriage with two or three wheels, drawn (pulled) or driven by a human being

ric•o•chet /ˈrɪkəʃeɪ/ verb, i. (**ricocheted**) *The ball hit the batsman's glove and ricocheted into the air.* = to change direction after hitting a surface (referring to a moving object)

rid /rɪd/ verb, t. *You won't find any mosquitoes here. We have managed to rid this place of mosquitoes.* = to make a place free of something harmful (e.g. rats, mosquitoes, cockroaches etc.) **riddance** noun, u. = the action of getting rid of something that is not wanted

to get rid of *I managed to get rid of my old radio. // It took me a long time to get rid of my cold.* = to make oneself free of something that is not wanted **Good riddance (to bad rubbish)** *We had a manager who kept everyone in this office in a state of terror for years. However, he has been dismissed this morning and all of us feel so relieved. Good riddance to bad rubbish!* = an expression of relief or happiness because an unpleasant situation caused by someone or something has ended

rid•dle[1] /ˈrɪdl/ noun, c. **1** *Can you answer this riddle: What is it that flies but has no wings?* = a difficult question which one tries to answer as part of a game **2** *The police are trying to solve the riddle of the murder.* = a mystery; something that people are not able to understand

riddle[2] verb, t. *The board which we had been using for target practice was riddled with bullets holes.* = to make many holes in something

ride[1] /raɪd/ verb, t. or i. (**rode**, **ridden**) **1** *Can you ride a horse?*(t.) = to travel while sitting on and controlling a horse, bicycle, motorcycle etc. **2** *Can you ride?*(i.) = sit on and control a horse **3** *We'll get very tired if we ride in a rickshaw all the way.* = travel in a vehicle which one is not driving

ride[2] noun, c. *I am going for a ride in the new car.* = a journey (often a short journey taken for pleasure) in a vehicle or or on a horse, motorcycle etc.

to take someone for a ride = to cheat or make a fool of someone (informal) **to ride up** *His shirt rides up everytime he raises his hands.* = to go up one's body in a way that is not wanted or intended (referring to clothing)

ridge /rɪdʒ/ noun, c. *a mountain ridge* = a long, narrow and raised part of a surface, specially the top of a line of mountains

rid•i•cule[1] /ˈrɪdɪkjuːl/ verb, t. *I wanted to go to Mumbai and become a film star, but my friends ridiculed the idea.* = to make fun of someone or something

ridicule[2] noun, u. *His writings were generally held up to ridicule by other writers.* = the act of making fun of someone or something **ridiculous** adj. **1** *The clothes you wore for the formal meeting were ridiculous.* = foolish and in bad taste **2** *He asked a ridiculous price for his old car.* = so high that it cannot be taken seriously (derogatory)

rife /raɪf/ adj. *A severe form of flu is rife in our town.* = spreading everywhere (referring to something bad or unpleasant) (literary or old-fashioned)

ri•fle[1] /ˈraɪfəl/ noun, c. = a kind of gun, the barrel (front part) of which has a curved groove (a hollow cut) inside it, so that a bullet fired from the gun is made to spin round and round

rifle[2] verb, t. *The thief rifled my safe and took away all the gold jewellery.* = to steal after searching through something

rift /rɪft/ noun, c. **1** *There is a rift in the rocks here.* = a crack **2** *There is a rift between the two friends.* = a misunderstanding which spoils a good relationship

rig[1] /rɪg/ noun, c. *an oil rig* = a large machine which is used for a particular purpose (e.g. drilling or making a deep hole in the ground to take out water or oil)

rig[2] verb, t. (**rigged**) *We put up our play on a crude stage which we had rigged up with a few planks.* = to put up something temporarily, using materials that are easily available

to rig an election/match = to organize an event dishonestly, so that the results favour one

right[1] /raɪt/ adj. **1** *the right hand* = the side/direction of the hand which is used more often by most people (opposite **left**) **2** *Take a right turn here.*= in the direction of the right hand **3** *You have given the right answer to this question.* = correct **4** *We have found the right person for this job.* = proper or most suitable **5** *I wish you wouldn't tell lies. It is not right.* = morally acceptable (opposite **wrong**)

right[2] noun, u. or c. **1** *Her house is to your right.*(u.) = the right side (indicated or shown by one's right hand) **2** (u.) = political parties which favour private ownership of business (often **Right**) (also **right wing**) (opposite **Left**) **3** *You should know the difference between right and wrong.* = what is good and morally acceptable **4** *You have a right to vote in the election.* = a claim which is fair and just

right[3] verb, t. **1** *The car turned over on its side after it hit a tree but we managed to right it.* = to bring back to a correct position **2** *right all the wrongs that have been done* = to correct something wrong (some unjust action)

right[4] adv. **1** *The ball hit me right on the nose.* = exactly **2** *Please turn right, not left.* = towards the right (direction) (opposite **left**) **3** *I do hope I played my part right.* = in the correct or acceptable way **4** *Let's do this right from the beginning.* = totally, completely **5** *Let's start right after lunch.* = soon, immediately **6** *Can't you see the bird? It's right in front of you.* = exactly

right[5] interjec. *'Anil, you should meet the minister soon.' 'Right!'* = an expression of agreement **right angle** noun = an angle which measures 90 degrees [GEOMETRY] (see pic under **triangles**) **righteous** adj. *a righteous person* = morally good **rightful** adj. *He has a rightful claim to this property.* = legally correct **rightfully** adv. *Someone has built a house on property which is rightfully ours.* = by law, by right **right-handed** adj. *a right-handed batsman* = a person who does most things with the right hand **right-hand man (person)** noun *He is the minister's right-hand man.* = a trusted and useful follower **rightly** adv. *You rightly refused to accept money from him.* = properly

right now = at this moment **to get something right** = to repair something or to solve a problem **to be in the right** = to have done what is correct and fair **in one's**

R

own right *You are an excellent singer in your own right, not because your mother is a well-known singer.* = by yourself, not because of others **to be on the right track** = to have the right idea about something **to be in one's right mind** = in a balanced mental state **to be on the right side of someone** = to enjoy someone's favour **right, left and centre** *They had put up posters right, left and centre.* = in all places, everywhere **right of way** = the right to drive or walk first through traffic

rig•id /ˈrɪdʒɪd/ adj. **1** *We need a rigid framework of bamboos in order to build a hut.* = stiff; not easily bent (opposite **flexible**) **2** *He is very rigid and won't accept any new ideas.* = fixed in one's thinking or behaviour **rigidity** noun, u. = the quality of being rigid

rig•ma•role /ˈrɪgmərəʊl/ noun, u. *The security guard at the entrance made me go through the rigmarole of writing my name and address, as well as the name of the person I wanted to meet and the purpose of my visit.* = a series of actions which stretch out and sometimes do not have a purpose (derogatory)

rig•or mor•tis /rɪgə ˈmɔːtɪs/ noun (French) = the stiffening of the body after death [MEDICINE]

rig•o•rous /ˈrɪgərəs/ adj. **1** *When you are doing scientific research, you have to be rigorous. You can't be careless.* = careful and exact **2** *rigorous hard work* = very difficult, hard and painful **3** *rigorous imprisonment* = severe (very strict) and painful **rigour** noun, u. **1** *Scientific research demands a lot of rigour.* = exactness or precision **2** *The judge treated the man with unusual rigour.* = severity or strictness **rigours** noun, u. (always plural) *He is not used to the rigours of the desert.* = difficult or severe conditions that cause suffering

rile /raɪl/ verb, t. *His habit of tapping on the desk riles me.* = to annoy (to make someone angry)

rim[1] /rɪm/ noun, u. *the rim of the cycle wheel* = the outside edge of a circular object

rim[2] verb, t. (**rimmed**) *The lake was rimmed with a row of cottages.* = to lie around the rim (edge) of something that is round in shape

rind /raɪnd/ noun, u. *the rind of a lemon* = the thick outer covering of some kinds of fruit

ring[1] /rɪŋ/ noun, c. **1** *a gold ring* = a circular piece of metal (usually gold or silver) that is worn on the finger **2** = a circular object made from different kinds of material, e.g. the inflatable rubber ring used in a swimming pool **3** *There is a ring of trees around the house.* = a circular line or mark **4** *a ring of thieves* = a group of dishonest people working together for their own advantage **5** *Could you give the bell a ring?* = the act of making a bell ring **6** *Did you hear that ring?* = the sound of a bell **7** *I am expecting a ring from my sister.* = a telephone call **8** *a key ring* = any object having the shape of a ring **9** *rings under one's eyes* = dark marks under the eyes which come from lack of sleep, illness etc.

ring[2] verb, t. or i. (**rang, rung**) **1** *Please ring the bell.*(t.) = to cause a bell to make a sound **2** *Did you ring the doctor?*(t.) = to call someone on the telephone **3** *The house is ringed with trees.*(t.) = to form a circular line around something **4** *The sound made my ears ring.*(i.) = to cause a painful feeling in one's ears **5** *We rang for some coffee.*(i.) = to use a buzzer or make a telephone call to ask for some service e.g. a cup of coffee in a hotel **ring finger** noun = the third finger on the left or right hand, on which a ring is usually worn **ring leader** noun = the leader of a group of criminals or dishonest people **ringmaster** noun, c. = a person who trains animals to perform tricks in a circus **ring road** noun = a road that goes around the edge of a city, in order to avoid the traffic inside the city **ringworm** noun = a kind of skin disease that causes red marks to appear on the skin

to ring a bell *What you said in your speech rang a bell.* = to be reminded of something **to ring hollow** *She didn't like me, so when she said good things about me, her words rang hollow.* = to sound untrue **to not ring true** *Her story didn't ring true.* = to not sound convincing **to ring someone back** = to telephone someone because one wasn't present to receive his/her call **to ring in one's ears** *Her words of farewell rang in my ears for a long time.* = to be remembered (referring to a sound one hears) (disapproving)

rink /rɪŋk/ noun, c. *a skating rink* = an area set apart for the sport of skating (either ice-skating or roller-skating)

rinse[1] /rɪns/ verb, t. **1** *You should rinse your mouth with water after every meal.* = to clean with water **2** *Rinse the clothes.* = to wash with water

rinse[2] noun, c. **1** *Give the clothes another rinse. They don't look very clean.* = the act of rinsing something **2** *She uses a herbal rinse for her face.* = a liquid used to clean the face or to colour hair

ri•ot[1] /ˈraɪət/ noun, c. **1** *Several people have been injured in the riot.* = violent behaviour by a crowd of people (derogatory) **2** *You will enjoy Govinda's new film. It is really a riot!* = a very entertaining or humorous performance (informal, not derogatory) **3** *The garden is full of flowers now. It is really a riot of colours.* = a very bright and colourful scene (not derogatory)

riot[2] verb, i. *Many people were rioting in the streets.* = to take part in a riot **riotous** adj. *a riotous crowd* = wild and uncontrolled

rip[1] /rɪp/ verb, t. (**ripped**) *He ripped the envelope open with a knife.* = to tear

rip[2] noun, c. *a rip in the sari* = a long split, tear or cut in some material

to rip somebody off *When my neighbours told me she had paid Rs 10,000 for an ordinary cotton sari, I realized she had been ripped off.* = to cheat a person (informal) **rip apart** = to criticise heavily (informal) **rip-off** *The holiday tour was a rip off!* = an act of cheating someone by charging too much money, offering bad service etc (informal) **rip-roaring** *We had a rip-roaring time at the party.* = exciting and highly enjoyable (informal)

RIP abbr. of the Latin words for "Rest in Peace" = words written on tombs (the stone platforms put up over the place where a dead person has been buried)

ripe /raɪp/ adj. **1** *The mangoes are ripe. You can eat them.* = fully grown and ready to be eaten (used for fruits and crops) **2** *The time is ripe to start a new school.* = suitable for something to happen **ripen** verb, i. *The mangoes have ripened.* = to become ripe **ripeness** noun, u.

rip•ple /ˈrɪpəl/ noun, c. **1** *If you throw a stone into the water you will cause ripples.* = a gentle wave moving through the water **2** *a ripple of laughter* = a continuous sound which becomes louder and then fades away (like a wave)

rise[1] /raɪz/ verb, i. (**rose, risen**) **1** *The level of water in the river has risen after the heavy rains.* = to become higher **2** *She rose from a junior position to become the Managing Director.* = to move from a lower to a higher position **3** *The members of the audience rose to their feet when the Prime Minister entered the hall.* = to stand up in order to show respect (formal) **4** *We can watch the sun rise.* = to appear in the sky **5** *She rises at six o'clock every morning.* = to get out of bed **6** *We watched the bubbles rise.* = to come to the surface

rise[2] noun, u. **1** *There is a noticeable rise in the level of the water.* = upward movement **2** *There is a rise in the cost of food.* = increase **3** *The rise of Japanese technology after 1950 has been rapid.* = the act of becoming more developed

to rise to the occasion = to show that one is able to handle problems, challenges etc. **to give rise to** *The new system gave rise to many complaints.* = to cause (formal) **rise up against / rise up in arms** = rebel, oppose **on the rise** *Malaria is on the rise in our city.* = of something unpleasant or harmful, increasing in force or numbers

risk[1] /rɪsk/ noun, u. or c. **1** *Don't drive so fast on this busy road. There is a risk of accidents.*(u.) = danger; the possibility of something bad happening **2** *He likes to take risks.*(c.) = an action that may lead to some bad result but is done in the hope that something good will happen

risk[2] verb, t. **1** *Our soldiers are risking their lives every day to protect us.* = to put oneself in a dangerous situation **2** *If you don't get your licence you risk getting caught.* = to face the chance of something bad happening **risky** adj. *Taking photographs of wild animals in the forest is a risky business.* = dangerous; involving a lot of risk

at one's own risk = to agree to take the responsibility in case something unpleasant happens **to risk one's neck** = to decide to do something very risky

ris•que /ˈrɪskeɪ/ adj. *risque humour* = connected with sex and slightly rude and shocking (referring to a joke or a story) (disapproving)

rite /raɪt/ noun, c. *funeral rites* = a religious ceremony or act

rit•u•al /ˈrɪtʃuəl/ noun, c. or u. = a set of fixed actions, especially of a religious nature, that are performed regularly **ritualism** noun, u. = obedience to rituals without questioning them (disapproving)

ri•val[1] /ˈraɪvəl/ noun, c. *I defeated my rival in the election by more than 10,000 votes.* = a person against whom one is competing

rival[2] verb, t. (**rivalled**) *Many countries will soon rival America as centres of information technology.* = to be equal to someone, especially in a competition **rivalry** noun, u. *There is great rivalry between motorbike companies to sell two-wheelers.* = competition

ri•ver /ˈrɪvəʳ/ noun, c. = a large stream of fresh water flowing into a lake, another wide stream, or the sea **river-basin** noun, c. = an area of land surrounding a river, from which all the water flows into the river **river-bed** noun, c. = the ground below the water of a river

ri•vet[1] /ˈrɪvɪt/ noun,c. = a metal pin which is used to fasten (hold together) flat pieces of metal or some other material

rivet[2] verb, t. (**rivetted**) **1** *These metal plates have been rivetted together.* = to fasten (hold together) with rivets **2** *While the rest of us talked and laughed, the child's attention was rivetted on the ant crawling across the floor.* = to attract and hold someone's attention **riveting** adj. *This television programme is riveting. You will feel compelled to watch it.* = highly interesting; holding one's attention

RNA abbr.of **ribonucleic acid** noun = an important chemical that is present in all living cells

road /rəʊd/ noun, c. or u. *The engineers are building a new road to connect the two towns.*(c.) = a wide track with a hard surface on which people can walk, vehicles can run etc. **road block** noun, c. = a barrier or temporary wall put across a road by the police to stop traffic **road hog** noun, c. = a person who drives either too fast or too slowly on the road, without thinking of the problems he/she may be causing for

R

other drivers **road-worthy** adj. *This old car is not road-worthy* = fit to be driven on a road

on the road *He is a salesperson, and has to travel a lot. He is always on the road.* = travelling in connection with one's work **by road** *It will take us about three hours by road.* = in a car, bus, van, scooter etc. **to get the show on the road** = to get something that was planned, moving or happening (informal) **to hit the road** (American) = to begin a journey (informal) **All roads lead to Rome** = One can follow different beliefs, plans etc. and yet arrive at the same conclusion or result

roam /rəʊm/ verb, i. *I like to spend my Sundays roaming across the countryside.* = to wander or move about aimlessly

roar[1] /rɔːʳ/ noun, c. *I heard the roar of a tiger.* = the deep, loud sound produced by a tiger or lion, or any other sound of the same kind

roar[2] verb, i. *The crowd roared with excitement as Tendulkar hit a 'six' to complete his century.* = to produce a deep, loud sound, like that of a roar

roast[1] /rəʊst/ verb, t. = to cook something directly over a fire or in an oven

roast[2] noun, u. or c. or adj. *chicken roast* (noun) *roast chicken* (adj.) = something (usually meat) which has been roasted **roasting** noun, u. **1** = the process by which something is roasted **2** *The Principal gave us a roasting for coming late.* = a severe scolding (expression of anger) (informal)

rob /rɒb/ verb, t. (**robbed**) *to rob a bank* = to take money or property away from someone by using force **robber** noun, c. = a person who robs **robbery** noun, u. = the crime of robbing

to rob someone of something *My illness robbed me of the chance to act in the play.* = to take away from a person something valuable or important that he or she should have had (literary, old-fashioned)

robe[1] /rəʊb/ noun, c. (often in plural form **robes**) *a judge's robes* = a long, loose garment, like an overcoat, worn for official or ceremonial occasions

robe[2] verb, i. *You must be robed if you want to argue a case in court.* = to be dressed in a robe

rob•in /ˈrɒbɪn/ noun = a small bird with a red chest, commonly seen in Europe

ro•bot /ˈrəʊbɒt/ noun, c. = a machine, usually controlled by a computer, that can move and work like a human being **robotics** /rəʊˈbɒtɪks/ noun = the study of the making and use of robots [TECHNICAL]

ro•bust /rəˈbʌst/ adj. *You must be robust if you want to climb mountains.* = strong and healthy

rock[1] /rɒk/ noun, u. or c. **1** *The river Ganga comes down from the mountains with great force, cutting its way through solid rock.*(u.) = hard stone which forms part of the earth's surface **2** *A huge rock fell down the mountain, crushing many cars on the road.*(c.) = a large piece of stone **3** *rock music* = a type of popular music which uses drums and guitars and has a loud and strong rhythm

rock[2] verb, t. or i. **1** *The mother rocked the baby to sleep.*(t.) = to cause someone or something to move backwards and forwards, or from side to side, with a regular movement **2** *The whole town was rocked by the earthquake.*(t.) = to shake violently **3** *Loud music rocks.*(i.) = a way of saying that something is very good and that ones enjoys it (slang) **rock and roll** noun, u. = a type of music with a strong beat and rhythm that was very popular in the 1950s **rock bottom** noun *The price of cotton has hit rock bottom.* = the lowest point **rock-garden** noun = a garden in which beauty is created mainly through the use of rocks of different size, colour etc. (very popular in Japan) **rock solid** adj. *The financial position of the company is rock solid.* = very stable and safe

on the rocks = with only ice, not water or soda, added to an alcoholic drink (informal) **to be on the rocks** = to be in danger of breaking up (referring usually to a marriage) **to rock the boat** = to disturb or spoil a situation which is calm or comfortable or going well

rock•et[1] /ˈrɒkɪt/ noun, c. = a cylindrical object which moves very fast by forcing out burning gases, and can be used as a weapon or for space travel

rocket[2] verb, i. *The price of vegetables has rocketed because of poor rains.* = to increase very sharply (informal)

rod /rɒd/ noun, c. *The walls of this building have a lining of steel rods.* = a long thin pole or stick of wood or metal

ro•dent /ˈrəʊdənt/ noun, c. *Rats, squirrels and rabbits belong to the family of rodents.* = a small animal with very sharp teeth [BIOLOGY]

rodent

roe /rəʊ/ noun, u. *fish roe* = the eggs inside the stomach of a female fish

roent•gen /ˈrɒntgən/ noun = a unit used to measure the strength of x- rays (see **x-ray**)

Roger /ˈrɒdʒəʳ/ noun *'Can you read me?' 'Roger!'* = an exclamation used in radio communication to show that a message has been understood

rogue[1] /rəʊg/ noun, c. = a very dishonest person (derogatory)

rogue[2] adj. *a rogue elephant* = a wild elephant that lives alone and not with a herd in the forest, and can easily become violent **rogue state** = a country that supports terrorism and can cause problems for other countries

role /rəʊl/ noun, c. **1** *Hrithik Roshan plays the role of a terrorist in this film.* = a part played by an actor in a film or drama **2** *Many unknown people played a role in India's struggle for freedom.* = a duty performed by a person in a particular situation **title role** = the leading or most important role in a film **role model** noun = a person whose behaviour is so good that it should be copied by others **role play** noun, u. *Let us do a role play. You can be a doctor and I will be your patient.*= the activity of trying to behave like someone else, in an imaginary situation (often used by teachers and trainers)

roll[1] /rəʊl/ verb, i. or t. **1** *The dog rolled on its back on the grass.*(i.) = to turn over or from side to side **2** *The ball rolled along the ground.*(i.) = to move by turning over,like a wheel **3** *He rolled up the carpet.* (t.) = to cause something to curl into a cylindrical (tube-like) shape **4** *The cricket pitch has to be rolled every morning.*(t.) = to make something flat by pressing it down with force, or using a roller **5** *roll out a chapati* (t.) = to press out with a rolling-pin and make flat **6** *Please ask the actors to be ready before the cameras start rolling.*(i.) = to begin operating (used for cameras) **7** *This pudding is ice-cream and cake rolled into one.*(i.) = a combination of two or more things (sometimes disapproving)

roll[2] noun, c. **1** *a roll of bread* = a small of piece of bread shaped like a rounded tube **2** *a roll of cloth* = a piece of flat material that has been rolled (curled up) into a tube **3** *the student roll* = an official list of names **4** *The plane went into a roll.* = a rolling (turning) movement from side to side **5** *a roll of thunder* = a deep continuous noise as of drums, thunder etc. **6** *rolls of flab around his waist* = layers or 'rings', one on top of the other, caused by too much fat in the body **roll-call** noun *All students must be present during the roll-call.* = the act of reading out the names from a list **roller** noun, c. *a steam-roller* = a heavy machine used to make the surface of the ground flat **roller skates** noun = a frame with four small wheels, fixed under a shoe, allowing the wearer to move quickly over a smooth surface **rolling mill** noun = a factory in which steel is rolled by machines into flat sheets or plates **rolling pin** noun, c. = a long, tube-shaped piece of wood, used for rolling dough (flour mixed with water) into bread (e.g. chappaties) **rolling stock** noun, u. = carriages on wheels that are used by a railway

to call the rolls = calling out a list (in a classroom, the army etc.) of persons to see who is present/absent **to roll up one's sleeves** = to start a fight with someone **to roll one's eyes** = to express irritation, boredom or great surprise **to roll out the red carpet** = to make special arrangements for a visitor who is important **to be rolling in money** = to have much more money than is considered necessary (informal, disapproving) **A rolling stone gathers no moss.** = A proverb meaning that a person who changes jobs often, cannot prosper.

ROM abbr. of **Read Only Memory** = a kind of computer memory which holds information that can be used but cannot be changed or added to [COMPUTERS]

Roman Catholic noun = a member of the Church of Rome, one of the divisions within the Christian religion, of which the Pope is the head

Roman numeral noun = a sign such as I, II, IV, V, X etc. used to show different numbers (see also **Arabic numeral**)

ro•mance /rəʊ'mæns/ noun, c. or u. **1** (c.) = a relationship between people who are in love but not married to one another **2** *The new film is full of romance.*(u.) = the feeling of love **3** *He is writing a new romance.* = a story of love and adventure **romantic** adj. or noun **1** *a romantic film*(adj.) = having to do with romance (love and adventure) **2** (noun) = a person who has ideas that are not very practical **romantically** adv.

Ro•man•ti•cis•m /rəʊ'mæntɪsɪzəm/ noun = the idea, commonly found in the literature of Europe in the 19th century, that imagination and feelings are more important than reason (the power of thinking)

romp[1] /rɒmp/ verb, i. *The children are romping about in the garden.* = to run about and play noisily (informal)

romp[2] noun, c. *The children are going for a romp in the garden.* = the activity of romping

romp•ers /'rɒmpərz/ noun (always plural) = a one-piece garment for babies that combines a shirt with trousers

roof[1] /ru:f/ noun, c. **1** *The house has a tile roof.* = the outside covering on top of a building or a vehicle **2** *the roof of a person's mouth* = the curved upper part of the inside of the mouth

roof[2] verb, t. *This building will be roofed next month.* = to put a roof on a building **roof garden** noun = a garden on the roof of a building

to go through the roof (or to hit the roof) 1 = to react very angrily to something (informal) **2** *The prices of property have gone through the roof.* = to rise very sharply (referring to the price of something) (informal)

rook /rʊk/ noun = a bird that looks like a **crow**

rook•ie /'rʊki/ noun, c. (American) *a rookie driver* =

R

someone who is new to a certain activity and has no experience of it

room[1] /ru:m/ noun, c. or u. **1** *This house has five rooms.*(c.) = a part of a house, with its own walls, doors, ceiling etc. which is normally used for a specific purpose **2** *There is a lot of room in the car.*(u.) = space **3** *There is room for improvement in your work.*(u.) = the need or possibility for something to be done

room[2] verb, i. *I am rooming with one of my friends.* = to share living space (informal) **room-mate** noun, c. = a person with whom one shares a room **room service** noun, u. = the system which allows one to have food served in one's room in a hotel **roomy** adj. *a roomy car* = having a lot of space **roomie** noun, c. = a person with whom one shares a room in a hostel etc. (slang)

to make room for something = to remove something and make the space available for something else **room for improvement** *Your singing is quite good, but there is room for improvement.* = a polite way of saying that something is not good enough **to take up a lot of room** = to cover space in such a way that it is difficult to place anything else there

roost[1] /ru:st/ verb, i. *Many birds roost on this tree at night.* = to sit and rest at night (referring to birds)

roost[2] noun, c. *a chicken roost* = a place where birds can sit and rest **rooster** noun, c. (American) = a cock (male bird)

root[1] /ru:t/ noun, c. (often in plural form **roots**) **1** *the roots of a tree* = the part of a tree or plant that generally lies under the soil, helps to keep the tree or plant in place and carries food and water from the soil to other parts **2** *The root of this tooth has become weak.* = the part of a tooth or hair that joins it to the body **3** *The root of 49 is seven.* = a number which when multiplied by itself gives the other number (also **square root**) [MATHEMATICS] **4** *The word "polygon" comes from the Latin root "poly".* = the part of a word from which other words can be formed **5** *the root of the trouble* = the origin (the thing from which something begins)

root[2] verb, t. **1** *These plants have rooted themselves strongly.* = to form roots in the ground (referring to plants or trees) **2** *The habit of showing respect to teachers is rooted in our culture.* = to be a part of something for a very long time (figurative) **rooted** adj. *Our superstitions are deep-rooted.* = firmly fixed in the mind and not easily given up **root vegetable** noun, c. = a vegetable such as a carrot, which is the root of a plant

to take root = to become firm and accepted (referring usually to a new idea, belief etc.) **to root out something** = get rid of a problem by removing its source

rope /rəʊp/ noun, u. or c. *The cow was being led by a rope.*(u.) = a thick or stout cord made by winding together threads of cotton or some other material e.g. nylon or steel **rope ladder** noun = a light ladder made out of two long ropes, joined together by pieces of wood

to be roped into something = to be persuaded to join some activity against one's will (informal) **rope off** = to use ropes to separate an area so that only some people can enter it **to know the ropes** = to have deep knowledge of the rules or customs which are used to run an organisation (informal) **to give someone enough rope to hang themselves** = to give someone a lot of freedom, knowing that he/she will do something foolish

rose /rəʊz/ noun **1** = a kind of flower often grown in gardens which is known for its sweet smell **2** = a soft pink colour **rose-water** noun = a sweet-smelling liquid made from the petals of roses **rosewood** noun = a kind of wood found in the tropics which has a dark red colour **rosy** adj. **1** *rosy lips* = having a healthy pink colour **2** *When we started the new job conditions were not rosy.* = easy and comfortable (figurative)

to not be a bed of roses = used about something one is doing or a situation one is in) to be difficult and painful and not easy

ros•ter /ˈrɒstəʳ/ noun, c. *a duty roster* = a list of names of people, showing the duties they are expected to perform

ros•trum /ˈrɒstrəm/ noun, c. (**rostrums** or **rostra**) = a platform on which a speaker stands while speaking

rot[1] /rɒt/ verb, i. (**rotted**) *These apples have begun to rot. We can't eat them.* = to go bad

rot[2] noun, u. **1** *These fruits have been affected by rot.* = the process of rotting (going bad) **2** *The film was such a lot of rot!* = silly and mindless (informal, derogatory) **rotten** adj. *rotten eggs* = (something which has) gone bad **rotter** noun, c. = a bad person (informal, derogatory)

rot setting in *This was once a good hote,. before the rot set in.* = (of something once considered good), the stage of going wrong or bad **to stop the rot** = to stop the worsening of a situation which has started to go wrong

ro•tate /rəʊˈteɪt/ verb, i. or t. **1** *The earth rotates once in 24 hours.*(i.) = to turn round a fixed point or line, like a wheel **2** *We have decided to rotate the headship of the department.*(t.) = to allow the persons in a group to take turns at doing something **rotary** /ˈrəʊtəri/ adj. *a rotary pump.* = having a part that goes round and round **Rotary Club** noun = an international organization which tries to serve society in different ways **rotation** noun, u. **1** = movement around a fixed point **2** *The post will be held in rotation.* = by turns

rote /rəʊt/ noun, u. *He learnt the answers to all the*

questions by rote. = the use of memory, rather than one's power of thinking, to learn something

ro•tund /rəʊ'tʌnd/ adj. *a rotund person* = fat and round (humorous) **rotundity** noun, u. = the quality of being rotund

rou•ble /'ru:bəl/ noun = the unit of money used in Russia

rouge /ru:ʒ/ noun, u. = a red substance used for colouring the cheeks, to make the face look more healthy

rough[1] /rʌf/ adj. **1** *Sandpaper has a rough surface.* = not smooth **2** *The sea is rough.* = stormy; not calm **3** *a rough person* = lacking good manners and likely to become violent **4** *He led a rough life in the city.* = not comfortable and full of problems (informal) **5** *I don't know exactly how many people live here, but I have a rough idea.* = not exact; approximate **6** *You should make a rough copy of your essay before you write the final version.* = done without too much care and meant to be improved upon later

rough[2] verb, t. *The students were roughed up by the police.* = to be treated with violence **roughness** noun, u. **roughly** adv. **rough-and-tumble** noun *the rough-and-tumble of children's play* = activity that is full of noise and energy **rough diamond (a diamond in the rough)** noun *You may not be impressed with his appearance, but he is a rough diamond.* = a person who looks rough on the outside but has many good qualities **roughhouse** noun *He got into a roughhouse and was slightly injured.* = a fight without weapons

to rough it out = to live in a manner which is not comfortable **to take the rough with the smooth** = to accept difficult situations with easy ones **to be rough on someone 1** *The journey was very rough on the children.* = causing great discomfort, tiredness etc. **2** *I wish you wouldn't be so rough on me. I am trying to help.* = unpleasant and harsh **to ride roughshod over someone** = to be harsh and unkind **rough and ready** = of something which is being prepared, good enough to be accepted, though not perfect

rough•age /'rʌfɪdʒ/ noun, u. = thread-like substances present in food which help the bowels get rid of waste matter more easily

round[1] /raʊnd/ adj. **1** *His watch has a round face.* = shaped like a circle **2** *a round head* = shaped like a ball **3** *a round figure* = a number to the nearest 10,000 or 1,000

round[2] prep. **1** *We gathered round the teacher.* = on all sides of **2** *The earth moves round the sun.* = in a circular path in relation to an object in the centre

round[3] adv. *Let me show you round the building.* = into all parts of

round[4] noun, c. **1** *The two leaders had a round of talks.* = one event in a series of events **2** (always plural) *The doctor is going on her rounds.* = a regular journey made as part of one's duty **3** *The Indian players were defeated in the first round of the tournament.* = a stage in a sports tournament **4** *The police fired three rounds at the thieves who were trying to escape in their car.* = a single shot fired from a gun **5** *a round of cheese* = a soft substance made into a ball-like shape

round[5] verb, t. **1** *Round your lips!* = to give a round shape to something **2** *The bus rounded the corner at great speed.* = to go round a curve at a corner **roundabout** noun, c. or adj. **1** (noun) = a circular area at a place where several roads meet, round which the traffic is supposed to move **2** *I heard of the incident in a roundabout way.*(adj.) = not directly **roundness** noun, u. **round-robin** adj. *India, Sri Lanka and New Zealand are taking part in a round-robin tournament.* = a tournament in which each team has to play against each of the other teams **round-the-clock** adj. or adv. *You can get round-the-clock service at this fast-food restaurant.*(adj.) = at all times of the day and night **round trip** noun, c. *I am taking a round trip to Singapore.* = a journey to a place and back again

round up *The police rounded up the gang of thieves.* = to bring to one place people or animals (especially cows and sheep) things which are spread out or scattered **to round off** *We rounded off the party with a song.* = to conclude or bring a pleasant event to an end (informal) **the wrong/other way round** = facing in the wrong direction; starting at the end instead of at the beginning

round•ly /'raʊndlɪ/ adv. **1** *Our team was roundly defeated.* = completely, thoroughly **2** *We were scolded roundly for making a noise.* = strongly

rouse /raʊz/ verb, t. **1** *The noise roused him from his sleep.* = to wake up **2** *He made an angry speech which roused his audience into action.* = to make someone active or excited **rousing** adj. *She made a rousing speech.* = something that makes people excited

rout[1] /raʊt/ verb, t. *India routed Zimbabwe by an innings and 200 runs.* = to defeat completely

rout[2] noun, u. or c. *the rout of the other team*(u.) = complete defeat

route[1] /ru:t/ noun, c. *Vasco da Gama reached India by a sea route.* = path; a line of travel from one place to another

route[2] verb, t. *We will have to route the package through Assam.* = to send by a particular route

rou•tine[1] /ru:'ti:n/ noun, c. *The school will follow a new routine, starting next week.* = a regular or fixed

R

way of doing things; a time-table showing when different lessons are taught in a school

routine[2] adj. *The police will check your bags. This is just a routine check, so please don't be alarmed.* = something that is done regularly or always; nothing special

rove /rəʊv/ verb, i. *He spent many years roving through the forests of Africa.* = to wander about **rover** noun, c. = a wanderer (literary)

to have a roving eye = to have a weakness for other women, besides one's wife (disapproving)

row[1] /raʊ/ noun, c. **1** *He is sitting in the second row.* = a line of people or things **2** *He got into a row with a fellow-passenger on the bus.* = an angry, noisy quarrel

row[2] verb, t. *He rowed the boat slowly up the river.* = to move a boat through the water with the help of **oars**

row•dy /'raʊdi/ adj. *rowdy people* = noisy and rough **rowdyism** noun, u. *Rowdyism at football matches has become quite common. The police has to be ready to deal with it.* = noisy and violent behaviour

ro•yal /'rɔɪəl/ adj. *the royal family* = connected with a king or queen **royalty** noun, u. or c. **1** (u.) = people belonging to the royal family **2** (c.) = a share of the money earned by the publisher of a book through sales, which is paid to the writer each year

rpm = abbr. of **revolutions per minute** (a unit for measuring the speed at which an engine is working)

RSVP = abbr. of **repondez sil vous plait** (French) = reply if you please (a request to reply to a printed invitation)

rub[1] /rʌb/ verb, t. or i. (**rubbed**) **1** *She rubbed the blackboard with a piece of cloth in order to clean it.*(t.) = to press something against a surface and to move it backwards and forwards repeatedly **2** *Please rub some pain balm into my knee.*(t.) = to apply a substance to something with the purpose of making it seep through the surface **3** *The sandals I am wearing are tight and are rubbing.*(i.) = causing soreness by moving against the skin

rub[2] noun, u. **1** *He gave the table a good rub with a piece of cloth.* = the act of rubbing something **2** *He wants to become an actor, but no one will help him with a role. There's the rub!* = the cause of some difficulty or problem (literary)

to rub salt into a wound = to make a person who is feeling bad, feel even worse **to rub shoulders with** = to be on familiar terms with people who are famous **rub in** *I know I shouldn't have forgotten you, but don't rub in the fact that I should have remembered.* = to say something again and again in order to hurt **rub off** *Your habit of singing in the bathroom has rubbed off on her.* = to be passed on to another person because of close or constant contact **to rub someone up the wrong way** = to cause someone to feel annoyed as a result of one's careless way of dealing with them

rub•ber /'rʌbəʳ/ noun, u. or c. **1** *Car tyres are made of rubber.*(u.) = a solid substance made from the sap (juice) of the rubber tree, used for making tyres etc. **2** (c.) = a piece of rubber used to remove pencil marks from paper (also **eraser**) **3** *Let us play a rubber of bridge.*(c.) = a competition in games such as cricket or bridge **4** = condom (American, slang) **rubber band** noun, c. = a thin piece of rubber shaped like a circle **rubbery** adj.

rub•bish[1] /'rʌbɪʃ/ noun, u. **1** *Don't throw rubbish on the streets.* = waste material from the house **2** *You are talking rubbish!* = nonsense

rubbish[2] verb, t. *She rubbished all my ideas.*= to dismiss something as being of no impotance or value

rub•ble /'rʌbəl/ noun, u. *The earthquake reduced the building to rubble.* = broken pieces from a building that has been damaged

ru•by /'ru:bi/ noun, c. (**rubies**) = a precious stone which is deep red or pink in colour

ruck•sack /'rʌksæk/ noun, c. = a bag for carrying clothes etc. which is fixed to a light metal frame and fastened (tied) round the shoulders, used by travellers

ruck•us /'rʌkəs/ noun, u. *I don't want you to get into a ruckus with those people.* = a noisy argument (informal)

rud•der /'rʌdəʳ/ noun, c. = a metal or wooden blade fixed to the rear (back part) of a boat, ship or aircraft, which can move to the left or the right and control the direction in which the boat, ship or aircraft is moving

rude /ru:d/ adj. **1** *It was rude of you to leave the meeting without excusing yourself.* = not polite **2** *He had a rude shock when he was told that he had missed the last train.* = unpleasant and sudden **3** *a rude house* = crude (built in a simple and rough way)

ru•di•men•ta•ry /ru:dɪ'mentəri/ adj. *He does not have even a rudimentary knowledge of cricket.* = concerned with the first or the simplest facts (formal)

rudiments /'ru:dɪmənts/ noun, u. (always plural) *You don't know anything about geography. I will have to teach you the rudiments of the subject.* = the simplest facts, which must be learnt first

rue /ru:/ verb, t. *You were foolish to leave college in a hurry. You may rue the day you did that.* = to be sorry for something that one has done (formal, literary) **rueful** adj. *She had a rueful expression on her face after I told her she had made a mistake.* = showing that one is sorry for something (humourous)

ruf•fian /'rʌfiən/ noun, c. *He was beaten up by a gang of ruffians.* = a rough and violent person (informal)

ruf•fle /'rʌfəl/ verb, t. **1** *The wind ruffled the calm* *waters of the lake.* = to cause something to become uneven **2** *The actor was ruffled when someone in the audience started shouting at him.* = to be upset or disturbed

rug /rʌg/ noun, c. = a small carpet or blanket, usually made of wool

rug•by /ˈrʌgbi/ noun = a game somewhat like football, which is played with an egg-shaped ball and in which 13 or 15 players are allowed to carry the ball in their hands as well as kick it with their feet

rug•ged /ˈrʌgɪd/ adj. **1** *rugged mountains* = rough and uneven in surface **2** *He has a rugged body.* = strongly built (used about men) **3** *the rugged outdoors* = conditions requiring strength and good health

ruin[1] /ˈruːɪn/ noun, c. or u. **1** *The old palace is now a ruin.*(c.) = the remains of a building that has fallen down or been destroyed **2** *The company has lost a lot of money and is facing ruin.*(u.) = total loss or destruction

ruin[2] verb, t. **1** *The old palace was ruined in the fire.* = to be damaged or destroyed (referring to a building) **2** *He was ruined by the medical expenses for his operation.* = to be made poor **ruinous** adj. *ruinous floods* = leading to complete loss

rule[1] /ruːl/ noun, c. **1** *You must follow the library rules.* = an official principle which guides behaviour **2** *We are learning about Akbar's rule.* = the period during which someone (usually a king) is ruling

rule[2] verb, t. **1** *The judge ruled that the police must produce all their witnesses in the case.* = to give an official decision or to lay down a rule **2** *Akbar ruled (over) India in the sixteenth century.* = to be in control of a country **3** *You will have to rule this paper, or the child will not be able to write on it.* = to draw lines on paper **ruler** noun, c. **1** = a person who rules over a country **2** = a flat and narrow piece of wood or plastic, with a straight edge, which is used to draw lines on paper **ruling** adj. or noun **1** *the ruling party*(adj.) = with the power to govern **2** *The Speaker has given her ruling.*(noun) = an official decision **rule of thumb** noun = a simple rule based on common-sense

to rule out = to not consider possible

rum /rʌm/ noun = an alcoholic drink distilled from sugarcane juice

rum•ba /ˈrʌmbə/ noun = a kind of popular dance that started in Cuba

rum•ble[1] /ˈrʌmbəl/ verb, i. *The train rumbled across the bridge.* = to produce a loud, deep sound while moving

rumble[2] noun, u. *We heard the rumble of thunder.* = a loud, deep sound

ruminant /ˈruːmɪnənt/ noun, c. *Sheep and goats are ruminants.* = an animal that chews the cud (brings back food that has already been eaten from the stomach into the mouth and chews it a second time) [BIOLOGY]

ru•mi•nate /ˈruːmɪneɪt/ verb, i. **1** = to chew the cud (see also **ruminant**) **2** *She has been ruminating over the things that she wants to say at the meeting.* = to think carefully and repeatedly about something **rumination** noun

rum•mage /ˈrʌmɪdʒ/ verb, t. *He rummaged through the papers on the desk, trying to look for the letter he had received that morning.* = to search for something by moving things around, causing disorder

rum•my /ˈrʌmi/ noun = a kind of card game

ru•mour /ˈruːməʳ/ noun, u. or c. *When I heard that my colleague had resigned, I called him up on the telephone. But he told me the rumour was false.* = a piece of news or information, usually false, which spreads from one person to another **rumoured** verb, t. or adj. **1** *It is rumoured that war has broken out in Iraq.*(verb) = to be talked about as a rumour **2** *The rumoured war never took place.*(adj.) **rumour monger** noun, c. = a person who spreads rumour

rump /rʌmp/ noun, c. = the buttocks (the part of the body of an animal above the hind legs)

rum•ple /ˈrʌmpəl/ verb, t. *My father rumpled my hair with affection.* = to disarrange and make something untidy **rumpled** adj.

rum•pus /ˈrʌmpəs/ noun, u. *He created a rumpus when I told him he was not going to be included in the team.* = noisy argument (informal)

run[1] /rʌn/ verb, i. (**ran**, **run**) **1** *He ran down the hill.* = to move quickly on foot **2** *The Rajdhani Express runs at 120 kilometres an hour.* = to move **3** *This bus runs between the station and the university.* = to travel from one place to another **4** *The tears ran down his cheeks.* = to flow (referring to a liquid) **5** *The child's nose is running. Does she have a cold?* = to flow out in liquid form **6** *She runs this company.* = to control or be in charge of **7** *Do you know how to run this machine?* = to operate something, especially a machine **8** *The machines are running now.* = to be in operation **9** *This engine runs on kerosene.* = to operate a machine with the help of **10** *This highway runs from Mumbai to Pune.* = to continue in a certain direction **11** *The newspaper ran a story about the summit meeting in Agra.* = to publish in a newspaper **12** *The colour of his kurta ran and stained his trousers.* = of the colour (dye) of cloth to spread on to other garments or come off when wet **13** *The film ran for weeks in Jalandhar.* = to be shown to the public

run[2] noun, c. **1** *Let us go for a run.* = an act of running **2** *We took the car for a short run.* = a short journey

R

3 *India lost the match by six runs.* = a point scored in cricket or baseball, when two batsmen run from one end of the pitch to the other (cricket) or around the four bases (baseball) **4** *The film had a long run of fifty weeks.* = period of being performed or shown

run-of-the-mill *a run-of-the mill story* = very ordinary; not special in any way (derogatory) **to run someone down** = to speak against someone **to run one's eyes over something** *Could you run your eyes over the report?* = to look at something (e.g. a report) quickly (informal) **to run short/out of something** *At the dinner, I was expecting only four people and eight came, so we ran short of rice.* = to reach a point where something that is needed (e.g. money, oil) gets finished or used up **to run over** **1** = to flow out after boiling or being filled completely **2** = (used of a car, bus etc.) to cause a person to fall and go over his/her body **to be on the run** = to be trying to escape from the police **to run across/into someone** = to meet someone by chance **to run after** = to chase someone in order to catch them or meet them **to run into something** In the middle of the project, we ran into the problem of money. = to meet with a problem **to run through** **1** *run through a report* = to discuss a set of points quickly or rehearse a play, watch a film (when it is in preparation) very quickly **2** *We didn't realise you would run through the money so soon.* = to spend the money one has (disapproving, informal) **in the long run** *Our moving house seemed such a bad idea but, in the long run, it turned out to be worthwhile.* = in the longer period of time; in the end

runn•ing[1] /'rʌnɪŋ/ noun, u. = the action of running

running[2] adj. **1** *What are the running costs of this machine?* = the day-to-day cost of keeping something in order and working **2** *running water* = water that one gets when a tap is opened (a constant supply) **3** *There is a running battle between brother and sister for the use of the computer.* = continuous, non-stop

running[3] adv. *I missed the train three times running.* = in a continous sequence without a break

run•a•way /'rʌnə'weɪ/ adj. *a runaway horse* = out of control

runn•er•up /'rʌnərʌp/ noun, c. (runners-up) = the person or team that comes second in a competition

rung /rʌŋ/ noun, c. *the rungs of a ladder* = the short pieces of wood etc. that one can put one's feet on while climbing a ladder

run•way /'rʌnweɪ/ noun = a person-made surface on which aircraft land and take off

ru•pee /ru:'pi:/ noun = the unit of money used in India, Sri Lanka, Nepal and Pakistan

rup•ture[1] /'rʌptʃəʳ/ verb, t. *to rupture a blood vessel* = to cause something to burst

rupture[2] noun, c. **1** *There is a rupture in the pipeline. The water is leaking out.* = a burst (a place where something has come apart) **2** *There has been a rupture in the relationship between the two countries.* = a break-down in a relationship

ru•ral /'rʊərəl/ adj. *rural development* = having to do with a village (compare **urban**)

ruse /ru:z/ noun, c. *He pretended to be asleep as a ruse to escape doing his homework.* = a trick by which one deceives (cheats) someone (sometimes mildly derogatory)

rush[1] /rʌʃ/ verb, i. **1** *She rushed up the stairs as the meeting was about to begin.* = to move with great speed **2** *You can take your time to get dressed for the meeting. I don't want to rush you.* = to force someone to do something quickly

rush[2] noun, u. or c. **1** *There was a rush of people as the cinema opened.* = sudden and quick movement **2** *You can take your time. There is no rush.* = hurry (need to do things quickly) **3** *There is a lot of rush on the streets when the offices are closing.* = activity **4** = a kind of grass that grows near the water **rush hour** noun = the time of the day when the traffic on the streets is greatest

rust[1] /rʌst/ noun, u. *The iron pipe which was lying in the open is covered with rust.* = the orange-brown substance (an oxide of iron) that forms on the surface of iron, because of the effect of water and oxygen present in the air

rust[2] verb, i. *Iron rusts, but aluminium does not.* = to allow rust to form **rusty** adj. **1** = with rust formed on it **2** *I learnt Urdu when I was young, but my Urdu is rusty now.* = not capable of being used fluently (referring to a skill that one has not practised for a long time) **rust-proof** adj. *Stainless steel is rust-proof.* = which cannot rust

rus•tic /'rʌstɪk/ adj. **1** *a rustic manner* = crude and lacking in refinement, because of its connection with a village (derogatory, not respectful) (compare **urban, rural**) **2** *This village has a certain rustic charm.* = simple and unspoilt, because of its connection with a village (not derogatory)

rus•tic•ate /'rʌstɪkeɪt/ verb, t. *The Principal has decided to rusticate the student who was found dodging college.* = to send a student out of a school, college or university as a punishment [TECHNICAL]

rust•le /'rʌsəl/ verb, i. or t. *The wind caused the leaves to rustle.*(i.) = to make a soft sound, caused by gentle movement

rustle up *Can you rustle up a meal?* = to do something quickly and without careful planning or planning ahead (informal)

rut[1] /rʌt/ noun, c. **1** *The constant movement of carts has formed ruts on this road.* = a narrow and somewhat deep track left on a surface by the movement of a wheel **2** = the state of sexual excitement in animals during the mating season [TECHNICAL]

rut[2] verb, t. or i. *The movement of bullock carts has rutted this road.*= to cause ruts to form

to be in a rut = to be in a difficult situation one cannot get out of easily

ruth•less /'ru:θləs/ adj. *a ruthless leader* = having no mercy or pity; very hard and cruel

rye /raɪ/ noun, u. = a kind of foodgrain used for making bread or whisky (a strong alcoholic drink), grown in cold countries

R

sS

s, S /es/ the nineteenth letter of the English alphabet

's poss. pron., singular form **1** *Yusuf's son // Anita's bag* = of or belonging to **2** *He is going to the barber's.* = a shop or house belonging to someone

s' poss. pron., plural form *a girls' hostel* = for or belonging to

Sab•bath /'sæbəθ/ noun = the day of the week which is treated as a day of rest and worship (Sunday, for some Christians or Saturday for others) **sabbatical** /sə'bætɪkəl/ noun = a period of leave with full pay given to university teachers, usually once in seven years

sab•o•tage[1] /'sæbətɑːʒ/ noun, u. *A bridge has been blown up in the war zone. This is the third case of sabotage this month.* = damage caused by an enemy during a war or by dissatisfied people

sabotage[2] verb, t. *If the holiday is cancelled tomorrow, it will sabotage our plans for a picnic.* = to prevent something from happening or to spoil a plan

sa•bre /'seɪbə^r/ noun, c. = a heavy sword with a curved blade

sac /sæk/ noun, c. *The honey-bee carries honey in a sac. // the snake's poison sac* = a bag-like part inside the body of an animal or plant which produces or stores some kind of liquid

sac•cha•rin /'sækərɪn/ noun = a kind of chemical with a sweet taste that is used by some people in place of sugar

sach•et /'sæʃeɪ/ noun, c. = a very small bag, generally made of paper or plastic, containing a small quantity of some liquid or powder

sack[1] /sæk/ noun, c. = a large, strong bag made of jute, paper, plastic etc.used for storing food-grains, charcoal, potatoes etc.

sack[2] verb, t. **1** *I hope we won't be sacked for being absent.* = to dismiss from a job (informal) **2** *Delhi was sacked in the 14th century.* = to rob and destroy a city, using military force (in former times)

to be given the sack (**to get the sack**) = to be dismissed from a job (informal) **to hit the sack** = to go to bed (informal)

sac•ra•ment /'sækrəmənt/ noun, c. *A marriage is a sacrament in many societies.* = a religious ceremony which has spiritual value

sa•cred /'seɪkrɪd/ adj. *All places of worship are sacred.* = having religious importance or value; holy

sac•ri•fice[1] /'sækrɪfaɪs/ verb, t. **1** *Animals have been sacrificed as offerings to God from ancient times.* = to make an offering to God or to some divine being, often of an animal which is killed in a religious ceremony **2** *Many Indians sacrificed their lives during the freedom movement.* = to give up something of value for a cause

sacrifice[2] noun, c. or u. **1** (u.) = an offering made to God or some divine being **2** *Parents make many sacrifices in order to educate their children.*(c.) = something of value which is given up in order to help others

sac•ri•lege /'sækrɪlɪdʒ/ noun, c. or u. = the act of not showing respect to a holy place or object

sac•ro•sanct /'sækrəsæŋkt/ adj. *Most people consider holy books sacrosanct.* = of such importance or value that it cannot be criticised or changed

sad /sæd/ adj. **1** *I was sad to learn of your wife's illness.* = unhappy **2** *The sad news of India's defeat made us miserable.* = causing unhappiness **sadden** verb, t. *We were saddened by the news of the violence in our state.* = to cause someone to become unhappy **sadly** adv. **1** *She waved goodbye sadly to her child, who was going off to a boarding school.* = unhappily **2** *Sadly, there are no buses running today.* = unfortunately

sad•dle[1] /'sædl/ noun, c. **1** = a seat, usually made of leather, which is tied to the back of a horse and on which the rider sits **2** = the rider's seat on a bicycle or motor-cycle

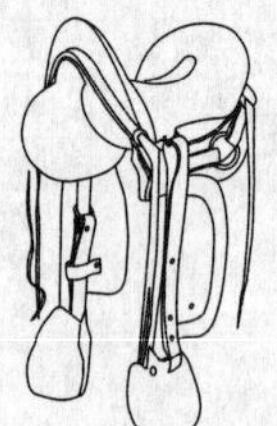

saddle

saddle[2] verb, t. **1** *He will saddle the horse for you.* = to put a saddle on the back of a horse **2** *How can you saddle me with work that everyone else refuses to do?* = to make someone carry a difficult or unpleasant responsibility; to burden someone with something

to be in the saddle = to be in control

sa•dis•m /'seɪdɪzəm/ noun = the practice of getting pleasure by causing pain to others **sadist** noun, c. = a person who gets pleasure by causing pain to others (opposite **masochist**)

sa•fa•ri /sə'fɑːri/ noun, u. or c. = a trip through a jungle, to hunt or photograph wild animals, specially in East Africa **safari park** noun, c. = a large area in which wild animals are allowed to move about freely and can be viewed by visitors from cars and buses **safari suit** noun, c. = an outfit consisting of a loose shirt-like, light weight jacket with two or four pockets in front, and matching trousers

safe[1] /seɪf/ adj. **1** *It is safe to swim here as the water is only three feet deep.* = free from danger or the chance of physical injury **2** *This doctor will cure you.You are in safe hands.* = which can be trusted **3** *Putting your money in a bank is a safe investment.* = free from risk **4** *a safe choice* = with little chance of one's making a mistake

safe[2] noun, c. *I keep my money in a steel safe.* = a cupboard or box made of strong, thick steel in which money or other things of value can be kept, protected from thieves **safely** adv. *We reached home safely although we set out in stormy weather.* = without any problem

to be on the safe side *When you are travelling with a baby, it is better to be on the safe side and take extra clothes.* = to take extra precautions **to be safe and sound** *The bus met with an accident, but the passengers are safe and sound.* = free from danger, well-protected (informal) **better safe than sorry** *I could have overtaken the bus, but I decided not to: better safe than sorry.* = 'It is better to be overcareful than to risk an accident, illness or failure.' **a safe bet** *If you want a moderately priced holiday with mountain-climbing and lots of fine weather, then the Nilgiris is a safe bet!* = something that one can be sure of (informal)

safeguard[1] /'seɪfgɑːd/ noun, c. *It is better to use a backup computer disk as a safeguard against mishaps.* = something that protects one from being harmed

safeguard[2] verb, t. *Vaccination against hepatitis safeguards people from getting the disease.* = to protect someone or something **safe-keeping** noun, u. *They have put all their gold ornaments in the bank for safe-keeping.* = the action of protecting something from loss or harm

safety /'seɪftɪ/ noun, u. *There is perfect safety in this house. No one can enter it as it is well guarded.* = freedom from danger or harm **safety belt** noun, c. *Wearing a safety belt can save your life in an accident.* = a strap attached to a seat in a car or a plane which holds you in place and protects you from injury in case of an accident (also **seat belt**) **safety pin** noun, c. = a bent metal pin for fastening things together that has a cover at one end so that the point cannot slip (see pic under **pin**) **safety razor** noun, c. = a razor (instrument used for removing hair from the face or body) with a blade which is covered, to prevent cutting the skin deeply **safety valve** noun, c. = a part of a machine which allows air or gas to escape when the pressure becomes too great, so that there is no danger of the machine exploding **safety in numbers** *The campers realised they were in unknown territory and that there was safety in numbers, so they kept together.* = expressing the belief that there is better protection if you are in a large group

saf•fron[1] /'sæfrən/ noun, u. = a spice (substance used to add taste to food) made from a kind of flower that has a deep orange colour and grows mainly in Kashmir and Spain

saffron[2] adj. = having the deep orange colour of saffron **saffron robes** noun (always plural) = clothes of a saffron colour, often worn by Buddhist/ Hindu monks

sag /sæg/ verb, i. (**sagged**) **1** *When people are young, their muscles are tight, but in old age their muscles begin to sag.* = to become loose and to come down to a lower position **2** *Over 10,000 motor-cycles were sold last month but the demand for cars is sagging. We have sold only 2,000 this month.* = to come down in number **3** *It is an interesting film, but it sags in the middle.* = to become uninteresting for a time (referring to a book, film etc.) (figurative)

sa•ga /'sɑːgə/ noun, u. *The new novel by Vinod Seth is a saga of three generations of Indians living in South Africa.* = a long heroic story about a particular place or group of people

sa•ga•cious /sə'geɪʃəs/ adj. *My grandfather's sagacious decision to sell the barren land solved a difficult problem.* = shrewd, with practical wisdom and good judgement (formal) **sagacity** noun, u. = wisdom; good judgement and understanding

sage[1] /seɪdʒ/ noun, c. or u. **1** *People came to the learned sage for advice.*(c.) = a wise old person **2** (u.) = a herb used in cooking

sage[2] adj. *The teacher has given you sage advice. You should follow it.* = wise (formal)

Sa•git•tar•i•us /sædʒɪ'teəriəs/ noun = one of the signs of the zodiac, represented by a creature that is half a horse and half a man with a bow and arrow (see pic under **zodiac**)

sa•go /'seɪgəʊ/ noun = a white powder produced from the trunk of a kind of palm tree that is used in puddings and as a thickener in sauces

sail[1] /seɪl/ verb, i. or t. *We sailed across the Atlantic Ocean on a cargo ship.*(i.) = to travel across a body of water in a boat or ship

sail[2] noun, c. **1** *The ships that carried people from England to India in the 18th century were driven by sails.* = a large piece of canvas (thick,strong cloth) or nylon fixed to a ship, which helps to drive it through the water by using the force of the wind **2** *We are going for a sail on the river in the new boat.* = a short journey in a boat, taken for pleasure

to set sail = to begin a journey by boat or ship **to sail through something** *Some of us found the exam hard,*

S

but Navin and Shaila sailed through it. = to do something (e.g. a test) which others find difficult, easily

sail•or /ˈseɪləʳ/ noun, c. = a person who works on a ship

saint /seɪnt/ noun, c. = a very good or holy person who is deeply respected **saintly** adj. *a saintly person* = very good and holy, like a saint

sake[1] /seɪk/ noun, u. **1** *I don't like going to the market, but I will go for your sake.* = in order to help someone **2** *For God's sake, will you stop making that noise?* = in the name of (used when telling or asking someone strongly to do something; an exclamation of annoyance)

Usage 'For God's sake!' is often used to express irritation (mild anger) but is considered offensive by some people. 'For goodness sake!' is more acceptable.

sake[2] /ˈsɑːki/ noun, u. = a kind of wine made from rice, popular in Japan

sa•la•cious /səˈleɪʃəs/ adj. *salacious writing* = indecent; relating to sex or causing strong sexual feelings

sal•ad /ˈsæləd/ noun, u. or c. = a mixture of raw leafy vegetables or fruit eaten as part of a meal **fruit salad** = a dish which combines different kinds of cut fruit, generally eaten raw

sa•la•man•der /ˈsæləmændəʳ/ noun = a small animal like a lizard that lives in water as well as on land

sa•la•mi /səˈlɑːmi/ noun, u. = a kind of sausage (meat, usually pork or beef, which has been cut up into very fine pieces, spiced and stuffed into a kind of edible tube)

sal•a•ry /ˈsæləri/ noun, u. or c. (**salaries**) *He earns a salary of Rs 3,000 a month.* = money paid to someone, usually once a month, for work done by him/her **salaried** adj. *a salaried person* = earning or getting a salary

sale /seɪl/ noun, u. or c. **1** *This car is for sale.* = an arrangement by which something is given in exchange for money **2** *This shop will have a sale of men's clothing next month.* = a special offering of goods at a price lower than usual **salesperson (salesman/ saleswoman)** noun, c. = a person whose job is to sell things to people **salesmanship (salespersonship)** noun, u. = skill in selling things **sales tax** noun = money which has to be paid to the government by a person who is buying something **sale or return** = an arrangement in which a large shop allows other shops to take goods and to return those which are not sold

to make a sales pitch = to try to talk someone into buying something

sal•a•ble (saleable) /ˈseɪləbəl/ adj. *a salable product* = which can be sold or is easy to sell (see **sell**)

sa•li•ent /ˈseɪliənt/ adj. *It was a dull match. The only salient feature was the century by Tendulkar.* = outstanding (most easily noticed or remembered)

sa•line /ˈseɪlaɪn/ adj. *the saline water of the sea* = containing salt

sa•li•va /səˈlaɪvə/ noun, u. = the natural liquid produced inside the mouth; spittle **salivary** adj. *salivary glands* = having to do with saliva **salivate** /ˈsælɪveɪt/ verb, i. *The sight of meat makes a dog salivate.* = to produce saliva in the mouth

sal•low /ˈsæləʊ/ adj. *a sallow complexion* = pale and not looking very healthy (referring to the colour of a person's face or body)

sal•ly[1] /ˈsæli/ noun, c. (**sallies**) **1** *The troops made a sally into an area held by the enemy.* = a quick attack followed by a return to the old position **2** *The girl's witty sallies made everyone laugh.* = a clever and humorous remark

sally[2] verb, i. *The candidate's followers sallied forth to ask the people to vote for him.* = to go out bravely to face some difficulty (humorous)

salm•on /ˈsæmən/ noun = a kind of fish with pink flesh that lives in the sea but returns to a river to lay its eggs **salmon-pink** adj. *She wore a salmon-pink saree for the get-together.* = having the colour of salmon

sal•mo•nel•la /sælməˈnelə/ noun, u. = a kind of bacteria (very tiny living creature) that causes food poisoning, typhoid and paratyphoid fever [MEDICINE]

sal•on /ˈsælɒn/ noun, c. **1** *a hair-dressing salon* = a shop where people can get their hair dressed etc. **2** = a shop selling clothes in fashion at a high price

sa•loon /səˈluːn/ noun, c. **1** = a motor-car with a closed body; sedan **2** = a place where alcoholic drinks are sold and drunk in the USA (also **bar**)

salt[1] /sɔːlt/ noun, u. or c. **1** (u.) = a white chemical, (sodium chloride) which is present in the human body as well as in the sea, and which gives flavour to food **2** (c.) = a compound that is formed when an acid and base combine [CHEMISTRY]

salt[2] adj. *salt water* = containing salt

salt[3] verb, t. *We first salt the water in which the vegetables are to be cooked.* = to flavour with salt **salty** adj. *Sea water is too salty to drink.* = having the taste of salt **salted** adj. *Salted nuts are very tasty.* = with salt added **saltpan** noun, c. = a layer of salt that is left behind in a sea or lake when all the water evaporates [GEOGRAPHY] **salt-water** adj. *salt-water fish* = found in the sea **salt-cellar** noun, c. = a small container with holes in the cover through which salt can be shaken out, used on the table during meals (also, **saltshaker**) **saltpetre** noun, u. = a chemical, (potassium nitrate) used in making gun-powder, in preserving meat and in medicine

to salt away *In the time of famine, while others suffered some people salted away a fortune.* = to save money and put it away secretly, usually dishonestly **to take something with a pinch/grain of salt** *He makes a lot of promises but rarely keeps them, so we have to take what he says with a pinch of salt!*= to have doubts about the truth of something **to (not) be worth one's salt** *No teacher worth her salt will expect her pupils to know everything.* = to be sincere and skilled in one's work

sal•u•ta•tion /sæljʊ'teɪʃən/ noun, u. or c. **1** *The salutation at the beginning of the letter read: 'My dear friend.'*(c.) = the standard form of words used at the beginning of a speech or a letter as a greeting **2** *The participants bowed in salutation.*(u.) = greeting

sa•lute[1] /sə'lu:t/ verb, t. or i. **1** *When the soldiers saw the general, they saluted.*(i.) = to show respect to a person who has a higher rank in a military service (army, navy or airforce) by raising the right hand stiffly and smartly to the forehead **2** *On this day, we salute the heroes who gave their lives to defend the country.* (t.) = to give honour to someone

salute[2] noun, c. *The soldier raised his hand in a salute.* = the action of saluting someone

to take the salute = to accept the salutes of those marching past in a parade

sal•vage[1] /'sælvɪdʒ/ verb, t. *The house was destroyed by the fire but we were able to salvage some of the furniture.* = to save something from loss or damage

salvage[2] noun, u. *This salvage from the sunken ship was worth millions.* = something that has been saved from being destroyed

sal•va•tion /sæl'veɪʃən/ noun, u. *He often got into trouble but his family helped him out each time. It proved to be his salvation.* = something that saves one from danger or from evil **Salvation Army** noun = a Christian missionary organization that works like an army but does charitable work among the poor

salve[1] /sælv/ noun, u. = an oily substance that helps to heal a cut, wound etc.

salve[2] verb, t. *The only way he can salve his guilty conscience is by apologizing to the people whom he has harmed.* = to make pain or suffering, especially in the mind, less (formal)

sal•ver /'sælvəʳ/ noun, c. = a large metal plate on which food is served

sal•vo /'sælvəʊ/ noun, c. (**salvos** or **salvoes**) = the firing of many guns or the dropping of many bombs at the same time

sam•ba /'sæmbə/ noun = a kind of popular dance that started in Brazil

same /seɪm/ adj. *This is the same story that you read to us last week.* = not different or not another **sameness** noun, u. *There is a certain sameness of plot in all his films.* = absence of variety

same old story *It is the same old story every time: he forgets to do his homework.* = something that happens usually (informal) **at the same time** **1** *The teacher said she couldn't understand us if we all talked at the same time.* = all together **2** *You have to correct them if they make mistakes, but at the same time you should praise them when they are right.* = however; on the other hand **all the same** *It is all the same to me which place we go to for our holiday.* = 'It makes no difference to me.' (expressing indifference or boredom) **the same here** *'I'll have a cup of coffee.' 'The same here.'* = me too (informal) **the same to you** *'Happy New Year!'. 'The same to you.'* = returning a greeting or replying to an expression of good wishes (informal)

sa•mo•sa /səməʊsə/ noun, c. or u. = a kind of Indian snack (food eaten between meals), made by filling a thin piece of dough, rolled into the shape of a triangle, with meat or vegetables, sealed and deep fried

sa•mo•var /'sæməvɑ:ʳ/ noun, c. = a large metal pot used for boiling tea, popular in Russia and countries in Central Asia

sam•pan /'sæmpæn/ noun, c. = a kind of small boat commonly used in China and countries in Southeast Asia

sam•ple[1] /'sɑ:mpəl/ noun, c. **1** *The doctor collected a sample of my blood for examination.* = a small part or a small quantity of something, from which one can get an idea of the whole **2** *a blood sample* = a small quantity of body fluid or waste which is tested in order to see if there is infection etc. **3** = a part (usually small) of a product which gives the buyer an idea of its qualities or features

sample[2] verb, t. *Would you like to sample the biryani we are cooking for tonight's dinner?* = to try out a small part or a small quantity of something in order to get an idea of the whole

sample[3] adj. *The teacher gave us some sample test papers for practice.* = of the same kind as the real thing

sam•u•rai /'sæmʊraɪ/ noun, c. = a professional soldier belonging to a military class in Japan (in former times)

san•a•to•ri•um /sænɪ'tɔ:riəm/ noun, c. (**sanatoriums** or **sanatoria**) = a kind of hospital, built in a place which has a good climate, where people with illness are sent to get back their health

sanc•ti•fy /'sæŋktɪfaɪ/ verb, t. *They wanted a priest*

S

to sanctify their new house. = to make something holy or sacred

sanc•tion[1] /'sæŋkʃən/ verb, t. *The government has sanctioned a new school for our village.* = to give permission for something

sanction[2] noun, u. or c. **1** *No solider can leave the barracks without the commanding officer's sanction.*(u.) = official permission **2** *The UN can impose sanctions against any country which does not follow the rules of international trade.*(c.) = action taken against a country which has broken some international law or agreement

sanc•ti•ty /'sæŋktɪti/ noun, u. *Bus drivers who drive rashly have no respect for the sanctity of human life.* = something of great value which deserves respect and protection (formal)

sanc•tu•a•ry /'sæŋktʃuəri/ noun, c. (**sanctuaries**) or u. **1** (c.) = the most sacred part of any place of worship (see **sanctum**) **2** *a bird sanctuary*(c.) = a place where birds or animals are protected by law and cannot be hunted **3** *Some people sought sanctuary in a foreign embassy when there was political unrest in the country.*(u.) = protection (usually of a political nature) or safety

sanc•tum /'sæŋktəm/ noun, c. = a holy area inside a place of worship

sand[1] /sænd/ noun, c. = loose material with very fine grains of worn-down rock, found in deserts and on seashores and river banks

sand[2] verb, t. *The surface of a wooden table has to be sanded before it is polished.* = to make a surface smooth by rubbing it with sandpaper (see **sandpaper**) **sand bank** noun, c. = a wall of sand which appears in a river **sand dune** noun, c. = a small hill made of sand, created by the wind, commonly found in deserts **sandpaper** noun, u. = paper covered with sand or other rough material, which is rubbed over wooden or metal surfaces to make them smooth **sandy** adj. **1** *a sandy beach* = having a lot of sand **2** *sandy hair* = having the colour of sand or full of sand

san•dal /'sændl/ noun, u. or c. **1** *a pair of leather sandals* (c.) = light, open shoes **2** (u.) = the wood of the sandalwood tree **3** = perfume (sweet-smelling liquid) made from oil obtained from a sandalwood tree **sandalwood** noun, u. = the wood of the sandalwood tree, which has a sweet smell

sand•piper /'sændpaɪpə^r/ noun = a small bird with long legs, often found in sandy places

sand•wich /'sændwɪdʒ/ noun, c. (**sandwiches**) = two or more pieces of bread with a layer of some food (meat, vegetables, cheese etc.) between them

sane /seɪn/ adj. **1** *a sane person* = having a healthy mind (opposite **insane**) **2** *sane advice* = wise and practical **sanity** noun, u. **1** *Could he have lost his sanity? He keeps talking to imaginary people all the time.* = the quality of being sane (having a healthy mind) **2** *There was total confusion at the meeting, but the President was able to bring some sanity into the proceedings.* = reasonableness, moderate behaviour (figurative)

san•guine /'sæŋgwɪn/ adj. *My friends think the city will never be able to solve its water problem, but I am sanguine.* = hopeful, confident (formal)

san•i•ta•ry /'sænɪtəri/ adj. **1** *Many of the food shops do not prepare food in a sanitary environment.* = clean and free from germs etc. (opposite **insanitary**) (formal) **2** *sanitary fittings/ware for the bathroom* = toilet bowls, wash basins, sinks, showers etc. **sanitary napkin** noun, c. = a padded piece of material worn by women to absorb blood during their menstrual period **sanitation** /sænɪ'teɪʃən/ noun, u. *People who live in a city must be careful about sanitation.* = removal of waste, especially sewage **sanitize (sanitise)** /'sænɪtaɪz/ verb, t. **1** *This building has been thoroughly sanitized. There is no risk to your health here.* = to make clean and free from germs **2** *a sanitized account of the incident* = to change something (e.g. a report) or leave out some parts, in order to make it more acceptable to people (derogatory)

Sans•krit /'sʌnskrɪt/ noun = the ancient, classical language in which most of the holy books of the Hindus were first written

San•ta•Claus /'sæntə klɔːz/ noun = an imaginary old man who is supposed to bring gifts for children at Christmas time, often shortened to Santa (also **Father Christmas**)

sap[1] /sæp/ noun, u. or c. **1** (u.) = the juice that flows inside a living plant **2** (c.) = a very stupid person (informal)

sap[2] verb, t. *Too much exposure to the sun will sap your energy.* = to weaken gradually

sap•ling /'sæplɪŋ/ noun, c. = a young tree

sap•per /'sæpə^r/ noun, c. = a soldier who carries out engineering duties (building roads, bridges etc.) during a war

sap•phire /'sæfaɪə^r/ noun = a transparent precious blue gemstone, used in making jewellery

sar•cas•tic /sɑː'kæstɪk/ adj. *They asked me for a loan but when I told them I could not give it to them, they made a sarcastic remark 'How generous of you!'* = saying something which is oppposite in meaning to what it seems to mean, in order to make fun of someone, express one's disappointment etc. **sarcasm** noun **sarcastically** adv.

sar•coph•a•gus /sɑːˈkɒfəgəs/ noun, c. (**sarcophagi**) = a kind of box in which a dead body was kept in former times [TECHNICAL]

sar•dine /sɑːˈdiːn/ noun, c. = a kind of small fish found in the sea

to be packed like sardines *The six of us were packed together like sardines in the back seat of the car.* = tightly crowded together (like sardines in a can)

sa•ri (saree) /ˈsɑːri/ noun, c. = a long piece of cloth wrapped around the body and worn as a dress by women in India, Nepal and other neighbouring countries

sa•rong /səˈrɒŋ/ noun, c. = a piece of cloth covering the waist and legs, used by men and women, specially in Malaysia, Indonesia and neighbouring countries

sarong

SAT abbr. of **Scholastic Aptitude Test** = a test which must be taken by students applying for admission to an American University

Sa•tan /ˈseɪtn/ noun = the Devil (the evil power which is the enemy of God, according to the Jewish, Christian and Islamic religions) **satanic** /seɪˈtænɪk/ adj. = very cruel and evil (like Satan)

sa•tay /sɑːˈteɪ/ noun, u. = pieces of meat which are cooked over an open fire and eaten with a spicy peanut sauce (popular in Indonesia and Malaysia)

satch•el /ˈsætʃəl/ noun, c. = a leather or cloth bag hung from one's shoulder or carried on one's back, specially used by school children for carrying books

sat•el•lite[1] /ˈsætɪlaɪt/ noun, c. **1** *The moon is a satellite of the earth.* = a heavenly body that revolves around a planet, especially around one of the nine major planets of the solar system **2** *India is sending a telecommunications satellite into space.* = an artificial object which moves in space around the earth and serves some useful purpose, such as sending radio signals

satellite[2] adj. *For many years the East European countries were satellite countries of Russia.* = a country that is controlled by another country which is more powerful

sa•ti•ate /ˈseɪʃieɪt/ verb, t. *The meal satiated us.* = to be very fully satisfied, especially after eating (formal) **satiated** adj.

sa•t•ire /ˈsætaɪəʳ/ noun, u. or c. = writing which shows the evil or foolishness of someone/something in a way that creates humour **satirical** /səˈtɪrɪkəl/ adj. *a satirical play* = containing satire

sat•is•fac•tion /sætɪsˈfækʃən/ noun, u. **1** *A teacher finds satisaction when her students do well.*(u.) = the feeling of happiness that one gets by doing something that one likes to do **2** *Every human being desires the satisfaction of some basic needs.* = the fulfillment of a need or desire **satisfactory** adj. *I asked him why he had come late to class but he could not give me a satisfactory reply.* = good enough to be accepted **satisfactorily** adv. *He performed satisfactorily in the test.* = fairly well

sat•is•fy /ˈsætɪsfaɪ/ verb, t. **1** *I looked after my guests as well as I could, but wasn't able to satisfy them.* = to please someone by giving him/her enough of something **2** *You will be selected for this job if you satisfy all the requirements.* = to be good enough for something

sat•u•rate /ˈsætʃəreɪt/ verb, t. **1** *His clothes were saturated with sweat after he had run a kilometre.* = to become completely wet **2** *You can't sell any more television sets in this city. The market for television is saturated.* = to be so completely full of something that there is no space for any more of it **saturated** adj. **1** = filled with so much liquid that it cannot take in any more (of a substance which absorbs water or some other liquid) **2** = containing chemicals which are harmful to the body (of certain kinds of food) **saturated fat** noun = a kind of fat (substance present in meat, milk etc.) which is solid at ordinary temperature and is believed to cause blocking of the arteries **saturation** /sætʃəˈreɪʃən/ noun, u. = the state of being saturated (completely full and unable to take in anymore of something)

Sat•ur•day /ˈsætədi/ noun, c. = the day of the week that comes just before Sunday and is named after the planet Saturn (see below)

Sat•urn /ˈsætən/ noun = the sixth planet from the sun and the second largest in the solar system

sat•yr /ˈsætəʳ/ noun = a god in Greek and Roman mythology who is half man and half goat (below the waist)

sauce /sɔːs/ noun, u. or c. **1** = a thick liquid containing some fruit, vegetables, fish etc. boiled with spices, used to give flavour to food **2** *Don't give me any of your sauce or you will be sorry!* = impolite talk or behaviour (informal) **saucy** adj. *'Don't be saucy!' the mother told the child.* = disrespectful in an impolite way

What's sauce for the goose is sauce for the gander = 'Rules which apply to one person should also apply to others'.

sau•cer /ˈsɔːsəʳ/ noun, c. = a flat, round plate, slightly

S

raised at the edge, on which a cup is put **flying saucer** noun = a saucer-shaped **Unidentified Flying Object (UFO)**

saucepan /ˈsɔːspən/ noun, c. = a deep, round cooking pot with a handle and a lid

sau•na /ˈsaʊnə/ noun = a room or building in which steam is produced by throwing water on hot stones and in which people sit before taking a bath, in order to allow sweat to run out of their bodies (also **sauna bath**)

saun•ter /ˈsɔːntəʳ/ verb, i. *The boy sauntered along the road with his hands in his pockets.* = to walk slowly, without any hurry, in an aimless manner

saus•age /ˈsɒsɪdʒ/ noun, c. or u. = meat, usually pork or beef, which is cooked with spices, minced and then pressed into an edible tube sealed at both ends

sau•te /ˈsəʊteɪ/ verb, t. = to fry (cook) something quickly using a small quantity of oil

sav•age[1] /ˈsævɪdʒ/ noun, c. = a word now considered offensive used to describe a person from a tribe living (usually) in the forest and depending mostly on hunting for food

savage[2] adj. **1** *a savage temper* = wild; fierce; cruel **2** *The robbers made a savage attack on the village.* = violent and cruel

savage[3] verb, t. *The tiger jumped on the man and savaged him.* = to attack and injure someone badly (referring to an attack by a wild animal), especially with the teeth

sa•van•na (savannah) /səˈvænə/ noun = a flat piece of grassland with scattered bushes or trees lying between equatorial forests and hot deserts

sav•ant /ˈsævənt/ noun, c. = a person who has deep knowledge of some subject; a person of great learning (formal)

save[1] /seɪv/ verb, t. or i. **1** *He was about to drown in the river but I saved his life.*(t.) = to make someone free from danger or harm **2** *I am trying to save some money for the education of my children.*(t.) = to keep money aside for future use instead of spending it **3** *Let's not have the ice cream now, let's save it for later.*(i.) = to set aside food or something useful, interesting etc. for a later/better time **4** *You must remember to save before you quit.*(i.) = to store a document on the hard disk of a computer so that it can be called up again (retrieved) (opposite **delete**) [COMPUTERS] **5** *If you walk, it will take you an hour to reach the station but you can save time by taking the bus.*(t.) = to prevent the waste of something

save[2] prep. *I have read all these books save one.* = except

save[3] noun, c. *Our goal-keeper made a good save.* = the act of preventing the ball from entering the goal, in the game of football or hockey **savings** noun, u. (always plural) *The man lost all his savings when the finance company in which he had invested closed down.* = money that has been saved and put aside in a bank or a financial organization **savings account** noun, c. = a bank or post office account where individuals, but not business companies, can deposit money, on which they get interest

to save the day/situation *Our school won the quiz only because one of our team-mates saved the day by answering the last question.* = to turn a likely defeat or failure into victory or success **to save one's own neck/skin** *When we were all being scolded, you could have explained things and helped everyone. Instead you spoke only for yourself and saved your own skin.* = to escape harm or punishment in a selfish way **saving grace** *She may be lazy and not very reliable but her saving grace is her honesty.* = the one good quality which makes up for all the bad ones **to save face** *We forgot to prepare lunch for our guests but saved face by getting some food from a restaurant.* = to be able to keep the respect of someone when one is in danger of losing it

sa•viour (Saviour) /ˈseɪvɪəʳ/ noun, c. **1** = a person who protects (saves) people from danger or harm **2** = (usually capital) a reference to Jesus Christ by people who follow the Christian religion

sa•vour[1] /ˈseɪvəʳ/ verb, t. *The food is excellent. I am going to savour this meal.* = to enjoy something (especially food)

savour[2] noun, u. *The food has lost its savour.* = taste

sa•vou•ry[1] /ˈseɪvəri/ adj. *This restaurant is famous for its savoury dishes.* = tasty

savoury[2] noun, c. (**savouries**) = different kinds of snacks which have a salty taste

sav•vy /ˈsævi/ noun, u. *He is smart, but has he got the savvy to make a success of his business?* = practical wisdom; commonsense (slang)

saw[1] /sɔː/ noun, c. = a tool used for cutting hard material such as wood, consisting of a flat steel blade with teeth (see pic under **tools**)

saw[2] verb, t. (**sawed, sawn**) **1** *The carpenter will saw these wooden logs into planks.* = to cut with a saw **2** = past tense of **see** **sawdust** noun, u. = the dust produced when wood is sawn, often used as packing material **saw-mill** noun, c. = a factory in which logs of wood are cut into flat boards with the help of saws that are driven by machines

Sax•on /ˈsæksən/ noun = a member of a Germanic tribe which conquered and lived in England in the fifth and sixth centuries AD

sax•o•phone /ˈsæksəfəʊn/ noun = a brass musical wind instrument

say[1] /seɪ/ verb, t. (**said**) **1** *You haven't spoken at all.*

Please say something. = to speak **2** *You must say your prayers before you go to bed.* = to express in words (aloud or silently) **3** *People say he was an honest man.* = to express a general opinion **4** *The expression on your face says you have some bad news.* = to show

say[2] adv. *Could you come back in, say, five minutes?* = about (used in speaking) **saying** noun, c. *Have you heard the saying 'Don't count your chickens before they are hatched'?* = a well-known statement or proverb which contains some wisdom

to have a say *If life in a family has to run smoothly, every member must have a say in matters of importance.* = the right to decide something or to express an opinion **It goes without saying** *I'm sorry I didn't invite you to the meeting, but it goes without saying that you are welcome.* = It should be understood, even if it is not said in words. **to save face** = to prevent oneself or others from being ashamed, embarrassed, or looking foolish **If I may say so** *The event went well, but if I may say so, it went on too long.* = if I am allowed to speak frankly (formal) **Let's just say** *Many things happened at the meeting. Let's just say it wasn't very satisfactory.* = an expression used to avoid going into details, often so that one does not give a negative picture **You can say that again!** *'What a difficult Physics test we had.' 'You can say that again!'* = I agree completely (informal)

scab /skæb/ noun, c. = a piece of skin, or a crust which forms over a cut or wound when it is getting better

scab•bard /'skæbəd/ noun, c. = a sheath or a case, usually made of leather, for the blade of a knife, dagger or sword

sca•bies /'skeɪbi:z/ noun = a skin disease which causes a lot of itching

scaf•fold /'skæfəld/ noun, c. **1** = a framework of bamboos, wooden poles or metal put up around a building that is being built, painted or repaired so that workers can go up and down (also **scaffolding**) **2** = a raised platform on which criminals were made to stand (in former times) before they were hanged

scaffolding see **scaffold**

scald /skɔ:ld/ verb, t. *He scalded his tongue when he tried to drink hot coffee.* = to burn some part of one's body with hot liquid or steam **scalding** adj. *How can you drink that scalding coffee?* = so hot that it can burn

scale[1] /skeɪl/ noun, c. or u. **1** *Marks for this test will be given on a scale of 0 to 10.*(c.) = a set of numbers which are used to measure something **2** (c.) = an instrument on which a set of numbers are marked at equal distances, used to measure the length of different objects **3** *This map is drawn to a scale of one centimetre to five kilometres.*(c.) = the relationship between the distances shown on a map and the actual distances(c.) **4** *The government is going to start the teaching of computer science on a large scale. This year it will start in 10,000 schools.*(c.) = the size or level, especially if it is very big, at which something is done **5** *Most fish have scales.*(c.) = a piece of hard skin which covers the body of a fish or snake **6** (usually plural) *Bathroom scales will help you keep a watch over your weight.* = an instrument for weighing **7** *Do you know the scale of damage in the accident?*(u.) = extent

scale[2] verb, t. **1** *The thief entered the house through a window upstairs, after scaling the wall.* = to climb up **2** *You will have to scale the fish before you can cook it.* = to remove the scales of a fish (also **de-scale**)

to scale up or scale down something = to increase or decrease the quantity of something that is being produced or the level at which something is being done

scalp /skælp/ noun, c. = the skin of the human head excluding the face

scal•pel /'skælpəl/ noun, c. = a kind of small, sharp knife used by surgeons for surgical operations

scam /skæm/ noun, c. *The newspapers have reported a scam.* = a dishonest action involving large sums of money (slang)

scamp /skæmp/ noun, c. = a mischievous child (informal)

scam•per /'skæmpə^r/ verb, i. *The children scampered out of the classroom when the bell rang.* = to run quickly and playfully

scan[1] /skæn/ verb, t. **1** *We scanned the countryside from the top of the hill, but could see no sign of the house.* = to search or look for something carefully **2** *He scanned the newspaper quickly, looking for the report on the School Day function.* = to read quickly through a newspaper or book, searching for something that one is interested in **3** *scan a text* = to look through a text in order to locate a specific part of it [TECHNICAL] **4** *The doctors will scan his brain to see if there is a tumour.* = to examine the inside of a person's body using a special computerised instrument **5** *Does this poem scan?*(i.) = to follow a regular rhythm of strong and weak sounds **6** *to scan a photograph* = to make a copy of a photograph or printed document which can be stored in a computer system, by using an electronic machine called a scanner [COMPUTERS]

scan[2] noun, c. or u. **1** *a brain scan*(c.) = an examination of the inside of the body **2** *Most people have a quick scan of the newspaper with their morning cup of tea.*(u.) = quick look

scanner /skænə^r/ noun, c. **1** = a machine which can make copies of photographs or documents for storing in a computer system [COMPUTERS] **2** *Air-traffic*

S

controllers depend on the radar scanner to keep track of planes coming in or going out. = an instrument which tracks flying aircraft and shows their movement on a radar screen

scan•dal /'skændl/ noun, c. **1** *The Director caused a scandal when he appointed his niece manager.* = an action that people find improper and shocking **2** *Some magazines print a lot of scandal about famous people to increase their sale.* = news which may be true or false, but harms the reputation of someone **scandalize (scandalise)** verb, t. *Our parents were scandalised when they saw us watching an adult film.* = to feel angry or shocked about something which seems improper **scandalous** adj. *The sudden and sharp rise in the price of cooking gas is scandalous.* = an action causing shock and anger

Scan•di•na•vi•an /skændɪ'neɪvɪən/ noun or adj. = belonging to or concerning Denmark, Norway, Sweden, Finland and Iceland (which form part of Scandinavia)

scant /skænt/ adj. *The government pays scant attention to education. Many schools are without teachers.* = very little **scanty** adj. *Most parts of Rajasthan receive scanty rainfall: only about 20 mm in a year.* = very little in quantity

scape•goat /'skeɪpgəʊt/ noun, u. *When our team lost, everyone started looking for a scapegoat.* = a person who is made to take the blame or is blamed for some mistake made by others

scap•u•la /'skæpjʊlə/ noun = the wide bone at the back, just below the shoulders (also known as **shoulder-blade**) [MEDICINE]

scar[1] /skɑːʳ/ noun, c. **1** *His right cheek was cut in an accident five years ago and you can still see the scar.* = a mark left on the skin as the result of a wound **2** *The children left scars on the furniture with their muddy shoes.* = marks

scar[2] verb, t. (**scarred**) *The accident has scarred him for life.* = to leave a scar or mark on somebody permanently (often figurative) **scarred** adj. *The tragedy of the earthquake left the residents scarred for life.* = an emotional mark left by a tragic experience

scarce /skeəs/ adj. *The economy of the country has to improve. Otherwise jobs will be scarce.* = not easily found, in short supply **scarcely** adv. *I spoke to him for half an hour but he said scarcely anything in reply.* = almost nothing **scarcity** noun, c. *There is a scarcity of vegetables because of the transport strike.* = the state of being scarce (not easily found)

scare[1] /skeəʳ/ verb, t. *The sound of crackers bursting scared the baby and it started to cry.* = to frighten (informal)

scare[2] noun, c. **1** *He gave me a scare by suddenly jumping out from behind the door.* = a sudden feeling of fear **2** *Most people were removed from the building because of a bomb scare.* = a feeling of fear shared by many people **scary** adj. *The horror film on television yesterday was very scary.* = frightening (informal)

to be scared stiff *He was scared stiff as he stood up to face the audience and began his speech.* = to be frightened, alarmed, nervous (informal) **to be scared to death / scared out of one's wits** *When the car that was following us suddenly bumped into ours, it scared me to death.* = to frighten, or make very anxious (informal)

scarecrow /skeəcrow/ noun, c. = a human figure made out of rags and straw, meant to frighten birds away in a field

scarf /skɑːf/ noun, c. (**scarves, scarfs**) a piece of cloth that is wrapped around the neck or head, often to keep oneself warm

scar•let /'skɑːlɪt/ adj. = of a bright red

scath•ing /'skeɪðɪŋ/ adj. *She is very sad because her new book received a scathing review in several newspapers.* = (about a piece of writing or speech) very unfavourable and hurting

scat•ter[1] /'skætəʳ/ verb, i. or t. **1** *The crowd scattered when the police threatened to open fire.*(i.) = to move away quickly in different directions **2** *When farmers plant rice in the fields, they scatter the seeds by hand.*(t.) = to throw something so as to spread it in all directions **scatterbrain** noun = a person who lacks concentration (mildly derogatory)

scav•enge /'skævɪndʒ/ verb, i. or t. **1** *The forest is kept clean by jackals and vultures who scavenge on the bodies of dead animals.*(i.) = to feed on waste matter and dead animals **2** *The stray dogs were scavenging the garbage heaps for scraps of waste food.*(t.) = to search through waste material, looking for food **scavenger** noun, c. **1** = an animal such as a jackal or vulture which feeds on dead animals **2** = a person whose job it is to remove garbage or waste material (not respectful, use **cleaner** instead)

sce•na•ri•o /sɪ'nɑːriəʊ/ noun, c. **1** *The director of the film that is being shot has a complete scenario.* = a detailed written description of the action that is planned for a new film or play **2** *What will life be like if someday human beings start living on other planets? No one knows, but there are several possible scenarios.* = a description of possible events or actions in the future

scene /siːn/ noun, c. **1** *We will show you a scene from our new film.* = a part of a film or play showing some action which takes place in a single place **2** *There were scenes of great joy at the airport when the victorious team returned.* = an action or event in real life that looks like something in a play or film **3** *The artist was painting a rural scene.* = a place seen in a painting or photograph **4** *The police arrived on the scene after the thieves had escaped.* = a place where some event has taken place **5** *Please leave quietly and don't make a scene.* = an expression of anger in public **scenery** /'si:nəri/ noun, u. *The scenery near Darjeeling, with the snow-covered mountains in the background, is wonderful.* = the natural surroundings of a place **scenic** adj. *The road that runs along the sea shore from Puri to Konark is very scenic.* = having beautiful views of nature

scent[1] /sent/ noun, u. or c. **1** *The room was filled with the scent of lilies.* = smell **2** *a bottle of scent* = perfume (old-fashioned)

scent[2] verb, t. **1** *The dogs started barking when they scented the leopard.* = to get the smell of something **2** *When I see all of you whispering, I scent something suspicious.* = to get a feeling that something bad is going on (often humorous) **3** *The flowers scented the air with their perfume.* = to fill with a pleasant smell

scep•tic /'skeptɪk/ noun, c. *He is a sceptic. He has no faith in our plans.* = a person who doubts the truth of something **sceptical** adj. *The experts tell us that the world economy is improving, but I am sceptical about this.* = not willing to believe **scepticism** noun, u. *Many people look at all advertisements with scepticism.* = unwillingness to believe something; doubt that something can be believed in or trusted

scep•tre /'septə[r]/ noun, c. = a small ornamental rod carried by a king or queen on special occasions as a sign of royal power

sched•ule[1] /'ʃedju:l/ or /'skedʒʊl/ (American English) noun, c. or u. **1** *The President of Russia is visiting India next week. A tight schedule of meetings with Indian leaders has been drawn up for him.*(c.) = a list of things that have been planned and have to be done **2** *The train is running behind schedule.*(u.) = the expected time **3** *The road-laying work has gone according to schedule.*(u.) = as was planned

schedule[2] verb, t. *The trip to Silent Valley has been scheduled for April.* = to plan or fix up something for the future

scheme[1] /ski:m/ noun, c. *The government has a new pension scheme for its employees.* = plan

scheme[2] verb, i. *Some criminals are scheming to rob the bank.* = to make plans for some dishonest action **schemer** noun *I don't trust him. He is a great schemer.* = a cunning person (derogatory)

schiz•o•phre•ni•a /skɪtsəʊ'fri:niə/ noun = a sickess of the mind in which a person appears to have two or more different personalities [MEDICINE]

schiz•o•phren•ic /skɪtsəʊ'frenɪk/ noun, c. = a person who suffers from schizophrenia

schol•ar /'skɒlə[r]/ noun, c. **1** *a Sanskrit scholar* = a person who has deep knowledge of some subject **2** = a student who is receiving a scholarship (see below) **scholarship** noun, c. = money given to a student as a prize to help him/her to study or money given by an individual or an institution to help pay for a person's studies **scholastic** /skə'læstik/ adj. *The teachers are proud of the scholastic achievements of their students.* = relating to schools, students and education (formal)

school[1] /sku:l/ noun, c. **1** = a place where children receive education **2** *The School of Life Sciences* = a part of a university which specialises in the teaching of a particular subject or group of subjects **3** *a driving school* = a place where a particular skill or trade is taught **4** *a school of dolphins* = a large group of fish or sea animals such as dolphins or whales which swim together **5** *My grandfather belongs to the school which believed in disciplining children firmly.* = a group of people who share the same ideas

school[2] verb, t. or i. **1** *He has been schooled in the art of public speaking.* = to teach or train (formal) **2** *My children are schooling in Sri Lanka.* = to receive education in a school **school fellow** noun, c. = a person who goes or went to school at the same time as another person (also **school mate**) **schooling** noun, u. *He had his schooling in Nainital.* = education at school **school leaver** noun, c. = a student who has just completed education at school (formal)

the old school *He belongs to the old school and does not care for modern theories of education.* = an old-fashioned or traditional style of living, thinking etc.

schoo•ner /'sku:nə[r]/ noun = a kind of high-speed sailing ship with two or more sails

sci•a•ti•ca /saɪ'ætɪkə/ noun = pain in the lower part of the back, hips and legs [MEDICINE]

sci•ence /'saɪəns/ noun, u. = knowledge which is based on observation (looking carefully at things), measurement and experiment from which conclusions are drawn and can be presented in the form of general theories or laws **sciences** noun, c. *the life sciences* = a group of scientific subjects which are related to each other e.g. Botany and Zoology **science fiction** noun, u. = writing (books etc.) about imaginary future developments in science and their effect on human life **science park** noun, c. = an area set aside for organizations which help in the development of science **scientific** /saɪən'tɪfɪk/ adj. **1** *scientific research* = connected with science **2** *We are trying to improve the fitness of our school cricket team but I don't think we are doing it in a scientific way.* = using a proper method or system

S

scientist /ˈsaɪəntɪst/ noun, c. = a person who studies one of the branches of science, or works on a problem connected with one of the sciences

scin•til•late /ˈsɪntɪleɪt/ verb, i. *The stars scintillate in the darkness.* = to shine or give out flashes as if throwing off sparks; twinkle **scintillating** adj. *Shah Rukh Khan has given a scintillating performance in his new film.* = exciting and full of life (figurative)

scis•sors /ˈsɪzəz/ noun, c. (always plural, generally used with 'a pair of') = a tool used for cutting paper, cloth etc., consisting of two sharp blades joined in the middle, each having a handle at one end **scissors-and-paste** adj. *The writer has taken bits and pieces from a number of books and produced a new book. It is only a scissors-and-paste job.* = produced by putting together parts from other writings (derogatory)

scle•ro•sis /sklɪˈrəʊsɪs/ noun = a kind of disease which causes soft parts of the body to become hard [MEDICINE]

scoff /skɒf/ verb, i. *When I told my friend we could make a fortune by growing lemon grass, he scoffed at the idea.* = to laugh at or make fun of something or someone

scold /skəʊld/ verb, t. *My mother scolds me if I wake up late on weekdays.* = to speak angrily to someone, especially a child, who has done something wrong **scolding** noun, c. (usually singular) *I got a scolding for not doing my work.* = the act of being scolded

scone /skɒn/ noun, c. = a kind of small cake

scoop[1] /skuːp/ noun, c. **1** *an icecream scoop* = a tool, shaped like a deep spoon, which is used to gather or take out any soft, powdery substance **2** *Give me just one scoop/scoopful of icecream.* = the amount of some substance which can be held in a scoop **3** *The story of the industrialist's kidnap was a scoop for the journalist.* = an exciting piece of news which a newspaper is able to publish before others (informal)

scoop[2] verb, t. *He scooped up some sand and put it in a flower-pot.* = to pick up with a scoop

scoot /skuːt/ verb, i. *The bell will ring any moment now. You'd better scoot.* = to leave a place quickly and suddenly (informal)

scoo•ter /ˈskuːtəʳ/ noun, c. = a kind of light motor-cycle with small wheels

scope /skəʊp/ noun, u. **1** *This is a book on Indian politics. It doesn't discuss the powers of the American president because that would be outside the scope of the book.* = the limits within which something can be discussed or studied **2** *There are only two people working in this office. There is no scope for any growth.* = opportunity or chance

scorch /skɔːtʃ/ verb, t. *The sun was so hot that it scorched the plants in my garden.* = to burn slightly or to dry up

score[1] /skɔːʳ/ noun, c. **1** *The Indian captain declared when the score was 250.* = the number of points, runs, goals etc. made in a game **2** *What was your score on the maths test?* = marks obtained in a test or competition **3** *He owns more than a score of houses.* = the number 20 **4** *There were scores of people on the street protesting against the shortage of drinking water.* = a large number (informal) **5** *A violinist puts the score on a stand in front of him/her while playing the instrument.* = a piece of music in written form

score[2] verb, t. or i. *Tendulkar scored a century in the last match.* = to gain points, runs, goals etc. in a game **score board** noun, c. = a large board on which the score is shown during a game **scorer** noun, c. = a person who keeps the score (record of runs, points etc.) during a game

to score out *The teacher scored out the names of the children who had not taken the test.* = to cross out or cancel by drawing a line through a piece of writing **on that score** *I have enough money now. I will not trouble you on that score.* = with regard to that particular problem **to settle scores** *They insulted me and I am going to settle scores very soon.* = to take revenge for some wrong done to one

scorn[1] /skɔːn/ noun, u. *They rejected our offer with scorn.* = a feeling of strong disrespect for someone, expressed through words, gestures or actions

scorn[2] verb, t. *She scorned all offers of help saying she was old enough now.* = to strongly refuse to accept, in a way that is hurtful

Scor•pi•o /ˈskɔːpiəʊ/ noun = one of the signs of the zodiac, represented by a scorpion (see pic under **zodiac**)

scor•pi•on /ˈskɔːpiən/ noun, c. = an eight-legged insect which has poison in its tail and can give a painful sting

Scot /skɒt/ adj. = (a person who is) from Scotland **Scottish** adj. = belonging to Scotland (not generally used to refer to persons)

scotch /skɒtʃ/ verb, t. *Someone went round telling everyone there is going to be a transport strike tomorrow, but we managed to scotch the rumour.* = to put an end to **Scotch** adj. *Scotch whisky* = made in Scotland (used to refer mainly to whisky) **Scotch** noun = whisky made in Scotland

scot•free /skɒtfriː/ adj. *The prisoner got off scot-free for lack of evidence against him.* = without any punishment (informal)

Scot•land Yard /skɒtlənd ˈjɑːd/ noun = the main office of the London police

scoun•drel /ˈskaʊndrəl/ noun, c. *The scoundrel duped people by talking to them pleasantly and then* *cheating them of their money.* = a wicked or dishonest person

scour /skaʊəʳ/ verb, t. **1** *The police are scouring the city for the thieves.* = to search carefully for someone or something **2** *You will have to scour these cooking pots.* = to clean a pot by rubbing it with some rough material

scourge /skɜːdʒ/ noun, c. **1** = a whip which was used in earlier times to hit people as a form of punishment **2** *Drought and famine have been a scourge in many countries.* = someone or something that causes great damage or harm

scout[1] /skaʊt/ noun, c. **1** = a soldier who is sent ahead of the army, during a war, to get information about the enemy **2** = a member of an international association (the Boy/Girl Scouts, also called Girl Guides) that trains young boys and girls in practical skills

scout[2] verb, i. *The government is scouting for a suitable place to set up a new factory.* = to search (informal)

scowl[1] /skaʊl/ noun, c. *The children were frightened when they saw a scowl on their father's face.* = an expression on the face showing anger or displeasure

scowl[2] verb, i. *Why are you scowling? Is something wrong?* = to show anger or displeasure through an expression on the face

Scrab•ble /'skræbəl/ noun = a game in which players try to form words out of individual letters which they pick up from a pool of letters

scrag•gly /'skrægli/ adj. *a scraggly and untidy beard* = growing in an untidy and irregular way

scrag•gy /'skrægi/ adj. *a scraggy horse // a scraggy neck* = weak-looking and with thin bones

scram•ble[1] /'skræmbəl/ verb, i. **1** *We scrambled up the hill quickly, anxious to reach the top.* = to move quickly but with difficulty over a steep or rough surface **2** *People were scrambling wildly for seats on the train which was already overcrowded.* = to struggle to get something **3** *I am going to scramble some eggs for breakfast.* = to mix together the white and yellow parts of an egg with a little milk, before cooking it in butter **4** *No one could understand the message that came over the radio because it had been scrambled.* = to mix up the sounds of a secret radio/telephone message, using a machine called a scrambler, so that it cannot be understood by someone who is not supposed to hear the message **5** *Our pilots were ordered to scramble as some enemy aircraft were seen in the sky.* = to take off (fly up from the ground in an aircraft) quickly before an attack [MILITARY]

scramble[2] noun, u. **1** *We reached the top of the hill after a painful scramble.* = the act of moving up over a rough surface **2** *There was a scramble for the best seats in the stadium.* = an effort made in a crowded situation to do or get something

scrap[1] /skræp/ noun, c. or u. **1** *Scraps of paper were lying all over the floor.*(c.) = a small piece **2** *He makes a lot of money by selling scrap.*(u.) = waste material (e.g. old newspapers) which can be re-used **3** *This man is always getting into scraps. You must keep him out of trouble.*(c.) = a fight or quarrel which is not very serious (informal)

scrap[2] verb, t. (**scrapped**) **1** *These old buses cannot be used now. They will have to be scrapped.* = to get rid of something which cannot be used any more **2** *I would advise you to stop scrapping with the other boys in your class.* = to fight or quarrel **scrap-book** noun, c. = a book with blank pages in which one can keep pictures, newspaper articles etc. that one has collected **scrap dealer** noun, c. = a person who buys and sells scrap (waste material) **scrapheap** noun, c. = a pile of waste material **scrap paper** noun = cheap paper used for writing things that are not important

scrappy adj. **1** *a scrappy child* = one who likes to fight **2** *a scrappy report* = (of writing) not detailed enough, or written in a disconnected way (derogatory)

scrape[1] /skreɪp/ verb, t. **1** *Scrape the carrots.* = to rub against a rough surface so as to remove the skin of a vegetable etc.; to cut into very thin pieces, or shred **2** *He scraped the car door while parking.* = to cause damage by making something rub hard against something else

scrape[2] noun, c. or u. **1** *The classroom was noisy because the children were having a scrape.* = a minor fight (slang) **2** *The scrape of heavy furniture being dragged across the floor is very disturbing.* = an unpleasant sound produced when two objects rub against each other

to scrape together *He has scraped together enough money to buy a bicycle.* = to collect with difficulty (figurative) **to scrape through** *I thought I wouldn't pass but managed to scrape through the examination.* = to get through or pass with difficulty (informal)

scratch[1] /skrætʃ/ verb, t. or i. **1** *The cat scratched the child's face with its claws.* = to cut or damage a surface with something sharp or rough, leaving marks or injuries **2** *He was bitten by mosquitoes and kept on scratching himself.* = to use one's fingernails to get over an itching feeling

scratch[2] noun, c. *The child's face was covered with scratches because she had walked through a thorny bush.* = a mark or injury made by something sharp or rough **scratch pad** noun = a pad of paper used for jotting down something quickly e.g. a phone number or someone's address

S

to do/start something from scratch *When all their personal belongings were destroyed in the flood, they had to start from scratch.* = to start from the beginning or with nothing (informal) **to scratch one's head** *She scratched her head but could not recall the title of the book.* = to try to remember or think of something (informal) **to not be up to scratch** *The experts tested her singing but it wasn't up to scratch.* = (only negative) to not be of the standard or level expected

scrawl[1] /skrɔːl/ verb, t. *He hurriedly scrawled a few lines across the sheet of paper.* = to write hurriedly or carelessly and therefore not clearly

scrawl[2] noun, c. *I hope you can read my scrawl!* = something written hurriedly or carelessly

scraw•ny /'skrɔːni/ adj. *How can that scrawny boy hope to become a fast bowler?* = thin and bony in an unattractive way (informal)

scream[1] /skriːm/ verb, t. or i. *I screamed when the man in the film jumped out suddenly from behind the door.* = to cry out loudly in a high-pitched/shrill voice, expressing fear, excitement, pain or anger

scream[2] noun, c. **1** *We heard a loud scream from the child's room.* = a loud, shrill cry expressing fear etc. **2** *The story you told us was a scream.* = something that makes people laugh a lot (informal)

screech[1] /skriːtʃ/ verb, t. or i. **1** *We screeched when a ghostly figure suddenly appeared out of the darkness.* = to cry out suddenly in a high-pitched voice because of extreme fear or pain **2** *The brakes of the car screeched as the driver tried to stop the car suddenly.* = to produce a shrill sound as a result of stopping suddenly from high speed

screech[2] noun, c. **1** *I heard the screech of an owl.* = a screeching sound **2** *There was a screech of tyres as she braked on the wet road.* = a high-pitched sound produced when something with wheels is moving fast and comes to a sudden stop

screen[1] /skriːn/ noun, c. **1** *My television set has a 29-inch screen.* = a flat surface in a television, computer system or cinema on which images or text can be seen **2** *He writes stories for the screen.* = the cinema or television industry (**the small screen** = television; **the big screen, the silver screen** = cinema) **3** *We can divide this large hall into two smaller rooms by putting up a screen across the middle.* = a movable wall, made of cloth, wood etc. which divides a room **4** *When she travels by bus, she uses a newspaper as a screen to keep the sun out.* = something that one can use to avoid strong light, dust etc. **5** *The restaurant they own is just a screen for smuggling activities.* = something that looks harmless but hides something bad

screen[2] verb, t. **1** *We are screening our new film at the Regal cinema.* = to show on a cinema or television screen (see meaning **1** for **screen**[1]) **2** *We will screen off the patient so that the doctor can examine her.* = to put up a screen (movable wall) so that someone or something is hidden from view **3** *We have received hundreds of applications for this job but we will screen them carefully before we call people for the interview.* = to examine someone or something in order to make sure that he/she satisfies the requirements for a job **4** *We'll have to screen the luggage.* = to put something through an x-ray machine to make sure that it does not have guns, knives, explosives etc. inside **screening** noun, c. or u. **1** *The first screening of the film will take place next week.* = the showing of a film **2** *Candidates will be called for an interview after the screening.* = a first examination **screenplay** noun, c. = the dialogue and camera directions written for a film **screen test** noun, c. = a test of a person's ability to act in films or television **screensaver** noun = the moving images that appear on a computer monitor when the computer is not in use [COMPUTERS]

screw[1] /skruː/ noun, c. = a straight, thin metal object, pointed at one end and flat at the other, which has a raised line going round and round it from top to bottom (called the thread) and is used to join pieces of wood or metal together

screw[2] verb, t. **1** *Can you screw these pieces of wood together.* = to join things together with screws (see pic under **tools**) **2** = to have sex with a person (slang) USE **screwdriver** noun, c. = a tool with a handle and a narrow metal blade which is used to turn a screw so that it moves forwards or backwards into a piece of wood, metal etc. (see pic under **tools**) **screw top** noun = a cover for a bottle which is made tight or loose by turning it around like a screw

to screw something up *He has screwed up the programme.* = to spoil something or to cause something to fail (slang)

scrib•ble[1] /'skrɪbəl/ verb, t. **1** *He scribbled a note to me just before rushing out of the house.* = to write something hurriedly and carelessly **2** *Some people have scribbled names and messages on the walls of the monument.* = to write something meaningless or to write something on a surface which is not meant to be written on

scribble[2] noun, c. or u. **1** *I can't read your scribble.* = careless writing which is difficult to read **2** *The walls are covered with childish scribbles.* = meaningless marks which look like writing

scribe /skraɪb/ noun, c. = a person who is paid to write something for others or a person who was paid to copy out books by hand before the invention of printing

scrimp /skrɪmp/ verb, i. *We will have to scrimp and save in order to buy a house.* = to save with great difficulty; to be forced to economize (informal)
script[1] /skrɪpt/ noun, c. **1** *Most Indian languages have their own script.* = the system of writing used by a language **2** *Do you have the script of the Prime Minister's speech?* = the written form of a speech (usually broadcast over the radio or television) or a story from which a film is to be made
script[2] verb, t. *Do you know who scripted the film?* = to write something which is to be used for a speech or for making a film etc. **scriptwriter** noun, c. = a person who produces the script for a speech or a film
scrip•ture /'skrɪptʃəʳ/ noun, c. = a holy book which has religious importance
scroll[1] /skrəʊl/ noun, c. *The poet received a scroll announcing that he had been given the title of 'Padma Vibhushan'.* = a long, narrow piece of paper or cloth with some official writing on it, which can be rolled up
scroll[2] verb, t. *You can scroll the file by pressing this key on the computer.* = to move computer text up or down so as to read it fully on the screen [COMPUTERS]
scro•tum /'skrəʊtəm/ noun = the loose bag of skin which holds the testicles (the parts of the body that produce sperm) in male animals or human beings [BIOLOGY]
scrounge /skraʊndʒ/ verb, i. **1** *He never buys any clothes; he just scrounges off his friends.* = to get things from others by begging and borrowing instead of buying them (derogatory) **2** *The cows shouldn't have to scrounge for food. We can feed them.* = to search for things which are not easily available
scrub[1] /skrʌb/ verb, t. *The floor is dirty. You must scrub it clean with a brush.* = to rub something hard in order to clean it
scrub[2] noun, u. **1** *Give the floor a good scrub.* = the act of rubbing hard in order to clean some surface **2** = low bushes growing in rocky soil
to scrub up *Surgeons have to scrub up before an operation.* = (of surgeons) to wash one's hands with antiseptic solution before surgery
scruff /skrʌf/ noun, c. = the back part of the neck **scruffy** adj. *He generally wears scruffy clothes.* = untidy (informal)
scrump•tious /'skrʌmpʃəs/ adj. *The food at the birthday party was scrumptious.* = delicious (informal)
scru•ple /'skru:pəl/ noun, c. (always plural) *He has no scruples about travelling without a ticket.* = a principle (something that one believes in) which stops one from doing something wrong **scrupulous** adj. *He is never late for work. He is always scrupulous about reaching the office on time.* = careful to do the right thing or guided by right principles **scrupulously** adv. *She has kept her room scrupulously clean.* = absolutely, very
scru•ti•nize (scrutinise) /'skru:tɪnaɪz/ verb, t. *The university authorities will scrutinize your certificates before they admit you.* = to examine or study very carefully (formal) **scrutiny** noun, u. *These papers need careful scrutiny. I cannot express an opinion about them now.* = careful study or examination
scu•ba•div•ing /'sku:bədaɪvɪŋ/ noun = the sport of swimming under water with special equipment for breathing
scud /skʌd/ verb, i. (**scudded**) *The clouds scudded across the sky, driven by the wind.* = to move quickly (referring usually to the movement of clouds or ships)
scuf•fle /'skʌfəl/ noun, c. *He got into a scuffle and was slightly hurt.* = a rough struggle or fight
scull /skʌl/ verb, t. = to row a light boat using small oars **sculling** noun = the sport of rowing
sculpt•or /'skʌlptəʳ/ noun, c. = a person who makes solid figures of human beings, animals etc. out of marble, stone, wood or other material
sculp•ture[1] /'skʌlptʃəʳ/ noun, u. or c. **1** = the art of making figures out of stone etc. **2** = a figure made out of stone etc.
sculpture[2] verb, t. *The artist sculptured a horse in bronze.* = to make a figure out of metal, stone etc. (also **sculpt**)
scum /skʌm/ noun, u. **1** = the dirty froth or foam often seen floating on top of a liquid **2** = a worthless person who deserves no respect (informal, derogatory)
scur•ri•lous /'skʌrɪləs/ adj. *The newspaper published an article making a scurrilous attack on the managing director of the company.* = false or unfair criticism which damages a person's reputation
scur•ry[1] /'skʌri/ noun, u. *We could hear the scurry of children's feet outside, along the corridor.* = to move with short, quick steps
scurry[2] verb, i. (**scurried**) *As soon as I turned on the light, the mouse scurried back into the hole in the wall.* = to run hurriedly
scur•vy /'skɜ:vi/ noun = a disease caused by the lack of vitamin C in the body, which sailors often suffered from in the old days
scut•tle /'skʌtl/ verb, t. or i. **1** *The children scuttled away when they saw their teacher coming.*(i.) = to move away with short quick steps in order to escape **2** *The committee scuttled our plans to build a swimming pool.*(t.) = to make someone give up some activity that has been planned (informal)
scythe /saɪð/ noun, c. = a tool with a long, sharp

S

curved blade and a long handle, used to cut grain or long grass

sea /siː/ noun, c. **1** = the body of salt water which covers the suface of the earth **2** *the Arabian Sea* = a particular body of salt water, smaller than an ocean, which lies near some country **sea-bed** noun = the land at the bottom of the sea **sea breeze** noun = a wind blowing from the sea to the land **sea change** noun *He was very short-tempered, but there is a sea change in him now.* = a complete change, usually for the better **sea dog** noun, c. = a sailor who has a lot of experience **sea-faring** adj. *a sea-faring person* = working or travelling on ships (formal) **seafood** noun, u. = fish and other animals from the sea (e.g. oysters) which can be eaten **sea horse** noun = a kind of small fish whose head and neck look like that of a horse **sea level** noun *Mount Everest is 5,000 feet above sea level.* = the average level of the surface of the sea, which is used to measure the height of places on land **sea lion** noun = a large kind of seal (sea animal) found in the Pacific Ocean **seasick** adj. *She hates travelling by boat as she becomes seasick.* = feeling nausea (the desire to vomit) because of the constant movement of the ship on water **seaweed** noun = plants growing in the sea, especially any one of the algae

to be all at sea *She was all at sea when I asked her a question in class.* = to not know something that one is expected to know **to go to sea** *Not many young people want to go to sea these days.* = to become a sailor

seal[1] /siːl/ noun, c. **1** = a sea animal, a mammal, found in cold climates **2** *This is an official document, carrying the President's seal.* = an official mark made on a document, letter etc. which proves that it is genuine or legal **3** *You will have to break the seal on the cap of the bottle before you can open it.* = a piece of wax, paper, plastic, metal etc., used to close an opening in an envelope, bottle etc., which must be broken before the contents can be taken out or used **4** *an oil seal in a car engine* = a piece of rubber or plastic fixed tightly around an opening (usually in a machine) to stop some liquid or gas from flowing through it

seal[2] verb, t. **1** *Seal the envelope before you post it.* = to close the flap, using gum etc. **2** *The agreement between the two countries has been sealed.* = to make an agreement final **sealing wax** noun, u. = a solid material which easily becomes liquid when heated and solid again when cooled, used to seal envelopes etc.

sealed off *The police sealed off the highway after the accident.* = to close all approaches to or exits from a place

my lips are sealed *I can't tell you what happened at the meeting this morning. My lips are sealed.* = to refuse to reveal a secret because one has promised not to reveal it

seam /siːm/ noun, c. **1** *Your shirt is coming apart at the seams.* = a line of stitches joining two pieces of cloth or other material **2** *Water is leaking into the boat through the seams.* = the place where two things are joined together **3** *a coal seam* = a long, thin layer of some mineral, specially coal, found between layers of other rocks

to be bursting at the seams *The shops were so crowded with shoppers that they were bursting at the seams.* = to be completely full (figurative)

seamy /ˈsɪːmi/ verb, t. *the seamy side of life* = (of life or conditions) unpleasant or immoral

sear /sɪəʳ/ verb, t. *The hot sun has seared the plants in my garden.* = to burn or dry up with heat **searing** adj. **1** *I cannot tolerate the searing heat.* = unpleasantly hot or burning **2** *He felt a searing pain in the leg when the stone hit him.* = very great pain which seems to burn (see **scorch**)

search[1] /sɜːtʃ/ verb, i. or t. *I searched for the letter on my desk but could not find it.*(i.) // *The police want to search your car.*(t.) = to look for something or someone; to examine something carefully in order to find something or somebody

search[2] noun, c. *The police are making a search of the house as they think the thieves may be hiding there.* = the act of searching (looking for something) **searching** adj. *The examiners asked me some searching questions to find out how well I knew the subject.* = intended to find out the truth about something or the extent of a person's knowledge **searchlight** noun, c. = a powerful light which can be turned around and used to see the movements of enemy aircraft in the sky at night **search engine** = an Internet-based programme which helps a person locate information on the Net [COMPUTERS] **search party** noun, c. = a group of people who are looking for someone who is lost **search warrant** noun, c. = a written order given by a court to the police, allowing them to search a place in order to find someone or something that may be hidden there [LAW]

in search of *The police went in search of the missing child.* = to look carefully for someone or something **to do/run a search** = to look for specific information or data or a file on the hard disk of a computer [COMPUTERS]

sea•son[1] /ˈsiːzən/ noun **1** *the four seasons of the year* = a period of time, extending over several months (e.g. spring, summer, winter), marked by a particular kind of weather **2** *The Christmas/music/apple season* = the period in a year when an event normally takes place or something is available in plenty

season[2] verb, t. **1** *You will have to season the curry by adding some more chillies.* = to give food better taste by adding salt, spices etc. to it **2** *This wood will have to be seasoned before we can use it to make furniture.* = to make wood fit for use (to make furniture etc.) by drying it **seasonal** adj. *We get seasonal rains here from July to September.* = happening during a particular time of the year only **seasoned** adj. *He is a seasoned teacher. He can teach any class.* = having a lot of experience **seasoning** noun, u. = salt, spices etc. which are added to food to give it taste **season ticket** noun, c. = a ticket which allows one to travel on a train or bus or to go to a theatre where plays, concerts etc. are being performed, which can be used over a period of time such as a month and is sold at a lower price than if one bought a ticket for each event

seat[1] /siːt/ noun, c. **1** *My seat is in the third row of the bus.* = a place where one can sit **2** *Your trousers are too tight at the seat.* = the part of the body on which one sits (the buttocks) or the part of a dress which covers this part of the body **3** *He lost his seat in the parliament as he was defeated in the election.* = a position in an official body or organization **4** *a seat of learning* = a centre where a particular kind of activity takes place

seat[2] verb, t. **1** *We were all seated in the first row.* = to get a seat (a place to sit) or to help someone to find a seat **2** *This bus seats 45 passengers.* = to have space where people can sit **seat belt** noun, c. = a belt worn around some part of the body by a person travelling in a car or aircraft which protects him/ her in case of an accident by preventing sudden movement of the body **-seater** adj. *a 16-seater bus* = having seats for the stated number of persons **seating** noun, u. *The seating in this cinema is very comfortable.* = the arrangement of seats

se•cede /sɪˈsiːd/ verb, t. *One of the states in the country threatened to secede unless some steps were taken to improve its economy.* = to separate from or to leave a group because of some disagreement (formal) **secession** /səˈsesən/ noun, u. = the act of separating from a group or organisation

sec•lude /sɪˈkluːd/ verb, t. *He has chosen to seclude himself as he does not like crowds.* = to keep away or to keep someone away from other people **secluded** adj. *They chose a secluded spot by the side of the lake to pitch their tent.* = lonely, away from the crowd **seclusion** noun, u. *The people of this village have no contact with the outside world. They live in complete seclusion.* = the state of being secluded (kept away from other people)

sec•ond[1] /ˈsekənd/ det. or pron. **1** *This is my second visit to Bangalore. I have come here once before.*(det.) // *He came first in the examination and I came second.*(pron.) = coming after the first **2** *This is the second largest building in the city.* = the one after the first **3** *Every second year, we visit Sri Lanka.* = every other (year, month etc.)

second[2] noun, c. **1** *It took him five seconds to reach the top of the stairs.* = a length of time equal to the sixtieth (1/60) part of a minute **2** *This angle measures 35 degrees, 4 minutes and 55 seconds.* = a unit for measuring an angle, equal to 1/3600 part of a degree [GEOMETRY] **3** *Any message sent by fax reaches the other end within seconds.* = very quickly

second[3] verb, t. (**seconded**) *When one of the members of the committee proposed that we should meet every week, I seconded the proposal.* = to support a proposal or an idea at a meeting **second-best** adj. *Rashmi won the first prize in the contest and Avinash was second-best.* = next after the best **second class** adj. *Most of our guests can afford only second class travel.* = not of the highest quality **second-class citizen** noun *I refuse to be treated like a second-class citizen in my own country.* = someone who is not treated as well as other members of a society **second-generation** adj. *There are many second-generation Indians living in the US now.* = the children of parents who were born in another country **second-hand** adj. *I can't afford a new one, so I will buy a second-hand car.* = previously owned or used **second language** noun *For many educated Indians, English is the second language.* = a language that is learnt after the mother tongue **second name** noun *Arundhati is her first name and Roy her second name.* = a less formal expression for **surname** **second rate** adj. *The music produced by the new group is second rate.* = of poor quality **second thoughts** noun (always plural) *I am having second thoughts about settling down in a large city.* = a change of plan, opinion etc.

sec•ond•a•ry /ˈsekəndəri/ adj. **1** *The government is taking steps to improve secondary education.* = the education given to children after the first six or seven years of school **2** *It is most important to give these people shelter. Building roads is only secondary.* = not as important as something else **3** *The patient caught a cold and then developed a secondary infection in the lungs.* = developing from (growing out of) something else

seconds /ˈsekənds/ noun (always plural) **1** *You can buy shirts very cheaply at this shop. They sell*

S

seconds. = an article, usually clothing, which is sold at a low price because it has some minor faults **2** *That pulao was really nice. I'll have seconds.* = a second helping of food or drink (informal)

se•cret[1] /ˈsiːkrɪt/ noun, c. **1** *I will tell you a secret, if you promise not to tell anyone. My sister is getting married to her boy-friend tomorrow!* = something which is kept hidden and not known to many people **2** *the secret of her success* = something that helps someone to become successful, but is not known to many people **3** *the secret of how the first living creatures on earth came into being* = a mystery that is not clearly understood or has yet to be explained

secret[2] adj. *I know of a secret place where we can hide.* = not known to many people **secrecy** noun, u. *This job has to be done in secrecy. No one should know about it.* = the state of being secret (not known to anyone) **secretive** adj. *They are so secretive that they won't talk to anyone about their plans to visit America next month.* = preferring to hide one's thoughts, plans etc. from others **secretly** adv. *My little brother reads in bed secretly by keeping his book hidden under his blanket!* = something kept from the knowledge of others **secret service** noun = the branch of the police or the government that collects secret information through spies

in secret *The children had planned the party in secret. No one knew about it until the actual day.* = in private, not openly **to keep a secret** *I don't know if I should tell you my plans because you just can't keep a secret.* = to not let a secret be known to anyone

sec•re•ta•ry /ˈsekrɪtəri/ noun, c. = a person who helps an important person by writing or typing letters, keeping records, arranging meetings etc. **secretarial** /sekrɪˈteərɪəl/ adj. *He has been trained for secretarial work.* = relating to the work of a secretary **secretariat** noun, u. **1** = the building in which the offices of the government are located **2** = the department that is responsible for the administration of a large organization

se•crete /sɪˈkriːt/ verb, t. *The bark of this tree secretes a sticky fluid.* = (of a living thing), to produce some substance, usually a liquid **secretion** noun, u. or c. **1** = a substance which is secreted or produced by some part of the body **2** = the act of secreting something in the body

sect /sekt/ noun, c. = a group which is part of a larger religious group **sectarian** /sekˈteərɪən/ adj. *a sectarian dispute* = having to do with one or more sects

sec•tion /ˈsekʃən/ noun, c. **1** *A section of the crowd was restless and demanded better seats. // He lives in the front section of the house.* = a part of something larger **2** *This computer table comes in sections. You will have to screw them together.* = a part of something which can be joined to other parts to make up a whole **3** *You are arrested under Section 420 of the Criminal Procedure Code.* = a law or rule forming a part of a set of laws or rules **4** *The scientist examined a section of the stem of the plant under the microscope.* = a view of what something would look like if cut across or cut through

sec•tor /ˈsektəʳ/ noun, c. **1** *The film industry is entirely in the private sector.* = one part of some field of activity, specially trade and industry **2** *The city has been divided into sectors for the purpose of taking a census of the population.* = a part into which an area is divided **3** = a part of a circle between two radii [TECHNICAL] **private/public sector** = used to refer to trade and industry—the public sector is controlled and run by the government, the private sector is controlled by private companies

sec•u•lar /ˈsekjʊləʳ/ adj. **1** *The country is governed by secular laws.* = connected with the world and its affairs, not connected with religion **2** *India is a secular country.* = not favouring any particular religion **secularism** noun, u. = the belief that all religions are to be treated as equal

se•cure[1] /sɪˈkjʊəʳ/ adj. **1** *This city is secure against enemy attack.* = safe; protected from danger or risk **2** *He has a secure job in a bank.* = free from risk or anxiety

secure[2] verb, t. **1** *The army will fight to secure the freedom of the country.* = to protect from burglary, danger etc. **2** *Please secure the door with a chain and lock.* = (of doors, windows, luggage etc.) to close tightly and make safe (formal) **3** *He has secured full marks in mathematics.* = to get something worthy of praise (formal)

security /sɪˈkjʊərɪtɪ/ noun, u. or c. (**securities**) **1** *We have employed guards for the security of this building.*(u.) = the state of being protected and safe **2** = protection (by guards etc.) against danger, fear etc. **3** *The bank is willing to give me a loan, but they want this house as a security.*(c.) = property which is kept by a bank or a person giving a loan to someone, to make sure that the loan is paid back

Security Council noun = the group of 15 countries within the United Nations Organization that tries to ensure peace in the world

se•dan /sɪˈdæn/ noun, c. = a large and often luxurious car with a closed body

se•date[1] /sɪˈdeɪt/ adj. **1** *The discussion at the meeting was very sedate. No one shouted or created a scene.* = calm and without excitement **2** *The child had a sedate manner.* = quiet and modest

sedate[2] verb, t. *The doctor had to sedate the patient* *as he was unable to sleep.* = to cause a person to become calm or to fall asleep, by using some medicine **sedation** noun, u. *The patient is relaxed and does not need sedation.* = the use of medicines to make a person calm **sedative** /'sedətɪv/ noun, c. = a medicine or drug that makes a person calm **sedately** adv.

sed•en•ta•ry /'sedəntəri/ adj. *He is a man of sedentary habits. I have never seen him going for a walk.* = staying in one place and not moving about (often disapproving)

sed•i•ment /'sedɪmənt/ noun, u. or c. *Rivers deposit sediment at the river-mouth where they enter the sea.*(u.) = small particles (pieces) of solid material that are often present at the bottom of a liquid **sedimentary** /sedɪ'mentəri/ adj. *sedimentary rocks* = left behind by some liquid as sediment

se•di•tion /sɪ'dɪʃən/ noun, u. *The writer of this book has been arrested for sedition.* = writing or speeches that may cause people to rise against the government **seditious** adj. *seditious literature* = likely to cause anger against the government

se•duce /sɪ'dju:s/ verb, t. **1** = to get someone to agree to have sex, usually through flattery **2** *They would not have moved to the city but were seduced by the offer of good jobs.* = to attract someone into doing something which he/she would not have done otherwise (figurative) **seduction** noun, u. or c. = the act of seducing someone **seductive** adj. = having the qualities needed to seduce someone

see /si:/ verb, i. or t. (**saw**, **seen**) **1** *Nobody can see a thing! Why don't you switch on the light?*(t.) = to be able to observe with the use of the eyes **2** *It's so dark! I can hardly see to write this letter.*(i.) = to make out with the use of the eyes **3** *I saw a film last night.*(t.) = to watch a film, play etc. **4** *We're going to see our grandmother over the week-end.*(t.) = to visit or meet someone **5** *I am not well. I'll be seeing the doctor this evening.*(t.) = to consult, visit **6** *They had to see a lawyer about the land dispute.*(t.) = to have a meeting with, over a serious matter **7** *Can you see the crack on the wall?*(t.) = to notice **8** *I can see why he is so upset.*(i.) = to understand or realize something **9** *I can't see the point of learning how to type when hardly anyone uses a typewriter these days!*(t.) = to understand the reason for something **10** *See if there are any more books in the cupboard.*(i.) = to look for a thing, information etc. **11** *Let's see what we can do about this problem.*(i.) = a way of offering help with a problem **12** *It'll be interesting to see if this film will do well considering that it deals with a totally new subject.*(i.) = to find out how something fares in the future **13** *We'll see.*(i.) = used when one cannot make a decision at once **14** *See you! // See you later.* (t.) = said when parting company when one knows that one will soon be meeting the person again (informal) **15** *Please see that the letter is posted today.*(i.) = to make sure that something is done without fail **16** *You test the thickness of the paper like this, see.*(t.) = used to check that someone listens, understands and follows what you are trying to explain/demonstrate **17** *Don't do that, see?* = a way of threatening or warning someone, or ensuring in an unpleasant way that something will be done **see-through** adj. = a garment, screen etc. which is transparent or so thin that one can see what is underneath

to see somebody off *I saw my friend off at the station.* = to go with someone to a place (a railway station etc.) from where they will leave **to see somebody across the road** *May I see you across the road?* = to help a person cross a road by going with them, holding their hand etc. **to see someone to the door** *I'll see you to the door.* = to go to the door with someone when the person is leaving your house, a building etc. after a visit **to see to something** *I'll pack the food for the journey. Could you see to the tickets?* = to arrange or to take responsibility for something **to see through something** *I saw through his game of cheating others.* = to understand/recognize the truth **to see something through** *I'm tired. Could you see the rest of the meeting through?* = to be in charge of something to the end **to see somebody through (an illness)** = to look after and help someone get over a period of difficulty until it has passed **to be seeing someone** = to be involved with someone in a romantic way and to meet him/her regularly **Seeing is believing!** *You've written this story? Seeing is believing!* = This is hard to believe. (The expression is a way of expressing doubt.) **I'll see about that!** *You're planning to go on holiday without me? I shall see about that!* = a way of mildly threatening someone (often humorous)

seed[1] /si:d/ noun, c. or u. **1** *Plant these seeds in the soil.* = a hard and small part of a fruit, from which it is usually possible to grow another plant **2** = the sperm of a male animal or human being (old-fashioned) **3** *the seeds of revolt* = the beginning of something that is expected to happen in the future **4** *Pete Sampras is the top seed in the tennis tournament.* = a player who is expected to do well in a competition (especially in tennis) and given a rank on the basis of some calculations

seed[2] verb, t. **1** *Pull up these plants before they start seeding.* = to produce seeds (referring to a plant) **2** *Can you seed these water-melons?* = to remove the seeds from a fruit **3** *Pete Sampras has been seeded for this tennis tournament.* = to place a player on a list of possible winners in a competition

S

seedling noun, c. = a young plant which has grown from a seed **seedy** adj. *This hotel looks rather seedy. I don't think we should stay here.* = dirty and in poor condition and appearing to be connected with dishonest activity

to go (run) to seed *He looked good a few years ago but he has run to seed now.* = to become unhealthy or unattractive in appearance because of old age, laziness or carelessness

seek /siːk/ verb, t. or i. (**sought**) **1** *The police are seeking clues which will help them find the murderer.*(i.) = to search or look for **2** *I sought his advice when I was in trouble.*(t.) = to ask for (formal) **3** *Seek and you will find happiness.*(i.) = to look for answers to spiritual questions **sought-after** adj. *She is a much sought-after actor.* = very popular, highly regarded

seem /siːm/ verb, i. *The patient seems to be improving, but we cannot be sure.* = to appear to be **seeming** adj. *Don't be misled by his seeming honesty. He is really a cheat.* = as seen on the surface but not really so

seep /siːp/ verb, i. *Water is seeping through the walls.* = to pass slowly through small holes or openings in some solid material (referring to the movement of a liquid or gas) **seepage** noun, u. *How can the seepage of water be stopped ?* = the slow movement of a liquid or gas through small openings in a solid material

seer /ˈsɪəʳ/ noun, c. *Sri Aurobindo was a great seer who had a grand vision of human progress.* = someone who is wise and can look into the future

see•saw[1] /ˈsiːsɔː/ noun, c. = a long, narrow plank of wood which is balanced in the middle and on which children can move up or down when they sit at the opposite ends

seesaw[2] verb, i. *The match between India and South Africa seesawed, with first one side and then the other being in a winning position.* = to move first in one direction and then in the opposite direction

seethe /siːð/ verb, i. *We are seething with anger over the rude remarks made against us.* = to be in a state of agitation, ready to fight

seg•ment /ˈsegmənt/ noun, c. **1** *The cake was cut into segments.* = one of the parts into which something circular can be divided or cut **2** *The Maruti 800 dominates the medium-price segment of the car market.* = a particular part of something larger **3** = a part of a circle formed by drawing a straight line across the circle [TECHNICAL]

seg•re•gate /ˈsegrɪgeɪt/ verb, t. *A good hospital segregates patients suffering from infectious diseases.* = to separate or keep people away from each other, ususally for medical reasons [TECHNICAL] **segregation** /segrɪˈgeɪʃən/ noun, u. = the act of segregating people (keeping them separated from each other) often for political reasons

seis•mic /ˈsaɪzmɪk/ adj. *Scientists continue to find some seismic disturbance near the area which experienced an earthquake yesterday.* = having to do with the movement of the earth's surface **seismograph** noun, = an instrument that can measure the force of an earthquake **seismology** /saɪzˈmɔːlədʒi/ noun = the scientific study of the movements of the earth's surface leading to earthquakes

seize /siːz/ verb, t. **1** *The man seized my hand and pulled me up the steps.* = to take hold of something forcefully and suddenly **2** *The government has seized all the documents and ornaments found in the locker of the accused.* = to take possession of something, usually through a government order **3** *When she was offered a free ticket to South Africa she seized the opportunity at once.* = to accept eagerly something which comes to you by chance **seizure** /ˈsiːzəʳ/ noun, c. **1** = the act of seizing something (taking possession of something) **2** = a sudden illness or attack which causes an organ to stop functioning, become paralysed etc.

sel•dom /ˈseldəm/ adv. *We seldom watch television because we find it dull.* = not often, rarely

se•lect[1] /sɪˈlekt/ verb, t. *We will select one of these three candidates for the job.* = to choose or take one or more persons or things out of a group

select[2] adj. *He belongs to a select group of artists.* = carefully chosen and belonging to a small or special group **selection** noun, u. or c. **1** *Her selection as the captain was approved by everyone.*(u.) = the act of selecting (choosing) someone or something **2** *We are studying a selection of Urdu short stories.*(c.) = something that has been selected (chosen) out of a larger number **selective** adj. *She is very selective about the books she reads.* = careful in choosing (sometimes disapproving)

self /self/ noun, c. (**selves**) or u. **1** *One must be in control of one's own self in order to find peace.*(c.) = body as well as mind **2** *This is not the time to put the self first. We must think of the nation.*(u.) = one's own interest or profit

self- prefix meaning 'of, by or for oneself or itself' e.g. **self-explanatory** adj. *Just follow this map and you will be able to reach the school easily. The map is self-explanatory.* = explaining itself and easy to understand

self-appointed adj. *He is the self-appointed leader of this group.* = chosen by oneself and not by others (derogatory)

self-assured adj. *He looked completely self-assured when he was asked to make a speech.* = very sure of one's own ability and therefore calm

self-centred adj. *He loves to talk about his own greatness. I have not seen a more self-centred person.* = interested only in oneself

self-confident adj. = (as in **self-assured** above) very sure of one's own ability and therefore calm

self-conscious adj. *She looked very self-conscious when she was asked to stand up and make a speech.* = feeling nervous and uncomfortable

self-contained adj. *a self-contained flat, with a kitchen and bathroom* = having everything that may be required, in one place

self-control noun, u. *He does not get angry easily. He has a lot of self-control.* = control over one's own feelings

self-defence noun *The law allows you to shoot someone who is trying to kill you. You have the right of self-defence.* = something done to save one's own life or property

self-destruct verb, i. *This plane will self-destruct if it falls into the hands of the enemy.* = to destroy itself, automatically

self-effacing adj. *Not many people know about her talent in writing because she is so self-effacing.* = very modest, not wishing to boast; unassuming

self-employed adj. *a self-employed motor-mechanic* = earning money from some business but not working for an employer

self-esteem noun, u. *He was very sure that he would get the job. His failure to do so was a blow to his self-esteem.* = the good opinion that one has of oneself

self-evident adj. *It should be self-evident that our city is getting over crowded.* = so clear that no proof is needed

self-government noun = the government or rule of a country or organization by its own people

self-help noun = the action of doing something without depending on others for help

self-knowledge noun = an understanding of one's own nature or character

self-locking adj. *a self-locking door* = able to lock itself (referring to a door)

self-made adj. *a self-made businessperson* = becoming successful without any help from others

self-preservation noun *All living creatures have the instinct of self-preservation.* = the desire to keep oneself alive and safe from harm

self-reliant adj. = not depending on others for help

self-respect noun *Once he started to drink heavily he lost all self-respect!* = the regard that one has for oneself, which makes a person behave in a way that gets respect from others

self-righteous adj. *She is so self-righteous that she will never admit her own mistakes.* = always believing that one's actions are correct

self-service adj. *a self-service restaurant* = a restaurant or a shop where there is no one to serve customers, who are expected to get what they want themselves

self-starter noun, c. = an electrical device (instrument) fitted to a machine or engine, which starts it when a button is pressed

self-sufficient adj. *India is self-sufficient in rice. We do not need to buy rice from any other country.* = not depending on anyone else for the things one needs

selfish /ˈselfɪʃ/ adj. *They spend all the money they earn on themselves. What selfish persons they are!* = thinking only of one's own interest, convenience, welfare etc. and not that of others **selfishness** noun *It was because of his selfishness that he lost all his friends.* = selfish behaviour **selfishly** adv.

self•less /ˈselflɪs/ adj. *Mother Teresa devoted her life to the selfless care of the sick.* = showing concern for others and not for oneself **selflessness** noun, u. *Every member of the rescue team acted out of pure selflessness in helping the accident victims.* = the quality of showing concern for others and not oneself

sell[1] /sel/ verb, t. or i. (**sold**) **1** *I have sold my old car to a doctor for Rs 20,000.*(t.) = to exchange something in return for money **2** *The farmers grow vegetables and sell them in the town.*(t.) = to offer something to a buyer **3** *This new book is not interesting. I don't think it will sell.*(i.) = to be able to find buyers **4** *The government has not been able to sell its new health programme to the people.*(t.) = to make people accept a new idea

sell[2] noun, c. *The car is so costly that it is proving to be a difficult sell.* = something that is offered to a buyer **seller** noun, c. = a person who has sold or is trying to sell something for money **seller's market** noun *If you try to buy a house in Mumbai, you will find that very few houses are available. It is a seller's market.* = a time when many people are trying to buy the same things, and prices are high **selling point** noun, c. *The strongest selling point for this car is that it uses very little petrol.* = a quality in a product which is expected to be liked by someone who may be interested in buying it **sell-out** noun, c. *The cricket match between Australia and India was a sell-out.* = an event (usually connected with sports, music etc.) that is so popular that it becomes difficult to get tickets **sell-by date** noun, c. = referring to an item (usually food or medicine) which, by an order, has a date on it by which time it must be sold

S

to sell like hot cakes *Books on yoga are selling like hot cakes.* = to be in great demand (informal) **to be sold on something** *He is totally sold on pop music.* = to be an enthusiastic believer in something (informal)

se•man•tic /sɪ'mæntɪk/ adj. = having to do with the meaning of words **semantics** noun = the scientific study of meaning in language

sem•blance /'sembləns/ noun, u. *There was no semblance of order at the meeting. Everyone was shouting at the top of his or her voice.* = outward appearance (formal)

se•men /'si:mən/ noun = the thick whitish fluid which carries the sperm or seed of a male animal or human being [BIOLOGY]

se•mes•ter /sɪ'mestəʳ/ noun, c. = one of the two or three periods into which a year is divided for purposes of teaching at a university

semi- /'semɪ/ prefix meaning **1** half e.g. **semi-circle** noun, c. = half a circle **2** almost e.g. **semi-automatic** adj. *a semi-automatic washing machine* = a (machine) which can almost run itself and needs little attention

semi-colon /semɪ'kəʊlən/ noun, c. = a mark of punctuation, shown by the sign (;), which is often used to separate the parts of a sentence

semi-conductor /semɪkən'dʌktəʳ/ noun, c. = a substance such as silicon which allows an electric current to pass through it with some resistance and is used for making transistors and other electronic parts, also used in computers

semi-detached /semɪdɪ'tætʃt/ adj. *a semi-detached house* = a house that is joined to the neighbouring house by a common wall

semi-final /semɪ'faɪnəl/ noun, c. = a match that is played just before the final (last) match in a tournament or competition

sem•i•nar /'semɪnɑ:ʳ/ noun, c. = a small group which meets to discuss or study a subject

sem•i•na•ry /'semɪnəri/ noun, c. (**seminaries**) **1** = a school (old-fashioned) **2** = a place where people are trained to become priests or nuns

semi-precious /semɪ'preʃəs/ adj. *a semi-precious stone* = a kind of stone, such as garnet or amethyst, which is used for making jewellery but is not as costly as a precious stone such as diamond

Se•mit•ic /sɪ'mɪtɪk/ adj. **1** *a Semitic religion* = belonging to the race, languages and cultures of the Jews and Arabs **2** = Jewish (connected with the Jewish race or religion)

sem•o•li•na /semə'li:nə/ noun, u. = a kind of powdered food made by crushing wheat (known as 'sooji' or 'rava' in India)

sen•ate /'senɪt/ noun, c. = a group of people who make laws or look after the affairs of a university **senator** noun, c. = a member of a senate

send /send/ verb, t. (**sent**) **1** *Please send this letter by registered post.* = to cause something or someone to go to a place, without going there oneself **2** *He gave the ball a kick which sent it flying.* = to cause something to move with force **3** *The film was so boring that it sent me to sleep.* = to cause something to happen **4** *The crowd sent out a roar of joy when Mahanama scored a century.* = to produce **5** *I don't feel like cooking today. Let us send for some food.* = to ask someone to bring something or to order something from some source **sender** noun, c. = a person who sends something to someone, usually by post **send-off** noun, c. *My friends gave me a grand send-off when I was leaving for Japan.* = a show of good wishes for someone who is going on a journey

to send in *When the doctor arrived, I was sent in first.* = to ask someone to enter a place **to send out 1** *If you make any more noise, you will be sent out.* = asked to leave a place **2** *This instrument sends out a lot of heat.* = to emit, give out **to send for someone/something** *We sent for the doctor.* = to ask someone to come; to place an order for **to send out for something** *I don't feel like cooking. Shall we send out for some food?* = to order food to be brought in from a restaurant (instead of going there to eat) **to send back** *As the address on the cover was incorrect, the post office sent the letter back to us.* = return **to send off** *There was a large crowd at the airport to send him off.* = to convey good wishes when someone is about to leave; to say good-bye **to send word (to somebody)** *The meeting had to be postponed because the chairperson sent word to say he was unwell.* = to send a message

se•nile /'si:naɪl/ adj. *Both my grandparents have become old and senile. They can't think clearly now.* = mentally or physically weak as a result of old age (technical or not respectful) **senility** /sɪ'nɪlɪti/ noun, u. = the condition of being senile

se•ni•or[1] /'si:niəʳ/ adj. *He is a senior officer in the government.* = having a high rank or a higher rank than someone else

senior[2] noun, c. *She is my senior by three years.* = older in age than someone else **senior citizen** noun, c. = a person who is (usually) more than 65 years of age; retired people, pensioners **seniority** /si:nɪ'ɔ:rɪti/ noun, u. *Promotions should be based not merely on seniority, but also on ability.* = the condition of being older or higher in rank than others

sen•sa•tion /sen'seɪʃən/ noun, u. or c. **1** *He has lost all sensation in his limbs after the accident he had last year.*(u.) = the ability to feel pain, heat etc. **2** *The famous actor caused a sensation by appearing* *in the role of a woman in a play.*(c.) = something that creates great excitement or interest **sensational** adj. *The bank robbery made sensational news.* = exciting or causing great wonder, shock etc.

sense[1] /sens/ noun, c. or u. **1** *He has lost the sense of smell.*(c.) = one of the five senses (the ability to see, hear, smell, taste, feel) **2** *How could you take a taxi when taxis are so expensive? I thought you had more sense!*(u.)= good judgement about practical things **3** *He had a sense of helplessness when he lost his father.* = feeling **4** *When I say she is 'clever', I am using the word in a positive sense.* = meaning

sense[2] verb, t. *Why don't you speak? I sense some kind of anger in you.* = to detect or notice **senseless** adj. **1** *Stop this senseless talk at once!* = meaningless, foolish **2** *The man became senseless because of the heat.* = unconscious **sense organ** noun, c. = a part of the body that is connected with one of the five senses (e.g. the eyes, ears, nose or tongue) **senses** noun (only plural) **1** = all or some of the five senses **2** *The man was not in his senses.* = in control of one's own actions

to talk sense *Come on! Talk sense!* = used to say that what is being suggested is impossible **beat/drive/knock some sense into someone** *Will you drive some sense into the boy? He is too young to start a business.* = to change someone's opinion, decision etc., in a forceful manner **to bring someone to their senses** *I don't know how I can bring her to her senses. She wants to take part in a cycle race so soon after her surgery!* = to stop someone from behaving foolishly **in one's right senses** (always plural) *Nobody in their right senses would want to see a film with so much violence.* = in a normal state of mind **to talk sense** *You are asking me to climb that tree! Will you talk sense?* = to not say something foolish or impossible **in a sense** *It is not fair, in a sense, to expect the government to solve every problem.* = if understood or thought about in a particular way **to make sense** *This letter doesn't make sense; the writer seems to have used words which don't exist in the language.* = to be easily understood

sen•si•bil•i•ty /sensəˈbɪlɪti/ noun, u. *They cannot understand art or music. They have no sensibility.* = the ability to understand art, music, poetry etc.

sen•si•ble /ˈsensəbəl/ adj. **1** *As we were all thirsty, he suggested that we should stop and have something to drink. I thought it was a very sensible suggestion.* = based on good judgement and understanding of practical matters **2** *We were asked to wear sensible footwear while hiking.* = practical and suitable rather than fashionable

sen•si•tive /ˈsensɪtɪv/ adj. **1** *Her skin is very sensitive. It is easily burnt by the sun.* = easily influenced, changed or damaged by something **2** *She is so sensitive that she may start crying if you shout at her.* = having feelings that are easily hurt or upset **3** *Madhuri Dixit has given a very sensitive performance in this film.* = showing delicate feelings **4** *You should be sensitive to the suffering of others.* = able to understand the feelings of others **5** *Don't tell anyone about the minister's illness. This is a sensitive matter.* = delicate; requiring careful handling **6** *This is a very sensitive thermometer. It can show even a slight change in the temperature.* = able to measure things exactly (referring to instruments) **sensitivity** /sensɪˈtɪvɪti/ noun, u. = the quality of being sensitive

sen•sor /ˈsensəʳ/ noun, c. *a heat sensor* = a device (part of a machine) that can show the presence of something such as heat etc. **sensory** adj. *sensory perception* = having to do with the five senses (sight, smell, taste, hearing, touch)

sen•su•al /ˈsenʃuəl/ adj. *sensual enjoyment* = having to do with physical or bodily, specially sexual, pleasure

sen•su•ous /ˈsenʃuəs/ adj. *I loved the sensuous touch of soft silk in my hands.* = giving pleasure to the senses (sight, taste, smell etc.)

sen•tence[1] /ˈsentəns/ noun, c. **1** *'He went home last night' is a sentence.* = a group of words that contains a finite verb and a subject [GRAMMAR] **2** *The judge passed sentence on the accused.* = an order given by a judge in court, declaring someone to be guilty of some crime and fixing the punishment to be given to him/her

sentence[2] verb, t. *The judge sentenced the accused to five years' imprisonment.* = to pass a sentence in court, declaring someone to be guilty and fixing the punishment to be given

sen•tient /ˈsenʃənt/ adj. *J.C. Bose, the famous scientist, showed that plants are sentient creatures and can feel pain as well as pleasure.* = living and able to feel pain, pleasure etc. (formal)

sen•ti•ment /ˈsentɪmənt/ noun, c. or u. **1** *Hindi films are full of sentiment. Several films have been made about the love between a mother and her sons.*(u.) = gentle feelings of sadness, caring, attachment etc. which are often thought to be unsuitable for the practical world (sometimes derogatory) **2** *The sentiments expressed by every speaker were the same: that the country should not go to war.*(c.) = idea or feeling expressed in words **sentimental** /sentɪˈmentəl/ adj. *This camera has sentimental value for me because it was given to me by a favourite uncle.* = based more on feelings than on practical judgement (see **sentiment**, meaning **1**)

sen•ti•nel /ˈsentɪnəl/ noun, c. *The Himalayas have always been India's sentinel against enemy attack.* =

S

a guard (literary, old-fashioned)

sen•try /ˈsentri/ noun, c. (**sentries**) = a guard, soldier or policeman

se•pal /ˈsepəl/ noun, c. = one of the small green leaves surrounding the coloured petals of a flower (see pic under **flower**) [BIOLOGY]

sep•a•rate[1] /ˈsepəreɪt/ verb, t. or i. **1** *There is a fence separating the two plots of land.*(t.) = to keep unconnected or apart **2** *The mother was separated from her children while they were moving through the crowd.*(i.) = to move apart or away from each other **3** *Let's separate the graduates from the undergraduates.* = to cause two or more people, groups or objects to move away from each other **4** *Mr Verma and his wife have separated.*(i.) = to live apart from each other while still married because of differences

separate[2] /ˈsepərɪt/ adj. **1** *The two brothers live in separate houses now, although they grew up in the same house.* = different **2** *The boys stayed in a separate hostel.* = not connected **separable** adj. *A country's economic progress is not separable from its political freedom.* = which can be seperated from something else (opposite **inseparable**) **separation** /sepəˈreɪʃən/ noun, u. **1** *My brother moved into a new house last year, although we had grown up in the same house. The separation was painful.* = the act of seperating or moving apart **2** *My son has returned after spending five years in America. The long separation has made us more fond of each other than before.* = the time of living apart **separatist** /ˈseprətɪst/ noun *The separatists want to break away from the country and form an independent state.* = someone who wants to break away from a state, a political union or a religious group

se•pi•a /ˈsiːpiə/ noun = a yellowish brown colour, found in old photographs

sep•sis /ˈsepsɪs/ noun = the poisoning of a wound in some part of the body, caused by harmful bacteria **septic** adj. *The wound in his leg has turned septic.* = infected by bacteria **septic tank** noun = a large tank or container, fixed below the ground, in which waste from lavatories is collected and turned into harmless matter by the action of bacteria

Sep•tem•ber /sepˈtembə^r/ noun = the ninth month of the year, between August and October

sep•tu•a•gen•a•ri•an /septʃuədʒɪˈneəriən/ noun, c. = a person who is between the ages of 70 and 79

sep•ul•chre /ˈsepəlkə^r/ noun, c. = a tomb or underground room in which dead bodies are kept (literary, old-fashioned)

se•quel /ˈsiːkwəl/ noun, c. **1** *A new film called 'Sholay II' has been made as a sequel to the famous Hindi film 'Sholay'.* = a film or book which continues the story of an earlier film or book (opposite **prequel**) **2** *The Prime Minister has decided to visit Britain, as a sequel to his visit to the USA* = some action which follows another action and is often its result

se•quence /ˈsiːkwəns/ noun, c. or u. **1** *India became independent in 1947 but became a republic only in 1950. Let us get the sequence right.* = the order in which a group of events or objects are arranged, one following the other **2** *The crowd sequence had to be re-shot.* = a part of a film showing a single episode/event **sequential** /sɪˈkwənʃəl/ adj. *sequential events* = forming a sequence

se•ren•di•pi•ty /serənˈdɪpɪti/ noun, u. *The old man stumbled into a ditch by the roadside and found he had discovered a gold-mine! What a wonderful case of serendipity!* = the making of a valuable or interesting discovery purely by accident (often humorous)

se•rene /sɪˈriːn/ adj. *You will admire the serene beauty of the mountains near Darjeeling.* = (of natural beauty, music etc.) clear, quiet and calm in a way which is pleasing **serenity** /sɪˈrenəti/ noun, u. *The serenity of the prayer hall helps us to concentrate.* = quiet, peace, calmness

serf /sɜːf/ noun, c. = a person working as a labourer on a farm belonging to a rich land-owner, in former times in Europe

serge /sɜːdʒ/ noun = a kind of woollen cloth used for making warm clothing

ser•geant /ˈsɑːdʒənt/ noun = an army or police officer of low rank

se•ri•al[1] /ˈsɪəriəl/ noun, c.*a television serial* = a play in many parts, presented on radio or television, in which the story continues from one episode or series of events to the next

serial[2] adj. *seats placed in serial order* = arranged in a series (one after the other) **serialize (serialise)** verb, t. *This novel will be serialized into a television programme.* = to make a radio or television serial out of a book

se•ries /ˈsɪəriːz/ noun (singular as well as plural) **1** *The Indian and Australian teams will play a series of one-day matches.* = a set of objects of the same kind which are arranged in order, one after the other **2** *The cultural organization arranged for a series of lectures on art and music.* = a set of programmes which are part of a theme or topic **in series** *Light bulbs in parallel require more electrical current than those connected in series.* = an electrical arrangement in which a number of batteries or capacitors are connected so that a current flows in turn through each one [TECHNICAL]

se•ri•ous /ˈsɪəriəs/ adj. **1** *The patient's condition is serious. His lungs have become infected.* = causing worry or anxiety **2** *Why do you look so serious? Is something wrong?* = worried **3** *This is a serious film. You won't find any humour in it.* = not meant to be funny; requiring intellectual effort **4** *We had a serious discussion about the war.* = thoughtful (requiring a lot of thinking) **5** *I have a serious interest in architecture.* = an activity on which one is willing to spend time in reading, practising etc. **seriousness** noun *I want you to understand the seriousness of the water problem. Soon we will have to buy every drop.* = the extent to which something causes one to feel anxious and to take action based on this

in all seriousness *In all seriousness, I think you are wasting your money on this course.* = frankly, honestly

> **Usage** When we want to say someone is very ill, we say, *'He/She is in a serious condition'* not *'He/She is serious'.*

ser•mon /ˈsɜːmən/ noun, c. **1** = a religious or moral talk, usually given in a church and based on a verse taken from the Bible **2** *Don't start sermonizing just because I didn't come home for lunch. I don't want to listen to any more of your sermons.* = a talk given, especially to advise (not respectful) **sermonize (sermonise)** verb, i. *Look, I know I should be more serious about my studies. Now don't start sermonizing!* = to talk seriously to someone, usually offering advice, in a way that is often found boring (disapproving)

ser•pent /ˈsɜːpənt/ noun, c. **1** = a large snake (formal and old fashioned; literary) **2** = a wicked person who cannot be trusted (figurative) **serpentine** adj. *a serpentine road, winding up the mountain* = turning and twisting from side to side, like a moving snake

ser•rat•ed /sɪˈreɪtɪd/ adj. *a knife with a serrated edge, used for cutting bread into slices* = having a row of small teeth with a saw-like edge

se•rum /ˈsɪərəm/ noun, u. or c. **1** *Anti-rabies serum should be given at once if a person has been bitten by a dog.* = a liquid used to prevent some disease, prepared from the blood of an animal into which the germs of the disease have been introduced earlier **2** = the thin, watery substance present in blood which separates when blood clots

ser•vant /ˈsɜːvənt/ noun, c. *a loyal government servant* = a person who works regularly for someone on a salary (pay)

serve /sɜːv/ verb, t. or i. **1** *He has served the government for 35 years and is going to retire soon.*(t.) = to work for someone **2** *This railway serves the people living along the east coast.* = to provide with something useful **3** *Who is going to serve food to the guests?* = distribute **4** *The criminal will serve a five-year sentence in jail.* = to pass a period of time in jail **5** *Now Venus Williams is going to serve to Serena.* = to begin play by hitting the ball to the opponent in a game such as tennis, badminton or volleyball **6** *This atlas will serve until I can find a more detailed one.* = to be sufficient for a given purpose

serve up *My father served up a very tasty meal at short notice.* = to make and serve food efficiently (informal) **Serve you right!** *So you have lost your keys and can't get into the house. Serve you right! Why are you so careless?* = a harsh way of telling someone they get what they deserve

serv•er /sɜːvəʳ/ noun, c. **1** = a computer which controls other computers in a network, or one which has a special function (e.g. a file-server) [COMPUTERS] **2** = the player who is serving (in the game of tennis, badminton or volleball)

ser•vice[1] /ˈsɜːvɪs/ noun, u. or c. **1** *He has been in government service for many years.*(u.)= work done regularly for someone **2** *The post office offers a number of services to the public.*(c.)= work done to meet a particular need **3** *The service in this restaurant is poor.*(u.) = attention given to customers in a shop, hotel etc. **4** *I have to send my car for service.* = work done to keep a machine in good condition **5** *Navratilova has a powerful service.* = the act of serving (hitting the ball to an opponent) in the game of tennis, badminton or volleyball

service[2] verb, t. *This mechanic will service my car.* = to work on a machine in order to keep it in good condition **serviceable** adj. *This old car is still serviceable. Don't sell it away.* = good enough to be used **service charge** noun *Many restaurants include a service charge in the bill.* = a percentage of the bill added on as a tip **service station** noun, c. = a workshop where cars are serviced or a petrol-filling station or a garage that sells fuel for vehicles

at your service *Don't hesitate to call me if you need help. I am always at your service.* = ready to help (formal but often humorous) **on active service** = engaged in fighting a war **out of service** *This lift (elevator) is often out of service.* = not working

ser•vi•ette /sɜːviˈet/ noun, c. = a table-napkin (a piece of cloth placed over the thighs while eating at a table, so as to prevent food from accidentally falling on one's clothes and making them dirty)

ser•vile /ˈsɜːvaɪl/ adj. *Why do you speak in such a servile tone when you talk to your seniors on the phone?* = showing too much humility, like a slave (derogatory)

ser•ving /ˈsɜːvɪŋ/ noun, c. *Please give me just a*

S

small serving of rice. = an amount of food which is offered to one person

se•sa•me /ˈsesəmi/ noun = a kind of plant which produces small white seeds, from which sesame oil is made

ses•sion /ˈseʃən/ noun, c. **1** *The winter session of the parliament begins on the sixth of December.* = a meeting or series of meetings of an official body, such as the parliament **2** *a question-and-answer session* = a period of time given to a particular kind of activity

set[1] /set/ verb, t. or i. (**set**) **1** *He set the suitcase down on the floor.*(t.) = to put something in a particular place or position **2** *The story of this film is set in Manipur.*(t.) = to fix the time and place of a story **3** *His question set me thinking.*(t.) = to cause some activity to start **4** *I have set the alarm on the clock to ring at 4.30 in the morning.*(t.) = to make something ready for use **5** *The date for the examination has not been set.*(i.) = to fix or establish a rule, time etc. **6** *The gold ring was set with diamonds and rubies.*(i.) = to fix a precious stone in a piece of jewellery **7** *He has broken his arm. It will take three months for the bones to set.*(i.) = to heal or join together (referring to a broken bone) **8** *The cement is still wet. It will set in three hours.*(i.) = to become hard (referring to soft cement) **9** *I have been asked to set the questions for the examination.*(t.) = to decide on a task to be given to somebody **10** *The sun sets very early in winter.*(i.) = to disappear from the sky (referring to the sun, moon or stars)

set[2] adj. **1** *I have no set time for meals. I eat whenever I feel hungry.* = fixed **2** *We are all set for the trek. The preparations are complete.* = ready **3** *'The Tempest' is a set text for the B.A. degree course.* = a textbook that has to be used by everyone doing a course of study

set[3] noun, c. **1** *I have bought a set of tools for the car.* = a group of connected things which form a whole **2** *a television set* = an instrument which receives television or radio signals or telephone messages **3** *This colourful set has been made for the new film.* = the scenery, buildings, furniture etc. made to show the place where the story of a film or play is supposed to take place **4** *Pete Sampras has won the first set in this match.* = a part of a match, in tennis, made up of at least six games **5** *The set of his jaws showed that he had made up his mind and would not listen to me.* = the position of some part of the body **setback** noun, c. *Our transport business has suffered a setback. One of our trucks has met with an accident.* = an event or accident that causes some loss **set square** noun, c. = a piece of plastic or metal in the shape of a triangle, having one angle of 90 degrees, used by students of geometry to make measurements **set theory** noun = a branch of mathematics that deals with sets of numbers etc. [MATHEMATICS] **set-up** noun *There is a new set-up in the office. We have a new manager and a new secretary.* = an arrangement for doing some work

to set about *After the party was over we set about cleaning up the mess.* = to start doing something **to set against** *Such a decision may set the people against the authorities.* = to make someone oppose a person **to set apart** *Her quick ways set her apart from the others in the class.* = to bring out the difference between two people (approving) **set aside 1** *Let's set aside these books. We may find use for them later.* = to put away for a while **2** *Our savings make us set aside some money for use in our old age.* = to keep for a special purpose **to set somebody back** *The expense on the surgery set him back quite a bit.* = to have to spend a lot of money on something **set down** *If you want to write an article, first set down your ideas on paper.* = to note in writing **to set forth** *The voyagers set forth on the first Sunday in December.* = to start on a journey or a voyage (old-fashioned) **to set in** *If the children don't work to a set time-table, confusion will set in. // We have to stock our supplies before the winter sets in.* = to start, become established **to set off 1** *We set off early in the morning.* = to start on a journey **2** *A remote-controlled device set off the alarm.* = to cause **to set out** *His arguments in the essay are clearly set out.* = to present or arrange/explain **to set up 1** *The highway authorities have set up road-blocks because some repair is going on.* = to put in place **2** *We set up the stage in readiness for the play.* = to make ready for use **3** *The authorities have set up a committee to go into the new system of examinations.* = to establish **to set someone/something free** *The bird was in a cage and I set it free.* = to give a person or an animal its freedom **to set a table** = to make a dining table ready for a meal by arranging plates etc. on it **to set a record** = to create a new standard in a race or competitive event e.g. swimming **to set something (things) right** *This whole matter is in such a mess. We need your help in setting it right.* = to bring order to a situation or to solve problems **to set an example** *You shouldn't behave so badly; in fact you should set an example for others.* = to act in such a way that others can follow your example **to set great store by something** *In my family, we set great store by punctuality.* = to have great respect for a quality, behaviour etc. **to be set in one's opinions/ways** = to have opinions/habits which are firm and difficult to change (often disapproving) **to set one's heart on something** *She set her heart on going to an art school.* = to want something very much and be determined to get it

set•ting /setɪŋ/ noun, c. **1** *The university is located in a beautiful setting, surrounded by a ring of mountains.* = the natural scenery (trees, mountains etc.) found in or near a place **2** *The setting for this film is a small village in Kashmir.* = the background (time and place) for the story of a film **3** *The diamond in my ring has come out of its setting.* = the piece of metal (usually gold or silver) in which a precious stone is fixed **4** *The air-conditioner will switch itself off after four hours as the timer setting is on 4.* = the position at which the controlling switches of a machine are set

set•tee /se'tiː/ noun, c. = a sofa (a long, comfortable chair on which more than one person can sit)

set•tle /'setl/ verb, i. or t. **1** *When the Parsis first came to India from Persia, they settled in Gujarat.*(i.) = to start living in a place **2** *The bird flew down and settled on the branch of a tree.*(i.) = to come to rest in some place **3** *The walls of the building are showing cracks because the earth is settling.*(i.) = to sink to a lower level **4** *We have to settle a date for our meeting.*(t.) = to decide or fix **5** *The two neighbours had been quarrelling for years, but now they have settled their dispute.* = to end a quarrel and reach an agreement **settlement** noun, c. or u. **1** *a refugee settlement* = an area into which people have moved from some other place and where they are living **2** *We have decided to end our dispute and reach a settlement.* = an agreement or understanding **settler** noun, c. *The first settlers in America faced many problems.* = one who settles in a new place, country etc.

to settle down = to make oneself comfortable or to become used to a new place or job **to settle for something** *He wanted to become a film star, but he finally had to settle for the job of a film star's secretary.* = to accept or agree to something which is not as good as something else that one expected **to settle on someone or something** *We took a long time to decide on whether we would live in Kolkata or Siliguri. In the end, we settled on Kolkata.* = to choose someone or something

sev•en /'sevən/ noun = the number shown by the sign **7** or **vii**, which comes between 6 and 8

seventh heaven *Don't disturb him now. He is in seventh heaven when he is watching a cricket match on television.* = the highest state of happiness (informal, humorous)

sev•en•teen /sevən'tiːn/ noun = the number represented by 17 (10+7)

sev•en•ty /'sevənti/ noun = the number represented by 70 (10x7)

sev•er /'sevəʳ/ verb, t. **1** *My father decided to sever all connections with his village after he moved to the city.* = to cut off (a relationship) completely (formal) **2** *One of my fingers got severed accidentally when I was working on a machine.* = to be cut off completely and separated from something

sev•e•ral[1] /'sevərəl/ det. *I have several friends living in America.* = more than a few in number

several[2] pron. *He has no friends in America but I have several.* = quite a few

se•vere /sɪ'vɪəʳ/ adj. **1** *The injuries he received in the accident were quite severe. // The winter has been severe this year.* = causing great harm, pain or discomfort **2** *My teacher was severe with me as I had not prepared for the test.* = strict and harsh in dealing with someone **severely** adv. *This district has been severely affected by viral fever.* = badly **severity** /sə'verɪti/ noun, u. **severities** (always plural) *The children were afraid of the new tutor because of her severity.* = strictness, harshness

sew /səʊ/ verb, i. or t. (**sewed**, **sewn**) *The boys are learning to sew.*(i.) // *The woman is sewing clothes for her baby.*(t.) = to join pieces of cloth together, using a needle and thread or a sewing machine

to sew on *Please sew on this button for me.* = to fix by using a needle and thread **to sew up** *The doctor had to sew up the wound.* = to bring torn parts of skin together by sewing them

sew•ing /'səʊɪŋ/ noun, u. *The woman carried her sewing in a basket.* = the material (cloth, thread etc.) used to sew something **sewing machine** noun, c. = a machine used for sewing clothes, generally used by tailors

sew•age /'sjuːɪdʒ/ noun, u. = waste matter, including body wastes, together with water, which is carried away from houses in sewers (drains) **sewer** /sjuːəʳ/ noun, c. = large pipes or drains, generally laid underground, which carry sewage (waste matter)

sewing, sewing machine see under **sew**

sex /seks/ noun, u. or c. **1** (u.) = the act of sexual intercourse (see below) **2** *Many of our films seem to be concerned only with sex.*(u.) = physical attraction between two people, which may lead to the act of sex **3** *The application form requires you to state your sex.*(u.) = the fact of being either male or female (also **gender**) **4** *separation of the sexes*(c.) = the two groups (male or female) into which humans and most animals can be divided **sex appeal** noun = the power of attracting someone belonging to the opposite sex, in a physical way **sexism** noun = the belief that women and girls are inferior to men and boys, which may lead to unfair treatment of women and girls **sexist** noun, c. = a person who believes that women are inferior to men **sexist** adj. *sexist attitude* = a way of thinking which is based on sexism **sex organ** noun, c. = some part of the body which is connected with the production of children or with sexual intercourse (see below) **sexual** adj. = connected with sex **sexual intercourse** noun, u. = the act of physical union

S

between two persons in which their sex organs are brought together (formal) **sexy** adj. **1** *a sexy scene in a film* = sexually exciting (informal) **2** *a sexy idea* = very clever (slang)

sex•tant /'sekstənt/ noun = an instrument used to calculate the position of a ship at sea by measuring the angles between stars

sex•tu•plet /sek'stjuːplɪt/ noun, c. = one of six children born to a woman at the same time

shab•by /'ʃæbi/ adj. **1** *They keep their house in a shabby condition. They should clean it at least once a week.* = having an appearance of neglect, lack of care **2** *The candidate was shabbily treated by the interviewing panel. They should have been more fair to him.* = unkind or unfair **3** *You have so many clean clothes, why are you wearing these shabby ones?* = crumpled, old-looking (usually said of clothes)

shack /ʃæk/ noun, c. = a small hut or house made of zinc sheets, cardboard, plastic sheets etc.

shack•le[1] /'ʃækəl/ noun, c. **1** *The prisoner was chained with a shackle.* = a heavy metal chain used to tie up a person so that he/she is unable to move **2** *We want our people to throw off their shackles and make themselves free.* = (usually plural) anything that checks the freedom of a person, specially freedom of the mind (figurative)

shackle[2] verb, t. *The government has passed a new law to shackle the freedom of the press.* = to check the freedom of a person or organization

shade[1] /ʃeɪd/ noun, u. or c. **1** *These plants grow better in the shade than in direct sunlight.*(u.) = a place where there is not too much sunlight **2** *Please get a new shade for the lamp.* = something that blocks light (stops too much light from passing through) **3** *I want a sari in a lighter shade of green.*(c.) = a difference in the brightness of a colour **4** *The word 'nice' carries many shades of meaning.* = a slight difference in meaning **5** *He uses black magic to communicate with shades.* = the spirit of a dead person (literary)

shade[2] verb, t. **1** *She shaded her eyes with her hand.* = to protect something from too much light **2** *The artist used a soft pencil to shade the face of the man in the picture.* = to show the effect of shadow in a picture

put somebody/something in the shade *His painting was so good that it put all the other paintings in the exhibition in the shade.* = to do or to be much better than the others (informal)

shad•ow[1] /'ʃædəʊ/ noun, c. or u. **1** *The trees cast their shadows on the grass.* = a dark area or a dark shape caused by the blocking of light by some object **2** *There were dark shadows under his eyes.* = a dark area on the skin **3** *That little boy is his father's shadow. He follows him everywhere.* = a person who follows some other person very closely

shadow[2] verb, t. *He has hired a private detective to shadow the suspect.* = to follow and watch someone closely **shadowy** adj. **1** *The shadowy garden was a perfect place for a picnic.* = full of shadows **2** *a shadowy person* = someone about whom not much is known

to chase shadows *You have to stop chasing shadows and start working.* = to have impossible ambitions **without a shadow of doubt** *With all the proof available there is not a shadow of doubt that he is the guilty person.* = without any doubt

shady /'ʃeɪdi/ adj. **1** *a shady place* = not receiving too much sunlight **2** *a shady character* = a person with a bad moral reputation (derogatory, informal)

shaft /ʃɑːft/ noun, c. **1** *the shaft of a spear* = the long, thin handle, usually made of wood, to which the head (sharp end) of a spear or arrow is fixed **2** *the drive shaft of a motor car* = a long piece of metal which connects the engine of a car to the wheels and causes them to turn **3** *the shaft of a coal mine* = a long underground passage in a mine, along which people move up or down

shag•gy /'ʃægi/ adj. *The dog has a shaggy coat.* = covered with long and thick hair

Shah /ʃɑː/ noun = the title given to the ruler of some Muslim countries such as Iran (in former times)

shake[1] /ʃeɪk/ verb, t. or i. (**shook, shaken**) **1** *The wind shook the trees.*(t.) = to cause something to move from side to side **2** *His hand shakes when he writes.*(i.) = to move very slightly from side to side **3** *The death of her father has shaken her badly.* = to trouble someone's mind or to upset someone **4** *My confidence was shaken when I lost the first game in the match.* = to become weak

shake[2] noun, c. **1** *She gave my hand a shake.* = The action of shaking (moving something quickly up and down or sideways) **2** *I will be with you in two shakes.* = a very short period of time (informal) **shake-up** noun, c. *Several senior managers lost their jobs last month when there was a shake-up in the company.* = a re-arrangement in an organization which produces a big change **shaky** adj. *My position in the company is shaky. I may be replaced soon.* = weak or uncertain

shall /ʃəl/ or /ʃæl/ aux. verb **1** *I shall visit my parents next week.* = showing that some action is to be performed in the future (generally used with 'I' or 'we') **2** *The traffic rule says that the driver of a car shall stop the car when the traffic signal is red.* = used, generally in official or legal writing, to show that something must be done (formal)

shal•lot /ʃə'lɒt/ noun = a kind of small onion

shal•low /ˈʃæləʊ/ adj. **1** *The river is shallow here: only three feet deep.* = not deep **2** *His writings on architecture are rather shallow. He should have spent more time studying the subject.* = not showing deep thinking or study

sham[1] /ʃæm/ noun, u. **1** *That man is not really a doctor. His medical degree is a sham.* = something or someone that is not really what it/he/she appears or claims to be (derogatory) **2** *He claimed to be a doctor and deceived everyone through his sham.* = false show or pretence

sham[2] verb, i. or t. (**shammed**) *We are shamming illness so that we can miss school.* = to pretend to have an illness, feelings etc. which one does not have

sham•bles /ˈʃæmbəlz/ noun (always plural) *The house is a shambles as no one looks after it now.* = a place which is in a state of disorder or confusion

shame[1] /ʃeɪm/ noun, u. **1** *I felt great shame when I was caught copying.* = the feeling of unhappiness or discomfort caused by the knowledge of having done something wrong or having failed to do something **2** *My family said I had brought shame on the family by becoming an actor.* = loss of honour **3** *It's a shame that you could not complete your studies.* = an unfortunate state of affairs; a pity

shame[2] verb, t. **1** *You have shamed the family by not telling the truth.* = to cause loss of honour **2** *When a poor woman gave away her gold earrings to help the flood victims, many of us were shamed into donating money for this cause.* = to persuade someone to do something by causing a feeling of shame **shamefaced** adj. *He looked shamefaced when I asked him why he had come late.* = showing shame because of something wrong that one has done **shameful** adj. *a shameful defeat in the match* = something that causes or should cause shame **shamefully** adv. **shameless** adj. *a shameless coward* = not showing the expected feeling of shame when one does something wrong **shamelessly** adv.

sham•poo[1] /ʃæmˈpuː/ noun, u. or c. = a kind of liquid soap used to clean the hair

shampoo[2] verb, t. = to wash the hair with shampoo

shan•ty /ˈʃænti/ noun, c. (**shanties**) = a small, rough hut built with cheap materials **shanty town** noun, c. = an area where poor people live in huts made of cheap materials

shape[1] /ʃeɪp/ noun, u. or c. **1** *The dining table has a round shape.* = the outer form of something **2** *the shape of the economy* = the nature or character of something **3** *We will not accept religious intolerance in any shape or form.* = (of any) sort or kind

shape[2] verb, t. **1** *The potter shaped the soft clay into beautiful vases.* = to give a particular form or shape to something **2** *His mind was shaped by the experiences he went through as a child.* = to have an influence on **shapely** adj. *shapely legs* = attractive, pleasing to the eye

shapes

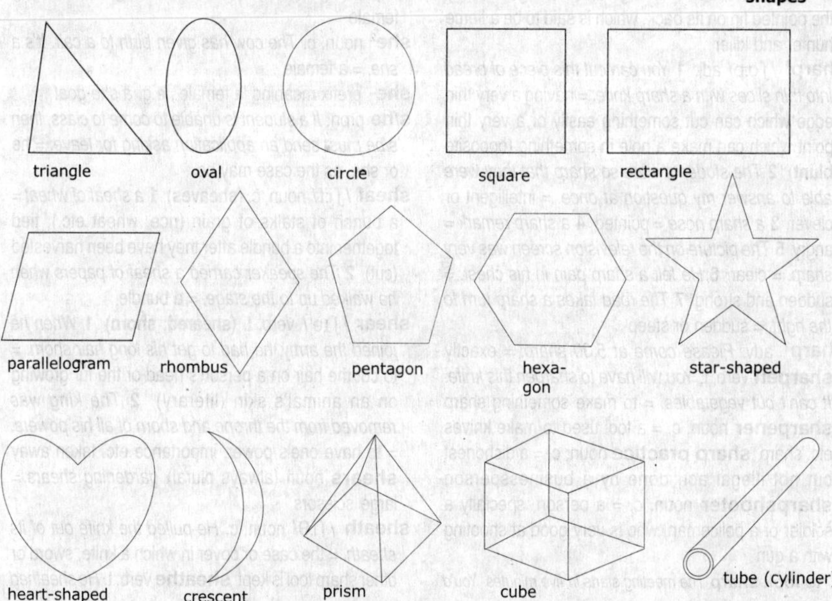

take shape *After many rehearsals the play is at last taking some shape.* = (of a plan, piece of writing etc.) to begin to look as one intends it to **shape up** *It is too early to say how the student will shape up in his new school.* = develop **to get (oneself) into shape** *If you are keen on a career in the army, you must be physically fit. Go to a gym and get yourself in shape.* = to become fit through exercise and shed body weight **out of shape** *We have not had any exercise for three months and are really out of shape.* = to become flabby and fat **to be in bad shape** *The animals in this zoo are in bad shape because they are not cared for.* = a poor condition (informal)

share[1] /ʃeəʳ/ noun, c. **1** *We have given each of our children a share of the property.* = one part out of several parts into which something (e.g. an amount of money or a piece of land) is divided **2** *I have bought 500 shares in this company.* = a part of the ownership of a company, which can be bought or sold by members of the public

share[2] verb, t. *When my mother and I travelled to Mumbai, we shared a berth as the train was full.* = to have or to use something together with someone else **share-cropper** noun, c. = a farmer who does not own the land on which he grows crops and who has to give a part of the crops to the owner of the land **share-holder** noun, c. = a person who owns part of a business or a company

sha•ri•a /ʃəˈriːə/ noun = the system of religious laws that is followed by most Muslims

shark /ʃɑːk/ noun = a large fish, distinguished by the pointed fin on its back, which is said to be a fierce hunter and killer

sharp[1] /ʃɑːp/ adj. **1** *You can cut this piece of bread into thin slices with a sharp knife.* = having a very thin edge which can cut something easily or a very thin point which can make a hole in something (opposite **blunt**) **2** *The students were so sharp that they were able to answer my question at once.* = intelligent or clever **3** *a sharp nose* = pointed **4** *a sharp remark* = angry **5** *The picture on the television screen was very sharp.* = clear **6** *He felt a sharp pain in his chest.* = sudden and strong **7** *The road takes a sharp turn to the right.* = sudden or steep

sharp[2] adv. *Please come at 5.30 sharp.* = exactly **sharpen** verb, t. *You will have to sharpen this knife. It can't cut vegetables.* = to make something sharp **sharpener** noun, c. = a tool used to make knives etc. sharp **sharp practice** noun, c. = a dishonest but not illegal act, done by a businessperson **sharpshooter** noun, c. = a person, specially a soldier or a policeman, who is very good at shooting with a gun

to look sharp *The meeting starts in five minutes. You'd better look sharp or else you may not be allowed in.* = to hurry up (informal)

shat•ter /ˈʃætəʳ/ verb, i. or t. **1** *The flower vase dropped from his hand and shattered.*(i.) = to break into very small pieces **2** *The sound of a gun shattered the silence.*(t.) = to disturb suddenly and violently **3** *I was shattered to hear the sad news of your father's death.* = to be shocked **shatter-proof** adj. *shatter-proof glass* = made of material which cannot break into small pieces (which can cut a person)

shave[1] /ʃeɪv/ verb, i. or t. *You look very untidy with all that stubble growing on your cheeks. You should shave.*(i.) // *He shaved off his moustaches to change his appearance.*(t.) = to remove hair growing on the body, especially the face, with a razor

shave[2] noun, c. *I asked the barber to give me a shave.* = the act of shaving **shaven** adj. *clean shaven* = with the hair shaved off **shaver** noun, c. *an electric shaver* = a machine used to remove hair from the face or body **shaving cream** noun, u. = a kind of soap used to make the hair on the face soft so that it can be shaved off easily

a close shave *The train went off the rails but no one was hurt. It was a close shave.* = a narrow escape from something dangerous or unpleasant

shawl /ʃɔːl/ noun, c. = a piece of warm material used to protect the upper part of the body from cold

she[1] /ʃiː/ pron. *My wife was ill but she is better now.* = referring to a girl/woman, a female animal or some object (e.g. a ship) that is often thought of as being female

she[2] noun, c. *The cow has given birth to a calf. It's a she.* = a female

she- prefix meaning 'a female', e.g. *a she-goat*

s/he pron. *If a student is unable to come to class, then s/he must send an application asking for leave.* = he or she, as the case may be

sheaf /ʃiːf/ noun, c. (**sheaves**) **1** *a sheaf of wheat* = a bunch of stalks of grain (rice, wheat etc.), tied together into a bundle after they have been harvested (cut) **2** *The speaker carried a sheaf of papers when he walked up to the stage.* = a bundle

shear /ʃɪəʳ/ verb, t. (**sheared**, **shorn**) **1** *When he joined the army, he had to get his long hair shorn.* = to cut the hair on a person's head or the fur growing on an animal's skin (literary) **2** *The king was removed from the throne and shorn of all his powers.* = to have one's power, importance etc. taken away **shears** noun (always plural) *gardening shears* = large scissors

sheath /ʃiːθ/ noun, c. *He pulled the knife out of its sheath.* = the case or cover in which a knife, sword or other sharp tool is kept **sheathe** verb, t. *He sheathed* *his sword.* = to put a knife or sword back into its sheath (cover) (opposite **un-sheathe**)

shed[1] /ʃid/ noun, c. *a cow or cycle shed* = a light one-storey structure, sometimes without walls, used to store things etc.

shed[2] verb, t. (**shed**) **1** *These trees shed their leaves in winter. // Snakes shed their skins every year.* = to lose leaves, skin, hair etc. as part of a natural process **2** *If you want to join our group, you will have to shed your prejudices.* = to give up in a determined way **3** *It is natural sometimes to shed tears when you are unhappy.* = to cause some liquid to flow **4** *She has shed a lot of weight after she went on a diet.* = to lose something or to have something removed, usually something you do not want

to shed light on *Can you shed some light on this problem so that we can easily find a solution?* = to provide more information about

sheen /ʃiːn/ noun, u. *The silk dress has lost its sheen.* = shine or brightness

sheep /ʃiːp/ noun, c. (**sheep**) (both singular and plural form) = an animal whose hair gives us wool **sheep-dog** noun = a kind of large dog which is trained to control sheep **sheepish** adj. *He looked sheepish when I caught him telling a lie.* = looking uncomfortable or foolish because one has been caught doing something wrong **black sheep** noun *You could call him the black sheep of the family as he is the only one who never went to school.* = someone who is thought of as having brought shame on a family or group

to separate the sheep from the goats *This examination at the end of the course is designed to separate the sheep from the goats.* = to separate those thought worthy or suitable enough from those who are thought unworthy or unsuitable

sheer /ʃɪər/ adj. **1** *He had no one to help him but he became successful through sheer hard work.* = pure; not mixed with something else **2** *She was wearing a sari of sheer silk.* = very thin and light material **3** *It was a sheer drop of several hundred metres and no one could come out alive.* = very steep and almost vertical (straight)

sheet /ʃiːt/ noun, c. **1** *a cotton bedsheet* = a piece of cloth which is spread on top of a bed **2** *a sheet of paper* = a thin, flat piece of some material **sheet anchor** noun *Sachin Tendulkar is the sheet anchor for the Indian team.* = someone who is the main support or who can be depended upon to help

as white as a sheet *He looked as white as a sheet when he realized his house had been burgled during his vacation.* = very frightened; shocked

shelf /ʃelf/ noun, c. (**shelves**) *a bookshelf* = a long, narrow and flat piece of wood, fixed to a wall or a cupboard (almirah), on which things can be stored **shelf life** noun *These canned vegetables have a shelf life of six months.* = the period of time for which some product, specially food, can be stored without its going bad

off the shelf *Can I buy the furniture off the shelf? I need it urgently.* = readily available in a shop, factory etc. so that it can be bought without one's having to wait or place an order

shell[1] /ʃel/ noun, c. or u. **1** *a coconut shell* = the hard outer covering of an egg, nut, crab etc. **2** *an artillery shell* = a large bullet fired from a gun **3** = any hard outer covering or outer structure e.g. of a building

shell[2] verb, t. *The boy is shelling peanuts.* = to remove the shell (outer covering) of a nut etc. **shell-fish** noun, u. = sea-animals such as lobsters or prawns, which are covered with shells (hard outer coverings) **shell-shock** noun = damage to the mind caused by the experience of war

to shell out = to pay money unwillingly (slang) **to come out of one's shell** *He came out of his shell once he left home and joined a hostel.* = to become less shy and more inclined to make friends **to withdraw into one's shell draw back into one's shell** *She is shy and has just begun to make friends. If you criticize her now, she will withdraw into her shell.* = to become unsociable and shy once again

shel•ter[1] /ˈʃeltər/ noun, u. or c. *The rain was so heavy that I had to take shelter under a tree.*(u.)= a place where one can be safe or protected

shelter[2] verb, t. *The police arrested him for sheltering a criminal.* = to give protection to someone or something

shelve /ʃelv/ verb, t. **1** *We will have to shelve these new books which have been bought for the library.* = to arrange something (especially books) on a shelf **2** *The government has shelved its plans to start new schools for girls.* = to give up for some time; to postpone

shep•herd[1] /ˈʃepəd/ noun, c. = a person who looks after sheep, specially when they are grazing

shepherd[2] verb, t. *The teacher shepherded the children into the bus.* = to lead or guide

sher•bet /ˈʃɜːbət/ noun, u. = a kind of sweet drink

sher•iff /ˈʃerɪf/ noun, c. = an officer who is in charge of keeping law and order, specially in an American town or city

sher•ry /ˈʃeri/ noun = a kind of wine, first made in Spain

Shi•a /ʃiːa/ noun = a member of a large group within the Muslim religion (also **Shi-ite**)

shield[1] /ʃiːld/ noun, c. **1** *A thousand years ago, soldiers fought with swords and shields.* = a large, heavy piece of metal carried by soldiers (in former

S

times) to protect themselves from being hit **2** = a prize in the shape of a shield, given to the winner of a sports tournament

shield[2] verb, t. *Society should shield children from violence.* = to see that someone is protected from harm

shift[1] /ʃɪft/ verb, t. or i. **1** *We have to shift this furniture to the bedroom.*(t.) = to move an object from where it is to another place **2** *The wind was blowing from the north but it has now shifted.*(i.) = to change direction **3** *Shift this bed to the other side of the room.* = to move to a different place **4** *When the car moves fast, you must shift into fourth gear.*(i.) = to change gears (in a motorcycle, car etc.)

shift[2] noun, u. or c. **1** *We are expecting a shift in the government's trade policy.* = a change in position or direction **2** *I am working in the night shift in the factory.* = a group of workers who do a job for a certain period during the day or night **shift key** noun = a key on the keyboard of a typewriter or computer which, when pressed down, prints a capital letter [COMPUTERS] **shifty** adj. *a shifty character who cannot be trusted* = dishonest

shil•ling /ˈʃɪlɪŋ/ noun = a unit of money used in Britain before 1971, equal to the twentieth part (1/20) of a pound

shilly-shally /ˈʃɪli ʃæli/ verb, i. *Stop shilly-shalling and decide what you want to do.* = to remain undecided (informal)

shim•mer[1] /ˈʃɪməʳ/ verb, i. *Her silk dress shimmered in the light.* = to shine gently with a soft light which seems to move rapidly

shimmer[2] noun, u. *the shimmer of the waves in the moonlight* = the action or effect of shimmering (shining)

shin[1] /ʃɪn/ noun, c. *He received a painful kick on the shin.* = the bony front part of the leg, below the knee

shin[2] verb, i. (**shinned**) *The boy shinned up the tree.* = to climb up/down a tree or pole

shin•dig (shindy) /ˈʃɪndɪɡ/ noun, c. *The young people are having a shindig in their room.* = a noisy party or celebration (slang)

shine[1] /ʃaɪn/ verb, i. or t. (**shone**) **1** *The sun is shining.*(i.) = to give out light **2** *The polished surface of the table shone.*(i.) = to reflect light **3** *I must shine my shoes.*(t.) = to polish **4** *He is an average student but he shines in cricket.* = to do well in something **5** *The corridor is very dark. Will you shine the torch?* = to point light in a certain direction

shine[2] noun, u. *He polished the table and gave it a lovely shine.* = brightness **shiny** adj. *a shiny new car* = bright **shining** adj. *Helen Keller is a shining example of a person with a positive attitude to life.* = greatly to be admired

shin•gle /ˈʃɪŋɡəl/ noun, u. *The beach is covered with shingle.* = small stone pebbles lying on the beach **shingles** (always plural) noun = a viral disease which causes red marks to appear on the skin

Shin•to•ism /ˈʃɪntəʊɪzəm/ noun = a religion practised in Japan, in which one worships one's ancestors (older members of the family who are dead)

shiny see under **shine**

ship[1] /ʃɪp/ noun, c. = a large vessel (boat) which carries people and goods

ship[2] verb, t. (**shipped**) *We are shipping our products to America.* = to send goods for trading by one of the main means of transport e.g. plane, ship, truck **shipment** noun, u. or c. **1** = the action of sending goods by ship **2** *A shipment of wheat has arrived from America.* = a large quantity of goods sent by ship or road **shipping** noun, u. *The Suez Canal was closed to shipping during the war.* = ships in general **ship-shape** adj. *The office was looking very untidy but now it is ship-shape.* = clean and neat **shipwreck** noun, u. or c. *There is great danger of shipwreck along this coast because of the presence of dangerous rocks in the sea.* = the destruction or sinking of a ship due to an accident **shipyard** noun, c. = a place where ships are built or repaired **'The ship of the desert'** = a name given to a camel

shire /ʃaɪəʳ/ noun, c. = a county (large area that includes several towns) in Britain

shirk /ʃɜːk/ verb, t. or i. = to avoid work out of a feeling of laziness or irresponsibility

shirt /ʃɜːt/ noun, c. = a garment (dress) for the upper half of the body

shit[1] /ʃɪt/ noun, u. = human excrement (solid waste matter) passed out of the bowels especially of humans (slang)

shit[2] verb, i. (**shat, shitted**) = to pass out solid waste matter from the bowels

shit[3] interjec. = an expression of anger or annoyance

shiv•er[1] /ˈʃɪvəʳ/ verb, i. *The poor man was shivering in the cold as he had no warm clothing.* = to shake because of fever, or because of fear or cold

shiver[2] noun, c. *The cold sent shivers down his body.* = an act of shivering

to give one the shivers (always plural) *The memory of the night I spent alone in a deserted house still gives me the shivers.* = to cause fear

shoal /ʃəʊl/ noun, c. **1** *Shoals of fish can be seen swimming up the river.* = a large group of fish swimming together **2** *You can find shoals of foreign tourists around the Taj Mahal.* = a large group of people (informal) **3** *Ships sailing along the Hoogli River are often damaged when they hit large shoals.* = underwater sandbanks which make a river dangerous for boats or ships

shock[1] /ʃɒk/ noun, u. or c. **1** *The news of his illness came to us as a shock.* = the feeling produced by an event which is unpleasant as well as unexpected **2** *We felt a shock as the cracker exploded not far from where we were standing.* = the pain or discomfort caused by an explosion or a blow **3** *The man received a shock when he accidentally touched a live electric wire.* = a painful blow to the body produced by an electric current

shock[2] verb, t. *The film was so full of violence that it shocked the audience.* = to cause offence or angry surprise **shock absorber** noun, c. = a device (machine) fitted to a motor vehicle (car or bus) which reduces the jolting (shaking) caused by moving over rough roads **shocking** adj. *a shocking piece of news* = something unpleasant that shocks one **shock-proof** adj. *a shock-proof watch* = not easily damaged by being dropped or hit **shock-treatment** noun, u. = treatment of diseases of the mind by giving electric shocks (not commonly practised now)

shod adj. **1** *The girl could not walk far on her badly shod feet.* = wearing shoes of a certain kind **2** *The bullock-cart has rubber-shod wheels.* = covered with rubber tyres (old-fashioned)

shod•dy /ˈʃɒdi/ adj. *She surprised everyone by coming to the party in shoddy clothes.* = cheap, badly-made and untidy **shoddily** adv. *a shoddily produced table* = badly, cheaply

shoe[1] /ʃuː/ noun, c. = a covering or protection for the foot (of a human being, horse or bullock)

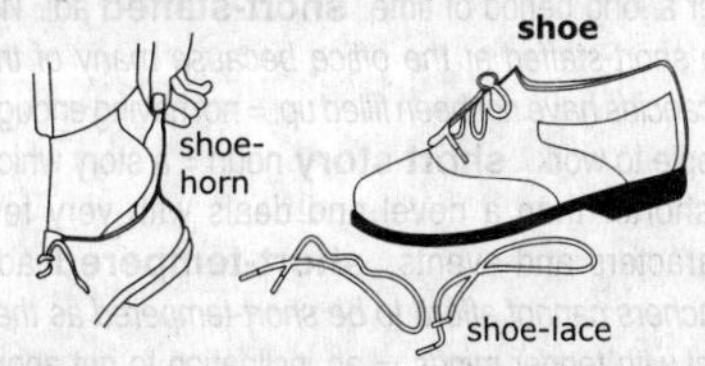

shoe[2] verb, t. (**shod** or **shoed**) *Our soldiers have been shod by the shoe factories in Agra.* = to provide shoes for a human being, horse or bullock (old-fashioned) **shoe-horn** noun = a curved piece of metal or plastic which is put inside the back of a shoe to help the wearer's foot to go in easily **shoelace** noun, c. = a long, thin piece of string which passes through holes in the front part of a shoe and keeps it in place on the wearer's foot **shoeshine** noun, c. **1** = the act of polishing shoes **2** = a person who earns money by polishing the shoes of people **shoestring budget** noun *We have to manage the school on a shoestring budget.* = a very small amount of money given to someone for some purpose (informal)

(where) the shoe pinches *I run this business year after year and know exactly where the shoe pinches.* = the difficulties that a person has to face **to (not want to) be in somebody's shoes** *If I were in your shoes, I'd accept the offer at once.* = to be in the position of some other person **to step into someone's shoes** *Ms Ahmad has been so successful as the Chairperson that it will not be easy for another person to step into her shoes.* = to take over a position from someone else

sho•gun /ˈʃəʊgʊn/ noun = a military leader in Japan, before the 19th century

shoo[1] /ʃuː/ interjec. *Shoo! Go away!* = an expression used to drive away an animal or a human being that is not welcome

shoo[2] verb, t. *I want you to shoo those noisy children away.* = to drive away, usually young children or animals

shoot[1] /ʃuːt/ verb, i. or t. (**shot**) **1** *These soldiers are being trained to shoot.*(i.) = to fire a gun **2** *The dangerous criminal has been shot by the police.* = to kill or injure someone with a gun **3** *In the old days people considered it brave to shoot and kill wild animals.* = to hunt animals with guns **4** *We will shoot the new film in Kashmir.* = to produce a film or a photograph by using a camera **5** *The centre-forward shot the ball into the open goal.* = to kick the ball in the game of football **6** *He shot past me at great speed in his car.* = to move very quickly

shoot[2] noun, c. **1** *The young plants have put out new shoots.* = a new stem that grows from a plant **2** = an occasion when animals were hunted (in the past) with guns **shooting**[1] noun, u. **1** *the noise of shooting* = the firing of guns to kill or injure someone **2** *The government has banned the shooting of wild animals.* = the act of hunting animals with guns **shooting**[2] adj. *a shooting pain in the chest* = sudden and sharp pain **shooting star** noun, c. = a meteor (a piece of material from some heavenly body in space) that burns brightly as it moves through the earth's atmosphere **shoot-out** noun, c. = an exchange of bullets fired from guns, between two groups of people

to shoot one's mouth off *He is always shooting his mouth off to impress others.* = to talk carelessly, without thinking of the result **shoot down** **1** *The plane was shot down when it entered enemy territory.* = to cause a plane to crash by firing at it **2** *All his suggestions were shot down by the committee as they were considered impractical.* = to reject what someone says **shoot up** **1** *The price of petroleum products keeps shooting up every now and then.* = to increase steeply **2** *At a certain stage of their growth, children shoot up in no time at all.* = to grow fast, especially in height

shop[1] /ʃɒp/ noun, c. **1** = a place where things are

S

sold **2** *He has set up shop as an electrician.* = a business

shop[2] verb, i. (**shopped**) *I shopped for clothes when I was in London.* = to visit a shop in order to buy something **shopper** noun, c. = a person who buys things from a shop **shopping** noun, u. **1** *I have to do some shopping this morning.* = the act of buying things from a shop **2** *Let me carry your shopping.* = the things bought in a shop **shop-floor** noun = the area in a factory where work is done **shop-lifting** noun *This man has been arrested for shop-lifting.* = the crime of taking things from a shop without paying **shopping centre** noun, c. = an area or building in which there are many shops **shop-soiled** adj. *We are selling these shirts cheaply because they are shop-soiled.* = slightly damaged or dirty as a result of being kept in a shop for a long time

to talk shop = to talk about subjects connected with one's work (informal)

shore[1] /ʃɔːʳ/ noun, c. = the land that borders a large body of water, such as a sea or lake

shore[2] verb, t. *The roof of this building is about to fall. It has to be shored up with concrete pillars.* = to support or hold up something that is falling

short[1] /ʃɔːt/ adj. **1** *The boy is rather short, although his parents are tall. // You have to travel only a short distance to reach the station.* = small in height or distance **2** *She made a short speech.* = lasting for a little time only **3** *'Phone' is the short form of 'telephone'* = smaller **4** *I wanted to buy this shirt but I am short of money. Can you lend me ten rupees?* = not having enough **5** *She was rather short with me when I spoke to her.* = rude and impatient

short[2] adv. *He cut me short when I was trying to explain the programme.* = to stop or interrupt someone while speaking **shortly** adv. *She will shortly be here to join us in our discussion.* = soon, in a little while **shortage** noun, u. *There is a shortage of sugar in the shops.* = a condition of not having enough of something **shortcoming** noun, c. *She has several shortcomings, but worst of all is her bad temper.* = a defect or fault **shortbread** noun = a kind of sweet biscuit **short-change** verb, t. *I use the shop often and I felt angry when the owner short-changed me.* = to cheat someone (informal) **short cut** noun *This road leads to the station, but you can take a short cut by walking across this field.* = a shorter and quicker way of reaching a place **shortfall** noun *We need Rs 500 crores for this new project but the government has given us only Rs 300 crores. We are trying to make up the shortfall by borrowing money from banks.* = the amount by which one is short of (has less than) an amount which is needed **shorthand** noun = a system of fast writing which uses symbols (signs) in place of words, allowing one to write down what is being said by someone else

short-circuit[1] /ʃɔːt'sɜːkɪt/ noun, c. *The television set was damaged because of a short circuit.* = a fault in an electrical connection which causes the current to flow along a wrong path and produces some damage

short circuit[2] verb, t. *It takes years to get permission to build a house, but you can short-circuit the process by making an appeal to the government.* = to cut down the time or effort required to do something

short list[1] /ʃɔːtlɪst/ noun = a list of people who may be offered a job or a contract etc., chosen out of a longer list of people who applied

shortlist[2] verb, t. *We have shortlisted you for this job.* = to include someone's name in a short list of the most likely candidates

short-lived /ʃɔːtlɪvəd/ adj. *This writer became famous after he won a prize for his first book, but his fame was short-lived. No one remembers him today.* = not lasting for a long time

shorts /ʃɔːts/ noun (always plural, used with 'a pair of') = a garment (dress) covering the legs from the waist to the knees **short shrift** noun, u. *I expected my boss to thank me for having defended him at the meeting, but he gave me short shrift.* = giving little time or attention to someone **short-sighted** adj. **1** *a short-sighted person* = unable to see clearly things which are at a distance **2** *the short-sighted policies of the company* = not thinking of the effect of some action over a long period of time **short-staffed** adj. *We are short-staffed at the office because many of the vacancies have not been filled up.* = not having enough people to work **short story** noun = a story which is shorter than a novel and deals with very few characters and events **short-tempered** adj. *Teachers cannot afford to be short-tempered as they deal with tender minds.* = an inclination to get angry very quickly **short-term** adj. *The bank has given me a short-term loan.* = for a short period of time **short-wave** adj. *a short-wave radio broadcast* = radio waves which are less than 60 metres in length and travel for long distances, carrying radio signals

shot[1] /spt/ noun, c. **1** *The policeman fired a shot at the thief, who was running away.* = a bullet from a gun which is fired at someone or something **2** *Pete Sampras hits a shot to Agassi's backhand.* = a hit or kick given to a ball in a game such as tennis, football, cricket etc. **3** *He is a very good shot.* = a person who knows how to shoot (aim and fire a gun) **4** *Let us have a shot of the hero singing a song.* = a photograph or a scene photographed for a film **5** *The doctor gave* *me a shot of penicillin.* = an injection (a medicine or drug injected into the body) **6** *He loaded the gun with lead shots.* = small pieces of metal which are put inside a bullet fired from a gun **7** *He must be a big shot, otherwise he can't be accompanied by a convoy of cars.* = a very important person (slang)

shot[2] verb, t. *The hunter shot a tiger.* = past tense of **shoot** **shotgun** noun, c. = a gun which fires bullets filled with shots (small pieces of metal) **shot put** noun = a sporting competition in which persons have to throw a heavy metal ball or shot, and the person throwing it farthest is the winner

should / ʃəd/ or / ʃʊd/ modal aux. verb **1** *You should always speak the truth.* = ought to (expressing the desirability of an action) **2** *My father has given me Rs 100 to buy a shirt. I think that should be enough.* = it is expected that (expressing probability) **3** *If you should need help, you can* telephone me. = in case (expressing possibility) **4** *As I was walking down the road, who should I meet but the minister himself, with a shopping bag in his hand!* = expressing surprise **5** *Should I go to the meeting?* = asking for advice **6** *Should it rain, the match will be cancelled.* = in case (expressing a condition) **7** *I have brought you here so that you should see this house.* = in order that (expressing purpose) **8** *I should tell you that this is your last chance.* = it is important to inform you that **9** *'It's midnight. I think we should stop working and go home now.' 'I should think so!'* = this is my opinion

shoul•der[1] /ˈʃəʊldəʳ/ noun, c. **1** = the part of the body below the neck, where the arms or front legs (in four-legged animals) meet the trunk (the upper part of the body) **2** *a shoulder of mutton* = meat from the shoulder (upper part of the front leg) of an animal

shoulder[2] verb, t. *Can you shoulder the responsibility of educating ten of the children in the village?* = to accept a responsibility or burden **shoulder bag** noun = a bag that hangs from one's shoulder **shoulder blade** noun, c. = the wide, flat bone on each side of the upper back (also **scapula**) **shoulder-high** adj. *The tiger stalked the animal through shoulder-high grass.* = as high as an average person's shoulder **shoulder length** adj. *She decided to have shoulder length hair which would be easier to manage.* = hanging up to the shoulder

an old head on young shoulders *Even as a child Mother Teresa had an old head on young shoulders.* = showing more maturity than is expected at a young age **to rub shoulders with** *When he was in Mumbai he had an opportunity to rub shoulders with actors and film people.* = to move socially with **head and shoulders above the rest** *Rima is head and shoulders above the rest in her ability to write.* = much better at something than all the others

shout[1] / ʃaʊt/ verb, i. or t. **1** *'Come home at once!' the man shouted to his son.*(i.) // *The officer shouted an order at his men.*(t.) = to speak in a loud voice **2** *Don't shout at me. I am not afraid of you.* = to speak angrily

shout[2] noun, c. *There were shouts of 'Goal!' from the crowd, but the ball went over the goal post.* = a loud cry or call **shout down** verb *The crowd shouted down when the Mayor began to speak because they disliked him.* = to shout in order to prevent someone from being heard

shove[1] / ʃʌv/ verb, i. or t. **1** *Everyone started pushing and shoving in order to get into the train.*(i.) = to push in a rough way **2** *He shoved the letter into his pocket and walked away.*(t.) = to put something away carelessly **3** *We shoved sand into the hole.* = to push something into an opening with force

shove[2] noun, c. *Give the car a good shove and it will start.* = a strong push

shov•el[1] /ˈʃʌvəl/ noun, c. = a tool with a broad, flat metal blade and a long handle, used for lifting or moving sand, coal etc.

shovel[2] verb, t. (**shovelled**) *His job is to shovel coal into the boiler of the engine.* = to lift or move something with a shovel

show[1] / ʃəʊ/ verb, t. (**showed**, **shown**) **1** *She showed the conductor her pass as he entered the bus.* = to allow someone to see something **2** *This book shows a very depressing picture of the country.* = to present or offer **3** *The poor sale of tickets shows that the film is not good.* = to indicate (tell what is happening) **4** *Can you show me Mr Roy's office?* = to point out **5** *The woman is in great pain but it doesn't show on her face.* = to be noticeable

show[2] noun, c. or u. **1** *Would you like to watch this show?* = a programme regularly shown on television **2** *Let us go to the flower show.* = a public exhibition **3** *The vote was taken by a show of hands.* = display **4** *Most people in the audience were bored with the speech, but they made a show of being interested.* = a pretence **5** *The man lives a simple life, without any show.* = the desire to let others know that one is rich or important **show business** noun = the profession of working in films, television etc. **show-case** **1** (noun, c.) *The gold chains are kept in a show case.* = a glass box in which objects meant to be sold are kept for people to see **2** (verb, t.) *We are arranging an exhibition to showcase our textiles.* = to help or encourage people to see something **show-down** noun *I was told that he had been talking against me to everyone, so I decided that we should have a show-down.* = a meeting at which a quarrel or disagreement can be settled or discussed openly **show-off** noun

= a person who likes to attract the attention of others (disapproving) **showman** (also **showperson**) noun **1** = a person who is in the profession of producing films, plays etc. **2** = a person who is good at getting the attention of the public **show-piece** noun = the best or finest object in a collection **showroom** noun = a shop or a large room in which things which are meant to be sold can be seen **showy** adj. *a showy dress* = attracting too much attention (derogatory)

for show *He organized a grand party on his sister's birthday, but it was only for show.* = only to impress others and to attract attention **to show one's (true) colours** *Many people show their true colours when they are under stress.* = to show the unpleasant side of oneself **to show one's face** *He made such a fool of himself yesterday that he wouldn't dare to show his face here again.* = to appear in public **to show off** *We know you can sing. Now stop showing off.* = to try to make a good impression on others **to show somebody the door** = to ask someone to leave (informal) **to show up** *We held up the lunch for a long time, waiting for her to join us, but she didn't show up.* = to arrive at a place where one is expected, especially after some delay (informal)

show•er[1] /ˈʃaʊəʳ/ noun, c. **1** *We had a heavy shower last night.* = a fall of rain **2** *I am getting a shower for the bathroom.* = a piece of metal or plastic with many small holes that is fitted to a water-pipe, through which water can flow out in tiny drops, like rain **3** *He is taking a shower now after a game of tennis.* = the act of taking a bath by standing under a shower

shower[2] verb, t. or i. **1** *We showered, changed into casual clothes, had dinner and then settled down to watch a film.*(i.) = to bath under a shower **2** *The audience showered him with congratulatory messages.*(t.) = to give a lot (of something, either pleasant or unpleasant)

shrap•nel /ˈʃræpnəl/ noun, u. = small pieces of metal scattered by an exploding bomb

shred[1] /ʃred/ noun, c. *His clothes are so old and wornout that they have been reduced to shreds.* = a small narrow piece torn out of some material

shred[2] verb, t. (**shredded**) *The vegetables have to be shredded to make salad.* = to cut something into long, thin pieces

a shred of *The authorities can't find a shred of evidence against him. He will be released soon.* = the smallest amount of

shrew /ʃruː/ noun, c. **1** = an insulting word for a bad-tempered woman (derogatory) Ⓖ **2** = a small animal that looks like a mouse

shrewd /ʃruːd/ adj. *The man tried to cheat me, but I was too shrewd to be tricked by him.* = having good practical sense and judgement; clever

shriek[1] /ʃriːk/ verb, t. or i. *'Please don't harm me!' the man shrieked in terror when the robbers caught him.*(i.) = to shout or cry out loudly in a high, thin voice because of anger, fear etc.

shriek[2] noun, c. *We heard a shriek of anger.* = a loud cry in a high-pitched voice

shrill /ʃrɪl/ adj. *The train gave a shrill whistle announcing that it was about to start.* = (a sound that is) thin, high and unpleasant to hear **shrillness** noun, u.

shrimp /ʃrɪmp/ noun, c. or u. **1** = a sea-animal with a hard shell (covering) and ten legs **2**= the meat of the shrimp, eaten as food

shrine /ʃraɪn/ noun, c. = a place of worship or a place that has religious importance

shrink[1] /ʃrɪŋk/ verb, i. or t. (**shrank, shrunk**) **1** *The shirt shrank when it was washed. It has become too tight now.*(i.) = to become smaller in size due to the action of water **2** *The number of students has shrunk from 70 to 25.*(i.) = to become smaller in number **3** *The man shouted so loudly that the child shrank back.*(i.) = to move back as a result of fear

shrink[2] noun, c. = a psychiatrist (a doctor who treats people with mental problems) (slang) **shrinkage** noun, u. *Buy some extra material as you must allow for shrinkage.* = the amount by which something shrinks

shriv•el /ˈʃrɪvəl/ verb, i. or t. (**shrivelled**) *The rose plants seem to be dying. They have shrivelled because of the heat.* = to dry up and lose shape or become smaller in size **shrivelled** adj.

shroud /ʃraʊd/ noun, c. **1** = a sheet of cloth used to cover a dead body **2** *No one knows who paid for these guns. The whole deal is covered in a shroud of secrecy.* = something that hides a situation which is secret or likely to cause criticism

shroud[2] verb, t. *Thick fog shrouded the trees and houses.* = to cover up and hide

shrub /ʃrʌb/ noun, c. or u. = a low bush or line of bushes

shrug[1] /ʃrʌg/ verb, i. *When I asked the boy where his sister was, he just shrugged.* = to move one's shoulders up and down to show lack of knowledge or interest

shrug noun, c. *He answered the question with only a shrug.* = a movement of the shoulders showing lack of knowledge or interest

shucks /ʃʌks/ interjec. *Oh shucks! I have lost my keys!* = an expression of mild annoyance or disappointment (slang)

shud•der[1] /ˈʃʌdəʳ/ verb, i. *The little child shuddered when the teacher shouted at her.* = to shake suddenly because of cold, fear or strong dislike

shudder² noun, u. *The roaring of the lions sent a shudder through the group of children.* = shivering/trembling of the body caused by fear etc.

shuf•fle /ˈʃʌfəl/ verb, t. or i. **1** *It is your turn to deal the cards. You should shuffle them well before you deal.*(t.) = to mix up a set of playing cards by moving them around quicky, so that the players cannot know the order in which they are arranged **2** *The prime minister plans to shuffle the ministers in his cabinet.* = to change the positions of people in a government or company **3** *You can see that the little girl is nervous from the way in which she keeps shuffling her feet.*(i.) = to move repeatedly from one position to another **4** *The sick man shuffled across the room slowly with the help of a support.* = to walk slowly, dragging the feet

shuffle² noun, u. **1** *Give the cards a good shuffle.* = mix (see meaning 1 above) **2** *One of my colleagues lost his job in a shuffle.* = the act of changing people's positions or jobs **3** *He walks with a painful shuffle.* = the act of shuffling (walking slowly)

shun /ʃʌn/ verb, t. *People shun them because they tell many lies.* = to avoid or keep away from in a determined and angry way

shunt¹ /ʃʌnt/ verb, t. **1** *The empty carriages of the train are being shunted from Platform 1 to Platform 13.* = to move the carriages of a train from one track to another **2** *The officer is going to be shunted out of office.* = to move someone or something to a less important position, usually as a punishment (informal, not respectful)

shunt² noun, c. = a machine which allows something (e.g. an electrical current) to flow in a different direction or along a different path

shush¹ /ʃʊʃ/ interjec. *Shush, everybody! The film is about to begin.* = an expression asking people to be quiet (informal)

shush² verb, t. (**shushed**) *She shushed the child, who was making a noise.* = to order someone to be quiet (informal)

shut /ʃʌt/ verb, t.or i. (**shut**) **1** *Shut the door as you go out.*(t.) = to close (to block or cover up an opening) **2** *She shut herself in the room and refused to come out.* = to stop someone from entering or leaving a place **3** *The company will shut down this factory.* = to cause something to stop working **shutdown** noun, c. *The factory is closed because of a shutdown.* = the action of stopping work

to shut (something) down *He has decided to shut down the factory.* = to cause work to stop **to shut off** *If you stop this pump, the water supply will be shut off.* = to stop the flow of a liquid or gas **to shut out** *He closed the windows to shut out the noise.* = to prevent from getting in **shut up** *Oh shut up!* = a rude way of asking someone to stop talking

shut•ter /ˈʃʌtəʳ/ noun, c. **1** *the shutter of a camera* = a part of a camera which opens for a short time to allow light to enter the camera **2** *the wooden shutters of a door* = one of a pair of covers, usually made of wood, which can be used to block the opening of a door or window

to put up the shutters = to stop trading or doing business

shut•tle /ˈʃʌtl/ noun, c. **1** *He uses the Mumbai-Pune shuttle to travel from his home to his office and back.* = a vehicle (bus, train or aircraft) which regularly runs from one place to another, not too far away, and back again **2** *a weaver's shuttle* = a device used in weaving cloth, which carries a thread across and between other threads **3** *a badminton shuttle* = a piece of cork to which feathers are attached, which is hit back and forth, across the net, in the game of badminton (also **shuttlecock**)

shuttle

shy¹ /ʃaɪ/ adj. **1** *The girl is so shy that she hardly speaks to anyone.* = nervous and uncomfortable in the company of people **2** *We are collecting money for charity and we have made a good collection. We are only a hundred rupees shy of 5,000.* = less than ; short of a certain amount (informal)

shy² verb, i. or t. (**shied**) **1** *The horse shied when the car sounded its horn.*(i.) = to move away suddenly in fear (referring to the movement of an animal) **2** *She shied the ball at me.*(t.) = to throw **shyly** adv. *The child looked at the stranger and smiled shyly.* = in a shy manner **shyness** noun.

to shy away from *'Don't shy away from hard work,' the teacher advised her class.* = avoid

sib•i•lant /ˈsɪbɪlənt/ noun, c. *The sound heard at the beginning of the word 'ship' is a sibilant.* = a speech-sound (sound used in speaking) in which a stream of air is allowed to escape with a light hiss [TECHNICAL]

sib•ling /ˈsɪblɪŋ/ noun, c. *He grew up in this house together with his three siblings.* = brother(s) and sister(s)

sic /sɪk/ adv. (Latin) *Samir writes in his letter that he is going to his vilig (sic) next week.* = a word given in brackets after a word or phrase which has been wrongly spelt or used, to show that it has been copied exactly as it was written, in its incorrect form

sick /sɪk/ adj. **1** *He is not playing in this match as he is sick.* = unwell (not in good health) **2** *I felt sick as the*

S

aircraft was moving up and down because of the strong air currents. = having the desire to vomit **3** *I am sick of your stupid jokes.* = feeling annoyed or irritated (angry) because there is too much of something **4** *a sick mind* = unhealthy and cruel **sicken** verb, i. or t. **1** *The man sickened and died.*(i.) = to become very sick **2** *Your jokes sicken me.*(t.) = to make someone feel disgusted **sickening** adj. *There was a sickening smell of rotten fish on the beach.* = causing nausea; disgusting **sickness** noun, u. *The bite of this fly can cause sleeping sickness.* = the condition of not being well or suffering from some disease **sickly** adj. *The child looks sickly. Perhaps it is not getting enough food.* = weak and in poor health **sick note/letter** = a letter written to inform someone in authority (e.g. a teacher, an employer) that one is ill and cannot come

to be sick and tired of something *I am sick and tired of your constant complaints.* = tired, weary, fed up with (slang) **to be worried sick** *After the accident she was worried sick until she got a message to say her child was safe.* = absolutely worried **to be off sick** = to be absent from work, school etc. because one is ill (informal) **to call in sick** = to phone one's school, place of work etc. to say one is ill and cannot come

sick•le /'sɪkəl/ noun, c. = a kind of knife with a curved blade, used for cutting grain or long grass

sickle

side[1] /saɪd/ noun, c. **1** *The house has two doors in front, one door at the back and a small door on each side.* = a surface of a solid object that is not the front or back, top or bottom **2** *The child was sitting by the side of the road.* = the edge or border of something **3** *Come and sit by my side.* = the place or area next to someone or something **4** *My room is on this side of the house and my sister's room is on the other side.* = part **5** *Our side is sure to win this match.* = team

side[2] verb, i. *My classmates sided with me against our seniors in the argument.* = to support someone in an argument etc. **sideboard** noun = a cupboard, usually kept next to the dining table in a house, in which cups, dishes etc. are kept **sideburns** noun (always plural) = hair growing on a man's face, in front of the ears **sidecar** noun = a small carriage with only one wheel, attached to the side of a motor-cycle **side dish** noun *I ordered chicken biryani and a vegetable side dish for lunch.* = a portion of food that is served with the main item **side-effect** noun *This new drug cures malaria, but it has a number of harmful side-effects.* = the harmful effect that a drug or medicine can have on a patient, in addition to the main effect for which it is given **sidekick** noun = a person who is always found in the company of someone important (informal) **to sideline** noun *It is quite obvious that Fouzia has been sidelined after she got into an argument with the other members of the team.* = to give less importance, remove (from a team etc.) (informal) **side-line** noun, c. = a line marking the limit of the playing area in a game such as tennis or football **side-splitting** adj. *side-splitting laughter* = something that is very funny **side-step** verb, t. *The reporter asked the actor a very awkward question, but he side-stepped it.* = to avoid cleverly **side-track** verb, i. *We were discussing the political situation but somehow we got side-tracked into talking about cricket.* = to move away from the main subject **sidewalk** noun, c. = a raised surface along the side of a street on which people can walk (also **pavement** or **foot-path**) **siding** noun, c. *The train was standing at a siding.* = a short railway track connected to but away from the main track, where trains can be taken for loading, unloading etc.

from all sides *The players were greeted from all sides with shouts of 'Well played!' as they walked through the crowd.* = from different directions **to do something on the side** = to be engaged in some activity, often dishonest or illegal, in additon to one's main occupation or profession **to be on the right side/wrong side of something** *He is on the right/wrong side of forty.* = to be less than or more than a certain age **the other side of the coin** = a different view or aspect of some question that one has been considering (thinking about) **to stand by someone's side** = to give someone help or support when it is needed

si•dle /'saɪdl/ verb, i. *He was ashamed that he was late and sidled up to a seat where he couldn't be seen.* = to move nervously and stealthily without attracting too much attention

siege[1] /si:dʒ/ noun, u. *The siege of the TV station by the rebel soldiers is over. Now the two groups ought to settle their differences.* = the surrounding of a place by an armed group in order to force the enemy to accept defeat

si•es•ta /si'estə/ noun, c. *We enjoy our siesta after lunch.* = a period of rest or sleep during the daytime, specially in a warm country

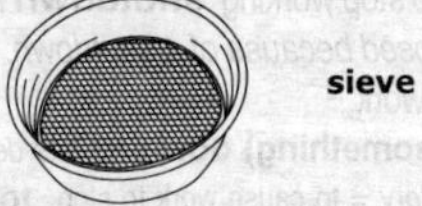
sieve

sieve[1] /sɪv/ noun, c. *The flour is passed through a sieve before it is used to make bread.* = a tool consisting of a metal frame with a wire or plastic net fixed to its bottom, used to separate solids from a liquid or large pieces of solid matter from something containing smaller pieces of matter

sieve[2] verb, t. *We will have to sieve the flour in order to remove the husk from it.* = to pass something through a sieve

to have a memory like a sieve (see **memory**)

sift /sɪft/ verb, t. or i. **1** *The flour has many small pieces of stone mixed with it. We will have to sift it.* = to put a solid substance through a sieve **2** *We have collected a lot of data (information) for our research, but we will have to sift through it before we prepare our report.* = to examine carefully in order to separate what is useful or valuable from something that is less useful or valuable

sigh[1] /saɪ/ verb, i. *'When shall we reach the end of this journey?' the man sighed as he sat down to rest in the shade of a tree.* = to let out a deep breath with a sound, expressing tiredness, sadness, boredom etc.

sigh[2] noun, c. *'I think we are going to lose again,' the man said with a sigh.* = the act of sighing or the sound made while sighing

to heave a sigh of relief *He heaved a sigh of relief when his interview was over.* = to express satisfaction when a difficult or unpleasant task has been completed

sight[1] /saɪt/ noun, u. or c. **1** *The man was hit in the eye by a cricket ball and lost his sight.*(u.) = the power of seeing **2** *The flowers in the garden presented a beautiful sight.*(c.) = something that is seen **3** (always plural) *Have you visited all the sights of this city?*(c.) = things that are worth seeing **4** *The car was travelling so fast that it was soon out of sight.*(u.) = the range or distance within which things can be seen **5** *When the animal was in his sights the man fired but missed.*(c.) = the part of a gun through which one looks at something that one is aiming at

sight[2] verb, t. *The sailors sighted land after spending more than a month at sea.* = to see something that one has been looking for **sighted** adj. *Most of the people in the group are blind, but a few are sighted.* = able to see **sightseeing** noun, u. *Most people went sight-seeing after we reached Delhi, but I was so tired that I went to bed.* = the act of visiting a famous or interesting place as a tourist **sightseer** noun, c. = a tourist who visits famous or interesting places

in sight *We are nearing the station. The platform is in sight.* = near enough to be seen **out of sight** = too far away to be seen **a sight for sore eyes** *How happy the parents were to see their daughter when she got off the train at Chennai! She was a sight for sore eyes.* = someone whom one is very happy to see **to lose sight of** *We lost sight of the boy whom we had been chasing.* = to be unable to see someone or something that one had been able to see earlier **to set one's sights on** *Kalpana Chawla set her sights on becoming an astronaut even when she was in school.* = to have an ambition to achieve something in the future

-sighted = suffix describing the way one sees things e.g. **short-sighted** = unable to see distant objects clearly, **far-sighted** = wise and able to plan for the future

sign[1] /saɪn/ noun, c. **1** *When you see a plus sign (+), you know that you have to add two numbers together.* = a mark, or **symbol**, which carries a meaning that can be understood **2** *The sign outside the doctor's clinic says 'Shoes not allowed inside.'* = a written notice or warning in a public place **3** *The man made a sign with his hand to inform us that he was going into a restaurant to eat.* = a movement of the body which carries a certain meaning; a gesture **4** *The red marks on the child's face are a sign of measles.* = something that serves as a warning

sign[2] verb, t. **1** *Please sign the contract.* = to write one's name on a document (official paper) etc. to show that one accepts or agrees to something **2** *He signed that he wanted me to return.* = to make a movement of the body in order to express some meaning; to gesture **3** *We have signed up a new manager.* = to get someone to work for you **sign- board** noun = a board carrying the name of a shop or business establishment **sign language** noun = a kind of language consisting of movements of the hands and fingers, used by people who are unable to talk or hear

to sign away something = to give up your rights to a piece of property etc. by signing a legal document **to sign for** = to sign a document to show that you have received something e.g. a registered letter **to sign in** = to put your signature in a register or book when you enter a hotel, club etc. **to sign off** = to end a letter or a radio broadcast **to sign up** = to show that you want to take part in some activity by signing a list **to sign on the dotted line** = to sign an agreement or contract **the signs of the Zodiac** = a sign or symbol used in astrology, showing the group of stars, present in the sky at the time of one's birth, which are supposed to influence a person's character and destiny (see pic under **zodiac**)

signatory /'sɪgnətəri/ noun, c. (**signatories**) *India is a signatory to the free-trade agreement.* = a person or a country that signs an agreement or a contract

signature noun, u. or c. *It is difficult to copy your signature.* = the form in which a person's name is written by himself/herself on a document etc. **signature tune** = a short piece of music played before and after a television or radio programme

sig•nal[1] /'sɪgnəl/ noun, c. **1** *The policeman made a signal with his hand, ordering us to stop.* = a movement

S

of the body or an action that carries a certain message or meaning **2** *a traffic signal* = some equipment, found by the side of a road or railway track, that uses lights to inform drivers whether to stop or move ahead **3** *The new satellite will carry television signals.* = magnetic waves that travel through the air carrying messages or pictures

signal[2] verb, i. or t. (**signalled**) **1** *The policeman signalled to us to stop.*(i.) = to make a signal **2** *The surrender of the soldiers signalled the end of the war.*(t.) = to show or indicate what is going to happen

sig•nif•i•cance /sɪɡˈnɪfɪkəns/ noun, u. *I was only five years old when India became free. I was too young to understand the significance of this event.* = the special importance or value of something **significant** adj. **1** *World Wars I and II were very significant events in world history.* = important **2** *The girl looked at me and gave me a significant smile.* = carrying a special meaning **signify** /ˈsɪɡnɪfaɪ/ verb, t. **1** *The red light signifies the presence of some danger ahead.* = to be a sign of **2** *He signified his agreement by raising his hand.* = to make known

Signor /siːˈnjɔːʳ/ noun = a title used to address a man in Italian **Signora** noun = a title used to address a lady in Italian

sign•post[1] /ˈsaɪnpəʊst/ noun, c. = a sign at a place where roads meet, showing the directions in which different places lie, and the distances to them

sign-post[2] verb, t. *We found our way to this place easily because the roads were clearly sign-posted.* = to provide information through sign-posts

Sikh /siːk/ noun = a person who follows the Sikh religion, founded by Guru Nanak in India in the 16th century

silage see **silo**

si•lence[1] /ˈsaɪləns/ noun, u. **1** *We expect complete silence in the library.* = the absence of sound or noise **2** *Your silence shows that you agree with me.* = the state of not saying anything

silence[2] verb, t. *The instructor silenced the noisy children with an angry look.* = to cause someone to stop speaking or making a noise **silencer** noun, c. = a device fitted to a gun that cuts down the sound produced by the firing of a bullet **silent** adj. **1** *We were so shocked by the news that everyone became silent.* = not making any sound **2** *The letter 'g' is silent in the word 'sign'.* = not pronounced (spoken aloud) **3** *The law is silent on this point.* = not expressing an opinion

sil•hou•ette[1] /sɪluːet/ noun, c. *I could see only the silhouette of the man standing behind the window. I did not see his face clearly.* = the dark shape or shadow of a person or object seen against a light background

silhouette[2] verb, t. *The tall building was silhouetted against the evening sky.* = to be seen as a silhouette (in outline)

sil•i•ca /ˈsɪlɪkə/ noun = a chemical substance that is present in sand and is used in making glass

sil•i•con /ˈsɪlɪkən/ noun = a chemical substance that is not a metal but is found in many different minerals, used in making glass **silicon chip** noun, c. = a small piece of silicon used in making parts for a computer and other electronic machines **Silicon Valley** noun = an area in California, U.S.A., where many famous computer companies have their offices and factories

sil•i•cone /ˈsɪlɪkəʊn/ noun = a group of chemicals which contain silicon and are used to manufacture paints,rubber etc.

silk /sɪlk/ noun **1** = a kind of fibre (thread-like material) produced by a larva known as the silk-worm **2** = cloth produced from this fibre **silken** adj. **1** *silken dresses* = made of silk **2** *silken hair* = like silk **silk-worm** noun = the larva which produces threads of silk **silky** adj. *silky hair* = like silk (also **silken**)

sill /sɪl/ noun, c. *window-sill* = a shelf-like structure made of wood or cement at the base of a window

sil•ly /ˈsɪli/ adj. *You want to become a writer? Don't be silly! You can't even write a page of composition!* = foolish or unreasonable

si•lo /ˈsaɪləʊ/ noun, c. *a grain silo* = a large building on a farm, shaped like a tower, in which grain or food for cattle is stored **silage** noun, u. = food for cattle stored in a silo

silt /sɪlt/ noun, u. *A lot of silt was left behind on the river bank after the flood.* = solid material (mud or soil) carried by a river and often deposited (dropped) on the banks or at the place where the river meets the sea

sil•ver[1] /ˈsɪlvəʳ/ noun **1** = a soft, white metal used for making jewellery, utensils (plates, spoons etc.) **2** *Let's put the silver away.* = things made of silver (referring usually to spoons, forks, etc. See **silverware**) **3** = a coin made of silver (old-fashioned)

silver[2] adj. **1** *a silver spoon* = made of silver **2** *a silver-haired man* = like silver in colour

silver[3] verb, t. *The back of the mirror has been silvered.* = to cover with a thin layer of silver **silverfish** noun = a kind of insect that often damages the paper of old books, cloth etc. **silver jubilee** noun, c. = a celebration of an important event, held exactly 25 years after the event took place **silver medal** noun, c. = a medal (prize) made of silver, given to a person who comes second in a competition **silver-tongued** adj. *a silver-tongued orator* = having great skill as a speaker **silverware**

noun, u. = things such as spoons, knives, dishes etc. made of silver or some other metal which looks like silver **silver wedding** noun = a celebration marking 25 years of the marriage of a man and his wife **silvery** adj. **1** *the silvery light of the moon* = looking like silver (literary) **2** *silvery laughter* = having a pleasant sound

sim•i•an[1] /'sɪmiən/ noun, c. = a monkey or animal belonging to the monkey family

simian[2] adj. *simian features* = like that of a monkey

sim•i•lar /'sɪmələʳ/ adj. **1** *Many of the metropolitan cities have similar problems because they all suffer from over-crowding.* = of the same kind **2** *The two brothers look so similar that I often mistake one for the other.* = resembling each other **3** *similar triangles* = triangles having exactly the same shape but not the same size [GEOMETRY] **similarity** /sɪmɪ'lærɪti/ noun, u. *There is a lot of similarity between Assamese and Oriya.* = the quality of being similar **similarly** adv. *Last Friday was a holiday. Similarly, next Friday is a holiday.* = in the same way

sim•i•le /'sɪmɪli/ noun, c. *When you say 'They worked like machines', you are using a simile.* = an expression which compares one thing to another directly, using words such as 'like' or 'as', often used in poetry [LITERATURE]

sim•mer /'sɪməʳ/ verb, i.or t. **1** *Allow the curry to simmer on the fire for ten minutes.*(t.) = to cook something containing a liquid at low heat (below the boiling point) **2** *The crowd was simmering with anger.*(i.) = to be in a state of anger or excitement **simmer down** verb *It was quite a task for the officer to ask the crowd to simmer down as they were angry about getting no piped water.*= to become quiet after a spell of anger

sim•per /'sɪmpəʳ/ verb, i. *Why are you simpering? Do you find something funny?* = to smile in a foolish way

sim•ple /'sɪmpəl/ adj. **1** *I eat simple food—only rice and daal. Nothing fancy!* = plain or very ordinary **2** *He leads a simple life.* = without any show **3** *This is a simple mathematical problem. You should be able to solve it easily.* = easy to understand or do **4** *This wooden 'charkha' is a simple machine for spinning thread, which was made popular by Mahatma Gandhi.* = something which is made up of very few parts **5** *'He eats rice' is a simple sentence.* = a sentence that has only one clause, with one finite verb [GRAMMAR] **simple fracture** noun, c. = a fracture (breaking of a bone) in which the bone does not cut through the flesh and skin **simple interest** noun = interest calculated only on the principal (the sum of money given as a loan) and not on the interest which has been earned **simple-minded** adj. *a simple-minded person* = not vey intelligent or clever **simpleton** noun, c. *She is such a simpleton that anyone can cheat her.* = a person who is not very clever and trusts people easily **simplicity** /sɪm'plɪsɪti/ noun, u. = the quality of being simple **simplify** /'sɪmplɪfaɪ/ verb, t. *This story is difficult for the children. Can you simplify it?* = to make something easier to understand **simplistic** /sɪm'plɪstɪk/ adj. *The problem of feeding millions of poor people is a difficult one. It cannot be solved by simplistic measures.* = treating something difficult as if it was simple (derogatory) **simply** adv. *Our teacher explains the meanings of words as simply as possible so that the whole class can understand easily.* = in a simple manner

sim•u•late /'sɪmjʊleɪt/ verb, t. *Cheap plastic is often used to simulate ivory.* = to imitate (to make something look like something else) **simulation** /sɪmjʊ'leɪʃən/ noun, u. or c. **1** = the act of imitating something **2** *a computer simulation* = the use of a computer programme to imitate and study a real event such as an earthquake **simulator** noun, c. = a machine used to train people to fly an aircraft

sim•ul•ta•ne•ous /sɪməl'teɪnəs/ adj. *The start of the meeting was simultaneous with the explosion of the bomb.* = happening at exactly the same time

sin[1] /sɪn/ noun, c. *Cruelty to living things is a sin.* = an action that is against God's laws or religion

sin[2] verb, i. (**sinned**) *You have sinned by telling a lie.* = to do something which is a sin **sinful** adj. *a sinful life* = guilty of sin **sinner** noun, c. = a person who commits a sin

since[1] /sɪns/ prep. *He has been working here since 15 July.* = after (referring to the period of time that has passed after a particular point of time)

since[2] adv. *I saw them last Friday but I haven't seen them since.* = after that time

since[3] conj. **1** *He has put on a lot of weight since we last met.* = after **2** *She ate the last samosa since it would have been wasted otherwise.* = because

sin•cere /sɪn'sɪəʳ/ adj. *He was not sincere when he said that he agrees with our views. I know that he has differences with us.* = honest or true **sincerely** adv. **1** *I sincerely hope you will attend the general body meetingon Monday.* = really (*sincerely* is here a way of telling the listener that something is important.) **2** *Please let's do this work sincerely, or not at all.* = in a sincere way **sincerity** noun, u. *I like that woman for her sincerity. You can always trust her.* = the quality of being sincere

sine /saɪn/ = the ratio between the length of the side which is opposite an angle of less than 90 degrees,

S

and the length of the hypotenuse in a right-angled triangle [MATHEMATICS]

si•ne•cure /ˈsaɪnɪkjʊəʳ/ noun, c. = a paid job with no or very few duties (derogatory)

sine•die /saɪni ˈdaɪ-iː/ adv. (Latin) *The examination has been postponed sine die.* = indefinitely (without a date being fixed)

sine•qua•non /sɪnikwɑːˈnəʊn/ noun, u. (Latin) *A knowledge of Kannada is a sine qua non for this job in Bangalore.* = a necessary condition for something to happen

sin•ew /ˈsɪnjuː/ noun, c. = a tendon (strong thread-like structure which attaches a muscle to a bone) **sinewy** adj. *a sinewy body* = muscular

sing /sɪŋ/ verb, i. *He has a fine voice and he sings beautifully.* = to produce music or musical sounds with the voice **sing-song** noun, u. *She spoke in a strange sing-song.* = a manner of speaking in which the voice rises and falls regularly

to sing a different song/tune *You are sure to sing a different song when you experience life abroad. Every luxury will seem a necessity!* = to change one's views

singe /sɪndʒ/ verb, t. *I was trying to iron my shirt and I have singed it.* = to burn slightly

sin•gle[1] /ˈsɪŋgəl/ adj. **1** *He managed to win the game in a single shot.* = only one **2** *He uttered only a single word when he was questioned, which was 'No'.* = only one **3** *He is still single. // a single parent* = used to describe someone who is unmarried, divorced, or whose married partner has died **4** *I want a single bed.* = for the use of one person only

single[2] verb, t. *He was singled out for criticism when the project failed.* = to separate or choose someone from a group **single-breasted** adj. *a single-breasted jacket* = a coat or jacket with buttons on only one side of the front **single-handed** adv. *I built this house single-handed.* = with no help from anyone **single-minded** adj. *She is single-minded when she is working.* = having only one clear aim or purpose **singles** noun *Hewitt has won the singles title at Wimbledon.* = a match in tennis or badminton in which only one player plays against another player

single out verb *Why do you always single me out for criticism?* = to choose one person/thing out of a group to blame, scold etc. **single file** noun *Classes have to walk to the quadrangle generally in single file.* = a line of people coming one behind the other

sin•g•let /ˈsɪŋglɪt/ noun, c. = a kind of shirt without sleeves, generally worn by men as an undergarment

singular /ˈsɪŋgjuləʳ/ noun or adj. **1** *'Boy' is singular while 'boys' is plural.* = the form of a word which shows that it is being used to refer to only one person or thing [GRAMMAR] **2** *a child with singular intelligence*(adj.) = unusually great

sin•is•ter /ˈsɪnɪstəʳ/ adj. *They were planning to steal money from the bank, but we were able to defeat their sinister plans.* = evil or dangerous (formal, literary)

sink[1] /sɪŋk/ verb, i. or t. (**sank**, **sunk**) **1** *The 'Titanic' hit an iceberg and sank in the Atlantic Ocean.*(t.) = to go down below the surface of water **2** *The river kept rising after the rains, but now the level of the water is slowly sinking.*(i.) = to fall to a lower level **3** *The patient is sinking. He may not live very long.*(i.) = to become weaker and close to death **4** *We have agreed to sink our differences and become friends.*(t.) = to give up **5** *We are planning to sink a well here.*(t.) = to dig into the earth

sink[2] noun, c. *a kitchen sink* = a container for water, fixed to a wall and connected to a water pipe, from which the water can be removed after pots and pans have been washed in it **sunken** adj. *The children in the famine-stricken area had sunken cheeks.* = hollow **sinker** noun, c. = a weight attached to a fishing line or net to keep it in place below the surface of the water **sinking fund** noun, c. = an amount of money set apart for repayment of debts

sink into *The accident victim sank into a coma.* = slowly become inactive **sink in** *The thought that my mother is no more is slowly sinking in.* = (referring to an idea or an experience) making itself felt; producing an effect on the mind **to have a sinking feeling** *He had a sinking feeling when he heard that some people in the office would lose their jobs.* = an uncomfortable feeling caused by fear, anxiety or nervousness **sink so low** *How could you sink so low as to cheat someone who's been so good to you?* = to behave in a worse manner than one could expect **sink or swim** *We are alone in running this business, and will either sink or swim.* = to fail (sink) or succeed (swim) in something in which one is on one's own **one's heart sank** *His heart sank when he realised he had not been selected for the job.* = to feel unhappy and disappointed

Sino- /ˈsaɪnəʊ/ prefix meaning connected with China e.g. *Sino-Indian relationships*

sin•u•ous /ˈsɪnjuəs/ adj. *The sinuous path led up*

the mountain. = twisting and turning like a snake, with many curves (literary)

si•nus /'saɪnəs/ noun c. (**sinuses**) *The doctor says my headache is caused by a blocked sinus.* = a hollow space, filled with air, inside the bones of the face, leading to the nose [MEDICINE]

sip[1] /sɪp/ verb, t. (**sipped**) *We sat on the verandah all evening, sipping lemonade from tall glasses.* = to drink some liquid in small amounts at a time

sip[2] noun, c. = a very small amount of some liquid that is drunk by someone

si•phon[1] (**syphon**) /'saɪfən/ noun, u. = a bent tube or pipe which is used to draw out water or other liquid from one container into another, using the pressure of air

siphon[2] verb, t. **1** *We siphoned some petrol from the petrol tank of the car into a plastic can.* = to draw out liquid with the help of a siphon **2** *to siphon off huge sums of money* = to take money dishonestly (derogatory)

Sir /səʳ/ noun **1** *Sir, may I be excused?* = a title commonly used by school children to address a male teacher **2** *Dear Sir,* = a salutation (words used to begin a letter) commonly used in writing to a man (formal) **3** *Sir Donald Bradman* = a title given as an honour by the King or Queen of England to a man who has become famous

sire[1] /saɪəʳ/ noun, c. *The sire of this colt (young horse) was a well-known race-horse.* = a male animal (usually a horse or a dog) which is the father of another animal (female **dame**)

sire[2] verb, t. *This horse has sired a number of champion race horses.* = to become the father of (generally used of horses and other animals)

si•ren /'saɪərən/ noun, c. **1** *a factory siren* = a machine which produces a long, high warning sound, commonly used in factories or on police cars or ambulances **2** = an imaginary sea-creature that was half-woman and half bird and sang so sweetly that sailors were charmed by its music (found in stories from ancient Greece)

sir•loin /'sɜːlɔɪn/ noun, c. *a sirloin of beef* = a piece of costly meat cut from the lower back of a cow

sis /sɪs/ noun = a form of address used for one's sister (informal)

si•sal /'saɪsəl/ noun = a kind of plant whose leaves produce a strong thread-like substance that is used for making ropes

sis•sy /'sɪsi/ noun, c. (**sissies**) *Don't be such a sissy!* = a boy who looks or acts like a girl (informal, derogatory) Ⓖ

sis•ter /'sɪstəʳ/ noun, c. **1** = a girl or woman who has the same father and mother as another person **2** = a title commonly used to address a nurse in a hospital or a nun (a woman who is a member of a Christian religious group) **sister-in-law** noun, c. (**sisters-in-law**) = a woman who is the sister of one's wife or husband or the wife of one's brother **sisterly** adj. *She gave me sisterly affection.* = as a sister would give/do

sit /sɪt/ verb, i. or t. (**sat** /sæt/) **1** = to rest on a chair or on the ground with the legs bent at the waist and the knees but the upper part of the body (above the waist) straight **2** *I am sitting on the Board of Directors of this company.*(i.) = to be a member of an official body **3** *The court will sit in the mornings only.*(i.) = to meet for official work **4** *He is sitting for the M.Sc. examination.*(t.) = to take a written examination (also **to sit an examination**) **5** *She is sitting for a portrait.*(i.) = to pose for a photograph or painting (to sit without moving while one's photograph is being taken or one's picture is being painted)

sit•ting[1] /'sɪtɪŋ/ noun, c. or adj. **1** *a sitting of the parliament*(noun) = a meeting of an official body **2** *He read the book in a single sitting.*(noun) = time spent in a chair, usually for reading a book **3** *a sitting for a portrait.*(noun) = the time spent in having one's photograph taken or one's picture painted **4** *a sitting member of the parliament*(adj.) = one who is already a member of an official body **sitting room** noun = the room in a house in which people meet guests but which is not used to sleep in (also **drawing-room** or **living-room**) **sit-down (strike)** noun = the stopping of work by workers in a factory or office who refuse to leave until their demands are met **a sit-down meal** noun = a meal during which people sit down at a table and have food served to them **sit-in** noun = a way of expressing dissatisfaction by entering a public place, stopping the work being done there and refusing to leave (**gherao**, in some Indian languages as well as Indian English) **sit-up** noun, c. = a form of exercise in which a person quickly and repeatedly sits down from a standing position

a sitting duck = a person who can be very easily cheated **to sit around** *It was so hot that we sat around doing nothing.* = to sit, together with others, in a relaxed way, not doing anything serious (often disapproving) **to sit in** *Although she wasn't a member of the committee, we asked her to sit in at the meeting.* = to attend a meeting etc. in order to listen and observe, not to take an active part **to sit in for someone** = to take someone's place in doing some work or attending a meeting **to be sitting pretty** **1** *Our business did very well last year and we are sitting pretty.* = (of business) to be in a good state **2** *I think we should help in the housework instead of sitting pretty.* = being idle and not helping **to sit on something** *I sent the newspaper an article, but they're just*

S

sitting on it. = to delay in reaching a decision (disapproving) **to sit something out** *We didn't like the film, but because Rehana did, we sat it out with her.* = to go through an experience of listening to or watching something, even if one does not like it **to sit through something** *It was a long and dull lecture but we sat through it patiently.* = to listen to or watch something e.g. a film, from beginning to end **to sit up** *We sat up to watch the film.* = to stay awake very late **to make someone sit up** *We went to the music performance not expecting much, but the singer made us really sit up and listen.* = to cause someone to feel a sudden interest which they didn't think they would feel

si•tar /'sɪtɑːr/ noun = an Indian musical instrument with many strings

sit-com /'sɪtkɒm/ noun, c. = the short form of **situational-comedy** (a drama shown on television in which humour is created through funny situations or events)

site[1] /saɪt/ noun, c. **1** *The police rushed to the site of the accident.* = the place where something happens **2** = short form for **website**

site[2] verb, t. *The company will site the new factory near a port.* = to put or build something at a particular place (formal)

sit•u•ate /'sɪtʃueɪt/ verb, t. *We have not decided where we will situate the new office.* = to put in a particular position. (also **site**[2]) **situated** /sɪtʃu'eɪtəd/ adj. *The school is situated on top of a hill.* = to be in a particular place or position **situation** noun, u. or c. **1** *When I got into the bus, I found I had no money to buy a ticket. It was a difficult situation.* = a set of events leading to a certain condition at a particular time **2** *This house has a wonderful situation.* = the place where something is built

six /sɪks/ noun **1** = the number shown by the sign 6, which comes after 5 **2** *He hit the ball for a six.* = a hit in the game of cricket which brings six runs (also **sixer**) **six-footer** noun, c. = a tall person who is more than six feet (1.83 metres) in height **six-shooter** noun, c. = a revolver (small gun) which holds six bullets and can fire them one after another

six•teen /sɪk'stiːn/ noun = the number represented by 16 (10 +6)

six•th /'sɪksθ/ det. *the sixth house on the road* = coming after five persons or objects **sixth sense** noun *His sixth sense told him he was in danger.* = an ability to know things without the use of the ordinary five senses (sight, smell, hearing, taste, feeling)

six•ty /'sɪksti/ noun = the number represented by 60 (10x6)

size[1] /saɪz/ noun, u. or c. **1** *This car is of just the right size—neither too big nor too small.* = the degree of bigness or smallness **2** *China's neighbours admire China because of its size.* = degree of bigness **3** *This shop stocks shoes in many different sizes.* = a set of standard measurements in which things are produced

size[2] verb, t. *The students were becoming restless and could easily turn violent. The chief of the police party sized up the situation immediately.* = to form an opinion or judgement after considering the facts **sizable** adj. *She won the election by a sizable number of votes.* = rather large

siz•zle /'sɪzəl/ verb, i. *The fish which the woman was frying sizzled in the frying-pan.* = to make the sound that is produced when something is being fried in hot oil **sizzler** noun, c. = a meat dish served in a restaurant, which is brought to the table while it is still hot and sizzling

skate[1] /skeɪt/ noun, c. **1** (usually plural) *roller skates* = a piece of metal like a shoe, with four small wheels attached to the bottom, which a person can wear on the foot and use to move very fast **2** *ice-skates* = a shoe or boot, to the bottom of which a steel blade is attached, to allow the wearer to move quickly over ice **3** = a kind of large, flat fish found in the sea

skate[2] verb, i. *He loves to skate.* = to move on skates **skate-board** noun, c. = a short, flat board with four small wheels attached to the bottom, on which one can stand and move quickly

skeet-shooting /'skiːt ʃuːtɪŋ/ noun = a sport in which one shoots at clay objects thrown into the air like flying birds

skein /skeɪn/ noun, c. *a skein of wool* = a length of thread or wool wound loosely into the shape of a large ring

skel•e•ton[1] /'skelɪtən/ noun, c. **1** = the framework of connected bones which supports the body **2** *the skeleton of a building* = the framework around which something is constructed **3** *He has become a skeleton after his long illness.* = an extremely thin and weak person (figurative)

skeleton[2] adj. *The company is running with only a skeleton staff.* = just enough to keep something going **skeleton key** noun, c. = a key which can open many different locks

a skeleton in the cupboard = a shameful event or fact which a person tries to keep secret

skeletal /'skelɪtəl/ adj. **1** *skeletal tissues* = belonging to a skeleton **2** *a skeletal report* = giving only the main points, without details

sketch[1] /sketʃ/ noun, c. **1** *a pencil sketch* = a simple drawing, often done quickly **2** = a short written or spoken description

sketch[2] verb, t. or i. **1** *The artist sketched the scene on a piece of paper.*(t.) = to draw quickly **2** *The Director* *sketched out the programmes planned for the next year.*(i.) = to describe only the main points, without details **sketchy** adj. *She gave us only a sketchy account of what happened at the meeting.* = not complete or not giving enough information (often derogatory)

skew /skjuː/ verb, t. *The facts in the report have been skewed. This is not what happened.* = to change the information in something written or spoken so that one does not get the correct picture

skew•er[1] /ˈskjuːəʳ/ noun, c. = a long metal or wooden stick which is put through pieces of meat being cooked on a fire

skewer[2] verb, t. = to pierce meat for cooking with a skewer

ski[1] /skiː/ noun, c. = a long, curved piece of metal that can be fixed to the bottom of a shoe and used for travelling over ice

ski[2] verb, i. (**skied**) = to move over ice by using skis, either as a sport or for going from one place to another **ski-lift** noun, c. = a machine used to carry people who want to ski down a hill to the top of the hill

skid /skɪd/ verb, i. (**skidded**) *The car skidded on the wet road and hit a tree on the side of the road.* = to slip or move sideways, out of control (describing the movement of a vehicle)

skill /skɪl/ noun, u. or c. *The skill of writing can be improved with practice.* = a special ability to do something which one develops through practice or training **skilful** adj. *a skilful writer* = having a lot of skill **skilled** adj. *skilled labour* = having skill

skil•let /ˈskɪlɪt/ noun, c. = a metal pan in which food is fried (also **frying-pan**)

skim /skɪm/ verb, t. or i. (**skimmed**) **1** *She skimmed the cream off the milk.*(t.) = to remove something solid which is floating on the surface of a liquid **2** *The birds skimmed across the lake.*(i.) = to move quickly just above the surface of water, without touching it or touching it only occasionally **3** *I skimmed through the documents in the file.*(i.) = to read something quickly to understand the main points **skimmed milk** noun, u. = milk from which the cream or fat has been removed

skimp /skɪmp/ verb, i. or t. *For the school play, we had to skimp on the lights because most of the money was spent on costumes.* = to spend less money on something than is required, often because there is not enough money **skimpy** adj. **1** *a skimpy meal* = using or providing less of something than is needed **2** *a skimpy dress* = clothes which barely cover the body (disapproving)

skin[1] /skɪn/ noun, u. or c. **1** *The bone in his arm was broken, but the skin was not damaged.*(u.) = the natural outer cover over the body of a human being or animal or a fruit or vegetable **2** (c.) = the covering over an animal's body, from which leather is made

skin[2] verb, t. (**skinned**) = to remove the skin from an animal **skingraft** noun *The skin on his chest and arms got badly burnt in the fire. The doctors will give him a skingraft next month.* = a surgical operation in which healthy skin from one part of the body is used to replace damaged skin in a different part **skinny** adj. *a skinny girl* = very thin and having little flesh on the body **skin-tight** adj. *a skin-tight dress* = fitting very tightly and showing the shape of the body clearly (referring to a dress)

skin-deep *The friendship between the two neighbours is only skin-deep. They don't really like each other.* = only on the surface; not deep or real **by the skin of one's teeth** *She escaped an accident by the skin of her teeth.* = narrowly; by a small margin **to jump out of one's skin** = to react to something with fear or shock **to get under someone's skin** *Their habit of boasting really gets under my skin.* = to cause someone to feel irritated or annoyed **to skin someone alive** = to punish someone harshly by scolding them etc. (informal, often humorous)

skip[1] /skɪp/ verb, i. or t. (**skipped**) **1** *The little girl skipped happily after her mother.*(i.)= to move lightly or quickly with small, dancing steps **2** *The children are practising skipping.*(i.) = to jump as an exercise, using a skipping rope **3** *The next five pages of the book are not interesting, so you can skip them.*(t.) = to leave out or pass over **4** *I am going to skip class and watch a film on television.*(t.) = to avoid doing something (informal)

skip[2] noun, c. *The little girl walked out of the room with a skip.* = a light jumping movement **skipping rope** noun = a light rope which is held in both hands and swung repeatedly over the head and then under the legs, as one jumps over it as an exercise

to skip out/off *I'm amazed that all of you skipped off without helping me to clean the house.* = to go away, often suddenly, without feeling any worry or anxiety or a sense of responsibility

skip•per /ˈskɪpəʳ/ noun, c. = the captain of a ship or a sports team

skir•mish[1] /ˈskɜːmɪʃ/ noun, c. *There was a skirmish between the two groups of students.* = a short fight which is not planned (formal)

skirmish[2] verb, i. *The two groups skirmished briefly and then became friends again.* = to take part in a skirmish

skirt[1] /skɜːt/ noun, c. **1** = a short dress for a woman or girl that covers the legs from the waist to the knees **2** = a covering for a machine that protects some of its parts

S

skirt[2] verb, t. or i. *The road skirts the house.* = to go around or along the edge of something

skit /skɪt/ noun, c. = a short humorous play **skittish** adj. *a playful and skittish child* = energetic and restless (disapproving)

skulk /skʌlk/ verb, i. *The policeman caught the man who was skulking in the bushes.* = to hide or move about stealthily in a suspicious manner

skull /skʌl/ noun, c. = the framework of bones inside the head **skull-and-crossbones** noun **1** = a sign, consisting of a skull with two long bones crossing each other below it, which shows the presence of some danger **2** = a flag, carrying the skull-and-crossbones sign, which was used in former times by pirates (sea robbers) **skullcap** noun, c. = a kind of cap which fits tightly on the head, often used by men who follow the Muslim or Jewish religion

skunk /skʌŋk/ noun, c. = an animal found in the U.S.A. which looks like a fox and gives out a liquid with a strong, bad smell when it is attacked

sky /skaɪ/ noun, u. or c. (**skies**) = the space above the earth in which the sun, moon and stars can be seen **sky-blue** *Their school uniform is sky-blue in colour.* = light blue **sky-diving** noun = a sport in which someone jumps from an aircraft and falls freely for several seconds or minutes before opening his/her parachute **sky-high** adv. *The price of onions has risen sky-high.* = very high **sky-jack** verb, t *The flight which took off from Kolkata for Bangkok has been sky-jacked.* = to take control of an aircraft by force (also **hi-jack**) **sky-lark** noun, c. = a kind of singing bird **sky-light** noun, c. = a high opening in a wall inside a house, covered with glass, which allows light to enter **sky-line** noun, u. or c. = the view of a city showing tall buildings with the sky as a background **sky-scraper** noun, c. = a very tall building

to praise someone to the skies = to shower great praise on someone (informal) **the sky's the limit** *If you are determined, you can achieve anything you want. The sky's the limit.* = 'There is nothing that one cannot achieve.'

slab /slæb/ noun, c. *The drain was covered with stone slabs.* = a thick, flat piece of some material

slack[1] /slæk/ adj. **1** *The telephone wires have become slack and are hanging loosely from the poles.* = not tight (referring to a rope or wire) **2** *Discipline in this school has become slack.* = not firm **3** *Business in hotels is slack here after the earthquake last month.* = not active

slack[2] noun, u. the part of a rope or wire that hangs loose

slack[3] verb, i. *Tell the workers not to slack off or they will be dismissed.* = to be lazy in doing work **slacken** verb, t. **1** *The ropes are too tight. Can you slacken them a bit?* = to make less tight **2** *The train has slackened speed.* = to cut down or decrease **slacks** noun, c. (always plural, often used with 'a pair of') = loose-fitting trousers

slag /slæg/ noun, u. = waste material that is left behind after a metal has been separated from the ore (rock) in which it was present **slag-heap** noun, c. = a pile of slag often found outside a factory

slake /sleɪk/ verb, t. *Animals come to this lake to slake their thirst.* = to drink some liquid in order to get rid of one's thirst (also **quench**) (formal, literary)

sla•lom /'slɑːləm/ noun, c. = a race for persons wearing **skis** (see **ski**), or for drivers of motor cars, in which competitors have to follow a route that winds in and out through a line of poles carrying flags [SPORTS]

slam[1] /slæm/ verb, t. or i. (**slammed**) **1** *He slammed the door angrily.*(t.) = to shut or close a door or window with force, making a loud noise **2** *He slammed the books down on the table.*(t.) = to put something down with force **3** *The car behind us slammed into us when we stopped the car suddenly.*(t.) = to hit with force **4** *The new film was slammed by all the reviewers.*(t.) = to attack in writing (informal)

slam[2] noun, c. *He shut the door with a slam.* = the loud noise produced when a door is closed with force **Grand Slam** *Venus Williams has won the French, Australian and American titles and is likely to complete the Grand Slam this year.* = to win all the important tournaments that one plays in (in tennis) or to win by a very big margin (in bridge)

slan•der[1] /'slɑːndəʳ/ noun, u. = a false report or news which damages someone's reputation

slander[2] verb, t. *He is doing so many good things for our town, why do you keep slandering him?* = to make a false statement about someone which damages his or her reputation

slanderous adj. *a slanderous report* = containing slander

slang[1] /slæŋ/ noun, u. *'Chamcha' is a slang word in Hindi used to refer to a person who follows an important person everywhere and flatters him or her all the time.* = highly informal and often rude or insulting language. Slang words are often used by groups of people (e.g. drug peddlers) who don't want others to know what they are saying (e.g. 'joint' for marijuana)

slang[2] verb, t. *The players in the fielding side slanged the umpire for not giving the batsman out.* = to attack with rude and angry words (informal)

a slanging match *It is not uncommon to see people on discussion panels getting into a slanging match, especially if they belong to different political parties.* = an angry argument where people insult each other (informal)

slant[1] /slɑːnt/ verb, i. **1** *In this sentence, all the letters* *slant to the right.* = to lean in a certain direction; to be at an angle instead of being perfectly straight **2** *The newspaper slanted its report in favour of the Indian team.* = to present facts in a way that favours or helps someone (disapproving)

slant[2] noun, u. **1** *The rain water falling on the tin roof flows down the slant.* = slope (going from a higher to a lower level) **2** *Your report has a slant against the government.* = the way in which a fact is presented **slanted** adj.

slap[1] /slæp/ verb, t. (**slapped**) **1** *Why did you slap me? What did I do? // We slapped each other on the back when our team won.* = to hit with the palm (the flat part of the hand) usually on the cheek, making a sound to express either anger or a feeling of friendship or joy **2** *The waves slapped against the rocks.* = to strike something with a sound like that of a slap **3** *The police slapped a fine on the driver of the car.* = to cause something unpleasant to happen (informal)

slap[2] noun, c. *a slap on the cheeks* = a quick hit with the flat part of the hand on the cheek, back etc. as a sign of either anger or friendship

slap[3] adv. *The car hit the wall slap in the middle.* = exactly (informal) **slap-dash** adj. *He has written the essay in a slap-dash manner.* = done in a hurry, in a careless manner **slapstick** noun = humorous acting in a play or film that makes use of action or jokes that are somewhat silly

to slap something on *I slapped some cold cream on my face as the skin was very dry.* = to place or apply quickly and carelessly on a surface (informal) **a slap in the face** *He did not even speak to me when he visisted our school, though we had been good friends once. It was a slap in the face for me.* = an insult

slash[1] /slæʃ/ verb, t. **1** *The tiger slashed the man's face with its claws.* = to cut with something sharp (e.g. a knife or the claws of an animal) **2** *The price of petrol has been slashed from Rs 30 a litre to Rs 12 a litre.* = to reduce (make less) by a large amount **3** *The people walking through the jungle had to slash their way through.* = to clear a way by cutting down bushes etc.

slash[2] noun, c. **1** *The slash that you see on my face was made by my cat when I was playing with her.* = a cut or a heavy blow with a sharp instrument **2** *The number of the house he lives in is 13 slash 2 (13/2).* = a sloping line used in writing or printing to separate two words or letters (also **oblique**)

slat /slæt/ noun, c. *He sleeps on a bed of wooden slats.* = a thin, narrow piece of wood used for making furniture etc.

slate[1] /sleɪt/ noun, u. or c. **1** *The house has a slate roof.*(u.) = a kind of dark grey stone that can be cut easily into flat pieces or sheets **2** *The teacher asked the children to write a word on their slates.*(c.) = a small, flat piece of slate (stone) on which children can write with a piece of chalk

slate[2] verb, t. **1** *The roof has been slated.* = to cover a roof with slate **2** *Rahul Dravid is slated to be the next captain of the Indian team.* = to choose someone or something for a future occasion **3** *Salman Rushdie's new book was slated by most critics.* = to attack with words

to wipe the slate clean *The two friends quarrelled but they have agreed to wipe the slate clean.* = to forgive and forget past happenings

slaugh•ter[1] /ˈslɔːtəʳ/ verb, t. **1** *Many innocent children were slaughtered during the riots.* = to kill in a cruel way **2** *These chickens will be slaughtered for the feast tomorrow.* = to kill animals for meat

slaughter[2] noun, u. **1** *The air-raids on the city caused terrible slaughter.* = killing **2** *These goats are being led to the slaughter.* = the act of killing animals for meat **slaughter-house** = a place where animals are killed for meat

slave[1] /sleɪv/ noun, c. = a person who works for someone without being paid, is said to be owned by that person and can be bought or sold

slave[2] verb, i. *I slaved for the government for 35 years.* = to work very hard on low pay **slaver** noun, c. = a ship which was used to carry slaves (in the old days) **slavish** adj. **1** *He shows a slavish obedience to his seniors.* = showing complete obedience to someone (derogatory) **2** *He produced a slavish translation of a Telugu novel.* = a translation of a book which is a close but unintelligent copy of the original **slave-driver** = someone who makes people work very hard (derogatory or humorous) **slave-labour** *The Egyptian pyramids were built with slave labour.* = work done by slaves, without any payment **slave-trade** = the buying and selling of slaves

slay /sleɪ/ verb, t. (**slew**, **slain**) *He slew the demon.* = to kill (literary)

slea•zy /ˈsliːzi/ adj. *The old part of the city is full of sleazy hotels.* = dirty, cheap and having a bad reputation

sled /sled/ = a carriage without wheels that can travel over ice, on long metal blades called runners, and is pulled by horses or dogs (also **sledge**)

sledge•ham•mer /ˈsledhæməʳ/ noun, c. = a large, heavy hammer that is swung with both hands

sledg•ing /sledʒɪŋ/ noun, u. = the action of abusing a player of the team against which you are playing in a cricket match, in order to make that person angry or nervous (slang)

sleek /sliːk/ adj. **1** *a cat with sleek fur* = neat and

S

shining; in very good condition or health (referring generally to hair or fur) **2** *a sleek car* = attractive and neat-looking

sleep[1] /sli:p/ verb, i. or t. (**slept**) **1** *He always sleeps in the afternoon.*(i.)= to be in a resting state **2** *This large bed can sleep three children.*(t.) = to provide space for sleeping **3** *Are they sleeping with each other?*(t.) = to have sex (informal, old-fashioned)

sleep[2] noun, u. **1** *You should get at least six hours of sleep every day.* = a state of deep rest in which the body and mind are not active **sleepy** adj. **1** *I am feeling sleepy* = ready to sleep **2** *a sleepy little town* = a place where there is very little activity **sleeper** noun, c. **1**= a person who is sleeping **2** = a carriage on a train in which people can sleep (also **sleeping-car**) **sleeping-bag** noun = a large, warm bag fitted with a zip which one can sleep in **sleeping-partner** noun = a partner in a business who is not active at all in looking after the business **sleeping-pill** noun = a medicine which helps a person to get sleep (also **sleeping tablet**) **sleeping-policeman** noun = a raised part across the road which prevents vehicles from speeding (also **speed-breaker**) **sleeping sickness** noun = a serious disease, common in Africa and caused by the biting of a kind of fly (the tse-tse fly) which causes a person to become weak with fever **sleepless** adj. *I spent a sleepless night.* = not able to sleep **sleep-walking** noun = a condition of the mind which causes a person to walk about during sleep without knowing what is happening (also **somnambulism**) **sleep-walker** noun = a person who walks in his/her sleep (also **somnambulist**)

to put something to sleep = to medically kill an animal that is old or ill so that it no longer suffers **to not sleep a wink** *The mother couldn't sleep a wink last night as her baby was very ill.* = to not sleep at all **to sleep on it** *Don't take a hasty decision. Why don't you sleep on it and give me a reply tomorrow?* = to not decide quickly about something important, but to take time until the next day (informal) **to not lose sleep** *If I were you, I wouldn't lose sleep over what he said; it is such a trivial matter!* = not to feel worried **to sleep rough** = to be in the open and not have a sheltered place where one can eat, sleep etc. as a result of being poor (informal)

sleet /sli:t/ noun, u. = rain which has turned into ice because of the cold weather

sleeve /sli:v/ noun, c. = the part of a dress which covers the arm of the person wearing it **sleeveless** adj. = without a sleeve

to have something up one's sleeve = to have a secret plan for use at the right time in the future

sleigh /sleɪ/ noun, u. = a sled or sledge (see **sled**)

sleight-of-hand /slaɪt əv ˈhænd/ noun *The magician used sleight-of-hand to make the girl disappear.* = the skill used by a magician to perform a magical trick

slen•der /ˈslendəʳ/ adj. **1** = slim (thin in an attractive way) **2** *My chances of getting leave are quite slender.* = slight; very small (often humorous)

by a slender majority *He won the elections by a slender majority.* = by a narrow margin (a small difference)

sleuth /slu:θ/ noun, c. = a detective (a person who is hired to find out who has committed a crime) (old-fashioned)

slew /slu:/ past tense of **slay**

slice[1] /slaɪs/ noun, c. *a slice of bread* = a flat, thin piece cut out of a larger piece

slice[2] verb, t. *You can slice the bread with this knife.* = to cut into slices

slice of life *The new film has been praised highly as it presents a slice of life.* = a film or book which shows life as it really is

slick[1] /slɪk/ adj. **1** *Kajol gives a slick performance in her new film.* = done with great skill but without much effort **2** *Don't be taken in by his slick talk. He is trying to cheat you.* = appearing to be friendly, but clever and dishonest (derogatory)

slick[2] noun, c. *an oil slick* = a large sheet of oil floating on the surface of the sea **slicker** noun, c. *a city slicker* = a person who is very slick (clever) in his or her talk and behaviour but is dishonest and cannot be trusted (derogatory)

slide[1] /slaɪd/ verb, i. or t. (**slid**) **1** *The boy slipped and fell while running and slid across the wet floor.*(i.) = to move quickly over a smooth surface such as ice **2** *The value of the rupee slid to its lowest level this week.* = to go down suddenly

slide[2] noun, c. **1** *The children are playing on the slide.* = a long, narrow and smooth piece of metal fixed to the top of a small ladder, generally found in a playground, on which children can play by sliding down from the top to the bottom **2** *The environmentalist spoke to the students with the help of slides.* = a picture on a transparent film mounted on a card, that is shown with the help of a projector **slide-rule** noun, c. = an instrument used by engineers for making mathematical calculations, consisting of a long wooden ruler or scale, down the middle of which a small movable piece can slide (move up and down)

to let things slide *If you continue to let things slide, you can't expect your results to improve.* = to allow things to become worse

slight[1] /slaɪt/ adj. **1** *I have a slight fever. It's not serious.* = not much or not serious **2** *The slight frame of the girl is ideal for a long-distance runner.* = small in size

slight² verb, t. *You slighted them by refusing to meet their leader.* = to insult or not show proper respect

slight³ noun, c. *It was a slight to have made the guests wait for so long.* = insult **slightly** adv. *The line you have drawn is not perfectly straight. It is slightly crooked.* = a little bit

slim¹ /slɪm/ adj. *The girl was tall and slim. She looked very graceful.* = thin in a way that is healthy and attractive

slim² verb, i. (**slimmed**) *I tried to slim down by eating less but didn't succeed.* = to become thin by eating less, taking exercise etc. **slimming** noun, u. *Slimming should be done only under a doctor's supervision.* = the process of trying to lose weight

slime /slaɪm/ noun, u. *The water in the pond has dried up, but the bottom is covered with thick slime.* = dirty and unpleasant matter which is partly solid and partly liquid and feels slippery when touched **slimy** adj. **1** *a slimy pond* = covered with slime **2** *a slimy person* = a person who talks or behaves in a way that seems friendly but is not sincere (derogatory)

sling¹ /slɪŋ/ verb, t. (**slung**) **1** *He took off his shirt and slung it over the chair.* = to hang something loosely **2** *He slung the letters into the waste-paper basket.* = to throw carelessly (often disapproving)

sling

sling² noun, c. **1** *The doctor plastered his arm and put it in a sling.* = a piece of cloth which is tied around the neck and used to support a damaged arm, in which a bone has been broken **2** *The pot of milk was kept in a sling hanging from the ceiling.* = a support, made of cloth, rope etc. which is hung up and used to lift or store heavy objects **3** *The gun is hanging by its sling.* = a thick piece of cloth tied to a gun, which is used to hang the gun from the shoulder **sling-shot** noun, c. = a simple weapon used in former times, consisting of a thick piece of cloth in which a stone could be placed and thrown with force (also **catapult**)

slink /slɪŋk/ verb, t. (**slunk**) *The wounded lion slunk back into its den after it had been defeated in a battle with a younger lion.* = to move quietly or secretly, as if in shame

slip¹ /slɪp/ verb, i. or t. (**slipped**) **1** *The man slipped on the wet floor and fell heavily.*(i.) = to slide (move quickly over a wet or smooth surface) without planning to do so **2** *He slipped out of the room while the meeting was going on.*(i.) = to move quickly and quietly without being noticed **3** *He slipped a 100-rupee note into my hand.*(t.) = to put or give quickly and secretly, so that one is not seen doing it **4** *I forgot to buy a present for you. It slipped my mind completely.*(t.) = to be forgotten or to escape one's attention **5** *Be careful! You are slipping in your work.*(i.) = to go down from an expected or usual standard

slip² noun, c. **1** *He had a slip in the bathroom and broke a leg.* = the act of slipping on a wet or smooth surface **2** *He made a slip while reading out the report.* = a small mistake **3** *She handed him a slip of paper while he was speaking.* = a small piece of paper **slip-on** = a shoe without laces which is worn by pushing the foot into it **slipped disc** = a painful medical condition caused by one of the bones in the spine (the long line of bones in the middle of the back) moving away from its usual place **slipper** noun, c. = a light, open shoe **slippery** adj. **1** *The floor is slippery. Be careful when you walk over it.* = very smooth or wet and likely to make one slip and fall **2** *a slippery customer* = a person who cannot be trusted **slip-shod** adj. *Your work has been done in a very slip-shod manner. You must do better next time.* = careless **slipstream** = an area of low pressure just behind a fast-moving vehicle, such as an aircraft **slip-up** = a careless but small mistake

to let slip **1** *She is unhappy because she let slip this chance to win a prize.* = to lose or miss an opportunity **2** *During our talk, he let slip that he was planning to resign.* = to give out a secret without intending to do so **to slip through one's fingers** *Because of one player's carelessness, victory in the finals slipped through our fingers.* = to miss an opportunity through carelessness **a slip of the tongue** = an unintended mistake made while speaking

slit¹ /slɪt/ noun, c. *He slipped the letter into the letter-box through the slit at the top.* = a narrow, long opening or cut

slit² verb, t. (**slit**) *The robber slit the man's throat and took his watch.* = to cut with a sharp knife

slith•er /ˈslɪðəʳ/ verb, i. *The snake slithered through the grass.* = to move with a smooth but twisting movement (like a snake)

sliv•er /ˈslɪvəʳ/ noun, c. *He cut the bamboo into thin slivers.* = a thin, sharp piece cut or broken out of something

slob•ber /ˈslɒbəʳ/ verb, i. **1** *The dog was ill and slobbered all over my clothes.* = to allow saliva (liquid) to run out of the mouth **2** *Yes, he is a good poet, but there is no need for you to slobber over him.* = to show too much admiration or liking for someone (informal, derogatory)

sloe /sləʊ/ noun = a kind of fruit, like a plum, with a slightly sour taste

slog¹ /slɒg/ verb, i. or t. (**slogged**) **1** *We had to slog*

S

15 hours a day for a month to complete the project. = to work very hard (informal) **2** *They really made us slog.* = to do boring and hard work **3** *He slogged the ball over long-on.* = to hit the ball hard but without skill, in cricket (informal)

slog[2] noun, u. *Writing all those invitation letters was a real slog.* = a piece of hard and boring work (informal) **slog overs** = (in cricket) the last few overs in a one-day match, when players are expected to hit the ball hard and score runs quickly

slo•gan /'sləʊgən/ noun, c. *The crowd shouted slogans of 'Down with smoking'. // The slogan for Amul Butter is 'Utterly butterly delicious'.* = a short phrase or expression which is easily remembered and is used for political or advertising purposes

sloop /slu:p/ noun, c. = a small sailing ship, often with a single mast

slop[1] /slɒp/ noun, u. or c. *How can we eat such slop?* = tasteless food or waste food often given to animals (informal)

slop[2] verb, i. (**slopped**) *He slopped coffee all over the carpet.* = to spill a liquid (to cause it to flow out of a container) because of carelessness (informal)

slope[1] /sləʊp/ verb, i. *The Gangetic plain slopes towards the east.* = to lie at an angle, from a higher to a lower height (also **slant**)

slope[2] noun, u. or c. *The bus went slowly down the slope.* = a surface that runs from a higher to a lower level

slop•py /'slɒpi/ adj. **1** *You should not have come to the party in those sloppy clothes.* = untidy and dirty-looking **2** *We cannot accept such sloppy work.* = carelessly done

slosh /slɒʃ/ verb, i. *The petrol sloshed around in the bottom of the tank.* = (referring to a liquid) to move around noisily in the bottom of a container **sloshed** adj. *At the end of the party we were completely sloshed.* = drunk (slang)

slot[1] /slɒt/ noun, c. **1** *You can get a cup of hot coffee from this machine when you drop a five-rupee coin into the slot.* = a long, narrow opening in a machine **2** *We will fit the new television programme in the 8.15 slot, after the news.* = a fixed position or place in a list, into which someone or something can be fitted

slot[2] verb, t. **1** *With great difficulty he slotted the car into the parking lot.* = to fit into a small space **2** *The doctor is busy but he will try to slot you in.* = to find a position or time for someone **slot-machine** noun = a machine into which one drops coins and which is used for a form of gambling

sloth /sləʊθ/ noun **1** = an animal found in South America that looks like a small bear, hangs upside down from the branches of trees and moves very slowly **2** *Your sloth makes you unfit for any responsible position.*(u.)= the quality of being very lazy **slothful** adj. = lazy

slouch[1] /slaʊtʃ/ verb, i. *Tired after the long journey, the man slouched over the table as he ate his lunch.* = to stand, sit or walk with the shoulders hanging forward and the head slightly bent, because of tiredness or boredom **slouch** noun, u. **1** = a slouching position in which one sits or stands **2** *He is no slouch when it comes to running between the wickets.* = a person who is lazy or slow to act (used in the negative only, to carry the opposite meaning)

slough[1] /slʌf/ verb, t. **1** *Snakes slough off their skin once a year.* = to throw off dead skin (referring to snakes) **2** *He has sloughed off all his old friends.* = to get rid of something or someone that one does not find useful any longer

slough[2] /slaʊ/ noun, u. **1** = a marsh (a wet and muddy place) **2** *She has got into a slough after the death of her husband and is unable to get out of it.* = a state of depression (sadness)

sloven•ly /'slʌvənli/ adj. **1** *He lives in very slovenly surroundings.* = dirty and untidy **2** *slovenly work* = done in a careless manner

slow[1] /sləʊ/ adj. **1** *a slow train* = moving at low speed **2** *Your watch is ten minutes slow.* = behind the correct time **3** *These students are rather slow.* = not able to understand something quickly **4** *Business is slow these days.* = not active

slow[2] verb, i. or t. **1** *Ask the driver to slow down the car.*(t.) = to make something move at a lower speed **2** *Business has slowed down.*(i.) = to become less active **slow coach** noun, c. = a person who is very slow to think or act **slow motion** noun, u. = a scene from a film which makes the action look much slower than in real life **slowly** adv. *Life came back to normal, although slowly.* = not happening quickly or moving fast

slowly but surely *Being a friendly person, he made new friends slowly but surely.* = making good progress though slowly

sludge /slʌdʒ/ noun, c. = dirty solid matter which settles at the bottom of a liquid

slug[1] /slʌg/ noun, c. **1** = a small animal that is like a snail, but has no shell **2** = a small piece of metal fired from a gun

slug[2] verb, t. (**slugged**) *I slugged him on the nose.* = to hit hard with the fist (closed hand) (informal)

slug•gard /'slʌgəd/ noun, c. = a very lazy person (derogatory, old-fashioned)

slug•gish /'slʌgɪʃ/ adj. **1** *the sluggish flow of the water* = very slow **2** *I feel sluggish because of the hot weather.* = less active than usual

sluice[1] /slu:s/ verb, t. *We sluiced out the verandah with hose pipes after everyone had finished eating.* = to wash and clean up with water

sluice[2] noun, c. = a channel or passage through which water can flow

sluice-gate noun, c. = a gate which can be raised or lowered to control the flow of water through a dam (see pic under **dam**)

slum[1] /slʌm/ noun, c. = a dirty and crowded area in or outside a city in which poor people generally live

slum[2] verb, i. *We had so little money when we were students in the U.S.A. that we were forced to slum.* = to live in conditions that are much poorer than one is used to (informal)

slum•ber /'slʌmbəʳ/ noun, u. or c. (**slumbers**) *We hope that one day he will wake up from his slumbers.*(c.) // *Don't wake the baby up. He seems to be in deep slumber.*(u.) = deep sleep or lack of activity (literary)

slumber[2] verb, i. *The country is slumbering now, but it will wake up and become active again.* = to be asleep and inactive (literary)

slump[1] /slʌmp/ verb, i. **1** *He was so tired that he slumped in his seat as he was speaking.* = to fall or drop back heavily **2** *The price of rice has slumped.* = to fall or come down suddenly in value

slump[2] noun, c *There is a slump in the car market.* = a fall in business

slur[1] /slɜ:ʳ/ noun, c. **1** *The article in today's paper is a slur on my reputation.* = a remark in speech or writing which damages the reputation of some person **2** *He speaks with a slur.* = an unclear way of speaking

slur[2] verb, i. (**slurred**) **1** *This article slurs many of the people in our group.* = to make damaging remarks about someone **2** *He was drunk and slurred many of the words in his speech.* = to speak in an unclear way

slurp /slɜ:p/ verb, t. *He slurped his tea noisily.* = to drink a liquid with an unpleasant sucking noise

slur•ry /'slʌri/ noun, u. *The coal slurry was pumped out of the mine.* = a mixture of water and some solid material such as coal [TECHNICAL]

slush /slʌʃ/ noun, u. **1** *We drove slowly as there was slush on the roads.* = snow which has partly melted **2** *The new film, which has a romantic story, is full of slush.* = immature and somewhat silly romantic feelings (derogatory) **slushy** adj. *With the heavy rains the roads have turned slushy.* = muddy **slush fund** = money set apart for secret and dishonest use (slang)

slut /slʌt/ noun, c. = an insulting way of referring to a woman who has had sex with many men (derogatory) USE G **sluttish** adj. = like a slut (derogatory)

sly /slaɪ/ adj. *He's a sly old fox!* = clever and not to be trusted

to do something on the sly = to do something bad secretly

smack[1] /smæk/ verb, t. **1** *Why did you smack the child?* = to hit someone with the flat part of the hand, producing a sound **2** *Let me smack you for bringing me flowers.* = a loud kiss (informal) **3** *He smacked his lips when he heard we were going to have icecream.* = to make a sound with the lips, expressing pleasure because one is about to eat something that one likes **4** *Your words smack of some mischief.* = to suggest

smack[2] noun, c. **1** *a smack on the jaw* = a hard blow **2** *He dropped the suitcase on the floor with a smack.* = the sound made when an object hits some surface **3** *The police arrested him for selling smack.* = heroin (a dangerous drug) (slang)

smack[3] adv. *He drove smack into a tree.* = directly; straight (informal)

small[1] /smɔ:l/ adj. **1** *The house is small. It has only one room.* = not big **2** *I'll have a small whisky and soda.* = in a small quantity (referring to a drink) **3** *Small children are not allowed to see this film.* = very young in age **4** *She is a small-minded person.* = mean or petty; not generous **5** *Use only small letters when you write my e-mail address.* = not capital (letters)

small[2] adv. *She writes so small that I can't read her writing.* = using letters that are small in size

small[3] noun, u. *He was hit in the small of the back.* = the narrow, middle part of the back **small arms** noun = guns which can be fired from the hand **small change** noun = coins of low value **small hours** noun *He returned home in the small hours.* = the early morning hours, after midnight **small intestine** noun = the long, narrow, twisting tube inside the body through which food passes **small pox** noun = a serious disease which leaves marks on the skin, specially the face **small print** noun *Read the small print carefully before you sign the agreement.* = the details in an agreement or a legal document, which one can miss unless one is careful **small screen** noun *Amitabh Bachchan will appear on the small screen for the first time.* = television **small talk** noun *I don't go to parties as I am not good at making small talk.* = light (not serious) conversation during social gatherings etc.

to cost a small fortune *The necklace cost us a small fortune.* = a great deal of money **with a small 'a', 'b' etc.** *I'm a director of the company with a small 'd'.* = used to say that one is not as important as others may think or that one's beliefs in something are not deep or strong (e.g. *a Marxist with a small 'm'*) **small fry** *Who cares about my opinion? I am only small fry.* = an unimportant person

smart[1] /smɑ:t/ adj. **1** *He looks smart in the checked*

S

shirt and blue jeans. = neat and stylish **2** *a smart reply* = clever or intelligent

smart[2] verb, i. *There was so much smoke in the room that my eyes began to smart.* = to get a burning feeling, specially in the eyes

smart[3] noun, u. *He burnt his finger on the glowing end of a cigarette and could feel the smart for a long time.* = pain or burning feeling **smartly** adv. *Everyone looked up when the smartly dressed candidate walked into the room.* = in a neat or stylish manner **smart aleck** noun, c. = a person who tries to impress people by pretending to know everything (informal, derogatory) **smartypants** *All right you smartypants, now let's see you repair this car.* = a humorous way of addressing someone who thinks she or he knows everything or is very clever (informal)

smash[1] /smæʃ/ verb, i. or t. **1** *The cup dropped from my hand and smashed.*(i.) // *The boy dropped the cup and smashed it.*(t.) = to break or cause to break into pieces **2** *The girl smashed the old record for the 100-metre race.*(t.) = to bring something to an end **3** *Our tanks smashed through the enemy's defences.* = to attack and destroy **4** *Pete Sampras smashed the ball to Agassi's backhand.*(t.) = to hit the ball downwards with force, in the game of tennis or badminton

smash[2] noun, u. or c. **1** *The car was badly damaged in the smash.* = accident **2** *We heard the smash of the car hitting a wall.* = the sound produced when something hits another object with force **smashing** adj. *You look smashing in that dress.* = very attractive (slang) **smash-up** noun, c. *Several people were killed in the smash-up.* = a serious accident

smat•ter•ing /'smætərɪŋ/ noun, u. *I can't claim to be an expert. I have only a smattering of French.* = a very limited knowledge of something

smear[1] /smɪəʳ/ verb, t. or i. **1** *During the Holi festival, people smear each other's faces with coloured powder.*(t.) = to cause a sticky material to spread over a surface **2** *The ink had not dried and so the words on the page got smeared and could not be read.*(i.) = to spread over a surface and lose clarity

smear[2] noun, c. **1** *There was a smear of paint across his face.* = a mark made by something spreading across a surface **2** *The doctor took a smear from the inside of the patient's mouth.* = a small amount of matter (e.g. skin) taken from some part of a person's body, which is examined under a microscope to test for certain diseases **smear campaign** noun, c. *The manager is not very good to us, but we don't have to start a smear campaign against her.* = an effort to damage someone's reputation by spreading false information **smear test** noun = a medical test of some matter taken from the body to see if a person has cancer (see **smear**[2], meaning **2**)

smell[1] /smel/ verb, t. or i. (**smelt** or **smelled**) **1** *I smell something burning in the kitchen.*(t.) = to be able to feel or know something by using the sense of smell, which is connected with the nose **2** *His breath smells of alcohol.*(i) = to have a particular quality which one can smell **3** *I want you to smell these flowers.* = to draw in air through the nose in order to get the smell of something

smell[2] noun, u.or c. **1** *Dogs use smell to track down criminals.*(u.) = the ability to smell something **2** *There's a foul smell coming from the kitchen.*(c.) = a particular smell that one can feel though the nose **smelling salts** noun = a chemical containing ammonia, which has a strong smell and is sometimes used to bring an unconscious person back to his/her senses **smelly** adj. *Throw away those smelly socks.* = having a bad smell (derogatory)

to smell a rat *When I asked him what he was doing in the office so late at night, he said he was looking for some papers. However, I smelt a rat.* = to suspect that something either wrong or dishonest is going on

smelt /smelt/ verb, t. *Iron ore is smelted in this furnace.* = to melt ore (rock or soil containing some metal) in order to separate the metal

smile[1] /smaɪl/ verb, i. **1** *He is smiling. He must have received some good news!* = to have a pleased or happy expression on one's face **2** *Fortune has smiled on us! We have won the lottery.* = to favour or help someone

smile[2] noun, c. *There's a smile on his face. He must be in a happy mood.* = an expression on the face in which the lips are usually stretched out, showing pleasure or amusement

all smiles *He was all smiles when he was proved correct!* = very happy, pleased

smirch /smɜːtʃ/ verb, t. *You have smirched the family's reputation by stealing.* = to bring dishonour to someone (formal)

smirk /smɜːk/ verb, t. *I saw the boys smirking when you were scolding me. They were enjoying the situation.* = to smile with pleasure at someone else's misfortune (bad luck) (derogatory)

smite /smaɪt/ verb, t. or i. (**smote, smitten**) **1** (t.) = to hit or strike someone hard (literary) **2** *Cricket fever has smitten the entire country.*(i.) = to have a powerful effect on someone **3** (i.) = To be smitten is to fall in love.

smith /smɪθ/ noun, c. *a blacksmith* = a person who is skilled in making things out of metal **smithy** noun, c. *Take these broken pans to the smithy for repair.* = a place where things are made from metal or where metal objects can be repaired

smith•e•reens /smɪðəˈriːnz/ noun (always plural) *The glass door was smashed to smithereens.* = very small pieces

smock /smɒk/ noun, c. = a loose dress that looks like a long shirt

smog /smɒg/ noun, u. *In winter the air in Delhi is polluted by thick smog.* = an unhealthy mixture of smoke and fog, often found during winter in cities where there are many motor vehicles

smoke[1] /sməʊk/ noun, u. or c. **1** *Thick black smoke rose from the burning huts.*(u.)= the hot gases produced when something is burning, usually grey or black because of the presence of very small particles (pieces) of some solid matter **2** *Would you like a smoke?*(c.) = a cigarette or some other form of tobacco that can be smoked (informal) **3** *I left the meeting for a smoke.* = the act of smoking tobacco

smoke[2] verb, i. or t. **1** *The doctor has advised me not to smoke.*(i.) = to breathe in smoke produced by burning tobacco in some form, e.g. a cigarette **2** *The wood which you used for the fire was wet. It is smoking.*(i.) = to produce a lot of smoke **3** *We can smoke the fish and store it away for a whole year.*(t.) = to hang up meat or fish in smoke from a fire so that it is preserved (does not go bad when kept for a long time) **smoke screen** noun, c. **1** *Our soldiers attacked the enemy under the cover of a smoke screen.* = a cloud of smoke created by firing a special kind of shell (large bullet) from a gun, so that the enemy cannot see what is going on **2** *The company's plans to distribute free books may be only a smoke screen for some new business activity.* = something used to hide one's real intentions (derogatory) **smoke-stack** noun, c. = a chimney or tall pipe through which smoke comes out **smoke-stack industry** noun = a factory which produces a lot of pollution (disapproving)

to smoke someone or something out *There are hundreds of rats living in tunnels below the ground. We will have to smoke them out.* = to force a dangerous or harmful animal or human being to come out of a hiding place **there's no smoke without fire** *The rumour is that train fares will go up. There can be no smoke without fire.* = every rumour has some truth in it **to go up in smoke** *All our plans went up in smoke as the Director did not support us.* = to come to an unhappy end (informal)

smooch /smuːtʃ/ verb, i. = to kiss (usually not openly) (slang)

smooth[1] /smuːð/ adj. **1** *The wooden table has a smooth surface.* = perfectly level and allowing something to move easily over it **2** *The new manager has taken up her duties. The changeover from the old administration to the new was smooth.* = happening in an orderly and peaceful manner **3** *a smooth batter* = without large pieces of something in it **4** *It was a smooth ride all the way to Agra.* = (of a journey in a vehicle) comfortable as a result of not going over bumps on the road etc. **5** *I don't trust this man. He is a smooth talker.* = so polite in talk or behaviour as to be insincere (derogatory)

smooth[2] verb, t. *The suface of this table is still rough. Ask the carpenter to smooth it.* = to make something smooth (also **smoothen**)

smoth•er /ˈsmʌðəʳ/ verb, t. **1** *The walls of her bedroom are smothered in posters of Hrithik Roshan.* = to cover up something almost completely **2** *If she wants to dance, you should encourage her. Don't smother her talent.* = to prevent something from developing or growing

smoul•der /ˈsməʊldəʳ/ verb, i. **1** *The fire had died down, but it went on smouldering for hours.* = to burn slowly with a low flame **2** *He was smouldering because he had been insulted, but he said nothing.* = to have strong or violent feelings which are not openly expressed

smudge[1] /smʌdʒ/ noun, c. *The little girl had been playing in the dust and there were smudges all over her face.* = a small mark made by rubbing something across a surface

smudge[2] verb, t. or i. *The little girl smudged the walls with her dirty fingers.* = to make something dirty by leaving smudges (marks) on it

smug /smʌg/ adj. *He thinks he is the world's greatest singer, although no one shares this opinion. I have never seen a more smug person!* = very pleased or satisfied with oneself (derogatory)

smug•gle /ˈsmʌgəl/ verb, t. **1** = to bring something from one country into another in an illegal way **2** *The boys tried to smuggle some cigarettes into the hostel though they were perfectly aware that they were breaking a rule.* = to bring in something which is against the rules **smuggler** noun, c. = a person who takes part in smuggling

smut /smʌt/ noun, u. **1** *He enjoys reading smut, but he is careful to hide it from his friends.* = magazines, books, films etc. that deal with sex (also **pornography**) (informal) **2** *We live very near the railway station and so our clothes are generally covered with smut.* = small particles of dust, coal etc. which leave dirty marks on faces or clothes **smutty** adj. *smutty jokes* = dirty; dealing with sex in a way which offends some people

snack[1] /snæk/ noun, c. *Potato chips are my favourite snack.* = light food eaten between meals

snack[2] verb, i. *You can find them snacking on potato chips any evening.* = to eat a snack (informal) **snack bar** noun = a restaurant that sells snacks

S

sna•fu /snæˈfuː/ noun *We had planned the meeting carefully, but unfortunately everything went snafu.* = a state of confusion and disorder (informal) USE

snag /snæg/ noun, c. *My classmate would like to join us on the trip to Ooty, but there is a snag. We haven't got a confirmed railway booking for her.* = a problem or difficulty that prevents something from happening

snail /sneɪl/ noun = a small creature with a hard shell on its back that moves very slowly along the ground **snail's pace** noun *The construction of the bridge is going on, but at a snail's pace.* = a very slow speed (derogatory)

snake[1] /sneɪk/ noun, c. **1** = a reptile (animal that lays eggs and has scales) with a long thin body and no limbs **2** = a dangerous person who cannot be trusted (figurative)

snake[2] verb, i. *The river snakes its way through the mountains.* = to move with twists and turns **snake-charmer** noun, c. = a person who can control snakes and make them perform tricks (found mostly in India) **snakes-and-ladders** noun = a game in which players throw a dice to move their pieces across a board on which there are pictures of snakes as well as ladders

snap[1] /snæp/ verb, i. or t. (**snapped**) **1** *We tied a rope to the car and tried to pull it out of the ditch, but the rope snapped.*(i.) = to break suddenly **2** *The door snapped shut.*(i.) = to move quickly into a certain position **3** *'You are late again!' the manager snapped as I entered the office.*(i.) = to speak quickly in an angry manner **4** *The photographer wants to snap you with the famous actor.*(t.) = to take a photograph of someone or something (informal)

snap[2] noun, c. **1** *The branch of the tree on which we were sitting broke with a snap.* = the sound produced when something breaks suddenly **2** *Take a look at this snap of our baby.*(c.) = photograph (informal) **snapdragon** noun = a small flower that looks like the head of an animal, which seems to open and close its mouth when its neck is pressed **snapper** noun = a kind of sea-fish **snapshot** noun, c. = a photograph taken quickly with a camera that is held in the hand

snappy adj. **1** *He was in such a snappy mood that no one dared to speak to him.* = irritable; getting angry for no reason at all **2** *He is a snappy dresser* = smart and fashionable (approving)

to snap one's fingers = to make a sound to attract someone's attention, by moving the thumb quickly against the next two fingers **to snap out of it** *You have been depressed ever since you failed the driving test. I want you to snap out of it!* = to get quickly out of an unhealthy state of mind (informal) **to snap up** *There is a sale on, and shirts are being sold very cheaply. You should snap up a few.* = to buy or take something quickly (informal) **Make it snappy!** = *You'll be late for class if you don't hurry. Come on, make it snappy!* = be quick (informal)

snare[1] /ˈsneəʳ/ noun, u. = a trap in which small animals are captured

snare[2] verb, t. *The bird-catcher snares pigeons in his net.* = to trap and catch an animal

snarl[1] /snɑːl/ noun, c. **1** *We heard the snarl of the leopard which was hiding in the bushes.* = the warning sound made by an angry dog or wild animal **2** *The accident caused a snarl-up in the traffic. No vehicle could move for hours.* = confusion, obstruction (of traffic)

snarl[2] verb, i. **1** *The leopard snarled at us, baring its teeth to warn us away.* = to make an angry, warning sound (referring to an animal) **2** *'Now get out!' he snarled.* = to speak angrily

snatch[1] /snætʃ/ verb, t. **1** *The eagle snatched the chapati from my hand.* = to take possession of something by pulling it away forcibly with a sudden movement **2** *We still have one hour before the meeting. We can snatch some sleep.* = to make use of an opportunity to get something (informal)

snatch[2] noun, c. (**snatches**) **1** *The thief made a snatch and got away with my gold chain.* = an act of snatching **2** (usually plural) *I heard only snatches of your speech.* = a short and incomplete part of something

sneak[1] /sniːk/ verb, i. **1** *The students sneaked past the Headmaster's office.* = to move away quietly without being seen **2** = to give information about something wrong done by others (referring to the habit, believed to be common among school-children, of informing their teachers about the activities of other children)

sneak[2] noun, c. *You should not be such a sneak.* = a person who sneaks (meaning **2**) **sneakers** noun, c. (commonly used with 'a pair of') = light canvas shoes used while playing or running **sneak preview** noun = a chance to see a new film before most people have seen it (informal) [TECHNICAL] **sneak thief** noun = a thief who steals things quietly and secretly

sneer[1] /snɪəʳ/ verb, i. *You may not like the customs of these people, but you have no right to sneer at them.* = to show strong dislike or lack of respect, especially through the expression on one's face

sneer[2] noun, c. *'You have a budget of only Rs 15,000 and you want to travel round the world!' said the travel agent with a sneer.* = a disrespectful look or remark

sneeze[1] /sniːz/ verb, t. *The smell of dry chillies made him sneeze.* = to send out air through the mouth and nose with great force, because of some feeling of discomfort in the nose

sneeze[2] noun, c. *We were startled by a loud sneeze.* = the sound of sneezing

not to be sneezed at *If they are offering you a salary of Rs 2000 a month, you should accept their offer. It's not to be sneezed at.* = something that should be considered seriously and not rejected at once

snick[1] /snɪk/ verb, t. *Tendulkar snicked the ball to a fielder.* = to hit the ball with the edge of the bat, without intending to do so (cricket)

snick[2] noun, c. *He was out to a snick.* = an act of snicking the ball in cricket

snicker see **snigger**

snide /snaɪd/ adj. *I know our school is not as grand as yours, but I don't like the snide remarks you have been making.* = containing unpleasant and indirect criticism (referring to a remark made by someone)

sniff[1] /snɪf/ verb, i. or t. **1** = to take in air noisily and repeatedly into the nose when one has a cold, in order to prevent the liquid inside the nose from running (flowing out) (also **sniffle**) **2** *He sniffed the curry carefully to find out if it had gone bad.*(t.) = to smell something by taking in air through the nose **3** *He sniffs heroin regularly.*(t.) = to use a harmful drug by taking it into the body through the nose

sniff[2] noun, c. *He took a sniff of the chicken curry and said 'This smells delicious!'* = an act of sniffing **sniffer dog** noun = a dog which has been trained to smell and find out drugs (such as opium) hidden in secret places

not to be sniffed at *His offer of Rs 2 million for this house is not to be sniffed at.* = something that should be considered seriously; not to be taken lightly (compare **not to be sneezed at**)

sniffle see **sniff**[1] (meaning **1**)

snig•ger[1] /ˈsnɪgəʳ/ verb, i. *When I'm on stage and I make a mistake, please don't snigger.* = to make unkind fun of someone by laughing, but not loudly or openly

snigger[2] noun, c. = the sound of sniggering (also **snicker**, in American English)

snip[1] /snɪp/ verb, t. (**snipped**) *He snipped off a corner of the plastic bag and poured out the sugar into a jar.* = to cut with a pair of scissors using short, quick strokes

snip[2] noun, c. = a short, quick cut made with a pair of scissors

snipe /snaɪp/ verb, i. **1** *The enemy soldiers who had hidden themselves in the trees sniped at our troops.* = to shoot at someone from a place of hiding **2** *It is quite silly of the two leaders to be sniping at each other all the time.* = to say unpleasant things attacking someone **sniper** = a soldier who shoots at someone from a place of hiding

snip•pet /ˈsnɪpɪt/ noun, c. *This website on the Internet gives us some interesting snippets of news.* = a small piece taken from a speech or piece of writing

sniv•el /ˈsnɪvəl/ verb, i. (**snivelled**) *He is snivelling because the teacher punished him.* = to cry softly in a complaining manner (derogatory)

snob /snɒb/ noun, c. *They are such snobs that they don't mix with people who don't own cars.* = a person who keeps away from people whom he considers to be of a lower social class (derogatory) **snobbery** noun, u. = the behaviour of a snob **snobbish** adj. *snobbish behaviour* = like that of a snob

snook /snu:k/ noun

to cock a snook at someone = to show openly that one has no respect for someone

snoo•ker /ˈsnu:kəʳ/ noun = a game in which small balls of different colours are hit across a table into holes or pockets, using a long stick called a cue

snoop /snu:p/ verb, i. *The guards caught him snooping around our factory.* = to look into someone else's property or affairs without permission, in order to discover something (derogatory)

snoot•y /ˈsnu:ti/ adj. *They are so snooty that they don't talk to any of their neighbours.* = showing through one's behaviour that one considers oneself as belonging to a higher social class than others (also **haughty, snobbish**) (informal)

snooze /snu:z/ verb, i. = to have a short, light sleep (informal)

snore /snɔ:ʳ/ verb, i. *Those who snore while sleeping disturb others.* = to breathe noisily through the mouth and nose during sleep

snor•kel /ˈsnɔ:kəl/ noun = a short tube which allows a swimmer to breathe under the surface of water

snort[1] /snɔ:t/ verb, i. **1** *He snorts like a horse when he laughs.* = to make a loud, rough sound by drawing in or forcing out air through the nose **2** *'I will not pay a single paisa for this rubbish,' the man snorted to the shopkeeper.* = to speak angrily, expressing strong feeling **3** *The police caught him snorting heroin.* = to take a harmful drug by breathing it in though the nose (slang)

snort[2] noun, c. *She gave a snort of annoyance.* = the sound produced when snorting

snot /snɒt/ noun, u. = the thick, dirty liquid produced inside the nose when one has a cold

snout /snaʊt/ noun, c. = the long mouth and nose of an animal such as a pig

snow[1] /snəʊ/ noun, u. = soft ice formed, because of the low temperature, from tiny drops of water present in the air

S

snow[2] verb, i. **1** *It sometimes snows in Chandigarh during winter.* = to fall from the sky in the form of snow **2** *For years there have been no plays in town, but this year it's snowing plays.* = to have a lot of something suddenly (figurative) **snow-ball** noun, c. = a round ball made by a child by pressing lumps of snow together, which is thrown at another child as a game **snowball effect** = a problem or a plan that grows bigger and more serious as more people join in **snow blindness** noun = a medical condition caused by looking at snow in bright sunlight, causing pain in the eyes or temporary loss of eyesight **snow-bound** adj. *The roads in Kashmir are snow-bound in winter.* = blocked by snow, so that traffic cannot move **snow-capped** adj. *snow-capped mountains* = covered with snow throughout the year **snowflake** noun, c. = a soft, light piece of snow that floats through the air **snowline** noun = the level or height on a mountain above which one can find snow at all times **snowman** noun = a figure of a man made out of soft snow by children, as a game **snowmobile** noun = a vehicle like a motorcycle which has no wheels but can move on metal blades over ice **snow-white** adj. = as white as snow

snub[1] /snʌb/ verb, t. (**snubbed**) *When I tried to settle a quarrel between two of my classmates they snubbed me by asking me to mind my own business.* = to insult someone by making him/her feel small

snub[2] noun, c. *I wasn't invited to the wedding and knew it was a snub.* = an act of snubbing someone

snub[3] adj. *a snub nose* = flat and short

snuff[1] /snʌf/ noun, u. = tobacco in the form of a powder which is used by putting it into the nose and and drawing it in by inhaling it

snuff[2] verb, t. **1** *Snuff out the candle!* = to put out the flame of a candle by pressing the wick **2** *A promising career was snuffed out when the young chess player was killed in an accident.* = to put a sudden end to something

snug /snʌg/ adj. **1** *He doesn't want to come out of that snug bed.* = a place that gives a feeling of warmth, comfort and protection **2** *I feel so snug in this house that I have no desire to go anywhere.* = feeling comfortable and protected (safe)

snug•gle /ˈsnʌgəl/ verb, i. *The child snuggled into its mother's bed.* = to move into a warm and comfortable position

so[1] /səʊ/ adv. **1** *Mysore was never so hot earlier.* = to such a degree **2** *He is so fat that he cannot run.* = leading to some result or effect **3** *'My father can sing,' Vishal said. 'So can my father,' said Rita.* = similarly (in the same way) **4** *He thinks that the Indian team is sure to win and I think so too.* = the same (referring to something that has already been mentioned) **5** *Fold down this sofa so, and it turns into a bed.* = in this way (in the manner described or shown)

so[2] conj. **1** *I was hungry, so I cooked some rice for myself.* = therefore **2** *Leave the window open, so you can get some fresh air.* = in order that **3** *So you are going to become an actor!* = used to prompt someone to speak on a subject, often unkindly

so[3] adj. **1** *He was smart as a student and is more so now.* = having the quality already mentioned **2** *He is very particular about his house. Everything has to be just so!* = neat and tidy **3** *How could you be so greedy as to eat up your sister's share!* = to this extent **4** *Mother Teresa picked up the abandoned children so that they could have a home.* = in order that **5** *I hope you will be ready in another half an hour or so.* = approximately **so-and-so** noun, c. **1** *A Mr So-and-so came to meet us. I can't recall his name.* = a person who is not being named (informal, sometimes not respectful) **2** *I don't like that man at all. He's a so-and-so.* = an unpleasant person (informal) **so-called** adj. *The government is asking some so-called experts to write the new textbooks.* = having a reputation which is not deserved (derogatory) **so-so** adj. *We expected him to do well in the examination but his performance was just so-so.* = very ordinary; not good, just average (informal)

soak[1] /səʊk/ verb, t. or i. *If you soak these dirty clothes overnight, you will be able to clean them easily.*(t.) = to cause something to remain covered by a liquid for some time so that the liquid enters into it

soak[2] noun, u. *Give the clothes a good soak in hot water.* = an act of soaking **soaking** adj. *He was soaking wet by the end of the walk as he had forgotten to take his umbrella.* = totally wet

soap[1] /səʊp/ noun, u. **1** = a substance used for cleaning clothes etc. which produces lather (foam) when mixed with water **2** *She enjoys watching soaps on television.* = soap opera (see below)

soap[2] verb, t. *He soaped himself before going under the shower.* = to rub soap over the body **soap opera** noun, c. = A serial play (a drama in many parts) shown regularly on television, in which events in the daily life of a few characters are shown. (They are called 'soap operas' because they used to be mainly sponsored by companies that manufactured cosmetics as well as soap.) **soapstone** noun, u. = a kind of soft stone which feels smooth when it is touched (like soap)

to soft-soap someone = to flatter someone (disapproving)

Usage A small piece of soap is called a 'cake' or a 'bar' of soap.

soar /sɔːʳ/ verb, i. **1** *My kite soared into the sky.* = to fly at a great height **2** *The price of onions has soared.* = to rise to a high level **soaring** adj. *Soaring prices pushed up the cost of living.* = sharply increasing

sob[1] /sɒb/ verb, i. (**sobbed**) *The athlete sobbed hysterically when she could not participate in the race because of an injury.* = to cry loudly out of sorrow, taking in deep breaths

sob[2] noun, c. *His sobs died down after some time.* = the sound of sobbing **sob story** noun, c. *They got some money out of me by making up a sob story.* = a story, generally not true, intended to make the hearer feel pity (derogatory)

so•ber /'səʊbəʳ/ adj. **1** *He is usually drunk but today he seems to be sober.* = not drunk **2** *We should have a sober discussion on this matter.* = serious and thoughtful **3** *He always wears sober clothes.* = not attracting too much attention (approving) **sobering** adj. *My son had all kinds of wild plans but the teacher gave him some sobering advice.* = having the effect of making someone think in a practical way **sobriety** /se'braɪəti/ adj. *He is a very successful person, but you will never find him boasting. We are all impressed by his sobriety.* = balanced behaviour (formal)

soc•cer /'sɒkəʳ/ noun = the game of football, as it is played in India and neighbouring countries

so•cial /'səʊʃəl/ adj. **1** *Drinking creates social problems.* = having to do with a society (a group) and relations within it **2** *He takes part in many social activities.* = relating to activities with friends and other people and not to one's profession **3** *Human beings are social animals.* = having a natural desire to live together with others of the same kind **4** *a social class* = based on rank and position within a society **sociable** adj. *He is a very sociable person. You will always find him surrounded by friends.* = fond of the company of other people **socially** adv. *His constant quarrels with others are not socially acceptable.* = according to the values of society **social climber** noun, c. = a person who tries to get into a higher social class by mixing with people belonging to that class (derogatory) **socialism** noun, u. = the political belief that all industries should be owned and controlled by the state and that the differences between social classes should be removed **socialist** noun, c. = a person who believes in socialism **socialite** noun, c. = a person who takes part in many social activities and can often be seen at parties etc. (disapproving)

socialize (socialise) verb, i. **1** *We like to socialize with our colleagues.* = to mix with others in a friendly way **2** *Children need to be socialized.* = to train someone to live with others as members of a society **social sciences** noun = the study of subjects such as history, economics and sociology which deal with social events or relationships **social security** noun = help from the government in the form of money, given to people who have no jobs or are in need of medical help etc. **social work** noun = work done by an organization or person to improve social conditions

so•ci•e•ty /sə'saɪəti/ noun, u. or c. (**societies**) **1** *Teachers are important members of society.*(u.) = an organization made up of groups of people who are controlled by certain rules and bound together by certain relationships **2** *Western society* = people belonging to a particular group, sharing a common religion, language etc. **3** *a film society* = a group of people with common interests

socio- /'səʊʃəʊ/ prefix meaning 'having to do with society' e.g. **socioeconomic** adj. *The two parties support each other, although they represent different socioeconomic classes.* = having to do with social groups that have different levels of income

so•ci•ol•o•gy /səʊsi'ɒlədʒi/ noun = the study of human behaviour in a society

sock[1] /sɒk/ noun, c. (usually plural **socks**, used together with 'a pair of') = a covering of soft material for the foot, worn inside shoes

sock[2] verb, t. *I was socked on the jaw.* = to hit someone with the fist (closed hand) (informal)

to pull up one's socks = to make an effort to improve one's work (informal)

sock•et /'sɒkɪt/ noun, c. *an electrical socket* = an opening or hollow space into which something fits (see pic under **plug**)

sod /sɒd/ noun, c. **1** *He moved the sods of earth with a spade.* = a small piece of earth to which grass is attached **2** *a silly sod* = an insulting word for a man who one thinks is foolish or difficult to tolerate (derogatory, slang) USE

so•da /'səʊdə/ noun, u. or c. **1** = water in which carbon di-oxide gas has been mixed under pressure, used to make an alcoholic drink strong, or taken by itself as a soft drink (also **soda-water**) **2** *washing soda* = a chemical containing sodium which is used as a cleaning agent

sod•den /'sɒdn/ adj. *The cricket field is sodden after the heavy rain.* = very wet and soft

so•di•um /'səʊdɪəm/ noun = a chemical that is a kind of metal and is commonly found in combination with other chemicals **sodium chloride** noun =

S

the chemical name for common salt, used in cooking

so•fa /'səʊfə/ noun, c. = a long, comfortable seat on which two or three people can sit

soft /sɒft/ adj. **1** *The earth was so soft after the rain that my feet sank into it as I walked.* = not hard or firm **2** *The baby's cheeks are as soft as silk.* = feeling pleasant and smooth to the touch; not rough **3** *He spoke in a soft whisper.* = not loud **4** *He gave the boy a soft push.* = gentle; not using much force **5** *Don't you think you are too soft on them?* = too kind and not able to control someone (disapproving) **6** *You have grown soft. You should take some exercise.* = not in a good physical condition **7** = something which is less difficult or less unpleasant (see **soft line**, **soft option** below) **softener** = a chemical which, when added to water, makes clothes or cloth feel soft when dry **softly** adv. **soften** verb, t. or i. **1** *These new curtains seem to soften the light.*(t.) =to make something look less bright **2** *I was angry with the children and wanted to scold them but when I saw them looking happy and friendly, I softened.*(i.) = to feel less angry and more kind or gentle **3** *The news that she had a rare disease upset her very much but we were able to soften the effect by telling her it could be treated.*(t.) = to make something less painful or unpleasant **soft ball** noun = a game which is like baseball, but is played with a soft ball **soft-boiled** adj. *a soft-boiled egg* = boiled for a short time only and soft to the touch (referring to one way of cooking an egg) **soft copy** noun = information stored on the hard disk of a computer or a floppy disk and not printed out on paper (see **hard copy**) **soft drink** = a non-alcoholic drink such as fruit juice **soft-hearted** adj. = very kind **soft landing** noun = the landing (coming down to earth) of a spacecraft or aircraft which does not cause any damage to it **soft palate** noun = the back of the palate (the bony part at the top of the mouth) **software** noun = the programs used in a computer system (and not the mechanical parts, or **hardware**) **softy** adj. = a person who is seen as being too kind or gentle and not able to handle a situation firmly (derogatory or humorous)

to have a soft spot for somebody *I have a soft spot for anyone who comes from Mumbai.*= to have a special liking for someone **to soft-pedal something** *They want to introduce the study of astrology in schools but are soft-pedalling this issue at present.* = to not be too active in doing something, because one finds that people are opposed to it **soft- spoken** *a soft-spoken person* = speaking in a gentle voice **to have a soft spot for somebody** *I have a soft spot for anyone who comes from Mumbai.* = to have a special liking for someone **to be soft in the head** = foolish or not in one's right mind (informal, derogatory, old-fashioned) **to soften someone up** *They wanted to soften Mira up before they asked her to lend them some money.* = to try to please someone (usually through flattery) in order to get something from him/her (informal, not respectful) **to take soft line (on something)** = to not be strict or harsh in reacting to something **a soft option** *I want to study art rather than computer science, not because it is a soft option but because I like art.* = something which is seen as being easier and requiring less effort than something else

sog•gy /'sɒgi/ adj. *The ground was so soggy after the rain that our car sank into it.* = completely wet and soft (see **sodden**)

soil[1] /sɔɪl/ noun, u. **1** *The soil is so fertile that you can grow anything you like on it.* = the material that covers the top of the earth's suface, in which plants grow **2** *I have decided to return to the soil.* = the profession of farming (figurative) **3** *Do you like living on this soil?* = country (literary)

soil[2] verb, t. *His clothes were soiled with mud.* = to cause something to become dirty

a son (daughter) of the soil = a person who belongs to a place because he/she was born there and has a special claim on the things it can offer, such as jobs

soi•ree /'swɑːreɪ/ noun, c. (French) = an evening party devoted to music, poetry etc.

so•journ /'sɒdʒɜːn/ noun, u. *He ended his sojourn in the U.S.A. and returned to India.* = a period of stay in a country or a place in which you do not live (literary)

sol•ace /'sɒlɪs/ noun, u. *When his wife died, he found solace in the company of his children.* = comfort or support when one is unhappy, especially because someone has died

so•lar /'səʊləʳ/ adj. *a solar eclipse* = having to do with the sun **solar cell** noun = a kind of battery (device or machine that produces electrical energy) which uses the sun's energy **solar panel** noun = a number of solar cells connected to each other, which can produce a large amount of electrical energy **solar plexus** noun = the network (group) of nerves in the body lying between the stomach and the backbone **solar system** noun = the sun, together with the planets that move around it **solar year** noun = the time taken by the earth to go around the sun once, equal to 365 days, 5 hours, 48 minutes and 46 seconds

sold /səʊld/ verb, t. = past tense of **sell**

solder[1] /'sɒldəʳ/ verb, t. *The electrician soldered two pieces of wire together.* = to join pieces of metal by using a mixture of lead and tin, which melts and becomes soft when it is heated

solder[2] noun, u. = a soft mixture of lead and tin, which is heated and used to join pieces of metal together

soldering iron noun = a tool which works on electricity, used for melting the mixture of lead and tin that is used in soldering

sol•dier[1] /ˈsəʊldʒəʳ/ noun, c. = a member of the army (the group of people who fight on land to defend their country) who generally is not an officer

soldier[2] verb, i. *These two men teach tribal children in a village. Although they get no help from anyone, they have been soldiering on for the last 25 years.* = to continue to work steadily in spite of difficulties **soldier of fortune** noun = a professional soldier who is ready to fight for anyone who will pay him (also **mercenary**)

sole[1] /səʊl/ adj. *He is the sole owner of this house.* = the only one

sole[2] noun, c. **1** *the sole of the foot* = the bottom surface of the foot or of the front part of a shoe **2** = a kind of sea fish

sole[3] verb, t. *I have to get my old shoes soled.* = to repair a shoe by putting a new sole on it

sol•emn /ˈsɒləm/ adj. **1** *The teacher likes to joke when she is outside the class, but she is always solemn when teaching.* = serious **2** *I will return the money next week. I give you my solemn promise.* = a promise etc. made seriously, which one intends to keep **solemnity** /səˈlemnɪti/ noun, u. *He spoilt the solemnity of the occasion by talking loudly while the marriage ceremony was going on.* = the quality of being solemn **solemnize (solemnise)** /səˈlemnaɪz/ verb, t. *The marriage will be solemnized by the priest.* = to perform a wedding (marriage) ceremony (formal)

sol•fa /sɒl ˈfɑː/ noun = the set of names given to the seven notes on a musical scale (do, re, mi, fa, so, la, ti, in Western music, and sa, re, ga, ma, pa, dha, ni, in Indian music)

so•li•cit /səˈlɪsɪt/ verb, t. *I am contesting an election next month, and am soliciting the support of the people in this city.* = to ask someone for help or support, in the form of votes, money, advice etc. (formal) **solicitor** noun, c. = a lawyer who gives advice or help to someone in connection with a law case but does not argue the case in court **solicitor general** noun = a lawyer who advises the government on legal matters **solicitous** adj. *She was very solicitous about you when she heard that you had financial problems.* = feeling anxious about someone and eager to help (formal)

sol•id[1] /ˈsɒlɪd/ adj. **1** *Water becomes solid when it freezes and turns into ice.* = hard and firm, with a clear shape of its own **2** *These gold bangles are so light because they are hollow. They are not solid.* = having some matter inside; not hollow **3** *These walls are solid.* = strongly made **4** *Shah Rukh Khan gives a solid performance as a poet in this film.* = of a very high standard (informal, approving) **5** *I have been waiting here for three solid hours.* = without a break or gap (informal)

solid[2] noun, c. **1** *Water can have different forms. It is usually a liquid but it becomes a solid when it is frozen.* = one of the forms in which matter exists, which is neither that of a liquid nor of a gas **2** (always plural) *When the baby is about six months old, you can start giving it solids.* = food which is not in liquid form

sol•i•dar•i•ty /sɒlɪˈdærɪti/ noun, u. *There is solidarity among the members of the team. Everyone supports the captain.* = agreement between the members of a group

so•lid•i•fy /səˈlɪdɪfaɪ/ verb, i. *Water solidifies when it is cooled to zero degrees Centigrade.* = to become solid or hard **solidity** noun, u. *It was the solidity of this old building that saved it during the earthquake.* = the quality of being solid (strong and dependable) **solid state** adj. *Computers use solid state circuits.* = having transistors, microchips or other advanced electronic parts and not valves [TECHNICAL]

so•lil•o•quy /səˈlɪləkwi/ noun, c. (**soliloquies**) = a speech in a play (drama) where a character is talking only to himself/herself **soliloquize (soliloquise)** /səˈlɪləkwaɪz/ verb, i. = to speak to oneself

sol•i•taire /sɒlɪˈteəʳ/ noun **1** = a piece of jewellery (usually a ring) that contains a single large diamond **2** = a card game played by one person (also **patience**)

sol•i•ta•ry /ˈsɒlɪtəri/ adj. **1** *He is the solitary official in the department who is 25. All the others are above forty.* = the only one **2** *We lead a solitary life on our farm.* = without friends or companions **solitary confinement** noun = a form of punishment in which one is locked up alone in a room (usually in a prison)

sol•i•tude /ˈsɒlɪtjuːd/ noun, u. = the state of being away from others

so•lo /ˈsəʊləʊ/ adj. *The pilot took off for a solo flight in his aircraft.* = done by only one person **soloist** noun, c. = a musician who sings or plays on some instrument alone and not together with others

sol•stice /ˈsɒlstɪs/ noun = a particular day, which is either the longest day of the year (the summer solstice, on June 22) or the shortest (the winter solstice, on December 22)

sol•u•ble /ˈsɒljʊbəl/ adj. *Sugar is soluble in water, but chalk is not soluble.* = able to dissolve (get completely mixed up) in some liquid (referring to a solid substance or a gas)

so•lu•tion /səˈluːʃən/ noun, u. or c. **1** *The doctor asked her to drink a solution of glucose in water.* = a liquid in which some solid substance or gas has been

S

dissolved (completely mixed up) **2** *He has found a job at last. That should provide the solution to most of his financial problems.* = an answer to a difficult problem

solve /sɒlv/ verb, t. *The teacher has given us a difficult mathematical problem to solve.* = to find a solution (answer) to a problem

sol•vent /ˈsɒlvənt/ noun, c. *Alcohol is often used as a solvent.* = a liquid in which solid substances can easily dissolve (get completely mixed up and form a solution) [TECHNICAL]

som•bre /ˈsɒmbəʳ/ adj. *The meeting opened on a sombre note, with the chanting of prayers.* = serious or solemn (not light-hearted)

som•bre•ro /sɒmˈbreərəʊ/ noun = a kind of hat commonly worn by men in Mexico

some[1] /səm/ det. **1** *There is some sugar in the jar.* = a certain quantity (not stated exactly, but usually understood as a small quantity) **2** *Some children are waiting for you.* = a certain number (not stated exactly, but usually understood as a small number) **3** *Some books are torn, but others are in good condition.* = not all

some[2] pron. **1** *There is no sugar but I am going to get some.* = a certain amount or number (not stated exactly) **2** *Some of the people are here.* = not all **3** *Some think he is nervous.* = some people (not all) **somebody** pron. **1** *Somebody has torn my book.* = a person whose identity is not known to the speaker **2** *He thinks he is somebody.* = an important person **somehow** adv. **1** *I haven't found a suitable job as yet, but I will find one somehow.* = using every means possible **2** *Somehow, I can't remember his name.* = for some unknown reason **someone** pron. *Someone has come to meet you.* = somebody (see **somebody** above) **something** noun *You will find something in your room.* = a thing that is not known **sometime** adv. *Come home sometime.* = at any time **somewhat** adv. *I find this problem somewhat difficult.* = a little/rather **somewhere** adv. *I can't find the house keys. I must have left them somewhere.* = at some unknown place

som•er•sault[1] /ˈsʌməsɔːlt/ noun, c. *He turned two complete somersaults before he dived into the water.* = a circular movement of the body (going round like a wheel), either forwards or backwards, in which the legs are first raised above the head and then lowered again

somersault[2] verb, i. *She somersaulted and landed on her feet.* = to turn a somersault

som•nam•bu•lism /sɒmˈnæmbjʊlɪzəm/ noun = sleep-walking (an unusual condition in which one walks in one's sleep) **somnambulist** noun, c. = a person who walks in his/her sleep

son /sʌn/ noun, c. *I have three sons.* = someone's male child **son-in-law** noun = the husband of one's daughter

so•nar abbr. of **Sonar Navigation and Ranging** noun = a device (machine) that uses sound waves to find the position of objects which are under water

so•na•ta /səˈnɑːtə/ noun, c. = a piece of music (in Western music) in three or four movements (parts), which are played at different speeds

son•et•lumiere /sɒn eɪ ˈluːmieəʳ/ noun (French) = 'sound and light' (a performance or show after sunset that uses sounds, usually recorded, as well as cinema pictures or living actors, to tell the story of a historical place)

song /sɒŋ/ noun, c. **1** = a poem or other text which is set to music (given a tune so that it can be sung) **2** *the cuckoo's song* = the musical sounds produced by a bird **song-and-dance** noun *I can understand your feelings were hurt when you were dropped from the team, but there was no need for you to make such a song-and-dance.* = an unnecessary show of anger or excitement (informal, derogatory) **song bird** noun, c. **1** = a bird that produces musical sounds **2** = a famous or skilled singer

to go for a song *You can buy this car for Rs 10,000. It is going for a song.* = to be on sale at a very low price

son•ic /ˈsɒnɪk/ adj. **1** *a sonic barrier* = having to do with sound **2** = travelling at the speed of sound in air (about 340 metres per second) (see also **subsonic** and **supersonic**) **sonic boom** noun = the loud sound created when an aircraft travels at a speed greater than the speed of sound

son•net /ˈsɒnɪt/ noun, c. = a poem which has 14 lines [LITERATURE]

so•nor•ous /ˈsɒnərəs/ adj. *a sonorous voice* = deep; musical and pleasant to hear

soon /suːn/ adv. *He will come back soon.* = within a short period of time **as soon as** adv. *I need help. Please come as soon as possible.* = quickly

soot /sʊt/ noun, u. *The smoke from the fire has covered the walls with soot.* = the black powder produced when something is burnt **sooty** adj. *The miners coming out of the coal-mine had sooty faces.* = blackened with soot

soothe /suːð/ verb, t. **1** *He is very upset and angry. We should try to soothe him.* = to calm; to make someone less angry or excited **2** *This ointment will soothe the pain in your back.* = to make the pain less **soothing** adj. *Soothing music can calm our nerves.* = comforting

sooth•sayer /ˈsuːθseɪəʳ/ noun, c. = a person who can tell the future

sop /sɒp/ noun, c. *They don't have proper drinking*

water, how can we give them television sets as a sop? = something, usually of little value, given to someone to make him/her less angry (derogatory) **soppy** adj. *I do not care for such soppy novels.* = sentimental in a way which is annoying

so•phis•ti•cat•ed /sə'fɪstɪkeɪtɪd/ adj. **1** *He doesn't listen to pop music. He has sophisticated tastes in music.* = having an understanding of art, literature etc. which is considered very high or very good **2** *These new computers are highly sophisticated machines.* = requiring high levels of skill and knowledge **sophistication** /səfɪstɪ'keɪʃən/ noun, u. = the quality of being sophisticated

soph•ist•ry /'sɒfɪstri/ noun, u. *The minister's speech on educational reform was full of sophistry.* = the use of clever arguments which seem reasonable but are really false (derogatory)

soph•o•more /'sɒfəmɔːʳ/ noun, c. = a second-year student at an American school or college

sop•o•rif•ic /sɒpə'rɪfɪk/ adj. *The cool breeze had a soporific effect on us and we fell asleep.* = causing one to fall asleep

sop•ping /'sɒpɪŋ/ adj. *She came in from the rain with her clothes sopping wet.* = soaking wet (very wet)

so•pra•no /sə'prɑːnəʊ/ noun = a woman singer who is required to sing in a very high voice [MUSIC]

sor•cer•er /'sɔːsərəʳ/ noun, c. = a person with supernatural powers who can perform black magic **sorcery** noun = the art practised by a sorcerer

sor•did /'sɔːdɪd/ adj. **1** *The newspaper can report the crime, but why does it have to give us all the sordid details?* = unpleasant because of its connection with dishonest or immoral behaviour **2** *sordid surroundings* = dirty and unhealthy

sore[1] /sɔːʳ/ noun, c. *He has a deep sore in his leg.* = a painful and infected wound

sore[2] adj. **1** *His shoulder felt sore because he had been carrying a heavy load.* = painful **2** *They are sore because you did not meet them when they came to town.* = angry and feeling unjustly treated (informal)

a sore point *His failure in the driving test is a sore point with him. Let's not bring it up.* = something in which one has not succeeded and which one doesn't want others to talk about. **to stick out like a sore thumb** *Our garden, unlike those of our neighbours, is dry and ugly, and sticks out like a sore thumb.* = to be clearly different from other things/persons of the same kind in a negative way, so that it or they can be noticed easily

sor•ghum /'sɔːgəm/ noun = a kind of foodgrain grown in tropical (hot) countries

so•ror•i•ty /sə'rɒrɪti/ noun = a group of women students at an American university who live together, forming a club

sor•row[1] /'sɒrəʊ/ noun, u. or c. *I felt great sorrow at the death of my dog.* = unhappiness which is connected with a death, a great loss or something very unfortunate which has happened

sorrow[2] verb, i. *She sorrowed over his death.* = to express sorrow (literary)

sor•ry[1] /'sɒri/ adj. **1** *I felt sorry when I heard of your illness.* = feeling of sadness or pity because something unfortunate has happened **2** *I hope you are sorry for your mistake.* = having a feeling of shame or unhappiness for doing something wrong or bad **3** *I am sorry, but I don't agree with you.* = expressing disagreement or refusal **4** *The house is in a sorry state. It must be repaired.* = in a poor or weak condition

sorry[2] interjec. **1** *Sorry, you can't go in. Everyone is at a meeting.* = an expression of refusal, disagreement etc. **2** *Sorry?* = an expression asking someone to repeat something, because one was unable to hear what was said

sort[1] /sɔːt/ noun, c. **1** *Penicillin is made from a sort of plant.* = type or kind **2** *We had a sort of holiday, although it was not very relaxing.* = a kind of (although not of the expected quality) (informal)

sort[2] verb, t. **1** *The post office has to sort the letters before they can be delivered.* = to arrange things in different groups **2** *Can you sort out the letters that have to be sent to Delhi?* = to separate from other things **3** *I had many problems but I have been able to sort them out.* = to put things in order **4** = the 'sort' command in a computer, which helps one arrange a list in a certain order [COMPUTERS]

out of sorts *Ever since he heard he had not been selected for the job, he has been out of sorts .* = upset, irritable **it takes all sorts to make a world** *I am not surprised so many impractical suggestions were made at the meeting. After all, it takes all sorts to make a world.* = 'People are not all alike.' (disapproving, humorous) **nothing of the sort** *'I'll sit up and work all night tonight.' 'You'll do nothing of the sort!'* = used to give someone an order not to do something (informal)

sor•tie /'sɔːti/ noun, c. *Our fighter planes have gone on a sortie.* = a quick attack made by a group of aircraft on an enemy

SOS noun = abbr. of **'Save Our Souls'** = a message sent out through radio or a distress signal sent by ships at sea which are in serious trouble and need help

sot /sɒt/ noun, c. = a person who is always drunk and cannot think clearly (derogatory)

sot•to vo•ce /sɒtəʊ 'veʊtʃi/ adv. (Latin) *He spoke to me sotto voce, so that others would not hear.* = in a very low voice

souf•fle /'suːfleɪ/ noun, c. or u. (French) = a kind of light pudding or cake made with eggs, flour, milk etc.

S

soul /səʊl/ noun, c. or u. **1** = the non-physical part of a human being that is believed to live on forever even after death **2** *Shah Rukh Khan's performance in the film was good, but it had no soul.* = deep and sincere feeling **soulful** adj. *The national anthem, if sung well, can be soulful music.* = expressing deep feeling **soul music** noun = music having deep religious feeling, usually produced by African American singers

the life and soul *She is the life and soul of the party.* = the most important or active part (informal, approving) **soul-destroying** *Working with a computer all your life can be soul-destroying.* = causing dullness and lack of activity **soul searching** *After years of soul-searching he decided to resign from politics.* = a deep examination of one's own conscience (mind)

sound[1] /saʊnd/ noun, u. or c. **1** *Sound travels though water as well as air.*(u.) // *I heard the sounds of people whispering.*(c.) = a kind of disturbance that moves through air or water in the form of waves and can be heard by the ears **2** *You say the doctor refused to examine the patient? I don't like the sound of it.* = the impression (feeling) that one gets after reading or hearing something (generally unpleasant)

sound[2] verb, i. or t. **1** *He sounded as if he had been crying* (i.) = to seem when heard **2** *The bell sounded to inform us that the class was over.*(i.) = to give out a sound **3** *You should sound the horn when you come to a busy street corner.*(t.) = to cause something to produce a sound

sound[3] adj. **1** *Don't worry. Your heart is perfectly sound.* = in good condition **2** *He made a sound decision by refusing the offer.* = showing good judgement **3** *Did you get sound sleep last night?* = deep and undisturbed (sleep) **soundly** adj. *The children slept soundly after the long journey.* = fully and deeply **sound barrier** noun = the force created by the air that acts on an object flying above the speed of sound (340 metres per second) **sound effects** noun = different sounds produced for a film or television show to give the effects of different kinds of natural sounds (e.g. the sound of waves striking the shore) **soundproof** adj. *You require a soundproof studio to record a song.* = (something) that sounds cannot get into **soundtrack** noun = a recording made of the different sounds in a film, including the words spoken by the actors

soup[1] /suːp/ noun, u. = liquid food made by boiling meat, vegetables etc. and removing the solid matter

soup[2] verb, t. *The engine of his car has been souped up from 65 to 150 horse power.* = to increase the power of an engine (slang)

to be in the soup *My little sister will really be in the soup when Mother returns because she hasn't completed any of the work that she was told to do.* = be in trouble (informal, often humorous)

sour[1] /saʊəʳ/ adj. **1** *We use lemon juice to give the curry a sour taste.* = having the taste of lemons, tamarind etc. (not sweet, bitter or salty) **2** *He has a sour temper.* = unfriendly

sour[2] verb, i. or t. **1** *The milk has soured.*(i.) = to become sour (in taste) **2** *The war has soured the relationship between our countries.*(t.) = to spoil

sour grapes *He told me he wasn't interested in the job, but I happen to know he wasn't selected. It may have been a case of sour grapes!* = pretending that you don't want or like something when you are not able to get it

source[1] /sɔːs/ noun, c. **1** *We walked up the mountain to Gangotri, where the river Ganga has its source.* = the place where something (usually a river or stream) begins or comes from **2** *This farm is the source of my income.* = the means from which one gets something **3** *I got this news from a reliable source.* = a person who gives information

source[2] verb, t. *This tyre factory sources its rubber from Malaysia.* = to get something from a certain source (place)

souse /saʊs/ verb, t. *He got completely soused in the rain.* = to become or to make something very wet (informal)

south (South)[1] /saʊθ/ noun **1** *Which is the south?* = the direction which is to the right of a person who is facing east (the direction in which the sun rises) **2** *He is from the south.* = the southern part of the country **3** *the countries of the South* = countries in Asia, Africa and South America, lying to the south of America and Europe, which are also known as 'developing countries' or 'third world countries' (terms which are now avoided as they offend some people)

south[2] adj. **1** *the south side of the building* = facing the south **2** *a south wind* = coming from the south

south[3] adv. *We are flying south.* = towards the south **south-east** noun = the direction which lies between the south and the east **south-eastern** adj. *the south-eastern corner of the building* = facing the south-east **southern** adj. *the southern part of the country* = in the south **Southerner** noun, c. = a person who is from the southern part of a country **south-west** noun = the direction which lies between the south and the west

sou•ve•nir /suːvəˈnɪəʳ/ noun, c. *This is a model of the Taj Mahal, which I brought back from Agra as a souvenir.* = an object which is kept as a reminder of an event, a visit to a place etc.

sove•reign[1] /ˈsɒvrɪn/ noun, c. = a king or queen who rules over a country

sovereign[2] adj. *a sovereign state* = having all the powers of an independent state
sow[1] /səʊ/ verb, t. (**sowed**, **sown**) *Farmers sow wheat after the rains.* = to plant seeds in the soil
sow[2] /saʊ/ noun, c. = a female pig (opposite **boar**)
soy•a bean /sɔɪbiːn/ noun = the seed of a kind of bean plant which is rich in protein and is commonly used as food (also soy) **soy sauce** noun = a thick, dark liquid made from soya beans, used to add taste to food, specially in Chinese cooking
soz•zled /ˈsɒzəld/ adj. *He was completely sozzled.* = drunk (slang, disapproving)
spa /spɑː/ noun, c. = a place where there is a natural spring of health-giving mineral water and where people come to improve their health
space[1] /speɪs/ noun, u. **1** *This car has enough space for six people.* = room or accommodation; an empty area or place which can be filled up by something **2** *This rocket will fly through space to the moon.* = the empty area between the earth and other heavenly bodies (also **outer space**) **3** *Leave some space between words when you write.* = an empty area between words or lines, in writing (also **single space, double space**)

outer space

space[2] verb, t. *The trees in the garden have been widely spaced.* = to leave some space (empty area) between two things **spacing** = the blank space between letters, words, lines etc. in printed text **spacious** adj. *a spacious house* = having a lot of space **spatial** /speɪʃəl/ adj. *To be a successful architect, you need excellent spatial judgement.* = dealing with space (the ability to judge how things should be related to each other within a large space) **space-age** adj. *This new car is a space-age machine.* = very modern **spacecraft** noun, c. = a vehicle that can travel through space **space-person (spaceman/spacewoman)** noun, c. = a person who is sent from earth into space in a spacecraft to carry out missions (also **astronaut**) **space suit** noun = a special kind of protective dress worn by people who are travelling through space, where there is no oxygen and no gravitation
spade /speɪd/ noun, c. **1** = a tool with a handle and a broad, flat metal blade, used for digging the earth or moving loose earth, sand etc. from one place to another **2** *I want you to play a spade.* = one of a set of 13 playing cards, marked with a black figure that looks like a pointed leaf **spadework** noun *We were able to set up the new school easily because the spadework had already been done by others.* = hard work done in preparation for the main event

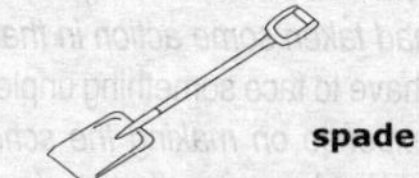
spade

to call a spade a spade *What you have done can only be described as cheating. You may not like the word, but I have to call a spade a spade.* = to speak frankly and truthfully, even when the truth is unpleasant
spa•ghet•ti /spəˈgeti/ noun, u. = food made from flour, in the shape of long threads which are cooked in boiling water, commonly eaten in Italy (see also **pasta**) **spaghetti junction** = a complicated road junction (a place where many roads meet) (informal)
spam /ˈspæm/ noun, u. = e-mail messages, usually sent as advertisments, that are not wanted or asked for [COMPUTERS]
span[1] /spæn/ noun, u. or c. **1** *The new bridge over the river has 13 spans.* = a part of a bridge or an arch that lies between two pillars or supports **2** *He became a first-rate swimmer within a span of three years.* = the period of time that separates two events **3** *Children have a short attention span.* = the period of time during which something can work
span[2] verb, t. (**spanned**) **1** *This new bridge spans the river Ganga near Patna.* = to cover or spread across or over something **2** *The story of this film spans three generations.* = to spread over
span•gle /ˈspæŋgəl/ noun = a shiny piece of metal stitched on a dress **spangled** adj. *The night sky was spangled with stars.* = covered with something that shines
span•iel /ˈspænjəl/ noun = a kind of dog with long ears and long hair
spank /spæŋk/ verb, t. = to punish by beating, especially on the bottom or buttocks **spanking** adj. *a spanking new car* = first rate, praiseworthy (slang)
span•ner /ˈspænəʳ/ noun, c. = a tool with fixed jaws, used for loosening or tightening a nut (see pic under **tools**)
spar[1] /spɑːʳ/ noun, c. = a thick pole made of wood or bamboo
spar[2] verb, i. **1** *The two boxers are sparring.* = to practise the sport of boxing by fighting against a partner [TECHNICAL] **2** *The two managers sparred with each other at the meeting.* = to exchange arguments in a somewhat friendly battle of words
spare[1] /speəʳ/ verb, t. **1** *I need your help in writing the report. Can you spare a couple of hours for me?* =

S

to give up something which is not needed or not being used, in order to help someone **2** *The robber said he would kill me, but I begged him to spare my life.* = not to hurt or harm someone, usually out of a feeling of pity **3** *The committee could have spared itself a lot of trouble if it had taken some action in the matter.* = to avoid or not have to face something unpleasant **4** *We spared no expense on making the school a happy place.* = to hold back money, effort etc. (generally used in negative sentences) **5** *We are glad you had a good holiday, but please spare us the details!* = to save someone the trouble, time or boredom of getting extra information on something (humorous)

spare[2] adj. **1** *You can stay in my house for the night. We have a spare bed.* = extra; (something) that is not being used but can be used when needed **2** *She likes to paint in her spare time.* = free; not being used **3** *He has the spare body of a long-distance runner.* = thin and without any extra fat (approving)

spare[3] noun, c. *The front tyre of my scooter is punctured, but I have a spare.* = an extra object that can be used to replace something when needed **sparing** adj. *In spite of his wonderful performance, the public was sparing in its praise.* = using or giving very little **sparingly** adv. *We use the car sparingly as petrol is very expensive.* = (of something that is used) very little, because of expense or worry that it will get spoilt or used up (often approving) **spare part** noun, c. = a part for a machine which can be used to replace a damaged or worn-out part **spare tyre** noun, c. **1** = an extra tyre carried on a vehicle which can be used to replace a tyre that is damaged **2** = the layer of fat round a person's waist (informal, humorous)

spark[1] /spɑːk/ noun, c. **1** *The straw roof of the hut was burnt after a spark from the fire fell on it.* = a small piece of burning material from a fire **2** *Petrol is made to burn inside the engine of a car by a small spark.* = a small flame caused by an electrical current jumping across a narrow space **3** *a spark of imagination* = a trace (a very small amount) of some quality in a person **4** *The shouting of slogans while the procession was going along the main road was the spark that caused the riot.* = something that starts trouble or violence **sparky** *a sparky speech* = lively (approving)

spark[2] verb, t. **1** *His writings sparked off a revolt.* = to cause something violent to happen **2** *His interest in cricket was sparked off by television broadcasts.* = to stimulate (cause something to grow or develop) **spark plug** noun, c. = a small part that fits into a petrol engine and produces an electrical spark which causes the petrol to burn

a bright spark = an intelligent person (informal)

spar•kle[1] /ˈspɑːkəl/ verb, i. **1** *The diamonds in the king's crown sparkled in the light.* = to shine brightly, with small flashes of light **2** *Her eyes sparkled with joy when she received her parents at the airport.* = to shine brightly

sparkle[2] noun, u. *These diamonds have lost their sparkle.* = the quality of sparkling **sparkling** adj. **1** *a sparkling clean house* = very (informal) **2** *'Sparkling results! Keep it up!' said the teacher.* = outstanding, shining **sparkler** noun = a type of fireworks which gives off sparks of fire when lit

spark plug see **spark**

spar•row /ˈspærəʊ/ noun, c. = a small bird commonly found in and around houses in many parts of the world

sparse /spɑːs/ adj. *The vegetation in this area is sparse. There are only a few small trees and bushes.* = small in number or quantity and scattered over a large area **sparsely** adv. *Since this is a sparsely populated area, there are very few shops here.* = thinly

spar•tan /ˈspɑːtn/ adj. *They lead a spartan life, without electricity or running water in the house. Many of us would find it difficult.* = (used of the way one chooses to live) very simple and not having comfort or luxury

spas•m /ˈspæzəm/ noun, c. **1** *His whole body was shaken with spasms.* = an uncontrollable tightening of the muscles which causes the body to shake **2** *a spasm of coughing* = a short period of suffering **spasmodic** /spæzˈmɒdɪk/ adj. *They make spasmodic attempts to clean up the house.* = irregular and lasting only for a short period of time; not continuous

spas•tic /ˈspæstɪk/ noun, c. = a person suffering from a condition which makes it difficult to control the muscles of the body [MEDICINE]

spat[1] /spæt/ verb, i. = past tense of **spit** (see **spit**)

spat[2] noun, c. *He often gets into a spat with other children.* = a short and not serious quarrel (informal)

spate /speɪt/ noun, u. **1** *The river is in spate after the heavy rains.* = a flooded condition **2** *We had a spate of cases of malaria.* = a very large number of unpleasant events coming at almost the same time

spatial see **space**

spat•ter[1] /ˈspætəʳ/ verb, t. *As we were walking along the road, a car drove past us at great speed, spattering us with mud.* = to cause drops of liquid to scatter (fall across) a surface

spatter[2] noun, u. *a spatter of rain* = a small amount of some liquid, falling in drops

spat•u•la /ˈspætjʊlə/ noun, c. = a kind of spoon with a flat blade, used in the kitchen to spread or mix food; also used by doctors to hold the tongue down so that the throat can be examined

spawn[1] /spɔːn/ verb, t. **1** *The fish in the lake are spawning.* = to produce eggs from which young ones will grow (referring to animals that live in water e.g. fish or frogs) **2** *The automobile industry has spawned a number of small trades, such as car-repairing.* = to give rise to something, in large quantities or numbers

spawn[2] noun, u. *fish spawn* = the eggs of fish or frogs, floating in the water

spay /speɪ/ = to surgically remove or block the sex organs of a female cat, dog etc. so that it cannot have young ones

speak /spiːk/ verb, i. or t. (**spoke, spoken**) **1** *She has a bad cold and has lost her voice. She can't speak.*(i.) = to use the voice to express one's thoughts aloud **2** *I will speak to the authorities about the condition of this road.*(i.) = to have a conversation (exchange of ideas and opinions) with someone usually in order to complain about something **3** *Can you speak French?*(t.) = to be able to talk in a language **4** *The President will speak on television tonight.*(i.) = to give a formal talk to a group of people **speaker** noun, c. **1** = a person who gives a talk **2** *a speaker of German/French etc.* = a person who knows a language and can speak it **Speaker** noun = the person who controls discussions in parliament

to speak up **1** *Please speak up, I can't hear you.* = to say something louder so that it can be heard clearly **2** *Everyone is afraid to speak about the pollution in the city. Well, I'm going to speak up.* = to be bold in stating one's opinion on something **to speak up for** *At the meeting, no one supported Alice Kohli, but I spoke up for her.* = to say something, usually strongly, in favour of someone or something **to speak out** *All the students in our class are going to speak out against cruelty to animals in laboratories.* = to state one's views strongly, usually against something which is wrong, unfair or dangerous **Speak for (your)self** **1** *'All of us love action films.' 'Speak for yourself!'* = a way of telling someone that a statement made or an opinion expressed by them is not shared by others (informal) **2** *We didn't need anyone to tell us how the animals were treated in the zoo. The place spoke for itself.* = something that can be clearly understood, without anyone's help **to speak highly/well/etc. of someone/something** *The way everyone works in this company speaks highly of your ability to manage people.* = to show that something good is happening **to not be on speaking terms** *After they insulted me in public, I am not on speaking terms with them.* = to not talk to someone, especially after a quarrel **to speak highly of** *Everyone I met spoke highly of the film.* = to praise

-speak a suffix used to refer to the terms and special language used in a subject e.g. armyspeak, computerspeak

spear[1] /spɪəʳ/ noun, c. **1** = a weapon used in former times in war or hunting, consisting of a long, thin pole (made of wood or bamboo) with a sharp metal point at one end **2** *a spear of grass* = the young stem of a plant

spear[2] verb, t. *The hunter speared a fish.* = to hunt an animal with a spear **spearhead**[1] noun, c. **1** = the sharp metal point at one end of a spear **2** *Dhanraj Pillay is the spearhead of the Indian hockey team.* = a person or group that leads an attack **spearhead**[2] verb, i. *Dhanraj will spearhead the attack.* = to lead an attack **spearmint** noun = a kind of plant which has a pleasant taste and is used in making chewing-gum

spec /spək/ noun, c. (always plural) **1** *These are the specs for the new machine we have to order.* = abbr. of 'specifications' (the details of something) **2** *I can't read this. I forgot my specs.* = spectacles (informal)

spe•cial[1] /'speʃəl/ adj. **1** *We use a special kind of sugar, made from the juice of palm trees, to prepare this sweet.* = not ordinary or usual **2** *We will take special care of your children.* = very great

special[2] noun, c. *We are going to watch the New Year's special on television.* = a programme meant for a special occasion **specialist** noun, c. **1** *Our professor is a specialist in European history.* = a person who has very great knowledge or skill in a limited area of study or work **2** *a child specialist* = a doctor who treats only certain kinds of diseases or patients **specialism** noun, c. or u. *His specialism is American literature.* = the limited area of study or work in which a person has special (very great) knowledge or skill (also **specialization, specialisation**) **speciality** /speʃi'ælɪti/ noun, u. or c. **1** = a special field of work or study (see **specialism**) **2** *Tandoori chicken is the speciality of this restaurant.* = a product for which a place is famous **specialize (specialise)** verb, i. *This lawyer specializes in income tax cases.* = to limit one's interests or work to a small area **special needs** = (always plural) the needs of people who have mental or physical problems **special school** noun = a school meant for children who have learning difficulties as a result of mental or physical problems

spe•cies /'spiːʃiːz/ noun, c. (always plural) *Whales are an endangered species.* = a group or family of animals or plants which have similar qualities and which can breed with each other (produce young ones)

specific[1] /spɪ'sɪfɪk/ adj. **1** *There is no one to teach physics to Class 12 students. We need a teacher for this specific job.* = particular (relating to one thing only)

S

2 *I have given the caretaker specific instructions to clean the office every morning.* = clear and exact

specific[2] noun, c. *This new drug is a specific for malaria.* = a drug that is used to treat a particular disease [MEDICINE]

s•pe•ci•fi•ca•tion /spesɪfɪˈkeɪʃən/ noun, c. or u. (often in plural form **specifications**) *The new laboratory has been built according to the director's specifications.* = a detailed and exact plan or description **specify** /ˈspesɪfaɪ/ verb, t. *The director had specified that she wanted the walls to be made of stone and not of any synthetic material.* = to state something exactly

spe•ci•men /ˈspesɪmen/ noun, c. **1** *This animal is a fine specimen of the Asiatic or Gir lion.* = a single thing which is shown as a typical example of the whole class of things to which it belongs **2** *The pathologist will examine a specimen of your urine.* = a small amount of some matter taken from the body, used for a test [MEDICINE]

spe•cious /ˈspiːʃəs/ adj. *specious arguments* = seeming to be true, but really false; clever in a dishonest way (derogatory)

speck /spek/ noun, c. *You will not find even a speck of dust in this room.* = a very tiny piece

speck•led /ˈspekəld/ adj. *Some snakes have speckled bodies.* = covered with many small marks or spots

spec•ta•cle /ˈspektəkəl/ noun, c. **1** *The Republic Day parade in Delhi is a colourful spectacle.* = a grand public show **2** *We witnessed the spectacle of a cat chasing a dog.* = an unusual sight

to make a spectacle of oneself *Don't make a spectacle of yourself by arguing so loudly in public.* = to behave in such a way that others notice one and laugh at one

spec•ta•cles /ˈspektəkəlz/ noun, c. (always plural used together with 'a pair of') = glasses worn to correct deficiencies in eyesight (see pic under **glass**)

spec•tac•u•lar /spekˈtækʊləʳ/ adj. *Aravinda scored a spectacular century, with five sixes and 20 hits to the boundary.* = exciting and worth seeing

spec•ta•tor /spekˈteɪtəʳ/ noun, c. = a person who watches a public event (usually a sports event) but does not take part in it

spec•tre /ˈspektəʳ/ noun, c. **1** = a ghost **2** *The spectre of unemployment haunts many countries.* = something fearful which may happen in the future

spec•trum /ˈspektrəm/ noun, c. (**spectra**) **1** = the bands of different colours into which a beam of light is divided when it passes through a prism **2** *The government's decision to fight terrorism has been supported by all sections of the political spectrum.* = a wide range of opinions, feelings etc. **spectroscope** /ˈspektrəskəʊp/ noun = an instrument used to examine the spectra formed by light coming from different sources

spec•u•late /ˈspekjʊleɪt/ verb, i. **1** *The newspapers are speculating about the results of the election. No one is sure who will win.* = to make guesses, without knowing all the facts **2** *We lost money by speculating on the stock market.* = to buy or sell something (specially business shares) in the hope that prices will go up or come down, resulting in a profit **speculation** /spekjʊˈleɪʃən/ noun, c. or u. **1** *The speculation is that New Zealand may lift the World Cup.* = a guess made by someone **2** *The shares of this company have gone down in value on account of heavy speculation.* = the act of buying or selling something in the hope of making a profit through the rise or fall of prices **speculative** /ˈspekjʊlətɪv/ adj. *a speculative remark* = based on speculation (trying to guess what will happen)

speech /spiːtʃ/ noun, u. or c. (**speeches**) **1** *He suffered loss of speech after the accident.*(u.) = the power of speaking **2** *Your speech sounds unnatural.*(u.) = the way in which someone speaks **3** *He made an emotional speech in parliament.*(c.) = a formal talk given to a group of people **speechify** verb, i. *They keep speechifying about falling standards.* = to speak as if one was making an important speech before an audience, causing others to feel annoyed or bored (informal, not respectful) **speechless** adj. *He was speechless with anger.* = unable to speak (for a short time) because of anger etc. **speech synthesizer (synthesiser)** = a machine, using a computer system, that can produce sounds similar to human speech [TECHNICAL] **speech therapy** noun = treatment given to help people who have difficulty in speaking

speed[1] /spiːd/ noun, u. *The car travelled at a speed of 80 kilometres an hour.* = the rate of movement, showing how far someone or something can travel in a given period of time

speed[2] verb, i. (**sped**) *The motorcycle sped away after it knocked down a cyclist.* = to move fast (at a high speed) **speedometer** /spɪˈdɒmɪtəʳ/ noun, c. = an instrument which can measure the speed of a vehicle **speedy** adj. **1** *a speedy motorcycle* = fast **2** *We wish her a speedy recovery.* = quick **speeding** *We were fined by a traffic policeman for speeding.* = going too fast (used of cars, buses etc.)

speedometer

speed up *We must ask the builders to speed up the work.* = do something faster **to speed something up** *We will need to speed the school concert up.* = to make something finish in a shorter period of time **at full speed** *He drove at full speed in order to reach the airport in time.* = at very high speed (usually in a special situation)

spell[1] /spel/ verb, t. or i. (**spelt** or **spelled**) **1** *Can you spell the word 'dinosaur'?*(t.) = to form a word by calling out or writing out the letters in the word in the correct order **2** *Has the child learnt how to spell?*(i.) = to be able to spell words **3** *The late monsoon may spell trouble for our farmers.* = to lead to or bring about some unpleasant result **4** *The principal spelt out his plans for the development of the school.* = to give someone the details of something

spell[2] noun, c. **1** *We had a long spell of rain.* = a period of time for which some activity goes on continuously **2** *The magician cast a spell on the young prince.* = a condition or effect caused by magic **3** *The audience was under the spell of the singer.* = the strong influence that a performer can have on an audience **spellbinding** adj. *Jennifer Kapoor gave a spellbinding performance in '36 Chowringhee Lane'.* = holding the complete attention of someone **spelling** noun, u. or c. *Have you learnt the spelling of this word?* = the set of letters forming a word

spend /spend/ verb, t. (**spent**) **1** *The government spends millions every month on this hospital.* = to give out money in payment for something **2** *I spent 15 days in Delhi last month.* = to pass time or use time in doing something **spending** noun, c. or adj. **1** *This money is for spending.*(noun, u.) = buying something, not keeping the money **2** *We were given very little spending money when we were children.*(adj.) = (money) to spend **spendthrift** noun, c. = a person who wastes money (disapproving)

spent /spent/ adj. *He looks completely spent after the long meeting.* = very tired

sperm /spɜːm/ noun, u. or c. = cells produced in the body of a male animal or human being which can produce new life when they unite with the eggs produced by a female **spermatozoa** /spɜːmətə'zəʊə/ noun, c. (plural form of **spermatozoon**) = sperm cells [BIOLOGY] **spermicide** /'spɜːmɪsaɪd/ noun, c. = a chemical substance used to prevent pregnancy by destroying sperm cells **sperm whale** noun = a kind of whale which produces a valuable kind of oil known as spermaceti and was often hunted for this oil

spew /spjuː/ verb, t. or i. *The volcano spewed out red-hot lava.* = to throw out with force in large amounts

sphere /sfɪə^r/ noun, c. **1** = a solid object which is round in shape, like a ball **2** *His fame in the sphere of economics is growing.* = an area of activity **spherical** /'sferɪkəl/ adj. = having the shape of a sphere **spheroid** noun, c. = a solid object that is almost round in shape, but slightly egg-shaped

sphinc•ter /'sfɪŋktə^r/ noun, c. = a muscle which controls an opening in the body and can either close or open it [BIOLOGY]

sphinx /sfɪŋks/ noun **1** = an imaginary creature with the body of a lion and the head of a woman **2** *the Sphinx* = a very old and large building in Egypt which is built in the shape of a sphinx

spice[1] /spaɪs/ noun, c. or u. **1** *Ginger is used as a spice.* = a substance, prepared from the fruits, seeds, roots or leaves of certain plants, which is used to add taste to food **2** *He added a lot of spice to his report.* = something, often not true, which is put into a speech or piece of writing to make it more interesting or exciting (sometimes derogatory)

spice[2] verb, t. *She forgot to spice the curry.* = to add spice to something **spicy** adj. **1** *spicy food* = containing a lot of spice **2** *a spicy story* = interesting and exciting

spick-and-span /spɪkən'spæn/ adj. *The house is spick-and-span.* = absolutely clean and tidy (informal)

spi•der /'spaɪdə^r/ noun = a kind of insect that produces silken threads and weaves them into webs (nets), in order to catch other insects **spidery** adj. *His spidery scrawl was difficult to read.* = (with reference to a person's handwriting) long and thin, bent writng like a spider's legs

spiel /ʃpiːl/ noun, u. *the travel agent's spiel* = fast and clever talk, used for a particular purpose (usually to sell something) (informal, not respectful)

spike[1] /spaɪk/ noun, c. *There are sharp iron spikes fitted to the top of the wall.* = something long and thin, having a sharp point

spike[2] verb, t. **1** *The wall has been spiked.* = to fit or drive a spike into something **2** *She did not know that her drink had been spiked.* = to add some alcohol to a non-alcoholic drink (informal) **spiky** adj. *a spiky plant* = having long, sharp spikes (thorns)

spill[1] /spɪl/ verb, t. or i. (**spilt** or **spilled**) **1** *The waiter spilt coffee on my trousers.*(t.) = to cause a liquid to pour out or flow out of a container accidentally **2** *His letter spilled over to the next page.*(i.) = to spread beyond the limit of something

spill[2] noun, c. **1** *The oil leaked from the ship, creating a huge spill across the sea.* = an amount of liquid that flows out accidentally **2** *He had a nasty spill when his motorcycle skidded on the road.* = a fall from a horse, bicycle etc. (informal) **spillover** noun, c. *Today's strike is a spillover from yesterday's failed talks*

S

between the manager and the workers. = the effect of some event which continues for some time, having an effect on other events

spin[1] /spɪn/ verb, i. or t. (**spun** or **span**, **spun**) **1** *The earth spins on its axis, making one complete revolution in 24 hours.*(i.) = to turn round and round fast **2** *Mahatma Gandhi used to spin for an hour every morning on his charkha.* = to make thread from cotton for the purpose of weaving cloth **3** *Muralitharan spun the ball from outside the leg stump to the off stump.* = to make the ball move in a different direction, in the game of cricket, by turning the fingers or wrist

spin[2] noun, u. **1** *The spin of the coin may decide the result of the match.* = the act of spinning (turning round and round) **2** *We are going for a spin in our new car.* = a short journey in a vehicle, taken for pleasure (informal) **3** *The aircraft went into a spin and crashed to the ground.* = a circular movement (turning round and round) **spin-dry** verb, t. *You can spin-dry these clothes.* = to remove water from washed clothes by allowing them to spin (turn round and round at high speed) in a drier (a machine used to dry clothes) **spinning-wheel** noun, c. = a simple machine used for spinning thread **spin-off** noun, c. or u. *These books for children were a useful spin-off from the school project.* = a by-product (something which is not planned but is produced during the process of producing or doing something else) **spinner** noun, c. **1** = a person who spins thread for a living **2**= a bowler who can make the ball spin [CRICKET]

to spin a yarn *Don't spin a yarn; tell us the truth!* = to tell a story, usually made up and untrue (informal)

spin•ach /ˈspɪnɪtʃ/ noun = a soft, green leafy vegetable, rich in iron

spin•dle /ˈspɪndl/ noun, c. **1** = a part inside a machine which turns round and round **2** = the part of a machine used for spinning thread, around which the thread is wound **spindly** adj. *a child with spindly arms and legs* = thin and weak-looking

spin dry, **spinner**, **spin-off** see **spin**

spine /spaɪn/ noun, c. **1** = the long, straight line of small bones which runs down the middle of the back (also **backbone**) **2** *The hedgehog's body is covered with sharp spines.* = a part of the body of an animal or plant which ends in a sharp point **3** *the spine of a book* = the narrow strip at the back of a book joining its pages to the cover **spinal cord** noun = the thick bundle of nerves inside the spine through which the brain controls the different parts of the body **spine-chilling** adj. *a spine-chilling ghost story* = very frightening **spineless** adj. *They knew what was happening was unfair but were afraid to protest. I never thought they were so spineless.* = having no courage

spiny adj. = full of spines (sharp, bony points)

spin•ster /ˈspɪnstəʳ/ noun, c. = a woman who is no longer young and who has remained unmarried (The word often takes on an insulting meaning.) (old-fashioned) Ⓖ

spi•ral[1] /ˈspaɪərəl/ noun, c. = a line which winds in a continuous curve, always moving further and further away, or higher and higher, from a central point

spiral[2] adj. *a spiral staircase* = having the shape of a spiral

spiral

spiral[3] verb, i. (**spiralled**) *The prices of cars are spiralling.* = to rise upwards continuously

spire /spaɪəʳ/ noun, c. = the tall, pointed roof of a building

spir•it[1] /ˈspɪrɪt/ noun, u. or c. **1** *I always feel that my father is present in spirit, though not in body.*(u.) = soul; the part of a human being that is separate from the body and is believed to exist even after death **2** *It doesn't matter if you lost the match. You should take the defeat in a sporting spirit.* = attitude; a particular way of thinking or feeling about something **3** *Dravid batted with great spirit.* = courage or determination **4** *The children sang the national anthem with spirit.* = enthusiasm (interest and energy) **5** *You have to use spirit to light this stove.* = a liquid (ethyl alcohol) used as a fuel or to dissolve solid substances **6** *He seems to be under the control of an evil spirit.*(c.) = a supernatural being **7** (always plural) *They did not serve spirits at the party.* = strong alcoholic drinks

spirit[2] verb, t. *The prisoner was spirited away to some unknown place.* = to take someone away in a secret or mysterious way **spirited** adj. *The Prime Minister made a spirited speech on the eve of Republic Day.* = full of determination and energy **spirit level** noun, c. = an instrument, consisting of a glass tube filled with some liquid and having an air bubble inside, used to test whether a surface (e.g. the floor of a building) is level or not **spiritual** adj. *After his retirement he has become interested in spiritual matters.* = having to do with the spirit (soul) and not the body; connected with religion

to be in high/good spirits *The children were in high spirits as the school declared a holiday.* = full of enthusiasm **to be in low spirits** *The children were in low spirits when they were told not to watch television.* = dejected, very unhappy **to take something in the right spirit** *He took his failure in the right spirit and decided to work harder.*

= to not feel either too sad or happy about something

spit[1] /spɪt/ verb, i. or t. (**spat**) **1** *You should not spit on the road.*(i.) = to throw out saliva (the thin liquid produced inside the mouth) with force **2** *'I hate you!' the girl spat out.*(t.) = to say something with anger

spit[2] noun, u. = saliva ('Spit' is used only in very informal situations.)

spit[3] *When you barbecue meat, you actually roast it on a spit.* = a pointed rod on which pieces of meat are strung and roasted **spit and polish** noun *The General is a great believer in spit and polish.* = great attention to neatness and order, specially in the army **to spit something out** *'What's on your mind? Why don't you spit it out?' my father told me.* = to come out with one's thoughts (informal)

spite[1] /spaɪt/ noun, u. *They knew I wanted to see the film but they went without me, just out of spite.* = the desire to harm or hurt someone in a small way

spite[2] verb, t. *He kept the information away from me just to spite me.* = to annoy, make angry **spiteful** adj. *a spiteful person* = full of spite (the desire to harm)

spit•fire /'spɪtfaɪə^r/ noun, c. = a person, especially a woman, who has a very bad temper Ⓖ

spitting image noun, c. *The baby is the spitting image of his mother.* = the exact likeness (copy) of someone (informal)

spit•tle /'spɪtl/ noun, u. = spit (liquid produced in the mouth) (formal, old-fashioned)

spit•toon /spɪ'tu:n/ noun, c. = a metal container into which one can spit

splash[1] /splæʃ/ verb, t. or i. **1** *I splashed cold water on the face of the man who had become unconscious.*(t.) = to throw a liquid against something with force **2** *The rain splashed down on the tin roof.*(i.)= to fall or hit noisily **3** *The children were splashing about in the water.*(i.) = to move noisily through water **4** *A film star was arrested last night and the newspaper splashed the story on its front page.*(t.) = to report a piece of news in such a way as to make it look important (informal)

splash[2] noun, c. **1** *We heard a splash as the rock fell into the river.* = the sound made by something hitting the surface of some liquid **2** *He poured out a splash of hot chocolate sauce over the ice cream.* = a small amount of some liquid **3** *The botanical garden was a splash of colours during the flower show.* = an area of brightness

splat•ter /'splætə^r/ verb, t. *His clothes were splattered with mud.* = to cover a surface with small drops of some thick liquid

spleen /spli:n/ noun = a small organ (working part) inside the body which produces certain kinds of blood cells and controls the quality of the blood [MEDICINE] **to vent one's spleen** = to express anger

splen•did /'splendɪd/ adj. **1** *The king wore splendid clothes.* = grand in appearance and attracting attention **2** *She made a splendid speech.* = of very good quality **splendour** noun, u. *The splendour of the king's palace filled us with wonder.* = great beauty which causes admiration (literary)

splice[1] /splaɪs/ verb, t. *The electrician spliced the two ends of the wire.* = to join together

splice[2] noun, c. *There is a splice in the rope.* = a place where two things are joined together

splint /splɪnt/ noun, c. *The surgeon placed my arm in splints.* = a flat piece of wood used for keeping a broken bone in position

splin•ter[1] /'splɪntə^r/ noun, c. *The windscreen of the car was broken in the accident and the glass splinters cut his face.* = a small, sharp piece of wood, glass, metal etc. broken from a larger piece

splinter[2] verb, i. *While she was chopping wood, it splintered and hurt her hand.* = to break into very small, thin pieces **splinter group** noun, c. = a group of people who leave a political party or other group and form one of their own

split[1] /splɪt/ verb, t. or i. (**split**) **1** *The British split India into two separate states in 1947.*(t.)= to divide or break into parts **2** *His trousers were so tight that they split when he sat down.*(i.) = to burst or break open **3** *Hilla and Navroz have decided to split.*(i.) = to end a marriage (informal) (also **split up**)

split[2] noun, c. *There is a split in the group.* = a division or break **split infinitive** noun, c. *The sentence 'I request you to kindly leave this room' contains a split infinitive.* = an expression (e.g. 'to kindly leave') in which a word or phrase is put between 'to' and the verb (e.g. 'leave') which usually follows it [GRAMMAR] **split level** adj. *a split-level drawing room* = a room or house which has floors at different heights [TECHNICAL] **split personality** noun = a disorder of the mind in which a person seems to behave like two or more different people (also **schizophrenia**) **split second** noun *In a split second, the plane turned and crashed into the World Trade Centre.* = a very short period of time **split up** verb **1** *In the P.T. class we were asked to split up into groups according to the houses we belonged to.* = divide **2** *The Titanic split up after it hit an iceberg.* = to break into two or more pieces **3** (see meaning **3** in **split**[1]) **splitting** adj. *Stop making that noise! I have a splitting headache.* = very painful

splurge /splɜ:dʒ/ verb, i. or t. *We have always been very careful with our money but this year we decided to splurge on a holiday.*(i.) = to spend a lot of money without caring about the expense (informal)

S

splut•ter[1] /ˈsplʌtəʳ/ verb, i. *Mustard splutters when it is added to hot oil.*(i.) = to produce short, explosive sounds **splutter**[2] noun, c. *the splutter of candles in the rain* = the sound made by a burning candle or fire when some water falls on it

spoil /spɔɪl/ verb, t. or i. (**spoilt** or **spoiled**) **1** *He spoilt the party by quarrelling with one of the guests.*(t.)= to cause harm or damage **2** *The meat will spoil if you don't keep it in the refrigerator.*(i.) = to go bad (referring to food) **3** *Don't spoil the child by giving her too much money.*(t.) = to cause someone, specially a child, to behave badly by giving him/her too much love, attention etc. **spoilage** noun, u. *We lost most of the fruits we had grown due to spoilage.* = the damage caused when something (specially food) goes bad (formal) **spoiler** noun, c. = a flat piece of metal attached to the back of a car which helps the car to travel at high speed by changing the direction of the flow of air **spoils** noun (always plural) *The robbers hid their spoils in a cave.* = things taken by thieves or by an army which wins a war **spoilsport** noun *Why don't you allow the children to go on a picnic? Don't be a spoilsport.* = a person who is very strict and does not want others to have fun (informal, disapproving)

spoke[1] /spəʊk/ noun, c. = a piece of wire or a thin metal rod which connects the rim (outer ring) of a wheel (specially of a bicycle or motor-cycle) to the centre

spoke[2] verb = past tense of **speak** **spokesperson** noun, c. *A government spokesperson told reporters that the Foreign Minister was expected to visit China.* = someone who speaks officially for a group

sponge[1] /spʌndʒ/ noun, c. **1** = a kind of sea-animal with a soft body full of small holes **2** = a piece of soft rubber, full of small holes, which can suck up water and is generally used for cleaning a surface with water

sponge[2] verb, t. or i. **1** *The doctor told the nurse to sponge the patient.*(t.) = to clean by rubbing with a wet cloth **2** *They do not work to earn a living but sponge on their friends.*(i.) = to live by getting everything free from friends, relatives etc (informal, derogatory) **spongy** adj. *This raincoat has a spongy feel to it.* = soft, like a sponge **sponge cake** noun = a very light and soft cake

spon•sor[1] /ˈspɒnsəʳ/ verb, t. *This film festival is being sponsored by a company which manufactures soap.* = to support or help someone or something (specially an event or activity) by providing money etc.

sponsor[2] noun, u. *Our hockey team is looking for a sponsor.* = a person or group that supports or helps someone or something

spon•ta•ne•ous /spɒnˈteɪnɪəs/ adj. *There was spontaneous applause when the Principal declared a holiday.* = happening because of some natural feeling, without any planning or preparation in advance **spontaneity** /spɒntəˈniːəti/ noun, u. *The visitors were impressed by the spontaneity of the children's dancing.* = the quality of being spontaneous (doing something in a natural way, without planning or preparation)

spoof[1] /spuːf/ noun, c. *The new film called 'Bollywood Calling' is a spoof on the Indian film industry.* = parody (a copy of something which creates humour but may not be entirely true) (informal)

spoof[2] verb, t. *The television serial 'Yes, Minister' spoofs the British government.* = to create humour through a spoof (slang)

spook /spuːk/ noun, c. = a ghost (informal) **spooky** adj. *a spooky house* = causing fear (like a ghost) (informal)

spool /spuːl/ noun, c. = a reel (a wheel-like object on which a length of thread, wire or film can be wound)

spoon[1] /spuːn/ noun, c. = a tool made of metal or plastic, consisting of a small bowl to which a handle is attached, used for carrying food to the mouth or for serving food

spoon[2] verb, t. *Spoon a small amount of the tomato sauce onto the roast meat.* = to move food with a spoon **spoon-feed** verb, t. **1** *The nurse spoon-fed the patient as he was very weak.* = to feed someone with the help of a spoon **2** *Don't spoon- feed your students. Let them solve their problems themselves.* = to give more help than is necessary, making things too easy (disapproving) **spoonful** noun, c. *a spoonful of sugar* = as much of something as can be carried in a spoon

born with a silver spoon in one's mouth *He does not have to work for a living as he was born with a silver spoon in his mouth.* = born into a wealthy family **to spoon out advice/ideas etc.** = to give someone advice etc. easily, as if it was wanted (informal, disapproving)

spoonerism /ˈspuːnərizm/ noun, c. *The absent-minded professor committed a spoonerism when he told his students 'You have hissed my mystery lecture' instead of 'You have missed my history lecture'.* = an expression in which the first sound of a word changes place with the first sound of another word, producing humour

spoor /spɔːʳ/ noun, c. *We tracked the tiger through the jungle by following its spoor.* = the marks or solid waste matter (dung or droppings) left by a wild animal as it moves through a forest, which help a person to follow it [TECHINICAL]

spo•rad•ic /spəˈrædɪk/ adj. *Things are usually*

peaceful in this state, but we have sporadic outbursts of violence. = happening now and then, not regularly (formal) **sporadically** adv. *We do not get news of him regularly. He sends us e-mails sporadically.* = occasionally, once in a way (formal)

spore /spɔːʳ/ noun, c. = a single cell by which flowerless plants such as moss, fungi and ferns reproduce themselves [BIOLOGY]

sport[1] /spɔːt/ noun, u. or c. **1** *Volleyball is a popular sport.*(c.) = a game **2** *When I called you a fool, I did not mean it seriously. It was said only in sport.*(u.) = something said or done as a joke, to create humour (literary, old-fashioned) **3** *Come on, be a sport! Don't be unhappy because you lost the match.* = a person who accepts defeat or something unpleasant in a cheerful manner, without complaining (informal)

sport[2] verb, t. **1** *He was sporting a bright red shirt when he came to class.* = to wear or show something in a manner which attracts attention **2** *The children were sporting in the field.* = to play (literary) **sporting** adj. *Gilchrist made a sporting gesture and walked away from the pitch when the ball hit his pad, although the umpire had not given him out.* = fair-minded, specially in sports **sportive** adj. *sportive children* = playful **sports** noun, u. (always plural) **1** *He is outstanding in all sports.* = games or activities in which one takes part for exercise or entertainment, or as part of a competition **2** *the school sports* = a meeting at which people take part in different physical activities such as running, jumping etc. **sportsperson (sportsman/sportswoman)** (plural **sportsmen/sportswomen**) noun, c. **1** = a person who takes part in games, physical activities etc. **2** = a person who is very fair-minded, specially in playing games (see **sport**, meaning **3**) **sportsmanship (sportspersonship)** noun, u. *Cricket has become so commercial that now you don't see much sportsmanship on the field.* = the spirit of being fair-minded and honest in sports **sportswear** noun = clothes worn during sports/ games **sporty** adj. *sporty clothes* = colourful and attractive (referring to clothes)

spot[1] /spɒt/ noun, c. **1** *Let us go to a quiet spot where no one will disturb us.* = a particular place **2** *There are some ink spots on your shirt.* = a small mark on a surface of a different colour **3** *The boy has got into a spot of trouble.* = a little bit (informal)

spot[2] verb, t. (**spotted**) **1** *I have spotted a few spelling mistakes in your essay.* = to see or find something by looking carefully **2** *The whole area was spotted with colourful flags.* = to place or spread something over a surface or area **spotless** adj. *His reputation as a forest officer is spotless.* = morally above blame **spotlight** noun, c. **1** = a lamp which lights up a small area with a very bright light **2** *Most film stars enjoy being in the spotlight.* = the attention of the public

in a tight spot *The foreign tourist was in a tight spot when she lost her passport.* = in a difficult situation (informal)

soft spot *He may be a problem child but everyone has a soft spot for him because he is so friendly.* = affection, warmth

spouse /spaʊs/ noun, c. = the person of the opposite sex to whom one is married (husband or wife) (formal)

spout[1] /spaʊt/ noun, c. **1** *the spout of a teapot* = a narrow opening through which some liquid is poured out **2** *The water rushed out of the broken pipe in a spout.* = a stream of water rushing out with force **3** *the whale's spout* = water which a whale causes to rise with force when it breathes out

spout[2] verb, i. or t. **1** *Water spouted from the damaged pipe.* = to rush out with force (referring to some liquid) **2** *He spouted nonsense for nearly two hours.* = to talk for a very long time (informal, derogatory)

sprain[1] /spreɪn/ verb, t. *He sprained his ankle while running.* = to damage or hurt a joint in the body by sudden twisting

sprain[2] noun, c. *He has a sprain in the left ankle.* = the damage caused by a sudden twisting movement [MEDICINE] **sprained** adj. *He was pulled out of the team because of his sprained wrist.* = injured

sprawl[1] /sprɔːl/ verb, i. or t. **1** *The man was injured and lay sprawled out on the floor.* = to sit or lie with the body spread out in an untidy manner which is not natural **2** *The college buildings sprawl across ten acres of land.* = to spread out in an untidy manner over a large area

sprawl[2] noun, c. *You will find a sprawl of buildings spreading all over the new town.* = a mass or group of things spreading in an untidy manner over a large area

spray[1] /spreɪ/ verb, t. *We sprayed insecticide all over the house, but it had no effect on the mosquitoes.* = to throw or force out liquid in very fine drops

spray[2] noun, u. **1** *The spray from the waves dashing against the rocks made him wet.* = water in very small drops **2** *a spray of flowers* = a bunch of flowers arranged in an attractive way

spread[1] /spred/ verb, t. or i. (**spread**) **1** *He spread some jam over the slice of bread.*(t.) = to cause something to cover a larger area **2** *The new town has spread across the river.*(i.) = to grow in such a manner as to cover a larger area **3** *Spread this bedsheet over the bed.*(t.) = to put a covering on a surface

spread[2] noun, u. or c. **1** *The government is trying to check the spread of malaria.*(u.)= the action of spreading (growing so as to cover a larger area) **2** *He*

S

served 15 different dishes for dinner. It was a huge spread.(c.)= a meal at which many different items of food are served (informal) **3** *cheese spread*(c.) = a kind of food which is spread over bread **spreadeagle** verb, t. *The injured man lay spreadeagled on the ground.* = to lie in a flat position with the arms and legs spread out **spreading** adj. *We took shelter under a spreading banyan tree.* = spread over a wide area **spreadsheet** noun, c. = a kind of computer program mostly used by businesspersons or companies to show sales, expenditure, profits etc. [COMPUTERS]

spree /spriː/ noun, c. *The two ladies went on a shopping spree when they were in Singapore.* = a period of uncontrolled activity, providing pleasure (humorous)

sprig /sprɪg/ noun, c. *a sprig of rose leaves* = a small branch to which leaves are attached

spright•ly /'spraɪtli/ adj. *The girls performed a sprightly dance which everyone enjoyed.* = lively; full of energy

spring[1] /sprɪŋ/ verb, i. or t. (**sprang, sprung**) **1** *The man sprang to his feet and started shouting.*(i.) = to jump or move upwards or forwards with force **2** *Many new colleges have sprung up in this state in the last five years.* = to appear or come into existence quickly **3** *He sprang a surprise on us by announcing that he was going to get married.* (t.) = to make something known unexpectedly **4** *The thought of home makes tears spring to my eyes.* = to be seen (in one's eyes) **5** *If you press this button the door will spring open.* = happen suddenly and quickly

spring[2] noun, c. **1** *The tiger took a spring and landed on the back of the elephant.* = the act of jumping with force **2** = the season that comes after winter, when new flowers and leaves appear on trees **3** *a hot spring* = an underground source of water which flows out naturally **4** *a coil spring* = a length of wire or thin metal, wound into a number of circles, which can be pressed into a smaller space but returns to its original shape and size when the pressure is removed **springboard** noun, c. **1** = a flat, narrow piece of wood, to which a spring is attached so that it can move up and down, from which a person can dive into a swimming pool (also **diving board**) **2** *His victory in the college elections became a springboard to a successful political career.* = a starting point for future success (figurative) **spring chicken** noun, c. **1** = a very young chicken which has soft meat **2** *I am no spring chicken.* = a very young person (generally used in negative form, to express the opposite meaning) **spring onion** noun, c. = a very young onion, to which a long green stem is attached **spring roll** noun, c. = an item of Chinese food, somewhat like a samosa, which has pieces of meat or vegetables inside a covering made of flour and eggs

to spring a leak *The boat sprang a leak and sank within a few minutes.* = to begin to leak (referring usually to a boat or ship) **to spring to someone's defence** = to quickly and strongly express one's support of a person or defend her/him

sprin•kle[1] /'sprɪŋkəl/ verb, t. *He sprinkled some salt into the soup.* = to scatter (throw) some liquid in small drops or some solid matter in very small pieces over a surface

sprinkle[2] noun, u. **1** *We were expecting rain today but we had only a sprinkle.* = light rain (informal) **2** *There was only a sprinkle of people in the audience.* = very few (people) **sprinkler** noun, c. **1** = a container for water with a spout having small holes, which is used to sprinkle water in small drops over the roots of plants in a garden **2** = a system of pipes having small holes in them, through which water can flow slowly in small drops and reach the roots of plants (also **sprinkler irrigation**)

sprint[1] /sprɪnt/ verb, i. *The runners sprinted down the track.* = to run at a fast speed

sprint[2] noun, c. *He is competing in the 100-metre sprint.* = a short race which is run at a very fast speed

sprite /spraɪt/ noun, c. = a fairy or a playful child (literary)

sprock•et /'sprɒkɪt/ noun, c. = a wheel fitted with small teeth, used to drive the chain of a bicycle or motor-cycle [TECHNICAL]

sprocket

sprout[1] /spraʊt/ verb, i. or t. *The rice plants are beginning to sprout from the seeds.* = to grow (referring specially to plants)

sprout[2] noun, c. = a very young plant that grows out of a seed

spruce[1] /spruːs/ adj. *The house looks spruce after it has been painted.* = neat and clean

spruce[2] noun = a kind of tree that grows in cold or high places

to spruce up *The house is very untidy. We will have to spruce it up.* = to make something neat and clean (informal)

spry /spraɪ/ adj. *The old man is still very spry. He goes for a long swim every day.* = active and full of energy (referring to an old person)

spunk /spʌŋk/ noun, u. *This soldier was shot in the leg but he managed to climb over a fence and capture the enemy position. He is full of spunk.* = courage (informal, not commonly used today because **spunk**

is also slang for *semen*) **spunky** adj. = courageous

spur[1] /spɜːʳ/ noun, c. **1** = a piece of metal with a sharp point, fitted to the heel of a shoe worn by the rider of a horse, which is pressed into the belly of the horse in order to control it or make it run faster **2** *the spur of a mountain* = a small hill or mountain which grows out of a longer, higher mountain [GEOGRAPHY]

spur[2] verb, t. (**spurred**) **1** *The rider spurred the horse onwards.* = to use spurs in order to control a horse **2** *The runner was tired and was about to give up the race, but the shouts of encouragement from the crowd spurred him on to greater effort.* = to encourage someone to try harder to do something (figurative) **to do something on the spur of the moment** = to do something without making any preparations in advance (informal) **to spur somebody on** *Your harsh words will not spur your child on to do any better.* = to encourage a person to do even better than before

spu•ri•ous /ˈspjʊəriəs/ adj. *This is a spurious letter. It does not have the Principal's signature.* = not real or genuine (formal, derogatory)

spurn /spɜːn/ verb, t. *My opponent offered to help me with money, but I spurned his offer.* = to refuse or reject something with anger or pride (formal, somewhat literary)

spurt[1] /spɜːt/ verb, i. *Blood spurted from his wound.* = to flow out with force

spurt[2] noun, c. **1** *There was a spurt of blood from the wound.* = a sudden flow of liquid **2** *No work was done in the office all month, but there was a sudden spurt of activity last week.* = a short and sudden period of activity **3** *He is not a steady worker. He works in spurts.* = in sudden short bursts

sput•ter /ˈspʌtəʳ/ verb, i. **1** *The engine of the car sputtered and then stopped completely.* = to make short explosive sounds **2** *"Wha … what's wrong?" he sputtered, when we woke him up suddenly.* = to speak in a confused way **3** *The mustard seeds sputtered when the cook added them to the hot oil.* = to make short, sharp sounds

spu•tum /ˈspjuːtəm/ noun, u. = the thick liquid that comes out of the lungs and mouth after coughing [MEDICINE]

spy[1] /spaɪ/ noun, c. (**spies**) = a person who collects secret information

spy[2] verb, i. or t. (**spied**) **1** = to work as a spy **2** *She spied her son in the middle of the crowd.* = to catch sight of someone (literary) **3** *The detective spied on the man to see what he was up to.* = to watch and gather information on someone secretly **spy-glass** noun = a small telescope (an instrument used to see things which are far away)

squab•ble[1] /ˈskwɒbəl/ verb, i. *The two children have been squabbling over who should have the window seat.* = to quarrel over something unimportant (informal)

squabble[2] noun, c. *They decided to end their squabble and become friends.* = quarrel

squad /skwɒd/ noun, c. **1** *a police squad* = a small group of soldiers or policepersons who are given some special duty **2** *The student squads went round the locality telling the residents not to use plastic bags.* = a small team of people selected to do a particular job

squad•ron /ˈskwɒdrən/ noun, c. *a fighter squadron* = a small group of aircraft or ships, in the air-force or navy, together with the men who fly them or sail in them and fight together as a team [TECHNICAL] **squadron leader** noun = an officer in the air-force

squal•id /ˈskwɒlɪd/ adj. *squalid surroundings* = dirty and unpleasant **squalor** noun, u. = the quality of being squalid (very dirty)

squall /skwɔːl/ noun, c. = a sudden storm or strong wind accompanied with rain

squan•der /ˈskwɒndəʳ/ verb, t. *He squandered all his money on gambling and horse-racing.* = to waste money or to spend it on wrong things

square[1] /skweəʳ/ noun, c. **1** = a geometrical figure (shape) having four sides of equal length and all its angles as right angles (measuring 90 degrees) [GEOMETRY] (see pic under **shapes**) **2** = a large open area in a city which has buildings on all four sides **3** *The square of 7 is 49.* = a number obtained by multiplying a certain number by itself [MATHEMATICS] **4** *He is a square. He never goes to the cinema.* = a person who is old-fashioned and dull in his/her thinking and behaviour (informal, mildly derogatory)

square[2] adj. **1** *a square table* = having the shape of a square **2** *The room is 15 square metres in area.* = a unit for the measurement of area **3** *India won the first match and Australia the second. Now the two teams are square.* = on equal terms (informal) **4** *He gave me a square deal.* = fair and honest (informal) **5** *Draw this graph on a sheet of squared paper.* = something that has been divided into squares

square[3] verb, t. or i. **1** *You have to square this number.* = to multiply a number by itself [MATHEMATICS] **2** *Your report does not square with the facts.* = to be in agreement with (informal) **square bracket** noun, c. = a bracket (sign used in writing or printing) having the shape [ ] **squarely** adv. *The responsibility for this accident lies squarely on the driver of the car.* = directly or completely **square meal** noun, c. = a meal that satisfies one's hunger **square root** noun *The square root of 49 is 7.* = a number, which when multiplied by itself, gives a certain number [MATHEMATICS] **to go back to square one** *The new shop had good*

S

sales last week, but now it is back to square one. = to go back to the starting point (which is usually disappointing) so that something has to be done all over again (informal) **a square peg in a round hole** = a person who does not fit a job or a responsibility

squash[1] /skwɒʃ/ verb, t. *He squashed the tomato between the palms of his hands.* = to crush; to press into a flat shape

squash[2] noun **1** = a game played with a small rubber ball and rackets, in a court having four walls **2** = a large fruit, like a pumpkin, that grows on a creeping plant and is eaten as a vegetable **3** *orange squash* = the flesh of an orange or other fruit which has been crushed (pressed) and from which a sweet drink can be made by adding water

squat[1] /skwɒt/ verb, i. (**squatted**) **1** = to sit on the ground with the knees bent and the weight of the body supported only by the feet **2** = to occupy an empty building or plot of land forcibly

squat[2] adj. *a squat building* = low, thick and ugly-looking **squatter** noun, c. = a person who occupies an empty building or plot of land without permission and gets a legal right, after some time, to own it [TECHNICAL]

squawk[1] /skwɔ:k/ verb, i. *The parrot squawked loudly.* = to make the loud, somewhat low and rough sound produced by certain birds

squawk[2] noun, c. *the squawk of a parrot* = the noise made by a bird when squawking

squeak[1] /skwi:k/ verb, i. *The wheels of the bullock cart squeaked when the cart moved.* = to make a short and high-pitched sound (like that produced by the wheel of a cart which needs oiling)

squeak[2] noun, c. *the squeak of cart wheels* = the sound produced by something that squeaks **squeaky** adj. *a squeaky door* = something that makes a squeaking sound **squeaky-clean** adj. *a squeaky-clean reputation* = extremely honest (informal, humorous)

squeal[1] /skwi:l/ verb, i. *The children squealed happily when I told them we were going on a picnic.* = to make a long, high pitched sound expressing excitement

squeal[2] noun, c. *We knew the children were enjoying themselves when we heard squeals of delight coming from the nursery.* = a long, high pitched sound made when a person or animal is gladly surprised, happy or in pain

squeam•ish /ˈskwi:mɪʃ/ adj. *You shouldn't visit a fish market if you are so squeamish.* = easily upset or shocked by things that are unpleasant (disapproving)

squeeze[1] /skwi:z/ verb, t. or i. **1** *The mother squeezed her daughter's arm affectionately.* = to press something with the whole hand curved round the object **2** *She squeezed some juice out of the lemon.*(t.) = to force a liquid or soft solid substance (e.g. toothpaste) out by pressing something between the fingers **3** *The car was small but all six of us managed to squeeze into it.*(i.) = to be able to get into a space with some difficulty, by using pressure **4** *The rat tried to squeeze through the narrow opening.* = to force one's way through a very small gap **5** *I don't know how they manage to squeeze so much into a day.*(i.) = do many things within a limited time

squeeze[2] noun, u. **1** *She gave the child's arm a gentle squeeze.* = the act of squeezing, usually to show affection or to encourage someone (see meaning **1** above) **2** *All six of us managed to get into the car, but it was a tight squeeze.* = a state of being crowded into a limited space (informal) **3** *The company is facing a credit squeeze.* = a difficult situation in business, caused by short supplies etc. **squeezer** noun, c. = a tool used to press juice out of a fruit such as an orange

squelch[1] /skweltʃ/ noun, u. *We heard the squelch of heavy shoes moving across the muddy fields.* = the sucking sound produced when one walks through mud

squelch[2] verb, i. *We squelched through the muddy fields.* = to move across soft, wet ground, making a squelching sound (also **squish**)

squib /skwɪb/ noun, c. = a kind of fire-cracker that hisses before producing a loud sound or a bright light when it is lit, used to celebrate a festival such as Deepavali

a damp squib *The producer expected the new film to do well, but it turned out to be a damp squib.* = something that is expected to succeed, but does not succeed (informal)

squid /skwɪd/ noun = a sea-creature with a long, tube-like body, having long, thin arms at one end

squint[1] /skwɪnt/ noun = a defect of the muscles that control the movement of the eyes, causing the eyes to look in different directions

squint[2] verb, i. **1** *The girl squints.* = to suffer from a squint **2** *The bright sunlight caused him to squint.* = to close the eyes partly because of too much light

squire /skwaɪəʳ/ noun, c. = a land-owner in England (in former times)

squirm /skwɜ:m/ verb, i. **1** *The thought of speaking to such a large audience made him squirm with nervousness.* = to move from side to side in an awkward way because of discomfort, shame, nervousness etc. **2** *I squirm to think that I will have to apologise in front of the whole class.* = to feel discomfort about doing something unpleasant

squir•rel /ˈskwɪrəl/ noun = a small animal with a long tail that climbs trees

squirt[1] /skwɜːt/ verb, t. *I squeezed the tube and the gel squirted out.* = to force out some liquid through a narrow opening or a container which can be squeezed

squirt[2] noun, c. *a squirt of oil* = a stream of liquid that is forced out through a narrow opening

squish /skwɪʃ/ noun, u. *We heard the squish of feet moving across the wet sand.* = the sound of feet moving over soft, wet ground (also **squelch**)

Sr. = abbr. of 'Senior' (American) (used after the name of a person to show that we are referring to the father and not to a son who has the same name e.g. George W. Bush, Sr.)

ss = abbr. of 'steam ship' (used before the name of a ship, e.g. *ss Titanic*)

Ssh /ʃ/ interjec. = a command ordering silence or less noise

St. 1 = abbr. of 'Saint' (used before the name of someone who is recognised as a holy person by the Roman Catholic Church e.g. *St. Francis Xavier*) 2 = abbr. of 'Street' (e.g. *Oxford St.*)

stab[1] /stæb/ verb, t. (**stabbed**) *The robber stabbed me with a knife.* = to injure someone with a sharp, pointed weapon e.g. the point of a knife

stab[2] noun, c. 1 = an injury caused by a pointed weapon 2 *He felt a stab of pain in the chest.* = a sudden, sharp pain

to stab someone in the back = to harm someone who trusts you or depends on you

sta•ble[1] /ˈsteɪbəl/ adj. 1 *a stable business* = (something that is) not easily moved, upset or changed; strongly in position 2 *The patient's condition was causing some worry but now it is stable.* = not changing for the worse

stable[2] noun, c. = a building in which horses are kept

stable[3] verb, t. *The horse has been stabled.* = to put a horse in a stable

sta•bil•i•ty /stəˈbɪlɪti/ noun, u. = the quality of being stable (steady and strong) **stabilize (stabilise)** /ˈsteɪbɪlaɪz/ verb, t. or i. *The price of petroleum has stabilized.* = to become stable (steady and not changing frequently) **stabilizer (stabiliser)** noun, c. 1 = a machine that helps to control the flow of electricity and keeps it at a steady level 2 = a device fitted to a ship which enables it to remain steady even when it is hit by large waves

stac•ca•to /stəˈkɑːtəʊ/ adj. *We heard the staccato sounds of motorcycle engines running at high speed.* = sounds which are sharp and heard at short intervals

stack[1] /stæk/ noun, c. 1 *There was a stack of papers on my desk.* = an orderly pile of things, kept one above another 2 *Users of the library are not allowed into the stacks.* = the place where books are stored in a library [TECHNICAL]

stack[2] verb, t. *Ask them to stack the chairs in a corner of the room.* = to arrange in a neat pile, one on top of the other **stackable chairs** noun = light chairs made of plastic or metal which can be arranged in stacks (piles), on top of each other, so that they do not take up much space when not being used

sta•di•um /ˈsteɪdɪəm/ noun, c. (**stadia** or **stadiums**) = a sports ground with seating arrangements for spectators (people who are watching but not taking part)

staff[1] /stɑːf/ noun, u. or c. (**staff/staffs**) 1 *This school has a staff of 40 teachers.*(only singular, used with plural or singular verbs) = the group of people working for an organisation 2 *The farmer carried a thick staff.*(c.) = a long, thick stick

staff[2] verb, t. *The new school has not been staffed yet.* = to provide or find people to work in an organization

stag /stæg/ noun, c. = a fully grown male deer **stag party** noun = a party to which only men are invited (slang)

stage[1] /steɪdʒ/ noun, c. or u. 1 *We are setting up a stage for the new play.*(c.)= an area, generally a raised platform, on which dramas are performed 2 *Nasiruddin Shah made his name on the stage before he came to cinema.*(u.) = the profession of acting in plays 3 *Children should be educated through the mother-tongue at the primary stage of education.*(c.) = a particular point or period of time in a series of events 4 *We will travel to Kolkata for the first stage of our journey.* = a part of a journey

stage[2] verb, t. 1 *We are staging a new play.* = to present a play to an audience 2 *The members who disagreed staged a walk-out in Parliament.* = to cause something to happen, mainly for some dramatic effect **stage direction** noun, c. = a written description of something that an actor is required to do when acting in a play on the stage **stage fright** noun, u. = the feeling of nervousness which some people have when appearing before an audience **stage-manage** verb, t. *Everyone thought the crowd was supporting the leader, but in fact the meeting had been stage-managed by his supporters.* = to control or manage an event in such a way that a certain effect is produced (derogatory)

stag•ger[1] /ˈstægəʳ/ verb, i. *He managed to stagger to his car after he was wounded and drove himself to the hospital.* =to walk with great difficulty

stagger[2] noun, u. = unsteady movement when one is tired, ill or drunk **staggering** adj. *The batsman scored a staggering 435 runs!* = very surprising and difficult to believe

stag•nant /ˈstægnənt/ adj. 1 *The river has got*

S

choked up with sand and is completely stagnant. = not moving or flowing (referring to a body of water) **2** *Our economy has been stagnant this year.* = not growing or developing **stagnate** /stæg'nəɪt/ verb, i. *I've been doing the same work for 30 years. Do you think I am stagnating?* = to become stagnant (to stop growing or developing) **stagnation** noun. *There has been a stagnation in building construction this year.* = a state of not growing or developing

staid /steɪd/ adj. *He works as a clerk in a bank and leads a staid life.* = somewhat dull and boring; not very exciting or interesting (formal)

stain[1] /steɪn/ verb, t. **1** *My teeth are stained black because of my habit of chewing tobacco.* = to leave a mark on something which is difficult to remove **2** *The weavers stain the thread in different colours before they start weaving a sari.* = to use a dye (colour) to colour something

stain[2] noun, c. or u. *The tea left a stain on the white table-cloth.* = a mark which is difficult to remove **stained glass** noun = glass of different colours used for making patterns in windows, often found in churches **stainless** adj. **1** *stainless steel* = something that cannot easily rust **2** *a stainless reputation* = not spoilt by behaviour which is morally wrong (literary)

stair /steəʳ/ noun, c. **1** (plural) *You will have to go up these stairs to reach the Principal's office, which is on the floor above.* = a set of steps which lead from one part of a building to another, up or down **2** *He slipped on the stair but managed to keep his balance.* = a step in a staircase **staircase** noun, c. = a set of stairs or steps

stake[1] /steɪk/ noun, c. or u. **1** *The cow was tied to a stake.*(c.) = a piece of wood or metal driven into the ground, to which something can be tied or which forms part of a fence **2** *We all have a stake in the welfare of this company.*(c.) = a share in something, specially a business company, which causes someone to take special interest in it **3** *He has put a stake on the result of this match.*(c.) = an amount of money which one bets on the result of some event **4** *If I lose this match, everyone will be disappointed. My reputation is at stake.* = a situation which carries a certain risk **5** = a post to which, in the old days, a person who had committed a crime was tied to

stake[2] verb, t. *He has staked a claim to the ancestral property.* = to claim ownership **stakeholder** noun, c. = a person who has a share or a great interest in something

high stakes = One plays a game for high stakes when one puts a lot of one's money into winning it. **to stake out a claim** *They have staked out a claim on the house after her death.* = to say openly that one has a right to something

stal•ac•tite /'stæləktaɪt/ noun = a kind of rock formed inside a cave by the slow deposit of minerals present in water leaking through the roof, which grows downwards like a pillar from the roof [GEOGRAPHY]

stal•ag•mite /'stæləgmaɪt/ noun, c. = a rock-formation similar to a stalactite, but growing upwards

stale[1] /steɪl/ adj. **1** *The chicken curry is stale. It was cooked two days ago.* = not fresh and therefore not good to eat (referring to food) **2** *stale news* = no longer new or interesting (figurative)

stale[2] verb, i. *News stales quickly.* = to become stale

stale•mate /'steɪlmeɪt/ noun, c. or u. *India and South Africa have reached a stalemate in this match. Neither side is likely to win.* = a situation in a fight or competition in which neither side can win

stalk[1] /stɔːk/ noun, c. *the stalk of a rice plant* = the stem of a plant (the long narrow part from which leaves and flowers grow)

stalk[2] verb, t. *The tiger stalked its prey.* = to follow someone or something quietly while remaining hidden, in order to hunt (kill) **stalker** noun, c. = a person, usually of an abnormal condition of mind, who follows a person (usually a woman) everywhere and is likely to harm the person **stalk out** *At the end of the argument she stalked out of the room in anger.* = walk in anger with long steps (informal)

stall[1] /stɔːl/ noun, c. **1** *He runs a bookstall on the railway platform.* = a small, open shop **2** *The cows are kept in stalls.* = a small enclosed place in which an animal is kept **3** (plural) = the seats in the main part of a cinema, a theatre etc.

stall[2] verb, i. or t. **1** *The car stalled as we were going up the hill.*(i.) = to stop running (referring to a vehicle or the engine of a vehicle) **2** *I have been asking him for a long time to fix a date for our meeting but he keeps stalling.*(i.) // *The committee member is trying to stall the election as he thinks he may lose.*(t.) = to put off or delay something

stal•li•on /'stælɪən/ noun, c. = a male horse kept for breeding (producing young ones)

stal•wart[1] /'stɔːlwət/ adj. *a stalwart supporter of the rights of women* = loyal; strong and determined

stalwart[2] noun, c. *He is a stalwart of the Congress Party who can always be depended on.* = a strong and loyal supporter of (usually) a political cause

sta•men /'steɪmən/ noun, c. = a long, hair-like part of a flower that produces pollen (the male cells which combine with the female cells to produce a new plant) (see pic under **flower**) [BIOLOGY]

stam•i•na /'stæmɪnə/ noun, u. *He has a lot of stamina. He can work all day without getting tired.* = strength and energy

stam•mer[1] /ˈstæməʳ/ verb, i. *He stammers while speaking.* = to suffer from some defect which causes one to pause (stop for a short time) between words while speaking or to have difficulty in producing certain sounds

stammer[2] noun, u. *He has a painful stammer.* = a speech defect which makes one unclear while speaking

stamp[1] /stæmp/ noun, c. **1** *a postage stamp* = a small piece of printed paper, usually with a picture on it, to be bought at a post office and fixed to letters etc. before they can be sent through the post **2** *a rubber-stamp* = a small tool used to print something, usually the name or rank of a person who is signing a document, to show that it is genuine (real) **3** *The manager put his stamp on the letter.* = the mark made on paper by a stamp (meaning **2**)

stamp[2] verb, t. **1** *He stamped his foot on the ground.* = to bring the foot down on the ground with force **2** *Have you stamped the letter?* = to fix a postage stamp on a letter before posting it **3** *I stamped the letter after I had signed it.* = to put an official stamp (meaning **3**) on a document

stam•pede[1] /stæmˈpiːd/ noun, c. *There was a stampede in the football stadium after two groups of spectators started fighting.* = a sudden rush or violent movement by a crowd of people or animals

stampede[2] verb, i. or t. *The cattle stampeded when someone exploded a fire-cracker.* = to rush suddenly out of fear

stance /stɑːns/ noun, u. **1** *The government has adopted a firm stance on tax-evaders.* = a way of thinking about or dealing with something that is happening **2** *Rahul Dravid was advised to change his batting stance.* = the way of standing while waiting to hit the ball, in the game of cricket [TECHNICAL]

stand[1] /stænd/ verb, i. or t. (**stood**) **1** *I'd like to stand for a while.*(i.) // *The boys stood up when their teacher entered the classroom.*(i.) = to be in or to come to an upright (straight) position, with the legs straight and the weight of the body supported by the feet **2** *He stood the book on the shelf.*(t.) = to make something rest in an upright position **3** *Our house stands on top of a hill.*(i.) = to be in a particular position or place **4** *Our collection now stands at Rs 5,000.*(i.) = to be at or to show a particular level **5** *He stood first in the test.*(i.) = to have a certain rank or position **6** *He is going to stand for election.*(i.) = to compete for an official position **7** *I can't stand the smell of tobacco.*(t.) = to tolerate or accept (generally used in negative sentences) **8** *The letters 'HRD' stand for 'Human Resource Development.'* = to represent

stand[2] noun, c. or u. **1** *What is your stand on the question of reservation of seats for women?* = an opinion that someone has **2** *Some teachers are making a stand against the government's decision to close down the school.* = an act of opposition **3** *All buses stop at the bus stand.* = a place where buses or taxis stop to allow people to get on or off **4** *Sachin Tendulkar hit the ball over the stands.* = rows of seats at a sports stadium **5** *He has a newspaper stand at the railway station.* = a small shop (also **stall**) **stand-by** noun, c. (**stand-bys**) *We have some candles as a stand-by in case there is no electricity.* = someone or something that can be used in case of need **stand-in** noun, c. *Rehana is a stand-in for Neha in the play.* = a person who can take the place of someone else when required to do so **stand-offish** adj. *His behaviour was rather stand-offish when I met him after ten years.* = not friendly **standpoint** noun, c. *You have to look at the Palestinian problem from a historical standpoint.* = a point of view **standstill** noun *Work in the factory has come to a standstill as the workers are ill.* = a total stop; a condition when there is no activity

to stand to attention *You have to stand to attention when you salute your national flag.* = to stand straight without any movement, as a mark of respect **to stand firm** *We must learn to stand firm even in the face of temptation.* = to stick to the same opinion and not waver **to (not) stand a chance** *We do stand a chance of winning the World Cup this time.* = have a possibility **to stand on one's own two feet** *Living in a hostel for many years has taught her to stand on her own two feet.* = to not depend on others for help (approving) **as things stand** *As things stand, you can expect the strike to end tomorrow.* = judging from the present situation **to stand aside** *He stood aside while the fight was on.* = to take no part in something **to stand by** **1** *No parent will stand by and watch his child suffer.* = to observe without doing anything **2** *The chief guest is coming. Please stand by.* = to move to one side for someone important **3** *I have a baby-sitter coming but please stand by in case she doesn't arrive.* = to wait to help in case help is needed **to stand down** *The actor should stand down and give others a chance.* = to withdraw from an activity in order to help someone else **to stand in** *The reserve player had to stand in for the injured fielder.* = to take the place of someone else **stand out** *Our national flag stood out because of its simplicity in design.* = be noticeable **to stand up for** *She has always stood up for the rights of animals.* = to support a cause or defend somebody in a quarrel

stan•dard[1] /ˈstændəd/ noun, c. **1** *This is one of our best schools. The teaching here is of a very high standard.* = level or quality **2** *The government has fixed a standard for the purity of gold.* = something that is used to measure or to compare other things

S

with **3** *My child is in the Third Standard.* = a class or level in a school **4** *The President's standard is flown over Rashtrapati Bhavan.* = a ceremonial flag

standard[2] adj. **1** *You will have to take the TOEFL test if you want to study in the U.S.A. This is standard procedure for all foreign students.* = usual **2** *Books produced by the government are generally regarded as standard textbooks for schools.* = of an acceptable quality which others are required to follow **standardize (standardise)** verb, t. *We have standardized the quality of Basmati rice being exported to the USA.* = to fix a standard or an acceptable level of quality for something **standard of living** noun, c. (**standards of living**) = a measure which allows us to judge how comfortably people are living

stan•ding[1] /ˈstændɪŋ/ noun, u. *She has a high standing as a writer.* = position or reputation

standing[2] adj. *I have left standing instructions that I should be informed whenever there is some trouble here.* = permanent or fixed until changed

stan•za /ˈstænzə/ noun, c. = a group of lines forming a division in a poem

staph•y•lo•coc•cus /stæfɪləʊˈkɒkəs/ noun = a kind of bacterium (tiny living creature) that causes infection [MEDICINE]

sta•ple[1] /ˈsteɪpəl/ adj. *Rice is the staple food of the people of this state.* = forming the main part

staple[2] noun, c. **1** = something (specially food) that is absolutely necessary **2** = a thin metal wire that is used to join pieces of paper together

staple[3] verb = to join pieces of paper together with staples **stapler** noun, c. = a small tool used for driving staples (pieces of metal) into paper

star[1] /stɑːʳ/ noun, c. **1** = a heavenly body that is made up of burning gas and is seen as a point of light in the sky **2** = a geometrical figure with five points, having the shape * (see pic under **shapes**) **3** *a film star* = a famous person who has been very successful in some profession **4** *the star of the match* = the person who plays the most important part **5** *His star sign is Aquarius. What is yours?* = the positions of the planets which are believed to decide the fate of a person [TECHNICAL]

star[2] verb, i. or t. (**starred**) *The new film stars Farida Jalal.*(t.) = to have as the main performer (referring to a film) **starboard** noun = the right side of a ship or aircraft (when one stands facing its front part) **starry** adj. *It is a clear starry night, excellent for star-gazing.* = full of stars **star-crossed** adj. *'Laila Majnu', like 'Romeo and Juliet' is the story of two star-crossed lovers.* = unlucky **star-fish** noun, c. = a sea-animal with five arms that looks like a star **star-gaze** verb, i. *She spends all her time star-gazing.* = to be imagining things in an impractical way (disapproving) **starlet** noun, c. = a young actress who hopes to become a star (a famous actress) Ⓖ **starry-eyed** adj. *a starry-eyed teenager* = full of hopes for the future **Stars and Stripes** noun = the flag of the USA **star-studded** adj. *a star-studded film* = having a large number of stars (famous performers)

starch[1] /stɑːtʃ/ noun, u. **1** *Rice contains a lot of starch.* = a chemical substance, also known as carbohydrate, present in certain kinds of food e.g. rice, potatoes etc. **2** *Put some starch in these clothes when you wash them.* = a product made from rice etc. which is used to make clothes stiff

starch[2] verb, t. *You should starch this sari.* = to use starch to make clothes stiff

stare /steəʳ/ verb, i. or t. *When I went out wearing a mask, everyone stared at me.* = to look at someone or something for a long time with eyes wide open, usually in surprise or admiration

to stare someone in the face *We were trying hard to find an answer to the question, while it was staring us in the face all the time.* = to be easily seen or difficult to miss

stark[1] /stɑːk/ adj. *stark poverty* = bare; without any decoration or addition

stark[2] adv. *stark naked* = completely

star•ling /ˈstɑːlɪŋ/ noun, c. = a kind of small bird, very common in Europe

start[1] /stɑːt/ verb, i. or t. **1** *The test-match starts on Wednesday and ends on Sunday.*(i.) = to begin **2** *He started the car.*(t.) = to cause something to begin moving or working **3** *He is starting for Kolkata in an hour.* = to begin a journey **4** *He started the book last year.* = to begin doing a piece of work

start[2] noun, c. or u. **1** *The runners got off to a good start.*(c.) = the beginning of an activity or a race **2** *They have a 25-minute start, but we should be able to catch up with them soon.*(c.) = the amount by which one person is ahead of another person in a race or a chase **3** *He gave a start when I told him someone was looking for him.*(c.) = a sudden movement of the body, usually caused by surprise **starter** noun, c. **1** *the starter in a race* = a person who gives the signal for some activity (e.g. a race) to begin **2** *a self-starter* = a small machine which is used to start an engine (e.g. the engine of a car) **3** = food which is served at the beginning of a meal **starting block** noun, c. = pieces of wood fixed to the ground at the point where a race begins, which support the feet of runners and help to give them a good start

start•le /ˈstɑːtl/ verb, t. *He startled me by walking up quietly behind my chair and suddenly shouting into my ear.* = to surprise or shock someone by doing something sudden and unexpected **startling** adj.

a startling piece of news = something that startles

starve /stɑːv/ verb, i. or t. **1** (i.) = to suffer from great hunger because of not getting food **2** *He is starving his guests.*(t.) = to cause someone to suffer great hunger **3** *The children in these schools are starved of books.*(i.) = to suffer from the lack of something, usually something one considers good

starv•a•tion /stɑːˈveɪʃən/ noun, u. *Fifteen people have died of starvation in this state.* = suffering or death caused by lack of food

stash /stæʃ/ verb, t. *He has stashed away a lot of money in a secret place inside his house.* = to store or hide something secretly (informal)

state[1] /steɪt/ noun, c. or u. **1** *The man was lying in an unconscious state.* = the condition in which someone or something is at a particular time **2** *The state must protect its citizens.* = the government of a country **3** *the state of Jharkhand* = one of the areas into which a country is divided

state[2] adj. *a state funeral* = something done or managed by the government

state[3] verb, t. *The magistrate ordered me to state my name, age and profession.* = to say or express clearly (formal) **statehood** noun, u. *Bangladesh acquired statehood in 1971.* = the condition of being an independent country **stateless** adj. *a stateless person* = not belonging to any country **stately** adj. *a stately home* = large and grand in appearance **statement** noun, c. *He made a statement before the police, admitting his crime.* = something that is expressed in speech or writing **state-of-the-art** adj. *They are constructing a state-of-the-art Communication Centre in New Delhi.* = using the latest technology **statesman** noun, c. (**statesmen**) = a political leader who is respected for his/her qualities (also **statesperson**)

stat•ic[1] /ˈstætɪk/ adj. **1** *The price of gold will never be static.* = stay the same (used of money or value) **2** *The organization we started was making great progress but is now static.* = stay the same without making progress (derogatory)

static[2] noun, u. *We could not hear your talk over the radio because of the static.* = noise caused by some disturbance in the air that spoils radio or television broadcasts [TECHNICAL]

stat•ics noun = the branch of physics that deals with objects which are not moving, because of different forces acting upon them [PHYSICS]

sta•tion[1] /ˈsteɪʃən/ noun, c. or u. **1** *the railway station* = the buildings and surrounding areas where trains or buses stop for people to get on or off **2** *a police station* = a building where a special kind of activity is carried on **3** *They thought I had married beneath my station.* = position in society (old-fashioned)

station[2] verb, t. *Several guards have been stationed in front of the building.* = to put someone at a place for some duty (formal) **stationmaster** noun = a person who is in charge of a railway station **station wagon** noun = a large car in which several passengers and a lot of luggage can be carried

sta•tion•a•ry /ˈsteɪʃənəri/ adj. *a stationary pump* = not moving from its place

sta•tion•er•y /ˈsteɪʃənəri/ noun, u. = paper, pens and other materials used in writing or doing office work

sta•tis•tic /stəˈtɪstɪk/ noun, c. (generally in plural form **statistics**) *The government is collecting statistics in order to prepare a new voters' list.* = numbers which reveal (show) the facts in a certain situation **statistics** noun = the branch of mathematics which deals with numbers **statistician** /stætɪˈstɪʃən/ noun, c. = a person who is an expert in statistics (the subject) or is required to collect and deal with statistics (facts)

stat•ue /ˈstætʃuː/ noun, c. = the figure of a human being/animal, made out of stone or metal [TECHNICAL]

stat•u•esque /stætʃʊˈesk/ adj. *a statuesque dancer* = tall and graceful, like a statue (literary)

stat•ure /ˈstætʃəʳ/ noun, u. **1** *He is 190 centimetres in stature.* = the height of a person **2** *Jayasuriya is a cricketer of world stature.* = the level to which a person is respected and admired

stat•us /ˈsteɪtəs/ noun, u. **1** *marital status* = legal position **2** *What is the present status of the World Cup matches?* = a state or situation at a particular time **3** *He thinks a small house is not in keeping with his status.* = the position or rank that a person has in society or at work

sta•tus quo /steɪtəs ˈkwəʊ/ noun (Latin) *The Supreme Court has directed the government not to disturb the status quo.* = the existing state of affairs (the state of things as they are)

stat•ute /ˈstætʃuːt/ noun, c. = a law that is in force **statutory** adj. *The girl has not reached the statutory age of marriage.* = controlled by law [LAW]

staunch[1] /stɔːntʃ/ adj. *Britain is a staunch ally of the USA.* = loyal and dependable

staunch[2] verb, t. = to stop the flow of blood from a wound

stave /steɪv/ noun, c. = a thin piece of wood

to stave off *The travellers were lost in the jungle and managed to stave off their hunger by eating the fruit and berries they found.* = to hold back for a while (somewhat literary)

stay[1] /steɪ/ verb, i. or t. **1** *I usually stay at Hotel Janpath when I am in New Delhi.*(i.) = to live for a

S

short time in a place as a visitor or guest **2** *I am sorry I can't stay. I must leave now.*(i.) = to stop or remain in a place **3** *He stayed alive for many years, although he was unable to speak or move.*(i.) = to remain in a certain condition or position **4** *The government had ordered his dismissal, but the High Court has stayed the matter.*(t.) = to delay something (referring to the decision of a court) [LAW]

stay[2] noun, c. or u. **1** *We had a short stay in New York.*(u.) = a limited time during which one stops in a place **2** *The High Court has ordered a stay in this case.*(u.) = an order by a court delaying something **3** *The new bridge is supported by stays.*(c.) = a strong rope or wire which supports something **stay after school** *Sheila was afraid that she might be asked to stay after school if she didn't finish her work.* = stay back at school (often as a form of punishment) after classes are over

stay away *Stay away from damp places. They are not good for you.* = keep oneself far from **stay behind** *Would you mind staying behind? I have something important to discuss with you.* = stay after others have left **to stay calm** *You must learn to stay calm during your exams.* = not get excited **stay out of** *Stay out of my affairs if you know what's good for you!* = to not get involved in something **stay put** *She decided to stay put while her husband went abroad on a short assignment.* = to remain in the same place **stay up** *I'll have to stay up late in order to finish my homework.* = not go to bed

std. abbr. of **'standard'** (e.g. Std III) = a class of students in a school

STD abbr. of **1 Subscriber Trunk Dialling** = a telephone system which allows telephone users to make a long-distance call directly, without having to take the help of a telephone operator **2 Sexually Transmitted Diseases** = diseases such as syphilis, which are passed on from one person to another through sexual activity

stead /sted/ noun, u. **1** *I cannot attend the meeting. Anita Batliwala will go in my stead.* = in place of someone (formal) **2** *The money you sent stood me in good stead. I could pay off my hospital bills.* = to be handy and useful at the right time (old-fashioned)

stead•fast /'stedfɑːst/ adj. *All his friends left him when he was in trouble; only his brother remained steadfast.* = faithful or loyal (literary, old-fashioned)

stead•y[1] /'stedi/ adj. **1** *Your hand should be steady when you are drawing a line.* = not shaking **2** *He drove the car at a steady speed of 50 kms an hour.* = not changing **3** *She has a steady job in a bank.* = not likely to come to an end suddenly **4** *a steady girlfriend/ boyfriend* = a person with whom one has a strong romantic relationship, often leading to marriage **5** *I trust his judgement because he is always steady.* = possessing good sense and remaining calm even in the face of difficulties

steady[2] verb, t. (**steadied**) **1** *He steadied the camera with one hand before he took the picture.* = to keep something firmly in place **2** *He steadied himself or he would have fallen off the horse.* = to be able to keep the balance of one's own body

steady[3] interjec. *Steady now! I am going to take your picture.* = a warning to someone to be careful or not to move

steak /steɪk/ noun, u. or c. = a flat piece of meat of good quality, cut from an animal or fish

steal[1] /stiːl/ verb, t. or i. (**stole, stolen**) **1** *Someone stole some money from my room last night while I was sleeping.*(t.) // *He has promised never to steal again.*(i.) = to take without permission something (e.g. money) that belongs to another person, and which she/he does not want you to have **2** *She stole out of the meeting quietly.* = to move quietly or secretly

steal[2] noun, c. *I paid only Rs 100 for this sari. At that price, it was a steal!* = something that one gets at a very cheap price (informal) **stealth** noun, u. *He removed the watch from the table by stealth.* = the action of doing something so quietly and secretly that no one is able to know about it (formal) **stealth bomber** = a military aircraft which cannot be traced by radar

to steal the show *They are sure to steal the show with their choral singing.* = to receive the greatest praise from the public **to steal someone's thunder** *We were thinking of organizing a blood-donation camp next month, but the people in the neighbouring village have stolen our thunder. They are organizing a camp this week.* = to do something good before someone else is able to do it, thereby getting all the credit **to steal a march on someone** = to do something which someone else was about to do, in a quiet way so as to get an advantage over him/her

steam[1] /stiːm/ noun, u. **1** = the gas that is formed when water boils **2** *This engine is driven by steam.* = the power produced by steam under pressure, used to make a machine work

steam[2] adj. *a steam engine* = driven by the power of steam

steam[3] verb, i. **1** *The ship steamed up the river.* = to use the power of steam to move **2** *You should steam these vegetables.* = to cook by using steam **steamer** noun, c. **1** = a ship or boat that is driven by the power of steam **2** = a vessel in which meat or vegetables can be cooked by steam **steaming** adv. *a cup of steaming hot coffee* = very hot with steam coming out of it **steamy** adj. **1** *I can't see what's happening as my glasses have become steamy.* = covered with moisture (tiny drops of water) as a result of condensation (see **condensation**) **2** *a steamy novel* = containing descriptions or scenes of sexual activity

steam roller noun, c. or verb, t. **1** (noun, c.) = a vehicle with large and heavy wheels used to level roads, driven by steam **2** *Our committee was steam rollered into taking action.*(verb, t.) = to use one's power to make someone do something they may not otherwise have done

to let off steam = to express a strong feeling (usually of anger) which one was forced to hold back earlier **to run out of steam** = to lose the energy or the will to do something that one had earlier **to be/get steamed up** *I don't know why she got so steamed-up about the quality of our work. It was not bad.* = to become angry, excited or worried (informal)

steed /sti:d/ noun, c. = a horse (literary)

steel[1] /sti:l/ noun, u. **1** = a hard metal produced by mixing iron with carbon and other metals **2** *She looks gentle, but she is all steel.* = having a strong mind, with great courage and determination (figurative)

steel[2] verb, t. *You must be brave when you are fighting a war. You will have to steel yourself.* = to make oneself hard in body and mind **steely** adj. *He spoke in a steely voice.* = hard and cold (without much emotion) (referring to a person's voice, expression etc.)

steep[1] /sti:p/ adj. *You have to climb a steep hill to reach the temple.* = rising at a sharp angle

steep[2] verb, t. *You have to steep the vegetables in vinegar for three or four days in order to make pickles.* = to keep something fully covered by a liquid

to be steeped in something *These ancient temples are steeped in history.* = to have so much of some quality that one seems to be filled with it

stee•ple /'sti:pəl/ noun, c. = a tall church tower rising to a point

stee•ple•chase /'sti:pəltʃeɪs/ noun = a race in which a horse or a human runner has to jump over various obstacles

steer[1] /'stɪəʳ/ verb, t. or i. *He steered the car carefully through the heavy traffic.*(t.) = to control the direction in which a ship or motor vehicle is moving

steer[2] noun, c. = a young ox or bullock (male animal which has had its sex organs removed) **steering committee** noun = a small group of people who control or guide some activity, usually of a political nature **steering wheel** noun = a wheel in a car or on a ship which one uses to control the direction in which it is moving

to steer clear (of) *He is so ill-tempered that I always steer clear of him.* = to avoid something unpleasant or someone who is nasty or difficult

stel•lar /'steləʳ/ adj. **1** *stellar orbit* = having to do with a star [TECHNICAL] **2** *The actor has a stellar role in this film.* = very prominent (as might be expected of a star actor etc.)

stem[1] /stem/ noun, c. **1** *the stem of a plant* = the part of a plant to which leaves and flowers are joined **2** *a wine glass with a narrow stem* = a narrow, straight part of something that supports some other part **3** *a word stem* = the part of a word from which other words can be made by adding different endings to it [TECHNICAL]

stem[2] verb, t. or i. (**stemmed**) **1** *The doctors tried to stem the bleeding from the man's wound.*(t.)= to stop the flow of blood **2** *Most of our social problems stem from the lack of education.*(i.) = to happen as the result of

to stem the tide/flow *Most parents are sending their children to private schools. The government will have to improve its own schools if it wants to stem the tide.* = to prevent something negative from spreading

stench /stentʃ/ noun, u. or c. = a very strong and bad smell

sten•cil[1] /'stensəl/ noun, c. *We used a stencil to print these slogans on the wall.* = a piece of metal or plastic in which patterns or letters have been cut out, which can be used to paint or print the pattern or letters on some surface

stencil[2] verb, t. = to paint or print something on a surface by using a stencil

sten gun /'sten gʌn/ noun = a light automatic gun which fires bullets continuously when the trigger is pressed

ste•nog•ra•pher /stə'nɒgrəfəʳ/ noun, c. = a person who takes dictation in shorthand while someone is speaking and later types out what is dictated

sten•to•ri•an /sten'tɔ:riən/ adj. *The sergeant shouted at the soldiers in a stentorian voice.* = loud and powerful (referring to a person's voice) (literary)

step[1] /step/ noun, c. **1** *She walked with small, quick steps.* = the action of raising a foot and bringing it down again in a different place, so as to cause the body to move **2** *The garage was only a few steps away from the house.* = the distance covered in a single step **3** *If you climb these steps you will reach the bed-room.* = a flat, narrow surface, forming one part of a series of such surfaces, leading to a higher or lower level **4** *If you want to make chapatis, the first step is to mix the flour with a little water.* = the first action in a series of actions which one has to go through in order to produce a certain result

step[2] verb, i. (**stepped**) **1** *The boy stepped forward to receive the prize from the president.* = to move the body by raising a foot and putting it down again

S

somewhere else **2** *She stepped across the road to a neighbour's house.* = to walk a short distance (informal) **stepping stone** noun, c. **1** = a row of stones placed at a little distance away from each other, which one can walk on while crossing a stream **2** *He joined as a cashier in the bank, but this was only a stepping stone to a successful career. He retired as the managing director.* = something that leads to success or improvement (figurative)

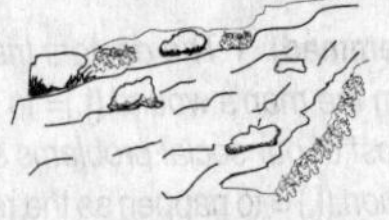
stepping stone

to step down = to give up a job or position **to step up something** = to increase the size or speed of some activity **to retrace one's steps** *We had to retrace our steps when we could not find the house.* = go back the same way by which one came **a step forward** *Educating the public about the seriousness of AIDS is a step forward in controlling the disease.* = an improvement **a step in the right direction** *Sohail's refusal to watch television because of the approaching examinations is a step in the right direction.* = a positive action which is likely to yield the expected results **step by step** *You cannot expect to learn a language overnight. You have to go step by step.* = slowly and in an orderly manner from one level to another

steppes /steps/ noun *the Siberian Steppes* = a large area of land without trees, specially in Russia or Central Asia

ster•e•o /'steriəʊ/ adj. *a stereo music system* = a tape recorder or other electronic instrument which produces sounds that seem to be coming from different places in the room (abbr. of 'stereophonic')

ster•e•o•scop•ic /steriə'skɒpɪk/ adj. *a stereoscopic picture* = a picture which seems to have depth, instead of being flat

ster•e•o•type /'sterɪətaɪp/ noun, c. *In Hindi films businessmen are always shown as dishonest people who make money by smuggling. But this is only a stereotype.* = a fixed set of ideas, generally believed to be true but often false, which people commonly have about something or someone, specially about the members of a group

ster•ile /'steraɪl/ adj. **1** = (of humans) unable to produce children **2** *sterile land* = unable to produce crops **3** *a sterile operating theatre in a hospital* = free from harmful bacteria **sterilize (sterlise)** verb, t. **1** *The instruments must be sterilized before the surgeon begins the operation.* = to make something free from germs **2** *These dogs have been sterilized.* = to make a person or an animal sterile (unable to produce young ones)

ster•ling[1] /'stɜːlɪŋ/ noun *This aircraft costs 50 million pounds sterling.* = the system of money used in Britain

sterling[2] adj. *He has sterling qualities as a leader and is therefore much respected.* = having very high value or quality

stern[1] /stɜːn/ adj. **1** *The teacher gave her students a stern look when she found them shouting in class.* = showing slight anger or displeasure **2** *a stern manager* = strict

stern[2] noun = the back part of a ship

ster•num /'stɜːnəm/ noun = the long, thick bone running down the middle of the chest, to which the ribs are attached (also **breast-bone**) [MEDICINE]

ste•roid /'stɪərɔɪd/ noun *The doctor is using steroids to treat my disease.* = a powerful chemical substance that is often used to treat certain diseases but can have a harmful effect on the body if taken in large quantities or for a long time [MEDICINE]

stet /stet/ verb = a sign used by a proof-reader (someone who is going through a book before it is printed in its final form) to say that something which was wrongly deleted or changed should be restored

steth•o•scope /'steθəskəʊp/ noun = an instrument used by a doctor to listen to the sound of a person's heart-beat

ste•ve•dore /'stiːvədɔːr/ noun, c. = a person whose job is to load or unload ships

stew[1] /stjuː/ noun, c. = a light dish made by cooking meat and vegetables together in a liquid, without using a lot of spices

stew[2] verb, t. = to cook into a stew

to be in a stew *The girls were in a stew because they had gone out without informing the hostel authorities.* = in a difficult situation (informal) **to stew in one's own juice** *I advised her to stop brooding over her misfortunes but she won't listen. She is determined to stew in her own juice.* = to keep on brooding over one's misfortunes or the mistakes one has made (informal, disapproving)

stew•ard /'stjuːəd/ noun, c. = a person who looks after the comfort of passengers on an aircraft or a ship or of guests in a hotel or restaurant

stick[1] /stɪk/ noun, c. **1** = a long, thin piece of wood **2** *a stick of chalk* = a long, thin piece of any material

stick[2] verb, t. or i. (**stuck**) **1** *Use glue to stick these pieces of paper together.*(t.) = to join things together using glue or some other substance **2** *Don't stick your hand out of the bus window.*(t.) = to push a long object through an opening **3** *I can't open this door. It has got stuck.*(i.) = to become fixed in position (informal) **4** *As a child we called my sister Ria 'Princess' and the name stuck.*(i.) = to stay or remain **sticker** noun, c. *The windscreen of his car is covered with stickers.* = a piece of paper or other material, on which a message or picture is printed, which can be stuck (fixed) to some surface **sticking plaster** noun, u. = a kind of bandage, made of cloth or other material, which sticks to a person's body and can be used to cover a wound **sticky** adj. **1** *The child's fingers are sticky with chocolate.* = covered with some thick liquid which sticks to a person's body **2** *The police is looking for you, but I will help you to get out of this sticky situation.* = difficult and dangerous **3** *When the rains come, Chennai becomes very sticky.* = humid (having a lot of moisture in the air) **4** *He was in a sticky situation when he missed the last train. He had to spend the night on the platform.* = unpleasant (informal)

to stick to something **1** *Let's stick to the plan we made and not change it.* = to not change a plan etc. **2** *In class we'll stick to English but outside the classroom, the children can stick to the use of Tamil.* = to keep doing something which has been decided on without changing it **to stick by someone** *She'll stick by her husband all her life.* = to be loyal to someone or something and not leave them **to stick at nothing** *They will stick at nothing to get the property.* = to not allow anything, even if it is not legal, to prevent one from doing something (informal, disapproving) **to stick it out** *She felt miserable working in a dusty office but she stuck it out for ten years.* = to face an unpleasant situation with courage and patience **to stick one's neck out** *No one liked the manager's plan, but they didn't have the courage to say so. Finally, I had to stick my neck out.* = to take a risk by saying or doing something, when others are afraid to do so **to stick to one's story** *We didn't believe his version of the incident, but he stuck to his story.* = to keep saying that something one said earlier is true, even if others doubt it (informal) **to stick up for someone** = to speak in support of someone (informal) **to be stuck with something/someone** **1** *Everyone else is going on the picnic, but I can't go. I am stuck with this homework.* = to be unable to give up something difficult or unpleasant that one has to do **2** *Rama is visiting us for the day. She is a terrible bore but I can't get rid of her. I am stuck with her.* = to be unable to get rid of a person whose company one doesn't enjoy **to get the wrong end of the stick** *This test is for adults, not children. You've got the wrong end of the stick!* = to understand something wrongly or differently (informal) **to stick in one's mind** *I have forgotten my school days, but the wonderful classrooms have stuck in my mind.* = to be remembered for a long time **stick it** *I cannot stick it any longer! How can she be so rude?* = to tolerate, bear **to stick fast to a belief** *In the old days people stuck fast to the belief that the sun went round the earth.* = to continue to hold on to a belief or an idea **to stick around** *Why don't you stick around? We are expecting Fred soon.* = to wait a little longer in the same place (informal, not respectful) **stick by (each other)** *They are childhood friends and will certainly stick by each other.* = to continue to support a friend, specially one who is in trouble

stick•ler /ˈstɪkləʳ/ noun, c. *Our new teacher is a stickler for discipline.* = a person who wants everyone to behave in a certain way or follow certain rules (informal)

stiff /stɪf/ adj. **1** *The box is made of stiff cardboard. You can use it to carry your books. // My fingers have become stiff because of the cold.* = not easily bent **2** *Our new neighbour is very stiff. He never smiles and doesn't like to mix with people.* = not friendly **3** *I will try to win the prize but the competition is going to be stiff.* = strong; difficult to deal with **4** *You will be forced to pay a stiff fine if you break the rule.* = more than one expects **stiffen** verb, t. *The tailor has put a lining inside the collar of the shirt to stiffen it.* = to make something stiff (hard), so that it will not bend or lose its shape easily **stiff-necked** adj. *a stiff-necked person* = stubborn and not willing to change one's mind **stiff upper lip** noun *He tries to keep a stiff upper lip though he has many problems.* = the ability to remain calm and not reveal one's feelings inspite of trouble or bad luck

sti•fle /ˈstaɪfəl/ verb, t. **1** *Someone dropped a burning cigarette on the carpet and started a fire but we were able to stifle it quickly.* = to prevent something from happening or growing **2** *It was so hot in the room that we felt stifled.* = to be unable to breathe properly because of the lack of fresh air

to stifle a yawn *The lecture was so boring that she was forced to stifle a yawn.* = to stop a yawn (so as not to let others know that one is feeling bored)

stig•ma /ˈstɪgmə/ noun, u. **1** *Not long ago there was a stigma attached to dancing as a profession. But now many girls are becoming dancers.* = a feeling of shame **2** = the central female part of a flower in which the seeds grow [BIOLOGY] (see pic under **flower**)

stile /staɪl/ noun, c. = steps which one has to climb in order to cross a fence or wall

sti•let•to /stɪˈletəʊ/ noun, c. (**stilettos**) = a long, narrow dagger used as a weapon **stiletto heels** noun, c. = a woman's shoes with very high and thin, pointed heels

still[1] /stɪl/ adj. **1** *The child is so restless that it cannot sit still even for a minute.* = without movement **2** *It was a hot, still day.* = without wind **3** *It was perfectly still inside the forest.* = quiet

still[2] verb, t. **1** *The mother rocked the baby in her arms to still its cries.* = to make quiet **2** *He tried to still the girl's fears by telling her some funny stories.* = to make someone calm

still[3] noun, c. = a photograph of a scene from a film

still[4] adv. **1** *It is 10 o'clock now and he is still sleeping.*

S

= up to now **2** *I went to meet him at 10 a.m. and found him still sleeping.* = up to that time **3** *I know he is busy; still, I must see him.* = even so **4** *Gold is costly now but will be still more costly next month.* = even **5** *I have still another joke to tell you.* = yet **still-born** adj. *a still-born child* = born dead **still life** noun, u. or c. = a painting of flowers, fruits or other lifeless objects

stilt /stɪlt/ noun, c. (usually plural) **1** *people walking on stilts* = one of a pair of long poles, with supports for the feet, which allow a person to stand and walk high above the ground **2** *a house built on stilts* = a set of poles supporting a house which is built above the ground or water

stilt•ed /ˈstɪltɪd/ adj. *He writes in a stilted style.* = a formal and unnatural style of speaking or writing (derogatory)

stim•u•late /ˈstɪmjʊleɪt/ verb, t. or i. **1** *The government is trying to stimulate trade by reducing taxes.*(t.) = to help or encourage something to grow or develop **2** *This book is sure to stimulate you.*(t.) = to make the mind more active and full of ideas **stimulating** adj. *a stimulating film* = helping to make the mind more active **stimulant** noun, c. *Coffee is a stimulant.* = a substance that makes the mind or body more active **stimulus** noun, c. (**stimuli**) **1** *The excellent monsoon should provide a stimulus to the economy.* = something that helps growth or activity **2** *All plants grow in the direction from which they receive light. Light acts as a stimulus for them.* = something that causes activity in a living thing [TECHNICAL]

sting[1] /stɪŋ/ verb, t. or i. (**stung**) **1** *A bee stung him in the arm.* = to cause a painful injury by making a small hole in the skin with a sharp, pointed part, through which some poisonous substance is pushed in (referring to an injury caused by certain insects, animals and plants) **2** *When I clean this wound with spirit, it will sting.* = to produce a sharp burning feeling **3** *He was stung by her words.* = to feel upset and angry by what is said (figurative)

sting[2] noun, c. *The scorpion carries a sting in its tail.* = a pointed part of an insect, animal or plant which is used to make a small hole in the skin of some human being or animal **sting ray** noun = a large, flat sea-fish with a long tail which carries a number of sharp, needle-like points or stings

stin•gy /ˈstɪndʒi/ adj. *Why are they so stingy? They have a lot of money.* = unwilling to spend money (derogatory)

stink[1] /stɪŋk/ verb, i. (**stank**, **stunk**) *The drain stinks as it is never cleaned.* = to have or to give out a strong, bad smell (informal)

stink[2] noun, u. *You can catch the stink of rotten fish from the fish market.* = a strong, bad smell **stinking** adj. *stinking rich* = extremely (rich) (strongly disapproving)

stint[1] /stɪnt/ noun, c. *He has just completed a 5-year stint in the army.* = a limited period of time spent in doing a particular job

stint[2] verb, t. or i. *He didn't stint on money to celebrate his brother's wedding.* = to provide or use a very small amount of something, which is not enough (generally used in negative sentences)

sti•pend /ˈstaɪpend/ noun, c. *The students receive stipends from the government.* = money paid as a kind of scholarship regularly to someone

stip•u•late /ˈstɪpjʊleɪt/ verb, t. *The customer ordered a new car, but stipulated that it had to be delivered within a week.* = to lay down a condition which must be fulfilled (formal) **stipulation** /stɪpjʊˈleɪʃən/ noun, u. or c. *The government is recruiting soldiers for the army, but the stipulation is that they must be at least 185 centimetres in height.* = a condition that must be fulfilled (formal)

stir[1] /stɜː/ verb, t. or i. (**stirred**) **1** *He put some sugar in his tea and stirred it with a spoon.*(t.)= to mix up a solid substance with a liquid by moving it around the liquid with a spoon or some other object **2** *The child stirred in her sleep.*(i.) = to move or to cause something to move slightly **3** *The leader's speech stirred the crowd to anger.* = to produce strong feelings **4** *He is trying to stir up trouble in the office.* = to cause trouble

stir[2] noun, c. **1** *Give the curry a stir.* = the act of moving liquid round (with a spoon etc.) **2** *My resignation caused a stir in the office.* = excitement **3** (American) *He landed in stir after he was caught stealing.* = jail (slang) **stir-fry** verb, t. = to cook something by frying it in a little oil and on high heat, by moving it around in the frying-pan **stirring** adj. *a stirring speech* = causing admiration or strong feeling

stir•rup /ˈstɪrəp/ noun, c. = a small D-shaped piece of metal on either side of a horse's saddle on which the rider of a horse can rest his/her feet

stitch[1] /stɪtʃ/ verb, t. **1** *The tailor is stitching the collar of the shirt.* = to sew (to join pieces of cloth together with the help of a needle and thread or a sewing machine in order to make a garment) **2** *The doctor had to stitch the wound with cat-gut.* = to join the edges of a wound together with a special kind of thread

stitch[2] noun, c. (**stitches**) **1** *The stitches in this dress have been made by a machine.* = a movement of a needle and thread through a piece of cloth, resulting in a piece of thread being fixed in place over the cloth **2** *She dropped a stitch while she was knitting a pull-*

over for me. = a turn of wool made around a knitting-needle **3** *The doctor had to put in six stitches to close the wound in his forehead.* = a piece of surgical thread used to close a wound **4** *He felt a stitch in his side.* = a sharp pain in the side of the body, often caused by running (informal) **5** *without a stitch on* = not wearing any clothes (used in negative sentences) (informal)

to have someone in stitches *Her funny jokes had all of us in stitches.* = to make someone laugh uncontrollably (by saying or doing something funny) **a stitch in time saves nine** *If you have problems with your homework, ask your teacher to help. Don't keep putting it off. Remember, a stitch in time saves nine.* = 'Deal with problems early before they get worse.'

stock[1] /stɒk/ noun, c. or u. **1** *We have just received a new stock of tea. We can sell you as much tea as you want.*(c.) = an amount or number of things kept for sale or use **2** *He has invested his money in company stocks.* = shares in a company, which one buys as an investment **3** *You should use chicken stock to make soup.*(u.) = a thick liquid made by boiling bones, vegetables etc. which can be used in cooking **4** = popularity **5** *She comes of good farmer stock. You can depend on her.* = the family from which a person comes (old-fashioned)

stock[2] verb, t. *This shop stocks paper.* = to keep a supply of something for sale or use

stock[3] adj. *a stock expression* = used very commonly **stock-broker** noun, c. = a person who sells or buys shares in companies **stock-exchange** noun, c. = a place where shares in companies are bought and sold (also **stock-market**) **stockist** noun, c. = a shopkeeper who keeps a supply of things that people buy **stockpile** noun, c. *a stockpile of nuclear weapons* = a large store of things, specially weapons, kept for possible future use **stock-still** adv. *He stood stock-still, trying to listen to the conversation inside the room.* = not moving at all **stock-taking** noun *The library is closed for stock-taking.* = a check or examination of the things that are supposed to be available in a place (e.g. the books in a library), to make sure if they are actually there **stocky** adj. *a person with a stocky build* = short, thick and strong

to build up a stock *The Food Corporation helps India build up a stock of foodgrains just in case the monsoon fails.* = to have a supply of something ready **to be the laughing stock** *He acted so foolishly that he has become the laughing stock of the entire office.* = a person who behaves in a foolish manner and is laughed at by everyone

stock•ing /ˈstɒkɪŋ/ noun, c. = a tight-fitting covering for a woman's leg, usually made of thin nylon or silk

stodg•y /ˈstɒdʒi/ adj. *He is such a stodgy person that no one wants to talk to him.* = dull and uninteresting; lacking imagination (derogatory)

sto•ic[1] /ˈstəʊɪk/ noun, c. = a person who never shows any emotion and does not complain when he/she has to suffer

stoic[2] adj. *a stoic attitude* = not complaining or showing any emotion (also stoical) **stoicism** noun = the belief that a person must not show any emotion or complain when suffering

stoke /stəʊk/ verb, t. *You will have to stoke the fire to keep it burning.* = to add coal or some other fuel to a fire so as to keep it burning **stoker** noun, c. = a person whose job it is to keep the fire in the boiler of a steam engine burning

to stoke up *She always reminds her brother of the unfair treatment he received as a child, just to stoke up his anger.* = to cause a feeling of anger etc. to grow in some/other person

STOL /stɒl/ abbr. of **Short Take-Off and Landing** an aircraft which needs little space for its take-off and landing [TECHNICAL]

stole[1] /stəʊl/ noun, c. = a kind of shawl which is wrapped around the shoulders of a woman

stole[2] verb, t. or i. = past tense of **steal**

stol•id /ˈstɒlɪd/ adj. *We thought he would smile when he received his award, but the stolid expression on his face never changed.* = showing little emotion or interest (slightly derogatory)

stom•ach[1] /ˈstʌmək/ noun **1** = the bag-like organ (working part) inside the body in which food is digested after it is eaten **2** = the abdomen (the front part of the body below the chest) **3** *He does not have the stomach for flying planes.* = the courage and determination needed to do something

stomach[2] verb, t. *I cannot stomach the kind of noisy programme that is being staged these days.* = to put up with, tolerate (often used with a negative meaning)

stomach ache noun = a pain in the stomach

stone[1] /stəʊn/ noun, u. or c. **1** *The wall is made of stone.*(u.)= the hard material of which rocks are made **2** *He threw a stone at the dog to drive it away.*(c.) = a small piece of rock **3** *He has stones in his kidney.* = a tiny piece of hard material which forms inside the body

stone[2] verb, t. *The angry crowd stoned the police jeep.* = to throw stones at something, usually in anger

Stone Age noun = the early period, many thousands of years ago, when human beings had not learnt the use of metals and made all their tools and weapons out of stone **stone-cold** adj. *stone-cold food* = very, very cold **stoned** adj. *The man was completely stoned when he came out of the bar.* = very drunk (informal) **stone dead** adj. = completely dead (informal) **stone's throw** noun, u. *The house is only a stone's throw away from the station.* = a very short distance **stonewall** verb, i. *The director*

S

stonewalled when he was questioned about the progress made by his department. = to block discussion by talking for a long time and refusing to answer questions **stoneware** noun, u. = pots, cups, plates etc. made out of a speciai kind of hard clay **stony** adj. **1** *stony ground* = full of stones **2** *He maintained a stony silence.* = showing unfriendliness and displeasure

stooge /stuːdʒ/ noun, c. = a person who follows some leader and obeys the leader's orders unquestioningly (informal, derogatory)

stool /stuːl/ noun, c. or u. **1** = a kind of low chair which has no back or arms (see pic under **chair**) **2** = (often plural, **stools**) solid waste matter passed out of the body [MEDICINE]

stoop[1] /stuːp/ verb, i. **1** *The door is so low that one has to stoop to pass through it.* = to bend the upper part of the body **2** *I never expected you to steal money from the students' fund. How could you stoop so low?* = to do something immoral or improper

stoop[2] noun, u. *He walks with a slight stoop.* = a position of the body in which the shoulders and back are always bent

stop[1] /stɒp/ verb, i. or t. (**stopped**) **1** *The train stopped at the station.*(i.) // *Please stop writing.*(t.) = to be no longer moving or doing something **2** *We were able to stop those boys from leaving.*(t.) = to prevent **3** *The rain has stopped.*(i.) = to come to an end **4** *We stopped at Kolkata for an hour on the way to Delhi.*(i.) = to pause or halt at a place

stop[2] noun, c. **1** *We worked for five hours without a stop.* = an act of stopping (not working) **2** *We waited for the bus at the bus stop.* = a place where a vehicle stops to allow passengers to get on or get off **stopcock** noun, c. = a valve which stops or allows the flow of liquid through a pipe **stopgap** noun *The Assistant Manager will look after the office as a stop-gap until a new Manager is appointed.* = something that meets a need for a limited period of time **stopover** noun, c. *We had a stopover at London on our way to New York.* = a short halt at a place, while travelling to some other place **stop press** noun = the last piece of news to be included in a newspaper, just as it is about to be printed **stop-watch** noun, c. = a watch which can be stopped and started again by pressing a button, and can be used to measure very short periods of time

store[1] /stɔːʳ/ verb, t. **1** *We have stored some rice and ghee for the wedding feast next month.* = to keep a supply of something for future use **2** *When winter is over, we will store our woollen clothes in a cupboard.* = to keep something in a special place when not in use

store[2] noun, c. or u. **1** *There is a store of vegetables in the fridge.* = a supply of something for future use **2** *We are going to a shoe store to buy shoes.* = a large shop **storekeeper** noun, c. = a shopkeeper **storeroom** noun, c. = a place where things are stored for future use

stores /stɔːz/ noun (always plural) = a supply of things for future use needed for a large group of people

sto•rey /'stɔːri/ noun, c. (**storeys**) *the second storey of the building* = a level or floor in a building

stork /stɔːk/ noun = a large white bird with long legs and a long neck and beak

storm[1] /stɔːm/ noun, c. **1** *The roofs of many houses were blown away by the storm.* = bad weather bringing strong winds and rain **2** *There was a storm of protest when the Director announced that the meeting had been cancelled.* = a show of strong feeling

storm[2] verb, t. *The police stormed the hotel in which the smugglers were hiding.* = to attack with force **stormy** adj. **1** *stormy seas* = having storms (strong winds) **2** *a stormy meeting* = full of expressions of anger and dissatisfaction

a storm in a tea-cup = a lot of worry over something that is not important

sto•ry /'stɔːri/ noun, c. (**stories**) **1** *I told my grandchild a story about a wicked giant.* = an account of events, often imaginary **2** *The reporter sent in a story for publication in the newspaper.* = an article or report written for a newspaper

stout[1] /staʊt/ adj. **1** *a stout person* = fat and heavy **2** *a stout stick* = thick and strong **3** *Our soldiers offered stout resistance to the enemy.* = brave and determined

stout[2] noun = a kind of strong beer (alcoholic drink) **stout-hearted** adj. *stout-hearted soldiers* = brave

stove /stəʊv/ noun, c. = a simple device which uses electricity, gas or kerosene to produce heat, generally for cooking

stow /stəʊ/ verb, t. *We stowed our clothes in suit-cases.* = to put or pack away neatly **stowaway** noun, c. = a person who hides on a ship or aircraft in order to get a free journey

strad•dle /'strædl/ verb, t. *straddle the horse* = to have a leg on either side of something

strafe /strɑːf/ verb, t. *Our aircraft strafed the enemy camp.* = to attack with heavy gun-fire from an aircraft [TECHNICAL]

strag•gle /'strægəl/ verb, i. **1** *His thick beard straggled all the way down to his chest.* = to grow or spread in an untidy way **2** *The elderly refugees straggled across the border with their belongings.* = to move slowly in small groups, away from the main group **straggler** noun, c. *Most of the birds had settled on the branches of trees, but a few stragglers* *were still flying.* = someone or something that remains behind the others in a group

straight[1] /streɪt/ adj. **1** *Join the points A and B with a straight line.* = not curved or bent; continuing in the same direction **2** *Make sure that the pictures hanging on the wall are straight.* = level; not sloping to either side **3** *His business deals are always straight.* = honest **4** *I must put everything in the house straight before everyone returns.* = tidy **5** = not a homosexual (opposite **gay**)

straight[2] adv. **1** *You will reach the station if you drive straight along this road.* = in a straight line, without turning anywhere **2** *I want you to go straight to bed.* = at once **3** *He was so drunk that he couldn't see straight.* = clearly **straighten** verb, t. *The picture is hanging crooked on the wall. Let me straighten it.* = to make something straight or to become straight **straightaway** adv. *You have been asked to meet him straightaway.* = at once (also straightway)

straight•for•ward /streɪt'fɔːwəd/ adj. **1** *He has told you to sweep the floor. That is a straightforward task.* = easy to do **2** *I like his straightforward way of doing business.* = direct and honest

to put the record straight *Mary thought I was angry with her but I was not, so I decided to put the record straight.* = to correct a wrong idea that someone has **to keep a straight face** *I don't know how she can keep a straight face and also tell us some of the funniest stories!* = to have a serious expression **to get something straight** *I am not going to help you, and that's final. You had better get this straight.* = to understand something clearly **to go straight** *He was once a criminal, but he has decided to go straight.* = to become honest after being a criminal

strain[1] /streɪn/ verb, t. or i. **1** *He strained his back while trying to lift a heavy box.*(t.) = to hurt some part of one's body through too much effort **2** *She strained her ears to hear what the old man was trying to say.* = to make a great effort to do something **3** *I am straining my resources by building this house.* = to stretch something beyond its limits **4** *He strained the liquid by pouring it out through a piece of thin cloth.* = to separate a liquid from any solid substance that may be in it by making it pass through tiny holes

strain[2] noun, u. or c. **1** *The office staff are under a lot of strain because of the conference next month.* = pressure or tension **2** *He has a strain in his back.* = damage to a part of the body caused by too much effort **3** *There is a strain in my relations with my neighbour after my dog bit him.* = a state of not being friendly **strained** adj. **1** *Relations between the two countries are somewhat strained.* = not friendly **2** *He looks strained after the rough time he has been through.* = showing the effects of working too hard or putting up with too many problems **strainer** noun, c. *a tea-strainer* = a tool used to separate a liquid from solids which may be present in it, having some net-like material fixed to its bottom **strenuous** /'strenjuəs/ adj. **1** *The doctor has advised me to avoid strenuous exercise.* = requiring a lot of strain (effort) **2** *The principal made strenuous efforts to improve the quality of teaching in the school.* = active

strait /streɪt/ noun, c. (usually in plural form **straits**) **1** *the Straits of Gibraltar* = a narrow stretch of water which connects two seas or oceans **2** *He is in difficult straits after he lost his job.* = a very difficult situation **straitjacket** noun, c. (**straightjacket**) **1** = a kind of coat that persons suffering from mental illness were made to wear in former times, which tied their arms down and prevented them from making violent movements **2** *Our economy will not grow unless the straitjacket of government controls is removed.* = something that prevents freedom or growth **strait-laced** adj. *They are very straitlaced and do not allow their children to read film magazines.* = very strict about morals

straits see **strait**

strand /strænd/ noun, c. **1** *a strand of hair* = a single thin thread or hair **2** *Let us walk along the strand.* = beach or shore (literary) **stranded** adj. *We were stranded in the middle of nowhere when our vehicle broke down.* = unable to get away from a difficult or unpleasant situation because of some inconvenience, such as lack of money or transport

strange /streɪndʒ/ adj. **1** *I lost my way when I was travelling to Bikaner and had to spend the night in a strange place.* = unknown or unfamiliar **2** *The man and the horse ate together in the stable. It was a strange sight.* = unusual and surprising **stranger** noun, c. **1** *The dog barks at strangers but not at persons he knows.* = a person who is unfamiliar or unknown **2** *I don't know the customs of these people as I am a stranger here.* = a person who is new to a place

stran•gle /'stræŋgəl/ verb, t. = to kill by pressing on the throat so as to prevent breathing **stranglehold** /'stræŋgəlhəʊld/ noun, c. **1** = a strong hold around the neck which stops a person from breathing **2** *A few oil-producing countries have a stranglehold on the world's supply of petroleum.* = almost total control over something, which gives one a great advantage (figurative)

stran•gu•late /'stræŋgjʊleɪt/ verb, t. or i. = to press some part of the body so tightly that the flow of blood or air is stopped **strangulation** /stræŋgjʊ'leɪʃən/ noun, u. *death by strangulation* = the act of killing someone by pressing the throat so

S

tightly that the flow of air is stopped

strap[1] /stræp/ noun, c. *He had to travel standing in the crowded bus, holding on to the strap.* = a long, narrow piece of leather, cloth etc. which is used to tie up or support something

strap[2] verb, t. (**strapped**) **1** *He strapped the bag after he had packed it.* = to close or tie up something (e.g. a bag) with a strap **2** *The doctor strapped up his leg.* = to tie a bandage around some part of the body **strapless** adj. *a strapless dress* = having no straps to support it (referring usually to a woman's dress) **strapped** adj. *The government had to close many schools as it is strapped for money.* = having little money **strapping** adj. *a strapping young man* = tall and strong

stra•ta /'strɑːtə/ noun = plural of **stratum** (see below)

stra•te•gy /'strætɪdʒi/ noun, c. (**strategies**) or u. **1** *The company has developed a new strategy to get customers.*(c.) = a plan for gaining success in some activity **2** *You can't win the war by just attacking the enemy. You have to use strategy.*(u.) = the art of planning in advance and doing different things to gain victory **strategic** /strə'tiːdʒɪk/ adj. *The chess player made a strategic move to win the match.* = done as part of a strategy (plan), specially in a war **strategist** /'strætɪdʒɪst/ noun, c. = a person who is very skilled in planning a strategy

strat•os•phere /'strætəsfɪəʳ/ noun = the upper part of the atmosphere (the air that surrounds the earth) [GEOGRAPHY]

stra•tum /'strɑːtəm/ noun, c. (**strata**) **1** = a layer (level) of earth or rock of a certain kind, above or below which there may be layers of a different kind **2** *a social stratum* = a class or group of people having a certain level of income, education etc. **stratify** verb, t. = to divide or arrange something in different strata (layers or levels) **stratification** /strætɪfɪ'keɪʃən/ noun, u. *the stratification of society* = the division or arrangement of something in different strata (layers)

straw /strɔː/ noun, u. **1** = the dried stems of plants of rice or other food grains, used to feed cattle or to cover the roofs of houses **2** = a small, thin tube made of paper or plastic, used for sucking up some liquid
the last straw (the straw that breaks the camel's back) *First, Ravi's pet dog died and then his mother fell ill. But when he lost his job, that was the last straw!* = the last of the problems in a series which makes one give up and lose hope

straw•ber•ry /'strɔːbəri/ noun = a kind of red, juicy fruit

stray[1] /streɪ/ verb, i. *The child strayed while he was going to school and got lost.* = to wander away from the right path (often figurative)

stray[2] noun, c. *This special hospital for animals has been set up to care for strays.* = an animal or child that has no home

stray[3] adj. **1** *a stray dog* = homeless **2** *He shared a few stray thoughts with us.* = random; not connected to other things of the same kind

streak[1] /striːk/ noun, c. **1** *She has a prominent grey streak in her black hair.* = a line or band which is different in colour from the surrounding areas **2** *He has a mean streak in his character.* = a particular quality (usually unpleasant) in a person which is different from the other qualities **3** *Our cricket team is going through a losing streak, but I am sure it will start winning again.* = a limited period during which something happens repeatedly

streak[2] verb, i. *The boy streaked across so fast that we couldn't catch him.* = to move very fast **streaker** noun = a person who appears without clothes at some public place (e.g. a sports stadium) in order to attract attention **a streak of lightning** *Did you see a streak of lightning across the sky just now? I am sure it is going to rain.* = a sudden burst of lightning

stream[1] /striːm/ noun, c. **1** = a small, narrow river **2** *a stream of visitors* = something flowing or moving continuously **3** *I would like to choose the fine arts stream after my schooling.* = a group of subjects that one has to study

stream[2] verb, i. **1** *The clouds streamed across the sky.* = to move fast in a continuous mass **2** *Blood streamed from the deep wound.* = to flow out with force **streamer** noun, c. = a long, narrow piece of coloured paper used as a decoration

stream•line /'striːmlaɪn/ verb, t. = to design a shape for something (e.g. a car or an aircraft) that allows it to move smoothly through air or water with very little disturbance or resistance **streamlined** adj. *a streamlined organization* = something which is designed to work smoothly

street /striːt/ noun, c. = a wide road inside a city or town, with shops and houses on both sides **street-car** = a tram (a vehicle running on tracks, like a train, along a street) **street-smart** adj. *a street-smart child* = clever and able to take care of oneself in all kinds of situations (generally approving)
the man in the street (the person in the street) *The man in the street expects the government of the day to improve the quality of life.* = the average person **streets ahead** *The computers they have in their office are streets ahead of ours.* = far better (informal)

strength /streŋθ/ noun, u. = the quality of being strong (see **strong**) **strengthen** = to make something strong or stronger (see **strong**)

strenuous see under **strain** (above)

stress[1] /stres/ noun, u. or c. **1** *Our cricket team was under great stress as many people expected them to win the championship.*(u.) = pressure on the mind as well as body causing serious discomfort **2** *An aircraft flying at a speed greater than that of sound has to overcome heavy stresses.*(c.) = the forces acting on an object which put pressure on it **3** *In his Independence Day speech, the President laid stress on self-reliance.* = the special importance or emphasis given to something **4** *You should put the stress on the second syllable of the word 'begin'.* = the force that one puts on a part of a word [TECHNICAL]

stress[2] verb, t. **1** *The teacher stressed the importance of regular study.* = to give special importance to something **2** *You should stress the first syllable in the word 'cataract'.* = to use greater force when speaking a part of a word **stressed** adj. *He feels stressed because of the nature of his work.* = under stress **stressful** adj. *The test which I had to go through was very stressful.* = causing stress (pressure on the body and mind)

stretch[1] /stretʃ/ verb, t. or i. **1** *The shoes feel tight now but they will stretch and become loose after you have worn them a few times.*(i.) = to become longer or wider or to cause something to become longer or wider **2** *This room has such a low ceiling that you can touch it easily if you stretch your arms.*(t.) = to extend something (to cause it to reach its full length or width) **3** *The Sunderban forest is so big that it stretches for hundreds of kilometres.* = to spread out

stretch[2] noun, c. or u. **1** *Give yourself a good stretch when you get out of bed every morning.* = an act of stretching the body (trying to make it reach its full length) **2** *This stretch of the road passes through a thick forest.* = an area or section of land or water **3** *He lived in the USA for a stretch of ten years.* = a continuous period of time **stretcher** noun, c. = a small, light bed made of canvas (thick cloth), with handles, in which a sick or injured person who is unable to walk can be carried

at a stretch *We worked for 12 hours at a stretch.* = continuously **by no stretch of imagination** *By no stretch of imagination can you call them poor.* = by no means **to stretch one's legs** = to walk around after sitting for some time (informal)

strew /struː/ verb, t. (**strewed**, **strewn**) *The guests at the wedding strewed rice and flower petals on the bride and bridegroom.* = to scatter or throw something in an irregular manner (literary)

stri•at•ed /straɪˈeɪtɪd/ adj. *a striated snake* = having narrow bands of different colours [TECHNICAL]

strick•en /ˈstrɪkən/ adj. *He was stricken with malaria last year.* = suffering from some illness, worry etc. (formal)

strict /strɪkt/ adj. **1** *The teacher is very strict with her students and expects them to be attentive in class.* = demanding obedience and not allowing people in one's control much freedom **2** *The judge is very strict in his interpretation of the law.* = exact **3** *She is a strict vegetarian.* = complete or total **strictest** adj. **1** = the most strict (person) **2** *It wasn't a story in the strictest sense of the word; it was a description.* = the most exact (meaning) **strictly** adv. **1** *She spoke to them strictly.* = in a strict way **2** *Strictly speaking, you shouldn't be allowed to attend this meeting as you are not a member.* = going by the rules

stric•ture /ˈstrɪktʃəʳ/ noun, c. *The High Court passed a stricture on the police for arresting an innocent person.* = the act of finding fault with someone for doing something wrong and criticizing the person strongly [TECHNICAL/LAW]

stride[1] /straɪd/ verb, i. (**strode**, **stridden**) *The general strode across the parade ground, followed by two junior officers.* = to walk with long steps

stride[2] noun, c. **1** *He crossed the hall with a few strides.* = a long step **2** *Sri Lanka has made great strides in Information Technology.* = advance or rapid progress (figurative)

to take something in one's stride *He has come across many hurdles in his life but he has always taken everything in his stride.* = to face problems calmly

stri•dent /ˈstraɪdənt/ adj. *The strident shouts of the people marching in procession drowned the sound of the music.* = loud and harsh (unpleasant to hear)

strife /straɪf/ noun, u. *Although the city looks peaceful now, there is strife among the people over political matters.* = trouble or violence (formal, literary)

strike[1] /straɪk/ verb, t. or i. (**struck**) **1** (t.) = to hit hard in order to hurt **2** *The American aircraft struck the caves in which the terrorists were hiding.*(t.) = to attack **3** *The workers are planning to strike for higher wages.*(i.) = to stop working **4** *He struck me as being very intelligent.*(t.) = to have an effect on someone **5** *The clock struck twelve.*(t.) = to show the time by ringing or chiming **6** *Your name has been struck off the list.*(t.) = to remove something that has been written or printed **7** *I struck a match to find my way in the dark.*(t.) = to produce a flame **8** *The solution to this problem struck me all of a sudden.*(t.) = to come to mind suddenly **9** *We had not dug very deep before we struck oil.* = to come suddenly in contact with **10** *I just hope we have some time before dengue fever strikes again.* = to happen (referring to a disease or something unpleasant)

strike[2] noun, c. or u. **1** *The workers are on strike.*(u.)= the act of stopping work or a period when work is

S

stopped because of some disagreement **2** *Our aircraft carried out a strike on the enemy position.*(c.) = attack **striker 1** = a person who takes part in a strike **2** = one of the important players in football whose responsibility it is to score goals (compare **stopper**)

to strike out *In her speech she struck out against smokers.* = to speak very strongly against something **to strike up (a conversation, a friendship)** = to start something interesting **to strike a balance** *You shouldn't sacrifice your home life for the sake of your work. You must learn to strike a balance.* = to be able to balance the different demands made on you **to strike at the roots of** *If we want to control the spread of AIDS, we must strike at the roots of the problem.* = go to the origin of a problem and remove it **to strike back** *If he attacks you, it doesn't mean that you have to strike back.* = to return an attack **to strike out on one's own** *When his partner left him, Mukesh decided to strike out on his own.* = to try to do something independently **to strike a pose** *I wish the photographer would take the picture naturally instead of asking us to strike a pose.* = to stand, sit etc. in a particular way for the camera **to strike gold 1** = to find gold (inside the earth) **2** = to have an idea which results in one's making a lot of money **to strike while the iron is hot** = to take action early, when the chances of success are high, rather than later when they are not likely to be good

strik•ing /'straɪkiŋ/ **1** *a striking picture // striking features* = specially interesting or attractive **2** *a striking person* = someone who is on strike

to be within striking distance *We were within striking distance of the city when our car had a flat tyre.* = to be very near a place

string[1] /strɪŋ/ noun, c. or u. **1** *The parcel had been tied with string.*(u.) = a number of threads twisted together and used to tie up something **2** *The strings of the sitar have to be tuned.*(c.) = a thin piece of wire used to produce sounds from a musical instrument **3** *The strings of the tennis racquet are loose.*(c.) = a length of nylon thread tied across the opening in the face of a tennis or badminton racquet **4** *She was wearing a string of pearls.*(c.) = a number of things joined together by a thread **5** *Our cricket team had a string of defeats in New Zealand.*(c.) = a number of similar events happening one after the other

string[2] verb, t. (**strung**) **1** *The beads of the necklace have to be strung.* = to join together with a string **2** *The tennis racquet will have to be strung.* = to replace the strings on a tennis racquet **stringed instrument** noun = a musical instrument such as a sitar or guitar, which uses strings to produce sounds

no strings attached *This scholarship is being awarded to you with no strings attached.* = without any conditions/ restrictions **to have someone on a string** = to be in a position of control where one can make a person do whatever one wants

strin•gent /'strɪndʒənt/ adj. *The government has introduced stringent laws to check smuggling.* = strict

strip[1] /strɪp/ noun, c. *He bandaged the wound with a strip of clean cloth.* = a narrow piece

strip[2] verb, t. or i. **1** *The electrician stripped the ends of the two pieces of wire and joined them together.*(t.) = to remove or take off the covering of something (e.g. the cotton or rubber covering of an electric wire) **2** *He stripped and got under the shower.*(i.) = to take off one's clothes (informal) **3** *The mechanic stripped the engine of the car.* = to open up an engine into its separate parts **stripper 1** = a chemical in liquid form which is used to remove old paint from walls etc. **2** = a person who takes off her or his clothes in a way which is sexually exciting, in order to entertain an audience (informal) **striptease** = a show in which a stripper (see above), generally a woman, takes part **cartoon strip** (also **comic strip**) = a row of cartoons (funny pictures) which tell a story

to strip someone of something *The officer was stripped of his rank as he was found to be incompetent.* = to take away a position given to someone, as a punishment

stripe /straɪp/ noun, c. *The tiger has black stripes on its yellow skin.* = a narrow band of colour on a background of different colour **striped** adj. *a striped shirt* = having stripes

strip•ling /'strɪplɪŋ/ noun, c. = a young man

strive /straɪv/ verb, i. (**strove**, **striven**) *You should strive to perfect your singing.* = to try very hard (literary)

stroke[1] /strəʊk/ verb, t. *The woman stroked her cat lovingly.* = to pass the hand gently over something, usually to show affection

stroke[2] noun, c. **1** *The woman gave her cat a loving stroke.* = the act of stroking (touching gently) **2** *The judge ordered 15 strokes with a whip as a punishment for the thief.* = a hit or blow to the body **3** *Tendulkar played a graceful stroke to square leg.* = an act of hitting the ball with a bat or racquet, in a game such as cricket or tennis **4** *She swam across the lake with powerful strokes.* = a movement of the arms in swimming **5** *He scribbled a note on the sheet of paper with a few strokes of his pen.* = a movement of a pen in writing **6** *suffer a stroke* = injury caused to a blood vessel in the brain because of high blood pressure **7** *The number of the house he lives in is 17 stroke 2 (17/2)* = a slanting line used in writing to show a division or separation

a stroke of luck = a piece of good luck **at one stroke** *The new law cancelled, at one stroke, the concessions that the farmers had been enjoying.* = in one single action **never/ not do a stroke of work** *I can't ask him to help. He* *never does a stroke of work!* = do no work at all **on the stroke of** *Cinderella had to rush back home on the stroke of twelve.* = punctually (at a stated time)

stroll[1] /strəʊl/ verb, i. *The old man strolled across the road to his neighbour's house.* = to walk slowly, without a particular purpose

stroll[2] noun, c. *Let us take a little stroll.* = a slow walk **stroller** noun, c. = a light, folding carriage in which a baby can be pushed along

strong /strɒŋ/ adj. **1** *He is so strong that he can pull a loaded truck with his teeth.* = powerful in body **2** *This old house, built of solid stone, is very strong.* = not easily damaged or broken **3** *a strong drink* = having a powerful effect **strongly** adv. **1** *We support the plan strongly.* = in a strong way **2** *I strongly believe that we should not let children watch too much television.* = used to stress something that is considered important **strong box** = a closed container in which valuable things are kept for safety **strong-minded** adj. = having great determination **stronghold** noun, c. *Varanasi is a stronghold of Sanskrit studies.* = a place where a particular activity is common **strong point** *He may not have brilliant ideas but his ability to work hard is his strong point.* = the best quality in a person **strong language** *I liked the book but it does have a lot of strong language!* = something spoken or written which contains a lot of swear-words and language which is not considered polite **a strong accent** *You can easily tell that he is a foreigner. He speaks Tamil with a strong accent.* = a way of speaking (in any language) which shows the influence of some other language (which is generally the speaker's mother-tongue) **to have a strong stomach for something** *They have a strong stomach for horror films.* = to be able to look at something which has violence etc without feeling upset **to be still going strong** *My friend is 96 and still going strong.* = to be in good health and leading an active life though old

stron•ti•um /'strɒntiəm/ noun = a kind of metal used to make fire crackers etc. [CHEMISTRY]

strop[1] /strɒp/ noun, c. = a narrow piece of leather on which a razor or knife is rubbed to give it a sharp edge

strop[2] verb, t. = to rub the edge of a razor or knife on a strop so as to make it more sharp

stroppy /strɒpi/ adj. *I wish you'd stop being stroppy and make this a pleasant occasion!* = behaving in an irritable and unpleasant manner (informal)

struc•ture[1] /'strʌktʃəʳ/ noun, c. or u. **1** *The new hotel will be a steel and glass structure.*(c.) = a building or other object made up of many parts **2** *We are studying the structure of the human brain.*(u.) = the arrangement of parts which make up some object

structure[2] verb, t. *You have not been able to structure your essay logically. The different parts of the essay are not connected to each other.* = to arrange or connect things together so that they form a whole **structural** adj. *The building suffered serious structural damage because of the earthquake.* = relating to the structure of something (the joining together of its parts)

strug•gle[1] /'strʌgəl/ verb, i. **1** *He has been struggling against poverty.* = to fight against someone or something **2** *He struggled against his attacker and was able to throw him off.* = to try one's best to get out of another's hold **3** *He has been struggling to understand this book.* = to make great efforts to do something

struggle[2] noun, c. *The police officer managed to overpower the thief after a hard struggle.* = a hard fight or a great effort

strum /strʌm/ verb, t. or i. (**strummed**) *He strummed a tune on his guitar.* = to play a tune on a musical instument with strings

strut[1] /strʌt/ verb, i. (**strutted**) *He strutted about proudly after his victory in the match.* = to walk proudly in a way which annoys the person watching (disapproving)

strut[2] noun, c. **1** *The roof of the bus is supported by struts.* = a long,thin rod, made of metal or wood, which supports something **2** *His proud strut to the stage was in bad taste.* = a proud way of walking

strychnine = a poisonous chemical substance, used in medical drugs in very small quantities

stub[1] /stʌb/ noun, c. *a cigarette stub // a ticket stub* = the short end of something which remains after it has been used or the main part torn out

stub[2] verb, t. (**stubbed**) *He stubbed his toe on a rock.* = to hurt one's toe by hitting it against a hard object

stub•ble /'stʌbəl/ noun, u. **1** *The fields are covered with stubble after the rice plants have been harvested.* = the short remains of plants above the ground after they have been cut **2** = the short, stiff hairs growing on a man's unshaven face

stub•born /'stʌbən/ adj. **1** *The child is so stubborn that he will not listen to anyone. He will do exactly what he wants to do.* = unwilling to change one's mind and generally unreasonable (derogatory) **2** *Our soldiers offered stubborn resistance to the enemy.* = determined and brave (not derogatory)

stub•by /'stʌbɪ/ adj. *stubby legs* = short and thick (derogatory)

stuck /stʌk/ verb, t. (see **stick**) **stuck-up** adj. *She is so stuck-up that she doesn't talk to her neighbours.* = proud (informal, derogatory)

stud[1] /stʌd/ noun, c. **1** *The thick wooden door of the old fort had large iron studs fixed to it.* = a thick iron nail with a large head **2** *The girl wore a diamond stud in her nose.* = a short piece of gold, usually holding one or more precious stones, worn through a hole in the nose or ear as a piece of jewellery **3** *The soles of his boots were covered with large studs.* = a piece of metal or hard rubber fixed to the sole (bottom) of a boot or shoe **4** = a man who is very active sexually (slang) Ⓖ

stud[2] adj. *a stud horse* = a male animal, specially a horse, that is used for breeding (producing young ones)

stud[3] verb, t. or i. (**studded**) *The sky was studded with stars.* = to cover with

stu•dent /ˈstjuːdənt/ noun *He is a student of Delhi University.* = a person who is studying at an educational institution e.g. a school, a college

stu•di•o /ˈstjuːdiəʊ/ noun, c. (**studios**) **1** *a film studio* = a place where cinema films are made, photographs taken by a professional photographer, video-or audio recordings made etc. with professional equipment **2** *an artist's studio* = a place where a painter works

stud•y[1] /ˈstʌdi/ verb, t. or i. **1** *He is studying law at the university.*(t.) = to spend time in learning a subject **2** *I can't play with you now as I am studying.* = busy in reading or doing other work related to school or college **3** *I will have to study the report before I can comment on it.*(t.) = to read and examine carefully **4** *Saras is in South America, studying the animals of the rain forest.* = to observe in order to understand something for research etc.

study[2] noun, u. or c. (**studies**) **1** *He has taken up the study of law.*(u.) = the act of studying (learning about) some subject **2** *He has published a number of studies on the Santhali language.*(c.) = a piece of research (something written on a topic or subject after a lot of study) **3** *The professor is in his study.*(c.) = a room in a house where one likes to read **studied** adj. *He gave a studied answer to the question.* = carefully thought out (formal) **studious** adj. *a studious child* = fond of study or always studying

stuff[1] /stʌf/ noun, u. **1** *This shirt is made of good stuff.* = material (informal) **2** *Carry all your stuff to the room upstairs.* = things in general (of different kinds) (informal) **3** *trekking stuff* = the equipment one needs for some activity (informal) **4** *Don't tell me you watch all that stuff on television!* = a way of referring to things of which one has a poor opinion (informal, disapproving) **5** *'What did you do in the holiday?' 'Stuff.'* = information you either don't want to give or are too lazy to give (very informal)

stuff[2] verb, t. **1** *We will stuff this pillow with some cotton.* = to fill up with some material **2** *The child stuffed himself with sweets.* = to eat as much as possible (disapproving) **stuffed** adj. **1** *stuffed potatoes* = having some kind of substance filled into it **2** *a stuffed bird* = an animal or bird which, after it is dead, is filled with materials and chemicals to preserve it **3** *The cupboard was stuffed with all kinds of clothes.* = completely full **stuffing** noun, u. *There is cotton stuffing inside the pillow.* = a material used to fill up something **stuffy** adj. **1** *The room has become stuffy. Please open the windows.* = having air which is not fresh **2** *His ideas on love are rather stuffy.* = old-fashioned **stuffed shirt** noun, c. = a person who pretends to be very important (disapproving)

to be stuffed *'Will you have some rice?' 'No thanks I'm stuffed.'* = to be very full (very informal) **Get stuffed!** *'You never seem to learn from your mistakes. How stupid can you be?' 'Get stuffed!'* = a rude expression used to say that you do not like what the other person has just said, and want him to shut up (slang) USE

stum•ble[1] /ˈstʌmbəl/ verb, i. **1** *He stumbled as he was coming down the stairs and almost fell.* = to lose one's balance because of a step badly taken while walking or running and almost fall **2** *He stumbled several times while reading out his speech.* = to stop or make a mistake while reading out something aloud

stumble[2] noun, u. or c. *He was able to regain his balance after his stumble.* = the act of stumbling **stumbling block** noun, c. *The Principal is trying hard to improve the school but the lack of funds is a stumbling block.* = something that prevents progress or action

stump[1] /stʌmp/ noun, c. **1** *The trees have been cut down but their stumps remain.* = the bottom part of a tree which remains in the ground after the tree has been cut down **2** *He lost both his legs in an accident but he can walk on the stumps.* = the remaining part of a limb which has been cut off **3** *The ball hit the middle stump.* = one of the three pieces of wood fixed to the ground, at which the ball is bowled in the game of cricket

stump[2] verb, t. **1** *His question was so unexpected that it stumped me.* = to leave one unable to reply **2** *Ganguly stepped out of the crease to hit the ball, missed and was stumped.* = to be given out (in cricket) when the wicket-keeper knocks down the stumps while the batsman is outside the crease (batting area) after trying to hit the ball

stun /stʌn/ verb, t. (**stunned**) **1** *The rider fell from the horse and was stunned.* = to become unconscious after being hit on the head or receiving a shock **2** *He was stunned when he heard that our team had lost.* =

to be shocked or greatly surprised by something **stunning** adj. *stunning looks* = causing great wonder and admiration (informal)

stunt[1] /stʌnt/ verb, t. *The lack of water has stunted the growth of these plants.* = to prevent the growth of something

stunt[2] noun, c. **1** *In this film you will see a number of exciting stunts, such as a man fighting a tiger with his bare hands.* = a dangerous act requiring great skill and courage **2** *In your speech, you made some grand promises but was that only a stunt?* = something said to attract attention but not meant sincerely (derogatory) **stuntman (stuntperson)** noun, c. = a person who is paid to perform stunts (dangerous actions) in films, in place of the actors

stu•pe•fy /'stju:pɪfaɪ/ verb, t. (**stupefied**) **1** *The beauty of theTaj Mahal stupefied me when I saw it for the first time.* = to make someone speechless with surprise or admiration (formal) **2** *The patient was in a stupefied state because the surgeon had given him some anesthetic to make him unconscious.* = to be unable to feel anything

stu•pen•dous /stju:'pendəs/ adj. *The dance competition attracted huge crowds and was a stupendous success.* = very great

stu•pid /'stju:pɪd/ adj. **1** = foolish; having a dull mind **2** *My car has a puncture again. It has those stupid radial tyres!* = an expression used to show annoyance or irritation (informal) **stupidity** /stju:'pɪdɪti/ noun, u. = the quality of being stupid

stu•por /'stju:pəʳ/ noun, u. *a drunken stupor* = the state of being unconscious, usually because of taking too much of some alcoholic drink

stur•dy /'stɜ:di/ adj. *You need sturdy shoes for climbing rocks.* = strong

stut•ter[1] /'stʌtəʳ/ verb, i. or t. *It is difficult to understand what he says as he stutters.*(i.) = to have difficulty in producing certain sounds while speaking (also **stammer**)

stutter[2] noun, u. *a bad stutter* = difficulty in producing certain sounds while speaking

sty /staɪ/ noun, c. (**sties**) **1** *a pig sty* = a small, low hut in which animals are kept **2** = an infection around the eyes that causes a small swelling to appear

style[1] /staɪl/ noun, c. or u. **1** *The Ashoka Hotel has been built in the Mughal style.*(c.) = the manner of doing something which is common at a particular time **2** *He spoke in a formal style.*(c.) = a particular manner of speaking or writing, depending mainly on the choice of words **3** *They live in great style.*(u) = spending a lot of money on expensive things in a manner that attracts attention or admiration **4** *Tight trousers are no longer in style.* = fashion (in clothes)

style[2] verb, t. **1** *His clothes are styled by a famous designer.* = to give a certain appearance or shape to something **2** *He styles himself the 'Management Guru.'* = to give a title to oneself or to someone else (not respectful, often humorous) **stylish** adj. *a stylish batsman* = doing things in an attractive manner **stylist** noun, c. **1** *a hair stylist* = a person who styles things (gives them a certain shape or appearance) **2** = a person who writes in an attractive style **stylize (stylise)** verb, t. *The gestures and expressions in Bharatnatyam dance are stylized.* = to represent (show) things not as they really are but in a symbolic and simplified manner

no longer in style *Brocade saris are no longer in style.* = out of fashion **not my style** *The colours are so flashy; this is just not my style.* = not according to one's liking (used of clothes or of one's way of approaching a problem)

sty•lus /'staɪləs/ noun, c. (**styluses**) **1** = a kind of large metal needle used, in former times, for writing on palm leaves or metal plates **2** = a small, thin needle used for playing records on a record-player (now rarely used)

sty•mie /'staɪmi/ verb, t. *My illness stymied my attempts to arrange a good dinner for my colleagues.* = to prevent (informal)

sty•ro•foam /'staɪərəfəʊm/ noun = a soft plastic material used as an insulator (to keep heat out) or as packing material

suave /swɑ:v/ adj. *Don't be taken in by his suave manners. He is not to be trusted.* = seeming to be very polite and polished in behaviour but not very sincere or honest

sub- /sʌb/ prefix meaning **1** under e.g. **sub•ed•i•tor** /sʌb'edɪtəʳ/ noun, c. = a person who works under the editor of a newspaper **2** below e.g. **sub-zero** /sʌb'zɪərəʊ/ adj. *sub-zero temperatures* = below 0 degrees **3** a part of e.g. **sub•cul•ture** /sʌb'kʌltʃəʳ/ noun, c. = the behaviour, customs etc. of a small group of people who form part of a larger group

sub•al•tern[1] /'sʌbəltən/ noun = a very junior officer in the army

subaltern[2] adj. *a subaltern culture* = under the control or influence of someone or something that is more powerful

sub•a•tom•ic /'sʌbə'tɒmɪk/ adj. *a sub-atomic particle* = smaller than an atom and forming a part of an atom

sub•com•mit•tee /'sʌbkə'mɪti/ noun, c. = a small group of persons that deals with a particular matter and forms part of a larger group (a committee)

sub•con•scious /'sʌb'kɒnʃəs/ noun = the part of the human mind that is not used deliberately to know or understand something

S

sub•con•ti•nent /ˈsʌbˈkɒnyɪnənt/ noun, c. *the Indian subcontinent.* = a large mass of land that forms part of a continent

sub•con•tract /ˈsʌbənˈtrækt/ verb, t. = to hire someone to do a part of some work which one has agreed to do

sub•divide /ˈsʌbdɪvaɪd/ verb, t. = to divide something that has already been divided

sub•due /səbˈdjuː/ verb, t. **1** *The Mughal rulers tried hard to subdue the Rajput kings but did not succeed. Most of them remained free.* = to conquer or defeat in order to control **2** *She had to subdue her tears.* = to keep under check **3** *After his defeat, he is somewhat subdued in his behaviour.* = less confident than before **4** *subdued lighting/music* = not too bright or loud

sub-human /sʌbˈhjuːmən/ adj. *The workers are living in sub-human conditions.* = less than human (very bad or poor)

sub•ject[1] /ˈsʌbdʒɪkt/ noun, u. **1** *Geography was my favourite subject at school.* = something that one studies as a branch of knowledge or a part of education **2** *The subject of his talk is 'Corruption in the army.'* = the topic **3** *In the sentence 'Prema likes sweets', the subject is 'Prema'.* = the noun or pronoun in a sentence that comes before the main verb and often refers to the 'doer' of some action [GRAMMAR] **4** *a loyal subject of the king* = a person who has to obey the ruler of the country, specially a ruling king or queen **5** *For my research I selected 50 subjects, who were school-children between the ages of 12 and 15.* = a person who is chosen for study in an experiment

subject[2] adj. **1** *The programme that has been announced is subject to change.* = can be changed if necessary **2** *The laws passed by the Parliament are subject to the President's approval.* = depending on **3** *a subject race* = ruled by someone else; not free

sub•ject[3] /sʌbˈdʒekt/ verb, t. or i. *Nowadays all passengers travelling by air are subjected to security checks.*(i.) = made to go through, often in a way that is not convenient or comfortable (formal) **subjection** noun, u. *They lived in subjection to their rulers.* = a state of being ruled by someone else **subjective** adj. *The decision of the judges who select the winner in a dance competition is generally subjective.* = influenced by personal feelings and therefore not likely to be very reliable (opposite **objective**)

sub•ju•gate /ˈsʌbdʒʊgeɪt/ verb, t. = to conquer and bring under one's control (used of rulers) (formal) [HISTORY]

sub•junc•tive /səbˈdʒʌŋktɪv/ adj. *In the sentence 'If he were to come here tomorrow, he would not find me', the verb 'were' is subjunctive.* = the form of a verb which shows that it is being used to express a possibility, a wish or hope and not a reality [GRAMMAR]

sub•let /sʌbˈlet/ verb, t. *As tenants we are not allowed to sub-let a house which we have taken on rent.* = to rent a property or a part of it, which one has taken on rent, to someone else

sub•li•mate /ˈsʌblɪmeɪt/ verb, t. **1** *In this poem, the poet tries to sublimate his love for a woman into a form of divine love.* = to change a natural feeling, such as love, into what is thought to be a higher or more refined kind of feeling or activity **2** = to change a solid substance into a gas by heating it and then changing it back into a solid, in order to make it more pure [CHEMISTRY] **sublimation** noun

sub•lime /səˈblaɪm/ adj. *sublime music* = very beautiful

sub•ma•rine /ˈsʌbməriːn/ noun = a kind of ship that can travel under the surface of the water

sub•merge /səbˈmɜːdʒ/ verb, t. *When a dam is built across this river, these villages will be submerged.* = to go under the surface of the water

sub•mit /səbˈmɪt/ verb, i. or t. (**submitted**) **1** *The wrestler threw his opponent on his back and the referee asked him to submit.*(i.) = to admit or accept defeat **2** *You have to submit your application before the end of the month.*(t.) = to send in; to offer something for a decision to be made by others (formal) **submission** noun, u. or c. **1** *an act of submission*(u.) = the act or state of accepting defeat **2** *The last date for submission of applications is 13 December.*(u.) = the act of offering something which will be analysed or judged and a decision taken **3** *The lawyer made a submission to the judge.*(c.) = a request or suggestion [LAW] **submissive** adj. *I expected them to put up a fight, but they were submissive.* = willing to accept defeat and to obey (sometimes disapproving)

sub•or•di•nate[1] /səˈbɔːdɪnət/ adj. *The High Court is subordinate to the Supreme Court.* = having a lower position than; bound to obey someone in a higher position

subordinate[2] noun, c. = a person who works with someone but in a lower position than them

subordinate[3] verb, t. *The interests of individuals must be subordinated to the interests of the whole nation.* = to give less importance to something than to something else (formal)

> **Usage** Other expressions are now preferred in place of **subordinate**. Some of these are 'my colleague (Nima)' // '(Nima) who works with me' // '(Nima), who assists me in my work'.

sub•poe•na /sə'pi:nə/ noun, c. = an order given to someone to attend a court of law [LAW]

sub•scribe /səb'skraɪb/ verb, i. or t. **1** *I subscribe to three newspapers.*(i.) = to pay money regularly in order to receive a magazine, newspaper etc. **2** *Each of us subscribed Rs 100 to buy a present for a colleague in the office.*(t.)= to give or pay money into a common fund (formal) **3** *My brother has changed his job three times this year. He does not subscribe to the belief that a rolling stone gathers no moss.* = to agree with or to support an idea (formal) **subscription** /səb'skrɪpʃən/ noun, u. *Have you paid your subscription for the club this month?* = money paid regularly for some product or service

sub•se•quent /'sʌbsɪkwənt/ adj. *In 1999 I was living in Mumbai, but in the subsequent year I moved to Delhi.* = following or coming after something else (formal) **subsequently** adv. *This used to be a school but was subsequently turned into a hospital.* = later; after some time (formal)

sub•ser•vi•ent /səb'sɜ:vɪənt/ adj. *Why must you be so subservient?* = always willing to obey and not having enough self-respect (derogatory)

sub•side /səb'saɪd/ verb, i. **1** *I had a swelling in the leg, but it has subsided now. // Has the violence subsided?* = to become less (referring to something unpleasant) **2** *We are afraid these old buildings may collapse as the soil has subsided after the rains.* = to sink to a lower level (formal)

sub•sid•i•a•ry[1] /səb'sɪdiəri/ adj. *In our factory project, the main objective is to create employment and the subsidary one is to make clothing from natural fibres.* = something that is less important than something else to which it is connected

subsidiary[2] noun, c. (**subsidiaries**) = a company which is owned and controlled by a larger company

sub•si•dize (subsidise) /'sʌbsɪdaɪz/ verb, t. *The supply of rice in many states is subsidized by the government. Each kilogram of rice costs the government Rs 5 but the buyer pays only Rs 2. The difference is made up by the government.* = to pay part of the cost of something that is sold to someone else, in order to keep its cost (to the buyer) less **subsidy** noun, c. (**subsidies**) or u. *The government provides a subsidy of Rs 100 on each bag of fertilizer, to make it cheaper for farmers.* = money paid, usually by the government, in order to make a product cheaper to buy

sub•sist /səb'sɪst/ verb, i. *When we were lost in the jungle we had to subsist on wild fruits for a week.* = to manage to live on a small amount of food or money (formal) **subsistence** noun, u. *money for subsistence* = staying alive with the least amount of food or money (formal) [TECHNICAL]

sub•soil /'sʌbsɔɪl/ noun, u. = the layer of earth below the surface

sub•son•ic /sʌb'sɒnɪk/ adj. *subsonic speed* = below the speed of sound (opposite **supersonic**)

sub•stance /'sʌbstəns/ noun, c. or u. **1** *Vinegar is a sour substance prepared from sugarcane*(c.) = material **2** *There is no substance in the report that they were caught stealing.*(u.) = truth **3** *I want only the substance of the chairperson's speech for my report.* = the main points, without any details **4** *She is a person of substance.* = wealth (literary)

sub•stan•dard /'sʌbstændəd/ adj. *It is quite clear that this house has been built with substandard materials.* = below average, not of an acceptable standard

sub•stan•tial /səb'stænʃəl/ adj. **1** *a substantial salary* = quite large **2** *Ever since the road was widened there has been a substantial increase in the flow of traffic.* = large enough to make a difference

sub•stan•ti•ate /səb'stænʃieɪt/ verb, t. *You will have to substantiate the charges you have made against the man before the police can arrest him.* = to prove; to support a statement with facts (formal)

sub•sta•tion /'sʌbsteɪʃən/ noun, c. *an electrical sub-station* = a place where electricity is converted from a higher voltage to a lower voltage before it can be used in homes etc.

sub•sti•tute[1] /'sʌbstɪtju:t/ noun, c. *The doctor has told me to avoid sugar. I am using saccharine as a substitute.* = something that can be used in place of something else or someone who takes the place of another person

substitute[2] verb, t. *You can substitute 2 for x and solve the problem.* = to use one thing in place of another

sub•tend /səb'tend/ verb, t. *In triangle ABC, side AB subtends an angle of 30 degrees.* = to have an angle opposite to it (referring to a side of a triangle) [TECHNICAL]

sub•ter•fuge /'sʌbtəfju:dʒ/ noun, u. or c. *I told my friend that there was a phone call for him. It was a lie but I had to use this subterfuge to pull him out of bed.* = a slightly dishonest trick used to get something that is considered necessary done (formal)

sub•ter•ra•ne•an /sʌbtə'reɪnɪən/ adj. *a subterranean river* = underground; existing below the surface of the earth [GEOGRAPHY]

sub•ti•tle /'sʌbtaɪtl/ noun, c. *The film was in Chinese but had English subtitles.* = words appearing on a cinema television screen to explain the meaning of something that is said in a different language

sub•tle /'sʌtl/ adj. **1** *The meaning of the poem is so* *subtle that it cannot be explained.* = delicate; not easy to understand or explain **2** *There is a subtle difference between the words 'huge' and 'enormous'.* = small but important **3** *a subtle mind* = clever and nothing fine things **subtlety** noun, u. or c. **1** *There is great subtlety in his ideas.*(u.)= the quality of being clever or difficult to understand **2** *I can't understand the subtleties of English grammar.*(c.) = the small details which are difficult to understand (somewhat literary)

sub•to•tal /'sʌbtəʊtl/ noun, c. = the number obtained by adding up a set of figures, which has to be added to some other number

sub•tract /səb'trækt/ verb, t. *If you subtract 3 from 7, the remainder is 4.* = to take away from a larger number **subtraction** noun = the act of subtracting [MATHEMATICS]

sub-trop•i•cal /sʌb'trɒpɪkəl/ adj. *Pune has a sub-tropical climate.* = almost like that of the tropics (places which are near the equator and therefore have a hot climate) [GEOGRAPHY]

sub•urb /'sʌbɜ:b/ noun, c. *Matunga is a suburb of Mumbai.* = an outer part of a city which is far away from the centre **suburban** /sə'bɜ:bən/ adj. *a suburban house* = belonging to a suburb

sub•vert /səb'vɜ:t/ verb, t. *The Naxalites are trying to subvert the government by arming the peasants and telling them to attack police stations.* = to work against a government or an established system

sub•ver•sive /səb'vɜ:sɪv/ adj. *subversive activities* = done with the intention of destroying or harming the government, a religion or an established system

sub•way /'sʌbweɪ/ noun, c. **1** = an underground railway system **2** = a path that passes under a road and allows pedestrians to cross the road safely

suc•ceed /sək'si:d/ verb, i. or t. **1** *He succeeded in growing the plants.* = to be able to do something that one planned or tried to do **2** *I expect her to succeed in life.* = to do well **3** *Jehangir succeeded his father Akbar to the throne.* = to follow; to be the next to take up a position **succeeding** adj. *Every succeeding generation thinks the previous generation was too old-fashioned.* = coming after another

suc•cess /sək'ses/ noun, u. **1** *I am delighted to hear of your success in the examination.* = the fact of being able to do what one had planned or tried to do **2** *He was a great success as a lawyer.* = a person who does well in life or in some profession **successful** adj. *a successful lawyer* = able to do well or to do what one had planned or tried to do **nothing succeeds like success** *If your first film proves to be a hit, people will love all your other films. Nothing succeeds like success!.* = 'A success often leads to even greater success.' **a success story** *The White Revolution which made India the world's largest producer of milk, is a great success story.* = something which proves to be a great success

suc•ces•sion /sək'seʃən/ noun, u. **1** *First Robin left the job, then Valsa, then four others in quick succession.* = the act of following something **2** *Salim changed his name to Jehangir after his succession to the throne.* = the act of following someone into a position **successive** adj. *I made cakes on two successive days, Thursday and Friday.* = coming one after the other **successor** noun, c. *The director will retire next week and hand over charge to his successor.* = the person who comes next into a certain position or office

suc•cint /sək'sɪŋkt/ adj. = expressed clearly and in a few words (approving)

suc•cour (succor) /'sʌkə^r/ noun, u. *I had no money for my business but my sister came to my succour by lending me some money.* = help given to someone who is in difficulty (formal, literary)

suc•cu•lent /'sʌkjʊlənt/ adj. *succulent fruits* = sweet and full of juice

suc•cumb /sə'kʌm/ verb, i. **1** *He had a serious accident last week and succumbed to his injuries.* = to die as a result of something **2** *At first I was quite determined not to eat the rich food in the restaurant, but it tasted very good and I finally succumbed to the temptation.* = to stop fighting against or resisting something

such /sʌtʃ/ det. **1** *She is always on time. I admire such people.* = of this kind **2** *He had cooked a number of dishes for us such as tandoori chicken and biriyani.* = for example **3** *They are such fans of Hindi music that they spend days listening to it.* = having some quality to an unusual degree **as such** noun *I don't have a job as such, but I work when I feel like it.* = in the exact sense (meaning) **such-and-such** det. *If he tells you he will pay back the money by such-and-such a day, you must believe him.* = a certain time, date etc. which is not named exactly **such-like** det. or pron. *This restaurant serves tandoori chicken, biryani and such-like.* = things of that kind (informal)

suck /sʌk/ verb, t. or i. **1** *The child sucked the juice through a straw.*(t.) = to draw or pull in some liquid into the mouth **2** *You should suck these cough lozenges slowly, not chew them.* = to keep something solid in the mouth and make it dissolve (melt away) slowly by moving it around with the tongue **3** *Waking up early in the morning sucks!*(i.) = is not pleasant (slang)

sucker noun, c. **1** *a blood sucker* = an animal that sucks something **2** *the sucker of a banana plant* = a young plant that grows out of the root or lower stem of an older plant [BIOLOGY] **3** *They are, looking for suckers whom they can cheat.* = a person who is easily cheated (American, slang)

suck•le /ˈsʌkəl/ verb, t. or i. **1** (t.)= to feed a baby or young one with milk from the mother's body **2** *The lion cubs were suckling.*(i.) = to suck milk from the mother's body **suckling** noun, c. = a very small human or animal baby which sucks milk from its mother (old-fashioned)

su•crose /ˈsu:krəʊz/ noun = the common form of sugar

suc•tion /ˈsʌkʃən/ noun, u. *A vacuum cleaner uses suction to suck up dust from the floor.* = the process of sucking or pulling up something by removing the air above it

sud•den /ˈsʌdn/ adj. *We were not prepared for the sudden downpour.* = happening unexpectedly and quickly, without any warning or information

all of a sudden *All of a sudden, they decided to move to Monghyr.* = happening all at once without any warning

suds /sʌdz/ noun (plural only) *soap suds* = small bubbles forming on the surface of water in which soap has been mixed

sue /sju:/ verb, t. or i. *We will sue the company for selling us a defective machine.*(t.) = to take someone to court for some loss or damage that he/she has caused

suede /sweɪd/ noun or adj. (*suede leather* = soft leather which is slightly rough to the touch and does not have a shine

suf•fer /ˈsʌfəʳ/ verb, i. or t. **1** *He suffered great pain when he was injured.*(t.) // *I am sorry to hear that you have been suffering.*(i.) // *They suffered a heavy loss in their business.*(t.) = to feel or experience pain, unhappiness, misfortune, loss etc. **2** *Are you suffering from typhoid?* = to have some illness or physical problem **suffering** noun, u. *It was a time of suffering, and I want to forget it.* = the experience of pain, unhappiness etc.

suf•fice /səˈfaɪs/ verb, i. *If you want to buy only fruit, the Rs 30 you have will suffice.* = to be enough for some purpose (formal) **sufficient** adj. *Rs 12 will be sufficient for a kilo of potatoes.* = enough (formal)

suf•fix /ˈsʌfɪks/ noun, c. *The word 'botheration' is formed from the word 'bother', by adding the suffix '-tion'.* = a letter or group of letters that is added to the end of a word to form a new word [GRAMMAR]

suf•fo•cate /ˈsʌfəkeɪt/ verb, i. or t. *You will suffocate if you keep a fire burning inside this room, with all the doors and windows closed.* = to die or suffer because of lack of air **suffocating** verb *It's suffocating to be sitting in this crowded room where there is no ventilation. I would rather be outside.* = to feel uneasy because of lack of air

suf•frage /ˈsʌfrɪdʒ/ noun, u. = the right to vote in an election

suf•fuse /səˈfju:z/ verb, t. *The clouds were suffused with the colours of the setting sun.* = to spread through something (literary)

sug•ar[1] /ˈʃʊgəʳ/ noun, u. = the sweet white or brown substance obtained from the juice of plants such as sugarcane, beet etc.

sugar[2] verb, t. *Have you sugared the pudding?* = to add sugar **sugarcane** noun = a tall plant from the juice of which sugar is made

sug•gest /səˈdʒest/ verb, t. or i. **1** *They were thinking of a place to hold the next meeting and I suggested the Park Hotel.* = to mention something for other people to consider (think about) **2** *The redness in your eyes suggests that you may have fever.* = to show indirectly **3** *The sight of a rabbit running through a meadow suggested an idea for a well-known children's book.* = to put an idea into a person's mind **suggestion** noun, c. or u. **1** *We will accept your suggestion and hold the next meeting at the Park Hotel.* = something that is suggested **2** *We have agreed to have a friendly match with the opponent at your suggestion.* = the act of suggesting something **suggestible** adj. *a very suggestible person* = easily influenced by what others suggest **suggestive** adj. **1** *This classical raga is suggestive of the coming of the rains.* = bringing a particular idea or feeling to the mind **2** *a suggestive dance* = bringing thoughts of sex to the mind

su•i•cide /ˈsu:ɪsaɪd/ noun = the act of killing oneself **suicidal** /suɪˈsaɪdəl/ adj. **1** *a suicidal tendency* = having the desire to commit suicide **2** *a suicidal policy* = unwise and likely to cause harm to one or to an organization (figurative)

suit[1] /su:t/ noun, c. **1** = a set of clothes, usually consisting of a jacket (coat) and trousers (or a skirt, if it is meant for a woman), often made out of the same cloth **2** = a full set of playing cards **3** *He has filed a suit in court.* = a law case

suit[2] verb, t. **1** *The time of the meeting does not suit me as I will be busy at that time.* = to be convenient or acceptable **2** *This pink sari does not suit you.* = to look good on someone

sui•ta•ble /ˈsu:təbəl/ adj. *We have found a suitable person to work with us as a computer operator.* = of the right kind; having the right qualities or skills

suit•case /ˈsu:tkeɪs/ noun, c. a large container, usually made of leather or plastic material, in which clothes and others things can be carried during a journey (see pic under **luggage**)

suite /swi:t/ noun, c. **1** *a hotel suite* = a set of rooms in a hotel **2** = a set of different pieces of furniture or fittings for a room **3** *a suite of dances* = a number of dances etc. which are usually performed during every programme

sui•tor /'su:təʳ/ noun, c. = a man who wishes to marry a certain woman (old-fashioned)

sulk[1] /sʌlk/ verb, i. *He can't always have what he wants. Let him sulk.* = to be in a bad mood and refuse to smile or talk in order to let someone know that you are unhappy about something (derogatory)

sulk[2] noun, c. *He went into a sulk.* = the state of sulking (showing unhappiness by refusing to talk etc.)

sul•len /'sʌlən/ adj. **1** *The little boy was sullen and angry with his mother.* = bad-tempered and refusing to smile or speak **2** *The sky looks sullen. There may be a storm coming.* = dark and unpleasant

sul•ly /'sʌli/ verb, t. (**sullied**) *The river has been sullied by the discharge from the drains.* = to make something dirty or impure (formal, literary)

sul•phate /'sʌlfeɪt/ noun *copper sulphate* = a salt (chemical) produced when some chemical reacts with sulphuric acid [CHEMISTRY]

sul•phur /'sʌlfəʳ/ noun = a chemical that is yellow in colour and has a strong smell **sulphuric acid** /sʌl'fjʊərɪk 'æsɪd/ noun = a powerful acid (a liquid chemical that can damage the things on which it falls) containing sulphur **sulphurous** /'sʌlfərəs/ adj. *sulphurous gases rising from a volcano* = containing or smelling of sulphur [CHEMISTRY]

sul•ta•na /sʊl'tɑ:nə/ noun = a seedless light brown variety of dried grape, used in sweets and cakes

sul•try /'sʌltri/ adj. *sultry weather* = hot and humid (with a lot of wetness in the air)

sum[1] /sʌm/ noun, c. **1** *I had to spend a large sum of money on my medical treatment.* = an amount of money **2** *Can you do this sum which our maths teacher gave us for homework?* = a simple mathematical problem **3** *The sum of 5 and 7 is 12.* = total

sum[2] verb, t. (**summed**) *The teacher summed up the Principal's speech.* = to state the main points of a speech or piece of writing

sum•ma•ry[1] /'sʌməri/ noun, c. *The teacher gave us a summary of the poem.* = a statement of the main points of a speech or piece of writing

summary[2] adj. *The judge carried out a summary trial.* = done suddenly, without delay and without going into details (referring to the way in which justice may be done in a court of law) **summarize (summarise)** verb, t. *Can you summarize the report?* = to make a summary of a speech or piece of writing

sum•mer /'sʌməʳ/ noun = the hottest season of the year **summery** adj. *Although it is not summer yet, the weather is getting summery.* = like summer (informal)

sum•mit /'sʌmɪt/ noun, c. **1** *We reached the summit of the mountain after a difficult climb.* = the top of a mountain **2** *This book was the summit of her achievement as a writer.* = the highest point **3** *a meeting of the summit* = the top political leaders of a country

sum•mon /'sʌmən/ verb, t. **1** *The judge summoned the accused persons to the court.* = to order someone officially to come (specially to a court of law) [LAW] **2** *A meeting has been summoned.* = to call or request people to come for a meeting etc. **summons** noun (always plural) *I have received a summons from the court.* = an official order to appear in a court of law [LAW]

sump /sʌmp/ noun, c. **1** = an underground tank in which water is stored **2** = the bottom part of an engine which holds a supply of oil, to make the engine run more smoothly

sump•tu•ous /'sʌmptʃʊəs/ adj. *a sumptuous dinner* = very grand and expensive

sun[1] /sʌn/ noun = the star which gives light and heat during the day and around which the earth moves

sun[2] verb, t. (**sunned**) *Let's sun ourselves on the beach.* = to sit or lie in the sunlight, so as to receive the sun's heat **sun-baked** adj. **1** *sun-baked bricks* = hardened by the heat of the sun **2** *the sun-baked plains of India* = receiving a lot of heat from the sun **sun-bathe** verb, i. = to lie or sit in the sunlight, so as to receive the sun's heat **sunbeam** noun = a narrow band of light from the sun **sunburn** noun, u. = damage to the skin caused by sitting or lying too long in strong sunlight **sundial** noun = an instrument used in former times to tell the time of the day from the moving shadow of a pointer **sun-flower** noun = a large yellow flower from which oil is produced **sun-glasses** noun (always plural, used with 'a pair of') = dark glasses used to protect the eyes from strong sunlight **sun god** noun = the god represented by the sun (in the religions of ancient Greece and Rome as well as India, Egypt and some other countries) **sunrise** noun = the time early in the morning when the sun is first seen in the sky **sunrise industry** noun, c. = a new industry which is growing and becoming more important than the older industries **sunset** noun = the time when the sun begins to disappear from the sky, bringing night **sunspot** noun, c. = a small, dark area on the surface of the sun which can be seen through a telescope **sunstroke** noun = fever caused by too much heat from the sun **sun-tan** noun = the turning of the skin (in a white man or woman) into a brown or dark colour, which is considered healthy, as a result of lying or sitting in strong sunlight **sunny** adj. **1** *a sunny verandah* = receiving a lot of sunlight **2** *a sunny temperament* = cheerful **sunnyside up** adj. = (an egg) fried in such a way that the yolk (yellow liquid inside the egg) remains liquid, forming a kind of bag on top of the egg

under the sun *Nowhere under the sun would you find such delicious mangoes.* = anywhere in the world, wherever one may go (used in negative sentences only)

sun•dae /'sʌndeɪ/ noun, c. = a sweet dish made by adding chocolate, fruits, nuts etc. to icecream

Sun•day /'sʌndi/ noun = the day of the week which comes between Saturday and Monday and is usually a day of rest

sun•dry /'sʌndri/ adj. *Keep some money for sundry expenses.* = miscellaneous (of several different kinds)

sunk•en /'sʌŋkən/ adj. *sunken cheeks* = at a lower level than the surrounding parts or areas

su•per /'su:pə^r/ adj. *That's a super idea!* = very good, (informal)

super- /'su:pə:/ prefix meaning **1** above e.g. **su•per•im•pose** /su:pərɪm'pəʊz/ verb, t. *If we superimpose a map of India over that of Russia, you can see how big Russia is.* = to put something, specially a picture, over or on top of something else, so that both can be seen **2** greater than e.g. **superhuman** /su:pə'hju:mən/ adj. *He was able to reach the top of Mt Everest by a superhuman effort.* = much greater than is possible for an ordinary human being

su•per•an•nu•ate /su:pər'ænjʊeɪt/ verb, i. = to retire or stop working after reaching a certain age

su•perb /su:'pɜ:b/ adj. *a superb piece of writing* = of the highest quality

su•per•charg•er /'su:pətʃɑ:dʒə^r/ noun = a part fitted to the engine of a car, truck or aircraft which increases the power of the engine

su•per•cil•i•ous /su:pə'sɪliəs/ adj. *a supercilious manner* = thinking oneself to be better than others

su•per-con•duc•tor /su:pəkən'dʌktə^r/ noun = a substance (usually a metal or a mixture of different metals) which allows electricity to pass through it with no resistance (does not check the flow of electricity at all), specially at a very low temperature

su•per•du•per /su:pə'du:pə^r/ adj. *a super-duper musical hit* = very good or very successful (informal)

su•per•ego /su:pər'i:gəʊ/ noun = one of the three parts into which the mind is thought to be divided, which tells us whether an action is right or wrong [TECHNICAL]

su•per•fi•cial /su:pə'fɪʃəl/ adj. **1** *He has only a superficial knowledge of computers. He hardly knows anything about them.* = not deep; only on the surface (disapproving) **2** *Don't worry. It's only a superficial injury.* = affecting only the top layers of the skin; not deep, therefore not serious

su•per•flu•ous /su:'pɜ:flʊəs/ adj. *Good athletes should have no superfluous fat on their bodies.* = extra or unnecessary

su•per•in•tend•ent /su:pərɪn'tendənt/ noun, c. *the superintendent of the hostel* = the person in charge of something

su•pe•ri•or[1] /su:'piəriə^r/ adj. **1** *This car is superior to the other one. It has a more powerful engine but uses less fuel.* = better than **2** *a superior person* = of a higher rank or position

superior[2] noun, c. *He respects his superiors.* = a person having a higher rank than someone else **superiority** /su:pɪərɪ'ɒrɪti/ noun, u. = the quality of being better than someone or something **superiority complex** noun = the belief, for which there is usually no reason, that one is better than others

su•per•la•tive /su:'pɜ:lətɪv/ adj. **1** *'Best' is the superlative form of 'good'.* = the form of an adjective which refers to the highest degree of comparison [GRAMMAR] **2** *Kajol gives a superlative performance in this film.* = of the highest quality

su•per•man (-woman) /'su:pəmæn/ noun, c. (**supermen**) (also a trademark) = a person who has much greater powers of the body and mind than an ordinary human being

su•per•mar•ket /'su:pəma:kɪt/ noun, c. = a very large shop in which many kinds of things are sold and where the customers have to serve themselves; a self-service market

su•per•nat•u•ral[1] /su:pə'nætʃərəl/ adj. *In very ancient times, people believed that a solar eclipse was a supernatural event.* = something which is above the laws of nature and is believed to be caused by gods, spirits etc.

supernatural[2] noun *He is a strong believer in the supernatural.* = the existence of gods, spirits, fairies etc.

su•per•no•va /su:pə'nəʊvə/ noun = a very large and bright star [PHYSICS]

su•per•nu•me•ra•ry /su:pə'nju:mərəri/ noun, c. or adj. = a person with no fixed duties, who is working in addition to the usual or required number (formal)

su•per•pow•er /'su:pəpaʊə^r/ noun, c. = a country with very great political, economic and military power

su•per•sede /su:pə'si:d/ verb, t. *This new rule for admission to the club supersedes the earlier rule.* = to replace something (formal) [LAW]

su•per•son•ic /su:pə'sɒnɪk/ adj. *supersonic aircraft // supersonic speed* = travelling at a speed greater than that of sound

S

su•per•sti•tion /suːpə'stɪʃən/ noun, u. or c. *Many people have the supersition that if a cat crosses your path, you will have bad luck.* = a belief that is not based on scientific thinking or reason and is generally connected with luck, magic, spirits etc. **superstitious** /suːpəstɪʃəs/ adj. *a superstitious person* = a believer in superstitions

su•per•struc•ture /'suːpəstrʌktʃər/ noun, u. *The new building has a very impressive superstructure.* = the upper parts of a building, ship etc. which rise above the base (the lower parts)

su•per•tank•er /'suːpətæŋkər/ noun, c. = a very large tanker (ship) that can carry oil or some other liquid or gas

su•per•vise /'suːpəvaɪz/ verb, t. or i. *He has been asked to supervise the arrangements for the meeting.* = to look after or be in charge of some activity **supervision** noun, u. *The meeting has been arranged under his supervision.* = the act of supervising (looking after) something/someone

su•pine[1] /'suːpaɪn/ adv. *He lay supine on the ground.* = in a flat position, on one's back (literary)

supine[2] adj. **1** *The beach is crowded with supine bodies.* = lying flat on the ground **2** *He attacked the committee for its supine acceptance of the new proposal.* = weak; not showing enough firmness

sup•per /'sʌpər/ noun = the last meal of the day, usually taken in the evening

sup•plant /sə'plɑːnt/ verb, t. *Typewriters have been supplanted by computers in this office.* = to take the place of (disapproving)

sup•ple /'sʌpəl/ adj. *Yoga keeps our bodies supple.* = able to bend or move easily

sup•ple•ment[1] /'sʌplɪment/ verb, t. *I get a small pension after retirement and supplement it by working part-time in a school.* = to add to something, in order to increase it or make it more complete

supplement[2] noun, c. **1** *You should take some vitamin supplements as you are not getting enough vitamins in your food.* = something that adds to or completes something else **2** *a newspaper supplement* = extra pages given out with a newspaper, magazine, book etc. **supplementary** /sʌplɪ'mentəri/ adj. **1** *a supplementary examination* = additional (in addition to the main thing) **2** *a supplementary angle* = an angle which, when taken together with another angle, makes up a total of 180 degrees [GEOMETRY]

sup•pli•cant /'sʌplɪkənt/ noun, c. *The emperor gave alms to supplicants each morning.* = a person who begs or asks for something, especially from God (formal, old-fashioned)

sup•ply[1] /sə'plaɪ/ verb, t. *This river supplies water to the whole city.* = to provide (give or bring) something that is needed

supply[2] noun, u. or c. **1** *When we went to Ladakh, we carried a large supply of medicines.*(c.) = a stock (amount) of something that is needed **2** *The government has stopped the supply of medicines to this hospital.*(u.) = the action or the system that provides something which is needed **supplier** noun, c. = a person or a company that sells something **supplies** noun (always plural) *Our supplies have been cut off because of the floods.* = the things that one needs and uses

to be in short supply *The relief workers have complained that although the government has given flood victims a lot of help, medicines are in short supply.* = not easily available **to cut off a supply** *With all the feeder lakes almost running dry this season, the corporation has cut off the water supply to the city on alternate days.* = to stop the supply of something

sup•port[1] /sə'pɔːt/ verb, t. **1** *These concrete pillars support the roof of the building.* = to bear (carry) the weight of something, to prevent it from falling **2** *I have to support a large family on my income.* = to look after all the needs of someone **3** *I support the demand of everyone in this office for better working conditions.* = to encourage or help

support[2] noun, u. or c. **1** *The roof of this building is very heavy. It needs more support.*(u.) // *We are putting up some additional supports for the roof.*(c.) = something that carries the weight of something else and prevents it from falling **2** *We have decided to withdraw our support to this club.* = encouragement and help **supporter** noun, c. = a person who encourages or helps a political party etc. **supportive** adj. *The school is very supportive of my efforts to improve the library.* = providing encouragement and help

sup•pose /sə'pəʊz/ verb, t. **1** *She is late for our meeting. I suppose she has been held up by the heavy traffic.* = to consider or imagine, sometimes in a displeased way, that something is likely **2** *Isn't he supposed to speak at this meeting?* = to remind someone that something had been planned or arranged, and should be done as expected **supposedly** adv. *He is supposedly the leader of the group.* = as believed by most people, but not necessarily true (disapproving) **supposition** /sʌpəʊ'zɪʃən/ *Your supposition that he was sincere in the speech he made may not be correct.* = something that one supposes (thinks to be likely) (formal)

sup•press /sə'pres/ verb, t. *We suppressed the news by refusing to meet the press.* = to stop something from being known

sup•pu•rate /ˈsʌpjʊreɪt/ verb, i. *The wound in my leg got infected and began to suppurate.* = to form pus (thick white or yellowish liquid that forms inside a wound) (referring to a wound) (formal)

su•pra /ˈsuːprə/ adv. *Refer to paragraph 2 (supra)* = above (describing the position, in a book or piece of writing, of something that is being referred to) (formal)

supra- prefix meaning 'above' or 'beyond' e.g. **supranational** = going beyond the boundaries of a country

su•preme /suːˈpriːm/ adj. **1** *When a soldier dies in battle, his family makes the supreme sacrifice.* = the highest or greatest in importance **2** *Music gives me supreme pleasure.* = of the highest or best kind (informal) **the Supreme (Being)** noun = God **supremacy** noun, u. *She was the best tennis player in the world, but now her supremacy is being challenged by younger players.* = the state of being supreme (the greatest) **Supreme Court** noun = the highest court in the country **supremo** noun = a ruler who has unlimited power

sur•charge /ˈsɜːtʃɑːdʒ/ noun, c. *We have to pay a surcharge of one rupee, in addition to the usual charge of Rs 2.50, on every unit of electricity that we use.* = money that has to be paid for something (usually to the government) in addition to the usual charge or payment

surd /sɜːd/ noun, c. *The square-root of 5 is a surd.* = a mathematical quantity that cannot be expressed as a whole number [MATHEMATICS]

sure[1] /ʃʊəʳ/ adj. **1** *I am sure that he is honest because I have proof of his honesty.* = certain; having no doubt about the truth of something **2** *He is sure to win the election.* = bound to happen

sure[2] adv. *'Will you sing for us?' 'Sure, I will.'* = certainly **sure-fire** adj. *a sure-fire winner* = certain to happen **sure-footed** adj. *a sure-footed mule* = able to walk in difficult places without slipping or falling **surely** adv. *It will surely rain this afternoon.* = without doubt **sure thing** interjec. *'Will you come with me?' 'Sure thing!'* = of course (an expression of willingness to do something) (informal) **surety** noun, c. (**sureties**) or u. **1** *I need a loan from the bank. Will you stand surety for me?* = a person who agrees to take the responsibility for the good behaviour of another person, her/his returning a loan etc. **2** *He was asked to deposit a surety of Rs 20,000.* = bail; money given to make sure that a person will appear in court

surf[1] /sɜːf/ noun, u. **1** *The children were paddling about happily in the surf.* = the foam (air bubbles) formed when sea-waves strike against the shore

surf[2] verb, i. **1** *Let us go surfing.* = to ride over the waves coming towards the shore, using a surf-board (see **surfboard**) **2** *to surf the Net* = to go from one web-site to another while using the Internet, without spending too much time at one web-site (see **Internet** and **web-site**) **surf-board** noun, c. = a long, narrow piece of wood or plastic on which one stands while riding across the tops of waves as they move towards the shore

sur•face[1] /ˈsɜːfɪs/ noun, c. **1** *The surface of the earth is hard and rocky.* = the topmost or outermost part or layer of an object **2** *There were dead leaves floating on the surface of the water.* = the top of a body of water **3** *There isn't enough surface here for us to work on.* = the surface or available area for one to use while working e.g. in a kitchen

surface[2] verb, i. **1** *The diver surfaced after a few minutes.* = to come to the surface of a body of water **2** *The road is being surfaced.* = to cover the surface of something with some material, so as to create a new surface **3** *Everyone thought he was honest, but many unpleasant facts have surfaced after the police investigation.* = to become known (referring to something unpleasant or negative that was not known earlier) **4** *It's so cold, I don't feel like surfacing in the morning!* = to come out of bed (humorous) **surface mail** = post that is carried over land or sea, not by air **surface tension** = the natural forces in the molecules of a liquid that hold them together at the surface [PHYSICS]

on the surface *On the surface he seems to be a nice person, but once you get to know him well, you will find he has many faults.* = judging from the things one can observe (see) easily, which do not give a complete picture **to rise to the surface** = see **surface**[2], meaning 3

sur•feit /ˈsɜːfɪt/ noun, u. *I am tired of watching cricket on television. We are getting a surfeit of cricket.* = too much of something (formal)

sur•ge[1] /sɜːdʒ/ verb, i. *The crowd surged forward to catch a glimpse of the great leader.* = to move or rush forward with force

surge[2] noun, u. **1** *There has been a surge in the sale of motor cars.* = a sudden and great increase **2** *He felt a surge of anger.* = a sudden rise of some feeling **3** *A surge in the voltage burnt out all the electric gadgets.* = a sudden increase in the flow of something (e.g. an electric current, or some liquid)

sur•geon /ˈsɜːdʒən/ noun, c. = a person who treats disease by operating on the body (cutting open the body to remove a diseased part or repair, replace a defective one) **surgery** noun **1** = the branch of medicine which deals with the treatment of disease through operations **2** *You will need surgery as you are suffering from appendicitis.* = an operation performed by a surgeon **3** *a doctor's surgery* = a room

S

where a doctor sees patients **surgical** adj. *a surgical knife* = connected with surgery

sur•ly /ˈsɜːli/ adj. *He was in a surly mood and refused to talk or smile.* = bad-tempered and showing bad manners (disapproving)

sur•mise[1] /səˈmaɪz/ verb, t. *I surmise that you are new to this country.* = to guess (formal)

surmise[2] noun, c. or u. *Your surmise is quite correct.* = guess

sur•mount /səˈmaʊnt/ verb, t. *I had to face many difficulties when I started my business, but I was able to surmount them.* = to overcome (get over) a difficult situation (formal)

sur•name /ˈsɜːneɪm/ noun, c. = the family name (the last part of a person's name, which one shares with other members of the family) (also **last name**)

sur•pass /səˈpɑːs/ verb, t. *Gangubai was a great singer, but many believe her daughter Kesarbai surpassed her.* = to be better or to do better than someone else **surpassing** adj. *Noor Jehan was a woman of surpassing beauty.* = very great (literary)

sur•plus[1] /ˈsɜːpləs/ adj. *This house has ten rooms but we need only two. We should rent out the surplus rooms.* = extra; more than what is needed

surplus[2] noun, u. **1** *The harvest was so good that we had a large surplus after meeting all our needs.* = something that is left over after use **2** = profit after tax [BUSINESS]

sur•prise[1] /səˈpraɪz/ verb, t. **1** *When we returned from Dinapur, my neighbour surprised me by cooking us a hot meal.* = to cause a feeling of wonder by doing something unexpected **2** *The police surprised the gang of robbers as they were about to rob a bank.* = to catch or attack someone when he/she is not prepared

surprise[2] noun, u. or c. **1** *Imagine my surprise when I heard you had applied for admission to a medical college. I thought you wanted to be a teacher.*(u.) = the feeling of wonder caused by some unexpected event **2** *This morning I met an old friend whom I had not seen for 20 years. It was a real surprise.*(c.) = an unexpected event, usually pleasant

surprise[3] adj. *We are planning a surprise welcome for them.* = something done without the other person's knowledge

sur•real•ism /səˈrɪəlɪzəm/ noun = the twentieth century practice of using art (specially painting) or literature to represent things in an unnatural or unreal way, as they might appear in a dream **surrealist** noun = a painter or writer who makes use of surrealism **surrealistic** /sərɪəˈlɪstɪk/ adj. *a surrealistic painting* = influenced by surrealism [TECHNICAL]

sur•ren•der /səˈrendəʳ/ verb, i. or t. **1** *When the enemy soldiers found they were sure to be killed, they surrendered.*(i.) = to accept defeat and stop fighting **2** *The king was defeated and surrendered his throne to the enemy.* = to give up control or possession of something

sur•rep•ti•tious /sʌrəpˈtɪʃəs/ adj. *a surreptitious meeting* = done secretly and stealthily for a dishonest purpose (formal)

sur•ro•gate /ˈsʌrəgeɪt/ adj. *I lost both my parents when I was a baby and was brought up by surrogate parents.* = substitute (someone or something that takes the place of another) (formal)

sur•round /səˈraʊnd/ verb, t. **1** *You can't enter the building as a high wall surrounds it.* = to be all around (on all sides of) something **2** *The police surrounded the house in which the thieves were hiding.* = to take up positions all around someone so that he/she cannot escape **surrounding** adj. *a surrounding wall* = found around (on all sides of) something **surroundings** noun (always plural) *He lives in pleasant surroundings.* = everything that is found near or around a place

sur•veil•lance /sɜːˈveɪləns/ noun, u. *They have been under police surveillance because of their suspicious activities.* = close watch kept on someone who may be a criminal

sur•vey[1] /səˈveɪ/ verb, t. **1** *We surveyed the countryside and finally decided to camp on the bank of a river nearby.* = to examine something as a whole, without going into details **2** *The government is surveying all the schools in the state to find out how many trained teachers there are.* = to carry out an examination or study of something for a particular purpose

survey[2] /ˈsɜːveɪ/ noun, c. *The government is doing a survey of the schools in the state.* = an official examination or study, carried out for some purpose **land survey** noun = a measurement of the land, in order to prepare maps and government records

sur•vive /səˈvaɪv/ verb, i. or t. **1** *She was badly injured in the accident, but the doctors think she will survive.*(i.) = to not die after going through an experience which threatens a person's life (e.g. an accident, disease etc.) (formal) **2** *This building survived the earthquake.*(t.) = to not be destroyed (in a fire, earthquake etc.) **survival** noun, u. *We had given up hopes of his survival.* = the fact of surviving **survivor** noun, c. **1** = a person who goes on living after coming close to death **2** *I am quite sure Ali will manage beautifully on his own. After all, he is a survivor.* = a person who can take care of himself or herself in difficult or dangerous situations, sometimes by using means which are not admired (sometimes derogatory) **to survive on** *With the cost of living going up by the month, I don't know how much longer we can survive on a fixed monthly income.* = to continue to live and be able to satisfy one's needs in spite of financial problems

sus•cep•ti•ble /sə'septɪbəl/ adj. **1** *She is highly susceptible to colds.* = likely to suffer from (formal) **2** *He is susceptible to pressure.* = easily influenced by (formal)

su•shi /'suːʃi/ noun = a Japanese dish prepared from raw fish and rice

sus•pect[1] /sə'spekt/ verb, t. **1** *Someone has stolen my ring. I am not sure whom to suspect.* = to have the feeling, without being sure or having enough proof, that someone is guilty (has done something wrong) **2** *According to the report, 200 new homes were built in this village after the earthquake. I suspect that this is not quite true.* = to doubt something that you are told **3** *She seems to be putting in a lot of hard work, but I suspect her motives.* = not to trust someone or something

sus•pect[2] /'sʌspekt/ noun, c. *A bank was robbed last night. The police have arrested two suspects.* = a person who is thought to be guilty of some crime **suspicion** /sə'spɪʃən/ noun, u. or c. **1** *I am not sure who stole our plans but our suspicion is that it may have been one of our rivals.*(u.) = the feeling that someone may be guilty (may have done something wrong) **2** *His strange behaviour aroused my suspicions.*(c.) = the fact of not trusting someone **suspicious** adj. **1** *Her behaviour looked suspicious.* = causing doubt or lack of trust **2** *I am suspicious of his behaviour.* = not trusting someone

to suspect someone of doing something *They are suspected of passing on some secret documents to a neighbouring country.* = to think that someone has done something that he or she should not have, though there is no proof

sus•pend /sə'spend/ verb, t. **1** *This bridge is suspended from the two towers which you see on each side of the river.* = to make something hang from a support **2** *We have decided to suspend you as you have been found to be dishonest.* = to take away someone's job or to prevent someone from taking part in some activity for a time, because of something wrong that he or she has done **3** *The law requiring all drivers of two-wheelers to wear helmets has been suspended, but it may be re-introduced next year.* = to make something ineffective for a time (formal) **suspenders** noun (only plural) = a pair of narrow bands of elastic material which pass over one's shoulders and hold up the trousers (also **braces**)

sus•pense /sə'spens/ noun, u. *There was suspense in the room as the Chairperson got up to announce the name of the winner.* = the feeling of excitement or anxiety that one has when waiting for something to happen, not knowing what it will be **suspension** noun, u. **1** = the act of taking away someone's job for a time **2** *The suspension of talks between the two leaders has created a fear that there may be trouble.* = the act of stopping something for a time (formal) **3** *the suspension of a car* = the parts that connect the wheels of a car to the body and reduce the discomfort caused by travelling over rough roads **4** = a liquid mixture consisting of very small pieces of solid that are mixed in the liquid but have not combined with it [CHEMISTRY] **suspension bridge** noun = a bridge that is not supported by pillars in the middle but is hung from steel cables (thick wires) fixed to towers at each end

to keep someone in suspense *A nurse came out to announce that a baby had been born, but did not tell us if it was a girl or a boy. She wanted to keep us in suspense!* = to keep someone in a state of excitement or anxiety by not giving out some information **The suspense is killing me.** *I wish they would tell us soon whether Shama had a baby boy or girl! The suspense is killing me!* = a way of saying that one is anxious because of not knowing what will happen or has happened (informal)

sus•tain /sə'steɪn/ verb, t. **1** *You should drink some milk every day. The food you are getting is not enough to sustain you.* = to nourish (make someone healthy and strong) (formal) **2** *The first half of the film was interesting, but the director was unable to sustain the interest till the end.* = to keep up something **3** *He sustained a serious injury in the accident.* = to suffer harm or loss (formal) **4** *Objection sustained!* = used by a judge to say that someone was right to object to the opponent's statement or argument [LAW] **sustenance** /'sʌstənəns/ noun, u. **1** *Milk will give you sustenance.* = the ability to remain strong and healthy (formal) **2** *The judge ordered the man to pay his old mother Rs 500 every month for her sustenance.* = money provided to keep a person alive

su•ture[1] /'suːtʃər/ noun, c. = a stitch made by a surgeon to join together the edges of a wound [MEDICINE]

suture[2] verb, t. = to join together or stitch up the edges of a wound

swab[1] /swɒb/ noun, c. = a small piece of cotton used to clean a wound or to take a small amount of some substance from the body for testing [MEDICINE]

swab[2] verb, t. (**swabbed**) = to clean with a swab **swab down** = clean, especially the floors of a ship

swad•dle /'swɒdl/ verb, t. *He swaddled the baby in a warm shawl.* = to wrap a baby in a piece of cloth (old-fashioned)

S

swag•ger[1] /ˈswægəʳ/ verb, i. *The young soldier swaggered across the parade ground.* = to walk proudly with a swinging movement, in order to show off one's importance (disapproving)

swagger[2] noun, u. *He walked with a swagger.* = a proud, swinging movement, indicating over-confidence

swal•low[1] /ˈswɒləʊ/ verb, t. **1** *The doctor told the girl to swallow the tablets he had given her, and not to chew them.* = to cause some liquid or solid substance to move down the throat towards the stomach by using the muscles of the throat **2** *I am not going to swallow this insult.* = to accept something unpleasant or painful patiently **3** *She swallowed her anger and kept calm.* = to hold back one's negative feelings

swallow[2] noun, c. **1** *He took a swallow of the strong drink.* = a small amount of some liquid that is swallowed **2** = a kind of small bird

hard to swallow *I find his story a little hard to swallow.* = difficult to believe (informal) **to swallow one's pride** *We knew how fiercely independent he was, but he had to swallow his pride and ask some of his relatives to help him pay the hospital bill.* = to be forced to do something that one would not normally do as it would hurt one's self-respect

swamp[1] /swɒmp/ noun, c. = a piece of land that is always covered with water

swamp[2] verb, t. **1** *The village was completely swamped when the flood came.* = to be covered with a large amount of water; to be flooded **2** *The actor was swamped with telephone calls from her fans after her new film was released.* = to receive such a large quantity of something that one is unable to deal with the situation; to be flooded with something **swampy** adj. *swampy ground* = like a swamp

swan /swɒn/ noun = a large white bird with a long neck which lives near the water **swan-song** noun, c. *This film proved to be Lalita Pawar's swan-song. She died a month after it was released.* = the last performance given or the last piece of work produced by an artist

swank[1] /swæŋk/ verb, i. *They love to swank by showing off their expensive cars to visitors whenever they get the chance.* = to behave or speak in a manner intended to show one's importance and attract other people's attention; to show off (informal, disapproving)

swank[2] noun, u. *When he talks to you about his wonderful adventures, it is nothing but swank.* = proud talk or behaviour that is intended to attract the attention of other people **swanky** adj. *He has a swanky office.* = fashionable and luxurious (informal)

swap[1] /swɒp/ verb, t. *My friend and I have decided to swap motorcycles. She likes my bike, and I am very fond of hers.* = to exchange (informal)

swap[2] noun, c. *You can have my car and I will take yours. That's a fair swap.* = an exchange

swarm[1] /swɔːm/ noun, c. **1** *a swarm of bees* = a large group of insects moving (usually through the air) together **2** *a swarm of tourists* = a large group of people (informal)

swarm[2] verb, i. *When Sachin Tendulkar arrived, hundreds of his admirers swarmed around him.* = to move together in a crowd

to be swarming with *The zoo was swarming with holiday makers.* = to be very crowded (with people or animals)

swar•thy /ˈswɔːði/ adj. *a swarthy complexion* = dark in colour (somewhat derogatory)

swas•ti•ka /ˈswɒstɪkə/ noun = a religious symbol, in the form of a cross with each of its arms bent at 90 degrees, which is used by Hindus and was also used by Hitler in Germany for his Nazi party

swastika

swat /swɒt/ verb, t. (**swatted**) *He swatted a fly with a newspaper rolled up to form a stick.* = to hit an insect with a flat object in order to kill it (informal)

swatch /swɒtʃ/ noun, c. (**swatches**) = a small piece of cloth cut out of a larger piece and used as a sample (example) of something that one needs

swath /swɒθ/ noun, c. *The mower cut a swath across the lawn.* = a line or area that has been cut (usually across a patch of grass) by a machine

swathe /sweɪð/ verb, t. *His head was swathed in bandages.* = to cover or wrap with cloth

sway[1] /sweɪ/ verb, i. or t. **1** *The branches of the trees swayed in the wind.* = to swing from side to side **2** *Your tears cannot sway me. I have made up my mind to go.* = to influence; to cause someone to change his or her mind

sway[2] noun, u. *Queen Elizabeth held sway in England at the time when Akbar was the emperor of India.* = political power or control (formal, literary)

swear /sweəʳ/ verb, t. or i. (**swore, sworn**) **1** *As a soldier, I have sworn to protect the freedom of my country.* = to make a promise to do something **2** *The witness swore that he would tell the truth and nothing but the truth.* = to make a formal declaration in a court of law in support of a statement **3** *The driver of the car in front swore at me angrily when I sounded the horn.* = to use language that is not used in polite conversation **swear words** noun = abusive or obscene words that are avoided in ordinary conversation (shown in this dictionary by the symbol USE)

to swear by *Most students swear by Dr Rao's coaching classes. They believe that with his training they are sure to* *find a place on a professional course.* = to have great confidence that something will work (informal) **to swear (someone) in** *The newly appointed governor was sworn in yesterday.* = to make someone who has been appointed to an important position make a promise in front of a gathering to say he/she will be loyal to the country

sweat[1] /swet/ noun, u. *Have you been running? Your body is covered with sweat.* = liquid which comes out of the body through tiny openings in the skin, after some exercise (informal) (also **perspiration**)

sweat[2] verb, i. **1** *He was sweating after the game of football.* = to give out sweat from the body **2** *The walls are sweating.* = to show liquid on the surface **sweaty** adj. *sweaty clothes* = covered with sweat **sweat-band** noun = a narrow elastic band worn around the forehead by tennis players etc. to prevent sweat from running into the eyes **sweat pants** = loose trousers made of soft (not stiff) cloth, generally cotton, for sports activities (also **sweats**) **sweater** noun, c. = a knitted woollen garment worn around the upper part of the body **sweat gland** noun = an organ (working part) in the body, lying under the skin, which produces sweat **sweat-shop** = a factory in which people are expected to work long hours in unpleasant conditions, for a very low salary

to sweat it out **1** *I know you are not happy with your job, but just sweat it out until you find something better.* = to carry on doing something in spite of its being unpleasant **2** *They are sweating it out in the field, practising for the sports day.* = to do hard physical exercise or work **no sweat** *'I'm so sorry, but could you bring all the books to my house tonight?' 'Sure, no sweat.'* = used to mean that something is no trouble and that you are willing to do it (informal) **to break out into a sweat** = to get very frightened or nervous suddenly (informal) **to be (or get into) a sweat about something** = to worry about something (informal)

sweep[1] /swi:p/ verb, t. or i. (**swept**) **1** *The floor is dirty. Let's sweep it clean.*(t.)= to clean a surface by removing dust or other things lying on it, using a broom or brush **2** *The flood water swept away many of the houses on the banks of the river.* = to carry away with force **3** *He never walks into a room, he sweeps in!*(i.) = to move quickly and with energy and confidence

sweep[2] noun **1** *She gave the floor a sweep.* = an act of sweeping **2** *In the film we saw last night the hero pushed away the men who were blocking his path with just a sweep of his arm!* = a powerful movement of the arm **3** *The police are carrying out a sweep of the area in an attempt to find the burglar.* = a search carried out over a large area **sweeper** noun, c. **1** = a person who is paid to keep a place clean by sweeping it regularly ('Cleaner' is the preferred term now.) **2** = a player, in the game of football or hockey, who is expected to be very active in the forward line as well as in defence [SPORTS] **sweeping** adj. **1** *The government will introduce sweeping changes in the system of education.* = relating to many different things and having a powerful effect **2** *You should not make such sweeping remarks unless you are sure of your facts.* = too general and made carelessly, without being sure of the facts (disapproving) **sweepstake** noun = a form of gambling in which the winner gets all the money that has been collected from bets

to sweep somebody off their feet = to make a person feel attracted to one strongly in a romantic way **to sweep something under the carpet** *Our company is facing many problems but the report does not mention them. Everything has been swept under the carpet.* = to hide unpleasant facts

sweet[1] /swi:t/ adj. **1** *Honey tastes sweet.* = having a taste like sugar **2** *sweet music // a sweet smell* = pleasing to the senses (the sense of hearing,smell, taste etc.) **3** *a sweet child* = lovable

sweet[2] noun, c. = food which has a sweet taste and is usually eaten at the end of a meal **sweeten** verb, t. = to make something sweet by adding sugar to it **sweetener** noun, u. or c. = a substance such as sugar which is added to something to make it sweet **sweetheart** noun, c. = a word used to address someone whom one loves (e.g. one's child, one's boyfriend) **sweetmeat** noun, c. = a food used as a sweet (old-fashioned) **sweet potato** noun = a kind of vegetable that is the fleshy root of a plant and has a sweet taste **sweet tooth** noun = a great fondness for sweets

sweet talk *Don't give me this sweet talk. I don't believe you!* = flattery; insincere talk intended to please someone (informal) **to sweet-talk someone into doing something** *He sweet-talked me into doing some work for him.* = to persuade someone to do something through flattery or pleasing words

swell[1] /swel/ verb, i. or t. (**swelled, swollen**) **1** *When the doctor saw him, the injured leg had swelled and was painful.*(i.) = to become larger and more round than before **2** *The excellent sale of cars has swelled the company's profits.*(t.) = to cause an increase in quantity or number

swell[2] noun, u. *We can't go for a swim in the sea today because there is a heavy swell.* = the presence of large waves in the sea **swelling** noun, u. or c. *There's a swelling in my foot because of an infection.*(c.) = a part of the body which has become swollen **swollen** adj. *He has a swollen neck.* = increased to a size greater than usual **to get a swollen head** noun *That is one of the best essays I have read, but don't get a swollen head!* = to have a

S

great sense of one's own importance, intelligence etc.
to swell with pride *Our hearts swelled with pride when we sang the college anthem.* = to feel very proud

swel•ter /ˈsweltəʳ/ verb, i. *There were no fans in the classroom and the boys had to swelter in the heat.* = to suffer because of heat (usually damp heat which caused sweating) **sweltering** adj. *We can't play football on such a sweltering day.* = having unpleasantly hot and humid weather which makes one sweat

swerve[1] /swɜːv/ verb, i. *The car swerved to avoid hitting a child who suddenly ran into the middle of the road.* = to turn suddenly to one side or change direction while moving

swerve[2] noun, c. *The car made a swerve to the right.* = a sudden movement or change of direction to one side
to swerve from *Once you have taken a decision about your future course of action, I do not expect you to swerve from your chosen path.* = to change one's course of action (formal)

swift[1] /swɪft/ adj. **1** *a swift horse* = able to run fast (literary) **2** *a swift reply* = given without delay

swift[2] noun = a kind of small bird that flies very fast

swig[1] /swɪg/ verb, t. (**swigged**) = to drink a large quantity of some alcoholic liquid (informal)

swig[2] noun, c. *a swig of whisky* = a large mouthful of (usually) an alcoholic drink (informal)

swill /swɪl/ verb, t. **1** *He was swilling beer all night.* = to drink a large quantity of some alcoholic liquid (informal) **2** *I had to swill out the verandah after we finished eating.* = to clean a place by pouring a large amount of water over it

swim[1] /swɪm/ verb, i. or t. (**swam, swum**) **1** *The river is deep. Can you swim?*(i.) = to move oneself through the water by using the arms and legs **2** *He swam the Palk Straits when he was a young man.*(t.) = to cross a body of water by swimming **3** *Her head swam and she thought she was going to fall.* = to feel dizzy (as if about to fall)

swim[2] noun, c. (always singular) *We are going for a swim in the lake.* = the act of swimming for exercise or pleasure **swimming** noun = the sport of swimming in the water **swimming costume** noun = a short, light dress for a woman or girl which is worn while swimming **swimming pool** noun, c. = a large tank (container) made by digging into the ground and filling up the sides and bottom with concrete, which is filled with water and in which people can swim for exercise or pleasure **swimming trunks** noun (always plural) = a short dress for a man or boy, covering the body from the waist to the top part of the thighs, worn while swimming
to swimwith/against the tide = to do or not do what everyone else is doing because it seems wise to do so **to be swimming in (something)** **1** *His business is so successful that he is swimming in wealth.* = to have a lot of money (usually expressing jealousy on the part of the speaker) **2** *I am sorry, but I have no time for you now. I am swimming in work.* = to be extremely busy in doing something

swin•dle[1] /ˈswɪndl/ verb, t. *They swindled my parents out of a lot of money.* = to cheat someone by taking money dishonestly (strongly disapproving)

swindle[2] noun, c. *I have become the victim of a swindle.* = an act of swindling (cheating) **swindler** noun, c. = a person who swindles

swine /swaɪn/ noun (**swine**) **1** = a pig (old-fashioned use) **2** = a word used in anger to address or describe an unpleasant person USE

swing[1] /swɪŋ/ verb, i. or t. (**swung**) **1** *The monkey swung from the branch of a tree.*(i.) // *The cadets swung their arms during the parade.*(t.) = to move or to cause something to move forwards and backwards from a fixed point above **2** *Ganguly swung his bat but missed the ball.* = to move something in a curve **3** *He swung around and faced his enemy.* = to turn around quickly **4** *They want us to swing this deal for them.* = to arrange for something to happen, using dishonest means if necessary (informal)

swing[2] noun, c. **1** *We are putting up a swing for the children.* = a seat which hangs by ropes or metal chains from the branch of a tree or some other high, fixed point, in which someone (usually a child) can sit and move backwards and forwards for pleasure **2** *He took a swing at the ball but missed.* = a swinging movement **3** *a swing in public opinion* = a change in the way people think or feel **mood swings** = (usually plural) a situation in which, one experiences changes in emotions e.g. from sad to happy, especially when one is physically or mentally unwell **swinger** noun, c. **1** = a person who lives an active social life (goes frequently to parties, clubs etc.) (informal) **2** = a ball bowled in the game of cricket which moves quickly to one side after hitting the ground (**in-swinger** or **out-swinger**)
to swing by *Please swing by on your way home from work.* = to call on someone on one's way somewhere else (informal) **to take a swing at someone** = to make a swinging movement with one's hand in order to hit someone (informal) **to be in full swing** *School was closed for the holidays but classes are in full swing now.* = to happen in the busiest possible way (informal) **to get into the swing of things** = to start to do something with the expected speed and skill (e.g. in a job) after not being able to do this at first **What one loses on the swings, one gains on the roundabouts** = used to say that there are always

things gained and things lost and these gains and losses balance out equally in the end

swipe[1] /swaɪp/ noun, c. **1** *The batsman took a swipe at the ball but missed.* = a forceful, sweeping blow **2** *The article takes a swipe at people who visit shopping malls.* = an attack in words, criticizing someone for something (informal)

swipe[2] verb, i. or t. **1** *The batsman swiped at the ball but missed.*(i.)= to hit or try to hit hard **2** *Someone has swiped my watch.*(t.) = to steal (informal) **3** *The cashier swiped the credit card through the scanner.* = to pull a credit card through a **scanner** so that a computer can tell whether the card can be accepted

swirl[1] /swɜːl/ verb, t. *The children swirled across the stage, presenting an energetic folk dance.* = to move quickly with a circular movement

swirl[2] noun, c. *The truck raised a swirl of dust as it rushed along the village roads.* = a mass of dust, leaves, etc. carried along by the wind or water with a fast, turning movement **swirling** adj. *the swirling waters of the flooded river* = moving forward very fast, with a turning movement

swish /swɪʃ/ verb, i. or t. **1** *The cows swished their tails to drive the flies away.*(t.) = to move or to cause something to move fast through the air, making a whistling sound **2** *Her silk sari swished as she made a quick exit through the door.*(i.) = to make a sound while moving fast

Swiss /swɪs/ adj. = from or belonging to Switzerland

switch[1] /swɪtʃ/ noun, c. **1** *an electrical switch* = a device (simple machine) which is used to stop the flow of electricity or turn it on again **2** *There is a switch in our plans. We will start tomorrow and not today.* = a complete change (informal) **3** = a thin stick used to drive an animal (make it move)

switch[2] verb, t. **1** *We have switched our plans.* = to change **2** *Let us switch coats. You can put on my coat and I will wear yours.* = to exchange

to switch (something) off/on **1** = to stop electricity from flowing or to make it flow again by using a switch **2** *I switch off whenever she starts talking about her illness!* = to stop listening because of boredom or lack of interest (informal) **to switch over** *He started his speech in Hindi but soon switched over to English.* = to change from one thing to another **to make a switch** *Art critics are certain that this is not the original painting by Van Gogh. They wonder who made the switch!* = the removal of one object and the putting of a similar looking one in its place (informal)

swiv•el /ˈswɪvəl/ verb, i. *He was working on his computer, facing the wall, but when I entered he swivelled around to face me.* = to turn around quickly **swivel-chair** noun, c. = a chair with a seat which is fixed on a central screw and can be turned in a circle (see pic under **chair**)

swollen see **swell**

swoon /swuːn/ verb, i. = to faint; to become unconscious because of a powerful shock

swoop[1] /swuːp/ verb, i. *Gabbar Singh and his gang of dacoits swooped on the village, creating terror.* = to attack suddenly

swoop[2] noun, c. *Five terrorists were arrested by the police in a pre-dawn swoop.* = a sudden attack

sword /sɔːd/ noun, c. = a long knife with a sharp point and either one or two sharp edges, used as a weapon in fighting **swordfish** noun = a large fish with a long, pointed upper jaw that looks like a sword **sword of Damocles** noun *The danger of a nuclear attack hangs over us like the sword of Damocles.* = something bad that may happen at any time

to put to the sword = to kill (formal) **to cross swords (with someone)** *Ratin and I crossed swords at the meeting.* = to get into a serious disagreement or argument

swot /swɒt/ verb, i. (**swotted**) *The students are swotting for their exams which begin next week.* = to study hard for an examination (informal)

sy•ca•more /ˈsɪkəmɔːʳ/ noun = a kind of large tree found in Europe and America (belonging to the maple family)

syc•o•phant /ˈsɪkəfənt/ noun, c. = a flatterer; a person who says pleasant things to make one feel happy, but is always looking for some benefit for himself or herself **sycophancy** noun **sycophantic** adj.

syl•la•ble /ˈsɪləbəl/ noun, c. *The word 'nation' has two syllables.* = a part of a word which contains a vowel and one or more consonants

syl•la•bus /ˈsɪləbəs/ noun, c. (**syllabuses** or **syllabi**) = a course of studies; the different subjects, books and topics which have to be studied in order to pass an examination

syl•lo•gis•m /ˈsɪlədʒɪzəm/ noun, c. = a set of two arguments or reasons which lead to a certain conclusion, in the study of logic [TECHNICAL]

syl•van /ˈsɪlvən/ adj. *The new hotel has been built in sylvan surroundings,in the middle of a small pine forest.* = having natural beauty because of the presence of many trees (literary)

sym•bi•o•sis /sɪmbiˈəʊsɪs/ noun *Bees pollinate flowers and flowers produce nectar, from which bees make honey. This illustrates the symbiosis between bees and flowers.* = a natural condition or arrangement in which animals or plants live together, helping and depending on each other [BIOLOGY] **symbiotic** adj. *a symbiotic relationship* = a relationship of symbiosis

S

sym•bol /ˈsɪmbəl/ noun, c. *A dove is a symbol of peace.* = something that represents (stands for) something else **symbolic** /sɪmˈbɒlɪk/ adj. *a symbolic gesture in a dance* = used as or making use of symbols **symbolize (symbolise)** /ˈsɪmbəlaɪz/ verb, t. *The rising sun in the Japanese flag symbolizes the hopes of the nation.* = to be a symbol of something

sym•met•ri•cal /sɪˈmetrɪkəl/ adj. *The Taj Mahal is a perfectly symmetrical building.* = having sides which are exactly similar (alike) (opposite **asymmetrical**) **symmetry** /ˈsɪmətri/ noun, u. *The Taj Mahal has perfect symmetry.* = the quality of being symmetrical (where the two halves look exactly alike)

sym•pa•thy /ˈsɪmpəθi/ noun, u. **1** *Many people came to express their sympathy when our father died.* = the kindness and understanding shown to someone who is suffering, in an attempt to share his or her suffering **2** *I am in sympathy with your views but I cannot support you publicly.* = to share or to be in agreement with the ideas or feelings of someone **sympathetic** /sɪmpəˈθetɪk/ adj. *She spoke with great feeling to a sympathetic audience.* = sharing the feelings and ideas of someone else and therefore willing to listen **sympathize (sympathise)** /ˈsɪmpəθaɪz/ verb, i. *I sympathize with you in your great loss.* = to feel or show sympathy

sym•pho•ny /ˈsɪmfəni/ noun, c. (**symphonies**) = a long piece of music created for a large orchestra (a number of musicians playing together on different musical instruments) usually in three or four parts [TECHNICAL]

sym•po•si•um /sɪmˈpəʊziəm/ noun, c. (**symposiums** or **symposia**) = a meeting of scholars at which some serious subject or topic is discussed

symp•tom /ˈsɪmptəm/ noun, c. *Do you see those red marks on the child's face? That's a symptom of measles.* = an outward sign (which can be easily seen) of some disease that a person may be suffering from **symptomatic** /sɪmptəˈmætɪk/ adj. *Loss of appetite is often symptomatic of jaundice.* = being a symptom (sign) of something undesirable, such as a disease

syn•a•gogue /ˈsɪnəgɒg/ noun, c. = a place of worship for Jewish people

sync /sɪŋk/ noun abbr. of **synchrony** (see below) *The views of those in the Sales Department are not in sync with those of who are manufacturing the goods.* = a state of harmony (good understanding of each other) (informal)

syn•chro•nize (synchronise) /ˈsɪŋkrənaɪz/ verb, t. or i. **1** *The two umpires synchronized their watches before the start of the match.* = to adjust a watch or clock so that it shows exactly the same time as another watch or clock **2** *We synchronized our travel plans so that we could reach Delhi at the same time.* = to make two things happen at the same time **synchrony** = the state of being in perfect harmony or agreement with someone (see **sync**)

syn•di•cate[1] /ˈsɪndɪkət/ noun, c. = a group of people or companies that join together for a common purpose

syndicate[2] /ˈsɪndɪkeɪt/ verb, t. *Khushwant Singh writes a weekly column called 'With Malice Towards All' which is syndicated to many newspapers.* = to arrange for the same article to be published in a number of newspapers [TECHNICAL]

syn•drome /ˈsɪndrəʊm/ noun, c. **1** *The child is suffering from Down's Syndrome.* = a combination of medical problems or symptoms (see **symptom** above) which shows some physical or mental disorder [MEDICINE] **2** *Unemployment and high prices are part of an economic syndrome.* = a set of events or conditions which are found together with or as parts of a particular problem

syn•er•gy /ˈsɪnədzɪ/ noun, u. *We hope to create synergy between the government and private organizations.* = the combined power of different groups of people working together, which is greater than the power of the same groups working separately [TECHNICAL]

syn•o•nym /ˈsɪnənɪm/ noun, c. *'Die' and 'expire' are synonyms.* = a word having the same meaning as another word **synonymous** /sɪˈnɒnɪməs/ adj. *The IIT's are synonymous with world-class technical education.* = closely connected with something; having almost the same meaning

sy•nop•sis /sɪˈnɒpsɪs/ noun, c. (**synopses**) *I have prepared a synopsis of the President's speech in 150 words.* = a summary; the main points without the details

syn•tax /ˈsɪntæks/ noun **1** = the rules of grammar which decide how words combine together to form sentences [GRAMMAR] **2** = the rules used in computer languages [TECHNICAL] **syntactic** /sɪnˈtæktɪk/ adj. *There is a syntactic error in the sentence 'The child icecream likes'.* = having to do with syntax (the rules for forming sentences from words)

syn•the•sis /ˈsɪnθɪsɪs/ noun, u. or c. **1** *The Constitution of India is a synthesis of the British, American and French constitutions.* = something created by joining or combining different things to form a whole **synthesize (synthesise)** verb, t. *We wish to create a new kind of Asian culture by synthesizing several different cultures.* = to join or combine different things together to form a whole **2** =

the act of combining things together into a whole **synthesizer (synthesiser)** /sɪnθɪ'saɪzə[r]/ noun, c. = an electronic machine which can produce the sounds of many different musical instruments **synthetic** /sɪn'θetɪk/ adj. *This is not natural orange juice. It tastes synthetic. // synthetic rubber* = artificial; made by combining several different chemicals or substances so that it has the qualities of a natural product

syph•i•lis /'sɪfəlɪs/ noun = a disease which affects the sex organs and is passed on from one person to another through sexual contact **syphilitic** /sɪfə'lɪtɪk/ **1** *a syphilitic infection*(adj.) = having to do with syphilis **2** (noun, c.) = a person suffering from syphilis

syphon see **siphon**

sy•ringe[1] /sɪ'rɪndʒ/ noun, c. *The doctor used a syringe to remove some blood so that it could be tested.* = a glass or metal tube to which a needle is attached, which can be used to push or take out some liquid into the body (see pic under **laboratory equipment**, **needles**)

syringe[2] verb, t. = to clean with some liquid, through a syringe

syr•up /'sɪrəp/ noun, u. or c. = a very sweet, thick liquid (see pic under **medicine**) **syrupy** adj. *syrupy words* = too sweet or pleasant and therefore likely to be insincere (informal, derogatory)

sys•tem /'sɪstəm/ noun, c. or u. **1** *the digestive system* = something (often a machine) that is made up of a number of connected parts which work together **2** *The British brought their system of justice to India.*(c.) = a set of related ideas or methods for doing something **3** *There seems to be no system in your work.*(u.) = proper methods of working **systematic** /sɪstɪ'mætɪk/ adj. *We carried out a systematic search of all the files in the program.* = doing things in an organised manner **systematize (systematise)** /'sɪstɪmətaɪz/ verb, t. *We will have to systematize your methods of keeping accounts.* = to arrange things in an orderly manner, so as to form a system **systemic** /sɪs'temɪk/ adj. *The swelling in your stomach seems to be systemic.* = relating to a whole system and not just a part of it [TECHNICAL]

systems analyst noun = a person who makes a study of the different systems (methods of working) in a company and then uses computers to plan improved systems

S

tT

t,T /tiː/ the twentieth letter of the English alphabet

T- = a prefix to indicate that something is in the shape of the letter 'T' **T- junction** /'tiːdʒʌŋkʃən/ noun, c. = a place where one road meets another road without crossing it, forming the shape of the letter T **T-shirt** /'tiːʃɜːt/ noun, c. = a shirt without a collar, generally used for informal wear (not on serious or important occasions) (also tee-shirt) **T-square** /'tiːskweəʳ/ noun, c. = an instrument consisting of two flat pieces of wood joined together in the shape of the letter T, used for drawing parallel lines on paper

to a T *The dress suits her to a T.* = perfectly

't /t/ abbr. of **'it'** (e.g. *think on't*) (literary)

ta /tɑː/ interjec. (British) = thank you (informal)

TA noun, abbr. of **Travelling Allowance** = money paid to a person to meet the cost of travelling

tab /tæb/ noun, c. = a small strip of paper or metal fixed to something to help in handling or finding it

to keep a tab on someone = to watch someone (specially a wrong doer) closely **to pick up the tab** = to pay the bill (the money that has to be paid for something)

ta•bas•co /tə'bæskəʊ/ noun = a kind of hot sauce made from red chillies, used to add taste to food

tab•by /'tæbi/ noun, c. = a female cat with dark stripes

ta•ble[1] /'teɪbəl/ noun, c. **1** *a dining table* = a piece of furniture with legs and a flat top, used for placing things or writing etc. **2** *a table in a book* = a set of facts or numbers printed or written in rows or blocks

table[2] verb, t. *The new Income Tax Act was tabled last week.* = to present a report or a new law etc. for discussion, especially in the parliament **tablecloth** noun, c. = a piece of cloth, plastic etc. used to cover the top of a table, specially during a meal **table-knife** noun, c. (**-knives**) = a knife used for cutting up food into small pieces while eating **table manners** noun (always plural) = the kind of behaviour that a person is expected to show during a meal **tablemat** noun, c. = a small piece of cloth, plastic etc. which is placed under a plate containing hot food, so that the heat does not spoil the surface of the table **tablespoon** noun, c. **1** = a large spoon used to move food from a plate to the mouth **2** = the amount of food held in this (see also **teaspoon**) **tableware** /'teɪbəlweəʳ/ noun,u. = all the things (plates, knives, spoons etc.) used during a meal served on a table

table-land noun, c. = a large area of high land which is flat at the top (also **plateau** or table-mountain) [GEOGRAPHY]

tabletennis noun, u. = an indoor game played on a table with small bats and a ball, by two or four players

tab•u•late /'tæbjʊleɪt/ verb, t. *We have tabulated the results of the Pollution Board's report on water quality.* = to arrange in the form of a table (**table**[1] meaning **2**) **tabular** /'tæbjʊləʳ/ adj. *The growth of population during the last five years is shown here in tabular form.* = having the form (shape) of a table (see **table**[1] meaning **2**)

tab•leau /'tæbləʊ/ noun, c. (**tableaux** or **tableaus**) = a scene presented by a group of people on a stage, in which the people do not move or speak

tab•let /'tæblɪt/ noun, c. = a small, hard piece of some medicine which is usually swallowed (also pill) (see pic under **medicine**)

tab•loid /'tæblɔɪd/ noun or adj. = a newspaper printed on pages of small size, containing many pictures and short, simple reports, which is popular with people who do not have the time to read full-length newspapers (noun)

ta•boo[1] /tə'buː/ adj. *Certain kinds of food are taboo for some groups of people.* = prohibited or forbidden (not allowed) by religious or social custom

taboo[2] noun, c. *There is a taboo in some religions on the eating of pork.* = a religious or social custom forbidding something

taboo[3] verb, t. *The film censors have tabooed the use of vulgar words in films.* = to forbid strongly

ta•chom•e•ter /tæ'kɒmɪtəʳ/ noun, c. = an instrument fitted to the engine of a car which measures the speed at which the engine is turning, in revolutions per minute (rpm) [TECHNICAL]

ta•cit /'tæsɪt/ adj. *There is a tacit understanding between the teachers in our school that they will hold the tests at the same time.* = (an agreement that is) understood or accepted without being clearly written down

tack[1] /tæk/ noun, c. or u. **1** (c.) = a small nail with a flat head **2** *The tailor attached the collar to the shirt with a few tacks.*(c.) = a long, loose stitch which holds two pieces of cloth together before they are stitched (joined) properly **3** *The ship followed a southern tack.*(u.) = the direction in which a boat or ship is sailing, driven by the wind **4** *The speaker started on a new tack in the middle of his talk.*(c.) = a line of thinking or action

tack[2] verb, t. **1** *He tacked the picture to the wall.* = to fasten with a tack (see pic under **pin**) **2** *She tacked on an additional piece of cloth to the skirt to make it longer.* = to join two pieces of cloth with long stitches

to tack on something *This last paragraph was tacked*

on to the report. = to add or join something which was not there earlier

tack•le[1] /ˈtækəl/ verb, t. **1** *The shortage of water is creating a problem. We must tackle it in such a way that there is enough water for all.* = to deal with a problem by taking some action **2** *Our defenders tackled the forwards of the opposing team.* = to try to take the ball away from an opposing player (in the game of football, hockey or rugby)

tackle[2] noun, c. or u. **1** *The defender made a determined tackle.*(c.) = the act of trying to take the ball away from an opposing player, in football, hockey or rugby **2** *We need some fishing tackle.*(u.) = equipment (things needed for a particular job)

tack•y /ˈtæki/ adj. *tacky clothes* = of poor quality or carelessly made (of clothes, ornaments etc.)

ta•co /ˈtɑːkəʊ/ noun, c. (**tacos**) = a kind of Mexican bread made from flour and filled with meat, vegetables etc.

tact /tækt/ noun, u. *You should use tact to inform your friend that she has been dropped from the team.* = the ability to say or do the right thing without making someone angry or unhappy; skill in dealing with people **tactful** adj. *a tactful speech* = showing tact (opposite tactless)

tac•tics /ˈtæktɪk/ noun, c. (usually plural) *military tactics* = plans drawn up to win a battle or a war **tactical** adj. *Sri Lanka decided to field after winning the toss. This turned out to be a clever tactical move.* = done as part of a tactic, in order to get a desired result **tactician** /tækˈtɪʃən/ noun, c. = a person who is skilled at tactics

tac•tile /ˈtæktɪl/ adj. *Snakes have a highly developed tactile sense. They can pick up faint vibrations from the ground.* = related to the sense of touch [BIOLOGY]

tad /ˈtæd/ noun, u. *The food was good but a tad too spicy.* = slightly; a little (informal)

tad•pole /ˈtædpəʊl/ noun, c. = a very young frog, which lives in the water and looks like a small fish with a round head and long tail

tag[1] /tæg/ noun, c. **1** *The price of the shirt is printed on the price tag.* = a small piece of paper, cloth or metal which is attached to some object and on which there is some information about the object (e.g. its price) **2** *In the sentence, 'It's warm, isn't it?', the expression 'isn't it' is a tag.* = a group of words added to a sentence to ask a question, ask for agreement etc. (also question-tag) [GRAMMAR] **3** *The children are playing a game of tag.* = a children's game in which one player has to chase and touch the other players

tag[2] verb, t. (**tagged**) **1** *The turtles which come to this beach to lay eggs have been tagged.* = to attach a tag to something so that it may be easily studied over a period of time **2** *This actor has been tagged as greedy because she asked for more money to act in the TV serial.* = to describe or think of someone in a particular way, usually in a negative way

to tag along *When the scientist left for a lecture, his secretary tagged along.* = to go together with someone especially when you are not wanted (informal) **to tag on** *You can tag on this quotation to your speech.* = to add or join to something (informal)

taichi /ˈtaɪtʃiː/ noun, u. = a system of exercise which uses slow body movements and was first practised in China

tail[1] /teɪl/ noun, c. **1** *Monkeys have tails.* = the movable part of an animal's body which is joined to it **2** *The CBI has put a tail on the man, who is suspected of being a smuggler.* = a person who is employed to follow someone closely and keep a watch on his/her movements (informal) **3** = the raised outer part at the end of the aircraft **4** *My seat is at the tail of the aircraft.* = the back part of something **5** *shirt tails* = the lower part of the shirt which is tucked inside the trousers

tail[2] verb, t. *The police have been tailing the criminal for a long time.* = to follow closely in order to keep a watch on someone **tailbone** noun = the last piece of bone in the backbone (also **coccyx**) **tail-end** noun, c. *We reached the cinema so late that we could see only the tail-end of the film.* = the very last part **tail-gate** noun, c. or verb t. **1** = a door at the back of a vehicle (car or truck) which can be raised or lowered to allow things to be loaded or unloaded (noun) **2** *It is dangerous to tail-gate a vehicle. You should always keep a safe distance between it and yourself.* = to drive too close to a vehicle which is ahead of you (verb) **tail-light** noun, c. = the red lights at the back of a vehicle **tail-piece** noun, c. *the tail-piece to a story* = something added on at the end **tailspin** noun, c. = an uncontrolled fall by an aircraft, in which the tail spins (goes round and round at speed) **tailwind** noun, c. = a wind which blows from behind and pushes a flying aircraft forward

to turn tail = to run away from an unpleasant situation **to tail off** **1** *The music tailed off.* = to become quieter, weaker **2** *My visits to the gym have tailed off.* = to gradually become less frequent **with one's tail between one's legs** = to lose one's courage or high spirits and feel defeated

tails /teɪlz/ noun (always plural) = the side of a coin which is opposite the head (see also **heads**)

tai•lor[1] /ˈteɪləʳ/ noun, c. = a person who stitches (makes) clothes

tailor[2] verb, t. **1** *Can you tailor these clothes for me?* = to stitch clothes for someone (formal) **2** *We can tailor a computer programme for your bank.* = to make

T

or prepare something specially for someone, to suit his/her needs **tailor-made** adj. *a tailor-made work schedule* = specially prepared for someone

taint[1] /teɪnt/ verb, t. *His reputation has been tainted by his refusal to pay tax.* = to spoil; to make something unclean or impure (formal)

taint[2] noun, u. *taint of greed* = the mark left behind by something bad or immoral

take[1] /teɪk/ verb, t. (**took, taken**) **1** *Take this child to the hospital.* = to move something or someone from one place to another **2** *I am taking the night train to Kolkata.* = to use some means to travel from one place to another **3** *If you take (away) 5 from 7, the remainder is 2.* = to remove **4** *Who took my pen (away)?* = to remove without permission **5** *The doctor has asked me to take this medicine.* = to introduce (put) into the body by eating or drinking **6** *He took a pen and scribbled his name across the sheet of paper.* = to hold something in the hand **7** *The flight to Kolkata will take 45 minutes.* = to require or need **8** *The professor is taking a class.* = to perform an action (which is mentioned) **9** *He took pity on the dog.* = to show or experience some feeling **10** *She took some excellent photographs of the Puja festival.* = to use a camera to produce a photograph **11** *to take one's blood pressure* = to measure **12** *The British took Bengal in 1757.* = to gain possession of **13** *He took my criticism well.* = to receive **14** *'Do you take this woman as your wife?' the priest asked.* = to accept (formal)

take[2] noun, c. *The director filmed the dance sequence with a single take.* = the action of filming (photographing) a scene for a film **take-away** adj. *a take-away dinner* = a meal ordered from a restaurant, which is not eaten inside the restaurant but somewhere else **take-home pay** noun = the amount that remains out of one's salary after all taxes etc. have been paid **take-off** noun, c. **1** *The passengers on an aircraft must remain seated during a take-off.* = the action of rising from the ground at the beginning of a flight in an aircraft **2** *The well-known television programme 'Yes, Minister' is a take-off on the way in which a government works.* = a funny copy (or parody) of the way in which someone usually behaves (informal) **take-over** noun, c. *Some workers lost their jobs after the take-over of the company by the government.* = the act of taking control of a company by a new owner **taker** noun, c. *I want to sell my farm but there are no takers.* = someone who is willing to buy something (informal) **takings** noun (always plural) *The takings from the new play have been good during the first week.* = money received from the sale of something, specially tickets

to take something apart *While repairing the clock, do you really need to take it apart?* = to separate into pieces **to take down** = to write down something that is being spoken **to take it out on someone** = to express anger at someone who may not have done anything wrong **to take someone up on something** *I took Salim up on his invitation to visit him in Nainital.* = to accept an offer made by someone **to be taken with someone/something** = to like someone or something very much **to take a lot out of someone** = to feel very tired after going through some experience **to take a lot of doing (to take some doing)** *Making arrangements for all the tourists took a lot of doing.* = to require a lot of effort **to be taken in by someone/something** *I trusted them. I was taken in by their friendly talk.* = to be deceived by someone on something **take after** = to look or act like an older member of your family **take it from me** = believe me

talcum powder /'tælkəmpaʊdə[r]/ noun, u. = a sweet-smelling powder made from talc (a kind of mineral which is dug out of the earth and feels like soap) which is put on the body to dry it, after a bath or when one has been sweating

tale /teɪl/ noun, c. **1** *a fairy tale* = a story about imaginary people and events **2** *When I asked him why he was late he told us a tale about having to visit someone in the hospital.* = a false report or description (disapproving)

to carry tales = to say false things about someone in order to get them into trouble **a tall tale** = something that is difficult to believe

tal•ent /'tælənt/ noun, u. or c. **1** *His talent will make him a great singer.*(u.) = an ability to do something well that one is usually born with **2** *The swimming coach is looking for new talent.*(u.) = persons who have talent **talent scout** noun, c. = a person whose job it is to look for talented actors, singers, musicians etc. **talented** adj. *a talented singer* = having talent

ta•lis•man /'tælɪzmən/ noun, c.= an object which is supposed to have magical or spiritual powers to protect someone from harm

talk[1] /tɔːk/ verb, i. or t. **1** *The baby can talk now.*(i.) = to communicate through words **2** *She is talking to her friend on the phone.*(t.) = to speak to someone, usually in a friendly way, in order to express one's ideas and feelings; to carry on a conversation **3** *People will talk if you are seen with that person very often.*(i.) = to gossip; to speak in an unpleasant manner about someone's private actions **4** *I forced my friend to talk because she was looking unhappy.*(i.) = to give out information unwillingly **5** *The parrot talks.*(i.) = to imitate or copy human speech **6** *You and I need to talk.*(i.) = to discuss a problem in a serious way **7** *Mr. Guhan will talk on science and religion.*(t.) = to give a lecture on a subject

talk[2] noun, u. or c. **1** *I had a long talk with an old friend.*(u.) = a conversation (the act of speaking to as well as listening to someone) **2** *He gave us a talk on western music.*(c.) = a lecture given to an audience **3** *His rude behaviour caused a lot of talk.*(u.) = discussion resulting from surprise or shock **4** *Don't be frightened by his threat. It is just talk!*(u.) = empty or meaningless speech **5** *There was a lot of talk when he decided to leave his well-paid job to take care of homeless children.*(u.) = gossip **talkative** /'tɔ:kətɪv/ adj. *a talkative child* = fond of talking **talkie** /'tɔ:ki/ noun, c. = a film in which the characters speak (old-fashioned) **talking point** noun, c. = a subject which is being discussed by a group

to talk back = to answer someone, especially someone who should be respected, in a rude way **to talk down to somebody** = to speak to somebody as if they were inferior to you **to talk someone around/into doing something** *She talked me around into diving her to the station.* = to get someone to agree to do somthing they are not willing to do **to talk something out/through** = to discuss a problem fully **to talk somebody out of doing something** = to persuade someone not to do something they were planning to do **to talk things over** = to discuss a problem **to be all talk** *He said he would give us all the help we needed, but we found he was all talk.* = to not really do something that one promises to do **the talk of the town** = something or someone that attracts a lot of attention and causes people to talk **to talk shop** = to talk about one's work or business in a way that others do not like (informal, disapproving) **to talk through one's hat** = to say something without knowing enough about what one is saying **talking-to** noun *The Principal gave the students a good talking-to.* = a scolding (an angry talk in order to criticize or point out some mistake) **to talk nineteen to the dozen** = to talk continuously and very fast **Now you're talking!** = an expression used to show that something you consider acceptable has been said after a lot of discussion (informal) **Look who's talking!** *'It's good to be up bright and early every morning.' 'Look who's talking!'* = used to express a lack of belief in what someone says because of your knowledge of the speaker's character, habits etc. (informal, humorous)

tall /tɔ:l/ adj. **1** *He is 185 centimetres tall.* = having a certain height **2** *a tall building* = having a greater height than the average (of people, trees, buildings etc.)

to walk tall = to behave with pride and confidence because one knows one has done nothing wrong **a tall order** *You are asking me to write a book in just one week. That's a tall order!* = a request or order to do something very difficult (informal) **a tall story** *He says his father takes his advice on all important matters. That's a tall story!* = something that is difficult to believe (informal)

tally[1] /'tæli/ verb, i. or t. **1** *The reports on the accident which the two of you have sent me don't tally.*(i.) = to match or to agree with each other **2** *Can you tally (up) the boy's marks in the different subjects?* (t.) = to add up or to calculate

tally[2] noun, c. (**tallies**) *We asked her to keep the tally while we were playing a game of cards.* = a record of the points scored in a game etc.

tal•on /'tælən/ noun, c. (usually plural) *The hawk picked up the mouse in its talons.* = the long, sharp, curved claws or nails on the feet of hunting birds

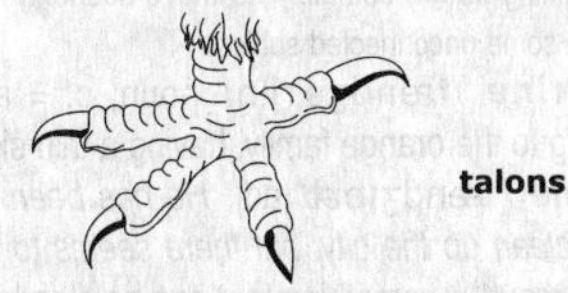
talons

tam•a•rind /'tæmərɪnd/ noun = a kind of fruit which has a sour taste and is often used in cooking

tame[1] /teɪm/ adj. **1** *a tame tiger in a circus* = not wild or fierce and used to living with human beings (referring to an animal) **2** *The film had a tame ending.* = not exciting; dull (informal)

tame[2] verb, t. *The horse was difficult to control at first, but the rider has tamed it.* = to bring under control

tam•per /'tæmpə[r]/ verb, i. *The computer was working perfectly this morning but it is not working now. Someone must have tampered with it.* = to touch or change something (e.g. a machine) without permission, so as to cause damage to it **tamper-proof** adj. *a bottle of milk with a tamper-proof cap.* = made in such a way that it cannot be tampered with

tam•pon /'tæmpɒn/ noun, c. = a piece of soft material which can absorb (draw in) liquids and is worn inside the vagina by women who are having their period (see **menses**)

tan[1] /tæn/ verb, t. (**tanned**) **1** = to change animal skin into leather by treating it with certain chemicals **2** *The sun has tanned him.* = to make the colour of a person's skin brown, through the action of the sun's rays

tan[2] adj. *tan trousers* = brown

tan[3] noun, u. **1** *He has developed a tan as he is out in the sun often.* = the brown colour that a person's skin gets because of the action of sunlight **2** *tan 45* = abbr. of **tangent** (the ratio between the length of the side that is opposite an angle of less than 90 degrees, in a right-angled triangle, and the length of the side next to it) [MATHEMATICS] (compare **cosine** and **sine**)

tan•dem /'tændəm/ noun, u. **1** *a tandem bicycle* = a bicycle which two riders can sit on, one behind the other, and pedal together **2** *The two scriptwriters are* *working in tandem.* = partnership (an arrangement which allows two people to work together closely)

tang /tæŋ/ noun, u. *The lemon juice will add tang to the salad.* = a taste or smell which is sharp and strong but pleasant

tan•gent /'tændʒənt/ noun, c. **1** = a straight line that touches the curve of a circle but does not cut it [GEOMETRY] **2** = a ratio in trigonometry (see **tan**³, meaning **2**) [MATHEMATICS]

to go off at a tangent *The speaker was talking about the fim 'Lagaan' when he suddenly went off at a tangent and started talking about football.* = to move suddenly from a subject to some unconnected subject

tan•ge•rine /tændʒə'ri:n/ noun, c. = a fruit belonging to the orange family, having a thin skin

tan•gi•ble /'tændʒɪbəl/ adj. *He has been trying hard to clean up the city, but there seems to be no tangible result.* = something that can be clearly seen or felt

tan•gle¹ /'tæŋgəl/ verb, i. **1** *My mother was knitting a pullover, but the wool has got all tangled (up).* = to form an untidy, confused mass of twisted threads or thread-like substances (opposite **un-tangle**) **2** *The end of her sari got tangled among the bushes.* = to get caught in something **3** *Don't tangle with that man. He is dangerous.* = to get into a fight or quarrel with someone

tangle² noun, c. **1** *It is difficult to walk through this tangle of bushes.* = an untidy mass of things **2** *This cupboard is in a tangle. I can't find any of the important papers.* = a confused state

tan•go /'tæŋgəʊ/ noun = a kind of South American dance in which men and women dance in pairs

tan•in /'tænɪn/ noun, u. = a chemical produced from the bark of certain trees, used in tanning (the process of making leather out of animal skins)

tank /tæŋk/ noun, c. **1** *a water tank* = a large container in which water or some other liquid or gas can be stored **2** *the fuel tank of a car* = a container fitted to a vehicle (car, motorcycle etc.) in which the petrol, diesel, or gas which is burnt in the engine can be stored **3** *There is a large tank outside the village in which people bathe.* = a pond or artificial lake in which water is stored **4** *a fish tank* = a box, usually made of glass and filled with water, in which fish are kept **5** *a battle tank* = a military vehicle used to attack enemy positions in a battle, protected by thick steel plates and running on metal tracks (chains) instead of wheels **tanker** noun, c. = a vehicle (truck or railway carriage), ship or aircraft which is fitted with large metal tanks in which some liquid or gas can be stored and carried from one place to another **tanked** adj. *The man was so heavily tanked that he couldn't walk.* = drunk (on alcohol) (slang)

tan•ne•ry /'tænəri/ noun, c. (**tanneries**) = a factory in which leather is made out of animal skins

tan•trum /'tæntrəm/ noun, c. *The little girl threw a tantrum when her parents refused to let her go on the school picnic.* = a sudden attack of uncontrolled and unreasonable anger

tap¹ /tæp/ verb, t. (**tapped**) **1** *There is a lot of oil lying under the Arabian Sea, which has not been tapped.* = to obtain (take) something from a source in order to make use of it **2** *People tap rubber trees to make rubber.* = to take out juice from a tree by making a cut in its trunk **3** *My telephone is being tapped.* = to listen secretly to messages which are sent over a telephone line **4** *I tapped him on the shoulder to catch his attention.* = to hit lightly

tap² noun, c. **1** *a water tap* = a device (simple machine) used to control the flow of liquid or gas through a pipe **2** *The police suspect him of being a spy. They are carrying out a telephone tap.* = the action of tapping a telephone (listening secretly to messages) **3** *a tap on the hand* = a light blow **tap-dance** noun, c. = a kind of dance in which the dancer produces sounds by striking the floor lightly with his/her shoes while dancing

to be on tap *I'm thirsty. I wish we had some coffee on tap.* = to be available whenever needed (of information, water, drinks etc.)

tape¹ /teɪp/ noun, u. or c. **1** *The papers were tied together with tape.*(u.) = a piece of thin, narrow material (usually cloth, plastic or metal) used for different purposes **2** *a measuring tape*(c.) = a long, narrow flexible piece of cloth, metal or plastic, marked in centimetres and metres or inches and feet, used to measure the length of something **3** *audio- / video-tape*(c.) = a thin, narrow piece of plastic coated (covered) with special material, on which sounds or pictures, or both, can be recorded **4** *sticky tape* (u.) = a thin piece of plastic ribbon which is sticky on one side and is used for joining things together

tape² verb, t. **1** *We will tape the song and play it back later.* = to record sounds or pictures on tape **2** *Please tape this packet of books.* = to hold together with tape **tape deck** noun, c. = a machine which records and plays back sounds and forms part of a **music system** (also tape recorder) **tape measure** noun, c. = a length of tape used to measure the length of something **tapeworm** /'teɪpwɜ:m/ noun, c. = a kind of flat worm that is sometimes found inside the intestines of human beings and animals as a parasite (see also **parasite**)

ta•per /'teɪpəʳ/ verb, i. or t. **1** *Crocodiles have long tails which are thick at the base and gradually taper to* *a point.*(i.) = to gradually become narrower **2** *The doctor asked me to take six tablets of this medicine every day for a week, then four tablets for the next two weeks, and gradually taper off the dose to just one tablet a day.*(t.) = to gradually reduce a certain quantity

tap•es•try /ˈtæpɪstri/ noun, u. or c. (**tapestries**) = thick cloth with colourful designs woven into it, which is used to make curtains, covers for sofas etc. or hung up on walls for decoration

tap•i•o•ca /tæpiˈəʊkə/ noun, u. = the dried roots of the cassava plant used in different forms as food

ta•pir /ˈteɪpəʳ/ noun, c. = an animal found in parts of Southeast Asia and South America, which looks like a pig but has a long snout (nose)

tap•pet /ˈtæpɪt/ noun, c. = a part of a machine (e.g. the engine of a car) which causes some other part to move by striking against it [TECHNICAL]

tap-root /ˈtæpruːt/ noun, c. = the main root of a plant, from which other side-roots grow [BIOLOGY]

tar[1] /tɑːʳ/ noun, u. *The workers are spreading tar on the new road.* = a thick and sticky black liquid, produced from coal, which is used to prepare the surface of roads

tar[2] verb, t. (**tarred**) *Drive carefully on that road. It has just been tarred.* = to cover with tar

ta•ran•tu•la /təˈræntjʊlə/ noun = a kind of large, hairy spider found in South America, the bite of which is poisonous

tar•dy /ˈtɑːdi/ adj. *She is tardy in replying to letters. I got her reply after six months.* = slow or late in doing something

tar•get[1] /ˈtɑːgɪt/ noun, c. **1** *His arrow hit the target in the centre.* = a circular piece of wood on which circles are drawn in different colours, at which people aim and shoot in order to practise and improve their skill in using a gun or a bow and arrows **2** *The government has set a target of building 20,000 houses this month.* = a quantity or level that one tries to reach while carrying out some task

target[2] verb, t. *The company has started a new campaign to sell television sets, which is targeted at people living in villages.* = to try to reach a certain group of people

tar•iff /ˈtærɪf/ noun, c. = a tax collected by the government on goods entering a country (also duty or customs duty)

tar•mac /ˈtɑːmæk/ noun, u. *The plane could not take off because of fog and had to wait for half an hour on the tarmac.* = the hard surface, covered with tar, which aircraft can land on or use for take-offs

tar•nish /ˈtɑːnɪʃ/ verb, t. **1** *The brass statues have to be polished as they have tarnished.* = to become dull (to lose brightness) **2** *His reputation was tarnished after he was arrested.* = to spoil a person's reputation

ta•rot /ˈtærəʊ/ noun, u. *tarot cards* = a set of 22 cards with different pictures on them, used to tell someone's fortune (luck)

tar•pau•lin /tɑːˈpɔːlɪn/ noun, c. = a piece of thick water-proof canvas (thick cloth) used to protect things from rain

tar•sus /ˈtɑːsəs/ noun, u. = the set of 7 small bones in the ankle [MEDICINE]

tart[1] /tɑːt/ noun, c. **1** = a small cake filled with something sweet **2** = a derogatory way of referring to a woman who is, or seems to be, a sex worker (slang) USE G

tart[2] adj. **1** *Use some lemon juice to give the curry a tart taste.* = slighly sour **2** *She gave me a tart reply when I asked her for some help.* = sharp and unpleasant (in behaviour)

tart[3] verb, t. *They have tarted up the old cinema hall by painting it purple on the outside.* = to try to make something look attractive, but in a cheap way (informal, derogatory)

tar•tan /ˈtɑːtn/ noun, u. = a printed or woven design of coloured checks (straight lines crossing each other), originally used by people in Scotland

tar•tar /ˈtɑːtəʳ/ noun, u. *The dentist removed the tartar from his teeth.* = a hard substance that forms on the surface of teeth

tar•ta•ric a•cid /tɑːtærɪk ˈæsɪd/ noun = a kind of chemical substance with a sour taste, found in tomatoes and some other fruit [CHEMISTRY]

tar•tar sauce noun = a kind of white sauce (thick liquid that adds taste to food) usually eaten with fish

task[1] /tɑːsk/ noun, c. *I must go to the market and buy some vegetables. That is my first task this morning.* = a duty; a piece of work that must be done

task[2] verb, t. *The government has tasked us with the responsibility of checking the fire escapes in all the buildings in this area.* = to give someone a task (duty) (formal) **task force** noun, c. = a group of people (usually soldiers) who are ordered to carry out a particular task **taskmaster** noun, c. *Our new coach is a hard taskmaster.* = a person who makes people work very hard (generally approving)

to take someone to task = to speak angrily to someone for doing something wrong

tas•sel /ˈtæsəl/ noun, c. **1** = a bunch of threads tied together, forming a hanging decoration **2** = a bunch of threads woven together to look like the plaits in a woman's hair, used to make the plaits look longer or thicker than they really are (see also **plait**)

taste[1] /teɪst/ noun, u. **1** *Honey has a sweet taste.* = flavour; the sensation (feeling) or effect produced inside the mouth, specially around the tongue, by a

T

particular kind of food or drink **2** *She has lost her sense of taste after her long illness.* = the ability to feel the effect that a particular food or drink has **3** *I want you to have a taste of this curry.* = a small quantity of food or drink, taken in order to find out if it has the right taste or flavour **4** *Some people think he has excellent taste.* = the ability to judge correctly whether something has beauty, value etc., especially in matters relating to art, literature, music etc. **5** *I have bought some religious books for you as I know your taste.* = a personal liking for something

taste[2] verb, t. **1** *I want you to taste this pudding and tell me if it is sweet enough.* = to take a small quantity of food or drink in the mouth in order to judge its taste **2** *This cake tastes a little too sweet. You must have put a lot of sugar in it.* = to have a particular taste (referring to food or drink) **taste bud** noun, c. = a group of special cells in the tongue which have the ability to feel the taste of something **tasteful** adj. *The choice of curtains for the room is tasteful.* = showing good taste (see **taste**[1] meaning **4**) **tasteless** adj. **1** *The curry is tasteless. You should add some spices to it.* = having no taste (see **taste**[1] meaning **1**) **2** *The remarks he made at the meeting were tasteless.* = showing poor taste (see **taste**[1] meaning **4**) **taster** noun, c. *a tea-taster* = a person whose job it is to taste (see **taste**[2], meaning **1**) food or drink, to test if the taste is good **tasty** adj. *a tasty curry* = having good taste (see **taste**[1] meaning **1**)

to leave a bad taste in someone's mouth = to have an unpleasant feeling that remains for a long time

tat /tæt/ noun see **tit** for **tat** (below)

ta-ta /tæ'tɑː/ interjec. *Say ta-ta to your friend* = good-bye (an expression mostly used by children when saying good-bye to someone) (informal)

tat•ters /'tætəz/ noun (always plural) *She refused to give up her old shirt although it was in tatters.* = torn or worn-out old clothing **tattered** adj. *He wore tattered clothes.* = old and torn (referring to clothes)

tat•too[1] /tə'tuː/ noun, c. *The gypsy woman had tattoos all over her arms and hands.* = a pattern or design made on the skin of the body

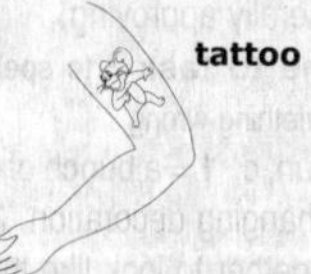
tattoo

tattoo[2] verb, t. = to make a design on the skin by using a needle **tattooist** noun, c. = a person whose job is to tattoo others

tat•ty /'tæti/ adj. *The furniture in the room was tatty.* = in poor condition (informal)

taught /tɔːt/ verb, t. past tense of **teach**

taunt[1] /tɔːnt/ verb, t. *The crowd taunted the members of the team after they lost the match.* = to make fun of someone or to say unkind things about someone, with the intention of making him/her angry

taunt[2] noun, c. *The taunt made the player so angry that he attacked a spectator.* = an unkind remark made to hurt someone's feelings

Tau•rus /'tɔːrəs/ noun, u. = a sign of the zodiac, in the form of a bull (see pic under **zodiac**)

taut /tɔːt/ adj. **1** *The strings of the sitar are loose. They should be taut.* = tight (fully stretched out) **2** *She had a taut expression on her face.* = showing worry or anxiety **tauten** verb, t. *You should tauten the strings of your sitar.* = to make something taut (tight)

tau•tol•o•gy /tɔː'tɒlədʒi/ noun, u. or c. (**tautologies**) *To say 'He lives alone, all by himself' is to use a tautology.*(c.) = an unnecessary use of a word, repeating an idea that has already been expressed through some other word

tav•ern /'tævən/ noun, c. = a place where alcoholic drinks are served (old-fashioned, literary) (also **pub**)

taw•ny /'tɔːni/ adj. *the lion's tawny fur* = having a brownish-yellow colour

tax[1] /tæks/ noun, c. or u. = money which is paid to the government, usually as a percentage of one's income or of the price of something that one buys

tax[2] verb, t. **1** *The government taxes people who own houses or cars.* = to charge a tax or to make someone pay a tax **2** *to tax someone's patience* = to make greater demands than usual on some quality that a person has **taxing** adj. *a taxing journey* = something that is difficult to go through **taxation** noun, u. *the government's policy on taxation* = the act of making someone pay tax **tax-free** adj. *a tax-free salary* = on which no tax needs to be paid **tax haven** noun, c. = a country which attracts rich businessmen by charging very low taxes **tax holiday** noun, c. = a period during which a new business company is not required to pay tax to the government, so that it can grow **tax-payer** noun, c. = a person who pays tax to the government

tax•i[1] /'tæksi/ noun, c. = a car which can be hired for a journey (also **cab**)

taxi[2] verb, i. (**taxiing, taxied**) *The aircraft taxied to a stop.* = to move slowly on the ground

tax•i•der•my /'tæksɪdɜːmi/ noun, u. = the art of cleaning and preparing the skins of wild animals and filling them up with special materials so that they look as if they are alive **taxidermist** noun, c. = a person who practises the art of taxidermy

tax•on•o•my /tæk'sɒnəmi/ noun, c. (**taxonomies**) or u. = a system used for naming and organizing things (e.g. plants and animals) into groups or classes, for the purpose of studying them [SCIENCE]

TB abbr. used for **tuberculosis** noun, u. = a disease caused by a type of bacillus which usually attacks the lungs

tea /tiː/ noun, u. **1** = a kind of drink prepared from the dried leaves of the tea-plant **2** = a meal, usually light, usually taken in the afternoon or early evening **tea-bag** noun, c. = a small paper bag filled with tea leaves, which is dipped in hot water to prepare a cup of tea **tea break** noun,c. = a period of rest during which people stop work to drink tea **tea-cosy** noun, c. (**cosies**) = a cover made of thick cloth which is put over a teapot to keep the tea inside it warm **tea cup** noun, c. = a cup in which one drinks tea, coffee, milk and other hot beverages **tea garden** noun, c. = land on which tea is farmed (also **tea plantation**) **tea leaves** noun = the leaves of the tea plant used to make tea **tea-house** noun, c. = a restaurant where tea is served (in China or Japan) **tea-party** noun, c. = a social gathering at which tea is served, usually in the afternoon **teapot** noun, c. = a container from which tea can be poured out and served to people **tea-trolley** noun, c. = a small table fitted with wheels, used to carry food and drinks to people

teach /tiːtʃ/ verb, t. (**taught**) **1** *She teaches English to little children.* = to help someone to learn something **2** *Buddhism teaches people to be kind to animals.* = to make something known and accepted **teacher** noun, c. = a person whose job is to teach, especially children in a school **teaching** noun, u. or c. **1** *She loves teaching.*(u.) = the work or profession of a teacher **2** *We should follow the teachings of Mahatma Gandhi.*(c.) = the ideas or principles taught by someone

to teach someone a lesson = to make someone understand through a punishment that something should not be done **to teach an old dog new tricks** = teach a person who is used to something, a different way of doing things

tea cup see **tea**

teak /tiːk/ noun, u. = a hard and expensive kind of wood, used for making furniture, which is obtained from the teak tree

teal /tiːl/ noun, c. = a kind of bird that looks like a duck and is found near lakes etc.

team[1] /tiːm/ noun, c. (used with either a singular or plural form of a verb) *a cricket team* = a group of people who work or play together, helping and supporting each other in a competition or in doing something

team[2] verb, t. *The two sisters teamed up for the doubles match.* = to work or play together or to make people work or play together as a team **team-mate** noun, c. = a person who is in the same team as someone else **team spirit** noun = the attitude of wanting to work together as a team **team-work** noun, u. *There is excellent team-work among the Bangladeshi players.* = the ability to work or play together as a team, helping and supporting each other

tear[1] /teəʳ/ verb, t. or i. (**tore, torn**) **1** *The girl tore a page out of her notebook and wrote her name and address on it.*(t.) = to separate or divide something by pulling it apart **2** *This paper is so thin that it tears easily. Write on it carefully.*(i.) = to become damaged by use **3** *He was torn between his desire to see the film and to go for the lecture.* = to feel the effect of opposite forces **4** *He tore along at great speed.* = to move very fast or in a hurry

to tear at something = to pull something strongly **tear off/away/out** *He tore off/out/away a page from the notebook.* = to separate something by pulling it away from something else **tear open** = to open a cover made of paper or cloth by pulling it with force **to tear down** = to bring a building down **to tear someone or something into shreds/pieces** = to criticise severely **a tearing hurry** = a great hurry (informal) **a tearaway bowler** = a very fast bowler (in the game of cricket)

tear[2] noun, c. *There is a tear in my shirt. Can you mend it?* = a torn place in a piece of cloth or paper

tear[3] /tɪəʳ/ noun, c. *He wiped the tears from his eyes.* = a drop of the liquid that flows out of the eyes when one is unhappy or in pain **tear-drop** **1** = a single tear **2** *a tear-drop shape* = having the shape of a tear drop **tearful** *a tearful scene from a film* = full of sad feelings **tear-gas** = a kind of gas which causes tears to flow from the eyes and is often used by the police to control crowds **tear-jerker** *The new film is a tear-jerker.* = a very sad film that makes people cry (often derogatory)

to burst into tears = to start crying suddenly **to be close to tears** = almost crying **to fight back tears** = to try hard not to cry **tears of joy/laughter** = a certain kind of strong emotion

tease[1] /tiːz/ verb, t. **1** *The girls tease Shobha because she usually goes to sleep in class.* = to make fun of someone or to do something to hurt or annoy someone **2** *Don't tease the animals in the zoo.* = to be cruel to animals by throwing stones at them etc.

tease[2] noun, c. (usually singular) **1** *The other children are afraid of him as he is a terrible tease.* = someone who likes to tease others **2** *The woman is a tease.* = someone who likes to excite others sexually (slang, approving) Ⓖ **teaser** noun, c. *The question you asked me was a real teaser. I couldn't think of an answer.* = a difficult question that forces one to think

to tease out = to find meaning, information etc. that is difficult to get

tea spoon see **tea**

teat /ti:t/ noun, c. **1** = a piece of rubber fitted to the end of a bottle, through which a baby can suck milk **2** = one of several raised parts along the chest of a female animal through which its young ones can suck milk (also **nipple**)

tech•ni•cal /'teknɪkəl/ adj. **1** *Computer science is a highly technical subject.* = requiring special knowledge or skill **2** *The word 'program' has a technical meaning when we use it to talk about computers.* = belonging to or related to a technical subject **3** *Jayasuriya's batting has technical brilliance.* = showing special skill or technique (see also **techique**) **technicality** /teknɪ'kælɪti/ noun, u. or c. (**technicalities**) *Despite her excellent record, she was not awarded the prize because of a technicality—she was six months older than her classmates.* = a small detail which may seem unimportant **technician** /tek'nɪʃən/ noun, c. *a laboratory technician* = a worker who has special skills, developed through special training

tech•nique /tek'ni:k/ noun, u. or c. **1** *This surgeon has excellent technique.*(u.) = special skill which has been developed carefully and can be, seen in the way one does something **2** *We have developed a new technique for recycling old plastic bags.* = a method used to perform a certain task, based on special knowledge (see also **technology**)

tech•no•crat /'teknəkræt/ noun, c. = a person with special knowledge who is put in charge of an organization and has administrative powers

tech•nol•o•gy /tek'nɒlədʒi/ noun, u. or c. (**technologies**) **1** *software technology*(u.) = special knowledge relating to the practical application (use) of science in industry **2** *Our scientists use the latest technologies to develop our telecommunication systems.*(c.) = an application (use) of scientific knowledge, for a particular purpose **technological** /teknə'lɒdʒɪkəl/ adj. *technological development* = relating to technology

ted•dy-bear /'tedi-beəʳ/ noun, c. = a child's toy which looks like a small bear

te•di•ous /'ti:diəs/ adj. *The lecture was so tedious that many people walked away while it was going on.* = long and boring **tedium** /'ti:diəm/ noun, u. *Many people read books while waiting for trains at a railway station, to reduce the tedium.* = boredom (the effect of something that is tedious)

tee[1] /ti:/ noun, c. = a small cup-like instrument, used in the game of golf, in which the ball is placed before it is hit with the golf club (stick)

tee[2] verb, i. *The oldest player taking part in the golf tournament was the first to tee off.* = to start a game of golf by hitting the ball

teem (with) /ti:m/ verb, i. *These rivers teem with fish.* = to be full (of living creatures) **teeming** adj. *food for our teeming millions* = overcrowded; filling up a lot of space

teens /ti:nz/ noun (always plural) *boys and girls in their teens* = the period in one's life between the ages of 13 and 19 (informal) **teenage** adj. *teenage fashion* = relating to people who are in their teens **teenager** /'ti:neɪdʒəʳ/ noun, c. = a person who is in his/her teens

tee•ny-wee•ny /ti:ni-'wi:ni/ adj. *a teeny-weeny dress* = very small (informal)

tee-shirt see **T-shirt**

tee•ter /'ti:təʳ/ verb, i. *The Indian team had scored 297 runs for 9 wickets, in reply to Australia's total of 300. They teetered on the brink of defeat, but managed to draw the match.* = to be balanced unsteadily; to be about to fall or suffer a defeat, loss etc.

teeth /ti:θ/ noun **1** = plural of tooth **2** *The new law has given the government the teeth it needed to deal with crimes against women.* = power

teethe /ti:ð/ verb, i. *The baby is teething.* = to grow teeth **teething troubles** noun *The school faced teething troubles during the first two years, but is doing well now.* = the problems faced in the early period of doing something new

tee•to•tal•ler /ti:'təʊtələʳ/ noun, c. = a person who does not take alcoholic drinks

tef•lon /'teflɒn/ noun (trademark)= a plastic material to which things do not stick, used in making cooking pots which allow one to cook without using much oil

tele- /telə/ prefix meaning **'far'** e.g. telephone

tel•e•cast[1] /'telikɑ:st/ noun, c. = a programme shown on television

telecast[2] verb, t. *The cricket match is being telecast.* = to show something on television

tel•e•com•mu•ni•ca•tions /telikəmju:nɪ'keɪʃənz/ noun (always plural) = the processes or systems that allow people to send and receive messages by telephone, telegraph, radio etc.

te•le•con•fer•ence noun, c. = a meeting among people in different places, using telephones and television cameras (also **video conferencing**)

tel•e•gram /'telɪgræm/ noun, c.= a written message sent by telegraph **telegraph** /'telɪgrɑ:f/ noun, u. = a system of sending written messages by using electrical signals along a wire, which print out sets of dots and dashes that are later converted into words

te•lep•a•thy /tɪ'lepəθi/ noun, u. = the ability to know the thoughts of another person and to communicate (exchange ideas) without speaking or using language often from a distance

tel•e•phone[1] /'telɪfəʊn/ noun, c. or u. **1** (u.) = a system by which people can speak to each other from a distance, using electrical signals sent along a wire or through space **2** (c.) = an instrument used for speaking to another person from a distance

telephone[2] verb, t. *You can telephone me at this number.* = to speak to someone over the telephone **telephone booth** noun, c. = a small, closed room containing a telephone which can be used by someone on payment of money **telephone directory** noun, c. = a printed book containing the names and telephone numbers of people living in a certain area **telephone exchange** noun, c. = a central place where connections can be made between people wishing to speak to each other by telephone

tel•e•prompt•er /'telɪprɒmptə[r]/ noun, c. = a machine used by newsreaders on television, which allows the printed words on a sheet of paper to appear on a large screen facing the newsreader, so that he or she seems to be speaking directly to the audience and not reading from a sheet of paper

tel•e•scope[1] /'telɪskəʊp/ noun, c. = an instrument which allows one to see clearly objects which are far away, consisting of metal tubes which can slide inside each other, making the instrument shorter or longer

telescope[2] verb, i. **1** *Three carriages in the middle part of the train telescoped in the accident because of the pressure from the carriages which were behind them.* = to become shorter in length; to run into each other **2** *The film telescopes a long story into fifteen minutes.* = to make short

tel•e•vi•sion /'telvɪʒən/ noun, u. or c. **1** (u.) = a system by which pictures and sounds can be sent and received between places which are far apart and not connected to each other by wires **2** = an instrument which allows one to see pictures and hear sounds being sent by television **televize** /'telɪvaɪz/ verb, t. *The cricket match will be televized.* = to show over television (also **telecast**)

tell /tel/ verb, t. or i. (**told**) **1** *Tell me your name.* = to make something known to someone by speaking **2** *The teacher told the child to stand up.* = to order or command **3** *These words in the poem tell you that the poet was very unhappy.* = to suggest (to allow a certain meaning to be understood **4** *There were so many people in the room that I couldn't tell who was shouting.* = to recognize or to know for certain **5** *I told you it would rain.* = to warn **teller** noun, c. = a person who works in a bank and receives or pays out money **telling** adj. *Pillai's excellent running was the most telling factor in India's victory.* = having a strong effect **telltale** adj. *There were some telltale bloodstains on the murderer's clothes.* = something that allows a secret to become known

to tell off = to speak angrily to someone for doing something wrong **to tell on** *Staying up late is telling on me.* = to have a harmful effect on someone **to tell on someone** = to carry stories/information about someone to another person (see also **to tell tales**) **to tell against someone** *His poor health will tell against him.* = to make it difficult for someone to succeed **to tell apart (to tell the difference)** *The puppies looked so similar, we could not tell them apart.* = to be able to recognize the difference between two people, animals or things which are similiar **to tell tales** (always plural) = to carry information which is not favourable about a person, to another person (informal, disapproving) **all told** *I will pay you Rs 500 a month all told.* = everything included **I'll tell you what** *I'll tell you what. Let's stay at home and watch television.* = words which are followed by a suggestion **Tell me another!** *'I scored nine goals in a match today.' 'Tell me another!'* = used when one does not believe something that is being said (informal) **to tell somebody where to get off** *When his friend tried to tell Arjun what to do with his new exercise cycle, he told him where he got off.* = to tell someone rudely that you are not interested in what they are saying (not respectful) **You're telling me!** *'She loves to argue.' 'You're telling me!'* = used to express agreement (informal)

te•me•ri•ty /te'meriti/ noun, u. *You have the temerity to argue with me when you have made such a stupid mistake?* = excessive courage, especially in an inappropriate situation (disapproving)

tem•per[1] /'tempə[r]/ noun, u. **1** *Be careful when you speak to the coach. He has a bad temper.* = the quality of a person's mind which causes him/her to become angry easily **2** *Let's not try to meet her now. She is in a temper.* = a temporary condition of being angry **3** *This steel spring has lost its temper.* = the ability of a piece of metal to stand up to rough treatment without breaking [TECHNICAL]

temper[2] verb, t. **1** *Atul was disappointed when he lost the match. However, his disappointment was tempered by the realization that he had lost to a better player.* = to reduce (make less) the effect of something **2** *These steel swords are tempered by making them red-hot and then dipping them in ice-cold water.* = to heat and then cool a piece of metal in order to make it hard and strong [TECHNICAL]

tem•pe•ra•ment /'tempərəmənt/ noun, u. *The manager of a large company should have a calm temperament.* = nature or character, which controls one's behaviour **temperamental** /tempərə'məntəl/ adj. *a temperamental actor* =

moody (having frequent changes of mood or temper and easily made angry)

tem•pe•rance /'tempərəns/ noun, u. **1** *Although he was being abused, he remained calm. His temperance surprised everyone.* = self-control, specially in eating or drinking **2** *a temperance society* = being opposed to the use of alcohol

tem•pe•rate /'tempərɪt/ adj. **1** *temperate climate* = neither too hot nor too cold **2** *The Prime Minister is known to be temperate in her speech and never uses harsh language.* = calm and controlled

tem•pe•ra•ture /'tempərətʃəʳ/ noun, u. or c. **1** *The temperature in Delhi today was 32 degrees Celsius.* = the degree of heat in a place or an object **2** *The child has a temperature.* = fever

tem•pest /'tempɪst/ noun, c. = a violent storm **tem•pes•tu•ous** /tem'pestʃuəs/ adj. *There were tempestuous scenes at the meeting.* = charged with emotion (usually anger)

tem•plate /'templeɪt/ noun, c. = a thin piece of metal, plastic etc., which has been cut into a certain shape or pattern and is used to make copies of some object

tem•ple /'tempəl/ noun, c. **1** = a place of worship, specially for Hindus, Sikhs or Buddhists **2** = the flat area on each side of the forehead

tem•po /'tempəʊ/ noun, c. (**tempos** or **tempi**) **1** *The music is played at a fast tempo.* = speed (of music) **2** *The tempo of life in the city has become hectic.* = the speed at which things happen

tem•po•ral /'tempərəl/ adj. *People are more interested in temporal advancement than in spiritual progress.* = belonging to the world of material objects

tem•po•ra•ry /'tempərəri/ adj. *a temporary arrangement* = lasting only for a short time

tem•po•rize /'tempəraɪz/ verb, i. *The government seems to be temporizing in deciding whether or not a new dam should be built.* = to delay in taking a decision, in order to gain time (disapproving)

tempt /tempt/ verb, t. **1** *When I saw my uncle's motorcycle, I was tempted to drive it without telling him.* = to feel the desire to do something which one knows to be wrong **2** *We want him as our new manager. Maybe we could tempt him with an attractive salary.* = to offer something to someone in order to persuade him/her to do something **temptation** /temp'teɪʃən/ noun, c. or u. **1** *Chicken curry is a great temptation for me, although the doctor has advised me to avoid meat.* = something that tempts (attracts one into doing something unwise) **2** *I felt a strong temptation when I found all that money lying on the street.* = a desire to do something which one knows to be wrong

ten /ten/ noun, c. = the number represented by the figure 10 **ten-pin** noun, c. = one of the wooden pins that one tries to knock down in the game of bowling

ten•a•ble /'tenəbəl/ adj. *You want Sanskrit to be our national language, but the arguments you have offered in support of Sanskrit are not tenable.* = (arguments or opinions) which can be supported or defended

te•na•cious /tɪ'neɪʃəs/ adj. *He wants to take the test again, though he has failed it three times. He is really tenacious!* = not ready to give up trying

ten•ant /'tenənt/ noun, c. = a person who pays rent to someone for the use of a building or a piece of land **tenancy** noun, u. = the period of time during which one has a right to use a building etc., as a tenant **tenant-farmer** noun, c. = a person who cultivates land owned by someone else

tend /tend/ verb, i. **1** *She tends to speak very fast when she is excited.* = to be likely to behave in a certain way **2** *My brother tends his rose plants with great affection.* = to take care of something or someone (old-fashioned) **tendency** /'tendənsi/ noun, u. or c. (tendencies) **1** *He has a tendency to get involved in arguments unnecessarily.*(c.) = a natural quality which makes a person likely to behave in a certain way **2** *There is a tendency for prices to come down when there is a good monsoon.*(c.) = a likelihood that something will happen

ten•der[1] /'tendəʳ/ adj. **1** *a baby's tender skin* = soft **2** *The wound in my leg has healed, but the skin is still tender.* = sensitive; causing one to feel pain when touched **3** *tender meat* = easy to cut, bite or chew (referring to meat or vegetables) **4** *tender feelings* = loving and kind **5** *a tender age* = very young

tender[2] noun, c. **1** *I have submitted my tender for a government contract.* = a formal written offer to supply goods or services for a certain price **2** *the tender of a steam locomotive* = a small carriage attached to the locomotive (engine) of a train, which carries extra coal or water

tender[3] verb, i. or t. **1** *Five companies have tendered for the contract to build a new hospital.*(i.) = to make a formal offer to do something or sell something for a certain price **2** *I would like to tender my apologies for not coming to the meeting yesterday.*(t.) = to offer **tender-foot** noun, c. (**tender-foots**) = a young person without any experience of doing something (informal) **tender-hearted** adj. *a tender-hearted person* = kind **tenderize** /'tendəraɪz/ verb, t. *You can use the juice of a papaya to tenderize meat.* = to make something (specially meat) soft

ten•don /'tendən/ noun, c. = the thick, strong cord-like parts of the body which connect a large muscle to a bone [BIOLOGY]

ten•dril /ˈtendrɪl/ noun, c. *The rose creeper attached itself to the wall by means of its many tendrils.* = a thin stem-like part of a climbing plant which grows on to walls etc. for support [BIOLOGY]

ten•e•ment /ˈtenɪmənt/ noun, c. = a large building divided into flats, usually built for people who are not very rich

ten•et /ˈtenɪt/ noun, c. *He follows the tenets of his religion faithfully.* = a teaching or principle on which a religion or philosophy is based

ten•ner /ˈtenəʳ/ noun, c. *Take this 50-rupee note and give me five tenners.* = a ten-rupee note (slang)

ten•nis /ˈtenɪs/ noun, u. = a game played between two or four players, who use racquets to hit a ball over a net stretched across the middle of a court **tennis-elbow** noun, c. = a painful swelling near the elbow, caused by frequent twisting of the hand and arm

ten•or /ˈtenəʳ/ noun, c. or u. **1** (c.) = a male singer with a high pitched voice **2** *I could follow the general tenor of his speech but not all his ideas.*(u.) = the general meaning **3** *The earthquake has disturbed the tenor of our lives.*(c.) = the character or pattern

tense[1] /tens/ adj. **1** *The girl was very tense before the interview, so the chairperson of the selection committee asked her to relax.* = nervous and anxious and unable to relax **2** *The situation in the college became tense when a student was arrested by the police.* = causing anxiety **3** *The muscles of your arm are tense. Can you loosen them?* = stretched tight and stiff (hard)

tense[2] verb, t. *She tensed the muscles of her arm.* = to stretch out and make something stiff and hard

tense[3] noun, c. *'Eat' is in the present tense whereas 'ate' is in the past tense.* = the form of a verb which shows the period of time (past or present) during which an action is supposed to have taken place [GRAMMAR]

ten•sile /ˈtensaɪl/ adj. *Steel is tensile but wood is not.* = the ability of a material to be stretched beyond its normal length [TECHNICAL]

ten•sion /ˈtenʃən/ noun, u. **1** *Ejaz has to deal with so many problems at work that he is always suffering from tension.* = a state of anxiety and pressure on the mind **2** *There is tension in the city after the police firing.* = a dangerous condition which may lead to violence **3** *You should reduce the tension in the strings of the sitar.* = the degree of tightness of a wire or rope (see also **taut**)

tent /tent/ noun, c. = a movable shelter made of canvas (strong, thick cloth) or nylon, which is supported by poles and held in position by ropes

ten•ta•cle /ˈtentɪkəl/ noun, c. *the tentacles of an octopus* = the long, snake-like arms of certain sea-creatures, used for holding prey

ten•ta•tive /ˈtentətɪv/ adj. **1** *The date for my marriage has not been fixed, but the tentative date is the 4 March.* = not fully certain **2** *He gave a tentative reply to my question, which showed that he was not sure of the facts.* = done or said without confidence

ten•ter-hooks /ˈtentəhʊks/ noun (always plural) *The girl was on tenter-hooks before her exam.* = a nervous state of mind

tenth /tenθ/ det. *the tenth day of the month* = coming after nine objects or people; the ordinal form of ten

ten•ure /ˈtenjəʳ/ noun, u. **1** *During his tenure as Vice Chancellor of the university, he brought about many changes.* = the period of time during which one holds a job or occupies a piece of land etc. **2** *The professor holds a tenure in the English Department.* = a permanent position

te•pid /ˈtepɪd/ adj. **1** *tepid water* = used to describe a liquid which is slightly warm but not hot **2** *The new film got a tepid reception from critics.* = not very enthusiastic (not showing much liking for something)

term[1] /tɜːm/ verb, t. *The head of this village is termed the 'sarpanch'.* = to name or describe someone by a particular word

term[2] noun, c. **1** *The consultant was appointed for a three-year term.* = a fixed or limited period of time for which something lasts **2** *The professor taught poetry during the last term.* = a period of time (usually about 4 months) into which a year is divided for the purposes of teaching at a university **3** *'Subjunctive' is a grammatical term.* = a word or expression having a particular meaning in relation to a particular subject **4** *'Rascal' is a term of abuse as well as endearment.* = a word used to express a certain feeling **terms** noun (always plural) **1** *Under the terms of the new agreement, Pakistani traders will move about freely in India.* = the conditions of an agreement or contract **2** *Binaifer and Naina have always been on good terms.* = the relationship between two persons, countries etc. **3** *Switzerland is an important country, though it is not a big country in terms of size.* = some quality that is used to judge or decide something

to come to terms with *I wasn't happy with my new job at first, but I have come to terms with it.* = to accept something or someone that one did not like at first **to be on equal terms** = to be someone's equal in something (e.g. money) **in the long/short term** *This new law may help us in the short term, but not in the long term.* = the length or period of time for which something has an effect

ter•mi•nal[1] /ˈtɜːmɪnəl/ adj. **1** *a terminal examination* = coming at the end of a term (a period of teaching) **2** *terminal cancer* = (an illness) which leads to death

T

terminal[2] noun, c. *an airport terminal* = a large building (at an airport, railway station etc.) for the use of passengers

ter•mi•nate /'tɜːmɪneɪt/ verb, t. *Your services will be terminated next month.* = to come to or bring to an end (formal) **termination** /tɜːmɪ'neɪʃən/ noun, u. *He returned to his village after the termination of his services.* = the act of coming to an end

ter•mi•nol•o•gy /tɜːmɪ'nɒlədʒi/ noun, u. or c. (**terminologies**) *medical terminology*(u.) = the system of terms (words with special meanings) used for talking or writing about a particular subject

ter•mi•nus /'tɜːmɪnəs/ noun, c. (**terminuses** or **termini**) *a train terminus* = a station or stop at the end of a railway or bus line

ter•mite /'tɜːmaɪt/ noun, c. = an ant-like insect that builds and lives in large mounds of hard earth (called ant-hills) and eats and destroys wood

terms = see **term**

tern /tɜːn/ noun, c. = a sea-bird with black and white wings

ter•race /'terɪs/ noun, c. **1** *He likes to sleep on the terrace at night.* = the flat area on the top of a house **2** *The hill-side has been cut into terraces for cultivation.* = a flat, level area cut from the side of a hill, in order to grow crops **terraced house** noun, c. = a row of houses joined to each other

ter•ra-cot ta /terə'kɒtə/ noun, u. *a terra-cotta statue* = a kind of hard, red material, produced by baking clay (mud)

ter•ra fir•ma /terə 'fɜːmə/ noun, u. (Latin) *It was good to be back on terra-firma after our long journey in a boat.* = dry land (literary or humorous)

ter•rain /te'reɪn/ noun, u. or c. *Our army does not use tanks to fight on the mountains. Tanks are not useful in this kind of terrain.*(u.) = an area of land which has a particular natural quality (sandy, hilly, rocky etc.) [TECHNICAL]

ter•ra•pin /'terəpɪn/ noun, c. = a kind of turtle that lives in fresh water

ter•res•tri•al /tɪ'restriəl/ noun, c. *Some scientists believe that whales, which now live in the sea, were once terrestrial creatures.* = belonging to the land (and not the sea)

ter•ri•ble /'terɪbəl/ adj. **1** *terrible earthquake* = causing much destruction and suffering **2** *These forests are full of terrible snakes.* = causing fear **3** *I made a terrible mistake when introducing the musician.* = very bad

ter•rier /'teriəʳ/ noun, c. = a kind of dog used (in earlier times) in hunting

ter•rif•fic /tə'rɪfɪk/ adj. **1** *The new book has been a terrific success. We sold 1,000 copies on the first day.* = very great (in a good sense) **2** *He drove off at a terrific speed.* = great (not necessarily in a good sense)

ter•ri•fy /'terɪfaɪ/ verb, t. *A gang of robbers terrified the city for years.* = to keep someone in a state of fear **terrified** adj. *He is terrified of reptiles.* = very frightened

ter•ri•to•ry /'terɪtəri/ noun, u. or c. (**territories**) **1** *Some enemy soldiers were captured when they crossed over into Indian territory.*(c.) = an area of land which belongs to or is controlled by a particular country **2** *The tiger marked off its territory by spraying the bushes with its urine.*(u.) = an area which an animal considers as belonging to it alone, and is prepared to defend against others **3** *He is managing the northern territory.*(c.) = an area which is looked after by a particular branch of a company **territorial** /terɪ'tɔːriəl/ adj. **1** *We hope India and China will soon settle their territorial disputes.* = relating to territory (the ownership of an area of land) **2** *a territorial tiger* = (an animal which is) guarding its own territory **territorial waters** noun (always plural) = the part of the sea which lies along the coastline of a country, over which that country has a legal right

ter•ror /'terəʳ/ noun, u. or c. **1** *The people of the Sunderban forests live in terror of man-eating tigers.*(u.) = extreme fear **2** *Her strictness makes her a terror in the office.*(c.) = someone who causes great fear (not formal) **terrorism** noun, u. = the use of violence, particularly against innocent people, to obtain political demands **terrorist** noun, c. = one who takes part in terrorism **terrorize** verb, t. = to create terror (great fear) in the minds of people

ter•ry-cloth /'terіklɒθ/ noun, u. = thick cotton cloth with threads hanging from the surface, used for making towels

terse /tɜːs/ adj. *his terse reply* = using as few words as possible, brief, in a way that seems rude or unfriendly

ter•tia•ry /'tɜːʃəri/ adj. *a tertiary branch of a tree* = belonging to the third level or stage (formal) **tertiary education** noun, u. = education given at the college level, after the primary and secondary (school) levels

TESOL /'tesɒl/ abbr. of **Teaching English to Speakers of Other Languages** noun **1** = an American organization which is interested in problems related to the teaching of English to people for whom it is not the mother-tongue or first language **2** = the study of the principles used in teaching English such people

test[1] /test/ noun, c. **1** *a language test* = a set of questions or practical activities used to find out whether someone has the knowledge or skill required for some purpose **2** *a blood test* = a medical examination of some part of the body to find out if one is suffering from some disease **3** *The car was put through a road test.* = the act of using something (e.g. a machine) to see if it works properly

test[2] verb, t. **1** *The teachers will test all students applying for admission to the school.* = to ask someone to answer questions etc. as part of a test **2** *This new wicket will test the skill of the batsmen.* = to challenge; to put someone in a situation which will prove if he/she has the required skill **testing** adj. *We are going through testing times. We must be very patient.* = difficult to deal with **test ban** noun = an agreement between countries to stop the testing of nuclear weapons **test match** noun, c. (**matches**) = a cricket match usually played over five days between the national teams of two countries **test pilot** noun, c. = a person whose job is to test new aircraft by flying them, to make sure that they fly properly **test-tube** noun, c. = a thin tube made of glass, closed at one end, which is used for scientific tests **test-tube baby** noun, c. = a baby which is developed outside the mother's body from an egg and sperms taken from the parents, and then placed inside the mother's body where it grows into a fully-formed baby

tes•ta•ment /ˈtestəmənt/ noun, c. **1** *a person's last will and testament* = a legal document signed by a person before his/her death, which tells how that person's property is to be divided **2** *This beautiful painting is a testament to your artistic talent.* = a proof of something **testate** adj. *He died testate.* = having made a will or testament, deciding how one's property will be divided (opposite **intestate**) [LAW]

tes•ti•cle /ˈtestɪkəl/ noun, c. = one of the two round organs in a male animal or human being which produce **sperms** and lie inside a loose bag of skin, called the scrotum, behind and below the **penis** [BIOLOGY]

tes•ti•fy /ˈtestɪfaɪ/ verb, t. **1** *The witness testified that he had seen the accused entering the room in which a man had been murdered.* = to provide evidence (a statement of what one knows or has seen and believes to be true) in court [LAW] **2** *The clothes lying all over the floor testified to the fact that the man had left in a hurry.* = to prove; to show clearly

tes•ti•mo•ni•al /testɪˈməʊniəl/ noun, c. **1** *The candidates who had been called for the interview were asked to produce testimonials from people who knew them personally.* = a statement about the character or qualities of someone who is being considered for a job etc. **2** *a testimonial match* = something done to show honour to someone (e.g. a well-known player who is no longer playing)

tes•ti•mo•ny /ˈtestɪməni/ noun, u. *The testimony given by this witness proves that the accused is innocent.* = evidence given by a witness in court (see also **testify**) [LAW]

testing = see **test**

tes•tis /ˈtestɪs/ noun, c. (**testes**) = testicle [BIOLOGY]

tes•tos•ter•one /tesˈtɒstərəʊn/ noun, u. = the male hormone (chemical substance produced inside the body) that gives a person the qualities of a male

tes•ty /ˈtesti/ adj. *a testy gatekeeper* = bad-tempered

tet•a•nus /ˈtetənəs/ noun, u. = a serious disease, caused by bacteria which enter the blood through a wound, that leads to paralysis of the muscles, specially around the mouth and death (also **lock-jaw**) [MEDICINE]

tete-a-tete /teɪt ɑː ˈteɪt/ noun (French) *The leaders of the two countries had a tete-a-tete.* = a private conversation

teth•er[1] /ˈteðəʳ/ noun, c. *The horse was tied with a tether.* = a rope or chain used to tie an animal to a post

tether[2] verb, t. *The horse was tethered to a tree.* = to tie with a tether

to be at (to come to) the end of one's tether = to reach the end of one's patience, or one's ability to deal with a difficult situation

text /tekst/ noun, c. **1** = a piece of language, spoken or written, which is made up of a number of connected sentences and has a definite meaning **2** *This book contains 150 pages of text.* = written or printed material **3** *We will print the full text of the President's speech.* = the exact words used by someone **4** *We have discovered a number of ancient history texts.* = a book which has high literary or religious value **5** *The text for this year's examination was Tagore's 'Geetanjali.'* = a book which has to be studied for an examination (see also **textbook**) **textbook** noun, c. or adj. **1** *We have to study two history textbooks.*(noun, c.) = a book used to study a subject **2** *a textbook example* (adj.) = ideal or perfect; good enough to be used as an example in a text-book on the subject **textual** /ˈtekstʃuəl/ adj. *the textual study of a play* = having to do with a text (usually in its printed form)

tex•tile /ˈtekstaɪl/ noun, c. (usually plural **textiles**) *cotton textiles* = a material produced by weaving

tex•ture /ˈtekstʃəʳ/ noun, u. or c. *This silk sari has a smooth texture.*(u.) = the quality of being rough, smooth etc., that can be felt by touching something

than[1] /ðən/ or /ðæn/ prep. **1** *He is taller than his father.* = when compared to **2** *He has more than twenty books of stamps.* = a number or amount compared to another number or amount

than[2] conj. *There are more TV watchers now than there were before.* = joining the two parts of a comparison

T

thank /θæŋk/ verb, t. **1** *I must thank you for helping me.* = to let someone know that you feel grateful for and have appreciated something that the person did for you **2** *We have our neighbours to thank for the mess in this corridor.* = to blame someone (hold someone responsible for something bad)

thanks[1] /θæŋks/ noun (always plural) *We would like to express our thanks for this help.* = the feeling of being grateful to someone for something that he/she has done for you

thanks[2] interjec. *That was a lovely meal. Thanks!* = an informal expression meaning 'thank you!' **thankful** adj. *We are thankful to our teacher for arranging this picnic.* = grateful; appreciating something that someone has done to help **thankless** adj. *Writing addresses on invitation cards is a thankless job.* = not likely to be appreciated **thanksgiving** noun, u. = the formal act of thanking someone, especially God **Thanksgiving Day** noun = a North American festival celebrated on the fourth Thursday in November each year, to thank God for providing a good harvest

that[1] /ðət/ det. (plural **those**) **1** *This book is for you, but that book over there is for your brother.* = referring to something or someone that is at some distance from the speaker **2** *Have you ever played badmiton? That is my favourite game!* = referring to something that has just been mentioned

that[2] pron. **1** *This book is mine, but that is yours.* = referring to something that is at some distance **2** *'I believe Tagore is the greatest of all Indian writers.' 'I will accept that.'* = referring to something that has just been mentioned or is understood

that[3] conj. **1** *He says that he cannot come now.* = introducing, in reported (indirect) speech, what a speaker says **2** *She knows that you are here.* = introducing a noun clause which is the object of the verb coming before 'that' **3** *This is the book that he wrote last year. // He is the man that I spoke to you about.* = which or who (introducing a relative clause) **4** *I am happy that you could come.* = because **5** *That she is going to win is certain.* = introducing a noun clause which is the subject of a sentence

that[4] adv. *She runs fast, but not that fast.* = so much (to such a degree)

that is to say *I love cricket. That is to say, I love watching cricket on television.* = an exression used to explain or correct a statement that one has just made **and all that** *I need to buy soap, toothpaste and all that.* = things of the same kind **That's that!** *I've told you I am not coming to your party, and that's that!* = what I have said is final

thatch[1] /θætʃ/ noun, c. *The rain dripped through the thatch.* = the straw covering over the roof of a house

thatch[2] verb, t. *The roof will be thatched this year.* = to cover the roof of a house with straw

thaw[1] /θɔː/ verb, i. or t. **1** *The ice on the mountains thaws (out) when summer comes.*(i.) // *You will have to remove the meat from the freezer and thaw it out before you can cook it.*(t.) = to change from a frozen, solid state (e.g. ice) to a liquid state (e.g. water) or a less hard state because of an increase in temperature **2** *He was quite unfriendly at first and refused to talk to us, but after some time he thawed.*(i.) = to become more friendly and relaxed (figurative)

thaw[2] noun, u. **1** *It is June now, and the thaw has set in.* = the period of warm weather when snow begins to melt **2** *Rose and Meena were not on friendly terms, but now there is a thaw in their relationship.* = an improvement in relationships after a period of unfriendliness

the[1] /ðə/ or /ði/ det. (definite article) **1** *One of your students wants to meet you. The boy is waiting outside.* = referring to a particular person or thing which has just been mentioned **2** *The sun has risen, but you can't see it because there are clouds in the sky.* = referring to something which is the only one in existence **3** *The man whom you met last night is my brother.* = referring to someone in particular about whom more is going to be said **4** *He was hurt on the arm.* = one's **5** *The city person is used to public transport.* = referring to a whole class of people, animals or things **6** *The old and the sick will be looked after.* = used to change an adjective into a noun **7** *Pop music started in the seventies.* = a particular period of time

the[2] adv. *The sooner he comes, the better it will be for him.* = used with comparative forms of adverbs and adjectives

thea•tre /ˈθɪətəʳ/ noun, c. or u. **1** *Kolkata has a number of theatres where plays are performed every evening.*(c.)= a special building in which plays (dramas) are performed or films shown **2** *a lecture theatre*(c.) = a large room meant for some special purpose **3** *He writes for the theatre.*(u.) = the profession of producing or acting in plays (dramas) **theatrical** /θiˈætrɪkəl/ adj. **1** *a theatrical performance* = connected with the theatre **2** *a theatrical speech* = done in an unnatural manner to attract attention (derogatory) **theatre-goer** noun, c. = a person who regularly watches plays in a theatre

thee /ðiː/ pron. = old form of 'you' (used as the object of a verb or preposition)

theft /θeft/ noun, u. or c. *He was arrested while trying to steal money and will be tried for theft.*(u.) = the act of stealing

their /ðəʳ/ det. (possessive form of 'they') **1** *They* *have sold their house.* = belonging to them **2** *Everyone must remember to bring their textbook to class.* = used to avoid saying 'his' or 'her' **theirs** /ðeəz/ pron. (possessive form of 'they') *This house was mine but now it is theirs.* = belonging to them

the•is•m /'θi:ɪzəm/ noun, u. = belief in God (opposite **atheism**)

them /ðəm/ pron. **1** *'Have you invited Mr and Mrs Verma to your party?' 'No, I don't know them.'* = object form of 'they' **2** *If anyone wants to see me, tell them I am not at home.* = used to avoid saying 'him' or 'her'

theme /θi:m/ noun, c. *She has written a novel on the theme of war.* = the main subject of a talk, piece of writing, film etc. **theme song** noun, c. = a song which is repeated several times in a film

them•selves /ðəm'selvz/ pron. **1** *They hid themselves in a cave.* = reflexive form of 'they' **2** *They built this house themselves.* = by their own efforts without anyone's help (used for emphasis)

all by themselves *They like to wander through the forest all by themselves.* = alone

then[1] /ðen/ adv. **1** *My father started his medical practice in Bhubaneswar in 1945. There were very few doctors in the city then.* = at that time **2** *He had his dinner and then he went to bed.* = afterwards **3** *If you can't come today, then you may come tomorrow.* = in that case **4** *You should ring the bell twice, then somebody will open the door.* = as a result

then[2] adj. *My grandfather received the title of 'Rai Bahadur in 1925, from the then Governor of Bengal.* = at that time

then and there *When the police tell you to pay a fine, it must be paid then and there.* = at once

thence /ðens/ adv. *We travelled first to Kolkata and thence to Dhaka.* = from that place (old-fashioned) **thenceforth** adv. *The Queen died in 1880, and thenceforth the country was ruled by a line of kings.* = after that time (old-fashioned)

theo- /θɪɔ/ prefix meaning 'having to do with God' **the•ol•o•gy** /θɪ'ɒlədʒi/ noun = the study of religion, in particular beliefs about the relationships between God and man **theo•lo•gian** /θɪə'ləʊdʒən/ noun, c. = a person who has studied or taught theology

the•o•cra•cy /θɪ'ɒkrəsi/ noun = a political system or government which is based on a particular religion **theocratic** /θɪə'krætɪk/ adj. *a theocratic state* = following theocratic principles

the•od•o•lite /θi'ɒdəlaɪt/ noun, c. = an instrument used for surveying (measuring) land

theo•rem /'θɪərəm/ noun, c. *One of the theorems I learnt in geometry was 'The sum of the angles of a triangle is equal to two right angles.'* = a statement (specially in mathematics) that can be proved to be true through logical reasoning [MATHEMATICS]

theo•ry /'θɪəri/ noun, u. or c. (**theories**) **1** *Einstein's Theory of Relativity says that matter can be converted into energy and energy into matter.*(u.) = a formal statement of some rule or principle which helps to explain something and has been proved to be true [SCIENCE] **2** *The theory of the police is that the woman was killed by someone who was known to her, as she offered no resistance.*(c.) = a possible explanation for a fact or event, which has not been proved **in theory** *In theory, men are stronger than women, but in practice you will find that men are weaker.* = what is commonly believed to be true but is not necessarily true **theoretical** /θɪə'retɪkəl/ adj. **1** *theoretical physics* = concerned with the study of theories (see **theory** meaning **1**) **2** *There is a theoretical possibility that India's economy could grow by 6 percent this year, if conditions are right.* = something which could happen but is not very likely to happen **3** *His ideas are all theoretical, but they won't work in practice.* = something that cannot be used for a practical purpose (slightly derogatory) **theorist** /'θɪərɪst/ noun, c. = a person who contributes a new theory to the study of some subject **theorize (theorise)** /θɪə'raɪz/ verb, i. = *Some people are trying to theorize why cricket has suddenly become the most popular game.* = to try to find a possible explanation for a fact

ther•a•py /'θerəpi/ noun, u. or c. (**therapies**) = a process or a method used to treat illness **therapist** noun, c. = a person who offers therapy (treatment to cure illness) **therapeutic** /θerə'pju:tɪk/ adj. *This plant possesses therapeutic qualities.* = relating to therapy (the treatment of illness)

there[1] /ðeəʳ/ adv. **1** *I went to Mumbai last week and met Shankar Mahadevan there.* = in that place **2** *You say he is honest but there I must disagree with you.* = at that point **3** *There she goes!* = used to draw attention to someone or something

there[2] pron. *There is a man waiting to see you.* = a word used at the beginning of a sentence, often followed by verbs such as 'is', 'are' etc., to introduce a topic (idea) that is going to be mentioned

there[3] interjec. *There! My task is done!* = an expression of satisfaction, sympathy etc. **thereabouts** adv. **1** *You can find me in the library or thereabouts.* = near that place **2** *I'll reach your house at 7.00 or thereabouts.* = near that time **thereafter** adv. *He moved to Kolkata five years ago and we have had no contact thereafter.* = after that time **thereby** adv. *He resigned after working for only two years, thereby giving up his claim to a pension.* = by doing or saying that **therefore** adv. *You invited me to come and*

T

therefore I am here. = so; for that reason (formal) **therein** adv. *He wrote a letter to the Director, stating therein that he had decided to resign.* = in that place or in that piece of writing (formal, old-fashioned) **thereupon** adv. *Everyone agreed that he should be asked to preside, and thereupon he took the chair.* = just after that

to be there for someone *Whenever you need help, I'll be there for you.* = to be ready to help **There you are!** *You asked for a cup of tea, didn't you? There you are!* = a polite way of saying 'Take it (what you asked for)'

therm- /θɜːm/ prefix meaning **'heat'**

ther•mal[1] /ˈθɜːməl/ adj. *a thermal spring* = producing heat or caused by heat

thermal[2] noun, c. = a rising current of warm air which can cause a flying aircraft to rise up **thermodynamics** /θɜːməʊdaɪˈnæmɪks/ noun = the branch of physics that deals with the connection between heat energy and its use in different kinds of machines [PHYSICS] **thermometer** /θəˈmɒmɪtəʳ/ noun, c. = an instrument that can measure temperature (the degree of heat) **thermonuclear** /θɜːməʊˈnjuːkliəʳ/ adj. *a thermo-nuclear bomb* = having to do with some nuclear process (the splitting up or joining together of atoms, see also **nuclear**) which produces a great deal of heat **thermos (flask)** /ˈθɜːməs/ noun (trademark) = a kind of container which keeps the contents (the things kept inside it) at either a higher or lower temperature than the temperature outside

ther•mo•stat /ˈθɜːməstæt/ noun, c. = a device (instrument) fitted to an electrical machine used for heating or cooling something, which switches off the supply of electricity when the temperature rises above or falls below a certain temperature

the•sau•rus /θɪˈsɔːrəs/ noun, c. (**thesauruses**) = a book in which words are arranged in groups based on their meanings and which lists together words having similar or opposite meanings

these /ðiːz/ det. *Can you put these books back on the shelf?* = plural of **'this'**

the•sis /ˈθiːsɪs/ noun, c. (**theses**) **1** *The main thesis in his book is that India's problems are not because of over-population.* = the main idea or opinion expressed in a talk or a piece of writing, which is supported by arguments, examples etc. **2** *Your doctoral thesis has been accepted by the examiners.* = a long piece of writing which puts forward a new idea and for which a university awards a higher degree

thes•pi•an /ˈθespiən/ noun, c. = an actor, specially one who acts in plays (dramas) (formal)

they /ðeɪ/ pron. (plural of 'he' or 'she') **1** *I have invited Akhil and Shamshad to my party. They are my best friends.* = the persons or things mentioned earlier **2** *They say Beckham is the best striker in the world.* = people in general **they'd** *The people were starving. They'd eaten nothing for a week.* = abbr. of 'they had' or 'they would' **they'll** = abbr. of 'they will'

thick[1] /θɪk/ adj. **1** *He has written a thick book of about 900 pages.* = having a large distance between opposite surfaces (opposite **thin**) **2** *a thick wire* = having a large diameter (referring to a round object) **3** *Add corn flour to the gravy to make it thick.* = not watery; not flowing very easily (referring to a liquid) **4** *thick jungle* = closely packed; having a large number of things or persons within a space **5** *thick smoke* = difficult to see through **6** *He is so thick that he won't understand your joke.* = stupid (informal, derogatory) **7** *He and the minister's secretary are very thick.* = friendly (informal)

thick[2] adv. *The bushes grow thick in the jungle.* = very close together

thick[3] noun, u. *You will always find the general in the thick of the battle.* = the most busy or active part of something **thicken** verb, t. *You can thicken the gravy by adding some flour.* = to make something more thick (less watery) **thickener** noun, c. *Flour is used as a thickener for soups.* = something that thickens a liquid **thick-set** adj. *a thick-set person* = having a broad and strong body **thick-headed** adj. = stupid (not very intelligent) **thick-skinned** adj. *a thick-skinned person* = not sensitive; unable to understand an insult (derogatory)

to have a thick skin *Everyone criticised but he didn't seem to mind. He really has a thick skin.* = not worried if people criticize you **to be thick with someone** = to have a friendly relationship with someone **through thick and thin** *He has been my friend for thirty years and has stayed close to me through thick and thin.* = through difficult times **as thick as thieves** = to be very friendly

thick•et /ˈθɪkɪt/ noun, c. = a place where bushes or trees grow very close together

thief /θiːf/ noun, c. (**thieves**) = a person who steals (takes away the belongings of other people without letting them know) **thieve** /θiːv/ verb, i. = to steal **thieving** noun, u. *a life of thieving* = stealing

thigh /θaɪ/ noun, c. = the part of a person's leg above the knee

thim•ble /ˈθɪmbəl/ noun, c. = a small cap (cover) worn over the finger to protect it while using a needle to stitch clothes **thimbleful** noun, c.= a very small amount of some liquid

thin[1] /θɪn/ adj. **1** *a thin book of only 15 pages* = having a small distance between opposite surfaces (opposite **thick**) **2** *a thin and sickly child* = having very little fat on the body **3** *thin soup* = watery **4** *thin* *hair* = having a few objects widely separated **5** *a thin voice* = high-pitched **6** *a thin speech* = (of ideas), not satisfactory; not having enough substance (derogatory)

thin[2] verb, i. or t. (**thinned**) **1** *The crowd thinned after the main speakers left the meeting.*(i.) = to become thin (less closely packed) **2** *You can thin this paint by adding some turpentine.*(t.)= to make a liquid more watery **thinner** noun, c. *Turpentine is used as a thinner for paint.* = something that makes a liquid more watery **thin-skinned** adj. *a thin-skinned person* = sensitive; easily hurt or offended

to vanish into thin air = to disappear completely **thin on the ground** *Good computer operators are rather thin on the ground.* = not easily available

thine /ðaɪn/ pron. *This house is thine. Thou art its master.* = belonging to you (old-fashioned)

thing /θɪŋ/ noun, c. **1** *All the things in this room belong to my brother.* = an object that cannot be named or does not have to be named exactly **2** *The next thing I want to discuss is your wife's health.* = idea, subject, event etc. **3** *I don't have a thing to wear!* = anything (used for emphasis) **4** *The whole thing is that he is too old to run.* = a word used to introduce a topic **5** *She couldn't reply because she was unprepared, poor thing!* = used to refer affectionately or sympathetically to a person or an animal

thing-a-ma-jig noun, c. *'What's that thingamajig you use to open a program on the computer?' 'Oh, you mean 'mouse'!'* = a word used to refer to something whose name one has forgotten (informal)

things /ðɪŋz/ noun (always plural) **1** *Put your things in the back of the car.* = belongings **2** *Things in this company are better now than they were last year.* = the situation or state of affairs at a particular time

to do one's own thing *You don't have to wear a tie if you don't want to. You should do your own thing.* = to do what one likes to do, instead of copying others (informal) **to have a thing about someone or something** *He's got a thing about Hindi film songs. He can't stand anyone talking ill of them.* = to have a very strong liking or dislike for something (informal) **to be all things to all people** *When they are in the city, they wear western clothes. But when they go to the village, they put on traditional clothes. They believe in being all things to all people.* = to try to keep everyone pleased (often derogatory) **the done thing** *You must invite all your friends to dinner when you get married. That's the done thing.* = what one is supposed or expected to do (informal) **the shape of things to come** = an indication of how things will be in the future **all things considered** *All things considered, the meeting didn't go off too badly.* = taking all the facts into account **of all things** *He invited everybody for dinner and then gave us just a cup of tea, of all things!* = an expression of surprise and shock

think[1] /θɪŋk/ verb, t. or i. (**thought**) **1** *As a human being you should be able to think when you are faced with a problem.*(i.) = to use the mind to form an idea, reach a solution, make a decision etc. **2** *He thinks that Mrs Singh can be our next Prime Minister.*(t.) = to have an opinion; to believe **3** *I can't think why she married that horrible man.*(t.) = to understand or imagine **4** *I want you to think. Where did you meet him last?*(i.) = to try to remember **5** *I think I'll have a cup of tea.*(t.) = to have as a plan, but not very strongly

think[2] noun, u. *I can't decide who I should vote for. Let me have a think.* = an act of thinking, in order to decide something **thinking**[1] noun, u. *What's the minister's thinking on this subject?* = opinion **thinking**[2] adj. *He is a thinking person.* = describing a person who is in the habit of using his/her mind to think about problems etc.; intelligent **think-tank** noun, u. *the government's think-tank* = a group of experts who advise the government etc.

to think back = to remember or think about the past **to think out (think through)** = to think very carefully and in great detail about something **to think up** = to get a new idea or plan in one's mind **to think the better of something** *I was planning to challenge him to a game of tennis, but when I heard he had been a champion, I thought the better of it.* = to not do or say something you had planned, because you realize it would be a mistake **to think twice before doing something** *You should think twice before you go on such a long strenuous journey.* = to think carefully before doing something risky **to think the world of someone** = to have a very good opinion of someone (informal) **to think on one's feet** = to be able to think of something quickly, without much preparation **That's what you think!** *'You won't agree with us because you want to have your own way.' 'That's what you think.'* = a way of telling someone, in an unfriendly or humorous way, that what they think about you is wrong

thinner see **thin**

third[1] /θɜːd/ det. *a seat in the third row* = coming after the first two (objects or people)

third[2] noun, u. or c. **1** *I'll give each of you a third of my property.*(u.) = one part out of three equal parts **2** *I got a third in the examination.*(u.) = a third class degree from a university **third degree**[1] noun, u. = rough or cruel treatment; torture **third-degree**[2] adj. *She has suffered third-degree burns and is in a critical condition.* = very serious (referring to burn injuries) **third party** (**insurance**) noun, u. = a person who is not named but who is protected by an insurance policy in case of an accident **third person** noun *The pronoun 'he' is third person, singular number, masculine gender.* = the pronoun that refers to a

T

person other than the speaker or the person being spoken to (the listener) [GRAMMAR] **third-rate** adj. *He gave a third-rate performance in this film.* = of poor quality **Third World** noun or adj. *a Third World Country* = a country which is not very developed economically or industrially (usually referring to the poorer countries in Asia, Africa and South America) (The preferred term now is countries of the South.)

thirst[1] /θɜːst/ noun, u. or c. **1** *My thirst was so great that I drank six glasses of water.*(u.) = a great need or desire to drink some liquid (usually water) **2** *The poor bird died of thirst.*(u.) = lack of water **3** *Their thirst for adventure took them to many strange places.*(u.) = great desire

thirst[2] (**for**) verb, t. *She thirsts for fame.* = to have a very strong desire for something (formal, literary)

thir•teen /θɜːˈtiːn/ noun = the number after 12, represented by 13 (10+3)

thir•ty /ˈθɜːti/ noun = the number represented by 30 (10x3) **thirtieth** det. *the thirtieth day* = related to the number 30

this[1] /ðɪs/ det. (plural **these**) **1** *I like this painting, but not the other one.* = the object or person that one is referring to, talking about or pointing at, at the time of speaking **2** *I am going home this week.* = a time that is most near

this[2] pron. **1** *Do you want this?* = some object that one has been talking about or is pointing at **2** *This is my colleague, Roshan.* = used to introduce a person to someone else **3** *This is Mohan speaking.* = used to refer to oneself when speaking on the telephone

this[3] adv. *She was only this high when I saw her last.* = as much as shown (by using a gesture etc.)

this and that (this, that and the other) *We have been talking of this and that.* = various subjects (informal)

this•tle /ˈθɪsəl/ noun = a wild plant with pointed leaves, which is the national symbol of Scotland

thith•er /ˈðɪðəʳ/ adv. *Ram went to the forest and Sita followed him thither.* = to that place (old-fashioned)

thong /θɒŋ/ noun, c. *The dog was tied up with a leather thong.* = a narrow piece of leather used to tie up something

tho•rax /ˈθɔːræks/ noun, u. = the upper front part of the body (the chest) [BIOLOGY]

thorn /θɔːn/ noun, c. *Rose plants have thorns.* = a sharp,pointed growth on the stem of a plant **thorny** adj. **1** *a thorny bush* = having many thorns **2** *a thorny problem* = difficult to deal with

thor•ough /ˈθʌrə/ adj. **1** *He made a thorough study of the Santhali language, which took about 20 years of hard work.*= detailed and carefully done **2** *The meeting was a thorough waste of time. Nothing useful was done.* = complete **thoroughbred** noun, c. or adj. *a thoroughbred horse* = pure-bred; an animal, specially a horse, born of parents of the same breed, having the best qualities **thoroughfare** noun, c. = a busy public road **thorough-going** adj. *The police made a thorough-going search of the house.* = done very carefully

those /ðəʊz/ det. (plural **that**) *Ask those boys to come here.* = referring to persons or objects at a distance from the speaker

thou /ðaʊ/ pron. *Wilt thou marry me?* = you (used as the subject of a verb) (old-fashioned)

though[1] /ðəʊ/ conj. *You will like the old city, though it is rather dirty and overcrowded.* = in spite of the fact that

though[2] adv. *The old city is dirty and over-crowded. You will like it though.* = however; in spite of what has been said earlier

thought[1] /θɔːt/ verb, t. = past tense of **think**

thought[2] noun, c. **1** *want to share my thoughts on poetry with you.* = an idea or opinion that one forms by thinking **2** *We want you to contest this election. Please give it some thought.* = consideration; the action of thinking about something **3** *He was lost in thought.* = the act of thinking **thoughtful** adj. **1** *You look thoughtful. Is something wrong?* = thinking deeply **2** *a thoughtful person* = one who is careful to respect the wishes or feelings of others **thoughtless** adj. *Why didn't you offer him a seat? That was thoughtless of you.* = showing not enough respect for the feelings of others

to be deep in thought (to be lost in thought) = to be so busy thinking that one doesn't notice what is happening around one **on second thoughts** *I think I'll go to Ranchi. On second thoughts, I don't think I will.* = saying that one is changing one's mind about something **Don't give it another thought!** *'I'm sorry, I was so rude.' 'Don't give it another thought!'* = to forget something that one has done or said and not feel unhappy about it **That's a thought!** = that's a very good idea or suggestion

thou•sand /ˈθaʊzənd/ noun, c. = the number represented by 1000 (100x10) **thousands (of)** noun = a very large number

thrash /θræʃ/ verb, t. **1** = to beat or hit, usually as a punishment **2** *Australia thrashed India in this match.* = to defeat badly in a game or competition **3** *He couldn't get any sleep and thrashed about in his bed all night.* = to move restlessly or violently

to thrash out verb *We should discuss the matter in detail and thrash out our differences.* = to discuss a matter in detail in order to find a solution

thread[1] /θred/ noun, u. or c. **1** (u.) = a length of thin material made by spinning some fibre such as cotton, silk, nylon etc., from which cloth can be woven **2** *the* *thread of a screw*(c.) = a raised line that runs around the outside of a screw **3** *I have lost the thread of your argument.*(u.) = the line of reasoning that holds together the parts of an argument or story

thread[2] verb, t. *Can you thread this needle for me?* = to put something thin (e.g. a thread) through a hole or narrow opening **threadbare** adj. *He has been wearing the same clothes for so many years that they have become threadbare.* = worn out through use

to thread one's way *The driver threaded his way through the crowded street.* = to move carefully through a crowded place, avoiding people etc. who may be in your way **to hang by a thread** *My father had cerebral malaria and his life hung by a thread.* = to be in great danger

threat /θret/ noun, c. **1** *The people said they would take the woodcutters to court . This threat kept the neighbourbood trees safe!* = an expression of an intention to harm or punish someone or something if a certain condition is fulfilled or a certain action is not carried out **2** *Wild elephants pose a threat to the safety of these villagers.* = a source of danger **threaten** verb, t. **1** *The gatekeeper threatened to lock the gates if the students came late.* = to make a threat (to say that one will harm someone if something is not done) **2** *The dark clouds in the sky threaten rain.* = to give warning of something bad

three /θriː/ det. or noun, c. = the number represented by 3 (2+1) **three-cornered** adj. *The tournament is a three-cornered contest between Australia, New Zealand and Sri Lanka* = having three competitors **three-dimensional** adj. *a three-dimensional picture* = appearing to have depth as well as length and breadth; looking very life-like (real) **three-legged race** noun, c. = a race in which which pairs of runners take part, with one leg of each runner tied together **three-piece (suit)** noun, u. = a set of clothes, usually for a man, made up of a pair of trousers, a jacket (coat) and a waistcoat **three-quarters** noun, u. *The children have eaten three-quarters of the cake.* = three parts out of four equal parts into which something is divided **three R's** noun *The children are learning the three R's in school.* = reading, writing and (a)rithmetic (considered the three most important parts of a child's education) **three-wheeler** = a vehicle with three wheels

thresh /θreʃ/ verb, t. = to separate grain (rice, wheat etc.) from the plant after it has been harvested

thresh•old /'θreʃhəʊld/ noun, c. **1** = a piece of wood or stone fixed to the ground or floor at the entrance to a door **2** *With the arrival of independence. India entered the threshold of a new age.* = the start of something new **3** *The threshold for admission to this course is a B.A. degree.* = the lowest level which can be accepted, or at which something begins

to have a high pain threshold = to be able to bear a lot of pain **to be on the threshold of** = to be about to begin something new and important

thrice /θraɪs/ adv. *He came to see me thrice, but he has not been back after the third visit.* = three times (old-fashioned)

thrift /θrɪft/ noun, u. *He manages to save at least Rs 1,000 out of his salary each month. I am impressed by his thrift.* = careful use of money, without wasting it or spending too much (old-fashioned) **thrifty** adj. *a thrifty person* = one who does not overspend

thrill[1] /θrɪl/ noun, u. or c. *My first elephant ride was quite a thrill.* = an event that produces a feeling of excitement mixed with pleasure

thrill[2] verb, t. **1** *Yuvraj Singh thrilled the crowd by hitting three sixers in one over.* = to cause a thrill (a feeling of excitement and pleasure) **2** *We thrilled to the sound of the drums.* = to feel excited by something **thriller** noun, c. = a novel or film which contains a lot of exciting action

thrive /θraɪv/ verb, i. (**thrived** or **throve**) *These plants were weak and sickly at first but now they are healthy. They seem to be thriving.* = to become healthy and strong and grow well; to be successful (formal)

throat /θrəʊt/ noun, c. **1** = the front part of the neck **2** *A fish bone has got stuck in his throat.* = the passage inside the neck through which food and air pass **throaty** adj. *a throaty voice* = a low, rough voice

to be at each other's throats = to be fighting or arguing with great excitement **to bring a lump to someone's throat** *The story he told us of his childhood brought a lump to my throat.* = to make one feel emotional and want to cry **to force something down one's throat** = to force someone to listen to and accept your ideas

throb[1] /θrɒb/ verb, i. (**throbbed**) **1** *His heart throbbed wildly as he neared the finish of the 10,000 metres race.* = to beat fast **2** *The drums throbbed.* = to produce a regular, fast sound (referring to the sound of a drum) **3** *My shoulder throbbed with pain.* = to feel a sharp, continuous pain

throb[2] noun, u. *the steady throb of the car's engine* = the regular sound produced by a machine etc.

throes /θrəʊz/ noun (always plural) **1** *The woman was passing through the throes of childbirth.* = sudden and violent pain **2** *The country is going through the throes of unemployment.* = a difficult or painful experience or situation

throm•bo•sis (thromboses) /θrɒm'bəʊsɪs/ noun, c. *coronary thrombosis* = a blockage in a blood vessel, preventing the flow of blood, caused by a blood clot (a half-solid lump of blood) [MEDICINE]

throne /θrəʊn/ noun, c. **1** = the ceremonial chair

on which a king or queen sits **2** *Akbar came to the throne after Babar's death.* = the position of a king or queen

throng[1] /θrɒŋ/ noun, c. *There were at least 5000 people in the stadium and I could not find my friend in the throng.* = a large crowd (literary)

throng[2] verb, t. *Thousands of cricket fans thronged the airport when the Sri Lankan team arrived.* = to fill up or crowd a place

throt•tle[1] /'θrɒtl/ verb, t. **1** *The robber caught hold of me by the throat and tried to throttle me.* = to kill someone by pressing on his/her throat and stopping the supply of air **2** *The new tax laws are throttling trade.* = to check and stop something from growing (figurative)

throttle[2] noun, c. = a valve which allows or prevents the flow of fuel to an engine

through[1] /θru:/ prep. **1** *He walked through the corridor and entered the room.* = from one side of something to the other **2** *We drove to Mumbai through Pune.* = by way of **3** *He won the prize through hard work.* = as a result of **4** *I have read through your essay.* = from the beginning to the end **5** *He is going through a difficult time.* = from the beginning to the end of a period of time or a process or event **6** *He got through the test.* = having completed something successfully

through[2] adv. **1** *When I showed my pass to the guards at the gate, they let me through.* = from one side to the other **2** *I have read the essay through.* = from the beginning to the end **3** *The results of the examination are out. I got through!* = to be successful (in an examination)

through[3] adj. **1** *We took the through train to Kolkata.* = going directly to some place **2** *I am almost through the book.* = completing something **3** *I don't want to work for you any longer. We are through!* = at the end of a relationship **throughout** adv. **1** *He slept throughout the lecture.* = during the whole period of time **2** *People are starving throughout the state.* = in every part of **through-put** noun = the amount of work done in a given period of time [TECHNICAL]

to come through (get through) *He is very worried about his exams but I am sure he will come (get) through easily.* = to be successful in dealing with a difficult situation **to pull through** = to be successful in dealing with a different situation, but only with great effort **(to be something) through and through** *He is an artist through and through.* = completely **Monday through Friday** (American English) *You will have your exams Monday through Friday.* = starting on a certain day and ending on another

throw[1] /θrəʊ/ verb, t. (**threw, thrown**) **1** *The fielder threw the ball to the wicket-keeper.* = to cause something to move quickly through the air or along the ground by a sudden movement of the arm **2** *She threw the bag on the table.* = to handle something carelessly **3** *He threw the door open.* = to move or act quickly **4** *Can you throw some light on this matter?* = to give or send out **5** *The wrestler threw his opponent.* = to cause to fall to the ground **6** *He plans to throw a party next week.* = to arrange (a party) (informal) **7** *He was thrown out of his job.* = to take away someone's job suddenly **8** *He was the thrown into jail.* = to be sent to jail (informal) **9** *He threw up his hands.* = to move quickly (informal)

throw[2] noun, c. *The fielder's throw reached the wicket-keeper.* = an act of throwing **throw-away** adj. *a throw-away paper plate* = something that is meant to be thrown away after a single use (also **disposable**)

throw away *He threw his old clothes away.* = to get rid of something that is not needed **throw in** *If you buy a computer, the dealer will throw in a printer along with the computer.* = to add to something that is being sold, without increasing the price (informal) **to throw off** *He has been able to throw off his fever.* = to get rid of something unpleasant or something that has been troubling you (informal) **to throw on (a shirt)** = to put on some clothes (informal) **to throw up (threw up)** *The food was so bad that I threw up at once.* = to vomit **to throw good money after bad** *You shouldn't have bought that old car and you shouldn't waste money in trying to repair it. You are throwing good money after bad.* = to waste money over some useless thing **to throw light on something** = to explain something clearly **to throw one's weight around** = to use one's power or authority in a way that other people do not like (informal) **to throw the book at somebody** = to punish someone by using the rules in a very strict manner **to throw out the baby with the bath-water** = to lose something useful or valuable in trying to get rid of something that you do not want

thru /θru:/ prep. *He works Monday thru Friday.* = from one day or time to the other (American English) (informal)

thrush /θrʌʃ/ noun, c. **1** = a kind of singing bird **2** = an infectious disease that causes white sores in the mouth, specially of young children

thrust[1] /θrʌst/ verb, t. (**thrust**) *He thrust the letter into my hand and ordered me to read it.* = to push something suddenly and with force

thrust[2] noun, u. or c. **1** *He made a sudden thrust at me with his knife.*(u.) = a sudden forward movement **2** *I have not been able to understand the thrust of your argument.*(c.) = the central point that one is trying to put across **3** *The engines of this jet aircraft develop*

100,000 pounds of thrust.(u.) = the force produced by the engine of an aircraft which pushes it forward [TECHNICAL]

thud[1] /θʌd/ noun, c. *The book fell to the floor with a thud.* = the dull sound caused by a heavy object hitting a hard surface

thud[2] verb, i. (**thudded**) *The cricket ball thudded into his head.*= to hit a hard surface, producing a dull sound

thug /θʌd/ noun, c. = a person who commits violent crimes (informal)

thumb[1] /θʌm/ noun, c. = the thickest finger on the hand of a human being, which is set apart from the other fingers

thumb[2] verb, t. *The student who was going home on vacation thumbed a ride in a truck.* = to ask the driver of a passing vehicle for a free ride by holding out one's hand, with the thumb pointing in the direction in which one wants to travel (informal) **thumb index** noun, u. = a series of cuts in the pages of a book which help you to find a page you want quickly **thumb-nail** **1** (noun, c.) = the nail on the end of the thumb **2** *a thumb-nail biography*(adj.) = a very short piece of writing **thumb-screw** noun, c. = an instrument used in former times to torture a person by putting great pressure on the thumb

to thumb through something = to go quickly through a book or magazine **to be under someone's thumb** = to be completely under someone's control **to be all thumbs** = to be clumsy in doing something **to thumb your nose at someone** = to show lack of respect

thump[1] /θʌmp/ verb, t. *The teacher thumped the boy on his back.*= to hit someone or something once or repeatedly, producing a loud sound

thump[2] noun, c. **1** *If you don't do as I say, I'll give you a thump.* = a blow **2** *We heard a loud thump.* = the sound of a blow **thumping** adj. *Our party won the election by a thumping majority.* = very great

thun•der[1] /'θʌndə^r/ noun, u. = the loud noise, often accompanied by lightning, produced due to electrical disturbance in the sky, before or during a storm

thunder[2] verb, i. *The guns thundered all night.* = to produce a sound like that of thunder **thunderbolt** noun, c. **1** = a flash of lightning accompanied by thunder **2** *The news of her defeat came to us like a thunderbolt.* = a piece of news that shocks one **thunderclap** noun, c. = the loud sound of thunder **thunderous** /'θʌndərəs/ adj. *The Prime Minister received a thunderous ovation when he finished his speech.* = very loud **thunderstorm** noun, c. = a storm during which there is a lot of thunder **thunderstruck** adj. *I was thunderstruck by the news of our defeat.* = shocked; greatly surprised

Thurs•day /'θɜːzdi/ noun, c. = the day of the week that comes between Wednesday and Friday

thus /ðʌs/ adv. **1** *You should hold the pen thus, between your thumb and the first two fingers.* = in this manner (as shown) **2** *We have appointed two new teachers, thus bringing the total staff strength to six.* = by this means; by so doing

thwart /θwɔːt/ verb, t. *The bus strike thwarted my plans to visit my village.* = to stop something from happening; to prevent (old-fashioned)

thy /ðaɪ/ pron. (possessive form of **thou**) *How many crimes are committed in thy name!* = your (old-fashioned)

thyme /taɪm/ noun, u. = a kind of plant, the leaves of which are used to give taste to food

thy•roid (gland) /'θaɪrɔɪd/ noun, c. = a gland (an organ) inside the neck which produces a chemical that has a powerful effect on the working of the body [MEDICINE]

thyself /ðaɪ'self/ pron. *Physician, heal thyself!* = yourself (old-fashioned)

ti•a•ra /ti'ɑːrə/ noun, c. = a piece of jewellery worn by women, that looks like a small crown

tib•i•a /'tɪbiə/ noun, c. = the thicker of the two bones inside the leg, in the front part of the leg, below the knee [MEDICINE]

tic /tɪk/ noun, c. *a nervous tic* = a small, uncontrolled movement of the muscles in the face, caused by a nervous illness

tick[1] /tɪk/ noun, c. **1** *the tick of the clock* = the low, regular sound produced by a clock or watch **2** *Put a tick against his name.* = a mark that looks like (✓), put against an answer to show that it is correct, or against a name on a list, to show that the person is present **3** = a small insect that lives on the skin of animals (such as dogs and cows) and sucks their blood

tick[2] verb, i. **1** *The clock ticked away steadily.* = to make the sound produced by a watch or clock **2** *Have you ticked my name?* = to put a tick mark against something

to tick somebody off = to speak angrily to someone, expressing displeasure

tick•et /'tɪkɪt/ noun, c. *a bus ticket* = a printed piece of paper or card given to a person to show that he/she has paid for something (e.g. to travel in a bus or to watch a film show in a cinema)

tick•ing /'tɪkɪŋ/ noun, u. = thick cotton cloth used for making mattresses or pillows

tick•le /'tɪkəl/ verb, t. or i. **1** *We tickled him under the arm-pit to make him laugh.*(t.) = to touch someone lightly in a sensitive part of the body, causing him/her to laugh **2** *I was tickled to receive the invitation to his party.* = to be pleased **ticklish** adj. **1** *You can't*

T

make him laugh by tickling him. He is not ticklish. = sensitive to being tickled **2** *These people are angry because the match was cancelled. You should be careful in dealing with them, as it is a ticklish matter.* = sensitive; needing special care (referring to a difficult situation or problem)

tick-tack-toe noun = the game of noughts-and-crosses (American English)

tide[1] /taɪd/ noun, c. **1** *The tide is rising.* = the regular rise and fall in the level of the water in the sea because of the moon's gravitational attraction (see also **gravity**) **2** *tide of public opinion* = a strong feeling that can easily change

tide[2] **(over)** verb, t. *The money which you lent me tided me over (through) a difficult time.* = to help someone during a period of difficulty **tidal** /'taɪdl/ adj. *a tidal current* = caused by a tide **tidal wave** noun, c. = a large and dangerous wave in the sea caused by a movement of the earth under the water

to swim with the tide = to follow the opinion that most people have **to stem the tide** = to check something (prevent it from happening)

tid-bit /'tɪdbɪt/ noun, c. see **tit-bit**

tid•ings /'taɪdɪŋz/ noun (always plural) *I have received tidings of your victory in the election.* = news (old-fashioned)

ti•dy[1] /'taɪdi/ adj. *She keeps her desk tidy. You won't find a speck of dust on it.* = clean and neat (having everything in order)

tidy[2] verb, t. (**tidied**) *She tidied (up) the house when she heard that guests were expected.* = to make something tidy (clean and neat)

tie[1] /taɪ/ verb, t. (**tied**) **1** *She tied up the parcel of books with a piece of string.* = to fasten (bind) something or someone using a rope or string **2** *His coming to the movie is tied to his finding someone to take care of his baby.* = to connect to something **3** *These two boys tied for second place in the contest.* = to get the same number of points as someone else in a competition, or to finish a race at the same time as someone else

tie[2] noun, c. **1** *He wore a shirt without a tie.* = a long, thin piece of material worn round the neck, usually by men, under the collar of a shirt and tied into a knot in front (also neck-tie) **2** *Use this tie to close the bag.* = a piece of string or rope used to tie (fasten) something **3** *I return to my village every summer because I have strong ties with my family.* = something that unites people and keeps them together **4** *There is a tie for second place between these two boys.* = an equal result in a competition, race etc. as someone else **tie-breaker** noun, c. = something done to speed up a game (in tennis, hockey or foot-ball) when no one is winning, so as to get a quick result **tie-and-dye** noun *a tie-and-dye design for a sari* = a method used to create coloured designs in a piece of cloth by tying up some parts with thread before dipping it in dye (colour) **tie-up** noun, c. *Our company has a tie-up with a Japanese company to produce motorcycles.* = an agreement or partnership between two companies

to be tied up *I can't come this evening. I'm very tied up.* = to be very busy with something (informal) **to have one's hands tied** *I wanted to speak at the meeting and save you but my hands were tied.* = to not be free to do what one wants **to tie the knot** = to get married (informal, humorous) **to tie oneself up in knots** = to become confused and not be able to speak clearly

tier /tɪəʳ/ noun, c. *I have a middle berth in a three-tier coach on the train.* = one out of a number of rows or levels, one above the other

tiff[1] /tɪf/ noun, c. *My wife and I had a tiff this evening. She wanted to go to the cinema but I wanted to watch television at home.* = a slight quarrel (informal)

tiff[2] verb, i. (**tiffed**) *My brother and I tiffed regularly when we were young.* = to have a slight quarrel

tif•fin /'tɪfɪn/ noun, u. = a light snack or meal eaten late in the morning (old-fashioned)

ti•ger /'taɪgəʳ/ noun, c. = a large and fierce animal belonging to the cat family, which has a yellow skin with black stripes on it **tigress** noun, c. = a female tiger

tight[1] /taɪt/ adj. **1** *These shoes are too tight for you. You need shoes of a larger size.* = fitting some part of the body very closely **2** *He held her hand in such a tight grip that she was unable to pull it away.* = held or kept together firmly (strongly) **3** *Security at the airport is tight.* = firmly controlled **4** *The minister cannot see you today as he has a tight schedule.* = having no free time **5** *There are very few seats available for this course so competition is tight.* = close

tight[2] adv. *The mother held her baby tight.* = closely and firmly **tighten** verb, t. *These trousers are too loose for you. Ask the tailor to tighten them a bit at the waist.* = to make something more tight **tight-fisted** adj. *a tight-fisted person* = one who does not like to spend money; miserly (disapproving) **tight-lipped** adj. *The reporters asked the girl many questions, but she remained tight-lipped.* = unwilling to talk **tight-rope** noun, u. = a length of rope or wire stretched tightly high above the ground, on which an acrobat (someone who performs difficult actions requiring a lot of skill, usually in a circus) has to walk **tights** noun (always plural) = a close-fitting garment or under-garment, usually worn by girls and women, covering the legs and hips

to walk a tightrope = to face a difficult situation in

which one has to make decisions between two opposite plans of action **to keep a tight rein on someone** = to keep someone under one's control **to run a tight ship** = to be very strict in maintaining discipline and seeing that money is spent very carefully **to tighten one's belt** = to prepare to face a difficult time by cutting down on expenses

tile[1] /taɪl/ noun, c. = a small, flat piece of some material, used for covering the floor or roof of a building

tile[2] verb, t. *The floor has been tiled.* = to cover with tiles

till[1] /tɪl/ prep. or conj. **1** *The examination will start on Monday and continue till Friday.*(prep.) = until (upto a certain time) **2** *He will look after the office till a new Manager is appointed.*(conj.) = upto the time when something happens or is done

Usage Note that the clause following 'till' is not negative. It is a common mistake to say 'He will look after the office till a new manager is not appointed'.

till[2] noun, c. = a locked drawer in a desk, in which money is kept

till[3] verb, t. = to cultivate land (old-fashioned) **tiller** noun, c. **1** *a tiller of the soil* = a farmer **2** *a power-tiller* = a small machine used to plough the land, which is controlled by someone who walks behind it **3** *the tiller of a boat* = a long handle tied to the rudder of boat (the piece of wood which is turned to control the direction in which the boat is moving)

tilt[1] /tɪlt/ verb, t. or i. **1** *He tilted the glass and poured out some of the water.*(t.)= to cause something to move into a sloping position (not upright or straight, but leaning to one side **2** *The wall is tilting to one side.*(i.) = to lean to one side instead of being straight **3** *Opinion has tilted in favour of Rekha's winning the race.*(i.) = to turn in someone's favour

tilt[2] noun, u. **1** *There is a slight tilt in the wall.* = a slope to one side **2** *a tilt in the public opinion* = a turn or change which favours someone **at full tilt** = at full speed

tim•ber[1] /'tɪmbəʳ/ noun, u. = wood used for making furniture, building houses etc.

timber[2] adj. *He has planted timber trees on the land.* = trees which can be cut down and used for timber

tim•bre /'tæmbəʳ/ noun, u. (French) *The sound produced by a sarod has a special timbre.* = the special quality that a musical sound has [MUSIC]

time[1] /taɪm/ noun, u. **1** *Time is measured in years, months and days as well as hours, minutes and seconds.* = the entire period that makes up the past, present and future **2** *He was once strong, but time has made him weak.* = the passing of time **3** *I will need time to complete this job.* = a period (of time) in the future, the length of which is not specified (mentioned) **4** *The time taken to complete this job was exactly 200 days.* = a period of time measured in days, hours etc. **5** *It's 9.30 now—time for you to go to school.* = a particular point of time **6** *I will speak next time, but not now.* = an occasion **7** *My great grand-father lived in Kolkata in the time(s) of Queen Victoria.* = a period of time associated with a particular person or event

time[2] verb, t. **1** *I have timed my visit to Pune to coincide with the marriage of your daughter.* = to choose or arrange the time for something **2** *Rahul can hit the ball hard without using much force as he times his shots beautifully.* = to hit the ball (in a game such as cricket or tennis) at just the right moment **3** *He ran the 100-metre race in 10.85 seconds. I timed him.*= to measure the time taken to do something **time-bomb** noun, c. **1** = a bomb that is fitted with a timer (see also **timer**) and can be set to explode (burst) at a particular time **2** *The bridge across this river is half-broken and has not been repaired. It is a time-bomb waiting to explode.* = something that can create danger in the future **time capsule** noun, c. = a container in which objects representing a particular period of time are stored and buried in the ground, so that they can be dug up and examined in the future, to let people know about the past **time-consuming** adj. *a time-consuming process* = something that takes up a lot of time **time exposure** noun, c. = a photograph taken in poor light, in which the lens of the camera is kept open for several seconds **time-honoured** adj. *Dancing to celebrate a wedding is a time-honoured custom.* = done by everyone over a long period of time **time immemorial** noun *The oldest teacher in our school speaks on opening day. This has been the custom in the school since time immemorial.* = a very, very long period in the past **time-keeper** noun, c. = a person who keeps record of time (e.g. in a sports competition or a factory where people are working) **time lag** noun, u. *There is a time lag of at least three months between the end of the examination and the declaration of results.* = the period of time that separates two connected events **timeless** adj. *the timeless beauty of the Taj Mahal* = not affected by the passage of time **time-limit** noun, u. *The time-limit for answering this question is 5 seconds.* = the period of time within which something must be done **timely** adj. *Your timely help enabled me to write my essay.* = done at just the right time **timepiece** noun, c. = a clock or watch (old-fashioned) **timer** noun, c. *The oven has a timer which switches it off after 30 seconds.* = a machine that can measure time (like a watch) and be set to perform a certain operation at a selected time (see also **time-bomb**) **time-server** /ˈtaɪmsɜːvəʳ/ noun, c. = someone who changes his or her opinions and behaviour in order to please those who are in power **time-sharing** noun, u. = a system by which people can share the ownership of a building so that they can live in it at different times in the year **time-table** noun, c. *a railway time-table* = a list of the times at which trains, buses etc. arrive at a place or leave it **time-worn** adj. *time-worn customs* = no longer interesting or useful because of having been in use for too long a period **time zone** noun, c. *When it is 7.30 a.m. in New York, it is only 6.30 a.m. in Chicago. These cities fall in different time zones.* = an area over all parts of which the time is the same **timing** noun, u. *You should not have asked the boss to raise your salary just when he had broken his leg in an accident. Your timing was bad.* = the choice of a suitable time to do something

time-out 1 *The players asked for a time-out.* = a short break requested in a game [TECHNICAL] **2** *She took some time-out from her busy schedule.* = a short break to do something that one wants to do **time up** = an expression to indicate that the alloted time is over **to pass the time of day** = to greet someone and have a friendly chat **about time** *'The train that has arrived at last.' 'It's about time!'* = an expression used to show displeasure about something that has not happened at the expected time or to show the importance of doing something at the correct time (informal) **all the time** *The telephone is ringing all the time.* = very often **at times** *We need a break from work at times.* = not very often **at one time** *It was a beautiful city at one time.* = in the past but not now **for a time** *We worked together for a time.* = for a short period of time in the past **for the time being** *You can use the room for the time being but you must move out tomorrow morning.* = for a short period of time following the present time **in time** *You must come in time for the start of the match.* = early enough to be able to do something **on time** *The train is supposed to arrive at 10.15, but it is seldom on time.* = happening at the correct or expected time **in the nick of time** *The burglars were about to drive off with all the money they had looted from the bank, but the police arrived in the nick of time.* = just in time to prevent something bad from happening **to have the time of one's life** *She was not keen on going on a holiday but she had the time of her life.* = to spend time in a very enjoyable manner (informal)

times[1] /taɪmz/ prep. (always plural) *Three times seven is twentyone.* (3x7= 21)= multiplied by

times[2] noun (always plural) **1** *He is poor now, but he has seen better times.* = a period in one's life **2** *He earns three times as much money as I do.* = multiplied by a certain number

tim•id /ˈtɪmɪd/ adj. *The children are so timid that they ran away as soon as they saw the visitors.* = shy and nervous; having no courage

tin /tɪn/ noun, u. or c. **1** *Tin can be mixed with other metals.*(u.) = a soft, silver-coloured metal **2** *a tin of pickled mangoes* (c.) = a container made of tin or some other metal (also **can**) **tin god** noun *He is only the class monitor, but he behaves as if he was the headboy. What a tin god he is!* = someone who gives himself/herself more importance than he/she deserves (derogatory) **tinned** adj. *tinned fruit* = (food) that has been packed in a tin (also canned) **tinny** adj. **1** *The body of the car looks tinny.* = as if made of tin (or some cheap and light metal) **2** *This sitar produces a tinny sound.* = having a thin metallic sound (both meanings are derogatory) **tin opener** noun, c. = a tool used for opening tins (see **tin** meaning **2**) (also **can opener**)

tinc•ture /ˈtɪŋktʃəʳ/ noun, u. *tincture of iodine* = a liquid prepared by mixing some medicinal substance with alcohol [TECHNICAL]

tin•der /ˈtɪndəʳ/ noun, u. *You can use some of the dry leaves as tinder to light the fire.* = a substance that burns easily and can be used to start a fire

tinge[1] /tɪndʒ/ noun, u. *At sunset the sky looks red, with a tinge of orange. // There was a tinge of sadness in her voice as she sang.* = a very slight (small) amount of colour or feeling

tinge[2] verb, t. *The sky looks grey in your painting. Can you tinge it with a little red?* = to give a slight colour to something

tin•gle[1] /ˈtɪŋgəl/ verb, i. *His whole body tingled after he had a bath in the ice-cold water.* = to have a light stinging feeling (as if many needles were being gently pressed into your skin)

tingle[2] noun, u. *He felt a tingle all over his body.* = a light, stinging feeling

tin•ker[1] /ˈtɪŋkəʳ/ noun, c. = a person who repairs pots and pans

tinker[2] verb, i. *There is something wrong with the computer but I don't want you to tinker with it. Send it to the dealer for servicing.* = to try to make some change or improvement that is not effective e.g. when repairing a machine

tin•kle[1] /ˈtɪŋkəl/ verb, i. *The little bells on the dancer's feet tinkled.* = to make a light metallic sound, like that of a small bell

tinkle[2] noun, u. *the tinkle of little bells* = the sound made by a small bell

to give someone a tinkle = to call up someone on the telephone

tin•sel /ˈtɪnsəl/ noun, u. **1** *The room where the wedding was performed was decorated with tinsel.* = shiny material which is cut into small pieces or strips and hung up as decoration, on some special occasion **2** *the tinsel world of Bollywood films* = something cheap that looks attractive but has no value (derogatory)

tint[1] /tɪnt/ noun, u. or c. *The glass fitted in the window has a light blue tint.*(u.) = a light shade of some colour

tint[2] verb, t. *She got her hair tinted orange in a beauty parlour.* = to give a slight colour to something

ti•ny /ˈtaɪni/ adj. *The bed is so tiny that only a baby could sleep in it.* = very small

tip[1] /tɪp/ noun, c. **1** *Kanyakumari forms the southern tip of India. // the tip of the tongue* = the pointed end of something **2** *I gave the waiter Rs 50 as a tip.* = an additional amount of money given to someone as a reward for doing something **3** *Let me give you a tip. You should never phone him in the morning.* = a piece of useful advice or information **4** a *garbage tip* = a place where waste material is thrown (also dump)

tip[2] verb, t. (**tipped**) **1** *The wooden arrow was tipped with steel.* = to cover the tip (end) of something **2** *He tipped some of the water in the glass to the floor.* = to pour something out of a container by making it tilt (see **tilt**) **3** *He tipped the table over.* = to knock something over **4** *Have you tipped the waiter?* = to give a tip (reward) to someone for doing something (see **tip**[1] meaning **2**) **5** *He is tipped to be our next coach.* = to consider something as being likely to happen **tip-off** noun, u. *The smuggler received a tip-off from someone in the police force and escaped.* = a warning or piece of secret information **tip-toe**[1] noun, u. *The child stood on tip-toe and tried to peep out through the window.* = the ends or tips of the toes' **tip-toe**[2] verb, i. *He tip-toed out of the room, taking care not to make any sound.* = to walk on the tips of the toes only, to avoid making a sound while walking

to tip someone off *The thief escaped just as the police arrived. Someone must have tipped him off.* = to give someone some secret information **to be on the tip of one's tongue** *I can't remember his name now but it is on the tip of my tongue.* = a word or name that you know but cannot remember **the tip of the iceberg** *The manager was shocked to find an expensive watch missing from the shop. But this was only the tip of the iceberg.* = a small part of a much larger problem **to tip-toe around (a subject)** = to avoid dealing directly with something (figurative)

tip•ple /ˈtɪpəl/ verb, i. *His favourite tipple is brandy.* = an alcoholic drink that someone takes regularly (informal) **tippler** noun, c. = someone who loves to take alcoholic drinks (informal)

tip•sy /ˈtɪpsi/ adj. *He became tipsy after drinking a bottle of beer.* = slightly drunk (informal)

tip-top /ˈtɪp tɔːp/ adj. *His house was repaired and painted only last week and it is in tip-top condition now.* = excellent (informal)

ti•rade /taɪˈreɪd/ noun, c. = a long and angry speech (formal)

tired /taɪəd/ adj. **1** *He feels tired after taking part in the 10,000 metres race.* = having little energy or strength to do anything, as a result of taking part in some activity **2** *I have been sitting here for the last six hours, and I am tired of waiting.* = having lost patience or interest

tire[1] /taɪəˈ/ verb, t. *The game of tennis I played this evening has tired me.* = to make someone tired or to become tired (formal)

tire[2] (American English) see **tyre**

tireless /ˈtaɪəles/ adj. *He is a tireless walker.* = one who never gets tired **tiresome** adj. *I find your stupid jokes rather tiresome.* = boring or annoying; causing one to lose patience (derogatory)

tis•sue /ˈtɪʃuː/ noun, u. or c. **1** *bone tissue*(u.) = a group of connected cells of the same kind, forming one part of a plant or animal **2** *tissue paper*(c.) = light, thin paper, used for wrapping things or for cleaning the nose etc. **3** *a Banarasi tissue sari*(u.) = expensive cloth woven from silk, gold thread etc.

tit /tɪt/ noun, c. **1** = a kind of small bird **2** = a woman's breast (slang) (USE)

ti•tan /ˈtaɪtn/ noun, c. *Prof Amartya Sen, who won the Nobel prize a few years ago, is an intellectual titan.* = a person of very great strength or importance or a person having some outstanding quality **titanic** /taɪˈtænɪk/ adj. = very large, powerful or important

ti•ta•ni•um /taɪˈteɪniəm/ noun, u. = a very light but strong metal that is used for making parts for aircraft

tit-bit /ˈtɪtbɪt/ noun, c. **1** *He offered his guests sweets and other tit-bits after the meal.* = a small bit of food with a pleasant taste **2** *I collected some interesting tit-bits of information from him.* = an interesting item of information (also **tidbit**)

tit for tat noun *My neighbour stole my dog last week so I am going to steal his cat. I believe in tit for tat.* = something unpleasant done as a punishment for something unpleasant that was done to you (informal)

tit•il•late /ˈtɪtɪleɪt/ verb, t. = to excite someone pleasantly, specially with thoughts of sex

ti•tle /ˈtaɪtl/ noun, c. **1** *The title of Tagore's novel is 'Gora'.* = the name given to a book, film etc. **2** *Pandit Jasraj was given the title of 'Padma Vibhushan' by the government.* = an honour which can be used as a part of one's name **3** *Sampras won the tennis singles title at Wimbledon.* = the honour of being the winner in a sports competition **4** *The court has given me the title to this property.* = a legal right to possess something [LAW] **title-deed** noun, c. = a legal document showing that a person owns a piece of

T

property [LAW] **title-holder** noun, c. **1** = a person who has won a sports competition **2** = a person who has a legal right to own a piece of property **title-page** noun, c. = the page at the front of a book on which the name of the book and the author are printed **title-role** noun, c. = the main role (part) in a film or play, of the person whose name also becomes the title of the film or play **titular** /'tɪtʃʊləʳ/ adj. *The President is the titular head of the government , but the real power is in the hands of the Prime Minister.* = holding a title or position only in name, without having much power

tit•ter /'tɪtəʳ/ verb, i. *When the police officer asked the girl why she ran across the road dodging traffic, she could only titter.* = to laugh in a nervous way when one does not know what to say

tittle-tattle /'tɪtl tætl/ noun, u. *When neighbours meet, they often indulge in a little tittle-tattle.* = gossip; idle talk about other people (informal)

titular see **title**

tiz•zy /'tɪzi/ noun, u. *Don't get into such a tizzy; everything will be all right.* = a state of nervous excitement (informal)

T-junction see under **T**

TNT noun = abbr. of tri-nitro toluene, (a powerful explosive used to blow up rocks etc.,

to[1] /tə/ or /tu:/ prep. **1** *I am going to the market.* = with the intention of reaching a certain place **2** *He was taken to the hospital.* = so as to be in a certain place **3** *He pointed to a house in the distance.* = in the direction of **4** *The water came to her waist.* = as far as **5** *The child went to sleep.* = so as to be in a certain state **6** *He pinned the notice to the wall.* = against **7** *The time is 5 minutes to 8.* = short of (less than) **8** *He works from Monday to Friday.* = until **9** *I will give this money to my wife.* = for the possession of **10** *He is the personal secretary to the minister.* = of **11** *To my surprise, she accepted the invitation.* = causing **12** *There are 100 paise to a rupee.* = for each **13** *There were three to four hundred people in the crowd.* = between

to[2] infinitive (used before a verb in its root form e.g. to eat) **1** *He plans to go now.* = the object of a verb **2** *To hear him sing is an unforgettable experience.* = the subject of a verb **3** *He has come here to study.* = for the purpose of **4** *He has asked me to work for him, but I don't want to.* = used to avoid repetition of a phrase

to[3] adv. *He was unconscious for some time, but now he has come to.* = return to a conscious state

toad /təʊd/ noun, c. = an animal that looks like a frog but has a rough skin

toad-stool /'təʊdstu:l/ noun, c. = a kind of poisonous fungus (mushroom)

toa•dy[1] /'təʊdi/ noun, c. (**toadies**) *Film stars are followed everywhere by their toadies.* = a person who flatters someone in power to gain a personal advantage (derogatory)

toady[2] verb, i. *He is in the habit of toadying to his boss.* = to flatter someone in power to gain a personal advantage

to-and-fro adj. *The pendulum of a clock makes a steady to-and-fro movement.* = from one side to the other and back

toast[1] /təʊst/ noun, u. or c. **1** (u.) = bread which has been lightly burnt so that it becomes brown and crisp **2** *We drank a toast to the bride and the bridegroom.*(c.) = an expression of good wishes or respect for someone, shown by drinking some liquid (usually containing alcohol) out of a glass, after a short speech

toast[2] verb, t. **1** *I will toast some bread for your breakfast.* = to prepare toast by burning bread lightly **2** *Let us toast the young couple.* = to drink a toast to express good wishes to someone (see **toast**[1], meaning **2**) **toaster** noun, c. = a machine which makes toast by heating bread

to•bac•co /tə'bækəʊ/ noun, u. = the dried leaves of the tobacco plant, smoked in the form of cigarettes etc. or chewed **tobacconist** noun, c. = a person who sells cigarettes etc.

to•bog•gan /tə'bɒgən/ noun, c. = a light cart which has no wheels but is fitted with metal blades, on which a person can sit or lie down and slide down an ice-covered slope, as a form of sport

to•day[1] /tə'deɪ/ noun, u. **1** *Today is Sunday, 17 February.* = this day (on which I am speaking or writing) **2** *The students of today are more intelligent than the students of our time.* = the present time or age

today[2] adv. **1** *He is coming here today and will leave tomorrow.* = on this day **2** *Schools are much better today than they were in our time.* = at the present time

tod•dle /'tɒdl/ verb, i. **1** *The baby can't walk yet but is just beginning to toddle.* = to walk with short, unsteady steps, trying to balance the body (referring to the movements of a baby) **2** *My friend and I toddled over to the book-shop next door.* = to walk in a relaxed way (informal) **toddler** noun, c. = a little baby who is beginning to toddle

tod•dy /'tɒdi/ noun, u. or c. (**toddies**) **1** (u.) = an alcoholic drink produced from the juice of a kind of palm tree **2** (c.) = a mixture of whisky and warm water

to-do /tə'du:/ noun, u. *There was quite a to-do when it was time for the minister to leave but his car and driver were missing.* = a state of unnecessary confusion

toe[1] /təʊ/ noun, c. **1** = the finger-like parts at the end of each foot (see pic under **foot**) **2** *the toe of a shoe* = the front part of a shoe, which covers the toes

toe[2] verb, t. *You are expected to toe the line and do whatever the boss says.* = to obey orders or rules (informal) **toe-hold** noun, c. **1** = a small place on a rock etc. which provides a climber with just enough space on which to put the toe (front part of the foot), so as to climb higher **2** *Chinese computer manufacturers are trying to gain a toe-hold in the Indian market.* = a position from which one can make a further advance **toe-nail** noun, c. = the nail covering the end of a toe (see pic under **foot**)

tof•fee /ˈtɒfi/ noun, u. or c. = a kind of hard and sticky sweet made by boiling sugar and butter with water

to•fu /ˈtəʊfuː/ noun, u. = a kind of solid food made from soya beans, popular in Chinese cooking (also **bean curd**)

to•ga /ˈtəʊgə/ noun, c. = a piece of cloth hanging loosely from the shoulders, worn by men in ancient Rome

to•geth•er /təˈgeðəʳ/ adv. **1** *My wife and I went to the cinema together.* = with each other **2** *The boys shouted 'We want a holiday!' together.* = at the same time **3** *The electrician joined the two pieces of wire together.* = so as to form a single object or group **4** *The old boys of the school come together in December each year.* = in the same place **5** *You must repay the loan together with the interest.* = and also

tog•gle /ˈtɒgəl/ noun, c. = a button or key on a computer which is used as a switch, to turn something on or off [COMPUTERS]

togs /tɒgʒ/ noun, c. (always plural) *Put on your togs. We are going to a party.* = clothes (informal)

toil[1] /tɔɪl/ verb, i. **1** *My father toiled hard to build this house.* = to work hard for a long time (literary) **2** *The pilgrims going to Amarnath toiled up the mountain slowly.* = to move slowly, with great effort

toil[2] noun, u. *We managed to lift the cement slab after a great deal of toil.* = hard work (literary)

toi•let /ˈtɔɪlɪt/ noun, c. or u. **1** *We have to fit a new toilet in the bathroom.*(c.) = a kind of seat having the shape of a bowl, fitted to a pipe, on which one can sit while getting rid of waste matter from the body (also **commode**) **2** *This house has three toilets.*(c.) = a room which contains a toilet (see meaning **1**) (also **lavatory** or **bath-room**) **3** *The lady has not completed her toilet yet.*(u.) = the act of washing up and dressing (old-fashioned) **toilet-paper** noun, u. = thin and soft paper which is used to clean oneself after passing out waste matter from the body (also toilet tissue) **toilet-trained** adj. *The child has not been toilet-trained. He still uses the floor to pass urine.* = a child who has not learnt when and how to use a toilet (see meaning **1**)

toi•let•ries /ˈtɔɪlɪtriz/ noun, u.(always plural) = things that are used to clean and dress oneself e.g. soap, tooth-paste, hair-oil etc.

to•ken[1] /ˈtəʊkən/ noun, u. or c. **1** *When there is a death in the family, people wear white clothes as a token of their grief.*(u.) = an action or an object which represents (shows) a certain feeling **2** *a bank token*(c.) = a small piece of metal given to a person who wants to take some money out of his/her account in a bank, which is later exchanged for money

token[2] adj. *The workers went on a token strike for one day.* = having little practical effect, but done to express a certain feeling

told /təʊld/ verb, t. = past tense of **tell**

tol•e•rance /ˈtɒlərəns/ noun, u. **1** *In a democracy, people are free to express their opinions. There is a lot of tolerance on the part of the government.* = willingness to accept beliefs or behaviour that one does not like or does not agree with (also **toleration**) **2** *When I went to Darjeeling last month I caught cold and fell ill. I have very little tolerance to cold.* = the ability to bear pain or discomfort without being harmed **3** *The parts used in the engine of a jet plane are made to a tolerance of 0.001 mm.* = the amount by which the measurement of an object is allowed to be more or less than the correct measurement [TECHNICAL] **tolerate** /ˈtɒləreɪt/ verb, t. **1** *The manager of the office hates the smell of tobacco, but he tolerates our smoking in the office.* = to allow someone to have beliefs that one does not agree with or to behave in a way that one does not like **2** *The woman was in pain, but she still looked cheerful. She can tolerate a lot of pain.* = to suffer pain or discomfort without complaining **tolerable** adj. *The quality of the food in this restaurant is only tolerable, not very good.* = acceptable, though not very good **toleration** /tɒləˈreɪʃən/ noun, u. (see **tolerance** meaning **1**)

toll[1] /təʊl/ verb, t. or i. *The church bells are tolling in honour of those who died in the war.*(i.) = to ring a bell slowly and repeatedly (formal, literary)

toll[2] noun, u. or c. **1** *The drivers of cars using these highways have to pay toll.*(c.) = a tax paid for using a road, bridge etc. **2** *The death toll in this railway accident is more than 100.*(u.) = the suffering, loss or damage caused by an accident, disease etc. **toll-booth** /ˈtəʊlbuːθ/ noun, c. = a place by the side of a road where toll (tax) is collected from the people using a road **toll-free** adj. *You can make a toll-free call to this number.* = a telephone call for which money is not charged **toll-gate** noun, c. = a gate, built across a road, at which people have to stop to pay toll

tom•a•hawk /'tɒməhɔːk/ noun, c. = a light axe used as a weapon, in former times, by people belonging to the Red Indian tribes in North America (see **Red-Indians**)

to•ma•to /tə'mɑːtəʊ/ or /to'meɪtoʊ/ noun = a soft fleshy fruit, red when ripe, and generally eaten as a vegetable

tomb /tuːm/ noun, c. *The Taj Mahal is a tomb built by the emperor Shah Jehan for his wife, Mumtaz Mahal.* = a large, decorative building built over the place where a dead body is buried

tom•bo•la /tɒm'bəʊlə/ noun, c. = a game in which numbered tickets are bought and small prizes may be won if numbers on the tickets are the same as the ones called out

tom-boy /'tɒmbɔɪ/ noun, c. = a girl who acts and dresses like a boy (often derogatory) **tom cat** noun, c. = a male cat **tomfoolery** /tɒm'fuːləri/ noun, u. *The teacher told the boys to stop their tomfoolery and return to their studies.* = playful and often foolish behaviour **tom-tom** noun, c. = a long, narrow drum

tommy gun /'tɒmi gʌn/ noun, c. = a kind of light machine-gun

to•mor•row[1] /tə'mɒrəʊ/ noun, u. *Today is the 17 February. Tomorrow is the 18.* = the day which follows today

tomorrow[2] adv. *He is coming here tomorrow.* = on the day following today

ton /tʌn/ noun, c. **1** = a unit of weight, equal to 2800 pounds, or 0.9 tonnes (see also **tonne**) **2** *Jayasuriya scored a ton in this match.* = 100 (informal) **tonnage** noun, u. *Indian shipping companies are growing in size, and India's tonnage is rapidly increasing.* = the total number of ships belonging to a country [TECHNICAL]

tone /təʊn/ noun, u. or c. **1** *The tone of his voice showed that his feelings had been hurt.*(u.) = a quality in the voice which expresses the speaker's feelings or a particular meaning **2** *The sarod is a musical instrument with a rich tone.*(u.) = the quality of a musical sound **3** *Even though she was smiling, the tone of her actions suggested that she was angry.*(u.). = the general mood or feeling **4** *She loves light colours. Most of her saris are in different tones of pink.*(c.) = a variety of a particular colour **5** *The muscles of your body have lost their tone. You need more exercise.*(u.) = firmness (of muscles) **tonal** adj. *Her voice has a rich tonal quality.* = having to do with tone (the musical quality of a sound) **tone-deaf** adj. *a tone-deaf person* = one who is unable to tell the difference between different musical sounds **tone language** noun, c. = a language in which a word can have different meanings when spoken with a different tone (that is, with a rise or fall in the level of the voice) e.g. Chinese

to tone down (**something**) *This letter to your father is very disrespectful. You must tone it down so that he does not feel hurt.* = to reduce the forcefulness of something **to tone up** (something) *Exercise will tone up your body.* = to make something healthier or stronger

tongs /tɒŋz/ noun, c. (always plural, often used with 'a pair of') = a tool used to hold or lift something, consisting of a pair of movable arms joined together (see pic under **laboratory equipment**)

tongue /tʌŋ/ noun, c. or u. **1** *The doctor asked me to put out my tongue so that he could examine it.*(c.) = the movable, fleshy part inside the mouth, which plays an important part in tasting food as well as in speaking **2** *Sanskrit is a classical tongue, not spoken by many people now.*(u.) = language (formal, literary) **3** *He has a sharp tongue.*(u.) = style of speaking **4** *the tongue of a shoe*(c.) = a piece of leather, in the shape of the tongue, that lies under the lace in a shoe **tongue-tied** adj. *We became tongue-tied when we saw our teacher on the train.* = unable to speak freely **tongue-twister** noun, c. *The sentence 'She sells sea-shells by the seashore' is a tongue twister.* = a word or sentence that is difficult to pronounce, specially when spoken quickly, which someone may be asked to say as a game

to speak tongue in cheek = to say something without meaning it seriously **to speak with a forked tongue** = to tell lies or to say two clearly opposite things at the same time in order to trick or deceive **silver tongue** = the ability to use a language beautifully **a slip of the tongue** = an unintended mistake made while speaking

ton•ic /'tɒnɪk/ noun, c. *The doctor has asked me to take some tonic containing Vitamin B.* = something that is taken to improve one's health

to•night /tə'naɪt/ adv. *We are expecting a guest tonight.* = this night

tonn•age see **ton**

tonne /tʌn/ noun = a unit of weight equal to 1000 kilograms (see also **ton**)

ton•sil /'tɒnsəl/ noun, c. (usually plural form **tonsils**) *The doctor is going to remove my tonsils.* = the two small, soft pieces of flesh at the back of the mouth **tonsilitis** /tɒnsɪ'laɪtɪs/ noun, u. = infection of the tonsils causing pain and swelling [MEDICINE] **tonsillectomy** noun, u. = an operation done to remove the tonsils

ton•sure /'tɒnʃəʳ/ noun, u. = a religious ceremony during which all the hair on the head is removed

too /tuː/ adv. **1** *I am going to Delhi and Avinash is going too.* = also **2** *The food is too hot. I can't eat it.* = more than is necessary or good **3** *You are really too kind.* = very

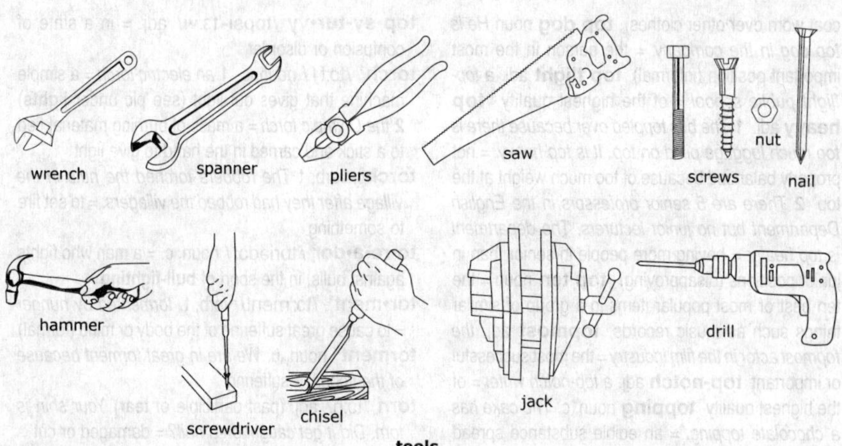

tools

took /tʊk/ verb, t. = past tense of **take**

tool[1] /tu:l/ noun, c. **1** *The mechanic uses a screwdriver, spanner and other tools to repair cars.* = an instrument that is held in the hand and used for doing special jobs, such as repairing a machine **2** *She became a tool for their dishonest plans.* = someone who is used by someone else for his/her own advantage (derogatory)

tool[2] verb, t. **1** *These shoes are tooled by hand.* = to make something by hand, using tools **2** *We were tooling along at 80 kilometres an hour in our car.* = to drive (informal)

toot[1] /tu:t/ verb, t. *The driver of the car tooted his horn to warn people to move out of the way.* = to make a warning sound on a horn (informal)

toot[2] noun, c. *He sounded a toot on the car's horn.* = the sound made by a horn

tooth /tu:θ/ noun, c. (**teeth**) **1** *A baby gets its first tooth at about the age of six months.* = one of the hard, white objects in the mouth that grows from the upper and lower jaws, and is used for biting or chewing food **2** *The teeth of a comb* = one of the narrow, pointed parts that stands out from a comb **toothache** noun, u. or c.= pain in a tooth **toothpick** noun, c. = a short, thin piece of wood or plastic used for removing pieces of food from between the teeth, specially after a meal **toothpowder** noun, u. = a powder used for cleaning the teeth **toothsome** adj. *a toothsome chicken curry* = having a good taste **toothy** adj. *a toothy smile* = showing a lot of teeth (when smiling)

to fight tooth and nail = to try to do something with great determination (informal) **to be long in the tooth** = to become old (informal, not respectful) **to get (sink) one's teeth into something** = to find a piece of work which is interesting and which one enjoys doing **in the teeth of** *We carried out our plan in the teeth of opposition.* = in spite of **to have a sweet tooth** = to have a great fondness for sweets **to escape by the skin of one's teeth** = to have a narrow escape from a dangerous situation (informal)

toot•le /'tu:tl/ verb, i. *The old couple were tootling along slowly in their old car.* = to drive at a very slow speed (informal, humorous)

toot•sie /'tʊtsi/ noun, c. (**tootsies**) *Did you hurt your tootsies?* = foot (an expression used when talking to a child)

top[1] /tɒp/ noun, c. or u. **1** *He reached the top of the mountain after a difficult climb.*(c.) = the highest point or part **2** *He is at the top of his class.*(u.) = the most important or desirable place **3** *The bottle has a screw top.*(c.) = a lid or cover for a container **4** *She wore a blue skirt and a pink top.*(c.) = a garment worn on the upper part of the body, specially by a girl or woman **5** *The child was playing with a large wooden top.*(c.) = a child's toy which can be made to spin (turn round and round) very fast

top[2] adj. **1** *He lives on the top floor.* = the highest **2** *She is the top student in the class.* = the best

top[3] verb, t. (**topped**) **1** *She has topped the list of successful candidates.* = to be the best or most successful **2** *My uncle promised me an ice cream if I finished my homework by 6 p.m. My father topped the offer and promised to buy me a book and a cricket bat.* = to do better than someone else **3** *The ice-cream was topped with a red cherry.* = to form the top part of something **top brass** noun, u. *You will find the top brass of the Indian army watching the Republic Day parade.* = the people in the highest positions, specially in the army **top coat** noun, c. = an overcoat (warm

T

coat worn over other clothes) **top dog** noun *He is top dog in the company.* = the person in the most important position (informal) **top flight** adj. *a top-flight public school* = of the highest quality **top heavy** adj. **1** *The bus toppled over because there is too much luggage piled on top. It is top heavy.* = not properly balanced because of too much weight at the top **2** *There are 5 senior professors in the English Department but no junior lecturers. The department is top heavy.* = having more people in senior than in junior positions (disapproving) **top ten** noun = the ten best or most popular items in a group of similar things such as music records **topmost** adj. *the topmost actor in the film industry* = the most successful or important **top-notch** adj. *a top-notch writer* = of the highest quality **topping** noun, c. *The cake has a chocolate topping.* = an edible substance spread on top of some food, to give it a better look or taste **tops** adj. *Zora Sehgal is still tops, though she is more than 90 years old.* = the best (informal) **top secret** adj. *a top-secret plan* = something that has been kept secret, usually because it has military importance **top soil** noun, u. = the layer of soil lying on the surface of an area of land, in which small plants have their roots **top spin** noun, u. **1** = a shot hit (in the game of tennis or table-tennis) with the racket or bat held at an angle, so that the ball is made to spin forward in the air **2** = a ball bowled (in cricket) in such a way that it spins forward through the air

top off *We topped off a wonderful evening at the cinema with a meal in a good restaurant.* = to bring something to a successful end (informal) **top up** *Let us fill 10 litres of petrol in the car's tank and top it up.* = to make a partly empty container (of some liquid) full

topaz /ˈtəʊpæz/ noun = a semi-precious stone having a yellow colour

to•pi•a•ry /ˈtəʊpjri/ noun, u. = the art of cutting bushes into the shape of animals etc. [TECHNICAL]

top•ic /ˈtɒpɪk/ noun, c. *He is going to speak on the topic of political equality for women.* = a subject for a talk or a piece of writing **topical** adj. *A book on wild life is of great topical interest now.* = being of interest at the present time

to•pog•ra•phy /təˈpɒgrəfi/ noun, u. *The government is surveying the topography of the coastal areas in order to prepare a new map.* = the shape of the surface (hills, valleys, plains etc.) of an area of land

top•ple /ˈtɒpəl/ verb, i. **1** *It is dangerous for a bus to have too many people in it as it might topple over.* = to roll over or fall because of being unsteady **2** *This government is likely to topple soon.* = to fall or be defeated (referring to a government in power)

top•sy-tur•vy /tɒpsi-ˈtɜːvi/ adj. = in a state of confusion or disorder

torch[1] /tɔːtʃ/ noun, c. **1** *an electric torch* = a simple machine that gives out light (see pic under **lights**) **2** *the Olympic torch* = a mass of burning material tied to a stick and carried in the hand to give light

torch[2] verb, t *The robbers torched the huts in the village after they had robbed the villagers.* = to set fire to something

to•re•a•dor /ˈtɒriədɔːʳ/ noun, c. = a man who fights against bulls, in the sport of **bull-fighting**

tor•ment[1] /tɔːˈment/ verb, t. *tormented by hunger* = to cause great suffering of the body or mind (formal)

torment[2] noun, u. *We are in great torment because of the floods.* = suffering

torn /tɔːn/ adj. (past participle of **tear**) *Your shirt is torn. Did it get caught on a nail?* = damaged or cut

tor•na•do /tɔːˈneɪdəʊ/ noun, c. = a very powerful wind that turns round and round at high speed, causing great damage

tor•pe•do /tɔːˈpiːdəʊ/ noun, c. = an explosive weapon fired from a submarine (a fighting ship that can travel under the surface of water), which can strike and blow up an enemy ship

tor•que /tɔːk/ noun, u. *The jeep got stuck in the mud, but it was able to come out easily as it has a high-torque engine.* = the force produced by an engine which causes a turning or twisting movement, causing the wheels of a vehicle to rotate [TECHNICAL]

tor•rent /ˈtɒrənt/ noun, c. *When the Ganga flows through the mountains above Hardwar, it is a rushing torrent.* = a powerful and fast-flowing stream of water (literary) **torrential** /tɒˈrenʃəl/ adj. *torrential rain* = like a torrent

tor•rid /ˈtɒrɪd/ adj. *In June, the temperature here rises to 42 degrees Celsius.The weather is torrid.* = very hot

tor•sion /ˈtɔːʃən/ noun, u. *He twisted his knee while playing football and damaged the knee-joint. It could not take so much torsion.* = the action of twisting something (see also **twist**)

tor•so /ˈtɔːsəʊ/ noun, u. = the human body, without the head, arms and legs [TECHNICAL]

tort /tɔːt/ noun, c. = a wrong act which cannot be considered a crime [LAW]

tor•til•la /tɔːˈtiːjə/ noun, c. = a kind of flat bread which is eaten in Mexico

tor•toise /ˈtɔːtəs/ noun, c. = a slow-moving animal that lives on land and has a hard, round shell covering its body (see also **turtle**)

tor•tu•ous /ˈtɔːtʃuəs/ adj. *The car climbed slowly along the tortuous mountain road.* = turning and twisting frequently; full of bends (formal, literary)

tor•ture[1] /ˈtɔːtʃəʳ/ verb, t. *The prisoner told the judge that the police had tortured him by giving him electric shocks.* = to cause great pain or suffering to someone, as a punishment or to force someone to give information

torture[2] noun, u. **1** *The police is not allowed to use torture to get information from prisoners.* = the act of torturing someone (causing pain and suffering to get information etc.) **2** *It was sheer torture to hear him speak.* = something that causes suffering (humorous)

To•ry /ˈtɔːri/ noun, c. (**Tories**) = a member of the Conservative Party (the political party that favours private industries etc.) in Britain

toss[1] /tɒs/ verb, t. or i. **1** *The children tossed their school-bags away as soon as they reached home after school, and dashed off to play.*(t.)= to throw something carelessly **2** *I was unable to sleep and tossed about in my bed all night.*(i.) = to move about continuously in a violent manner **3** *The two captains tossed, and the Indian team was asked to bat first.*(i.) = to decide something by tossing (throwing) a coin up in the air and correctly naming, in advance, the side of the coin which will be on top when it lands

toss[2] noun, c. **1** *The Indian captain won the toss.* = an act of tossing a coin **2** *He was unable to control the horse and took a toss.* = a fall

toss-up noun *Who is going to win the election? Both parties are equally strong, and it will be a toss-up between them.* = an equal contest, the result of which is uncertain

tot[1] /tɒt/ noun, c. **1** *a tiny tot* = child (informal) **2** *Give him a tot of rum.* = a small amount of some alcoholic drink

tot[2] verb, t. (**totted**) *We have to tot up the number of votes you got in the election.* = to add up (informal)

to•tal[1] /ˈtəʊtl/ noun, c. *The Indian team scored a total of 365 runs.* = a number obtained by adding together a number of separate numbers

total[2] adj. *There was total silence in the room when the Prime Minister got up to speak.* = complete

total[3] verb, t. (**totalled**) **1** *Mohini scored 95 in Mathematics, 82 in English and 78 in History. Can you total up her marks?* = to add up different numbers **2** *Mohini's marks in Mathematics, English and History totalled 255.* = to reach a number when added up together **totality** noun, u. *We have to look at the economy of the country in its totality.* = the whole of something

to•tal•i•tar•i•an•is•m /təʊtælɪˈteəriənɪzəm/ noun = a political system in which the state (government) has total power and control over the people **totalitarian** adj. *a totalitarian government* = based on a system of totalitarianism

to•tem /ˈtəʊtəm/ noun, c. = an object (often an animal) which is respected by the members of a tribe or group as a religious symbol or sign [TECHNICAL]

tot•ter /ˈtɒtəʳ/ verb, i. **1** *The man was so drunk that he tottered as he tried to cross the road.* = to walk unsteadily **2** *The government is tottering and will not last very long.* = to become weak and helpless

tou•can /ˈtuːkən/ noun, c. = a kind of bird, found in America, which has a large beak and brightly-coloured feathers

touch[1] /tʌtʃ/ verb, t or i. **1** *You may look at these paintings from a distance, but you are not allowed to touch them.*(t.)= to bring the fingers in contact with something **2** *They were sitting so close to each other on the train that their knees almost touched.*(i.) = to be in contact with something **3** *Thank you for the flowers you sent me. I am so touched.*(i.) = to have a feeling of happiness when one is remembered, or when something is done that shows one is loved or cared for **4** *He told the story of the wounded tiger with great feeling. No one could fail to be touched.*(i.) = to cause a feeling of pity **5** *Who says I drink? I never touch alcohol!* = to take some drink or food (used in negative sentences only) **6** *She sings well, but she can't touch Gangubai Hangal!* = to be equal to someone in some quality (used in negative sentences only)

touch[2] noun, u. **1** *Blind people are able to read books by touch.* = the ability to feel, specially with the finger-tips **2** *I felt the touch of a hand on my shoulder.* = an act of touching **3** *He is a good player, but he hasn't won many tournaments this season. He seems to be out of touch.* = a condition in which one can perform well **4** *His speech was good, but too serious. He should have added a touch of humour.* = a small amount (informal) **5** *He had a touch of influenza, but he is better now.* = a slight attack of some illness (informal) **touch-and-go** *He had such a severe attack of typhoid that the doctors had given up hope. For a while it was touch-and-go, but then he improved.* = a dangerous or risky situation in which one can die, lose an important opportunity etc. **touch-down** noun = the landing of a flying aircraft on the ground **touching** adj. *a touching story of human suffering* = causing a feeling of pity **touch screen** noun = the screen of a computer monitor which can be operated by touching it [COMPUTERS] **touchstone** noun **1** = a kind of stone which was used, in former times, to test the purity of gold, by rubbing a piece of gold against it and examining the colour of the mark left by the gold on the stone **2** *The touchstone of your ability as a writer is the number of readers that your books attract.* = the test or standard by which

T

something can be judged (figurative) **touch-type** verb. = the ability to type, using a type-writer or computer keyboard, without looking at the keyboard **touchy** adj. *He is very touchy if you remind him what a cry-baby he was as a child.* = sensitive; easily upset by something

to touch on (upon) *He touched on the subject of film music while talking about popular culture.* = to mention something in a talk or a piece of writing without going deeply into it **to touch off** *A simple argument between friends touched off a deep misunderstanding between the families.* = to cause some unpleasant events **to touch up** *I have sent my book to a well-known writer, who has promised to touch it up.* = to improve something by making small changes **to be (get) in touch** = to write to someone or speak to someone often **to be in touch with something or someone** = to have the latest information or some subject **to lose one's touch** 1 *Wasim scored less than ten runs in his last three matches. He seems to be losing his touch.* = to lose a skill or ability that one had 2 *Have you met Rehana recntly? 'No, actually we've lost touch.'* = to be in the position of not having met or communicated with someone for a long time **to not touch something with a barge-pole** *I don't think you should take up that job. I wouldn't touch it with a barge-pole.* = to have such a poor opinion of something that you do not wish to have anything to do with it

tou•che /ˈtuːʃeɪ/ interjec. (French) *'You claim to be a good writer but no one seems to be buying your books.' 'Touche!'* = an expression used to admit the correctness of something that has just been said (humorous)

tough[1] /tʌf/ adj. 1 *Many farmers are so tough that they can work for 20 hours a day without getting tired.* = strong; able to bear hardship 2 *People are of disposing of their garbage any way that suits them. Unless we take a tough stand on this things will go out of control.* = determined and bold and unpleasant if necessary 3 *The bread was so tough that I couldn't chew it.* = hard; difficult to cut or eat 4 *Unemployment is a tough problem for the government.* = difficult to deal with 5 *He has had tough luck and has lost a lot of money.* = bad luck

tough[2] noun, c. *The toughs who live in this neighbourhood keep the people terrorized.* = a criminal or violent person (informal) **toughen** verb, t. *You should allow your son to join the army. Army life will toughen him.* = to make someone tough (strong)

tou•pee /ˈtuːpeɪ/ noun, c. = a wig (artificial hair which can be fitted on the head)

tour[1] /tʊəʳ/ noun, c. 1 *The doctor made a tour of the three districts where people are reported to be suffering from malaria.* = a journey made in connection with one's work, during which one usually visits a number of places 2 *We are planning a holiday tour.* = a journey to several places, for pleasure 3 *We were taken on a tour of the museum.* = a short trip around a place of interest

tour[2] verb, t. *The teachers will be touring the western part of the state to see the way schools are run there.* = to go on a tour **tourist** noun, c. = a person who visits a place for pleasure or for a holiday **tourism** noun, u. *Singapore earns billions of dollars each year through tourism.* = the business of bringing tourists to a place **tourist class** noun = the cheapest class in which one can travel on an aircraft or ship, usually during the holiday season **touristy** adj. *Rajasthan has many beautiful places, but unfortunately some of them have become rather touristy.* = designed to earn money by attracting tourists (derogatory)

tour-de-force /tʊədəˈfɔːs/ noun, c. (French) *The villain's speech at the climax of the play was a tour-de-force. Everyone in the audience was impressed.* = a performance requiring or made with great skill

tour•na•ment /ˈtʊənəmənt/ noun, c. *the tennis tournament at Wimbledon* = a competition, usually in sports, in which a number of matches are played, and the player or team that wins a match goes on to play the next match **tourney** /ˈtʊəni/ noun, c. = tournament (old-fashioned)

tour•ni•quet /ˈtʊənɪkeɪ/ noun, c. = a tight bandage put on some part of the body to stop bleeding [TECHNICAL]

tou•sled /ˈtaʊzəld/ adj. *a school-boy with tousled hair* = untidy looking

tout[1] /taʊt/ noun, c. *If you visit the market you will run into touts who will try to make you buy things from a particular shop.* = a person who tries to persuade someone, often by using dishonest means, to buy something being sold or offered by someone else (derogatory)

tout[2] verb, t. *The company uses television to tout its products.* = to advertise in a dishonest manner

tow[1] /təʊ/ verb, t. *When our car broke down on the road it had to be towed by a truck.* = to pull (usually a vehicle, boat or ship) along, using a rope or chain

tow[2] noun (only singular) *Our car has broken down. Can you give us a tow?* = an act of towing (pulling)

to•wards /təˈwɔːdz/ prep. 1 *He was going towards the market.* = in the direction of 2 *He sat with his back towards the speaker.* = facing 3 *You seem to have changed your attitude towards English.* = in relation to 4 *I am sending you Rs 500 towards the examination fee.* = for the purpose of meeting a certain expenditure (formal)

tow•el /ˈtaʊəl/ noun, c. = a piece of cloth or paper used to dry something which is wet **towelling** noun, u. = special cloth used to make towels

tow•er[1] /ˈtaʊəʳ/ noun, c. *the Qutub Minar near Delhi is a tower built hundreds of years ago.* = a very tall and narrow building

tower[2] verb, i. **1** *He is so tall that he towers over all the other boys in the class.* = to be much taller or higher than someone or something else **2** *Rabindranath Tagore towers over other writers of the time.* = to be much better than others (figurative) **tower block** noun, c. = a tall building containing a number of flats or apartments **towering** adj. *a towering personality* = very great

tower of strength = someone or something that one can always depend on for protection, help etc.

town /taʊn/ noun, c. **1** = an area containing many houses, shops, offices etc. which is smaller than a **city** but larger than a **village** **2** *I am leaving town for a week.* = the place where one lives or works **3** *I am going to town to do some shopping.* = the main business area in a city **town planning** noun = the art and science of planning a new town or city in such a way that people can live and work in it comfortably **township** noun, c. = an area, usually part of a city, where people live

to go to town on something *She felt she had to welcome her old friends, whom she was meeting after years and she really went to town on that.* = to do something with great eagerness, often spending a lot of money (informal) **to paint the town red** *We have won the World Cup and tonight we plan to paint the town red.* = to celebrate something and enjoy oneself by feasting, dancing etc.

tox•in /ˈtɒksɪn/ noun, c. *It is dangerous to eat meat which is not fresh as it sometimes contains toxins.* = a poisonous substance formed by bacteria, which may produce disease **toxic** adj. *The chemical factory should be closed down as it produces toxic wastes.* = poisonous or harmful **toxaemia** /tɒkˈsiːmiə/ noun *If the wound is not treated at once, you may get toxaemia.* = a medical condition in which the blood gets poisoned [MEDICINE]

tox•i•col•o•gy /ˈtɒksɪˈkɒlədʒi/ noun = the scientific study of poisons, their effects on the body and their treatment [TECHNICAL]

toy[1] /tɔɪ/ noun, c. or adj. **1** *a toy bus for a child*(adj.) = an object that a child can play with **2** *This new music system is his latest toy.*(noun.) = something that an adult uses to amuse himself/herself

toy[2] verb, t. **1** *I am toying with the idea of starting a bookshop.* = to think about something in not a serious way **2** *If you are serious about marrying her, you should tell her. Don't toy with her emotions.* = to play with someone or something without being serious; to handle someone or something in a careless manner (disapproving)

trace[1] /treɪs/ verb, t. **1** *The police detectives are trying to trace the criminals who robbed the bank last night.* = to find someone or something by following and examining marks or other evidence **2** *He says he can trace his family back to the last Moghul emperor.* = to find the origin of something (the point from which something began) through evidence **3** *This book traces the development of English education in India.* = to follow the history of something **4** *The girl is tracing the picture of a flower from a book.* = to copy a picture etc. by drawing its outline on **tracing paper**

trace[2] noun, c. **1** *Historians have found traces of an ancient city which existed here 5000 years ago.* = marks or signs showing the presence of something **2** *There is just a trace of sugar in your urine.* = a very small amount of something **tracing paper** noun, u. = strong transparent paper through which one can see pictures etc. from a book, in order to trace (copy) them **trace chemical** noun = a chemical which is injected into the arteries of a person so that doctors can follow the path of the blood through the body by watching a picture on a screen [TECHNICAL]

tra•che•a /trəˈkiːə/ noun = the wind-pipe (the pipe-like part of the body inside the throat through which air is carried to the lungs) [BIOLOGY]

tra•cho•ma /trəˈkəʊmə/ noun, u. = a painful disease of the eyes [MEDICINE]

track[1] /træk/ noun, c. **1** *a mountain track* = a narrow path or road **2** *The hunters followed the tracks of the wounded leopard through the jungle.* = the marks left by a moving person, animal or vehicle **3** *a railway track* = a set of steel rails on which trains run (see also **rail**) **4** *a race track // running track* = an area, usually circular or oval in shape, which is specially prepared for races in which human beings or animals (e.g. horses, dogs) take part **5** *This audio cassette has five tracks.* = a piece of recorded music on a tape

track[2] verb, t. *The hunters tracked the wounded leopard.* = to follow the tracks (marks) left by a moving person, animal etc. **track event** noun, c. = an event in a sports competition that is performed on a running track e.g. the 100-metre race **trackless** adj. *a trackless desert* = having no roads or paths **track-suit** noun, c. = a set of loose-fitting and warm clothes worn by persons while practising for a sports competition

to be on track *We've solved the problems we had using the computer program and are now on track.* = going ahead in the right direction **to have a one-track mind** = to follow a single idea or plan and not allow oneself to move away from it **off the beaten track** *No one ever comes to this village as it is off the beaten track.* = far away from the places that people usually visit

T

tract /trækt/ noun, c. **1** *a religious tract* = a short piece of writing, specially on a religious subject **2** *a barren tract* = a large area of land

trac•tion /'trækʃən/ noun, u. **1** *Trains were pulled by steam locomotives earlier but now they are pulled by electric locomotives.The railways changed over to electric traction last year.* = the power used to pull a heavy load along a surface **2** *Our car got stuck in the sand and was unable to move. The wheels lost traction.* = the force which allows the wheels of a vehicle to grip (hold) the road and pull the vehicle forward [TECHNICAL] **3** *The doctor has prescribed traction for her as she has a pain in the back.* = medical treatment requiring the pulling or stretching of the backbone by the use of weights [MEDICINE]

trac•tor /'træktər/ noun, c. = a powerful vehicle with large wheels, used to plough the land or to pull heavy loads

trade[1] /treɪd/ noun, u. or c. **1** *India sells foodgrains to Nepal and buys timber from Nepal. There is a lot of trade between the two countries.*(u.) = the buying and selling or exchanging of goods **2** *Thousands of people in Surat work in the diamond-cutting trade.*(c.) = a particular business or industry

trade[2] verb, i. or t. **1** *His family trades in silk saris.*(i.) = to be engaged in some business; to buy and sell something **2** *I traded my old car for a new one.*(t.) = to exchange (give something away and get something in return) **trade-in** noun, c. *When I bought a new television set, I gave the dealer my old set as a trade-in.* = something that one gives away in exchange while buying something new, as part of the price that is paid **trademark** noun, c. *The trademark of the His Master's Voice company was a dog sitting near an old-fashioned gramophone.* = a particular sign or name which a company uses to sell its products (also **logo**) **trade-off** noun, c. *If you leave Nepal and settle in Japan you may earn more money but you will have to give up all your friends. There has to be trade-off.* = a loss of some kind that one must suffer in order to gain something (informal) **trade-price** noun, c. = a lower price charged to someone who buys goods wholesale (in large quantities) **trader** noun, c. *a trader in children's clothes* = one who buys and sells things **trade route** noun, c. *Vasco da Gama discovered a new trade route between Europe and India.* = a route (path) that is used for purposes of trade **tradesman** noun, c. = a person who travels from place to place, selling and buying things (old-fashioned) **trade union** noun, c. = a group of people who protect the interests of the workers (e.g. make sure that they are paid the wages due to them etc.) **trade wind** noun, c. = a strong wind blowing in a particular direction across the sea which drove sailing ships to the countries which they wanted to visit for trade (in former times, when ships were driven by wind)

tra•di•tion /trə'dɪʃən/ noun, u. or c. *For hundreds of years, most of the young men of this village have been serving in the army. The village has a long military tradition.*(u.) = a belief, or a way of thinking or behaving which the people in a particular society or group have been following for a long time **traditional** /trə'dɪʃənəl/ adj. *Kathakali is the traditional dance of Kerala.* = (something) which has been commonly practised (done) for a long time

traf•fic /'træfɪk/ noun, u. **1** *Thousands of cars use this road everyday, but the traffic is specially heavy in the mornings.* = the movement of people, vehicles, etc. along roads **2** *There is heavy traffic in drugs across the Afghan border.* = illegal trade **traffic jam** noun, c. = a halt in the traffic (movement of vehicles along a road) caused by over-crowding **traffic lights** noun (always plural) = a set of red, yellow and green lights used to control the movement of traffic (see pic under **lights**)

traf•fick•ing /'træfɪkɪŋ/ noun, u. *The police have been ordered to check trafficking in opium.* = illegal trade (buying and selling) (see **traffic** meaning **2**) **trafficker** noun, c. = a person who buys and sells things in an illegal way (disapproving)

tra•ge•dy /'trædʒɪdi/ noun, u. or c. (**tragedies**) **1** *'Romeo and Juliet' is a tragedy.*(c.) = a play (drama) or film that has a sad ending, usually in the death of the main characters **2** *The death of so many people in a bus accident is a great tragedy.* = a very sad or unfortunate event **tragedian** noun, c. *Dilip Kumar became famous as a tragedian.* = an actor who acts in tragedies **tragic** /'trædʒɪk/ adj. **1** *a tragic accident* = very sad or unfortunate **2** *tragic circumstances* = connected with death or something very sad **tragi-comedy** noun, c. = a drama or film that is very sad in parts but has a happy ending

trail[1] /treɪl/ verb, t. or i. **1** *As the woman walked across the room, the end of her sari trailed along the floor.*(i.)= to follow or come after someone or something slowly **2** *The police trailed the criminals to their hiding place.*(t.) = to follow a person or animal, often in order to capture (catch) or kill, with the help of tracks (marks that can be seen or found) (see **track**[2]) **3** *Holland scored 9 goals, and now Pakistan have scored 7 goals. They are trailing Holland by 2 goals.*(t.) = to be behind someone in a competition

trail[2] noun, c. **1** *The wounded tiger left a trail of blood across the jungle.*= the marks left behind by a person or animal which can be used to follow it (see also **track**[1] meaning **2**) **2** *The people walking across the* *field everyday have created a trail.* = a path created on the ground by the passing of people or animals **3** *The car raced along the village road, leaving a trail of dust.* = a stream of dust or smoke that follows a train, car etc. moving at speed **trailer** noun, c. **1** = a vehicle that is pulled by some other vehicle **2** = a short part of a film shown to attract the audience

train[1] /treɪn/ noun, c. **1** *a railway train* = a line of carriages attached to each other **2** *The painter arrived with a train of followers.* = a large number (of people who follow an important person) **3** *You have interrupted the train of my thoughts by singing loudly.* = a chain of related events, thoughts etc.

train[2] /treɪn/ verb, t. or i. **1** *The Police Academy at Hyderabad trains policeofficers.*(t.) **2** *He is training to become a teacher.*(i.) = to prepare someone or oneself for a job or profession by giving or receiving special knowledge or skills **3** *He is training for the Olympics.*(i.) = to strengthen the body through exercise **4** *The policeman trained his gun at the thief.*(t.) = to aim a gun at someone (formal) **trainee** /treɪˈniː/ noun, c. *a trainee policeofficer* = a person who is being trained **trainer** noun, c. = a person who gives training to others **training college** noun, c. = a college where teachers are trained

trait /treɪt/ noun, c. *He becomes talkative when he is nervous. This is his worst trait.* = a quality in one's character

trai•tor /ˈtreɪtəʳ/ noun, c. *These traitors have been giving secret military information to the enemy.* = a person who does something to harm his/her own country or a cause (political belief etc.)

tra•jec•to•ry /trəˈdʒektəri/ noun, c. (**trajectories**) = the curved path that an object follows when it is flying through the air [TECHNICAL]

tram /træm/ noun, c. = a carriage that runs on steel tracks or rails (like a railway train) along the streets of a city **tram-lines** noun (always plural) = the tracks or rails on which a tram runs

tramp[1] /træmp/ verb, i. *He was unable to sleep and tramped up and down the corridor all night.* = to walk with heavy steps

tramp[2] noun, c. = a person without a home or job who wanders from place to place (disapproving)

tram•ple /ˈtræmpəl/ verb, t. or i. *The herd of wild elephants trampled the rice plants growing in the fields.* (t.)= to step heavily on someone or something, causing damage or injury

tram•po•line /ˈtræmpəliːn/ noun, c. = a sheet of thick canvas stretched tightly across a metal frame, on which a person can jump up and down, as a form of exercise or sport

trance /trɑːns/ noun (only singular) *It is said that the woman goes into a trance every evening and communicates with the spirits of the dead.* = a temporary mental condition in which one is not aware of what is happening or not in control of his/her actions

tran•quil /ˈtræŋkwɪl/ adj. *The city is crowded and noisy, but life in my village is tranquil.* = quiet and peaceful (literary) **tranquilize (tranquilise)** /ˈtræŋkwɪlaɪz/ verb, t. *The tiger in the zoo was ill and had to be treated, but first it had to be tranquilized.* = to make someone (specially a fierce animal) calm by using a drug [TECHNICAL] **tranquilizer (tranquiliser)** noun, c. = a drug or medicine that is used to make a person calm

trans- /træns/ prefix meaning 'across' (e.g. a trans-Atlantic flight) **trans-atlantic** /trænzətˈlæntɪk/ adj. = from one side of the Atlantic Ocean to the other **trans•con•ti•nen•tal** /trænzkɒntɪˈnentl/ adj. *We flew to America on a transcontinental flight.* = from one continent to another

trans•act /trænˈzækt/ verb, t. *I am going to Japan as I have some important business to transact.* = to carry out a piece of business (formal) **transaction** /trænˈzækʃən/ noun, c. *a business transaction* = a piece of business in which more than one person takes part

tran•scend /trænˈsend/ verb, t. *You should love all human beings, not just those who belong to your family. Your love should transcend all barriers.* = to rise above or to go beyond the limits of something (formal, literary) **transcendent** /trænˈsendənt/ adj. *the transcendent power of music* = rising above or going beyond ordinary limits (literary) **transcendental** /trænsenˈdentl/ adj. *The truths which are revealed through religion are transcendental.* = going beyond human reasoning

trans•cribe /trænˈskraɪb/ verb, t. *Kathy will transcribe all that is said at this meeting.* = to copy in writing or to put into written form **transcript** noun, c. *The newspaper published a transcript of the Prime Minister's speech.* = a written or printed copy of a speech **transcription** /trænˈskrɪpʃən/ noun, u. or c. **1** (u.) = the act of transcribing (putting something in written form) **2** (c.) = a written form of something that is spoken

trans•fer[1] /trænsˈfɜːʳ/ verb, t. (**transferred**) *The government has transferred several officials from Nagpur to other districts.* = to move from one place or position to another

transfer[2] noun, u. or c. *I am being sent to Kolkata on transfer.* (u.) = the act of being transferred (sent from one place or position to another)

trans•fig•ure /trænsˈfɪgəʳ/ verb, t. *He is a very ordinary person, but when he dances on the stage he*

T

is completely transfigured. = to become completely changed in appearance and look more beautiful (literary)

trans•fix /træns'fɪks/ verb, t. *When the powerful headlights of the car fell on the deer, it stood transfixed.* = to become unable to move

trans•form /træns'fɔ:m/ verb, t. *In a nuclear reactor, the energy obtained by splitting atoms is transformed into electrical energy.* = to change something from one form into another **transformer** noun, c. = a device or machine that changes an electric current from a higher to a lower, or a lower to a higher voltage [TECHNICAL]

trans•fu•sion /træns'fju:ʒən/ noun, c. or u. *a blood transfusion* = the act of putting blood from one person into the body of another person [MEDICINE]

trans•gress /trænz'gres/ verb, t. *You have transgressed the law by making a false declaration and you will be punished.* = to break a law or rule (formal)

tran•si•ent /'trænziənt/ adj. **1** *transient peace* = lasting for only a short time **2** *Mumbai has a large transient population. Thousands of people come here everday from nearby places and return home after work.* = staying in a place for only a short time (also **transitory**)

tran•sis•tor /træn'zɪstə^r/ noun, c. = a small electrionic device, used in radios, television sets etc. that controls the flow of an electric current [TECHNICAL]

tran•sit[1] /'trænsɪt/ noun, u. *I sent my furniture from Ranchi to Kolkata by truck, but a number of things were damaged in transit.* = the process of moving people or goods from one place to another

transit[2] verb, i. *I am not going to stay long in Bangalore; I am only transiting on my way to Mumbai.* = to pass through a place without staying or stopping there for a long time **transition** /træn'zɪʃən/ noun, u. *Nepal is passing through a transition. Many of our old customs are changing.* = a period of change

tran•si•tive /'trænsɪtɪv/ adj. *In the sentence 'He is reading a novel', the verb 'read' is transitive.* = a verb which is followed by an object [GRAMMAR]

tran•si•to•ry /'trænzɪtəri/ adj. = something that will not last long (see **transient**)

trans•late /træns'leɪt/ verb, t. *Arnold translated 'The Odyssey' from Greek to English.* = to change something, spoken or written, from one language into another **translation** noun, u. or c. **1** *I have read 'War and Peace' only in translation.*(u.) = a translated form (in a language different from that of the original) **2** *This is a new translation of the novel 'Devadas'.*(c.) = something that has been translated from one language to another **translator** noun, c. = a person who translates a book from one language into another

trans•lit•e•rate /trænz'lɪtəreɪt/ verb, t. *The signboards on all the shops were in English but now the government has ordered people to transliterate them into Tamil.* = to change from one script (system of writing) to another (formal)

trans•lu•cent /trænz'lu:sənt/ adj. *The glass fitted in the bathroom window is translucent. You can't peep through it.* = something that one cannot see through, although it allows light to pass through it (compare **transparent**)

trans•mi•gra•tion /trænzmaɪ'greɪʃən/ noun, u. *transmigration of the soul* = the passing of the soul from one body into another after death (formal)

trans•mit /trænz'mɪt/ verb, t. **1** *The sun transmits light and heat to the earth.* = to give out or send out **2** *Doordarshan transmits news in all the regional languages.* = to broadcast (send out over radio or television) **3** *Mosquitoes transmit malaria.* = to carry (a disease) from one person to another **transmission** /træz'mɪʃən/ noun, u. or c. **1** *the transmission of heat* (u.) = the act of transmitting **2** *a news transmission*(c.) = something that is broadcast **3** *the transmission of a car.* = the parts of a car that carry power from the engine to the wheels [TECHNICAL]

trans•mute /trænz'mju:t/ verb, t. = to transform (change completely)

trans•par•ent /træn'spærənt/ adj. *transparent glass* = which one can see through (compare **translucent**)

tran•spi•ra•tion /trænspɪ'reɪʃən/ noun, u. = the process by which plants give up excess water through their leaves [BIOLOGY]

trans•pire /træn'spaɪə^r/ verb, i. **1** *The prime ministers of the two countries are meeting. Let us see what transpires at this meeting.* = to happen (with some worry about the outcome) (formal) **2** *The doctor said he had examined the patient and found nothing wrong. It later transpired that he had not seen the patient at all.* = to become known (formal) **3** = to give up excess water (see **transpiration**)

trans•plant[1] /træns'plɑ:nt/ verb, t. **1** *The seedlings of rice are transplanted when they are about six weeks old.* = to take a young plant out of the soil and plant it in another place **2** *His heart has been transplanted.* = to take an organ (body part) from one person's body and put it in place in the body of another person

transplant[2] noun, c. **1** *He has undergone a kidney transplant.* = the surgical operation by which an organ is transplanted **2** *His body has rejected the transplant.* = an organ that has been transplanted

trans•pond•er /træn'spɒndə^r/ noun, c. = an electronic device that gives out a radio signal on receiving another signal [TECHNICAL]

trans•port[1] /'trænspɔ:t/ verb, t. *Railway wagons transport iron ore from mines to the steel plant in Jamshedpur.* = to carry or move goods or people from one place to another

transport[2] noun, u. **1** *The transport of goods has been stopped as the roads are in poor condition.* = the act of transporting (carrying goods and people) **2** *Boats provide the only transport for people living on this island.* = a means by which people or goods can be moved or carried from one place to another (also transportation)

trans•pose /træn'spəʊz/ verb, t. *When I am typing, the word 'and' often gets transposed to 'nad'.* = to exchange the positions of two things (putting something in place of another)

trans•verse /trænz'vɜ:s/ adj. *Most motor cars now have transverse engines.* = in a position which is at 90 degrees to something else [TECHNICAL]

trans•ves•tite /trænz'vestaɪt/ noun, c. = a man who wears the clothes of a woman and behaves like a woman [TECHNICAL]

trap[1] /træp/ noun, c. **1** *a mouse trap* = a device used for capturing (catching) an animal **2** *I want to give up this job, but I can't because I need the money. I am trapped.* = a dangerous, difficult or unpleasant situation that one cannot get out of easily

trap[2] verb, t. (**trapped**) **1** *The mouse has been trapped.* = to catch an animal in a trap **2** *It was terrible to be trapped inside the burning building.* = to be caught in a dangerous situation, with no means of escape **3** *The clever lawyer trapped the prisoner into confessing his guilt.* = to trick or deceive someone **trap-door** noun, c. = a small door covering an opening in a roof or floor **trapper** noun, c. = a person who catches wild animals in traps, usually for their fur

tra•peze /trə'pi:z/ noun, c. = a piece of equipment used by **acrobats** in a circus, consisting of a short bar hanging from ropes high above the ground, on which a person can swing backwards and forwards

tra•pe•zi•um /trə'pi:ziəm/ noun, c. = a four-sided geometrical figure in which two of the sides are parallel [GEOMETRY]

trap•pings /'træpɪŋz/ noun (always plural) *The new minister has acquired all the trappings of power, including a bullet-proof car and a security guard with a machine-gun.* = the things that are a part of a particular job or position and become its outward signs

trap-shooting noun, u. = a sport in which a person shoots (with a gun) at clay plates thrown up into the air

trash[1] /træʃ/ noun, u. **1** *The trash from the kitchen should be deposited in the trash-can.* = waste matter (also **garbage**) **2** *The new film is pure trash. No one wants to see it.* = something of very poor quality

trash[2] verb, t. *My neighbour drove his new car into a tree and trashed it.* = to damage or destroy something **trash-can** noun, c. = a large container into which trash (waste matter) is thrown **trashy** adj. *He has produced a trashy film--the worst I have ever seen.* = of very poor quality (informal)

trau•ma /'trɔ:mə/ noun, u. *She was unable to bear the trauma of her child's accidental death.* = mental shock and pain (formal) [MEDICINE] **traumatic** /trɔ:'mætɪk/ adj. *a traumatic experience* = causing trauma (shock) **traumatize** /'trɔ:mətaɪz/ verb, t. *She was traumatized by the death of her son.* = to cause trauma (shock)

trav•ail /'træveɪl/ noun, u. (usually plural **travails**) *The teachers have not been paid for a year and their travails have attracted the sympathy of the government.* = the difficulties experienced by someone (literary)

tra•vel[1] /'trævəl/ verb, i. (**travelled**) **1** *He is travelling to Kolkata by bus.*(u.) = to make a journey; to go from one place to another, usually at some distance **2** *The train is travelling at 100 kilometres an hour.* = to move at a certain speed

travel[2] noun, u. or c. **1** *I hate travel.*(u.) = the act of travelling (going from one place to another) **2** *Has he told you about his travels in the Himalayas?* = journeys (usually plural) **travel-agent** noun, c. = a person who makes arrangements for people to travel (by buying tickets for them etc.) **traveller** noun, c. = a person who goes on a journey or travels to some place **traveller's cheque** noun, c. = a cheque (piece of printed paper) that a person can buy from a bank and exchange for money while travelling, so that there is no need to carry a lot of cash (money) **travelogue** /'trævəlɒg/ noun, c. = a book describing a person's travels **travel-sickness** noun, u.= the feeling of being unwell (usually wanting to vomit) that some people have when travelling in a vehicle or aircraft

tra•ver•se /'trævɜ:s/ verb, t. *He has traversed the entire Himalayan region on foot.* = to move or travel across a large area (formal)

tra•ves•ty /'trævɪsti/ noun, c. (**travesties**) *It would be a travesty of the truth to call him a musician. The sounds he produces when singing are not musical at all.* = something that does not represent or show things as they really are (a misrepresentation); (formal, often humorous)

trawl /trɔ:l/ verb, i. *The fishermen are trawling the river.* = to try to catch fish by dragging a net across the bottom of a sea or river [TECHNICAL] **trawler** noun, c. = a small ship or boat used by fishermen to catch fish

T

tray /treɪ/ noun, c. *a tea tray* = a flat piece of metal, plastic or wood, held in the hands and used for carrying small objects such as cups and plates on which food is served

treach•e•rous /ˈtretʃərəs/ adj. **1** *They are so treacherous that they are sure to deceive you if you trust them.* = unfaithful; not to be trusted **2** *treacherous climb* = difficult; dangerous

treachery /ˈtretʃəri/ noun, u. = the quality of being treacherous (unfaithful)

trea•cle /ˈtri:kəl/ noun, u. = a thick, sticky liquid made from sugar

tread[1] /tred/ verb, i. (**trod**, **trodden**) *Don't tread on the grass.* = to step on something heavily while walking

tread[2] noun, c. **1** *We heard the policeman's heavy tread on the verandah.* = the sound of the feet on the ground while walking **2** *the treads of a car's tyres* = the pattern of raised lines on the part of a tyre that meets the surface of the road **3** = the flat part of a step on which the foot is placed **treadmill** noun, c. = an exercise machine which has a moving rubber belt on which one can walk without moving forward **treadmill test** noun, c. = a medical test, using a treadmill, to test the condition of a person's heart

treadle /ˈtredl/ noun, c. *the treadle of a sewing machine* = a part of a machine that is pressed down with the feet to make the machine work

trea•son /ˈtri:zən/ noun, u. *This man, who has been giving away secret military information to the enemy, will be tried fo treason.* = the crime of working against and harming one's own country (see also **traitor**) **treasonable** adj. *a treasonable offence* = which can be considered to be treason

trea•sure[1] /ˈtreʒəʳ/ noun, u. **1** *The farmer found a pot full of gold coins while he was digging up his fields. No one knows where the treasure came from.* = wealth in the form of gold etc. **2** *The Taj Mahal is considered to be a national treasure.* = something or someone that has of very great value

treasure[2] verb, t. *I shall always treasure this pen which I received from my father.* = to consider or treat something as precious (valuable) **treasurer** = a person who has charge of the money belonging to an organization **treasure trove** noun, c.= treasure (gold etc.) found hidden somewhere, usually inside the earth, the owner of which is not known **treasury** noun = the place where the money of the government is kept

treat[1] /tri:t/ verb, t. **1** *I treat him with respect because of his age and wisdom.* = to behave towards someone in a certain way, showing a certain kind of feeling **2** *You should treat my letter as a warning.* = to consider in a certain way **3** *The doctors are treating my brother for typhoid.* = to try to cure an illness **4** *This piece of steel has been chemically treated so that it will not rust.*= to put something through a chemical process **5** *I treated my friend to a meal at a five-star restaurant.* = to give someone a special present or favour

treat[2] noun, c. **1** *She sings so beautifully that it is a treat to hear her.* = something that gives pleasure **2** *This meal in a restaurant is a birthday treat from me.* = something that someone pays for, as a present for someone else **treatment** noun, u. **1** *I shall never forget the kind treatment I received from you.* = the manner in which someone behaves towards you **2** *The doctor's treatment has cured me of filaria.* = the medical care or help that one receives from a doctor

trea•tise /ˈtri:tɪs/ noun, c. *He has written a treatise on the temple architecture of Tamil Nadu.* = a learned book or article written on some subject (formal)

treat•y /ˈtri:ti/ noun, c. (**treaties**) *India and Pakistan signed a treaty at Shimla, under which India returned 90,000 prisoners-of-war to Pakistan.* = an agreement between two countries

treb•le[1] /ˈtrebəl/ adj. *I bought this motorcycle for only 5,000 rupees but sold it for 15,000-- treble the amount.* = multiplied by 3; three times as great (old-fashioned)

treble[2] verb, t. *He offered me 1 lakh for the house but I wanted him to treble the offer to 3 lakhs.* = to make something three times as big

treble[3] noun, c. or u. **1** (c.) = a boy who sings the higher notes in a group of singers **2** (u.) = the higher notes in music (compare **bass**)

tree /tri:/ noun, c. **1** = a tall, thick plant that has reached a certain age **2** *a tree diagram* = a drawing in which branching lines show how things are related to each other **tree-line** noun = the height (on a mountain) beyond which trees will not grow

seasons

summer autumn winter spring

trek[1] /trek/ noun, c. *We are going on a trek through the Sahyadris.* = a long and difficult journey on foot

trek[2] verb, i. (**trekked**) *We plan to trek through the Sahyadris.* = to go on a trek

trel•lis /ˈtrelɪs/ noun, c. = a wooden frame used to support a climbing plant

trellis

trem•ble[1] /ˈtrembəl/ verb, i. **1** *His hand trembled so much that he was unable to hold a pen.* = to shake in an uncontrollable manner **2** *The fear of being attacked by robbers makes us tremble.* = to feel great fear or excitement

tremble[2] noun, c. *We felt a tremble in the earth, beneath our feet.* = an act of trembling (shaking)

tre•men•dous /trɪˈmendəs/ adj. *He has tremendous strength in his arms. He can easily lift a 250 kilogram weight.* = very great

trem•o•lo /ˈtremələʊ/ noun, u. = a pleasant shaking effect produced by the voice of a singer or the sound of a musical instrument [TECHNICAL]

trem•or /ˈtreməʳ/ noun, c. **1** *We felt a tremor in the earth and knew that an earthquake was coming.* = a shaking movement of the earth **2** *The tremor in his limbs is caused by a nervous disease.* = a shaking movement of the body **tremulous** /ˈtremjʊləs/ adj. *'Please don't hurt me!' the child said in a tremulous voice to the robber.* = shaking because of fear or unhappiness (literary)

trench /trentʃ/ noun, c. (**trenches**) = a long, narrow hole dug into the ground **trench-coat** noun, c. = a loose coat made of waterproof material

tren•chant /ˈtrenʃənt/ adj. *The new film is so bad that it has received trenchant criticism from all reviewers.* = forceful and direct in expressing one's views or opinions

trend /trend/ noun, u. or c. *These days many women are joining the army or police. This is a new trend.*(c.) = a development or change in a situation or in the way in which people are behaving **trend-setter** noun, c. *Rabindranath Tagore was a trend-setter in Bangla literature.* = one who begins a new trend (a new development) **trendy** adj. *He always wears trendy clothes.* = in the latest fashion (informal)

trep•i•da•tion /trepɪˈdeɪʃən/ noun, u. *Usually, I am not nervous before an interview, but this time I faced the interview with great trepidation.* = a state of anxiety, mixed with fear (formal)

tres•pass[1] /ˈtrespəs/ noun, u. *If you enter my property without my permission, I will take you to the court for trespass.* = the act of entering private property without permission [LAW]

trespass[2] verb, i. *You have trespassed into my property.* = to commit trespass

tress•es /ˈtresɪz/ noun (always plural) *Everyone admired Draupadi's dark tresses.* = a woman's long hair (literary)

tres•tle /ˈtresəl/ noun, c. = a supporting structure for a wooden table or a bridge

tri- /traɪ/ prefix meaning 'three' (e.g. 'tri-cycle')

triad /ˈtraɪæd/ noun, c. = a group made up of three people

tri•al /ˈtraɪəl/ noun, u. or c. **1** *The suspected murderer has been put on trial.*(u.) = the judging of a person in a law court **2** *The trial of the new rocket system has ended.*(c.) = a test of a new product, to make sure of its quality **trial-run** noun, c. = an act of testing a new product before it is put to use

tri•an•gle /ˈtraɪæŋgəl/ noun, c. = a geometrical figure with three sides and three angles **triangular** /traɪˈæŋgjʊləʳ/ adj. **1** *a triangular park.* = having the shape of a triangle **2** *a triangular tournament* = in which three people or three teams take part

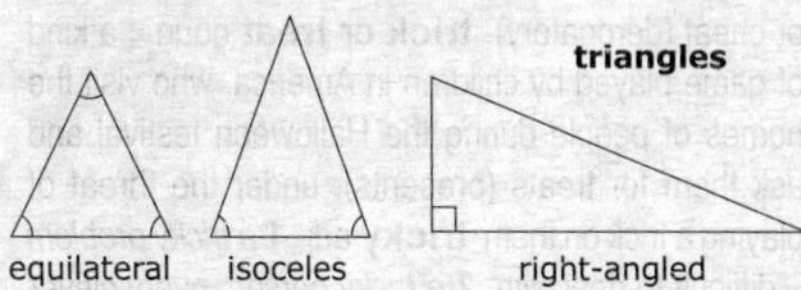

tribe /traɪb/ noun, c. *a member of the Santhal tribe* = a group of people having common customs and beliefs and a common language, often led by a chief **tribal**[1] adj. *tribal customs* = belonging to a tribe **tribal**[2] noun, c. *He is a tribal.* = a member of a tribe (also **tribesman**) **tribesman** noun, c. = a member of a tribe

trib•u•la•tion /trɪbjʊˈleɪʃən/ noun, c. or u. *The book describes the trials and tribulations of the first settlers who went to Australia.*(u.) = troubles and suffering (literary)

tri•bu•nal /traɪˈbjuːnəl/ noun, c. *The complaint made by the workers will be examined by the industrial tribunal.* = a court set up the government to deal with special matters [LAW]

trib•ute /ˈtrɪbjuːt/ noun, u. or c. **1** *Several important people paid tribute to Mahatma Gandhi on the occasion of his birth anniversary.*(u.) = something said in praise of someone **2** *Most of the kings of ancient India paid tribute to Emperor Chandragupta.*(u.) = money paid regularly by the ruler of a kingdom to the ruler of a more powerful kingdom, in former times, as a sign of his/her authority **3** *All the children love her even though she scolds them when they misbehave. This is a tribute to her good intentions.*(c.) = a sign of some good quality

trib•u•ta•ry /ˈtrɪbjʊtəri/ noun, c. (**tributaries**) **1** *The river Gandak is a tributary of the Ganga.* = a river or stream that flows into a larger river **2** *a tributary state* = a state or country that pays tribute to a more powerful state (see **tribute**, meaning **2**)

trice /traɪs/ noun, u. *Please wait for me. I will be back in a trice.* = a vey short time (old-fashioned)

tri•ceps /ˈtraɪseps/ noun (always plural) = the large muscle that runs along the back of the upper arm (compare **biceps**) [BIOLOGY]

T

trick[1] /trɪk/ noun, c. **1** *Let me show you a trick. I will make your pen disappear without touching it.* = a set of clever actions, leading to a surprising result, done to entertain people **2** *He cheated me of a lot of money by playing a trick on me.* = a dishonest plan or action meant to cheat someone (derogatory) **3** *People like to play tricks on their friends on April Fool's Day.* = a playful act which may be slightly unpleasant

trick[2] verb, t. (**tricked**) *He tricked me into giving him a thousand rupees.* = to deceive or cheat someone **trickery** noun, u. *He got a thousand rupees from me by trickery.* = actions which are meant to deceive or cheat (derogatory) **trick or treat** noun = a kind of game played by children in America, who visit the homes of people during the Halloween festival and ask them for treats (presents), under the threat of playing a trick on them **tricky** adj. **1** *a tricky problem* = difficult to deal with **2** *a tricky person* = very clever and somewhat dishonest (derogatory)

trick•le[1] /ˈtrɪkəl/ verb, i. *The water trickled slowly through a hole in the pipe.* = to flow slowly, in drops or in a thin stream

trickle[2] noun, c. *At first there was only a trickle of refugees entering the country, but now it has grown into a flood.* = small and slow flow or movement (of a liquid, or people or things)

tri-colour /ˈtrɪkələʳ/ noun **1** = a flag having three colours **2** *the national tri-colour* = India's national flag

tri•cy•cle /ˈtraɪsɪkəl/ noun, c. = a carriage with three wheels (usually meant for a child)

tri•dent /ˈtraɪdənt/ noun, c. = a weapon consisting of a stick having a metal head with three sharp points

tried /traɪd/ verb, i. or t. past tense of **try**

tri•en•ni•al /traɪˈeniəl/ adj. *a triennial conference* = happening once in three years

trier see **try**

tri•fle[1] /ˈtraɪfəl/ noun, c. or u. *Does it matter which kind of ice-cream you serve your guests? Don't waste your time over such trifles.*(c.) = something which has no importance or value (literary)

trifle[2] verb, i. *You should never trifle with a king cobra. You will be sorry if you do!* = to treat someone or something without proper seriousness or respect

trifle[3] adv. *He came to the meeting a trifle late.* = a little **trifling** adj. *You need not return the two rupees which you borrowed from me last night. This is only a trifling amount.* = very small and unimportant

trig•ger[1] /ˈtrɪgəʳ/ noun, c. = a small piece of metal fitted to the lower side of a gun which is pressed to fire the gun

trigger[2] verb, t. *He spoke angrily to the child who broke his window, and that triggered off a quarrel among the neighbours.* = to start a series of events, usually unpleasant **trigger-happy** adj. *a trigger-happy police-officer* = too ready or quick to shoot or to react to a situation

trig•o•nom•e•try /trɪgəˈnɒmɪtri/ noun = the branch of mathematics that deals with the relationships between the sides and the angles of triangles

trilin•gu•al /traɪˈlɪŋgwəl/ adj. **1** *a trilingual publication* = in three languages **2** *a trilingual person* = knowing three languages

trill /trɪl/ noun, c. *the trill of a nightingale* = a musical sound which is repeated a number of times very quickly

tril•lion /ˈtrɪljən/ noun = one million millions; the number 1,000,000,000,000 or 10^{12}

tril•o•gy /ˈtrɪlədʒi/ noun, c. (**trilogies**) = a group of three related books, plays or films

trim[1] /trɪm/ verb, t. (**trimmed**) **1** *Your hair is too long. Ask the barber to trim it.* = to make something look more neat by making it shorter or removing the unwanted parts **2** *Her dress was trimmed with lace.* = to decorate

trim[2] noun, u. **1** *Your hair needs a trim.* = the act of trimming (cutting) **2** *Our team should win the match. It is in good trim.* = a condition of being fit and ready to do something

trim[3] adj. *He has a trim figure.* = neat in appearance

tri•mes•ter /trɪˈmestəʳ/ noun, c. = one of the three equal parts (of about 3 months) into which a year is divided for purposes of teaching at a school or university

trin•i•ty /ˈtrɪnɪti/ noun, c. (**trinities**) = a group of three persons **Trinity** noun = the three different aspects or qualities of God, in the Hindu religion (Brahma, the Creator; Vishnu, the Preserver and Shiva, the Destroyer) or in Christianity (the Father, the Son and the Holy Ghost)

trin•ket /ˈtrɪŋkɪt/ noun, c. = a piece of cheap jewellery

tri•o /ˈtriːəʊ/ noun, c. *trio of fast bowlers* = a group of three people or things

trip[1] /trɪp/ noun, c. **1** *I am going on a trip to Chennai.* = a journey, specially a short one, for pleasure or some special purpose **2** *He is on a trip.* = a dream-like state produced by a drug such as heroin (slang) **3** *a trip of the tongue* = a mistake

trip[2] verb, i. or t. (**tripped**) **1** *He tripped on the door-mat and almost fell.*(i.) = to catch one's foot on something and lose one's balance **2** *The people who interviewed me tried to trip me up, but I was able to answer all their questions.*(t.) = to try to confuse someone and get him/her to make a mistake **3** *The little girl tripped down the stairs.*(i.) = to move quickly, with light steps **4** *The electric lights have gone out. The main switch must have tripped.*(i.) = to shut off the flow of electricity by causing a switch to operate (work) **trip-wire** noun, c. = a piece of wire stretched out along the ground, which causes a bomb to explode when someone trips on it (catches his/her foot on it)

tri•par•tite /traɪ'pɑːtaɪt/ adj. *a tripartite agreement* = in which three countries, groups or people are taking part

tripe /traɪp/ noun, u. **1** *I found him reading 'The Adventures of a Pickpocket.' He shouldn't be reading such tripe.* = writing or talk of extremely poor quality **2** = a meat dish, made by cooking the stomach of a cow or sheep

trip•le[1] /'trɪpəl/ verb, t. *My boss was paying me only Rs 200 a month but now he will pay me Rs 600 a month. He has tripled my salary.* = to make something or to become three times the previous size or quantity

triple[2] adj. *A triple murder has been committed.* = involving (having to do with) three people or things **triple jump** noun,c. = a sports event, also known as 'hop, step and jump', in which a competitor has to jump three times **triplet** noun, c. = one child out of three children born to a mother at almost the same time

trip•li•cate /'trɪplɪkɪt/ noun or adj. *You will have to send in your application in triplicate.*(noun) = requiring three copies of the same thing

tri•pod /'traɪpɒd/ noun, c. *the tripod of a camera* = a frame with three legs which supports a camera or a gun (see pic under **laboratory equipment**)

tri•pos /'traɪpɒs/ noun, u. = the course for the B.A. degree given by Cambridge University in England, for which one has to study three different subjects

tri•sect /traɪ'sekt/ verb, t. = to divide something into three equal parts

trite /traɪt/ adj. *The film is about two friends who fall in love with the same girl. It is such a trite theme that everyone found it boring.* = repeated so many times that it is no longer interesting or meaningful (derogatory)

tri•umph[1] /'traɪəmf/ verb, i. *India triumphed over Australia by defeating them by an innings and 150 runs.* = to gain victory over someone

triumph[2] noun, u. or c. **1** *The victory of the English team will be remembered as a triumph for Beckham, who scored 3 goals in the match.*(u.) = a great success or victory **2** *The Indian team returned home in triumph after defeating Kenya in all three test matches.*(u.) = the joy or satisfaction caused by winning **triumphant** adj. *the triumphant Australian team* = victorious or successful

tri•um•vir•ate /traɪ'ʌmvɪrɪt/ noun, c. = a group of three, specially a group of three powerful people who rule a country

triv•i•a /'trɪviə/ noun, u. (always plural) *The two leaders sat together discussing the weather and other such trivia.*= unimportant matters or details (formal)

tri•vi•al /'trɪviəl/ adj. *Why are you so worried about the colour of the cover for your new book? It's quite a trivial matter.* = unimportant

trod /trɒd/ verb, i. past tense of **tread**

trog•lo•dyte /'trɒglədaɪt/ noun, c. = a cave-dweller (a person who lived in a cave, in very ancient times)

troi•ka /'trɔɪkə/ noun, c. (Russian) **1** = a carriage drawn by three horses **2** = a group of three powerful people leading a government

trol•ley /'trɒli/ noun, c. *a tea-trolley* = a small cart with two or four wheels **trolley-bus** noun, c. = a bus that is driven by electricity and draws power from an electric wire running above it

trom•bone /trɒm'bəʊn/ noun, c. = a large musical instrument made of brass which is played by blowing air through it (see also **trumpet**)

troop[1] /truːp/ noun, c. **1** *a troop of monkeys* = a large group of wild animals or people **2** *a troop of soldiers* = a group of soldiers, specially those riding on horses or in motor vehicles

troop[2] verb, i. *Several people trooped into the hall when the famous scholar got up to speak.* = to move together in a group **troops** noun (always plural) *troops of the country* = soldiers **troop-carrier** noun, c. = a ship or large aircraft in which soldiers are sent out to fight

trope /trəʊp/ noun, c. *When the poet says 'The moon was a ghostly ship, sailing across cloudy seas', he is using a trope.* = a figure of speech (a special use of language in poetry, to create a striking effect) [LITERATURE]

tro•phy /'trəʊfi/ noun, c. (**trophies**) *The Australian team won the World Cup and brought the silver trophy home.* = a prize given to the winner of a competition

tro•pic /'trɒpɪk/ noun, c. *the tropic of Cancer* = one of the two imaginary lines drawn around the earth, north and south of the equator, and at equal distances from it [GEOGRAPHY] (see pic under **earth**) **tropical** adj. *a tropical climate* = found in the tropics (the areas or countries that lie not too far fom the equator) **tropics** noun (always plural) *Mango trees are found only in the tropics.* = the warm countries on both sides of the equator, between the two tropics

trot[1] /trɒt/ verb, i. or t. (**trotted**) **1** *The horse trotted along the road.*(i.)= to move at a speed which is not too fast and not too slow, between a walk and a run (referring to the movement of a horse) **2** *He is trotting the horse.*(t.) = to cause a horse to trot **3** *I should be trotting along now. It's getting late.*(i.) = to walk at a

T

fast speed (referring to the movement of a human being) (humorous)

trot[2] noun, u. *The riders set off at a trot.* = a somewhat fast, but not very fast, movement **trotter** noun, c. *pig's trotters* = the foot an animal, cooked and used as food (informal)

to trot out something = to repeat an idea or a statement that has been used many times before (not respectful)

trou•ba•dor /'tru:bədɔ:'/ noun, c.= a poet and singer who travelled around the royal courts of Europe, in the 12th and 13th centuries

trouble[1] /'trʌbəl/ noun, u. or c. **1** *My friend is in trouble. His wife is seriously ill and he has no money to pay the hospital bills.*(u.) = a difficult or dangerous situation which causes worry, suffering etc. **2** *I am sorry to give you this trouble.*(u.) = inconvenience **3** *You should have taken the trouble to write to me regularly.*(u.) = effort **4** *We are expecting some trouble in the city.*(u.) = disorder **5** *There is some trouble with the engine of my car.*(c.) = defect

trouble[2] verb, t. **1** *He has been troubled by stomach ailments.* = to cause pain or suffering **2** *The thought of defeat troubled him.* = to cause worry **3** *I am sorry to trouble you, but could you tell me how to get to the station?* = to cause inconvenience to someone (used when making a request) **trouble-maker** noun, c.= a person who causes trouble **trouble-shooter** noun, c. = a person whose job is to solve problems (informal) **troublesome** adj. *a troublesome person* = causing trouble **trouble-spot** noun, c. = a place where there is likely to be trouble (disorder)

trough /trɒf/ noun, c. **1** *The horses drink water out of this trough.* = a long, narrow container from which animals can drink water **2** = a hollow area between the high waves on the sea

trounce /traʊns/ verb, t. *The Indian hockey team trounced the American team by 6 goals to 1.* = to defeat badly

troupe /tru:p/ noun, c. *a dance troupe* = a group of singers, actors or dancers

trou•sers /'traʊzəz/ noun, u. (always plural, often used with 'a pair of') = a garment covering the body from the waist to the ankles, with a separate part for each leg

trous•seau /'tru:səʊ/ noun, c. (**trousseaux** or **trousseaus**) (French) *a bride's trousseau* = the collection of clothes and other personal belongings that a woman takes with her to her new home after she gets married

trout /traʊt/ noun = a kind of fish, found in rivers where the water is cold

trow•el /'traʊəl/ noun, c. = a tool with a flat blade, used for spreading mortar (a mixture of sand and cement)

tru•ant /'tru:ənt/ adj. or noun. **1** *a truant school-boy* (adj.) = one who deliberately stays away from school or work **2** *a habitual truant* (noun)

to play truant = to stay away from school

truce /tru:s/ noun, u. = an agreement to stop fighting during a war, usually for a short time

truck[1] /trʌk/ noun, c. or u. = a large motor vehicle used to carry goods (also **lorry**)

truck[2] verb, t. *We will truck these vegetables to Kolkata.* = to transport (send) goods by truck **trucker** noun, c. **1** = a person who owns trucks and hires them out **2** = a truck-driver **trucking** noun, u. = the business of transporting goods by truck

to have no truck with someone = to have nothing to do with someone

truc•u•lent /'trʌkjʊlənt/ adj. *He is a very truculent person. He loves to argue and quarrel with people.* = fond of arguing or quarrelling (formal, literary)

trudge[1] /trʌdʒ/ verb, i. *The workers are trudging back home after the day's work.* = to walk slowly, in a tired manner

trudge[2] noun, u. *It's a long trudge from the rice-fields to our home.* = a tiring walk over a long distance

true /tru:/ adj. **1** *Is it true that you went to the beach today?* = a fact; correct **2** *There is true love between parents and their children.* = genuine; real **3** *You should be true to your beliefs.* = faithful or loyal **4** *A whale is a true mammal, though it lives in water.* = having all the necessary qualities of something **5** *He missed the target because his aim was not true.* = accurate **true-blue** *adj. He is a true-blue environmentalist.* = loyal to the principles of a party or group **true-life** adj. *a true-life adventure* = based on fact **truism** noun, c. *To say that life in the cities is full of tension is a truism.* = a statement which is clearly true **truly** adv. **1** *She is a truly generous woman.* = really, (used for emphasis in both positive and negative sentences) **2** *I am truly sorry for what I have done.* = sincerely **3** *Yours truly* = salutation used at the end of a formal letter

truf•fle /'trʌfəl/ noun, c. = a kind of edible fungus (flowerless plant) that grows under the ground and is very expensive because it is not commonly found

trump[1] /trʌmp/ noun, c. *The trump is diamonds.* = any card in a game of cards, out of a set of 13 cards having the same sign (clubs, diamonds, hearts or spades), which is chosen to have a higher value than cards having some other sign in a particular game [TECHNICAL]

trump[2] verb, t. *He played the ace of clubs, but I trumped his ace by playing a spade, which was the* *trump.* = to win a trick (one round in a game of cards) by playing a trump **trump card** noun, c. *When the Sri Lankan team needed some quick wickets, the captain asked Muralitharan to bowl. He was their trump card.* = something that makes victory certain (figurative)

trum•pet[1] /ˈtrʌmpɪt/ noun, c. **1** = a musical instrument made of brass, played by blowing air through it **2** *The wounded elephant gave out a trumpet to call the other elephants in the herd for help.* = the loud cry of an elephant

trumpet[2] verb, t. **1** *He loves to trumpet his own achievements.* = to announce or state something proudly to a lot of people (disapproving) **2** *The elephants were trumpeting in the distance.* = to make a loud cry

trun•cate /trʌŋˈkeɪt/ verb, t. *The book was 600 pages in length, but it has now been truncated by removing the last 150 pages.* = to make something shorter by cutting out the last part (formal)

trun•cheon /ˈtrʌnʃən/ noun, c. *a policeman's truncheon* = a short stick carried by the police as a weapon

trun•dle /ˈtrʌndl/ verb, i. *The heavy trucks loaded with coal trundled slowly up the hill.* = to move slowly and unevenly on wheels

trunk /trʌŋk/ noun, c. **1** *the trunk of a tree* = the thick main part of a tree which grows out of the earth and supports the branches **2** *the trunk of a person* = the body, without the head, arms and legs **3** *a steel trunk* = a large box in which things are stored **4** *the trunk of an elephant* = the long, tube-like nose of an elephant **trunk-call** noun, c. = a long-distance telephone call **trunk road** noun, c.= a main road, usually connecting cities **trunk route** noun, c. = a main railway or air route, connecting cities

trunks /trʌŋks/ noun, u. (always plural) *swimming trunks* = short, tight pants worn while swimming

truss[1] /trʌs/ verb, t. *The robbers trussed up the man with ropes after they had robbed him.* = to tie up strongly with ropes

truss[2] noun, c. (**trusses**) **1** = a metal frame which supports a roof or building **2** = a special belt worn by someone who is suffering from **hernia**

trust[1] /trʌst/ verb, t. **1** *I trust him when he says he locked hte gates before he left.* = to believe someone (to accept something that he/she says as the truth) **2** *The manager is completely honest. The company trusts him.*= to be sure of the honesty, ability etc. of someone **3** *You can't trust these trains to run on time.* = to depend on or be sure about **4** *I trust you had a good holiday in Goa.* = to hope

trust[2] noun, u. or c. **1** *He abused my trust by joining the company with whom we were competing.*(u.) = confidence or faith (in the honesty of someone) **2** *After my death, the lawyer will hold my property in trust until my children have reached the age of 21.*(u.) = an arrangement for holding and protecting money, property etc. for the benefit of someone else **3** *We are setting up a trust to manage this school.*(c.) = a group of people who control and manage an organization **trustee** /trʌsˈtiː/ noun, c. **1** = a person who looks after someone else's money or property **2** = a person who helps to control and manage an organization **trust fund** noun, u. = money which belongs to someone else but is being looked after by another person **trustworthy** adj. *a trustworthy person* = whom you can trust (believe or depend on) **trusty** adj. *I will use my trusty motor-cycle to go to your village.* = which can be depended on (old-fashioned, humorous)

truth /truːθ/ noun, u. or c. **1** *The boy says he did not steal the money but found it lying by the road-side. I feel he is telling us the truth.*(u.) = that which is a fact **2** *The witness says he was not in the city when the murder took place. The police will examine the truth of his statement.* = the quality of being true (correct) **3** *Buddha meditated on the truths of human existence.*(c.) = the principles on which something is based **truthful** adj. **1** *a truthful person* = one who always speaks the truth **2** *a truthful account of all that happened* = correct or accurate

the gospel truth = something which is completely true

to tell you the truth *To tell you the truth, I think we are sure to lose.* = an expression used while giving one's opinion

try[1] /traɪ/ verb, i. or t. **1** *I don't think I can jump over this wall, but I will try.*(i.) = to make an attempt or effort to do something **2** *If you can't get him on e-mail, try calling him up on the phone.*(t.) = to attempt to get a result by using a different means **3** *My wife has cooked some chicken curry. Will you try it?*(t.) // *She has bought a new shirt for you. I want you to try it on.*(t.) = to test something by tasting or using it in order to make sure of its quality, correct size etc. **4** *The magistrate will try your case.*(t.) = to examine and judge in a court of law **5** *I have answered all your questions. Please go now and don't try my patience.*(t.) = to annoy someone

try[2] noun, c. (**tries**) *He was not able to jump over the fence, but he made a good try.* = attempt **trier** noun, c. *He has not been doing too well in studies, but he works hard. He is a trier.* = one who always tries to do well **trying** adj. *He has lost all his property and is going through trying times.* = difficult or worrying **try-out** noun, c. *The new textbook will be adopted by the school only after a try-out.* = a trial or test to see if some new thing can be used

T

to try for something *She is trying for a job at the U.N.* = to make efforts to get something **to try on something** *Will you try this shirt on?* = to test whether a piece of clothing etc. fits you **to try out** *I want you to try out the new computer.* = to test whether a machine works **to try one's hand at something** *I want to try my hand at pottery.* = to try to do something for the first time, in order to test how well one can do it **to try one's luck** *It is difficult to find your friend in this crowd, but you can try your luck.* = to make an effort to achieve something

tryst /trɪst/ noun, c. **1** = an arrangement between lovers to meet at a secret place **2** = a place where lovers meet

tsar /zɑːʳ/ noun, c. = the title given to the king of Russia, before the country became a republic in 1917 (also **czar** or tzar) **tsarina** /zɑːˈriːnə/ noun, c. = the title given to the queen of Russia before 1917

tse•tse-fly /ˈtetsi flaɪ/ noun, c. = a kind of large African insect which sucks blood and causes sleeping-sickness

tub /tʌb/ noun, c. **1** *a tub of water* = a large, open container in which water is kept for washing etc. **2** *a bath tub* = a large container in which one can sit down or lie down while having a bath **3** *a tub of butter* = a small container in which food can be stored **tubby** /ˈtʌbi/ adj. *a tubby person* = short and fat (informal, not respectful)

tube /tjuːb/ noun, c. **1** *Water is flowing along the tube.* = a hollow, round pipe, usually not very wide, made of metal, plastic or glass, through which a liquid or gas can pass (see pic under **shapes**) **2** *a pneumatic tube for a car's tyre* = a circular (round) and hollow container made of rubber, which fits inside the tyre of a car and into which air is pumped **3** *a tube of toothpaste* = a soft, hollow container, made of metal or plastic, closed at one end and having a cap (cover) at the other end, in which some liquid or soft solid substance is kept **4** *the London tube* = underground railway running below the streets of a city **tubeless** adj. *a tubeless tyre* = a tyre (for a motor car) for which a tube is not needed, as it can hold air directly **tubular** adj. *tubular furniture* = having the shape of a tube or made out of metal tubes

tu•ber /ˈtjuːbəʳ/ noun, c. = the fleshy, underground stem of a plant, such as the potato plant

tu•ber•cu•lo•sis /tjuːbɜːkjʊˈləʊsɪs/ noun = a serious disease of the lungs caused by a kind of bacteria (also **TB**) [MEDICINE]

tuck[1] /tʌk/ verb, t. **1** *Your shirt is hanging out. You should tuck it into your trousers.* = to push the edge or end of a garment or piece of material into a particular position, so as to make it look tidy **2** *He tucked the book under his arm.* = to put something in a safe or convenient position

tuck[2] noun, c. or u. **1** *The shirt was too loose for me, so I asked the tailor to to put a tuck in the waist.*(c.)= a narow fold sewn into a garment for decoration or to change its shape or size **2** *School boys are fond of tuck.*(u.) = food (cakes, sweets etc.) eaten by school-children (informal)

to tuck into 1 *He tucked into a big meal.*(i.) = to eat eagerly (informal) **2** *It's time for the child to go to bed. I'll tuck her in.*(t.) = to make a child comfortable in bed by covering it with sheets etc.

Tues•day /ˈtjuːzdi/ noun = the day of the week which comes between Monday and Wednesday

tuft /tʌft/ noun, c. *a tuft of hair* = a bunch of hair, feathers, grass etc. growing closely together

tug[1] /tʌg/ verb, t. or i. (**tugged**) *The little girl tugged at the end her mother's sari to attract her attention.*(t.) = to pull with gentle force

tug[2] noun, c. **1** *The child gave her mother's sari a tug.* = a gentle pull **2** *The ship was towed into the harbour by a tug.* = a small but powerful ship which is used to tow (pull) large ships into a harbour **tug-of-war** noun, u. = a sport in which the members of two teams test their strength by holding a rope near its two ends, facing each other, and trying to pull each other across a line

tu•i•tion /tjuːˈɪʃən/ noun, u. **1** *He earns some money by giving tuition to students.* = the act of teaching students in small groups **2** *He paid the year's tuition in advance.* = the fee for a course of study

tu•lip /ˈtjuːlɪp/ noun = a kind of cup-shaped flower, for which Holland is famous

tum•ble[1] /ˈtʌmbəl/ verb, i. **1** *The stream tumbles from the top of the high rock into the valley below.* = to fall with force **2** *The children tumbled out of the bus.* = to move quickly, in an uncontrolled way, as if about to fall **3** *The prices of shares tumbled in the stock market.* = to fall in value

tumble[2] noun, c. *He lost his balance as he was walking up the hill and took a nasty tumble.* = a fall from a height **tumble-down** adj. *a tumble-down hut* = in very poor condition (about to fall to pieces) **tumble-dryer** noun, c. = a machine which dries clothes after washing by making them spin round and round in a metal drum **tumbler** noun, c. = a drinking glass with a flat bottom

tu•mes•cent /tjuːˈmesənt/ adj. swollen up because of the flow of blood (referring to some part of the body) [BIOLOGY]

tum•my /ˈtʌmi/ noun, c. (**tummies**) = the stomach, or the lower front part of the body (in baby-talk, the kind of language in which people speak to very young children)

tu•mour /'tju:mə^r/ noun, c. *He has a tumour inside his stomach.* = a mass of diseased cells in the body which form a kind of swelling or lump [MEDICINE]

tu•mult /'tju:mʌlt/ noun, u. *When he got up to speak, everyone in the audience started clapping and shouting and his voice was drowned in the tumult.* = the loud noise produced by a large and excited crowd (formal, literary) **tumultuous** adj. *He received a tumultuous welcome from the large crowd.* = very noisy

tu•na /'tju:nə/ noun = a kind of large fish found in the sea

tun•dra /'tʌndrə/ noun, u. or c. = a large area of land, in Northern Asia, Europe or America, where trees do not grow because of the cold

tune[1] /tju:n/ noun, c. **1** *The song has an attractive tune.* = a pattern of musical sounds **2** *The sitar is out of tune.* = the correct pitch (level of sound) which a musical instrument or singer's voice is expected to produce **3** *Your ideas are not in tune with those of other economists.* = agreement **4** *The engine of the car is out of tune.* = proper working condition

tune[2] verb, t. **1** *You will have to tune the sitar.* = to adjust a musical instrument so that it gives out the correct pitch (level of sound) **2** *The mechanic will tune the engine of your car.* = to put an engine in proper working order **3** *Can you tune to my favourite channel?* = to adjust a television or radio set so that it receives a particular programme **tuneful** adj. *a tuneful song* = pleasing to listen to **tuneless** adj. = not pleasant to hear **tuner** noun, c. = the part of a radio or television set that receives signals and changes them into sounds or pictures **tuning-fork** noun, c. = an instrument which is used to produce a pure musical sound having a certain pitch (level), consisting of a handle to which a U-shaped fork is attached

tung•sten /'tʌŋstən/ noun = a kind of hard metal

tu•nic /'tju:nɪk/ noun, c. = a kind of loose-fitting dress without sleeves, reaching to the knees

tun•nel[1] /'tʌnəl/ noun, c. *The trains run through a tunnel which cuts through the mountain.* = a long underground passage, cut into or through the earth or a mountain

tunnel[2] verb, i. (**tunnelled**) *The railway engineers tunnelled through the mountain.* = to cut or dig a tunnel **tunnel vision** noun, u. **1** = a defect in the eyes which allows one to see only straight ahead, without seeing anything on either side of the eyes **2** *He thinks only of the money that will have to be spent on his child's education, not of the benefits it will bring. He seems to suffer from tunnel vision.* = the habit of considering only one part of a question or problem, and not others

tur•ban /'tɜ:bən/ noun, c. = a long piece of cloth wound around the head to form a covering

tur•bid /'tɜ:bɪd/ adj. *The water of the lake has become so turbid that you can't see anything below the surface.* = not allowing one to see through it (referring to a liquid) [TECHNICAL]

tur•bine /'tɜ:baɪn/ noun, c. = an engine in which the pressure of a liquid or gas drives a wheel fitted with blades

tur•bo-char•ger /tɜ:bəʊʃa:dʒə^r/ noun, c. = a turbine (wheel) fitted to the engine of a car which is driven by the waste gases from the engine and increases the power of the engine **turbo-jet** noun, c. = an aircraft engine fitted with a turbine (wheel) which drives the aircraft forward by forcing out a powerful jet (stream) of hot air and gases **turbo-prop** noun, c.= an aircraft engine which uses a turbine to drive a propeller

tur•bu•lence /'tɜ:bjʊləns/ noun, u. *Our aircraft is rocking/shaking because of the turbulence in the air.* = violent movement of the air (formal) **turbulent** adj. *It looks like we will have turbulent weather. Let's not go out.* = violent; not peaceful

turd /tɜ:d/ noun, c. = a piece of solid waste matter passed out of the body (informal)

turf[1] /tɜ:f/ noun, u. **1** *the turf on a cricket pitch* = the top surface of the earth, on which grass is growing **2** *No politician wants a rival to visit his city. Each one wants to defend his own turf.* = the territory (area) which one considers as belonging to him or her and does not like to share with others (informal)

turf[2] verb, t. *The football ground has been newly turfed.* = to cover a piece of land with turf (grass)

tur•gid /'tɜ:dʒɪd/ adj. **1** *The book is written in such a turgid style that I find it unreadable.* = too serious and therefore boring (referring to a piece of writing or speech) **2** = swollen (referring to some part of the body)

tur•key /'tɜ:ki/ noun = a large bird, with a lot of flesh, which is eaten specially at Christmas time

Turkish bath noun = a way of cleaning the body by using steam

tur•me•ric /'tɜ:mərɪk/ noun = a yellow spice made from the roots of a plant

tur•moil /'tɜ:mɔɪl/ noun, u. *The city was in turmoil after the recent violence.* = a state of excitement and confusion

turn[1] /tɜ:n/ verb, t. **1** *The wheels of the car are turning, but the car is not moving.* = to move round or in a circle, around a central point **2** *He turned the page of the book.* = to move something so that a different side faces upwards **3** *Turn right when you reach the cross-*

T

roads. = to change direction **4** *The weather has turned cold.* = to change so as to become **5** *Water turns into steam at 100 degrees Celsius.* = to change into a different form **6** *The legs of this chair have been turned on a lathe.* = to shape wood or metal on a **lathe** (machine) **7** *Can you turn on the light?* = to switch on

turn[2] noun, c. **1** *He gave the screw a couple of turns with the screw-driver.* = a circular movement **2** *We made a left turn on reaching the main road.* = a change of direction **3** *It is my turn to bat now.* = an opportunity to do something at a certain time or in a certain order **4** *She was improving in health, but she has taken a turn for the worse.* = a change from an existing situation **turnaround** noun *The company was losing money, but it has had a turnaround.* = a change in a situation, usually an improvement **turn-coat** noun, c. = a person who changes his or her political beliefs and joins a different party (derogatory) **turning** noun, c. = a place where a road branches out from another road **turning-circle** noun, c. *The car has a very small turning-circle.* = the space that a vehicle occupies when it is turning **turning-point** noun, c. *She lost the third game 0-40 and that was the turning point in the match.* = a point when an important change takes place **turnkey** adj. *A Japanese company has been given a turn-key project to build a new steel plant.* = completed and handed over ready to work (referring to a new factory etc.) **turnout** noun *There was good turnout at the Prime Minister's election meeting.* = the number of people attending a meeting etc. **turnover** noun, u. *The shop has a good turnover every month.* = the amount of business done in a certain period of time **turnpike** noun, c. = a highway which one can use on payment of money **turnstile** noun, c. = a gate with which four arms spinning around on a central post, allows only one person to pass **turntable** noun, c. = a flat surface on which a gramophone record is placed, so that it can be played **turn-up** noun, c. = a narrow fold of cloth at the bottom of each leg of a pair of trousers

turn against *Public opinion has turned against our players.* = to stop supporting or helping someone **turn away** = to refuse to give help to someone **turn down** = to refuse an offer or invitation (informal) **turn in** *It's late, let's turn in.* = to go to bed **to be turned off** *The smell of the food in the restaurant was good, but the dirty floor turned me off.* = to lose the desire to do something **turn off** = to stop the flow or supply of water etc. **to turn the corner** = to go through a bad situation successfully **to turn the other cheek** = to not try to stop someone who is harming you **to turn someone's head** *All the good things we said about him have turned his head.* = to spoil someone through too much praise or affection **to turn (a business etc.)** = to make a business etc. that was losing money and doing badly, start doing well

tur•nip /'tɜːnɪp/ noun = a kind of vegetable which is the fleshy root of a plant

tur•pen•tine /'tɜːpəntaɪn/ noun = a kind of oil made from the wood of a tree, which is mixed with paint as a thinner (see **thinner**)

tur•pi•tude /'tɜːpɪtjuːd/ noun, u. *He made a false declaration of his income and will be charged with moral turpitude.* = improper behaviour, which is not morally or socially acceptable (formal, old-fashioned)

tur•quoise[1] /'tɜːkwɔːz/ noun = a precious stone which has a bluish-green colour

turquoise[2] adj. *a turquoise sari* = having the colour of turquoise

tur•ret /'tʌrɪt/ noun, c. **1** = a small tower which is part of a building **2** *a gun turret* = a part of a tank (military vehicle) which contains a large gun, and which can be turned around to aim the gun in a particular direction

tur•tle /'tɜːtl/ noun = an animal that lives in the water and has a hard, bony covering or shell over its body **to turn turtle** *The bus turned turtle when it was going up the hill.* = to turn upside down **turtle dove** noun = a small bird which makes a very pleasant sound **turtleneck** noun or adj. *a turtleneck sweater* = having a round neck which can be folded over (referring to a garment for the upper part of the body)

tusk /tʌsk/ noun, c. = one of the two long, pointed teeth which stick out of the mouths of elephants and some other animals **tusker** noun, c. = a male elephant with large tusks

tus•sle[1] /'tʌsəl/ noun, u. *The policeman caught hold of the robber and managed to pin him to the ground after a long tussle.* = fight

tussle[2] verb, i. *The policeman tussled with the robber.* = to fight

tut tut /tʌt 'tʌt/ interjec. *Tut, tut! How could you forget to bring a pen when you are writing an examination?* = an expression expressing disapproval (slight unhappiness over something)

tu•te•lage /'tjuːtɪlɪdʒ/ noun, u. *My son's education is being supervised by a professor of mathematics; the boy is making excellent progress under his tutelage.* = the teaching and care given by a teacher to a pupil

tu•tor[1] /'tjuːtəʳ/ noun, c. = a teacher who teaches a single student or a small group of students

tutor[2] verb, t. *I am tutoring Ali's son.* = to act as a tutor **tutorial** noun, c. *a tutorial class* = a class taken by a tutor, meeting a small group of students

tutti fruti /tu:ti ˈfru:ti/ noun, u. = ice-cream containing different kinds of fruits and nuts

tux•e•do /tʌkˈsi:dəʊ/ noun, c. = dinner-jacket (a black or white jacket worn by a man on a formal occasion)

TV /ti:ˈvi:/ noun = abbr. of **television**

twad•dle /ˈtwɒdl/ noun, c. *You should keep quiet if you can't talk sense. I am tired of twaddle.* = foolish talk (slang, not respectful)

twain /tweɪn/ noun *East is East and West is West, and the twain shall never meet.* = two; a pair (old-fashioned, poetic)

twang[1] /twæŋ/ noun, u. **1** *the twang of a bow-string* = the sharp, nasal sound (as if coming from a person's nose) made by pulling a string which has been tightly stretched **2** *He spoke with a nasal twang.* = a particular quality of the human voice, which is the result of air passing through the nose as one speaks

twang[2] verb, t. *The singer twanged his guitar as he sang.* = to make the sound of a twang

'twas /twɒz/ = short form of 'it was' (literary)

tweak /twi:k/ verb, t. **1** *The teacher tweaked Paro's ear beacause she didn't bring her notebook.* = to pull lightly with a twisting (turning) movement **2** = to make a small change to the engine of a car or a computer programme, so as to make it work better (informal) [TECHNICAL]

tweed /twi:d/ noun = rough woollen cloth woven from threads of different colour

tweet[1] /twi:t/ noun, u. *the tweet of a bird* = the soft sound made by a young bird

tweet[2] verb, i. *The birds tweeted in the branches of trees.* = to make the sound of a tweet **tweeter** noun, c. = a loud-speaker that gives out high sounds

twee•zers /ˈtwi:zəz/ noun (only plural, often used with 'a pair of') = a small metal instrument with two long arms, used to pull out unwanted hair from the face or body or to pick up small objects

twelve /twelv/ noun = the number represented by 12 (10+2) **twelfth** /twelfθ/ det. *the twelfth house in the row* = coming after 11 objects or people

twen•ty /ˈtwenti/ noun = the number represented by 20 (10x2) **twenty-twenty vision** noun *A pilot must have twenty-twenty vision.* = perfect eye-sight

twerp /twɜ:p/ noun, c. = a foolish person (slang, disrespectful)

twice /twaɪs/ adv. *I have been to his house only twice so far.* = two times **twice-told** adj. *a twice-told tale* = well-known

twid•dle /ˈtwɪdl/ verb, t. *She sat twiddling the pencil between her fingers, thinking of something.* = to move something repeatedly between the fingers, as a kind of play (informal)

to twiddle one's thumbs = to waste time without doing anything useful

twig /twɪg/ noun, c. *Sparrows build their nests with twigs.* = a very small piece of wood from the branch of a tree

twi•light /ˈtwaɪlaɪt/ noun = the period just before night, when the light of the sun is about to disappear

twin[1] /twɪn/ noun, c. or adj. **1** = one of two children born to a mother at almost the same time **2** *Hyderabad and Secunderabad are twin cities.*(adj.) = two things or people that are closely related or connected

twin[2] verb, t. (**twinned**) *Delhi University is being twinned with London University.* = to join or connect two organizations together through an agreement **twin bed** noun, c. = one of two beds in a room, in each of which only one person can sleep

twine /twaɪn/ noun, u. *The parcel was tied up with twine.* = strong, thick thread or string

twinge /twɪndʒ/ noun (no plural) *She felt a twinge of pain in her back.* = a sudden, sharp pain

twin•kle[1] /ˈtwɪŋkəl/ verb, i. *Twinkle, twinkle little star.* = to shine with a soft light that seems to go out and then come back repeatedly

twinkle[2] noun, c. *I see a twinkle in your eyes. Are you planning some mischief?* = a brightness in the eyes, showing pleasure etc.

twink•ling noun *I will be back in a twinkling.* = a very short period of time (informal)

twirl[1] /twɜ:l/ verb, t. *He sat admiring himself in the mirror, twirling the ends of his moustaches with his fingers.* = to cause something to turn or spin round and round

twirl[2] noun, c. *He gave his moustaches a twirl.* = a quick circular movement

twist[1] /twɪst/ verb, t. **1** *He twisted the metal rod into a U-shape.* = to change the shape of something by bending or turning it **2** *The narrow road twisted and turned as it went up the mountain.* = to move in a winding way, from one side to another **3** *I have twisted my ankle.It may be broken.* = to hurt a limb (part of the body) by causing it to turn sharply

twist[2] noun, c. **1** *He gave the cap of the bottle a twist.* = a turning movement **2** *There was a twist to the story. The woman's husband, whom everyone believed to be dead, suddenly returned.* = an unexpected change or development **twisted** adj. *a twisted mind* = wicked in an unnatural way

twit[1] /twɪt/ noun, c. *Don't take him seriously. He's a twit!* = a foolish person (informal, derogatory)

twit[2] verb, t. (**twitted**) *Her friends twitted her about her habit of forgetting things.* = to make fun of someone in a gentle way (informal)

twitch[1] /twɪtʃ/ verb, i. *I feel my right eye twitching.*

T

I am going to have some good luck. = to make a sudden but not conscious movement

twitch[2] noun, c. *I felt a twitch in the muscles of my shoulders.* = a sudden, brief movement

twit•ter[1] /ˈtwɪtəʳ/ verb, i. **1** *The birds are twittering.* = to make short sounds repeatedly (referring to the sound made by birds) **2** *The girls kept on twittering about the picnic they were planning.* = to talk quickly in an excited way

twitter[2] noun, u. **1** *the twitter of birds* = short sounds made by birds **2** *The children are in a twitter about their picnic.* = a state of excitement which makes someone talk quickly

twixt /twɪkst/ prep. *twixt land and water* = between (old-fashioned)

two[1] /tuː/ noun = the number represented by 2

two[2] det. *The man has two wives.* **two-bit** adj. *I don't want to be insulted by a two-bit writer.* = having no importance or respect **two-handed** adj. *He played a two-handed backhand shot.* = using both hands **two-piece** adj. *a two-piece suit* = a suit of clothes consisting of a pair of trousers and a jacket, without a waistcoat **twosome** noun, c. *He and I made a twosome for a game of cards.* = a team or group of two people **two-star** adj. *a two-star hotel* = of medium quality

two-time verb, t. *They were planning to get married but she two-timed him and married a millionaire.* = to be unfaithful (in love) to someone (disapproving, informal) **two-tone** adj. *a two-tone car* = painted in two different colours **two-way** adj. *a two-way street* = allowing movement in both directions

ty•coon /taɪˈkuːn/ noun, c. *a shipping tycoon* = a rich and powerful businessman (informal)

tym•pa•num /ˈtɪmpənəm/ noun = the eardrums; thin pieces of skin inside the ears which help people to hear sounds [BIOLOGY]

type[1] /taɪp/ noun, c. **1** *A 'naan' is a type of bread.* = a particular kind of thing (belonging to a class of similar things) **2** *The invitation card was printed in Gothic type.* = printed letters

type[2] verb, t. or i. *Please type this letter for me.*(t.) // *Do you know how to type?* = to use a typewriter or word-processor (computer) to produce a piece of writing **type-cast** verb, t. *He is an excellent actor, but unfortunately he has been type-cast as a villain.* = to give an actor the same kind of role always **type-face** noun = the size and shape of the letters used in printing **typescript** noun, c. *a typescript of a novel* = a piece of writing produced on a type-writer, but not printed **typesetter** noun, c. = a person who arranges the letters from which a book is printed **typewriter** noun, c. = a machine that is used to print out pieces of writing **typewritten** adj. *a type-written letter* = done on a type-writer

ty•phoid /ˈtaɪfɔɪd/ noun, u. = a serious disease caused by bacteria that attacks the bowels (intestines) [MEDICINE]

ty•phoon /taɪˈfuːn/ noun, c. = a very violent storm

ty•phus /ˈtaɪfəs/ noun, u. = an infectious disease caused by fleas (small insects)

typ•i•cal /ˈtɪpɪkəl/ adj. **1** *The pointed ears and thick, bushy tail of this dog are typical of Alsatians.* = showing the signs or qualities of an entire class of animals or things **2** *Did he repeat 'Know what I mean?' after every sentence? That's typical of him.* = showing the usual behaviour or manner of a person **typify** /ˈtɪpɪfaɪ/ verb, t. *Hard work and the ambition to become rich typify all Chinese businessmen.* = to be a typical sign of something

ty•pist /ˈtaɪpɪst/ noun, c. = a person whose job is to type letters etc. on a typewriter **typing-pool** noun, c. = a group of typists in a large office who share the work of typing

ty•pog•ra•phy /taɪˈpɒgrəfi/ noun = the arrangement of the type (letters) used for printing books etc.

ty•rant /ˈtaɪərənt/ noun, c. *It is said the emperor Aurangzeb was a tyrant.* = a powerful ruler who is very cruel **tyranny** /ˈtɪrəni/ noun, u. *The Marathas revolted against the tyranny of Aurangzeb's rule.* = the cruel use of power by a ruler **tyrannical** /tɪˈrænɪkəl/ adj. *Stalin's tyrannical rule* = cruel **tyrannize (tyrannise)** /ˈtɪrənaɪz/ verb, t. *Mussolini tyrannized his subjects.* = to keep someone in fear through the use of power

ty•ran•no•sau•rus /tɪrænəˈsɔːrəs/ noun = a very large, flesh-eating dinosaur (a large animal belonging to the same family as lizards, which lived millions of years ago and is not found now)

tyre /taɪəʳ/ noun, c. *a motor car tyre* = a thick band of rubber, either solid or filled with air, which is fitted to the edge of the wheel of a vehicle (also **tire**, in American English)

ty•ro /ˈtaɪərəʊ/ noun, s. = a person with no experience (informal)

uU

u, U /juː/ = the twenty-first letter of the English alphabet

u *How r u?* = sometimes used in place of 'you', specially in e-mail messages (informal)

u•biq•ui•tous /juːˈbɪkwɪtəs/ adj. *Ten years ago, there were hardly any computers in this country, but now they seem to be ubiquitous.* = found everywhere (formal)

U-boat /ˈjuːbəʊt/ noun = a kind of submarine (a ship that can travel under the surface of the water) used by the German navy during World War II (1939-1945)

ud•der /ˈʌdəʳ/ noun, c. = the bag of skin found between the hind (back) legs of a cow or goat, in which milk is stored

UFO abbr. of **Unidentified Flying Object** = a mysterious flying object which some people claim to have seen in the sky, believed to be flown by creatures from some other planet

ug•ly /ˈʌgli/ adj. **1** *an ugly building* = not good to look at; unattractive **2** *an ugly scene // an ugly temper* = very unpleasant or violent **ugliness** noun **ugly duckling** noun, c. = a person who is quite ordinary as a child but grows up to be beautiful, skilled, popular etc.

UHF abbr. of **Ultra High Frequency** = radio or television signals sent out at very high speed (between 300 and 3000 megahertz), which allow excellent sound quality

UK abbr. of **United Kingdom** = England, Scotland and Wales

ul•cer /ˈʌlsəʳ/ noun, c. = a sore (break in the skin) on the body or in some organ inside the body (e.g. the stomach or intestines) through which bleeding may take place **ulcerate** verb, i. = to develop into an ulcer

ul•na /ˈʌlnə/ noun = the thinner of the two bones inside the lower arm [BIOLOGY]

ul•te•ri•or /ʌlˈtɪərɪəʳ/ adj. *Why were they suddenly so kind to us? I am sure they had some ulterior motive.* = secret and kept hidden (derogatory)

ul•ti•mate[1] /ˈʌltɪmɪt/ adj. *He hopes to do well in the geography quiz, but his ultimate aim is to win the national geography talent prize.* = final; happening at the end of a process or series of actions

ultimate[2] noun *This new car provides the ultimate in luxury.* = the highest point

ul•ti•ma•tum /ʌltɪˈmeɪtəm/ noun, c. *The tenants were given an ultimatum. They would either pay the rent or vacate the house.* = a threat to do something unpleasant if a certain condition is not fulfilled

ul•tra- /ˈʌltrə/ prefix meaning 'above' or 'beyond' e.g. **ul•tra•son•ic** /ʌltrəˈsɒnɪk/ adj. *an ultrasonic scan* = (sound waves) which have such a high frequency (speed) that they cannot be heard by human ears (are beyond our ability to hear)

ultra high frequency see **UHF**

ul•tra•ma•rine[1] /ʌltrəməˈriːn/ noun = a bright blue colour

ultramarine[2] adj. = of an ultramarine colour

ul•tra•sound /ˈʌltrəsaʊnd/ noun = sound which is beyond the hearing of human ears

ul•tra•vi•o•let /ʌltrəˈvaɪəlɪt/ adj. *Sunglasses will protect your eyes against ultraviolet rays from the sun.* = waves of light which have a very high wavelength and therefore cannot be seen by human eyes, but can harm them

um•ber[1] /ˈʌmbəʳ/ noun = a dark brown colour (the colour of the earth)

umber[2] adj. = having an umber colour

um•bil•i•cus /ʌmˈbɪlɪkəs/ noun = the tube of flesh which connects the embryo (the baby before it is born) to the mother (also umbilical cord or placenta) [BIOLOGY]

um•brel•la /ʌmˈbrelə/ noun, c. **1** = a device that protects a person from rain or the sun, consisting of a stick to which a folding metal frame, covered with some waterproof material, is attached **2** *These NGOs work under the umbrella of the government.* = protection or support **nuclear umbrella** = an agreement between countries by which a powerful country which possesses nuclear weapons promises to protect another country which does not have nuclear weapons (see **nuclear**) **umbrella organization** = a large organization that includes many smaller groups

um•laut /ˈʊmlaʊt/ noun, c. = a mark, in the form of two dots placed over the vowel in some word, (e.g. Göthe) which shows how the word is to be pronounced (in languages such as German)

um•pire[1] /ˈʌmpaɪəʳ/ noun, c. *a cricket umpire* = a person who is responsible for making sure that the rules are followed in a game

umpire[2] verb, t. *I have been asked to umpire this match.* = to act as an umpire

ump•teen /ʌmpˈtiːn/ det. *I have seen umpteen Hindi films but I can't remember their names now.* = a large number, which is not mentioned exactly (informal)

UN abbr. of **United Nations** noun = an organization of nearly all the countries in the world, working together to bring peace to the world

un- /ʌn/ prefix meaning **1** not e.g. **unabashed** /ʌnəˈbæʃt/ adj. *He is unabashed, even after he was caught stealing.* = not ashamed; feeling no shame

2 the opposite of e.g. **unabated** /ʌnə'beɪtɪd/ adj. *The storm continued unabated for two days.* = without going down in force or strength

un•a•ble /ʌn'eɪbəl/ adj. *I will be unable to go to the meeting as I have fever.* = not able to do something

un•a•bridged /ʌnə'brɪdʒd/ adj. *an unabridged novel* = not abridged (made shorter in length)

un•ac•cep•ta•ble /ʌnə'kseptəbəl/ adj. *The essay you have written is unacceptable. It has too many spelling mistakes.* = not good enough to be accepted

un•ac•coun•ta•ble /ʌnə'kaʊntəbəl/ adj. *The Indian team's defeat in this match was unaccountable. Everyone expected them to win.* = very surprising and difficult to explain

un•a•dul•te•rat•ed /ʌnə'dʌltəreɪtɪd/ adj. **1** *We must make sure that the milk given to these babies is unadulterated.* = pure; not mixed with any other substance **2** *He writes unadulterated nonsense.* = complete

un•af•fect•ed /ʌnə'fektɪd/ adj. **1** *The people in this village were unaffected by the earthquake.* = not influenced or made to suffer by something **2** *The child behaved in a very unaffected manner when she received the prize.* = natural; without any false show of feeling (approving)

un•am•big•u•ous /ʌnəm'bɪgjʊəs/ adj. *I would like an unambiguous reply to my question. Please say 'yes' or 'no'.* = having a clear meaning which cannot be missed by anyone (referring to a statement)

u•nan•i•mous /juː'nænɪməs/ adj. *Everyone wants him as our leader. The choice is unanimous.* = without any differences of opinion **unanimity** /juːnə'nɪmɪti/ noun, u. = the fact of being unanimous

un•an•nounced /ʌnə'naʊnst/ adj. or adv. *The famous actor came to our film club meeting unannounced.* = unexpectedly; without any information or warning being given earlier

un•ap•proa•cha•ble /ʌnə'prəʊtʃəbəl/ adj. **1** *I am sorry, but I cannot request the Managing Director to help you in this matter. He is unapproachable.* = not willing to listen to anyone, especially someone who wants a favour (generally referring to a person in power) (generally disapproving) **2** *Shimla is unapproachable in winter, because of the heavy snow.* = difficult to reach

un•armed /ʌn'ɑːmd/ adj. **1** *unarmed policemen* = not carrying weapons **2** *unarmed combat* = without the use of weapons

un•as•sum•ing /ʌnə'sjuːmɪŋ/ adj. *She is so unassuming that you would never know from her behaviour that she was a famous writer.* = modest; not wishing to attract attention

un•at•tached /ʌnə'tætʃt/ adj. **1** *He is 35 and unattached.* = not married **2** *Send us your photograph along with the letter, but leave it unattached.* = not joined to something

un•at•tend•ed /ʌnə'tendɪd/ adj. *Don't leave the baby unattended.* = with no one to look after something or someone

un•av•oid•a•ble /ʌnə'vɔɪdəbəl/ adj. *We were forced to cancel the meeting for unavoidable reasons.* = (something) that one cannot avoid (escape or get away from)

un•a•ware /ʌnə'weəʳ/ adj. *I was unaware of the change in the programme. No one informed me.* = not having knowledge of something **unawares** adv. (always plural) *Your question took me unawares. I need some time to think of an answer.* = unprepared; without warning

un•bal•anced /ʌn'bælənst/ adj. *She has become unbalanced after the loss of her parents.* = not fully in control of one's mind

un•bear•a•ble /ʌn'beərəbəl/ adj. *The heat is unbearable today.* = too unpleasant to be tolerated

un•be•lie•va•ble /ʌnbɪ'liːvəbəl/ adj. *Your story is unbelievable. It can't be true.* = which cannot be believed

un•blem•ished /ʌn'blemɪʃt/ adj. *She has an unblemished record of honesty.* = not spoilt by any fault or wrong action (formal)

un•born /ʌn'bɔːn/ adj. *the unborn child* = not yet born

un•bound•ed /ʌn'baʊndɪd/ adj. *Her ambition is unbounded.* = having no limits

un•called for /ʌn'kɔːld fɔːʳ/ adj. *Your remarks at the meeting were uncalled for. You should have been more polite.* = not proper or justified (not supported by any good reason)

un•can•ny /ʌn'kæni/ adj. *She has an uncanny understanding of animals.* = mysterious; not natural or usual (approving)

un•ce•re•mo•ni•ous /ʌnserɪ'məʊnɪəs/ adj. *The captain's exit from the team was unceremonious.* = happening suddenly and in an unpleasant manner (derogatory)

un•cer•tain /ʌn'sɜːtn/ adj. *The result of this match is uncertain.* = (something) that one cannot be sure of

un•cha•ri•ta•ble /ʌn'tʃærɪtəbəl/ adj. *I am hurt by your uncharitable remarks about my book.* = not kind

un•chart•ed /ʌn'tʃɑːtɪd/ adj. *He plans to travel to the uncharted areas of Tibet.* = not known to anyone (referring to a place or a situation)

un•checked /ʌn'tʃekt/ adj. *Hundreds of people have died of cholera. Many more will die if the disease remains unchecked.* = not stopped or prevented from growing (referring to something unpleasant)

un•cle /ˈʌŋkəl/ noun = the brother of one's father or mother

unclean /ʌnˈkliːn/ **1** adj. *This case is unclean. You cannot store your contact lenses in it.* = not clean **2** = not in a proper state to take part in some religious ceremony

Un•cle Sam /ʌŋkəl ˈsæm/ noun = a name sometimes used for the American nation or government (informal)

un•com•for•ta•ble /ʌnˈkʌmftəbəl/ adj. **1** *This is a very uncomfortable chair.* = not providing comfort **2** *I felt uncomfortable when my friend's uncle shouted at him in my presence.* = uneasy; not finding a situation to one's liking

un•com•mon /ʌnˈkɒmən/ adj. *It is uncommon for a young person of 15 to become a famous writer.* = not happening or seen often

un•con•cerned /ʌnkənˈsɜːnd/ adj. *The doctors have warned him that he may have a heart attack if he doesn't give up smoking but he remains unconcerned.* = not worried about something that one should be worried about

un•con•di•tion•al /ʌnkənˈdɪʃənəl/ adj. *an unconditional promise* = complete; not limited by any conditions

un•con•scious[1] /ʌnˈkɒnʃəs/ adj. **1** *He was unconscious for a while after he was hit on the head.* = not having consciousness (not able to know or feel anything) **2** *It was an unconscious remark. I didn't mean to hurt you.* = not done knowingly

unconscious[2] noun *These ancient traditions are rooted in our unconscious.* = the part of the human mind which controls actions that one does not perform knowingly [TECHNICAL]

un•con•sti•tu•tional /ʌnkɒnstɪˈtjʊʃənəl/ adj. *an unconstitutional act* = against the constitution (the laws of the country)

un•con•ven•tion•al /ʌnkənˈvenʃənəl/ adj. *He has unconventional habits. He sleeps all day and works all night.* = different from what is usual (often approving)

un•con•vin•cing /ʌnkənˈvɪnsɪŋ/ adj. *I asked him why he was late, but his answer was unconvincing.* = not easily believed

un•co•op•e•ra•tive /ʌnkəʊˈɒpərətɪv/ adj. *I asked him to help me in preparing the report but he was uncooperative.* = not willing to help

un•count•a•ble /ʌnˈkaʊntəbəl/ adj. *'Information' is an uncountable noun.* = a noun which cannot have a plural form as it refers to something that cannot be counted [GRAMMAR]

un•couth /ʌnˈkuːθ/ adj. *Don't sit in the library with your legs on the table. We don't like such uncouth behaviour.* = crude; not polite

un•cov•er /ʌnˈkʌvəʳ/ verb, t. **1** *He removed the bedsheet and uncovered the bed.* = to remove the cover from something **2** *The investigation by the CBI has uncovered a lot of corruption in the organization.* = to make things which were hidden or secret known to people

un•crit•i•cal /ʌnˈkrɪtɪkəl/ adj. *I find that you always support your friend, even when he does something wrong. You should not be so uncritical.* = not using one's judgement properly to decide whether something is good or bad

un•crowned (king/queen) /ʌnˈkraʊnd/ noun *He is the uncrowned king of Asian tennis.* = a person who is supposed to be the best in some field of activity, though he/she may have no official position

un•de•cid•ed /ʌndɪˈsaɪdɪd/ adj. **1** *The case has been in court for five years, but it is still undecided.* = without a result **2** *Should I or should I not call the doctor? I am undecided.* = not able to decide

undemocratic /ʌndeməˈkrætɪk/ adj. = acting against the system of equal rights for all people

un•de•ni•a•ble /ʌndɪˈnaɪəbəl/ adj. *His ability as a teacher is undeniable. I have not seen a better teacher.* = (something) that cannot be doubted

un•der[1] /ˈʌndəʳ/ prep. **1** *The box is under the bed.* = below; in a lower place than **2** *Children under five are not allowed to come.* = less than **3** *She works under the Director.* = controlled by (slightly old-fashioned) **4** *You will find his name under 'D' in the telephone directory.* = in the class of **5** *Under the rules, you cannot be selected for the post.* = according to **6** *I cannot be made to sign this paper under pressure.* = feeling the effects of something

under[2] adv. **1** *He was unable to swim in the stormy sea and went under for a while.* = below the surface of the water **2** *This book is meant for children of the age of seven and under.* = less than

under- prefix meaning **1** 'below' e.g. **underclothes** /ˈʌndəkləʊðz/ noun, u. = clothes worn below a dress (also **undergarment** or **underwear**) **2** 'too little' e.g. **underdeveloped** /ʌndədɪˈveləpt/ adj. **1** *an underdeveloped country* = having little economic or industrial growth (see note below) **2** *an underdeveloped child* = not properly or fully developed physically according to the standard

Usage The term 'underdeveloped' is no longer acceptable to countries which are described thus. A more acceptable term is 'developing'.

un•der•a•chiev•er /ʌndərəˈtʃiːvəʳ/ noun, c. = a

U

person who does less well, specially at studies, than he or she is expected to do

un•der•act /ʌndər'ækt/ verb, i. *Aamir Khan underacts in this film.* = to put less feeling into acting (in a film or play) than may be expected, often resulting in acting which is appreciated (also **underplay**)

un•der•age /ʌndər'eɪdʒ/ adj. *You can't join the army as you are underage.* = below the age required for some purpose

un•der•arm[1] /'ʌndərɑːm/ adj. *underarm hair* = growing in the arm-pit (the hollow area below the shoulder)

underarm[2] adv. (or adj.) *He bowled underarm as he had a sprained shoulder.* = with the arm not rising above the shoulder (in a game such as tennis or cricket)

un•der•brush /'ʌndəbrʌʃ/ noun, u. = the plants growing to a low height under the tall trees in a forest (also **undergrowth**)

un•der•car•riage /'ʌndəkærɪdʒ/ noun, c. = the framework that supports the wheels of an aircraft or a railway carriage

un•der•charge /ʌndə'tʃɑːdʒ/ verb, i. or t. = to ask a person to pay less than the correct amount that should be paid

un•der•coat /'ʌndəkəʊt/ noun = the layer of paint put directly on a surface, over which another layer of paint is put

un•der•cov•er /ʌndə'kʌvə[r]/ adj. *an undercover agent* = working in a secret manner (usually as a spy)

un•der•cur•rent /'ʌndəkʌrənt/ noun, c. **1** *It is dangerous to swim in the sea at Chennai as there is a strong undercurrent.* = a hidden current of water below the surface (also undertow) **2** *He congratulated me, but there was an undercurrent of unhappiness in his voice.* = a feeling or opinion that is not openly expressed

un•der•cut /ʌndə'kʌt/ verb, t. *I was hoping to sell 5,000 tonnes of rice to the government but another trader undercut me.* = to quote (ask for) a lower price for something than someone else, often using dishonest means

un•der•dog /'ʌndədɒg/ noun, c. *Kenya was the underdog in the match against Australia.* = a person or group that is considered weaker than another person or group in a competition or fight and is expected to lose, often getting sympathy because of being weaker

un•der•done /ʌndə'dʌn/ adj. *The fish is underdone.* = not cooked enough (slightly raw)

un•der•es•ti•mate /ʌndər'estɪmɪt/ verb, t. **1** *I took only Rs 150 with me, but the taxi cost me Rs 200. I had underestimated the expense.* = to calculate too low an amount **2** *Don't underestimate the Bangladesh team. They have some very good players.* = to have a lower opinion of someone or something than one should have (also **underrate**)

un•der•foot /ʌndə'fʊt/ adv. **1** *Walk carefully. The road is very slippery underfoot.* = to walk on **2** *We trampled the poppy plants underfoot.* = with the feet

undergarment see **underclothes**

un•der•go /ʌndə'gəʊ/ verb, t. (**underwent**, **undergone**) *He underwent surgery last year.* = to experience (go through) something difficult or unpleasant (formal)

un•der•grad•u•ate[1] /ʌndə'grædʒuɪt/ noun = a person (usually a student) who has not passed the first degree examination (B.A., B.Sc., B.Com. etc.)

undergraduate[2] adj. *an undergraduate course* = leading to a first degree (B.A. etc.)

un•der•ground[1] /ʌndə'graʊnd/ adj. *an underground room* = below the surface of the ground

underground[2] adv. *He has gone underground as the police are looking for him.* = into a hidden or secret place

undergrowth see **underbrush**

un•der•hand /ʌndə'hænd/ adj. *an underhand deal* = dishonest and secret

un•der•lie /ʌndə'laɪ/ verb, t. (**underlay**, **underlain**) *Love for nature underlies all her writings.* = to be a hidden cause or meaning for something

underlying adj. *The underlying theme in this novel is the need for peace.* = present but not immediately seen or understood

un•der•line /ʌndə'laɪn/ verb, t. **1** *The most important word in this <u>sentence</u> has been underlined.* = to draw a line below a word to draw attention to it (also **underscore**) **2** *The speaker underlined the importance of agricultural reform.* = to draw special attention to something

un•der•ling /'ʌndəlɪŋ/ noun, c. = a person of low rank who works under someone's orders

un•der•man /ʌndə'mæn/ verb, t. *We need at least 20 teachers for this school but we have only five. We are badly undermanned.* = to not have enough people required for some purpose

> **Usage** It is preferable to use the gender-free term **understaffed**.

un•der•mine /ʌndə'maɪn/ verb, t. *Our attempts to discourage the use of plastic bags were undermined by the manufacturers of the bags.* = to make something weaker or less effective

un•der•neath[1] /ʌndə'niːθ/ prep. *The floor underneath the carpet is covered with dust.* = below

underneath[2] adv. *He looks rough on the surface, but he has a heart of gold underneath.* = inside (in the part that is hidden)

un•der•nour•ished /ʌndəˈnʌrɪʃt/ adj. *an undernourished child* = not healthy because of lack of healthy food

un•der•pass /ˈʌndəpɑːs/ = a road built below another road or a railway track, for people to cross in safety

under•pay /ʌndəˈpeɪ/ verb, t. (**underpaid**) = to pay a person less money than he/she should be paid

un•der•play /ʌndəˈpleɪ/ verb, t. *Don't underplay the importance of exercise in physical fitness.* = to make something seem less important than it really is

un•der•priv•i•leged /ʌndəˈprɪvɪlɪdʒd/ adj. *underprivileged children* = lacking the things that more fortunate people have (e.g. money, food, housing etc.)

un•der•rate see **underestimate** (meaning **2**) (also **undervalue**)

underscore see **underline**

un•der•sell /ʌndəˈsel/ verb, t. = to sell something at a lower price than someone else (see also **undercut**)

un•der•side /ˈʌndəsaɪd/ noun *The underside of the car has to be painted.* = the lower side or surface of something

un•der•signed /ˈʌndəsaɪnd/ noun *We, the undersigned, earnestly request you to look into this matter.* = the person or persons whose signature appears below this writing (formal)

un•der•sized /ʌndəˈsaɪzd/ adj. *an undersized apple* = smaller in size than the average (derogatory when referring to a person)

un•der•stand /ʌndəˈstænd/ verb, t. or i. **1** *I can't understand this poem. The meaning is not clear.*(t.) = to not be able to know the meaning of something **2** *I am afraid I can't come to your party as the doctor has ordered me to stay in bed. I hope you will understand.*(i.) = to be able to judge a situation correctly and not feel hurt, offended etc. **3** *I understand you are moving to Nagpur.*(t.) = to hear about something **understandable** adj. *Your unwillingness to go on this long journey is understandable.* = which can be understood as there are clear reasons for it **understanding** noun, u. **1** *This book is too difficult. It is beyond my understanding.* = the ability to understand something **2** *He has no understanding of modern literature.* = knowledge **3** *Three of us who share a flat have reached an understanding. No loud music will be played.* = an agreement between people to do or not do something

un•der•state /ʌndəˈsteɪt/ verb, t. *The water problem is getting worse but your report understates the seriousness of the situation.* = to make something look less serious or important than it really is **understated** adj. *The writers' description of the woman's sorrow is understated.* = to deliberately put less feeling into something (e.g. a piece of writing) than may be expected, so as to produce an artistic effect **understatement** noun, u. or c. *He said the building needed a little repair, but that was an understatement. It was in a very bad state.*(c.) = a statement which does not bring out the full facts or the importance of something

to make oneself understood *I can't speak Tamil very well but I can make myself understood.* = to be able to express oneself, although not very well or clearly **Do you understand? 1** = an expression used to check that the other person understands one's orders or instructions **2** *I don't want anyone phoning me tonight. Do you understand?* = an expression used to check that someone has understood something as well as to warn them

un•der•stud•y[1] /ˈʌndəstʌdi/ noun, c. (**understudies**) = an actor who can replace another actor in a play (drama) if required to do so; anyone who may be asked to replace another person

understudy[2] verb, t. = to replace an actor in a play

un•der•take /ʌndəˈteɪk/ verb, t. (**undertook, undertaken**) **1** *The parents have undertaken the responsibility of improving the library.* = to accept a certain duty or responsibility **2** *I undertake to repay this loan by the end of the month.* = to promise to do something **undertaking** noun, c. **1** *The Indian Oil Company is a government undertaking.* = a piece of work or a business which someone is doing **2** *He has given us an undertaking to complete this building in a month.* = a promise

undertaker /ˈʌndəteɪkəʳ/ noun = a person whose job it is to make arrangements for the funeral of dead people [TECHNICAL]

under-the-counter adj. *He expects you to make an under-the-counter payment for helping you to get the contract.* = done secretly and in an illegal manner (disapproving)

un•der•tone /ˈʌndətəʊn/ noun, c. **1** *He spoke in an undertone because he did not want the others to hear.* = a quiet, low voice **2** *There are undertones of sadness in this song.* = a quality which is present but not openly or clearly

un•der•val•ue /ʌndəˈvæljuː/ verb, t. = to put too low a value or price on something (see **under-rate**)

un•der•wa•ter /ʌndəˈwɔːtəʳ/ adj. *underwater photography* = done below the surface of the water

underwear see **underclothes** (also **undergarments**)

U

un•der•weight /ʌndəˈweɪt/ adj. *The man was not selected for the army as he was underweight. He is only 48 kilos.* = below the weight required for some purpose
underwent verb, t. = past tense of **undergo** (see **undergo**)
un•der•world /ˈʌndəwɜːld/ noun **1** *a member of the underworld* = gangs of criminals who work very secretly **2** = the place where the spirits of the dead are taken (specially in stories from ancient Greece)
un•der•write /ʌndəˈraɪt/ verb, t. **1** *The government will underwrite this new company.* = to support with money and to take responsibility for the failure of a business **2** *The insurance company has underwritten this ship.* = to insure (to promise to pay money in case of an accident etc.) [TECHNICAL]
un•de•si•ra•ble /ʌndɪˈzaɪərəbəl/ adj. *an undesirable person* = not wanted or liked
un•de•vel•oped /ʌndɪˈveləpt/ adj. *Many areas of this region are still undeveloped.* = not having any buildings, industry, farming activity etc.; not fully or properly grown when referring to an unborn child or animal (foetus)
un•dies /ˈʌndiːz/ noun = women's underwear (slang)
un•di•vid•ed /ʌndɪˈvaɪdɪd/ adj. *an undivided country* = not broken up into parts; complete
un•do /ʌnˈduː/ verb, t. (**undid, undone**) **1** *The chemical factories have caused a lot of damage to the environment but we must try to undo some of it.* = to remove the effects of something **2** *He undid the buttons of his coat.* = to unfasten (to cause something that is tied to open up or become loose) **undoing** noun, u. *My refusal to work hard was my undoing.* = the cause of someone's downfall or failure
un•doubt•ed /ʌnˈdaʊtɪd/ adj. *a person who has undoubted talent* = of which one can be certain (also **unquestioned, unquestionable**)
un•dreamed-of /ʌnˈdriːmd əv/ adj. *undreamed-of wealth* = more than one can imagine
un•dress /ʌnˈdres/ verb, i. or t. *He undressed and went to bed.*(i.) // *The mother undressed her baby and put her to sleep.*(t.) = to remove (take off) one's own clothes or the clothes that someone else is wearing **a state of undress** noun = having no clothes on
un•due /ʌnˈdjuː/ adj. **1** *You are giving him undue importance.* = more than one deserves **2** *You are asking for an undue favour.* = (something) which one does not deserve **unduly** adv. *He is not unduly worried about the result of the examination as he knows he will pass.* = too much
un•dy•ing /ʌnˈdaɪ-ɪŋ/ adj. *You have earned our undying gratitude by building this hospital.* = which will never end
un•earth /ʌnˈɜːθ/ verb, t. **1** *He unearthed a pot full of old coins while digging up his garden.* = to dig up something that was buried inside the earth **2** *He has unearthed a lot of musical talent among these children.* = to discover something by making a lot of effort
un•earth•ly /ʌnˈɜːθli/ adj. **1** *He heard an unearthly scream of terror.* = unnatural; ghostly **2** *She dropped in to see us at an unearthly hour.* = very inconvenient (see also **ungodly**)
un•eas•y /ʌnˈiːzi/ adj. **1** *The patient is feeling uneasy.* = not comfortable or well **2** *There is an uneasy calm in the city.* = likely to change
un•e•co•nom•ic /ʌniːkəˈnɒmɪk/ adj. *It will be uneconomic to set up a factory here, as there are no transport facilities.* = not providing any profit or likely to lead to a loss (also uneconomical)
un•ed•u•cat•ed /ʌnˈedjʊkeɪtɪd/ adj. = having little or no education
un•em•ployed /ʌnɪmˈplɔɪd/ aj. = having no job **unemployment** /ʌnɪmˈplɔɪmənt/ noun, u. = the state of not having a job
un•end•ing /ʌnˈendɪŋ/ adj. *an unending speech* = going on for too long a time (referring to something unpleasant)
un•e•qual /ʌnˈiːkwəl/ adj. **1** *an unequal contest* = not fair; between people or groups that are not equal in strength or size **2** *He was unequal to the task.* = not having enough strength or ability to do something **unequalled** adj. *The beauty of the Taj Mahal is unequalled.* = having no equal; better than anything else
UNESCO /jʊˈneskəʊ/ abbr. of **United Nations Educational, Scientific and Cultural Organization** = a part of the United Nations Organization that looks after educational and cultural activities
un•eth•i•cal /ʌneθɪkəl/ adj. *It is unethical to offer bribes.* = not morally good or right
un•e•ven /ʌnˈiːvən/ adj. **1** *The road has an uneven surface.* = not smooth or level **2** *His breathing is uneven.* = not regular **3** *Her performance has been uneven this year.* = varying (changing) in quality **4** *The match between South Africa and India proved to be an uneven contest.* = not equal in talent, ability etc.
un•e•vent•ful /ʌnɪˈventfəl/ adj. *We were expecting some excitement at the meeting but it was quite uneventful.* = without any exciting events
un•fail•ing /ʌnˈfeɪlɪŋ/ adj. *He is popular because of his unfailing sense of humour.* = always present (referring to something good)
un•fair /ʌnˈfeəʳ/ adj. *It was unfair of you to blame only him when so many of us made the same mistake.* = not just or right
un•faith•ful /ʌnˈfeɪθfəl/ adj. **1** *an unfaithful*

husband = having sexual relations with someone to whom one is not married **2** *an unfaihful friend* = not loyal or supporting one in the way expected

un•fal•ter•ing /ʌn'fɔːltərɪŋ/ adj. *His loyalty to his leader is unfaltering.* = steady; not losing strength

un•fath•o•ma•ble /ʌn'fæðəməbəl/ adj. *For some unfathomable reason he thinks of his own brother as his worst enemy.* = difficult to understand

un•fa•vou•ra•ble /ʌn'feɪvərəbəl/ adj. *You should not think of starting a new business now, as conditions are unfavourable.* = not helpful

un•fazed /ʌnfeɪzd/ adj. *There have been many insulting reports about him in the newspapers, but he remains unfazed.* = not worried by problems or difficulties (approving)

un•feel•ing /ʌn'fiːlɪŋ/ adj. *When I was lying in hospital with a broken leg, my friends did not visit me even once. I never thought they would be so unfeeling.* = not feeling any sympathy for others

un•fi•nished /'ʌnfiniʃt/ adj. *an unfinished novel* = not completed

un•fit /ʌn'fɪt/ adj. **1** *If you can't control your temper, you are unfit to be a teacher.* = not having the right qualities needed for something **2** *Wasim is not playing in this match as he is unfit.* = not in good health or good physical condition

un•flap•pa•ble /ʌn'flæpəbəl/ adj. *She remains unflappable even when there are problems.* = never losing one's calm

un•fold /ʌn'fəʊld/ verb, t. or i. **1** *He took the letter out of the envelope, unfolded it and read it out to his wife.*(t.) = to open or spread out something **2** *As the story of the film unfolds, you realize how true to life it is.*(i.) = to develop and become more clear

un•fore•seen /ʌnfɔː'siːn/ adj. *If no unforeseen problems arise, we should be able to complete this task in a week.* = not expected

un•for•get•ta•ble /ʌnfə'getəbəl/ adj. *My meeting with her grandmother will always remain unforgettable for me.* = (something) that one cannot forget because of the strong effect it has

un•for•tu•nate /ʌn'fɔːtənɪt/ adj. **1** *These unfortunate people lost their homes in the earthquake.* = having bad luck **2** *It is unfortunate that you did not follow my instructions.* = something that one should feel sorry about (disapproving)

un•found•ed /ʌn'faʊndɪd/ adj. *The rumour that the company will shut down is unfounded. It is doing well.* = not supported by facts

un•furl /ʌn'fɜːl/ verb, t. *The President will unfurl the national flag on Republic Day.* = to open up a flag from a rolled-up position

un•gain•ly /ʌn'geɪnli/ adj. *Even though he has an ungainly body, he is very graceful when he dances.* = clumsy

un•god•ly /ʌn'gɒdli/ adj. *I had to go to the airport at the ungodly hour of 4.00 a.m. to receive my friend.* = very inconvenient (see also **unearthly**, meaning **2**)

un•gram•ma•ti•cal /ʌngrə'mætɪkl/ adj. *an ungrammatical sentence* = not in keeping with the rules of grammar

un•grate•ful /ʌn'greɪtfəl/ adj. *Have you forgotten that I helped you when you were in trouble? How can you be so ungrateful?* = not thankful (not showing appreciation of help received from someone)

un•guard•ed /ʌn'gɑːdɪd/ adj. **1** *If the house is left unguarded, thieves are sure to break in.* = not protected by guards **2** *In an unguarded moment he told me that he had never been to college.* = careless

un•hap•pi•ly /ʌn'hæpɪli/ adv. **1** *Unhappily, she fell ill on the day of the examination.* = unfortunately **2** *He walked to the examination hall unhappily.* = in an unhappy mood

un•health•y /ʌn'helθi/ adj. **1** *The children look unhealthy.* = not in good health **2** *He lives in unhealthy surroundings.* = likely to cause disease or health problems **3** *He takes an unhealthy interest in the activities of smugglers.* = not proper

un•heard /ʌn'hɜːd/ adj. *My prayer remained unheard.* = not listened to **unheard of** /ʌn'hɜːd/ adj. *For anyone to become a professor at the age of 18 is unheard of.* = (something) that has never happened before

un•hinge /ʌn'hɪndʒ/ verb, t. *The death of his wife in an accident has unhinged him.* = to cause someone to lose control of the mind

u•ni- /'juːnɪ/ prefix meaning one or single e.g. **unicellular** = having only one cell

UNICEF abbr. of **United Nations International Children's Fund** = an organization which is a part of the United Nations and helps suffering children

u•ni•corn /'juːnɪkɔːn/ noun = an imaginary animal that looks like a white horse but has a single horn growing from its forehead

un•i•den•ti•fied /ʌnaɪ'dentɪfaɪd/ adj. *Some unidentified people have given the police a clue about where to find the criminal.* = (someone) whose name etc. is not known

u•ni•form[1] /'juːnɪfɔːm/ noun, u. or c. *a police officer in uniform* = a type of clothing worn by all the members of a group or profession, specially the army or police

uniform[2] adj. *The temperature here remains at a uniform 32 degrees Celsius throughout the year.* = always the same; not changing or different

u•ni•fy /'juːnɪfaɪ/ verb, t. or i. *Some people would like to unify the countries in Europe into a single large*

U

state. = to join separate things together to form a whole **unification** /juːnɪfɪ'keɪʃən/ noun, u. *The unification of East Germany and West Germany into a single state took place not many years ago.* = the act of joining separate things together into a whole

u•ni•lat•e•ral /juːnɪ'lætərəl/ adj. *India has made a unilateral declaration that it will not be the first to use nuclear weapons in the case of a war.* = done by or having an effect on only one group or country [TECHNICAL]

un•in•hab•i•ta•ble /ʌnɪn'hæbɪtəbəl/ adj. *Some of the islands in the Indian Ocean are uninhabitable as they have no fresh water.* = on which no one can live

un•in•hib•it•ed /ʌnɪn'hɪbɪtɪd/ adj. *These days young people talk freely about love and sex when taking part in discussions. They are quite uninhibited.* = free and natural in behaviour and not worried about what other people may think

un•in•spired /ʌnɪn'spaɪəd/ adj. *Shah Rukh Khan, who usually acts well, gives an uninspired performance in this film.* = dull; done without imagination **uninspiring** adj. *an uninspiring speech* = not able to inspire (to create special interest in something)

un•in•te•rest•ed /ʌn'ɪntrɪstɪd/ adj. *I tried to sell him my car, but he was uninterested.* = not showing interest

un•in•ter•rupt•ed /ʌnɪntə'rʌptɪd/ adj. *We have had an uninterrupted week of rain. It has not stopped raining at all during this period.* = continuous; without a halt

u•ni•on /'juːnɪən/ noun, c. or u. **1** *I am a member of the teacher's union.*(c.)= a group of people, generally belonging to the same profession, that looks after the rights and interests of its members **2** *We are happy at the union of these two families.* = the act of being joined together (formal) **3** *Their union has been blessed at last, after ten long years.* = marriage (old-fashioned) **unionize (unionise)** /'juːnjənaɪz/ verb, t. *The workers employed in this factory have been unionized.* = to form a union of workers [TECHNICAL]

Union Jack noun = the national flag of Great Britain (formed by the union of England, Scotland and Wales)

u•nique /juː'niːk/ adj. *She has a unique style of singing. No one can copy her style.* = the only one of its kind; unusual

u•ni•sex /'juːnɪseks/ adj. *unisex clothes* = for both men and women

u•ni•son /'juːnɪsən/ noun, u. *'We want a holiday!' the school-boys shouted in unison.* = the act of doing something together, at the same time

u•nit /'juːnɪt/ noun, c. **1** *The most widely used unit of weight is the kilogramme.* = an amount or quantity used in measuring something **2** *He is an officer in a naval unit.* = a group of people living or working together for a special purpose **3** *This chapter is divided into six units.* = a division in a book **unit trust** noun, c. *the Unit Trust of India* = a business company which collects money from the public and uses it to buy shares in different kinds of business [TECHNICAL]

u•nite /juː'naɪt/ verb, t. or i. **1** *The government plans to unite these two departments into a single department.*(t.)= to join together to form a whole **2** *The teachers united to demand higher pay.*(i.) = to come together for some purpose

United Nations see **UN**

unit trust see **unit**

u•ni•ty /'juːnɪti/ noun, u. *There is perfect unity among the workers.* = the state of being united and working together in agreement

u•ni•ver•sal /juːnɪ'vɜːsəl/ adj. *Peace is the universal wish of all nations.* = common to everyone; found everywhere **universal joint** noun = a joint in a machine which connects two parts and allows movement in all directions [TECHNICAL]

u•ni•verse /'juːnɪvɜːs/ noun, c. = everything that exists, including the stars, planets etc.

u•ni•ver•si•ty /juːnɪ'vɜːsɪti/ noun = a place where higher education (after the school level) is given

un•just /ʌn'dʒʌst/ adj. *The prize was not given to the best student because she was below the minimum age. This was unjust.* = not right or fair

un•kempt /ʌn'kempt/ adj. *You should not come to class looking so unkempt.* = untidy (old-fashioned)

un•kind /ʌn'kaɪnd/ adj. *How can you be so unkind to those animals?* = cruel

un•know•ing /ʌn'nəʊɪŋ/ adj. *I didn't know she was ill when I asked her to come with me. It was an unknowing thing I did.* = not aware of a particular situation or problem **unknowingly** adv. *He was unknowingly spreading infection by travelling in a crowded bus.* = without knowing that one is doing something

un•known /ʌn'nəʊn/ adj. *a book by an unknown author* = whose name, etc. no one knows

un•law•ful /ʌn'lɔːfəl/ adj. *The government has declared this meeting unlawful.* = against the law

un•learn /ʌn'lɜːn/ verb, t. *I have to unlearn the grammar I was taught in school and start all over again.* = to forget or give up deliberately something that one has already learnt

un•leash /ʌn'liːʃ/ verb, t. *The enemy unleashed a violent attack on our soldiers.* = to release (set free) some strong force or feeling suddenly

un•leav•ened /ʌn'levənd/ adj. *unleavened bread*

= flat bread made without yeast (a substance that makes bread soft)

un•less /ʌn'les/ conj. *You can't leave the class unless your teacher allows you to go.* = except on the condition that

un•like[1] /ʌn'laɪk/ prep. **1** *He is quite unlike his brother. His brother is tall and fat whereas he is short and thin.* = different from **2** *It is unlike her to be late. There must be a good reason.* = not what one expects from someone

unlike[2] adj. *His brother and he are quite unlike.* = different from each other **unlikely** adv. *It is unlikely that you will win this election. Not many people have heard of you.* = not expected

un•list•ed /ʌn'lɪstɪd/ adj. *an unlisted telephone number* = not included in an official list and therefore not known to many people

un•load /ʌn'ləʊd/ verb, t. **1** *Please unload the machines from the trucks.* = to remove a load, usually something heavy, from something **2** *unload the camera* = to remove the bullets from a gun or a film from a camera **3** *The shopkeeper managed to unload a consignment of rotten apples on us.* = to get rid of something that is not wanted (using dishonest means) (derogatory)

un•lock /ʌn'lɒk/ verb, t. *Unlock the door.* = to remove the lock from something

un•luck•y /ʌn'lʌki/ adj. *The batsman was unlucky to be run out when his score was 99.* = having or bringing bad luck

un•manned /ʌn'mænd/ adj. *an unmanned aircraft* = not having or not requiring someone to look after it or to control it (referring to a machine e.g. an aircraft)

un•man•age•able /ʌn'mænɪdʒəbəl/ adj. *unmanageable crowds // an unmanageable task* = something which is difficult to control or complete

un•mar•ried /ʌn'mærid/ adj. = not married

un•mask /ʌn'mɑːsk/ verb, t. *Everyone thought he was an honest man, but your report proves that he is dishonest. I am glad you have unmasked him.* = to expose someone (to let people know the unpleasant truth about someone, which had been kept hidden)

un•matched /ʌn'mætʃt/ adj. *Her greatness as a leader is unmatched.* = having no equal (also **unparalleled**)

un•men•tio•na•ble /ʌn'menʃənəbəl/ adj. *unmentionable facts* = too shocking or unpleasant to be spoken about

un•mind•ful /ʌn'maɪndfəl/ adj. *Please don't be unmindful when crossing the street or a car will hit you.* = careless; not paying attention to something

un•mis•ta•ka•ble /ʌnmɪ'steɪkəbəl/ adj. *This letter has certainly been written by him. The handwriting is unmistakable.* = clearly recognizable

un•moved /ʌn'muːvd/ adj. *The man begged the policeman to let him go but the policeman remained unmoved.* = showing no pity

un•nat•u•ral /ʌn'nætʃərəl/ adj. *It seems unnatural for him to hate his parents.* = not natural or usual

un•ne•ces•sa•ry /ʌn'nesəsəri/ adj. **1** *It is unnecessary to bring paper with you when you come for the examination. Paper will be provided.* = not required or wanted **2** *Your cruel remarks were quite unnecessary.* = not welcome, not right

un•nerve /ʌn'nɜːv/ verb, t. *She felt so unnerved when she was at the interview that she could not answer a single question.* = to lose courage or confidence or to cause someone to lose courage

un•ob•tru•sive /ʌnəb'truːsɪv/ adj. *I want my entry at the meeting to be unobtrusive. I don't want anyone to see me coming in.* = not easily noticed (seen)

un•of•fi•cial /ʌnə'fɪʃəl/ adj. **1** *India is playing an unofficial test match against the Australian team.* = not official **2** = not known to people in a formal way

un•or•tho•dox /ʌn'ɔːθədɒks/ adj. *He has an unorthodox style of singing. He mixes western tunes with Indian ragas.* = different from what is usual or expected

un•pack /ʌn'pæk/ verb, t. *You can unpack your suitcase and hang your clothes in the wardrobe.* = to remove things from a container

un•pal•at•a•ble /ʌn'pælətəbəl/ adj. *What I have to say may be unpalatable to you, but I must point out the weaknesses in your writing.* = unpleasant and difficult to accept (referring to a fact etc.)

un•par•al•leled /ʌn'pærəleld/ adj. *Shakespeare's plays are unparalleled.* = having no equal (also **unmatched**)

un•par•lia•men•ta•ry /ʌnpɑːlə'mentəri/ adj. *unparliamentary language* = not in keeping with the rules or traditions of the parliament; not acceptable

un•play•a•ble /ʌn'pleɪəbəl/ adj. *Tendulkar was out to an unplayable ball from Wasim Akram.* = too difficult to hit (in the game of tennis, cricket etc.)

un•pleas•ant /ʌn'plezənt/ adj. *There was an unpleasant incident in the office today. Two people quarreled.* = which causes some bad or unhappy feelings

un•pre•ce•dent•ed /ʌn'presɪdentɪd/ adj. *When Amitabh Bachchan arrived, there were unprecedented crowds waiting to greet him at the airport.* = which has never happened or been seen before

un•pre•dict•a•ble /ʌnprɪ'dɪktəbəl/ adj. *The weather in Shillong is unpredicatable. You may suddenly get rain when it is not expected.* = which one cannot know about in advance or cannot be sure of

un•pro•fes•sion•al /ʌnprəˈfeʃənəl/ adj. *unprofessional behaviour* = not in keeping with the rules or traditions followed in a particular profession

un•pro•voked /ʌnprəˈvəʊkt/ adj. *an unprovoked attack* = done without any provocation (something that might make a person angry and cause him or her to behave in a certain way)

un•pun•ished /ʌnˈpʌnɪʃt/ adj. *The rule has been broken, and we cannot allow them to go unpunished.* = without getting punishment

un•qual•i•fied /ʌnˈkwɒlɪfaɪd/ adj. **1** *As he does not have a medical degree he is unqualified to treat patients.* = not having the knowledge or ability required to do something **2** *The programme was an unqualified success.* = complete (approving)

un•ques•tio•na•ble /ʌnˈkwestʃənəbəl/ adj. *His honesty is unquestionable.* = which cannot be doubted **unquestioning** adj. *You must give the Prime Minister your unquestioning support.* = without expressing any doubts

un•qui•et /ʌnˈkwaɪət/ adj. *The situation in the city is unquiet. We are expecting some trouble.* = not calm or peaceful

un•quote /ʌnˈkwəʊt/ adv. *They said they were quote busy unquote so I could not meet them.* = a word used while speaking to show that one has come to the end of a quotation (a statement made by someone else which one is repeating) (The words quote–unquote, except when used in formal speeches, are often used to create a special effect e.g. sarcasm, lack of belief.)

un•rav•el /ʌnˈrævəl/ verb, t. *No one knows how she happened to be at the scene of the crime but we expect the police to unravel this mystery.* = to solve or make clear a mystery

un•real /ʌnˈrɪəl/ adj. *Everyone in the audience started weeping loudly when the film star announced he was going to give up acting. The whole situation was so unreal!* = strange and difficult to believe (somewhat derogatory)

un•rea•so•na•ble /ʌnˈriːzənəbəl/ adj. *How can I sell you my car for a thousand rupees? Don't be unreasonable!* = not fair or not showing reason

un•re•served /ʌnrɪˈzɜːvd/ adj. **1** *He has promised me his unreserved support.* = without limits or conditions **2** *He travelled in an unreserved compartment.* = without a reservation (a seat or berth on a train which no one else is allowed to use)

un•rest /ʌnˈrest/ noun, u. *We had a period of unrest, but now the city is peaceful.* = a state of trouble (when there is no peace)

un•ri•valled /ʌnˈraɪvəld/ adj. *Many think that the beauty of the Taj Mahal is unrivalled.* = not having anything to equal it (also **unequalled**, **unmatched**, **unparalleled**)

un•roll /ʌnˈrəʊl/ verb, t. *He unrolled the carpet so that I could see the design.* = to open from a rolled-up position

un•ru•ly /ʌnˈruːli/ adj. *an unruly mob* = difficult to control

un•said /ʌnˈsed/ adj. *You have helped me so much that I don't know how to thank you. I will leave my thanks unsaid.* = not expressed

un•sa•vour•y /ʌnˈseɪvəri/ adj. *an unsavoury reputation* = bad or unpleasant

un•scathed /ʌnˈskeðd/ adj. *Many people in the crowd were injured, but he came out unscathed.* = not harmed

un•scram•ble /ʌnˈskræmbəl/ verb, t. *We have received a message from the commander but it is in code. We will have to unscamble it.* = to put back a message which is in code (secret language which cannot be understood) into ordinary language, so that it can be understood [TECHNICAL]

un•screw /ʌnˈskruː/ verb, t. *Can you unscrew the cap of this bottle of medicine?* = to take the lid (cover) off something by twisting it around

un•scru•pu•lous /ʌnˈskruːpjʊləs/ adj. *They are so unscrupulous that they will do anything to win.* = completely without moral principles and willing to do anything in order to get what one wants

un•seat /ʌnˈsiːt/ verb, t. *unseat a person* = to cause someone to lose a position of power

un•seed•ed /ʌnˈsiːdɪd/ adj. *an unseeded player* = a player who has not been seeded (given a special position because he/she is likely to win) in a tournament

un•seem•ly /ʌnˈsiːmli/ adj. *Your conduct at the meeting was unseemly. Why did you shout so much?* = not proper

un•seen /ʌnˈsiːn/ adj. **1** *There is an unseen hand guiding me.* = which cannot be seen **2** *The examination will include an unseen passage for comprehension.* = which has not been studied before

un•set•tle /ʌnˈsetl/ verb, t. *Your question was so unexpected that it unsettled me.* = to upset someone (to make someone less calm) **unsettled** /ʌnˈsetld/ adj. **1** *The dispute between the two sides is still unsettled.* = which has not reached a settlement (a peaceful or acceptable end or solution) **2** *unsettled weather* = likely to change

un•shav•en /ʌnˈʃeɪvən/ adj. = not having shaved (removed the hairs growing on the face)

un•sight•ly /ʌnˈsaɪtli/ adj. *The room has not been cleaned. There are unsightly stains on the floor.* = not pleasant to look at

un•skilled /ʌn'skɪld/ adj. **1** *unskilled labour* = without the special training required to do something **2** *an unskilled job* = not requiring any special skill or training

un•so•cia•ble /ʌn'səʊʃəbəl/ adj. *an unsociable person* = one who does not enjoy the company of others and prefers to be alone

un•sound /ʌn'saʊnd/ adj. **1** *His ideas on economics are unsound.* = not based on correct or good reasoning **2** *His health is unsound.* = not good **3** *a person of unsound mind* = mentally unwell

un•spa•ring /ʌn'speərɪŋ/ adj. **1** *He was unsparing in his criticism of our mistakes.* = holding nothing back; hiding nothing **2** *We would like to thank the people who have been so unsparing with their help.* = generous with money, help etc. (also unstinting)

un•spea•ka•ble /ʌn'spi:kəbəl/ adj. *unspeakable crimes* = too bad or unpleasant to be described

un•sta•ble /ʌn'steɪbəl/ adj. **1** *an unstable government* = not firmly in position and in danger of falling (losing power) **2** *an unstable person* = mentally unwell

un•stuck /ʌn'stʌk/ adj. **1** *The labels on the parcel have become unstuck.* = not sticking to something **2** *All my plans are unstuck.* = becoming unsuccessful

un•sung /ʌn'sʌŋ/ adj. *Let us honour the unsung heroes of the army.* = not praised, although deserving praise

un•tan•gle /ʌn'tæŋgəl/ verb, t. **1** *He untangled the threads.* = to remove the knots from an untidy mass of string etc. **2** *Everything here is in a confused state. Can you untangle this situation?* = to put something in order

un•tapped /ʌn'tæpt/ adj. *These children can become excellent musicians. They have a lot of untapped talent.* = which has not been discovered and put to use

un•thin•ka•ble /ʌn'θɪŋkəbəl/ adj. *It is unthinkable that I should settle in America. I love my country too much.* = which cannot be imagined or thought of

un•tie /ʌn'taɪ/ verb, t. *Untie the dog. He needs some exercise.* = to open a knot in a rope or piece of string or to set free something that has been tied with a rope

un•til /ʌn'tɪl/ prep. or conj. *I waited on the platform until the departure of the train.*(prep.) // *I waited until the train had left.*(conj.) = up to the time that (also **till**)

> **Usage** 'Until' is often used incorrectly, as in the following sentence: *You should keep on trying until you don't succeed.* The sentence should be: *You should keep on trying until you succeed.*

un•time•ly /ʌn'taɪmli/ adj. **1** *We were shocked by his untimely death. He was only 27.* = happening too early; premature **2** *Your remarks are untimely.* = done or made at a time which is not suitable

un•to /'ʌntu:/ prep. *Do unto others as you would want them to do unto you.* = to [old-fashioned use]

un•told /ʌn'təʊld/ adj. **1** *an untold story of heroism* = which has never been told **2** *He had to face untold dangers.* = too great or too many to be described

un•touch•ed /ʌn'tʌtʃt/ adj. **1** *These biscuits are packed by machines. They are untouched by hands.* = not touched **2** *The glass of milk lay untouched.* = not eaten or drunk (referring to food or drink)

un•to•ward /ʌntə'wɔ:d/ adj. *The meeting went off without any untoward incident.* = undesirable (formal)

un•true /ʌn'tru:/ adj. *The reports of increasing crime are untrue.* = false

un•used /ʌn'ju:zd/ adj. **1** *I bought this shirt a month ago but it is still unused.* = not used **2** *I am unused to such spicy food.* = having no experience of something

un•u•su•al /ʌn'ju:ʒuəl/ adj. *It is unusual to have rain in January in Bhubaneswar.* = not common; rare

un•veil /ʌn'veɪl/ verb, t. **1** *unveil a statue* = to remove the covering from something at a formal ceremony **2** *The latest model of the car will be unveiled at the exhibition.* = to show something for the first time

un•war•rant•ed /ʌn'wɒrəntɪd/ adj. *The leader said that the criticism of her work was unwarranted.* = not justified; done without good reason

un•well /ʌn'wel/ adj. *He cannot come for the meeting as he is unwell.* = not in good health

un•weil•dy /ʌn'wi:ldi/ adj. *The system of justice in this country is extremely unweildy.* = too big, heavy or complicated to be used effectively

un•will•ing /ʌn'wɪlɪŋ/ adj. **1** *He is unwilling to contest the election as he thinks he is sure to lose.* = not wishing to do something **2** *She gave her unwilling consent to the marriage.* = doing something under pressure without wanting to do it

un•wind /ʌn'waɪnd/ verb, t. or i. (unwound) **1** *The nurse unwound the bandage which was tied around the soldier's leg.*(t.) = to undo (take off) something that has been wound (wrapped around) some object **2** *He has come to the seaside to unwind.*(i.) = to relax and take one's mind away from work etc.

un•wit•ting /ʌn'wɪtɪŋ/ adj. *These children have been made the unwitting victims of drug abuse.* = not having knowledge of what is going on (formal)

un•zip /ʌn'zɪp/ verb, t. (**unzipped**) *He unzipped the bag.* = to open something by using a zip

up[1] /ʌp/ prep. **1** *They walked up the hill.* = to a higher place **2** *Her house is up the road.* = further along (at a greater distance than something else) **3** *We sailed*

U

up the river. = against the direction of the current (in a river or stream)

up[2] adv. **1** *He stood up.* = to an upright position **2** *The glacier is 1,000 feet up.* = at a higher position or place **3** *Prices are going up.* = to a higher level **4** *She has just got up.* = out of bed

up[3] adj. **1** *He caught the up train to Delhi.* = going towards a certain destination (away from the place where one started) **2** *The prices of most things are up.* = rising higher **3** *Your time is up.* = finished **4** *This road is up.* = being repaired and therefore not in use **5** *I've hurt my foot and can't go out, but the upside is that I can rest, read and watch television!* = the good part of something

up[4] verb, t. or i. (upped) **1** *My senior has upped my salary by Rs 100.*(t.)= to increase or raise to a higher level (informal) **2** *He was so angry that he just upped and left.*(i.) = to do something suddenly, in an unexpected way

to be up *Call me at seven. I'll be up by then.* = to be awake **to be up and about** = to be active (usually after a period of not being active **to be up against something** = to face a difficult situation **to be up to something** *You are creeping around the house. What are you up to?* = to be planning something mischievous or secret (informal) **to be up to one's ears/neck in something** *I am up to my ears in work.* = to be in a situation which is full of something **It's up to you.** **1** *I've done everything I can. It's up to you now.* = an expression meaning, 'You must continue now. We are all depending on you.' **2** *'Shall we eat now?' 'It's up to you.'* = an expression meaning, 'You decide.' **to be well up on something** *'What's the capital of Fiji?' 'Ask Amit. He's well up on geography.'* = to have good knowledge about something **up yours** = a very offensive and disrespectful way of replying to someone to show you don't care or are angry (USE) **ups and downs** *We have gone through many ups and downs.* = good as well as bad periods in one's life

up- prefix meaning 'higher' or 'improved' (e.g. *up-market* = things of higher value, meant to be sold at a high price) **up-and-coming** adj. *an up-and-coming pop singer* = becoming famous **up•beat** /'ʌpbiːt/ adj. *The atmosphere in this office is very upbeat.* = cheerful and full of hope (informal)

up•bring•ing /'ʌpbrɪŋɪŋ/ noun *I am very careful with my money because of my upbringing. I grew up in a family where money was always scarce.* = the training that one receives from one's parents while growing up

up•com•ing /'ʌpkʌmɪŋ/ adj. *He plans to contest the up-coming election.* = about to happen soon

up•coun•try /ʌp'kʌntri/ adj. *up-country manners* = belonging to a part of a country which is far away from the coast or from any important city, and therefore less advanced (sometimes derogatory)

up•date /ʌp'deɪt/ verb **1** *Let me update you on some recent events.* = to supply with the latest information **2** *This textbook needs to be updated.* = to make something more modern

up•front /ʌp'frʌnt/ adj. *He was upfront about his reasons for wanting a job in Delhi.* = speaking or behaving in a direct and open manner, hiding nothing (informal)

up•grade /ʌpgreɪd/ verb, t. **1** *The company has decided to upgrade you.* = to give someone a better position, more money etc. **2** *I want my computer upgraded.* = to get an improved, more recent version of a machine, with more features etc.

up•heav•al /ʌp'hiːvəl/ noun, c. or u. *When war broke out, there was an upheaval in the whole country.* = a great change, usually leading to confusion and violence

up•hill[1] /ʌp'hɪl/ adv. *We are going uphill.* = towards the top of a hill

uphill[2] adj. *Teaching these boys English is an uphill task.* = very difficult

up•hold /ʌp'həʊld/ verb, t. (**upheld**) **1** *The President of India has to swear to uphold the Indian Constitution.* = to defend and protect something (specially a principle or law) **2** *The Supreme Court has upheld the decision of the High Court.* = to confirm; to declare that a judgement is correct [LAW]

up•hol•ster•y /ʌp'həʊlstəri/ noun, u. *This sofa needs new upholstery.* = the material used to cover a seat (e.g. a sofa) as well as to fill it so as to make it more comfortable to sit on **upholster** verb, t. *The sofa has been upholstered.* = to cover and fill a seat with some material

up•keep /'ʌpkiːp/ noun, u. *He spends a thousand rupees a month on the upkeep of the house.* = the cost or the act of keeping a house or a machine in good condition

up•land /'ʌplənd/ noun, c. = an area or part of a country which is at a height

up•lift[1] /ʌp'lɪft/ verb, t. **1** *Your encouraging words have helped to uplift our spirits.* = to bring hope to **2** *The earthquake has uplifted this area, which used to be quite low.* = to raise to a higher position

uplift[2] noun, u. *These people are working for the uplift of the village.* = improvement

up•mar•ket /ʌp'mɑːkət/ adj. *He designs upmarket furniture.* = costly and meant for people with a lot of money to spend

up•on /ə'pɒn/ prep. *The little girl sat down upon the sofa.* = on (formal)

up•per /'ʌpə[r]/ adj. *His room is on the upper floor.* =

in a higher position than something else **upper case** noun = capital letters (e.g. A, B, C and not a, b, c)

upper class[1] noun, c. **1** = the highest social class, having money and social importance **2** = the higher classes in a school or college

upper class[2] adj. *an upper class school* = meant for rich people in high social positions **upper crust** noun, c. = the upper class **upper-cut** noun, c. *He knocked out his opponent with an upper-cut.* = a blow (in the sport of boxing) which moves upwards to the head **Upper House** noun = one of the two divisions in a parliament, the members of which are generally not elected directly by the people and therefore have less political power than the members of the Lower House (In India, the Rajya Sabha is the Upper House.)

uppermost adv. or adj. *The thought of your happiness is uppermost in my mind.* = most important; in the highest position

to have (keep) a stiff upper lip = to show no emotion or weakness when you are in trouble **to have the upper hand** = to have an advantage over someone

up•pi•ty /ˈʌpɪti/ adj. *He has been behaving in an uppity manner.* = thinking oneself to be better than others (informal, disapproving)

up•right[1] /ˈʌp-raɪt/ adj. **1** *He was sitting in an upright position.* = with the back straight, not bent **2** *an upright person* = honest

upright[2] adv. *You should sit upright.* = in a straight position, not bent

upright[3] noun, c. *The roof is supported by uprights.* = a supporting post or pillar which is vertical (straight)

up•ris•ing /ˈʌpraɪzɪŋ/ noun, c. *an armed uprising* = a revolt; violent opposition against those who are in power

up•roar /ˈʌprɔːʳ/ noun, u. *When the crowd heard that the transport strike would continue, there was an uproar.* = a state of confusion, with people shouting angrily **uproarious** /ʌpˈrɔːriəs/ adj. **1** *uproarious scenes in the crowded compartment of the train* = full of shouting and confusion **2** *an uproarious comedy* = very humorous and causing a lot of laughter

up•root /ʌpˈruːt/ verb, t. **1** *The elephants have uprooted many of the young trees in the forest.* = to pull up a plant so that its roots come out of the ground **2** *The family was uprooted after the war.* = to remove someone from his/her home or usual surroundings

up•set[1] /ʌpˈset/ verb, t. (**upset**) **1** *He upset the table while trying to clean it and all the papers were scattered on the floor.* = to cause something to fall or turn over on its side by accident **2** *The rain has upset all our plans for a picnic.* = to cause some confusion **3** *The news of his child's illness has upset him.* = to cause unhappiness, worry or anxiety

upset[2] noun, c. or u. **1** *The defeat of the Australian team was a major upset in the tournament.* = a surprising or unexpected event **2** *He has a stomach upset.* = slight illness

to upset the apple cart = to spoil someone's plans

up•shot /ˈʌpʃɒt/ noun, u. *The upshot of the discussion is that we will work longer hours.* = the immediate result of something

up•side /ˈʌpsaɪd/ noun, u. **upside down** adv. or adj. **1** *You are holding the book upside down.*(adv.) = having the top part where the bottom part should be **2** *Everything in the office is upside down at the moment.*(adj.) = in a state of disorder or confusion

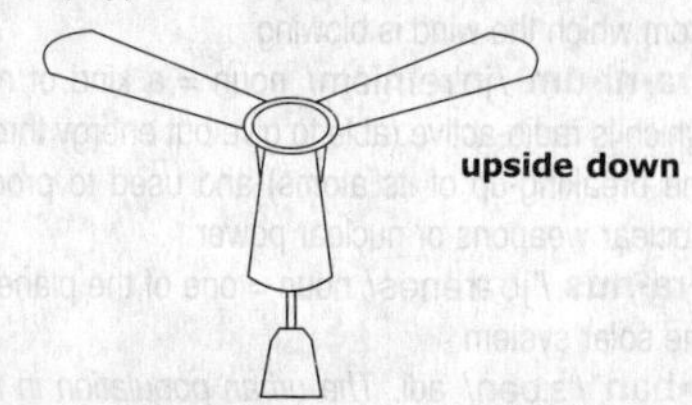

upside down

up•stage[1] /ʌpˈsteɪdʒ/ adv. *The actor moved upstage.* = towards the back of the stage on which a drama is being performed

upstage[2] verb, t. *They are always trying to upstage us by wearing more fashionable clothes.* = to take attention away from someone else to oneself (informal, often disapproving)

up•stairs /ʌpˈsteəz/ adv. *He has gone upstairs.* = to the upper floor of a building, usually reached by climbing a set of stairs

up•start /ˈʌpstɑːt/ noun, c. *Your new leader is an upstart with very little education or ability.* = a person who suddenly rises to an important position and takes advantage of it (derogatory)

up•stream /ʌpˈstriːm/ adv. *We have to row the boat upstream.* = against the flow of the current

up•surge /ˈʌpsɜːdʒ/ noun, u. *There has been an upsurge in the number of students joining computer courses.* = a sudden and large increase

up•take /ˈʌpteɪk/ noun, u. **1** *I tried to tell him how to make money quickly, but he was slow on the uptake.* = ability to understand something **2** *The uptake of oxygen by young plants increases during the daytime.* = the rate at which something is taken in or used

up•tight /ˈʌptaɪt/ adj. *Don't be so uptight about the surprise test. We'll all pass.* = reacting with anger because one is nervous or worried about something

up-to-date /ʌptəˈdeɪt/ adj. *We use the most up-to-date methods of training.* = modern; using the latest ideas etc.

to bring someone up-to-date = to give the latest

U

information to someone **to bring something up-to-date** = to change something in order to make it modern

up•turned /ʌpˈtɜːnd/ adj. *He sat down on the beach to rest, leaning against an upturned boat.* = turned upside down, with the bottom facing up

up•ward /ˈʌpwəd/ adj. *We are observing an upward movement of prices in the market.* = going up **upwardly-mobile** adj. *upwardly-mobile people* = wanting or trying to move to a higher level of income and a higher social class

up•wards /ˈʌpwədz/ adv. *Prices are moving upwards.* = towards a higher level

up•wind /ʌpˈwɪnd/ adv. *The deer caught the scent of the tiger, which was lying upwind.* = in the direction from which the wind is blowing

u•ra•ni•um /jʊˈreɪniəm/ noun = a kind of metal which is radio-active (able to give out energy through the breaking-up of its atoms) and used to produce nuclear weapons or nuclear power

U•ra•nus /ˈjʊərənəs/ noun = one of the planets in the solar system

ur•ban /ˈɜːbən/ adj. *The urban population in most parts of the country is growing rapidly.* = belonging to a town or city (opposite **rural**)

ur•bane /ɜːbeɪn/ adj. *He makes friends easily because of his urbane manners.* = polite and confident in dealing with others

ur•chin /ˈɜːtʃɪn/ noun, c. *a street urchin* = a young child who is poor and homeless and usually dirty

ur•e•thra /jʊərˈiːθrə/ noun = the narrow tube inside the body which carries urine out of the body [BIOLOGY]

urge[1] /ɜːdʒ/ verb, t. *I urge you to vote for her, she's really capable.* = to ask someone strongly to do something

urge[2] noun, u. or c. *I felt the urge to slap him on the face when he insulted my brother.* = a strong wish or need to do something

ur•gent /ˈɜːdʒənt/ adj. *I received an urgent phone call from my boss asking me to come at once.* = very important and requiring immediate attention or action **urgency** noun = the state of being urgent

u•rine /ˈjʊərɪn/ noun = waste liquid passed out of the body **urinate** verb, i. = to pass urine **urinal** noun, c. **1** = a kind of pot, fitted to a wall, into which men can urinate **2** = a building containing a number of urinals **urinary** adj. *the urinary bladder* = having to do with urine or the parts of the body connected with the production and passing of urine

urn /ɜːn/ noun, c. = a large container used to collect the ashes from the body of a dead person who has been cremated (burnt)

Ur•sa Ma•jor /ɜːsə ˈmeɪdʒəʳ/ noun = a constellation (group) of seven bright stars seen in the northern part of the sky at night

us /əs/ pron. *He called out to us as we were getting out of the bus.* = the object form of the pronoun 'we'

US (**USA**) abbr. of **United States** (**of America**)

usable, **usage** see **use**

use[1] /juːz/ verb, t. **1** *I use this car to go to the office every morning.* = to put into action or service for some purpose **2** *All the bread has been used.* = to finish; to consume (reduce the amount of something) **3** *He is trying to use you.* = to take unfair advantage of someone (disapproving)

use[2] noun, u. or c. **1** *The use of private cars has decreased with the rise in the price of petrol.*(u.) = the act of using something **2** *Many uses can be found for old newspapers.*(c.) = a way of using something **3** *He has lost the use of one arm.* = the ability to use something **4** *This old pump is of no use now.* = a purpose for which something can be used

to use up *He has used up all the water. There is nothing left.* = to use all of something **to be of use** *This pen may be of use to you.* = useful **to have no use for someone or something** = to have no respect or liking for someone, or use for something **What's the use?** = an expression meaning 'Let us not waste our time in talking about or doing something.'

u•sa•ble /ˈjuːzɪbəl/ adj. *The car is very old, but still usable.* = fit to be used

us•age /ˈjuːzɪdʒ/ noun, u. **1** *'You must be knowing him' is common in Indian English usage, but it is not acceptable in standard English.* = the manner in which a language, or a particular word in the language, is commonly used **2** *This car can stand rough usage.* = the way of using something

used /juːzd/ adj. *a used car* = something which was owned and used by someone else earlier (also **second-hand**)

used to[1] aux. verb *I used to smoke 20 cigarettes a day when I was a student, but I have given up smoking now.* = referring to some habitual activity in the past (something that happened regularly) which has stopped or been discontinued

used to[2] adj. *I am quite used to life in a big city.* = accustomed to (having a lot of experience of something)

use•ful /ˈjuːsfəl/ adj. *People want to learn English because they find it useful.* = able to help or to bring some advantage **useless** adj. *This old car has become useless as spare parts are not available.* = not fit for use

us•er /ˈjuːzəʳ/ noun, c. *We want to serve all computer users.* = one who uses something **user-friendly** adj. *a user-friendly machine* = easy to use

ush•er[1] /ˈʌʃəʳ/ verb, t. **1** *We have a visitor. Will you* *please usher him in?* = to bring someone to a place by showing him/her the way **2** *These winds from the south will usher in the monsoon.* = to call in; to bring

usher[2] noun, c. *an usher in a cinema* = a person who works in a cinema, whose job it is to lead people to their seats

USSR abbr. of **Union of Soviet Socialist Republics** = a political union (which no longer exists) of Russia and some neighbouring countries, which were all communist states

u•su•al /'ju:ʒuəl/ adj. *The office will start work at the usual time, which is 10.00 a.m.* = happening or done always or very often **usually** adv. *The train usually comes on time but is late today.* = in most cases or on most days

u•su•ry /'ju:ʒəri/ noun = the practice of lending money at very high rates of interest [LAW]

u•surp /ju:'zɜ:p/ verb, t. *The state government has accused the central government of usurping some of its powers.* = to take away in an illegal manner the power or position that belongs to someone else

u•ten•sil /ju:'tensəl/ noun, c. *cooking utensils* = a tool or a container (pot etc.) which has some practical use

u•te•rus /'ju:tərəs/ noun = the womb (the organ in the body of a female animal or human being in which the baby grows before it is born) [MEDICINE] **uterine** /'ju:təraɪn/ *uterine cancer* = of the uterus

u•til•i•ty /ju:'tɪlɪti/ noun, u. or c.(**utilities**) **1** *This land has no utility for us. We should sell it.*(u.) = the quality of being useful **2** *The government manages most utilities, such as the supply of water and electricity.*(c.) = a useful service offered to the public **utilitarian** /ju:tɪlɪ'teəriən/ adj. *This factory building is strictly utilitarian.* = useful but lacking beauty (often derogatory) **utilitarianism** noun = a philosophy (system of belief) which states that the value of something should be judged by its utility (usefulness)

u•til•ize (utilise) /'ju:tɪlaɪz/ verb, t. *We will utilize these holidays to complete our work.* = to make good use of something (formal)

ut•most[1] /'ʌtməʊst/ adj. *She performed her task with the utmost efficiency.* = greatest; to the highest degree

utmost[2] noun, u. *I will try my utmost to complete this report today.* = the most that can be done

u•to•pi•a /ju:'təʊpiə/ noun = a perfect or ideal society (which does not exist) **utopian** adj. *utopian plans* = ideal but not practical

ut•ter[1] /'ʌtə^r/ verb, t. *He did not utter a word when he was asked why he was late.* = to speak

utter[2] adj. *You are an utter fool!* = complete (referring to something bad) **utterly** adv.

ut•ter•ance /'ʌtərəns/ noun, c. or u. **1** *Every utterance of the great historian was written down by his eager students.*(c.) = something that is spoken **2** *The utterance of this mantra will create a magical spell.*(u.) = the act of saying something

u-turn /'ju: tɜ:n/ noun, c. **1** *The car made a u-turn.* = a complete turn which takes a vehicle back in the direction from which it had come **2** *My friend always thought of sports as a waste of time, but now he is actively participating in them. He seems to have made a u-turn!* = a complete change in opinion or behaviour, leading to the very opposite of what had been said or done before

u•vu•la /'ju:vjʊlə/ noun = the small, soft piece of flesh hanging from the top of the mouth, at the back [BIOLOGY] **uvular** adj. *a uvular consonant* = a sound produced with the back part of the tongue nearly touching the uvula [TECHNICAL]

U

vV

v, V /viː/ the twentysecond letter of the English alphabet

v. abbr. of **versus** (see **versus**)

va•can•cy /ˈveɪkənsi/ noun, c. (**vacancies**) *We have a vacancy in the company as one of our managers has retired.* = a position (job) that needs to be filled **vacant** adj. **1** *One of the rooms in the hotel is vacant.* = empty; not being used **2** *The Manager's post is vacant.* = not filled or taken up **3** *a vacant expression* = blank (used to describe a face which shows no reaction, intelligence or emotion)

to fall vacant *A job has fallen vacant in our company.* = to become available because the person who had it earlier has left (referring to a job, house etc.) (formal)

va•ca•te /vəˈkeɪt/ verb, t. *You will have to vacate this room as we are expecting an important guest tomorrow.* = to give up or stop using a house, room etc. **vacation** noun, u. or c. **1** *The school has its summer vacation in June and July.* = the period when a school or college is not working **2** *We are going to Kerala for a vacation.*(c.) = holiday **3** = the act of vacating (leaving or giving up) something (e.g. a job, a room etc.) (formal)

vac•cine /ˈvæksiːn/ noun, u. or c. *The doctor uses small-pox vaccine to protect children from small-pox.*(u.) = a kind of medicine prepared from the bacteria or virus (tiny living creatures that cause disease) of some disease and given, in a weaker form, to a person so that he/she can be protected from that disease [MEDICINE] **vaccinate** verb, t. *The doctor vaccinated the children against small-pox.* = to protect someone against a disease by putting vaccine into his/her body **vaccination** /væksɪnˈeɪʃən/ noun, u. = the act of giving someone a vaccine

vac•il•late /ˈvæsɪleɪt/ verb, i. *You didn't want to buy the house, but now you do. Why are you vacillating?* = to change one's views or opinions frequently (derogatory)

vac•u•um[1] /ˈvækjuəm/ noun, u. **1** = a space which is completely empty and from which all the air has been taken out [TECHNICAL] **2** *His wife's death created a vacuum in his life.* = a feeling of emptiness

vacuum[2] verb, t. *This carpet is very dirty. You should vacuum it.* = to clean something with the help of a vacuum cleaner (informal) **vacuum cleaner** noun, c. = a machine which sucks up dirt from floors, carpets etc. **vacuum flask** noun, c. = a glass container with a double wall which can keep things hot or cold for a long time as there is no air between the two walls for the heat to escape or get in (also **thermos flask**, trademark)

vag•a•bond /ˈvægəbɒnd/ noun, c. = a person who is always wandering from one place to another or one job to another (derogatory)

va•gi•na /vəˈdʒaɪnə/ noun = the passage leading from the outer sex organ of a woman or female animal to the uterus or womb [MEDICINE]

va•grant /ˈveɪgrənt/ noun or adj. = a person who does not have a steady home or job (see **vagabond**)

vague /veɪg/ adj. **1** *There was a thick mist and we could not see the trees or houses clearly. Everything looked vague.* = not clear in shape **2** *I want to go on a holiday but I have not decided where I will go. My plans are still vague.* = not clearly known

vain[1] /veɪn/ adj. **1** *He is a vain person and always wants people to praise him.* = proud; thinking very highly of oneself (derogatory) **2** *He made a vain attempt to catch the thief, who was able to get away.* = unsuccessful

(in) vain[2] noun, u. *I tried to persuade him to come to class but it was in vain.* = without a successful result

vale /veɪl/ noun, c. = valley (literary)

val•e•dic•tion /vælɪˈdɪkʃən/ noun, c. *We have arranged a valediction for our accountant, who is retiring tomorrow.* = the act of saying farewell to someone on a formal occasion **valedictory** adj. *a valedictory speech* = used as a valediction, to say farewell to someone (formal)

va•len•cy /ˈveɪlənsi/ noun *Hydrogen has a valency of 2.* = a measure of the power of the atoms of different substances to combine with each other to form compounds [CHEMISTRY]

va•len•tine /ˈvæləntain/ noun = a person to whom one sends a greeting card on St.Valentine's Day (February 14) to show one's love or to show that one is attracted to that person

val•et /ˈvælɪt/ or /væleɪ/ noun, c. = a person who serves another by taking care of their things

val•i•ant /ˈvæliant/ adj. *a valiant soldier* = brave in war

val•id /ˈvælɪd/ adj. **1** *A cheque is valid for only six months.* = effective (can be used or accepted legally) **2** *Do you have a valid excuse for coming late to this important meeting?* = reasonable; something that can be accepted **validate** verb, t. *This cheque will have to be validated after six months.* = to make something valid (legally acceptable)

val•ley /ˈvæli/ noun, c. = an area lying between hills or mountains, at a lower height [GEOGRAPHY]

valour /væləʳ/ noun, u. = (generally describing a

man) courage or bravery, usually in war; the quality of being valiant

value[1] /'vælju:/ noun, u. **1** *The value of this piece of land is Rs 5 lakh.* = the worth of something in money (the price that it should fetch if it is sold) **2** *His experience as a manager is of great value to the company.* = usefulness or importance

value[2] verb, t. **1** *I have asked the manager of the bank to value this property before I sell it.* = to calculate the correct price of something **2** *The company values your services greatly.* = to consider very important or useful **values** noun (always plural) *You should respect the values of this society.* = the ideas and qualities considered important by a group of people **valuable** adj. *a valuable piece of property* = having great value

valve /vælv/ noun, c. *Water is not flowing into the tank as the valve is closed.* = a device which can be opened or closed so as to allow or prevent the flow of some liquid or gas through a pipe or tube

va•moose /væ'mu:s/ verb, i. (American) *You should vamoose before the police finds you here.* = to disappear or go away quickly (informal, often humorous)

vamp /væmp/ noun, c. = a woman who uses her charm to make a man do something morally wrong or bad; an evil woman character in a film or play

vam•pire /'væmpaɪə^r/ noun, c. = an evil spirit which lives in a dead body and sucks the blood of human beings (found in horror stories which people sometimes read for entertainment) **vampire bat** noun = a kind of large bat (flying mammal) found in South America which sucks the blood of other animals

van /væn/ noun,c. = a small truck with a closed body, used for carrying goods as well as passengers

va•na•di•um /və'neɪdɪəm/ noun = a metal used for making special kinds of steel [CHEMISTRY]

van•dal /'vændl/ noun,c. *The cushions of the seats on the train have been damaged by vandals.* = a person who intentionally damages public property or things belonging to others (derogatory) **vandalism** noun, u. = the destruction caused by a vandal **vandalize (vandalise)** verb, t. *These buses have been vandalized.* = to damage or destroy public property intentionally

van•guard /'vængɑ:d/ noun, u. **1** *The Jat Regiment will form the vanguard of the army, with the other regiments coming behind them.* = the leading position at the front of an army **2** *America has been in the vanguard to promote free trade among nations.* = in a leading position

van•il•la /və'nɪlə/ noun = a sweet-smelling substance obtained from the seeds of a plant, used to improve the taste of food, specially sweets and ice-cream

va•nish /'vænɪʃ/ verb, i. *The beautiful fairy vanished after singing a song to the prince.* = to disappear (to be no longer seen) quickly, as if by magic

va•ni•ty /'vænɪti/ noun, u. = the quality of being vain (proud) **vanity bag** noun = a small bag used by a woman to carry things needed for her make-up (also **vanity case**)

van•quish /'væŋkwɪʃ/ verb, t. *Our army is certain to vanquish the enemy.* = to defeat completely, specially in a war (formal/literary)

vantage (point) /'vɑ:ntɪdʒ/ noun, c. = a high point from which one can have a clear view of things (formal)

vap•id /'væpɪd/ adj. *I find this book boring because of the author's vapid style of writing.* = dull and uninteresting

va•pour /'veɪpə^r/ noun, u. *Clouds are made up of water vapour.* = gas or very tiny drops into which a liquid, such as water, can change because of the action of heat **vaporize (vaporise)** verb, t. or i. *All the water in the pot has vaporized.* = to turn into vapour (also **evaporate**)

var•i•a•ble[1] /'veərɪəbəl/ adj. *The weather in the hills is variable.* = changing frequently

variable[2] noun,c. *When the government calculates the economic growth expected during a year, one of the variables is the monsoon.* = something which can change and have an important effect on a situation **variant** noun, c. *Haryanvi, the language spoken in Haryana, is a variant of Hindi.* = a form of something which is a little different from other forms **variation** /veərɪ'eɪʃən/ noun, u. *There is great variation between the temperature in the day and at night.* = change

var•i•cose veins /værɪkəʊs 'veɪnz/ noun = a medical condition in which the veins (blood vessels or tubes carrying blood) in the legs become swollen [MEDICINE]

variety /və'rɑɪəti/ noun, u. or c. (**varieties**) **1** *We eat rice and dal everyday. There is no variety in the food.*(u.)= a change or difference from time to time that makes things interesting **2** *This is a new variety of rice from Taiwan.*(c.) = a type or kind of something, which is different from other kinds **variety entertainment** noun = a programme of entertainment, shown to an audience which contains a number of different items (songs, dances etc.) **variety store** = a shop which sells many different things **various** /'veərɪəs/ adj. *Various languages are spoken in this part of India.* = of different kinds

var•nish[1] /'vɑ:nɪʃ/ noun, u. *This old table needs a coat of varnish.* = a kind of colourless liquid paint which

V

gives a bright surface to wood or metal

varnish[2] verb, t. *You will have to varnish the table.* = to cover with varnish

var•si•ty /ˈvɑːsɪti/ noun = university (old-fashioned, informal)

vary /ˈveəri/ verb, i. or t. (**varied**) **1** *The weather varies almost every day. On some days it is hot and on other days it is cold.*(i.) = to change **2** *He thinks cricket should be banned but I think it should be encouraged. Our opinions on this subject vary.*(i.) = to be different from each other **3** *A good bowler should be able to vary the speed at which he is bowling.*(t.) = to change and make things different from each other

vas•cu•lar /ˈvæskjʊləʳ/ adj. = having to do with the blood vessels or other kinds of tubes through which liquids flow inside the body of an animal or a plant [BIOLOGY]

vase /vɑːz/ noun, c. *a flower vase* = a decorative container or pot in which flowers are kept

vas /vɑːs/ noun = a thin tube which carries sperm (male seed) from the testes to the penis (the male sex organ) [MEDICINE] **vasectomy** /vəˈsektəmi/ noun = a surgical operation by which the vas is cut off, so that a man cannot produce any more children [MEDICINE]

vas•e•line /ˈvæsɪliːn/ noun, u. = a soft yellowish substance produced from petroleum (oil taken out of the earth) which is used for medicinal and other purposes (trademark)

vast /vɑːst/ adj. *She owns a vast estate (piece of land) in Uttaranchal.* = very large

vat /væt/ noun, c. = a large tub (container in which water or some other liquid is kept)

VAT /viːeɪˈtiː/ noun abbr. of **Value Added Tax** = a tax added to the price of an article and paid by the buyer to the seller

vault[1] /vɔːlt/ noun, c. *a bank vault* **1**= a strong room (a room in a bank, with thick, strong walls and heavy steel doors, where money, gold etc. can be kept, protected from robbery) **2** = an underground room in a church where the bodies of dead persons are kept

vault[2] verb, i. *He vaulted over the wall and ran across the road.* = to jump over a high wall etc. **pole vault** noun = a sport in which persons are required to vault (jump) over a high bar, using a pole [SPORTS]

VC abbr. of **Vice Chancellor** (see below)

VCD abbr. of **Video Compact Disc** = a small, circular piece of metal coated with plastic, on which pictures as well as sounds have been recorded and can be played back through a machine called a VCD player

VCR abbr. of **Video Cassette Recorder** noun = a machine which records pictures as well as sounds on plastic tape, which can be played back

vd abbr. of **venereal diseases** (see **venereal** below)

veal /viːl/ noun, u. = the meat from a calf (the young of a cow)

vec•tor /ˈvektəʳ/ noun, c. **1** = a quantity which has direction as well as size [MATHEMATICS] **2** = an insect which can carry a disease e.g. a mosquito [MEDICINE]

veer /vɪəʳ/ verb, i. *The bus veered from one side of the road to the other, as the driver tried to avoid a scooter.* = to change direction suddenly

vegan /vɪːgən/ noun, c. = a person who does not eat any kind of food that comes from an animal (e.g. meat, eggs, milk, cheese) (compare **vegetarian**)

vege•ta•ble[1] /ˈvedʒtəbəl/ noun, u. or c. **1** = some part of a plant (the fruit, root, leaf etc.) that is eaten as food **2** = a descriptive word for a person who, because of damage to the brain, limbs etc. cannot move and needs looking after for everything (informal)

vegetable[2] adj. *vegetable oil* = made from a plant **vegetarian** /vedʒɪˈteəriən/ noun, c. = a person who does not eat meat or fish **vegetate** /ˈvedʒɪteɪt/ verb, i. *He used to be very active but now he is just vegetating at home.* = to lead a dull and useless life, without any activity (like a vegetable) **vegetation** /vedʒɪˈteɪʃən/ noun *There is very little vegetation in a desert.* = plants in general **veggie** /vedʒɪ/ vegetable (informal)

vehe•ment /ˈvɪəmənt/ adj. *The Leader of the Opposition made a vehement attack on the government's policies.* = showing strong feelings, specially of anger (formal)

ve•hi•cle /ˈviːɪkəl/ noun, c. **1** = any kind of carriage that runs on wheels and can carry people or goods e.g. a bicycle, scooter or car **2** *Television is an excellent vehicle for educating people on the dangers of smoking.* = something that can be used to spread a message (figurative) **vehicular** /viːˈhɪkjʊləʳ/ adj. *vehicular traffic* = having to do with vehicles

veil /veɪl/ noun, c. = a covering of thin material used by a woman to hide her face

veiled adj. **1** *veiled criticism* = expressed indirectly, so as not to offend someone **2** *a veiled threat* = hidden or covered

a veil of secrecy/mystery *This story is shrouded in a veil of secrecy.* = something that does not allow the truth to be known fully

vein /veɪn/ noun, c. **1** = a blood vessel (tube through which blood flows inside the body) which carries blood from the heart to some part of the body (compare **artery**) **2** *A vein of gold runs through these rocks.* = a crack or line running through a rock, which contains a valuable metal such as gold **3** *The marble has greenish veins running through it.* = an irregular line of a different colour which runs through a rock **4** *All* *his books are written in a serious vein.* = mood or style

vel•cro /ˈvelkrəʊ/ noun = a kind of material, made from thin nylon threads which can stick to each other, used for fastening things (holding them together) (trademark)

veldt /velt/ noun, u. = a flat piece of land in South Africa covered with grass but without any trees

ve•loc•i•ty /vɪˈlɒsɪti/ *The car was moving at a high velocity.* = speed [PHYSICS]

vel•vet /ˈvelvɪt/ noun, u. = soft cotton or silk material with very short hair-like threads on the surface

vend /vend/ verb, t. *He made a lot of money by vending sweets.* = to sell (formal) **vendor** noun, c. = a person who sells something **vending machine** noun, c. = a machine from which one can get hot or cold drinks etc. by dropping a coin into the machine

ven•det•ta /venˈdetə/ noun, u. = a situation in which someone deliberately tries to harm another person or to take revenge for some harm that was done earlier

ve•neer[1] /vɪˈnɪəʳ/ noun, u. **1** *There is a veneer of teak wood over the surface of the table.* = a thin covering of wood or plastic on top of a wooden surface **2** *He has a cunning mind behind that veneer of politeness.* = an outer appearance which covers an unpleasant reality (figurative, derogatory)

veneer[2] verb, t. *The door has been veneered with plastic.* = to cover with a veneer

ve•ne•re•al /vɪˈnɪəriəl/ adj. *venereal disease* = diseases such as syphilis that are passed on from one person to another through sexual activity

ve•ne•tian (blind) /vəniːʃən/ noun = a blind (covering for a window) made of thin, flat pieces of wood or plastic fixed to strings which can be raised or lowered so as to allow light to enter

ven•geance /ˈvendʒəns/ noun, u. **1** = the act of punishing someone in return for some harm that he/she had done to you earlier (formal) (see **revenge**) **2** *We had no rain for the last six weeks and today it rained with a vengeance.* = with greater force than usual **vengeful** adj. *She seems to be in a vengeful mood today.* = showing a desire for vengeance

to do something with a vengence = with greater force or energy than usual

ven•om /ˈvenəm/ noun, u. **1** = the poison from a snake, scorpion etc. **2** *There is a lot of venom in the articles he writes.* = feelings of anger or hatred (figurative) **venomous** adj. **1** *a venomous snake* = containing or able to produce poison [TECHNICAL] **2** *a venomous article* = expressing anger or hatred

to draw somebody's venom = to make someone unable to harm you

venous /ˈviːnəs/ adj. *venous blood* = having to do with the veins in the body [BIOLOGY]

vent[1] /vent/ verb, t. *The manager shouted at Anil in the office, and Anil vent his anger by shouting at his friend when he went home.* = to give expression to a strong feeling of anger etc.

vent[2] noun, c. *an air vent* = a small opening through which air or smoke can pass

to give vent to something = to express a feeling strongly or openly

ven•ti•late /ˈventɪleɪt/ verb, t. *There are no windows in this room. We will have to construct at least one window in order to ventilate the room properly.* = to allow fresh air to come in **ventilation** /ventɪˈleɪʃən/ noun, u. *The ventilation in this room is excellent because there are many doors and windows.* = the flow of fresh air into a room **ventilator** noun, c. = an opening in a wall etc. that allows or helps ventilation

ven•tri•cle /ˈventrɪkəl/ noun, c. = a chamber (hollow space) in the heart into which blood flows from different parts of the body through the arteries [BIOLOGY]

ven•tril•o•qui•sm /venˈtrɪləkwɪzəm/ noun, u. = the art of speaking without moving one's lips, so that the sounds seem to come from somewhere else **ventriloquist** noun, c. = a person who entertains people through tricks of ventriloquism

ven•ture[1] /ˈventʃəʳ/ verb, t. *He did not venture to speak during the serious discussion.* = to have the courage to do or say something

venture[2] noun, c. *These two companies have started a joint venture to produce computer software.* = a course of action, especially in business, in which there is some risk (specially of losing money) **venture capital** noun = money which one borrows (usually from a bank) to start a business

to venture an opinion = to express an opinion with some hesitation

venue /venjuː/ noun, c. *the venue for the meeting* = a place where some event is organized (formal)

Ve•nus /ˈviːnəs/ noun **1** = the Roman goddess of love and beauty **2** = the planet nearest to the earth **venus fly-trap** noun = a kind of plant that traps and eats insects

ve•rac•i•ty /vəˈræsɪti/ noun, u. *The witness said that he had seen two people entering the house just before the murder. The police are now examining the veracity of this statement.* = truthfulness; the extent to which one can be believed (formal) [LAW]

verb /vɜːb/ noun *In the sentence 'The boys have been playing cricket', the verb is 'have been playing'.* = a word or group of words used to refer to an action or state (condition) [GRAMMAR]

V

verb•al /ˈvɜːbəl/ adj. **1** *He has excellent verbal skills.* = having to do with the use of language **2** *I have given you a verbal report now. Later, I will write it out.* = in spoken (not written) form **3** *a verbal noun* = having to do with a verb [GRAMMAR] **verbalize (verbalise)** verb, t. *He was not able to verbalize his feelings.* = to express oneself through words

ver•ba•tim /vɜːˈbeɪtɪm/ adj. *What did the man say about me? Can you give me a verbatim report?* = repeating the actual words used by someone

ver•bi•age /ˈvɜːbɪədʒ/ noun, u. *There is too much verbiage in this book. You will have to cut out most of it.* = the use of unnecessary words (derogatory)

ver•bose /vɜːˈbəʊz/ adj. *a verbose speech* = containing too many words

ver•dict /ˈvɜːdɪkt/ noun, c. **1** *The verdict given by the judge was that the accused is not guilty.* = the decision or judgement given by a judge at the end of a trial [LAW] **2** *Well, you have seen the film. What is your verdict?* = opinion

verge[1] /vɜːdʒ/ noun, u. *He was on the verge of tears after he lost his favourite cap.* = edge; a point or condition that is very near to something

verge[2] verb, i. *He used strong language verging on abuse.* = being or coming very close to something

ver•i•fy /ˈverɪfaɪ/ verb, t. *She says she has a First class M.A. degree. We will have to verify this statement from her certificates.* = to confirm (to make certain whether something is correct or true) **verification** /verɪfɪˈkeɪʃən/ noun, u. = the act of verifying something

ver•i•ta•ble /ˈverɪtəbəl/ adj. *He owns a huge house. It is so grand that it is a veritable palace.* = may be described as (used to add force to an expression) (formal)

ver•mi•cel•li /vɜːmɪˈseli/ noun = food made from wheat flour, in the shape of very thin threads, eaten in India as a kind of sweet but also popular in Italy

ver•mil•ion[1] /vəˈmɪljən/ noun, u. = a kind of powder of reddish-orange colour, used by as a sign of marriage by many Hindu women

vermilion[2] adj. *a vermilion sari* = having a reddish-brown colour (the colour of vermillion)

ver•min /ˈvɜːmɪn/ noun, u. (no plural form, but used with plural verbs) *The dog's fur is full of vermin.* = small insects that often suck the blood of animals and can cause disease

ver•nac•u•lar /vəˈnækjʊləʳ/ noun, u. or c. *Let's speak in the vernacular and not in English.*(u.) = the language spoken by the common people living in a region

ver•sa•tile /ˈvɜːsətaɪl/ adj. **1** *He is a versatile person. He can cook; he can play the sitar and he is also an excellent painter.* = having many different skills (referring to a person) **2** *Nylon is a versatile material. It can be used to make clothing as well as small parts for motor cars.* = having many different uses (referring to a material)

verse /vɜːs/ noun, u. or c. **1** *Shakespeare's plays are written in verse.*(u.) = poetry (language written or printed in the form of poetry and having the musical quality that one expects in poetry) **2** *Can you read out the last verse of this poem?*(c.) = a part of a poem, usually consisting of two or four lines **versification** /vɜːsɪfɪˈkeɪʃən/ noun, u. **1** = the arrangement of lines in a poem **2** = the art of writing poetry

to quote chapter and verse = to know all the details of some rule or law

versed /vɜːst/ adj. *A professor is expected to be well versed in her subject.* = having deep knowledge of something

ver•sion /ˈvɜːʃən/ noun, c. **1** *I've read 'David Copperfield' but not seen the film version.* = a form or copy of a book which is generally a little different from the original work **2** *Anil tells me that you shouted at him for no reason at all. Now I want to hear your version of what happened.* = one person's account of an event, as compared to another person's account of the same event

ver•sus /ˈvɜːsəs/ prep. *The India versus West Indies match will be played tomorrow in Chennai.* = against (abbr. as **vs.** or **v.**)

ver•te•bra /ˈvɜːtɪbrə/ noun, c. (**vertebrae**) = one of the bones forming the backbone or spine (the long chain of bones which runs down the middle of the back) **vertebrate** noun, c. *A bird is a vertebrate, but an insect is not.* = an animal which possesses a backbone (opposite **invertebrate**) [BIOLOGY]

ver•tex /ˈvɜːteks/ noun, c. (**vertices**) *the vertex of a triangle* = the angle lying opposite to the base of a triangle or pyramid [GEOMETRY]

ver•ti•cal /ˈvɜːtɪkəl/ adj. *The flag-post should be perfectly vertical.* = making an angle of 90 degrees with the ground [GEOMETRY]

ver•ti•go /ˈvɜːtɪgəʊ/ noun = a medical condition which causes a feeling of unsteadiness and loss of balance especially when one looks down from a height [MEDICINE]

verve /vɜːv/ noun, u. *He sings beautifully, with a lot of verve in his singing.*= the expression of energy and enjoyment in doing something

ve•ry[1] /ˈveri/ adv. *He is a very honest person.* = to a great degree (used to add force to an expression)

very[2] adj. *This is the very tree under which the Buddha meditated, 5,000 years ago.* = exact (used to add force to an expression)

the very thing *This report is the very thing I need to prove my case.* = the right thing needed for some purpose **The very idea!** *How could you imagine that I would harm you? The very idea!* = an expression suggesting shock at something

ves•sel /'vesəl/ noun, c. **1** = ship **2** = a pot used to hold some liquid **3** *a blood vessel* = a tube through which blood or some other liquid flows

vest[1] /vest/ noun, c. **1** = an undergarment, worn under a shirt **2** = a waistcoat (short coat without sleeves, worn under a jacket)

vest[2] verb, t. *The people have vested parliament with the power to make new laws.* = to give some right or power to someone [LAW] **vested interest** noun *She has a vested interest in not allowing her children to watch television, because then they will develop a love for reading.* = a personal reason for doing or not doing something because of the benefit one hopes to get

ves•ti•bule /'vestɪbju:l/ noun, c. *The coaches on this train are connected by vestibules.*= a corridor or passage through which one can walk from one part of a building or train to another part

ves•tige /'vestɪdʒ/ noun, c. *A powerful king once ruled over this part of India. But today you do not find even a vestige of his kingdom.* = sign or trace; a small part which remains behind when something is gone

vet[1] /vet/ noun, c. = short form of **veterinarian** (a doctor who treats the diseases of animals) (informal)

vet[2] verb, t. **(vetted)** *We will have to vet these reports carefully before we can send them on to the Director.* = to examine carefully or to correct and improve something (informal)

vet•e•ran[1] /'vetərən/ noun,c. *He is a veteran of the war of 1962.* = an old person with a lot of past experience, specially of fighting in the army

veteran[2] adj. *She is a veteran writer. She has written more than 50 books.* = having a great deal of experience

vet•e•ri•na•ry /'vetərɪnəri/ adj. *a veterinary hospital* = having to do with the care and treatment of animals **veterinarian** /vetərɪ'neəriən/ noun, c. = a doctor who treats animals (see **vet**[1])

ve•to[1] /'vi:təʊ/ verb, t. **(vetoed)** *In 1956, England and France wanted to attack Egypt but America vetoed this proposal.* = to prevent some action by refusing permission

veto[2] noun, u. or c. *the power of veto // exercise one's veto* = the power given to someone to refuse permission for some action or to turn down a proposal made by someone

vex /veks/ verb, t. *Don't vex the customer by constantly asking if she would like to buy something.* = to annoy (displease) or trouble someone (old-fashioned) **vexation** noun

VHF abbr. of **Very High Frequency** = a measure of the frequency (speed) at which radio waves travel through the air

vi•a /'vaɪə/ prep. (Latin) *We will go to New York via London.* = through; by way of

vi•a•ble /'vaɪəbəl/ adj. *An engineer has sent us a plan for cleaning up the river, but we do not think it is a viable plan.* = possible; something that can be carried out successfully

vi•a•duct /'vaɪədʌkt/ noun, c. = a long, high bridge built to carry a road or railway across a valley

vi•al /'vaɪəl/ noun, c. = a small bottle used as a container for medicine

vibes see under **vibrate** (below)

vi•brate /vaɪ'breɪt/ verb, i. or t. *The loud sound of the drums made the glass window vibrate.*(i.) = to cause something to shake continuously, producing a sound **vibration** noun, u. or c. *Can you feel the vibration in the glass windows?* = the action or effect of vibrating **vibes** noun, u. (always plural) *There are excellent vibes between the manager and myself.* = a feeling of friendship or a good relationship between two or more people that is often not expressed in words (informal; short form of **vibrations**) **vibrant** adj. *Malaysia has a vibrant economy, which is growing at 10 per cent every year.* = active and full of life

vic•ar /'vɪkə^r/ noun, c.= a Christian priest who is in charge of an area

vi•car•i•ous /vɪ'keəriəs/ adj. *He is too old to dance, but he gets vicarious pleasure by watching other people dance.* = indirect; something that one experiences or feels through others

vice /vaɪs/ noun, c. **1** *the vice of smoking* = a fault in one's character or a bad habit that one has **2** = a tool with metal jaws that can be tightened, used to hold something firmly in place

vice- prefix meaning 'in place of' e.g. **vice-captain** noun, c. = a senior member of a team who takes the place of the captain when the captain is not playing

vice-chancellor noun,c. = the person in charge of a university, who is supposed to be acting in place of the Chancellor (usually the Governor of the state, in India) **vice-president** noun, c. = a person who is next in importance or position to the president **viceroy** noun, c. *the Viceroy of India* = a person who rules a country in place of the king or queen

vice versa /vaɪs 'vɜ:sə/ adv. (Latin) *Remember the saying 'God is Truth, and vice versa.'* = the opposite is also true (i.e. 'Truth is God'.)

vi•cin•i•ty /vɪ'sɪnɪti/ noun, u. *I can't get any books here as there are no bookshops in the vicinity.* =

V

neighbourhood (the area surrounding a place) (formal)

vi•cious /ˈvɪʃəs/ adj. *He is a vicious criminal who has committed many murders.* = dangerous and violent **vicious circle** noun *When people do not have education, they cannot find jobs; and when they do not have jobs, they cannot send their children to school. In this way, a vicious circle is formed.* = a chain of undesirable events, in which one event leads to another, which leads back to the first, and the whole process is repeated

vi•cis•si•tudes /vɪˈsɪsɪtjuːdz/ noun, c. (plural form only) *Our state has gone through a number of vicissitudes recently; first, the cyclone and now the floods.* = events that cause suffering; misfortunes (formal, literary)

vic•tim /ˈvɪktɪm/ noun, c. *Many innocent people were killed in the bomb attack. Some of the victims have not been identified.* = a person who suffers harm or damage as a result of some action done by someone or some natural event **victimize (victimise)** verb, t. *She says she is being victimized because she is not afraid to express her opinions freely.* = to cause someone to suffer unfairly

vic•to•ry /ˈvɪktəri/ noun, u. or c. (**victories**) *India defeated the New Zealand team by 250 runs.We did not expect this victory.* = the act of winning in a war or competition **victor** noun, c. = a person who has won in a war or competition **victorious** /vɪkˈtɔːrɪəs/ adj. *the victorious Australian team* = which has won a victory

Vic•to•ri•an /vɪkˈtɔːriən/ adj. *a Victorian poet* = belonging to the time when Queen Victoria reigned in England (1837-1901)

vid•e•o /ˈvɪdiəʊ/ noun, c. or adj. **1** = moving pictures with sound which have been recorded on videotape (noun) **2** *video recording*(adj.) = having both pictures and sound **video disc** noun = a round piece of metal covered with plastic, on which pictures and sounds have been recorded and can be played back (see **VCD**) **video tape** noun = a narrow, flat piece of plastic on which video recording has been done

vie /vaɪ/ verb, i. (**vied, vying**) *Pakistan and Australia are vying for the championship in the World Cup.* = to compete (formal)

view[1] /vjuː/ noun, u. or c. **1** *The car was moving so fast that it disappeared from view in a few seconds.*(u.) = sight (the ability to be seen) **2** *You can get an excellent view of the Taj Mahal from this room.*(c.) = something seen from a particular place **3** *In my view, this plan will not work. // Your views on religion are different from mine.*(c.) = opinion or belief

view[2] verb, t. **1** *You can view the Taj Mahal from this room.* = to look at **2** *The Chairperson views your remarks as being offensive.* = to think of something in a particular way (formal) **point of view** = how one thinks about something; opinion **view-finder** noun = a small window in a camera through which one can get a picture of the person or object whose photograph is being taken **viewpoint** *We should try to look at this textbook from the student's viewpoint.* = the way in which a particular person thinks about a matter **to take a dim view of something** = to have a poor opinion of something **in full view of** *They took out their gold jewellery in full view of all the people present.* = being watched or seen clearly by everyone (used of something that is not normally done in public) **on view** *Anjolie Ela Menon's recent paintings are on view at the Taj Gallery.* = displayed, arranged (used in the context of an exhibition) **in view of** *In view of your long years of service, we wish to give you this award.* = because of or recognising something (formal) **with something in view** *I designed this door with safety in view.* = as the main aim (formal)

vig•il /ˈvɪdʒɪl/ noun, u. or c. *My mother was very ill last week, so I kept a vigil by her bedside all night.* = an act of staying awake and keeping watch over someone or something (literary) **vigilance** noun, u. **1** *No thieves can enter this building, thanks to the vigilance of the guards.*= the quality of being careful in keeping watch over or guarding someone or something (formal) **2** = the department of the government which keeps watch over the actions of government officials and tries to check corruption [TECHNICAL] **vigilant** adj. *The guards have been told to remain vigilant as theft is very common in this area.* = always watchful or prepared for danger

vi•gnette /vɪˈnjet/ noun, c = a short, well-written description of a person or scene (literary)

vi•gour /ˈvɪgə[r]/ noun, u. *Although he is old, he still has a lot of vigour.* = energy or strength **vigorous** adj. *vigorous exercise* = showing or requiring a lot of vigour (energy and strength)

Vi•king /ˈvaɪkɪŋ/ noun = a person belonging to one of the tribes living in Scandinavia (Denmark, Sweden and Norway) about 1,200 years ago, who sailed across the seas in wooden ships and often attacked and plundered other people

vile /vaɪl/ adj. **1** *Why do you want to harm them by spreading vile rumours about them?* = evil and unpleasant **2** *She has a vile temper.* = very bad

vil•i•fy /ˈvɪlɪfaɪ/ *The newspapers have vilified him, although he is an honest person.* = to give someone a bad name

vil•la /ˈvɪlə/ noun, c. **1** = a large house in a place which one goes to for a holiday **2** = a large old-style house with a garden

vil•lage /ˈvɪlɪdʒ/ noun, c. **1** = a group of houses in a place away from a city or town **2** *The entire village celebrated the festival.* = the people of a village (meaning **1**)

vil•lain /ˈvɪlən/ noun, c. = an evil person or a bad character in a film or drama

vim /vɪm/ noun, u. *She acted in her last film with a lot of vim and vigour.* = energy

vin•di•cate /ˈvɪndɪkeɪt/ verb, t. *I always believed that Yuvraj Singh would become a great player and now he has scored a century. My faith in him has been vindicated.*= to prove that something is true or correct

vin•dic•tive /vɪnˈdɪktɪv/ adj. *a vindictive nature* = unwilling to forgive someone for some harm that may have been done in the past (derogatory)

vine /vaɪn/ noun,c. = a climbing plant, specially one that produces grapes **vineyard** /ˈvɪnjəd/ noun, c. = a garden or farm in which grapes are grown to produce wine

vin•e•gar /ˈvɪnɪgəʳ/ noun, u. = a liquid with a sour taste, often made from wine, used to add taste to food

vin•tage /ˈvɪntɪdʒ/ adj. *This is a vintage Satyajit Ray film.* = of the highest quality, which is usually found in the work of the person named **a vintage car** noun = an old car having a famous name, which is treated with a lot of respect by car lovers

vi•nyl /ˈvaɪnɪl/ noun, u. = a kind of plastic material used for making floors etc. [CHEMISTRY]

vi•o•late /ˈvaɪəleɪt/ verb, t. *The police will arrest you if you violate the laws of the country. // He had agreed to pay me half the amount last month but he violated the agreement.* = to break (go against) a law or an agreement

vi•o•lence /ˈvaɪələns/ noun, u. *When the crowd started burning buses, the police had to open fire in order to control the violence.* = the use of physical force leading to damage, injury etc. **violent** adj. *The violent crowd burnt a number of cars.* = acting with great physical force leading to damage etc.

vi•o•let[1] /ˈvaɪəlɪt/ noun = a kind of small flower having a dark purple colour

violet[2] adj. *a violet dress* = having a dark purple colour

vi•o•lin /vaɪəˈlɪn/ noun = a musical instrument with a number of strings, played by drawing a bow across the strings

VIP abbr. of **Very Important Person** (a person in a high position who has to be given special treatment)

vi•per /ˈvaɪpəʳ/ noun, c. = a kind of poisonous snake with a broad v-shaped head

vi•ra•go /vɪˈrɑːgəʊ/ noun, c. = an insulting word for a woman with a very bad temper who is feared or disliked by everyone (derogatory) (originally a word for a woman who is wise and brave) Ⓖ

vi•ral /ˈvaɪərəl/ adj. see **virus**

vir•gin[1] /ˈvɜːdʒɪn/ noun, c. = a person who has never had sex

virgin[2] adj. **1** *virgin land/forest* = something that has not been used or spoilt by human beings and has remained in a natural condition **2** *With this new way of printing books cheaply, we are on virgin territory.* = (of an idea, plan etc.) not tried out or known before

Vir•go /ˈvɜːgəʊ/ noun = one of the signs of the zodiac, represented by a virgin (see pic under **zodiac**)

vi•rile /ˈvɪraɪl/ adj. = strong and active, specially in matters of sex (referring to a man) **virility** /vɪˈrɪlɪti/ noun,u. = the quality of being strong and active, specially in sex

vir•tu•al /ˈvɜːtʃuəl/ adj. **1** *The company is in a state of virtual closure.* = in effect, though not officially or legally **2** *a virtual image seen in a mirror* = something that is not real [PHYSICS] **virtual reality** noun = pictures created by computers that seem completely real **virtually** adv. *He is virtually the owner of this building, although it belongs to his sister.* = for all practical purposes, though not legally or officially

vir•tue /ˈvɜːtʃuː/ noun, c. **1** *Honesty is his greatest virtue.* = a good quality in a person's character **2** *His plan has the virtue of being simple.* = something that offers an advantage **virtuous** adj. *a virtuous person* = having many virtues (good qualities)

to make a virtue of something *He is poor, but he makes a virtue of poverty.* = to turn something which should be a disadvantage into an advantage

vir•tu•o•so[1] /vɜːtʃuˈəʊsəʊ/ noun, c. *Pandit Ravi Shankar is a famous sitar virtuoso.* = a person with very great skill in some form of art, specially music

virtuoso[2] adj. *He gave a virtuoso performance.* = showing very great skill **virtuosity** noun, u. = the skill or ability that a virtuoso has

vir•u•lent /ˈvɪrʊlənt/ adj. **1** *Cholera is a virulent disease.* = dangerous or harmful **2** *She wrote a virulent article attacking the organization.* = full of anger or hatred **virulence** adj. = the quality of being virulent

vi•rus /ˈvaɪərəs/ noun, c. **1** *AIDS is caused by a virus.* = a very tiny living substance that can cause diseases [BIOLOGY] **2** *My computer has picked up a virus.* = a set of instructions for a computer, which someone has created mischievously, which can prevent it from working [COMPUTERS] **viral** adj. *viral fever* = caused by a virus

vi•sa /ˈviːzə/ noun, c. *You will need a visa to go to Japan.* = permission to enter a foreign country, which is shown on a person's passport

vis-à-vis /viːzɑːˈviː/ prep. (Latin) *I want to know what you have decided, vis-à-vis the discussion we had last week.* = with reference to; in connection with (formal)

V

vis•ce•ra /'vɪsərə/ noun, u. = the main organs (inner parts of the body) such as the heart, lungs, stomach, intestines etc. [MEDICINE/LAW]

vis•count /'vaɪkaʊnt/ noun = a title sometimes given to a British nobleman (a person belonging to a rich or important family)

vis•cous /'vɪskəs/ adj. *When the flood was over, the banks of the river were covered with viscous mud.* = thick and sticky (referring usually to a thick liquid) [TECHNICAL]

visible /'vɪzibəl/ adj. *The moon is sometimes visible during the day.* = can be seen **visibility** /vɪzɪ'bɪlɪti/ noun, u. = the quality of being visible

vi•sion /'vɪʒən/ noun, u. **1** *You need excellent vision to become a pilot.* = the ability to see **2** *Jawaharlal Nehru was a leader with vision.* = the ability to look ahead and plan for the future (see **visionary**) **3** *Nehru had a vision of a great and prosperous India.* = an idea or a picture in the mind **4** *God appeared to him in a vision.* = a dream or a religious experience **20-20 vision** = perfect eyesight [TECHNICAL] **visionary** /'vɪʒənərɪ/ noun, c. **1** = a person who can think or plan ahead and has a clear idea of what the future will be like **2** = a person who has ideas but is not practical

vis•it[1] /'vɪzɪt/ verb, t. *I visit my brother's house once a week.* = to go to a place to spend some time or to meet someone

visit[2] noun, c. *I have come here on a visit.* = the act of visiting a place, usually for a short time **visiting card** noun,c. = a small card with one's name, address etc. printed on it, which one gives to people one meets (also **business card**) **visiting hours** noun = the time during which one is allowed to go to a hosital in order to see a person who is there for medical reasons **visitor** noun, c. = a person who is visiting a place **visitor's book** noun, c. = a book in which important visitors (people visiting a place) are asked to write their opinions on the place they are visiting

to pay someone a visit = to go somewhere in order to meet someone (formal) **a flying visit** = a very short visit (informal)

vi•sor /'vaɪzə[r]/ noun, c. = a part of a helmet which can be lowered or raised to protect the face

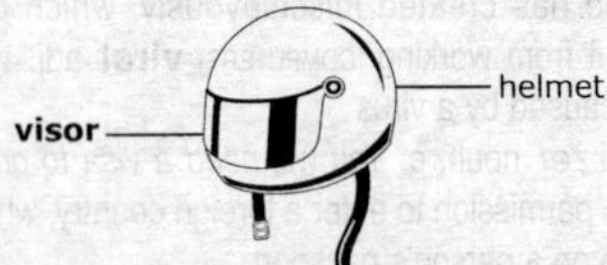

vis•ta /'vɪstə/ noun, c. *As you drive up to this building, you can see a wonderful vista of tall trees.* = an attractive view of something seen from a distance, usually through a line of trees on each side

vi•su•al /'vɪʒuəl/ adj. *This lovely rose garden is a visual delight.* = something that is meant to be seen **visual aid** noun = something (e.g. a picture, map, photograph etc.) that can be shown to a person to help him/her learn something **visual arts** noun = painting, sculpture etc. through which one can create objects that can be seen **visualize (visualise)** verb, t. *I cannot visualize from this drawing what the new building will look like when it is complete.* = to imagine or form a picture of something in the mind **visually impaired** adj. = someone who is unable to see (an expression that is often used in place of 'blind')

vi•tal /'vaɪtl/ adj. *Your support is vital for my victory in the election.* = very necessary or important **vitality** /vaɪ'tælɪti/ noun, c. *He is old, but he still has a lot of vitality.* = energy or spirit **vital statistics** noun = the measurements of the body of a woman around her chest, waist and hips (often used to draw attention to a woman's physical beauty) (generally humourous)

vi•ta•min /'vɪtəmɪn/ noun, c. or u. *Milk contains many important vitamins.* = a chemical substance which is very important for health and is present in small quantities in different foods

vi•va•cious /vɪ'veɪʃəs/ adj. *She has such a vivacious nature that anyone who meets her is charmed.* = full of life and high spirits

viv•a voc•e /vaɪvə 'vəʊsi/ noun, u. or adj. *a viva-voce test* = an oral (spoken) examination or test (sometimes abbreviated to **viva**)

viv•id /'vɪvɪd/ adj. *The book presents such a vivid picture of life in a small American town that you can imagine you are actually living there.* = very clear; leaving a strong impression (effect) on the mind

viz. abbr. of **videlicet** *The entire town depends on only one profession, viz., carpet weaving.* = namely (that is to say) (also **i.e.**)

vo•cab•u•la•ry /və'kæbjʊləri/ noun, u. *A high-school student is expected to have a vocabulary of at least 4,000 words of English.*(u.) = the stock of words (in a language) which a person knows and can use [TECHNICAL]

vo•cal /'vəʊkəl/ adj. **1** *vocal organs* = connected with the voice or with speech **2** *Students are very vocal in today's world. They are not afraid to speak out.* = willing or able to express oneself freely, specially in speech **vocal cords** noun, c. = thin pieces of muscle inside the throat, with the help of which we are able to produce the sounds we use while speaking **vocalist** noun, c. = a musician who sings, often as part of a band (together with musical instruments) **vocal music** noun = music produced by the human voice (and not instruments)

vo•ca•tion /vəʊ'keɪʃən/ noun, c. **1** *He is being trained for a vocation.*(c.) = a job for which one requires some special skill **2** *She will make a good teacher because she has a vocation for teaching.* = a particular ability that one has for a certain kind of work **vocational** adj. *vocational education* = having to do with some job **vocational training** noun = training which prepares someone for a particular job

vo•cif•er•ous /və'sɪfərəs/ adj. *a vociferous crowd* = noisy (making a lot of noise)

vod•ka /'vɒdkə/ noun = a strong, colourless alcoholic drink, made originally in Russia

vogue /vəʊg/ noun, u. *The latest vogue in western countries is transcendental meditation.* = a fashion which lasts for a short time

to be in vogue = to be popular or in fashion

voice[1] /vɔɪs/ noun, c. **1** *This singer has a sweet voice.* = the sounds that one makes in speaking or singing **2** *He does not have much of a voice in the running of this school.* = the ability to express an opinion or influence other people **3** *'The policeman arrested the thief' is in the active voice while 'The thief was arrested' is in the passive voice.* = the form of the verb (in a sentence) which tells us whether the subject of the sentence is the doer of an action (active voice) or the person or thing on which some action is done (passive voice) [GRAMMAR]

voice[2] verb, t. *He has voiced the feelings of all of us about this school.* = to express in words **voice box** noun, c. = the larynx (hollow box inside the throat which contains the vocal cords) **voice mail** noun = a system used to record spoken messages when someone is not there to answer the telephone **voiceless** adj. *'p', 't' and 'k' are voiceless consonants.* = a speech sound produced without any vibration (movement) of the vocal cords [TECHNICAL] **voiceover** noun = the voice of an unseen person in a film or television programme, who describes what is happening, speaking directly to the audience [TECHNICAL] **voice print** noun = a recording of a person's voice which can be used to recognize who that person is

to have a voice = to have the power or right to express one's opinion **to give voice to something (to voice something)** = to express an opinion or feeling openly **to speak in one voice** = to express an opinion which everyone shares **a dissenting voice** = a person whose opinion is different from that of others

void[1] /vɔɪd/ adj. **1** *The new book he has written is void of interest.* = empty; lacking in some quality (formal) **2** *The agreement that we had signed is now void.* = without any legal force [LAW]

void[2] noun, u. **1** *The death of the Prime Minister has created a void.* = a feeling of emptiness **2** *The sun's rays travel through a void before reaching the earth.* = empty space

void[3] verb, t. *The patient is unable to void his bladder.* = to make something empty by getting rid of something that is not wanted [TECHNICAL]

voile /vɔɪl/ noun, u. = very thin material for a dress, made out of cotton or silk

vol•a•tile /'vɒlətaɪl/ adj. **1** *Alcohol is a volatile liquid.* = a liquid that easily changes into a gas **2** *He has a volatile temper.* = quick to turn into anger

vol•ca•no /vɒl'keɪnəʊ/ noun, c. (**volcanoes** or **volcanos**) = a mountain that has an opening at the top, through which lava (hot, liquid rock) is sometimes poured out with great force **volcanic** adj. *volcanic rocks* = having to do with a volcano

vo•li•tion /və'lɪʃən/ noun, u. *No one forced her to come here; she came of her own volition.* = free will (the right or power that one has to decide on some course of action) (formal)

vol•ley[1] /'vɒli/ noun,c. **1** *The soldiers fired a volley into the air as a mark of respect to the officer who had died.* = a number of shots fired at the same time **2** *The tennis player hit a powerful volley into the opponent's court.* = the act of hitting or kicking a ball before it has touched the ground, in the game of tennis or football

volley[2] verb, i. **1** *The guns volleyed out together.* = (of firearms) to fire at the same time **2** *The centre-forward volleyed the ball into the net.* = to hit or kick a ball before it has touched the ground (in tennis or football) **volley ball** noun = a game in which two teams of players have to hit a ball with their hands across a net without allowing it to touch the ground

volt /vəʊlt/ noun = a unit used to measure the strength of an electrical current **voltage** noun, u. = the strength of an electrical current measured in volts

volte face /vɒlt 'fæs/ noun *My brother told everyone he was going to take music lessons. Then he suddenly did a volte face and declared that music was a waste of time.* = to do something completely opposite to what one had said or done before (see also **U-turn**)

vol•u•ble /'vɒljʊbəl/ adj. *He is a voluble person. Once he starts talking, it is difficult to make him shut up.* = very fond of talking at length (formal) (disapproving)

vol•ume /'vɒlju:m/ noun, u. or c. **1** *The volume of a box 3 metres long, 2 metres wide and 2 metres deep is 12 cubic metres.*(u.) = the amount of space that a solid object occupies, calculated by multiplying its length by its width and then by its height or depth **2** *Can you please turn down the volume of the sound from the radio? It is too loud.*(u.) = the degree of

V

loudness of a sound **3** (c.) = a large book, or one out of a set of books **voluminous** /vəjuːmɪnəs/ adj. *a voluminous trunk* = having a lot of space inside

vol•un•ta•ry /ˈvɒləntəri/ adj. *An army officer usually retires at the age of 50, but he is taking voluntary retirement at 45.* = done out of one's own choice and not because of some rule or pressure

vol•un•teer[1] /vɒlənˈtɪəʳ/ noun, c. *Milk is being distributed to sick children by volunteers.* = a person who chooses or offers to do something without expecting any payment

volunteer[2] verb, t. *He volunteered to help in the setting up of the school library.* = to offer to do something without payment

vo•lup•tu•ous /vəˈlʌptʃuəs/ adj. *a voluptuous figure* = attractive in a sexual manner

vom•it[1] /ˈvɒmɪt/ verb, i. = to throw up, through the mouth, food that one has eaten

vomit[2] noun, u. *His clothes were covered with vomit.*= food that has been vomitted (thrown up)

vo•ra•cious /vəˈreɪʃəs/ adj. **1** *a voracious eater* = having a large appetite for food **2** *a voracious reader* = very keen or eager

vor•tex /ˈvɔːteks/ noun, c. (**vortexes** or **vertices**) = the centre of a whirlwind or whirlpool (a column of air or water, moving round and round at great speed), where there is usually little movement

vo•ta•ry /ˈvəʊtəri/ noun, c. (**votaries**) **1** *He is a votary of the Buddha.* = a person who regularly worships a god or goddess **2** *a votary of music* = a person who is very fond of some form of art (literature, music etc.)

vote[1] /vəʊt/ verb, i. or t. *I make it a point to vote in the election.* = to show one's choice or preference for someone or something through some action such as raising one's hand or marking a piece of paper

vote[2] noun, u. or c. **1** *How many of us think we should go to Mahabalipuram for our picnic? Let us take a vote.*= the act of choosing or showing one's preference **2** *I have cast my vote in favour of the candidate from Bidar.* = the choice or preference shown by a particular person **3** *Many votes were cancelled because the voters did not put any marks on the ballot papers.* = the piece of paper on which a choice is expressed **voter** noun, c. = a person who takes part in voting or has the right to vote

to cast one's vote = a vote given by a person in charge of a meeting, which is used to reach a decision when the number of votes on each side is equal **vote of no-confidence** = a vote taken (in a parliament etc.) to show that most people do not support the party or person in power (opposite **vote of confidence**) **vote of thanks** = a short formal speech made at the end of a meeting to thank various people for their help etc. **voting booth** = a closed space where one can vote in secrecy (so that no one can see who you have voted for) **voting machine** = an electronic machine which can count up the number of votes which each person has received

vouch /vaʊtʃ/ verb, i. *He is an honest worker. I can vouch for his honesty.* = to guarantee something (to declare that one is certain of something) **voucher** noun, c. = a receipt given to prove that money has been paid for something

vow[1] /vaʊ/ verb, t. *I have vowed to serve my country faithfully.* = to make a serious promise

vow[2] noun, c. *He had made a vow that he would not visit the football field for a month if he lost this match.* = the act of making a promise, especially to God

to keep (fulfill) a vow = to do something that one has vowed (promised) to do (opposite **to break a vow**)

vo•wel /ˈvaʊəl/ noun, c. *The vowel in the word 'can' is different from the vowel in the word 'jaw', although it is represented by the same letter, 'a'.* = a sound used in human speech which is produced without blocking the flow of air through the mouth or throat

voy•age[1] /ˈvɔɪ-ɪdʒ/ noun, c. *I am going on a voyage to the North Pole.* = a long journey made by boat or ship

voyage[2] verb, i. *Some European sailors had voyaged to America long before Columbus went there.* = to go on a voyage (formal)

vul•can•ize (vulcanise) /ˈvʌlkənaɪz/ verb, t. *The tube inside the front tyre of my car has a big puncture. I will have to vulcanize it.* = to seal up (close) a hole in a piece of rubber by using some chemicals and heating it

vul•gar /ˈvʌlgəʳ/ adj. **1** *Don't use vulgar language.* = rude or offensive (derogatory) **2** *The bright colours he has used to paint his house look rather vulgar.* = not in good taste **vulgar fraction** noun, c. *7/8 is a vulgar fraction.* = a number smaller than 1, in which the denominator (the number below the line) is greater than the numerator (number above the line) **vulgarize (vulgarise)** verb,t. *This film is based on a story by Premchand, but the story has been vulgarized in the film.* = to spoil the quality of something

vul•ne•ra•ble /ˈvʌlnərəbəl/ adj. *The captain of the team is in a vulnerable position. Anyone can criticize him.* = weak; open to attack

vul•ture /ˈvʌltʃəʳ/ noun, c. = a large, heavy bird which feeds on dead animals or human beings (see pic under **bird**)

vul•va /ˈvʌlvə/ noun = the opening of the female sex organ [MEDICINE]

wW

w, W /ˈdʌbəljuː/ the twenty-third letter of the English alphabet; abbr. of **watt,** a unit that measures electrical energy

wack•y /ˈwæki/ adj. *He's such a wacky person that one never knows what he will do next.* = slightly mad (informal, American English)

wad /wɒd/ noun, c. **1** *wad of 100-rupee notes* = a thick bundle of paper etc. tied together **2** *He stuffed a wad of cotton into his ears.* = a mass of some soft material such as cotton

wad•dle /ˈwɒdl/ verb, i. *The ducks waddled across the field on their way to the pond.* = to walk in an awkward manner, with slow, short steps

wade /weɪd/ verb, i. *As the water in the stream was only about three feet deep, we were able to wade across.* = to walk through water which is not very deep

wa•fer /ˈweɪfəʳ/ noun, c. = a very thin biscuit or a thin slice of fried potato

waf•fle[1] /ˈwɒfəl/ noun, c. = a kind of sweet pancake

waffle[2] verb, i. *Say what you have to say in a few words, don't waffle.* = to talk or write at great length without much meaning (informal, disapproving)

waft /wɑːft/ verb, t. *The wind wafted the sheet of paper across the room.* = to carry something light across an open space (referring to something that can be carried by the wind)

wag[1] /wæg/ verb, t. (**wagged**) *The dog wagged its tail when it saw the children.* = to shake or move quickly from side to side, often to show friendliness

wag[2] noun, c. **1** *The dog gave its tail a wag.* = the act of shaking or moving from side to side **2** *He is quite a wag and can keep people amused.* = a person who makes clever and humorous remarks (informal)

to wag one's finger at someone = to shake one's finger at someone as a sign of warning

wage[1] /weɪdʒ/ noun, c. (usually plural **wages**) = payment made for work calculated on the number of days, hours etc. that one works

wage[2] verb, t. *Napoleon waged war against Russia.* = to start and fight a war

wa•ger[1] /ˈweɪdʒəʳ/ verb, t. *I wager a hundred rupees that our train will be late!* = to make a bet

wager[2] noun, c. *He has made a wager.* = the act of making a bet

wa•gon /ˈwægən/ noun, c. **1** *a railway wagon* = a railway carriage used to carry goods **2** = a large covered cart, drawn by horses or bullocks (in former times)

wagon

waif /weɪf/ noun, c. *She found the little kitten crying by the roadside and brought it home. The poor waif had lost its mother.* = a word used to expresss pity for a homeless child or animal (informal)

wail[1] /weɪl/ verb, i. = to cry out or weep loudly

wail[2] noun, c. = the sound of loud weeping

waist /weɪst/ noun, c. **1** = the part of the body just below the chest and above the hips **2** *These trousers are very loose at the waist.* = the part of a garment (dress) that goes round the waist **waistcoat** /ˈweɪskəʊt/ noun, c. = a short coat without arms, worn under a man's jacket (coat) **waistline** noun *You should watch your waistline. It's not healthy to put on so much weight.* = the measurement of the body around the waist which shows whether a person is overweight

wait /weɪt/ verb, i. *The doctor will see you after ten minutes. Please wait.* = to stay in a place, doing nothing, until something happens **waiter** noun, c. = a person who serves food to customers at a restaurant **waiting list** noun,c. *You cannot get a reserved berth on this train as there is a long waiting list.* = a list of people who want or have asked for something but cannot get it at once **waiting room** noun, c. **1** = a room at a railway station in which people can wait for a train to arrive **2** = a room in which people can wait for their turn to see a doctor

to wait up *I'll be very late getting back tonight. Don't wait up for me.* = to stay awake at night waiting for someone to return etc. **to wait on someone** *You are old enough to cook and clean and not have someone wait on you.* = to serve someone and look after their needs **wait and watch** *We won't do anything now. We'll just wait and watch.* = to observe without doing anything **to lie in wait for someone** *The lion lay in wait behind the bush and pounced on the deer when it went past.* = to hide in a place with the purpose of harming or killing a person or an animal **to wait one's turn** = to not push ahead of others in a queue, crowd etc. and to wait patiently until one's turn comes **What are you waiting for?** *They've invited you to Ranikhet and even offered to take you round. What are you waiting for?* = a way of telling someone to act soon and not miss an opportunity

waive /weɪv/ verb, t. **1** *Usually, this college does not admit students below the age of 18 but we will*

W

waive that rule in your case. = to allow a rule not to be used **2** *He should have been made the next Principal as he was the seniormost teacher, but he has waived his claim to the Principal's post.* = to give up a right or a claim **waiver** noun, u. = the act of waiving (giving up) a right or claim

wake[1] /weɪk/ verb, t. (**woke, woken**) *He has been sleeping since 8.00 this morning. Please wake him up.* = to make someone stop sleeping

wake[2] noun, c. **1** *The ship moved quickly through the water, leaving a long wake.* = the track left by a moving ship in the water **2** *The storm continued for two whole days, leaving a great deal of destruction in its wake.* = the result or effect of some event **waken** verb, t. = to cause someone to wake up (formal) **wakeful** adj. **1** = lying in a state in which one is unable to sleep **2** *Be wakeful. Anything can happen.* = alert and prepared to act fast

walk[1] /wɔːk/ verb, i. or t. **1** *He usually walks to his office instead of taking a bus.*(i.) = to travel to a place on foot, moving at a natural speed **2** *He walked the streets all night.*(t.) = to move along a street etc. on foot **3** *I want you to walk the dogs.*(t.) = to take a horse or a dog out for exercise

walk[2] noun, c. or u. **1** *Let us go for a walk.*(c.) = a short journey on foot, taken for pleasure or exercise **2** *a graceful walk*(u.) = the movement of the body while walking **3** *The college is only a short walk from my house.*(u.) = a distance to be walked **4** *There are some lovely walks around this park.*(c.) = a place where one can walk **walk-in** adj. = *a walk-in interview* = an event that one can take part in without advance notice or permission **walk-out** noun *Some of the members of the opposition staged a walk-out.* = the action of leaving a meeting as a form of protest (to show that one does not agree with what is happening) **walk-over** noun, c. **1** *Our team won by an innings and 200 runs. The match was a walkover for us.* = a very easy victory, especially in a sporting contest **2** *The Mohun Bagan team was given a walkover as their opponents, East Bengal, did not turn up for the match.* = a victory given to a player or a team when the opponent is unable or unwilling to play

to walk away *You have to help me clear up. You can't just walk away!* = leave someone to do something on their own **to walk away with** *She walked away with all the prizes.* = to achieve something easily, in one's opinion (informal) **to walk (right) into it** *She didn't know about their quarrel and walked right into it.* = to get into trouble because of carelessness or not knowing about something (informal) **to walk off with** *Somebody walked off with my books.* = to take without permission (informal, not respectful) **to walk on air** = to be very happy **to walk out on someone** **1** = leave one's wife or husband without warning **2** *The main actor in the play walked out on us two days before we were due to perform.* = to let someone down by going away suddenly **Take a walk!** *You expect me to do your homework for you? Take a walk!* = a way of telling someone that you are not going to do what they expect you to do (informal, humorous or not respectful)

walk•ie-talk•ie /wɔːkɪˈtɔːkɪ/ noun, c. = a kind of telephone which uses radio waves and allows one to talk to someone from a distance

walk•man /wɔːkmən/ noun, c. = (trademark) a small tape-recorder which can be carried in the pocket and on which one can listen to music while walking

wall[1] /wɔːl/ noun, c. **1** = a line of bricks or stone built around a house or an open area to protect it **2** *The walls of her bedroom have been painted pink.*= one side of a building or room

wall[2] verb, t. *The owner of the house has walled up the entrance.*= to put up a wall in order to cover or close something **wallpaper** noun, c. = thick paper used to cover (to decorate) the walls of a room **wall-to-wall** *wall-to-wall carpeting* = stretching from one end of a room to the other

to have one's back to the wall = to be forced to fight and defend oneself as there is no means of avoiding a situation **to be driven up the wall** *This music is driving me up the wall.* = to be made very angry or upset by something (informal)

wal•la•by /ˈwɒləbi/ noun, c. (**wallabies**) = an animal found in Australia, which is like a kangaroo but smaller

wallet /ˈwɒlɪt/ noun, c. = a small foldable case in which money, cards etc. may be carried

wal•lop /ˈwɒləp/ verb, t. **1** = to hit hard **2** *The Australian team walloped the Indian side.* = to defeat badly (informal)

wal•low /ˈwɒləʊ/ verb, i. **1** *Buffaloes like to wallow in mud.* = to roll or lie happily **2** *He loves to wallow in self-pity.* = to find pleasure in some emotion (derogatory)

wal•nut /ˈwɔːlnʌt/ noun = a kind of nut (fruit covered by a hard shell) which is commonly grown in Kashmir

wal•rus /ˈwɔːlrəs/ noun, c. = a large animal that lives in the sea and has two long pointed tusks (teeth)

waltz[1] /wɔːls/ noun = a kind of dance popular in western countries, in which a man and a woman dance slowly together to the sound of a special kind of music

waltz[2] verb, t. or i. = to take part in a waltz

wand /wɒnd/ noun, c. *a magician's wand* = a thin stick carried by a magician (a person who performs magic tricks), which is supposed to have magical powers

wan•der /ˈwɒndəʳ/ verb, i. **1** *He lost his way and wandered through the forest for many days before he* *reached a town.* = to walk aimlessly **2** *He was supposed to speak on football, but he wandered away from the topic and spoke about films.* = to move away from a topic or subject **wanderlust** /ˈwɒndəlʌst/ noun, u. (German) *His wanderlust has taken him to many distant lands.* = love of travelling (literary)

wane /weɪn/ verb, i. *He was famous as a poet 50 years ago, but his reputation is waning.* = to become less

wan•gle /ˈwæŋgəl/ verb, t. *I wanted to meet the famous sportsman who was coming to the party, so I managed to wangle an invitation.* = to get something that one wants through cleverness or through a trick (informal)

want[1] /wɒnt/ verb, t. **1** *I am thirsty and I want a glass of water.* = to have a need or strong desire for something **2** *The Principal wants you.* = to express a desire to meet someone who is usually junior **3** *He is wanted by the police.* = to have one's name on a list of criminals whom the police is trying to arrest **4** *The people of this village are wanting in the spirit of adventure.* = to lack something

want[2] noun, u. or c. **1** *I have to take care of my family"s wants.*(c.) = the things that one needs or wishes to have **2** *He lives in great want.*(u.) = lack of the things that one needs; poverty **wanted** adj. **1** *The criminal was on the police 'wanted' list.* = a person who is being searched for by the police **2** *I found my assistant through the 'wanted' advertisment placed in the newspaper.* = the title of an advertisment in a newspaper or magazine placed by a person who is looking for or wants something

to be (found) wanting *As a nurse we found her wanting in patience.* = to not fulfil expectations **for want of anything better (to do)** *For want of anything better to do, we watched television.* = because one has nothing else to do

wan•ton /ˈwɒntən/ adj. **1** *wanton cruelty* = unjustified (done without any good reason) and unnecessary **2** *There are very few tigers left in the country, because of wanton killing.* = uncontrolled and done without pity

war /wɔːʳ/ noun, u. or c. **1** = an armed fight between countries **2** *The government has started a war against malaria.* = an attempt to oppose and check something evil or unpleasant **war crime** = a crime committed during a war which breaks the international rules of war **warfare** noun, u. *We cannot use warfare to solve our political problems.* = the act of fighting a war **warhead** noun, c. = the front part of a bomb or rocket which can cause damage by exploding (bursting) **warhorse** noun, c. = a person who has a lot of experience of politics or some other profession and is still active (often humorous) **warlike** adj. **1** *a warlike nation* = brave and skilled in war (literary) **2** = always ready to go to war (derogatory) **warship** = an armed ship used during war

to be on the warpath = to be ready to start a fight because one is very angry (informal, humorous)

war•rior /ˈwɒriəʳ/ noun, c. = a soldier or famous fighter (in former times)

war•ble /ˈwɔːbəl/ verb, i. or t. *Can you hear the birds warbling in the trees?*(i.) = to sing (referring usually to the song of birds)

ward[1] /wɔːd/ noun, c. **1** *a hospital ward* = a large room in a hospital where usually people suffering from the same kind of disease are kept **2** *a prison ward* = a part of a prison (jail) in which several prisoners are kept **3** *a municipal ward* = a division or part of a city **4** *This orphan is now my brother's ward.* = a person placed under somebody's legal care

ward[2] verb, t. *You should use a mosquito net to ward off the danger of malaria.* = to prevent or keep away something unpleasant

-ward /wəd/ suffix meaning **1** towards a place e.g. **homeward** /ˈhəʊmwəd/ adv. = towards home **2** moving towards e.g. **downward** /ˈdʌunwəd/ *a downward spiral* = moving down or decreasing **3** towards a certain direction e.g. **northward** /ˈnɑθwəd/ = towards the north

war•den /ˈwɔːdn/ noun, c. *the warden of a hostel* = a person who looks after a place and the people living in it

war•der /ˈwɔːdəʳ/ noun, c. *a jail warder* = a person who guards a prison (**ward**[1] meaning **2**)

ward•robe /ˈwɔːdrəʊb/ noun, u. or c. **1** (c.) = a cupboard (almirah) in which one hangs or keeps one's clothes **2** *He has a large wardrobe.*(u.) = a collection of clothes

ware•house /ˈweəhaʊs/ noun, c. = a large building in which things are stored before they are sold, used etc.

wares /weəz/ noun, u. (always plural) *household wares* = small things which are kept for sale

warm[1] /wɔːm/ adj. **1** *The doctor has asked me to wash my face with warm, not hot, water.* = having heat but not too much (just enough to feel comfortable) (also **tepid**) **2** *It is rather cold today. You should put on some warm clothes.* = able to keep out the cold **3** *I received a warm welcome from the teachers when I visited the college.* = friendly

warm[2] verb, t. *Please warm some milk for the baby.* = to make something warm (to heat it to a comfortable temperature) **warmth** noun, u. *I was touched by the warmth of his feelings when we met last night after many years.* = the quality of being friendly **warm-**

W

blooded adj. *Birds are warm-blooded animals but fish are cold-blooded.* = having a body temperature that remains warm even when the outside temperature is low [BIOLOGY] **warm-hearted** adj. *a warm-hearted person* = kind and friendly **house warming** noun = celebration of one's moving into a new house **global warming** = the rise in the temperature experienced round the world as a result of polllution, careless treatment of plant and animal life etc. **warm-up** noun = a series of exercises done before one prepares to play, run, dance, do more energetic exercises etc.

warn /wɔːn/ verb, t. *I warn you: don't drive so fast or you'll be fined for speeding.* = to tell someone of something bad that might happen if something is done or not done **warning** noun, u. or c. **1** *The teacher gave the student a warning that if he missed any more classes, he would not be allowed to take the exam.*(c.) = the act of telling someone that something bad might happen **2** *The chair on the merry-go-round tilted violently, without warning.*(u.) = a sign indicating in advance that something is going to happen

warp[1] /wɔːp/ verb, i. *The doors have warped because the wood from which they were made was not properly seasoned.* = to become twisted out of shape (referring usually to things made of wood)

warp[2] noun, u. = the threads used to weave a piece of cloth which run along its length (see also **weft**)

war•rant[1] /'wɒrənt/ noun, c. *Before searching the house, the police got a search warrant from the magistrate.* = a written order signed by a magistrate, allowing the police to take a certain action

warrant[2] verb, t. **1** *I warrant that this motorcycle has no defects.* = to guarantee something (to promise that it is free from defect etc.) **2** *This building is in very poor condition and warrants the spending of at least Rs 50,000 on repairs.* = to justify something (to provide a good reason for doing something) (formal) **warranty** noun, u. *This refrigerator is sold under a 12-month warranty and will be repaired free of charge during this period.* = a written guarantee (see **warrant**[2] meaning **1**)

war•ren /'wɒrən/ noun, c. **1** = a hole in the ground in which a rabbit lives **2** = a small and crowded building (derogatory)

wart /wɔːt/ noun, c. = a small, hard lump of flesh on the face of a person **wart-hog** noun, c. = a kind of wild pig found in Africa which seems to have warts all over its head

wa•ry /'weəri/ adj. *The health centre promised that I would lose weight in five days, but as I was wary I did not join their fitness programme.* = careful and not easily tricked **warily** adv. *You should walk warily through these fields as there may be some snakes in the grass.* = carefully (literary)

was /wəz/ verb, i. = past tense of '**is**'

wash[1] /wɒʃ/ verb, t. or i. **1** *You should wash your shirt. There is some mud on it.*(t.) = to clean with water **2** *This shirt washes quite easily.*(i.) = to be easy to clean with water **3** *Many large trees were washed away during the flood.*(i.) = to be carried away by flowing water **4** *I am afraid the story which you have told the police will not wash.*(i.) = to be something that can be believed (generally used in negative sentences) (informal)

wash[2] noun, c. *Give the shirt a good wash.* = the act of washing with water **washable** adj. *a washable silk sari* = something that can be cleaned with water **face wash** = a lotion or liquid used to clean the face **washing** noun, u. **1** *I have a lot of washing to do.* = the task of washing clothes **2** *He hung out the washing to dry.* = clothes that have been washed **wash-basin** noun, c. = a container fitted with a tap, in which one can wash one's face or hands **washing machine** noun, c. = a machine which operates on electricity and washes clothes **wash-room** noun, c. = a bath-room or toilet in a public building

wash off **1** *Wash off the dirt on your trousers.* = to get rid of mud etc. by washing the garment, object etc **2** *Will the ink stain on this shirt wash off?* = go away as a result of washing **wash up** *There are lots of plates and glasses, Can you help me wash up?* = to clean used plates etc. usually in a sink **to wash one's hands of something** = to decide to stop being responsible for the success, progress etc of something **to wash (one's) dirty linen in public** = to talk about something unpleasant happening in one's family to others **to feel washed out** *I feel completely washed out after the hard work I have done today.* = to feel very tired (informal) **to be a wash-out** *The film show proved to be a wash-out as none of the invited guests came.* = a total failure (informal)

> **Usage** The expressions 'Would you like to wash?' or 'Would you like to have a quick wash?' are polite ways of asking someone if they would like to use the bathroom. We don't say 'Would you like a wash?' Someone or something needs a wash when it is dirty and you think it is time to clean them/it with water.

washer /'wɒʃə[r]/ **1** = a flat disc, made of rubber, metal etc. with a hole in the middle, fitted over a bolt to make it tight and secure **2** = a washing machine (informal)

wasp /wɒsp/ noun, c. = a flying insect, usually yellow or red in colour, that can give people a painful sting

wastage = see **waste**

waste[1] /weɪst/ verb, t. or i. **1** *They wasted all their money on gambling. Now they have no money left.*(t.) = to use wrongly or to use too much of something **2** *The muscles of his body are wasting away because of some unknown disease.*(i.) = to lose flesh or muscle from the body slowly

waste[2] noun, u. or c. **1** *I tried to repair the electric iron, but it was a waste of time since I didn't have the proper tools.* = a wrong or unsuccessful use of something **2** *The factories near the city release a lot of poisonous waste into the river.* = unwanted matter **wastage** noun, u. *There is a huge wastage of electricity as many people forget to switch off the fans and lights.* = loss caused by wrong or bad use of something **wasteland** noun, u. or c. = land which cannot be used **waste-paper** noun, u. = paper which has already been used or cannot be used and must be thrown away **waste product** noun, c. *Urine is a waste product from the body.* = some material that is produced as a result of some activity but cannot be used and needs to be thrown away or got rid of

to go waste *Please let's finish this rice. Otherwise it'll go waste.* = (of food) be left over and wasted; (of effort) to become purposeless **wasted on someone** *The poem you read out was wasted on us. We don't enjoy poetry.* = to not have an effect or serve a purpose **to not waste one's breath** *Don't waste your breath. They won't follow your advice.* = to not offer advice to someone who will not take it

watch[1] /wɒtʃ/ noun, c. **1** *His watch keeps perfect time.* = a machine, usually worn on the wrist, that shows the time **2** *The police are keeping a close watch on his movements.* = the act of observing someone

watch[2] verb, t. **1** *I like to watch cricket matches.* = to look at something that is happening with interest, usually for entertainment **2** *The mother watched her baby crawling across the room.* = to observe (look at someone or something carefully) **3** *You need to watch what you are saying.* = be careful about **4** *Could you watch my children for an hour while I get their lunch ready?* = to look after and keep someone or something safe from harm **5** *I don't feel comfortable while writing the exam. I feel I'm being watched.* = to observe with the intention of finding fault with or punishing someone **watch-dog** noun, c. = a dog that guards a house **watchful** adj. *The police have become very watchful after the theft last night.* = careful and paying close attention to things **watch-maker** noun, c. = a person who repairs watches **watchword** noun, c. *Let your watchword in business be 'Honesty'.* = a word or phrase that guides a person's actions

to watch one's step *You can speak frankly at the meeting but watch your step!* = a way of warning someone not to say or do something which could cause trouble **to watch the clock** = to keep looking at the time in order to leave or stop what one is doing and therefore not doing one's work properly (informal, derogatory) **to watch the time** *You'd better watch the time. We are so busy enjoying ourselves that we may miss the last bus home.* = to take care to see that one is not late for something; to take care to see that one finishes something in time **to watch it 1** *Watch it! You're going to fall into that ditch.* = used to alert someone to danger (informal) **2** *You'd better watch it. You're making us very angry.* = a way of warning someone that one may cause them harm if they are not careful

wa•ter[1] /'wɔːtə[r]/ noun, u. **1** = the colourless liquid which living beings (animals or plants) need in order to live **2** *The water of this river has become poisonous.* = the liquid that is found in seas, rivers, lakes etc **3** *The water was too shallow for us to swim in.* = a quantity of water such as one would find in a river, swimming pool, pond etc. **4** (always plural) *the waters of the Bay of Bengal* = the entire volume of water in an ocean, river or sea

water[2] verb, t. **1** *He is watering the plants.* = to pour water over a piece of land or to supply water to a plant or animal **2** *The smell of food makes my mouth water.* = to cause water to form and flow out of the mouth or eyes in the form of saliva or tears **watery** /'wɔːtərɪ/ adj. *The chicken curry was watery and tasteless.* = containing too much water **water-bird** noun, c. = any kind of bird that lives in or near water **water-borne** adj. *Cholera is a water-borne disease* = carried by water **water-closet** noun, c. = a toilet or lavatory that is flushed (cleaned out) by using water (also **WC**) **water colour** = a kind of paint used on paper that dissolves in water **watering hole** noun, c. **1** = a small pool or lake in a forest where wild animals come to drink water **2** = a place where alcoholic drinks are available and which is very popular (informal) **water-logged** adj. *The roads are water-logged after the heavy rain and it is not possible to travel over them.* = full of water and therefore not usable **water-soluble** adj. = something (e.g. a pill, powder) which dissolves when water is added to it **waterworks** noun (always plural) = the systems of pumps, pipes etc. which supplies water to a city

to water something down = to make something (e.g. a report) less strong by removing something that may not be liked (disapproving) **to keep one's head above water** = to keep out of difficulties, especially those which are connected with money **to be in (or get into) hot water** *They are always getting into hot water.* = to be in trouble (informal) **to pour cold water over something** *I suggested many exciting ideas to my parents but they poured cold water over them.* = to say something discouraging about one's ideas when one is expecting praise, enthusiasm etc. **to test the waters** *Let's not move to Birganj permanently. Let's test the waters first.* = to test or try out an idea before taking a decision **to feel like a fish out of water** *At the party, I was the only one who didn't know anyone. I felt like a fish out of water.* = to feel uncomfortable and out of place because one is different in some way from others **like water off a duck's back** *I kept offering him advice, but he paid no attention. It was like water off a duck's back.* = having no effect on someone

waterfall /'wɔ:təfɔ:l/ noun, c. = a place where a river or stream falls from a height over the side of a mountain or hill

watermark /'wɔ:təmɑ:k/ noun, u. **1** = a mark made on paper (especially bank notes) which is visible only when it is held up against light **2** = the markings showing the level of water in a river etc.

water-melon /'wɔ:təmelən/ noun, c. = a large green fruit with juicy pink and white flesh inside and many seeds

waterproof /'wɔ:təpru:f/ adj. *a waterproof watch* = something that does not allow water to enter

watershed /'wɔ:təʃed/ noun, c. **1** = a line of mountains which separates an area through which rivers flow from another such area **2** *The arrival of the East India Company proved to be a watershed in India's history.* = an event that marks an important change (figurative)

watt /wɒt/ noun = a unit for measuring the amount of electrical power used **wattage** noun, u. *a high-wattage electric heater* = electrical power measured in watts

wave[1] /weɪv/ noun, c. **1** *There are huge waves in the sea today.* = a mass (quantity) of water, on the surface of a sea, which is raised up in the form of a small hill and moves across the water, followed by other waves **2** *Light travels in the form of waves.* = the path along which forms of energy such as light, heat, sound etc. travel through space or through the air, which cannot be seen by the eyes but is said to act like waves in the sea **3** *The film star greeted the crowd with a wave.* = a movement of the hand to greet or call someone **4** *He lost the last election but hopes to win this time as the new wave is in his favour.* = a sudden feeling or pattern of behaviour that is shared by many people

wave[2] verb, i. or t. **1** *The traffic policeman waved his hand, signalling to the drivers of the vehicles to drive on.*(t.) // *The film star waved to the crowd.*(i.) = to move one's hand quickly from side to side, as a sign of greeting or to express some other meaning **2** *wave a flag* = to move something that one is holding from one side to the other to draw attention, ask for help etc.

wavy adj. *a wavy line* = in the form of a wave

wavelength noun, u. or c. **1** = the distance between waves of sound or light [PHYSICS] **2** *He and I seem to be on the same wavelength. We agree on most things.* = the ability among two or more people to understand each other's minds (figurative)

wa•ver /'weɪvə^r/ verb, i. *If you once make up your mind to do something, you should not waver.* = to be changing one's mind frequently; to hesitate

wax[1] /wæks/ noun, u. *Candles are made of wax.* = a solid material, usually made from petroleum (oil taken out of the earth) which becomes soft and turns into a liquid when heated and can be used to make candles etc.

wax[2] verb, t. or i. **1** *I want you to wax the car.*(t.) = to rub wax or a polish containing wax on some surface, so as to make it shine **2** *The moon waxes and wanes every month.*(i.) = to become larger (referring to the regular changes in the moon's size and appearance)

waxy adj. = made of wax or feeling like wax

to wax eloquent *He waxed eloquent when asked to describe his trip to Kerala.* = to speak at great length, usually in praise of someone

way[1] /weɪ/ noun, c. **1** *Is this the way to the station?* = the path or road which leads to some place **2** *Come this way, please.* = in a certain direction **3** *We have a long way to go before we reach Kolkata.* = the distance one must travel **4** *I will show you the way to make dosas.*= a method of doing something **5** *They have a nice way of welcoming their guests.* = habit or manner

way[2] adv. *The new fridge was way more expensive than I thought. // I can't walk with you to the shops. It's way too far.* = much more than expected (informal)

to be (get) in the way 1 *Can you move a little to your left please? I can't see the speaker because you are in the way.* = to be in such a position that one prevents someone from seeing something **2** *I would like to buy a television set, but he is in the way.* = to prevent someone from doing or becoming something which he/she wants **to have a way with someone or something** *Sarah has a way with young children. They love to play with her.* = to be good at managing someone or something (e.g. an animal, a machine) **the other way round** *I didn't beg him to marry me. It was the other way round!* = in exactly the opposite manner **to give way** *Our father was unwilling at first to let us watch television, but he gave way in the end when he saw how keen we were.* = to allow someone to do something after not allowing them at first **to mend one's ways** = to correct those parts of one's behaviour which others do not like or support **by the way** *I really like Sam. By the way, have you seen him today?* = an expression used when one moves away from the main thing one is talking about (informal) **to rub someone up the wrong way** = to annoy someone who is important (informal) **to work one's way through something** *She didn't have the money to continue her studies, so she worked her way through college.* = to work in order to earn the money to fulfil a goal **No way!** *'Can I borrow your bike?' 'No way!'* = a way of strongly refusing to do what someone wants you to do (informal, not respectful) **way out** *Your answer was way out and we couldn't give you any marks. // Her clothes were way out.* = completely wrong; different in way that causes either disapproval or admiration (slang) **to have it both ways** = to want all the benefits of a situation and none of the risks/ disadvantages **to have one's way** *None of us wanted to see a film that evening, but my sister had her way and we went to the cinema.* = to get what one intends/plans **to go all the way** *We only expected them to meet us at the station but they went all the way and took us home, cooked for us and took us round the city.* = to do much more than one is expected to do **to make way** *When people in cars hear the siren of an ambulance, they make way for it.* = to yield to somebody **ways and means** (always plural) *The police have ways and means of collecting information.* = methods of doing or getting something which may not always be legal

way•lay /weɪˈleɪ/ verb, t. = to rob someone while he/she is travelling

way•side /weɪˈsaɪd/ adj. *We stopped at a wayside shop to buy some bread.* = by the side of a road

way•ward /ˈweɪwəd/ adj. *He has been spoilt by having too much money, and has become completely wayward.* = not willing to listen to or be guided by anyone

WC (**water**) see **water-closet**

we /wi/ pron. **1** *We are learning English.* = the plural form of 'I' **2** *We will now discuss the causes of the French Revolution.* = used by a writer or speaker to include the audience **3** *We will make you the Prince of York.* = used by a king or queen to refer to himself/ herself

weak /wiːk/ adj. **1** *He has become so weak after his illness that he cannot walk. // a weak leader* = not strong in body or mind **2** *He is weak in mathematics.* = not able to do well in something **3** *The tea has no taste. It is weak.* = containing too much water **4** *The past tense of the verb 'ask' is 'asked', which is a weak form.* = the past tense form of a verb which is produced by adding '-ed' to the present tense form [GRAMMAR] **weaken** verb, t. *My mother was quite strong, but the fever has weakened her.* = to become weak or to make someone or something weak **weakness** noun, u. or c. **1** *I am drinking plenty of milk to help me get over my weakness.*(u.) = the condition of being weak in body or mind **2** *Drinking is his greatest weakness.*(c.) = a fault in one's character or a bad habit that one is unable to check **the weaker sex** noun = used to refer to women in general (considered offensive, but sometimes used humorously) (derogatory, not respectful) Ⓖ **weakling** noun, c. = a person who is weak in body or mind (derogatory, not respectful) **weakly** adv. **1** *She was ill and held out her hand weakly when I went to see her.* = in a way which shows one does not have strength (as a result of illness etc.) **2** *When I asked him if he liked his new school, he smiled weakly.* = not wishing to say that something is bad

weak point *He has no understanding of music, but he gets upset when people make fun of him. That is his weak point.* = a part of one's personality or behaviour which others can find fault with or make fun of **a weak moment** *In a weak moment, I let twenty of them stay with me, but it was a mistake.* = a time when, instead of being wise or careful, one feels pity or is tempted to do something out of kindness **to be weak in the head** *You're planning to go for a walk at this late hour? You must be weak in the head!* = mad or foolish (informal, not respectful)

weal /wiːl/ noun, c. = a raised mark on the skin caused by a hard blow (see also **welt**)

wealth /welθ/ noun, u. *The people of a country are its greatest wealth.* = money or other things of value that one has **wealthy** adj. = rich

wean /wiːn/ verb, t. **1** = to make a baby form the habit of giving up its mother's milk and start taking other kinds of food **2** *This boy had started smoking but his teacher has been able to wean him away from the habit.* = to persuade a person to give up a bad habit

weap'on /ˈwepən/ noun, c. *We were not allowed to carry any weapons.* = an instrument or tool, such as a sword, that is used in fighting **weaponry** noun, u. *The army is trying to get modern weaponry from other countries.* = weapons in general

wear[1] /weəʳ/ verb, t. (**wore, worn**) **1** *He wears only white clothes.* = to put on clothes **2** *He wore an angry look on his face.* = to have a certain expression on one's face **3** *If you use these shoes to walk through the fields you will wear them out quickly.* = to make something weaker through use or to become weaker through use **4** *She wears her hair loose.* = to have a certain style for one's hair

wear[2] noun, u. **1** *These shoes are showing signs of wear. They will not last very long.* = damage or weakness caused by use **2** *This shop sells men's wear.* = clothes **wear and tear** noun, u. *His car is ten years old and it is showing a lot of wear and tear.* = damage or weakness caused by long use

to wear one's heart on one's sleeve = to show one's feelings openly, making no attempt to hide them **to**

W

wear away/off *The stone steps under the water have worn away because the water is constantly flowing over them.* = to show damage because of long use **to wear (oneself) out** *We wore ourselves out working all night.* = to be very tired after something and unable to to do any more or anything else

wear•y[1] /ˈwɪəri/ adj. *I have been working for six hours and I am weary.* = tired (literary)

weary[2] verb, t. *This book is written in an old-fashioned style. It will soon weary you.* = to make one feel tired or bored (old-fashioned)

wea•sel /ˈwiːzəl/ noun, c. = a small animal, like a fox, that hunts other small animals

wea•ther[1] /ˈweðəʳ/ noun, u. *It has been raining every day for the last three months. I wonder when the weather will change.* = the condition produced by wind, rain, sunshine etc. over a period of time

weather[2] verb, t. *Everyone criticized him when he gave up his job and went into business, but he weathered the criticism and proved to be a success.* = to come out of a difficult situation without suffering much harm or damage **weather-beaten** adj. *The old farmer had a weather-beaten face* = showing the effects of a hard life **weather forecast** noun, c. *'What's the weather forecast for today?' 'Heavy rain.'* = a description of the weather that may be expected, usually published in a newspaper or broadcast over the radio or television

weave[1] /wiːv/ verb, t. (**wove**, **woven**) = to produce cloth by using threads, passing one set of threads over or under another set, using a simple machine called a loom

weave[2] noun, u. *This sari has an attractive weave.* = the patterns produced in a piece of cloth by weaving **weaver** noun, c. = a person who weaves cloth

web /web/ noun, c. **1** *a spider's web* = a net made by spiders out of thin threads, to catch insects **2** (always capital) *the World-Wide Web* = the various **websites** which can be accessed (reached) through the Internet [COMPUTERS] **3** = the thin skin between the toes on the feet of some animals (e.g. ducks) **webbed** adj. *webbed feet* = having webs **website** noun, c. = a page or place on the Internet which belongs to a particular individual or company and can be visited by typing in the name [COMPUTERS]

wed /wed/ verb, t. (**wedded**) *Shaheen Wansi will wed her childhood friend next month.* = to marry (formal) **wedding** noun, c. = a marriage ceremony

wedge[1] /wedʒ/ noun, c. = a solid piece of wood or other material in the shape of a triangle, one end of which is wider than the other

wedge[2] verb, t. *The door has been wedged open.* = to fix a wedge in a narrow space, usually to prevent something from moving or closing

the thin edge of the wedge *Our new neighbour asked me to water his plants while he is away. This may be the thin edge of the wedge. We can expect many other requests.* = the beginning of an unpleasant situation

weed[1] /wiːd/ noun, c. *The garden is full of weeds.*= wild plants which are not wanted and which prevent crops from growing properly

weed[2] verb, t. *We will have to weed the garden.* = to pull out and remove the weeds growing in a garden or field

week /wiːk/ noun, c. = a period of seven days, starting on Monday and ending on Sunday **weekday** noun, c. = any day of the week other than Saturday or Sunday **weekend** noun, c. = the last two days of a week (Saturday and Sunday) which are usually holidays **long weekend** either Friday or Monday being a holiday, in additon to Saturday and Sunday, thus making it three consecutive holidays **weekly** adj. or noun, c. (**weeklies**) **1** *a weekly meeting*(adj.) = happening once a week **2** (noun) = a magazine that appears once a week

weep /wiːp/ verb, i. (**wept**) *The sight of his first grandchild made him weep happy tears.* = to express sorrow or happiness by producing tears **weepy** noun, c. = a film or television programme that makes people weep (informal, usually disapproving) **weeping willow** noun, c. = a tree with thin leaves that hang downwards

wee•vil /ˈwiːvəl/ noun, c. = a kind of insect that gets into and spoils rice and other kinds of grain

wee-wee /ˈwiːwiː/ verb, i. = to urinate (used by small children or by parents while talking to their children) (slang)

weft /weft/ noun, u. = the shorter threads used in weaving a piece of cloth, which run across the **warp** (the long threads) (also **woof**)

weigh /weɪ/ verb, i. or t. **1** *He weighs 75 kilograms.*(i.)= to have a certain weight **2** *We will have to weigh this rice before we can sell it.*(t.) = to measure the weight of something **weighbridge** noun, c. = a machine used to measure the weight of large vehicles such as trucks

to be weighed down by *He is weighed down by the responsibility of looking after the school.* = to have to carry a heavy responsibility **to weigh on one's mind** *The little child's unhappiness weighed on our minds and we could not sleep.* = to be troubled by an idea etc. **to weigh one's words carefully** = to be very careful in selecting the words that one uses

weight[1] /weɪt/ noun, u. or c. **1** *His weight is 75 kilograms.* = the measurement of how heavy a person or thing is **2** *Put a 500-gramme weight on one pan of* *the scale.* = a piece of metal whose weight is known and which is used to measure the weight of something **3** *Her words carry a lot of weight with the senior manager.* = importance or value **4** *After the surgery on my arm, I am not allowed to lift heavy weights.*(c.) = things that are heavy **5** *weights* = (always plural) pieces of metal used for exercise or sport

weight[2] verb, t. *The basket will have to be weighted with stones.* = to make something heavier by adding weights to it **weighty** adj. *a weighty argument* = having importance **weight-lifting** noun, u. = a sport in which people compete by lifting weights

to pull one's weight *If everyone pulls their weight, we can finish this job soon.* = to share properly in doing a piece of work **to throw one's weight around** *Stop throwing your weight around.* = to offend people by behaving in a superior way, giving them orders etc. (informal, derogatory)

weir /wɪəʳ/ noun, c. = a dam (a wall built across a stream to control the flow of water)

weird /wɪəd/ adj. *Some people keep snakes as pets. They seem weird to some of us.* = very strange or unusual (disapproving) **weirdo** noun = a person who is thought to be weird (informal, not respectful)

wel•come[1] /'welkəm/ verb, t. **1** *When my sister returned from her trip to Iceland, we went to welcome her at the airport.* = to meet a guest or visitor (someone who comes to a place) happily and in a spirit of friendliness **2** *We welcome new ideas.* = to receive or accept something (e.g. a new idea) happily

welcome[2] noun, c. *I received a warm welcome when I visited Pakistan.* = the act of welcoming a guest

welcome[3] adj. *We had some rain last night after two months of dry weather. It was a welcome change!* = something that one accepts with pleasure

welcome[4] interjec. *'Welcome!' said the little girl, as she presented the visitor with a garland of flowers.* = an expression of happiness on meeting a guest or visitor

to be welcome to do something *We have a small house, but you're welcome to stay with us.* = a way of offering someone something **to overstay one's welcome** *I think we overstayed our welcome in their house. They never invited us again!* = to stay somewhere so long that one's hosts find it unpleasant or difficult

weld[1] /weld/ verb, t. *This door is made of steel plates which have been welded together.* = to join two pieces of metal together after heating them to a high temperature, causing them to melt at the edges

weld[2] noun, c. *The weld on this metal plate is rather weak.*= the place where two pieces of metal are welded (joined) together **welder** noun, c. = a person whose profession is to weld metal

wel•fare /'welfeəʳ/ noun, u. **1** *You must look after the welfare of your children.* = health and happiness **2** *Our hospitals provide free medical treatment to the poor, under the government's welfare programme.* = help given to poor people or to people with special needs or problems **welfare state** noun, c. = a country which has a government that provides special help to people in need of help

well[1] /wel/ adv. **1** *He writes well, but he is not a good speaker.* = in a good manner **2** *Shake the bottle well before you drink the medicine.* = thoroughly **3** *The project was completed well within the time limit of one year.* = much **4** *She was well aware that we were arriving today, but didn't come to receive us.* = certainly, completely (used to stress something)

well[2] adj. **1** *She had fever last week, but she is quite well now.* = in good health **2** *Don't worry, all is well here.* = in a satisfactory state

well[3] noun, c. = a deep hole dug in the ground, from which water can be taken out

well[4] interjec. **1** *Well, well! I didn't expect to see you here.* = an expression of surprise **2** *I've lost the book you lent me.' 'Well!'* = an expression of annoyance **3** *'I went to the office late today and ...' 'Well?'* = a way of asking someone to continue to speak. (Sometimes a nervous tone is used to show that one is worried about what is to follow.) **4** *'How did you do in the test?' 'Well...'* = a way of showing that one is not happy to give someone the information they want, usually because it is unpleasant

well[5] verb, i. *Tears welled up in the child's eyes when she was scolded.* = to flow (referring to some liquid) **well-adjusted** adj. *a well-adjusted person* = feeling comfortable with the surroundings **well-advised** adj. *You would be well-advised to consult your doctor regularly.* = doing the proper or correct thing **well-appointed** adj. *a well-appointed library* = having everything necessary **wellbeing** noun, u. = the state of being healthy or comfortable **well-balanced** adj. *a well-balanced person* = sensible and not controlled too much by feelings **well-bred** adj. = thought of as belonging to a good family **well-connected** adj. = known to many important people **well-earned** adj. *well-earned praise* = deserved **well-heeled** adj. = rich (informal) **well-informed** *Let's ask him what kind of food the local restaurants serve. He is quite well-informed.* = to have a wide knowledge of things **well-off** adj. = rich **well-preserved** adj. = looking young, though not very young (humorous or not respectful) **well-rounded** adj. *a well-rounded personality* = combining many good qualities **well-read** adj. = having read many books and being aware of many things **well-thought-of** adj. *a well-thought-of person* = respected by everyone **well-to-**

do adj. = rich (informal) **well-wisher** noun, c. = a person who has good wishes or feelings towards another **well-worn** adj. *a well-worn pair of shoes* = used for a long time and not in very good condition

to know something full well *Why did you ask him to come to work? You knew full well that he was ill.* = to do something that one should not have done, inspite of knowing that it should not have been done (an expression of annoyance) **to be well out of something** *Thank goodness I'm well out of that project.* = to feel relieved because one no longer has to do something that one did not like doing (informal) **to be well up on something** *She's really well up on the geography of Russia.* = to have good knowledge of a subject (informal) **It's just as well...** *It's just as well that we didn't go to the station. The train was cancelled.* = a way of saying 'It is a good thing that ..' **All's well that ends well** = a saying which means that if something ends happily (even if it did not begin or go on happily), that is a good thing **Oh well** *'I haven't brought the book you wanted.' 'Oh well, we'll manage without it.'* = a way of responding to something that has not happened as expected, and expressing willingness to find a way out **Ah well** *The village is not as lovely as it used to be. Ah well.* = a way of accepting calmly that something is different, or worse than one expected it to be

Welsh[1] /welʃ/ adj. = belonging to the country known as Wales

Welsh[2] noun, u. = the language or the people of Wales

welt /welt/ noun, c. **1** = a piece of leather used to join the upper and lower parts of a shoe **2** = a raised mark on the skin caused by a hard blow (see also **weal**)

wend /wend/ verb, t. (**wended**) *He wended his way slowly through the countryside.* = to move or travel slowly (literary)

were•wolf /'weəwʊlf/ noun, c. (**werewolves**) = a person (in fairy stories) who is believed to have the power to turn into a wolf

west[1] /west/ noun *The sun sets in the west.* = the direction in which the sun sets

west[2] adv. *We are now travelling west.* = towards the west

west[3] adj. *The west wind is blowing.* = from the west **West** noun = the western part of the world, especially Europe and North America **westbound** adj. *a west-bound train* = travelling towards the west **West End** noun = the western part of the centre of London, which is famous as a centre of fashion **westerly** adj. *travelling in a westerly direction* = towards the west **westerlies** noun (always plural) = the winds that blow from the west towards the east **western** adj. *the western part of the city* = belonging to the west **westernize (westernise)** verb, t. *westernize the system of education* = to introduce new ideas, habits etc. taken from the West (Europe or America) **West Indies** noun (always plural) = a group of islands lying between Europe and America

wet[1] /wet/ adj. **1** *My clothes have become wet in the rain.* = covered with water or some other liquid (opposite **dry**) **2** *We are expecting wet weather today.* = rainy **3** *Careful! There's wet paint on the chair.* = not dry **4** *You don't want to come with us? What a wet person you are!* = cowardly and generally unwilling to do what others are interested in doing (informal)

wet[2] verb, t. (**wet** or **wetted**) *wet one's bed* = to make wet, specially by passing urine

a wet blanket *If the children want to go on a picnic, you should let them go. Don't be such a wet blanket!* = a person who does not want others to have fun or to enjoy themselves **to be wet behind the ears** = to be young and without much experience

whack[1] /wæk/ verb, t. *The batsman whacked the ball over the boundary.* = to hit hard (informal)

whack[2] noun, c. *The boy's mother gave him a whack for telling a lie.* = a hard blow **whacking** noun, c. = a beating **whacking** adj. *He has a whacking big house.* = very big (informal, slang)

whale /weɪl/ noun, c. = a very large mammal (animal that feeds its young ones with milk) which lives in the sea and is hunted for its fat, from which a kind of oil is produced **whaler** noun, c. = a kind of ship that is used for hunting whales at sea **whaling** noun, u. = the industry or business of hunting whales

wharf /wɔːf/ noun, c. (**wharves**) = a kind of platform that projects (sticks out) into a sea or river, to which ships can be tied in order to unload goods

a whale of a time = a very enjoyable time (informal)

what[1] /wɒt/ det. *What is your name?* = used to ask a question about something to which the answer is not known

what[2] pron. *I will do what you ask me to do.* = the thing that **whatever** det. or pron. **1** *I did whatever I could do to help him.* = everything possible **2** *Whatever happens, I will stay here.* = it is not important what **3** *Whatever took you so long?* = an expression used instead of 'what', to express surprise

wheat /wiːt/ noun, u. = a kind of foodgrain from which bread etc. is made

whee•dle /'wiːdl/ verb, t. or i. *Ali wheedled his brother into giving him the new toy.* = to get what one wants from someone by using flattery (false praise) or a trick (derogatory)

wheel[1] /wiːl/ noun, c. *A bicycle has two wheels.* = a circular (round) object on which a vehicle (e.g. a bicycle) moves

wheel[2] verb, t. **1** *He wheeled the motor-cycle along the* *road.* = to move a vehicle with wheels by pushing it **2** *The driver of the motor-cycle wheeled sharply left.* = to turn or change direction **wheeler** suffix *a three-wheeler* = a vehicle having a specific number of wheels **wheel-barrow** noun, c. = a small cart with two wheels, which is pushed by hand and used to carry small loads **wheel-base** noun *The car has a wheel-base of 1.5 metres.* = the distance between the front wheels and the rear (back) wheels of a vehicle **wheel-chair** noun = a chair with wheels which is used by people who are unable to walk and which can often be moved by the user's hands (see pic under **chair**)

wheeze[1] /wi:z/ verb, i. = to make a whistling sound because of difficulty in breathing

wheeze[2] noun, c. *His wheezes are painful to hear.* = the act or sound of wheezing

when /wen/ adv. **1** *When will the meeting begin?* = at what time (used in questions) **2** *I was sleeping when the fire broke out.* = at the time that **3** *Why do you want to resign when you have such a good job?* = considering that **whenever** adv. *I can come to meet you whenever you ask me to come.* = at any time

whence /wens/ adv. *I often return to the village whence my family came.* = from where (old-fashioned, literary)

where /weəʳ/ adv. **1** *Where are you going?* = to which place (used in questions) **2** *I like to visit the town where I was born.* = at which place **3** *Where possible, you should use the local language to speak to these people.* = whenever **whereabouts** noun, u. (plural form only) *The police are looking for the man, but his whereabouts are not known.* = the place where a thing or person can be found **whereas** conj. *They were looking for the child outside the house, whereas he was inside the house, in his grandmother's bed.* = but; on the other hand **whereupon** conj. *The player argued with the referee, whereupon the referee ordered him to leave the field.* = following which (because of which)

whet /wet/ verb, t. (**whetted**) **1** *This knife is not very sharp. We will have to whet it.* = to make a knife or sword sharp by rubbing it against a stone **2** *What you have told me about the new film has whetted my desire to see it.* = to increase one's desire to do something **whetstone** noun, c. = a stone used for sharpening knives, scissors etc.

wheth•er /'weðəʳ/ conj. **1** *Ask him whether he would like to meet us now.* = if **2** *I will go to the meeting anyhow, whether you come with me or not.* = not depending on something

whew /hju:/ interjec. *Whew! It's really hot today!* = an expression of tiredness or relief (also **phew**) (informal)

whey /weɪ/ noun, u. = the watery part of milk from which the solid part has been taken out in the form of curds (yogurt)

which[1] /wɪtʃ/ det. *Which shirt are you going to wear?* = expressing the possibility of choosing one out of several things or people (used in questions)

which[2] pron. **1** *Show me the pen which you bought yesterday.* = referring to the particular thing which is being talked about **2** *He asked me to come back next year, which I had expected him to do.* = adding more information to something that has been said earlier **whichever** det. **1** *Take whichever book you like.* = any one of several things **2** *This is a very bad situation, whichever way you look at it.* = no matter which

> **Usage** **who** is used to refer to human beings (e.g. *the boy who won*)
> **which** refers to non-living things or non-human creatures (e.g. *the house which you built* or *the horse which you ride*)
> **that** refers to non-living things as well as human and non-human creatures (e.g. *the car that broke down; the bird that flew away; the child that goes to school*)

whiff /wɪf/ noun, u. or c. *She is cooking chicken curry. I caught just a whiff of it as I was coming in.*(u.) = a smell of something good, lasting for a short time only

While[1] /waɪl/ conj. **1** *You can read a book while I am writing this letter.* = during the time that **2** *Anu likes apples, while I like guavas.* = but; on the other hand **3** *While I like your plan I don't think it will work.* = although

while[2] noun, u. *I haven't seen you for a while.* = a period of time

while[3] verb, t. *He paints pictures to while away the time.* = to pass time in a pleasant and interesting manner

to while away (time) = to spend time (usually in a way that is not useful) **worth the while (worthwhile)** *I had to work very hard for a whole year. But it was worth the while and I learnt a lot.* = something that gives satisfactory results for the time/effort spent

whim /wɪm/ noun, c. *We changed our plans on a sudden whim and went to the cinema instead of the chess competition.* = a sudden wish or desire, which is usually not sensible **whimsical** adj. *a whimsical person* = having strange ideas or behaving in a strange way

whim•per[1] /'wɪmpəʳ/ verb, i. *The baby whimpered with fright when someone shouted at it.* = to make low sounds of fear or pain

whimper[2] noun, c. *The boy never made a whimper when he was hurt.* = a cry of pain

W

whine[1] /waɪn/ verb, i. *The dog had been chained all day and it whined when it saw its master, begging to be set free.* = to make a long high sound (referring commonly to the sound made by a dog)
whine[2] noun, c. *We heard the whine of the engines of the plane which was about to take off.* = a high sound produced by an animal or a machine
whin•ny /ˈwɪni/ verb,i. *The horse whinnied.* = to make the gentle sound that a horse makes when it is feeling comfortable
whip[1] /wɪp/ noun, c. = a long piece of rope or leather tied to a handle, used to drive an animal or to punish someone
whip[2] verb, t. (**whipped**) **1** = to strike with a whip **2** *The Australian team whipped the Indian team by an innings and 200 runs.* = to defeat badly **3** *You should whip the white of the egg with a fork until it is full of air bubbles.* = to beat cream or the white of an egg so as to make it rise due to the presence of air bubbles **whipping boy** noun, c. = someone who gets the blame for other people's mistakes (generally used to express sympathy)
to whip up (anger) = to raise the level of someone's emotions strongly (disapproving)
whirl[1] /wɜːl/ verb, i. or t. *All the fans in the room were whirling at top speed.*(i.) = to turn round and round very fast
whirl[2] noun, u. *My head was in a whirl and I felt I was about to fall.* = the sensation (feeling) of turning round and round or of feeling confused **whirlpool** noun, c. = a place in a river or sea where the water goes round and round and sucks objects down **whirlwind** noun, c. = a pillar of air that turns round and round and moves at great speed
whirr /wɜːʳ/ noun, u. *the whirr of an electric fan* = the sound made by a machine (e.g. the blades of a fan) turning round and round at speed and causing the air to move fast
whisk[1] /wɪsk/ verb, t. *The cow whisked the flies away with its tail.* = to remove or drive away with a quick sideways movement
whisk[2] noun, u. **1** *The cow drove the flies away with a whisk of its tail.* = a quick sideways movement **2** *a fly whisk* = a small brush with a long handle, used for driving away flies etc.
to whisk away *I was planning to stay at home but my friends whisked me away to the cinema.* = to take away with speed and without allowing one to think (informal, humorous)
whis•ker /ˈwɪskəʳ/ noun, c. *a cat's whiskers* = one of the long hairs growing on either side of the mouth of a cat, tiger etc. **whiskers** noun (always plural) = hair growing on a man's face
to be the cat's whiskers = to be greatly admired by others (informal)
whis•ky /ˈwɪski/ noun = a strong alcoholic drink made from barley
whis•per[1] /ˈwɪspəʳ/ verb, t. *The little girl whispered something into her mother's ear.* = to say something in a very low voice, so that only the person to whom it is said can hear it
whisper[2] noun, c. *They were speaking in whispers.* = the low sound produced when someone whispers
whis•tle[1] /ˈwɪsəl/ noun, c. **1** *The referee blew his whistle to signal the end of the match.* = an instrument which produces a high, loud sound when air is blown through it **2** *The train gave a whistle and started.* = the high sound produced when air is blown through a whistle
whistle[2] verb, i. or t. **1** *The boy whistled to attract the attention of his friend.*(i.) = to make a high sound by forcing air through a narrow hole formed between the lips, sometimes by putting two fingers into the mouth **2** *The man whistled a tune as he walked along.*(t.) = to produce a musical sound by blowing out air through rounded lips **3** *The train whistled.*(i.) = to make a high sound by forcing air or steam through a whistle
a whistle-stop tour = a quick journey round several places **to blow the whistle on someone** *The robber's family blew the whistle on him and he was caught.* = to reveal a secret so that someone is punished for it **to whistle in the dark** = to do something to keep one's courage high when one is actually feeling afraid
white[1] /waɪt/ adj. **1** *a white shirt* = having the colour of milk **2** *Her face turned white with nervousness* = pale (not having much blood) **3** *a white person* = belonging to the pale-skinned Caucasian race, to which most Europeans and Americans belong **4** *white coffee* = coffee with milk in it
white[2] noun, c. **1** = a member of the white (Caucasian) race **2** *the white of an egg* = the colourless part of the egg **3** = the part of the eye which surrounds the pupil **4** *Let's separate the whites from the other clothes.* = (always plural) white clothes, linen etc. **whiten** verb, t. = to make something white **white ant** noun, c. = an insect that looks like an ant and eats and destroys wood (also **termite**) **white blood cell** noun, c. = a type of cell present in the blood which fights against germs that cause disease **white-board** = a board used by a teacher etc. to write on **white collar worker** = a person who works in an office, not in a factory **white elephant** noun = something that costs a lot of money but is not very useful **white flag** noun, c. = a sign that one has surrendered (accepted defeat) **White House** noun = the official home of the President of America **white goods** noun (always plural) = large machines

which are used in the home, specially in the kitchen (e.g. refrigerators, washing machines) **white meat** noun, c. = the flesh of a chicken or fish, which is considered to be more healthy than 'red meat' (flesh from a large animal such as a sheep, pig or cow) **white paper** noun, c. = an official report put out by the government about something that the government plans to do **whitewash[1]** noun, c. = a mixture of lime (calcium carbonate) and water, used to paint the walls of houses **whitewash[2]** verb, t. **1** *The house will be whitewashed next month.* = to paint a house with whitewash **2** *The report tries to whitewash the mistakes that were made by the government.* = to try to cover up or hide something bad **white water** = water flowing swiftly down a river among rocks, causing foam to form

white lie = a harmless lie **to show the white flag** = to give up and accept that one has lost a war etc. (figurative)

whith•er /'wɪðə^r/ adv. *Whither did the man disappear?* = where; to which place (old-fashioned, literary)

whittle /'wɪtl/ verb, t. or i. *He was whittling away at a piece of wood, trying to shape it into a boat.*(i.) = to cut away pieces of wood in order to make something

whiz (**whizz**) /wɪz/ verb, i. (**whizzed**) *His car whizzed past us on the road.* = to move at great speed, making a rushing sound **whiz kid** noun, c. = a person who shows great intelligence or skill at a very early age (informal, approving)

who /hu:/ pron. **1** *Who is that man?* = which person (used in questions) **2** *I know the man who came to see you.* = referring to the particular person being talked about **3** *I sent the new book to my son, who had not heard of it.* = adding more information on the person being talked about **whodunit** /hu:'dʌnɪt/ noun, c. = a novel or film about a murder or other serious crime, which leaves everyone wondering till the end who has committed the crime (informal) **whoever** pron. *Whoever wants to go to the station can get into the bus.* = anyone who

> **Usage** **whom** is the object form of **who**, used in sentences such as *He is the man whom you met yesterday* or in questions such as *Whom do you want?* In modern usage **whom** is often replaced by **who**, specially when speaking (*the person who you met* or *Who do you want?*)

WHO abbr. of **World Health Organization** = a branch of the United Nations Organization (UNO) which fights disease in different parts of the world

whole[1] /həul/ adj. **1** *He ate the whole chicken.* = entire (all of something) **2** *Tell me the whole story.* = complete **3** *The whole point of my coming here was to be with you.* = main, important

whole[2] noun, u. or c. **1** *The whole of the class was able to fit into one bus.*(u.) = the entire or complete amount **2** *Do these two parts of a cake make a whole?* = a complete unit of something **whole-hearted** adj. *whole-hearted support* = total (complete) and sincere **wholemeal** noun, u. *wholemeal bread* = rough flour made from grains of wheat from which the outer covering has not been removed **whole number** noun, c. = a number which has not been divided by another number (e.g. 3½ is a fraction but 3 is a whole number) **wholesale** adj. or adv. **1** *I bought these notebooks from a wholesale shop.*(adj.) = selling things in large quantities and at a cheaper price (opposite **retail**) **2** *I bought these notebooks wholesale.*(adv.) = in large quantities **wholesome** adj. *You can get wholesome food at this restaurant.* = healthy (good for the body or mind) **wholeness** noun

on the whole *We had a few unpleasant experiences on the way, but on the whole it was a good trip.* = largely or generally **to go the whole hog** *For the school play, the teachers went the whole hog and hired costumes and lights.* = to try and make a success of something by doing everything possible and not letting anything stop one (informal)

whom /hu:m/ pron. **1** *Whom do you want?* = which person (used in questions) (often replaced by 'who', specially in speech) **2** *I gave the money to the man whom you wanted to help.* = the particular person being referred to (talked about)

whoop /wu:p/ noun, c. *He gave a whoop when he was told that he had won.* = a loud shout expressing joy **whoopee** interjec. *'Whoopee!' he shouted. 'We have won!'* = a shout of joy (informal)

whooping cough /'hu:pɪŋ kɒf/ noun = a disease that children sometimes suffer from, causing painful attacks of coughing

whoosh[1] /wʊʃ/ verb, i. *The train whooshed past us.* = to move very fast, producing a rushing sound (informal)

whoosh[2] noun, u. *The air escaped from the balloon with a whoosh.* = the soft sound produced by air moving very fast

whop•per /'wɒpə^r/ noun, c. *He caught a whopper of a fish, weighing about 20 kilograms.* = something unusually big in size (informal, American English) **whopping** adj. *He caught a whopping fish.* = very big (informal)

whore /hɔ:^r/ noun, c. = a term of contempt for a sex-worker USE G

whorl /wɜ:l/ noun, c. = a circle made by the leaves of a plant or the petals of a flower

whose[1] /hu:z/ det. *Whose house is that?* = belonging to which person (used in questions)

W

whose[2] pron. *She's the person whose sister is an actor.* = a word showing that someone is connected to someone else or that something belongs to someone

why[1] /waɪ/ adv. or conj. *Why did you run away when I called you?*(adv.) // *I want to know why you did it.*(conj.) = for what reason (used in questions or indirect questions)

why[2] noun, c. (**whys**) *He is always interested in the why of things.* = the reasons or causes that make things happen (informal)

why[3] interject. *Why! You have actually come to visit me!* = an expression of surprise

Why on earth... *Why on earth must I wear formal clothes?* = a way of expressing surprise and asking for an explanation (informal, not respectful) **Why me ...** **1** = a way of asking with annoyance why one has been asked to do something **2** = a way of asking why something unlucky or unfortunate should happen to one

wick /wɪk/ noun, c. *the wick of a candle* = the piece of thread inside a candle which burns to give out light (see pic under **candle**)

wick•ed /ˈwɪkɪd/ adj. **1** *a wicked person* = bad or evil **2** *What a wicked idea!* = very good (slang)

wicker /ˈwɪkəʳ/ adj. *a wicker chair* = made by weaving cane or thin, long pieces of bamboo

wicket /ˈwɪkɪt/ noun, c. **1** *leg before wicket* = the set of three sticks (stumps) at each end of a cricket pitch (the area within which the ball is supposed to be bowled) **2** *India has lost three wickets in ten minutes.* = (in cricket) the turn of a player to bat [SPORTS] **wicket gate** noun, c. = a small gate or door which forms part of a larger gate or door **wicket-keeper** noun, c. = the player who stands behind the wicket and stops the ball (in cricket) [SPORTS]

wide[1] /waɪd/ adj. **1** *a wide river* = having a large distance between one side and the other **2** *He is a person with wide experience.* = covering a large range of things **3** *The guards were asked to remain wide awake.* = alert (watching carefully)

wide[2] adv. *The two houses are wide apart.* = a great distance away from each other

wide[3] noun, c.= a ball that is bowled so far away from the wicket that the batsman cannot reach it (in cricket) [SPORTS] **widen** verb, t. *The engineers are widening the road* = to make wider **width** /wɪdθ/ noun, u. *The river is two kilometres in width.* = the measurement of how wide a thing is from one side to another (see pic under **dimension**) **wide-angle lens** noun, u. = a lens for a camera that can give a wider view than is usual **wide-eyed** adj. *The child stared wide-eyed at the beautiful palace.* = with eyes fully open because of wonder or surprise **widespread** adj. *Malaria is widespread in this part of the country.* = common; found in many places

wid•ow /ˈwɪdəʊ/ noun, c. = a woman whose husband is dead **widower** noun, c. = a man whose wife is dead

wield /wiːld/ verb, t. **1** *The bat is so heavy that the batsman cannot wield it easily.* = to cause some object e.g. a weapon, to move fast by a movement of the hands holding it **2** *The Prime Minister weilded great power during the reign of Queen Victoria.* = to have and use power, influence etc.

wife /waɪf/ noun, c. (**wives**) = the woman to whom a man is married

wig /wɪg/ noun, c. = a covering of artificial (false) hair worn on the head, usually by a person who has lost his/her natural hair

wig•gle /ˈwɪgəl/ verb, t. *Can you wiggle your toes?* = to cause some part of the body to move or shake slightly

wild /waɪld/ adj. **1** *a wild animal* = living in natural conditions and not controlled by man **2** *wild with anger* = showing very strong feelings **3** *My children are wild about your books.* = extremely fond of something (informal) **4** *I didn't know the answer. It was just a wild guess.* = without thinking carefully about something **wildly** adv. **wildboar** noun, c. = a kind of large pig, living in the forest, that was often hunted **wildcat strike** noun = a sudden stopping of work by the workers in a factory or office **wildlife** noun, u. *The Corbett National Park is full of all kinds of wildlife.* = animals and plants found in natural conditions

to go wild over something = to be filled with strong feelings of joy, anger, excitement etc. (informal) **to run wild** = to behave in an uncontrolled manner **to spread like wildfire** *The news of his victory spread like wildfire.* = very fast **a wild-goose chase** *The search for the Yeti or the Abominable Snowman proved to be a wild-goose chase. No such creature exists.* = a useless search for something that does not exist **wild oats** (**to sow wild oats**) *He sowed his wild oats in his youth, but now he has settled down to a steady life.* = to lead a wild and exciting life during one's youth

wil•der•ness /ˈwɪldənɪs/ noun, u. **1** *The Gobi Desert in Central Asia is a wilderness.* = a place where no human beings live or can live **2** *Mr Patnaik lost the election in 1970 and spent the next ten years in the political wilderness.* = the state of being away from power or public attention

wil•de•beest /ˈwɪldəbiːst/ noun, c. = a kind of large deer found in Africa (also **gnu**)

wiles /waɪlz/ noun (always plural) *That man is known to be very cunning. Beware of his wiles.* = clever tricks (literary)

wil•y /'wɪli/ adj. *He is wily and cannot be trusted.* = cunning (clever and not to be trusted) (disapproving)

wil•ful /'wɪlfəl/ adj. **1** *a wilful child* = doing whatever one wants **2** *He was arrested on a charge of wilful murder* = (of a bad deed) done deliberately (knowingly)

will[1] /wɪl/ aux. (modal) verb **1** *I will meet you next week.* = referring to an action in the future **2** *He will generally do what he is ordered to do.* = to be willing or ready to do something **3** *Will you answer the phone, please? I am busy.* = used to make a command or request in the form of a question **4** *A piece of metal will expand when it is heated.* = expressing a universal truth (something that always happens) **5** *Will the glass hold all the tea in the pan?* = used to show that something is possible **6** *Will you be staying with us on your next visit?* = are you likely to

will[2] noun, c. **1** *He made a will, leaving all his property to their daughter.* = a legal document signed by a person, stating how his/her property and other belongings are to be shared after his/her death **2** *He has such a strong will that he will always succeed in doing something that he wants to do.* = determination (the ability to make decisions and act according to them) (also **will power**) **3** *The will of the people is expressed through the vote in an election.* = desire or wish

will[3] verb, t. **1** *He has willed his property to his daughter and son.* = to give one's property to someone through a will **2** *The people have willed that you should be their leader.* = to express a desire **3** *I willed myself not to burst into tears.* = to force oneself into doing something

will o' the wisp noun = a kind of bluish flame seen in marshes (wet lands) where methane gas, formed by the rotting of dead plants, sometimes catches fire

at will *In the film, the alien could disappear at will.* = whenever he/she/it wants or chooses **Where there's a will there's a way** = If you are determined enough about something, you will succeed. **against one's will** *I'm sorry I went against your will and built a high wall round the house.* = doing something against one's own or someone's wishes

wil•low /'wɪləʊ/ noun, u. = a kind of tree with tall, thin branches that grows near water and has soft wood, from which cricket bats are made **willowy** adj. *a willowy dancer* = tall, thin and graceful, like a willow tree (referring to a woman)

wil•ly-nil•ly /wɪli'nɪli/ adv. *There are no buses running today so you will have to walk to school, willy-nilly.* = whether you like it or not (informal)

wilt[1] /wɪlt/ verb, i. *The plants are wilting because they did not get enough water.* = to dry up and begin to die (referring to plants)

wilt[2] aux. verb *Thou wilt do as I command.* = (you) will (old-fashioned)

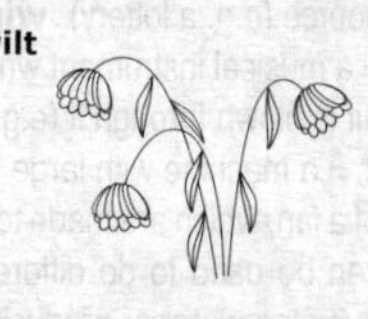
wilt

wimp /wɪmp/ noun, c. *They were afraid to speak the truth. What wimps they are!* = a weak person or someone who is afraid to do something (informal, derogatory)

win[1] /wɪn/ verb, t. or i. (**won**) **1** *Australia has won the match against Holland.*(t.) = to defeat an opponent in a competition or fight **2** *Who has won the first prize?*(t.)= to gain something in a competition **3** *She won everyone's respect through her gentle behaviour.*(t.) = to gain something through one's efforts or good qualities etc.

win[2] noun, c. *Our school is celebrating its win in the quiz competition.* = victory or success **winner** noun, c. = a person or team that has won something (a prize or a competition etc.)

to win over = to bring somebody around to one's way of thinking, through one's good deeds, behaviour etc. **You can't win with him/her** = you can never satisfy that person, whatever you do (informal)

wince /wɪns/ verb, i. *He winced when he thought of the unfair treatment he had received from his employer.* = to suffer pain in the mind which is shown in the expression on the face

winch[1] /wɪntʃ/ noun, c. = a machine that is used to lift or pull up heavy objects by means of a rope or chain that is wound around a turning part, called the drum

winch[2] verb, t. *The bus which fell into the river has been winched out.* = to lift with the help of a winch

wind[1] /wɪnd/ noun, c. or u. **1** *The wind is blowing from the east.*(c.) = air which is moving **2** *The baby is crying because it has wind.*(u.) = gas in the stomach **3** *The speech contained nothing but wind.*(u.) = words which sound good but mean little **4** *He ran out of breath and we thought he would not be able to complete the race, but he was able to recover his wind.*(u.) = breath **windy** adj. **1** *a windy place* = open to the wind (see **wind-swept**) **2** *a windy speech* = very long and containing too many words (derogatory) **wind-bag** noun, c. = a person who talks too much (derogatory) **wind-break** noun, c. = a line of trees planted (usually near the sea-shore) to check the force of the wind **wind-cheater** noun, c. = a short coat, usually made of nylon, which keeps out the wind and keeps the body warm **windfall** noun, c. = money which one gets from an unexpected

W

source (e.g. a lottery) **wind instrument** noun, c. = a musical instrument which produces sounds when air is blown through it (e.g. a flute) **windmill** noun, c. = a machine with large metal arms, like the blades of a fan, which are made to turn by the wind and which can be used to do different kinds of work, such as pumping water or producing electricity **wind-pipe** noun = the tube inside the throat through which air passes as we breathe in or out **windscreen** noun, c. = a piece of glass or plastic fixed in front of a car, bus etc. to keep out the wind **windscreen wiper** noun, c. = pieces of metal with rubber blades that are attached to the windscreen of a car, bus etc. to wipe away the water when it rains, so that the road ahead is clearly visible **wind surf** verb, i. *We went wind-surfing on the beach yesterday.* = to ride the waves on a flat wooden or plastic board **wind-swept** adj. *a wind-swept meadow* = open to the wind **wind-tunnel** noun, c. = an artificial tunnel in which scientific tests are carried out to study the effect of the wind on the movement of aircraft, motor cars etc. **windward** adv. or adj. = in the direction from which the wind is blowing

to get wind of something = to find out something that was meant to be a secret **to take the wind out of someone's sails** = to take away someone's confidence or determination by saying or doing something unexpected

wind[2] /wɪnd/ verb, t. *The man received a blow in the stomach which winded him.* = to lose one's breath or have difficulty in breathing

wind[3] /waɪnd/ verb, t. or i. (**wound**) **1** *The clock has stopped. You will have to wind it up.*(t.) = to make the spring inside a clock, watch or toy tight by turning a handle round and round **2** *The narrow road wound up the hill.*(i.)= to follow a twisting (not straight) course, with many turns or changes in direction

wind (something) up **1** = to pull a curtain or blind down or up **2** *We are putting up some one-act plays for the school programme, but we will wind up with a group song.* = to end **3** *I'm tired now. Let's wind up and go home.* = stop doing whatever one is doing (informal) **4** *We wound up the business as we were losing money.* = to close a business enterprise **wind (something) down** **1** *Since the exams are near, I think you should wind down your sports activities.* = to cut down or reduce an activity **2** *We are winding down the project which started three years ago.* = to start the process of bringing some activity to a stop **to wind someone up** = to annoy someone, often in order to get pleasure from doing so (informal)

win•dow /'wɪndəʊ/ noun, c. **1** = an opening in the wall of a building or the side of a vehicle, intended to allow light and air to enter, which can be closed when required **2** *You can open a new window if you want to view this file.* = an area on a computer screen where one can look at a part of a program that one is working on [COMPUTERS] **window-dressing** noun, u. **1** = the act of decorating the front (visible) part of a shop **2** *He seems to be a successful lawyer, but don't be taken in by the glittering office. This is all window dressing.* = something done to give people a good impression or opinion, often hiding the reality (disapproving) **window pane** noun, c. = a piece of glass fixed to a window (which can be opened or closed) (see pic under **glass**) **window shop** verb, i. (**window shopped**) *We went to the market but bought nothing. We just window shopped.* = to look at the goods inside a shop without buying anything **window sill** noun, c. = a shelf or space in the wall near the lower edge of a window

go out of the window **1** *I was on a diet but when I saw all the good food on the table, my diet went out of the window!* = to suddenly give up something that one has been doing (informal, humorous) **2** *Shikha's plan was accepted and ours went out of the window.* = to be rejected (informal)

wine /waɪn/ noun, u. or c. = an alcoholic drink made from grapes or other kinds of fruit

wing[1] /wɪŋ/ noun, c. **1** *a bird with large wings* = the front limbs of a bird which can move up and down and are used to fly **2** *the wings of an aircraft* = the long, flat pieces of metal sticking out from the sides of an aircraft, like the wings of a bird, which support the aircraft while it is flying through the air **3** *This is the new wing of the college, where we have our library.* = a part of a building which stands out from the central part **4** *These politicians belong to the left wing parties.* = a group within a political party or some other organization

wing[2] verb, t. **1** *The eagle winged down from the mountain top.* = to fly (literary) **2** *We tried to shoot the bird down but succeeded only in winging it.* = to wound a bird in its wing **winger** noun, c. = a player, in the game of football or hockey, who plays in the forward line, in the extreme left or right position **wing span** noun, u. *The Boeing 747 aircraft has a wing span of 65 metres.* = the distance from the tip (end) of one wing of an aircraft to the tip of the other wing

to take someone under one's wing = to protect or support someone and guide them

wink[1] /wɪŋk/ verb, i. *'You are late again!' my employer shouted at me. I thought he was angry, but when he winked I knew he was only joking.* = to close and open one eye quickly, as a signal of some kind, usually meant to be humorous

wink[2] noun, c. = the act of winking (closing and opening one eye quickly)

to not get a wink of sleep = to not be able to sleep at

all **forty winks** = a very short nap (period of sleep), usually in the afternoon **to wink at something** *Our teacher was not happy that we were singing loudly when she entered the class, but she winked at it.* = to allow something to happen which should not be allowed

win•now /'wɪnəʊ/ verb,t. *Farmers use a large basket as a fan, to winnow the grain after the harvest.* = to separate the husk (outer covering) from the grain by blowing it away

win•ter[1] /'wɪntə^r/ noun, c. = the cold part of the year, which usually lasts from November to January in countries that are north of the equator

winter[2] verb, i. *These birds from Siberia winter in the warm waters of the Chilika Lake.* = to spend the winter in some place **winter sports** noun (always plural) = sports such as skiing (moving across the snow on skis) which take place on snow during winter **wintry** adj. **1** *wintry winds* = cold **2** *a wintry welcome* = unfriendly and cold (also **frosty**)

wipe[1] /waɪp/ verb, t. *There are some ink stains on the table. Can you wipe them away with this piece of cloth?* = to rub a surface with a piece of cloth or against another surface in order to remove dirt, mud or marks etc. from it

wipe[2] noun, u. *Give the table a good wipe.*= the act of wiping (rubbing) something to clean it

to wipe off *When I restarted my computer I found that all my important files had been wiped off.* = to lose information etc. [COMPUTERS] **to wipe out** **1** *wipe out the enemy* = to destroy completely **2** *The disease has now been wiped out in the region.* = to end or destroy something so that it will not occur again **to wipe the slate clean** = to make a new beginning by forgetting the past **to wipe the floor with someone** *The other team wiped the floor with us in the debate.* = to defeat badly (informal) **to feel wiped out** = to feel very tired (informal)

wire[1] /waɪə^r/ noun, c. or u. **1** *We need some barbed wire for this fence.* = a piece of metal in the shape of a long thread, often used to carry electrical currents **2** *I have received a wire from my friend in Delhi.* = a telegram (message sent by telegraph)

wire[2] verb, t. **1** *This house has just been wired.* = to fix or set up a system of wires, specially to carry electricity **2** *My friend has wired to say he is arriving next week.* = to send a telegram **wireless** noun or adj. *a wireless message* = sent by radio, without the use of wires **wire-tapping** noun = the act of listening secretly to telephone conversations between other people (also **phone tapping**) **wiring** noun, u. *The wiring in this house is old and needs to be changed.* = the system of wires in a building by which electricity is carried to its different parts **wiry** adj. *a person with a wiry body* = thin but strong (like a wire)

wis•dom /'wɪzdəm/ noun, u. *He is a man of great wisdom. You should follow his advice.* = knowledge gained through experience or learning, which gives a person the ability to understand a situation correctly and to decide on the right course of action **wisdom tooth** noun, c. (**wisdom teeth**) = the four large teeth at the corners of the upper and lower jaws, which appear later than the other teeth

wise /waɪz/ adj. **1** *a wise lady* = having wisdom **2** *Earlier, he was able to fool me, but now I am wise to his tricks.* = able to understand and deal with the cleverness of someone **wisecrack** noun, c. *As the speaker was about to begin his talk, someone in the audience made a wisecrack. 'Be quiet, everyone!' he said, 'or you will miss these pearls of wisdom'.* = a humorous or clever remark that is not always liked (often disapproving)

-wise suffix meaning **1** showing that a thing is placed in a certain way e.g. **lengthwise** adv. *Let's lay the tablecloth lengthwise.* = in a particular way or direction **2** with reference to something e.g. **agewise** adv. *Agewise, we have no problem with you.* = with reference to your age (informal)

wish[1] /wɪʃ/ verb, t. **1** *I wish to buy a sari for my wife.* = to want (formal) **2** *'I wish we could fly off to the moon!' he said.* = to want or ask for something which one cannot have or do **3** *I wish you a long and prosperous life.* = to express a hope for someone else, as a kind of greeting

wish[2] noun, c. *'I will grant your wish!' the kind fairy told the poor woman.* = something that one wants, but is difficult to get **wishbone** noun, c. = the V-shaped bone in the breast of a chicken **wishful thinking** noun *He believes that his son has become a fine cricketer and will soon be playing for the country, but this is only wishful thinking on his part.* = the false belief that something that one wishes for is really going to happen

wish•y-wash•y /'wɪʃiwɒʃi/ adj. *All his ideas on making society better are wishy-washy.* = confused and unclear (derogatory)

wisp /wɪsp/ noun, c. *He saw a wisp of cloud in the sky.* = a small, thin piece of something

wist•ful /'wɪstfəl/ adj. *The little child stood outside the toy shop, gazing at the toys with a wistful look on her face.* = looking sad because one cannot get something that one wants

wit /wɪt/ noun, u. or c. **1** *She is popular as a speaker because of her ready wit.*(u.) = the ability to say things which are clever as well as humorous **2** *He is a famous wit.*(c.) = a person who possesses wit **3** (always plural) *He lives by his wits alone.* = cleverness

witch /wɪtʃ/ noun, c. (**witches**) = a woman who is

W

believed to have evil or magical powers (masculine **wizard**) **witchcraft** noun,u. = the use of magical powers by witches **witch-doctor** noun, c. = a person (usually a man belonging to a tribe that lives in a forest) who is believed to have magical powers and can cure diseases **witch-hunt** noun, c. = action taken by someone in power to harm those who are thought to be enemies

with /wɪð/ prep. **1** *Anne came to my house with her uncle.* = in the company of **2** *I peel oranges with my fingers.* = by means of **3** *The house with green doors is Vijay's.* = having **4** *India's trade with its neighbours should grow further.* = in relation to **5** *The pavement was littered with peanut shells.* = showing **6** *I can't study with all that noise around me.* = caused by **7** *We have to compete with our friends in the quiz.* = against **8** *With all the support from her parents, she still failed to learn swimming.* = in spite of **9** *Pran has replaced his old bedsheets with new ones.* = used to compare two things

with•draw /wɪð'drɔː/ verb, t. or i. (**withdrew, withdrawn**) **1** *The government has withdrawn the laws that were passed last year against trade with China.* (t.)= to take back **2** *I want to withdraw Rs 1,000 out of my account in this bank.*(t.) = to take money out of a bank account **3** *The protesters withdrew when they saw the police jeep and went back to their homes.*(i.) = to go back **4** *I had agreed to contest the election but now I have decided to withdraw.*(i.) = not to take part in some activity **withdrawal** noun, u. **1** = the act of withdrawing **2** = the amount of money that one takes out of a bank account (see **withdraw** meaning **2**) **withdrawn** adj. *He used to be very friendly and sociable but now he has become withdrawn.* = quiet and unwilling to communicate (talk)

with•er /ˈwɪðə^{r}/ verb, i. or t. *The plants withered because they were not looked after properly.*(i.) = to become weak (referring commonly to plants) **withering** adj. *He gave me such a withering look that I did not have the courage to speak to him.* = something that takes away one's courage and makes one feel small

with•hold /wɪð'həʊld/ verb, t. (**withheld**) *She had promised to help me during the election but she withheld her support.* = not to give something that one has the power to give

with•in /wɪð'ɪn/ prep. **1** *It was hot outside but cool within the room.* = inside **2** *We have ordered some food from a restaurant. It should arrive within 15 minutes.* = in not more than

with•out /wɪð'aʊt/ prep. or adv. **1** *You should not leave the classroom without the teacher's permission.* (prep.) = not having **2** *His books are selling very well, both within the country and without.*(adv.) = outside (old-fashioned)

with•stand /wɪð'stænd/ verb, t. (**withstood**) *The storm was so severe that it blew down most of the trees. But this old peepul tree was able to withstand the storm.* = to oppose (fight against) something successfully and remain unharmed

wit•ness[1] /ˈwɪtnɪs/ verb, t. **1** *Did you witness the Republic Day parade this year?* = to be present at some event and to see what happens (formal) **2** *I want you to witness this document by signing it.* = to sign a document as proof that it is genuine (real) [LAW]

witness[2] noun, c. (**witnesses**) **1** *Call the next witness.* = a person who is asked to state in court what he/she knows about a case that is being tried **2** *He was a witness to the rude behaviour of the salesperson.* = a person who is present when something happens and sees it happening **witness box** = an enclosed area in a court room in which the witness stands/sits

wiz•ard /ˈwɪzəd/ noun, c. = a man who has magical powers (see **witch**)

wiz•ened /ˈwɪzənd/ adj. *an old man with a wizened face* = dried up and looking old

wob•ble /ˈwɒbəl/ verb, i. **1** *The old man is so weak that he wobbles when he walks.* = to move unsteadily (as if about to fall) **2** *The organization is wobbling.* = to be unable to stay in control or power **wobbly** adj. *The baby tried to walk on its wobbly legs.* = shaking and unable to remain steady

woe /wəʊ/ noun, u. or c. **1** *His financial woes are increasing.*(c.) = problems or difficulties **2** *His heart was full of woe when his wife died.*(u.) = sorrow (old-fashioned, literary) **woeful** adj. **1** *a woeful story* = very sad **2** *The house was in a state of woeful neglect.* = very bad; something that one should feel unhappy about (literary)

wok /wɒk/ noun, c. = a metal pot with a round bottom, used specially in Chinese cooking

wolf[1] /wʊlf/ noun, c. (**wolves**) = a wild animal that looks like a large dog and lives and hunts with other wolves in a pack (group)

wolf[2] verb, t. *They were so hungry that they wolfed down the food I placed before them.* = to eat very quickly and hungrily (informal)

to keep the wolf from the door *The money she earns is not enough for them but it keeps the wolf from the door.* = to have just enough money for basic needs so that one is able to manage **to cry wolf** = to pretend to be in danger when there is no danger, thereby losing the sympathy of people **a wolf in sheep's clothing** = referring to a person who pretends to be good but has evil intentions

wom•an /ˈwʊmən/ noun, c. (**women** /ˈwɪmɪn/) or

u. **1** (c.)= a fully grown female human being **2** *In several aboriginal tribes the woman builds the houses.* = women in general **3** *I need a woman to help us with the cooking.* = a helper who is a woman **womanhood** noun, u. *The girl will reach womanhood in a few years.* = the state of being a woman (old-fashioned) **womanish** adj. *a womanish voice* = like that of a woman (referring to a quality that should not be found in a man) (derogatory) Ⓖ (compare with **womanly**) **womanize (womanise)** verb, i. *He has a reputation for womanizing.* = to become sexually involved with many women (disapproving) **womanly** adj. *womanly qualities* = qualities that people expect to find in a woman Ⓖ (compare with **manly**) **women's studies** noun = the study of history or literature with the aim of studying issues connected with women (also **feminist studies**)

> **Usage** Modern usage recognizes the need to refer to women without reference to social position, or women as distinct from men.
> - *woman/women* can be used instead of *lady/ladies*, e.g. *Could all the women put their hands up, please?*
> - Use *a woman teacher, a woman driver* instead of *a lady teacher* etc. but only if there is a need to show that it is a woman and not a man.

womb /wu:m/ noun, c. = the part of a woman's body in which a baby grows before it is born (also **uterus**)

wom•bat /'wɒmbæt/ noun = a small animal that looks like a bear, found in Australia

won•der[1] /'wʌndəʳ/ verb, i. or t. **1** *I wonder how you can write so well.* = to express admiration or surprise at something **2** *I wonder what the two managers are discussing at their meeting.* = to feel curious about something (to want to know) **3** *I wonder if she understood what I was trying to say.* = to doubt something **4** *I wonder if you could tell me how I could get to the station.* = used to make a polite request

wonder[2] noun, u. or c. **1** *The beauty of the Taj Mahal fills us with wonder.*(u.) = the feeling of surprise, mixed with admiration, that is caused by something unusually beautiful **2** *The Taj Mahal is one of the seven wonders of the world.*(c.) = something that causes a feeling of wonder (surprise and admiration)

wonder[3] adj. *a wonder drug* = something that is unusually good or effective

wont[1] /wəʊnt/ noun, u. *He ate too much at the feast, as is his wont, and fell ill.* = habit (formal and old-fashioned)

wont[2] adj. *She is wont to fall asleep while studying at night.* = in the habit of doing something (old-fashioned)

won't /wəʊnt/ aux. verb *I won't be able to come.* = shortened form of 'will not'

woo /wu:/ verb, t. **1** *He wooed the girl for years and finally married her.* = to try to win the love of a woman or man in order to marry him or her **2** *The banks are trying hard to woo customers with new schemes.* = to try to win someone over or to gain the support of

wood /wʊd/ noun, u. or c. **1** *The chair is made of teak wood.*(u.) = the hard substance of which trees are made and from which furniture etc. can be made **2** (c.) = a place where many trees grow (usually plural **woods**) **wooden** adj. **1** *a wooden bench* = made of wood **2** *a wooden expression* = dull **wooded** adj. = having woods (many trees) **woodland** = an area that has woods **woodpecker** noun, c. = a kind of small bird with a long beak that can make holes in trees to pull out insects **woodwork** noun, u. = the parts of a house that are made of wood (e.g. doors etc.) **wood worm** noun, c. = a kind of worm that lives in and eats wood

woof /wʊf/ noun **1** = the shorter threads used in weaving cloth which run across the long threads (also **weft**) **2** = the low, soft sound sometimes produced by a dog while barking **woofer** noun, c. = a loud-speaker that gives out deep sounds (opposite **tweeter**)

wool /wʊl/ noun, u. **1** = the thick hair produced by sheep **2** = the threads and the cloth made from the hair of sheep **wool-gathering** noun *You should pay attention to the teacher when she is talking. Stop wool-gathering!* = thinking of other things instead of paying attention to what is being said or done **woollen** adj. *a woollen shirt* = made of wool **woollens** noun, u. (always plural) *You should put on some woollens. It is rather cold today.* = warm clothes made of wool, usually knitted from threads (e.g. a sweater) **woolly** adj. *His ideas are somewhat woolly.* = confused (not very clear) (referring to the way in which a person thinks) (derogatory)

to pull the wool over someone's eyes = to deceive (fool) someone by telling them things which are not true

woozy /'wʊ:zɪ/ adj. = feeling weak and unsteady on one's feet (informal)

word[1] /wɜ:d/ noun, c. **1** *The word 'chef' means 'a cook'.* = a group of sounds, that can be written as a group of letters of the alphabet, which carries a certain meaning **2** *I would like to have a word with you.* = a short conversation (talk) **3** *There has been no word from my daughter in Nagpur for more than a month.* = message **4** *He has given me his word and I am sure he will keep it.* = promise

word[2] verb, t. *How should I word this letter?* = to express through words **word-blindness** noun,

W

u. = the inability to recognize the difference between certain letters e.g. 'b', 'd', 'p' etc. which causes difficulty in reading (also **dyslexia**) **wordless** adj. *Her expression conveyed wordless thanks.* = expressed without the use of words or language **word-play** noun, u. *You can find a lot of word-play in the plays of Shakespeare, for example in the line 'Not upon my soul but upon my sole'.* = playing with the sounds and meanings of words to create humour (also **pun**) **wordy** adj. *a wordy speech* = using too many words (slightly derogatory)

in other words *He said your idea was good, but people were not ready for it. In other words, he thought the idea would not work.* = saying the same thing using different words **in your own words** *Tell me in your own words what the actor said.* = expressing /describing something using one's own terms/words **to give/keep your word** *I hope you'll keep your word and not spend so much time on the telephone.* = to make/keep a promise **word-for-word** *The reports in the two newspapers were the same, word-for-word. They must have been written by the same person.* = identical in every respect **word by word** *This is a word by word translation of the book from English into Tamil. I just wanted a general translation.* = exact, based on each word (often derogatory when referring to a translation) **Take my word for it** = an expression meaning 'You don't have to ask others to check if it is true. Believe me.' **to have a word with someone** *We need to take a decision about the school holidays. I'll have a word with the Principal and let you know.* = to discuss a matter with someone **to take someone at their word** *I wasn't sure Amit would do what he had promised but I took him at his word.* = to trust that someone will do something that has been promised **to send word** *We have sent word to him to come as soon as possible.* = to send someone a message, usually asking them to do something **to put in a good word for someone** *She doesn't have a very high opinion of me. Please put in a good word for me.* = to say something favourable about a person to another person **by word of mouth** *Publicity for the new restaurant by word of mouth is better than an advertisment in the newspaper.* = an opinion about someone or something which spreads when people talk to each other **to (not) get a word in edgeways** *Whenever we meet, she speaks such a lot that I am not able to get a word in edgeways.* = to not be able to express your opinion because the other person does not give you a chance to speak **to be the last word in comfort etc.** = to have very high standards for which something is admired (informal) **from the word go** *Our journey was bad from the word go.* = from the beginning (said about events, relationships etc.) (informal)

word-processor /wɜːdˈprəʊsesəʳ/ noun, c. = a computer used for typing letters, documents etc.

work[1] /wɜːk/ verb, i. or t. **1** *Don't disturb me now. I am working.*(i.) = to do something which is part of one's job **2** *We worked hard on the essay we had to write.*(t.) = to put a lot of effort into something **3** *This pump does not work.*(i.) = to be in a proper condition, so that it can be used for the purpose for which it was intended (referring to a machine etc.) **4** *Show me how to work this machine.*(t.) = to make something work (operate) **5** *Today we tried out a new method of saving water, and it worked!*(i.) = to be successful

work[2] noun, u. or c. **1** *I have to do a lot of work in the office.*(u.) = activity which is done as part of one's job **2** *I hope this essay is your own work and not copied from the book?*(u.) = something that one has produced through one's own efforts **3** *I can't leave work until nine tonight.*(u.) = the office or place where one works **4** *All the artist's works were displayed at the exhibition.*(c.) = things that one has produced **5** *We don't know much about her writing. Let's ask her to read us some examples of her work.*(u.) = writing, music etc. that one produces as a part of one's work **workable** adj. *She has given us a workable plan.* = something which can be put into practice **workaday** adj. *He has a wonderful imagination but he is not suited to the workaday world.* = ordinary **workaholic** noun, c. *He works 15 hours a day. He is a workaholic.* = a person who loves hard work and feels unhappy when he/she is not working (usually disapproving) **workbook** noun, c. = a book with exercises or questions to which the answers have to be written in the book **worker** noun, c. **1** = a person who works in a business house or factory etc. and is generally not asked to make important decisions **2** = a female bee that collects food for the other bees living in the hive **workforce** noun, u. = the group of people working for a factory **work-horse** noun, c. **1** = a person who is often made to do most of the work in an office etc. **2** *The Ambassador car remains an excellent work-horse even after 50 years of production.* = a vehicle or machine that is very useful **working class** noun, u. (often plural **working classes**) = the class (group) of people who are required to work with their hands, specially in factories (The term **factory workers** is now preferred.) **work-load** noun, c. = the amount of work that one is required to do in a given period of time **workman** noun, c. (**workmen**) = a person who does skilled work with his/her hands (e.g. a carpenter) **workmanship** noun, u. *The workmanship on this furniture is really excellent.* = the skill used in producing something with one's hands **workout** noun, u. or c. *He has gone to the gymnasium (gym) for a workout.* = exercise done to keep oneself healthy **workplace** noun, u.= the factory or place where one works **works** noun (always plural) *The government has taken up a new programme of works.* = the construction of roads, buildings, bridges etc. usually paid for by the government (also **public works**) **workshop** noun, c. **1** *a motor workshop* = a place where machines are used to produce something or to carry out repairs **2** *a workshop for teachers* = a meeting of people working in the same profession where ideas for practical use are discussed or developed **workstation** noun, c. = a computer that is connected to a more powerful computer, used for additional work [COMPUTERS]

at work *I called her at ten in the night and she was still at work.* = busy in the office or workplace **to work out (something)** **1** *Before we go on the journey, we have to work out the details.* = to calculate or get a clear picture of something **2** *I know it's a difficult time for you. Don't worry, things will work out.* = (of a difficult situation) to move gradually towards a solution which is acceptable, peaceful etc. **3** *I have put on a lot of weight. I must start working out.* = to do exercises in order to keep fit **to work out to something** *Our expenses work out to roughly Rs 500.* = the result when calculated **to be worked up** *Our teacher was really worked up about our poor performance in the exam.* = to be upset/angry about something (informal) **to work something out for oneself** = to find an answer or solution on one's own **to have one's work cut out** = to have a specific task that is waiting to be done **to work well** *I try to sleep in the mornings and work at night. It works well for me.* = to be suitable/effective; to yield results **to work wonders** *The new school worked wonders for my child's happiness.* = to be very successful in achieving something **out of work** = to be without employment **'people at work'** = a sign put up to show that repair/maintenance work is taking place **working knowledge** noun, u. *He has only a working knowledge of Chinese.* = just enough knowledge of something to be able to manage **the works** *'Did you enjoy the party?' 'Oh yes. We had music and dancing and food—the works!'* = everything (informal)

world /wɜːld/ noun, u. or c. **1** *the seven wonders of the world* = the Earth (the planet on which we live) **2** *the countries of the Third World* = a part or area of the world that has some special quality **3** *The animal world and the plant world are closely linked.* = a group of living things **4** *the world of sports* = a particular area or branch of human activity **5** *Buddha renounced the world at a very early age.* = things that are connected with everyday life **world-class** adj. *We have several world-class players.*= of the highest international class **wordly** adj. *I am able to meet all my worldly needs.* = connected with the material world (see meaning **5** for **world**) **wordly-wise** adj. = clever in dealing with people and everyday situations **world-power** noun, c. = a country which has a powerful influence on the rest of the world **world-wide** adj. or adv. *Indian textiles are famous world-wide.* = all over the world **World Cup** = an international competition in football/cricket which takes place once in four years **World War** (I or II) = fought during 1914-18 (World War I) and 1939-45 (World War II), in which many of the countries of the world took part

to have the best of both worlds *She's getting paid for the work she is doing, but she can work from home. She is having the best of both worlds.* = to enjoy a double advantage (often disapproving) **out of this world** *The music was out of this world.* = so good that it cannot be described (informal) **to be on top of the world** = to be or feel very happy (informal) **to do someone a world of good** *He was very tired and the rest did him a world of good.* = something which helps someone a lot (informal)

worm[1] /wɜːm/ noun, c. **1** *an earthworm* = a kind of insect (an animal without bones) with a long, thin body **2** = a weak person who gets no respect **3** = the thread or curving line on the outside of a screw [TECHNICAL] **4** = a kind of computer-related virus which creates problems by making copies of itself, causing the computer to shut down etc. [COMPUTERS]

worm[2] verb, i. *They managed to worm their way into our confidence.* = to get into a favourable position after making a lot of effort, often using dishonest means (derogatory) **worm-eaten** adj. *worm-eaten books* = old and in poor condition

to worm out = to extract information from somebody (derogatory)

worn /wɔːn/ verb, t. (past tense of **wear**) *Are saris worn only in India?* = used as part of one's dress

worn out **1** *These shirts are worn out. You should give them away.* = in poor condition as a result of long use (referring to clothes, shoes etc.) **2** *I feel completely worn out after the match.* = tired

wor•ry[1] /ˈwʌri/ verb, i. or t. **1** *You should not worry so much about your health. There is nothing wrong with you.*(i.) = to feel anxious or uneasy in the mind over something, or to fear that something bad will happen, over a long period **2** *He wants me to help him find a job and he has been worrying me with his requests.*(t.) = to trouble someone or to make someone feel uneasy or anxious

worry[2] noun, u. or c. (**worries**) **1** *Worry will cause your blood pressure to go up.*(u.) = anxiety (uneasy feelings in the mind) **2** *They have many financial worries.*(c.) = something that causes worry (anxiety)

worse[1] /wɜːs/ adj. (comparative degree of **bad**) *They told me your health was better, but I find it worse. You have become very weak.* = more bad than before

W

worse[2] adv. *He played badly in the last game but he played even worse this time.* = more badly

worse[3] noun, u. *The day was the hottest day of the season but worse was to follow. There was no electricity all night.* = something that is more bad than something else

to take a turn for the worse = when one is ill, to become more ill **to make matters worse** *I returned late from work last night. To make matters worse, I missed the last bus.* = used when describing two bad situations which happen one after the other, the second of which is worse than the first

wor•ship[1] /ˈwɜːʃɪp/ verb, t. (**worshipped**) **1** *The people of this tribe worship the spirits that live in the forest.* = to pray to a supernatural power or being as part of one's religion **2** *He worships the ground that she walks on.* = to have very great love or affection for someone (figurative)

worship[2] noun, u. *The church is open for worship all day.* = the act of showing respect to God or to a god as part of one's religion

worst[1] /wɜːst/ adj. (superlative form of **bad**) *This is one of the worst films I have seen.* = most bad

worst[2] adv. *Of all the players in the team, he played the worst.* = most badly

worst[3] noun, u. *I have had some illnesses, but this is the worst.*= the most bad thing or person

at (the) worst *Don't worry. At worst you will lose some marks if you miss these tests.* = the most bad outcome or result **to fear the worst** = to have the fear that someone may have died, met with an accident etc.

wor•sted /ˈwʊstɪd/ noun, u. = a kind of heavy woollen cloth

worth[1] /wɜːθ/ prep. **1** *This ring is worth Rs 5,000.* = having the value or price that is stated (mentioned) **2** *He looks simple but is worth a lot of money.* = to possess (have) money, property etc. of the value stated

worth[2] noun, u. *The present worth of the Kohinoor diamond is difficult to calculate.*= value **worthless** adj. *No one wants to buy that house. It is in such poor condition that it is worthless.* = having no value **worthwhile** adj. *We had to miss our dinner to listen to the concert, but it was worthwhile. She sang beautifully.* = providing good value (worth the money or time spent) **worthy** *Queen Elizabeth I proved to be a worthy queen.* = deserving respect

would /wʊd/ aux. (modal) verb **1** *He said he would come here on Friday.* = used as the past tense form of 'will' in reported speech (a sentence which reports what someone else said, without using the speaker's actual words. The actual words, in this case, were 'I will go there on Friday.') **2** *I thought you would bring us some food.* = used to refer to some future action or event which is probable (likely to happen) but not certain **3** *My grandmother would tell me stories every night.* = referring to habitual action in the past (something that happened regularly, over a long period of time) **4** *I would rather stay at home than go to the market.* = expressing a preference or choice **would-be** adj. *a would-be teacher* = something that one is preparing to become but has not yet become

wound[1] /wuːnd/ verb, t. *He was wounded in the leg during the battle.* = to cause damage to someone's body by using a weapon such as a gun or a knife

wound[2] noun, c. *He received a wound in the leg.* = a place where the body has been damaged as the result of some accident, injury etc.

wow[1] /waʊ/ interjec. *Wow! What a beautiful shirt you are wearing!* = an expression of admiration or surprise (informal)

wow[2] verb, t. (**wowed**) *This shirt is sure to wow your friends.*= to cause admiration in someone (informal)

wraith /reɪθ/ noun, c. = a ghost or spirit (literary)

wran•gle[1] /ˈræŋgəl/ verb, i. *Prem said the capital of Holland was Amsterdam while Aziz said it was The Hague. They wrangled for a long time before Aziz admitted he was wrong.*= to argue noisily for a long time

wrangle[2] noun, c. = a noisy argument

wran•gler /ˈræŋgləʳ/ noun, c. = a cowboy (a person whose job it is to take care of cattle on an American ranch or farm)

wrap[1] /ræp/ verb, t. (**wrapped**) *He wrapped the book in an old newspaper so that the cover would not become dirty.* = to fold some soft material such as paper around an object, so as to cover it up

wrap[2] noun, c. *It is rather cold today. You should get a wrap.* = a garment that one can wrap (fold) around one's body e.g. a shawl **wrapper** noun, c. = a loose cover for a book or some other object **wrap-around** adj. *a wrap-around skirt* = a garment, usually a skirt or a sarong, which is passed round the waist and tied with an overlapping fold **wrapping (paper)** = something that is used to cover a gift etc. to make it look attractive

to wrap up (something) **1** *We had better wrap up. It's cold outside.* = to wear suitably warm clothing to protect oneself against cold weather **2** *It's almost nine o' clock. Let's wrap up the meeting.* = to bring some activity to a close (informal) **to be wrapped up in something** = to be so completely involved in an activity, a hobby, one's work etc. that one cannot think of anything else (informal, mildly disapproving) **to keep something under wraps** *Let's keep the matter under wraps for the moment.* = to keep something secret (informal)

wrath /rɒθ/ noun, u. = great anger (formal and old-fashioned)

wreak /riːk/ verb, t. *The storm wreaked great damage in most parts of the state.* = to cause destruction or damage (literary)

wreath[1] /riːθ/ noun, c. = a circle made of flowers and leaves, often used to show respect to a dead person

wreath[2] verb, t. **1** *We could not see the top of the mountain because it was wreathed in clouds.* = to cover something up by forming a circle around it **2** *Her face was wreathed in smiles.* = to cover up almost completely

wreck[1] /rek/ verb, t. **1** *The ship was wrecked when it hit an iceberg floating in the sea.* = to cause a ship to be destroyed **2** *We had hoped to win this match but the rain wrecked our hopes of victory.* = to destroy completely

wreck[2] noun, c. **1** *The wreck of the 'Titanic' sank slowly to the bottom of the ocean.* = a ship that has been badly damaged in a storm etc. and is unable to sail **2** *He has become a wreck after he lost his wife.* = a person whose health or mind has been badly damaged (figurative)

wren /ren/ noun, c. = a kind of small bird

wrench[1] /rentʃ/ verb, t. **1** *The man was about to strike the dog but I wrenched the stick out of his hand.* = to pull something out by using a twisting or turning motion **2** *She wrenched her knee while playing volleyball.* = to twist and damage a limb or a part of a limb

wrench[2] noun, c. **1** *The dentist gave my rotten tooth a wrench and pulled it out.* = the act of pulling out something by using a twisting motion **2** *You will have to use a wrench to loosen this nut.* = a tool used to hold and tighten or loosen (make tight or loose) a nut (see pic under **tools**) **3** *It was such a wrench to see the children being separated from their parents.* = causing great sadness and pain

wrest /rest/ verb, t. **1** *I wouldn't give her the book, so she had to wrest it from my hand.* = to pull (formal) **2** *It is difficult to make money through farming, but we manage to wrest a living out of the soil.* = to get something after a hard struggle (old-fashioned)

wres•tle /'resəl/ verb, i. or t. **1** = to take part in the sport of wrestling **2** *He has to wrestle with a lot of problems.*(i.) = to struggle or fight against **wrestling** noun, u. = a sport in which two opponents try to throw each other to the ground

wretch /retʃ/ noun, c. (**wretches**) **1** *poor wretch* = an unfortunate person for whom one feels pity **2** *What a wretch!* = someone who makes you angry by doing something bad, dishonest etc. (informal) **wretched** adj. **1** *The Indian players are feeling wretched after losing the match.* = very unhappy **2** *It was a wretched film, without a story or any interesting scenes.* = very bad

wrig•gle /'rɪgəl/ verb, i. **1** *We saw a worm wriggling along the ground.* = to make short, quick movements from side to side while moving forward slowly **2** *Now the hero of this film has been surrounded by ten armed robbers. Let's see how he wriggles out of this situation.* = to escape a difficult situation by using some clever trick (informal)

wring /rɪŋ/ verb, t. (**wrung**) **1** *Tigers kill their prey by wringing the animal's neck.* = to twist **2** *The towel is wet. Can you wring it dry?* = to squeeze or press water out of a piece of cloth by twisting it between the hands **3** *When he found that the money in the cupboard had gone, he wrung his hands and wept.* = to move one's hands loosely up and down in a way that shows one is shocked or sad or helpless

wrin•kle[1] /'rɪŋkəl/ noun, c. = a line or fold on the skin, caused by age, worry, tiredness etc; an uneven line or fold on paper etc. **wrinkled** adj.

wrinkle[2] verb, t. *Age has wrinkled his face.* = to cause lines or folds to appear on the skin

wrist /rɪst/ noun, c. = the place where the hand joins the lower arm **wristwatch** noun, c. = a watch that is worn on the wrist by means of a band or strap **wristy** adj. *The batsman scored a boundary with a wristy cover-drive.* = done with a movement of the wrist (referring to a stroke or hit in tennis or cricket)

writ[1] /rɪt/ noun, c. *The High Court issued a writ, ordering the college to admit the student who had been refused admission.*= an order issued by a court [LAW]

writ[2] adj. *Disappointment was writ large on his face.* = clearly visible (old-fashioned)

write /raɪt/ verb, i. or t. (**wrote, written**) **1** *The children are learning to write.*(i.)= to make marks that represent letters or words on paper, using a pencil or pen **2** *Shakespeare has written a large number of plays.*(t.) = to create (produce) a book or something else that is read by people **3** *My son writes to me every week.*(i.) = to produce and send a letter **4** *Does this pen write?*(i.) = to make marks on paper etc. (used of a writing instrument such as a pen) **write-up** noun, c. *The new play has received very good write-ups in the newspapers.* = a written report that expresses an opinion about something e.g. a new film **writings** noun (always plural) = a collection of things written by a person

to write back *Did you write back to thank them for the card?* = to reply to someone's letters **to write down** *Please write down my message, otherwise you'll forget the details.* = to note something by writing it on paper **to write (something) off** 1 *The new car is so badly damaged in*

W

the accident that it will have to be written off. = to treat something as having no value **2** *Since they can't pay the loan, let's write it off.* = to agree or accept that someone who owes one money does not have to pay it **to be nothing to write home about** *The play was good, but nothing to write home about.* = (about an event) to not deserve great praise or attention (informal)

writhe /raɪð/ verb, i. *He writhed in pain after he was hit in the stomach.* = to make twisting movements of the body because of great pain

wrong[1] /rɒŋ/ adj. **1** *You said the capital of Madhya Pradesh is Nagpur. That statement is wrong.* = not correct or true **2** *It is wrong to steal.* = evil; against the rules of morality **3** *There is something wrong with this machine.* = some defect **4** *He is the wrong person for this job.* = not suitable

wrong[2] adv. **1** *Don't get me wrong. I support your proposal.* = in a wrong manner or with a wrong meaning **2** *The leader went wrong in his calculations.* = to make a mistake

wrong[3] noun, u. **1** *I hope you can understand the difference between right and wrong.* = behaviour that is not morally right **2** *He has done me no wrong.* = harm

wrong[4] verb, t. *You wrong me when you say that I am responsible for the defeat of the team.* = to be unjust or unfair to someone (formal) **wrong-doing** noun, c. *We find he is not guilty of any wrong-doing.* = bad or illegal behaviour **wrongful** adj. *wrongful action* = unjust

to get on the wrong side of someone = to do something which turns a person against one **to get out of the wrong side of one's bed** = to be in a bad mood (informal, often humorous) **to get off on the wrong foot** *It's a good film he's acting in. It's a pity he annoyed the director and got off on the wrong foot.* = to spoil a new relationship by doing something foolish or careless **to be on the wrong side of sixty etc.** *She should slow down because she's on the wrong side of sixty.* = to be in the late part of the stated age (and therefore unable to do something) (informal) **You can't go wrong** *If you do exactly what she says, you can't go wrong.* = nothing will go wrong **to have something all wrong** *You've got the instructions all wrong.* = to make a mistake because one hasn't understood something properly **(Please) don't get me wrong** = '(Please) don't misunderstand me.' (informal) **Correct me if I'm wrong** *Correct me if I'm wrong, but isn't this the house you lived in first?* = a way of saying one hopes one is correct (informal)

wrought /'rɔːt/ adj. *These beautiful chairs are wrought by hand.* = made (old-fashioned, literary) **wrought-iron** noun, u. or adj. *wrought-iron furniture* = things made from pieces of iron which are shaped by hand

wry /raɪ/ adj. *The man gave me a wry smile when I told him he was likely to get the job.* = showing that one is amused, displeased, and not ready to believe what is said

WWF abbr. of **Worldwide Fund for Nature**

www abbr. of **World Wide Web**

WYSIWYG abbr. of **What You See Is What You Get** = to say that something will look exactly the same when printed as when it is seen on the computer screen [COMPUTERS]

x, X /eks/ the twentyfourth letter of the English alphabet

x noun *3x–2 = 7.* = the sign that stands for some unknown quantity [MATHEMATICS]

X- prefix meaning 'extra' especially when referring to size (specially of clothes) e.g. XL, XS

x-chro•mo•some noun, c. = see **chromosome**

x-rated /eks-'reɪtid/ *an x-rated film* = A film with an X certificate is one which persons under the age of 18 are not allowed to see, because it has scenes of sex and violence.

xenon /'zenɒn/ noun, u. = a kind of gas which has no colour or smell and is sometimes used in light bulbs

xen•o•pho•bi•a /zenə'fəʊbiə/ noun, u. *He doesn't want any foreigners in this country. He seems to suffer from xenophobia.* = unnatural fear of foreign people, their customs etc.

xe•rox /'zɪərɒks/ noun, c. = (trademark) a photographic copy of a printed document, produced by a special copying machine (also **photocopy**)

X•mas /'krɪsməs/ noun, c. = Christmas

x-ray[1] /'eks reɪ/ noun, c. = a kind of invisible light that can pass through many solid sustances and is often used to photograph the inside of the body, for treating certain diseases [SCIENCE]

x-ray[2] verb, t. *The doctor x-rayed my hand to check if there was a fracture.* = to x-ray something

xy•lo•phone /'zaɪləfəʊn/ noun, c. = a kind of musical instrument consisting of a number of flat wooden or metal bars of different length which produce musical sounds when they are hit with a pair of wooden sticks

yY

y, Y /waɪ/ the twentyfifth letter of the English alphabet

Y abbr. for 'Yes' in forms etc.

yacht /jɒt/ noun, c. = a kind of sail-boat used for racing or a large private ship used for leisure travel

yak /jæk/ noun, c. **1** = an animal that looks like a cow but has long hair, found in Central Asia (Tibet and neighbouring areas) **2** *We often meet for a yak about the old days.* = an informal conversation (slang)

yam /jæm/ noun = the root of a kind of plant used as food

yang /jæŋ/ noun = the male force or power which combines with yin, the female force, to form the entire universe, according to Chinese philosophy (see also **yin**)

yank[1] /jæŋk/ verb, t. *He yanked the alarm cord on the train, making the train come to a halt.* = to pull suddenly with force

yank[2] noun, c. **1** *He gave the rope a yank.* = a sudden and strong pull (informal) **2** = a term sometimes used to describe an American humorously

yap /jæp/ verb, i. (**yapped**) **1** *The little dog yapped angrily at the stranger.* = to bark in a thin, sharp voice (referring to the sound produced by a dog of small size) **2** *The girls yapped away all night.* = to talk in an excited manner about unimportant things (humourous)

yard /jɑːd/ noun, c. **1** = a unit for the measurement of length, equal to three feet (a little less than one metre) **2** *backyard* = an enclosed area next to a building **yardstick** noun, c. *He can be considered a great writer by any yardstick.* = a standard by which a quality or ability might be judged or compared

yarn /jɑːn/ noun, u. or c. **1** *We buy silk yarn from China to make these saris.*(u.) = thread used to make cloth **2** *He told us a yarn about meeting a ghost.*(c.) = a story about an adventure etc. which is not entirely true

to spin a yarn = to make up a false story

yaw /jɔː/ verb, i. *The aircraft yawed suddenly to the left, driven by the wind.* = to move suddenly to one side, out of control (referring to the movement of an aircraft or ship) [TECHNICAL]

yawn[1] /jɔːn/ verb, i. *The child is yawning. He must be sleepy.* = to breathe in or out deeply with the mouth wide open, as a result of feeling of tired, sleepy or bored

yawn[2] noun, c. **1** *The child suppressed a yawn.*= the action of yawning **2** *The film was a yawn. I couldn't sit through it.* = very boring (informal)

yaws /jɔːz/ noun (always plural) = a kind of skin disease [MEDICINE]

Y-chromosome noun, c. = see **chromosome**

yea /jeɪ/ adv. = yes (expressing consent or agreement) (old-fashioned)

yeah /jeə/ adv. *'Will you come to my party?' 'Yeah, sure!'* = yes (informal)

year /jɪə^r/ noun, c. **1** = a period of 365 (sometimes 366) days or 12 months **2** *She is in the second year of college.* = a particular part of a school or college course that a person is studying **yearly** adj. *a yearly meeting* = happening once a year (also **annual**) **calendar year** noun = the period starting in January and ending in December **leap year** noun = (see **leap**) **light year** noun = the distance covered by light in 365 days **year book** noun = a book published by an organization, school etc. presenting facts and events relating to the past year

yearn /jɜːn/ verb, i. *I often yearn to go back to the village where I was born.* = to wish very strongly to have or do something (often something that one cannot have or do) (literary) **yearning** noun, c. or u. *Although he has given up smoking, he often has a yearning for cigarettes.*(c.) = a strong desire for something

yeast /jiːst/ noun, u. = a type of **fungus** (tiny plant) which is used to produce alcohol and also to make bread soft

yell[1] /jel/ verb, i. *The captain yelled at one of the players when he missed an easy catch.* = to shout at someone loudly and angrily

yell[2] noun, c. *Anita let out an angry yell when a man stepped on her guitar.* = a loud and angry shout

yel•low[1] /'jeləʊ/ noun = a colour which is like that of a lemon

yellow[2] adj. **1** *a yellow dress* = having a yellow colour **2** *Are you afraid to ask for permission to join the protest march? I didn't know you were so yellow!* = cowardly (afraid to do something) (slang, derogatory)

yellow[3] verb, i. (**yellowed**) *The pages of the old book have yellowed with age.* = to become yellow **Yellow Pages** noun, u. (always plural) = the pages in a telephone directory (a book containing names and telephone numbers) which have a list of business companies and the kinds of business they do **yellow fever** noun = a dangerous tropical disease that makes the body turn yellow

yelp /jelp/ verb, i. *A man on a bicycle ran over a dog accidentally, making it yelp.* = to make a sharp cry expressing pain or excitement (see also **yowl**)

yen /jen/ noun **1** = the unit of money used in Japan **2** (only singular) *He has a yen for studying foreign languages.* = a strong desire or talent

yeo•man /ˈjəʊmən/ noun, c. (**yeomen**) = a farmer in Britain (in former times) **yeoman service** noun *The community is honouring the old teacher for having done yeoman service.* = valuable and loyal service given over a long period (old-fashioned)

yes /jes/ adv. **1** *'Can you see the ship?' 'Yes.'* = an expression of agreement or acceptance in answer to something that has been said **2** *'Can you hear me?' 'Yes, I can.'* = used to show that one has heard what someone is saying **3** *'Could I borrow your coat?' 'Yes, certainly.'* = used to allow someone to do something **yes-man** noun, c. *a loyal yes-man* = someone who always agrees with his/her leader (derogatory)

yet[1] /jet/ adv. **1** *He was supposed to come at nine o'clock. It is 9.25 now, but he hasn't come yet.* = so far; until this time **2** *The song is sad yet appealing.* = but (in spite of)

yet[2] conj. *He is careless and lazy, yet he has earned a name as a writer.* = but even so

ye•ti /ˈjeti/ noun = a mysterious animal that looks like a hairy human being and is believed to live in the Himalayas (also **abominable snowman**)

yew /juː/ noun = a kind of tree that grows in high altitudes

Yid•dish /ˈjɪdɪʃ/ noun, u. = a language somewhat like German which is spoken by Jewish people in some countries of eastern Europe

yield[1] /jiːld/ verb, t. or i. **1** *These mango trees yielded a lot of fruit this year.*(t.) = to produce **2** *He was not happy to do what we wanted, but finally yielded to our request.*(t.) = to give way and agree to do something after expressing strong unwillingness to do it **3** *The soldier was surrounded and had to yield to the enemy.*(i.) = to surrender (to accept defeat)

yield[2] noun, u. or c. *The yield from the farm has been very good this year.*(u.) = something that is produced **yielding** adj. **1** *A good leader should be strong, not yielding.* = ready to give way and agree with others, flexible (often disapproving) **2** *a yielding platform* = a surface which becomes lower in height when pressure is put on it

yin /jɪn/ noun, c. = the female force that combines with yang, the male force, to produce the universe, according to Chinese philosophy (see also **yang**)

yip•pee /jɪˈpiː/ interjec. *The results are out, and I have passed. Yippee!* = a cry expressing great happiness (informal)

yo•del /ˈjəʊdl/ verb, i. (**yodelled**) *Kishore Kumar, the famous singer, could yodel beautifully.* = to sing in a way that requires fast changes between one's normal voice and a very high voice (commonly used by folksingers in Switzerland)

yo•ga /ˈjəʊgə/ noun, u. **1** = an aspect of Hindu philosophy that aims to bring about union between human beings and God through control of the mind and body **2** = a set of physical exercises which form part of yoga **yogi** noun, c. = a person who practises yoga

yog•urt (yoghurt) /ˈjɒgət/ noun, u. = a product of milk which is thick, smooth and a little sour (also **curds**)

yoke[1] /jəʊk/ noun, c. **1** = a wooden pole or bar used to join a pair of animals, usually bullocks or horses, to a plough or a vehicle which the animals pull **2** *Large parts of Asia were once under foreign yoke.* = control or power which is not liked **3** = the front part of a dress just above the pleats

yoke[2] verb, t. *The cart-driver yoked his bullocks to the cart.* = to join a pair of animals (usually bullocks) to a vehicle or plough by using a yoke

yo•kel /ˈjəʊkəl/ noun, c. = a simple and somewhat foolish person from a village (derogatory, not respectful)

yolk /jəʊk/ noun, c. or u. = the yellow part of an egg (compare the **white** of an egg)

yon•der[1] /ˈjɒndəʳ/ adj. *Let us sit under yonder tree and enjoy Nature's beauty.* = that (old-fashioned, literary)

yonder[2] adv. *There's a house yonder where we can find shelter.* = over there; nearby (old-fashioned, literary)

you /juː/ or /jə/ pron. **1** *You and I will join together to start a business.* = the person to whom one is speaking **2** *You have to know the right people if you want to be successful in business.* = anyone (any person) **3** *This shirt is not you.* = a way of saying that something (e.g. a dress, music) is not suitable because it is not something the person normally wears, hears, does etc.

young[1] /jʌŋ/ adj. **1** *a young child // a young nation* = in an early stage of life or growth **2** *You are too young to watch this film.* = not old or mature enough **3** *This colour is too young for me.* = not suitable because one feels it is better for younger people

young[2] noun, u. *The lioness takes good care of her young.* = offspring (child or baby produced by a parent)

yours /jɔːz/ poss. pron. *This house is yours.* = belonging to you (the person spoken to) **Yours faithfully** = an expression used to end a formal or business letter **Yours sincerely** = an expression used to end a less formal letter

your•self /jəˈself/ reflexive pron. **1** *Be careful! You may hurt yourself.* = you (showing that an action performed by someone has an effect on the same person) **2** *You will have to do this yourself. No one is going to help you.* = showing that an action must be performed by someone without help from any other

Y

person **3** *You want us to wear ties, but you haven't worn one yourself.* = used to make the word 'you' stronger

all by oneself **1** *The baby can now drink from the bottle all by herself.* = on one's own and without help **2** *Did you make the journey all by yourself?* = alone **to keep something to oneself** *I'm going to tell you a secret. Please keep it to yourself.* = 'Do not tell anyone.'

youth /juːθ/ noun, u. or c. **1** *I was a good cricket player in my youth.*(u.) = younger days (the period of life when one is young) **2** (u.) = young people **3** *an ambitious youth*(c.) = young man **youthful** adj.

yowl /jaʊl/ verb, i. *The cat yowled angrily.* = to cry out loudly in anger or pain (referring to the sound made by a cat or dog) (see also **yelp**)

yo-yo /'jəʊ jəʊ/ noun, c. = a toy, consisting of a circular piece of wood or plastic, attached to a string, which can be made to run up and down the string

yuck•y /'jʌki/ adj. *The ice-cream is absolutely yucky. You won't be able to eat it.* = very bad or unpleasant (used mostly by children) (slang/derogatory)

yule•tide /'juːltaɪd/ noun = Christmas (formal)

yummy /'jʌmi/ adj. *The spiced rice is yummy.* = very tasty (slang)

yup /'jʌp/ interjec. = yes (very informal)

yup•pie /'jʌpi/ noun = an expression used as an abbreviation for 'young upwardly mobile professional' (a young person in a professional job who is seen as making and spending a lot of money)

zZ

z, Z /zed/ /zi:/ the twentysixth and last letter of the English alphabet

za•ny /ˈzeɪni/ adj. *Everyone made fun of his zany ideas.* = strange in an amusing kind of way

zap /zæp/ verb, t. **1** *The soldiers zapped the enemy.* = to destroy by force (informal) **2** *I have only 10 minutes. Let us zap through these files.* = to do something at a fast pace (informal) **3** *She zapped the television while we were watching something.* = to switch off a television, a radio etc. **4** *Let me zap these documents for you.* = to make a photocopy (informal)

zeal /zi:l/ noun, u. *She has been helping the people of this village for the last 10 years. I admire the zeal with which she works.* = the quality of showing great interest in doing something **zealous** adj. = full of zeal **zealously** adv. **zealousness** noun

zealot /ˈzelət/ noun, u. *A few zealots want to ban television as they think it can harm children.* = a person with very strong beliefs which he/she tries to force on others (derogatory, old-fashioned)

ze•bra /ˈzi:brə/ noun = an animal found in Africa that looks like a horse and has black and white stripes (lines) all over its body **zebra crossing** noun, c. = a broad band of black and white (or yellow) lines painted across a busy street, showing that pedestrians may cross the street at this point

zeit•geist /ˈzaɪtgaɪst/ noun, u. (German) = the spirit of the age (the ideas, emotions etc. that most people in a society share during a particular time)

Zen /zen/ noun = a form of Buddhism that is very popular in Japan, which gives great importance to meditation

zen•ith /ˈzenɪθ/ noun, u. **1** *The sun was at the zenith.* = the highest point in the sky reached by the sun **2** *The athlete was at her zenith that season. She won four gold medals.* = the highest point of achievement, power, influence etc.

zeph•yr /ˈzefəʳ/ noun, c. = a soft and gentle wind (literary)

zep•pe•lin /ˈzepəlɪn/ noun, c. = a kind of flying machine, used by the German army during World War I (1914–1918), that had no wings and was filled with hydrogen gas

ze•ro[1] /ˈzɪərəʊ/ noun, c. (**zeros** or **zeroes**) **1** = the number represented by the sign 0; nothing (having no quantity or value), also referred to as **nil**, **nought** or **O** ('Oh') **2** = the temperature (in celsius) at which water freezes **3** *Our hopes dipped to zero.* = a way of saying 'very low' to describe one's feelings (informal)

zero[2] verb, i. (**zeroed**) *The plumber zeroed in on the problem that was causing the water to overflow.* = to focus or fix one's attention on a particular person or thing (informal) **zero hour** noun, u. *The presentation was to be at two o'clock in the afternoon. The men looked nervous as zero hour approached.* = the time fixed for some action, specially by the military

zero[3] adj. *I did zero work during the holidays.* = no or not any (informal)

zest /zest/ noun, u. *These actors have been presenting the same play for two years. There is no zest in their acting now.* = enthusiasm or eagerness; the pleasure that one gets from doing something (formal)

zig-zag[1] /ˈzɪgzæg/ noun, c. (**zig-zags**) *We planted the flowers in a zig-zag.* = a line that moves like the letter 'z'; from left to right and not in a straight line

zig-zag[2] verb, i. *The tiger was chasing the deer but was unable to catch it as the deer kept zig-zagging all the time.* = to run in a zig-zag (from side to side) instead of running in a straight line

zinc /zɪŋk/ noun = a kind of metal that is often mixed with other metals to make special kinds of steel

Zi•on•ism /ˈzaɪənɪzəm/ noun = the political movement that led to the formation of Israel as a homeland for the Jewish people

zip[1] /zɪp/ noun, c. **1** = a fastener with two sets of metal or plastic teeth which are brought together by pulling a small sliding piece over them, used for closing openings in a dress, bag etc. (also zipper or zip fastener) **2** *Can you put a little zip into your movements? You are very slow!* = energy or speed (informal)

zip[2] verb, t. or i. **1** *Please zip up the bag.*(t.) = to close something with a zip **2** *He zipped through the town on his motor-cycle.*(i.) = to move at speed or to do something with speed (informal) **3** *Zip up your mouth.*(t.) = to keep silent (slang, not polite) **zippy** adj. *a zippy centre-forward* (in a game of football) = fast and lively (full of energy) (informal) **zip code** noun, c. = a number at the end of an address which indicates the area that the letter has to be delivered to (also **pincode**)

zith•er /ˈzɪðəʳ/ noun, c. = a musical instrument with strings

zo•di•ac /ˈzəʊdiæk/ noun, u. = *the 12 signs of the zodiac* = the area of the sky through which the sun, moon and different planets are believed to move (in astrology), which is divided into 12 equal parts, each of which is given a sign, named after a constellation (group of stars)

zom•bie /ˈzɒmbi/ noun, c. *He sits like a zombie in*

Z

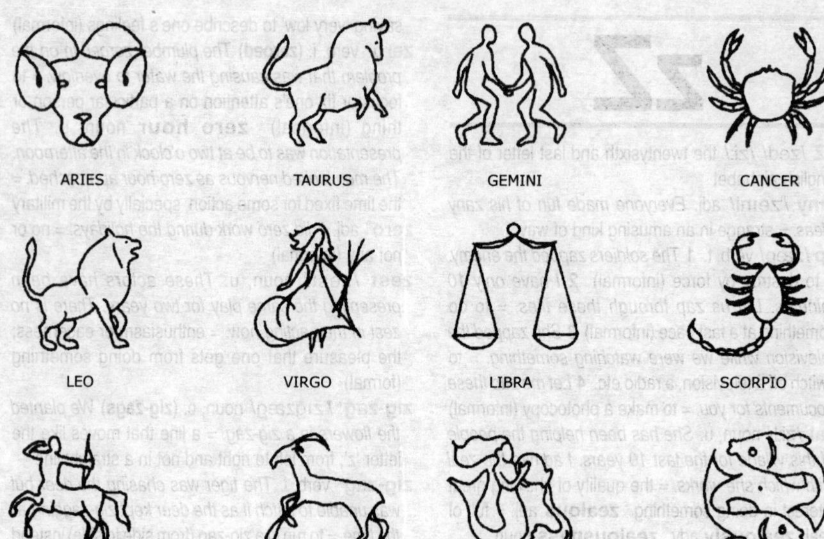

zodiac signs

front of the television. = a person who has no energy or who is not thinking (informal, derogatory)

zone /zəʊn/ noun, c. **1** *This city lies in an earthquake zone.* = an area which is different from other areas because of some special quality that it has or because it is used for a special purpose **2** *India lies in the torrid zone.* = one of the five divisions into which the surface of the earth has been divided, according to climate [GEOGRAPHY] **zonal** adj. *We are playing a zonal match.* = having to do with a particular zone or area **zoning** noun. = dividing an area into zones

zoo /zuː/ noun, c. = a kind of park in which animals of different kinds, including wild animals, are kept so that people can learn about them

zo•ol•o•gy /zuːˈɒlədʒi/ noun = the scientific study of different kinds of animals, their characteristics, habitat, behaviour etc. **zoologist** /zuːˈɒlədʒəst/ noun, c. = a person who studies animals

zoom¹ /zuːm/ verb, i. (**zoomed**) *Anil zoomed past us on his new bicycle.* = to move quickly and with a loud noise (informal)

zoom² noun, u. *He rushed past us with a zoom.* = a loud noise, caused by fast movement **zoom lens** noun = a special kind of lens for a camera which can move quickly from a distant view of a person or object to a close-up (very near) view

zuc•chi•ni /zʊˈkiːni/ noun = a vegetable of the cucumber family

zzz = often used in cartoons (humorous drawings) to show a person enjoying a sleep

PAST AND PARTICIPLE FORMS OF IRREGULAR VERBS

verb	past tense	participle
arise	arose	arisen
awake	awoke / awakened	awoken
bear	bore	borne
beat	beat	beaten
become	became	become
begin	began	begun
bend	bent	bent
bet	bet / betted	bet / betted
bid	bade / bid	bid / bidden
bind	bound	bound
bite	bit	bitten
bleed	bled	bled
blow	blew	blown
break	broke	broken
breed	bred	bred
bring	brought	brought
broadcast	broadcast	broadcast
build	built	built
burn	burned / burnt	burned / burnt
burst	burst	burst
buy	bought	bought
cast	cast	cast
catch	caught	caught
choose	chose	chosen
cling	clung	clung
come	came	come
cost	cost	cost
creep	crept	crept
cut	cut	cut
deal	dealt / delt	dealt
dig	dug	dug
dive	dived / (AmE dove)	dived
do	did	done
draw	drew	drawn
dream	dreamed / dreamt	dreamed / dreamt
drink	drank	drunk
drive	drove	driven
eat	ate	eaten
fall	fell	fallen
feed	fed	fed
feel	felt	felt
fight	fought	fought
find	found	found
fling	flung	flung
fly	flew	flown
forbid	forbade / forbad	forbidden
forget	forgot	forgotten
forgive	forgave	forgiven

verb	past tense	participle
freeze	froze	frozen
get	got	got / (AmE gotten)
give	gave	given
go	went	gone
grind	ground	ground
grow	grew	grown
hang	hung / hanged	hung / hanged
have	had	had
hear	heard	heard
hide	hid	hidden / hid
hit	hit	hit
hold	held	held
hurt	hurt	hurt
keep	kept	kept
kneel	knelt / kneeled (esp. AmE kneeled)	knelt / kneeled (esp. AmE kneeled)
knit	knitted / knit	knitted / knit
know	knew	known
lay	laid	laid
lead	led	led
lean	leaned / leant (esp. BrE leant)	leaned / leant (esp. BrE leant)
leap	leapt / leaped (esp. AmE leaped)	leapt / leaped (esp. AmE leaped)
learn	learned / learnt	learned / learnt
leave	left	left
lend	lent	lent
let	let	let
lie	lay	lain
light	lit / lighted	lit / lighted
lose	lost	lost
make	made	made
mean	meant	meant
meet	met	met
mistake	mistook	mistaken
mow	mowed	mowed / mown
pay	paid	paid
put	put	put
read /ri:d/	read /red/	read /red/
ride	rode	ridden
ring	rang	rung
rise	rose	risen
run	ran	run
saw	sawed	sawn / sawed
say	said	said
see	saw	seen
sell	sold	sold
send	sent	sent
set	set	set
sew	sewed	sewn / sewed
shake	shook	shaken
shave	shaved	shaved

verb	past tense	participle
shine	shone / shined	shone / shined
shoot	shot	shot
show	showed	shown / showed
shrink	shrank / shrunk	shrunk
shut	shut	shut
sing	sang	sung
sink	sank / sunk	sunk
sit	sat	sat
sleep	slept	slept
smell	smelt / smelled (esp. AmE smelled)	smelt / smelled (esp. AmE smelled)
speak	spoke	spoken
spell	spelt	speeded
spend	spent	spent
spin	spun / span	spun
spit	spat / (AmE spit)	spat / (AmE spit)
spoil	spoilt	spoiled
spread	spread	spread
spring	sprang / (AmE sprung)	sprung
stand	stood	stood
steal	stole	stolen
stick	stuck	stuck
sting	stung	stung
stink	stank / stunk	stunk
strike	struck	struck
swear	swore	sworn
sweep	swept	swept
swell	swelled	swollen / swelled
swim	swam	swum
swing	swung	swung
take	took	taken
teach	taught	taught
tear	tore	torn
tell	told	told
think	thought	thought
throw	threw	thrown
upset	upset	upset
wake	woke / waked	waked / woken
wear	wore	worn
weave	wove	woven
wed	wedded / wed	wedded / wed
weep	wept	wept
wet	wetted	wetted, wet
win	won	won
wind /waɪnd/	wound	wound
wring	wrung	wrung
write	wrote	written

SOME COMMON WORDS AND THEIR DERIVATIVES

Note: The plus sign (+) shows that the verb can be made passive. The minus sign (–) shows that it cannot be made passive.

Noun	Verb	Passive	Adjective	Adverb
A				
ability	–	–	able	ably
absence	absent	+ (self)	absent	–
abuse	abuse	+	abusive	abusively
acceptance	accept	+	accepting	–
achievement	achieve	+	–	–
action	act	+	active	actively
addition	add	+	additional	additionally
admission	admit	+	admissible	admittedly
advice	advise	+	advisory	–
age	age	+	ageing / aged	–
agreement	agree	+	agreeable	agreeably
anger	anger	+	angry	angrily
appearance	appear	–	apparent	apparently
arrangement	arrange	+	arranged	–
attention	attend	+	attentive	attentively
attraction	attract	+	attractive	attractively
B				
bag	bag	+	baggy	–
base	base	+	based / basic	basically
bath	bath, bathe	+	bathed	–
beating	beat	+	beaten	–
beauty	beautify	+	beautiful	beautifully
beginning	begin	+	–	–
belief	believe	+	believable	–
bend	bend	+	bent	–
better	better	+	better	better
bite	bite	+	bitten	–
blood	bleed	–	bleeding / bloody	–
blessing	bless	+	blessed	–
block	block	+	blocked	–
–	blind	+	blind / blinding	–
–	boil	+	boiled / boiling	–
bottle	bottle	+	bottled	–
breadth	broaden	+	broad	broadly
break	break	+	brokenly / breakable	–
breath	breathe	–	breathy / breathlessly	–
brush	brush	+	brushed	–
building	build	+	built	–
burial	bury	+	buried	–
buy	buy	–	bought	–
C				
calculation	calculate	+	calculated	–

Noun	Verb	Passive	Adjective	Adverb
call	call	+	–	–
calm	calm	+	calm	calmly
care	care	–	caring / careful	carefully
catch	catch	+	catchy	–
centre	centre	+	central	centrally
chain	chain	+	chained	–
change	change	+	changed / changing	–
charm	charm	+	charmed / charming	charmingly
chase	chase	+	–	–
–	cheapen	+	cheap	cheaply
cheat	cheat	+	cheating	–
cheer	cheer	+	cheerful	cheerfully
child	–	–	childish	childishly
choice	choose	+	choice / choosy	choosily
circle	circle	+	circular	–
class	classify	+	classy	–
climb	climb	+	–	–
–	close	+	close	closely
clothes	clothe	+	clothed	–
coat	coat	+	coated	–
collection	collect	+	collective	collectively
colour	colour	+	coloured / colourful	colourfully
combination	combine	+	combined	–
comfort	comfort	+	comfortable	comfortably
command	command	+	commanding	commandingly
comparison	compare	+	comparative	comparatively
competition	compete	–	competitive	competitively
complaint	complain	+	complaining	complainingly
computer	compute	+	–	–
concern	concern	+	concerned	–
confidence	confide	+	confident	confidently
confusion	confuse	+	confusing	confusingly
connection	connect	+	connecting / connective	–
consideration	consider	+	considerate / considerable	considerably
content	contain	+	containing	–
control	control	+	controlled	–
cook	cook	+	cooked	–
copy	copy	+	copied	–
corner	corner	+	corner	–
correction	correct	+	correct	correctly
cost	cost	+	costly	–
count	count	+	counted	–
cover	cover	+	covered	–
crack	crack	+	cracked	–
crash	crash	–	crashing	–
cross	cross	+	cross / crossed	crossly
crowd	crowd	+	crowded	–
cruelty	–	–	cruel	cruelly
crush	crush	+	crushed / crushing	crushingly
cry	cry	–	crying	–

Noun	Verb	Passive	Adjective	Adverb
cure	cure	+	curative	–
curl	curl	+	curly	–
curse	curse	+	cursed	–
cut	cut	+	cut / cutting	–
D				
damage	damage	+	damaged	–
danger	–	–	dangerous	dangerously
daring	dare	+	daring	daringly
dark	darken	+	dark	darkly
date	date	+	dated	–
dead	deaden	+	dead / deadly	–
decay	decay	–	decaying / decadent	–
decision	decide	+	decisive	decisively
declaration	declare	+	declarative	–
decrease	decrease	+	decreasing	–
defeat	defeat	+	defeated	–
defence	defend	+	defensive	defensively
delay	delay	+	delayed	–
delight	delight	+	delightful	delightfully
demand	demand	+	demanding	demandingly
description	describe	+	descriptive	descriptively
desire	desire	+	desirable	desirably
destruction	destroy	+	destructive	destructively
difference	differentiate	+	different	differently
direction	direct	+	direct	directly
disappointment	disappoint	+	disappointing	disappointingly
discovery	discover	+	–	–
dismissal	dismiss	+	–	–
distance	distance	+ (self)	distant	distantly
division	divide	+	divided / divisible	–
doing	do	+	done	–
dot	dot	+	dotted	–
double	double	+	doubled	–
doubt	doubt	+	doubtful / doubting	doubtfully
drag	drag	+	dragging	–
draw	draw	+	drawn	–
dream	dream	+	dreamy	dreamily
dress	dress	+	dressy	–
drink	drink	+	drunk / drunken	drunkenly
drive	drive	+	driven	–
drop	drop	+	dropped	–
drug	drug	+	drugged	–
drum	drum	+	drummed	–
–	dry	+	dry	drily
–	dull	+	dull	dully
E				
earning	earn	+	earned	–
east	–	–	eastern	–

Noun	Verb	Passive	Adjective	Adverb
ease	ease	+	easy	easily
education	educate	+	educated	–
effect	effect	+	effective	effectively
election	elect	+	elective	–
employment	employ	+	employed	–
enclosure	enclose	+	enclosed	–
end	end	+	ended	–
enjoyment	enjoy	+	enjoyable	–
entertainment	entertain	+	entertaining	–
equal	equal	+	equal	equally
examination	examine	+	–	–
excellence	excel	+	excellent	excellently
excitement	excite	+	exciting	excitingly
exercise	exercise	+	–	–
existence	exist	–	existing	–
experience	experience	+	experienced	–
explanation	explain	+	explanatory	–
explosion	explode	+	explosive	explosively
expression	express	+	expressive	expressively
F				
face	face	+	facial	–
failure	fail	+	failing	–
faith	–	–	faithful	faithfully
fall	fall	–	falling	–
falsehood	falsify	+	false	falsely
–	fancy	+	fancy / fanciful	fancifully
farm	farm	+	farm	–
fashion	fashion	+	fashionable	fashionably
father	father	+	fatherly	–
fault	fault	+	faulty	–
favour	favour	+	favourable / favourite	favourably
fear	fear	+	fearsome, fearful	fearfully
feeling	feel	+	feeling	feelingly
fence	fence	+	fenced	–
field	field	+	–	–
fight	fight	+	fighting	–
figure	figure	–	–	–
fill	fill	+	filled	–
find	find	+	–	–
finish	finish	+	finished	–
fire	fire	+	fiery	–
fish	fish	+	fishy	–
fit	fit	+	fit	–
fixture	fix	+	fixed	–
flame	flame	–	flaming	–
flash	flash	+	flashy	flashily
flat	flatten	+	flat	flatly
flesh	flesh out	+	fleshy	–
flight	fly	+	flying	–

Noun	Verb	Passive	Adjective	Adverb
–	float	+	floating	–
flood	flood	+	flooded	–
flow	flow	–	flowing	–
flower	flower	–	flowery	–
fold	fold	+	folded	–
fool	fool	+	foolish	foolishly
–	forbid	+	forbidding	–
force	force	+	forceful	forcefully
forgetfulness	forget	+	forgotten	–
forgiveness	forgive	+	forgiving	–
form	form	+	formal	formally
fox	fox	+	foxy	–
freedom	free	+	free	freely
freeze	freeze	+	frozen / freezing	–
frequency	frequent	+	frequent	frequently
fright	frighten	+	frightening	frighteningly
fulfillment	fulfil	+	fulfilling	–
furnishing	furnish	+	furnished	–
G				
gain	gain	+	gainful	gainfully
garden	garden	–	–	–
gas	gas	+	–	–
gathering	gather	+	gathered	–
generosity	generous	generously	–	–
gift	gift	+	gifted	–
–	gladden	+	glad	gladly
glue	glue	+	gluey / glued	–
government	govern	+	–	–
grace	grace	+	graceful / gracious	gracefully / graciously
gratitude	–	–	grateful	gratefully
greenery	green	+	green	–
greeting	greet	+	–	–
grief	grieve	–	grieving	–
–	grind	+	ground	–
group	group	+	grouped	–
growth	grow	+	growing	–
guard	guard	+	guarded	–
guess	guess	+	–	–
H				
habit	habituate	–	habitual	habitually
hammer	hammer	+	hammered	–
handle	handle	+	handled	–
hanging	hang	+	hanged / hung	–
–	harden	+	hard	–
harm	harm	+	harmful	harmfully
haste	hasten	+	hasty	hastily
hatred	hate	+	hated / hateful	hatefully

Noun	Verb	Passive	Adjective	Adverb
head	head	+	head	–
heat	heat	+	hot	hotly
help	help	+	helpful	helpfully
hide	hide	+	hidden	–
height	heighten	+	high	high
hire	hire	+	hired	–
hit	hit	+	hit	–
hold	hold	+	held	–
hollow	hollow	+	hollow	–
home	home	–	homely	–
honour	honour	+	honourable	honourably
hope	hope	+	hopeful	hopefully
host	host	+	–	–
house	house	+	–	–
humour	humour	+	humorous	humorously
hunger	hunger	–	hungry	hungrily
hunt	hunt	+	hunted	–
hurry	hurry	+	hurried	hurriedly
hurt	hurt	+	hurtful	hurtingly
I				
ice	ice	+	iced / icy	icily
imagination	imagine	+	imaginary	–
improvement	improve	+	improved	–
inclusion	include	+	inclusive	–
increase	increase	+	increasing	increasingly
infection	infect	+	infectious	–
influence	influence	+	influential	–
information	inform	+	–	–
ink	ink	+	inky	–
inquiry	inquire	+	–	–
instruction	instruct	+	instructive	–
intention	intend	+	intended / intentional	intentionally
interest	interest	+	interesting	interestingly
interruption	interrupt	+	interrupted	–
introduction	introduce	+	introductory	–
invention	invent	+	inventive	–
invitation	invite	+	invite	–
J				
join	join	+	joined / jointed	–
joke	joke	–	jocular	jocularly
joy	–		joyful / joyous	joyfully
judgement	judge	+	judgemental	judgementally
jump	jump	+	jumping	–
K				
key	key	+	keyed	–
kick	kick	+	kicked	–
kill	kill	+	killing	–

Noun	Verb	Passive	Adjective	Adverb
kiss	kiss	+	kissed	–
knife	knife	+	knifed	–
knock	knock	+	knocked	–
knowledge	know	+	knowledgeable	knowledgeably
L				
labour	labour	+	laboured / laborious	laboriously
lack	lack	+	–	–
land	land	+	landed	–
–	last	–	lasting	–
laughter	laugh	–	laughable	laughably
–	laze	–	lazy	lazily
lead	lead	+	led / leading	–
learning	learn	+	learned	–
–	leave	+	left	–
–	lend	+	lent	–
length	lengthen	+	length / long	–
less	lessen	+	less	less
level	level	+	level	level
lie	lie	–	–	–
life	live	–	lifeless / lively	lifelessly
lift	lift	+	–	–
light	light	+	lit	–
–	lighten	+	light	–
liking	like	+	liked	–
limit	limit	+	limited	–
line	line	+	lined	–
liquid	liquidize	+	liquid	–
list	list	+	listed	–
load	load	+	loaded	–
lock	lock	+	locked	–
look	look	–	–	–
–	loosen	+	loose	loosely
loss	lose	+	lost	–
love	love	+	loving / loved / beloved	lovingly
–	lower	+	low	–
M				
machine	machine	+	machined	–
–	madden	+	mad	madly
mail	mail	+	mailed	–
make	make	+	made	–
man	man	+	manned / manly	manfully
management	manage	+	managerial	–
map	map	+	mapped	–
mark	mark	–	marked	markedly
marriage	marry	+	married	–
master	master	+	mastered	–
match	match	+	matching / marched	–
material	materialize	–	material	materially

Noun	Verb	Passive	Adjective	Adverb
meaning	mean	+	meaningful	meaningfully
measure	measure	+	measured	–
medicine	medicate	+	medical / medicinal	medically
meeting	meet	–	–	–
–	melting	+	melting / molten	–
memory	memorize	+	memorized	–
–	mend	+	mended	–
mention	mention	+	mentionable	–
method	–	–	methodical	methodically
microscope	–	–	microscopic	microscopically
middle	middle	+	middle / middling	–
milk	milk	+	milked	–
mind	mind	+	minded	–
mirror	mirror	+	mirrored	–
miss	miss	+	missed / missing	–
mistake	mistake	+	mistaken	–
mixture	mix	+	mixed	–
model	model	+	model	–
mother	mother	+	mothered / motherly	–
motor	motor	+	motorable	–
mouth	mouth	+	–	–
movement	move	+	moving / movable	–
multiplication	multiply	+	multiplying	–
murder	murder	+	murdered	–
mystery	mystify	+	mysterious	mysteriously
N				
nail	nail	+	nailed	–
name	name	+	named	–
near	near	+	near	nearly
necessity	–	–	necessary	necessarily
need	need	+	needed	–
nerve	nerve	+	nervous	nervously
notice	notice	+	noticable	noticably
O				
obedience	obey	+	obedient	obediently
objection	object	+	objectionable	–
–	obtain	+	obtainable	–
occasion	–	–	occasional	occasionally
offence	offend	+	offensive	offensively
office	–	–	official	officially
opening	open	+	open	openly
operation	operate	+	operative / operational	–
opponent / opposition	oppose	+	opposite	–
order	order	+	ordered	orderly
organization	organize	+	organized	–
origin	originate	+	original	originally
ownership	own	+	own	–

Noun	Verb	Passive	Adjective	Adverb
P				
pack	pack	+	packed	–
pain	pain	+	painful	painfully
painting	paint	+	painted	–
–	pale	–	pale	–
paper	paper	+	papered	–
park	park	+	parked	–
part	part	–	parted	–
partner	partner	+	partnered	–
passage	pass	+	passing	–
payment	pay	+	paid	–
performance	perform	+	–	–
permission	permit	+	permitted / permissible	–
persuasion	persuade	+	persuasive	persuasively
photograph	photograph	+	photographic	
photographically				
picture	picture	+	pictorial	pictorially
pile	pile	+	piled	–
pilot	pilot	+	piloted	–
pin	pin	+	pinned	–
plan	plan	+	planned	–
play	play	+	playful	playfully
pleasure	please	+	pleasant	pleasantly
plural	pluralize	+	plural	–
point	point	+	pointed	pointedly
poison	poison	+	poisonous	–
polish	polish	+	polished	–
possession	possess	+	possessed	–
possibility	–	–	possible	possibly
powder	powder	+	powdery	–
practice	practise	+	practical	practically
prepartion	pepare	+	prepared	–
presence	present	+	present	presently
print	print	+	printed	–
prize	prize	+	prized	–
process	process	+	processed	–
production	produce	+	produced	–
pronunciation	pronounce	+	pronounced	–
protection	protect	+	protective	protectively
proof	prove	+	proved	–
punishment	punish	+	punished	–
push	push	+	pushed	–
Q				
quarrel	quarrel	–	quarrelsome	–
question	question	+	questioning	questioningly
quiet	quieten	+	quiet	quietly
R				
race	race	+	racing	–

Noun	Verb	Passive	Adjective	Adverb
rain	rain	+	rainy	–
raise	raise	+	raised	–
rank	rank	+	ranking	–
rate	rate	+	rated	–
reach	reach	+	reachable	–
reading	read	+	readable	–
–	ready	+	ready	readily
reason	reason	+	reasonable	reasonably
recognition	recognize	+	recognized / recognizable	recognizably
record	record	+	recorded	–
reduction	reduce	+	reduced	–
refusal	refuse	+	–	–
relation	relate	+	related, relative	relatively
religion	–	–	religious	religiously
remainder	remain	–	remaining	–
remark	remark	+	remarkable	remarkably
remembrance	remember	+	remembered	–
removal	remove	+	removable	–
rent	rent	+	rented	–
repair	repair	+	repaired	–
repetition	repeat	+	repetitive	repetitively
reply	reply	+	–	–
report	report	+	reported	reportedly
representation	represent	+	representative	–
request	request	+	requested	–
respect	respect	+	respectful	respectfully
rest	rest	+	restful	restfully
result	result	+	resulting / resultant	–
return	return	+	returning	–
reward	reward	+	rewarding	rewardingly
rise	rise	+	rising	–
risk	risk	+	risky	riskily
robbery	rob	+	–	–
ruin	ruin	+	ruinous	ruinously
ruler	rule	+	–	–
S				
sadness	sadden	+	sad	sadly
sail	sail	–	sailing	–
sale	sell	+	sold	–
salt	salt	+	salted	–
satisfaction	satisfy	+	satisfactory	satisfactorily
saying	say	+	said	–
scene	–	–	scenic	–
screw	screw	+	screwed	–
search	search	+	searched	searchingly
seat	seat	+	seated	–
secrecy	–	–	secret	secretly
sentence	sentence	+	sentenced	–
seaparation	separate	+	separate	separately

Noun	Verb	Passive	Adjective	Adverb
service	serve	+	serving / serviceable	–
settlement	settle	+	settled	–
sewing	sew	+	sewn	–
sex	–	–	sexual	sexually
shade	shade	+	shady	–
shadow	shadow	+	shadowy	–
shake	shake	+	shaky	shakily
shame	shame	+	shameful	shamefully
shape	shape	+	shapely	–
share	share	+	shared	–
sharp	sharpen	+	sharp	sharply
shell	shell	+	shelled	–
shelter	shelter	+	sheltered	–
shine	shine	+	shiny	–
ship	ship	+	shipped	–
shock	shock	+	shocked	shockingly
shooting	shoot	+	shot	–
shoulder	shoulder	+	shouldered	–
show	show	+	showy	–
sickness	sicken	+	sick / sickly	–
signal	signal	+	signalled	–
silence	silence	+	silent	silently
simplicity	simplify	+	simple	simply
song	sing	+	sung	–
sinking	sink	+	sunk	–
skin	skin	+	skinned	–
sleep	sleep	–	sleepy	sleepily
slip	slip	+	slippery	–
smell	smell	+	smelly	–
smile	smile	-	smiling	smilingly
soil	soil	+	soiled	–
sound	sound	+	sounded	–
space	space	+	spacious	spaciously
speech	speak	+	spoken	–
speed	speed	+	speedy	speedily
spelling	spell	+	spelt	–
split	split	+	split	–
spread	spread	+	spreading	–
stamp	stamp	+	stamp	–
standard	standardize	+	standard	–
start	start	+	starting	–
statement	state	+	stated	–
stealth	steal	+	stolen / stealthy	stealthily
steam	steam	+	steamed	–
stick	stick	+	sticky	stickily
sting	sting	+	stinging	–
strength	strengthen	+	strong	strongly
study	study	+	studied	–
style	style	+	stylish	stylishly
subtraction	subtract	+	subtracted	–

Noun	Verb	Passive	Adjective	Adverb
success	succeed	–	successful	successfully
suggestion	suggest	+	suggestive	suggestively
–	suit	+	suitable	suitably
support	support	+	supportive	supportively
surprise	surprise	+	surprising	surprisingly
–	sweep	+	swept / sweeping	–
sweet	sweeten	+	sweet	sweetly
sympathy	sympathize	–	sympathetic	sympathetically
T				
table	table	+	tabular	–
taking	take	+	taken	–
talk	talk	–	talkative	talkatively
taste	taste	+	tasty	tastefully
tax	tax	+	taxed	–
teaching	teach	+	taught	–
tear	tear	+	torn	–
tendency	tend	+	tending	–
terror	terrorize	+	terrorized	–
thought	think	+	thoughtful	thoughtfully
thirst	thirst	+	thirsty	thirstily
threat	threaten	+	threatening	threateningly
thunder	thunder	+	thundering / thunderous	thunderously
touch	touch	+	touchy	–
tower	tower	–	towering	–
travel	travel	+	travelled	–
treatment	treat	+	treated	–
trick	trick	+	tricked / tricky	trickily
trouble	trouble	+	troubled / troublesome	–
trust	trust	+	trusted / trusty	–
trial	try	+	tried	–
U				
understanding	understand	+	understood	–
undoing	undo	+	undone	–
union	unite	+	united / unified	unitedly
upset	upset	+	upset / upsetting	–
V				
value	value	+	valuable	–
variation	vary	+	variable	variably
view	view	+	–	–
violence	–	–	violent	violently
visit	visit	+	–	–
voice	voice	+	voiced	–
vote	vote	+	–	–
W				
wait	wait	–	waiting	–
walk	walk	–	–	–

Noun	Verb	Passive	Adjective	Adverb
want	want	+	wanted	–
warmth	warm	+	warm	warmly
warning	warn	+	warning	–
wash	wash	+	washed	–
waste	waste	+	wasted	–
water	water	+	watered	–
wear	wear	+	worn	–
weave	weave	+	woven	–
wedding	wed	+	wedded	–
weight	weigh	+	weighed	–
whip	whip	+	whipped	–
width	widen	+	wide	widely
win	win	+	winning	winningly
Y				
yellow	yellow	+	yellow	–

SOME PROBLEM AREAS FOR SOUTH ASIAN LEARNERS OF ENGLISH

1. The 'double possessive'

In English, possession is commonly shown by the use of the **apostrophe s ('s).** e.g. (1) *Roy is Vimal's son.* However, the apostrophe **s** is not used when the 'possessor' is a lifeless object. It is incorrect to say (2) * *Raghu is painting the house's door.* Here, we use the preposition **of** to show possession. So Sentence 2 becomes (3) *Raghu is painting the door of the house.*

However, the use of the **double possessive** (using both **'s** and **of**) is common. e.g. (4) *Roy is a son of Vimal's.* The double possessive is used to highlight the 'possessor' (Vimal) and not the 'possessed' (Roy). Sentence 4 has the meaning ' Vimal has several sons and Roy is one of them'.

2. Using the possessive form before a gerund (verb used as a noun)

Look at these two sentences. (1a) *Ravi goes to the cinema every day.* (1b) *I don't like it* (the fact that he goes to the cinema every day). If we combine these two sentences, we get (2) *I don't like Ravi's going to the cinema every day.* The verb 'goes' changes into 'going', which is a **gerund** (a verb used as a noun). Just before 'going' we have the word 'Ravi's', which is in the **possessive** form.

Some grammar books tell you that the possessive (Ravi's) must be used here and not 'Ravi' (which is the 'object form'). But in modern English, specially in spoken English, you are allowed to use the object form and say, *I don't like Ravi going to the cinema every day* or *I don't like him going to the cinema every day.*

3. The 'double future'

In many Indian languages, it is possible to say something like (1) * *When I shall go to Kolkata, I shall meet my niece.* The use of 'shall' shows that we are talking about an action in the future. But notice that 'shall' has been used twice. This is called the '**double future**', and English does not allow it. So Sentence 1 must be changed to (2) *When I go to Kolkata, I shall meet my niece.*

4. The double future with 'if'

The '**double future**' is frequently (and incorrectly) used in '**conditional sentences**' containing 'if'. e.g. (1) * *If you will look after me, I will work for you.* This sentence has to be changed to (2) *If you look after me, I will work for you.* (avoiding the double future)

5. Verbs which do not take the progressive (-ing) form

Look at the following sentence (1) *The child is crying for its mother.* The verb 'cry' is in the **progressive (be + -ing)** form, showing '**action in progress' at the present time.** However, many English verbs cannot normally be used in the progressive form. For example, we cannot say (2) * *My friend is knowing your sister.* The verb 'know' is a '**mental verb**'.

Other verbs which cannot be used in the progressive form (except in special cases) include (a) **verbs of sensation:** *see, touch, smell, hear, feel* (b) **mental verbs:** *understand, know, believe, imagine* (c) **stative verbs:** *like, love, contain, have, own, possess, prefer.*

Note: Incorrect sentences are marked by an asterisk (*) placed at the beginning of the sentence.

6. Nouns which do not take plural forms (by adding –s)

accommodation, advice, ammunition, baggage, blame, chalk, equipment, furniture, information, intelligence, jewellery, luggage, machinery, mail, poetry, scenery, slang, staff, stationery
[Common error: * *I have got all the equipments for my laboratory.*]

7. Nouns ending in –s which do not have singular forms

forceps, news, pants, pliers, pyjamas, series, species, spectacles (glasses), trousers, whereabouts
[Common error: * *I have sent my trouser to the laundry.*]

8. Nouns which are plural in meaning but take the indefinite article 'a'

a dozen, a hundred, a thousand, a million
[Common error: * *There are hundred students in this class.*]

9. Nouns which are uncountable but take the indefinite article 'a'

a headache, a stomachache, a pain, a fever, a noise
[Common errors: * *He has headache.* * *Don't make noise.*]

10. Words which are commonly misused

1 He has found a room in the *boarding.* (hostel)
2 There is no *place* in this bus. (room)
3 I have done the exercise in my *copy.* (exercise book)
4 I saw the *joker* at the circus. (clown)
5 He is acting in a *drama.* (play)
6 Meet my *cousin sister.* (cousin)

11. Verbs which are commonly followed by reflexive pronouns

enjoy (enjoy oneself) avail (avail oneself of something)
hurt (hurt oneself)
[Common errors: * *When you visit Goa, you should enjoy.* * *I am availing a concession.*]

12. Unnecessary use of the pronoun after a relative clause

Incorrect	***Correct***
The boy whom you met yesterday he is my brother.	The boy (whom) you met yesterday is my brother.

13. Starting a sentence with a relative clause

Incorrect	***Correct***
That pen you bought yesterday is broken.	The pen (that) you bought yesterday is broken.

14 . Incorrect use of the reflexive ponoun (with –self)

Incorrect	***Correct***
'Who brought these flowers?' 'Myself.'	'Who brought these flowers?' 'I.'

Reflexive pronouns are used only to indicate (a) **emphasis**: *I did this myself.* (= I alone, with no help from anyone); (b) **the effect of an action on the doer:** *I cut myself with the knife.*

15. Wrong use of a noun as a determiner (before another noun)

Incorrect	*Correct*
I need a matchbox to light the stove.	a box of matches ('matchbox' means just the box, without the marches)
I have bought an ink bottle.	a bottle of ink
My family members enjoyed the picnic.	the members of my family

16. Some common verbs and adjectives and the prepositions they are used with

accuse **of**	accustomed **to**	afraid **of**	aim **at**	angry **with**
arrive **at**	ashamed **of**	believe **in**	benefit **by**	boast **of**
careful **of**	complain **of**	conform **to**	consist **of**	cure **of**
depend **on**	deprive **of**	different **from**	doubtful **of**	fail **in**
full **of**	good **at**	guard **against from**	guilty **of**	independent **of**
indifferent **to**	insist **on**	interested **in**	jealous **of**	look **at**
married **to**	pleased **with**	prefer **to**	proud **of**	related **to**
satisfied **with**	succeed **in**	superior **to**	sure **of**	surprised **at**
suspect **of**	tired **of**	translate **into**	warn **of**	

17. Some common errors with determiners (words which are used before nouns in noun phrases)

Incorrect	*Correct*
I have lost my both parents.	both my parents
I washed my some clothes.	some of my clothes
These all books belong to the library.	all these books
I met him after long five years.	five long years
Give me his these books.	these books of his
I have bought a round big table.	big round table

WEIGHT

	Imperial	Metric
	1 ounce (oz)	= 28.35 grams (g)
16 ounces	= 1 pound (lb)	= 0.454 kilograms (kg)
14 pounds	= 1 stone (st)	= 6.356 kilograms
112 pounds	= 1 hundredweight (cwt)	= 50.8 kilograms
20 hundredweight	= 1 ton (t)	= 1.016 tonnes

Note: In the United States, 1 hundredweight is equal to 100 pounds and 1 ton is 2000 lb or 0.907 tonne. Americans do not use stones, so they talk about their weight in pounds.

LENGTH

	Imperial	Metric
	1 inch (in)	= 25.4 millimetres (mm)
12 inches	= 1 foot (ft)	= 30.48 centimetres (cm)
3 feet	= 1 yard (yd)	= 0.914 metre (m)
1760 yards	= 1 mile	= 1.609 kilometres (km)

AREA

	Imperial	Metric
	1 square inch (sq in)	= 6.452 square centimetres (sq cm)
144 square inches	= 1 square foot (sq ft)	= 929.03 square centimetres
9 square feet	= 1 square yard (sq yd)	= 0.836 square metre (sq m)
4840 square yards	= 1 acre	= 0.405 hectare (ha)
640 acres	= 1 square mile	= 2.59 square kilometres (sq km) or 259 hectares

CUBIC MEASURE

	Imperial	Metric
	1 cubic inch (cu in)	= 16.39 cubic centimetres (cc)
1727 cubic inches	= 1 cubic foot (cu ft)	= 0.028 cubic metre (cu m)
27 cubic feet	= 1 cubic yard	= 0.765 cubic metre

CAPACITY

	UK	US	Metric
20 fluid ounces (fl oz)	= 1 pint (pt)	= 1.201 pints	= 0.568 litre (l)
2 pints	= 1 quart (qt)	= 1.201 quarts	= 1.136 litres
4 quarts	= 1 gallon (gal)	= 1.201 gallons	= 4.546 litres

Note: Quart is not often used in British English.

Units

	physical quantity	name	symbol
Base units	length	metre	m
	mass	kilogram	kg
	time	second	s
	electric current	ampere	A
	temperature	Celsius	C
	thermodynamic temperature	kelvin	K
	luminous intensity	candela	cd
	amount of substance	mole	mol
Supplementary units	plane angle	radian	rad
	solid angle	steradian	sr

Affixes

Multiple	Affix	Symbol	Multiple	Affix	Symbol
10	deca-	da	10^{-1}	deci-	d
10^{2}	hecto-	h	10^{-2}	centi-	c
10^{3}	kilo-	k	10^{-3}	milli-	m
10^{6}	mega-	M	10^{-6}	micro-	µ
10^{9}	giga-	G	10^{-9}	nano-	n
10^{12}	tera-	T	10^{-12}	pico-	p
10^{15}	peta-	P	10^{-15}	femto-	f
10^{18}	exa-	E	10^{-18}	atto-	a

COUNTRIES AND NATIONALITIES

Country	Nationality (Adjective form)
Afghanistan	Afghan
Albania	Albanian
Algeria	Algerian
Andorra	Andorran
Angola	Angolan
Argentina	Argentine or Argentinian
Armenia	Armenian
Australia	Australian
Austria	Austrian
Azerbaijan	Azerbaijani
Bahamas	Bahamian
Bahrain	Bahraini
Bangladesh	Bangladeshi
Barbados	Barbadian
Belarus	Belorussian or Byelorussian
Belgium	Belgian
Belize	Belizian
Benin	Beninese
Bhutan	Bhutanese
Bolivia	Bolivian
Bosnia Herzegovina	Bosnian
Botswana	Botswanan
Brazil	Brazilian
Brunei	Bruneian
Bulgaria	Bulgarian
Burkina Faso	Burkinese
Burundi	Burundian
Cambodia	Cambodian
Cameroon	Cameroonian
Canada	Canadian
Cape Verde	Cape Verdean
Chad	Chadian
Chile	Chilean
China	Chinese
Colombia	Colombian
Congo	Congolese
Costa Rica	Costa Rican
Croatia	Croat or Croatian

Country	Nationality (Adjective form)
Cuba	Cuban
Cyprus	Cypriot
Czech Republic	Czech
Democratic Republic of Congo	Congolese
Denmark	Danish
Djibouti	Djiboutian
Dominican Republic	Dominican
Ecuador	Ecuadorean
Egypt	Egyptian
El Salvador	Salvadorean
Eritrea	Eritrean
Estonia	Estonian
Ethiopia	Ethiopian
Fiji	Fijian
Finland	Finnish or Finn
France	French
Gabon	Gabonese
Gambia	Gambian
Georgia	Georgian
Germany	German
Ghana	Ghanaian
Greece	Greek
Greenland	Greenlander
Grenada	Grenadian
Guatemala	Guatemalan
Guinea	Guinean
Guyana	Guyanese
Haiti	Haitian
Honduras	Honduran
Hungary	Hungarian
Iceland	Icelander or Icelandic
Ireland	Irish
India	Indian
Indonesia	Indonesian
Iran	Iranian
Iraq	Iraqi
Ireland	Irish
Israel	Israeli
Italy	Italian
Jamaica	Jamaican
Japan	Japanese

Country	Nationality (Adjective form)
Jordan	Jordanian
Kazakhstan	Kazakh
Kenya	Kenyan
Kuwait	Kuwaiti
Laos	Laotian
Latvia	Latvian
Lebanon	Lebanese
Liberia	Liberian
Libya	Libyan
Liechtenstein	Liechtensteiner
Lithuania	Lithuanian
Luxembourg	Luxembourger
Macao	Macaoan
Macedonia	Macedonian
Madagascar	Malagasay or Madagascan
Malawi	Malawian
Malaysia	Malaysian
Maldives	Maldivian
Mali	Malian
Malta	Maltese
Mauritania	Mauritanian
Mauritius	Mauritian
Mexico	Mexican
Moldova	Moldovan
Monaco	Monégasque or Monacan
Mongolia	Mongolian
Montenegro	Montenegrin
Morocco	Moroccan
Mozambique	Mozambican
Myanmar	Myanmarese
Namibia	Namibian
Nepal	Nepalese
Netherlands (Holland)	Dutch
New Zealand	New Zealander or Kiwi
Nicaragua	Nicaraguan
Niger	Nigerien
Nigeria	Nigerian
North Korea	North Korean
Norway	Norwegian
Oman	Omani
Pakistan	Pakistani